A to Zoo

Recent Titles in the
Children's and Young Adult Literature Reference Series

Catherine Barr, Series Editor

A to Zoo: Subject Access to Children's Picture Books, 8th Edition
Carolyn W. Lima and Rebecca L. Thomas

Literature Links to American History, 7–12: Resources to Enhance and Entice
Lynda G. Adamson

Literature Links to American History, K–6: Resources to Enhance and Entice
Lynda G. Adamson

Celebrating Cuentos: Promoting Latino Children's Literature and Literacy in Classrooms and Libraries
Jamie Campbell Naidoo, Editor

The Family in Literature for Young Readers: A Resource Guide for Use with Grades 4 to 9
John T. Gillespie

Best Books for High School Readers, Grades 9–12: Supplement to the Second Edition
Catherine Barr

Best Books for Middle School and Junior High Readers, Grades 6–9: Supplement to the Second Edition
Catherine Barr

Rainbow Family Collections: Selecting and Using Children's Books with Lesbian, Gay, Bisexual, Transgender, and Queer Content
Jamie Campbell Naidoo

A to Zoo: Subject Access to Children's Picture Books, Supplement to the 8th Edition
Rebecca L. Thomas

Best Books for Children: Preschool Through Grade 6, Supplement to the 9th Edition
Catherine Barr

Best Books for Middle School and Junior High Readers, Grades 6–9: Third Edition
Catherine Barr

Best Books for High School Readers, Grades 9–12: Third Edition
Catherine Barr

Ninth Edition

Rebecca L. Thomas
Carolyn W. Lima

A to Zoo

Subject Access to Children's Picture Books

Children's and Young Adult Literature Reference
Catherine Barr, Series Editor

LIBRARIES UNLIMITED

AN IMPRINT OF ABC-CLIO, LLC
Santa Barbara, California • Denver, Colorado • Oxford, England

Library of Congress Cataloging-in-Publication Data

Thomas, Rebecca L.
A to zoo : subject access to children's picture books / Rebecca L. Thomas and Carolyn W. Lima (in memoriam). — Ninth edition.
pages cm — (Children's and young adult literature reference)
Includes bibliographical references and indexes.
ISBN 978-1-61069-353-0 (hardback)
1. Picture books for children—Indexes. I. Lima, Carolyn W. II. Title. III. Title: Subject access to children's picture books. IV. Series: Children's and young adult literature reference series.
Z1037.L715 2014
011.62—dc23 2014004143

ISBN: 978-1-61069-353-0

18 17 16 15 14 1 2 3 4 5

Libraries Unlimited
An Imprint of ABC-CLIO, LLC

ABC-CLIO, LLC
130 Cremona Drive, P.O. Box 1911
Santa Barbara, California 93116-1911

This book is printed on acid-free paper ♾
Manufactured in the United States of America

6/16

Contents

Preface

In the early 1980s, John and Carolyn Lima had a vision to create a reference book to provide better subject access to picture books for children. That vision became *A to Zoo,* now one of the most highly regarded reference books in school and public libraries. Even with today's computerized library catalogs, the specialized subjects in *A to Zoo* give librarians and teachers easy access to books that will meet the needs of their patrons and of their programs. John and Carolyn Lima's creation has served generations of readers and provides the foundation for future editions and users. Rebecca Thomas continues the tradition established by the Limas. Dr. Thomas worked as an elementary school librarian for 35 years in the Shaker Heights City Schools, retiring in 2011. She has also been a university teacher and author in the field of children's literature. Her work to revise and update earlier editions has returned the focus of *A to Zoo* to books that are readily accessible for reading as well as for programs and curriculum use.

The importance of the picture book, long a source of delight and learning for young readers, continues today with the increasing emphasis on early childhood education and on reading, and with the need for supervised childcare for working parents. Teachers, librarians, and parents are finding the picture book an important learning and entertainment tool. Choosing the right book for a particular situation or need can be time-consuming and frustrating without some guidance. Many responsible professionals and parents have neither the time nor the materials to develop an intimate familiarity with the field. Rather than simply choosing the first title that appears to treat a specific subject from among the many thousands of books available, the user can now confidently identify a book that will cover the desired subject using this 9th edition of *A to Zoo: Subject Access to Children's Picture Books.* The new edition has 17,025 titles cataloged under 1,225 subjects.

Several library collections served as guides in the selection process, including the San Diego Public Library—the collection that served as the original resource for early editions of *A to Zoo.* Also examined was the catalog of the CLEVNET libraries in Ohio, which includes the Cleveland Public Library along with numerous independent libraries in northeastern Ohio. School library collections were also explored, including those of the Shaker Heights (Ohio) City schools and other schools in the North Coast Council consortium.

Titles with copyright dates in the 2000s are generally included, while titles with earlier dates have been checked for availability. Out-of-print titles are retained because public and school library collections are largely retrospective. Folktales, poetry, and informational picture books in particular are maintained in many libraries along with books about holidays and seasons. Popular titles from beloved authors and illustrators will still be found here, regardless of the copyright date. However, books featuring issues such as divorce, disabilities, and illnesses have been examined to remove dated titles and include newer ones with more contemporary approaches to these issues.

New titles from 2012 and 2013 have been added to this edition along with the titles in the *Supplement to the 8th Edition* (2012). Many sources were consulted to select titles for inclusion, including the library collections mentioned above, along with published reviews and review copies from publishers.

The picture book, as it is broadly defined within the scope of this book, is a fiction or nonfiction title with illustrations occupying as much or more space than the text and with text, vocabulary, or concepts suitable for preschool through grade two. It is noted, however that picture books appeal to a wider audience; adults, older children, and others often find picture books enjoyable, useful, and informative.

HOW TO USE THIS BOOK

A to Zoo can be used to obtain information about children's picture books in two ways: to learn the titles, authors, and illustrators of books on a particular subject, such as "dragons" or "weddings"; or to ascertain the subject (or subjects) when only the title, author and title, or illustrator and title are known. For example, if the title *Suppose You Meet a Dinosaur* is known, this volume will enable the user to discover that *Suppose You Meet a Dinosaur: A First Book of Manners* is written by Judy Sierra, illustrated by Tim Bowers, published by Knopf in 2012, and that the subject areas are Dinosaurs; Etiquette; Rhyming text; Shopping; and Stores.

For ease and convenience of reference use, *A to Zoo* is divided into five sections:

Subject Headings
Subject Guide
Bibliographic Guide
Title Index
Illustrator Index

Subject Headings: This section contains an alphabetical list of the subjects cataloged in this book. The subject headings reflect the established terms used commonly in public libraries, originally based on questions asked by parents and teachers and then modified and adapted by librarians. To facilitate reference use, and because subjects are requested in a variety of terms, the list of subject headings contains numerous cross-references. Subheadings are arranged alphabetically under each general topic, for example:

Animals (general topic)
Animals – aardvarks (subheading)
Animals – anteaters (subheading)
Animals – apes see Animals – baboons; Animals – chimpanzees; Animals – gorillas; Animals – monkeys (cross-reference)

SUBJECT GUIDE: This guide to 17,025 picture books for preschool children through second graders is cataloged under 1,225 subjects. The guide reflects the arrangement in the Subject Headings—alphabetical by subject heading and subheading. Many books, of course, relate to more than one subject, and this comprehensive list provides a means of identifying all those books that may contain any information or material on a particular subject.

If, for example, the user wants books on crabs (crustaceans), the Subject Headings section will show that Crustaceans is a subject classification. A look in the Subject Guide reveals that under Crustaceans there are 2 titles listed alphabetically by author, plus an additional 17 titles under 4 related subheadings.

For ease of access to the extensive list of subjects, many headings are organized in groupings:

Activities	Emotions	Musical instruments
Anatomy	Ethnic groups in the U.S.	Mythical creatures
Animals	Family life	Religion
Behavior	Foreign lands	Reptiles
Birds	Format, unusual	Royalty
Careers	Furniture	Seasons
Character traits	Holidays	Senses
Clothing	Illness	Sports
Concepts	Indians of North America	Toys
Disabilities	Insects	Weather

Using the list of Subject Headings, a teacher can examine the general subject Activities and see topics such as driving, flying, hiking, jumping, running, traveling, and walking to select books for a program on motion. Or a parent can look through the list of Careers to plan a home-schooling lesson on jobs and work. A librarian might explore the books in Ethnic Groups in the U.S. and find African Americans and then organize programming for Black History Month.

Two of the most-used groupings in the Subject Headings list are Behavior and Character Traits. These two areas contain subtopics such as Behavior – boredom, Behavior – bullying, teasing, Behavior – fighting, arguing, Behavior – sharing, Character traits – helpfulness, Character traits – individuality, Character traits – shyness, and Character traits – vanity. They are the "go to" headings for programs on character development and conduct. Cross-references have been generated for all of the subtopics for Behavior and Character Traits.

BIBLIOGRAPHIC GUIDE: Each book is listed with full bibliographic information. This section is arranged alphabetically by author, or by title when the author is unknown, or by uniform (classic) title. Each entry contains bibliographic information in order: author, title, illustrator, publisher and date of publication, miscellaneous notes when given, International Standard Book Number (ISBN), and subjects, listed according to the alphabetical classification in the Subject Headings section.

The user can consult the Bibliographic Guide to find complete data on each of the titles listed in the Subject Guide. Turning from the Subject Guide subheading of Insects – bees to consult the Bibliographic Guide, for example, the user will find the following entry:

Formento, Alison. *These bees count!* ill. by Sarah Snow. Whitman, 2012. ISBN 978-080757868-1
Subj: Counting, numbers. Insects – bees. School – field trips.

In the case of joint authors, the second author is listed in alphabetical order, followed by the book title and the name of the primary author or main entry. The user can then locate the primary author for complete bibliographic information. For example:

Hamilton, Emma Walton. *The very fairy princess* (Andrews, Julie)

Bibliographic information for this title will be found in the Bibliographic Guide section under Andrews, Julie.

Titles for an author who is both a single author and a joint author are interfiled alphabetically. Where the author is not known, the entry is listed alphabetically by title with complete bibliographic information following the same format as given above.

TITLE INDEX: This section contains an alphabetical list of all titles in the book with authors in parentheses where appropriate, followed by the page number of the full listing in the Bibliographic Guide, such as:

Duck sock hop (Kohuth, Jane), 763

For books with the same title, for example, *The Three Bears,* one title is listed as a guide to the page in the Bibliographic Guide with all of the matching titles and full bibliographic information.

The three bears (The three bears), 1014

Variant titles are included with the relevant page numbers in the Bibliographic Guide. And, in this example, users would also want to check for related books beginning with Goldilocks.

The three bears [board book] (The three bears), 1014
The three bears ABC (Maccarone, Grace), 803
The 3 bears and Goldilocks (The three bears), 1014
The Three Bears' Christmas (Duval, Kathy), 624
The Three Bears' Halloween (Duval, Kathy), 624
The three bears holiday rhyme book (Yolen, Jane), 1070

Ultimately, the Title Index guides the reader to the full bibliographic information in the Bibliographic Index.

ILLUSTRATOR INDEX: This section contains an alphabetical list of illustrators with titles, author names in parentheses, and the page number of the full listing in the Bibliographic Guide. For example:

Porter, Jane. *Duck sock hop* (Kohuth, Jane), 763

Titles listed under an illustrator's name appear in alphabetical sequence. When the author is the same as the illustrator the author's name is not repeated.

Acknowledgments

The author wishes to express her thanks for the assistance provided by many people in bringing this book together. Special thanks to Barbara Ittner of Libraries Unlimited, to series editor Catherine Barr, and to Christine McNaull, who looked after the database, sorting, and typesetting and provided invaluable help with the editing.

Subject Headings

Main headings, subheadings, and cross-references are arranged alphabetically and provide a quick reference to the subjects used in the Subject Guide section, where author and title names appear under appropriate headings. For more information on how subjects are grouped, see Preface p. ix.

Animals – donkeys
Animals – elephants
Animals – endangered animals
Animals – ferrets
Animals – foxes
Animals – gerbils
Animals – giraffes
Animals – goats
Animals – gorillas
Animals – groundhogs
Animals – guinea pigs
Animals – hamsters
Animals – hedgehogs
Animals – hippopotamuses
Animals – horses, ponies
Animals – hyenas
Animals – jackals
Animals – jaguars
Animals – kangaroos
Animals – kindness to *see* Character traits – kindness to animals
Animals – koalas
Animals – lemurs
Animals – leopards
Animals – lions
Animals – llamas
Animals – lorises
Animals – lynx
Animals – manatees
Animals – marsupials
Animals – meerkats
Animals – mice
Animals – migration *see* Migration
Animals – moles
Animals – mongooses
Animals – monkeys
Animals – moose
Animals – mountain lions *see* Animals – cougars
Animals – mules
Animals – muskoxen
Animals – muskrats
Animals – octopuses *see* Octopuses
Animals – opossums *see* Animals – possums
Animals – orangutans
Animals – otters
Animals – oxen
Animals – pack rats
Animals – pandas
Animals – panthers *see* Animals – leopards
Animals – pigs
Animals – platypuses
Animals – polar bears
Animals – porcupines
Animals – possums
Animals – prairie dogs
Animals – prairie wolves *see* Animals – coyotes
Animals – pumas *see* Animals – cougars
Animals – rabbits
Animals – raccoons
Animals – rats
Animals – reindeer
Animals – rhinoceros
Animals – salamanders *see* Reptiles – salamanders
Animals – sea lions
Animals – seals
Animals – service animals
Animals – sheep
Animals – shrews
Animals – skunks
Animals – sloths
Animals – slugs
Animals – snails
Animals – snow leopards *see* Animals – leopards
Animals – squid *see* Squid
Animals – squirrels
Animals – swine *see* Animals – pigs
Animals – Tasmanian devils
Animals – tigers
Animals – voles
Animals – wallabies
Animals – walruses
Animals – warthogs
Animals – weasels
Animals – whales
Animals – wolves
Animals – wombats
Animals – woolly mammoths
Animals – worms
Animals – yaks
Animals – zebras
Anti-violence *see* Violence, nonviolence
Apartments *see* Homes, houses
Appearance *see* Character traits – appearance
Aquariums
Arachnids *see* Spiders
Arithmetic *see* Counting, numbers
Art
Assertiveness *see* Character traits – assertiveness
Astrology *see* Zodiac
Astronauts *see* Careers – astronauts; Space & space ships
Astronomy
Aurora Borealis *see* Northern lights
Australian aborigines
Authors *see* Careers – writers
Authors, children *see* Children as authors
Automobiles
Autumn *see* Seasons – fall
Award-winning books *see* Caldecott award books; Caldecott award honor books

Babies *see also* Animals – babies
Babies, new *see* Family life – new sibling
Bad day *see* Behavior – bad day
Ballerinas *see* Ballet; Careers – dancing
Ballet
Balloons *see* Toys – balloons
Balls *see* Toys – balls
Barns
Beaches *see* Sea & seashore – beaches
Beasts *see* Monsters
Beauty shops
Bedtime
Bedwetting *see* Behavior – bedwetting
Behavior
Behavior – animals, dislike of
Behavior – arguing *see* Behavior – fighting, arguing
Behavior – bad day
Behavior – bedwetting
Behavior – boasting
Behavior – boredom
Behavior – bossy
Behavior – bullying, teasing
Behavior – carelessness
Behavior – cheating
Behavior – collecting things
Behavior – disbelief
Behavior – dissatisfaction
Behavior – fidgeting
Behavior – fighting, arguing
Behavior – forgetfulness
Behavior – forgiving
Behavior – gossip
Behavior – greed
Behavior – growing up
Behavior – hiding
Behavior – hiding things
Behavior – hurrying
Behavior – imitation
Behavior – indecision
Behavior – indifference
Behavior – lost
Behavior – lost & found possessions
Behavior – lying
Behavior – messy
Behavior – misbehavior
Behavior – mistakes
Behavior – misunderstanding
Behavior – name calling

Careers – harpists
Careers – housekeepers
Careers – illustrators
Careers – inventors
Careers – janitors *see* Careers – custodians, janitors
Careers – jockeys
Careers – journalists
Careers – judges
Careers – lawyers
Careers – librarians
Careers – lifeguards
Careers – lumberjacks
Careers – magicians
Careers – mail carriers *see* Careers – postal workers
Careers – mathematicians
Careers – mayors
Careers – mechanics
Careers – messengers
Careers – meteorologists
Careers – migrant workers
Careers – military
Careers – miners
Careers – motion picture producers
Careers – musicians
Careers – nuns
Careers – nurses
Careers – oceanographers
Careers – opticians, optometrists
Careers – ornithologists
Careers – painters *see* Careers – artists
Careers – paleontologists
Careers – park rangers
Careers – peddlers
Careers – pharmacists
Careers – photographers
Careers – physicians *see* Careers – doctors
Careers – plasterers
Careers – poets
Careers – police officers
Careers – postal workers
Careers – potters
Careers – preachers *see* Careers – clergy
Careers – principals *see* Careers – school principals
Careers – printers
Careers – race car drivers
Careers – railroad engineers
Careers – ranchers
Careers – rangers *see* Careers – park rangers
Careers – sailors *see* Careers – military; Sailors
Careers – salespeople
Careers – sanitation workers
Careers – school principals
Careers – scientists
Careers – sculptors
Careers – seamstresses
Careers – shepherds
Careers – sheriffs
Careers – shoe shiners
Careers – shoemakers
Careers – singers
Careers – soldiers *see* Careers – military
Careers – storekeepers
Careers – tailors
Careers – teachers
Careers – toy makers
Careers – train engineers *see* Careers – railroad engineers
Careers – truck drivers
Careers – veterinarians
Careers – waiters, waitresses
Careers – weather reporters *see* Careers – meteorologists
Careers – weavers
Careers – window cleaners
Careers – woodcarvers
Careers – writers
Careers – zookeepers
Carelessness *see* Behavior – carelessness
Caribou *see* Animals – reindeer
Carnivals *see* Fairs, festivals
Carousels *see* Merry-go-rounds
Cars *see* Automobiles
Castles
Caterpillars *see* Insects – butterflies, caterpillars
Cave drawings *see* Petroglyphs
Cave dwellers
Caves
Centipedes *see* Crustaceans – centipedes, millipedes
Chanukah *see* Holidays – Hanukkah
Character traits
Character traits – ambition
Character traits – appearance
Character traits – assertiveness
Character traits – being different
Character traits – bravery
Character traits – cleanliness
Character traits – cleverness
Character traits – clumsiness
Character traits – completing things
Character traits – compromising
Character traits – conceit
Character traits – confidence
Character traits – cooperation
Character traits – courage *see* Character traits – bravery
Character traits – cruelty to animals *see* Character traits – kindness to animals
Character traits – curiosity
Character traits – flattery
Character traits – foolishness
Character traits – fortune *see* Character traits – luck
Character traits – freedom
Character traits – generosity
Character traits – helpfulness
Character traits – honesty
Character traits – hopefulness
Character traits – incentive *see* Character traits – ambition
Character traits – individuality
Character traits – kindness
Character traits – kindness to animals
Character traits – laziness
Character traits – loyalty
Character traits – luck
Character traits – meanness
Character traits – optimism
Character traits – orderliness
Character traits – ostracism *see* Character traits – being different
Character traits – patience
Character traits – perfectionism
Character traits – perseverance
Character traits – persistence
Character traits – practicality
Character traits – pride
Character traits – questioning
Character traits – responsibility
Character traits – selfishness
Character traits – shyness
Character traits – smallness
Character traits – stubbornness
Character traits – vanity
Character traits – willfulness
Character traits – wisdom
Cheating *see* Behavior – cheating
Cheerleading
Cherubs *see* Angels
Child abuse
Children as authors
Children as illustrators
Children as inventors
Circular tales
Circus
Cities, towns
Cleanliness *see* Character traits – cleanliness
Cleverness *see* Character traits – cleverness
Cloaks *see* Clothing – coats
Clocks, watches
Clothing

Emotions – sadness
Emotions – unhappiness *see* Emotions – happiness; Emotions – sadness
Engineered books *see* Format, unusual – toy & movable books
Entertainment *see* Theater
Environment *see* Ecology
Eskimos *see also* Indians of North America – Inuit
Ethnic groups in the U.S.
Ethnic groups in the U.S. – Acadians *see* Ethnic groups in the U.S. – Cajuns
Ethnic groups in the U.S. – African Americans
Ethnic groups in the U.S. – Amish
Ethnic groups in the U.S. – Arab Americans
Ethnic groups in the U.S. – Asian Americans
Ethnic groups in the U.S. – Black Americans *see* Ethnic groups in the U.S. – African Americans
Ethnic groups in the U.S. – Cajuns
Ethnic groups in the U.S. – Cambodian Americans
Ethnic groups in the U.S. – Chinese Americans
Ethnic groups in the U.S. – Cuban Americans
Ethnic groups in the U.S. – East Indian Americans
Ethnic groups in the U.S. – Filipino Americans
Ethnic groups in the U.S. – French Americans
Ethnic groups in the U.S. – German Americans
Ethnic groups in the U.S. – Greek Americans
Ethnic groups in the U.S. – Guatemalan Americans
Ethnic groups in the U.S. – Hispanic Americans
Ethnic groups in the U.S. – Hmong Americans
Ethnic groups in the U.S. – Hungarian Americans
Ethnic groups in the U.S. – Irish Americans
Ethnic groups in the U.S. – Italian Americans
Ethnic groups in the U.S. – Jamaican Americans
Ethnic groups in the U.S. – Japanese Americans
Ethnic groups in the U.S. – Jewish Americans *see* Jewish culture
Ethnic groups in the U.S. – Korean Americans
Ethnic groups in the U.S. – Lebanese Americans
Ethnic groups in the U.S. – Mexican Americans
Ethnic groups in the U.S. – Pakistani Americans
Ethnic groups in the U.S. – Puerto Rican Americans
Ethnic groups in the U.S. – Russian Americans
Ethnic groups in the U.S. – Shakers
Ethnic groups in the U.S. – Sudanese Americans
Ethnic groups in the U.S. – Swedish Americans
Ethnic groups in the U.S. – Tibetan Americans
Ethnic groups in the U.S. – Vietnamese Americans
Etiquette
Evening *see* Twilight
Exercise *see* Health & fitness – exercise
Experiments *see* Science
Extraterrestrial beings *see* Aliens
Eye glasses *see* Glasses
Eyes *see* Anatomy – eyes; Glasses; Disabilities – blindness; Senses – sight

Fables *see* Folk & fairy tales
Fairies
Fairs, festivals
Fairy tales *see* Folk & fairy tales
Family life
Family life – aunts, uncles
Family life – brothers *see also* Family life; Family life – brothers & sisters; Sibling rivalry
Family life – brothers & sisters
Family life – cousins
Family life – daughters
Family life – fathers
Family life – grandfathers
Family life – grandmothers
Family life – grandparents
Family life – great-grandparents
Family life – mothers
Family life – new sibling
Family life – only child
Family life – parents
Family life – same-sex parents
Family life – single-parent families
Family life – sisters *see also* Family life; Family life – brothers & sisters; Sibling rivalry
Family life – sons
Family life – stepchildren *see* Divorce; Family life – stepfamilies
Family life – stepfamilies
Family life – stepparents *see* Divorce; Family life – stepfamilies
Farms
Feathers
Feeling *see* Senses – touch
Feelings *see* Emotions
Fidgeting *see* Behavior – fidgeting
Fighting, arguing *see* Behavior – fighting, arguing
Fingers *see* Anatomy – hands
Finishing things *see* Character traits – completing things
Fire
Fire engines *see* Careers – firefighters; Trucks
Fish
Fish – seahorses
Fish – sharks
Fitness *see* Health & fitness
Flags
Flattery *see* Character traits – flattery
Flowers
Flowers – roses
Fold-out books *see* Format, unusual – toy & movable books
Folk & fairy tales
Folk & fairy tales – pourquoi tales
Food
Foolishness *see* Character traits – foolishness
Foreign lands
Foreign lands – Afghanistan
Foreign lands – Africa
Foreign lands – Antarctic
Foreign lands – Arabia
Foreign lands – Arctic
Foreign lands – Argentina
Foreign lands – Armenia
Foreign lands – Asia
Foreign lands – Australia
Foreign lands – Austria
Foreign lands – Bangladesh
Foreign lands – Bavaria *see* Foreign lands – Austria; Foreign lands – Germany
Foreign lands – Belarus

Handicaps *see* Disabilities
Hares *see* Animals – rabbits
Hawaii
Health & fitness
Health & fitness – exercise
Health & safety
Hearing *see* Anatomy – ears; Disabilities – deafness; Senses – hearing
Heat *see* Concepts – cold & heat
Heavy equipment *see* Machines
Helicopters
Helpfulness *see* Character traits – helpfulness
Hens *see* Birds – chickens
Hibernation
Hiccups
Hiding *see* Behavior – hiding
Hiding things *see* Behavior – hiding things
Hieroglyphics
Hobby horses *see* Toys – rocking horses
Hogs *see* Animals – pigs
Holidays
Holidays – April Fools' Day
Holidays – Chanukah *see* Holidays – Hanukkah
Holidays – Chinese New Year
Holidays – Christmas
Holidays – Cinco de Mayo
Holidays – Day of the Dead
Holidays – Divali
Holidays – Earth Day
Holidays – Easter
Holidays – Father's Day
Holidays – Fourth of July
Holidays – Groundhog Day
Holidays – Halloween
Holidays – Hanukkah
Holidays – Independence Day *see* Holidays – Fourth of July
Holidays – Juneteenth
Holidays – Kwanzaa
Holidays – Mardi Gras *see* Mardi Gras
Holidays – May Day
Holidays – Memorial Day
Holidays – Mother's Day
Holidays – New Year's
Holidays – Passover
Holidays – Purim
Holidays – Ramadan
Holidays – Rosh Hashanah
Holidays – Rosh Kodesh
Holidays – Seder
Holidays – Shavuot
Holidays – St. Patrick's Day
Holidays – Sukkot
Holidays – Thanksgiving
Holidays – Tu B'Shevat
Holidays – Valentine's Day
Holidays – Yom Kippur
Holocaust
Homeless
Homes, houses
Homework
Homosexuality
Honesty *see* Character traits – honesty
Honey bees *see* Insects – bees
Hope *see* Character traits – hopefulness
Hopefulness *see* Character traits – hopefulness
Horses, rocking *see* Toys – rocking horses
Hospitals
Hotels
Hugging
Humorous stories
Hurrying *see* Behavior – hurrying
Hygiene *see also* Character traits – cleanliness; Health & fitness

Identity *see* Self-concept
Illness
Illness – AIDS
Illness – alcoholism
Illness – allergies
Illness – Alzheimer's
Illness – asthma
Illness – cancer
Illness – chicken pox
Illness – cold (disease)
Illness – diabetes
Illness – epilepsy
Illness – influenza
Illness – mental illness
Illness – poliomyelitis
Illness – tonsillectomy
Imagination
Imagination – imaginary friends
Imitation *see* Behavior – imitation
Immigrants
Incentive *see* Character traits – ambition
Indecision *see* Behavior – indecision
Independence Day *see* Holidays – Fourth of July
Indians of Central America – Maya
Indians of Central America – Taino
Indians of North America
Indians of North America – Algonquin
Indians of North America – Aztec
Indians of North America – Blackfoot
Indians of North America – Cherokee
Indians of North America – Cheyenne (Sioux)
Indians of North America – Chippewa
Indians of North America – Choctaw
Indians of North America – Chumash
Indians of North America – Comanche
Indians of North America – Cree
Indians of North America – Creek
Indians of North America – Crow
Indians of North America – Dakota (Sioux)
Indians of North America – Goshute
Indians of North America – Great Basin
Indians of North America – Great Plains
Indians of North America – Haida
Indians of North America – Hopi
Indians of North America – Huichol
Indians of North America – Inuit
Indians of North America – Iroquois
Indians of North America – Kato
Indians of North America – Lakota
Indians of North America – Lakota (Sioux)
Indians of North America – Lenape
Indians of North America – Metis
Indians of North America – Miwok
Indians of North America – Mohawk
Indians of North America – Muskogee
Indians of North America – Narragansett
Indians of North America – Navajo
Indians of North America – Nez Perce
Indians of North America – Ojibwa

Mistakes *see* Behavior – mistakes
Misunderstanding *see* Behavior – misunderstanding
Mittens *see* Clothing – gloves, mittens
Money
Monsters
Months of the year *see* Days of the week, months of the year
Moon
Mopeds *see* Motorcycles
Morning
Mother Goose *see* Nursery rhymes
Motion picture producers *see* Careers – motion picture producers
Motorcycles
Mountain climbing *see* Sports – mountain climbing
Mountain lions *see* Animals – cougars
Mountains
Moving
Multi-ethnic *see* Ethnic groups in the U.S.
Multiple births – triplets
Multiple births – twins
Mummies
Muppets *see* Puppets
Museums
Music
Musical instruments
Musical instruments – accordions
Musical instruments – bagpipes
Musical instruments – bands
Musical instruments – banjos
Musical instruments – cellos
Musical instruments – drums
Musical instruments – Fiddles *see* Musical instruments – violins
Musical instruments – flutes
Musical instruments – guitars
Musical instruments – harmonicas
Musical instruments – harps
Musical instruments – lutes
Musical instruments – orchestras
Musical instruments – pianos
Musical instruments – saxophones
Musical instruments – trombones
Musical instruments – trumpets
Musical instruments – tubas
Musical instruments – violins
Mystery stories
Mythical creatures
Mythical creatures – aliens *see* Aliens
Mythical creatures – elves
Mythical creatures – genies
Mythical creatures – gnomes
Mythical creatures – goblins
Mythical creatures – leprechauns
Mythical creatures – lutins
Mythical creatures – mermaids, mermen
Mythical creatures – ogres
Mythical creatures – Pegasus
Mythical creatures – phoenix
Mythical creatures – pixies
Mythical creatures – pooka spirit
Mythical creatures – trolls
Mythical creatures – unicorns
Mythical creatures – werewolves

Name calling *see* Behavior – name calling
Names
Napping *see* Sleep
Native Americans *see* Eskimos; Indians of Central America; Indians of North America; Indians of South America
Nature
Naughty *see* Behavior – misbehavior
Needing someone *see* Behavior – needing someone
Negotiation *see* Activities – trading
Neighborhoods *see* Communities, neighborhoods
Netherlands *see* Foreign lands – Holland
Night
Nightmares *see also* Bedtime; Monsters; Mythical creatures – goblins; Night; Sleep
No text *see* Wordless
Noise, sounds
Noise, sounds – snoring *see* Sleep – snoring
Nomads
North Pole *see* Foreign lands – Arctic
Northern lights
Noses *see* Anatomy – noses; Senses – smell
Numbers *see* Counting, numbers
Nursery rhymes
Nursery school *see* School – nursery
Occupations *see* Careers
Oceans *see* Sea & seashore
Octopuses
Odors *see* Senses – smell
Oil
Old age
Opossums *see* Animals – possums
Optical illusions
Optimism *see* Character traits – optimism
Orderliness *see* Character traits – orderliness
Orphans
Outer space *see* Space & space ships

Pageants *see* Theater
Painters *see* Activities – painting; Careers – artists
Panthers *see* Animals – leopards
Paper
Parades
Parks
Parks – amusement
Parrots *see* Birds – parakeets, parrots
Participation
Parties
Patience *see* Character traits – patience
Pen pals
Perfectionism *see* Character traits – perfectionism
Perseverance *see* Character traits – perseverance
Persistence *see* Character traits – persistence
Petroglyphs
Petroleum *see* Oil
Pets
Physicians *see* Careers – doctors
Picture puzzles
Pilgrims
Pioneer life *see* U.S. history – frontier & pioneer life
Pirates
Planes *see* Airplanes, airports
Planets
Plants
Plays *see* Theater
Pockets *see* Clothing
Poetry
Poltergeists *see* Ghosts
Ponds *see* Lakes, ponds
Ponies *see* Animals – horses, ponies
Poor *see* Homeless; Poverty
Pop-up books *see* Format, unusual – toy & movable books

Siblings *see* Family life – brothers; Family life – brothers & sisters; Family life – sisters; Family life – stepfamilies
Sickness *see* Health & fitness; Illness
Sight *see* Anatomy – eyes; Glasses; Disabilities – blindness; Senses – sight
Sign language
Signs
Singers *see* Careers – singers
Sioux Indians *see* Indians of North America – Cheyenne (Sioux); Indians of North America – Dakota (Sioux); Indians of North America – Sioux
Sisters *see* Family life – brothers; Family life – brothers & sisters; Family life – sisters; Sibling rivalry
Skating *see* Sports – ice skating; Sports – hockey; Sports – roller skating
Sky
Slavery
Sleep
Sleep – snoring
Sleepovers
Sleight-of-hand *see* Magic
Smallness *see* Character traits – smallness
Smell *see* Anatomy – noses; Senses – smell
Smiles, smiling *see* Anatomy – faces
Snoring *see* Noise, sounds; Sleep – snoring
Snow *see* Weather – blizzards; Weather – snow
Snow plows *see* Machines
Snowmen
Society Islands *see* Foreign lands – South Sea Islands
Soldiers *see* Careers – military
Soldiers, toy *see* Toys – soldiers
Solitude *see* Behavior – solitude
Songs
Sorcerers *see* Wizards
Sounds *see* Noise, sounds
South Pole *see* Foreign lands – Antarctic
Space & space ships
Spectacles *see* Glasses
Speech *see* Disabilities – stuttering; Language
Spelunking *see* Caves
Spiders
Split page books *see* Format, unusual
Spooks *see* Ghosts; Mythical creatures – goblins
Sports
Sports – archery
Sports – baseball
Sports – basketball
Sports – bicycling
Sports – bowling
Sports – boxing
Sports – camping *see* Camps, camping
Sports – fishing
Sports – football
Sports – golf
Sports – gymnastics
Sports – hiking
Sports – hockey
Sports – hunting
Sports – ice skating
Sports – jumping rope
Sports – karate
Sports – martial arts
Sports – mountain climbing
Sports – Olympics
Sports – racing
Sports – roller skating
Sports – sailing
Sports – skateboarding
Sports – skiing
Sports – skin diving
Sports – sledding
Sports – soccer
Sports – Special Olympics
Sports – surfing
Sports – swimming
Sports – T-ball
Sports – Tae Kwon Do
Sports – tennis
Sports – volleyball
Sports – wrestling
Sportsmanship
Squid
Stage *see* Theater
Stars
Stealing *see* Behavior – stealing; Crime
Steam shovels *see* Machines
Steamrollers *see* Machines
Step families *see* Divorce; Family life – stepfamilies
Stepchildren *see* Divorce; Family life – stepfamilies
Stepparents *see* Divorce; Family life – stepfamilies
Stones *see* Rocks
Stores
Stories in rhyme *see* Rhyming text
Strangers *see* Behavior – talking to strangers
Streams *see* Rivers
Streets *see* Roads
String
Stubbornness *see* Character traits – stubbornness
Submarines *see* Boats, ships
Sullivan Islands *see* Foreign lands – South Sea Islands
Sun
Superstition
Swamps
Swapping *see* Activities – trading
Symbiosis

Talking to strangers *see* Behavior – talking to strangers
Tall tales
Tardiness *see* Behavior – promptness, tardiness
Taxis
Teasing *see* Behavior – bullying, teasing
Teddy bears *see* Toys – bears
Teeth
Telephone
Television
Telling stories *see* Activities – storytelling
Telling time *see* Clocks, watches; Time
Temper tantrums *see* Emotions – anger
Texas
Textless *see* Wordless
Theater
Thieves *see* Crime
Thumb sucking
Thunder *see* Weather – lightning, thunder; Weather – storms
Time
Tin soldiers *see* Toys – soldiers
Toads *see* Frogs & toads
Toilet training
Toilets
Tongue twisters
Tools
Tooth fairy *see* Fairies; Teeth
Tortoises *see* Reptiles – turtles, tortoises
Towns *see* Cities, towns
Toy & movable books *see* Format, unusual – toy & movable books
Toys
Toys – balloons
Toys – balls
Toys – bears
Toys – blocks
Toys – dolls
Toys – rocking horses
Toys – soldiers

Subject Guide

This is a subject-arranged guide to picture books. Under appropriate subject headings and subheadings, titles appear alphabetically by author name, or by title when author is unknown. Complete bibliographic information for each title cited will be found in the Bibliographic Guide.

ABC books

ABC school riddles
Abrams, Pam. *Now I eat my ABC's*
Ada, Alma Flor. *Gathering the sun*
Agee, Jon. *Z goes home*
Alberti, Theresa Jarosz. *Vietnam ABCs*
Alda, Arlene. *Arlene Alda's ABC*
Alko, Selina. *B is for Brooklyn*
Allen, Susan. *Read anything good lately?*
Used any numbers lately?
Anno, Mitsumasa. *Anno's alphabet*
Archer, Peggy. *Name that dog!*
Arnosky, Jim. *Mouse letters*
Mouse numbers and letters
Mouse writing
Ashley Bryan's ABC of African American poetry
Ashman, Linda. *M is for mischief*
Aylesworth, Jim. *The folks in the valley*
Little Bitty Mousie
Old Black Fly
Azarian, Mary. *A gardener's alphabet*
Babypants, Caspar. *Augie to zebra*
Baker, Alan. *Black and White Rabbit's ABC*
Baker, Keith. *LMNO peas*
Barron, Rex. *Fed up!*
Base, Graeme. *Animalia*
Basher, Simon. *ABC kids*
Baskin, Leonard. *Hosie's alphabet*
Bataille, Marion. *ABC3D*
Bayer, Jane. *A my name is Alice*
Bea, Holly. *My spiritual alphabet book*
Beaton, Clare. *Zoë and her zebra*
Belle, Jennifer. *Animal stackers*
Berenstain, Stan and Jan. *The Berenstains' B book*
Bingham, Kelly. *Z is for Moose*
Blackstone, Stella. *Alligator alphabet*
Cleo's alphabet book
Bleiman, Andrew. *ABC zooborns!*
Boldt, Mike. *123 versus ABC*
Bottner, Barbara. *An annoying ABC*
Brennan-Nelson, Denise. *J is for jack-o-lantern*
Bridwell, Norman. *Clifford's ABC*
Bronson, Linda. *The circus alphabet*
Brown, Marc. *Arthur's animal adventure*
Brown, Margaret Wise. *Goodnight moon ABC*
Sleepy ABC, ill. by Karen Katz
Sleepy ABC, ill. by Esphyr Slobodkina
Bruchac, Joseph. *Many nations*
Bruel, Nick. *Bad Kitty*
Poor puppy
Brunhoff, Laurent de. *B is for Babar*
Babar's ABC
Bryant, Megan E. *Alphasaurus*
Burnard, Damon. *I spy in the ocean*
Burningham, John. *First steps*
Butler, Dori Hillestad. *F is for firefighting*
C is for caboose
Cabatingan, Erin. *A is for Musk Ox*
Caldicott, Chris. *World food alphabet*
Capucilli, Alyssa Satin. *Mrs. McTats and her houseful of cats*
Carlson, Nancy. *ABC, I like me!*
Catalanotto, Peter. *Matthew A.B.C.*
Charlip, Remy, et al. *Handtalk*
Chin-Lee, Cynthia. *A is for Asia*
Chung, Hyechong. *K is for Korea*
Cleary, Beverly. *The hullabaloo ABC*
Cleary, Brian P. *Peanut butter and jellyfishes*
Cline-Ransome, Lesa. *Quilt alphabet*
Compestine, Ying Chang. *D is for dragon dance*
Crane, Carol. *D is for dancing dragon*
Crews, Donald. *We read*
Cronin, Doreen. *Click, clack, quackity-quack*
Czekaj, Jef. *A call for a new alphabet*
Day, Nancy Raines. *A is for alliguitar*
Delessert, Etienne. *A was an apple pie*
Demarest, Chris L. *All aboard! a traveling alphabet*
Alpha Bravo Charlie
Firefighters A to Z
DeRubertis, Barbara. *Alexander Anteater's amazing act*
Bobby Baboon's banana be-bop
Dilly Dog's dizzy dancing
De Vicq de Cumptich, Roberto. *Bembo's zoo*
DiTerlizzi, Tony. *G is for one gzonk!*
Dodd, Emma. *Dog's ABC*
Domeniconi, David. *M is for masterpiece*
Doodler, Todd H. *The zoo I drew*
Downie, Mary Alice. *A pioneer ABC*
Downing, Johnette. *Amazon alphabet*

Doyle, Charlotte Lackner. *The bouncing, dancing, galloping ABC*
Dragonwagon, Crescent. *All the awake animals are almost asleep*
Dugan, Joanne. *ABC NYC*
Eastman, P. D. *The alphabet book*
Ehlert, Lois. *Eating the alphabet*
Eichenberg, Fritz. *Ape in cape*
Elya, Susan Middleton. *F is for fiesta*
N is for Navidad
Engelbreit, Mary. *Mary Engelbreit's A merry little Christmas*
Ernst, Lisa Campbell. *The letters are lost!*
Eschbacher, Roger. *Nonsense! He yelled*
Evans, Nate. *Bang! Boom! Roar!*
Farley, Carol J. *The king's secret*
Faulkenberry, Lauren. *What do animals do on the weekend?*
Feelings, Muriel. *Jambo means hello*
Fisher, Valorie. *Ellsworth's extraordinary electric ears and other amazing alphabet anecdotes*
Fleming, Denise. *Alphabet under construction*
Shout! Shout it out!
Ford, Juwanda G. *K is for Kwanzaa*
Frampton, David. *My beastie book of ABC*
Franceschelli, Christopher. *Alphablock*
Frasier, Debra. *A fabulous fair alphabet*
Freymann, Saxton. *Food for thought*
Fuge, Charles. *Astonishing animal ABC*
Gaiman, Neil. *The dangerous alphabet*
Geisert, Arthur. *Country road ABC*
Gerstein, Mordicai. *The absolutely awful alphabet*
Girnis, Margaret. *ABC for you and me*
Golenbock, Peter. *ABCs of baseball*
Green, Dan. *Wild alphabet*
Grossman, Bill. *My little sister hugged an ape*
Haas, Jessie. *Appaloosa zebra*
Hague, Kathleen. *Alphabears*
Heder, Thyra. *Fraidyzoo*
Heller, Lora. *Sign language ABC*
Hepworth, Catherine. *ANTics! an alphabetical anthology*
Herzog, Brad. *G is for gold medal*
R is for race
Hoban, Tana. *A B See!*
26 letters and 99 cents
Hobbie, Holly. *Toot and Puddle, Puddle's ABC*
Hopkins, Lee Bennett. *Alphathoughts*
April, bubbles, chocolate
Horowitz, Dave. *Twenty-six pirates*
Twenty-six princesses
Howell, Will C. *Zoo flakes ABC*
Howland, Naomi. *ABCDrive!*
Hudes, Quiara Alegría. *Welcome to my neighborhood!*
Hughes, Langston. *The sweet and sour animal book*
Hughes, Shirley. *Alfie's ABC*
Hyman, Trina Schart. *A little alphabet*
Inkpen, Mick. *Kipper's A to Z*
Isadora, Rachel. *ABC pop!*
Janovitz, Marilyn. *A, B, see!*
Jocelyn, Marthe. *ABC x 3*
Johnson, Stephen T. *Alphabet city*
Johnston, Tony. *P is for piñata*
Jonas, Ann. *Aardvarks, disembark!*
Joubert, Beverly. *African animal alphabet*
Joyce, Susan. *ABC nature riddles*
Kabakov, Vladimir. *R is for Russia*
Kalman, Maira. *What Pete ate from A-Z*
Katz, Susan B. *ABC, baby me!*
Kelley, Marty. *Summer stinks*
Kellogg, Steven. *Aster Aardvark's alphabet adventures*
Kirk, David. *Miss Spider's ABC*
Kontis, Alethea. *Alpha oops!*
AlphaOops!
Krull, Kathleen. *M is for music*
Kutner, Merrily. *Z is for zombie*
Lauture, Denizé. *Running the road to ABC*
Lawlor, Laurie. *Muddy as a duck puddle and other American similes*
Layne, Steven L. *T is for teachers*
Lester, Mike. *A is for salad*
Lichtenheld, Tom. *E-mergency!*
Lindbergh, Reeve. *The awful aardvarks go to school*
Lionni, Leo. *The alphabet tree*
Lobel, Anita. *Alison's zinnia*
Animal antics: A to Z
Lobel, Arnold. *On Market Street*
London, Jonathan. *Do your ABC's, Little Brown Bear*
Maass, Robert. *A is for autumn*
McArthur, Meher. *An ABC of what art can be*
Maccarone, Grace. *The three bears ABC*
MacDonald, Ross. *Achoo! Bang! Crash!*
MacDonald, Suse. *Alphabatics*
Edward Lear's A was once an apple pie
McDonnell, Flora. *Flora McDonnell's ABC*
McGuirk, Leslie. *If rocks could sing*
McLean, Dirk. *Play mas'! a carnival ABC*
McLeod, Bob. *Super hero ABC*
McLimans, David. *Gone wild*
McNamara, Margaret. *Apples A to Z*
Major, Kevin. *Eh to zed?*
Marino, Gianna. *Zoopa*
Markes, Julie. *Sidewalk ABC*
Martin, Bill, Jr. *Chicka chicka boom boom*
Chicka chicka boom boom [board book]
Marzollo, Jean. *Baby's alphabet*
I spy A to Z
I spy little letters
Melmed, Laura Krauss. *Capital! Washington D.C. from A to Z*
New York, New York!
Merriam, Eve. *Halloween ABC*
Michaels, Pat. *W is for wind*
Milich, Zoran. *The city ABC book*
Minor, Wendell. *Yankee Doodle America*
Miranda, Anne. *Alphabet fiesta*
Pignic
Mitter, Matt. *ABC: alphabet rhymes*
Mora, Pat. *Marimba!*
Morales, Yuyi. *Just in case: a trickster tale and Spanish alphabet book*
Most, Bernard. *ABC T-Rex*
Moxley, Sheila. *ABCD an alphabet book of cats and dogs*
Mullins, Patricia. *V for vanishing*
Munari, Bruno. *ABC*
Murphy, Liz. *ABC doctor*
Murphy, Mary. *The Alphabet Keeper*
Murray, Alison. *Apple pie ABC*
Musgrove, Margaret. *Ashanti to Zulu*
Napier, Matt. *Z is for zamboni*
Nichol, Barbara. *Trunks all aboard*
Nickle, John. *Alphabet explosion!*
O'Connell, Rebecca. *Danny is done with diapers*
O'Connor, Jane. *Fancy Nancy's collection of fancy words*
O'Keefe, Susan Heyboer. *Hungry monster ABC*
Pallotta, Jerry. *The airplane alphabet book*

The construction alphabet book
F is for Fenway
The jet alphabet book
Parker, Marjorie Blain. *A paddling of ducks*
Paul, Ann Whitford. *Eight hands round*
Everything to spend the night . . . from A to Z
Pearle, Ida. *A child's day*
Pearson, Debora. *Alphabeep*
Pelham, David. *A is for animals*
Pelletier, David. *The graphic alphabet*
Petersham, Maud. *An American ABC*
Pfister, Marcus. *Animal ABC*
Rainbow fish ABC
Pomeroy, Diana. *Wildflower ABC*
Potter, Beatrix. *Peter Rabbit's ABC*
Raczka, Bob. *3-D ABC*
Raschka, Chris. *Talk to me about the alphabet*
Rash, Andy. *Agent A to Agent Z*
Reed, Lynn Rowe. *Pedro, his perro, and the alphabet sombrero*
Rey, H. A. *Curious George learns the alphabet*
Riehle, Mary Ann McCabe. *A is for airplane*
Rodriguez, Sonia. *T is for tutu*
Rogalski, Mark. *Tickets to ride*
Rogers, Jacqueline. *Kindergarten ABC*
Rose, Deborah Lee. *Into the A, B, sea*
Rosen, Michael J. *Avalanche*
Rosenberg, Liz. *A big and little alphabet*
Rosenthal, Amy Krouse. *Al Pha's bet*
Roth, Ruby. *V is for vegan*
Rumford, James. *Sequoyah*
There's a monster in the alphabet
Sabuda, Robert. *The Christmas alphabet*
Sanders, Marilyn. *What's your name?*
Sanders, Nancy. *D is for drinking gourd*
Sandved, Kjell Bloch. *The butterfly alphabet*
Schaefer, Carole Lexa. *ABCers*
Schaefer, Lola M. *Homes ABC*
Schafer, Kevin. *Penguins A B C*
Schnur, Steven. *Autumn*
Spring
Summer
Winter
Seeger, Laura Vaccaro. *The hidden alphabet*
Walter was worried
Sendak, Maurice. *Alligators all around*
Shahan, Sherry. *The jazzy alphabet*
Shannon, George. *Tomorrow's alphabet*
Shapiro, Zachary. *We're all in the same boat*
Shelby, Anne. *Potluck*
Shindler, Ramon. *Found alphabet*
Shoulders, Michael. *The ABC book of American homes*
D is for drum
Shulman, Mark. *A is for zebra*
Aa is for Aardvark
Siddals, Mary McKenna. *Compost stew*
Sierra, Judy. *Sleepy little alphabet*
There's a zoo in room 22
Slate, Joseph. *Miss Bindergarten celebrates the last day of kindergarten*
Miss Bindergarten gets ready for kindergarten
Miss Bindergarten has a wild day in kindergarten
Miss Bindergarten stays home from kindergarten
Miss Bindergarten takes a field trip with kindergarten
Sloat, Teri. *Patty's pumpkin patch*
Smith, Marie. *N is for our nation's capital*
S is for Smithsonian
Z is for zookeeper
Sneed, Brad. *Picture a letter*
Sobel, June. *Shiver me letters*
Spirin, Gennady. *A apple pie*
Spradlin, Michael P. *Baseball from A to Z*
Staake, Bob. *My little ABC book*
Stevenson, James. *Grandpa's great city tour*
Stewig, John Warren. *The animals watched*
Stock, Catherine. *Alexander's midnight snack*
Stone, Tanya Lee. *D is for dreidel*
Stutson, Caroline. *Prairie primer A to Z*
Sweet, Melissa. *Carmine*
Tapahonso, Luci. *Navajo ABC*
Teyssèdre, Fabienne. *Joseph wants to read*
Thurlby, Paul. *Paul Thurlby's alphabet*
Todd, Traci. *T is for tugboat*
Troll, Ray. *Sharkabet*
Tryon, Leslie. *Albert's alphabet*
Ulmer, Wendy. *A isn't for fox*
Vamos, Samantha R. *Alphabet trucks*
Van Allsburg, Chris. *The Z was zapped*
van Lieshout, Maria. *Backseat A-B-see*
Verstraete, Larry. *S is for scientists*
Vidrine, Beverly Barras. *Easter Day alphabet*
Viorst, Judith. *The alphabet from Z to A*
Waber, Bernard. *An anteater named Arthur*
Wallace, Nancy Elizabeth. *Alphabet house*
Walton, Rick. *So many bunnies*
Watson, Clyde. *Applebet*
Watterson, Carol. *An edible alphabet*
Wells, Rosemary. *Letters and sounds*
Max's ABC
Werner, Sharon. *Alphasaurs and other prehistoric types*
Wethered, Peggy. *Touchdown Mars!*
Whitehouse, Patricia. *Seasons ABC*
What's awake? A B C
Wilbur, Helen L. *Z is for Zeus*
Wilbur, Richard. *The disappearing alphabet*
Williams, Laura E. *ABC kids*
Wilner, Isabel. *A garden alphabet*
Winnie-the-Pooh's A B C
Wishinsky, Frieda. *Where are you, Bear?*
Wood, Audrey. *Alphabet adventure*
Alphabet rescue
Wormell, Christopher. *The new alphabet of animals*
Yolen, Jane. *All in the woodland early*
Young, Judy. *H is for hook*
Ziefert, Harriet. *ABC dentist*
Lights on Broadway
Zuckerman, Andrew. *Creature abc*

Aborigines, Australian *see* Australian aborigines

Abused children *see* Child abuse

Accidents

Bauer, Marion Dane. *Uh-oh! a lift-the-flap story*
Bond, Michael. *Paddington Bear goes to the hospital*
Brown, Marc. *D. W. thinks big [board book]*
Hurd, Thacher. *Santa Mouse and the ratdeer*
Lange, Willem. *John and Tom*
Luján, Jorge. *Sky blue accident / Accidente celeste*
Polacco, Patricia. *In Enzo's splendid gardens*
Proimos, James. *The best bike ride ever*

Pulver, Robin. *Axle Annie and the speed grump*
Rand, Gloria. *Baby in a basket*
Little Flower
Rylant, Cynthia. *Silver packages*
Singer, Marilyn. *Boo hoo boo-boo*
Sykes, Julie. *Careful, Santa*
Timmers, Leo. *Bang*
Wardlaw, Lee. *The chair where bear sits*
Weller, Frances Ward. *The angel of Mill Street*
Wild, Margaret. *The pocket dogs*
Wood, Audrey. *A cowboy Christmas*

Activities

Ajmera, Maya. *To be a kid*
Aliki. *All by myself!*
Overnight at Mary Bloom's
Allard, Harry. *The Stupids step out*
Arquette, Kerry. *What did you do today?*
Asch, Frank. *Like a windy day*
Barasch, Lynne. *Radio rescue*
Blackstone, Stella. *You and me*
Bowie, C. W. *Busy toes*
Boyd, Lizi. *I love Daddy*
I love Mommy
Bridges, Margaret Park. *Edna elephant*
Bush, Timothy. *Teddy bear, teddy bear*
Carle, Eric. *From head to toe*
Carlson, Nancy. *Look out kindergarten, here I come!*
Carluccio, Maria. *The sounds around town*
Carr, Jan. *Frozen noses*
Cauley, Lorinda Bryan. *Clap your hands*
Cocca-Leffler, Maryann. *Let it rain*
Time to say bye-bye
Crews, Nina. *A high, low, near, far, loud, quiet story*
Cronin, Doreen. *Wiggle*
Day, Alexandra. *Carl's sleepy afternoon*
Denim, Sue. *Make way for Dumb Bunnies*
Doyle, Malachy. *Well, a crocodile can!*
Falconer, Ian. *Olivia*
Faulkenberry, Lauren. *What do animals do on the weekend?*
Fitz-Gibbon, Sally. *Two shoes, blue shoes, new shoes!*
Franco, Betsy. *Summer beat*
Friend, Catherine. *Eddie the raccoon*
Funny Ruby
Gay, Marie-Louise. *Read me a story, Stella*
Gentieu, Penny. *Baby! Talk!*
George, Jean Craighead. *Morning, noon, and night*
Gerstein, Mordicai. *The man who walked between the towers*
Gibbons, Gail. *The missing maple syrup sap mystery*
Grindley, Sally. *Mucky Duck*
Haley, Amanda. *It's a baby's world*
Harper, Dan. *Sit, Truman*
Hayles, Marsha. *He saves the day*
Heidbreder, Robert. *Noisy poems for a busy day*
Hennessy, B. G. *Busy Dinah Dinosaur*
Herkert, Barbara. *Birds in your backyard*
Hindley, Judy. *What's in baby's morning*
Hines, Anna Grossnickle. *What can you do in the rain?*
What can you do in the snow?
What can you do in the sun?
What can you do in the wind?
Hooks, Bell. *Be boy buzz*
Hop a little, jump a little!
Hughes, Shirley. *Annie Rose is my little sister*
Isadora, Rachel. *Peekaboo morning [board book]*
Johnson, Angela. *Lottie Paris lives here*
Johnson, Doug. *Substitute teacher plans*
Johnson, Paul Brett. *The pig who ran a red light*
Jonas, Ann. *When you were a baby*
Kavanagh, Peter. *I love my mama*
Kerley, Barbara. *The world is waiting for you*
Koller, Jackie French. *Bouncing on the bed*
Kroll, Virginia L. *Boy, you're amazing!*
Lachner, Dorothea. *Smoky's special Easter present*
Lavis, Steve. *Jump!*
Lee, Ho Baek. *While we were out*
Levine, Abby. *Daddies give you horsey rides*
Lionni, Leo. *Let's make rabbits*
McGuirk, Leslie. *Tucker off his rocker*
McPhail, David. *Those can-do pigs*
McQuade, Jacqueline. *Good times with Teddy Bear*
Maitland, Barbara. *My bear and me*
Markes, Julie. *Good thing you're not an octopus!*
Martin, David. *Piggy and Dad*
Matheson, Christie. *Tap the magic tree*
Mayo, Margaret. *Stomp, dinosaur, stomp!*
Meyers, Susan. *Everywhere babies*
Mora, Pat. *Join hands!*
Most, Bernard. *A pair of protoceratops*
A trio of triceratops
Munsch, Robert N. *Up, up, down!*
Murkoff, Heidi Eisenberg. *What to expect at preschool*
Murphy, Mary. *I like it when . . .*
I like it when . . . [board book]
Some things change
My busy day
Newman, Lesléa. *Dogs, dogs, dogs*
Nobisso, Josephine. *The moon's lullaby*
Noble, Trinka Hakes. *The day Jimmy's boa ate the wash*
Numeroff, Laura Joffe. *Chimps don't wear glasses*
If you take a mouse to the movies
What puppies do best
O'Connor, Jane. *Ready, set, skip!*
O'Mara, Carmel. *Good morning*
Good night
Ormerod, Jan. *Who's whose?*
Paradis, Susan. *My Daddy*
Pearle, Ida. *A child's day*
Pilkey, Dav. *Make way for Dumb Bunnies*
Pomeroy, Diana. *Wildflower ABC*
Ray, Karen. *Sleep song*
Regan, Lara Jo. *A Winkle in time*
Reinen, Judy. *Bow wow*
Meow
Rhyme time around the day
Roberts, Bethany. *Fourth of July mice*
Rosenberry, Vera. *Run, jump, whiz, splash*
Rotner, Shelley. *What can you do?*
Rylant, Cynthia. *In November*
Samuels, Barbara. *Duncan and Dolores*
Scanlon, Elizabeth Garton. *All the world*
Schindel, John. *Busy penguins*
Schwartz, Amy. *The boys teams*
Senisi, Ellen B. *Hurray for pre-K!*
Seven spunky monkeys
Shields, Carol Diggory. *Day by day a week goes round*
Silbaugh, Elizabeth. *Raggedy Ann's birthday party book*
Simmons, Jane. *Daisy says, "Here we go round the mulberry bush"*
Simon, Francesca. *Toddler time*
Siomades, Lorianne. *Kangaroo and cricket*

Spetter, Jung-Hee. *Lily and Trooper's winter*
Spinelli, Eileen. *What do angels wear?*
Spinelli, Jerry. *My daddy and me*
Stanley, Mandy. *Bloomer, the dog you can play with*
Stevenson, James. *Rolling Rose*
Stock, Catherine. *Halloween monster*
Tafuri, Nancy. *Do not disturb*
Tirabosco, Tom. *At the same time*
Uff, Caroline. *Lulu's busy day*
Walsh, Melanie. *Do donkeys dance?*
Warnick, Elsa. *Bedtime*
Wells, Rosemary. *Night sounds, morning colors*
Willis, Jeanne. *Susan laughs*
Winch, John. *Keeping up with Grandma*
Wood, Audrey. *King Bidgood's in the bathtub*
Ziefert, Harriet. *A polar bear can swim*
Robin, where are you?
Rockheads
Toes have wiggles, kids have giggles
Zuckerberg, Randi. *Dot*

Activities – babysitting

Anderson, Peggy Perry. *Time for bed, the babysitter said*
Berenstain, Stan and Jan. *The Berenstain bears and the sitter*
Brown, Marc. *Arthur babysits*
Butler, M. Christina. *The special blankie*
Child, Lauren. *Clarice Bean, guess who's babysitting?*
Christelow, Eileen. *Five little monkeys trick-or-treat*
Day, Alexandra. *Carl's birthday*
Follow Carl!
Good dog, Carl
Fox, Mem. *Good night, sleep tight*
Gardner, Sally. *Mama, don't go out tonight*
Harris, Robie H. *Don't forget to come back*
Hughes, Shirley. *Don't want to go!*
Hunter, Dette. *38 ways to entertain your babysitter*
Johnson, Angela. *Shoes like Miss Alice's*
Joyce, William. *George shrinks*
Keller, Holly. *Geraldine and Mrs. Duffy*
Kromhout, Rindert. *Little Donkey and the baby-sitter*
McCourt, Lisa. *Chicken soup for little souls: The never-forgotten doll*
McNiff, Dawn. *Mommy's little monster*
Moss, Miriam. *A babysitter for Billy Bear*
Reagan, Jean. *How to babysit a grandpa*
Robbins, Beth. *Tom, Ally, and the baby-sitter*
Schwartz, Amy. *Willie and Uncle Bill*
Sendak, Maurice. *Outside over there*
Stewart, Amber. *No babysitters allowed*
Teague, Mark. *Baby tamer*
Urbanovic, Jackie. *Sitting duck*
Van Laan, Nancy. *Mama rocks, Papa sings*
Viorst, Judith. *The good-bye book*
Ward, Nick. *Don't eat the babysitter!*
Wardlaw, Lee. *Saturday night jamboree*
Wells, Rosemary. *Max's dragon shirt*
Shy Charles
Stanley and Rhoda
Weninger, Brigitte. *Davy in the middle*
Will you mind the baby, Davy?
Winthrop, Elizabeth. *Bear and Mrs. Duck*
Bear's Christmas surprise

Activities – baking, cooking

Ahlberg, Allan. *Hooray for bread*
Argueta, Jorge. *Arroz con leche / Rice pudding*
Guacamole
Sopa de frijoles: un poema para cocinar / Bean soup: a cooking poem
Tamalitos
Auch, Mary Jane. *The princess and the pizza*
Averbeck, Jim. *The market bowl*
Axelrod, Amy. *Pigs in the pantry*
Bailey, Linda. *Toads on toast*
Bastianich, Lidia. *Nonna tell me a story*
Nonna's birthday surprise
Beck, Andrea. *Elliot bakes a cake*
Best, Cari. *Easy as pie*
Blackstone, Stella. *Making minestrone*
Cartaya, Pablo. *Tina Cocolina*
Cazet, Denys. *The perfect pumpkin pie*
Chavarría-Cháirez, Becky. *Magda's tortillas / Las tortillas de Magada*
Christelow, Eileen. *Don't wake up Mama!*
Coffelt, Nancy. *Aunt Ant leaves through the leaves*
Compestine, Ying Chang. *Boy dumplings*
The runaway wok
The story of noodles
Cooper, Helen. *Delicious!*
A pipkin of pepper
Cousins, Lucy. *Maisy makes gingerbread*
Denise, Anika. *Pigs love potatoes*
dePaola, Tomie. *Pancakes for breakfast*
The popcorn book
DeRubertis, Barbara. *Lulu's lemonade*
Donohue, Dorothy. *Veggie soup*
Dooley, Norah. *Everybody serves soup*
Edwards, Pamela Duncan. *Warthogs in the kitchen*
Elya, Susan Middleton. *Eight animals bake a cake*
Emberley, Ed. *The red hen*
Erdrich, Louise. *The range eternal*
Ericsson, Jennifer A. *Out and about at the bakery*
Ernst, Lisa Campbell. *Little Red Riding Hood: a newfangled prairie tale*
Evans, Lezlie. *The bunnies' picnic*
Everitt, Betsy. *Mean soup*
Falwell, Cathryn. *Feast for ten*
Rainbow Stew
Fearnley, Jan. *Mr. Wolf and the three bears*
Mr. Wolf's pancakes
Florence, Tyler. *Tyler makes pancakes!*
Tyler makes spaghetti!
Fox, Christyan. *Count to ten, PiggyWiggy!*
Gibbons, Gail. *Apples*
The berry book
The too-great bread bake book
Glaser, Linda. *Mrs. Greenberg's messy Hanukkah*
Goldin, Barbara Diamond. *Cakes and miracles*
Gourley, Robbin. *Bring me some apples and I'll make you a pie*
Grey, Mini. *Ginger bear*
Hall, Margaret. *Corn*
Peanuts
Hartland, Jessie. *Bon appetit!*
Hassett, Ann. *Too many frogs!*
Head, Judith. *Mud soup*
Heath, Amy. *Sofie's role*
Hill, Eric. *Spot bakes a cake*
Hill, Mary. *Let's make pizza*
Let's make tacos
Holub, Joan. *The pizza that we made*
Hopkinson, Deborah. *Fannie in the kitchen*
Howe, James. *Houndsley and Catina*
Hunter, Dette. *38 ways to entertain your babysitter*

38 ways to entertain your grandparents
Iwai, Melissa. *Soup day*
Jackson, Kathryn. *Pantaloon*
Katzler, Eva. *Florentine and Pig*
Kimmel, Eric A. *Jack and the giant barbecue*
Kneen, Maggie. *Chocolate moose*
Krause, Ute. *Oscar and the very hungry dragon*
Laminack, Lester L. *Saturdays and teacakes*
Leonard, Marcia. *Food is fun!*
Lewin, Ted. *Big Jimmy's Kum Kau Chinese take out*
Lin, Grace. *Dim sum for everyone*
Lipson, Eden Ross. *Applesauce season*
The little red hen. *The little red hen*, ill. by Byron Barton
The little red hen, ill. by Emily Bolam
The little red hen, ill. by Paul Galdone
Little red hen
The little red hen, ill. by Jerry Pinkney
The little red hen, ill. by Kate Slater
The little red hen, ill. by Annie West
The little red hen, ill. by Margot Zemach
The little red hen: an old fable
The Little Red Hen and the Passover matzah
The Little Red Hen makes a pizza
Lyons, Kelly Starling. *Tea cakes for Tosh*
McAlister, Caroline. *Holy Molé!*
McElligott, Matthew. *Even aliens need snacks*
McKissack, Patricia C. *Messy Bessey's holidays*
McMullan, Kate. *Bulldog's big day*
Malkin, Michele. *Pinky's sweet tooth*
Many, Paul. *The great pancake escape*
Martin, David. *All for pie, pie for all*
Meadows, Michelle. *Piggies in the kitchen*
Meddaugh, Susan. *Hog-eye*
Meister, Cari. *Skinny and fats, best friends*
Millen, C. M. *Blue bowl down*
Mora, Pat. *The bakery lady / La señora de la panadería*
Mother Goose *Pat-a-cake*, ill. by Olga Ivanov
Pat-a-cake, ill. by Annie Kubler
Mozelle, Shirley. *The bear upstairs*
Muir, Leslie. *The little bitty bakery*
Müller, Birte. *Finn cooks*
Murphy, Stuart J. *A fair bear share*
Murray, Alison. *Apple pie ABC*
Nakagawa, Chihiro. *Who made this cake?*
Nakagawa, Rieko. *Guri and Gura*
Guri and Gura's special gift
Neuschwander, Cindy. *Pastry school in Paris*
Newman, Lesléa. *A sweet Passover*
Nolen, Jerdine. *In my momma's kitchen*
Oxenbury, Helen. *It's my birthday*
Parish, Herman. *Amelia Bedelia's first apple pie*
Park, Frances. *Where on earth is my bagel?*
Park, Linda Sue. *Bee-bim bop!*
Parkhurst, Carolyn. *Cooking with Henry and Elliebelly*
Paschkis, Julie. *Apple cake*
Pelham, David. *Sam's pizza*
Platt, Cynthia. *A little bit of love*
Priceman, Marjorie. *How to make a cherry pie and see the U.S.A.*
How to make an apple pie and see the world
Reich, Susanna. *Minette's feast*
Rex, Michael. *The pie is cherry*
Reynolds, Aaron. *Buffalo wings*
Chicks and salsa
Rice, Eve. *Benny bakes a cake*
Robbins, Ken. *Apples*
Roberts, Bethany. *Cookie angel*
Rodman, Mary Ann. *Surprise soup*
Rosenthal, Amy Krouse. *Cookies*
One smart cookie: bite-size lessons for the school years and beyond
Rosoff, Meg. *Wild boars cook*
Rossell, Judith. *Ruby and Leonard and the great big surprise*
Rotner, Shelley. *Hold the anchovies!*
Rylant, Cynthia. *The cookie-store cat*
Sanders, Rob. *Cowboy Christmas*
Sanger, Amy Wilson. *First book of sushi*
Schubert, Leda. *The Princess of Borscht*
Shannon, George. *Who put the cookies in the cookie jar?*
Shulman, Lisa. *The moon might be milk*
Simmonds, Posy. *Baker cat*
Smalls, Irene. *My Pop Pop and me*
Smith, Linda. *Mrs. Biddlebox*
Smothers, Ethel Footman. *Auntee Edna*
Speed, Toby. *Brave potatoes*
Spilsbury, Louise. *Carrots*
Oranges
Peas
Staake, Bob. *The donut chef*
Stadler, Alexander. *Beverly Billingsly takes the cake*
Stevens, Jan Romero. *Carlos digs to China / Carlos excava hasta la China*
Stevens, Janet. *Cook-a-doodle-doo!*
Stewig, John Warren. *Making plum jam*
Stowell, Penelope. *The greatest potatoes*
Sylver, Adrienne. *Hot diggity dog*
Teevin, Toni. *What to do? What to do?*
Torres, Leyla. *Saturday sancocho*
Ungar, Richard. *Rachel's gift*
Urbanovic, Jackie. *Duck soup*
Vamos, Samantha R. *The cazuela that the farm maiden stirred*
VanHecke, Susan. *An apple pie for dinner*
Wallace, Nancy Elizabeth. *Apples, apples, apples*
Wellington, Monica. *Mr. Cookie Baker*
Pizza at Sally's
Wells, Rosemary. *Bunny cakes*
Max's apples
Wheeler, Lisa. *Ugly pie*
Whelan, Gloria. *The boy who wanted to cook*
Wilson, Karma. *Whopper cake*
Wolff, Nancy. *Tallulah in the kitchen*
Yamada, Utako. *The story of Cherry the pig*
Yorinks, Arthur. *Company's going*
Zepeda, Gwendolyn. *Growing up with tamales / Los tamales de Ana*
Zia, F. *Hot, hot roti for Dada-ji*
Zolkower, Edie Stoltz. *Too many cooks*

Activities – ballooning

Adams, Adrienne. *The great Valentine's Day balloon race*
Appelt, Kathi. *Elephants aloft*
Calhoun, Mary. *Hot-air Henry*
Curious George and the hot air balloon
De Beer, Hans. *Little Polar Bear and the big balloon*
Gibbons, Gail. *Flying*
Huneck, Stephen. *Sally's great balloon adventure*
Jahn-Clough, Lisa. *Felicity and Cordelia*
McGrory, Anik. *Mouton's impossible dream*
McPhail, David. *Henry Bear's park*
Moseley, Keith. *Where's the dinosaur?*

Priceman, Marjorie. *Hot air*
Rawlinson, Julia. *A surprise for Rosie*
Sakai, Komako. *Emily's balloon*

Activities – bargaining *see* Activities – trading

Activities – bartering *see* Activities – trading

Activities – bathing

Anderson, Peggy Perry. *To the tub*
Andreasen, Dan. *The treasure bath*
Andres, Kristina. *Elephant in the bathtub*
Arnold, Tedd. *No more water in the tub!*
Averbeck, Jim. *Oh no, Little Dragon!*
Barner, Bob. *Animal baths*
Beaumont, Karen. *Dini Dinosaur*
Beck, Andrea. *Elliot's bath*
Bedford, David. *Shaggy Dog and the terrible itch*
Brown, Alan James. *Love-a-Duck*
Brown, Margaret Wise. *The dirty little boy*
Capucilli, Alyssa Satin. *Bathtime for Biscuit*
Biscuit visits the pumpkin patch
Coffelt, Nancy. *Catch that baby!*
Conrad, Pam. *The Tub People*
Dodds, Dayle Ann. *Pet wash*
Ehrlich, Fred. *Does an elephant take a bath?*
Esbaum, Jill. *Estelle takes a bath*
Ficocelli, Elizabeth. *Kid tea*
The fish is me
Geisert, Arthur. *Hogwash*
Harper, Jamie. *Splish splash, Baby Bundt*
Jenkins, Steve. *Time for a bath*
Johansen, K. V. *Pippin takes a bath*
Jones, Sylvie. *Who's in the tub?*
Kay, Julia. *Gulliver Snip*
Krosoczka, Jarrett J. *Bubble bath pirates*
Landström, Lena. *A hippo's tale*
Lauber, Patricia. *What you never knew about tubs, toilets and showers*
Lindgren, Barbro. *Sam's bath*
Lobb, Janice. *Splish! Splosh! Why do we wash?*
McDonnell, Flora. *I love boats*
Mahy, Margaret. *The green bath*
Maizes, Sarah. *On my way to the bath*
Mortensen, Lori. *Cowpoke Clyde and Dirty Dawg*
Myers, Tim. *Down at the Dino Wash Deluxe*
Neubecker, Robert. *Beasty bath*
Noonan, Julia. *Bath day*
Palatini, Margie. *Tub-boo-boo*
Pallotta, Jerry. *Dory story*
Patricelli, Leslie. *Tubby*
Pattison, Darcy. *Desert baths*
Pelletier, Andrew T. *The amazing adventures of Bathman!*
Postgate, Daniel. *Smelly Bill: love stinks*
Puttock, Simon. *Squeaky clean*
Sayre, April Pulley. *Splish! splash! animal baths*
Schotter, Roni. *Captain Bob sets sail*
Segal, John. *Pirates don't take baths*
Shannon, Terry Miller. *Tub toys*
Slangerup, Erik Jon. *Dirt Boy*
Smith, Janice Lee. *Jess and the stinky cowboys*
Spinelli, Eileen. *Summerbath, winterbath*
Sykes, Julie. *I don't want to take a bath!*
Teckentrup, Britta. *Big smelly bear*
Thompson, Kay. *Kay Thompson's Eloise takes a bawth (sic)*
Weinert, Matthias. *No bath, no cake!*
Wells, Rosemary. *Max's bath*
Weninger, Brigitte. *"No bath! No way!"*
Wilson, Karma. *Hogwash!*
Wood, Audrey. *King Bidgood's in the bathtub*
Zion, Gene. *Harry, the dirty dog*

Activities – cooking *see* Activities – baking, cooking

Activities – dancing

Ackerman, Karen. *Song and dance man*
Allen, Debbie. *Brothers of the knight*
Dancing in the wings
Andreae, Giles. *Giraffes can't dance*
Andrews, Sylvia. *Dancing in my bones*
Appelt, Kathi. *The Alley Cat's Meow*
Bats around the clock
Arnosky, Jim. *Rattlesnake dance*
Asch, Frank. *Moondance*
Moongame
Asher, Sandy. *Stella's dancing days*
Auch, Mary Jane. *Hen lake*
Peeping Beauty
Axelrod, Amy. *Pigs in the corner*
Backx, Patsy. *Skippy and Jack*
Bansch, Helga. *Brava, Mimi!*
Baryshnikov, Mikhail. *Because . . .*
Bell, Cece. *Sock Monkey boogie-woogie*
Benzwie, Teresa. *Numbers on the move*
Bird, Betsy. *Giant dance party*
Bluemle, Elizabeth. *How do you wokka-wokka?*
Bonwill, Ann. *Naughty toes*
Bradley, Kimberly Brubaker. *Ballerino Nate*
Brandenberg, Alexa. *Ballerina flying*
Brown, Margaret Wise. *Sailor boy jig*
Burningham, John. *It's a secret!*
Callahan, Sean. *Shannon and the world's tallest leprechaun*
Capucilli, Alyssa Satin. *Katy Duck*
Katy Duck, big sister
Katy Duck is a caterpillar
Catrow, David. *Monster mash*
Chaconas, Dori. *Dancing with Katya*
Clarke, Jane. *Dancing with the Dinosaurs*
Collins, Pat Lowery. *I am a dancer*
Corey, Shana. *Ballerina bear*
Craig, Lindsey. *Dancing feet!*
Crimi, Carolyn. *Tessa's tip-tapping toes*
Cristaldi, Kathryn. *Baseball ballerina*
Baseball ballerina strikes out
Dawavendewa, Gerald. *The butterfly dance*
De Anda, Diane. *Dancing Miranda / Baila, Miranda, baila*
DePalma, Mary Newell. *The Nutcracker doll*
dePaola, Tomie. *Oliver Button is a sissy*
DeRubertis, Barbara. *Dilly Dog's dizzy dancing*
Durango, Julia. *Cha-cha chimps*
Duval, Kathy. *Take me to your BBQ*
Edwards, Pamela Duncan. *Bravo, Livingstone Mouse!*
Honk!
Elliott, David. *One little chicken*
French, Jackie. *Josephine wants to dance*
Gauch, Patricia Lee. *Bravo, Tanya*
Dance, Tanya
Presenting Tanya, the Ugly Duckling

Tanya and Emily in a dance for two
Geras, Adèle. *Giselle*
The nutcracker
Sleeping beauty
Swan Lake
Time for ballet
Gliori, Debi. *Polar Bolero*
Goble, Paul. *Star boy*
Gollub, Matthew. *Gobble, quack, moon*
Gorbachev, Valeri. *Catty Jane who loved to dance*
Greenberg, Jan. *Ballet for Martha*
Grimm, Jacob and Wilhelm. *Twelve dancing princesses*
The twelve dancing princesses, ill. by Lucy Corvino
The twelve dancing princesses, ill. by Kinuko Y. Craft
The twelve dancing princesses, ill. by Rachel Isadora
The twelve dancing princesses, ill. by Gerald McDermott
The twelve dancing princesses, ill. by Jane Ray
The twelve dancing princesses, ill. by Suçie Stevenson
The twelve princesses
Gruska, Denise. *The only boy in ballet class*
Gunnufson, Charlotte. *Halloween hustle*
Hager, Sarah. *Dancing Matilda*
Hague, Michael. *The nutcracker*
Hallworth, Grace. *Sing me a story*
Hannert, Todd. *Morning dance*
Hanson, Warren. *Bugtown Boogie*
Hayward, Linda. *A day in the life of a dancer*
Headley, Justina Chen. *The patch*
Heidbreder, Robert. *Drumheller dinosaur dance*
Hesse, Karen. *Come on, rain*
Hest, Amy. *Mabel dancing*
Hoffmann, E. T. A. *The nutcracker*, ill. by Renée Graef
The nutcracker, ill. by Alison Jay
The nutcracker, ill. by Peter Malone
The nutcracker, ill. by Maurice Sendak
The nutcracker, ill. by Lisbeth Zwerger
The Nutcracker and the Mouse King
The nutcracker ballet
Holabird, Katharine. *Angelina and the princess*
Angelina ballerina
Angelina dances
Angelina on stage
Angelina, star of the show
Angelina's ballet class
Christmas in Mouseland
Hudson, Cheryl Willis. *My friend Maya loves to dance*
Hueston, M. P. *The all-American jump and jive jig*
Hutchins, Pat. *Barn dance!*
Idle, Molly. *Flora and the flamingo*
Isadora, Rachel. *Lili at ballet*
Lili on stage
Not just tutus
Janni, Rebecca. *Every cowgirl needs dancing boots*
Jennings, Sharon. *Priscilla's paw de deux*
Jonas, Ann. *Color dance*
Kajikawa, Kimiko. *Yoshi's feast*
Kinerk, Robert. *Clorinda*
Kleven, Elisa. *The dancing deer and the foolish hunter*
Klingel, Cynthia Fitterer. *Dancers*
Knister. *Sophie's dance*
Kohuth, Jane. *Duck sock hop*
Kroll, Virginia L. *Can you dance, Dalila?*
Krosoczka, Jarrett J. *Ollie the purple elephant*
Lasky, Kathryn. *Starring Lucille*
Lee, Jeanne M. *Silent lotus*
Leiner, Katherine. *Mama does the mambo*
Lillegard, Dee. *The Big Bug Ball*
London, Jonathan. *Who bop*
Lynn, Sarah. *Tip-tap pop*
Maccarone, Grace. *Miss Lina's ballerinas and the prince*
Miss Lina's ballerinas and the wicked wish
McElmurry, Jill. *Mario makes a move*
McKissack, Patricia C. *Mirandy and Brother Wind*
Mahy, Margaret. *Mister Whistler*
Manning, Maurie J. *Kitchen dance*
Manson, Ainslie. *Ballerinas don't wear glasses*
Marshall, James. *The Cut-Ups carry on*
George and Martha encore
Swine lake
Martin, Bill, Jr. *Barn dance!*
Mayhew, James. *Ella Bella ballerina and The Nutcracker*
Medearis, Angela Shelf. *Dancing with the Indians*
Mills, Judith Christine. *The painted chest*
Mitton, Tony. *Dinosaurumpus*
Down by the cool of the pool
Murphy, Kelly. *The boll weevil ball*
Newsome, Jill. *Dream dancer*
Paraskevas, Betty. *Marvin, the tap-dancing horse*
Pavlova, Anna. *I dreamed I was a ballerina*
Paxton, Tom. *Engelbert the elephant*
Pinkney, Andrea Davis. *Alvin Ailey*
Pinkwater, Daniel. *Dancing Larry*
Pulver, Robin. *Alicia's tutu*
Puttock, Simon. *A ladder to the stars*
Quattlebaum, Mary. *Sparks fly high*
Rubin, Susan Goldman. *Matisse dance for joy*
Ryder, Joanne. *Big bear ball*
Dance by the light of the moon
Sauer, Tammi. *Bawk and roll*
Chicken dance
Schaefer, Carole Lexa. *Dragon dancing*
Schneider, Christine M. *Saxophone Sam and his snazzy jazz band*
Schomp, Virginia. *If you were a . . . ballet dancer*
Schroeder, Alan. *Ragtime Tumpie*
Schumaker, Ward. *Dance!*
Shannon, George. *April showers*
Shields, Carol Diggory. *Saturday night at the dinosaur stomp*
Silverman, Erica. *The Hanukkah hop!*
Singer, Marilyn. *Tallulah's toe shoes*
Sís, Peter. *Ballerina*
Smith, Charles R. *Dance with me*
Smith, Cynthia Leitich. *Jingle dancer*
Stanley, Mandy. *Lettice the dancing rabbit*
Stickland, Paul. *Dinosaur stomp!*
Stower, Adam. *Two left feet*
Stroud, Bettye. *Dance y'all*
Stutson, Caroline. *Cats' night out*
Symes, Ruth. *Harriet dancing*
Taylor, Ann. *Baby dance*
Thomas, Joyce Carol. *Shouting*
Thomas, Peggy. *Snow dance*
Thompson, Lauren. *Ballerina dreams*
Thorpe, Kiki. *Time to cha-cha-cha!*
Tricarico, Christine. *Cock-a-doodle dance!*
Tucker, Lindy. *Porkelia*
Waboose, Jan Bourdeau. *Firedancers*
Walton, Rick. *How can you dance?*

Noah's square dance
Wardlaw, Lee. *Saturday night jamboree*
Waters, Kate. *Lion dancer*
Welch, Willy. *Dancing with Daddy*
Wheeler, Lisa. *Hokey pokey*
Wild, Margaret. *Midnight babies*
Witte, Anna. *Lola's fandango*
Wood, Audrey. *Little Penguin's tale*
Yee, Wong Herbert. *The Officers' Ball*
Young, Amy. *Belinda and the glass slipper*
Belinda begins ballet
Belinda in Paris
Belinda, the ballerina

Activities – digging

Aliki. *Digging up dinosaurs*
Gay, Marie-Louise. *Roslyn Rutabaga and the biggest hole on earth!*
Gibbons, Gail. *Tunnels*
Hoban, Tana. *Dig, drill, dump, fill*
Krauss, Ruth. *A hole is to dig*
Paraskevas, Betty. *Maggie and the Ferocious Beast, the big carrot*
Stevens, Jan Romero. *Carlos digs to China / Carlos excava hasta la China*
Tyler, Jenny. *Big Pig on a dig*

Activities – drawing

Ahlberg, Allan. *The pencil*
Alexander, Martha G. *I'll never share you, Blackboard Bear*
Max and the dumb flower picture
Baker, Liza. *Dinosaur days*
Banks, Kate. *The eraserheads*
Becker, Aaron. *Journey*
Bloom, Becky. *Mice make trouble*
Carle, Eric. *Draw me a star*
Collins, Ross. *Doodleday*
Degen, Bruce. *I gotta draw*
Demi. *The girl who drew a phoenix*
Dormer, Frank W. *The obstinate pen*
Edwards, Pamela Duncan. *The neat line*
Emberley, Ed. *Ed Emberley's drawing book of trucks and trains*
Ed Emberley's fingerprint drawing book
Ericsson, Jennifer A. *A piece of chalk*
Falwell, Cathryn. *David's drawing*
Freedman, Deborah. *Scribble*
Gerstein, Mordicai. *The first drawing*
Gretz, Susanna. *Riley and Rose in the picture*
Hamsa, Bobbie. *Fast-draw Freddie*
Heap, Sue. *Danny's drawing book*
Hillenbrand, Will. *Louie!*
Hutchins, Hazel. *The sidewalk rescue*
Jagtenberg, Yvonne. *Jack's rabbit*
Johnson, D. B. *Eddie's kingdom*
Kleven, Elisa. *The paper princess*
Kroll, Steven. *Patches*
Patches lost and found
Lichtenheld, Tom. *Bridget's beret*
Lucas, David. *Something to do*
Ludwig, Trudy. *The invisible boy*
McCarty, Peter. *Jeremy draws a monster*
The monster returns
McDonnell, Patrick. *Art*
McPhail, David. *Drawing lessons from a bear*
Moony B. Finch, fastest draw in the West
Mills, Claudia. *Ziggy's blue-ribbon day*
Moss, Marissa. *Regina's big mistake*
Nikola-Lisa, W. *Can you top that?*
O'Connor, Jane. *Fancy Nancy: aspiring artist*
Pericoli, Matteo. *See the city*
Tommaso and the missing line
Poydar, Nancy. *Cool Ali*
Priest, Robert H. *The pirate's eye*
Reidy, Jean. *Time out for monsters!*
Rey, Margret. *Billy's picture*
Roslonek, Steve. *The shape song swingalong*
Russo, Marisabina. *Under the table*
Saltzberg, Barney. *Andrew drew and drew*
Say, Allen. *Emma's rug*
Tate, Don. *It jes' happened*
Thomson, Bill. *Chalk*
Tierney, Fiona. *Lion's lunch?*
Van Allsburg, Chris. *Bad day at Riverbend*
Wallner, Alexandra. *Beatrix Potter*
Watt, Mélanie. *Chester*
Chester's back!
Chester's masterpiece
Williams, Karen Lynn. *A beach tail*
Wilson, April. *April Wilson's magpie magic*
Wing, Natasha. *Go to bed, monster!*
Yates, Louise. *Dog loves drawing*
Zemach, Kaethe. *Ms. McCaw learns to draw*

Activities – driving

Pulver, Robin. *Axle Annie and the speed grump*
Timmers, Leo. *Who is driving?*
Wilson, Karma. *Sakes alive!*

Activities – eating *see* Food

Activities – flying

Aardema, Verna. *Jackal's flying lesson*
Allard, Harry. *The Stupids take off*
Bang, Molly. *Goose*
Berger, Melvin. *How do airplanes fly?*
Berkeley, Jon. *Chopsticks*
Berne, Jennifer. *Calvin can't fly*
Bildner, Phil. *The hallelujah flight*
Blake, Robert J. *Fledgling*
Breen, Steve. *Violet the pilot*
Brown, Tami Lewis. *Soar, Elinor!*
Cave, Kathryn. *The boy who became an eagle*
Church, Caroline Jayne. *Ping Pong Pig*
Clark, Leslie Ann. *Peepsqueak!*
Comden, Betty, et al. *Flying to Neverland with Peter Pan*
Conover, Chris. *The lion's share*
Crews, Donald. *Flying*
De Beer, Hans. *Little Polar Bear and the big balloon*
Demarest, Chris L. *Lindbergh*
Smokejumpers one to ten
Dollinger, Renate. *The rabbi who flew*
Dominguez, Angela. *Let's go, Hugo!*
Dorros, Arthur. *Abuela*
Edwards, Pamela Duncan. *The Wright brothers*
Fardell, John. *Jeremiah Jellyfish flies high!*
Finn, Isobel. *The very lazy ladybug*
Forler, Nan. *Bird child*
Fuge, Charles. *Three little dinosaurs*
Garland, Michael. *Icarus Swinebuckle*
Gibbons, Gail. *Flying*
Glass, Andrew. *The wondrous whirligig*

Gorbachev, Valeri. *The fool of the world and the flying ship: a Ukrainian folk tale*
Graham, Bob. *Max*
Gregorowski, Christopher. *Fly, eagle, fly!*
Grist, Julie. *Flying, just plane fun*
Heide, Florence Parry. *Princess Hyacinth*
Heller, Nicholas. *Elwood and the witch*
Hodgkins, Fran. *How people learned to fly*
Ichikawa, Satomi. *Come fly with me*
James, Simon. *George flies south*
Jeffers, Oliver. *Up and down*
Jenkins, Steve. *Animals in flight*
Jessell, Tim. *Falcon*
Johnson, Angela. *Wind flyers*
Johnson, Paul Brett. *The cow who wouldn't come down*
Joyce, William. *The fantastic flying books of Mr. Morris Lessmore*
Santa calls
Kinerk, Robert. *Clorinda takes flight*
Kleven, Elisa. *The paper princess*
Kotzwinkle, William. *Walter, the farting dog: rough weather ahead*
Kroll, Steven. *Super-dragon*
Lewis, Kim. *Here we go Harry*
Light, Steve. *Zephyr takes flight*
Lindbergh, Reeve. *Nobody owns the sky*
Loux, Lynn C. *The day I could fly*
Lund, Deb. *Dinosoaring*
McCarty, Peter. *Moon plane*
McDermott, Gerald. *Coyote*
McGhee, Alison. *Only a witch can fly*
McGill, Alice. *Way up and over everything*
McKee, David. *Elmer and the wind*
Elmer takes off
McLellan, Stephanie Simpson. *The chicken cat*
Mara, Wil. *Amelia Earhart*
Meade, Holly. *If I never forever endeavor*
Minshull, Evelyn White. *Eaglet's world*
Modarressi, Mitra. *Owlet's first flight*
Morison, Toby. *Little Louie takes off*
Munsch, Robert N. *Angela's airplane*
Myers, Christopher. *Wings*
O'Malley, Kevin. *Little Buggy*
Peet, Bill. *The kweeks of Kookatumdee*
Merle the high flying squirrel
Pinkney, Brian. *The adventures of sparrowboy*
Pomerantz, Charlotte. *Flap your wings and try*
Priceman, Marjorie. *Princess Picky*
Provensen, Alice. *The glorious flight*
Ransome, Arthur. *The fool of the world and the flying ship*
Rau, Dana Meachen. *Flying*
Ringgold, Faith. *Tar Beach*
Rosen, Michael. *Bear flies high*
Ryan, Pam Muñoz. *Amelia and Eleanor go for a ride*
Ryder, Joanne. *Rainbow wings*
Schomp, Virginia. *If you were a . . . pilot*
Schotter, Roni. *Captain Bob takes flight*
Seibold, J. Otto. *Penguin dreams*
Simont, Marc. *The goose that almost got cooked*
Spinelli, Eileen. *Buzz*
Stanley, Mandy. *Lettice the flying rabbit*
Stevenson, James. *The castaway*
Grandpa's great city tour
Tarpley, Natasha Anastasia. *Joe-Joe's first flight*
Thompson, Colin. *Falling angels*
Tibo, Gilles. *The cowboy kid*
Walter, Mildred Pitts. *Brother to the wind*
Ward, Helen. *The dragon machine*
The king of the birds
Whitaker, Suzanne George. *The daring Miss Quimby*
Wiesner, David. *Tuesday*
Willard, Nancy. *The flying bed*
Willis, Jeanne. *Fly, chick, fly!*
Winer, Yvonne. *Butterflies fly*
Yolen, Jane. *Wings*
Young, Ed. *Hook*
Zullo, Germano. *Little bird*

Activities – gardening *see* Gardens, gardening

Activities – hiking

Longstreth, Galen Goodwin. *Yes, let's*
Quattlebaum, Mary. *Jo MacDonald hiked in the woods*

Activities – jumping

Cronin, Doreen. *Bounce*
Fischer, Scott M. *Jump!*
King, Stephen Michael. *Emily loves to bounce*
Murphy, Stuart J. *Ready, set, hop!*
Scruggs, Afi. *Jump rope magic*

Activities – kissing *see* Kissing

Activities – knitting

Aber, Linda Williams. *Carrie measures up!*
Barnett, Mac. *Extra yarn*
Bunge, Daniela. *The scarves*
Campbell, K. G. *Lester's dreadful sweaters*
Clifton-Brown, Holly. *Annie Hoot and the knitting extravaganza*
Elliott, David. *Knitty Kitty*
Hopkinson, Deborah. *Knit your bit*
Martins, Isabel Minhós. *Little lamb, have you any wool?*
Mortimer, Rachael. *The three Billy Goats Fluff*
Shannon, Margaret. *The red wolf*
Waterton, Betty. *A bumblebee sweater*
Webster, Sheryl. *Noodle's knitting*
Wild, Margaret. *Mr. Nick's knitting*
Yoon, Salina. *Penguin in love*

Activities – making things

Alter, Anna. *What can you do with an old red shoe?*
Bastin, Marjolein. *Christmas with Vera*
Demas, Corinne. *Valentine surprise*
DiPucchio, Kelly. *Crafty Chloe*
Crafty Chloe: dress-up mess-up
Ehlert, Lois. *Hands*
Fleming, Denise. *Alphabet under construction*
Gibbons, Gail. *How a house is built*
Ginsburg, Mirra. *Clay boy*
Hall, Donald. *Lucy's Christmas*
Hoban, Tana. *Construction zone*
Howell, Will C. *Zoo flakes ABC*
Hunter, Dette. *38 ways to entertain your babysitter*
38 ways to entertain your grandparents
Inkpen, Mick. *Wibbly Pig can make a tent*
Jeffers, Oliver. *The great paper caper*
Johnson, Angela. *Those building men*

Johnson, Stephen T. *My little blue robot*
Kleven, Elisa. *The apple doll*
Knick knack paddy whack
Kroll, Steven. *Will you be my valentine?*
Lachenmeyer, Nathaniel. *The origami master*
Lin, Grace. *Lissy's friends*
Lovell, Patty. *Have fun, Molly Lou Melon*
Lum, Kate. *What! cried Granny*
McCain, Becky R. *Grandmother's dreamcatcher*
McDonald, Megan. *It's picture day today!*
Michelin, Linda. *Zuzu's wishing cake*
Moffatt, Judith. *Snow shapes*
Moon, Nicola. *Lucy's picture*
Moss, Marissa. *Knick knack paddywack*
Neitzel, Shirley. *The house I'll build for the wrens*
Ransom, Candice F. *The promise quilt*
Ray, Mary Lyn. *Basket moon*
Rockwell, Anne. *What we like*
Rylant, Cynthia. *If you'll be my Valentine*
Shaw, Mary. *Brady Brady and the great rink*
Smith, Danna. *Balloon trees*
Sturges, Philemon. *I love tools!*
Swinburne, Stephen R. *Swallows in the birdhouse*
Tafuri, Nancy. *Counting to Christmas*
Tryon, Leslie. *Albert's alphabet*
Wellington, Monica. *Riki's birdhouse*
Wood, Audrey. *The flying dragon room*
Ziefert, Harriet. *Grandma, it's for you!*
Knick-knack paddywhack

Activities – painting *see also* Careers – artists

Adams, Adrienne. *The Easter egg artists*
Agee, Jon. *The incredible painting of Felix Clousseau*
Arnold, Katya. *Elephants can paint, too!*
Baker, Alan. *Black and White Rabbit's ABC*
White Rabbit's color book
Beaumont, Karen. *I ain't gonna paint no more!*
Bilgrami, Shaheen. *Farmyard painting party*
Jungle art show
Black, Harley. *Magic art class*
Bridges, Shirin Yim. *The Umbrella Queen*
Caple, Kathy. *Worm gets a job*
Carle, Eric. *The artist who painted a blue horse*
Demi. *The boy who painted dragons*
dePaola, Tomie. *The legend of the Indian paintbrush*
Eaton, Maxwell. *The mystery*
Edwards, Pamela Duncan. *Warthogs paint*
Engle, Margarita. *Summer birds*
Flanagan, Alice K. *The Wilsons, a house-painting team*
Freedman, Deborah. *Blue chicken*
Geoghegan, Adrienne. *All your own teeth*
Haseley, Dennis. *Twenty heartbeats*
Hogrogian, Nonny. *Cool cat*
Hong, Chen Jiang. *The magic horse of Han Gan*
Hurd, Thacher. *Art dog*
Johnson, Angela. *Lily Brown's paintings*
Kelley, True. *Claude Monet*
Knapp, Ruthie. *Who stole Mona Lisa?*
Larsen, Andrew. *The imaginary garden*
Look, Lenore. *Brush of the gods*
MacLachlan, Patricia. *Painting the wind*
McPhail, David. *Something special*
Numeroff, Laura Joffe. *The Jellybeans and the big art adventure*
Parker, Marjorie Blain. *Colorful dreamer*
Partridge, Elizabeth. *Pig's eggs*
Pinkwater, Daniel. *The picture of Morty and Ray*
Reynolds, Peter H. *Sky color*
Rylant, Cynthia. *All I see*
Seeger, Laura Vaccaro. *One boy*
Segal, Lore Groszmann. *Morris the artist*
Snyder, Carol. *We're painting*
Spier, Peter. *Oh, were they ever happy!*
Sweet, Melissa. *Carmine*
Tafuri, Nancy. *Blue goose*
Tamar, Erika. *The garden of happiness*
Walsh, Ellen Stoll. *Mouse paint*
Walsh, Melanie. *Ned's rainbow*
Wiesner, David. *Art and Max*
Wilhelm, Hans. *Quacky Ducky's Easter fun*
Williams, Karen Lynn. *Painted dreams*
Winter, Jonah. *Just behave, Pablo Picasso!*
Ziefert, Harriet. *Lunchtime for a purple snake*
My dog thinks I'm a genius

Activities – photographing

Casteel, Seth. *Underwater dogs*
Davis, Jill. *Orangutans are ticklish*
Diesen, Deborah. *Picture day perfection*
Hest, Amy. *Guess who, Baby Duck*
Levinson, Riki. *I go with my family to Grandma's*
McPhail, David. *Pig Pig and the magic photo album*
Perkins, Lynne Rae. *Pictures from our vacation*
Pichon, Liz. *Penguins*
Plourde, Lynn. *School picture day*
Roche, Denis. *The best class picture ever*
Scotton, Rob. *Russell and the lost treasure*
Swinburne, Stephen R. *Guess whose shadow?*
Trimble, Marcia. *Hello sun*

Activities – picnicking

Alborough, Jez. *It's the bear*
Asch, Frank. *Sand cake*
Asher, Sandy. *Here comes Gosling!*
Ashforth, Camilla. *Willow on the river*
Bertrand, Diane Gonzales. *Uncle Chente's picnic / El picnic de Tío Chente*
Bunting, Eve. *A picnic in October*
Capucilli, Alyssa Satin. *Biscuit's picnic*
Christelow, Eileen. *Five little monkeys sitting in a tree*
Cronin, Doreen. *Click, clack, quackity-quack*
Crum, Shutta. *Dozens of cousins*
Eilenberg, Max. *Squeak's good idea*
Elya, Susan Middleton. *Oh no, gotta go #2*
Ets, Marie Hall. *In the forest*
Evans, Lezlie. *The bunnies' picnic*
Goode, Diane. *The most perfect spot*
Graham, Bob. *Jethro Byrd, fairy child*
Oscar's half birthday
Granowsky, Alvin. *Can I help?*
Hamilton, Richard. *Polly's picnic*
Harper, Charise Mericle. *Pink me up*
Inkpen, Mick. *Picnic*
Jarrett, Clare. *The best picnic ever*
Kasza, Keiko. *Ready for anything*
Katzler, Eva. *Florentine and Pig*
Keller, Holly. *Henry's Fourth of July*
Kennedy, Jimmy. *The teddy bears' picnic*, ill. by Alexandra Day
The teddy bears' picnic, ill. by Michael Hague
The teddy bears' picnic, ill. by Prue Theobalds
Kroll, Steven. *It's Groundhog Day!*
Kruusval, Catarina. *Franny's friends*
Landström, Olof. *Boo and Baa in the woods*

Lies, Brian. *Bats at the beach*
Livingston, Irene. *Finklehopper Frog cheers*
Lo, Ginnie. *Auntie Yang's great soybean picnic*
London, Jonathan. *Let's go, Froggy!*
Longstreth, Galen Goodwin. *Yes, let's*
McCully, Emily Arnold. *Picnic*
Mack, Jeff. *Good news, bad news*
Mahy, Margaret. *The rattlebang picnic*
Manzano, Sonia. *No dogs allowed*
Miranda, Anne. *Pignic*
Murphy, Mary. *Panda Foo and the new friend*
Murphy, Stuart J. *More or less*
Naylor, Phyllis Reynolds. *Please do feed the bears*
Numeroff, Laura Joffe. *What mommies do best*
Polacco, Patricia. *Picnic at Mudsock Meadow*
Schaap, Martine. *Mop and the birthday picnic*
Spetter, Jung-Hee. *Lily and Trooper's spring*
Steig, William. *Toby, who are you?*
Thomas, Jane Resh. *Celebration!*
Vincent, Gabrielle. *Ernest and Celestine's picnic*
Wardlaw, Lee. *Red, white, and boom!*
Webster, Christine. *Otter everywhere*
Wells, Rosemary. *Bunny mail*
McDuff saves the day
Woodson, Jacqueline. *We had a picnic this Sunday past*
Yolen, Jane. *Picnic with Piggins*

Activities – playing

Ahlberg, Janet. *Funnybones*
Playmates
Ajmera, Maya. *Come out and play*
Alda, Arlene. *Lulu's piano lesson*
Alexander, Martha G. *Blackboard Bear*
Aliki. *Overnight at Mary Bloom's*
Push button
Alko, Selina. *Every-day dress-up*
Allen, Joy. *Princess Palooza*
Anderson, Peggy Perry. *Joe on the go*
Anglund, Joan Walsh. *The brave cowboy*
Apperley, Dawn. *Flip and Flop*
Arnold, Caroline. *Playtime for zoo animals*
Splashtime for zoo animals
Arnosky, Jim. *Watching foxes*
Ashburn, Boni. *The fort that Jack built*
Ashman, Linda. *Rain!*
Ayres, Katherine. *Matthew's truck*
Baguley, Elizabeth. *Meggie moon*
Baillie, Marilyn. *Nose to toes*
Baker, Leslie A. *You bad dog!*
Bang, Molly. *Yellow ball*
Banks, Kate. *Max's dragon*
Barclay, Jane. *Going on a journey to the sea*
Beaty, Andrea. *When giants come to play*
Beck, Andrea. *Elliot's shipwreck*
Bently, Peter. *King Jack and the dragon*
Berger, Carin. *A perfect day*
Berger, Samantha. *Crankenstein*
Bergman, Mara. *Lively Elizabeth!*
Bloom, Suzanne. *A mighty fine time machine*
What about Bear?
Bottner, Barbara. *Bootsie Barker bites*
Boyd, Lizi. *Inside outside*
Brimner, Larry Dane. *The big, beautiful, brown box*
Brown, Jo. *Hoppity skip Little Chick*
Brown, Susan Taylor. *Oliver's must-do list*
Bruzzone, Catherine. *Puppy finds a friend / Cachorrito encuentra un amigo*
Puppy finds a friend / Le petit chien se trouve un ami
Butler, John. *Ten in the meadow*
Buxton, Jane. *The littlest llama*
Cabrera, Jane. *Monkey's play time*
Cader, Lisa Lebowitz. *When I wear my crown*
When I wear my tiara
Capucilli, Alyssa Satin. *Biscuit wants to play*
Little spotted cat
Castle, Caroline. *Naughty!*
Cauley, Lorinda Bryan. *Clap your hands*
Clarke, Jane. *Gilbert the hero*
Cole, Joanna. *Sharing is fun*
Come and play
Cotten, Cynthia. *Rain play*
Cousins, Lucy. *Doctor Maisy*
Crews, Donald. *Cloudy day/sunny day*
Crews, Nina. *Below*
Sky-high Guy
Snowball
Cronin, Doreen. *Bounce*
Crum, Shutta. *Dozens of cousins*
Cuyler, Margery. *Please play safe!*
Day, Alexandra. *Carl goes to daycare*
Follow Carl!
DeBear, Kirsten. *Be quiet, Marina!*
DePrisco, Dorothea. *Snowbear's winter day*
Dewan, Ted. *Baby gets the zapper*
Crispin, the pig who had it all
Doyle, Charlotte Lackner. *The bouncing, dancing, galloping ABC*
Duke, Kate. *One guinea pig is not enough*
Dunbar, Polly. *Where's Tumpty?*
Dunrea, Olivier. *Gideon*
Durand, Hallie. *Mitchell's license*
Eaton, Maxwell. *Superheroes*
Ehrlich, H. M. *Gotcha, Louie!*
Ellery, Amanda. *If I had a dragon*
Ets, Marie Hall. *Play with me*
Fitzpatrick, Marie-Louise. *I'm a tiger, too!*
Ford, Miela. *Follow the leader*
Mom and me
Fosberry, Jennifer. *Isabella*
Fucile, Tony. *Let's do nothing!*
Fuge, Charles. *I know a rhino*
Gammell, Stephen. *Mudkin*
Gardiner, Lindsey. *Here come Poppy and Max*
When Poppy and Max grow up
Gay, Marie-Louise. *Stella, queen of the snow*
George, Jean Craighead. *Snow bear*
Gibala-Broxholm, Scott. *Maddie's monster dad*
Gibbons, Gail. *Playgrounds*
Gibson, Amy. *Split! Splat!*
Gorbachev, Valeri. *Big Little Elephant*
Chicken chickens
Gravett, Emily. *Monkey and me*
Gray, Nigel. *Time to play!*
Greenfield, Eloise. *Big friend, little friend*
The friendly four
My doll, Keshia
Grindley, Sally. *Can we play too, Piglittle?*
Gudeon, Adam. *Me and Meow*
Gundersheimer, Karen. *Find cat, wear hat*
Gutierrez, Akemi. *The mummy and other adventures of Sam and Alice*
Guy, Ginger Foglesong. *¡Bravo!*
Hale, Christy. *Dreaming up*
Halpern, Julie. *Toby and the snowflakes*
Harper, Charise Mericle. *Mimi and Lulu*
Havill, Juanita. *Jamaica Tag-Along*

Heap, Sue. *What shall we play?*
Heidbreder, Robert. *I wished for a unicorn*
Heide, Iris van der. *The red chalk*
Henkes, Kevin. *Oh!*
A weekend with Wendell
Hill, Eric. *Spot at play*
Spot goes to the beach
Spot goes to the park
Spot sleeps over
Hines, Anna Grossnickle. *I am a backhoe*
Holmes, Janet A. *Me and you*
Hru, Dakari. *Tickle, tickle*
Hubbell, Patricia. *Pots and pans*
Snow happy!
Hudelhoff, Allen H. *Cats and kids*
Hughes, Sarah. *Let's play hopscotch*
Let's play jacks
Hunter, Sally. *Humphrey's corner*
Inkpen, Mick. *Kipper's snowy day*
Swing!
Wibbly Pig can make a tent
Janovitz, Marilyn. *Play baby play!*
Jarrett, Clare. *The best picnic ever*
Jocelyn, Marthe. *A day with Nellie*
Joosse, Barbara. *Old Robert and the sea-silly cats*
Sleepover at Gramma's house
Kasza, Keiko. *Dorothy and Mikey*
Keats, Ezra Jack. *The snowy day*
The snowy day [board book]
King, Stephen Michael. *Emily loves to bounce*
Konnecke, Ole. *Anthony and the girls*
Kraus, Robert. *Come out and play, little mouse*
Kvasnosky, Laura McGee. *Really truly Bingo*
Lacome, Julie. *Ruthie's big old coat*
Lakin, Patricia. *Rainy day*
Lawler, Janet. *A father's song*
Leslie, Amanda. *Who's that scratching at my door?*
Lewin, Betsy. *Thumpy Feet*
Lewis, Kim. *Floss*
Seymour and Henry
Lewison, Wendy Cheyette. *Mud*
Lia, Simone. *Red's great chase*
Liwska, Renata. *Red wagon*
London, Jonathan. *Puddles*
Sun dance, water dance
Loomis, Christine. *Cowboy bunnies*
Luenn, Nancy. *Otter play*
Lynn, Sarah. *1-2-3 va-va-vroom!*
McAllister, Angela. *Harry's box*
McClintock, Barbara. *Dahlia*
McCully, Emily Arnold. *First snow*
McDonnell, Christine. *Dog wants to play*
McGhee, Alison. *The case of the missing donut*
McGuirk, Leslie. *Tucker flips!*
McHenry, E. B. *Poodlena*
McKay, Hilary. *Pirates ahoy!*
McKee, David. *Elmer in the snow*
McLean, Janet. *Let's go, baby-o!*
MacLennan, Cathy. *Chicky Chicky Chook Chook*
McLerran, Alice. *Roxaboxen*
McPhail, David. *Emma in charge*
Pig Pig rides
McQuinn, Anna. *Lola loves stories*
Mallat, Kathy. *Just ducky*
Trouble on the tracks
Marley, Cedella. *Every little thing*
Martin, David. *Peep and Ducky*
Merz, Jennifer J. *Playground day*
Milgrim, David. *Time to get up, time to go*
Miller, Ruth. *I went to the farm*
Miller, Virginia. *In a minute!*
Mills, Judith Christine. *The painted chest*
Moers, Hermann. *Rufus and Max*
Morgan-Vanroyen, Mary. *Wild Rosie*
Morozumi, Atsuko. *Playing*
Morris, Ann. *Play*
Morrison, Toni. *Peeny butter fudge*
Morstad, Julie. *How to*
Moss, Miriam. *The snow bear*
Munsch, Robert N. *Mud puddle*
Murkoff, Heidi Eisenberg. *What to expect at a play date*
Murphy, Jill. *All for one*
Naylor, Phyllis Reynolds. *King of the playground*
Neitzel, Shirley. *I'm taking a trip on my train*
Neubecker, Robert. *What little boys are made of*
Newcome, Zita. *Pop-up toddlerobics*
Newman, Lesléa. *A fire engine for Ruthie*
Nikola-Lisa, W. *Bein' with you this way*
Ochiltree, Dianne. *Pillow pup*
O'Connor, George. *Ker-splash!*
Ohi, Ruth. *And you can come too*
O'Keefe, Susan Heyboer. *Baby day*
O'Mara, Carmel. *Rainy day*
Sunny day
Onyefulu, Ifeoma. *Omer's favorite place*
Ormerod, Jan. *Miss Mouse's day*
Patricelli, Leslie. *Tubby*
Paul, Ann Whitford. *Hello toes! Hello feet!*
Portis, Antoinette. *No es una caja / not a box*
Not a box
Not a stick
Princess Super Kitty
Powell, Alma. *My little wagon [board book]*
Poydar, Nancy. *Snip, snip . . . snow!*
Priest, Robert H. *The old pirate of Central Park*
Pringle, Laurence P. *Octopus hug*
Pritchett, Andy. *Stick!*
Purcell, Rebecca. *Super Chicken*
Ray, Mary Lyn. *Red rubber boot day*
Rayner, Catherine. *Solomon Crocodile*
Rim, Sujean. *Birdie's big-girl shoes*
Ritchie, Alison. *What Bear likes best!*
Rockwell, Anne. *At the beach*
Roddie, Shen. *Toes are to tickle*
Rodman, Mary Ann. *My best friend*
Rogers, Fred. *Making friends*
Roode, Daniel. *Little Bea and the snowy day*
Ross, Michael Elsohn. *Play with me*
Russo, Marisabina. *The big brown box*
Ryan, Pam Muñoz. *Mud is cake*
Rylant, Cynthia. *Brownie and Pearl get dolled up*
Sarcone-Roach, Julia. *The secret plan*
Schaap, Martine. *Mop's mountain adventure*
Schaefer, Carole Lexa. *ABCers*
Kids like us
Snow pumpkin
Scheffler, Axel. *The super scooter*
Schertle, Alice. *The adventures of old Bo Bear*
Schoenherr, Ian. *Cat and mouse*
Schwartz, Corey Rosen. *Hop! Plop!*
Schwartz, Roslyn. *The mole sisters and the fairy ring*
Schwarz, Viviane. *There are cats in this book*
Sendak, Maurice. *The sign on Rosie's door*
Sheridan, Sara. *I'm me!*
Shields, Gillian. *Library Lily*
Shirotani, Hideo. *Let's play*
Siddals, Mary McKenna. *I'll play with you*

Silverman, Erica. *Follow the leader*
Simmons, Jane. *Little Fern's first winter*
Simon, Francesca. *Calling all toddlers*
Singer, Marilyn. *A stick is an excellent thing*
Slegers, Liesbet. *Playing*
Smalls, Irene. *My Nana and me*
Smith, Lois T. *Carrie and Carl play*
Soman, David. *The amazing adventures of Bumblebee Boy*
Ladybug Girl
Ladybug Girl and Bumblebee Boy
Ladybug Girl and the big snow
Ladybug Girl and the Bug Squad
Spetter, Jung-Hee. *Lily and Trooper's fall*
Lily and Trooper's spring
Lily and Trooper's summer
Steig, William. *Pete's a pizza*
Toby, what are you?
Toby, where are you?
Stein, David Ezra. *Monster hug!*
Steptoe, John. *Baby says*
Stevenson, Robert Louis. *Where go the boats?*
Sullivan, Mary. *Ball*
Sykes, Julie. *Wait for me, Little Tiger*
Thomas, Jan. *Here comes the big, mean dust bunny!*
Thompson, Lauren. *Little Quack's new friend*
Tompert, Ann. *Just a little bit*
Van Allsburg, Chris. *Zathura*
Van der Meer, Mara. *Can we play?*
Vigna, Judith. *Boot weather*
Waber, Bernard. *Ira sleeps over*
Waddell, Martin. *Snow bears*
Squeak-a-lot
Tom Rabbit
Weatherford, Carole Boston. *Jazz baby*
Weeks, Sarah. *Bunny fun*
Overboard!
Weiss, Ellen. *Playtime for twins*
Wells, Rosemary. *A lion for Lewis*
Wewer, Iris. *My wild sister and me*
Whybrow, Ian. *Harry and the bucketful of dinosaurs*
Williams, Sherley Anne. *Girls together*
Wilson, Karma. *Horseplay*
Winter, Jeanette. *Cowboy Charlie*
Wishinsky, Frieda. *You're mean, Lily Jean!*
Wolff, Nancy. *It's time for school with Tallulah*
Wood, Audrey. *The Tickleoctopus*
Wood, Douglas. *Nothing to do*
Yolen, Jane. *Before the storm*
Dimity Duck
Romping monsters, stomping monsters
Soft house
Young, Ned. *Zoomer*
Zehler, Antonia. *Two fine ladies*
Two fine ladies have a tiff
Ziefert, Harriet. *Mighty Max*

Activities – reading *see* Books, reading

Activities – running

Cartier, Wesley. *Marco's run*
Golding, Theresa Martin. *Abby's asthma and the big race*
Grant, Brianna K. *We are girls who love to run / Somos chicas y a nosotras nos encanta correr*
Livingston, Irene. *Finklehopper Frog*
Mitton, Tony. *The Jungle Run*

Activities – sewing

Ashburn, Boni. *I had a favorite dress*
Beck, Andrea. *Elliot's emergency*
Cotten, Cynthia. *Abbie in stitches*
Edwards, Michelle. *Room for the baby*
Gibbons, Gail. *The quilting bee*
Gordon, Domenica More. *Archie*
Green, Stephanie. *Betsy Ross and the silver thimble*
Heo, Yumi. *Lady Hahn and her seven friends*
Hopkinson, Deborah. *Sweet Clara and the freedom quilt*
Johnston, Tony. *Levi Strauss gets a bright idea*
My best friend Bear
Kimmel, Eric A. *Stormy's hat*
Leedahl, Shelley A. *The bone talker*
McDonald, Megan. *The Hinky Pink*
McKee, David. *Elmer and Super El*
Marshall, Linda Elovitz. *Grandma Rose's magic*
Masini, Beatrice. *Here comes the bride*
Paul, Ann Whitford. *The seasons sewn*
Ransom, Candice F. *The promise quilt*
Sabuda, Robert. *The Blizzard's robe*
Shea, Pegi Deitz. *The whispering cloth*
Strauss, Linda Leopold. *The princess gown*
Wallner, Alexandra. *Betsy Ross*
White, Becky. *Betsy Ross*
Ziefert, Harriet. *My forever dress*

Activities – shopping *see* Shopping

Activities – singing

Andrews, Julie. *The very fairy princess sparkles in the snow*
Auch, Mary Jane. *Bantam of the opera*
Bolliger, Max. *The happy troll*
Bonwill, Ann. *The Frazzle family finds a way*
Cave, Kathryn. *Henry's song*
Crimi, Carolyn. *Tessa's tip-tapping toes*
Crow, Kristyn. *The middle-child blues*
Cunnane, Kelly. *Chirchir is singing*
Daly, Niki. *Ruby sings the blues*
D'Arc, Karen Scourby. *My grandmother is a singing Yaya*
dePaola, Tomie. *The song of Francis*
Elya, Susan Middleton. *Sophie's trophy*
Gray, Luli. *Ant and Grasshopper*
Howe, James. *Horace and Morris join the chorus (but what about Dolores?)*
Kushner, Tony. *Brundibar*
Litwin, Eric. *Pete the cat: rocking in my school shoes*
Pete the cat and his four groovy buttons
Ljungkvist, Laura. *Pepi sings a new song*
Lucado, Max. *Alabaster's song*
Martin, Jacqueline Briggs. *Chicken joy on Redbean Road*
Mitchell, Margaree King. *When Grandmama sings*
Peterson, Jeanne Whitehouse. *My mama sings*
Raposo, Joe. *Sing!*
Schotter, Roni. *Doo-Wop Pop*
Sproule, Gail. *Singing the dark*
Taylor, Ann. *Baby dance*
Watts, Leslie Elizabeth. *The Baabaasheep Quartet*
Weaver, Tess. *Opera cat*
Wright, Catherine. *Steamboat Annie and the thousand-pound catfish*

Activities – storytelling

Ahlberg, Allan. *The snail house*
Ahlberg, Janet. *It was a dark and stormy night*
Aska, Warabe. *Tapicero tap tap*
Banks, Kate. *Max's words*
Blackstone, Stella. *How big is a pig?*
Bouchard, Dave. *The song within my heart*
Brutschy, Jennifer. *Just one more story*
Carlson, Nancy. *Henry's amazing imagination!*
Cazet, Denys. *The octopus*
Davol, Marguerite W. *The snake's tales*
Donaldson, Julia. *The fish who cried wolf*
Downey, Lynn. *Matilda's humdinger*
Fagan, Carl. *Mr. Zinger's hat*
Fleming, Candace. *Clever Jack takes the cake*
Freedman, Deborah. *The Story of Fish and Snail*
Gonzalez, Lucia. *The storyteller's candle / La velita de los cuentos*
Grey, Mini. *Toys in space*
Hanlon, Abby. *Ralph tells a story*
Hanson, Regina. *A season for mangoes*
Hest, Amy. *The babies are coming!*
Hughes, Vi. *Aziz, the story teller*
Johnston, Tony. *My abuelita*
Joosse, Barbara. *Grandma calls me Beautiful*
Kasza, Keiko. *Silly Goose's big story*
Kroll, Steven. *The Tyrannosaurus game*
Kurtz, Jane. *In the small, small night*
LaRochelle, David. *The haunted hamburger and other ghostly stories*
It's a tiger
Lyon, George Ella. *My friend, the starfinder*
McKinlay, Meg. *No bears*
McQuinn, Anna. *Lola loves stories*
Mahoney, Daniel J. *The Saturday escape*
Martin, Rafe. *The storytelling princess*
Mayr, Diane. *Littlebat's Halloween story*
Mortimer, Rachael. *Song for a princess*
Muth, Jon J. *Zen ghosts*
Zen shorts
Nash, Scott. *Tuff Fluff*
Nolan, Janet. *The St. Patrick's Day shillelagh*
O'Malley, Kevin. *Velcome*
Paschkis, Julie. *Mooshka*
Reiser, Lynn. *Little clam*
Robberecht, Thierry. *Sam tells stories*
Roberts, Bethany. *Gramps and the fire dragon*
Rochelle, Belinda. *Jewels*
Rosenthal, Eileen. *I'll save you Bobo!*
Say, Allen. *Kamishibai man*
Schaefer, Carole Lexa. *Down in the woods at sleepytime*
Down in the woods at sleepytime [board book]
Schwartz, Amy. *Some babies*
Scrimger, Richard. *Eugene's story*
Shannon, David. *Jangles*
Sierra, Judy. *Tell the truth, B. B. Wolf*
Simms, Laura. *Rotten teeth*
Slate, Joseph. *Story time for Little Porcupine*
Spalding, Andrea. *Solomon's tree*
Stead, Philip C. *Bear has a story to tell*
Sullivan, Sarah. *Once upon a baby brother*
Taback, Simms. *Kibitzers and fools*
Van Leeuwen, Jean. *The tickle stories*
Velasquez, Eric. *Grandma's records*
Wallen, Ila. *The moon in my room*
Wyeth, Sharon Dennis. *The granddaughter necklace*
Yeh, Kat. *The magic brush*
Yolen, Jane. *Miz Berlin walks*

Activities – swapping *see* Activities – trading

Activities – swimming *see* Sports – swimming

Activities – swinging

Patricelli, Leslie. *Higher! Higher!*
Tusa, Tricia. *Follow me*

Activities – talking

Cruise, Robin. *Bartleby speaks!*
Hindley, Judy. *Baby talk*
Jones, Christianne. *Lacey Walker, nonstop talker*
Ziefert, Harriet. *Talk, baby!*

Activities – trading

Chorao, Kay. *Pig and Crow*
Dick Whittington and his cat. *Dick Whittington and his cat*
Gardella, Tricia. *Blackberry booties*
Heide, Iris van der. *The red chalk*
Jennings, Sharon. *Franklin makes a deal*
Johnson, Paul Brett. *Bearhide and crow*
Martin, Jacqueline Briggs. *On Sand Island*
Murphy, Stuart J. *Dinosaur deals*
O'Neill, Alexis. *Estela's swap*
Steig, Jeanne. *Fleas!*
Suen, Anastasia. *Window music*
Torres, Leyla. *Saturday sancocho*
VanHecke, Susan. *An apple pie for dinner*

Activities – traveling

Aardema, Verna. *Traveling to Tondo*
Alsenas, Linas. *Mrs. Claus takes a vacation*
Axelrod, Amy. *Pigs on the move*
Aylesworth, Jim. *My sister's rusty bike*
Bailey, Linda. *Stanley at sea*
Baillie, Allan. *Dragonquest*
Banks, Kate. *City cat*
Barnett, Mac. *Oh no! Not again!*
Barracca, Debra. *Maxi, the star*
Bart, Kathleen. *Town Teddy and Country Bear go global*
Bateman, Teresa. *Gus, the pilgrim turkey*
Bauer, Sepp. *The Christmas rose*
Becker, Aaron. *Journey*
Best, Cari. *When Catherine the Great and I were eight!*
Blackstone, Stella. *Bear takes a trip*
Brown, Laurie Krasny. *Dinosaurs travel*
Brown, Marc. *Arthur meets the president*
Brunhoff, Jean de. *The travels of Babar*
Brunhoff, Laurent de. *Babar's USA*
Babar's world tour
Brutschy, Jennifer. *Just one more story*
Bunting, Eve. *Ducky*
Peepers
Burleigh, Robert. *Hit the road, Jack*
Carle, Eric. *Friends*
The rooster who set out to see the world
Rooster's off to see the world
Chancellor, Deborah. *Traveling on land*
Clifton-Brown, Holly. *Annie Hoot and the knitting extravaganza*

Cocca-Leffler, Maryann. *Bus route to Boston*
Codell, Esme Raji. *Seed by seed*
Conrad, Donna. *See you soon, Moon*
Cooney, Barbara. *Miss Ramphius*
Cooper, Elisha. *Train*
Cora, Cat. *A suitcase surprise for Mommy*
Coy, John. *Vroomaloom zoom*
Crampton, Gertrude. *Scuffy the tugboat*
Crowley, Ned. *Nanook and Pryce*
Cummings, Pat. *My aunt came back*
Davis, Kenneth C. *Don't know much about the pioneers*
Deacon, Alexis. *A place to call home*
Dickson, Louise. *The vanishing cat*
Docherty, Thomas. *To the beach*
Dunbar, Joyce. *Shoe baby*
Dupre, Kelly. *The raven's gift*
Egan, Tim. *Dodsworth in London*
Dodsworth in New York
Dodsworth in Paris
Dodsworth in Rome
Elissa, Barbara. *The remarkable journey of Josh's kippah*
Eschbacher, Roger. *Road trip*
Evans, Lezlie. *The bunnies' trip*
Evert, Lori. *The Christmas wish*
Faller, Regis. *The adventures of Polo*
Polo
Polo and the magician!
Fitzpatrick, Marie-Louise. *You, me and the big blue sea*
Foreman, Michael. *Fortunately, unfortunately*
Fox, Mem. *Possum magic*
Gaiman, Neil. *Instructions*
Gammell, Stephen. *How about going for a ride*
Gerstein, Mordicai. *How to bicycle to the moon to plant sunflowers*
Gravett, Emily. *Meerkat mail*
Gutman, Anne. *Lisa's airplane trip*
Handford, Martin. *Find Waldo now*
The great Waldo search
Where's Waldo?
Where's Waldo? In Hollywood
Where's Waldo? The fantastic journey
Where's Waldo? The wonder book
Where's Waldo now?
Hawkes, Kevin. *The wicked big toddlah goes to New York*
Helldorfer, M. C. *Hog music*
Hobbie, Holly. *Toot and Puddle*
Toot and Puddle: wish you were here
Toot and Puddle, I'll be home for Christmas
Toot and Puddle, top of the world
Hodgkinson, Leigh. *Boris and the snoozebox*
Holmes, Mary Tavener. *A giraffe goes to Paris*
Horowitz, Dave. *Duck, duck, moose*
Howland, Naomi. *ABCDrive!*
Hubbell, Patricia. *My first airplane ride*
Hume, Stephen Eaton. *Red moon follows truck*
Hutchins, Hazel. *Beneath the bridge*
Isadora, Rachel. *Over the green hills*
Jahn-Clough, Lisa. *Felicity and Cordelia*
Jonas, Ann. *Round trip*
Joslin, Mary. *The shore beyond*
Kaczman, James. *A bird and his worm*
Kasparavicius, Kestutis. *The bear family's world tour Christmas*
Kay, Verla. *Covered wagons, bumpy trails*
Kellogg, Steven. *Johnny Appleseed: a tall tale*
Kelly, Mij. *William and the night train*
Kerby, Mona. *Owney, the mail-pouch pooch*
Kimmel, Eric A. *Pumpkinhead*
Kirk, Daniel. *Honk honk! Beep beep!*
Krebs, Laurie. *Off we go to Mexico*
We're riding on a caravan
We're sailing down the Nile
We're sailing to Galapagos
Lawlor, Laurie. *Old Crump*
Lazo, Caroline. *Someday when my cat can talk*
Lester, Alison. *Sophie Scott goes south*
Levitin, Sonia. *Nine for California*
Lin, Grace. *Olvina flies*
Lindbergh, Reeve. *Johnny Appleseed*
London, Jonathan. *Froggy goes to Hawaii*
Moshi moshi
Loth, Sebastian. *Clementine*
Louis, Catherine. *Liu and the bird*
McCarthy, Meghan. *The adventures of Patty and the big red bus*
McCarty, Peter. *Little bunny on the move*
McClintock, Barbara. *Adele and Simon in America*
McCourt, Lisa. *I miss you, Stinky Face*
McPhail, David. *Pig Pig returns*
Margolin, H. Ellen. *Goin' to Boston*
Mauner, Claudia. *Zoe Sophia's scrapbook*
Miller, Sara Swan. *Cat in the bag*
Moss, Miriam. *Matty takes off!*
Munro, Roxie. *The inside-outside book of Texas*
The inside-outside book of Washington, D.C.
Mazescapes
Neitzel, Shirley. *The bag I'm taking to Grandma's*
Neubecker, Robert. *Courage of the blue boy*
Norling, Beth. *The stone baby*
Nye, Naomi Shihab. *Come with me*
Ohi, Ruth. *A trip with Grandma*
Ormerod, Jan. *Miss Mouse takes off*
Orona-Ramirez, Kristy. *Kiki's journey*
Pattison, Darcy. *The journey of Oliver K. Woodman*
Searching for Oliver K. Woodman
Piepmeier, Charlotte. *Lucy's journey to the wild west*
Pinkney, Gloria Jean. *The Sunday outing*
Potter, Giselle. *The year I didn't go to school*
Priceman, Marjorie. *How to make a cherry pie and see the U.S.A.*
How to make an apple pie and see the world
Ramsey, Calvin Alexander. *Ruth and the Green Book*
Reibstein, Mark. *Wabi Sabi*
Rockwell, Anne. *Whoo! whoo! goes the train*
Rogers, Fred. *Going on an airplane*
Rohmann, Eric. *Pumpkinhead*
Rosen, Michael J. *A drive in the country*
Rubin, Adam. *Those darn squirrels fly south*
Rumford, James. *Chee-lin*
The Island-below-the-star
Rylant, Cynthia. *The relatives came*
Tulip sees America
Say, Allen. *Grandfather's journey*
Segal, John. *Alistair and Kip's great adventure*
Seuss, Dr. *I had trouble getting to Solla Sollew*
Siegel, Randy. *Grandma's smile*
Silvano, Wendi. *Just one more*
Sís, Peter. *Tibet through the red box*
Skinner, Daphne. *All aboard!*
Smath, Jerry. *Sammy Salami*
Smith, Maggie. *Counting our way to Maine*
Sorensen, Henri. *New Hope*
Stanley, Diane. *Joining the Boston Tea Party*
Thanksgiving on Plymouth Plantation

Stead, Philip C. *Jonathan and the big blue boat*
Steggall, Susan. *Rattle and rap*
Stem, J. David. *Kay Thompson's Eloise in Hollywood*
Steptoe, Javaka. *The Jones family express*
Stevenson, James. *All aboard!*
Stoop, Naoko. *Red Knit Cap Girl to the rescue*
Suen, Anastasia. *Road work ahead*
Swain, Gwenyth. *Johnny Appleseed*
Thomas, Joyce Carol. *In the land of milk and honey*
Thompson, Emma. *The further tale of Peter Rabbit*
Thompson, Kay. *Kay Thompson's Eloise in Moscow*
Tibo, Gilles. *The grand journey of Mr. Man*
Tonatiuh, Duncan. *Pancho Rabbit and the coyote*
Trimble, Marcia. *Hello sun*
Turner, Ann Warren. *Nettie's trip south*
Uhlberg, Myron. *Lemuel, the fool*
Van Leeuwen, Jean. *Across the wide dark sea*
van Lieshout, Maria. *Backseat A-B-see*
Verburg, Bonnie. *The kiss box*
Waddell, Martin. *Small Bear lost*
Wallace, Ivy. *Pookie*
Walters, Virginia. *Are we there yet, Daddy?*
Waugh, Peter. *The great cannon beach mouse caper*
Wiesmüller, Dieter. *The adventures of Marco and Polo*
Wild, Margaret. *Going home*
Willems, Mo. *Knuffle Bunny free*
Wishinsky, Frieda. *What's up, bear?*
Wong, Janet S. *The trip back home*
Wood, Audrey. *Silly Sally*
Silly Sally [board book]
Wright, Courtni Crump. *Wagon train*
Yolen, Jane. *Johnny Appleseed: the legend and the truth*
Ziefert, Harriet. *From Kalamazoo to Timbuktu!*
Zullo, Germano. *Line 135*

Activities – vacationing

Adams, Adrienne. *The Easter egg artists*
Alsenas, Linas. *Mrs. Claus takes a vacation*
Becker, Suzy. *Manny's cows*
Berenstain, Stan and Jan. *The Berenstain bears and too much vacation*
Breen, Steve. *The secret of Santa's island*
Brown, Marc. *Arthur's family vacation*
Chapra, Mimi. *Sparky's bark / El ladrido de Sparky*
Cocca-Leffler, Maryann. *A vacation for Pooch*
Cottle, Joan. *Miles away from home*
Cousins, Lucy. *Maisy goes on vacation*
Davies, Jacqueline. *The house takes a vacation*
Day, Alexandra. *Carl's summer vacation*
dePaola, Tomie. *Strega Nona takes a vacation*
Falconer, Ian. *Olivia goes to Venice*
Frazee, Marla. *A couple of boys have the best week ever*
Gutman, Anne. *Gaspard on vacation*
Hundal, Nancy. *Camping*
Jocelyn, Marthe. *Mayfly*
Joyce, William. *Dinosaur Bob*
Kellogg, Steven. *Ralph's secret weapon*
Koch, Ed. *Eddie's little sister makes a splash*
Korda, Lerryn. *It's vacation time*
Laden, Nina. *Clowns on vacation*
McPhail, David. *Emma's pet*
Emma's vacation
Marshall, James. *George and Martha 'round and 'round*
Maynard, Bill. *Santa's time off*
Meddaugh, Susan. *Martha calling*
Murphy, Stuart J. *The best vacation ever*
Perkins, Lynne Rae. *Pictures from our vacation*
Perret, Delphine. *The Big Bad Wolf goes on vacation*
Pulver, Robin. *Punctuation takes a vacation*
Puttock, Simon. *Goat and Donkey in the great outdoors*
Reiss, Mike. *Santa claustrophobia*
Samuels, Barbara. *Aloha, Dolores*
Smath, Jerry. *Sammy Salami*
Stephens, Helen. *Ahoyty-toyty*
Stevenson, James. *The castaway*
The Sea View Hotel
Stock, Catherine. *A porc in New York*
Tafuri, Nancy. *The brass ring*
Teague, Mark. *LaRue across America*
Thomas, Shelley Moore. *A Good Knight's rest*
Van Leeuwen, Jean. *Touch the sky summer*
Yoon, Salina. *Penguin on vacation*
Ziefert, Harriet. *Pushkin minds the bundle*

Activities – walking

Arnosky, Jim. *Crinkleroot's guide to walking in wild places*
Outdoors on foot
Best, Cari. *When we go walking*
Briggs, Raymond. *The puddleman*
Cooper, Elisha. *A good night walk*
Devine, Monica. *Carry me, Mama*
Duncan, Lois. *I walk at night*
Edwards, Pamela Duncan. *The worrywarts*
Frazee, Marla. *Walk on!*
George, Lindsay Barrett. *In the woods*
Graham, Bob. *The silver button*
Haughton, Emma. *Rainy day*
Hertz, Grete Janus. *Olie's bedtime walk*
Hill, Eric. *Spot's first walk*
Hoban, Tana. *I walk and read*
Hubbell, Patricia. *Sidewalk trip*
Inches, Alison. *Corduroy's hike*
Johnson, D. B. *Henry hikes to Fitchburg*
Henry works
Jonas, Ann. *The trek*
Watch William walk
Kimmelman, Leslie. *The Shabbat puppy*
Lewis, Kim. *One summer day*
London, Jonathan. *Wiggle, waggle*
Luenn, Nancy. *Squish!*
Monroe, Chris. *Cookie, the walker*
Pfister, Marcus. *Penguin Pete and Little Tim*
Rockwell, Anne. *Willy can count*
Sattler, Jennifer. *Uh-oh, Dodo!*
Schindler, S. D. *Spike and Ike take a hike*
Shirotani, Hideo. *Let's take a walk / Vamos a caminar*
Showers, Paul. *The listening walk*
Singer, Marilyn. *Didi and Daddy on the Promenade*
Smalls-Hector, Irene. *Jonathan and his mommy*
Stevenson, James. *Rolling Rose*
Sullivan, Paula. *Todd's box*
Waber, Bernard. *Lyle walks the dogs*
White, Kathryn. *Ruby's school walk*
Williams, Sue. *I went walking*
I went walking [board book]
Yolen, Jane. *Miz Berlin walks*
Zolotow, Charlotte. *Say it!*

Activities – weaving

Bang, Molly. *Dawn*

Blood, Charles L. *The goat in the rug*
Bodkin, Odds. *The crane wife*
Brill, Marlene Targ. *Margaret Knight, girl inventor*
Castaneda, Omar S. *Abuela's weave*
Francis, Lee DeCora. *Kunu's basket*
Hamilton, Virginia. *The girl who spun gold*
Heyer, Marilee. *The weaving of a dream*
Hurd, Thacher. *The weaver*
Medearis, Angela Shelf. *Seven spools of thread*
Musgrove, Margaret. *The spider weaver*
Oughton, Jerrie. *The magic weaver of rugs*
Perrow, Angeli. *Many hands*
San Souci, Robert D. *The enchanted tapestry*
A weave of words
Schubert, Leda. *Feeding the sheep*
Shah, Idries. *Fatima the spinner and the tent*
Tseng, Grace. *White tiger, blue serpent*
Yagawa, Sumiko. *The crane wife*

Activities – whistling

Egielski, Richard. *Three magic balls*
Keats, Ezra Jack. *Whistle for Willie*
Mahy, Margaret. *Mister Whistler*

Activities – wood carving

Dorros, Arthur. *Julio's magic*
Martín, Hugo C. *Pablo's Christmas*

Activities – working

Ackerman, Karen. *By the dawn's early light*
Aesop. *The ant and the grasshopper*, ill. by Amy Lowry Poole
The ant and the grasshopper, ill. by Sara Rojo
Altman, Linda Jacobs. *Amelia's road*
Ancona, George. *Mis quehaceres / My chores*
Asim, Jabari. *Daddy goes to work*
Bair, Sheila. *Isabel's car wash*
Ballard, Robin. *My day, your day*
Banks, Kate. *Mama's coming home*
The night worker
Barton, Byron. *Machines at work*
Batt, Tanya Robyn. *The faerie's gift*
Bloom, Becky. *Crackers*
Bunting, Eve. *A day's work*
Burton, Virginia Lee. *Mike Mulligan and his steam shovel*
Carle, Eric. *Walter the baker*
Cordsen, Carol Foskett. *The milkman*
Dahl, Roald. *The giraffe and the pelly and me*
dePaola, Tomie. *Boss for a day*
Emberley, Rebecca. *The ant and the grasshopper*
Ericsson, Jennifer A. *Home to me, home to you*
Gershator, Phillis. *Sky sweeper*
Gibbons, Gail. *Deadline!*
Zoo
Gray, Luli. *Ant and Grasshopper*
Haley, Gail E. *Two bad boys*
Hall, Donald. *Ox-cart man*
Hartland, Jessie. *Night shift*
Heide, Florence Parry. *The day of Ahmed's secret*
Hertz, Grete Janus. *Olie's bedtime walk*
Johnson, Angela. *I dream of trains*
Johnson, D. B. *Henry works*
Levine, Arthur A. *Monday is one day*
Lewis, Kim. *Floss*
Look, Lenore. *Love as strong as ginger*
Lum, Kate. *Princesses are not quitters!*
Lyon, George Ella. *Mama is a miner*
McPhail, David. *Pig Pig gets a job*
Markel, Michelle. *Brave girl*
Mills, Judith Christine. *The painted chest*
Morck, Irene. *Old bird*
Morris, Ann. *Work*
Murphy, Stuart J. *Sluggers' car wash*
Paulsen, Gary. *Worksong*
Pedersen, Marika. *Mommy works, Daddy works*
Pilkey, Dav. *The paperboy*
Pryor, Bonnie. *The dream jar*
Purmell, Ann. *Christmas tree farm*
Reichert, Amy. *Take your mama to work today*
Rotner, Shelley. *Everybody works*
Rylant, Cynthia. *Mr. Griggs' work*
San Souci, Robert D. *The hired hand*
Shaw, Mary. *Brady Brady and the great rink*
Spinelli, Eileen. *Night shift daddy*
Stolz, Mary. *Zekmet, the stone carver*
Taber, Tory. *Rufus at work*
Thayer, Tanya. *Earning money*
Thomas, Mark. *Work in Colonial America*
Waber, Bernard. *Lyle at the office*
Warwick, Dionne. *Little Man*
Wells, Rosemary. *Love waves*
Wheeler, Lisa. *Jam and jelly by Holly and Nellie*
Williams, Sherley Anne. *Working cotton*
Yee, Wong Herbert. *Hamburger Heaven*
Yu, Li-Qiong. *A New Year's reunion*

Activities – writing

Aliki. *Communication*
Arnosky, Jim. *Mouse writing*
Asch, Frank. *The Daily Comet*
Auch, Mary Jane. *The plot chickens*
Banks, Kate. *The eraserheads*
Barnett, Mac. *Chloe and the lion*
Battle-Lavert, Gwendolyn. *Papa's mark*
Best, Cari. *Beatrice spells some lulus and learns to write a letter*
Brown, Marc. *Arthur writes a story*
Brown, Monica. *My name is Gabito / Me llamo Gabito*
Burleigh, Robert. *If you spent a day with Thoreau at Walden pond*
Carlson, Nancy. *Henry's amazing imagination!*
Christelow, Eileen. *The desperate dog writes again*
Letters from a desperate dog
Cline-Ransome, Lesa. *Words set me free*
Clinton, Catherine. *Phillis's big test*
Crimi, Carolyn. *Dear Tabby*
Henry and the Crazed Chicken Pirates
Cronin, Doreen. *Click, clack, moo*
Click, clack, quackity-quack
Diary of a fly
Diary of a spider
Diary of a worm
Danneberg, Julie. *Cowboy Slim*
Darbyshire, Kristen. *Put it on the list!*
de Las Casas, Dianne. *The Little "Read" Hen*
Dormer, Frank W. *The obstinate pen*
Dubosarsky, Ursula. *Rex*
Esbaum, Jill. *Stanza*
Farley, Brianne. *Ike's incredible ink*
French, Jackie. *Diary of a baby wombat*
Gerstein, Mordicai. *A book*
Gorbachev, Valeri. *What's the big idea, Molly?*
Hanlon, Abby. *Ralph tells a story*

Heide, Florence Parry. *The day of Ahmed's secret*
Hills, Tad. *Rocket writes a story*
Hobbie, Holly. *Fanny and Annabelle*
Holub, Joan. *Little red writing*
Hopkins, Lee Bennett. *Full moon and star*
Howe, James. *Houndsley and Catina*
Inches, Alison. *Corduroy writes a letter*
Johnson, D. B. *Henry works*
Kempter, Christa. *Dear Little Lamb*
Kirk, Daniel. *Library mouse*
Library mouse: a friend's tale
Library mouse: a museum adventure
Ten things I love about you
Leedy, Loreen. *The Furry News*
Messages in the mailbox
Linch, Tanya. *My duck*
Lionni, Leo. *The alphabet tree*
Long, Ethan. *The book that Zack wrote*
Look, Lenore. *Polka Dot Penguin Pottery*
Louis, Catherine. *Liu and the bird*
McAnulty, Stacy. *Dear Santasaurus*
McElroy, Lisa Tucker. *Meet my grandmother. She's a children's book author*
Matsuoka, Mei. *Footprints in the snow*
Morgan, Michaela. *Dear bunny*
Muntean, Michaela. *Do not open this book!*
Murphy, Stuart J. *Write on, Carlos!*
Niemann, Christoph. *The pet dragon*
O'Connor, Jane. *Fancy Nancy: poet extraordinaire!*
O'Malley, Kevin. *Once upon a cool motorcycle dude*
Once upon a royal superbaby
Pearson, Susan. *Slugs in love*
Pulver, Robin. *The case of the incapacitated capitals*
Thank you, Miss Doover
Puttock, Simon. *Yours truly, Louisa*
Rockwell, Anne. *Father's Day*
Rumford, James. *Silent music*
Rylant, Cynthia. *Best wishes*
Schubert, Leda. *Reading to Peanut*
Scieszka, Jon. *Battle Bunny*
Seabrooke, Brenda. *'Twas the day before Christmas*
Shipton, Jonathan. *Baby baby blah blah blah!*
Solheim, James. *Born yesterday*
Spinelli, Eileen. *The best story*
Stanton, Melissa. *My pen pal, Santa*
Stein, David Ezra. *Love, Mouserella*
Stevens, Janet. *Help me, Mr. Mutt!*
Stewart, Sarah. *The journey*
Sullivan, Sarah. *Once upon a baby brother*
Sutton, Jane. *Don't call me Sidney*
Taback, Simms. *Postcards from camp*
Teague, Mark. *Dear Mrs. LaRue*
Detective LaRue
LaRue across America
Tonatiuh, Duncan. *Dear Primo*
Van Nutt, Julia. *Skyrockets and snickerdoodles*
Wallner, Alexandra. *Lucy Maud Montgomery*
Watt, Mélanie. *Chester*
Chester's back!
Chester's masterpiece
Wells, Rosemary. *Yoko writes her name*
Yeh, Kat. *The magic brush*
Yorinks, Arthur. *Homework*

Adoption

Bunting, Eve. *Jin Woo*
Carlson, Nancy. *My family is forever*
Clark, Karen Henry. *Sweet moon baby*
Cole, Joanna. *How I was adopted*
Coste, Marion. *Finding Joy*
Curtis, Jamie Lee. *Tell me again about the night I was born*
Czech, Jan M. *An American face*
D'Antonio, Nancy. *Our baby from China*
dePaola, Tomie. *A new Barker in the house*
Foggo, Cheryl. *Dear baobab*
Friedman, Darlene. *Star of the Week: a story of love, adoption, and brownies with sprinkles*
Friedrich, Molly. *You're not my real mother!*
Garden, Nancy. *Molly's family*
Heo, Yumi. *Ten days and nine nights*
Hodge, Deborah. *Emma's story*
Höjer, Dan. *Heart of mine*
Joosse, Barbara. *Nikolai, the only bear*
Kasza, Keiko. *A mother for Choco*
Katz, Karen. *Over the moon*
Keller, Holly. *Horace*
Krishnaswami, Uma. *Bringing Asha home*
Lears, Laurie. *Megan's birthday tree*
Lewis, Rose A. *Every year on your birthday*
I love you like crazy cakes
Orange Peel's pocket
Lin, Grace. *The red thread*
López, Susana. *The best family in the world*
Lottridge, Celia Barker. *Berta, a remarkable dog*
McCully, Emily Arnold. *My real family*
McCutcheon, John. *Happy adoption day!*
McDonnell, Christine. *Goyangi means cat*
McMahon, Patricia. *Just add one Chinese sister*
Mora, Pat. *Pablo's tree*
Oelschlager, Vanita. *Made in China*
Okimoto, Jean Davies. *The White Swan express*
Parr, Todd. *We belong together*
Peacock, Carol Antoinette. *Mommy far, Mommy near*
Pettitt, Linda. *Yafi's family*
Rogers, Fred. *Adoption*
Rosenberg, Liz. *We wanted you*
Rotner, Shelley. *I'm adopted!*
Say, Allen. *Allison*
Schreck, Karen Halvorsen. *Lucy's family tree*
Stoeke, Janet Morgan. *Waiting for May*
Sugarman, Brynn Olenberg. *Rebecca's journey home*
Thisdale, François. *Nini*
Thomas, Eliza. *The red blanket*
Turner, Ann Warren. *Through moon and stars and night skies*
Wynne-Jones, Tim. *The boat in the tree*
Xinran, Xue. *Motherbridge of love*
Young, Ed. *My Mei Mei*

Aged *see* Old age

Airplanes, airports

Barton, Byron. *Airplanes*
Airport
Berger, Melvin. *How do airplanes fly?*
Bingham, Caroline. *DK big book of airplanes*
Blechman, Nicholas. *Night light*
Brown, Don. *Ruth Law thrills a nation*
Bunting, Eve. *Fly away home*
Buzzeo, Toni. *Lighthouse Christmas*
Crews, Donald. *Flying*
Demarest, Chris L. *Lindbergh*
Edwards, Pamela Duncan. *The Wright brothers*

Fardell, John. *Jeremiah Jellyfish flies high!*
Flanagan, Alice K. *Flying an agricultural plane with Mr. Miller*
Floca, Brian. *Five trucks*
Ford, Gilbert. *Flying lessons*
Gibbons, Gail. *Flying*
Gordon, David. *The ugly truckling*
Grist, Julie. *Flying, just plane fun*
Gutman, Anne. *Lisa's airplane trip*
Hodgkins, Fran. *How people learned to fly*
Hubbell, Patricia. *Airplanes: soaring! diving! turning!*
My first airplane ride
Ichikawa, Satomi. *Come fly with me*
Joseph, Lynn. *Fly, Bessie, fly*
Lenski, Lois. *The little airplane*
Lin, Grace. *Olvina flies*
Lindbergh, Reeve. *Nobody owns the sky*
London, Jonathan. *A plane goes ka-zoom!*
Lund, Deb. *Dinosoaring*
Lyon, George Ella. *Planes fly!*
McCarty, Peter. *Moon plane*
Meadows, Michelle. *Pilot pups*
Munsch, Robert N. *Angela's airplane*
Ormerod, Jan. *Miss Mouse takes off*
Pallotta, Jerry. *The airplane alphabet book*
The jet alphabet book
Pett, Mark. *The boy and the airplane*
Provensen, Alice. *The glorious flight*
Raven, Margot Theis. *Mercedes and the chocolate pilot*
Reynolds, Peter H. *I'm here*
Riehle, Mary Ann McCabe. *A is for airplane*
Rockwell, Anne. *Planes*
Rogers, Fred. *Going on an airplane*
Rogers, Hal. *Airplanes*
Ryan, Pam Muñoz. *Amelia and Eleanor go for a ride*
Schaefer, Lola M. *Airport*
The Wright brothers
Siebert, Diane. *Plane song*
Spier, Peter. *Bored — nothing to do!*
Stanley, Mandy. *Lettice the flying rabbit*
Sturges, Philemon. *I love planes*
Suen, Anastasia. *Air show*
Van Lieshout, Maria. *Flight 1-2-3*
Wells, Rosemary. *Yoko finds her way*
Williams, Treat. *Air show!*
Yolen, Jane. *My brothers' flying machine*

Alaska

Aillaud, Cindy Lou. *Recess at 20 below*
Blake, Robert J. *Painter and Ugly*
Chamberlin-Calamar, Pat. *Alaska's twelve days of summer*
Claflin, Willy. *The uglified ducky*
Crummel, Susan Stevens. *Ten-Gallon Bart beats the heat*
Gill, Shelley. *Up on Denali*
Guenther, James. *Turnagain, Ptarmigan, where did you go?*
Joosse, Barbara. *Wind-wild dog*
Laverde, Arlene. *Alaska's three pigs*
London, Jonathan. *Sled dogs run*
McCarthy, Meghan. *The incredible life of Balto*
Miller, Debbie S. *A caribou journey*
River of life
Rand, Gloria. *Baby in a basket*
Prince William
Schoenherr, John. *Bear*
Seibert, Patricia. *Mush!*
Senshu, Noriko. *Sonny's dream*
Stihler, Chérie B. *The giant cabbage turnip*

Aliens

Agee, Jon. *The other side of town*
Arnold, Tedd. *Green Wilma, frog in space*
Bartram, Simon. *Bob's best-ever friend*
Breathed, Berkeley. *Edwurd Fudwupper fibbed big*
Mars needs moms!
Corey, Shana. *First graders from Mars: Horus's horrible day*
First graders from Mars: Nergal and the Great Space Race
First graders from Mars: Tera, star student
First graders from Mars: The problem with Pelly
Donovan, Sandy. *Bob the Alien discovers the Dewey Decimal System*
Duval, Kathy. *Take me to your BBQ*
Jeffers, Oliver. *The way back home*
Karas, G. Brian. *Bebe's bad dream*
Kirk, Daniel. *Hush, little alien*
Layton, Neal. *Smile if you're human*
McElligott, Matthew. *Even aliens need snacks*
McNamara, Margaret. *The three little aliens and the big bad robot*
McNaughton, Colin. *Here come the aliens!*
We're off to look for aliens
McPhail, David. *Tinker and Tom and the Star Baby*
O'Malley, Kevin. *Captain Raptor and the moon mystery*
Pallotta, Jerry. *Twizzlers percentages book*
Passen, Lisa. *Attack of the 50-foot teacher*
Porto, Tony. *Blue aliens*
Get red
Schories, Pat. *Jack and the night visitors*
When Jack goes out
Scieszka, Jon. *Baloney, Henry P.*
Shields, Carol Diggory. *Martian rock*
Singer, Marilyn. *The boy who cried alien*
Smallcomb, Pam. *Earth to Clunk*
Viva, Frank. *A long way away*
Whatley, Bruce. *Captain Pajamas*
Wiesner, David. *Mr. Wuffles!*
Wood, Audrey. *The Christmas adventure of Space Elf Sam*
Yaccarino, Dan. *First day on a strange new planet*
New pet
Yorinks, Arthur. *Company's going*
Young, Ned. *Zoomer's out-of-this-world Christmas*

Alphabet books *see* ABC books

Ambition *see* Character traits – ambition

American Indians *see* Indians of Central America; Indians of North America; Indians of South America

Amphibians *see also* Frogs & toads; Reptiles

Florian, Douglas. *Lizards, frogs, and polliwogs*

Amusement parks *see* Parks – amusement

Anatomy

Andrews, Sylvia. *Dancing in my bones*
Arnold, Tedd. *More parts*
Parts
Baker, Keith. *My octopus arms*
Bang, Molly. *All of me!*
Barnett, Mac. *Mustache!*
Bauer, Marion Dane. *If you had a nose like an elephant's trunk*
Thank you for me!
Toes, ears, and nose!
Bennett, Artie. *The butt book*
The best part of me
Bilgrami, Shaheen. *Amazing dinosaur discovery*
Incredible animal discovery
Brown, Laurie Krasny. *What's the big secret?*
Carle, Eric. *From head to toe*
My very first book of heads and tails
Cole, Joanna. *The magic school bus inside the human body*
Collard, Sneed B. *Beaks!*
Davick, Linda. *I love you, nose! I love you, toes!*
Harper, Charise Mericle. *Henry's heart*
Harris, Robie H. *Who has what?*
Henderson, Kathy. *Look at you!*
Hickling, Meg. *Boys, girls and body science*
Hindley, Judy. *Eyes, nose, fingers and toes*
Jenkins, Steve. *Actual size*
Prehistoric actual size
What do you do with a tail like this?
Maloney, Peter. *His mother's nose*
Martin, Bill, Jr. *Here are my hands*
Martin, David. *We've all got bellybuttons*
Menchin, Scott. *What if everything had legs?*
Moore, Julianne. *Freckleface Strawberry*
Freckleface Strawberry: best friends forever
Pratt, Pierre. *I see . . . my mom / I see . . . my dad*
I see . . . my sister / I see . . . my cat
Rotner, Shelley. *The body book*
Saltz, Gail. *Amazing you*
Schwartz, Amy. *A beautiful girl*
Seuling, Barbara. *From head to toe*
Showers, Paul. *A drop of blood*
Hear your heart
How you talk
Singer, Marilyn. *The one and only me*
Zoboli, Giovanna. *I wish I had . . .*

Anatomy – belly buttons *see* Anatomy – navels

Anatomy – brain

O'Connor, Teddy. *A new brain for Igor*

Anatomy – ears

Genechten, Guido van. *Flop-Ear*
Hartley, Karen, et al. *Hearing in living things*
Harvey, Amanda. *Dog-eared*
Miles, Elizabeth J. *Ears*
Nelson, Robin. *Hearing*
Rowe, Jeannette. *Whose ears?*
Showers, Paul. *Ears are for hearing*
Slegers, Liesbet. *Funny ears*

Anatomy – eyes

Barclay, Eric. *I can see just fine*
Cobb, Vicki. *Open your eyes*
Fielding, Beth. *Animal eyes*
Glaser, Jason. *Pinkeye*
Gordon, Sharon. *Pinkeye*
Seeing
Hartley, Karen. *Seeing in living things*
Kostecki-Shaw, Jenny Sue. *My travelin' eye*
Lyon, George Ella. *The pirate of kindergarten*
Nelson, Robin. *Seeing*
Priest, Robert H. *The pirate's eye*
Showers, Paul. *Look at your eyes*
Wiesmüller, Dieter. *In the blink of an eye*

Anatomy – faces

Alda, Arlene. *Here a face, there a face*
Ehrlich, Fred. *Does a seal smile?*
Hodgkinson, Leigh. *Smile!*
Miller, Margaret. *Baby faces*
Piven, Hanoch. *Let's make faces*
Rayner, Catherine. *Augustus and his smile*
Rotner, Shelley. *Faces*
Siegel, Randy. *Grandma's smile*

Anatomy – feet

Aliki. *My feet*
Crocker, Nancy. *Betty Lou Blue*
Ellis, Sarah. *The queen's feet*
Gow, Nancy. *Ten big toes and a prince's nose*
Hayles, Marsha. *Bunion Burt*
Hulbert, Laura. *Who has these feet?*
Konagaya, Kiyomi. *Beach feet*
O'Connor, George. *Uncle Bigfoot*
O'Hair, Margaret. *Sweet baby feet*
Paul, Ann Whitford. *Hello toes! Hello feet!*
Pearson, Susan. *Hooray for feet!*
Rowe, Jeannette. *Whose feet?*
Slegers, Liesbet. *Funny feet*
Vail, Rachel. *Righty and Lefty*
Walton, Rick. *My two hands, my two feet*
Whittaker, Nicola. *Feet*
Young, Amy. *Belinda and the glass slipper*
Belinda begins ballet
Belinda in Paris
Belinda, the ballerina

Anatomy – fins

Miles, Elizabeth J. *Wings, fins, and flippers*

Anatomy – hands

Aliki. *My hands*
Bowie, C. W. *Busy fingers*
Clements, Andrew. *The handiest things in the world*
Ehlert, Lois. *Hands*
Emberley, Ed. *Ed Emberley's fingerprint drawing book*
Fox, Mem. *Ten little fingers and ten little toes*
Hendra, Sue. *Barry, the fish with fingers*
Kroll, Virginia L. *Hands!*
Lasky, Kathryn. *Mommy's hands*
Mason, Margaret H. *These hands*
Price, Hope Lynne. *These hands*
Ryder, Joanne. *My father's hands*
Walton, Rick. *My two hands, my two feet*

Anatomy – heads

Kimmel, Eric A. *Pumpkinhead*

Miller, Margaret. *What's on my head?*
Swanson, Diane. *Headgear that hides and plays*

Anatomy – mouths

Brown, Heather. *Chomp!*
Miles, Elizabeth J. *Mouths and teeth*

Anatomy – navels

Batten, Mary. *Who has a belly button?*
Maloney, Peter. *Belly button boy*
Martin, David. *We've all got bellybuttons*
Pringle, Laurence P. *Everybody has a bellybutton*
Willis, Jeanne. *The boy who lost his bellybutton*

Anatomy – noses

Brown, Marc. *Arthur's nose*
Conway, David. *Errol and his extraordinary nose*
Cullen, Lynn. *Little Scraggly Hair*
Eaton, Jason Carter. *The day my runny nose ran away*
Flesher, Vivienne. *Alfred's nose*
Freymann, Saxton. *Dr. Pompo's nose*
Gordon, Sharon. *Smelling*
Gow, Nancy. *Ten big toes and a prince's nose*
Hartley, Karen. *Smelling in living things*
Johnston, Tony. *The badger and the magic fan*
Kipling, Rudyard. *How the elephant got his trunk*
Levine, Deb. *Parker picks*
Lucke, Deb. *Sneezenesia*
May, Robert Lewis. *Rudolph the red-nosed reindeer*
Miles, Elizabeth J. *Noses*
Nelson, Robin. *Smelling*
Rowe, Jeannette. *Whose nose?*
Samuels, Jenny. *A nose like a hose*
Schwarz, Viviane. *The adventures of a nose*
Swanson, Diane. *Noses that plow and poke*
Warrick, Karen Clemens. *Who needs that nose?*
Whittaker, Nicola. *Noses*

Anatomy – skeletons

Ahlberg, Janet. *Funnybones*
Bunting, Eve. *The bones of Fred McFee*
Crow, Kristyn. *Skeleton cat*
Cuyler, Margery. *Skeleton for dinner*
Skeleton hiccups
Glaser, Byron. *Bonz, inside-out*
Gunnufson, Charlotte. *Halloween hustle*
Heidbreder, Robert. *Black and bittern was night*
Johansen, K. V. *Pippin and the bones*
Johnston, Tony. *The ghost of Nicholas Greebe*
Soup bone
Levine, Sara. *Bone by bone*
Lucas, David. *The skeleton pirate*
Morales, Yuyi. *Just in case: a trickster tale and Spanish alphabet book*
Pickering, Jimmy. *Skelly the skeleton girl*
Rohmann, Eric. *Bone dog*
San Souci, Robert D. *Cinderella Skeleton*
Schertle, Alice. *The skeleton in the closet*
Stevenson, James. *The most amazing dinosaur*

Anatomy – skin

Iyengar, Malathi Michelle. *Tan to tamarind*
Pinkney, Sandra L. *A rainbow all around me*
Rotner, Shelley. *Shades of people*
Showers, Paul. *Your skin and mine*
Swanson, Diane. *Skin that slimes and scares*
Tyler, Michael. *The skin you live in*

Anatomy – tails

Ashman, Linda. *The tale of Wagmore Gently*
Bechtold, Lisze. *Edna's tale*
Duvall, Deborah L. *The opossum's tale*
Feiffer, Kate. *Henry, the dog with no tail*
Fielding, Beth. *Animal tails*
Hatkoff, Craig, et al. *Winter's tail*
Hulbert, Laura. *Who has this tail?*
Kawata, Ken. *Animal tails*
Kleven, Elisa. *A carousel tale*
McDonnell, Patrick. *Wag!*
Milne, A. A. *Eeyore loses a tail*
Slegers, Liesbet. *Funny tails*
Warrick, Karen Clemens. *If I had a tail*
Whittaker, Nicola. *Tails*

Anatomy – teeth *see* Teeth

Anatomy – thumbs *see* Thumb sucking

Anatomy – toes

Bowie, C. W. *Busy toes*
Crum, Shutta. *Who took my hairy toe?*
Fox, Mem. *Ten little fingers and ten little toes*
Harrington, Tim. *This little piggy*
Madison, Alan. *The littlest grape stomper*
Paul, Ann Whitford. *Hello toes! Hello feet!*
Tarpley, Todd. *Ten tiny toes*

Anatomy – tongues

Bonsignore, Joan. *Stick out your tongue*
Hartley, Karen. *Tasting in living things*
Nelson, Robin. *Tasting*

Anatomy – wings

Miles, Elizabeth J. *Wings, fins, and flippers*
Myers, Christopher. *Wings*
Tanaka, Shinsuke. *Wings*

Angels

Arrigan, Mary. *Mario's angels*
Clements, Andrew. *Bright Christmas*
Cole, Brock. *Larky Mavis*
dePaola, Tomie. *Angels, angels everywhere*
Durango, Julia. *Angels watching over me*
Greenfield, Eloise. *Angels*
I imagine angels
Judd, Naomi. *Naomi Judd's guardian angels*
Kleven, Elisa. *The friendship wish*
Lester, Julius. *What a truly cool world*
Why heaven is far away
Lucado, Max. *Alabaster's song*
Magnier, Thierry. *Isabelle and the angel*
Marzollo, Jean. *Snow angel*
Morpurgo, Michael. *On angel wings*
Myers, Walter Dean. *Brown angels*
Norris, Leslie. *Albert and the angels*
Pienkowski, Jan. *Bel and Bub and the baby bird*
Bel and Bub and the bad snowball

Bel and Bub and the big brown box
Bel and Bub and the black hole
Pittman, Helena Clare. *The angel tree*
Randall, Angel. *Snow angels*
Roberts, Bethany. *Cookie angel*
Rylant, Cynthia. *Dog Heaven*
Sloat, Teri. *Hark! The aardvark angels sing*
Spinelli, Eileen. *City angel*
What do angels wear?
Tazewell, Charles. *The littlest angel*, ill. by Deborah Lanino
The littlest angel, ill. by Paul Micich
The littlest angel, ill. by Rebecca Thornburgh
Tolan, Stephanie S. *Bartholomew's blessing*
Turner, Ann Warren. *Angel hide and seek*
Vainio, Pirkko. *The Christmas angel*
Wangerin, Walter. *Probity Jones and the Fear Not Angel*
Weller, Frances Ward. *The angel of Mill Street*
Williams, Sam. *Angel's Christmas cookies*
Snowy magic

Animals *see also* Birds; Frogs & toads; Reptiles

Aardema, Verna. *Princess Gorilla and a new kind of water*
Rabbit makes a monkey of lion
Traveling to Tondo
The vingananee and the tree toad
What's so funny, Ketu?
Who's in Rabbit's house?
Why mosquitoes buzz in people's ears
Ada, Alma Flor. *Dear Peter Rabbit*
Adler, Victoria. *Baby, come away*
Adlerman, Daniel. *Africa calling*
Aesop. *Animal fables from Aesop*
Bat's big game
Belling the cat and other Aesop fables
Doctor Coyote
The donkey in the lion's skin
Fox tails
The lion and the mouse and other Aesop fables
Road signs
Agee, Jon. *Dmitri the astronaut*
Mr. Putney's quacking dog
Ajmera, Maya. *Animal friends: a global celebration of children and their animals*
Alborough, Jez. *Captain Duck*
Duck in the truck
Fix-it Duck
Hug
Super Duck
Tall
Watch out! Big Bro's coming!
Alda, Arlene. *Sheep, sheep, sheep, help me fall asleep*
Alexander, Cecil Frances. *All creatures great and small*
Alexander, Claire. *Back to front and upside down*
Lucy and the bully
Aliki. *My visit to the aquarium*
My visit to the zoo
Wild and woolly mammoths
Allard, Harry. *Bumps in the night*
Allen, Jonathan. *"I'm not cute!"*
I'm not reading!
The little rabbit who liked to say moo
Allen, Pamela. *Who sank the boat?*
Alter, Anna. *Disappearing Desmond*
American Museum of Natural History. *Spot the animals*
Amusing moments in the wild
Anastas, Margaret. *A hug for you*
Mommy's best kisses
Anaya, Rudolfo A. *Roadrunner's dance*
Ancona, George. *Handtalk zoo*
Andersen, Hans Christian. *The emperor's new clothes*
Anderson, Derek. *Story county*
Anderson, Peggy Perry. *Chuck's band*
Chuck's truck
Anderson, Stephen Axel. *I know the moon*
Andreae, Giles. *Cock-a-doodle-doo!*
The pop-up Rumble in the jungle
Rumble in the jungle
Anholt, Catherine. *Chimp and Zee's noisy book*
Animal I spy
Animal 123
Apperley, Dawn. *Good night, sleep tight, little bunnies*
Santa Claus will come tonight
Arnold, Caroline. *Australian animals*
Mealtime for zoo animals
Mother and baby zoo animals
Noisytime for zoo animals
Playtime for zoo animals
Sleepytime for zoo animals
Splashtime for zoo animals
Arnold, Katya. *The adventures of Snowwoman*
Let's find it!
Meow!
Arnosky, Jim. *At this very moment*
Babies in the bayou
Crinkleroot's guide to knowing animal habitats
Crinkleroot's 25 mammals every child should know
Every autumn comes the bear
Gobble it up!
I see animals hiding
Wild and swampy
Wild tracks!
Arquette, Kerry. *What did you do today?*
Artell, Mike. *Petite Rouge*
Aruego, José. *We hide, you seek*
Weird friends
Asch, Frank. *Barnyard lullaby*
Moonbear's dream
Asher, Sandy. *Here comes Gosling!*
Ashforth, Camilla. *Willow by the sea*
Ashman, Linda. *Castles, caves, and honeycombs*
Askani, Tanja. *A friend like you*
Aston, Dianna Hutts. *Loony Little*
Auch, Mary Jane. *The nutquacker*
Poultrygeist
Souperchicken
Auld, Mary. *Noah's ark*
Austin, Margot. *A friend for Growl Bear*
Averbeck, Jim. *Except if*
Aylesworth, Jim. *Cock-a-doodle-doo, creak, pop-pop, moo*
The mitten
One crow
Azore, Barbara. *Wanda and the wild hair*
Babypants, Caspar. *Augie to zebra*
Baddiel, Ivor. *Cock-a-doodle quack! Quack!*
Badescu, Ramona. *Big Rabbit's bad mood*
Bailey, Linda. *The farm team*
Baillie, Marilyn. *Nose to toes*
Baker, Alan. *Gray Rabbit's one, two, three*
Baker, Ken. *Old MacDonald had a dragon*
Banks, Kate. *What's coming for Christmas?*

Barasch, Lynne. *First come the zebra*
Barner, Bob. *Animal baths*
Barnes, Laura T. *Ernest's special Christmas*
Barnett, Mac. *Count the monkeys*
Barrett, Judi. *Animals should definitely not act like people*
Animals should definitely not wear clothing
Never take a shark to the dentist and other things not to do
Barretta, Gene. *Dear deer*
Bartoletti, Susan Campbell. *Naamah and the ark at night*
Barton, Byron. *Zoo animals*
Base, Graeme. *Animalia*
Jungle drums
The water hole
Bateman, Donna M. *Out on the prairie*
Bateman, Teresa. *Farm flu*
The frog with the big mouth
Bates, Ivan. *All by myself*
Batten, Mary. *Please don't wake the animals*
Who has a belly button?
Battut, Eric. *The fox and the hen*
Little Mouse's big secret
Bauer, Marion Dane. *Frog's best friend*
If frogs made the weather
If you had a nose like an elephant's trunk
If you were born a kitten
The longest night
My mother is mine
Sleep, little one, sleep
Why do kittens purr?
Bayer, Jane. *A my name is Alice*
Beames, Margaret. *Night cat*
Beaton, Clare. *Clare Beaton's bedtime rhymes*
Clare Beaton's farmyard rhymes
How loud is a lion?
One moose, twenty mice
One moose, twenty mice [board book]
Beaumont, Karen. *Duck, duck, goose!*
No sleep for the sheep!
Who ate all the cookie dough?
Beautiful moments in the wild
Beaver steals fire
Beck, Andrea. *Elliot bakes a cake*
Elliot digs for treasure
Elliot gets stuck
Elliot's bath
Elliot's Christmas surprise
Elliot's emergency
Elliot's shipwreck
Becker, Bonny. *An ant's day off*
Tickly prickly
Becker, Helaine. *Mama likes to mambo*
Beeke, Jemma. *The Rickety Barn show*
Beeke, Tiphanie. *Roar like a lion!*
Behrens, Janice. *Let's find rain forest animals*
Belle, Jennifer. *Animal stackers*
Benevelli, Alberto. *The colors of the chameleon*
Berger, Melvin. *Brrr! a book about polar animals*
Dive! a book of deep sea creatures
Bergman, Mara. *Yum yum! What fun!*
Bergstein, Rita M. *Your own big bed*
Berkes, Marianne. *Animalogy*
Going home: the mystery of animal migration
Marsh music
Over in a river
Over in the Arctic
Over in the forest
Over in the jungle
Bernhard, Durga. *Earth, sky, wet, dry*
Big, bad, and a little bit scary
Bilgrami, Shaheen. *Amazing dinosaur discovery*
Farmyard painting party
Incredible animal discovery
Jungle art show
Black, Harley. *Amazing magic school*
Blackaby, Susan. *Brownie Groundhog and the wintry surprise*, ill. by Carmen Segovia
Brownie Groundhog and the wintry surprise, ill. by Carmen Segovia
Blackstone, Stella. *Alligator alphabet*
How big is a pig?
Octopus opposites
Secret seahorse
Secret seahorse [board book]
Blaich, Ute. *The star*
Blake, Quentin. *Fantastic Daisy Artichoke*
Bleiman, Andrew. *ABC zooborns!*
Bless the beasts
Bloom, Suzanne. *A mighty fine time machine*
Bock, Lee. *Oh, crumps! / Ay, caramba!*
Bolam, Emily. *Animals talk*
Bond, Felicia. *Big hugs, little hugs*
Bonnett-Rampersaud, Louise. *How do you sleep?*
Bosca, Francesca. *The apple king*
Bourgeois, Paulette. *Franklin and Harriet*
Franklin and the thunderstorm
Franklin rides a bike
Franklin's class trip
Franklin's secret club
Boutignon, Beatrice. *Not all animals are blue*
Boyle, Bob. *Hugo and the really, really, really long string*
Boynton, Sandra. *Christmas parade*
Bracken, Beth. *The little bully*
Brenner, Barbara A. *One small place by the sea*
Brenner, Emily. *On the first day of grade school*
Brett, Jan. *Annie and the wild animals*
Armadillo rodeo
Berlioz the bear
The hat
The three little dassies
Brett, Jessica. *Animals on the go*
Bright, Paul. *Quiet!*
Brisson, Pat. *Hobbledy-clop*
Broach, Elise. *Gumption!*
Brooks, Alan. *Frogs jump*
Brooks, Erik. *Slow days, fast friends*
Brown, Heather. *Chomp!*
Brown, James. *Farm*
Brown, Jo. *Where's my mommy?*
Brown, Ken. *What's the time, Grandma Wolf?*
Brown, Lisa. *How to be*
Brown, Marc. *Arthur and the true Francine*
Arthur goes to camp
Arthur's animal adventure
Arthur's April fool
Arthur's Christmas
Arthur's eyes
Arthur's Halloween
Arthur's perfect Christmas
Arthur's teacher moves in
Arthur's teacher trouble
Arthur's Thanksgiving
Arthur's tooth
Arthur's underwear
Arthur's Valentine

The bionic bunny show
Brown, Marcia. *Once a mouse . . .*
Brown, Margaret Wise. *A child's good morning book*
The dirty little boy
The fathers are coming home
The friendly book
The Golden sleepy book
Where have you been?
Brown, Ruth. *Monkey's friends*
Browne, Anthony. *Animal fair*
Browne, Eileen. *Handa's hen*
Bruchac, Joseph. *The great ball game*
Bruss, Deborah. *Book! book! book!*
Bunting, Eve. *Happy birthday, dear duck*
Have you seen my new blue socks?
Hey diddle diddle
Hurry! Hurry!
Little Badger's just-about birthday
Night tree
Our library
Swan in love
We were there
Burnard, Damon. *I spy in the jungle*
I spy in the ocean
Burningham, John. *Mr. Gumpy's outing*
The shopping basket
Burns, Diane L., et al *Backyard beasties*
Butler, John. *Bedtime in the jungle*
Can you growl like a bear?
Ten in the den
Ten in the meadow
While you were sleeping
Butler, M. Christina. *Mouse and the moon*
One snowy night
One special Christmas
One winter's day
The smiley snowman
Butterworth, Nick. *One snowy night*
Cabatingan, Erin. *A is for Musk Ox*
Musk Ox counts
Cabrera, Jane. *If you're happy and you know it*
Monkey's play time
Twinkle, twinkle, little star
Callahan, Sean. *A wild Father's Day*
Callery, Sean. *Hide and seek in the jungle*
Calmenson, Stephanie. *Birthday at the Panda Palace*
Jazzmatazz!
Campbell, Rod. *Dear zoo*
Caple, Kathy. *Worm gets a job*
Capucilli, Alyssa Satin. *Biscuit visits the pumpkin patch*
Inside a zoo in the city
Carle, Eric. *The artist who painted a blue horse*
Does a kangaroo have a mother, too?
From head to toe
Hello, red fox
1, 2, 3 to the zoo
"Slowly, slowly, slowly," said the sloth
10 little rubber ducks
Today is Monday
The very busy spider
Carlson, Nancy. *Arnie and the skateboard gang*
Get up and go!
Henry and the bully
How about a hug?
Think happy!
Carlstrom, Nancy White. *The way to Wyatt's house*
Carrick, Carol. *Patrick's dinosaurs*
Carryl, Charles E. *The camel's lament*
Carter, David A. *Old MacDonald had a farm: a pop-up book*
Whoo? Whoo?
Cartwright, Reg. *What we do*
Casanova, Mary. *One-dog canoe*
One-dog sleigh
Casey, Dawn. *The great race: the story of the Chinese zodiac*
Casey, Patricia. *One day at Wood Green Animal Shelter*
Cash, Megan Montague. *I saw the sea and the sea saw me*
Cassie, Brian. *Say it again*
Cave, Kathryn. *Henry's song*
Cazet, Denys. *Never poke a squid*
Never spit on your shoes
Nothing at all
Ceelen, Vicky. *Baby! baby!*
Chaconas, Dori. *Don't slam the door!*
Looking for Easter
Chamberlin-Calamar, Pat. *Alaska's twelve days of summer*
Chapman, Jane. *Very special friends*
Chedru, Delphine. *Spot it!*
Chernaik, Judith. *Carnival of the animals: poems inspired by Saint-Saëns' music*
Cherry, Lynne. *The great kapok tree*
Chichester Clark, Emma. *Follow the leader!*
Little Miss Muffet counts to ten
Chicken Little. *Chicken Little*
Henny Penny, ill. by Emily Bolam
Henny Penny, ill. by Paul Galdone
Henny Penny, ill. by Sophie Windham
Henny-Penny
The sky is falling
Child, Lauren. *I am not sleepy and I will not go to bed*
Chin, Oliver. *The year of the tiger*
Chitwood, Suzanne Tanner. *Wake up, big barn!*
Chivers, Natalie. *Rhino's great big itch!*
Christelow, Eileen. *Where's the big bad wolf?*
Clark, Leslie Ann. *Peepsqueak!*
Cneut, Carll. *The amazing love story of Mr. Morf*
Cocca-Leffler, Maryann. *Jungle Halloween*
Coffelt, Nancy. *Aunt Ant leaves through the leaves*
Big, bigger, biggest!
Cohen, Caron Lee. *Digger Pig and the turnip*
Cohen, Peter Zachary. *Boris's glasses*
Cohn, Diana. *Dream carver*
Colato Laínez, René. *Señor Pancho had a rancho*
Collard, Sneed B. *Animals asleep*
Making animal babies
Collicott, Sharleen. *Toestomper and the caterpillars*
Comden, Betty. *What's new at the zoo?*
Conover, Chris. *The lion's share*
Conway, David. *The most important gift of all*
Cooper, Helen. *Delicious!*
A pipkin of pepper
Costello, David Hyde. *I can help*
Côté, Geneviève. *With you always, Little Monday*
Cotten, Cynthia. *At the edge of the woods*
Cousins, Lucy. *Doctor Maisy*
Happy birthday, Maisy
I'm the best
Maisy at the fair
Maisy, Charley, and the wobbly tooth
Maisy dresses up
Maisy's amazing big book of learning
Maisy's bedtime
Maisy's book of things that go

Maisy's farm
Maisy's Halloween
Maisy's morning on the farm
Maisy's noisy day
Maisy's pool
Noah's ark
Noah's ark [board book]
Cowan, Charlotte. *Katie caught a cold*
Peeper has a fever
Sadie's sore throat
Cowell, Cressida. *What shall we do with the Boo-Hoo Baby?*
Cowley, Joy. *Mrs. Wishy-Washy's Christmas*
Coxe, Molly. *Bunny and the beast*
Craig, Lindsey. *Dancing feet!*
Farmyard beat
Crawford, Laura. *In arctic waters*
Crawford, Sheryl Ann. *The baby who changed the world*
Crimi, Carolyn. *Dear Tabby*
Don't need friends
Crisp, Marty. *Black and white*
Cronin, Doreen. *Click, clack, boo!*
Click, clack, quackity-quack
Click, clack, splish, splash
Dooby dooby moo
Duck for President
Giggle, giggle, quack
Thump, quack, moo
Cruickshank, Margrit. *We're going to feed the ducks*
Crum, Shutta. *The bravest of the brave*
A family for Old Mill Farm
Cullen, Lynn. *Little Scraggly Hair*
Cummings, Pat. *Ananse and the lizard*
Cummings, Phil. *Boom bah!*
Cusimano, Maryann K. *You are my wonders*
Cuyler, Margery. *The biggest, best snowman*
That's good! That's bad!
Czekaj, Jef. *Oink-a-doodle-moo*
Dahl, Michael. *Hippo says "excuse me."*
One giant splash
Starry arms
Dahl, Roald. *The enormous crocodile*
The giraffe and the pelly and me
Dale, Penny. *The boy on the bus*
Dallas-Conte, Juliet. *Cock-a-moo-moo*
Daly, Catherine. *Whiskers*
Daly, Niki. *Next stop — Zanzibar Road!*
Welcome to Zanzibar Road
Davis, Jill. *Orangutans are ticklish*
Davis, Katie. *Who hoots?*
Davis, Lee. *Feeding time*
Day, Alexandra. *Special deliveries*
Day, Trevor. *Youch! it bites!*
Deacon, Alexis. *Slow Loris*
Deady, Kathleen W. *It's time!*
Out and about at the zoo
deGroat, Diane. *Happy birthday to you, you belong in a zoo*
Jingle bells, homework smells
Roses are pink, your feet really stink
Trick or treat, smell my feet
de Las Casas, Dianne. *The Little "Read" Hen*
Demers, Dominique. *Every single night*
De Monfreid, Dorothee. *Dark night*
Dempsey, Kristy. *Mini racer*
Denim, Sue. *The Dumb Bunnies go to the zoo*
Dennard, Deborah. *Bullfrog at Magnolia Circle*
Koala country
Denslow, Sharon Phillips. *In the snow*
DePalma, Mary Newell. *The perfect gift*
dePaola, Tomie. *Bill and Pete to the rescue*
Jingle, the Christmas clown
DePrisco, Dorothea. *Snowbear's winter day*
Who lives here?
De Regniers, Beatrice Schenk. *May I bring a friend?*
What did you put in your pocket?
Derrick, Patricia. *Riley the rhinoceros*
Desmoinaux, Christel. *Mrs. Hen's big surprise*
De Vicq de Cumptich, Roberto. *Bembo's zoo*
Díaz, Katacha. *Badger at Sandy Ridge Road*
Dijs, Carla. *Mommy, what if—?*
DiPucchio, Kelly. *What's the magic word?*
DiTerlizzi, Angela. *Say what?*
Dobbins, Jan. *Driving my tractor*
Docherty, Helen. *The Snatchabook*
Dodd, Emma. *Dog's noisy day*
Meow said the cow
Dodd, Lynley. *Find me a tiger*
Dodds, Dayle Ann. *Pet wash*
Donahue, Shari Faden. *The zebra-striped whale with the polka-dot tail*
Donaldson, Julia. *Room on the broom*
What the ladybug heard
Where's my mom?
Doner, Kim. *On a road in Africa*
Donohue, Dorothy. *Veggie soup*
Doolittle, Bev. *Reading the wild*
Doray, Malika. *One more Wednesday*
Doremus, Gaetan. *Bear despair*
Dorros, Arthur. *City chicken*
Downey, Lynn. *The flea's sneeze*
Matilda's humdinger
Downing, Johnette. *Down in Louisiana*
Downs, Mike. *Pig giggles and rabbit rhymes*
Doyle, Malachy. *Well, a crocodile can!*
Dragonwagon, Crescent. *All the awake animals are almost asleep*
Drummond, Ree. *Charlie goes to school*
Du Bois, William Pène. *Bear party*
Dubuc, Marianne. *Animal masquerade*
Dudley, Rebecca. *Hank finds an egg*
Dunbar, Polly. *Hello Tilly*
Pretty Pru
Where's Tumpty?
Dunnick, Regan. *Sweet dreams, Douglas*
Dunrea, Olivier. *Bear Noel*
Dupasquier, Philippe. *1 2 3, follow me!*
Du Quette, Keith. *They call me Woolly*
Dutton, Sandra. *Dear Miss Perfect*
Duvoisin, Roger Antoine. *Petunia*
Dyer, Sarah. *Clementine and Mungo*
Dylan, Bob. *Man gave names to all the animals*
Edens, Cooper. *The Animal Mall*
Edwards, Pamela Duncan. *Bravo, Livingstone Mouse!*
The grumpy morning
McGillycuddy could
Ms. Bitsy Bat's kindergarten
Roar
Some smug slug
While the world is sleeping
The worrywarts
Edwards, Richard. *Good night, Copycub*
Egan, Tim. *Dodsworth in London*
Dodsworth in New York
Dodsworth in Paris
Dodsworth in Rome

The pink refrigerator
Serious farm
The trial of Cardigan Jones
Ehlert, Lois. *Lots of spots*
Oodles of animals
Ehrlich, Fred. *Does a baboon sleep in a bed?*
Does a camel cook?
Does a chimp wear clothes?
Does a duck have a daddy?
Does a giraffe drive?
Does a mouse have a mommy?
Does a seal smile?
Does an elephant take a bath?
Ellery, Amanda. *If I were a jungle animal*
Elliott, David. *And here's to you!*
In the sea
In the wild
Elliott, Laura Malone. *A string of hearts*
Thanksgiving Day thanks
Elya, Susan Middleton. *Eight animals bake a cake*
Eight animals on the town
No more, por favor
Emberley, Barbara. *One wide river to cross*
Emberley, Ed. *The red hen*
Thanks, Mom!
Where's my sweetie pie?
Emberley, Rebecca. *Chicken Little*
My animals / Mis animales
Emmett, Jonathan. *The best gift of all*
Bringing down the moon
No place like home
Erdrich, Liselotte. *Bears make rock soup and other stories*
Ericsson, Jennifer A. *Whoo goes there?*
Eriksson, Eva. *A crash course for Molly*
Ernst, Lisa Campbell. *Wake up, it's Spring!*
Ets, Marie Hall. *In the forest*
Just me
Mister Penny
Play with me
Eure, Wesley. *A fish out of water*
Evert, Lori. *The Christmas wish*
Farber, Norma. *How the hibernators came to Bethlehem*
Fardell, John. *Jeremiah Jellyfish flies high!*
Faulkenberry, Lauren. *What do animals do on the weekend?*
Faulkner, Keith. *Do you have my quack?*
The giraffe who cock-a-doodle-doo'd
Jumbled jungle
The tallest shortest longest greenest brownest animal in the jungle!
Fearnley, Jan. *Arthur and the meanies*
A perfect day for it
Feiffer, Kate. *Which puppy?*
Felix, Monique. *The rumor*
Fernandes, Eugenie. *Busy little mouse*
Kitten's winter
Fielding, Beth. *Animal eyes*
Animal tails
Finn, Isobel. *The very lazy ladybug*
Fischer, Scott M. *Jump!*
Fisher, Aileen Lucia. *Do rabbits have Christmas?*
Know what I saw?
Fisher, Carolyn. *A twisted tale*
Fitzgerald, Joanne. *Yum! Yum!*
Fitzpatrick, Marie-Louise. *I'm a tiger, too!*
Fitzsimmons, David. *Curious critters*
Flack, Marjorie. *Ask Mr. Bear*
Flanagan, Alice K. *Dr. Friedman helps animals*
Soil
Fleming, Candace. *Gator gumbo*
Oh, no!
Who invited you?
Fleming, Denise. *Barnyard banter*
Count!
The cow who clucked
In the small, small pond
Sleepy, oh so sleepy
Underground
Where once there was a wood
Florian, Douglas. *Zoo's who*
Flynn, Kitson. *Carrot in my pocket*
Foley, Greg. *Don't worry Bear*
Good luck Bear
Purple Little Bird
Thank you, Bear
Ford, Christine. *Ocean's child*
Foster, John. *Pet poems*
Fox, Mem. *Hattie and the fox*
Hello, baby!
Time for bed
Wombat divine
Zoo-looking
Frampton, David. *My beastie book of ABC*
Franco, Betsy. *Pond circle*
Fraser, Mary Ann. *Where are the night animals?*
Fredericks, Anthony D. *In one tidepool*
Freedman, Claire. *One magical day*
One magical morning
Snuggle up, sleepy ones
Where's your smile, crocodile?
Freeman, Mylo. *Potty*
Freeman, Tor. *Hooray! I'm five today!*
Olive and the big secret
Fries, Claudia. *A pig is moving in*
A frog he would a-wooing go [folk-song]. *Frog went a-courtin'*
Frog went a-courting
Froggie went a courting
Froggy went a-courtin'
Fuge, Charles. *Astonishing animal ABC*
I know a rhino
Galdone, Paul. *Cat goes fiddle-i-fee*
Galko, Francine. *Cave animals*
Gallo, Frank. *Night sounds*
Gamble, Isobel. *Who's that?*
Gannij, Joan. *Hidden hippo*
Garelli, Cristina. *Farm friends clean up*
Garland, Michael. *Last night at the zoo*
Gay, Marie-Louise. *On my island*
Stella, fairy of the forest
Geist, Ken. *Who's who?*
Genechten, Guido van. *Guess what?*
Guess where?
Geoghegan, Adrienne. *All your own teeth*
George, Jean Craighead. *Morning, noon, and night*
George, Lindsay Barrett. *Around the pond*
In the garden: who's been here?
In the woods
The secret
George, William T. *Christmas at Long Pond*
Fishing at Long Pond
Geraghty, Paul. *Help me!*
The hoppameleon
Geras, Adèle. *My wishes for you*
Gershator, Phillis. *Moo, moo, brown cow! Have you any milk?*

When it starts to snow
Who's awake in springtime?
Who's in the farmyard?
Who's in the forest?
Gerstein, Mordicai. *The absolutely awful alphabet*
Leaving the nest
Gibbons, Gail. *Nature's green umbrella*
Prehistoric animals
Say woof!
Zoo
Gibbs, Edward. *I spy on the farm*
I spy under the sea
I spy with my little eye
Gibert, Bruno. *The king is naked!*
Gibson, Ginger Foglesong. *Tiptoe Joe*
Gillham, Bill. *How many sharks in the bath?*
Gilman, Rita Golden. *Mole in a hole*
Rice is life
Ginsburg, Mirra. *Mushroom in the rain*
Giogas, Valarie. *In my backyard*
Gliori, Debi. *Mr. Bear to the rescue*
Goble, Paul. *The great race of the birds and animals*
Godwin, Laura. *Barnyard prayers*
Little white dog
Goembel, Ponder. *Animal fair*
Goldin, David. *Go-Go-Go!*
Gollub, Matthew. *Gobble, quack, moon*
The Jazz Fly
Goodhart, Pippa. *Noah makes a boat*
Goodman, Susan E. *What do you do — at the zoo?*
Gorbachev, Valeri. *Chicken chickens*
Chicken chickens go to school
Dragon is coming!
Molly who flew away
One rainy day
Red red red
What's the big idea, Molly?
Where is the apple pie?
Whose hat is it?
Gore, Leonid. *The wonderful book*
Worms for lunch?
Gottfried, Maya. *Our farm*
Graham Barber, Lynda. *Spy hops and belly flops*
Grahame, Kenneth. *The wind in the willows*
A wind in the willows Christmas
Grambling, Lois G. *This whole Tooth Fairy thing's nothing but a big rip-off!*
Gravett, Emily. *Monkey and me*
Gray, Kes. *The "Get well soon" book*
Green, Alison. *The fox in the dark*
Green, Dan. *Wild alphabet*
Greene, Rhonda Gowler. *Barnyard song*
Jamboree day
Noah and the mighty ark
Grey, Mini. *Three by the sea*
Griessman, Annette. *Like a hundred drums*
Grimes, Nikki. *Minnie's new friend*
Grimm, Jacob and Wilhelm. *Battle of the beasts*
The Bremen town band
The Bremen town musicians, ill. by Bill Dickson
The Bremen town musicians, ill. by Ilse Plume
The Bremen town musicians, ill. by Bernadette Watts
The Bremen town musicians, ill. by Lisbeth Zwerger
Musicians of Bremen
Musicians of Bremen / Los musicos de Bremner
Snow White
Grindley, Sally. *Where are my chicks?*
Grobler, Piet. *Hey, frog!*
Grupper, Jonathan. *Destination — Rocky Mountains*
Guarino, Deborah. *Is your mama a llama?*
Gugler, Laurel Dee. *There's a billy goat in the garden*
Haas, Rick de. *Peter and the winter sleepers*
Hacohen, Dean. *Tuck me in!*
Hague, Michael. *Animal friends: a collection of poems for children*
Hall, Michael. *My heart is like a zoo*
Hamburg, Jennifer. *A moose that says mooooooooooo*
Hamilton, Martha. *The hidden feast*
Hamilton, Richard. *Polly's picnic*
Hamilton, Virginia. *Jaguarundi*
Hargrove, Linda. *Wings across the moon*
Harker, Lesley. *Annie's ark*
Harley, Bill. *Bear's all-night party*
Harper, Jamie. *Miss Mingo and the fire drill*
Miss Mingo and the first day of school
Miss Mingo weathers the storm
Harper, Jessica. *A place called Kindergarten*
Harper, Jo. *I could eat you up!*
Harris, Joel Chandler. *Jump! the adventures of Brer Rabbit*
Jump again!
Harris, Robie H. *Maybe a bear ate it!*
Harris, Trudy. *The clock struck one*
Harrison, David L. *A perfect home for a family*
Hartley, Karen. *The sixth sense and other special senses*
Hartman, Gail. *As the crow flies*
Hassett, John. *Mouse in the house*
Hayashi, Leslie Ann. *Fables from the sea*
Hayles, Marsha. *A pet of a pet*
Hays, Anna Jane. *The pup speaks up*
Hayward, Linda. *The King's chorus*
Heinz, Brian J. *Butternut Hollow Pond*
Helmer, Marilyn. *Three barnyard tales*
Three tales of three
Henkes, Kevin. *A good day*
Oh!
Hennessy, B. G. *Corduroy at the zoo*
Henry, Jed. *Cheer up, Mouse!*
Hewitt, Sally. *All year round*
Animal homes
Face to face safari
Woods and meadows
Hickman, Pamela. *It's moving day!*
Hill, Eric. *Spot at play*
Spot at the fair
Spot counts from 1 to 10
Spot goes to the farm
Spot on the farm
Hill, Susanna Leonard. *Can't sleep without sheep*
Hillenbrand, Will. *Fiddle-i-fee*
Himmelman, John. *Mouse in a meadow*
Hindley, Judy. *Does a cow say boo?*
Sleepy places
Hines, Anna Grossnickle. *Miss Emma's wild garden*
Hirschi, Ron. *Fall*
Spring
Summer
When morning comes
When night comes
Winter
Hiscock, Bruce. *Coyote and badger*
Ho, Minfong. *Brother Rabbit*
Hush!
Hoban, Tana. *A children's zoo*
Who are they?

Hoberman, Mary Ann. *"It's simple," said Simon*
Hodgkins, Fran. *Who's been here?*
Hodgkinson, Leigh. *Limelight Larry*
Hogg, Gary. *Beautiful Buehla and the zany zoo makeover*
Holmes, Anita. *Can you find us?*
Who dug that hole?
Holub, Joan. *Turkeys never gobble*
Hood, Susan. *Spike, the mixed-up monster*
Hooper, Patricia. *Where do you sleep, little one?*
Horacek, Petr. *Animal opposites*
Look out, Suzy Goose
One spotted giraffe
Silly Suzy Goose
Suzy Goose and the Christmas star
When the moon smiled
Horn, Peter. *The best father of all*
Horowitz, Dave. *Buy my hats!*
Soon, Baboon, soon
Horowitz, Ruth. *Crab moon*
Hort, Lenny. *We're going on a treasure hunt*
We're going on safari
Horton, Joan. *Hippopotamus stew*
Hosta, Dar. *I love the night*
Howell, Will C. *Zoo flakes ABC*
Hruby, Emily. *Counting in the garden*
Hubbell, Patricia. *Earthmates*
Hughes, Langston. *The sweet and sour animal book*
Hulbert, Laura. *Who has these feet?*
Who has this tail?
Huling, Jan. *Ol' Bloo's boogie-woogie band and blues ensemble*
Hull, Rod. *Mr. Betts and Mr. Potts*
Huneck, Stephen. *Sally goes to the farm*
Hunter, Anne. *Possum and the peeper*
Possum's harvest moon
What's in the meadow?
What's in the tide pool?
Hurwitz, Johanna. *Ethan out and about*
Hutchins, Pat. *Barn dance!*
Little pink pig
1 hunter
Rosie's walk [board book]
Shrinking mouse
The surprise party
Ten red apples
What game shall we play?
Ichikawa, Satomi. *My little train*
Inkpen, Mick. *The great pet sale*
Kipper's A to Z
Kipper's book of numbers
Meow!
Picnic
Splosh!
Ipcizade, Catherine. *'Twas the Day before Zoo Day*
Isaacs, Anne. *Pancakes for supper!*
Isadora, Rachel. *Old Mikamba had a farm*
A South African night
Isop, Laurie. *How do you hug a porcupine?*
Jacobs, Joseph. *The three sillies*
Jahn-Clough, Lisa. *On the hill*
Jamieson, Victoria. *Olympig!*
Janovitz, Marilyn. *A, B, see!*
Jarrett, Clare. *The best picnic ever*
Jay, Alison. *Welcome to the zoo*
Jeffers, Oliver. *The great paper caper*
Jenkins, Steve. *Actual size*
Animals in flight
Animals upside down
Big and little
Biggest, strongest, fastest
How to clean a hippopotamus
I see a kookaburra
Living color
Move!
Never smile at a monkey
Prehistoric actual size
Slap, squeak, and scatter
Time for a bath
Time to eat
Time to sleep
What do you do when something wants to eat you?
What do you do with a tail like this?
Jennewein, Lenore. *Chick-o-Saurus Rex*
Jennings, Linda. *Hide and seek birthday treat*
Jennings, Sharon. *Franklin forgives*
Franklin makes a deal
Franklin wants a badge
Jocelyn, Marthe. *Eats*
Johnson, Amy Crane. *Cinnamon and the April shower / Canela y el aguacero de abril*
Johnson, Angela. *The girl who wore snakes*
Johnson, D. B. *Four legs bad, two legs good!*
Johnson, Paul Brett. *On top of spaghetti*
Johnston, Tony. *Desert song*
Jolivet, Joëlle. *Zoo-ology*
Jonas, Ann. *Aardvarks, disembark!*
Splash!
The trek
Jones, Sylvie. *Who's in the tub?*
Jordan, Mary Ellen. *Lazy Daisy, cranky Frankie*
Jordan, Sandra. *Frog hunt*
Jorgensen, Gail. *Crocodile beat*
Gotcha!
Joubert, Beverly. *African animal alphabet*
Juan, Ana. *The pet shop revolution*
Judge, Lita. *Red hat*
Red sled
Kajikawa, Kimiko. *Sweet dreams: how animals sleep*
Kaner, Etta. *And the winner is . . .*
Kangas, Juli. *The surprise visitor*
Kasza, Keiko. *A mother for Choco*
Silly Goose's big story
Kaufmann, Nancy. *Bye, Bye*
Kawata, Ken. *Animal tails*
Keats, Ezra Jack. *Pet show!*
Keller, Emily Snowell. *Sleeping Bunny*
Keller, Holly. *Cecil's garden*
Help!
That's mine, Horace
Keller, Laurie. *Do unto otters*
Kellogg, Steven. *Aster Aardvark's alphabet adventures*
Chicken Little
Kelly, Irene. *Even an octopus needs a home*
Kelly, Mij. *Achoo!*
A bed of your own!
Friendly Day
Where's my darling daughter?
Kenah, Katharine. *Predator attack!*
Kennedy, Marge M. *The book of boo!*
Kepes, Juliet. *Five little monkeys*
Kherdian, David. *Come back, Moon*
Khing, T. T. *Where is the cake?*
Where is the cake now?
Kimmel, Eric A. *Anansi and the moss-covered rock*
Anansi and the talking melon
I took my frog to the library
Kinerk, Robert. *Clorinda takes flight*

King, Thomas. *Coyote sings to the moon*
Kipling, Rudyard. *The elephant's child*
How the camel got his hump
How the elephant got his trunk
Klausmeier, Jesse. *Open this little book*
Kleven, Elisa. *Sun bread*
Klingel, Cynthia Fitterer. *Deserts*
Forests
Oceans
Klise, Kate. *Why do you cry?*
Koponen, Libby. *Mmm . . . let's eat!*
Korda, Lerryn. *Into the wild*
It's vacation time
Kranking, Kathy. *The ocean is . . .*
Krebs, Laurie. *We're roaming in the rainforest*
We're sailing to Galapagos
Krensky, Stephen. *Mother's Day surprise*
Noah's bark
Krilanovich, Nadia. *Chicken, chicken, duck!*
Moon child
Kroll, Steven. *It's Groundhog Day!*
Jungle bullies
Krosoczka, Jarrett J. *Punk Farm*
Punk Farm on tour
Kudlinski, Kathleen V. *The sunset switch*
Kumin, Maxine. *Mites to astodons*
Kurtz, Jane. *Do kangaroos wear seat belts?*
LaMarche, Jim. *The raft*
Landa, Norbert. *The great monster hunt*
Langstaff, John M. *Over in the meadow*
Larios, Julie. *Yellow elephant*
LaRochelle, David. *It's a tiger*
Larson, Bonnie. *When animals were people / Cuando los animales eran personas*
Lass, Bonnie. *Who took the cookies from the cookie jar?*
Latimer, Alex. *Lion vs Rabbit*
Penguin's hidden talent
Lavis, Steve. *Cock-a-doodle-doo*
Jump!
On the farm
Lawler, Janet. *Ocean counting*
Lawrence, John. *This little chick*
Lawrence, Michael. *The caterpillar that roared*
Layton, Neal. *Hot, hot, hot*
Smile if you're human
Ledwon, Peter. *Midnight math twelve terrific math games*
Lee, Chinlun. *Good dog, Paw*
Lee, Jeanne M. *Toad is the uncle of heaven*
Leedy, Loreen. *Fraction action*
The Furry News
The great trash bash
Missing math
Mission — addition
There's a frog in my throat
Leeson, Christine. *Molly and the storm*
Lenski, Lois. *The Easter Rabbit's parade*
Leonard, Marcia. *Animal talk*
Léonard, Marie. *Tibili, the little boy who didn't want to go to school*
Leslie, Amanda. *Alfie and Betty Bug*
Are chickens stripy?
Do crocodiles moo?
Flappy, waggy, wiggly
Who's that scratching at my door?
Lesser, Carolyn. *What a wonderful day to be a cow*
Lester, Alison. *Noni the pony*
Lester, Helen. *Hooway for Wodney Wat*
It wasn't my fault
Wodney Wat's wobot
Lester, Julius. *Ackamarackus*
Albidaro and the mischievous dream
Levine, Sara. *Bone by bone*
Lewandowski, Frrich. *It's Christmas again*
Lewis, J. Patrick. *Earth and me, our family tree*
Good mousekeeping
A hippopotamusn't
Long was the winter road they traveled
Tulip at the bat
What's looking at you, kid?
Lewis, Kevin. *Not inside this house!*
Lewis, Kim. *Here we go Harry*
Lewison, Wendy Cheyette. *"Buzz," said the bee*
Going to sleep on the farm
Lillegard, Dee. *Tortoise brings the mail*
Lindbergh, Reeve. *The day the goose got loose*
Midnight farm
North country spring
Lionni, Leo. *The biggest house in the world*
Frederick's fables
Lithgow, John. *Carnival of the animals*
Never play music right next to the zoo
Little Bear's Valentine
Little, Jean. *Pippin the Christmas pig*
Little old lady who swallowed a fly. *There was an old monkey who swallowed a frog*
The little red hen. *The little red hen*, ill. by Byron Barton
The little red hen, ill. by Emily Bolam
The little red hen, ill. by Paul Galdone
Little red hen
The little red hen, ill. by Jerry Pinkney
The little red hen, ill. by Kate Slater
The little red hen, ill. by Annie West
The little red hen, ill. by Margot Zemach
The little red hen: an old fable
The Little Red Hen and the Passover matzah
The Little Red Hen makes a pizza
Livingston, Myra Cohn. *Valentine poems*
Livinson, Nancy Smiler. *North Pole, South Pole*
Liwska, Renata. *Red wagon*
Ljungkvist, Laura. *Follow the line around the world*
Lloyd-Jones, Sally. *Being a pig is nice*
Old MacNoah had an ark
Time to say goodnight
The ultimate guide to grandmas and grandpas!
Lobel, Anita. *Animal antics: A to Z*
Hello, day!
Lobel, Arnold. *Fables*
Lobel, Gillian. *Little Honey Bear and the smiley moon*
Lodge, Jo. *Happy birthday, Moo Moo*
Logue, Mary. *Sleep like a tiger*
London, Jonathan. *Crunch munch*
Fireflies, fireflies, light my way
Froggy plays in the band
Froggy plays soccer
Froggy's first Christmas
Gone again ptarmigan
Loon Lake
The owl who became the moon
What the animals were waiting for
Who bop
Wiggle, waggle
Long, Steffanie. *Such a silly baby!*
Loomis, Christine. *Scuba bunnies*
Lottridge, Celia Barker. *Berta, a remarkable dog*
Louise, Tina. *When I grow up*
Lowell, Susan. *The tortoise and the jackrabbit*

Lumry, Amanda. *Safari in South Africa*
Lyon, George Ella. *Mother to tigers*
Sleepsong
McBratney, Sam. *Just you and me*
McCall, Francis X. *A huge hog is a big pig*
Maccarone, Grace. *Oink! moo! how do you do?*
McCarthy, Michael. *The story of Noah and the ark*
McCarty, Peter. *Little bunny on the move*
McClements, George. *Dinosaur Woods*
McCurry, Kristen. *Ocean babies*
Safari babies
MacDonald, Alan. *Wilfred to the rescue*
MacDonald, Elizabeth. *The wolf is coming!*
MacDonald, Margaret Read. *Give up, Gecko!*
A hen, a chick, and a string guitar
The squeaky door
McDonald, Megan. *Hen hears gossip*
When the library lights go out
MacDonald, Suse. *Look whooo's counting*
McDonnell, Christine. *Dog wants to play*
McDonnell, Flora. *Giddy-up! Let's ride!*
I love animals
Splash!
McDonnell, Patrick. *Me . . . Jane*
McFarlane, Sheryl. *On the farm*
McGee, Marni. *The noisy farm*
McGill, Alice. *Sure as sunrise*
McGinley-Nally, Sharon. *The friendly beasts*
McGrath, Barbara Barbieri. *The little gray bunny*
McKee, David. *Elmer and Super El*
Elmer's special day
MacLennan, Cathy. *Chicky Chicky Chook Chook*
McMullan, Kate. *Supercat*
McNamara, Margaret. *Apples A to Z*
McPhail, David. *Edward in the jungle*
Farm morning
The puddle
McQuade, Jacqueline. *At the petting zoo with Teddy Bear*
Big babies
Small babies
Snow babies
Maggi, María Elena. *The great canoe*
Mahoney, Daniel J. *The perfect clubhouse*
The Saturday escape
Mahy, Margaret. *Boom Baby boom, boom*
The Christmas tree tangle
17 kings and 42 elephants
Simply delicious!
A summery Saturday morning
Maitland, Barbara. *Moo in the morning*
Manceau, Edouard. *Windblown*
Manning, Mick. *Supermom*
Marino, Gianna. *One too many*
Zoopa
Markes, Julie. *Good thing you're not an octopus!*
Marshall, James. *Eugene*
Marshall, Janet Perry. *A honey of a day*
Martin, Bill, Jr. *Baby bear, baby bear, what do you see?*
Chicken Chuck
Polar bear, polar bear, what do you hear?
Martin, David. *Let's have a tree party!*
We've all got bellybuttons
Martin, Emily Winfield. *Dream animals*
Martin, Francesca. *Clever Tortoise*
Martin, Rafe. *Will's mammoth*
Martins, Isabel Minhós. *My neighbor is a dog*
Marzollo, Jean. *I spy little animals*
Mama, Mama
Papa, Papa
Pretend you're a cat
Sun song
Ten cats have hats
Ten little Christmas presents
Mathers, Petra. *A cake for Herbie*
Mathews, Judith. *Nathaniel Willy, scared silly*
Mayer, Marianna. *Beauty and the beast*
Mayer, Mercer. *What do you do with a kangaroo?*
Mayo, Margaret. *Roar!*
Meade, Holly. *A place to sleep*
Meadows, Michelle. *Hibernation station*
Meddaugh, Susan. *The best place*
Melmed, Laura Krauss. *I love you as much . . .*
Meng, Cece. *Tough chicks*
Meres, Jonathan. *The big bad rumor*
Merz, Jennifer J. *Playground day*
Meschenmoser, Sebastian. *Waiting for winter*
Messner, Kate. *Over and under the snow*
Metaxas, Eric. *It's time to sleep, my love*
Meyers, Susan. *This is the way a baby rides*
Michelson, Richard. *Ten times better*
Miles, Elizabeth J. *Ears*
Mouths and teeth
Noses
Wings, fins, and flippers
Milgrim, David. *Santa Duck*
Young MacDonald
Miller, David. *Just like you and me*
Miller, Edna. *Mousekin's Thanksgiving*
Miller, Margaret. *I love colors*
Miller, Pat. *Squirrel's New Year's resolution*
Substitute Groundhog
Miller, Ruth. *I went to the farm*
Minarik, Else Holmelund. *Am I beautiful?*
Minor, Wendell. *My farm friends*
Miranda, Anne. *Alphabet fiesta*
To market, to market
Mitchell, Susan K. *The rainforest grew all around*
Mitter, Matt. *ABC: alphabet rhymes*
Once upon a rhyme
1, 2, 3, counting rhymes
Mitton, Tony. *All afloat on Noah's boat!*
Down by the cool of the pool
Farmer Joe and the music show
The Jungle Run
Modesitt, Jeanne. *Oh, what a beautiful day!*
Mollel, Tololwa M. *Rhinos for lunch and elephants for supper*
To dinner, for dinner
Montanari, Eva. *The crocodile's true colors*
Montes, Marisa. *Egg-napped!*
Moore, Inga. *A house in the woods*
Moore, Raina. *How do you say good night?*
Mora, Pat. *Delicious hullabaloo / Pachanga deliciosa*
Listen to the desert / Oye al desierto
Marimba!
The race of toad and deer
The song of Francis and the animals
Sweet dreams / Dulces suenos
This big sky
Moran, Alex. *Boots for Beth*
Come here, tiger
Moreton, Daniel. *La Cucaracha Martina*
Morlock, Lisa. *Track that scat!*
Morozumi, Atsuko. *One gorilla*
Morpurgo, Michael. *Wombat goes walkabout*
Morrow, Tara Jaye. *Mommy loves her baby; Daddy loves his baby*

Moss, Miriam. *Bad hare day*
This is the tree
Most, Bernard. *Cock-a-doodle-moo!*
The cow that went oink
Mother Goose. *Hey, diddle, diddle,* ill. by Linda Bronson
Hey, diddle, diddle, ill. by Heather Collins
Hickory, dickory, dock
Mozelle, Shirley. *The pig is in the pantry, the cat is on the shelf*
Munari, Bruno. *Bruno Munari's zoo*
Munsch, Robert N. *Alligator baby*
Murphy, Mary. *How kind*
Koala and the flower
Murphy, Stuart J. *Animals on board*
Freda is found
Write on, Carlos!
Muth, Jon J. *The three questions*
Myers, Walter Dean. *The story of the three kingdoms*
Na, Il Sung. *A book of sleep*
Hide and seek
Snow rabbit, spring rabbit
Nakamura, Katherine Riley. *Song of night*
Nakawaki, Hatsue. *Wait! wait!*
Nelson, Robert Lyn. *Ocean friends*
Newman, Jeff. *Reginald*
Newman, Lesléa. *Skunk's spring surprise*
Nikola-Lisa, W. *Can you top that?*
Norman, Kim. *If it's snowy and you know it, clap your paws!*
Ten on the sled
Numeroff, Laura Joffe. *The Chicken sisters*
Chimps don't wear glasses
The hope tree
The Jellybeans and the big art adventure
The Jellybeans and the big book bonanza
The Jellybeans and the big camp kickoff
The Jellybeans and the big dance
What grandmas do best; What grandpas do best
When sheep sleep
Nygaard, Elizabeth. *Snake alley band*
Odanaka, Barbara. *A crazy day at the Critter Café*
Ohmura, Tomoko. *The long, long line*
Old MacDonald had a farm. *Old MacDonald*
Old MacDonald had a farm, ill. by Holly Berry
Old MacDonald had a farm, ill. by Jane Cabrera
Old MacDonald had a farm, ill. by Carol Jones
Old MacDonald had a farm, ill. by Tracey Campbell Pearson
Old MacDonald had a farm, ill. by Glen Rounds
Old MacDonald had a farm, ill. by Jessica Souhami
Old MacDonald had a farm, ill. by Prue Theobalds
Oldland, Nicholas. *Up the creek*
Olson, David J. *The thunderstruck stork*
Olson, Nathan. *Animal patterns*
O'Malley, Kevin. *Animal crackers fly the coop*
Onishi, Satoru. *Who's hiding*
Oram, Hiawyn. *Badger's bad mood*
Orgel, Doris. *The cat's tale*
Ormerod, Jan. *If you're happy and you know it!*
Ms. MacDonald has a class
When we went to the zoo
Otto, Carolyn. *What color is camouflage?*
Over in the meadow
Owens, Mary Beth. *Panda whispers*
Oxenbury, Helen. *It's my birthday*
Page, Robin. *How many ways can you catch a fly?*
Sisters and brothers
Palatini, Margie. *Earthquack*
Moo who?
Paley, Joan. *One more river*
Pallotta, Jerry. *Dory story*
A giraffe did one
Ocean counting: odd numbers
Who will see their shadows this year?
Park, Linda Sue. *Xander's panda party*
Parker, Kim. *Counting in the garden*
Parker, Marjorie Blain. *A paddling of ducks*
Your kind of mommy
Parker, Victoria. *Bearum scarum*
Partridge, Elizabeth. *Moon glowing*
Patent, Dorothy Hinshaw. *Bold and bright, black-and-white animals*
Paterson, Brian. *Zigby camps out*
Patkau, Karen. *Creatures*
Patricelli, Leslie. *Faster! Faster!*
Patten, Brian. *The big snuggle-up*
Pattison, Darcy. *Desert baths*
Paul, Ann Whitford. *Fiesta fiasco*
If animals kissed goodnight
Paul, Ruth. *Hedgehog's magic tricks*
Paxton, Tom. *Going to the zoo*
Peaceful moments in the wild
Pearson, Tracey Campbell. *Bob*
Elephant's story
Peck, Jan. *Way up high in a tall green tree*
Peek, Merle. *Mary wore her red dress and Henry wore his green sneakers*
Peet, Bill. *The ant and the elephant*
Cock-a-doodle Dudley
Farewell to Shady Glade
The gnats of knotty pine
No such things
Pelham, David. *A is for animals*
Crawlies creep
Perrin, Martine. *Cock-a-doodle who?*
Look who's there!
Petersen, David. *Snowy Valentine*
Pfister, Marcus. *Animal ABC*
Charlie at the zoo
Hopper hunts for spring
How Leo learned to be king
Just the way you are
Phillips, Mildred. *And the cow said, "moo"!*
Pienkowski, Jan. *Pizza!*
Piers, Helen. *Who's in my bed?*
Pilkey, Dav. *The Moonglow Roll-O-Rama*
Pinder, Eric. *If all the animals came inside*
Pinkney, Jerry. *Noah's ark*
Pinkwater, Daniel. *Rainy morning*
Pipe, Jim. *Farm animals*
Pitcher, Caroline. *Are you spring?*
Pittau, Francisco. *Out of sight*
Piven, Hanoch. *The perfect purple feather*
Plourde, Lynn. *Only cows allowed!*
Polacco, Patricia. *Mommies say shhh!*
Potter, Beatrix. *Appley Dapply's nursery rhymes*
Cecily Parsley's nursery rhymes
Ginger and Pickles
More tales from Beatrix Potter
Peter Rabbit's ABC
The tale of Jemima Puddle-Duck and other farmyard tales
The tale of Peter Rabbit and other stories
A treasury of Peter Rabbit and other stories
Yours affectionately, Peter Rabbit

Pow, Tom. *Who is the world for?*
Prap, Lila. *Animal lullabies*
Animals speak
Daddies
Prater, John. *On top of the world*
Pratt, Pierre. *Car*
Park
Prelutsky, Jack. *Behold the bold umbrellaphant and other poems*
Beneath a blue umbrella
The pack rat's day and other poems
Stardines swim high across the sky
Price, Kathy. *The Bourbon Street musicians*
Pritchett, Andy. *Stick!*
Provensen, Alice. *The year at Maple Hill Farm*
Puttock, Simon. *The baby that roared*
Big bad wolf is good
Quattlebaum, Mary. *Jo MacDonald hiked in the woods*
Rankin, Joan. *First day*
You're somebody special, Walliwigs!
Raschka, Chris. *Moosey Moose*
Rash, Andy. *Are you a horse?*
Rathmann, Peggy. *Good night, Gorilla*
Raye, Rebekah. *The very best bed*
Rayner, Catherine. *Abigail*
Rechner, Amy. *Out and about at the aquarium*
Regan, Dian Curtis. *Barnyard slam*
The Snow Blew Inn
Reibstein, Mark. *Wabi Sabi*
Reider, Katja. *The big little sneeze*
Snail started it!
Reinhart, Matthew. *Animal popposites*
Reiser, Lynn. *Little clam*
Rempt, Fiona. *Snail's birthday wish*
Rex, Michael. *Dunk skunk*
Rey, Margret. *Billy's picture*
Reynolds, Aaron. *Buffalo wings*
Rice, Eve. *Sam who never forgets*
Riley, Linda Capus. *Elephants swim*
Rinck, Maranke. *I feel a foot!*
Rinker, Sherri Duskey. *Steam train, dream train*
Riphagen, Loes. *Animals home alone*
Robberecht, Thierry. *I can't do anything!*
Sam's new friend
Robbins, Beth. *Tom's first day at school*
Tom's new haircut
Roberts, Bethany. *Birthday mice*
Valentine mice!
Robinson, Fiona. *What animals really like*
Robinson, Michelle. *What to do if an elephant stands on your foot*
Rock, Brian. *The deductive detective*
Rockwell, Anne. *Chip and the karate kick*
Katie Catz makes a splash
Morgan plays soccer
Root, Barry. *Gumbrella*
Root, Phyllis. *One duck stuck*
One duck stuck [board book]
Toot toot zoom!
Rose, Deborah Lee. *Birthday zoo*
Into the A, B, sea
Rosen, Michael. *How the animals got their colors*
Tiny little fly
Rosen, Michael J. *With a dog like that, a kid like me . . .*
Rosenberg, Liz. *A big and little alphabet*
Rosenberry, Vera. *Who is in the garden?*
Rosoff, Meg. *Wild boars cook*
Ross, Eileen. *The Halloween showdown*
Ross, Michael Elsohn. *Mama's milk*
Play with me
Roth, Carol. *All aboard to work — choo-choo!*
The little school bus
Will you still love me?
Rotner, Shelley. *Pick a pet*
Rouillard, Wendy. *Barnaby's bunny*
Rowe, Jeannette. *Whose ears?*
Whose feet?
Whose nose?
Ruddell, Deborah. *A whiff of pine, a hint of skunk*
Rueda, Claudia. *Let's play in the forest while the wolf is not around*
Rumford, James. *Nine animals and the well*
Ruurs, Margriet. *In my backyard*
Ryan, Pam Muñoz. *Armadillos sleep in dugouts*
Ryder, Joanne. *Big bear ball*
Dance by the light of the moon
Each living thing
A fawn in the grass
Rylant, Cynthia. *Night in the country*
Puppies and piggies
Sabuda, Robert. *Beauty and the beast: a pop-up book of the classic fairy tale*
The movable Mother Goose
Sage, Angie. *Monkeys in the jungle*
St. Pierre, Stephanie. *What the sea saw*
Salley, Coleen. *Epossumondas*
Epossumondas saves the day
San Souci, Robert D. *Two bear cubs: a Miwok legend from California's Yosemite Valley*
Santore, Charles. *A stowaway on Noah's Ark*
Sauer, Tammi. *Me want pet!*
Mr. Duck means business
Saunders, Dave. *So slow!*
Sayre, April Pulley. *Dig, wait, listen*
Home at last
If you should hear a honey guide
If you're hoppy
Splish! splash! animal baths
Schaefer, Carole Lexa. *Big Little Monkey*
Cool time song
Down in the woods at sleepytime
Down in the woods at sleepytime [board book]
Schaefer, Lola M. *Just one bite*
Lifetime
Schertle, Alice. *Advice for a frog and other poems*
Button up!
Schindel, John. *What did they see?*
Schindler, S. D. *Spike and Ike take a hike*
Schoenherr, Ian. *Read it, don't eat it!*
Schofield, Jennifer. *Animal babies in grasslands*
Animal babies in polar lands
Animal babies in ponds and rivers
Animal babies in rain forests
Schomp, Virginia. *If you were a . . . veterinarian*
If you were a . . . zookeeper
Schubert, Ingrid. *There's always room for one more*
Schulman, Janet. *Countdown to spring*
Schultz, Sam. *Animal antics: the beast jokes ever*
Schumaker, Ward. *Dance!*
Schwartz, Amy. *A beautiful girl*
Starring Miss Darlene
Schwartz, David M. *If you hopped like a frog*
Where else in the wild?
Where in the wild
Schwartz, Roslyn. *The mole sisters and the cool breeze*
The mole sisters and the question

Tales from Parc la Fontaine
Scieszka, Jon. *Battle Bunny*
Sebe, Masayuki. *100 animals on parade!*
Seder, Rufus Butler. *Waddle!*
Seeger, Laura Vaccaro. *Bully*
I had a rooster
Selkowe, Valrie M. *Happy birthday to me!*
Selsam, Millicent E. *How to be a nature detective*
Keep looking!
Sendak, Maurice. *Very far away*
Sensel, Joni. *Bears barge in*
Serfozo, Mary. *Whooo's there?*
Seuling, Barbara. *Spring song*
Winter lullaby
Shahan, Sherry. *Cool cats counting*
Shannon, David. *Duck on a bike*
Shannon, George. *Rabbit's gift*
Turkey Tot
Shapiro, Zachary. *We're all in the same boat*
Sharmat, Marjorie Weinman. *The 329th friend*
Sharratt, Nick. *Shark in the park*
Shaskan, Stephen. *A dog is a dog*
Shea, Kitty. *Out and about at the vet clinic*
Showers, Paul. *Sleep is for everyone*
Shulman, Lisa. *The moon might be milk*
Sidman, Joyce. *Just us two*
Sierra, Judy. *Preschool to the rescue*
There's a zoo in room 22
We love our school!
Wild about books
Zoozical
Sill, Cathryn. *About mammals*
Siminovich, Lorena. *Monkey see, look at me!*
Simmons, Jane. *Daisy and the Beastie*
Daisy says coo!
Daisy's favorite things
Daisy's hide-and-seek
Little Fern's first winter
Simple gifts
Singer, Isaac Bashevis. *Why Noah chose the dove*
Singer, Marilyn. *Creature carnival*
Fred's bed
Quiet night
Turtle in July
Siomades, Lorianne. *Cuckoo can't find you*
Kangaroo and cricket
My box of color
Slack, Michael. *Monkey truck*
Slate, Joseph. *Little Porcupine's Christmas*
Miss Bindergarten celebrates the last day of kindergarten
Miss Bindergarten celebrates the 100th day of kindergarten
Miss Bindergarten gets ready for kindergarten
Miss Bindergarten has a wild day in kindergarten
Miss Bindergarten stays home from kindergarten
Miss Bindergarten takes a field trip with kindergarten
Who is coming to our house?
Slegers, Liesbet. *Funny ears*
Funny feet
Funny tails
Slingsby, Janet. *Hush-a-bye babies*
Sloat, Teri. *Farmer Brown goes round and round*
Pieces of Christmas
Rib-ticklers
There was an old lady who swallowed a trout
The thing that bothered Farmer Brown
Small, David. *George Washington's cows*
Imogene's antlers
Smath, Jerry. *The animals' Christmas carol*
Smee, Nicola. *Clip-clop*
Jingle-jingle
Smith, Lane. *It's a book*
Sockabasin, Allen. *Thanks to the animals*
Souhami, Jessica. *Foxy!*
No dinner!
Soule, Jean Conder. *Never tease a weasel*
Spafford, Suzy. *Witzy's colors*
Spence, Robert, III. *Clickety clack*
Spier, Peter. *Gobble, growl, grunt*
Noah's ark
Spinelli, Eileen. *Peace Week in Miss Fox's class*
Polar bear, arctic hare
Silly Tilly
Spurling, Margaret. *Bilby moon*
Spurr, Elizabeth. *Two bears beneath the stairs*
Srinivasan, Divya. *Little Owl's night*
Staake, Bob. *My little opposites book*
Stadler, John. *What's so scary?*
Staines, Bill. *All God's critters*
Staub, Leslie. *Bless this house*
Stead, Philip C. *Bear has a story to tell*
A sick day for Amos McGee
Steig, William. *Sylvester and the magic pebble*
Toby, what are you?
Toby, where are you?
Toby, who are you?
Stein, David Ezra. *The nice book*
Stern, Ellen. *I saw a bullfrog*
Stevens, Janet. *And the dish ran away with the spoon*
Cook-a-doodle-doo!
Old bag of bones
Stevenson, Emma. *Hide-and-seek science*
Stevenson, James. *Christmas at Mud Flat*
Don't make me laugh
Happy Valentine's Day, Emma!
Heat wave at Mud Flat
The most amazing dinosaur
Mr. Hacker
National worm day
No need for Monty
A village full of valentines
We can't sleep
Which one is Whitney?
Yard sale
Stewart, Melissa. *Under the snow*
When rain falls
Stewig, John Warren. *The animals watched*
Stihler, Chérie B. *The giant cabbage turnip*
Sting [Musician]. *Rock steady*
Stock, Catherine. *A porc in New York*
Stoeke, Janet Morgan. *Hide and seek*
Stojic, Manya. *Rain*
Snow
Stone, Lynn M. *Getting around*
Partners
Stoop, Naoko. *Red Knit Cap Girl*
Straaten, Harmen van. *Duck's tale*
For me?
Strete, Craig Kee. *How the Indians bought the farm*
Sutton, Jane. *Don't call me Sidney*
Swanson, Diane. *Headgear that hides and plays*
Noses that plow and poke
Skin that slimes and scares
Sweeney, Jacqueline. *What about Bettie?*
Sweet, Melissa. *Fiddle-i-fee*
Swenson, Jamie A. *Boom! Boom! Boom!*

Swinburne, Stephen R. *Lots and lots of zebra stripes*
Safe, warm, and snug
Water for one, water for everyone
Sykes, Julie. *Careful, Santa*
Dora's chicks
Dora's eggs
I don't want to take a bath!
Smudge
Symes, Sally. *Yawn*
Taback, Simms. *Simms Taback's city animals*
Simms Taback's farm animals
Simms Taback's safari animals
Tafuri, Nancy. *All kinds of kisses*
The barn party
The big storm
Counting to Christmas
Do not disturb
The donkey's Christmas song
I love you, little one
Junglewalk
Rabbit's morning
Silly little goose!
This is the farmer
Where we sleep
Who's counting?
Tang, Greg. *Math fables too*
Tankard, Jeremy. *Boo hoo Bird*
Grumpy Bird
Me hungry!
Tarlow, Ellen. *Pinwheel days*
Taylor, Eleanor. *Beep, beep, let's go!*
Taylor, Harriet Peck. *Secrets of the stone*
Ulaq and the northern lights
Taylor, Theodore. *Hello, Arctic!*
Tebbs, Victoria. *Noah's Ark story*
Terry, Michael. *Rhino's horns*
Teyssèdre, Fabienne. *Joseph wants to read*
Thimmesh, Catherine. *Friends: true stories of extraordinary animal friendships*
Thomas, Jan. *A birthday for Cow!*
The doghouse
Thompson, Lauren. *One starry night*
Wee little lamb
Thomson, Pat. *The squeaky, creaky bed*
Thomson, Sarah L. *Around the neighborhood*
Thornhill, Jan. *The rumor*
Wild in the city
Thorpe, Kiki. *A comfy, cozy Thanksgiving*
Time to cha-cha-cha!
Thurlby, Paul. *Paul Thurlby's wildlife*
Tildes, Phyllis Limbacher. *Animals in camouflage*
Eye guess
Tillman, Nancy. *The crown on your head*
Timmers, Leo. *Bang*
Who is driving?
Todd, Mark. *Start your engines*
Toft, Kim Michelle. *Neptune's nursery*
The world that we want
Tolman, Marije. *The tree house*
Tolstoy, Aleksey Nikolayevich. *The enormous turnip*
Tomlinson, Jill. *The owl who was afraid of the dark*
Trapani, Iza. *Baa baa black sheep*
Baa baa black sheep [board book]
Row, row, row your boat
What am I?
Trenc, Milan. *Another night at the museum*
Tresselt, Alvin R. *The mitten: an old Ukrainian folktale*
Wake up, farm!
Tricarico, Christine. *Cock-a-doodle dance!*
Trumbauer, Lisa. *The great reindeer rebellion*
Tryon, Leslie. *Albert's birthday*
Albert's Christmas
Albert's Halloween
Albert's play
Patsy says
Tudor, Tasha. *A tale for Easter*
Tulloch, Shirley. *Who made me?*
Underwood, Deborah. *The quiet book*
Urban, Linda. *Mouse was mad*
Urbanovic, Jackie. *Duck soup*
Uribe, Verónica. *Buzz buzz buzz*
Vagin, Vladimir. *The enormous carrot*
Vail, Rachel. *Over the moon*
Vamos, Samantha R. *The cazuela that the farm maiden stirred*
Van Eerbeek. *The world of farm animals*
The world of wild animals
Van Fleet, Matthew. *Fuzzy yellow ducklings*
Heads
Moo
One yellow lion
Spotted yellow frogs
Van Kampen, Vlasta. *It couldn't be worse*
Van Laan, Nancy. *Little Fish lost*
Moose tales
Sleep, sleep, sleep
This is the hat
A tree for me
When winter comes: a lullaby
Van Woerkom, Dorothy. *The rat, the ox and the zodiac*
Vaughan, Marcia Kapok. *Snap!*
Whistling Dixie
Verboven, Agnes. *Ducks like to swim*
Vestergaard, Hope. *Hillside lullaby*
Potty animals
Voce, Louise. *Over in the meadow*
Votaw, Carol. *Good morning, little polar bear*
Waking up down under
Vrombaut, An. *Clarabella's teeth*
Waber, Bernard. *Bearsie Bear and the surprise sleepover party*
Fast food! gulp! gulp!
Waddell, Martin. *Farmer Duck*
The pig in the pond
Webster J. Duck
Wadsworth, Ginger. *One tiger growls*
Waldron, Kevin. *Mr. Peek and the misunderstanding at the zoo*
Wallace, Ivy. *Pookie*
Pookie believes in Santa Claus
Pookie puts the world right
Wallen, Ila. *The moon in my room*
Wallner, Alexandra. *Beatrix Potter*
Walsh, Ellen Stoll. *Pip's magic*
Walsh, Joanna. *The perfect hug*
Walsh, Melanie. *Do donkeys dance?*
Do lions live on lily pads?
Do monkeys tweet?
Walter, Virginia. *"Hi, pizza man!"*
Walters, Eric. *The matatu*
Walton, Rick. *Little dogs say "Rough!"*
Noah's square dance
Wan, Joyce. *Hug you, kiss you, love you*
Wang, Gabrielle. *The race for the Chinese zodiac*
Ward, Helen. *Old shell, new shell*
The tin forest

Ward, Jennifer. *Forest bright, forest night*
Way up in the Arctic
Wardlaw, Lee. *The chair where bear sits*
Warhola, James. *If you're happy and you know it: jungle edition*
Warnes, Tim. *Daddy hug*
Warrick, Karen Clemens. *If I had a tail*
Who needs that nose?
Wayne-von Königslöw, Andrea. *How do you read to a rabbit?*
Weeks, Sarah. *Catfish Kate and the sweet swamp band*
Crocodile smile
My somebody special
Wegerif, Gay. *Up close*
Weigelt, Udo. *Bear's last journey*
Old Beaver
Who stole the gold?
Weinstein, Ellen Slusky. *Everywhere the cow says "Moo!"*
Weiss, Nicki. *Where does the brown bear go?*
Where does the brown bear go? [board book]
Welch, Willy. *Dancing with Daddy*
Welling, Peter J. *Shawn O'Hisser, the last snake in Ireland*
Wellington, Monica. *Bunny's first snowflake*
Wells, Rosemary. *Hazel's amazing mother*
Miracle melts down
My kindergarten
Weninger, Brigitte. *Bye-bye, Binky*
The elf's hat
Merry Christmas, Davy!
West, Colin. *One day in the jungle*
West, Judy. *Have you got my purr?*
Westcott, Nadine Bernard. *There's a hole in the bucket*
Wheeler, Lisa. *The pet project*
Whippo, Walt. *Little white duck*
Whitehouse, Patricia. *What's awake? A B C*
What's awake? 1 2 3
Whitfield, Susan. *The animals of the Chinese zodiac*
Whittaker, Nicola. *Feet*
Hair
Noses
Tails
Whybrow, Ian. *Good night, monster*
Hello! Is this grandma?
Wick, Walter. *Can you see what I see? cool collections*
Can you see what I see? Seymour and the juice box boat
Wiesmüller, Dieter. *In the blink of an eye*
Wild, Margaret. *Nighty night*
Wildsmith, Brian. *Goat's trail*
Jungle party
Willems, Mo. *Naked mole rat gets dressed*
Willey, Margaret. *Clever Beatrice and the best little pony*
Williams, Brenda. *Home for a tiger, home for a bear*
Williams, Linda. *Horse in the pigpen*
Williams, Sue. *I went walking*
I went walking [board book]
Let's go visiting
Williams, Suzanne. *Old MacDonald in the city*
Willis, Jeanne. *The boy who lost his bellybutton*
Hippospotamus
That's not funny!
The wheels on the bus: a read-along sing-along trip to the zoo
Wilner, Isabel. *A garden alphabet*
Wilson, Anna. *Over in the grasslands*
Wilson, Anne. *Noah's ark*
Wilson, Karma. *Animal strike at the zoo, it's true!*
Bear feels scared
Bear feels sick
Bear says thanks
Bear stays up for Christmas
Mama always comes home
Moose tracks!
Wilson, Sarah. *Love and kisses*
Winnick, Karen B. *Barn sneeze*
Winters, Kay. *Wolf watch*
Wise, William. *Zany zoo*
Witte, Anna. *The parrot Tico Tango*
Wojtowycz, David. *Animal antics from 1 to 10*
Wolf, Jake. *Daddy, could I have an elephant?*
Wolff, Ferida. *It is the wind*
Wolkstein, Diane. *Little Mouse's painting*
Wood, Audrey. *Little Penguin's tale*
The napping house
The napping house wakes up
Silly Sally
Silly Sally [board book]
Wood, Douglas. *Old Turtle*
When a dad says "I love you"
Wood, Jakki. *Moo moo, brown cow*
Never say boo to a goose!
Wormell, Christopher. *Blue Rabbit and friends*
Blue Rabbit and the runaway wheel
The new alphabet of animals
Puff, puff, chugga-chugga
Wormell, Mary. *Bernard the angry rooster*
Hilda Hen's happy birthday
Why not?
Worth, Valerie. *Pug and other animal poems*
Wright, Maureen. *Barnyard fun*
Earth Day, birthday!
Yaccarino, Dan. *Deep in the jungle*
Five little ducks
Lawn to lawn
An octopus followed me home
So big
Yamaguchi, Kristi. *It's a big world, little pig!*
Yarrow, Peter. *Day is done*
Yee, Wong Herbert. *Detective Small in the amazing banana caper*
Eek! There's a mouse in the house
Fireman Small
Fireman Small, fire down below
Fireman Small to the rescue
Hamburger Heaven
Mrs. Brown went to town
The Officers' Ball
A small Christmas
Tracks in the snow
Yolen, Jane. *Jane Yolen's Old MacDonald songbook*
Picnic with Piggins
Piggins
Sleep, black bear, sleep
Welcome to the icehouse
Welcome to the river of grass
Welcome to the sea of sand
Yoon, Salina. *Do cows meow?*
Do crocs kiss?
Yorinks, Arthur. *Quack!*
Young, Ruth. *Who says moo?*
Zane, Alexander. *The wheels on the race car*
Zelch, Patti R. *Ready, set . . . wait!*
Ziefert, Harriet. *Animal music*
Be fair, share!

Beach party!
A bunny is funny
I swapped my dog
A polar bear can swim
What do ducks dream?
Wiggle like an octopus
You and me: we're opposites
Zoboli, Giovanna. *I wish I had . . .*
Zoehfeld, Kathleen Weidner. *What lives in a shell?*
What's alive?
Zolotow, Charlotte. *The sleepy book*
Sleepy book
Zuckerman, Andrew. *Creature abc*

Animals – aardvarks

Brown, Marc. *Arthur babysits*
Arthur goes to school
Arthur lost and found
Arthur meets the president
Arthur tricks the tooth fairy
Arthur turns green
Arthur writes a story
Arthur's animal adventure
Arthur's baby
Arthur's birthday
Arthur's chicken pox
Arthur's computer disaster
Arthur's family vacation
Arthur's first sleepover
Arthur's neighborhood
Arthur's new puppy
Arthur's new puppy [board book]
Arthur's nose
Arthur's perfect Christmas
Arthur's pet business
Arthur's really helpful word book
Arthur's spookiest Halloween
Arthur's teacher moves in
Arthur's TV trouble
Arthur's underwear
D. W., go to your room!
D. W. rides again!
D. W., the picky eater
D. W. thinks big [board book]
D. W.'s library card
D. W.'s lost blankie
Glasses for D. W.
The true Francine
Kellogg, Steven. *Aster Aardvark's alphabet adventures*
Lindbergh, Reeve. *The awful aardvarks go to school*
The awful aardvarks shop for school
Moodie, Fiona. *Noko and the night monster*
Sloat, Teri. *Hark! The aardvark angels sing*

Animals – anteaters

Brown, Marc. *D. W. all wet*
D. W. flips!
DeRubertis, Barbara. *Alexander Anteater's amazing act*
Dewdney, Anna. *Roly Poly pangolin*
Waber, Bernard. *An anteater named Arthur*

Animals – apes *see* Animals – baboons; Animals – chimpanzees; Animals – gorillas; Animals – monkeys

Animals – armadillos

Arnosky, Jim. *Armadillo's orange*
Brett, Jan. *Armadillo rodeo*
Brimner, Larry Dane. *Trick or treat, Old Armadillo*
David, Lawrence. *The land of the hungry armadillos*
Fearnley, Jan. *Milo Armadillo*
Ketteman, Helen. *Armadillo tattletale*
Armadilly chili
Kipling, Rudyard. *The beginning of the armadillos*
Radunsky, Vladimir. *One: a nice story about an awful braggart*
Ten
Swinburne, Stephen R. *Armadillo trail*

Animals – babies

Abercrombie, Barbara. *Bad dog, Dodger*
Alexander, Martha G. *When the new baby comes, I'm moving out*
Aliki. *At Mary Bloom's*
Arnold, Caroline. *Mother and baby zoo animals*
Asch, Frank. *Baby Bird's first nest*
Ashman, Linda. *Babies on the go*
Babies on the go [board book]
Asper-Smith, Sarah. *I would tuck you in*
Baby animals
Baby animals at the zoo
Baddiel, Ivor. *Cock-a-doodle quack! Quack!*
Baillie, Marilyn. *Small wonders*
Bauer, Marion Dane. *The cutest critter*
If you were born a kitten
Blomgren, Jennifer. *Where do I sleep?*
Bogue, Gary. *There's an opossum in my backyard*
Bourguignon, Laurence. *Heart in the pocket*
Brenner, Barbara A. *What the elephant told*
Bruzzone, Catherine. *Puppy finds a friend / Cachorrito encuentra un amigo*
Puppy finds a friend / Le petit chien se trouve un ami
Bunting, Eve. *The baby shower*
Sing a song of piglets
Butler, John. *Hush, little ones*
Pi-shu, the little panda
Whose baby am I?
Buzzeo, Toni. *Just like my Papa*
Stay close to Mama
Cabrera, Jane. *Mommy, carry me please!*
Calmenson, Stephanie. *Perfect puppy*
Capucilli, Alyssa Satin. *Biscuit wants to play*
Biscuit's new trick
Biscuit's Valentine's Day
Castle, Caroline. *Naughty!*
Chaconas, Dori. *Christmas mouseling*
Chwast, Seymour. *Harry, I need you!*
Clark, Leslie Ann. *Peepsqueak!*
Clements, Andrew. *Slippers at home*
Cole, Babette. *Lady Lupin's book of etiquette*
Collard, Sneed B. *Leaving home*
Costello, Emily. *Realm of the panther*
Cowen-Fletcher, Jane. *Hello, puppy!*
Davies, Nicola. *Dolphin baby!*
Davis, Kate. *Barnyard babies*
Deady, Kathleen W. *It's time!*
DePrisco, Dorothea. *What will I become?*
Doepker, David. *Animal babies*
Farm babies
Dowson, Nick. *Tigress*
Doyle, Malachy. *Baby see, baby do!*
Dunrea, Olivier. *Little cub*
Edwards, Nicola. *Goodnight Baxter*

Edwards, Pamela Duncan. *Wake-up kisses*
Evans, Lezlie. *Who loves the little lamb?*
Falconer, Ian. *Olivia counts*
  Olivia's opposites
Falwell, Cathryn. *Pond babies*
Fearnley, Jan. *Just like you*
Fernandes, Eugenie. *Kitten's spring*
Fisher, Aileen Lucia. *You don't look like your mother*
Fisher, Doris. *Happy birthday to whooo?*
Fleming, Denise. *Mama cat has three kittens*
Fraggalosch, Audrey. *Trails above the tree line*
Fraser, Mary Ann. *How animal babies stay safe*
French, Jackie. *Diary of a baby wombat*
French, Vivian. *Growing frogs*
Freymann, Saxton. *Baby food*
Friedman, Mel. *Kitten castle*
Genechten, Guido van. *Kai-Mook*
Gentle, Victor. *Baby sharks*
George, Jean Craighead. *Look to the north*
Gibson, Ginger Foglesong. *Tiptoe Joe*
Godwin, Laura. *What the baby hears*
Goodhart, Pippa. *Pudgy, a puppy to love*
Gréban, Quentin. *Nestor*
Grindley, Sally. *Little Elephant Thunderfoot*
Guion, Melissa. *Baby penguins everywhere!*
Gulbis, Stephen. *Cowgirl Rosie and her five baby bison*
Halfmann, Janet. *Eggs 1, 2, 3*
Halls, Kelly Milner. *I bought a baby chicken*
Henkes, Kevin. *Kitten's first full moon*
Heos, Bridget. *What to expect when you're expecting joeys*
Hewett, Joan. *A flamingo chick grows up*
  A giraffe calf grows up
  A harbor seal pup grows up
  A kangaroo joey grows up
  A koala joey grows up
  A monkey baby grows up
  A penguin chick grows up
  A tiger cub grows up
Hindley, Judy. *The best thing about a puppy*
Holt, Sharon. *Did my mother do that?*
Houran, Lori Haskins. *I will keep you safe and sound*
Hulme, Joy N. *Easter babies*
Hutchins, Hazel. *One dark night*
James, Betsy. *Tadpoles*
Jenkins, Steve. *My first day*
Johnson, Paul Brett. *The goose who went off in a huff*
Jonovitz, Marilyn. *Maybe, my baby*
Joosse, Barbara. *Higgledy-piggledy chicks*
Kajikawa, Kimiko. *Close to you*
Kessler, Cristina. *Jubela*
Kimmelman, Leslie. *The three bully goats*
Kirk, David. *Oh So Tiny bunny*
Krauss, Ruth. *The growing story*
Kuiper, Nannie. *Bailey the bear cub*
Kunhardt, Katharine. *Let's count the puppies*
Lang, Aubrey. *The adventures of Baby Bear*
  Baby elephant
  Baby fox
  Baby lion
  Baby penguin
Lawrence, John. *This little chick*
Levine, Ellen. *Seababy*
Lewis, Kim. *Just like Floss*
  Little Baa
  Little calf
  Little lamb
  Little puppy
Llewellyn, Claire. *Crocodile*
  Duck
London, Jonathan. *Baby whale's journey*
  Little penguin
  Snuggle wuggle
McAllister, Angela. *Little Mist*
McClure, Nikki. *How to be a cat*
McCurry, Kristen. *Ocean babies*
  Safari babies
McLellan, Stephanie Simpson. *The chicken cat*
McMullan, Kate. *If you were my bunny*
  Supercat
McQuade, Jacqueline. *Big babies*
  Farm babies
  Small babies
  Snow babies
Magloff, Lisa. *Bear*
  Butterfly
  Duckling
  Elephant
  Frog
  Kitten
  Penguin
  Rabbit
Marciano, John Bemelmans. *Delilah*
Markle, Sandra. *Creepy, crawly baby bugs*
Morton-Shaw, Christine. *Wake up, sleepy bear!*
Murphy, Mary. *A kiss like this*
Murphy, Stuart J. *Pepper's journal*
Murray, Marjorie Dennis. *Little Wolf and the moon*
Nakamura, Katherine Riley. *Song of night*
Nolan, Lucy A. *Jack Quack*
Numeroff, Laura Joffe. *What puppies do best*
Nyeu, Tao. *Bunny days*
O'Hair, Margaret. *My kitten*
Olson, David J. *The thunderstruck stork*
Otto, Carolyn. *Our puppies are growing*
Partis, Joanne. *Stripe*
Pfeffer, Wendy. *Mallard duck at Meadow View Pond*
Pipe, Jim. *Baby animals*
Porter, Sue. *Parsnip*
Purmell, Ann. *Where wild babies sleep*
Radcliffe, Theresa. *Bashi, elephant baby*
Reasoner, Charles. *Animal babies!*
Robinson, Sue. *I want to play*
Roddie, Shen. *Not now, Mrs. Wolf*
Root, Phyllis. *Flip, flap, fly!*
  Oliver finds his way
Rose, Deborah Lee. *Ocean babies*
Rostoker-Gruber, Karen. *Bandit's surprise*
Ryder, Joanne. *Little panda*
Saltzberg, Barney. *Baby animal kisses*
Schneider, Howie. *Chewy Louie*
Schofield, Jennifer. *Animal babies in grasslands*
  Animal babies in polar lands
  Animal babies in ponds and rivers
  Animal babies in rain forests
Shoulders, Michael. *Say Daddy!*
Sidman, Joyce. *Just us two*
Sierra, Judy. *Wild about you!*
Stone, Lynn M. *Chickens have chicks*
  Pigs and piglets
Sturges, Philemon. *How do you make a baby smile?*
Swinburne, Stephen R. *Safe, warm, and snug*
Tafolla, Carmen. *Baby Coyote and the old woman / El coyotito y la viejita*
Tafuri, Nancy. *Five little chicks*
  I love you, little one
Talbott, Hudson. *It's all about me-ow*

Tanner, Suzy-Jane. *Tinyflock Nursery School*
Tatham, Betty. *Baby Sea Otter*
Penguin chick
Tender moments in the wild
Thompson, Lauren. *Little Quack*
Little Quack [board book]
Wee little bunny
Van Eerbeek. *The world of baby animals*
Volkmann, Roy. *Curious kittens*
Waddell, Martin. *It's quacking time*
Walters, Catherine. *Are you there, Baby Bear?*
Ward, Jennifer. *Somewhere in the ocean*
Wilson, Karma. *What's in the egg, Little Pip?*
Where is home, Little Pip?
Wormell, Mary. *Why not?*
Yolen, Jane. *Off we go!*
Zenz, Aaron. *Chuckling ducklings and baby animal friends*
Ziefert, Harriet. *A dozen ducklings lost and found*

Animals – baboons

Bustos, Eduardo. *Going ape!*
Bynum, Janie. *Altoona up north*
DeRubertis, Barbara. *Bobby Baboon's banana be-bop*
Horowitz, Dave. *Soon, Baboon, soon*
Olaleye, Isaac. *Bitter bananas*

Animals – badgers

Brett, Jan. *Honey, honey — lion!*
Bright, Paul. *Grumpy Badger's Christmas*
Bunting, Eve. *Can you do this, Old Badger?*
Little Badger, terror of the seven seas
Little Badger's just-about birthday
Díaz, Katacha. *Badger at Sandy Ridge Road*
Grahame, Kenneth. *The wind in the willows*
Hiscock, Bruce. *Coyote and badger*
Hoban, Russell. *A baby sister for Frances*
A bargain for Frances
Bedtime for Frances
Best friends for Frances
A birthday for Frances
Bread and jam for Frances
Johnston, Tony. *The badger and the magic fan*
Kasza, Keiko. *Badger's fancy meal*
Linders, Clara. *The very best door of all*
Muller, Robin. *Badger's new house*
Odone, Jamison. *Honey badgers*
Oram, Hiawyn. *Badger's bad mood*
Potter, Beatrix. *The tale of Mr. Tod*
Saunders, Karen. *Baby Badger's wonderful night*
Schuurmans, Hilde. *Sydney won't swim*
Varley, Susan. *Badger's parting gifts*
Wells, Rosemary. *Hazel's amazing mother*
Weninger, Brigitte. *Davy, soccer star!*

Animals – bandicoots

Fox, Mem. *Hunwick's egg*

Animals – bats

Aesop. *Bat's big game*
Appelt, Kathi. *Bats around the clock*
Bats on parade
Berk, Ari. *Nightsong*
Cannon, Janell. *Stellaluna*
Stellaluna: a pop-up book and mobile
Davies, Nicola. *Bat loves the night*
Dyer, Sarah. *Batty*
Edwards, Pamela Duncan. *Ms. Bitsy Bat's kindergarten*
Gerber, Carole. *Little red bat*
Gibbons, Gail. *Bats*
Jennings, Patrick. *Bat and Rat*
Laschütza, Susanne. *Nat the bat*
Lies, Brian. *Bats at the ballgame*
Bats at the beach
Bats at the library
Lunde, Darrin. *Hello, bumblebee bat*
Maestro, Betsy. *Bats*
Markle, Sandra. *Bats: biggest! littlest!*
Little lost bat
Mayr, Diane. *Littlebat's Halloween story*
Mitchard, Jacquelyn. *Baby bat's lullaby*
Quackenbush, Robert M. *Batbaby*
Waring, Geoff. *Oscar and the bat*
Whitehouse, Patricia. *Bats*

Animals – bears

Abbott, Bud. *Who's on first?*
Agee, Jon. *Milo's hat trick*
Alborough, Jez. *Ice cream bear*
It's the bear
My friend bear
Where's my teddy?
Alexander, Martha G. *And my mean old mother will be sorry, Blackboard Bear*
Blackboard Bear
I sure am glad to see you, Blackboard Bear
I'll never share you, Blackboard Bear
We're in big trouble, Blackboard Bear
You're a genius, Blackboard Bear
Alter, Anna. *Abigail spells*
Altes, Marta. *My grandpa*
Anglund, Joan Walsh. *The cowboy's Christmas*
Appelt, Kathi. *Where, where is Swamp Bear?*
Apperley, Dawn. *Blossom and Boo*
Blossom and Boo stay up late
Arnosky, Jim. *Every autumn comes the bear*
Aruego, José. *Splash!*
Asch, Frank. *Bear shadow*
Bear's bargain
Good night, Baby Bear
Goodbye house
Happy birthday, moon!
Just like daddy
Moonbear
Moonbear's books
Moonbear's canoe
Moonbear's dream
Moonbear's friend
Moonbear's pet
Mooncake
Moondance
Moongame
Popcorn
Sand cake
Skyfire
Austin, Margot. *A friend for Growl Bear*
Banks, Kate. *The bear in the book*
Bardill, Linard. *The great golden thing*
Barner, Bob. *Bears! bears! bears!*
Bauer, Marion Dane. *Jason's bears*
The bear
Beaty, Andrea. *Artist Ted*
Doctor Ted

Firefighter Ted
Becker, Bonny. *A bedtime for Bear*
A birthday for Bear
The sniffles for Bear
A visitor for Bear
Bedford, David. *Big bears can!*
I've seen Santa!
Bentley, Dawn. *Fuzzy bear*
Fuzzy Bear's potty book
Berenstain, Jan. *The Berenstain bears trim the tree*
Berenstain, Stan and Jan. *The bear detectives*
Bears in the night
Bears on wheels
The Berenstain bears and mama's new job
The Berenstain bears and the bad dream
The Berenstain bears and the bad habit
The Berenstain bears and the big road race
The Berenstain bears and the double dare
The Berenstain bears and the ghost of the forest
The Berenstain bears and the messy room
The Berenstain bears and the missing dinosaur bone
The Berenstain bears and the missing honey
The Berenstain bears and the prize pumpkin
The Berenstain bears and the real Easter eggs
The Berenstain bears and the sitter
The Berenstain bears and the slumber party
The Berenstain bears and the spooky old tree
The Berenstain bears and the trouble with friends
The Berenstain bears and the truth
The Berenstain bears and the week at grandma's
The Berenstain bears and the wild, wild honey
The Berenstain bears and too much birthday
The Berenstain bears and too much junk food
The Berenstain bears and too much TV
The Berenstain bears and too much vacation
The Berenstain bears blaze a trail
The Berenstain bears' Christmas tree
The Berenstain bears' counting book
The Berenstain bears don't pollute anymore
The Berenstain bears forget their manners
The Berenstain bears get in a fight
The Berenstain bears get stage fright
The Berenstain bears get the gimmies
The Berenstain bears go out for the team
The Berenstain bears go to camp
The Berenstain bears go to school
The Berenstain bears go to the doctor
The Berenstain bears in the dark
The Berenstain bears learn about strangers
The Berenstain bears meet Santa Bear
The Berenstain bears' moving day
The Berenstain bears no girls allowed
The Berenstain bears on the moon
The Berenstain bears ready, set, go!
The Berenstain bears' report card trouble
The Berenstain bears' science fair
The Berenstain bears' that stump must go!
The Berenstain bears trick or treat
The Berenstain bears' trouble at school
The Berenstain bears' trouble with money
The Berenstain bears' trouble with pets
The Berenstain bears visit the dentist
The Berenstains' B book
He bear, she bear
Inside outside upside down
Old hat, new hat
Blackaby, Susan. *Rembrandt's hat*
Blackstone, Stella. *Bear at home*
Bear at work
Bear in a square
Bear in sunshine
Bear on a bike
Bear takes a trip
Bear's birthday
Bear's busy family
Bloom, Suzanne. *Fox forgets*
Oh! What a surprise!
What about Bear?
Boelts, Maribeth. *Looking for Sleepy*
Bond, Michael. *Paddington Bear*
Paddington Bear and the Busy Bee Carnival
Paddington Bear and the Christmas surprise
Bonnett-Rampersaud, Louise. *Never ask a bear*
Bonwill, Ann. *Bug and Bear*
Braun, Sebastien. *I love my daddy*
Brett, Jan. *Berlioz the bear*
Brian, Janeen. *Where does Thursday go?*
Bright, Paul. *The bears in the bed and the great big storm*
Brown, Margaret Wise. *Love songs of the little bear*
Brown, Peter. *Children make terrible pets*
You will be my friend!
Browne, Anthony. *Me and you*
Bruins, David. *The call of the cowboy*
Bryan, Sean. *A bear and his boy*
Bunting, Eve. *Big Bear's big boat*
The Valentine bears
Butler, M. Christina. *Snow friends*
Cabrera, Jane. *Bear's good night*
Capucilli, Alyssa Satin. *Bear hugs*
What kind of kiss?
Carlstrom, Nancy White. *Better not get wet, Jesse Bear*
Guess who's coming, Jesse Bear
Happy birthday, Jesse Bear!
How do you say it today, Jesse Bear?
It's about time, Jesse Bear
Jesse Bear, what will you wear?
Let's count it out, Jesse Bear
What a scare, Jesse Bear!
Where is Christmas, Jesse Bear?
Carrick, Carol. *The polar bears are hungry*
Catalano, Dominic. *Santa and the three bears*
Chapman, Jane. *Is it Christmas yet?*
Chaud, Benjamin. *The bear's song*
Chen, Chih-Yuan. *The best Christmas ever*
Cleminson, Katie. *Otto the book bear*
Cocca-Leffler, Maryann. *Bravery soup*
Collins, Billy. *Daddy's little boy*
Conover, Chris. *The Christmas bears*
Cooper, Elisha. *Bear dreams*
Corey, Shana. *Ballerina bear*
Cowan, Charlotte. *Katie caught a cold*
Cusimano, Maryann K. *You are my wish*
Dahl, Michael. *Bear says "thank you"*
Day, Alexandra. *Frank and Ernest*
Frank and Ernest on the road
Frank and Ernest play ball
DePrisco, Dorothea. *Snowbear's winter day*
DeRubertis, Barbara. *Corky Cub's crazy caps*
Dierssen, Andreas. *Timmy's new friend*
Dodd, Emma. *Just like you*
Doodler, Todd H. *Bear in long underwear*
Doremus, Gaetan. *Bear despair*
Dunbar, Joyce. *The very small*
Dunrea, Olivier. *Bear Noel*
Little cub
Old Bear and his cub

Durant, Alan. *Brown Bear gets in shape*
Duval, Kathy. *The Three Bears' Christmas*
The Three Bears' Halloween
Dyckman, Ame. *Tea party rules*
Dyer, Jane. *Little Brown Bear and the bundle of joy*
Edwards, Richard. *Always Copycub*
Copy me, Copycub
Good night, Copycub
Egan, Tim. *A mile from Ellington Station*
Elya, Susan Middleton. *Rubia and the three osos*
Ernst, Lisa Campbell. *Goldilocks returns*
Faglia, Matteo. *Happy birthday, I'm 4*
Fearnley, Jan. *Mr. Wolf and the three bears*
A perfect day for it
Flack, Marjorie. *Ask Mr. Bear*
Fleming, Denise. *Time to sleep*
Foley, Greg. *Don't worry Bear*
Good luck Bear
I miss you Mouse
Make a wish Bear
Thank you, Bear
Fox, Mem. *Sleepy bears*
Fraggalosch, Audrey. *Great grizzly wilderness*
Grizzly bear family
Freedman, Claire. *Follow that bear if you dare!*
One magical morning
Freeman, Don. *Bearymore*
Gabriel, Ashala. *Night night toes*
Gammell, Stephen. *Wake up, bear . . . It's Christmas!*
Gibbons, Gail. *Grizzly bears*
Gibson, Ginger Foglesong. *Tiptoe Joe*
Glass, Andrew. *Bewildered for three days*
Glicksman, Caroline. *Eric the math bear*
Gliori, Debi. *Can I have a hug?*
Mr. Bear to the rescue
Mr. Bear's new baby
Goodings, Lennie. *When you grow up*
Goossens, Philippe. *Knock! Knock! Knock! Who's there?*
Gorbachev, Valeri. *Me too!*
Gravett, Emily. *Orange pear apple bear*
Greene, Rhonda Gowler. *Firebears*
Grimm, Jacob and Wilhelm. *As luck would have it*
Rose Red and the bear prince
Grindley, Sally. *What are friends for?*
What will I do without you?
Guiberson, Brenda Z. *Moon bear*
Hague, Kathleen. *Calendarbears*
Ten little bears
Hansen, Felicity. *The first bear*
Harley, Bill. *Bear's all-night party*
Harrison, Joanna. *Grizzly dad*
Haseley, Dennis. *A story for Bear*
Hayes, Geoffrey. *Patrick at the circus*
Hayes, Karel. *The summer visitors*
The winter visitors
Heap, Sue. *Four friends in the garden*
Helquist, Brett. *Bedtime for Bear*
Henkes, Kevin. *Old Bear*
Hest, Amy. *Kiss good night*
When you meet a bear on Broadway
You can do it, Sam
Hillenbrand, Will. *Kite day*
Off we go! a Bear and Mole story
Spring is here
Hirschi, Ron. *Our three bears*
Hodgkinson, Leigh. *Goldilocks and just one bear*
Horvath, David. *Bossy bear*
Just like Bossy Bear
Irwin, Michael. *Bears in my bed*
Itaya, Satoshi. *Buttons and Bo*
Janice. *Little Bear marches in the St. Patrick's Day parade*
Little Bear's Christmas
Little Bear's Thanksgiving
Jeffers, Oliver. *The great paper caper*
Jennings, Sharon. *Bearcub and Mama*
Johnson, D. B. *Henry builds a cabin*
Henry climbs a mountain
Henry works
Henry's night
Jonas, Ann. *Two bear cubs*
Joosse, Barbara. *Nikolai, the only bear*
Roawr!
Jorgensen, Gail. *Gotcha!*
Jukes, Mavis. *You're a bear*
Kasparavicius, Kestutis. *The bear family's world tour Christmas*
Kasza, Keiko. *Don't laugh, Joe*
The mightiest
Keller, Holly. *Jacob's tree*
Kempter, Christa. *Wally and Mae*
Ketteman, Helen. *If Beaver had a fever*
Kherdian, David. *Come back, Moon*
Kimmel, Eric A. *Hanukkah bear*
Kinsey-Warnock, Natalie. *The bear that heard crying*
Klassen, Jon. *I want my hat back*
Klingel, Cynthia Fitterer. *Grizzly bears*
Kolar, Bob. *Big kicks*
Kornell, Max. *Bear with me*
Krauss, Ruth. *Bears*
Kroll, Virginia L. *On the way to kindergarten*
Kuiper, Nannie. *Bailey the bear cub*
Lamb, Albert. *The abandoned lighthouse*
Sam's winter hat
Tell me the day backwards
Landa, Norbert. *Little Bear and the wishing tree*
Lang, Aubrey. *The adventures of Baby Bear*
Langreuter, Jutta. *Little Bear and the big fight*
Little Bear brushes his teeth
Little Bear goes to kindergarten
Little Bear won't go to bed
Langsen, Richard C. *When someone in the family drinks too much*
Lansky, Vicki. *It's not your fault, KoKo Bear*
Lasky, Kathryn. *Fourth of July bear*
Lewis, Paeony. *I'll always love you*
Little Bear's Valentine
Lobel, Gillian. *Little Honey Bear and the smiley moon*
London, Jonathan. *Count the ways, Little Brown Bear*
Do your ABC's, Little Brown Bear
Honey Paw and Lightfoot
Lowell, Susan. *Dusty Locks and the three bears*
Lucas, David. *Something to do*
McBratney, Sam. *There, there*
Maccarone, Grace. *The three bears ABC*
McCloskey, Robert. *Blueberries for Sal*
McCully, Emily Arnold. *My real family*
MacDonald, Alan. *Beware of the bears!*
McGinness, Suzanne. *My bear Griz*
McKinlay, Meg. *No bears*
McMullan, Kate. *Papa's song*
McPhail, David. *The bear's toothache*
Big Brown Bear goes to town
Big Brown Bear's birthday surprise
Big brown bear's up and down day
Budgie and Boo

Drawing lessons from a bear
Emma in charge
Emma's pet
Emma's vacation
Henry Bear's Christmas
Henry Bear's park
Lost
Tinker and Tom and the Star Baby
Magloff, Lisa. *Bear*
Mahoney, Daniel J. *A really good snowman*
Martin, Bill, Jr. *Baby bear, baby bear, what do you see?*
Brown bear, brown bear, what do you see?
Marzollo, Jean. *Little Bear, you're a star!*
Melling, David. *Don't worry, Douglas!*
Hugless Douglas
Merlin, Christophe. *Under the hood*
Miles, Victoria. *Old Mother Bear*
Miller, Ruth. *The bear on the bed*
Miller, Virginia. *Be gentle!*
I love you just the way you are
In a minute!
On your potty!
Ten red apples
Minarik, Else Holmelund. *Little Bear's new friend*
Mitton, Tony. *A very curious bear*
Monari, Manuela. *Zero kisses for me!*
Moss, Miriam. *A babysitter for Billy Bear*
Bare bear
Matty in a mess!
Matty takes off!
Mozelle, Shirley. *The bear upstairs*
Murphy, Jill. *Peace at last*
Murphy, Stuart J. *A fair bear share*
Nash, Ogden. *The adventures of Isabel*, ill. by James Marshall
The adventures of Isabel, ill. by Bridget Starr Taylor
Naylor, Phyllis Reynolds. *Please do feed the bears*
Nesbitt, Kenn. *More bears!*
Nolan, Janet. *A Father's Day thank you*
Novak, Matt. *Jazzbo and Googy*
Jazzbo goes to school
Numeroff, Laura Joffe. *Otis and Sydney and the best birthday ever*
Nyeu, Tao. *Bunny days*
O'Keefe, Susan Heyboer. *Baby day*
Oldland, Nicholas. *Big bear hug*
O'Mara, Carmel. *Good morning*
Good night
Rainy day
Sunny day
Oram, Hiawyn. *Going to Grandpa's*
Kiss it better
Ørdal, Stina Langlo. *Princess Aasta*
Ormerod, Jan. *Maudie and Bear*
Pamintuan, Macky. *Twelve haunted rooms of Halloween*
Parenteau, Shirley. *Bears in beds*
Bears on chairs
Parker, Victoria. *Bearum scarum*
Peek, Merle. *Mary wore her red dress and Henry wore his green sneakers*
Peet, Bill. *Big bad Bruce*
Peters, Lisa Westberg. *Sleepyhead bear*
Petty, Dini. *The queen, the bear and the bumblebee*
Pfister, Marcus. *Make a wish, Honey Bear!*
Pinkwater, Daniel. *Bear in love*
Bear's Picture
Bongo Larry
Pitcher, Caroline. *Are you spring?*
Poppy Bear
Powell, Alma. *My little wagon [board book]*
Prater, John. *Hold tight!*
Pringle, Laurence P. *Bear hug*
Rayner, Catherine. *The bear who shared*
Reider, Katja. *The big little sneeze*
Ritchie, Alison. *Me and my dad!*
Me and my mom!
What Bear likes best!
Rock, Brian. *With all my heart*
Rockwell, Anne. *Backyard bear*
Boats
First comes spring
Morgan plays soccer
Roddie, Shen. *Sandbear*
Rodman, Mary Ann. *Surprise soup*
Rogers, Gregory. *The boy, the bear, the baron, the bard*
Midsummer knight
Root, Phyllis. *Oliver finds his way*
Rosales, Melodye Benson. *Leola and the honeybears*
Rosen, Michael. *Bear flies high*
Bear's day out
We're going on a bear hunt
Rouillard, Wendy. *Barnaby's bunny*
Rueda, Claudia. *No*
Russo, Marisabina. *Peter is just a baby*
Ruzzier, Sergio. *Bear and Bee*
Ryder, Joanne. *Bear of my heart*
Big bear ball
Rylant, Cynthia. *Bear day*
San Souci, Robert D. *Two bear cubs: a Miwok legend from California's Yosemite Valley*
Sayre, April Pulley. *Eat like a bear*
Scheffler, Ursel. *Taking care of Sister Bear*
Who has time for Little Bear?
Schertle, Alice. *Very hairy bear*
Schoenherr, Ian. *Don't spill the beans!*
Schoenherr, John. *Bear*
Schubert, Ingrid. *Bear's eggs*
Senshu, Noriko. *Sonny's dream*
Shannon, George. *Lizard's song*
Sharmat, Marjorie Weinman. *I'm terrific*
Sherry, Kevin. *Acorns everywhere!*
Shoulders, Michael. *Goodnight Baby Bear*
Say Daddy!
Smallman, Steve. *My dad!*
Spelman, Cornelia Maude. *Mama and Daddy Bear's divorce*
When I care about others
When I feel scared
Spohn, Kate. *Snow play*
Stanley, Diane. *Goldie and the three bears*
Stead, Philip C. *Bear has a story to tell*
Stein, David Ezra. *Leaves*
Ol' Mama Squirrel
Stevens, Janet. *Tops and bottoms*
Stewart, Amber. *Bedtime for Button*
Stewart, Joel. *Addis Berner Bear forgets*
Stickland, Paul. *Bears*
Stower, Adam. *Silly doggy*
Tafuri, Nancy. *Mama's little bears*
Taylor, Sean. *The grizzly bear with the frizzly hair*
Teckentrup, Britta. *Big smelly bear*
Thorpe, Kiki. *A comfy, cozy Thanksgiving*
Time to cha-cha-cha!
The three bears. *Goldilocks*
Goldilocks and the three bears, ill. by Jan Brett

Goldilocks and the three bears, ill. by Mark Buehner
Goldilocks and the three bears, ill. by Lorinda Bryan Cauley
Goldilocks and the three bears, ill. by Emma Chichester Clark
Goldilocks and the three bears, ill. by Valeri Gorbachev
Goldilocks and the three bears, ill. by Steven Guarnaccia
Goldilocks and the three bears, ill. by David McPhail
Goldilocks and the three bears, ill. by James Marshall
Goldilocks and the three bears, ill. by Gerda Muller
Goldilocks and the three bears, ill. by Gennady Spirin
Goldilocks and the three bears, ill. by Janet Stevens
The three bears, ill. by Byron Barton
The three bears, ill. by Paul Galdone
The three bears [board book]
The 3 bears and Goldilocks
Tolhurst, Marilyn. *Somebody and the three Blairs*
Trapani, Iza. *The bear went over the mountain*
Row, row, row your boat
Turkle, Brinton. *Deep in the forest*
Vainio, Pirkko. *The best of friends*
Van Buren, David. *I love you as big as the world*
Van Kampen, Vlasta. *Bear tales*
van Lieshout, Maria. *Tumble!*
Van Woerkom, Dorothy. *Becky and the bear*
Verburg, Bonnie. *The kiss box*
Vincent, Gabrielle. *Ernest and Celestine at the circus*
Ernest and Celestine's picnic
Merry Christmas, Ernest and Celestine
Waddell, Martin. *Can't you sleep, Little Bear?*
Good job, Little Bear!
Let's go home, Little Bear
Night night Cuddly Bear
Sleep tight, Little Bear
Snow bears
Yum, yum, yummy
Wallace, John. *Anything for you*
Wallace, Nancy Elizabeth. *Pond walk*
Rocks! rocks! rocks!
Seeds! Seeds! Seeds!
Shells! Shells! Shells!
Wallen, Ila. *The moon in my room*
Walters, Catherine. *Are you there, Baby Bear?*
Play gently, Alfie Bear
When will it be spring?
Walton, Rick. *The bear came over to my house*
Ward, Lynd. *The biggest bear*
Wardlaw, Lee. *The chair where bear sits*
Wargin, Kathy-jo. *Scare a bear*
Watanabe, Shigeo. *Ice cream is falling!*
Let's go swimming
Where's my daddy?
Watts, Frances. *Kisses for Daddy*
Weigelt, Udo. *Bear's last journey*
Weinberg, Larry. *The Forgetful Bears help Santa*
Wells, Rosemary. *The bear went over the mountain*
Weston, Carrie. *The new bear at school*
Wheeler, Lisa. *Ugly pie*
Williams, Sam. *Angel's Christmas cookies*
Wilson, Karma. *Bear feels scared*
Bear feels sick
Bear says thanks
Bear stays up for Christmas
Bear's loose tooth
Winters, Kay. *The bears go to school*
Winthrop, Elizabeth. *Bear and Mrs. Duck*
Bear's Christmas surprise
Wolff, Ashley. *Baby Bear counts one*
Baby Bear sees blue
Wood, Audrey. *Oh my baby bear!*
Wright, Cliff. *Bear and ball*
Bear and kite
Wright, Maureen. *Sleep, Big Bear, sleep!*
Sneeze, Big Bear, sneeze
Yee, Wong Herbert. *Big black bear*
Yektai, Niki. *Bears at the beach*
Bears in pairs
Yolen, Jane. *Baby Bear's big dreams*
Baby Bear's books
Baby Bear's chairs
Sister Bear
The three bears holiday rhyme book
Zalben, Jane Breskin. *Beni's first Chanukah*
Beni's first wedding
Zehler, Antonia. *Two fine ladies*
Zoehfeld, Kathleen Weidner. *Apples, apples*

Animals – beavers

Arnosky, Jim. *Beaver pond, moose pond*
Bentley, Dawn. *Busy little beaver*
Cooper, Elisha. *Beaver is lost*
George, William T. *Beaver at Long Pond*
Gibbons, Gail. *Beavers*
Harper, Charise Mericle. *When Randolph turned rotten*
Johnson, Amy Crane. *Mason moves away / Mason se muda*
Kuiper, Nannie. *Bravo, brave beavers*
Long, Heather. *Max & Milo go to sleep!*
Oldland, Nicholas. *The busy beaver*
Schubert, Ingrid. *There's always room for one more*
Van Laan, Nancy. *Moose tales*
Weigelt, Udo. *Old Beaver*

Animals – bison *see* Animals – buffaloes

Animals – bonobos

Napoli, Donna Jo. *Bobby the bold*

Animals – brush wolves *see* Animals – coyotes

Animals – buffaloes

Arnosky, Jim. *Grandfather Buffalo*
Baker, Olaf. *Where the buffaloes begin*
Bruchac, Joseph. *Buffalo song*
Fern, Tracey E. *Buffalo music*
George, Jean Craighead. *The buffalo are back*
Goble, Paul. *Her seven brothers*
The return of the buffaloes
Gulbis, Stephen. *Cowgirl Rosie and her five baby bison*
Ravishankar, Anushka. *Elephants never forget!*
Vernick, Audrey. *Is your buffalo ready for kindergarten?*
Teach your buffalo to play drums
Waldman, Neil. *They came from the Bronx*
Wiebe, Rudy. *Hidden buffalo*

Animals – bulls, cows

Aliki. *Milk from cow to carton*
Alsdurf, Phyllis. *It's milking time*
Baehr, Patricia. *Boo Cow*
Becker, Suzy. *Manny's cows*
Borgo, Lacy. *Big Mama's baby*
Bunting, Eve. *The baby shower*
Chaconas, Dori. *When cows come home for Christmas*
Chambers, Angela. *How now, cow?*
Climo, Shirley. *The Irish Cinderlad*
Cordsen, Carol Foskett. *Market day*
Cronin, Doreen. *Click, clack, moo*
Cutbill, Andy. *The cow that laid an egg*
First week at cow school
Ditchfield, Christin. *Cowlick!*
Doyle, Malachy. *Cow*
Duffield, Katy. *Farmer McPeepers and his missing milk cows*
Flanagan, Alice K. *Raising cows on the Koebels' farm*
Fleming, Denise. *The cow who clucked*
Fox, Mem. *A particular cow*
Gibbons, Gail. *Yippee-yay!*
Gollub, Matthew. *Gobble, quack, moon*
Gomi, Taro. *Spring is here*
Hamilton, Arlene. *Only a cow*
Helakoski, Leslie. *Fair cow*
Hill, Ros. *Shamoo*
Himmelman, John. *Cows to the rescue*
Hoberman, Mary Ann. *Mrs. O'Leary's cow*
Hume, Lachie. *Clancy the courageous cow*
Hurd, Thacher. *Moo Cow Kaboom!*
Johnson, Paul Brett. *The cow who wouldn't come down*
Ketteman, Helen. *Bubba the cowboy prince*
Kinerk, Robert. *Clorinda*
Clorinda plays baseball!
Clorinda takes flight
Korchek, Lori. *Adventures of Cow, too*
LaRochelle, David. *Moo!*
Leaf, Munro. *The story of Ferdinand the bull*
Lewis, Kim. *Little calf*
Lodge, Jo. *Moo Moo goes to the city*
Lowell, Susan. *Little Red Cowboy Hat*
Macaulay, David. *Black and white*
Milgrim, David. *Cows can't fly*
Milway, Katie Smith. *Cappuccina goes to town*
Mortensen, Lori. *Cindy Moo*
Murphy, Andy. *Out and about at the dairy farm*
Neubecker, Robert. *Courage of the blue boy*
Newman, Jeff. *Reginald*
Newman, Marlene. *Myron's magic cow*
Ohi, Ruth. *Chicken, Pig, Cow and the class pet*
Chicken, Pig, Cow horse around
Chicken, Pig, Cow's first fight
Palatini, Margie. *Boo-hoo moo*
Moo who?
Pedersen, Janet. *Millie wants to play*
Peterson, Cris. *Amazing grazing*
Extra cheese, please!
Plourde, Lynn. *Only cows allowed!*
Rogers, Hal. *Milking machines*
Root, Phyllis. *Kiss the cow*
Ross, Fiona. *Chilly Milly Moo*
Schertle, Alice. *How now, brown cow?*
Schnitzler, Pattie L. *Widdermaker*
Schuh, Mari C. *Cows on the farm*
Seeger, Laura Vaccaro. *Bully*
Shannon, George. *The Secret Chicken Club*
Smith, Linda. *When Moon fell down*
Souders, Taryn. *Whole-y cow!*
Speed, Toby. *Two cool cows*
Steffensmeier, Alexander. *Millie and the big rescue*
Millie in the snow
Millie waits for the mail
Stevens, Janet. *Find a cow now!*
Thomas, Jan. *A birthday for Cow!*
Is everyone ready for fun?
Weis, Carol. *When the cows got loose*
Wheeler, Lisa. *Sixteen cows*
Willis, Jeanne. *Misery Moo*
Wilson, Karma. *The cow loves cookies*
Sakes alive!

Animals – camels

Alsenas, Linas. *Peanut*
Carryl, Charles E. *The camel's lament*
Kipling, Rudyard. *How the camel got his hump*
Manuel, Lynn. *Camels always do*
Peet, Bill. *Pamela Camel*
Thury, Frederick. *The last straw*

Animals – caribou *see* Animals – reindeer

Animals – cats

Abley, Mark. *Ghost cat*
Adoff, Arnold. *Daring Dog and Captain Cat*
Aesop. *Belling the cat*
Town mouse, country mouse
Alexander, Lloyd. *The house Gobbaleen*
How the cat swallowed thunder
Aliki. *Tabby*
Almond, David. *Kate, the cat and the moon*
Alter, Anna. *Estelle and Lucy*
Appelt, Kathi. *The Alley Cat's Meow*
Apple, Margot. *Brave Martha*
Aralan, Haydé. *Milton*
Milton's Christmas
Arnold, Katya. *Meow!*
Arnold, Marsha Diane. *Metro cat*
Asch, Frank. *Mr. Maxwell's mouse*
Mrs. Marlowe's mice
Asher, Sandy. *Stella's dancing days*
Austin, Mike. *Countdown with Milo*
Austin, Patricia. *The cat who loved Mozart*
Aylesworth, Jim. *Mother Halverson's new cat*
Baeten, Lieve. *Happy birthday, Little Witch!*
Bailey, Linda. *Stanley's little sister*
Bailey, Mary Bryant. *Jeoffry's Christmas*
Balian, Lorna. *Leprechauns never lie*
Banks, Kate. *City cat*
Barbero, Maria. *The bravest mouse*
Bartoletti, Susan Campbell. *Nobody's nosier than a cat*
Barton, Byron. *The wee little woman*
Beames, Margaret. *Night cat*
Beaton, Clare. *One moose, twenty mice*
One moose, twenty mice [board book]
Bechtold, Lisze. *Edna's tale*
Berger, Joe. *My special one and only*
Bergman, Tamar. *Where is?*
Berry, Lynne. *The curious demise of a contrary cat*
The best cat in the world
Bibbel, Mark. *Oh, Harry!*
Birnbaum, Abe. *Green eyes*
Blackstone, Stella. *Cleo and Caspar*

Cleo in the snow
Cleo on the move
Cleo the cat
Cleo's alphabet book
Cleo's color book
Cleo's counting book
Come here, Cleo
Bloom, Becky. *Crackers*
Bogan, Paulette. *Momma's magical purse*
Bowman, Patty. *The amazing Hamweenie*
Boxall, Ed. *Francis the scaredy cat*
Boyer, Cécile. *Woof meow tweet-tweet*
Bradford, Karleen. *You can't rush a cat*
Bramsen, Carin. *Hey, duck!*
Brett, Jan. *Annie and the wild animals*
Comet's nine lives
Brimner, Larry Dane. *Cat on wheels*
Brown, Margaret Wise. *Sneakers, the seaside cat*
Brown, Ruth. *Gracie the lighthouse cat*
Holly, the true story of a cat
The tale of two mice
Browne, Anthony. *Little Beauty*
Bruel, Nick. *Bad Kitty*
A Bad Kitty Christmas
Poor puppy
Bryan, Ashley. *The cat's purr*
Bunting, Eve. *Mouse island*
Burningham, John. *It's a secret!*
Butterworth, Nick. *Jasper's beanstalk*
Jingle bells
Cabrera, Jane. *Kitty's cuddles*
Calhoun, Mary. *Blue-ribbon Henry*
Cross-country cat
Henry the Christmas cat
Henry the sailor cat
High-wire Henry
Hot-air Henry
Caple, Kathy. *Hillary to the rescue*
Capucilli, Alyssa Satin. *Biscuit wants to play*
Happy birthday, Biscuit!
Little spotted cat
Mrs. McTats and her houseful of cats
Only my mom and me
Carle, Eric. *Have you seen my cat?*
Carlson, Nancy. *Arnie and the skateboard gang*
Carmody, Isobelle. *Magic night*
Casanova, Mary. *Some cat!*
Cash, Megan Montague. *What makes the seasons?*
Catalanotto, Peter. *Kitten red, yellow, blue*
Cazet, Denys. *Never spit on your shoes*
Cecka, Melanie. *Violet comes to stay*
Violet goes to the country
Chichester Clark, Emma. *Will and Squill*
Chorao, Kay. *Knock at the door and other baby action rhymes*
Christian, Mary Blount. *If not for the calico cat*
Chwast, Seymour. *Harry, I need you!*
Clements, Andrew. *Dolores and the big fire*
Coffey, Maria. *A cat adrift*
Cole, Joanna. *My new kitten*
Collington, Peter. *Clever cat*
Cooper, Elisha. *Magic thinks big*
Cooper, Helen. *Delicious!*
A pipkin of pepper
Cox, Judy. *One is a feast for Mouse*
Crawley, Dave. *Cat poems*
Crimi, Carolyn. *Dear Tabby*
Tessa's tip-tapping toes
Crow, Kristyn. *Skeleton cat*
Crum, Shutta. *Thunder-Boomer!*
Cushman, Doug. *Space cat*
Czekaj, Jef. *Cat secrets*
da Costa, Deborah. *Snow in Jerusalem*
Dahl, Michael. *Nap time for Kitty*
Davis, Anne. *No dogs allowed!*
Davis, David. *Jazz cats*
Day, Nancy Raines. *A kitten's year*
Dean, James. *Valentine's Day is cool*
Demas, Corinne. *Here comes trouble!*
Desmond, Jenni. *Red cat blue cat*
Dick Whittington and his cat. *Dick Whittington and his cat*, ill. by Marcia Brown
Dick Whittington and his cat, ill. by Mélisande Potter
Dickson, Louise. *The vanishing cat*
Dodd, Emma. *I don't want a cool cat!*
Donaldson, Julia. *Tabby McTat, the musical cat*
Downey, Lynn. *Matilda's humdinger*
Doyle, Malachy. *Storm cats*
Duncan, Lois. *I walk at night*
Egan, Tim. *Roasted peanuts*
Egielski, Richard. *Slim and Jim*
Ehlert, Lois. *Boo to you!*
Feathers for lunch
Top cat
Einhorn, Edward. *A very improbable story*
Elliott, David. *Knitty Kitty*
Elschner, Geraldine. *Mark's messy room*
Elsdale, Bob. *Mac side up*
Emberley, Rebecca. *Mice on ice*
Esbaum, Jill. *Tom's tweet*
Ets, Marie Hall. *Mr. T. W. Anthony Woo*
Faglia, Matteo. *Happy birthday, I'm 3*
Farish, Terry. *The cat who liked potato soup*
Fernandes, Eugenie. *Kitten's spring*
Kitten's winter
Fleming, Denise. *Buster*
Mama cat has three kittens
Fletcher, Ashlee. *My dog, my cat*
Florian, Douglas. *Bow wow meow meow, it's rhyming cats and dogs*
Ford, Bernette. *Ballet Kitty*
Foreman, Michael. *Cat in the manger*
Friends
Franco, Betsy. *A curious collection of cats*
Freeman, Tor. *Olive and the bad mood*
Olive and the big secret
French, Vivian. *A present for mom*
Friedman, Mel. *Kitten castle*
Friend, Catherine. *The perfect nest*
Fuller, Sandy F. *My cat, coon cat*
Gág, Wanda. *Millions of cats*
Gantos, Jack. *Back to school for Rotten Ralph*
Happy birthday, Rotten Ralph
The nine lives of Rotten Ralph
Not so Rotten Ralph
Rotten Ralph
Rotten Ralph's rotten Christmas
Rotten Ralph's rotten romance
Rotten Ralph's show and tell
Rotten Ralph's trick or treat
Wedding bells for Rotten Ralph
Worse than Rotten Ralph
Gay, Marie-Louise. *Caramba*
Caramba and Henry
Geras, Adèle. *Sleep tight, Ginger Kitten*
Gerstein, Mordicai. *Minifred goes to school*
Gibbons, Gail. *Cats*

Giff, Patricia Reilly. *Good luck, Ronald Morgan*
Godwin, Laura. *One moon, two cats*
Going, K. L. *Dog in charge*
Goodwin-Sturges, Judy Sue. *Construction Kitties*
Gorbachev, Valeri. *The best cat*
Catty Jane who hated the rain
Catty Jane who loved to dance
Graham-Yooll, Liz. *Timothy Tib*
Grant, Joan. *Cat and Fish*
Gravdahl, John. *Curious catwalk*
Greene, Carol. *Where is that cat?*
Gretz, Susanna. *Riley and Rose in the picture*
Grimes, Nikki. *When Gorilla goes walking*
Grimm, Jacob and Wilhelm. *The fisherman and his wife*
Gudeon, Adam. *Me and Meow*
Hafner, Marylin. *Molly and Emmett's camping adventure*
Molly and Emmett's surprise garden
Hall, Michael. *Cat tale*
Hamilton, Martha. *Priceless gifts*
Harjo, Joy. *The good luck cat*
Harper, Anita. *It's not fair!*
Harper, Charise Mericle. *The best birthday ever!*
Harper, Dan. *Telling time with Big Mama Cat*
Harper, Jessica. *I'm not going to chase the cat today*
Harris, Trudy. *Tally cat keeps track*
Harvey, Amanda. *Dog days*
Hassett, John. *The nine lives of Dudley Dog*
Havill, Juanita. *Jamaica is thankful*
Helmer, Diana Star. *The cat who came for tacos*
Helmer, Marilyn. *Three cat and mouse tales*
Henkes, Kevin. *Kitten's first full moon*
Henrichs, Wendy. *I am Tama, lucky cat*
Henry, Steve. *Nobody asked me!*
Hicks, Barbara Jean. *The secret life of Walter Kitty*
Himmelman, John. *Katie loves the kittens*
Hoberman, Mary Ann. *The looking book*
The two sillies
Hodgkins, Fran. *The cat of Strawberry Hill*
Hodgkinson, Leigh. *Boris and the snoozebox*
Boris and the wrong shadow
Hogg, Gary. *Look what the cat dragged in!*
Hogrogian, Nonny. *Cool cat*
Holub, Joan. *Cinderdog and the wicked stepcat*
Scat cats
Why do cats meow?
Hood, Susan. *Meet Trouble*
Hooper, Meredith. *Celebrity cat*
Horn, Emily. *Excuse me — are you a witch?*
Howe, James. *Houndsley and Catina*
Houndsley and Catina and the birthday surprise
Hubbell, Patricia. *Wrapping paper romp*
Hudelhoff, Allen H. *Cats and kids*
Hughes, Shirley. *Alfie and the birthday surprise*
Huling, Jan. *Puss in cowboy boots*
Hurd, Thacher. *Cat's pajamas*
Hutchins, Hazel. *One dark night*
Inkpen, Mick. *Meow!*
Jackson, Shelley. *Mimi's Dada Catifesto*
Jacobs, Joseph. *King of the cats*
Jane, Pamela. *Milo and the greatest trick ever*
Janovitz, Marilyn. *We love school!*
Jarka, Jeff. *Love that kitty!*
Jenkins, Emily. *Five creatures*
Love you when you whine
Jenkins, Steve. *Dogs and cats*
Perros y gatos / dogs and cats
Jennings, Sharon. *Priscilla's paw de deux*
Jobling, Curtis. *Frankenstein's cat*
Johansen, K. V. *Pippin and Pudding*
Johnson, Paul Brett. *Mr. Persnickety and Cat Lady*
Johnston, Tony. *The cat with seven names*
Jonathan, Langley. *Missing*
Jones, Elizabeth. *Sunshine and Storm*
Jonovitz, Marilyn. *Three little kittens*
Joosse, Barbara. *Nugget and Darling*
Old Robert and the sea-silly cats
Keats, Ezra Jack. *Hi, cat!*
Kitten for a day
Kellogg, Steven. *A rose for Pinkerton*
Tallyho, Pinkerton!
Khalsa, Dayal Kaur. *Green cat*
Kirk, Daniel. *Library mouse: a museum adventure*
Kitamura, Satoshi. *Comic adventures of Boots*
Me and my cat?
Kleven, Elisa. *The wishing ball*
Krasnesky, Thad. *That cat can't stay*
Kraus, Robert. *Come out and play, little mouse*
Krauss, Ruth. *And I love you*
Kroll, Steven. *It's April Fools' Day!*
Krosoczka, Jarrett J. *Ollie the purple elephant*
Kuskin, Karla. *So, what's it like to be a cat?*
Toots the cat
Kwon, Yoon-duck. *My cat copies me*
Lakin, Patricia. *Clarence the copy cat*
Larson, Kirby. *Two Bobbies*
Lawson, Janet. *Audrey and Barbara*
Lazo, Caroline. *Someday when my cat can talk*
Lear, Edward. *The owl and the pussycat*, ill. by Jan Brett
The owl and the pussycat, ill. by Paul Galdone
The owl and the pussycat, ill. by Anne Mortimer
Le Guin, Ursula K. *Cat dreams*
Lent, Blair. *Ruby and Fred*
Lewin, Betsy. *Thumpy Feet*
Where is Tippy Toes?
Lewis, J. Patrick. *Kindergarten cat*
Lindbergh, Reeve. *Homer the library cat*
Lindgren, Barbro. *Sam's ball*
Litwin, Eric. *Pete the cat: I love my white shoes*
Pete the cat: rocking in my school shoes
Pete the cat and his four groovy buttons
Pete the cat saves Christmas
Lloyd, Sam. *Doctor Meow's big emergency*
Mr. Pusskins
Mr. Pusskins and Little Whiskers
Lobel, Anita. *Nini here and there*
Nini lost and found
One lighthouse, one moon
Lord, Janet. *Where is Catkin?*
Luxbacher, Irene. *Mattoo, let's play!*
McBratney, Sam. *The dark at the top of the stairs*
McCarty, Peter. *Fabian escapes*
Henry in love
Hondo and Fabian
McClure, Gillian. *Tom Finger*
McClure, Nikki. *How to be a cat*
McCully, Emily Arnold. *Four hungry kittens*
MacDonald, Margaret Read. *Fat cat*
Mabela the clever
MacDonald, Maryann. *The Christmas cat*
McDonnell, Christine. *Goyangi means cat*
McDonnell, Patrick. *The gift of nothing*
Just like Heaven
South
Wag!
McFarland, Lyn Rossiter. *Widget and the puppy*

McGraw, Sheila. *Pussycats everywhere*
McGuinness-Kelly, Tracy-Lee. *Bad Cat puts on his top hat*
McKinlay, Penny. *Flabby Tabby*
MacLachlan, Patricia. *Bittle*
Cat talk
Who loves me?
McLaren, Chesley. *Zat cat!*
McLellan, Stephanie Simpson. *The chicken cat*
McMullan, Kate. *Supercat*
Supercat to the rescue
McQuade, Jacqueline. *Good times with Teddy Bear*
Mader, C. Roger. *Lost cat*
Magloff, Lisa. *Kitten*
Mahy, Margaret. *The Christmas tree tangle*
Mallat, Kathy. *Trouble on the tracks*
Manning, Jane. *Cat nights*
Manzano, Sonia. *A box full of kittens*
Marciano, John Bemelmans. *Madeline and the cats of Rome*
Martin, Bill, Jr. *Kitty Cat, Kitty Cat, are you going to school?*
Kitty Cat, Kitty Cat, are you going to sleep?
Kitty Cat, Kitty Cat, are you waking up?
Martin, David. *All for pie, pie for all*
Marzollo, Jean. *Thanksgiving cats*
Valentine cats
Masurel, Claire. *A cat and a dog*
Meggs, Libby Phillips. *Go home!*
Merriam, Eve. *Where's that cat?*
Meyers, Susan. *Kittens! Kittens! Kittens!*
Miller, Sara Swan. *Cat in the bag*
Miller, Virginia. *Be gentle!*
Ten red apples
Minarik, Else Holmelund. *It's spring!*
Monks, Lydia. *The cat barked?*
Monson, A. M. *Wanted . . . best friend*
Montes, Marisa. *Los gatos black on Halloween*
Moore, Inga. *Captain Cat*
Mora, Pat. *A birthday basket for Tía*
Here, kitty, kitty! / ¡Ven, gatita, ven!
Moran, Alex. *Come here, tiger*
Sam and Jack
Morris, Bob. *Crispin the Terrible*
Morris, Dewi. *Sandy's street*
Morris, Jackie. *I am Cat*
Mortimer, Anne. *Pumpkin cat*
Moss, Miriam. *Matty in a mess!*
Matty takes off!
Mother Goose. *The three little kittens*
Moxley, Sheila. *ABCD an alphabet book of cats and dogs*
Murphy, Stuart J. *Pepper's journal*
Murray, Alison. *Princess Penelope and the runaway kitten*
Murray, Andrew. *Have you seen Chester?*
Myers, Tim. *Looking for Luna*
Myron, Vicki. *Dewey*
Napoli, Donna Jo. *Rocky, the cat who barks*
Nelson-Schmidt, Michelle. *Cats, cats!*
Newberry, Clare Turlay. *April's kittens*
Marshmallow
Newbery, Linda. *Posy*
Newman, Lesléa. *Cats, cats, cats*
Nishimura, Kae. *Dinah*
Nishizuka, Koko. *The beckoning cat*
Norwich, William D. *Molly and the magic dress*
Numeroff, Laura Joffe. *If you give a cat a cupcake*
Oh, Jiwon. *Cat and mouse*
O'Hair, Margaret. *My kitten*
Oller, Erika. *The cabbage soup solution*
Oram, Hiawyn. *Just Dog*
Oxley, Jennifer. *The chicken problem*
Page, Gail. *How to be a good cat*
Partridge, Elizabeth. *Big Cat Pepper*
Peacock, Carol Antoinette. *Pilgrim cat*
Peet, Bill. *Jennifer and Josephine*
Pelley, Kathleen T. *Raj the bookstore tiger*
Penner, Fred. *The cat came back*
Perkins, Lynne Rae. *The broken cat*
Perrault, Charles. *Puss in boots*, ill. by Marcia Brown
Puss in boots, ill. by Lorinda Bryan Cauley
Puss in boots, ill. by Paul Galdone
Puss in boots, ill. by Steve Light
Puss in boots, ill. by Giuliano Lunelli
Puss in boots, ill. by Fred Marcellino
Puss in boots, ill. by Fred Marcellino
Puss in boots, ill. by Bernhard Oberdieck
Puss in boots, ill. by Jerry Pinkney
Puss in boots, ill. by Alain Vaës
Pete the cat: the wheels on the bus
Peters, Lisa Westberg. *Frankie works the night shift*
Pilkey, Dav. *Dragon's fat cat*
When cats dream
Pinkney, Jerry. *Three little kittens*
Plecas, Jennifer. *Olive's perfect world*
Polacco, Patricia. *Mrs. Katz and Tush*
Tikvah means hope
Potter, Beatrix. *The pie and the patty-pan*
Roly-Poly pudding
The sly old cat
The story of Miss Moppet
The tale of Tom Kitten
Prap, Lila. *Doggy whys*
Pratt, Pierre. *I see . . . my sister / I see . . . my cat*
Priceman, Marjorie. *My nine lives / by Clio*
Pringle, Laurence P. *Naming the cat*
Protopopescu, Orel. *Thelonious Mouse*
Pullman, Philip. *Puss in boots: the adventures of that most enterprising feline*
Pulver, Robin. *Christmas for a kitten*
Christmas kitten, home at last
Radzinski, Kandy. *Where to sleep*
Raschka, Chris. *John Coltrane's giant steps*
Rathmann, Peggy. *Ruby the copycat*
Regan, Dian Curtis. *The Snow Blew Inn*
Reibstein, Mark. *Wabi Sabi*
Reich, Susanna. *Minette's feast*
Reinen, Judy. *Meow*
Reiser, Lynn. *My cat Tuna*
Reynolds, Marilynn. *A present for Mrs. Kazinski*
Richard, Françoise. *On Cat Mountain*
Ritz, Karen. *Windows with birds*
Robbins, Beth. *Tom, Ally, and the baby-sitter*
Tom, Ally, and the new baby
Tom and Ally visit the doctor
Tom's afraid of the dark
Tom's first day at school
Tom's new haircut
Roberts, Bethany. *Christmas mice*
Robinson, Sue. *I want to play*
Robledo, Honorio. *Nico visits the moon*
Rockwell, Anne. *Katie Catz makes a splash*
Space vehicles
Rohmann, Eric. *The cinder-eyed cats*
Root, Phyllis. *Lucia and the light*
Scrawny cat

Rose, Deborah Lee. *All the seasons of the year*
Rosenthal, Eileen. *Bobo the sailor man!*
I must have Bobo!
I'll save you Bobo!
Ross, Eileen. *The Halloween showdown*
Rostoker-Gruber, Karen. *Bandit*
Bandit's surprise
Ferret fun
Roth, Carol. *Where's my mommy?*
Rubin, Adam. *Those darn squirrels and the cat next door*
Rueda, Claudia. *Is it big or is it little?*
Rylant, Cynthia. *Brownie and Pearl get dolled up*
Brownie and Pearl go for a spin
Brownie and Pearl grab a bite
Brownie and Pearl hit the hay
Brownie and Pearl make good
Brownie and Pearl see the sights
Brownie and Pearl take a dip
The cookie-store cat
Moonlight, the Halloween cat
Rymond, Lynda Gene. *Oscar and the mooncats*
Sage, James. *Farmer Smart's fat cat*
Saltzberg, Barney. *I love cats*
Samuels, Barbara. *Aloha, Dolores*
Dolores meets her match
Duncan and Dolores
Happy Valentine's Day, Dolores
The trucker
Sanderson, Ruth. *Papa Gatto*
San Souci, Robert D. *The white cat*
Santoro, Scott. *Farm-fresh cats*
Sarcone-Roach, Julia. *The secret plan*
Saul, Carol P. *Barn cat*
Say, Allen. *Allison*
Schachner, Judith Byron. *Bits and pieces*
The Grannyman
Skippyjon Jones and the big bones
Skippyjon Jones Cirque de Olé
Skippyjon Jones class action
Skippyjon Jones in mummy trouble
Skippyjon Jones, lost in spice
Schertle, Alice. *I am the cat*
Schoenherr, Ian. *Cat and mouse*
Schoonmaker, Elizabeth. *Square cat*
Schwarz, Viviane. *There are cats in this book*
There are no cats in this book
Scillian, Devin. *Memoirs of a hamster*
Scotton, Rob. *Love, Splat*
Merry Christmas, Splat
Secret Agent Splat!
Splat and the cool school trip
Splat says thank you!
Splat the cat
Splat the cat: on with the show
Splish, splash, Splat!
Segal, John. *Alistair and Kip's great adventure*
Seki, Sunny. *The tale of the lucky cat*
Shea, Bob. *Cheetah can't lose*
Shireen, Nadia. *Hey, Presto!*
Sidman, Joyce. *Meow ruff*
Siminovich, Lorena. *Alex and Lulu*
Simmonds, Posy. *Baker cat*
Siomades, Lorianne. *Three little kittens*
Skinner, Daphne. *The right place for Albert*
Smath, Jerry. *Sammy Salami*
Smiley, Norene. *That stripy cat*
Smith, Maggie. *Desser, the best ever cat*
So, Meilo. *Gobble, gobble, slip, slop*
Soto, Gary. *Chato and the party animals*
Chato goes cruisin'
Chato's kitchen
Spinelli, Eileen. *Callie Cat, ice skater*
Do you have a cat?
Hero cat
Spires, Elizabeth. *The big meow*
Stadler, John. *Catilda*
The cats of Mrs. Calamari
Stainton, Sue. *The chocolate cat*
I love cats
The lighthouse cat
Santa's snow cat
Steig, William. *Solomon the rusty nail*
Stephens, Helen. *I'm too busy*
What about me?
Stevens, Janet. *My big dog*
Sturges, Philemon. *Waggers*
Stutson, Caroline. *Cats' night out*
Surovec, Yasmine. *I see Kitty*
Sykes, Julie. *This and that*
Taber, Tory. *Rufus at work*
Talbott, Hudson. *It's all about me-ow*
Tan, Amy. *The Chinese Siamese cat*
Teague, Mark. *Detective LaRue*
LaRue across America
Teckentrup, Britta. *Grumpy cat*
Thomas, Jan. *Here comes the big, mean dust bunny!*
Thomas, Shelley Moore. *Take care, Good Knight*
Thomas, Valerie. *Winnie the witch*
Winnie's midnight dragon
Thompson, Lauren. *How many cats?*
Thornhill, Jan. *Wild in the city*
Tillman, Nancy. *Tumford the terrible*
Tumford's rude noises
Titus, Eve. *Anatole and the cat*
Townsend, Michael. *Cute and cuter*
Turkle, Brinton. *Do not open*
Turner, Ann Warren. *Pumpkin cat*
Uchida, Yoshiko. *The two foolish cats*
Umansky, Kaye. *I don't like Gloria!*
Ungerer, Tomi. *Flix*
Vagin, Vladimir. *Here comes the cat*
Varon, Sara. *Chicken and Cat*
Chicken and Cat clean up
Viorst, Judith. *The tenth good thing about Barney*
Vischer, Frans. *Fuddles*
A very Fuddles Christmas
Voake, Charlotte. *Ginger*
Ginger and the mystery visitor
Pizza kittens
Volkmann, Roy. *Curious kittens*
Waber, Bernard. *Lyle at Christmas*
Waddell, Martin. *A kitten called Moonlight*
Who do you love?
Wade, Mary Dodson. *No year of the cat*
Wahman, Wendy. *A cat like that*
Waite, Judy. *Mouse, look out!*
The stray kitten
Walton, Rick. *The remarkable friendship of Mr. Cat and Mr. Rat*
Ward, B. J. *Farty Marty*
Ward, Cindy. *Cookie's week*
Wardlaw, Lee. *Won Ton*
Warhola, James. *Uncle Andy's cats*
Waring, Geoff. *Oscar and the bat*
Oscar and the cricket
Oscar and the moth
Warner, Sunny. *The moon quilt*

Washington, Donna L. *A big, spooky house*
Watson, Wendy. *Happy Easter day!*
Watt, Mélanie. *Chester*
Chester's back!
Chester's masterpiece
Weaver, Tess. *Cat jumped in!*
Opera cat
Weeks, Sarah. *Woof*
Wellington, Monica. *Squeaking of art, the mice go to the museum*
Wells, Rosemary. *McDuff's wild romp*
Yoko
Yoko finds her way
Yoko learns to read
Yoko's paper cranes
Weninger, Brigitte. *Good night, Nori*
West, Judy. *Have you got my purr?*
Wethered, Peggy. *Touchdown Mars!*
Wheeler, Lisa. *Castaway cats*
Wiesner, David. *Mr. Wuffles!*
Willard, Nancy. *The mouse, the cat and Grandmother's hat*
Wilson, Karma. *Hello, Calico!*
Sleepyhead
Wiviott, Meg. *Benno and the night of broken glass*
Woelfle, Gretchen. *Katje the windmill cat*
Wojtusik, Elizabeth. *Kitty up!*
Wolff, Nancy. *It's time for school with Tallulah*
Tallulah in the kitchen
Wood, Jakki. *Moo moo, brown cow*
Never say boo to a goose!
Wormell, Mary. *Why not?*
Yokococo. *Matilda and Hans*
Yolen, Jane. *The day Tiger Rose said goodbye*
Soft house
Young, Ed. *Cat and Rat*
Ziefert, Harriet. *No kiss for Grandpa!*

Animals – cheetahs

St. Pierre, Stephanie. *Cheetahs*
Shea, Bob. *Cheetah can't lose*

Animals – chimpanzees

Alborough, Jez. *Hug*
Yes
Anholt, Catherine. *Chimp and Zee and the big storm*
Chimp and Zee's noisy book
Happy birthday, Chimp and Zee
Monkey around with Chimp and Zee [board book]
Browne, Anthony. *How do you feel?*
I like books
I like books [board book]
One gorilla: a counting book
Willy and Hugh
Willy the champ
Willy the dreamer
Willy the wimp
Willy the wizard
Willy's pictures
Bustos, Eduardo. *Going ape!*
Durango, Julia. *Cha-cha chimps*
Durant, Alan. *Brown Bear gets in shape*
Faulkner, Keith. *Charlie Chimp's Christmas*
McDonnell, Patrick. *Me . . . Jane*
Napoli, Donna Jo. *Bobby the bold*
Oram, Hiawyn. *The wrong overcoat*
Watson, Richard Jesse. *The boy who went ape*
Winter, Jeanette. *The watcher*

Animals – chipmunks

Bruchac, Joseph. *How Chipmunk got his stripes*
Gorbachev, Valeri. *Me too!*
Ryder, Joanne. *Chipmunk song*
Sauer, Tammi. *Oh, nuts!*
Stevenson, James. *Wilfred the rat*
Taylor, Jane. *Twinkle, twinkle, little star*
Williams, Barbara. *Chester Chipmunk's Thanksgiving*

Animals – coatis

Schindler, S. D. *Spike and Ike take a hike*

Animals – cougars

Costello, Emily. *Realm of the panther*
London, Jonathan. *Panther, shadow of the swamp*
Mora, Pat. *Doña Flor*

Animals – cows *see* Animals – bulls, cows

Animals – coyotes

Aardema, Verna. *Borreguita and the coyote*
Aesop. *Doctor Coyote*
Arnosky, Jim. *Coyote raid in Cactus Canyon*
Beaumont, Karen. *Duck, duck, goose!*
Beaver steals fire
Czernecki, Stefan. *Huevos rancheros*
The gingerbread boy. *The Gingerbread Cowboy*
Goble, Paul. *Iktomi and the ducks*
Hausman, Gerald. *Coyote walks on two legs*
Hiscock, Bruce. *Coyote and badger*
Hopkins, Jackie Mims. *Prairie chicken little*
Johnston, Tony. *The tale of Rabbit and Coyote*
King, Thomas. *Coyote sings to the moon*
Lowell, Susan. *Josefina javelina*
The three little javelinas
McDermott, Gerald. *Coyote*
Paul, Ann Whitford. *Tortuga in trouble*
Pia Toya
Puttock, Simon. *Little lost cowboy*
Stevens, Janet. *Old bag of bones*
Tafolla, Carmen. *Baby Coyote and the old woman / El coyotito y la viejita*
Taylor, Harriet Peck. *Coyote and the laughing butterflies*
Tonatiuh, Duncan. *Pancho Rabbit and the coyote*
Whitehouse, Patricia. *Coyotes*

Animals – deer

Arnosky, Jim. *All about deer*
Deer at the brook
Collins, Pat Lowery. *The deer watch*
Gordon, Gus. *Herman and Rosie*
Kleven, Elisa. *The dancing deer and the foolish hunter*
Marzollo, Jean. *Once upon a springtime*
Puttock, Simon. *The baby that roared*
Scott, Nathan Kumar. *Mangoes and bananas*
The sacred banana leaf
Soros, Barbara. *Tenzin's deer*
Springett, Martin. *Kate and Pippin*
Townsend, Emily Rose. *Deer*

Animals – dislike of *see* Behavior – animals, dislike of

Animals – dogs

Abercrombie, Barbara. *Bad dog, Dodger*
Abramson, Jill. *Ready or not, here comes Scout*
Adoff, Arnold. *Daring Dog and Captain Cat*
Aesop. *The dog and the wolf*
Smog, the city dog
Ajmera, Maya. *A kid's best friend*
Alexander, Claire. *Back to front and upside down*
Archer, Peggy. *Name that dog!*
Arnold, Katya. *Meow!*
Asare, Meshack. *Sosu's call*
Asch, Frank. *The last puppy*
Ashman, Linda. *Stella, unleashed*
The tale of Wagmore Gently
Autry, Gene. *Here comes Santa Claus*
Backx, Patsy. *Josie and Mr. Fernandez*
Skippy and Jack
Baek, Matthew J. *Be gentle with the dog, dear*
Bailey, Linda. *Stanley at sea*
Stanley's beauty contest
Stanley's little sister
Stanley's party
Stanley's wild ride
Baker, Leslie A. *You bad dog!*
Barracca, Debra. *Maxi, the hero*
Maxi, the star
A taxi dog Christmas
Barracca, Sal. *The adventures of taxi dog*
Barry, Holly M. *Helen Keller's best friend Belle*
Bartoletti, Susan Campbell. *Nobody's diggier than a dog*
Beaumont, Karen. *Doggone dogs!*
Move over, Rover
Where's my t-r-u-c-k?
Bedford, David. *Shaggy Dog and the terrible itch*
The way I love you
Beil, Karen Magnuson. *Jack's house*
Bell, Cece. *Itty Bitty*
Belton, Robyn. *Herbert*
Bemelmans, Ludwig. *Madeline's rescue*
Berenstain, Stan and Jan. *The Berenstain bears on the moon*
Bergen, Lara Rice. *Blue's world of words*
Berger, Lou. *Dream dog*
Birdsall, Jeanne. *Lucky and Squash*
Blackstone, Stella. *Cleo and Caspar*
Cleo in the snow
Cleo on the move
An island in the sun
Blades, Ann. *Mary of mile 18*
Blake, Quentin. *Mrs. Armitage*
Blake, Robert J. *Painter and Ugly*
Bliss, Harry. *Bailey*
Bailey at the museum
Bluemle, Elizabeth. *Dogs on the bed*
My father the dog
Blumenthal, Deborah. *The blue house dog*
Boase, Susan. *Lucky boy*
Boelts, Maribeth. *Before you were mine*
Bogan, Paulette. *Momma's magical purse*
Spike in the city
Boldt, Claudia. *Odd dog*
Bowen, Anne. *Scooter in the outside*
Boyer, Cécile. *Woof meow tweet-tweet*
Bradley, Kimberly Brubaker. *Ballerino Nate*
Braeuner, Shellie. *The great dog wash*
Breen, Steve. *Pug and Doug*
Brennan, Eileen. *Bad Astrid*
Brett, Jan. *Comet's nine lives*
The first dog
The trouble with trolls
Bridwell, Norman. *Clifford counts bubbles*
Clifford goes to Hollywood
Clifford the champion
Clifford's ABC
Clifford's good deeds
Clifford's Halloween
Clifford's neighborhood
Glow-in-the-dark Halloween
Broach, Elise. *Wet dog!*
Brown, Marc. *Arthur's new puppy*
Arthur's new puppy [board book]
Arthur's pet business
Brown, Margaret Wise. *Sailor boy jig*
Brown, Peter. *Chowder*
Browne, Anthony. *Voices in the park*
Bruce, Lisa. *Fran's friend*
Bruel, Nick. *Poor puppy*
Bruzzone, Catherine. *Puppy finds a friend / Cachorrito encuentra un amigo*
Puppy finds a friend / Le petit chien se trouve un ami
Buckley, Carol. *Tarra and Bella*
Buehner, Caralyn. *Superdog, the heart of a hero*
Bunge, Daniela. *Cherry time*
Bunting, Eve. *Ghost's hour, spook's hour*
My dog Jack is fat
Burleigh, Robert. *Good-bye, Sheepie*
Butler, Kristi T. *Rip's secret spot*
Cabrera, Jane. *Here we go round the mulberry bush*
Calhoun, Mary. *High-wire Henry*
Calmenson, Stephanie. *May I pet your dog?*
Perfect puppy
Capucilli, Alyssa Satin. *Bathtime for Biscuit*
Biscuit
Biscuit finds a friend
Biscuit gives a gift
Biscuit goes to school
Biscuit loves school
Biscuit wants to play
Biscuit wins a prize
Biscuit's big friend
Biscuit's new trick
Biscuit's picnic
Biscuit's Valentine's Day
Happy birthday, Biscuit!
Happy Hanukkah, Biscuit
Hello, Biscuit!
Merry Christmas, from Biscuit
Carbone, Elisa. *Night running*
Carlin, Patricia. *Alfie is not afraid*
Carlson, Nancy. *Harriet and George's Christmas treat*
Harriet and the garden
Harriet and the roller coaster
Harriet and Walt
Harriet's Halloween candy
Carlstrom, Nancy White. *It's your first day of school, Annie Claire*
Carnesi, Monica. *Little dog lost*
Casanova, Mary. *Some cat!*
Some dog!
Casteel, Seth. *Underwater dogs*
Catalano, Dominic. *Mr. Bassett plays*
Catalanotto, Peter. *Ivan the terrier*

Catusanu, Mircea. *The strange case of the missing sheep*
Cazet, Denys. *The octopus*
Chall, Marsha Wilson. *Bonaparte*
One pup's up
Pick a pup
Chapman, Nancy Kapp. *Doggie dreams*
Chapra, Mimi. *Sparky's bark / El ladrido de Sparky*
Chess, Victoria. *The costume party*
Chichester Clark, Emma. *Melrose and Croc*
Piper
Child, Lauren. *Who wants to be a poodle*
Chorao, Kay. *Bad boy, good boy*
Christelow, Eileen. *The desperate dog writes again*
The five-dog night
Letters from a desperate dog
Not until Christmas, Walter!
Church, Caroline Jayne. *Digby takes charge*
Ruff!
Clements, Andrew. *Brave Norman*
Circus family dog
Dogku
Naptime for Slippers
Slippers at home
Slippers at School
Slippers loves to run
Tara and Tiree, fearless friends
Cneut, Carll. *The amazing love story of Mr. Morf*
Cocca-Leffler, Maryann. *A vacation for Pooch*
Cochran, Bill. *The forever dog*
Coffelt, Nancy. *Fred stays with me!*
Pug in a truck
Cohen, Miriam. *Jim's dog Muffins*, ill. by Ronald Himler
Jim's dog Muffins, ill. by Lillian Hoban
Cole, Babette. *Lady Lupin's book of etiquette*
Truelove
Cole, Barbara Hancock. *Anna and Natalie*
Cole, Joanna. *My puppy is born*
Conahan, Carolyn. *The twelve days of Christmas dogs*
Consentino, Ralph. *The story of Honk-Honk-Ashoo and Swella-Bow-Wow*
Cooper, Elisha. *Homer*
Cooper, Helen. *Dog biscuit*
Cottle, Joan. *Miles away from home*
Cousins, Lucy. *I'm the best*
Cowen-Fletcher, Jane. *Hello, puppy!*
Crimi, Carolyn. *Don't need friends*
Pugs in a Bug
Crisp, Marty. *Black and white*
The most precious gift
Cronin, Doreen. *Bounce*
Stretch
Wiggle
Crosby, Jeff. *Wiener Wolf*
Crummel, Susan Stevens. *Sherlock Bones and the missing cheese*
Ten-Gallon Bart
Ten-Gallon Bart and the Wild West Show
Ten-Gallon Bart beats the heat
Crunk, Tony. *Grandpa's overalls*
Cullen, Lynn. *Little Scraggly Hair*
The mightiest heart
Moi and Marie Antoinette
Curious George and the puppies
Dalgleish, Sharon. *Working dogs*
Daly, Niki. *Pretty Salma*
Davis, Anne. *No dogs allowed!*
Day, Alexandra. *Carl goes shopping*
Carl goes to daycare
Carl's birthday
Carl's sleepy afternoon
Carl's snowy afternoon
Carl's summer vacation
The fairy dogfather
Follow Carl!
Good dog, Carl
Deady, Kathleen W. *It's time!*
De Beer, Hans. *Oh no, Ono!*
Degen, Bruce. *I gotta draw*
deGroat, Diane. *Homer*
Demas, Corinne. *Always in trouble*
Here comes trouble!
Demers, Dominique. *Old Thomas and the little fairy*
Dennis, Major Brian. *Nubs*
DePalma, Mary Newell. *Bow-wow wiggle-waggle*
dePaola, Tomie. *Boss for a day*
Hide-and-seek all week
Meet the Barkers
A new Barker in the house
DeRubertis, Barbara. *Dilly Dog's dizzy dancing*
Desimini, Lisa. *Dot the Firedog*
Desrosiers, Sylvie. *Hocus Pocus*
Dewdney, Anna. *Grumpy Gloria*
Dickson, Louise. *The vanishing cat*
Dodd, Emma. *Dog's ABC*
Dog's colorful day
Dog's noisy day
I don't want a posh dog
Dodd, Lynley. *A dragon in a wagon*
Dodds, Dayle Ann. *The Kettles get new clothes*
Where's Pup?
Doyle, Malachy. *Sleepy Pendoodle*
Drummond, Ree. *Charlie goes to school*
Charlie the ranch dog
Dunbar, Polly. *Dog Blue*
Dunnick, Regan. *Sweet dreams, Douglas*
Edwards, Nicola. *Goodnight Baxter*
Edwards, Pamela Duncan. *Muldoon*
Egan, Tim. *A mile from Ellington Station*
Ehlert, Lois. *Rrralph*
Wag a tail
Ellwand, David. *Alfred's camera*
Alfred's party
Esbaum, Jill. *Stanza*
Estefan, Gloria. *Noelle's treasure tale*
Ets, Marie Hall. *Mr. T. W. Anthony Woo*
Faglia, Matteo. *Happy birthday, I'm 2*
Faller, Regis. *The adventures of Polo*
Polo
Polo and Lily
Polo and the dragon
Polo and the magician!
Falwell, Cathryn. *P.J. and Puppy*
Fearnley, Jan. *The search for the perfect child*
Feiffer, Jules. *Bark, George*
Feiffer, Kate. *Henry, the dog with no tail*
President Pennybaker
Which puppy?
Figley, Marty Rhodes. *Emily and Carlo*
Fleming, Denise. *Buster*
Buster goes to Cowboy Camp
Flesher, Vivienne. *Alfred's nose*
Fletcher, Ashlee. *My dog, my cat*
Florian, Douglas. *Bow wow meow meow, it's rhyming cats and dogs*
Foreman, Jack. *Say hello*
Foreman, Michael. *Mia's story*

Oh! if only . . .
Fox, Mem. *Night noises*
Franco, Betsy. *A dazzling display of dogs*
Frank, John. *The toughest cowboy, Or, How the Wild West was tamed*
Frasier, Debra. *Spike*
Frazee, Marla. *Boot and Shoe*
French, Jackie. *Pete the sheep-sheep*
Freymann, Saxton. *Dog food*
Fuge, Charles. *Yip! Snap! Yap!*
Furstinger, Nancy. *Maggie's second chance*
Gal, Susan. *Please take me for a walk*
Gardiner, Lindsey. *Good night, Poppy and Max*
Here come Poppy and Max
When Poppy and Max grow up
Gardner, Carol. *Princess Zelda and the frog*
Gay, Marie-Louise. *What are you doing, Sam?*
George, Jean Craighead. *Cliff hanger*
George, Kristine O'Connell. *Little Dog and Duncan*
George, Lindsay Barrett. *Maggie's ball*
That pup!
Gibbons, Gail. *Dogs*
Gibson, Amy. *Split! Splat!*
Giff, Patricia Reilly. *Good luck, Ronald Morgan*
Giglio, Judy. *The tapping tale*
Gill-Brown, Vanessa. *Rufferella*
Gliori, Debi. *The snow lambs*
Going, K. L. *Dog in charge*
Goldfinger, Jennifer P. *My dog Lyle*
Goode, Diane. *Mama's perfect present*
The most perfect spot
Tiger trouble
Goodhart, Pippa. *Pudgy, a puppy to love*
Goodman, Susan E. *It's a dog's life*
Goodrich, Carter. *Say hello to Zorro!*
Zorro gets an outfit
Gordon, Domenica More. *Archie*
Gormley, Greg. *Dog in boots*
Gottfried, Maya. *Good dog*
Graham, Bob. *"Let's get a pup!" said Kate*
"The trouble with dogs," said Dad
Grambling, Lois G. *Big Dog*
Granowsky, Alvin. *At the park*
Gravett, Emily. *Dogs*
Gregory, Nan. *How Smudge came*
Gretz, Susanna. *Riley and Rose in the picture*
Grogan, John. *Bad dog, Marley!*
Marley goes to school
Trick or treat, Marley!
A very Marley Christmas
Grover, Jan Zitz. *A home for Dakota*
Gutman, Anne. *Gaspard and Lisa, friends forever*
Gaspard and Lisa's Christmas surprise
Gaspard and Lisa's rainy day
Gaspard at the seashore
Gaspard in the hospital
Gaspard on vacation
Lisa in New York
Lisa in the jungle
Lisa's airplane trip
Lisa's baby sister
Guy, Ginger Foglesong. *Perros! perros! dogs! dogs!*
Haber, Tiffany Strelitz. *Ollie and Claire*
Hall, Marcellus. *Everyone sleeps*
Harper, Charise Mericle. *Henry's heart*
Harper, Dan. *Sit, Truman*
Harper, Jessica. *I'm not going to chase the cat today*
Harper, Lee. *Snow! Snow! Snow!*
Harrison, David L. *Farmer's garden*
Harvey, Amanda. *Dog days*
Dog-eared
Dog gone
Hassett, John. *The nine lives of Dudley Dog*
Haughton, Chris. *Oh no, George!*
Hayes, Sarah. *Dog day*
Hays, Anna Jane. *The pup speaks up*
Heiligman, Deborah. *Cool dog, school dog*
Fun dog, sun dog
Snow dog, go dog
Helakoski, Leslie. *Doggone feet!*
Henkes, Kevin. *Circle dogs*
Henry, Rohan. *The gift box*
Herman, R. A. *Gomer and Little Gomer*
Hernandez, Leeza. *Dog gone!*
Hest, Amy. *Charley's first night*
The dog who belonged to no one
The reader
When Charley met Grampa
Hewitt, Kathryn. *No dogs here!*
Hill, Eric. *Spot at home*
Spot at play
Spot at the fair
Spot bakes a cake
Spot counts from 1 to 10
Spot goes to a party
Spot goes to school
Spot goes to the beach
Spot goes to the circus
Spot goes to the farm
Spot goes to the park
Spot looks at colors
Spot looks at opposites
Spot looks at shapes
Spot looks at weather
Spot on the farm
Spot sleeps over
Spot visits his grandparents
Spot's baby sister
Spot's big book of words / El libro grande de las palabras de Spot
Spot's first Christmas
Spot's first Easter
Spot's first walk
Spot's first words
Spot's magical Christmas
Hill, Meggan. *Nico and Lola*
Hills, Tad. *How Rocket learned to read*
Rocket writes a story
Rocket's mighty words
Himmelman, John. *Katie and the puppy next door*
Katie loves the kittens
10 little hot dogs
Hindley, Judy. *The best thing about a puppy*
Hines, Anna Grossnickle. *No, no Jack!*
Hoberman, Mary Ann. *One of each*
Hodge, Marie. *Are you sleepy yet, Petey?*
Holt, Kimberly Willis. *Skinny brown dog*
Holub, Joan. *Cinderdog and the wicked stepcat*
Why do dogs bark?
Hooks, William H. *A dozen dizzy dogs*
Hooper, Meredith. *Dogs' Night*
Hornsey, Chris. *Why do I have to eat off the floor?*
Horvath, James. *Dig, dogs, dig*
Howard, Arthur. *Cosmo zooms*
Howe, James. *Houndsley and Catina*
Houndsley and Catina and the birthday surprise
Hubbell, Patricia. *Shaggy dogs, waggy dogs*
Hume, Stephen Eaton. *Red moon follows truck*

Huneck, Stephen. *Sally gets a job*
Sally goes to the beach
Sally goes to the farm
Sally goes to the mountains
Sally's great balloon adventure
Sally's snow adventure
Hurd, Thacher. *Art dog*
Hutchins, Hazel. *Up dog*
Ichikawa, Satomi. *Come fly with me*
Imai, Ayano. *Chester*
Inkpen, Mick. *Hissss!*
Honk!
Kipper
Kipper and Roly
Kipper's A to Z
Kipper's birthday
Kipper's book of colors
Kipper's book of numbers
Kipper's book of opposites
Kipper's book of weather
Kipper's Christmas eve
Kipper's monster
Kipper's rainy day
Kipper's snowy day
Kipper's sunny day
Kipper's toybox
Meow!
Picnic
Splosh!
Swing!
Thing
Jackson, Emma. *A home for Dixie*
Jackson, Kathryn. *Pantaloon*
Jahn-Clough, Lisa. *Little dog*
James, Brian. *The Supertwins meet the bad dogs from space*
Jane, Pamela. *Milo and the fire engine parade*
Jarka, Jeff. *Love that puppy!*
Jenkins, Emily. *Skunkdog*
That new animal
Jenkins, Steve. *Dogs and cats*
Perros y gatos / dogs and cats
Jennings, Linda. *Little puppy lost*
Jennings, Sharon. *C'mere, boy!*
Jobling, Curtis. *Frankenstein's cat*
Johansen, K. V. *Pippin and Pudding*
Pippin takes a bath
Johnson, D. B. *Magritte's marvelous hat*
Johnson, Gillian. *My sister Gracie*
Johnson, Paul Brett. *Lost*
Johnston, Lynn. *Farley follows his nose*
Johnston, Tony. *Desert dog*
The ghost of Nicholas Greebe
Jonas, Ann. *Watch William walk*
Jonell, Lynne. *It's my birthday, too!*
Jones, Elizabeth. *Sunshine and Storm*
Joosse, Barbara. *Bad dog school*
Dog parade
Nugget and Darling
Wind-wild dog
Jordan, Sandra. *Mr. and Mrs. Portly and their little dog Snack*
Kalman, Maira. *What Pete ate from A-Z*
Kastner, Jill. *Princess Dinosaur*
Kasza, Keiko. *The dog who cried wolf*
Katschke, Judy. *Take a hike, Snoopy*
Katz, Bobbi. *Nothing but a dog*
Katz, Jon. *Lenore finds a friend*
Meet the dogs of Bedlam Farm
Keats, Ezra Jack. *Kitten for a day*
My dog is lost!
Whistle for Willie
Keller, Holly. *Sophie's window*
Kelley, True. *The dog who saved Santa*
Kellogg, Steven. *Best friends*
Give the dog a bone
A penguin pup for Pinkerton
Pinkerton, behave!
Prehistoric Pinkerton
A rose for Pinkerton
Tallyho, Pinkerton!
Kerby, Johanna. *Little pink pup*
Kerby, Mona. *Owney, the mail-pouch pooch*
Kimmel, Haven. *Orville, a dog story*
Kimmelman, Leslie. *The Shabbat puppy*
Kinch, Devon. *Pretty Penny cleans up*
Kinerk, Robert. *Timothy Cox will not change his socks*
King, Stephen Michael. *Mutt dog!*
You
Kirk, Daniel. *Moondogs*
Kirk, Katie. *Eli, no!*
Kirwan, Wednesday. *Minerva the monster*
Nobody notices Minerva
Kleven, Elisa. *The friendship wish*
Knudsen, Michelle. *Big Mean Mike*
Kolar, Bob. *Racer dogs*
Könnecke, Ole. *Anton and the battle*
Kotzwinkle, William. *Walter, the farting dog*
Walter, the farting dog: rough weather ahead
Walter, the farting dog: trouble at the yard sale
Kovacs, Deborah. *Katie Copley*
Kroll, Steven. *Oh, Tucker!*
Pooch on the loose
Kroll, Virginia L. *Selvakumar knew better*
Kumin, Maxine. *What color is Caesar?*
Kunhardt, Katharine. *Let's count the puppies*
Kvasnosky, Laura McGee. *Really truly Bingo*
Lacombe, Benjamin. *Cherry and Olive*
Laden, Nina. *Bad dog*
LaMarche, Jim. *Lost and found: three dog stories*
Lang, Glenna. *Looking out for Sarah*
Langdo, Bryan. *The dog who loved the good life*
Larson, Kirby. *Two Bobbies*
Laschütza, Susanne. *Nat the bat*
Lawrence, Jennifer B. *Sad doggy*
Lears, Laurie. *Ben has something to say*
Lee, Chinlun. *Good dog, Paw*
The very kind rich lady and her one hundred dogs
Lee, Spike. *Please, puppy, please*
Leedy, Loreen. *It's probably Penny*
Mapping Penny's world
Lendroth, Susan. *Calico Dorsey*
L'Engle, Madeleine. *The other dog*
Lenski, Lois. *The little sailboat*
Lent, Blair. *Ruby and Fred*
Leslie, Amanda. *Who's that scratching at my door?*
Let me call you sweetheart
Lewis, Kim. *First snow*
Floss
Just like Floss
Little puppy
A puppy for Annie
Lewis, Wendy A. *In Abby's hands*
Lindgren, Barbro. *Sam's bath*
Sam's wagon
Lipkind, William. *Finders keepers*
Lish, Ted. *The three little puppies and the big bad flea*
Lithgow, John. *I got two dogs*

Lloyd, David. *Polly Molly Woof Woof*
London, Jonathan. *Sled dogs run*
What do you love?
What do you love? [board book]
Long, Loren. *Otis and the puppy*
Lord, Cynthia. *Hot rod Hamster*
Lottridge, Celia Barker. *Berta, a remarkable dog*
Loupy, Christophe. *Don't worry, Wags*
Wiggles
Lupton, David. *Goodbye, Brecken*
Lyon, Tammie. *Olive and Snowflake*
McAllister, Angela. *Harry's box*
McCarthy, Meghan. *The incredible life of Balto*
McCarty, Peter. *Fabian escapes*
Hondo and Fabian
McCue, Lisa. *Quiet Bunny and Noisy Puppy*
MacDonald, Margaret Read. *The great smelly, slobbery small-toothed dog*
McDonnell, Christine. *Dog wants to play*
McDonnell, Flora. *Sparky*
McDonnell, Patrick. *The gift of nothing*
Just like Heaven
Wag!
McFarland, Lyn Rossiter. *Widget and the puppy*
McGhee, Alison. *Always*
McGuirk, Leslie. *Ho, ho, ho, Tucker!*
Lucky Tucker
Tucker flips!
Tucker off his rocker
Tucker over the top
Tucker's spooky Halloween
McHenry, E. B. *Has anyone seen Winnie and Jean?*
Poodlena
MacLachlan, Patricia. *Bittle*
Three names
Who loves me?
McMullan, Kate. *Bulldog's big day*
Macomber, Debbie. *The yippy, yappy Yorkie in the green doggy sweater*
McPhail, David. *Weezer changes the world*
Magoon, Scott. *Hugo and Miles in I've painted everything!*
Manuel, Lynn. *The trouble with Tilly Trumble*
Manzano, Sonia. *No dogs allowed*
Marcus, Kimberly. *Scritch-scratch a perfect match*
Martin, Sarah Catherine. *Old Mother Hubbard*
Old Mother Hubbard and her wonderful dog
Martins, Isabel Minhós. *My neighbor is a dog*
Mason, Adrienne. *Lu and Clancy sound off*
Lu and Clancy's spy stuff
Masurel, Claire. *A cat and a dog*
Domino
Mauner, Claudia. *Zoe Sophia's scrapbook*
Mayer, Mercer. *A boy, a dog, a frog and a friend*
A boy, a dog and a frog
Meadows, Michelle. *Pilot pups*
Traffic pups
Meddaugh, Susan. *Martha and Skits*
Martha blah blah
Martha calling
Martha says it with flowers
Martha speaks
Martha walks the dog
Perfectly Martha
The witches' supermarket
Menchin, Scott. *Harry goes to dog school*
Meserve, Adria. *No room for Napoleon*
Meyers, Susan. *Puppies! Puppies! Puppies!*
Milgrim, David. *Dog brain*
My friend Lucky
Why Benny barks
Moers, Hermann. *Rufus and Max*
Monks, Lydia. *The cat barked?*
Monroe, Chris. *Cookie, the walker*
Sneaky sheep
Moore, Elaine. *Roly-poly puppies*
Mortensen, Lori. *Cowpoke Clyde and Dirty Dawg*
Moss, Marissa. *Knick knack paddywack*
Moxley, Sheila. *ABCD an alphabet book of cats and dogs*
Murphy, Mary. *Here comes spring, and summer and fall and winter*
I feel happy, and sad, and angry, and glad
You smell and taste and feel and see and hear
Murphy, Stuart J. *Get up and go!*
Henry the fourth
Murray, Alison. *Apple pie ABC*
One two that's my shoe!
Murray, Andrew. *Have you seen Chester?*
Myers, Walter Dean. *The blues of Flats Brown*
Mystery manor
Napoli, Donna Jo. *Rocky, the cat who barks*
Nelson, Marilyn. *Snook alone*
Nelson-Schmidt, Michelle. *Dogs, dogs!*
Newberry, Clare Turlay. *Barkis*
Newgarden, Mark. *Bow-Wow bugs a bug*
Bow-Wow orders lunch
Newman, Lesléa. *Dogs, dogs, dogs*
Nez, John. *One smart Cookie*
Noble, Sheilagh. *More*
Noonan, Julia. *Bath day*
Breakfast time
Norris, Leslie. *Albert and the angels*
North, Sherry. *Champ's story*
Noullet, Georgette. *Bed hog*
Novak, Matt. *The Pillow War*
Numeroff, Laura Joffe. *If you give a dog a donut*
Sherman Crunchley
What puppies do best
Ochiltree, Dianne. *Pillow pup*
O'Connor, Jane. *Fancy Nancy and the posh puppy*
The perfect puppy for me
O'Hair, Margaret. *My pup*
Oppel, Kenneth. *The king's taster*
Oram, Hiawyn. *Just Dog*
My friend Fred
Otto, Carolyn. *Our puppies are growing*
Page, Gail. *Bobo and the new neighbor*
How to be a good cat
Paraskevas, Betty. *Chocolate at the Four Seasons*
Parker, Marjorie Blain. *Jasper's day*
Parr, Todd. *Otto goes to school*
Patricelli, Leslie. *The Patterson puppies and the midnight monster party*
Paul, Ann Whitford. *Hello toes! Hello feet!*
Peet, Bill. *The Whingdingdilly*
Perkins, Lynne Rae. *Snow music*
Perrow, Angeli. *Lighthouse dog to the rescue*
Sirius, the dog star
Peters, Bernadette. *Stella is a star!*
Pfister, Marcus. *Snow puppy*
Pickering, Jimmy. *It's fall*
It's winter
Skelly the skeleton girl
Piepmeier, Charlotte. *Lucy's journey to the wild west*
Pilkey, Dav. *The Hallo-wiener*
Pinfold, Levi. *Black dog*
Pinkwater, Daniel. *I am the dog*

Pipe, Jim. *Dogs*
Pitzer, Susanna. *Not afraid of dogs*
Postgate, Daniel. *Smelly Bill*
Smelly Bill: love stinks
Posthuma, Sieb. *Benny*
Potter, Beatrix. *The pie and the patty-pan*
Powell, Consie. *Old dog Cora and the Christmas tree*
Prap, Lila. *Doggy whys*
Price, Mathew. *Patch and the rabbits*
Pritchett, Andy. *Stick!*
Radunsky, Vladimir. *You?*
Rankin, Joan. *First day*
Rankin, Laura. *Fluffy and Baron*
Raschka, Chris. *A ball for Daisy*
Can't sleep
Daisy gets lost
Hip Hop Dog
Rathmann, Peggy. *Officer Buckle and Gloria*
Ray, Mary Lyn. *Boom!*
Reed, Lynn Rowe. *Pedro, his perro, and the alphabet sombrero*
Regan, Lara Jo. *What is Mr. Winkle?*
A Winkle in time
Reinen, Judy. *Bow wow*
Reiser, Lynn. *Any kind of dog*
Hardworking puppies
My dog Truffle
Two dogs swimming
Rey, Margret. *Pretzel*
Rice, Eve. *Benny bakes a cake*
Richardson, Bill. *Sally Dog Little*
Ries, Lori. *Aggie and Ben*
Roberton, Fiona. *The perfect present*
Rockwell, Anne. *Fire engines*
Rohmann, Eric. *Bone dog*
Rosen, Michael. *Howler*
Rosen, Michael J. *Avalanche*
The dog who walked with God
With a dog like that, a kid like me . . .
Rowe, John A. *Moondog*
Rubinger, Ami. *Dog number 1 dog number 10*
Ruelle, Karen Gray. *Bark park*
Russell, Joan Plummer. *Aero and Officer Mike*
Ruzzier, Sergio. *Amandina*
Rylant, Cynthia. *The bookshop dog*
Dog Heaven
The great Gracie chase
Tulip sees America
Sadler, Judy Ann. *Sandwiches for Duke*
Saltzberg, Barney. *I love dogs*
Sampson, Michael R. *Caddie, the golf dog*
San Souci, Robert D. *The Hobyahs*
The silver charm
Sattler, Jennifer. *Chick 'n' Pug*
Chick 'n' Pug meet the Dude
Sayre, April Pulley. *Hush, little puppy*
Schaap, Martine. *Mop and the birthday picnic*
Mop's backyard concert
Mop's mountain adventure
Mop's treasure hunt
Schachner, Judith Byron. *Skippyjon Jones and the big bones*
Skippyjon Jones Cirque de Olé
Skippyjon Jones class action
Skippyjon Jones in mummy trouble
Skippyjon Jones, lost in spice
Schmidt, Karen Lee. *Carl's nose*
Schneider, Christine M. *I'm bored!*
Schneider, Howie. *Chewy Louie*
Schories, Pat. *Jack and the night visitors*
Jack wants a snack
When Jack goes out
Schubert, Ingrid. *The umbrella*
Schubert, Leda. *Reading to Peanut*
Winnie all day long
Winnie plays ball
Schwartz, Amy. *Oma and Bobo*
Schweninger, Ann. *Autumn days*
Seeber, Dorothea P. *A pup just for me . . . A boy just for me*
Seeger, Laura Vaccaro. *Dog and Bear: three to get ready*
Dog and Bear: two friends, three stories
Dog and Bear: two's company
Segal, John. *Alistair and Kip's great adventure*
Seibert, Patricia. *Mush!*
Serfozo, Mary. *What's what?*
Shannon, David. *Good boy, Fergus!*
Shannon, George. *Tippy-toe chick, go*
Sharmat, Marjorie Weinman. *I'm the best*
Shaskan, Stephen. *A dog is a dog*
Shields, Carol Diggory. *I wish my brother was a dog*
Shireen, Nadia. *Hey, Presto!*
Sidman, Joyce. *Meow ruff*
Siminovich, Lorena. *Alex and Lulu*
Simmons, Jane. *Ebb and Flo and the greedy gulls*
Ebb and Flo and the new friend
Together
Simon, Charnan. *Big bad Buzz*
Simont, Marc. *The stray dog*
Singer, Marilyn. *Every day's a dog's day*
What is your dog doing?
Slater, Teddy. *Smooch your pooch*
Slonim, David. *Patch*
Smith, Charles R. *Loki and Alex*
Smith, Janice Lee. *Jess and the stinky cowboys*
Smith, Linda. *The inside tree*
Snicket, Lemony. *13 words*
Soman, David. *Ladybug Girl and Bingo*
Soto, Gary. *Chato goes cruisin'*
Chato's kitchen
Spetter, Jung-Hee. *Lily and Trooper's fall*
Lily and Trooper's spring
Lily and Trooper's summer
Lily and Trooper's winter
Spinelli, Eileen. *Do you have a dog?*
Spires, Elizabeth. *The big meow*
Springett, Martin. *Kate and Pippin*
Staake, Bob. *The first pup*
Stadler, John. *The cats of Mrs. Calamari*
Stanley, Mandy. *Bloomer, the dog you can play with*
Steig, William. *Caleb and Kate*
Tiffky Doofky
Stephens, Helen. *Fleabag*
Poochie-poo
Ruby and the muddy dog
Stevens, Janet. *Find a cow now!*
Help me, Mr. Mutt!
My big dog
Stevenson, James. *Worse than the worst*
Stohner, Anu. *Brave Charlotte*
Sturges, Philemon. *Waggers*
Stuve-Bodeen, Stephanie. *A small brown dog with a wet pink nose*
Sullivan, Mary. *Ball*
Swaim, Jessica. *The hound from the pound*
Sweeney, Joan. *Suzette and the puppy*
Sweet, Melissa. *Carmine*

Tupelo rides the rails
Sykes, Julie. *Smudge*
Tafuri, Nancy. *Who's counting?*
Tanaka, Shinsuke. *Wings*
Taylor, Alastair. *Swollobog*
Taylor, Eleanor. *Beep, beep, let's go!*
Teague, Mark. *Dear Mrs. LaRue*
Detective LaRue
Firehouse!
Funny farm
LaRue across America
LaRue for mayor
Tellis, Annabel. *If my dad were a dog*
Thayer, Jane. *Part-time dog*
The puppy who wanted a boy
Thomas, Jan. *The doghouse*
Thomas, Jane Resh. *Scaredy dog*
Thompson, Colin. *Unknown*
Thomson, Bill. *Fossil*
Townsend, Michael. *Cute and cuter*
Trapani, Iza. *How much is that doggie in the window?*
Trimble, Marcia. *Peppy's shadow*
Turner, Pamela S. *Hachiko*
Turner, Sandy. *Silent night*
Uhlberg, Myron. *Mad Dog McGraw*
Umansky, Kaye. *I don't like Gloria!*
Ungerer, Tomi. *Flix*
Urbanovic, Jackie. *Sitting duck*
U'Ren, Andrea. *Pugdog*
Van Allsburg, Chris. *The garden of Abdul Gasazi*
Van Dusen, Chris. *Down to the sea with Mr. Magee*
Learning to ski with Mr. Magee
Van Leeuwen, Jean. *The strange adventures of Blue Dog*
Van Steenwyk, Elizabeth. *First dog Fala*
Waber, Bernard. *Lyle walks the dogs*
Waddell, Martin. *The Super Hungry Dinosaur*
We love them
Wahman, Wendy. *Don't lick the dog*
Waite, Judy. *Mouse, look out!*
Waite, Michael P. *Jojofu*
Walton, Rick. *Bertie was a watchdog*
Ward, Helen. *Little Moon Dog*
Watt, Mélanie. *Scaredy Squirrel makes a friend*
Weeks, Sarah. *Oh my gosh, Mrs. McNosh!*
Woof
Weller, Frances Ward. *The angel of Mill Street*
Wells, Rosemary. *Bingo*
Lucy comes to stay
McDuff and the baby
McDuff comes home
McDuff goes to school
McDuff moves in
McDuff saves the day
McDuffs hide-and-seek
McDuff's new friend
McDuff's wild romp
Otto runs for President
Otto se presenta para presidente / Otto runs for President
Whatley, Bruce. *Captain Pajamas*
White, Ellen Emerson. *Santa paws*
White, Marsha. *Hooper has lost his owner*
Wild, Margaret. *Fox*
Harry and Hopper
The pocket dogs
Wildsmith, Brian. *Give a dog a bone*
Wilhelm, Hans. *I'll always love you*
Schnitzel's first Christmas
Willems, Mo. *City dog, country frog*
The pigeon wants a puppy!
Williams, Suzanne. *My dog never says please*
Willis, Jeanne. *The boy who lost his bellybutton*
Winthrop, Elizabeth. *I'm the Boss!*
Wishinsky, Frieda. *Please, Louise!*
Wojtusik, Elizabeth. *Kitty up!*
Wolff, Ashley. *When Lucy goes out walking*
Wood, Audrey. *A dog needs a bone*
It's Duffy time!
Yaccarino, Dan. *Oswald*
Unlovable
Yates, Louise. *Dog loves books*
Dog loves counting
Dog loves drawing
Yorinks, Arthur. *Harry and Lulu*
Hey, Al
Young, Ned. *Zoomer*
Zoomer's out-of-this-world Christmas
Zoomer's summer snowstorm
Zarins, Kim. *The helpful puppy*
Ziefert, Harriet. *I swapped my dog*
Knick-knack paddywhack
Lucy rescued
Mommy, I want to sleep in your bed!
Murphy jumps a hurdle
My dog thinks I'm a genius
Pushkin meets the bundle
Pushkin minds the bundle
Zimmerman, Andrea Griffing. *My dog Toby*
Zion, Gene. *Harry, the dirty dog*
No roses for Harry
Zolotow, Charlotte. *The old dog*
The poodle who barked at the wind

Animals – dolphins

Allen, Judy. *Whales and dolphins*
Arnosky, Jim. *Dolphins on the sand*
Canyon, Christopher. *John Denver's Ancient rhymes*
Davies, Nicola. *Dolphin baby!*
Edgemon, Darcie. *Seamore, the very forgetful porpoise*
Hatkoff, Craig, et al. *Winter's tail*
Nelson, Robert Lyn. *Ocean friends*
Pfeffer, Wendy. *Dolphin talk*
Winton, Tim. *The deep*
Wood, Audrey. *The rainbow bridge*

Animals – donkeys

Aesop. *The donkey in the lion's skin*
Arnosky, Jim. *Little Burro*
Barnes, Laura T. *Ernest and the big itch*
Ernest's special Christmas
Teeny tiny Ernest
Twist and Ernest
Barton, Bob. *Paul Gallico's The small miracle*
Brown, Monica. *Waiting for the Biblioburro*
Byrd, Robert. *Saint Francis and the Christmas donkey*
Clanton, Ben. *Vote for me!*
Crawford, Sheryl Ann. *The baby who changed the world*
Kennedy, Kim. *Hee-Haw-Dini and the Great Zambini*
Kromhout, Rindert. *Little Donkey and the baby-sitter*
Little Donkey and the birthday present
McGee, Marni. *The colt and the king*
Mandell, Muriel. *A donkey reads*
Newton, Jill. *Crash bang donkey!*

Puttock, Simon. *Goat and Donkey in strawberry sunglasses*
Goat and Donkey in the great outdoors
Seim, Donna Marie. *Where is Simon, Sandy?*
Smith, Kathryn. *Little Donkey's Christmas story*
Spang, Günter. *The ox and the Donkey*
Steig, William. *Farmer Palmer's wagon ride*
Sylvester and the magic pebble
Tafuri, Nancy. *The donkey's Christmas song*
Tarlow, Ellen. *Pinwheel days*
Taylor, Sean. *Crocodiles are the best animals of all*
Van Woerkom, Dorothy. *Abu Ali counts his donkeys*
Donkey Ysabel
Wildsmith, Brian. *A Christmas story*
The Easter story
Winter, Jeanette. *Biblioburro*
Young, Ed. *Donkey trouble*
Ziefert, Harriet. *Buzzy had a little lamb*

Animals – elephants

Alsenas, Linas. *Peanut*
Andreasen, Dan. *Saturday with Daddy*
Andres, Kristina. *Elephant in the bathtub*
Appelt, Kathi. *Elephants aloft*
Arnold, Katya. *Elephants can paint, too!*
Bachelet, Gilles. *My cat, the silliest cat in the world*
When the silliest cat was small
Badescu, Ramona. *Pomelo begins to grow*
Pomelo's opposites
Barclay, Eric. *Hiding Phil*
Base, Graeme. *Little elephants*
Bates, Ivan. *All by myself*
Beake, Lesley. *Home now*
Beeler, Selby B. *How many Elephants?*
Blackford, Harriet. *Elephant's story*
Brenner, Barbara A. *What the elephant told*
Bridges, Margaret Park. *Edna elephant*
Brunhoff, Jean de. *Babar and Father Christmas*
Babar and his children
Babar the king
Babar the king [facsimile ed.]
The story of Babar, the little elephant
The travels of Babar
Brunhoff, Laurent de. *B is for Babar*
Babar and the ghost
Babar and the ghost [easy-to-read ed.]
Babar and the succotash bird
Babar and the Wully-Wully
Babar's ABC
Babar's battle
Babar's birthday surprise
Babar's little girl
Babar's Museum of Art
Babar's USA
Babar's world tour
Meet Babar and his family
Buckley, Carol. *Tarra and Bella*
Bunting, Eve. *Tweak tweak*
Burningham, John. *Tug-of-war*
Clanton, Ben. *Vote for me!*
Clarke, Jane. *Trumpet*
Conway, David. *Errol and his extraordinary nose*
Côté, Geneviève. *What elephant?*
Cousins, Lucy. *Maisy makes lemonade*
Cowcher, Helen. *Desert elephants*
Daly, Niki. *Next stop — Zanzibar Road!*
Welcome to Zanzibar Road
D'Amico, Carmela. *Ella sets sail*
Ella sets the stage
Ella takes the cake
Ella, the elegant elephant
Davies, Gill. *Tiny's big wish*
Day, Alexandra. *Frank and Ernest*
Frank and Ernest on the road
Frank and Ernest play ball
Dijs, Carla. *Mommy, what if—?*
Dodd, Emma. *Cinderelephant*
No matter what
Dunbar, Polly. *Where's Tumpty?*
Eilenberg, Max. *Squeak's good idea*
Fearnley, Jan. *Arthur and the meanies*
Genechten, Guido van. *Kai-Mook*
Gibbons, Gail. *Elephants of Africa*
Ginkel, Anne. *I've got an elephant*
Goodhart, Pippa. *Little Nelly's big book*
Goodman, Joan Elizabeth. *Bernard goes to school*
Gorbachev, Valeri. *Big Little Elephant*
Gréban, Quentin. *Nestor*
Grindley, Sally. *Little Elephant Thunderfoot*
Hänel, Wolfram. *Little elephant's song*
Hart, Christopher. *Merwin, master of disguise*
Henrichs, Wendy. *When Anju loved being an elephant*
Henry, Rohan. *The gift box*
Hillenbrand, Will. *My book box*
Hoberman, Mary Ann. *Miss Mary Mack*
Horacek, Petr. *My elephant*
Hunter, Sally. *Humphrey's bedtime*
Humphrey's birthday
Humphrey's Christmas
Humphrey's corner
Jackson, Kathryn. *The saggy baggy elephant*
Johnson, Paul Brett. *The goose who went off in a huff*
Joosse, Barbara. *Sleepover at Gramma's house*
Judge, Lita. *Pennies for elephants*
Kasza, Keiko. *The mightiest*
Kavanagh, Peter. *I love my mama*
Kilaka, John. *True friends*
Kimmel, Eric A. *Anansi and the talking melon*
Kipling, Rudyard. *The elephant's child*
How the elephant got his trunk
Kitamura, Satoshi. *Pablo the artist*
Kleven, Elisa. *Welcome home, Mouse*
Krosoczka, Jarrett J. *Ollie the purple elephant*
Lang, Aubrey. *Baby elephant*
Leslie, Amanda. *Alfie and Betty Bug*
Lester, Helen. *Hurty feelings*
Tacky in trouble
Levitin, Sonia. *When Elephant goes to a party*
Lewis, Kim. *Good night, Harry*
Here we go Harry
Hooray for Harry
My friend Harry
MacDonald, Suse. *Elephants on board*
McDonnell, Flora. *Splash!*
McGrory, Anik. *Kidogo*
McKee, David. *Elmer*
Elmer again
Elmer and Rose
Elmer and Snake
Elmer and Super El
Elmer and the big bird
Elmer and the hippos
Elmer and the kangaroo
Elmer and the lost teddy
Elmer and the wind
Elmer and Wilbur
Elmer in the snow

Elmer takes off
Elmer's Christmas
Elmer's special day
Magloff, Lisa. *Elephant*
Magoon, Scott. *Hugo and Miles in I've painted everything!*
Marino, Gianna. *Meet me at the moon*
Melmed, Laura Krauss. *Jumbo's lullaby*
Monroe, Chris. *Monkey with a tool belt and the seaside shenanigans*
Mueller, Doris L. *Small One's adventure*
Muir, Leslie. *The little bitty bakery*
Murphy, Jill. *Mr. Large in charge*
A piece of cake
A quiet night in
Na, Il Sung. *Hide and seek*
The thingamabob
Nichol, Barbara. *Trunks all aboard*
Ormerod, Jan. *When an elephant comes to school*
Oyibo, Papa. *Big brother, little sister*
Paxton, Tom. *Engelbert the elephant*
Pearson, Tracey Campbell. *Elephant's story*
Peet, Bill. *The ant and the elephant*
Ella
Encore for Eleanor
Polacco, Patricia. *Emma Kate*
Pratt, Pierre. *Car*
Home
Park
Shopping
Price, Mathew. *Dumbo*
Prince, April Jones. *Twenty-one elephants and still standing*
Radcliffe, Theresa. *Bashi, elephant baby*
Ravishankar, Anushka. *Elephants never forget!*
Robinson, Bruce. *The obvious elephant*
Root, Barry. *Gumbrella*
Rubinger, Ami. *I dream of an elephant*
Samuels, Jenny. *A nose like a hose*
Sarcone-Roach, Julia. *The secret plan*
Schubert, Leda. *Ballet of the elephants*
Schwartz, Amy. *A beautiful girl*
How to catch an elephant
Tiny and Hercules
Schwartz, Corey Rosen. *Hop! Plop!*
Seuss, Dr. *Horton hatches the egg*
Horton hears a Who!
Shields, Gillian. *Elephantantrum!*
Slack, Michael. *Elecopter*
Slobodkina, Esphyr. *Circus caps for sale*
Smith, Maggie. *Paisley*
Steig, William. *Doctor De Soto goes to Africa*
Stock, Catherine. *Alexander's midnight snack*
Tompert, Ann. *Just a little bit*
Turner, Sandy. *Otto's trunk*
van Lieshout, Maria. *Hopper and Wilson*
Vere, Ed. *Everyone's little*
The getaway
Wallace, Joseph E. *Big and noisy Simon*
Wells, Robert E. *Why do elephants need the sun?*
Westcott, Nadine Bernard. *Peanut butter and jelly*
Whitehouse, Patricia. *Elephants*
Wilson-Max, Ken. *Max's starry night*
Wojtowycz, David. *Elephant Joe, Brave Knight!*
Young, Ed. *Seven blind mice*

Animals – endangered animals

Aliki. *My visit to the zoo*
Barry, Frances. *Let's save the animals*
Beard, Alex. *Crocodile's tears*
Beeke, Tiphanie. *Roar like a lion!*
Blackford, Harriet. *Elephant's story*
Butler, John. *Pi-shu, the little panda*
Coville, Bruce. *The prince of butterflies*
Dewdney, Anna. *Roly Poly pangolin*
George, Jean Craighead. *The buffalo are back*
The eagles are back
The wolves are back
Gibbons, Gail. *Giant pandas*
Grizzly bears
Guiberson, Brenda Z. *Moon bear*
Hamilton, Virginia. *Jaguarundi*
Hatkoff, Craig, et al. *Leo the snow leopard*
Looking for Miza
Heinz, Brian J. *The wolves*
Jacobs, Francine. *Lonesome George, the giant tortoise*
Jenkins, Martin. *Can we save the tiger?*
Jenkins, Priscilla Belz. *Falcons nest on skyscrapers*
Jenkins, Steve. *Almost gone*
Jonas, Ann. *Aardvarks, disembark!*
Lunde, Darrin. *Hello, bumblebee bat*
McCully, Emily Arnold. *Hurry!*
McLimans, David. *Gone wild*
Markle, Sandra. *Family pack*
Martin, Jacqueline Briggs. *The chiru of High Tibet*
Mullins, Patricia. *V for vanishing*
Noonan, Diana. *The crocodile*
Raffi. *Baby beluga*
Schertle, Alice. *Advice for a frog and other poems*
Slade, Suzanne. *What's the difference?*
Theodorou, Rod. *Bengal tiger*
Black rhino
Blue whale
Florida manatee
Giant panda
Mountain gorilla
Thomson, Sarah L. *Tigers*
Weeks, Sarah. *Crocodile smile*

Animals – ferrets

Elsdale, Bob. *Mac side up*
Jenkins, Emily. *Num, num, num!*
Plonk, plonk, plonk!
Up, up, up!
Rostoker-Gruber, Karen. *Ferret fun*
Weigelt, Udo. *It wasn't me*

Animals – foxes

Aesop. *Anno's Aesop*
The donkey in the lion's skin
The fox and the grapes
Fox tails
Three Aesop fox fables
Alborough, Jez. *Six little chicks*
Arnosky, Jim. *Watching foxes*
Auch, Mary Jane. *Peeping Beauty*
Bailey, Linda. *Toads on toast*
Baker, Liza. *I love you because you're you*
Banks, Kate. *Fox*
Battut, Eric. *The fox and the hen*
Blackaby, Susan. *Brownie Groundhog and the February Fox*
Bloom, Suzanne. *Fox forgets*
Oh! What a surprise!
What about Bear?

Bonning, Tony. *Fox tale soup*
Campoy, F. Isabel. *Rosa Raposa*
Carlstrom, Nancy White. *Mama, will it snow tonight?*
Chaucer, Geoffrey. *Chanticleer and the fox*
Church, Caroline Jayne. *One smart goose*
Cocca-Leffler, Maryann. *Bravery soup*
Cox, Phil Roxbee. *Fox on a box*
Crum, Shutta. *Fox and Fluff*
Dodd, Emma. *Foxy*
Foxy in love
Ehlert, Lois. *Mole's hill*
Moon rope / Un lazo a la luna
Ernst, Lisa Campbell. *The Gingerbread Girl goes animal crackers*
The fox went out on a chilly night
Ginsburg, Mirra. *Across the stream*
Mushroom in the rain
Gliori, Debi. *No matter what*
Stormy weather
Grindley, Sally. *Silly Goose and Dizzy Duck play hide-and-seek*
What are friends for?
What will I do without you?
Hawkins, Emily. *Little snow goose*
Heinz, Brian J. *Red Fox at McCloskey's farm*
Hindley, Judy. *Do like a duck does*
Hogrogian, Nonny. *One fine day*
Hutchins, Pat. *Rosie's walk*
Rosie's walk [board book]
Jonovitz, Marilyn. *Good morning, Little Fox*
Keller, Holly. *Nosy Rosie*
Keller, John G. *The rubber-legged ducky*
Lang, Aubrey. *Baby fox*
Leedy, Loreen. *Crazy like a fox*
Levine, Michelle. *Red foxes*
Liwska, Renata. *Red wagon*
Lobel, Gillian. *Too small for honey cake*
London, Jonathan. *Ice Bear and Little Fox*
McBratney, Sam. *I'll always be your friend*
McKissack, Patricia C. *Flossie and the fox*
Marshall, James. *Wings: a tale of two chickens*
Myers, Tim. *Basho and the fox*
Numeroff, Laura Joffe. *What daddies do best*
Palatini, Margie. *Lousy rotten stinkin' grapes*
Three French hens
Zoom Broom
Pauli, Lorenz. *The fox in the library*
Potter, Beatrix. *The tale of Mr. Tod*
Puttock, Simon. *Miss Fox*
Rankin, Joan. *Wow! It's great being a duck*
Rankin, Laura. *Ruthie and the (not so) teeny tiny lie*
Rave, Friederike. *Outfoxing the fox*
Rawlinson, Julia. *Fletcher and the falling leaves*
Fletcher and the snowflake Christmas
Fletcher and the springtime blossoms
Rodriguez, Béatrice. *The chicken thief*
Fox and hen together
Root, Phyllis. *Toot toot zoom!*
Salzano, Tammi. *One windy day*
San Souci, Robert D. *The silver charm*
Sharmat, Marjorie Weinman. *The best Valentine in the world*
Smith, Alex T. *Foxy and Egg*
Souhami, Jessica. *Foxy!*
Spinelli, Eileen. *Miss Fox's class earns a field trip*
Miss Fox's class gets it wrong
Miss Fox's class goes green
Miss Fox's class shapes up
Peace Week in Miss Fox's class
Steig, William. *Doctor De Soto*
Roland, the minstrel pig
Taylor, Harriet Peck. *Ulaq and the northern lights*
The three little pigs *The three little pigs and the fox*
Tolan, Stephanie S. *Bartholomew's blessing*
Tompert, Ann. *Grandfather Tang's story*
Little Fox goes to the end of the world
Townsend, Emily Rose. *Arctic foxes*
Twohy, Mike. *Outfoxed*
Walsh, Ellen Stoll. *You silly goose*
Ward, Helen. *The rooster and the fox*
Waring, Richard. *Hungry hen*
Watson, Clyde. *Valentine foxes*
Watt, Mélanie. *Have I got a book for you!*
Weston, Carrie. *If a chicken stayed for supper*
Wild, Margaret. *Fox*
Wilhelm, Hans. *More bunny trouble*
Willems, Mo. *That is not a good idea!*
Williams, Sue. *Dinnertime*
Yerkes, Jennifer. *A funny little bird*

Animals – gerbils

Roth, Susan L. *Cinnamon's day out*

Animals – giraffes

Andreae, Giles. *Giraffes can't dance*
Bracken, Beth. *Too shy for show-and-tell*
Buzzeo, Toni. *Stay close to Mama*
Cowan, Charlotte. *Sadie's sore throat*
Cronin, Doreen. *Rescue bunnies*
De Vries, Anke. *Raf*
Hewett, Joan. *A giraffe calf grows up*
Holmes, Mary Tavener. *A giraffe goes to Paris*
Horowitz, Dave. *A monkey among us*
Lin, Grace. *Okie-dokie, Artichokie*
McEvoy, Anne. *Betsy B. Little*
Ommen, Sylvia van. *The surprise*
Rayner, Catherine. *Abigail*
Rey, H. A. *Cecily G and the nine monkeys*
Rumford, James. *Chee-lin*
St. George, Judith. *Zarafa*
Spanyol, Jessica. *Carlo likes counting*
Tourville, Amanda Doering. *A giraffe grows up*
A jaguar grows up

Animals – goats

Alakija, Polly. *Catch that goat!*
Andrews, Julie. *Dumpy to the rescue!*
Asbjørnsen, P. C. *The three billy goats Gruff*, ill. by Stephen Carpenter
The three billy goats Gruff, ill. by Paul Galdone
The three billy goats Gruff, ill. by Glen Rounds
The three billy goats Gruff, ill. by Janet Stevens
Berry, Lynne. *What floats in a moat?*
Blood, Charles L. *The goat in the rug*
Burks, James. *Beep and Bah*
Church, Caroline Jayne. *Little Apple Goat*
Cole, Henry. *Trudy*
Crummel, Susan Stevens. *Ten-Gallon Bart*
Dewdney, Anna. *Llama Llama and the bully goat*
Elschner, Geraldine. *Pashmina the little Christmas goat*
Emberley, Rebecca. *Three cool kids*
Ford, Bernette. *No more biting for Billy Goat!*
Fox, Mem. *Let's count goats!*
Garland, Michael. *King Puck*

Gorbachev, Valeri. *One rainy day*
That's what friends are for
Gugler, Laurel Dee. *There's a billy goat in the garden*
Hale, Dean. *Scapegoat*
Helquist, Brett. *Grumpy Goat*
Hoberman, Mary Ann. *Bill Grogan's goat*
Johnston, Tony. *Desert dog*
Keefer, Janice Kulyk. *Anna's goat*
Kimmel, Eric A. *The three cabritos*
Kimmelman, Leslie. *The three bully goats*
Kimura, Yuichi. *One stormy night . . .*
One sunny day . . .
McBrier, Page. *Beatrice's goat*
Miller, Heather. *My goats*
Mortimer, Rachael. *The three Billy Goats Fluff*
Palatini, Margie. *The three silly billies*
Polacco, Patricia. *Oh, look!*
Puttock, Simon. *Goat and Donkey in strawberry sunglasses*
Goat and Donkey in the great outdoors
Salley, Coleen. *Who's that tripping over my bridge?*
Schrock, Jan West. *Give a goat*
Sharmat, Mitchell. *Gregory, the terrible eater*
Shea, Bob. *Unicorn thinks he's pretty great*
Shepard, Aaron. *One-eye! Two-eyes! Three-eyes!*
Taylor, Sean. *Huck runs amuck!*
Waddell, Martin. *Captain Small Pig*
Wildsmith, Brian. *Goat's trail*
Wolkstein, Diane. *The banza*
Youngquist, Cathrene Valente. *The three Billygoats Gruff and Mean Calypso Joe*
Ziefert, Harriet. *Pumpkin Pie*

Animals – gorillas

Aardema, Verna. *Princess Gorilla and a new kind of water*
Adams, Sarah. *Gary and Ray*
Anderson, Derek. *Gladys goes out to lunch*
Browne, Anthony. *Gorilla*
Little Beauty
One gorilla: a counting book
Voices in the park
Willy and Hugh
Willy the champ
Willy the wimp
Bustos, Eduardo. *Going ape!*
Durango, Julia. *Go-go gorillas*
Gibbons, Gail. *Gorillas*
Harvey, Damian. *Just the thing!*
Hatkoff, Craig, et al. *Looking for Miza*
Howe, James. *The day the teacher went bananas*
Layton, Neal. *Smile if you're human*
Morozumi, Atsuko. *My friend gorilla*
One gorilla
OHora, Zachariah. *No fits, Nilson!*
Palatini, Margie. *Ding dong ding dong*
Rex, Michael. *Furious George goes bananas*
Robinson, Michelle. *Ding dong! Gorilla!*
Shulman, Mark. *Gorilla Garage*
Theodorou, Rod. *Mountain gorilla*
Willis, Jeanne. *Gorilla! Gorilla!*

Animals – groundhogs

Bang, Molly. *Goose*
Blackaby, Susan. *Brownie Groundhog and the February Fox*
Brownie Groundhog and the wintry surprise
Cherry, Lynne. *How Groundhog's garden grew*
Cox, Judy. *Go to sleep, Groundhog*
Cuyler, Margery. *Groundhog stays up late*
Freeman, Don. *Gregory's Shadow*
Groundhog at Evergreen Road
Hill, Susanna Leonard. *April Fool, Phyllis!*
Punxsutawney Phyllis
Hiskey, Iris. *The secret of the first one up*
Holub, Joan. *Groundhog weather school*
Johnson, Crockett. *Will spring be early or will spring be late?*
Levine, Abby. *Gretchen Groundhog, it's your day!*
Lewin, Betsy. *Groundhog day*
Miller, Pat. *Substitute Groundhog*
Olson, Julie. *Tickle, tickle! itch, twitch!*
Pallotta, Jerry. *Who will see their shadows this year?*
Roberts, Bethany. *Double trouble Groundhog Day*
Swallow, Pamela Curtis. *Groundhog gets a say*
Tompert, Ann. *Nothing sticks like a shadow*
Welling, Peter J. *Andrew McGroundhog and his shady shadow*

Animals – guinea pigs

Berenzy, Alix. *Sammy*
Blumenthal, Deborah. *Charlie hits it big*
Child, Lauren. *I completely know about guinea pigs*
Cuyler, Margery. *Guinea pigs add up*
Duke, Kate. *One guinea pig is not enough*
Ready for pumpkins
Twenty is too many
Katz, Susan. *Oh, Theodore!*
Knutson, Barbara. *Love and roast chicken*
Kroll, Steven. *Patches*
Patches lost and found
Liersch, Anne. *Nell and Fluffy*
McGinty, Alice B. *Eliza's kindergarten pet*
Meade, Holly. *John Willy and Freddy McGee*
John Willy and Freddy McGee [board book]
Middleton, Charlotte. *Nibbles*
Nibbles' garden
Nelson, Robin. *Pet guinea pig*
Ohi, Ruth. *Clara and the Bossy*
The couch was a castle
A trip with Grandma
Potter, Beatrix. *The tale of Tuppeny*
Roth, Susan L. *Great big guinea pigs*
Rylant, Cynthia. *Little Whistle*
Little Whistle's Christmas
Little Whistle's dinner party
Little Whistle's medicine
Shannon, Margaret. *Gullible's troubles*
Spelman, Cornelia Maude. *When I feel sad*
When I feel worried
When I miss you
Surplice, Holly. *Guinea pig party*
Weigelt, Udo. *Super Guinea Pig to the rescue*

Animals – hamsters

Bateman, Teresa. *Hamster Camp*
Cohen, Peter Zachary. *Boris's glasses*
Deacon, Alexis. *A place to call home*
Fraser, Mary Ann. *Pet shop lullaby*
Hill, Susanna Leonard. *Not yet, Rose*
Inkpen, Deborah. *Harriet and the little fat fairy*
Inkpen, Mick. *Kipper and Roly*
Kimmel, Elizabeth Cody. *Glamsters*
Kimmel, Eric A. *The great Texas hamster drive*

Kirk, Daniel. *Bus stop, bus go*
Lord, Cynthia. *Happy birthday, Hamster*
Hot rod Hamster
Nelson, Robin. *Pet hamster*
Norac, Carl. *Hello, sweetie pie*
I love to cuddle
I love you so much
Ohi, Ruth. *Chicken, Pig, Cow and the class pet*
Rathmann, Peggy. *10 minutes till bedtime*
Rockwell, Anne. *My pet hamster*
Rubel, Nicole. *Ham and Pickles*
Saltzberg, Barney. *Crazy hair day*
Scillian, Devin. *Memoirs of a hamster*
Walsh, Ellen Stoll. *Hamsters to the rescue*
Weigelt, Udo. *Who stole the gold?*

Animals – hedgehogs

Anderson, Lena. *The hedgehog, the pig, and their little friend*
Brett, Jan. *Christmas trolls*
The hat
Hedgie blasts off!
Hedgie's surprise
Butler, M. Christina. *One special Christmas*
One winter's day
The special blankie
Dennard, Deborah. *Hedgehog haven*
Dumont, Jean-François. *The chickens build a wall*
Falkenstern, Lisa. *A dragon moves in*
Grimm, Jacob and Wilhelm. *Hans my hedgehog*
Muir, Leslie. *C.R. Mudgeon*
Paul, Ruth. *Hedgehog's magic tricks*
Petz, Moritz. *Wish you were here*
Pfister, Marcus. *The happy hedgehog*
Potter, Beatrix. *The tale of Mrs. Tiggy-Winkle*
Schindler, S. D. *Spike and Ike take a hike*
Schubert, Ingrid. *Bear's eggs*
Stewart, Paul. *The birthday presents*
A little bit of winter
Rabbit's wish
Sutton, Benn. *Hedgehug*
Symes, Ruth. *Harriet dancing*
Wheeler, Lisa. *Hokey pokey*
Porcupining

Animals – hippopotamuses

Bauer, Marion Dane. *A mama for Owen*
Bonwill, Ann. *I am not a copycat!*
Burningham, John. *Tug-of-war*
Castle, Caroline. *Naughty!*
Coat, Janik. *Hippopposites*
Dahl, Michael. *Hippo says "excuse me."*
Fliess, Sue. *Shoes for me!*
Grambling, Lois G. *This whole Tooth Fairy thing's nothing but a big rip-off!*
Hill, Eric. *Spot's baby sister*
Horowitz, Dave. *A monkey among us*
Jenkins, Emily. *Num, num, num!*
Plonk, plonk, plonk!
Up, up, up!
Kasza, Keiko. *Dorothy and Mikey*
Landström, Lena. *A hippo's tale*
The little hippos' adventure
Lester, Helen. *Hurty feelings*
London, Jonathan. *Here comes Doctor Hippo*
Here comes firefighter Hippo
Loomis, Christine. *Hattie hippo*
McKee, David. *Elmer and the hippos*
Marshall, James. *George and Martha*
George and Martha back in town
George and Martha encore
George and Martha one fine day
George and Martha rise and shine
George and Martha 'round and 'round
George and Martha, tons of fun
Meng, Cece. *The wonderful thing about hiccups*
Minarik, Else Holmelund. *Am I beautiful?*
Neugebauer, Charise. *The real winner*
Paxton, Tom. *The jungle baseball game*
Pfister, Marcus. *Bertie*
Bertie at bedtime
Happy birthday, Bertie!
Questions, questions
Plourde, Lynn. *You're wearing that to school?!*
Puttock, Simon. *A story for Hippo*
Raschka, Chris. *The blushful hippopotamus*
Rox, John. *I want a hippopotamus for Christmas*
Saltzberg, Barney. *Hip, hip, hooray day!*
The problem with pumpkins
Schwartz, Amy. *Starring Miss Darlene*
Shea, Bob. *Oh, Daddy!*
Shipton, Jonathan. *How to be a happy hippo*
Stephens, Helen. *Ruby and the noisy hippo*
Waber, Bernard. *Evie and Margie*
Whitehouse, Patricia. *Hippopotamus*
Wild, Margaret. *Hush, hush!*
Willis, Jeanne. *Hippospotamus*
Winter, Jeanette. *Mama: a true story, in which a baby hippo loses his mama during a tsunami, but finds a new home*
Yee, Wong Herbert. *The Officers' Ball*

Animals – horses, ponies

Addy, Sharon Hart. *When wishes were horses*
Ammon, Richard. *Amish horses*
Anderson, Peggy Perry. *We go in a circle*
Angleberger, Tom. *Crankee Doodle*
Armstrong, Jennifer. *Magnus at the fire*
Barnes, Laura T. *Twist and Ernest*
Bemelmans, Ludwig. *Madeline in London*
Bradley, Kimberly Brubaker. *The perfect pony*
Brett, Jan. *Fritz and the beautiful horses*
Brill, Marlene Targ. *Bronco Charlie and the Pony Express*
Cantrell, Charlie. *A friend for Einstein*
Chan, Chin-Yi. *Good luck horse*
Clayton, Elaine. *A blue ribbon for Sugar*
Clement-Davies, David. *Spirit*
Cohen, Caron Lee. *The mud pony*
Cotten, Cynthia. *Snow ponies*
Cowley, Joy. *Where horses run free*
Darrow, Sharon. *Old Thunder and Miss Raney*
Dockray, Tracy. *The lost and found pony*
Doyle, Malachy. *Horse*
Egan, Tim. *Roasted peanuts*
Ets, Marie Hall. *Mr. Penny's race horse*
Goble, Paul. *Adopted by the eagles*
The gift of the sacred dog
The girl who loved wild horses
Mystic horse
Gray, Rita. *The wild little horse*
Haas, Jessie. *Appaloosa zebra*
Hamilton, Arlene. *Only a cow*
Hammerle, Susa. *Let's try horseback riding*
Haseley, Dennis. *Twenty heartbeats*

Havill, Juanita. *Call the horse lucky*
Hayden, Kate. *Horse show*
High, Linda Oatman. *The girl on the high-diving horse*
Winter shoes for Shadow Horse
Hoban, Russell. *Rosie's magic horse*
Hobbie, Holly. *Everything but the horse*
Hoffman, Mary. *Clever Katya*
Hong, Chen Jiang. *The magic horse of Han Gan*
Hubbell, Patricia. *Horses: trotting! prancing! racing!*
Isaacs, Anne. *Dust Devil*
Jeffers, Susan. *My Chincoteague pony*
Jeppson, Ann-Sofie. *Here comes Pontus*
You're growing up, Pontus
Kay, Verla. *Whatever happened to the Pony Express?*
Kumin, Maxine. *Oh, Harry!*
Lange, Willem. *John and Tom*
Lester, Alison. *Noni the pony*
Running with the horses
Lester, Julius. *Black cowboy, wild horses*
Lewin, Ted. *Horse song*
Libby, Barbara. *I rode the red horse*
London, Jonathan. *Mustang canyon*
Long, Loren. *An Otis Christmas*
McCarthy, Meghan. *Seabiscuit*
McCully, Emily Arnold. *Wonder horse*
McDonnell, Flora. *Giddy-up! Let's ride!*
Martin, Bill, Jr. *Chicken Chuck*
Miller, Heather. *My horses*
Morck, Irene. *Old bird*
Mullins, Patricia. *One horse waiting for me*
Murphy, Stuart J. *Same old horse*
Nelson, S. D. *Gift horse*
Numeroff, Laura Joffe. *Ponyella*
Ohi, Ruth. *Chicken, Pig, Cow horse around*
Otsuka, Yuzo. *Suho's white horse*
Paraskevas, Betty. *Marvin, the tap-dancing horse*
Peet, Bill. *Cowardly Clyde*
Pipe, Jim. *Horses*
Polacco, Patricia. *Mrs. Mack*
Rosenberg, Liz. *The carousel*
Rounds, Glen. *Once we had a horse*
Sanderson, Ruth. *The golden mare, the firebird, and the magic ring*
Schnitzler, Pattie L. *Widdermaker*
Stein, David Ezra. *Cowboy Ned and Andy*
Ned's new friend
Stockland, Patricia M. *In the horse stall*
Tibo, Gilles. *The cowboy kid*
Trollinger, Patsi B. *Perfect timing*
Willey, Margaret. *Clever Beatrice and the best little pony*
Wilson, Karma. *Horseplay*
Winnick, Karen B. *Sybil's night ride*
Yolen, Jane. *Hush, little horsie*
Sky dogs
Young, Ed. *The lost horse*

Animals – hyenas

Kimmel, Eric A. *Anansi and the magic stick*
Prelutsky, Jack. *The mean old mean hyena*
Willis, Jeanne. *That's not funny!*

Animals – jackals

Aardema, Verna. *Jackal's flying lesson*

Animals – jaguars

Campoy, F. Isabel. *Rosa Raposa*
Hamilton, Virginia. *Jaguarundi*
Ryder, Joanne. *Jaguar in the rain forest*
St. Pierre, Stephanie. *Jaguars*

Animals – kangaroos

Beaumont, Karen. *Who ate all the cookie dough?*
Bonnett-Rampersaud, Louise. *Polly Hopper's pouch*
Bourguignon, Laurence. *Heart in the pocket*
Chichester Clark, Emma. *Where are you, Blue Kangaroo?*
Edwards, Pamela Duncan. *McGillycuddy could*
French, Jackie. *Josephine wants to dance*
Hewett, Joan. *A kangaroo joey grows up*
Levitin, Sonia. *When Kangaroo goes to school*
Lithgow, John. *Marsupial Sue*
Marsupial Sue presents "The Runaway Pancake"
McAllister, Angela. *Mama and Little Joe*
McBratney, Sam. *Yes we can!*
McKee, David. *Elmer and the kangaroo*
Murphy, Stuart J. *Too many kangaroo things to do!*
Numeroff, Laura Joffe. *Nighty-night, Cooper*
Payne, Emmy. *Katy no-pocket*
Stein, David Ezra. *Pouch!*
Vaughan, Marcia Kapok. *Snap!*

Animals – kindness to *see* Character traits – kindness to animals

Animals – koalas

Backker, Vera de. *Coco the koala*
Dennard, Deborah. *Koala country*
Du Bois, William Pène. *Bear party*
Fox, Mem. *Koala Lou*
Hewett, Joan. *A koala joey grows up*
Markle, Sandra. *Finding home*
Murphy, Mary. *Koala and the flower*
Sutton, Jane. *The trouble with cauliflower*

Animals – lemurs

Browne, Anthony. *One gorilla: a counting book*
Dennard, Deborah. *Lemur landing*
Lester, Helen. *Something might happen*

Animals – leopards

Aardema, Verna. *Half-a-ball-of-kenki*
Fox, Mem. *Two little monkeys*
Frampton, David. *The whole night through*
Hatkoff, Craig, et al. *Leo the snow leopard*
Jennings, Linda. *Hide and seek birthday treat*
Keller, Holly. *Brave Horace*
Horace
Kipling, Rudyard. *How the leopard got his spots*
McAllister, Angela. *Little Mist*
Mollel, Tololwa M. *To dinner, for dinner*
Nagda, Anne Whitehead. *World above the clouds*
Orr, Wendy. *The princess and her panther*
Poppenhäger, Nicole. *Snow leopards*
St. Pierre, Stephanie. *Leopards*
Souhami, Jessica. *The leopard's drum*

Animals – lions

Aardema, Verna. *The lonely lioness and the ostrich chicks*
Aesop. *Androcles and the lion*, ill. by Dennis Nolan
Androcles and the lion, ill. by Janet Stevens
Androcles and the lion: and other Aesop fables
The lion and the mouse, ill. by Lisa McCue
The lion and the mouse, ill. by Sara Rojo
The lion and the mouse, ill. by Bernadette Watts
Mouse and lion
Auld, Mary. *Daniel in the lions' den*
Bennett, Barbara. *Lion's precious gift*
Bright, Paul. *Quiet!*
Buzzeo, Toni. *Just like my Papa*
Cohen, Caron Lee. *Martin and the giant lions*
Conover, Chris. *The lion's share*
Cuyler, Margery. *We're going on a lion hunt*
Daugherty, James Henry. *Andy and the lion*
Day, Nancy Raines. *The lion's whiskers*
Dineen, Jacqueline. *Lions*
Du Bois, William Pène. *Lion*
Edwards, Pamela Duncan. *Roar*
Foley, Greg. *Willoughby and the lion*
Freeman, Don. *Dandelion*
Gibert, Bruno. *The king is naked!*
Goldsboro, Bobby. *Jonah and the whale; and, Daniel in the lion's den*
Hartman, Bob. *Dinner in the lions' den*
Horacek, Petr. *Silly Suzy Goose*
Kanevsky, Polly. *Sleepy boy*
Kasza, Keiko. *The mightiest*
Knudsen, Michelle. *Library lion*
Lang, Aubrey. *Baby lion*
Latimer, Alex. *Lion vs Rabbit*
McCarthy, Michael. *The story of Daniel in the lions' den*
McElligott, Matthew. *The lion's share*
McPhail, David. *Pig Pig meets the lion*
Markham, Beryl. *The good lion*
Marzollo, Jean. *Daniel in the lion's den*
Peet, Bill. *Eli*
Hubert's hair-raising adventures
Randy's dandy lions
Pfister, Marcus. *How Leo learned to be king*
Pinkney, Jerry. *The lion and the mouse*
Reynolds, Aaron. *Carnivores*
Richardson, Justin. *Christian, the hugging lion*
Stephens, Helen. *How to hide a lion*
Tierney, Fiona. *Lion's lunch?*
Trimble, Marcia. *Hello sun*
Waber, Bernard. *A lion named Shirley Williamson*
Yaccarino, Dan. *Deep in the jungle*

Animals – llamas

Buxton, Jane. *The littlest llama*
Dewdney, Anna. *Llama Llama and the bully goat*
Llama Llama home with Mama
Llama Llama mad at Mama
Llama Llama misses Mama
Llama, Llama red pajama
Llama Llama time to share
Dominguez, Angela. *Maria had a little llama/Maria tenia una llama pequena*
Guarino, Deborah. *Is your mama a llama?*
Horowitz, Dave. *Chico the brave*
Livingstone, Star. *Harley*

Animals – lorises

Deacon, Alexis. *Slow Loris*

Animals – lynx

St. Pierre, Stephanie. *Lynx*

Animals – manatees

Arnosky, Jim. *All about manatees*
A manatee morning
Slow down for manatees
Klingel, Cynthia Fitterer. *Manatees*
Lithgow, John. *I'm a manatee*
Theodorou, Rod. *Florida manatee*

Animals – marsupials

Heos, Bridget. *What to expect when you're expecting joeys*
Sill, Cathryn. *About marsupials*

Animals – meerkats

Gravett, Emily. *Meerkat mail*
Lunde, Darrin. *Meet the meerkat*
Paterson, Brian. *Zigby camps out*
Zigby hunts for treasure

Animals – mice

Ada, Alma Flor. *Friend frog*
Aesop. *Belling the cat*
The country mouse and the city mouse
The lion and the mouse, ill. by Lisa McCue
The lion and the mouse, ill. by Sara Rojo
The lion and the mouse, ill. by Bernadette Watts
Milly and Tilly
Mouse and lion
The town mouse and the country mouse, ill. by Lorinda Bryan Cauley
The town mouse and the country mouse, ill. by Janet Stevens
The town mouse and the country mouse: an Aesop fable, ill. by Helen Ward
The town mouse and the country mouse: an Aesop fable, ill. by Bernadette Watts
Town mouse, country mouse, ill. by Jan Brett
Town mouse, country mouse, ill. by Carol Jones
Alborough, Jez. *Watch out! Big Bro's coming!*
Aliki. *At Mary Bloom's*
Alter, Anna. *Estelle and Lucy*
Arnosky, Jim. *Mouse letters*
Mouse numbers and letters
Mouse writing
Asch, Frank. *Mr. Maxwell's mouse*
Mrs. Marlowe's mice
Austin, Mike. *Countdown with Milo*
Aylesworth, Jim. *The completed hickory dickory dock*
Little Bitty Mousie
Two terrible frights
Baker, Keith. *Hickory dickory dock*
Balian, Lorna. *Mother's Mother's Day*
Bansch, Helga. *Brava, Mimi!*
Barbero, Maria. *The bravest mouse*
Barringer, William. *Gregory and Alexander*
Bastin, Marjolein. *Christmas with Vera*
Battut, Éric. *Little Mouse's big secret*
Baum, Louis. *The mouse who braved bedtime*

Becker, Bonny. *A bedtime for Bear*
A birthday for Bear
The sniffles for Bear
A visitor for Bear
Bedford, David. *Ella's games*
Benjamin, A. H. *Mouse, mole and the falling star*
Berkeley, Jon. *Chopsticks*
Bernheimer, Kate. *The girl who wouldn't brush her hair*
Billingsley, Franny. *Big bad bunny*
Bloom, Becky. *Crackers*
Mice make trouble
Bond, Felicia. *The Halloween play*
Bonnett-Rampersaud, Louise. *Bubble and Squeak*
Bottner, Barbara. *Wallace's lists*
Braun, Sebastien. *Back to bed, Ed!*
Brooks, Nigel. *Country mouse cottage*
Town mouse house
Brown, Ruth. *The tale of two mice*
Bunting, Eve. *The Mother's Day mice*
Mouse island
Butler, M. Christina. *Mouse and the moon*
Butterworth, Nick. *Jingle bells*
Bynum, Janie. *Nutmeg and Barley*
Cain, Sheridan. *By the light of the moon*
Calmenson, Stephanie. *Birthday at the Panda Palace*
Carle, Eric. *Do you want to be my friend?*
Carlson, Nancy. *First grade, here I come!*
Henry and the bully
Henry and the Valentine surprise
Henry's 100 days of kindergarten
I don't like to read!
Look out kindergarten, here I come!
Start saving, Henry!
Carlstrom, Nancy White. *I'm not moving, Mama!*
Chaconas, Dori. *Christmas mouseling*
Chapman, Jane. *Very special friends*
Church, Caroline Jayne. *One more hug for Madison*
Ruff!
Collicott, Sharleen. *Mildred and Sam*
Corderoy, Tracey. *I want my mommy!*
Monty and Milli
Cousins, Lucy. *Count with Maisy*
Doctor Maisy
Ha ha, Maisy!
Happy birthday, Maisy
Happy Easter, Maisy!
Maisy at the fair
Maisy at the farm
Maisy big, Maisy small
Maisy, Charley, and the wobbly tooth
Maisy cleans up
Maisy dresses up
Maisy goes on vacation
Maisy goes shopping
Maisy goes to preschool
Maisy goes to the hospital
Maisy goes to the library
Maisy goes to the museum
Maisy learns to swim
Maisy makes gingerbread
Maisy makes lemonade
Maisy's amazing big book of learning
Maisy's amazing big book of words
Maisy's bedtime
Maisy's book of things that go
Maisy's colors
Maisy's farm
Maisy's first clock
Maisy's Halloween
Maisy's morning on the farm
Maisy's noisy day
Maisy's pirate treasure hunt
Maisy's pool
Maisy's rainbow dream
Maisy's twinkly, crinkly counting book
Maisy's wonderful weather book
More fun with Maisy!
Stop and go, Maisy
Sweet dreams, Maisy
With love from Maisy
Cox, Judy. *Cinco de Mouse-o!*
Haunted house, haunted Mouse
One is a feast for Mouse
Snow day for Mouse
Crimi, Carolyn. *Tessa's tip-tapping toes*
Currey, Anna. *Truffle's Christmas*
Dahlie, Elizabeth. *Bernelly and Harriet*
Deedy, Carmen Agra. *Martina the beautiful cockroach*
Demas, Corinne. *Two Christmas mice*
dePaola, Tomie. *Charlie needs a cloak*
Donofrio, Beverly. *Mary and the mouse, the mouse and Mary*
Doyen, Denise. *Once upon a twice*
Duke, Kate. *The tale of Pip and Squeak*
Edwards, Pamela Duncan. *Bravo, Livingstone Mouse!*
Egielski, Richard. *Slim and Jim*
Ehlert, Lois. *Boo to you!*
Ellwand, David. *Midas Mouse*
Emberley, Ed. *Thanks, Mom!*
Emberley, Rebecca. *Mice on ice*
Emmett, Jonathan. *I love you always and forever*
Engelbreit, Mary. *Mary Engelbreit's A merry little Christmas*
Esbaum, Jill. *Estelle takes a bath*
Ets, Marie Hall. *Mr. T. W. Anthony Woo*
Fearnley, Jan. *Just like you*
Martha in the middle
Watch out!
Fernandes, Eugenie. *Big week for little mouse*
Busy little mouse
Sleepy little mouse
Fleming, Denise. *Alphabet under construction*
Lunch
Shout! Shout it out!
Foley, Greg. *I miss you Mouse*
Thank you, Bear
Fontes, Justine Korman. *Signs of spring*
Forward, Toby. *Ben's Christmas carol*
Fraser, Mary Ann. *I.Q. gets fit*
I.Q. goes to school
I.Q. goes to the library
I.Q., it's time
Frederick, Heather Vogel. *Hide and squeak*
Fyleman, Rose. *Mice*
Garland, Michael. *Hooray José!*
How many mice?
Geras, Adèle. *The nutcracker*
Gerritsen, Paula. *Nuts*
Goldsboro, Bobby. *Noah and the ark; and, David and Goliath*
Goodall, John S. *Creepy castle*
Goodhart, Pippa. *Little Nelly's big book*
Gorbachev, Valeri. *Dragon is coming!*
Molly who flew away
What's the big idea, Molly?

Gore, Leonid. *Mommy, where are you?*
Guest, C. Z. *Tiny green thumbs*
Hague, Michael. *The nutcracker*
Harper, Jessica. *I'm not going to chase the cat today*
Harris, Robie H. *Goodbye, Mousie*
Heling, Kathryn. *Mouse makes magic*
Mouse's hide-and-seek words
Helmer, Marilyn. *Three cat and mouse tales*
Henkes, Kevin. *Chester's way*
Chrysanthemum
El gran día de Lily / Lilly's big day
Julius, the baby of the world
Lilly's big day
Lilly's chocolate heart
Lilly's purple plastic purse
Owen
Sheila Rae, the brave
Sheila Rae's peppermint stick
A weekend with Wendell
Wemberly worried
Henry, Jed. *Cheer up, Mouse!*
Good night, Mouse!
Hines, Anna Grossnickle. *Whose shoes?*
Hoberman, Mary Ann. *The two sillies*
Hodgkinson, Leigh. *Boris and the wrong shadow*
Hoffman, Elizabeth Stokes. *Miss Renée's mice*
Miss Renée's mice go to an exhibition
Hoffmann, E. T. A. *The nutcracker,* ill. by Renée Graef
The nutcracker, ill. by Alison Jay
The nutcracker, ill. by Peter Malone
The nutcracker, ill. by Maurice Sendak
The nutcracker, ill. by Lisbeth Zwerger
The Nutcracker and the Mouse King
The nutcracker ballet
Holabird, Katharine. *Angelina and Alice*
Angelina and Henry
Angelina and the princess
Angelina and the royal wedding
Angelina at the fair
Angelina at the palace
Angelina ballerina
Angelina dances
Angelina ice skates
Angelina on stage
Angelina, star of the show
Angelina's baby sister
Angelina's ballet class
Angelina's Christmas
Angelina's Halloween
Christmas in Mouseland
Christmas with Angelina
Holmes, Janet A. *Me and you*
Hood, Susan. *The Tooth Mouse*
Howe, James. *Horace and Morris but mostly Dolores*
Horace and Morris join the chorus (but what about Dolores?)
Horace and Morris say cheese (which makes Dolores sneeze!)
Hucke, Johannes. *Pip in the Grand Hotel*
Hurd, Thacher. *Little Mouse's big Valentine*
Santa Mouse and the ratdeer
Inkpen, Mick. *Kipper's toybox*
Irving, John. *A sound like someone trying not to make a sound*
Ivimey, John William. *The complete story of the three blind mice*
Three blind mice
Johnson, Paul Brett. *Mr. Persnickety and Cat Lady*
Kangas, Juli. *The surprise visitor*
Keller, Holly. *Help!*
Kelley, True. *Blabber Mouse*
Kellogg, Steven. *The island of the skog*
Kelly, Mark. *Mousetronaut*
Mousetronaut goes to Mars
Kennedy, Kim. *Hee-Haw-Dini and the Great Zambini*
Kirk, Daniel. *Library mouse*
Library mouse: a friend's tale
Library mouse: a museum adventure
Library mouse: a world to explore
Library mouse: home sweet home
Kleven, Elisa. *Welcome home, Mouse*
Kneen, Maggie. *Chocolate moose*
Knight, Hilary. *A firefly in a fir tree*
Kolanovic, Dubravka. *Everyone needs a friend*
Kraus, Robert. *Another mouse to feed*
Come out and play, little mouse
Mouse in love
Where are you going, little mouse?
Whose mouse are you?
Kroll, Steven. *The Hanukkah mice*
Krupinski, Loretta. *Christmas in the city*
Pirate treasure
Lakin, Patricia. *Clarence the copy cat*
Leeson, Christine. *Molly and the storm*
Lionni, Leo. *Alexander and the wind-up mouse*
A busy year
Frederick
Geraldine, the music mouse
The greentail mouse
Matthew's dream
Mr. McMouse
Nicolas, where have you been?
Theodore and the talking mushroom
Tillie and the wall
Lithgow, John. *Mahalia Mouse goes to college*
Lord, Cynthia. *Hot rod Hamster*
Low, Joseph. *Mice twice*
McBratney, Sam. *The dark at the top of the stairs*
McCully, Emily Arnold. *The Christmas gift*
First snow
Monk camps out
Mouse practice
New baby
Picnic
School
MacDonald, Alan. *Wilfred to the rescue*
MacDonald, Margaret Read. *Fat cat*
Mabela the clever
McFarland, Lyn Rossiter. *Mouse went out to get a snack*
Mack, Jeff. *Good news, bad news*
McMillan, Bruce. *Mouse views*
McMullan, Kate. *Supercat to the rescue*
Martin, Bill, Jr. *A beasty story*
Martin, David. *All for pie, pie for all*
Masters, Anthony. *Ricky's rat gang*
May, Eleanor. *Albert is not scared*
Albert's amazing snail
The mousier the merrier
Mayer, Mercer. *The little drummer mouse*
Meadows, Michelle. *Itsy-bitsy baby mouse*
Medoff, Francine. *The mouse in the matzah factory*
Merski, P. K. *Roaring, boring, Alice*
Miller, Edna. *Mousekin's Christmas eve*
Mousekin's Easter basket
Mousekin's frosty friend
Mousekin's golden house

Mousekin's Thanksgiving
Modesitt, Jeanne. *Little Mouse's happy birthday*
Mollel, Tololwa M. *Kitoto the mighty*
Monson, A. M. *Wanted . . . best friend*
Moore, Clement Clarke. *The night before Christmas*
Moran, Alex. *Sam and Jack*
Morgan, Michaela. *Brave, brave mouse*
Bunny wishes
Dear bunny
Morgan-Vanroyen, Mary. *Curious Rosie*
Gentle Rosie
Patient Rosie
Sleep tight, little mouse
Wild Rosie
Morrissey, Dean. *The wizard mouse*
Mortimer, Anne. *Pumpkin cat*
Moser, Lisa. *Perfect soup*
Moss, Miriam. *I'll be your friend, Smudge*
It's my turn, Smudge
A new house for Smudge
Muir, Leslie. *The little bitty bakery*
Muller, Robin. *Badger's new house*
Nakagawa, Rieko. *Guri and Gura*
Guri and Gura's special gift
Nikola-Lisa, W. *Magic in the margins*
Nivola, Claire A. *The forest*
Noonan, Julia. *Mouse by mouse*
Numeroff, Laura Joffe. *If you give a mouse a cookie*
If you take a mouse to school
If you take a mouse to the movies
Merry Christmas, Mouse!
What mommies do best
Oh, Jiwon. *Cat and mouse*
Olson, Julie. *Tickle, tickle! itch, twitch!*
Ormerod, Jan. *Miss Mouse's day*
Oyibo, Papa. *Big brother, little sister*
Papineau, Lucie. *Lulu's pajamas*
Paraskevas, Betty. *Maggie and the Ferocious Beast, the big carrot*
Maggie and the Ferocious Beast, the big scare
Pauli, Lorenz. *The fox in the library*
Pennypacker, Sara. *Pierre in love*
Petz, Moritz. *Wish you were here*
Pfister, Marcus. *Milo and the magical stones*
Milo and the mysterious island
Pinkney, Jerry. *The lion and the mouse*
Platt, Cynthia. *A little bit of love*
Plourde, Lynn. *You're wearing that to school?!*
Pomerantz, Charlotte. *The mousery*
Potter, Beatrix. *The tailor of Gloucester*
The tale of Johnny Town-Mouse
The tale of Mrs. Tittlemouse
The tale of Mrs. Tittlemouse and other mouse stories
The tale of two bad mice
The two bad mice
Pratt, Pierre. *Car*
Home
Park
Shopping
Protopopescu, Orel. *Thelonious Mouse*
Provencher, Rose-Marie. *Mouse cleaning*
Pryor, Bonnie. *The porcupine mouse*
Rand, Gloria. *Prince William*
Randall, Ronne. *The Hanukkah mice*
Rayner, Catherine. *The bear who shared*
Reiser, Lynn. *Two mice in three fables*
Reitman, Andrea. *Mouse in the house*
Reynolds, Peter H. *Sydney's star*
Riddell, Chris. *Wendel's workshop*
Riley, Linnea Asplind. *Mouse mess*
Roberts, Bethany. *Birthday mice*
Christmas mice
Easter mice
Fourth of July mice
Valentine mice!
Rogers, Paul. *Ruby's dinnertime*
Ruby's potty
Rohmann, Eric. *My friend Rabbit*
Rossell, Judith. *Ruby and Leonard and the great big surprise*
Rueda, Claudia. *Is it big or is it little?*
Ryan, Pam Muñoz. *Mice and beans*
Ryder, Joanne. *Mouse tail moon*
Sage, James. *Farmer Smart's fat cat*
San Souci, Robert D. *The silver charm*
Santore, Charles. *A stowaway on Noah's Ark*
Scheffler, Axel. *The big balloon*
The little puddle
The scary monster
The snowy day
The super scooter
Schoenherr, Ian. *Cat and mouse*
Pip and Squeak
Schwartz, Amy. *Tiny and Hercules*
Schwartz, Corey Rosen. *Hop! Plop!*
Scotton, Rob. *Splat says thank you!*
Splat the cat
Shepard, Aaron. *The princess mouse*
Sierra, Judy. *The beautiful butterfly*
'Twas the fright before Christmas
Simmonds, Posy. *Baker cat*
Siomades, Lorianne. *Three little kittens*
Skinner, Daphne. *Albert keeps score*
The right place for Albert
Slate, Joseph. *Who is coming to our house?*
Smith, Mavis. *'Twas the day after Thanksgiving*
Snell, Gordon. *'Twas the day after Christmas*
Soto, Gary. *Chato's kitchen*
Spinelli, Eileen. *Now it is summer*
Together at Christmas
Spohn, Kate. *By word of mouse*
Springman, I. C. *More*
Spurling, Margaret. *Bilby moon*
Steig, William. *Doctor De Soto*
Doctor De Soto goes to Africa
Stein, David Ezra. *Love, Mouserella*
Steptoe, John. *The story of jumping mouse*
Stevenson, James. *All aboard!*
The castaway
The Sea View Hotel
The stowaway
Summers, Kate. *Milly's wedding*
Szekeres, Cyndy. *The mouse that Jack built*
Toby!
Toby's please and thank you
Tashiro, Chisato. *Five nice mice*
Taylor, Thomas. *Little Mouse and the big cupcake*
Thomas, Jan. *Pumpkin trouble*
Thompson, Lauren. *Mouse's first Christmas*
Mouse's first Christmas [board book]
Mouse's first fall
Mouse's first Halloween
Mouse's first snow
Mouse's first spring
Wee little lamb
Titus, Eve. *Anatole*
Anatole and the cat
Tolan, Stephanie S. *Bartholomew's blessing*

Tompert, Ann. *A carol for Christmas*
Just a little bit
The pied piper of Peru
Trapani, Iza. *Shoo fly!*
Urban, Linda. *Mouse was mad*
Vagin, Vladimir. *Here comes the cat*
van Lieshout, Maria. *Hopper and Wilson*
Vere, Ed. *The getaway*
Vincent, Gabrielle. *Ernest and Celestine at the circus*
Ernest and Celestine's picnic
Merry Christmas, Ernest and Celestine
Viva, Frank. *A trip to the bottom of the world with Mouse*
Vulliamy, Clara. *Small*
Waber, Bernard. *Do you see a mouse?*
The mouse that snored
Waddell, Martin. *Mimi's Christmas*
Sam Vole and his brothers
Squeak-a-lot
Wagner, Karen. *Bravo, Mildred and Ed!*
A friend like Ed
Wahl, Jan. *The field mouse and the dinosaur named Sue*
Waite, Judy. *Mouse, look out!*
Wallace, Nancy Elizabeth. *Look! Look! Look!*
Look! Look! Look! at sculpture
Walsh, Ellen Stoll. *Balancing act*
Dot and Jabber and the great acorn mystery
Dot and Jabber and the mystery of the missing stream
Mouse count
Mouse magic
Mouse paint
Mouse shapes
You silly goose
Waugh, Peter. *The great cannon beach mouse caper*
Wax, Wendy. *A very mice Christmas*
Webster, Sheryl. *Noodle's knitting*
Weigelt, Udo. *It wasn't me*
Wellington, Monica. *Squeaking of art, the mice go to the museum*
Wells, Rosemary. *Noisy Nora*
Shy Charles
Stanley and Rhoda
Time-out for Sophie
Weninger, Brigitte. *Double birthday*
Miko goes on vacation
Miko wants a dog
"Mom, wake up and play!"
"No bath! No way!"
Willard, Nancy. *The mouse, the cat and Grandmother's hat*
Willems, Mo. *Time to pee*
Time to say "please"!
Willis, Jeanne. *Cottonball Colin*
Gorilla! Gorilla!
Wilson, Karma. *Mortimer's Christmas manger*
Mortimer's first garden
Who goes there?
Wisniewski, David. *Sumo Mouse*
Wolkstein, Diane. *Little Mouse's painting*
Wood, Don. *Merry Christmas, big hungry bear*
Yamashita, Haruo. *Seven little mice go to school*
Seven little mice have fun on the ice
Yolen, Jane. *Beneath the ghost moon*
Young, Ed. *Mouse match*
Seven blind mice
Zalben, Jane Breskin. *Mousterpiece*
Zelinsky, Paul O. *The maid and the mouse and the odd-shaped house*
Ziefert, Harriet. *Messy Bessie*

Animals – migration *see* Migration

Animals – moles

Bedford, David. *Mole's in love*
Benjamin, A. H. *Mouse, mole and the falling star*
Crimi, Carolyn. *Rock 'n' roll Mole*
Delessert, Etienne. *Alert!*
Ehlert, Lois. *Mole's hill*
Moon rope / Un lazo a la luna
Emmett, Jonathan. *The best gift of all*
Bringing down the moon
Diamond in the snow
No place like home
Gilman, Rita Golden. *Mole in a hole*
Grahame, Kenneth. *The wind in the willows*
A wind in the willows Christmas
Hillenbrand, Jane. *What a treasure!*
Hillenbrand, Will. *Kite day*
Off we go! a Bear and Mole story
Spring is here
McAllister, Angela. *Take a kiss to school*
McPhail, David. *Mole music*
Moon, Nicola. *Tick-tock, drip-drop*
Newman, Marjorie. *Mole and the baby bird*
Mole and the baby bird [board book]
Odone, Jamison. *Mole had everything*
Oram, Hiawyn. *Badger's bad mood*
Schwartz, Roslyn. *The mole sisters and the cool breeze*
The mole sisters and the fairy ring
The mole sisters and the piece of moss
The mole sisters and the question
The mole sisters and the rainy day
Shannon, George. *Heart to heart*
Villeneuve, Anne. *The red scarf*

Animals – mongooses

Aardema, Verna. *The lonely lioness and the ostrich chicks*
Kipling, Rudyard. *Rikki-tikki-tavi*, ill. by Lambert Davis
Rikki-tikki-tavi, ill. by Jerry Pinkney

Animals – monkeys

Alborough, Jez. *Tall*
Barnett, Mac. *Count the monkeys*
Bell, Cece. *Sock Monkey boogie-woogie*
Sock Monkey goes to Hollywood
Sock Monkey rides again
Black, Michael Ian. *The purple kangaroo*
Brown, Ruth. *Monkey's friends*
Browne, Anthony. *Animal fair*
One gorilla: a counting book
Bustos, Eduardo. *Going ape!*
Bynum, Janie. *Kiki's blankie*
Cabrera, Jane. *Monkey's play time*
Christelow, Eileen. *Don't wake up Mama!*
Five little monkeys go shopping
Five little monkeys jumping on the bed
Five little monkeys reading in bed
Five little monkeys sitting in a tree
Five little monkeys trick-or-treat
Five little monkeys wash the car
Five little monkeys with nothing to do
Curious George and the dinosaur

Curious George and the dump truck (1984)
Curious George and the dump truck (1999)
Curious George and the hot air balloon
Curious George and the pizza
Curious George and the puppies
Curious George at the fire station
Curious George goes camping
Curious George goes hiking
Curious George goes sledding
Curious George goes to a chocolate factory
Curious George goes to a movie
Curious George goes to an ice cream shop
Curious George goes to school
Curious George goes to the aquarium
Curious George goes to the circus
Curious George goes to the dentist
Curious George in the big city
Curious George in the snow
Curious George makes pancakes
Curious George takes a train
Curious George visits a toy store
Curious George visits the zoo
Curious George's 1 to 10 and back again
DePalma, Mary Newell. *The strange egg*
Diakité, Baba Wagué. *The hatseller and the monkeys*
DiCamillo, Kate. *Great joy*
Donaldson, Julia. *Where's my mom?*
Du Quette, Keith. *Little Monkey lost*
Durant, Alan. *I love you, little monkey*
Elliott, George. *The boy who loved bananas*
Fox, Mem. *Two little monkeys*
Franco, Betsy. *Double play!*
Gravett, Emily. *Monkey and me*
Gréban, Quentin. *Nestor*
Hapka, Cathy. *Margret and H. A. Rey's Merry Christmas, Curious George*
Heck, Ed. *Monkey lost*
Heide, Florence Parry. *The one and only Marigold*
Hewett, Joan. *A monkey baby grows up*
Horowitz, Dave. *A monkey among us*
Jeyaveeran, Ruth. *The road to Mumbai*
Jiang, Ji-li. *The magical Monkey King, mischief in heaven*
Kepes, Juliet. *Five little monkeys*
Koller, Jackie French. *One monkey too many*
Landström, Lena. *A hippo's tale*
LaReau, Kara. *Rocko and Spanky have company*
Lehrhaupt, Adam. *Warning: do not open this book!*
Lin, Grace. *Okie-dokie, Artichokie*
Lunde, Darrin. *Monkey colors*
McDermott, Gerald. *Monkey*
Mangan, Anne. *The monkey who wanted the moon*
Martin, David. *Monkey business*
Monkey trouble
Metzger, Steve. *The dancing clock*
Monroe, Chris. *Monkey with a tool belt and the seaside shenanigans*
Myers, Walter Dean. *Looking for the easy life*
Oxenbury, Helen. *Tom and Pippo go shopping*
Tom and Pippo in the garden
Tom and Pippo on the beach
Tom and Pippo see the moon
Patricelli, Leslie. *Be quiet, Mike!*
Paxton, Tom. *The jungle baseball game*
Peet, Mal. *Cloud tea monkeys*
Perez, Monica. *Curious George plants a tree*
Curious George saves his pennies
Phillipps, J. C. *Monkey Ono*
Phillips, Betty Lou. *Emily goes wild*
Puttock, Simon. *A story for Hippo*
Regan, Dana. *Monkey see, monkey do*
Rey, H. A. *Cecily G and the nine monkeys*
Curious George
Curious George gets a medal
Curious George learns the alphabet
Curious George rides a bike
Curious George takes a job
The original Curious George
Rey, Margret. *Curious George flies a kite*
Curious George goes to the hospital
Rosenthal, Marc. *Archie and the pirates*
San Souci, Robert D. *Pedro and the monkey*
Sayre, April Pulley. *Meet the howlers!*
Schaefer, Carole Lexa. *Big Little Monkey*
Schwartz, Amy. *Oscar*
Scott, Nathan Kumar. *Mangoes and bananas*
Seven spunky monkeys
Sierra, Judy. *Counting crocodiles*
Silvano, Wendi. *Counting coconuts / Contando cocos*
Siminovich, Lorena. *Monkey see, look at me!*
Slack, Michael. *Monkey truck*
Slobodkina, Esphyr. *Caps for sale*
Souhami, Jessica. *Rama and the demon king*
Temple, Frances. *Tiger soup*
Teyssèdre, Fabienne. *Joseph wants to read*
Van Laan, Nancy. *So say the little monkeys*
Vere, Ed. *Banana!*
Wiesmüller, Dieter. *The adventures of Marco and Polo*
Williams, Suzanne. *Ten naughty little monkeys*
Wright, Maureen. *Earth Day, birthday!*
Young, Ed. *Monkey King*

Animals – moose

Allen, Jonathan. *Mucky moose*
Arnosky, Jim. *Beaver pond, moose pond*
Beck, Andrea. *Elliot bakes a cake*
Elliot digs for treasure
Elliot gets stuck
Elliot's bath
Elliot's Christmas surprise
Elliot's emergency
Elliot's great big lift-the-flap book
Elliot's noisy night
Elliot's shipwreck
Bingham, Kelly. *Z is for Moose*
Bloxam, Frances. *Antlers forever!*
Bourgeois, Paulette. *Franklin's new friend*
Bunting, Eve. *A turkey for Thanksgiving*
Capucilli, Alyssa Satin. *Biscuit visits the pumpkin patch*
Claflin, Willy. *The uglified ducky*
Egan, Tim. *The trial of Cardigan Jones*
Gannij, Joan. *Elusive moose*
Green, Stephanie. *Not just another moose*
Haseley, Dennis. *The invisible moose*
Horowitz, Dave. *Duck, duck, moose*
Jeffers, Oliver. *This moose belongs to me*
Kneen, Maggie. *Chocolate moose*
Love, Pamela. *A moose's morning*
Murray, Martine. *A moose called Mouse*
Numeroff, Laura Joffe. *If you give a moose a muffin*
Oldland, Nicholas. *Making the moose out of life*
Palatini, Margie. *Moosetache*
Raschka, Chris. *Moosey Moose*
Rayner, Catherine. *Ernest, the moose who doesn't fit*
Root, Phyllis. *Looking for a moose*

Segal, John. *The lonely moose*
Seuss, Dr. *Thidwick, the big-hearted moose*
Stihler, Chérie B. *The giant cabbage turnip*
Van Laan, Nancy. *Moose tales*
Wilson, Karma. *Moose tracks!*

Animals – mountain lions *see* Animals – cougars

Animals – mules

Bishop, Brett. *Clayton's path*
Edwards, Pamela Duncan. *Rude mule*
Ramsey, Calvin Alexander. *Belle, the last mule at Gee's Bend*
Rawlinson, Julia. *Mule school*
Sharmat, Marjorie Weinman. *Hooray for Father's Day!*

Animals – muskoxen

Cabatingan, Erin. *A is for Musk Ox*
Musk Ox counts

Animals – muskrats

Arnosky, Jim. *Come out, muskrats*

Animals – octopuses *see* Octopuses

Animals – opossums *see* Animals – possums

Animals – orangutans

Browne, Anthony. *One gorilla: a counting book*
Bustos, Eduardo. *Going ape!*
Daddo, Andrew. *Goodnight, me*

Animals – otters

Bedford, David. *Little Otter's big journey*
Berger, Samantha. *Martha doesn't say sorry*
Martha doesn't share!
Casanova, Mary. *Utterly otterly day*
Utterly otterly night
Galvin, Laura Gates. *River Otter at Autumn Lane*
Howe, James. *Otter and odder*
Levine, Ellen. *Seababy*
Luenn, Nancy. *Otter play*
Ohora, Zachariah. *Stop snoring, Bernard!*
Stewart, Amber. *Little by little*
Tatham, Betty. *Baby Sea Otter*
Webster, Christine. *Otter everywhere*

Animals – oxen

Balcziak, Bill. *Paul Bunyan*
Kellogg, Steven. *Paul Bunyan: a tall tale*
Lawlor, Laurie. *Old Crump*
Luckhurst, Matt. *Paul Bunyan and Babe the Blue Ox*
Spang, Günter. *The ox and the Donkey*

Animals – pack rats

Kroll, Steven. *Stuff!*
Mariconda, Barbara. *Sort it out!*
Ruzzier, Sergio. *The room of wonders*

Animals – pandas

Baek, Matthew J. *Panda and polar bear*
Briant, Ed. *A day at the beach*
Butler, John. *Pi-shu, the little panda*
Calmenson, Stephanie. *Birthday at the Panda Palace*
Carr, Jan. *Sweet hearts*
Dowson, Nick. *Tracks of a panda*
Gaiman, Neil. *Chu's day*
Gibbons, Gail. *Giant pandas*
Granfield, Linda. *The legend of the panda*
Jarman, Julia. *Two shy pandas*
Kraus, Robert. *Milton the early riser*
Liwska, Renata. *Little panda*
Markle, Sandra. *How many baby pandas?*
Morrow, Tara Jaye. *Panda goes to school*
Murphy, Mary. *Panda Foo and the new friend*
Muth, Jon J. *Zen ghosts*
Zen shorts
Zen ties
Nagda, Anne Whitehead. *A home for panda*
Park, Linda Sue. *Xander's panda party*
Perry, Phyllis J. *Pandas' earthquake escape*
Potter, Alicia. *Mrs. Harkness and the panda*
Ryder, Joanne. *Little panda*
Panda kindergarten
Theodorou, Rod. *Giant panda*
Wild, Margaret. *Tom goes to kindergarten*

Animals – panthers *see* Animals – leopards

Animals – pigs

Addy, Sharon Hart. *Lucky Jake*
Ahlberg, Allan. *Half a pig*
Alexander, Claire. *Small Florence*
Anderson, Lena. *The hedgehog, the pig, and their little friend*
Asch, Frank. *Happy birthday, Big Bad Wolf*
Ziggy Piggy and the three little pigs
Axelrod, Amy. *Pigs in the corner*
Pigs in the pantry
Pigs on a blanket
Pigs on the ball
Pigs on the move
Pigs will be pigs
Bailey, Linda. *Goodnight, sweet pig*
Bardhan-Quallen, Sudipta. *Hampire!*
Bassède, Francine. *A day with the Bellyflops*
Beck, Scott. *A mud pie for mother*
Bendall-Brunello, Tiziana. *I wish I could read!*
Black, Michael Ian. *A pig parade is a terrible idea*
Bloom, Suzanne. *No place for a pig*
Piggy Monday
Bond, Felicia. *Poinsettia and her family*
Poinsettia and the firefighters
The book of Pooh
Branford, Henrietta. *Little Pig Figwort can't get to sleep*
Brown, Marc. *Perfect pigs*
Brown, Margaret Wise. *The good little bad little pig*
Bunting, Eve. *Sing a song of piglets*
Bynum, Janie. *Otis*
Carlson, Nancy. *Get up and go!*
How about a hug?
Louanne Pig in the mysterious Valentine
Cazet, Denys. *Will you read to me?*
Chataway, Carol. *The perfect pet*
Chorao, Kay. *Pig and Crow*

Christelow, Eileen. *The great pig escape*
The great pig search
Church, Caroline Jayne. *Ping Pong Pig*
Cordell, Matthew. *Trouble gum*
Cort, Ben. *Pigs can't fly!*
Costello, David Hyde. *Little Pig joins the band*
Côté, Geneviève. *Me and you*
Without you
Dahl, Michael. *Pie for piglets*
Dakos, Kalli. *Our principal promised to kiss a pig*
Denise, Anika. *Pigs love potatoes*
Dewan, Ted. *Crispin and the 3 little piglets*
Crispin, the pig who had it all
Dorros, Arthur. *When the pigs took over*
Dotlich, Rebecca Kai. *Mama loves*
Papa loves
Downey, Lynn. *The tattletale*
Dunbar, Polly. *Happy Hector*
Eaton, Maxwell. *Best buds*
The mystery
Superheroes
Edwards, Pamela Duncan. *Princess Pigtoria and the pea*
Egan, Tim. *The experiments of Doctor Vermin*
Elliot, David. *Henry's map*
Elya, Susan Middleton. *Adiós, tricycle*
Emmett, Jonathan. *The princess and the pig*
Ernst, Lisa Campbell. *Sylvia Jean, drama queen*
Sylvia Jean, scout supreme
Falconer, Ian. *Olivia*
Olivia and the fairy princesses
Olivia — and the missing toy
Olivia counts
Olivia forms a band
Olivia goes to Venice
Olivia saves the circus
Olivia's opposites
Fine, Howard. *A piggie Christmas*
Folgueira, Rodrigo. *Ribbit!*
Ford, Bernette. *No more pacifier for Piggy!*
Fox, Christyan. *Astronaut PiggyWiggy*
Count to ten, PiggyWiggy!
Fire fighter PiggyWiggy
What color is that, PiggyWiggy?
What shape is that, PiggyWiggy?
Gal, Susan. *Day by day*
Garland, Michael. *Icarus Swinebuckle*
Geisert, Arthur. *The giant ball of string*
The giant seed
Hogwash
Ice
Lights out
Mystery
Nursery crimes
Oops
Pigaroons
Gibbons, Gail. *Pigs*
Gliori, Debi. *What's the time, Mr. Wolf?*
Gorbachev, Valeri. *One rainy day*
That's what friends are for
Gravett, Emily. *Wolf won't bite!*
Grindley, Sally. *Can we play too, Piglittle?*
Griswell, Kim T. *Rufus goes to school*
Guarnaccia, Steven. *The three little pigs: an architectural tale*
Harris, Trudy. *Twenty hungry piggies*
Harrison, David L. *Piggy Wiglet*
Heller, Nicholas. *Elwood and the witch*
Hillenbrand, Will. *Louie!*
Himmelman, John. *Pigs to the rescue*
Hobbie, Holly. *Toot and Puddle: let it snow*
Toot and Puddle
Toot and Puddle: wish you were here
Toot and Puddle, a present for Toot
Toot and Puddle, I'll be home for Christmas
Toot and Puddle, Puddle's ABC
Toot and Puddle, top of the world
Toot and Puddle, you are my sunshine
Horning, Sandra. *The giant hug*
Hutchins, Pat. *Little pink pig*
Inkpen, Mick. *Kipper and Roly*
Kipper's A to Z
Wibbly Pig can make a tent
Wibbly Pig is upset
Wibbly Pig likes bananas
Wibbly Pig opens his presents
Jacobs, Joseph. *The three sillies*
Jamieson, Victoria. *Olympig!*
Johnson, Angela. *Julius*
Johnson, Paul Brett. *The pig who ran a red light*
Johnston, Tony. *Farmer Mack measures his pig*
Kasza, Keiko. *My lucky birthday*
Katzler, Eva. *Florentine and Pig*
Kaufmann, Nancy. *Bye, Bye*
Keller, Holly. *Geraldine and Mrs. Duffy*
Geraldine first
Geraldine's baby brother
Geraldine's big snow
Geraldine's blanket
Merry Christmas, Geraldine
Kerby, Johanna. *Little pink pup*
Kinney, Jessica. *The pig scramble*
Kirk, Daniel. *Ten things I love about you*
Kirk, David. *Little pig, Biddle pig*
Kneen, Maggie. *The Christmas surprise*
Lasky, Kathryn. *Lucille camps in*
Lucille's snowsuit
Starring Lucille
Laverde, Arlene. *Alaska's three pigs*
Lester, Helen. *All for me and none for all*
Me first
Score one for the sloths
Lin, Grace. *Olvina flies*
Lindgren, Barbro. *Benny and the binky*
Benny's had enough
Oink, oink, Benny
Little, Jean. *Pippin the Christmas pig*
Lobel, Arnold. *Odd owls and stout pigs*
Lowell, Susan. *Josefina javelina*
The three little javelinas
McDermott, Gerald. *Pig-Boy*
MacDonald, Alan. *The pig in a wig*
McLarey, Kristina Thermaenius. *When you take a pig to a party*
MacLean, Kerry Lee. *Peaceful piggy meditation*
McNaughton, Colin. *Boo!*
Little boo!
Little goal!
Little oops!
Little suddenly!
Oomph!
Oops!
Preston's goal!
Suddenly!
McPhail, David. *Pig Pig and the magic photo album*
Pig Pig gets a job
Pig Pig goes to camp
Pig Pig grows up

Pig Pig meets the lion
Pig Pig returns
Pig Pig rides
Pigs ahoy
Pigs aplenty, pigs galore!
Those can-do pigs
Magnier, Thierry. *Isabelle and the angel*
Mansfield, Howard. *Hogwood steps out*
Marshall, James. *Portly McSwine*
Swine lake
Yummers!
Yummers too
Martin, David. *Five little piggies*
Piggy and Dad
Piggy and Dad go fishing
Martin, Jacqueline Briggs. *The water gift and the pig of the pig*
Martín Larrañaga, Ana. *Pepo and Lolo and the red apple*
Pepo and Lolo are friends
Meadows, Michelle. *Piggies in pajamas*
Piggies in the kitchen
Meddaugh, Susan. *Hog-eye*
Meister, Cari. *Skinny and fats, best friends*
Miller, Heather. *My pigs*
Milord, Susan. *Willa the wonderful*
Miranda, Anne. *Pignic*
To market, to market
Moran, Alex. *Boots for Beth*
Most, Bernard. *Z-Z-Zoink!*
Munsch, Robert N. *Pigs*
Muntean, Michaela. *Do not open this book!*
Newman, Lesléa. *Pigs, pigs, pigs*
Norac, Carl. *Monster, don't eat me!*
Norman, Kim. *I know a wee piggy*
Novak, Matt. *Jazzbo and Googy*
Numeroff, Laura Joffe. *If you give a pig a pancake*
If you give a pig a party
Odanaka, Barbara. *Smash! Mash! Crash! There goes the trash!*
Ohi, Ruth. *Chicken, Pig, Cow and the class pet*
Chicken, Pig, Cow horse around
Chicken, Pig, Cow's first fight
Oxenbury, Helen. *Pig tale*
Palatini, Margie. *Hogg, Hogg, and Hog*
Oink?
Piggie pie
Paraskevas, Betty. *Maggie and the Ferocious Beast, the big carrot*
Maggie and the Ferocious Beast, the big scare
Partridge, Elizabeth. *Pig's eggs*
Peet, Bill. *Chester the worldly pig*
Petach, Heidi. *Wee three pigs*
Peterson, Mary. *Piggies in the pumpkin patch*
Philpot, Graham. *Where is Little Harry?*
Pichon, Liz. *The three horrid little pigs*
Plourde, Lynn. *Pigs in the mud in the middle of the rud*
Polacco, Patricia. *Ginger and Petunia*
Pomerantz, Charlotte. *The piggy in the puddle*
Portis, Antoinette. *Not a stick*
Potter, Beatrix. *The tale of Little Pig Robinson*
The tale of Pigling Bland
Pryor, Bonnie. *Amanda and April*
Merry Christmas, Amanda and April
Puttock, Simon. *Squeaky clean*
Yours truly, Louisa
Rader, Laura. *Tea for me, tea for you*
Rand, Gloria. *Little Flower*
Ransom, Jeanie Franz. *Don't squeal unless it's a big deal*
Richardson, John. *Grunt*
Roche, Denis. *Little Pig is capable*
Rockwell, Anne. *Brendan and Belinda and the slam dunk!*
Root, Phyllis. *Mrs. Potter's pig*
Rosenthal, Amy Krouse. *Little Oink*
Roth, Carol. *Ten dirty pigs / Ten clean pigs*
Ruddell, Deborah. *Who said coo?*
Rueda, Claudia. *Huff and puff*
Rusackas, Francesca. *Daddy all day long*
I love you all day long
Saltzberg, Barney. *Cornelius P. Mud, are you ready for baby?*
Cornelius P. Mud, are you ready for bed?
Cornelius P. Mud, are you ready for school?
Santore, Charles. *Three hungry pigs and the wolf who came to dinner*
Sattler, Jennifer. *Pig kahuna*
Schroeder, Alan. *Smoky Mountain Rose*
Schuh, Mari C. *Pigs on the farm*
Schwartz, Corey Rosen. *The three ninja pigs*
Scieszka, Jon. *The true story of the three little pigs by A. Wolf, as told to Jon Scieszka*
Segal, John. *Far far away!*
Pirates don't take baths
Sendak, Maurice. *Bumble-ardy*
Shaw, Natalie. *Olivia plans a tea party*
Sillifant, Alec. *Farmer Ham*
Simon, Charnan. *A greedy little pig*
Smith, Maggie. *Pigs in pajamas*
Snyder, Laurel. *Baxter, the pig who wanted to be kosher*
Spinelli, Eileen. *Princess Pig*
Six hogs on a scooter
Spurr, Elizabeth. *A pig named Perrier*
Steig, William. *The amazing bone*
Farmer Palmer's wagon ride
Roland, the minstrel pig
Zeke Pippin
Stein, Mathilde. *Monstersong*
Stockland, Patricia M. *In the pig pen*
Stolz, Mary. *Emmett's pig*
Stone, Lynn M. *Pigs and piglets*
Sturges, Philemon. *This little pirate*
Sutton, Jane. *Don't call me Sidney*
Teague, Mark. *Pigsty*
The three little pigs and the somewhat bad wolf
Thaler, Mike. *Pig Little*
Thomas, Jan. *Pumpkin trouble*
The three little pigs. *The three little pigs*, ill. by Gavin Bishop
The three little pigs, ill. by Paul Galdone
The three little pigs, ill. by Rob Hefferan
The three little pigs, ill. by Steven Kellogg
The three little pigs, ill. by David McPhail
The three little pigs, ill. by James Marshall
The three little pigs, ill. by Bernadette Watts
The three little pigs, ill. by Margot Zemach
The three little pigs [board book]
The three little pigs / Los tres cerditos
The three little pigs and the big bad wolf
The three little pigs and the fox
Thurman, Kathryn K. *A garden for Pig*
Trivizas, Eugenios. *The three little wolves and the big bad pig*
Tryon, Leslie. *Patsy says*
Tucker, Lindy. *Porkelia*

Twohy, Mike. *Poindexter makes a friend*
Tyler, Jenny. *Big Pig on a dig*
Vail, Rachel. *Piggy Bunny*
Van Nutt, Julia. *The mystery of Mineral Gorge*
Pignapped!
Pumpkins from the sky?
Vischer, Phil. *Sidney and Norman*
Waddell, Martin. *Captain Small Pig*
The pig in the pond
Waldron, Jan L. *Angel Pig and the hidden Christmas*
John Pig's Halloween
Walton, Rick. *Pig, pigger, piggest*
Weeks, Sarah. *Ella, of course!*
I'm a pig
Wells, Rosemary. *The little lame prince*
Weston, Martha. *Tuck in the pool*
Tuck's haunted house
Whatley, Bruce. *Wait! No paint!*
Whybrow, Ian. *Wish, change, friend*
Wiesner, David. *The three pigs*
Wild, Margaret. *Old Pig*
Piglet and Granny
Piglet and Mama
Piglet and Papa
Wilson, Karma. *Hogwash!*
Wood, Audrey. *Piggy Pie Po*
Wood, Don. *Piggies*
Piggies [board book]
Yamada, Utako. *The story of Cherry the pig*
Yamaguchi, Kristi. *Dream big, little pig!*
It's a big world, little pig!
Yee, Wong Herbert. *Fireman Small*
Fireman Small, fire down below
Fireman Small to the rescue
Hamburger Heaven
Yolen, Jane. *Picnic with Piggins*
Piggins

Animals – platypuses

Arnold, Caroline. *A platypus' world*
Clarke, Ginjer L. *Platypus!*
Collard, Sneed B. *A platypus, probably*
Fuge, Charles. *Swim, Little Wombat, swim!*
Riddell, Chris. *Platypus*
Platypus and the lucky day

Animals – polar bears

Anderson, Derek. *Romeo and Lou blast off*
Baek, Matthew J. *Panda and polar bear*
Bedford, David. *Touch the sky, my little bear*
Bergren, Lisa Tawn. *God gave us Easter*
Bloom, Suzanne. *A splendid friend, indeed*
Brett, Jan. *The three snow bears*
Brooks, Erik. *Polar opposites*
The practically perfect pajamas
Bushey, Jeanne. *The polar bear's gift*
Carrick, Carol. *The polar bears are hungry*
Cleminson, Katie. *Magic box*
Davies, Nicola. *Ice bear*
De Beer, Hans. *Little Polar Bear and the big balloon*
Little Polar Bear and the submarine
Little Polar Bear and the whales
Dodd, Emma. *Forever*
Floyd, Madeleine. *Cold paws, warm heart*
Ford, Miela. *Follow the leader*
Mom and me
Genechten, Guido van. *Because you are my friend*
George, Jean Craighead. *The last polar bear*
Snow bear
Gibbons, Gail. *Polar bears*
Gliori, Debi. *Polar Bolero*
Graber, Janet. *Jacob and the polar bears*
Guiberson, Brenda Z. *Ice bears*
Hatkoff, Isabella, et al. *Knut*
Cabrera, Jane. *The lonesome polar bear*
Just like father
Karas, G. Brian. *Skidamarink*
Kern, Noris. *I love you with all my heart*
London, Jonathan. *Ice Bear and Little Fox*
Lumry, Amanda. *Polar bear puzzle*
Markle, Sandra. *Waiting for ice*
Mercer, Lynn. *Schubert's snowflakes*
Modugno, Maria. *Santa Claus and the three bears*
Moss, Miriam. *The snow bear*
Murphy, Yannick. *Baby Polar*
Ørdal, Stina Langlo. *Princess Aasta*
Pinkwater, Daniel. *At the Hotel Larry*
Bad bear detectives
Bad bears and a bunny
Bad bears go visiting
Bad bears in the big city
Bongo Larry
Dancing Larry
Ice-cream Larry
Irving and Muktuk
Sleepover Larry
Young Larry
Rives. *If I were a polar bear*
Rockhill, Dennis. *Polar slumber / Sueño polar*
Rueda, Claudia. *My little polar bear*
Ryder, Joanne. *A pair of polar bears*
White bear, ice bear
Stafford, Liliana. *The snow bear*
Steven, Kenneth. *The biggest thing in the world*
Stoop, Naoko. *Red Knit Cap Girl to the rescue*
Thompson, Lauren. *Polar bear morning*
Thomson, Sarah L. *Cub's big world*
Where do polar bears live?
Townsend, Emily Rose. *Polar bears*
Ward, Lindsay. *Please bring balloons*
Wild, Margaret. *Thank you, Santa*
Wilson, Karma. *Mama, why?*
Wojtowycz, David. *A cuddle for Claude*

Animals – porcupines

Czekaj, Jef. *Yes, yes, Yaul!*
Haines, Mike. *Countdown to bedtime*
LaReau, Kara. *Mr. Prickles*
Lester, Helen. *A porcupine named Fluffy*
Linders, Clara. *The very best door of all*
Moodie, Fiona. *Noko and the night monster*
Pfister, Marcus. *Where is my friend?*
Rowe, John A. *I want a hug*
Schmid, Paul. *Hugs from Pearl*
Perfectly Percy
Slate, Joseph. *Little Porcupine's Christmas*
Story time for Little Porcupine
Stevenson, James. *The castaway*
Underwood, Deborah. *A balloon for Isabel*
Wheeler, Lisa. *Hokey pokey*
Porcupining
Wilson, Karma. *Sweet Briar goes to camp*

Animals – possums

Bogue, Gary. *There's an opossum in my backyard*
deGroat, Diane. *Ants in your pants, worms in your plants!*
Brand-new pencils, brand-new books
Good night, sleep tight, don't let the bedbugs bite
Jingle bells, homework smells
Last one in is a rotten egg!
Liar, liar, pants on fire
Lola the elf
Mother, you're the best! (but Sister, you're a pest!)
Duvall, Deborah L. *The opossum's tale*
Fox, Mem. *Possum magic*
Hunter, Anne. *Possum and the peeper*
Possum's harvest moon
Hurd, Thacher. *Mama don't allow*
Kasza, Keiko. *Don't laugh, Joe*
Keller, Holly. *Henry's Fourth of July*
Henry's happy birthday
Salley, Coleen. *Epossumondas*
Epossumondas plays possum
Epossumondas saves the day
Van Laan, Nancy. *Possum come a-knocking*
Whitehouse, Patricia. *Opossums*

Animals – prairie dogs

Stevens, Janet. *The great fuzz frenzy*

Animals – prairie wolves *see* Animals – coyotes

Animals – pumas *see* Animals – cougars

Animals – rabbits

Abbott, Bud. *Who's on first?*
Adams, Adrienne. *The Christmas party*
The Easter egg artists
The great Valentine's Day balloon race
Aesop. *The hare and the tortoise*, ill. by Paul Galdone
The hare and the tortoise, ill. by Carol Jones
The hare and the tortoise, ill. by Helen Ward
The hare and the tortoise / La liebre y la tortuga
The race
Road signs
The tortoise and the hare, ill. by Jerry Pinkney
The tortoise and the hare, ill. by Sara Rojo
The tortoise and the hare: an Aesop fable
Allen, Jonathan. *"I'm not Santa!"*
The little rabbit who liked to say moo
Amant, Kathleen. *Little Rabbit gets messy*
On your potty, Little Rabbit
Anderson, Derek. *How the Easter Bunny saved Christmas*
Apperley, Dawn. *Blossom and Boo*
Blossom and Boo stay up late
Araki, Mie. *The magic toolbox*
Arnosky, Jim. *Rabbits and raindrops*
Asher, Sandy. *Too many frogs!*
Badescu, Ramona. *Big Rabbit's bad mood*
Baguley, Elizabeth. *A long way from home*
Baker, Alan. *Black and White Rabbit's ABC*
Brown Rabbit's shape book
Gray Rabbit's one, two, three
Little Rabbit's first number book
Little Rabbit's first word book
White Rabbit's color book
Balian, Lorna. *Humbug rabbit*
Bardill, Linard. *The great golden thing*
Bate, Lucy. *Little rabbit's loose tooth*
Battersby, Katherine. *Brave Squish Rabbit*
Squish Rabbit
Bauer, Marion Dane. *One brown bunny*
Becker, John Leonard. *Seven little rabbits*
Berger, Barbara. *Thunder Bunny*
Berger, Carin. *Forever friends*
Berlin, Irving. *Easter parade*
Bianco, Margery Williams. *The velveteen rabbit*, ill. by David Jorgensen
The velveteen rabbit, ill. by Thea Kliros
The velveteen rabbit, ill. by Komako Sakai
The velveteen rabbit, ill. by Gennady Spirin
The velveteen rabbit: or, How toys became real, ill. by Allen Atkinson
The velveteen rabbit: or, How toys became real, ill. by Steve Johnson
Birchall, Mark. *Rabbit's birthday surprise*
Rabbit's wooly sweater
Blake, Stephanie. *I don't want to go to school!*
Boelts, Maribeth. *Sweet dreams, Little Bunny!*
You're a brother, Little Bunny!
Bottner, Barbara. *Raymond and Nelda*
Brett, Jan. *The Easter egg*
Brown, Marc. *The bionic bunny show*
Brown, Margaret Wise. *Bunny's noisy book*
Bunny's noisy book [board book]
The golden egg book
Goodnight moon
Goodnight moon ABC
Goodnight moon 123: a counting book
Goodnight moon 123: a counting book [board book]
My world
The runaway bunny
The runaway bunny [board book]
Bruchac, James. *Rabbit's snow dance*
Burg, Sarah Emmanuelle. *One more egg*
Burke, Bobby. *Daddy's little girl*
Burleigh, Robert. *Hit the road, Jack*
Burningham, John. *Tug-of-war*
Capucilli, Alyssa Satin. *Only my dad and me*
Carlson, Nancy. *Harriet and George's Christmas treat*
Loudmouth George and the cornet
Loudmouth George and the fishing trip
Loudmouth George and the new neighbors
Loudmouth George and the sixth-grade bully
Loudmouth George earns his allowance
Carlstrom, Nancy White. *Mama, will it snow tonight?*
Carrer, Chiara. *Otto Carrotto*
Cate, Annette LeBlanc. *The magic rabbit*
Cazet, Denys. *December 24th*
Chaconas, Dori. *Looking for Easter*
Cooper, Helen. *Tatty-Ratty*
Côté, Geneviève. *Me and you*
With you always, Little Monday
Without you
Cowell, Cressida. *Emily Brown and the Thing*
That rabbit belongs to Emily Brown
Crimi, Carolyn. *Henry and the Buccaneer Bunnies*
Henry and the Crazed Chicken Pirates
Cronin, Doreen. *Rescue bunnies*
Crummel, Susan Stevens. *Tumbleweed stew*
Czekaj, Jef. *Hip and Hop, don't stop!*
Yes, yes, Yaul!
D'Amico, Carmela. *Suki and Mirabella*

Suki the very loud bunny
Denim, Sue. *The Dumb Bunnies*
The Dumb Bunnies' Easter
The Dumb Bunnies go to the zoo
Make way for Dumb Bunnies
Desrosiers, Sylvie. *Hocus Pocus*
Hocus Pocus takes the train
Dewdney, Anna. *Nobunny's perfect*
Diakité, Baba Wagué. *The magic gourd*
Dierssen, Andreas. *Timid Timmy*
Timmy's new friend
Dieterlé, Nathalie. *I am the king!*
Dijkstra, Lida. *Cute*
Donohue, Dorothy. *Veggie soup*
Downard, Barry. *The Race of the Century*
Dubosarsky, Ursula. *The terrible plop*
Durant, Alan. *Big Bad Bunny*
Brown Bear gets in shape
Edvall, Lilian. *The rabbit who longed for home*
Empson, Jo. *Rabbityness*
Escoffier, Michael. *Rabbit and the Not-So-Big-Bad Wolf*
Evans, Lezlie. *The bunnies' picnic*
The bunnies' trip
Faglia, Matteo. *Happy birthday, I'm 1*
Falkenstern, Lisa. *A dragon moves in*
Faller, Regis. *Polo and Lily*
Feeney, Tatyana. *Small Bunny's blue blanket*
Fleming, Candace. *Muncha! Muncha! Muncha!*
Tippy-tippy-tippy, hide!
Ford, Bernette. *First snow*
No more bottles for Bunny!
Freedman, Claire. *Follow that bear if you dare!*
Hushabye Lily
Galbraith, Kathryn O. *Boo, bunny!*
Gay, Marie-Louise. *Roslyn Rutabaga and the biggest hole on earth!*
Genechten, Guido van. *Flop-Ear*
Ricky and the squirrel
Ricky is brave
George, Lindsay Barrett. *My bunny and me*
Geras, Adèle. *My wishes for you*
Gershator, Phillis. *Time for a hug*
Glaser, Linda. *Hoppy Passover!*
Gliori, Debi. *Flora's blanket*
Flora's surprise
The scariest thing of all
Goodman, Joan Elizabeth. *Ballet Bunnies*
Gorbachev, Valeri. *Christopher counting*
Nicky and the big, bad wolves
Nicky and the fantastic birthday gift
Nicky and the rainy day
Gore, Leonid. *Danny's first snow*
Got, Yves. *Sam's big book of words*
Sam's little sister
Grambling, Lois G. *Here comes T. Rex Cottontail*
Gravett, Emily. *The rabbit problem*
Wolves
Gretz, Susanna. *Rabbit food*
Griffith, Helen V. *Moonlight*
Grimm, Jacob and Wilhelm. *The rabbit's bride*
Grossman, Virginia. *Ten little rabbits*
Guest, C. Z. *Tiny green thumbs*
Hample, Stoo. *I will kiss you (lots and lots and lots!)*
Harper, Charise Mericle. *Pink me up*
Harry, Rebecca. *Snow Bunny's Christmas wish*
Hayes, Geoffrey. *The bunny's night-light*
Heap, Sue. *Four friends in the garden*
Henkes, Kevin. *Bailey goes camping*
Little white rabbit
So happy!
Heyward, Du Bose. *The country bunny and the little gold shoes*
Ho, Minfong. *Brother Rabbit*
Hoban, Tana. *Where is it?*
Holmes, Janet A. *Me and you*
Horse, Harry. *Little rabbit lost*
Little Rabbit runaway
Little Rabbit's new baby
Hubbell, Patricia. *Rabbit moon*
Ichikawa, Satomi. *La La Rose*
Ives, Penny. *Rabbit pie*
Jackson, Ellen. *The seven seas*
Jagtenberg, Yvonne. *Jack's rabbit*
Jahn-Clough, Lisa. *Felicity and Cordelia*
Jeram, Anita. *I love my little storybook*
Johnson, Paul Brett. *Little Bunny Foo Foo*
Johnston, Tony. *Little Rabbit goes to sleep*
The tale of Rabbit and Coyote
Julian, Alison. *Brave as a bunny can be*
Kaplan, Michael B. *Betty Bunny didn't do it*
Betty Bunny loves chocolate cake
Betty Bunny wants everything
Keller, Emily Snowell. *Sleeping Bunny*
Keller, Holly. *Cecil's garden*
Pearl's new skates
Kempter, Christa. *Wally and Mae*
Kenyon, Tony. *Hyacinth Hop has the hic-hops*
Kirk, Daniel. *Ten things I love about you*
Kirk, David. *Little bunny, Biddle bunny*
Oh So Tiny bunny
Klise, Kate. *Imagine Harry*
Little Rabbit and the Meanest Mother on Earth
Little Rabbit and the Night Mare
Why do you cry?
Knudsen, Michelle. *Big Mean Mike*
Kortepeter, Paul. *Oliver's red toboggan*
Krensky, Stephen. *Milo and the really big bunny*
Krishnaswami, Uma. *Remembering Grandpa*
Kroll, Steven. *The big bunny and the Easter eggs*
The big bunny and the magic show
Kroll, Virginia L. *Really rabbits*
Lachner, Dorothea. *Smoky's special Easter present*
Lacome, Julie. *Ruthie's big old coat*
Larsen, Andrew. *Bella and the bunny*
Lasky, Kathryn. *Lunch bunnies*
Science fair bunnies
Show and tell bunnies
Tumble bunnies
Latimer, Alex. *Lion vs Rabbit*
Layne, Steven L. *Love the baby*
Leathers, Philippa. *The black rabbit*
Lee, Ho Baek. *While we were out*
Lester, Helen. *Listen, Buddy*
Lewis, Rob. *Friends*
Lillegard, Dee. *Balloons, balloons, balloons*
Lionni, Leo. *Let's make rabbits*
Livingston, Irene. *Finklehopper Frog*
Finklehopper Frog cheers
Lobel, Anita. *Ten hungry rabbits*
London, Jonathan. *Jackrabbit*
Long, Sylvia. *Deck the hall*
Loomis, Christine. *Astro Bunnies*
Cowboy bunnies
Scuba bunnies
Lowell, Susan. *The tortoise and the jackrabbit*
Luthardt, Kevin. *You're weird!*
McAllister, Angela. *The little blue rabbit*

Night-night, little one
McBratney, Sam. *Guess how much I love you*
McCarty, Peter. *Chloe*
Henry in love
Little bunny on the move
McCue, Lisa. *Quiet Bunny*
Quiet Bunny and Noisy Puppy
McCullough, Sharon Pierce. *Bunbun at bedtime*
Bunbun, the middle one
McDermott, Gerald. *Zomo the rabbit*
MacDonald, Elizabeth. *The wolf is coming!*
MacDonald, Margaret Read. *Conejito*
Pickin' peas
McGrath, Barbara Barbieri. *The little gray bunny*
Mack, Jeff. *Good news, bad news*
McPhail, David. *Bella loves Bunny*
Budgie and Boo
Sylvie and True
Magloff, Lisa. *Rabbit*
Marino, Gianna. *Too tall houses*
Marlow, Layn. *Hurry up and slow down*
Martin, David. *Little Bunny and the magic Christmas tree*
Marzollo, Jean. *I spy little bunnies*
Meister, Cari. *Skinny and fats, best friends*
Minters, Frances. *Too big, too small, just right*
Modesitt, Jeanne. *Little Bunny's Easter surprise*
Molk, Laurel. *Good job, Oliver!*
Mollel, Tololwa M. *To dinner, for dinner*
Montanari, Eva. *A very full morning*
Moon, Nicola. *Tick-tock, drip-drop*
Morgan, Michaela. *Bunny wishes*
Dear bunny
Moroney, Trace. *When I'm feeling angry*
When I'm feeling happy
When I'm feeling sad
When I'm feeling scared
Morrison, Toni. *The tortoise or the hare*
Mortimer, Anne. *Bunny's Easter egg*
Moss, Miriam. *Bad hare day*
Müller, Birte. *I can dress myself!*
Murphy, Stuart J. *Just enough carrots*
Rabbit's pajama party
Na, Il Sung. *Snow rabbit, spring rabbit*
Newberry, Clare Turlay. *Marshmallow*
Nishimura, Kae. *Bunny Lune*
Noonan, Julia. *Hare and Rabbit, friends forever*
Novak, Matt. *Too many bunnies*
Nyeu, Tao. *Bunny days*
O'Keefe, Susan Heyboer. *Love me, love you*
Oller, Erika. *The cabbage soup solution*
O'Malley, Kevin. *The great race*
O'Mara, Carmel. *Rainy day*
Sunny day
Palatini, Margie. *Goldie and the three hares*
Stuff
Paraskevas, Betty. *Maggie and the Ferocious Beast, the big carrot*
Nibbles O'Hare
Park, Linda Sue. *What does Bunny see?*
Peet, Bill. *Huge Harold*
Pennypacker, Sara. *Pierre in love*
Petach, Heidi. *Goldilocks and the three hares*
Petersen, David. *Snowy Valentine*
Pfister, Marcus. *Hang on, Hopper!*
Hopper
Hopper hunts for spring
Hopper's treetop adventure
Pilkey, Dav. *The Dumb Bunnies*
The Dumb Bunnies' Easter
The Dumb Bunnies go to the zoo
Make way for Dumb Bunnies
Pinkwater, Daniel. *Bad bears and a bunny*
Bear in love
Irving and Muktuk
Portis, Antoinette. *No es una caja / not a box*
Not a box
Posey, Lee. *Night rabbits*
Potter, Beatrix. *The complete adventures of Peter Rabbit*
Peter Rabbit's one two three
The story of fierce bad rabbit
The tale of Benjamin Bunny
The tale of Mr. Tod
The tale of Peter Rabbit, ill. by Margot Apple
The tale of Peter Rabbit, ill. by Beatrix Potter
The tale of the Flopsy Bunnies, ill. by Beatrix Potter
The tale of the Flopsy Bunnies, ill. by Wendy Rasmussen
Where's Peter Rabbit?
Price, Mathew. *Patch and the rabbits*
Rand, Betseygail. *Big Bunny*
Raschka, Chris. *Five for a little one*
Rawlinson, Julia. *A surprise for Rosie*
Ray, Mary Lyn. *All aboard*
Reidy, Jean. *All through my town*
Rey, Margret. *Spotty*
Reynolds, Aaron. *Creepy carrots!*
Robbins, Beth. *Tom, Ally, and the baby-sitter*
Roberts, Bethany. *Waiting-for-Christmas stories*
Waiting-for-Papa stories
Waiting-for-spring stories
Rockwell, Anne. *Chip and the karate kick*
Roddie, Shen. *Sandbear*
Rohmann, Eric. *My friend Rabbit*
Rosenthal, Amy Krouse. *Duck! Rabbit!*
Roth, Carol. *Little Bunny's sleepless night*
Russell, Natalie. *Brown Rabbit in the city*
Moon rabbit
Russo, Marisabina. *The bunnies are not in their beds*
A very big bunny
Ruzzier, Sergio. *Hey, Rabbit!*
Ryan, Candace. *Ribbit rabbit*
Rylant, Cynthia. *Bunny bungalow*
Sakai, Komako. *Mad at Mommy*
The snow day
Saltzberg, Barney. *Hi, Blueberry!*
Hip, hip, hooray day!
The problem with pumpkins
San Souci, Daniel. *The rabbit and the dragon king*
Scanlon, Elizabeth Garton. *Happy birthday, Bunny!*
Scheffler, Axel. *The big balloon*
The little puddle
The scary monster
The snowy day
The super scooter
Schmid, Eleonore. *Hare's Christmas gift*
Schoenherr, Ian. *Pip and Squeak*
Schulman, Janet. *A bunny for all seasons*
Schwartz, Amy. *Oscar*
Schweninger, Ann. *Halloween surprises*
Valentine friends
Scieszka, Jon. *Battle Bunny*
Segal, John. *Carrot soup*
Selkowe, Valrie M. *Happy birthday to me!*
Shannon, George. *Rabbit's gift*
Shields, Gillian. *When the world was waiting for you*

Simmons, Jane. *Little Fern's first winter*
Slegers, Liesbet. *Happy Easter!*
Smee, Nicola. *What's the matter, Bunny Blue?*
Smythe, Theresa. *Chester's colorful Easter eggs*
Soto, Gary. *Lucky Luis*
Spelman, Cornelia Maude. *When I feel angry*
Spinelli, Eileen. *A big boy now*
Stadler, John. *Wilson and Miss Lovely*
Stalder, Päivi. *Ernest's first Easter*
Stanley, Mandy. *Lettice the dancing rabbit*
Lettice the flower girl
Lettice the flying rabbit
Steig, William. *Solomon the rusty nail*
Which would you rather be?
Stein, Janet. *This little bunny can bake*
Stevens, Janet. *Tops and bottoms*
Stevenson, James. *Monty*
Stewart, Amber. *I'm big enough*
No babysitters allowed
Rabbit ears
Stewart, Paul. *The birthday presents*
A little bit of winter
Rabbit's wish
Stiegemeyer, Julie. *Seven little bunnies*
Stills, Caroline. *The house of 12 bunnies*
Szekeres, Cyndy. *Cyndy Szekeres' learn to count, funny bunnies*
I can count 100 bunnies, and so can you!
Tafuri, Nancy. *Rabbit's morning*
Where did Bunny go?
Will you be my friend?
Taylor, Sean. *The grizzly bear with the frizzly hair*
Taylor, Shirley. *The cross in the egg*
Tegen, Katherine Brown. *The story of the Easter Bunny*
Thomas, Jan. *The Easter Bunny's assistant*
Thompson, Emma. *The further tale of Peter Rabbit*
Thompson, Lauren. *Wee little bunny*
Thornhill, Jan. *The rumor*
Tingle, Tim. *When Turtle grew feathers*
Tompert, Ann. *Nothing sticks like a shadow*
Tonatiuh, Duncan. *Pancho Rabbit and the coyote*
Tone, Satoe. *The very big carrot*
Vainio, Pirkko. *The best of friends*
Van Leeuwen, Jean. *Five funny bunnies*
Van Woerkom, Dorothy. *Harry and Shelburt*
Waddell, Martin. *Tom Rabbit*
We love them
Waechter, Phillip. *Rosie and the nightmares*
Wakeman, Daniel. *Ben's bunny trouble*
Wallace, Ivy. *Pookie*
Pookie believes in Santa Claus
Pookie puts the world right
Wallace, John. *Tiny Rabbit goes to a birthday party*
Wallace, Nancy Elizabeth. *Alphabet house*
Apples, apples, apples
Count down to clean up
Fly, monarch! Fly!
Paperwhite
Planting seeds
Pumpkin day
Rabbit's bedtime
Ready, set, 100th day!
Recycle every day!
Snow
Snow [board book]
Stars! Stars! Stars!
Tell-a-bunny
The Valentine Express
Walters, Catherine. *The magical snowman*
Walton, Rick. *Bunny school*
One more bunny
What do we do with the baby?
Washington, Donna L. *Li'l Rabbit's Kwanzaa*
Watson, Wendy. *Bedtime bunnies*
Watt, Mélanie. *You're finally here!*
Weeks, Sarah. *Bunny fun*
Overboard!
Weigelt, Udo. *The Easter Bunny's baby*
Weil, Lisl. *The candy egg bunny*
Welch, Willy. *Grumpy Bunnies*
Wellington, Monica. *Bunny's first snowflake*
Night rabbits
Wells, Rosemary. *Bunny cakes*
Bunny mail
Bunny money
Bunny party
Carry me!
Clean-up time
Emily's first 100 days of school
First tomato
Goodnight Max
The island light
Love waves
McDuffs hide-and-seek
Max and Ruby's bedtime book
Max and Ruby's Midas
Max and Ruby's treasure hunt
Max cleans up
Max counts his chickens
Max's ABC
Max's apples
Max's bath
Max's bedtime
Max's birthday
Max's breakfast
Max's bunny business
Max's chocolate chicken
Max's Christmas
Max's dragon shirt
Max's Easter surprise
Max's first word
Max's new suit
Max's ride
Max's toys
Max's worm cake
Morris's disappearing bag
Moss pillows
My kindergarten
Peek-a-boo
Read to your bunny
Red boots
Ruby's beauty shop
Shopping
Weninger, Brigitte. *Davy in the middle*
Davy, soccer star!
Happy birthday, Davy
Happy Easter, Davy
Merry Christmas, Davy!
What's the matter, Davy?
Why are you fighting, Davy?
Will you mind the baby, Davy?
Whybrow, Ian. *Bella gets her skates on*
Wild, Margaret. *Rosie and Tortoise*
Wilhelm, Hans. *Bunny trouble*
More bunny trouble
Willems, Mo. *Knuffle Bunny*
Knuffle Bunny free

Knuffle Bunny too
Williams, Garth. *Benjamin's treasure*
Williams, Sue. *Dinnertime*
Winget, Susan. *Tucker's four-carrot school day*
Wolf, Winfried. *The Easter bunny*
Wormell, Christopher. *Blue Rabbit and friends*
Blue Rabbit and the runaway wheel
Wright, Joanna. *Bunnies on ice*
Ziefert, Harriet. *Bunny's lessons*
Zolotow, Charlotte. *The bunny who found Easter*
Mr. Rabbit and the lovely present

Animals – raccoons

Arnosky, Jim. *Raccoon on his own*
Raccoons and ripe corn
Bunting, Eve. *Our library*
Cocca-Leffler, Maryann. *Bravery soup*
Elliott, David. *Hunter's best friend at school*
Elliott, Laura Malone. *Hunter and Stripe and the soccer showdown*
Hunter's big sister
Friend, Catherine. *Eddie the raccoon*
Glass, Andrew. *Bewildered for three days*
Guest, Elissa Haden. *Harriet's had enough!*
Haines, Mike. *Countdown to bedtime*
Harrison, David L. *A perfect home for a family*
Hubery, Julia. *A friend for all seasons*
Kasza, Keiko. *Ready for anything*
McPhail, David. *Henry Bear's Christmas*
The Searcher and Old Tree
Something special
Waddles
Milord, Susan. *If I could*
Mitchard, Jacquelyn. *Ready, set, school!*
Modarressi, Mitra. *Stay awake, Sally*
Taking care of Mama
Nelson, Kristin L. *Clever raccoons*
Neugebauer, Charise. *The real winner*
Penn, Audrey. *A bedtime kiss for Chester Raccoon*
A color game for Chester Raccoon
Rayner, Catherine. *The bear who shared*
Rubin, Adam. *Secret pizza party*
Sharmat, Marjorie Weinman. *The 329th friend*
Shaw, Hannah. *School for bandits*
Shaw, Nancy. *Raccoon tune*
Wells, Rosemary. *Timothy goes to school*
Yoko
Whitehouse, Patricia. *Raccoons*

Animals – rats

Browning, Robert. *The pied piper of Hamelin*, ill. by Mercer Mayer
The pied piper of Hamelin, ill. by Drahos Zak
Bryan, Ashley. *The cat's purr*
Child, Lauren. *That pesky rat*
Coffey, Maria. *A cat adrift*
Covell, David. *Rat and Roach*
Rat and Roach rock on!
Crimi, Carolyn. *Don't need friends*
Crow, Kristyn. *Cool Daddy Rat*
Deacon, Alexis. *Cheese belongs to you!*
Donaldson, Julia. *The Highway Rat*
Egielski, Richard. *Slim and Jim*
Emberley, Rebecca. *Three cool kids*
Grahame, Kenneth. *The wind in the willows*
A wind in the willows Christmas
Hamilton, Martha. *Priceless gifts*
Jennings, Patrick. *Bat and Rat*
Jennings, Sharon. *Priscilla and Rosy*
Priscilla's paw de deux
Kellogg, Steven. *The Pied Piper's magic*
Kilaka, John. *True friends*
Lester, Helen. *Hooway for Wodney Wat*
Wodney Wat's wobot
McPhail, David. *Big Brown Bear goes to town*
Big Brown Bear's birthday surprise
Big brown bear's up and down day
Meddaugh, Susan. *Cinderella's rat*
Moore, Inga. *Captain Cat*
Potter, Beatrix. *The sly old cat*
Stevenson, James. *The most amazing dinosaur*
Wilfred the rat
Van Woerkom, Dorothy. *The rat, the ox and the zodiac*
Wade, Mary Dodson. *No year of the cat*
Walton, Rick. *Just me and 6,000 rats*
The remarkable friendship of Mr. Cat and Mr. Rat
Whitehouse, Patricia. *Rats*
Young, Ed. *Cat and Rat*

Animals – reindeer

Brett, Jan. *The wild Christmas reindeer*
McCaughrean, Geraldine. *How the reindeer got their antlers*
May, Robert Lewis. *Rudolph the red-nosed reindeer*
Miller, Debbie S. *A caribou journey*
Moulton, Mark Kimball. *Reindeer Christmas*
Root, Phyllis. *If you want to see a caribou*
Trumbauer, Lisa. *The great reindeer rebellion*

Animals – rhinoceros

Agee, Jon. *My rhinoceros*
Araki, Mie. *The magic toolbox*
Brown, Susan Taylor. *Oliver's must-do list*
Brunhoff, Laurent de. *Babar's battle*
Chivers, Natalie. *Rhino's great big itch!*
Derrick, Patricia. *Riley the rhinoceros*
Kessler, Cristina. *Jubela*
Lloyd, Sam. *Chief Rhino to the rescue!*
Mammano, Julie. *Rhinos who play baseball*
Rhinos who play soccer
Rhinos who rescue
Rhinos who surf
Moser, Lisa. *Cowboy Boyd and Mighty Calliope*
Newman, Jeff. *Hippo! No, rhino!*
O'Malley, Kevin. *Bud*
Terry, Michael. *Rhino's horns*
Theodorou, Rod. *Black rhino*

Animals – salamanders *see* Reptiles – salamanders

Animals – sea lions

Schreiber, Georges. *Bambino the clown*
Tafuri, Nancy. *Follow me!*
Whitehouse, Patricia. *Sea lion*

Animals – seals

Butterworth, Chris. *See what a seal can do*
Haas, Rick de. *Peter and the seal*
Hewett, Joan. *A harbor seal pup grows up*
Hollenbeck, Kathleen M. *Islands of ice*

Mitton, Tony. *Playful little penguins*
Rotter, Charles. *Seals*
Rumford, James. *Dog-of-the-Sea-Waves*
Seeger, Laura Vaccaro. *What if?*
Townsend, Emily Rose. *Seals*
van Lieshout, Maria. *Splash: a little book about bouncing back*

Animals – service animals

Dalgleish, Sharon. *Working dogs*
Kovacs, Deborah. *Katie Copley*
Lang, Glenna. *Looking out for Sarah*
Russell, Joan Plummer. *Aero and Officer Mike*

Animals – sheep

Aardema, Verna. *Borreguita and the coyote*
Aesop. *The wolf in sheep's clothing*
Alborough, Jez. *The gobble gobble moooooo tractor book*
Alda, Arlene. *Sheep, sheep, sheep, help me fall asleep*
Beaty, Andrea. *Hide and sheep*
Beaumont, Karen. *No sleep for the sheep!*
Belloni, Giulia. *Anything is possible*
Bently, Peter. *The great sheep shenanigans*
Brown, Margaret Wise. *Sheep don't count sheep*
Calhoun, Mary. *Henry the Christmas cat*
Carrick, Carol. *Valentine*
Catusanu, Mircea. *The strange case of the missing sheep*
Church, Caroline Jayne. *Digby takes charge*
Cordell, Matthew. *Another brother*
dePaola, Tomie. *Charlie needs a cloak*
De Sève, Randall. *Mathilda and the orange balloon*
Edwards, David. *The pen that Pa built*
Ford, Bernette. *No more blanket for Lambkin!*
Fox, Mem. *Where is the green sheep?*
Fraggalosch, Audrey. *Trails above the tree line*
French, Jackie. *Pete the sheep-sheep*
Friend, Catherine. *Funny Ruby*
Gliori, Debi. *The snow lambs*
Goodings, Christina. *Lost sheep story*
Hale, Sarah Josepha Buell. *Mary had a little lamb*, ill. by Tomie dePaola
Mary had a little lamb, ill. by Laura Huliska-Beith
Mary had a little lamb, ill. by Salley Mavor
Mary had a little lamb, photos by Bruce McMillan
Heap, Sue. *Four friends in the garden*
Helakoski, Leslie. *Woolbur*
Hill, Susanna Leonard. *Can't sleep without sheep*
Hoberman, Mary Ann. *Mary had a little lamb*
Imai, Ayano. *The 108th sheep*
Kelly, Mij. *One more sheep*
Kempter, Christa. *Dear Little Lamb*
Klise, Kate. *Grammy Lamby and the secret handshake*
Landström, Lena. *Boo and Baa have company*
Landström, Olof. *Boo and Baa get wet*
Boo and Baa in the woods
Lang, Aubrey. *Baby mountain sheep*
Lester, Helen. *The sheep in wolf's clothing*
Levine, Gail Carson. *Betsy Red Hoodie*
Betsy who cried wolf
Lewis, Kim. *Emma's lamb*
First snow
Little Baa
Little lamb
The shepherd boy
Livingstone, Star. *Harley*
Lobel, Anita. *Lena's sleep sheep*
Lunge-Larsen, Lise. *Noah's mittens*
McCully, Emily Arnold. *My real family*
McGinty, Alice B. *Ten little lambs*
McGrory, Anik. *Mouton's impossible dream*
McQuinn, Anna. *The sleep sheep*
Marciano, John Bemelmans. *Delilah*
Marshall, Linda Elovitz. *The passover lamb*
Martins, Isabel Minhós. *Little lamb, have you any wool?*
Monroe, Chris. *Sneaky sheep*
Moses, Will. *Mary and her little lamb*
Numeroff, Laura Joffe. *When sheep sleep*
Olsen, Sylvia. *Yetsa's sweater*
Ommen, Sylvia van. *The surprise*
Peet, Bill. *Buford the little bighorn*
Porter, Sue. *Parsnip*
Puttock, Simon. *Miss Fox*
Root, Phyllis. *Ten sleepy sheep*
Rothstein, Gloria. *Sheep asleep*
Sanders, Scott R. *Warm as wool*
Schroeder, Lisa. *Baby can't sleep*
Schubert, Leda. *Feeding the sheep*
Schuh, Mari C. *Sheep on the farm*
Scotton, Rob. *Russell and the lost treasure*
Russell the sheep
Russell's Christmas magic
Shaw, Nancy. *Sheep blast off!*
Sheep in a jeep
Sheep in a shop
Sheep on a ship
Sheep out to eat
Sheep take a hike
Sheep trick or treat
Sloat, Teri. *Farmer Brown shears his sheep*
Smallman, Steve. *The lamb who came for dinner*
Smith, Kathryn. *Little Lamb's Christmas story*
Stickland, Paul. *Bears*
Stockland, Patricia M. *In the sheep pasture*
Stohner, Anu. *Brave Charlotte*
Brave Charlotte and the wolves
Sundgaard, Arnold. *The lamb and the butterfly*
Tanner, Suzy-Jane. *Tinyflock Nursery School*
Taylor-Butler, Christine. *Lamb's Easter surprise*
Thompson, Lauren. *Wee little lamb*
Trapani, Iza. *Baa baa black sheep*
Baa baa black sheep [board book]
Urbigkit, Cat. *A young shepherd*
Watts, Leslie Elizabeth. *The Baabaasheep Quartet*
Weeks, Sarah. *Counting Ovejas*
Wheeler, Lisa. *Wool gathering*
Wiley, Thom. *One sheep, blue sheep*
Willis, Jeanne. *Misery Moo*
Wright, Maureen. *Barnyard fun*
Zalben, Jane Breskin. *Pearl's eight days of Chanukah*
Pearl's marigolds for grandpa

Animals – shrews

Goodall, John S. *Shrewbettina's birthday*
Weiss, Ellen. *The taming of Lola*

Animals – skunks

Crum, Shutta. *The bravest of the brave*
Greenberg, David. *Skunks*
Jenkins, Emily. *Skunkdog*
Newman, Lesléa. *Skunk's spring surprise*
Reed, Lynn Rowe. *Please don't upset P.U. Zorilla!*

Schmid, Paul. *A pet for Petunia*
Stevens, Jan Romero. *Carlos and the skunk / Carlos y el zorrillo*
Wells, Rosemary. *Fritz and the mess fairy*
Wilson, Karma. *Sweet Briar goes to camp*

Animals – sloths

Carle, Eric. *"Slowly, slowly, slowly," said the sloth*
Lester, Helen. *Score one for the sloths*
Seibold, J. Otto. *Lost sloth*

Animals – slugs

Colborn, Mary Palenick. *Rainy day slug*
Edwards, Pamela Duncan. *Some smug slug*
Krosoczka, Jarrett J. *My buddy, Slug*
Pearson, Susan. *How to teach a slug to read*
Slugs in love
Raschka, Chris. *Sluggy Slug*

Animals – snails

Ahlberg, Allan. *The snail house*
Allen, Judy. *Are you a snail?*
Base, Graeme. *The legend of the Golden Snail*
Dorros, Arthur. *When the pigs took over*
Foley, Greg. *Willoughby and the moon*
Freedman, Deborah. *The Story of Fish and Snail*
Leedy, Loreen. *The great graph contest*
Loomis, Christine. *The best Father's Day present ever*
Loth, Sebastian. *Clementine*
McGuirk, Leslie. *Snail boy*
May, Eleanor. *Albert's amazing snail*
Murguia, Bethanie Deeney. *Snippet the early riser*
Murphy, Mary. *Slow snail*
Reider, Katja. *Snail started it!*
Rempt, Fiona. *Snail's birthday wish*
Rosoff, Meg. *Jumpy Jack and Googily*
Saunders, Dave. *So slow!*
Veit, Barbara. *Who stole my house?*

Animals – snow leopards *see* Animals – leopards

Animals – squid *see* Squid

Animals – squirrels

Apperley, Dawn. *Don't wake the baby*
Bottner, Barbara. *Raymond and Nelda*
Bowers, Tim. *A new home*
Braun, Sebastien. *I love my mommy*
Bynum, Janie. *Nutmeg and Barley*
Cherry, Lynne. *How Groundhog's garden grew*
Chichester Clark, Emma. *Will and Squill*
Cooper, Helen. *Delicious!*
A pipkin of pepper
Ehlert, Lois. *Nuts to you!*
Emmett, Jonathan. *Leaf trouble*
Frazee, Marla. *Boot and Shoe*
Freeman, Don. *Earl the squirrel*
One more acorn
Genechten, Guido van. *Ricky and the squirrel*
George, Lindsay Barrett. *That pup!*
Glaser, Linda. *Hello, squirrels!*
Glass, Beth Raisner. *Blue-ribbon dad*
Grindley, Sally. *What will I do without you?*
Guthrie, James. *Last song*
Harper, Charise Mericle. *The trouble with normal*
Hawcock, Claire. *Mine, all mine!*
Iwamura, Kazuo. *Bedtime in the forest*
Hooray for fall!
Hooray for snow!
Hooray for spring!
Hooray for summer!
Kimmel, Eric A. *Pumpkinhead*
Kroll, Steven. *The squirrels' Thanksgiving*
Lithgow, John. *Micawber*
Lloyd-Jones, Sally. *Just because you're mine*
McElmurry, Jill. *Mario makes a move*
Miller, Pat. *Squirrel's New Year's resolution*
Muir, Leslie. *C.R. Mudgeon*
Peet, Bill. *Merle the high flying squirrel*
Pfister, Marcus. *Hopper's treetop adventure*
Potter, Beatrix. *The tale of Squirrel Nutkin*
The tale of Timmy Tiptoes
Quackenbush, Robert M. *Batbaby*
Raye, Rebekah. *The very best bed*
Roberts, Bethany. *Rosie to the rescue*
Rubin, Adam. *Those darn squirrels!*
Those darn squirrels and the cat next door
Those darn squirrels fly south
Shannon, George. *Heart to heart*
The surprise
Sherry, Kevin. *Acorns everywhere!*
Shore, Diane Z. *Look both ways*
Stein, David Ezra. *Ol' Mama Squirrel*
Stevenson, James. *Wilfred the rat*
Tafuri, Nancy. *The busy little squirrel*
Townsend, Emily Rose. *Squirrels*
Vainio, Pirkko. *Who hid the Easter eggs?*
Walsh, Ellen Stoll. *Dot and Jabber and the great acorn mystery*
Watt, Mélanie. *Scaredy Squirrel*
Scaredy Squirrel at night
Scaredy Squirrel at the beach
Scaredy Squirrel goes camping
Scaredy Squirrel has a birthday party
Scaredy Squirrel makes a friend
Scaredy Squirrel prepares for Christmas
Scaredy Squirrel prepares for Halloween
White, Alexina B. *Frisky brisky hippity hop*

Animals – swine *see* Animals – pigs

Animals – Tasmanian devils

Blake, Robert J. *Little devils*

Animals – tigers

Banks, Kate. *Close your eyes*
Bannerman, Helen. *The story of Little Babaji*
The story of Little Black Sambo (1990), ill. by Helen Bannerman
The story of Little Black Sambo (1996), ill. by Helen Bannerman
The story of Little Black Sambo, ill. by Christopher Bing
Bee, William. *Whatever*
Blackford, Harriet. *Tiger's story*
Brown, Peter. *Mr. Tiger goes wild*
Bunting, Eve. *Riding the tiger*
Chichester Clark, Emma. *Follow the leader!*
Child, Lauren. *Maude*
Chin, Oliver. *The year of the tiger*

Davies, Gill. *Wilbur waited*
Derrick, David G., Jr. *I'm the scariest thing in the jungle!*
Dowson, Nick. *Tigress*
Duncan, Lois. *Song of the circus*
Fore, S. J. *Read to Tiger*
Tiger can't sleep
Gliori, Debi. *Where did that baby come from?*
Goode, Diane. *Tiger trouble*
Hewett, Joan. *A tiger cub grows up*
Hoberman, Mary Ann. *"It's simple," said Simon*
Hoffman, Eric. *No fair to tigers / No es justo para los tigres*
Hogrogian, Nonny. *The tiger of Turkestan*
Kraus, Robert. *Leo the late bloomer*
Little Louie the baby bloomer
LaRochelle, David. *It's a tiger*
Lester, Julius. *Sam and the tigers*
London, Jonathan. *Little lost tiger*
Nagda, Anne Whitehead. *A tiger tale*
O'Brien, Patrick. *Sabertooth*
Partis, Joanne. *Stripe*
Stripe's naughty sister
Prelutsky, Jack. *The terrible tiger*
Rayner, Catherine. *Augustus and his smile*
Rumford, James. *Tiger and turtle*
St. Pierre, Stephanie. *Siberian tigers*
Seuss, Dr. *I can lick 30 tigers today and other stories*
Sheth, Kashmira. *Tiger in my soup*
Stewart, Amber. *Too small for my big bed*
Sykes, Julie. *I don't want to take a bath!*
Little Tiger's big surprise
Wait for me, Little Tiger
Temple, Frances. *Tiger soup*
Theodorou, Rod. *Bengal tiger*
Thomson, Sarah L. *Tigers*
Tseng, Grace. *White tiger, blue serpent*
Whitehouse, Patricia. *Tiger*
Winters, Kay. *Tiger trail*
Wolkstein, Diane. *The banza*
Xiong, Blia. *Nine-in-one Grr! Grr!*
Yep, Laurence. *Auntie Tiger*

Animals – voles

Schwartz, Roslyn. *The Vole brothers*

Animals – wallabies

Wild, Margaret. *Bobbie Dazzler*

Animals – walruses

Rotter, Charles. *Walruses*
Savage, Stephen. *Where's Walrus?*

Animals – warthogs

Base, Graeme. *Jungle drums*
Edwards, Pamela Duncan. *Slop goes the soup*
Warthogs in a box
Warthogs in the kitchen
Warthogs paint

Animals – weasels

George, Jean Craighead. *Frightful's daughter meets the Baron Weasel*
Grant, Rose Marie. *Andiamo, Weasel*
Shaw, Hannah. *Sneaky Weasel*

Animals – whales

Allen, Judy. *Whales and dolphins*
Auld, Mary. *The story of Jonah*
Barnett, Mac. *Billy Twitters and his big blue whale problem*
Bible. Old Testament. Jonah. *The Book of Jonah*
De Beer, Hans. *Little Polar Bear and the whales*
Edwardson, Debby Dahl. *Whale snow*
Fogliano, Julie. *If you want to see a whale*
Gentle, Victor. *Orcas, killer whales*
Gibbons, Gail. *Whales*
Goldsboro, Bobby. *Jonah and the whale; and, Daniel in the lion's den*
Hill, Ros. *Shamoo*
Hodson, Sally. *Granny's clan*
Horacek, Petr. *Puffin Peter*
James, Simon. *Dear Mr. Blueberry*
London, Jonathan. *Baby whale's journey*
Lucas, David. *The skeleton pirate*
Whale
Lunde, Darrin. *Hello, baby beluga*
O'Neill, Alexis. *Loud Emily*
Oppel, Kenneth. *Peg and the whale*
Pfister, Marcus. *Rainbow fish and the big blue whale*
Pinkney, Andrea Davis. *Peggony-Po*
Raff, Courtney Granet. *Giant of the sea*
Raffi. *Baby beluga*
Raschka, Chris. *Whaley Whale*
Robinson, Fiona. *Whale shines*
Rylant, Cynthia. *The whales*
Sayre, April Pulley. *Here come the humpbacks!*
Schuch, Steve. *A symphony of whales*
Siberell, Anne. *Whale in the sky*
Sís, Peter. *An ocean world*
Sobol, Richard. *Adelina's whales*
Spinelli, Eileen. *Jonah's whale*
Theodorou, Rod. *Blue whale*
Thomson, Sarah L. *Amazing whales*
Tokuda, Wendy. *Humphrey the lost whale*
Van Dusen, Chris. *Down to the sea with Mr. Magee*
Wood, Audrey. *Little Penguin's tale*

Animals – wolves

Aesop. *The boy who cried wolf*
The dog and the wolf
The wolf in sheep's clothing
Allen, Jonathan. *Mucky moose*
Alley, Zoe B. *There's a wolf at the door*
Andres, Kristina. *Good Little Wolf*
Asch, Frank. *Happy birthday, Big Bad Wolf*
Ziggy Piggy and the three little pigs
Bedard, Michael. *The wolf of Gubbio*
Belloni, Giulia. *Anything is possible*
Bently, Peter. *The great sheep shenanigans*
Bevis, Mary. *Wolf song*
Blades, Ann. *Mary of mile 18*
Brett, Jan. *The first dog*
Brimner, Larry Dane. *The littlest wolf*
Brown, Ken. *What's the time, Grandma Wolf?*
Brun-Cosme, Nadine. *Big Wolf and Little Wolf*
Big Wolf and Little Wolf, such a beautiful orange!
Burgess, Mark. *Where teddy bears come from*
Catusanu, Mircea. *The strange case of the missing sheep*
Child, Lauren. *Beware of the storybook wolves*
Christelow, Eileen. *Where's the big bad wolf?*
Cohn, Scotti. *One wolf howls*
Conway, David. *The great fairy tale disaster*

Crosby, Jeff. *Wiener Wolf*
Egan, Tim. *The experiments of Doctor Vermin*
Egielski, Richard. *St. Francis and the wolf*
Ernst, Lisa Campbell. *Little Red Riding Hood: a newfangled prairie tale*
Escoffier, Michael. *Rabbit and the Not-So-Big-Bad Wolf*
Fearnley, Jan. *Mr. Wolf and the three bears*
Mr. Wolf's pancakes
Felix, Monique. *The rumor*
George, Jean Craighead. *Look to the north*
Nutik and Amaroq play ball
Nutik, the wolf pup
The wolves are back
Gliori, Debi. *What's the time, Mr. Wolf?*
Godkin, Celia. *Wolf island*
Gorbachev, Valeri. *Nicky and the big, bad wolves*
Grant, Rose Marie. *Andiamo, Weasel*
Gravett, Emily. *Wolf won't bite!*
Wolves
Grimm, Jacob and Wilhelm. *Little red cap*
Little Red Riding Hood, ill. by Célia Chauffrey
Little Red Riding Hood, ill. by Gwen Connelly
Little Red Riding Hood, ill. by Trina Schart Hyman
Little Red Riding Hood, ill. by Jerry Pinkney
Little Red Riding Hood, ill. by Gennady Spirin
Little Red Riding Hood, ill. by Bernadette Watts
Little Red Riding Hood, ill. by Andrea Wisnewski
The story of Little Red Riding Hood
Guarnaccia, Steven. *The three little pigs: an architectural tale*
Hartman, Bob. *The wolf who cried boy*
Heinz, Brian J. *The wolves*
Helakoski, Leslie. *Big chickens*
Hennessy, B. G. *The boy who cried wolf*
Jagtenberg, Yvonne. *Jack the wolf*
Judes, Marie-Odile. *Max, the stubborn little wolf*
Kasza, Keiko. *The dog who cried wolf*
The wolf's chicken stew
Kelly, Mij. *One more sheep*
Kempter, Christa. *Dear Little Lamb*
Kimmel, Eric A. *Little Red Hot*
The three little tamales
Kimura, Yuichi. *One stormy night . . .*
One sunny day . . .
Klingel, Cynthia Fitterer. *Timber wolves*
Kolanovic, Dubravka. *Everyone needs a friend*
Krensky, Stephen. *Big bad wolves at school*
Kulka, Joe. *Wolf's coming*
Lairla, Sergio. *Abel and the wolf*
Lallemand, Orianne. *The wolf who wanted to change his color*
Langton, Jane. *Saint Francis and the wolf*
Lester, Helen. *The sheep in wolf's clothing*
Tacky the penguin
Levine, Gail Carson. *Betsy Red Hoodie*
Betsy who cried wolf
Lindbergh, Reeve. *Bridget and the gray wolves*
London, Jonathan. *Red wolf country*
Lowell, Susan. *Little Red Cowboy Hat*
MacDonald, Elizabeth. *The wolf is coming!*
McGee, Marni. *Winston the book wolf*
Machado, Ana Maria. *Wolf wanted*
McNaughton, Colin. *Oomph!*
Oops!
Preston's goal!
Suddenly!
Mallat, Kathy. *Papa pride*
Markle, Sandra. *Family pack*
Marshall, James. *Red Riding Hood*
Swine lake
Matsuoka, Mei. *Footprints in the snow*
Meddaugh, Susan. *The best place*
Hog-eye
Melling, David. *The Scallywags*
Moore, Maggie. *Little Red Riding Hood*
Mortimer, Rachael. *Red Riding Hood and the sweet little wolf*
Murphy, Yannick. *Ahwoooooooo!*
Murray, Marjorie Dennis. *Little Wolf and the moon*
Palatini, Margie. *Bad boys get cookie!*
Bad boys get henpecked!
Piggie pie
Perret, Delphine. *The Big Bad Wolf and me*
The Big Bad Wolf goes on vacation
Pichon, Liz. *The three horrid little pigs*
Pinkwater, Daniel. *Wolf Christmas*
Prokofiev, Sergei Sergeievitch. *Peter and the wolf*, ill. by Charles Mikolaycak
Peter and the wolf, ill. by Josef Palecek
Peter and the wolf, ill. by Chris Raschka
Peter and the wolf, ill. by Vladimir Vagin
Puttock, Simon. *Big bad wolf is good*
Ramos, Mario. *I am so handsome*
I am so strong
Reynolds, Aaron. *Carnivores*
Rocco, John. *Wolf! Wolf!*
Roche, Denis. *Little Pig is capable*
Roddie, Shen. *Not now, Mrs. Wolf*
Ross, Gayle. *How Turtle's back was cracked*
Ross, Tony. *The boy who cried wolf*
Roth, Susan L. *Kanahena*
Rueda, Claudia. *Huff and puff*
Let's play in the forest while the wolf is not around
Santangelo, Colony Elliott. *Brother Wolf of Gubbio*
Santore, Charles. *Three hungry pigs and the wolf who came to dinner*
Scieszka, Jon. *The true story of the three little pigs by A. Wolf, as told to Jon Scieszka*
Shireen, Nadia. *Good little wolf*
Sierra, Judy. *Mind your manners, B. B. Wolf*
Tell the truth, B. B. Wolf
Smallman, Steve. *The lamb who came for dinner*
Souhami, Jessica. *No dinner!*
Spinelli, Eileen. *Thanksgiving at the Tappletons'*
Stevenson, Harvey. *Big scary wolf*
Stohner, Anu. *Brave Charlotte and the wolves*
Sweet, Melissa. *Carmine*
Teague, Mark. *The three little pigs and the somewhat bad wolf*
Teckentrup, Britta. *Little Wolf's song*
The three little pigs. *The three little pigs*, ill. by Gavin Bishop
The three little pigs, ill. by Paul Galdone
The three little pigs, ill. by Rob Hefferan
The three little pigs, ill. by Steven Kellogg
The three little pigs, ill. by David McPhail
The three little pigs, ill. by James Marshall
The three little pigs, ill. by Bernadette Watts
The three little pigs, ill. by Margot Zemach
The three little pigs [board book]
The three little pigs / Los tres cerditos
The three little pigs and the big bad wolf
Trivizas, Eugenios. *The three little wolves and the big bad pig*
Vozar, David. *Yo, hungry wolf!*
Whatley, Bruce. *Wait! No paint!*

Whybrow, Ian. *Badness for beginners*
Wiesner, David. *The three pigs*
Winters, Kay. *Wolf watch*
Young, Ed. *Lon Po Po*
Yum, Hyewon. *There are no scary wolves*

Animals – wombats

Arnold, Caroline. *A wombat's world*
Churchill, Vicki. *Sometimes I like to curl up in a ball*
Fox, Mem. *Wombat divine*
French, Jackie. *Christmas wombat*
Diary of a baby wombat
Diary of a wombat
Fuge, Charles. *Swim, Little Wombat, swim!*
Where to, Little Wombat?
Lester, Helen. *Batter up Wombat*
McAllister, Angela. *Found you, Little Wombat!*
Morpurgo, Michael. *Wombat goes walkabout*
Shields, Carol Diggory. *Wombat walkabout*

Animals – woolly mammoths

Grambling, Lois G. *Can I bring Woolly to the library, Ms. Reeder?*
Hall, Algy Craig. *Mammoth and me*
Manning, Mick. *Woolly mammoth*
Miller, Debbie S. *Woolly mammoth journey*
Wheeler, Lisa. *Mammoths on the move*

Animals – worms

Bruel, Robert O. *Bob and Otto*
Caple, Kathy. *Worm gets a job*
Cronin, Doreen. *Diary of a worm*
French, Vivian. *Yucky worms*
Hemingway, Edward. *Bad apple*
Horacek, Petr. *Jonathan and Martha*
James, Brian. *Supertwins and the sneaky, slimy book worms*
Kaczman, James. *A bird and his worm*
Lackner, Michelle Myers. *Toil in the soil*
Martin, David. *Piggy and Dad go fishing*
Pfeffer, Wendy. *Wiggling worms at work*
Pinczes, Elinor J. *Inchworm and a half*
Raschka, Chris. *Wormy Worm*
Runton, Andy. *Owly and Wormy: bright lights and starry nights!*
Owly and Wormy: friends all aflutter!
San Souci, Robert D. *Two bear cubs: a Miwok legend from California's Yosemite Valley*
Scanlon, Elizabeth Garton. *Noodle and Lou*
Wells, Rosemary. *Max's worm cake*

Animals – yaks

Berger, Barbara. *All the way to Lhasa*
Johnston, Tony. *Go track a yak*
Kromhout, Rindert. *Little Donkey and the birthday present*
Stryer, Andrea Stenn. *Kami and the yaks*

Animals – zebras

Bingham, Kelly. *Z is for Moose*
Cabatingan, Erin. *A is for Musk Ox*
Musk Ox counts
Castle, Caroline. *Naughty!*
Gay, Michel. *Zee is not scared*
Miranda, Anne. *Alphabet fiesta*

Paterson, Brian. *Zigby camps out*
Zigby dives in
Zigby hunts for treasure
Peet, Bill. *Zella, Zack, and Zodiac*
Walker, Anna. *I love birthdays*
I love my dad
I love my mom

Anti-violence *see* Violence, nonviolence

Apartments *see* Homes, houses

Appearance *see* Character traits – appearance

Aquariums

Aliki. *My visit to the aquarium*
Buzzeo, Toni. *One cool friend*
Curious George goes to the aquarium
Levine, Ellen. *Seababy*
Poydar, Nancy. *Fish school*
Rechner, Amy. *Out and about at the aquarium*

Arachnids *see* Spiders

Arithmetic *see* Counting, numbers

Art

Agee, Jon. *The incredible painting of Felix Clousseau*
Alexander, Martha G. *Max and the dumb flower picture*
Andrews-Goebel, Nancy. *The pot that Juan built*
Angelou, Maya. *My painted house, my friendly chicken, and me*
Arrigan, Mary. *Mario's angels*
Auch, Mary Jane. *Eggs mark the spot*
Baylor, Byrd. *When clay sings*
Bilgrami, Shaheen. *Jungle art show*
Black, Harley. *Amazing magic school*
Brennan-Nelson, Denise. *Willow*
Brett, Jan. *The first dog*
Brown, Laurie Krasny. *Visiting the art museum*
Browne, Anthony. *The shape game*
Willy's pictures
Brunhoff, Laurent de. *Babar's Museum of Art*
Bryant, Jen. *A splash of red*
Carle, Eric. *The artist who painted a blue horse*
Hello, red fox
Cohen, Miriam. *No good in art*
Cohn, Diana. *Dream carver*
Compos, Tito. *Muffler man / El hombre mofle*
Court, Rob. *Color*
Cressy, Judith. *Can you find it?*
Can you find it, too?
Dawes, Kwame Senu Neville. *I saw your face*
Degen, Bruce. *I gotta draw*
dePaola, Tomie. *The art lesson*
Domeniconi, David. *M is for masterpiece*
Emberley, Ed. *Ed Emberley's big green drawing book*
Ed Emberley's big orange drawing book
Ed Emberley's big purple drawing book
Ed Emberley's drawing book
Engle, Margarita. *Summer birds*
Falken, Linda. *Can you find it?*

FitzGerald, Dawn. *Vinnie and Abraham*
Friedland, Katy. *Art museum opposites*
Gibbons, Gail. *The art box*
Hale, Christy. *Dreaming up*
Hartland, Jessie. *How the sphinx got to the museum*
Harvey, Jeanne Walker. *My hands sing the blues*
Haseley, Dennis. *Twenty heartbeats*
Hill, Laban Carrick. *Dave the potter*
Hillenbrand, Will. *Louie!*
Hogrogian, Nonny. *Cool cat*
Holub, Joan. *Vincent van Gogh*
Hong, Chen Jiang. *The magic horse of Han Gan*
Hooper, Meredith. *Celebrity cat*
Dogs' Night
Hopkins, Lee Bennett. *Behind the museum door*
Howell, Will C. *Zoo flakes ABC*
Hughes, Langston. *The sweet and sour animal book*
Hurd, Thacher. *Art dog*
Hutchins, Hazel. *The sidewalk rescue*
Hyde, Margaret E. *Matisse for kids*
Van Gogh for kids
I imagine angels
Isadora, Rachel. *ABC pop!*
Jackson, Shelley. *Mimi's Dada Catifesto*
Johnson, Crockett. *Harold and the purple crayon*
A picture for Harold's room
Johnson, D. B. *Magritte's marvelous hat*
Palazzo inverso
Jordan, Sandra. *Mr. and Mrs. Portly and their little dog Snack*
Kamm, Katja. *Invisible*
Kirk, Daniel. *Library mouse: a museum adventure*
Kitamura, Satoshi. *Pablo the artist*
Kleven, Elisa. *A carousel tale*
Knapp, Ruthie. *Who stole Mona Lisa?*
Larsen, Andrew. *The imaginary garden*
Lee-Tai, Amy. *A place where sunflowers grow / Sabaku ni saita himawari*
Lefebvre, Jason. *Too much glue*
Lin, Grace. *Robert's snowflakes*
Lionni, Leo. *Let's make rabbits*
Look, Lenore. *Brush of the gods*
McArthur, Meher. *An ABC of what art can be*
McCully, Emily Arnold. *The secret cave*
McDonald, Megan. *It's picture day today!*
McDonnell, Patrick. *Art*
Maestro, Betsy. *The story of the Statue of Liberty*
Magoon, Scott. *Hugo and Miles in I've painted everything!*
Maltbie, P. I. *Claude Monet: the painter who stopped the trains*
Markel, Michelle. *The fantastic jungles of Henri Rousseau*
Mayhew, James. *Katie and the Mona Lisa*
Katie and the sunflowers
Katie meets the Impressionists
Merberg, Julie. *In the garden with Van Gogh*
A magical day with Matisse
Metropolitan Museum of Art, NY. *Museum shapes*
Micklethwait, Lucy. *In the picture*
Moffatt, Judith. *Snow shapes*
Moon, Nicola. *Lucy's picture*
Moss, Marissa. *Regina's big mistake*
Napoli, Donna Jo. *Ready to dream*
Nikola-Lisa, W. *Magic in the margins*
The year with Grandma Moses
Nolan, Janet. *A Father's Day thank you*
O'Connor, Jane. *Fancy Nancy: aspiring artist*
Parker, Marjorie Blain. *Colorful dreamer*
Peet, Bill. *Encore for Eleanor*
Pilkey, Dav. *When cats dream*
Pinkwater, Daniel. *Bear's Picture*
Piven, Hanoch. *Let's make faces*
Polacco, Patricia. *The art of Miss Chew*
Raczka, Bob. *Art is . . .*
No one saw
Rey, Margret. *Billy's picture*
Reynolds, Aaron. *Metal man*
Reynolds, Peter H. *The dot*
Ish
Ringgold, Faith. *Dinner at Aunt Connie's house*
Robinson, Fiona. *Whale shines*
Rodríguez, Rachel Victoria. *Through Georgia's eyes*
Rogers, Gregory. *The hero of Little Street*
Rubin, Susan Goldman. *Matisse dance for joy*
The yellow house
Rylant, Cynthia. *All I see*
Scanlon, Elizabeth Garton. *Think big!*
Schaefer, A. R. *Alexander Calder*
Diego Rivera
Grandma Moses
Shapiro, J. H. *Magic trash*
Sherry, Kevin. *I'm the best artist in the ocean*
Sierra, Judy. *Ballyhoo Bay*
Spinelli, Eileen. *Sophie's masterpiece*
Stone, Tanya Lee. *Sandy's circus*
Tate, Don. *It jes' happened*
Taylor, Harriet Peck. *Secrets of the stone*
Tonatiuh, Duncan. *Diego Rivera: his world and ours*
Tougas, Chris. *Art's supplies*
Tusa, Tricia. *Bunnies in my head*
Stay away from the junkyard!
Vande Griek, Susan. *The art room*
Velasquez, Eric. *Grandma's gift*
Verde, Susan. *The museum*
Wahl, Jan. *The art collector*
Waldman, Neil. *The starry night*
Wallace, Nancy Elizabeth. *Look! Look! Look!*
Look! Look! Look! at sculpture
Wallner, Alexandra. *Beatrix Potter*
Weitzman, Jacqueline Preiss. *You can't take a balloon into the Metropolitan Museum*
You can't take a balloon into the National Gallery
Wellington, Monica. *Squeaking of art, the mice go to the museum*
Wheatley, Nadia. *Luke's way of looking*
Whitman, Candace. *Lines that wiggle*
Wiesner, David. *Art and Max*
Williams, Vera B. *Cherries and cherry pits*
Winter, Jeanette. *Cowboy Charlie*
Henri's scissors
My baby
Winter, Jonah. *Diego*
Just behave, Pablo Picasso!
Wood, Michele. *Going back home*
Yolleck, Joan. *Paris in the spring with Picasso*
Zalben, Jane Breskin. *Mousterpiece*
Ziarnik, Natalie. *Madeleine's light*
Zuffi, Stefano. *Art 123*

Assertiveness *see* Character traits – assertiveness

Astrology *see* Zodiac

Astronauts *see* Careers – astronauts; Space & space ships

Astronomy

Alberti, Theresa Jarosz. *Out and about at the planetarium*
Asch, Frank. *The sun is my favorite star*
Barner, Bob. *Stars, stars, stars*
Gibbons, Gail. *The planets*
Stargazers
Hirst, Robin. *My place in space*
Holland, Simon. *Space*
Leedy, Loreen. *Postcards from Pluto*
Parker, Michael. *You are a star!*
Pettenati, Jeanne K. *Galileo's journal, 1609–1610*
Sís, Peter. *Starry messenger*
Sykes, Julie. *Little Rocket's special star*
Tomecek, Steve. *Stars*

Aurora Borealis *see* Northern lights

Australian aborigines

Lester, Alison. *Ernie dances to the didgeridoo*
Wolkstein, Diane. *Sun Mother wakes the world*

Authors *see* Careers – writers

Authors, children *see* Children as authors

Automobiles

Bair, Sheila. *Isabel's car wash*
Barton, Byron. *My car*
Bee, William. *And the cars go . . .*
Bell, Babs. *The bridge is up!*
Sputter, sputter, sput!
Best, Cari. *When Catherine the Great and I were eight!*
Biggs, Brian. *123 beep beep beep!*
Blake, Quentin. *Mrs. Armitage*
Blechman, Nicholas. *Night light*
Braithwaite, Jill. *Police cars*
Bridwell, Norman. *Clifford's good deeds*
Burningham, John. *Mr. Gumpy's motor car*
Christelow, Eileen. *Five little monkeys wash the car*
Collicutt, Paul. *This car*
Coy, John. *Vroomaloom zoom*
Crimi, Carolyn. *Pugs in a Bug*
Dahl, Michael. *One checkered flag*
Dale, Penny. *Dinosaur zoom!*
Drummond, Allan. *Tin Lizzie*
Ernst, Lisa Campbell. *This is the van that Dad cleaned*
Flanagan, Alice K. *Mr. Yee fixes cars*
Gammell, Stephen. *How about going for a ride*
Gibbons, Gail. *Fill it up!*
Harper, Jamie. *Miles to go*
Herzog, Brad. *R is for race*
Horacek, Petr. *Beep beep*
Howland, Naomi. *ABCDrive!*
Hubbell, Patricia. *Cars: rushing! honking! zooming!*
Hurd, Thacher. *Sleepy Cadillac*
Zoom City
Kenney, Sean. *Cool cars and trucks*
Kirk, Daniel. *Honk honk! Beep beep!*
Kirk, David. *Miss Spider's new car*
Kolar, Bob. *Racer dogs*
LaReau, Kara. *Otto: the boy who loved cars*
LaRochelle, David. *Moo!*
Lord, Cynthia. *Hot rod Hamster*
Lynn, Sarah. *1-2-3 va-va-vroom!*
Maccarone, Grace. *Cars! Cars! Cars!*
McMullan, Kate. *I'm fast*
Mahy, Margaret. *The rattlebang picnic*
Manzano, Sonia. *No dogs allowed*
Marshall, James. *The Cut-Ups crack up*
Medina, Meg. *Tía Isa wants a car*
Meister, Cari. *Busy, busy city street*
Merlin, Christophe. *Under the hood*
Milusich, Janice. *Off go their engines, off go their lights*
Miranda, Anne. *Beep! beep!*
Vroom, chugga, vroom-vroom
Mitton, Tony. *Cool cars*
Murphy, Stuart J. *Beep beep, vroom vroom!*
Nobles, Kristen M. *Drive this book*
Pearson, Debora. *Alphabeep*
Peet, Bill. *Jennifer and Josephine*
Perry, Michael. *Daniel's ride*
Pratt, Pierre. *Car*
Rex, Michael. *My race car*
Rockwell, Anne. *Cars*
Rogers, Hal. *Cars*
Root, Phyllis. *Rattletrap car*
Rattletrap car [board book]
Toot toot zoom!
Rylant, Cynthia. *Brownie and Pearl go for a spin*
Tulip sees America
The scrubbly-bubbly car wash
Shulman, Mark. *Gorilla Garage*
Shuter, Jane. *Henry Ford*
Soto, Gary. *My little car / Mi carrito*
Stanley, Mandy. *On the move*
Steen, Sandra. *Car wash*
Steggall, Susan. *The life of a car*
Stein, Peter. *Cars galore*
Stille, Darlene R. *Police cars*
Suen, Anastasia. *Red light, green light*
Timmers, Leo. *Who is driving?*
Todd, Mark. *Start your engines*
van Lieshout, Maria. *Backseat A-B-see*
Walters, Virginia. *Are we there yet, Daddy?*
Weston, Mark. *Honda*
Zane, Alexander. *The wheels on the race car*

Autumn *see* Seasons – fall

Award-winning books *see* Caldecott award books; Caldecott award honor books

Babies *see also* Animals – babies

Adler, Victoria. *All of baby nose to toes*
Baby, come away
Ahlberg, Janet. *The baby's catalogue*
Peek-a-boo!
Alexander, Martha G. *Nobody asked me if I wanted a baby sister*
Aliki. *Welcome, little baby*
Alko, Selina. *I'm your peanut butter big brother*
American babies
Andreae, Giles. *There's a house inside my mommy*
Anholt, Catherine. *What makes me happy?*
Anholt, Laurence. *Sophie and the new baby*
Appelt, Kathi. *Brand-new baby blues*
Apperley, Dawn. *Don't wake the baby*
Archer, Peggy. *From dawn to dreams*
Arnosky, Jim. *Babies in the bayou*
Asher, Sandy. *Here comes Gosling!*
Ashman, Linda. *Mama's day*
When I was king
Aston, Dianna Hutts. *Mama Outside, Mama Inside*
Baek, Matthew J. *Be gentle with the dog, dear*
Baicker, Karen. *Pea pod babies*
Ballard, Robin. *I used to be the baby*
Banks, Kate. *This baby*
Bauer, Marion Dane. *Grandmother's song*
Bennett, Barbara. *Lion's precious gift*
Bennett, Kelly. *Vampire baby*
Bertrand, Lynne. *Granite baby*
Boelts, Maribeth. *You're a brother, Little Bunny!*
Bourgeois, Paulette. *Franklin's baby sister*
Bowen, Anne. *I loved you before you were born*
When you visit Grandma and Grandpa
Brenner, Barbara A. *What the elephant told*
Broach, Elise. *What the no-good baby is good for*
Brown, Marc. *Arthur's baby*
Brownlow, Mike. *Way out West — with a baby!*
Bunting, Eve. *Baby can*
Will it be a baby brother?
Burell, Sarah. *Diamond Jim Dandy and the sheriff*
Burningham, John. *There's going to be a baby*
Calmenson, Stephanie. *Good for you!*
Welcome, baby!
Carlstrom, Nancy White. *Before you were born*
Carter, Alden R. *Big brother Dustin*
Ceelen, Vicky. *Baby! baby!*
Charlip, Remy. *Baby hearts and baby flowers*
Sleepytime rhyme
Chichester Clark, Emma. *Will and Squill*
Chorao, Kay. *Knock at the door and other baby action rhymes*
Cocca-Leffler, Maryann. *Theo's mood*
Time to say bye-bye
Cocovini, Abby. *What's inside your tummy, Mommy?*
Coffelt, Nancy. *Catch that baby!*
Cohen, Caron Lee. *Happy to you!*
Cole, Babette. *Truelove*
Cole, Brock. *Larky Mavis*
Cole, Joanna. *How you were born*
I'm a big brother
I'm a big sister
The new baby at your house
When you were inside mommy
Collicott, Sharleen. *Mildred and Sam*
Cooke, Trish. *So much*
Cowell, Cressida. *What shall we do with the Boo-Hoo Baby?*
Creech, Sharon. *Who's that baby?*
Crum, Shutta. *Mine!*
Cuetara, Mittie. *Baby business*
Cullen, Catherine Ann. *Thirsty baby*
Cummings, Pat. *Angel baby*
Curtis, Jamie Lee. *Tell me again about the night I was born*
When I was little
Davies, Gill. *Wilbur waited*
Dempsey, Sheena. *Bye-bye baby brother!*
dePaola, Tomie. *The baby sister*
Baby's first Christmas
Dewan, Ted. *Baby gets the zapper*
Crispin and the 3 little piglets
Diesen, Deborah. *The barefooted, bad-tempered baby brigade*
Dixon, Ann. *Waiting for Noël*
Doerrfeld, Cori. *Penny loves pink*
Douglas, Ann. *Before you were born*
Downes, Belinda. *Baby days*
Doyle, Malachy. *Baby see, baby do!*
Dunbar, Joyce. *Shoe baby*
Dunrea, Olivier. *It's snowing*
Dyer, Jane. *Little Brown Bear and the bundle of joy*
Elkin, Mark. *Samuel's baby*
Elya, Susan Middleton. *Bebé goes shopping*
Bebé goes to the beach
Enersen, Adele. *When my baby dreams*
English, Karen. *The baby on the way*
Falwell, Cathryn. *We have a baby*
Fearnley, Jan. *A special something*
Feiffer, Kate. *But I wanted a baby brother!*
No go sleep!
Fleming, Candace. *Seven hungry babies*
Ford, Bernette. *No more pacifier for Piggy!*
Fox, Mem. *Hello, baby!*
Ten little fingers and ten little toes
Frasier, Debra. *On the day you were born*
Frazee, Marla. *The boss baby*
Hush, little baby: a folk song with pictures
Walk on!
Frederick, Heather Vogel. *Babyberry pie*
French, Simon. *Guess the baby*
Gentieu, Penny. *Baby! Talk!*
Grow! babies!
Gershator, Phillis. *This is the day!*
Gliori, Debi. *Mr. Bear's new baby*
Penguin post
Where did that baby come from?
Graham, Bob. *The silver button*
Grambling, Lois G. *Grandma tells a story*
Green, Jen. *Our new baby*
Greenstein, Elaine. *As big as you*

Grimes, Nikki. *Welcome, Precious*
Gutman, Anne. *Lisa's baby sister*
Haley, Amanda. *It's a baby's world*
Hanson, Mary Elizabeth. *The difference between babies and cookies*
Harris, Robie H. *Hi, new baby*
What's in there?
Havill, Juanita. *Just like a baby*
Hawkes, Kevin. *The wicked big toddlah*
The wicked big toddlah goes to New York
Heiligman, Deborah. *Babies*
Henderson, Kathy. *Baby knows best*
Look at you!
Heos, Bridget. *Mustache baby*
Hest, Amy. *The babies are coming!*
Off to school, Baby Duck
You're the boss, Baby Duck
Hiatt, Fred. *Baby talk*
Hill, Susanna Leonard. *Not yet, Rose*
Hillenbrand, Will. *Fiddle-i-fee*
Hindley, Judy. *Baby talk*
What's in baby's morning
Hines, Anna Grossnickle. *Big like me*
Höjer, Dan. *Heart of mine*
Holabird, Katharine. *Angelina's baby sister*
Holt, Kimberly Willis. *Waiting for Gregory*
Hop a little, jump a little!
Horse, Harry. *Little Rabbit's new baby*
Hort, Lenny. *We're going on a treasure hunt*
We're going on safari
Hru, Dakari. *Tickle, tickle*
Hubbell, Patricia. *Bouncing time*
Wrapping paper romp
Hughes, Shirley. *Olly and me*
Hurwitz, Johanna. *Russell's secret*
Hush, little baby
Hutchins, Hazel. *Two so small*
Hutchins, Pat. *Where's the baby?*
Intrater, Roberta Grobel. *Peek-a-boo!*
Smile!
Isadora, Rachel. *Peekaboo morning [board book]*
James, Simon. *Baby Brains and RoboMom*
Janovitz, Marilyn. *Baby, Baby, Baby!*
Play baby play!
Jenkins, Emily. *That new animal*
Johnston, Tony. *Laugh-out-loud baby*
Kallok, Emma. *Gem*
Katz, Karen. *The babies on the bus*
Baby loves winter!
Now I'm big
Over the moon
Princess Baby
Princess Baby, night-night
Ten tiny babies
Ten tiny tickles
Where is baby's mommy?
Katz, Susan B. *ABC, baby me!*
Keats, Ezra Jack. *Peter's chair*
Keller, Holly. *Geraldine's baby brother*
Kleven, Elisa. *A monster in the house*
Koller, Jackie French. *Baby for sale*
Krishnaswami, Uma. *Bringing Asha home*
Landolf, Diane Wright. *What a good big brother!*
Lasky, Kathryn. *Baby love*
Lawrence, Michael. *Baby loves*
Layne, Steven L. *Love the baby*
Leigh, Heather. *Hey little baby!*
L'Engle, Madeleine. *The other dog*
Leonard, Marcia. *Babies help out*
Peek-a-boo, baby!
Lester, J. D. *Mommy calls me Monkeypants*
Lewis, Rose A. *I love you like crazy cakes*
Lindgren, Barbro. *Benny and the binky*
Lloyd-Jones, Sally. *How to be a baby — by me, the big sister*
Lobel, Gillian. *Too small for honey cake*
Lohans, Alison. *Waiting for the sun*
Long, Steffanie. *Such a silly baby!*
Look, Lenore. *Henry's first-moon birthday*
Lund, Deb. *Tell me my story, Mama*
Lyon, George Ella. *Sleepsong*
McCarty, Peter. *Baby steps*
McCormick, Wendy. *The night you were born*
MacDonald, Ross. *Bad baby*
McElmurry, Jill. *I'm not a baby!*
Mackall, Dandi Daley. *There's a baby in there!*
Macken, JoAnn Early. *Baby says "moo!"*
MacLachlan, Patricia. *All the places to love*
Before you came
Bittle
You were the first
McLean, Janet. *Let's go, baby-o!*
McMullan, Kate. *If you were my bunny*
Papa's song
Rock-a-baby band
Supercat to the rescue
McNaughton, Colin. *Captain Abdul's little treasure*
McQuinn, Anna. *Lola reads to Leo*
Mahy, Margaret. *Boom Baby boom, boom*
Manning, Jane. *My first baby games*
Manzano, Sonia. *A box full of kittens*
Margalith, Joan. *The babies are landing*
Marzollo, Jean. *Baby's alphabet*
Do you know new?
Melmed, Laura Krauss. *The rainbabies*
Mendes, Valerie. *Look at me, Grandma!*
Meyers, Susan. *Everywhere babies*
Rock-a-bye room
This is the way a baby rides
Michels-Gualtieri, Akaela S. *I was born to be a sister*
Milgrim, David. *Best baby ever*
Miller, Margaret. *Baby faces*
I love colors
Now I'm big
Milord, Susan. *Love that baby*
Moon, Nicola. *Something special*
Morris, Richard. *Bye-bye, baby!*
Morrow, Tara Jaye. *Mommy loves her baby; Daddy loves his baby*
Moses, Will. *Silent night*
Munsch, Robert N. *Alligator baby*
Murkoff, Heidi Eisenberg. *What to expect when the new baby comes home*
Newman, Marjorie. *Just like me*
Nichols, Grace. *Whoa, Baby, whoa!*
North, Sherry. *Because you are my baby*
Novak, Matt. *A wish for you*
Oborne, Martine. *One beautiful baby*
O'Connell, Rebecca. *Baby parade*
O'Hair, Margaret. *Star baby*
Sweet baby feet
O'Keefe, Susan Heyboer. *Baby day*
Okimoto, Jean Davies. *The White Swan express*
O'Malley, Kevin. *Once upon a royal superbaby*
Orlean, Susan. *Lazy little loafers*
Osofsky, Audrey. *Dreamcatcher*
Overend, Jenni. *Welcome with love*
Palatini, Margie. *Goldie is mad*

Patricelli, Leslie. *Baby happy, baby sad*
Binky
Blankie
Fa la la
No no, yes yes
Patz, Nancy. *Babies can't eat kimchee!*
Peddicord, Jane Ann. *That special little baby*
Pinkney, Brian. *Hush, little baby*
Puttock, Simon. *The baby that roared*
Radunsky, Vladimir. *Ten*
Rand, Gloria. *Baby in a basket*
Reiser, Lynn. *My baby and me*
Reynolds, Marilynn. *The name of the child*
Rheingrover, Jean Sasso. *Veronica's first year*
Richards, Laura Elizabeth Howe. *Jiggle joggle jee*
Robberecht, Thierry. *Back into Mommy's tummy*
Robbins, Beth. *Tom, Ally, and the new baby*
Rock, Lois. *Now we have a baby*
Rockwell, Anne. *Long ago yesterday*
Once upon a time this morning
Rockwell, Lizzy. *Hello baby!*
Roddie, Shen. *Toes are to tickle*
Rogers, Fred. *The new baby*
Root, Phyllis. *Mrs. Potter's pig*
What Baby wants
Roper, Janice M. *Dancing on the moon*
Rosen, Michael. *Howler*
Rosenberg, Maxine B. *Mommy's in the hospital having a baby*
Ross, Michael Elsohn. *Mama's milk*
Russo, Marisabina. *Come back, Hannah*
Hannah's baby sister
Peter is just a baby
Rylant, Cynthia. *Baby face: a book of love for baby*
Salariya, David. *All about me!*
Saltzberg, Barney. *Cornelius P. Mud, are you ready for baby?*
Sartell, Debra. *Time for bed, Baby Ted*
Savadier, Elivia. *Time to get dressed!*
Schaefer, Lola M. *One special day*
Scheffler, Ursel. *Taking care of Sister Bear*
Schroeder, Lisa. *Baby can't sleep*
Sears, William, M.D. *Baby on the way*
Sears, William, M.D., et al. *What baby needs*
Sendak, Maurice. *Outside over there*
Shannon, David. *David smells*
Oh, David!
Oops! a diaper David book
Shapiro, Jody Fickes. *Family lullaby*
Shapiro, Lawrence E. *It's time to give up your pacifier*
Shea, Pegi Deitz. *I see me!*
Sheldon, Annette. *Big sister now*
Shields, Carol Diggory. *I wish my brother was a dog*
Shipton, Jonathan. *Baby baby blah blah blah!*
Singer, Marilyn. *City lullaby*
Slater, Dashka. *Baby shoes*
Smith, Charles R. *I'll be there*
My gal
Smith, Maggie. *One naked baby*
Sockabasin, Allen. *Thanks to the animals*
Solheim, James. *Born yesterday*
Springstubb, Tricia. *Phoebe and Digger*
Stanley, Malaika Rose. *Baby Ruby bawled*
Steptoe, John. *Baby says*
Stevens, April. *Edwin speaks up*
Stevenson, James. *Rolling Rose*
Worse than Willy!
Stoeke, Janet Morgan. *A friend for Minerva Louise*
Stuve-Bodeen, Stephanie. *Mama Elizabeti*
Suen, Anastasia. *Baby born*
Baby born [board book]
Sullivan, Sarah. *Dear Baby*
Tabby, Abigail. *Baby face*
Tafolla, Carmen. *Fiesta babies*
Tafuri, Nancy. *The ball bounced*
Tarpley, Todd. *Ten tiny toes*
Taylor, Ann. *Baby dance*
Taylor, Sean. *When a monster is born*
Thomas, Joyce Carol. *You are my perfect baby*
Thomas, Shelley Moore. *A baby's coming to your house*
Thong, Roseanne. *Tummy girl*
Titherington, Jeanne. *Baby's boat*
A place for Ben
Vamos, Samantha R. *Before you were here, mi amor*
Van Laan, Nancy. *Mama rocks, Papa sings*
Van Leeuwen, Jean. *Benny and beautiful baby Delilah*
Vulliamy, Clara. *Ellen and Penguin and the new baby*
Waddell, Martin. *When the teddy bears came*
Wahl, Jan. *Mabel ran away with the toys*
Waiting for baby
Walton, Rick. *Baby's first year!*
What do we do with the baby?
Wangerin, Walter. *Water come down*
Wardlaw, Lee. *The chair where bear sits*
Weeks, Sarah. *Bite me, I'm a book*
Bite me, I'm a shape
Overboard!
Sophie Peterman tells the truth!
Wells, Rosemary. *McDuff and the baby*
Max cleans up
Weninger, Brigitte. *Will you mind the baby, Davy?*
Wheeler, Lisa. *Jazz baby*
Whybrow, Ian. *A baby for Grace*
Wigersma, Tanneke. *Baby brother*
Wild, Margaret. *Itsy-bitsy babies*
Midnight babies
Williams, Vera B. *A chair for always*
"More more more," said the baby
Willis, Jeanne. *What did I look like when I was a baby?*
Wilner, Isabel. *The baby's game book*
Winter, Jeanette. *My baby*
Withrow, Sarah. *Be a baby*
Wong, Janet S. *Grump*
Woodson, Jacqueline. *Pecan pie baby*
Yolen, Jane. *Grandma's hurrying child*
Young, Amy. *Don't eat the baby!*
Zalben, Jane Breskin. *Baby Babka*
Ziefert, Harriet. *Pushkin meets the bundle*
Pushkin minds the bundle
Talk, baby!
Waiting for baby
Zolotow, Charlotte. *Do you know what I'll do?*

Babies, new *see* Family life – new sibling

Bad day *see* Behavior – bad day

Ballerinas *see* Ballet; Careers – dancing

Ballet

Allen, Debbie. *Dancing in the wings*
Auch, Mary Jane. *Hen lake*
Peeping Beauty

Bansch, Helga. *Brava, Mimi!*
Bonwill, Ann. *Naughty toes*
Bradley, Kimberly Brubaker. *Ballerino Nate*
Brandenberg, Alexa. *Ballerina flying*
Capucilli, Alyssa Satin. *My first ballet class*
Chaconas, Dori. *Dancing with Katya*
Corey, Shana. *Ballerina bear*
Cristaldi, Kathryn. *Baseball ballerina*
Baseball ballerina strikes out
Crow, Kristyn. *Zombelina*
DePalma, Mary Newell. *The Nutcracker doll*
dePaola, Tomie. *Oliver Button is a sissy*
Edwards, Pamela Duncan. *Honk!*
Ellwand, David. *Cinderlily*
Ferguson, Sarah. *Ballerina Rosie*
The firebird. *The firebird*, ill. by Demi
The firebird, ill. by Rachel Isadora
The tale of the firebird
Ford, Bernette. *Ballet Kitty*
French, Jackie. *Josephine wants to dance*
Gauch, Patricia Lee. *Bravo, Tanya*
Dance, Tanya
Presenting Tanya, the Ugly Duckling
Tanya and Emily in a dance for two
Geras, Adèle. *Giselle*
Little ballet star
The nutcracker
Sleeping beauty
Swan Lake
Time for ballet
Goodman, Joan Elizabeth. *Ballet Bunnies*
Gorbachev, Valeri. *Catty Jane who loved to dance*
Greenberg, Jan. *Ballet for Martha*
Gruska, Denise. *The only boy in ballet class*
Hague, Michael. *The nutcracker*
Hayward, Linda. *A day in the life of a dancer*
Headley, Justina Chen. *The patch*
Hoffmann, E. T. A. *The nutcracker*, ill. by Renée Graef
The nutcracker, ill. by Alison Jay
The nutcracker, ill. by Peter Malone
The nutcracker, ill. by Maurice Sendak
The nutcracker, ill. by Lisbeth Zwerger
The Nutcracker and the Mouse King
The nutcracker ballet
Holabird, Katharine. *Angelina and the princess*
Angelina at the palace
Angelina ballerina
Angelina dances
Angelina on stage
Angelina's ballet class
Christmas in Mouseland
Howe, James. *Brontorina*
Isadora, Rachel. *Bea at ballet*
Lili at ballet
Lili on stage
Not just tutus
Jennings, Sharon. *Priscilla's paw de deux*
Kent, Allegra. *Ballerina swan*
Kinerk, Robert. *Clorinda*
Kroll, Virginia L. *Can you dance, Dalila?*
Lasky, Kathryn. *Starring Lucille*
Lowell, Susan. *Josefina javelina*
Maccarone, Grace. *Miss Lina's ballerinas*
Miss Lina's ballerinas and the prince
Miss Lina's ballerinas and the wicked wish
McEvoy, Anne. *Betsy B. Little*
Manson, Ainslie. *Ballerinas don't wear glasses*
Marshall, James. *Swine lake*
Mayhew, James. *Ella Bella ballerina and Swan Lake*
Ella Bella ballerina and The Nutcracker
Ella Bella ballerina and The sleeping beauty
Mills, Elaine. *Marinetta at the ballet*
Nelson, Marilyn. *Beautiful ballerina*
Newman, Lesléa. *Miss Tutu's star*
Newsome, Jill. *Dream dancer*
Numeroff, Laura Joffe. *The Jellybeans and the big dance*
Pace, Anne Marie. *Vampirina ballerina*
Vampirina ballerina hosts a sleepover
Pavlova, Anna. *I dreamed I was a ballerina*
Pennypacker, Sara. *Pierre in love*
Peters, Bernadette. *Stella is a star!*
Pinkwater, Daniel. *Dancing Larry*
Polacco, Patricia. *Rotten Richie and the ultimate dare*
Pulver, Robin. *Alicia's tutu*
Rodriguez, Sonia. *T is for tutu*
Schomp, Virginia. *If you were a . . . ballet dancer*
Schubert, Leda. *Ballet of the elephants*
Shulman, Lisa. *Over in the meadow at the big ballet*
Singer, Marilyn. *Tallulah's Nutcracker*
Tallulah's solo
Tallulah's toe shoes
Tallulah's tutu
Sís, Peter. *Ballerina*
Skeers, Linda. *Tutus aren't my style*
Stanley, Mandy. *Lettice the dancing rabbit*
Thompson, Lauren. *Ballerina dreams*
Weeks, Sarah. *Ella, of course!*
Yolen, Jane. *The firebird*
Young, Amy. *Belinda and the glass slipper*
Belinda begins ballet
Belinda in Paris
Belinda, the ballerina

Balloons *see* Toys – balloons

Balls *see* Toys – balls

Barns

Atwell, Debby. *Barn*
Johnston, Tony. *The barn owls*
Martin, Bill, Jr. *Barn dance!*
Schubert, Leda. *Here comes Darrell*
Tafuri, Nancy. *The barn party*
Yolen, Jane. *Raising Yoder's barn*

Beaches *see* Sea & seashore – beaches

Beasts *see* Monsters

Beauty shops

Buehner, Caralyn. *The queen of style*
Caseley, Judith. *In style with Grandma Antoinette*
Choung, Euh-hee. *Minji's Salon*
Daly, Niki. *A song for Jamela*
Munsch, Robert N. *Makeup mess*
O'Connor, Jane. *Fancy Nancy: ooh la la! it's beauty day*
Schotter, Roni. *Mama, I'll give you the world*
Wells, Rosemary. *Ruby's beauty shop*

Bedtime

Adams, Diane. *I can do it myself!*
Adler, David A. *It's time to sleep, it's time to dream*
Alborough, Jez. *Yes*
Alda, Arlene. *Sheep, sheep, sheep, help me fall asleep*
Allen, Elanna. *Itsy Mitsy runs away*
Anderson, Christine. *Bedtime!*
Anderson, Peggy Perry. *Time for bed, the babysitter said*
Appelt, Kathi. *Cowboy dreams*
Apperley, Dawn. *Blossom and Boo stay up late*
Good night, sleep tight, little bunnies
Apple, Margot. *Brave Martha*
Arnold, Marsha Diane. *Roar of a snore*
Arnold, Tedd. *No jumping on the bed!*
Asch, Frank. *Good night, Baby Bear*
Ashman, Linda. *How to make a night*
Starry safari
Asper-Smith, Sarah. *I would tuck you in*
Averbeck, Jim. *In a blue room*
Aylesworth, Jim. *Teddy bear tears*
Baguley, Elizabeth. *A long way from home*
Bailey, Linda. *Goodnight, sweet pig*
Baker, Ken. *Brave little monster*
Baker, Roberta. *Olive's first sleepover*
Ballard, Robin. *Tonight and tomorrow*
Bang, Molly. *Ten, nine, eight*
Banks, Kate. *The bear in the book*
Bardhan-Quallen, Sudipta. *Chicks run wild*
Baring-Gould, S. *Now the day is over*
Bauer, Marion Dane. *Sleep, little one, sleep*
Baum, Louis. *The mouse who braved bedtime*
Bea, Holly. *Bless your heart*
Bean, Jonathan. *At night*
Beaton, Clare. *Clare Beaton's bedtime rhymes*
Beaty, Andrea. *Hush, Baby Ghostling*
Beaumont, Karen. *Dini Dinosaur*
No sleep for the sheep!
Beck, Andrea. *Elliot's noisy night*
Becker, Bonny. *A bedtime for Bear*
Berenstain, Stan and Jan. *Bears in the night*
The Berenstain bears and the slumber party
Bergman, Mara. *Musical beds*
Oliver who would not sleep!
Blackall, Sophie. *Are you awake?*
Bluemle, Elizabeth. *Dogs on the bed*
Boelts, Maribeth. *Looking for Sleepy*
Sweet dreams, Little Bunny!
Bogan, Paulette. *Goodnight Lulu*
Bond, Felicia. *Poinsettia and the firefighters*
Bonnett-Rampersaud, Louise. *Bubble and Squeak*
Boudreau, Hélène. *I dare you not to yawn*
Bradley, Kimberly Brubaker. *Favorite things*
Branford, Henrietta. *Little Pig Figwort can't get to sleep*
Braun, Sebastien. *Back to bed, Ed!*
Briggs, Kelly Paul. *Lighthouse lullaby*
Bright, Paul. *The bears in the bed and the great big storm*
Brisson, Pat. *Star blanket*
Brown, Margaret Wise. *Goodnight moon*
Goodnight moon ABC
Goodnight moon 123: a counting book
Goodnight moon 123: a counting book [board book]
Sleepy ABC, ill. by Karen Katz
Sleepy ABC, ill. by Esphyr Slobodkina
Brunelle, Nicholas. *Snow moon*
Burnell, Heather Ayris. *Bedtime monster / ¡A dormir, pequeño monstruo!*
Butler, John. *Bedtime in the jungle*
Can you growl like a bear?
While you were sleeping
Cabrera, Jane. *Bear's good night*
Ten in the bed
Cain, Sheridan. *By the light of the moon*
Camp, Lindsay. *The biggest bed in the world*
Capucilli, Alyssa Satin. *Biscuit*
Castle, Caroline. *Naughty!*
Chapman, Jane. *I'm not sleepy!*
Charlip, Remy. *Baby hearts and baby flowers*
Child, Lauren. *I am not sleepy and I will not go to bed*
Christelow, Eileen. *Five little monkeys jumping on the bed*
Five little monkeys reading in bed
Church, Caroline Jayne. *One more hug for Madison*
Cocca-Leffler, Maryann. *Time to say bye-bye*
Cousins, Lucy. *Maisy's bedtime*
Sweet dreams, Maisy
Cowell, Cressida. *Emily Brown and the Thing*
Coy, John. *Vroomaloom zoom*
Craig, Lindsey. *Farmyard beat*
Crimi, Carolyn. *Principal Fred won't go to bed*
Where's my mummy?
Crow, Kristyn. *Bedtime at the swamp*
Crum, Shutta. *All on a sleepy night*
Cushman, Doug. *Christmas Eve good night*
Halloween good night
DaCosta, Barbara. *Nighttime Ninja*
Daddo, Andrew. *Goodnight, me*
Dahl, Michael. *Goodnight baseball*
Davey, Owen. *Night Knight*
Davies, Jacqueline. *The night is singing*
Demers, Dominique. *Every single night*
De Vries, Maggie. *How sleep found Tabitha*
Dewdney, Anna. *Llama, Llama red pajama*
Docherty, Helen. *The Snatchabook*
Dodd, Emma. *Best bear*
Dodds, Dayle Ann. *The prince won't go to bed*
Donaldson, Julia. *One Ted falls out of bed*
Dragonwagon, Crescent. *All the awake animals are almost asleep*
The drowsy hours
Dunbar, Joyce. *The monster who ate darkness*
Dunnick, Regan. *Sweet dreams, Douglas*
Durand, Hallie. *Mitchell's license*
Durango, Julia. *Dream hop*
Edwards, Nicola. *Goodnight Baxter*
Edwards, Pamela Duncan. *While the world is sleeping*
Edwards, Richard. *Good night, Copycub*
Egielski, Richard. *The sleepless little vampire*
Eilenberg, Max. *Cowboy Kid*
Emberley, Ed. *Go away, big green monster!*
Nighty night Little Green Monster
Fancher, Lou. *Star climbing*
Faulkner, Keith. *The scared little bear*
Fearnley, Jan. *Just like you*
Feiffer, Kate. *No go sleep!*
Ferreri, Della Ross. *How will I ever sleep in this bed?*
Flattinger, Hubert. *Stormy night*
Fleming, Denise. *Sleepy, oh so sleepy*
Ford, Christine. *Ocean's child*
Fore, S. J. *Tiger can't sleep*
Fox, Mem. *Good night, sleep tight*
Tell me about your day today
Time for bed

Where the giant sleeps
Fraser, Mary Ann. *Pet shop lullaby*
Frederick, Heather Vogel. *Babyberry pie*
Hide and squeak
Freedman, Claire. *Hushabye Lily*
Night-night, Emily
Snuggle up, sleepy ones
Gabriel, Ashala. *Night night toes*
Gal, Susan. *Night lights*
Gamble, Isobel. *Who's that?*
Gardiner, Lindsey. *Good night, Poppy and Max*
Gay, Michel. *Zee is not scared*
Geisert, Arthur. *Lights out*
Genechten, Guido van. *No ghost under my bed*
Geringer, Laura. *Boom boom go away!*
Gershator, Phillis. *Moo, moo, brown cow! Have you any milk?*
Who's awake in springtime?
Ginsburg, Mirra. *Asleep, asleep*
Glass, Beth Raisner. *Noises at night*
Gliori, Debi. *Flora's blanket*
Polar Bolero
Stormy weather
Gorbachev, Valeri. *Nicky and the big, bad wolves*
Gravett, Emily. *Again!*
Greenstein, Elaine. *Dreaming*
Griffith, Helen V. *Moonlight*
Gurney, John Steven. *Dinosaur train*
Guthrie, James. *Last song*
Hächler, Bruno. *What does my teddy bear do all night?*
Hacohen, Dean. *Tuck me in!*
Hague, Kathleen. *Good night, fairies*
Haines, Mike. *Countdown to bedtime*
Hall, Marcellus. *Everyone sleeps*
Harby, Melanie. *All aboard for Dreamland!*
Harper, Jamie. *Night night, Baby Bundt*
Harris, Peter. *The night pirates*
Harris, Robie H. *Maybe a bear ate it!*
Harshman, Marc. *All the way to morning*
Hayes, Geoffrey. *The bunny's night-light*
Heller, Nicholas. *This little piggy*
Hemingway, Edward. *Bump in the night*
Henry, Jed. *Good night, Mouse!*
Hest, Amy. *Kiss good night*
Mabel dancing
Hicks, Barbara Jean. *Jitterbug jam*
Hill, Susanna Leonard. *Can't sleep without sheep*
Hindley, Judy. *Sleepy places*
Hines, Anna Grossnickle. *Rumble thumble boom!*
Hissey, Jane. *Hoot*
Hoban, Russell. *Bedtime for Frances*
Hodge, Marie. *Are you sleepy yet, Petey?*
Holt, Sharon. *Did my mother do that?*
Hoppe, Paul. *The woods*
Howland, Naomi. *Princess says goodnight*
Hunter, Sally. *Humphrey's bedtime*
Hurd, Thacher. *Sleepy Cadillac*
Hutchins, Pat. *Little pink pig*
Imai, Ayano. *The 108th sheep*
Imbody, Amy. *Snug as a bug?*
Inches, Alison. *The stuffed animals get ready for bed*
Irving, John. *A sound like someone trying not to make a sound*
Isadora, Rachel. *Peekaboo bedtime*
Ives, Penny. *Rabbit pie*
Iwamura, Kazuo. *Bedtime in the forest*
Jadoul, Émile. *Good night, Chickie*
Jennings, Sharon. *No monsters here*
Jewel. *Sweet dreams*
That's what I'd do
Johnson, D. B. *Henry's night*
Johnson, Lindan Lee. *The dream jar*
Johnston, Tony. *Little Rabbit goes to sleep*
Jonas, Ann. *The quilt*
Joosse, Barbara. *Lovabye dragon*
Roawr!
Joyce, William. *The Sandman: the story of Sanderson Mansnoozie*
Sleepy time Olie
Kanevsky, Polly. *Sleepy boy*
Katz, Karen. *Princess Baby, night-night*
Kellogg, Steven. *A-hunting we will go!*
Kelly, Mij. *A bed of your own!*
William and the night train
Kempter, Christa. *When Mama can't sleep*
Ketteman, Helen. *Goodnight, Little Monster*
Kirk, Daniel. *Hush, little alien*
Kloske, Geoffrey. *Once upon a time, the end (asleep in 60 seconds)*
Koller, Jackie French. *No such thing*
Kono, Erin Eitter. *Hula lullaby*
Kramer, Andrew. *Pajama pirates*
Krauss, Ruth. *Goodnight, goodnight, sleepyhead*
Krilanovich, Nadia. *Moon child*
Krosoczka, Jarrett J. *Good night, Monkey Boy*
Kurtz, Jane. *In the small, small night*
Lamb, Albert. *Tell me the day backwards*
Landry, Leo. *Space boy*
Langreuter, Jutta. *Little Bear won't go to bed*
LaReau, Kara. *Snowbaby could not sleep*
LaRochelle, David. *The haunted hamburger and other ghostly stories*
Lesynski, Loris. *Night school*
Leuck, Laura. *Goodnight, baby monster*
Levine, Joan. *Topsy-turvy bedtime*
Lewis, Anne Margaret. *Fly blanky fly*
Lewis, Kim. *Good night, Harry*
Lewis, Paeony. *No more yawning!*
Lewis, Rose A. *Sweet dreams*
Lewison, Wendy Cheyette. *Going to sleep on the farm*
Lloyd-Jones, Sally. *Just because you're mine*
Time to say goodnight
Lobel, Anita. *Lena's sleep sheep*
Logue, Mary. *Sleep like a tiger*
London, Jonathan. *Froggy goes to bed*
Long, Heather. *Max & Milo go to sleep!*
Long, Kathy. *Christopher sat straight up in bed*
Lum, Kate. *What! cried Granny*
Lundgren, Mary Beth. *Seven scary monsters*
Lyon, George Ella. *Sleepsong*
McAllister, Angela. *Night-night, little one*
McBratney, Sam. *The caterpillow fight*
The dark at the top of the stairs
Guess how much I love you
In the light of the moon and other bedtime stories
Maccarone, Grace. *A child's good night prayer*
McCourt, Lisa. *Good night, Princess Pruney Toes*
I love you, Stinky Face
McCullough, Sharon Pierce. *Bunbun at bedtime*
MacDonald, Margaret Read. *The squeaky door*
Tuck-me-in tales
McGee, Marni. *Sleepy me*
Mack, Jeff. *Hush little polar bear*
McMullan, Kate. *If you were my bunny*
McQuinn, Anna. *The sleep sheep*
Maitland, Barbara. *My bear and me*
Maizes, Sarah. *On my way to bed*

Manning, Maurie J. *Kitchen dance*
Markes, Julie. *Shhhhh! Everybody's sleeping*
Marlow, Layn. *Hurry up and slow down*
Martin, Bill, Jr. *Kitty Cat, Kitty Cat, are you going to sleep?*
Martin, Emily Winfield. *Dream animals*
Matheis, Mickie. *Bedtime for Boo*
Mathews, Judith. *Nathaniel Willy, scared silly*
Mayer, Mercer. *There's a nightmare in my closet*
There's an alligator under my bed
Meade, Holly. *A place to sleep*
Meadows, Michelle. *Piggies in pajamas*
Melmed, Laura Krauss. *The first song ever sung*
Jumbo's lullaby
Meng, Cece. *Bedtime is canceled*
I will not read this book
Meserve, Jessica. *Bedtime without Arthur*
Metaxas, Eric. *It's time to sleep, my love*
Meyers, Susan. *Rock-a-bye room*
Mitchard, Jacquelyn. *Baby bat's lullaby*
Modarressi, Mitra. *Stay awake, Sally*
Monari, Manuela. *Zero kisses for me!*
Moon, Nicola. *Tick-tock, drip-drop*
Moore, Raina. *How do you say good night?*
Mora, Pat. *Sweet dreams / Dulces suenos*
Morales, Yuyi. *Little night*
Morgan, Mary. *My good night book*
Morgan-Vanroyen, Mary. *Sleep tight, little mouse*
Morozumi, Atsuko. *Time for bed*
Morrissey, Dean. *The crimson comet*
Morton, Lone. *Hurry up, Molly / Apúrate, Molly*
Hurry up, Molly / Dépêche-toi, Molly
Munsch, Robert N. *Mortimer*
Murphy, Jill. *A quiet night in*
Murray, Alison. *Little Mouse*
Nakamura, Katherine Riley. *Song of night*
Newman, Lesléa. *Daddy's song*
Nobisso, Josephine. *The moon's lullaby*
Noll, Amanda. *I need my monster*
Numeroff, Laura Joffe. *Nighty-night, Cooper*
When sheep sleep
Ohi, Ruth. *Pants off first*
O'Keefe, Susan Heyboer. *Good night, God bless*
Otto, Carolyn. *Dinosaur chase*
Owens, Mary Beth. *Panda whispers*
Papineau, Lucie. *Lulu's pajamas*
Parenteau, Shirley. *Bears in beds*
Patricelli, Leslie. *The Patterson puppies and the midnight monster party*
Paul, Ann Whitford. *Everything to spend the night . . . from A to Z*
If animals kissed goodnight
Peck, Jan. *Way up high in a tall green tree*
Peck, Richard. *Monster night at Grandma's house*
Pedersen, Judy. *When night time comes near*
Penn, Audrey. *A bedtime kiss for Chester Raccoon*
Perlman, Willa. *Good night, world*
Pfister, Marcus. *Bertie at bedtime*
Good night, little rainbow fish
Piers, Helen. *Who's in my bed?*
Plourde, Lynn. *Wild child*
Pomerantz, Charlotte. *All asleep*
Porter, Pamela. *Yellow moon, apple moon*
Pow, Tom. *Tell me one thing, Dad*
Prap, Lila. *Daddies*
Pumphrey, Jerome. *Creepy things are scaring me*
Purmell, Ann. *Where wild babies sleep*
Quackenbush, Robert M. *Batbaby*
Raschka, Chris. *Can't sleep*
Rathmann, Peggy. *10 minutes till bedtime*
Ray, Karen. *Sleep song*
Raye, Rebekah. *The very best bed*
Reidy, Jean. *Light up the night*
Reiser, Lynn. *Little clam*
Rex, Michael. *Goodnight goon*
You can do anything, Daddy!
Rice, Eve. *Goodnight, goodnight*
Richardson, Bill. *But if they do*
Richmond, Marianne. *I'm not tired yet!*
Rinker, Sherri Duskey. *Goodnight, goodnight, construction site*
Robbins, Beth. *Tom's afraid of the dark*
Robbins, Maria Polushkin. *Mother, Mother, I want another*
Roberts, Bethany. *Gramps and the fire dragon*
Waiting-for-Christmas stories
Rock, Lois. *God bless me, God bless you*
Rockwell, Anne. *Here comes the night*
Rohmann, Eric. *The cinder-eyed cats*
Clara and Asha
Root, Phyllis. *Ten sleepy sheep*
Rose, Deborah Lee. *Someone's sleepy*
Rosenberg, Liz. *Eli's night-light*
Rosenthal, Amy Krouse. *Bedtime for Mommy*
Little Hoot
Ross, Tony. *I want my light on!*
Roth, Carol. *Ten dirty pigs / Ten clean pigs*
Roth, Susan L. *Night-time numbers*
Rothstein, Gloria. *Sheep asleep*
Ruddell, Deborah. *Who said coo?*
Rueda, Claudia. *No*
Rusackas, Francesca. *Daddy all day long*
Russo, Marisabina. *The bunnies are not in their beds*
Rylant, Cynthia. *Brownie and Pearl hit the hay*
Puppies and piggies
Saltzberg, Barney. *Cornelius P. Mud, are you ready for bed?*
Sanromán, Susana. *Señora Reganoña*
Sarcone-Roach, Julia. *The secret plan*
Sartell, Debra. *Time for bed, Baby Ted*
Saudo, Coralie. *My dad is big and strong, but . . .*
Sayles, Elizabeth. *The goldfish yawned*
Sayre, April Pulley. *Hush, little puppy*
Sayres, Brianna Caplan. *Where do diggers sleep at night?*
Schaefer, Carole Lexa. *Down in the woods at sleepytime*
Down in the woods at sleepytime [board book]
Someone says
Who's there?
Schertle, Alice. *Goodnight, Hattie, my dearie, my dove*
Schneider, Josh. *Bedtime monsters*
Schroeder, Lisa. *Baby can't sleep*
Schubert, Ingrid. *There's a crocodile under my bed!*
Schwartz, Amy. *Lucy can't sleep*
Some babies
Scotton, Rob. *Russell the sheep*
Selig, Josh. *Red & Yellow's noisy night*
Shannon, David. *David gets in trouble*
Shea, Bob. *Dinosaur vs. bedtime*
Race you to bed
Shoulders, Michael. *Goodnight Baby Bear*
Showers, Paul. *Sleep is for everyone*
Sierra, Judy. *Sleepy little alphabet*
Silverman, Erica. *Follow the leader*
Simmons, Jane. *The dreamtime fairies*
Go to sleep, Daisy
Slater, Dashka. *Firefighters in the dark*

Slingsby, Janet. *Hush-a-bye babies*
Smee, Nicola. *No bed without Ted*
Snyder, Betsy E. *Sweet dreams lullaby*
Sobel, June. *The goodnight train*
Sperring, Mark. *Mermaid dreams*
Spinelli, Eileen. *When Mama comes home tonight*
When Papa comes home tonight
Sproule, Gail. *Singing the dark*
Stanley, Malaika Rose. *Baby Ruby bawled*
Staub, Leslie. *Bless this house*
Stein, David Ezra. *Interrupting chicken*
Stein, Mathilde. *Monstersong*
Stevenson, Harvey. *Big scary wolf*
Stevenson, James. *We can't sleep*
What's under my bed?
Stewart, Amber. *Bedtime for Button*
Too small for my big bed
Stickland, Paul. *Bears*
Stiegemeyer, Julie. *Seven little bunnies*
Stills, Caroline. *The house of 12 bunnies*
Stock, Catherine. *Alexander's midnight snack*
Swenson, Jamie A. *Boom! Boom! Boom!*
Symes, Sally. *Yawn*
Tafuri, Nancy. *Goodnight, my duckling*
What the sun sees / What the moon sees
Taylor, Sean. *The world champion of staying awake*
Teague, David. *Franklin's big dreams*
Thomas, Jan. *Let's sing a lullaby with the Brave Cowboy*
Thomas, Shelley Moore. *Good night, Good Knight*
Putting the world to sleep
Thompson, Lauren. *Little Quack's bedtime*
Titherington, Jeanne. *Baby's boat*
Underwood, Deborah. *Part-time princess*
Vail, Rachel. *Jibberwillies at night*
Van Leeuwen, Jean. *The tickle stories*
Vere, Ed. *Bedtime for monsters*
Vestergaard, Hope. *Hillside lullaby*
Viorst, Judith. *My mama says there aren't any zombies, ghosts, vampires, creatures, demons, monsters, fiends, goblins, or things*
Waber, Bernard. *Bearsie Bear and the surprise sleepover party*
Ira sleeps over
Waddell, Martin. *Can't you sleep, Little Bear?*
Night night Cuddly Bear
Sleep tight, Little Bear
Tom Rabbit
Who do you love?
Wahl, Jan. *Elf night*
Wallace, John. *Anything for you*
Wallace, Nancy Elizabeth. *Rabbit's bedtime*
Wallen, Ila. *The moon in my room*
Walsh, Melanie. *Hide and sleep*
Walty, Margaret. *Rock-a-bye baby*
Warnick, Elsa. *Bedtime*
Watson, Wendy. *Bedtime bunnies*
Watts, Frances. *Kisses for Daddy*
Weeks, Sarah. *Counting Ovejas*
Weiss, Nicki. *Where does the brown bear go?*
Where does the brown bear go? [board book]
Wells, Rosemary. *Clean-up time*
Goodnight Max
Max's bedtime
Weninger, Brigitte. *Good night, Nori*
"No bath! No way!"
Whatley, Bruce. *Clinton Gregory's secret*
Wick, Walter. *Can you see what I see? dream machine*
Wiesner, David. *Free fall*
Wild, Margaret. *Hush, hush!*
Nighty night
Willems, Mo. *Don't let the pigeon stay up late!*
Wilson, Karma. *Mama, why?*
Sleepyhead
Wing, Natasha. *Go to bed, monster!*
Withrow, Sarah. *Be a baby*
Wolfe, Myra. *Charlotte Jane battles bedtime*
Wolff, Ferida. *It is the wind*
Wood, Audrey. *Moonflute*
Oh my baby bear!
Sweet dream pie
Wright, Michael. *Jake stays awake*
Yaccarino, Dan. *Good night, Mr. Night*
Yarrow, Peter. *Day is done*
Yates, Louise. *Dog loves counting*
Yolen, Jane. *Baby Bear's chairs*
Creepy monsters, sleepy monsters
How do dinosaurs say good night?
Hush, little horsie
Moon ball
Sleep, black bear, sleep
Ziefert, Harriet. *Clara Ann Cookie go to bed!*
Mommy, I want to sleep in your bed!
What do ducks dream?
Zolotow, Charlotte. *The sleepy book*
Sleepy book
When the wind stops

Bedwetting *see* Behavior – bedwetting

Behavior

Andres, Kristina. *Good Little Wolf*
Auch, Mary Jane. *Poultrygeist*
Bauer, Marion Dane. *Why do kittens purr?*
Bennett, Kelly. *Your daddy was just like you*
Berenstain, Stan and Jan. *The Berenstain bears' trouble at school*
Birchall, Mark. *Rabbit's wooly sweater*
Bond, Felicia. *Poinsettia and her family*
Brown, Marc. *The true Francine*
Carle, Eric. *The grouchy ladybug*
Chorao, Kay. *Pig and Crow*
Collard, Sneed B. *Leaving home*
Collicott, Sharleen. *Toestomper and the bad butterflies*
Cooper, Ilene. *The golden rule*
Corey, Shana. *First graders from Mars: Tera, star student*
Cowell, Cressida. *What shall we do with the Boo-Hoo Baby?*
Curious George and the hot air balloon
Curtis, Jamie Lee. *I'm gonna like me*
Czekaj, Jef. *Yes, yes, Yaul!*
David, Lawrence. *Peter Claus and the naughty list*
Donnelly, Jennifer. *Humble pie*
Doyle, Malachy. *Get happy*
Well, a crocodile can!
Dutton, Sandra. *Dear Miss Perfect*
Edwards, Pamela Duncan. *Rude mule*
Elliott, David. *Hunter's best friend at school*
Ets, Marie Hall. *Play with me*
Falconer, Ian. *Olivia*
Olivia's opposites
Fearnley, Jan. *The search for the perfect child*
Watch out!
Fernandes, Eugenie. *Sleepy little mouse*
Gary, Meredith. *Sometimes you get what you want*

Gibbons, Gail. *Bats*
Graham Barber, Lynda. *Spy hops and belly flops*
Griffin, Kitty. *The foot-stomping adventures of Clementine Sweet*
Gutman, Anne. *Lisa's baby sister*
Harley, Bill. *Dear Santa*
Harper, Jamie. *Don't grown-ups ever have fun?*
Harper, Jessica. *Lizzy's do's and don'ts*
Harris, Robie H. *Don't forget to come back*
Helakoski, Leslie. *Woolbur*
Heos, Bridget. *Mustache baby*
Hubbard, Woodleigh Marx. *Whoa, jealousy*
Huget, Jennifer LaRue. *Thanks a lot, Emily Post!*
Hutchins, Pat. *Tidy Titch*
James, Betsy. *Tadpoles*
Javernick, Ellen. *What if everybody did that?*
Johnson, Angela. *Lottie Paris lives here*
Johnson, Paul Brett. *The pig who ran a red light*
Kasza, Keiko. *Don't laugh, Joe*
Keller, Holly. *That's mine, Horace*
Keller, Laurie. *Do unto otters*
Kelley, Marty. *The rules*
Kelly, Mij. *Achoo!*
Knowlton, Laurie Lazzaro. *Why cowgirls are such sweet talkers*
Kopelke, Lisa. *Excuse me!*
Kroll, Steven. *That makes me mad*
Kroll, Virginia L. *Cristina keeps a promise*
Good citizen Sarah
Good neighbor Nicholas
Kurtz, Jane. *Rain romp*
Lester, Helen. *Hurty feelings*
Me first
Tacky in trouble
Lester, Julius. *Albidaro and the mischievous dream*
Levine, Deb. *Parker picks*
Levine, Gail Carson. *Forgive me, I meant to do it*
Lloyd-Jones, Sally. *Being a pig is nice*
Lucado, Max. *All you ever need*
McCarthy, Meghan. *George upside down*
MacDonald, Amy. *Quentin Fenton Herter three*
McGee, Marni. *Wake up, me!*
Mahoney, Daniel J. *The Saturday escape*
Marlowe, Sara. *No ordinary apple*
Monster, be good!
Mora, Pat. *Abuelos*
Morgan-Vanroyen, Mary. *Gentle Rosie*
Wild Rosie
Morstad, Julie. *How to*
Murkoff, Heidi Eisenberg. *What to expect at a play date*
Muth, Jon J. *The three questions*
Naylor, Phyllis Reynolds. *Sweet strawberries*
Niner, Holly L. *Mr. Worry*
Parr, Todd. *Do's and don'ts*
Patricelli, Leslie. *No no, yes yes*
Pfister, Marcus. *How Leo learned to be king*
Milo and the magical stones
Pilkey, Dav. *The Silly Gooses*
Pinkwater, Daniel. *Bad bears and a bunny*
Puttock, Simon. *Big bad wolf is good*
Reider, Katja. *Snail started it!*
Reidy, Jean. *Too pickley!*
Roberts, David. *Dirty Bertie*
Rosenthal, Amy Krouse. *Christmas cookies*
Cookies
One smart cookie: bite-size lessons for the school years and beyond
This plus that
Rotner, Shelley. *The A.D.D. book for kids*
Shannon, David. *A bad case of stripes*
The rain came down
Spelman, Cornelia Maude. *When I feel angry*
Stem, J. David. *Kay Thompson's Eloise in Hollywood*
Stevenson, James. *Don't make me laugh*
Sweetland, Nancy Rose. *Yelly Kelly*
Teague, Mark. *Baby tamer*
Thomas, Joan G. *If Jesus came to my house*
Thompson, Kay. *Kay Thompson's Eloise*
Torrey, Richard. *Because*
Wahl, Jan. *Little Johnny Buttermilk*
Walker, Alice. *Finding the green stone*
Wallace, Joseph E. *Big and noisy Simon*
Wheeler, Lisa. *Old Cricket*
Willis, Jeanne. *Do little mermaids wet their beds*
Winer, Yvonne. *Frogs sing songs*
Wisdom, Jude. *Whatever Wanda wanted*
Yaccarino, Dan. *If I had a robot*
Yolen, Jane. *How do dinosaurs play with their friends?*
How do dinosaurs say good night?
Ziefert, Harriet. *Bunny's lessons*
Zimmett, Debbie. *Eddie enough*

Behavior – animals, dislike of

Bemelmans, Ludwig. *Madeline and the bad hat*
Pitzer, Susanna. *Not afraid of dogs*
Simon, Charnan. *Big bad Buzz*

Behavior – arguing *see* Behavior – fighting, arguing

Behavior – bad day

Agee, Jon. *Terrific*
Badescu, Ramona. *Big Rabbit's bad mood*
Berenstain, Stan and Jan. *The Berenstain bears get in a fight*
Breznak, Irene. *Sneezy Louise*
Corey, Shana. *First graders from Mars: Horus's horrible day*
Everitt, Betsy. *Mean soup*
Freeman, Tor. *Olive and the bad mood*
Friday, Mary Ellen. *It's a bad day*
Gammell, Stephen. *Is that you, winter?*
Giff, Patricia Reilly. *Today was a terrible day*
Grindley, Sally. *The sulky vulture*
Harrison, Joanna. *Grizzly dad*
Henkes, Kevin. *A good day*
Hodgkinson, Leigh. *Smile!*
Hurd, Thacher. *Santa Mouse and the ratdeer*
Jackson, Ellen. *Sometimes bad things happen*
Lubner, Susan. *Ruthie Bon Bair, do not go to bed with wringing wet hair!*
Mack, Jeff. *Good news, bad news*
Miller, Virginia. *I love you just the way you are*
Moss, Miriam. *Smudge's grumpy day*
Murphy, Stuart J. *Probably pistachio*
Oram, Hiawyn. *Badger's bad mood*
Kiss it better
Palatini, Margie. *Gone with the wand*
Patterson, Rebecca. *My no, no, no day!*
Pippin-Mathur, Courtney. *Maya was grumpy*
Riddell, Chris. *Platypus and the lucky day*
Rockwell, Anne. *No! No! No!*
Rodman, Mary Ann. *First grade stinks!*
Rosen, Michael. *Totally wonderful Miss Plumberry*

Rosenthal, Amy Krouse. *One of those days*
Slate, Joseph. *Miss Bindergarten has a wild day in kindergarten*
Tankard, Jeremy. *Grumpy Bird*
van Lieshout, Maria. *Splash: a little book about bouncing back*
Viorst, Judith. *Alexander and the terrible, horrible, no good, very bad day*
Wight, Tamra. *The three grumpies*
Wormell, Mary. *Bernard the angry rooster*

Behavior – bedwetting

Clarke, Jane. *Dippy's sleepover*
Willis, Jeanne. *Do little mermaids wet their beds*

Behavior – boasting

Auch, Mary Jane. *Beauty and the beaks*
Braun, Sebastien. *Toot and Pop!*
Butterworth, Nick. *My dad is awesome*
Carlson, Nancy. *Loudmouth George and the cornet*
Loudmouth George and the fishing trip
Loudmouth George and the new neighbors
Loudmouth George and the sixth-grade bully
Cohen, Deborah Bodin. *Engineer Ari and the Rosh Hashana ride*
Cousins, Lucy. *I'm the best*
Heo, Yumi. *Lady Hahn and her seven friends*
Hodgkinson, Leigh. *Limelight Larry*
Johnston, Tony. *Farmer Mack measures his pig*
Kulka, Joe. *My crocodile does not bite*
Ludwig, Trudy. *Better than you*
Ross, Gayle. *How Turtle's back was cracked*
Shea, Bob. *Cheetah can't lose*
Taylor, Sean. *Crocodiles are the best animals of all*
Van Dusen, Chris. *King Hugo's huge ego*
Wortche, Allison. *Rosie Sprout's time to shine*

Behavior – boredom

Anholt, Catherine. *Come back, Jack!*
Arqués, Isabel M. *Ken's cloud*
Black, Michael Ian. *I'm bored*
Brown, Peter. *Mr. Tiger goes wild*
Buehner, Caralyn. *The queen of style*
Christelow, Eileen. *Five little monkeys with nothing to do*
Coh, Smiljana. *Princesses on the run*
Cordell, Matthew. *Trouble gum*
Donovan, Sandy. *Bored Bella learns about fiction and nonfiction*
Elschner, Geraldine. *Max's magic seeds*
Gall, Chris. *There's nothing to do on Mars*
Gay, Marie-Louise. *On my island*
Graves, Keith. *Pet boy*
Gutman, Anne. *Gaspard and Lisa's rainy day*
Haber, Tiffany Strelitz. *Ollie and Claire*
Heide, Florence Parry. *Princess Hyacinth*
Heide, Iris van der. *The red chalk*
Kvasnosky, Laura McGee. *Really truly Bingo*
Lakin, Patricia. *Rainy day*
Levert, Mireille. *The princess who had almost everything*
McKee, David. *Elmer again*
Murray, Alison. *Princess Penelope and the runaway kitten*
Myer, Andy. *Delia's dull day*
Rosenthal, Marc. *Phooey!*
Schneider, Christine M. *I'm bored!*
Spier, Peter. *Bored — nothing to do!*
Stevenson, James. *There's nothing to do!*
Szekeres, Cyndy. *Toby!*
Yolen, Jane. *Soft house*

Behavior – bossy

Choldenko, Gennifer. *Louder, Lili*
D'Amico, Carmela. *Suki and Mirabella*
deGroat, Diane. *Last one in is a rotten egg!*
dePaola, Tomie. *Boss for a day*
Escoffier, Michaël. *Me first!*
Frazee, Marla. *The boss baby*
Horvath, David. *Bossy bear*
Just like Bossy Bear
Ohi, Ruth. *Clara and the Bossy*
Palatini, Margie. *Shelly*
Ritchie, Alison. *Duck says don't!*
Zemach, Margot. *Eating up Gladys*

Behavior – bullying, teasing

Alexander, Claire. *Lucy and the bully*
Small Florence
Alexander, Martha G. *I sure am glad to see you, Blackboard Bear*
Amato, Mary. *The chicken of the family*
Anaya, Rudolfo A. *Roadrunner's dance*
Anderson, Laurie Halse. *The big cheese of Third Street*
Aruego, José. *The last laugh*
Aston, Dianna Hutts. *Not so tall for six*
Bateman, Teresa. *The Bully Blockers Club*
Bottner, Barbara. *Bootsie Barker bites*
Bowles, Paula. *Scary Mary*
Bracken, Beth. *The little bully*
Brennan, Eileen. *Bad Astrid*
Brooks, Erik. *The practically perfect pajamas*
Browne, Anthony. *Willy the champ*
Buehner, Caralyn. *Would I ever lie to you?*
Burningham, John. *Tug-of-war*
Button, Lana. *Willow finds a way*
Calvert, Pam. *Princess Peepers*
Carlson, Nancy. *Henry and the bully*
Loudmouth George and the sixth-grade bully
Carter, Anne Laurel. *The F team*
Caseley, Judith. *Bully*
Christelow, Eileen. *Jerome camps out*
Church, Caroline Jayne. *One smart goose*
Cohen, Miriam. *Tough Jim*
Cole, Joanna. *Bully trouble*
Collicott, Sharleen. *Toestomper and the caterpillars*
Cooper, Ilene. *Jake's best thumb*
Couric, Katie. *The brand new kid*
Cristaldi, Kathryn. *Baseball ballerina strikes out*
Crocker, Nancy. *Betty Lou Blue*
Cuyler, Margery. *Bullies never win*
D'Amico, Carmela. *Ella, the elegant elephant*
Davies, Matt. *Ben rides on*
Dewdney, Anna. *Llama Llama and the bully goat*
Diggs, Taye. *Chocolate me!*
Docherty, Thomas. *Big scary monster*
Dolenz, Micky. *Gakky Two-Feet*
Eaton, Maxwell. *Two dumb ducks*
Emberley, Ed. *Ed Emberley's bye-bye, big bad bullybug!*
Fearnley, Jan. *Arthur and the meanies*
Finlay, Lizzie. *Little Croc's purse*
Forler, Nan. *Bird child*
Frankel, Erin. *Dare!*

Tough!
Weird!
Garden, Nancy. *Molly's family*
Haber, Tiffany Strelitz. *The monster who lost his mean*
Hassett, John. *The three silly girls Grubb*
Henkes, Kevin. *Chester's way*
High, Linda Oatman. *Tenth Avenue cowboy*
Hilton, Perez. *The boy with pink hair*
Javaherbin, Mina. *Goal!*
Jennewein, Lenore. *Chick-o-Saurus Rex*
Keats, Ezra Jack. *Goggles*
Keller, Holly. *Nosy Rosie*
Kilodavis, Cheryl. *My princess boy*
Kimmelman, Leslie. *The three bully goats*
Kling, Kevin. *Big little brother*
Kliphuis, Christine. *Robbie and Ronnie*
Kroll, Steven. *It's April Fools' Day!*
Jungle bullies
Kroll, Virginia L. *Ryan respects*
Kushner, Tony. *Brundibar*
Lacombe, Benjamin. *Cherry and Olive*
LaReau, Kara. *Ugly fish*
Latimer, Alex. *Lion vs Rabbit*
Lester, Helen. *Hooway for Wodney Wat*
Wodney Wat's wobot
Levert, Mireille. *Eddie Longpants*
Lovell, Patty. *Stand tall, Molly Lou Melon*
McBratney, Sam. *Yes we can!*
McCain, Becky R. *Nobody knew what to do*
McKee, David. *Elmer and the big bird*
Masters, Anthony. *Ricky's rat gang*
Mayer, Mercer. *Just big enough*
Meddaugh, Susan. *Martha walks the dog*
Montanari, Eva. *Dino bikes*
Moore, Julianne. *Freckleface Strawberry and the dodgeball bully*
Morrison, Toni. *The book of mean people*
Moss, Peggy. *Say something*
Naylor, Phyllis Reynolds. *King of the playground*
Nickle, John. *The ant bully*
Nolen, Jerdine. *Plantzilla goes to camp*
O'Connor, George. *Ker-splash!*
O'Neill, Alexis. *The Recess Queen*
Otoshi, Kathryn. *One*
Peet, Bill. *Big bad Bruce*
Pendziwol, Jean E. *The tale of Sir Dragon*
Pienkowski, Jan. *Bel and Bub and the bad snowball*
Pinkney, Brian. *The adventures of sparrowboy*
Pinkwater, Daniel. *Yo-yo man*
Polacco, Patricia. *Mr. Lincoln's way*
Rotten Richie and the ultimate dare
Ramos, Mario. *I am so strong*
Recorvits, Helen. *Yoon and the jade bracelet*
Rickards, Lynne. *Pink!*
Robberecht, Thierry. *Stolen smile*
Robbins, Jacqui. *Two of a kind*
Roche, Denis. *Mim, gym, and June*
Sauer, Tammi. *Cowboy camp*
Schaefer, Lola M. *Frankie Stein starts school*
Schafer, Milton. *That crazy Barb'ra*
Seeger, Laura Vaccaro. *Bully*
Shaw, Hannah. *Sneaky Weasel*
Shipton, Jonathan. *No biting, horrible crocodile!*
Smith, Stu. *The bubble gum kid*
Sorel, Edward. *The Saturday kid*
Soule, Jean Conder. *Never tease a weasel*
Springstubb, Tricia. *Phoebe and Digger*
Staake, Bob. *Bluebird*
Teckentrup, Britta. *Little Wolf's song*
Tierney, Fiona. *Lion's lunch?*
Waddell, Martin. *Yum, yum, yummy*
Wells, Rosemary. *Yoko writes her name*
Weninger, Brigitte. *Davy, soccer star!*
Weulersse, Odile. *Nasreddine*
Winstead, Rosie. *Ruby and Bubbles*
Woodson, Jacqueline. *Each kindness*

Behavior – carelessness

Bergman, Mara. *Lively Elizabeth!*
Brett, Jan. *Comet's nine lives*
Brimner, Larry Dane. *Cat on wheels*
Brunhoff, Laurent de. *Babar's little girl*
dePaola, Tomie. *The quicksand book*
Strega Nona's magic lessons
Oldland, Nicholas. *The busy beaver*
Whatley, Bruce. *Wait! No paint!*

Behavior – cheating

Bailey, Linda. *The farm team*
Cuyler, Margery. *I repeat, don't cheat!*
Fox, Kathleen. *The pirates of plagiarism*
Havill, Juanita. *Jamaica and the substitute teacher*

Behavior – collecting things

Armstrong-Ellis, Carey. *Prudy's problem and how she solved it*
Banks, Kate. *Max's words*
Best, Cari. *When we go walking*
Blumenthal, Deborah. *Aunt Claire's yellow beehive hair*
Bunting, Eve. *Anna's table*
Côté, Geneviève. *Mr. King's things*
Delessert, Etienne. *Alert!*
DiPucchio, Kelly. *Alfred Zector, book collector*
Fleischman, Paul. *The matchbox diary*
Gall, Chris. *Awesome Dawson*
Hughes, Ted. *My brother Bert*
Hurst, Carol Otis. *Rocks in his head*
Jocelyn, Marthe. *Hannah's Collections*
Kleven, Elisa. *The puddle pail*
Kroll, Steven. *Stuff!*
McDonald, Megan. *Insects are my life*
McGinty, Alice B. *Eliza's kindergarten surprise*
Major, Kevin. *Aunt Olga's Christmas postcards*
Manuel, Lynn. *The trouble with Tilly Trumble*
Mariconda, Barbara. *Sort it out!*
Palatini, Margie. *Stuff*
Reid, Margarette S. *Lots and lots of coins*
Ruzzier, Sergio. *The room of wonders*
Slingsby, Janet. *Hetty's 100 hats*
Springman, I. C. *More*
Sullivan, Paula. *Todd's box*
Thompson, Richard. *The night walker*
Tusa, Tricia. *Stay away from the junkyard!*
Wahl, Jan. *The art collector*
Wimmer, Sonja. *The word collector*

Behavior – disbelief

Turner, Ann Warren. *Nettie's trip south*
Waber, Bernard. *Do you see a mouse?*

Behavior – dissatisfaction

Agee, Jon. *Terrific*

Aliki. *The twelve months*
Baguley, Elizabeth. *A long way from home*
Berger, Samantha. *Crankenstein*
Butterworth, Nick. *Jasper's beanstalk*
Child, Lauren. *Who wants to be a poodle*
Cronin, Doreen. *Click, clack, moo*
Crosby, Jeff. *Wiener Wolf*
Daywalt, Drew. *The day the crayons quit*
Grindley, Sally. *The sulky vulture*
Helquist, Brett. *Grumpy Goat*
Hosford, Kate. *Big birthday*
Keats, Ezra Jack. *Jennie's hat*
Kornell, Max. *Bear with me*
Laminack, Lester L. *Three hens and a peacock*
MacDonald, Margaret Read. *The old woman who lived in a vinegar bottle*
Meddaugh, Susan. *The best place*
Palatini, Margie. *Good as Goldie*
Peet, Bill. *The caboose who got loose*
The luckiest one of all
The Whingdingdilly
Reynolds, Peter H. *The smallest gift of Christmas*
Rosenthal, Amy Krouse. *It's not fair!*
Roth, Carol. *Little Bunny's sleepless night*
White, Linda. *Too many pumpkins*
Yaccarino, Dan. *Deep in the jungle*

Behavior – fidgeting

Carlson, Nancy. *Sit still!*

Behavior – fighting, arguing

Alborough, Jez. *Yes*
Angleberger, Tom. *Crankee Doodle*
Barasch, Lynne. *First come the zebra*
Bruchac, Joseph. *The great ball game*
Burdett, Lois. *Macbeth for kids*
Romeo and Juliet for kids
Burg, Sarah Emmanuelle. *Do you still love me?*
Burningham, John. *Mr. Gumpy's outing*
Clanton, Ben. *Vote for me!*
Côté, Geneviève. *Without you*
Desmond, Jenni. *Red cat blue cat*
Dorros, Alex. *Número uno*
Edwards, Pamela Duncan. *Gigi and Lulu's gigantic fight*
Gretz, Susanna. *Riley and Rose in the picture*
Grimm, Jacob and Wilhelm. *Battle of the beasts*
Harris, Robie H. *The day Leo said I hate you!*
Heo, Yumi. *Lady Hahn and her seven friends*
Horacek, Petr. *Jonathan and Martha*
Johnson, D. B. *Eddie's kingdom*
Keller, Holly. *Cecil's garden*
Könnecke, Ole. *Anton and the battle*
Kortepeter, Paul. *Oliver's red toboggan*
Lionni, Leo. *It's mine!*
Lyon, George Ella. *No dessert forever!*
McBratney, Sam. *I'm sorry*
McFarland, Lyn Rossiter. *The pirate's parrot*
Masurel, Claire. *A cat and a dog*
Mayer, Pamela. *The Grandma cure*
Morrison, Toni. *The book of mean people*
Murray, Andrew. *Have you seen Chester?*
Novak, Matt. *The Pillow War*
Ohi, Ruth. *Chicken, Pig, Cow's first fight*
O'Malley, Kevin. *Little Buggy runs away*
Pfister, Marcus. *Rainbow fish and the big blue whale*
Ransom, Jeanie Franz. *Don't squeal unless it's a big deal*
Rumford, James. *Tiger and turtle*
Schmid, Paul. *Peanut and Fifi have a ball*
Selig, Josh. *Red & Yellow's noisy night*
Souhami, Jessica. *Mrs. McCool and the giant Cuhullin*
Strauss, Linda Leopold. *The Elijah door*
Udry, Janice May. *Let's be enemies*
Van Kampen, Vlasta. *It couldn't be worse*
Van Leeuwen, Jean. *Sorry*
Weninger, Brigitte. *Why are you fighting, Davy?*
White, Kathryn. *When they fight*
Zehler, Antonia. *Two fine ladies have a tiff*
Zolotow, Charlotte. *The quarreling book*

Behavior – forgetfulness

Aliki. *Use your head, dear*
Ashman, Linda. *To the beach!*
Birdseye, Tom. *Soap! Soap! Don't forget the soap!*
Bloom, Suzanne. *Fox forgets*
Bonwill, Ann. *The Frazzle family finds a way*
Cordsen, Carol Foskett. *Market day*
Cruise, Robin. *Little Mama forgets*
dePaola, Tomie. *Strega Nona*
Edgemon, Darcie. *Seamore, the very forgetful porpoise*
Fox, Mem. *Wilfrid Gordon McDonald Partridge*
Galdone, Paul. *The magic porridge pot*
Hutchins, Pat. *Don't forget the bacon!*
Lindbergh, Reeve. *My little grandmother often forgets*
Plourde, Lynn. *Pajama day*
Sherry, Kevin. *Acorns everywhere!*
Van Allsburg, Chris. *The stranger*
Weinberg, Larry. *The Forgetful Bears help Santa*

Behavior – forgiving

Bower, Gary. *Ivy's icicle*
Dierssen, Andreas. *Timmy's new friend*
Jennings, Sharon. *Franklin forgives*
Kroll, Virginia L. *Forgiving a friend*
Thompson, Lauren. *The forgiveness garden*
Tutu, Archbishop Desmond. *Desmond and the very mean word*

Behavior – gossip

Andersen, Hans Christian. *It's perfectly true!*
Aston, Dianna Hutts. *Loony Little*
Bowen, Anne. *The great math tattle battle*
Chicken Little. *Chicken Little*
Henny Penny, ill. by Emily Bolam
Henny Penny, ill. by Paul Galdone
Henny Penny, ill. by Sophie Windham
Henny-Penny
The sky is falling
Downey, Lynn. *The tattletale*
Emberley, Rebecca. *Chicken Little*
Felix, Monique. *The rumor*
Gorbachev, Valeri. *Dragon is coming!*
Hopkins, Jackie Mims. *Prairie chicken little*
Hutchins, Pat. *The surprise party*
Ketteman, Helen. *Armadillo tattletale*
McDonald, Megan. *Hen hears gossip*
Madonna. *Mr. Peabody's apples*
Meres, Jonathan. *The big bad rumor*
Ransom, Jeanie Franz. *Don't squeal unless it's a big deal*
Spinelli, Eileen. *Miss Fox's class gets it wrong*

Waldman, Debby. *A sack full of feathers*
Zolotow, Charlotte. *The hating book*

Behavior – greed

Aardema, Verna. *Sebgugugu the glutton*
Aesop. *The goose that laid the golden egg*
Ahmed, Said Salah. *The lion's share / Qayb Libaax*
Andersen, Hans Christian. *The princess and the pea*
The woman with the eggs
Bardhan-Quallen, Sudipta. *The Mine-o-saur*
Berenstain, Stan and Jan. *The Berenstain bears get the gimmies*
Bolliger, Max. *The happy troll*
Brett, Jan. *Honey, honey — lion!*
The brothers gruesome
Buckley, Richard. *The greedy python*
Carlson, Nancy. *Harriet's Halloween candy*
Carr, Jan. *Greedy apostrophe*
Cox, Judy. *One is a feast for Mouse*
David, Lawrence. *The land of the hungry armadillos*
Diakité, Baba Wagué. *The magic gourd*
Donnelly, Jennifer. *Humble pie*
Edwards, Pamela Duncan. *The leprechaun's gold*
Forward, Toby. *Ben's Christmas carol*
Gerson, Mary-Joan. *Why the sky is far away*
Gregory, Nan. *Pink*
Grimm, Jacob and Wilhelm. *The fisherman and his wife*, ill. by Eleanor Hubbard
The fisherman and his wife, ill. by Rachel Isadora
The fisherman and his wife, ill. by Todd Ouren
The fisherman and the turtle
The golden goose
Grobler, Piet. *Hey, frog!*
Hamilton, Virginia. *The girl who spun gold*
Hausman, Gerald. *Coyote walks on two legs*
Hawthorne, Nathaniel. *King Midas and the golden touch*
Johnson, Paul Brett. *Bearhide and crow*
Kaplan, Michael B. *Betty Bunny wants everything*
Kasbarian, Lucine. *The greedy sparrow*
Krudop, Walter Lyon. *The man who caught fish*
Lasky, Kathryn. *Pirate Bob*
Lepp, Bil. *The King of Little Things*
Lester, Helen. *All for me and none for all*
Lind, Michael. *Bluebonnet girl*
Lionni, Leo. *The biggest house in the world*
MacDonald, Margaret Read. *Little Rooster's diamond button*
Mangan, Anne. *The monkey who wanted the moon*
Marshall, James. *Yummers too*
Metz, Lorijo. *Floridius Bloom and the planet of Gloom*
Mollel, Tololwa M. *The flying tortoise*
Norac, Carl. *Monster, don't eat me!*
Oxenbury, Helen. *Pig tale*
Peet, Bill. *Kermit the hermit*
The kweeks of Kookatumdee
Reiss, Mike. *The boy who wouldn't share*
Rohmer, Harriet, et al. *The invisible hunters*
Sanderson, Ruth. *Papa Gatto*
San Souci, Robert D. *The enchanted tapestry*
Schlessinger, Laura. *But I waaannt it!*
Schroeder, Alan. *The stone lion*
Scott, Nathan Kumar. *Mangoes and bananas*
Simon, Charnan. *A greedy little pig*
Smallman, Steve. *The very greedy bee*
Smath, Jerry. *The animals' Christmas carol*
So, Meilo. *Gobble, gobble, slip, slop*
Stanley, Diane. *Rumpelstiltskin's daughter*
Stevens, Janet. *The great fuzz frenzy*
Stewig, John Warren. *King Midas*
Waddell, Martin. *Yum, yum, yummy*
Wells, Rosemary. *The little lame prince*
Max and Ruby's Midas
Willard, Nancy. *The flying bed*
Witte, Anna. *The parrot Tico Tango*

Behavior – growing up

Adoff, Jaime. *Small fry*
Aliki. *I'm growing!*
Anholt, Laurence. *Billy and the big new school*
Atkins, Jeannine. *Robin's home*
Badescu, Ramona. *Pomelo begins to grow*
Banks, Kate. *Fox*
Beaty, Daniel. *Knock knock*
Bedford, David. *Touch the sky, my little bear*
Bentley, Dawn. *Fuzzy Bear's potty book*
Bergstein, Rita M. *Your own big bed*
Berk, Ari. *Nightsong*
Best, Cari. *Sally Jean, the Bicycle Queen*
Blackford, Harriet. *Tiger's story*
Brimner, Larry Dane. *The littlest wolf*
Brown, Margaret Wise. *Another important book*
Cannon, Janell. *Verdi*
Carle, Eric. *My very first book of growth*
Carluccio, Maria. *I'm 3! Look what I can do*
Cohen, Miriam. *Jim meets the thing*
Cole, Joanna. *My big boy potty*
My big girl potty
Collard, Sneed B. *Leaving home*
Cote, Nancy. *Jackson's blanket*
Cruise, Robin. *Bartleby speaks!*
Curtis, Jamie Lee. *It's hard to be five*
My brave year of firsts
When I was little
Davies, Gill. *Tiny's big wish*
Devine, Monica. *Carry me, Mama*
Dowson, Nick. *Tigress*
Dungy, Tony. *You can do it!*
Emmett, Jonathan. *I love you always and forever*
Ferri, Giuliano. *Little Tad grows up*
Ford, Bernette. *No more bottles for Bunny!*
No more pacifier for Piggy!
Fox, Mem. *Shoes from grandpa*
Fraggalosch, Audrey. *Grizzly bear family*
Frazee, Marla. *Walk on!*
Freeman, Mylo. *Potty*
Galvin, Laura Gates. *River Otter at Autumn Lane*
Gay, Marie-Louise. *When Stella was very, very small*
Gentieu, Penny. *Grow! babies!*
George, Jean Craighead. *Look to the north*
Gerstein, Mordicai. *Leaving the nest*
Goodings, Lennie. *When you grow up*
Gore, Leonid. *When I grow up*
Greenstein, Elaine. *As big as you*
Groundhog at Evergreen Road
Hänel, Wolfram. *Little elephant's song*
Harper, Charise Mericle. *When I grow up*
Harris, Robie H. *Go! Go! Maria!*
Harris, Teresa E. *Summer Jackson*
Heiligman, Deborah. *Babies*
Henkes, Kevin. *Owen*
Hewett, Joan. *A flamingo chick grows up*
A giraffe calf grows up
A harbor seal pup grows up
A kangaroo joey grows up
A koala joey grows up

A monkey baby grows up
A penguin chick grows up
A tiger cub grows up
Hines, Anna Grossnickle. *Big like me*
Hoffman, Don. *Billy is a big boy*
Horn, Peter. *When I grow up . . .*
Howard, Arthur. *When I was five*
Jadoul, Emile. *All by myself!*
James, Simon. *George flies south*
Jeppson, Ann-Sofie. *You're growing up, Pontus*
Johnson, Marion. *Caillou, new shoes*
Jonas, Ann. *When you were a baby*
Jorgensen, Richard. *Reading with Dad*
Joslin, Mary. *The shore beyond*
Joyce, William. *Big time Olie*
Karon, Jan. *The trellis and the seed*
Katz, Karen. *Now I'm big*
Keller, Holly. *Jacob's tree*
Kelly, Luke. *Blanket and bear, a remarkable pair*
Kerley, Barbara. *The world is waiting for you*
Kirk, Daniel. *Bigger*
Kraus, Robert. *Leo the late bloomer*
Krauss, Ruth. *The growing story*
Kroll, Virginia L. *On the way to kindergarten*
Kuiper, Nannie. *Bailey the bear cub*
Laden, Nina. *Once upon a memory*
Lane, Adam J. B. *Stop thief!*
Lewison, Wendy Cheyette. *The princess and the potty*
Lindgren, Barbro. *Sam's potty*
Louise, Tina. *When I grow up*
McCarty, Peter. *Baby steps*
MacDonald, Amy. *Cousin Ruth's tooth*
McElmurry, Jill. *I'm not a baby!*
McGhee, Alison. *Bye-bye, crib*
Little boy
Someday
McPhail, David. *Pig Pig grows up*
Magloff, Lisa. *Bear*
Butterfly
Duckling
Elephant
Frog
Kitten
Penguin
Rabbit
Mayer, Marianna. *The prince and the pauper*
Mayer, Mercer. *Bun Bun's birthday*
Just big enough
Meddaugh, Susan. *Martha and Skits*
Milgrim, David. *How you got so smart*
Miller, Virginia. *On your potty!*
Minshull, Evelyn White. *Eaglet's world*
Monnier, Miriam. *Just right*
Morgan, Richard. *Zoo poo*
Moss, Thylias. *I want to be*
Mueller, Doris L. *Small One's adventure*
Munsch, Robert N. *Andrew's loose tooth*
I have to go!
My potty book for boys
My potty book for girls
Nelson, S. D. *Gift horse*
Nicholls, Judith. *Billywise*
Otto, Carolyn. *Our puppies are growing*
Oud, Pauline. *Ian's new potty*
Parker, Marjorie Blain. *Mama's little duckling*
When dads don't grow up
Patz, Nancy. *Babies can't eat kimchee!*
Pearson, Debora. *Leo's tree*
Sophie's wheels
Pfeffer, Wendy. *Mallard duck at Meadow View Pond*
Piggy and Bear in their underwear
Pinkwater, Daniel. *Young Larry*
Rockwell, Anne. *Growing like me*
Rogers, Fred. *Going to the potty*
Rogers, Paul. *Ruby's dinnertime*
Ruby's potty
Rueda, Claudia. *My little polar bear*
Schlessinger, Laura. *Dr. Laura Schlessinger's Growing up is hard*
Schwartz, Amy. *Begin at the beginning*
Things I learned in second grade
Sears, William, M.D., et al. *You can go to the potty*
Senior, Olive. *Birthday suit*
Senshu, Noriko. *Sonny's dream*
Shapiro, Lawrence E. *It's time to give up your pacifier*
Shavick, Andrea. *You'll grow soon, Alex*
Shea, Bob. *New socks*
Shea, Susan A. *Do you know which one will grow?*
Sís, Peter. *Madlenka*
Slater, Dashka. *The sea serpent and me*
Sloat, Teri. *I'm a duck!*
Spinelli, Eileen. *A big boy now*
Stein, David Ezra. *Pouch!*
Stevenson, James. *Higher on the door*
I meant to tell you
Stewart, Amber. *I'm big enough*
Stott, Ann. *I'll be there*
Suen, Anastasia. *Baby born*
Baby born [board book]
Tarpley, Todd. *Ten tiny toes*
Tavares, Matt. *Becoming Babe Ruth*
Taylor, Sean. *When a monster is born*
Teckentrup, Britta. *Little Wolf's song*
Thermes, Jennifer. *Sam Bennett's new shoes*
Thong, Roseanne. *Tummy girl*
Tildes, Phyllis Limbacher. *Billy's big-boy bed*
Torrey, Richard. *Almost*
Turner, Sandy. *Grow up*
Vande Griek, Susan. *Loon*
Van Leeuwen, Jean. *"Wait for me!" said Maggie McGee*
Waite, Judy. *The stray kitten*
Wells, Rosemary. *Timothy goes to school*
Weninger, Brigitte. *Bye-bye, Binky*
Davy in the middle
Wild, Margaret. *Puffling*
Willis, Jeanne. *Cottonball Colin*
Fly, chick, fly!
What did I look like when I was a baby?
Wilson, Gina. *Ignis*
Winter, Jeanette. *My baby*
Winters, Kay. *Tiger trail*
Wolf watch
Wood, Audrey. *Oh my baby bear!*
Yolen, Jane. *Baby Bear's big dreams*
Zagwÿn, Deborah Turney. *The pumpkin blanket*
Zolotow, Charlotte. *Do you know what I'll do?*
I like to be little

Behavior – hiding

Adler, David A. *Hiding from the Nazis*
Alter, Anna. *Disappearing Desmond*
Arnosky, Jim. *I see animals hiding*
Aruego, José. *We hide, you seek*
Asch, Frank. *Moongame*
Braun, Sebastien. *Who's hiding?*
Butler, John. *Ten in the meadow*

Dodd, Lynley. *Find me a tiger*
Dunbar, Polly. *Where's Tumpty?*
Egan, Tim. *Dodsworth in New York*
Fleming, Candace. *Tippy-tippy-tippy, hide!*
Greene, Carol. *Where is that cat?*
Grifalconi, Ann. *The village that vanished*
Hutchins, Pat. *Titch and Daisy*
Jahn-Clough, Lisa. *Missing Molly*
Jennings, Linda. *Hide and seek birthday treat*
Lewis, Kim. *Seymour and Henry*
Love, Pamela. *A loon alone*
Mayr, Diane. *Run, Turkey, run*
Mazer, Norma Fox. *Has anyone seen my Emily Greene?*
Na, Il Sung. *Hide and seek*
Oliver, Narelle. *Twilight hunt*
Panzieri, Lucia. *The kindhearted crocodile*
Paquette, Ammi-Joan. *The tiptoe guide to tracking fairies*
Philpot, Graham. *Where is Little Harry?*
Polacco, Patricia. *The butterfly*
Raschka, Chris. *Whaley Whale*
Santore, Charles. *A stowaway on Noah's Ark*
Schertle, Alice. *Jeremy Bean's St. Patrick's Day*
Steffensmeier, Alexander. *Millie and the big rescue*
Steig, William. *Toby, where are you?*
Stoeke, Janet Morgan. *Hide and seek*
Tafuri, Nancy. *Where did Bunny go?*
Van Leeuwen, Jean. *Chicken soup*
Walsh, Ellen Stoll. *Mouse paint*
Walsh, Melanie. *Hide and sleep*
Wong, Janet S. *Hide and seek*

Behavior – hiding things

Barclay, Eric. *Hiding Phil*
Beck, Andrea. *Elliot digs for treasure*
Dunrea, Olivier. *Ollie's Easter eggs [board book]*
Ollie's Easter eggs
Hines, Anna Grossnickle. *No, no Jack!*
Modesitt, Jeanne. *Little Bunny's Easter surprise*
Stephens, Helen. *How to hide a lion*
Vainio, Pirkko. *Who hid the Easter eggs?*

Behavior – hurrying

Alda, Arlene. *Hurry Granny Annie*
Egan, Kate. *Kate and Nate are running late!*
McCully, Emily Arnold. *Hurry!*
Marlow, Layn. *Hurry up and slow down*
Pfister, Marcus. *Wake up, Santa Claus!*

Behavior – imitation

Allen, Jonathan. *Don't copy me!*
Asch, Frank. *Just like daddy*
Barrett, Judi. *Animals should definitely not act like people*
Animals should definitely not wear clothing
Bonwill, Ann. *I am not a copycat!*
Brown, Lisa. *How to be*
Chou, Yih-Fen. *Mimi loves to mimic*
Clanton, Ben. *Mo's mustache*
Cordell, Matthew. *Another brother*
Cort, Ben. *Pigs can't fly!*
Dicmas, Courtney. *Harold finds a voice*
Elliott, George. *The boy who loved bananas*
Gauch, Patricia Lee. *Dance, Tanya*
Gill-Brown, Vanessa. *Rufferella*
Harper, Jamie. *Me too!*
Harrison, David L. *Dylan, the eagle-hearted chicken*
Inkpen, Mick. *Kipper*
Kellogg, Steven. *A rose for Pinkerton*
Lavis, Steve. *Jump!*
Lawrence, Michael. *The caterpillar that roared*
Marzollo, Jean. *Pretend you're a cat*
Merz, Jennifer J. *Playground day*
Meyers, Susan. *This is the way a baby rides*
Munsch, Robert N. *Stephanie's ponytail*
Numeroff, Laura Joffe. *If you give a mouse a cookie*
Pfister, Marcus. *Bertie*
Rathmann, Peggy. *Ruby the copycat*
Schwartz, Amy. *Bea and Mr. Jones*
Shields, Carol Diggory. *I am really a princess*
Siminovich, Lorena. *Monkey see, look at me!*
Steig, William. *Toby, what are you?*

Behavior – indecision

Cooper, Elisha. *Magic thinks big*
Reidy, Jean. *Too purpley!*

Behavior – indifference

Bee, William. *Whatever*
Konnecke, Ole. *Anthony and the girls*
Kroll, Steven. *Will you be my valentine?*
Sendak, Maurice. *Pierre*

Behavior – lost

Alborough, Jez. *Hug*
Anderson, Lena. *The hedgehog, the pig, and their little friend*
Anholt, Catherine. *Chimp and Zee and the big storm*
Arnosky, Jim. *Armadillo's orange*
Baeten, Lieve. *Happy birthday, Little Witch!*
Bauer, Marion Dane. *A mama for Owen*
Beck, Ian. *Home before dark*
Teddy's snowy day
Bedford, David. *Little Otter's big journey*
Bemelmans, Ludwig. *Madeline and the gypsies*
Billingsley, Franny. *Big bad bunny*
Blake, Robert J. *Little devils*
Brennan-Nelson, Denise. *Grady the goose*
Brett, Jan. *Daisy comes home*
Brown, Marc. *Arthur lost and found*
Brown, Ruth. *Gracie the lighthouse cat*
Browne, Anthony. *Me and you*
Brunhoff, Laurent de. *Babar's little girl*
Buckingham, Matt. *Bright Stanley*
Bush, Timothy. *Teddy bear, teddy bear*
Buzzeo, Toni. *Adventure Annie goes to work*
Carle, Eric. *Have you seen my cat?*
Chaud, Benjamin. *The bear's song*
Cohen, Miriam. *Lost in the museum*
Cooper, Elisha. *Beaver is lost*
Côté, Geneviève. *With you always, Little Monday*
D'Amico, Carmela. *Suki the very loud bunny*
Davis, Jerry. *Little Chicken's big day*
Donovan, Gail. *Lost at sea*
Doyle, Malachy. *Too noisy!*
Dunbar, Joyce. *The very small*
Du Quette, Keith. *Little Monkey lost*
Edwards, Richard. *Always Copycub*
Emmett, Jonathan. *This way, Ruby!*
Empson, Jo. *Rabbityness*
Fitzpatrick, Marie-Louise. *Lizzy and Skunk*
Fleischman, Paul. *Lost!*
Fletcher, Ralph. *The circus surprise*

Freschet, Gina. *Naty's parade*
Gomi, Taro. *I lost my dad*
Goodings, Christina. *Lost sheep story*
Gorbachev, Valeri. *The missing chick*
Grimm, Jacob and Wilhelm. *Hansel and Gretel*, ill. by Jen Corace
Hansel and Gretel, ill. by Rachel Isadora
Hansel and Gretel (1980), ill. by Susan Jeffers
Hansel and Gretel (2011), ill. by Susan Jeffers
Hansel and Gretel, ill. by Jane Ray
Hansel and Gretel, ill. by Claudia Wolf
Hansel and Gretel, ill. by Paul O. Zelinsky
Hansel and Gretel, ill. by Lisbeth Zwerger
Hansel and Gretel / Hansel y Gretel
Hansel and Gretel: a retelling from the original tale by the Brothers Grimm
Grindley, Sally. *Where are my chicks?*
Gutman, Anne. *Lisa in New York*
Hänel, Wolfram. *Little elephant runs away*
Hatkoff, Craig, et al. *Looking for Miza*
Haughton, Chris. *Little Owl lost*
Hawkes, Kevin. *The wicked big toddlah goes to New York*
Heck, Ed. *Monkey lost*
Heiligman, Deborah. *Snow dog, go dog*
Henkes, Kevin. *Sheila Rae, the brave*
Hest, Amy. *When you meet a bear on Broadway*
Hill, Eric. *Where's Spot?*
Hodgkins, Fran. *The cat of Strawberry Hill*
Holabird, Katharine. *Angelina and Henry*
Holt, Kimberly Willis. *The adventures of Granny Clearwater and Little Critter*
Horacek, Petr. *Puffin Peter*
Suzy Goose and the Christmas star
Horse, Harry. *Little rabbit lost*
Huneck, Stephen. *Sally's snow adventure*
Hutchins, Pat. *Where's the baby?*
Ichikawa, Satomi. *La La Rose*
Inches, Alison. *Corduroy's hike*
Itaya, Satoshi. *Buttons and Bo*
Jeffers, Oliver. *Lost and found*
Jennings, Linda. *Little puppy lost*
Johnson, Paul Brett. *Lost*
Johnston, Lynn. *Farley follows his nose*
Jonas, Ann. *Two bear cubs*
Jonathan, Langley. *Missing*
Kato, Yukiko. *In the meadow*
Keane, Michael. *The night Santa got lost*
Keats, Ezra Jack. *My dog is lost!*
Kelly, Mij. *Where's my darling daughter?*
Kimmel, Eric A. *Rip Van Winkle's return*
Kinsey-Warnock, Natalie. *The bear that heard crying*
Kleven, Elisa. *Glasswings*
Kroll, Steven. *Pooch on the loose*
LaMarche, Jim. *Lost and found: three dog stories*
Lambert, Martha Lewis. *I won't get lost*
Lears, Laurie. *Ian's walk*
Levine, Ellen. *Seababy*
Lindbergh, Reeve. *Bridget and the gray wolves*
Lobel, Gillian. *Little Honey Bear and the smiley moon*
London, Jonathan. *Ali, child of the desert*
Little lost tiger
Long, Loren. *Drummer boy*
Loupy, Christophe. *Don't worry, Wags*
McAllister, Angela. *Found you, Little Wombat!*
Mama and Little Joe
McCloskey, Robert. *Blueberries for Sal*
McCully, Emily Arnold. *Picnic*
MacDonald, Alan. *Wilfred to the rescue*
McDonald, Megan. *When the library lights go out*
McFarland, Lyn Rossiter. *Widget and the puppy*
McGraw, Sheila. *Pussycats everywhere*
McHenry, E. B. *Has anyone seen Winnie and Jean?*
McKee, David. *Elmer and Wilbur*
McMullan, Kate. *I'm big!*
McPhail, David. *Lost*
Mader, C. Roger. *Lost cat*
Marshall, James. *Hansel and Gretel*
Marzollo, Jean. *Snow angel*
Mauner, Claudia. *Zoe Sophia's scrapbook*
Meadows, Michelle. *Itsy-bitsy baby mouse*
Melmed, Laura Krauss. *Little Oh*
Minarik, Else Holmelund. *Little Bear's new friend*
Mitton, Tony. *Playful little penguins*
Moerbeek, Kees. *The diary of Hansel and Gretel*
Morpurgo, Michael. *Wombat goes walkabout*
Moss, Miriam. *The snow bear*
Murphy, Stuart J. *Freda is found*
Nishimura, Kae. *Dinah*
Peet, Bill. *Ella*
Pfister, Marcus. *Snow puppy*
Pinkwater, Daniel. *Beautiful Yetta*
Puttock, Simon. *Little lost cowboy*
Ramsden, Ashley. *Seven fathers*
Raschka, Chris. *Daisy gets lost*
Rey, Margret. *Curious George goes to the hospital*
Root, Phyllis. *Oliver finds his way*
Scrawny cat
Rosenberry, Vera. *Vera's Halloween*
Salat, Cristina. *Peanut's emergency*
Scheffler, Ursel. *Taking care of Sister Bear*
Schertle, Alice. *Little Frog's song*
Simmons, Jane. *Come along, Daisy!*
Quack, Daisy, quack!
Skalak, Barbara Anne. *Waddle, waddle, quack, quack, quack*
Smath, Jerry. *Sammy Salami*
Smee, Nicola. *What's the matter, Bunny Blue?*
Sockabasin, Allen. *Thanks to the animals*
Stead, Philip C. *Jonathan and the big blue boat*
Stevenson, James. *Howard*
Stoop, Naoko. *Red Knit Cap Girl to the rescue*
Sykes, Julie. *Dora's chicks*
Tafuri, Nancy. *Goodnight, my duckling*
Titherington, Jeanne. *Where are you going, Emma?*
Tokuda, Wendy. *Humphrey the lost whale*
Uhlberg, Myron. *A storm called Katrina*
Vischer, Frans. *Fuddles*
Waddell, Martin. *A kitten called Moonlight*
Sailor Bear
Small Bear lost
Webster J. Duck
Waite, Judy. *The stray kitten*
Waring, Richard. *Alberto the dancing alligator*
Watanabe, Shigeo. *Where's my daddy?*
Wells, Rosemary. *McDuff comes home*
Max's dragon shirt
Wheeler, Lisa. *Castaway cats*
Whybrow, Ian. *Harry and the dinosaurs at the museum*
Wild, Margaret. *The pocket dogs*
Wilson, Karma. *Bear feels scared*
Where is home, Little Pip?

Behavior – lost & found possessions

Alborough, Jez. *Duck's key where can it be?*
Andrews, Julie. *Dumpy to the rescue!*

Aylesworth, Jim. *The mitten*
Beaumont, Karen. *Where's my t-r-u-c-k?*
Who ate all the cookie dough?
Berger, Joe. *My special one and only*
Birchall, Mark. *Rabbit's birthday surprise*
Blackaby, Susan. *Rembrandt's hat*
Blankenship, Lee Ann. *Mr. Tuggle's troubles*
Bogan, Paulette. *Spike in the city*
Bottner, Barbara. *Pish and Posh*
Brandle, Bine. *Flusi, the sock monster*
Brett, Jan. *The mitten*
Briere-Haquet, Alice. *Zebedee's balloon*
Brown, Alan James. *Love-a-Duck*
Brown, Marc. *D. W.'s lost blankie*
Bunting, Eve. *Have you seen my new blue socks?*
Burks, James. *Beep and Bah*
Butler, Kristi T. *Rip's secret spot*
Butler, M. Christina. *The special blankie*
Bynum, Janie. *Kiki's blankie*
Calmenson, Stephanie. *Oopsy, teacher!*
Carmichael, Clay. *Lonesome bear*
Cate, Annette LeBlanc. *The magic rabbit*
Chessa, Francesca. *Holly's red boots*
Child, Lauren. *I completely know about guinea pigs*
Cooper, Helen. *Tatty-Ratty*
Crimi, Carolyn. *Principal Fred won't go to bed*
Davis, Aubrey. *A hen for Izzy Pippik*
Derby, Sally. *Two fools and a horse*
De Sève, Randall. *Mi barco / Toy boat*
Toy boat
Desrosiers, Sylvie. *Hocus Pocus takes the train*
De Vries, Anke. *Raf*
Diesen, Deborah. *The pout-pout fish in the big-big dark*
DiFiori, Lawrence. *Jackie and the Shadow Snatcher*
Donaldson, Julia. *Room on the broom*
Dornbusch, Erica. *Finding Kate's shoes*
Dunbar, Joyce. *Where's my sock?*
Dunrea, Olivier. *Gideon & Otto*
Edgemon, Darcie. *Seamore, the very forgetful porpoise*
Ellwand, David. *Alfred's camera*
Alfred's party
Ernst, Lisa Campbell. *Stella Louella's runaway book*
Falconer, Ian. *Olivia — and the missing toy*
Feeney, Tatyana. *Little Owl's orange scarf*
Feiffer, Jules. *I lost my bear*
Findlay, Lisa. *What's in Oscar's trashcan?*
Fitzgerald, Ella. *A-tisket, a-tasket*
Flynn, Kitson. *Carrot in my pocket*
Freedman, Claire. *Night-night, Emily*
Geisert, Arthur. *The giant ball of string*
George, Lindsay Barrett. *Maggie's ball*
George, Margaret. *Lucille lost*
Geser, Gretchen. *One bright ring*
Gliori, Debi. *Flora's blanket*
Gorbachev, Valeri. *Whose hat is it?*
Grey, Mini. *Traction Man meets Turbodog*
Gulbis, Stephen. *Cowgirl Rosie and her five baby bison*
Handford, Martin. *Where's Waldo?*
Where's Waldo? The wonder book
Harley, Bill. *Lost and found*
Harvey, Matthea. *Cecil the pet glacier*
Havill, Juanita. *Jamaica's find*
Hayes, Sarah. *Lucy Anna and the Finders*
Hernandez, Leeza. *Dog gone!*
Hoberman, Mary Ann. *The looking book*
Hodgkinson, Leigh. *Smile!*
Holmes, Janet A. *Have you seen Duck?*
Hoppe, Paul. *Hat*
The woods
Hughes, Shirley. *Bobbo goes to school*
Ichikawa, Satomi. *The first bear in Africa!*
Jesset, Aurore. *Loopy*
Johnson, G. Francis. *Has anybody lost a glove?*
Jonas, Ann. *Where can it be?*
Jonovitz, Marilyn. *Three little kittens*
Kako, Satoshi. *Little Daruma and little Kaminari*
Kellogg, Steven. *The mystery of the magic green ball*
The mystery of the missing red mitten
Kelly, Luke. *Blanket and bear, a remarkable pair*
Klassen, Jon. *I want my hat back*
Kovacs, Deborah. *Katie Copley*
Kroll, Steven. *Patches*
Patches lost and found
Kruusval, Catarina. *Franny's friends*
LaMarche, Jim. *Lost and found: three dog stories*
Lamb, Albert. *Sam's winter hat*
Lewis, Kim. *First snow*
Hooray for Harry
Lobel, Anita. *Nini lost and found*
London, Jonathan. *Let's go, Froggy!*
Long, Loren. *Otis and the puppy*
Low, Alice. *Aunt Lucy went to buy a hat*
Luciani, Brigitte. *Those messy Hempels*
McClintock, Barbara. *Adele and Simon*
Adele and Simon in America
McCourt, Lisa. *Chicken soup for little souls: The never-forgotten doll*
MacDonald, Amy. *Cousin Ruth's tooth*
McDonnell, Christine. *Goyangi means cat*
McElmurry, Jill. *Mad about plaid*
McGinty, Alice B. *Eliza's kindergarten pet*
McKee, David. *Elmer and the lost teddy*
McPhail, David. *The teddy bear*
Mahy, Margaret. *Down the back of the chair*
Mister Whistler
Maidment, Stella. *Cowboy puzzles*
Manning, Maurie J. *Laundry day*
Meserve, Jessica. *Bedtime without Arthur*
Meyers, Susan. *Bear in the air*
Montes, Marisa. *Egg-napped!*
Moss, Miriam. *Bare bear*
Matty takes off!
Wibble wobble
Mother Goose. *The three little kittens*
Myers, Tim. *Looking for Luna*
Norris, Leslie. *Albert and the angels*
Ohi, Ruth. *Kenta and the big wave*
Pericoli, Matteo. *Tommaso and the missing line*
Perkins, Lynne Rae. *Snow music*
Pett, Mark. *The boy and the airplane*
Pinkney, Jerry. *Three little kittens*
Plourde, Lynn. *A mountain of mittens*
Polacco, Patricia. *Bun Bun Button*
Poydar, Nancy. *Busy Bea*
Priest, Robert H. *The pirate's eye*
Quattlebaum, Mary. *Winter friends*
Randall, Alison L. *The wheat doll*
Rickert, Janet Elizabeth. *Russ and the almost perfect day*
Rosen, Michael. *Red Ted and the lost things*
Rosenthal, Eileen. *Bobo the sailor man!*
I must have Bobo!
Schachner, Judith Byron. *Bits and pieces*
Scotton, Rob. *Secret Agent Splat!*
Shaw, Mary. *Brady Brady and the big mistake*
Siegel, Randy. *Grandma's smile*

Simhaee, Rebeka. *Sara finds a mitzva*
Simon, Charnan. *Messy Molly*
Siomades, Lorianne. *Cuckoo can't find you*
Three little kittens
Slonim, David. *Oh, Ducky*
Smee, Nicola. *No bed without Ted*
Soman, David. *Ladybug Girl and Bingo*
Springstubb, Tricia. *Phoebe and Digger*
Stadler, John. *Catilda*
Stainton, Sue. *Santa's snow cat*
Stephens, Helen. *The big adventure of the Smalls*
Teague, Mark. *The lost and found*
Trewin, Trudie. *I lost my kisses*
Villeneuve, Anne. *The red scarf*
Walsh, Ellen Stoll. *Hamsters to the rescue*
Weninger, Brigitte. *What's the matter, Davy?*
West, Judy. *Have you got my purr?*
White, Marsha. *Hooper has lost his owner*
Willems, Mo. *Knuffle Bunny*
Knuffle Bunny free
Wood, Audrey. *Alphabet adventure*
Yoon, Salina. *Penguin in love*
Yorinks, Arthur. *Christmas in July*

Behavior – lying

Abercrombie, Barbara. *The show-and-tell lion*
Aesop. *The boy who cried wolf*
Berenstain, Stan and Jan. *The Berenstain bears and the truth*
Brown, Marc. *Arthur and the true Francine*
Buehner, Caralyn. *Would I ever lie to you?*
Cocca-Leffler, Maryann. *Princess K.I.M. and the lie that grew*
Cuyler, Margery. *I repeat, don't cheat!*
deGroat, Diane. *Liar, liar, pants on fire*
Diakité, Baba Wagué. *The hunterman and the crocodiles*
Hale, Dean. *Scapegoat*
Hayes, Joe. *Juan Verdades, the man who could not tell a lie*
Hennessy, B. G. *The boy who cried wolf*
Kaplan, Michael B. *Betty Bunny didn't do it*
Latimer, Alex. *The boy who cried ninja*
McKissack, Patricia C. *The honest-to-goodness truth*
Magoon, Scott. *The boy who cried bigfoot!*
Poydar, Nancy. *Zip, zip . . . homework*
Rankin, Laura. *Ruthie and the (not so) teeny tiny lie*
Robberecht, Thierry. *Sam tells stories*
Sarah's little ghosts
Rocco, John. *Wolf! Wolf!*
Ross, Tony. *The boy who cried wolf*
Singer, Marilyn. *The boy who cried alien*

Behavior – messy

Amant, Kathleen. *Little Rabbit gets messy*
Blankenship, Lee Ann. *Mr. Tuggle's troubles*
Brennan, Eileen. *Dirtball Pete*
Cuyler, Margery. *Monster mess!*
Diesen, Deborah. *Picture day perfection*
Dunrea, Olivier. *Jasper & Joop*
Elschner, Geraldine. *Mark's messy room*
Ericsson, Jennifer A. *She did it!*
Gay, Marie-Louise. *What are you doing, Sam?*
Harris, Robie H. *I love messes!*
Keane, Dave. *Sloppy Joe*
Killen, Nicola. *Not me!*
Klise, Kate. *Little Rabbit and the Meanest Mother on Earth*
Lichtenheld, Tom. *What's with this room?*
McKissack, Patricia C. *Messy Bessey*
Messy Bessey / Ada, la desordenada
Messy Bessey's closet
Modan, Rutu. *Maya makes a mess*
Moss, Miriam. *Matty in a mess!*
Provencher, Rose-Marie. *Mouse cleaning*
Riley, Linnea Asplind. *Mouse mess*
Robinson, Michelle. *Ding dong! Gorilla!*
Simon, Charnan. *Messy Molly*
Stein, Janet. *This little bunny can bake*
Waldman, Debby. *Room enough for Daisy*
Ziefert, Harriet. *Messy Bessie*

Behavior – misbehavior

Abramson, Jill. *Ready or not, here comes Scout*
Alexander, Lloyd. *How the cat swallowed thunder*
Alexander, Martha G. *We're in big trouble, Blackboard Bear*
Allard, Harry. *Miss Nelson is back*
Miss Nelson is missing!
Anderson, Laurie Halse. *The hair of Zoe Fleefenbacher goes to school*
Anderson, Peggy Perry. *Out to lunch*
Aralan, Haydé. *Milton's Christmas*
Arnold, Tedd. *Huggly takes a bath*
No jumping on the bed!
Asch, Frank. *Moonbear's dream*
Ashman, Linda. *Desmond and the naughtybugs*
M is for mischief
Baek, Matthew J. *Be gentle with the dog, dear*
Baker, Leslie A. *You bad dog!*
Bardhan-Quallen, Sudipta. *Chicks run wild*
Barnett, Mac. *Billy Twitters and his big blue whale problem*
Bemelmans, Ludwig. *Madeline and the bad hat*
Berenstain, Stan and Jan. *The Berenstain bears and the truth*
Bottner, Barbara. *An annoying ABC*
Brennan-Nelson, Denise. *He's been a monster all day!*
Brown, Marc. *Arthur's computer disaster*
Arthur's first sleepover
Brown, Margaret Wise. *Sneakers, the seaside cat*
Bruel, Nick. *Bad Kitty*
A Bad Kitty Christmas
Burningham, John. *Edwardo*
Buzzeo, Toni. *No T. Rex in the library*
Carlson, Nancy. *Loudmouth George earns his allowance*
Catalanotto, Peter. *Ivan the terrier*
Cecka, Melanie. *Violet comes to stay*
Chamberlain, Margaret. *Please don't tease Tootsie*
Chorao, Kay. *Bad boy, good boy*
Christelow, Eileen. *Five little monkeys jumping on the bed*
Five little monkeys sitting in a tree
Letters from a desperate dog
Church, Caroline Jayne. *Digby takes charge*
Cohen, Miriam. *Starring first grade*
Collins, Ross. *Doodleday*
Cordell, Matthew. *Trouble gum*
Curious George and the puppies
Curious George goes to a chocolate factory
Curious George goes to a movie
Curious George in the snow

Davies, Gill. *Can't, don't, won't*
Day, Alexandra. *Carl's birthday*
Debecker, Benoît. *The naughty prince*
deGroat, Diane. *Roses are pink, your feet really stink*
Demas, Corinne. *Always in trouble*
DePalma, Mary Newell. *Uh-oh!*
Devlin, Jane. *Hattie the bad*
Dewdney, Anna. *Nobunny's perfect*
Dieterlé, Nathalie. *I am the king!*
Dodds, Dayle Ann. *The prince won't go to bed*
Durant, Alan. *Big Bad Bunny*
Elliott, David. *Finn throws a fit!*
Emmett, Jonathan. *The Santa trap*
Esbaum, Jill. *Stanza*
Fergus, Maureen. *The day my mom came to kindergarten*
Flack, Marjorie. *The story about Ping*
Ford, Bernette. *No more biting for Billy Goat!*
Fredrickson, Lane. *Watch your tongue, Cecily Beasley*
Funke, Cornelia. *Princess Pigsty*
Gall, Chris. *Revenge of the Dinotrux*
Gantos, Jack. *Happy birthday, Rotten Ralph*
The nine lives of Rotten Ralph
Not so Rotten Ralph
Rotten Ralph
Rotten Ralph's rotten romance
Wedding bells for Rotten Ralph
Worse than Rotten Ralph
Gassman, Julie. *Crabby pants*
Gerstein, Mordicai. *Minifred goes to school*
Going, K. L. *Dog in charge*
Grogan, John. *Bad dog, Marley!*
Gutman, Anne. *Gaspard and Lisa's rainy day*
Hale, Bruce. *Clark the Shark*
Haughton, Chris. *Oh no, George!*
Havill, Juanita. *Jamaica and the substitute teacher*
Heide, Florence Parry. *Always listen to your mother*
Henkes, Kevin. *A weekend with Wendell*
Henry, Jed. *I speak dinosaur*
Heo, Yumi. *The green frogs*
Hodgkinson, Leigh. *Goldilocks and just one bear*
Holabird, Katharine. *Angelina, star of the show*
Hood, Susan. *Meet Trouble*
Horacek, Petr. *My elephant*
Hurd, Thacher. *Bad frogs*
Hutchins, Pat. *Three-star Billy*
Where's the baby?
Isadora, Rachel. *Uh-oh!*
Isol. *Petit, the monster*
Jenkins, Emily. *Love you when you whine*
Johnson, Paul Brett. *Little Bunny Foo Foo*
Joosse, Barbara. *Please is a good word to say*
Juster, Norton. *Sourpuss and sweetie pie*
Kaplan, Bruce Eric. *Monsters eat whiny children*
Kellogg, Steven. *Prehistoric Pinkerton*
Kerley, Barbara. *What to do about Alice?*
Kipling, Rudyard. *How the camel got his hump*
Kirk, Katie. *Eli, no!*
Kirwan, Wednesday. *Nobody notices Minerva*
Kumin, Maxine. *Oh, Harry!*
Laden, Nina. *Bad dog*
Langreuter, Jutta. *Little Bear and the big fight*
LaRochelle, David. *Moo!*
Lindbergh, Reeve. *The awful aardvarks go to school*
The awful aardvarks shop for school
The day the goose got loose
Lindgren, Barbro. *Oink, oink, Benny*
London, Jonathan. *Froggy eats out*
McAnulty, Stacy. *Dear Santasaurus*
McBratney, Sam. *The caterpillow fight*
McClements, George. *Baron von Baddie and the ice ray incident*
Night of the Veggie Monster
MacDonald, Amy. *Quentin Fenton Herter three*
McDonnell, Patrick. *The monsters' monster*
McElligott, Matthew. *The lion's share*
McNaughton, Colin. *Captain Abdul's pirate school*
Manning, Jane. *Millie Fierce*
Mansfield, Howard. *Hogwood steps out*
Marshall, James. *The Cut-Ups*
The Cut-Ups at Camp Custer
The Cut-Ups crack up
The Cut-Ups cut loose
George and Martha back in town
Martin, David. *Monkey trouble*
Milgrim, David. *Dog brain*
Monroe, Chris. *Sneaky sheep*
Moss, Miriam. *Bad hare day*
Mozelle, Shirley. *The pig is in the pantry, the cat is on the shelf*
Munsch, Robert N. *Angela's airplane*
Moira's birthday
Murphy, Patti Beling. *Elinor and Violet*
O'Connor, Jane. *Fancy Nancy: fanciest doll in the universe*
Offill, Jenny. *17 things I'm not allowed to do anymore*
Palatini, Margie. *Goldie and the three hares*
Pallotta, Jerry. *A giraffe did one*
Partis, Joanne. *Stripe*
Patterson, Rebecca. *My no, no, no day!*
Pearce, Clemency. *Frangoline and the midnight dream*
Phillips, Betty Lou. *Emily goes wild*
Pichon, Liz. *The three horrid little pigs*
Pinfold, Levi. *The Django*
Pinkwater, Daniel. *Bad bears in the big city*
Ice-cream Larry
Irving and Muktuk
The picture of Morty and Ray
Potter, Beatrix. *The complete adventures of Peter Rabbit*
The tale of Benjamin Bunny
The tale of Peter Rabbit, ill. by Margot Apple
The tale of Peter Rabbit, ill. by Beatrix Potter
The tale of two bad mice
The two bad mice
Where's Peter Rabbit?
Redmond, E. S. *The Unruly Queen*
Reidy, Jean. *Time out for monsters!*
Rice, Eve. *Benny bakes a cake*
Robberecht, Thierry. *I can't do anything!*
Robinson, Michelle. *Ding dong! Gorilla!*
Rockwell, Anne. *The boy who wouldn't obey*
Rosoff, Meg. *Wild boars cook*
Russo, Marisabina. *The bunnies are not in their beds*
Under the table
Sattler, Jennifer. *Uh-oh, Dodo!*
Say, Allen. *Allison*
Schmid, Paul. *Petunia goes wild*
Schneider, Josh. *You'll be sorry*
Schotter, Roni. *When the Wizzy Foot goes walking*
Scotton, Rob. *Merry Christmas, Splat*
Sendak, Maurice. *Where the wild things are*
Shannon, David. *David gets in trouble*
David goes to school
Good boy, Fergus!
No, David!
Oh, David!

Shannon, Molly. *Tilly the trickster*
Shaw, Hannah. *School for bandits*
Shaw, Mary. *Brady Brady and the big mistake*
Shea, Bob. *Big plans*
Shields, Gillian. *Elephantantrum!*
Simmons, Steven J. *Alice and Greta's color magic*
Greta's revenge
Stephens, Helen. *Poochie-poo*
Stevenson, James. *Worse than the worst*
The three bears. *The 3 bears and Goldilocks*
Tillman, Nancy. *Tumford the terrible*
Tumford's rude noises
Tobin, Jim. *The very inappropriate word*
Trivizas, Eugenios. *The three little wolves and the big bad pig*
Urdahl, Catherine. *Polka-dot fixes kindergarten*
Van Allsburg, Chris. *The garden of Abdul Gasazi*
Vidal, Beatriz A. *Federico and the Magi's gift*
Viorst, Judith. *Nobody here but me*
Walton, Rick. *I need my own country!*
Warburton, Tom. *1000 times no*
Ward, Cindy. *Cookie's week*
Watson, Richard Jesse. *The boy who went ape*
Watt, Mélanie. *You're finally here!*
We wish you a merry Christmas
Weaver, Tess. *Cat jumped in!*
Weis, Carol. *When the cows got loose*
Weiss, Ellen. *The taming of Lola*
Wells, Rosemary. *Fritz and the mess fairy*
Hands off, Harry!
Hazel's amazing mother
Time-out for Sophie
Yoko's show-and-tell
Weston, Carrie. *If a chicken stayed for supper*
Whybrow, Ian. *Badness for beginners*
Willems, Mo. *Goldilocks and the three dinosaurs*
Wood, Audrey. *Elbert's bad word*
Yee, Wong Herbert. *Big black bear*
Yokococo. *Matilda and Hans*
Ziefert, Harriet. *The princess and the peas and carrots*
There was a little girl who had a little curl

Behavior – mistakes

Aliki. *Jack and Jake*
Becker, Bonny. *The Christmas crocodile*
Bedford, David. *Mole's in love*
Brett, Jan. *Armadillo rodeo*
Bridwell, Norman. *Clifford's good deeds*
Burdett, Lois. *Twelfth night for kids*
Dodd, Emma. *Foxy*
Dubosarsky, Ursula. *The terrible plop*
Inkpen, Mick. *Kipper's birthday*
McFarland, Lyn Rossiter. *The pirate's parrot*
Medearis, Angela Shelf. *Poppa's new pants*
Root, Phyllis. *Contrary bear*
Rylant, Cynthia. *Brownie and Pearl make good*
Saltzberg, Barney. *Crazy hair day*
Scheffler, Axel. *The little puddle*
Schwartz, Amy. *Starring Miss Darlene*
Singer, Marilyn. *Tallulah's Nutcracker*
Spinelli, Eileen. *Somebody loves you, Mr. Hatch*
Stoeke, Janet Morgan. *A friend for Minerva Louise*
Minerva Louise at the fair
Weigelt, Udo. *The Easter Bunny's baby*

Behavior – misunderstanding

Allard, Harry. *The Stupids die*
Breen, Steve. *Pug and Doug*
Brown, Don. *Odd boy out*
Cottle, Joan. *Miles away from home*
Cuyler, Margery. *Skeleton for dinner*
Henkes, Kevin. *Kitten's first full moon*
Lionni, Leo. *Fish is fish*
Mayer, Marianna. *The prince and the pauper*
Mayer, Mercer. *Bun Bun's birthday*
Salley, Coleen. *Epossumondas*
Shannon, David. *The rain came down*
Sharmat, Marjorie Weinman. *Gila monsters meet you at the airport*
Simmons, Jane. *Ebb and Flo and the greedy gulls*
Stoeke, Janet Morgan. *A hat for Minerva Louise*
Minerva Louise
Minerva Louise at school
Thornhill, Jan. *The rumor*
Waber, Bernard. *Funny, funny Lyle*
Waldron, Kevin. *Mr. Peek and the misunderstanding at the zoo*
Willis, Jeanne. *Gorilla! Gorilla!*
Yorinks, Arthur. *Company's coming*
Young, Ed. *Donkey trouble*

Behavior – name calling

Clanton, Ben. *Vote for me!*
Eaton, Maxwell. *Two dumb ducks*
Luthardt, Kevin. *You're weird!*

Behavior – naughty *see* Behavior – misbehavior

Behavior – needing someone

Aardema, Verna. *The lonely lioness and the ostrich chicks*
Alborough, Jez. *Hug*
Aruego, José. *Weird friends*
Austin, Margot. *A friend for Growl Bear*
Boase, Susan. *Lucky boy*
Casanova, Mary. *Utterly otterly day*
Chichester Clark, Emma. *I love you, Blue Kangaroo!*
Crimi, Carolyn. *Don't need friends*
Folgueira, Rodrigo. *Ribbit!*
Godard, Alex. *Mama, across the sea*
Goodhart, Pippa. *Pudgy, a puppy to love*
Cabrera, Jane. *The lonesome polar bear*
Jonell, Lynne. *Bravemole*
Mom pie
Keats, Ezra Jack. *Louie's search*
Lewis, Kim. *Emma's lamb*
Lottridge, Celia Barker. *Berta, a remarkable dog*
McAllister, Angela. *The little blue rabbit*
McBratney, Sam. *Once there was a Hoodie*
McCormick, Wendy. *Daddy, will you miss me?*
McGuirk, Leslie. *Snail boy*
McPhail, David. *Emma's pet*
Meggs, Libby Phillips. *Go home!*
Peet, Bill. *Zella, Zack, and Zodiac*
Pelton, Mindy L. *When Dad's at sea*
Robertson, M. P. *The egg*
Schneider, Christine M. *Horace P. Tuttle, magician extraordinaire*
Scott, Ann Herbert. *On mother's lap*
On mother's lap [board book]
Seeber, Dorothea P. *A pup just for me . . . A boy just for me*
Sendak, Maurice. *Very far away*
Smith, Maggie. *Paisley*

Thompson, Colin. *Unknown*
Tibo, Gilles. *The grand journey of Mr. Man*
Tokuda, Wendy. *Humphrey the lost whale*
Viorst, Judith. *Nobody here but me*
Wells, Rosemary. *McDuff moves in*
Noisy Nora
Wheeler, Lisa. *Porcupining*
Wilhelm, Hans. *Schnitzel's first Christmas*
Wyeth, Sharon Dennis. *Always my dad*

Behavior – potty training *see* Toilet training

Behavior – promptness, tardiness

Axelrod, Amy. *Pigs on a blanket*
Burningham, John. *John Patrick Norman McHennessy — the boy who was always late*
Calmenson, Stephanie. *Late for school!*
Edwards, Pamela Duncan. *The grumpy morning*
Egan, Kate. *Kate and Nate are running late!*
Gregory, Nan. *Amber waiting*
Hines, Anna Grossnickle. *What Joe saw*
Hutchins, Pat. *Little pink pig*
Lachtman, Ofelia Dumas. *Pepita takes time / Pepita, siempre tarde*
Reiss, Mike. *Late for school*
Sykes, Julie. *Hurry, Santa!*
Teague, Mark. *The secret shortcut*

Behavior – resourcefulness

Boelts, Maribeth. *Happy like soccer*
Bouler, Olivia. *Olivia's birds*
Breen, Steve. *Violet the pilot*
Button, Lana. *Willow's whispers*
Divakaruni, Chitra Banerjee. *Grandma and the great gourd*
Foreman, Michael. *Fortunately, unfortunately*
Geisert, Arthur. *The giant seed*
Hayes, Sarah. *Lucy Anna and the Finders*
Juster, Norton. *Neville*
Kamkwamba, William. *The boy who harnessed the wind*
Keller, Holly. *Help!*
Latimer, Alex. *Penguin's hidden talent*
Layton, Neal. *Hot, hot, hot*
McAllister, Angela. *Trust me, Mom!*
McMillan, Bruce. *How the ladies stopped the wind*
The problem with chickens
Medina, Meg. *Tía Isa wants a car*
Meisel, Paul. *Zara's hats*
Ørdal, Stina Langlo. *Princess Aasta*
Perrow, Angeli. *Sirius, the dog star*
Phillipps, J. C. *Monkey Ono*
Rayner, Catherine. *Ernest, the moose who doesn't fit*
Rees, Douglas. *Jeannette Claus saves Christmas*
Rosenthal, Amy Krouse. *Yes Day!*
Sauer, Tammi. *Nugget and Fang*
Stohner, Anu. *Brave Charlotte*
Stuve-Bodeen, Stephanie. *A small brown dog with a wet pink nose*
Van Dusen, Chris. *Randy Riley's really big hit*
Young, Cybèle. *A few blocks*

Behavior – running away

Ahlberg, Allan. *The runaway dinner*
Alexander, Martha G. *And my mean old mother will be sorry, Blackboard Bear*
Allen, Elanna. *Itsy Mitsy runs away*
Bailey, Linda. *Stanley's wild ride*
Barton, Byron. *The wee little woman*
Bogan, Paulette. *Lulu the big little chick*
Brett, Jan. *Home for Christmas*
Brown, Margaret Wise. *The runaway bunny*
The runaway bunny [board book]
Brunhoff, Jean de. *The story of Babar, the little elephant*
Bunting, Eve. *Emma's turtle*
Cadow, Kenneth M. *Alfie runs away*
Chichester Clark, Emma. *Piper*
Christelow, Eileen. *The great pig escape*
The great pig search
Coh, Smiljana. *Princesses on the run*
Davies, Gill. *Can't, don't, won't*
Dyer, Heather. *Tina and the penguin*
Eaton, Jason Carter. *The day my runny nose ran away*
Edwards, Pamela Duncan. *Barefoot: escape on the Underground Railroad*
Ernst, Lisa Campbell. *The Gingerbread Girl goes animal crackers*
Fearnley, Jan. *Martha in the middle*
Fleming, Denise. *Buster*
Freeman, Don. *Beady Bear*
Garland, Michael. *Last night at the zoo*
The gingerbread boy. *Can't catch me*
Gingerbread baby
The gingerbread boy, ill. by Emily Bolam
The gingerbread boy, ill. by Richard Egielski
The gingerbread boy, ill. by Paul Galdone
The Gingerbread Cowboy
The gingerbread girl
The gingerbread man, ill. by Carol Jones
The gingerbread man, ill. by Megan Lloyd
The gingerbread man, ill. by Barbara McClintock
The gingerbread man, ill. by Béatrice Rodriguez
The Gingerbread Man loose in the school
The Gingerbread Man loose on the fire truck
The Library Gingerbread Man
The pancake boy
Señorita Gordita
Whiff, sniff, nibble and chew
Goodhart, Pippa. *Pudgy, a puppy to love*
Hänel, Wolfram. *Little elephant runs away*
Harrison, David L. *Piggy Wiglet*
Hernandez, Leeza. *Dog gone!*
Hoban, Russell. *A baby sister for Frances*
Horse, Harry. *Little Rabbit runaway*
Howland, Naomi. *The matzah man*
Huget, Jennifer LaRue. *The beginner's guide to running away from home*
Ichikawa, Satomi. *I am Pangoo the penguin*
Imai, Ayano. *Chester*
Jagtenberg, Yvonne. *Jack's rabbit*
Johnson, Angela. *The day Ray got away*
Johnston, Lynn. *Farley follows his nose*
Kimmel, Eric A. *The runaway tortilla*
The three little tamales
Kimmelman, Leslie. *The runaway latkes*
Kraus, Robert. *Where are you going, little mouse?*
Lindgren, Barbro. *Benny's had enough*
Lloyd, Sam. *Mr. Pusskins*
Lobel, Gillian. *Does anybody love me?*
Long, Kathy. *The runaway shopping cart*
McCully, Emily Arnold. *My real family*
McHenry, E. B. *Has anyone seen Winnie and Jean?*

Macomber, Debbie. *The yippy, yappy Yorkie in the green doggy sweater*
Martín Larrañaga, Ana. *Woo! The not-so-scary Ghost*
Massini, Sarah. *Trixie ten*
Meade, Holly. *John Willy and Freddy McGee*
John Willy and Freddy McGee [board book]
Moss, Miriam. *Smudge's grumpy day*
Munsch, Robert N. *Aaron's hair*
Murray, Andrew. *Have you seen Chester?*
Ohi, Ruth. *And you can come too*
O'Malley, Kevin. *Little Buggy runs away*
Peet, Bill. *Pamela Camel*
Rand, Betseygail. *Big Bunny*
Rex, Michael. *Runaway mummy*
Rosen, Michael. *Crow and Hawk*
Rosenberry, Vera. *Vera runs away*
Rostoker-Gruber, Karen. *Bandit*
Roth, Susan L. *Cinnamon's day out*
Savage, Stephen. *Where's Walrus?*
Scieszka, Jon. *Walt Disney's Alice in Wonderland*
Segal, John. *Far far away!*
Sendak, Maurice. *Very far away*
Shulman, Goldie. *Way too much challah dough*
Slangerup, Erik Jon. *Dirt Boy*
Steig, William. *Zeke Pippin*
Stevens, Janet. *And the dish ran away with the spoon*
My big dog
Sykes, Julie. *I don't want to take a bath!*
Urbanovic, Jackie. *Duck and cover*
Van Laan, Nancy. *Little baby Bobby*
Villeneuve, Anne. *Loula is leaving for Africa*
Voake, Charlotte. *Ginger*
Waber, Bernard. *A lion named Shirley Williamson*
Waddell, Martin. *Bee frog*
Wahl, Jan. *Mabel ran away with the toys*
Weeks, Sarah. *Oh my gosh, Mrs. McNosh!*
Wojtowycz, David. *A cuddle for Claude*
Yorinks, Arthur. *Hey, Al*
Zion, Gene. *Harry, the dirty dog*

Behavior – saving things

Carlson, Nancy. *Start saving, Henry!*
Child, Lauren. *But I've used all my pocket change*
Perez, Monica. *Curious George saves his pennies*
Thayer, Tanya. *Saving money*

Behavior – secrets

Aardema, Verna. *What's so funny, Ketu?*
Allard, Harry. *Miss Nelson has a field day*
Asch, Frank. *Mrs. Marlowe's mice*
Bang, Molly. *Dawn*
Battut, Éric. *Little Mouse's big secret*
Coombs, Kate. *The secret-keeper*
Farley, Carol J. *The king's secret*
Freeman, Tor. *Olive and the big secret*
George, Lindsay Barrett. *The secret*
Gray, Kes. *006 and a half*
Griffin, Kitty. *Cowboy Sam and those confounded secrets*
Heide, Florence Parry. *The day of Ahmed's secret*
Hines, Anna Grossnickle. *The secret keeper*
Kelley, True. *Blabber Mouse*
Lehman, Barbara. *The secret box*
Naylor, Phyllis Reynolds. *Keeping a Christmas secret*
Polacco, Patricia. *The butterfly*
Rappaport, Doreen. *The long-haired girl*
Riggio, Anita. *Secret signs*
San Souci, Robert D. *The snow wife*
Schoenherr, Ian. *Don't spill the beans!*
Winter, Jeanette. *Nasreen's secret school*

Behavior – seeking better things

Adler, David A. *A picture book of Cesar Chavez*
Alter, Anna. *What can you do with an old red shoe?*
Altman, Linda Jacobs. *Amelia's road*
Asim, Jabari. *Fifty cents and a dream*
Bradby, Marie. *More than anything else*
Buckley, Richard. *The foolish tortoise*
DiPucchio, Kelly. *Grace for president*
Feiffer, Kate. *President Pennybaker*
Hamilton, Virginia. *Jaguarundi*
Hopkinson, Deborah. *Sweet Clara and the freedom quilt*
Kraus, Robert. *Where are you going, little mouse?*
Lionni, Leo. *Tillie and the wall*
McGinty, Alice B. *Gandhi*
McPhail, David. *Weezer changes the world*
Markel, Michelle. *Brave girl*
Martin, Jacqueline Briggs. *Farmer Will Allen and the growing table*
Milway, Katie Smith. *One hen*
Mortenson, Greg. *Listen to the wind*
Myers, Walter Dean. *Looking for the easy life*
Odone, Jamison. *Mole had everything*
Parish, Herman. *Amelia Bedelia's first vote*
Proimos, James. *Paulie Pastrami achieves world peace*
Schrock, Jan West. *Give a goat*
Shulevitz, Uri. *How I learned geography*
Smith, Lane. *Madam President*
Spinelli, Eileen. *Peace Week in Miss Fox's class*
Stone, Tanya Lee. *Elizabeth leads the way*
Warren, Sarah. *Dolores Huerta*
Wells, Rosemary. *Otto runs for President*
Otto se presenta para presidente / Otto runs for President
Williams, Vera B. *A chair for my mother*
Yolen, Jane. *Naming Liberty*

Behavior – sharing

Aesop. *Smog, the city dog*
Alexander, Martha G. *I'll never share you, Blackboard Bear*
Arnold, Katya. *That apple is mine!*
Backx, Patsy. *Josie and Mr. Fernandez*
Bardhan-Quallen, Sudipta. *The Mine-o-saur*
Battut, Éric. *Little Mouse's big secret*
Beaumont, Karen. *Move over, Rover*
Benjamin, A. H. *Mouse, mole and the falling star*
Berger, Samantha. *Martha doesn't share!*
Blegvad, Lenore. *First friends*
Boldt, Claudia. *Odd dog*
Bosca, Francesca. *The apple king*
Brett, Jan. *Christmas trolls*
Bryant, Jen. *Abe's fish*
Cameron, C. C. *One for me, one for you*
Caudill, Rebecca. *A pocketful of cricket*
Chaconas, Dori. *Looking for Easter*
Cohen, Caron Lee. *Digger Pig and the turnip*
Cohen, Miriam. *Don't eat too much turkey!*
Cole, Joanna. *Sharing is fun*
Cote, Nancy. *It feels like snow*
Cousins, Lucy. *Maisy makes lemonade*
Crum, Shutta. *Mine!*
Deacon, Alexis. *Cheese belongs to you!*

deGroat, Diane. *Last one in is a rotten egg!*
Devlin, Wende. *Cranberry Christmas*
Dewdney, Anna. *Llama Llama time to share*
Dunbar, Joyce. *The very small*
Dunbar, Polly. *Happy Hector*
Ehlert, Lois. *Top cat*
Emberley, Ed. *The red hen*
Forest, Heather. *Stone soup*
Forward, Toby. *Ben's Christmas carol*
Freeman, Tor. *Olive and the bad mood*
Galdone, Paul. *The magic porridge pot*
Grimm, Jacob and Wilhelm. *The star child*
Grindley, Sally. *Can we play too, Piglittle?*
Hamilton, Richard. *Polly's picnic*
Hawcock, Claire. *Mine, all mine!*
Henkes, Kevin. *Sheila Rae's peppermint stick*
Himmelman, John. *Katie and the puppy next door*
Hoberman, Mary Ann. *One of each*
Horacek, Petr. *Jonathan and Martha*
Hutchins, Pat. *The doorbell rang*
It's my birthday!
Keats, Ezra Jack. *Peter's chair*
Ketteman, Helen. *Armadilly chili*
Kirsch, Vincent X. *Forsythia and me*
Kortepeter, Paul. *Oliver's red toboggan*
Kroll, Steven. *Jungle bullies*
Landa, Norbert. *Little Bear and the wishing tree*
LaReau, Kara. *Ugly fish*
Lester, Helen. *All for me and none for all*
Lindgren, Barbro. *Sam's car*
Sam's cookie
Lister, Mary. *The Winter King and the Summer Queen*
The little red hen. *The little red hen*, ill. by Byron Barton
The little red hen, ill. by Emily Bolam
The little red hen, ill. by Paul Galdone
Little red hen
The little red hen, ill. by Jerry Pinkney
The little red hen, ill. by Kate Slater
The little red hen, ill. by Annie West
The little red hen, ill. by Margot Zemach
The little red hen: an old fable
The Little Red Hen and the Passover matzah
The Little Red Hen makes a pizza
Luthardt, Kevin. *Mine*
McDaniels, Preston. *A perfect snowman*
McKissack, Patricia C. *The all-I'll-ever-want Christmas doll*
Martin, David. *All for pie, pie for all*
Martins, Isabel Minhós. *Little lamb, have you any wool?*
Masurel, Claire. *Christmas is coming*
Medina, Tony. *Christmas makes me think*
Meserve, Adria. *No room for Napoleon*
Mills, Lauren A. *The rag coat*
Moss, Miriam. *It's my turn, Smudge*
Munsch, Robert N. *We share everything!*
Murphy, Stuart J. *Give me half!*
Let's fly a kite
Seaweed soup
Nakagawa, Rieko. *Guri and Gura*
Guri and Gura's special gift
Nanji, Shenaaz. *Treasure for lunch*
Oram, Hiawyn. *My friend Fred*
Orloff, Karen Kaufman. *I wanna new room*
Pacilio, V. J. *Ling Cho and his three friends*
Parenteau, Shirley. *Bears on chairs*
Parkinson, Kathy. *The enormous turnip*
Paschkis, Julie. *Mooshka*
Patten, Brian. *The big snuggle-up*
Peck, Jan. *The giant carrot*
Perlman, Janet. *The delicious bug*
Pfister, Marcus. *The rainbow fish*
Pienkowski, Jan. *Bel and Bub and the big brown box*
Pinkwater, Daniel. *Bear in love*
Proimos, James. *Paulie Pastrami achieves world peace*
Ransome, James. *New red bike!*
Rathmann, Peggy. *Officer Buckle and Gloria*
Rayner, Catherine. *The bear who shared*
Rockliff, Mara. *My heart will not sit down*
Rosen, Michael. *This is our house*
Rosenthal, Amy Krouse. *Plant a kiss*
Rostoker-Gruber, Karen. *Bandit's surprise*
Russo, Marisabina. *The big brown box*
Ruzzier, Sergio. *Bear and Bee*
Rylant, Cynthia. *Birthday presents*
Sasso, Sandy Eisenberg. *God said amen*
Savadier, Elivia. *Will Sheila share?*
Sawyer, Ruth. *The remarkable Christmas of the cobbler's sons*
Schmid, Paul. *Peanut and Fifi have a ball*
Seeger, Laura Vaccaro. *What if?*
Shannon, George. *Rabbit's gift*
Simmons, Jane. *Ebb and Flo and the new friend*
Siomades, Lorianne. *A place to bloom*
Smallman, Steve. *The very greedy bee*
Smalls-Hector, Irene. *Because you're lucky*
Spelman, Cornelia Maude. *When I care about others*
Spinelli, Eileen. *Thanksgiving at the Tappletons'*
Stein, Mathilde. *Mine!*
Stewart, Paul. *The birthday presents*
Stone, Lynn M. *Partners*
Taylor, Thomas. *Little Mouse and the big cupcake*
Thayer, Jane. *Part-time dog*
Toscano, Charles. *Papa's pastries*
van Lieshout, Maria. *Tumble!*
Vere, Ed. *Banana!*
Waldman, Debby. *Room enough for Daisy*
Weninger, Brigitte. *Merry Christmas, Davy!*
Willems, Mo. *The duckling gets a cookie!?*
Wilson, Karma. *Bear says thanks*
Wolff, Ferida. *The story blanket*
Wood, Don. *Merry Christmas, big hungry bear*
Yum, Hyewon. *The twins' blanket*
Ziefert, Harriet. *Be fair, share!*

Behavior – solitude

Asher, Sandy. *Too many frogs!*
Doyle, Malachy. *Too noisy!*
Guion, Melissa. *Baby penguins everywhere!*
Horacek, Petr. *Look out, Suzy Goose*
Lemniscates. *Silence*
Sif, Birgitta. *Oliver*
Underwood, Deborah. *The quiet book*
van Lieshout, Elle. *The wish*

Behavior – stealing

Ada, Alma Flor. *The gold coin*
Ahlberg, Janet. *Jeremiah in the dark wood*
Alborough, Jez. *It's the bear*
Amado, Elisa. *Tricycle*
Arabian Nights. *The tale of Ali Baba and the forty thieves*
Barton, Byron. *The wee little woman*
Beaver steals fire
Brett, Jan. *Christmas trolls*

Bromley, Anne C. *The lunch thief*
Carlson, Nancy. *Loudmouth George and the sixth-grade bully*
dePaola, Tomie. *Bill and Pete go down the Nile*
Devlin, Wende. *Cranberry Halloween*
The firebird. *The firebird*, ill. by Demi
The firebird, ill. by Rachel Isadora
The tale of the firebird
Hennessy, B. G. *The missing tarts*
Khing, T. T. *Where is the cake?*
Where is the cake now?
MacDonald, Margaret Read. *Tunjur! Tunjur! Tunjur!*
Pinkwater, Daniel. *Bad bear detectives*
Vere, Ed. *The getaway*
Weigelt, Udo. *It wasn't me*
Who stole the gold?
Yolen, Jane. *Piggins*

Behavior – talking to strangers

Berenstain, Stan and Jan. *The Berenstain bears learn about strangers*
Ernst, Lisa Campbell. *Little Red Riding Hood: a newfangled prairie tale*
Grimm, Jacob and Wilhelm. *Little red cap*
Little Red Riding Hood, ill. by Célia Chauffrey
Little Red Riding Hood, ill. by Gwen Connelly
Little Red Riding Hood, ill. by Trina Schart Hyman
Little Red Riding Hood, ill. by Jerry Pinkney
Little Red Riding Hood, ill. by Gennady Spirin
Little Red Riding Hood, ill. by Bernadette Watts
Little Red Riding Hood, ill. by Andrea Wisnewski
The story of Little Red Riding Hood
Kaczman, James. *A bird and his worm*
Kevi. *Don't talk to strangers*
Marshall, James. *Red Riding Hood*
Moore, Maggie. *Little Red Riding Hood*
Potter, Beatrix. *The tale of Little Pig Robinson*
Wood, Audrey. *Heckedy Peg*

Behavior – tardiness *see* Behavior – promptness, tardiness

Behavior – teasing *see* Behavior – bullying, teasing

Behavior – toilet training *see* Toilet training

Behavior – trickery

Aardema, Verna. *Anansi finds a fool*
Borreguita and the coyote
Jackal's flying lesson
Rabbit makes a monkey of lion
Aesop. *The boy who cried wolf*
The donkey in the lion's skin
Fox tails
Three Aesop fox fables
The wolf in sheep's clothing
Alexander, Lloyd. *The house Gobbaleen*
Bateman, Teresa. *Keeper of soles*
Beaver steals fire
Bently, Peter. *The great sheep shenanigans*
Blackaby, Susan. *Brownie Groundhog and the February Fox*
Brown, Marc. *Arthur tricks the tooth fairy*
Browning, Robert. *The pied piper of Hamelin*, ill. by Mercer Mayer
The pied piper of Hamelin, ill. by Drahos Zak
Burdett, Lois. *Twelfth night for kids*
Burningham, John. *Tug-of-war*
Campoy, F. Isabel. *Rosa Raposa*
Chicken Little. *Chicken Little*
Henny Penny, ill. by Emily Bolam
Henny Penny, ill. by Paul Galdone
Henny Penny, ill. by Sophie Windham
Henny-Penny
The sky is falling
Christelow, Eileen. *Five little monkeys trick-or-treat*
Crummel, Susan Stevens. *Tumbleweed stew*
Daly, Niki. *Pretty Salma*
Davis, David. *Fandango stew*
DeFelice, Cynthia C. *Cold feet*
DeSpain, Pleasant. *The dancing turtle*
Divakaruni, Chitra Banerjee. *Grandma and the great gourd*
Emberley, Rebecca. *Chicken Little*
The crocodile and the scorpion
Friend, Catherine. *The perfect nest*
Goble, Paul. *Iktomi and the buffalo skull*
Iktomi and the buzzard
Iktomi and the coyote
Iktomi and the ducks
Greene, Rhonda Gowler. *Eek! Creak! Snicker, sneak*
Hausman, Gerald. *Coyote walks on two legs*
Helmer, Marilyn. *Three tales of trickery*
Hennessy, B. G. *The boy who cried wolf*
Janisch, Heinz. *The merry pranks of Till Eulenspiegel*
Johnson, Paul Brett. *Jack outwits the giants*
Johnston, Tony. *The badger and the magic fan*
Kasbarian, Lucine. *The greedy sparrow*
Kasza, Keiko. *My lucky birthday*
Kellogg, Steven. *Chicken Little*
Kelly, Mij. *One more sheep*
Kimmel, Eric A. *Anansi and the moss-covered rock*
Anansi and the talking melon
Anansi goes fishing
Anansi's party time
Knutson, Barbara. *Love and roast chicken*
Kraus, Robert. *Come out and play, little mouse*
Krause, Ute. *Oscar and the very hungry dragon*
Latimer, Alex. *Lion vs Rabbit*
McCaughrean, Geraldine. *One bright Penny*
McDermott, Gerald. *Jabutí the tortoise*
Monkey
Pig-Boy
Raven
Tim O'Toole and the wee folk
Zomo the rabbit
MacDonald, Amy. *Please, Malese!*
MacDonald, Margaret Read. *Conejito*
Pickin' peas
McGuinness-Kelly, Tracy-Lee. *Bad Cat puts on his top hat*
McKee, David. *Elmer and Snake*
Mahy, Margaret. *The great white man-eating shark*
Martin, Bill, Jr. *Trick or treat?*
Mollel, Tololwa M. *Ananse's feast*
The flying tortoise
Mora, Pat. *The race of toad and deer*
Morales, Yuyi. *Just a minute: a trickster tale and counting book*
Just in case: a trickster tale and Spanish alphabet book

Munsch, Robert N. *Mmm, cookies!*
Nadimi, Suzan. *The rich man and the parrot*
Oram, Hiawyn. *Baba Yaga and the wise doll*
Pauli, Lorenz. *The fox in the library*
Potter, Beatrix. *The pie and the patty-pan*
The story of Miss Moppet
Rocco, John. *Wolf! Wolf!*
Root, Phyllis. *Aunt Nancy and Old Man Trouble*
Ross, Tony. *The boy who cried wolf*
San Souci, Robert D. *Feathertop*
Scott, Nathan Kumar. *Mangoes and bananas*
The sacred banana leaf
Shannon, Margaret. *Gullible's troubles*
Shea, Bob. *Cheetah can't lose*
Singleton, Debbie. *The king who wouldn't sleep*
Smith, Alex T. *Foxy and Egg*
Snyder, Dianne. *The boy of the three-year nap*
Souhami, Jessica. *Foxy!*
No dinner!
Steig, William. *Solomon the rusty nail*
Stevens, Janet. *Tops and bottoms*
Stevenson, James. *Emma*
Fried feathers for Thanksgiving
Strete, Craig Kee. *How the Indians bought the farm*
Sunami, Kitoba. *How the fisherman tricked the genie*
Taylor, Sean. *The grizzly bear with the frizzly hair*
Temple, Frances. *Tiger soup*
Tingle, Tim. *When Turtle grew feathers*
Turkle, Brinton. *Do not open*
Twohy, Mike. *Outfoxed*
Willems, Mo. *That is not a good idea!*
Yep, Laurence. *The man who tricked a ghost*
Young, Ed. *Monkey King*

Behavior – unnoticed, unseen

Bridges, Shirin Yim. *Mary Wrightly, so politely*
Ludwig, Trudy. *The invisible boy*
Scott, Ann Herbert. *Hi!*

Behavior – wishing

Addy, Sharon Hart. *When wishes were horses*
Allard, Harry. *Starlight goes to town*
Base, Graeme. *Jungle drums*
Baumgart, Klaus. *Laura's secret*
Brett, Jan. *Fritz and the beautiful horses*
Brown, Margaret Wise. *The fierce yellow pumpkin*
Callahan, Sean. *Shannon and the world's tallest leprechaun*
Cleminson, Katie. *Magic box*
Clifton, Lucille. *Three wishes*
Conahan, Carolyn. *The big wish*
Davis, Aubrey. *Kishka for Koppel*
Ellwand, David. *Midas Mouse*
Fagan, Cary. *Ella May and the wishing stone*
Foley, Greg. *Make a wish Bear*
Willoughby and the lion
Fox, Mem. *Possum magic*
Geras, Adèle. *My wishes for you*
Hächler, Bruno. *Anna's wish*
Heidbreder, Robert. *I wished for a unicorn*
Holub, Joan. *Twinkle, star of the week*
Horn, Sandra Ann. *The dandelion wish*
Howe, James. *I wish I were a butterfly*
Hru, Dakari. *Joshua's Masai mask*
Jackson, Shirley. *9 magic wishes*
Kimmel, Eric A. *Joha makes a wish*
Kirk, Daniel. *Jack and Jill*
Kleven, Elisa. *The wishing ball*
Klinting, Lars. *What do you want?*
Krensky, Stephen. *The youngest fairy godmother ever*
Landa, Norbert. *Little Bear and the wishing tree*
Lesynski, Loris. *Rocksy*
Lipp, Frederick. *The caged birds of Phnom Penh*
McClintock, Barbara. *Molly and the magic wishbone*
McGrory, Anik. *Mouton's impossible dream*
Meddaugh, Susan. *The witch's walking stick*
Michelin, Linda. *Zuzu's wishing cake*
Morgan, Michaela. *Bunny wishes*
Moser, Lisa. *Watermelon wishes*
Munsch, Robert N. *Wait and see*
Murphy, Mary. *Caterpillar's wish*
Napoli, Donna Jo. *The wishing club*
Newman, Marlene. *Myron's magic cow*
Petty, Dini. *The queen, the bear and the bumblebee*
Pfister, Marcus. *Make a wish, Honey Bear!*
Polacco, Patricia. *Luba and the wren*
Primavera, Elise. *The house at the end of Ladybug Lane*
Proimos, James. *Joe's wish*
Pulver, Robin. *Alicia's tutu*
Puttock, Simon. *A ladder to the stars*
Reynolds, Peter H. *The smallest gift of Christmas*
Robertson, M. P. *The sandcastle*
Rock, Lois. *I wish tonight*
Rose, Marion. *The Christmas tree fairy*
Rosenthal, Amy Krouse. *Yes Day!*
Roth, Susan L. *Happy birthday Mr. Kang*
Shepard, Aaron. *The gifts of Wali Dad*
Shields, Carol Diggory. *I wish my brother was a dog*
Souhami, Jessica. *Sausages*
Stanley, Diane. *The trouble with wishes*
Stevenson, James. *The wish card ran out!*
Tan, Amy. *The moon lady*
Thong, Roseanne. *Wish*
Tobias, Tobi. *Wishes for you*
Turkle, Brinton. *Do not open*
van Lieshout, Elle. *The wish*
Vigna, Judith. *I wish my daddy didn't drink so much*
Wallace, Ivy. *Pookie puts the world right*
Washington, Ned. *When you wish upon a star*
Whybrow, Ian. *Wish, change, friend*
Williams, Suzanne. *My dog never says please*
Wishinsky, Frieda. *Please, Louise!*
Wood, Audrey. *Jubal's wish*
Wooldridge, Connie Nordhielm. *Wicked Jack*
Zemach, Margot. *The three wishes*
Zoboli, Giovanna. *I wish I had . . .*

Behavior – worrying

Borden, Louise. *Off to first grade*
Bourgeois, Paulette. *Franklin says "I love you"*
Brown, Marc. *Arthur's underwear*
Browne, Anthony. *Silly Billy*
Brun-Cosme, Nadine. *Big Wolf and Little Wolf, such a beautiful orange!*
Burg, Sarah Emmanuelle. *Do you still love me?*
Cannon, A. E. *Sophie's fish*
Carlstrom, Nancy White. *It's your first day of school, Annie Claire*
Clarke, Jane. *The best of both nests*
Cocca-Leffler, Maryann. *Jack's talent*
Collet, Géraldine. *All by myself!*
Cooper, Helen. *Dog biscuit*
Corey, Dorothy. *You go away*
Cuyler, Margery. *Bullies never win*

Hooray for Reading Day!
Stop drop and roll
Devlin, Wende. *Cranberry Easter*
Dodd, Emma. *Foxy*
Edwards, Pamela Duncan. *Dinosaur starts school*
The worrywarts
Foley, Greg. *Don't worry Bear*
Gavril, David. *Penelope Nuthatch and the big surprise*
George, Lucy M. *Back to school Tortoise*
Graves, Keith. *The unexpectedly bad hair of Barcelona Smith*
Griffin, Molly Beth. *Loon baby*
Hartt-Sussman, Heather. *Noni is nervous*
Henkes, Kevin. *Wemberly worried*
Horton, Joan. *Math attack!*
Jackson, Kathryn. *The saggy baggy elephant*
Jacobs, Julie. *My heart is a magic house*
Jadoul, Émile. *Good night, Chickie*
Johnson, Neil. *The falling raindrop*
Kasza, Keiko. *Ready for anything*
Kelley, Marty. *Winter woes*
Kempter, Christa. *When Mama can't sleep*
Klise, Kate. *Little Rabbit and the Night Mare*
Lasky, Kathryn. *Lunch bunnies*
Leijten, Aileen. *Hugging hour!*
Lester, Helen. *Something might happen*
Lewis, Paeony. *I'll always love you*
Loupy, Christophe. *Don't worry, Wags*
Lyon, Tammie. *Olive and Snowflake*
McGinty, Alice B. *Eliza's kindergarten pet*
McPhail, David. *Pig Pig returns*
Mahoney, Daniel J. *Monstergarten*
Marshall, James. *Portly McSwine*
Milord, Susan. *Happy school year!*
Montanari, Eva. *A very full morning*
Moss, Miriam. *A babysitter for Billy Bear*
Ohi, Ruth. *A trip with Grandma*
Pennypacker, Sara. *Stuart's cape*
Pett, Mark. *The girl who never made mistakes*
Pizzoli, Greg. *The watermelon seed*
Poydar, Nancy. *The bad-news report card*
The biggest test in the universe
Quackenbush, Robert M. *First grade jitters*
Raschka, Chris. *Waffle*
Ray, Jane. *The dollhouse fairy*
Roche, Denis. *Little Pig is capable*
Scieszka, Jon. *Melvin might?*
Spelman, Cornelia Maude. *When I feel worried*
Stadler, Alexander. *Beverly Billingsly borrows a book*
Urdahl, Catherine. *Emma's question*
Viorst, Judith. *Just in case*
Waddell, Martin. *Mimi's Christmas*
Wagner, Anke. *Tim's big move!*
Waldron, Kevin. *Mr. Peek and the misunderstanding at the zoo*
Whybrow, Ian. *Bella gets her skates on*
Yin. *Dear Santa, please come to the 19th floor*
Yum, Hyewon. *Mom, it's my first day of kindergarten!*

Being different *see* Character traits – being different

Bereavement *see* Death; Emotions – grief

Bible *see* Religion

Bigotry *see* Prejudice

Birds

Aardema, Verna. *Jackal's flying lesson*
Adams, Sarah. *Gary and Ray*
Aesop. *Bat's big game*
Feed me!
Aliki. *My visit to the zoo*
Amann, Jürg. *Ten birds*
Anholt, Laurence. *Billy and the big new school*
Apperley, Dawn. *Good night, sleep tight, little bunnies*
Arnosky, Jim. *Crinkleroot's 25 birds every child should know*
Mouse writing
Asch, Frank. *Baby Bird's first nest*
Bear's bargain
Moonbear
Moonbear's dream
Moonbear's pet
Mooncake
Aston, Dianna Hutts. *Mama Outside, Mama Inside*
Baker, Keith. *Just how long can a long string be?!*
No two alike
Barnes, Laura T. *Ernest and the big itch*
Bash, Barbara. *Urban roosts*
Bauer, Marion Dane. *The longest night*
Beck, Scott. *Pepito the brave*
Berger, Carin. *Forever friends*
Berkes, Marianne. *Marsh music*
Berne, Jennifer. *Calvin can't fly*
Bonwill, Ann. *I am not a copycat!*
Bouler, Olivia. *Olivia's birds*
Boyer, Cécile. *Woof meow tweet-tweet*
Brett, Jan. *Honey, honey — lion!*
Brian, Janeen. *Where does Thursday go?*
Bruchac, Joseph. *The great ball game*
Brunhoff, Laurent de. *Babar and the succotash bird*
Buchanan, Jane. *Seed magic*
Cannon, Janell. *Stellaluna*
Stellaluna: a pop-up book and mobile
Carney, Margaret. *Where does a tiger-heron spend the night?*
Charles, Veronika Martenova. *The birdman*
Chast, Roz. *Marco goes to school*
Chivers, Natalie. *Rhino's great big itch!*
Climo, Shirley. *Tuko and the birds*
Collard, Sneed B. *Beaks!*
Cousins, Lucy. *Doctor Maisy*
Cronin, Doreen. *Click, clack, moo*
Crowther, Kitty. *Jack and Jim*
Cruickshank, Margrit. *We're going to feed the ducks*
Davies, Jacqueline. *The boy who drew birds*
DePalma, Mary Newell. *The strange egg*
dePaola, Tomie. *The birds of Bethlehem*
The song of Francis
DiPucchio, Kelly. *What's the magic word?*
Dominguez, Angela. *Let's go, Hugo!*
Doolittle, Bev. *Reading the wild*
Dunning, Joan. *Seabird in the forest*
Ehlert, Lois. *Cuckoo, a Mexican folktale / Cucú: un cuento folklórico mexicano*
Feathers for lunch
Elliott, David. *And here's to you!*
Esbaum, Jill. *Tom's tweet*
Eure, Wesley. *A fish out of water*
Fleming, Candace. *Seven hungry babies*
When Agnes caws
Foley, Greg. *Purple Little Bird*

Franco, Betsy. *Birdsongs*
Frazier, Craig. *Bee and Bird*
Fredrickson, Lane. *Watch your tongue, Cecily Beasley*
Friend, Catherine. *The perfect nest*
Gallo, Frank. *Bird calls*
Gavril, David. *Penelope Nuthatch and the big surprise*
Genechten, Guido van. *The big woods orchestra*
Goble, Paul. *The great race of the birds and animals*
Goodall, Jane. *The eagle and the wren*
Graham, Bob. *How to heal a broken wing*
Gray, Samantha. *Birds*
Green, Jen. *Birds*
Grimm, Jacob and Wilhelm. *Battle of the beasts*
Haas, Irene. *Bess and Bella*
Harper, Charise Mericle. *Amy and Ivan*
Hayles, Marsha. *The feathered crown*
Helmer, Marilyn. *Three barnyard tales*
Henkes, Kevin. *Birds*
Herkert, Barbara. *Birds in your backyard*
Hills, Tad. *How Rocket learned to read*
Rocket writes a story
Rocket's mighty words
Hines, Anna Grossnickle. *Miss Emma's wild garden*
Hirschi, Ron. *When morning comes*
When night comes
Hoban, Tana. *A children's zoo*
Hunter, Anne. *What's in the meadow?*
Iwamura, Kazuo. *Hooray for snow!*
James, Simon. *The birdwatchers*
George flies south
Jenkins, Steve. *Animals in flight*
Jonas, Ann. *Bird talk*
Kaczman, James. *A bird and his worm*
Kasza, Keiko. *A mother for Choco*
Katschke, Judy. *Take a hike, Snoopy*
Kellogg, Steven. *Aster Aardvark's alphabet adventures*
Kelly, Irene. *Even an ostrich needs a nest*
Kimmel, Eric A. *The birds' gift*
King, Stephen Michael. *You*
Kirk, David. *Little bird, Biddle bird*
Kleven, Elisa. *The dancing deer and the foolish hunter*
Kono, Erin Eitter. *Caterina and the perfect party*
Krilanovich, Nadia. *Chicken, chicken, duck!*
Lachenmeyer, Nathaniel. *The origami master*
Lavis, Steve. *Jump!*
Lent, Blair. *Ruby and Fred*
Lerner, Harriet Goldhor. *Franny B. Kranny, there's a bird in your hair*
Lionni, Leo. *Inch by inch*
Tico and the golden wings
Lipp, Frederick. *The caged birds of Phnom Penh*
Long, Ethan. *Bird and Birdie in a fine day*
Up, tall and high
Louie, Therese On. *Raymond's perfect present*
McDonnell, Patrick. *South*
McGrory, Anik. *Mouton's impossible dream*
McKee, David. *Elmer and the big bird*
McPhail, David. *Farm morning*
Malnor, Carol L. *The Blues go birding across America*
Marley, Cedella. *Every little thing*
Mathers, Petra. *Herbie's secret Santa*
Lottie's new friend
Mazzola, Frank. *Counting is for the birds*
Mead, Alice. *Billy and Emma*
Meade, Holly. *If I never forever endeavor*
Meddaugh, Susan. *Tree of birds*
Melvin, Alice. *Counting birds*
Meres, Jonathan. *The big bad rumor*
Mollel, Tololwa M. *Song bird*
Mortimer, Rachael. *Song for a princess*
Munari, Bruno. *Bruno Munari's zoo*
Munro, Roxie. *Hatch!*
Myers, Christopher. *Sparrows*
Napoli, Donna Jo. *Albert*
Nathan, Emma. *What do you call a group of turkeys?*
Neitzel, Shirley. *The house I'll build for the wrens*
Newman, Marjorie. *Mole and the baby bird*
Mole and the baby bird [board book]
Norling, Beth. *The stone baby*
Oberman, Sheldon. *The wisdom bird*
O'Connor, Jane. *Fancy Nancy: explorer extraordinaire!*
Palatini, Margie. *Gorgonzola*
Paulsen, Gary. *Canoe days*
Pearson, Tracey Campbell. *The purple hat*
Peet, Bill. *The kweeks of Kookatumdee*
The pinkish, purplish, bluish egg
Perry, Andrea. *The Bicklebys' birdbath*
Pienkowski, Jan. *Bel and Bub and the baby bird*
Polacco, Patricia. *Mr. Lincoln's way*
Pomerantz, Charlotte. *Flap your wings and try*
Potter, Beatrix. *The tale of Jemima Puddle-Duck and other farmyard tales*
Pratt, Pierre. *Car*
Prosek, James. *Bird, butterfly, eel*
Reed, Lynn Rowe. *Basil's birds*
Riddle, Tohby. *The singing hat*
Robey, Katharine Crawford. *Where's the party?*
Robinson, Tim. *Tobias, the quig, and the rumplenut tree*
Rockwell, Anne. *Our yard is full of birds*
Rohmann, Eric. *Time flies*
Roth, Susan L. *Happy birthday Mr. Kang*
Rubin, Adam. *Those darn squirrels!*
Those darn squirrels and the cat next door
Those darn squirrels fly south
Ruddell, Deborah. *Today at the Bluebird Cafe*
Runton, Andy. *Owly and Wormy: friends all aflutter!*
Ryder, Joanne. *Wild birds*
Rylant, Cynthia. *The bird house*
San Souci, Robert D. *The birds of Killingworth*
Sayre, April Pulley. *If you should hear a honey guide*
Sazaklis, John. *Fowl play*
Scanlon, Elizabeth Garton. *Noodle and Lou*
Schaefer, Carole Lexa. *Two scarlet songbirds*
Segal, John. *The lonely moose*
Seuss, Dr. *Horton hatches the egg*
Thidwick, the big-hearted moose
Sharratt, Nick. *Shark in the park*
Shulevitz, Uri. *What is a wise bird like you doing in a silly tale like this?*
Simple gifts
Snicket, Lemony. *13 words*
Stead, Philip C. *Hello, my name is Ruby*
A home for Bird
Stevens, Janet. *Find a cow now!*
Stewart, Melissa. *A place for birds*
Stileman, Kali. *Roly-poly egg*
Snack time for Confetti
Stockdale, Susan. *Bring on the birds*
Tafuri, Nancy. *Where did Bunny go?*
Whose chick are you?
Will you be my friend?
Tankard, Jeremy. *Boo hoo Bird*
Grumpy Bird
Teevin, Toni. *What to do? What to do?*
Thong, Roseanne. *Fly free!*
Thornhill, Jan. *Is this Panama?*

Wild in the city
Timmers, Leo. *Crow*
Valckx, Catharina. *Lizette's green sock*
Van Fleet, Matthew. *Fuzzy yellow ducklings*
Ward, Helen. *The king of the birds*
Ward, Lindsay. *When Blue met Egg*
Wellington, Monica. *Riki's birdhouse*
Winer, Yvonne. *Birds build nests*
Winstead, Rosie. *Ruby and Bubbles*
Wood, Audrey. *Birdsong*
Little Penguin's tale
Yerkes, Jennifer. *A funny little bird*
Yolen, Jane. *Welcome to the river of grass*
Young, Cybèle. *Ten birds*
Ten birds meet a monster
Ziefert, Harriet. *Robin, where are you?*
Zoehfeld, Kathleen Weidner. *Did dinosaurs have feathers?*
Zullo, Germano. *Little bird*

Birds – blackbirds

Bryan, Ashley. *Beautiful blackbird*

Birds – bluebirds

Ketteman, Helen. *Armadilly chili*
Kirby, Pamela F. *What bluebirds do*
Lucas, David. *The robot and the bluebird*
Martin, David. *Peep and Ducky*
Staake, Bob. *Bluebird*

Birds – bluejays

Rockwell, Anne. *Two blue jays*

Birds – buzzards

Goble, Paul. *Iktomi and the buzzard*

Birds – canaries

Freeman, Don. *Quiet! There's a canary in the library*
Yolen, Jane. *Elsie's bird*

Birds – cardinals

Preller, James. *Cardinal and sunflower*

Birds – chickadees

Ziefert, Harriet. *Birdhouse for rent*

Birds – chickens

Ada, Alma Flor. *The rooster who went to his uncle's wedding*
Alborough, Jez. *Six little chicks*
Alexander, Kwame. *Acoustic Rooster and his barnyard band*
Allard, Harry. *Starlight goes to town*
Allen, Jonathan. *I'm not reading!*
Alter, Anna. *Abigail spells*
Amato, Mary. *The chicken of the family*
Arnold, Tedd. *The twin princes*
Auch, Mary Jane. *Bantam of the opera*
Beauty and the beaks
Chickerella
The Easter egg farm
Eggs mark the spot
Hen lake
Peeping Beauty
The plot chickens
Poultrygeist
Souperchicken
Baddiel, Ivor. *Cock-a-doodle quack! Quack!*
Baehr, Patricia. *Boo Cow*
Bardhan-Quallen, Sudipta. *Chicks run wild*
Battut, Eric. *The fox and the hen*
Berry, Lynne. *What floats in a moat?*
Birchall, Mark. *Hen goes shopping*
Bogan, Paulette. *Goodnight Lulu*
Lulu the big little chick
Bowles, Paula. *Scary Mary*
Brett, Jan. *Daisy comes home*
Hedgie's surprise
Brown, Jo. *Hoppity skip Little Chick*
Where's my mommy?
Brown, Ken. *The scarecrow's hat*
Browne, Eileen. *Handa's hen*
Bunting, Eve. *Hurry! Hurry!*
Burg, Sarah Emmanuelle. *One more egg*
Carle, Eric. *The rooster who set out to see the world*
Rooster's off to see the world
Cazet, Denys. *Elvis the rooster almost goes to heaven*
Chaconas, Dori. *Dori the contrary hen*
Chambers, Angela. *Follow that chicken!*
Chaucer, Geoffrey. *Chanticleer and the fox*
Chen, Chih-Yuan. *The featherless chicken*
Chicken Little. *Chicken Little*
Henny Penny, ill. by Emily Bolam
Henny Penny, ill. by Paul Galdone
Henny Penny, ill. by Sophie Windham
Henny-Penny
The sky is falling
Chukovskii, Kornei Ivanovich. *Good morning, chick*
Clark, Leslie Ann. *Peepsqueak!*
Clarke, Jane. *Stuck in the mud*
Collet, Géraldine. *All by myself!*
Crimi, Carolyn. *Henry and the Crazed Chicken Pirates*
Crum, Shutta. *Fox and Fluff*
Czernecki, Stefan. *Huevos rancheros*
Dallas-Conte, Juliet. *Cock-a-moo-moo*
Daly, Niki. *Welcome to Zanzibar Road*
What's cooking, Jamela?
Darbyshire, Kristen. *Put it on the list!*
Davis, Aubrey. *A hen for Izzy Pippik*
Davis, Jerry. *Little Chicken's big day*
de Las Casas, Dianne. *The Little "Read" Hen*
Dempsey, Kristy. *Surfer chick*
Denchfield, Nick. *Charlie Chick*
Desmoinaux, Christel. *Mrs. Hen's big surprise*
Diakité, Penda. *I lost my tooth in Africa*
DiCamillo, Kate. *Louise*
Dorros, Arthur. *City chicken*
Dumont, Jean-François. *The chickens build a wall*
Edwards, Pamela Duncan. *The mixed-up rooster*
Elliott, David. *One little chicken*
Emberley, Ed. *The red hen*
Emberley, Rebecca. *Chicken Little*
Feldman, Thea. *Who you callin' chicken?*
Fox, Mem. *Hattie and the fox*
Franceschelli, Christopher. *(Oliver)*
Freedman, Deborah. *Blue chicken*
Ginsburg, Mirra. *Across the stream*
The chick and the duckling
Golan, Avirama. *Little Naomi, Little Chick*
Golson, Terry. *Tillie lays an egg*

Gorbachev, Valeri. *Chicken chickens*
Chicken chickens go to school
The missing chick
Graves, Keith. *Chicken Big*
Grindley, Sally. *Where are my chicks?*
Hader, Berta Hoerner. *Cock-a-doodle doo*
Halls, Kelly Milner. *I bought a baby chicken*
Harrington, Janice N. *Busy-busy Little Chick*
The chicken-chasing queen of Lamar County
Harrison, David L. *Dylan, the eagle-hearted chicken*
Hayward, Linda. *The King's chorus*
Helakoski, Leslie. *Big chickens*
Big chickens fly the coop
Big chickens go to town
Hest, Amy. *Little chick*
Himmelman, John. *Chickens to the rescue*
Hopkins, Jackie Mims. *Prairie chicken little*
Horowitz, Dave. *Chico the brave*
Hutchins, Pat. *Bumpety bump*
Rosie's walk
Rosie's walk [board book]
Jadoul, Émile. *Good night, Chickie*
Jennewein, Lenore. *Chick-o-Saurus Rex*
Johnston, Tony. *Chicken in the kitchen*
Joosse, Barbara. *Higgledy-piggledy chicks*
Kasza, Keiko. *The wolf's chicken stew*
Kelley, Ellen A. *My life as a chicken*
Kellogg, Steven. *Chicken Little*
Kimmel, Eric A. *Medio Pollito*
Knudsen, Michelle. *Argus*
Kromhout, Rindert. *Little Donkey and the baby-sitter*
Laminack, Lester L. *Three hens and a peacock*
Latter, Jill. *Mama Hen's big day*
Lawrence, John. *This little chick*
Leslie, Amanda. *Are chickens stripy?*
Lester, Helen. *The revenge of the magic chicken*
Lin, Grace. *Olvina flies*
Olvina swims
The little red hen. *The little red hen,* ill. by Byron Barton
The little red hen, ill. by Emily Bolam
The little red hen, ill. by Paul Galdone
Little red hen
The little red hen, ill. by Jerry Pinkney
The little red hen, ill. by Kate Slater
The little red hen, ill. by Annie West
The little red hen, ill. by Margot Zemach
The little red hen: an old fable
The Little Red Hen and the Passover matzah
The Little Red Hen makes a pizza
Lottridge, Celia Barker. *The little rooster and the diamond button*
MacDonald, Margaret Read. *Little Rooster's diamond button*
McDonald, Megan. *Hen hears gossip*
MacLachlan, Patricia. *Nora's chicks*
McLellan, Stephanie Simpson. *The chicken cat*
McMillan, Bruce. *The problem with chickens*
Maguire, Gregory. *Crabby Cratchitt*
Manning, Mick. *Cock-a-doodle hooooooo!*
Marshall, James. *Wings: a tale of two chickens*
Martin, Bill, Jr. *Chicken Chuck*
Martin, Jacqueline Briggs. *Chicken joy on Redbean Road*
Martín Larrañaga, Ana. *Pepo and Lolo and the red apple*
Pepo and Lolo are friends
Mathers, Petra. *Lottie's new beach towel*
Matthews, Tina. *Out of the egg*
Meng, Cece. *Tough chicks*
Miller, Heather. *My chickens*
Milway, Katie Smith. *One hen*
Mollel, Tololwa M. *Kele's secret*
Most, Bernard. *Cock-a-doodle-moo!*
Murphy, Patti Beling. *Elinor and Violet*
Nimmo, Jenny. *Something wonderful*
Numeroff, Laura Joffe. *The Chicken sisters*
Ohi, Ruth. *Chicken, Pig, Cow and the class pet*
Chicken, Pig, Cow horse around
Chicken, Pig, Cow's first fight
O'Malley, Kevin. *Gimme cracked corn and I will share*
Oxley, Jennifer. *The chicken problem*
Palatini, Margie. *Bad boys get henpecked!*
Shelly
Three French hens
Partridge, Elizabeth. *Pig's eggs*
Pauli, Lorenz. *The fox in the library*
Paye, Won-Ldy. *Mrs. Chicken and the hungry crocodile*
Pearson, Tracey Campbell. *Bob*
Peet, Bill. *Cock-a-doodle Dudley*
Perl, Erica S. *Chicken Butt's back!*
Pinkwater, Daniel. *Beautiful Yetta*
Pomerantz, Charlotte. *Here comes Henny*
Poole, Amy Lowry. *How the rooster got his crown*
Purcell, Rebecca. *Super Chicken*
Rankin, Joan. *You're somebody special, Walliwigs!*
Rave, Friederike. *Outfoxing the fox*
Reiser, Lynn. *The surprise family*
Reynolds, Aaron. *Buffalo wings*
Chicks and salsa
Rodriguez, Béatrice. *The chicken thief*
Fox and hen together
Ruurs, Margriet. *Wake up, Henry Rooster!*
Sattler, Jennifer. *Chick 'n' Pug*
Chick 'n' Pug meet the Dude
Sauer, Tammi. *Bawk and roll*
Chicken dance
Schuh, Mari C. *Chickens on the farm*
Scillian, Devin. *Brewster the rooster*
Shah, Idries. *The silly chicken*
Shannon, George. *The Secret Chicken Club*
Tippy-toe chick, go
Sharmat, Marjorie Weinman. *Hooray for Mother's Day!*
Shea, Bob. *New socks*
Sidjanski, Brigitte. *Little Chicken and Little Duck*
Sklansky, Amy E. *Where do chicks come from?*
Stampler, Ann Redisch. *The rooster prince of Breslov*
Stein, David Ezra. *Interrupting chicken*
Stevens, Janet. *Cook-a-doodle-doo!*
Stoeke, Janet Morgan. *A friend for Minerva Louise*
A hat for Minerva Louise
Hide and seek
The Loopy Coop hens
The Loopy Coop hens: letting go
Minerva Louise
Minerva Louise and the colorful eggs
Minerva Louise and the red truck
Minerva Louise at school
Minerva Louise at the fair
Minerva Louise on Christmas Eve
Minerva Louise on Halloween
Pip's trip
Stone, Lynn M. *Chickens have chicks*
Stuchner, Joan Betty. *Can hens give milk?*
Sykes, Julie. *Dora's chicks*
Dora's eggs
Tafuri, Nancy. *Five little chicks*

Thomas, Jan. *Is everyone ready for fun?*
Thompson, Lauren. *Wee little chick*
The three little pigs *The three little pigs and the fox*
Valentina, Marina. *Lost in the roses*
Van Leeuwen, Jean. *Chicken soup*
van Lieshout, Maria. *Peep!*
Varon, Sara. *Chicken and Cat*
  Chicken and Cat clean up
Vere, Ed. *Chick*
Ward, Helen. *The rooster and the fox*
Waring, Richard. *Hungry hen*
Weston, Carrie. *If a chicken stayed for supper*
Why did the chicken cross the road?
Willis, Jeanne. *Mommy do you love me?*
Wormell, Christopher. *Henry and the fox*
Wormell, Mary. *Bernard the angry rooster*
  Hilda Hen's happy birthday
  Hilda Hen's search
Young, Ed. *Hook*

Birds – cranes

Bang, Molly. *Dawn*
  The paper crane
Bodkin, Odds. *The crane wife*
Chen, Kerstin. *Lord of the cranes*
Coerr, Eleanor. *Sadako*
George, Jean Craighead. *Luck*
Say, Allen. *The boy in the garden*
Wells, Rosemary. *Yoko's paper cranes*
Yagawa, Sumiko. *The crane wife*

Birds – crows

Aesop. *The crow and the pitcher*
Appelt, Kathi. *Merry Christmas, merry crow*
Chorao, Kay. *Pig and Crow*
Goble, Paul. *Crow chief*
Grant, Rose Marie. *Andiamo, Weasel*
Johnson, Paul Brett. *Bearhide and crow*
Kleven, Elisa. *The wishing ball*
Lionni, Leo. *Six crows*
Loux, Lynn C. *The day I could fly*
Lowry, Lois. *Crow call*
McDermott, Gerald. *Coyote*
Paul, Alison. *The crow (a not so scary story)*
Pringle, Laurence P. *Crows*
Raschka, Chris. *Little black crow*
Rosen, Michael. *Crow and Hawk*
Sillifant, Alec. *Farmer Ham*
Singer, Marilyn. *The company of crows*
Spirin, Gennady. *Martha*
Timmers, Leo. *Crow*
Van Laan, Nancy. *Rainbow crow*
Wheeler, Lisa. *Old Cricket*

Birds – cuckoos

Ehlert, Lois. *Cuckoo, a Mexican folktale / Cucú: un cuento folklórico mexicano*

Birds – dodos

Mathers, Petra. *Dodo gets married*
Sattler, Jennifer. *Uh-oh, Dodo!*

Birds – doves

Ford, Gilbert. *Flying lessons*
Peet, Bill. *The pinkish, purplish, bluish egg*
Potter, Beatrix. *The tale of the faithful dove*
Singer, Isaac Bashevis. *Why Noah chose the dove*
Wells, Rosemary. *The language of doves*
Yang, Belle. *Always come home to me*

Birds – ducks

Abrahams, Peter. *Quacky baseball*
Alborough, Jez. *Captain Duck*
  Duck in the truck
  Duck's key where can it be?
  Fix-it Duck
  Hit the ball Duck
  Super Duck
Anastas, Margaret. *A hug for you*
Andersen, Hans Christian. *The ugly duckling*, ill. by Adrienne Adams
  The ugly duckling, ill. by Sebastien Braun
  The ugly duckling, ill. by Lorinda Bryan Cauley
  The ugly duckling, ill. by Charlene Delage
  The ugly duckling, ill. by Robert Ingpen
  The ugly duckling, ill. by Rachel Isadora
  The ugly duckling, ill. by Steve Johnson
  The ugly duckling, ill. by Jerry Pinkney
  The ugly duckling, ill. by Meilo So
  The ugly duckling, ill. by Pirkko Vainio
  The ugly duckling, ill. by Bernadette Watts
  The ugly duckling, ill. by Roberta Wilson
Arnosky, Jim. *All night near the water*
Aruego, José. *The last laugh*
Asch, Frank. *Baby Duck's new friend*
Auch, Mary Jane. *The nutquacker*
Bardhan-Quallen, Sudipta. *Hampire!*
Barry, Frances. *Duckie's ducklings*
  Duckie's rainbow
Bates, Ivan. *Five little ducks*
Bechtold, Lisze. *Sally and the purple socks*
Berry, Lynne. *Duck dunks*
  Duck skates
  Duck tents
  Ducking for apples
Bramsen, Carin. *Hey, duck!*
Bromley, Nick. *Open very carefully*
Brown, Alan James. *Love-a-Duck*
Brown, Margaret Wise. *The golden egg book*
Bunting, Eve. *Happy birthday, dear duck*
  Have you seen my new blue socks?
Capucilli, Alyssa Satin. *Biscuit finds a friend*
  Katy Duck
  Katy Duck, big sister
  Katy Duck is a caterpillar
Carle, Eric. *10 little rubber ducks*
Chae, In Seon. *How do you count a dozen ducklings?*
Chen, Chih-Yuan. *Guji Guji*
Church, Caroline Jayne. *Ruff!*
Claflin, Willy. *The uglified ducky*
Cooper, Helen. *Delicious!*
  A pipkin of pepper
Costello, David Hyde. *I can help*
Cronin, Doreen. *Click, clack, quackity-quack*
  Duck for President
  Giggle, giggle, quack
  Thump, quack, moo
Cruickshank, Margrit. *We're going to feed the ducks*
Curious George and the dump truck
Davies, Nicola. *Just ducks!*
Duckling
Eaton, Maxwell. *Two dumb ducks*
Egan, Tim. *Dodsworth in London*

Dodsworth in New York
Dodsworth in Paris
Dodsworth in Rome
Emmett, Jonathan. *Ruby in her own time*
This way, Ruby!
Escoffier, Michaël. *Me first!*
Faulkner, Keith. *Do you have my quack?*
Fierstein, Harvey. *The sissy duckling*
Flack, Marjorie. *The story about Ping*
Ford, Bernette. *No more blanket for Lambkin!*
No more diapers for Ducky!
Gibbons, Gail. *Ducks*
Ginsburg, Mirra. *Across the stream*
The chick and the duckling
Goble, Paul. *Iktomi and the ducks*
Goldin, Augusta. *Ducks don't get wet*
Goldsboro, Bobby. *Noah and the ark; and, David and Goliath*
Gravett, Emily. *The odd egg*
Grimm, Jacob and Wilhelm. *The twelve princesses*
Grindley, Sally. *Mucky Duck*
Silly Goose and Dizzy Duck play hide-and-seek
Hader, Berta Hoerner. *Cock-a-doodle doo*
Hest, Amy. *Baby Duck and the bad eyeglasses*
Baby Duck and the cozy blanket
Guess who, Baby Duck
Make the team, Baby Duck
Off to school, Baby Duck
You're the boss, Baby Duck
Hills, Tad. *Duck and Goose*
Duck and Goose find a pumpkin
Duck and Goose, how are you feeling?
Duck and Goose, 1, 2, 3
Duck, Duck, Goose
What's up, Duck?
Hindley, Judy. *Do like a duck does*
Holmes, Janet A. *Have you seen Duck?*
Horowitz, Dave. *Duck, duck, moose*
Ives, Penny. *Celestine, drama queen*
James, Simon. *Little One Step*
Johansen, Hanna. *The duck and the owl*
Jonas, Ann. *Watch William walk*
Joyce, William. *Bently and egg*
Kasza, Keiko. *Ready for anything*
Keller, John G. *The rubber-legged ducky*
Kohuth, Jane. *Duck sock hop*
Lewis, Kim. *Seymour and Henry*
Linch, Tanya. *My duck*
Llewellyn, Claire. *Duck*
Long, Ethan. *The Wing Wing brothers carnival de math*
The Wing Wing brothers math spectacular!
McCloskey, Robert. *Make way for ducklings*
McMillan, Bruce. *Days of the ducklings*
McPhail, David. *Waddles*
Magloff, Lisa. *Duckling*
Mallat, Kathy. *Just ducky*
Martin, David. *Peep and Ducky*
Mathers, Petra. *A cake for Herbie*
Milgrim, David. *Santa Duck*
Santa Duck and his merry helpers
Moore, Eva. *Lucky ducklings*
Murphy, Mary. *Quick Duck!*
Nedwidek, John. *Ducks don't wear socks*
Nolan, Lucy A. *Jack Quack*
Palatini, Margie. *Earthquack*
Parker, Marjorie Blain. *Mama's little duckling*
Paterson, Katherine. *The tale of the Mandarin ducks*
Peters, Lisa Westberg. *Cold little duck, duck, duck*
Pfeffer, Wendy. *Mallard duck at Meadow View Pond*
Pfister, Marcus. *Charlie at the zoo*
Pomerantz, Charlotte. *One duck, another duck*
Potter, Beatrix. *The tale of Jemima Puddle-Duck*
Rankin, Joan. *Wow! It's great being a duck*
Rankin, Laura. *Fluffy and Baron*
Reiser, Lynn. *The surprise family*
Reynolds, Adrian. *Pete and Polo's farmyard adventure*
Ritchie, Alison. *Duck says don't!*
Roberton, Fiona. *The perfect present*
Wanted: the perfect pet
Rock, Brian. *The deductive detective*
Roddie, Shen. *Not now, Mrs. Wolf*
Root, Phyllis. *One duck stuck*
One duck stuck [board book]
Rosenthal, Amy Krouse. *Duck! Rabbit!*
Salzano, Tammi. *One rainy day*
Sauer, Tammi. *Mr. Duck means business*
Shannon, David. *Duck on a bike*
Sidjanski, Brigitte. *Little Chicken and Little Duck*
Simmons, Jane. *Bouncy bouncy Daisy*
Come along, Daisy!
Daisy and the Beastie
Daisy and the egg
Daisy says coo!
Daisy says, "Here we go round the mulberry bush"
Daisy says, "If you're happy and you know it"
Daisy, the little duck with big feet
Daisy's day out
Daisy's favorite things
Daisy's hide-and-seek
Go to sleep, Daisy
Quack, Daisy, quack!
Splish splash Daisy
Skalak, Barbara Anne. *Waddle, waddle, quack, quack, quack*
Sklansky, Amy E. *The duck who played the kazoo*
Sloat, Teri. *I'm a duck!*
Sones, Sonya. *Violet and Winston*
Stevenson, James. *Howard*
Monty
Stewart, Amber. *Puddle's new school*
Straaten, Harmen van. *Duck's tale*
For me?
Sweeney, Jacqueline. *What about Bettie?*
Tafuri, Nancy. *Goodnight, my duckling*
Have you seen my duckling?
Thomas, Jan. *Pumpkin trouble*
Thompson, Lauren. *Little Quack*
Little Quack [board book]
Little Quack: dial-a-duck
Little Quack's bedtime
Little Quack's hide and seek
Little Quack's hide and seek [board book]
Little Quack's new friend
Tryon, Leslie. *Albert's alphabet*
Albert's birthday
Albert's Christmas
Albert's Halloween
Twohy, Mike. *Outfoxed*
Urbanovic, Jackie. *Duck and cover*
Duck at the door
Duck soup
Sitting duck
Van Laan, Nancy. *Shingebiss*
Verboven, Agnes. *Ducks like to swim*
Verdick, Elizabeth. *Peep leap*
Waddell, Martin. *Farmer Duck*
It's quacking time

Webster J. Duck
Ward, Nick. *Come on Baby Duck*
Wells, Rosemary. *The itsy-bitsy spider*
Whippo, Walt. *Little white duck*
Wildsmith, Brian. *The little wood duck*
Wilhelm, Hans. *Quacky Ducky's Easter egg*
Quacky Ducky's Easter fun
Willems, Mo. *The duckling gets a cookie!?*
The pigeon finds a hot dog!
Winthrop, Elizabeth. *Bear and Mrs. Duck*
Bear's Christmas surprise
Yaccarino, Dan. *Five little ducks*
Yolen, Jane. *Dimity Duck*
Yorinks, Arthur. *Quack!*
Ziefert, Harriet. *A dozen ducklings lost and found*

Birds – eagles

Bardhan-Quallen, Sudipta. *Flying eagle*
The bear
Brett, Jan. *The three little dassies*
George, Jean Craighead. *The eagles are back*
Gibbons, Gail. *Soaring with the wind*
Goble, Paul. *Adopted by the eagles*
Gregorowski, Christopher. *Fly, eagle, fly!*
Harrison, David L. *Dylan, the eagle-hearted chicken*
Hausman, Gerald. *Eagle boy*
Hodge, Deborah. *Eagles*
Martin-James, Kathleen. *Soaring bald eagles*
Minshull, Evelyn White. *Eaglet's world*
Vaughan, Richard Lee. *Eagle boy*
Young, Ed. *Hook*

Birds – falcons

George, Jean Craighead. *Frightful's daughter*
Frightful's daughter meets the Baron Weasel
Jenkins, Priscilla Belz. *Falcons nest on skyscrapers*
Jessell, Tim. *Falcon*

Birds – finches

Pericoli, Matteo. *The true story of Stellina*

Birds – flamingos

Grambling, Lois G. *Miss Hildy's missing cape caper*
Guiberson, Brenda Z. *Mud city*
Harper, Jamie. *Miss Mingo and the fire drill*
Miss Mingo and the first day of school
Hewett, Joan. *A flamingo chick grows up*
Idle, Molly. *Flora and the flamingo*
London, Jonathan. *Flamingo sunset*
Sattler, Jennifer. *Sylvie*
Walsh, Ellen Stoll. *For Pete's sake*
Whitehouse, Patricia. *Flamingo*

Birds – geese

Aesop. *The goose that laid the golden egg*
Asher, Sandy. *Here comes Gosling!*
Bang, Molly. *Goose*
Bloom, Suzanne. *Fox forgets*
Oh! What a surprise!
A splendid friend, indeed
What about Bear?
Brennan-Nelson, Denise. *Grady the goose*
Church, Caroline Jayne. *One smart goose*
Cox, Phil Roxbee. *Goose on the loose*
Dunrea, Olivier. *Gideon*
Gideon & Otto
Gossie's busy day
Jasper & Joop
Merry Christmas, Ollie!
Ollie
Ollie the stomper
Ollie's Easter eggs
Ollie's Easter eggs [board book]
Ollie's Halloween
Peedie
Duvoisin, Roger Antoine. *Petunia*
Fox, Mem. *Boo to a goose*
Fredericks, Anthony D. *In one tidepool*
Greenstein, Elaine. *The goose man*
Grimm, Jacob and Wilhelm. *The golden goose*
Grindley, Sally. *Silly Goose and Dizzy Duck play hide-and-seek*
Harper, Charise Mericle. *When Randolph turned rotten*
Hawkins, Emily. *Little snow goose*
Hills, Tad. *Duck and Goose*
Duck and Goose find a pumpkin
Duck and Goose, how are you feeling?
Duck and Goose, 1, 2, 3
Duck, Duck, Goose
What's up, Duck?
Horacek, Petr. *Look out, Suzy Goose*
Silly Suzy Goose
Suzy Goose and the Christmas star
Inkpen, Mick. *Honk!*
Jackson, Chris. *The Gaggle sisters river tour*
Johnson, Paul Brett. *The goose who went off in a huff*
Kasza, Keiko. *Silly Goose's big story*
Kindermans, Martine. *You and me*
Lears, Laurie. *Waiting for Mr. Goose*
Lindbergh, Reeve. *The day the goose got loose*
Loth, Sebastian. *Remembering Crystal*
Zelda the Varigoose
McBratney, Sam. *Just you and me*
Mahy, Margaret. *A summery Saturday morning*
Montes, Marisa. *Egg-napped!*
Mraz, David. *Little Goose*
Oram, Hiawyn. *Gerda the goose*
Pilkey, Dav. *The Silly Gooses*
Polacco, Patricia. *I can hear the sun*
Rechenka's eggs
Ritchie, Alison. *Duck says don't!*
Rong, Yu. *A lovely day for Amelia Goose*
Root, Phyllis. *Grandmother Winter*
Sansone, Adele. *The little green goose*
Sayre, April Pulley. *Honk, honk, goose!*
Schoenherr, John. *Rebel*
Schubert, Ingrid. *Bear's eggs*
Simmons, Jane. *Ebb and Flo and the new friend*
Simont, Marc. *The goose that almost got cooked*
Spinelli, Eileen. *Silly Tilly*
Strand, Keith. *Grandfather's Christmas tree*
Tafuri, Nancy. *Silly little goose!*
Walsh, Ellen Stoll. *You silly goose*
Wild, Margaret. *Lucy Goosey*
Willems, Mo. *That is not a good idea!*
Wood, Jakki. *Never say boo to a goose!*

Birds – guinea fowl

Paterson, Brian. *Zigby camps out*

Birds – hawks

Baylor, Byrd. *Hawk, I'm your brother*
Hayes, Joe. *Little Gold Star / Estrellita de oro*
Kimura, Ken. *999 tadpoles*
McCarthy, Meghan. *City hawk*
Pia Toya
Rosen, Michael. *Crow and Hawk*
Schulman, Janet. *Pale Male*
Winter, Jeanette. *The tale of Pale Male*

Birds – herons

Gorbachev, Valeri. *Heron and Turtle*
McGaw, Wayne T. *T-boy of the bayou*
Quigley, Mary. *Granddad's fishing buddy*
Yolen, Jane. *An egret's day*

Birds – hummingbirds

Dudley, Rebecca. *Hank finds an egg*
Sayre, April Pulley. *The hungry hummingbird*
Sill, Cathryn. *About hummingbirds*
Yahgulanaas, Michael Nicoll. *The little hummingbird*

Birds – kestrels

Blake, Robert J. *Fledgling*

Birds – larks

Nelson, Marilyn. *Ostrich and Lark*

Birds – loons

Aston, Dianna Hutts. *Loony Little*
Griffin, Molly Beth. *Loon baby*
London, Jonathan. *Loon Lake*
Love, Pamela. *A loon alone*
Santucci, Barbara. *Loon summer*
Vande Griek, Susan. *Loon*

Birds – macaws

Mead, Alice. *Billy and Emma*

Birds – magpies

Springman, I. C. *More*
Wild, Margaret. *Fox*
Wilson, April. *April Wilson's magpie magic*

Birds – nightingales

Andersen, Hans Christian. *The nightingale,* ill. by Nancy Ekholm Burkert
The nightingale, ill. by Pirkko Vainio
The nightingale, ill. by Lisbeth Zwerger

Birds – ostriches

Aardema, Verna. *The lonely lioness and the ostrich chicks*
Nelson, Marilyn. *Ostrich and Lark*
Peet, Bill. *Zella, Zack, and Zodiac*
Weigelt, Udo. *The Easter Bunny's baby*
Whitehouse, Patricia. *Ostrich*

Birds – owls

Aesop. *Town mouse, country mouse*
Ainsworth, Kimberly. *Hootenanny!*
Allen, Jonathan. *"I'm not cute!"*
I'm not reading!
"I'm not Santa!"
"I'm not scared!"
Blaich, Ute. *The star*
Brown, Alan James. *Hoot and Holler*
Brunelle, Nicholas. *Snow moon*
Chapman, Jane. *I'm not sleepy!*
Clifton-Brown, Holly. *Annie Hoot and the knitting extravaganza*
Corderoy, Tracey. *The little white owl*
Davies, Nicola. *White owl, barn owl*
Edwards, Pamela Duncan. *While the world is sleeping*
Ericsson, Jennifer A. *Whoo goes there?*
Feeney, Tatyana. *Little Owl's orange scarf*
Gibbons, Gail. *Owls*
Haughton, Chris. *Little Owl lost*
Hills, Tad. *Rocket writes a story*
Hiscock, Bruce. *Ookpik*
Hissey, Jane. *Hoot*
Hopgood, Tim. *Wow! said the owl*
Hutchins, Pat. *Good-night owl*
Iwamura, Kazuo. *Bedtime in the forest*
Johansen, Hanna. *The duck and the owl*
Johnston, Tony. *The barn owls*
Jones, Christianne. *Lacey Walker, nonstop talker*
Lear, Edward. *The owl and the pussycat,* ill. by Jan Brett
The owl and the pussycat, ill. by Paul Galdone
The owl and the pussycat, ill. by Anne Mortimer
Lears, Laurie. *Nathan's wish*
Lionni, Leo. *Six crows*
Lobel, Arnold. *Odd owls and stout pigs*
London, Jonathan. *The owl who became the moon*
McDonald, Megan. *Whoo-oo is it?*
Manning, Mick. *Cock-a-doodle hooooooo!*
Marino, Gianna. *Too tall houses*
Modarressi, Mitra. *Owlet's first flight*
Most, Bernard. *Z-Z-Zoink!*
Na, Il Sung. *A book of sleep*
Nicholls, Judith. *Billywise*
Oliver, Narelle. *Twilight hunt*
Potter, Beatrix. *The tale of Squirrel Nutkin*
Rosenthal, Amy Krouse. *Little Hoot*
Ruddell, Deborah. *Who said coo?*
Runton, Andy. *Owly and Wormy: bright lights and starry nights!*
Serfozo, Mary. *Whooo's there?*
Srinivasan, Divya. *Little Owl's night*
Tomlinson, Jill. *The owl who was afraid of the dark*
Townsend, Emily Rose. *Owls*
Waddell, Martin. *Owl babies*
Whitehouse, Patricia. *Barn owls*
Willis, Jeanne. *Fly, chick, fly!*
Yolen, Jane. *Owl moon*

Birds – parakeets, parrots

Agee, Jon. *Terrific*
Bee, William. *And the train goes . . .*
Best, Cari. *Ava and the real Lucille*
Davis, Patricia Anne. *Brian's bird*
DePalma, Mary Newell. *The perfect gift*
Dicmas, Courtney. *Harold finds a voice*
Fox, Mem. *Tough Boris*
Harris, Trudy. *Say something, Perico*
Javaherbin, Mina. *The secret message*

Kennedy, Kim. *Pirate Pete's giant adventure*
Lester, Helen. *Princess Penelope's parrot*
Ljungkvist, Laura. *Pepi sings a new song*
McFarland, Lyn Rossiter. *The pirate's parrot*
Meddaugh, Susan. *Martha walks the dog*
Nadimi, Suzan. *The rich man and the parrot*
Pinkwater, Daniel. *Beautiful Yetta*
Rankin, Joan. *You're somebody special, Walliwigs!*
Rawson, Katherine. *If you were a parrot*
Roth, Susan L. *Parrots over Puerto Rico*
Steig, William. *Wizzil*
Witte, Anna. *The parrot Tico Tango*

Birds – peacocks, peahens

Auch, Mary Jane. *Hen lake*
Hodgkinson, Leigh. *Limelight Larry*
Laminack, Lester L. *Three hens and a peacock*
Peet, Bill. *The spooky tail of Prewitt Peacock*
Polacco, Patricia. *Just plain Fancy*

Birds – pelicans

Johnson, Rebecca. *The proud pelican's secret*
Reed, Lynn Rowe. *Roscoe and the pelican rescue*

Birds – penguins

Anderson, Derek. *Romeo and Lou blast off*
Apperley, Dawn. *Flip and Flop*
Arnold, Caroline. *A penguin's world*
Barner, Bob. *Penguins, penguins, everywhere!*
Brooks, Erik. *Polar opposites*
Buzzeo, Toni. *One cool friend*
Cuyler, Margery. *Please play safe!*
Davies, Gill. *Can't, don't, won't*
Dodd, Emma. *I am small*
Dunbar, Polly. *Penguin*
Pingüino / penguin
Duquennoy, Jacques. *North Pole, South Pole*
Dyer, Heather. *Tina and the penguin*
Fromental, Jean-Luc. *365 penguins*
Genechten, Guido van. *No ghost under my bed*
Gibbons, Gail. *Penguins!*
Gliori, Debi. *Penguin post*
Gorbachev, Valeri. *Turtle's penguin day*
Guiberson, Brenda Z. *The emperor lays an egg*
Guion, Melissa. *Baby penguins everywhere!*
Harper, Lee. *The Emperor's cool clothes*
Hewett, Joan. *A penguin chick grows up*
Horacek, Petr. *Flip's day*
Ichikawa, Satomi. *I am Pangoo the penguin*
Jadoul, Emile. *All by myself!*
Jeffers, Oliver. *Lost and found*
Up and down
Karas, G. Brian. *Skidamarink*
Kellogg, Steven. *A penguin pup for Pinkerton*
Kimmel, Elizabeth Cody. *My penguin Osbert*
My penguin Osbert in love
Lang, Aubrey. *Baby penguin*
Latimer, Alex. *Penguin's hidden talent*
Lester, Helen. *Happy birdday, Tacky!*
Tacky and the Emperor
Tacky and the Winter Games
Tacky goes to camp
Tacky in trouble
Tacky the penguin
Tackylocks and the three bears
Tacky's Christmas
Three cheers for Tacky
Lin, Grace. *Olvina swims*
London, Jonathan. *Little penguin*
McDonald, Megan. *Penguin and Little Blue*
McMillan, Bruce. *Puffins climb, penguins rhyme*
Magloff, Lisa. *Penguin*
Markle, Sandra. *A mother's journey*
Marzollo, Jean. *Pierre the penguin*
Minor, Florence. *If you were a penguin*
Mitton, Tony. *Playful little penguins*
Morison, Toby. *Little Louie takes off*
Murphy, Mary. *I like it when . . .*
I like it when . . . [board book]
Please be quiet!
Some things change
Perlman, Janet. *The Emperor Penguin's new clothes*
The penguin and the pea
Pfister, Marcus. *Penguin Pete and Little Tim*
Pichon, Liz. *Penguins*
Portis, Antoinette. *A penguin story*
Radcliffe, Theresa. *Nanu, penguin chick*
Richardson, Justin. *And Tango makes three*
Rickards, Lynne. *Pink!*
Rodriguez, Edel. *Sergio makes a splash*
Sergio saves the game!
Ryan, Pam Muñoz. *Tony Baloney*
Schafer, Kevin. *Penguins A B C*
Penguins 1 2 3
Schindel, John. *Busy penguins*
Seibold, J. Otto. *Penguin dreams*
Shields, Carol Diggory. *Martian rock*
Sill, Cathryn. *About penguins*
Tatham, Betty. *Penguin chick*
Townsend, Emily Rose. *Penguins*
Weeks, Sarah. *Without you*
Whybrow, Ian. *Wish, change, friend*
Wiesmüller, Dieter. *The adventures of Marco and Polo*
Wilson, Karma. *Don't be afraid, Little Pip*
What's in the egg, Little Pip?
Where is home, Little Pip?
Wood, Audrey. *Little Penguin's tale*
Yoon, Salina. *Penguin and Pinecone*
Penguin in love
Penguin on vacation

Birds – pigeons

Eitzen, Ruth. *Tara's flight*
Farmer, Nancy. *Clever Ali*
Keller, Holly. *Sophie's window*
Macaulay, David. *Angelo*
Peet, Bill. *Fly, Homer, fly*
Ruddell, Deborah. *Who said coo?*
San Souci, Daniel. *The Mighty Pigeon Club*
Wells, Rosemary. *The language of doves*
Willems, Mo. *Don't let the pigeon drive the bus*
Don't let the pigeon stay up late!
The duckling gets a cookie!?
The pigeon finds a hot dog!
The pigeon has feelings, too!
The pigeon loves things that go!
The pigeon wants a puppy!

Birds – plovers

dePaola, Tomie. *Bill and Pete*
Bill and Pete go down the Nile
Bill and Pete to the rescue

Birds – ptarmigans

Guenther, James. *Turnagain, Ptarmigan, where did you go?*
London, Jonathan. *Gone again ptarmigan*

Birds – puffins

Allen, Jonathan. *Don't copy me!*
Bentley, Dawn. *Welcome back, Puffin*
De Beer, Hans. *Little Polar Bear and the big balloon*
Horacek, Petr. *Puffin Peter*
McMillan, Bruce. *Nights of the pufflings*
Puffins climb, penguins rhyme
Soltis, Sue. *Nothing like a puffin*
Wild, Margaret. *Puffling*
Zecca, Katherine. *A puffin's year*

Birds – ravens

Bansch, Helga. *Odd bird out*
Battle-Lavert, Gwendolyn. *The shaking bag*
Dupre, Kelly. *The raven's gift*
Johnson, Amy Crane. *Cinnamon and the April shower / Canela y el aguacero de abril*
Mason moves away / Mason se muda
McDermott, Gerald. *Raven*
Weigelt, Udo. *It wasn't me*

Birds – roadrunners

Anaya, Rudolfo A. *Roadrunner's dance*

Birds – robins

Atkins, Jeannine. *Robin's home*
Fisher, Aileen Lucia. *You don't look like your mother*
Holmes, Anita. *Where robins fly*
Jenkins, Priscilla Belz. *A nest full of eggs*
Ketcham, Sallie. *The Christmas bird*
Mackall, Dandi Daley. *The story of the Easter robin*
Posada, Mia. *Robins*
Rockwell, Anne. *My spring robin*
Schwartz, Amy. *A beautiful girl*

Birds – sandpipers

Willis, Nancy Carol. *Red knot*

Birds – seagulls

Allen, Jonathan. *Don't copy me!*
Clark, Katie. *Seagull Sam*
Eaton, Maxwell. *Two dumb ducks*
Engels-Fietzek, Petra. *Sophie and the seagull*
Gibbons, Gail. *Gulls — gulls — gulls*
Simmons, Jane. *Ebb and Flo and the greedy gulls*
Turkle, Brinton. *Thy friend, Obadiah*
Walsh, Ellen Stoll. *Hamsters to the rescue*
Waugh, Peter. *The great cannon beach mouse caper*

Birds – sparrows

Kasbarian, Lucine. *The greedy sparrow*
Lee, Y. J. *The little moon princess*
Myers, Christopher. *Sparrows*

Birds – storks

Brown, Margaret Wise. *Wheel on the chimney*
Clarke, Jane. *The best of both nests*
Olson, David J. *The thunderstruck stork*

Birds – swallows

Politi, Leo. *Song of the swallows*
Ryan, Pam Muñoz. *Nacho and Lolita*
Swinburne, Stephen R. *Swallows in the birdhouse*

Birds – swans

Andersen, Hans Christian. *The ugly duckling*, ill. by Adrienne Adams
The ugly duckling, ill. by Sebastien Braun
The ugly duckling, ill. by Lorinda Bryan Cauley
The ugly duckling, ill. by Charlene Delage
The ugly duckling, ill. by Robert Ingpen
The ugly duckling, ill. by Rachel Isadora
The ugly duckling, ill. by Steve Johnson
The ugly duckling, ill. by Jerry Pinkney
The ugly duckling, ill. by Meilo So
The ugly duckling, ill. by Pirkko Vainio
The ugly duckling, ill. by Bernadette Watts
The ugly duckling, ill. by Roberta Wilson
The wild swans, ill. by Anne Yvonne Gilbert
The wild swans, ill. by Susan Jeffers
Bunting, Eve. *Swan in love*
Edwards, Pamela Duncan. *Honk!*
Geras, Adèle. *Swan Lake*
Grimm, Jacob and Wilhelm *The six swans*
Kent, Allegra. *Ballerina swan*
London, Jonathan. *Little swan*
Morpurgo, Michael. *The silver swan*
Shulman, Lisa. *Over in the meadow at the big ballet*
Sones, Sonya. *Violet and Winston*
Tafuri, Nancy. *Whose chick are you?*

Birds – toucans

Lehrhaupt, Adam. *Warning: do not open this book!*

Birds – turkeys

Anderson, Derek. *Over the river*
Archer, Peggy. *Turkey surprise*
Arnosky, Jim. *All about turkeys*
I'm a turkey!
Auch, Mary Jane. *Beauty and the beaks*
Balian, Lorna. *Sometimes it's turkey*
Bateman, Teresa. *Gus, the pilgrim turkey*
A plump and perky turkey
Bunting, Eve. *A turkey for Thanksgiving*
Cole, Brock. *The money we'll save*
Cowley, Joy. *Gracias, the Thanksgiving turkey*
Falwell, Cathryn. *Gobble gobble*
Kroll, Steven. *One tough turkey*
Mayr, Diane. *Run, Turkey, run*
Nathan, Emma. *What do you call a group of turkeys?*
Pilkey, Dav. *'Twas the night before Thanksgiving*
Pollock, Penny. *The turkey girl*
Reed, Lynn Rowe. *Thelonius Turkey lives!*
Shannon, George. *Turkey Tot*
Silvano, Wendi. *Turkey Claus*
Turkey trouble
Stiegemeyer, Julie. *Gobble gobble crash!*
Sturgis, Brenda Reeves. *10 turkeys in the road*
Waddell, Martin. *Captain Small Pig*
Wheeler, Lisa. *Turk and Runt*
White, Linda. *Too many turkeys*

Birds – vultures

Grindley, Sally. *The sulky vulture*
Peet, Bill. *Eli*
Sayre, April Pulley. *Vulture view*

Birds – woodpeckers

Cousins, Lucy. *Peck, peck, peck*
Townsend, Emily Rose. *Woodpeckers*

Birds – wrens

Polacco, Patricia. *Luba and the wren*

Birth

Alexander, Sue. *One more time, Mama*
Andreae, Giles. *There's a house inside my mommy*
Anholt, Laurence. *Sophie and the new baby*
Aston, Dianna Hutts. *Mama Outside, Mama Inside*
Batten, Mary. *Who has a belly button?*
Bauer, Marion Dane. *Grandmother's song*
Carlstrom, Nancy White. *Before you were born*
Cocovini, Abby. *What's inside your tummy, Mommy?*
Cole, Joanna. *How you were born*
My puppy is born
When you were inside mommy
Dixon, Ann. *Waiting for Noël*
Douglas, Ann. *Before you were born*
Fearnley, Jan. *A special something*
Fox, Mem. *Sophie*
Frasier, Debra. *On the day you were born*
Grambling, Lois G. *Grandma tells a story*
Harris, Robie H. *What's in there?*
Holt, Kimberly Willis. *Waiting for Gregory*
Holt, Sharon. *Did my mother do that?*
Kallok, Emma. *Gem*
Lohans, Alison. *Waiting for the sun*
Lund, Deb. *Tell me my story, Mama*
Mackall, Dandi Daley. *There's a baby in there!*
MacLachlan, Patricia. *All the places to love*
Overend, Jenni. *Welcome with love*
Pringle, Laurence P. *Everybody has a bellybutton*
Radunsky, Vladimir. *Ten*
Rockwell, Lizzy. *Hello baby!*
Rosenberg, Maxine B. *Mommy's in the hospital having a baby*
Saltz, Gail. *Amazing you*
Sears, William, M.D. *Baby on the way*
Simpson-Enock, Sarah. *Mommy, Mommy, what's in your tummy?*
Sykes, Julie. *Dora's eggs*
This and that
Tillman, Nancy. *On the night you were born*
Van Steenwyk, Elizabeth. *Prairie Christmas*
Waiting for baby
Yolen, Jane. *Grandma's hurrying child*

Birthdays

Aliki. *Use your head, dear*
Allen, Nancy Kelly. *"Happy Birthday"*
Anholt, Catherine. *Happy birthday, Chimp and Zee*
Asch, Frank. *Happy birthday, Big Bad Wolf*
Happy birthday, moon!
Asher, Sandy. *What a party!*
Ashman, Linda. *Maxwell's magic mix-up*
Avraham, Kate Aver. *What will you be, Sara Mee?*
Awdry, W. *Happy birthday, Thomas!*
Badescu, Ramona. *Big Rabbit's bad mood*
Baeten, Lieve. *Happy birthday, Little Witch!*
Baker, Roberta. *Olive's pirate party*
Bastianich, Lidia. *Nonna's birthday surprise*
Beck, Andrea. *Elliot bakes a cake*
Beck, Scott. *Happy birthday, Monster!*
A mud pie for mother
Becker, Bonny. *A birthday for Bear*
Bemelmans, Ludwig. *Madeline in London*
Berenstain, Stan and Jan. *The Berenstain bears and too much birthday*
Bergel, Colin. *Mail by the pail*
Bertrand, Diane Gonzales. *The last doll / La última muñeca*
The party for Papa Luis / La fiesta para Papa Luis
Best, Cari. *Three cheers for Catherine the Great!*
Blackstone, Stella. *Bear's birthday*
Borden, Louise. *A. Lincoln and me*
Bourgeois, Paulette. *Franklin says "I love you"*
Postal workers
Breen, Steve. *Pug and Doug*
Brown, Marc. *Arthur's birthday*
Browne, Anthony. *Gorilla*
Brunhoff, Laurent de. *Babar's birthday surprise*
Bunting, Eve. *Flower garden*
Happy birthday, dear duck
Little Badger's just-about birthday
A picnic in October
The Wednesday surprise
Cabrera, Jane. *One, two, buckle my shoe*
Calmenson, Stephanie. *Birthday at the Panda Palace*
Capucilli, Alyssa Satin. *Happy birthday, Biscuit!*
Carle, Eric. *Hello, red fox*
The secret birthday message
Carlstrom, Nancy White. *Happy birthday, Jesse Bear!*
Cazet, Denys. *December 24th*
A fish in his pocket
Charlip, Remy. *Handtalk birthday*
Chavarría-Cháirez, Becky. *Magda's piñata magic / Magda y la piñata mágica*
Magda's tortillas / Las tortillas de Magada
Cheng, Andrea. *The lemon sisters*
Chodos-Irvine, Margaret. *Best best friends*
Christelow, Eileen. *Don't wake up Mama!*
Clarke, Jane. *Trumpet*
Cleminson, Katie. *Magic box*
Coats, Lucy. *Neil's numberless world*
Cooke, Trish. *So much*
Cousins, Lucy. *Happy birthday, Maisy*
Cox, Judy. *Happy birthday, Mrs. Millie!*
Dale, Penny. *Dinosaur zoom!*
Daly, Niki. *Happy birthday, Jamela!*
Day, Alexandra. *Carl's birthday*
deGroat, Diane. *Happy birthday to you, you belong in a zoo*
Demas, Corinne. *The boy who was generous with salt*
The disappearing island
Díaz, Katacha. *Carolina's gift*
DiPucchio, Kelly. *Crafty Chloe*
Dixon, Ann. *Waiting for Noël*
Edwards, Pamela Duncan. *Rosie's roses*
Ellwand, David. *Alfred's party*
Elya, Susan Middleton. *F is for fiesta*
Evans, Cambria. *Martha Moth makes socks*
Faglia, Matteo. *Happy birthday, I'm 1*
Happy birthday, I'm 2
Happy birthday, I'm 3
Happy birthday, I'm 4
Fearnley, Jan. *Mr. Wolf and the three bears*

Fernandes, Eugenie. *Big week for little mouse*
Flack, Marjorie. *Ask Mr. Bear*
Fleming, Candace. *Clever Jack takes the cake*
Fliess, Sue. *A gluten-free birthday for me!*
Foreman, George. *Let George do it!*
Fox, Mem. *Night noises*
Frasier, Debra. *A birthday cake is no ordinary cake*
Freeman, Tor. *Hooray! I'm five today!*
Gantos, Jack. *Happy birthday, Rotten Ralph*
Gibbons, Gail. *Happy birthday!*
Gillmor, Don. *Yuck, a love story*
Glass, Julie. *A dollar for Penny*
Gliori, Debi. *What's the time, Mr. Wolf?*
Goble, Paul. *Iktomi and the boulder*
Goodall, John S. *Shrewbettina's birthday*
Goode, Diane. *Mama's perfect present*
Gorbachev, Valeri. *Nicky and the fantastic birthday gift*
What's the big idea, Molly?
Graham, Bob. *Oscar's half birthday*
Hardy, Sarah Frances. *Puzzled by pink*
Harper, Charise Mericle. *The best birthday ever!*
When Randolph turned rotten
Hennessy, B. G. *Corduroy's birthday*
Hest, Amy. *Nana's birthday party*
Hill, Eric. *Spot bakes a cake*
Spot's birthday party
Hoban, Russell. *A birthday for Frances*
Hobbie, Holly. *Everything but the horse*
Toot and Puddle, a present for Toot
Hoberman, Mary Ann. *The seven silly eaters*
Hosford, Kate. *Big birthday*
Howe, James. *Houndsley and Catina and the birthday surprise*
Huget, Jennifer LaRue. *The best birthday party ever*
Hughes, Shirley. *Alfie and the birthday surprise*
Hunter, Sally. *Humphrey's birthday*
Hutchins, Pat. *Happy birthday, Sam*
It's my birthday!
Inkpen, Mick. *Kipper and Roly*
Kipper's birthday
Janni, Rebecca. *Every cowgirl needs a horse*
Jennings, Linda. *Hide and seek birthday treat*
Jocelyn, Marthe. *Hannah and the seven dresses*
Jonas, Ann. *The thirteenth clue*
Jonell, Lynne. *It's my birthday, too!*
Jorgensen, Gail. *Gotcha!*
Kasza, Keiko. *My lucky birthday*
Keller, Holly. *Henry's happy birthday*
Khan, Rukhsana. *Big red lollipop*
Kirk, David. *Miss Spider's ABC*
Kleven, Elisa. *Ernst*
Kroll, Virginia L. *Jason takes responsibility*
Kromhout, Rindert. *Little Donkey and the birthday present*
Kulka, Joe. *Wolf's coming*
Lasky, Kathryn. *Starring Lucille*
Lears, Laurie. *Megan's birthday tree*
Leedy, Loreen. *Crazy like a fox*
Lester, Helen. *Happy birdday, Tacky!*
Levine, Gail Carson. *Betsy Red Hoodie*
Lewin, Ted. *Amazon boy*
Lewis, Rose A. *Every year on your birthday*
Linders, Clara. *The very best door of all*
Lodge, Jo. *Happy birthday, Moo Moo*
Look, Lenore. *Henry's first-moon birthday*
Lord, Cynthia. *Happy birthday, Hamster*
Lucas, David. *Cake girl*
McClatchy, Lisa. *Dear Tyrannosaurus Rex*
McClure, Wendy. *The princess and the peanut allergy*
McCormack, Caren McNelly. *The fiesta dress*
McCourt, Lisa. *Chicken soup for little souls: The never-forgotten doll*
McCourt, Lisa, et al. *Chicken soup for little souls: Della Splatnuk birthday girl*
McElligott, Matthew. *Backbeard and the birthday suit*
Machado, Ana Maria. *What a party!*
Mackintosh, David. *Marshall Armstrong is new to our school*
McKissack, Patricia C. *Messy Bessey and the birthday overnight*
McNamara, Margaret. *George Washington's birthday*
McNaughton, Colin. *Not last night but the night before*
McPhail, David. *Big Brown Bear's birthday surprise*
Madrigal, Antonio Hernandez. *Erandi's braids*
Martin, Bill, Jr. *Fire! Fire! said Mrs. McGuire*
"Fire! Fire!" said Mrs. McGuire
Martin, David. *Monkey business*
Mayer, Mercer. *Bun Bun's birthday*
Meddaugh, Susan. *Martha says it with flowers*
Milord, Susan. *Happy 100th day!*
Miranda, Anne. *Alphabet fiesta*
Monster math
Modell, Frank. *Ice cream soup*
Modesitt, Jeanne. *Little Mouse's happy birthday*
Mora, Pat. *A birthday basket for Tía*
One, two, three / Uno, dos, tres
Pablo's tree
Morales, Yuyi. *Just in case: a trickster tale and Spanish alphabet book*
Moss, Miriam. *I'll be your friend, Smudge*
Muir, Leslie. *The little bitty bakery*
Munsch, Robert N. *Moira's birthday*
Wait and see
Murphy, Stuart J. *Too many kangaroo things to do!*
Myller, Rolf. *How big is a foot?*
Neuschwander, Cindy. *Sir Cumference and all the king's tens*
Noble, Trinka Hakes. *Jimmy's boa and the big splash birthday bash*
Numeroff, Laura Joffe. *Otis and Sydney and the best birthday ever*
O'Connor, Jane. *Bonjour, butterfly*
Fancy Nancy: ooh la la! it's beauty day
Oxenbury, Helen. *It's my birthday*
Patricelli, Leslie. *The birthday box*
Paul, Ann Whitford. *Fiesta fiasco*
Peek, Merle. *Mary wore her red dress and Henry wore his green sneakers*
Pfister, Marcus. *Happy birthday, Bertie!*
Make a wish, Honey Bear!
Pilgrim, Elza. *The china doll*
Polacco, Patricia. *Some birthday!*
Pomerantz, Charlotte. *You're not my best friend anymore*
Reed, Lynn Rowe. *Pedro, his perro, and the alphabet sombrero*
Rempt, Fiona. *Snail's birthday wish*
Reynolds, Marilynn. *A present for Mrs. Kazinski*
Rice, Eve. *Benny bakes a cake*
Rim, Sujean. *Birdie's big-girl dress*
Roberton, Fiona. *The perfect present*
Roberts, Bethany. *Birthday mice*
Rodman, Mary Ann. *A tree for Emmy*
Rollings, Susan. *New shoes, red shoes*
Rose, Deborah Lee. *Birthday zoo*
Ross, Tony. *I want two birthdays!*

Rossell, Judith. *Ruby and Leonard and the great big surprise*
Ryan, Pam Muñoz. *Mice and beans*
Rylant, Cynthia. *Birthday presents*
Sáenz, Benjamin Alire. *A gift from papá Diego / Un regalo de papá Diego*
Grandma Fina and her wonderful umbrellas / La abuelita Fina y sus sombrillas maravillosas
Sage, Angie. *Molly and the birthday party*
Saltzberg, Barney. *Hi, Blueberry!*
Hip, hip, hooray day!
Samuels, Barbara. *Happy birthday, Dolores*
Sayre, April Pulley. *It's my city*
Scanlon, Elizabeth Garton. *Happy birthday, Bunny!*
Schaap, Martine. *Mop and the birthday picnic*
Schachner, Judith Byron. *Yo, Vikings*
Schoenherr, Ian. *Don't spill the beans!*
Pip and Squeak
Schotter, Roni. *Mama, I'll give you the world*
Schubert, Leda. *Winnie plays ball*
Scieszka, Jon. *Battle Bunny*
Segal, Lore Groszmann. *Morris the artist*
Selkowe, Valrie M. *Happy birthday to me!*
Sendak, Maurice. *Bumble-ardy*
Seuss, Dr. *Happy birthday to you!*
Shannon, George. *The surprise*
Silbaugh, Elizabeth. *Raggedy Ann's birthday party book*
Simpson, Lesley. *The Purim surprise*
Slingsby, Janet. *Hetty's 100 hats*
Soto, Gary. *Chato and the party animals*
Sperring, Mark. *The fairytale cake*
Spinelli, Eileen. *In my new yellow shirt*
Stanton, Karen. *Papi's gift*
Starr, Meg. *Alicia's happy day*
Stevens, April. *Edwin speaks up*
Stewart, Paul. *The birthday presents*
Stewart, Sarah. *The journey*
Stock, Catherine. *The birthday present*
Stolz, Mary. *Emmett's pig*
Swanson, Susan Marie. *The first thing my mama told me*
Sykes, Julie. *Little Rocket's special star*
Tafuri, Nancy. *The barn party*
Tatcheva, Eva. *Witch Zelda's birthday cake*
Thomas, Jan. *A birthday for Cow!*
Thomas, Naturi. *Uh-oh! It's Mama's birthday!*
Tryon, Leslie. *Albert's birthday*
Uff, Caroline. *Happy birthday, Lulu*
Vigna, Judith. *My two uncles*
Waber, Bernard. *Lyle and the birthday party*
Walker, Anna. *I love birthdays*
Wallace, John. *Tiny Rabbit goes to a birthday party*
Wallace, Nancy Elizabeth. *Tell-a-bunny*
Watt, Mélanie. *Scaredy Squirrel has a birthday party*
Wells, Rosemary. *Bunny party*
Max's birthday
Yoko's paper cranes
Weninger, Brigitte. *Double birthday*
Happy birthday, Davy
White, Linda Arms. *Comes a wind*
Wilcox, Brian. *Full moon*
Willard, Nancy. *The mouse, the cat and Grandmother's hat*
Williams, Barbara. *Albert's gift for grandmother*
Williams, Vera B. *Something special for me*
Wilson, Karma. *Whopper cake*
Witte, Anna. *Lola's fandango*
Wood, Audrey. *The Birthday Queen*
Wormell, Mary. *Hilda Hen's happy birthday*
Wright, Betty Ren. *The blizzard*
Wright, Maureen. *Earth Day, birthday!*
Yaccarino, Dan. *The birthday fish*
Yashima, Taro. *Umbrella*
Yezerski, Thomas. *Queen of the world*
Yolen, Jane. *Picnic with Piggins*
Zolotow, Charlotte. *Mr. Rabbit and the lovely present*

Blackouts *see* Power failures

Blindness *see* Disabilities – blindness; Senses – sight

Board books *see* Format, unusual – board books

Boasting *see* Behavior – boasting

Boats, ships

Alborough, Jez. *Captain Duck*
Allen, Pamela. *Who sank the boat?*
Arnosky, Jim. *Parrotfish and sunken ships*
Arro, Lena. *By geezers and galoshes!*
Auld, Mary. *Noah's ark*
Bartoletti, Susan Campbell. *Naamah and the ark at night*
Barton, Byron. *Boats*
Base, Graeme. *The legend of the Golden Snail*
Beck, Andrea. *Elliot's shipwreck*
Bergel, Colin. *Mail by the pail*
Berger, Melvin. *Dive! a book of deep sea creatures*
Blackstone, Stella. *Ship shapes*
Braun, Sebastien. *Toot and Pop!*
Bunting, Eve. *Big Bear's big boat*
Swan in love
Burdett, Lois. *Twelfth night for kids*
Burningham, John. *Mr. Gumpy's outing*
Calhoun, Mary. *Henry the sailor cat*
Carbone, Elisa. *Heroes of the surf*
Chan, Arlene. *Awakening the dragon*
Christian, Mary Blount. *If not for the calico cat*
Clark, Mary Higgins. *Ghost ship*
Corey, Shana. *Boats!*
Cotten, Cynthia. *The book boat's in*
Cousins, Lucy. *Noah's ark*
Noah's ark [board book]
Crampton, Gertrude. *Scuffy the tugboat*
Crews, Donald. *Harbor*
Sail away
Cullen, Lynn. *Little Scraggly Hair*
Cumming, Hannah. *The red boat*
De Beer, Hans. *Little Polar Bear and the submarine*
Demas, Corinne. *The disappearing island*
Dickson, Louise. *The vanishing cat*
Duke, Kate. *Twenty is too many*
Dunbar, Polly. *Arthur's dream boat*
Fitzpatrick, Marie-Louise. *You, me and the big blue sea*
Flanagan, Alice K. *Riding the ferry with Captain Cruz*
Fleming, Candace. *Papa's mechanical fish*
Floca, Brian. *Lightship*
Garland, Sherry. *My father's boat*
Gibbons, Gail. *Boat book*
Exploring the deep, dark sea

Goldsboro, Bobby. *Noah and the ark; and, David and Goliath*
Goodhart, Pippa. *Noah makes a boat*
Gorbachev, Valeri. *The fool of the world and the flying ship: a Ukrainian folk tale*
Gramatky, Hardie. *Little Toot*
Greene, Rhonda Gowler. *Noah and the mighty ark*
Gutman, Anne. *Gaspard on vacation*
Haas, Rick de. *Peter and the seal*
Harker, Lesley. *Annie's ark*
Harrison, Troon. *The floating orchard*
Holabird, Katharine. *Angelina, star of the show*
Hubbell, Patricia. *Boats: speeding! sailing! cruising!*
Hutchins, Hazel. *Beneath the bridge*
Hyde, Heidi Smith. *Emanuel and the Hanukkah rescue*
Jonas, Ann. *Aardvarks, disembark!*
Kellogg, Steven. *The island of the skog*
Mike Fink
Kimmel, Eric A. *The Erie Canal pirates*
Krensky, Stephen. *Noah's bark*
LaMarche, Jim. *The raft*
Lamb, Albert. *The abandoned lighthouse*
Lenski, Lois. *The little sailboat*
Lewin, Ted. *Amazon boy*
Lloyd-Jones, Sally. *Old MacNoah had an ark*
London, Jonathan. *Where the big fish are*
Maass, Robert. *Tugboats*
McCarthy, Michael. *The story of Noah and the ark*
McCully, Emily Arnold. *The pirate queen*
McDonnell, Flora. *I love boats*
McNeil, Florence. *Sail away*
McPhail, David. *Pigs ahoy*
Martin, Jacqueline Briggs. *On Sand Island*
Matteson, George. *The Christmas tugboat*
Meddaugh, Susan. *Harry on the rocks*
Mitton, Tony. *All afloat on Noah's boat!*
Morrissey, Dean. *The Christmas ship*
O'Neill, Alexis. *Loud Emily*
Oppel, Kenneth. *Peg and the whale*
Paley, Joan. *One more river*
Pallotta, Jerry. *Dory story*
Peacock, Carol Antoinette. *Pilgrim cat*
Pelton, Mindy L. *When Dad's at sea*
Perrow, Angeli. *Sirius, the dog star*
Philip, Neil. *Noah and the devil*
Pinkney, Jerry. *Noah's ark*
Potter, Beatrix. *The tale of Little Pig Robinson*
Priest, Robert H. *The old pirate of Central Park*
Rand, Gloria. *Sailing home*
Ransome, Arthur. *The fool of the world and the flying ship*
Rappaport, Doreen. *Freedom ship*
Reynolds, Peter H. *Sydney's star*
Rockwell, Anne. *Boats*
Ferryboat ride!
Rohmann, Eric. *The cinder-eyed cats*
Rotner, Shelley. *Boats afloat*
Rumford, James. *The Island-below-the-star*
San Souci, Robert D. *Brave Margaret*
Santore, Charles. *A stowaway on Noah's Ark*
Savage, Stephen. *Little Tug*
Schachner, Judith Byron. *Yo, Vikings*
Schaefer, Lola M. *Tugboats*
Segal, John. *Alistair and Kip's great adventure*
Shapiro, Zachary. *We're all in the same boat*
Shaw, Nancy. *Sheep on a ship*
Singer, Isaac Bashevis. *Why Noah chose the dove*
Sís, Peter. *Ship ahoy!*
Soto, Gary. *Chato goes cruisin'*
Spier, Peter. *Noah's ark*
Stafford, Liliana. *Just dragon*
Stead, Philip C. *Jonathan and the big blue boat*
Steggall, Susan. *Busy boats*
Stephens, Helen. *Ahoyty-toyty*
Stevenson, James. *The stowaway*
Stewig, John Warren. *The animals watched*
Sting [Musician]. *Rock steady*
Swift, Hildegarde Hoyt. *The little red lighthouse and the great gray bridge*
Tebbs, Victoria. *Noah's Ark story*
Titherington, Jeanne. *Baby's boat*
Todd, Traci. *T is for tugboat*
Trapani, Iza. *Row, row, row your boat*
Van Allsburg, Chris. *The wreck of the Zephyr*
Van Dusen, Chris. *The circus ship*
Down to the sea with Mr. Magee
Van Leeuwen, Jean. *Across the wide dark sea*
Waddell, Martin. *Captain Small Pig*
Sailor Bear
Walton, Rick. *Noah's square dance*
Wick, Walter. *Can you see what I see? Seymour and the juice box boat*
Can you see what I see? treasure ship
Williams, Vera B. *Three days on a river in a red canoe*
Wilson, Anne. *Noah's ark*
Winter, Jeanette. *The Christmas tree ship*
Winter, Jonah. *Here comes the garbage barge!*
Wynne-Jones, Tim. *The boat in the tree*
Zagwÿn, Deborah Turney. *The sea house*

Bombs *see* Weapons

Boogy man *see* Monsters

Books, reading *see also* Libraries

Aliki. *How a book is made*
Allen, Jonathan. *I'm not reading!*
Allen, Susan. *Read anything good lately?*
Amado, Elisa. *What are you doing?*
Anholt, Catherine. *Come back, Jack!*
Asch, Frank. *Moonbear's books*
Asim, Jabari. *Fifty cents and a dream*
Auch, Mary Jane. *The plot chickens*
Souperchicken
Banks, Kate. *The bear in the book*
Barnett, Mac. *Chloe and the lion*
Battle-Lavert, Gwendolyn. *Papa's mark*
Bendall-Brunello, Tiziana. *I wish I could read!*
Berne, Jennifer. *Calvin can't fly*
Bernheimer, Kate. *The lonely book*
Bertram, Debbie. *The best book to read*
The best place to read
The best time to read
Boatfield, Jonny. *The twilight book*
Borden, Louise. *The day Eddie met the author*
Bottner, Barbara. *Miss Brooks loves books! (and I don't)*
Bradby, Marie. *More than anything else*
Briant, Ed. *Seven stories*
Bromley, Nick. *Open very carefully*
Brown, Ken. *The scarecrow's hat*
Brown, Marc. *Arthur's really helpful word book*
D. W.'s library card
Brown, Monica. *Waiting for the Biblioburro*
Browne, Anthony. *I like books*

I like books [board book]
Bruss, Deborah. *Book! book! book!*
Buitrago, Jairo. *Jimmy the greatest*
Bunting, Eve. *Our library*
The Wednesday surprise
Burgess, Mark. *Where teddy bears come from*
Burleigh, Robert. *I love going through this book*
Bush, Laura. *Read all about it!*
Buzzeo, Toni. *Inside the books*
Penelope Popper book doctor
Carlson, Nancy. *I don't like to read!*
Carnavas, Peter. *The children who loved books*
Casanova, Mary. *The day Dirk Yeller came to town*
Caseley, Judith. *Sophie and Sammy's library sleepover*
Cazet, Denys. *Will you read to me?*
Charlip, Remy. *Why I will never ever ever ever have enough time to read this book*
Cheng, Andrea. *Anna the bookbinder*
Child, Lauren. *But, excuse me, that is my book*
Who's afraid of the big bad book?
Chin, Jason. *Coral reefs*
Christelow, Eileen. *Five little monkeys reading in bed*
Cleminson, Katie. *Otto the book bear*
Cline-Ransome, Lesa. *Light in the darkness*
Words set me free
Cohen, Miriam. *When will I read?*
Colandro, Lucille. *There was an old lady who swallowed some books!*
Conover, Chris. *The lion's share*
Cotten, Cynthia. *The book boat's in*
Cousins, Lucy. *Maisy goes to the library*
Cowley, Joy. *Mrs. Goodstory*
Crimi, Carolyn. *Henry and the Buccaneer Bunnies*
Henry and the Crazed Chicken Pirates
Cuyler, Margery. *Hooray for Reading Day!*
Dakos, Kalli. *Our principal promised to kiss a pig*
Daly, Niki. *Once upon a time*
Deedy, Carmen Agra. *Return of the library dragon*
DeFelice, Cynthia C. *The real, true Dulcie Campbell*
de Las Casas, Dianne. *There's a dragon in the library*
DePalma, Mary Newell. *The perfect gift*
DiPucchio, Kelly. *Alfred Zector, book collector*
Docherty, Helen. *The Snatchabook*
Donaldson, Julia. *Charlie Cook's favorite book*
Donovan, Sandy. *Bob the Alien discovers the Dewey Decimal System*
Bored Bella learns about fiction and nonfiction
Karl and Carolina uncover the parts of a book
Pingpong Perry experiences how a book is made
Duvoisin, Roger Antoine. *Petunia*
Edwards, Pamela Duncan. *The neat line*
Elya, Susan Middleton. *Fairy trails*
Faulkner, Keith. *The monster who loved books*
Finchler, Judy. *Miss Malarkey leaves no reader behind*
Flanagan, Alice K. *Librarians*
Ms. Davison, our librarian
Fore, S. J. *Read to Tiger*
Fosberry, Jennifer. *Isabella star of the story*
Fox, Kathleen. *The pirates of plagiarism*
Freedman, Deborah. *The Story of Fish and Snail*
Gall, Chris. *Revenge of the Dinotrux*
Garland, Michael. *King Puck*
Miss Smith and the haunted library
Miss Smith reads again!
Miss Smith's incredible storybook
Gay, Marie-Louise. *Read me a story, Stella*
Gerstein, Mordicai. *A book*
Goodhart, Pippa. *Little Nelly's big book*
Gore, Leonid. *The wonderful book*
Gravett, Emily. *Again!*
Spells
Greene, Rhonda Gowler. *No pirates allowed! said Library Lou*
Griswell, Kim T. *Rufus goes to school*
Hall, Patricia. *Hooray for reading!*
Harris, Robie H. *Maybe a bear ate it!*
Haseley, Dennis. *A story for Bear*
Hayward, Linda. *I am a book*
Hector, Julian. *The gentleman bug*
Hest, Amy. *The reader*
Hillenbrand, Will. *My book box*
Hills, Tad. *How Rocket learned to read*
Rocket writes a story
Hoban, Tana. *I read signs*
I read symbols
I walk and read
Hodge, Deborah. *Lily and the mixed-up letters*
Hood, Susan. *Look! I can read!*
Hopkins, Lee Bennett. *Good books, good times*
Houston, Gloria. *Miss Dorothy and her bookmobile*
Hubbell, Patricia. *Check it out! reading, finding, helping*
Ivey, Randall. *Jay and the bounty of books*
Jeffers, Oliver. *The incredible book eating boy*
Jeram, Anita. *I love my little storybook*
Johnson, Angela. *Lottie Paris and the best place*
Jorgensen, Richard. *Reading with Dad*
Joyce, William. *The fantastic flying books of Mr. Morris Lessmore*
Kanninen, Barbara. *A story with pictures*
Kirk, Daniel. *Library mouse*
Library mouse: a friend's tale
Library mouse: home sweet home
Klausmeier, Jesse. *Open this little book*
Kloske, Geoffrey. *Once upon a time, the end (asleep in 60 seconds)*
Krull, Kathleen. *The boy on Fairfield Street*
Lakin, Patricia. *Fat chance Thanksgiving*
Rainy day
Lamm, C. Drew. *Pirates*
Lehman, Barbara. *The red book*
Lehrhaupt, Adam. *Warning: do not open this book!*
Léonard, Marie. *Tibili, the little boy who didn't want to go to school*
Lies, Brian. *Bats at the library*
Long, Ethan. *The book that Zack wrote*
Lyon, George Ella. *Book*
McGee, Marni. *Winston the book wolf*
McGill, Alice. *Molly Bannaky*
Mack, Jeff. *The things I can do*
McNaughton, Colin. *Not last night but the night before*
McPhail, David. *Edward and the pirates*
Fix-it
Santa's book of names
McQuinn, Anna. *Lola at the library*
Lola loves stories
Lola reads to Leo
Mahoney, Daniel J. *The Saturday escape*
Marshall, James. *Wings: a tale of two chickens*
Meddaugh, Susan. *Hog-eye*
Meng, Cece. *I will not read this book*
Miller, Pat. *We're going on a book hunt*
Miller, William. *Richard Wright and the library card*
Milord, Susan. *Happy 100th day!*
Montanari, Eva. *My first . . .*

Mora, Pat. *Book fiesta! celebrate Children's Day/Book Day / Celebremos El día de los niños/El día de los libros*
A library for Juana
Tomás and the library lady
Morris, Carla. *The boy who was raised by librarians*
Muntean, Michaela. *Do not open this book!*
Nez, John. *One smart Cookie*
Nikola-Lisa, W. *Magic in the margins*
Numeroff, Laura Joffe. *The Jellybeans and the big book bonanza*
Olofsson, Helena. *The little jester*
Orozco, Jose-Luis. *Rin, rin, rin / do, re, mi*
Palatini, Margie. *The three silly billies*
Panzieri, Lucia. *The kindhearted crocodile*
Parish, Herman. *Amelia Bedelia's first library card*
Parlato, Stephen. *The world that loved books*
Parr, Todd. *Reading makes you feel good*
Paschkis, Julie. *Apple cake*
Patschke, Steve. *The spooky book*
Pauli, Lorenz. *The fox in the library*
Pearson, Susan. *How to teach a slug to read*
Pearson, Tracey Campbell. *Elephant's story*
Perry, John. *The book that eats people*
Pinczes, Elinor J. *My full moon is square*
Pinkney, Sandra L. *Read and rise*
Plourde, Lynn. *Book Fair Day*
Polacco, Patricia. *Aunt Chip and the great Triple Creek dam affair*
Thank you, Mr. Falker
Radabaugh, Melinda Beth. *Going to the library*
Rahaman, Vashanti. *Read for me, Mama*
Rau, Dana Meachen. *The secret code*
Robb, Diane Burton. *The alphabet war*
Rockwell, Anne. *Father's Day*
Rogers, Jacqueline. *Kindergarten ABC*
Rosenstock, Barb. *Thomas Jefferson builds a library*
Roth, Susan L. *Hands around the library*
Schoenherr, Ian. *Read it, don't eat it!*
Schubert, Leda. *Reading to Peanut*
Scieszka, Jon. *Battle Bunny*
Sheth, Kashmira. *Tiger in my soup*
Shields, Gillian. *Library Lily*
Shoulders, Michael. *Goodnight Baby Bear*
Say Daddy!
Sierra, Judy. *Born to read*
Wild about books
Smalls, Irene. *Don't say ain't*
Smith, Lane. *It's a book*
Sperring, Mark. *The fairytale cake*
Staake, Bob. *Look! A book!*
Look! Another book!
Stadler, Alexander. *Beverly Billingsly borrows a book*
Stadler, John. *What's so scary?*
Stanley, Diane. *Raising Sweetness*
Stewart, Sarah. *The library*
Straaten, Harmen van. *Duck's tale*
Thomas, Shelley Moore. *Take care, Good Knight*
Tirabosco, Tom. *At the same time*
Tobin, Jim. *Sue MacDonald had a book*
Twohy, Mike. *Poindexter makes a friend*
Viorst, Judith. *The good-bye book*
Waller, Curt. *Baby's first signs*
More baby's first signs
Wallner, Alexandra. *Lucy Maud Montgomery*
Watt, Mélanie. *Have I got a book for you!*
You're finally here!
Wayne-von Königslöw, Andrea. *How do you read to a rabbit?*
Weeks, Sarah. *Bite me, I'm a book*
Catfish Kate and the sweet swamp band
Wells, Rosemary. *Read to your bunny*
Yoko learns to read
Whybrow, Ian. *Wish, change, friend*
Wiesner, David. *Free fall*
The three pigs
Williams, Suzanne. *Library Lil*
Winter, Jeanette. *Biblioburro*
Winters, Kay. *Abe Lincoln, the boy who loved books*
Yates, Louise. *Dog loves books*
Dog loves counting
Yolen, Jane. *Baby Bear's books*

Boredom *see* Behavior – boredom

Bossy *see* Behavior – bossy

Bravery *see* Character traits – bravery

Bridges

Bell, Babs. *The bridge is up!*
Prince, April Jones. *Twenty-one elephants and still standing*
Swift, Hildegarde Hoyt. *The little red lighthouse and the great gray bridge*

Brothers *see* Family life – brothers; Family life – brothers & sisters; Sibling rivalry

Brownies *see* Mythical creatures – elves

Bubbles

Bradley, Kimberly Brubaker. *Pop!*
Bridwell, Norman. *Clifford counts bubbles*
dePaola, Tomie. *Strega Nona takes a vacation*
Inkpen, Mick. *Thing*
Mahy, Margaret. *Bubble trouble*
Van Camp, Katie. *Harry and Horsie*

Bugs *see* Insects

Buildings

Beaty, Andrea. *Iggy Peck, architect*
Cooper, Elisha. *Building*
Curlee, Lynn. *Skyscraper*
Edwards, Pamela Duncan. *Jack and Jill's treehouse*
Gibbons, Gail. *Up goes the skyscraper!*
Hale, Christy. *Dreaming up*
Hill, Isabel. *Building stories*
Hudson, Cheryl Willis. *Construction zone*
Johnson, D. B. *Palazzo inverso*
Kirk, Daniel. *Library mouse: home sweet home*
Lewis, Kevin. *The lot at the end of my block*
Merriam, Eve. *Bam, bam, bam*
Newhouse, Maxwell. *The house that Max built*
Numeroff, Laura Joffe. *What daddies do best*
Rockliff, Mara. *Me and Momma and Big John*
Slade, Suzanne. *The house that George built*
Smith, Charles R. *Brick by brick*
Stone, Lynn M. *Farm buildings*

Suen, Anastasia. *Raise the roof*
Tarsky, Sue. *The busy building book*
Vila, Laura. *Building Manhattan*

Bulldozers *see* Machines

Bullying *see* Behavior – bullying, teasing

Burros *see* Animals – donkeys

Buses

Brillhart, Julie. *Molly rides the school bus*
Brown, Marc. *Arthur lost and found*
Bus-a-saurus bop
Cabrera, Jane. *The wheels on the bus*
Cocca-Leffler, Maryann. *Bus route to Boston*
Cole, Joanna. *The magic school bus and the science fair expedition*
The magic school bus in the time of the dinosaurs
The magic school bus inside a beehive
The magic school bus lost in the solar system
The magic school bus on the ocean floor
Crews, Donald. *School bus*
School bus [board book]
Dale, Penny. *The boy on the bus*
Graham, Bob. *A bus called Heaven*
Grandits, John. *Ten rules you absolutely must not break if you want to survive the school bus*
Helakoski, Leslie. *The smushy bus*
Hirst, Robin. *My place in space*
Katz, Karen. *The babies on the bus*
Kirk, Daniel. *Bus stop, bus go*
Kovalski, Maryann. *The wheels on the bus*
Liu, Julia. *Gus, the dinosaur bus*
McCarthy, Meghan. *The adventures of Patty and the big red bus*
Moore, Mary-Alice. *The wheels on the school bus*
Owen, Ann. *Taking your places*
Pete the cat: the wheels on the bus
Redeker, Kent. *Don't squish the sasquatch!*
Rogers, Hal. *Buses*
Roth, Carol. *The little school bus*
Silvano, Wendi. *Just one more*
Singer, Marilyn. *I'm your bus*
Stoeke, Janet Morgan. *The bus stop*
Walters, Eric. *The matatu*
Willis, Jeanne. *The wheels on the bus: a read-along sing-along trip to the zoo*
Zelinsky, Paul O. *The wheels on the bus*

Cabs *see* Taxis

Cafés *see* Restaurants

Caldecott award books

Aardema, Verna. *Why mosquitoes buzz in people's ears*
Ackerman, Karen. *Song and dance man*
Alger, Leclaire Gowans. *Always room for one more*
Aulaire, Ingri Mortenson d'. *Abraham Lincoln*
Bemelmans, Ludwig. *Madeline's rescue*
Brown, Marcia. *Once a mouse . . .*
Brown, Margaret Wise. *The little island*
Bunting, Eve. *Smoky night*
Burton, Virginia Lee. *The little house*
Cendrars, Blaise. *Shadow*
Chaucer, Geoffrey. *Chanticleer and the fox*
De Regniers, Beatrice Schenk. *May I bring a friend?*
Emberley, Barbara. *Drummer Hoff*
Ets, Marie Hall. *Nine days to Christmas*
Field, Rachel Lyman. *Prayer for a child*
Floca, Brian. *Locomotive*
A frog he would a-wooing go [folk-song]. *Frog went a-courtin'*
Gerstein, Mordicai. *The man who walked between the towers*
Goble, Paul. *The girl who loved wild horses*
Grimm, Jacob and Wilhelm *Rapunzel*
Hader, Berta Hoerner. *The big snow*
Haley, Gail E. *A story, a story*
Hall, Donald. *Ox-cart man*
Handforth, Thomas. *Mei Li*
Henkes, Kevin. *Kitten's first full moon*
Hodges, Margaret. *Saint George and the dragon*
Hogrogian, Nonny. *One fine day*
Juster, Norton. *The hello, goodbye window*
Keats, Ezra Jack. *The snowy day*
The snowy day [board book]
Klassen, Jon. *This is not my hat*
Lawson, Robert. *They were strong and good*
Lipkind, William. *Finders keepers*
Lobel, Arnold. *Fables*
Macaulay, David. *Black and white*
McCloskey, Robert. *Make way for ducklings*
Time of wonder
McCully, Emily Arnold. *Mirette on the high wire*
McDermott, Gerald. *Arrow to the sun*
Martin, Jacqueline Briggs. *Snowflake Bentley*
Milhous, Katherine. *The egg tree*
Mosel, Arlene. *The funny little woman*
Musgrove, Margaret. *Ashanti to Zulu*
Ness, Evaline. *Sam, Bangs, and moonshine*
Perrault, Charles. *Cinderella: or, the little glass slipper*
Petersham, Maud. *The rooster crows*
Pinkney, Jerry. *The lion and the mouse*
Politi, Leo. *Song of the swallows*
Provensen, Alice. *The glorious flight*
Ransome, Arthur. *The fool of the world and the flying ship*
Raschka, Chris. *A ball for Daisy*
Rathmann, Peggy. *Officer Buckle and Gloria*
Robbins, Ruth. *Baboushka and the three kings*
Rohmann, Eric. *My friend Rabbit*
St. George, Judith. *So you want to be president?*
Say, Allen. *Grandfather's journey*
Selznick, Brian. *The invention of Hugo Cabret*
Sendak, Maurice. *Where the wild things are*
Spier, Peter. *Noah's ark*
Stead, Philip C. *A sick day for Amos McGee*
Steig, William. *Sylvester and the magic pebble*
Swanson, Susan Marie. *The house in the night*
Taback, Simms. *Joseph had a little overcoat*
Thurber, James. *Many moons*

Tresselt, Alvin R. *White snow, bright snow*
Udry, Janice May. *A tree is nice*
Van Allsburg, Chris. *Jumanji*
The polar express
Ward, Lynd. *The biggest bear*
Wiesner, David. *Flotsam*
The three pigs
Tuesday
Wisniewski, David. *Golem*
Yolen, Jane. *Owl moon*
Yorinks, Arthur. *Hey, Al*
Young, Ed. *Lon Po Po*
Zemach, Harve. *Duffy and the devil*

Caldecott award honor books

Alger, Leclaire Gowans. *All in the morning early*
Andersen, Hans Christian. *The ugly duckling*
Artzybasheff, Boris. *Seven Simeons*
Baker, Olaf. *Where the buffaloes begin*
Bang, Molly. *The grey lady and the strawberry snatcher*
Ten, nine, eight
When Sophie gets angry — really, really angry . . .
Barnett, Mac. *Extra yarn*
Bartone, Elisa. *Peppe the lamplighter*
Baskin, Leonard. *Hosie's alphabet*
Baylor, Byrd. *The desert is theirs*
Hawk, I'm your brother
The way to start a day
When clay sings
Becker, Aaron. *Journey*
Belting, Natalia Maree. *The sun is a golden earring*
Bemelmans, Ludwig. *Madeline*
Birnbaum, Abe. *Green eyes*
Brown, Marcia. *Stone soup*
Brown, Margaret Wise. *Wheel on the chimney*
Bryant, Jen. *A river of words*
Buzzeo, Toni. *One cool friend*
Caudill, Rebecca. *A pocketful of cricket*
Chan, Chin-Yi. *Good luck horse*
A child's calendar
Chodos-Irvine, Margaret. *Ella Sarah gets dressed*
Clark, Ann Nolan. *In my mother's house*
Crews, Donald. *Freight train*
Truck
Cronin, Doreen. *Click, clack, moo*
Dalgliesh, Alice. *The Thanksgiving story*
Daugherty, James Henry. *Andy and the lion*
Dayrell, Elphinstone. *Why the sun and the moon live in the sky*
dePaola, Tomie. *Strega Nona*
Dick Whittington and his cat. *Dick Whittington and his cat*
Domanska, Janina. *If all the seas were one sea*
Du Bois, William Pène. *Bear party*
Lion
Ehlert, Lois. *Color zoo*
Eichenberg, Fritz. *Ape in cape*
Emberley, Barbara. *One wide river to cross*
Ets, Marie Hall. *In the forest*
Just me
Mister Penny
Mr. Penny's race horse
Mr. T. W. Anthony Woo
Play with me
Falconer, Ian. *Olivia*
Feelings, Muriel. *Jambo means hello*
Moja means one
Fleming, Denise. *In the small, small pond*
Ford, Lauren. *The ageless story*
The fox went out on a chilly night
Frazee, Marla. *A couple of boys have the best week ever*
Giovanni, Nikki. *Rosa*
Goudey, Alice E. *The day we saw the sun come up*
Houses from the sea
Grifalconi, Ann. *The village of round and square houses*
Grimm, Jacob and Wilhelm. *Hansel and Gretel*
Little Red Riding Hood
Snow White and the seven dwarfs
Hader, Berta Hoerner. *Cock-a-doodle doo*
The mighty hunter
Henkes, Kevin. *Owen*
Hill, Laban Carrick. *Dave the potter*
Ho, Minfong. *Hush!*
Hodges, Margaret. *The wave*
Hogrogian, Nonny. *The contest*
Holbrook, Stewart. *America's Ethan Allen*
Holling, Holling C. *Paddle-to-the-sea*
Howitt, Mary Botham. *Mary Howitt's The spider and the fly*
Idle, Molly. *Flora and the flamingo*
Isaacs, Anne. *Swamp Angel*
Isadora, Rachel. *Ben's trumpet*
Jenkins, Steve. *What do you do with a tail like this?*
Johnson, Stephen T. *Alphabet city*
Keats, Ezra Jack. *Goggles*
Kepes, Juliet. *Five little monkeys*
Kimmel, Eric A. *Hershel and the Hanukkah goblins*
Krauss, Ruth. *The happy day*
A very special house
Leaf, Munro. *Wee Gillis*
Lehman, Barbara. *The red book*
Lester, Julius. *John Henry*
Levine, Ellen. *Henry's freedom box*
Lionni, Leo. *Alexander and the wind-up mouse*
Frederick
Inch by inch
Swimmy
Little old lady who swallowed a fly. *There was an old lady who swallowed a fly*
Lobel, Arnold. *Frog and Toad are friends*
On Market Street
Logue, Mary. *Sleep like a tiger*
Low, Joseph. *Mice twice*
Macaulay, David. *Castle*
Cathedral
McCarty, Peter. *Hondo and Fabian*
McCloskey, Robert. *Blueberries for Sal*
One morning in Maine
McDermott, Gerald. *Anansi the spider*
Raven
MacDonald, Suse. *Alphabatics*
McDonnell, Patrick. *Me . . . Jane*
McKissack, Patricia C. *Mirandy and Brother Wind*
McLimans, David. *Gone wild*
Moss, Lloyd. *Zin! zin! zin! A violin*
Mother Goose. *Mother Goose*
The three jovial huntsmen
Muth, Jon J. *Zen shorts*
Myers, Walter Dean. *Harlem*
Newberry, Clare Turlay. *April's kittens*
Barkis
Marshmallow
Peet, Bill. *Bill Peet*
Pelletier, David. *The graphic alphabet*
Perrault, Charles. *Puss in boots*, ill. by Marcia Brown

Puss in boots, ill. by Fred Marcellino
Petersham, Maud. *An American ABC*
Pilkey, Dav. *The paperboy*
Pinkney, Andrea Davis. *Duke Ellington*
Pinkney, Jerry. *Noah's ark*
Politi, Leo. *Juanita*
Pedro, the angel of Olvera Street
Priceman, Marjorie. *Hot air*
Rappaport, Doreen. *Martin's big words*
Raschka, Chris. *Yo! Yes?*
Reyher, Rebecca. *My mother is the most beautiful woman in the world*
Reynolds, Aaron. *Creepy carrots!*
Ringgold, Faith. *Tar Beach*
Rocco, John. *Blackout*
Rohmann, Eric. *Time flies*
Ryan, Cheli Durán. *Hildilid's night*
Rylant, Cynthia. *The relatives came*
When I was young in the mountains
San Souci, Robert D. *The faithful friend*
The talking eggs
Sawyer, Ruth. *Journey cake, ho!*
Scanlon, Elizabeth Garton. *All the world*
Scheer, Julian. *Rain makes applesauce*
Schreiber, Georges. *Bambino the clown*
Scieszka, Jon. *The Stinky Cheese Man and other fairly stupid tales*
Seeger, Laura Vaccaro. *First the egg*
Green
Sendak, Maurice. *In the night kitchen*
Outside over there
Seuss, Dr. *Bartholomew and the Oobleck*
If I ran the zoo
McElligot's pool
Shannon, David. *No, David!*
Shulevitz, Uri. *How I learned geography*
Snow
The treasure
Sidman, Joyce. *Red sings from treetops*
Song of the water boatman
Simont, Marc. *The stray dog*
Sís, Peter. *Starry messenger*
Tibet through the red box
The wall: growing up behind the Iron Curtain
Sleator, William. *The angry moon*
Smith, Lane. *Grandpa Green*
Snyder, Dianne. *The boy of the three-year nap*
Steig, William. *The amazing bone*
Stein, David Ezra. *Interrupting chicken*
Steptoe, John. *Mufaro's beautiful daughters*
The story of jumping mouse
Stevens, Janet. *Tops and bottoms*
Stewart, Sarah. *The gardener*
Tafuri, Nancy. *Have you seen my duckling?*
Thayer, Ernest Lawrence. *Casey at the bat: a ballad of the Republic, sung in the year 1888*
The three bears. *Goldilocks and the three bears*
Titus, Eve. *Anatole*
Anatole and the cat
Tom Tit Tot. *Tom Tit Tot*
Tresselt, Alvin R. *Hide and seek fog*
Rain drop splash
Tudor, Tasha. *1 is one*
Turkle, Brinton. *Thy friend, Obadiah*
Udry, Janice May. *The moon jumpers*
Van Allsburg, Chris. *The garden of Abdul Gasazi*
Weatherford, Carole Boston. *Moses: when Harriet Tubman led her people to freedom*
Wheeler, Opal. *Sing in praise*
Sing Mother Goose
Wiese, Kurt. *Fish in the air*
You can write Chinese
Wiesner, David. *Free fall*
Mr. Wuffles!
Sector 7
Willard, Nancy. *A visit to William Blake's inn*
Willems, Mo. *Don't let the pigeon drive the bus*
Knuffle Bunny
Knuffle Bunny too
Williams, Sherley Anne. *Working cotton*
Williams, Vera B. *A chair for my mother*
"More more more," said the baby
Wilson, Anne. *Noah's ark*
Wood, Audrey. *King Bidgood's in the bathtub*
Woodson, Jacqueline. *Coming on home soon*
Yashima, Taro. *Crow boy*
Umbrella
Yolen, Jane. *The emperor and the kite*
Young, Ed. *Seven blind mice*
Zemach, Harve. *The judge*
Zemach, Margot. *It could always be worse*
Zolotow, Charlotte. *Mr. Rabbit and the lovely present*
The storm book

Calendars

A child's calendar
Frasier, Debra. *A birthday cake is no ordinary cake*
Hague, Kathleen. *Calendarbears*
Livingston, Myra Cohn. *Calendar*
Murphy, Stuart J. *Pepper's journal*

Camouflages *see* Disguises

Camps, camping

Bateman, Teresa. *Hamster Camp*
The bear
Berenstain, Stan and Jan. *The Berenstain bears go to camp*
Berry, Lynne. *Duck tents*
Birdseye, Tom. *Oh yeah!*
Brown, Marc. *Arthur goes to camp*
Arthur's first sleepover
Carlin, Patricia. *Alfie is not afraid*
Christelow, Eileen. *Jerome camps out*
Clements, Andrew. *Because your mommy loves you*
Cummins, Julie. *Country kid, city kid*
Curious George goes camping
deGroat, Diane. *Good night, sleep tight, don't let the bedbugs bite*
Fleming, Denise. *Buster goes to Cowboy Camp*
Genechten, Guido van. *Ricky is brave*
Gifaldi, David. *Ben, king of the river*
Gutman, Anne. *Gaspard at the seashore*
Hafner, Marylin. *Molly and Emmett's camping adventure*
Henkes, Kevin. *Bailey goes camping*
Holabird, Katharine. *Angelina and Henry*
Hume, Stephen Eaton. *Red moon follows truck*
Hundal, Nancy. *Camping*
Huneck, Stephen. *Sally goes to the mountains*
Inkpen, Mick. *Kipper's monster*
Wibbly Pig can make a tent
Jagtenberg, Yvonne. *Jack's kite*
Johnson, Paul Brett. *Lost*
Jules, Jacqueline. *Picnic at Camp Shalom*
Katschke, Judy. *Take a hike, Snoopy*

Korda, Lerryn. *Into the wild*
Lakin, Patricia. *Camping day*
Lasky, Kathryn. *Lucille camps in*
Lester, Helen. *Tacky goes to camp*
London, Jonathan. *Froggy goes to camp*
McCully, Emily Arnold. *Monk camps out*
McPhail, David. *Pig Pig goes to camp*
Marshall, James. *The Cut-Ups at Camp Custer*
Mayer, Mercer. *Just me and my dad*
You're the scaredy cat
Nolen, Jerdine. *Plantzilla goes to camp*
Numeroff, Laura Joffe. *The Jellybeans and the big camp kickoff*
Orr, Wendy. *The princess and her panther*
Paterson, Brian. *Zigby camps out*
Pringle, Laurence P. *Bear hug*
Rosenstock, Barb. *The camping trip that changed America*
Ross, Tony. *I want to do it myself!*
Ruurs, Margriet. *When we go camping*
Sauer, Tammi. *Cowboy camp*
Princess in training
Schwartz, Henry. *How I captured a dinosaur*
Shulevitz, Uri. *Dawn*
Singer, Marilyn. *Quiet night*
Snyder, Laurel. *Good night, laila tov*
Soman, David. *Ladybug Girl and Bingo*
Taback, Simms. *Postcards from camp*
Tafuri, Nancy. *Do not disturb*
Watt, Mélanie. *Scaredy Squirrel goes camping*
Williams, Vera B. *Three days on a river in a red canoe*
Wilson, Karma. *Sweet Briar goes to camp*
Wolff, Ashley. *Stella and Roy go camping*

Canoes & canoeing

Asch, Frank. *Moonbear's canoe*
Casanova, Mary. *One-dog canoe*
Drawson, Blair. *All along the river*
Ford, Christine. *Ocean's child*
London, Jonathan. *Loon Lake*
Maggi, María Elena. *The great canoe*
Oldland, Nicholas. *Up the creek*
Paterson, Brian. *Zigby hunts for treasure*
Paulsen, Gary. *Canoe days*

Canyons

Cameron, Eileen. *Canyon*
London, Jonathan. *Mustang canyon*

Cards *see* Letters, cards

Careers

Baker, Keith. *LMNO peas*
Berenstain, Stan and Jan. *The Berenstain bears and mama's new job*
Berne, Jennifer. *Manfish*
Blackstone, Stella. *Bear at work*
Bond, Michael. *Paddington Bear and the Christmas surprise*
Bond, Rebecca. *Bravo, Maurice!*
Bunting, Eve. *Girls A to Z*
Buzzeo, Toni. *Adventure Annie goes to work*
Catalanotto, Peter. *Kitten red, yellow, blue*
Cordsen, Carol Foskett. *The milkman*
DiPucchio, Kelly. *Grace for president*
Ericsson, Jennifer A. *Home to me, home to you*
Gardiner, Lindsey. *When Poppy and Max grow up*
Gibbons, Gail. *Emergency!*
Farming
Fill it up!
The pottery place
Gibson, Karen Bush. *Child care workers*
Emergency medical technicians
Glassman, Peter. *My dad's job*
Goodings, Lennie. *When you grow up*
Hartland, Jessie. *Night shift*
Havill, Juanita. *Just like a baby*
Heling, Kathryn. *Clothesline clues to jobs people do*
High, Linda Oatman. *The last chimney of Christmas eve*
Horton, Joan. *Working mummies*
Jordan, Deloris. *Salt in his shoes*
Judes, Marie-Odile. *Max, the stubborn little wolf*
Karas, G. Brian. *The village garage*
Kerley, Barbara. *The world is waiting for you*
Krensky, Stephen. *How Santa got his job*
How Santa lost his job
Liebman, Daniel. *I want to be a cowboy*
Lloyd-Jones, Sally. *How to get a job — by me, the boss*
McMullan, Kate. *Bulldog's big day*
McNaughton, Colin. *When I grow up*
McPhail, David. *Pig Pig gets a job*
Mara, Wil. *Jackie Robinson*
Mellage, Nanette. *Coming home*
Miller, Heather. *Cowboy*
Miller, Margaret. *Who uses this?*
Whose hat?
Morris, Ann. *Work*
Nettleton, Pamela Hill. *George Washington*
Nolen, Jerdine. *Raising dragons*
Paulsen, Gary. *Worksong*
Ray, Mary Lyn. *Basket moon*
Reed, Lynn Rowe. *Please don't upset P.U. Zorilla!*
Reichert, Amy. *Take your mama to work today*
Reiser, Lynn. *Hardworking puppies*
Rockliff, Mara. *Me and Momma and Big John*
Rockwell, Anne. *Career day*
Roth, Carol. *All aboard to work — choo-choo!*
Rotner, Shelley. *Everybody works*
Sava, Donna Lynn. *Teddy bear dreams*
Schaefer, Lola M. *Airport*
Schomp, Virginia. *If you were a . . . ballplayer*
Spinelli, Jerry. *I can be anything!*
Stevenson, James. *Sam the Zamboni man*
Swinburne, Stephen R. *Whose shoes? a shoe for every job*
Turner, Sandy. *Grow up*
Wax, Wendy. *Even firefighters go to the potty*
Yankovic, Al. *When I grow up*
Ziefert, Harriet. *The biggest job of all*

Careers – acrobats

Filleul, Liz. *Tumbler*
Schachner, Judith Byron. *Skippyjon Jones Cirque de Olé*

Careers – actors

Ackerman, Karen. *Bean's big day*
Bell, Cece. *Sock Monkey boogie-woogie*
Sock Monkey goes to Hollywood
Sock Monkey rides again
Blumenthal, Deborah. *Charlie hits it big*

Dunrea, Olivier. *Appearing tonight! Mary Heather Elizabeth Livingstone*
Francis, Pauline. *Sam stars at Shakespeare's Globe*
LaChanze. *Little diva*
Littlesugar, Amy. *Tree of hope*
McLean, Dirk. *Curtain up!*
Milgrim, David. *Amelia makes a movie*
Schwartz, Amy. *Starring Miss Darlene*
Waber, Bernard. *Evie and Margie*

Careers – aerialists

Gerstein, Mordicai. *The man who walked between the towers*
McCully, Emily Arnold. *Mirette and Bellini cross Niagara Falls*
Mirette on the high wire

Careers – airplane pilots

Adler, David A. *A picture book of Amelia Earhart*
Barton, Byron. *Airport*
Bildner, Phil. *The hallelujah flight*
Breen, Steve. *Violet the pilot*
Brown, Don. *Ruth Law thrills a nation*
Brown, Tami Lewis. *Soar, Elinor!*
Duble, Kathleen Benner. *Pilot mom*
Edwards, Pamela Duncan. *The Wright brothers*
Flanagan, Alice K. *Flying an agricultural plane with Mr. Miller*
Johnson, Angela. *Wind flyers*
Joseph, Lynn. *Fly, Bessie, fly*
Lenski, Lois. *The little airplane*
Mara, Wil. *Amelia Earhart*
Meadows, Michelle. *Pilot pups*
Moss, Marissa. *Sky high*
Pelton, Mindy L. *When Dad's at sea*
Raven, Margot Theis. *Mercedes and the chocolate pilot*
Schomp, Virginia. *If you were a . . . pilot*
Tarpley, Natasha Anastasia. *Joe-Joe's first flight*
Whitaker, Suzanne George. *The daring Miss Quimby*
Yolen, Jane. *My brothers' flying machine*

Careers – architects

Beaty, Andrea. *Iggy Peck, architect*
Cooper, Elisha. *Building*
Guarnaccia, Steven. *The three little pigs: an architectural tale*
Laden, Nina. *Roberto, the insect architect*

Careers – artists *see also* Activities – painting; Art

Adams, Adrienne. *The great Valentine's Day balloon race*
Arrigan, Mary. *Mario's angels*
Beaty, Andrea. *Artist Ted*
Belton, Sandra. *Pictures for Miss Josie*
Browne, Anthony. *Willy's pictures*
Browning, Diane. *Signed, Abiah Rose*
Bryant, Jen. *A splash of red*
Carle, Eric. *The artist who painted a blue horse*
Catalanotto, Peter. *Emily's art*
Christelow, Eileen. *Letters from a desperate dog*
What do authors do?
Davies, Jacqueline. *The boy who drew birds*
Demi. *The boy who painted dragons*
DeNoble, Augustine. *Brother Joseph*
Domney, Alexis. *Splish, splat!*
Flanagan, Alice K. *Mrs. Scott's beautiful art*
The Wilsons, a house-painting team
Freedman, Deborah. *Blue chicken*
Frith, Margaret. *Frida Kahlo*
Gibbons, Gail. *The art box*
Harvey, Jeanne Walker. *My hands sing the blues*
Haseley, Dennis. *Twenty heartbeats*
Hershenhorn, Esther. *Fancy that*
Hest, Amy. *Nana's birthday party*
Holub, Joan. *Vincent van Gogh*
Hong, Chen Jiang. *The magic horse of Han Gan*
Hyde, Margaret E. *Matisse for kids*
Van Gogh for kids
Jahn-Clough, Lisa. *Little dog*
Johnson, Angela. *Daddy calls me man*
Johnson, D. B. *Magritte's marvelous hat*
Palazzo inverso
Kelley, True. *Claude Monet*
Kirk, Daniel. *Library mouse: a museum adventure*
Kitamura, Satoshi. *Pablo the artist*
Lakin, Patricia. *Subway sonata*
Lichtenheld, Tom. *Bridget's beret*
Lionni, Leo. *Matthew's dream*
Lithgow, John. *Micawber*
Look, Lenore. *Brush of the gods*
MacLachlan, Patricia. *Painting the wind*
MacLean, Kerry Lee. *Peaceful piggy meditation*
McPhail, David. *Drawing lessons from a bear*
Magnier, Thierry. *Isabelle and the angel*
Maltbie, P. I. *Claude Monet: the painter who stopped the trains*
Markel, Michelle. *The fantastic jungles of Henri Rousseau*
Mayhew, James. *Katie and the Mona Lisa*
Katie meets the Impressionists
Merberg, Julie. *In the garden with Van Gogh*
A magical day with Matisse
Moss, Marissa. *Regina's big mistake*
Napoli, Donna Jo. *Ready to dream*
Nikola-Lisa, W. *The year with Grandma Moses*
Novesky, Amy. *Georgia in Hawaii*
Parker, Marjorie Blain. *Colorful dreamer*
Pinkwater, Daniel. *Bear's Picture*
Raczka, Bob. *No one saw*
Reynolds, Peter H. *Sky color*
Ringgold, Faith. *Henry Ossawa Tanner*
Robinson, Fiona. *Whale shines*
Rodríguez, Rachel Victoria. *Through Georgia's eyes*
Ross, Tom. *Eggbert, the slightly cracked egg*
Rubin, Susan Goldman. *The yellow house*
Rusch, Elizabeth. *A day with no crayons*
Schaefer, A. R. *Alexander Calder*
Diego Rivera
Grandma Moses
Segal, Lore Groszmann. *Morris the artist*
Shapiro, J. H. *Magic trash*
Sherry, Kevin. *I'm the best artist in the ocean*
Sierra, Judy. *Ballyhoo Bay*
Sís, Peter. *The wall: growing up behind the Iron Curtain*
Spohn, Kate. *By word of mouse*
Stadler, John. *What's so scary?*
Stevenson, James. *Fun, no fun*
I meant to tell you
Stock, Catherine. *Gugu's house*
Stone, Tanya Lee. *Sandy's circus*
Sweeney, Joan. *Suzette and the puppy*

Tonatiuh, Duncan. *Diego Rivera: his world and ours*
Tunnell, Michael O. *The joke's on George*
Vande Griek, Susan. *The art room*
Waldman, Neil. *The starry night*
Warhola, James. *Uncle Andy's*
Uncle Andy's cats
Wheatley, Nadia. *Luke's way of looking*
Wiesner, David. *Art and Max*
Willard, Nancy. *Pish posh, said Hieronymous Bosch*
Winter, Jeanette. *Cowboy Charlie*
Henri's scissors
Winter, Jonah. *Diego*
Just behave, Pablo Picasso!
Wolkstein, Diane. *Little Mouse's painting*
Wood, Michele. *Going back home*
Zalben, Jane Breskin. *Mousterpiece*
Ziefert, Harriet. *Lunchtime for a purple snake*

Careers – astronauts

Agee, Jon. *Dmitri the astronaut*
Aldrin, Buzz. *Look to the stars*
Reaching for the moon
Barrett, Judi. *Cloudy with a chance of meatballs 3*
Barton, Byron. *I want to be an astronaut*
Bartram, Simon. *Bob's best-ever friend*
Man on the moon: a day in the life of Bob
Branley, Franklyn M. *Floating in space*
Brett, Jan. *Hedgie blasts off!*
Brown, Don. *One giant leap: the story of Neil Armstrong*
Burleigh, Robert. *One giant leap*
Floca, Brian. *Moonshot*
Fox, Christyan. *Astronaut PiggyWiggy*
Hilliard, Richard. *Godspeed, John Glenn*
Kelly, Mark. *Mousetronaut*
Mousetronaut goes to Mars
McCarthy, Meghan. *Astronaut handbook*
McReynolds, Linda. *Eight days gone*
Mayo, Margaret. *Zoom, rocket, zoom!*
Naden, Corinne J. *Ron's big mission*
Nettleton, Pamela Hill. *Sally Ride*
Rau, Dana Meachen. *Neil Armstrong*
Schomp, Virginia. *If you were an . . . astronaut*

Careers – astronomers

Gerber, Carole. *Annie Jump Cannon, astronomer*
Hopkinson, Deborah. *Maria's comet*
Pettenati, Jeanne K. *Galileo's journal, 1609–1610*
Pinkney, Andrea Davis. *Dear Benjamin Banneker*
Sís, Peter. *Starry messenger*

Careers – authors *see* Careers – writers

Careers – bakers

Carle, Eric. *Walter the baker*
dePaola, Tomie. *Tony's bread*
Ericsson, Jennifer A. *Out and about at the bakery*
Flanagan, Alice K. *Mr. Santizo's tasty treats!*
Heath, Amy. *Sofie's role*
Holt, Kimberly Willis. *Skinny brown dog*
Jackson, Kathryn. *Pantaloon*
Kleven, Elisa. *Sun bread*
Kneen, Maggie. *Chocolate moose*
Levitin, Sonia. *Boom town*
McMullan, Kate. *Bulldog's big day*
Mathers, Petra. *Herbie's secret Santa*
O'Callahan, Jay. *Raspberries!*
Ogburn, Jacqueline K. *The bake shop ghost*
Rylant, Cynthia. *The cookie-store cat*
Shepard, Aaron. *The baker's dozen*
Simmonds, Posy. *Baker cat*
Stewart, Sarah. *The gardener*
Wellington, Monica. *Mr. Cookie Baker*
Westcott, Nadine Bernard. *Peanut butter and jelly*
Willard, Nancy. *The flying bed*
Willey, Margaret. *Clever Beatrice and the best little pony*

Careers – barbers

Burnard, Damon. *Dave's haircut*
Cole, Kenneth, Dr. *No bad news*
Hamilton, Martha. *The ghost catcher*
Koren, Edward. *Very hairy Harry*
McElligott, Matthew. *Even monsters need haircuts*
Mitchell, Margaree King. *Uncle Jed's barbershop*
Peet, Bill. *Hubert's hair-raising adventures*
Radabaugh, Melinda Beth. *Getting a haircut*
Robbins, Beth. *Tom's new haircut*
Rocco, John. *Super Hair-o and the barber of doom*
Tarpley, Natasha Anastasia. *Bippity Bop barbershop*

Careers – beekeepers

Flanagan, Alice K. *Learning about bees from Mr. Krebs*
Kessler, Cristina. *The best beekeeper of Lalibela*
Krebs, Laurie. *The beeman*, ill. by Valeria Cis
The beeman, ill. by Melissa Iwai
Nargi, Lela. *The honeybee man*

Careers – beggars

Oppenheim, Shulamith Levey. *Ali and the magic stew*

Careers – blacksmiths

High, Linda Oatman. *Winter shoes for Shadow Horse*

Careers – bookbinders

Cheng, Andrea. *Anna the bookbinder*

Careers – bus drivers

Brown, Marc. *Arthur lost and found*
Flanagan, Alice K. *Riding the school bus with Mrs. Kramer*
Helakoski, Leslie. *The smushy bus*
Marin, Cheech. *Cheech and the spooky ghost bus*
Owen, Ann. *Taking your places*
Poydar, Nancy. *First day, hooray!*
Pulver, Robin. *Axle Annie*
Axle Annie and the speed grump
Willems, Mo. *Don't let the pigeon drive the bus*

Careers – butchers

Yorinks, Arthur. *Louis the fish*

Careers – carpenters

Lucado, Max. *Jacob's gift*
Pickthall, Marjorie L. C. *The worker in sandalwood*

Careers – cartographers

Chancellor, Deborah. *Maps and mapping*

Careers – chauffeurs

Villeneuve, Anne. *Loula is leaving for Africa*

Careers – chefs, cooks

Barasch, Lynne. *Hiromi's hands*
Demas, Corinne. *The boy who was generous with salt*
Egan, Tim. *The experiments of Doctor Vermin*
Hartland, Jessie. *Bon appetit!*
Medearis, Angela Shelf. *The ghost of Sifty-Sifty Sam*
Ochiltree, Dianne. *Molly, by golly!*
Radabaugh, Melinda Beth. *Going to a restaurant*
Reich, Susanna. *Minette's feast*
Staake, Bob. *The donut chef*
Stein, Janet. *This little bunny can bake*
Stimpson, Colin. *Jack and the baked beanstalk*
Stowell, Penelope. *The greatest potatoes*
Wellington, Monica. *Pizza at Sally's*
Whelan, Gloria. *The boy who wanted to cook*

Careers – clergy

DeNoble, Augustine. *Brother Joseph*
Dollinger, Renate. *The rabbi who flew*
I've seen the promised land
Johnson, Paul Brett. *Old Dry Fry*
Kimmel, Eric A. *Zigazak!*
Muth, Jon J. *Stone soup*
Nettleton, Pamela Hill. *Martin Luther King, Jr*
Norris, Kathleen. *The holy twins*
Olofsson, Helena. *The little jester*
Rappaport, Doreen. *Martin's big words*
Sexton, Colleen A. *Let's meet Martin Luther King, Jr*
Swain, Gwenyth. *I wonder as I wander*

Careers – coaches

Finchler, Judy. *You're a good sport, Miss Malarkey*
Flanagan, Alice K. *Coach John and his soccer team*

Careers – composers

Anderson, M. T. *Strange Mr. Satie*
Celenza, Anna Harwell. *The farewell symphony*
Costanza, Stephen. *Vivaldi and the invisible orchestra*
Robinson, Fiona. *What animals really like*
Schaefer, Carole Lexa. *Two scarlet songbirds*
Swain, Gwenyth. *I wonder as I wander*

Careers – conductors (music)

Costello, David Hyde. *Little Pig joins the band*
Devernay, Laetitia. *The conductor*
Lithgow, John. *The remarkable Farkle McBride*
Robinson, Fiona. *What animals really like*

Careers – construction workers

Ashburn, Boni. *Builder Goose*
Banks, Kate. *The night worker*
Bean, Jonathan. *Building our house*
Beil, Karen Magnuson. *Jack's house*
Big noisy trucks and diggers
Clement, Nathan. *Job site*
Copeland, Cynthia L. *What are you waiting for?*
Dale, Penny. *Dinosaur dig!*
Evans, Nate. *Bang! Boom! Roar!*
Flanagan, Alice K. *Mr. Paul and Mr. Luecke build communities*
Goodwin-Sturges, Judy Sue. *Construction Kitties*
Hayward, Linda. *A day in the life of a builder*
Hennessy, B. G. *Road builders*
Hill, Lee Sullivan. *Earthmovers*
Horvath, James. *Dig, dogs, dig*
Hudson, Cheryl Willis. *Construction zone*
Johnson, Angela. *Those building men*
Kilby, Don. *At a construction site*
Lewis, Kevin. *The lot at the end of my block*
Liebman, Daniel. *I want to be a builder*
Lund, Deb. *Monsters on machines*
McMullan, Kate. *I'm dirty!*
Mandel, Peter. *Jackhammer Sam*
Meltzer, Lynn. *The construction crew*
Nevius, Carol. *Building with Dad*
Newhouse, Maxwell. *The house that Max built*
Paul, Ann Whitford. *Word builder*
Schaefer, Lola M. *Construction site*
Schomp, Virginia. *If you were a . . . construction worker*
Skultety, Nancy. *From here to there*
Steggall, Susan. *The diggers are coming!*
Stoeke, Janet Morgan. *Minerva Louise and the red truck*
Suen, Anastasia. *Raise the roof*
Sutton, Sally. *Demolition*
Roadwork
Wood, Jakki. *A hole in the road*

Careers – cooks *see* Careers – chefs, cooks

Careers – custodians, janitors

Brett, Jan. *Hedgie blasts off!*
Flanagan, Alice K. *Call Mr. Vasquez, he'll fix it!*
Harley, Bill. *Lost and found*
Reed, Lynn Rowe. *Basil's birds*
Schotter, Roni. *Doo-Wop Pop*

Careers – dancers

Crow, Kristyn. *Zombelina*
Ferguson, Sarah. *Ballerina Rosie*
Hayward, Linda. *A day in the life of a dancer*
Isadora, Rachel. *Lili on stage*
Klingel, Cynthia Fitterer. *Dancers*
Pace, Anne Marie. *Vampirina ballerina*
Vampirina ballerina hosts a sleepover
Pavlova, Anna. *I dreamed I was a ballerina*
Pinkney, Andrea Davis. *Alvin Ailey*
Schomp, Virginia. *If you were a . . . ballet dancer*
Sís, Peter. *Ballerina*

Careers – dentists

Berenstain, Stan and Jan. *The Berenstain bears visit the dentist*
Cousins, Lucy. *Maisy, Charley, and the wobbly tooth*
Curious George goes to the dentist
Davis, Katie. *Mabel the Tooth Fairy and how she got her job*
Dungy, Tony. *You can do it!*
Flanagan, Alice K. *Dr. Kanner, dentist with a smile*
Gomi, Taro. *The crocodile and the dentist*
Keller, Laurie. *Open wide*

Murkoff, Heidi Eisenberg. *What to expect when you go to the dentist*
Rockwell, Harlow. *My dentist*
Rosenberry, Vera. *Vera goes to the dentist*
Schaefer, Lola M. *Dental office*
Steig, William. *Doctor De Soto goes to Africa*
Swanson, Diane. *The dentist and you*
Whybrow, Ian. *Harry and the dinosaurs say "Raahh"*
Ziefert, Harriet. *ABC dentist*

Careers – detectives

Berenstain, Stan and Jan. *The bear detectives*
Biedrzycki, David. *Ace Lacewing, Bug Detective*
Christelow, Eileen. *Where's the big bad wolf?*
Crummel, Susan Stevens. *Sherlock Bones and the missing cheese*
Dickson, Louise. *The vanishing cat*
Geisert, Arthur. *Mystery*
Levinthal, David. *Who pushed Humpty Dumpty?*
Mason, Adrienne. *Lu and Clancy sound off*
Lu and Clancy's spy stuff
Meddaugh, Susan. *Perfectly Martha*
Metzger, Steve. *Detective Blue*
Nash, Scott. *Tuff Fluff*
Palatini, Margie. *The web files*
Pinkwater, Daniel. *Bad bear detectives*
Rash, Andy. *Agent A to Agent Z*
Schaefer, Lola M. *Police station*
Scotton, Rob. *Secret Agent Splat!*
Teague, Mark. *Detective LaRue*
Tryon, Leslie. *Albert's Halloween*
Yee, Wong Herbert. *Detective Small in the amazing banana caper*

Careers – doctors

Beaty, Andrea. *Doctor Ted*
Berenstain, Stan and Jan. *The Berenstain bears go to the doctor*
Charlip, Remy. *"Mother, mother I feel sick"*
Cole, Joanna. *My friend the doctor*
Freeman, Don. *Corduroy's busy street and Corduroy goes to the doctor*
Grimm, Jacob and Wilhelm. *Doctor All-Knowing*
Harness, Cheryl. *Mary Walker wears the pants*
Ketteman, Helen. *If Beaver had a fever*
Liebman, Daniel. *I want to be a doctor*
Lloyd, Sam. *Doctor Meow's big emergency*
London, Jonathan. *Froggy goes to the doctor*
Here comes Doctor Hippo
Murkoff, Heidi Eisenberg. *What to expect when you go to the doctor*
Murphy, Liz. *ABC doctor*
My doctor's bag
Oelschlager, Vanita. *Bonyo Bonyo*
Owen, Ann. *Keeping you healthy*
Piumini, Roberto. *Doctor Me Di Cin*
Robbins, Beth. *Tom and Ally visit the doctor*
Rockwell, Harlow. *My doctor*
Rogers, Fred. *Going to the doctor*
Rylant, Cynthia. *Silver packages*
Schaefer, Lola M. *Hospital*
Schomp, Virginia. *If you were a . . . doctor*
Singer, Marilyn. *I'm getting a checkup*
Slegers, Liesbet. *Katie goes to the doctor*
Stone, Tanya Lee. *Who says women can't be doctors?*
Swanson, Diane. *The doctor and you*
Viorst, Judith. *The tenth good thing about Barney*

Careers – doormen

Grimm, Edward. *The doorman*

Careers – electricians

Cole, Joanna. *The magic school bus and the electric field trip*

Careers – emergency medical technicians

Levine, Michelle. *Ambulances*
Mayo, Margaret. *Emergency!*

Careers – engineers

Beaty, Andrea. *Rosie Revere, engineer*
Drummond, Allan. *Casey Jones*
Highet, Alistair. *The yellow train*
Moss, Marissa. *True heart*
Shuter, Jane. *Henry Ford*

Careers – entertainers

Newman, Lesléa. *Pigs, pigs, pigs*

Careers – explorers

Brown, Don. *Uncommon traveler*
Hopkinson, Deborah. *Keep on!*
Kirk, Daniel. *Library mouse: a museum adventure*
Library mouse: a world to explore
Kroll, Steven. *Lewis and Clark*
St. George, Judith. *So you want to be an explorer?*
Schachner, Judith Byron. *Yo, Vikings*
Sís, Peter. *Follow the dream*
Thomas, Frances. *One day, Daddy*
Weatherford, Carole Boston. *I, Matthew Henson*
Yorinks, Arthur. *The Miami giant*

Careers – farmers

Aesop. *The goose that laid the golden egg*
Aliki. *Milk from cow to carton*
Asch, Frank. *Barnyard lullaby*
Baker, Ken. *Old MacDonald had a dragon*
Barbour, Karen. *Mr. Williams*
Bock, Lee. *Oh, crumps! / Ay, caramba!*
Carlson, Melody. *Farmer Brown's field trip*
Carney, Margaret. *At Grandpa's sugar bush*
Carter, David A. *Old MacDonald had a farm: a pop-up book*
Carter, Don. *Old MacDonald drives a tractor*
Christelow, Eileen. *The great pig escape*
Cordsen, Carol Foskett. *Market day*
Cronin, Doreen. *Click, clack, moo*
Dooby dooby moo
Thump, quack, moo
Crunk, Tony. *Grandpa's overalls*
Douglas, Erin. *Get that pest!*
Duffield, Katy. *Farmer McPeepers and his missing milk cows*
Egan, Tim. *Serious farm*
The farmer in the dell. *The farmer in the dell*, ill. by John O'Brien
The farmer in the dell, ill. by Alexandra Wallner
Fitz-Gibbon, Sally. *On Uncle John's farm*
Flanagan, Alice K. *Farmers*
Raising cows on the Koebels' farm
A visit to the Gravesens' farm

The Zieglers and their apple orchard
Goodhart, Pippa. *Arthur's tractor*
Haas, Jessie. *Hurry!*
Klingel, Cynthia Fitterer. *Farmers*
Lasky, Kathryn. *The emperor's old clothes*
Maccarone, Grace. *Oink! moo! how do you do?*
Maguire, Gregory. *Crabby Cratchitt*
Marciano, John Bemelmans. *Delilah*
Most, Bernard. *Cock-a-doodle-moo!*
Nettleton, Pamela Hill. *George Washington*
Old MacDonald had a farm. *Old MacDonald*
Old MacDonald had a farm, ill. by Holly Berry
Old MacDonald had a farm, ill. by Jane Cabrera
Old MacDonald had a farm, ill. by Carol Jones
Old MacDonald had a farm, ill. by Tracey Campbell Pearson
Old MacDonald had a farm, ill. by Glen Rounds
Old MacDonald had a farm, ill. by Jessica Souhami
Old MacDonald had a farm, ill. by Prue Theobalds
Palatini, Margie. *The cheese*
Parks, Carmen. *Farmers market*
Pelletier, Andrew T. *The toy farmer*
Peterson, Cris. *Extra cheese, please!*
Plourde, Lynn. *Grandpappy snippy snappies*
Powell, Consie. *Amazing apples*
Purmell, Ann. *Apple cider making days*
Christmas tree farm
Sandburg, Carl. *The Huckabuck family and how they raised popcorn in Nebraska and quit and came back*
Schomp, Virginia. *If you were a . . . farmer*
Sillifant, Alec. *Farmer Ham*
Skrypuch, Marsha Forchuk. *Enough*
Slate, Joseph. *The great big wagon that rang*
Sloat, Teri. *The thing that bothered Farmer Brown*
Steig, William. *Wizzil*
Stock, Catherine. *A porc in New York*
Sturgis, Brenda Reeves. *10 turkeys in the road*
Tafuri, Nancy. *This is the farmer*
Taylor, Joanne. *Full moon rising*
Trent, Shanda. *Farmers' market day*
Van Leeuwen, Jean. *Nothing here but trees*
Sorry
Waddell, Martin. *Farmer Duck*
The pig in the pond
Wellington, Monica. *Apple farmer Annie*
Wilson, Karma. *Horseplay*
Yee, Wong Herbert. *Fireman Small to the rescue*
Yolen, Jane. *The flying witch*
Harvest home

Careers – firefighters

Armstrong, Jennifer. *Magnus at the fire*
Beaty, Andrea. *Firefighter Ted*
Bingham, Caroline. *Big book of rescue vehicles*
Bourgeois, Paulette. *Fire fighters*
Bridwell, Norman. *Clifford's good deeds*
Butler, Dori Hillestad. *F is for firefighting*
Carabine, Sue. *A firefighter's night before Christmas*
Child, Lauren. *Clarice Bean, guess who's babysitting?*
Curious George at the fire station
Cutlip, Kimbra L. *Firefighter's night before Christmas*
Demarest, Chris L. *Firefighters A to Z*
Hotshots!
Smokejumpers one to ten
Desimini, Lisa. *Dot the Firedog*
Dubois, Muriel L. *Out and about at the fire station*
Elya, Susan Middleton. *Fire! ¡Fuego! Brave bomberos*
Emergency!
Flanagan, Alice K. *Ms. Murphy fights fires*
Fox, Christyan. *Fire fighter PiggyWiggy*
Frampton, David. *Mr. Ferlinghetti's poem*
Gergely, Tibor. *The great big fire engine book*
Gibbons, Gail. *Fire! Fire!*
Godwin, Laura. *This is the firefighter*
Gorbachev, Valeri. *The missing chick*
Graham, Tom. *Five little firefighters*
Grambling, Lois G. *My mom is a firefighter*
Greene, Rhonda Gowler. *Firebears*
Hamilton, Kersten. *Firefighters to the rescue!*
Harper, Jamie. *Miss Mingo and the fire drill*
Hayward, Linda. *A day in the life of a firefighter*
Hubbell, Patricia. *Firefighters!*
Jane, Pamela. *Milo and the fire engine parade*
Klingel, Cynthia Fitterer. *Firefighters*
Krensky, Stephen. *Spark the firefighter*
Lenski, Lois. *The little fire engine*
Liebman, Daniel. *I want to be a firefighter*
Lloyd, Sam. *Chief Rhino to the rescue!*
London, Jonathan. *Here comes firefighter Hippo*
Lukasewich, Lori. *The night fire*
Mammano, Julie. *Rhinos who rescue*
Martin, Bill, Jr. *Fire! Fire! said Mrs. McGuire*
"Fire! Fire!" said Mrs. McGuire
Mayo, Margaret. *Emergency!*
Miller, Edward. *Fireboy to the rescue!*
Mitton, Tony. *Flashing fire engines*
Munsch, Robert N. *The fire station*
Nolan, Janet. *The firehouse light*
Ochiltree, Dianne. *Molly, by golly!*
Osborne, Mary Pope. *New York's bravest*
Owen, Ann. *Protecting your home*
Rex, Michael. *My fire engine*
Rey, H. A. *Curious George*
The original Curious George
Rockwell, Anne. *At the firehouse*
Fire engines
Santoro, Scott. *Isaac the Ice Cream Truck*
Sís, Peter. *Fire truck*
Slater, Dashka. *Firefighters in the dark*
Teague, Mark. *Firehouse!*
Whiting, Sue. *The firefighters*
Wood, Audrey. *Alphabet rescue*
Yee, Wong Herbert. *Fireman Small*
Fireman Small, fire down below
Fireman Small to the rescue
A small Christmas
Zimmerman, Andrea Griffing. *Fire engine man*

Careers – fishermen

Bateman, Teresa. *The merbaby*
Demas, Corinne. *The boy who was generous with salt*
Demers, Dominique. *Old Thomas and the little fairy*
Garland, Sherry. *My father's boat*
Gibbons, Gail. *Surrounded by sea*
LaMarche, Jim. *Up*
McGaw, Wayne T. *T-boy of the bayou*
Pennypacker, Sara. *Pierre in love*
San Souci, Robert D. *Nicholas Pipe*
Sunami, Kitoba. *How the fisherman tricked the genie*

Careers – forest rangers *see* Careers – park rangers

Careers – fortune tellers

Alexander, Lloyd. *Fortune tellers*
Shepard, Aaron. *Forty fortunes*

Careers – fur traders

Pendziwol, Jean E. *The red sash*

Careers – garbage collectors *see* Careers – sanitation workers

Careers – geologists

Cole, Joanna. *The magic school bus inside the earth*

Careers – handymen

Flanagan, Alice K. *Call Mr. Vasquez, he'll fix it!*

Careers – harpists

Edwards, Pamela Duncan. *The leprechaun's gold*

Careers – housekeepers

Hanson, Warren. *It's Monday, Mrs. Jolly Bones!*
McKissack, Patricia C. *Ma Dear's aprons*
Polacco, Patricia. *Gifts of the heart*

Careers – illustrators

Browne, Anthony. *The shape game*
Kanninen, Barbara. *A story with pictures*
Krull, Kathleen. *The boy on Fairfield Street*
Myers, Walter Dean. *Harlem*
Rau, Dana Meachen. *Dr. Seuss*
Steig, William. *When everybody wore a hat*
Whatley, Bruce. *Wait! No paint!*

Careers – inventors

Barretta, Gene. *Neo Leo*
Now and Ben
Timeless Thomas
Brill, Marlene Targ. *Margaret Knight, girl inventor*
Brown, Don. *A wizard from the start*
Fleming, Candace. *Papa's mechanical fish*
Gall, Chris. *Awesome Dawson*
Glass, Andrew. *The wondrous whirligig*
Kelly, David A. *Miracle mud*
Krensky, Stephen. *Ben Franklin and his first kite*
Kulling, Monica. *All aboard! Elijah McCoy's steam engine*
McCall, Bruce. *Marveltown*
Milgrim, David. *Young MacDonald*
Nettleton, Pamela Hill. *Benjamin Franklin*
Pelley, Kathleen T. *Inventor McGregor*
Priceman, Marjorie. *Hot air*
It's me, Marva!
Reynolds, Peter H. *Sydney's star*
Schaefer, Lola M. *The Wright brothers*
Schanzer, Rosalyn. *How Ben Franklin stole the lightning*
Taylor, Barbara. *I wonder why zippers have teeth and other questions about inventions*
Weston, Mark. *Honda*
Yolen, Jane. *My brothers' flying machine*

Careers – janitors *see* Careers – custodians, janitors

Careers – jockeys

Trollinger, Patsi B. *Perfect timing*

Careers – journalists

Dray, Philip. *Yours for justice, Ida B. Wells*
Hawkins, Colin. *Fairytale news*
Leedy, Loreen. *The Furry News*
Shea, Kitty. *Out and about at the newspaper*

Careers – judges

Winter, Jonah. *Sonia Sotomayor*
Zemach, Harve. *The judge*

Careers – lawyers

Flanagan, Alice K. *A day in court with Mrs. Trinh*
McKissack, Patricia C. *Ol' Clip-Clop*

Careers – librarians

Deedy, Carmen Agra. *Return of the library dragon*
Ernst, Lisa Campbell. *Stella Louella's runaway book*
Flanagan, Alice K. *Librarians*
Ms. Davison, our librarian
Gonzalez, Lucia. *The storyteller's candle / La velita de los cuentos*
Grambling, Lois G. *Can I bring Woolly to the library, Ms. Reeder?*
Greene, Rhonda Gowler. *No pirates allowed! said Library Lou*
King, M. G. *Librarian on the roof!*
Liebman, Daniel. *I want to be a librarian*
Miller, Heather. *Librarian*
Mora, Pat. *Tomás and the library lady*
Morris, Carla. *The boy who was raised by librarians*
Radabaugh, Melinda Beth. *Going to the library*
Ruurs, Margriet. *My librarian is a camel*
Shea, Kitty. *Out and about at the public library*
Sierra, Judy. *Wild about books*
Stadler, Alexander. *Beverly Billingsly borrows a book*
Williams, Suzanne. *Library Lil*
Winter, Jeanette. *The librarian of Basra*

Careers – lifeguards

Bingham, Caroline. *Big book of rescue vehicles*
Pinkwater, Daniel. *At the Hotel Larry*
Young Larry

Careers – lumberjacks

Balcziak, Bill. *Paul Bunyan*
Bateman, Teresa. *Paul Bunyan vs. Hals Halson*
Kellogg, Steven. *Paul Bunyan: a tall tale*
Lange, Willem. *John and Tom*
Luckhurst, Matt. *Paul Bunyan and Babe the Blue Ox*

Careers – magicians

Adler, David A. *A picture book of Harry Houdini*
Agee, Jon. *Milo's hat trick*
Ashman, Linda. *Maxwell's magic mix-up*
Bardill, Linard. *The great golden thing*

Baynton, Martin. *Jane and the magician*
Cate, Annette LeBlanc. *The magic rabbit*
Desrosiers, Sylvie. *Hocus Pocus takes the train*
Faller, Regis. *Polo and the magician!*
Geras, Adèle. *Swan Lake*
Kennedy, Kim. *Hee-Haw-Dini and the Great Zambini*
Many, Paul. *The great pancake escape*
Paul, Ruth. *Hedgehog's magic tricks*
Schneider, Christine M. *Horace P. Tuttle, magician extraordinaire*
Seeger, Pete. *Abiyoyo returns*
Villeneuve, Anne. *The red scarf*

Careers – mail carriers *see* Careers – postal workers

Careers – mathematicians

Heiligman, Deborah. *The boy who loved math*

Careers – mayors

Flanagan, Alice K. *Mayors*

Careers – mechanics

Flanagan, Alice K. *Mr. Yee fixes cars*
Liebman, Daniel. *I want to be a mechanic*
Merlin, Christophe. *Under the hood*
Shulman, Mark. *Gorilla Garage*

Careers – messengers

Burleigh, Robert. *Messenger, messenger*

Careers – meteorologists

Bahr, Mary. *My brother loved snowflakes*
Kespert, Deborah. *Rain and shine*
Schmidt, Karen Lee. *Carl's nose*

Careers – migrant workers

Adler, David A. *A picture book of Cesar Chavez*
Altman, Linda Jacobs. *Amelia's road*
Dorros, Arthur. *Radio Man / Don Radio*
Mora, Pat. *Tomás and the library lady*
Pérez, L. King. *First day in grapes*
Stanton, Karen. *Papi's gift*
Thomas, Jane Resh. *Lights on the river*
Tonatiuh, Duncan. *Pancho Rabbit and the coyote*
Warren, Sarah. *Dolores Huerta*
Williams, Sherley Anne. *Working cotton*

Careers – military

Andersen, Hans Christian. *The tinderbox*
Biden, Jill. *Don't forget, God bless our troops*
Brisson, Pat. *Sometimes we were brave*
Brown, Marcia. *Stone soup*
Bunting, Eve. *My red balloon*
The wall
Collins, Suzanne. *Year of the jungle*
Demarest, Chris L. *Alpha Bravo Charlie*
Dennis, Major Brian. *Nubs*
Dewan, Ted. *One true bear*
Duble, Kathleen Benner. *Pilot mom*
Emberley, Barbara. *Drummer Hoff*
Hardin, Melinda. *Hero dad*
Keane, Michael. *The night Santa got lost*
Lee, Jeanne M. *The song of Mu Lan*
Littlesugar, Amy. *Lisette's angel*
McElroy, Lisa Tucker. *Love, Lizzie*
Mackintosh, David. *The Frank show*
Nadel, Carolina. *Daddy's home*
Nelson, S. D. *Quiet hero*
Nettleton, Pamela Hill. *George Washington*
Norman, Geoffrey. *Stars above us*
Pelton, Mindy L. *When Dad's at sea*
Seeger, Pete. *Some friends to feed*
Tomp, Sarah Wones. *Red, white, and blue goodbye*

Careers – miners

Addy, Sharon Hart. *Lucky Jake*
Amsden, Janet. *Grizzly Pete and the ghosts*
Kay, Verla. *Gold fever*
Levitin, Sonia. *Boom town*
Lyon, George Ella. *Mama is a miner*
Provensen, Alice. *Klondike gold*

Careers – motion picture producers

Brown, Don. *Mack made movies*
Milgrim, David. *Amelia makes a movie*

Careers – musicians

Alexander, Kwame. *Acoustic Rooster and his barnyard band*
Andrews, Julie. *Simeon's gift*
Battle-Lavert, Gwendolyn. *The music in Derrick's heart*
Burleigh, Robert. *Lookin' for Bird in the big city*
Carter, Don. *Heaven's all-star jazz band*
Celenza, Anna Harwell. *Duke Ellington's Nutcracker Suite*
Christensen, Bonnie. *Woody Guthrie, poet of the people*
Cox, Judy. *My family plays music*
DeFelice, Cynthia C. *Cold feet*
Dillon, Leo. *Jazz on a Saturday night*
Francis, Panama. *David gets his drum*
Grimm, Jacob and Wilhelm. *The Bremen town band*
The Bremen town musicians, ill. by Bill Dickson
The Bremen town musicians, ill. by Ilse Plume
The Bremen town musicians, ill. by Bernadette Watts
The Bremen town musicians, ill. by Lisbeth Zwerger
Musicians of Bremen
Musicians of Bremen / Los musicos de Bremner
Huling, Jan. *Ol' Bloo's boogie-woogie band and blues ensemble*
Ingalls, Ann. *The little piano girl*
Johnson, Angela. *Violet's music*
Liebman, Daniel. *I want to be a musician*
Lithgow, John. *The remarkable Farkle McBride*
Long, Loren. *Drummer boy*
Manders, John. *The really awful musicians*
Marsalis, Wynton. *Squeak, rumble, whomp! Whomp! Whomp!*
Martin, Bill, Jr. *Maestro plays*
Orgill, Roxane. *If I only had a horn*
Parker, Robert Andrew. *Piano starts here*
Pinkney, Andrea Davis. *Duke Ellington*
Pinkwater, Daniel. *Bongo Larry*
Price, Kathy. *The Bourbon Street musicians*
Raschka, Chris. *Charlie Parker played be bop*

Mysterious Thelonious
Schomp, Virginia. *If you were a . . . musician*
Seeger, Pete. *The deaf musicians*
Shepard, Aaron. *The sea king's daughter*
Sís, Peter. *Play, Mozart, play*
Stinson, Kathy. *The man with the violin*
Troupe, Quincy. *Little Stevie Wonder*
Turner, Barbara J. *Out and about at the orchestra*
Weatherford, Carole Boston. *Before John was a jazz giant*
Weller, Frances Ward. *The angel of Mill Street*
Winter, Jeanette. *Once upon a time in Chicago*
Winter, Jonah. *Dizzy*

Careers – nuns

Mora, Pat. *A library for Juana*
Norris, Kathleen. *The holy twins*
Ransom, Candice F. *Mother Teresa*

Careers – nurses

Flanagan, Alice K. *Ask Nurse Pfaff, she'll help you!*
James, Simon. *Nurse Clementine*
Liebman, Daniel. *I want to be a nurse*
Schaefer, Lola M. *Hospital*
Wohlrabe, Sarah C. *Helping you heal, a book about nurses*

Careers – oceanographers

Nivola, Claire A. *Life in the ocean*
Yaccarino, Dan. *The fantastic undersea life of Jacques Cousteau*

Careers – opera singers *see* Careers – singers

Careers – opticians, optometrists

Barclay, Eric. *I can see just fine*
Flanagan, Alice K. *Choosing eyeglasses with Mrs. Koutris*

Careers – ornithologists

Davies, Jacqueline. *The boy who drew birds*

Careers – painters *see* Careers – artists

Careers – paleontologists

Atkins, Jeannine. *Mary Anning and the sea dragon*
Barner, Bob. *Dinosaur bones*
Brown, Don. *Rare treasure*
Hartland, Jessie. *How the dinosaur got to the museum*
Houran, Lori Haskins. *Dig those dinosaurs*

Careers – park rangers

Flanagan, Alice K. *Exploring parks with Ranger Dockett*

Careers – peddlers

Derby, Sally. *Two fools and a horse*
Diakité, Baba Wagué. *The hatseller and the monkeys*
Johnson, Angela. *The Rolling Store*
Miller, William. *Jenny and the peddler*
Slobodkina, Esphyr. *Caps for sale*
Circus caps for sale

Careers – pharmacists

Gibson, Karen Bush. *Pharmacists*

Careers – photographers

Alter, Anna. *A photo for Greta*
Bahr, Mary. *My brother loved snowflakes*
Bibbons, Faye. *The day the picture man came*
Davis, Jill. *Orangutans are ticklish*
High, Linda Oatman. *The girl on the high-diving horse*
Martin, Jacqueline Briggs. *Snowflake Bentley*

Careers – physicians *see* Careers – doctors

Careers – plasterers

Carle, Eric. *My apron*

Careers – poets

Burleigh, Robert. *Langston's train ride*
Gollub, Matthew. *Cool melons — turn to frogs*
Malaspina, Ann. *Phillis sings out freedom*
Perdorno, Willie. *Visiting Langston*
Yolen, Jane. *My Uncle Emily*

Careers – police officers

Bourgeois, Paulette. *Police officers*
Braithwaite, Jill. *Police cars*
Carter, Anne Laurel. *Under a prairie sky*
Flanagan, Alice K. *Officer Brown keeps neighborhoods safe*
Police officers
Gorbachev, Valeri. *The missing chick*
Hamilton, Kersten. *Police officers on patrol*
Hubbell, Patricia. *Police*
Keats, Ezra Jack. *My dog is lost!*
Lenski, Lois. *Policeman Small*
Liebman, Daniel. *I want to be a police officer*
McCloskey, Robert. *Make way for ducklings*
Meadows, Michelle. *Traffic pups*
Mortensen, Denise Dowling. *Bug Patrol*
Niemann, Christoph. *The police cloud*
Numeroff, Laura Joffe. *Sherman Crunchley*
Owen, Ann. *Keeping you safe*
Rathmann, Peggy. *Officer Buckle and Gloria*
Russell, Joan Plummer. *Aero and Officer Mike*
Schaefer, Lola M. *Police station*
Schomp, Virginia. *If you were a . . . police officer*
Smith, Janice Lee. *Jess and the stinky cowboys*
Stille, Darlene R. *Police cars*
Whitehead, Kathy. *Looking for Uncle Louie on the Fourth of July*
Yee, Wong Herbert. *The Officers' Ball*

Careers – postal workers

Ahlberg, Janet. *The jolly Christmas postman*
The jolly pocket postman
The jolly postman
Blackstone, Stella. *Bear at work*
Bottner, Barbara. *Raymond and Nelda*
Bourgeois, Paulette. *Postal workers*

Bradby, Marie. *The longest wait*
Brill, Marlene Targ. *Bronco Charlie and the Pony Express*
Carter, Don. *Send it!*
Day, Alexandra. *Special deliveries*
Flanagan, Alice K. *Here comes Mr. Eventoff with the mail!*
Letter carriers
Gibbons, Gail. *The post office book*
Grindley, Sally. *The giant postman*
Henkes, Kevin. *Good-bye, Curtis*
Holabird, Katharine. *Angelina's Christmas*
Horning, Sandra. *The giant hug*
Kay, Verla. *Whatever happened to the Pony Express?*
Kerby, Mona. *Owney, the mail-pouch pooch*
Klingel, Cynthia Fitterer. *Postal workers*
Lendroth, Susan. *Calico Dorsey*
Lillegard, Dee. *Tortoise brings the mail*
Olshan, Matthew. *The mighty Lalouche*
Owen, Ann. *Delivering your mail*
Rylant, Cynthia. *Mr. Griggs' work*
Salzano, Tammi. *One windy day*
Schneider, Howie. *Fast 'n Snappy*
Shea, Kitty. *Out and about at the post office*
Spinelli, Eileen. *Somebody loves you, Mr. Hatch*
Spradlin, Michael P. *Off like the wind!*
Steffensmeier, Alexander. *Millie waits for the mail*
Tunnell, Michael O. *Mailing May*

Careers – potters

Andrews-Goebel, Nancy. *The pot that Juan built*
Hill, Laban Carrick. *Dave the potter*

Careers – preachers *see* Careers – clergy

Careers – principals *see* Careers – school principals

Careers – printers

Fisher, Leonard Everett. *Gutenberg*
Nettleton, Pamela Hill. *Benjamin Franklin*

Careers – race car drivers

Clement, Nathan. *Speed*
Rex, Michael. *My race car*

Careers – railroad engineers

Kimmel, Eric A. *Stormy's hat*
Lenski, Lois. *The little train*
Moser, Lisa. *Railroad Hank*
Rex, Michael. *My freight train*

Careers – ranchers

Drummond, Ree. *Charlie the ranch dog*
Lawson, Dorie McCullough. *Tex*
Moser, Lisa. *Cowboy Boyd and Mighty Calliope*
Parish, Herman. *Go west, Amelia Bedelia!*
Peterson, Cris. *Amazing grazing*
Urbigkit, Cat. *A young shepherd*

Careers – rangers *see* Careers – park rangers

Careers – sailors *see* Careers – military; Sailors

Careers – salespeople

Horowitz, Dave. *Buy my hats!*
Palatini, Margie. *Ding dong ding dong*
Rozen, Anna. *The merchant of noises*
Watt, Mélanie. *Have I got a book for you!*

Careers – sanitation workers

Bourgeois, Paulette. *Garbage collectors*
Kirk, Daniel. *Trash trucks!*
Maass, Robert. *Garbage*
McMullan, Kate. *I stink!*
Odanaka, Barbara. *Smash! Mash! Crash! There goes the trash!*
Showers, Paul. *Where does the garbage go?*
Steig, William. *Tiffky Doofky*
Ward, D. J. *What happens to our trash?*
Winter, Jonah. *Here comes the garbage barge!*
Zimmerman, Andrea Griffing. *Trashy town*

Careers – school principals

Calmenson, Stephanie. *The frog principal*
The principal's new clothes
Cocca-Leffler, Maryann. *Mr. Tanen's ties rule!*
Creech, Sharon. *A fine, fine school*
Crimi, Carolyn. *Principal Fred won't go to bed*
Dakos, Kalli. *Our principal promised to kiss a pig*
Griswell, Kim T. *Rufus goes to school*
Polacco, Patricia. *Mr. Lincoln's way*
Poydar, Nancy. *First day, hooray!*

Careers – scientists

Berne, Jennifer. *On a beam of light*
Brown, Don. *Odd boy out*
Chambers, Roland. *Rooftop rocket party*
Elliott, David. *Hazel Nutt, mad scientist*
Greenstein, Elaine. *The goose man*
James, Brian. *Supertwins meet the dangerous dino-robots*
Krensky, Stephen. *Ben Franklin and his first kite*
A man for all seasons
Lawlor, Laurie. *Rachel Carson and her book that changed the world*
Lehn, Barbara. *What is a scientist?*
McCully, Emily Arnold. *Marvelous Mattie*
McDonnell, Patrick. *Me . . . Jane*
Martin, Jacqueline Briggs. *Snowflake Bentley*
Marzollo, Jean. *The little plant doctor*
Nettleton, Pamela Hill. *Benjamin Franklin*
O'Connor, Teddy. *A new brain for Igor*
Offill, Jenny. *11 experiments that failed*
Pettenati, Jeanne K. *Galileo's journal, 1609–1610*
Schanzer, Rosalyn. *How Ben Franklin stole the lightning*
Verstraete, Larry. *S is for scientists*
Winter, Jeanette. *The watcher*

Careers – sculptors

Rappaport, Doreen. *Lady Liberty*
Schaefer, A. R. *Alexander Calder*
Stanley, Diane. *The trouble with wishes*
Stevenson, Harvey. *Looking at liberty*
Ziarnik, Natalie. *Madeleine's light*

Careers – seamstresses

Brown, Margaret Wise. *Bunny's noisy book*
Bunny's noisy book [board book]
Heo, Yumi. *Lady Hahn and her seven friends*

Careers – shepherds

Calhoun, Mary. *A shepherd's gift*
Daly, Niki. *The herd boy*
Levine, Gail Carson. *Betsy Red Hoodie*
Betsy who cried wolf
Lewis, Kim. *The shepherd boy*
Moser, Barry. *Psalm 23*
Urbigkit, Cat. *A young shepherd*

Careers – sheriffs

Crummel, Susan Stevens. *Ten-Gallon Bart*
Rumford, James. *Don't touch my hat!*
Sneed, Brad. *Deputy Harvey and the ant cow caper*
Yorinks, Arthur. *Whitefish Will rides again*

Careers – shoe shiners

Quattlebaum, Mary. *The shine man*

Careers – shoemakers

Barrett, Mary Brigid. *Shoebox Sam*
Bateman, Teresa. *Keeper of soles*
Dollinger, Renate. *The rabbi who flew*
Grimm, Jacob and Wilhelm. *The elves and the shoemaker*, ill. by Kirill Chelushkin
The elves and the shoemaker, ill. by Paul Galdone
The elves and the shoemaker, ill. by Margaret Walty
The shoemaker and his elves
The shoemaker and the elves, ill. by Adrienne Adams
The shoemaker and the elves, ill. by Ilse Plume
Johnson, Grace. *The candle in the window*
Light, Steve. *The shoemaker extraordinaire*
Lowell, Susan. *The bootmaker and the elves*
Madonna. *Yakov and the seven thieves*
San Souci, Robert D. *The red heels*
Stampler, Ann Redisch. *The wooden sword*
Tegen, Katherine Brown. *The story of the leprechaun*

Careers – singers

Fisher, Mary M. *Rosita's bridge*
Orgill, Roxane. *Skit-scat raggedy cat*
Pinkney, Andrea Davis. *Martin and Mahalia*
Ryan, Pam Muñoz. *When Marian sang*
Schroeder, Alan. *Baby Flo*
Sciurba, Katie. *Oye, Celia!*
Watson, Renée. *Harlem's little blackbird*
Weaver, Tess. *Opera cat*

Careers – soldiers *see* Careers – military

Careers – storekeepers

Flanagan, Alice K. *A busy day at Mr. Kang's grocery store*
Buying a pet from Ms. Chavez
Choosing eyeglasses with Mrs. Koutris
Heo, Yumi. *Father's rubber shoes*
Schaefer, Lola M. *Supermarket*
Shea, Kitty. *Out and about at the supermarket*
Wisniewski, David. *Sumo Mouse*
Yorinks, Arthur. *The invisible man*

Careers – tailors

Calmenson, Stephanie. *The principal's new clothes*
Charles, Veronika Martenova. *The birdman*
Green, Stephanie. *Betsy Ross and the silver thimble*
Grimm, Jacob and Wilhelm. *The brave little tailor*, ill. by Olga Dugina
The brave little tailor, ill. by David Shaw
Seven at one blow
Hest, Amy. *The purple coat*
Oddino, Licia. *Finn and the fairies*
Osborne, Mary Pope. *The brave little seamstress*
Potter, Beatrix. *The tailor of Gloucester*

Careers – teachers

Allard, Harry. *Miss Nelson is back*
Miss Nelson is missing!
Anderson, Laurie Halse. *The hair of Zoe Fleefenbacher goes to school*
Bowen, Anne. *I know an old teacher*
Brandt, Amy. *When Katie was our teacher / Cuando Katie era nuestra maestra*
Brennan-Nelson, Denise. *Willow*
Brenner, Emily. *On the first day of grade school*
Brisson, Pat. *I remember Miss Perry*
Brown, Marc. *Arthur's teacher moves in*
Calmenson, Stephanie. *Late for school!*
Oopsy, teacher!
The teeny tiny teacher
Carlson, Nancy. *Henry and the Valentine surprise*
Cole, Joanna. *The magic school bus and the science fair expedition*
The magic school bus in the time of the dinosaurs
The magic school bus inside a beehive
The magic school bus lost in the solar system
The magic school bus on the ocean floor
Cook, Lisa Broadie. *Peanut butter and homework sandwiches*
Cox, Judy. *Happy birthday, Mrs. Millie!*
Pick a pumpkin, Mrs. Millie!
Cusimano, Maryann K. *You are my wonders*
Cuyler, Margery. *Kindness is cooler, Mrs. Ruler*
Danneberg, Julie. *First day jitters*
First year letters
Last day blues
deGroat, Diane. *No more pencils, no more books, no more teacher's dirty looks!*
Dodds, Dayle Ann. *Teacher's pets*
Edwards, Pamela Duncan. *Ms. Bitsy Bat's kindergarten*
Ferris, Jeri Chase. *Noah Webster and his words*
Figley, Marty Rhodes. *The schoolchildren's blizzard*
Finchler, Judy. *Congratulations, Miss Malarkey!*
Miss Malarkey leaves no reader behind
Miss Malarkey won't be in today
Testing Miss Malarkey
You're a good sport, Miss Malarkey
Flanagan, Alice K. *Learning is fun with Mrs. Perez*
Teachers
Gall, Chris. *Substitute creacher*
Garland, Michael. *Miss Smith and the haunted library*
Miss Smith reads again!
Miss Smith's incredible storybook

George, Lucy M. *Back to school Tortoise*
Harper, Jamie. *Miss Mingo and the first day of school*
Havill, Juanita. *Jamaica and the substitute teacher*
Hayes, Sarah. *Dog day*
Hayward, Linda. *A day in the life of a teacher*
Henkes, Kevin. *El gran día de Lily / Lilly's big day*
Lilly's big day
Lilly's purple plastic purse
Hennessy, B. G. *Mr. Ouchy's first day*
Hopkinson, Deborah. *Annie and Helen*
Houston, Gloria. *My Great-Aunt Arizona*
Hubbell, Patricia. *Teacher!*
James, Simon. *Dear Mr. Blueberry*
Johnson, Doug. *Substitute teacher plans*
Krensky, Stephen. *My teacher's secret life*
Laminack, Lester L. *Snow day!*
Layne, Steven L. *T is for teachers*
Lehn, Barbara. *What is a teacher?*
Liebman, Daniel. *I want to be a teacher*
Linch, Tanya. *My duck*
McKissack, Robert L. *Try your best*
McNaughton, Colin. *Once upon an ordinary school day*
Marshall, James. *Eugene*
Montanari, Eva. *A very full morning*
Munsch, Robert N. *Thomas' snowsuit*
Passen, Lisa. *Attack of the 50-foot teacher*
The incredible shrinking teacher
Pattou, Edith. *Mrs. Spitzer's garden*, ill. by Tricia Tusa
Mrs. Spitzer's garden, ill. by Tricia Tusa
Polacco, Patricia. *The art of Miss Chew*
The junkyard wonders
The lemonade club
Thank you, Mr. Falker
Poydar, Nancy. *First day, hooray!*
Priceman, Marjorie. *Emeline at the circus*
Primavera, Elise. *Louise the big cheese and the back-to-school smarty-pants*
Pulver, Robin. *The case of the incapacitated capitals*
Mrs. Toggle and the dinosaur
Mrs. Toggle's beautiful blue shoe
Mrs. Toggle's zipper
Puttock, Simon. *Miss Fox*
Radabaugh, Melinda Beth. *Going to school*
Ransome, James. *My teacher*
Rappaport, Doreen. *Helen's big world*
Reynolds, Marilynn. *The magnificent piano recital*
Roche, Denis. *The best class picture ever*
Rosen, Michael. *Totally wonderful Miss Plumberry*
Schomp, Virginia. *If you were a . . . teacher*
Slate, Joseph. *Miss Bindergarten celebrates the last day of kindergarten*
Miss Bindergarten celebrates the 100th day of kindergarten
Miss Bindergarten gets ready for kindergarten
Miss Bindergarten has a wild day in kindergarten
Miss Bindergarten stays home from kindergarten
Miss Bindergarten takes a field trip with kindergarten
Spinelli, Eileen. *Miss Fox's class gets it wrong*
Miss Fox's class shapes up
Stadler, John. *Wilson and Miss Lovely*
Teyssèdre, Fabienne. *Joseph wants to read*
Wheatley, Nadia. *Luke's way of looking*
Wohlrabe, Sarah C. *Helping you learn, a book about teachers*
Wood, Douglas. *What teachers can't do*
Woodson, Jacqueline. *Each kindness*
Yankovic, Al. *My new teacher and me!*
Zemach, Kaethe. *Ms. McCaw learns to draw*

Careers – toy makers

Geras, Adèle. *The nutcracker*
Hague, Michael. *The nutcracker*
Hoffmann, E. T. A. *The nutcracker*, ill. by Renée Graef
The nutcracker, ill. by Alison Jay
The nutcracker, ill. by Peter Malone
The nutcracker, ill. by Maurice Sendak
The nutcracker, ill. by Lisbeth Zwerger
The Nutcracker and the Mouse King
The nutcracker ballet
Thurber, James. *The great Quillow*

Careers – train engineers *see* Careers – railroad engineers

Careers – truck drivers

Clement, Nathan. *Drive*
Coffelt, Nancy. *Pug in a truck*
Cowley, Joy. *Gracias, the Thanksgiving turkey*
Day, Alexandra. *Frank and Ernest on the road*
Gibson, Karen Bush. *Truck drivers*
Liebman, Daniel. *I want to be a truck driver*
London, Jonathan. *I'm a truck driver*
Mitchell, Joyce Slayton. *Tractor-trailer trucker*
Schomp, Virginia. *If you were a . . . truck driver*
Sturges, Philemon. *I love trucks!*
Wellington, Monica. *Truck driver Tom*

Careers – veterinarians

Flanagan, Alice K. *Dr. Friedman helps animals*
Gibbons, Gail. *Say woof!*
Hull, Rod. *Mr. Betts and Mr. Potts*
Lee, Chinlun. *Good dog, Paw*
Liebman, Daniel. *I want to be a vet*
McCully, Emily Arnold. *Wonder horse*
Owen, Ann. *Caring for your pet*
Perkins, Lynne Rae. *The broken cat*
Schomp, Virginia. *If you were a . . . veterinarian*
Shea, Kitty. *Out and about at the vet clinic*

Careers – waiters, waitresses

Downey, Lynn. *Matilda's humdinger*
Radabaugh, Melinda Beth. *Going to a restaurant*

Careers – weather reporters *see* Careers – meteorologists

Careers – weavers

Musgrove, Margaret. *The spider weaver*

Careers – window cleaners

Dahl, Roald. *The giraffe and the pelly and me*
Rey, H. A. *Curious George takes a job*

Careers – woodcarvers

Cohn, Diana. *Dream carver*
Dorros, Arthur. *Julio's magic*

Rosen, Michael J. *Elijah's angel*
Wojciechowski, Susan. *The Christmas miracle of Jonathan Toomey*

Careers – writers

Borden, Louise. *The day Eddie met the author*
Brown, Monica. *My name is Gabito / Me llamo Gabito*
Browne, Anthony. *The shape game*
Bunting, Eve. *My special day at third street school*
Christelow, Eileen. *What do authors do?*
Clinton, Catherine. *Phillis's big test*
Corpi, Lucha. *Where fireflies dance / Ahí, donde bailan las luciérnagas*
Davidson, Rebecca Piatt. *All the world's a stage*
Dunlap, Julie. *Louisa May and Mr. Thoreau's flute*
Fagan, Carl. *Mr. Zinger's hat*
Kanninen, Barbara. *A story with pictures*
Kirk, Daniel. *Library mouse*
Library mouse: a friend's tale
Krull, Kathleen. *The boy on Fairfield Street*
Lester, Helen. *Author*
McElroy, Lisa Tucker. *Meet my grandmother. She's a children's book author*
MacLean, Kerry Lee. *Peaceful piggy meditation*
Mara, Wil. *Laura Ingalls Wilder*
Mora, Pat. *A library for Juana*
Myers, Walter Dean. *Harlem*
Nesbitt, Kenn. *More bears!*
Pulver, Robin. *Author day for room 3T*
Rau, Dana Meachen. *Dr. Seuss*
Rylant, Cynthia. *Best wishes*
Steig, William. *When everybody wore a hat*
Stevenson, James. *Fun, no fun*
I meant to tell you
Wallner, Alexandra. *Beatrix Potter*
Yaccarino, Dan. *All the way to America*

Careers – zookeepers

Goodman, Susan E. *What do you do — at the zoo?*
Liebman, Daniel. *I want to be a zookeeper*
Lyon, George Ella. *Mother to tigers*
Miller, Heather. *Zookeeper*
Rathmann, Peggy. *Good night, Gorilla*
Savage, Stephen. *Where's Walrus?*
Schomp, Virginia. *If you were a . . . zookeeper*

Carelessness *see* Behavior – carelessness

Caribou *see* Animals – reindeer

Carnivals *see* Fairs, festivals

Carousels *see* Merry-go-rounds

Cars *see* Automobiles

Castles

Ashburn, Boni. *Over at the castle*
Bernheimer, Kate. *The girl in the castle inside the museum*
Berry, Lynne. *What floats in a moat?*
Brunhoff, Laurent de. *Babar and the ghost*
Clavel, Bernard. *Castle of books*
Hawkins, Colin. *Creepy castle*
Kenney, Sean. *Cool castles*
Walton, Rick. *Pig, pigger, piggest*
Yee, Brenda Shannon. *Sand castle*

Caterpillars *see* Insects – butterflies, caterpillars

Cave drawings *see* Petroglyphs

Cave dwellers

Sauer, Tammi. *Me want pet!*
Winter, Jeanette. *Kali's song*
Wood, Audrey. *The Tickleoctopus*

Caves

Brett, Jan. *The first dog*
Galko, Francine. *Cave animals*
Galloway, Ruth. *Fidgety fish*
Harrison, David L. *Caves*
McCully, Emily Arnold. *The secret cave*
Pfister, Marcus. *Rainbow fish and the sea monsters' cave*
Rau, Dana Meachen. *Explore in a cave*
Siebert, Diane. *Cave*
Taylor, Harriet Peck. *Secrets of the stone*

Centipedes *see* Crustaceans – centipedes, millipedes

Chanukah *see* Holidays – Hanukkah

Character traits

Burdett, Lois. *Twelfth night for kids*
Javernick, Ellen. *What if everybody did that?*
Lee, Spike. *Giant steps to change the world*
Lucas, David. *The robot and the bluebird*
McPhail, David. *No!*
Mora, Pat. *Gracias / Thanks*
Morstad, Julie. *How to*
Obama, Barack. *Of thee I sing*
Parr, Todd. *The thankful book*
Rosenthal, Amy Krouse. *Christmas cookies*
Cookies
One smart cookie: bite-size lessons for the school years and beyond
Thomas, Joan G. *If Jesus came to my house*
Walker, Alice. *Finding the green stone*
Yahgulanaas, Michael Nicoll. *The little hummingbird*

Character traits – ambition

Aska, Warabe. *Tapicero tap tap*
Barton, Byron. *I want to be an astronaut*
Clanton, Ben. *Vote for me!*
Cronin, Doreen. *Duck for President*
Daly, Niki. *The herd boy*
DiPucchio, Kelly. *Grace for president*
Dungy, Tony. *You can do it!*
Evans, Richard Paul. *The spyglass*
Feiffer, Kate. *President Pennybaker*
Gramatky, Hardie. *Little Toot*

Lester, Helen. *Score one for the sloths*
Palatini, Margie. *Hogg, Hogg, and Hog*
Pavlova, Anna. *I dreamed I was a ballerina*
Primavera, Elise. *Louise the big cheese and the back-to-school smarty-pants*
Louise the big cheese and the Ooh-la-la Charm School
Rappaport, Doreen. *To dare mighty things*
Smith, Lane. *Madam President*
Spirin, Gennady. *Philipok*
Teague, Mark. *LaRue for mayor*
Tucker, Lindy. *Porkelia*
Wells, Rosemary. *Otto runs for President*
Otto se presenta para presidente / Otto runs for President
Yamaguchi, Kristi. *Dream big, little pig!*

Character traits – appearance

Allen, Jonathan. *"I'm not cute!"*
Andersen, Hans Christian. *The ugly duckling*, ill. by Adrienne Adams
The ugly duckling, ill. by Sebastien Braun
The ugly duckling, ill. by Lorinda Bryan Cauley
The ugly duckling, ill. by Charlene Delage
The ugly duckling, ill. by Robert Ingpen
The ugly duckling, ill. by Rachel Isadora
The ugly duckling, ill. by Steve Johnson
The ugly duckling, ill. by Jerry Pinkney
The ugly duckling, ill. by Meilo So
The ugly duckling, ill. by Pirkko Vainio
The ugly duckling, ill. by Bernadette Watts
The ugly duckling, ill. by Roberta Wilson
Barnett, Mac. *Mustache!*
Beaumont, Karen. *Shoe-la-la!*
Bell, Cece. *Bee-Wigged*
Billstrom, Dianne. *You can't go to school naked!*
Boelts, Maribeth. *Those shoes*
Brisson, Pat. *Melissa Parkington's beautiful, beautiful hair*
Brown, Jeff. *Flat Stanley*
Carlson, Nancy. *Think big!*
Chen, Chih-Yuan. *The featherless chicken*
Choldenko, Gennifer. *How to make friends with a giant*
Claflin, Willy. *The uglified ducky*
Crocker, Nancy. *Betty Lou Blue*
dePaola, Tomie. *Big Anthony and the magic ring*
Ditchfield, Christin. *Cowlick!*
Duke, Shirley Smith. *No bows!*
Dunbar, Polly. *Arthur's dream boat*
Pretty Pru
Fox, Mem. *The goblin and the empty chair*
Freeman, Don. *Dandelion*
Gaiman, Neil. *Crazy hair*
Glass, Eleri. *The red shoes*
Goble, Paul. *Star boy*
Greenfield, Eloise. *Grandpa's face*
Harper, Charise Mericle. *Cupcake*
Harper, Lee. *The Emperor's cool clothes*
Heos, Bridget. *Mustache baby*
Hogg, Gary. *Beautiful Buehla and the zany zoo makeover*
Hosford, Kate. *Big bouffant*
Hovland, Henrik. *John Jensen feels different*
Hume, Lachie. *Clancy the courageous cow*
Johnson, Rebecca. *The proud pelican's secret*
Kochan, Vera. *What if your best friend were blue?*
Krensky, Stephen. *Milo and the really big bunny*
Langen, Annette. *I won't comb my hair!*
LaReau, Kara. *Ugly fish*
Long, Ethan. *Chamelia*
MacDonald, Margaret Read. *The great smelly, slobbery small-toothed dog*
Mayer, Marianna. *Beauty and the beast*
Meddaugh, Susan. *Just Teenie*
Montserrat, Pep. *Ms. Rubinstein's beauty*
Munsch, Robert N. *Makeup mess*
The paper bag princess
Stephanie's ponytail
Murguia, Bethanie Deeney. *Zoe gets ready*
Napoli, Donna Jo. *Bobby the bold*
Newman, Barbara Johansen. *Glamorous glasses*
Numeroff, Laura Joffe. *Why a disguise?*
O'Connor, Jane. *Fancy Nancy and the posh puppy*
Ormondroyd, Edward. *Theodore*
Otto, Carolyn. *What color is camouflage?*
Palatini, Margie. *Piggie pie*
Pfister, Marcus. *The rainbow fish*
Rainbow fish to the rescue!
Pichon, Liz. *The very ugly bug*
Primavera, Elise. *Louise the big cheese and the la-di-da shoes*
Reidy, Jean. *Too purpley!*
Rickards, Lynne. *Pink!*
Rylant, Cynthia. *Brownie and Pearl get dolled up*
Sabuda, Robert. *Beauty and the beast: a pop-up book of the classic fairy tale*
Schwartz, Amy. *A beautiful girl*
Skeers, Linda. *Tutus aren't my style*
Small, David. *Imogene's antlers*
Stern, Ellen. *I saw a bullfrog*
Willis, Jeanne. *What did I look like when I was a baby?*
Yerkes, Jennifer. *A funny little bird*
Ziefert, Harriet. *There was a little girl who had a little curl*

Character traits – assertiveness

Bridges, Shirin Yim. *Mary Wrightly, so politely*
Button, Lana. *Willow finds a way*
Chou, Yih-Fen. *Mimi says no*
Dodd, Emma. *I don't want a posh dog*
Dunklee, Annika. *My name is Elizabeth!*
Fleming, Candace. *Imogene's last stand*
Fradin, Dennis. *The price of freedom*
Harness, Cheryl. *Mary Walker wears the pants*
Henkes, Kevin. *Lilly's big day*
Latimer, Alex. *Penguin's hidden talent*
Lindgren, Astrid. *Pippi Longstocking's after-Christmas party*
Meade, Holly. *If I never forever endeavor*
Milgrim, David. *Eddie gets ready for school*
Novesky, Amy. *Georgia in Hawaii*
Stein, David Ezra. *Ol' Mama Squirrel*
Stone, Tanya Lee. *Elizabeth leads the way*
Who says women can't be doctors?
Urdahl, Catherine. *Polka-dot fixes kindergarten*
Winthrop, Elizabeth. *I'm the Boss!*

Character traits – being different

Andersen, Hans Christian. *The ugly duckling*, ill. by Adrienne Adams
The ugly duckling, ill. by Sebastien Braun
The ugly duckling, ill. by Lorinda Bryan Cauley
The ugly duckling, ill. by Charlene Delage
The ugly duckling, ill. by Robert Ingpen

The ugly duckling, ill. by Rachel Isadora
The ugly duckling, ill. by Steve Johnson
The ugly duckling, ill. by Jerry Pinkney
The ugly duckling, ill. by Meilo So
The ugly duckling, ill. by Pirkko Vainio
The ugly duckling, ill. by Bernadette Watts
The ugly duckling, ill. by Roberta Wilson
Arnold, Tedd. *Green Wilma*
Baek, Matthew J. *Panda and polar bear*
Bansch, Helga. *Odd bird out*
Bar-el, Dan. *Not your typical dragon*
Baryshnikov, Mikhail. *Because . . .*
Bradley, Kimberly Brubaker. *Ballerino Nate*
Brown, Margaret Wise. *Robin's room*
Brown, Peter. *Chowder*
Cannon, Janell. *Stellaluna*
Stellaluna: a pop-up book and mobile
Carle, Eric. *The mixed-up chameleon*
Chen, Chih-Yuan. *The featherless chicken*
Child, Lauren. *Maude*
Claflin, Willy. *The uglified ducky*
Cohen, Miriam. *It's George!*
Corderoy, Tracey. *The little white owl*
Côté, Geneviève. *Me and you*
Dumont, Jean-François. *The chickens build a wall*
Dyer, Sarah. *Batty*
Edwards, Pamela Duncan. *The mixed-up rooster*
Empson, Jo. *Rabbityness*
Fleming, Denise. *Mama cat has three kittens*
Ford, Gilbert. *Flying lessons*
Gerstein, Mordicai. *Minifred goes to school*
Graves, Keith. *Chicken Big*
Harness, Cheryl. *Mary Walker wears the pants*
Harris, Robie H. *Who's in my family?*
Hilton, Perez. *The boy with pink hair*
Howe, James. *Otter and odder*
Johnson, D. B. *Henry climbs a mountain*
Kaczman, James. *A bird and his worm*
Keller, Holly. *Horace*
Keller, John G. *The rubber-legged ducky*
Kilodavis, Cheryl. *My princess boy*
Klise, Kate. *Stand straight, Ella Kate*
Kochan, Vera. *What if your best friend were blue?*
Le Neouanic, Lionel. *Little smudge*
Levert, Mireille. *Eddie Longpants*
Lionni, Leo. *Cornelius*
McAllister, Angela. *Yuck! That's not a monster*
McKee, David. *Elmer*
Elmer and Rose
Maclear, Kyo. *Spork*
Martins, Isabel Minhós. *My neighbor is a dog*
Milgrim, David. *Some monsters are different*
Monroe, Chris. *Cookie, the walker*
Mora, Pat. *The rainbow tulip*
Mortimer, Rachael. *Red Riding Hood and the sweet little wolf*
Myers, Christopher. *Wings*
Nanji, Shenaaz. *An alien in my house*
Napoli, Donna Jo. *Bobby the bold*
Nimmo, Jenny. *Something wonderful*
O'Connor, George. *Uncle Bigfoot*
Peet, Bill. *The spooky tail of Prewitt Peacock*
Polacco, Patricia. *I can hear the sun*
Portis, Antoinette. *A penguin story*
Pulver, Robin. *Never say boo!*
Rania, Queen, consort of Abdullah II, King of Jordan. *The sandwich swap*
Rankin, Joan. *You're somebody special, Walliwigs!*
Rawlinson, Julia. *Mule school*
Rey, Margret. *Spotty*
Reynolds, Peter H. *I'm here*
Rickards, Lynne. *Pink!*
Rohmann, Eric. *Pumpkinhead*
Rosenthal, Amy Krouse. *Exclamation mark*
Ross, Fiona. *Chilly Milly Moo*
Russo, Marisabina. *A very big bunny*
Saltzberg, Barney. *Star of the week*
Sansone, Adele. *The little green goose*
Sauer, Tammi. *Mostly monsterly*
Say, Allen. *The favorite daughter*
Schaefer, Lola M. *Frankie Stein*
Frankie Stein starts school
Schertle, Alice. *Jeremy Bean's St. Patrick's Day*
Schotter, Roni. *Captain Snap and the children of Vinegar Lane*
Sif, Birgitta. *Oliver*
Siminovich, Lorena. *Alex and Lulu*
Simon, Norma. *Why am I different?*
Smith, Cynthia Leitich. *Holler Loudly*
Spires, Ashley. *Larf*
Small Saul
Sweeney, Jacqueline. *What about Bettie?*
Thurber, James. *The great Quillow*
Timmers, Leo. *Crow*
Uegaki, Chieri. *Suki's kimono*
Underwood, Deborah. *A balloon for Isabel*
Valdivia, Paloma. *Up above and down below*
Wallace, Ivy. *Pookie*
Walsh, Ellen Stoll. *For Pete's sake*
Watt, Mélanie. *Leon the chameleon*
Wood, Audrey. *Weird parents*
Woodson, Jacqueline. *Each kindness*
Yorinks, Arthur. *The invisible man*
Young, Amy. *The mud fairy*
Young, Ed. *Hook*

Character traits – bravery

Andersen, Hans Christian. *The snow queen*, ill. by Angela Barrett
The snow queen, ill. by Sally Holmes
The snow queen, ill. by Susan Jeffers
The snow queen: a retelling of the fairy tale
Anglund, Joan Walsh. *The brave cowboy*
Arnold, Marsha Diane. *The bravest of us all*
Asare, Meshack. *Sosu's call*
Bailey, Linda. *The farm team*
Barbero, Maria. *The bravest mouse*
Battersby, Katherine. *Brave Squish Rabbit*
Beck, Scott. *Pepito the brave*
Biden, Jill. *Don't forget, God bless our troops*
Birdseye, Tom. *Oh yeah!*
Buckley, Michael. *Kel Gilligan's daredevil stunt show*
Bynum, Janie. *Kiki's blankie*
Carlson, Nancy. *Arnie and the skateboard gang*
Harriet and the roller coaster
Coles, Robert. *The story of Ruby Bridges*
Cowell, Cressida. *Hiccup the seasick Viking*
Crum, Shutta. *The bravest of the brave*
Curtis, Jamie Lee. *My brave year of firsts*
Danticat, Edwidge. *Eight days*
Deedy, Carmen Agra. *The yellow star*
Demi. *The boy who painted dragons*
Dierssen, Andreas. *Timid Timmy*
Doyen, Denise. *Once upon a twice*
Duncan, Lois. *Song of the circus*
Ehlert, Lois. *Cuckoo, a Mexican folktale / Cucú: un cuento folklórico mexicano*

Foreman, Michael. *The littlest dinosaur*
Fradin, Dennis. *The price of freedom*
Frasier, Debra. *Spike*
Genechten, Guido van. *Ricky is brave*
Giovanni, Nikki. *Rosa*
Gliori, Debi. *The scariest thing of all*
Golenbock, Peter. *Hank Aaron*
Griffin, Kitty. *The ride*
Grimm, Jacob and Wilhelm. *The brave little tailor,* ill. by Olga Dugina
The brave little tailor, ill. by David Shaw
Seven at one blow
Harrison, Troon. *Courage to fly*
Hearne, Betsy Gould. *Seven brave women*
Henkes, Kevin. *Sheila Rae, the brave*
Hood, Susan. *The Tooth Mouse*
Hopkinson, Deborah. *Abe Lincoln crosses a creek*
Hoppe, Paul. *The woods*
Horowitz, Dave. *Chico the brave*
Humpty Dumpty climbs again
Jakes, John. *Susanna of the Alamo*
Jennewein, Lenore. *Chick-o-Saurus Rex*
Jordan, Sandra. *Mr. and Mrs. Portly and their little dog Snack*
Julian, Alison. *Brave as a bunny can be*
Keller, Holly. *Brave Horace*
Kelly, Mark. *Mousetronaut*
Kipling, Rudyard. *Rikki-tikki-tavi,* ill. by Lambert Davis
Rikki-tikki-tavi, ill. by Jerry Pinkney
Kirk, Daniel. *Library mouse: a world to explore*
Krensky, Stephen. *Sisters of Scituate Light*
Lears, Laurie. *Becky the brave*
Lee, Jeanne M. *The song of Mu Lan*
Lester, Alison. *Running with the horses*
Lloyd, Sam. *Chief Rhino to the rescue!*
Long, Loren. *An Otis Christmas*
McDonald, Megan. *Beetle McGrady eats bugs!*
McGhee, Alison. *A very brave witch*
McKissack, Patricia C. *Precious and the Boo Hag*
Markel, Michelle. *Brave girl*
Martin, Bill, Jr. *Knots on a counting rope*
Masini, Beatrice. *A brave little princess*
Mayer, Marianna. *The unicorn and the lake*
Mayer, Mercer. *Liza Lou and the Yeller Belly Swamp*
Meade, Holly. *If I never forever endeavor*
Mitchell, Margaree King. *Granddaddy's gift*
Morgan, Michaela. *Brave, brave mouse*
Nash, Ogden. *The adventures of Isabel,* ill. by James Marshall
The adventures of Isabel, ill. by Bridget Starr Taylor
Custard the dragon and the wicked knight
Nobisso, Josephine. *John Blair and the great Hinckley fire*
Osborne, Mary Pope. *The brave little seamstress*
New York's bravest
Otoshi, Kathryn. *One*
Peet, Bill. *Cowardly Clyde*
Pienkowski, Jan. *Bel and Bub and the black hole*
Pryor, Bonnie. *The porcupine mouse*
Rappaport, Doreen. *Freedom river*
Jack's path of courage
The long-haired girl
The secret seder
Raschka, Chris. *Waffle*
Ray, Mary Lyn. *Boom!*
Reynolds, Aaron. *Back of the bus*
Reynolds, Marilynn. *The name of the child*
Robinson, Sharon. *Testing the ice*
Rockwell, Anne. *Big George*
San Souci, Robert D. *The enchanted tapestry*
The samurai's daughter
Sazaklis, John. *Fowl play*
Schmid, Eleonore. *Hare's Christmas gift*
Schwarz, Viviane. *Timothy and the strong pajamas*
Scieszka, Jon. *Melvin might?*
Shannon, George. *Tippy-toe chick, go*
Simon, Charnan. *Big bad Buzz*
Spinelli, Eileen. *Hero cat*
Steig, William. *Brave Irene*
Stein, Mathilde. *Brave Ben*
Stoeke, Janet Morgan. *Pip's trip*
Stohner, Anu. *Brave Charlotte*
Brave Charlotte and the wolves
Stone, Tanya Lee. *Elizabeth leads the way*
Stryer, Andrea Stenn. *Kami and the yaks*
Sweet, Melissa. *Tupelo rides the rails*
Tessler, Manya. *Yuki's ride home*
Thompson, Lauren. *Little Quack*
Little Quack [board book]
Titus, Eve. *Anatole and the cat*
Uchida, Yoshiko. *The magic purse*
Van Allsburg, Chris. *Queen of the falls*
Van Woerkom, Dorothy. *Becky and the bear*
Waber, Bernard. *Courage*
Watt, Mélanie. *Scaredy Squirrel*
Weitzman, Jacqueline Preiss. *Superhero Joe*
Willems, Mo. *Knuffle Bunny free*
Wolkstein, Diane. *The banza*
Yolen, Jane. *Beneath the ghost moon*

Character traits – cleanliness

Allen, Jonathan. *Mucky moose*
Bell, Cece. *Sock Monkey goes to Hollywood*
Bernheimer, Kate. *The girl who wouldn't brush her hair*
Bradford, Wade. *Why do I have to make my bed?*
Braeuner, Shellie. *The great dog wash*
Brennan, Eileen. *Dirtball Pete*
Brown, Margaret Wise. *The dirty little boy*
Bynum, Janie. *Otis*
Child, Lauren. *Say cheese!*
Church, Caroline Jayne. *One smart goose*
Cohen, Caron Lee. *Broom, zoom!*
Cummings, Pat. *Clean your room, Harvey Moon!*
Cuyler, Margery. *Monster mess!*
Dunrea, Olivier. *Jasper & Joop*
Ehrlich, Fred. *Does an elephant take a bath?*
Elschner, Geraldine. *Mark's messy room*
Ernst, Lisa Campbell. *This is the van that Dad cleaned*
Funke, Cornelia. *Princess Pigsty*
Garelli, Cristina. *Farm friends clean up*
Geisert, Arthur. *Hogwash*
Grindley, Sally. *Mucky Duck*
Hanson, Warren. *It's Monday, Mrs. Jolly Bones!*
Harris, Robie H. *I love messes!*
Howie, Betsy. *The Block Mess Monster*
Huget, Jennifer LaRue. *How to clean your room in 10 easy steps*
Hutchins, Pat. *Where's the baby?*
Kamish, Daniel. *Diggy Dan*
Keane, Dave. *Sloppy Joe*
Kempter, Christa. *Wally and Mae*
Kirk, David. *Little pig, Biddle pig*
Krensky, Stephen. *What a mess!*

Kroll, Virginia L. *Really rabbits*
Lattimore, Deborah Nourse. *Cinderhazel*
Lauber, Patricia. *What you never knew about tubs, toilets and showers*
Lichtenheld, Tom. *What's with this room?*
Lobb, Janice. *Splish! Splosh! Why do we wash?*
Luciani, Brigitte. *Those messy Hempels*
McElligott, Matthew. *Backbeard and the birthday suit*
McElmurry, Jill. *Mess pets*
McHenry, E. B. *Poodlena*
McKissack, Patricia C. *Messy Bessey*
Messy Bessey / Ada, la desordenada
Messy Bessey and the birthday overnight
Messy Bessey's family reunion
Messy Bessey's holidays
Maloney, Peter. *Belly button boy*
Milway, Katie Smith. *Mimi's village and how basic health care transformed it*
Moss, Miriam. *Matty in a mess!*
Munsch, Robert N. *Mud puddle*
Myers, Tim. *Down at the Dino Wash Deluxe*
Nelson, Robin. *Staying clean*
Noonan, Julia. *Hare and Rabbit, friends forever*
Novak, Matt. *The everything machine*
Papineau, Lucie. *Lulu's pajamas*
Potter, Beatrix. *The tale of Mrs. Tittlemouse*
Primavera, Elise. *The house at the end of Ladybug Lane*
Provencher, Rose-Marie. *Mouse cleaning*
Puttock, Simon. *Yours truly, Louisa*
Riddell, Chris. *Wendel's workshop*
Roberts, David. *Dirty Bertie*
Root, Phyllis. *Mrs. Potter's pig*
Rosenthal, Amy Krouse. *Little Oink*
Sayre, April Pulley. *Stars beneath your bed*
Schertle, Alice. *The adventures of old Bo Bear*
Sloat, Teri. *This is the house that was tidy and neat*
Smith, Janice Lee. *Jess and the stinky cowboys*
Stephens, Helen. *Ruby and the muddy dog*
Stewart, Amber. *Rabbit ears*
Taylor, Sean. *Robomop*
Teague, Mark. *Pigsty*
Teckentrup, Britta. *Big smelly bear*
Varon, Sara. *Chicken and Cat clean up*
Viorst, Judith. *Super-completely and totally the messiest*
Wallace, Nancy Elizabeth. *Count down to clean up*
Weinert, Matthias. *No bath, no cake!*
Wells, Rosemary. *Clean-up time*
Fritz and the mess fairy
Max cleans up
Wilson, Karma. *Hogwash!*

Character traits – cleverness

Aesop. *The crow and the pitcher*
Ahlberg, Janet. *It was a dark and stormy night*
Andersen, Hans Christian. *The swineherd*
Asbjørnsen, P. C. *The three billy goats Gruff*, ill. by Stephen Carpenter
The three billy goats Gruff, ill. by Paul Galdone
The three billy goats Gruff, ill. by Glen Rounds
The three billy goats Gruff, ill. by Janet Stevens
Asch, Frank. *Ziggy Piggy and the three little pigs*
Bang, Molly. *Wiley and the hairy man*
Bannerman, Helen. *The story of Little Babaji*
The story of Little Black Sambo, ill. by Helen Bannerman
The story of Little Black Sambo, ill. by Helen Bannerman
The story of Little Black Sambo, ill. by Christopher Bing
Birdsall, Jeanne. *Lucky and Squash*
Birtha, Becky. *Lucky beans*
Bishop, Claire Huchet. *The five Chinese brothers*
Bonning, Tony. *Fox tale soup*
Brett, Jan. *Fritz and the beautiful horses*
Hedgie's surprise
The trouble with trolls
Brown, Marcia. *Stone soup*
Buchanan, Sue. *Mud Pie Annie*
Burningham, John. *The shopping basket*
Calhoun, Mary. *Cross-country cat*
Cole, Brock. *Good enough to eat*
Collington, Peter. *Clever cat*
Compestine, Ying Chang. *The real story of stone soup*
Czernecki, Stefan. *Huevos rancheros*
Davis, David. *Fandango stew*
Dee, Ruby. *Two ways to count to ten*
Demi. *One grain of rice*
Desrosiers, Sylvie. *Hocus Pocus*
Forest, Heather. *Stone soup*
Galdone, Paul. *What's in fox's sack?*
Geisert, Arthur. *Ice*
Lights out
Gorbachev, Valeri. *The fool of the world and the flying ship: a Ukrainian folk tale*
Grimm, Jacob and Wilhelm. *The rabbit's bride*
Guarnaccia, Steven. *The three little pigs: an architectural tale*
Hood, Susan. *The Tooth Mouse*
Huck, Charlotte S. *Princess Furball*
Huling, Jan. *Puss in cowboy boots*
Isaacs, Anne. *Pancakes for supper!*
Johnson, Rebecca. *Sea turtle's clever plan*
Johnson-Davies, Denys. *Goha, the wise fool*
Kimmel, Eric A. *The three cabritos*
Kipling, Rudyard. *Rikki-tikki-tavi*, ill. by Lambert Davis
Rikki-tikki-tavi, ill. by Jerry Pinkney
Krause, Ute. *Oscar and the very hungry dragon*
Lester, Julius. *Sam and the tigers*
Lowell, Susan. *The three little javelinas*
McDermott, Gerald. *Monkey*
McMillan, Bruce. *The problem with chickens*
McNaughton, Colin. *Oops!*
Maddern, Eric. *Nail soup*
Mahy, Margaret. *The seven Chinese brothers*
Mandell, Muriel. *A donkey reads*
Mathers, Petra. *Lottie's new beach towel*
Muth, Jon J. *Stone soup*
Olaleye, Isaac. *Bitter bananas*
Perrault, Charles. *Puss in boots*, ill. by Marcia Brown
Puss in boots, ill. by Lorinda Bryan Cauley
Puss in boots, ill. by Paul Galdone
Puss in boots, ill. by Steve Light
Puss in boots, ill. by Giuliano Lunelli
Puss in boots, ill. by Fred Marcellino
Puss in boots, ill. by Fred Marcellino
Puss in boots, ill. by Bernhard Oberdieck
Puss in boots, ill. by Jerry Pinkney
Puss in boots, ill. by Alain Vaës
Potter, Beatrix. *The sly old cat*
The tale of the Flopsy Bunnies, ill. by Beatrix Potter
The tale of the Flopsy Bunnies, ill. by Wendy Rasmussen

Prokofiev, Sergei Sergeievitch. *Peter and the wolf*, ill. by Charles Mikolaycak
Peter and the wolf, ill. by Josef Palecek
Peter and the wolf, ill. by Chris Raschka
Peter and the wolf, ill. by Vladimir Vagin
Pullman, Philip. *Puss in boots: the adventures of that most enterprising feline*
Ransome, Arthur. *The fool of the world and the flying ship*
Rozen, Anna. *The merchant of noises*
Rueda, Claudia. *Huff and puff*
Salley, Coleen. *Who's that tripping over my bridge?*
San Souci, Robert D. *Callie Ann and Mistah Bear*
Little Pierre
Seeger, Pete. *Some friends to feed*
Shannon, George. *Lizard's home*
Shea, Bob. *Cheetah can't lose*
Sierra, Judy. *Wiley and the Hairy Man*
Singleton, Debbie. *The king who wouldn't sleep*
Souhami, Jessica. *Mrs. McCool and the giant Cuhullin*
Steig, William. *Doctor De Soto*
Stevens, Janet. *Tops and bottoms*
Stewart, Joel. *Dexter Bexley and the big blue beastie*
Stewig, John Warren. *Clever Gretchen*
Stone soup
Taylor, Sean. *The grizzly bear with the frizzly hair*
Tchana, Katrin. *Sense Pass King*
The three little pigs. *The three little pigs*, ill. by Gavin Bishop
The three little pigs, ill. by Paul Galdone
The three little pigs, ill. by Rob Hefferan
The three little pigs, ill. by Steven Kellogg
The three little pigs, ill. by David McPhail
The three little pigs, ill. by James Marshall
The three little pigs, ill. by Bernadette Watts
The three little pigs, ill. by Margot Zemach
The three little pigs [board book]
The three little pigs / Los tres cerditos
The three little pigs and the big bad wolf
The three little pigs and the fox
Thurber, James. *The great Quillow*
Twohy, Mike. *Outfoxed*
Van Dusen, Chris. *Randy Riley's really big hit*
Van Woerkom, Dorothy. *The rat, the ox and the zodiac*
Wahl, Jan. *Little Johnny Buttermilk*
Ward, Helen. *The king of the birds*
The rooster and the fox
Wheeler, Lisa. *Turk and Runt*
Wiesner, David. *The three pigs*
Willey, Margaret. *Clever Beatrice, an Upper Peninsula conte*
Clever Beatrice and the best little pony
Clever Beatrice Christmas
Wood, Audrey. *Heckedy Peg*
Yamashita, Haruo. *Seven little mice go to school*
Yolen, Jane. *The flying witch*
Young, Ed. *Little Plum*
Youngquist, Cathrene Valente. *The three Billygoats Gruff and Mean Calypso Joe*

Character traits – clumsiness

Aruego, José. *Splash!*
Edwards, Pamela Duncan. *Slop goes the soup*
Fox, Mem. *Harriet, you'll drive me wild*
Kleven, Elisa. *Welcome home, Mouse*
Kroll, Steven. *Oh, Tucker!*
McNaughton, Colin. *Preston's goal!*
Rodriguez, Edel. *Sergio saves the game!*
Simon, Charnan. *Jeremy Jones, clumsy guy*
Stower, Adam. *Two left feet*
Wardlaw, Lee. *The chair where bear sits*

Character traits – completing things

Alda, Arlene. *Lulu's piano lesson*
Mortenson, Greg. *Listen to the wind*

Character traits – compromising

Covell, David. *Rat and Roach rock on!*
Eure, Wesley. *A fish out of water*
Janni, Rebecca. *Every cowgirl needs dancing boots*
Sauer, Tammi. *Mr. Duck means business*
Weeks, Sarah. *Catfish Kate and the sweet swamp band*

Character traits – conceit

Goble, Paul. *Iktomi and the boulder*
Iktomi and the buffalo skull
Martin, Ann M. *Rachel Parker, kindergarten show-off*
Peet, Bill. *Ella*
Sauer, Tammi. *Oh, nuts!*
Sharmat, Marjorie Weinman. *I'm terrific*

Character traits – confidence

Alexander, Claire. *Small Florence*
Aliki. *All by myself!*
Asch, Frank. *Baby Duck's new friend*
Boyce, Katie. *Hector the hermit crab*
Corey, Shana. *Ballerina bear*
Cumming, Hannah. *The red boat*
Curtis, Jamie Lee. *My brave year of firsts*
Dempsey, Kristy. *Surfer chick*
Esham, Barbara. *Last to finish*
Gorbachev, Valeri. *Chicken chickens*
Grant, Rose Marie. *Andiamo, Weasel*
Hest, Amy. *Make the team, Baby Duck*
You can do it, Sam
Hillenbrand, Jane. *What a treasure!*
Kerley, Barbara. *What to do about Alice?*
Krensky, Stephen. *I know a lot!*
Latifah, Queen. *Queen of the scene*
Lewis, Wendy A. *In Abby's hands*
Mack, Jeff. *The things I can do*
Milgrim, David. *Eddie gets ready for school*
Pérez, L. King. *First day in grapes*
Reynolds, Peter H. *The dot*
Robinson, Fiona. *Whale shines*
Schotter, Roni. *Doo-Wop Pop*
Shea, Bob. *New socks*
Thompson, Lauren. *Wee little chick*
Waddell, Martin. *Good job, Little Bear!*
Wagner, Karen. *Bravo, Mildred and Ed!*
Wormell, Christopher. *Henry and the fox*
Wright, Joanna. *Bunnies on ice*

Character traits – cooperation

Aliki. *A play's the thing*
Barasch, Lynne. *First come the zebra*
Belloni, Giulia. *Anything is possible*
Braun, Sebastien. *Digger and Tom!*
Brimner, Larry Dane. *The big, beautiful, brown box*
Brooks, Jeremy. *Let there be peace*
Bunting, Eve. *Our library*

Cecil, Randy. *Horsefly and Honeybee*
Cohen, Caron Lee. *Broom, zoom!*
Conahan, Carolyn. *The big wish*
Cowcher, Helen. *Desert elephants*
Dorros, Alex. *Número uno*
Fraser, Mary Ann. *Pet shop follies*
Gainer, Cindy. *I'm like you, you're like me*
Geisert, Arthur. *The giant ball of string*
Ice
Goodall, Jane. *The eagle and the wren*
Graham, Bob. *A bus called Heaven*
Grey, Mini. *Three by the sea*
Heide, Florence Parry. *Always listen to your mother*
Hester, Denia Lewis. *Grandma Lena's big ol' turnip*
Hiscock, Bruce. *Coyote and badger*
Hopkins, Lee Bennett. *Full moon and star*
Hudelhoff, Allen H. *Cats and kids*
Hutchins, Hazel. *Mattland*
Jackson, Jill. *Let there be peace on earth*
Jennings, Sharon. *Priscilla's paw de deux*
Kako, Satoshi. *Little Daruma and little Daikoku*
Klausmeier, Jesse. *Open this little book*
Kuiper, Nannie. *Bravo, brave beavers*
McKee, David. *Elmer and the big bird*
Elmer and the hippos
Mahoney, Daniel J. *The perfect clubhouse*
Marino, Gianna. *Too tall houses*
Martín Larrañaga, Ana. *Pepo and Lolo and the red apple*
Martins, Isabel Minhós. *Little lamb, have you any wool?*
Numeroff, Laura Joffe. *The Jellybeans and the big art adventure*
The Jellybeans and the big camp kickoff
The Jellybeans and the big dance
Otoshi, Kathryn. *Zero*
Parkinson, Kathy. *The enormous turnip*
Paye, Won-Ldy. *Head, body, legs*
Peck, Jan. *Giant peach yodel!*
Reid, Barbara. *Perfect snow*
Roberts, Bethany. *Double trouble Groundhog Day*
Rouss, Sylvia A. *The littlest pair*
Ruddell, Deborah. *Who said coo?*
Scheffler, Axel. *The snowy day*
Singer, Marilyn. *Let's build a clubhouse*
Soman, David. *Ladybug Girl and the Bug Squad*
Stevens, Janet. *The little red pen*
Stihler, Chérie B. *The giant cabbage turnip*
Swann, Rick. *Our school garden!*
Tolstoy, Aleksey Nikolayevich. *The enormous turnip*
The gigantic turnip
Vail, Rachel. *Righty and Lefty*
Wallace, Nancy Elizabeth. *Ready, set, 100th day!*

Character traits – courage *see* Character traits – bravery

Character traits – cruelty to animals *see* Character traits – kindness to animals

Character traits – curiosity

Adler, David A. *Things that float and things that don't*
Arnosky, Jim. *Raccoon on his own*
Bang, Molly. *Dawn*
Bonnett-Rampersaud, Louise. *Polly Hopper's pouch*
Bryan, Ashley. *Can't scare me!*
Bunting, Eve. *Tweak tweak*
Catalanotto, Peter. *Question Boy meets Little Miss Know-It-All*
Cecka, Melanie. *Violet goes to the country*
Chou, Yih-Fen. *Mimi loves to mimic*
Curious George and the dump truck
Curious George and the pizza
Curious George at the fire station
Curious George goes hiking
Curious George goes sledding
Curious George goes to the aquarium
Curious George goes to the circus
Curious George in the big city
Curious George takes a train
Curious George visits a toy store
Curious George visits the zoo
Curtis, Jamie Lee. *Is there really a human race?*
De Beer, Hans. *Oh no, Ono!*
Gorbachev, Valeri. *Red red red*
Gravdahl, John. *Curious catwalk*
Hapka, Cathy. *Margret and H. A. Rey's Merry Christmas, Curious George*
Henkes, Kevin. *Little white rabbit*
Hopgood, Tim. *Wow! said the owl*
Kipling, Rudyard. *The elephant's child*
How the elephant got his trunk
Lamb, Rosy. *Paul meets Bernadette*
Lewis, Kevin. *Not inside this house!*
Loupy, Christophe. *Wiggles*
McBratney, Sam. *The dark at the top of the stairs*
Mitton, Tony. *A very curious bear*
Morgan-Vanroyen, Mary. *Curious Rosie*
Murphy, Mary. *Koala and the flower*
Rey, H. A. *Curious George*
Curious George gets a medal
Curious George learns the alphabet
Curious George rides a bike
Curious George takes a job
The original Curious George
Rey, Margret. *Curious George flies a kite*
Curious George goes to the hospital
Rylant, Cynthia. *Miss Maggie*
Schoenherr, John. *Rebel*
Torrey, Richard. *Why?*
Waber, Bernard. *Lorenzo*

Character traits – flattery

Aesop. *Three Aesop fox fables*
Chaucer, Geoffrey. *Chanticleer and the fox*

Character traits – foolishness

Aardema, Verna. *Sebgugugu the glutton*
Alexander, Lloyd. *The house Gobbaleen*
Carlson, Nancy. *Arnie and the skateboard gang*
Davis, Aubrey. *Kishka for Koppel*
Hurston, Zora Neale. *The six fools*
Jacobs, Joseph. *The three sillies*
Johnson-Davies, Denys. *Goha, the wise fool*
Pilkey, Dav. *The Dumb Bunnies*
The Dumb Bunnies' Easter
The Dumb Bunnies go to the zoo
Make way for Dumb Bunnies
San Souci, Robert D. *Six foolish fishermen*
Souhami, Jessica. *Sausages*
Spinelli, Eileen. *Silly Tilly*
Uhlberg, Myron. *Lemuel, the fool*

Van Nutt, Julia. *Pignapped!*
Zemach, Margot. *The three wishes*

Character traits – fortune *see* Character traits – luck

Character traits – freedom

Aesop. *The dog and the wolf*
Amnesty International. *We are all born free*
Andersen, Hans Christian. *The nightingale*, ill. by Nancy Ekholm Burkert
The nightingale, ill. by Pirkko Vainio
The nightingale, ill. by Lisbeth Zwerger
Baylor, Byrd. *Hawk, I'm your brother*
Bryant, Jen. *Abe's fish*
Bunting, Eve. *How many days to America?*
Drummond, Allan. *Liberty*
Evans, Shane W. *Underground: finding the light to freedom*
Grady, Cynthia. *I lay my stitches down*
Grifalconi, Ann. *Ain't nobody a stranger to me*
Levine, Ellen. *Henry's freedom box*
Lyons, Kelly Starling. *Hope's gift*
Meade, Holly. *John Willy and Freddy McGee*
John Willy and Freddy McGee [board book]
Murphy, Mary. *The Alphabet Keeper*
Nadimi, Suzan. *The rich man and the parrot*
Nelson, Vaunda Micheaux. *Almost to freedom*
Park, Frances. *My freedom trip*
Pinkney, Andrea Davis. *Sojourner Truth's step-stomp stride*
Polacco, Patricia. *The butterfly*
Rappaport, Doreen. *Freedom river*
Freedom ship
Roth, Susan L. *Happy birthday Mr. Kang*
Sanders, Scott R. *A place called Freedom*
Shange, Ntozake. *Freedom's a-callin me*
Shulevitz, Uri. *What is a wise bird like you doing in a silly tale like this?*
Siegelson, Kim L. *In the time of the drums*
Stroud, Bettye. *The patchwork path*
Sundgaard, Arnold. *The lamb and the butterfly*
Walker, Sally M. *Freedom song*
Wright, Courtni Crump. *Journey to freedom*

Character traits – generosity

Aliki. *The story of Johnny Appleseed*
Anglund, Joan Walsh. *Christmas is a time of giving*
Barrett, Mary Brigid. *Shoebox Sam*
Battle-Lavert, Gwendolyn. *The shaking bag*
Beck, Scott. *A mud pie for mother*
Blackwood, Freya. *Ivy loves to give*
Bouler, Olivia. *Olivia's birds*
Brisson, Pat. *Melissa Parkington's beautiful, beautiful hair*
Butler, M. Christina. *One snowy night*
Chamberlin, Mary. *Mama Panya's pancakes*
Child, Lauren. *But I've used all my pocket change*
Chinn, Karen. *Sam and the lucky money*
Compestine, Ying Chang. *The runaway rice cake*
Demas, Corinne. *The magic apple*
DiSalvo, DyAnne. *A castle on Viola Street*
Fleming, Candace. *Boxes for Katje*
Frazee, Marla. *Hush, little baby: a folk song with pictures*
Gibfried, Diane. *Brother Juniper*
Grimm, Jacob and Wilhelm. *The star child*
Hamilton, Martha. *The ghost catcher*
Hayes, Joe. *Don't say a word, Mamá/No digas nada, Mamá*
Heller, Linda. *How Dalia put a big yellow comforter inside a tiny blue box*
Hughes, Shirley. *Giving*
Hush, little baby
Janice. *Little Bear's Christmas*
Kasza, Keiko. *The wolf's chicken stew*
Kromhout, Rindert. *Little Donkey and the birthday present*
Lionni, Leo. *Tico and the golden wings*
Lucado, Max. *All you ever need*
McCourt, Lisa. *Chicken soup for little souls: The best night out with Dad*
McGinley, Phyllis. *The year without a Santa Claus*
Marshall, Linda Elovitz. *Grandma Rose's magic*
Mitchell, Marianne. *Gullywasher gulch*
Munsch, Robert N. *Ribbon rescue*
O'Connor, Jane. *Fancy Nancy and the fabulous fashion boutique*
Patten, Brian. *The big snuggle-up*
Pilkey, Dav. *Dragon's merry Christmas*
Pinkney, Brian. *Hush, little baby*
Pomerantz, Charlotte. *The mousery*
Priest, Robert H. *The pirate's eye*
Quattlebaum, Mary. *The shine man*
Rockliff, Mara. *My heart will not sit down*
Rylant, Cynthia. *Silver packages*
Sacre, Antonio. *A mango in the hand*
Sandman, Rochel. *Perfect porridge*
Schotter, Roni. *Captain Snap and the children of Vinegar Lane*
Schrock, Jan West. *Give a goat*
Shepard, Aaron. *The baker's dozen*
Shollar, Leah. *A thread of kindness*
Silverstein, Shel. *The giving tree*
Tada, Joni Eareckson. *The incredible discovery of Lindsey Renee*
Toscano, Charles. *Papa's pastries*
Tutu, Archbishop Desmond. *God's dream*
Villnave, Erica Pelton. *Sophie's lovely locks*
Williams, Laura E. *The can man*
Winget, Susan. *Sam the Snowman*
Young, Ned. *Zoomer's out-of-this-world Christmas*
Ziefert, Harriet. *Surprise!*

Character traits – helpfulness

Adams, Diane. *I want to help!*
Aesop. *Androcles and the lion*, ill. by Dennis Nolan
Androcles and the lion, ill. by Janet Stevens
Androcles and the lion: and other Aesop fables
The lion and the mouse, ill. by Lisa McCue
The lion and the mouse, ill. by Sara Rojo
The lion and the mouse, ill. by Bernadette Watts
Mouse and lion
Aliki. *The two of them*
Ancona, George. *Mis quehaceres / My chores*
Anderson, Derek. *How the Easter Bunny saved Christmas*
Asch, Frank. *Baby Bird's first nest*
Monsieur Saguette and his baguette
Barnes, Laura T. *Ernest's special Christmas*
Bogacki, Tomasz. *Circus girl*
Bouler, Olivia. *Olivia's birds*
Bourgeois, Paulette. *Franklin and Harriet*
Brett, Jan. *Home for Christmas*

Bridwell, Norman. *Clifford's good deeds*
Bunting, Eve. *December*
Burningham, John. *Harvey Slumfenburger's Christmas present*
Bushey, Jeanne. *The polar bear's gift*
Calhoun, Mary. *Blue-ribbon Henry*
Cannon, Janell. *Crickwing*
Clarke, Jane. *Stuck in the mud*
Coffelt, Nancy. *Aunt Ant leaves through the leaves*
Costello, David Hyde. *I can help*
Cousins, Lucy. *Maisy makes lemonade*
Cunnane, Kelly. *Chirchir is singing*
D'Amico, Carmela. *Ella takes the cake*
Day, Alexandra. *Frank and Ernest*
deGroat, Diane. *Lola the elf*
Mother, you're the best! (but Sister, you're a pest!)
Devlin, Wende. *Cranberry autumn*
Cranberry Christmas
DiCamillo, Kate. *Great joy*
Emberley, Ed. *The red hen*
Ernst, Lisa Campbell. *Sylvia Jean, scout supreme*
Esbaum, Jill. *To the big top*
Ethan, Eric. *Helicopters*
Fackelmayer, Regina. *The gifts*
Freedman, Deborah. *Blue chicken*
Garland, Sarah. *Eddie's toolbox and how to make and mend things*
Gibbons, Gail. *Emergency!*
Graham, Tom. *Five little firefighters*
Grambling, Lois G. *Here comes T. Rex Cottontail*
Granowsky, Alvin. *Can I help?*
Grimm, Jacob and Wilhelm. *The elves and the shoemaker*, ill. by Kirill Chelushkin
The elves and the shoemaker, ill. by Paul Galdone
The elves and the shoemaker, ill. by Margaret Walty
The shoemaker and his elves
The shoemaker and the elves, ill. by Adrienne Adams
The shoemaker and the elves, ill. by Ilse Plume
Hamilton, Kersten. *Red truck*
Heide, Iris van der. *A strange day*
Hill, Elizabeth Starr. *Evan's corner*
Himmelman, John. *Chickens to the rescue*
Pigs to the rescue
Jackson, Ellen. *Sometimes bad things happen*
Jackson, Kathryn. *Pantaloon*
Jeffers, Oliver. *The way back home*
Jenkins, Emily. *Up, up, up!*
Joyce, William. *Bently and egg*
The Leaf Men and the brave good bugs
Keller, Holly. *Nosy Rosie*
Kinch, Devon. *Pretty Penny makes ends meet*
Kinerk, Robert. *Clorinda plays baseball!*
Kirsch, Vincent X. *Forsythia and me*
Natalie and Naughtily
Klise, Kate. *Grammy Lamby and the secret handshake*
Knudsen, Michelle. *Library lion*
Kroll, Virginia L. *Good citizen Sarah*
Makayla cares about others
Krosoczka, Jarrett J. *Giddy up, Cowgirl*
Laminack, Lester L. *Saturdays and teacakes*
Lehman, Barbara. *Trainstop*
Loki. *Jake Greenthumb*
Lord, Janet. *Albert the fix-it man*
Lowell, Susan. *The bootmaker and the elves*
McKissack, Patricia C. *Messy Bessey and the birthday overnight*
McPhail, David. *Santa's book of names*
Mahoney, Daniel J. *A really good snowman*
Manning, Mick. *Cock-a-doodle hooooooo!*
Manzano, Sonia. *A box full of kittens*
Mayer, Mercer. *Just for you*
Melling, David. *Don't worry, Douglas!*
Miller, Pat. *Squirrel's New Year's resolution*
Muth, Jon J. *Zen ties*
Nolen, Jerdine. *Pitching in for Eubie*
Numeroff, Laura Joffe. *What brothers do best; What sisters do best*
Oyibo, Papa. *Big brother, little sister*
Panzieri, Lucia. *The kindhearted crocodile*
Paraskevas, Betty. *Maggie and the Ferocious Beast, the big carrot*
Peet, Bill. *The ant and the elephant*
Cyrus the unsinkable sea serpent
Petrillo, Genevieve. *Keep your ear on the ball*
Pinkney, Jerry. *The lion and the mouse*
Potter, Beatrix. *The tailor of Gloucester*
Randall, Angel. *Snow angels*
Rau, Dana Meachen. *In the yard*
Reider, Katja. *The big little sneeze*
Ries, Lori. *Fix it, Sam*
Sauer, Tammi. *Nugget and Fang*
Savage, Stephen. *Little Tug*
Schubert, Leda. *Here comes Darrell*
Schuch, Steve. *A symphony of whales*
Schwartz, Roslyn. *The mole sisters and the piece of moss*
Scieszka, Jon. *Melvin might?*
Scotton, Rob. *Russell's Christmas magic*
Seuss, Dr. *Horton hatches the egg*
Shah, Idries. *The clever boy and the terrible, dangerous animal*
Shaw, Hannah. *School for bandits*
Sierra, Judy. *Preschool to the rescue*
Slack, Michael. *Monkey truck*
Soto, Gary. *The old man and his door*
Stead, Philip C. *Bear has a story to tell*
Steffensmeier, Alexander. *Millie in the snow*
Stevenson, James. *Will you please feed our cat?*
Stoop, Naoko. *Red Knit Cap Girl to the rescue*
Strauss, Anna. *Hush, Mama loves you*
Thomas, Shelley Moore. *Somewhere today*
Take care, Good Knight
Thorpe, Kiki. *A comfy, cozy Thanksgiving*
Toten, Teresa. *Bright red kisses*
Tutu, Archbishop Desmond. *God's dream*
Verdick, Elizabeth. *On-the-go time*
Waber, Bernard. *Lyle, Lyle Crocodile*
Waddell, Martin. *Farmer Duck*
Good job, Little Bear!
Watson, Wendy. *Holly's Christmas eve*
Weninger, Brigitte. *Davy in the middle*
Wheeler, Lisa. *Old Cricket*
White, Ellen Emerson. *Santa paws*
Ziefert, Harriet. *Ode to Humpty Dumpty*

Character traits – honesty

Aardema, Verna. *Pedro and the padre*
Abercrombie, Barbara. *The show-and-tell lion*
Breathed, Berkeley. *Edwurd Fudwupper fibbed big*
Bunting, Eve. *A day's work*
Cocca-Leffler, Maryann. *Princess K.I.M. and the lie that grew*
Princess Kim and too much truth
Cuyler, Margery. *I repeat, don't cheat!*
deGroat, Diane. *Liar, liar, pants on fire*
Demi. *The empty pot*

Dierssen, Andreas. *Timid Timmy*
Donovan, Gail. *A fishy story*
Earnhardt, Donna W. *Being Frank*
Finlay, Lizzie. *Little Croc's purse*
Geser, Gretchen. *One bright ring*
Grambling, Lois G. *The witch who wanted to be a princess*
Gutman, Anne. *Lisa in the jungle*
Havill, Juanita. *Jamaica's find*
Hesse, Karen. *Spuds*
Hobbie, Holly. *Fanny and Annabelle*
Hood, Susan. *The Tooth Mouse*
Kaplan, Michael B. *Betty Bunny didn't do it*
Keller, Holly. *That's mine, Horace*
Kroll, Virginia L. *Honest Ashley*
Latimer, Alex. *The boy who cried ninja*
McKissack, Patricia C. *The honest-to-goodness truth*
Madonna. *Mr. Peabody's apples*
Mathers, Petra. *Herbie's secret Santa*
Poydar, Nancy. *Zip, zip . . . homework*
Rahaman, Vashanti. *Divali rose*
Rankin, Laura. *Ruthie and the (not so) teeny tiny lie*
Robberecht, Thierry. *Sam tells stories*
Schroeder, Alan. *The stone lion*
Sierra, Judy. *Tell the truth, B. B. Wolf*
Singer, Marilyn. *The boy who cried alien*
Stephens, Helen. *Ruby and the muddy dog*

Character traits – hopefulness

Cocca-Leffler, Maryann. *Rain brings frogs*
Daly, Niki. *The herd boy*
Kittinger, Jo S. *The house on Dirty-Third Street*
MacLachlan, Patricia. *Snowflakes fall*
Our children can soar
Sasso, Sandy Eisenberg. *Butterflies under our hats*
Watson, Jesse Joshua. *Hope for Haiti*

Character traits – incentive *see* Character traits – ambition

Character traits – individuality

Alexander, Martha G. *Max and the dumb flower picture*
Aliki. *All by myself!*
Jack and Jake
Andreae, Giles. *Giraffes can't dance*
Appelt, Kathi. *Incredible me!*
Azore, Barbara. *Wanda and the wild hair*
Baicker, Karen. *Pea pod babies*
Baker, Keith. *No two alike*
Baker, Roberta. *No ordinary Olive*
Banks, Kate. *That's Papa's way*
Bar-el, Dan. *Not your typical dragon*
Bates, Ivan. *All by myself*
Battut, Éric. *The little pea*
Berne, Jennifer. *On a beam of light*
Blabey, Aaron. *Pearl Barley and Charlie Parsley*
Boutignon, Beatrice. *Not all animals are blue*
Boynton, Sandra. *Yay, you!*
Breen, Steve. *Violet the pilot*
Bridges, Shirin Yim. *The Umbrella Queen*
Brooks, Erik. *Polar opposites*
Brown, Don. *Odd boy out*
Brown, Peter. *Mr. Tiger goes wild*
Brumbeau, Jeff. *Miss Hunnicutt's hat*
Bynum, Janie. *Otis*
Carlson, Nancy. *I like me*
Carrer, Chiara. *Otto Carrotto*
Cartaya, Pablo. *Tina Cocolina*
Cave, Kathryn. *Henry's song*
Child, Lauren. *Who wants to be a poodle*
Chodos-Irvine, Margaret. *Ella Sarah gets dressed*
Clanton, Ben. *Mo's mustache*
Cochran, Bill. *My parents are divorced, my elbows have nicknames, and other facts about me*
Collington, Peter. *Clever cat*
Corderoy, Tracey. *Hubble bubble, Granny trouble*
Corey, Shana. *First graders from Mars: The problem with Pelly*
Côté, Geneviève. *Me and you*
dePaola, Tomie. *Oliver Button is a sissy*
Dicmas, Courtney. *Harold finds a voice*
Diggs, Taye. *Chocolate me!*
Dolenz, Micky. *Gakky Two-Feet*
Duke, Shirley Smith. *No bows!*
Ehlert, Lois. *Oodles of animals*
Evans, Kristina. *What's special about me, Mama?*
Falconer, Ian. *Olivia and the fairy princesses*
Frankel, Erin. *Weird!*
Friedman, Laurie. *A style all her own*
Gainer, Cindy. *I'm like you, you're like me*
Genechten, Guido van. *Flop-Ear*
Gilbert, Jane. *Indescribably Arabella*
Goodhart, Pippa. *You choose*
Hall, Michael. *Perfect square*
Hardy, Sarah Frances. *Puzzled by pink*
Harris, Robie H. *I'm all dressed!*
Heide, Florence Parry. *The one and only Marigold*
Heiligman, Deborah. *The boy who loved math*
Helakoski, Leslie. *Fair cow*
Woolbur
Henderson, Alicia Terry. *Call me black, call me beautiful*
Himmelman, John. *Tudley didn't know*
Hines, Anna Grossnickle. *What Joe saw*
Hobbie, Holly. *Fanny*
Hogrogian, Nonny. *The tiger of Turkestan*
Horacek, Petr. *Look out, Suzy Goose*
Silly Suzy Goose
Hosford, Kate. *Big birthday*
Big bouffant
Hovland, Henrik. *John Jensen feels different*
Hughes, Susan. *Earth to Audrey*
Hume, Lachie. *Clancy the courageous cow*
Iyengar, Malathi Michelle. *Romina's rangoli*
Jeffers, Oliver. *The Hueys in The new sweater*
Jenkins, Emily. *Daffodil*
Daffodil, crocodile
Kann, Victoria. *Purplicious*
Katz, Karen. *The colors of us*
Keane, Dave. *Sloppy Joe*
Keller, John G. *The rubber-legged ducky*
Kilodavis, Cheryl. *My princess boy*
Kostecki-Shaw, Jenny Sue. *My travelin' eye*
Kuskin, Karla. *I am me*
Leaf, Munro. *The story of Ferdinand the bull*
Lester, Helen. *Tacky the penguin*
Three cheers for Tacky
Lionni, Leo. *A color of his own*
Pezzettino
Tico and the golden wings
Livingston, Irene. *Finklehopper Frog*
Long, Ethan. *Chamelia*
Lucas, David. *Halibut Jackson*
McAllister, Angela. *Yuck! That's not a monster*

McBratney, Sam. *Yes we can!*
McCarthy, Meghan. *George upside down*
McCaughrean, Geraldine. *How the reindeer got their antlers*
McCue, Lisa. *Quiet Bunny*
McKee, David. *Elmer and Rose*
Mackintosh, David. *Marshall Armstrong is new to our school*
Maclear, Kyo. *Spork*
Maguire, John. *People*
Maloney, Peter. *His mother's nose*
Manning, Jane. *Cat nights*
Marciano, John Bemelmans. *Delilah*
Martin, Bill, Jr. *Chicken Chuck*
Mayer, Marianna. *The prince and the pauper*
Milgrim, David. *Some monsters are different*
Mitchell, Lori. *Different just like me*
Montserrat, Pep. *Ms. Rubinstein's beauty*
Morris, Ann. *Families*
Morrison, Toni. *Little Cloud and Lady Wind*
Moss, Peggy. *One of us*
Murguia, Bethanie Deeney. *Zoe gets ready*
Numeroff, Laura Joffe. *Sherman Crunchley*
Oram, Hiawyn. *The wrong overcoat*
Parkinson, Curtis. *Emily's eighteen aunts*
Parr, Todd. *The okay book*
Peet, Bill. *Buford the little bighorn*
The spooky tail of Prewitt Peacock
Pham, LeUyen. *Big sister, little sister*
Phinn, Gervase. *Who am I?*
Player, Micah. *Chloe, instead*
Plourde, Lynn. *You're wearing that to school?!*
Polacco, Patricia. *The art of Miss Chew*
Prelutsky, Jack. *Me I am!*
Primavera, Elise. *The house at the end of Ladybug Lane*
Rankin, Joan. *You're somebody special, Walliwigs!*
Richardson, John. *Grunt*
Robbins, Jacqui. *Two of a kind*
Rockwell, Anne. *Show and tell day*
Rogers, Fred. *If we were all the same*
Rohmann, Eric. *Pumpkinhead*
Rosenthal, Amy Krouse. *Exclamation mark*
Spoon
Ross, Tom. *Eggbert, the slightly cracked egg*
Rotner, Shelley. *Faces*
What can you do?
Saltzberg, Barney. *Star of the week*
Sauer, Tammi. *Cowboy camp*
Mostly monsterly
Princess in training
Savadier, Elivia. *Time to get dressed!*
Schoonmaker, Elizabeth. *Square cat*
Schotter, Roni. *All about grandmas*
Sendak, Maurice. *Pierre*
Seskin, Steve. *Don't laugh at me*
Shannon, David. *A bad case of stripes*
Shireen, Nadia. *Good little wolf*
Silverstein, Shel. *The missing piece*
Simon, Norma. *All kinds of children*
Why am I different?
Simont, Marc. *The goose that almost got cooked*
Singer, Marilyn. *The one and only me*
Skeers, Linda. *Tutus aren't my style*
Smallcomb, Pam. *I'm not*
Tafuri, Nancy. *Have you seen my duckling?*
Thomas, Joyce Carol. *Cherish me*
Tillman, Nancy. *The crown on your head*
Urbanovic, Jackie. *Duck at the door*
Vail, Rachel. *Piggy Bunny*
Valdivia, Paloma. *Up above and down below*
Walsh, Ellen Stoll. *For Pete's sake*
Weaver, Tess. *Frederick Finch, loudmouth*
Wells, Rosemary. *Shy Charles*
Weninger, Brigitte. *Why are you fighting, Davy?*
Wheatley, Nadia. *Luke's way of looking*
Willems, Mo. *Naked mole rat gets dressed*
Winans, CeCe, et al. *Colorful world*
Winter, Jeanette. *Kali's song*
Woo, Alan. *Maggie's chopsticks*
Yolen, Jane. *Not all princesses dress in pink*
Yum, Hyewon. *The twins' blanket*

Character traits – kindness

Aesop. *The lion and the mouse*
Mouse and lion
Aliki. *The story of William Penn*
Andreasen, Dan. *The giant of Seville*
Aston, Dianna Hutts. *Not so tall for six*
Bang, Molly. *The paper crane*
Barrett, Mary Brigid. *Shoebox Sam*
Blaich, Ute. *The star*
Bloom, Becky. *Crackers*
Bromley, Anne C. *The lunch thief*
Butler, M. Christina. *One winter's day*
Caraballo, Samuel. *My big sister / Mi hermana mayor*
Cazet, Denys. *A fish in his pocket*
Church, Caroline Jayne. *Ruff!*
Compton, Joanne. *Ashpet*
Cuyler, Margery. *Kindness is cooler, Mrs. Ruler*
Dewan, Ted. *One true bear*
Dudley, Rebecca. *Hank finds an egg*
Earnhardt, Donna W. *Being Frank*
Edwards, Nancy. *Glenna's seeds*
Evans, Richard Paul. *The light of Christmas*
Fackelmayer, Regina. *The gifts*
Gainer, Cindy. *I'm like you, you're like me*
Grimm, Jacob and Wilhelm. *The golden goose*
Harry, Rebecca. *Snow Bunny's Christmas wish*
Hasler, Eveline. *A tale of two brothers*
Hennessy, B. G. *Because of you*
Heyward, Du Bose. *The country bunny and the little gold shoes*
Holmquist, Delano. *SantaSaurus*
Jiménez, Francisco. *The Christmas gift / El regalo de Navidad*
Johnson, Grace. *The candle in the window*
Jules, Jacqueline. *No English*
Juster, Norton. *The odious ogre*
Kasza, Keiko. *Ready for anything*
Kelly, Mij. *Friendly Day*
Kroll, Virginia L. *Good neighbor Nicholas*
Lamstein, Sarah Marwil. *I like your buttons!*
McCourt, Lisa. *Chicken soup for little souls: The Goodness Gorillas*
Chicken soup for little souls: The never-forgotten doll
MacDonald, Margaret Read. *Slop!*
McKinley, Cindy. *One smile*
McNaughton, Janet. *Brave Jack and the unicorn*
Munsch, Robert N. *David's father*
Murphy, Mary. *How kind*
O'Callahan, Jay. *Raspberries!*
Ormondroyd, Edward. *Theodore*
Proimos, James. *Paulie Pastrami achieves world peace*
Richard, Françoise. *On Cat Mountain*
Robberecht, Thierry. *Sam's new friend*
Rohmer, Harriet. *Atariba and Niguayona*

Rylant, Cynthia. *If you'll be my Valentine*
San Souci, Robert D. *The talking eggs*
Say, Allen. *The boy in the garden*
Schnur, Steven. *The tie man's miracle*
Schotter, Roni. *Captain Snap and the children of Vinegar Lane*
Schroeder, Alan. *The stone lion*
Schwartz, Howard. *Gathering sparks*
Scotton, Rob. *Splat says thank you!*
Seuss, Dr. *Horton hears a Who!*
Silverman, Erica. *Gittel's hands*
Simmons, Steven J. *Alice and Greta*
Spelman, Cornelia Maude. *When I care about others*
Steig, William. *Wizzil*
Stein, David Ezra. *Because Amelia smiled*
Steptoe, John. *Mufaro's beautiful daughters*
Stock, Catherine. *Secret Valentine*
Stroud, Bettye. *Down home at Miss Dessa's*
Thong, Roseanne. *Fly free!*
Toscano, Charles. *Papa's pastries*
Ungar, Richard. *Rachel's gift*
Wallace, Nancy Elizabeth. *The kindness quilt*
Wheeler, Eliza. *Miss Maple's seeds*
Wilde, Oscar. *The selfish giant,* ill. by S. Saelig Gallagher
The selfish giant, ill. by Fabian Negrin
The selfish giant, ill. by Lisbeth Zwerger
Wojciechowski, Susan. *A fine St. Patrick's Day*
Zolotow, Charlotte. *I know a lady*

Character traits – kindness to animals

Aardema, Verna. *Koi and the kola nuts*
Aesop. *Androcles and the lion,* ill. by Dennis Nolan
Androcles and the lion, ill. by Janet Stevens
Androcles and the lion: and other Aesop fables
Arnosky, Jim. *Slow down for manatees*
Baek, Matthew J. *Be gentle with the dog, dear*
Bodkin, Odds. *The crane wife*
Brett, Jan. *Mossy*
Brunhoff, Laurent de. *Babar's little girl*
Bunting, Eve. *Night tree*
Butterworth, Nick. *One snowy night*
Chall, Marsha Wilson. *Pick a pup*
Chamberlain, Margaret. *Please don't tease Tootsie*
Chichester Clark, Emma. *Piper*
Church, Caroline Jayne. *Digby takes charge*
Collicott, Sharleen. *Toestomper and the caterpillars*
Cowcher, Helen. *Desert elephants*
Daugherty, James Henry. *Andy and the lion*
Davis, Anne. *No dogs allowed!*
Dennis, Major Brian. *Nubs*
Dockray, Tracy. *The lost and found pony*
Federspiel, Jurg. *Alligator Mike*
Furstinger, Nancy. *Maggie's second chance*
Gottfried, Maya. *Our farm*
Graham, Bob. *How to heal a broken wing*
Grover, Jan Zitz. *A home for Dakota*
Hatkoff, Craig, et al. *Winter's tail*
Havill, Juanita. *Call the horse lucky*
Henrichs, Wendy. *When Anju loved being an elephant*
Hest, Amy. *Charley's first night*
Hill, Meggan. *Nico and Lola*
Hoose, Philip M. *Hey little ant*
Jackson, Ellen. *Abe Lincoln loved animals*
Jackson, Emma. *A home for Dixie*
Joosse, Barbara. *Nugget and Darling*
Juan, Ana. *The pet shop revolution*
Keats, Ezra Jack. *Jennie's hat*
Kimmel, Eric A. *The birds' gift*
Knudsen, Michelle. *Big Mean Mike*
Lamstein, Sarah Marwil. *Big night for salamanders*
Lears, Laurie. *Waiting for Mr. Goose*
London, Jonathan. *Jackrabbit*
Luján, Jorge. *Stephen and the beetle*
Macaulay, David. *Angelo*
McDonnell, Flora. *I love animals*
McMillan, Bruce. *Nights of the pufflings*
McPhail, David. *The bear's toothache*
Martin, Rafe. *The language of birds*
The Shark God
Marzollo, Jean. *Pierre the penguin*
Meddaugh, Susan. *Tree of birds*
Miller, Edna. *Mousekin's frosty friend*
Moore, Eva. *Lucky ducklings*
Mora, Pat. *The song of Francis and the animals*
Numeroff, Laura Joffe. *If you give a cat a cupcake*
If you give a dog a donut
If you give a moose a muffin
If you give a mouse a cookie
If you give a pig a pancake
Peet, Bill. *Huge Harold*
Peet, Mal. *Cloud tea monkeys*
Pericoli, Matteo. *The true story of Stellina*
Pinkwater, Daniel. *Rainy morning*
Reed, Lynn Rowe. *Roscoe and the pelican rescue*
Root, Barry. *Gumbrella*
Roth, Ruby. *V is for vegan*
Rumford, James. *Dog-of-the-Sea-Waves*
Ryder, Joanne. *Each living thing*
Rylant, Cynthia. *The bookshop dog*
Sampson, Michael R. *Caddie, the golf dog*
Sayre, April Pulley. *Turtle, turtle, watch out!,* ill. by Lee Christiansen
Turtle, turtle, watch out!, ill. by Annie Patterson
Simont, Marc. *The stray dog*
Soros, Barbara. *Tenzin's deer*
Soule, Jean Conder. *Never tease a weasel*
Strand, Keith. *Grandfather's Christmas tree*
Tada, Satoshi. *Mr. Beetle*
Thayer, Jane. *Part-time dog*
Thomas, Jane Resh. *Scaredy dog*
Tompert, Ann. *The pied piper of Peru*
Turkle, Brinton. *Thy friend, Obadiah*
Ward, Lynd. *The biggest bear*
Wardlaw, Lee. *Won Ton*
Yagawa, Sumiko. *The crane wife*

Character traits – laziness

Cohen, Caron Lee. *Digger Pig and the turnip*
Davies, Gill. *Can't, don't, won't*
dePaola, Tomie. *Jamie O'Rourke and the big potato*
Jamie O'Rourke and the pooka
Egan, Tim. *The pink refrigerator*
Finn, Isobel. *The very lazy ladybug*
Grimm, Jacob and Wilhelm. *The three spinning fairies*
Hogg, Gary. *Look what the cat dragged in!*
Johnson, D. B. *Four legs bad, two legs good!*
Jordan, Mary Ellen. *Lazy Daisy, cranky Frankie*
Ketteman, Helen. *Armadilly chili*
Lester, Helen. *Score one for the sloths*
The little red hen. *The little red hen,* ill. by Byron Barton
The little red hen, ill. by Emily Bolam
The little red hen, ill. by Paul Galdone
Little red hen

The little red hen, ill. by Jerry Pinkney
The little red hen, ill. by Kate Slater
The little red hen, ill. by Annie West
The little red hen, ill. by Margot Zemach
The little red hen: an old fable
The Little Red Hen and the Passover matzah
The Little Red Hen makes a pizza
McGrath, Barbara Barbieri. *The little gray bunny*
The little green witch
Murphy, Jim. *Fergus and the Night-Demon*
Paul, Ann Whitford. *Mañana Iguana*
Root, Phyllis. *Aunt Nancy and Cousin Lazybones*
San Souci, Robert D. *The hired hand*
Snyder, Dianne. *The boy of the three-year nap*
Stampler, Ann Redisch. *Shlemazel and the remarkable spoon of Pohost*

Character traits – loyalty

Aliki. *The two of them*
Bridwell, Norman. *Clifford goes to Hollywood*
Cullen, Lynn. *The mightiest heart*
Gregory, Nan. *How Smudge came*
Hautzig, Deborah. *Beauty and the beast*
Jennings, Sharon. *Priscilla and Rosy*
Lester, Alison. *Running with the horses*
McGhee, Alison. *Always*
Mayer, Marianna. *Beauty and the beast*
Nelson, Marilyn. *Snook alone*
Pollock, Penny. *The turkey girl*
Potter, Beatrix. *The tale of the faithful dove*
Sabuda, Robert. *Beauty and the beast: a pop-up book of the classic fairy tale*
Waite, Michael P. *Jojofu*

Character traits – luck

Addy, Sharon Hart. *Lucky Jake*
Alexander, Lloyd. *The house Gobbaleen*
Aliki. *Three gold pieces*
Bateman, Teresa. *Fiona's luck*
Brown, Margaret Wise. *Wheel on the chimney*
Christian, Mary Blount. *If not for the calico cat*
D'Amico, Carmela. *Ella sets sail*
Foley, Greg. *Good luck Bear*
Friday, Mary Ellen. *It's a bad day*
Harjo, Joy. *The good luck cat*
Lin, Grace. *Fortune cookie fortunes*
McGuirk, Leslie. *Lucky Tucker*
Nishizuka, Koko. *The beckoning cat*
Polacco, Patricia. *Bun Bun Button*
Riddell, Chris. *Platypus and the lucky day*
Sasso, Sandy Eisenberg. *Butterflies under our hats*
Seibold, J. Otto. *Lost sloth*
Seki, Sunny. *The tale of the lucky cat*
Seuss, Dr. *Did I ever tell you how lucky you are?*
Soto, Gary. *Lucky Luis*
Stampler, Ann Redisch. *Shlemazel and the remarkable spoon of Pohost*
Sutton, Jane. *The trouble with cauliflower*

Character traits – meanness

Brown, Marc. *D. W., go to your room!*
Debecker, Benoît. *The naughty prince*
Gantos, Jack. *Rotten Ralph's rotten Christmas*
Rotten Ralph's show and tell
Rotten Ralph's trick or treat
Worse than Rotten Ralph
Goble, Paul. *The lost children*
Hasler, Eveline. *A tale of two brothers*
McKissack, Patricia C. *Ol' Clip-Clop*
Morrison, Toni. *The book of mean people*
O'Malley, Kevin. *Humpty Dumpty egg-splodes*
Prelutsky, Jack. *The mean old mean hyena*
Roberts, Lynn. *Rapunzel, a groovy fairy tale*
San Souci, Robert D. *Sootface*
Seuss, Dr. *How the Grinch stole Christmas*
Silverman, Erica. *Gittel's hands*
Simmons, Steven J. *Alice and Greta*
Somers, Kevin. *Meaner than meanest*
Steptoe, John. *Mufaro's beautiful daughters*
Stevenson, James. *Fried feathers for Thanksgiving*
Happy Valentine's Day, Emma!
The worst person's Christmas
Wooldridge, Connie Nordhielm. *Wicked Jack*

Character traits – optimism

Aliki. *The twelve months*
Carlson, Nancy. *Smile a lot!*
Cocca-Leffler, Maryann. *Rain brings frogs*
Hubbard, Woodleigh Marx. *All that you are*
Krauss, Ruth. *The carrot seed*
Lionni, Leo. *Theodore and the talking mushroom*
Mack, Jeff. *Good news, bad news*
Peet, Bill. *The Whingdingdilly*
Schwartz, Roslyn. *The mole sisters and the piece of moss*

Character traits – orderliness

Blankenship, Lee Ann. *Mr. Tuggle's troubles*
Bottner, Barbara. *Wallace's lists*
Braybrooks, Ann. *Plenty of pockets*
Elliot, David. *Henry's map*
Glaser, Linda. *Mrs. Greenberg's messy Hanukkah*
Guest, Elissa Haden. *Harriet's had enough!*
Harris, Robie H. *I love messes!*
Hassett, John. *Mouse in the house*
Kamish, Daniel. *Diggy Dan*
MacDonald, Alan. *Beware of the bears!*
McElmurry, Jill. *Mess pets*
McKissack, Patricia C. *Messy Bessey*
Mariconda, Barbara. *Sort it out!*
Odone, Jamison. *Mole had everything*
O'Malley, Kevin. *Bud*
Piers, Helen. *Who's in my bed?*
Prigger, Mary Skillings. *Aunt Minnie McGranahan*
Root, Phyllis. *Mrs. Potter's pig*
Schotter, Roni. *Captain Bob takes flight*
Schwab, Eva. *Robert and the Robot*
Simon, Charnan. *Messy Molly*
Teague, Mark. *Pigsty*
Viorst, Judith. *Super-completely and totally the messiest*
Yolen, Jane. *How do dinosaurs clean their rooms?*

Character traits – ostracism *see* Character traits – being different

Character traits – patience

Barton, Bethany. *This monster cannot wait!*
Dunrea, Olivier. *Ollie*
Ehrlich, Amy. *Baby Dragon*
Fogliano, Julie. *If you want to see a whale*
Himmelman, John. *Katie loves the kittens*
Horowitz, Dave. *Soon, Baboon, soon*
Kaplan, Michael B. *Betty Bunny loves chocolate cake*

Lemniscates. *Silence*
Leonetti, Mike. *Swinging for the fences*
MacKay, Elly. *If you hold a seed*
Marlowe, Sara. *No ordinary apple*
May, Eleanor. *Albert's amazing snail*
Mollel, Tololwa M. *Subira subira*
Morgan-Vanroyen, Mary. *Patient Rosie*
Poydar, Nancy. *Mailbox magic*
Rockwell, Anne. *Chip and the karate kick*
Train, Mary. *Time for the fair*
Walters, Catherine. *When will it be spring?*
Wells, Rosemary. *Max's breakfast*
Ziefert, Harriet. *Robin, where are you?*

Character traits – perfectionism

Fearnley, Jan. *The search for the perfect child*
Harris, Peter. *Perfect Prudence*
Kono, Erin Eitter. *Caterina and the perfect party*
Pett, Mark. *The girl who never made mistakes*
Ziefert, Harriet. *The princess and the peas and carrots*

Character traits – perseverance

Aliki. *A weed is a flower*
Asim, Jabari. *Fifty cents and a dream*
Balcziak, Bill. *John Henry*
Barber, Tiki, et al. *Teammates*
Beaty, Andrea. *Rosie Revere, engineer*
Belloni, Giulia. *Anything is possible*
Best, Cari. *Sally Jean, the Bicycle Queen*
Blades, Ann. *Mary of mile 18*
Braver, Vanita. *Madison and the two wheeler*
Brown, Don. *Teedie*
Bryant, Jen. *A splash of red*
Carle, Eric. *The very clumsy click beetle*
Carter, Anne Laurel. *The F team*
Curtis, Jamie Lee. *My brave year of firsts*
Cutler, Jane. *Guttersnipe*
Davis, Aubrey. *A hen for Izzy Pippik*
Dempsey, Kristy. *Surfer chick*
Francis, Lee DeCora. *Kunu's basket*
Garland, Michael. *Hooray José!*
Hodge, Deborah. *Lily and the mixed-up letters*
Hubbard, Crystal. *Catching the moon: the story of a young girl's baseball dream*
Isadora, Rachel. *Luke goes to bat*
Jordan, Deloris. *Dream big*
Keats, Ezra Jack. *John Henry*
Kessler, Cristina. *The best beekeeper of Lalibela*
Kinerk, Robert. *Clorinda*
Clorinda takes flight
Timothy Cox will not change his socks
Kurtz, Jane. *In the small, small night*
Lee, Spike. *Giant steps to change the world*
Lester, Julius. *John Henry*
London, Jonathan. *Where the big fish are*
MacDonald, Margaret Read. *Give up, Gecko!*
McGinty, Alice B. *Gandhi*
Malaspina, Ann. *Touch the sky*
Markel, Michelle. *The fantastic jungles of Henri Rousseau*
Mitchell, Margaree King. *Uncle Jed's barbershop*
Mortenson, Greg. *Listen to the wind*
O'Brien, Anne Sibley. *A path of stars*
O'Callahan, Jay. *Raspberries!*
Pace, Anne Marie. *Vampirina ballerina*
Pinkney, Brian. *Jojo's flying side kick*
Piper, Watty. *The little engine that could*, ill. by George Hauman
The little engine that could, ill. by Loren Long
Potter, Alicia. *Mrs. Harkness and the panda*
Rappaport, Doreen. *Eleanor, quiet no more*
To dare mighty things
Ruzzier, Sergio. *Amandina*
Saunders, Dave. *So slow!*
Schubert, Leda. *Reading to Peanut*
Seim, Donna Marie. *Where is Simon, Sandy?*
Singer, Marilyn. *Tallulah's toe shoes*
Tallulah's tutu
Spinelli, Eileen. *Sophie's masterpiece*
Steig, William. *Brave Irene*
Stewart, Amber. *Little by little*
Stone, Tanya Lee. *Who says women can't be doctors?*
Thomas, Jane Resh. *Scaredy dog*
Warwick, Dionne. *Little Man*
Watanabe, Shigeo. *Where's my daddy?*
Wild, Margaret. *Bobbie Dazzler*
Winters, Kari-Lynn. *Gift days*
Ziefert, Harriet. *Murphy jumps a hurdle*

Character traits – persistence

Adler, David A. *Helen Keller*
Anderson, Laurie Halse. *The big cheese of Third Street*
Braun, Sebastien. *Digger and Tom!*
Czernecki, Stefan. *Paper lanterns*
Daly, Cathleen. *Prudence wants a pet*
Dudley, Rebecca. *Hank finds an egg*
Egielski, Richard. *Itsy bitsy spider*
Gray, Kes. *Eat your peas*
Hopkins, H. Joseph. *The tree lady*
Howe, James. *Horace and Morris join the chorus (but what about Dolores?)*
Jordan, Deloris. *Michael's golden rules*
Keller, Holly. *Pearl's new skates*
Kennedy, Kim. *Hee-Haw-Dini and the Great Zambini*
Krull, Kathleen. *Hillary Rodham Clinton*
McCully, Emily Arnold. *Mouse practice*
McGhee, Alison. *Only a witch can fly*
Mortensen, Lori. *Cindy Moo*
Murphy, Stuart J. *Same old horse*
O'Connor, Jane. *Ready, set, skip!*
Palatini, Margie. *The perfect pet*
Paul, Chris. *Long shot*
Penner, Fred. *The cat came back*
Poydar, Nancy. *No fair science fair*
Ramsden, Ashley. *Seven fathers*
Raschka, Chris. *Everyone can learn to ride a bicycle*
Rockliff, Mara. *Me and Momma and Big John*
Rodriguez, Alex. *Out of the ballpark*
Schachner, Judith Byron. *Yo, Vikings*
Shannon, George. *Turkey Tot*
Siomades, Lorianne. *The itsy bitsy spider*
Trapani, Iza. *The itsy bitsy spider*
Van Allsburg, Chris. *Queen of the falls*
Van Leeuwen, Jean. *Sorry*
Woo, Alan. *Maggie's chopsticks*
Yamaguchi, Kristi. *Dream big, little pig!*
Young, Ed. *Hook*
Zagwÿn, Deborah Turney. *Apple batter*

Character traits – practicality

Aylesworth, Jim. *Mother Halverson's new cat*
Gág, Wanda. *Millions of cats*

Modell, Frank. *One zillion valentines*
Wells, Rosemary. *Otto runs for President*
Otto se presenta para presidente / Otto runs for President

Character traits – pride

Andersen, Hans Christian. *The dinosaur's new clothes*
The emperor's new clothes, ill. by Angela Barrett
The emperor's new clothes, ill. by Virginia Lee Burton
The emperor's new clothes, ill. by Robert Byrd
The emperor's new clothes, ill. by Serena Curmi
The emperor's new clothes, ill. by Charlene DeLage
The emperor's new clothes, ill. by Jack Delano
The emperor's new clothes, ill. by Anne Rockwell
The emperor's new clothes, ill. by Janet Stevens
The emperor's new clothes, ill. by Eve Tharlet
The emperor's new clothes: a tale set in China
Balcziak, Bill. *John Henry*
Calmenson, Stephanie. *The principal's new clothes*
Cousins, Lucy. *I'm the best*
Duvoisin, Roger Antoine. *Petunia*
Evans, Richard Paul. *The tower*
Grimm, Jacob and Wilhelm. *The water of life*
Hillenbrand, Jane. *What a treasure!*
Hughes, Langston. *My people*
Jackson, Chris. *The Gaggle sisters river tour*
Johnson, Rebecca. *The proud pelican's secret*
Keats, Ezra Jack. *John Henry*
Kirk, Daniel. *Keisha Ann can!*
Lester, Julius. *John Henry*
McCaughrean, Geraldine. *How the reindeer got their antlers*
Perlman, Janet. *The Emperor Penguin's new clothes*
Quattlebaum, Mary. *Sparks fly high*
Radunsky, Vladimir. *One: a nice story about an awful braggart*
Ramos, Mario. *I am so handsome*
Rumford, James. *Nine animals and the well*
Rylant, Cynthia. *Mr. Griggs' work*
Sasso, Sandy Eisenberg. *God said amen*
Schwartz, Amy. *Annabelle Swift, kindergartner*
Sharmat, Marjorie Weinman. *I'm terrific*
Ward, Helen. *The rooster and the fox*
Yolen, Jane. *King Long Shanks*

Character traits – questioning

Adler, David A. *A little at a time*
Blackall, Sophie. *Are you awake?*
Brown, Calef. *Boy wonders*
Calmenson, Stephanie. *Ollie's school day*
Carter, David A. *Whoo? Whoo?*
Catalanotto, Peter. *Question Boy meets Little Miss Know-It-All*
Coyle, Carmela LaVigna. *Do princesses really kiss frogs?*
Do super heroes have teddy bears?
Crumpacker, Bunny. *Alexander's pretending day*
Erlbruch, Wolf. *The big question*
Gonyea, Mark. *The spooky box*
Goodhart, Pippa. *You choose*
Gorbachev, Valeri. *Where is the apple pie?*
Hines, Anna Grossnickle. *Even if I spill my milk?*
Holub, Joan. *Why do cats meow?*
Why do dogs bark?
Hornsey, Chris. *Why do I have to eat off the floor?*
Kuskin, Karla. *Green as a bean*
Laden, Nina. *Once upon a memory*
Lionni, Leo. *Tico and the golden wings*
Luthardt, Kevin. *Flying*
McClure, Nikki. *Mama, is it summer yet?*
Mamada, Mineko. *Which is round? which is bigger?*
Marshall, Linda Elovitz. *The passover lamb*
Menchin, Scott. *Taking a bath with the dog and other things that make me happy*
What if everything had legs?
Miller, Margaret. *Can you guess?*
Mitton, Tony. *A very curious bear*
Munro, Roxie. *Hatch!*
Murphy, Mary. *Koala and the flower*
Offill, Jenny. *11 experiments that failed*
Pfister, Marcus. *Questions, questions*
Phillips, Christopher. *Ceci Ann's day of why*
Raab, Brigitte. *Where does pepper come from?*
Raschka, Chris. *Little black crow*
Reibstein, Mark. *Wabi Sabi*
Rosenthal, Amy Krouse. *It's not fair!*
Yes Day!
Rossell, Judith. *Oliver*
Simpson-Enock, Sarah. *Mommy, Mommy, what's in your tummy?*
Steven, Kenneth. *The biggest thing in the world*
Stott, Ann. *Always*
Taylor, Barbara. *I wonder why zippers have teeth and other questions about inventions*
Torrey, Richard. *Why?*
Tucker, Kathy. *Do cowboys ride bikes?*
Vega, Denise. *Grandmother, have the angels come?*
Walsh, Melanie. *Do lions live on lily pads?*
Weeks, Sarah. *My somebody special*
Wheeler, Valerie. *Yes, please! No, thank you!*
Wilson, Karma. *Mama, why?*
Wormell, Mary. *Why not?*
Young, Ruth. *Who says moo?*

Character traits – responsibility

Bowen, Anne. *Scooter in the outside*
Cutler, Jane. *Guttersnipe*
Davies, Stephen. *Don't spill the milk!*
Graves, Keith. *Pet boy*
Hawkins, Emily. *Little snow goose*
Johnson, Jen Cullerton. *Seeds of change*
Killen, Nicola. *Not me!*
Kroll, Virginia L. *Cristina keeps a promise*
Jason takes responsibility
Liersch, Anne. *Nell and Fluffy*
Mahoney, Daniel J. *The Saturday escape*
Napoli, Donna Jo. *Mama Miti*
Park, Linda Sue. *The firekeeper's son*
Schachner, Judith Byron. *The Grannyman*
Schwartz, Howard. *Gathering sparks*
Stephens, Helen. *Ruby and the muddy dog*
Winter, Jeanette. *Wangari's trees of peace*

Character traits – selfishness

Andersen, Hans Christian. *The swineherd*
Davidson, Ellen Dee. *Princess Justina Albertina*
Deacon, Alexis. *Cheese belongs to you!*
Demi. *One grain of rice*
Gantos, Jack. *Back to school for Rotten Ralph*
Grindley, Sally. *Can we play too, Piglittle?*
Henkes, Kevin. *A weekend with Wendell*
Kimmel, Eric A. *The mysterious guests*

Lester, Helen. *Me first*
Princess Penelope's parrot
Lipkind, William. *Finders keepers*
Meserve, Adria. *No room for Napoleon*
Peet, Bill. *The ant and the elephant*
Rosen, Michael. *This is our house*
Schroeder, Alan. *The stone lion*
Stein, Mathilde. *Mine!*
Wilde, Oscar. *The selfish giant*, ill. by S. Saelig Gallagher
The selfish giant, ill. by Fabian Negrin
The selfish giant, ill. by Lisbeth Zwerger
Wisdom, Jude. *Whatever Wanda wanted*

Character traits – shyness

Adams, Sarah. *Dave and Violet*
Alter, Anna. *Disappearing Desmond*
Bracken, Beth. *Too shy for show-and-tell*
Bunge, Daniela. *Cherry time*
Button, Lana. *Willow's whispers*
Child, Lauren. *Maude*
Choldenko, Gennifer. *A giant crush*
Louder, Lili
D'Amico, Carmela. *Ella sets the stage*
Devlin, Wende. *Cranberry Valentine*
Goble, Paul. *Love flute*
Gorbachev, Valeri. *Chicken chickens go to school*
Graham, Bob. *Dimity Dumpty*
Haseley, Dennis. *The invisible moose*
Hurwitz, Johanna. *Mighty Monty*
Hutchins, Pat. *Titch and Daisy*
Jarman, Julia. *Two shy pandas*
Keats, Ezra Jack. *Louie*
Kirk, Daniel. *Library mouse*
Library mouse: a friend's tale
Lin, Grace. *Lissy's friends*
Lucas, David. *Halibut Jackson*
Maccarone, Grace. *Miss Lina's ballerinas and the prince*
McCourt, Lisa. *Chicken soup for little souls: The new kid and the cookie thief*
Montenegro, Laura Nyman. *A bird about to sing*
Morgan, Michaela. *Dear bunny*
Newman, Jeff. *The boys*
Paraskevas, Betty. *Chocolate at the Four Seasons*
Pearson, Susan. *Slugs in love*
Rappaport, Doreen. *Eleanor, quiet no more*
Rockwell, Anne. *Big George*
Rosenberry, Vera. *Vera's first day of school*
Ruzzier, Sergio. *Amandina*
Schmid, Paul. *Oliver and his alligator*
Spinelli, Eileen. *When no one is watching*
Srinivasan, Divya. *Octopus alone*
Thompson, Lauren. *Wee little lamb*
Twohy, Mike. *Poindexter makes a friend*
Udry, Janice May. *What Mary Jo shared*
Yashima, Taro. *Crow boy*
Zolotow, Charlotte. *A tiger called Thomas*, ill. by Diana Cain Bluthenthal
A tiger called Thomas, ill. by Catherine Stock

Character traits – smallness

Adoff, Jaime. *Small fry*
Alborough, Jez. *Tall*
Andersen, Hans Christian. *Sylvia Long's Thumbelina*
Thumbelina, ill. by Charlene Delage
Thumbelina, ill. by Demi
Thumbelina, ill. by Arlene Graston
Thumbelina, ill. by Bagram Ibatoulline
Thumbelina, ill. by Susan Jeffers
Thumbelina, ill. by Lauren A. Mills
Thumbeline
Aston, Dianna Hutts. *Not so tall for six*
Balouch, Kristen. *The little little girl with the big big voice*
Base, Graeme. *Little elephants*
Battersby, Katherine. *Brave Squish Rabbit*
Squish Rabbit
Bell, Cece. *Itty Bitty*
Bogan, Paulette. *Lulu the big little chick*
Braun, Sebastien. *Toot and Pop!*
Cantrell, Charlie. *A friend for Einstein*
Carlson, Nancy. *Think big!*
Clark, Katie. *Seagull Sam*
Costello, David Hyde. *Little Pig joins the band*
Dodd, Emma. *I am small*
Durant, Alan. *A dinosaur called Tiny*
Emmett, Jonathan. *Ruby in her own time*
This way, Ruby!
Foreman, Michael. *The littlest dinosaur*
Gay, Marie-Louise. *When Stella was very, very small*
Hosford, Kate. *Infinity and me*
Kirk, David. *Oh So Tiny bunny*
LaMarche, Jim. *Up*
Lepp, Bil. *The King of Little Things*
Lichtenheld, Tom. *Cloudette*
McGrory, Anik. *Kidogo*
Martin, David. *Little Bunny and the magic Christmas tree*
Marx, Patricia. *Dot in Larryland*
Masurel, Claire. *Domino*
Meserve, Jessica. *Small sister*
Miura, Taro. *The tiny king*
Nakagawa, Chihiro. *Who made this cake?*
Nolen, Jerdine. *Hewitt Anderson's great big life*
O'Leary, Sara. *When you were small*
Palatini, Margie. *Shelly*
Paul, Chris. *Long shot*
Schwarz, Viviane. *Timothy and the strong pajamas*
Silverman, Erica. *There was a wee woman . . .*
Spires, Ashley. *Small Saul*
Stead, Philip C. *Hello, my name is Ruby*
Stewart, Amber. *Too small for my big bed*
Symes, Ruth. *Little Rex, big brother*
Thompson, Lauren. *Wee little chick*
Watts, Bernadette. *The smallest snowflake*
Yolen, Jane. *The emperor and the kite*
Young, Ed. *Little Plum*

Character traits – stubbornness

Berger, Samantha. *Martha doesn't say sorry*
Chaconas, Dori. *Dori the contrary hen*
Chou, Yih-Fen. *Mimi says no*
Dormer, Frank W. *The obstinate pen*
Keller, Holly. *Merry Christmas, Geraldine*
Langen, Annette. *I won't comb my hair!*
Plourde, Lynn. *Pigs in the mud in the middle of the rud*
Priceman, Marjorie. *Princess Picky*
Steig, William. *Spinky sulks*
Tarbescu, Edith. *The boy who stuck out his tongue*
Tyler, Anne. *Timothy Tugbottom says no!*
Viorst, Judith. *Alexander, who's not (do you hear me? I mean it!) going to move*

Character traits – vanity

Andersen, Hans Christian. *The dinosaur's new clothes*
The emperor's new clothes, ill. by Angela Barrett
The emperor's new clothes, ill. by Virginia Lee Burton
The emperor's new clothes, ill. by Robert Byrd
The emperor's new clothes, ill. by Serena Curmi
The emperor's new clothes, ill. by Charlene DeLage
The emperor's new clothes, ill. by Jack Delano
The emperor's new clothes, ill. by Anne Rockwell
The emperor's new clothes, ill. by Janet Stevens
The emperor's new clothes, ill. by Eve Tharlet
The emperor's new clothes: a tale set in China
It's perfectly true!
Barnett, Mac. *Mustache!*
Braun, Sebastien. *Toot and Pop!*
Brown, Marcia. *Once a mouse . . .*
Calmenson, Stephanie. *The principal's new clothes*
Cousins, Lucy. *I'm the best*
Evans, Richard Paul. *The tower*
Harper, Lee. *The Emperor's cool clothes*
Hausman, Gerald. *Coyote walks on two legs*
Heo, Yumi. *Lady Hahn and her seven friends*
MacDonald, Margaret Read. *The girl who wore too much*
Marshall, James. *George and Martha, tons of fun*
Perlman, Janet. *The Emperor Penguin's new clothes*
Primavera, Elise. *Louise the big cheese and the la-di-da shoes*
Radunsky, Vladimir. *One: a nice story about an awful braggart*
Ramos, Mario. *I am so handsome*
Rumford, James. *Nine animals and the well*
Sasso, Sandy Eisenberg. *God said amen*
Shields, Carol Diggory. *I am really a princess*
Ward, Helen. *The rooster and the fox*
Yolen, Jane. *King Long Shanks*
Pegasus, the flying horse

Character traits – willfulness

Carlson, Nancy. *Loudmouth George earns his allowance*
Davidson, Ellen Dee. *Princess Justina Albertina*

Character traits – wisdom

Hoffman, Mary. *Three wise women*
Kajikawa, Kimiko. *Tsunami!*
Marlowe, Sara. *No ordinary apple*
Oberman, Sheldon. *The wisdom bird*
Uchida, Yoshiko. *The wise old woman*
Wisniewski, David. *The warrior and the wise man*

Cheating *see* Behavior – cheating

Cheerleading

Lester, Helen. *Three cheers for Tacky*

Cherubs *see* Angels

Child abuse

Clifton, Lucille. *One of the problems of Everett Anderson*
Kleven, Sandy. *The right touch*
Riggs, Shannon. *Not in Room 204*
Sherman, Joanne. *Because it's my body*
Spelman, Cornelia Maude. *Your body belongs to you*
Starishevsky, Jill. *My body belongs to me*
Trottier, Maxine. *A safe place*

Children as authors

Baskin, Leonard. *Hosie's alphabet*
The best part of me
Burdett, Lois. *Hamlet for kids*
Macbeth for kids
A midsummer night's dream for kids
Romeo and Juliet for kids
The tempest for kids
Twelfth night for kids
Kallok, Emma. *Gem*
Kroll, Steven. *Patches*
Michels-Gualtieri, Akaela S. *I was born to be a sister*
Noah, build your boat
The palm of my heart
Pia Toya
Poems for the very young
Wiener, Lori S., et al *Be a friend*

Children as illustrators

Burdett, Lois. *Hamlet for kids*
Macbeth for kids
A midsummer night's dream for kids
Romeo and Juliet for kids
The tempest for kids
Twelfth night for kids
Hughes, Langston. *The sweet and sour animal book*
Kamish, Daniel. *Diggy Dan*
Kroll, Steven. *Patches*
Miranda, Anne. *Alphabet fiesta*
Noah, build your boat
Pia Toya
Tusa, Tricia. *Bunnies in my head*
Wiener, Lori S., et al *Be a friend*

Children as inventors

Brill, Marlene Targ. *Margaret Knight, girl inventor*

Circular tales

Ada, Alma Flor. *The gold coin*
Carle, Eric. *Draw me a star*
Czekaj, Jef. *Oink-a-doodle-moo*
Fagan, Carl. *Mr. Zinger's hat*
Gorbachev, Valeri. *Where is the apple pie?*
Johnston, Tony. *Big red apple*
McKinley, Cindy. *One smile*
Murphy, Mary. *How kind*
Numeroff, Laura Joffe. *If you give a cat a cupcake*
If you give a dog a donut
If you give a moose a muffin
If you give a mouse a cookie
If you give a pig a pancake
If you give a pig a party
Shaskan, Stephen. *A dog is a dog*
Van Laan, Nancy. *This is the hat*
Ziefert, Harriet. *A polar bear can swim*

Circus

Alsenas, Linas. *Peanut*

Andreasen, Dan. *The giant of Seville*
Bogacki, Tomasz. *Circus girl*
Bronson, Linda. *The circus alphabet*
Brown, Marc. *Arthur's chicken pox*
Campbell, K. G. *Lester's dreadful sweaters*
Carlson, Melody. *The day the circus came to town*
Carter, Anne Laurel. *Circus play*
Clements, Andrew. *Circus family dog*
Cneut, Carll. *The amazing love story of Mr. Morf*
Coerr, Eleanor. *Circus day in Japan*
Curious George goes to the circus
dePaola, Tomie. *Jingle, the Christmas clown*
Dockray, Tracy. *The lost and found pony*
Dodds, Dayle Ann. *Where's Pup?*
Downs, Mike. *You see a circus, I see —*
Duncan, Lois. *Song of the circus*
Ehlert, Lois. *Circus*
Emberley, Ed. *Thanks, Mom!*
Esbaum, Jill. *To the big top*
Falconer, Ian. *Olivia saves the circus*
Faller, Regis. *Polo and the magician!*
Fleischman, Paul. *Sidewalk circus*
Fletcher, Ralph. *The circus surprise*
Freeman, Don. *Bearymore*
Gottfried, Maya. *Last night I dreamed a circus*
Graham, Bob. *Dimity Dumpty*
Gravett, Emily. *Wolf won't bite!*
Hayes, Geoffrey. *Patrick at the circus*
Henrichs, Wendy. *When Anju loved being an elephant*
Hill, Eric. *Spot goes to the circus*
Jackson, Kathryn. *The golden circus book*
Klise, Kate. *Little Rabbit and the Meanest Mother on Earth*
Krosoczka, Jarrett J. *Ollie the purple elephant*
Landry, Leo. *Eat your peas, Ivy Louise!*
Littlesugar, Amy. *Clown child*
Lobel, Anita. *Animal antics: A to Z*
McCourt, Lisa. *Chicken soup for little souls: The best night out with Dad*
MacDonald, Suse. *Circus opposites*
Elephants on board
McGuirk, Leslie. *Tucker over the top*
Martin, Bill, Jr. *Chicken Chuck*
Millman, Isaac. *Moses goes to the circus*
Montserrat, Pep. *Ms. Rubinstein's beauty*
Munro, Roxie. *Circus*
Murphy, Stuart J. *Circus shapes*
Nimmo, Jenny. *Esmeralda and the children next door*
Noonan, Julia. *Hare and Rabbit, friends forever*
Peet, Bill. *Chester the worldly pig*
Ella
Randy's dandy lions
Pinkwater, Daniel. *Rainy morning*
Prelutsky, Jack. *Circus*
Price, Mathew. *Dumbo*
Priceman, Marjorie. *Emeline at the circus*
Rau, Dana Meachen. *Clown around*
Rey, H. A. *Curious George rides a bike*
Robertson, Patrisha Grainger. *Cirque du Soleil*
Schachner, Judith Byron. *Skippyjon Jones Cirque de Olé*
Seuss, Dr. *If I ran the circus*
Slobodkina, Esphyr. *Circus caps for sale*
Smith, Joseph A. *Circus train*
Spier, Peter. *Peter Spier's circus!*
Stone, Tanya Lee. *Sandy's circus*
Sturgis, Brenda Reeves. *10 turkeys in the road*
Teague, Mark. *Baby tamer*
Van Dusen, Chris. *The circus ship*
Villeneuve, Anne. *The red scarf*
Vincent, Gabrielle. *Ernest and Celestine at the circus*
Weis, Carol. *When the cows got loose*
Yaccarino, Dan. *Deep in the jungle*
Ziefert, Harriet. *Circus parade*

Cities, towns

Ackerman, Karen. *Bean's big day*
Adoff, Arnold. *Street music*
Aesop. *The country mouse and the city mouse*
Milly and Tilly
The town mouse and the country mouse, ill. by Lorinda Bryan Cauley
The town mouse and the country mouse, ill. by Janet Stevens
The town mouse and the country mouse: an Aesop fable, ill. by Helen Ward
The town mouse and the country mouse: an Aesop fable, ill. by Bernadette Watts
Town mouse, country mouse, ill. by Jan Brett
Town mouse, country mouse, ill. by Carol Jones
Alko, Selina. *B is for Brooklyn*
Barracca, Debra. *Maxi, the hero*
A taxi dog Christmas
Barracca, Sal. *The adventures of taxi dog*
Bartone, Elisa. *Peppe the lamplighter*
Bash, Barbara. *Urban roosts*
Berger, Barbara. *Angels on a pin*
Berner, Rotraut Susanne. *In the town all year 'round*
Bernhard, Durga. *To and fro, fast and slow*
Blake, Robert J. *Fledgling*
Bloom, Suzanne. *No place for a pig*
Bogan, Paulette. *Spike in the city*
Bradby, Marie. *Momma, where are you from?*
Brooks, Nigel. *Town mouse house*
Brown, Peter. *The curious garden*
Brown, Tameka Fryer. *Around our way on Neighbors' Day*
Browne, Anthony. *Me and you*
Buchanan, Jane. *Seed magic*
Buitrago, Jairo. *Jimmy the greatest*
Bunting, Eve. *Riding the tiger*
Smoky night
Burleigh, Robert. *Clang-clang! beep-beep!*
Lookin' for Bird in the big city
Messenger, messenger
Burton, Virginia Lee. *Katy and the big snow*
The little house
Chall, Marsha Wilson. *Prairie train*
Chaud, Benjamin. *The bear's song*
Chocolate, Deborah. *El barrio*
Cocca-Leffler, Maryann. *Bus route to Boston*
Cole, Henry. *On Meadowview Street*
Cole, Kenneth, Dr. *No bad news*
Collier, Bryan. *Uptown*
Corey, Shana. *Milly and the Macy's Parade*
Crews, Donald. *Parade*
Crews, Nina. *One hot summer day*
Cummins, Julie. *Country kid, city kid*
Curious George in the big city
Curlee, Lynn. *Skyscraper*
Dahlie, Elizabeth. *Bernelly and Harriet*
Daly, Niki. *Not so fast Songololo*
Donnelly, Liza. *Dinosaurs' Halloween*
Dorros, Arthur. *Abuela*
City chicken
Dugan, Joanne. *ABC NYC*
Emberley, Rebecca. *My city / Mi cuidad*

Three cool kids
Fitzgerald, Joanne. *This is me and where I am*
Flanagan, Alice K. *Mayors*
Fleischman, Paul. *Sidewalk circus*
Garhan Attebury, Nancy. *Out and about at city hall*
Geisert, Bonnie. *Desert town*
Mountain town
Geser, Gretchen. *One bright ring*
Gibbons, Gail. *Up goes the skyscraper!*
Godwin, Laura. *Central Park serenade*
One moon, two cats
Goode, Diane. *Tiger trouble*
Gordon, Gus. *Herman and Rosie*
Graham, Bob. *The silver button*
Greenfield, Eloise. *Night on Neighborhood Street*
Grimes, Nikki. *A pocketful of poems*
Harrison, Troon. *Courage to fly*
Helakoski, Leslie. *Big chickens go to town*
Heo, Yumi. *One afternoon*
One Sunday morning
Hest, Amy. *Nana's birthday party*
When you meet a bear on Broadway
High, Linda Oatman. *Tenth Avenue cowboy*
Under New York
Hoban, Tana. *Is it red? Is it yellow? Is it blue?*
Hodge, Deborah. *Watch me grow!*
Hodgkinson, Leigh. *Goldilocks and just one bear*
Hopkins, H. Joseph. *The tree lady*
Hopkins, Lee Bennett. *City I love*
Hubbell, Patricia. *City kids*
Sidewalk trip
Hurd, Thacher. *Zoom City*
Isadora, Rachel. *Listen to the city*
Say hello!
Jack and the beanstalk. *Jack and the beanstalk*
Jenkins, Priscilla Belz. *Falcons nest on skyscrapers*
Jocelyn, Marthe. *Mayfly*
Joel, Billy. *New York state of mind*
Johnson, Stephen T. *Alphabet city*
Jonas, Ann. *Round trip*
Karas, G. Brian. *The village garage*
Keats, Ezra Jack. *Apt. 3*
Goggles
Hi, cat!
Pet show!
Kenney, Sean. *Cool city*
Kilby, Don. *In the city*
Kleven, Elisa. *Glasswings*
Kroll, Steven. *Mary McLean and the St. Patrick's Day parade*
Kroll, Virginia L. *Faraway drums*
Krupinski, Loretta. *Christmas in the city*
Lakin, Patricia. *Subway sonata*
Lenski, Lois. *Policeman Small*
Levitin, Sonia. *Boom town*
Lewin, Ted. *Amazon boy*
Lodge, Jo. *Moo Moo goes to the city*
Low, William. *Machines go to work in the city*
McCloskey, Robert. *Make way for ducklings*
McDermott, Gerald. *Tim O'Toole and the wee folk*
McFarlane, Sheryl. *In the city*
Maitland, Barbara. *Moo in the morning*
Mak, Kam. *My Chinatown*
Martin, Jacqueline Briggs. *Farmer Will Allen and the growing table*
Medina, Tony. *DeShawn days*
Meister, Cari. *Busy, busy city street*
Melmed, Laura Krauss. *Capital! Washington D.C. from A to Z*
New York, New York!
Merriam, Eve. *Bam, bam, bam*
Milich, Zoran. *The city ABC book*
City colors
City 1 2 3
City signs
Milway, Katie Smith. *Cappuccina goes to town*
Moreton, Daniel. *La Cucaracha Martina*
Munro, Roxie. *The inside-outside book of London*
The inside-outside book of New York City
The inside-outside book of Paris
The inside-outside book of Texas
The inside-outside book of Washington, D.C.
Mazescapes
Myers, Christopher. *Sparrows*
Myers, Walter Dean. *Harlem*
Neubecker, Robert. *Wow! City!*
Niemann, Christoph. *Subway*
Numeroff, Laura Joffe. *What daddies do best*
Osborne, Mary Pope. *New York's bravest*
Palatini, Margie. *Hogg, Hogg, and Hog*
Pearson, Debora. *Big city song*
Peet, Bill. *Fly, Homer, fly*
Pericoli, Matteo. *See the city*
Pinkwater, Daniel. *Bad bears in the big city*
Beautiful Yetta
Poffenberger, Nancy M. *September 11, 2001*
Poydar, Nancy. *Cool Ali*
Proimos, James. *The loudness of Sam*
Provensen, Alice. *Town and country*
Pryor, Bonnie. *The dream jar*
Raschka, Chris. *New York is English, Chattanooga is Creek*
Reidy, Jean. *All through my town*
Reiss, Mike. *Late for school*
Reynolds, Peter H. *Rose's garden*
Ringgold, Faith. *Tar Beach*
Roth, Susan L. *Happy birthday Mr. Kang*
Rotner, Shelley. *Citybook*
Senses in the city
Russell, Natalie. *Brown Rabbit in the city*
Moon rabbit
Russo, Marisabina. *Mama talks too much*
Santangelo, Colony Elliott. *Brother Wolf of Gubbio*
Sayre, April Pulley. *It's my city*
Schertle, Alice. *Little Blue Truck leads the way*
Schulman, Janet. *Pale Male*
Shapiro, J. H. *Magic trash*
Shewchuk, Pat. *In Lucia's neighborhood*
Shulevitz, Uri. *Dusk*
One Monday morning
Snow
Singer, Marilyn. *City lullaby*
Smalls-Hector, Irene. *Jonathan and his mommy*
Smith, Marie. *N is for our nation's capital*
Soto, Gary. *Chato's kitchen*
Spinelli, Eileen. *City angel*
Stadler, John. *The cats of Mrs. Calamari*
Stainton, Sue. *Santa's snow cat*
Stevenson, James. *Grandpa's great city tour*
Stewart, Joel. *Addis Berner Bear forgets*
Stewart, Sarah. *The journey*
Stolz, Mary. *Emmett's pig*
Stutson, Caroline. *Cats' night out*
Taback, Simms. *Simms Taback's city animals*
Tafolla, Carmen. *What can you do with a paleta?*
Takabayashi, Mari. *I live in Brooklyn*
I live in Tokyo
Tamar, Erika. *The garden of happiness*

Tauss, Marc. *Superhero*
Thornhill, Jan. *Wild in the city*
Uhlberg, Myron. *Lemuel, the fool*
Ungar, Richard. *Rachel's library*
Van Nutt, Julia. *Skyrockets and snickerdoodles*
Vila, Laura. *Building Manhattan*
Watson, Renée. *A place where hurricanes happen*
Watts, Leslie Elizabeth. *The Baabaasheep Quartet*
Weitzman, Jacqueline Preiss. *You can't take a balloon into the Metropolitan Museum*
You can't take a balloon into the National Gallery
Wilcox, Brian. *Full moon*
Wilde, Oscar. *The happy prince*
Wilder, Laura Ingalls. *Going to town*
Williams, Karen Lynn. *Beatrice's dream*
Williams, Sherley Anne. *Girls together*
Williams, Suzanne. *Old MacDonald in the city*
Woodson, Jacqueline. *The other side*
Wyeth, Sharon Dennis. *Something beautiful*
Yaccarino, Dan. *Doug unplugged*
Yashima, Taro. *Umbrella*
Zimmerman, Andrea Griffing. *Trashy town*
Zullo, Germano. *Line 135*

Cleanliness *see* Character traits – cleanliness

Cleverness *see* Character traits – cleverness

Cloaks *see* Clothing – coats

Clocks, watches

Appelt, Kathi. *Bats around the clock*
Axelrod, Amy. *Pigs on a blanket*
Aylesworth, Jim. *The completed hickory dickory dock*
Baker, Keith. *Hickory dickory dock*
Blackstone, Stella. *Bear takes a trip*
Coats, Lucy. *Neil's numberless world*
Fraser, Mary Ann. *I.Q., it's time*
Gibbons, Gail. *Clocks and how they go*
Harper, Dan. *Telling time with Big Mama Cat*
Hutchins, Pat. *Clocks and more clocks*
McCaughrean, Geraldine. *My grandmother's clock*
McMillan, Bruce. *Time to . . .*
Metzger, Steve. *The dancing clock*
Mother Goose. *Hickory, dickory, dock*
Murphy, Stuart J. *Game time*
It's about time!
Older, Jules. *Telling time*
Pilegard, Virginia Walton. *The warlord's alarm*
Richards, Kitty. *It's about time, Max!*
Stead, Philip C. *A home for Bird*
Verdet, Andre. *All about time*
Wood, Audrey. *It's Duffy time!*

Clothing

Aesop. *The donkey in the lion's skin*
The wolf in sheep's clothing
Ajmera, Maya, et al. *What we wear*
Alko, Selina. *Every-day dress-up*
Andersen, Hans Christian. *The dinosaur's new clothes*
The emperor's new clothes, ill. by Angela Barrett
The emperor's new clothes, ill. by Virginia Lee Burton
The emperor's new clothes, ill. by Robert Byrd
The emperor's new clothes, ill. by Serena Curmi
The emperor's new clothes, ill. by Charlene DeLage
The emperor's new clothes, ill. by Jack Delano
The emperor's new clothes, ill. by Anne Rockwell
The emperor's new clothes, ill. by Janet Stevens
The emperor's new clothes, ill. by Eve Tharlet
The emperor's new clothes: a tale set in China
Arnold, Tedd. *Huggly gets dressed*
Bae, Hyun-Joo. *New clothes for New Year's day*
Barrett, Judi. *Animals should definitely not wear clothing*
Beaton, Clare. *Daisy gets dressed*
Beaumont, Karen. *Dini Dinosaur*
Bentley, Dawn. *Fuzzy bear*
Billstrom, Dianne. *You can't go to school naked!*
Blankenship, Lee Ann. *Mr. Tuggle's troubles*
Brett, Jan. *The hat*
The trouble with trolls
Brown, Marc. *Arthur's underwear*
Calmenson, Stephanie. *The principal's new clothes*
Carlstrom, Nancy White. *Jesse Bear, what will you wear?*
Carter, David A. *Who's under that hat?*
Catchpool, Michael. *The cloud spinner*
Chocolate, Deborah. *Kente colors*
Chodos-Irvine, Margaret. *Ella Sarah gets dressed*
Chwast, Seymour. *Get dressed!*
Cole, Brock. *Buttons*
Corey, Shana. *You forgot your skirt, Amelia Bloomer*
Cullen, Catherine Ann. *The magical, mystical, marvelous coat*
Cunnane, Kelly. *Deep in the Sahara*
Cuyler, Margery. *Princess Bess gets dressed*
De Regniers, Beatrice Schenk. *What did you put in your pocket?*
Dodds, Dayle Ann. *Hello, sun!*
The Kettles get new clothes
Ehrlich, Fred. *Does a chimp wear clothes?*
Emberley, Rebecca. *My clothes / Mi ropa*
Fox, Mem. *Shoes from grandpa*
Freeman, Don. *Corduroy*
A pocket for Corduroy
Gay, Marie-Louise. *Good morning Sam*
Gibert, Bruno. *The king is naked!*
Gordon, Domenica More. *Archie*
Harley, Bill. *Dirty Joe, the pirate*
Harper, Lee. *The Emperor's cool clothes*
Harris, Robie H. *I'm all dressed!*
Heling, Kathryn. *Clothesline clues to jobs people do*
Hickox, Rebecca. *The golden sandal*
Hoberman, Mary Ann. *I like old clothes*
Hopkinson, Deborah. *Knit your bit*
Hutchins, Pat. *You'll soon grow into them, Titch*
Jocelyn, Marthe. *Ready for autumn*
Ready for spring
Ready for summer
Ready for winter
Kuskin, Karla. *The Philharmonic gets dressed*
Under my hood I have a hat
Larson, Kirby. *The magic kerchief*
Lasky, Kathryn. *The emperor's old clothes*
Lucille's snowsuit
Lester, Helen. *The sheep in wolf's clothing*
Tacky and the Emperor
Lester, Julius. *Sam and the tigers*
Lewis, Rose A. *Orange Peel's pocket*
Lindaman, Jane. *Zip it!*
Litwin, Eric. *Pete the cat and his four groovy buttons*
London, Jonathan. *Froggy gets dressed*

Froggy goes to school
Long, Ethan. *Chamelia*
Lottridge, Celia Barker. *The little rooster and the diamond button*
Lucas, David. *Halibut Jackson*
Lunge-Larsen, Lise. *Noah's mittens*
MacDonald, Margaret Read. *The girl who wore too much*
Little Rooster's diamond button
McElligott, Matthew. *Backbeard and the birthday suit*
McKee, David. *Elmer and Super El*
McKissack, Patricia C. *Nettie Jo's friends*
Makhijani, Pooja. *Mama's saris*
Markel, Michelle. *Brave girl*
Martins, Isabel Minhós. *Little lamb, have you any wool?*
Medearis, Angela Shelf. *Poppa's itchy Christmas*
Poppa's new pants
Mills, Lauren A. *The rag coat*
Morris, Ann. *Weddings*
Moss, Miriam. *Bare bear*
Mould, Wendy. *Ants in my pants*
Müller, Birte. *I can dress myself!*
Munsch, Robert N. *Thomas' snowsuit*
Murguia, Bethanie Deeney. *Zoe gets ready*
Nedwidek, John. *Ducks don't wear socks*
Neitzel, Shirley. *The dress I'll wear to the party*
The jacket I wear in the snow
Oberman, Sheldon. *The always prayer shawl*
O'Connor, Jane. *Fancy Nancy*
Nancy la elegante / Fancy Nancy
Ohi, Ruth. *Pants off first*
Parr, Todd. *Underwear do's and don'ts*
Perlman, Janet. *The Emperor Penguin's new clothes*
Plourde, Lynn. *Grandpappy snippy snappies*
You're wearing that to school?!
Potter, Beatrix. *The tale of Mrs. Tiggy-Winkle*
Rao, Sandhya. *My mother's sari*
Reidy, Hannah. *All sorts of clothes*
Reidy, Jean. *Too purpley!*
Rothenberg, Joan Keller. *Inside-out grandma*
Sanders, Scott R. *Warm as wool*
Savadier, Elivia. *Time to get dressed!*
Schertle, Alice. *Button up!*
The skeleton in the closet
Schnur, Steven. *The tie man's miracle*
Scott, Janine. *Let's get dressed*
Senior, Olive. *Birthday suit*
Sheth, Kashmira. *My Dadima wears a sari*
Stoeke, Janet Morgan. *A hat for Minerva Louise*
Szekeres, Cyndy. *The mouse that Jack built*
Tafolla, Carmen. *What can you do with a rebozo?*
Thomas, Mark. *Clothes in Colonial America*
Vigil-Piñón, Evangelina. *Marina's muumuu / El muumuu de Marina*
Weiss, Nicki. *The world turns round and round*
Wells, Rosemary. *Max's dragon shirt*
Max's new suit
Wild, Margaret. *The pocket dogs*
Willems, Mo. *Naked mole rat gets dressed*
Winter, Jeanette. *My baby*
Wright, Maureen. *Sneezy the snowman*
Yolen, Jane. *King Long Shanks*
Yorinks, Arthur. *Christmas in July*
Ziefert, Harriet. *Clara Ann Cookie*
Zion, Gene. *No roses for Harry*

Clothing – aprons

Carle, Eric. *My apron*
McKissack, Patricia C. *Ma Dear's aprons*
Payne, Emmy. *Katy no-pocket*

Clothing – boots

Chessa, Francesca. *Holly's red boots*
DeFelice, Cynthia C. *Cold feet*
Dunrea, Olivier. *Ollie the stomper*
Havill, Juanita. *Jamaica and Brianna*
Huling, Jan. *Puss in cowboy boots*
Lewison, Wendy Cheyette. *So many boots*
London, Jonathan. *Puddles*
Lowell, Susan. *The bootmaker and the elves*
Millard, Glenda. *And red galoshes*
Mitchell, Marianne. *Joe Cinders*
Moran, Alex. *Boots for Beth*
Olson-Brown, Ellen. *Ooh la la polka-dot boots*
Perrault, Charles. *Puss in boots*, ill. by Steve Light
Puss in boots, ill. by Jerry Pinkney
Ray, Mary Lyn. *Red rubber boot day*
Wells, Rosemary. *Red boots*

Clothing – coats

David, Ryan. *The magic raincoat*
dePaola, Tomie. *Charlie needs a cloak*
Hest, Amy. *The purple coat*
Kassirer, Sue. *Joseph and his coat of many colors*
Lacome, Julie. *Ruthie's big old coat*
Milligan, Bryce. *Brigid's cloak*
Oram, Hiawyn. *The wrong overcoat*
Pulver, Robin. *Mrs. Toggle's zipper*
Taback, Simms. *Joseph had a little overcoat*
Wheeler, Lisa. *Jam and jelly by Holly and Nellie*
Woodruff, Elvira. *The memory coat*
Ziefert, Harriet. *A new coat for Anna*

Clothing – costumes

Biedrzycki, David. *Me and my dragon: scared of Halloween*
Billingsley, Franny. *Big bad bunny*
Bollinger, Peter. *Algernon Graeves is scary enough*
Chess, Victoria. *The costume party*
Christelow, Eileen. *Five little monkeys trick-or-treat*
Cousins, Lucy. *Maisy dresses up*
David, Lawrence. *Superhero Max*
deGroat, Diane. *Trick or treat, smell my feet*
Demas, Corinne. *Halloween surprise*
DiPucchio, Kelly. *Crafty Chloe: dress-up mess-up*
Ernst, Lisa Campbell. *Sylvia Jean, drama queen*
Flesher, Vivienne. *Alfred's nose*
Goodrich, Carter. *Zorro gets an outfit*
Grey, Mini. *Traction Man is here*
Hennessy, B. G. *Corduroy's Halloween*
Hort, Lenny. *We're going on a treasure hunt*
We're going on safari
Joosse, Barbara. *Dog parade*
Kovalski, Maryann. *Omar's Halloween*
Landry, Leo. *Trick or treat*
Lobel, Anita. *Lena's sleep sheep*
London, Jonathan. *Froggy's Halloween*
McCue, Lisa. *Corduroy's best Halloween ever!*
McDonald, Megan. *Ant and Honey Bee, what a pair!*
McGuirk, Leslie. *Tucker's spooky Halloween*
Mayer, Pamela. *The scariest monster in the whole wide world*

Neitzel, Shirley. *Who will I be?*
O'Connell, Jennifer. *It's Halloween night!*
Poydar, Nancy. *The perfectly horrible Halloween*
Rockwell, Anne. *Halloween Day*
Saltzberg, Barney. *The problem with pumpkins*
Soccer mom from outer space
Scheffler, Axel. *The scary monster*
Silvano, Wendi. *Turkey Claus*
Turkey trouble
Todd, Mark. *What will you be for Halloween?*
Winter, Jeanette. *Niño's mask*
Wojciechowski, Susan. *The best Halloween of all*
Wolff, Ferida. *On Halloween night*

Clothing – dresses

Ashburn, Boni. *I had a favorite dress*
Bertrand, Diane Gonzales. *Sofía and the purple dress / Sofía y el vestido morado*
Daly, Niki. *Jamela's dress*
Friedman, Laurie. *A style all her own*
Jenkins, Emily. *Daffodil*
Jocelyn, Marthe. *Hannah and the seven dresses*
McCormack, Caren McNelly. *The fiesta dress*
McDonald, Megan. *The Hinky Pink*
Masini, Beatrice. *Here comes the bride*
Munsch, Robert N. *Ribbon rescue*
Norwich, William D. *Molly and the magic dress*
Rim, Sujean. *Birdie's big-girl dress*
Schaefer, Carole Lexa. *The Bora-Bora dress*
Seymour, Dorothy Z. *Ann likes red*
Strauss, Linda Leopold. *The princess gown*
Yolen, Jane. *Come to the fairies' ball*
Ziefert, Harriet. *My forever dress*

Clothing – gloves, mittens

Johnson, G. Francis. *Has anybody lost a glove?*
Jonovitz, Marilyn. *Three little kittens*
Kellogg, Steven. *The mystery of the missing red mitten*
Mother Goose. *The three little kittens*
Pinkney, Jerry. *Three little kittens*
Plourde, Lynn. *A mountain of mittens*
Quattlebaum, Mary. *Winter friends*
Siomades, Lorianne. *Three little kittens*
Yoon, Salina. *Penguin in love*

Clothing – handbags, purses

Bogan, Paulette. *Momma's magical purse*
Dunbar, Polly. *Pretty Pru*
Finlay, Lizzie. *Little Croc's purse*
Hansen, P. *My granny's purse*
Henkes, Kevin. *Lilly's purple plastic purse*
McElmurry, Jill. *Mad about plaid*
Uchida, Yoshiko. *The magic purse*
Westcott, Nadine Bernard. *The lady with the alligator purse*

Clothing – hats

Blackaby, Susan. *Rembrandt's hat*
Brown, Ken. *The scarecrow's hat*
Brumbeau, Jeff. *Miss Hunnicutt's hat*
Butler, M. Christina. *One snowy night*
Chaconas, Dori. *Virginnie's hat*
D'Amico, Carmela. *Ella, the elegant elephant*
DeRubertis, Barbara. *Corky Cub's crazy caps*
Diakité, Baba Wagué. *The hatseller and the monkeys*
Dunrea, Olivier. *Peedie*
Fagan, Carl. *Mr. Zinger's hat*
Gorbachev, Valeri. *Whose hat is it?*
Grifalconi, Ann. *Tiny's hat*
Harley, Bill. *Lost and found*
Holm, Sharon Lane. *Zoe's hats*
Hoppe, Paul. *Hat*
Horowitz, Dave. *Buy my hats!*
Howard, Elizabeth Fitzgerald. *Aunt Flossie's hats (and crab cakes later)*
Johnson, D. B. *Magritte's marvelous hat*
Judge, Lita. *Red hat*
Katz, Karen. *Twelve hats for Lena*
Keats, Ezra Jack. *Jennie's hat*
Kimmel, Eric A. *Stormy's hat*
Klassen, Jon. *I want my hat back*
This is not my hat
Könnecke, Ole. *Anton can do magic*
Lamb, Albert. *Sam's winter hat*
Langdo, Bryan. *Tornado Slim and the magic cowboy hat*
Lear, Edward. *The Quangle Wangle's hat*
Lichtenheld, Tom. *Bridget's beret*
Low, Alice. *Aunt Lucy went to buy a hat*
Lowell, Susan. *Little Red Cowboy Hat*
Luthardt, Kevin. *Hats*
Meisel, Paul. *Zara's hats*
Melling, David. *Don't worry, Douglas!*
Miller, Margaret. *What's on my head?*
Whose hat?
Moore, Lilian. *While you were chasing a hat*
Morris, Ann. *Hats, hats, hats*
Numeroff, Laura Joffe. *Sherman Crunchley*
Pearson, Tracey Campbell. *The purple hat*
Reed, Lynn Rowe. *Pedro, his perro, and the alphabet sombrero*
Riddle, Tohby. *The singing hat*
Rumford, James. *Don't touch my hat!*
Sadler, Judy Ann. *Sandwiches for Duke*
Savage, Stephen. *Where's Walrus?*
Slingsby, Janet. *Hetty's 100 hats*
Slobodkina, Esphyr. *Caps for sale*
Circus caps for sale
Steig, William. *When everybody wore a hat*
Which would you rather be?
Stephens, Helen. *How to hide a lion*
Stoop, Naoko. *Red Knit Cap Girl*
Tafuri, Nancy. *Silly little goose!*
Turner-Denstaedt, Melanie. *The hat that wore Clara B.*
Van Laan, Nancy. *This is the hat*
Weninger, Brigitte. *The elf's hat*
Williams, Karen Lynn. *Tap-tap*
Winthrop, Elizabeth. *Halloween hats*
Ziefert, Harriet. *Grandma, it's for you!*
Hats off for the Fourth of July!

Clothing – kimonos

Uegaki, Chieri. *Suki's kimono*

Clothing – neckties

Cocca-Leffler, Maryann. *Mr. Tanen's ties rule!*

Clothing – pajamas

Brooks, Erik. *The practically perfect pajamas*
Graber, Janet. *Jacob and the polar bears*
Hayles, Marsha. *Pajamas anytime*
Jackson, Isaac. *Somebody's new pajamas*

Papineau, Lucie. *Lulu's pajamas*
Plourde, Lynn. *Pajama day*
Schwarz, Viviane. *Timothy and the strong pajamas*

Clothing – pants

Andreae, Giles. *Pants*
Crunk, Tony. *Grandpa's overalls*
Gassman, Julie. *Crabby pants*
Gilani-Williams, Fawzia. *Nabeel's new pants*
Good, Merle, et al. *Dan's pants*
Johnston, Tony. *Levi Strauss gets a bright idea*
Medearis, Angela Shelf. *Poppa's new pants*
Raschka, Chris. *Moosey Moose*
Rice, Eve. *Peter's pockets*

Clothing – pockets

Braybrooks, Ann. *Plenty of pockets*
Payne, Emmy. *Katy no-pocket*
Rice, Eve. *Peter's pockets*
Scanlon, Elizabeth Garton. *A sock is a pocket for your toes*

Clothing – scarves

Bunge, Daniela. *The scarves*
Feeney, Tatyana. *Little Owl's orange scarf*
Villeneuve, Anne. *The red scarf*
Wright, Dare. *A gift from the lonely doll*

Clothing – shirts

Spinelli, Eileen. *In my new yellow shirt*

Clothing – shoes

Barrett, Mary Brigid. *Shoebox Sam*
Bateman, Teresa. *Keeper of soles*
Beaumont, Karen. *Shoe-la-la!*
Blessing, Charlotte. *New old shoes*
Boelts, Maribeth. *Those shoes*
Browne, Anthony. *Willy the wizard*
Colato Laínez, René. *My shoes and I*
Daly, Niki. *Happy birthday, Jamela!*
Dornbusch, Erica. *Finding Kate's shoes*
Dunbar, Joyce. *Shoe baby*
Fitz-Gibbon, Sally. *Two shoes, blue shoes, new shoes!*
Fliess, Sue. *Shoes for me!*
Fullerton, Alma. *A good trade*
Glass, Eleri. *The red shoes*
Gormley, Greg. *Dog in boots*
Grimes, Nikki. *Shoe magic*
Hayles, Marsha. *Bunion Burt*
Heo, Yumi. *Father's rubber shoes*
Hines, Anna Grossnickle. *Whose shoes?*
Hoe, Susan. *Which shoes would you choose?*
Johnson, Angela. *Shoes like Miss Alice's*
Johnson, Marion. *Caillou, new shoes*
Light, Steve. *The shoemaker extraordinaire*
Lipp, Frederick. *Running shoes*
Litwin, Eric. *Pete the cat: I love my white shoes*
Pete the cat: rocking in my school shoes
Lodge, Bernard. *Shoe Shoe Baby*
Mader, C. Roger. *Lost cat*
Meunier, Brian. *Bravo, Tavo!*
Miller, Margaret. *Whose shoe?*
Morris, Ann. *Shoes, shoes, shoes*
Novak, Matt. *Flip flop bop*
Paul, Ann Whitford. *Hello toes! Hello feet!*
Pratt, Pierre. *Shopping*
Primavera, Elise. *Louise the big cheese and the la-di-da shoes*
Pulver, Robin. *Mrs. Toggle's beautiful blue shoe*
Rim, Sujean. *Birdie's big-girl shoes*
Rollings, Susan. *New shoes, red shoes*
Rosenthal, Betsy R. *Which shoes would you choose?*
Ross, Tony. *Centipede's 100 shoes*
Silverman, Erica. *There was a wee woman . . .*
Singer, Marilyn. *Shoe bop!*
Tallulah's toe shoes
Slater, Dashka. *Baby shoes*
Swinburne, Stephen R. *Whose shoes? a shoe for every job*
Thermes, Jennifer. *Sam Bennett's new shoes*
Tucker, Kathy. *The leprechaun in the basement*
Uff, Caroline. *Hello, Lulu*
Vigna, Judith. *Boot weather*
Winthrop, Elizabeth. *Shoes*
Young, Amy. *Belinda in Paris*

Clothing – socks

Bechtold, Lisze. *Sally and the purple socks*
Brandle, Bine. *Flusi, the sock monster*
Bunting, Eve. *Have you seen my new blue socks?*
Burks, James. *Beep and Bah*
Dormer, Frank W. *Socksquatch*
Dunbar, Joyce. *Where's my sock?*
Evans, Cambria. *Martha Moth makes socks*
Kinerk, Robert. *Timothy Cox will not change his socks*
Kohuth, Jane. *Duck sock hop*
Murphy, Stuart J. *A pair of socks*
Shea, Bob. *New socks*
Valckx, Catharina. *Lizette's green sock*

Clothing – suits

Rader, Laura. *Santa's new suit*

Clothing – sweaters

Birchall, Mark. *Rabbit's wooly sweater*
Campbell, K. G. *Lester's dreadful sweaters*
Jeffers, Oliver. *The Hueys in The new sweater*
Larsen, Andrew. *Bella and the bunny*
Olsen, Sylvia. *Yetsa's sweater*
Waterton, Betty. *A bumblebee sweater*

Clothing – underwear

Escoffier, Michaël. *Brief thief*
Freedman, Claire. *Dinosaurs love underpants*
Pirates love underpants
Piggy and Bear in their underwear
Sendelbach, Brian. *The underpants zoo*
Swain, Ruth Freeman. *Underwear*

Clowns, jesters

Baynton, Martin. *Jane and the dragon*
Campbell, K. G. *Lester's dreadful sweaters*
dePaola, Tomie. *Jingle, the Christmas clown*
Dodds, Dayle Ann. *Where's Pup?*
Fletcher, Ralph. *The circus surprise*
Fox, Christyan. *What color is that, PiggyWiggy?*
Harper, Jo. *Ollie Jolly, rodeo clown*
Hayes, Geoffrey. *Patrick at the circus*
Kotzwinkle, William. *Walter, the farting dog: trouble at the yard sale*

Laden, Nina. *Clowns on vacation*
Littlesugar, Amy. *Clown child*
Olofsson, Helena. *The little jester*
Rau, Dana Meachen. *Clown around*
Salley, Coleen. *Epossumondas*
Schreiber, Georges. *Bambino the clown*
Schubert, Leda. *Monsieur Marceau*
Thurber, James. *Many moons*, ill. by Marc Simont
Many moons, ill. by Louis Slobodkin

Clubs, gangs

Bateman, Teresa. *The Bully Blockers Club*
Berenstain, Stan and Jan. *The Berenstain bears no girls allowed*
Bourgeois, Paulette. *Franklin's secret club*
Bunting, Eve. *Riding the tiger*
Collicott, Sharleen. *Toestomper and the caterpillars*
Corey, Shana. *Here come the Girl Scouts!*
Ernst, Lisa Campbell. *Sylvia Jean, scout supreme*
Howe, James. *Horace and Morris but mostly Dolores*
McCourt, Lisa. *Chicken soup for little souls: The Goodness Gorillas*
Mahoney, Daniel J. *The perfect clubhouse*
Murphy, Stuart J. *Treasure map*
O'Connor, Jane. *Fancy Nancy: explorer extraordinaire!*
Powell, Alma. *America's promise*
San Souci, Daniel. *The Mighty Pigeon Club*
Shannon, George. *The Secret Chicken Club*
Singer, Marilyn. *Let's build a clubhouse*
Stohner, Anu. *Brave Charlotte and the wolves*

Clumsiness *see* Character traits – clumsiness

Cold *see* Concepts – cold & heat; Weather – cold

Collecting things *see* Behavior – collecting things

Communication

Acredolo, Linda P. *My first baby signs*
Allen, Kathryn Madeline. *A kiss means I love you*
Ancona, George. *Handtalk zoo*
Beeke, Tiphanie. *Roar like a lion!*
Charlip, Remy, et al. *Handtalk*
Cheng, Andrea. *Grandfather counts*
Cruise, Robin. *Bartleby speaks!*
de Lestrade, Agnès. *Phileas's fortune*
Dorros, Arthur. *Radio Man / Don Radio*
Ehrlich, Fred. *Does a seal smile?*
Felix, Monique. *The rumor*
Fisher, Leonard Everett. *Gutenberg*
Gibbons, Gail. *The post office book*
Puff — flash — bang!
Heelan, Jamee Riggio. *Can you hear a rainbow?*
Hoban, Tana. *I read signs*
I read symbols
Jenkins, Steve. *Slap, squeak, and scatter*
Leedy, Loreen. *The Furry News*
Meres, Jonathan. *The big bad rumor*
Milich, Zoran. *City signs*
Millman, Isaac. *Moses goes to a concert*
Moses goes to the circus
Mortimer, Rachael. *Song for a princess*
Pfeffer, Wendy. *Dolphin talk*
Potter, Beatrix. *Yours affectionately, Peter Rabbit*
Reynolds, Aaron. *Pirates vs. cowboys*
Seuss, Dr. *Gerald McBoing Boing*
Gerald McBoing Boing sound book
Sherman, Joanne. *Because it's my body*
Showers, Paul. *How you talk*
Van Woerkom, Dorothy. *Hidden messages*
Walton, Rick. *My two hands, my two feet*
Wells, Rosemary. *Letters and sounds*
Williams, Karen Lynn. *My name is Sangoel*

Communities, neighborhoods

Alda, Arlene. *Morning glory Monday*
Alko, Selina. *B is for Brooklyn*
Ancona, George. *Barrio*
Best, Cari. *When Catherine the Great and I were eight!*
Block party today
Bluemle, Elizabeth. *How do you wokka-wokka?*
Boelts, Maribeth. *Happy like soccer*
Bourgeois, Paulette. *Fire fighters*
Garbage collectors
Police officers
Postal workers
Brown, Marc. *Arthur's neighborhood*
Brown, Tameka Fryer. *Around our way on Neighbors' Day*
Bunting, Eve. *Smoky night*
Caseley, Judith. *On the town*
Chocolate, Deborah. *El barrio*
Christensen, Bonnie. *Plant a little seed*
Cole, Kenneth, Dr. *No bad news*
Cooper, Elisha. *A good night walk*
Cumpiano, Ina. *Quinito's neighborhood / El vecindario de Quinito*
De Anda, Diane. *The patchwork garden / pedacitos de huerto*
DiSalvo, DyAnne. *Grandpa's corner store*
Dooley, Norah. *Everybody brings noodles*
Eclare, Melanie. *A harvest of color*
Edwards, Nancy. *Glenna's seeds*
Flanagan, Alice K. *A busy day at Mr. Kang's grocery store*
Buying a pet from Ms. Chavez
Coach John and his soccer team
Here comes Mr. Eventoff with the mail!
Letter carriers
Mayors
Ms. Davison, our librarian
Ms. Murphy fights fires
Officer Brown keeps neighborhoods safe
Police officers
Riding the school bus with Mrs. Kramer
A visit to the Gravesens' farm
Forman, Ruth. *Young Cornrows callin out the moon*
Freeman, Don. *Corduroy's busy street and Corduroy goes to the doctor*
Fries, Claudia. *A pig is moving in*
Gal, Susan. *Day by day*
Garland, Sarah. *Eddie's toolbox and how to make and mend things*
Geras, Adèle. *The Cats of Cuckoo Square, Geejay the Hero*
Gibson, Karen Bush. *Child care workers*
Emergency medical technicians
Pharmacists
Truck drivers
Graham, Bob. *A bus called Heaven*
Greenfield, Eloise. *Night on Neighborhood Street*

Harshman, Marc. *Only one neighborhood*
Henkes, Kevin. *Good-bye, Curtis*
Heo, Yumi. *One afternoon*
Herrera, Juan Felipe. *Grandma and Me at the flea / Los meros meros remateros*
Hubbell, Patricia. *Sidewalk trip*
Hudes, Quiara Alegría. *Welcome to my neighborhood!*
Isadora, Rachel. *Over the green hills*
Say hello!
Yo, Jo!
Johnson, D. B. *Eddie's kingdom*
Johnson, G. Francis. *Has anybody lost a glove?*
Johnson, Paul Brett. *Mr. Persnickety and Cat Lady*
Johnston, Tony. *The cat with seven names*
Keats, Ezra Jack. *Pet show!*
Kittinger, Jo S. *The house on Dirty-Third Street*
Kraus, Robert. *Mouse in love*
Krensky, Stephen. *My teacher's secret life*
Lakin, Patricia. *Fat chance Thanksgiving*
Leedahl, Shelley A. *The bone talker*
Leedy, Loreen. *The Furry News*
Lewis, Rob. *Friends*
Liebman, Daniel. *I want to be a firefighter*
I want to be a police officer
Lord, Janet. *Albert the fix-it man*
Louie, Therese On. *Raymond's perfect present*
Lyon, George Ella. *You and me and home sweet home*
Machado, Ana Maria. *What a party!*
Manning, Maurie J. *Laundry day*
Marsalis, Wynton. *Squeak, rumble, whomp! Whomp! Whomp!*
Martin, Jacqueline Briggs. *Farmer Will Allen and the growing table*
Medearis, Angela Shelf. *Rum-a-tum-tum*
Modarressi, Mitra. *Yard sale*
Nielsen, Laura. *Mrs. Muddle's holidays*
Novak, Matt. *The Robobots*
Owen, Ann. *Taking your places*
Pedersen, Judy. *When night time comes near*
Pinkney, Brian. *The adventures of sparrowboy*
Pittman, Helena Clare. *The angel tree*
Powell, Alma. *America's promise*
Rockwell, Anne. *Backyard bear*
Rogers, Fred. *Moving*
Rose, Naomi C. *Tashi and the Tibetan flower cure*
Rosen, Michael. *A Thanksgiving wish*
Russo, Marisabina. *Mama talks too much*
SanAngelo, Ryan. *Eddie spaghetti*
Schubert, Leda. *Here comes Darrell*
Shewchuk, Pat. *In Lucia's neighborhood*
Sís, Peter. *Madlenka, soccer star*
Smalls-Hector, Irene. *Jonathan and his mommy*
Spinelli, Eileen. *Cold snap*
Somebody loves you, Mr. Hatch
Stevens, April. *Waking up Wendell*
Sutherland, Marc. *MacMurtrey's wall*
Tamar, Erika. *The garden of happiness*
Taulbert, Clifton L. *Little Cliff and the porch people*
Thayer, Jane. *Part-time dog*
Thomson, Sarah L. *Around the neighborhood*
Watson, Renée. *A place where hurricanes happen*
Wells, Rosemary. *McDuff goes to school*
Wong, Janet S. *The dumpster diver*
Wyeth, Sharon Dennis. *Something beautiful*
Yolen, Jane. *Raising Yoder's barn*

Competition *see* Contests; Sibling rivalry; Sports, Sportsmanship

Completing things *see* Character traits – completing things

Compromising *see* Character traits – compromising

Computers

Brown, Marc. *Arthur's computer disaster*
Carrick, Carol. *Patrick's dinosaurs on the Internet*
Collins, Suzanne. *When Charlie McButton lost power*
Gutch, Michael. *Sticky, sticky, stuck!*
Zuckerberg, Randi. *Dot*

Conceit *see* Character traits – conceit

Concepts

Adler, David A. *Perimeter, area, and volume*
Things that float and things that don't
Anno, Mitsumasa. *Anno's math games*
Anno's math games II
Anno's math games III
Berenstain, Stan and Jan. *Inside outside upside down*
Berry, Lynne. *What floats in a moat?*
Boutignon, Beatrice. *Not all animals are blue*
Boyd, Lizi. *Inside outside*
Brown, Margaret Wise. *Sailor boy jig*
Burningham, John. *First steps*
Carle, Eric. *My very first book of motion*
Cousins, Lucy. *Maisy's amazing big book of learning*
Crews, Donald. *Light*
We read
Dunn, Todd. *We go together*
Ehlert, Lois. *In my world*
Einhorn, Edward. *A very improbable story*
Fisher, Valorie. *Everything I need to know before I'm five*
Fleming, Denise. *The everything book*
The everything book [board book]
Goldstone, Bruce. *Great estimations*
That's a possibility!
Hammersmith, Craig. *Patterns*
Hays, Anna Jane. *Ready, set, preschool!*
Hoban, Tana. *All about where*
Black on white
Dots, spots, speckles, and stripes
Is it rough? Is it smooth? Is it shiny?
Look! Look! Look!
More, fewer, less
Over, under and through
White on black
Jenkins, Steve. *Biggest, strongest, fastest*
Jocelyn, Marthe. *Same same*
Johnson, Stephen T. *Alphabet city*
Jonas, Ann. *Reflections*
Killion, Bette. *Just think!*
Leedy, Loreen. *Seeing symmetry*
McCarthy, Mary. *A closer look*
McMillan, Bruce. *Dry or wet?*
One, two, one pair!
Sense suspense
Maloney, Peter. *One foot two feet*
Mamada, Mineko. *Which is round? which is bigger?*
Marzollo, Jean. *I love you*
May, Eleanor. *Albert's amazing snail*
Montanari, Eva. *The crocodile's true colors*

Murphy, Mary. *Quick Duck!*
Slow snail
Murphy, Stuart J. *The greatest gymnast of all*
Let's fly a kite
Missing mittens
Probably pistachio
Neuschwander, Cindy. *Pastry school in Paris*
Pelletier, David. *The graphic alphabet*
Pinto, Sara. *Apples and oranges*
Pipe, Jim. *What makes it swing?*
Rockwell, Anne. *What we like*
Rosenthal, Amy Krouse. *This plus that*
Ross, Michael Elsohn. *Earth cycles*
Rotner, Shelley. *Parts*
Scarry, Richard. *Richard Scarry's best first book ever!*
Schwartz, David M. *If you hopped like a frog*
Seuss, Dr. *Gerald McBoing Boing*
Gerald McBoing Boing sound book
Shannon, George. *Tomorrow's alphabet*
Sís, Peter. *Beach ball*
Spohn, Kate. *The wet dry book*
Swinburne, Stephen R. *What's a pair? What's a dozen?*
Tompert, Ann. *Just a little bit*
Walsh, Ellen Stoll. *Balancing act*
Wells, Rosemary. *How many? How much?*
Yektai, Niki. *Bears in pairs*

Concepts – change

McPhail, David. *Weezer changes the world*
Murphy, Mary. *Some things change*
Seeger, Laura Vaccaro. *First the egg*
Shea, Susan A. *Do you know which one will grow?*
Wagner, Anke. *Tim's big move!*

Concepts – cold & heat

Arnold, Caroline. *Too hot? too cold?*
Best, Cari. *When Catherine the Great and I were eight!*
Bynum, Janie. *Altoona up north*
Chambers, Catherine. *Heat wave*
Floyd, Madeleine. *Cold paws, warm heart*
Rau, Dana Meachen. *Chilly Charlie*
Schwartz, Roslyn. *The mole sisters and the cool breeze*
Taulbert, Clifton L. *Little Cliff and the cold place*

Concepts – color

Alda, Arlene. *Except the color grey*
Anderson, Brian. *The prince's new pet*
Austin, Mike. *Monsters love colors*
Averbeck, Jim. *In a blue room*
Baker, Alan. *White Rabbit's color book*
Barnes, Brynne. *Colors of me*
Barnett, Mac. *Extra yarn*
Barry, Frances. *Duckie's rainbow*
Bauer, Marion Dane. *One brown bunny*
Beautiful moments in the wild
Beck, Andrea. *Elliot's great big lift-the-flap book*
Benevelli, Alberto. *The colors of the chameleon*
Bilgrami, Shaheen. *Farmyard painting party*
Jungle art show
Black, Harley. *Amazing magic school*
Magic art class
Blackstone, Stella. *Bear's busy family*
Cleo's color book
Briggs, Raymond. *The snowman [a lift-the-flap board book]*
Brocket, Jane. *Ruby, violet, lime*
Brown, Margaret Wise. *My world of color*
Brown, Tameka Fryer. *My cold plum lemon pie bluesy mood*
Bryant, Megan E. *Colorasaurus*
Burningham, John. *First steps*
Carle, Eric. *The artist who painted a blue horse*
Hello, red fox
The mixed-up chameleon
My very first book of colors
Catalanotto, Peter. *Kitten red, yellow, blue*
Chichester Clark, Emma. *Eliza and the moonchild*
Chocolate, Deborah. *Kente colors*
Cottin, Menena. *The black book of colors*
Court, Rob. *Color*
Cousins, Lucy. *Maisy's colors*
Maisy's rainbow dream
Crowther, Robert. *Colors*
Daywalt, Drew. *The day the crayons quit*
Delessert, Etienne. *Full color*
dePaola, Tomie. *Marcos*
Dodd, Emma. *Dog's colorful day*
Doerrfeld, Cori. *Penny loves pink*
Dunbar, Polly. *Dog Blue*
Flyaway Katie
Edwards, Pamela Duncan. *Warthogs paint*
Ehlert, Lois. *Color farm*
Color zoo
Fish eyes
Emberley, Rebecca. *My colors / Mis colores*
Ericsson, Jennifer A. *A piece of chalk*
Feiffer, Kate. *Double pink*
Ficocelli, Elizabeth. *Kid tea*
Fleming, Denise. *Lunch*
Foley, Greg. *Purple Little Bird*
Fontes, Justine Korman. *Black meets White*
Fox, Christyan. *What color is that, PiggyWiggy?*
Freedman, Deborah. *Blue chicken*
Freymann, Saxton. *Food for thought*
Gibbs, Edward. *I spy on the farm*
I spy with my little eye
Godwin, Laura. *Little white dog*
Gold-Vukson, Marji E. *The colors of my Jewish Year*
Gonyea, Mark. *A book about color*
Gorbachev, Valeri. *Red red red*
Gravett, Emily. *Blue chameleon*
Orange pear apple bear
Gregory, Nan. *Pink*
Gunzi, Christiane. *Colors*
Harper, Charise Mericle. *Pink me up*
Harshman, Marc. *Red are the apples*
Hassett, John. *Father Sun, Mother Moon*
Heller, Ruth. *Color, color, color, color*
Henkes, Kevin. *Birds*
Hest, Amy. *The purple coat*
Hicks, Barbara Jean. *I like black and white*
Hill, Eric. *Spot looks at colors*
Hoban, Tana. *Colors everywhere*
Dots, spots, speckles, and stripes
Is it red? Is it yellow? Is it blue?
Of colors and things
Holm, Sharon Lane. *Zoe's hats*
Hopgood, Tim. *Wow! said the owl*
Horacek, Petr. *Butterfly butterfly*
Strawberries are red
What is black and white?
Horwood, Annie. *Butterfly, butterfly what colors do you see?*
Houblon, Marie. *A world of colors*
Hubbard, Patricia. *My crayons talk*

Inkpen, Mick. *Kipper's book of colors*
Iyengar, Malathi Michelle. *Tan to tamarind*
Jackson, Ellen. *The seven seas*
Jay, Alison. *Red green blue*
Jenkins, Steve. *Living color*
Jonas, Ann. *Color dance*
Kaiser, Ruth. *The smiley book of colors*
Kann, Victoria. *Pinkalicious*
Purplicious
Katz, Karen. *The colors of us*
Klausmeier, Jesse. *Open this little book*
Kumin, Maxine. *What color is Caesar?*
Lallemand, Orianne. *The wolf who wanted to change his color*
Larios, Julie. *Yellow elephant*
Leonard, Marcia. *Favorite colors*
Leslie, Amanda. *Do crocodiles moo?*
Lionni, Leo. *A color of his own*
Little blue and little yellow
Litwin, Eric. *Pete the cat: I love my white shoes*
Liu, Jae Soo. *Yellow umbrella*
Lobb, Janice. *Color and noise! Let's play with toys!*
Lobel, Anita. *Ten hungry rabbits*
Lottridge, Celia Barker. *One watermelon seed*
Luján, Jorge. *Colors! / ¡Colores!*
Macdonald, Maryann. *The pink party*
McGrath, Barbara Barbieri. *Kellogg's froot loops color fun book*
Teddy bear counting
McMillan, Bruce. *Growing colors*
Marcos, subcomandante. *The story of colors / La historia de los colores*
Martin, Bill, Jr. *Brown bear, brown bear, what do you see?*
Milich, Zoran. *City colors*
Miller, Margaret. *I love colors*
Munsch, Robert N. *Purple, green and yellow*
Neubecker, Robert. *Courage of the blue boy*
Norman, Kim. *I know a wee piggy*
Otoshi, Kathryn. *One*
Pantone
Park, Linda Sue. *What does Bunny see?*
Parr, Todd. *Black and white*
Patent, Dorothy Hinshaw. *Bold and bright, black-and-white animals*
Peek, Merle. *Mary wore her red dress and Henry wore his green sneakers*
Penn, Audrey. *A color game for Chester Raccoon*
Pinkney, Sandra L. *A rainbow all around me*
Pinkwater, Daniel. *Bear's Picture*
Portis, Antoinette. *A penguin story*
Porto, Tony. *Blue aliens*
Get red
Priceman, Marjorie. *It's me, Marva!*
Raschka, Chris. *Mysterious Thelonious*
Rau, Dana Meachen. *Lots of balloons*
Reasoner, Charles. *One blue fish*
Reed, Lynn Rowe. *Color chaos!*
Reynolds, Peter H. *Sky color*
Rickards, Lynne. *Pink!*
Robertson, Patrisha Grainger. *Cirque du Soleil*
Rosen, Michael. *How the animals got their colors*
Rotner, Shelley. *Shades of people*
Rubinger, Ami. *I dream of an elephant*
Rusch, Elizabeth. *A day with no crayons*
Ryan, Pam Muñoz. *The crayon counting book*
Salzano, Tammi. *One rainy day*
Seeger, Laura Vaccaro. *Green*
Lemons are not red
Selig, Josh. *Red & Yellow's noisy night*
Serfozo, Mary. *Who said red?*
Seymour, Dorothy Z. *Ann likes red*
Shannon, George. *White is for blueberry*
Shirotani, Hideo. *What color? / Qué color?*
Siddals, Mary McKenna. *Tell me a season*
Sidman, Joyce. *Red sings from treetops*
Simmons, Steven J. *Alice and Greta's color magic*
Siomades, Lorianne. *My box of color*
Slater, Dashka. *Baby shoes*
Smith, Danna. *Pirate nap*
Smythe, Theresa. *Chester's colorful Easter eggs*
Snyder, Carol. *We're painting*
Spafford, Suzy. *Witzy's colors*
Spier, Peter. *Oh, were they ever happy!*
Spinelli, Eileen. *In my new yellow shirt*
Staake, Bob. *My little color book*
Steggall, Susan. *Red car, red bus*
Strete, Craig Kee. *They thought they saw him*
Sweet, Melissa. *Carmine*
Swinburne, Stephen R. *Lots and lots of zebra stripes*
What color is nature?
Tafuri, Nancy. *Blue goose*
Thomas, Valerie. *Winnie the witch*
Trimble, Marcia. *Flower Green*
Tusa, Tricia. *Follow me*
Van Fleet, Matthew. *Fuzzy yellow ducklings*
One yellow lion
Spotted yellow frogs
Van Laan, Nancy. *Rainbow crow*
Walsh, Ellen Stoll. *Mouse magic*
Mouse paint
Watt, Mélanie. *Leon the chameleon*
Weeks, Sarah. *Counting Ovejas*
Wellington, Monica. *Colors for Zena*
Wiley, Thom. *One sheep, blue sheep*
Williams, Sue. *I went walking*
I went walking [board book]
Wilson, April. *April Wilson's magpie magic*
Winne, Joanne. *Blue in my world*
Green in my world
Red in my world
Wolff, Ashley. *Baby Bear sees blue*
Wood, Audrey. *The deep blue sea*
Wood, Jakki. *Moo moo, brown cow*
Yolen, Jane. *How do dinosaurs learn their colors?*
Young, Jessica. *My blue is happy*
Ziefert, Harriet. *Lunchtime for a purple snake*
Zolotow, Charlotte. *Mr. Rabbit and the lovely present*

Concepts – counting *see* Counting, numbers

Concepts – distance

Axelrod, Amy. *Pigs on the move*

Concepts – left & right

Barrett, Judi. *The marshmallow incident*
May, Eleanor. *Albert is not scared*
Murphy, Stuart J. *Left, right, Emma!*

Concepts – measurement

Aber, Linda Williams. *Carrie measures up!*
Adler, David A. *Perimeter, area, and volume*
Axelrod, Amy. *Pigs on the move*
DeRubertis, Barbara. *Lulu's lemonade*
Lionni, Leo. *Inch by inch*

Murphy, Stuart J. *Bigger, better, best*
Polly's pen pal
Myller, Rolf. *How big is a foot?*
Pelley, Kathleen T. *Magnus Maximus, a marvelous measurer*
Pinczes, Elinor J. *Inchworm and a half*
Schwartz, David M. *Ready! set! measure!*
Sweeney, Joan. *Me and the measure of things*
Me counting time

Concepts – motion

Dotlich, Rebecca Kai. *In the spin of things*
Ehrlich, Fred. *Does a giraffe drive?*
Jenkins, Steve. *Move!*
Lillegard, Dee. *Go! poetry in motion: poems*
Rau, Dana Meachen. *Rolling*
Seder, Rufus Butler. *Waddle!*
Waring, Geoff. *Oscar and the cricket*
Ziefert, Harriet. *Beach party!*

Concepts – opposites

Alda, Arlene. *Hello, good-bye*
Badescu, Ramona. *Pomelo's opposites*
Bernhard, Durga. *Earth, sky, wet, dry*
To and fro, fast and slow
Biggs, Brian. *Stop! go!*
Blackstone, Stella. *Octopus opposites*
You and me
Brooks, Erik. *Polar opposites*
Burningham, John. *First steps*
Chambers, Angela. *Follow that chicken!*
Child, Lauren. *Charlie and Lola's opposites*
Coat, Janik. *Hippopposites*
Cousins, Lucy. *Maisy big, Maisy small*
Crews, Nina. *A high, low, near, far, loud, quiet story*
Crowther, Robert. *Opposites*
Cumpiano, Ina. *Quinito, day and night / Quinito, dia y noche*
Davis, Nancy. *A garden of opposites*
Deegan, Kim. *My first book of opposites*
Emberley, Rebecca. *My opposites / Mis opuestos*
Falconer, Ian. *Olivia's opposites*
Fernandes, Eugenie. *Big week for little mouse*
Freymann, Saxton. *Food for thought*
Friedland, Katy. *Art museum opposites*
Guy, Ginger Foglesong. *Perros! perros! dogs! dogs!*
High, Linda Oatman. *Under New York*
Hill, Eric. *Spot looks at opposites*
Hills, Tad. *What's up, Duck?*
Hoban, Tana. *Exactly the opposite*
Horacek, Petr. *Animal opposites*
Hunter, Tom. *Build it up and knock it down*
Inkpen, Mick. *Kipper's book of opposites*
Intriago, Patricia. *Dot*
Krensky, Stephen. *I know a lot!*
Lewis, J. Patrick. *Big is big and little little*
MacDonald, Suse. *Circus opposites*
Milgrim, David. *My friend Lucky*
Miller, Margaret. *Big and little*
Minters, Frances. *Too big, too small, just right*
Reinhart, Matthew. *Animal poppposites*
Rueda, Claudia. *Is it big or is it little?*
Salzano, Tammi. *One windy day*
Seeger, Laura Vaccaro. *Black? White! Day? Night!*
Serfozo, Mary. *What's what?*
Siminovich, Lorena. *I like vegetables*
Staake, Bob. *My little opposites book*
Stevenson, James. *Fun, no fun*
Stickland, Paul. *Dinosaur roar!*
Swinburne, Stephen R. *What's opposite?*
Wagner, Karen. *A friend like Ed*
Wishinsky, Frieda. *What's up, bear?*
Yoon, Salina. *Opposnakes*
Ziefert, Harriet. *You and me: we're opposites*

Concepts – patterns

Beaton, Clare. *Daisy gets dressed*
Brocket, Jane. *Spotty, stripy, swirly*
Harris, Trudy. *Pattern bugs*
Pattern fish
Harvey, Jayne. *Busy bugs*
Holm, Sharon Lane. *Zoe's hats*
Kassirer, Sue. *What's next, Nina?*
McElmurry, Jill. *Mad about plaid*
Masini, Beatrice. *A brave little princess*
Olson, Nathan. *Animal patterns*
Stockdale, Susan. *Stripes of all types*
Swinburne, Stephen R. *Lots and lots of zebra stripes*

Concepts – perspective

Berry, Matt. *Up on Daddy's shoulders*
Hutchins, Pat. *Shrinking mouse*
Yolen, Jane. *All those secrets of the world*

Concepts – self *see* Self-concept

Concepts – shape

Axelrod, Amy. *Pigs on the ball*
Baker, Alan. *Brown Rabbit's shape book*
Baranski, Joan Sullivan. *Round is a pancake*
Basher, Simon. *Go! Go! Bobo*
Beck, Andrea. *Elliot's great big lift-the-flap book*
Berenstain, Stan and Jan. *Old hat, new hat*
Blackstone, Stella. *Bear in a square*
Ship shapes
Brocket, Jane. *Circles, stars, and squares*
Bryant, Megan E. *Shapeasaurus*
Carle, Eric. *Little cloud*
Little cloud [board book]
My very first book of shapes
Chavarría-Cháirez, Becky. *Magda's tortillas / Las tortillas de Magada*
Chernesky, Felicia Sanzari. *Pick a circle, gather squares*
Crews, Donald. *Ten black dots*
Crowther, Robert. *Shapes*
Demas, Corinne. *Valentine surprise*
Dotlich, Rebecca Kai. *What is a triangle?*
What is round?
What is square?
Ehlert, Lois. *Color farm*
Color zoo
Emberley, Ed. *The wing on a flea*
Emberley, Rebecca. *My shapes / Mis formas*
Falwell, Cathryn. *Shape capers*
Franco, Betsy. *Bees, snails, and peacock tails*
Frazier, Craig. *Lots of dots*
Freymann, Saxton. *Food for thought*
Friedman, Mel. *Kitten castle*
Godwin, Laura. *Little white dog*
Gravett, Emily. *Blue chameleon*
Orange pear apple bear
Gunzi, Christiane. *Shapes*

Hall, Michael. *My heart is like a zoo*
Perfect square
Henkes, Kevin. *The biggest boy*
Birds
Circle dogs
Hill, Eric. *Spot looks at shapes*
Hoban, Tana. *Circles, triangles, and squares*
Cubes, cones, cylinders and spheres
Dots, spots, speckles, and stripes
Is it red? Is it yellow? Is it blue?
Shapes, shapes, shapes
So many circles, so many squares
Spirals, curves, fanshapes and lines
Joyce, William. *Rolie Polie Olie*
Kassirer, Sue. *Math fair blues*
Le Neouanic, Lionel. *Little smudge*
Lionni, Leo. *Pezzettino*
Loth, Sebastian. *Clementine*
MacDonald, Suse. *Shape by shape*
McGrath, Barbara Barbieri. *Teddy bear counting*
MacKinnon, Debbie. *Eye spy shapes*
McMillan, Bruce. *Fire engine shapes*
Manceau, Edouard. *Windblown*
Metropolitan Museum of Art, NY. *Museum shapes*
Murphy, Stuart J. *Captain Invincible and the space shapes*
Circus shapes
Nagel, Karen. *Shapes that roll*
Onyefulu, Ifeoma. *A triangle for Adaora*
Pilegard, Virginia Walton. *The warlord's puzzle*
Poydar, Nancy. *Cool Ali*
Rau, Dana Meachen. *Rectangles*
Ray, Mary Lyn. *Stars*
Reisberg, Joanne A. *Zachary Zormer shape transformer*
Ribke, Simone T. *The shapes we eat*
Roslonek, Steve. *The shape song swingalong*
Schoonmaker, Elizabeth. *Square cat*
Serfozo, Mary. *There's a square*
Shaw, Charles Green. *It looked like spilt milk*
Sidman, Joyce. *Swirl by swirl*
Silverstein, Shel. *The missing piece*
Simon, Annette. *Robot zombie Frankenstein!*
Snyder, Carol. *We're painting*
Sperring, Mark. *The shape of my heart*
Tafuri, Nancy. *The brass ring*
Thong, Roseanne. *Round is a mooncake*
Round is a tortilla
Van Fleet, Matthew. *Fuzzy yellow ducklings*
Spotted yellow frogs
Walsh, Ellen Stoll. *Mouse shapes*
Weeks, Sarah. *Bite me, I'm a shape*
Wildsmith, Brian. *Brian Wildsmith 1 2 3*
Wilson, April. *April Wilson's magpie magic*
Ziefert, Harriet. *Squarehead*

Concepts – size

Ahlberg, Allan. *The snail house*
Alborough, Jez. *Tall*
Watch out! Big Bro's coming!
Alexander, Martha G. *Blackboard Bear*
Alter, Anna. *Estelle and Lucy*
Anderson, Laurie Halse. *The big cheese of Third Street*
Barnes, Laura T. *Teeny tiny Ernest*
Bechtold, Lisze. *Sally and the purple socks*
Bedford, David. *Big bears can!*
Berenstain, Stan and Jan. *Old hat, new hat*
Berger, Barbara. *Angels on a pin*
Blackstone, Stella. *Bear in a square*
Blades, Ann. *Too small*
Bogan, Paulette. *Lulu the big little chick*
Bogart, Jo Ellen. *Big and small, room for all*
The book of Pooh
Bridges, Margaret Park. *Am I big or little?*
Brown, Marcia. *Once a mouse . . .*
Brownlow, Mike. *Mickey Moonbeam*
Buehner, Caralyn. *Superdog, the heart of a hero*
Callahan, Sean. *Shannon and the world's tallest leprechaun*
Carlson, Nancy. *Think big!*
Choldenko, Gennifer. *How to make friends with a giant*
Clements, Andrew. *Big Al and Shrimpy*
Cuyler, Margery. *The biggest, best snowman*
Docherty, Thomas. *Big scary monster*
Dunbar, Joyce. *The very small*
Durant, Alan. *A dinosaur called Tiny*
Emmett, Jonathan. *Someone bigger*
Florian, Douglas. *A pig is big*
Garland, Michael. *Hooray José!*
Goodhart, Pippa. *Little Nelly's big book*
Gorbachev, Valeri. *Big Little Elephant*
Graves, Keith. *Chicken Big*
Grindley, Sally. *The giant postman*
Gunzi, Christiane. *Sizes*
Hall, Algy Craig. *Dino bites!*
Helmer, Marilyn. *Three teeny tiny tales*
Henkes, Kevin. *The biggest boy*
Birds
Hoban, Tana. *Is it larger? Is it smaller?*
Is it red? Is it yellow? Is it blue?
Spirals, curves, fanshapes and lines
Hosford, Kate. *Infinity and me*
Howe, James. *Brontorina*
Hutchins, Hazel. *Two so small*
Hutchins, Pat. *Shrinking mouse*
Titch
Jenkins, Emily. *Small medium large*
Jenkins, Steve. *Actual size*
Big and little
Prehistoric actual size
Jordan, Deloris. *Salt in his shoes*
Joyce, William. *Big time Olie*
George shrinks
Judge, Lita. *How big were dinosaurs?*
Kalan, Robert. *Blue sea*
Keller, Holly. *Jacob's tree*
Kirk, Daniel. *Bigger*
Kliphuis, Christine. *Robbie and Ronnie*
Klise, Kate. *Stand straight, Ella Kate*
Lepp, Bil. *The King of Little Things*
Lichtenheld, Tom. *Cloudette*
Long, Ethan. *Up, tall and high*
MacDonald, Ross. *Bad baby*
McEvoy, Anne. *Betsy B. Little*
McGrory, Anik. *Kidogo*
McGuirk, Leslie. *Snail boy*
Markle, Sandra. *Bats: biggest! littlest!*
Sharks: biggest! littlest!
Marks, Jennifer L. *Sorting by size*
Marx, Patricia. *Dot in Larryland*
Masurel, Claire. *Too big!*
Mayer, Mercer. *Just big enough*
Meddaugh, Susan. *Just Teenie*
Miller, Margaret. *Big and little*
Now I'm big

Most, Bernard. *How big were the dinosaurs?*
Mueller, Doris L. *Small One's adventure*
Murphy, Kelly. *The boll weevil ball*
Murphy, Stuart J. *Bigger, better, best*
Nickle, John. *The ant bully*
Nimmo, Jenny. *Esmeralda and the children next door*
Nolen, Jerdine. *Hewitt Anderson's great big life*
Norac, Carl. *My daddy is a giant*
O'Brien, Patrick. *Gigantic!*
Ohmura, Tomoko. *The long, long line*
O'Leary, Sara. *When you were small*
Packard, Edward. *Big numbers*
Parr, Todd. *Big and little*
Passen, Lisa. *Attack of the 50-foot teacher*
The incredible shrinking teacher
Peet, Bill. *Huge Harold*
Pinfold, Levi. *Black dog*
Poydar, Nancy. *Cool Ali*
Rand, Betseygail. *Big Bunny*
Rayner, Catherine. *Ernest, the moose who doesn't fit*
Rueda, Claudia. *Is it big or is it little?*
Russo, Marisabina. *A very big bunny*
Ruzzier, Sergio. *The little giant*
San Souci, Robert D. *Little Pierre*
Schotter, Roni. *When the Wizzy Foot goes walking*
Schwartz, David M. *How much is a million?*
Sherry, Kevin. *I'm the biggest thing in the ocean*
Tafuri, Nancy. *The brass ring*
Turner, Sandy. *Otto's trunk*
Van Leeuwen, Jean. *"Wait for me!" said Maggie McGee*
Vere, Ed. *Everyone's little*
Walton, Rick. *Bertie was a watchdog*
Wheeler, Lisa. *Turk and Runt*
Willems, Mo. *Big Frog can't fit in*
Wilson, April. *April Wilson's magpie magic*
Yaccarino, Dan. *So big*
Ziefert, Harriet. *Bigger than Daddy*
Zoehfeld, Kathleen Weidner. *Dinosaurs big and small*

Concepts – speed

Cartier, Wesley. *Marco's run*
Munro, Roxie. *Go! go! go!*
Munsch, Robert N. *Zoom*
Patricelli, Leslie. *Faster! Faster!*
Saunders, Dave. *So slow!*
Smee, Nicola. *Clip-clop*

Concepts – up & down

George, Kristine O'Connell. *Up!*
Harris, Trudy. *Up bear, down bear*
Hoban, Tana. *Look up, look down*
May, Eleanor. *Albert is not scared*
Redding, Sue. *Up above and down below*

Concepts – weight

Cobb, Vicki. *I fall down*
Schwartz, David M. *Ready! set! measure!*
Sweeney, Joan. *Me and the measure of things*

Confidence *see* Character traits – confidence

Conservation *see* Ecology

Contests

Aesop. *The contest between the Sun and the Wind*
Alexander, Kwame. *Acoustic Rooster and his barnyard band*
Alter, Anna. *Abigail spells*
Arnold, Tedd. *The twin princes*
Bailey, Linda. *Stanley's beauty contest*
Barton, Chris. *Shark vs. train*
Bateman, Teresa. *Paul Bunyan vs. Hals Halson*
Best, Cari. *Ava and the real Lucille*
Birtha, Becky. *Lucky beans*
Bond, Michael. *Paddington Bear and the Busy Bee Carnival*
Brett, Jan. *The Easter egg*
Bridwell, Norman. *Clifford the champion*
Callahan, Sean. *Shannon and the world's tallest leprechaun*
Calvert, Pam. *Princess Peepers picks a pet*
Caple, Kathy. *Worm gets a job*
Cartaya, Pablo. *Tina Cocolina*
Catalanotto, Peter. *Emily's art*
Clayton, Elaine. *A blue ribbon for Sugar*
Cole, Barbara Hancock. *Anna and Natalie*
Conahan, Carolyn. *The big wish*
Czekaj, Jef. *Hip and Hop, don't stop!*
Darrow, Sharon. *Old Thunder and Miss Raney*
Demas, Corinne. *Nina's waltz*
Dorros, Alex. *Número uno*
Dorros, Arthur. *Julio's magic*
Durango, Julia. *Pest fest*
Esbaum, Jill. *Stanza*
Frasier, Debra. *Spike*
Grigsby, Susan. *First peas to the table*
Heide, Iris van der. *A strange day*
Helmore, Jim. *Oh no, monster tomato!*
Kaner, Etta. *And the winner is . . .*
Khan, Rukhsana. *King for a day*
Kinney, Jessica. *The pig scramble*
Kroll, Steven. *Super-dragon*
Kulka, Joe. *My crocodile does not bite*
Leedy, Loreen. *The great graph contest*
London, Jonathan. *Froggy plays in the band*
McMullan, Kate. *I'm fast*
Mahoney, Daniel J. *A really good snowman*
Marshall, James. *The Cut-Ups carry on*
Mathers, Petra. *A cake for Herbie*
Munsch, Robert N. *More pies*
Neugebauer, Charise. *The real winner*
Olaleye, Isaac. *In the Rainfield*
Park, Frances. *The royal bee*
Polacco, Patricia. *Rotten Richie and the ultimate dare*
Quattlebaum, Mary. *Pirate vs. pirate*
Sparks fly high
Reynolds, Peter H. *Sydney's star*
Root, Phyllis. *Rosie's fiddle*
Rose, Deborah Lee. *The spelling bee before recess*
Rosen, Michael J. *Night of the pumpkinheads*
Ross, Tony. *I want to win!*
Sage, James. *Farmer Smart's fat cat*
Samuels, Barbara. *Aloha, Dolores*
Sauer, Tammi. *Chicken dance*
Shannon, George. *A very witchy spelling bee*
Shea, Bob. *Cheetah can't lose*
Shields, Carol Diggory. *The bugliest bug*
Spinelli, Eileen. *The best story*
Callie Cat, ice skater
Stower, Adam. *Two left feet*
Wallace, Nancy Elizabeth. *Recycle every day!*

Weaver, Tess. *Frederick Finch, loudmouth*
Weninger, Brigitte. *Davy, soccer star!*
White, Linda Arms. *Comes a wind*
Winters, Kay. *The teeny tiny ghost and the monster*
Wojciechowski, Susan. *A fine St. Patrick's Day*
Yamada, Utako. *The story of Cherry the pig*
Yamaguchi, Kristi. *It's a big world, little pig!*

Cooks *see* Careers – bakers; Careers – chefs, cooks

Cooperation *see* Character traits – cooperation

Counting, numbers

Adler, David A. *Fun with Roman numerals*
Millions, billions, and trillions
Money madness
Ainsworth, Kimberly. *Hootenanny!*
Alakija, Polly. *Catch that goat!*
Alda, Arlene. *Arlene Alda's 1 2 3*
Allen, Susan. *Used any numbers lately?*
Amann, Jürg. *Ten birds*
Animal 123
Anno, Mitsumasa. *Anno's counting book*
Anno's counting house
Anno's hat tricks
Anno's magic seeds
Anno's math games
Anno's math games II
Anno's math games III
Appelt, Kathi. *Bats on parade*
Rain dance
Arena, Jennifer. *100 snowmen*
Armstrong-Ellis, Carey. *Ten creepy monsters*
Arnold, Tedd. *Five ugly monsters*
Arnosky, Jim. *Mouse numbers and letters*
Ashburn, Boni. *Over at the castle*
Austin, Mike. *Countdown with Milo*
Axelrod, Amy. *Pigs in the pantry*
Pigs on the ball
Aylesworth, Jim. *The completed hickory dickory dock*
One crow
Bailey, Linda. *Goodnight, sweet pig*
Bair, Sheila. *Isabel's car wash*
Baker, Alan. *Gray Rabbit's one, two, three*
Little Rabbit's first number book
Baker, Keith. *1-2-3 peas*
Potato Joe
Bang, Molly. *Ten, nine, eight*
Barber, Patti. *First number book*
Barnett, Mac. *Count the monkeys*
Barry, Frances. *Duckie's ducklings*
Base, Graeme. *The water hole*
Bateman, Donna M. *Deep in the swamp*
Bates, Ivan. *Five little ducks*
Bauer, Marion Dane. *One brown bunny*
Beaton, Clare. *One moose, twenty mice*
One moose, twenty mice [board book]
Beaty, Andrea. *Hide and sheep*
Beaumont, Karen. *Doggone dogs!*
Beck, Andrea. *Elliot's great big lift-the-flap book*
Becker, John Leonard. *Seven little rabbits*
Beeler, Selby B. *How many Elephants?*
Benzwie, Teresa. *Numbers on the move*
Berenstain, Stan and Jan. *Bears on wheels*
The Berenstain bears' counting book
Berkes, Marianne. *Over in a river*
Over in Australia
Over in the Arctic
Over in the forest
Over in the jungle
Seashells by the seashore
Berry, Lynne. *Duck dunks*
Biggs, Brian. *123 beep beep beep!*
Billin-Frye, Paige. *One, two, buckle my shoe*
Birtha, Becky. *Lucky beans*
Blackstone, Stella. *Bear in a square*
Bear's birthday
Cleo's counting book
Blechman, Nicholas. *Night light*
Boldt, Mike. *123 versus ABC*
Bowen, Anne. *The great math tattle battle*
Bridwell, Norman. *Clifford counts bubbles*
Briggs, Raymond. *The snowman [a lift-the-flap board book]*
Brooks, Alan. *Frogs jump*
Brown, Margaret Wise. *Goodnight moon 123: a counting book*
Goodnight moon 123: a counting book [board book]
Browne, Anthony. *One gorilla: a counting book*
Browne, Eileen. *Handa's hen*
Bruce, Lisa. *Engines, engines*
Bruel, Nick. *Poor puppy*
Bryant, Megan E. *Countasaurus*
Burningham, John. *First steps*
Butler, John. *Bedtime in the jungle*
Ten in the den
While you were sleeping
Cabatingan, Erin. *Musk Ox counts*
Cabrera, Jane. *One, two, buckle my shoe*
Ten in the bed
Cameron, C. C. *One for me, one for you*
Capucilli, Alyssa Satin. *Mrs. McTats and her houseful of cats*
Carle, Eric. *My very first book of numbers*
1, 2, 3 to the zoo
The rooster who set out to see the world
Rooster's off to see the world
10 little rubber ducks
Carlson, Nancy. *Henry's 100 days of kindergarten*
Carlstrom, Nancy White. *Let's count it out, Jesse Bear*
Carter, David A. *One red dot*
Cave, Kathryn. *One child, one seed*
Chae, In Seon. *How do you count a dozen ducklings?*
Chall, Marsha Wilson. *One pup's up*
Chamberlin-Calamar, Pat. *Alaska's twelve days of summer*
Chichester Clark, Emma. *Little Miss Muffet counts to ten*
Child, Lauren. *Charlie and Lola's numbers*
Christelow, Eileen. *Five little monkeys go shopping*
Five little monkeys jumping on the bed
Five little monkeys sitting in a tree
Clements, Andrew. *A million dots*
Cline-Ransome, Lesa. *Quilt counting*
Coats, Lucy. *Neil's numberless world*
Cobb, Annie. *The long wait*
Cohn, Scotti. *One wolf howls*
Cotten, Cynthia. *At the edge of the woods*
Cousins, Lucy. *Count with Maisy*
Maisy's twinkly, crinkly counting book
Crews, Donald. *Bicycle race*
Ten black dots
Crimi, Carolyn. *Pugs in a Bug*
Cronin, Doreen. *Click, clack, splish, splash*

Crum, Shutta. *The bravest of the brave*
Curious George's 1 to 10 and back again
Cuyler, Margery. *Guinea pigs add up*
  100th day worries
Dahl, Michael. *Downhill fun*
  Eggs and legs
  Footprints in the snow
  From the garden
  Hands down
  Lots of ladybugs!
  On the launch pad
  One big building
  One checkered flag
  One giant splash
  Pie for piglets
  Starry arms
Dale, Penny. *Dinosaur dig!*
Daniels, Teri. *Math man*
Davies, Jacqueline. *Tricking the Tallyman*
Deegan, Kim. *My first book of numbers*
Degman, Lori. *1 zany zoo*
Delessert, Etienne. *Hungry for numbers*
Demarest, Chris L. *Smokejumpers one to ten*
Demi. *One grain of rice*
Denega, Danielle. *Numbers*
Denise, Anika. *Pigs love potatoes*
DeRubertis, Barbara. *Bobby Baboon's banana be-bop*
Dickinson, Rebecca. *Over in the Hollow*
DiTerlizzi, Tony. *G is for one gzonk!*
Dobbins, Jan. *Driving my tractor*
Dodd, Emma. *Dog's colorful day*
Donaldson, Julia. *One mole digging a hole*
  One Ted falls out of bed
Downing, Johnette. *Down in Louisiana*
Duckling
Duke, Kate. *One guinea pig is not enough*
  Twenty is too many
Dupasquier, Philippe. *1 2 3, follow me!*
Durango, Julia. *Cha-cha chimps*
Edwards, Pamela Duncan. *Roar*
  Warthogs in the kitchen
Ehlert, Lois. *Fish eyes*
Elliott, David. *One little chicken*
Ellwand, David. *Ten in the bed*
Elya, Susan Middleton. *Eight animals on the town*
Emberley, Rebecca. *My numbers / Mis números*
  Ten little beasties
Esham, Barbara. *Last to finish*
Evans, Lezlie. *Can you count ten toes?*
Falconer, Ian. *Olivia counts*
Falwell, Cathryn. *Christmas for 10*
  Feast for ten
  Turtle splash!
Faulkner, Keith. *Pop! went another balloon!*
Fearrington, Ann. *Who sees the lighthouse?*
Feelings, Muriel. *Moja means one*
Fisher, Aileen Lucia. *Know what I saw?*
Fisher, Doris. *My even day*
  One odd day
Fisher, Valorie. *Everything I need to know before I'm five*
  How high can a dinosaur count?
Five little pumpkins, ill. by Ben Mantle
  Five little pumpkins, ill. by Dan Yaccarino
Fleming, Candace. *Seven hungry babies*
  Who invited you?
Fleming, Denise. *Count!*
  The first day of winter
  Shout! Shout it out!
Formento, Alison. *These bees count!*
  These seas count!
  This tree counts!
  This tree, 1, 2, 3
Fox, Christyan. *Count to ten, PiggyWiggy!*
Fox, Mem. *Let's count goats!*
Franco, Betsy. *Birdsongs*
  Double play!
Freymann, Saxton. *Food for thought*
  One lonely seahorse
Fromental, Jean-Luc. *365 penguins*
Fry, Jenny. *Building numbers*
Gardiner, Lindsey. *Good night, Poppy and Max*
Garland, Michael. *How many mice?*
George, Bobby. *Montessori number work*
George, Kristine O'Connell. *The great frog race and other poems*
Gershator, Phillis. *Zoo day, olé!*
Geser, Gretchen. *One bright ring*
Gibbs, Edward. *I spy under the sea*
Giganti, Paul. *Each orange had eight slices*
  How many blue birds flew away?
  How many snails?
Gill, Shelley. *The big buck adventure*
Gillham, Bill. *How many sharks in the bath?*
Ginkel, Anne. *I've got an elephant*
Giogas, Valarie. *In my backyard*
Girnis, Margaret. *1, 2, 3 for you and me*
Glicksman, Caroline. *Eric the math bear*
Goldstone, Bruce. *Great estimations*
  That's a possibility!
Gollub, Matthew. *Ten oni drummers*
Gorbachev, Valeri. *Christopher counting*
  One rainy day
Gravett, Emily. *The rabbit problem*
Greenstein, Elaine. *Dreaming*
Grindley, Sally. *Where are my chicks?*
Grossman, Bill. *My little sister ate one hare*
Grossman, Virginia. *Ten little rabbits*
Gunzi, Christiane. *Numbers*
Guy, Ginger Foglesong. *Fiesta*
Hague, Kathleen. *Numbears*
  Ten little bears
Halfmann, Janet. *Eggs 1, 2, 3*
Halls, Kelly Milner. *I bought a baby chicken*
Harper, Charise Mericle. *Amy and Ivan*
Harrington, Tim. *This little piggy*
Harris, Trudy. *Jenny found a penny*
  100 days of school
  Tally cat keeps track
  Twenty hungry piggies
Harshman, Marc. *Only one neighborhood*
Harvey, Jayne. *Busy bugs*
Haskins, Jim. *Count your way through Afghanistan*
  Count your way through Africa
  Count your way through Brazil
  Count your way through Canada
  Count your way through China
  Count your way through France
  Count your way through Germany
  Count your way through Greece
  Count your way through India
  Count your way through Iran
  Count your way through Ireland
  Count your way through Israel
  Count your way through Italy
  Count your way through Japan
  Count your way through Korea
  Count your way through Mexico

Count your way through Russia
Count your way through the Arab world
Hawk, Fran. *Count down to fall*
Hawkins, Colin. *One, two, guess who?*
Hays, Anna Jane. *Kindergarten countdown*
Heiligman, Deborah. *The boy who loved math*
Helakoski, Leslie. *The smushy bus*
Hennessy, B. G. *Mr. Ouchy's first day*
One little, two little, three little pilgrims
Hill, Eric. *Spot counts from 1 to 10*
Hill, Susanna Leonard. *Can't sleep without sheep*
Hills, Tad. *Duck and Goose, 1, 2, 3*
Himmelman, John. *10 little hot dogs*
Hoban, Tana. *Count and see*
Let's count
More, fewer, less
26 letters and 99 cents
Hoberman, Mary Ann. *The looking book*
Hoffman, Don. *A counting book with Billy and Abigail*
Holub, Joan. *Apple countdown*
Pumpkin countdown
Zero the hero
Hooks, William H. *A dozen dizzy dogs*
Horacek, Petr. *One spotted giraffe*
When the moon smiled
Horton, Joan. *Math attack!*
Hosford, Kate. *Infinity and me*
Hruby, Emily. *Counting in the garden*
Hubbard, Patricia. *Trick or treat countdown*
Huck, Charlotte S. *A creepy countdown*
Hughes, Shirley. *Olly and me 1-2-3*
Hulme, Joy N. *Easter babies*
Hutchins, Pat. *1 hunter*
Ten red apples
Imai, Ayano. *The 108th sheep*
Inkpen, Mick. *Kipper's book of numbers*
Kipper's toybox
Isadora, Rachel. *123 pop!*
Jane, Pamela. *Little goblins ten*
Monster countdown
Jay, Alison. *1 2 3*
Jenkins, Emily. *Lemonade in winter*
Jocelyn, Marthe. *Ones and twos*
Johnson, Stephen T. *City by numbers*
Jonas, Ann. *Splash!*
Kassirer, Sue. *Math fair blues*
Katz, Karen. *Counting kisses*
Ten tiny babies
Ten tiny tickles
Keats, Ezra Jack. *One red sun*
Keller, Laurie. *Grandpa Gazillion's number yard*
Kellogg, Steven. *Give the dog a bone*
Kerr, Judith. *One night in the zoo*
Kimmelman, Leslie. *How do I love you?*
Kinch, Devon. *Pretty Penny makes ends meet*
Knick knack paddy whack
Koller, Jackie French. *One monkey too many*
Krebs, Laurie. *We all went on safari*
Kroll, Virginia L. *Equal shmequal*
Uno, dos, tres, posada!
Kunhardt, Katharine. *Let's count the puppies*
Laminack, Lester L. *Jake's 100th day of school*
Langstaff, John M. *Over in the meadow*
Larochelle, David. *1+1=5*
Lavis, Steve. *Cock-a-doodle-doo*
Law, Diane. *Come out and play: count around the world in five languages*
Lawler, Janet. *Ocean counting*
Ledwon, Peter. *Midnight math twelve terrific math games*
Lee, Huy Voun. *1, 2, 3 go!*
Lee, Mark. *20 big trucks in the middle of the street*
Leedy, Loreen. *Fraction action*
The great graph contest
Missing math
Mission — addition
2 x 2 = boo!
Lessac, Frané. *Island Counting 123*
Leuck, Laura. *One witch*
Levine, Arthur A. *Monday is one day*
Lewis, J. Patrick. *Arithme-tickle*
Lewison, Wendy Cheyette. *Two is for twins*
Lindbergh, Reeve. *Midnight farm*
Litwin, Eric. *Pete the cat and his four groovy buttons*
Ljungkvist, Laura. *Follow the line*
Lobel, Anita. *One lighthouse, one moon*
Ten hungry rabbits
Lodge, Bernard. *How scary*
London, Jonathan. *Count the ways, Little Brown Bear*
Long, Ethan. *One drowsy dragon*
Soup for one
The Wing Wing brothers carnival de math
The Wing Wing brothers math spectacular!
Lottridge, Celia Barker. *One watermelon seed*
Lynn, Sarah. *1-2-3 va-va-vroom!*
Lyon, George Ella. *Counting on the woods*
Maccarone, Grace. *Miss Lina's ballerinas*
MacDonald, Margaret Read. *A hen, a chick, and a string guitar*
How many donkeys?
MacDonald, Suse. *Fish, swish! splash, dash!*
Look whooo's counting
McElligott, Matthew. *Bean thirteen*
The lion's share
McFarland, Lyn Rossiter. *Mouse went out to get a snack*
McGinty, Alice B. *Ten little lambs*
McGrath, Barbara Barbieri. *Kellogg's froot loops counting fun book*
Teddy bear counting
McMillan, Bruce. *Counting wildflowers*
Eating fractions
Jelly beans for sale
One, two, one pair!
McMullan, Kate. *I'm dirty!*
McNamara, Margaret. *How many seeds in a pumpkin?*
McQuinn, Anna. *The sleep sheep*
Maestro, Betsy. *Dollars and cents for Harriet*
Maloney, Peter. *One foot two feet*
Manning, Maurie J. *The aunts go marching*
Mannis, Celeste Davidson. *One leaf rides the wind*
Mariconda, Barbara. *Sort it out!*
Marino, Gianna. *One too many*
Markel, Michelle. *Tyrannosaurus math*
Markes, Julie. *Sidewalk 1 2 3*
Markle, Sandra. *How many baby pandas?*
Martin, Bill, Jr. *Rock it, sock it, number line*
Ten little caterpillars
Marzollo, Jean. *Help me learn addition*
Help me learn numbers 0-20
Help me learn subtraction
I spy little numbers
Ten cats have hats
Ten little Christmas presents
May, Eleanor. *The mousier the merrier*

Mazzola, Frank. *Counting is for the birds*
Melmed, Laura Krauss. *This first Thanksgiving*
Melvin, Alice. *Counting birds*
Menotti, Andrea. *How many jelly beans?*
Merriam, Eve. *12 ways to get to 11*
Michelson, Richard. *Ten times better*
Milich, Zoran. *City 1 2 3*
Miller, Virginia. *Ten red apples*
Milord, Susan. *Happy 100th day!*
Miranda, Anne. *Monster math*
Vroom, chugga, vroom-vroom
Mitter, Matt. *1, 2, 3, counting rhymes*
Modesitt, Jeanne. *Oh, what a beautiful day!*
Moore, Elaine. *Roly-poly puppies*
Mora, Pat. *One, two, three / Uno, dos, tres*
Morales, Yuyi. *Just a minute: a trickster tale and counting book*
Morozumi, Atsuko. *One gorilla*
Moseley, Keith. *Where's the dinosaur?*
Moss, Lloyd. *Zin! zin! zin! A violin*
Moss, Marissa. *Knick knack paddywack*
Mother Goose. *Mother Goose numbers on the loose*
1, 2, buckle my shoe
Mullins, Patricia. *One horse waiting for me*
Murphy, Stuart J. *Animals on board*
Beep beep, vroom vroom!
The best bug parade
Betcha!
Bug dance
Captain Invincible and the space shapes
Dave's down-to-earth rock shop
Dinosaur deals
Earth Day — hooray!
Elevator magic
Every buddy counts
A fair bear share
Give me half!
The greatest gymnast of all
Henry the fourth
Jack the builder
Just enough carrots
Leaping lizards
Mall mania
Missing mittens
Monster musical chairs
More or less
100 days of cool
The penny pot
Ready, set, hop!
Same old horse
Seaweed soup
Sluggers' car wash
The sundae scoop
Too many kangaroo things to do!
Murray, Alison. *One two that's my shoe!*
Napoli, Donna Jo. *The wishing club*
Neuschwander, Cindy. *Amanda Bean's amazing dream*
Sir Cumference and all the king's tens
Newman, Lesléa. *Dogs, dogs, dogs*
Nickle, John. *Alphabet explosion!*
Nikola-Lisa, W. *Can you top that?*
One hole in the road
One, two, three Thanksgiving!
Noonan, Julia. *Mouse by mouse*
Norman, Kim. *Ten on the sled*
Numeroff, Laura Joffe. *Merry Christmas, Mouse!*
When sheep sleep
Ohmura, Tomoko. *The long, long line*
O'Keefe, Susan Heyboer. *One hungry monster*
Oldland, Nicholas. *Dinosaur countdown*
One, two, skip a few!
Orozco, Jose-Luis. *Rin, rin, rin / do, re, mi*
Otoshi, Kathryn. *One*
Zero
Over in the meadow
Oxley, Jennifer. *The chicken problem*
Packard, Edward. *Big numbers*
Paley, Joan. *One more river*
Pallotta, Jerry. *Ocean counting: odd numbers*
Twizzlers percentages book
Pamintuan, Macky. *Twelve haunted rooms of Halloween*
Paquette, Ammi-Joan. *Ghost in the house*
Parenteau, Shirley. *One frog sang*
Parker, Kim. *Counting in the garden*
Parker, Mary Jessie. *The deep, deep puddle*
Parker, Victoria. *Bearum scarum*
Paul, Ann Whitford. *Count on Culebra*
Peek, Merle. *Roll over!*
Pelley, Kathleen T. *Magnus Maximus, a marvelous measurer*
Perl, Erica S. *Ninety-three in my family*
Peters, Lisa Westberg. *Frankie works the night shift*
Philpot, Lorna. *Find Anthony Ant*
Pierce, Terry. *Counting your way*
Pilegard, Virginia Walton. *The warlord's beads*
Pinczes, Elinor J. *Inchworm and a half*
A remainder of one
Pistoia, Sara. *Counting*
Money
Pomerantz, Charlotte. *One duck, another duck*
Pomeroy, Diana. *One potato*
Potter, Beatrix. *Peter Rabbit's one two three*
Prelutsky, Jack. *Halloween countdown*
Wild witches' ball
Rader, Laura. *Tea for me, tea for you*
Rankin, Laura. *The handmade counting book*
Raschka, Chris. *Five for a little one*
Rayner, Catherine. *Abigail*
Reasoner, Charles. *One blue fish*
Reid, Margarette S. *Lots and lots of coins*
Reisberg, Joanne A. *Zachary Zormer shape transformer*
Reiser, Lynn. *Christmas counting*
Hardworking puppies
Reynolds, Aaron. *Superhero School*
Reynolds, Adrian. *Pete and Polo's farmyard adventure*
Ribke, Simone T. *The shapes we eat*
Rockwell, Anne. *100 school days*
Willy can count
Roop, Peter. *Down east in the ocean*
Root, Phyllis. *One duck stuck*
One duck stuck [board book]
Rose, Deborah Lee. *The twelve days of kindergarten*
The twelve days of springtime
The twelve days of winter
Rosen, Michael J. *Chanukah lights everywhere*
Rosenthal, Amy Krouse. *This plus that*
Wumbers
Roth, Carol. *Ten dirty pigs / Ten clean pigs*
Roth, Susan L. *Night-time numbers*
Rothstein, Gloria. *Sheep asleep*
Rubinger, Ami. *Dog number 1 dog number 10*
Rumford, James. *Nine animals and the well*
Rusackas, Francesca. *Daddy all day long*
Ryan, Pam Muñoz. *The crayon counting book*
Salzano, Tammi. *One little blueberry*

Saul, Carol P. *Barn cat*
Savage, Stephen. *Ten orange pumpkins*
Schaefer, Lola M. *Homes 123*
Lifetime
Schafer, Kevin. *Penguins 1 2 3*
Schertle, Alice. *Goodnight, Hattie, my dearie, my dove*
Schnur, Steven. *Night lights*
Schroeder, Lisa. *Baby can't sleep*
Schulman, Janet. *Countdown to spring*
10 Easter egg hunters
10 trick-or-treaters
10 Valentine friends
Schumaker, Ward. *In my garden*
Schwartz, David M. *How much is a million?*
If you hopped like a frog
Ready! set! measure!
Scotton, Rob. *Russell the sheep*
Sebe, Masayuki. *Let's count to 100!*
100 animals on parade!
Seeger, Laura Vaccaro. *One boy*
Sendak, Maurice. *One was Johnny*
Seven little monsters
Serfozo, Mary. *Who wants one?*
Seven spunky monkeys
Shahan, Sherry. *Cool cats counting*
Sharmat, Marjorie Weinman. *The 329th friend*
Shields, Carol Diggory. *Wombat walkabout*
Sierra, Judy. *Counting crocodiles*
Silvano, Wendi. *Counting coconuts / Contando cocos*
Silverman, Erica. *The Halloween house*
Siminovich, Lorena. *I like bugs*
Singer, Marilyn. *City lullaby*
Quiet night
Singleton, Debbie. *The king who wouldn't sleep*
Sís, Peter. *Fire truck*
Waving
Siy, Alexandra. *One tractor*
Skinner, Daphne. *Albert keeps score*
Henry keeps score
The right place for Albert
Tightwad Tod
Slade, Suzanne. *What's new at the zoo? an animal adding adventure*
What's the difference?
Slate, Joseph. *Miss Bindergarten celebrates the 100th day of kindergarten*
Slingsby, Janet. *Hetty's 100 hats*
Smith, David J. *If America were a village*
Smith, Maggie. *Counting our way to Maine*
Dear Daisy, get well soon
One naked baby
Souders, Taryn. *Whole-y cow!*
Spanyol, Jessica. *Carlo likes counting*
Sper, Emily. *Hanukkah: a counting book in English, Hebrew, and Yiddish*
Spinelli, Eileen. *Miss Fox's class earns a field trip*
Together at Christmas
Spurr, Elizabeth. *Two bears beneath the stairs*
Staake, Bob. *My little 1 2 3 book*
Stevens, April. *Waking up Wendell*
Stickland, Paul. *A number of dinosaurs*
Ten terrible dinosaurs
Stiegemeyer, Julie. *Gobble gobble crash!*
Seven little bunnies
Stills, Caroline. *The house of 12 bunnies*
Sturges, Philemon. *Ten flashing fireflies*
Sturgis, Brenda Reeves. *10 turkeys in the road*
Surplice, Holly. *Guinea pig party*
Swinburne, Stephen R. *Water for one, water for everyone*
What's a pair? What's a dozen?
Sykes, Julie. *Dora's chicks*
Szekeres, Cyndy. *Cyndy Szekeres' learn to count, funny bunnies*
I can count 100 bunnies, and so can you!
Tafuri, Nancy. *The big storm*
Counting to Christmas
Who's counting?
Tang, Greg. *Math appeal*
Math fables
Math fables too
Thayer, Tanya. *Counting money*
Thompson, Lauren. *How many cats?*
Little Quack
Little Quack [board book]
Little Quack: dial-a-duck
Little Quack's hide and seek
Little Quack's hide and seek [board book]
One riddle, one answer
Thomson, Sarah L. *Around the neighborhood*
Todd, Mark. *Start your engines*
Toft, Kim Michelle. *One less fish*
Trapani, Iza. *Haunted party*
Tudor, Tasha. *1 is one*
Two little eyes and other action rhymes
Van Fleet, Matthew. *One yellow lion*
Van Laan, Nancy. *Mama rocks, Papa sings*
A tree for me
Van Lieshout, Maria. *Flight 1-2-3*
Van Woerkom, Dorothy. *Abu Ali counts his donkeys*
Vega, Denise. *Build a burrito*
Verdick, Elizabeth. *Peep leap*
Voce, Louise. *Over in the meadow*
Waber, Bernard. *Lyle walks the dogs*
Wadsworth, Ginger. *One tiger growls*
Wahman, Joe. *Snowboy 1, 2, 3*
Wallace, Nancy Elizabeth. *Count down to clean up*
Planting seeds
Ready, set, 100th day!
Walsh, Ellen Stoll. *Mouse count*
Walton, Rick. *One more bunny*
So many bunnies
Ward, Jennifer. *Over in the garden*
Somewhere in the ocean
Way up in the Arctic
Weeks, Sarah. *Counting Ovejas*
Wells, Rosemary. *Emily's first 100 days of school*
How many? How much?
Max counts his chickens
Max's toys
Weston, Carrie. *If a chicken stayed for supper*
Whitehouse, Patricia. *Seasons 1 2 3*
What's awake? 1 2 3
Wildsmith, Brian. *Brian Wildsmith 1 2 3*
Wiley, Thom. *One sheep, blue sheep*
Williams, Brenda. *The real princess*
Williams, Rozanne Lanczak. *The coin counting book*
Williams, Sue. *Dinnertime*
Let's go visiting
Williams, Suzanne. *Old MacDonald in the city*
Ten naughty little monkeys
Wilson, Anna. *Over in the grasslands*
Wojtowycz, David. *Animal antics from 1 to 10*
Wolff, Ashley. *Baby Bear counts one*
Wolff, Ferida. *On Halloween night*
Wong, Janet S. *Hide and seek*
Wood, Audrey. *Ten little fish*

Wood, Jakki. *Moo moo, brown cow*
Yates, Louise. *Dog loves counting*
Yates, Philip. *Ten little mummies*
Yektai, Niki. *Bears at the beach*
Yolen, Jane. *How do dinosaurs count to ten?*
Young, Cybèle. *Ten birds*
Ten birds meet a monster
Ziefert, Harriet. *Counting chickens*
A dozen ducklings lost and found
Knick-knack paddywhack
Rockheads
Two little witches
You can't buy a dinosaur with a dime
Zuffi, Stefano. *Art 123*

Countries, foreign *see* Foreign lands

Country

Aesop. *The country mouse and the city mouse*
Milly and Tilly
The town mouse and the country mouse, ill. by Lorinda Bryan Cauley
The town mouse and the country mouse, ill. by Janet Stevens
The town mouse and the country mouse: an Aesop fable, ill. by Helen Ward
The town mouse and the country mouse: an Aesop fable, ill. by Bernadette Watts
Town mouse, country mouse, ill. by Jan Brett
Town mouse, country mouse, ill. by Carol Jones
Bernhard, Durga. *To and fro, fast and slow*
Brooks, Nigel. *Country mouse cottage*
Burton, Virginia Lee. *The little house*
Carlstrom, Nancy White. *The snow speaks*
Cecka, Melanie. *Violet goes to the country*
Chall, Marsha Wilson. *Prairie train*
Cline-Ransome, Lesa. *Quilt alphabet*
Quilt counting
Cummins, Julie. *Country kid, city kid*
Dahlie, Elizabeth. *Bernelly and Harriet*
Davies, Jacqueline. *The night is singing*
Dennard, Deborah. *Hedgehog haven*
Dorros, Arthur. *City chicken*
Gibbons, Gail. *County fair*
Gray, Rita. *Nonna's porch*
Hesse, Karen. *Spuds*
Hoffman, Elizabeth Stokes. *Miss Renée's mice go to an exhibition*
Jocelyn, Marthe. *Mayfly*
Johnson, Angela. *Down the winding road*
Kilby, Don. *In the country*
Lawrence, Mary. *What's that sound?*
Lewin, Ted. *Fair!*
Lewis, Kim. *One summer day*
Loomis, Christine. *Cowboy bunnies*
MacLachlan, Patricia. *All the places to love*
Martin, Bill, Jr. *Barn dance!*
Miller, William. *Jenny and the peddler*
Mollel, Tololwa M. *Ananse's feast*
Munro, Roxie. *The inside-outside book of Texas*
Mazescapes
Parks, Carmen. *Farmers market*
Polacco, Patricia. *Meteor!*
Provensen, Alice. *Town and country*
Rockwell, Anne. *Willy can count*
Rylant, Cynthia. *Appalachia*
Christmas in the country
Night in the country
Scarecrow
Schertle, Alice. *Down the road*
Southwell, Jandelyn. *The little country town*
Tucker, Kathy. *Do cowboys ride bikes?*
Van Allsburg, Chris. *The stranger*
Wyeth, Sharon Dennis. *Always my dad*
Yolen, Jane. *Letting Swift River go*
Zullo, Germano. *Line 135*

Courage *see* Character traits – bravery

Cowboys, cowgirls

Anglund, Joan Walsh. *The brave cowboy*
The cowboy's Christmas
Appelt, Kathi. *Cowboy dreams*
Balcziak, Bill. *Pecos Bill*
Bell, Cece. *Sock Monkey rides again*
Brownlow, Mike. *Way out West — with a baby!*
Bruins, David. *The call of the cowboy*
Cowley, Joy. *Where horses run free*
Danneberg, Julie. *Cowboy Slim*
Elya, Susan Middleton. *Cowboy Jose*
Fleming, Denise. *Buster goes to Cowboy Camp*
Frank, John. *The toughest cowboy, Or, How the Wild West was tamed*
Gibbons, Gail. *Yippee-yay!*
The gingerbread boy. *The Gingerbread Cowboy*
Greathouse, Carol. *The dinosaur tamer*
Gulbis, Stephen. *Cowgirl Rosie and her five baby bison*
Harper, Jo. *Ollie Jolly, rodeo clown*
High, Linda Oatman. *Tenth Avenue cowboy*
Hill, Eric. *Spot goes to a party*
Holub, Joan. *Cinderdog and the wicked stepcat*
Janni, Rebecca. *Every cowgirl goes to school*
Every cowgirl loves a rodeo
Every cowgirl needs a horse
Every cowgirl needs dancing boots
Johnston, Tony. *The cowboy and the black-eyed pea*
Kellogg, Steven. *Pecos Bill*
Ketteman, Helen. *Bubba the cowboy prince*
Kimmel, Eric A. *Little Britches and the rattlers*
Knowlton, Laurie Lazzaro. *Why cowgirls are such sweet talkers*
Langdo, Bryan. *Tornado Slim and the magic cowboy hat*
Lawson, Dorie McCullough. *Tex*
Lawson, Julie. *Arizona Charlie and the Klondike Kid*
Lester, Julius. *Black cowboy, wild horses*
Liebman, Daniel. *I want to be a cowboy*
Loomis, Christine. *Cowboy bunnies*
Lowell, Susan. *The bootmaker and the elves*
McClements, George. *Ridin' dinos with Buck Bronco*
Maidment, Stella. *Cowboy puzzles*
Miller, Heather. *Cowboy*
Mitchell, Marianne. *Joe Cinders*
Montijo, Rhode. *The Halloween Kid*
Mortensen, Lori. *Cowpoke Clyde and Dirty Dawg*
Moser, Lisa. *Cowboy Boyd and Mighty Calliope*
Munro, Roxie. *The inside-outside book of Texas*
Pinkney, Andrea Davis. *Bill Pickett, rodeo ridin' cowboy*
Rash, Andy. *Are you a horse?*
Reynolds, Aaron. *Pirates vs. cowboys*
Roberts, Bethany. *Birthday mice*
Rounds, Glen. *Cowboys*

Rubel, Nicole. *A cowboy named Ernestine*
Sanders, Rob. *Cowboy Christmas*
Sauer, Tammi. *Cowboy camp*
Schanzer, Rosalyn. *The Old Chisholm Trail*
Schnitzler, Pattie L. *Widdermaker*
Scieszka, Jon. *Cowboy and Octopus*
Smith, Janice Lee. *Jess and the stinky cowboys*
Stein, David Ezra. *Cowboy Ned and Andy*
Ned's new friend
Stutson, Caroline. *Cowpokes*
Thomas, Jan. *Let's sing a lullaby with the Brave Cowboy*
Tibo, Gilles. *The cowboy kid*
Tucker, Kathy. *Do cowboys ride bikes?*
Wheeler, Lisa. *Sixteen cows*
Winter, Jeanette. *Cowboy Charlie*
Wood, Audrey. *A cowboy Christmas*

Cows *see* Animals – bulls, cows

Crafts *see* Activities – making things

Creation

Alexander, Cecil Frances. *All creatures great and small*
All things bright and beautiful, ill. by Ashley Bryan
All things bright and beautiful, ill. by Anna Vojtech
All things bright and beautiful, ill. by Bruce Whatley
Anaya, Rudolfo A. *Roadrunner's dance*
Bible. Old Testament. Genesis. *Genesis*
The Genesis of it all
Boroson, Martin. *Becoming me*
Brown, Kerry. *Tupag the dreamer*
Cohen, Deborah Bodin. *The seventh day*
dePaola, Tomie. *Let the whole earth sing praise*
Downey, Lynn. *This is the earth that God made*
Fisher, Leonard Everett. *The seven days of creation*
Goble, Paul. *The great race of the birds and animals*
Remaking the earth
Goodings, Christina. *Creation story*
Greene, Rhonda Gowler. *The beautiful world that God made*
Grimes, Nikki. *At break of day*
Haley, Gail E. *Two bad boys*
Hansen, Felicity. *The first bear*
Hofmeyr, Dianne. *The star-bearer*
Jaffe, Nina. *The golden flower*
Johnson, James Weldon. *The Creation*
King, Thomas. *Coyote sings to the moon*
Lester, Julius. *What a truly cool world*
Lewis, Jacqueline Janette. *You are so wonderful*
Lindbergh, Reeve. *The circle of days*
Pia Toya
Poole, Amy Lowry. *How the rooster got his crown*
Rodanas, Kristina. *Follow the stars*
Rohmer, Harriet. *How we came to the fifth world*
Root, Phyllis. *Big Momma makes the world*
Rosen, Michael J. *The dog who walked with God*
Slate, Joseph. *Story time for Little Porcupine*
Strauss, Susan. *When woman became the sea*
Van Kampen, Vlasta. *Bear tales*
Van Laan, Nancy. *Rainbow crow*
Wolkstein, Diane. *Sun Mother wakes the world*
Wood, Audrey. *The rainbow bridge*
Wood, Nancy C. *Mr. and Mrs. God in the creation kitchen*
Ziefert, Harriet. *First He made the sun*

Creatures *see* Monsters; Mythical creatures

Creeks *see* Rivers

Crime

Ada, Alma Flor. *The gold coin*
Agee, Jon. *My rhinoceros*
Ahlberg, Janet. *It was a dark and stormy night*
Auch, Mary Jane. *Eggs mark the spot*
Balouch, Kristen. *The king and the three thieves*
Barracca, Debra. *Maxi, the hero*
Base, Graeme. *The Jewel Fish of Karnak*
Biedrzycki, David. *Ace Lacewing, Bug Detective*
Burdett, Lois. *Hamlet for kids*
Macbeth for kids
Casanova, Mary. *The day Dirk Yeller came to town*
Crummel, Susan Stevens. *Sherlock Bones and the missing cheese*
Dahl, Roald. *The giraffe and the pelly and me*
Davies, Matt. *Ben rides on*
Delessert, Etienne. *Alert!*
Derby, Sally. *Two fools and a horse*
DiFiori, Lawrence. *Jackie and the Shadow Snatcher*
Docherty, Helen. *The Snatchabook*
Donaldson, Julia. *The Highway Rat*
Douglas, Erin. *Get that pest!*
Durant, Alan. *Big Bad Bunny*
Egan, Tim. *The trial of Cardigan Jones*
Escoffier, Michaël. *Brief thief*
Flanagan, Alice K. *A day in court with Mrs. Trinh*
Officer Brown keeps neighborhoods safe
Police officers
Geisert, Arthur. *Mystery*
Nursery crimes
Pigaroons
Glicksman, Caroline. *Eric the math bear*
Goode, Diane. *Tiger trouble*
Grey, Mini. *The adventures of the dish and the spoon*
Grimm, Jacob and Wilhelm. *The Bremen town band*
The Bremen town musicians, ill. by Bill Dickson
The Bremen town musicians, ill. by Ilse Plume
The Bremen town musicians, ill. by Bernadette Watts
The Bremen town musicians, ill. by Lisbeth Zwerger
Musicians of Bremen
Musicians of Bremen / Los musicos de Bremner
Hoffman, Eric. *Play Lady / La Señora Juguetona*
Hogrogian, Nonny. *The contest*
Huling, Jan. *Ol' Bloo's boogie-woogie band and blues ensemble*
James, Brian. *The Supertwins and tooth trouble*
Jordan, Sandra. *Mr. and Mrs. Portly and their little dog Snack*
Klassen, Jon. *This is not my hat*
Knapp, Ruthie. *Who stole Mona Lisa?*
Kotzwinkle, William. *Walter, the farting dog: trouble at the yard sale*
Krall, Dan. *The great lollipop caper*
Lane, Adam J. B. *Stop thief!*
Lawson, Julie. *Arizona Charlie and the Klondike Kid*
McCully, Emily Arnold. *An outlaw Thanksgiving*

McPhail, David. *Moony B. Finch, fastest draw in the West*
Madonna. *Yakov and the seven thieves*
Magoon, Scott. *The boy who cried bigfoot!*
Marciano, John Bemelmans. *Madeline and the cats of Rome*
Mead, Alice. *Billy and Emma*
Moss, P. Buckley. *Reuben and the quilt*
Poffenberger, Nancy M. *September 11, 2001*
Price, Kathy. *The Bourbon Street musicians*
Rock, Brian. *The deductive detective*
Rubin, Adam. *Secret pizza party*
SanAngelo, Ryan. *Eddie spaghetti*
Sazaklis, John. *Fowl play*
Schneider, Howie. *Fast 'n Snappy*
Skolsky, Mindy Warshaw. *Hannah and the whistling tea kettle*
Slobodkina, Esphyr. *Circus caps for sale*
Sneed, Brad. *Deputy Harvey and the ant cow caper*
Stephens, Helen. *How to hide a lion*
Ungerer, Tomi. *The three robbers*
Van Nutt, Julia. *The monster in the shadows*
Walton, Rick. *Bertie was a watchdog*
Weigelt, Udo. *It wasn't me*
Wisniewski, David. *Sumo Mouse*
Yee, Wong Herbert. *Detective Small in the amazing banana caper*
The Officers' Ball

Crippled *see* Disabilities – physical Disabilities

Crocodiles *see* Reptiles – alligators, crocodiles

Cruelty to animals *see* Character traits – kindness to animals

Crustaceans

Himmelman, John. *A pill bug's life*
Tokuda, Yukihisa. *I'm a pill bug*

Crustaceans – centipedes, millipedes

Greenaway, Theresa. *Centipedes and millipedes*
Ross, Tony. *Centipede's 100 shoes*

Crustaceans – crabs

Boyce, Katie. *Hector the hermit crab*
Carle, Eric. *A house for Hermit Crab*
Galloway, Ruth. *Clumsy crab*
Horowitz, Ruth. *Crab moon*
Kalan, Robert. *Moving day*
McDonald, Megan. *Is this a house for Hermit Crab?*
Mason, Janeen I. *Ocean commotion*
Nelson, Robin. *Pet hermit crab*
Peet, Bill. *Kermit the hermit*
Riddell, Chris. *Platypus*
Tafuri, Nancy. *Follow me!*
Walsh, Ellen Stoll. *Hamsters to the rescue*
Ward, Helen. *Old shell, new shell*

Crustaceans – lobsters

Schwarz, Viviane. *Shark and Lobster's amazing undersea adventure*

Crustaceans – shrimp

McGaw, Wayne T. *T-boy of the bayou*

Crying *see* Emotions

Cumulative tales

Aardema, Verna. *Bringing the rain to Kapiti Plain*
The riddle of the drum
Ada, Alma Flor. *The Christmas tree / El arbol de Navidad*
The gold coin
The rooster who went to his uncle's wedding
Alexander, Lloyd. *Fortune tellers*
Alger, Leclaire Gowans. *Always room for one more*
Arnold, Tedd. *No more water in the tub!*
Asbjørnsen, P. C. *The three billy goats Gruff*, ill. by Paul Galdone
The three billy goats Gruff, ill. by Glen Rounds
The three billy goats Gruff, ill. by Janet Stevens
Aston, Dianna Hutts. *Loony Little*
Azore, Barbara. *Wanda and the wild hair*
Baker, Alan. *Black and White Rabbit's ABC*
Baker, Ken. *Old MacDonald had a dragon*
Barton, Byron. *Buzz, buzz, buzz*
Beil, Karen Magnuson. *Jack's house*
Bell, Babs. *The bridge is up!*
Bertrand, Diane Gonzales. *The party for Papa Luis / La fiesta para Papa Luis*
Birdseye, Tom. *Soap! Soap! Don't forget the soap!*
Blackstone, Stella. *An island in the sun*
Bond, Rebecca. *The great doughnut parade*
Bowen, Anne. *I know an old teacher*
Brenner, Emily. *On the first day of grade school*
Brett, Jan. *Berlioz the bear*
Brisson, Pat. *Hobbledy-clop*
Brown, Ruth. *A dark, dark tale*
Bryan, Ashley. *Beat the story-drum, pum-pum*
Burningham, John. *Mr. Gumpy's outing*
Burton, Virginia Lee. *Katy and the big snow*
Capucilli, Alyssa Satin. *Inside a zoo in the city*
Carle, Eric. *Pancakes, pancakes*
Carter, David A. *Old MacDonald had a farm: a pop-up book*
Cazet, Denys. *Nothing at all*
Chaconas, Dori. *Don't slam the door!*
Chicken Little. *Chicken Little*
Henny Penny, ill. by Emily Bolam
Henny Penny, ill. by Paul Galdone
Henny Penny, ill. by Sophie Windham
Henny-Penny
The sky is falling
Clarke, Jane. *Stuck in the mud*
Cohen, Caron Lee. *Digger Pig and the turnip*
Colandro, Lucille. *There was a cold lady who swallowed some snow!*
There was an old lady who swallowed a clover!
There was an old lady who swallowed some books!
Cooke, Trish. *So much*
Davidson, Rebecca Piatt. *All the world's a stage*
Deacon, Alexis. *Cheese belongs to you!*
de Las Casas, Dianne. *The house that Witchy built*
De Regniers, Beatrice Schenk. *What did you put in your pocket?*
Downey, Lynn. *This is the earth that God made*
Downing, Johnette. *There was an old lady who swallowed some bugs*
Dunrea, Olivier. *Bear Noel*

Old MacDonald had a farm, ill. by Tracey Campbell Pearson
Old MacDonald had a farm, ill. by Glen Rounds
Old MacDonald had a farm, ill. by Jessica Souhami
Old MacDonald had a farm, ill. by Prue Theobalds
The old woman and her pig. *The old woman and her pig*
The old woman and her pig: an Appalachian folktale
Ormerod, Jan. *Ms. MacDonald has a class*
Oxenbury, Helen. *It's my birthday*
Paquette, Ammi-Joan. *Ghost in the house*
Parkinson, Kathy. *The enormous turnip*
Peck, Jan. *Giant peach yodel!*
Peet, Bill. *The ant and the elephant*
Perry, Andrea. *The Bicklebys' birdbath*
Piers, Helen. *Who's in my bed?*
Pinkney, Brian. *Hush, little baby*
Polacco, Patricia. *In Enzo's splendid gardens*
Prelutsky, Jack. *The terrible tiger*
Reider, Katja. *Snail started it!*
Reidy, Jean. *Light up the night*
Reiser, Lynn. *Christmas counting*
Robart, Rose. *The cake that Mack ate*
Root, Phyllis. *Creak! said the bed*
Rose, Deborah Lee. *The twelve days of kindergarten*
The twelve days of springtime
Rosenthal, Marc. *Phooey!*
Rylant, Cynthia. *The great Gracie chase*
Sawyer, Ruth. *Journey cake, ho!*
Schaefer, Lola M. *This is the sunflower*
Scieszka, Jon. *The book that Jack wrote*
Sierra, Judy. *The house that Drac built*
'Twas the fright before Christmas
Silverstein, Shel. *A giraffe and a half*
Sloat, Teri. *There was an old lady who swallowed a trout*
Snell, Gordon. *Twelve days, a Christmas countdown*
Steig, Jeanne. *Fleas!*
Stevens, Jan Romero. *Twelve lizards leaping*
Stihler, Chérie B. *The giant cabbage turnip*
Stojic, Manya. *Rain*
Stutson, Caroline. *By the light of the Halloween moon*
Sweet, Melissa. *Fiddle-i-fee*
Szekeres, Cyndy. *The mouse that Jack built*
Tafuri, Nancy. *This is the farmer*
Taylor, Sean. *The ring went zing!*
Thomas, Shelley Moore. *Putting the world to sleep*
Thompson, Lauren. *The apple pie that Papa baked*
Thompson, Richard. *The follower*
Thomson, Pat. *The squeaky, creaky bed*
Thornhill, Jan. *The rumor*
Tolstoy, Aleksey Nikolayevich. *The enormous turnip*
The gigantic turnip
Tompert, Ann. *Just a little bit*
Tresselt, Alvin R. *Rain drop splash*
The twelve days of Christmas. English folk song.
The twelve days of Christmas
The 12 days of Christmas
The twelve days of Christmas
Twelve days of Christmas
The twelve days of Christmas, ill. by Laurel Long
The twelve days of Christmas, ill. by Ilse Plume
The twelve days of Christmas, ill. by Jane Ray
The twelve days of Christmas, ill. by Gennady Spirin
The twelve days of Christmas, ill. by Vladimir Vagin
The twelve days of Christmas [board book]
Vagin, Vladimir. *The enormous carrot*
Vamos, Samantha R. *The cazuela that the farm maiden stirred*
Van Laan, Nancy. *Mama rocks, Papa sings*
Possum come a-knocking
Vasilovich, Guy. *The 13 nights of Halloween*
Waddell, Martin. *The pig in the pond*
Wardlaw, Lee. *The chair where bear sits*
Weninger, Brigitte. *The elf's hat*
West, Colin. *One day in the jungle*
Wildsmith, Brian. *Goat's trail*
Williams, Linda. *The little old lady who was not afraid of anything*
Witte, Anna. *The parrot Tico Tango*
Wolff, Ferida. *On Halloween night*
Wood, Audrey. *The napping house*
Silly Sally
Silly Sally [board book]
Yee, Brenda Shannon. *Sand castle*
Yee, Wong Herbert. *Eek! There's a mouse in the house*
Yolen, Jane. *Jane Yolen's Old MacDonald songbook*
Young, Ed. *What about me?*
Ziefert, Harriet. *I swapped my dog*
Knick-knack paddywhack
When I first came to this land
Zolotow, Charlotte. *The quarreling book*

Curiosity *see* Character traits – curiosity

Currency *see* Money

Cycles *see* Motorcycles; Sports – bicycling

Dark *see* Night; Power failures

Darkness – fear *see* Emotions – fear

Dawn *see* Morning

Day

Andreasen, Dan. *Saturday with Daddy*
Ashman, Linda. *Just another morning*
Ballard, Robin. *My day, your day*
Berger, Carin. *A perfect day*
Bernhard, Durga. *While you are sleeping: a lift-the-flap book of time around the world*
Bradley, Kimberly Brubaker. *Favorite things*
Braun, Sebastien. *I love my daddy*
Calmenson, Stephanie. *Ollie's school day*
Carluccio, Maria. *The sounds around town*
Charlip, Remy. *A perfect day*

Why I will never ever ever ever have enough time to read this book
Cocca-Leffler, Maryann. *Time to say bye-bye*
Freedman, Claire. *One magical day*
George, Jean Craighead. *Morning, noon, and night*
Geras, Adèle. *My wishes for you*
Haley, Amanda. *It's a baby's world*
Heidbreder, Robert. *Noisy poems for a busy day*
Hopgood, Tim. *Wow! said the owl*
Jenkins, Emily. *Water in the park*
What happens on Wednesdays
Johnson, Angela. *Lottie Paris lives here*
Kavanagh, Peter. *I love my mama*
Kerley, Barbara. *One world, one day*
Lamb, Albert. *Tell me the day backwards*
Lobel, Anita. *Hello, day!*
McGee, Marni. *The noisy farm*
Marley, Cedella. *Every little thing*
Martin, Ruth. *Moon dreams*
Melmed, Laura Krauss. *A hug goes around*
Modesitt, Jeanne. *Oh, what a beautiful day!*
Munro, Roxie. *Desert days, desert nights*
Murphy, Stuart J. *It's about time!*
Nelson, Robin. *A day*
Rong, Yu. *A lovely day for Amelia Goose*
Ross, Michael Elsohn. *Earth cycles*
Rylant, Cynthia. *All in a day*
Schaefer, Carole Lexa. *Someone says*
Seven spunky monkeys
Turner, Ann Warren. *In the heart*
Underwood, Deborah. *The loud book!*
Waring, Geoff. *Oscar and the moth*
Yee, Wong Herbert. *Summer days and nights*

Day care *see* School – nursery

Days of the week, months of the year

Boling, Katherine. *New year be coming!*
Boling, Ruth L. *Come worship with me*
Brian, Janeen. *Where does Thursday go?*
Bunting, Eve. *Sing a song of piglets*
Butterworth, Nick. *Jasper's beanstalk*
Carle, Eric. *Today is Monday*
The very hungry caterpillar
Carlstrom, Nancy White. *How do you say it today, Jesse Bear?*
A child's calendar
Cohn, Scotti. *One wolf howls*
Day, Nancy Raines. *A kitten's year*
Demas, Corinne. *Valentine surprise*
De Regniers, Beatrice Schenk. *What did you put in your pocket?*
Downing, Johnette. *Today is Monday in Louisiana*
Downing, Julie. *No hugs till Saturday*
Elya, Susan Middleton. *A year full of holidays*
Fernandes, Eugenie. *Big week for little mouse*
Ficocelli, Elizabeth. *Kid tea*
Firmin, Josie. *My week*
Gershator, Phillis. *This is the day!*
Glenn, Sharlee. *Just what Mama needs*
Gravett, Emily. *The rabbit problem*
Hague, Kathleen. *Calendarbears*
Hanson, Warren. *It's Monday, Mrs. Jolly Bones!*
Harness, Cheryl. *Our colonial year*
Hayles, Marsha. *Pajamas anytime*
Hewitt, Kathryn. *No dogs here!*
Hubbell, Patricia. *Rabbit moon*
Jackson, Ellen. *April*
August
December
February
January
July
June
March
May
November
October
September
Katz, Bobbi. *Once around the sun*
Katz, Karen. *Twelve hats for Lena*
Lesser, Carolyn. *What a wonderful day to be a cow*
Levine, Arthur A. *Monday is one day*
Livingston, Myra Cohn. *Calendar*
Lobel, Anita. *One lighthouse, one moon*
McCurdy, Michael. *An Algonquian year*
McGowan, Michael. *Sunday is for God*
Martin, Bill, Jr. *The turning of the year*
Marzollo, Jean. *I spy, year-round challenger!*
Nelson, Robin. *A day*
Months
A week
Newman, Jeff. *The boys*
Obed, Ellen Bryan. *Who would like a Christmas tree?*
Otten, Charlotte F. *January rides the wind*
Peters, Lisa Westberg. *October smiled back*
Provensen, Alice. *The year at Maple Hill Farm*
Rau, Dana Meachen. *I'll make you a card*
Rosenberg, Madelyn. *The Schmutzy Family*
Rylant, Cynthia. *Bless us all*
Give me grace
Santos, Rosa. *Play date*
Sayre, April Pulley. *Eat like a bear*
Scarry, Richard. *Richard Scarry's best first book ever!*
Sendak, Maurice. *Chicken soup with rice*
Seven, John. *A year with friends*
Shahan, Sherry. *Fiesta!*
Shields, Carol Diggory. *Day by day a week goes round*
Month by month a year goes round
Shulevitz, Uri. *One Monday morning*
Singer, Marilyn. *Turtle in July*
Smith, Maggie. *Dear Daisy, get well soon*
Spinelli, Eileen. *Heat wave*
Here comes the year
Tafuri, Nancy. *Snowy flowy blowy*
Taylor, Joanne. *Full moon rising*
Thomas, Joyce Carol. *Gingerbread days*
Thompson, Richard. *The follower*
Van der Meer, Mara. *Can we play?*
Verdet, Andre. *All about time*
Wang, Xiaohong. *One year in Beijing*
Ward, Cindy. *Cookie's week*
Wells, Rosemary. *My kindergarten*
Winnick, Karen B. *A year goes round*
Wolff, Ashley. *When Lucy goes out walking*
Wood, Audrey. *Heckedy Peg*
Young, Ed. *Seven blind mice*

Deafness *see* Anatomy – ears; Disabilities – deafness; Senses – hearing

Death

Abley, Mark. *Ghost cat*
Aliki. *Mummies made in Egypt*

Anaya, Rudolfo A. *Farolitos for Abuelo*
Andersen, Hans Christian. *It's perfectly true!*
The little match girl, ill. by Rachel Isadora
The little match girl, ill. by Blair Lent
The little match girl, ill. by Jerry Pinkney
The little matchstick girl
Anholt, Laurence. *Seven for a secret*
Barron, T. A. *Where is Grandpa?*
Bateman, Teresa. *Keeper of soles*
The best cat in the world
Bley, Anette. *And what comes after a thousand?*
Blumenthal, Deborah. *The blue house dog*
Boyden, Linda. *The blue roses*
Brisson, Pat. *I remember Miss Perry*
Brown, Laurie Krasny. *When dinosaurs die*
Bunting, Eve. *Rudi's pond*
Burleigh, Robert. *Good-bye, Sheepie*
Burrowes, Adjoa J. *Grandma's purple flowers*
Castellucci, Cecil. *Grandma's gloves*
Cazet, Denys. *A fish in his pocket*
Clifton, Lucille. *Everett Anderson's goodbye*
Cobb, Rebecca. *Missing Mommy*
Cochran, Bill. *The forever dog*
Coerr, Eleanor. *Sadako*
Cohen, Miriam. *Jim's dog Muffins*, ill. by Ronald Himler
Jim's dog Muffins, ill. by Lillian Hoban
Cooke, Trish. *The grandad tree*
Crowe, Carole. *Turtle girl*
dePaola, Tomie. *Nana Upstairs and Nana Downstairs*
Doray, Malika. *One more Wednesday*
Fletcher, Ralph. *Grandpa never lies*
Fox, Mem. *Sophie*
Fraustino, Lisa Rowe. *The hickory chair*
Fritts, Mary Bahr. *If Nathan were here*
Genechten, Guido van. *Ricky and the squirrel*
Goble, Paul. *Beyond the ridge*
Goldman, Judy. *Uncle Monarch and the Day of the Dead*
Gregory, Nan. *Wild Girl and Gran*
Grimm, Edward. *The doorman*
Hanson, Regina. *A season for mangoes*
Harris, Robie H. *Goodbye, Mousie*
Haynes, Max. *Grandma's gone to live in the stars*
Hill, Frances. *The bug cemetery*
Hopkinson, Deborah. *Bluebird summer*
Jeffers, Oliver. *The heart and the bottle*
Jeffs, Stephanie. *Jenny*
Josh
Johnston, Tony. *That summer*
Joosse, Barbara. *Ghost wings*
Keats, Ezra Jack. *Maggie and the pirate*
Kerner, Susan. *Always by my side*
Krishnaswami, Uma. *Remembering Grandpa*
Londner, Renee. *Stones for Grandpa*
Loth, Sebastian. *Remembering Crystal*
Luenn, Nancy. *A gift for Abuelita*
Lunde, Stein Erik. *My father's arms are a boat*
Lupton, David. *Goodbye, Brecken*
Maier, Inger. *Ben's flying flowers*
Monk, Isabell. *Blackberry stew*
Moundlic, Charlotte. *The scar*
Murphy, Sally. *Pearl verses the world*
Napoli, Donna Jo. *Flamingo dream*
Nobisso, Josephine. *Grandpa loved*
O'Brien, Anne Sibley. *A path of stars*
Onyefulu, Ifeoma. *Saying goodbye*
Parker, Marjorie Blain. *Jasper's day*
Partridge, Elizabeth. *Big Cat Pepper*
Pitcher, Caroline. *Nico's octopus*
Portnoy, Mindy Avra. *Where do people go when they die?*
Puttock, Simon. *A story for Hippo*
Rappaport, Doreen. *The new king*
Raschka, Chris. *The purple balloon*
Rogers, Fred. *When a pet dies*
Rohmann, Eric. *Bone dog*
Roper, Janice M. *Dancing on the moon*
Rosen, Michael. *A Thanksgiving wish*
Rosenberg, Liz. *The carousel*
Russo, Marisabina. *Grandpa Abe*
Rylant, Cynthia. *Dog Heaven*
Santucci, Barbara. *Anna's corn*
Schick, Eleanor. *Mama*
Schotter, Roni. *In the piney woods*
Simon, Norma. *The saddest time*
Sinykin, Sheri. *Zayde comes to live*
Smith, Maggie. *Desser, the best ever cat*
Staake, Bob. *Bluebird*
Stafford, Liliana. *Just dragon*
Thomas, Jane Resh. *Saying good-bye to grandma*
Tibo, Gilles. *The grand journey of Mr. Man*
Turner, Pamela S. *Hachiko*
Varley, Susan. *Badger's parting gifts*
Vigna, Judith. *Saying goodbye to daddy*
Viorst, Judith. *The tenth good thing about Barney*
Walker, Alice. *To hell with dying*
Warner, Sunny. *The moon quilt*
Weigelt, Udo. *Bear's last journey*
Weitzman, Elizabeth. *Let's talk about when a parent dies*
Wells, Rosemary. *The language of doves*
Wild, Margaret. *Harry and Hopper*
Old Pig
Wilhelm, Hans. *I'll always love you*
Wood, Douglas. *Aunt Mary's rose*
Grandad's prayers of the earth
Woodson, Jacqueline. *Sweet, sweet memory*
Yeh, Kat. *The magic brush*
Yolen, Jane. *The day Tiger Rose said goodbye*
Zalben, Jane Breskin. *Pearl's marigolds for grandpa*
Zolotow, Charlotte. *My grandson Lew*
The old dog

Demons *see* Devil; Monsters

Department stores *see* Shopping; Stores

Desert

Anaya, Rudolfo A. *Roadrunner's dance*
Arnosky, Jim. *Coyote raid in Cactus Canyon*
Bash, Barbara. *Desert giant*
Baylor, Byrd. *The desert is theirs*
Brett, Jan. *The three little dassies*
Geisert, Bonnie. *Desert town*
Guiberson, Brenda Z. *Cactus hotel*
Hiscock, Bruce. *Coyote and badger*
Johnson, Paul Brett. *Lost*
Johnston, Tony. *Desert dog*
Desert song
Keats, Ezra Jack. *Clementina's cactus*
Klingel, Cynthia Fitterer. *Deserts*
Lawlor, Laurie. *Old Crump*
Levinson, Nancy Smiler. *Death Valley*
London, Jonathan. *Ali, child of the desert*

Lowell, Susan. *The tortoise and the jackrabbit*
McLerran, Alice. *Roxaboxen*
Mora, Pat. *Delicious hullabaloo / Pachanga deliciosa*
The desert is my mother / El desierto es mi madre
Listen to the desert / Oye al desierto
This big sky
Moss, Miriam. *This is the oasis*
Munro, Roxie. *Desert days, desert nights*
Pattison, Darcy. *Desert baths*
Paul, Ann Whitford. *Count on Culebra*
Fiesta fiasco
Mañana Iguana
Tortuga in trouble
Reynolds, Jan. *Sahara*
Sayre, April Pulley. *Dig, wait, listen*
Serafini, Frank. *Looking closely across the desert*
Siebert, Diane. *Mojave*
Spurling, Margaret. *Bilby moon*
Yolen, Jane. *Welcome to the sea of sand*
Young, Ed. *Donkey trouble*

Detective stories *see* Careers – detectives; Mystery stories; Problem solving

Devil

Philip, Neil. *Noah and the devil*
Quattlebaum, Mary. *Sparks fly high*
Root, Phyllis. *Rosie's fiddle*
Stewig, John Warren. *Clever Gretchen*
Wooldridge, Connie Nordhielm. *The legend of Strap Buckner*
Wicked Jack
Zemach, Harve. *Duffy and the devil*

Dictionaries

Bergen, Lara Rice. *Blue's world of words*
Day, Alexandra. *Frank and Ernest play ball*
Ferris, Jeri Chase. *Noah Webster and his words*
Got, Yves. *Sam's big book of words*
Stanley, Mandy. *First word book*

Diggers *see* Careers – construction workers; Machines

Diners *see* Restaurants

Dinosaurs

Aliki. *Digging up dinosaurs*
Dinosaur bones
Dinosaurs are different
Fossils tell of long ago
My visit to the dinosaurs
Alphin, Elaine Marie. *Dinosaur hunter*
Andersen, Hans Christian. *The dinosaur's new clothes*
Andreae, Giles. *Captain Flinn and the pirate dinosaurs*
Captain Flinn and the pirate dinosaurs: missing treasure!
Dinosaurs galore!
Atkins, Jeannine. *Mary Anning and the sea dragon*
Baker, Liza. *Dinosaur days*
Bardhan-Quallen, Sudipta. *The Mine-o-saur*
Barner, Bob. *Dinosaur bones*
Dinosaurs roar, butterflies soar!
Barry, Frances. *Let's look at dinosaurs*
Barton, Byron. *Bones, bones, dinosaur bones*
Dinosaurs, dinosaurs
Bateman, Teresa. *Hunting the daddyosaurus*
Bauer, Marion Dane. *Dinosaur thunder*
Beaumont, Karen. *Dini Dinosaur*
Berger, Melvin. *Why did the dinosaurs disappear?*
Bilgrami, Shaheen. *Amazing dinosaur discovery*
Blackstone, Stella. *I dreamt I was a dinosaur*
Bourgeois, Paulette. *Franklin's class trip*
Broach, Elise. *When dinosaurs came with everything*
Brockenbrough, Martha. *The Dinosaur Tooth Fairy*
Brown, Laurie Krasny. *Dinosaurs alive and well*
Dinosaurs divorce
Dinosaurs to the rescue
Dinosaurs travel
How to be a friend
When dinosaurs die
Brown, Marc. *Dinosaurs, beware!*
Bryant, Megan E. *Alphasaurus*
Colorasaurus
Countasaurus
Shapeasaurus
Buzzeo, Toni. *No T. Rex in the library*
Carrick, Carol. *Big old bones*
Patrick's dinosaurs
Patrick's dinosaurs on the Internet
What happened to Patrick's dinosaurs?
Carter, David A. *Flapdoodle dinosaurs*
Casalis, Anna. *Dinosaurs [board book]*
Clarke, Jane. *Dancing with the Dinosaurs*
Dippy's sleepover
Cohen, Daniel. *Apatosaurus*
Pteranodon
Stegosaurus
Triceratops
Tyrannosaurus rex
Velociraptor
Cole, Joanna. *The magic school bus in the time of the dinosaurs*
Curious George and the dinosaur
Cyrus, Kurt. *Tadpole Rex*
The voyage of turtle Rex
Dale, Penny. *Dinosaur dig!*
Dinosaur rescue!
Dinosaur zoom!
Daniels, Teri. *G-Rex*
DePalma, Mary Newell. *Uh-oh!*
dePaola, Tomie. *Little Grunt and the big egg*
Desmoinaux, Christel. *Mrs. Hen's big surprise*
DiPucchio, Kelly. *Dinosnores*
Donaldson, Julia. *Tyrannosaurus Drip*
Donnelly, Liza. *Dinosaurs' Halloween*
Drehsen, Britta. *Flip-o-storic*
Durant, Alan. *A dinosaur called Tiny*
Edwards, Pamela Duncan. *Dinosaur starts school*
Edwards, Wallace. *The extinct files*
Evans, Nate. *Bang! Boom! Roar!*
Faulkner, Keith. *Rexerella*
Florian, Douglas. *Dinothesaurus*
Foreman, Michael. *The littlest dinosaur*
Fox, Diane. *Tyson the terrible*
Freedman, Claire. *Dinosaurs love underpants*
Fuge, Charles. *Three little dinosaurs*
Gall, Chris. *Dinotrux*
Revenge of the Dinotrux
Garland, Michael. *Miss Smith reads again!*
Gibbons, Gail. *Dinosaur discoveries*

Dinosaurs!
Goecke, Michael P. *Diplodocus*
Grambling, Lois G. *Big Dog*
Here comes T. Rex Cottontail
T. Rex and the Mother's Day hug
T. Rex trick-or-treats
Granowsky, Alvin. *Dinosaurs*
Greathouse, Carol. *The dinosaur tamer*
Greenfield, Eloise. *I can draw a weeposaur and other dinosaurs*
Gurney, John Steven. *Dinosaur train*
Hall, Algy Craig. *Dino bites!*
Halls, Kelly Milner. *Dinosaur parade*
Harrison, Carol. *Dinosaurs everywhere!*
Hartland, Jessie. *How the dinosaur got to the museum*
Hartmann, Wendy. *The dinosaurs are back and it's all your fault, Edward!*
Heidbreder, Robert. *Drumheller dinosaur dance*
Hennessy, B. G. *Busy Dinah Dinosaur*
The dinosaur who lived in my backyard
Meet Dinah Dinosaur
Henry, Jed. *I speak dinosaur*
Hines, Anna Grossnickle. *I am a Tyrannosaurus*
Holmquist, Delano. *SantaSaurus*
Hort, Lenny. *Did dinosaurs eat pizza?*
Houran, Lori Haskins. *Dig those dinosaurs*
Howe, James. *Brontorina*
Idle, Molly. *Tea Rex*
James, Brian. *Supertwins meet the dangerous dino-robots*
Jenkins, Steve. *Animals in flight*
Jennewein, Lenore. *Chick-o-Saurus Rex*
Joyce, William. *Dinosaur Bob*
Judge, Lita. *How big were dinosaurs?*
Kastner, Jill. *Merry Christmas, Princess Dinosaur*
Princess Dinosaur
Kellogg, Steven. *Prehistoric Pinkerton*
Kirsch, Vincent X. *Freddie and Gingersnap*
Kroll, Steven. *The Tyrannosaurus game*
Kudlinski, Kathleen V. *Boy, were we wrong about dinosaurs!*
Lawler, Janet. *Tyrannoclaus*
Lewis, Kevin. *Dinosaur dinosaur*
Liu, Julia. *Gus, the dinosaur bus*
Lund, Deb. *All aboard the dinotrain*
Dinosailors
Dinosoaring
McAnulty, Stacy. *Dear Santasaurus*
McClatchy, Lisa. *Dear Tyrannosaurus Rex*
McClements, George. *Dinosaur Woods*
Ridin' dinos with Buck Bronco
MacDonald, Suse. *Shape by shape*
MacLeod, Elizabeth. *What did dinosaurs eat?*
McMullan, Kate. *I'm bad!*
I'm big!
Manning, Mick. *Dino-dinners*
Markel, Michelle. *Tyrannosaurus math*
Masurel, Claire. *Too big!*
Mayer, Mercer. *Too many dinosaurs*
Mayo, Margaret. *Stomp, dinosaur, stomp!*
Middleton, Julie. *Are the dinosaurs dead, Dad?*
Mitton, Tony. *Dinosaurumpus*
Rumble, roar, dinosaur!
Montanari, Eva. *Dino bikes*
Moseley, Keith. *Where's the dinosaur?*
Most, Bernard. *ABC T-Rex*
A dinosaur named after me
Dinosaur questions
How big were the dinosaurs?
If the dinosaurs came back
A pair of protoceratops
A trio of triceratops
Whatever happened to the dinosaurs?
Muecke, Anne. *The dinosaurs' night before Christmas*
Munro, Roxie. *Inside-outside dinosaurs*
Murphy, Stuart J. *Dinosaur deals*
Myers, Tim. *Down at the Dino Wash Deluxe*
Neubecker, Robert. *Linus the vegetarian T. rex*
O'Brien, Patrick. *Gigantic!*
Sabertooth
Oldland, Nicholas. *Dinosaur countdown*
O'Malley, Kevin. *Captain Raptor and the moon mystery*
Captain Raptor and the space pirates
Otto, Carolyn. *Dinosaur chase*
Palatini, Margie. *Gorgonzola*
Pfister, Marcus. *Dazzle the dinosaur*
Plourde, Lynn. *Dino pets*
Dino pets go to school
Prap, Lila. *Dinosaurs?!*
Prelutsky, Jack. *Tyrannosaurus was a beast*
Pulver, Robin. *Mrs. Toggle and the dinosaur*
Rennert, Laura Joy. *Buying, training and caring for your dinosaur*
Rohmann, Eric. *Time flies*
Rosenberg, Liz. *Tyrannosaurus dad*
Ryder, Joanne. *Tyrannosaurus time*
Sabuda, Robert. *Encyclopedia prehistorica: dinosaurs*
Sansone, Adele. *The little green goose*
Schachner, Judith Byron. *Skippyjon Jones and the big bones*
Schwartz, Henry. *How I captured a dinosaur*
Sedaka, Marc. *Dinosaur pet*
Sharkey, Niamh. *Santasaurus*
Shea, Bob. *Dinosaur vs. bedtime*
Dinosaur vs. Santa
Dinosaur vs. the library
Dinosaur vs. the potty
Shields, Carol Diggory. *Saturday night at the dinosaur stomp*
Sierra, Judy. *Suppose you meet a dinosaur*
Sís, Peter. *Dinosaur!*
Stein, David Ezra. *Dinosaur kisses*
Stevenson, James. *The most amazing dinosaur*
Stickland, Paul. *Dinosaur roar!*
Dinosaur stomp!
A number of dinosaurs
Ten terrible dinosaurs
Symes, Ruth. *Little Rex, big brother*
Waddell, Martin. *The Super Hungry Dinosaur*
Wahl, Jan. *The field mouse and the dinosaur named Sue*
I met a dinosaur
Wallace, Karen. *I am an ankylosaurus*
Werner, Sharon. *Alphasaurs and other prehistoric types*
Wheeler, Lisa. *Dino-baseball*
Dino-basketball
Dino-football
Dino-hockey
Dino-soccer
Dino-wrestling
Whybrow, Ian. *Harry and the bucketful of dinosaurs*
Harry and the dinosaurs at the museum
Harry and the dinosaurs go to school
Harry and the dinosaurs say "Raahh"
Wick, Walter. *Can you see what I see? cool collections*

Willems, Mo. *Edwina, the dinosaur who didn't know she was extinct*
Goldilocks and the three dinosaurs
Willis, Jeanne. *I'm sure I saw a dinosaur*
Wilson, Karma. *Dinos in the snow!*
Wing, Natasha. *How to raise a dinosaur*
Wise, William. *Dinosaurs forever*
Wood, Douglas. *What teachers can't do*
Yolen, Jane. *How do dinosaurs clean their rooms?*
How do dinosaurs count to ten?
How do dinosaurs eat their food?
How do dinosaurs get well soon?
How do dinosaurs go to school?
How do dinosaurs learn their colors?
How do dinosaurs play with their friends?
How do dinosaurs say good night?
How do dinosaurs say Happy Chanukah?
How do dinosaurs say I love you?
How do dinosaurs say I'm mad?
How do dinosaurs say Merry Christmas?
Zoehfeld, Kathleen Weidner. *Did dinosaurs have feathers?*
Dinosaur tracks
Dinosaurs big and small
Where did dinosaurs come from?

Disabilities

Anderson, Peggy Perry. *We go in a circle*
Asare, Meshack. *Sosu's call*
Carter, Alden R. *Seeing things my way*
Eisner, Will. *Sundiata*
Lears, Laurie. *Waiting for Mr. Goose*
Lester, Helen. *Author*
Hooway for Wodney Wat
Wodney Wat's wobot
Lester, Julius. *Shining*
Niner, Holly L. *I can't stop!*
Polacco, Patricia. *The art of Miss Chew*
The junkyard wonders
Thank you, Mr. Falker
Pulver, Robin. *Way to go, Alex!*
Rogers, Fred. *Extraordinary friends*
Senisi, Ellen B. *Just kids*
Wisniewski, David. *Sundiata: lion king of Mali*
Zemach, Kaethe. *Ms. McCaw learns to draw*

Disabilities – ADD

Bishop, Brett. *Clayton's path*
Rotner, Shelley. *The A.D.D. book for kids*
Zimmett, Debbie. *Eddie enough*

Disabilities – autism

Altman, Alexandra Jessup. *Waiting for Benjamin*
Amenta, Charles A., III. *Russell's world*
Ely, Lesley. *Looking after Louis*
Lears, Laurie. *Ian's walk*
Lehman-Wilzig, Tami. *Nathan blows out the Hanukkah candles*
Moore-Mallinos, Jennifer. *My brother is autistic*
Mueller, Dagmar H. *David's world*
Niekerk, Clarabelle van. *Understanding Sam and Asperger syndrome*
Peete, Holly Robinson. *My brother Charlie*
Reynolds, Peter H. *I'm here*

Disabilities – blindness *see also* Anatomy – eyes

Adler, David A. *Helen Keller*
Barry, Holly M. *Helen Keller's best friend Belle*
Clements, Andrew. *Brave Norman*
Cole, Barbara Hancock. *Anna and Natalie*
Cottin, Menena. *The black book of colors*
Davis, Patricia Anne. *Brian's bird*
Fraustino, Lisa Rowe. *The hickory chair*
Goldin, Barbara Diamond. *Cakes and miracles*
Hopkinson, Deborah. *Annie and Helen*
Keats, Ezra Jack. *Apt. 3*
Lang, Glenna. *Looking out for Sarah*
Liao, Jimmy. *The sound of colors*
Martin, Bill, Jr. *Knots on a counting rope*
Moon, Nicola. *Lucy's picture*
Petrillo, Genevieve. *Keep your ear on the ball*
Rappaport, Doreen. *Helen's big world*
Rau, Dana Meachen. *The secret code*
Rodriguez, Bobbie. *Sarah's sleepover*
Troupe, Quincy. *Little Stevie Wonder*
Wisniewski, David. *Elfwyn's saga*
Young, Ed. *Seven blind mice*

Disabilities – cerebral palsy

DeBear, Kirsten. *Be quiet, Marina!*
Heelan, Jamee Riggio. *Rolling along, the story of Taylor and his wheelchair*
Lears, Laurie. *Nathan's wish*
Thompson, Lauren. *Ballerina dreams*

Disabilities – deafness *see also* Anatomy – ears

Acredolo, Linda P. *My first baby signs*
Adler, David A. *Helen Keller*
Ancona, George. *Handtalk zoo*
Barry, Holly M. *Helen Keller's best friend Belle*
Charlip, Remy. *Handtalk birthday*
Charlip, Remy, et al. *Handtalk*
Domney, Alexis. *Splish, splat!*
Heelan, Jamee Riggio. *Can you hear a rainbow?*
Hopkinson, Deborah. *Annie and Helen*
Lee, Jeanne M. *Silent lotus*
McCully, Emily Arnold. *My heart glow*
Millman, Isaac. *Moses goes to a concert*
Moses goes to school
Moses goes to the circus
Nijssen, Elfi. *Laurie*
Rankin, Laura. *The handmade counting book*
Rappaport, Doreen. *Helen's big world*
Seeger, Pete. *The deaf musicians*
Stryer, Andrea Stenn. *Kami and the yaks*
Uhlberg, Myron. *Dad, Jackie, and me*
The printer
Waller, Curt. *Baby's first signs*
More baby's first signs
Winnie-the-Pooh's A B C
Wise, Bill. *Silent star*

Disabilities – Down syndrome

Carter, Alden R. *Big brother Dustin*
DeBear, Kirsten. *Be quiet, Marina!*
Girnis, Margaret. *ABC for you and me*
1, 2, 3 for you and me
Gregory, Nan. *How Smudge came*
Ling, Nancy Tupper. *My sister, Alicia May*
Rheingrover, Jean Sasso. *Veronica's first year*

Rickert, Janet Elizabeth. *Russ and the almost perfect day*
Stuve-Bodeen, Stephanie. *We'll paint the octopus red*

Disabilities – dyslexia

Alexander, Claire. *Back to front and upside down*
Hodge, Deborah. *Lily and the mixed-up letters*
Robb, Diane Burton. *The alphabet war*

Disabilities – mental Disabilities

Gifaldi, David. *Ben, king of the river*
Rickert, Janet Elizabeth. *Russ and the almost perfect day*
Shriver, Maria. *What's wrong with Timmy?*

Disabilities – physical disabilities

Adler, David A. *Campy*
Buchanan, Jane. *Seed magic*
Burnett, Frances Hodgson. *The secret garden*
Cowen-Fletcher, Jane. *Mama zooms*
De Anda, Diane. *Dancing Miranda / Baila, Miranda, baila*
Elliott, Rebecca. *Just because*
Emmons, Chip. *Sammy wakes his dad*
Heelan, Jamee Riggio. *The making of my special hand, Madison's story*
Rolling along, the story of Taylor and his wheelchair
Hines, Anna Grossnickle. *Gramma's walk*
Hoffman, Eric. *No fair to tigers / No es justo para los tigres*
Hudson, Cheryl Willis. *My friend Maya loves to dance*
Khan, Rukhsana. *King for a day*
Lee, Jeanne M. *Silent lotus*
Moore, Genevieve. *Catherine's story*
Moore-Mallinos, Jennifer. *It's ok to be me!*
Munsch, Robert N. *Zoom*
Senisi, Ellen B. *All kinds of friends, even green*
Stewart, Shannon. *Sea crow*
Wells, Rosemary. *The little lame prince*
Willis, Jeanne. *Susan laughs*
Yin. *Dear Santa, please come to the 19th floor*

Disabilities – stuttering

Lears, Laurie. *Ben has something to say*

Disbelief *see* Behavior – disbelief

Diseases *see* Illness

Disguises

Aesop. *The donkey in the lion's skin*
The wolf in sheep's clothing
Bell, Cece. *Bee-Wigged*
Cannon, Janell. *Little Yau*
Ehlert, Lois. *Lots of spots*
Ernst, Lisa Campbell. *Sylvia Jean, scout supreme*
Fenton, Joe. *Boo!*
Gentle, Victor. *Shark camouflage and armor*
Holmes, Anita. *Can you find us?*
Hutchins, Hazel. *I'd know you anywhere*
Lester, Helen. *The sheep in wolf's clothing*
McNaughton, Colin. *Boo!*
Mason, Adrienne. *Lu and Clancy's spy stuff*
Oliver, Narelle. *Twilight hunt*
Onishi, Satoru. *Who's hiding*
Peters, Bernadette. *Stella is a star!*
Roberton, Fiona. *Wanted: the perfect pet*
Savage, Stephen. *Where's Walrus?*
Schwartz, David M. *Where else in the wild?*
Where in the wild
Shaskan, Stephen. *A dog is a dog*
Stevenson, Emma. *Hide-and-seek science*
Swinburne, Stephen R. *Lots and lots of zebra stripes*
Tildes, Phyllis Limbacher. *Animals in camouflage*
Weigelt, Udo. *Super Guinea Pig to the rescue*
Yep, Laurence. *Auntie Tiger*

Dissatisfaction *see* Behavior – dissatisfaction

Diving *see* Sports – skin diving

Divorce

Adams, Eric J. *On the day his daddy left*
Bernhard, Durga. *To and fro, fast and slow*
Brown, Laurie Krasny. *Dinosaurs divorce*
Bunting, Eve. *The days of summer*
My mom's wedding
Clarke, Jane. *The best of both nests*
Cochran, Bill. *My parents are divorced, my elbows have nicknames, and other facts about me*
Coffelt, Nancy. *Fred stays with me!*
Cook, Julia. *The "D" word*
Coy, John. *Two old potatoes and me*
Grindley, Sally. *A new room for William*
Haughton, Emma. *Rainy day*
Holmberg, Bo R. *A day with Dad*
Lansky, Vicki. *It's not your fault, KoKo Bear*
Levins, Sandra. *Do you sing Twinkle?*
Masurel, Claire. *Two homes*
Moore-Mallinos, Jennifer. *When my parents forgot how to be friends*
Portnoy, Mindy Avra. *A tale of two seders*
Ransom, Jeanie Franz. *I don't want to talk about it*
Rogers, Fred. *Divorce*
Santucci, Barbara. *Loon summer*
Schotter, Roni. *Room for Rabbit*
Shreeve, Elizabeth. *Oliver at the window*
Smet, Marian De. *I have two homes*
Spelman, Cornelia Maude. *Mama and Daddy Bear's divorce*
Thomas, Pat. *My family's changing*
Walsh, Melanie. *Living with Mom and living with Dad*
Weninger, Brigitte. *Good-bye, Daddy!*
Willhoite, Michael. *Daddy's roommate*
Winthrop, Elizabeth. *As the crow flies*

Down & up *see* Concepts – up & down

Dragons

Adams, Sarah. *Dave and Violet*
Ashburn, Boni. *Over at the castle*
Atkins, Jeannine. *Mary Anning and the sea dragon*
Averbeck, Jim. *Oh no, Little Dragon!*
Baillie, Allan. *Dragonquest*
Baker, Ken. *Old MacDonald had a dragon*
Banks, Kate. *Max's dragon*

Bar-el, Dan. *Not your typical dragon*
Baynton, Martin. *Jane and the dragon*
Jane and the magician
Beck, Scott. *Happy birthday, Monster!*
Berkeley, Jon. *Chopsticks*
Biedrzycki, David. *Me and my dragon*
Me and my dragon: scared of Halloween
Calvert, Pam. *Princess Peepers picks a pet*
Cave, Kathryn. *You've got dragons*
Deedy, Carmen Agra. *Return of the library dragon*
de Las Casas, Dianne. *There's a dragon in the library*
Demi. *The boy who painted dragons*
The dragon's tale and other animal fables of the Chinese zodiac
dePaola, Tomie. *The knight and the dragon*
Donaldson, Julia. *A gold star for Zog*
Room on the broom
Downing, Julie. *No hugs till Saturday*
Ehrlich, Amy. *Baby Dragon*
Ellery, Amanda. *If I had a dragon*
Eversole, Robyn. *East Dragon, West Dragon*
Falkenstern, Lisa. *A dragon moves in*
Faller, Regis. *Polo and the dragon*
Fletcher, Ralph. *The Sandman*
Gliori, Debi. *The trouble with dragons*
Goodhart, Pippa. *Arthur's tractor*
Gorbachev, Valeri. *How to be friends with a dragon*
Grahame, Kenneth. *The reluctant dragon*
Gravett, Emily. *Again!*
Hale, Bruce. *Snoring Beauty*
Hodges, Margaret. *Saint George and the dragon*
Howe, James. *There's a dragon in my sleeping bag*
Hunter, Jana Novotny. *Little ones do*
Joosse, Barbara. *Lovabye dragon*
Kaufman, Jeanne. *Young Henry and the dragon*
Kirsch, Vincent X. *Freddie and Gingersnap*
Knudsen, Michelle. *Argus*
Kraegel, Kenneth. *King Arthur's very great grandson*
Krause, Ute. *Oscar and the very hungry dragon*
Krensky, Stephen. *Spark the firefighter*
Kroll, Steven. *Super-dragon*
Lambert, Martha Lewis. *I won't get lost*
Leedy, Loreen. *The dragon Halloween party*
The dragon Thanksgiving feast
Long, Ethan. *One drowsy dragon*
Mayhew, James. *The knight who took all day*
Meddaugh, Susan. *Harry on the rocks*
Moore, Jodi. *When a dragon moves in*
Moore, Lilian. *Beware, take care*
Morgan, Mary. *Dragon pizzeria*
Munsch, Robert N. *The paper bag princess*
Nash, Ogden. *Custard the dragon and the wicked knight*
Niemann, Christoph. *The pet dragon*
Nolen, Jerdine. *Raising dragons*
Nunes, Susan Miho. *The last dragon*
Peet, Bill. *How Droofus the dragon lost his head*
Pendziwol, Jean E. *No dragons for tea*
The tale of Sir Dragon
A treasure at sea for dragon and me
Pienkowski, Jan. *Bel and Bub and the black hole*
Pilkey, Dav. *Dragon's fat cat*
Dragon's merry Christmas
A friend for Dragon
Ramos, Mario. *I am so strong*
Robertson, M. P. *The dragon snatcher*
The egg
Roth, Judith L. *Goodnight, dragons*
Rubin, Adam. *Dragons love tacos*
San Souci, Daniel. *The rabbit and the dragon king*
Schaefer, Carole Lexa. *Dragon dancing*
Sierra, Judy. *'Twas the fright before Christmas*
Smallman, Steve. *Dragon stew*
Sperring, Mark. *The sunflower sword*
Thayer, Jane. *The popcorn dragon*
Thomas, Shelley Moore. *A cold winter's Good Knight*
A Good Knight's rest
Good night, Good Knight
Take care, Good Knight
Thomas, Valerie. *Winnie's midnight dragon*
Tucker, Kathy. *The seven Chinese sisters*
Ward, Helen. *The dragon machine*
Wiesner, David. *Free fall*
The loathsome dragon
Wilson, Gina. *Ignis*
Wojtowycz, David. *Elephant Joe, Brave Knight!*
Wong, Benedict Norbert. *Lo and behold*
Lo and behold, good enough to eat
Yarrow, Peter. *Puff, the magic dragon*
Yep, Laurence. *Dragon prince*
Yolen, Jane. *Waking dragons*
Ziefert, Harriet. *William and the dragon*

Dreams *see also* Nightmares

Adlerman, Daniel. *Africa calling*
Alborough, Jez. *Ice cream bear*
Alexander, Martha G. *You're a genius, Blackboard Bear*
Anholt, Laurence. *Jack and the dreamsack*
Appelt, Kathi. *Cowboy dreams*
Argueta, Jorge. *Trees are hanging from the sky*
Arnold, Tedd. *Green Wilma*
No jumping on the bed!
Asch, Frank. *Moonbear's dream*
Banks, Kate. *Close your eyes*
Berenstain, Stan and Jan. *The Berenstain bears and the bad dream*
Blackstone, Stella. *I dreamt I was a dinosaur*
The book of Pooh
Browne, Anthony. *Willy the dreamer*
Burdett, Lois. *A midsummer night's dream for kids*
Burningham, John. *The magic bed*
Byun, You. *Dream friends*
Carlson, Nancy. *It's going to be perfect*
Chapman, Nancy Kapp. *Doggie dreams*
Cohen, Caron Lee. *Martin and the giant lions*
Cousins, Lucy. *Maisy's bedtime*
Maisy's rainbow dream
deGroat, Diane. *Homer*
Demi. *The magic pillow*
Dunbar, Polly. *Arthur's dream boat*
Dunnick, Regan. *Sweet dreams, Douglas*
Durango, Julia. *Dream hop*
Enersen, Adele. *When my baby dreams*
Farmer, Bonnie. *Isaac's dreamcatcher*
Ginsburg, Mirra. *Across the stream*
Gorbachev, Valeri. *Nicky and the big, bad wolves*
When someone is afraid
Gottfried, Maya. *Last night I dreamed a circus*
Henkes, Kevin. *Old Bear*
Hoban, Russell. *Rosie's magic horse*
Hurd, Thacher. *The weaver*
Hutchins, Hazel. *Beneath the bridge*
Isadora, Rachel. *Caribbean dream*
Jay, Alison. *1 2 3*
Johnson, Angela. *I dream of trains*
Johnson, Lindan Lee. *The dream jar*

Jonas, Ann. *The quilt*
Joyce, William. *The Sandman: the story of Sanderson Mansnoozie*
Keats, Ezra Jack. *Dreams*
Kenah, Katharine. *The dream shop*
King, Martin Luther, Jr. *I have a dream*
Kirk, David. *Oh So Tiny bunny*
Lawson, Dorie McCullough. *Tex*
Le Guin, Ursula K. *Cat dreams*
Lester, Julius. *Albidaro and the mischievous dream*
Lithgow, John. *Never play music right next to the zoo*
London, Jonathan. *Froggy goes to school*
McCain, Becky R. *Grandmother's dreamcatcher*
McDermott, Gerald. *Daniel O'Rourke*
MacDonald, Ross. *Another perfect day*
Mack, Jeff. *Hush little polar bear*
Maconie, Robin. *Alice and her fabulous teeth*
McPhail, David. *Boy on the brink*
Martin, Bill, Jr. *Barn dance!*
Little granny quarterback
Martin, Emily Winfield. *Dream animals*
Martin, Ruth. *Moon dreams*
Melmed, Laura Krauss. *Jumbo's lullaby*
Mendes, Valerie. *Look at me, Grandma!*
Milgrim, David. *Another day in the Milky Way*
Nahas, Sylvaine. *Nicolo's unicorn*
Napoli, Donna Jo. *Ready to dream*
Neuschwander, Cindy. *Amanda Bean's amazing dream*
Osofsky, Audrey. *Dreamcatcher*
Owens, Mary Beth. *Panda whispers*
Pfister, Marcus. *Wake up, Santa Claus!*
Pilkey, Dav. *When cats dream*
Polacco, Patricia. *Appelemando's dreams*
Price, Mathew. *Patch and the rabbits*
Ringgold, Faith. *My dream of Martin Luther King*
Tar Beach
Rock, Lois. *I wish tonight*
Rockhill, Dennis. *Polar slumber / Sueño polar*
Rohmann, Eric. *The cinder-eyed cats*
Roper, Janice M. *Dancing on the moon*
Sava, Donna Lynn. *Teddy bear dreams*
Say, Allen. *A river dream*
Sayles, Elizabeth. *The goldfish yawned*
Schaefer, Carole Lexa. *Down in the woods at sleepytime*
Down in the woods at sleepytime [board book]
Schuch, Steve. *A symphony of whales*
Seibold, J. Otto. *Penguin dreams*
Sendak, Maurice. *In the night kitchen*
Senshu, Noriko. *Sonny's dream*
Shah, Idries. *The boy without a name*
Sheldon, Dyan. *Under the moon*
Showers, Paul. *Sleep is for everyone*
Shulevitz, Uri. *The treasure*
Simmons, Jane. *Go to sleep, Daisy*
Slater, Dashka. *Firefighters in the dark*
Steig, William. *The Zabajaba Jungle*
Stewart, Amber. *Bedtime for Button*
Tafuri, Nancy. *Junglewalk*
What the sun sees / What the moon sees
Teague, David. *Franklin's big dreams*
Tudor, Tasha. *A tale for Easter*
Wahl, Jan. *Elf night*
Ward, Helen. *The tin forest*
Washington, Ned. *When you wish upon a star*
Watt, Mélanie. *Scaredy Squirrel at night*
Weber, Linda Kay. *Louie Larkey and the bad dream patrol*
Wick, Walter. *Can you see what I see? dream machine*
Wiebe, Rudy. *Hidden buffalo*
Wiesner, David. *Free fall*
Wild, Margaret. *Going home*
Wood, Audrey. *Sweet dream pie*
Yaccarino, Dan. *Good night, Mr. Night*
Yolen, Jane. *Moon ball*
Yorinks, Arthur. *Hey, Al*
Young, Ed. *Night visitors*
Yum, Hyewon. *Last night*
Zalben, Jane Breskin. *Baby shower*
Ziefert, Harriet. *Squarehead*
What do ducks dream?

Dwarfs, midgets

Delessert, Etienne. *The seven dwarfs*
Grimm, Jacob and Wilhelm. *Rose Red and the bear prince*
Snow White, ill. by Melinda Copper
Snow White, ill. by Quentin Gréban
Snow White, ill. by Trina Schart Hyman
Snow White, ill. by Charles Santore
Snow White and the seven dwarfs, ill. by Wanda Gág
Snow White and the seven dwarfs, ill. by Laura Ljungkvist
Ruzzier, Sergio. *The little giant*

Dwellings *see* Buildings; Homes, houses

Dying *see* Death

Ears *see* Anatomy – ears; Disabilities – deafness; Senses – hearing

Earth

Asch, Frank. *The earth and I*
Branley, Franklyn M. *Earthquakes*
The sun, our nearest star
What makes day and night
Cameron, Eileen. *Canyon*
Cole, Joanna. *The magic school bus inside the earth*
Elschner, Geraldine. *Moonchild, star of the sea*
Ernst, Lisa Campbell. *Round like a ball!*
Flanagan, Alice K. *Rocks*
Soil
Water
Glaser, Linda. *Our big home*
Greene, Rhonda Gowler. *The beautiful world that God made*
Guiberson, Brenda Z. *Earth*
Jenkins, Steve. *Hottest, coldest, highest, deepest*
Karas, G. Brian. *On Earth*
Lauber, Patricia. *You're aboard spaceship Earth*

Lewis, J. Patrick. *Earth and me, our family tree*
Earth and you, a closer view
Luenn, Nancy. *Mother earth*
Martin, Bill, Jr. *I love our Earth*
Milgrim, David. *Here in space*
Munro, Roxie. *Ecomazes*
Parr, Todd. *The earth book*
Reiser, Lynn. *Earthdance*
Rockwell, Anne. *What's so bad about gasoline?*
Ross, Michael Elsohn. *Earth cycles*
Siomades, Lorianne. *A place to bloom*
Staub, Leslie. *Bless this house*
Wells, Robert E. *What's so special about planet Earth?*
Zoehfeld, Kathleen Weidner. *How mountains are made*

Earthquakes

Danticat, Edwidge. *Eight days*
Harrison, David L. *Earthquakes*
Lee, Milly. *Earthquake*
Oelschlager, Vanita. *I came from the water*
Palatini, Margie. *Earthquack*
Perry, Phyllis J. *Pandas' earthquake escape*
Prager, Ellen J. *Earthquakes*
Watson, Jesse Joshua. *Hope for Haiti*

Eating *see* Food

Ecology

Alexander, Sue. *Behold the trees*
Aliki. *My visit to the zoo*
Alter, Anna. *What can you do with an old red shoe?*
Appelt, Kathi. *Miss Lady Bird's wildflowers*
Armentrout, David. *John Muir*
Arnold, Caroline. *A warmer world*
Arnosky, Jim. *Crinkleroot's guide to giving back to nature*
Crinkleroot's visit to Crinkle Cove
Atwell, Debby. *River*
Baker, Jeannie. *The story of rosy dock*
Where the forest meets the sea
Window
Bateman, Donna M. *Deep in the swamp*
Out on the prairie
Baylor, Byrd. *The desert is theirs*
Beard, Alex. *Crocodile's tears*
Berenstain, Stan and Jan. *The Berenstain bears don't pollute anymore*
Berger, Carin. *OK go*
Berger, Melvin. *Oil spill!*
Brenner, Barbara A. *One small place by the sea*
Brett, Jan. *Mossy*
Brown, Laurie Krasny. *Dinosaurs to the rescue*
Brown, Marc. *Arthur turns green*
Brown, Peter. *The curious garden*
Brown, Ruth. *The old tree*
Burton, Virginia Lee. *The little house*
Catchpool, Michael. *The cloud spinner*
Cherry, Lynne. *The great kapok tree*
A river ran wild
Child, Lauren. *What planet are you from Clarice Bean?*
Chin, Jason. *Coral reefs*
Cole, Henry. *The littlest evergreen*
On Meadowview Street
Cole, Joanna. *The magic school bus and the climate challenge*
Corr, Christopher. *Whole world*
Côté, Geneviève. *Mr. King's things*
Crowe, Carole. *Turtle girl*
Davies, Nicola. *Oceans and seas*
deGroat, Diane. *Ants in your pants, worms in your plants!*
Dennard, Deborah. *Hedgehog haven*
DePalma, Mary Newell. *A grand old tree*
Flanagan, Alice K. *Soil*
Formento, Alison. *These seas count!*
Franco, Betsy. *Pond circle*
Galko, Francine. *Cave animals*
Gall, Chris. *Awesome Dawson*
George, Jean Craighead. *The buffalo are back*
The eagles are back
Everglades
The last polar bear
The wolves are back
Gerardi, Jan. *The little recycler*
Gibbons, Gail. *Coral reefs*
Exploring the deep, dark sea
Nature's green umbrella
Recycle!
Glaser, Linda. *Garbage helps our garden grow*
Gliori, Debi. *The trouble with dragons*
Grupper, Jonathan. *Destination — Rocky Mountains*
Destination, rain forest
Guiberson, Brenda Z. *Cactus hotel*
Earth
Hader, Berta Hoerner. *The mighty hunter*
Hamilton, Virginia. *Drylongso*
Jaguarundi
Heinz, Brian J. *Butternut Hollow Pond*
Hewitt, Sally. *All year round*
Woods and meadows
Himmelman, John. *Mouse in a meadow*
Hines, Gary. *A Christmas tree in the White House*
Hobbie, Holly. *Gem*
Jackson, Ellen. *Earth Mother*
Jeffers, Oliver. *The great paper caper*
Jenkins, Steve. *I see a kookaburra*
Johanasen, Heather. *About the rain forest*
Johnson, Amy Crane. *Mason moves away / Mason se muda*
Johnson, Jen Cullerton. *Seeds of change*
Johnston, Tony. *The whole green world*
Kann, Victoria. *Emeraldalicious*
Keister, Douglas. *Fernando's gift / El regalo de Fernando*
Kleven, Elisa. *The dancing deer and the foolish hunter*
Glasswings
Klingel, Cynthia Fitterer. *Underground*
Kroll, Steven. *Stuff!*
Kudlinski, Kathleen V. *The seaside switch*
Kurtz, Kevin. *A day in the salt marsh*
Lamstein, Sarah Marwil. *Big night for salamanders*
Lauber, Patricia. *Be a friend to trees*
Who eats what?
Lawlor, Laurie. *Rachel Carson and her book that changed the world*
Leedy, Loreen. *The great trash bash*
Levinson, Nancy Smiler. *Death Valley*
Rain forests
Lewin, Ted. *Amazon boy*
Lewis, J. Patrick. *Earth and you, a closer view*
London, Jonathan. *Gone again ptarmigan*
Luenn, Nancy. *Mother earth*
Squish!
Lumry, Amanda. *Polar bear puzzle*

Safari in South Africa
Maass, Robert. *Garbage*
McClements, George. *Dinosaur Woods*
MacDonald, Margaret Read. *Surf war!*
McMillan, Bruce. *Days of the ducklings*
McPhail, David. *The family tree*
Markle, Sandra. *Waiting for ice*
Mazer, Anne. *The salamander room*
Middleton, Charlotte. *Nibbles*
Miller, Debbie S. *Are trees alive?*
River of life
Moss, Miriam. *This is the tree*
Muldrow, Diane. *We planted a tree*
Munro, Roxie. *Desert days, desert nights*
Ecomazes
Murphy, Stuart J. *Earth Day — hooray!*
Napoli, Donna Jo. *Mama Miti*
Nivola, Claire A. *Life in the ocean*
Planting the trees of Kenya
Oldland, Nicholas. *Big bear hug*
Pandell, Karen. *I love you sun, I love you moon*
Parr, Todd. *The earth book*
Peet, Bill. *The caboose who got loose*
Farewell to Shady Glade
Fly, Homer, fly
The gnats of knotty pine
The wump world
Perez, Monica. *Curious George plants a tree*
Peterson, Cris. *Amazing grazing*
Poppy Bear
Quattlebaum, Mary. *Jo MacDonald had a garden*
Rand, Gloria. *Prince William*
Reed, Lynn Rowe. *Roscoe and the pelican rescue*
Reed-Jones, Carol. *The tree in the ancient forest*
Reynolds, Aaron. *Carnivores*
Robinson, Tim. *Tobias, the quig, and the rumplenut tree*
Rockwell, Anne. *What's so bad about gasoline?*
Roop, Connie. *Let's celebrate Earth Day*
Root, Phyllis. *Big belching bog*
Rosenberg, Madelyn. *Happy birthday, tree!*
Rosenstock, Barb. *The camping trip that changed America*
Roth, Susan L. *Parrots over Puerto Rico*
Rotner, Shelley. *The buzz on bees*
Rowe, John A. *Moondog*
Ryder, Joanne. *The waterfall's gift*
St. Pierre, Stephanie. *What the sea saw*
Sanders, Scott R. *Crawdad Creek*
San Souci, Robert D. *The birds of Killingworth*
Sayre, April Pulley. *The shape of Betts Meadow*
Trout are made of trees
Sazaklis, John. *Fowl play*
Seattle, Chief. *Brother eagle, sister sky*
Sensel, Joni. *Bears barge in*
Seuss, Dr. *The Lorax*
Seven, John. *The ocean story*
Showers, Paul. *Where does the garbage go?*
Siddals, Mary McKenna. *Compost stew*
Sierra, Judy. *Ballyhoo Bay*
Siomades, Lorianne. *A place to bloom*
Sirett, Dawn. *Love your world*
Spinelli, Eileen. *Miss Fox's class goes green*
Staub, Leslie. *Bless this house*
Stewart, Melissa. *A place for birds*
A place for frogs
Stone, Lynn M. *Life of the kelp forest*
Partners
Suzuki, David. *Salmon forest*
Swamp, Jake. *Giving thanks*
Tafolla, Carmen. *Baby Coyote and the old woman / El coyotito y la viejita*
Thornhill, Jan. *Wild in the city*
Toft, Kim Michelle. *The world that we want*
Tresselt, Alvin R. *The gift of the tree*
Waldman, Neil. *They came from the Bronx*
Wallace, Nancy Elizabeth. *Recycle every day!*
Walsh, Melanie. *10 things I can do to help my world*
Ward, D. J. *What happens to our trash?*
Ward, Helen. *The tin forest*
Weninger, Brigitte. *Precious water*
Winer, Yvonne. *Frogs sing songs*
Winkelman, Barbara Gaines. *Sockeye's journey home*
Winter, Jeanette. *Wangari's trees of peace*
Wong, Janet S. *The dumpster diver*
Wood, Douglas. *Old Turtle*
Wright, Maureen. *Earth Day, birthday!*
Yahgulanaas, Michael Nicoll. *The little hummingbird*
Yezerski, Thomas. *Meadowlands*
Yolen, Jane. *Welcome to the river of grass*
Welcome to the sea of sand
Where have the unicorns gone?
Ziefert, Harriet. *My forever dress*
Zoehfeld, Kathleen Weidner. *Secrets of the garden*

Education *see* School

Eggs

Aesop. *The goose that laid the golden egg*
Andersen, Hans Christian. *The woman with the eggs*
Aston, Dianna Hutts. *An egg is quiet*
Auch, Mary Jane. *The Easter egg farm*
Eggs mark the spot
Averbeck, Jim. *Except if*
Balian, Lorna. *Humbug rabbit*
Bateson-Hill, Margaret. *Masha and the firebird*
Battut, Eric. *The fox and the hen*
Berenstain, Stan and Jan. *The Berenstain bears and the real Easter eggs*
Brett, Jan. *The Easter egg*
Hedgie's surprise
Brown, Margaret Wise. *The golden egg book*
Burg, Sarah Emmanuelle. *One more egg*
Carter, David A. *Easter bugs*
Cutbill, Andy. *The cow that laid an egg*
Dahl, Michael. *Eggs and legs*
DePalma, Mary Newell. *The strange egg*
Desmoinaux, Christel. *Mrs. Hen's big surprise*
Douglas, Erin. *Get that pest!*
Dudley, Rebecca. *Hank finds an egg*
Dunrea, Olivier. *Ollie*
Ollie's Easter eggs
Ollie's Easter eggs [board book]
Fox, Mem. *Hunwick's egg*
Franceschelli, Christopher. *(Oliver)*
Friend, Catherine. *The perfect nest*
Gill, Shelley. *The egg*
Golson, Terry. *Tillie lays an egg*
Graham, Bob. *Dimity Dumpty*
Grambling, Lois G. *Here comes T. Rex Cottontail*
Gravett, Emily. *The odd egg*
Halfmann, Janet. *Eggs 1, 2, 3*
Hartmann, Wendy. *The dinosaurs are back and it's all your fault, Edward!*
Heller, Ruth. *Chickens aren't the only ones*
Hill, Eric. *Spot's first Easter*

Horowitz, Dave. *Humpty Dumpty climbs again*
Howard, Reginald. *The big, big wall*
Jenkins, Priscilla Belz. *A nest full of eggs*
Joyce, William. *Bently and egg*
Kangas, Juli. *The surprise visitor*
Kellogg, Steven. *A penguin pup for Pinkerton*
Kimmel, Eric A. *The birds' gift*
Latter, Jill. *Mama Hen's big day*
Lionni, Leo. *An extraordinary egg*
Meddaugh, Susan. *Harry on the rocks*
Milhous, Katherine. *The egg tree*
Montes, Marisa. *Egg-napped!*
Mortimer, Anne. *Bunny's Easter egg*
Mother Goose. *Humpty Dumpty*
Munro, Roxie. *Hatch!*
Nakagawa, Rieko. *Guri and Gura*
Nolen, Jerdine. *Raising dragons*
Partridge, Elizabeth. *Pig's eggs*
Peet, Bill. *The pinkish, purplish, bluish egg*
Polacco, Patricia. *Chicken Sunday*
Just plain Fancy
Rechenka's eggs
Polhemus, Coleman. *The crocodile blues*
Posada, Mia. *Guess what is growing inside this egg*
Potter, Beatrix. *The tale of Jemima Puddle-Duck*
Rand, Betseygail. *Big Bunny*
Roberts, Bethany. *Easter mice*
Robertson, M. P. *The dragon snatcher*
The egg
Ross, Tom. *Eggbert, the slightly cracked egg*
Rouillard, Wendy. *Barnaby's bunny*
San Souci, Robert D. *The talking eggs*
Schertle, Alice. *Down the road*
Schubert, Ingrid. *Bear's eggs*
Schulman, Janet. *10 Easter egg hunters*
Seuss, Dr. *Horton hatches the egg*
Simmons, Jane. *Daisy and the egg*
Singer, Marilyn. *Eggs*
Sklansky, Amy E. *Where do chicks come from?*
Slegers, Liesbet. *Happy Easter!*
Smith, Alex T. *Foxy and Egg*
Smythe, Theresa. *Chester's colorful Easter eggs*
Stalder, Päivi. *Ernest's first Easter*
Stevenson, James. *The great big especially beautiful Easter egg*
Stileman, Kali. *Roly-poly egg*
Stoeke, Janet Morgan. *Minerva Louise and the colorful eggs*
Sykes, Julie. *Dora's eggs*
Tafuri, Nancy. *Whose chick are you?*
Taylor, Shirley. *The cross in the egg*
Thomas, Jan. *The Easter Bunny's assistant*
Tudor, Tasha. *A tale for Easter*
Vainio, Pirkko. *Who hid the Easter eggs?*
Waddell, Martin. *It's quacking time*
Ward, Lindsay. *When Blue met Egg*
Weigelt, Udo. *The Easter Bunny's baby*
Wilhelm, Hans. *More bunny trouble*
Quacky Ducky's Easter egg
Wilson, Karma. *What's in the egg, Little Pip?*
Wormell, Mary. *Hilda Hen's search*

Egyptian language *see* Hieroglyphics

Elderly *see* Old age

Elevators, escalators

Murphy, Stuart J. *Elevator magic*

Emotions

Aliki. *Feelings*
Allen, Kathryn Madeline. *A kiss means I love you*
Alrawi, Karim. *The girl who lost her smile*
Anderson, Stephen Axel. *I know the moon*
Anholt, Catherine. *What makes me happy?*
Berger, Samantha. *Crankenstein*
Berkner, Laurie. *The story of my feelings*
Bluthenthal, Diana Cain. *I'm not invited?*
Boyden, Linda. *The blue roses*
Brisson, Pat. *Sometimes we were brave*
Brown, Alan James. *Hoot and Holler*
Brown, Laurie Krasny. *When dinosaurs die*
Brown, Tameka Fryer. *My cold plum lemon pie bluesy mood*
Browne, Anthony. *How do you feel?*
Burdett, Lois. *The tempest for kids*
Burrowes, Adjoa J. *Grandma's purple flowers*
Cain, Janan. *The way I feel*
Carter, David A. *If you're happy and you know it, clap your hands*
Cocca-Leffler, Maryann. *Theo's mood*
Cowell, Cressida. *What shall we do with the Boo-Hoo Baby?*
Curtis, Jamie Lee. *Today I feel silly and other moods that make my day*
Daly, Niki. *What's cooking, Jamela?*
Dewdney, Anna. *Grumpy Gloria*
Llama Llama misses Mama
DiCamillo, Kate. *Great joy*
Doughty, Rebecca. *Oh no! Time to go!*
Dunbar, Polly. *Flyaway Katie*
Edvall, Lilian. *The rabbit who longed for home*
Edwards, Becky. *My first day at nursery school*
Emberley, Ed. *Glad monster, sad monster*
Fernandes, Eugenie. *Sleepy little mouse*
Frame, Jeron Ashford. *Yesterday I had the blues*
Freedman, Claire. *Where's your smile, crocodile?*
Freymann, Saxton. *How are you peeling?*
Galdone, Paul. *The teeny-tiny woman*
Got, Yves. *Sam loves kisses*
Grossman, Bill. *My little sister hugged an ape*
Hall, Michael. *My heart is like a zoo*
Harper, Charise Mericle. *Henry's heart*
Harper, Jessica. *Lizzy's ups and downs*
Hills, Tad. *Duck and Goose, how are you feeling?*
Hines, Anna Grossnickle. *Even if I spill my milk?*
Hobbie, Holly. *Toot and Puddle, you are my sunshine*
Hodgkinson, Leigh. *Smile!*
Hopkinson, Deborah. *Bluebird summer*
Hout, Mies van. *Happy*
Inkpen, Mick. *Wibbly Pig is upset*
Isadora, Rachel. *At the crossroads*
Jackson, Ellen. *Sometimes bad things happen*
Johnson, Angela. *The leaving morning*
Kimmel, Haven. *Orville, a dog story*
Klise, Kate. *Why do you cry?*
Konnecke, Ole. *Anthony and the girls*
Krauss, Ruth. *You're just what I need*
Krosoczka, Jarrett J. *My buddy, Slug*
Lairla, Sergio. *Abel and the wolf*
Lester, Helen. *Hurty feelings*
Lewin, Hugh. *Jafta*
Jafta — the homecoming
Lodge, Jo. *Happy Snappy!*

McAllister, Angela. *The little blue rabbit*
Maclear, Kyo. *Virginia Wolf*
Melmed, Laura Krauss. *A hug goes around*
Munsch, Robert N. *Aaron's hair*
Murphy, Mary. *I feel happy, and sad, and angry, and glad*
Napoli, Donna Jo. *Flamingo dream*
Nemiroff, Marc A. *Shy spaghetti and excited eggs*
Nicholls, Judith. *Someone I like*
Norling, Beth. *The stone baby*
Numeroff, Laura Joffe. *The hope tree*
Otoshi, Kathryn. *One*
Parr, Todd. *The feelings book*
Things that make you feel good, things that make you feel bad
Patricelli, Leslie. *Baby happy, baby sad*
Patterson, Rebecca. *My no, no, no day!*
Peacock, Carol Antoinette. *Mommy far, Mommy near*
Proimos, James. *The loudness of Sam*
Raschka, Chris. *Ring! Yo?*
Yo! Yes?
Robberecht, Thierry. *Stolen smile*
Rogers, Fred. *Adoption*
Making friends
Moving
Ross, Dave. *A book of hugs*
A book of kisses
Rotner, Shelley. *Feeling thankful*
Say, Allen. *Allison*
Seeger, Laura Vaccaro. *Walter was worried*
Senisi, Ellen B. *Hurray for pre-K!*
Simon, Norma. *How do I feel?*
Smith, Linda. *Mrs. Biddlebox*
Smith, Maggie. *Desser, the best ever cat*
Spelman, Cornelia Maude. *Mama and Daddy Bear's divorce*
When I care about others
Spinelli, Eileen. *When you are happy*
Stanley, Malaika Rose. *Baby Ruby bawled*
Stevenson, James. *Fun, no fun*
Strauss, Anna. *Hush, Mama loves you*
Tabby, Abigail. *Baby face*
Tankard, Jeremy. *Grumpy Bird*
Thomas, Jane Resh. *Lights on the river*
Vigna, Judith. *Saying goodbye to daddy*
Waber, Bernard. *Ira says goodbye*
Walter, Mildred Pitts. *Two too much*
Weeks, Sarah. *My somebody special*
Weninger, Brigitte. *Good-bye, Daddy!*
Wight, Tamra. *The three grumpies*
Willems, Mo. *The pigeon has feelings, too!*
Willis, Jeanne. *Susan laughs*
Winthrop, Elizabeth. *Promises*
Young, Jessica. *My blue is happy*
Yum, Hyewon. *Last night*
Ziefert, Harriet. *Bunny's lessons*

Emotions – anger

Alexander, Martha G. *And my mean old mother will be sorry, Blackboard Bear*
Aliki. *We are best friends*
Bang, Molly. *When Sophie gets angry — really, really angry . . .*
Bunting, Eve. *Smoky night*
Burnell, Heather Ayris. *Bedtime monster / ¡A dormir, pequeño monstruo!*
Clarke, Jane. *Trumpet*
Demers, Dominique. *Old Thomas and the little fairy*
Dewdney, Anna. *Llama Llama mad at Mama*
Du Bois, William Pène. *Bear party*
Elliott, David. *Finn throws a fit!*
Everitt, Betsy. *Mean soup*
Fox, Mem. *Harriet, you'll drive me wild*
Gassman, Julie. *Crabby pants*
Gilmore, Rachna. *Making grizzle grow*
Harrington, Janice N. *Roberto walks home*
Harris, Robie H. *The day Leo said I hate you!*
Henkes, Kevin. *Lilly's big day*
Lilly's purple plastic purse
Hooks, Bell. *Grump groan growl*
Howe, James. *Horace and Morris join the chorus (but what about Dolores?)*
Hughes, Shirley. *Don't want to go!*
Jonell, Lynne. *When Mommy was mad*
Jones, Elizabeth. *Sunshine and Storm*
Kaplan, Michael B. *Betty Bunny wants everything*
Kroll, Steven. *That makes me mad*
Lachner, Dorothea. *Danny, the angry lion*
Landa, Norbert. *Little Bear and the wishing tree*
Langreuter, Jutta. *Little Bear and the big fight*
Lester, Helen. *Princess Penelope's parrot*
Lewis, Kim. *Friends*
Lyon, George Ella. *No dessert forever!*
McBratney, Sam. *I'll always be your friend*
I'm sorry
Moroney, Trace. *When I'm feeling angry*
Morrison, Toni. *The book of mean people*
Moss, Miriam. *Smudge's grumpy day*
Nadel, Carolina. *Daddy's home*
OHora, Zachariah. *No fits, Nilson!*
O'Malley, Kevin. *Humpty Dumpty egg-splodes*
Palatini, Margie. *Goldie is mad*
Perl, Erica S. *Dotty*
Pienkowski, Jan. *Bel and Bub and the bad snowball*
Sakai, Komako. *Mad at Mommy*
Sasso, Sandy Eisenberg. *Cain and Abel*
Seeger, Laura Vaccaro. *Bully*
Shannon, David. *The amazing Christmas extravaganza*
Shea, Pegi Deitz. *The boy and the spell*
Shields, Carol Diggory. *I wish my brother was a dog*
Shields, Gillian. *Elephantantrum!*
Spelman, Cornelia Maude. *When I feel angry*
Sunami, Kitoba. *How the fisherman tricked the genie*
Sykes, Julie. *Little Tiger's big surprise*
Tutu, Archbishop Desmond. *Desmond and the very mean word*
Urban, Linda. *Mouse was mad*
Vail, Rachel. *Flabbersmashed about you*
Sometimes I'm Bombaloo
Waddell, Martin. *The Super Hungry Dinosaur*
Weiss, Ellen. *The taming of Lola*
Wells, Rosemary. *Miracle melts down*
Wormell, Mary. *Bernard the angry rooster*
Yolen, Jane. *How do dinosaurs say I'm mad?*
Yorinks, Arthur. *Harry and Lulu*
Zolotow, Charlotte. *The quarreling book*

Emotions – embarrassment

Altman, Alexandra Jessup. *Waiting for Benjamin*
Baryshnikov, Mikhail. *Because . . .*
Brown, Marc. *Arthur's underwear*
Bunting, Eve. *A picnic in October*
Feiffer, Kate. *My mom is trying to ruin my life*
Foreman, Michael. *Oh! if only . . .*

Freeman, Don. *Quiet! There's a canary in the library*
Goodrich, Carter. *Zorro gets an outfit*
Moore-Mallinos, Jennifer. *My brother is autistic*
Raschka, Chris. *The blushful hippopotamus*
Singer, Marilyn. *Tallulah's Nutcracker*
Wood, Audrey. *Weird parents*

Emotions – envy, jealousy

Alexander, Martha G. *Nobody asked me if I wanted a baby sister*
When the new baby comes, I'm moving out
Asch, Frank. *Bear's bargain*
Calhoun, Mary. *High-wire Henry*
Cole, Joanna. *The new baby at your house*
Desmond, Jenni. *Red cat blue cat*
Dierssen, Andreas. *The old red tractor*
Egan, Tim. *A mile from Ellington Station*
Enderle, Judith Ross. *Smile, Principessa!*
Fleming, Denise. *Buster*
Gantos, Jack. *Back to school for Rotten Ralph*
Rotten Ralph's rotten Christmas
Grimm, Jacob and Wilhelm. *Snow White,* ill. by Melinda Copper
Snow White, ill. by Quentin Gréban
Snow White, ill. by Trina Schart Hyman
Snow White, ill. by Charles Santore
Snow White and the seven dwarfs, ill. by Wanda Gág
Snow White and the seven dwarfs, ill. by Laura Ljungkvist
Hamilton, Arlene. *Only a cow*
Harper, Anita. *It's not fair!*
Hartt-Sussman, Heather. *Here comes Hortense!*
Havill, Juanita. *Jamaica and Brianna*
Hest, Amy. *You're the boss, Baby Duck*
Hoban, Russell. *A baby sister for Frances*
A birthday for Frances
Howe, James. *I wish I were a butterfly*
Hubbard, Woodleigh Marx. *Whoa, jealousy*
Joosse, Barbara. *Nugget and Darling*
Keller, Holly. *Geraldine's baby brother*
Kellogg, Steven. *Best friends*
Layne, Steven L. *Love the baby*
Lindenbaum, Pija. *Mini Mia and her darling uncle*
Lionni, Leo. *Alexander and the wind-up mouse*
Macdonald, Maryann. *The pink party*
Martin, Ann M. *Rachel Parker, kindergarten show-off*
Mathers, Petra. *Lottie's new friend*
Mayer, Mercer. *One frog too many*
Milligan, Bryce. *The prince of Ireland and the three magic stallions*
Moore, Liz. *Zizi and Tish*
Peet, Bill. *The luckiest one of all*
Reynolds, Peter H. *The best kid in the world*
Robberecht, Thierry. *Back into Mommy's tummy*
Roper, Janice M. *Dancing on the moon*
Rosen, Michael. *Howler*
Russo, Marisabina. *The trouble with baby*
San Souci, Robert D. *Peter and the blue witch baby*
Satoshi, Kako. *Little Daruma and little Tengu*
Shea, Bob. *Unicorn thinks he's pretty great*
Smalls-Hector, Irene. *Because you're lucky*
Stein, David Ezra. *Ned's new friend*
Stephens, Helen. *What about me?*
Sykes, Julie. *Little Tiger's big surprise*
Townsend, Michael. *Cute and cuter*
Umansky, Kaye. *I don't like Gloria!*
Voake, Charlotte. *Ginger*
Waber, Bernard. *Evie and Margie*
Lyle and the birthday party
Wahl, Jan. *Mabel ran away with the toys*
Wewer, Iris. *My wild sister and me*
Wild, Margaret. *Fox*
Wortche, Allison. *Rosie Sprout's time to shine*
Yep, Laurence. *Dragon prince*

Emotions – fear

Alborough, Jez. *It's the bear*
Watch out! Big Bro's coming!
Alexander, Martha G. *I'll protect you from the jungle beasts*
Allen, Jonathan. *"I'm not scared!"*
Apple, Margot. *Brave Martha*
Arnold, Marsha Diane. *The bravest of us all*
Aylesworth, Jim. *Teddy bear tears*
Two terrible frights
Baker, Ken. *Brave little monster*
Baker, Roberta. *Olive's first sleepover*
Battersby, Katherine. *Brave Squish Rabbit*
Bauer, Marion Dane. *Dinosaur thunder*
Halloween forest
Jason's bears
Baum, Louis. *The mouse who braved bedtime*
Beaty, Andrea. *Hush, Baby Ghostling*
Beck, Scott. *Pepito the brave*
Bently, Peter. *King Jack and the dragon*
Berenstain, Stan and Jan. *The Berenstain bears get stage fright*
The Berenstain bears learn about strangers
Bergman, Mara. *Snip snap!*
Bird, Betsy. *Giant dance party*
Blake, Stephanie. *I don't want to go to school!*
Bonnett-Rampersaud, Louise. *Bubble and Squeak*
Bourgeois, Paulette. *Franklin and the thunderstorm*
Franklin in the dark
Boxall, Ed. *Francis the scaredy cat*
Bradbury, Ray. *Switch on the night*
Bright, Paul. *The bears in the bed and the great big storm*
Bunting, Eve. *Ghost's hour, spook's hour*
Capucilli, Alyssa Satin. *Katy Duck*
Carlin, Patricia. *Alfie is not afraid*
Carlson, Melody. *When the creepy things come out*
Carlson, Nancy. *There's a big, beautiful world out there!*
Carman, William. *What's that noise?*
Case, Chris. *Sophie and the next-door monsters*
Cave, Kathryn. *You've got dragons*
Chaconas, Dori. *Pennies in a jar*
Chorao, Kay. *Shadow night*
Cocca-Leffler, Maryann. *Bravery soup*
Cohen, Miriam. *Jim meets the thing*
The real-skin rubber monster mask
Collins, Suzanne. *Year of the jungle*
Covell, David. *Rat and Roach rock on!*
Cowell, Cressida. *Hiccup the seasick Viking*
Crimi, Carolyn. *Rock 'n' roll Mole*
Where's my mummy?
Crum, Shutta. *The bravest of the brave*
Cuyler, Margery. *Stop drop and roll*
Danneberg, Julie. *The big test*
Davis, Katie. *Kindergarten rocks!*
Scared stiff
Day, Nancy Raines. *On a windy night*
Demi. *The boy who painted dragons*
De Monfreid, Dorothee. *Dark night*

Derrick, David G., Jr. *I'm the scariest thing in the jungle!*
Dewdney, Anna. *Roly Poly pangolin*
Diesen, Deborah. *The pout-pout fish in the big-big dark*
Dominguez, Angela. *Let's go, Hugo!*
Dubosarsky, Ursula. *The terrible plop*
Dunbar, Joyce. *The monster who ate darkness*
Dunrea, Olivier. *Little cub*
Edwards, Michelle. *What's that noise?*
Egan, Tim. *The experiments of Doctor Vermin*
Ellis, Sarah. *Ben over night*
Emberley, Ed. *Go away, big green monster!*
Engelbreit, Mary. *Queen of Halloween*
Farmer, Bonnie. *Isaac's dreamcatcher*
Faulkner, Keith. *The scared little bear*
Fitzpatrick, Marie-Louise. *Lizzy and Skunk*
Flattinger, Hubert. *Stormy night*
Foley, Greg. *Willoughby and the moon*
Fore, S. J. *Tiger can't sleep*
Fox, Diane. *Tyson the terrible*
Frankel, Erin. *Dare!*
Frazee, Marla. *Roller coaster*
Funke, Cornelia. *The wildest brother*
Gaiman, Neil. *The dangerous alphabet*
Galbraith, Kathryn O. *Boo, bunny!*
Gantos, Jack. *Back to school for Rotten Ralph*
Gay, Michel. *Zee is not scared*
Geisert, Arthur. *Lights out*
Genechten, Guido van. *No ghost under my bed*
Ricky is brave
Gliori, Debi. *The scariest thing of all*
Goldin, Barbara Diamond. *Night lights*
Gonyea, Mark. *The spooky box*
Goossens, Philippe. *Knock! Knock! Knock! Who's there?*
Gorbachev, Valeri. *Dragon is coming!*
Nicky and the big, bad wolves
When someone is afraid
Grandits, John. *Ten rules you absolutely must not break if you want to survive the school bus*
Green, Alison. *The fox in the dark*
Greene, Rhonda Gowler. *Eek! Creak! Snicker, sneak*
Harris, Robie H. *When lions roar*
Heder, Thyra. *Fraidyzoo*
Heide, Florence Parry. *Some things are scary*
Helakoski, Leslie. *Big chickens*
Big chickens go to town
Hest, Amy. *Off to school, Baby Duck*
Hicks, Barbara Jean. *Jitterbug jam*
Hines, Anna Grossnickle. *My own big bed*
Rumble thumble boom!
Hoban, Russell. *Bedtime for Frances*
Hoppe, Paul. *The woods*
Horowitz, Dave. *Chico the brave*
Howe, James. *There's a monster under my bed*
Hughes, Shirley. *Don't want to go!*
Ives, Penny. *Celestine, drama queen*
Jennings, Sharon. *No monsters here*
Priscilla's paw de deux
Johnston, Tony. *Little Rabbit goes to sleep*
Jonas, Ann. *Holes and peeks*
Julian, Alison. *Brave as a bunny can be*
Keller, Holly. *Brave Horace*
Help!
Sophie's window
Kimura, Yuichi. *One stormy night . . .*
One sunny day . . .
Kirk, Daniel. *Library mouse: a world to explore*
Kirk, David. *Miss Spider's tea party*
Klise, Kate. *Little Rabbit and the Night Mare*
Koller, Jackie French. *No such thing*
Krensky, Stephen. *Spark the firefighter*
Kroll, Virginia L. *Makayla cares about others*
Lamm, C. Drew. *Pirates*
Landa, Norbert. *The great monster hunt*
Layne, Steven L. *My brother Dan's delicious*
Lears, Laurie. *Ben has something to say*
Lester, Helen. *Something might happen*
Lin, Grace. *Olvina flies*
Olvina swims
Lindbergh, Reeve. *Bridget and the gray wolves*
London, Jonathan. *Froggy learns to swim*
Lucke, Deb. *The boy who wouldn't swim*
Lyon, George Ella. *Cecil's story*
McAllister, Angela. *Trust me, Mom!*
McBratney, Sam. *The dark at the top of the stairs*
McCully, Emily Arnold. *Mirette on the high wire*
MacDonald, Margaret Read. *The squeaky door*
McGhee, Alison. *Countdown to kindergarten*
Song of middle C
McPhail, David. *Water boy*
Martín Larrañaga, Ana. *Woo! The not-so-scary Ghost*
Mathews, Judith. *Nathaniel Willy, scared silly*
May, Eleanor. *Albert is not scared*
Mayer, Mercer. *There are monsters everywhere*
There's a nightmare in my closet
There's an alligator under my bed
You're the scaredy cat
Meserve, Jessica. *Bedtime without Arthur*
Michelson, Richard. *Oh no, not ghosts!*
Miller, William. *A house by the river*
Milord, Susan. *Happy school year!*
Modarressi, Mitra. *Owlet's first flight*
Mollel, Tololwa M. *Rhinos for lunch and elephants for supper*
Moodie, Fiona. *Noko and the night monster*
Moore, Lilian. *Beware, take care*
Morgan, Michaela. *Brave, brave mouse*
Moroney, Trace. *When I'm feeling scared*
Murphy, Jim. *Fergus and the Night-Demon*
Nash, Ogden. *The adventures of Isabel*, ill. by James Marshall
The adventures of Isabel, ill. by Bridget Starr Taylor
Newman, Lesléa. *Miss Tutu's star*
Nivola, Claire A. *The forest*
Norman, Geoffrey. *Stars above us*
Paraskevas, Betty. *Maggie and the Ferocious Beast, the big scare*
Patricelli, Leslie. *The Patterson puppies and the midnight monster party*
Patschke, Steve. *The spooky book*
Paul, Alison. *The crow (a not so scary story)*
Peck, Richard. *Monster night at Grandma's house*
Penn, Audrey. *A bedtime kiss for Chester Raccoon*
Pfister, Marcus. *Rainbow fish to the rescue!*
Pinfold, Levi. *Black dog*
Pitzer, Susanna. *Not afraid of dogs*
Polacco, Patricia. *Thunder cake*
Powell, Polly. *Just dessert*
Pryor, Bonnie. *The porcupine mouse*
Pumphrey, Jerome. *Creepy things are scaring me*
Raschka, Chris. *Can't sleep*
Daisy gets lost
Waffle
Ray, Mary Lyn. *Boom!*
Reynolds, Aaron. *Creepy carrots!*

Reynolds, Marilynn. *The name of the child*
Riggs, Shannon. *Not in Room 204*
Robberecht, Thierry. *Sam is never scared*
Robbins, Beth. *Tom, Ally, and the baby-sitter*
Tom and Ally visit the doctor
Tom's afraid of the dark
Tom's new haircut
Rockwell, Anne. *Katie Catz makes a splash*
Welcome to kindergarten
Rodriguez, Edel. *Sergio makes a splash*
Rosenberry, Vera. *Vera's first day of school*
Rosoff, Meg. *Jumpy Jack and Googily*
Ross, Tony. *I want my light on!*
Runton, Andy. *Owly and Wormy: bright lights and starry nights!*
Salley, Coleen. *Epossumondas plays possum*
Sanromán, Susana. *Señora Reganoña*
Sattler, Jennifer. *Pig kahuna*
Saunders, Karen. *Baby Badger's wonderful night*
Savadier, Elivia. *No haircut today!*
Schaefer, Carole Lexa. *Who's there?*
Schmid, Paul. *Oliver and his alligator*
Schneider, Josh. *Bedtime monsters*
Schuurmans, Hilde. *Sydney won't swim*
Schwarz, Viviane. *Shark and Lobster's amazing undersea adventure*
Scotton, Rob. *Splish, splash, Splat!*
Senshu, Noriko. *Sonny's dream*
Seuss, Dr. *The Sneetches, and other stories*
Shah, Idries. *The clever boy and the terrible, dangerous animal*
Shea, Bob. *I'm a shark*
Simon, Charnan. *Big bad Buzz*
Snicket, Lemony. *The dark*
Soman, David. *Ladybug Girl at the beach*
Spelman, Cornelia Maude. *When I feel scared*
Spinelli, Eileen. *A safe place called home*
Wanda's monster
Stein, Mathilde. *Brave Ben*
Stevenson, Harvey. *Big scary wolf*
Stevenson, James. *What's under my bed?*
Stewart, Amber. *No babysitters allowed*
Stewart, Shannon. *Sea crow*
Stock, Catherine. *Halloween monster*
Stroud, Bettye. *Dance y'all*
Taulbert, Clifton L. *Little Cliff's first day of school*
Tessler, Manya. *Yuki's ride home*
Thach, James Otis. *A child's guide to common household monsters*
This place I know
Thomas, Jan. *The doghouse*
Let's sing a lullaby with the Brave Cowboy
Thompson, Richard. *The night walker*
Thornhill, Jan. *The rumor*
Tomlinson, Jill. *The owl who was afraid of the dark*
Tyger, Rory. *Newton*
Vail, Rachel. *Jibberwillies at night*
van Lieshout, Maria. *Peep!*
Viorst, Judith. *My mama says there aren't any zombies, ghosts, vampires, creatures, demons, monsters, fiends, goblins, or things*
Waddell, Martin. *Can't you sleep, Little Bear?*
Let's go home, Little Bear
Owl babies
Owl babies [board book]
Tom Rabbit
Waechter, Phillip. *Rosie and the nightmares*
Waldron, Jan L. *John Pig's Halloween*
Wallace, Ian. *Chin Chiang and the dragon's dance*
Wallen, Ila. *The moon in my room*
Walsh, Ellen Stoll. *Pip's magic*
Ward, Nick. *Come on Baby Duck*
Watt, Mélanie. *Scaredy Squirrel*
Scaredy Squirrel at night
Scaredy Squirrel at the beach
Scaredy Squirrel goes camping
Scaredy Squirrel has a birthday party
Scaredy Squirrel makes a friend
Scaredy Squirrel prepares for Christmas
Scaredy Squirrel prepares for Halloween
Weitzman, Jacqueline Preiss. *Superhero Joe*
Superhero Joe and the creature next door
Weston, Martha. *Tuck in the pool*
Whybrow, Ian. *Harry and the dinosaurs say "Raahh"*
Williams, Linda. *The little old lady who was not afraid of anything*
Willis, Jeanne. *Fly, chick, fly!*
Wilson, Karma. *Bear feels scared*
Don't be afraid, Little Pip
Who goes there?
Wilson-Max, Ken. *Max's starry night*
Winters, Kay. *The teeny tiny ghost*
Whooo's haunting the teeny tiny ghost?
Winton, Tim. *The deep*
Wormell, Christopher. *Henry and the fox*
Wright, Michael. *Jake starts school*
Yum, Hyewon. *There are no scary wolves*
Zolotow, Charlotte. *The storm book*

Emotions – grief

Barron, T. A. *Where is Grandpa?*
The best cat in the world
Bley, Anette. *And what comes after a thousand?*
Blumenthal, Deborah. *The blue house dog*
Boase, Susan. *Lucky boy*
Brisson, Pat. *I remember Miss Perry*
Bunting, Eve. *The memory string*
Rudi's pond
Charles, Veronika Martenova. *The birdman*
Clifton, Lucille. *Everett Anderson's goodbye*
Cobb, Rebecca. *Missing Mommy*
Cochran, Bill. *The forever dog*
Cohen, Miriam. *Jim's dog Muffins*, ill. by Ronald Himler
Jim's dog Muffins, ill. by Lillian Hoban
Cooke, Trish. *The grandad tree*
dePaola, Tomie. *Nana Upstairs and Nana Downstairs*
Doray, Malika. *One more Wednesday*
Edwards, Michelle. *Papa's latkes*
Ewart, Claire. *The giant*
Fletcher, Ralph. *Grandpa never lies*
Fritts, Mary Bahr. *If Nathan were here*
Gregory, Nan. *Wild Girl and Gran*
Grifalconi, Ann. *Tiny's hat*
Grimm, Edward. *The doorman*
Hanson, Regina. *A season for mangoes*
Harris, Robie H. *Goodbye, Mousie*
Haynes, Max. *Grandma's gone to live in the stars*
Hill, Frances. *The bug cemetery*
Jeffers, Oliver. *The heart and the bottle*
Jeffs, Stephanie. *Jenny*
Josh
Johnston, Tony. *That summer*
Kerner, Susan. *Always by my side*
Krishnaswami, Uma. *Remembering Grandpa*
Leiner, Katherine. *Mama does the mambo*

Lunde, Stein Erik. *My father's arms are a boat*
Maier, Inger. *Ben's flying flowers*
Monk, Isabell. *Blackberry stew*
Moundlic, Charlotte. *The scar*
Murphy, Sally. *Pearl verses the world*
Napoli, Donna Jo. *Flamingo dream*
Nickle, John. *TV Rex*
Nobisso, Josephine. *Grandpa loved*
O'Brien, Anne Sibley. *A path of stars*
Onyefulu, Ifeoma. *Saying goodbye*
Parker, Marjorie Blain. *Jasper's day*
Puttock, Simon. *A story for Hippo*
Rappaport, Doreen. *The new king*
Raschka, Chris. *The purple balloon*
Rogers, Fred. *When a pet dies*
Roper, Janice M. *Dancing on the moon*
Rosenberg, Liz. *The carousel*
Russo, Marisabina. *Grandpa Abe*
Santucci, Barbara. *Anna's corn*
Schick, Eleanor. *Mama*
Simon, Norma. *The saddest time*
Stafford, Liliana. *Just dragon*
This place I know
Thomas, Jane Resh. *Saying good-bye to grandma*
Tibo, Gilles. *The grand journey of Mr. Man*
Vigna, Judith. *Saying goodbye to daddy*
Viorst, Judith. *The tenth good thing about Barney*
Weigelt, Udo. *Bear's last journey*
Weitzman, Elizabeth. *Let's talk about when a parent dies*
Wild, Margaret. *Harry and Hopper*
Wilhelm, Hans. *I'll always love you*
Wood, Douglas. *Grandad's prayers of the earth*
Woodson, Jacqueline. *Sweet, sweet memory*
Zalben, Jane Breskin. *Pearl's marigolds for grandpa*
Ziefert, Harriet. *Ode to Humpty Dumpty*
Zolotow, Charlotte. *My grandson Lew*
The old dog

Emotions – happiness

Cabrera, Jane. *If you're happy and you know it*
Carlson, Nancy. *Think happy!*
Cohen, Caron Lee. *Happy to you!*
Doyle, Malachy. *Get happy*
Emberley, Rebecca. *If you're a monster and you know it*
Hall, Michael. *Perfect square*
Jackson, Ellen. *Sometimes bad things happen*
Kaiser, Ruth. *The smiley book of colors*
Lloyd, David. *Polly Molly Woof Woof*
McBratney, Sam. *Once there was a Hoodie*
Menchin, Scott. *Taking a bath with the dog and other things that make me happy*
Miura, Taro. *The tiny king*
Moroney, Trace. *When I'm feeling happy*
Ormerod, Jan. *If you're happy and you know it!*
Parr, Todd. *The feel good book*
Rayner, Catherine. *Augustus and his smile*
Rylant, Cynthia. *The wonderful happens*
Schwarz, Viviane. *The adventures of a nose*
Starr, Meg. *Alicia's happy day*
Steig, William. *Spinky sulks*
Stein, David Ezra. *Because Amelia smiled*
Thomas, Joyce Carol. *Joy*
Warhola, James. *If you're happy and you know it: jungle edition*
Wilcox, Brad. *Hip, hip, hooray for Annie McRae!*
Willis, Jeanne. *Misery Moo*
Wood, Douglas. *The secret of saying thanks*

Emotions – hate

Harris, Robie H. *The day Leo said I hate you!*
Thompson, Lauren. *The forgiveness garden*
Udry, Janice May. *Let's be enemies*
Zolotow, Charlotte. *The hating book*

Emotions – jealousy *see* Emotions – envy, jealousy

Emotions – loneliness

Aardema, Verna. *The lonely lioness and the ostrich chicks*
Abley, Mark. *Ghost cat*
Ahlberg, Allan. *The pencil*
Alborough, Jez. *My friend bear*
Aliki. *We are best friends*
Battersby, Katherine. *Squish Rabbit*
Bernheimer, Kate. *The girl in the castle inside the museum*
The lonely book
Bowles, Paula. *Scary Mary*
Brett, Jan. *Annie and the wild animals*
Brun-Cosme, Nadine. *Big Wolf and Little Wolf*
Byun, You. *Dream friends*
Chichester Clark, Emma. *Melrose and Croc*
Cort, Ben. *Pigs can't fly!*
Cumming, Hannah. *The red boat*
Daly, Niki. *Welcome to Zanzibar Road*
DiPucchio, Kelly. *Zombie in love*
Dunrea, Olivier. *Little cub*
Esbaum, Jill. *Tom's tweet*
Floyd, Madeleine. *Cold paws, warm heart*
Foggo, Cheryl. *Dear baobab*
Foreman, Jack. *Say hello*
Fox, Mem. *The goblin and the empty chair*
Ginkel, Anne. *I've got an elephant*
Gorbachev, Valeri. *Big Little Elephant*
Gordon, Gus. *Herman and Rosie*
Grey, Mini. *Ginger bear*
Haas, Irene. *Bess and Bella*
Halpern, Julie. *Toby and the snowflakes*
Hest, Amy. *The dog who belonged to no one*
Jahn-Clough, Lisa. *On the hill*
James, J. Alison. *The bears' Christmas surprise*
Janni, Rebecca. *Every cowgirl needs dancing boots*
Jeffers, Oliver. *The heart and the bottle*
Lost and found
Johnston, Tony. *The cat with seven names*
Joosse, Barbara. *Lovabye dragon*
Jules, Jacqueline. *No English*
Juster, Norton. *Neville*
Keats, Ezra Jack. *The trip*
Kleven, Elisa. *The friendship wish*
Kohara, Kazuno. *Here comes Jack Frost*
Kolanovic, Dubravka. *Everyone needs a friend*
Kroll, Steven. *The hand-me-down doll*
Lacombe, Benjamin. *Cherry and Olive*
LaReau, Kara. *Mr. Prickles*
Snowbaby could not sleep
Ugly fish
Le Neouanic, Lionel. *Little smudge*
Lerch. *Swim! swim!*
Lucas, David. *Cake girl*
Ludwig, Trudy. *The invisible boy*

McCarty, Peter. *Jeremy draws a monster*
McCormick, Wendy. *Daddy, will you miss me?*
McDonnell, Christine. *Goyangi means cat*
McDonnell, Patrick. *South*
McElroy, Lisa Tucker. *Love, Lizzie*
MacLachlan, Patricia. *Nora's chicks*
Marx, Patricia. *Dot in Larryland*
Morison, Toby. *Little Louie takes off*
Mortimer, Rachael. *Song for a princess*
Murphy, Sally. *Pearl verses the world*
Norac, Carl. *I love to cuddle*
Norwich, William D. *Molly and the magic dress*
Pfister, Marcus. *The rainbow fish*
Pilkey, Dav. *A friend for Dragon*
Radunsky, Vladimir. *You?*
Root, Phyllis. *Scrawny cat*
Rowe, John A. *I want a hug*
Segal, John. *The lonely moose*
Spelman, Cornelia Maude. *When I miss you*
Spinelli, Eileen. *Somebody loves you, Mr. Hatch*
Staake, Bob. *Bluebird*
Stevenson, James. *Mr. Hacker*
Swaim, Jessica. *The hound from the pound*
Swann, Rick. *Our school garden!*
Taback, Simms. *I miss you every day*
Teckentrup, Britta. *Grumpy cat*
Teevin, Toni. *What to do? What to do?*
Titherington, Jeanne. *A place for Ben*
Vail, Rachel. *Flabbersmashed about you*
Viorst, Judith. *Nobody here but me*
Waber, Bernard. *Gina*
Waddell, Martin. *Sam Vole and his brothers*
Sleep tight, Little Bear
Wallner, Alexandra. *Beatrix Potter*
Walter, Mildred Pitts. *My mama needs me*
Ward, Helen. *The dragon machine*
Watt, Mélanie. *Scaredy Squirrel makes a friend*
Wells, Rosemary. *Small world of Binky Braverman*
Wheeler, Lisa. *Porcupining*
Wild, Margaret. *Fox*
Wilson, Karma. *Sweet Briar goes to camp*
Winter, Jeanette. *Angelina's island*
Wright, Dare. *A gift from the lonely doll*
The lonely doll
Yashima, Taro. *Crow boy*
Yerkes, Jennifer. *A funny little bird*
Yolen, Jane. *Elsie's bird*
Zolotow, Charlotte. *The bunny who found Easter*
A tiger called Thomas, ill. by Diana Cain Bluthenthal
A tiger called Thomas, ill. by Catherine Stock

Emotions – love

Adoff, Arnold. *Love letters*
Aigner-Clark, Julie. *You are the best medicine*
Anastas, Margaret. *A hug for you*
Mommy's best kisses
Andersen, Hans Christian. *The snow queen*, ill. by Angela Barrett
The snow queen, ill. by Sally Holmes
The snow queen, ill. by Susan Jeffers
The snow queen: a retelling of the fairy tale
Anholt, Laurence. *Seven for a secret*
Appelt, Kathi. *Oh my baby, little one*
Ashman, Linda. *What could be better than this*
Baker, Liza. *I love you because you're you*
Bang, Molly. *In my heart*
Bedford, David. *Mole's in love*
The way I love you
Bianco, Margery Williams. *The velveteen rabbit*, ill. by David Jorgensen
The velveteen rabbit, ill. by Thea Kliros
The velveteen rabbit, ill. by Komako Sakai
The velveteen rabbit, ill. by Gennady Spirin
The velveteen rabbit: or, How toys became real, ill. by Allen Atkinson
The velveteen rabbit: or, How toys became real, ill. by Steve Johnson
Bible. New Testament. Corinthians 1st, XIII. *Love is*
Bright, Rachel. *Love Monster*
Bunting, Eve. *Baby can*
Swan in love
You were loved before you were born
Burdett, Lois. *Romeo and Juliet for kids*
Calmenson, Stephanie. *Perfect puppy*
Capucilli, Alyssa Satin. *Bear hugs*
Cheshire, Marc. *Love and kisses, Eloise*
Clayton, Dallas. *An awesome book of love!*
Clements, Andrew. *Because your daddy loves you*
Because your mommy loves you
Clifton, Lucille. *Everett Anderson's goodbye*
Cole, Babette. *Truelove*
Conway, David. *The most important gift of all*
Cruise, Robin. *Only you*
Davies, Stephen. *Don't spill the milk!*
Delacre, Lulu. *How far do you love me?*
Dodd, Emma. *Forever*
Foxy in love
No matter what
Duncan, Alice Faye. *Honey baby sugar child*
Dunrea, Olivier. *Old Bear and his cub*
Durant, Alan. *I love you, little monkey*
Edwards, Nicola. *Goodnight Baxter*
Elffers, Joost. *Do you love me?*
Emmett, Jonathan. *I love you always and forever*
Eure, Wesley. *A fish out of water*
Evans, Kristina. *What's special about me, Mama?*
Evans, Lezlie. *Who loves the little lamb?*
Ferber, Brenda A. *The yuckiest, stinkiest, best Valentine ever*
Flack, Marjorie. *Ask Mr. Bear*
Fox, Mem. *Koala Lou*
Sophie
Freeman, Don. *Corduroy*
George, Lindsay Barrett. *The secret*
Gliori, Debi. *No matter what*
Goble, Paul. *Love flute*
Hample, Stoo. *I will kiss you (lots and lots and lots!)*
Hautzig, Deborah. *Beauty and the beast*
Hesse, Karen. *Spuds*
Hines, Anna Grossnickle. *When we married Gary*
Howe, James. *Otter and odder*
Jacobs, Julie. *My heart is a magic house*
Jaffe, Nina. *The way meat loves salt*
Jenkins, Emily. *Love you when you whine*
Joosse, Barbara. *Grandma calls me Beautiful*
Love is a good thing to feel
Mama, do you love me?
Papa do you love me?
Jordan, Deloris. *Baby blessings*
Juster, Norton. *Sourpuss and sweetie pie*
Karas, G. Brian. *Skidamarink*
Kasza, Keiko. *A mother for Choco*
Katz, Karen. *Daddy hugs 1 2 3*
Kern, Noris. *I love you with all my heart*
Kimmel, Elizabeth Cody. *My penguin Osbert in love*

Kimmelman, Leslie. *How do I love you?*
Kindermans, Martine. *You and me*
Kirk, David. *Little Miss Spider*
Kraus, Robert. *Mouse in love*
Krauss, Ruth. *And I love you*
Kuklin, Susan. *Families*
Laird, Elizabeth. *A book of promises*
Lawler, Janet. *A father's song*
Lawrence, Michael. *Baby loves*
Lee, Chinlun. *Good dog, Paw*
Lloyd-Jones, Sally. *Just because you're mine*
London, Jonathan. *Count the ways, Little Brown Bear*
Froggy's first kiss
What do you love?
What do you love? [board book]
McAllister, Angela. *Mama and Little Joe*
McBratney, Sam. *Guess how much I love you*
There, there
McCarty, Peter. *Henry in love*
McCaughrean, Geraldine. *Beauty and the beast*
McCourt, Lisa. *I love you, Stinky Face*
MacDonald, Margaret Read. *The great smelly, slobbery small-toothed dog*
MacLachlan, Patricia. *Who loves me?*
McNaughton, Colin. *Oomph!*
McPhail, David. *The teddy bear*
Marley, Cedella. *One love*
Martin, Bill, Jr. *Knots on a counting rope*
Marzollo, Jean. *I love you*
Masurel, Claire. *Two homes*
Mayer, Marianna. *Beauty and the beast*
Mayer, Mercer. *Just for you*
Milord, Susan. *If I could*
Love that baby
Morgan, Michaela. *Dear bunny*
Morris, Ann. *Loving*
Morrow, Tara Jaye. *Mommy loves her baby; Daddy loves his baby*
Munsch, Robert N. *Love you forever*
Newman, Lesléa. *Daddy's song*
Newman, Marjorie. *Mole and the baby bird*
Mole and the baby bird [board book]
Nobisso, Josephine. *Grandpa loved*
Norac, Carl. *I love you so much*
North, Sherry. *Because you are my baby*
O'Keefe, Susan Heyboer. *Love me, love you*
Oppenheim, Shulamith Levey. *I love you, Bunny Rabbit*
Oram, Hiawyn. *Kiss it better*
Otsuka, Yuzo. *Suho's white horse*
Paradis, Susan. *My mommy*
Parr, Todd. *The I Love You Book*
Paschkis, Julie. *Apple cake*
Pearson, Susan. *Slugs in love*
Pennypacker, Sara. *Pierre in love*
Pham, LeUyen. *All the things I love about you*
Pow, Tom. *Tell me one thing, Dad*
Price, Leontyne. *Aïda*
Quattlebaum, Mary. *Pirate vs. pirate*
Rankin, Joan. *You're somebody special, Walliwigs!*
Ransom, Jeanie Franz. *I don't want to talk about it*
Reiser, Lynn. *The surprise family*
Ritchie, Alison. *Me and my dad!*
Me and my mom!
Rock, Brian. *With all my heart*
Rock, Lois. *Now we have a baby*
Rohmer, Harriet. *Mother scorpion country*
Rose, Deborah Lee. *All the seasons of the year*
Rosenthal, Amy Krouse. *Plant a kiss*
Rossetti-Shustak, Bernadette. *I love you through and through*
Roth, Carol. *Will you still love me?*
Rotner, Shelley. *Lots of grandparents*
What's love?
Rueda, Claudia. *My little polar bear*
Rusackas, Francesca. *Daddy all day long*
Ryder, Joanne. *Bear of my heart*
Rylant, Cynthia. *Baby face: a book of love for baby*
If you'll be my Valentine
Puppies and piggies
Sabuda, Robert. *Beauty and the beast: a pop-up book of the classic fairy tale*
Saltzberg, Barney. *Kisses*
Samuels, Barbara. *Faye and Dolores*
San Souci, Robert D. *Nicholas Pipe*
Schlessinger, Laura. *Why do you love me?*
Scott, Ann Herbert. *On mother's lap*
On mother's lap [board book]
Shapiro, Jody Fickes. *Family lullaby*
Sheehan, Monica. *Love is you and me*
Slonim, David. *I loathe you*
Snyder, Betsy E. *I haiku you*
Spelman, Cornelia Maude. *Mama and Daddy Bear's divorce*
Steig, William. *Potch and Polly*
Tiffky Doofky
Steven, Kenneth. *The biggest thing in the world*
Stott, Ann. *Always*
I'll be there
Stuve-Bodeen, Stephanie. *Elizabeti's doll*
Summers, Kate. *Milly's wedding*
Taback, Simms. *I miss you every day*
Tafuri, Nancy. *I love you, little one*
Thomas, Eliza. *The red blanket*
Thompson, Kay. *Kay Thompson's Eloise's what I absolutely love love love*
Tillman, Nancy. *Wherever you are*
Tinkham, Kelly A. *Hair for Mama*
Trotter, Deborah W. *How do you know?*
Van Buren, David. *I love you as big as the world*
van Lieshout, Elle. *The wish*
Verburg, Bonnie. *The kiss box*
Vischer, Phil. *Sidney and Norman*
Waddell, Martin. *Who do you love?*
Walton, Rick. *What do we do with the baby?*
Wan, Joyce. *Hug you, kiss you, love you*
Watson, Wendy. *A Valentine for you*
Weeks, Sarah. *Woof*
Weiss, Ellen. *I love you, Little Monster*
Wells, Rosemary. *Carry me!*
Love waves
Wild, Margaret. *Piglet and Mama*
Piglet and Papa
Williams, Sam. *That's love*
Willis, Jeanne. *Mommy do you love me?*
Wilson, Sarah. *Love and kisses*
Wood, Douglas. *When a dad says "I love you"*
Xinran, Xue. *Motherbridge of love*
Yolen, Jane. *How do dinosaurs say I love you?*
Yoon, Salina. *Penguin in love*
Yorinks, Arthur. *Harry and Lulu*
Young, Ed. *My Mei Mei*
Zolotow, Charlotte. *Do you know what I'll do?*
Say it!
Some things go together
Zuckerman, Linda. *I will hold you 'til you sleep*

Emotions – sadness

Abley, Mark. *Ghost cat*
Beaty, Daniel. *Knock knock*
Cobb, Rebecca. *Missing Mommy*
Cora, Cat. *A suitcase surprise for Mommy*
Diesen, Deborah. *The pout-pout fish*
Havill, Juanita. *Jamaica's blue marker*
Henry, Jed. *Cheer up, Mouse!*
Kerner, Susan. *Always by my side*
Lawrence, Jennifer B. *Sad doggy*
Levis, Caron. *Stuck with the Blooz*
Maier, Inger. *Ben's flying flowers*
Medina, Sarah. *Sad*
Monk, Isabell. *Blackberry stew*
Moroney, Trace. *When I'm feeling sad*
Plecas, Jennifer. *Olive's perfect world*
Pulver, Robin. *Saturday is Dadurday*
Spelman, Cornelia Maude. *When I feel sad*
Willis, Jeanne. *Misery Moo*

Emotions – unhappiness *see* Emotions – happiness; Emotions – sadness

Engineered books *see* Format, unusual – toy & movable books

Entertainment *see* Theater

Environment *see* Ecology

Eskimos *see also* Indians of North America – Inuit

Brown, Kerry. *Tupag the dreamer*
Edwardson, Debby Dahl. *Whale snow*
George, Jean Craighead. *Nutik and Amaroq play ball*
Nutik, the wolf pup
Snow bear
Joosse, Barbara. *Mama, do you love me?*
Luenn, Nancy. *Nessa's fish*
Nessa's story
Munsch, Robert N. *A promise is a promise*
San Souci, Robert D. *Song of Sedna*
Scott, Ann Herbert. *On mother's lap*
On mother's lap [board book]
Sís, Peter. *A small tall tale from the far Far North*

Ethnic groups in the U.S.

Alko, Selina. *I'm your peanut butter big brother*
Bunting, Eve. *Smoky night*
Cohen, Miriam. *Will I have a friend?*, ill. by Ronald Himler
Will I have a friend?, ill. by Lillian Hoban
Dooley, Norah. *Everybody brings noodles*
Everybody cooks rice
Everybody serves soup
Dorros, Arthur. *Abuela*
Edwards, Nancy. *Glenna's seeds*
Golding, Theresa Martin. *Memorial Day surprise*
Graham, Bob. *Oscar's half birthday*
Harris, Robie H. *Who's in my family?*
Kallok, Emma. *Gem*
Katz, Karen. *The colors of us*
Keats, Ezra Jack. *My dog is lost!*
Lester, Julius. *Let's talk about race*
Maestro, Betsy. *Coming to America*
Miller, J. Philip. *We all sing with the same voice*
Moss, Jenny Jackson. *Cajun night after Christmas*
Nikola-Lisa, W. *Bein' with you this way*
Pinkney, Sandra L. *A rainbow all around me*
Polacco, Patricia. *In our mothers' house*
Rotner, Shelley. *Lots of moms*
Shades of people
Schaefer, Carole Lexa. *Snow pumpkin*
Shelby, Anne. *Potluck*
Smith, Charles R. *I am the world*
Stowell, Penelope. *The greatest potatoes*
Udry, Janice May. *What Mary Jo shared*
Vigil-Piñón, Evangelina. *Marina's muumuu / El muumuu de Marina*
Washington, Kathy Gates. *Three colors of Katie*
Weiss, Nicki. *The world turns round and round*
Williams, Vera B. *"More more more," said the baby*
Wing, Natasha. *Jalapeño bagels*
Wong, Janet S. *This next New Year*

Ethnic groups in the U.S. – Acadians *see* Ethnic groups in the U.S. – Cajuns

Ethnic groups in the U.S. – African Americans

Ackerman, Karen. *By the dawn's early light*
Adler, David A. *Campy*
Heroes for civil rights
Joe Louis
A picture book of Martin Luther King, Jr
Satchel Paige
Adoff, Arnold. *In for winter, out for spring*
Alexander, Elizabeth. *Praise song for the day*
Aliki. *A weed is a flower*
All night, all day
Allen, Debbie. *Dancing in the wings*
Altman, Linda Jacobs. *The legend of Freedom Hill*
Singing with Momma Lou
Altman, Susan. *Followers of the north star*
Armand, Glenda. *Love twelve miles long*
Ashley Bryan's ABC of African American poetry
Asim, Jabari. *Daddy goes to work*
Fifty cents and a dream
Aston, Dianna Hutts. *The moon over Star*
Baicker, Karen. *You can do it too!*
Balcziak, Bill. *John Henry*
Bandy, Michael S. *White water*
Bang, Molly. *Ten, nine, eight*
Wiley and the hairy man
Barber, Tiki. *Game day*
Barber, Tiki, et al. *By my brother's side*
Teammates
Barbour, Karen. *Mr. Williams*
Barnwell, Ysaye M. *No mirrors in my Nana's house*
Barrett, Mary Brigid. *Shoebox Sam*
Battle-Lavert, Gwendolyn. *The music in Derrick's heart*
Papa's mark
The shaking bag
Bauer, Marion Dane. *Harriet Tubman*
Beaty, Daniel. *Knock knock*
Belton, Sandra. *Pictures for Miss Josie*
Bennett, Kelly. *Not Norman*
Bible. New Testament. *The Lord's prayer*

Bildner, Phil. *The hallelujah flight*
Birtha, Becky. *Grandmama's pride*
  Lucky beans
Blackstone, Stella. *Bear on a bike*
Boelts, Maribeth. *Happy like soccer*
  Those shoes
Bolden, Tonya. *Rock of ages*
Boswell, Addie. *The rain stomper*
Bradby, Marie. *Momma, where are you from?*
  More than anything else
  Once upon a farm
Brooks, Gwendolyn. *Bronzeville boys and girls*
Brown, Tameka Fryer. *My cold plum lemon pie bluesy mood*
Broyles, Anne. *Priscilla and the hollyhocks*
Bryant, Jen. *A splash of red*
Buchanan, Jane. *Seed magic*
Bunting, Eve. *The blue and the gray*
  The cart that carried Martin
Burleigh, Robert. *Langston's train ride*
  Lookin' for Bird in the big city
  Stealing home
Campbell, Bebe Moore. *I get so hungry*
Carbone, Elisa. *Night running*
Carter, Don. *Heaven's all-star jazz band*
Cash, Megan Montague. *What makes the seasons?*
Celenza, Anna Harwell. *Duke Ellington's Nutcracker Suite*
Chocolate, Deborah. *Kwanzaa*
Clifton, Lucille. *Everett Anderson's goodbye*
  One of the problems of Everett Anderson
  Three wishes
Cline-Ransome, Lesa. *Light in the darkness*
  Words set me free
Clinton, Catherine. *Phillis's big test*
  When Harriet met Sojourner
Cole, Henry. *Unspoken*
Cole, Kenneth, Dr. *No bad news*
Coles, Robert. *The story of Ruby Bridges*
Collier, Bryan. *Uptown*
Cooper, Floyd. *Coming home: from the life of Langston Hughes*
  Max and the tag-along moon
  Willie and the All-Stars
Crews, Donald. *Cloudy day/sunny day*
  Shortcut
Crews, Nina. *A ghost story*
  One hot summer day
  You are here
Crowe, Chris. *Just as good*
Cummings, Pat. *Angel baby*
  Clean your room, Harvey Moon!
  My aunt came back
Curtis, Gavin. *The bat boy and his violin*
Dawes, Kwame Senu Neville. *I saw your face*
Deans, Karen. *Playing to win*
Derby, Sally. *No mush today*
Diggs, Taye. *Chocolate me!*
Dray, Philip. *Yours for justice, Ida B. Wells*
DuBurke, Randy. *The moon ring*
Duncan, Alice Faye. *Honey baby sugar child*
Dungy, Tony. *You can do it!*
Edwards, Pamela Duncan. *Barefoot: escape on the Underground Railroad*
  The bus ride that changed history
Ehrhardt, Karen. *This jazz man*
Elster, Jean Alicia. *Just call me Joe Joe*
English, Karen. *The baby on the way*
  Hot day on Abbott Avenue
Evans, Kristina. *What's special about me, Mama?*
Evans, Shane W. *Underground: finding the light to freedom*
  We march
Falwell, Cathryn. *Christmas for 10*
  David's drawing
  Feast for ten
Farris, Christine King. *March on!*
  My brother Martin
Feiffer, Kate. *Which puppy?*
Fishman, Cathy Goldberg. *When Jackie and Hank met*
Flournoy, Valerie. *The patchwork quilt*
Ford, Juwanda G. *K is for Kwanzaa*
  Together for Kwanzaa
Forman, Ruth. *Young Cornrows callin out the moon*
Fradin, Dennis. *The price of freedom*
Frame, Jeron Ashford. *Yesterday I had the blues*
Freeman, Don. *Corduroy*
  A pocket for Corduroy
Giovanni, Nikki. *Lincoln and Douglass*
  Rosa
  The sun is so quiet
Golenbock, Peter. *Hank Aaron*
Gourley, Robbin. *Bring me some apples and I'll make you a pie*
Grady, Cynthia. *I lay my stitches down*
Greenfield, Eloise. *Angels*
  Big friend, little friend
  Brothers and sisters
  Daydreamers
  Easter parade
  First pink light
  I make music
  Me and Neesie
  My doll, Keshia
  Nathaniel talking
  Night on Neighborhood Street
  Water, water
Greenfield, Monica. *Waiting for Christmas*
Grifalconi, Ann. *Ain't nobody a stranger to me*
  Tiny's hat
  The village that vanished
Grigsby, Susan. *In the garden with Dr. Carver*
Grimes, Nikki. *Barack Obama*
  Danitra Brown, class clown
  Welcome, Precious
  When Daddy prays
  When Gorilla goes walking
Hamilton, Virginia. *Drylongso*
Harrington, Janice N. *The chicken-chasing queen of Lamar County*
Harris, Teresa E. *Summer Jackson*
Harrison, Troon. *Courage to fly*
Harvey, Jeanne Walker. *My hands sing the blues*
Haskins, Jim. *Delivering justice*
Havill, Juanita. *Jamaica and Brianna*
  Jamaica and the substitute teacher
  Jamaica is thankful
  Jamaica Tag-Along
  Jamaica's blue marker
  Jamaica's find
Heath, Amy. *Sofie's role*
Henderson, Alicia Terry. *Call me black, call me beautiful*
Hesse, Karen. *Come on, rain*
Hester, Denia Lewis. *Grandma Lena's big ol' turnip*
Hill, Elizabeth Starr. *Evan's corner*
Hill, Laban Carrick. *Dave the potter*

Hoffman, Mary. *Amazing Grace*
Grace at Christmas
Princess Grace
Hood, Susan. *Look! I can read!*
Hooks, Bell. *Be boy buzz*
Happy to be nappy
Hopkinson, Deborah. *Keep on!*
Sweet Clara and the freedom quilt
Howard, Elizabeth Fitzgerald. *Aunt Flossie's hats (and crab cakes later)*
Chita's Christmas tree
Virgie goes to school with us boys
Hru, Dakari. *Joshua's Masai mask*
Hubbard, Crystal. *Catching the moon: the story of a young girl's baseball dream*
Hudson, Cheryl Willis. *Bright eyes, brown skin*
My friend Maya loves to dance
Hudson, Wade. *Pass it on*
Hughes, Langston. *Carol of the brown king*
I, too, am America
Lullaby (for a Black mother)
My people
The Negro speaks of rivers
Hurston, Zora Neale. *The six fools*
Hush songs
Hutchins, Pat. *My best friend*
In daddy's arms I am tall
Ingalls, Ann. *The little piano girl*
Isadora, Rachel. *Ben's trumpet*
Bring on that beat
Luke goes to bat
Peekaboo bedtime
Peekaboo morning
Peekaboo morning [board book]
Uh-oh!
Yo, Jo!
Issa, Kai Jackson. *Howard Thurman's Great Hope*
I've seen the promised land
Jackson, Isaac. *Somebody's new pajamas*
Johnson, Angela. *Daddy calls me man*
Do like Kyla
Down the winding road
The girl who wore snakes
Joshua by the sea
Joshua's night whispers
Julius
The leaving morning
Lily Brown's paintings
Lottie Paris and the best place
Lottie Paris lives here
One of three
Rain feet
The Rolling Store
Shoes like Miss Alice's
A sweet smell of roses
The wedding
When I am old with you
Wind flyers
Johnson, Dinah. *Black magic*
Quinnie Blue
Johnson, Dolores. *Now let me fly*
Johnson, James Weldon. *The Creation*
Lift every voice and sing
Lift ev'ry voice and sing
Johnston, Tony. *The wagon*
Jonas, Ann. *Splash!*
Jordan, Deloris. *Baby blessings*
Dream big
Michael's golden rules
Joseph, Lynn. *Fly, Bessie, fly*
Keats, Ezra Jack. *Apt. 3*
Dreams
Goggles
Hi, cat!
John Henry
A letter to Amy
Louie
Pet show!
Peter's chair
The snowy day
The snowy day [board book]
The trip
Whistle for Willie
King, Martin Luther, III. *My daddy, Dr. Martin Luther King, Jr.*
King, Martin Luther, Jr. *I have a dream*
Kirk, Daniel. *Keisha Ann can!*
Kittinger, Jo S. *Rosa's bus*
Klingel, Cynthia Fitterer. *Rosa Parks*
Krensky, Stephen. *I know a lot!*
A man for all seasons
Play ball, Jackie!
Kroll, Virginia L. *Africa brothers and sisters*
Can you dance, Dalila?
Faraway drums
Masai and I
Kulling, Monica. *All aboard! Elijah McCoy's steam engine*
Kurtz, Jane. *Faraway home*
Lang, Heather. *Queen of the track*
Latifah, Queen. *Queen of the scene*
Lee, Spike. *Please, puppy, please*
Lester, Julius. *Black cowboy, wild horses*
John Henry
What a truly cool world
Why heaven is far away
Levine, Ellen. *Henry's freedom box*
Levy, Debbie. *We shall overcome*
Lindbergh, Reeve. *Nobody owns the sky*
Littlesugar, Amy. *Freedom school, yes!*
Tree of hope
Livingston, Myra Cohn. *Keep on singing*
Lorbiecki, Marybeth. *Jackie's bat*
Luthardt, Kevin. *Flying*
Lyon, George Ella. *You and me and home sweet home*
Lyons, Kelly Starling. *Ellen's broom*
Hope's gift
One million men and me
Tea cakes for Tosh
McCully, Emily Arnold. *Wonder horse*
MacDonald, Margaret Read. *Pickin' peas*
McGhee, Alison. *In the hollow of your hand*
McGill, Alice. *Molly Bannaky*
Sure as sunrise
Way up and over everything
McGowan, Michael. *Sunday is for God*
McKissack, Patricia C. *Flossie and the fox*
Goin' someplace special
The honest-to-goodness truth
Ma Dear's aprons
Messy Bessey
Messy Bessey / Ada, la desordenada
Messy Bessey's closet
Messy Bessey's family reunion
Messy Bessey's holidays
Mirandy and Brother Wind
Precious and the Boo Hag
Stitchin' and pullin'

McLellan, Stephanie Simpson. *The chicken cat*
McQuinn, Anna. *Lola at the library*
Lola loves stories
Lola reads to Leo
My friend Mei Jing
Malaspina, Ann. *Finding Lincoln*
Phillis sings out freedom
Touch the sky
Mandel, Peter. *Say hey*
Mara, Wil. *Jackie Robinson*
Marsalis, Wynton. *Squeak, rumble, whomp! Whomp! Whomp!*
Martin, Ann M. *Rachel Parker, kindergarten show-off*
Martin, Jacqueline Briggs. *Farmer Will Allen and the growing table*
Marzollo, Jean. *The little plant doctor*
Mason, Margaret H. *These hands*
May, Kathy. *Molasses man*
Mayer, Mercer. *Liza Lou and the Yeller Belly Swamp*
Medearis, Angela Shelf. *Annie's gifts*
Dancing with the Indians
The freedom riddle
The ghost of Sifty-Sifty Sam
Poppa's new pants
Rum-a-tum-tum
Tailypo
Medearis, Michael. *Daisy and the doll*
Medina, Tony. *Christmas makes me think*
DeShawn days
Meister, Cari. *Follow the drinking gourd: an Underground Railroad story*
Mellage, Nanette. *Coming home*
Michelson, Richard. *Across the alley*
Busing Brewster
Twice as good
Miller, William. *The bus ride*
A house by the river
Jenny and the peddler
The piano
Rent party jazz
Richard Wright and the library card
Mitchell, Margaree King. *Granddaddy's gift*
Susie Mae
Uncle Jed's barbershop
When Grandmama sings
Mitchell, Rhonda. *The talking cloth*
Monk, Isabell. *Family*
Hope
Morris, Ann. *Grandma Lois remembers*
Morrison, Toni. *Peeny butter fudge*
Moss, Thylias. *I want to be*
Myers, Christopher. *Sparrows*
Myers, Walter Dean. *Brown angels*
Harlem
Muhammad Ali: the people's champion
Young Martin's promise
Naden, Corinne J. *Ron's big mission*
Nash, Sarah. *Purrfect!*
Nelson, Vaunda Micheaux. *Almost to freedom*
Who will I be, Lord?
Nettleton, Pamela Hill. *Martin Luther King, Jr*
Newton, Vanessa. *Let freedom sing*
Nikola-Lisa, W. *Bein' with you this way*
Hallelujah!
Summer sun risin'
Nobisso, Josephine. *John Blair and the great Hinckley fire*
Nolen, Jerdine. *Big Jabe*
Pitching in for Eubie
Thunder Rose
Obama, Barack. *Change has come*
Ochiltree, Dianne. *Molly, by golly!*
Oppenheim, Shulamith Levey. *Fireflies for Nathan*
Orgill, Roxane. *If I only had a horn*
Skit-scat raggedy cat
Our children can soar
The palm of my heart
Parker, Robert Andrew. *Piano starts here*
Paul, Chris. *Long shot*
Peete, Holly Robinson. *My brother Charlie*
Pegram, Laura. *Daughter's Day blues*
Peña, Matt de la. *A nation's hope*
Perdorno, Willie. *Visiting Langston*
Perry, Elizabeth. *Think cool thoughts*
Peterson, Jeanne Whitehouse. *My mama sings*
Phillips, Christopher. *Ceci Ann's day of why*
Piernas-Davenport, Gail. *Shanté Keys and the New Year's peas*
Pinkney, Andrea Davis. *Alvin Ailey*
Bill Pickett, rodeo ridin' cowboy
Boycott blues
Dear Benjamin Banneker
Duke Ellington
Martin and Mahalia
Mim's Christmas jam
Sit-in
Sojourner Truth's step-stomp stride
Pinkney, Brian. *The adventures of sparrowboy*
Pinkney, Gloria Jean. *Back home*
The Sunday outing
Pinkney, Sandra L. *Read and rise*
Shades of black
Polacco, Patricia. *Chicken Sunday*
I can hear the sun
Mrs. Katz and Tush
Poydar, Nancy. *Busy Bea*
Rhyme time Valentine
Price, Hope Lynne. *These hands*
Ramsey, Calvin Alexander. *Belle, the last mule at Gee's Bend*
Ruth and the Green Book
Rappaport, Doreen. *Freedom river*
Freedom ship
Martin's big words
The school is not white!
Raschka, Chris. *Charlie Parker played be bop*
Mysterious Thelonious
Yo! Yes?
Raven, Margot Theis. *Night boat to freedom*
Reynolds, Aaron. *Back of the bus*
Metal man
Richards, Beah E. *Keep climbing, girls*
Riggio, Anita. *Secret signs*
Ringgold, Faith. *Cassie's word quilt*
Dinner at Aunt Connie's house
Henry Ossawa Tanner
If a bus could talk
The invisible princesses
My dream of Martin Luther King
Tar Beach
Robbins, Jacqui. *The new girl . . . and me*
Robinson, Sharon. *Testing the ice*
Rochelle, Belinda. *Jewels*
Rockliff, Mara. *Me and Momma and Big John*
Rodman, Mary Ann. *My best friend*
Romain, Trevor. *Jemma's journey*
Rosales, Melodye Benson. *Leola and the honeybears*
'Twas the night b'fore Christmas

Rosen, Michael J. *Elijah's angel*
Ryan, Pam Muñoz. *When Marian sang*
Sadu, Itah. *Christopher changes his name*
Saint James, Synthia. *The gifts of Kwanzaa*
Salat, Cristina. *Peanut's emergency*
Sanders, Nancy. *D is for drinking gourd*
Sanders, Scott R. *A place called Freedom*
San Souci, Robert D. *The boy and the ghost*
Callie Ann and Mistah Bear
The hired hand
The secret of the stones
Sukey and the mermaid
Schaefer, Lola M. *Kwanzaa*
Schertle, Alice. *Down the road*
Schroeder, Alan. *Baby Flo*
Minty
Ragtime Tumpie
Scruggs, Afi. *Jump rope magic*
Serfozo, Mary. *What's what?*
Seskin, Steve. *A chance to shine*
Sexton, Colleen A. *Let's meet Martin Luther King, Jr*
Shange, Ntozake. *Coretta Scott*
Ellington was not a street
Freedom's a-callin me
Whitewash
Shapiro, J. H. *Magic trash*
Shelton, Paula Young. *Child of the civil rights movement*
Shore, Diane Z. *This is the dream*
Showers, Paul. *Look at your eyes*
Your skin and mine
Siegelson, Kim L. *In the time of the drums*
Sierra, Judy. *Wiley and the Hairy Man*
Skead, Robert. *Something to prove*
Slade, Suzanne. *Climbing Lincoln's steps*
Slate, Joseph. *I want to be free*
Smalls, Irene. *Don't say ain't*
My Nana and me
My Pop Pop and me
Smalls-Hector, Irene. *Because you're lucky*
Beginning school
Jenny Reen and the Jack Muh Lantern
Jonathan and his mommy
Kevin and his dad
Smith, Charles R. *Brick by brick*
Loki and Alex
Smothers, Ethel Footman. *Auntee Edna*
Stauffacher, Sue. *Nothing but trouble*
Steggall, Susan. *Rattle and rap*
Stephens, Helen. *What about me?*
Steptoe, Javaka. *The Jones family express*
Steptoe, John. *Creativity*
Stevie
Stolz, Mary. *Storm in the night*
Stroud, Bettye. *Dance y'all*
Down home at Miss Dessa's
The leaving
The patchwork path
Swain, Gwenyth. *Riding to Washington*
Tarpley, Natasha Anastasia. *Bippity Bop barbershop*
I love my hair!
Joe-Joe's first flight
Tate, Don. *It jes' happened*
Taulbert, Clifton L. *Little Cliff and the porch people*
Little Cliff's first day of school
Tauss, Marc. *Superhero*
Tavares, Matt. *Henry Aaron's dream*
Taylor, Ann. *Baby dance*
Teague, Mark. *Baby tamer*
Temple, Charles A. *Train*
This little light of mine
Thomas, Jane Resh. *Celebration!*
Thomas, Joyce Carol. *The blacker the berry*
Brown honey in broomwheat tea
Cherish me
Crowning glory
Gingerbread days
The gospel Cinderella
In the land of milk and honey
Joy
You are my perfect baby
Thomas, Naturi. *Uh-oh! It's Mama's birthday!*
Tinkham, Kelly A. *Hair for Mama*
Tokunbo, Dimitrea. *The sound of Kwanzaa*
Trice, Linda. *Kenya's word*
Trollinger, Patsi B. *Perfect timing*
Troupe, Quincy. *Little Stevie Wonder*
Turner, Ann Warren. *Nettie's trip south*
Turner, Glennette Tilley. *An apple for Harriet Tubman*
Turner-Denstaedt, Melanie. *The hat that wore Clara B.*
Udry, Janice May. *What Mary Jo shared*
Uhlberg, Myron. *Dad, Jackie, and me*
A storm called Katrina
Vernick, Audrey. *She loved baseball*
Walker, Alice. *Finding the green stone*
To hell with dying
Walker, Sally M. *Freedom song*
Walter, Mildred Pitts. *My mama needs me*
Two too much
Wangerin, Walter. *Probity Jones and the Fear Not Angel*
Warwick, Dionne. *Little Man*
Washington, Donna L. *The story of Kwanzaa*
Watkins, Angela Farris. *My Uncle Martin's big heart*
My Uncle Martin's words for America
Watson, Renée. *Harlem's little blackbird*
Weatherford, Carole Boston. *The Beatitudes*
Before John was a jazz giant
Champions on the bench
Freedom on the menu
I, Matthew Henson
Juneteenth jamboree
Moses: when Harriet Tubman led her people to freedom
Wiles, Debbie. *Freedom summer*
Williams, Karen Lynn. *A beach tail*
Williams, Sherley Anne. *Girls together*
Working cotton
Williams, Vera B. *Cherries and cherry pits*
Williams-Garcia, Rita. *Catching the wild waiyuuzee*
Wilson-Max, Ken. *Max's starry night*
Winne, Joanne. *Let's get ready for Kwanzaa*
Winter, Jeanette. *Follow the drinking gourd*
Winter, Jonah. *Barack*
Dizzy
Muhammad Ali: champion of the world
Winthrop, Elizabeth. *Squashed in the middle*
Wood, Michele. *Going back home*
Woodson, Jacqueline. *Coming on home soon*
Each kindness
Pecan pie baby
Show way
Sweet, sweet memory
This is the rope
We had a picnic this Sunday past
Wright, Courtni Crump. *Journey to freedom*

Jumping the broom
Wagon train
Wyeth, Sharon Dennis. *Always my dad*
The granddaughter necklace
Something beautiful
Yolen, Jane. *Miz Berlin walks*
Young, Ruth. *Golden Bear*
Ziefert, Harriet. *Bigger than Daddy*
Zolotow, Charlotte. *Do you know what I'll do?*
A father like that
The old dog

Ethnic groups in the U.S. – Amish

Ammon, Richard. *An Amish Christmas*
Amish horses
An Amish wedding
An Amish year
Moss, P. Buckley. *Reuben and the quilt*
Stewart, Sarah. *The journey*
Turkle, Brinton. *Thy friend, Obadiah*
Yolen, Jane. *Raising Yoder's barn*

Ethnic groups in the U.S. – Arab Americans

Bunting, Eve. *One green apple*
Nye, Naomi Shihab. *Sitti's secrets*

Ethnic groups in the U.S. – Asian Americans

Carlson, Nancy. *My family is forever*
Havill, Juanita. *Jamaica and Brianna*
Yee, Wong Herbert. *Summer days and nights*
Who likes rain?
Yoo, Paula. *Sixteen years in sixteen seconds*

Ethnic groups in the U.S. – Black Americans *see* Ethnic groups in the U.S. – African Americans

Ethnic groups in the U.S. – Cajuns

Collins, Sheila Hebert. *'T Pousette et 't Poulette*

Ethnic groups in the U.S. – Cambodian Americans

O'Brien, Anne Sibley. *A path of stars*

Ethnic groups in the U.S. – Chinese Americans

Chen, Yong. *A gift*
Cheng, Andrea. *Grandfather counts*
Chinn, Karen. *Sam and the lucky money*
Compestine, Ying Chang. *Crouching tiger*
D'Antonio, Nancy. *Our baby from China*
Flanagan, Alice K. *Chinese New Year*
Friedman, Darlene. *Star of the Week: a story of love, adoption, and brownies with sprinkles*
Isadora, Rachel. *Happy belly, happy smile*
Lee, Milly. *Earthquake*
Landed
Nim and the war effort
Lewis, Rose A. *Every year on your birthday*
Orange Peel's pocket
Lin, Grace. *Dim sum for everyone*
Fortune cookie fortunes
Thanking the moon
The ugly vegetables
Lo, Ginnie. *Auntie Yang's great soybean picnic*
Look, Lenore. *Henry's first-moon birthday*
Love as strong as ginger
Polka Dot Penguin Pottery
Uncle Peter's amazing Chinese wedding
Louie, Therese On. *Raymond's perfect present*
McMahon, Patricia. *Just add one Chinese sister*
McQuinn, Anna. *My friend Mei Jing*
Mak, Kam. *My Chinatown*
Mochizuki, Ken. *Be water, my friend*
Morris, Ann. *Grandma Lai Goon remembers*
Moss, Marissa. *Sky high*
Nunes, Susan Miho. *The last dragon*
Oelschlager, Vanita. *Made in China*
Okimoto, Jean Davies. *The White Swan express*
Partridge, Elizabeth. *Oranges on Golden Mountain*
Peacock, Carol Antoinette. *Mommy far, Mommy near*
Pomeranc, Marion Hess. *The American Wei*
Roth, Susan L. *Happy birthday Mr. Kang*
Schaefer, Lola M. *Chinese New Year*
Seto, Loretta. *Mooncakes*
Silverhardt, Lauryn. *Happy Chinese New Year, Kai-lan!*
Thomas, Eliza. *The red blanket*
Thong, Roseanne. *Gai see*
Round is a mooncake
Wallace, Ian. *Chin Chiang and the dragon's dance*
Waters, Kate. *Lion dancer*
Wong, Benedict Norbert. *Lo and behold*
Lo and behold, good enough to eat
Woo, Alan. *Maggie's chopsticks*
Yeh, Kat. *The magic brush*
Yin. *Brothers*
Coolies
Young, Ed. *My Mei Mei*

Ethnic groups in the U.S. – Cuban Americans

Ada, Alma Flor. *With love, Little Red Hen*
Chapra, Mimi. *Amelia's show-and-tell fiesta / Amelia y la fiesta de "muestra y cuenta"*
Sacre, Antonio. *La Noche Buena*

Ethnic groups in the U.S. – East Indian Americans

Iyengar, Malathi Michelle. *Romina's rangoli*
Krishnaswami, Uma. *Bringing Asha home*
Chachaji's cup
The happiest tree
Makhijani, Pooja. *Mama's saris*
Rao, Sandhya. *My mother's sari*
Sheth, Kashmira. *My Dadima wears a sari*
Zia, F. *Hot, hot roti for Dada-ji*

Ethnic groups in the U.S. – Filipino Americans

Giles, Almira Astudillo. *Willie wins*

Ethnic groups in the U.S. – French Americans

McCully, Emily Arnold. *Mirette and Bellini cross Niagara Falls*

Ethnic groups in the U.S. – German Americans

Bodkin, Odds. *The Christmas cobwebs*
Jaspersohn, William. *The two brothers*

Ethnic groups in the U.S. – Greek Americans

D'Arc, Karen Scourby. *My grandmother is a singing Yaya*

Ethnic groups in the U.S. – Guatemalan Americans

Flanagan, Alice K. *Mr. Santizo's tasty treats!*

Ethnic groups in the U.S. – Hispanic Americans

Aliki. *Tabby*
Ancona, George. *Barrio*
Mi música / My music
Mis abuelos / My grandparents
Mis comidas / My foods
Mis fiestas / My celebrations
Mis juegos / My games
Mis quehaceres / My chores
Caraballo, Samuel. *My big sister / Mi hermana mayor*
Carlson, Lori Marie. *Hurray for Three Kings' Day*
Chapra, Mimi. *Sparky's bark / El ladrido de Sparky*
Chocolate, Deborah. *El barrio*
Cumpiano, Ina. *Quinito, day and night / Quinito, dia y noche*
Quinito's neighborhood / El vecindario de Quinito
De Anda, Diane. *Dancing Miranda / Baila, Miranda, baila*
A day without sugar / Un dia sin azucar
dePaola, Tomie. *A new Barker in the house*
Dorros, Arthur. *Mama and me*
Papa and me
Elya, Susan Middleton. *Adiós, tricycle*
Tooth on the loose
English, Karen. *Speak English for us, Marisol*
Griessman, Annette. *The fire*
Harrington, Janice N. *Roberto walks home*
Hayes, Joe. *Don't say a word, Mamá/No digas nada, Mamá*
Hudes, Quiara Alegría. *Welcome to my neighborhood!*
Kroll, Virginia L. *Uno, dos, tres, posada!*
Lachtman, Ofelia Dumas. *Pepita takes time / Pepita, siempre tarde*
Lomas Garza, Carmen. *In my family*
McCormack, Caren McNelly. *The fiesta dress*
Manning, Maurie J. *Kitchen dance*
Medina, Meg. *Tía Isa wants a car*
Miller, Elizabeth I. *Just like home / Como en mi tierra*
Mora, Pat. *Abuelos*
Gracias / Thanks
Morris, Ann. *Grandma Francisca remembers*
Pinkney, Sandra L. *I am Latino*
San Souci, Robert D. *Little gold star*
Shea, Pegi Deitz. *New moon*
Starr, Meg. *Alicia's happy day*
Thong, Roseanne. *Round is a tortilla*
Winter, Jonah. *Sonia Sotomayor*
Witte, Anna. *Lola's fandango*
Yin. *Dear Santa, please come to the 19th floor*
Zepeda, Gwendolyn. *Growing up with tamales / Los tamales de Ana*

Ethnic groups in the U.S. – Hmong Americans

Gerdner, Linda. *Grandfather's story cloth / Yawg daim paj ntaub dab neeg*
Shea, Pegi Deitz. *The whispering cloth*

Ethnic groups in the U.S. – Hungarian Americans

Couric, Katie. *The brand new kid*

Ethnic groups in the U.S. – Irish Americans

Connor, Leslie. *Miss Bridie chose a shovel*
Dillon, Jana. *Lucky O'Leprechaun comes to America*
Hazen, Barbara Shook. *Katie's wish*
Kroll, Steven. *Mary McLean and the St. Patrick's Day parade*
Nolan, Janet. *The St. Patrick's Day shillelagh*
Weller, Frances Ward. *The angel of Mill Street*

Ethnic groups in the U.S. – Italian Americans

Akin, Sara Laux. *Three scoops and a fig*
Alda, Arlene. *Morning glory Monday*
Bartone, Elisa. *Peppe the lamplighter*
Bastianich, Lidia. *Nonna tell me a story*
Nonna's birthday surprise
Bunting, Eve. *A picnic in October*
Fleischman, Paul. *The matchbox diary*
Yaccarino, Dan. *All the way to America*

Ethnic groups in the U.S. – Jamaican Americans

Winter, Jeanette. *Angelina's island*

Ethnic groups in the U.S. – Japanese Americans

Barasch, Lynne. *Hiromi's hands*
Bunting, Eve. *So far from the sea*
DaCosta, Barbara. *Nighttime Ninja*
Kroll, Virginia L. *Pink paper swans*
Lee-Tai, Amy. *A place where sunflowers grow / Sabaku ni saita himawari*
Meshon, Aaron. *Take me out to the Yakyu*
Mochizuki, Ken. *Baseball saved us*
Noguchi, Rick. *Flowers from Mariko*
Sanger, Amy Wilson. *First book of sushi*
Say, Allen. *Emma's rug*
The favorite daughter
Grandfather's journey
Tea with milk
Terasaki, Stanley Todd. *Ghosts for breakfast*
Uchida, Yoshiko. *The bracelet*
Uegaki, Chieri. *Suki's kimono*
Wells, Rosemary. *Yoko learns to read*

Yoko writes her name
Yoko's paper cranes
Yoko's show-and-tell
Yamasaki, Katie. *Fish for Jimmy*
Yashima, Taro. *Umbrella*

Ethnic groups in the U.S. – Jewish Americans *see* Jewish culture

Ethnic groups in the U.S. – Korean Americans

Avraham, Kate Aver. *What will you be, Sara Mee?*
Bercaw, Edna Coe. *Halmoni's day*
Bunting, Eve. *Jin Woo*
Choi, Sook Nyul. *Halmoni and the picnic*
Choi, Yangsook. *Behind the mask*
The name jar
Choung, Euh-hee. *Minji's Salon*
Czech, Jan M. *An American face*
Flanagan, Alice K. *A busy day at Mr. Kang's grocery store*
Heo, Yumi. *Father's rubber shoes*
Ten days and nine nights
McDonnell, Christine. *Goyangi means cat*
Pak, Soyung. *Dear Juno*
A place to grow
Sumi's first day of school ever
Park, Frances. *Good-bye, 382 Shin Dang Dong*
The Have a Good Day Cafe
Patz, Nancy. *Babies can't eat kimchee!*
Recorvits, Helen. *My name is Yoon*
Yoon and the Christmas mitten
Yoon and the jade bracelet
Williams, Laura E. *The best winds*
Wong, Janet S. *The trip back home*

Ethnic groups in the U.S. – Lebanese Americans

Khan, Hena. *The night of the moon*

Ethnic groups in the U.S. – Mexican Americans

Ada, Alma Flor. *I love Saturdays y domingos*
Adler, David A. *A picture book of Cesar Chavez*
Anaya, Rudolfo A. *Farolitos for Abuelo*
Bertrand, Diane Gonzales. *Family / familia*
The last doll / La última muñeca
The party for Papa Luis / La fiesta para Papa Luis
Sofía and the purple dress / Sofia y el vestido morado
Uncle Chente's picnic / El picnic de Tío Chente
Brown, Monica. *Chavela and the magic bubble*
Side by side / Lado a lado
Bunting, Eve. *A day's work*
Going home
Colato Laínez, René. *The Tooth Fairy meets El Ratón Pérez*
Compos, Tito. *Muffler man / El hombre mofle*
Cox, Judy. *Carmen learns English*
Cruise, Robin. *Little Mama forgets*
da Costa, Deborah. *Hanukkah moon*
Dorros, Arthur. *Radio Man / Don Radio*
When the pigs took over
Ets, Marie Hall. *Gilberto and the wind*
Nine days to Christmas
Fisher, Mary M. *Rosita's bridge*
Flanagan, Alice K. *Cinco de Mayo*
Freschet, Gina. *Beto and the bone dance*
Galindo, Mary Sue. *Icy watermelon / Sandía fría*
Head, Judith. *Mud soup*
Herrera, Juan Felipe. *Grandma and Me at the flea / Los meros meros remateros*
Iyengar, Malathi Michelle. *Romina's rangoli*
Jiménez, Francisco. *The Christmas gift / El regalo de Navidad*
Johnston, Tony. *My abuelita*
Luenn, Nancy. *A gift for Abuelita*
Mora, Pat. *The bakery lady / La señora de la panadería*
A birthday basket for Tía
Confetti
Pablo's tree
The rainbow tulip
Tomás and the library lady
Morales, Yuyi. *Nino wrestles the world*
O'Neill, Alexis. *Estela's swap*
Pérez, Amada Irma. *My diary from here to there / Mi diario de aquí hasta allá*
My very own room / Mi propio cuartito
Pérez, L. King. *First day in grapes*
Politi, Leo. *Juanita*
Pedro, the angel of Olvera Street
Song of the swallows
Price, Mara. *Grandma's chocolate / El chocolate de Abuelita*
Roe, Eileen. *With my brother / Con mi hermano*
Ruiz-Flores, Lupe. *Alicia's fruity drinks / Las aguas frescas de Alicia*
Sáenz, Benjamin Alire. *A gift from papá Diego / Un regalo de papá Diego*
Grandma Fina and her wonderful umbrellas / La abuelita Fina y sus sombrillas maravillosas
Schaefer, Lola M. *Cinco de Mayo*
Schreck, Karen Halvorsen. *Lucy's family tree*
Soto, Gary. *Chato goes cruisin'*
Lucky Luis
My little car / Mi carrito
The old man and his door
Snapshots from the wedding
Too many tamales
Stewart, Sarah. *The quiet place*
Tafolla, Carmen. *Fiesta babies*
What can you do with a paleta?
What can you do with a rebozo?
Thomas, Jane Resh. *Lights on the river*
Tonatiuh, Duncan. *Dear Primo*
Warren, Sarah. *Dolores Huerta*

Ethnic groups in the U.S. – Pakistani Americans

English, Karen. *Nadia's hands*
Khan, Rukhsana. *Big red lollipop*

Ethnic groups in the U.S. – Puerto Rican Americans

Cowley, Joy. *Gracias, the Thanksgiving turkey*
Gonzalez, Lucia. *The storyteller's candle / La velita de los cuentos*
Keats, Ezra Jack. *My dog is lost!*
Manzano, Sonia. *A box full of kittens*
No dogs allowed
Steptoe, John. *Creativity*
Velasquez, Eric. *Grandma's gift*

Grandma's records

Ethnic groups in the U.S. – Russian Americans

Best, Cari. *When Catherine the Great and I were eight!*
Broyles, Anne. *Shy Mama's Halloween*
Polacco, Patricia. *The trees of the dancing goats*
Pryor, Bonnie. *The dream jar*
Tarbescu, Edith. *Annushka's voyage*
Woodruff, Elvira. *The memory coat*
Yolen, Jane. *Naming Liberty*

Ethnic groups in the U.S. – Shakers

Ray, Mary Lyn. *Shaker boy*

Ethnic groups in the U.S. – Sudanese Americans

Williams, Karen Lynn. *My name is Sangoel*

Ethnic groups in the U.S. – Swedish Americans

Peterson, Melissa. *Hanna's Christmas*

Ethnic groups in the U.S. – Tibetan Americans

Rose, Naomi C. *Tashi and the Tibetan flower cure*

Ethnic groups in the U.S. – Vietnamese Americans

Garland, Sherry. *The lotus seed*
My father's boat
Jules, Jacqueline. *Duck for Turkey Day*
Surat, Michele Maria. *Angel child, dragon child*

Etiquette

Ainslie, Tamsin. *I can say please*
I can say thank you
Aliki. *Manners*
Anderson, Peggy Perry. *Out to lunch*
Berenstain, Stan and Jan. *The Berenstain bears forget their manners*
Best, Cari. *Are you going to be good?*
Bloom, Suzanne. *Piggy Monday*
Breznak, Irene. *Sneezy Louise*
Bridges, Shirin Yim. *Mary Wrightly, so politely*
Brown, Marc. *Perfect pigs*
Cole, Babette. *Lady Lupin's book of etiquette*
Dahl, Michael. *Bear says "thank you"*
Hippo says "excuse me."
Dewdney, Anna. *Nobunny's perfect*
Dutton, Sandra. *Dear Miss Perfect*
Dyckman, Ame. *Tea party rules*
Edwards, Pamela Duncan. *Rude mule*
Ferguson, Sarah. *Tea for Ruby*
Fredrickson, Lane. *Watch your tongue, Cecily Beasley*
Gibbs, Lynne. *Don't slurp your soup!*
Goldberg, Whoopi. *Whoopi's big book of manners*
Gorbachev, Valeri. *How to be friends with a dragon*
Greenberg, David. *Don't forget your etiquette!*
Hamilton, Martha. *The hidden feast*
Harper, Charise Mericle. *The best birthday ever!*
Helmer, Diana Star. *The cat who came for tacos*
Henry, Jed. *I speak dinosaur*
Holub, Joan. *Turkeys never gobble*
Hood, Susan. *Just say boo!*
Huget, Jennifer LaRue. *Thanks a lot, Emily Post!*
Idle, Molly. *Tea Rex*
Jones, Christianne. *Lacey Walker, nonstop talker*
Joosse, Barbara. *Please is a good word to say*
Katz, Alan. *Don't say that word!*
Keller, Laurie. *Do unto otters*
Kelly, Mij. *Achoo!*
Kopelke, Lisa. *Excuse me!*
Levitin, Sonia. *When Elephant goes to a party*
When Kangaroo goes to school
Lloyd-Jones, Sally. *Being a pig is nice*
McElligott, Matthew. *The lion's share*
Manners mash-up
Marciano, John Bemelmans. *Madeline says merci*
Melling, David. *The Scallywags*
Metzger, Steve. *Will Princess Isabel ever say please?*
Miller, Virginia. *On your potty!*
Modan, Rutu. *Maya makes a mess*
Monster, be good!
Montanari, Donata. *Children around the world*
Morris, Jennifer E. *May I please have a cookie?*
Parr, Todd. *Do's and don'ts*
Paxton, Tom. *Engelbert the elephant*
Post, Peggy. *Emily's everyday manners*
Potter, Beatrix. *The sly old cat*
Primavera, Elise. *Louise the big cheese and the Ooh-la-la Charm School*
Robberecht, Thierry. *I can't do anything!*
Rosenthal, Amy Krouse. *Cookies*
Scarry, Richard. *Richard Scarry's please and thank you book*
Senning, Cindy Post. *Emily's out and about book*
Shaw, Hannah. *School for bandits*
Sierra, Judy. *Mind your manners, B. B. Wolf*
Suppose you meet a dinosaur
Stein, David Ezra. *The nice book*
Stephens, Helen. *Ahoyty-toyty*
Sweetland, Nancy Rose. *Yelly Kelly*
Szekeres, Cyndy. *Toby's please and thank you*
Thomas, Shelley Moore. *A cold winter's Good Knight*
Tillman, Nancy. *Tumford's rude noises*
Tryon, Leslie. *Patsy says*
Vestergaard, Hope. *Potty animals*
Watt, Mélanie. *You're finally here!*
Wheeler, Valerie. *Yes, please! No, thank you!*
Willems, Mo. *The duckling gets a cookie!?*
Time to say "please"!
Wilson, Karma. *Bear says thanks*
Yee, Wong Herbert. *Big black bear*
Yolen, Jane. *How do dinosaurs eat their food?*
Ziefert, Harriet. *Mother Goose manners*
Someday we'll have very good manners

Evening *see* Twilight

Exercise *see* Health & fitness – exercise

Experiments *see* Science

Extraterrestrial beings *see* Aliens

Eye glasses *see* Glasses

Eyes *see* Anatomy – eyes; Glasses; Disabilities – blindness; Senses – sight

Fables *see* Folk & fairy tales

Fairies

Bar-el, Dan. *Such a prince*
Bate, Lucy. *Little rabbit's loose tooth*
Batt, Tanya Robyn. *The faerie's gift*
Bottner, Barbara. *Pish and Posh*
Bouchard, Dave. *Fairy*
Bowen, Anne. *Tooth Fairy's first night*
Brockenbrough, Martha. *The Dinosaur Tooth Fairy*
Brown, Marc. *Arthur tricks the tooth fairy*
Cash, Rosanne. *Penelope Jane*
Clibbon, Meg. *Imagine you're a fairy!*
Climo, Shirley. *The Persian Cinderella*
Colato Laínez, René. *The Tooth Fairy meets El Ratón Pérez*
Davis, Katie. *Mabel the Tooth Fairy and how she got her job*
Demers, Dominique. *Old Thomas and the little fairy*
Durant, Alan. *Dear tooth fairy*
Edwards, Pamela Duncan. *Dear Tooth Fairy*
Fairies, trolls and goblins galore
Garland, Michael. *King Puck*
Gay, Marie-Louise. *Stella, fairy of the forest*
Graham, Bob. *April and Esme, tooth fairies*
Jethro Byrd, fairy child
Grambling, Lois G. *This whole Tooth Fairy thing's nothing but a big rip-off!*
Grimm, Jacob and Wilhelm. *Sleeping Beauty*
The sleeping beauty
The three spinning fairies
Hague, Kathleen. *Good night, fairies*
Hundal, Nancy. *Twilight fairies*
Inkpen, Deborah. *Harriet and the little fat fairy*
James, Brian. *The Supertwins and tooth trouble*
Jay, Betsy. *Jane vs. the Tooth Fairy*
Johnson, Paul Brett. *Little Bunny Foo Foo*
Kann, Victoria. *Silverlicious*
Kaye, Marilyn. *The real tooth fairy*
Krensky, Stephen. *The youngest fairy godmother ever*
Lowell, Susan. *Cindy Ellen*
McClintock, Barbara. *Molly and the magic wishbone*
MacDonald, Margaret Read. *Slop!*
Too many fairies
Maconie, Robin. *Alice and her fabulous teeth*
Milord, Susan. *Willa the wonderful*
Munsch, Robert N. *Andrew's loose tooth*
Numeroff, Laura Joffe. *Ponyella*
Oddino, Licia. *Finn and the fairies*
Olson, Mary. *Nice try, Tooth Fairy*
Palatini, Margie. *Gone with the wand*
Paquette, Ammi-Joan. *The tiptoe guide to tracking fairies*
Paxton, Tom. *The story of the Tooth Fairy*
Peters, Stephanie True. *Raggedy Ann and Andy and the magic potion*
Pomeranc, Marion Hess. *The American Wei*
Prelutsky, Jack. *Monday's troll*
Ray, Jane. *The dollhouse fairy*
Reinhart, Matthew. *Fairies and magical creatures*
Rose, Marion. *The Christmas tree fairy*
Sabuda, Robert. *Peter Pan*
Sierra, Judy. *The gift of the crocodile*
Simmons, Jane. *The dreamtime fairies*
Smith, Lane. *Pinocchio, the boy*
Taylor, Jane. *Twinkle, twinkle little star,* ill. by Heather Collins
Twinkle, twinkle, little star, ill. by Michael Hague
Wallace, Ivy. *Pookie*
Ward, Helen. *Little Moon Dog*
Wells, Rosemary. *Fritz and the mess fairy*
Weninger, Brigitte. *The elf's hat*
Yolen, Jane. *Come to the fairies' ball*
Young, Amy. *The mud fairy*

Fairs, festivals

Blumenthal, Deborah. *Ice palace*
Bond, Michael. *Paddington Bear and the Busy Bee Carnival*
Browne, Anthony. *Animal fair*
Bunting, Eve. *The pumpkin fair*
Calhoun, Mary. *Blue-ribbon Henry*
Castaneda, Omar S. *Abuela's weave*
Cave, Kathryn. *The boy who became an eagle*
Chaconas, Dori. *Hurry down to Derry Fair*
Chan, Arlene. *Awakening the dragon*
Colato Laínez, René. *Playing lotería / El juego de la lotería*
Cousins, Lucy. *Maisy at the fair*
Crews, Donald. *Night at the fair*
D'Amico, Carmela. *Ella sets sail*
Darrow, Sharon. *Old Thunder and Miss Raney*
Dorros, Arthur. *Tonight is carnaval*
Dubuc, Marianne. *Animal masquerade*
Ets, Marie Hall. *Mr. Penny's race horse*
Flanagan, Alice K. *Chinese New Year*
Fraser, Mary Ann. *Heebie-Jeebie Jamboree*
Frasier, Debra. *A fabulous fair alphabet*
Geisert, Arthur. *Pigaroons*
Gibbons, Gail. *County fair*
Goembel, Ponder. *Animal fair*
Gorbachev, Valeri. *Molly who flew away*
Greenwood, Mark. *Drummer boy of John John*
Guy, Ginger Foglesong. *Fiesta*
Hamilton, Arlene. *Only a cow*
Helakoski, Leslie. *Fair cow*
Hill, Eric. *Spot at the fair*
Himmelman, John. *Cows to the rescue*
Hoffman, Elizabeth Stokes. *Miss Renée's mice go to an exhibition*
Holabird, Katharine. *Angelina at the fair*
Horn, Sandra Ann. *The dandelion wish*
Jackson, Ellen. *The autumn equinox*
Janni, Rebecca. *Every cowgirl loves a rodeo*
Kassirer, Sue. *Math fair blues*
Khan, Rukhsana. *King for a day*
Kinney, Jessica. *The pig scramble*
Krishnaswami, Uma. *Holi*
Lasky, Kathryn. *Science fair bunnies*
Lewin, Ted. *Fair!*
Lin, Grace. *Thanking the moon*
McLean, Dirk. *Play mas'! a carnival ABC*

Murphy, Stuart J. *The penny pot*
Norman, Kim. *I know a wee piggy*
O'Malley, Kevin. *Roller coaster*
Paraskevas, Betty. *Marvin, the tap-dancing horse*
Polacco, Patricia. *Oh, look!*
Reynolds, Jan. *Celebrate!*
Rosen, Michael. *Bear flies high*
Seto, Loretta. *Mooncakes*
Shireen, Nadia. *Hey, Presto!*
Speed, Toby. *Brave potatoes*
Stevenson, James. *All aboard!*
Stihler, Chérie B. *The giant cabbage turnip*
Stoeke, Janet Morgan. *Minerva Louise at the fair*
Tafolla, Carmen. *Fiesta babies*
Train, Mary. *Time for the fair*
Van Nutt, Julia. *Pumpkins from the sky?*
Watson, Clyde. *Applebet*
Weaver, Tess. *Frederick Finch, loudmouth*
Winter, Jeanette. *Niño's mask*
Yacowitz, Caryn. *Pumpkin fiesta*
Ziefert, Harriet. *Pumpkin Pie*

Fairy tales *see* Folk & fairy tales

Family life

Adams, Eric J. *On the day his daddy left*
Adler, David A. *Hiding from the Nazis*
It's time to sleep, it's time to dream
Adoff, Arnold. *Black is brown is tan*
In for winter, out for spring
Ahlberg, Janet. *The baby's catalogue*
Peek-a-boo!
Ajmera, Maya. *To be a kid*
Akin, Sara Laux. *Three scoops and a fig*
Alcott, Louisa May. *An old-fashioned Thanksgiving*
Alda, Arlene. *Iris has a virus*
Aliki. *Christmas tree memories*
Jack and Jake
Marianthe's story one: painted words; Marianthe's story two: spoken memories
Those summers
Welcome, little baby
Allard, Harry. *The Stupids have a ball*
The Stupids step out
The Stupids take off
Altman, Linda Jacobs. *Amelia's road*
Anderson, Laurie Halse. *Turkey pox*
Anderson, Peggy Perry. *Out to lunch*
Andrews, Julie. *Dumpy to the rescue!*
Asch, Frank. *Good night, Baby Bear*
Goodbye house
Ashburn, Boni. *The fort that Jack built*
Ashman, Linda. *Creaky old house*
Stella, unleashed
To the beach!
Atwell, Debby. *Pearl*
Auld, Mary. *My aunt and uncle*
My brother
My dad
My grandparents
My mom
My sister
Avraham, Kate Aver. *What will you be, Sara Mee?*
Axelrod, Amy. *Pigs on the ball*
Pigs will be pigs
They'll believe me when I'm gone
Bang, Molly. *In my heart*
Banks, Kate. *Mama's coming home*
Bannerman, Helen. *The story of Little Babaji*
The story of Little Black Sambo, ill. by Helen Bannerman
The story of Little Black Sambo, ill. by Helen Bannerman
The story of Little Black Sambo, ill. by Christopher Bing
Barbour, Karen. *Little Nino's pizzeria*
Barnett, Mac. *Billy Twitters and his big blue whale problem*
Bean, Jonathan. *Building our house*
Bentley, Dawn. *Busy little beaver*
Welcome back, Puffin
Berenstain, Stan and Jan. *The Berenstain bears and the truth*
The Berenstain bears and too much TV
The Berenstain bears' Christmas tree
The Berenstain bears forget their manners
The Berenstain bears in the dark
The Berenstain bears learn about strangers
The Berenstain bears' moving day
The Berenstain bears' report card trouble
Bergman, Mara. *Musical beds*
Bernhard, Durga. *To and fro, fast and slow*
Bertrand, Diane Gonzales. *Family / familia*
Sofía and the purple dress / Sofía y el vestido morado
Best, Cari. *When we go walking*
Biden, Jill. *Don't forget, God bless our troops*
Bildner, Phil. *Turkey Bowl*
Billingsley, Franny. *Big bad bunny*
Birtha, Becky. *Grandmama's pride*
Bishop, Claire Huchet. *The five Chinese brothers*
Blades, Ann. *Too small*
Blume, Judy. *The one in the middle is a green kangaroo*
The Pain and The Great One
Blumenthal, Deborah. *Aunt Claire's yellow beehive hair*
Bodkin, Odds. *The Christmas cobwebs*
Bond, Felicia. *Poinsettia and her family*
Bond, Rebecca. *Bravo, Maurice!*
Bonwill, Ann. *The Frazzle family finds a way*
Brett, Jan. *Armadillo rodeo*
Bridges, Shirin Yim. *Mary Wrightly, so politely*
Bright, Robert. *Georgie*
Brisson, Pat. *Sometimes we were brave*
Brown, Jeff. *Flat Stanley*, ill. by Scott Nash
Flat Stanley, ill. by Tomi Ungerer
Brown, Laurie Krasny. *What's the big secret?*
When dinosaurs die
Brown, Marc. *Arthur's chicken pox*
Arthur's family vacation
D. W., the picky eater
D. W.'s lost blankie
Brown, Margaret Wise. *My world*
Robin's room
Broyles, Anne. *Shy Mama's Halloween*
Brunhoff, Laurent de. *Meet Babar and his family*
Bunting, Eve. *Ghost's hour, spook's hour*
Going home
Night tree
The wall
The Wednesday surprise
You were loved before you were born
Burdett, Lois. *Romeo and Juliet for kids*
Caffey, Donna. *Yikes-lice!*
Camp, Lindsay. *The biggest bed in the world*
Capucilli, Alyssa Satin. *Bear hugs*

Carling, Amelia Lau. *Mama and Papa have a store*
Carlson, Nancy. *It's going to be perfect*
My family is forever
Carlstrom, Nancy White. *Before you were born*
Jesse Bear, what will you wear?
Thanksgiving Day at our house
Casanova, Mary. *Utterly otterly day*
Caseley, Judith. *Witch mama*
Chaconas, Dori. *Hurry down to Derry Fair*
Chall, Marsha Wilson. *Happy Birthday, America!*
Sugarbush spring
Charlip, Remy. *A perfect day*
Cheng, Andrea. *Anna the bookbinder*
Child, Lauren. *Clarice Bean, that's me*
Maude
What planet are you from Clarice Bean?
Chocolate, Deborah. *Kwanzaa*
Chodos-Irvine, Margaret. *Ella Sarah gets dressed*
Chorao, Kay. *Shadow night*
Christelow, Eileen. *Five little monkeys with nothing to do*
Clark, Ann Nolan. *In my mother's house*
Clavel, Bernard. *Castle of books*
Clements, Andrew. *Slippers loves to run*
Clifton, Lucille. *Everett Anderson's goodbye*
Coffelt, Nancy. *Fred stays with me!*
Cole, Brock. *The money we'll save*
Cole, Joanna. *How I was adopted*
How you were born
Collicott, Sharleen. *Mildred and Sam*
Cooke, Trish. *So much*
Cooney, Barbara. *Eleanor*
Cooper, Floyd. *Coming home: from the life of Langston Hughes*
Corey, Dorothy. *You go away*
Corpi, Lucha. *Where fireflies dance / Ahí, donde bailan las luciérnagas*
Coste, Marion. *Finding Joy*
Cox, Judy. *My family plays music*
Crews, Donald. *Sail away*
Crews, Nina. *A ghost story*
You are here
Cruise, Robin. *Only you*
Crum, Shutta. *Dozens of cousins*
Cumpiano, Ina. *Quinito, day and night / Quinito, dia y noche*
Cunnane, Kelly. *Chirchir is singing*
Curtis, Jamie Lee. *Tell me again about the night I was born*
Today I feel silly and other moods that make my day
da Costa, Deborah. *Hanukkah moon*
D'Antonio, Nancy. *Our baby from China*
Darbyshire, Kristen. *Put it on the list!*
DeFelice, Cynthia C. *The real, true Dulcie Campbell*
Denim, Sue. *The Dumb Bunnies*
The Dumb Bunnies' Easter
The Dumb Bunnies go to the zoo
Make way for Dumb Bunnies
dePaola, Tomie. *The art lesson*
The family Christmas tree book
Devine, Monica. *Carry me, Mama*
Dewey, Jennifer Owings. *Once I knew a spider*
Dieterlé, Nathalie. *I am the king!*
Dixon, Ann. *Waiting for Noël*
Dodd, Emma. *I am small*
What pet to get?
Dooley, Norah. *Everybody cooks rice*
Dotlich, Rebecca Kai. *A family like yours*
Doughty, Rebecca. *Oh no! Time to go!*
Douglas, Ann. *Before you were born*
Downing, Julie. *No hugs till Saturday*
Downs, Mike. *You see a circus, I see —*
Doyle, Malachy. *Too noisy!*
Dungy, Tony. *You can do it!*
Ehlert, Lois. *Hands*
Elliott, David. *Knitty Kitty*
Elvgren, Jennifer Riesmeyer. *Josias, hold the book*
Elya, Susan Middleton. *N is for Navidad*
Emerman, Ellen. *Just right: the story of a Jewish home*
English, Karen. *Nadia's hands*
Eschbacher, Roger. *Road trip*
Falwell, Cathryn. *Feast for ten*
We have a baby
Fearnley, Jan. *A special something*
Feiffer, Jules. *I lost my bear*
Feiffer, Kate. *No go sleep!*
Which puppy?
Fishman, Cathy Goldberg. *On Purim*
On Shabbat
Flanagan, Alice K. *A visit to the Gravesens' farm*
Fleming, Candace. *Papa's mechanical fish*
Foggo, Cheryl. *Dear baobab*
Foreman, George. *Let George do it!*
Fox, Mem. *Time for bed*
Fraggalosch, Audrey. *Great grizzly wilderness*
Frame, Jeron Ashford. *Yesterday I had the blues*
Francis, Panama. *David gets his drum*
Friedman, Ina R. *How my parents learned to eat*
Friedrich, Molly. *You're not my real mother!*
Gal, Susan. *Day by day*
Galvin, Laura Gates. *River Otter at Autumn Lane*
Gilani-Williams, Fawzia. *Nabeel's new pants*
Gleeson, Libby. *Cuddle time*
Gliori, Debi. *Mr. Bear's new baby*
No matter what
Goodman, Susan E. *Chopsticks for my noodle soup*
Goudey, Alice E. *The day we saw the sun come up*
Gourley, Robbin. *Bring me some apples and I'll make you a pie*
Graham, Bob. *"Let's get a pup!" said Kate*
Oscar's half birthday
Gray, Nigel. *Time to play!*
Greenfield, Eloise. *I make music*
Me and Neesie
Greenfield, Monica. *Waiting for Christmas*
Gregory, Nan. *Pink*
Grey, Mini. *Traction Man is here*
Griessman, Annette. *The fire*
Grindley, Sally. *A new room for William*
Guest, Elissa Haden. *Harriet's had enough!*
Guiberson, Brenda Z. *The emperor lays an egg*
Gutch, Michael. *Sticky, sticky, stuck!*
Guy, Ginger Foglesong. *My grandma / Mi abuelita*
Hall, Donald. *Lucy's Christmas*
Hammersmith, Craig. *What is a family?*
Hänel, Wolfram. *Little elephant's song*
Harris, Robie H. *Don't forget to come back*
Go! Go! Maria!
Who's in my family?
Harris, Teresa E. *Summer Jackson*
Hartman, Bob. *Granny Mae's Christmas play*
Havill, Juanita. *Just like a baby*
Hazen, Barbara Shook. *Who is your favorite monster, mama?*
Hearne, Betsy Gould. *Seven brave women*
Heath, Amy. *Sofie's role*
Heide, Florence Parry. *Sami and the time of the troubles*

Helakoski, Leslie. *Doggone feet!*
Helmer, Marilyn. *One splendid tree*
Henkes, Kevin. *Bailey goes camping*
Julius, the baby of the world
Shhhh
Heo, Yumi. *Ten days and nine nights*
Herman, Charlotte. *The memory cupboard*
Hesse, Karen. *Spuds*
Hest, Amy. *The purple coat*
Hill, Elizabeth Starr. *Evan's corner*
Hill, Eric. *Spot goes to the beach*
Hindley, Judy. *What's in baby's morning*
Hines, Anna Grossnickle. *Big like me*
Daddy makes the best spaghetti
Even if I spill my milk?
The secret keeper
Whose shoes?
Hoban, Julia. *Amy loves the rain*
Amy loves the snow
Amy loves the sun
Hoban, Russell. *A baby sister for Frances*
Hoberman, Mary Ann. *All kinds of families*
Hodge, Deborah. *Emma's story*
Hodges, Margaret. *Silent night: the song and its story*
Hodgkinson, Leigh. *Smile!*
Hoffman, Don. *Good morning, good night Billy and Abigail*
Hoffman, Mary. *Grace at Christmas*
Höjer, Dan. *Heart of mine*
Hopkinson, Deborah. *Maria's comet*
Houston, Gloria. *The year of the perfect Christmas tree*
Howard, Ellen. *The log cabin Christmas*
The log cabin church
Hubbell, Patricia. *Bouncing time*
Huget, Jennifer LaRue. *The beginner's guide to running away from home*
Hughes, Shirley. *Giving*
Olly and me
Out and about
Hundal, Nancy. *Camping*
Hutchins, Pat. *The doorbell rang*
It's my birthday!
Tidy Titch
Titch
You'll soon grow into them, Titch
Intrater, Roberta Grobel. *Peek-a-boo!*
Smile!
Isadora, Rachel. *At the crossroads*
What a family!
Jackson, Isaac. *Somebody's new pajamas*
Jadoul, Emile. *All by myself!*
James, Simon. *Nurse Clementine*
Jarka, Jeff. *Love that kitty!*
Love that puppy!
Jenkins, Emily. *Five creatures*
What happens on Wednesdays
Johnson, Angela. *Daddy calls me man*
Down the winding road
The leaving morning
Johnson, Suzanne C. *Fribbity ribbit*
Johnston, Tony. *Laugh-out-loud baby*
The quilt story
Sunsets of the West
That summer
Joosse, Barbara. *A houseful of Christmas*
Snow day!
Jordan, Deloris. *Salt in his shoes*
Joyce, William. *Big time Olie*
A day with Wilbur Robinson
Dinosaur Bob
George shrinks
Julian, Alison. *Brave as a bunny can be*
Kaplan, Michael B. *Betty Bunny didn't do it*
Betty Bunny wants everything
Keane, Dave. *Sloppy Joe*
Keats, Ezra Jack. *Apt. 3*
Louie's search
Keister, Douglas. *Fernando's gift / El regalo de Fernando*
Keller, Holly. *Geraldine first*
Geraldine's blanket
Jacob's tree
Kellogg, Steven. *Can I keep him?*
Kempter, Christa. *When Mama can't sleep*
Kerner, Susan. *Always by my side*
Kimmelman, Leslie. *Hanukkah lights, Hanukkah nights*
Hooray! it's Passover!
How do I love you?
Round the turkey
King, Dedie. *I see the sun in Afghanistan*
I see the sun in Russia
Kinkade, Sheila. *My family*
Kinsey-Warnock, Natalie. *A Christmas like Helen's*
From dawn till dusk
Kirwan, Wednesday. *Minerva the monster*
Nobody notices Minerva
Kleven, Sandy. *The right touch*
Koda-Callan, Elizabeth. *The squiggly Wigglys*
Kornell, Max. *Bear with me*
Kosofsky, Chaim. *Much, much better*
Kraus, Robert. *Another mouse to feed*
Krauss, Ruth. *And I love you*
Krishnaswami, Uma. *Bringing Asha home*
Kroll, Steven. *Happy Mother's Day*
The squirrels' Thanksgiving
Kroll, Virginia L. *Masai and I*
Krosoczka, Jarrett J. *Ollie the purple elephant*
Kuiper, Nannie. *Bravo, brave beavers*
Kuklin, Susan. *Families*
Kurtz, Jane. *River friendly, river wild*
Kuskin, Karla. *A great miracle happened there*
I am me
Laird, Elizabeth. *A book of promises*
Langreuter, Jutta. *Little Bear brushes his teeth*
Langsen, Richard C. *When someone in the family drinks too much*
Lansky, Vicki. *It's not your fault, KoKo Bear*
LaRochelle, David. *How Martha saved her parents from green beans*
Lasky, Kathryn. *Lucille camps in*
Sophie and Rose
Lawrence, Mary. *What's that sound?*
Lawson, Robert. *They were strong and good*
Layton, Neal. *Smile if you're human*
Lears, Laurie. *Megan's birthday tree*
Lee, Milly. *Nim and the war effort*
Lendroth, Susan. *Ocean wide, ocean deep*
Lenski, Lois. *The little family*
Papa Small
Lerner, Harriet Goldhor. *Franny B. Kranny, there's a bird in your hair*
Lester, Julius. *Sam and the tigers*
Levine, Abby. *This is the turkey*
Levine, Arthur A. *Monday is one day*
Levinson, Riki. *I go with my family to Grandma's*
Watch the stars come out
Levitin, Sonia. *Nine for California*

Lewin, Hugh. *Jafta*
Lewis, Rose A. *I love you like crazy cakes*
Lin, Grace. *Thanking the moon*
Lindsay, Jeanne Warren. *Do I have a daddy?*
Lloyd-Jones, Sally. *Just because you're mine*
Lo, Ginnie. *Auntie Yang's great soybean picnic*
Lobel, Gillian. *Too small for honey cake*
Lomas Garza, Carmen. *In my family*
London, Jonathan. *Hurricane!*
Long, Melinda. *Hiccup snickup*
Longstreth, Galen Goodwin. *Yes, let's*
Loomis, Christine. *Across America, I love you*
López, Susana. *The best family in the world*
Lyon, George Ella. *Cecil's story*
Come a tide
No dessert forever!
One lucky girl
McAllister, Angela. *Yuck! That's not a monster*
Macaulay, David. *Black and white*
McCarty, Peter. *Chloe*
McCloskey, Robert. *Blueberries for Sal*
One morning in Maine
McCully, Emily Arnold. *Monk camps out*
My real family
McCutcheon, John. *Happy adoption day!*
MacDonald, Amy. *Cousin Ruth's tooth*
McDonald, Megan. *Insects are my life*
McGowan, Michael. *Sunday is for God*
McKissack, Patricia C. *Messy Bessey's family reunion*
Nettie Jo's friends
Stitchin' and pullin'
MacLachlan, Patricia. *All the places to love*
Who loves me?
You were the first
McPhail, David. *Emma's pet*
Emma's vacation
McQuade, Jacqueline. *Good times with Teddy Bear*
Mahy, Margaret. *The rattlebang picnic*
The seven Chinese brothers
Maloney, Peter. *His mother's nose*
Manning, Maurie J. *Kitchen dance*
Manning, Peyton. *Family huddle*
Manzano, Sonia. *No dogs allowed*
Markle, Sandra. *A mother's journey*
Martin, David. *Five little piggies*
Martín, Hugo C. *Pablo's Christmas*
Martin, Jacqueline Briggs. *On Sand Island*
Matteson, George. *The Christmas tugboat*
Mauner, Claudia. *Zoe Sophia in New York*
May, Kathy. *Molasses man*
Mayhew, James. *Where's my hug?*
Medina, Tony. *DeShawn days*
Melmed, Laura Krauss. *A hug goes around*
Little Oh
Meltzer, Amy. *The Shabbat Princess*
Meng, Cece. *I will not read this book*
Messinger, Carla. *When the shadbush blooms*
Miller, Margaret. *I love colors*
Modesitt, Jeanne. *Little Mouse's happy birthday*
Monk, Isabell. *Family*
Moore, Raina. *How do you say good night?*
Moore-Mallinos, Jennifer. *When my parents forgot how to be friends*
Moorman, Margaret. *Light the lights!*
Mora, Pat. *Let's eat! / A comer!*
Morozumi, Atsuko. *Helping daddy*
Morris, Ann. *Families*
Loving
Moses, Will. *Silent night*
Munsch, Robert N. *I have to go!*
Mmm, cookies!
Murguia, Bethanie Deeney. *Snippet the early riser*
Murphy, Jill. *A quiet night in*
Murphy, Stuart J. *The best vacation ever*
Nicholls, Judith. *Someone I like*
Nikola-Lisa, W. *One, two, three Thanksgiving!*
Summer sun risin'
Nolen, Jerdine. *Hewitt Anderson's great big life*
In my momma's kitchen
Pitching in for Eubie
Norac, Carl. *I love you so much*
Novak, Matt. *A wish for you*
O'Connell, Rebecca. *Baby parade*
O'Connor, Jane. *Fancy Nancy*
Fancy Nancy and the posh puppy
Fancy Nancy splendiferous Christmas
Nancy la elegante / Fancy Nancy
The snow globe family
Oelschlager, Vanita. *Made in China*
Ohi, Ruth. *And you can come too*
O'Keefe, Susan Heyboer. *Baby day*
Onyefulu, Ifeoma. *Omer's favorite place*
Orloff, Karen Kaufman. *I wanna new room*
Ormerod, Jan. *Who's whose?*
Orona-Ramirez, Kristy. *Kiki's journey*
Osborne, Mary Pope. *Happy birthday, America*
Osofsky, Audrey. *Dreamcatcher*
Overend, Jenni. *Welcome with love*
Palatini, Margie. *Tub-boo-boo*
Parr, Todd. *We belong together*
Paterson, Diane. *Hurricane wolf*
Pelley, Kathleen T. *Inventor McGregor*
Pérez, Amada Irma. *My diary from here to there / Mi diario de aquí hasta allá*
My very own room / Mi propio cuartito
Perkins, Lynne Rae. *The broken cat*
Home lovely
Pictures from our vacation
Perl, Erica S. *Ninety-three in my family*
Peterson, Jeanne Whitehouse. *Don't forget Winona*
Pfeffer, Wendy. *Mallard duck at Meadow View Pond*
Piernas-Davenport, Gail. *Shanté Keys and the New Year's peas*
Pilkey, Dav. *The Dumb Bunnies*
The Dumb Bunnies' Easter
The Dumb Bunnies go to the zoo
The Hallo-wiener
Make way for Dumb Bunnies
Pinfold, Levi. *Black dog*
Pinkney, Andrea Davis. *Mim's Christmas jam*
Pinkney, Brian. *Jojo's flying side kick*
Pinkney, Gloria Jean. *Back home*
The Sunday outing
Polacco, Patricia. *The blessing cup*
Gifts of the heart
Portnoy, Mindy Avra. *A tale of two seders*
Where do people go when they die?
Postgate, Daniel. *The snagglegrollop*
Powell, Consie. *Old dog Cora and the Christmas tree*
Pringle, Laurence P. *Everybody has a bellybutton*
Octopus hug
Prochovnic, Dawn Babb. *Hip hip hooray! It's Family Day!*
Pryor, Bonnie. *The dream jar*
Pulver, Robin. *Alicia's tutu*
Purmell, Ann. *Maple syrup season*
Raffi. *One light, one sun*
Rand, Gloria. *Baby in a basket*

Sailing home
Reid, Barbara. *The party*
Reynolds, Marilynn. *The new land*
Reynolds, Peter H. *My very big little world*
The smallest gift of Christmas
Richardson, John. *Grunt*
Ries, Lori. *Punk wig*
Riggs, Shannon. *Not in Room 204*
Ringgold, Faith. *Dinner at Aunt Connie's house*
The invisible princesses
Robberecht, Thierry. *I can't do anything!*
Rocco, John. *Blackout*
Rock, Lois. *Now we have a baby*
Rockwell, Anne. *Long ago yesterday*
No! No! No!
Once upon a time this morning
Rogers, Fred. *Adoption*
Divorce
Moving
Rogers, Paul. *Ruby's dinnertime*
Root, Phyllis. *Creak! said the bed*
Rattletrap car
Rattletrap car [board book]
What Baby wants
Rosen, Michael J. *A drive in the country*
Rosenberg, Liz. *On Christmas eve*
Rosenberry, Vera. *Vera runs away*
Rounds, Glen. *Sod houses on the Great Plains*
Rubin, C. M. *Eleanor, Ellatony, Ellencake, and me*
Russo, Marisabina. *Under the table*
When mama gets home
Ruurs, Margriet. *When we go camping*
Rylant, Cynthia. *Best wishes*
Birthday presents
Bunny bungalow
The relatives came
When I was young in the mountains
Sacre, Antonio. *A mango in the hand*
Safran, Sheri. *All kinds of families: a lift-the-flap book*
Salley, Coleen. *Epossumondas*
Sandburg, Carl. *The Huckabuck family and how they raised popcorn in Nebraska and quit and came back*
Sansone, Adele. *The little green goose*
Santiago, Esmeralda. *A doll for Navidades*
Santos, Rosa. *Play date*
Sasso, Sandy Eisenberg. *Naamah, Noah's wife*
Say, Allen. *Allison*
Grandfather's journey
A river dream
Scanlon, Elizabeth Garton. *All the world*
Schaefer, Lola M. *Frankie Stein*
Loose tooth
Scheffler, Ursel. *Who has time for Little Bear?*
Schertle, Alice. *Down the road*
Schoenherr, John. *Rebel*
Schreck, Karen Halvorsen. *Lucy's family tree*
Schwartz, Amy. *Some babies*
Schweninger, Ann. *Valentine friends*
Scott, Ann Herbert. *On mother's lap*
On mother's lap [board book]
Senisi, Ellen B. *For my family, love, Allie*
Seto, Loretta. *Mooncakes*
Shannon, David. *Demasiados juguetes / too many toys*
Too many toys
Shannon, Margaret. *Gullible's troubles*
Shapiro, Jody Fickes. *Family lullaby*
Shea, Pegi Deitz. *I see me!*
Shelby, Anne. *Homeplace*
Shields, Carol Diggory. *I am really a princess*
Shoulders, Michael. *Goodnight Baby Bear*
Simmons, Jane. *Come along, Daisy!*
Simon, Norma. *All families are special*
All kinds of families
How do I feel?
Simpson-Enock, Sarah. *Mommy, Mommy, what's in your tummy?*
Singer, Marilyn. *The one and only me*
Smalls, Irene. *Don't say ain't*
Smet, Marian De. *I have two homes*
Smith, Cynthia Leitich. *Jingle dancer*
Snyder, Laurel. *Good night, laila tov*
Sobol, Richard. *Adelina's whales*
Sorensen, Henri. *New Hope*
Soto, Gary. *Snapshots from the wedding*
Spinelli, Eileen. *Now it is summer*
The perfect Christmas
Six hogs on a scooter
Summerbath, winterbath
Thanksgiving at the Tappletons'
When you are happy
Stanley, Malaika Rose. *Baby Ruby bawled*
Steig, William. *Spinky sulks*
Sylvester and the magic pebble
Toby, what are you?
Toby, where are you?
Stein, Mathilde. *The child cruncher*
Stevenson, James. *"Could be worse!"*
When I was nine
Stevenson, Robert Louis. *The moon*
Stone, Lynn M. *Farms old and new*
Stutson, Caroline. *Prairie primer A to Z*
Stuve-Bodeen, Stephanie. *Elizabeti's school*
Suen, Anastasia. *Raise the roof*
Sugarman, Brynn Olenberg. *Rebecca's journey home*
Sweeney, Joan. *Me and my family tree*
Tafuri, Nancy. *Do not disturb*
Takabayashi, Mari. *I live in Brooklyn*
I live in Tokyo
Taulbert, Clifton L. *Little Cliff and the porch people*
Thermes, Jennifer. *Sam Bennett's new shoes*
When I was built
Thomas, Jane Resh. *Celebration!*
Lights on the river
Thomas, Joyce Carol. *Crowning glory*
Thomas, Pat. *My family's changing*
Thompson, Colin. *Falling angels*
Tortillas and lullabies / Tortillas y cancioncitas
Trapani, Iza. *How much is that doggie in the window?*
Row, row, row your boat
Shoo fly!
Trewin, Trudie. *I lost my kisses*
Turner, Ann Warren. *The Christmas house*
Nettie's trip south
Uff, Caroline. *Hello, Lulu*
Lulu's busy day
Underwood, Deborah. *Part-time princess*
Vamos, Samantha R. *Before you were here, mi amor*
Van Buren, David. *I love you as big as the world*
Van der Meer, Mara. *Can we play?*
Van Kampen, Vlasta. *It couldn't be worse*
Van Laan, Nancy. *Possum come a-knocking*
Van Leeuwen, Jean. *Going west*
Papa and the pioneer quilt
The tickle stories
Touch the sky summer
Van Steenwyk, Elizabeth. *Prairie Christmas*
Viau, Nancy. *Storm song*

Villa, Alvaro F. *Flood*
Viorst, Judith. *Alexander and the terrible, horrible, no good, very bad day*
Alexander, who's not (do you hear me? I mean it!) going to move
I'll fix Anthony
Nobody here but me
Voake, Charlotte. *Here comes the train*
Pizza kittens
Waber, Bernard. *Funny, funny Lyle*
Waddell, Martin. *Mimi's Christmas*
Night night Cuddly Bear
Walker, Rob D. *Mama says*
Wallace, Nancy Elizabeth. *Apples, apples, apples*
Ready, set, 100th day!
Walter, Mildred Pitts. *My mama needs me*
Wan, Joyce. *Hug you, kiss you, love you*
Wangerin, Walter. *Water come down*
Wardlaw, Lee. *Saturday night jamboree*
Warhola, James. *Uncle Andy's*
Warner, Sunny. *The moon quilt*
Washington, Kathy Gates. *Three colors of Katie*
Watson, Clyde. *Valentine foxes*
Watson, Wendy. *Boo! It's Halloween*
Happy Easter day!
Hurray for the Fourth of July
Thanksgiving at our house
Waugh, Peter. *The great cannon beach mouse caper*
Weitzman, Elizabeth. *Let's talk about when a parent dies*
Wells, Rosemary. *Carry me!*
The house in the mail
McDuff and the baby
McDuff saves the day
Moss pillows
Night sounds, morning colors
Shy Charles
Time-out for Sophie
Weninger, Brigitte. *Davy in the middle*
Westcott, Nadine Bernard. *Peanut butter and jelly*
Wheeler, Lisa. *Wool gathering*
Whelan, Gloria. *The boy who wanted to cook*
White, Kathryn. *When they fight*
Whiteley, Opal Stanley. *Only Opal*
Whybrow, Ian. *Harry and the snow king*
Wickstrom, Sylvie. *I love you, Mister Bear*
Wild, Margaret. *Tom goes to kindergarten*
Wilder, Laura Ingalls. *Santa comes to little house*
Williams, Karen Lynn. *When Africa was home*
Williams, Sherley Anne. *Working cotton*
Williams, Suzanne. *My dog never says please*
Williams, Vera B. *A chair for always*
A chair for my mother
"More more more," said the baby
Music, music for everyone
Something special for me
Wilner, Isabel. *The baby's game book*
Wing, Natasha. *Jalapeño bagels*
Winthrop, Elizabeth. *I'm the Boss!*
Squashed in the middle
Wohl, Lauren L. *Matzoh mouse*
Wolff, Ashley. *Stella and Roy go camping*
Wong, Benedict Norbert. *Lo and behold*
Lo and behold, good enough to eat
Wong, Janet S. *Buzz*
This next New Year
The trip back home
Woo, Alan. *Maggie's chopsticks*
Wood, Audrey. *A cowboy Christmas*
Elbert's bad word
The Tickleoctopus
Weird parents
Woodruff, Elvira. *Small beauties*
Woodson, Jacqueline. *This is the rope*
We had a picnic this Sunday past
Yaccarino, Dan. *If I had a robot*
Yum, Hyewon. *This is our house*
Zagwÿn, Deborah Turney. *Apple batter*
Zalben, Jane Breskin. *Baby Babka*
Beni's first Chanukah
Beni's first wedding
Pearl's Passover
Zamorano, Ana. *Let's eat!*
Ziefert, Harriet. *Birdhouse for rent*
Families have together
A new coat for Anna
The princess and the peas and carrots
Pushkin meets the bundle
Pushkin minds the bundle
Zolotow, Charlotte. *Do you know what I'll do?*
If it weren't for you
My grandson Lew
Some things go together
William's doll
Zuckerman, Linda. *I will hold you 'til you sleep*
Zweibel, Alan. *Our tree named Steve*

Family life – aunts, uncles

Arro, Lena. *By geezers and galoshes!*
Auld, Mary. *My aunt and uncle*
Austin, Heather. *Visiting Aunt Sylvia's*
Baker, Roberta. *Olive's pirate party*
Beake, Lesley. *Home now*
Bertrand, Diane Gonzales. *Uncle Chente's picnic / El picnic de Tío Chente*
Bevis, Mary. *Wolf song*
Blake, Quentin. *Mrs. Armitage*
Boelts, Maribeth. *Happy like soccer*
Bottner, Barbara. *Flower girl*
Brannen, Sarah S. *Uncle Bobby's wedding*
Broach, Elise. *Gumption!*
Bynum, Janie. *Altoona up north*
Carle, Eric. *My apron*
Child, Lauren. *Clarice Bean, guess who's babysitting?*
Crews, Nina. *A ghost story*
Cummings, Pat. *My aunt came back*
Daly, Niki. *No more kisses for Bernard!*
De Anda, Diane. *A day without sugar / Un dia sin azucar*
Dillon, Jana. *Lucky O'Leprechaun comes to America*
Edwards, Pamela Duncan. *Rosie's roses*
Fagan, Cary. *Oy, feh, so?*
Foggo, Cheryl. *Dear baobab*
Garland, Michael. *Americana adventure*
Super snow day seek and find
Geras, Adèle. *Little ballet star*
Go tell Aunt Rhody
Goldman, Judy. *Uncle Monarch and the Day of the Dead*
Gretz, Susanna. *Rabbit food*
Gutman, Anne. *Lisa in New York*
Helldorfer, M. C. *Hog music*
Holabird, Katharine. *Angelina and Henry*
Houston, Gloria. *My Great-Aunt Arizona*
Howard, Elizabeth Fitzgerald. *Aunt Flossie's hats (and crab cakes later)*
Johnson, Angela. *The girl who wore snakes*

Johnston, Tony. *A Kenya Christmas*
Jordan, Deloris. *Michael's golden rules*
Kimmelman, Leslie. *Sound the shofar!*
Kinsey-Warnock, Natalie. *A farm of her own*
Krishnaswami, Uma. *Chachaji's cup*
Lester, Helen. *Something might happen*
Lindenbaum, Pija. *Mini Mia and her darling uncle*
Lo, Ginnie. *Auntie Yang's great soybean picnic*
Look, Lenore. *Uncle Peter's amazing Chinese wedding*
McClintock, Barbara. *Adele and Simon in America*
Dahlia
McCormick, Wendy. *The night you were born*
Major, Kevin. *Aunt Olga's Christmas postcards*
Manning, Maurie J. *The aunts go marching*
Mauner, Claudia. *Zoe Sophia's scrapbook*
Medina, Meg. *Tía Isa wants a car*
Mendes, Valerie. *Look at me, Grandma!*
Mitchell, Margaree King. *Uncle Jed's barbershop*
Mitchell, Rhonda. *The talking cloth*
Monk, Isabell. *Hope*
Mora, Pat. *A birthday basket for Tía*
Moss, Miriam. *Bad hare day*
Nunes, Susan Miho. *The last dragon*
O'Connor, George. *Uncle Bigfoot*
Parish, Herman. *Go west, Amelia Bedelia!*
Parkinson, Curtis. *Emily's eighteen aunts*
Partridge, Elizabeth. *Oranges on Golden Mountain*
Perry, Elizabeth. *Think cool thoughts*
Prigger, Mary Skillings. *Aunt Minnie and the twister*
Aunt Minnie McGranahan
Primavera, Elise. *Auntie Claus*
Auntie Claus and the key to Christmas
Proimos, James. *The loudness of Sam*
Roberts, Bethany. *Rosie to the rescue*
Roberts, Lynn. *Rapunzel, a groovy fairy tale*
Schwartz, Amy. *Willie and Uncle Bill*
Scrimger, Richard. *Princess Bun Bun*
Sheridan, Sara. *I'm me!*
Steptoe, Javaka. *The Jones family express*
Stevenson, James. *Worse than the worst*
Stewart, Sarah. *The gardener*
The quiet place
Stewig, John Warren. *Making plum jam*
Vigna, Judith. *My two uncles*
Warhola, James. *Uncle Andy's*
Watkins, Angela Farris. *My Uncle Martin's big heart*
Wells, Rosemary. *Small world of Binky Braverman*
Whitehead, Kathy. *Looking for Uncle Louie on the Fourth of July*
Willey, Margaret. *Thanksgiving with me*
Wood, Douglas. *Aunt Mary's rose*
Yolen, Jane. *My Uncle Emily*
Zagwÿn, Deborah Turney. *The sea house*
Zalben, Jane Breskin. *Baby Babka*

Family life – brothers *see also* Family life; Family life – brothers & sisters; Sibling rivalry

Alko, Selina. *I'm your peanut butter big brother*
Allen, Debbie. *Brothers of the knight*
Altman, Alexandra Jessup. *Waiting for Benjamin*
Andreae, Giles. *There's a house inside my mommy*
Apperley, Dawn. *Flip and Flop*
Auld, Mary. *My brother*
Ballard, Robin. *I used to be the baby*
Banks, Kate. *Max's castle*
Barber, Tiki. *Game day*
Barber, Tiki, et al. *By my brother's side*
Teammates
Bateman, Teresa. *Hunting the daddyosaurus*
The merbaby
Bauer, Marion Dane. *Jason's bears*
Bedford, David. *Big bears can!*
Boelts, Maribeth. *You're a brother, Little Bunny!*
Borden, Louise. *Big brothers don't take naps*
Bunting, Eve. *Jin Woo*
Clarke, Jane. *Gilbert the hero*
Cole, Joanna. *I'm a big brother*
Cordell, Matthew. *Another brother*
Trouble gum
Crews, Nina. *Sky-high Guy*
Daniels, Teri. *G-Rex*
Davis, Patricia Anne. *Brian's bird*
Dempsey, Sheena. *Bye-bye baby brother!*
Edwards, Michelle. *What's that noise?*
Fisher, Valorie. *My big brother*
Gay, Marie-Louise. *Caramba and Henry*
Gifaldi, David. *Ben, king of the river*
Gorbachev, Valeri. *Shhh!*
Gordon, David. *The three little rigs*
Grandits, John. *Ten rules you absolutely must not break if you want to survive the school bus*
Harrington, Janice N. *Roberto walks home*
Harris, Robie H. *Mail Harry to the moon!*
Hartmann, Wendy. *The dinosaurs are back and it's all your fault, Edward!*
Henry, Steve. *Nobody asked me!*
Hiatt, Fred. *Baby talk*
Hoban, Russell. *Best friends for Frances*
Howe, James. *There's a dragon in my sleeping bag*
Itaya, Satoshi. *Buttons and Bo*
James, Simon. *Little One Step*
Jaspersohn, William. *The two brothers*
Johnston, Tony. *The iguana brothers, a perfect day*
That summer
Jonell, Lynne. *It's my birthday, too!*
Joosse, Barbara. *I love you the purplest*
Kirsch, Vincent X. *Two little boys from Toolittle Toys*
Kleven, Elisa. *A monster in the house*
The puddle pail
Kling, Kevin. *Big little brother*
Kraus, Robert. *Little Louie the baby bloomer*
Kushner, Donn. *Peter's pixie*
Larsen, Andrew. *In the tree house*
Layne, Steven L. *My brother Dan's delicious*
Lehman-Wilzig, Tami. *Nathan blows out the Hanukkah candles*
Leuck, Laura. *My beastly brother*
Lindgren, Barbro. *Oink, oink, Benny*
London, Jonathan. *Moshi moshi*
Long, Ethan. *The Wing Wing brothers carnival de math*
The Wing Wing brothers math spectacular!
Long, Heather. *Max & Milo go to sleep!*
Luthardt, Kevin. *Mine*
Moore-Mallinos, Jennifer. *My brother is autistic*
Numeroff, Laura Joffe. *What brothers do best*
Olson, Mary. *An alligator ate my brother*
Palatini, Margie. *Tub-boo-boo*
Perry, Michael. *Daniel's ride*
Pinkwater, Daniel. *Young Larry*
Rodman, Mary Ann. *Surprise soup*
Roe, Eileen. *With my brother / Con mi hermano*
Rossiter, Nan Parson. *Sugar on snow*
Rumford, James. *Dog-of-the-Sea-Waves*
The Island-below-the-star
Russo, Marisabina. *The big brown box*

Saltzberg, Barney. *Cornelius P. Mud, are you ready for baby?*
San Souci, Robert D. *The enchanted tapestry*
Little Pierre
Sasso, Sandy Eisenberg. *Cain and Abel*
Schaefer, Lola M. *One special day*
Schertle, Alice. *Witch Hazel*
Schwartz, Roslyn. *The Vole brothers*
Shields, Carol Diggory. *I wish my brother was a dog*
Silverman, Erica. *Follow the leader*
Soman, David. *The amazing adventures of Bumblebee Boy*
Steig, William. *The toy brother*
Stevenson, James. *That's exactly the way it wasn't*
Stuve-Bodeen, Stephanie. *Mama Elizabeti*
Symes, Ruth. *Little Rex, big brother*
Titherington, Jeanne. *A place for Ben*
Van Allsburg, Chris. *Zathura*
Van Leeuwen, Jean. *Sorry*
Vernick, Audrey. *Brothers at bat*
Vulliamy, Clara. *Ellen and Penguin and the new baby*
Waddell, Martin. *Sam Vole and his brothers*
Wheeler, Lisa. *Turk and Runt*
White, Linda Arms. *Comes a wind*
Wilhelm, Hans. *More bunny trouble*
Wilson, Sarah. *Friends and pals and brothers, too*
Yin. *Coolies*
Yolen, Jane. *My brothers' flying machine*
Zimmerman, Andrea Griffing. *Train man*

Family life – brothers & sisters

Alborough, Jez. *Watch out! Big Bro's coming!*
Archer, Peggy. *Turkey surprise*
Baicker, Karen. *You can do it too!*
Barclay, Eric. *Hiding Phil*
Bartone, Elisa. *Peppe the lamplighter*
Bassède, Francine. *A day with the Bellyflops*
Baumgart, Klaus. *Laura's secret*
Bedford, David. *Ella's games*
Bennett, Kelly. *Vampire baby*
Berenstain, Stan and Jan. *The Berenstain bears no girls allowed*
Bergman, Mara. *Snip snap!*
Birdsall, Jeanne. *Flora's very windy day*
Boelts, Maribeth. *You're a brother, Little Bunny!*
Bonnett-Rampersaud, Louise. *Bubble and Squeak*
Bourgeois, Paulette. *Franklin and Harriet*
Franklin's baby sister
Bowen, Anne. *When you visit Grandma and Grandpa*
Bower, Gary. *Ivy's icicle*
Breathed, Berkeley. *Edwurd Fudwupper fibbed big*
Broach, Elise. *What the no-good baby is good for*
Brown, Marc. *Arthur tricks the tooth fairy*
Arthur turns green
Arthur's first sleepover
D. W. rides again!
D. W. thinks big [board book]
D. W.'s library card
Glasses for D. W.
Browne, Anthony. *My brother*
Buzzeo, Toni. *Lighthouse Christmas*
Capucilli, Alyssa Satin. *Katy Duck, big sister*
Caraballo, Samuel. *My big sister / Mi hermana mayor*
Carter, Alden R. *Big brother Dustin*
Caseley, Judith. *Sophie and Sammy's library sleepover*
Chaconas, Dori. *Dancing with Katya*
Chavarría-Cháirez, Becky. *Magda's piñata magic / Magda y la piñata mágica*
Cheng, Andrea. *The lemon sisters*
Chessa, Francesca. *The mysterious package*
Child, Lauren. *But, excuse me, that is my book*
But I've used all my pocket change
Charlie and Lola's numbers
Charlie and Lola's opposites
I am too absolutely small for school
I completely know about guinea pigs
I really, really need actual ice skates
I will never not ever eat a tomato
I will never not ever eat a tomato [pop-up]
My best, best friend
Say cheese!
Snow is my favorite and my best
Clark, Katie. *Seagull Sam*
Collins, Suzanne. *When Charlie McButton lost power*
Corderoy, Tracey. *Monty and Milli*
Corpi, Lucha. *Where fireflies dance / Ahí, donde bailan las luciérnagas*
Crews, Nina. *A high, low, near, far, loud, quiet story*
Crow, Kristyn. *The middle-child blues*
Cummings, Pat. *Angel baby*
Cuyler, Margery. *The bumpy little pumpkin*
David, Lawrence. *The land of the hungry armadillos*
Davies, Gill. *Wilbur waited*
Dealey, Erin. *Goldie Locks has chicken pox*
deGroat, Diane. *Mother, you're the best! (but Sister, you're a pest!)*
Trick or treat, smell my feet
dePaola, Tomie. *Boss for a day*
Marcos
Meet the Barkers
A new Barker in the house
Dewan, Ted. *Crispin and the 3 little piglets*
Dixon, Ann. *Winter is . . .*
Doerrfeld, Cori. *Penny loves pink*
Downey, Lynn. *The tattletale*
Duke, Kate. *The tale of Pip and Squeak*
Dyer, Sarah. *Clementine and Mungo*
Ellery, Amanda. *If I had a dragon*
Elliott, Laura Malone. *Hunter's big sister*
Elliott, Rebecca. *Just because*
Ellis, Sarah. *Big Ben*
Elya, Susan Middleton. *Sophie's trophy*
Escoffier, Michaël. *Me first!*
Farris, Christine King. *My brother Martin*
Fearnley, Jan. *Martha in the middle*
Feiffer, Kate. *But I wanted a baby brother!*
Fleming, Denise. *Mama cat has three kittens*
Ford, Juwanda G. *Together for Kwanzaa*
Fraser, Mary Ann. *Heebie-Jeebie Jamboree*
Freedman, Deborah. *Scribble*
Funke, Cornelia. *The wildest brother*
Gammell, Stephen. *How about going for a ride*
Gary, Meredith. *Sometimes you get what you want*
Gay, Marie-Louise. *Good morning Sam*
Read me a story, Stella
Stella, fairy of the forest
Stella, queen of the snow
Stella, star of the sea
What are you doing, Sam?
When Stella was very, very small
George, Jean Craighead. *Nutik, the wolf pup*
Goode, Diane. *Mama's perfect present*
Gorbachev, Valeri. *The best cat*
How to be friends with a dragon
Nicky and the rainy day
Gordon, David. *The ugly truckling*
Got, Yves. *Sam's little sister*

Graham, Bob. *Dimity Dumpty*
Green, Jen. *Our new baby*
Greenfield, Eloise. *Brothers and sisters*
Grimm, Jacob and Wilhelm *The six swans*
Grindley, Sally. *It's my school*
Gutierrez, Akemi. *The mummy and other adventures of Sam and Alice*
Guy, Ginger Foglesong. *Siesta*
Hänel, Wolfram. *Little elephant runs away*
Harley, Bill. *Dirty Joe, the pirate*
Harper, Anita. *It's not fair!*
Harper, Jamie. *Me too!*
Harris, Robie H. *Hi, new baby*
Hasler, Eveline. *A tale of two brothers*
Havill, Juanita. *Jamaica is thankful*
Jamaica Tag-Along
Heller, Linda. *How Dalia put a big yellow comforter inside a tiny blue box*
Hershenhorn, Esther. *Fancy that*
Hest, Amy. *You're the boss, Baby Duck*
Hoberman, Mary Ann. *And to think that we thought that we'd never be friends*
The seven silly eaters
Hooks, William H. *The legend of the Christmas rose*
Hughes, Shirley. *Alfie's ABC*
Annie Rose is my little sister
Olly and me
Olly and me 1-2-3
Rhymes for Annie Rose
Hunter, Sally. *Humphrey's bedtime*
Humphrey's Christmas
Hurwitz, Johanna. *Russell's secret*
Hutchins, Pat. *Silly Billy!*
Isadora, Rachel. *Yo, Jo!*
Jalali, Reza. *Moon watchers*
James, Brian. *Supertwins and the sneaky, slimy book worms*
The Supertwins and tooth trouble
The Supertwins meet the bad dogs from space
Supertwins meet the dangerous dino-robots
Jeffs, Stephanie. *Jenny*
Jenkins, Emily. *Lemonade in winter*
Johnson, Angela. *Do like Kyla*
Johnson, Gillian. *My sister Gracie*
Johnson, Lindan Lee. *The dream jar*
Joyce, William. *Santa calls*
Kann, Victoria. *Silverlicious*
Kaplan, Bruce Eric. *Monsters eat whiny children*
Karas, G. Brian. *Bebe's bad dream*
Kay, Verla. *Orphan train*
Keller, Holly. *Geraldine and Mrs. Duffy*
Knudsen, Michelle. *A moldy mystery*
Koch, Ed. *Eddie's little sister makes a splash*
Koller, Jackie French. *Baby for sale*
Kortepeter, Paul. *Oliver's red toboggan*
Kurtz, Jane. *In the small, small night*
Kushner, Tony. *Brundibar*
LaMarche, Jim. *Up*
Lamm, C. Drew. *Pirates*
Landa, Norbert. *Little Bear and the wishing tree*
Landolf, Diane Wright. *What a good big brother!*
LaRochelle, David. *The haunted hamburger and other ghostly stories*
Lasky, Kathryn. *Lucille's snowsuit*
Starring Lucille
Lazar, Tara. *The Monstore*
Lears, Laurie. *Ian's walk*
Lloyd-Jones, Sally. *How to be a baby — by me, the big sister*
Look, Lenore. *Henry's first-moon birthday*
Lucke, Deb. *The boy who wouldn't swim*
McClintock, Barbara. *Adele and Simon*
Adele and Simon in America
Molly and the magic wishbone
McCormick, Wendy. *The night you were born*
McCullough, Sharon Pierce. *Bunbun, the middle one*
McDonald, Rae A. *A fishing surprise*
MacDonald, Ross. *Bad baby*
McKissack, Patricia C. *The all-I'll-ever-want Christmas doll*
McKy, Katie. *Pumpkin town!*
McQuinn, Anna. *Lola reads to Leo*
Mahoney, Daniel J. *A really good snowman*
Mair, Samia J. *The perfect gift*
Manson, Ainslie. *Ballerinas don't wear glasses*
Massini, Sarah. *Trixie ten*
Meade, Holly. *Inside, inside, inside*
Meddaugh, Susan. *Cinderella's rat*
Mendes, Valerie. *Look at me, Grandma!*
Meng, Cece. *The wonderful thing about hiccups*
Meserve, Jessica. *Bedtime without Arthur*
Small sister
Michels-Gualtieri, Akaela S. *I was born to be a sister*
Michelson, Richard. *Oh no, not ghosts!*
Milgrim, David. *Amelia makes a movie*
Santa Duck and his merry helpers
Moon, Nicola. *Something special*
Morales, Yuyi. *Nino wrestles the world*
Morrissey, Dean. *The crimson comet*
Munsch, Robert N. *Alligator baby*
Murkoff, Heidi Eisenberg. *What to expect when the new baby comes home*
Muth, Jon J. *Zen ghosts*
Zen shorts
Zen ties
Napoli, Donna Jo. *The wishing club*
Nelson, S. D. *The Star People*
Neubecker, Robert. *Winter is for snow*
Neuschwander, Cindy. *Pastry school in Paris*
Newman, Marjorie. *Just like me*
Norris, Kathleen. *The holy twins*
Novak, Matt. *The Pillow War*
Numeroff, Laura Joffe. *What brothers do best; What sisters do best*
Ohi, Ruth. *The couch was a castle*
Me and my brother
Me and my sister
A trip with Grandma
Palatini, Margie. *Goldie is mad*
Good as Goldie
Parkhurst, Carolyn. *Cooking with Henry and Elliebelly*
Partis, Joanne. *Stripe's naughty sister*
Patz, Nancy. *Babies can't eat kimchee!*
Peete, Holly Robinson. *My brother Charlie*
Pegram, Laura. *Daughter's Day blues*
Pelham, David. *Sam's pizza*
Sam's sandwich
Pham, LeUyen. *Big sister, little sister*
Polacco, Patricia. *My rotten redheaded older brother*
Rotten Richie and the ultimate dare
Prigger, Mary Skillings. *Aunt Minnie McGranahan*
Pulver, Robin. *Way to go, Alex!*
Raschka, Chris. *The blushful hippopotamus*
Reiser, Lynn. *My baby and me*
Reiss, Mike. *The boy who wouldn't share*
Reynolds, Peter H. *The best kid in the world*

Ish
Ries, Lori. *Fix it, Sam*
Robbins, Beth. *Tom, Ally, and the new baby*
Tom and Ally visit the doctor
Roberts, Bethany. *Double trouble Groundhog Day*
Robertson, M. P. *Hieronymous Betts and his unusual pets*
Rockwell, Anne. *Brendan and Belinda and the slam dunk!*
Rockwell, Lizzy. *Hello baby!*
Roddie, Shen. *Toes are to tickle*
Rogers, Jacqueline. *Tiptoe into kindergarten*
Roper, Janice M. *Dancing on the moon*
Rossell, Judith. *Ruby and Leonard and the great big surprise*
Rubel, Nicole. *Ham and Pickles*
Russo, Marisabina. *Hannah's baby sister*
Peter is just a baby
The trouble with baby
Ryan, Pam Muñoz. *Mud is cake*
Tony Baloney
Samuels, Barbara. *Dolores meets her match*
Happy Valentine's Day, Dolores
Sanders, Scott R. *Crawdad Creek*
Sanders-Wells, Linda. *Maggie's monkeys*
Sayre, April Pulley. *It's my city*
Scheffler, Ursel. *Taking care of Sister Bear*
Schneider, Christine M. *Saxophone Sam and his snazzy jazz band*
Schneider, Josh. *You'll be sorry*
Scrimger, Richard. *Eugene's story*
Princess Bun Bun
Shea, Pegi Deitz. *New moon*
Sheldon, Annette. *Big sister now*
Sheth, Kashmira. *Tiger in my soup*
Simmons, Jane. *Daisy and the Beastie*
Daisy and the egg
Little Fern's first winter
Singer, Marilyn. *Tallulah's solo*
Skinner, Daphne. *Henry keeps score*
Smallcomb, Pam. *Earth to Clunk*
Smith, Linda. *Sir Cassie to the rescue*
Stewart, Amber. *Little by little*
Stewart, Shannon. *Sea crow*
Stiegemeyer, Julie. *Under the baobab tree*
Stoeke, Janet Morgan. *Waiting for May*
Sturges, Philemon. *I love school*
Stuve-Bodeen, Stephanie. *We'll paint the octopus red*
Sullivan, Sarah. *Dear Baby*
Sweeney, Jacqueline. *What about Bettie?*
Sykes, Julie. *Wait for me, Little Tiger*
Vail, Rachel. *Sometimes I'm Bombaloo*
Van Leeuwen, Jean. *Five funny bunnies*
"Wait for me!" said Maggie McGee
Voake, Charlotte. *Hello twins*
Waddell, Martin. *When the teddy bears came*
Walter, Mildred Pitts. *Two too much*
Walters, Catherine. *Play gently, Alfie Bear*
Ward, Nick. *Don't eat the babysitter!*
Wells, Rosemary. *Bunny cakes*
Bunny mail
Bunny money
Bunny party
Clean-up time
Goodnight Max
Max and Ruby's bedtime book
Max and Ruby's Midas
Max and Ruby's treasure hunt
Max cleans up
Max's apples
Max's bunny business
Max's dragon shirt
Max's Easter surprise
Max's worm cake
Peek-a-boo
Red boots
Ruby's beauty shop
Shopping
Weninger, Brigitte. *Davy in the middle*
Weston, Martha. *Tuck's haunted house*
Wewer, Iris. *My wild sister and me*
Whybrow, Ian. *Badness for beginners*
Wiesner, David. *Hurricane*
Winters, Kari-Lynn. *Gift days*
Wishinsky, Frieda. *Please, Louise!*
Wynne-Jones, Tim. *The boat in the tree*
Yin. *Brothers*
Yolen, Jane. *Soft house*
Young, Cybèle. *A few bites*
A few blocks
Young, Ed. *My Mei Mei*
Zalben, Jane Breskin. *Baby Babka*
Zemach, Margot. *Eating up Gladys*
Zimmerman, Andrea Griffing. *Fire engine man*

Family life – cousins

Brownlee, Sophia Grace. *Tea time with Sophia Grace and Rosie*
Buehner, Caralyn. *Would I ever lie to you?*
Campbell, K. G. *Lester's dreadful sweaters*
Carlstrom, Nancy White. *Guess who's coming, Jesse Bear*
Crum, Shutta. *Dozens of cousins*
My mountain song
Dahlie, Elizabeth. *Bernelly and Harriet*
D'Amico, Carmela. *Suki and Mirabella*
deGroat, Diane. *Last one in is a rotten egg!*
Greenfield, Eloise. *Easter parade*
Hest, Amy. *Nana's birthday party*
Holabird, Katharine. *Angelina's Christmas*
Holt, Kimberly Willis. *Waiting for Gregory*
Kinsey-Warnock, Natalie. *A farm of her own*
McKay, Hilary. *Pirates ahoy!*
Newman, Barbara Johansen. *Glamorous glasses*
Rodriguez, Bobbie. *Sarah's sleepover*
Root, Phyllis. *Aunt Nancy and Cousin Lazybones*
Schaefer, Carole Lexa. *The little French whistle*
Smalls-Hector, Irene. *Because you're lucky*
Thomassie, Tynia. *Cajun through and through*
Tonatiuh, Duncan. *Dear Primo*
Weiss, Ellen. *The taming of Lola*

Family life – daughters

Baker, Roberta. *No ordinary Olive*
Bartoletti, Susan Campbell. *The Christmas promise*
Burke, Bobby. *Daddy's little girl*
Campbell, Ann-Jeanette. *Queenie Farmer had fifteen daughters*
Cole, Brock. *Buttons*
Coy, John. *Two old potatoes and me*
Day, Jan. *The pirate, Pink*
Pirate Pink and treasures of the reef
De Anda, Diane. *Dancing Miranda / Baila, Miranda, baila*
Duble, Kathleen Benner. *Pilot mom*
Feiffer, Jules. *The daddy mountain*

Fruisen, Catherine Myler. *My mother's pearls*
Gilmore, Rachna. *Making grizzle grow*
Gray, Kes. *Eat your peas*
006 and a half
Hesse, Karen. *Come on, rain*
Krosoczka, Jarrett J. *Giddy up, Cowgirl*
McCourt, Lisa. *Good night, Princess Pruney Toes*
Makhijani, Pooja. *Mama's saris*
Newman, Lesléa. *Heather has two mommies*
Pow, Tom. *Tell me one thing, Dad*
Rao, Sandhya. *My mother's sari*
Santucci, Barbara. *Loon summer*
Say, Allen. *The favorite daughter*
Simpson, Lesley. *The Purim surprise*
Singer, Marilyn. *Didi and Daddy on the Promenade*
Slawson, Michele Benoit. *Signs for sale*
Stephens, J. Moria. *Persephone, the ladybug*
Stevenson, James. *I meant to tell you*
Thiesing, Lisa. *Me and you: a mother-daughter album*
Winthrop, Elizabeth. *Promises*

Family life – fathers

Allen, Elanna. *Itsy Mitsy runs away*
Alter, Anna. *A photo for Greta*
Anderson, Peggy Perry. *To the tub*
Andreae, Giles. *I love my daddy*
Andreasen, Dan. *Saturday with Daddy*
Asch, Frank. *Just like daddy*
Asim, Jabari. *Daddy goes to work*
Auld, Mary. *My dad*
Banks, Kate. *The night worker*
That's Papa's way
Bartoletti, Susan Campbell. *The Christmas promise*
Bartone, Elisa. *Peppe the lamplighter*
Bateman, Teresa. *Hunting the daddyosaurus*
Battle-Lavert, Gwendolyn. *Papa's mark*
Bauer, Marion Dane. *Sleep, little one, sleep*
Beaty, Daniel. *Knock knock*
Bee, William. *Whatever*
Bennett, Kelly. *Dad and Pop*
Your daddy was just like you
Bergel, Colin. *Mail by the pail*
Berger, Lou. *Dream dog*
Berry, Matt. *Up on Daddy's shoulders*
Bildner, Phil. *The greatest game ever played*
Black, Birdie. *Just right for Christmas*
Bluemle, Elizabeth. *My father the dog*
Boelts, Maribeth. *Big Daddy, frog wrestler*
Looking for Sleepy
Boyd, Lizi. *I love Daddy*
Bradman, Tony. *Daddy's lullaby*
Braun, Sebastien. *I love my daddy*
Briant, Ed. *A day at the beach*
Brisson, Pat. *Star blanket*
Brown, Margaret Wise. *The fathers are coming home*
Browne, Anthony. *Gorilla*
My dad
Bruchac, Joseph. *My father is taller than a tree*
Brutschy, Jennifer. *Just one more story*
Bunting, Eve. *Fly away home*
My red balloon
A perfect Father's Day
Burke, Bobby. *Daddy's little girl*
Burleigh, Robert. *Good-bye, Sheepie*
Butterworth, Nick. *My dad is awesome*
Buzzeo, Toni. *Just like my Papa*
Capucilli, Alyssa Satin. *Only my dad and me*
Chaconas, Dori. *On a wintry morning*
Chaud, Benjamin. *The bear's song*
Cheng, Andrea. *Anna the bookbinder*
Clements, Andrew. *Because your daddy loves you*
Colato Laínez, René. *My shoes and I*
Cole, Brock. *Buttons*
Collins, Billy. *Daddy's little boy*
Collins, Pat Lowery. *The deer watch*
Collins, Suzanne. *Year of the jungle*
Compos, Tito. *Muffler man / El hombre mofle*
Cousins, Lucy. *Peck, peck, peck*
Cowley, Joy. *Gracias, the Thanksgiving turkey*
Coy, John. *Two old potatoes and me*
Coyle, Carmela LaVigna. *Do princesses really kiss frogs?*
Creech, Sharon. *Fishing in the air*
Crum, Shutta. *Fox and Fluff*
Dahl, Michael. *Goodnight baseball*
Day, Jan. *The pirate, Pink*
Pirate Pink and treasures of the reef
Demas, Corinne. *Nina's waltz*
Demers, Dominique. *Every single night*
DiTerlizzi, Tony. *Ted*
Dodd, Emma. *Just like you*
Dorros, Arthur. *Papa and me*
Dotlich, Rebecca Kai. *Papa loves*
Dunrea, Olivier. *A Christmas tree for Pyn*
Old Bear and his cub
Durand, Hallie. *Mitchell goes bowling*
Mitchell's license
Dyer, Sarah. *Monster day at work*
Eckart, Edana. *I can bowl*
Edwards, Michelle. *Papa's latkes*
Ehrlich, Fred. *Does a duck have a daddy?*
Eilenberg, Max. *Cowboy Kid*
Emmons, Chip. *Sammy wakes his dad*
Ernst, Lisa Campbell. *This is the van that Dad cleaned*
Ewart, Claire. *The giant*
Farmer, Nancy. *Clever Ali*
Feiffer, Jules. *The daddy mountain*
Feiffer, Kate. *My side of the car*
Frederick, Heather Vogel. *Hide and squeak*
Galbraith, Kathryn O. *Arbor Day square*
Gay, Marie-Louise. *Roslyn Rutabaga and the biggest hole on earth!*
George, Jean Craighead. *Cliff hanger*
George, Kristine O'Connell. *Up!*
George, William T. *Christmas at Long Pond*
Germein, Katrina. *My dad thinks he's funny*
Gibala-Broxholm, Scott. *Maddie's monster dad*
Giles, Almira Astudillo. *Willie wins*
Gilmore, Rachna. *Making grizzle grow*
Glass, Beth Raisner. *Blue-ribbon dad*
Glassman, Peter. *My dad's job*
Gomi, Taro. *I lost my dad*
Gore, Leonid. *When I grow up*
Granowsky, Alvin. *At the park*
Greene, Rhonda Gowler. *Daddy is a cozy hug*
Greenfield, Eloise. *First pink light*
Grifalconi, Ann. *Tiny's hat*
Grimes, Nikki. *When Daddy prays*
Grossmann-Hensel, Katharina. *Papa is a pirate*
Hardin, Melinda. *Hero dad*
Harper, Charise Mericle. *Pink me up*
Harper, Lee. *Snow! Snow! Snow!*
Harrison, Joanna. *Grizzly dad*
Haughton, Emma. *Rainy day*
Hazen, Barbara Shook. *Katie's wish*
Heo, Yumi. *Father's rubber shoes*

One Sunday morning
High, Linda Oatman. *The girl on the high-diving horse*
Winter shoes for Shadow Horse
Hines, Anna Grossnickle. *Daddy makes the best spaghetti*
Holmberg, Bo R. *A day with Dad*
Hooks, William H. *Moss gown*
Horn, Peter. *The best father of all*
When I grow up . . .
Hru, Dakari. *Tickle, tickle*
Hughes, Vi. *Aziz, the story teller*
Hundal, Nancy. *Number 21*
Hunter, Jana Novotny. *When Daddy's truck picks me up*
Hurwitz, Johanna. *Ethan out and about*
Hutchins, Hazel. *I'd know you anywhere*
Ichikawa, Satomi. *My father's shop*
In daddy's arms I am tall
Irving, John. *A sound like someone trying not to make a sound*
Jaffe, Nina. *The way meat loves salt*
Jennings, Sharon. *No monsters here*
Jiang, Ji-li. *Red kite, blue kite*
Johnson, Angela. *I dream of trains*
Joshua's night whispers
Lottie Paris lives here
Jonovitz, Marilyn. *Good morning, Little Fox*
Joosse, Barbara. *Papa do you love me?*
Jorgensen, Richard. *Reading with Dad*
Judes, Marie-Odile. *Max, the stubborn little wolf*
Just like father
Kanevsky, Polly. *Sleepy boy*
Katz, Karen. *Daddy hugs 1 2 3*
Kaufmann, Nancy. *Bye, Bye*
Keane, Dave. *Daddy adventure day*
Keillor, Garrison. *Daddy's girl*
King, Martin Luther, III. *My daddy, Dr. Martin Luther King, Jr.*
Kinsey-Warnock, Natalie. *When spring comes*
Kroll, Steven. *Happy Father's Day*
Kroll, Virginia L. *Africa brothers and sisters*
Kurtz, Jane. *Faraway home*
Lakin, Patricia. *Hurricane!*
Langley, Karen. *Shine*
Lawler, Janet. *A father's song*
Lenski, Lois. *Papa Small*
Leuck, Laura. *I love my pirate papa*
Levine, Abby. *Daddies give you horsey rides*
Lewin, Hugh. *Jafta — the homecoming*
Jafta's father
Lewin, Ted. *Big Jimmy's Kum Kau Chinese take out*
Lindaman, Jane. *Zip it!*
Lindsay, Jeanne Warren. *Do I have a daddy?*
London, Jonathan. *Do your ABC's, Little Brown Bear*
Loon Lake
Long, Ethan. *My dad, my hero*
Loomis, Christine. *The best Father's Day present ever*
Lowry, Lois. *Crow call*
Lunde, Stein Erik. *My father's arms are a boat*
Luthardt, Kevin. *Flying*
McBratney, Sam. *Guess how much I love you*
There, there
McCain, Meghan. *My dad, John McCain*
McCaughrean, Geraldine. *Father and son*
One bright Penny
McCormick, Wendy. *Daddy, will you miss me?*
McCourt, Lisa. *Chicken soup for little souls: The best night out with Dad*
Good night, Princess Pruney Toes
McCully, Emily Arnold. *Popcorn at the palace*
McGee, Marni. *Sleepy me*
McGhee, Alison. *Little boy*
MacLachlan, Patricia. *The sick day*
McMullan, Kate. *Papa's song*
McPhail, David. *Henry Bear's park*
McQuade, Jacqueline. *At preschool with Teddy Bear*
Mahy, Margaret. *Down the dragon's tongue*
Mallat, Kathy. *Papa pride*
Many, Paul. *Dad's bald head*
Markell, Denis. *Hush, Little Monster*
Martin, David. *Piggy and Dad*
Piggy and Dad go fishing
Marzollo, Jean. *Papa, Papa*
Mayer, Mercer. *Just me and my dad*
Shibumi and the kitemaker
Mazer, Norma Fox. *Has anyone seen my Emily Greene?*
Meisel, Paul. *Zara's hats*
Micklos, John. *Daddy poems*
Middleton, Julie. *Are the dinosaurs dead, Dad?*
Moore, Genevieve. *Catherine's story*
Morton, Lone. *Hurry up, Molly / Apúrate, Molly*
Hurry up, Molly / Dépêche-toi, Molly
Munsch, Robert N. *Something good*
Where is Gah-Ning?
Munson, Derek. *Enemy pie*
Murphy, Jill. *Mr. Large in charge*
Myers, Tim. *Looking for Luna*
Nadel, Carolina. *Daddy's home*
Nakawaki, Hatsue. *Wait! wait!*
Napoli, Donna Jo. *Flamingo dream*
Newman, Lesléa. *Daddy, Papa, and me*
Daddy's song
Niemann, Christoph. *Subway*
Nolan, Janet. *A Father's Day thank you*
Norac, Carl. *My daddy is a giant*
Norman, Geoffrey. *Stars above us*
North, Sherry. *Because I am your daddy*
Numeroff, Laura Joffe. *What daddies do best*
Ochiltree, Dianne. *It's a firefly night*
Oelschlager, Vanita. *A tale of two daddies*
O'Leary, Sara. *When you were small*
O'Malley, Kevin. *Little Buggy*
Little Buggy runs away
O'Neill, Alexis. *Estela's swap*
Oppenheim, Shulamith Levey. *Ali and the magic stew*
Ormerod, Jan. *Molly and her dad*
Pak, Soyung. *A place to grow*
Paradis, Susan. *My Daddy*
Snow princess
Park, Linda Sue. *The firekeeper's son*
The third gift
Parker, Marjorie Blain. *When dads don't grow up*
Parr, Todd. *The daddy book*
Patricelli, Leslie. *Faster! Faster!*
Pelton, Mindy L. *When Dad's at sea*
Pfister, Marcus. *Bertie*
Penguin Pete and Little Tim
Plecas, Jennifer. *Pretend*
Plourde, Lynn. *Dad, aren't you glad?*
Polacco, Patricia. *My ol' man*
Some birthday!
Posey, Lee. *Night rabbits*
Pow, Tom. *Tell me one thing, Dad*
Prap, Lila. *Daddies*
Pringle, Laurence P. *Bear hug*

Pullen, Zachary. *Friday my Radio Flyer flew*
Pulver, Robin. *Saturday is Dadurday*
Rappaport, Doreen. *The new king*
Raschka, Chris. *Everyone can learn to ride a bicycle*
Ray, Jane. *The dollhouse fairy*
Ray, Mary Lyn. *Basket moon*
Rex, Michael. *You can do anything, Daddy!*
Rice, Eve. *Swim!*
Ritchie, Alison. *Me and my dad!*
Roberts, Bethany. *Waiting-for-Papa stories*
Robinson, Sharon. *Testing the ice*
Rockwell, Anne. *Ducklings and pollywogs*
Father's Day
Root, Phyllis. *Contrary bear*
Rosenberg, Liz. *Tyrannosaurus dad*
Rusackas, Francesca. *Daddy all day long*
Ryder, Joanne. *My father's hands*
San Souci, Robert D. *The samurai's daughter*
Santucci, Barbara. *Loon summer*
Saudo, Coralie. *My dad is big and strong, but . . .*
Saunders, Karen. *Baby Badger's wonderful night*
Savadier, Elivia. *Time to get dressed!*
Schaefer, Lola M. *Toolbox twins*
Schlessinger, Laura. *Dr. Laura Schlessinger's Growing up is hard*
Schotter, Roni. *Room for Rabbit*
Schwartz, Amy. *Bea and Mr. Jones*
The scrubbly-bubbly car wash
Shahan, Sherry. *That's not how you play soccer, Daddy*
Shannon, David. *Jangles*
Shea, Bob. *Oh, Daddy!*
Shipton, Jonathan. *How to be a happy hippo*
Sidman, Joyce. *Just us two*
Singer, Marilyn. *Didi and Daddy on the Promenade*
Sitomer, Alan Lawrence. *Daddies do it different*
Slate, Joseph. *Story time for Little Porcupine*
Slawson, Michele Benoit. *Signs for sale*
Smallman, Steve. *My dad!*
Smalls-Hector, Irene. *Kevin and his dad*
Smith, Will. *Just the two of us*
Sockabasin, Allen. *Thanks to the animals*
Spinelli, Eileen. *A big boy now*
Night shift daddy
When Papa comes home tonight
Spinelli, Jerry. *My daddy and me*
Stanton, Karen. *Papi's gift*
Steen, Sandra. *Car wash*
Steig, William. *Pete's a pizza*
Stevenson, James. *I meant to tell you*
Sam the Zamboni man
Stewart, Amber. *Bedtime for Button*
Stock, Catherine. *Christmas time*
Tarbescu, Edith. *Annushka's voyage*
Tarpley, Natasha Anastasia. *Bippity Bop barbershop*
Taylor, Ann. *Baby dance*
Tellis, Annabel. *If my dad were a dog*
Thompson, Lauren. *Mouse's first snow*
Tomp, Sarah Wones. *Red, white, and blue goodbye*
Tonatiuh, Duncan. *Pancho Rabbit and the coyote*
Trottier, Maxine. *A safe place*
Udry, Janice May. *What Mary Jo shared*
Uhlberg, Myron. *Dad, Jackie, and me*
The printer
Vigna, Judith. *I wish my daddy didn't drink so much*
Saying goodbye to daddy
Waboose, Jan Bourdeau. *Morning on the lake*
Waddell, Martin. *Can't you sleep, Little Bear?*
Let's go home, Little Bear
Walker, Anna. *I love my dad*
Walters, Virginia. *Are we there yet, Daddy?*
Warnes, Tim. *Daddy hug*
Watanabe, Shigeo. *Let's go swimming*
Where's my daddy?
Watts, Frances. *Kisses for Daddy*
Weigel, Jeff. *Atomic Ace (he's just my dad)*
Welch, Willy. *Dancing with Daddy*
Wells, Rosemary. *The island light*
Weninger, Brigitte. *Good-bye, Daddy!*
Weulersse, Odile. *Nasreddine*
Wild, Margaret. *Piglet and Papa*
Willhoite, Michael. *Daddy's roommate*
Winthrop, Elizabeth. *As the crow flies*
Wolf, Jake. *Daddy, could I have an elephant?*
Wood, Douglas. *What dads can't do*
When a dad says "I love you"
Wyeth, Sharon Dennis. *Always my dad*
Yaccarino, Dan. *Every Friday*
Yolen, Jane. *All those secrets of the world*
Baby Bear's chairs
The emperor and the kite
My father knows the names of things
Owl moon
Young, Ed. *Mouse match*
Yu, Li-Qiong. *A New Year's reunion*
Zappa, Ahmet. *Because I'm your dad*
Ziefert, Harriet. *Bigger than Daddy*
Zolotow, Charlotte. *A father like that*

Family life – grandfathers

Acheson, Alison. *Grandpa's music*
Ackerman, Karen. *Song and dance man*
Adler, David A. *A little at a time*
Aliki. *The two of them*
Altes, Marta. *My grandpa*
Anaya, Rudolfo A. *Farolitos for Abuelo*
Andrews, Julie. *Dumpy the dump truck*
Anholt, Laurence. *Seven for a secret*
Appelt, Kathi. *Where, where is Swamp Bear?*
Asher, Sandy. *What a party!*
Aska, Warabe. *Tapicero tap tap*
Balouch, Kristen. *Mystery bottle*
Barrett, Judi. *Cloudy with a chance of meatballs*
Cloudy with a chance of meatballs 3
Barron, T. A. *Where is Grandpa?*
Beardshaw, Rosalind. *Grandpa's surprise*
Boyden, Linda. *The blue roses*
Bradford, Karleen. *You can't rush a cat*
Briggs, Raymond. *The puddleman*
Bunting, Eve. *Butterfly house*
A day's work
So far from the sea
Butler, Dori Hillestad. *My grandpa had a stroke*
Callahan, Sean. *The leprechaun who lost his rainbow*
Carney, Margaret. *The biggest fish in the lake*
Carter, Don. *Heaven's all-star jazz band*
Cazet, Denys. *December 24th*
Cheng, Andrea. *Grandfather counts*
Choi, Yangsook. *Behind the mask*
Cocca-Leffler, Maryann. *A vacation for Pooch*
Cohen, Deborah Bodin. *Papa Jethro*
Compestine, Ying Chang. *Crouching tiger*
Cooke, Trish. *The grandad tree*
Cooper, Floyd. *Max and the tag-along moon*
Crunk, Tony. *Grandpa's overalls*
Cumberbatch, Judy. *Can you hear the sea?*
Daly, Niki. *Old Bob's brown bear*

Davies, Nicola. *White owl, barn owl*
Davis, Aubrey. *Bagels from Benny*
dePaola, Tomie. *Now one foot, now the other*
Tom
DiSalvo, DyAnne. *Grandpa's corner store*
Drawson, Blair. *All along the river*
Drummond, Allan. *Tin Lizzie*
Earnhardt, Donna W. *Being Frank*
Falwell, Cathryn. *Rainbow Stew*
Fletcher, Ralph. *Grandpa never lies*
Fox, Mem. *Shoes from grandpa*
Sophie
Francis, Lee DeCora. *Kunu's basket*
Fry, Stella. *Grandpa's garden*
Garland, Michael. *Grandpa's tractor*
Geisert, Arthur. *Mystery*
George, William T. *Fishing at Long Pond*
Gerdner, Linda. *Grandfather's story cloth / Yawg daim paj ntaub dab neeg*
Gillard, Denise. *Music from the sky*
Gold-Vukson, Marji E. *Grandpa and me on Tu B'Shevat*
Golding, Theresa Martin. *Memorial Day surprise*
Gower, Catherine. *Long-Long's new year*
Greenfield, Eloise. *Grandpa's face*
Grifalconi, Ann. *Ain't nobody a stranger to me*
Grist, Julie. *Flying, just plane fun*
Henkes, Kevin. *Grandpa and Bo*
Henson, Heather. *Grumpy Grandpa*
Hest, Amy. *Baby Duck and the bad eyeglasses*
Guess who, Baby Duck
Make the team, Baby Duck
Off to school, Baby Duck
The purple coat
When Charley met Grampa
You're the boss, Baby Duck
Highet, Alistair. *The yellow train*
Hopkinson, Deborah. *Bluebird summer*
Hurst, Carol Otis. *Terrible storm*
Hutchins, Pat. *Bumpety bump*
Happy birthday, Sam
Isadora, Rachel. *Happy belly, happy smile*
Yo, Jo!
James, Simon. *The birdwatchers*
Johnson, Angela. *Julius*
The Rolling Store
When I am old with you
Johnston, Tony. *Little Rabbit goes to sleep*
Kasza, Keiko. *Grandpa Toad's last secret*
Kimmelman, Leslie. *The Shabbat puppy*
Krebs, Laurie. *The beeman*, ill. by Valeria Cis
The beeman, ill. by Melissa Iwai
LeBox, Annette. *Wild bog tea*
Liwska, Renata. *Little panda*
Lobel, Gillian. *Does anybody love me?*
Locker, Thomas. *Where the river begins*
Londner, Renee. *Stones for Grandpa*
Lynn, Sarah. *Tip-tap pop*
McCully, Emily Arnold. *The Christmas gift*
McDonald, Megan. *The great pumpkin switch*
McKenna, Sharon. *Good morning, sunshine*
Mackintosh, David. *The Frank show*
Martin, Bill, Jr. *Knots on a counting rope*
Martin, Jacqueline Briggs. *The water gift and the pig of the pig*
Mason, Margaret H. *These hands*
May, Kathy. *Molasses man*
Mayer, Mercer. *Just big enough*
Meshon, Aaron. *Take me out to the Yakyu*
Michelson, Richard. *Too young for Yiddish*
Mitchell, Margaree King. *Granddaddy's gift*
Monk, Isabell. *Blackberry stew*
Moon, Nicola. *Lucy's picture*
Moore, Lilian. *While you were chasing a hat*
Mora, Pat. *Pablo's tree*
Moseley, Keith. *Where's the dinosaur?*
Moser, Lisa. *Watermelon wishes*
Murphy, Yannick. *Ahwooooooooo!*
Nanji, Shenaaz. *An alien in my house*
Newman, Lesléa. *A sweet Passover*
Nickle, John. *TV Rex*
Nobisso, Josephine. *Grandpa loved*
Numeroff, Laura Joffe. *What grandmas do best; What grandpas do best*
Oberman, Sheldon. *The always prayer shawl*
By the Hanukkah light
O'Malley, Kevin. *Bud*
Oram, Hiawyn. *Going to Grandpa's*
Otto, Carolyn. *That sky, that rain*
Parr, Todd. *The grandpa book*
Paul, Ann Whitford. *Everything to spend the night . . . from A to Z*
Perret, Delphine. *The Big Bad Wolf goes on vacation*
Pfister, Marcus. *The happy hedgehog*
Prater, John. *Hold tight!*
Proimos, James. *Joe's wish*
Purmell, Ann. *Apple cider making days*
Quigley, Mary. *Granddad's fishing buddy*
Rahaman, Vashanti. *Divali rose*
Reagan, Jean. *How to babysit a grandpa*
Reynolds, Adrian. *Pete and Polo's farmyard adventure*
Roberts, Bethany. *Gramps and the fire dragon*
Rose, Naomi C. *Tashi and the Tibetan flower cure*
Rosenberry, Vera. *Vera's baby sister*
Roth, Susan L. *Happy birthday Mr. Kang*
Russo, Marisabina. *Grandpa Abe*
Sáenz, Benjamin Alire. *A gift from papá Diego / Un regalo de papá Diego*
Santucci, Barbara. *Anna's corn*
Say, Allen. *Grandfather's journey*
Schaap, Martine. *Mop's treasure hunt*
Schaefer, Carole Lexa. *The little French whistle*
Schlessinger, Laura. *Dr. Laura Schlessinger's Where's God?*
Schotter, Roni. *In the piney woods*
Schwartz, Howard. *Gathering sparks*
Sheth, Kashmira. *Monsoon afternoon*
Shields, Carol Diggory. *Lucky pennies and hot chocolate*
Shulevitz, Uri. *Dawn*
Dusk
Sinykin, Sheri. *Zayde comes to live*
Smalls, Irene. *My Pop Pop and me*
Soto, Gary. *My little car / Mi carrito*
Stafford, Liliana. *Just dragon*
Stevenson, James. *Brr!*
"Could be worse!"
Grandpa's great city tour
Grandpa's too-good garden
The great big especially beautiful Easter egg
No friends
That dreadful day
That terrible Halloween night
That's exactly the way it wasn't
There's nothing to do!
We can't sleep
What's under my bed?
Will you please feed our cat?

Worse than Willy!
Stiles, Martha Bennett. *Island magic*
Stock, Catherine. *Thanksgiving treat*
Stolz, Mary. *Storm in the night*
Tavares, Matt. *Oliver's game*
Titherington, Jeanne. *Where are you going, Emma?*
Tompert, Ann. *Grandfather Tang's story*
Van Leeuwen, Jean. *The tickle stories*
Vigna, Judith. *My two uncles*
Wallace, Ian. *Chin Chiang and the dragon's dance*
Wallace, Nancy Elizabeth. *Seeds! Seeds! Seeds!*
Snow
Walters, Eric. *The matatu*
Wells, Rosemary. *The language of doves*
Williams, Laura E. *The best winds*
Winch, John. *Keeping up with Grandma*
Wolff, Ashley. *I call my grandpa Papa*
Wood, Douglas. *Grandad's prayers of the earth*
Woodruff, Elvira. *Can you guess where we're going?*
Yeh, Kat. *The magic brush*
Zalben, Jane Breskin. *Pearl's marigolds for grandpa*
Zia, F. *Hot, hot roti for Dada-ji*
Ziefert, Harriet. *Lunchtime for a purple snake*
No kiss for Grandpa!
Robin, where are you?
That's what grandpas are for
Zolotow, Charlotte. *My grandson Lew*

Family life – grandmothers

Abeele, Veronique van den. *Still my Grandma*
Aber, Linda Williams. *Carrie measures up!*
Ackerman, Karen. *By the dawn's early light*
Addasi, Maha. *Time to pray*
Ahlberg, Allan. *The snail house*
Alcott, Louisa May. *An old-fashioned Thanksgiving*
Alda, Arlene. *Hurry Granny Annie*
Altman, Linda Jacobs. *Singing with Momma Lou*
Anderson, Laurie Halse. *Turkey pox*
Anderson, Peggy Perry. *Joe on the go*
Balian, Lorna. *Humbug rabbit*
Barnwell, Ysaye M. *No mirrors in my Nana's house*
Baryshnikov, Mikhail. *Because . . .*
Bastianich, Lidia. *Nonna tell me a story*
Nonna's birthday surprise
Bauer, Marion Dane. *Grandmother's song*
Beardshaw, Rosalind. *Grandma's beach*
Bercaw, Edna Coe. *Halmoni's day*
Berenstain, Stan and Jan. *The Berenstain bears and the week at grandma's*
Best, Cari. *Beatrice spells some lulus and learns to write a letter*
Three cheers for Catherine the Great!
When Catherine the Great and I were eight!
Biro, Maureen Boyd. *Walking with Maga*
Bootman, Colin. *Fish for the Grand Lady*
Borgo, Lacy. *Big Mama's baby*
Bouchard, Dave. *Nokum is my teacher*
Bourgeois, Paulette. *Oma's quilt*
Bowen, Anne. *I loved you before you were born*
Bower, Gary. *Ivy's icicle*
Brenner, Barbara A. *Beef stew*
Brisson, Pat. *Hobbledy-clop*
Brown, Ken. *What's the time, Grandma Wolf?*
Brown, Monica. *Chavela and the magic bubble*
Browne, Anthony. *Silly Billy*
Bryan, Ashley. *Can't scare me!*
Turtle knows your name
Bunting, Eve. *A picnic in October*
The Wednesday surprise
Burrowes, Adjoa J. *Grandma's purple flowers*
Busse, Sarah Martin. *Banjo granny*
Carrick, Carol. *Valentine*
Caseley, Judith. *In style with Grandma Antoinette*
Castaneda, Omar S. *Abuela's weave*
Castellucci, Cecil. *Grandma's gloves*
Chall, Marsha Wilson. *Prairie train*
Chapman, Jane. *I'm not sleepy!*
Choi, Sook Nyul. *Halmoni and the picnic*
Colato Laínez, René. *Playing lotería / El juego de la lotería*
Collins, Ross. *Alvie eats soup*
Conrad, Donna. *See you soon, Moon*
Corderoy, Tracey. *Hubble bubble, Granny trouble*
I want my mommy!
Crowe, Carole. *Turtle girl*
Cruise, Robin. *Little Mama forgets*
Crunk, Tony. *Big Mama*
Daly, Niki. *Not so fast Songololo*
D'Arc, Karen Scourby. *My grandmother is a singing Yaya*
De Anda, Diane. *The patchwork garden / pedacitos de huerto*
Demas, Corinne. *The disappearing island*
DePalma, Mary Newell. *The perfect gift*
dePaola, Tomie. *The baby sister*
Nana Upstairs and Nana Downstairs
Derby, Sally. *No mush today*
Devlin, Wende. *Cranberry autumn*
Díaz, Katacha. *Carolina's gift*
Divakaruni, Chitra Banerjee. *Grandma and the great gourd*
Doray, Malika. *One more Wednesday*
Dorros, Arthur. *Abuela*
Doyle, Malachy. *Splash, Joshua, splash!*
DuBurke, Randy. *The moon ring*
Dwyer, Mindy. *Quilt of dreams*
English, Karen. *The baby on the way*
Eriksson, Eva. *A crash course for Molly*
Ernst, Lisa Campbell. *Little Red Riding Hood: a newfangled prairie tale*
Fearnley, Jan. *Milo Armadillo*
Fletcher, Ralph. *Grandpa never lies*
Flournoy, Valerie. *The patchwork quilt*
Fraustino, Lisa Rowe. *The hickory chair*
French, Vivian. *Yucky worms*
Garland, Sherry. *The lotus seed*
George, Jean Craighead. *Dear Rebecca, winter is here*
Godard, Alex. *Mama, across the sea*
Gray, Rita. *Nonna's porch*
Greene, Rhonda Gowler. *At grandma's*
Gregory, Nan. *Wild Girl and Gran*
Griessman, Annette. *Like a hundred drums*
Guback, Georgia. *Luka's quilt*
Guest, C. Z. *Tiny green thumbs*
Hansen, P. *My granny's purse*
Hanson, Regina. *A season for mangoes*
Harley, Bill. *Lost and found*
Hartman, Bob. *Granny Mae's Christmas play*
Hartt-Sussman, Heather. *Here comes Hortense!*
Nana's getting married
Hassett, Ann. *Too many frogs!*
Hassett, John. *Mouse in the house*
Haynes, Max. *Grandma's gone to live in the stars*
Heller, Nicholas. *This little piggy*
Henderson, Kathy. *And the good brown earth*
Herman, Charlotte. *The memory cupboard*

Herrera, Juan Felipe. *Grandma and Me at the flea / Los meros meros remateros*
Hest, Amy. *The Friday nights of Nana*
Nana's birthday party
Hines, Anna Grossnickle. *Gramma's walk*
My grandma is coming to town
Holt, Kimberly Willis. *The adventures of Granny Clearwater and Little Critter*
Horning, Sandra. *The giant hug*
Howard, Ellen. *The log cabin quilt*
Isadora, Rachel. *Luke goes to bat*
Over the green hills
Johnson, Dinah. *Quinnie Blue*
Johnston, Tony. *My abuelita*
Joosse, Barbara. *Ghost wings*
Grandma calls me Beautiful
Hooray Parade
A houseful of Christmas
Sleepover at Gramma's house
Keister, Douglas. *To grandmother's house*
Kessler, Cristina. *My great-grandmother's gourd*
Klise, Kate. *Grammy Lamby and the secret handshake*
Knister. *Sophie's dance*
Kovalski, Maryann. *Take me out to the ball game*
The wheels on the bus
Kroll, Virginia L. *Jason takes responsibility*
The Thanksgiving bowl
LaMarche, Jim. *The raft*
Laminack, Lester L. *Saturdays and teacakes*
Leedahl, Shelley A. *The bone talker*
Leijten, Aileen. *Hugging hour!*
Levine, Gail Carson. *Betsy Red Hoodie*
Levinson, Riki. *I go with my family to Grandma's*
Watch the stars come out
Lindbergh, Reeve. *The hippie grandmother*
My little grandmother often forgets
London, Jonathan. *The sugaring-off party*
Look, Lenore. *Henry's first-moon birthday*
Love as strong as ginger
Lord, Janet. *Here comes Grandma!*
Love to mamá
Lovell, Patty. *Have fun, Molly Lou Melon*
Stand tall, Molly Lou Melon
Lowell, Susan. *Little Red Cowboy Hat*
Luenn, Nancy. *A gift for Abuelita*
Nessa's fish
Nessa's story
Lum, Kate. *What! cried Granny*
Lyons, Kelly Starling. *Tea cakes for Tosh*
McCain, Becky R. *Grandmother's dreamcatcher*
McCaughrean, Geraldine. *My grandmother's clock*
MacDonald, Margaret Read. *The squeaky door*
McElroy, Lisa Tucker. *Meet my grandmother. She's a children's book author*
Mackall, Dandi Daley. *The story of the Easter robin*
McKay, Hilary. *Pirates ahoy!*
MacLachlan, Patricia. *Your moon, my moon*
McLeod, Elaine. *Lessons from Mother Earth*
Manushkin, Fran. *How mama brought the spring*
Marshall, Linda Elovitz. *Grandma Rose's magic*
Martin, Bill, Jr. *Little granny quarterback*
Mathews, Judith. *Nathaniel Willy, scared silly*
Mayer, Pamela. *The Grandma cure*
The scariest monster in the whole wide world
Mayhew, James. *Katie and the sunflowers*
Meddaugh, Susan. *Martha says it with flowers*
Mendes, Valerie. *Look at me, Grandma!*
Mitchell, Lori. *Different just like me*
Mitchell, Margaree King. *When Grandmama sings*
Moore, Maggie. *Little Red Riding Hood*
Mora, Pat. *Sweet dreams / Dulces suenos*
Morris, Ann. *Grandma Esther remembers*
Grandma Francisca remembers
Grandma Lai Goon remembers
Grandma Lois remembers
Grandma Maxine remembers
Morrison, Toni. *Peeny butter fudge*
Mortimer, Rachael. *Red Riding Hood and the sweet little wolf*
Moser, Lisa. *Railroad Hank*
Murphy, Patti Beling. *Elinor and Violet*
Murphy, Sally. *Pearl verses the world*
Nelson, S. D. *The Star People*
Newman, Lesléa. *Matzo ball moon*
Newman, Nanette. *What will you be, Grandma?*
Newsome, Jill. *Dream dancer*
Numeroff, Laura Joffe. *What grandmas do best; What grandpas do best*
Nye, Naomi Shihab. *Sitti's secrets*
O'Brien, Anne Sibley. *A path of stars*
Ogburn, Jacqueline K. *The magic nesting doll*
Ohi, Ruth. *A trip with Grandma*
Older, Effin. *My two grandmothers*
Onyefulu, Ifeoma. *Grandma comes to stay*
Pak, Soyung. *Dear Juno*
Park, Frances. *The Have a Good Day Cafe*
Parr, Todd. *The grandma book*
Paul, Ann Whitford. *Tortuga in trouble*
Pearce, Philippa. *Amy's three best things*
Peck, Richard. *Monster night at Grandma's house*
Pegram, Laura. *Daughter's Day blues*
Perrow, Angeli. *Many hands*
Pippin-Mathur, Courtney. *Maya was grumpy*
Polacco, Patricia. *Babushka's Mother Goose*
Bun Bun Button
Chicken Sunday
Someone for Mr. Sussman
Thunder cake
Poydar, Nancy. *Busy Bea*
Preus, Margi. *The Peace Bell*
Price, Mara. *Grandma's chocolate / El chocolate de Abuelita*
Pulver, Robin. *Alicia's tutu*
Romain, Trevor. *Jemma's journey*
Root, Phyllis. *The name quilt*
Rothenberg, Joan Keller. *Inside-out grandma*
Russo, Marisabina. *I will come back for you*
Ryan, Pam Muñoz. *Mice and beans*
Rylant, Cynthia. *The ticky-tacky doll*
Sacre, Antonio. *La Noche Buena*
Sáenz, Benjamin Alire. *Grandma Fina and her wonderful umbrellas / La abuelita Fina y sus sombrillas maravillosas*
Sasso, Sandy Eisenberg. *For heaven's sake*
Savadier, Elivia. *Will Sheila share?*
Schotter, Roni. *All about grandmas*
Schubert, Leda. *The Princess of Borscht*
Schwartz, Amy. *Oma and Bobo*
Shea, Pegi Deitz. *The whispering cloth*
Shelby, Anne. *Homeplace*
Sheth, Kashmira. *My Dadima wears a sari*
Shulman, Lisa. *The moon might be milk*
Siegel, Randy. *Grandma's smile*
Simhaee, Rebeka. *Sara finds a mitzva*
Smalls, Irene. *My Nana and me*
Smee, Nicola. *What's the matter, Bunny Blue?*
Spinelli, Eileen. *Wanda's monster*
Spinner, Stephanie. *It's a miracle*

Spohn, Kate. *Snow play*
Stein, David Ezra. *Love, Mouserella*
Stock, Catherine. *Gugu's house*
Sweet, Melissa. *Carmine*
Tan, Amy. *The moon lady*
Tessler, Manya. *Yuki's ride home*
Thomas, Jane Resh. *Saying good-bye to grandma*
Thompson, Colin. *Falling angels*
Torres, Leyla. *Liliana's grandmothers*
Saturday sancocho
Turner-Denstaedt, Melanie. *The hat that wore Clara B.*
Uegaki, Chieri. *Suki's kimono*
Urdahl, Catherine. *Emma's question*
VanHecke, Susan. *An apple pie for dinner*
Vega, Denise. *Grandmother, have the angels come?*
Velasquez, Eric. *Grandma's gift*
Grandma's records
Vulliamy, Clara. *Small*
Waboose, Jan Bourdeau. *Firedancers*
Waldman, Neil. *They came from the Bronx*
Weiss, Ellen. *The taming of Lola*
Weitzman, Jacqueline Preiss. *You can't take a balloon into the Metropolitan Museum*
You can't take a balloon into the National Gallery
Wells, Rosemary. *Bunny cakes*
Bunny mail
Bunny money
Bunny party
Max and Ruby's bedtime book
Max and Ruby's treasure hunt
Ruby's beauty shop
Yoko's paper cranes
Whybrow, Ian. *Sammy and the robots*
Wigersma, Tanneke. *Baby brother*
Wilcox, Brian. *Full moon*
Wild, Margaret. *Old Pig*
Our granny
Piglet and Granny
Willard, Nancy. *The mouse, the cat and Grandmother's hat*
Williams, Barbara. *Albert's gift for grandmother*
Williams, Vera B. *Music, music for everyone*
Winch, John. *Keeping up with Grandma*
Wojtowycz, David. *A cuddle for Claude*
Wolff, Ashley. *I call my grandma Nana*
Wood, Audrey. *The napping house*
The napping house wakes up
Wood, Douglas. *What grandmas can't do*
Woodson, Jacqueline. *Coming on home soon*
Yolen, Jane. *Grandma's hurrying child*
Zagwÿn, Deborah Turney. *The winter gift*
Zelinsky, Paul O. *The wheels on the bus*
Ziefert, Harriet. *Grandma, it's for you!*
My forever dress
That's what grandmas are for
Zolotow, Charlotte. *William's doll*

Family life – grandparents

Ada, Alma Flor. *I love Saturdays y domingos*
Ajmera, Maya, et al. *Our grandparents*
Ancona, George. *Mis abuelos / My grandparents*
Auld, Mary. *My grandparents*
Barrett, Judi. *Pickles to Pittsburgh*
Bateman, Teresa. *April foolishness*
Bergman, Tamar. *Where is?*
Bowen, Anne. *When you visit Grandma and Grandpa*
Bryne, Gayle. *Sometimes it's grandmas and grandpas, not mommies and daddies*
Bunge, Daniela. *The scarves*
Bunting, Eve. *The days of summer*
Carlson, Nancy. *Hooray for Grandparent's Day!*
Cazet, Denys. *The octopus*
Child, Lydia Maria. *Over the river and through the wood*
Over the river and through the wood: the New England boy's song about Thanksgiving Day
Crum, Shutta. *All on a sleepy night*
My mountain song
Cusimano, Maryann K. *You are my wish*
Frazee, Marla. *A couple of boys have the best week ever*
Galindo, Mary Sue. *Icy watermelon / Sandía fría*
Grambling, Lois G. *Grandma tells a story*
A grand celebration
Haas, Jessie. *Hurry!*
Hazen, Barbara Shook. *Katie's wish*
Hill, Eric. *Spot visits his grandparents*
Hoberman, Mary Ann. *I'm going to Grandma's*
Holabird, Katharine. *Angelina, star of the show*
Horacek, Petr. *My elephant*
Horrocks, Anita. *Silas' seven grandparents*
Hunter, Dette. *38 ways to entertain your grandparents*
Hutchins, Hazel. *One dark night*
Jennings, Sharon. *Franklin's Thanksgiving*
Juster, Norton. *The hello, goodbye window*
Sourpuss and sweetie pie
Kinsey-Warnock, Natalie. *Nora's ark*
Krishnaswami, Uma. *Remembering Grandpa*
Kropf, Latifa Berry. *It's Hanukkah time!*
Lloyd-Jones, Sally. *The ultimate guide to grandmas and grandpas!*
Long, Kathy. *Christopher sat straight up in bed*
Long, Melinda. *When Papa snores*
Look, Lenore. *Polka Dot Penguin Pottery*
Mollel, Tololwa M. *Kele's secret*
Oppenheim, Shulamith Levey. *Fireflies for Nathan*
Palacios, Argentina. *A Christmas surprise for Chabelita*
Parish, Herman. *Amelia Bedelia's first apple pie*
Polacco, Patricia. *My rotten redheaded older brother*
The trees of the dancing goats
Rice, Eve. *At Grammy's house*
Rosen, Michael. *A Thanksgiving wish*
Rotner, Shelley. *Lots of grandparents*
Rylant, Cynthia. *Christmas in the country*
Schwartz, Joanne. *Our corner grocery store*
Shapiro, Jody Fickes. *Up, up, up! It's apple-picking time*
Shulimson, Sarene. *Lights out Shabbat*
Skolsky, Mindy Warshaw. *Hannah and the whistling tea kettle*
Stevenson, James. *Higher on the door*
July
Stojic, Manya. *Wet pebbles under our feet*
Thomson, Pat. *The squeaky, creaky bed*
Tsubakiyama, Margaret. *Mei-Mei loves the morning*
Tunnell, Michael O. *Mailing May*
Uslander, Arlene. *That's what grandparents are for*
Van Leeuwen, Jean. *Touch the sky summer*
Woodson, Jacqueline. *Sweet, sweet memory*
Wyeth, Sharon Dennis. *Always my dad*
Yolen, Jane. *Off we go!*
Ziefert, Harriet. *Grandma's wedding album*

Family life – great-grandparents

dePaola, Tomie. *Nana Upstairs and Nana Downstairs*
Fleischman, Paul. *The matchbox diary*
Judd, Naomi. *Naomi Judd's guardian angels*
MacLachlan, Patricia. *Three names*
Rochelle, Belinda. *Jewels*
Smith, Lane. *Grandpa Green*
Taulbert, Clifton L. *Little Cliff's first day of school*

Family life – mothers

Ackerman, Karen. *By the dawn's early light*
Aigner-Clark, Julie. *You are the best medicine*
Alborough, Jez. *Hug*
It's the bear
Alda, Arlene. *Morning glory Monday*
Alexander, Sue. *One more time, Mama*
Anastas, Margaret. *Mommy's best kisses*
Anderson, Laurie Halse. *No time for Mother's Day*
Andreae, Giles. *I love my mommy*
There's a house inside my mommy
Appelt, Kathi. *Oh my baby, little one*
Armand, Glenda. *Love twelve miles long*
Ashman, Linda. *Mama's day*
Aston, Dianna Hutts. *Mama Outside, Mama Inside*
Auld, Mary. *My mom*
Averbeck, Jim. *Oh no, Little Dragon!*
Baker, Liza. *I love you because you're you*
Balian, Lorna. *Mother's Mother's Day*
Banks, Kate. *The bear in the book*
Close your eyes
Mama's coming home
Bardhan-Quallen, Sudipta. *Chicks run wild*
Bassède, Francine. *A day with the Bellyflops*
Bauer, Marion Dane. *Grandmother's song*
A mama for Owen
My mother is mine
Beaty, Andrea. *Hush, Baby Ghostling*
Beck, Scott. *A mud pie for mother*
Bedford, David. *Little Otter's big journey*
Touch the sky, my little bear
Bergman, Tamar. *Where is?*
Bertram, Debbie. *The best place to read*
Black, Sonia. *Hanging out with Mom*
Blackall, Sophie. *Are you awake?*
Blake, Robert J. *Little devils*
Bogan, Paulette. *Goodnight Lulu*
Lulu the big little chick
Momma's magical purse
Bottner, Barbara. *Rosa's room*
Bourgeois, Paulette. *Franklin says "I love you"*
Bourguignon, Laurence. *Heart in the pocket*
Boyd, Lizi. *I love Mommy*
Bradby, Marie. *Momma, where are you from?*
Bradford, Wade. *Why do I have to make my bed?*
Bradley, Kimberly Brubaker. *Favorite things*
Brami, Elisbeth. *Mommy time*
Brandt, Amy. *Benjamin comes back / Benjamin regresa*
Braun, Sebastien. *I love my mommy*
Breathed, Berkeley. *Mars needs moms!*
Bridges, Margaret Park. *Am I big or little?*
Brisson, Pat. *Sometimes we were brave*
Brown, Jo. *Where's my mommy?*
Brown, Margaret Wise. *The runaway bunny*
The runaway bunny [board book]
Brown, Susan Taylor. *Oliver's must-do list*
Browne, Anthony. *My mom*
Bulion, Leslie. *Fatuma's new cloth*
Bunting, Eve. *Flower garden*
My mom's wedding
Pirate boy
Tweak tweak
Buzzeo, Toni. *Adventure Annie goes to work*
Stay close to Mama
Cabrera, Jane. *Mommy, carry me please!*
Cadow, Kenneth M. *Alfie runs away*
Campbell, Ann-Jeanette. *Queenie Farmer had fifteen daughters*
Cannon, Janell. *Stellaluna*
Stellaluna: a pop-up book and mobile
Capucilli, Alyssa Satin. *Only my mom and me*
What kind of kiss?
Carle, Eric. *Does a kangaroo have a mother, too?*
Carlstrom, Nancy White. *It's your first day of school, Annie Claire*
Mama, will it snow tonight?
Carrick, Carol. *Valentine*
Chaconas, Dori. *Christmas mouseling*
Charlip, Remy. *Sleepytime rhyme*
Christelow, Eileen. *Don't wake up Mama!*
Church, Caroline Jayne. *One more hug for Madison*
Clements, Andrew. *Because your mommy loves you*
Cobb, Rebecca. *Missing Mommy*
Cocovini, Abby. *What's inside your tummy, Mommy?*
Cohen, Caron Lee. *Happy to you!*
Cole, Joanna. *When you were inside mommy*
Collet, Géraldine. *All by myself!*
Collins, Ross. *Doodleday*
Cora, Cat. *A suitcase surprise for Mommy*
Côté, Geneviève. *With you always, Little Monday*
Cousins, Lucy. *Hooray for fish!*
Cowen-Fletcher, Jane. *Mama zooms*
Crimi, Carolyn. *Where's my mummy?*
Cronin, Doreen. *M.O.M. (Mom Operating Manual)*
Crumpacker, Bunny. *Alexander's pretending day*
Curtis, Jamie Lee. *My mommy hung the moon*
DaCosta, Barbara. *Nighttime Ninja*
Dahl, Michael. *Bear says "thank you"*
Davis, Jerry. *Little Chicken's big day*
De Anda, Diane. *Dancing Miranda / Baila, Miranda, baila*
de Las Casas, Dianne. *Mama's bayou*
dePaola, Tomie. *My mother is so smart*
Dewdney, Anna. *Llama Llama home with Mama*
Llama Llama mad at Mama
Llama Llama misses Mama
Llama, Llama red pajama
Diggs, Taye. *Chocolate me!*
Dijs, Carla. *Mommy, what if—?*
Dodd, Emma. *Forever*
No matter what
Donaldson, Julia. *Where's my mom?*
Dornbusch, Erica. *Finding Kate's shoes*
Dorros, Arthur. *Mama and me*
Dotlich, Rebecca Kai. *Mama loves*
Douglas, Ann. *Before you were born*
Dowson, Nick. *Tigress*
Duble, Kathleen Benner. *Pilot mom*
Duncan, Alice Faye. *Honey baby sugar child*
Dunrea, Olivier. *It's snowing*
Dwyer, Mindy. *Quilt of dreams*
Eckart, Edana. *I can swim*
Edwards, Richard. *Copy me, Copycub*
Ehrlich, Amy. *Baby Dragon*
Ehrlich, Fred. *Does a mouse have a mommy?*
Ehrlich, H. M. *Gotcha, Louie!*

Emberley, Ed. *Thanks, Mom!*
Ericsson, Jennifer A. *Home to me, home to you*
Evans, Kristina. *What's special about me, Mama?*
Evans, Lezlie. *Who loves the little lamb?*
Falwell, Cathryn. *P.J. and Puppy*
Fearnley, Jan. *Watch out!*
Feeney, Tatyana. *Little Owl's orange scarf*
Fergus, Maureen. *The day my mom came to kindergarten*
Fitzpatrick, Marie-Louise. *You, me and the big blue sea*
Flack, Marjorie. *Ask Mr. Bear*
Flattinger, Hubert. *Stormy night*
Fleming, Denise. *Sleepy, oh so sleepy*
Ford, Christine. *Ocean's child*
Ford, Miela. *Mom and me*
Fox, Mem. *Harriet, you'll drive me wild*
Koala Lou
Fraggalosch, Audrey. *Grizzly bear family*
Trails above the tree line
Frasier, Debra. *Out of the ocean*
Freedman, Claire. *One magical morning*
Fruisen, Catherine Myler. *My mother's pearls*
Gal, Susan. *Night lights*
Garden, Nancy. *Molly's family*
Gardner, Sally. *Mama, don't go out tonight*
Genechten, Guido van. *Because you are my friend*
Gershator, Phillis. *This is the day!*
Time for a hug
Gerstein, Mordicai. *Leaving the nest*
Glenn, Sharlee. *Just what Mama needs*
Gliori, Debi. *Stormy weather*
Godard, Alex. *Mama, across the sea*
Goode, Diane. *Mama's perfect present*
The most perfect spot
Goodings, Lennie. *When you grow up*
Gorbachev, Valeri. *Nicky and the fantastic birthday gift*
Gore, Leonid. *Mommy, where are you?*
Grambling, Lois G. *My mom is a firefighter*
Gray, Kes. *Eat your peas*
006 and a half
Greene, Rhonda Gowler. *Mommy is a soft, warm kiss*
Greenstein, Elaine. *As big as you*
Hague, Kathleen. *Good night, fairies*
Hample, Stoo. *I will kiss you (lots and lots and lots!)*
Harper, Jessica. *Lizzy's do's and don'ts*
Lizzy's ups and downs
Harris, Robie H. *The day Leo said I hate you!*
Heo, Yumi. *One afternoon*
Hesse, Karen. *Come on, rain*
Hest, Amy. *Kiss good night*
When you meet a bear on Broadway
You can do it, Sam
Ho, Minfong. *Hush!*
Hoberman, Mary Ann. *The seven silly eaters*
Horton, Joan. *Working mummies*
Howie, Betsy. *The Block Mess Monster*
Hubbell, Patricia. *Sea, sand, me!*
Sidewalk trip
Huget, Jennifer LaRue. *Thanks a lot, Emily Post!*
Hughes, Langston. *Lullaby (for a Black mother)*
Hunter, Sally. *Humphrey's corner*
Iwai, Melissa. *Soup day*
Jadoul, Émile. *Good night, Chickie*
Janowitz, Tama. *Hear that?*
Jenkins, Emily. *Love you when you whine*
Jennings, Sharon. *Bearcub and Mama*
Jewel. *That's what I'd do*
Johnson, Angela. *Tell me a story, mama*
Johnson, Marion. *Caillou, new shoes*
Johnson, Paul Brett. *The goose who went off in a huff*
Johnston, Tony. *My best friend Bear*
Jonas, Ann. *Two bear cubs*
Jonell, Lynne. *Bravemole*
I need a snake
Mom pie
When Mommy was mad
Joosse, Barbara. *I love you the purplest*
Mama, do you love me?
Kasza, Keiko. *A mother for Choco*
Katz, Karen. *Mommy hugs*
Where is baby's mommy?
Kavanagh, Peter. *I love my mama*
Keller, Holly. *Miranda's beach day*
Kempter, Christa. *When Mama can't sleep*
Kern, Noris. *I love you with all my heart*
Ketteman, Helen. *If Beaver had a fever*
Killion, Bette. *Just think!*
Kindermans, Martine. *You and me*
Kirk, David. *Little Miss Spider*
Klise, Kate. *Little Rabbit and the Meanest Mother on Earth*
Koller, Jackie French. *No such thing*
Kono, Erin Eitter. *Hula lullaby*
Krauss, Ruth. *You're just what I need*
Kroll, Steven. *That makes me mad*
Krosoczka, Jarrett J. *Bubble bath pirates*
Giddy up, Cowgirl
Good night, Monkey Boy
Kuiper, Nannie. *Bailey the bear cub*
Kuskin, Karla. *A boy had a mother who bought him a hat*
LaChanze. *Little diva*
Lamb, Albert. *Tell me the day backwards*
Lasky, Kathryn. *Mommy's hands*
Lawler, Janet. *A mother's song*
Lee, Tae-Jun. *Waiting for Mama*
Leuck, Laura. *My monster mama loves me so*
Lewin, Hugh. *Jafta's mother*
Lewis, Kim. *Seymour and Henry*
Lewis, Paeony. *I'll always love you*
Lindgren, Barbro. *Benny's had enough*
Lindsay, Jeanne Warren. *Do I have a daddy?*
Lish, Ted. *The three little puppies and the big bad flea*
Little Bear's Valentine
Lobel, Gillian. *Little Honey Bear and the smiley moon*
London, Jonathan. *Count the ways, Little Brown Bear*
Here comes Doctor Hippo
What do you love?
What do you love? [board book]
Love to mamá
Lyon, George Ella. *Mama is a miner*
McAllister, Angela. *My mom has x-ray vision*
Night-night, little one
Trust me, Mom!
McBratney, Sam. *I'll always be your friend*
McCourt, Lisa. *Happy Halloween, Stinky Face*
I love you, Stinky Face
I miss you, Stinky Face
It's time for school, Stinky Face
Merry Christmas, Stinky Face
McElroy, Lisa Tucker. *Love, Lizzie*
McGhee, Alison. *Someday*
McGinty, Alice B. *Eliza's kindergarten surprise*
Macken, JoAnn Early. *Waiting out the storm*
MacLachlan, Patricia. *Before you came*

Lala salama
McMullan, Kate. *If you were my bunny*
McNiff, Dawn. *Mommy's little monster*
Madrigal, Antonio Hernandez. *Erandi's braids*
Mahy, Margaret. *Boom Baby boom, boom*
Makhijani, Pooja. *Mama's saris*
Manning, Mick. *Supermom*
Marino, Gianna. *Meet me at the moon*
Martin, David. *Monkey business*
Marzollo, Jean. *Mama, Mama*
Matthies, Janna. *The goodbye cancer garden*
Mayer, Mercer. *Just for you*
Melmed, Laura Krauss. *I love you as much . . .*
Micklos, John. *Mommy poems*
Miller, William. *A house by the river*
Milord, Susan. *If I could*
Minarik, Else Holmelund. *Am I beautiful?*
Mitchard, Jacquelyn. *Baby bat's lullaby*
Modarressi, Mitra. *Taking care of Mama*
Monnier, Miriam. *Just right*
Moore, Eva. *Lucky ducklings*
Moore-Mallinos, Jennifer. *Mom has cancer!*
Morgan-Vanroyen, Mary. *Sleep tight, little mouse*
Morris, Ann. *The mommy book*
Morrow, Tara Jaye. *Panda goes to school*
Moss, Miriam. *The snow bear*
Moundlic, Charlotte. *The scar*
Mraz, David. *Little Goose*
Müller, Birte. *Finn cooks*
Munsch, Robert N. *Love you forever*
Murphy, Mary. *Please be quiet!*
Murphy, Stuart J. *Rabbit's pajama party*
Murphy, Yannick. *Baby Polar*
Murray, Alison. *Little Mouse*
Neitzel, Shirley. *We're making breakfast for mother*
Newman, Lesléa. *Donovan's big day*
Heather has two mommies
Just like Mama
Mommy, Mama, and Me
Nicholls, Judith. *Billywise*
Noble, Sheilagh. *More*
Norac, Carl. *My mommy is magic*
North, Sherry. *Because you are my baby*
Numeroff, Laura Joffe. *The hope tree*
Nighty-night, Cooper
Oelschlager, Vanita. *A tale of two mommies*
Ohi, Ruth. *Pants off first*
O'Keefe, Susan Heyboer. *Love me, love you*
Palacios, Argentina. *A Christmas surprise for Chabelita*
Palatini, Margie. *Zak's lunch*
Paradis, Susan. *My mommy*
Parker, Marjorie Blain. *Mama's little duckling*
Your kind of mommy
Parr, Todd. *The mommy book*
Patrick, Jean L. S. *If I had a snowplow*
Peacock, Carol Antoinette. *Mommy far, Mommy near*
Peet, Mal. *Cloud tea monkeys*
Peterson, Jeanne Whitehouse. *My mama sings*
Pham, LeUyen. *All the things I love about you*
Pinkwater, Daniel. *Young Larry*
Platt, Cynthia. *A little bit of love*
Polacco, Patricia. *Betty Doll*
In our mothers' house
Mommies say shhh!
Posthuma, Sieb. *Benny*
Price, Hope Lynne. *These hands*
Pulver, Robin. *Nobody's mother is in second grade*
Radcliffe, Theresa. *Bashi, elephant baby*
Raff, Courtney Granet. *Giant of the sea*
Rahaman, Vashanti. *Read for me, Mama*
Ransom, Candice F. *The Christmas dolls*
Rao, Sandhya. *My mother's sari*
Reichert, Amy. *Take your mama to work today*
Reiser, Lynn. *Any kind of dog*
Rex, Michael. *Runaway mummy*
Reyher, Rebecca. *My mother is the most beautiful woman in the world*
Reynolds, Marilynn. *The magnificent piano recital*
Richmond, Marianne. *I'm not tired yet!*
Oh, the things my mom will do . . .
Ritchie, Alison. *Me and my mom!*
Robberecht, Thierry. *Back into Mommy's tummy*
Robbins, Maria Polushkin. *Mother, Mother, I want another*
Robinson, Sue. *I want to play*
Rock, Brian. *With all my heart*
Rockliff, Mara. *Me and Momma and Big John*
Rockwell, Anne. *Willy can count*
Roddie, Shen. *Not now, Mrs. Wolf*
Rose, Deborah Lee. *All the seasons of the year*
Someone's sleepy
Rosenberg, Liz. *The carousel*
Rosenthal, Amy Krouse. *Bedtime for Mommy*
Ross, Michael Elsohn. *Mama's milk*
Roth, Carol. *Where's my mommy?*
Will you still love me?
Rotner, Shelley. *Lots of moms*
Rubel, Nicole. *No more vegetables!*
Rueda, Claudia. *My little polar bear*
Ruiz-Flores, Lupe. *Alicia's fruity drinks / Las aguas frescas de Alicia*
Rusackas, Francesca. *I love you all day long*
Russo, Marisabina. *Come back, Hannah*
Mama talks too much
When mama gets home
Ryder, Joanne. *Bear of my heart*
Sakai, Komako. *Mad at Mommy*
The snow day
Saltzberg, Barney. *Soccer mom from outer space*
Sattler, Jennifer. *Uh-oh, Dodo!*
Say, Allen. *Tree of cranes*
Sayre, April Pulley. *Here come the humpbacks!*
Schaefer, Carole Lexa. *Down in the woods at sleepytime*
Down in the woods at sleepytime [board book]
Schick, Eleanor. *Mama*
Schlessinger, Laura. *Why do you love me?*
Schotter, Roni. *Mama, I'll give you the world*
Schubert, Leda. *Feeding the sheep*
Scott, Ann Herbert. *On mother's lap*
On mother's lap [board book]
Segal, John. *Far far away!*
Senning, Cindy Post. *Emily's out and about book*
Simpson, Lesley. *The Purim surprise*
Slangerup, Erik Jon. *Dirt Boy*
Slonim, David. *I loathe you*
Smalls-Hector, Irene. *Jonathan and his mommy*
Smith, Maggie. *Dear Daisy, get well soon*
Sperring, Mark. *The shape of my heart*
Spinelli, Eileen. *When Mama comes home tonight*
Stampler, Ann Redisch. *Go home, Mrs. Beekman!*
Stephens, J. Moria. *Persephone, the ladybug*
Steven, Kenneth. *The biggest thing in the world*
Stinson, Kathy. *The man with the violin*
Stock, Catherine. *Easter surprise*
Stott, Ann. *Always*

I'll be there
Strauss, Anna. *Hush, Mama loves you*
Suen, Anastasia. *Window music*
Sullivan, Paula. *Todd's box*
Swanson, Susan Marie. *The first thing my mama told me*
Sykes, Julie. *I don't want to take a bath!*
Tafuri, Nancy. *All kinds of kisses*
I love you, little one
Mama's little bears
Whose chick are you?
Tarpley, Natasha Anastasia. *I love my hair!*
Thiesing, Lisa. *Me and you: a mother-daughter album*
Thomas, Jane Resh. *Scaredy dog*
Thomas, Joyce Carol. *Joy*
Thomas, Naturi. *Uh-oh! It's Mama's birthday!*
Thompson, Lauren. *Leap back home to me*
Little Quack's bedtime
Little Quack's hide and seek
Little Quack's hide and seek [board book]
Mouse's first spring
Thomson, Sarah L. *Cub's big world*
The three little pigs. *The three little pigs*
Tompert, Ann. *Little Fox goes to the end of the world*
Toten, Teresa. *Bright red kisses*
Trotter, Deborah W. *How do you know?*
Trottier, Maxine. *A safe place*
Van Laan, Nancy. *Little Fish lost*
Tickle tum
Verburg, Bonnie. *The kiss box*
Viorst, Judith. *My mama says there aren't any zombies, ghosts, vampires, creatures, demons, monsters, fiends, goblins, or things*
Vulliamy, Clara. *Ellen and Penguin and the new baby*
Waber, Bernard. *Lyle finds his mother*
Waddell, Martin. *The big big sea*
A kitten called Moonlight
Owl babies
Owl babies [board book]
Rosie's babies
Snow bears
Webster J. Duck
Yum, yum, yummy
Walker, Anna. *I love my mom*
Wallace, John. *Anything for you*
Walters, Catherine. *Play gently, Alfie Bear*
When will it be spring?
Watters, Debbie, et al. *Where's Mom's hair?*
Weiss, Ellen. *I love you, Little Monster*
Wells, Rosemary. *Hazel's amazing mother*
Yoko learns to read
Weninger, Brigitte. *"Mom, wake up and play!"*
"No bath! No way!"
Special delivery
Wheeler, Lisa. *Jam and jelly by Holly and Nellie*
White, Kathryn. *Ruby's school walk*
White, Linda Arms. *Comes a wind*
Wild, Margaret. *Lucy Goosey*
Piglet and Mama
Williams, Karen Lynn. *Tap-tap*
Williams, Linda. *Horse in the pigpen*
Willis, Jeanne. *Cottonball Colin*
Wilson, Karma. *Mama always comes home*
Winter, Jeanette. *Mama: a true story, in which a baby hippo loses his mama during a tsunami, but finds a new home*
Winthrop, Elizabeth. *Promises*
Witte, Anna. *Lola's fandango*
Wong, Janet S. *Grump*
Wood, Audrey. *The Birthday Queen*
Wood, Douglas. *What moms can't do*
Woodson, Jacqueline. *Coming on home soon*
Show way
Wyeth, Sharon Dennis. *The granddaughter necklace*
Xinran, Xue. *Motherbridge of love*
Yamashita, Haruo. *Seven little mice go to school*
Seven little mice have fun on the ice
Yang, Belle. *Always come home to me*
Yezerski, Thomas. *Queen of the world*
Yolen, Jane. *Mama's kiss*
Yum, Hyewon. *Mom, it's my first day of kindergarten!*
Ziefert, Harriet. *The biggest job of all*
Clara Ann Cookie
Home for Navidad
Mommies are for counting stars
Mommy, I want to sleep in your bed!
Surprise!
Zolotow, Charlotte. *I like to be little*
Mr. Rabbit and the lovely present
Say it!
This quiet lady

Family life – new sibling

Alexander, Martha G. *Nobody asked me if I wanted a baby sister*
When the new baby comes, I'm moving out
Anholt, Laurence. *Sophie and the new baby*
Appelt, Kathi. *Brand-new baby blues*
Apperley, Dawn. *Don't wake the baby*
Ashman, Linda. *When I was king*
Banks, Kate. *This baby*
Boelts, Maribeth. *You're a brother, Little Bunny!*
Borden, Louise. *Big brothers don't take naps*
Bradman, Tony. *The perfect baby*
Broach, Elise. *What the no-good baby is good for*
Brown, Marc. *Arthur's baby*
Bunting, Eve. *Baby can*
Will it be a baby brother?
Burningham, John. *There's going to be a baby*
Cocca-Leffler, Maryann. *Theo's mood*
Cole, Joanna. *I'm a big sister*
The new baby at your house
Conway, David. *The most important gift of all*
Cote, Nancy. *It's all about me!*
Davies, Gill. *Wilbur waited*
Dempsey, Sheena. *Bye-bye baby brother!*
dePaola, Tomie. *The baby sister*
Derby, Sally. *No mush today*
Dewan, Ted. *Crispin and the 3 little piglets*
Doerrfeld, Cori. *Penny loves pink*
Dunrea, Olivier. *Ollie*
Dyer, Jane. *Little Brown Bear and the bundle of joy*
Elkin, Mark. *Samuel's baby*
Enderle, Judith Ross. *Smile, Principessa!*
Fearnley, Jan. *A special something*
Gliori, Debi. *Where did that baby come from?*
Gutman, Anne. *Lisa's baby sister*
Hall, Algy Craig. *Fine as we are*
Hanson, Mary Elizabeth. *The difference between babies and cookies*
Harper, Anita. *It's not fair!*
Harris, Robie H. *Hi, new baby*
Mail Harry to the moon!
What's in there?
Henry, Steve. *Nobody asked me!*
Hill, Susanna Leonard. *Not yet, Rose*
Holabird, Katharine. *Angelina's baby sister*

Horse, Harry. *Little Rabbit's new baby*
Huget, Jennifer LaRue. *The beginner's guide to running away from home*
Jacobs, Julie. *My heart is a magic house*
Kallok, Emma. *Gem*
Keats, Ezra Jack. *Peter's chair*
Keller, Holly. *Geraldine's baby brother*
Kushner, Donn. *Peter's pixie*
Layne, Steven L. *Love the baby*
Lohans, Alison. *Waiting for the sun*
McCormick, Wendy. *The night you were born*
MacDonald, Ross. *Bad baby*
Mackall, Dandi Daley. *There's a baby in there!*
McQuinn, Anna. *Lola reads to Leo*
Mendes, Valerie. *Look at me, Grandma!*
Morris, Richard. *Bye-bye, baby!*
Munsch, Robert N. *Alligator baby*
Murkoff, Heidi Eisenberg. *What to expect when the new baby comes home*
My new baby
Newman, Marjorie. *Just like me*
Paschkis, Julie. *Mooshka*
Patz, Nancy. *Babies can't eat kimchee!*
Rheingrover, Jean Sasso. *Veronica's first year*
Robberecht, Thierry. *Back into Mommy's tummy*
Robbins, Beth. *Tom, Ally, and the new baby*
Rock, Lois. *Now we have a baby*
Rockwell, Lizzy. *Hello baby!*
Rodman, Mary Ann. *Surprise soup*
Rogers, Fred. *The new baby*
Rosenberg, Maxine B. *Mommy's in the hospital having a baby*
Rosenberry, Vera. *Vera's baby sister*
Roth, Carol. *Will you still love me?*
Russo, Marisabina. *Hannah's baby sister*
Schaefer, Lola M. *One special day*
Schindel, John. *Frog face, my little sister and me*
Sears, William, M.D., et al. *What baby needs*
Sheldon, Annette. *Big sister now*
Shields, Carol Diggory. *I wish my brother was a dog*
Shields, Gillian. *When the world was waiting for you*
Shipton, Jonathan. *Baby baby blah blah blah!*
Simmons, Jane. *Daisy and the egg*
Springstubb, Tricia. *Phoebe and Digger*
Stevenson, James. *Worse than Willy!*
Stinson, Kathy. *A pocket can have a treasure in it*
Stuve-Bodeen, Stephanie. *Mama Elizabeti*
Sullivan, Sarah. *Once upon a baby brother*
Sykes, Julie. *Little Tiger's big surprise*
Thomas, Joyce Carol. *You are my perfect baby*
Thomas, Shelley Moore. *A baby's coming to your house*
Titherington, Jeanne. *A place for Ben*
Van Leeuwen, Jean. *Benny and beautiful baby Delilah*
Vulliamy, Clara. *Ellen and Penguin and the new baby*
Waddell, Martin. *Rosie's babies*
When the teddy bears came
Wahl, Jan. *Mabel ran away with the toys*
Walters, Catherine. *Are you there, Baby Bear?*
Weeks, Sarah. *Sophie Peterman tells the truth!*
Weninger, Brigitte. *Will you mind the baby, Davy?*
Whybrow, Ian. *A baby for Grace*
Wigersma, Tanneke. *Baby brother*
Wild, Margaret. *Rosie and Tortoise*
Wilson, Karma. *What's in the egg, Little Pip?*
Woodson, Jacqueline. *Pecan pie baby*
You and me
Young, Amy. *Don't eat the baby!*
Zagwÿn, Deborah Turney. *Turtle spring*
Ziefert, Harriet. *Talk, baby!*
Waiting for baby

Family life – only child

Best, Cari. *What's so bad about being an only child?*

Family life – parents

Alko, Selina. *Daddy Christmas and Hanukkah Mama*
Anastas, Margaret. *A hug for you*
Ashman, Linda. *What could be better than this*
Baker, Roberta. *No ordinary Olive*
Ballard, Robin. *My day, your day*
Burg, Sarah Emmanuelle. *Do you still love me?*
Carlstrom, Nancy White. *Before you were born*
Cole, Joanna. *When Mommy and Daddy go to work*
Cusimano, Maryann K. *You are my I love you*
Elya, Susan Middleton. *No more, por favor*
Fearnley, Jan. *Just like you*
Feiffer, Kate. *My mom is trying to ruin my life*
Fraser, Mary Ann. *How animal babies stay safe*
Gay, Michel. *Zee is not scared*
Geras, Adèle. *My wishes for you*
Godwin, Laura. *What the baby hears*
Harper, Jamie. *Don't grown-ups ever have fun?*
Harper, Jo. *I could eat you up!*
Hest, Amy. *Mabel dancing*
Houran, Lori Haskins. *I will keep you safe and sound*
Hunter, Jana Novotny. *Little ones do*
Iijima, Geneva Cobb. *The way we do it in Japan*
Johnston, Tony. *Go track a yak*
Jonovitz, Marilyn. *Maybe, my baby*
Jordan, Deloris. *Baby blessings*
Kerley, Barbara. *You and me together*
Kirk, Daniel. *Snow family*
Kurtz, Jane. *Rain romp*
Lerman, Josh. *How to raise Mom and Dad*
Lobel, Gillian. *Does anybody love me?*
London, Jonathan. *Froggy eats out*
Lund, Deb. *Tell me my story, Mama*
McGee, Marni. *Wake up, me!*
Mack, Todd. *Princess Penelope*
Masurel, Claire. *Two homes*
Milgrim, David. *Best baby ever*
Mitchard, Jacquelyn. *Ready, set, school!*
Modarressi, Mitra. *Stay awake, Sally*
Morrow, Tara Jaye. *Mommy loves her baby; Daddy loves his baby*
Murphy, Mary. *I like it when . . .*
I like it when . . . [board book]
Numeroff, Laura Joffe. *Would I trade my parents?*
Okimoto, Jean Davies. *The White Swan express*
O'Mara, Carmel. *Good morning*
Good night
Parks, Carmen. *Farmers market*
Pedersen, Marika. *Mommy works, Daddy works*
Pow, Tom. *Who is the world for?*
Pratt, Pierre. *I see . . . my mom / I see . . . my dad*
I see . . . my sister / I see . . . my cat
Proimos, James. *Todd's TV*
Ramos, Jorge. *I'm just like my mom / Me parezco tanto a mi mamá; I'm just like my dad / Me parezco tanto a mi papá*
Ransom, Jeanie Franz. *I don't want to talk about it*
What do parents do? (. . . When you're not home)
Rau, Dana Meachen. *In the yard*
Roberts, Bethany. *Rosie to the rescue*
Robledo, Honorio. *Nico visits the moon*

Rockwell, Anne. *Two blue jays*
Root, Phyllis. *Oliver finds his way*
Rosenberg, Liz. *Nobody*
We wanted you
Ross, Michael Elsohn. *Play with me*
Schmid, Paul. *Petunia goes wild*
Spelman, Cornelia Maude. *When I miss you*
Steig, William. *Toby, who are you?*
Swinburne, Stephen R. *Safe, warm, and snug*
Tender moments in the wild
Thomas, Frances. *One day, Daddy*
Tobias, Tobi. *Wishes for you*
Wadham, Tim. *The queen of France*
Walsh, Melanie. *Living with Mom and living with Dad*
Weeks, Sarah. *My somebody special*
Without you
Weigelt, Udo. *The Easter Bunny's baby*
Wells, Rosemary. *Love waves*
Wild, Margaret. *Puffling*

Family life – same-sex parents

Newman, Lesléa. *Daddy, Papa, and me*
Heather has two mommies
Mommy, Mama, and Me
Polacco, Patricia. *In our mothers' house*
Richardson, Justin. *And Tango makes three*
Willhoite, Michael. *Daddy's roommate*

Family life – single-parent families

Beaty, Daniel. *Knock knock*
Edwards, Michelle. *Papa's latkes*
Egan, Kate. *Kate and Nate are running late!*
Moore, Genevieve. *Catherine's story*
Polacco, Patricia. *Something about Hensley's*
Schotter, Roni. *Mama, I'll give you the world*
Thomas, Eliza. *The red blanket*
Woodson, Jacqueline. *Pecan pie baby*
Zolotow, Charlotte. *A father like that*

Family life – sisters *see also* Family life; Family life – brothers & sisters; Sibling rivalry

Alcott, Louisa May. *Little women*
Alexander, Claire. *Small Florence*
Alexander, Martha G. *Nobody asked me if I wanted a baby sister*
Alter, Anna. *Estelle and Lucy*
Amato, Mary. *The chicken of the family*
Arnold, Marsha Diane. *The bravest of us all*
Auld, Mary. *My sister*
Bang, Molly. *When Sophie gets angry — really, really angry . . .*
Barasch, Lynne. *The reluctant flower girl*
Best, Cari. *Ava and the real Lucille*
Blumenthal, Deborah. *Don't let the peas touch!*
Bonwill, Ann. *Naughty toes*
Brown, Marc. *Arthur meets the president*
D. W., go to your room!
Bunting, Eve. *The days of summer*
Cole, Joanna. *I'm a big sister*, ill. by Maxie Chambliss
I'm a big sister, ill. by Rosalinda Kightley
Cox, Judy. *Carmen learns English*
Demas, Corinne. *The magic apple*
dePaola, Tomie. *The baby sister*
Ericsson, Jennifer A. *She did it!*
Figley, Marty Rhodes. *The schoolchildren's blizzard*
Fraser, Mary Ann. *Mermaid sister*
George, Kristine O'Connell. *Emma dilemma*
Graham, Bob. *April and Esme, tooth fairies*
Gritton, Steve. *The trouble with sisters and robots*
Grossman, Bill. *My little sister hugged an ape*
Gutman, Anne. *Lisa's baby sister*
Hanson, Mary Elizabeth. *The difference between babies and cookies*
Hardy, Sarah Frances. *Puzzled by pink*
Hayes, Joe. *Don't say a word, Mamá/No digas nada, Mamá*
Henkes, Kevin. *Sheila Rae, the brave*
Sheila Rae's peppermint stick
Hoban, Russell. *Best friends for Frances*
Holabird, Katharine. *Angelina's baby sister*
Jackson, Chris. *The Gaggle sisters river tour*
Jenkins, Emily. *Daffodil*
Daffodil, crocodile
Johnson, Angela. *One of three*
A sweet smell of roses
The wedding
Kassirer, Sue. *What's next, Nina?*
Keefer, Janice Kulyk. *Anna's goat*
Khan, Rukhsana. *Big red lollipop*
Kirsch, Vincent X. *Natalie and Naughtily*
Krensky, Stephen. *Sisters of Scituate Light*
Kroll, Virginia L. *Faraway drums*
Lears, Laurie. *Becky the brave*
Ling, Nancy Tupper. *My sister, Alicia May*
McCarthy, Meghan. *The adventures of Patty and the big red bus*
McCormack, Caren McNelly. *The fiesta dress*
McElmurry, Jill. *Mess pets*
Maclear, Kyo. *Virginia Wolf*
Martin, Rafe. *The rough-face girl*
Montanari, Eva. *Tiff, Taff, and Lulu*
Moore, Liz. *Zizi and Tish*
Murguia, Bethanie Deeney. *Zoe's room (no sisters allowed)*
Norling, Beth. *Sister night and sister day*
Numeroff, Laura Joffe. *The Chicken sisters*
O'Connor, Jane. *Fancy Nancy: fanciest doll in the universe*
Fancy Nancy and the fabulous fashion boutique
Orr, Wendy. *The princess and her panther*
Peterson, Jeanne Whitehouse. *Don't forget Winona*
Player, Micah. *Chloe, instead*
Plourde, Lynn. *Spring's sprung*
Pryor, Bonnie. *Amanda and April*
Merry Christmas, Amanda and April
Rheingrover, Jean Sasso. *Veronica's first year*
Rosenberg, Liz. *The carousel*
Rothenberg, Joan Keller. *Matzah ball soup*
Samuels, Barbara. *Aloha, Dolores*
Duncan and Dolores
What's so great about Cindy Snappleby?
San Souci, Robert D. *Sootface*
Schindel, John. *Frog face, my little sister and me*
Schmid, Paul. *Peanut and Fifi have a ball*
Schwartz, Amy. *Dee Dee and me*
Schwartz, Roslyn. *The mole sisters and the cool breeze*
The mole sisters and the fairy ring
The mole sisters and the piece of moss
The mole sisters and the question
The mole sisters and the rainy day
Spohn, Kate. *By word of mouse*
Stewig, John Warren. *Mother Holly*
Stroud, Bettye. *Down home at Miss Dessa's*

Tarbescu, Edith. *Annushka's voyage*
Tuck, Justin. *Home-field advantage*
Tucker, Kathy. *The seven Chinese sisters*
Viorst, Judith. *Super-completely and totally the messiest*
Waboose, Jan Bourdeau. *SkySisters*
Whybrow, Ian. *A baby for Grace*
Wilder, Laura Ingalls. *Going to town*
Wilhelm, Hans. *More bunny trouble*
Wishinsky, Frieda. *You're mean, Lily Jean!*
Yep, Laurence. *Auntie Tiger*
Dragon prince
Yezerski, Thomas. *Queen of the world*
Yum, Hyewon. *The twins' blanket*
Zehler, Antonia. *Two fine ladies*
Two fine ladies have a tiff

Family life – sons

Boelts, Maribeth. *Looking for Sleepy*
Boyd, Lizi. *I love Daddy*
I love Mommy
Braun, Sebastien. *I love my daddy*
Collins, Billy. *Daddy's little boy*
Compos, Tito. *Muffler man / El hombre mofle*
Creech, Sharon. *Fishing in the air*
Dorros, Arthur. *Papa and me*
Granowsky, Alvin. *At the park*
Jennings, Sharon. *Bearcub and Mama*
Jonovitz, Marilyn. *Good morning, Little Fox*
Krosoczka, Jarrett J. *Good night, Monkey Boy*
Lewin, Ted. *Big Jimmy's Kum Kau Chinese take out*
London, Jonathan. *Loon Lake*
Rusackas, Francesca. *Daddy all day long*
Schlessinger, Laura. *Dr. Laura Schlessinger's Growing up is hard*
Why do you love me?
Smith, Will. *Just the two of us*
Spinelli, Jerry. *My daddy and me*
Sullivan, Paula. *Todd's box*
Tarpley, Natasha Anastasia. *Bippity Bop barbershop*
Thomas, Joyce Carol. *Joy*

Family life – stepchildren *see* Divorce; Family life – stepfamilies

Family life – stepfamilies

Bennett, Kelly. *Dad and Pop*
Bullard, Lisa. *Trick-or-treat on Milton Street*
Bunting, Eve. *The memory string*
Cinderella
Climo, Shirley. *The Egyptian Cinderella*
The Korean Cinderella
The Persian Cinderella
Coburn, Jewell Reinhart. *Angkat*
Jouanah
Daly, Jude. *Fair, brown and trembling*
Day, Nancy Raines. *The lion's whiskers*
Geras, Adèle. *Sleeping beauty*
Hickox, Rebecca. *The golden sandal*
Hines, Anna Grossnickle. *When we married Gary*
Horrocks, Anita. *Silas' seven grandparents*
Levins, Sandra. *Do you sing Twinkle?*
Lowell, Susan. *Cindy Ellen*
McCaughrean, Geraldine. *Grandma Chickenlegs*
Manna, Anthony L. *The orphan*
Perrault, Charles *Cinderella,* ill. by Nicoletta Ceccoli
Cinderella, ill. by Susan Jeffers
Cinderella, ill. by Loek Koopmans
Cinderella, ill. by James Marshall
Cinderella, ill. by Barbara McClintock
Cinderella / Cenicienta
Cinderella: a pop-up fairy tale
Cinderella: or, the little glass slipper
Roberts, Lynn. *Cinderella, an Art Deco love story*
Sanderson, Ruth. *Cinderella*
San Souci, Robert D. *Cinderella Skeleton*
Little gold star
Schotter, Roni. *Room for Rabbit*
Schroeder, Alan. *Smoky Mountain Rose*
Shaskan, Trisha Speed. *Seriously, Cinderella is so annoying!*
Sierra, Judy. *The gift of the crocodile*
Stewig, John Warren. *Mother Holly*
Thomas, Joyce Carol. *The gospel Cinderella*

Family life – stepparents *see* Divorce; Family life – stepfamilies

Farms

Adler, David A. *A picture book of Cesar Chavez*
Alborough, Jez. *The gobble gobble moooooo tractor book*
Alsdurf, Phyllis. *It's milking time*
Amato, Mary. *The chicken of the family*
Ammon, Richard. *Amish horses*
Anderson, Derek. *Story county*
Anderson, Peggy Perry. *Chuck's band*
Andrews, Julie. *Dumpy the dump truck*
Arnosky, Jim. *Raccoons and ripe corn*
Ashforth, Camilla. *Willow at Christmas*
Auch, Mary Jane. *The nutquacker*
Aylesworth, Jim. *Cock-a-doodle-doo, creak, pop-pop, moo*
One crow
Baddiel, Ivor. *Cock-a-doodle quack! Quack!*
Bailey, Linda. *The farm team*
Baker, Ken. *Old MacDonald had a dragon*
Banks, Kate. *What's coming for Christmas?*
Barbour, Karen. *Mr. Williams*
Base, Graeme. *Little elephants*
Bateman, Teresa. *April foolishness*
Farm flu
Battut, Eric. *The fox and the hen*
Beaton, Clare. *Clare Beaton's farmyard rhymes*
Beaumont, Karen. *Duck, duck, goose!*
No sleep for the sheep!
Beeke, Jemma. *The Rickety Barn show*
Bibbons, Faye. *The day the picture man came*
Bilgrami, Shaheen. *Farmyard painting party*
Blackstone, Stella. *How big is a pig?*
Blades, Ann. *Mary of mile 18*
Bock, Lee. *Oh, crumps! / Ay, caramba!*
Bonning, Tony. *Fox tale soup*
Bradby, Marie. *Once upon a farm*
Bright, Robert. *Georgie*
Brown, James. *Farm*
Brown, Margaret Wise. *Christmas in the barn*
Bunting, Eve. *Hurry! Hurry!*
Burg, Sarah Emmanuelle. *One more egg*
Carle, Eric. *Dream snow*
Carlstrom, Nancy White. *The way to Wyatt's house*
Carr, Jan. *Big Truck and Little Truck*

Carter, David A. *Old MacDonald had a farm: a pop-up book*
Carter, Don. *Old MacDonald drives a tractor*
Caudill, Rebecca. *A pocketful of cricket*
Cazet, Denys. *Nothing at all*
Chaconas, Dori. *Dori the contrary hen*
Chaucer, Geoffrey. *Chanticleer and the fox*
Chernesky, Felicia Sanzari. *Pick a circle, gather squares*
Child, Lydia Maria. *Over the river and through the wood*
Over the river and through the wood: the New England boy's song about Thanksgiving Day
Chitwood, Suzanne Tanner. *Wake up, big barn!*
Church, Caroline Jayne. *Digby takes charge*
One smart goose
Ping Pong Pig
Clark, Leslie Ann. *Peepsqueak!*
Clarke, Jane. *Stuck in the mud*
Cleary, Beverly. *The hullabaloo ABC*
Cocca-Leffler, Maryann. *A vacation for Pooch*
Colato Laínez, René. *Señor Pancho had a rancho*
Cooper, Elisha. *Farm*
Cordsen, Carol Foskett. *Market day*
Cousins, Lucy. *Maisy at the farm*
Maisy's farm
Maisy's morning on the farm
Cowley, Joy. *Mrs. Wishy-Washy's Christmas*
Craig, Lindsey. *Farmyard beat*
Crisp, Marty. *Black and white*
Cronin, Doreen. *Click, clack, boo!*
Click, clack, moo
Click, clack, quackity-quack
Click, clack, splish, splash
Dooby dooby moo
Duck for President
Giggle, giggle, quack
Thump, quack, moo
Crum, Shutta. *My mountain song*
Thunder-Boomer!
Crunk, Tony. *Grandpa's overalls*
Cummins, Julie. *Country kid, city kid*
Czekaj, Jef. *Oink-a-doodle-moo*
Dalgleish, Sharon. *Working dogs*
Dallas-Conte, Juliet. *Cock-a-moo-moo*
Deady, Kathleen W. *It's time!*
De Beer, Hans. *Oh no, Ono!*
Dodd, Emma. *Dog's noisy day*
Meow said the cow
Doepker, David. *Farm babies*
Donaldson, Julia. *What the ladybug heard*
Dorros, Arthur. *Radio Man / Don Radio*
Tonight is carnaval
Douglas, Erin. *Get that pest!*
Downey, Lynn. *The flea's sneeze*
Doyle, Malachy. *Cow*
Horse
Duffield, Katy. *Farmer McPeepers and his missing milk cows*
Dunrea, Olivier. *Gideon*
Duvoisin, Roger Antoine. *Petunia*
Edwards, David. *The pen that Pa built*
Edwards, Pamela Duncan. *The grumpy morning*
McGillycuddy could
Egan, Tim. *Serious farm*
Ehlert, Lois. *Market day*
Elliot, David. *Henry's map*
Elliott, David. *On the farm*
Ets, Marie Hall. *Mister Penny*
Mr. Penny's race horse
Ewart, Claire. *The giant*
The farmer in the dell. *The farmer in the dell*, ill. by John O'Brien
The farmer in the dell, ill. by Alexandra Wallner
Faulkner, Keith. *Do you have my quack?*
Fernandes, Eugenie. *Busy little mouse*
Kitten's spring
Fisher, Carolyn. *A twisted tale*
Fitz-Gibbon, Sally. *On Uncle John's farm*
Flanagan, Alice K. *Farmers*
Flying an agricultural plane with Mr. Miller
Raising cows on the Koebels' farm
A visit to the Gravesens' farm
The Zieglers and their apple orchard
Fleming, Denise. *Barnyard banter*
Flynn, Kitson. *Carrot in my pocket*
Fox, Mem. *Hattie and the fox*
Friend, Catherine. *The perfect nest*
Galdone, Paul. *Cat goes fiddle-i-fee*
Garelli, Cristina. *Farm friends clean up*
Garland, Michael. *Grandpa's tractor*
Geisert, Arthur. *Country road ABC*
Nursery crimes
Gershator, Phillis. *Moo, moo, brown cow! Have you any milk?*
Who's in the farmyard?
Gibbons, Gail. *Farming*
The milk makers
Gibbs, Edward. *I spy on the farm*
Godwin, Laura. *One moon, two cats*
Golan, Avirama. *Little Naomi, Little Chick*
Golson, Terry. *Tillie lays an egg*
Gottfried, Maya. *Our farm*
Gourley, Robbin. *Bring me some apples and I'll make you a pie*
Greene, Rhonda Gowler. *Barnyard song*
Hader, Berta Hoerner. *Cock-a-doodle doo*
Hall, Donald. *Ox-cart man*
Hall, Margaret. *Corn*
Peanuts
Hamilton, Martha. *The hidden feast*
Hamilton, Virginia. *Drylongso*
Harper, Jessica. *A place called Kindergarten*
Harrington, Janice N. *The chicken-chasing queen of Lamar County*
Hayles, Marsha. *A pet of a pet*
Hayward, Linda. *The King's chorus*
Heinz, Brian J. *Red Fox at McCloskey's farm*
Helakoski, Leslie. *Big chickens*
Big chickens fly the coop
Helquist, Brett. *Grumpy Goat*
Hester, Denia Lewis. *Grandma Lena's big ol' turnip*
Hill, Eric. *Spot goes to the farm*
Spot on the farm
Hillenbrand, Will. *Fiddle-i-fee*
Himmelman, John. *Chickens to the rescue*
Cows to the rescue
Pigs to the rescue
Hindley, Judy. *Does a cow say boo?*
Hobbie, Holly. *Everything but the horse*
Holub, Joan. *Pumpkin countdown*
Hopkinson, Deborah. *Bluebird summer*
Hulme, Joy N. *Easter babies*
Huneck, Stephen. *Sally goes to the farm*
Huntington, Amy. *One Monday*
Hurd, Thacher. *Moo Cow Kaboom!*
Hutchins, Pat. *Barn dance!*
Bumpety bump

Rosie's walk
Rosie's walk [board book]
Isadora, Rachel. *Old Mikamba had a farm*
Jaspersohn, William. *The two brothers*
Jeppson, Ann-Sofie. *Here comes Pontus*
Johnson, D. B. *Four legs bad, two legs good!*
Johnson, Paul Brett. *The cow who wouldn't come down*
Johnston, Tony. *Farmer Mack measures his pig*
Joosse, Barbara. *Higgledy-piggledy chicks*
Jordan, Mary Ellen. *Lazy Daisy, cranky Frankie*
Kalz, Jill. *An a-maze-ing farm adventure*
Katz, Jon. *Lenore finds a friend*
Meet the dogs of Bedlam Farm
Kelly, Mij. *A bed of your own!*
Where's my darling daughter?
Kimmel, Haven. *Orville, a dog story*
Kinsey-Warnock, Natalie. *A Christmas like Helen's*
A farm of her own
From dawn till dusk
Nora's ark
When spring comes
Klingel, Cynthia Fitterer. *Farmers*
Krilanovich, Nadia. *Chicken, chicken, duck!*
Krosoczka, Jarrett J. *Punk Farm*
Punk Farm on tour
Krupinski, Loretta. *Pirate treasure*
Laminack, Lester L. *Three hens and a peacock*
Landman, Tanya. *Mary's penny*
Lavis, Steve. *On the farm*
Lee, Huy Voun. *In the leaves*
Lesser, Carolyn. *What a wonderful day to be a cow*
Lester, Alison. *Noni the pony*
Lewis, Kim. *Emma's lamb*
First snow
Friends
Just like Floss
Little Baa
Little calf
Little lamb
Little puppy
Lewison, Wendy Cheyette. *Going to sleep on the farm*
Lindbergh, Reeve. *The day the goose got loose*
Midnight farm
Lionni, Leo. *Six crows*
The little red hen. *The little red hen*, ill. by Byron Barton
The little red hen, ill. by Emily Bolam
The little red hen, ill. by Paul Galdone
Little red hen
The little red hen, ill. by Jerry Pinkney
The little red hen, ill. by Kate Slater
The little red hen, ill. by Annie West
The little red hen, ill. by Margot Zemach
The Little Red Hen makes a pizza
London, Jonathan. *Like butter on pancakes*
Long, Loren. *Otis*
Otis and the puppy
Otis and the tornado
An Otis Christmas
Lottridge, Celia Barker. *Berta, a remarkable dog*
Loupy, Christophe. *Wiggles*
Maccarone, Grace. *Oink! moo! how do you do?*
McDonnell, Flora. *I love animals*
McFarlane, Sheryl. *On the farm*
McGee, Marni. *The noisy farm*
McGill, Alice. *Molly Bannaky*
McGrath, Barbara Barbieri. *The little gray bunny*
MacLachlan, Patricia. *All the places to love*
McPhail, David. *Farm morning*
McQuade, Jacqueline. *Farm babies*
Maguire, Gregory. *Crabby Cratchitt*
Maitland, Barbara. *Moo in the morning*
Manning, Mick. *Cock-a-doodle hooooooo!*
Mansfield, Howard. *Hogwood steps out*
Marciano, John Bemelmans. *Delilah*
Marshall, Linda Elovitz. *The passover lamb*
Martin, Bill, Jr. *Chicken Chuck*
Martín, Hugo C. *Pablo's Christmas*
Martin, Jacqueline Briggs. *Chicken joy on Redbean Road*
Mayr, Diane. *Out and about at the apple orchard*
Milgrim, David. *Young MacDonald*
Miller, Heather. *My chickens*
My goats
My horses
My pigs
Miller, Ruth. *I went to the farm*
Milord, Susan. *The ghost on the hearth*
Milway, Katie Smith. *Cappuccina goes to town*
Minor, Wendell. *My farm friends*
Mitter, Matt. *1, 2, 3, counting rhymes*
Mitton, Tony. *Farmer Joe and the music show*
Mortensen, Denise Dowling. *Ohio thunder*
Moser, Lisa. *Railroad Hank*
Moses, Will. *Mary and her little lamb*
Most, Bernard. *Cock-a-doodle-moo!*
Moulton, Mark Kimball. *The very best pumpkin*
Mozelle, Shirley. *The pig is in the pantry, the cat is on the shelf*
Murphy, Andy. *Out and about at the dairy farm*
Murphy, Mary. *How kind*
My first farm
Nelson, Kristin L. *Farm tractors*
Newton, Jill. *Crash bang donkey!*
Nikola-Lisa, W. *Summer sun risin'*
Nolen, Jerdine. *Harvey Potter's balloon farm*
Raising dragons
Numeroff, Laura Joffe. *The Chicken sisters*
Old MacDonald had a farm. *Old MacDonald*
Old MacDonald had a farm, ill. by Holly Berry
Old MacDonald had a farm, ill. by Jane Cabrera
Old MacDonald had a farm, ill. by Carol Jones
Old MacDonald had a farm, ill. by Tracey Campbell Pearson
Old MacDonald had a farm, ill. by Glen Rounds
Old MacDonald had a farm, ill. by Jessica Souhami
Old MacDonald had a farm, ill. by Prue Theobalds
Oller, Erika. *The cabbage soup solution*
Ormerod, Jan. *Ms. MacDonald has a class*
Otto, Carolyn. *That sky, that rain*
Oxley, Jennifer. *The chicken problem*
Palatini, Margie. *The cheese*
Oink?
The web files
Parish, Herman. *Amelia Bedelia's first field trip*
Peet, Bill. *Cock-a-doodle Dudley*
Pelletier, Andrew T. *The toy farmer*
Perrin, Martine. *Cock-a-doodle who?*
Peterson, Cris. *Extra cheese, please!*
Fantastic farm machines
Peterson, Mary. *Piggies in the pumpkin patch*
Pfeffer, Wendy. *The big flood*
Phillips, Mildred. *And the cow said, "moo"!*
Piers, Helen. *Who's in my bed?*
Pinkney, Gloria Jean. *Back home*

The Sunday outing
Pipe, Jim. *Farm animals*
Plourde, Lynn. *Field trip day*
Only cows allowed!
Polacco, Patricia. *Just plain Fancy*
Potter, Beatrix. *The tale of Peter Rabbit*
Prigger, Mary Skillings. *Aunt Minnie and the twister*
Provensen, Alice. *The year at Maple Hill Farm*
Purmell, Ann. *Apple cider making days*
Christmas tree farm
Puttock, Simon. *Yours truly, Louisa*
Ransom, Candice F. *Tractor day*
Reed, Lynn Rowe. *Thelonius Turkey lives!*
Regan, Dian Curtis. *Barnyard slam*
Reynolds, Aaron. *Chicks and salsa*
Reynolds, Adrian. *Pete and Polo's farmyard adventure*
Reynolds, Marilynn. *The new land*
The prairie fire
Robart, Rose. *The cake that Mack ate*
Robbins, Ken. *Apples*
Rogers, Hal. *Combines*
Milking machines
Plows
Root, Phyllis. *What Baby wants*
Rossiter, Nan Parson. *Sugar on snow*
Roth, Carol. *Where's my mommy?*
Ryder, Joanne. *Dance by the light of the moon*
Rylant, Cynthia. *Scarecrow*
Sadler, Judy Ann. *Sandwiches for Duke*
Sage, James. *Farmer Smart's fat cat*
Sandburg, Carl. *From daybreak to good night*
The Huckabuck family and how they raised popcorn in Nebraska and quit and came back
Santoro, Scott. *Farm-fresh cats*
Schnur, Steven. *Spring thaw*
Schomp, Virginia. *If you were a . . . farmer*
Schubert, Leda. *Feeding the sheep*
Schuh, Mari C. *Chickens on the farm*
Cows on the farm
Pigs on the farm
Sheep on the farm
Selsam, Millicent E. *Keep looking!*
Shannon, George. *Turkey Tot*
Shapiro, Jody Fickes. *Up, up, up! It's apple-picking time*
Sillifant, Alec. *Farmer Ham*
Silvano, Wendi. *Turkey trouble*
Simmons, Jane. *Daisy and the Beastie*
Simont, Marc. *The goose that almost got cooked*
Sloat, Teri. *Farmer Brown goes round and round*
Farmer Brown shears his sheep
Spinelli, Eileen. *Princess Pig*
Silly Tilly
Staines, Bill. *All God's critters*
Steffensmeier, Alexander. *Millie and the big rescue*
Millie waits for the mail
Stevens, Jan Romero. *Carlos and the skunk / Carlos y el zorrillo*
Stevens, Janet. *Find a cow now!*
Stevenson, James. *"Could be worse!"*
Stewig, John Warren. *Making plum jam*
Stiegemeyer, Julie. *Gobble gobble crash!*
Stinson, Kathy. *A pocket can have a treasure in it*
Stockland, Patricia M. *In the horse stall*
In the pig pen
In the sheep pasture
Stoeke, Janet Morgan. *Hide and seek*
The Loopy Coop hens
Pip's trip
Stone, Lynn M. *Farm buildings*
Farms old and new
Strete, Craig Kee. *How the Indians bought the farm*
Stroud, Bettye. *Dance y'all*
Stuchner, Joan Betty. *Can hens give milk?*
Stutson, Caroline. *Prairie primer A to Z*
Sweet, Melissa. *Fiddle-i-fee*
Sykes, Julie. *Dora's eggs*
This and that
Taback, Simms. *Simms Taback's farm animals*
Tafuri, Nancy. *Blue goose*
Early morning in the barn
This is the farmer
Who's counting?
Teague, Mark. *Funny farm*
Terasaki, Stanley Todd. *Ghosts for breakfast*
Thermes, Jennifer. *Sam Bennett's new shoes*
Thomas, Jane Resh. *Lights on the river*
Thompson, Lauren. *Wee little chick*
Tolstoy, Aleksey Nikolayevich. *The enormous turnip*
The gigantic turnip
Tresselt, Alvin R. *Sun up*
Wake up, farm!
Tricarico, Christine. *Cock-a-doodle dance!*
Tudor, Tasha. *Pumpkin moonshine*
Turner, Ann Warren. *Dakota dugout*
Vagin, Vladimir. *The enormous carrot*
Vamos, Samantha R. *The cazuela that the farm maiden stirred*
Van Eerbeek. *The world of farm animals*
Van Fleet, Matthew. *Moo*
Van Leeuwen, Jean. *Chicken soup*
The strange adventures of Blue Dog
Verboven, Agnes. *Ducks like to swim*
Waddell, Martin. *Farmer Duck*
Tom Rabbit
Wallace, Nancy Elizabeth. *Apples, apples, apples*
Pumpkin day
Ward, Helen. *The rooster and the fox*
Watterson, Carol. *An edible alphabet*
Wellington, Monica. *Apple farmer Annie*
Westcott, Nadine Bernard. *Skip to my Lou*
There's a hole in the bucket
White, Linda. *Too many turkeys*
Whybrow, Ian. *Faraway farm*
Wild, Margaret. *Piglet and Granny*
Piglet and Mama
Piglet and Papa
Wiley, Thom. *One sheep, blue sheep*
Williams, Linda. *Horse in the pigpen*
Wilson, Karma. *The cow loves cookies*
Hogwash!
Horseplay
Wood, Jakki. *Moo moo, brown cow*
Never say boo to a goose!
Wormell, Mary. *Hilda Hen's happy birthday*
Hilda Hen's search
Why not?
Wright, Maureen. *Barnyard fun*
Yolen, Jane. *Harvest home*
Jane Yolen's Old MacDonald songbook
Raising Yoder's barn
Yoon, Salina. *Do cows meow?*
Zarins, Kim. *The helpful puppy*
Ziefert, Harriet. *I swapped my dog*
Pumpkin Pie
What do ducks dream?

Feathers

Piven, Hanoch. *The perfect purple feather*

Feeling *see* Senses – touch

Feelings *see* Emotions

Fidgeting *see* Behavior – fidgeting

Fighting, arguing *see* Behavior – fighting, arguing

Fingers *see* Anatomy – hands

Finishing things *see* Character traits – completing things

Fire

Beaver steals fire
Bourgeois, Paulette. *Fire fighters*
Cash, Rosanne. *Penelope Jane*
Cuyler, Margery. *Stop drop and roll*
Demarest, Chris L. *Firefighters A to Z*
Hotshots!
Dubois, Muriel L. *Out and about at the fire station*
Ehlert, Lois. *Cuckoo, a Mexican folktale / Cucú: un cuento folklórico mexicano*
Elya, Susan Middleton. *Fire! ¡Fuego! Brave bomberos*
Emergency!
Flanagan, Alice K. *Ms. Murphy fights fires*
Griessman, Annette. *The fire*
Hayward, Linda. *A day in the life of a firefighter*
Hoberman, Mary Ann. *Mrs. O'Leary's cow*
Jacobs, Paul DuBois. *Fire drill*
Kaufman, Jeanne. *Young Henry and the dragon*
Klingel, Cynthia Fitterer. *Firefighters*
Liebman, Daniel. *I want to be a firefighter*
London, Jonathan. *Little lost tiger*
Markle, Sandra. *Finding home*
Martin, Bill, Jr. *Fire! Fire! said Mrs. McGuire*
"Fire! Fire!" said Mrs. McGuire
Nelson, S. D. *The Star People*
Nez, John. *One smart Cookie*
Nobisso, Josephine. *John Blair and the great Hinckley fire*
Nolan, Janet. *The firehouse light*
Owen, Ann. *Protecting your home*
Pendziwol, Jean E. *No dragons for tea*
Polacco, Patricia. *Tikvah means hope*
Rex, Michael. *My fire engine*
Reynolds, Marilynn. *The prairie fire*
Roberts, Bethany. *Gramps and the fire dragon*
Sandburg, Carl. *The Huckabuck family and how they raised popcorn in Nebraska and quit and came back*
Spinelli, Eileen. *Hero cat*
Thompson, Colin. *Unknown*
Uhlberg, Myron. *The printer*
Van Laan, Nancy. *Rainbow crow*
Wilson, Gina. *Ignis*
Yee, Wong Herbert. *Fireman Small*
Fireman Small, fire down below
Fireman Small to the rescue

Fire engines *see* Careers – firefighters; Trucks

Fish

Aliki. *The long lost coelacanth and other living fossils*
My visit to the aquarium
Arenson, Roberta. *Manu and the talking fish*
Arnosky, Jim. *Crinkleroot's 25 fish every child should know*
Aruego, José. *Weird friends*
Asch, Frank. *Moonbear's pet*
Bennett, Kelly. *Not Norman*
Berger, Melvin. *Dive! a book of deep sea creatures*
Blackstone, Stella. *Secret seahorse*
Secret seahorse [board book]
Buckingham, Matt. *Bright Stanley*
Bunting, Eve. *Finn McCool and the great fish*
Gleam and Glow
Cannon, A. E. *Sophie's fish*
Clements, Andrew. *Big Al and Shrimpy*
Cook, Bernadine. *The little fish that got away*
Cousins, Lucy. *Hooray for fish!*
Curious George goes to the aquarium
Dahl, Michael. *One giant splash*
Diesen, Deborah. *The pout-pout fish*
The pout-pout fish in the big-big dark
DiPucchio, Kelly. *Gilbert goldfish wants a pet*
Donaldson, Julia. *The fish who cried wolf*
Donovan, Gail. *The copycat fish*
A fishy story
Hidden treasures
Lost at sea
Ehlert, Lois. *Fish eyes*
Elschner, Geraldine. *Fritz's fish*
Eure, Wesley. *A fish out of water*
Foreman, Michael. *Friends*
Freedman, Deborah. *The Story of Fish and Snail*
Galloway, Ruth. *Fidgety fish*
Geist, Ken. *The three little fish and the big bad shark*
Goldfinger, Jennifer P. *A fish named Spot*
Grant, Joan. *Cat and Fish*
Harris, Trudy. *Pattern fish*
Hendra, Sue. *Barry, the fish with fingers*
Hodge, Deborah. *Salmon*
Hout, Mies van. *Happy*
Howe, James. *Otter and odder*
Jonas, Ann. *Splash!*
Kalan, Robert. *Blue sea*
Klassen, Jon. *This is not my hat*
Krykorka, Ian. *Carl, the Christmas carp*
Lamb, Rosy. *Paul meets Bernadette*
LaReau, Kara. *Ugly fish*
LeBox, Annette. *Salmon Creek*
Lerch. *Swim! swim!*
Lionni, Leo. *Fish is fish*
Swimmy
Little old lady who swallowed a fly. *There was an old pirate who swallowed a fish*
London, Jonathan. *Where the big fish are*
MacDonald, Suse. *Fish, swish! splash, dash!*
McGaw, Wayne T. *T-boy of the bayou*
Martin, David. *Piggy and Dad go fishing*
Nelson, Robin. *Pet fish*
Pallotta, Jerry. *Dory story*
Paulsen, Gary. *Canoe days*
Pfeffer, Wendy. *What's it like to be a fish?*

Pfister, Marcus. *Good night, little rainbow fish*
The rainbow fish
Rainbow fish ABC
Rainbow fish and the big blue whale
Rainbow fish and the sea monsters' cave
Rainbow fish to the rescue!
Poydar, Nancy. *Fish school*
Prosek, James. *Bird, butterfly, eel*
Raschka, Chris. *Arlene sardine*
Rechner, Amy. *Out and about at the aquarium*
Rohmann, Eric. *Clara and Asha*
Sauer, Tammi. *Nugget and Fang*
Sayre, April Pulley. *Trout are made of trees*
Trout, trout, trout
Schwartz, Amy. *A beautiful girl*
Seuss, Dr. *McElligot's pool*
Shannon, David. *Jangles*
Shields, Gillian. *Dogfish*
Sill, Cathryn. *About fish*
Simeon, Jean-Pierre. *This is a poem that heals fish*
Sloat, Teri. *There was an old lady who swallowed a trout*
Stevenson, James. *Which one is Whitney?*
Stockdale, Susan. *Fabulous Fishes*
Suzuki, David. *Salmon forest*
Toft, Kim Michelle. *One less fish*
Van Laan, Nancy. *Little Fish lost*
Waber, Bernard. *Lorenzo*
Weeks, Sarah. *Catfish Kate and the sweet swamp band*
Winkelman, Barbara Gaines. *Puffer's surprise*
Sockeye's journey home
Wood, Audrey. *Ten little fish*
Wright, Catherine. *Steamboat Annie and the thousand-pound catfish*
Yaccarino, Dan. *The birthday fish*
Yoo, Taeeun. *The little red fish*
Yorinks, Arthur. *Louis the fish*

Fish – seahorses

Blackstone, Stella. *Secret seahorse*
Secret seahorse [board book]
Butterworth, Chris. *Sea horse*
Curtis, Jennifer Keats. *Seahorses*
Damjan, Mischa. *The little seahorse and the Christmas pearl*
Freymann, Saxton. *One lonely seahorse*

Fish – sharks

Arnold, Caroline. *Giant shark*
Barton, Chris. *Shark vs. train*
Clarke, Ginjer L. *Sharks!*
Clarke, Jane. *Gilbert the hero*
Cox, Phil Roxbee. *Shark in the park*
Diffily, Deborah. *Jurassic shark*
Geist, Ken. *The three little fish and the big bad shark*
Gentle, Victor. *Baby sharks*
Killer sharks, killer people
Shark camouflage and armor
Very big sharks
The world's strangest shark
Gibbons, Gail. *Sharks*
Griff. *Shark-mad Stanley*
Hale, Bruce. *Clark the Shark*
Mahy, Margaret. *The great white man-eating shark*
Markle, Sandra. *Sharks: biggest! littlest!*
Martin, Rafe. *The Shark God*
O'Brien, Patrick. *Megatooth*
Pfister, Marcus. *Rainbow fish to the rescue!*
Reynolds, Aaron. *Carnivores*
Rockwell, Anne. *Little shark*
Sabuda, Robert. *Encyclopedia prehistorica: sharks and other seamonsters*
Sauer, Tammi. *Nugget and Fang*
Schwarz, Viviane. *Shark and Lobster's amazing undersea adventure*
Sharratt, Nick. *Shark in the park*
Shea, Bob. *I'm a shark*
Troll, Ray. *Sharkabet*
Ward, Nick. *Don't eat the babysitter!*

Fitness *see* Health & fitness

Flags

Bartoletti, Susan Campbell. *The flag maker*
Cohan, George M. *You're a grand old flag*
Green, Stephanie. *Betsy Ross and the silver thimble*
White, Becky. *Betsy Ross*

Flattery *see* Character traits – flattery

Flowers

Alda, Arlene. *Morning glory Monday*
Appelt, Kathi. *Miss Lady Bird's wildflowers*
Bardill, Linard. *The great golden thing*
Blackstone, Stella. *What's this?*
Blossom tales
Bruce, Lisa. *Fran's flower*
Bunting, Eve. *Flower garden*
Sunflower house
Cooney, Barbara. *Miss Ramphius*
dePaola, Tomie. *The legend of the bluebonnet*
The legend of the Indian paintbrush
Eclare, Melanie. *A handful of sunshine*
Ehlert, Lois. *Planting a rainbow*
Ellwand, David. *Cinderlily*
Elschner, Geraldine. *Max's magic seeds*
Ford, Miela. *Sunflower*
Foreman, Michael. *Mia's story*
Gerber, Carole. *Spring blossoms*
Heller, Ruth. *The reason for a flower*
Himmelman, John. *A dandelion's life*
Hines, Anna Grossnickle. *Miss Emma's wild garden*
Hoban, Julia. *Amy loves the sun*
Holmes, Anita. *Flowers and friends*
Karon, Jan. *The trellis and the seed*
Lee-Tai, Amy. *A place where sunflowers grow / Sabaku ni saita himawari*
Lin, Grace. *The ugly vegetables*
Lind, Michael. *Bluebonnet girl*
Lobel, Anita. *Alison's zinnia*
Louie, Therese On. *Raymond's perfect present*
McMillan, Bruce. *Counting wildflowers*
Marshall, Janet Perry. *A honey of a day*
Maurer, Tracy. *Growing flowers*
Milne, A. A. *The magic hill*
Murphy, Mary. *Koala and the flower*
Noda, Takayo. *Song of the flowers*
Park, Linda Sue. *What does Bunny see?*
Pfister, Marcus. *Ava's poppy*
Pomeroy, Diana. *Wildflower ABC*
Posada, Mia. *Dandelions, stars in the grass*
Preller, James. *Cardinal and sunflower*

Ramirez, Melissa Bourbon. *The flight of the sunflower*
Rawlinson, Julia. *Fletcher and the springtime blossoms*
Reynolds, Peter H. *Rose's garden*
Rockwell, Anne. *Bumblebee, bumblebee, do you know me?*
My spring robin
Schaefer, Lola M. *This is the sunflower*
Stephens, J. Moria. *Persephone, the ladybug*
Swanson, Susan Marie. *To be like the sun*
Tamar, Erika. *The garden of happiness*
Taylor, Sean. *Huck runs amuck!*
Trimble, Marcia. *Flower Green*
Waber, Bernard. *A lion named Shirley Williamson*
Wallace, Nancy Elizabeth. *Paperwhite*
Wellington, Monica. *Zinnia's flower garden*
Wood, Audrey. *Birdsong*
When the root children wake up

Flowers – roses

Edwards, Pamela Duncan. *Rosie's roses*
Hooks, William H. *The legend of the Christmas rose*
Valentina, Marina. *Lost in the roses*
Wood, Douglas. *Aunt Mary's rose*

Fold-out books *see* Format, unusual – toy & movable books

Folk & fairy tales

Aardema, Verna. *Anansi does the impossible!*
Anansi finds a fool
Bimwili and the Zimwi
Borreguita and the coyote
Bringing the rain to Kapiti Plain
Half-a-ball-of-kenki
Jackal's flying lesson
Ji-nongo-nongo means riddles
Koi and the kola nuts
The lonely lioness and the ostrich chicks
Misoso
Oh, Kojo! How could you!
Pedro and the padre
Princess Gorilla and a new kind of water
The riddle of the drum
Sebgugugu the glutton
Traveling to Tondo
The vingananee and the tree toad
Who's in Rabbit's house?
Why mosquitoes buzz in people's ears
Ada, Alma Flor. *Dear Peter Rabbit*
The rooster who went to his uncle's wedding
Aesop. *Aesop's fables*, ill. by Piet Grobler
Aesop's fables, ill. by Michael Hague
Aesop's fables, ill. by Heidi Holder
Aesop's fables, ill. by Martin Jarrie
Aesop's fables, ill. by Jerry Pinkney
Aesop's fables, ill. by Fulvio Testa
Androcles and the lion, ill. by Dennis Nolan
Androcles and the lion, ill. by Janet Stevens
Androcles and the lion: and other Aesop fables
Animal fables from Aesop
Anno's Aesop
The ant and the grasshopper, ill. by Amy Lowry Poole
The ant and the grasshopper, ill. by Sara Rojo
Bat's big game
Belling the cat
Belling the cat and other Aesop fables
The best of Aesop's fables
The boy who cried wolf
The contest between the Sun and the Wind
The country mouse and the city mouse
The crow and the pitcher
Doctor Coyote
The dog and the wolf
Fables from Aesop
Feed me!
The fox and the grapes
Fox tails
The goose that laid the golden egg
The hare and the tortoise, ill. by Paul Galdone
The hare and the tortoise, ill. by Carol Jones
The hare and the tortoise, ill. by Helen Ward
The hare and the tortoise / La liebre y la tortuga
The lion and the mouse, ill. by Lisa McCue
The lion and the mouse, ill. by Sara Rojo
The lion and the mouse, ill. by Bernadette Watts
The lion and the mouse and other Aesop fables
Milly and Tilly
Mouse and lion
The race
Road signs
Smog, the city dog
Three Aesop fox fables
The tortoise and the hare, ill. by Jerry Pinkney
The tortoise and the hare, ill. by Sara Rojo
The tortoise and the hare: an Aesop fable
The town mouse and the country mouse, ill. by Lorinda Bryan Cauley
The town mouse and the country mouse, ill. by Janet Stevens
The town mouse and the country mouse: an Aesop fable, ill. by Helen Ward
The town mouse and the country mouse: an Aesop fable, ill. by Bernadette Watts
Town mouse, country mouse, ill. by Jan Brett
Town mouse, country mouse, ill. by Carol Jones
The wolf in sheep's clothing
Ahlberg, Allan. *The Goldilocks variations*
Previously
Ahmed, Said Salah. *The lion's share / Qayb Libaax*
Aleichem, Sholem. *Hanukah money*
Alger, Leclaire Gowans. *All in the morning early*
Always room for one more
Aliki. *Three gold pieces*
The twelve months
Allen, Debbie. *Brothers of the knight*
Alley, Zoe B. *There's a princess in the palace*
There's a wolf at the door
Alvarez, Julia. *The secret footprints*
Andersen, Hans Christian. *The dinosaur's new clothes*
The emperor's new clothes, ill. by Angela Barrett
The emperor's new clothes, ill. by Virginia Lee Burton
The emperor's new clothes, ill. by Robert Byrd
The emperor's new clothes, ill. by Serena Curmi
The emperor's new clothes, ill. by Charlene DeLage
The emperor's new clothes, ill. by Jack Delano
The emperor's new clothes, ill. by Anne Rockwell
The emperor's new clothes, ill. by Janet Stevens
The emperor's new clothes, ill. by Eve Tharlet
The emperor's new clothes: a tale set in China
The fir tree, ill. by Diane Goode
The fir tree, ill. by Bernadette Watts

It's perfectly true!
The little match girl, ill. by Rachel Isadora
The little match girl, ill. by Blair Lent
The little match girl, ill. by Jerry Pinkney
The little matchstick girl
The little mermaid, ill. by Charlene Delage
The little mermaid, ill. by Michael Hague
The little mermaid, ill. by Rachel Isadora
The nightingale, ill. by Nancy Ekholm Burkert
The nightingale, ill. by Pirkko Vainio
The nightingale, ill. by Lisbeth Zwerger
The princess and the pea, ill. by Emily Bolam
The princess and the pea, ill. by Charlene Delage
The princess and the pea, ill. by Dorothée Duntze
The princess and the pea, ill. by Maja Dusíková
The princess and the pea, ill. by Paul Galdone
The princess and the pea, ill. by Rachel Isadora
The princess and the pea, ill. by Bernhard Oberdieck
The princess and the pea, ill. by Janet Stevens
The princess and the pea, ill. by Alain Vaës
The princess and the pea in miniature
The snow queen, ill. by Angela Barrett
The snow queen, ill. by Sally Holmes
The snow queen, ill. by Susan Jeffers
The snow queen: a retelling of the fairy tale
The steadfast tin soldier, ill. by Jen Corace
The steadfast tin soldier, ill. by Charlene Delage
The steadfast tin soldier, ill. by Paul Galdone
The steadfast tin soldier, ill. by Rachel Isadora
The steadfast tin soldier, ill. by P. J. Lynch
The steadfast tin soldier, ill. by Fred Marcellino
The swineherd
Sylvia Long's Thumbelina
Thumbelina, ill. by Charlene Delage
Thumbelina, ill. by Demi
Thumbelina, ill. by Arlene Graston
Thumbelina, ill. by Bagram Ibatoulline
Thumbelina, ill. by Susan Jeffers
Thumbelina, ill. by Lauren A. Mills
Thumbeline
The tinderbox, ill. by Warwick Hutton
The tinderbox, ill. by Bagram Ibatoulline
The tinderbox, ill. by Barry Moser
The ugly duckling, ill. by Adrienne Adams
The ugly duckling, ill. by Sebastien Braun
The ugly duckling, ill. by Lorinda Bryan Cauley
The ugly duckling, ill. by Charlene Delage
The ugly duckling, ill. by Robert Ingpen
The ugly duckling, ill. by Rachel Isadora
The ugly duckling, ill. by Steve Johnson
The ugly duckling, ill. by Jerry Pinkney
The ugly duckling, ill. by Meilo So
The ugly duckling, ill. by Pirkko Vainio
The ugly duckling, ill. by Bernadette Watts
The ugly duckling, ill. by Roberta Wilson
The wild swans, ill. by Anne Yvonne Gilbert
The wild swans, ill. by Susan Jeffers
The woman with the eggs
Arabian Nights. *The tale of Ali Baba and the forty thieves*
Arenson, Roberta. *Manu and the talking fish*
Arnold, Katya. *That apple is mine!*
Artell, Mike. *Petite Rouge*
Asbjørnsen, P. C. *The three billy goats Gruff*, ill. by Stephen Carpenter
The three billy goats Gruff, ill. by Paul Galdone
The three billy goats Gruff, ill. by Glen Rounds
The three billy goats Gruff, ill. by Janet Stevens
Asch, Frank. *Ziggy Piggy and the three little pigs*
Auch, Mary Jane. *Chickerella*
The princess and the pizza
Aylesworth, Jim. *The full belly bowl*
The mitten
Baker, Olaf. *Where the buffaloes begin*
Balcziak, Bill. *John Henry*
Balducci, Rita. *Little Bear's timeless tales*
Balian, Lorna. *Leprechauns never lie*
Balouch, Kristen. *The king and the three thieves*
Bang, Molly. *Dawn*
The paper crane
Wiley and the hairy man
Bar-el, Dan. *Such a prince*
Bateman, Teresa. *Harp o' gold*
Leprechaun gold
The princesses have a ball
Traveling Tom and the leprechaun
Bateson-Hill, Margaret. *Masha and the firebird*
Batt, Tanya Robyn. *The faerie's gift*
Baylor, Byrd. *The desert is theirs*
The way to start a day
Beaver steals fire
Bedard, Michael. *The wolf of Gubbio*
Beeler, Selby B. *Throw your tooth on the roof*
Begin, Mary Jane. *The sorcerer's apprentice*
Belting, Natalia Maree. *The sun is a golden earring*
Bennett, Jill. *Teeny tiny*
Berger, Barbara. *All the way to Lhasa*
Grandfather Twilight
Bianco, Margery Williams. *The velveteen rabbit*, ill. by David Jorgensen
The velveteen rabbit, ill. by Thea Kliros
The velveteen rabbit, ill. by Komako Sakai
The velveteen rabbit, ill. by Gennady Spirin
The velveteen rabbit: or, How toys became real, ill. by Allen Atkinson
The velveteen rabbit: or, How toys became real, ill. by Steve Johnson
Birdseye, Tom. *Look out, Jack! The giant is back*
Soap! Soap! Don't forget the soap!
Bishop, Claire Huchet. *The five Chinese brothers*
Blossom tales
Bodkin, Odds. *The crane wife*
Bonning, Tony. *Fox tale soup*
Bower, Tamara. *The shipwrecked sailor*
Braun, Eric. *Trust me, Jack's beanstalk stinks*
Brett, Jan. *Fritz and the beautiful horses*
The mitten
The three little dassies
The three snow bears
Briant, Ed. *Seven stories*
Briggs, Raymond. *Jim and the beanstalk*
Bromley, Nick. *Open very carefully*
Brown, Marcia. *Once a mouse . . .*
Stone soup
Browne, Anthony. *Me and you*
Browning, Robert. *The pied piper of Hamelin*, ill. by Mercer Mayer
The pied piper of Hamelin, ill. by Drahos Zak
Bruchac, Joseph. *The circle of thanks*
The great ball game
Thirteen moons on turtle's back
Bryan, Ashley. *Beat the story-drum, pum-pum*
Beautiful blackbird
The cat's purr
The story of lightning and thunder
Turtle knows your name
Buckley, Richard. *The foolish tortoise*

The greedy python
Bunting, Eve. *Finn McCool and the great fish*
Calmenson, Stephanie. *The principal's new clothes*
The teeny tiny teacher
Casanova, Mary. *The hunter*
Casey, Dawn. *The great race: the story of the Chinese zodiac*
Catalanotto, Peter. *Ivan the terrier*
Cendrars, Blaise. *Shadow*
Charles, Veronika Martenova. *The maiden of the mist*
Chaucer, Geoffrey. *Chanticleer and the fox*
Chen, Kerstin. *Lord of the cranes*
Chicken Little. *Chicken Little*
Henny Penny, ill. by Emily Bolam
Henny Penny, ill. by Paul Galdone
Henny Penny, ill. by Sophie Windham
Henny-Penny
The sky is falling
Child, Lauren. *Beware of the storybook wolves*
Who's afraid of the big bad book?
Cinderella
Claflin, Willy. *The uglified ducky*
Climo, Shirley. *The Egyptian Cinderella*
The Irish Cinderlad
The Korean Cinderella
The Persian Cinderella
Tuko and the birds
Coburn, Jewell Reinhart. *Angkat*
Jouanah
Cohen, Caron Lee. *Digger Pig and the turnip*
The mud pony
Cole, Babette. *Prince Cinders*
Cole, Joanna. *Bony-legs*
Collins, Sheila Hebert. *'T Pousette et 't Poulette*
Compestine, Ying Chang. *The real story of stone soup*
Compton, Joanne. *Ashpet*
Conway, David. *The great fairy tale disaster*
Coppinger, Tom. *Curse in reverse*
Coxe, Molly. *Bunny and the beast*
Croll, Carolyn. *The little snowgirl*
Crum, Shutta. *Who took my hairy toe?*
Cullen, Catherine Ann. *Thirsty baby*
Cullen, Lynn. *The mightiest heart*
Cummings, E. E. *Fairy tales*
Dahlie, Elizabeth. *Bernelly and Harriet*
Daly, Jude. *Fair, brown and trembling*
Daly, Niki. *Pretty Salma*
Why the sun and moon live in the sky
Davis, Aubrey. *Bagels from Benny*
A hen for Izzy Pippik
Kishka for Koppel
Davis, David. *Fandango stew*
Day, Nancy Raines. *The lion's whiskers*
Dayrell, Elphinstone. *Why the sun and the moon live in the sky*
Dee, Ruby. *Two ways to count to ten*
Deedy, Carmen Agra. *Martina the beautiful cockroach*
DeFelice, Cynthia C. *Nelly May has her say*
de Las Casas, Dianne. *Blue frog*
The Little "Read" Hen
Delessert, Etienne. *The seven dwarfs*
Demas, Corinne. *The magic apple*
Demi. *The dragon's tale and other animal fables of the Chinese zodiac*
The empty pot
The greatest treasure
One grain of rice
dePaola, Tomie. *Big Anthony, his story*
Favorite nursery tales
Fin M'Coul
Jamie O'Rourke and the big potato
The legend of Old Befana
The legend of the bluebonnet
The legend of the Indian paintbrush
Little Grunt and the big egg
Strega Nona meets her match
Tony's bread
DeSpain, Pleasant. *The dancing turtle*
Diakité, Baba Wagué. *The hatseller and the monkeys*
The hunterman and the crocodiles
The magic gourd
Mee-an and the magic serpent
Dick Whittington and his cat. *Dick Whittington and his cat*, ill. by Marcia Brown
Dick Whittington and his cat, ill. by Mélisande Potter
Divakaruni, Chitra Banerjee. *Grandma and the great gourd*
Dodd, Emma. *Cinderelephant*
Donnelly, Jennifer. *Humble pie*
Downing, Johnette. *There was an old lady who swallowed some bugs*
Duvall, Deborah L. *The opossum's tale*
Edwards, Pamela Duncan. *Princess Pigtoria and the pea*
Ehlert, Lois. *Cuckoo, a Mexican folktale / Cucú: un cuento folklórico mexicano*
Mole's hill
Moon rope / Un lazo a la luna
Eisner, Will. *Sundiata*
Ellwand, David. *Cinderlily*
Elya, Susan Middleton. *Rubia and the three osos*
Emberley, Barbara. *One wide river to cross*
Emberley, Ed. *The red hen*
Emberley, Rebecca. *Chicken Little*
The crocodile and the scorpion
Three cool kids
Ernst, Lisa Campbell. *Goldilocks returns*
Little Red Riding Hood: a newfangled prairie tale
Evans, Cambria. *Bone soup*
The firebird. *The firebird*, ill. by Demi
The firebird, ill. by Rachel Isadora
The tale of the firebird
Fisher, Leonard Everett. *Cyclops*
Theseus and the Minotaur
William Tell
Fleischman, Paul. *Glass slipper, gold sandal*
Fleming, Candace. *Clever Jack takes the cake*
Forest, Heather. *Stone soup*
The fox went out on a chilly night
Franco, Betsy. *Why the frog has big eyes*
Galdone, Paul. *The magic porridge pot*
The teeny-tiny woman
What's in fox's sack?
Geras, Adèle. *The nutcracker*
Sleeping beauty
Swan Lake
Gershator, Phillis. *Only one cowry*
Zzzng! zzzng! zzzng!
Gerson, Mary-Joan. *Why the sky is far away*
The gingerbread boy. *Gingerbread baby*
The gingerbread boy, ill. by Emily Bolam
The gingerbread boy, ill. by Richard Egielski
The gingerbread boy, ill. by Paul Galdone
The Gingerbread Cowboy
The gingerbread girl

The gingerbread man, ill. by Carol Jones
The gingerbread man, ill. by Megan Lloyd
The gingerbread man, ill. by Barbara McClintock
The gingerbread man, ill. by Béatrice Rodriguez
The Gingerbread Man loose in the school
The Gingerbread Man loose on the fire truck
The pancake boy
Señorita Gordita
Whiff, sniff, nibble and chew
Ginsburg, Mirra. *Clay boy*
Go tell Aunt Rhody
Goble, Paul. *Adopted by the eagles*
Buffalo woman
Crow chief
The dream wolf
The gift of the sacred dog
The great race of the birds and animals
Her seven brothers
Iktomi and the berries
Iktomi and the boulder
Iktomi and the buffalo skull
Iktomi and the buzzard
Iktomi and the coyote
Iktomi and the ducks
The legend of the White Buffalo Woman
The lost children
Love flute
Mystic horse
Remaking the earth
The return of the buffaloes
Star boy
Goodall, Jane. *The eagle and the wren*
Goode, Diane. *Diane Goode's book of silly stories and songs*
Gorbachev, Valeri. *The fool of the world and the flying ship: a Ukrainian folk tale*
Grambling, Lois G. *The witch who wanted to be a princess*
Granfield, Linda. *The legend of the panda*
Gray, Luli. *Ant and Grasshopper*
Gregorowski, Christopher. *Fly, eagle, fly!*
Grey, Mini. *The very smart pea and the princess-to-be*
Grifalconi, Ann. *The village of round and square houses*
Grimm, Jacob and Wilhelm. *As luck would have it*
Battle of the beasts
The brave little tailor, ill. by Olga Dugina
The brave little tailor, ill. by David Shaw
The Bremen town band
The Bremen town musicians, ill. by Bill Dickson
The Bremen town musicians, ill. by Ilse Plume
The Bremen town musicians, ill. by Bernadette Watts
The Bremen town musicians, ill. by Lisbeth Zwerger
Doctor All-Knowing
The elves and the shoemaker, ill. by Kirill Chelushkin
The elves and the shoemaker, ill. by Paul Galdone
The elves and the shoemaker, ill. by Margaret Walty
The fisherman and his wife, ill. by Eleanor Hubbard
The fisherman and his wife, ill. by Rachel Isadora
The fisherman and his wife, ill. by Todd Ouren
The fisherman and the turtle
The frog prince, ill. by Anne Yvonne Gilbert
The frog prince, ill. by Todd Ouren
The glass mountain
The golden goose
The goose girl
Hans my hedgehog
Hansel and Gretel, ill. by Jen Corace
Hansel and Gretel, ill. by Rachel Isadora
Hansel and Gretel (1980), ill. by Susan Jeffers
Hansel and Gretel (2011), ill. by Susan Jeffers
Hansel and Gretel, ill. by Jane Ray
Hansel and Gretel, ill. by Claudia Wolf
Hansel and Gretel, ill. by Paul O. Zelinsky
Hansel and Gretel, ill. by Lisbeth Zwerger
Hansel and Gretel / Hansel y Gretel
Hansel and Gretel: a retelling from the original tale by the Brothers Grimm
Iron John, ill. by Trina Schart Hyman
Iron John, ill. by Winslow Pels
Jorinda and Jorindel
Little red cap
Little Red Riding Hood, ill. by Célia Chauffrey
Little Red Riding Hood, ill. by Gwen Connelly
Little Red Riding Hood, ill. by Trina Schart Hyman
Little Red Riding Hood, ill. by Jerry Pinkney
Little Red Riding Hood, ill. by Gennady Spirin
Little Red Riding Hood, ill. by Bernadette Watts
Little Red Riding Hood, ill. by Andrea Wisnewski
Musicians of Bremen
Musicians of Bremen / Los musicos de Bremner
The rabbit's bride
Rapunzel, ill. by Sarah Gibb
Rapunzel, ill. by Trina Schart Hyman
Rapunzel, ill. by Rachel Isadora
Rapunzel, ill. by Joma
Rapunzel, ill. by Kris Waldherr
Rapunzel, ill. by Paul O. Zelinsky
Rapunzel: a fairy tale
Rose Red and the bear prince
Rumpelstiltskin, ill. by Paul Galdone
Rumpelstiltskin, ill. by David Shaw
Rumpelstiltskin, ill. by Paul O. Zelinsky
Seven at one blow
The shoemaker and his elves
The shoemaker and the elves, ill. by Adrienne Adams
The shoemaker and the elves, ill. by Ilse Plume
The six swans
Sleeping Beauty
The sleeping beauty
Snow White, ill. by Melinda Copper
Snow White, ill. by Quentin Gréban
Snow White, ill. by Trina Schart Hyman
Snow White, ill. by Charles Santore
Snow White and the seven dwarfs, ill. by Wanda Gág
Snow White and the seven dwarfs, ill. by Laura Ljungkvist
The star child
The story of Little Red Riding Hood
The three spinning fairies
Twelve dancing princesses
The twelve dancing princesses, ill. by Lucy Corvino
The twelve dancing princesses, ill. by Kinuko Y. Craft
The twelve dancing princesses, ill. by Rachel Isadora
The twelve dancing princesses, ill. by Gerald McDermott
The twelve dancing princesses, ill. by Jane Ray
The twelve dancing princesses, ill. by Suçie Stevenson

The twelve princesses
The water of life
Grindley, Sally. *The sorcerer's apprentice*
Who is it?
Guarnaccia, Steven. *The three little pigs: an architectural tale*
Gugler, Laurel Dee. *There's a billy goat in the garden*
Hague, Michael. *The nutcracker*
Hale, Bruce. *Snoring Beauty*
Haley, Gail E. *A story, a story*
Hallworth, Grace. *Sing me a story*
Hamilton, Martha. *The ghost catcher*
The hidden feast
Priceless gifts
Hamilton, Virginia. *The girl who spun gold*
Harper, Charise Mericle. *There was a bold lady who wanted a star*
Harper, Lee. *The Emperor's cool clothes*
Harrington, Janice N. *Busy-busy Little Chick*
Harris, Joel Chandler. *Jump! the adventures of Brer Rabbit*
Jump again!
Harrison, David L. *The book of giant stories*
Hasler, Eveline. *A tale of two brothers*
Hassett, John. *The three silly girls Grubb*
Hausman, Gerald. *Coyote walks on two legs*
Eagle boy
Hautzig, Deborah. *Beauty and the beast*
Hawkins, Colin. *Fairytale news*
One, two, guess who?
Hawthorne, Nathaniel. *King Midas and the golden touch*
Hayes, Joe. *Juan Verdades, the man who could not tell a lie*
Little Gold Star / Estrellita de oro
Hayward, Linda. *Pepe and Papa*
The Helen Oxenbury nursery collection
Helmer, Marilyn. *Three barnyard tales*
Three cat and mouse tales
Three prince charming tales
Three royal tales
Three tales of enchantment
Three tales of three
Three tales of trickery
Three teeny tiny tales
Three tuneful tales
Hennessy, B. G. *The boy who cried wolf*
Henrichs, Wendy. *I am Tama, lucky cat*
Heo, Yumi. *The green frogs*
Heyer, Marilee. *The weaving of a dream*
Hickox, Rebecca. *The golden sandal*
Hill, Eric. *Spot's birthday party*
Where's Spot?
Ho, Minfong. *Brother Rabbit*
Hodges, Margaret. *Saint George and the dragon*
The wave
Hodgkinson, Leigh. *Goldilocks and just one bear*
Hoffman, Mary. *Clever Katya*
Hoffmann, E. T. A. *The nutcracker,* ill. by Renée Graef
The nutcracker, ill. by Alison Jay
The nutcracker, ill. by Peter Malone
The nutcracker, ill. by Maurice Sendak
The nutcracker, ill. by Lisbeth Zwerger
The Nutcracker and the Mouse King
The nutcracker ballet
Hogrogian, Nonny. *The contest*
Hong, Chen Jiang. *The magic horse of Han Gan*
Hooks, William H. *Moss gown*
Hopkins, Jackie Mims. *The gold miner's daughter*
Prairie chicken little
Horn, Sandra Ann. *Babushka*
Howland, Naomi. *Latkes, latkes, good to eat*
Huck, Charlotte S. *Princess Furball*
Huling, Jan. *Ol' Bloo's boogie-woogie band and blues ensemble*
Puss in cowboy boots
Hurst, Margaret M. *Grannie and the Jumbie*
Hurston, Zora Neale. *The six fools*
Irving, Washington. *The legend of Sleepy Hollow,* ill. by R. W. Alley
The legend of Sleepy Hollow, ill. by Daniel San Souci
Jack and the beanstalk. *Jack and the beanstalk,* ill. by Aljoscha Blau
Jack and the beanstalk, ill. by Steve Cox
Jack and the beanstalk, ill. by Nina Crews
Jack and the beanstalk, ill. by Julek Heller
Jack and the beanstalk, ill. by John Howe
Jack and the beanstalk, ill. by Steven Kellogg
Jack and the beanstalk, ill. by Albert Lorenz
Jack and the beanstalk, ill. by Niamh Sharkey
Jack and the beanstalk, ill. by Gennady Spirin
Jack and the beanstalk, ill. by Matt Tavares
Jacques and de beanstalk
Jackson, Alison. *I know an old lady who swallowed a pie*
Thea's tree
Jackson, Ellen. *Cinder Edna*
Jacobs, Joseph. *King of the cats*
The three sillies
Jaffe, Nina. *The golden flower*
In the month of Kislev
Tales for the seventh day
The way meat loves salt
Janisch, Heinz. *The merry pranks of Till Eulenspiegel*
Javaherbin, Mina. *The secret message*
Jay, Alison. *1 2 3*
Jiang, Ji-li. *The magical Monkey King, mischief in heaven*
Johnson, Paul Brett. *Jack outwits the giants*
Old Dry Fry
Johnson-Davies, Denys. *Goha, the wise fool*
Johnston, Tony. *The badger and the magic fan*
Bigfoot Cinderrrrrella
The cowboy and the black-eyed pea
Go track a yak
The tale of Rabbit and Coyote
Kajikawa, Kimiko. *Tsunami!*
Yoshi's feast
Kasbarian, Lucine. *The greedy sparrow*
Keats, Ezra Jack. *John Henry*
Keens-Douglas, Richardo. *Anancy and the haunted house*
Keller, Emily Snowell. *Sleeping Bunny*
Kellogg, Steven. *Chicken Little*
I was born about 10,000 years ago
The Pied Piper's magic
Ketcham, Sallie. *The Christmas bird*
Ketteman, Helen. *Bubba the cowboy prince*
The three little gators
Waynetta and the cornstalk
Kilaka, John. *True friends*
Kimmel, Eric A. *Anansi and the magic stick*
Anansi and the moss-covered rock
Anansi and the talking melon
Anansi goes fishing
Anansi's party time

The birds' gift
Easy work!
The Erie Canal pirates
The frog princess: a Tlingit legend from Alaska
Gershon's monster
Joseph and the Sabbath fish
Little Red Hot
The magic dreidels
Medio Pollito
Rip Van Winkle's return
The runaway tortilla
The three cabritos
The three little tamales
The three princes
The two mountains
King, Thomas. *Coyote sings to the moon*
Kloske, Geoffrey. *Once upon a time, the end (asleep in 60 seconds)*
Knutson, Barbara. *Love and roast chicken*
Kosofsky, Chaim. *Much, much better*
Krensky, Stephen. *Too many leprechauns*
Krudop, Walter Lyon. *The man who caught fish*
Kurtz, Jane. *In the small, small night*
Langstaff, John M. *Oh, a-hunting we will go*
Over in the meadow
Langton, Jane. *Saint Francis and the wolf*
LaRochelle, David. *The end*
Larson, Kirby. *The magic kerchief*
Lasky, Kathryn. *The emperor's old clothes*
LaTeef, Nelda. *The hunter and the ebony tree*
Laverde, Arlene. *Alaska's three pigs*
Lee, Jeanne M. *The song of Mu Lan*
Toad is the uncle of heaven
Lendler, Ian. *An undone fairy tale*
Lester, Julius. *Ackamarackus*
John Henry
Levine, Gail Carson. *Betsy Red Hoodie*
Forgive me, I meant to do it
Levinthal, David. *Who pushed Humpty Dumpty?*
Lewis, Jill. *Don't read this book!*
Light, Steve. *The shoemaker extraordinaire*
Lin, Grace. *The red thread*
Lind, Michael. *Bluebonnet girl*
Lionni, Leo. *Tico and the golden wings*
Little old lady who swallowed a fly. *I know an old lady*
I know an old lady who swallowed a fly, ill. by Stephen Gulbis
I know an old lady who swallowed a fly, ill. by Glen Rounds
I know an old lady who swallowed a fly, ill. by Nadine Bernard Westcott
There was an old lady who swallowed a fly, ill. by Pam Adams
There was an old lady who swallowed a fly, ill. by Simms Taback
There was an old monkey who swallowed a frog
The little red hen. *The little red hen*, ill. by Byron Barton
The little red hen, ill. by Emily Bolam
The little red hen, ill. by Paul Galdone
Little red hen
The little red hen, ill. by Jerry Pinkney
The little red hen, ill. by Kate Slater
The little red hen, ill. by Annie West
The little red hen, ill. by Margot Zemach
The little red hen: an old fable
The Little Red Hen and the Passover matzah
The Little Red Hen makes a pizza
Loo, Sanne te. *Ping-Li's kite*
Lottridge, Celia Barker. *The little rooster and the diamond button*
Louie, Ai-Ling. *Yeh Shen*
Lowell, Susan. *The bootmaker and the elves*
Cindy Ellen
Little Red Cowboy Hat
The three little javelinas
The tortoise and the jackrabbit
Lunge-Larsen, Lise. *The race of the Birkebeiners*
Lupton, Hugh. *Pirican Pic and Pirican Mor*
McAlister, Caroline. *Holy Molé!*
Maccarone, Grace. *The three bears ABC*
McCaughrean, Geraldine. *Beauty and the beast*
Grandma Chickenlegs
McDermott, Gerald. *Anansi the spider*
Arrow to the sun
Coyote
Daniel O'Rourke
Monkey
Musicians of the sun
Pig-Boy
Raven
Tim O'Toole and the wee folk
MacDonald, Amy. *Please, Malese!*
MacDonald, Margaret Read. *Conejito*
Fat cat
The girl who wore too much
Give up, Gecko!
The great smelly, slobbery small-toothed dog
A hen, a chick, and a string guitar
How many donkeys?
Little Rooster's diamond button
Mabela the clever
The old woman who lived in a vinegar bottle
Pickin' peas
Slop!
The squeaky door
Surf war!
Teeny Weeny Bop
Too many fairies
Tuck-me-in tales
Tunjur! Tunjur! Tunjur!
McDonald, Megan. *The Hinky Pink*
McGill, Alice. *Sure as sunrise*
Way up and over everything
Machado, Ana Maria. *Wolf wanted*
McKissack, Patricia C. *A million fish . . . more or less*
Mirandy and Brother Wind
McLeod, Heather. *Kiss me!*
McNaughton, Janet. *Brave Jack and the unicorn*
Maddern, Eric. *Nail soup*
Maggi, María Elena. *The great canoe*
Mahy, Margaret. *The seven Chinese brothers*
Mandell, Muriel. *A donkey reads*
Manna, Anthony L. *The orphan*
Marshall, James. *Hansel and Gretel*
Red Riding Hood
Martin, Francesca. *Clever Tortoise*
Martin, Rafe. *The language of birds*
The rough-face girl
The Shark God
Masini, Beatrice. *A brave little princess*
Mathews, Judith. *Nathaniel Willy, scared silly*
Matthews, Tina. *Out of the egg*
Mayer, Marianna. *Baba Yaga and Vasilisa the Brave*
Beauty and the beast
Pegasus
Perseus

Medearis, Angela Shelf. *The freedom riddle*
Seven spools of thread
The singing man
Tailypo
Too much talk
Melmed, Laura Krauss. *Moishe's miracle*
The rainbabies
Milligan, Bryce. *Brigid's cloak*
The prince of Ireland and the three magic stallions
Milne, A. A. *The magic hill*
Minters, Frances. *Cinder-Elly*
Sleepless Beauty
Mitchell, Marianne. *Joe Cinders*
Moerbeek, Kees. *The diary of Hansel and Gretel*
Mollel, Tololwa M. *Ananse's feast*
The flying tortoise
Kitoto the mighty
Orphan boy
Song bird
Subira subira
Montes, Marisa. *Juan Bobo goes to work*
Moore, Maggie. *Little Red Riding Hood*
Moore, Marian. *Dear Cinderella*
Mora, Pat. *The night the moon fell*
The race of toad and deer
Morales, Yuyi. *Just a minute: a trickster tale and counting book*
Just in case: a trickster tale and Spanish alphabet book
Moreton, Daniel. *La Cucaracha Martina*
Morgan, Mary. *Dragon pizzeria*
Morrison, Toni. *The tortoise or the hare*
Mortimer, Rachael. *Red Riding Hood and the sweet little wolf*
Mosel, Arlene. *Tikki Tikki Tembo*
Muller, Robin. *The lucky old woman*
Munsch, Robert N. *A promise is a promise*
Musgrove, Margaret. *The spider weaver*
Muth, Jon J. *Stone soup*
Zen shorts
Nadimi, Suzan. *The rich man and the parrot*
Newman, Marlene. *Myron's magic cow*
Nishizuka, Koko. *The beckoning cat*
Noble, Trinka Hakes. *A Christmas spider's miracle*
Norling, Beth. *Sister night and sister day*
Numeroff, Laura Joffe. *Ponyella*
Oberman, Sheldon. *The wisdom bird*
Ogburn, Jacqueline K. *The magic nesting doll*
Olaleye, Isaac. *In the Rainfield*
The old woman and her pig. *The old woman and her pig*
The old woman and her pig: an Appalachian folktale
O'Malley, Kevin. *The great race*
Onyefulu, Obi. *Chinye*
Oppenheim, Joanne. *The Christmas witch*
Oram, Hiawyn. *Baba Yaga and the wise doll*
Orgel, Doris. *The cat's tale*
Osborne, Mary Pope. *The brave little seamstress*
Kate and the beanstalk
Sleeping Bobby
Osofsky, Audrey. *Dreamcatcher*
Otsuka, Yuzo. *Suho's white horse*
Oughton, Jerrie. *How the stars fell into the sky*
The magic weaver of rugs
Over in the meadow
Palatini, Margie. *Lousy rotten stinkin' grapes*
Parkinson, Kathy. *The enormous turnip*
Paterson, Katherine. *The tale of the Mandarin ducks*
Paul, Ann Whitford. *Tortuga in trouble*
Paxton, Tom. *The story of Santa Claus*
The story of the Tooth Fairy
Paye, Won-Ldy. *Head, body, legs*
Mrs. Chicken and the hungry crocodile
Peck, Jan. *The giant carrot*
Giant peach yodel!
Perlman, Janet. *The Emperor Penguin's new clothes*
The penguin and the pea
Perrault, Charles *Cinderella*, ill. by Nicoletta Ceccoli
Cinderella, ill. by Susan Jeffers
Cinderella, ill. by Loek Koopmans
Cinderella, ill. by James Marshall
Cinderella, ill. by Barbara McClintock
Cinderella / Cenicienta
Cinderella: a pop-up fairy tale
Cinderella: or, the little glass slipper
Puss in boots, ill. by Marcia Brown
Puss in boots, ill. by Lorinda Bryan Cauley
Puss in boots, ill. by Paul Galdone
Puss in boots, ill. by Steve Light
Puss in boots, ill. by Giuliano Lunelli
Puss in boots, ill. by Fred Marcellino
Puss in boots, ill. by Fred Marcellino
Puss in boots, ill. by Bernhard Oberdieck
Puss in boots, ill. by Jerry Pinkney
Puss in boots, ill. by Alain Vaës
Petach, Heidi. *Goldilocks and the three hares*
Philip, Neil. *Noah and the devil*
Pia Toya
Pilegard, Virginia Walton. *The warlord's puzzle*
Pinkney, Jerry. *The lion and the mouse*
Pitcher, Caroline. *Mariana and the merchild*
Polacco, Patricia. *Babushka's Mother Goose*
Luba and the wren
Rechenka's eggs
Pollock, Penny. *The turkey girl*
When the moon is full
Poole, Amy Lowry. *The pea blossom*
Price, Kathy. *The Bourbon Street musicians*
Prokofiev, Sergei Sergeievitch. *Peter and the wolf*, ill. by Charles Mikolaycak
Peter and the wolf, ill. by Josef Palecek
Peter and the wolf, ill. by Chris Raschka
Peter and the wolf, ill. by Vladimir Vagin
Pullman, Philip. *Puss in boots: the adventures of that most enterprising feline*
Quattlebaum, Mary. *Sparks fly high*
Radunsky, Vladimir. *Manneken pis*
Ramos, Mario. *I am so handsome*
Ramsden, Ashley. *Seven fathers*
Ransome, Arthur. *The fool of the world and the flying ship*
Rappaport, Doreen. *The long-haired girl*
The new king
Ray, Jane. *The apple-pip princess*
Richard, Françoise. *On Cat Mountain*
Riggio, Anita. *Beware the Brindlebeast*
Ringgold, Faith. *The invisible princesses*
Robbins, Ruth. *Baboushka and the three kings*
Roberts, Lynn. *Cinderella, an Art Deco love story*
Rapunzel, a groovy fairy tale
Robins, Arthur. *The teeny tiny woman*
Rocco, John. *Wolf! Wolf!*
Rockwell, Anne. *The boy who wouldn't obey*
Rodanas, Kristina. *The dragonfly's tale*
Follow the stars
Rohmer, Harriet. *How we came to the fifth world*
Mother scorpion country

Rohmer, Harriet, et al. *The invisible hunters*
Root, Phyllis. *Aunt Nancy and Old Man Trouble*
Grandmother Winter
Rosales, Melodye Benson. *Leola and the honeybears*
Rosen, Michael. *Crow and Hawk*
Ross, Gayle. *How Turtle's back was cracked*
The legend of the Windigo
Ross, Tony. *The boy who cried wolf*
Roth, Susan L. *Kanahena*
Rothenberg, Joan Keller. *Inside-out grandma*
Rumford, James. *Nine animals and the well*
Ryan, Pam Muñoz. *Nacho and Lolita*
Sabuda, Robert. *Beauty and the beast: a pop-up book of the classic fairy tale*
Peter Pan
Sahagun, Bernardino de. *Spirit child*
Salley, Coleen. *Epossumondas*
Epossumondas saves the day
Sanderson, Ruth. *Cinderella*
The enchanted wood
The golden mare, the firebird, and the magic ring
Papa Gatto
San Souci, Daniel. *The rabbit and the dragon king*
San Souci, Robert D. *Brave Margaret*
Callie Ann and Mistah Bear
Cendrillon
Cinderella Skeleton
The enchanted tapestry
The faithful friend
The hired hand
The Hobyahs
The house in the sky
The legend of Scarface
Little gold star
Little Pierre
Nicholas Pipe
Pedro and the monkey
Peter and the blue witch baby
The red heels
Robin Hood and the golden arrow
The samurai's daughter
The secret of the stones
The silver charm
The snow wife
Song of Sedna
Sootface
Sukey and the mermaid
The talking eggs
Two bear cubs: a Miwok legend from California's Yosemite Valley
A weave of words
The white cat
Sawyer, Ruth. *Journey cake, ho!*
The remarkable Christmas of the cobbler's sons
Say, Allen. *Once under the cherry blossom tree*
Schmidt, Gary D. *The Great Stone Face*
Schroeder, Alan. *Smoky Mountain Rose*
The stone lion
Scieszka, Jon. *The frog prince, continued*
The Stinky Cheese Man and other fairly stupid tales
The true story of the three little pigs by A. Wolf, as told to Jon Scieszka
Scott, Nathan Kumar. *Mangoes and bananas*
The sacred banana leaf
Seeger, Pete. *Abiyoyo*
Abiyoyo returns
Some friends to feed
Seki, Sunny. *The tale of the lucky cat*
Seto, Loretta. *Mooncakes*
Shah, Idries. *The boy without a name*
The clever boy and the terrible, dangerous animal
Fatima the spinner and the tent
The silly chicken
Shannon, George. *Rabbit's gift*
Shannon, Margaret. *The red wolf*
Shaskan, Trisha Speed. *Seriously, Cinderella is so annoying!*
Shepard, Aaron. *The baker's dozen*
The crystal heart
Forty fortunes
The gifts of Wali Dad
One-eye! Two-eyes! Three-eyes!
The princess mouse
The sea king's daughter
Shulevitz, Uri. *The treasure*
Shute, Linda. *Clever Tom and the leprechaun*
Siberell, Anne. *Whale in the sky*
Sierra, Judy. *The beautiful butterfly*
The gift of the crocodile
Mind your manners, B. B. Wolf
Tasty baby belly buttons
Tell the truth, B. B. Wolf
Wiley and the Hairy Man
Skrypuch, Marsha Forchuk. *Enough*
Slate, Joseph. *Story time for Little Porcupine*
Sleator, William. *The angry moon*
Sloat, Teri. *There was an old lady who swallowed a trout*
Smith, Lane. *Pinocchio, the boy*
Snyder, Dianne. *The boy of the three-year nap*
So, Meilo. *Gobble, gobble, slip, slop*
Souhami, Jessica. *Foxy!*
The leopard's drum
The little, little house
Mrs. McCool and the giant Cuhullin
No dinner!
Rama and the demon king
Sausages
Stampler, Ann Redisch. *The rooster prince of Breslov*
Shlemazel and the remarkable spoon of Pohost
The wooden sword
Stanley, Diane. *The Giant and the beanstalk*
Rumpelstiltskin's daughter
Steptoe, John. *Mufaro's beautiful daughters*
The story of jumping mouse
Stevens, Janet. *Old bag of bones*
Tops and bottoms
Stewig, John Warren. *Clever Gretchen*
King Midas
Mother Holly
Stone soup
Stimpson, Colin. *Jack and the baked beanstalk*
Strauss, Susan. *When woman became the sea*
Sunami, Kitoba. *How the fisherman tricked the genie*
Swann, Brian. *The house with no door*
Sweet, Melissa. *Carmine*
Sylvester, Kevin. *Splinters*
Taback, Simms. *Kibitzers and fools*
Tan, Amy. *The moon lady*
Tarbescu, Edith. *The boy who stuck out his tongue*
Tchana, Katrin. *Sense Pass King*
Teague, Mark. *The three little pigs and the somewhat bad wolf*
Temple, Frances. *Tiger soup*
Thomas, Joyce Carol. *Gingerbread days*
The gospel Cinderella
Thornhill, Jan. *The rumor*
The three bears. *Goldilocks*

Goldilocks and the three bears, ill. by Jan Brett
Goldilocks and the three bears, ill. by Mark Buehner
Goldilocks and the three bears, ill. by Lorinda Bryan Cauley
Goldilocks and the three bears, ill. by Emma Chichester Clark
Goldilocks and the three bears, ill. by Valeri Gorbachev
Goldilocks and the three bears, ill. by Steven Guarnaccia
Goldilocks and the three bears, ill. by David McPhail
Goldilocks and the three bears, ill. by James Marshall
Goldilocks and the three bears, ill. by Gerda Muller
Goldilocks and the three bears, ill. by Gennady Spirin
Goldilocks and the three bears, ill. by Janet Stevens
The three bears, ill. by Byron Barton
The three bears, ill. by Paul Galdone
The three bears [board book]
The 3 bears and Goldilocks
The three little pigs. *The three little pigs*, ill. by Gavin Bishop
The three little pigs, ill. by Paul Galdone
The three little pigs, ill. by Rob Hefferan
The three little pigs, ill. by Steven Kellogg
The three little pigs, ill. by David McPhail
The three little pigs, ill. by James Marshall
The three little pigs, ill. by Bernadette Watts
The three little pigs, ill. by Margot Zemach
The three little pigs [board book]
The three little pigs / Los tres cerditos
The three little pigs and the big bad wolf
The three little pigs and the fox
Tingle, Tim. *When Turtle grew feathers*
Tolhurst, Marilyn. *Somebody and the three Blairs*
Tolstoy, Aleksey Nikolayevich. *The enormous turnip*
The gigantic turnip
Tom Thumb. *The adventures of Tom Thumb*
Tom Thumb
Tom Tit Tot. *Tom Tit Tot*
Tompert, Ann. *Saint Nicholas*
Tresselt, Alvin R. *The mitten: an old Ukrainian folktale*
Trivizas, Eugenios. *The three little wolves and the big bad pig*
Tseng, Grace. *White tiger, blue serpent*
Turkle, Brinton. *Deep in the forest*
Uchida, Yoshiko. *The magic purse*
The two foolish cats
The wise old woman
Ungar, Richard. *Rachel captures the moon*
Vagin, Vladimir. *The enormous carrot*
Vallverdu, Josep. *Aladdin and the magic lamp / Aldino y la lampara maravillosa*
Van Kampen, Vlasta. *Bear tales*
It couldn't be worse
Van Laan, Nancy. *The magic bean tree*
Rainbow crow
Shingebiss
So say the little monkeys
Van Woerkom, Dorothy. *The rat, the ox and the zodiac*
Vaughan, Richard Lee. *Eagle boy*
Verma, Jatinder Nath. *The story of Divaali*
Volkmer, Jane Anne. *Song of Chirimia / La Musica de la Chirimia*
Vozar, David. *Yo, hungry wolf!*
Wade, Mary Dodson. *No year of the cat*
Wahl, Jan. *Little Johnny Buttermilk*
Waite, Michael P. *Jojofu*
Walburg, Lori. *The legend of the candy cane*
Waldman, Debby. *A sack full of feathers*
Walter, Mildred Pitts. *Ty's one-man band*
Walters, Eric. *The matatu*
Wang, Gabrielle. *The race for the Chinese zodiac*
Wells, Rosemary. *The little lame prince*
Westcott, Nadine Bernard. *Skip to my Lou*
Weulersse, Odile. *Nasreddine*
Wick, Walter. *Can you see what I see? once upon a time*
Wiesner, David. *The loathsome dragon*
The three pigs
Wilcox, Leah. *Waking Beauty*
Wilde, Oscar. *The happy prince*
The selfish giant, ill. by S. Saelig Gallagher
The selfish giant, ill. by Fabian Negrin
The selfish giant, ill. by Lisbeth Zwerger
Willard, Nancy. *Shadow story*
Willems, Mo. *Goldilocks and the three dinosaurs*
Willey, Margaret. *Clever Beatrice, an Upper Peninsula conte*
Clever Beatrice and the best little pony
Williams, Brenda. *The real princess*
Wilson, Tony. *The princess and the packet of frozen peas*
Winthrop, Elizabeth. *Vasilissa the beautiful*
Wisniewski, David. *Elfwyn's saga*
Golem
Sundiata: lion king of Mali
The warrior and the wise man
Wolkstein, Diane. *The banza*
Sun Mother wakes the world
Wood, Audrey. *Heckedy Peg*
The rainbow bridge
Wooldridge, Connie Nordhielm. *The legend of Strap Buckner*
Wicked Jack
Xiong, Blia. *Nine-in-one Grr! Grr!*
Yagawa, Sumiko. *The crane wife*
Yahgulanaas, Michael Nicoll. *The little hummingbird*
Yee, Paul. *Bamboo*
Yep, Laurence. *Auntie Tiger*
Dragon prince
The Khan's daughter
The shell woman and the king
Yolen, Jane. *The firebird*
The flying witch
The girl in the golden bower
King Long Shanks
Pegasus, the flying horse
Sister Bear
Sky dogs
Young, Ed. *Cat and Rat*
Donkey trouble
Little Plum
Lon Po Po
The lost horse
Night visitors
What about me?
Youngquist, Cathrene Valente. *The three Billygoats Gruff and Mean Calypso Joe*
Zacharias, Ravi. *The merchant and the thief*
Zelinsky, Paul O. *The maid and the mouse and the odd-shaped house*
Zemach, Harve. *Duffy and the devil*
Zemach, Margot. *It could always be worse*

The three wishes
Zeman, Ludmila. *Sindbad*
Ziefert, Harriet. *When I first came to this land*

Folk & fairy tales – pourquoi tales

Alexander, Lloyd. *How the cat swallowed thunder*
Bruchac, James. *Rabbit's snow dance*
Bruchac, Joseph. *How Chipmunk got his stripes*
Cummings, Pat. *Ananse and the lizard*
Kipling, Rudyard. *How the camel got his hump*
How the elephant got his trunk
How the leopard got his spots
Larson, Bonnie. *When animals were people / Cuando los animales eran personas*
Lester, Julius. *Why heaven is far away*
McDermott, Gerald. *Jabutí the tortoise*
Marcos, subcomandante. *The story of colors / La historia de los colores*
Poole, Amy Lowry. *How the rooster got his crown*
Rosen, Michael. *How the animals got their colors*
Shepard, Aaron. *Master man*
Sherman, Pat. *The sun's daughter*
Wolkstein, Diane. *The day Ocean came to visit*

Food

Abrams, Pam. *Now I eat my ABC's*
Aesop. *The fox and the grapes*
Ahlberg, Allan. *Hooray for bread*
The runaway dinner
Akin, Sara Laux. *Three scoops and a fig*
Alalou, Elizabeth. *The butter man*
Alborough, Jez. *Ice cream bear*
It's the bear
Alcott, Louisa May. *An old-fashioned Thanksgiving*
Aliki. *Milk from cow to carton*
Ancona, George. *Mis comidas / My foods*
Anderson, Derek. *Gladys goes out to lunch*
Andrews, Julie. *Dumpy's apple shop*
Angelou, Maya. *Angelina of Italy*
Argueta, Jorge. *Arroz con leche / Rice pudding*
Guacamole
Sopa de frijoles: un poema para cocinar / Bean soup: a cooking poem
Tamalitos
Armstrong, Jennifer. *Once upon a banana*
Arnold, Caroline. *Mealtime for zoo animals*
Arnosky, Jim. *Gobble it up!*
Raccoons and ripe corn
Asch, Frank. *Monsieur Saguette and his baguette*
Moonbear
Popcorn
Aston, Dianna Hutts. *An orange in January*
Auch, Mary Jane. *The princess and the pizza*
Averbeck, Jim. *The market bowl*
Axelrod, Amy. *Pigs in the pantry*
Pigs will be pigs
Aylesworth, Jim. *The burger and the hot dog*
Backx, Patsy. *Josie and Mr. Fernandez*
Bailey, Linda. *Toads on toast*
Baker, Keith. *LMNO peas*
1-2-3 peas
Baranski, Joan Sullivan. *Round is a pancake*
Barasch, Lynne. *Hiromi's hands*
Barbour, Karen. *Little Nino's pizzeria*
Bardhan-Quallen, Sudipta. *Hampire!*
Barrett, Judi. *Cloudy with a chance of meatballs*
Cloudy with a chance of meatballs 3
The marshmallow incident
Pickles to Pittsburgh
Barron, Rex. *Fed up!*
Bastianich, Lidia. *Nonna tell me a story*
Nonna's birthday surprise
Baum, Maxie. *I have a little dreidel*
Berenstain, Stan and Jan. *The Berenstain bears and too much junk food*
Bergman, Mara. *Yum yum! What fun!*
Berry, Lynne. *Ducking for apples*
Bertrand, Diane Gonzales. *Sofía and the purple dress / Sofía y el vestido morado*
Best, Cari. *Easy as pie*
Black, Michael Ian. *I'm bored*
Blackstone, Stella. *Making minestrone*
Bloch, Serge. *You are what you eat*
Bloom, Suzanne. *Feeding friendsies*
Boldt, Claudia. *Odd dog*
Bond, Rebecca. *The great doughnut parade*
Bonning, Tony. *Fox tale soup*
Brenner, Barbara A. *Beef stew*
Brett, Jan. *Hedgie's surprise*
Brokamp, Elizabeth. *The picky little witch*
Brown, Marc. *D. W., the picky eater*
Brown, Marcia. *Stone soup*
Bruel, Nick. *Bad Kitty*
Bunting, Eve. *One green apple*
Butterworth, Chris. *How did that get in my lunchbox?*
Caldicott, Chris. *World food alphabet*
Capucilli, Karen. *The jelly bean fun book*
Carle, Eric. *My very first book of food*
Pancakes, pancakes
Today is Monday
Walter the baker
Carlson, Nancy. *Harriet and George's Christmas treat*
Carney, Margaret. *At Grandpa's sugar bush*
Carrer, Chiara. *Otto Carrotto*
Cartaya, Pablo. *Tina Cocolina*
Catalanotto, Peter. *The secret lunch special*
Cazet, Denys. *The perfect pumpkin pie*
Chall, Marsha Wilson. *Sugarbush spring*
Chamberlin, Mary. *Mama Panya's pancakes*
Chavarría-Cháirez, Becky. *Magda's tortillas / Las tortillas de Magada*
Chen, Chih-Yuan. *On my way to buy eggs*
Cherry, Lynne. *How Groundhog's garden grew*
Child, Lauren. *I will never not ever eat a tomato*
I will never not ever eat a tomato [pop-up]
Christelow, Eileen. *Don't wake up Mama!*
Church, Caroline Jayne. *Little Apple Goat*
Collins, Ross. *Alvie eats soup*
Compestine, Ying Chang. *Boy dumplings*
The real story of stone soup
The runaway rice cake
The story of chopsticks
The story of noodles
Cooper, Elisha. *Ice cream*
Cooper, Helen. *Dog biscuit*
Cordsen, Carol Foskett. *The milkman*
Cousins, Lucy. *Maisy makes gingerbread*
Coy, John. *Two old potatoes and me*
Cruickshank, Margrit. *We're going to feed the ducks*
Curious George and the pizza
Curious George goes to a chocolate factory
Curious George goes to an ice cream shop
Curious George makes pancakes
Curtis, Andrea. *What's for lunch?*
Dahl, Michael. *From the garden*
Darrow, Sharon. *Old Thunder and Miss Raney*

Davis, Aubrey. *Bagels from Benny*
Davis, David. *Fandango stew*
Davis, Lee. *Feeding time*
Deacon, Alexis. *Cheese belongs to you!*
Dealey, Erin. *Deck the walls!*
De Anda, Diane. *A day without sugar / Un dia sin azucar*
DeFelice, Cynthia C. *One potato, two potato*
de Las Casas, Dianne. *Blue frog*
Delessert, Etienne. *Hungry for numbers*
Denise, Anika. *Pigs love potatoes*
dePaola, Tomie. *Pancakes for breakfast*
The popcorn book
Tony's bread
De Regniers, Beatrice Schenk. *What did you put in your pocket?*
DeRubertis, Barbara. *Lulu's lemonade*
DiTerlizzi, Tony. *Jimmy Zangwow's out-of-this-world, moon pie adventure*
Donnelly, Jennifer. *Humble pie*
Donnio, Sylviane. *I'd really like to eat a child*
Donohue, Dorothy. *Veggie soup*
Dooley, Norah. *Everybody brings noodles*
Everybody cooks rice
Everybody serves soup
Downing, Johnette. *Today is Monday in Louisiana*
Doyle, Malachy. *Hungry! Hungry! Hungry!*
Drescher, Henrik. *Hubert the Pudge*
Durant, Alan. *Burger boy*
Duval, Kathy. *Take me to your BBQ*
Eaton, Maxwell. *Best buds*
Eclare, Melanie. *A harvest of color*
Egan, Tim. *The trial of Cardigan Jones*
Ehlert, Lois. *Eating the alphabet*
Growing vegetable soup
Ehrlich, Fred. *Does a camel cook?*
Elliott, George. *The boy who loved bananas*
Elvgren, Jennifer Riesmeyer. *Josias, hold the book*
Elya, Susan Middleton. *No more, por favor*
Emberley, Ed. *Thanks, Mom!*
Emberley, Rebecca. *My food / Mi comida*
Ernst, Lisa Campbell. *The Gingerbread Girl goes animal crackers*
Evans, Cambria. *Bone soup*
Evans, Lezlie. *The bunnies' picnic*
Everitt, Betsy. *Mean soup*
Faglia, Matteo. *Happy birthday, I'm 1*
Happy birthday, I'm 2
Happy birthday, I'm 3
Happy birthday, I'm 4
Falwell, Cathryn. *Mystery vine*
Rainbow Stew
Farish, Terry. *The cat who liked potato soup*
Fearnley, Jan. *Mr. Wolf's pancakes*
Fitzgerald, Joanne. *Yum! Yum!*
Flaherty, A. W. *The luck of the Loch Ness monster*
Flanagan, Alice K. *The Zieglers and their apple orchard*
Fleming, Candace. *Clever Jack takes the cake*
Gator gumbo
Fleming, Denise. *Lunch*
Fliess, Sue. *A gluten-free birthday for me!*
Florence, Tyler. *Tyler makes pancakes!*
Tyler makes spaghetti!
Forest, Heather. *Stone soup*
Fox, Christyan. *Count to ten, PiggyWiggy!*
Fox, Mem. *Possum magic*
Freymann, Saxton. *Baby food*
Dog food
Fast food
Food for thought
Food play
How are you peeling?
Friedman, Caitlin. *How do you feed a hungry giant?*
Galdone, Paul. *The magic porridge pot*
Garland, Michael. *The President and Mom's apple pie*
Gibbons, Gail. *Apples*
The berry book
Corn
The honey makers
Ice cream: the full scoop
The milk makers
The missing maple syrup sap mystery
The seasons of Arnold's apple tree
The vegetables we eat
Gilman, Rita Golden. *Rice is life*
The gingerbread boy. *Gingerbread baby*
The gingerbread boy, ill. by Richard Egielski
The gingerbread boy, ill. by Paul Galdone
The Gingerbread Cowboy
The gingerbread girl
The gingerbread man, ill. by Carol Jones
The gingerbread man, ill. by Barbara McClintock
The gingerbread man, ill. by Béatrice Rodriguez
The Gingerbread Man loose in the school
The Gingerbread Man loose on the fire truck
The Library Gingerbread Man
The pancake boy
Señorita Gordita
Glaser, Linda. *Mrs. Greenberg's messy Hanukkah*
Goble, Paul. *The return of the buffaloes*
Goldin, Barbara Diamond. *A mountain of blintzes*
Gore, Leonid. *Worms for lunch?*
Gourley, Robbin. *Bring me some apples and I'll make you a pie*
First garden
Gray, Kes. *Eat your peas*
Gretz, Susanna. *Rabbit food*
Grey, Mini. *Ginger bear*
Grigsby, Susan. *First peas to the table*
Hafner, Marylin. *Molly and Emmett's surprise garden*
Hall, Margaret. *Corn*
Peanuts
Hall, Zoe. *The apple pie tree*
Harper, Charise Mericle. *Cupcake*
Hart, Caryl. *The princess and the peas*
Hartland, Jessie. *Bon appetit!*
Hartman, Bob. *The wolf who cried boy*
Head, Judith. *Mud soup*
Heller, Nicholas. *Ogres! ogres! ogres!*
Helmer, Marilyn. *Yummy riddles*
Hemingway, Edward. *Bad apple*
Henkes, Kevin. *Sheila Rae's peppermint stick*
Hesse, Karen. *Spuds*
Hest, Amy. *You can do it, Sam*
Hester, Denia Lewis. *Grandma Lena's big ol' turnip*
Hicks, Barbara Jean. *Monsters don't eat broccoli*
Hill, Eric. *Spot bakes a cake*
Hill, Mary. *Let's make pizza*
Let's make tacos
Hirsh, Marilyn. *Potato pancakes all around*
Hoban, Russell. *Bread and jam for Frances*
Hoberman, Mary Ann. *The seven silly eaters*
Holub, Joan. *Apple countdown*
The pizza that we made
Pumpkin countdown
Hopkins, Lee Bennett. *Yummy! eating through a day*
Horacek, Petr. *Strawberries are red*

Horowitz, Dave. *The ugly pumpkin*
Hot potato
Howe, James. *Horace and Morris say cheese (which makes Dolores sneeze!)*
Howland, Naomi. *The matzah man*
Hurwitz, Johanna. *Ethan out and about*
Hutchins, Pat. *Don't forget the bacon!*
Ten red apples
Inkpen, Mick. *Wibbly Pig likes bananas*
Isaacs, Anne. *Pancakes for supper!*
Isadora, Rachel. *Happy belly, happy smile*
Iwai, Melissa. *Soup day*
Jackson, Alison. *I know an old lady who swallowed a pie*
Jeffers, Oliver. *The incredible book eating boy*
Jenkins, Steve. *Time to eat*
Jocelyn, Marthe. *Eats*
Johnson, Paul Brett. *On top of spaghetti*
Jonovitz, Marilyn. *Good morning, Little Fox*
Kalz, Jill. *Fruits*
Kann, Victoria. *Pinkalicious*
Kaplan, Michael B. *Betty Bunny loves chocolate cake*
Kasza, Keiko. *Badger's fancy meal*
The wolf's chicken stew
Keller, Laurie. *Arnie the doughnut*
Ketteman, Helen. *Armadilly chili*
Khing, T. T. *Where is the cake?*
Where is the cake now?
Kimmel, Eric A. *Hanukkah bear*
Jack and the giant barbecue
Little Red Hot
The three little tamales
Kirk, David. *Little bird, Biddle bird*
Kladstrup, Kristin. *The gingerbread pirates*
Kleven, Elisa. *The apple doll*
Sun bread
Koda-Callan, Elizabeth. *The squiggly Wigglys*
Koponen, Libby. *Mmm . . . let's eat!*
Koster, Gloria. *The peanut-free cafe*
Krall, Dan. *The great lollipop caper*
Krull, Kathleen. *Supermarket*
Landry, Leo. *Eat your peas, Ivy Louise!*
LaRochelle, David. *How Martha saved her parents from green beans*
Lass, Bonnie. *Who took the cookies from the cookie jar?*
Lauber, Patricia. *Who eats what?*
Leedy, Loreen. *The dragon Thanksgiving feast*
The edible pyramid
Jack and the hungry giant eat right with MyPlate
Lendler, Ian. *An undone fairy tale*
Leonard, Marcia. *Food is fun!*
Levert, Mireille. *An island in the soup*
Lewis, Paeony. *No more cookies!*
Lin, Grace. *Dim sum for everyone*
Fortune cookie fortunes
Thanking the moon
The ugly vegetables
Lipson, Eden Ross. *Applesauce season*
Ljungkvist, Laura. *Toni's topsy-turvy telephone day*
Llewellyn, Claire. *Tree*
Lo, Ginnie. *Auntie Yang's great soybean picnic*
Lobel, Anita. *Ten hungry rabbits*
Loehr, Patrick. *Mucumber McGee and the lunch lady's liver*
London, Jonathan. *Crunch munch*
Froggy eats out
The sugaring-off party
Long, Ethan. *Soup for one*
Luciani, Brigitte. *Those messy Hempels*
Luckhurst, Matt. *Paul Bunyan and Babe the Blue Ox*
McAlister, Caroline. *Holy Molé!*
McClements, George. *Night of the Veggie Monster*
McCloskey, Robert. *Blueberries for Sal*
McClure, Nikki. *Apple*
McCully, Emily Arnold. *Popcorn at the palace*
McCurdy, Michael. *An Algonquian year*
McDonald, Megan. *Beetle McGrady eats bugs!*
McDonald, Rae A. *A fishing surprise*
McElligott, Matthew. *Even aliens need snacks*
McFarland, Lyn Rossiter. *Mouse went out to get a snack*
McGhee, Alison. *The case of the missing donut*
McGrath, Barbara Barbieri. *Kellogg's froot loops color fun book*
Kellogg's froot loops counting fun book
Machado, Ana Maria. *What a party!*
McNamara, Margaret. *The apple orchard riddle*
Apples A to Z
How many seeds in a pumpkin?
McPhail, David. *Pigs aplenty, pigs galore!*
Madison, Alan. *The littlest grape stomper*
Madonna. *Mr. Peabody's apples*
Maestro, Betsy. *How do apples grow?*
Mahy, Margaret. *Boom Baby boom, boom*
Simply delicious!
Manning, Mick. *Snap!*
Manushkin, Fran. *How mama brought the spring*
Many, Paul. *The great pancake escape*
Marcellino, Fred. *I, crocodile*
Marchon, Benoit. *Spoonful!*
Marino, Gianna. *Zoopa*
Marlowe, Sara. *No ordinary apple*
Marshall, James. *Yummers!*
Yummers too
Marshall, Linda Elovitz. *Talia and the rude vegetables*
Martin, Bill, Jr. *Rock it, sock it, number line*
Trick or treat?
Martin, David. *All for pie, pie for all*
Martin, Jacqueline Briggs. *Chicken joy on Redbean Road*
Martín Larrañaga, Ana. *Pepo and Lolo and the red apple*
Mayer, Mercer. *Frog goes to dinner*
Mayr, Diane. *Out and about at the apple orchard*
Meddaugh, Susan. *Martha blah blah*
Medoff, Francine. *The mouse in the matzah factory*
Menotti, Andrea. *How many jelly beans?*
Michelin, Linda. *Zuzu's wishing cake*
Micucci, Charles. *The life and times of corn*
Millen, C. M. *Blue bowl down*
Miller, Edna. *Mousekin's frosty friend*
Miller, Pat Zietlow. *Sophie's squash*
Miller, Virginia. *Ten red apples*
Milway, Katie Smith. *The good garden*
Minor, Wendell. *How big could your pumpkin grow?*
Modan, Rutu. *Maya makes a mess*
Monk, Isabell. *Family*
Mora, Pat. *The bakery lady / La señora de la panadería*
Let's eat! / A comer!
Yum! Mmmm! Que rico!
Morgan, Mary. *Dragon pizzeria*
Morris, Ann. *Bread, bread, bread*
Morris, Jennifer E. *May I please have a cookie?*
Morrison, Toni. *Peeny butter fudge*
Moser, Lisa. *Perfect soup*
Watermelon wishes

Foolishness *see* Character traits – foolishness

Foreign lands

Play
Work
Raffi. *Like me and you*
Reynolds, Jan. *Celebrate!*
Rogers, Gregory. *The hero of Little Street*
Seim, Donna Marie. *Where is Simon, Sandy?*
Shah, Idries. *Fatima the spinner and the tent*
Singer, Marilyn. *Nine o'clock lullaby*
Sís, Peter. *Madlenka*
Soto, Gary. *The old man and his door*
Stein, David Ezra. *Because Amelia smiled*
Trapani, Iza. *I'm a little teapot*
Van Laan, Nancy. *Sleep, sleep, sleep*

Foreign lands – Afghanistan

Haskins, Jim. *Count your way through Afghanistan*
King, Dedie. *I see the sun in Afghanistan*
Stampler, Ann Redisch. *The wooden sword*
Winter, Jeanette. *Nasreen's secret school*

Foreign lands – Africa

Aardema, Verna. *Anansi does the impossible!*
Bimwili and the Zimwi
Bringing the rain to Kapiti Plain
Half-a-ball-of-kenki
Jackal's flying lesson
Ji-nongo-nongo means riddles
The lonely lioness and the ostrich chicks
Misoso
Oh, Kojo! How could you!
Princess Gorilla and a new kind of water
Rabbit makes a monkey of lion
Sebgugugu the glutton
The vingananee and the tree toad
What's so funny, Ketu?
Who's in Rabbit's house?
Why mosquitoes buzz in people's ears
Adlerman, Daniel. *Africa calling*
Aesop. *Aesop's fables*
Alakija, Polly. *Catch that goat!*
Alexander, Lloyd. *Fortune tellers*
Andersen, Hans Christian. *The princess and the pea*
The ugly duckling
Appelt, Kathi. *Elephants aloft*
Aruego, José. *We hide, you seek*
Asare, Meshack. *Sosu's call*
Base, Graeme. *Jungle drums*
Beake, Lesley. *Home now*
Beard, Alex. *Crocodile's tears*
Blackford, Harriet. *Elephant's story*
Blessing, Charlotte. *New old shoes*
Brett, Jan. *Honey, honey — lion!*
The three little dassies
Brown, Don. *Uncommon traveler*
Bryan, Ashley. *Beat the story-drum, pum-pum*
The story of lightning and thunder
Bulion, Leslie. *Fatuma's new cloth*
Buzzeo, Toni. *Just like my Papa*
Stay close to Mama
Cabrera, Jane. *The wheels on the bus*
Cendrars, Blaise. *Shadow*
Chocolate, Deborah. *Kente colors*
Conway, David. *The most important gift of all*
Daly, Niki. *Next stop — Zanzibar Road!*
Not so fast Songololo
Pretty Salma
Welcome to Zanzibar Road
Davies, Stephen. *Don't spill the milk!*
Dawes, Kwame Senu Neville. *I saw your face*
Dayrell, Elphinstone. *Why the sun and the moon live in the sky*
Dee, Ruby. *Two ways to count to ten*
dePaola, Tomie. *Bill and Pete*
De Vries, Anke. *Raf*
Diakité, Baba Wagué. *The hatseller and the monkeys*
The hunterman and the crocodiles
Diouf, Sylviane A,. *Bintou's braids*
Eisner, Will. *Sundiata*
Ellis, Veronica Freeman. *Afro-Bets, first book about Africa*
Faundez, Anne. *The day the rains fell*
Feelings, Muriel. *Jambo means hello*
Moja means one
Foggo, Cheryl. *Dear baobab*
Gannij, Joan. *Hidden hippo*
Geraghty, Paul. *Help me!*
Gershator, Phillis. *Only one cowry*
Zzzng! zzzng! zzzng!
Gibbons, Gail. *Elephants of Africa*
Gravett, Emily. *Meerkat mail*
Gregorowski, Christopher. *Fly, eagle, fly!*
Grifalconi, Ann. *The village of round and square houses*
The village that vanished
Grimm, Jacob and Wilhelm. *The fisherman and his wife*
Hansel and Gretel
Rapunzel
The twelve dancing princesses
Haley, Gail E. *A story, a story*
Harrington, Janice N. *Busy-busy Little Chick*
Haskins, Jim. *Count your way through Africa*
Heap, Sue. *Danny's drawing book*
House, Catherine. *A stork in a baobab tree*
Ichikawa, Satomi. *The first bear in Africa!*
Isadora, Rachel. *Old Mikamba had a farm*
A South African night
There was a tree
Joosse, Barbara. *Papa do you love me?*
Joubert, Beverly. *African animal alphabet*
Kessler, Cristina. *Jubela*
Kimmel, Eric A. *Anansi and the magic stick*
Anansi and the talking melon
Anansi goes fishing
Anansi's party time
Kipling, Rudyard. *The elephant's child*
How the camel got his hump
How the elephant got his trunk
Knight, Margy Burns. *Africa is not a country*
Kroll, Virginia L. *Africa brothers and sisters*
Faraway drums
Jaha and Jamil went down the hill
Masai and I
Landström, Lena. *A hippo's tale*
LaTeef, Nelda. *The hunter and the ebony tree*
Latimer, Alex. *Lion vs Rabbit*
Léonard, Marie. *Tibili, the little boy who didn't want to go to school*
Lester, Julius. *Shining*
Lewin, Hugh. *Jafta*
Jafta's father
Jafta's mother
London, Jonathan. *What the animals were waiting for*
McCormick, Wendy. *Daddy, will you miss me?*
McDermott, Gerald. *Anansi the spider*

Zomo the rabbit
MacDonald, Margaret Read. *Mabela the clever*
McGrory, Anik. *Kidogo*
MacLachlan, Patricia. *Your moon, my moon*
Marino, Gianna. *Meet me at the moon*
Markham, Beryl. *The good lion*
Melmed, Laura Krauss. *Jumbo's lullaby*
Mitchell, Rhonda. *The talking cloth*
Mollel, Tololwa M. *Kitoto the mighty*
To dinner, for dinner
Montanari, Eva. *The crocodile's true colors*
Moore, Clement Clarke. *The night before Christmas*
Morozumi, Atsuko. *My friend gorilla*
Moss, Miriam. *This is the mountain*
This is the oasis
This is the tree
Musgrove, Margaret. *Ashanti to Zulu*
Nelson, Marilyn. *Ostrich and Lark*
Oberman, Sheldon. *The wisdom bird*
Olaleye, Isaac. *Bitter bananas*
Lake of the Big Snake
Onyefulu, Ifeoma. *An African Christmas*
A triangle for Adaora
Onyefulu, Obi. *Chinye*
Pritchett, Dylan. *The first music*
Radcliffe, Theresa. *Bashi, elephant baby*
San Souci, Robert D. *The secret of the stones*
Sayre, April Pulley. *If you should hear a honey guide*
Schaefer, Carole Lexa. *Cool time song*
Souhami, Jessica. *The leopard's drum*
Steig, William. *Doctor De Soto goes to Africa*
Steptoe, John. *Mufaro's beautiful daughters*
Stiegemeyer, Julie. *Under the baobab tree*
Stojic, Manya. *Rain*
Swann, Brian. *The house with no door*
Swinburne, Stephen R. *Water for one, water for everyone*
Trimble, Marcia. *Hello sun*
Tulloch, Shirley. *Who made me?*
Unobagha, Uzoamaka Chinyelu. *Off to the sweet shores of Africa and other talking drum rhymes*
Van Laan, Nancy. *Little Fish lost*
Wallace, Joseph E. *Big and noisy Simon*
Walter, Mildred Pitts. *Brother to the wind*
Williams, Karen Lynn. *Galimoto*
When Africa was home
Wilson, Anna. *Over in the grasslands*
Winter, Jeanette. *My baby*
Wolkstein, Diane. *The day Ocean came to visit*

Foreign lands – Antarctic

Brooks, Erik. *Polar opposites*
Duquennoy, Jacques. *North Pole, South Pole*
Dyer, Heather. *Tina and the penguin*
Gibbons, Gail. *Penguins!*
Jeffers, Oliver. *Lost and found*
Kimmel, Elizabeth Cody. *My penguin Osbert in love*
Lester, Alison. *Sophie Scott goes south*
Livinson, Nancy Smiler. *North Pole, South Pole*
London, Jonathan. *Little penguin*
McDonald, Megan. *Penguin and Little Blue*
McQuade, Jacqueline. *Snow babies*
Radcliffe, Theresa. *Nanu, penguin chick*
Schofield, Jennifer. *Animal babies in polar lands*
Seibold, J. Otto. *Penguin dreams*
Townsend, Emily Rose. *Penguins*
Viva, Frank. *A trip to the bottom of the world with Mouse*
Wilson, Karma. *Where is home, Little Pip?*
Wood, Audrey. *Little Penguin's tale*

Foreign lands – Arabia

Haskins, Jim. *Count your way through the Arab world*
Kimmel, Eric A. *The three princes*
Vallverdu, Josep. *Aladdin and the magic lamp / Aldino y la lampara maravillosa*
Zeman, Ludmila. *Sindbad*

Foreign lands – Arctic

Agee, Jon. *Little Santa*
Aston, Dianna Hutts. *Loony Little*
Berger, Melvin. *Brrr! a book about polar animals*
Berkes, Marianne. *Over in the Arctic*
Blaikie, Lynn. *Beyond the northern lights*
Brett, Jan. *The three snow bears*
Brooks, Erik. *Polar opposites*
Brown, Kerry. *Tupag the dreamer*
Crawford, Laura. *In arctic waters*
Crowley, Ned. *Nanook and Pryce*
De Beer, Hans. *Little Polar Bear and the whales*
Duquennoy, Jacques. *North Pole, South Pole*
Ford, Christine. *Ocean's child*
Ford, Miela. *Mom and me*
George, Jean Craighead. *The last polar bear*
Nutik and Amaroq play ball
Nutik, the wolf pup
Snow bear
Guiberson, Brenda Z. *Ice bears*
Hopkinson, Deborah. *Keep on!*
Livinson, Nancy Smiler. *North Pole, South Pole*
London, Jonathan. *Gone again ptarmigan*
Ice Bear and Little Fox
Luenn, Nancy. *Nessa's story*
McQuade, Jacqueline. *Snow babies*
Merski, P. K. *Roaring, boring, Alice*
Moss, Miriam. *The snow bear*
Primavera, Elise. *Auntie Claus*
Auntie Claus and the key to Christmas
Raffi. *Baby beluga*
Reynolds, Jan. *Far north*
Rives. *If I were a polar bear*
Rueda, Claudia. *My little polar bear*
Ryder, Joanne. *White bear, ice bear*
Sabuda, Robert. *The Blizzard's robe*
Schofield, Jennifer. *Animal babies in polar lands*
Sís, Peter. *A small tall tale from the far Far North*
Spinelli, Eileen. *Polar bear, arctic hare*
Taulbert, Clifton L. *Little Cliff and the cold place*
Taylor, Harriet Peck. *Ulaq and the northern lights*
Taylor, Theodore. *Hello, Arctic!*
Thompson, Lauren. *Polar bear morning*
Thomson, Sarah L. *Where do polar bears live?*
Townsend, Emily Rose. *Arctic foxes*
Polar bears
Votaw, Carol. *Good morning, little polar bear*
Wallace, Mary. *I is for Inuksuk*
Ward, Jennifer. *Way up in the Arctic*
Ward, Lindsay. *Please bring balloons*
Weatherford, Carole Boston. *I, Matthew Henson*
Wild, Margaret. *Thank you, Santa*
Yolen, Jane. *Welcome to the icehouse*

Foreign lands – Argentina

Lamm, C. Drew. *Gauchada*
Van Laan, Nancy. *The magic bean tree*

Foreign lands – Armenia

Hogrogian, Nonny. *The contest*
San Souci, Robert D. *A weave of words*

Foreign lands – Asia

Chin-Lee, Cynthia. *A is for Asia*
Sierra, Judy. *Counting crocodiles*

Foreign lands – Australia

Arnold, Caroline. *Australian animals*
A platypus' world
A wombat's world
Baker, Jeannie. *Mirror*
The story of rosy dock
Where the forest meets the sea
Window
Berkes, Marianne. *Over in Australia*
Bonnett-Rampersaud, Louise. *Polly Hopper's pouch*
Brown, Marc. *Arthur's animal adventure*
Cheng, Christopher. *Python*
Dennard, Deborah. *Koala country*
Fox, Mem. *Possum magic*
French, Jackie. *Josephine wants to dance*
Lester, Alison. *Ernie dances to the didgeridoo*
Markle, Sandra. *Finding home*
Hip-pocket papa
Morpurgo, Michael. *Wombat goes walkabout*
Napoli, Donna Jo. *Ready to dream*
Pettitt, Linda. *Yafi's family*
Reynolds, Jan. *Down under*
Roth, Susan L. *The biggest frog in Australia*
Shields, Carol Diggory. *Wombat walkabout*
Spurling, Margaret. *Bilby moon*
Votaw, Carol. *Waking up down under*
Ward, Helen. *Old shell, new shell*
Wild, Margaret. *Bobbie Dazzler*
Thank you, Santa
Wolkstein, Diane. *Sun Mother wakes the world*

Foreign lands – Austria

Greenstein, Elaine. *The goose man*
Lester, Alison. *Running with the horses*
Tompert, Ann. *A carol for Christmas*

Foreign lands – Bangladesh

Malaspina, Ann. *Yasmin's hammer*

Foreign lands – Bavaria *see* Foreign lands – Austria; Foreign lands – Germany

Foreign lands – Belarus

Manushkin, Fran. *How mama brought the spring*

Foreign lands – Belgium

Radunsky, Vladimir. *Manneken pis*

Foreign lands – Bosnia-Herzegovina

Bunting, Eve. *Gleam and Glow*

Foreign lands – Brazil

Brown, Monica. *Pelé, king of soccer / Pelé, el rey del fútbol*
Cherry, Lynne. *The great kapok tree*
Cline-Ransome, Lesa. *Young Pelé*
DeSpain, Pleasant. *The dancing turtle*
Haskins, Jim. *Count your way through Brazil*
Lewin, Ted. *Amazon boy*
Van Laan, Nancy. *So say the little monkeys*

Foreign lands – British Columbia

Manuel, Lynn. *Camels always do*
Olsen, Sylvia. *Yetsa's sweater*

Foreign lands – Cambodia

Coburn, Jewell Reinhart. *Angkat*
Ho, Minfong. *Brother Rabbit*
Lee, Jeanne M. *Silent lotus*
Lipp, Frederick. *Running shoes*

Foreign lands – Cameroon

Alexander, Lloyd. *Fortune tellers*
Averbeck, Jim. *The market bowl*
Rockliff, Mara. *My heart will not sit down*
Tchana, Katrin. *Sense Pass King*

Foreign lands – Canada

Becker, Helaine. *Mama likes to mambo*
Blades, Ann. *Mary of mile 18*
Too small
Brebeuf, Jean de. *The Huron carol*
Bushey, Jeanne. *The polar bear's gift*
Butler, Geoff. *Ode to Newfoundland*
Carney, Margaret. *At Grandpa's sugar bush*
Carter, Anne Laurel. *My home bay*
Under a prairie sky
Clements, Andrew. *Tara and Tiree, fearless friends*
Cutler, Jane. *Guttersnipe*
Downie, Mary Alice. *A pioneer ABC*
Grassby, Donna. *A seaside alphabet*
Gregory, Nan. *Wild Girl and Gran*
Haskins, Jim. *Count your way through Canada*
Hodge, Deborah. *Emma's story*
Holling, Holling C. *Paddle-to-the-sea*
Hume, Stephen Eaton. *Red moon follows truck*
Lawson, Julie. *Arizona Charlie and the Klondike Kid*
Lee, Dennis. *Bubblegum delicious*
Lipp, Frederick. *The caged birds of Phnom Penh*
Little old lady who swallowed a fly. *There was an old lady who swallowed a fly*
London, Jonathan. *The sugaring-off party*
Lumry, Amanda. *Polar bear puzzle*
McNaughton, Janet. *Brave Jack and the unicorn*
Major, Kevin. *Eh to zed?*
Miles, Victoria. *Old Mother Bear*
Milord, Susan. *The ghost on the hearth*
Munsch, Robert N. *Love you forever*
Mud puddle
A promise is a promise
Thomas' snowsuit
Wait and see
Where is Gah-Ning?
Pendziwol, Jean E. *The red sash*
Perkins, Lynne Rae. *Pictures from our vacation*
Pickthall, Marjorie L. C. *The worker in sandalwood*

Pinkwater, Daniel. *Young Larry*
Reynolds, Marilynn. *The name of the child*
Stuchner, Joan Betty. *The Kugel Valley Klezmer Band*
Thien, Madeleine. *The Chinese violin*
Ward, Lynd. *The biggest bear*
Wiebe, Rudy. *Hidden buffalo*
Wishinsky, Frieda. *Where are you, Bear?*
Zagwÿn, Deborah Turney. *The pumpkin blanket*

Foreign lands – Caribbean Islands

Bryan, Ashley. *Can't scare me!*
Sing to the sun
Godard, Alex. *Mama, across the sea*
Hallworth, Grace. *Sing me a story*
Hurst, Margaret M. *Grannie and the Jumbie*
Isadora, Rachel. *Caribbean dream*
Lessac, Frané. *Island Counting 123*
McLean, Dirk. *Play mas'! a carnival ABC*
McMillan, Bruce. *Sense suspense*
Moreton, Daniel. *La Cucaracha Martina*
Moser, Barry. *Psalm 23*
Rahaman, Vashanti. *O Christmas tree*
San Souci, Robert D. *Cendrillon*
The faithful friend
The house in the sky
Youngquist, Cathrene Valente. *The three Billygoats Gruff and Mean Calypso Joe*

Foreign lands – Central America

Ada, Alma Flor. *The gold coin*
Tortillas and lullabies / Tortillas y cancioncitas
Wisniewski, David. *Rain player*

Foreign lands – Chad

Rumford, James. *Rain school*

Foreign lands – Chile

Foreman, Michael. *Mia's story*
Pitcher, Caroline. *Mariana and the merchild*
Rand, Gloria. *A pen pal for Max*

Foreign lands – China

Aesop. *The ant and the grasshopper*
Andersen, Hans Christian. *The emperor's new clothes*
The emperor's new clothes: a tale set in China
The nightingale, ill. by Nancy Ekholm Burkert
The nightingale, ill. by Pirkko Vainio
The nightingale, ill. by Lisbeth Zwerger
Berkeley, Jon. *Chopsticks*
Bishop, Claire Huchet. *The five Chinese brothers*
Brett, Jan. *Daisy comes home*
Bridges, Shirin Yim. *Ruby's wish*
Casanova, Mary. *The hunter*
Chan, Arlene. *Awakening the dragon*
Chen, Kerstin. *Lord of the cranes*
Clark, Karen Henry. *Sweet moon baby*
Compestine, Ying Chang. *Boy dumplings*
D is for dragon dance
The real story of stone soup
The runaway rice cake
The runaway wok
The story of chopsticks
The story of noodles
The story of paper
Coste, Marion. *Finding Joy*
Crane, Carol. *D is for dancing dragon*
Czernecki, Stefan. *Paper lanterns*
D'Antonio, Nancy. *Our baby from China*
Demi. *The dragon's tale and other animal fables of the Chinese zodiac*
The empty pot
The girl who drew a phoenix
The greatest treasure
The magic pillow
Flack, Marjorie. *The story about Ping*
Gibbons, Gail. *Giant pandas*
Granfield, Linda. *The legend of the panda*
Handforth, Thomas. *Mei Li*
Haskins, Jim. *Count your way through China*
Heyer, Marilee. *The weaving of a dream*
Hodge, Deborah. *Emma's story*
Hong, Chen Jiang. *The magic horse of Han Gan*
Jiang, Ji-li. *The magical Monkey King, mischief in heaven*
Red kite, blue kite
Keister, Douglas. *To grandmother's house*
Krebs, Laurie. *We're riding on a caravan*
Lee, Jeanne M. *The song of Mu Lan*
Lewis, Rose A. *I love you like crazy cakes*
Lin, Grace. *The red thread*
Lobel, Arnold. *Ming Lo moves the mountain*
Loo, Sanne te. *Ping-Li's kite*
Look, Lenore. *Brush of the gods*
Louie, Ai-Ling. *Yeh Shen*
Louis, Catherine. *Liu and the bird*
Mahy, Margaret. *The seven Chinese brothers*
Maples in the mist
Markle, Sandra. *How many baby pandas?*
Marx, Trish. *Kindergarten day USA and China*
Morris, Ann. *Grandma Lai Goon remembers*
Mosel, Arlene. *Tikki Tikki Tembo*
Muth, Jon J. *Stone soup*
Nagda, Anne Whitehead. *A home for panda*
Niemann, Christoph. *The pet dragon*
Okimoto, Jean Davies. *The White Swan express*
Orgel, Doris. *The cat's tale*
Pacilio, V. J. *Ling Cho and his three friends*
Partridge, Elizabeth. *Oranges on Golden Mountain*
Perry, Phyllis J. *Pandas' earthquake escape*
Pilegard, Virginia Walton. *The warlord's alarm*
The warlord's beads
The warlord's puzzle
Piumini, Roberto. *Doctor Me Di Cin*
Poole, Amy Lowry. *How the rooster got his crown*
The pea blossom
Potter, Alicia. *Mrs. Harkness and the panda*
Rappaport, Doreen. *The long-haired girl*
Rocco, John. *Wolf! Wolf!*
Rumford, James. *Chee-lin*
Ryder, Joanne. *Panda kindergarten*
San Souci, Robert D. *The enchanted tapestry*
Schaefer, Lola M. *Chinese New Year*
So, Sungwan. *Shanyi goes to China*
Stevens, Jan Romero. *Carlos digs to China / Carlos excava hasta la China*
Stoeke, Janet Morgan. *Waiting for May*
Tan, Amy. *The Chinese Siamese cat*
The moon lady
Thisdale, François. *Nini*
Tompert, Ann. *Grandfather Tang's story*
Tseng, Grace. *White tiger, blue serpent*
Tsubakiyama, Margaret. *Mei-Mei loves the morning*
Tucker, Kathy. *The seven Chinese sisters*

Van Woerkom, Dorothy. *The rat, the ox and the zodiac*
Wade, Mary Dodson. *No year of the cat*
Wang, Gabrielle. *The race for the Chinese zodiac*
Wang, Xiaohong. *One year in Beijing*
Whitfield, Susan. *The animals of the Chinese zodiac*
Wiese, Kurt. *Fish in the air*
Yang, Belle. *Always come home to me*
Yee, Paul. *Bamboo*
Yep, Laurence. *Auntie Tiger*
Dragon prince
The man who tricked a ghost
The shell woman and the king
Yi, Hu Yong. *Good morning China*
Yolen, Jane. *The emperor and the kite*
Young, Ed. *Cat and Rat*
Little Plum
Lon Po Po
The lost horse
Monkey King
Mouse match
Night visitors
Yu, Li-Qiong. *A New Year's reunion*
Zhang, Song Nan. *The ballad of Mulan*

Foreign lands – Colombia

Brown, Monica. *My name is Gabito / Me llamo Gabito*
Waiting for the Biblioburro
Torres, Leyla. *Saturday sancocho*
Winter, Jeanette. *Biblioburro*

Foreign lands – Congo (Democratic Republic)

Aardema, Verna. *Traveling to Tondo*
Hatkoff, Craig, et al. *Looking for Miza*

Foreign lands – Costa Rica

Keister, Douglas. *Fernando's gift / El regalo de Fernando*
Strauss, Susan. *When woman became the sea*

Foreign lands – Cuba

Deedy, Carmen Agra. *Martina the beautiful cockroach*
Leiner, Katherine. *Mama does the mambo*
Sacre, Antonio. *A mango in the hand*
Sciurba, Katie. *Oye, Celia!*

Foreign lands – Czechoslovakia

Krykorka, Ian. *Carl, the Christmas carp*
Marshak, S. *The Month-Brothers*
Sís, Peter. *The wall: growing up behind the Iron Curtain*
Van Kampen, Vlasta. *Bear tales*
Wisniewski, David. *Golem*

Foreign lands – Denmark

Burdett, Lois. *Hamlet for kids*
Deedy, Carmen Agra. *The yellow star*
Drummond, Allan. *Energy island*
MacDonald, Margaret Read. *Fat cat*

Foreign lands – Dominican Republic

Alvarez, Julia. *The secret footprints*

Foreign lands – Egypt

Aliki. *Mummies made in Egypt*
Auld, Mary. *Exodus from Egypt*
Base, Graeme. *The Jewel Fish of Karnak*
Bower, Tamara. *The shipwrecked sailor*
Climo, Shirley. *The Egyptian Cinderella*
dePaola, Tomie. *Bill and Pete go down the Nile*
Farmer, Nancy. *Clever Ali*
Hartland, Jessie. *How the sphinx got to the museum*
Heide, Florence Parry. *The day of Ahmed's secret*
Hofmeyr, Dianne. *The star-bearer*
Krebs, Laurie. *We're sailing down the Nile*
Marcellino, Fred. *I, crocodile*
Price, Leontyne. *Aïda*
Roth, Susan L. *Hands around the library*
Rouss, Sylvia A. *The littlest frog*
Sabuda, Robert. *Tutankhamen's gift*
St. George, Judith. *Zarafa*
Stolz, Mary. *Zekmet, the stone carver*
Yates, Philip. *Ten little mummies*

Foreign lands – El Salvador

Argueta, Jorge. *Trees are hanging from the sky*
Colato Laínez, René. *My shoes and I*

Foreign lands – England

Ahlberg, Allan. *The baby in the hat*
Anno, Mitsumasa. *Anno's Britain*
Atkins, Jeannine. *Mary Anning and the sea dragon*
Beardshaw, Rosalind. *Grandpa's surprise*
Bemelmans, Ludwig. *Madeline in London*
Bennett, Jill. *Teeny tiny*
Brooks, Nigel. *Country mouse cottage*
Town mouse house
Brown, Don. *Rare treasure*
Uncommon traveler
Brown, Ruth. *A dark, dark tale*
Burnett, Frances Hodgson. *A little princess*, ill. by Barbara McClintock
A little princess, ill. by Graham Rust
The secret garden
DeFelice, Cynthia C. *Nelly May has her say*
Dennard, Deborah. *Hedgehog haven*
Dick Whittington and his cat. *Dick Whittington and his cat*, ill. by Marcia Brown
Dick Whittington and his cat, ill. by Mélisande Potter
Egan, Tim. *Dodsworth in London*
Francis, Pauline. *Sam stars at Shakespeare's Globe*
Grahame, Kenneth. *The wind in the willows*
Hodges, Margaret. *Saint George and the dragon*
Hopkinson, Deborah. *The humblebee hunter*
Hughes, Shirley. *Alfie and the big boys*
Out and about
Jack and the beanstalk. *Jack and the beanstalk*
Kennedy, Cindy. *The star of Christmas*
Ketcham, Sallie. *The Christmas bird*
Little old lady who swallowed a fly. *I know an old lady*
I know an old lady who swallowed a fly, ill. by Stephen Gulbis
I know an old lady who swallowed a fly, ill. by Glen Rounds

I know an old lady who swallowed a fly, ill. by Nadine Bernard Westcott
Long, Sylvia. *Deck the hall*
McCully, Emily Arnold. *Popcorn at the palace*
MacDonald, Alan. *Wilfred to the rescue*
MacDonald, Margaret Read. *The old woman who lived in a vinegar bottle*
Munro, Roxie. *The inside-outside book of London*
Richardson, Justin. *Christian, the hugging lion*
Riggio, Anita. *Beware the Brindlebeast*
Robins, Arthur. *The teeny tiny woman*
Rogers, Gregory. *The boy, the bear, the baron, the bard*
Midsummer knight
San Souci, Robert D. *The Hobyahs*
Robin Hood and the golden arrow
Wahl, Jan. *Little Johnny Buttermilk*
Zemach, Harve. *Duffy and the devil*

Foreign lands – Ethiopia

Day, Nancy Raines. *The lion's whiskers*
Kessler, Cristina. *The best beekeeper of Lalibela*
Kurtz, Jane. *Faraway home*
Onyefulu, Ifeoma. *Omer's favorite place*
Pettitt, Linda. *Yafi's family*
Schur, Maxine Rose. *Day of delight*

Foreign lands – Europe

Banks, Kate. *City cat*
Jaffe, Nina. *The way meat loves salt*
Keefer, Janice Kulyk. *Anna's goat*

Foreign lands – Finland

Shepard, Aaron. *The princess mouse*

Foreign lands – France

Anderson, M. T. *Strange Mr. Satie*
Arnold, Marsha Diane. *Metro cat*
Bemelmans, Ludwig. *Madeline*
Madeline and the bad hat
Madeline and the gypsies
Madeline's Christmas
Madeline's rescue
Brunhoff, Jean de. *The story of Babar, the little elephant*
Chall, Marsha Wilson. *Bonaparte*
Chaud, Benjamin. *The bear's song*
Coxe, Molly. *Bunny and the beast*
Demi. *Joan of Arc*
Dicmas, Courtney. *Harold finds a voice*
Dominguez, Angela. *Let's go, Hugo!*
Egan, Tim. *Dodsworth in Paris*
Ellwand, David. *Cinderlily*
Goode, Diane. *Mama's perfect present*
Hartland, Jessie. *Bon appetit!*
Haskins, Jim. *Count your way through France*
Hobbie, Holly. *Toot and Puddle, top of the world*
Holmes, Mary Tavener. *A giraffe goes to Paris*
Huling, Jan. *Puss in cowboy boots*
Ichikawa, Satomi. *Come fly with me*
La La Rose
Johnson, D. B. *Magritte's marvelous hat*
Kelley, True. *Claude Monet*
Kimmelman, Leslie. *Everybody bonjours!*
Littlesugar, Amy. *Lisette's angel*
McCaughrean, Geraldine. *Beauty and the beast*
McClintock, Barbara. *Adele and Simon*
McCully, Emily Arnold. *Mirette on the high wire*
McLaren, Chesley. *Zat cat!*
Magoon, Scott. *Hugo and Miles in I've painted everything!*
Marcellino, Fred. *I, crocodile*
Marciano, John Bemelmans. *Madeline and the old house in Paris*
Markel, Michelle. *The fantastic jungles of Henri Rousseau*
Munro, Roxie. *The inside-outside book of Paris*
Neuschwander, Cindy. *Pastry school in Paris*
Olofsson, Helena. *The little jester*
Olshan, Matthew. *The mighty Lalouche*
Palatini, Margie. *Three French hens*
Parker, Marjorie Blain. *Colorful dreamer*
Perrault, Charles. *Cinderella / Cenicienta*
Polacco, Patricia. *The butterfly*
Poole, Josephine. *Joan of Arc*
Pullman, Philip. *Puss in boots: the adventures of that most enterprising feline*
Raffi. *Wheels on the bus*
Rappaport, Doreen. *The secret seder*
Reich, Susanna. *Minette's feast*
Rubin, Susan Goldman. *The yellow house*
St. George, Judith. *Zarafa*
Schubert, Leda. *Monsieur Marceau*
Selznick, Brian. *The invention of Hugo Cabret*
Stevenson, Harvey. *Looking at liberty*
Sweeney, Joan. *Suzette and the puppy*
Titus, Eve. *Anatole*
Anatole and the cat
Wells, Rosemary. *The miraculous tale of the two Maries*
Whelan, Gloria. *The boy who wanted to cook*
Winter, Jeanette. *Henri's scissors*
Yolleck, Joan. *Paris in the spring with Picasso*
Yorinks, Arthur. *Harry and Lulu*
Young, Amy. *Belinda in Paris*
Ziarnik, Natalie. *Madeleine's light*

Foreign lands – French Guiana

Ryder, Joanne. *Jaguar in the rain forest*

Foreign lands – Galapagos Islands

Jacobs, Francine. *Lonesome George, the giant tortoise*
Krebs, Laurie. *We're sailing to Galapagos*
Winkelman, Barbara Gaines. *Puffer's surprise*

Foreign lands – Germany

Allen, Debbie. *Brothers of the knight*
Bauer, Sepp. *The Christmas rose*
Browning, Robert. *The pied piper of Hamelin*, ill. by Mercer Mayer
The pied piper of Hamelin, ill. by Drahos Zak
Delessert, Etienne. *The seven dwarfs*
Grimm, Jacob and Wilhelm. *As luck would have it*
The brave little tailor, ill. by Olga Dugina
The brave little tailor, ill. by David Shaw
The elves and the shoemaker, ill. by Kirill Chelushkin
The elves and the shoemaker, ill. by Paul Galdone
The elves and the shoemaker, ill. by Margaret Walty
Hans my hedgehog
Iron John, ill. by Trina Schart Hyman
Iron John, ill. by Winslow Pels
The rabbit's bride
Seven at one blow

The shoemaker and his elves
The shoemaker and the elves, ill. by Adrienne Adams
The shoemaker and the elves, ill. by Ilse Plume
The three spinning fairies
Haskins, Jim. *Count your way through Germany*
Janisch, Heinz. *The merry pranks of Till Eulenspiegel*
Johnson, Grace. *The candle in the window*
Moore, Maggie. *Little Red Riding Hood*
Norling, Beth. *Sister night and sister day*
Raven, Margot Theis. *Mercedes and the chocolate pilot*
Root, Phyllis. *Grandmother Winter*
Seeger, Pete. *Some friends to feed*
Stewig, John Warren. *Mother Holly*
Ungerer, Tomi. *Otto: the autobiography of a teddy bear*
Wiviott, Meg. *Benno and the night of broken glass*

Foreign lands – Ghana

Angelou, Maya. *Kofi and his magic*
Cumberbatch, Judy. *Can you hear the sea?*
Cummings, Pat. *Ananse and the lizard*
Kurtz, Jane. *In the small, small night*
Medearis, Angela Shelf. *Seven spools of thread*
Too much talk
Milway, Katie Smith. *One hen*
Mollel, Tololwa M. *Ananse's feast*
Musgrove, Margaret. *The spider weaver*
Onyefulu, Ifeoma. *Deron goes to nursery school*
Grandma comes to stay

Foreign lands – Gilbert Islands *see* Foreign lands – South Sea Islands

Foreign lands – Great Britain

Browne, Anthony. *The shape game*

Foreign lands – Greece

Aliki. *Three gold pieces*
The twelve months
Haskins, Jim. *Count your way through Greece*
Manna, Anthony L. *The orphan*
Mayer, Marianna. *Pegasus*
Perseus
Rumford, James. *There's a monster in the alphabet*
Stewig, John Warren. *King Midas*

Foreign lands – Greenland

Dupre, Kelly. *The raven's gift*

Foreign lands – Guatemala

Carling, Amelia Lau. *Mama and Papa have a store*
Castaneda, Omar S. *Abuela's weave*
Mora, Pat. *The race of toad and deer*

Foreign lands – Haiti

Danticat, Edwidge. *Eight days*
Elvgren, Jennifer Riesmeyer. *Josias, hold the book*
Lauture, Denizé. *Running the road to ABC*
MacDonald, Amy. *Please, Malese!*
Oelschlager, Vanita. *I came from the water*
Van Laan, Nancy. *Mama rocks, Papa sings*
Watson, Jesse Joshua. *Hope for Haiti*
Williams, Karen Lynn. *Painted dreams*
Tap-tap

Foreign lands – Himalayas

Fleming, Candace. *When Agnes caws*
Nagda, Anne Whitehead. *World above the clouds*
Peet, Mal. *Cloud tea monkeys*

Foreign lands – Holland

Fleming, Candace. *Boxes for Katje*
Woelfle, Gretchen. *Katje the windmill cat*

Foreign lands – Honduras

Milway, Katie Smith. *The good garden*

Foreign lands – Hungary

Brown, Margaret Wise. *Wheel on the chimney*
Heiligman, Deborah. *The boy who loved math*
Lottridge, Celia Barker. *The little rooster and the diamond button*
MacDonald, Margaret Read. *Little Rooster's diamond button*

Foreign lands – Iceland

McMillan, Bruce. *Days of the ducklings*
How the ladies stopped the wind
Nights of the pufflings
The problem with chickens
Wisniewski, David. *Elfwyn's saga*

Foreign lands – India

Appelt, Kathi. *Elephants aloft*
Arenson, Roberta. *Manu and the talking fish*
Bannerman, Helen. *The story of Little Babaji*
The story of Little Black Sambo, ill. by Helen Bannerman
The story of Little Black Sambo, ill. by Helen Bannerman
The story of Little Black Sambo, ill. by Christopher Bing
Brown, Marcia. *Once a mouse . . .*
Bruce, Lisa. *Engines, engines*
Charles, Veronika Martenova. *The birdman*
Divakaruni, Chitra Banerjee. *Grandma and the great gourd*
Gardeski, Christina Mia. *Diwali*
Hamilton, Martha. *The ghost catcher*
Haskins, Jim. *Count your way through India*
Jeyaveeran, Ruth. *The road to Mumbai*
Kipling, Rudyard. *Rikki-tikki-tavi,* ill. by Lambert Davis
Rikki-tikki-tavi, ill. by Jerry Pinkney
Kostecki-Shaw, Jenny Sue. *Same, same but different*
Kroll, Virginia L. *Selvakumar knew better*
Lester, Julius. *Sam and the tigers*
McDermott, Gerald. *Monkey*
McGinty, Alice B. *Gandhi*
Noyes, Deborah. *When I met the wolf girls*
Rumford, James. *Nine animals and the well*
Shepard, Aaron. *The gifts of Wali Dad*
Sheth, Kashmira. *Monsoon afternoon*
So, Meilo. *Gobble, gobble, slip, slop*
Souhami, Jessica. *No dinner!*
Rama and the demon king

Thornhill, Jan. *The rumor*
Verma, Jatinder Nath. *The story of Divaali*
Young, Ed. *Seven blind mice*
Zacharias, Ravi. *The merchant and the thief*

Foreign lands – Indonesia

Gilman, Rita Golden. *Rice is life*
Henrichs, Wendy. *When Anju loved being an elephant*
Scott, Nathan Kumar. *Mangoes and bananas*
The sacred banana leaf
Sierra, Judy. *The gift of the crocodile*

Foreign lands – Iran

Balouch, Kristen. *The king and the three thieves*
Mystery bottle
Haskins, Jim. *Count your way through Iran*
Javaherbin, Mina. *The secret message*
Oppenheim, Shulamith Levey. *Ali and the magic stew*
Shepard, Aaron. *Forty fortunes*

Foreign lands – Iraq

Alrawi, Karim. *The girl who lost her smile*
Dennis, Major Brian. *Nubs*
Hickox, Rebecca. *The golden sandal*
Kosofsky, Chaim. *Much, much better*
Rumford, James. *Silent music*
Winter, Jeanette. *The librarian of Basra*

Foreign lands – Ireland

Balian, Lorna. *Leprechauns never lie*
Bateman, Teresa. *Fiona's luck*
Traveling Tom and the leprechaun
Bunting, Eve. *Ballywhinney Girl*
Finn McCool and the great fish
Walking to school
Climo, Shirley. *The Irish Cinderlad*
Daly, Jude. *Fair, brown and trembling*
dePaola, Tomie. *Fin M'Coul*
Jamie O'Rourke and the big potato
Jamie O'Rourke and the pooka
Patrick
Edwards, Pamela Duncan. *The leprechaun's gold*
Esckelson, Laura. *The copper braid of Shannon O'Shea*
Garland, Michael. *King Puck*
Haskins, Jim. *Count your way through Ireland*
Hazen, Barbara Shook. *Katie's wish*
Krensky, Stephen. *Too many leprechauns*
McCully, Emily Arnold. *The pirate queen*
McDermott, Gerald. *Daniel O'Rourke*
Milligan, Bryce. *Brigid's cloak*
The prince of Ireland and the three magic stallions
Murphy, Jim. *Fergus and the Night-Demon*
Nolan, Janet. *The St. Patrick's Day shillelagh*
San Souci, Robert D. *Brave Margaret*
Souhami, Jessica. *Mrs. McCool and the giant Cuhullin*
Taylor, Alice. *A child's treasury of Irish rhymes*
Tompert, Ann. *Saint Patrick*
Welling, Peter J. *Shawn O'Hisser, the last snake in Ireland*
Woodruff, Elvira. *Small beauties*

Foreign lands – Israel

Abraham, Michelle Shapiro. *My cousin Tamar lives in Israel*
Adler, David A. *A picture book of Israel*
Alexander, Sue. *Behold the trees*
Auld, Mary. *David and Goliath*
Biers-Ariel, Matt. *Solomon and the trees*
Cohen, Deborah Bodin. *Engineer Ari and the Rosh Hashana ride*
da Costa, Deborah. *Snow in Jerusalem*
Fisher, Leonard Everett. *David and Goliath*
Goldsboro, Bobby. *Noah and the ark; and, David and Goliath*
Haskins, Jim. *Count your way through Israel*
Herman, Charlotte. *First rain*
Oberman, Sheldon. *The wisdom bird*
Ofanansky, Allison. *Harvest of light*

Foreign lands – Italy

Aesop. *Androcles and the lion*, ill. by Dennis Nolan
Androcles and the lion, ill. by Janet Stevens
Androcles and the lion: and other Aesop fables
Angelou, Maya. *Angelina of Italy*
Anno, Mitsumasa. *Anno's Italy*
Barton, Bob. *Paul Gallico's The small miracle*
Costanza, Stephen. *Vivaldi and the invisible orchestra*
dePaola, Tomie. *Big Anthony, his story*
The clown of God
Jingle, the Christmas clown
The legend of Old Befana
Merry Christmas, Strega Nona
Tony's bread
Egan, Tim. *Dodsworth in Rome*
Egielski, Richard. *St. Francis and the wolf*
Falconer, Ian. *Olivia goes to Venice*
Fleming, Candace. *Gabriella's song*
Gibfried, Diane. *Brother Juniper*
Grant, Rose Marie. *Andiamo, Weasel*
Gutman, Anne. *Gaspard on vacation*
Hamilton, Martha. *Priceless gifts*
Haskins, Jim. *Count your way through Italy*
Marciano, John Bemelmans. *Madeline and the cats of Rome*
Mauner, Claudia. *Zoe Sophia's scrapbook*
Nivola, Claire A. *Orani*
Norris, Kathleen. *The holy twins*
Pericoli, Matteo. *Tommaso and the missing line*
Potter, Giselle. *The year I didn't go to school*
Russo, Marisabina. *I will come back for you*
Sanderson, Ruth. *Papa Gatto*
Weaver, Tess. *Opera cat*
Willard, Nancy. *The flying bed*
Yorinks, Arthur. *The Miami giant*

Foreign lands – Jamaica

Hanson, Regina. *A season for mangoes*
Temple, Frances. *Tiger soup*

Foreign lands – Japan

Bang, Molly. *Dawn*
Bauld, Jane Scoggins. *Journey of the third seed*
Bodkin, Odds. *The crane wife*
Christian, Mary Blount. *If not for the calico cat*
Coerr, Eleanor. *Circus day in Japan*
Sadako
Gershator, Phillis. *Sky sweeper*

Gollub, Matthew. *Cool melons — turn to frogs*
Ten oni drummers
Haskins, Jim. *Count your way through Japan*
Henrichs, Wendy. *I am Tama, lucky cat*
Hodges, Margaret. *The wave*
Iijima, Geneva Cobb. *The way we do it in Japan*
Issa, Kobayashi. *Today and today*
Johnston, Tony. *The badger and the magic fan*
Kajikawa, Kimiko. *Tsunami!*
Yoshi's feast
Kako, Satoshi. *Little Daruma and little Daikoku*
Little Daruma and little Kaminari
Kimura, Yuichi. *One stormy night . . .*
One sunny day . . .
Lachenmeyer, Nathaniel. *The origami master*
London, Jonathan. *Moshi moshi*
Mayer, Mercer. *Shibumi and the kitemaker*
Melmed, Laura Krauss. *The first song ever sung*
Meshon, Aaron. *Take me out to the Yakyu*
Mosel, Arlene. *The funny little woman*
Namioka, Lensey. *Hungriest boy in the world*
Nishizuka, Koko. *The beckoning cat*
Ohi, Ruth. *Kenta and the big wave*
Parot, Annelore. *Kimonos*
Paterson, Katherine. *The tale of the Mandarin ducks*
Preus, Margi. *The Peace Bell*
Richard, Françoise. *On Cat Mountain*
San Souci, Robert D. *The samurai's daughter*
The silver charm
The snow wife
Satoshi, Kako. *Little Daruma and little Tengu*
Say, Allen. *The bicycle man*
The boy in the garden
Erika-San
Grandfather's journey
Kamishibai man
Once under the cherry blossom tree
Tea with milk
Tree of cranes
Seki, Sunny. *The tale of the lucky cat*
Shannon, George. *Spring: a haiku story*
Sierra, Judy. *Tasty baby belly buttons*
Takabayashi, Mari. *I live in Tokyo*
Turner, Pamela S. *Hachiko*
Uchida, Yoshiko. *The magic purse*
The wise old woman
Waite, Michael P. *Jojofu*
Wells, Rosemary. *Yoko finds her way*
Yoko's paper cranes
Weston, Mark. *Honda*
Wisniewski, David. *Sumo Mouse*
The warrior and the wise man
Wright, Danielle. *Japanese nursery rhymes*
Yagawa, Sumiko. *The crane wife*
Yamada, Utako. *The story of Cherry the pig*
Yashima, Taro. *Crow boy*

Foreign lands – Kenya

Barasch, Lynne. *First come the zebra*
Browne, Eileen. *Handa's hen*
Chamberlin, Mary. *Mama Panya's pancakes*
Conway, David. *Lila and the secret of rain*
Cunnane, Kelly. *Chirchir is singing*
For you are a Kenyan child
Doner, Kim. *On a road in Africa*
Johnson, Jen Cullerton. *Seeds of change*
Johnston, Tony. *A Kenya Christmas*
Milway, Katie Smith. *Mimi's village and how basic health care transformed it*
Mollel, Tololwa M. *Orphan boy*
Rhinos for lunch and elephants for supper
Napoli, Donna Jo. *Mama Miti*
Nivola, Claire A. *Planting the trees of Kenya*
Oelschlager, Vanita. *Bonyo Bonyo*
Richardson, Justin. *Christian, the hugging lion*
Walters, Eric. *The matatu*
Williams, Karen Lynn. *Beatrice's dream*
Wilson-Max, Ken. *Fuhara means happy*
Winter, Jeanette. *Wangari's trees of peace*

Foreign lands – Korea

Bae, Hyun-Joo. *New clothes for New Year's day*
Chung, Hyechong. *K is for Korea*
Climo, Shirley. *The Korean Cinderella*
Farley, Carol J. *The king's secret*
Haskins, Jim. *Count your way through Korea*
Heo, Yumi. *The green frogs*
Lady Hahn and her seven friends
Lee, Tae-Jun. *Waiting for Mama*
Park, Frances. *Good-bye, 382 Shin Dang Dong*
The royal bee
Where on earth is my bagel?
Park, Linda Sue. *Bee-bim bop!*
The firekeeper's son
San Souci, Daniel. *The rabbit and the dragon king*
Wong, Janet S. *The trip back home*

Foreign lands – Korea (North)

Park, Frances. *My freedom trip*

Foreign lands – Laos

Xiong, Blia. *Nine-in-one Grr! Grr!*
Youme. *Mali under the night sky*

Foreign lands – Lapland

Reynolds, Jan. *Far north*

Foreign lands – Latin America

Mora, Pat. *A piñata in a pine tree*
Shahan, Sherry. *Fiesta!*
Stanton, Karen. *Papi's gift*
Torres, Leyla. *Liliana's grandmothers*
Vidal, Beatriz A. *Federico and the Magi's gift*

Foreign lands – Lebanon

Heide, Florence Parry. *Sami and the time of the troubles*

Foreign lands – Liberia

Aardema, Verna. *Koi and the kola nuts*
The vingananee and the tree toad
Paye, Won-Ldy. *Head, body, legs*
Mrs. Chicken and the hungry crocodile

Foreign lands – Madagascar

Dennard, Deborah. *Lemur landing*
Rappaport, Doreen. *The new king*

Foreign lands – Malawi

Kamkwamba, William. *The boy who harnessed the wind*

Foreign lands – Malaysia

Goodman, Susan E. *Chopsticks for my noodle soup*

Foreign lands – Mali

Cowcher, Helen. *Desert elephants*
Diakité, Baba Wagué. *The magic gourd*
Mee-an and the magic serpent
Diakité, Penda. *I lost my tooth in Africa*
Eisner, Will. *Sundiata*
Wisniewski, David. *Sundiata: lion king of Mali*

Foreign lands – Martinique

San Souci, Robert D. *The faithful friend*

Foreign lands – Mauritania

Cunnane, Kelly. *Deep in the Sahara*

Foreign lands – Mexico

Aardema, Verna. *Borreguita and the coyote*
Pedro and the padre
The riddle of the drum
Alarcón, Francisco X. *From the bellybutton of the moon and other summer poems / Del ombligo de la luna y otros poemas de verano*
Amado, Elisa. *What are you doing?*
Bernier-Grand, Carmen T. *Our Lady of Guadalupe*
Bullard, Lisa. *Marco's Cinco de Mayo*
Bunting, Eve. *Going home*
Cohn, Diana. *Dream carver*
Colato Laínez, René. *Playing lotería / El juego de la lotería*
Corpi, Lucha. *Where fireflies dance / Ahí, donde bailan las luciérnagas*
de Las Casas, Dianne. *Blue frog*
dePaola, Tomie. *The Lady of Guadalupe*
Dorros, Arthur. *Julio's magic*
Ehlert, Lois. *Cuckoo, a Mexican folktale / Cucú: un cuento folklórico mexicano*
Elya, Susan Middleton. *N is for Navidad*
Ets, Marie Hall. *Nine days to Christmas*
Flanagan, Alice K. *Cinco de Mayo*
Frith, Margaret. *Frida Kahlo*
Goldman, Judy. *Uncle Monarch and the Day of the Dead*
Grimm, Jacob and Wilhelm *The fisherman and the turtle*
Grossman, Patricia. *Saturday market*
Guy, Ginger Foglesong. *Fiesta*
Haskins, Jim. *Count your way through Mexico*
Johnston, Tony. *Day of the Dead*
The iguana brothers, a perfect day
My Mexico / México mío
P is for piñata
The tale of Rabbit and Coyote
Joosse, Barbara. *Ghost wings*
Keep, Linda Lowery. *Day of the Dead*
Kimmel, Eric A. *The two mountains*
Krebs, Laurie. *Off we go to Mexico*
Larson, Bonnie. *When animals were people / Cuando los animales eran personas*
Levy, Janice. *Celebrate! It's cinco de mayo! / Celebremos! Es el cinco de mayo!*
McAlister, Caroline. *Holy Molé!*
McDermott, Gerald. *Musicians of the sun*
Madrigal, Antonio Hernandez. *Erandi's braids*
Marcos, subcomandante. *The story of colors / La historia de los colores*
Martín, Hugo C. *Pablo's Christmas*
Meunier, Brian. *Bravo, Tavo!*
Mora, Pat. *The beautiful lady*
The gift of the poinsettia / El regalo de la flor de nochebuena
A library for Juana
The night the moon fell
Morales, Yuyi. *Just a minute: a trickster tale and counting book*
Rohmer, Harriet. *How we came to the fifth world*
Ross, Michael Elsohn. *Mexican Christmas*
Ryan, Pam Muñoz. *Mice and beans*
Sahagun, Bernardino de. *Spirit child*
Sanromán, Susana. *Señora Reganoña*
Schaefer, A. R. *Diego Rivera*
Schaefer, Lola M. *Cinco de Mayo*
Sobol, Richard. *Adelina's whales*
Swope, Sam. *Gotta go! Gotta go!*
Tafolla, Carmen. *What can you do with a rebozo?*
Tonatiuh, Duncan. *Dear Primo*
Diego Rivera: his world and ours
Van Laan, Nancy. *La boda*
Volkmer, Jane Anne. *Song of Chirimia / La Musica de la Chirimia*
Wade, Mary Dodson. *Cinco de Mayo*
Winter, Jeanette. *Niño's mask*
Wisniewski, David. *Rain player*
Yacowitz, Caryn. *Pumpkin fiesta*
Ziefert, Harriet. *Home for Navidad*

Foreign lands – Middle East

Addasi, Maha. *Time to pray*
Arabian Nights. *The tale of Ali Baba and the forty thieves*
Johnson-Davies, Denys. *Goha, the wise fool*
Kimmel, Eric A. *Joha makes a wish*
Shah, Idries. *The boy without a name*
The clever boy and the terrible, dangerous animal
The silly chicken
Weulersse, Odile. *Nasreddine*
Young, Ed. *What about me?*

Foreign lands – Mongolia

Baasansuren, Bolormaa. *My little round house*
Lewin, Ted. *Horse song*
Otsuka, Yuzo. *Suho's white horse*
Yep, Laurence. *The Khan's daughter*

Foreign lands – Morocco

Alalou, Elizabeth. *The butter man*
Baker, Jeannie. *Mirror*
Ichikawa, Satomi. *My father's shop*
London, Jonathan. *Ali, child of the desert*

Foreign lands – Namibia

Aardema, Verna. *Jackal's flying lesson*

Foreign lands – Nepal

Hobbie, Holly. *Toot and Puddle, top of the world*
Nagda, Anne Whitehead. *A tiger tale*
Reynolds, Jan. *Himalaya*
Stryer, Andrea Stenn. *Kami and the yaks*

Foreign lands – Netherlands *see* Foreign lands – Holland

Foreign lands – Nicaragua

Rohmer, Harriet. *Mother scorpion country*
Rohmer, Harriet, et al. *The invisible hunters*

Foreign lands – Nigeria

Daly, Niki. *Why the sun and moon live in the sky*
Gerson, Mary-Joan. *Why the sky is far away*
Medearis, Angela Shelf. *The singing man*
Mollel, Tololwa M. *The flying tortoise*
Olaleye, Isaac. *Bikes for rent!*
Bitter bananas
The distant talking drum
In the Rainfield
Onyefulu, Ifeoma. *Ogbo*
Saying goodbye
Shepard, Aaron. *Master man*

Foreign lands – Norway

Brett, Jan. *Who's that knocking on Christmas eve?*
Harvey, Matthea. *Cecil the pet glacier*
Kimmel, Eric A. *Easy work!*
Lunge-Larsen, Lise. *The race of the Birkebeiners*
Reynolds, Jan. *Far north*

Foreign lands – Pakistan

Khan, Rukhsana. *King for a day*
Mortenson, Greg. *Listen to the wind*
Shepard, Aaron. *The gifts of Wali Dad*

Foreign lands – Palestine

MacDonald, Margaret Read. *Tunjur! Tunjur! Tunjur!*
Nye, Naomi Shihab. *Sitti's secrets*

Foreign lands – Panama

MacDonald, Margaret Read. *Conejito*
Palacios, Argentina. *A Christmas surprise for Chabelita*
Sayre, April Pulley. *Army ant parade*

Foreign lands – Persia

Climo, Shirley. *The Persian Cinderella*
Nadimi, Suzan. *The rich man and the parrot*

Foreign lands – Peru

Díaz, Katacha. *Carolina's gift*
Dominguez, Angela. *Maria had a little llama/Maria tenia una llama pequena*
Dorros, Arthur. *Tonight is carnaval*
Ehlert, Lois. *Moon rope / Un lazo a la luna*
Horowitz, Dave. *Chico the brave*
Krebs, Laurie. *Up and down the Andes*
Tompert, Ann. *The pied piper of Peru*

Foreign lands – Philippines

Climo, Shirley. *Tuko and the birds*
San Souci, Robert D. *Pedro and the monkey*

Foreign lands – Poland

Carnesi, Monica. *Little dog lost*
Sasso, Sandy Eisenberg. *Butterflies under our hats*
Ungar, Richard. *Rachel's library*

Foreign lands – Puerto Rico

Gugler, Laurel Dee. *There's a billy goat in the garden*
Jaffe, Nina. *The golden flower*
London, Jonathan. *Hurricane!*
Montes, Marisa. *Juan Bobo goes to work*
Rohmer, Harriet. *Atariba and Niguayona*
Roth, Susan L. *Parrots over Puerto Rico*
Santiago, Esmeralda. *A doll for Navidades*

Foreign lands – Romania

Philip, Neil. *Noah and the devil*

Foreign lands – Russia

Arnold, Katya. *That apple is mine!*
Bateson-Hill, Margaret. *Masha and the firebird*
Brown, Marcia. *Stone soup*
Cole, Joanna. *Bony-legs*
Croll, Carolyn. *The little snowgirl*
The firebird. *The firebird,* ill. by Demi
The firebird, ill. by Rachel Isadora
The tale of the firebird
Ginsburg, Mirra. *Clay boy*
Haskins, Jim. *Count your way through Russia*
Hoffman, Mary. *Clever Katya*
Horn, Sandra Ann. *Babushka*
Howland, Naomi. *Latkes, latkes, good to eat*
Joosse, Barbara. *Nikolai, the only bear*
Kabakov, Vladimir. *R is for Russia*
King, Dedie. *I see the sun in Russia*
London, Jonathan. *Little lost tiger*
McCaughrean, Geraldine. *Grandma Chickenlegs*
Martin, Rafe. *The language of birds*
Mayer, Marianna. *Baba Yaga and Vasilisa the Brave*
Oram, Hiawyn. *Baba Yaga and the wise doll*
Parkinson, Kathy. *The enormous turnip*
Pavlova, Anna. *I dreamed I was a ballerina*
Peck, Jan. *The giant carrot*
Polacco, Patricia. *Babushka's Mother Goose*
Prokofiev, Sergei Sergeievitch. *Peter and the wolf,* ill. by Charles Mikolaycak
Peter and the wolf, ill. by Josef Palecek
Peter and the wolf, ill. by Chris Raschka
Peter and the wolf, ill. by Vladimir Vagin
Robbins, Ruth. *Baboushka and the three kings*
Sanderson, Ruth. *The golden mare, the firebird, and the magic ring*
San Souci, Robert D. *Peter and the blue witch baby*
Schuch, Steve. *A symphony of whales*
Shepard, Aaron. *The sea king's daughter*
Spirin, Gennady. *Martha*
Philipok
Thompson, Kay. *Kay Thompson's Eloise in Moscow*
Tolstoy, Aleksey Nikolayevich. *The enormous turnip*

The gigantic turnip
Vagin, Vladimir. *The enormous carrot*
Van Kampen, Vlasta. *Bear tales*
Winthrop, Elizabeth. *Vasilissa the beautiful*
Yolen, Jane. *The firebird*
The flying witch

Foreign lands – Rwanda

Aardema, Verna. *Sebgugugu the glutton*

Foreign lands – Sahara Desert

Reynolds, Jan. *Sahara*

Foreign lands – Saudi Arabia

MacDonald, Margaret Read. *How many donkeys?*

Foreign lands – Scandinavia

Manning, Mick. *What a Viking!*

Foreign lands – Scotland

Alger, Leclaire Gowans. *All in the morning early*
Always room for one more
Burdett, Lois. *Macbeth for kids*
Leaf, Munro. *Wee Gillis*
Lupton, Hugh. *Pirican Pic and Pirican Mor*
Thompson, Emma. *The further tale of Peter Rabbit*

Foreign lands – Siam *see* Foreign lands – Thailand

Foreign lands – Somalia

Ahmed, Said Salah. *The lion's share / Qayb Libaax*
McQuinn, Anna. *My friend Jamal*

Foreign lands – South Africa

Angelou, Maya. *My painted house, my friendly chicken, and me*
Cave, Kathryn. *One child, one seed*
Daly, Niki. *Happy birthday, Jamela!*
The herd boy
Jamela's dress
Not so fast Songololo
Once upon a time
A song for Jamela
What's cooking, Jamela?
Isadora, Rachel. *At the crossroads*
Over the green hills
A South African night
Javaherbin, Mina. *Goal!*
Lewin, Hugh. *Jafta — the homecoming*
Lumry, Amanda. *Safari in South Africa*
Nelson, Kadir. *Nelson Mandela*
Seeger, Pete. *Abiyoyo returns*
Tutu, Archbishop Desmond. *Desmond and the very mean word*
Wilson-Max, Ken. *Halala means welcome*

Foreign lands – South America

Bateman, Teresa. *The frog with the big mouth*
Buxton, Jane. *The littlest llama*
Campoy, F. Isabel. *Rosa Raposa*
Downing, Johnette. *Amazon alphabet*
Knutson, Barbara. *Love and roast chicken*
McDermott, Gerald. *Jabutí the tortoise*
Reynolds, Jan. *Amazon*
Silvano, Wendi. *Just one more*
Yahgulanaas, Michael Nicoll. *The little hummingbird*

Foreign lands – South Sea Islands

Blackstone, Stella. *Secret seahorse*
Secret seahorse [board book]
Wood, Audrey. *Ten little fish*

Foreign lands – Spain

Aska, Warabe. *Tapicero tap tap*
Davis, Aubrey. *Bagels from Benny*
Kimmel, Eric A. *Medio Pollito*
Leaf, Munro. *The story of Ferdinand the bull*
Sierra, Judy. *The beautiful butterfly*
Zamorano, Ana. *Let's eat!*

Foreign lands – Sudan

Aardema, Verna. *What's so funny, Ketu?*
Kessler, Cristina. *My great-grandmother's gourd*

Foreign lands – Sweden

Hooks, William H. *The legend of the Christmas rose*
Lindgren, Astrid. *Pippi Longstocking's after-Christmas party*
Maddern, Eric. *Nail soup*

Foreign lands – Switzerland

Fisher, Leonard Everett. *William Tell*
Hasler, Eveline. *A tale of two brothers*

Foreign lands – Taiwan

Chen, Chih-Yuan. *On my way to buy eggs*

Foreign lands – Tanzania

Bardhan-Quallen, Sudipta. *Flying eagle*
Kilaka, John. *True friends*
Krebs, Laurie. *We all went on safari*
MacLachlan, Patricia. *Lala salama*
Martin, Francesca. *Clever Tortoise*
Mollel, Tololwa M. *Kele's secret*
My rows and piles of coins
Song bird
Subira subira
Stuve-Bodeen, Stephanie. *Elizabeti's doll*
Elizabeti's school
Mama Elizabeti
Winter, Jeanette. *The watcher*

Foreign lands – Tasmania

Baker, Jeannie. *The hidden forest*

Foreign lands – Thailand

Arnold, Katya. *Elephants can paint, too!*
Bridges, Shirin Yim. *The Umbrella Queen*
Ho, Minfong. *Hush!*
Krudop, Walter Lyon. *The man who caught fish*

MacDonald, Margaret Read. *The girl who wore too much*
Shea, Pegi Deitz. *The whispering cloth*

Foreign lands – Tibet

Berger, Barbara. *All the way to Lhasa*
Martin, Jacqueline Briggs. *The chiru of High Tibet*
Schroeder, Alan. *The stone lion*
Sís, Peter. *Tibet through the red box*
Soros, Barbara. *Tenzin's deer*

Foreign lands – Trinidad

Bootman, Colin. *Fish for the Grand Lady*
Greenwood, Mark. *Drummer boy of John John*
Joseph, Lynn. *Coconut kind of day*
An island Christmas
Rahaman, Vashanti. *Divali rose*

Foreign lands – Turkey

Gilani-Williams, Fawzia. *Nabeel's new pants*
Mandell, Muriel. *A donkey reads*

Foreign lands – Tyrol

Sawyer, Ruth. *The remarkable Christmas of the cobbler's sons*

Foreign lands – Uganda

Fullerton, Alma. *A good trade*
McBrier, Page. *Beatrice's goat*
MacDonald, Margaret Read. *Give up, Gecko!*
Schrock, Jan West. *Give a goat*
Winters, Kari-Lynn. *Gift days*

Foreign lands – Ukraine

Aylesworth, Jim. *The mitten*
Brett, Jan. *The mitten*
Gorbachev, Valeri. *The fool of the world and the flying ship: a Ukrainian folk tale*
Kimmel, Eric A. *The birds' gift*
Polacco, Patricia. *Luba and the wren*
Ransome, Arthur. *The fool of the world and the flying ship*
Skrypuch, Marsha Forchuk. *Enough*
Tresselt, Alvin R. *The mitten: an old Ukrainian folktale*

Foreign lands – Uzbekistan

Sandman, Rochel. *Perfect porridge*

Foreign lands – Venezuela

Nazoa, Aquiles. *A small Nativity*

Foreign lands – Vietnam

Alberti, Theresa Jarosz. *Vietnam ABCs*
Garland, Sherry. *The lotus seed*
Shepard, Aaron. *The crystal heart*
Sugarman, Brynn Olenberg. *Rebecca's journey home*
Thong, Roseanne. *Fly free!*
Vander Zee, Ruth. *Always with you*

Foreign lands – Wales

Cullen, Lynn. *The mightiest heart*
MacDonald, Margaret Read. *Slop!*

Foreign lands – West Indies

Hamilton, Virginia. *The girl who spun gold*
Rahaman, Vashanti. *O Christmas tree*

Foreign lands – Yukon Territory

Provensen, Alice. *Klondike gold*

Foreign lands – Zaire

Aardema, Verna. *Traveling to Tondo*

Foreign lands – Zambia

Bryan, Ashley. *Beautiful blackbird*

Foreign lands – Zanzibar

Aardema, Verna. *Bimwili and the Zimwi*

Foreign lands – Zimbabwe

Stock, Catherine. *Gugu's house*

Foreign languages

Ada, Alma Flor. *The Christmas tree / El arbol de Navidad*
Gathering the sun
I love Saturdays y domingos
¡Muu, moo!
Pio peep!
Addasi, Maha. *Time to pray*
Aesop. *The hare and the tortoise / La liebre y la tortuga*
Ahmed, Said Salah. *The lion's share / Qayb Libaax*
Aigner-Clark, Julie. *Language nursery*
Alarcón, Francisco X. *From the bellybutton of the moon and other summer poems / Del ombligo de la luna y otros poemas de verano*
Iguanas in the snow and other winter poems / Iguanas en la nieve y otros poemas de invierno
Ancona, George. *Mi música / My music*
Mis abuelos / My grandparents
Mis comidas / My foods
Mis fiestas / My celebrations
Mis juegos / My games
Mis quehaceres / My chores
Argueta, Jorge. *Arroz con leche / Rice pudding*
Guacamole
Moony Luna / Luna, Lunita Lunera
Sopa de frijoles: un poema para cocinar / Bean soup: a cooking poem
Tamalitos
Barner, Bob. *The Day of the Dead / El Día de los Muertos*
Beaton, Clare. *At home / A la maison*
Bertrand, Diane Gonzales. *Family / familia*
The last doll / La última muñeca
Sofía and the purple dress / Sofia y el vestido morado
Uncle Chente's picnic / El picnic de Tío Chente
Bloom, Suzanne. *Nuestro autobús / The bus for us*
Bock, Lee. *Oh, crumps! / Ay, caramba!*
Bouchard, Dave. *Nokum is my teacher*

Brandt, Amy. *Benjamin comes back / Benjamin regresa*
When Katie was our teacher / Cuando Katie era nuestra maestra
Brimner, Larry Dane. *Trick or treat, Old Armadillo*
Brown, Monica. *My name is Gabito / Me llamo Gabito*
Pelé, king of soccer / Pelé, el rey del fútbol
Side by side / Lado a lado
Bruzzone, Catherine. *Puppy finds a friend / Cachorrito encuentra un amigo*
Puppy finds a friend / Le petit chien se trouve un ami
Burnell, Heather Ayris. *Bedtime monster / ¡A dormir, pequeño monstruo!*
Caraballo, Samuel. *My big sister / Mi hermana mayor*
Chapra, Mimi. *Amelia's show-and-tell fiesta / Amelia y la fiesta de "muestra y cuenta"*
Sparky's bark / El ladrido de Sparky
Chavarría-Cháirez, Becky. *Magda's piñata magic / Magda y la piñata mágica*
Magda's tortillas / Las tortillas de Magada
Chen, Yong. *A gift*
Coerr, Eleanor. *Circus day in Japan*
Colato Laínez, René. *Playing lotería / El juego de la lotería*
Señor Pancho had a rancho
Compos, Tito. *Muffler man / El hombre mofle*
Corpi, Lucha. *Where fireflies dance / Ahí, donde bailan las luciérnagas*
Cox, Judy. *Carmen learns English*
Cumpiano, Ina. *Quinito, day and night / Quinito, dia y noche*
Quinito's neighborhood / El vecindario de Quinito
De colores / Bright with colors
De Anda, Diane. *Dancing Miranda / Baila, Miranda, baila*
A day without sugar / Un dia sin azucar
The patchwork garden / pedacitos de huerto
Delacre, Lulu. *Arroz con leche*
Las Navidades
dePaola, Tomie. *Brava Strega Nona!*
Marcos
De Sève, Randall. *Mi barco / Toy boat*
Dominguez, Angela. *Maria had a little llama/Maria tenia una llama pequena*
Dorros, Alex. *Número uno*
Dorros, Arthur. *Abuela*
Mama and me
Papa and me
Radio Man / Don Radio
Dunbar, Polly. *Pingüino / penguin*
Ehlert, Lois. *Cuckoo, a Mexican folktale / Cucú: un cuento folklórico mexicano*
Moon rope / Un lazo a la luna
Elya, Susan Middleton. *Adiós, tricycle*
Bebé goes shopping
Bebé goes to the beach
Cowboy Jose
Eight animals bake a cake
Eight animals on the town
F is for fiesta
Fairy trails
Fire! ¡Fuego! Brave bomberos
N is for Navidad
No more, por favor
Oh no, gotta go #2
Rubia and the three osos
Say hola to Spanish
Sophie's trophy
Tooth on the loose
Emberley, Rebecca. *My animals / Mis animales*
My big book of Spanish words
My city / Mi cuidad
My clothes / Mi ropa
My colors / Mis colores
My food / Mi comida
My garden / Mi jardin
My house / Mi casa
My numbers / Mis números
My opposites / Mis opuestos
My room / Mi cuarto
My school / Mi escuela
My shapes / Mis formas
My toys / Mi juguetes
English, Karen. *Speak English for us, Marisol*
Evans, Lezlie. *Can you count ten toes?*
Can you greet the whole wide world?
Farley, Carol J. *The king's secret*
Feelings, Muriel. *Jambo means hello*
Moja means one
Flanagan, Alice K. *Learning is fun with Mrs. Perez*
Galindo, Mary Sue. *Icy watermelon / Sandía fría*
Gershator, Phillis. *Zoo day, olé!*
The gingerbread boy. *Señorita Gordita*
Gollub, Matthew. *Jazz Fly 2*
Ten oni drummers
Gonzalez, Lucia. *The storyteller's candle / La velita de los cuentos*
Grant, Brianna K. *We are girls who love to run / Somos chicas y a nosotras nos encanta correr*
Grimm, Jacob and Wilhelm. *Hansel and Gretel / Hansel y Gretel*
Musicians of Bremen / Los musicos de Bremner
Groner, Judyth Saypol. *My first Hebrew word book*
Guy, Ginger Foglesong. *¡Bravo!*
Fiesta
My grandma / Mi abuelita
My school / Mi escuela
Perros! perros! dogs! dogs!
Siesta
Harris, Trudy. *Say something, Perico*
Haskins, Jim. *Count your way through Afghanistan*
Count your way through Africa
Count your way through Brazil
Count your way through China
Count your way through France
Count your way through Germany
Count your way through Greece
Count your way through India
Count your way through Iran
Count your way through Israel
Count your way through Italy
Count your way through Japan
Count your way through Korea
Count your way through Mexico
Count your way through Russia
Count your way through the Arab world
Hayes, Joe. *Don't say a word, Mamá/No digas nada, Mamá*
Juan Verdades, the man who could not tell a lie
Little Gold Star / Estrellita de oro
Head, Judith. *Mud soup*
Henderson, Kathy. *Hush, baby, hush!*
Henkes, Kevin. *El gran día de Lily / Lilly's big day*
Herrera, Juan Felipe. *Grandma and Me at the flea / Los meros meros remateros*
Hill, Eric. *Spot's big book of words / El libro grande de las palabras de Spot*

Hoffman, Eric. *No fair to tigers / No es justo para los tigres*
Play Lady / La Señora Juguetona
Hood, Susan. *Spike, the mixed-up monster*
Hoshino, Felicia. *Sora and the cloud*
Hudes, Quiara Alegría. *Welcome to my neighborhood!*
Iijima, Geneva Cobb. *The way we do it in Japan*
Isadora, Rachel. *Say hello!*
Jenkins, Steve. *Perros y gatos / dogs and cats*
Jiménez, Francisco. *The Christmas gift / El regalo de Navidad*
Jocelyn, Marthe. *ABC x 3*
Johnson, Amy Crane. *Cinnamon and the April shower / Canela y el aguacero de abril*
Mason moves away / Mason se muda
Johnston, Tony. *My abuelita*
My Mexico / México mío
Katz, Karen. *Can you say peace?*
Keats, Ezra Jack. *My dog is lost!*
Keister, Douglas. *Fernando's gift / El regalo de Fernando*
Kimmelman, Leslie. *Everybody bonjours!*
King, Dedie. *I see the sun in Afghanistan*
I see the sun in Russia
Krebs, Laurie. *Off we go to Mexico*
We all went on safari
Lachtman, Ofelia Dumas. *Pepita takes time / Pepita, siempre tarde*
Larson, Bonnie. *When animals were people / Cuando los animales eran personas*
Law, Diane. *Come out and play: count around the world in five languages*
Lee, Huy Voun. *In the leaves*
1, 2, 3 go!
Lee-Tai, Amy. *A place where sunflowers grow / Sabaku ni saita himawari*
Levy, Janice. *Celebrate! It's cinco de mayo! / Celebremos! Es el cinco de mayo!*
Ljungkvist, Laura. *Pepi sings a new song*
Lomas Garza, Carmen. *In my family*
Love to mamá
Luenn, Nancy. *A gift for Abuelita*
Luján, Jorge. *Colors! / ¡Colores!*
Sky blue accident / Accidente celeste
MacDonald, Margaret Read. *Conejito*
How many donkeys?
McKissack, Patricia C. *Messy Bessey / Ada, la desordenada*
McLean, Dirk. *Play mas'! a carnival ABC*
Marcos, subcomandante. *The story of colors / La historia de los colores*
Meshon, Aaron. *Take me out to the Yakyu*
Miller, Elizabeth I. *Just like home / Como en mi tierra*
Montes, Marisa. *Los gatos black on Halloween*
Mora, Pat. *The bakery lady / La señora de la panadería*
Book fiesta! celebrate Children's Day/Book Day / Celebremos El día de los niños/El día de los libros
Confetti
Delicious hullabaloo / Pachanga deliciosa
The desert is my mother / El desierto es mi madre
The gift of the poinsettia / El regalo de la flor de nochebuena
Gracias / Thanks
Here, kitty, kitty! / ¡Ven, gatita, ven!
Let's eat! / A comer!
Listen to the desert / Oye al desierto
Marimba!
One, two, three / Uno, dos, tres
A piñata in a pine tree
The race of toad and deer
Sweet dreams / Dulces suenos
Morales, Yuyi. *Just in case: a trickster tale and Spanish alphabet book*
Nino wrestles the world
Moreton, Daniel. *La Cucaracha Martina*
Morton, Lone. *Hurry up, Molly / Apúrate, Molly*
Hurry up, Molly / Dépêche-toi, Molly
Niemann, Christoph. *The pet dragon*
Nye, Naomi Shihab. *Sitti's secrets*
O'Connor, Jane. *Nancy la elegante / Fancy Nancy*
Ogburn, Jacqueline K. *Little treasures*
Orozco, Jose-Luis. *Pancho Claus*
Rin, rin, rin / do, re, mi
Pak, Soyung. *Dear Juno*
Park, Linda Sue. *Yum! Yuck!*
Paul, Ann Whitford. *Count on Culebra*
Fiesta fiasco
Mañana Iguana
Tortuga in trouble
Pérez, Amada Irma. *My diary from here to there / Mi diario de aquí hasta allá*
My very own room / Mi propio cuartito
Perrault, Charles. *Cinderella / Cenicienta*
Pinkwater, Daniel. *Beautiful Yetta*
Portis, Antoinette. *No es una caja / not a box*
Prap, Lila. *Animals speak*
Price, Mara. *Grandma's chocolate / El chocolate de Abuelita*
Reed, Lynn Rowe. *Pedro, his perro, and the alphabet sombrero*
Reiser, Lynn. *My way / A mi manera*
Roe, Eileen. *With my brother / Con mi hermano*
Rosa-Mendoza, Gladys. *What time is it? / Qué hora es?*
Ruiz-Flores, Lupe. *Alicia's fruity drinks / Las aguas frescas de Alicia*
Rumford, James. *Dog-of-the-Sea-Waves*
Sequoyah
There's a monster in the alphabet
Russo, Marisabina. *Peter is just a baby*
Ryan, Pam Muñoz. *Hello ocean / Hola mar*
Mice and beans
Sacre, Antonio. *A mango in the hand*
Sáenz, Benjamin Alire. *A gift from papá Diego / Un regalo de papá Diego*
Grandma Fina and her wonderful umbrellas / La abuelita Fina y sus sombrillas maravillosas
San Souci, Robert D. *Little gold star*
Schotter, Roni. *All about grandmas*
Shannon, David. *Demasiados juguetes / too many toys*
Shirotani, Hideo. *Let's eat / Vamos a comer*
Let's take a walk / Vamos a caminar
What color? / Qué color?
Silvano, Wendi. *Counting coconuts / Contando cocos*
Soto, Gary. *Chato goes cruisin'*
Chato's kitchen
My little car / Mi carrito
Too many tamales
Sper, Emily. *Hanukkah: a counting book in English, Hebrew, and Yiddish*
Stevens, Jan Romero. *Carlos and the skunk / Carlos y el zorrillo*
Carlos digs to China / Carlos excava hasta la China
Sweetland, Nancy Rose. *If I could / Si yo pudiera*
Tafolla, Carmen. *Baby Coyote and the old woman / El coyotito y la viejita*

The three little pigs *The three little pigs / Los tres cerditos*
Tortillas and lullabies / Tortillas y cancioncitas
Vagin, Vladimir. *Here comes the cat*
Vallverdu, Josep. *Aladdin and the magic lamp / Aldino y la lampara maravillosa*
Vamos, Samantha R. *Before you were here, mi amor*
The cazuela that the farm maiden stirred
Van Laan, Nancy. *La boda*
Sleep, sleep, sleep
Vega, Denise. *Build a burrito*
Grandmother, have the angels come?
Velasquez, Eric. *Grandma's gift*
Vidal, Beatriz A. *Federico and the Magi's gift*
Vigil-Piñón, Evangelina. *Marina's muumuu / El muumuu de Marina*
Volkmer, Jane Anne. *Song of Chirimia / La Musica de la Chirimia*
Walker, Rob D. *Mama says*
Wallace, Mary. *I is for Inuksuk*
Warburton, Tom. *1000 times no*
Weeks, Sarah. *Counting Ovejas*
Weinstein, Ellen Slusky. *Everywhere the cow says "Moo!"*
Wells, Rosemary. *McDuff goes to school*
Otto se presenta para presidente / Otto runs for President
Wiese, Kurt. *You can write Chinese*
Wilson-Max, Ken. *Fuhara means happy*
Halala means welcome
Winter, Jonah. *Diego*
Sonia Sotomayor
Wolff, Ashley. *I call my grandma Nana*
I call my grandpa Papa
Wu, Faye-Lynn. *Chinese and English nursery rhymes*
Yeh, Kat. *The magic brush*
Zepeda, Gwendolyn. *Growing up with tamales / Los tamales de Ana*
Ziefert, Harriet. *Home for Navidad*

Forest, woods

Adler, David A. *Redwoods are the tallest trees in the world*
Ahlberg, Janet. *Jeremiah in the dark wood*
Alborough, Jez. *Where's my teddy?*
Arnosky, Jim. *Crinkleroot's guide to knowing the trees*
Baker, Jeannie. *Where the forest meets the sea*
Bauer, Marion Dane. *Halloween forest*
Berenstain, Stan and Jan. *The Berenstain bears and the ghost of the forest*
Berkes, Marianne. *Over in the forest*
Collins, Pat Lowery. *The deer watch*
Cotten, Cynthia. *At the edge of the woods*
Crum, Shutta. *The bravest of the brave*
Delessert, Etienne. *The seven dwarfs*
Demarest, Chris L. *Hotshots!*
Smokejumpers one to ten
Dennard, Deborah. *Koala country*
Lemur landing
DePrisco, Dorothea. *Snowbear's winter day*
Docherty, Helen. *The Snatchabook*
Ets, Marie Hall. *In the forest*
Fredericks, Anthony D. *In one tidepool*
Frost, Robert. *Stopping by woods on a snowy evening*
Gay, Marie-Louise. *Stella, fairy of the forest*
Genechten, Guido van. *The big woods orchestra*
George, Lindsay Barrett. *In the woods*
George, William T. *Christmas at Long Pond*
Gershator, Phillis. *Who's in the forest?*
Gliori, Debi. *Mr. Bear to the rescue*
Gore, Leonid. *The wonderful book*
Graham Barber, Lynda. *Spy hops and belly flops*
Grimm, Jacob and Wilhelm. *Hansel and Gretel*, ill. by Jen Corace
Hansel and Gretel, ill. by Rachel Isadora
Hansel and Gretel (1980), ill. by Susan Jeffers
Hansel and Gretel (2011), ill. by Susan Jeffers
Hansel and Gretel, ill. by Jane Ray
Hansel and Gretel, ill. by Claudia Wolf
Hansel and Gretel, ill. by Paul O. Zelinsky
Hansel and Gretel, ill. by Lisbeth Zwerger
Hansel and Gretel / Hansel y Gretel
Hansel and Gretel: a retelling from the original tale by the Brothers Grimm
Hewitt, Sally. *Woods and meadows*
Himmelman, John. *A wood frog's life*
Holabird, Katharine. *Angelina and Henry*
Itaya, Satoshi. *Buttons and Bo*
Johnson, Amy Crane. *Cinnamon and the April shower / Canela y el aguacero de abril*
Johnston, Tony. *Bigfoot Cinderrrrrella*
Judge, Lita. *Red hat*
Keister, Douglas. *Fernando's gift / El regalo de Fernando*
Kherdian, David. *Come back, Moon*
Kleven, Elisa. *The dancing deer and the foolish hunter*
Klingel, Cynthia Fitterer. *Forests*
Lairla, Sergio. *Abel and the wolf*
Landström, Olof. *Boo and Baa in the woods*
Lyon, George Ella. *Counting on the woods*
McClements, George. *Dinosaur Woods*
Marshall, James. *Hansel and Gretel*
Martin, Bill, Jr. *A beasty story*
Martin, David. *Let's have a tree party!*
Miller, Debbie S. *Are trees alive?*
Miller, Edna. *Mousekin's Thanksgiving*
Moerbeek, Kees. *The diary of Hansel and Gretel*
Nivola, Claire A. *The forest*
Olaleye, Isaac. *Lake of the Big Snake*
Pearson, Tracey Campbell. *The purple hat*
Peet, Bill. *Big bad Bruce*
Quattlebaum, Mary. *Jo MacDonald hiked in the woods*
Reed-Jones, Carol. *The tree in the ancient forest*
Ryder, Joanne. *The waterfall's gift*
Sayre, April Pulley. *Army ant parade*
Schaefer, Carole Lexa. *Down in the woods at sleepytime*
Down in the woods at sleepytime [board book]
Schofield, Jennifer. *Animal babies in rain forests*
Schotter, Roni. *In the piney woods*
Serafini, Frank. *Looking closely through the forest*
Serfozo, Mary. *Whooo's there?*
Sharratt, Nick. *The foggy, foggy forest*
Simple gifts
Stojic, Manya. *Snow*
Stoop, Naoko. *Red Knit Cap Girl*
Tresselt, Alvin R. *The gift of the tree*
Waddell, Martin. *Let's go home, Little Bear*
Wallen, Ila. *The moon in my room*
Ward, Helen. *The tin forest*
Ward, Jennifer. *Forest bright, forest night*
Wells, Rosemary. *Moss pillows*
Wilson, Karma. *Bear stays up for Christmas*
Yolen, Jane. *All in the woodland early*
Owl moon

Forgetfulness *see* Behavior – forgetfulness

Forgiving *see* Behavior – forgiving

Format, unusual

Ahlberg, Janet. *The jolly Christmas postman*
Aliki. *Marianthe's story one: painted words; Marianthe's story two: spoken memories*
Baeten, Lieve. *The clever little witch*
The curious little witch
Barnett, Mac. *Guess again!*
Behrens, Janice. *Let's find rain forest animals*
Blechman, Nicholas. *Night light*
Boyd, Lizi. *Inside outside*
Bridwell, Norman. *Glow-in-the-dark Halloween*
Brown, Ruth. *The tale of two mice*
Budnitz, Paul. *The hole in the middle*
Capucilli, Alyssa Satin. *My first soccer game*
Carle, Eric. *My very first book of colors*
My very first book of growth
My very first book of homes
My very first book of motion
My very first book of numbers
My very first book of shapes
My very first book of touch
My very first book of words
10 little rubber ducks
The very hungry caterpillar
The very quiet cricket
Carter, David A. *If you're happy and you know it, clap your hands*
Chedru, Delphine. *Spot it again!*
Dennard, Deborah. *Hedgehog haven*
Donovan, Gail. *The copycat fish*
A fishy story
Lost at sea
Ehlert, Lois. *Color farm*
Color zoo
In my world
Leaf man
Franceschelli, Christopher. *(Oliver)*
Goodall, John S. *Creepy castle*
Shrewbettina's birthday
Gore, Leonid. *Worms for lunch?*
Gravett, Emily. *Spells*
Halfmann, Janet. *Eggs 1, 2, 3*
Hoban, Tana. *Look! Look! Look!*
26 letters and 99 cents
Horacek, Petr. *Butterfly butterfly*
Jonathan and Martha
Jenkins, Steve. *Dogs and cats*
Perros y gatos / dogs and cats
Johnson, D. B. *Palazzo inverso*
Jonas, Ann. *Reflections*
The thirteenth clue
Little old lady who swallowed a fly. *There was an old lady who swallowed a fly*
Llewellyn, Claire. *Crocodile*
Duck
Ladybug
Tree
Long, Ethan. *The book that Zack wrote*
Loth, Sebastian. *Clementine*
Zelda the Varigoose
MacDonald, Suse. *Fish, swish! splash, dash!*
Shape by shape
MacKinnon, Debbie. *Eye spy shapes*
Marx, Trish. *Kindergarten day USA and China*
Menotti, Andrea. *How many jelly beans?*
Moffatt, Judith. *Trick-or-treat faces*
Morrow, Tara Jaye. *Mommy loves her baby; Daddy loves his baby*
Mother Goose. *Hickory dickory dock and other nursery rhymes*
My busy day
My doctor's bag
Nelson-Schmidt, Michelle. *Cats, cats!*
Dogs, dogs!
Numeroff, Laura Joffe. *What grandmas do best; What grandpas do best*
Old MacDonald had a farm. *Old MacDonald had a farm*
Olson-Brown, Ellen. *Ooh la la polka-dot boots*
Pericoli, Matteo. *See the city*
Perrin, Martine. *Cock-a-doodle who?*
Pfister, Marcus. *Charlie at the zoo*
Potter, Beatrix. *Where's Peter Rabbit?*
Pratt, Pierre. *I see . . . my mom / I see . . . my dad*
I see . . . my sister / I see . . . my cat
Ramos, Jorge. *I'm just like my mom / Me parezco tanto a mi mamá; I'm just like my dad / Me parezco tanto a mi papá*
Rasmussen, Halfdan. *The ladder*
Roth, Carol. *Ten dirty pigs / Ten clean pigs*
Seeger, Laura Vaccaro. *One boy*
Seuss, Dr. *Gerald McBoing Boing sound book*
Sharratt, Nick. *The foggy, foggy forest*
Siminovich, Lorena. *I like vegetables*
Simmons, Jane. *Daisy, the little duck with big feet*
Taback, Simms. *Postcards from camp*
Tafuri, Nancy. *What the sun sees / What the moon sees*
Toft, Kim Michelle. *The world that we want*
Tullet, Hervé. *The book with a hole*
Press here
Viva, Frank. *A long way away*
Wildsmith, Brian. *Give a dog a bone*
Goat's trail
Young, Ed. *Mouse match*
Ziefert, Harriet. *Counting chickens*
Hanukkah haiku
Messy Bessie

Format, unusual – board books

Abrams, Pam. *Now I eat my ABC's*
Acredolo, Linda P. *My first baby signs*
Aigner-Clark, Julie. *Language nursery*
Ajmera, Maya. *Animal friends: a global celebration of children and their animals*
Alborough, Jez. *Tall*
Alexander, Cecil Frances. *All creatures great and small*
Alley, R. W. *There once was a witch*
American babies
Anholt, Catherine. *Chimp and Zee's noisy book*
Monkey around with Chimp and Zee [board book]
Animal I spy
Animal 123
Asch, Frank. *Moonbear's books*
Moonbear's canoe
Ashman, Linda. *Babies on the go [board book]*
Austin, Mike. *Countdown with Milo*
Baby animals at the zoo
Barack, Marcy. *Season song*
Basher, Simon. *Go! Go! Bobo*

Beall, Pamela Conon. *Wee Sing if you're happy and you know it*
Beaton, Clare. *Clare Beaton's action rhymes*
Clare Beaton's bedtime rhymes
Clare Beaton's farmyard rhymes
Clare Beaton's nursery rhymes
One moose, twenty mice [board book]
Biggs, Brian. *123 beep beep beep!*
Stop! go!
Blackstone, Stella. *Secret seahorse [board book]*
Boelts, Maribeth. *Sweet dreams, Little Bunny!*
Bolam, Emily. *Animals talk*
I go potty
Brett, Jan. *The mitten*
Brown, James. *Farm*
Brown, Marc. *Arthur goes to school*
Arthur's animal adventure
Arthur's new puppy [board book]
D. W. thinks big [board book]
Brown, Margaret Wise. *Bunny's noisy book [board book]*
Goodnight moon 123: a counting book [board book]
The runaway bunny [board book]
Browne, Anthony. *I like books [board book]*
Brunhoff, Laurent de. *B is for Babar*
Bryant, Megan E. *Alphasaurus*
Colorasaurus
Countasaurus
Shapeasaurus
Buehner, Caralyn. *Snowmen at night [board book]*
Burg, Ann. *Autumn walk*
Burnard, Damon. *I spy in the jungle*
I spy in the ocean
Cabrera, Jane. *Monkey's play time*
Callery, Sean. *Hide and seek in the jungle*
Capucilli, Alyssa Satin. *Biscuit gives a gift*
Katy Duck
Katy Duck, big sister
Carle, Eric. *From head to toe*
Little cloud [board book]
Casalis, Anna. *Dinosaurs [board book]*
Chambers, Angela. *Follow that chicken!*
How now, cow?
Child, Lauren. *Charlie and Lola's numbers*
Charlie and Lola's opposites
Chwast, Seymour. *Get dressed!*
Cole, Joanna. *Sharing is fun*
Cousins, Lucy. *Count with Maisy*
Happy Easter, Maisy!
Maisy's Halloween
Maisy's noisy day
Noah's ark [board book]
Crews, Donald. *School bus [board book]*
Curious George's 1 to 10 and back again
Dahl, Michael. *Bear says "thank you"*
Hippo says "excuse me."
Nap time for Kitty
Dann, Penny. *Eensy weensy spider*
Davis, Caroline. *My little rocking horse lullabies*
My little rowboat
Deegan, Kim. *My first book of numbers*
My first book of opposites
dePaola, Tomie. *Get dressed, Santa!*
Marcos
Diehl, David. *Goal! my soccer book*
Doepker, David. *Animal babies*
Farm babies
Duckling
Dunrea, Olivier. *Ollie's Easter eggs [board book]*
Dupasquier, Philippe. *1 2 3, follow me!*
Edwards, Pamela Duncan. *Warthogs in a box*
Ellwand, David. *Ten in the bed*
Emberley, Ed. *Where's my sweetie pie?*
Emberley, Rebecca. *My animals / Mis animales*
My city / Mi cuidad
My clothes / Mi ropa
My colors / Mis colores
My food / Mi comida
My garden / Mi jardin
My house / Mi casa
My numbers / Mis números
My opposites / Mis opuestos
My room / Mi cuarto
My school / Mi escuela
My shapes / Mis formas
My toys / Mi juguetes
Emergency!
Faglia, Matteo. *Happy birthday, I'm 1*
Happy birthday, I'm 2
Happy birthday, I'm 3
Happy birthday, I'm 4
Falconer, Ian. *Olivia — and the missing toy*
Olivia counts
Olivia's opposites
Five little pumpkins, ill. by Ben Mantle
Five little pumpkins, ill. by Dan Yaccarino
Fleming, Denise. *The everything book [board book]*
Ford, Bernette. *No more diapers for Ducky!*
Formento, Alison. *This tree, 1, 2, 3*
Fox, Christyan. *Count to ten, PiggyWiggy!*
What color is that, PiggyWiggy?
What shape is that, PiggyWiggy?
Frazee, Marla. *Hush, little baby: a folk song with pictures*
Freeman, Don. *Corduroy's busy street and Corduroy goes to the doctor*
Freymann, Saxton. *Baby food*
Dog food
Food for thought
Fuge, Charles. *Where to, Little Wombat?*
Gardiner, Lindsey. *Good night, Poppy and Max*
George, Bobby. *Montessori number work*
Gerardi, Jan. *The little recycler*
Gergely, Tibor. *The great big fire engine book*
Gliori, Debi. *Can I have a hug?*
Gold-Vukson, Marji E. *The colors of my Jewish Year*
Good morning
Got, Yves. *Sam loves kisses*
Sam's little sister
Greenfield, Eloise. *Big friend, little friend*
I make music
My doll, Keshia
Gundersheimer, Karen. *Find cat, wear hat*
Harper, Jamie. *Night night, Baby Bundt*
Splish splash, Baby Bundt
Harris, Trudy. *Up bear, down bear*
Henkes, Kevin. *Lilly's chocolate heart*
Sheila Rae's peppermint stick
Hest, Amy. *Baby Duck and the cozy blanket*
Hill, Eric. *Spot at home*
Spot at the fair
Spot counts from 1 to 10
Spot goes to the circus
Spot goes to the farm
Spot looks at colors
Spot looks at opposites
Spot looks at shapes
Spot looks at weather

Spot on the farm
Spot visits his grandparents
Spot's first words
Spot's magical Christmas
Hills, Tad. *Duck and Goose find a pumpkin*
Duck and Goose, how are you feeling?
Duck and Goose, 1, 2, 3
Rocket's mighty words
What's up, Duck?
Hines, Anna Grossnickle. *What can you do in the rain?*
What can you do in the snow?
What can you do in the sun?
What can you do in the wind?
Hissey, Jane. *Old Bear [board book]*
Hoban, Tana. *What is that?*
White on black
Who are they?
Hoe, Susan. *Which shoes would you choose?*
Hoffman, Don. *A counting book with Billy and Abigail*
Good morning, good night Billy and Abigail
Holabird, Katharine. *Angelina dances*
Holub, Joan. *Turkeys never gobble*
Hop a little, jump a little!
Horacek, Petr. *Beep beep*
Choo choo
Hubbell, Patricia. *Pots and pans*
Wrapping paper romp
Hurd, Thacher. *Cat's pajamas*
Hutchins, Hazel. *Up dog*
Hutchins, Pat. *Rosie's walk [board book]*
Hyde, Margaret E. *Matisse for kids*
Van Gogh for kids
Imershein, Betsy. *Trucks*
Inkpen, Mick. *Wibbly Pig can make a tent*
Wibbly Pig is upset
Wibbly Pig likes bananas
Wibbly Pig opens his presents
Intrater, Roberta Grobel. *Peek-a-boo!*
Smile!
Isadora, Rachel. *Peekaboo morning [board book]*
Jackson, Kathryn. *The golden circus book*
Janovitz, Marilyn. *Baby, Baby, Baby!*
Jenkins, Emily. *Num, num, num!*
Plonk, plonk, plonk!
Up, up, up!
Jocelyn, Marthe. *Ready for autumn*
Ready for spring
Ready for summer
Ready for winter
Johnson, Angela. *Joshua by the sea*
Joshua's night whispers
Rain feet
Just like father
Katz, Karen. *Baby loves winter!*
Katz, Susan B. *ABC, baby me!*
Keats, Ezra Jack. *One red sun*
The snowy day [board book]
Kim, Sue. *How does a seed grow?*
Konnecke, Ole. *The big book of words and pictures*
Krensky, Stephen. *I know a lot!*
Laden, Nina. *Peek-a-who?*
Lawrence, Michael. *Baby loves*
Lester, J. D. *Mommy calls me Monkeypants*
Libney, Varda. *What I like about Passover*
Light, Steve. *Diggers go*
Trains go
Lister, Clare. *My first Passover [board book]*
Lodge, Jo. *Happy Snappy!*
Logan, Bob. *Rocket town*
London, Jonathan. *What do you love? [board book]*
Look at me!
McCurry, Kristen. *Ocean babies*
Safari babies
McFarlane, Sheryl. *In the city*
On the farm
McGrath, Barbara Barbieri. *Kellogg's froot loops color fun book*
McMullan, Kate. *Supercat*
McPhail, David. *Bella loves Bunny*
Ben loves Bear
McQuade, Jacqueline. *At preschool with Teddy Bear*
At the petting zoo with Teddy Bear
Marchon, Benoit. *Spoonful!*
Markes, Julie. *Sidewalk ABC*
Sidewalk 1 2 3
Marshall, James. *Eugene*
Martin, Bill, Jr. *Chicka chicka boom boom [board book]*
I pledge allegiance
Martin, David. *Hanukkah lights*
Marzollo, Jean. *Do you know new?*
I spy little animals
I spy little book
I spy little wheels
Mama, Mama
Papa, Papa
Mayo, Margaret. *Choo choo clickety-clack*
Meade, Holly. *John Willy and Freddy McGee [board book]*
Melmed, Laura Krauss. *I love you as much . . .*
Merberg, Julie. *In the garden with Van Gogh*
A magical day with Matisse
Miller, Margaret. *Baby faces*
Guess who?
I love colors
What's on my head?
Morozumi, Atsuko. *Helping daddy*
In the park
Playing
Time for bed
Mother Goose. *Hickory, dickory, dock*
Humpty Dumpty
Humpty Dumpty and other rhymes
Jack and Jill
Little Boy Blue and other rhymes
Little Miss Muffet, ill. by Heather Collins
Little Miss Muffet, ill. by Tracey Campbell Pearson
My first real Mother Goose [board book]
Pat-a-cake, ill. by Olga Ivanov
Pat-a-cake, ill. by Annie Kubler
Pat-a-cake [board book]
Pussycat, pussycat and other rhymes
Rock-a-bye baby [board book]
This little piggy [board book]
Wee Willie Winkie [board book]
Wee Willie Winkie and other rhymes
Murphy, Mary. *I like it when . . . [board book]*
Quick Duck!
Slow snail
My big book of trucks and diggers
My first farm
My first word, touch and feel
My new baby
Nelson, Steve. *Frosty the snowman [board book]*
Newgarden, Mark. *Bow-Wow orders lunch*
Newman, Lesléa. *Daddy, Papa, and me*

The pigeon loves things that go!
Williams, Sue. *I went walking [board book]*
Wilson, Karma. *Hello, Calico!*
Wood, Audrey. *Silly Sally [board book]*
Wood, Don. *Piggies [board book]*
Wright, Cliff. *Bear and ball*
Bear and kite
Yaccarino, Dan. *Five little ducks*
Yolen, Jane. *How do dinosaurs clean their rooms?*
How do dinosaurs count to ten?
Yoon, Salina. *At the beach*
You and me
Ziefert, Harriet. *Beach party!*
Knick-knack paddywhack
Wiggle like an octopus
Zoehfeld, Kathleen Weidner. *Apples, apples*

Format, unusual – graphic novels

Desrosiers, Sylvie. *Hocus Pocus takes the train*
Modan, Rutu. *Maya makes a mess*
Nordling, Lee. *The bramble*
Sazaklis, John. *Fowl play*
Viva, Frank. *A trip to the bottom of the world with Mouse*

Format, unusual – toy & movable books

Aesop. *The hare and the tortoise*
Ahlberg, Allan. *The Goldilocks variations*
Ahlberg, Janet. *The jolly pocket postman*
The jolly postman
Peek-a-boo!
Playmates
Alborough, Jez. *Duck's key where can it be?*
Allen, Judy. *Whales and dolphins*
American Museum of Natural History. *Spot the animals*
Andreae, Giles. *The pop-up Rumble in the jungle*
Arnosky, Jim. *Wild and swampy*
Baby animals
Baeten, Lieve. *Happy birthday, Little Witch!*
Baker, Jeannie. *Mirror*
Barry, Frances. *Duckie's rainbow*
Let's look at dinosaurs
Let's save the animals
Bataille, Marion. *ABC3D*
Bauer, Marion Dane. *Christmas lights*
I'm not afraid of Halloween!
Toes, ears, and nose!
Uh-oh! a lift-the-flap story
Beck, Andrea. *Elliot's great big lift-the-flap book*
Beeler, Selby B. *How many Elephants?*
Bentley, Dawn. *Fuzzy bear*
Fuzzy Bear's potty book
Berenstain, Jan. *The Berenstain bears trim the tree*
Berger, Melvin. *Early humans*
Bernhard, Durga. *In the fiddle is a song*
While you are sleeping: a lift-the-flap book of time around the world
Big noisy trucks and diggers
Bilgrami, Shaheen. *Amazing dinosaur discovery*
Farmyard painting party
Incredible animal discovery
Jungle art show
Birchall, Mark. *Hen goes shopping*
Black, Harley. *Amazing magic school*
Magic art class
Blum, Mark. *Big trucks and diggers in 3-D*
Braun, Sebastien. *Who's hiding?*
Bridwell, Norman. *Clifford's neighborhood*
Briggs, Raymond. *The snowman [a lift-the-flap board book]*
Brown, Heather. *Chomp!*
Brown, Marc. *Arthur goes to school*
Arthur's neighborhood
Arthur's spookiest Halloween
Brown, Ruth. *Monkey's friends*
The old tree
Browne, Anthony. *Animal fair*
Brownlow, Mike. *The big white book with almost nothing in it*
Butler, M. Christina. *One snowy night*
Butterfield, Moira. *Magic world of learning*
Cabrera, Jane. *Bear's good night*
Campbell, Rod. *Dear zoo*
Cannon, Janell. *Stellaluna: a pop-up book and mobile*
Capucilli, Alyssa Satin. *Biscuit loves school*
Biscuit's Valentine's Day
Happy Hanukkah, Biscuit
My first ballet class
Only my dad and me
Only my mom and me
Carle, Eric. *Dream snow*
My very first book of food
My very first book of heads and tails
My very first book of sounds
My very first book of tools
Papa, please get the moon for me
The secret birthday message
The very lonely firefly
Watch out! A giant!
Carney, Margaret. *Where does a tiger-heron spend the night?*
Carter, David A. *Blue 2*
Chanukah bugs
Easter bugs
Flapdoodle dinosaurs
How many bugs in a box?
In a dark, dark wood
Old MacDonald had a farm: a pop-up book
One red dot
Peekaboo bugs
600 black spots
Whoo? Whoo?
Who's under that hat?
Yellow square
Chambers, Angela. *Follow that chicken!*
How now, cow?
Cheshire, Marc. *Here comes Eloise!*
Merry Christmas, Eloise!
Child, Lauren. *I will never not ever eat a tomato [pop-up]*
My dream bed
Chwast, Seymour. *Get dressed!*
Ciboul, Adele. *The five senses*
Comden, Betty. *What's new at the zoo?*
Cousins, Lucy. *Ha ha, Maisy!*
Happy birthday, Maisy
Maisy at the farm
Maisy's amazing big book of learning
Maisy's amazing big book of words
Maisy's book of things that go
Maisy's farm
Maisy's first clock
Maisy's pirate treasure hunt
Maisy's twinkly, crinkly counting book
Maisy's wonderful weather book

More fun with Maisy!
Stop and go, Maisy
With love from Maisy
Cox, Phil Roxbee. *Fox on a box*
Goose on the loose
Shark in the park
Crews, Donald. *Inside freight train*
Crowther, Robert. *Amazing pop-up trucks*
Colors
Opposites
Shapes
Curtis, Jamie Lee. *Today I feel silly and other moods that make my day*
Davis, Kate. *Barnyard babies*
Davis, Nancy. *A garden of opposites*
Day, Trevor. *Youch! it bites!*
deGroat, Diane. *Lola the elf*
Denchfield, Nick. *Charlie Chick*
Denega, Danielle. *Numbers*
Rain or shine
dePaola, Tomie. *Brava Strega Nona!*
DePrisco, Dorothea. *Snowbear's winter day*
What will I become?
Who lives here?
Dijs, Carla. *Mommy, what if—?*
Dodds, Dayle Ann. *Where's Pup?*
Dowley, Tim. *The shepherds' tale*
The wise men's tale
Doyle, Malachy. *Baby see, baby do!*
Well, a crocodile can!
Drehsen, Britta. *Flip-o-storic*
Dunrea, Olivier. *Gossie's busy day*
Durant, Alan. *Dear tooth fairy*
Egielski, Richard. *Itsy bitsy spider*
Ehlert, Lois. *Hands*
Waiting for wings
Emberley, Ed. *Ed Emberley's bye-bye, big bad bullybug!*
Glad monster, sad monster
Go away, big green monster!
Nighty night Little Green Monster
Where's my sweetie pie?
Faulkner, Keith. *Charlie Chimp's Christmas*
Do you have my quack?
The giraffe who cock-a-doodle-doo'd
Jumbled jungle
The monster who loved books
Pop! went another balloon!
Rexerella
The scared little bear
The tallest shortest longest greenest brownest animal in the jungle!
A trick or a treat?
Findlay, Lisa. *What's in Oscar's trashcan?*
Firmin, Josie. *My week*
Fischer, Scott M. *Twinkle*
Foley, Greg. *I miss you Mouse*
Fontes, Justine Korman. *Black meets White*
Fox, Diane. *Tyson the terrible*
Franceschelli, Christopher. *Alphablock*
Friedman, Caitlin. *How do you feed a hungry giant?*
Gabriel, Ashala. *Night night toes*
Gallo, Frank. *Bird calls*
Night sounds
Gamble, Isobel. *Who's that?*
Genechten, Guido van. *Guess what?*
Guess where?
Gerstein, Mordicai. *The man who walked between the towers*
Gibbs, Edward. *I spy on the farm*
I spy pets
I spy under the sea
I spy with my little eye
The gingerbread boy. *Gingerbread baby*
Gonyea, Mark. *The spooky box*
Gore, Leonid. *Mommy, where are you?*
Gravett, Emily. *Meerkat mail*
The rabbit problem
Gray, Nigel. *Time to play!*
Green, Dan. *Wild alphabet*
Gukova, Julia. *All mixed-up!*
Hacohen, Dean. *Tuck me in!*
Haines, Mike. *Countdown to bedtime*
Hamilton, Libby. *The monstrous book of monsters*
Hansen, P. *My granny's purse*
Harper, Charise Mericle. *Amy and Ivan*
Harper, Dan. *Telling time with Big Mama Cat*
Hawkins, Colin. *Creepy castle*
One, two, guess who?
Hennessy, B. G. *Corduroy at the zoo*
Corduroy's birthday
Corduroy's Christmas
Corduroy's Easter
Corduroy's Halloween
Hernandez, Keith. *First-base hero*
Hewitt, Sally. *Face to face safari*
Hill, Eric. *Spot bakes a cake*
Spot goes to a party
Spot goes to school
Spot goes to the beach
Spot goes to the park
Spot sleeps over
Spot's baby sister
Spot's birthday party
Spot's first Christmas
Spot's first Easter
Spot's first walk
Where's Spot?
Hill, Susanna Leonard. *The house that Mack built*
Hines, Anna Grossnickle. *No, no Jack!*
Whose shoes?
Hoban, Tana. *Just look*
Look book
Horacek, Petr. *Animal opposites*
Flip's day
One spotted giraffe
Strawberries are red
Horwood, Annie. *Butterfly, butterfly what colors do you see?*
How much does God love me?
Hutchins, Hazel. *Two so small*
Idle, Molly. *Flora and the flamingo*
Inkpen, Mick. *Kipper's Christmas eve*
Kipper's rainy day
Kipper's sunny day
Janovitz, Marilyn. *A, B, see!*
Jenkins, Steve. *Animals upside down*
Johnson, Stephen T. *My little blue robot*
Jonas, Ann. *Where can it be?*
Kaner, Etta. *Who likes the rain?*
Who likes the sun?
Who likes the wind?
Karas, G. Brian. *Skidamarink*
Katz, Karen. *A potty for me!*
Where is baby's mommy?
Klausmeier, Jesse. *Open this little book*
Koda-Callan, Elizabeth. *The squiggly Wigglys*
Koponen, Libby. *Mmm . . . let's eat!*
Lavis, Steve. *On the farm*

Lawrence, Jennifer B. *Sad doggy*
Leslie, Amanda. *Alfie and Betty Bug*
Are chickens stripy?
Do crocodiles moo?
Flappy, waggy, wiggly
Who's that scratching at my door?
Lewin, Betsy. *Where is Tippy Toes?*
Lewis, Anne Margaret. *What am I? Christmas*
Lithgow, John. *The remarkable Farkle McBride*
Little old lady who swallowed a fly. *I know an old lady who swallowed a fly*
There was an old lady who swallowed a fly
Lobel, Arnold. *The frog and toad pop-up book*
Lodge, Jo. *Happy birthday, Moo Moo*
Happy Snappy!
Moo Moo goes to the city
Long, Ethan. *Up, tall and high*
Low, William. *Machines go to work*
Machines go to work in the city
MacDonald, Suse. *Circus opposites*
McNamara, Margaret. *The whistle on the train*
Martin, Ruth. *Santa's on his way*
Merlin, Christophe. *Under the hood*
Michelson, Richard. *Ten times better*
Mitton, Tony. *Rumble, roar, dinosaur!*
Moerbeek, Kees. *The diary of Hansel and Gretel*
Moore, Clement Clarke. *The night before Christmas: a pop-up*
Morgan, Mary. *My good night book*
Morris, Dewi. *Sandy's street*
Munro, Roxie. *Circus*
Go! go! go!
Murphy, Mary. *A kiss like this*
Mystery manor
Nobles, Kristen M. *Drive this book*
Noonan, Julia. *Mouse by mouse*
Novak, Matt. *Too many bunnies*
Old MacDonald had a farm. *Old MacDonald had a farm*
Park, Linda Sue. *Yum! Yuck!*
Parot, Annelore. *Kimonos*
Pelham, David. *A is for animals*
Crawlies creep
Sam's pizza
Sam's sandwich
Perrault, Charles. *Cinderella: a pop-up fairy tale*
Perrin, Martine. *Look who's there!*
Pfister, Marcus. *Just the way you are*
Milo and the magical stones
Philpot, Graham. *Where is Little Harry?*
Pienkowski, Jan. *Good night, a pop-up lullaby*
Haunted house
Pizza!
Piers, Helen. *Who's in my bed?*
Piggy and Bear in their underwear
Pittau, Francisco. *Out of sight*
Porter, Sue. *Parsnip*
Potter, Beatrix. *The two bad mice*
Price, Mathew. *Patch and the rabbits*
Rayner, Catherine. *Ernest, the moose who doesn't fit*
Reasoner, Charles. *One blue fish*
Regan, Dian Curtis. *How do you know it's Halloween?*
Reinhart, Matthew. *Animal popposites*
Fairies and magical creatures
Gods and heroes
Reiser, Lynn. *My cat Tuna*
My dog Truffle
Play ball with me!
Reitman, Andrea. *Mouse in the house*
Rives. *If I were a polar bear*
Rosen, Michael J. *Chanukah lights*
Rowe, Jeannette. *Whose ears?*
Whose feet?
Whose nose?
Rueda, Claudia. *Huff and puff*
Sabuda, Robert. *Beauty and the beast: a pop-up book of the classic fairy tale*
The Christmas alphabet
Encyclopedia prehistorica: dinosaurs
Encyclopedia prehistorica: mega-beasts
Encyclopedia prehistorica: sharks and other seamonsters
The movable Mother Goose
Peter Pan
Winter in white
Winter's tale
Safran, Sheri. *All kinds of families: a lift-the-flap book*
Sage, Angie. *Molly and the birthday party*
Saltzberg, Barney. *Andrew drew and drew*
Baby animal kisses
Hi, Blueberry!
Kisses
Santa Claus is coming to town
Santoro, Lucio. *Wild oceans*
Scarry, Huck. *Looking into the Middle Ages*
Schindel, John. *What did they see?*
Schwartz, David M. *Where else in the wild?*
Where in the wild
Schwarz, Viviane. *There are cats in this book*
There are no cats in this book
Seder, Rufus Butler. *Waddle!*
The Wizard of Oz
Seeber, Dorothea P. *A pup just for me . . . A boy just for me*
Seeger, Laura Vaccaro. *Black? White! Day? Night!*
First the egg
The hidden alphabet
Lemons are not red
Sendak, Maurice. *Mommy?*
Sharratt, Nick. *Shark in the park*
What's in the witch's kitchen?
Shea, Susan A. *Do you know which one will grow?*
Simmons, Jane. *Bouncy bouncy Daisy*
Daisy's hide-and-seek
Simpson-Enock, Sarah. *Mommy, Mommy, what's in your tummy?*
Sís, Peter. *Fire truck*
Trucks, trucks, trucks
Smee, Nicola. *No bed without Ted*
Smith, Kathryn. *Little Donkey's Christmas story*
Little Lamb's Christmas story
Smith, Lois T. *Carrie and Carl play*
Smith, Mavis. *'Twas the day after Thanksgiving*
Spafford, Suzy. *Witzy's colors*
Sper, Emily. *The Passover seder*
Spurr, Elizabeth. *Two bears beneath the stairs*
Stadler, John. *Take me out to the ball game: a pop-up book*
Stanley, Mandy. *Bloomer, the dog you can play with*
Steele, Philip. *A knight's city*
Trains: the slide-out, see-through story of world-famous trains and railroads
Stickland, Paul. *Dinosaur stomp!*
A number of dinosaurs
Truck jam
Stileman, Kali. *Roly-poly egg*
Taback, Simms. *Simms Taback's city animals*

Simms Taback's farm animals
Simms Taback's safari animals
Tabby, Abigail. *Baby face*
Tatcheva, Eva. *Witch Zelda's birthday cake*
Thompson, Lauren. *Little Quack: dial-a-duck*
Tildes, Phyllis Limbacher. *Eye guess*
Torres, Melissa A. *The great Christmas tree celebration*
Van der Meer, Mara. *Can we play?*
Van Fleet, Matthew. *Fuzzy yellow ducklings*
Heads
Moo
One yellow lion
Spotted yellow frogs
Verdet, Andre. *All about time*
Vere, Ed. *Everyone's little*
Walsh, Melanie. *Living with Mom and living with Dad*
Monster, monster
Wax, Wendy. *Even firefighters go to the potty*
Weeks, Sarah. *Be mine, be mine, sweet valentine*
Wells, Rosemary. *Goodnight Max*
McDuffs hide-and-seek
Max and Ruby's treasure hunt
Weninger, Brigitte. *Special delivery*
White, Marsha. *Hooper has lost his owner*
Whybrow, Ian. *Good night, monster*
Hello! Is this grandma?
Sammy and the robots
Willems, Mo. *Big Frog can't fit in*
Time to say "please"!
Wing, Natasha. *How to raise a dinosaur*
Wood, Audrey. *The napping house wakes up*
Yaccarino, Dan. *So big*
Yoon, Salina. *Do cows meow?*
Do crocs kiss?
Opposnakes
Zelinsky, Paul O. *The wheels on the bus*
Ziefert, Harriet. *Mommies are for counting stars*
Robin, where are you?
Talk, baby!

Fortune *see* Character traits – luck

Fossils

Aliki. *Fossils tell of long ago*
The long lost coelacanth and other living fossils
Alphin, Elaine Marie. *Dinosaur hunter*
Atkins, Jeannine. *Mary Anning and the sea dragon*
Barner, Bob. *Dinosaur bones*
Dinosaurs roar, butterflies soar!
Brown, Don. *Rare treasure*
Cohen, Daniel. *Apatosaurus*
Pteranodon
Stegosaurus
Triceratops
Tyrannosaurus rex
Velociraptor
Diffily, Deborah. *Jurassic shark*
Houran, Lori Haskins. *Dig those dinosaurs*
Johansen, K. V. *Pippin and the bones*
Pellant, Chris. *The best book of fossils, rocks, and minerals*
Sabuda, Robert. *Encyclopedia prehistorica: mega-beasts*
Encyclopedia prehistorica: sharks and other seamonsters
Thomson, Bill. *Fossil*
Zoehfeld, Kathleen Weidner. *Dinosaur tracks*

Freedom *see* Character traits – freedom

Friendship

Ada, Alma Flor. *Friend frog*
Adams, Sarah. *Dave and Violet*
Gary and Ray
Alborough, Jez. *My friend bear*
Aliki. *Best friends together again*
Feelings
Overnight at Mary Bloom's
We are best friends
Alter, Anna. *Abigail spells*
Amado, Elisa. *Tricycle*
Anastas, Margaret. *A hug for you*
Anderson, Derek. *Romeo and Lou blast off*
Anglund, Joan Walsh. *A friend is someone who likes you*
Apperley, Dawn. *Blossom and Boo*
Armstrong, Matthew S. *Jane and Mizmow*
Arnosky, Jim. *Armadillo's orange*
Asch, Frank. *Moonbear's friend*
Moonbear's pet
Askani, Tanja. *A friend like you*
Bailey, Linda. *Stanley's little sister*
Baker, Roberta. *Olive's first sleepover*
Barasch, Lynne. *The reluctant flower girl*
Bardhan-Quallen, Sudipta. *The Mine-o-saur*
Barnes, Laura T. *Ernest and the big itch*
Ernest's special Christmas
Twist and Ernest
Barringer, William. *Gregory and Alexander*
Bateman, Teresa. *The leprechaun under the bed*
Battersby, Katherine. *Squish Rabbit*
Bauer, Marion Dane. *Frog's best friend*
Baumgart, Klaus. *Laura's star*
Beck, Andrea. *Elliot's Christmas surprise*
Elliot's emergency
Elliot's shipwreck
Becker, Bonny. *A bedtime for Bear*
A birthday for Bear
The sniffles for Bear
A visitor for Bear
Bell, Cece. *Bee-Wigged*
Belloni, Giulia. *Anything is possible*
Belton, Sandra. *Pictures for Miss Josie*
Bendall-Brunello, Tiziana. *I wish I could read!*
Benjamin, A. H. *Mouse, mole and the falling star*
Bennett, Kelly. *Not Norman*
Berenstain, Stan and Jan. *The Berenstain bears and the trouble with friends*
The Berenstain bears' moving day
Berger, Carin. *Forever friends*
Birdsall, Jeanne. *Lucky and Squash*
Blabey, Aaron. *Pearl Barley and Charlie Parsley*
Blackaby, Susan. *Brownie Groundhog and the February Fox*
Brownie Groundhog and the wintry surprise
Blackstone, Stella. *Cleo and Caspar*
Cleo in the snow
Cleo on the move
Cleo the cat
Blake, Quentin. *Fantastic Daisy Artichoke*
Blake, Robert J. *Painter and Ugly*
Blegvad, Lenore. *First friends*
Bley, Anette. *A friend*

Block party today
Bloom, Suzanne. *A splendid friend, indeed*
What about Bear?
Bluthenthal, Diana Cain. *I'm not invited?*
Bogacki, Tomasz. *Circus girl*
Boldt, Claudia. *Odd dog*
Bonwill, Ann. *Bug and Bear*
I am not a copycat!
Bosca, Francesca. *The three grasshoppers*
Bottner, Barbara. *Raymond and Nelda*
Rosa's room
Wallace's lists
Bourgeois, Paulette. *Franklin's new friend*
Franklin's secret club
Bowers, Tim. *A new home*
Boyce, Katie. *Hector the hermit crab*
Bracken, Beth. *The little bully*
Bradbury, Ray. *Switch on the night*
Bramsen, Carin. *Hey, duck!*
Breen, Steve. *Pug and Doug*
Brenner, Barbara A. *Beef stew*
Briggs, Raymond. *The snowman*
Brooks, Erik. *Slow days, fast friends*
Brown, Alan James. *Hoot and Holler*
Brown, Laurie Krasny. *How to be a friend*
Brown, Marc. *Arthur's birthday*
The true Francine
Brown, Peter. *You will be my friend!*
Browne, Anthony. *Willy and Hugh*
Brownlee, Sophia Grace. *Tea time with Sophia Grace and Rosie*
Bruce, Lisa. *Fran's friend*
Bruel, Robert O. *Bob and Otto*
Bruins, David. *The call of the cowboy*
Brun-Cosme, Nadine. *Big Wolf and Little Wolf*
Big Wolf and Little Wolf, such a beautiful orange!
Bruzzone, Catherine. *Puppy finds a friend / Cachorrito encuentra un amigo*
Puppy finds a friend / Le petit chien se trouve un ami
Buckingham, Matt. *Bright Stanley*
Budnitz, Paul. *The hole in the middle*
Bunge, Daniela. *Cherry time*
Bunting, Eve. *The blue and the gray*
Mouse island
Rudi's pond
Bushey, Jeanne. *The polar bear's gift*
Butler, M. Christina. *Mouse and the moon*
Snow friends
Butterworth, Nick. *Albert the bear*
Button, Lana. *Willow finds a way*
Buzzeo, Toni. *One cool friend*
Bynum, Janie. *Nutmeg and Barley*
Otis
Byun, You. *Dream friends*
Calmenson, Stephanie. *May I pet your dog?*
Cannon, Janell. *Stellaluna*
Stellaluna: a pop-up book and mobile
Capucilli, Alyssa Satin. *Biscuit finds a friend*
Biscuit's big friend
Carle, Eric. *Do you want to be my friend?*
Friends
Carlson, Nancy. *Hooray for Grandparent's Day!*
My best friend moved away
Snowden
Carlstrom, Nancy White. *The way to Wyatt's house*
Carr, Jan. *Frozen noses*
Carter, Anne Laurel. *My home bay*
Case, Chris. *Sophie and the next-door monsters*
Caseley, Judith. *Field Day Friday*
Catalano, Dominic. *Mr. Bassett plays*
Catalanotto, Peter. *The secret lunch special*
Cazet, Denys. *Never poke a squid*
Chapman, Jane. *Very special friends*
Chast, Roz. *Marco goes to school*
Chichester Clark, Emma. *Melrose and Croc*
Will and Squill
Child, Lauren. *My best, best friend*
Chodos-Irvine, Margaret. *Best best friends*
Ella Sarah gets dressed
Choldenko, Gennifer. *How to make friends with a giant*
Louder, Lili
Church, Caroline Jayne. *Ruff!*
Clements, Andrew. *Big Al and Shrimpy*
Clifton, Lucille. *Three wishes*
Cneut, Carll. *The amazing love story of Mr. Morf*
Cohen, Caron Lee. *Broom, zoom!*
Cohen, Miriam. *Best friends*
First grade takes a test, ill. by Ronald Himler
First grade takes a test, ill. by Lillian Hoban
See you in second grade!
Will I have a friend?, ill. by Ronald Himler
Will I have a friend?, ill. by Lillian Hoban
Cole, Joanna. *My new kitten*
Consentino, Ralph. *The story of Honk-Honk-Ashoo and Swella-Bow-Wow*
Cooper, Helen. *Delicious!*
A pipkin of pepper
Corderoy, Tracey. *The little white owl*
Côté, Geneviève. *Without you*
Cousins, Lucy. *I'm the best*
Maisy cleans up
Covell, David. *Rat and Roach*
Rat and Roach rock on!
Coyle, Carmela LaVigna. *Do princesses have best friends forever?*
Crimi, Carolyn. *Don't need friends*
Crowther, Kitty. *Jack and Jim*
Cuyler, Margery. *Bullies never win*
I repeat, don't cheat!
Daly, Niki. *Once upon a time*
Davis, Anne. *No dogs allowed!*
Day, Marie. *Edward the "crazy man"*
DeBear, Kirsten. *Be quiet, Marina!*
deGroat, Diane. *Happy birthday to you, you belong in a zoo*
No more pencils, no more books, no more teacher's dirty looks!
Demas, Corinne. *Here comes trouble!*
DePalma, Mary Newell. *The strange egg*
dePaola, Tomie. *My first Thanksgiving*
Tom
De Regniers, Beatrice Schenk. *May I bring a friend?*
DeRubertis, Barbara. *Corky Cub's crazy caps*
de Varennes, Monique. *The jewel box ballerinas*
Dewdney, Anna. *Roly Poly pangolin*
Dierssen, Andreas. *Timmy's new friend*
Diesen, Deborah. *The pout-pout fish*
DiPucchio, Kelly. *Crafty Chloe: dress-up mess-up*
Donofrio, Beverly. *Mary and the mouse, the mouse and Mary*
Donohue, Dorothy. *Veggie soup*
Dorros, Arthur. *Julio's magic*
Doyle, Malachy. *Storm cats*
Dunbar, Polly. *Happy Hector*
Hello Tilly
Pretty Pru
Where's Tumpty?

Dunrea, Olivier. *Jasper & Joop*
Duvoisin, Roger Antoine. *Petunia*
Dyckman, Ame. *Boy + Bot*
Eaton, Maxwell. *Best buds*
The mystery
Superheroes
Edgemon, Darcie. *Seamore, the very forgetful porpoise*
Edwards, Nicola. *Goodnight Baxter*
Edwards, Pamela Duncan. *Gigi and Lulu's gigantic fight*
The old house
Warthogs in a box
Egan, Tim. *Roasted peanuts*
Elliott, David. *Hunter's best friend at school*
Elliott, Laura Malone. *Hunter and Stripe and the soccer showdown*
A string of hearts
Emmett, Jonathan. *The best gift of all*
Engels-Fietzek, Petra. *Sophie and the seagull*
English, Karen. *Hot day on Abbott Avenue*
Esbaum, Jill. *To the big top*
Tom's tweet
Fagan, Cary. *Ella May and the wishing stone*
Faller, Regis. *Polo and Lily*
Falwell, Cathryn. *David's drawing*
Farish, Terry. *The cat who liked potato soup*
Faulkner, Keith. *The tallest shortest longest greenest brownest animal in the jungle!*
Fearnley, Jan. *Arthur and the meanies*
A perfect day for it
Floyd, Madeleine. *Cold paws, warm heart*
Foley, Greg. *I miss you Mouse*
Make a wish Bear
Thank you, Bear
Willoughby and the lion
Folgueira, Rodrigo. *Ribbit!*
Ford, Bernette. *No more blanket for Lambkin!*
Foreman, Michael. *Friends*
The littlest dinosaur
Fox, Diane. *Tyson the terrible*
Fox, Mem. *Hunwick's egg*
Frankel, Erin. *Tough!*
Frazee, Marla. *Boot and Shoe*
Freeman, Tor. *Olive and the bad mood*
Freymann, Saxton. *One lonely seahorse*
Fritts, Mary Bahr. *If Nathan were here*
Fuge, Charles. *Swim, Little Wombat, swim!*
Gantos, Jack. *Back to school for Rotten Ralph*
Garland, Sarah. *Eddie's toolbox and how to make and mend things*
Gauch, Patricia Lee. *Tanya and Emily in a dance for two*
Genechten, Guido van. *Because you are my friend*
Geraghty, Paul. *The hoppameleon*
Gillmor, Don. *Yuck, a love story*
Giovanni, Nikki. *Lincoln and Douglass*
Glaser, Linda. *Hannah's way*
Gleeson, Libby. *Clancy and Millie and the very fine house*
Half a world away
Goodhart, Pippa. *Pudgy, a puppy to love*
Goossens, Philippe. *Knock! Knock! Knock! Who's there?*
Gorbachev, Valeri. *Big Little Elephant*
Catty Jane who hated the rain
Catty Jane who loved to dance
Chicken chickens go to school
Heron and Turtle
Me too!
That's what friends are for
Gordon, Gus. *Herman and Rosie*
Grant, Joan. *Cat and Fish*
Gray, Luli. *Ant and Grasshopper*
Greenfield, Eloise. *Big friend, little friend*
Gregory, Nan. *Wild Girl and Gran*
Gretz, Susanna. *Riley and Rose in the picture*
Grey, Mini. *Ginger bear*
Three by the sea
Grimes, Nikki. *Danitra Brown, class clown*
Minnie's new friend
When Gorilla goes walking
Grindley, Sally. *The giant postman*
What are friends for?
What will I do without you?
Gutman, Anne. *Gaspard and Lisa, friends forever*
Gaspard and Lisa's rainy day
Haas, Irene. *Bess and Bella*
Haber, Tiffany Strelitz. *Ollie and Claire*
Hall, Algy Craig. *Mammoth and me*
Halpern, Julie. *Toby and the snowflakes*
Harper, Charise Mericle. *Cupcake*
Mimi and Lulu
When Randolph turned rotten
Harris, Trudy. *Tally cat keeps track*
Harrison, Troon. *Courage to fly*
Havill, Juanita. *Jamaica and Brianna*
Jamaica Tag-Along
Hawkins, Emily. *Little snow goose*
Heap, Sue. *Four friends in the garden*
Hegg, Tom. *Peef and his best friend*
Heide, Florence Parry. *The one and only Marigold*
Helquist, Brett. *Grumpy Goat*
Hemingway, Edward. *Bad apple*
Henkes, Kevin. *Jessica*
Henry, Jed. *Cheer up, Mouse!*
Good night, Mouse!
Henry, Rohan. *The gift box*
Higgins, Ryan. *Wilfred*
Hill, Eric. *Spot sleeps over*
Hills, Tad. *Duck and Goose*
Duck, Duck, Goose
Himmelman, John. *Katie loves the kittens*
Tudley didn't know
Hissey, Jane. *Old Bear*
Old Bear [board book]
Hoban, Russell. *A bargain for Frances*
Best friends for Frances
Hobbie, Holly. *Toot and Puddle: let it snow*
Toot and Puddle
Toot and Puddle: wish you were here
Toot and Puddle, top of the world
Toot and Puddle, you are my sunshine
Hoberman, Mary Ann. *And to think that we thought that we'd never be friends*
One of each
Holabird, Katharine. *Angelina and Alice*
Angelina at the fair
Holmes, Anita. *Flowers and friends*
Holmes, Janet A. *Me and you*
Hopkins, Lee Bennett. *Full moon and star*
Hopkinson, Deborah. *Abe Lincoln crosses a creek*
Horacek, Petr. *Puffin Peter*
Horowitz, Dave. *Buy my hats!*
Hout, Mies van. *Friends*
Howard, Arthur. *When I was five*
Howard, Reginald. *The big, big wall*
Howe, James. *Horace and Morris but mostly Dolores*

Horace and Morris join the chorus (but what about Dolores?)
Houndsley and Catina
Houndsley and Catina and the birthday surprise
Howell, Will C. *I call it sky*
Hughes, Susan. *Earth to Audrey*
Hunter, Tom. *Build it up and knock it down*
Hutchins, Hazel. *Mattland*
Hutchins, Pat. *The doorbell rang*
My best friend
Titch and Daisy
Idle, Molly. *Flora and the flamingo*
Inkpen, Mick. *Kipper's Christmas eve*
Kipper's snowy day
Swing!
Jackson, Isaac. *Somebody's new pajamas*
Jahn-Clough, Lisa. *Alicia's best friends*
Felicity and Cordelia
Missing Molly
Simon and Molly plus Hester
Cabrera, Jane. *The lonesome polar bear*
Janni, Rebecca. *Every cowgirl goes to school*
Every cowgirl needs dancing boots
Javaherbin, Mina. *Goal!*
Jeffers, Oliver. *Lost and found*
Up and down
The way back home
Jeffs, Stephanie. *Josh*
Jenkins, Emily. *Num, num, num!*
Plonk, plonk, plonk!
Skunkdog
Up, up, up!
Jennings, Patrick. *Bat and Rat*
Jennings, Sharon. *Franklin wants a badge*
Priscilla and Rosy
Jocelyn, Marthe. *Ones and twos*
Johansen, Hanna. *The duck and the owl*
Johansen, K. V. *Pippin and Pudding*
Johnson, Angela. *Down the winding road*
Lottie Paris and the best place
Johnston, Tony. *Soup bone*
Jones, Elizabeth. *Sunshine and Storm*
Joosse, Barbara. *Friends (mostly)*
Lovabye dragon
Joyce, William. *Santa calls*
Jules, Jacqueline. *No English*
Picnic at Camp Shalom
Jurmain, Suzanne Tripp. *Worst of friends*
Kajikawa, Kimiko. *Yoshi's feast*
Kako, Satoshi. *Little Daruma and little Daikoku*
Little Daruma and little Kaminari
Kasza, Keiko. *Dorothy and Mikey*
Silly Goose's big story
Katz, Jon. *Lenore finds a friend*
Katzler, Eva. *Florentine and Pig*
Keats, Ezra Jack. *A letter to Amy*
Peter's chair
Keller, Holly. *Help!*
Sophie's window
Kellogg, Steven. *Best friends*
Ketteman, Helen. *Armadilly chili*
Kilaka, John. *True friends*
Kimura, Yuichi. *One stormy night . . .*
One sunny day . . .
Kinerk, Robert. *Clorinda plays baseball!*
King, Stephen Michael. *You*
Kirk, Daniel. *Library mouse: a world to explore*
Ten things I love about you
Kirsch, Vincent X. *Forsythia and me*
Freddie and Gingersnap
Kitamura, Satoshi. *Pablo the artist*
Kleven, Elisa. *The friendship wish*
Welcome home, Mouse
Kliphuis, Christine. *Robbie and Ronnie*
Kochan, Vera. *What if your best friend were blue?*
Kolanovic, Dubravka. *Everyone needs a friend*
Korda, Lerryn. *Into the wild*
It's vacation time
Kostecki-Shaw, Jenny Sue. *Same, same but different*
Kraegel, Kenneth. *King Arthur's very great grandson*
Kroll, Virginia L. *Forgiving a friend*
Krosoczka, Jarrett J. *Max for president*
My buddy, Slug
Lairla, Sergio. *Abel and the wolf*
Lakin, Patricia. *Camping day*
Langreuter, Jutta. *Little Bear and the big fight*
Little Bear goes to kindergarten
LaReau, Kara. *Mr. Prickles*
Lasky, Kathryn. *Fourth of July bear*
Leeson, Christine. *Molly and the storm*
Lehman, Barbara. *The red book*
Le Neouanic, Lionel. *Little smudge*
Lerch. *Swim! swim!*
Lester, Helen. *Three cheers for Tacky*
Lewis, Kim. *Friends*
Good night, Harry
Here we go Harry
Hooray for Harry
Lewis, Rob. *Friends*
Light, Steve. *The Christmas giant*
Lin, Grace. *Lissy's friends*
Okie-dokie, Artichokie
Linders, Clara. *The very best door of all*
Lionni, Leo. *Alexander and the wind-up mouse*
An extraordinary egg
Fish is fish
Little blue and little yellow
Mr. McMouse
Nicolas, where have you been?
Livingston, Irene. *Finklehopper Frog cheers*
Lobel, Arnold. *Days with Frog and Toad*
Frog and Toad all year
Frog and Toad are friends
Frog and Toad together
Long, Ethan. *Bird and Birdie in a fine day*
Long, Loren. *Otis and the puppy*
Lovell, Patty. *Have fun, Molly Lou Melon*
Lucas, David. *Cake girl*
Ludwig, Trudy. *Better than you*
The invisible boy
Lundy, Charlotte. *Thank you, Ruth and Naomi*
Luthardt, Kevin. *Hats*
You're weird!
Macaulay, David. *Angelo*
McBratney, Sam. *I'm sorry*
Yes we can!
McCarty, Peter. *The monster returns*
McCourt, Lisa. *Chicken soup for little souls: The new kid and the cookie thief*
McCourt, Lisa, et al. *Chicken soup for little souls: Della Splatnuk birthday girl*
McCue, Lisa. *Quiet Bunny and Noisy Puppy*
Macdonald, Maryann. *The pink party*
McDonald, Megan. *Reptiles are my life*
McDonnell, Patrick. *The gift of nothing*
McGhee, Alison. *Making a friend*
McKee, David. *Elmer and Wilbur*
Elmer in the snow

McKissack, Patricia C. *Messy Bessey and the birthday overnight*
MacLachlan, Patricia. *Nora's chicks*
McLellan, Stephanie Simpson. *The chicken cat*
McPhail, David. *Bella loves Bunny*
Ben loves Bear
Big Brown Bear goes to town
Big Brown Bear's birthday surprise
Big brown bear's up and down day
Budgie and Boo
Pig Pig meets the lion
Sylvie and True
Waddles
McQuinn, Anna. *My friend Jamal*
My friend Mei Jing
Mahoney, Daniel J. *The perfect clubhouse*
Mallat, Kathy. *Just ducky*
Marciano, John Bemelmans. *Delilah*
Marshall, James. *The Cut-Ups cut loose*
George and Martha
George and Martha back in town
George and Martha encore
George and Martha one fine day
George and Martha rise and shine
George and Martha 'round and 'round
Martin, Ann M. *Rachel Parker, kindergarten show-off*
Martin, David. *Peep and Ducky*
Martín Larrañaga, Ana. *Pepo and Lolo are friends*
Martins, Isabel Minhós. *Little lamb, have you any wool?*
Marx, Patricia. *Dot in Larryland*
Masurel, Claire. *A cat and a dog*
Mathers, Petra. *Herbie's secret Santa*
Lottie's new friend
Matsuoka, Mei. *Footprints in the snow*
Mayer, Mercer. *A boy, a dog, a frog and a friend*
A boy, a dog and a frog
Frog, where are you?
Mead, Alice. *Billy and Emma*
Meister, Cari. *Skinny and fats, best friends*
Meserve, Adria. *No room for Napoleon*
Metz, Lorijo. *Floridius Bloom and the planet of Gloom*
Michelin, Linda. *Zuzu's wishing cake*
Michelson, Richard. *Across the alley*
Miller, Pat Zietlow. *Sophie's squash*
Mills, Lauren A. *The rag coat*
Minarik, Else Holmelund. *Little Bear's new friend*
Monson, A. M. *Wanted . . . best friend*
Moore, Julianne. *Freckleface Strawberry*
Freckleface Strawberry: best friends forever
Mora, Pat. *Join hands!*
Moran, Alex. *Sam and Jack*
Morck, Irene. *Old bird*
Morgan, Michaela. *Bunny wishes*
Dear bunny
Morozumi, Atsuko. *My friend gorilla*
Moss, Miriam. *I'll be your friend, Smudge*
Moss, Peggy. *One of us*
Moulton, Mark Kimball. *The very best pumpkin*
Muir, Leslie. *C.R. Mudgeon*
Munsch, Robert N. *Wait and see*
Munson, Derek. *Enemy pie*
Murkoff, Heidi Eisenberg. *What to expect at a play date*
What to expect at preschool
Murphy, Jill. *All for one*
Murphy, Mary. *Panda Foo and the new friend*
Murphy, Patti Beling. *Elinor and Violet*
Murphy, Stuart J. *Betcha!*
Give me half!
Murray, Martine. *A moose called Mouse*
Napoli, Donna Jo. *Rocky, the cat who barks*
Narahashi, Keiko. *Two girls can!*
Naylor, Phyllis Reynolds. *King of the playground*
Nelson, Marilyn. *Snook alone*
Newberry, Clare Turlay. *Marshmallow*
Newman, Lesléa. *Skunk's spring surprise*
Nicholls, Judith. *Someone I like*
Nikola-Lisa, W. *Bein' with you this way*
Nimmo, Jenny. *Esmeralda and the children next door*
Nolen, Jerdine. *Raising dragons*
Noonan, Julia. *Hare and Rabbit, friends forever*
Novak, Matt. *Jazzbo and Googy*
Numeroff, Laura Joffe. *The Jellybeans and the big art adventure*
The Jellybeans and the big book bonanza
The Jellybeans and the big camp kickoff
Otis and Sydney and the best birthday ever
Nyeu, Tao. *Squid and Octopus*
Ó Flatharta, Antoine. *Hurry and the monarch*
O'Connor, George. *Sally and the Some-Thing*
Oh, Jiwon. *Cat and mouse*
Ohi, Ruth. *Clara and the Bossy*
Oldland, Nicholas. *Making the moose out of life*
O'Mara, Carmel. *Rainy day*
Oram, Hiawyn. *Badger's bad mood*
My friend Fred
Ørdal, Stina Langlo. *Princess Aasta*
Ormerod, Jan. *Maudie and Bear*
Oyibo, Papa. *Big brother, little sister*
Pacilio, V. J. *Ling Cho and his three friends*
Palatini, Margie. *Stuff*
Paraskevas, Betty. *Marvin, the tap-dancing horse*
Parr, Todd. *The best friends book*
Paul, Ruth. *Hedgehog's magic tricks*
Paxton, Tom. *The story of the Tooth Fairy*
Peet, Bill. *Eli*
Pendziwol, Jean E. *No dragons for tea*
Perkins, Lynne Rae. *The cardboard piano*
Petty, Dini. *The queen, the bear and the bumblebee*
Petz, Moritz. *Wish you were here*
Pfister, Marcus. *Rainbow fish to the rescue!*
Where is my friend?
Pienkowski, Jan. *Bel and Bub and the black hole*
Pilkey, Dav. *A friend for Dragon*
Pinkwater, Daniel. *Bear in love*
Pittman, Helena Clare. *The angel tree*
The snowman's path
Plecas, Jennifer. *Olive's perfect world*
Polacco, Patricia. *Chicken Sunday*
Emma Kate
Mrs. Katz and Tush
Pomerantz, Charlotte. *You're not my best friend anymore*
Postgate, Daniel. *The richest crocodile in the world*
The snagglegrollop
Pratt, Pierre. *Home*
Preus, Margi. *The Peace Bell*
Primavera, Elise. *Louise, the big cheese*
Louise the big cheese and the Ooh-la-la Charm School
Puttock, Simon. *Big bad wolf is good*
Goat and Donkey in strawberry sunglasses
Goat and Donkey in the great outdoors
A story for Hippo
Quattlebaum, Mary. *Winter friends*
Rand, Gloria. *A pen pal for Max*
Rania, Queen, consort of Abdullah II, King of Jordan. *The sandwich swap*

Rankin, Laura. *Fluffy and Baron*
Raschka, Chris. *Ring! Yo?*
Yo! Yes?
Rawlinson, Julia. *Fletcher and the snowflake Christmas*
Rayner, Catherine. *The bear who shared*
Solomon Crocodile
Reiser, Lynn. *My way / A mi manera*
Two mice in three fables
Reynolds, Peter H. *I'm here*
Ritchie, Alison. *What Bear likes best!*
Ritz, Karen. *Windows with birds*
Robberecht, Thierry. *Sam tells stories*
Sam's new friend
Robbins, Jacqui. *The new girl . . . and me*
Two of a kind
Robinson, Sue. *I want to play*
Roche, Denis. *Mim, gym, and June*
Roddie, Shen. *Sandbear*
Rodman, Mary Ann. *My best friend*
Rodriguez, Béatrice. *Fox and hen together*
Rogers, Fred. *Extraordinary friends*
Making friends
Moving
Rohmann, Eric. *My friend Rabbit*
Root, Phyllis. *Toot toot zoom!*
Rosen, Michael. *Bear's day out*
Rosen, Michael J. *Elijah's angel*
Rosenthal, Amy Krouse. *Chopsticks*
Rosenthal, Marc. *Archie and the pirates*
Rosoff, Meg. *Jumpy Jack and Googily*
Roth, Carol. *Little Bunny's sleepless night*
Roth, Roger. *Fishing for Methuselah*
Rumford, James. *Dog-of-the-Sea-Waves*
Tiger and turtle
Runton, Andy. *Owly and Wormy: bright lights and starry nights!*
Owly and Wormy: friends all aflutter!
Russell, Natalie. *Brown Rabbit in the city*
Moon rabbit
Russo, Marisabina. *A very big bunny*
Ruzzier, Sergio. *Hey, Rabbit!*
The little giant
Ryan, Candace. *Ribbit rabbit*
Rylant, Cynthia. *All I see*
The bookshop dog
Miss Maggie
Sakai, Komako. *Emily's balloon*
Saltzberg, Barney. *Hip, hip, hooray day!*
The problem with pumpkins
Sanromán, Susana. *Señora Reganoña*
Sasso, Sandy Eisenberg. *For heaven's sake*
Satoshi, Kako. *Little Daruma and little Tengu*
Scanlon, Elizabeth Garton. *Noodle and Lou*
Schaefer, Lola M. *Frankie Stein starts school*
Scheer, Julian. *By the light of the captured moon*
Scheffler, Axel. *The scary monster*
The snowy day
The super scooter
Scheffler, Ursel. *Who has time for Little Bear?*
Schertle, Alice. *Little Blue Truck*
Schick, Eleanor. *My Navajo sister*
Schubert, Ingrid. *There's always room for one more*
Schwartz, Amy. *Tiny and Hercules*
Schwartz, Corey Rosen. *Hop! Plop!*
Scieszka, Jon. *Cowboy and Octopus*
Smash! Crash!
Scott, Elaine. *Friends!*
Scotton, Rob. *Splat says thank you!*
Splish, splash, Splat!
Seeger, Laura Vaccaro. *Dog and Bear: three to get ready*
Dog and Bear: two friends, three stories
Dog and Bear: two's company
What if?
Segal, John. *The lonely moose*
Seven, John. *A year with friends*
Shannon, George. *Heart to heart*
Rabbit's gift
Sharmat, Marjorie Weinman. *The 329th friend*
Shaw, Hannah. *Sneaky Weasel*
Shaw, Mary. *Brady Brady and the Twirlin' Torpedo*
Shea, Bob. *Unicorn thinks he's pretty great*
Shields, Gillian. *Library Lily*
Shireen, Nadia. *Hey, Presto!*
Shriver, Maria. *What's wrong with Timmy?*
Sidjanski, Brigitte. *Little Chicken and Little Duck*
Sif, Birgitta. *Oliver*
Silverhardt, Lauryn. *Happy Chinese New Year, Kai-lan!*
Siminovich, Lorena. *Alex and Lulu*
Simmons, Jane. *Together*
Sklansky, Amy E. *The duck who played the kazoo*
Slonim, David. *He came with the couch*
Smallcomb, Pam. *I'm not*
Smallman, Steve. *The lamb who came for dinner*
Smalls-Hector, Irene. *Because you're lucky*
Smith, Maggie. *Dear Daisy, get well soon*
Soman, David. *Ladybug Girl and Bumblebee Boy*
Ladybug Girl and the Bug Squad
Sones, Sonya. *Violet and Winston*
Sperring, Mark. *The sunflower sword*
Spinelli, Eileen. *Somebody loves you, Mr. Hatch*
When no one is watching
Spires, Ashley. *Larf*
Srinivasan, Divya. *Octopus alone*
Staake, Bob. *Bluebird*
Stafford, Liliana. *The snow bear*
Stanley, Diane. *Goldie and the three bears*
Stead, Philip C. *Hello, my name is Ruby*
Stein, David Ezra. *Cowboy Ned and Andy*
Ned's new friend
Stephens, Helen. *Ahoyty-toyty*
How to hide a lion
What about me?
Steptoe, John. *Creativity*
Stevie
Stevens, Janet. *My big dog*
Stevenson, James. *Howard*
National worm day
No friends
The stowaway
Wilfred the rat
The worst person in the world
The worst person in the world at Crab Beach
Stewart, Joel. *Dexter Bexley and the big blue beastie*
Stewart, Paul. *A little bit of winter*
Rabbit's wish
Stihler, Chérie B. *The giant cabbage turnip*
Straaten, Harmen van. *Duck's tale*
For me?
Strauss, Linda Leopold. *The Elijah door*
Sutton, Jane. *The trouble with cauliflower*
Tada, Joni Eareckson. *Forever friends*
Tada, Satoshi. *Mr. Beetle*
Tafuri, Nancy. *Where did Bunny go?*
Will you be my friend?
Tarlow, Ellen. *Pinwheel days*

Taulbert, Clifton L. *Little Cliff and the porch people*
Teague, Mark. *The three little pigs and the somewhat bad wolf*
Tegen, Katherine Brown. *Dracula and Frankenstein are friends*
Thayer, Jane. *The popcorn dragon*
Thimmesh, Catherine. *Friends: true stories of extraordinary animal friendships*
Thomas, Jan. *A birthday for Cow!*
Thomas, Shelley Moore. *A Good Knight's rest*
Thompson, Lauren. *Little Quack's new friend*
Polar bear morning
Trapani, Iza. *Baa baa black sheep*
Baa baa black sheep [board book]
Tunnell, Michael O. *The joke's on George*
Twohy, Mike. *Poindexter makes a friend*
Uchida, Yoshiko. *The bracelet*
Udry, Janice May. *Let's be enemies*
Uff, Caroline. *Hello, Lulu*
Urbanovic, Jackie. *Duck soup*
Urdahl, Catherine. *Polka-dot fixes kindergarten*
Vail, Rachel. *Flabbersmashed about you*
Vainio, Pirkko. *The best of friends*
Van Laan, Nancy. *Moose tales*
van Lieshout, Maria. *Hopper and Wilson*
Van Woerkom, Dorothy. *Harry and Shelburt*
Varley, Susan. *Badger's parting gifts*
Varon, Sara. *Chicken and Cat*
Vincent, Gabrielle. *Merry Christmas, Ernest and Celestine*
Viorst, Judith. *Rosie and Michael*
Vrombaut, An. *Clarabella's teeth*
Waber, Bernard. *Evie and Margie*
Gina
Ira says goodbye
Ira sleeps over
Lovable Lyle
Waddell, Martin. *We love them*
Wagner, Anke. *Tim's big move!*
Wagner, Karen. *Bravo, Mildred and Ed!*
A friend like Ed
Walker, Alice. *To hell with dying*
Wallace, Nancy Elizabeth. *Paperwhite*
Walsh, Ellen Stoll. *Hamsters to the rescue*
Walton, Rick. *The remarkable friendship of Mr. Cat and Mr. Rat*
Ward, Helen. *Little Moon Dog*
Watson, Wendy. *Holly's Christmas eve*
Watt, Mélanie. *Scaredy Squirrel makes a friend*
Weigelt, Udo. *Who stole the gold?*
Weitzman, Jacqueline Preiss. *Superhero Joe and the creature next door*
Weninger, Brigitte. *Miko goes on vacation*
Why are you fighting, Davy?
Wheeler, Lisa. *Hokey pokey*
White, Linda. *Too many pumpkins*
Wick, Walter. *Can you see what I see? Seymour makes new friends*
Wild, Margaret. *Fox*
Mr. Nick's knitting
Wiles, Debbie. *Freedom summer*
Wilhelm, Hans. *Quacky Ducky's Easter egg*
Willems, Mo. *City dog, country frog*
Leonardo the terrible monster
Williams, Karen Lynn. *When Africa was home*
Williams, Sherley Anne. *Girls together*
Willis, Jeanne. *Misery Moo*
Wilson, Karma. *Bear feels scared*
Bear feels sick
Wilson, Sarah. *Friends and pals and brothers, too*
Winget, Susan. *Tucker's four-carrot school day*
Winstead, Rosie. *Ruby and Bubbles*
Wishinsky, Frieda. *You're mean, Lily Jean!*
Wojciechowski, Susan. *The Christmas miracle of Jonathan Toomey*
Wolff, Ferida. *The story blanket*
Wolkstein, Diane. *Little Mouse's painting*
Step by step
Wood, Audrey. *Jubal's wish*
Wormell, Christopher. *Blue Rabbit and friends*
Yaccarino, Dan. *Unlovable*
Yin. *Brothers*
Yolen, Jane. *Dimity Duck*
How do dinosaurs play with their friends?
Yoon, Salina. *Penguin and Pinecone*
Penguin on vacation
Young, Ruth. *Golden Bear*
Zalben, Jane Breskin. *Beni's first Chanukah*
Zehler, Antonia. *Two fine ladies*
Two fine ladies have a tiff
Ziefert, Harriet. *Bunny's lessons*
Fun Land fun!
39 uses for a friend
Zolotow, Charlotte. *The hating book*
My friend John

Frogs & toads

Ada, Alma Flor. *Friend frog*
Allchin, Rosalind. *The frog princess*
Anderson, Peggy Perry. *Joe on the go*
Out to lunch
Time for bed, the babysitter said
To the tub
Arnold, Tedd. *Green Wilma*
Green Wilma, frog in space
Arnosky, Jim. *All about frogs*
Asch, Frank. *Baby Bird's first nest*
Moonbear's pet
Asher, Sandy. *Here comes Gosling!*
Too many frogs!
What a party!
Azore, Barbara. *Wanda and the frogs*
Bailey, Linda. *Toads on toast*
Bateman, Teresa. *The frog with the big mouth*
Bauer, Marion Dane. *Frog's best friend*
Berkes, Marianne. *Marsh music*
Boelts, Maribeth. *Big Daddy, frog wrestler*
Bonning, Tony. *Snog the frog*
Boyd, Lizi. *I love Daddy*
I love Mommy
Breen, Steve. *Stick*
Bynum, Janie. *Otis*
Calmenson, Stephanie. *The frog principal*
Carle, Eric. *Hello, red fox*
Carlson, Nancy. *Smile a lot!*
Think big!
Think happy!
Cecil, Randy. *Horsefly and Honeybee*
Chrustowski, Rick. *Hop frog*
Cooper, Susan. *Frog*
Cowan, Charlotte. *Peeper has a fever*
Cyrus, Kurt. *Tadpole Rex*
Debecker, Benoît. *The naughty prince*
Dennard, Deborah. *Bullfrog at Magnolia Circle*
Downing, Johnette. *There was an old lady who swallowed some bugs*
Elya, Susan Middleton. *Sophie's trophy*

Fearnley, Jan. *Martha in the middle*
Ferri, Giuliano. *Little Tad grows up*
Fitzsimmons, David. *Curious critters*
Fleming, Denise. *In the small, small pond*
Florian, Douglas. *Lizards, frogs, and polliwogs*
Folgueira, Rodrigo. *Ribbit!*
Franco, Betsy. *Why the frog has big eyes*
French, Vivian. *Growing frogs*
A frog he would a-wooing go [folk-song]. *Frog went a-courtin'*
Frog went a-courting
Froggie went a courting
Froggy went a-courtin'
Gardner, Carol. *Princess Zelda and the frog*
Geraghty, Paul. *The hoppameleon*
Gibbons, Gail. *Frogs*
Grahame, Kenneth. *The wind in the willows*
Gravett, Emily. *Spells*
Grimm, Jacob and Wilhelm. *The frog prince*, ill. by Anne Yvonne Gilbert
The frog prince, ill. by Todd Ouren
Grobler, Piet. *Hey, frog!*
Guiberson, Brenda Z. *Frog song*
Hall, Algy Craig. *Fine as we are*
Hassett, Ann. *Too many frogs!*
Heo, Yumi. *The green frogs*
Himmelman, John. *Noisy frog sing-along*
A wood frog's life
Hobbie, Holly. *Gem*
Hunter, Anne. *Possum and the peeper*
Hurd, Thacher. *Bad frogs*
Isherwood, Shirley. *Flora the frog*
James, Betsy. *Tadpoles*
Johnson, Rebecca. *Tree frog hears a sound*
Johnson, Suzanne C. *Fribbity ribbit*
Jordan, Sandra. *Frog hunt*
Joyce, William. *Bently and egg*
Kalan, Robert. *Jump, frog, jump!*
Kasza, Keiko. *Grandpa Toad's last secret*
Kellogg, Steven. *The mysterious tadpole*
Ketteman, Helen. *Armadilly chili*
Kimmel, Eric A. *The frog princess: a Tlingit legend from Alaska*
Kimura, Ken. *999 frogs wake up*
999 tadpoles
Kopelke, Lisa. *Excuse me!*
Lee, Jeanne M. *Toad is the uncle of heaven*
Leedy, Loreen. *The great graph contest*
Lionni, Leo. *An extraordinary egg*
Fish is fish
It's mine!
Little old lady who swallowed a fly. *There was an old monkey who swallowed a frog*
Livingston, Irene. *Finklehopper Frog*
Finklehopper Frog cheers
Lobel, Arnold. *Days with Frog and Toad*
Frog and Toad all year
Frog and Toad are friends
The frog and toad pop-up book
Frog and Toad together
The frogs and toads all sang
London, Jonathan. *Froggy eats out*
Froggy gets dressed
Froggy goes to bed
Froggy goes to camp
Froggy goes to Hawaii
Froggy goes to school
Froggy goes to the doctor
Froggy learns to swim
Froggy plays in the band
Froggy plays soccer
Froggy plays T-ball
Froggy rides a bike
Froggy's first Christmas
Froggy's first kiss
Froggy's Halloween
Let's go, Froggy!
Long, Ethan. *The croaky pokey!*
Mack, Jeff. *Ah ha!*
Frog and Fly
McLeod, Heather. *Kiss me!*
Magloff, Lisa. *Frog*
Markle, Sandra. *Hip-pocket papa*
Mayer, Mercer. *A boy, a dog, a frog and a friend*
A boy, a dog and a frog
Frog goes to dinner
Frog on his own
Frog, where are you?
One frog too many
Mitton, Tony. *Down by the cool of the pool*
Murphy, Stuart J. *Ready, set, hop!*
Nelson, Robin. *Pet frog*
Northey, Lawrence. *I'm a hop hop hoppity frog*
Parenteau, Shirley. *One frog sang*
Pfeffer, Wendy. *From tadpole to frog*
Pfister, Marcus. *Hopper hunts for spring*
Pinczes, Elinor J. *My full moon is square*
Potter, Beatrix. *The tale of Mr. Jeremy Fisher*, ill. by David Jorgensen
The tale of Mr. Jeremy Fisher, ill. by Beatrix Potter
Rong, Yu. *A lovely day for Amelia Goose*
Roth, Susan L. *The biggest frog in Australia*
Rouss, Sylvia A. *The littlest frog*
Ryan, Candace. *Ribbit rabbit*
Ryder, Joanne. *Toad by the road*
Samuels, Barbara. *What's so great about Cindy Snappleby?*
Sayre, April Pulley. *Dig, wait, listen*
Schertle, Alice. *Advice for a frog and other poems*
Little Frog's song
Schneider, Howie. *Fast 'n Snappy*
Scieszka, Jon. *The frog prince, continued*
Shannon, George. *April showers*
Frog legs
Sill, Cathryn. *About amphibians*
Stead, Philip C. *A home for Bird*
Steig, William. *Gorky rises*
Steptoe, John. *The story of jumping mouse*
Stevenson, James. *Monty*
Stewart, Melissa. *A place for frogs*
Straaten, Harmen van. *Duck's tale*
For me?
Tagholm, Sally. *The frog*
Tashiro, Chisato. *Five nice mice*
Thomas, Jan. *Can you make a scary face?*
Thompson, Lauren. *Leap back home to me*
Little Quack's new friend
Tripp, Paul. *Tubby the tuba*
Vern, Alex. *Where do frogs come from?*
Waddell, Martin. *Bee frog*
Wiesner, David. *Tuesday*
Willems, Mo. *Big Frog can't fit in*
City dog, country frog
Willis, Jeanne. *Tadpole's promise*
Winer, Yvonne. *Frogs sing songs*
Wood, Audrey. *Jubal's wish*
Yolen, Jane. *Dimity Duck*
King Long Shanks

Young, Amy. *The mud fairy*

Frontier life *see* U.S. history – frontier & pioneer life

Furniture

Lillegard, Dee. *Wake up house!*
Slonim, David. *He came with the couch*

Furniture – beds

Arnold, Tedd. *No jumping on the bed!*
Bergstein, Rita M. *Your own big bed*
Bibbel, Mark. *Oh, Harry!*
Bluemle, Elizabeth. *Dogs on the bed*
Bottner, Barbara. *Rosa's room*
Burningham, John. *The magic bed*
Camp, Lindsay. *The biggest bed in the world*
Child, Lauren. *My dream bed*
Ferreri, Della Ross. *How will I ever sleep in this bed?*
Hines, Anna Grossnickle. *My own big bed*
Howe, James. *There's a monster under my bed*
Lum, Kate. *What! cried Granny*
McGhee, Alison. *Bye-bye, crib*
Pulver, Robin. *Alicia's tutu*
Root, Phyllis. *Creak! said the bed*
Singer, Marilyn. *Fred's bed*
Stevenson, James. *What's under my bed?*
Thomson, Pat. *The squeaky, creaky bed*
Willard, Nancy. *The flying bed*

Furniture – chairs

Bertram, Debbie. *The best place to read*
Keats, Ezra Jack. *Peter's chair*
Mahy, Margaret. *Down the back of the chair*
Manuel, Lynn. *The trouble with Tilly Trumble*
Parenteau, Shirley. *Bears on chairs*
Williams, Vera B. *A chair for always*
A chair for my mother

Games

Agee, Jon. *Mr. Putney's quacking dog*
Ahlberg, Janet. *Each peach pear plum*
Peek-a-boo!
Ancona, George. *Mis juegos / My games*
Anglund, Joan Walsh. *The brave cowboy*
Anno, Mitsumasa. *Anno's Britain*
Anno's counting house
Anno's Italy
Anno's journey
Anno's U.S.A.
Aruego, José. *We hide, you seek*
Barnett, Mac. *Guess again!*
Beaton, Clare. *Clare Beaton's action rhymes*
Behrens, Janice. *Let's find rain forest animals*
Boatfield, Jonny. *The twilight book*
Brown, Marc. *Finger rhymes*
Hand rhymes
Play rhymes
Burnard, Damon. *I spy in the jungle*
Burningham, John. *Tug-of-war*
Butler, John. *Ten in the meadow*
Butterfield, Moira. *Magic world of learning*
Carter, David A. *Peekaboo bugs*
Whoo? Whoo?
Cauley, Lorinda Bryan. *Clap your hands*
Chichester Clark, Emma. *Follow the leader!*
Cuyler, Margery. *We're going on a lion hunt*
Dann, Penny. *Eensy weensy spider*
Davenier, Christine. *It's raining, it's pouring*
Delacre, Lulu. *Arroz con leche*
dePaola, Tomie. *Hide-and-seek all week*
Edwards, Richard. *Always Copycub*
Einhorn, Edward. *A very improbable story*
The farmer in the dell. *The farmer in the dell*, ill. by John O'Brien
The farmer in the dell, ill. by Alexandra Wallner
Go tell Aunt Rhody
Grindley, Sally. *Silly Goose and Dizzy Duck play hide-and-seek*
Hague, Michael. *Teddy bear, teddy bear*
Handford, Martin. *Find Waldo now*
The great Waldo search
Where's Waldo?
Where's Waldo? In Hollywood
Where's Waldo? The fantastic journey
Where's Waldo? The wonder book
Where's Waldo now?
Hays, Anna Jane. *Ready, set, preschool!*
Hines, Anna Grossnickle. *What can you do in the wind?*
Hort, Lenny. *We're going on a treasure hunt*
Hru, Dakari. *Tickle, tickle*
Hughes, Sarah. *Let's play hopscotch*
Let's play jacks
Hunter, Dette. *38 ways to entertain your babysitter*
38 ways to entertain your grandparents
Hutchins, Pat. *What game shall we play?*
Which witch is which?
Intrater, Roberta Grobel. *Peek-a-boo!*
Isadora, Rachel. *Peekaboo bedtime*
Peekaboo morning
Peekaboo morning [board book]
Jahn-Clough, Lisa. *Missing Molly*
James, Simon. *Little One Step*
Jenkins, Steve. *What do you do with a tail like this?*
Jennings, Linda. *Hide and seek birthday treat*
Jonas, Ann. *The trek*
Katz, Karen. *Where is baby's mommy?*
Kraus, Robert. *Mort the sport*
Krauss, Ruth. *You're just what I need*
Krilanovich, Nadia. *Chicken, chicken, duck!*
Kroll, Steven. *The Tyrannosaurus game*
Ledwon, Peter. *Midnight math twelve terrific math games*
Leonard, Marcia. *Peek-a-boo, baby!*
Lewis, J. Patrick. *The bookworm's feast*
McCall, Francis X. *A huge hog is a big pig*
Manning, Jane. *My first baby games*
Meade, Holly. *Inside, inside, inside*
Miller, Margaret. *Whose shoe?*
Monson, A. M. *Wanted . . . best friend*
Moore, Julianne. *Freckleface Strawberry and the dodgeball bully*

Mother Goose *Pat-a-cake*
Munro, Roxie. *Mazescapes*
Murphy, Stuart J. *Monster musical chairs*
More or less
Murray, Martine. *A moose called Mouse*
Na, Il Sung. *Hide and seek*
Newman, Lesléa. *Runaway dreidel*
Palatini, Margie. *The cheese*
Petrillo, Genevieve. *Keep your ear on the ball*
Philpot, Graham. *Where is Little Harry?*
Pow, Tom. *Tell me one thing, Dad*
Ray, Karen. *Sleep song*
Robberecht, Thierry. *Sam is not a loser*
Roddie, Shen. *Toes are to tickle*
Rodriguez, Bobbie. *Sarah's sleepover*
Root, Phyllis. *Looking for a moose*
Rosen, Michael. *We're going on a bear hunt*
Rueda, Claudia. *Let's play in the forest while the wolf is not around*
Russo, Marisabina. *The big brown box*
Scruggs, Afi. *Jump rope magic*
Shaw, Charles Green. *It looked like spilt milk*
Simmons, Jane. *Daisy's hide-and-seek*
Little Fern's first winter
Steffensmeier, Alexander. *Millie and the big rescue*
Steig, William. *Pete's a pizza*
Toby, what are you?
Stoeke, Janet Morgan. *Hide and seek*
Tafuri, Nancy. *Where did Bunny go?*
Thomas, Mark. *Fun and games in Colonial America*
Thompson, Lauren. *Little Quack's hide and seek*
Little Quack's hide and seek [board book]
Trapani, Iza. *What am I?*
Van Allsburg, Chris. *Jumanji*
Zathura
Van Laan, Nancy. *Tickle tum*
Viorst, Judith. *The alphabet from Z to A*
Walsh, Melanie. *Hide and sleep*
Wells, Rosemary. *McDuffs hide-and-seek*
Peek-a-boo
Weninger, Brigitte. *Special delivery*
Westcott, Nadine Bernard. *The lady with the alligator purse*
Wick, Walter. *Can you see what I see? cool collections*
Wildsmith, Brian. *Brian Wildsmith's puzzles*
Wilner, Isabel. *The baby's game book*
Wisniewski, David. *Rain player*
Wood, Don. *Piggies*
Piggies [board book]
Yaccarino, Dan. *So big*
Yee, Wong Herbert. *Who likes rain?*

Gangs *see* Clubs, gangs

Garage sales, rummage sales

Devlin, Wende. *Cranberry autumn*
Elya, Susan Middleton. *Adiós, tricycle*
Kotzwinkle, William. *Walter, the farting dog: trouble at the yard sale*
Kroll, Steven. *Stuff!*
Stevenson, James. *Yard sale*

Garbage collectors *see* Careers – sanitation workers

Gardens, gardening

Aliki. *Corn is maize*
Quiet in the garden
The story of Johnny Appleseed
Ancona, George. *It's our garden*
Anno, Mitsumasa. *Anno's magic seeds*
Ayres, Katherine. *Up, down, and around*
Azarian, Mary. *A gardener's alphabet*
Baicker, Karen. *Pea pod babies*
Bauld, Jane Scoggins. *Journey of the third seed*
Beames, Margaret. *Night cat*
Beck, Andrea. *Elliot digs for treasure*
Blackstone, Stella. *What's this?*
Bogacki, Tomasz. *My first garden*
Bond, Michael. *Paddington Bear in the garden*
Boyden, Linda. *The blue roses*
Braun, Sebastien. *Who's hiding?*
Brenner, Barbara A. *Good morning, garden*
Brett, Jan. *Mossy*
Brown, Peter. *The curious garden*
Bruce, Lisa. *Fran's flower*
Bunting, Eve. *A day's work*
Flower garden
Sunflower house
Burnett, Frances Hodgson. *The secret garden*
Castellucci, Cecil. *Grandma's gloves*
Cherry, Lynne. *How Groundhog's garden grew*
Christensen, Bonnie. *Plant a little seed*
Codell, Esme Raji. *Seed by seed*
Dahl, Michael. *From the garden*
Davis, Nancy. *A garden of opposites*
De Anda, Diane. *The patchwork garden / pedacitos de huerto*
Demi. *The empty pot*
dePaola, Tomie. *Strega Nona's harvest*
Donaldson, Julia. *One mole digging a hole*
Duke, Kate. *Ready for pumpkins*
Eclare, Melanie. *A handful of sunshine*
A harvest of color
Ehlert, Lois. *Growing vegetable soup*
Planting a rainbow
Elvgren, Jennifer Riesmeyer. *Josias, hold the book*
Emberley, Rebecca. *My garden / Mi jardin*
Falwell, Cathryn. *Mystery vine*
Fine, Edith Hope. *Water, weed, and wait*
Fleischman, Paul. *Weslandia*
Fleming, Candace. *Muncha! Muncha! Muncha!*
Fogliano, Julie. *And then it's spring*
Ford, Miela. *Sunflower*
French, Vivian. *Yucky worms*
Fry, Stella. *Grandpa's garden*
George, Lindsay Barrett. *In the garden: who's been here?*
Gershator, Phillis. *Sky sweeper*
Gibbons, Gail. *Corn*
The pumpkin book
Glaser, Linda. *Garbage helps our garden grow*
Gliori, Debi. *Flora's surprise*
Gourley, Robbin. *First garden*
Grigsby, Susan. *First peas to the table*
In the garden with Dr. Carver
Guest, C. Z. *Tiny green thumbs*
Hafner, Marylin. *Molly and Emmett's surprise garden*
Hall, Zoe. *The surprise garden*
Harrison, David L. *Farmer's garden*
Harshman, Marc. *Red are the apples*
Hayes, Joe. *Don't say a word, Mamá/No digas nada, Mamá*

Heap, Sue. *Four friends in the garden*
Helmore, Jim. *Oh no, monster tomato!*
Henderson, Kathy. *And the good brown earth*
Henkes, Kevin. *My garden*
Henterly, Jamichael. *Good night, garden gnome*
Hest, Amy. *Little chick*
Hines, Anna Grossnickle. *Miss Emma's wild garden*
Hodge, Deborah. *Watch me grow!*
Hoffman, Eric. *Play Lady / La Señora Juguetona*
Holmes, Anita. *Flowers and friends*
Honey, Elizabeth. *That's not a daffodil!*
Hopkins, H. Joseph. *The tree lady*
Hruby, Emily. *Counting in the garden*
Hubbell, Patricia. *Black earth, gold sun*
Inches, Alison. *Corduroy's garden*
Jordan, Helene J. *How a seed grows*
Joyce, William. *The Leaf Men and the brave good bugs*
Kann, Victoria. *Emeraldalicious*
Kellogg, Steven. *Johnny Appleseed: a tall tale*
Krauss, Ruth. *The carrot seed*
Larsen, Andrew. *The imaginary garden*
Levenson, George. *Pumpkin circle*
Lin, Grace. *The ugly vegetables*
Lindbergh, Reeve. *Johnny Appleseed*
Lobel, Anita. *Ten hungry rabbits*
Loki. *Jake Greenthumb*
Lottridge, Celia Barker. *One watermelon seed*
Maass, Robert. *Garden*
MacDonald, Margaret Read. *Pickin' peas*
McLeod, Elaine. *Lessons from Mother Earth*
Mannis, Celeste Davidson. *One leaf rides the wind*
Marshall, Linda Elovitz. *Talia and the rude vegetables*
Martin, Jacqueline Briggs. *Farmer Will Allen and the growing table*
Matthies, Janna. *The goodbye cancer garden*
Maurer, Tracy. *Growing flowers*
Middleton, Charlotte. *Nibbles*
Nibbles' garden
Millard, Glenda. *Isabella's garden*
Miller, Pat Zietlow. *Sophie's squash*
Milway, Katie Smith. *The good garden*
Molk, Laurel. *Good job, Oliver!*
Mortimer, Anne. *Pumpkin cat*
Moulton, Mark Kimball. *The very best pumpkin*
Noguchi, Rick. *Flowers from Mariko*
O'Malley, Kevin. *Bud*
Oxenbury, Helen. *Tom and Pippo in the garden*
Pak, Soyung. *A place to grow*
Paraskevas, Betty. *Maggie and the Ferocious Beast, the big carrot*
Park, Linda Sue. *What does Bunny see?*
Parker, Kim. *Counting in the garden*
Pattou, Edith. *Mrs. Spitzer's garden*, ill. by Tricia Tusa
Mrs. Spitzer's garden, ill. by Tricia Tusa
Perkins, Lynne Rae. *Home lovely*
Peterson, Cris. *Seed soil sun*
Pinczes, Elinor J. *Inchworm and a half*
Poppy Bear
Quattlebaum, Mary. *Jo MacDonald had a garden*
Ray, Deborah Kogan. *Lily's garden*
Reynolds, Peter H. *Rose's garden*
Robbins, Ken. *Pumpkins*
Roberts, Bethany. *The wind's garden*
Rosenberry, Vera. *Who is in the garden?*
Rubel, Nicole. *No more vegetables!*
Ryder, Joanne. *My father's hands*
Rylant, Cynthia. *This year's garden*
Say, Allen. *The boy in the garden*
Schulman, Janet. *A bunny for all seasons*
Schumaker, Ward. *In my garden*
Segal, John. *Carrot soup*
Selkowe, Valrie M. *Happy birthday to me!*
Serafini, Frank. *Looking closely inside the garden*
Shannon, George. *Busy in the garden*
Siminovich, Lorena. *I like vegetables*
Smith, Lane. *Grandpa Green*
Smith, Maggie. *This is your garden*
Spurr, Elizabeth. *In the garden*
Stevens, Janet. *Tops and bottoms*
Stevenson, James. *Grandpa's too-good garden*
Stewart, Sarah. *The gardener*
Swain, Gwenyth. *Johnny Appleseed*
Swann, Rick. *Our school garden!*
Tamar, Erika. *The garden of happiness*
Thompson, Lauren. *The forgiveness garden*
Thurman, Kathryn K. *A garden for Pig*
Titherington, Jeanne. *Pumpkin pumpkin*
Trapani, Iza. *Here we go 'round the mulberry bush*
Voake, Steve. *Insect detective*
Waldherr, Kris. *Harvest*
Wallace, Karen. *Scarlette Beane*
Wallace, Nancy Elizabeth. *Paperwhite*
Planting seeds
Ward, Jennifer. *Over in the garden*
Weeks, Sarah. *Mrs. McNosh and the great big squash*
Wellington, Monica. *Zinnia's flower garden*
Wells, Rosemary. *First tomato*
Max's worm cake
White, Linda. *Too many turkeys*
Wilde, Oscar. *The selfish giant*, ill. by S. Saelig Gallagher
The selfish giant, ill. by Fabian Negrin
The selfish giant, ill. by Lisbeth Zwerger
Wilner, Isabel. *A garden alphabet*
Wilson, Karma. *Mortimer's first garden*
Wood, Douglas. *Aunt Mary's rose*
Wortche, Allison. *Rosie Sprout's time to shine*
Yacowitz, Caryn. *Pumpkin fiesta*
Yolen, Jane. *Johnny Appleseed: the legend and the truth*
Zagwÿn, Deborah Turney. *Apple batter*
The pumpkin blanket
Zoehfeld, Kathleen Weidner. *Secrets of the garden*

Gender roles

Baguley, Elizabeth. *Meggie moon*
Banks, Kate. *Mama's coming home*
Bridges, Shirin Yim. *Ruby's wish*
Brown, Don. *Rare treasure*
Brown, Tami Lewis. *Soar, Elinor!*
Browning, Diane. *Signed, Abiah Rose*
Codell, Esmé Raji. *The basket ball*
Corey, Shana. *You forgot your skirt, Amelia Bloomer*
Cristaldi, Kathryn. *Baseball ballerina*
DiPucchio, Kelly. *Grace for president*
Dray, Philip. *Yours for justice, Ida B. Wells*
Fierstein, Harvey. *The sissy duckling*
Gerber, Carole. *Annie Jump Cannon, astronomer*
Grant, Brianna K. *We are girls who love to run / Somos chicas y a nosotras nos encanta correr*
Harness, Cheryl. *Mary Walker wears the pants*
Hill, Susanna Leonard. *Punxsutawney Phyllis*
Hines, Anna Grossnickle. *Daddy makes the best spaghetti*
Hooks, Bell. *Be boy buzz*
Hopkins, H. Joseph. *The tree lady*

Hopkinson, Deborah. *Knit your bit*
Howard, Elizabeth Fitzgerald. *Virgie goes to school with us boys*
Hubbard, Crystal. *Catching the moon: the story of a young girl's baseball dream*
Kessler, Cristina. *The best beekeeper of Lalibela*
Kilodavis, Cheryl. *My princess boy*
Kroll, Virginia L. *Girl, you're amazing!*
Krull, Kathleen. *Hillary Rodham Clinton*
Landman, Tanya. *Mary's penny*
Lawlor, Laurie. *Rachel Carson and her book that changed the world*
Lyon, George Ella. *Mama is a miner*
Mackall, Dandi Daley. *A girl named Dan*
Milgrim, David. *Time to get up, time to go*
Moore, Julianne. *Freckleface Strawberry: best friends forever*
Mortenson, Greg. *Listen to the wind*
Moss, Marissa. *Sky high*
True heart
Numeroff, Laura Joffe. *What daddies do best*
What mommies do best
Ochiltree, Dianne. *Molly, by golly!*
Plourde, Lynn. *Margaret Chase Smith*
San Souci, Robert D. *Brave Margaret*
A weave of words
Shaw, Mary. *Brady Brady and the Twirlin' Torpedo*
Sierra, Judy. *Tasty baby belly buttons*
Smith, Jada Pinkett. *Girls hold up this world*
Smith, Lane. *Madam President*
Stone, Tanya Lee. *Elizabeth leads the way*
Who says women can't be doctors?
U'Ren, Andrea. *Pugdog*
Vernick, Audrey. *She loved baseball*
Wallner, Alexandra. *Susan B. Anthony*
Whitaker, Suzanne George. *The daring Miss Quimby*
Winter, Jeanette. *Nasreen's secret school*
Wooldridge, Connie Nordhielm. *When Esther Morris headed west*
Yolen, Jane. *Not all princesses dress in pink*
Zhang, Song Nan. *The ballad of Mulan*
Ziarnik, Natalie. *Madeleine's light*

Genealogy

Schreck, Karen Halvorsen. *Lucy's family tree*
Sweeney, Joan. *Me and my family tree*
Wyeth, Sharon Dennis. *The granddaughter necklace*

Generosity *see* Character traits – generosity

Geography

Cuyler, Margery. *That's good! That's bad! In Washington, D.C.*
Holub, Joan. *Geogra-fleas*
Jackson, Ellen. *The seven seas*
Jenkins, Steve. *Hottest, coldest, highest, deepest*
Keller, Laurie. *The scrambled states of America*
The scrambled states of America talent show
Lewis, J. Patrick. *Earth and you, a closer view*
Ljungkvist, Laura. *Follow the line around the world*
National Geographic Society [U.S.]. *National Geographic our world*
Piepmeier, Charlotte. *Lucy's journey to the wild west*
Schuett, Stacey. *Somewhere in the world right now*
Shulevitz, Uri. *How I learned geography*
Vyner, Tim. *World team*

Ghosts

Ahlberg, Janet. *Funnybones*
Allard, Harry. *Bumps in the night*
Amsden, Janet. *Grizzly Pete and the ghosts*
Auch, Mary Jane. *Poultrygeist*
Baehr, Patricia. *Boo Cow*
Beaty, Andrea. *Hush, Baby Ghostling*
Bennett, Jill. *Teeny tiny*
Berenstain, Stan and Jan. *The Berenstain bears and the ghost of the forest*
Bright, Robert. *Georgie*
Georgie's Christmas carol
Georgie's Halloween
Brunhoff, Laurent de. *Babar and the ghost [easy-to-read ed.]*
Babar and the ghost
Calmenson, Stephanie. *The teeny tiny teacher*
Carter, David A. *In a dark, dark wood*
Cazet, Denys. *The perfect pumpkin pie*
Chase, Mary. *The wicked, wicked ladies in the haunted house*
Clark, Mary Higgins. *Ghost ship*
Compestine, Ying Chang. *Boy dumplings*
Crews, Nina. *A ghost story*
Cuyler, Margery. *Skeleton hiccups*
deGroat, Diane. *Good night, sleep tight, don't let the bedbugs bite*
Diviny, Sean. *Halloween Motel*
Eeckhout, Emmanuelle. *There's no such thing as ghosts!*
Evans, Cambria. *Bone soup*
Fenton, Joe. *Boo!*
Galdone, Joanna. *The tailypo*
Galdone, Paul. *The teeny-tiny woman*
Goldie, Sonia. *Ghosts*
Goodhart, Pippa. *Three little ghosties*
Hamilton, Martha. *The ghost catcher*
Hawkins, Colin. *Creepy castle*
Irving, Washington. *The legend of Sleepy Hollow*
Jacobs, Joseph. *King of the cats*
Johnston, Tony. *The ghost of Nicholas Greebe*
Kohara, Kazuno. *Ghosts in the house!*
Landry, Leo. *The snow ghosts*
Trick or treat
LaRochelle, David. *The haunted hamburger and other ghostly stories*
Lester, Julius. *The hungry ghosts*
Lewis, J. Patrick. *The house of Boo*
McKissack, Patricia C. *Ol' Clip-Clop*
Marciano, John Bemelmans. *Madeline and the old house in Paris*
Marin, Cheech. *Cheech and the spooky ghost bus*
Martin, Bill, Jr. *Old devil wind*
Martín Larrañaga, Ana. *Woo! The not-so-scary Ghost*
Marzollo, Jean. *I spy spooky night*
Matheis, Mickie. *Bedtime for Boo*
Medearis, Angela Shelf. *The ghost of Sifty-Sifty Sam*
Milord, Susan. *The ghost on the hearth*
Moore, Lilian. *Beware, take care*
Murphy, Jim. *Fergus and the Night-Demon*
Muth, Jon J. *Zen ghosts*
Mystery manor
Ogburn, Jacqueline K. *The bake shop ghost*
Paquette, Ammi-Joan. *Ghost in the house*
Pearson, Susan. *We're going on a ghost hunt*
Pienkowski, Jan. *Haunted house*
Prelutsky, Jack. *Halloween countdown*
Pulver, Robin. *Never say boo!*

Reiner, Carl. *Tell me a scary story — but not too scary!*
Richardson, Bill. *Sally Dog Little*
Robberecht, Thierry. *Sarah's little ghosts*
Robins, Arthur. *The teeny tiny woman*
Rocklin, Joanne. *This book is haunted*
Ross, Tony. *I want my light on!*
San Souci, Robert D. *The boy and the ghost*
Silverman, Erica. *The Halloween house*
Smith, Lane. *Abe Lincoln's dream*
Stein, Mathilde. *Mine!*
Terasaki, Stanley Todd. *Ghosts for breakfast*
Trapani, Iza. *Haunted party*
Vaughan, Marcia Kapok. *We're going on a ghost hunt*
Winters, Kay. *The teeny tiny ghost*
The teeny tiny ghost and the monster
Whooo's haunting the teeny tiny ghost?
Yep, Laurence. *The man who tricked a ghost*

Giants

Andreasen, Dan. *The giant of Seville*
Auld, Mary. *David and Goliath*
Balian, Lorna. *A sweetheart for Valentine*
Beaty, Andrea. *When giants come to play*
Bertrand, Lynne. *Granite baby*
Bird, Betsy. *Giant dance party*
Birdseye, Tom. *Look out, Jack! The giant is back*
Braun, Eric. *Trust me, Jack's beanstalk stinks*
Briggs, Raymond. *Jim and the beanstalk*
Bryan, Ashley. *Can't scare me!*
Bunting, Eve. *Finn McCool and the great fish*
Carle, Eric. *Watch out! A giant!*
dePaola, Tomie. *Fin M'Coul*
Fisher, Leonard Everett. *David and Goliath*
Friedman, Caitlin. *How do you feed a hungry giant?*
Goldsboro, Bobby. *Noah and the ark; and, David and Goliath*
Grimm, Jacob and Wilhelm. *The brave little tailor*, ill. by Olga Dugina
The brave little tailor, ill. by David Shaw
Seven at one blow
Harrison, David L. *The book of giant stories*
Hawkes, Kevin. *The wicked big toddlah*
The wicked big toddlah goes to New York
Higgins, Ryan. *Wilfred*
Hutchins, Hazel. *Two so small*
Ivey, Randall. *Jay and the bounty of books*
Jack and the beanstalk. *Jack and the beanstalk*, ill. by Aljoscha Blau
Jack and the beanstalk, ill. by Steve Cox
Jack and the beanstalk, ill. by Nina Crews
Jack and the beanstalk, ill. by Julek Heller
Jack and the beanstalk, ill. by John Howe
Jack and the beanstalk, ill. by Steven Kellogg
Jack and the beanstalk, ill. by Albert Lorenz
Jack and the beanstalk, ill. by Niamh Sharkey
Jack and the beanstalk, ill. by Gennady Spirin
Jack and the beanstalk, ill. by Matt Tavares
Jacques and de beanstalk
Johnson, Paul Brett. *Jack outwits the giants*
Kasza, Keiko. *The mightiest*
Kennedy, Kim. *Pirate Pete's giant adventure*
Ketteman, Helen. *Waynetta and the cornstalk*
Kimmel, Eric A. *Jack and the giant barbecue*
Klausmeier, Jesse. *Open this little book*
Klise, Kate. *Stand straight, Ella Kate*
Leedy, Loreen. *Jack and the hungry giant eat right with MyPlate*
Light, Steve. *The Christmas giant*
The shoemaker extraordinaire
Mora, Pat. *Doña Flor*
Munsch, Robert N. *David's father*
Nash, Ogden. *The adventures of Isabel*, ill. by James Marshall
The adventures of Isabel, ill. by Bridget Starr Taylor
Nolen, Jerdine. *Hewitt Anderson's great big life*
O'Connor, George. *Uncle Bigfoot*
O'Malley, Kevin. *Once upon a cool motorcycle dude*
Osborne, Mary Pope. *The brave little seamstress*
Kate and the beanstalk
Ruzzier, Sergio. *The little giant*
San Souci, Robert D. *Brave Margaret*
Peter and the blue witch baby
Schotter, Roni. *When the Wizzy Foot goes walking*
Seeger, Pete. *Abiyoyo returns*
Souhami, Jessica. *Mrs. McCool and the giant Cuhullin*
Spalding, Andrea. *It's raining, it's pouring*
Stanley, Diane. *The Giant and the beanstalk*
Stimpson, Colin. *Jack and the baked beanstalk*
Thurber, James. *The great Quillow*
Tom Thumb. *The adventures of Tom Thumb*
Wilde, Oscar. *The selfish giant*, ill. by S. Saelig Gallagher
The selfish giant, ill. by Fabian Negrin
The selfish giant, ill. by Lisbeth Zwerger
Willey, Margaret. *Clever Beatrice, an Upper Peninsula conte*
Yorinks, Arthur. *The Miami giant*

Gifts

Anderson, Laurie Halse. *No time for Mother's Day*
Beck, Andrea. *Elliot's Christmas surprise*
Beck, Scott. *A mud pie for mother*
Best, Cari. *Three cheers for Catherine the Great!*
Black, Birdie. *Just right for Christmas*
Blackwood, Freya. *Ivy loves to give*
Bloom, Suzanne. *Oh! What a surprise!*
Bourgeois, Paulette. *Franklin says "I love you"*
Franklin's Christmas gift
Bridges, Shirin Yim. *Mary Wrightly, so politely*
Brown, Marc. *Arthur's Christmas*
Bruce, Lisa. *Fran's friend*
Buehner, Caralyn. *Snowmen at Christmas*
Bunting, Eve. *The baby shower*
Butler, M. Christina. *One snowy night*
One special Christmas
Calhoun, Mary. *A shepherd's gift*
Calmenson, Stephanie. *Birthday at the Panda Palace*
Capucilli, Alyssa Satin. *Happy Hanukkah, Biscuit*
Chen, Chih-Yuan. *The best Christmas ever*
Conway, David. *The most important gift of all*
Cousins, Lucy. *With love from Maisy*
Danneberg, Julie. *Last day blues*
deGroat, Diane. *Happy birthday to you, you belong in a zoo*
DePalma, Mary Newell. *The perfect gift*
Díaz, Katacha. *Carolina's gift*
DiPucchio, Kelly. *Crafty Chloe*
Dooley, Norah. *Everybody serves soup*
Dunrea, Olivier. *A Christmas tree for Pyn*
Edwards, Pamela Duncan. *Rosie's roses*
Elya, Susan Middleton. *Tooth on the loose*
Emmett, Jonathan. *The best gift of all*
Engelbreit, Mary. *Queen of Christmas*
Evans, Cambria. *Martha Moth makes socks*

Foley, Greg. *Thank you, Bear*
Frazee, Marla. *Santa Claus*
French, Vivian. *A present for mom*
Friedman, Laurie. *Love, Ruby Valentine*
Gardella, Tricia. *Blackberry booties*
Gliori, Debi. *What can I give him?*
Goble, Paul. *The gift of the sacred dog*
Gorbachev, Valeri. *What's the big idea, Molly?*
Gutman, Anne. *Gaspard and Lisa's Christmas surprise*
Hamilton, Martha. *Priceless gifts*
Harper, Charise Mericle. *Amy and Ivan*
Hayles, Marsha. *The feathered crown*
Helldorfer, M. C. *Hog music*
Hobbie, Holly. *Toot and Puddle: let it snow*
Toot and Puddle, a present for Toot
Hubbell, Patricia. *Wrapping paper romp*
Hughes, Shirley. *Alfie and the birthday surprise*
Hutchins, Pat. *It's my birthday!*
Inkpen, Mick. *Kipper and Roly*
Wibbly Pig opens his presents
Jeffers, Susan. *The twelve days of Christmas*
Keats, Ezra Jack. *The little drummer boy*
Keister, Douglas. *Fernando's gift / El regalo de Fernando*
Kimmel, Elizabeth Cody. *My penguin Osbert*
Krensky, Stephen. *Mother's Day surprise*
Kromhout, Rindert. *Little Donkey and the birthday present*
Linders, Clara. *The very best door of all*
Little, Jean. *Pippin the Christmas pig*
Louie, Therese On. *Raymond's perfect present*
McClure, Gillian. *Tom Finger*
McCourt, Lisa. *Chicken soup for little souls: The never-forgotten doll*
McCully, Emily Arnold. *The Christmas gift*
McDonnell, Patrick. *The gift of nothing*
McGinley, Phyllis. *The year without a Santa Claus*
Mair, Samia J. *The perfect gift*
Marzollo, Jean. *Ten little Christmas presents*
Mathers, Petra. *Lottie's new beach towel*
Meddaugh, Susan. *Martha says it with flowers*
Medearis, Angela Shelf. *Annie's gifts*
Montanari, Eva. *My first . . .*
Mora, Pat. *A birthday basket for Tía*
The gift of the poinsettia / El regalo de la flor de nochebuena
Morales, Yuyi. *Just in case: a trickster tale and Spanish alphabet book*
Morrissey, Dean. *The Christmas ship*
Naylor, Phyllis Reynolds. *Keeping a Christmas secret*
Nolan, Janet. *A Father's Day thank you*
Ommen, Sylvia van. *The surprise*
Paul, Ann Whitford. *Fiesta fiasco*
Pett, Mark. *The boy and the airplane*
Pilgrim, Elza. *The china doll*
Polacco, Patricia. *Gifts of the heart*
Pomerantz, Charlotte. *You're not my best friend anymore*
Price, Mara. *Grandma's chocolate / El chocolate de Abuelita*
Rempt, Fiona. *Snail's birthday wish*
Reynolds, Peter H. *The smallest gift of Christmas*
Roberton, Fiona. *The perfect present*
Rodanas, Kristina. *The little drummer boy*
Rumford, James. *Nine animals and the well*
Rylant, Cynthia. *Birthday presents*
Sabuda, Robert. *Tutankhamen's gift*
Sage, Angie. *Molly and the birthday party*
Saint James, Synthia. *The gifts of Kwanzaa*
Santiago, Esmeralda. *A doll for Navidades*
Segal, Lore Groszmann. *Morris the artist*
Shepard, Aaron. *The gifts of Wali Dad*
Skolsky, Mindy Warshaw. *Hannah and the whistling tea kettle*
Speirs, John. *The little boy's Christmas gift*
Spinelli, Eileen. *In my new yellow shirt*
Stanton, Karen. *Papi's gift*
Steptoe, Javaka. *The Jones family express*
Stewart, Paul. *The birthday presents*
Tazewell, Charles. *The littlest angel*, ill. by Deborah Lanino
The littlest angel, ill. by Paul Micich
The littlest angel, ill. by Rebecca Thornburgh
Thomas, Naturi. *Uh-oh! It's Mama's birthday!*
Thury, Frederick. *The last straw*
Uff, Caroline. *Happy birthday, Lulu*
Varley, Susan. *Badger's parting gifts*
Velasquez, Eric. *Grandma's gift*
Wallace, John. *Tiny Rabbit goes to a birthday party*
Walton, Rick. *The remarkable friendship of Mr. Cat and Mr. Rat*
Weeks, Sarah. *Be mine, be mine, sweet valentine*
Wells, Rosemary. *Morris's disappearing bag*
Yoko's show-and-tell
Weninger, Brigitte. *Double birthday*
Happy Easter, Davy
Williams, Barbara. *Albert's gift for grandmother*
Williams, Vera B. *Something special for me*
Wood, Don. *Merry Christmas, big hungry bear*
Wright, Dare. *A gift from the lonely doll*
Ziefert, Harriet. *Grandma, it's for you!*

Gilbert Islands *see* Foreign lands – South Sea Islands

Glasses *see also* Careers – opticians, optometrists

Barclay, Eric. *I can see just fine*
Bedford, David. *Mole's in love*
Brown, Marc. *Arthur's eyes*
Glasses for D. W.
Calvert, Pam. *Princess Peepers*
Princess Peepers picks a pet
Carlson, Melody. *Farmer Brown's field trip*
Cohen, Peter Zachary. *Boris's glasses*
Duffield, Katy. *Farmer McPeepers and his missing milk cows*
Flanagan, Alice K. *Choosing eyeglasses with Mrs. Koutris*
Headley, Justina Chen. *The patch*
Hest, Amy. *Baby Duck and the bad eyeglasses*
Newman, Barbara Johansen. *Glamorous glasses*
Scillian, Devin. *Brewster the rooster*
Smith, Lane. *Glasses . . . who needs 'em?*
Stadler, John. *The cats of Mrs. Calamari*

Gossip *see* Behavior – gossip

Grammar *see* Language

Greed *see* Behavior – greed

Grocery stores *see* Shopping; Stores

Growing up *see* Behavior – growing up

Guns *see* Weapons

Gypsies

Bemelmans, Ludwig. *Madeline and the gypsies*
Kellogg, Steven. *The mystery of the magic green ball*
Pinfold, Levi. *The Django*

Habits *see* Thumb sucking

Hair

Anderson, Laurie Halse. *The hair of Zoe Fleefenbacher goes to school*
Azore, Barbara. *Wanda and the wild hair*
Barton, Bethany. *This monster needs a haircut*
Bernheimer, Kate. *The girl who wouldn't brush her hair*
Brisson, Pat. *Melissa Parkington's beautiful, beautiful hair*
Burnard, Damon. *Dave's haircut*
Daly, Catherine. *Whiskers*
Diouf, Sylviane A,. *Bintou's braids*
Ditchfield, Christin. *Cowlick!*
Esckelson, Laura. *The copper braid of Shannon O'Shea*
Fisher, Jeff. *The hair scare*
Fox, Lee. *Ella Kazoo will not brush her hair*
Gaiman, Neil. *Crazy hair*
Graves, Keith. *The unexpectedly bad hair of Barcelona Smith*
Grimm, Jacob and Wilhelm. *Rapunzel*, ill. by Sarah Gibb
Rapunzel, ill. by Trina Schart Hyman
Rapunzel, ill. by Rachel Isadora
Rapunzel, ill. by Joma
Rapunzel, ill. by Kris Waldherr
Rapunzel, ill. by Paul O. Zelinsky
Rapunzel: a fairy tale
Higgins, Ryan. *Wilfred*
Hilton, Perez. *The boy with pink hair*
Hooks, Bell. *Happy to be nappy*
Hosford, Kate. *Big bouffant*
Koren, Edward. *Very hairy Harry*
Krosoczka, Jarrett J. *Baghead*
Krull, Kathleen. *Big wig*
Langen, Annette. *I won't comb my hair!*
Lerner, Harriet Goldhor. *Franny B. Kranny, there's a bird in your hair*
Lubner, Susan. *Ruthie Bon Bair, do not go to bed with wringing wet hair!*
MacDonald, Alan. *The pig in a wig*
McElligott, Matthew. *Backbeard and the birthday suit*
Madrigal, Antonio Hernandez. *Erandi's braids*
Many, Paul. *Dad's bald head*
Moss, Miriam. *Bad hare day*
Munsch, Robert N. *Aaron's hair*
Stephanie's ponytail
Napoli, Donna Jo. *Bobby the bold*
Palatini, Margie. *Bedhead*
Moosetache
Parr, Todd. *This is my hair*
Radabaugh, Melinda Beth. *Getting a haircut*
Ries, Lori. *Punk wig*
Robbins, Beth. *Tom's new haircut*
Roberts, Lynn. *Rapunzel, a groovy fairy tale*
Rocco, John. *Super Hair-o and the barber of doom*
Saltzberg, Barney. *Crazy hair day*
Savadier, Elivia. *No haircut today!*
Shannon, David. *Bugs in my hair!*
Tarpley, Natasha Anastasia. *Bippity Bop barbershop*
I love my hair!
Thomas, Joyce Carol. *Crowning glory*
Tinkham, Kelly A. *Hair for Mama*
Tuck, Justin. *Home-field advantage*
Villnave, Erica Pelton. *Sophie's lovely locks*
Watters, Debbie, et al. *Where's Mom's hair?*
Whittaker, Nicola. *Hair*
Williams-Garcia, Rita. *Catching the wild waiyuuzee*
Ziefert, Harriet. *There was a little girl who had a little curl*

Handicaps *see* Disabilities

Hares *see* Animals – rabbits

Hawaii

Guback, Georgia. *Luka's quilt*
Hayashi, Leslie Ann. *Fables from the sea*
Joosse, Barbara. *Grandma calls me Beautiful*
Kono, Erin Eitter. *Hula lullaby*
Lin, Grace. *Olvina swims*
London, Jonathan. *Froggy goes to Hawaii*
McDermott, Gerald. *Pig-Boy*
Martin, Rafe. *The Shark God*
Novesky, Amy. *Georgia in Hawaii*
Rumford, James. *Dog-of-the-Sea-Waves*
The Island-below-the-star
Samuels, Barbara. *Aloha, Dolores*
Stanley, Fay. *The last princess*
Vigil-Piñón, Evangelina. *Marina's muumuu / El muumuu de Marina*

Health & fitness

Ajmera, Maya, et al. *Healthy kids*
Bridge, Chris. *Andrew's story*
Brown, Laurie Krasny. *Dinosaurs alive and well*
Bunting, Eve. *My dog Jack is fat*
Butterworth, Chris. *How did that get in my lunchbox?*
Campbell, Bebe Moore. *I get so hungry*
Cleland, Jo. *Getting your zzzzs*
Cole, Joanna. *My friend the doctor*
Corey, Shana. *First graders from Mars: Nergal and the Great Space Race*
De Anda, Diane. *A day without sugar / Un dia sin azucar*
Drescher, Henrik. *Hubert the Pudge*
Fraser, Mary Ann. *I.Q. gets fit*
Glaser, Jason. *Pinkeye*
Gordon, Sharon. *Asthma*

Bruises
Pinkeye
Seeing
Smelling
Harper, Charise Mericle. *Flush!*
Henry's heart
Kalz, Jill. *Fruits*
Keller, Laurie. *Open wide*
Kelly, Mij. *Achoo!*
Kostecki-Shaw, Jenny Sue. *My travelin' eye*
Krishnaswami, Uma. *The happiest tree*
Leedy, Loreen. *The edible pyramid*
Jack and the hungry giant eat right with MyPlate
Lobb, Janice. *Splish! Splosh! Why do we wash?*
McElmurry, Jill. *Mess pets*
Miller, Edward. *The tooth book*
Milway, Katie Smith. *Mimi's village and how basic health care transformed it*
Müller, Birte. *Finn cooks*
Murkoff, Heidi Eisenberg. *What to expect when you go to the dentist*
What to expect when you go to the doctor
Murphy, Liz. *ABC doctor*
Nelson, Robin. *Staying clean*
Newcome, Zita. *Pop-up toddlerobics*
Owen, Ann. *Keeping you healthy*
Rockwell, Harlow. *My doctor*
Rosenberry, Vera. *Vera goes to the dentist*
Roth, Ruby. *V is for vegan*
Ruiz-Flores, Lupe. *Alicia's fruity drinks / Las aguas frescas de Alicia*
Sears, William, M.D., et al. *Eat healthy, feel great*
Showers, Paul. *Sleep is for everyone*
Singer, Marilyn. *I'm getting a checkup*
Slangerup, Erik Jon. *Dirt Boy*
Spelman, Cornelia Maude. *Your body belongs to you*
Swanson, Diane. *The dentist and you*
The doctor and you
Taylor, Sean. *Boing!*
Wells, Rosemary. *The gulps*
Whitford, Rebecca. *Little yoga*
Sleepy little yoga
Yoo, Taeeun. *You are a lion!*
Zamorano, Ana. *Let's eat!*

Health & fitness – exercise

Bateman, Teresa. *Hamster Camp*
Bertrand, Diane Gonzales. *Sofía and the purple dress / Sofía y el vestido morado*
Carlson, Nancy. *Get up and go!*
Cronin, Doreen. *Stretch*
McKinlay, Penny. *Flabby Tabby*
Rockwell, Lizzy. *The busy body book*
Spinelli, Eileen. *Miss Fox's class shapes up*
Thompson, Lauren. *Hop, hop, jump!*
Tsubakiyama, Margaret. *Mei-Mei loves the morning*
Wells, Rosemary. *The gulps*
Ziefert, Harriet. *Murphy meets the treadmill*

Health & safety

Gordon, Sharon. *Cuts and scrapes*

Hearing *see* Anatomy – ears; Disabilities – deafness; Senses – hearing

Heat *see* Concepts – cold & heat

Heavy equipment *see* Machines

Helicopters

Ethan, Eric. *Helicopters*
Glass, Andrew. *The wondrous whirligig*
Kimmel, Elizabeth Cody. *My penguin Osbert in love*
Slack, Michael. *Elecopter*

Helpfulness *see* Character traits – helpfulness

Hens *see* Birds – chickens

Hibernation

Arnosky, Jim. *Every autumn comes the bear*
Banks, Kate. *The bear in the book*
Bright, Paul. *Grumpy Badger's Christmas*
Cooper, Elisha. *Bear dreams*
Cox, Judy. *Go to sleep, Groundhog*
Cuyler, Margery. *Groundhog stays up late*
Fleming, Denise. *Time to sleep*
Fraggalosch, Audrey. *Grizzly bear family*
Freeman, Don. *Bearymore*
Gammell, Stephen. *Wake up, bear . . . It's Christmas!*
Gerber, Carole. *Little red bat*
Grindley, Sally. *What will I do without you?*
Helquist, Brett. *Bedtime for Bear*
Henkes, Kevin. *Old Bear*
Janice. *Little Bear's Christmas*
Krauss, Ruth. *The happy day*
London, Jonathan. *Froggy gets dressed*
Meadows, Michelle. *Hibernation station*
Messner, Kate. *Over and under the snow*
Miller, Edna. *Mousekin's golden house*
Partridge, Elizabeth. *Moon glowing*
Rueda, Claudia. *No*
Sayre, April Pulley. *Eat like a bear*
Schertle, Alice. *Very hairy bear*
Senshu, Noriko. *Sonny's dream*
Stead, Philip C. *Bear has a story to tell*
Stein, David Ezra. *Leaves*
Stewart, Paul. *A little bit of winter*
Walters, Catherine. *When will it be spring?*
Welling, Peter J. *Andrew McGroundhog and his shady shadow*
Wilson, Karma. *Bear stays up for Christmas*
Wolff, Ashley. *Baby Bear counts one*
Wright, Maureen. *Sleep, Big Bear, sleep!*
Yolen, Jane. *Sleep, black bear, sleep*
Zagwÿn, Deborah Turney. *Turtle spring*

Hiccups

Berger, Melvin. *Why I sneeze, shiver, hiccup, and yawn*
Cuyler, Margery. *Skeleton hiccups*
Kenyon, Tony. *Hyacinth Hop has the hic-hops*
Long, Melinda. *Hiccup snickup*
Meng, Cece. *The wonderful thing about hiccups*

Hiding *see* Behavior – hiding

Hiding things *see* Behavior – hiding things

Hieroglyphics

Bower, Tamara. *The shipwrecked sailor*

Hobby horses *see* Toys – rocking horses

Hogs *see* Animals – pigs

Holidays

Adler, David A. *The children's book of Jewish holidays*
A picture book of Jewish holidays
Ancona, George. *Mis fiestas / My celebrations*
Biers-Ariel, Matt. *Solomon and the trees*
Bullard, Lisa. *Rashad's Ramadan and Eid al-Fitr*
Capucilli, Alyssa Satin. *Biscuit gives a gift*
Carle, Eric. *Hello, red fox*
Carlson, Lori Marie. *Hurray for Three Kings' Day*
Cazet, Denys. *December 24th*
Chancellor, Deborah. *Holidays!*
Cooney, Barbara. *The story of Christmas*
dePaola, Tomie. *Strega Nona's gift*
Elya, Susan Middleton. *A year full of holidays*
Emerman, Ellen. *Is it Shabbos yet?*
Fishman, Cathy Goldberg. *On Shabbat*
Freschet, Gina. *Naty's parade*
Galbraith, Kathryn O. *Arbor Day square*
Gold-Vukson, Marji E. *Grandpa and me on Tu B'Shevat*
Hubbell, Patricia. *Rabbit moon*
Jackson, Ellen. *April*
August
The autumn equinox
December
February
January
July
June
March
May
November
October
September
The spring equinox
The summer solstice
The winter solstice
Kimmelman, Leslie. *Dance, sing, remember*
Lewis, J. Patrick. *World Rat Day*
Lin, Grace. *Thanking the moon*
Livingston, Myra Cohn. *Celebrations*
McGee, Marni. *The colt and the king*
Mair, Samia J. *The perfect gift*
Mobin-Uddin, Asma. *The best Eid ever*
Mora, Pat. *The bakery lady / La señora de la panadería*
Book fiesta! celebrate Children's Day/Book Day / Celebremos El día de los niños/El día de los libros
Morris, Ann. *Light the candle! Bang the drum!*
Murphy, Stuart J. *Earth Day — hooray!*
Nielsen, Laura. *Mrs. Muddle's holidays*
Pandya, Meenal. *Here comes Diwali*
Podwal, Mark H. *A sweet year*
Rau, Dana Meachen. *I'll make you a card*
Reiss, Mike. *Santa claustrophobia*
Reynolds, Jan. *Celebrate!*
Rockwell, Anne. *President's Day*
Rosenfeld, Dina Herman. *Five alive*
Rosenthal, Amy Krouse. *Yes Day!*
Shahan, Sherry. *Fiesta!*
Shulimson, Sarene. *Lights out Shabbat*
Singer, Marilyn. *Every day's a dog's day*
Tunnell, Michael O. *Halloween pie*
Yolen, Jane. *The three bears holiday rhyme book*

Holidays – April Fools' Day

Bateman, Teresa. *April foolishness*
Brown, Marc. *Arthur's April fool*
deGroat, Diane. *April Fool! watch out at school!*
Hill, Susanna Leonard. *April Fool, Phyllis!*
Kroll, Steven. *It's April Fools' Day!*
Modell, Frank. *Look out, it's April Fools' Day*
Morton, Carlene. *The library pages*
Wright, Maureen. *Barnyard fun*

Holidays – Chanukah *see* Holidays – Hanukkah

Holidays – Chinese New Year

Chen, Yong. *A gift*
Chinn, Karen. *Sam and the lucky money*
Compestine, Ying Chang. *Crouching tiger*
D is for dragon dance
The runaway rice cake
The runaway wok
Flanagan, Alice K. *Chinese New Year*
Gower, Catherine. *Long-Long's new year*
Handforth, Thomas. *Mei Li*
Schaefer, Lola M. *Chinese New Year*
Silverhardt, Lauryn. *Happy Chinese New Year, Kai-lan!*
Wallace, Ian. *Chin Chiang and the dragon's dance*
Waters, Kate. *Lion dancer*
Wong, Janet S. *This next New Year*
Yu, Li-Qiong. *A New Year's reunion*

Holidays – Christmas

Ada, Alma Flor. *The Christmas tree / El arbol de Navidad*
Adams, Adrienne. *The Christmas party*
Agee, Jon. *Little Santa*
Ahlberg, Janet. *The jolly Christmas postman*
Aliki. *Christmas tree memories*
Alko, Selina. *Daddy Christmas and Hanukkah Mama*
Allen, Jonathan. *"I'm not Santa!"*
Alsenas, Linas. *Mrs. Claus takes a vacation*
Ammon, Richard. *An Amish Christmas*
Anaya, Rudolfo A. *Farolitos for Abuelo*
Andersen, Hans Christian. *The fir tree*, ill. by Diane Goode
The fir tree, ill. by Bernadette Watts
Anderson, Derek. *How the Easter Bunny saved Christmas*
Angelou, Maya. *Amazing peace*
Anglund, Joan Walsh. *Christmas is a time of giving*
The cowboy's Christmas
Appelt, Kathi. *Merry Christmas, merry crow*
Apperley, Dawn. *Santa Claus will come tonight*
Aralan, Haydé. *Milton's Christmas*
Arnold, Katya. *The adventures of Snowwoman*
Ashforth, Camilla. *Willow at Christmas*
Auch, Mary Jane. *The nutquacker*
Autry, Gene. *Here comes Santa Claus*
Axelrod, Amy. *Pigs on the move*
Bailey, Mary Bryant. *Jeoffry's Christmas*

Balian, Lorna. *Bah! Humbug?*
Banks, Kate. *What's coming for Christmas?*
Barracca, Debra. *A taxi dog Christmas*
Barrett, Judi. *Santa from Cincinnati*
Bartoletti, Susan Campbell. *The Christmas promise*
Bastianich, Lidia. *Nonna tell me a story*
Bastin, Marjolein. *Christmas with Vera*
Bauer, Marion Dane. *Christmas lights*
Bauer, Sepp. *The Christmas rose*
Baumgart, Klaus. *Laura's Christmas star*
Beck, Andrea. *Elliot's Christmas surprise*
Becker, Bonny. *The Christmas crocodile*
Bedford, David. *I've seen Santa!*
Bemelmans, Ludwig. *Madeline's Christmas*
Berenstain, Jan. *The Berenstain bears trim the tree*
Berenstain, Stan and Jan. *The Berenstain bears' Christmas tree*
The Berenstain bears meet Santa Bear
Bible. New Testament. Gospels. *Bethlehem*
The Christmas story: from the Gospel according to St. Luke from the King James Bible
The story of Christmas
Biedrzycki, David. *Santa retires*
Black, Birdie. *Just right for Christmas*
Blaich, Ute. *The star*
Bodkin, Odds. *The Christmas cobwebs*
Bond, Michael. *Paddington Bear and the Christmas surprise*
Bond, Rebecca. *A city Christmas tree*
Bourgeois, Paulette. *Franklin's Christmas gift*
Bowen, Anne. *Christmas is coming*
Boynton, Sandra. *Christmas parade*
Brebeuf, Jean de. *The Huron carol*
Breen, Steve. *The secret of Santa's island*
Brett, Jan. *Christmas trolls*
Home for Christmas
Who's that knocking on Christmas eve?
The wild Christmas reindeer
Briggs, Raymond. *Father Christmas*
Bright, Paul. *Grumpy Badger's Christmas*
Bright, Robert. *Georgie's Christmas carol*
Brown, Marc. *Arthur's Christmas*
Arthur's perfect Christmas
Brown, Margaret Wise. *A child is born*
Christmas in the barn
The little fir tree
Brown, Ruth. *Holly, the true story of a cat*
Bruel, Nick. *A Bad Kitty Christmas*
Brunhoff, Jean de. *Babar and Father Christmas*
Buck, Nola. *A Christmas goodnight*
Buehner, Caralyn. *Snowmen at Christmas*
Bunting, Eve. *Christmas cricket*
December
Going home
Night tree
We were there
Who was born this special day?
Burgess, Mark. *Where teddy bears come from*
Burningham, John. *Harvey Slumfenburger's Christmas present*
Butler, M. Christina. *One snowy night*
One special Christmas
Butterworth, Nick. *Jingle bells*
Buzzeo, Toni. *Lighthouse Christmas*
Byrd, Robert. *Saint Francis and the Christmas donkey*
Calhoun, Mary. *Henry the Christmas cat*
A shepherd's gift
Capucilli, Alyssa Satin. *Merry Christmas, from Biscuit*
Carabine, Sue. *A firefighter's night before Christmas*
Carle, Eric. *Dream snow*
Carlson, Nancy. *Harriet and George's Christmas treat*
Carlstrom, Nancy White. *Where is Christmas, Jesse Bear?*
Catalano, Dominic. *Santa and the three bears*
Chaconas, Dori. *Christmas mouseling*
When cows come home for Christmas
Chapman, Jane. *Is it Christmas yet?*
Chen, Chih-Yuan. *The best Christmas ever*
Cheshire, Marc. *Merry Christmas, Eloise!*
Chichester Clark, Emma. *Melrose and Croc*
Chorao, Kay. *The Christmas story*
Christelow, Eileen. *Not until Christmas, Walter!*
Christmas presents
Clements, Andrew. *Bright Christmas*
Cole, Brock. *The money we'll save*
Cole, Henry. *The littlest evergreen*
Conahan, Carolyn. *The twelve days of Christmas dogs*
Conover, Chris. *The Christmas bears*
Conrad, Pam. *The Tub People's Christmas*
Cooney, Barbara. *The story of Christmas*
Corey, Shana. *Milly and the Macy's Parade*
Cowley, Joy. *Mrs. Wishy-Washy's Christmas*
Croll, Carolyn. *The little snowgirl*
Crossley-Holland, Kevin. *How many miles to Bethlehem?*
Currey, Anna. *Truffle's Christmas*
Cushman, Doug. *Christmas Eve good night*
Cutlip, Kimbra L. *Firefighter's night before Christmas*
Daly, Niki. *What's cooking, Jamela?*
Damjan, Mischa. *The little seahorse and the Christmas pearl*
David, Lawrence. *Peter Claus and the naughty list*
Deacon, Alexis. *While you are sleeping*
Dealey, Erin. *Deck the walls!*
deGroat, Diane. *Jingle bells, homework smells*
Lola the elf
Delacre, Lulu. *Las Navidades*
Demas, Corinne. *Two Christmas mice*
Demi. *The legend of Saint Nicholas*
Denim, Sue. *The Dumb Bunnies' Easter*
DePalma, Mary Newell. *The Nutcracker doll*
dePaola, Tomie. *Baby's first Christmas*
The clown of God
An early American Christmas
The family Christmas tree book
Get dressed, Santa!
Jingle, the Christmas clown
Merry Christmas, Strega Nona
The night of Las Posadas
The story of the three wise kings
Devlin, Wende. *Cranberry Christmas*
Dewan, Ted. *Crispin, the pig who had it all*
DiCamillo, Kate. *Great joy*
Dixon, Ann. *Waiting for Noël*
Donaldson, Julia. *Stick Man*
Dowley, Tim. *The shepherds' tale*
The wise men's tale
Dunrea, Olivier. *Bear Noel*
A Christmas tree for Pyn
Merry Christmas, Ollie!
Duquennoy, Jacques. *North Pole, South Pole*
Duval, Kathy. *The Three Bears' Christmas*
Elschner, Geraldine. *Pashmina the little Christmas goat*
Elya, Susan Middleton. *N is for Navidad*
Emmett, Jonathan. *The Santa trap*

Engelbreit, Mary. *Mary Engelbreit's A merry little Christmas*
Queen of Christmas
Ets, Marie Hall. *Nine days to Christmas*
Evans, Richard Paul. *The light of Christmas*
Evert, Lori. *The Christmas wish*
Fackelmayer, Regina. *The gifts*
Falwell, Cathryn. *Christmas for 10*
Farber, Norma. *How the hibernators came to Bethlehem*
Faulkner, Keith. *Charlie Chimp's Christmas*
Fine, Howard. *A piggie Christmas*
Fisher, Aileen Lucia. *Do rabbits have Christmas?*
Flanagan, Alice K. *Christmas*
Foreman, Michael. *Cat in the manger*
Forward, Toby. *Ben's Christmas carol*
Fox, Mem. *Wombat divine*
Frazee, Marla. *Santa Claus*
French, Jackie. *Christmas wombat*
Gammell, Stephen. *Wake up, bear . . . It's Christmas!*
Gantos, Jack. *Rotten Ralph's rotten Christmas*
Garland, Michael. *Christmas City*
Christmas magic
George, William T. *Christmas at Long Pond*
Geras, Adèle. *The nutcracker*
Gliori, Debi. *What can I give him?*
Godden, Rumer. *The story of Holly and Ivy*
Grahame, Kenneth. *A wind in the willows Christmas*
Greene, Rhonda Gowler. *The stable where Jesus was born*
Greenfield, Monica. *Waiting for Christmas*
Grimes, Nikki. *Voices of Christmas*
Grogan, John. *A very Marley Christmas*
Gutman, Anne. *Gaspard and Lisa's Christmas surprise*
Hächler, Bruno. *Anna's wish*
Hague, Michael. *The nutcracker*
Hale, Bruce. *Santa on the loose!*
Hall, Donald. *Lucy's Christmas*
Hapka, Cathy. *Margret and H. A. Rey's Merry Christmas, Curious George*
Harley, Bill. *Dear Santa*
Harness, Cheryl. *Papa's Christmas gift*
Harry, Rebecca. *Snow Bunny's Christmas wish*
Hartman, Bob. *Granny Mae's Christmas play*
Harvey, Brett. *My prairie Christmas*
Hassett, Ann. *The finest Christmas tree*
Hayles, Marsha. *The feathered crown*
Heath, Amy. *Sofie's role*
Helmer, Marilyn. *One splendid tree*
Hennessy, B. G. *Corduroy's Christmas*
The first night
Hickman, Martha Whitmore. *A baby born in Bethlehem*
High, Linda Oatman. *The last chimney of Christmas eve*
Hill, Eric. *Spot's first Christmas*
Spot's magical Christmas
Hines, Anna Grossnickle. *The secret keeper*
Hines, Gary. *A Christmas tree in the White House*
Hobbie, Holly. *Toot and Puddle: let it snow*
Toot and Puddle, I'll be home for Christmas
Hodges, Margaret. *Silent night: the song and its story*
Hoffman, Mary. *Grace at Christmas*
Three wise women
Hoffmann, E. T. A. *The nutcracker*, ill. by Renée Graef
The nutcracker, ill. by Alison Jay
The nutcracker, ill. by Peter Malone
The nutcracker, ill. by Maurice Sendak
The nutcracker, ill. by Lisbeth Zwerger
The Nutcracker and the Mouse King
The nutcracker ballet
Hogrogian, Nonny. *The first Christmas*
Holabird, Katharine. *Angelina's Christmas*
Christmas in Mouseland
Christmas with Angelina
Holmquist, Delano. *SantaSaurus*
Hooks, William H. *The legend of the Christmas rose*
Hooper, Maureen Brett. *Silent night: a Christmas carol is born*
Horacek, Petr. *Suzy Goose and the Christmas star*
Horn, Sandra Ann. *Babushka*
House, Catherine. *A stork in a baobab tree*
Houston, Gloria. *The year of the perfect Christmas tree*
Howard, Elizabeth Fitzgerald. *Chita's Christmas tree*
Howard, Ellen. *The log cabin Christmas*
Hughes, Langston. *Carol of the brown king*
Hughes, Shirley. *The Christmas Eve ghost*
Hunter, Sally. *Humphrey's Christmas*
Hurd, Thacher. *Santa Mouse and the ratdeer*
Ichikawa, Satomi. *What the little fir tree wore to the Christmas party*
Inkpen, Deborah. *Harriet and the little fat fairy*
Inkpen, Mick. *Kipper's Christmas eve*
James, J. Alison. *The bears' Christmas surprise*
Janice. *Little Bear's Christmas*
Jay, Alison. *Christmastime*
Jeffers, Susan. *The twelve days of Christmas*
Jiménez, Francisco. *The Christmas gift / El regalo de Navidad*
Johnson, Crockett. *Harold at the North Pole*
Johnson, David. *Snow sounds*
Johnson, Grace. *The candle in the window*
Johnston, Tony. *A Kenya Christmas*
Noel
Joosse, Barbara. *A houseful of Christmas*
Joseph, Lynn. *An island Christmas*
Joslin, Mary. *On that Christmas night*
Kasparavicius, Kestutis. *The bear family's world tour Christmas*
Kastner, Jill. *Merry Christmas, Princess Dinosaur*
Keane, Michael. *The night Santa got lost*
Keats, Ezra Jack. *The little drummer boy*
Keller, Holly. *Merry Christmas, Geraldine*
Kelley, True. *The dog who saved Santa*
Kellogg, Steven. *The Christmas witch*
Santa Claus is comin' to town
Kennedy, Cindy. *The star of Christmas*
Ketcham, Sallie. *The Christmas bird*
Kidslabel. *Spot 7: Christmas*
Kimmel, Elizabeth Cody. *My penguin Osbert*
Kinsey-Warnock, Natalie. *A Christmas like Helen's*
Kladstrup, Kristin. *The gingerbread pirates*
Kneen, Maggie. *The Christmas surprise*
Knight, Hilary. *A firefly in a fir tree*
Krensky, Stephen. *How Santa got his job*
How Santa lost his job
Kroll, Steven. *Pooch on the loose*
Santa's crash-bang Christmas
Kroll, Virginia L. *Uno, dos, tres, posada!*
Krupinski, Loretta. *Christmas in the city*
Krykorka, Ian. *Carl, the Christmas carp*
Lachner, Dorothea. *The gift from Saint Nicholas*
Langley, Karen. *Shine*
Lawler, Janet. *Tyrannoclaus*
Lee, Quinlan B. *Crazy Christmas chaos*
Lee, Stan. *Stan Lee's superhero Christmas*

LeSourd, Nancy. *Christy, Christmastime at Cutter Gap*
Lester, Helen. *Tacky's Christmas*
Lewandowski, Frrich. *It's Christmas again*
Lewis, Anne Margaret. *What am I? Christmas*
Lewis, J. Patrick. *Long was the winter road they traveled*
Light, Steve. *The Christmas giant*
Lin, Grace. *Okie-dokie, Artichokie*
Lindgren, Astrid. *Pippi Longstocking's after-Christmas party*
Little, Jean. *Pippin the Christmas pig*
Litwin, Eric. *Pete the cat saves Christmas*
Lloyd-Jones, Sally. *Song of the stars*
London, Jonathan. *Froggy's first Christmas*
Long, Loren. *Drummer boy*
  An Otis Christmas
Long, Sylvia. *Deck the hall*
Lucado, Max. *Alabaster's song*
Lucas, David. *Christmas at the toy museum*
McAnulty, Stacy. *Dear Santasaurus*
Maccarone, Grace. *A child was born*
McCaughrean, Geraldine. *Father and son*
  How the reindeer got their antlers
McCourt, Lisa. *Merry Christmas, Stinky Face*
McCully, Emily Arnold. *The Christmas gift*
McGinley, Phyllis. *The year without a Santa Claus*
McGinley-Nally, Sharon. *The friendly beasts*
McGuirk, Leslie. *Ho, ho, ho, Tucker!*
McKee, David. *Elmer's Christmas*
McKissack, Patricia C. *The all-I'll-ever-want Christmas doll*
  Messy Bessey's holidays
McPhail, David. *Henry Bear's Christmas*
  Santa's book of names
McQuade, Jacqueline. *Christmas with Teddy Bear*
Mahy, Margaret. *The Christmas tree tangle*
Major, Kevin. *Aunt Olga's Christmas postcards*
Marshall, James. *Merry Christmas, space case*
Martin, David. *Little Bunny and the magic Christmas tree*
Martín, Hugo C. *Pablo's Christmas*
Martin, Ruth. *Santa's on his way*
Marzollo, Jean. *I see a star*
  I spy Christmas
  I spy little Christmas
  Ten little Christmas presents
Masurel, Claire. *Christmas is coming*
Mathers, Petra. *Herbie's secret Santa*
Matteson, George. *The Christmas tugboat*
May, Robert Lewis. *Rudolph the red-nosed reindeer*
Mayer, Mercer. *The little drummer mouse*
Mayhew, James. *Ella Bella ballerina and The Nutcracker*
Mayper, Monica. *Come and see*
Medearis, Angela Shelf. *Poppa's itchy Christmas*
Medina, Tony. *Christmas makes me think*
Milgrim, David. *Santa Duck*
  Santa Duck and his merry helpers
Miller, Edna. *Mousekin's Christmas eve*
Minor, Wendell. *Christmas tree!*
Modugno, Maria. *Santa Claus and the three bears*
Mohr, Joseph. *Silent night*
Moore, Clement Clarke. *A creature was stirring*
  The night before Christmas
  The night before Christmas, ill. by Jan Brett
  The night before Christmas, ill. by Tomie dePaola
  The night before Christmas, ill. by Mary Engelbreit
  The night before Christmas, ill. by Holly Hobbie
  The night before Christmas, ill. by Rachel Isadora
  The night before Christmas, ill. by Raquel Jaramillo
  The night before Christmas, ill. by Anita Lobel
  The night before Christmas, ill. by James Marshall
  The night before Christmas, ill. by Will Moses
  The night before Christmas, ill. by Ted Rand
  The night before Christmas, ill. by Ruth Sanderson
  The night before Christmas, ill. by Gennady Spirin
  The night before Christmas, ill. by Tasha Tudor
  The night before Christmas, ill. by Richard Jesse Watson
  The night before Christmas, ill. by Wendy Watson
  The night before Christmas, ill. by Bruce Whatley
  The night before Christmas, ill. by Lisbeth Zwerger
  The night before Christmas: a pop-up
  The teddy bears' night before Christmas
  'Twas the night before Christmas, ill. by Matt Tavares
  'Twas the night before Christmas, ill. by Christopher Wormell
Moorman, Margaret. *Light the lights!*
Mora, Pat. *The gift of the poinsettia / El regalo de la flor de nochebuena*
  A piñata in a pine tree
Morpurgo, Michael. *On angel wings*
Morrissey, Dean. *The Christmas ship*
Moses, Will. *Silent night*
Moss, Jenny Jackson. *Cajun night after Christmas*
Moulton, Mark Kimball. *Reindeer Christmas*
Muecke, Anne. *The dinosaurs' night before Christmas*
Naylor, Phyllis Reynolds. *Keeping a Christmas secret*
Nazoa, Aquiles. *A small Nativity*
Nikola-Lisa, W. *Hallelujah!*
  To hear the angels sing
Noble, Trinka Hakes. *A Christmas spider's miracle*
Norris, Leslie. *Albert and the angels*
Novak, Matt. *The last Christmas present*
Numeroff, Laura Joffe. *If you take a mouse to the movies*
  Merry Christmas, Mouse!
Obed, Ellen Bryan. *Who would like a Christmas tree?*
O'Connor, Jane. *Fancy Nancy splendiferous Christmas*
Older, Effin. *My two grandmothers*
Onyefulu, Ifeoma. *An African Christmas*
Oppenheim, Joanne. *The Christmas witch*
Orozco, Jose-Luis. *Pancho Claus*
Park, Linda Sue. *The third gift*
Pasquali, Elena. *Ituku's Christmas journey*
Patricelli, Leslie. *Fa la la*
Paxton, Tom. *The story of Santa Claus*
Peet, Bill. *Countdown to Christmas*
Petach, Heidi. *Wee three pigs*
Peterson, Melissa. *Hanna's Christmas*
Pfister, Marcus. *The Christmas star*
  Wake up, Santa Claus!
Pickthall, Marjorie L. C. *The worker in sandalwood*
Pilkey, Dav. *Dragon's merry Christmas*
  The Dumb Bunnies' Easter
Pinkney, Andrea Davis. *Mim's Christmas jam*
Pinkwater, Daniel. *Wolf Christmas*
Pittman, Helena Clare. *The angel tree*
Polacco, Patricia. *Gifts of the heart*
  The trees of the dancing goats
  Welcome Comfort
Politi, Leo. *Pedro, the angel of Olvera Street*
Powell, Consie. *Old dog Cora and the Christmas tree*
Primavera, Elise. *Auntie Claus*

Auntie Claus and the key to Christmas
Pryor, Bonnie. *Merry Christmas, Amanda and April*
Pulver, Robin. *Christmas for a kitten*
Christmas kitten, home at last
Purmell, Ann. *Christmas tree farm*
Quattlebaum, Mary. *The shine man*
Rader, Laura. *Santa's new suit*
Rahaman, Vashanti. *O Christmas tree*
Ransom, Candice F. *The Christmas dolls*
Rawlinson, Julia. *Fletcher and the snowflake Christmas*
Ray, Mary Lyn. *Christmas farm*
Recorvits, Helen. *Yoon and the Christmas mitten*
Rees, Douglas. *Jeannette Claus saves Christmas*
Reiser, Lynn. *Christmas counting*
Reiss, Mike. *How Murray saved Christmas*
Merry un-Christmas
Santa claustrophobia
Reynolds, Peter H. *The smallest gift of Christmas*
Robbins, Ruth. *Baboushka and the three kings*
Roberts, Bethany. *Christmas mice*
Cookie angel
Waiting-for-Christmas stories
Rodanas, Kristina. *The little drummer boy*
Root, Phyllis. *All for the newborn baby*
Rosales, Melodye Benson. *'Twas the night b'fore Christmas*
Rose, Marion. *The Christmas tree fairy*
Rosen, Michael J. *Elijah's angel*
Rosenberg, Liz. *On Christmas eve*
Rosenthal, Amy Krouse. *Christmas cookies*
Ross, Michael Elsohn. *Mexican Christmas*
Rox, John. *I want a hippopotamus for Christmas*
Ryan, Pam Muñoz. *There was no snow on Christmas Eve*
Rylant, Cynthia. *Christmas in the country*
Little Whistle's Christmas
Silver packages
Sabuda, Robert. *The Christmas alphabet*
Sacre, Antonio. *La Noche Buena*
Sahagun, Bernardino de. *Spirit child*
Sanders, Rob. *Cowboy Christmas*
Santa Claus is coming to town
Santa's little library of Christmas stories
Santiago, Esmeralda. *A doll for Navidades*
Sawyer, Ruth. *The remarkable Christmas of the cobbler's sons*
Say, Allen. *Tree of cranes*
Scarry, Richard. *Richard Scarry's best Christmas book ever!*
Scotton, Rob. *Merry Christmas, Splat*
Russell's Christmas magic
Seabrooke, Brenda. *'Twas the day before Christmas*
Seuss, Dr. *How the Grinch stole Christmas*
Shannon, David. *The amazing Christmas extravaganza*
Sharkey, Niamh. *Santasaurus*
Shea, Bob. *Dinosaur vs. Santa*
Sierra, Judy. *'Twas the fright before Christmas*
Silvano, Wendi. *Turkey Claus*
Singer, Marilyn. *Tallulah's Nutcracker*
Slate, Joseph. *Little Porcupine's Christmas*
Slegers, Liesbet. *The child in the manger*
Sleigh bells and snowflakes
Sloat, Teri. *Hark! The aardvark angels sing*
Pieces of Christmas
Smath, Jerry. *The animals' Christmas carol*
Smith, Cynthia Leitich. *Santa knows*
Smith, Kathryn. *Little Donkey's Christmas story*
Little Lamb's Christmas story
Snell, Gordon. *'Twas the day after Christmas*
Twelve days, a Christmas countdown
Solheim, James. *Santa's secrets revealed*
Soto, Gary. *Too many tamales*
Spang, Günter. *The ox and the Donkey*
Speirs, John. *The little boy's Christmas gift*
Spier, Peter. *Peter Spier's Christmas!*
Spinelli, Eileen. *Coming through the blizzard*
The perfect Christmas
Together at Christmas
Spirin, Gennady. *We three kings*
Stainton, Sue. *Santa's snow cat*
Stanton, Melissa. *My pen pal, Santa*
Steffensmeier, Alexander. *Millie in the snow*
Stevens, Jan Romero. *Twelve lizards leaping*
Stevenson, James. *Christmas at Mud Flat*
The worst person's Christmas
Stock, Catherine. *Christmas time*
Stoeke, Janet Morgan. *Minerva Louise on Christmas Eve*
Strand, Keith. *Grandfather's Christmas tree*
Sykes, Julie. *Careful, Santa*
Hurry, Santa!
Tafuri, Nancy. *Counting to Christmas*
The donkey's Christmas song
Taylor, Jane. *Twinkle, twinkle little star*
Tazewell, Charles. *The littlest angel*, ill. by Deborah Lanino
The littlest angel, ill. by Paul Micich
The littlest angel, ill. by Rebecca Thornburgh
Thayer, Jane. *The puppy who wanted a boy*
Thompson, Kay. *Kay Thompson's Eloise at Christmastime*
Thompson, Lauren. *The Christmas magic*
Mouse's first Christmas
Mouse's first Christmas [board book]
One starry night
Thury, Frederick. *The last straw*
Tillman, Nancy. *The spirit of Christmas*
Tolan, Stephanie S. *Bartholomew's blessing*
Tompert, Ann. *A carol for Christmas*
Torres, Melissa A. *The great Christmas tree celebration*
Trapani, Iza. *Jingle bells*
Trimble, Marcia. *Moonbeams for Santa*
Trumbauer, Lisa. *The great reindeer rebellion*
Tryon, Leslie. *Albert's Christmas*
Tudor, Tasha. *The doll's Christmas*
Turner, Ann Warren. *The Christmas house*
Turner, Sandy. *Silent night*
The twelve days of Christmas. English folk song.
The twelve days of Christmas
The 12 days of Christmas
The twelve days of Christmas
Twelve days of Christmas
The twelve days of Christmas, ill. by Laurel Long
The twelve days of Christmas, ill. by Ilse Plume
The twelve days of Christmas, ill. by Jane Ray
The twelve days of Christmas, ill. by Gennady Spirin
The twelve days of Christmas, ill. by Vladimir Vagin
The twelve days of Christmas [board book]
Underwood, Deborah. *The Christmas quiet book*
Vainio, Pirkko. *The Christmas angel*
Van Allsburg, Chris. *The polar express*
Van Steenwyk, Elizabeth. *Prairie Christmas*
Velasquez, Eric. *Grandma's gift*
Vidal, Beatriz A. *Federico and the Magi's gift*

Vincent, Gabrielle. *Merry Christmas, Ernest and Celestine*
Vischer, Frans. *A very Fuddles Christmas*
Waber, Bernard. *Lyle at Christmas*
Waddell, Martin. *Mimi's Christmas*
Walburg, Lori. *The legend of the candy cane*
Waldron, Jan L. *Angel Pig and the hidden Christmas*
Wallace, Ivy. *Pookie believes in Santa Claus*
Wangerin, Walter. *Angels and all children*
Probity Jones and the Fear Not Angel
Watson, Wendy. *Holly's Christmas eve*
Watt, Mélanie. *Scaredy Squirrel prepares for Christmas*
Wax, Wendy. *A very mice Christmas*
We wish you a merry Christmas
Weinberg, Larry. *The Forgetful Bears help Santa*
Weller, Frances Ward. *The angel of Mill Street*
Wells, Rosemary. *McDuff's new friend*
Max's Christmas
Morris's disappearing bag
Weninger, Brigitte. *A letter to Santa Claus*
Merry Christmas, Davy!
What a morning!
White, Ellen Emerson. *Santa paws*
Wick, Walter. *Can you see what I see? the night before Christmas*
Wild, Margaret. *Thank you, Santa*
Wilder, Laura Ingalls. *Santa comes to little house*
Wildsmith, Brian. *A Christmas story*
Wilhelm, Hans. *Schnitzel's first Christmas*
Willey, Margaret. *Clever Beatrice Christmas*
Williams, Sam. *Angel's Christmas cookies*
Snowy magic
Wilson, Karma. *Bear stays up for Christmas*
Mortimer's Christmas manger
Wing, Natasha. *The night before the night before Christmas*
Winter, Jeanette. *The Christmas tree ship*
Winthrop, Elizabeth. *Bear's Christmas surprise*
A child is born: the Christmas story
Wojciechowski, Susan. *The Christmas miracle of Jonathan Toomey*
Wolff, Patricia Rae. *A new, improved Santa*
Wood, Audrey. *The Christmas adventure of Space Elf Sam*
A cowboy Christmas
Wood, Don. *Merry Christmas, big hungry bear*
Wright, Dare. *A gift from the lonely doll*
Yee, Wong Herbert. *A small Christmas*
Yin. *Dear Santa, please come to the 19th floor*
Yolen, Jane. *How do dinosaurs say Merry Christmas?*
Sister Bear
Yorinks, Arthur. *Christmas in July*
Young, Ned. *Zoomer's out-of-this-world Christmas*
Zagwÿn, Deborah Turney. *The winter gift*
Zepeda, Gwendolyn. *Growing up with tamales / Los tamales de Ana*
Ziefert, Harriet. *Home for Navidad*
Zolotow, Charlotte. *The beautiful Christmas tree*

Holidays – Cinco de Mayo

Bullard, Lisa. *Marco's Cinco de Mayo*
Cox, Judy. *Cinco de Mouse-o!*
Flanagan, Alice K. *Cinco de Mayo*
Levy, Janice. *Celebrate! It's cinco de mayo! / Celebremos! Es el cinco de mayo!*
Schaefer, Lola M. *Cinco de Mayo*
Wade, Mary Dodson. *Cinco de Mayo*

Holidays – Day of the Dead

Barner, Bob. *The Day of the Dead / El Día de los Muertos*
Freschet, Gina. *Beto and the bone dance*
Goldman, Judy. *Uncle Monarch and the Day of the Dead*
Johnston, Tony. *Day of the Dead*
Joosse, Barbara. *Ghost wings*
Keep, Linda Lowery. *Day of the Dead*
Luenn, Nancy. *A gift for Abuelita*
Montes, Marisa. *Los gatos black on Halloween*

Holidays – Divali

Gardeski, Christina Mia. *Diwali*
Pandya, Meenal. *Here comes Diwali*
Rahaman, Vashanti. *Divali rose*
Verma, Jatinder Nath. *The story of Divaali*

Holidays – Earth Day

deGroat, Diane. *Ants in your pants, worms in your plants!*
Roop, Connie. *Let's celebrate Earth Day*
Wright, Maureen. *Earth Day, birthday!*

Holidays – Easter

Adams, Adrienne. *The Easter egg artists*
Auch, Mary Jane. *The Easter egg farm*
Balian, Lorna. *Humbug rabbit*
Berenstain, Stan and Jan. *The Berenstain bears and the real Easter eggs*
Bergren, Lisa Tawn. *God gave us Easter*
Berlin, Irving. *Easter parade*
Bible. New Testament. Gospels. *Easter: from the King James Bible*
Brett, Jan. *The Easter egg*
Brown, Margaret Wise. *The golden egg book*
The runaway bunny
Burg, Sarah Emmanuelle. *One more egg*
Carlson, Melody. *The Easterville miracle*
Carter, David A. *Easter bugs*
Chaconas, Dori. *Looking for Easter*
Cousins, Lucy. *Happy Easter, Maisy!*
deGroat, Diane. *Last one in is a rotten egg!*
Denim, Sue. *The Dumb Bunnies' Easter*
Devlin, Wende. *Cranberry Easter*
Dunrea, Olivier. *Ollie's Easter eggs*
Ollie's Easter eggs [board book]
Friedrich, Priscilla. *The Easter bunny that overslept*
Garland, Michael. *The great Easter egg hunt*
Gibbons, Gail. *Easter*
Grambling, Lois G. *Here comes T. Rex Cottontail*
Greenfield, Eloise. *Easter parade*
Hennessy, B. G. *Corduroy's Easter*
Heyward, Du Bose. *The country bunny and the little gold shoes*
Hill, Eric. *Spot's first Easter*
Hulme, Joy N. *Easter babies*
Kimmel, Eric A. *The birds' gift*
Krensky, Stephen. *Milo and the really big bunny*
Kroll, Steven. *The big bunny and the Easter eggs*
The big bunny and the magic show
Lachner, Dorothea. *Smoky's special Easter present*
Lenski, Lois. *The Easter Rabbit's parade*
McGrath, Barbara Barbieri. *The little gray bunny*
Mackall, Dandi Daley. *The story of the Easter robin*

Marciano, John Bemelmans. *Madeline at the White House*
Milhous, Katherine. *The egg tree*
Miller, Edna. *Mousekin's Easter basket*
Modesitt, Jeanne. *Little Bunny's Easter surprise*
Mortimer, Anne. *Bunny's Easter egg*
Murphy, Elspeth Campbell. *Happy Easter, God*
Paraskevas, Betty. *Nibbles O'Hare*
Pienkowski, Jan. *Easter*
Pilkey, Dav. *The Dumb Bunnies' Easter*
Polacco, Patricia. *Chicken Sunday*
Rand, Betseygail. *Big Bunny*
Roberts, Bethany. *Easter mice*
Schulman, Janet. *10 Easter egg hunters*
Slegers, Liesbet. *Happy Easter!*
Smythe, Theresa. *Chester's colorful Easter eggs*
Stalder, Päivi. *Ernest's first Easter*
Stock, Catherine. *Easter surprise*
Stoeke, Janet Morgan. *Minerva Louise and the colorful eggs*
Stohs, Anita. *An Easter alleluia*
Taylor, Shirley. *The cross in the egg*
Taylor-Butler, Christine. *Lamb's Easter surprise*
Tegen, Katherine Brown. *The story of the Easter Bunny*
Thomas, Jan. *The Easter Bunny's assistant*
Thompson, Lauren. *Love one another*
Tudor, Tasha. *A tale for Easter*
Vail, Rachel. *Piggy Bunny*
Vainio, Pirkko. *Who hid the Easter eggs?*
Vidrine, Beverly Barras. *Easter Day alphabet*
Watson, Wendy. *Happy Easter day!*
Wedeven, Carol. *The Easter cave*
Weigelt, Udo. *The Easter Bunny's baby*
Weil, Lisl. *The candy egg bunny*
Wells, Rosemary. *Max counts his chickens*
Max's chocolate chicken
Max's Easter surprise
Weninger, Brigitte. *Happy Easter, Davy*
Wildsmith, Brian. *The Easter story*
Wilhelm, Hans. *More bunny trouble*
Quacky Ducky's Easter egg
Quacky Ducky's Easter fun
Winthrop, Elizabeth. *He is risen*
Wolf, Winfried. *The Easter bunny*
Zolotow, Charlotte. *The bunny who found Easter*
Mr. Rabbit and the lovely present

Holidays – Father's Day

Bunting, Eve. *A perfect Father's Day*
Butterworth, Nick. *My dad is awesome*
Callahan, Sean. *A wild Father's Day*
Kroll, Steven. *Happy Father's Day*
Loomis, Christine. *The best Father's Day present ever*
Nolan, Janet. *A Father's Day thank you*
Rockwell, Anne. *Father's Day*
Sharmat, Marjorie Weinman. *Hooray for Father's Day!*

Holidays – Fourth of July

Bertrand, Diane Gonzales. *Uncle Chente's picnic / El picnic de Tío Chente*
Chall, Marsha Wilson. *Happy Birthday, America!*
Keller, Holly. *Henry's Fourth of July*
Lasky, Kathryn. *Fourth of July bear*
Malnor, Carol L. *The Blues go birding across America*
Osborne, Mary Pope. *Happy birthday, America*
Roberts, Bethany. *Fourth of July mice*
Roosa, Karen. *Pippa at the parade*
Thomas, Jane Resh. *Celebration!*
Van Nutt, Julia. *Skyrockets and snickerdoodles*
Wardlaw, Lee. *Red, white, and boom!*
Watson, Wendy. *Hurray for the Fourth of July*
Wells, Rosemary. *McDuff saves the day*
Whitehead, Kathy. *Looking for Uncle Louie on the Fourth of July*
Ziefert, Harriet. *Hats off for the Fourth of July!*

Holidays – Groundhog Day

Blackaby, Susan. *Brownie Groundhog and the February Fox*
Cox, Judy. *Go to sleep, Groundhog*
Cuyler, Margery. *Groundhog stays up late*
Freeman, Don. *Gregory's Shadow*
Gibbons, Gail. *Groundhog Day*
Hill, Susanna Leonard. *Punxsutawney Phyllis*
Hiskey, Iris. *The secret of the first one up*
Holub, Joan. *Groundhog weather school*
Johnson, Crockett. *Will spring be early or will spring be late?*
Kroll, Steven. *It's Groundhog Day!*
Levine, Abby. *Gretchen Groundhog, it's your day!*
Lewin, Betsy. *Groundhog day*
Miller, Pat. *Substitute Groundhog*
Pallotta, Jerry. *Who will see their shadows this year?*
Roberts, Bethany. *Double trouble Groundhog Day*
Swallow, Pamela Curtis. *Groundhog gets a say*
Tompert, Ann. *Nothing sticks like a shadow*
Welling, Peter J. *Andrew McGroundhog and his shady shadow*

Holidays – Halloween

Adams, Adrienne. *A Halloween happening*
A woggle of witches
Agran, Rick. *Pumpkin shivaree*
Alexander, Sue. *Who goes out on Halloween?*
Alley, R. W. *There once was a witch*
Asch, Frank. *Popcorn*
Auch, Mary Jane. *Poultrygeist*
Balian, Lorna. *Humbug witch*
Bauer, Marion Dane. *Halloween forest*
I'm not afraid of Halloween!
Berenstain, Stan and Jan. *The Berenstain bears trick or treat*
Biedrzycki, David. *Me and my dragon: scared of Halloween*
Bollinger, Peter. *Algernon Graeves is scary enough*
Bond, Felicia. *The Halloween play*
Brennan-Nelson, Denise. *J is for jack-o-lantern*
Brenner, Tom. *And then comes Halloween*
Bridwell, Norman. *Clifford's Halloween*
Glow-in-the-dark Halloween
Bright, Robert. *Georgie's Halloween*
Brimner, Larry Dane. *Trick or treat, Old Armadillo*
Brokamp, Elizabeth. *The picky little witch*
Brown, Lisa. *Vampire boy's good night*
Brown, Marc. *Arthur's Halloween*
Arthur's spookiest Halloween
Brown, Margaret Wise. *The fierce yellow pumpkin*
Broyles, Anne. *Shy Mama's Halloween*
Bullard, Lisa. *Trick-or-treat on Milton Street*
Bunting, Eve. *The bones of Fred McFee*
Scary, scary Halloween
Carlson, Melody. *When the creepy things come out*

Carlstrom, Nancy White. *What a scare, Jesse Bear!*
Who said boo?
Caseley, Judith. *Witch mama*
Cazet, Denys. *Never poke a squid*
The perfect pumpkin pie
Chetkowski, Emily. *Pumpkin smile*
Choi, Yangsook. *Behind the mask*
Christelow, Eileen. *Five little monkeys trick-or-treat*
Christian, Cheryl. *Witches*
Cocca-Leffler, Maryann. *Jungle Halloween*
Cohen, Miriam. *The real-skin rubber monster mask*
Cousins, Lucy. *Maisy's Halloween*
Cox, Judy. *Haunted house, haunted Mouse*
Cronin, Doreen. *Click, clack, boo!*
Crum, Shutta. *Who took my hairy toe?*
Cushman, Doug. *Halloween good night*
Cuyler, Margery. *The bumpy little pumpkin*
David, Lawrence. *Superhero Max*
Day, Nancy Raines. *On a windy night*
deGroat, Diane. *Trick or treat, smell my feet*
de Las Casas, Dianne. *The house that Witchy built*
Demas, Corinne. *Halloween surprise*
Desmoinaux, Christel. *"Hallo-what?"*
Devlin, Wende. *Cranberry Halloween*
Dickinson, Rebecca. *Over in the Hollow*
Diviny, Sean. *Halloween Motel*
Donnelly, Liza. *Dinosaurs' Halloween*
Druce, Arden. *Halloween night*
Dunrea, Olivier. *Ollie's Halloween*
Duval, Kathy. *The Three Bears' Halloween*
Egan, Tim. *The experiments of Doctor Vermin*
Engelbreit, Mary. *Queen of Halloween*
Faulkner, Keith. *A trick or a treat?*
Five little pumpkins, ill. by Ben Mantle
Five little pumpkins, ill. by Dan Yaccarino
Flanagan, Alice K. *Halloween*
Fraser, Mary Ann. *Heebie-Jeebie Jamboree*
Galbraith, Kathryn O. *Boo, bunny!*
Gantos, Jack. *Rotten Ralph's trick or treat*
Gibbons, Gail. *Halloween*
Halloween is . . .
Grambling, Lois G. *Miss Hildy's missing cape caper*
T. Rex trick-or-treats
Grogan, John. *Trick or treat, Marley!*
Gunnufson, Charlotte. *Halloween hustle*
Hall, Zoe. *It's pumpkin time!*
Halloweena
Hatch, Elizabeth. *Halloween night*
Heidbreder, Robert. *Black and bittern was night*
Heinz, Brian J. *The monsters' test*
Hennessy, B. G. *Corduroy's Halloween*
Hines, Anna Grossnickle. *When the goblins came knocking*
Holabird, Katharine. *Angelina's Halloween*
Holub, Joan. *The Halloween Queen*
Hood, Susan. *Just say boo!*
Hopkins, Lee Bennett. *Ragged shadows*
Horowitz, Dave. *The ugly pumpkin*
Hubbard, Patricia. *Trick or treat countdown*
Hubbell, Patricia. *Boo! Halloween poems and limericks*
Wrapping paper romp
Hubbell, Will. *Pumpkin Jack*
Huck, Charlotte S. *A creepy countdown*
Hutchins, Pat. *Which witch is which?*
Irving, Washington. *The legend of Sleepy Hollow*, ill. by R. W. Alley
The legend of Sleepy Hollow, ill. by Daniel San Souci
Jane, Pamela. *Little goblins ten*
Monster mischief
Johnston, Tony. *Soup bone*
The vanishing pumpkin
Keats, Ezra Jack. *The trip*
Keens-Douglas, Richardo. *Anancy and the haunted house*
Kellogg, Steven. *The mystery of the flying orange pumpkin*
Klingel, Cynthia Fitterer. *Halloween*
Kontis, Alethea. *AlphaOops!*
Kovalski, Maryann. *Omar's Halloween*
Krieb, Mr. *We're off to find the witch's house*
Krosoczka, Jarrett J. *Annie was warned*
Kutner, Merrily. *Z is for zombie*
Landry, Leo. *Trick or treat*
Leedy, Loreen. *The dragon Halloween party*
2 x 2 = boo!
Leuck, Laura. *One witch*
Levine, Abby. *This is the pumpkin*
Lewis, J. Patrick. *The house of Boo*
Lewis, Kevin. *The runaway pumpkin*
London, Jonathan. *Froggy's Halloween*
McCourt, Lisa. *Happy Halloween, Stinky Face*
McCue, Lisa. *Corduroy's best Halloween ever!*
McGhee, Alison. *Only a witch can fly*
A very brave witch
McGuirk, Leslie. *Tucker's spooky Halloween*
Marshall, Edward. *Space case*
Martin, Bill, Jr. *The magic pumpkin*
Old devil wind
Trick or treat?
Marzollo, Jean. *I spy spooky night*
Mayer, Pamela. *The scariest monster in the whole wide world*
Mayr, Diane. *Littlebat's Halloween story*
Meddaugh, Susan. *The witches' supermarket*
Melmed, Laura Krauss. *Fright night flight*
Merriam, Eve. *Halloween ABC*
Miller, Edna. *Mousekin's golden house*
Minor, Wendell. *Pumpkin heads*
Moffatt, Judith. *The pumpkin man*
Trick-or-treat faces
Montes, Marisa. *Los gatos black on Halloween*
Montijo, Rhode. *The Halloween Kid*
Mortimer, Anne. *Pumpkin cat*
Murray, Marjorie Dennis. *Halloween night*
Muth, Jon J. *Zen ghosts*
Neitzel, Shirley. *Who will I be?*
Nikola-Lisa, W. *Shake dem Halloween bones*
Novak, Matt. *No zombies allowed*
O'Connell, Jennifer. *It's Halloween night!*
O'Malley, Kevin. *Velcome*
Palatini, Margie. *Piggie pie*
Pamintuan, Macky. *Twelve haunted rooms of Halloween*
Passen, Lisa. *Attack of the 50-foot teacher*
Pearson, Susan. *We're going on a ghost hunt*
Pilkey, Dav. *The Hallo-wiener*
Polacco, Patricia. *Picnic at Mudsock Meadow*
Poydar, Nancy. *The perfectly horrible Halloween*
Prelutsky, Jack. *Halloween countdown*
Wild witches' ball
Preston, Tim. *Pumpkin moon*
Reeves, Howard W. *There was an old witch*
Regan, Dian Curtis. *How do you know it's Halloween?*
Rex, Michael. *Brooms are for flying*
Riggio, Anita. *Beware the Brindlebeast*

Rocklin, Joanne. *This book is haunted*
Rockwell, Anne. *Apples and pumpkins*
Halloween Day
Rohmann, Eric. *Bone dog*
Rosen, Michael J. *Night of the pumpkinheads*
Rosenberry, Vera. *Vera's Halloween*
Ross, Eileen. *The Halloween showdown*
Rylant, Cynthia. *Moonlight, the Halloween cat*
Saltzberg, Barney. *The problem with pumpkins*
San Souci, Robert D. *Cinderella Skeleton*
Savage, Stephen. *Ten orange pumpkins*
Schulman, Janet. *10 trick-or-treaters*
Schweninger, Ann. *Halloween surprises*
Seibold, J. Otto. *Vunce upon a time*
Seinfeld, Jerry. *Halloween*
Shaw, Nancy. *Sheep trick or treat*
Shute, Linda. *Halloween party*
Sierra, Judy. *The house that Drac built*
Silverman, Erica. *The Halloween house*
Smalls-Hector, Irene. *Jenny Reen and the Jack Muh Lantern*
Spurr, Elizabeth. *Pumpkin hill*
Stevenson, James. *That terrible Halloween night*
Stock, Catherine. *Halloween monster*
Stoeke, Janet Morgan. *Minerva Louise on Halloween*
Stutson, Caroline. *By the light of the Halloween moon*
Tatcheva, Eva. *Witch Zelda's birthday cake*
Teague, Mark. *One Halloween night*
Tegen, Katherine Brown. *Dracula and Frankenstein are friends*
Thomas, Jan. *Pumpkin trouble*
Thompson, Lauren. *Mouse's first Halloween*
Titherington, Jeanne. *Pumpkin pumpkin*
Todd, Mark. *What will you be for Halloween?*
Trapani, Iza. *Haunted party*
Tryon, Leslie. *Albert's Halloween*
Tudor, Tasha. *Pumpkin moonshine*
Turner, Ann Warren. *Pumpkin cat*
Van Rynbach, Iris. *Five little pumpkins*
Vasilovich, Guy. *The 13 nights of Halloween*
Vaughan, Marcia Kapok. *We're going on a ghost hunt*
Waldron, Jan L. *John Pig's Halloween*
Walker, Sally M. *Druscilla's Halloween*
Watson, Wendy. *Boo! It's Halloween*
Watt, Mélanie. *Scaredy Squirrel prepares for Halloween*
Weston, Martha. *Tuck's haunted house*
Williams, Suzanne. *The witch casts a spell*
Winters, Kay. *The teeny tiny ghost*
Whooo's haunting the teeny tiny ghost?
Winthrop, Elizabeth. *Halloween hats*
Wojciechowski, Susan. *The best Halloween of all*
Wolff, Ferida. *On Halloween night*
Yolen, Jane. *Beneath the ghost moon*
Ziefert, Harriet. *Two little witches*
Zolotow, Charlotte. *A tiger called Thomas*, ill. by Diana Cain Bluthenthal
A tiger called Thomas, ill. by Catherine Stock

Holidays – Hanukkah

Adler, David A. *A picture book of Hanukkah*
A picture book of Jewish holidays
The story of Hanukkah
Aleichem, Sholem. *Hanukah money*
Alko, Selina. *Daddy Christmas and Hanukkah Mama*
Baum, Maxie. *I have a little dreidel*
Bunting, Eve. *One candle*
Capucilli, Alyssa Satin. *Happy Hanukkah, Biscuit*
Carter, David A. *Chanukah bugs*
Chwast, Seymour. *The miracle of Hanukkah*
Cleary, Brian P. *Eight wild nights*
da Costa, Deborah. *Hanukkah moon*
Edwards, Michelle. *The Hanukkah trike*
Papa's latkes
Room for the baby
Fishman, Cathy Goldberg. *On Hanukkah*
Glaser, Linda. *Mrs. Greenberg's messy Hanukkah*
Hanukkah lights
Hirsh, Marilyn. *Potato pancakes all around*
Howland, Naomi. *Latkes, latkes, good to eat*
Hyde, Heidi Smith. *Emanuel and the Hanukkah rescue*
Jaffe, Nina. *In the month of Kislev*
Kimmel, Eric A. *The Chanukkah guest*
Hanukkah bear
Hershel and the Hanukkah goblins
The magic dreidels
Zigazak!
Kimmelman, Leslie. *Hanukkah lights, Hanukkah nights*
The runaway latkes
Krensky, Stephen. *Hanukkah at Valley Forge*
Kroll, Steven. *The Hanukkah mice*
Kropf, Latifa Berry. *It's Hanukkah time!*
Krulik, Nancy E. *Is it Hanukkah yet?*
Kuskin, Karla. *A great miracle happened there*
Lehman-Wilzig, Tami. *Nathan blows out the Hanukkah candles*
McKissack, Patricia C. *Messy Bessey's holidays*
Manushkin, Fran. *Hooray for Hanukkah!*
Latkes and applesauce
Martin, David. *Hanukkah lights*
Melmed, Laura Krauss. *Eight winter nights*
Moishe's miracle
Moorman, Margaret. *Light the lights!*
Newman, Lesléa. *The eight nights of Chanukah*
Runaway dreidel
Oberman, Sheldon. *By the Hanukkah light*
Ofanansky, Allison. *Harvest of light*
Older, Effin. *My two grandmothers*
Podwal, Mark H. *The menorah story*
Polacco, Patricia. *The trees of the dancing goats*
Randall, Ronne. *The Hanukkah mice*
Rosen, Michael J. *Chanukah lights*
Chanukah lights everywhere
Elijah's angel
Our eight nights of Hanukkah
Rothenberg, Joan Keller. *Inside-out grandma*
Schaefer, Lola M. *Hanukkah*
Schnur, Steven. *The tie man's miracle*
Schotter, Roni. *Hanukkah!*
Silverman, Erica. *The Hanukkah hop!*
Simon, Norma. *The story of Hanukkah*
Smith, Dian G. *Hanukkah lights*
Sper, Emily. *Hanukkah: a counting book in English, Hebrew, and Yiddish*
Spinner, Stephanie. *It's a miracle*
Stone, Tanya Lee. *D is for dreidel*
Yolen, Jane. *How do dinosaurs say Happy Chanukah?*
Zalben, Jane Breskin. *Beni's first Chanukah*
Pearl's eight days of Chanukah
Ziefert, Harriet. *Hanukkah haiku*

Holidays – Independence Day *see* Holidays – Fourth of July

Holidays – Juneteenth

Weatherford, Carole Boston. *Juneteenth jamboree*

Holidays – Kwanzaa

Chocolate, Deborah. *Kente colors*
Kwanzaa
Ford, Juwanda G. *K is for Kwanzaa*
Together for Kwanzaa
McKissack, Patricia C. *Messy Bessey's holidays*
Medearis, Angela Shelf. *Seven spools of thread*
Saint James, Synthia. *The gifts of Kwanzaa*
Schaefer, Lola M. *Kwanzaa*
Tokunbo, Dimitrea. *The sound of Kwanzaa*
Washington, Donna L. *Li'l Rabbit's Kwanzaa*
The story of Kwanzaa
Winne, Joanne. *Let's get ready for Kwanzaa*

Holidays – Mardi Gras *see* Mardi Gras

Holidays – May Day

Mora, Pat. *The rainbow tulip*

Holidays – Memorial Day

Golding, Theresa Martin. *Memorial Day surprise*

Holidays – Mother's Day

Alexander, Martha G. *Max and the dumb flower picture*
Anderson, Laurie Halse. *No time for Mother's Day*
Balian, Lorna. *Mother's Mother's Day*
Bauer, Marion Dane. *My mother is mine*
Bunting, Eve. *The Mother's Day mice*
deGroat, Diane. *Mother, you're the best! (but Sister, you're a pest!)*
French, Vivian. *A present for mom*
Grambling, Lois G. *T. Rex and the Mother's Day hug*
Krensky, Stephen. *Mother's Day surprise*
Kroll, Steven. *Happy Mother's Day*
Rockwell, Anne. *Mother's Day*
Sharmat, Marjorie Weinman. *Hooray for Mother's Day!*

Holidays – New Year's

Andersen, Hans Christian. *The little match girl*, ill. by Rachel Isadora
The little match girl, ill. by Blair Lent
The little match girl, ill. by Jerry Pinkney
The little matchstick girl
Bae, Hyun-Joo. *New clothes for New Year's day*
Fromental, Jean-Luc. *365 penguins*
Holabird, Katharine. *Angelina ice skates*
Miller, Pat. *Squirrel's New Year's resolution*
Modell, Frank. *Goodbye old year, hello new year*
Piernas-Davenport, Gail. *Shanté Keys and the New Year's peas*
Preus, Margi. *The Peace Bell*
Ziefert, Harriet. *First Night*

Holidays – Passover

Adler, David A. *A picture book of Jewish holidays*
A picture book of Passover
Fishman, Cathy Goldberg. *On Passover*
Flanagan, Alice K. *Passover*
Geras, Adèle. *Rebecca's Passover*
Glaser, Linda. *Hoppy Passover!*
Hanft, Josh. *The miracles of Passover*
Howland, Naomi. *The matzah man*
Kimmelman, Leslie. *Hooray! it's Passover!*
Kropf, Latifa Berry. *It's seder time!*
Levine, Abby. *This is the matzah*
Libney, Varda. *What I like about Passover*
Lister, Clare. *My first Passover [board book]*
The little red hen. *The Little Red Hen and the Passover matzah*
Manushkin, Fran. *Miriam's cup*
Marshall, Linda Elovitz. *The passover lamb*
Newman, Lesléa. *Matzo ball moon*
A sweet Passover
Portnoy, Mindy Avra. *A tale of two seders*
Rappaport, Doreen. *The secret seder*
Rothenberg, Joan Keller. *Matzah ball soup*
Rouss, Sylvia A. *Sammy Spider's first Passover*
Schotter, Roni. *Passover!*
Passover magic
Shulevitz, Uri. *The magician*
Silverman, Erica. *Gittel's hands*
Simon, Norma. *The story of Passover*
Sper, Emily. *The Passover seder*
Strauss, Linda Leopold. *The Elijah door*
Ungar, Richard. *Rachel's gift*
Weber, Elka. *The Yankee at the seder*
Wohl, Lauren L. *Matzoh mouse*
Zalben, Jane Breskin. *Pearl's Passover*
Zolkower, Edie Stoltz. *Too many cooks*
Zucker, Jonny. *Four special questions*

Holidays – Purim

Fishman, Cathy Goldberg. *On Purim*
Goldin, Barbara Diamond. *Cakes and miracles*
Schotter, Roni. *Purim play*
Simpson, Lesley. *The Purim surprise*
Zucker, Jonny. *It's party time*

Holidays – Ramadan

Addasi, Maha. *The white nights of Ramadan*
Bullard, Lisa. *Rashad's Ramadan and Eid al-Fitr*
Ghazi, Suhaib Hamid. *Ramadan*
Gilani-Williams, Fawzia. *Nabeel's new pants*
Jalali, Reza. *Moon watchers*
Katz, Karen. *My first Ramadan*
Khan, Hena. *The night of the moon*
Mobin-Uddin, Asma. *A party in Ramadan*
Robert, Na'ima B. *Ramadan Moon*
Whitman, Sylvia. *Under the Ramadan moon*

Holidays – Rosh Hashanah

Cohen, Deborah Bodin. *Engineer Ari and the Rosh Hashana ride*
Fishman, Cathy Goldberg. *On Rosh Hashanah and Yom Kippur*
Kimmel, Eric A. *Gershon's monster*
Kimmelman, Leslie. *Sound the shofar!*
Kropf, Latifa Berry. *It's Shofar time!*
Marshall, Linda Elovitz. *Talia and the rude vegetables*
Schnur, Susan. *Tashlich at Turtle Rock*
Wayland, April Halprin. *New Year at the pier*
Zucker, Jonny. *Apples and honey*

Holidays – Rosh Kodesh

da Costa, Deborah. *Hanukkah moon*

Holidays – Seder

Kropf, Latifa Berry. *It's seder time!*
Levine, Abby. *This is the matzah*
Marshall, Linda Elovitz. *The passover lamb*
Weber, Elka. *The Yankee at the seder*

Holidays – Shavuot

Goldin, Barbara Diamond. *A mountain of blintzes*
Korngold, Jamie S. *Sadie and the big mountain*
Rouss, Sylvia A. *Sammy Spider's first Shavuot*

Holidays – St. Patrick's Day

Bunting, Eve. *St. Patrick's Day in the morning*
Callahan, Sean. *The leprechaun who lost his rainbow*
Shannon and the world's tallest leprechaun
Colandro, Lucille. *There was an old lady who swallowed a clover!*
Janice. *Little Bear marches in the St. Patrick's Day parade*
Kroll, Steven. *Mary McLean and the St. Patrick's Day parade*
McGuirk, Leslie. *Lucky Tucker*
Nolan, Janet. *The St. Patrick's Day shillelagh*
Rockwell, Anne. *St. Patrick's Day*
Schertle, Alice. *Jeremy Bean's St. Patrick's Day*
Tucker, Kathy. *The leprechaun in the basement*
Wojciechowski, Susan. *A fine St. Patrick's Day*

Holidays – Sukkot

Goldin, Barbara Diamond. *Night lights*
Kimmel, Eric A. *The mysterious guests*
Korngold, Jamie S. *Sadie's sukkah breakfast*
Polacco, Patricia. *Tikvah means hope*
Vorst, Rochel Groner. *The sukkah that I built*

Holidays – Thanksgiving

Alcott, Louisa May. *An old-fashioned Thanksgiving*
Allegra, Mike. *Sarah gives thanks*
Anderson, Derek. *Over the river*
Anderson, Laurie Halse. *Thank you, Sarah*
Turkey pox
Archer, Peggy. *Turkey surprise*
Atwell, Debby. *The Thanksgiving door*
Auch, Mary Jane. *Beauty and the beaks*
Balian, Lorna. *Sometimes it's turkey*
Bartlett, Robert Merrill. *The story of Thanksgiving*
Bateman, Teresa. *Gus, the pilgrim turkey*
A plump and perky turkey
Behrens, June. *The feast of Thanksgiving*
Berenstain, Stan and Jan. *The Berenstain bears and the prize pumpkin*
Bildner, Phil. *Turkey Bowl*
Borden, Louise. *Thanksgiving is . . .*
Brown, Marc. *Arthur's Thanksgiving*
Bruchac, Joseph. *Squanto's journey*
Bunting, Eve. *How many days to America?*
A turkey for Thanksgiving
Carlstrom, Nancy White. *Thanksgiving Day at our house*
Child, Lydia Maria. *Over the river and through the wood*
Over the river and through the wood: the New England boy's song about Thanksgiving Day
Corey, Shana. *Milly and the Macy's Parade*
Cowley, Joy. *Gracias, the Thanksgiving turkey*
Cox, Judy. *One is a feast for Mouse*
Dalgliesh, Alice. *The Thanksgiving story*
dePaola, Tomie. *My first Thanksgiving*
Devlin, Wende. *Cranberry Thanksgiving*
Elliott, Laura Malone. *Thanksgiving Day thanks*
Flanagan, Alice K. *Thanksgiving*
Friedman, Laurie. *Thanksgiving rules*
Geisert, Arthur. *Nursery crimes*
George, Jean Craighead. *The first Thanksgiving*
Gibbons, Gail. *Thanksgiving Day*
Greene, Rhonda Gowler. *The very first Thanksgiving Day*
Haugen, Brenda. *Thanksgiving*
Herman, Charlotte. *The memory cupboard*
Holub, Joan. *Turkeys never gobble*
Hopkins, Lee Bennett. *Merrily comes our harvest in*
Horowitz, Dave. *The ugly pumpkin*
Jackson, Alison. *I know an old lady who swallowed a pie*
Janice. *Little Bear's Thanksgiving*
Jennings, Sharon. *Franklin's Thanksgiving*
Jules, Jacqueline. *Duck for Turkey Day*
Kimmelman, Leslie. *Round the turkey*
Klingel, Cynthia Fitterer. *Thanksgiving*
Koller, Jackie French. *Nickommoh!*
Kroll, Steven. *Oh, what a Thanksgiving!*
One tough turkey
The squirrels' Thanksgiving
Kroll, Virginia L. *The Thanksgiving bowl*
Lakin, Patricia. *Fat chance Thanksgiving*
Leedy, Loreen. *The dragon Thanksgiving feast*
Levine, Abby. *This is the turkey*
McCully, Emily Arnold. *An outlaw Thanksgiving*
Markes, Julie. *Thanks for Thanksgiving*
Marzollo, Jean. *Thanksgiving cats*
Mayr, Diane. *Run, Turkey, run*
Melmed, Laura Krauss. *This first Thanksgiving*
Metaxas, Eric. *Squanto and the miracle of Thanksgiving*
Miller, Edna. *Mousekin's Thanksgiving*
Myra, Harold Lawrence. *Thanksgiving: what makes it special?*
Nikola-Lisa, W. *One, two, three Thanksgiving!*
Pilkey, Dav. *'Twas the night before Thanksgiving*
Pomeranc, Marion Hess. *The can-do Thanksgiving*
Rael, Elsa Okon. *Rivka's first Thanksgiving*
Reed, Lynn Rowe. *Thelonius Turkey lives!*
Rockwell, Anne. *Thanksgiving Day*
Rosen, Michael. *A Thanksgiving wish*
Shore, Diane Z. *This is the feast*
Silvano, Wendi. *Turkey trouble*
Smith, Mavis. *'Twas the day after Thanksgiving*
Spinelli, Eileen. *Thanksgiving at the Tappletons'*
Stanley, Diane. *Thanksgiving on Plymouth Plantation*
Stock, Catherine. *Thanksgiving treat*
Thorpe, Kiki. *A comfy, cozy Thanksgiving*
Tresselt, Alvin R. *Autumn harvest*
Watson, Wendy. *Thanksgiving at our house*
Wheeler, Lisa. *Turk and Runt*
Willey, Margaret. *Thanksgiving with me*
Williams, Barbara. *Chester Chipmunk's Thanksgiving*

Holidays – Tu B'Shevat

Rosenberg, Madelyn. *Happy birthday, tree!*

Rouss, Sylvia A. *Sammy Spider's first Tu B'Shevat*

Holidays – Valentine's Day

Adams, Adrienne. *The great Valentine's Day balloon race*
Andrews, Julie. *The very fairy princess follows her heart*
Balian, Lorna. *A sweetheart for Valentine*
Brown, Marc. *Arthur's Valentine*
Bunting, Eve. *The Valentine bears*
Capucilli, Alyssa Satin. *Biscuit's Valentine's Day*
Carlson, Nancy. *Henry and the Valentine surprise*
Louanne Pig in the mysterious Valentine
Carr, Jan. *Sweet hearts*
Carrick, Carol. *Valentine*
Casey, Tina. *The runaway Valentine*
Cheshire, Marc. *Love and kisses, Eloise*
Choldenko, Gennifer. *A giant crush*
Cohen, Miriam. *Bee my Valentine!*
Dean, James. *Valentine's Day is cool*
deGroat, Diane. *Roses are pink, your feet really stink*
Demas, Corinne. *Valentine surprise*
Devlin, Wende. *Cranberry Valentine*
Dodd, Emma. *Foxy in love*
Elliott, Laura Malone. *A string of hearts*
Ferber, Brenda A. *The yuckiest, stinkiest, best Valentine ever*
Flanagan, Alice K. *Valentine's Day*
Friedman, Laurie. *Love, Ruby Valentine*
Ruby Valentine saves the day
Gantos, Jack. *Rotten Ralph's rotten romance*
Gibbons, Gail. *Valentine's Day*
Valentine's Day is —
Henkes, Kevin. *Lilly's chocolate heart*
Hurd, Thacher. *Little Mouse's big Valentine*
Jackson, Alison. *The ballad of Valentine*
Kroll, Steven. *Will you be my valentine?*
Let me call you sweetheart
Little Bear's Valentine
Livingston, Myra Cohn. *Valentine poems*
London, Jonathan. *Froggy's first kiss*
Marzollo, Jean. *Valentine cats*
Modell, Frank. *One zillion valentines*
Parish, Herman. *Amelia Bedelia's first valentine*
Petersen, David. *Snowy Valentine*
Poydar, Nancy. *Rhyme time Valentine*
Roberts, Bethany. *Valentine mice!*
Rockwell, Anne. *Valentine's Day*
Rylant, Cynthia. *If you'll be my Valentine*
Sabuda, Robert. *St. Valentine*
Samuels, Barbara. *Happy Valentine's Day, Dolores*
Schulman, Janet. *10 Valentine friends*
Schweninger, Ann. *Valentine friends*
Scotton, Rob. *Love, Splat*
Shannon, George. *Heart to heart*
Sharmat, Marjorie Weinman. *The best Valentine in the world*
Spinelli, Eileen. *Somebody loves you, Mr. Hatch*
Stevenson, James. *Happy Valentine's Day, Emma!*
A village full of valentines
Stock, Catherine. *Secret Valentine*
Sutton, Benn. *Hedgehug*
Wallace, Nancy Elizabeth. *The Valentine Express*
Watson, Clyde. *Valentine foxes*
Watson, Wendy. *A Valentine for you*
Weeks, Sarah. *Be mine, be mine, sweet valentine*

Holidays – Yom Kippur

Fishman, Cathy Goldberg. *On Rosh Hashanah and Yom Kippur*
Kimmelman, Leslie. *Sound the shofar!*
Rouss, Sylvia A. *Sammy Spider's first Yom Kippur*

Holocaust

Adler, David A. *Hiding from the Nazis*
Lehman-Wilzig, Tami. *Keeping the promise*
Morris, Ann. *Grandma Esther remembers*
Oberman, Sheldon. *By the Hanukkah light*
Russo, Marisabina. *I will come back for you*
Schnur, Steven. *The tie man's miracle*
Ungerer, Tomi. *Otto: the autobiography of a teddy bear*
Wiviott, Meg. *Benno and the night of broken glass*

Homeless

Andersen, Hans Christian. *The little match girl*, ill. by Rachel Isadora
The little match girl, ill. by Blair Lent
The little match girl, ill. by Jerry Pinkney
The little matchstick girl
Barrett, Mary Brigid. *Shoebox Sam*
Bartoletti, Susan Campbell. *The Christmas promise*
Bromley, Anne C. *The lunch thief*
Bunting, Eve. *December*
Fly away home
Chinn, Karen. *Sam and the lucky money*
Cole, Brock. *Good enough to eat*
Day, Marie. *Edward the "crazy man"*
DiCamillo, Kate. *Great joy*
King, Stephen Michael. *Mutt dog!*
McPhail, David. *The teddy bear*
Meggs, Libby Phillips. *Go home!*
Myers, Christopher. *Sparrows*
Polacco, Patricia. *I can hear the sun*
Seskin, Steve. *A chance to shine*
Stewart, Joel. *Addis Berner Bear forgets*
Sweet, Melissa. *Tupelo rides the rails*
Tibo, Gilles. *The cowboy kid*
Vainio, Pirkko. *The Christmas angel*
Williams, Laura E. *The can man*

Homes, houses

Alger, Leclaire Gowans. *Always room for one more*
Altman, Linda Jacobs. *Amelia's road*
Angelou, Maya. *My painted house, my friendly chicken, and me*
Arnosky, Jim. *Armadillo's orange*
Ashman, Linda. *Castles, caves, and honeycombs*
Creaky old house
Banks, Kate. *The great blue house*
Barton, Byron. *Building a house*
Bean, Jonathan. *Building our house*
Beaton, Clare. *At home / A la maison*
Beil, Karen Magnuson. *Jack's house*
Blackstone, Stella. *Bear at home*
Bloom, Suzanne. *No place for a pig*
Brett, Jan. *The three little dassies*
Brown, Margaret Wise. *Robin's room*
Burton, Virginia Lee. *The little house*
Carle, Eric. *A house for Hermit Crab*
My very first book of homes
Carter, David A. *In a dark, dark wood*
Cecka, Melanie. *Violet comes to stay*
Clements, Andrew. *Slippers at home*

Collicott, Sharleen. *Mildred and Sam*
Crum, Shutta. *A family for Old Mill Farm*
Daly, Niki. *Welcome to Zanzibar Road*
Davies, Jacqueline. *The house takes a vacation*
Deacon, Alexis. *A place to call home*
DePrisco, Dorothea. *Who lives here?*
DiSalvo, DyAnne. *A castle on Viola Street*
Edwards, Pamela Duncan. *Jack and Jill's treehouse*
The old house
Emberley, Rebecca. *My house / Mi casa*
My room / Mi cuarto
Emerman, Ellen. *Just right: the story of a Jewish home*
Emmett, Jonathan. *No place like home*
Falkenstern, Lisa. *A dragon moves in*
Fitzgerald, Joanne. *This is me and where I am*
Flanagan, Alice K. *Call Mr. Vasquez, he'll fix it!*
Mr. Paul and Mr. Luecke build communities
The Wilsons, a house-painting team
Foley, Greg. *Purple Little Bird*
Fries, Claudia. *A pig is moving in*
Fuge, Charles. *Where to, Little Wombat?*
Gamble, Isobel. *Who's that?*
Gibbons, Gail. *How a house is built*
Gleeson, Libby. *Clancy and Millie and the very fine house*
Gliori, Debi. *Flora's surprise*
Mr. Bear to the rescue
Goode, Diane. *Tiger trouble*
Grahame, Kenneth. *A wind in the willows Christmas*
Grimm, Edward. *The doorman*
Grindley, Sally. *A new room for William*
Groundhog at Evergreen Road
Guthrie, Woody. *Bling blang*
Harper, Charise Mericle. *The trouble with normal*
Harrington, Janice N. *Busy-busy Little Chick*
Harrison, David L. *The alligator in the closet and other poems around the house*
A perfect home for a family
Hayward, Linda. *A day in the life of a builder*
Hewitt, Sally. *Animal homes*
Hickman, Pamela. *It's moving day!*
Hill, Lee Sullivan. *Homes keep us warm*
Hill, Susanna Leonard. *The house that Mack built*
Hindley, Judy. *Rosy's visitors*
Hoberman, Mary Ann. *A house is a house for me*
Hoffman, Elizabeth Stokes. *Miss Renée's mice*
Holmes, Anita. *Who dug that hole?*
Howard, Ginger. *William's house*
Hughes, Shirley. *Alfie gets in first*
Jackson, Alison. *If the shoe fits*
Jahn-Clough, Lisa. *On the hill*
Jocelyn, Marthe. *Mayfly*
Johnson, D. B. *Eddie's kingdom*
Henry builds a cabin
Kay, Verla. *Covered wagons, bumpy trails*
Keens-Douglas, Richardo. *Anancy and the haunted house*
Keister, Douglas. *To grandmother's house*
Kelly, Irene. *Even an octopus needs a home*
Even an ostrich needs a nest
Ketteman, Helen. *The three little gators*
Kirk, Daniel. *Library mouse: home sweet home*
Kittinger, Jo S. *The house on Dirty-Third Street*
Kleven, Elisa. *Welcome home, Mouse*
Kohara, Kazuno. *Ghosts in the house!*
Kooser, Ted. *House held up by trees*
Krauss, Ruth. *A very special house*
Krosoczka, Jarrett J. *Annie was warned*
Lakin, Patricia. *Fat chance Thanksgiving*
Laroche, Giles. *If you lived here*
Larsen, Andrew. *In the tree house*
Laverde, Arlene. *Alaska's three pigs*
Lewis, J. Patrick. *Good mousekeeping*
Lillegard, Dee. *Wake up house!*
Lin, Grace. *Okie-dokie, Artichokie*
Lindbergh, Reeve. *Our nest*
Lish, Ted. *The three little puppies and the big bad flea*
Ljungkvist, Laura. *Follow the line through the house*
Lyon, George Ella. *One lucky girl*
You and me and home sweet home
McCarty, Peter. *Little bunny on the move*
Marino, Gianna. *Too tall houses*
Masurel, Claire. *Two homes*
Meddaugh, Susan. *The best place*
Medearis, Angela Shelf. *The ghost of Sifty-Sifty Sam*
Meserve, Adria. *No room for Napoleon*
Miller, Elizabeth I. *Just like home / Como en mi tierra*
Miller, William. *A house by the river*
Moore, Inga. *A house in the woods*
Morris, Ann. *Houses and homes*
Moss, Miriam. *A new house for Smudge*
Mozelle, Shirley. *The kitchen talks*
The pig is in the pantry, the cat is on the shelf
Muller, Robin. *Badger's new house*
Nagda, Anne Whitehead. *A home for panda*
Napoli, Donna Jo. *Albert*
Neitzel, Shirley. *The house I'll build for the wrens*
Newhouse, Maxwell. *The house that Max built*
Nolen, Jerdine. *In my momma's kitchen*
Orloff, Karen Kaufman. *I wanna new room*
Patschke, Steve. *The spooky book*
Peaceful moments in the wild
Pérez, Amada Irma. *My very own room / Mi propio cuartito*
Petach, Heidi. *Wee three pigs*
Pienkowski, Jan. *Haunted house*
Pinkwater, Daniel. *Rainy morning*
Posey, Lee. *Night rabbits*
Pratt, Pierre. *Home*
Prigger, Mary Skillings. *Aunt Minnie and the twister*
Provencher, Rose-Marie. *Mouse cleaning*
Raye, Rebekah. *The very best bed*
Ritz, Karen. *Windows with birds*
Rocklin, Joanne. *This book is haunted*
Rosen, Michael. *This is our house*
Rounds, Glen. *Sod houses on the Great Plains*
Ryan, Pam Muñoz. *Armadillos sleep in dugouts*
Rylant, Cynthia. *The bird house*
Bunny bungalow
San Souci, Robert D. *The boy and the ghost*
The house in the sky
Schaefer, Lola M. *Apartment*
Homes ABC
Homes 123
House
Mobile home
Tugboats
Shannon, George. *Lizard's home*
Shoulders, Michael. *The ABC book of American homes*
Siegel, Mark. *Moving house*
Sierra, Judy. *The house that Drac built*
'Twas the fright before Christmas
Silverman, Erica. *There was a wee woman . . .*
Slade, Suzanne. *The house that George built*
Smith, Linda. *The inside tree*
Spinelli, Eileen. *A safe place called home*
Sophie's masterpiece

Stanley, Diane. *Goldie and the three bears*
Sturges, Philemon. *I love tools!*
Suen, Anastasia. *Raise the roof*
Swanson, Susan Marie. *The house in the night*
Swinburne, Stephen R. *Swallows in the birdhouse*
Tafuri, Nancy. *Silly little goose!*
Thermes, Jennifer. *When I was built*
Tolman, Marije. *The tree house*
Trivizas, Eugenios. *The three little wolves and the big bad pig*
Turner, Ann Warren. *The Christmas house*
Van Allsburg, Chris. *Two bad ants*
Veit, Barbara. *Who stole my house?*
Waite, Judy. *Mouse, look out!*
Walsh, Melanie. *Do lions live on lily pads?*
Weeks, Sarah. *Mrs. McNosh and the great big squash*
Wellington, Monica. *Riki's birdhouse*
Wells, Rosemary. *The house in the mail*
Weston, Martha. *Tuck's haunted house*
Williams, Brenda. *Home for a tiger, home for a bear*
Winer, Yvonne. *Birds build nests*
Wong, Janet S. *Homegrown house*
Wormell, Christopher. *Blue Rabbit and friends*
Yee, Wong Herbert. *Eek! There's a mouse in the house*
Mrs. Brown went to town
Yin. *Dear Santa, please come to the 19th floor*
Yum, Hyewon. *This is our house*
Zalben, Jane Breskin. *Hey, Mama Goose*
Zelinsky, Paul O. *The maid and the mouse and the odd-shaped house*
Ziefert, Harriet. *Birdhouse for rent*

Homework

Cook, Lisa Broadie. *Peanut butter and homework sandwiches*
deGroat, Diane. *Jingle bells, homework smells*
Kroll, Virginia L. *Honest Ashley*
Yorinks, Arthur. *Homework*

Homosexuality

Brannen, Sarah S. *Uncle Bobby's wedding*
Newman, Lesléa. *Daddy, Papa, and me*
Donovan's big day
Heather has two mommies
Mommy, Mama, and Me
Oelschlager, Vanita. *A tale of two daddies*
A tale of two mommies
Polacco, Patricia. *In our mothers' house*
Richardson, Justin. *And Tango makes three*
Vigna, Judith. *My two uncles*
Willhoite, Michael. *Daddy's roommate*

Honesty *see* Character traits – honesty

Honey bees *see* Insects – bees

Hope *see* Character traits – hopefulness

Hopefulness *see* Character traits – hopefulness

Horses, rocking *see* Toys – rocking horses

Hospitals

Bemelmans, Ludwig. *Madeline*
Bennett, Howard J. *Harry goes to the hospital*
Bond, Michael. *Paddington Bear goes to the hospital*
Cork, Barbara Taylor. *Katie goes to the hospital*
Cousins, Lucy. *Maisy goes to the hospital*
Curious George makes pancakes
Dooley, Virginia. *Tubes in my ears*
Flanagan, Alice K. *Ask Nurse Pfaff, she'll help you!*
Garhan Attebury, Nancy. *Out and about at the hospital*
Gutman, Anne. *Gaspard in the hospital*
Hapka, Cathy. *Margret and H. A. Rey's Merry Christmas, Curious George*
Hatkoff, Juliana Lee. *Good-bye tonsils*
Jennings, Sharon. *Franklin goes to the hospital*
Lloyd, Sam. *Doctor Meow's big emergency*
Pirner, Connie White. *Even little kids get diabetes*
Rey, Margret. *Curious George goes to the hospital*
Rogers, Fred. *Going to the hospital*
Rosenberg, Maxine B. *Mommy's in the hospital having a baby*
Ross, Tony. *I don't want to go to the hospital!*
Schaefer, Lola M. *Hospital*
Urdahl, Catherine. *Emma's question*
Whybrow, Ian. *Sammy and the robots*
Wild, Margaret. *Going home*
Mr. Nick's knitting
Zonta, Pat. *Jessica's x-ray*

Hotels

Cheshire, Marc. *Here comes Eloise!*
Diviny, Sean. *Halloween Motel*
Hucke, Johannes. *Pip in the Grand Hotel*
Kovacs, Deborah. *Katie Copley*
Paraskevas, Betty. *Chocolate at the Four Seasons*
Pinkwater, Daniel. *At the Hotel Larry*
Bad bears and a bunny
Stem, J. David. *Kay Thompson's Eloise in Hollywood*
Stevens, Jan Romero. *Carlos digs to China / Carlos excava hasta la China*
Stevenson, James. *The Sea View Hotel*
Thompson, Kay. *Kay Thompson's Eloise*
Kay Thompson's Eloise at Christmastime
Kay Thompson's Eloise in Moscow
Kay Thompson's Eloise takes a bawth (sic)
Kay Thompson's Eloise's what I absolutely love love love
Waber, Bernard. *Do you see a mouse?*
Wojtowycz, David. *Animal antics from 1 to 10*
Yee, Wong Herbert. *Fireman Small, fire down below*

Hugging

Bond, Felicia. *Big hugs, little hugs*
Cabrera, Jane. *Kitty's cuddles*
Church, Caroline Jayne. *One more hug for Madison*
Clements, Andrew. *Slippers loves to run*
Crandall, Court. *Hugville*
Downing, Julie. *No hugs till Saturday*
Gershator, Phillis. *Time for a hug*
Grambling, Lois G. *T. Rex and the Mother's Day hug*
Henry, Jed. *Cheer up, Mouse!*
Horning, Sandra. *The giant hug*
Isop, Laurie. *How do you hug a porcupine?*
Katz, Karen. *Daddy hugs 1 2 3*
Mommy hugs
McBratney, Sam. *There, there*

Macdonald, Maryann. *How to hug*
Mayhew, James. *Where's my hug?*
Melling, David. *Hugless Douglas*
Oldland, Nicholas. *Big bear hug*
Rowe, John A. *I want a hug*
Ryder, Joanne. *Won't you be my hugaroo?*
Saltzberg, Barney. *Cornelius P. Mud, are you ready for bed?*
Schmid, Paul. *Hugs from Pearl*
Spinelli, Eileen. *Hug a bug*
Stein, David Ezra. *Monster hug!*
Sutton, Benn. *Hedgehug*
Walsh, Joanna. *The perfect hug*
Warnes, Tim. *Daddy hug*

Humorous stories

Aardema, Verna. *Oh, Kojo! How could you!*
What's so funny, Ketu?
Who's in Rabbit's house?
Abbott, Bud. *Who's on first?*
Agee, Jon. *Nothing*
The retired kid
Ahlberg, Allan. *The adventures of Bert*
A bit more Bert
The Goldilocks variations
Half a pig
Aliki. *Digging up dinosaurs*
Allard, Harry. *Miss Nelson has a field day*
Miss Nelson is back
Miss Nelson is missing!
Starlight goes to town
The Stupids die
The Stupids have a ball
The Stupids step out
The Stupids take off
Andersen, Hans Christian. *The emperor's new clothes*, ill. by Virginia Lee Burton
The emperor's new clothes, ill. by Robert Byrd
The emperor's new clothes, ill. by Serena Curmi
The emperor's new clothes, ill. by Charlene DeLage
The emperor's new clothes, ill. by Jack Delano
The emperor's new clothes, ill. by Anne Rockwell
The emperor's new clothes, ill. by Janet Stevens
The emperor's new clothes, ill. by Eve Tharlet
The emperor's new clothes: a tale set in China
The princess and the pea
Anderson, Laurie Halse. *The hair of Zoe Fleefenbacher goes to school*
Andreae, Giles. *Pants*
Angleberger, Tom. *Crankee Doodle*
Apperley, Dawn. *Don't wake the baby*
Armstrong, Jennifer. *Once upon a banana*
Armstrong-Ellis, Carey. *Prudy's problem and how she solved it*
Arnold, Tedd. *Dirty Gert*
Arnosky, Jim. *Outdoors on foot*
Asch, Frank. *The Daily Comet*
Sand cake
Ashman, Linda. *To the beach!*
Auch, Mary Jane. *Bantam of the opera*
Chickerella
The plot chickens
The princess and the pizza
Axelrod, Amy. *They'll believe me when I'm gone*
Azore, Barbara. *Wanda and the frogs*
Bachelet, Gilles. *My cat, the silliest cat in the world*
When the silliest cat was small
Balian, Lorna. *Leprechauns never lie*
Bardhan-Quallen, Sudipta. *Hampire!*
Barnett, Mac. *Extra yarn*
Oh no!
Oh no! Not again!
Barrett, Judi. *The marshmallow incident*
Never take a shark to the dentist and other things not to do
Bell, Cece. *Bee-Wigged*
Bingham, Kelly. *Z is for Moose*
Black, Michael Ian. *A pig parade is a terrible idea*
The purple kangaroo
Bloch, Serge. *Butterflies in my stomach and other school hazards*
You are what you eat
Boldt, Mike. *123 versus ABC*
Braun, Eric. *Trust me, Jack's beanstalk stinks*
Bridwell, Norman. *The witch grows up*
Briggs, Raymond. *Jim and the beanstalk*
Broach, Elise. *When dinosaurs came with everything*
Brown, Jeff. *Flat Stanley*, ill. by Scott Nash
Flat Stanley, ill. by Tomi Ungerer
Brown, Peter. *Children make terrible pets*
Buckley, Michael. *Kel Gilligan's daredevil stunt show*
Burningham, John. *The shopping basket*
Buzzeo, Toni. *One cool friend*
Calmenson, Stephanie. *Oopsy, teacher!*
Carroll, Lewis. *Jabberwocky*
Castle, Caroline. *Naughty!*
Cazet, Denys. *Elvis the rooster almost goes to heaven*
Chaconas, Dori. *Don't slam the door!*
Charlip, Remy. *"Mother, mother I feel sick"*
Child, Lauren. *What planet are you from Clarice Bean?*
Christelow, Eileen. *The desperate dog writes again*
Letters from a desperate dog
Where's the big bad wolf?
Coffelt, Nancy. *Catch that baby!*
Cole, Babette. *Truelove*
Cole, Brock. *Buttons*
Collington, Peter. *Clever cat*
Collins, Ross. *Dear Vampa*
Conway, David. *The great fairy tale disaster*
The great nursery rhyme disaster
Cooper, Helen. *Dog biscuit*
Corey, Shana. *First graders from Mars: Horus's horrible day*
First graders from Mars: Nergal and the Great Space Race
First graders from Mars: Tera, star student
First graders from Mars: The problem with Pelly
Cosentino, Ralph. *The marvelous misadventures of — Fun-Boy*
Cox, Judy. *Happy birthday, Mrs. Millie!*
Pick a pumpkin, Mrs. Millie!
Crimi, Carolyn. *The Louds move in!*
Crisp, Marty. *Totally polar*
Cronin, Doreen. *Duck for President*
M.O.M. (Mom Operating Manual)
Cutbill, Andy. *The cow that laid an egg*
First week at cow school
Czekaj, Jef. *A call for a new alphabet*
Cat secrets
Daugherty, James Henry. *Andy and the lion*
Davis, Katie. *Mabel the Tooth Fairy and how she got her job*
Day, Alexandra. *The fairy dogfather*
De Beer, Hans. *Oh no, Ono!*
DeFelice, Cynthia C. *Nelly May has her say*
One potato, two potato

Demas, Corinne. *Always in trouble*
dePaola, Tomie. *Bill and Pete*
Merry Christmas, Strega Nona
Strega Nona
Strega Nona meets her match
Strega Nona's harvest
Strega Nona's magic lessons
De Regniers, Beatrice Schenk. *May I bring a friend?*
Diesen, Deborah. *The barefooted, bad-tempered baby brigade*
Dillon, Jana. *Lucky O'Leprechaun comes to America*
DiPucchio, Kelly. *Zombie in love*
Ditchfield, Christin. *Cowlick!*
Donaldson, Julia. *Tyrannosaurus Drip*
Dorros, Alex. *Número uno*
Dorros, Arthur. *City chicken*
When the pigs took over
Downard, Barry. *The Race of the Century*
Downs, Mike. *Pig giggles and rabbit rhymes*
Duffield, Katy. *Farmer McPeepers and his missing milk cows*
Durant, Alan. *Burger boy*
Duvoisin, Roger Antoine. *Petunia*
Edwards, Pamela Duncan. *Muldoon*
Princess Pigtoria and the pea
Edwards, Wallace. *The extinct files*
Egan, Tim. *Dodsworth in New York*
Ehlert, Lois. *Rrralph*
Elliott, David. *Hazel Nutt, Alien Hunter*
Hazel Nutt, mad scientist
Elliott, George. *The boy who loved bananas*
Elsdale, Bob. *Mac side up*
Ernst, Lisa Campbell. *Goldilocks returns*
Feiffer, Jules. *Bark, George*
Feiffer, Kate. *My mom is trying to ruin my life*
Ferber, Brenda A. *The yuckiest, stinkiest, best Valentine ever*
Fisher, Carolyn. *A twisted tale*
Foreman, George. *Let George do it!*
Fox, Mem. *A particular cow*
Frank, John. *The toughest cowboy, Or, How the Wild West was tamed*
Frazee, Marla. *A couple of boys have the best week ever*
French, Jackie. *Pete the sheep-sheep*
Gaiman, Neil. *Crazy hair*
Garriel, Barbara S. *I know a shy fellow who swallowed a cello*
Gay, Marie-Louise. *Good morning Sam*
Goode, Diane. *Diane Goode's book of silly stories and songs*
Goodhart, Pippa. *Arthur's tractor*
Graber, Janet. *Jacob and the polar bears*
Gravett, Emily. *Wolves*
Green, Stephanie. *Not just another moose*
Greenberg, David. *Crocs!*
Grey, Mini. *The adventures of the dish and the spoon*
Griffin, Kitty. *Cowboy Sam and those confounded secrets*
The foot-stomping adventures of Clementine Sweet
Grimm, Jacob and Wilhelm. *As luck would have it*
Grossman, Bill. *Timothy Tunny swallowed a bunny*
Hale, Bruce. *Snoring Beauty*
Hammill, Matt. *Sir Reginald's logbook*
Hanson, Warren. *It's Monday, Mrs. Jolly Bones!*
Hapka, Cathy. *Margret and H. A. Rey's Merry Christmas, Curious George*
Harper, Lee. *The Emperor's cool clothes*
Hart, Christopher. *Merwin, master of disguise*
Hawkes, Kevin. *The wicked big toddlah*
The wicked big toddlah goes to New York
Hayward, Linda. *Pepe and Papa*
Heide, Florence Parry. *Always listen to your mother*
Helakoski, Leslie. *Big chickens fly the coop*
Helmer, Marilyn. *Critter riddles*
Helquist, Brett. *Roger, the jolly pirate*
Hicks, Barbara Jean. *The secret life of Walter Kitty*
Himmelman, John. *Cows to the rescue*
Hoberman, Mary Ann. *"It's simple," said Simon*
Hodgkinson, Leigh. *Goldilocks and just one bear*
Holub, Joan. *Little red writing*
Zero the hero
Hornsey, Chris. *Why do I have to eat off the floor?*
Horowitz, Dave. *Humpty Dumpty climbs again*
Hort, Lenny. *Tie your socks and clap your feet*
Huget, Jennifer LaRue. *How to clean your room in 10 easy steps*
Hutchins, Pat. *Clocks and more clocks*
Don't forget the bacon!
Rosie's walk
I invited a dragon to dinner
Irving, Washington. *The legend of Sleepy Hollow*
Jackson, Alison. *I know an old lady who swallowed a pie*
Jagtenberg, Yvonne. *Jack the wolf*
James, Simon. *Baby Brains and RoboMom*
Jeffers, Oliver. *Stuck*
Jennings, Sharon. *C'mere, boy!*
Jobling, Curtis. *Frankenstein's cat*
Johnson, Crockett. *Harold and the purple crayon*
Harold at the North Pole
A picture for Harold's room
Johnson, Doug. *Substitute teacher plans*
Johnson, Paul Brett. *Bearhide and crow*
The goose who went off in a huff
Little Bunny Foo Foo
Johnson, Suzanne C. *Fribbity ribbit*
Johnston, Tony. *Go track a yak*
Jordan, Mary Ellen. *Lazy Daisy, cranky Frankie*
Katz, Alan. *Don't say that word!*
Keller, Laurie. *Arnie the doughnut*
Grandpa Gazillion's number yard
Kelley, Ellen A. *My life as a chicken*
Kelley, Marty. *Twelve terrible things*
Ketteman, Helen. *Bubba the cowboy prince*
Kimmel, Elizabeth Cody. *My penguin Osbert*
Kirk, Daniel. *Jack and Jill*
Klassen, Jon. *This is not my hat*
Könnecke, Ole. *Anton can do magic*
Krall, Dan. *The great lollipop caper*
Krosoczka, Jarrett J. *Baghead*
Kuszyk, R. Nicholas. *R Robot saves lunch*
Laden, Nina. *Bad dog*
Landström, Lena. *Boo and Baa have company*
Landström, Olof. *Boo and Baa get wet*
Boo and Baa in the woods
LaReau, Kara. *Otto: the boy who loved cars*
LaRochelle, David. *The end*
How Martha saved her parents from green beans
Lasky, Kathryn. *The emperor's old clothes*
Lear, Edward. *The Quangle Wangle's hat*
Lendler, Ian. *An undone fairy tale*
Lerman, Josh. *How to raise Mom and Dad*
Lester, Julius. *Sam and the tigers*
Levitin, Sonia. *When Elephant goes to a party*
Lewis, J. Patrick. *The bookworm's feast*
Tulip at the bat
Lewis, Kevin. *Not inside this house!*
Lichtenheld, Tom. *E-mergency!*

What's with this room?
Lindaman, Jane. *Zip it!*
Ljungkvist, Laura. *Toni's topsy-turvy telephone day*
Loehr, Patrick. *Mucumber McGee and the lunch lady's liver*
London, Jonathan. *Froggy goes to the doctor*
Long, Steffanie. *Such a silly baby!*
Low, Alice. *Aunt Lucy went to buy a hat*
Lowell, Susan. *The bootmaker and the elves*
Lubner, Susan. *Ruthie Bon Bair, do not go to bed with wringing wet hair!*
Lucke, Deb. *Sneezenesia*
McAllister, Angela. *My mom has x-ray vision*
McClements, George. *Baron von Baddie and the ice ray incident*
MacDonald, Amy. *Quentin Fenton Herter three*
McElmurry, Jill. *I'm not a baby!*
McGhee, Alison. *The case of the missing donut*
McGough, Roger. *What on earth can it be?*
McGovern, Ann. *Too much noise*
McGraw, Sheila. *Pussycats everywhere*
Mack, Jeff. *Frog and Fly*
McLarey, Kristina Thermaenius. *When you take a pig to a party*
McNamara, Margaret. *The three little aliens and the big bad robot*
McNaughton, Colin. *Preston's goal!*
Suddenly!
Madison, Alan. *Pecorino plays ball*
Pecorino's first concert
Mahy, Margaret. *Bubble trouble*
The man from the land of Fandango
A summery Saturday morning
Marcellino, Fred. *I, crocodile*
Marshall, James. *The Cut-Ups*
The Cut-Ups at Camp Custer
The Cut-Ups carry on
The Cut-Ups crack up
The Cut-Ups cut loose
Marx, Patricia. *Dot in Larryland*
Mayer, Mercer. *What do you do with a kangaroo?*
Meddaugh, Susan. *Cinderella's rat*
Melling, David. *The Scallywags*
Metzger, Steve. *Detective Blue*
Milgrim, David. *Eddie gets ready for school*
Minters, Frances. *Princess Fishtail*
Mitter, Matt. *Once upon a rhyme*
Moser, Lisa. *Railroad Hank*
Mould, Wendy. *Ants in my pants*
Muntean, Michaela. *Do not open this book!*
Myer, Andy. *Delia's dull day*
Myller, Rolf. *How big is a foot?*
Nedwidek, John. *Ducks don't wear socks*
Nesbitt, Kenn. *More bears!*
Newman, Jeff. *Hippo! No, rhino!*
Nishimura, Kae. *Dinah*
Noble, Trinka Hakes. *The day Jimmy's boa ate the wash*
Jimmy's boa and the big splash birthday bash
Jimmy's boa bounces back
Nolen, Jerdine. *Plantzilla goes to camp*
Novak, Matt. *The everything machine*
Numberman, Neil. *Do not build a Frankenstein!*
Numeroff, Laura Joffe. *Laura Numeroff's 10-step guide to living with your monster*
Sometimes I wonder if poodles like noodles
Oller, Erika. *The cabbage soup solution*
O'Malley, Kevin. *Animal crackers fly the coop*
Gimme cracked corn and I will share
Orlean, Susan. *Lazy little loafers*
Page, Gail. *Bobo and the new neighbor*
Palatini, Margie. *Boo-hoo moo*
Ding dong ding dong
Earthquack
Oink?
Three French hens
The three silly billies
The web files
Parish, Herman. *Amelia Bedelia's first apple pie*
Amelia Bedelia's first day of school
Amelia Bedelia's first field trip
Amelia Bedelia's first valentine
Go west, Amelia Bedelia!
Parkinson, Curtis. *Emily's eighteen aunts*
Parr, Todd. *Underwear do's and don'ts*
Passen, Lisa. *The incredible shrinking teacher*
Pearson, Tracey Campbell. *Bob*
Peet, Bill. *Big bad Bruce*
Buford the little bighorn
Chester the worldly pig
Countdown to Christmas
Cowardly Clyde
Eli
Hubert's hair-raising adventures
Huge Harold
Jennifer and Josephine
Jethro and Joel were a troll
Kermit the hermit
Merle the high flying squirrel
Randy's dandy lions
Perl, Erica S. *Chicken Butt's back!*
Pichon, Liz. *The three horrid little pigs*
Pilkey, Dav. *The Dumb Bunnies*
The Dumb Bunnies' Easter
The Dumb Bunnies go to the zoo
Make way for Dumb Bunnies
The Silly Gooses
Pinkney, Brian. *The adventures of sparrowboy*
Pinkwater, Daniel. *At the Hotel Larry*
Bad bear detectives
Bad bears and a bunny
Bad bears go visiting
Bad bears in the big city
Bongo Larry
Dancing Larry
I am the dog
Ice-cream Larry
The picture of Morty and Ray
Sleepover Larry
Young Larry
Plourde, Lynn. *Grandpappy snippy snappies*
Only cows allowed!
Pigs in the mud in the middle of the rud
Polacco, Patricia. *In Enzo's splendid gardens*
Potter, Beatrix. *The tale of Tom Kitten*
Prelutsky, Jack. *The baby uggs are hatching*
The queen of Eene
The Random House book of poetry for children
The snopp on the sidewalk and other poems
Primavera, Elise. *Thumb love*
Prince, Joshua. *I saw an ant in a parking lot*
I saw an ant on the railroad track
Pulver, Robin. *Mrs. Toggle's zipper*
Rader, Laura. *Santa's new suit*
Ransom, Jeanie Franz. *What do parents do? (. . . When you're not home)*
Rausch, Molly. *My cold went on vacation*
Redeker, Kent. *Don't squish the sasquatch!*

Regan, Dian Curtis. *How do you know it's Halloween?*
Regan, Lara Jo. *What is Mr. Winkle?*
Reichert, Amy. *Take your mama to work today*
Reiss, Mike. *Late for school*
Merry un-Christmas
Santa claustrophobia
Rennert, Laura Joy. *Buying, training and caring for your dinosaur*
Rex, Michael. *Furious George goes bananas*
Goodnight goon
You can do anything, Daddy!
Rey, H. A. *Cecily G and the nine monkeys*
Curious George
Curious George gets a medal
Curious George rides a bike
Curious George takes a job
Elizabite
The original Curious George
Rey, Margret. *Billy's picture*
Curious George flies a kite
Curious George goes to the hospital
Richardson, Bill. *But if they do*
Robinson, Bruce. *The obvious elephant*
Robinson, Fiona. *What animals really like*
Robinson, Michelle. *What to do if an elephant stands on your foot*
Root, Phyllis. *Rattletrap car*
Rattletrap car [board book]
Rosen, Michael. *Howler*
Rosenberg, Madelyn. *The Schmutzy Family*
Rosenthal, Amy Krouse. *Chopsticks*
Rosenthal, Marc. *Phooey!*
Rosoff, Meg. *Jumpy Jack and Googily*
Wild boars cook
Rovetch, Lissa. *Ook the book*
Salley, Coleen. *Epossumondas*
Epossumondas saves the day
Samuels, Barbara. *Dolores meets her match*
Duncan and Dolores
Happy Valentine's Day, Dolores
Sandburg, Carl. *The Huckabuck family and how they raised popcorn in Nebraska and quit and came back*
Sauer, Tammi. *Chicken dance*
Sayre, April Pulley. *Noodle Man*
Scheer, Julian. *Rain makes applesauce*
Schneider, Christine M. *Horace P. Tuttle, magician extraordinaire*
Schneider, Howie. *Fast 'n Snappy*
Schnitzler, Pattie L. *Widdermaker*
Scieszka, Jon. *Robot Zot!*
Scotton, Rob. *Splat the cat*
Sendak, Maurice. *Pierre*
Seuss, Dr. *And to think that I saw it on Mulberry Street*
Bartholomew and the Oobleck
Did I ever tell you how lucky you are?
Gerald McBoing Boing
Gerald McBoing Boing sound book
Happy birthday to you!
Horton hatches the egg
Horton hears a Who!
How the Grinch stole Christmas
I can lick 30 tigers today and other stories
I had trouble getting to Solla Sollew
If I ran the circus
If I ran the zoo
The king's stilts
The Lorax
McElligot's pool
On beyond zebra
Scrambled eggs super!
The Sneetches, and other stories
Thidwick, the big-hearted moose
Sharratt, Nick. *The foggy, foggy forest*
Shaskan, Trisha Speed. *Seriously, Cinderella is so annoying!*
Shea, Bob. *Big plans*
Sierra, Judy. *Mind your manners, B. B. Wolf*
Tell the truth, B. B. Wolf
Silverstein, Shel. *A giraffe and a half*
Singer, Marilyn. *Creature carnival*
Solomon sneezes
Sloat, Teri. *There was an old lady who swallowed a trout*
Slobodkina, Esphyr. *Caps for sale*
Circus caps for sale
Smith, Alex T. *Foxy and Egg*
Smith, Lane. *It's a book*
John, Paul, George and Ben
Madam President
Pinocchio, the boy
Smith, Linda. *The inside tree*
Snell, Gordon. *'Twas the day after Christmas*
Solheim, James. *Born yesterday*
Souhami, Jessica. *The little, little house*
Soule, Jean Conder. *Never tease a weasel*
Spier, Peter. *Bored — nothing to do!*
Oh, were they ever happy!
Spinelli, Eileen. *Six hogs on a scooter*
Thanksgiving at the Tappletons'
Stampler, Ann Redisch. *Go home, Mrs. Beekman!*
Stanley, Diane. *The Giant and the beanstalk*
Goldie and the three bears
Rumpelstiltskin's daughter
Steig, Jeanne. *Fleas!*
Steig, William. *Farmer Palmer's wagon ride*
Stein, David Ezra. *Interrupting chicken*
Stevens, Janet. *And the dish ran away with the spoon*
Help me, Mr. Mutt!
The little red pen
Stevenson, James. *Don't make me laugh*
Happy Valentine's Day, Emma!
The worst person in the world at Crab Beach
Stoeke, Janet Morgan. *The Loopy Coop hens: letting go*
Stuchner, Joan Betty. *Can hens give milk?*
Tankard, Jeremy. *Me hungry!*
Taxali, Gary. *This is silly!*
Taylor, Alastair. *Swollobog*
Taylor, Sean. *The ring went zing!*
Robomop
Teague, Mark. *Dear Mrs. LaRue*
Funny farm
Tellis, Annabel. *If my dad were a dog*
Terasaki, Stanley Todd. *Ghosts for breakfast*
Thomas, Jan. *Here comes the big, mean dust bunny!*
Is everyone ready for fun?
Rhyming dust bunnies
Tougas, Chris. *Art's supplies*
Trapani, Iza. *Baa baa black sheep*
Baa baa black sheep [board book]
Trenc, Milan. *Another night at the museum*
Ungerer, Tomi. *Crictor*
Urbanovic, Jackie. *Duck soup*
Van Kampen, Vlasta. *It couldn't be worse*
Van Laan, Nancy. *Little baby Bobby*
Van Woerkom, Dorothy. *Donkey Ysabel*

Walker, Sally M. *The Vowel family*
Walton, Rick. *Just me and 6,000 rats*
Weaver, Tess. *Frederick Finch, loudmouth*
Weeks, Sarah. *Bite me, I'm a book*
Mrs. McNosh hangs up her wash
Oh my gosh, Mrs. McNosh!
Weinberg, Larry. *The Forgetful Bears help Santa*
Welling, Peter J. *Shawn O'Hisser, the last snake in Ireland*
Westcott, Nadine Bernard. *The lady with the alligator purse*
Why did the chicken cross the road?
Wiese, Kurt. *Fish in the air*
Wilcox, Leah. *Waking Beauty*
Willems, Mo. *Don't let the pigeon drive the bus*
Don't let the pigeon stay up late!
The duckling gets a cookie!?
Goldilocks and the three dinosaurs
The pigeon finds a hot dog!
The pigeon has feelings, too!
Willis, Jeanne. *Hippospotamus*
That's not funny!
Wise, William. *Dinosaurs forever*
Wisniewski, David. *Tough cookie*
Wood, Audrey. *King Bidgood's in the bathtub*
Yankovic, Al. *My new teacher and me!*
Yorinks, Arthur. *Company's coming*
Company's going
What a trip!
Zemach, Margot. *It could always be worse*

Hurrying *see* Behavior – hurrying

Hygiene *see also* Character traits – cleanliness; Health & fitness

Bernheimer, Kate. *The girl who wouldn't brush her hair*
Brennan, Eileen. *Dirtball Pete*
Fox, Lee. *Ella Kazoo will not brush her hair*
Garelli, Cristina. *Farm friends clean up*
Kelly, Mij. *Achoo!*
Langreuter, Jutta. *Little Bear brushes his teeth*
Palatini, Margie. *Gorgonzola*
Puttock, Simon. *Squeaky clean*
Vestergaard, Hope. *Potty animals*
Weinert, Matthias. *No bath, no cake!*

Identity *see* Self-concept

Illness

Alda, Arlene. *Iris has a virus*
Bauer, Sepp. *The Christmas rose*
Bedford, David. *Shaggy Dog and the terrible itch*
Bemelmans, Ludwig. *Madeline's Christmas*
Bennett, Howard J. *Harry goes to the hospital*
Berger, Melvin. *Germs make me sick!*
Butler, Dori Hillestad. *My grandpa had a stroke*
Cannon, Janell. *Little Yau*
Carter, Alden R. *Seeing things my way*
Charlip, Remy. *"Mother, mother I feel sick"*
Coerr, Eleanor. *Sadako*
Cork, Barbara Taylor. *Katie goes to the hospital*
Cowan, Charlotte. *Peeper has a fever*
Sadie's sore throat
Cowell, Cressida. *Hiccup the seasick Viking*
dePaola, Tomie. *Now one foot, now the other*
Dewdney, Anna. *Llama Llama home with Mama*
Dooley, Virginia. *Tubes in my ears*
Finchler, Judy. *Miss Malarkey won't be in today*
Gaiman, Neil. *Chu's day*
Garhan Attebury, Nancy. *Out and about at the hospital*
Gibbons, Gail. *Say woof!*
Glaser, Jason. *Pinkeye*
Gordon, Sharon. *Cuts and scrapes*
Pinkeye
Gray, Kes. *The "Get well soon" book*
Greene, Rhonda Gowler. *Barnyard song*
Gretz, Susanna. *Teddy bears cure a cold*
Hobbie, Holly. *Toot and Puddle: wish you were here*
Hull, Rod. *Mr. Betts and Mr. Potts*
Inns, Christopher. *Next! please*
Jeffs, Stephanie. *Jenny*
Jennings, Sharon. *Franklin goes to the hospital*
Keane, Dave. *Sloppy Joe*
Ketteman, Helen. *If Beaver had a fever*
Kroll, Steven. *The big bunny and the Easter eggs*
Kroll, Virginia L. *Pink paper swans*
Louie, Therese On. *Raymond's perfect present*
Lyon, George Ella. *Cecil's story*
MacDonald, Amy. *Rachel Fister's blister*
McKissack, Patricia C. *Precious and the Boo Hag*
MacLachlan, Patricia. *The sick day*
McPhail, David. *The bear's toothache*
Madonna. *Yakov and the seven thieves*
Maier, Inger. *Ben's flying flowers*
Marshall, James. *Yummers!*
Martin, Jacqueline Briggs. *Chicken joy on Redbean Road*
Miller, Pat. *Substitute Groundhog*
Milway, Katie Smith. *Mimi's village and how basic health care transformed it*
Modarressi, Mitra. *Taking care of Mama*
Murphy, Jill. *Mr. Large in charge*
Neitzel, Shirley. *I'm not feeling well today*
Newsome, Jill. *Dream dancer*
Nimmo, Jenny. *Esmeralda and the children next door*
Oelschlager, Vanita. *I came from the water*
Oppenheim, Shulamith Levey. *Ali and the magic stew*
Peet, Mal. *Cloud tea monkeys*
Perkins, Lynne Rae. *The broken cat*
Raschka, Chris. *The purple balloon*
Ray, Jane. *The dollhouse fairy*
Rees, Douglas. *Jeannette Claus saves Christmas*
Reider, Katja. *The big little sneeze*
Rogers, Fred. *Going to the hospital*
Rohmer, Harriet. *Atariba and Niguayona*
Rose, Naomi C. *Tashi and the Tibetan flower cure*
Rosenfeld, Dina Herman. *Get well soon*
Rylant, Cynthia. *Little Whistle's medicine*
Silver packages
Say, Allen. *A river dream*
Schick, Eleanor. *Mama*

Schubert, Leda. *The Princess of Borscht*
Scotton, Rob. *Splat says thank you!*
Singer, Marilyn. *Boo hoo boo-boo*
Soros, Barbara. *Tenzin's deer*
Soto, Gary. *Chato goes cruisin'*
Spalding, Andrea. *It's raining, it's pouring*
Stead, Philip C. *A sick day for Amos McGee*
Stroud, Bettye. *Down home at Miss Dessa's*
Tankard, Jeremy. *Boo hoo Bird*
Thurber, James. *Many moons*, ill. by Marc Simont
Many moons, ill. by Louis Slobodkin
Urdahl, Catherine. *Emma's question*
Vigna, Judith. *I wish my daddy didn't drink so much*
Wells, Rosemary. *The island light*
Whybrow, Ian. *Sammy and the robots*
Wild, Margaret. *Mr. Nick's knitting*
Williams, Vera B. *Music, music for everyone*
Wilson, Karma. *Bear feels sick*
Winter, Jeanette. *Henri's scissors*
Yolen, Jane. *How do dinosaurs get well soon?*
Zonta, Pat. *Jessica's x-ray*

Illness – AIDS

Beake, Lesley. *Home now*
Wiener, Lori S., et al *Be a friend*

Illness – alcoholism

Langsen, Richard C. *When someone in the family drinks too much*

Illness – allergies

Berger, Lou. *Dream dog*
Berger, Melvin. *Why I sneeze, shiver, hiccup, and yawn*
Fliess, Sue. *A gluten-free birthday for me!*
Geras, Adèle. *The Cats of Cuckoo Square, Geejay the Hero*
Harrison, Troon. *Aaron's awful allergies*
Havill, Juanita. *Jamaica is thankful*
Howe, James. *Horace and Morris say cheese (which makes Dolores sneeze!)*
Koster, Gloria. *The peanut-free cafe*
McClure, Wendy. *The princess and the peanut allergy*
Pulver, Robin. *Christmas kitten, home at last*

Illness – Alzheimer's

Abeele, Veronique van den. *Still my Grandma*
Acheson, Alison. *Grandpa's music*
Altman, Linda Jacobs. *Singing with Momma Lou*
Gerdner, Linda. *Grandfather's story cloth / Yawg daim paj ntaub dab neeg*

Illness – asthma

Berger, Melvin. *Why I sneeze, shiver, hiccup, and yawn*
Carter, Alden R. *I'm tougher than asthma!*
Golding, Theresa Martin. *Abby's asthma and the big race*
Gordon, Sharon. *Asthma*
Hurwitz, Johanna. *Mighty Monty*
Matthies, Janna. *Peter, the knight with asthma*
Thomas, Pat. *Why is it so hard to breathe?*

Illness – cancer

Aigner-Clark, Julie. *You are the best medicine*
Bridge, Chris. *Andrew's story*
Lin, Grace. *Robert's snowflakes*
Matthies, Janna. *The goodbye cancer garden*
Moore-Mallinos, Jennifer. *Mom has cancer!*
Napoli, Donna Jo. *Flamingo dream*
North, Sherry. *Champ's story*
Numeroff, Laura Joffe. *The hope tree*
Polacco, Patricia. *Betty Doll*
The lemonade club
Ries, Lori. *Punk wig*
Tinkham, Kelly A. *Hair for Mama*
Tusa, Tricia. *Bunnies in my head*
Watters, Debbie, et al. *Where's Mom's hair?*
Winthrop, Elizabeth. *Promises*

Illness – chicken pox

Anderson, Laurie Halse. *Turkey pox*
Brown, Marc. *Arthur's chicken pox*
Cazet, Denys. *The octopus*
Dealey, Erin. *Goldie Locks has chicken pox*
Kelley, True. *I've got chicken pox*
Rosenberry, Vera. *When Vera was sick*
Smith, Maggie. *Dear Daisy, get well soon*

Illness – cold (disease)

Becker, Bonny. *The sniffles for Bear*
Breznak, Irene. *Sneezy Louise*
Cowan, Charlotte. *Katie caught a cold*
Emmett, Jonathan. *The best gift of all*
Hest, Amy. *Guess who, Baby Duck*
Mandel, Peter. *Zoo ah-choooo*
Mayer, Pamela. *The Grandma cure*
Posthuma, Sieb. *Benny*
Rausch, Molly. *My cold went on vacation*
Slate, Joseph. *Miss Bindergarten stays home from kindergarten*
Van Leeuwen, Jean. *Chicken soup*

Illness – diabetes

Carter, Alden R. *I'm tougher than diabetes!*
De Anda, Diane. *A day without sugar / Un dia sin azucar*
Pirner, Connie White. *Even little kids get diabetes*
Ruiz-Flores, Lupe. *Alicia's fruity drinks / Las aguas frescas de Alicia*

Illness – epilepsy

Lears, Laurie. *Becky the brave*

Illness – influenza

Bateman, Teresa. *Farm flu*
Reynolds, Marilynn. *The name of the child*

Illness – mental illness

Day, Marie. *Edward the "crazy man"*
Niner, Holly L. *Mr. Worry*

Illness – poliomyelitis

Chaconas, Dori. *Dancing with Katya*

De Anda, Diane. *Dancing Miranda / Baila, Miranda, baila*

Illness – tonsillectomy

Hatkoff, Juliana Lee. *Good-bye tonsils*

Imagination

Abercrombie, Barbara. *The show-and-tell lion*
Adlerman, Daniel. *Africa calling*
Agee, Jon. *The incredible painting of Felix Clousseau*
Ahlberg, Allan. *The pencil*
The shopping expedition
Alko, Selina. *Every-day dress-up*
Allen, Joy. *Princess Palooza*
Almond, David. *Kate, the cat and the moon*
Andersen, Hans Christian. *The dinosaur's new clothes*
The emperor's new clothes, ill. by Angela Barrett
The emperor's new clothes, ill. by Virginia Lee Burton
The emperor's new clothes, ill. by Robert Byrd
The emperor's new clothes, ill. by Serena Curmi
The emperor's new clothes, ill. by Charlene DeLage
The emperor's new clothes, ill. by Jack Delano
The emperor's new clothes, ill. by Anne Rockwell
The emperor's new clothes, ill. by Janet Stevens
Andreae, Giles. *Captain Flinn and the pirate dinosaurs*
Captain Flinn and the pirate dinosaurs: missing treasure!
Andreasen, Dan. *The treasure bath*
Anglund, Joan Walsh. *The brave cowboy*
Anno, Mitsumasa. *Anno's alphabet*
Anno's Britain
Anno's counting book
Anno's counting house
Anno's Italy
Anno's journey
Anno's U.S.A.
Arnold, Tedd. *No jumping on the bed!*
No more water in the tub!
Ashburn, Boni. *The fort that Jack built*
Ashman, Linda. *Just another morning*
Audet, Martine. *Martin on the moon*
Baguley, Elizabeth. *Meggie moon*
Baillie, Marilyn. *Nose to toes*
Baker, Roberta. *No ordinary Olive*
Bang, Molly. *The grey lady and the strawberry snatcher*
Banks, Kate. *The eraserheads*
Max's castle
Max's dragon
Barnett, Mac. *Extra yarn*
Barrett, Judi. *Cloudy with a chance of meatballs*
Base, Graeme. *The legend of the Golden Snail*
Beaty, Andrea. *Artist Ted*
Doctor Ted
Firefighter Ted
Becker, Aaron. *Journey*
Becker, Shari. *Maxwell's mountain*
Bently, Peter. *King Jack and the dragon*
Berenstain, Stan and Jan. *The Berenstain bears in the dark*
Berger, Lou. *Dream dog*
Bergman, Mara. *Oliver who would not sleep!*
Billingsley, Franny. *Big bad bunny*
Black, Michael Ian. *I'm bored*
The purple kangaroo
Bloom, Suzanne. *Feeding friendsies*
A mighty fine time machine
Bowman, Patty. *The amazing Hamweenie*
Bradley, Kimberly Brubaker. *Favorite things*
Brami, Elisbeth. *Mommy time*
Brennan-Nelson, Denise. *Willow*
Brimner, Larry Dane. *Cat on wheels*
Brown, Calef. *Tippintown*
Brown, Lisa. *How to be*
Browne, Anthony. *Gorilla*
Bunting, Eve. *Little Badger, terror of the seven seas*
Pirate boy
Burningham, John. *Come away from the water, Shirley*
John Patrick Norman McHennessy — the boy who was always late
Cader, Lisa Lebowitz. *When I wear my crown*
When I wear my tiara
Callahan, Sean. *A wild Father's Day*
Carle, Eric. *Little cloud*
Little cloud [board book]
Carlson, Nancy. *Henry's amazing imagination!*
Carman, William. *What's that noise?*
Carrick, Carol. *Patrick's dinosaurs*
Patrick's dinosaurs on the Internet
What happened to Patrick's dinosaurs?
Carter, Anne Laurel. *Circus play*
Cartier, Wesley. *Marco's run*
Chen, Chih-Yuan. *On my way to buy eggs*
Chessa, Francesca. *The mysterious package*
Child, Lauren. *I will never not ever eat a tomato*
Chin, Jason. *Coral reefs*
Redwoods
Choung, Euh-hee. *Minji's Salon*
Chwast, Seymour. *Get dressed!*
Harry, I need you!
Clayton, Dallas. *An awesome book!*
Clibbon, Meg. *Imagine you're a fairy!*
Imagine you're a mermaid!
Imagine you're a pirate!
Imagine you're a wizard!
Cohen, Caron Lee. *Martin and the giant lions*
Comden, Betty, et al. *Flying to Neverland with Peter Pan*
Cooper, Helen. *Tatty-Ratty*
Cosentino, Ralph. *The marvelous misadventures of — Fun-Boy*
Costanza, Stephen. *Vivaldi and the invisible orchestra*
Cowley, Joy. *Mrs. Goodstory*
Coy, John. *Vroomaloom zoom*
Coyle, Carmela Lavigna. *Do super heroes have teddy bears?*
Creech, Sharon. *Fishing in the air*
Crews, Nina. *Below*
I'll catch the moon
You are here
Crisp, Marty. *Totally polar*
Crumpacker, Bunny. *Alexander's pretending day*
Cumming, Hannah. *The red boat*
DaCosta, Barbara. *Nighttime Ninja*
Daly, Cathleen. *Prudence wants a pet*
Davey, Owen. *Night Knight*
Dematons, Charlotte. *Let's go*
Devernay, Laetitia. *The conductor*
De Vries, Maggie. *How sleep found Tabitha*
Dewan, Ted. *Baby gets the zapper*
DiTerlizzi, Tony. *Jimmy Zangwow's out-of-this-world, moon pie adventure*
Docherty, Thomas. *To the beach*

Dodd, Emma. *What pet to get?*
Dodd, Lynley. *A dragon in a wagon*
Donahue, Shari Faden. *The zebra-striped whale with the polka-dot tail*
Donaldson, Julia. *The fish who cried wolf*
Dornbusch, Erica. *Finding Kate's shoes*
Drawson, Blair. *All along the river*
Dubosarsky, Ursula. *Rex*
Dunbar, Polly. *Dog Blue*
Flyaway Katie
Dunnick, Regan. *Sweet dreams, Douglas*
Ellery, Amanda. *If I had a dragon*
If I were a jungle animal
Ets, Marie Hall. *In the forest*
Fagan, Carl. *Mr. Zinger's hat*
Faller, Regis. *The adventures of Polo*
Polo
Polo and the dragon
Falwell, Cathryn. *Word wizard*
Fancher, Lou. *Star climbing*
Fearnley, Jan. *A special something*
Fitzpatrick, Marie-Louise. *I'm a tiger, too!*
Fogliano, Julie. *If you want to see a whale*
Fosberry, Jennifer. *Isabella*
Isabella star of the story
Fox, Christyan. *Astronaut PiggyWiggy*
Fire fighter PiggyWiggy
Fox, Mem. *Tell me about your day today*
Freedman, Deborah. *Scribble*
Freeman, Don. *Quiet! There's a canary in the library*
Fuge, Charles. *I know a rhino*
Gammell, Stephen. *Mudkin*
Gardiner, Lindsey. *Here come Poppy and Max*
When Poppy and Max grow up
Gardner, Sally. *Mama, don't go out tonight*
Gay, Marie-Louise. *Caramba*
When Stella was very, very small
George, Lindsay Barrett. *My bunny and me*
Geras, Adèle. *The nutcracker*
Gerstein, Mordicai. *A book*
The first drawing
How to bicycle to the moon to plant sunflowers
Gibala-Broxholm, Scott. *Maddie's monster dad*
Gilmore, Rachna. *Making grizzle grow*
Glassman, Peter. *My dad's job*
Gleeson, Libby. *Clancy and Millie and the very fine house*
Glenn, Sharlee. *Just what Mama needs*
Godwin, Laura. *Little white dog*
Gorbachev, Valeri. *Turtle's penguin day*
Graham, Bob. *Max*
Gravett, Emily. *Spells*
Gray, Nigel. *Time to play!*
Greenfield, Eloise. *The friendly four*
I can draw a weeposaur and other dinosaurs
Gregory, Nan. *Wild Girl and Gran*
Grey, Mini. *Traction Man meets Turbodog*
Griff. *Shark-mad Stanley*
Gwynne, Fred. *A chocolate moose for dinner*
A little pigeon toad
Hague, Michael. *The nutcracker*
Hamburg, Jennifer. *A moose that says mooooooooooo*
Hammill, Matt. *Sir Reginald's logbook*
Handford, Martin. *Where's Waldo? The fantastic journey*
Harper, Charise Mericle. *The best birthday ever!*
Harper, Jamie. *Miles to go*
Harper, Jessica. *Nora's room*
Harris, Robie H. *Mail Harry to the moon!*
Maybe a bear ate it!
Hayles, Marsha. *He saves the day*
Heap, Sue. *Danny's drawing book*
What shall we play?
Heidbreder, Robert. *I wished for a unicorn*
Henkes, Kevin. *Little white rabbit*
My garden
Hennessy, B. G. *The dinosaur who lived in my backyard*
Hicks, Barbara Jean. *Monsters don't eat broccoli*
Hindley, Judy. *Rosy's visitors*
Hines, Anna Grossnickle. *Gramma's walk*
I am a backhoe
I am a Tyrannosaurus
Hoffmann, E. T. A. *The nutcracker,* ill. by Renée Graef
The nutcracker, ill. by Alison Jay
The nutcracker, ill. by Peter Malone
The nutcracker, ill. by Maurice Sendak
The nutcracker, ill. by Lisbeth Zwerger
The Nutcracker and the Mouse King
The nutcracker ballet
Honey, Elizabeth. *That's not a daffodil!*
Hoppe, Paul. *Hat*
Horacek, Petr. *My elephant*
Hoshino, Felicia. *Sora and the cloud*
Hughes, Susan. *Earth to Audrey*
Huneck, Stephen. *Sally gets a job*
Husband, Amy. *Dear Teacher*
Ichikawa, Satomi. *Come fly with me*
My little train
Imagine that! poems of never-was
Irwin, Michael. *Bears in my bed*
Jackson, Ellen. *The seven seas*
James, Simon. *Dear Mr. Blueberry*
Janni, Rebecca. *Every cowgirl needs a horse*
Jarka, Jeff. *Love that kitty!*
Love that puppy!
Jenkins, Emily. *Daffodil, crocodile*
Jennings, Sharon. *The happily ever afternoon*
Jeram, Anita. *I love my little storybook*
Jessell, Tim. *Falcon*
Jeyaveeran, Ruth. *The road to Mumbai*
Johnson, Angela. *Lily Brown's paintings*
Lottie Paris lives here
Johnson, Crockett. *Harold and the purple crayon*
Harold at the North Pole
Magic beach
A picture for Harold's room
Johnson, D. B. *Henry climbs a mountain*
Jonas, Ann. *The trek*
Jones, Sylvie. *Who's in the tub?*
Joosse, Barbara. *Roawr!*
Joyce, William. *The Man in the Moon*
Jukes, Mavis. *You're a bear*
Kamish, Daniel. *Diggy Dan*
Kanninen, Barbara. *A story with pictures*
Kay, Julia. *Gulliver Snip*
Keats, Ezra Jack. *Dreams*
The trip
Kellogg, Steven. *Ralph's secret weapon*
Kenney, Sean. *Cool creations in 35 pieces*
Kirk, Daniel. *Honk honk! Beep beep!*
Knight, Hilary. *Hilary Knight's the owl and the pussy-cat*
Krauss, Ruth. *A very special house*
Kroll, Steven. *Oh, what a Thanksgiving!*
The Tyrannosaurus game
Kroll, Virginia L. *Faraway drums*

Kruusval, Catarina. *Franny's friends*
Kwon, Yoon-duck. *My cat copies me*
Lamb, Rosy. *Paul meets Bernadette*
Landa, Norbert. *The great monster hunt*
Landry, Leo. *Eat your peas, Ivy Louise!*
LaRochelle, David. *It's a tiger*
1+1=5
Larsen, Andrew. *The imaginary garden*
Lawson, Dorie McCullough. *Tex*
Lawson, Janet. *Audrey and Barbara*
Lazo, Caroline. *Someday when my cat can talk*
Lee, Suzy. *Shadow*
Lehman, Barbara. *Museum trip*
Rainstorm
The secret box
Trainstop
Levert, Mireille. *An island in the soup*
The princess who had almost everything
Lewis, Anne Margaret. *Fly blanky fly*
Liao, Jimmy. *The sound of colors*
Light, Steve. *Zephyr takes flight*
Lionni, Leo. *Let's make rabbits*
Lithgow, John. *Carnival of the animals*
I'm a manatee
Liwska, Renata. *Red wagon*
Ljungkvist, Laura. *Follow the line*
Follow the line through the house
London, Jonathan. *Here comes Doctor Hippo*
Here comes firefighter Hippo
My big rig
Long, Melinda. *How I became a pirate*
Loth, Sebastian. *Zelda the Varigoose*
Loux, Lynn C. *The day I could fly*
Lovell, Patty. *Have fun, Molly Lou Melon*
Lucas, David. *Nutmeg*
Something to do
Luenn, Nancy. *Nessa's story*
Lynn, Sarah. *1-2-3 va-va-vroom!*
Lyon, George Ella. *Who came down that road?*
McAllister, Angela. *Harry's box*
McCarthy, Meghan. *The adventures of Patty and the big red bus*
McCarty, Peter. *Chloe*
Moon plane
McCourt, Lisa. *Good night, Princess Pruney Toes*
Happy Halloween, Stinky Face
I love you, Stinky Face
It's time for school, Stinky Face
Merry Christmas, Stinky Face
McGhee, Alison. *Song of middle C*
McKay, Hilary. *Pirates ahoy!*
McLerran, Alice. *Roxaboxen*
McNaughton, Colin. *Not last night but the night before*
McNeil, Florence. *Sail away*
McPhail, David. *Boy on the brink*
Edward and the pirates
Edward in the jungle
Emma in charge
Moony B. Finch, fastest draw in the West
Pig Pig and the magic photo album
Pig Pig rides
Tinker and Tom and the Star Baby
McQuinn, Anna. *Lola loves stories*
Mahy, Margaret. *The green bath*
The man from the land of Fandango
Maizes, Sarah. *On my way to bed*
On my way to the bath
Manceau, Edouard. *Windblown*
Manushkin, Fran. *The shivers in the fridge*
Marlowe, Pete. *One Arabian morning*
Marshall, James. *George and Martha 'round and 'round*
Martin, Rafe. *Will's mammoth*
Marzollo, Jean. *I spy fantasy*
Pretend you're a cat
Mayer, Mercer. *The bravest knight*
Mayhew, James. *Ella Bella ballerina and The Nutcracker*
Katie and the sunflowers
Mazer, Anne. *The salamander room*
Melanson, Luc. *Topsy-Turvy Town*
Menchin, Scott. *Harry goes to dog school*
What if everything had legs?
Merz, Jennifer J. *Playground day*
Milgrim, David. *Cows can't fly*
Minor, Wendell. *How big could your pumpkin grow?*
Miranda, Anne. *Beep! beep!*
Moers, Hermann. *Rufus and Max*
Moore, Jodi. *When a dragon moves in*
Morris, Ann. *Play*
Morris, Bob. *Crispin the Terrible*
Morstad, Julie. *How to*
Most, Bernard. *If the dinosaurs came back*
Mould, Wendy. *Ants in my pants*
Murphy, Stuart J. *Jack the builder*
Na, Il Sung. *The thingamabob*
Neitzel, Shirley. *I'm taking a trip on my train*
Ness, Evaline. *Sam, Bangs, and moonshine*
Neubecker, Robert. *Beasty bath*
What little boys are made of
Newman, Nanette. *What will you be, Grandma?*
Nickle, John. *TV Rex*
Niemann, Christoph. *That's how!*
Norwich, William D. *Molly and the magic dress*
Numeroff, Laura Joffe. *Chimps don't wear glasses*
O'Connor, George. *Ker-splash!*
Ohi, Ruth. *The couch was a castle*
O'Leary, Sara. *When you were small*
O'Malley, Kevin. *Straight to the pole*
Orr, Wendy. *The princess and her panther*
Palatini, Margie. *Zak's lunch*
Pallotta, Jerry. *Dory story*
Paolilli, Paul. *Silver seeds*
Paradis, Susan. *Snow princess*
Park, Frances. *Where on earth is my bagel?*
Parkhurst, Carolyn. *Cooking with Henry and Elliebelly*
Parlato, Stephen. *The world that loved books*
Patricelli, Leslie. *The birthday box*
Faster! Faster!
Higher! Higher!
Pearce, Philippa. *Amy's three best things*
Pearson, Susan. *We're going on a ghost hunt*
Peck, Jan. *Pirate treasure hunt!*
Way up high in a tall green tree
Pennypacker, Sara. *Stuart's cape*
Pericoli, Matteo. *Tommaso and the missing line*
Perlman, Janet. *The Emperor Penguin's new clothes*
Peters, Lisa Westberg. *Cold little duck, duck, duck*
Pinder, Eric. *If all the animals came inside*
Pinto, Sara. *Apples and oranges*
Piven, Hanoch. *Let's make faces*
Pizzoli, Greg. *The watermelon seed*
Plecas, Jennifer. *Pretend*
Polacco, Patricia. *Appelemando's dreams*
Emma Kate
My ol' man

Portis, Antoinette. *No es una caja / not a box*
Not a box
Not a stick
Princess Super Kitty
Postgate, Daniel. *The snagglegrollop*
Powell, Polly. *Just dessert*
Prelutsky, Jack. *The baby uggs are hatching*
Behold the bold umbrellaphant and other poems
Ride a purple pelican
The snopp on the sidewalk and other poems
Stardines swim high across the sky
Pringle, Laurence P. *Jesse builds a road*
Proimos, James. *The best bike ride ever*
Purcell, Rebecca. *Super Chicken*
Pym, Tasha. *Have you ever seen a sneep?*
Raschka, Chris. *Little black crow*
Rasmussen, Halfdan. *The ladder*
Reed, Neil. *The midnight unicorn*
Reidy, Jean. *Light up the night*
Time out for monsters!
Reiser, Lynn. *Any kind of dog*
Rex, Michael. *My fire engine*
Rinck, Maranke. *I feel a foot!*
Robbins, Beth. *Tom's afraid of the dark*
Roberts, Bethany. *Gramps and the fire dragon*
Rosie to the rescue
Roberts, Victoria. *The best pet ever*
Rogers, Gregory. *The hero of Little Street*
Rosen, Michael J. *With a dog like that, a kid like me . . .*
Rosenberg, Liz. *The carousel*
Rossell, Judith. *Oliver*
Russo, Marisabina. *The big brown box*
Ruzzier, Sergio. *Hey, Rabbit!*
Ryan, Pam Muñoz. *Mud is cake*
Ryder, Joanne. *Tyrannosaurus time*
Rymond, Lynda Gene. *Oscar and the mooncats*
Sabuda, Robert. *Peter Pan*
Salas, Laura Purdie. *A leaf can be . . .*
Saltzberg, Barney. *Andrew drew and drew*
SanAngelo, Ryan. *Eddie spaghetti*
Sanders-Wells, Linda. *Maggie's monkeys*
Sava, Donna Lynn. *Teddy bear dreams*
Say, Allen. *Emma's rug*
Schaap, Martine. *Mop's mountain adventure*
Schaefer, Carole Lexa. *Dragon dancing*
Kids like us
Someone says
Schmid, Paul. *Petunia goes wild*
Schotter, Roni. *Captain Bob sets sail*
Captain Bob takes flight
Scieszka, Jon. *Walt Disney's Alice in Wonderland*
Segal, John. *Pirates don't take baths*
Sendak, Maurice. *In the night kitchen*
The sign on Rosie's door
Where the wild things are
Seuss, Dr. *And to think that I saw it on Mulberry Street*
McElligot's pool
Shaw, Charles Green. *It looked like spilt milk*
Shea, Bob. *Big plans*
Sheldon, Dyan. *Unicorn dreams*
Sheridan, Sara. *I'm me!*
Sheth, Kashmira. *Tiger in my soup*
Shields, Carol Diggory. *I am really a princess*
Shipton, Jonathan. *What if?*
Shulevitz, Uri. *How I learned geography*
One Monday morning
So sleepy story
When I wore my sailor suit
Sif, Birgitta. *Oliver*
Sís, Peter. *Ballerina*
Dinosaur!
Madlenka
Madlenka, soccer star
Ship ahoy!
Slate, Jenny. *Marcel the shell with shoes on*
Smith, Dana Kessimakis. *A brave spaceboy*
Smith, Linda. *Sir Cassie to the rescue*
Soman, David. *The amazing adventures of Bumblebee Boy*
Ladybug Girl
Ladybug Girl and Bingo
Ladybug Girl and Bumblebee Boy
Ladybug Girl and the big snow
Ladybug Girl and the Bug Squad
Spalding, Andrea. *It's raining, it's pouring*
Spinelli, Eileen. *In my new yellow shirt*
Someday
Stadler, Alexander. *Beverly Billingsly takes the cake*
Steig, William. *Pete's a pizza*
Toby, who are you?
Stein, Mathilde. *The child cruncher*
Stern, Ellen. *I saw a bullfrog*
Stevenson, James. *Worse than Willy!*
Stevenson, Robert Louis. *Block city*, ill. by Daniel Kirk
Block city, ill. by Ashley Wolff
The little land
Stuve-Bodeen, Stephanie. *Elizabeti's doll*
Surovec, Yasmine. *I see Kitty*
Sweetland, Nancy Rose. *If I could / Si yo pudiera*
Tafuri, Nancy. *Junglewalk*
Tanaka, Shinsuke. *Wings*
Tarpley, Natasha Anastasia. *Joe-Joe's first flight*
Teague, Mark. *The lost and found*
Thomas, Jan. *Can you make a scary face?*
Thompson, Colin. *Falling angels*
Thompson, Richard. *The night walker*
Tibo, Gilles. *The cowboy kid*
Tompert, Ann. *Little Fox goes to the end of the world*
Tone, Satoe. *The very big carrot*
Tougas, Chris. *Art's supplies*
Trapani, Iza. *I'm a little teapot*
Tullet, Hervé. *The book with a hole*
Press here
Turner, Sandy. *Grow up*
Tusa, Tricia. *Bunnies in my head*
Follow me
Underwood, Deborah. *Part-time princess*
Van Allsburg, Chris. *Bad day at Riverbend*
The garden of Abdul Gasazi
Jumanji
The mysteries of Harris Burdick
The polar express
Probuditi!
Van Camp, Katie. *CookieBot!*
Harry and Horsie
Vaughan, Marcia Kapok. *We're going on a ghost hunt*
Vigna, Judith. *Boot weather*
Villeneuve, Anne. *Loula is leaving for Africa*
Viorst, Judith. *The good-bye book*
My mama says there aren't any zombies, ghosts, vampires, creatures, demons, monsters, fiends, goblins, or things
Waddell, Martin. *Bee frog*
Wadham, Tim. *The queen of France*
Wahl, Jan. *I met a dinosaur*
Waldman, Neil. *The starry night*

Wallner, Alexandra. *Beatrix Potter*
Walton, Rick. *I need my own country!*
Ward, Helen. *The dragon machine*
Weitzman, Jacqueline Preiss. *Superhero Joe*
Superhero Joe and the creature next door
Wells, Rosemary. *A lion for Lewis*
Small world of Binky Braverman
Whatley, Bruce. *Captain Pajamas*
Clinton Gregory's secret
Wheatley, Nadia. *Luke's way of looking*
White, Kathryn. *Ruby's school walk*
Whiting, Sue. *The firefighters*
Whybrow, Ian. *Harry and the bucketful of dinosaurs*
Wiesner, David. *Flotsam*
Hurricane
Willard, Nancy. *A visit to William Blake's inn*
Willems, Mo. *Leonardo the terrible monster*
Williams, Vera B. *Cherries and cherry pits*
Williams-Garcia, Rita. *Catching the wild waiyuuzee*
Willis, Jeanne. *Delilah D. at the library*
Wilson, Karma. *Princess me*
Wing, Natasha. *Go to bed, monster!*
Wood, Audrey. *The flying dragon room*
Yolen, Jane. *King Long Shanks*
Yoo, Taeeun. *You are a lion!*
Yorinks, Arthur. *Harry and Lulu*
Hey, Al
Louis the fish
What a trip!
Young, Cybèle. *A few blocks*
Young, Ned. *Zoomer*
Zoomer's summer snowstorm
Young, Ruth. *Golden Bear*
Yum, Hyewon. *There are no scary wolves*
Zalben, Jane Breskin. *Mousterpiece*
Ziefert, Harriet. *Mighty Max*
Zimmerman, Andrea Griffing. *Train man*
Zoboli, Giovanna. *I wish I had . . .*

Imagination – imaginary friends

Alexander, Martha G. *And my mean old mother will be sorry, Blackboard Bear*
Blackboard Bear
I sure am glad to see you, Blackboard Bear
I'll protect you from the jungle beasts
We're in big trouble, Blackboard Bear
You're a genius, Blackboard Bear
Anglund, Joan Walsh. *The cowboy's Christmas*
Byun, You. *Dream friends*
DiTerlizzi, Tony. *Ted*
Greenfield, Eloise. *Me and Neesie*
Henkes, Kevin. *Jessica*
Howe, James. *There's a dragon in my sleeping bag*
Klise, Kate. *Imagine Harry*
Kvasnosky, Laura McGee. *Really truly Bingo*
Perl, Erica S. *Dotty*
Pinfold, Levi. *The Django*
Rohmann, Eric. *Clara and Asha*
Rosenberg, Liz. *Nobody*

Imitation *see* Behavior – imitation

Immigrants

Atwell, Debby. *The Thanksgiving door*
Avi. *Silent movie*
Broyles, Anne. *Shy Mama's Halloween*
Bunting, Eve. *One green apple*
A picnic in October
Carling, Amelia Lau. *Mama and Papa have a store*
Colato Laínez, René. *My shoes and I*
Connor, Leslie. *Miss Bridie chose a shovel*
Corey, Shana. *Milly and the Macy's Parade*
Cutler, Jane. *Guttersnipe*
Fleischman, Paul. *The matchbox diary*
Hearne, Betsy Gould. *Seven brave women*
Hyde, Heidi Smith. *Mendel's accordion*
Jaspersohn, William. *The two brothers*
Jiménez, Francisco. *The Christmas gift / El regalo de Navidad*
Jules, Jacqueline. *No English*
Kurtz, Jane. *In the small, small night*
Lee, Milly. *Landed*
McCully, Emily Arnold. *Mirette and Bellini cross Niagara Falls*
McGill, Alice. *Molly Bannaky*
MacLachlan, Patricia. *Nora's chicks*
McQuinn, Anna. *My friend Jamal*
Mak, Kam. *My Chinatown*
Miller, Elizabeth I. *Just like home / Como en mi tierra*
Nolan, Janet. *The St. Patrick's Day shillelagh*
Oberman, Sheldon. *The always prayer shawl*
Pak, Soyung. *A place to grow*
Park, Frances. *The Have a Good Day Cafe*
My freedom trip
Partridge, Elizabeth. *Oranges on Golden Mountain*
Pérez, Amada Irma. *My diary from here to there / Mi diario de aquí hasta allá*
Polacco, Patricia. *The blessing cup*
The keeping quilt
Pomeranc, Marion Hess. *The American Wei*
Pryor, Bonnie. *The dream jar*
Rael, Elsa Okon. *Rivka's first Thanksgiving*
Recorvits, Helen. *My name is Yoon*
Yoon and the Christmas mitten
Reynolds, Marilynn. *The new land*
Sandman, Rochel. *Perfect porridge*
Steig, William. *When everybody wore a hat*
Stevenson, Harvey. *Looking at liberty*
Stewart, Sarah. *The quiet place*
Tarbescu, Edith. *Annushka's voyage*
Williams, Karen Lynn. *My name is Sangoel*
Winter, Jeanette. *Angelina's island*
Woodruff, Elvira. *The memory coat*
Small beauties
Yaccarino, Dan. *All the way to America*
Yin. *Brothers*
Coolies
Yolen, Jane. *Naming Liberty*
Ziefert, Harriet. *When I first came to this land*

Incentive *see* Character traits – ambition

Indecision *see* Behavior – indecision

Independence Day *see* Holidays – Fourth of July

Indians of Central America – Maya

Ehlert, Lois. *Cuckoo, a Mexican folktale / Cucú: un cuento folklórico mexicano*
Marcos, subcomandante. *The story of colors / La historia de los colores*
Mora, Pat. *The night the moon fell*

Price, Mara. *Grandma's chocolate / El chocolate de Abuelita*
Rockwell, Anne. *The boy who wouldn't obey*
Volkmer, Jane Anne. *Song of Chirimia / La Musica de la Chirimia*
Wisniewski, David. *Rain player*

Indians of Central America – Taino

Alvarez, Julia. *The secret footprints*

Indians of North America

Aliki. *Corn is maize*
Baker, Olaf. *Where the buffaloes begin*
Baylor, Byrd. *Hawk, I'm your brother*
When clay sings
Beaver steals fire
Bouchard, Dave. *The song within my heart*
Boyden, Linda. *The blue roses*
Brown, Don. *Bright path*
Bruchac, Joseph. *Buffalo song*
The circle of thanks
How Chipmunk got his stripes
Many nations
Thirteen moons on turtle's back
Clement-Davies, David. *Spirit*
Farmer, Bonnie. *Isaac's dreamcatcher*
Francis, Lee DeCora. *Kunu's basket*
Goble, Paul. *Buffalo woman*
The girl who loved wild horses
Grossman, Virginia. *Ten little rabbits*
Hader, Berta Hoerner. *The mighty hunter*
Harjo, Joy. *The good luck cat*
London, Jonathan. *Fireflies, fireflies, light my way*
Luenn, Nancy. *Nessa's fish*
McDermott, Gerald. *Raven*
McLeod, Elaine. *Lessons from Mother Earth*
Martin, Bill, Jr. *Knots on a counting rope*
Olsen, Sylvia. *Yetsa's sweater*
Perrow, Angeli. *Many hands*
Pollock, Penny. *When the moon is full*
Rappaport, Doreen. *We are the many*
Shoulders, Michael. *D is for drum*
Siberell, Anne. *Whale in the sky*
Smith, Cynthia Leitich. *Jingle dancer*
Strete, Craig Kee. *How the Indians bought the farm*
Taylor, Harriet Peck. *Coyote and the laughing butterflies*
Vaughan, Richard Lee. *Eagle boy*

Indians of North America – Algonquin

McCurdy, Michael. *An Algonquian year*
Martin, Rafe. *The rough-face girl*
Ross, Gayle. *The legend of the Windigo*

Indians of North America – Aztec

Aesop. *Doctor Coyote*
de Las Casas, Dianne. *Blue frog*
Kimmel, Eric A. *The two mountains*
McDermott, Gerald. *Musicians of the sun*
Mora, Pat. *The beautiful lady*

Indians of North America – Blackfoot

Goble, Paul. *The lost children*
San Souci, Robert D. *The legend of Scarface*
Yolen, Jane. *Sky dogs*

Indians of North America – Cherokee

Duvall, Deborah L. *The opossum's tale*
Flanagan, Alice K. *Mrs. Scott's beautiful art*
Haley, Gail E. *Two bad boys*
Ross, Gayle. *How Turtle's back was cracked*
Roth, Susan L. *Kanahena*
Rumford, James. *Sequoyah*

Indians of North America – Cheyenne (Sioux)

Goble, Paul. *Death of the iron horse*
The great race of the birds and animals
Her seven brothers

Indians of North America – Chippewa

McCain, Becky R. *Grandmother's dreamcatcher*

Indians of North America – Choctaw

Tingle, Tim. *When Turtle grew feathers*

Indians of North America – Chumash

Wood, Audrey. *The rainbow bridge*

Indians of North America – Comanche

dePaola, Tomie. *The legend of the bluebonnet*
Lind, Michael. *Bluebonnet girl*
Waldman, Neil. *They came from the Bronx*

Indians of North America – Cree

Bouchard, Dave. *Nokum is my teacher*
Wiebe, Rudy. *Hidden buffalo*

Indians of North America – Creek

Bruchac, Joseph. *The great ball game*

Indians of North America – Crow

Goble, Paul. *Crow chief*

Indians of North America – Dakota (Sioux)

Iktomi and the boulder
Iktomi and the buzzard
Love flute
Nelson, S. D. *Gift horse*

Indians of North America – Goshute

Pia Toya

Indians of North America – Great Basin

Pia Toya

Indians of North America – Great Plains

dePaola, Tomie. *The legend of the Indian paintbrush*
Erdrich, Liselotte. *Bears make rock soup and other stories*
Goble, Paul. *Beyond the ridge*
The dream wolf
The gift of the sacred dog

Iktomi and the berries
Iktomi and the boulder
Iktomi and the buffalo skull
Iktomi and the buzzard
Iktomi and the coyote
Iktomi and the ducks
Mystic horse
Remaking the earth
The return of the buffaloes

Indians of North America – Haida

Frantz, Jennifer. *Totem poles*

Indians of North America – Hopi

Dawavendewa, Gerald. *The butterfly dance*

Indians of North America – Huichol

Larson, Bonnie. *When animals were people / Cuando los animales eran personas*

Indians of North America – Inuit

Bushey, Jeanne. *The polar bear's gift*
Edwardson, Debby Dahl. *Whale snow*
Ford, Christine. *Ocean's child*
London, Jonathan. *Ice Bear and Little Fox*
Pasquali, Elena. *Ituku's Christmas journey*
Sís, Peter. *A small tall tale from the far Far North*
Stafford, Liliana. *The snow bear*

Indians of North America – Iroquois

Bruchac, James. *Rabbit's snow dance*
Longfellow, Henry Wadsworth. *Hiawatha*
Sherman, Pat. *The sun's daughter*

Indians of North America – Kato

Rosen, Michael J. *The dog who walked with God*

Indians of North America – Lakota

Nelson, S. D. *The Star People*

Indians of North America – Lakota (Sioux)

Bateson-Hill, Margaret. *Shota and the star quilt*
Bruchac, Joseph. *Crazy horse's vision*
Goble, Paul. *Adopted by the eagles*
The legend of the White Buffalo Woman
The return of the buffaloes

Indians of North America – Lenape

Messinger, Carla. *When the shadbush blooms*
Van Laan, Nancy. *Rainbow crow*

Indians of North America – Metis

Pendziwol, Jean E. *The red sash*

Indians of North America – Miwok

San Souci, Robert D. *Two bear cubs: a Miwok legend from California's Yosemite Valley*

Indians of North America – Mohawk

Swamp, Jake. *Giving thanks*

Indians of North America – Muskogee

Bruchac, Joseph. *The great ball game*

Indians of North America – Narragansett

Koller, Jackie French. *Nickommoh!*

Indians of North America – Navajo

Blood, Charles L. *The goat in the rug*
Hausman, Gerald. *Coyote walks on two legs*
Eagle boy
Oughton, Jerrie. *How the stars fell into the sky*
The magic weaver of rugs
Schick, Eleanor. *My Navajo sister*
Tapahonso, Luci. *Navajo ABC*

Indians of North America – Nez Perce

Kay, Verla. *Broken Feather*

Indians of North America – Ojibwa

Osofsky, Audrey. *Dreamcatcher*
Rodanas, Kristina. *Follow the stars*
San Souci, Robert D. *Sootface*
Van Laan, Nancy. *Shingebiss*
Waboose, Jan Bourdeau. *Firedancers*
Morning on the lake
SkySisters

Indians of North America – Papago

Baylor, Byrd. *The desert is theirs*

Indians of North America – Passamaquoddy

Sockabasin, Allen. *Thanks to the animals*

Indians of North America – Pawnee

Cohen, Caron Lee. *The mud pony*
Goble, Paul. *Mystic horse*

Indians of North America – Pima

Nelson, S. D. *Quiet hero*

Indians of North America – Powhatan

Krull, Kathleen. *Pocahontas: princess of the New World*
Nettleton, Pamela Hill. *Pocahontas*

Indians of North America – Pueblo

McDermott, Gerald. *Arrow to the sun*
Rosen, Michael. *Crow and Hawk*

Indians of North America – Seminole

Medearis, Angela Shelf. *Dancing with the Indians*

Indians of North America – Seneca

Charles, Veronika Martenova. *The maiden of the mist*
Ehlert, Lois. *Mole's hill*

Indians of North America – Shoshone

Morris, Ann. *Grandma Maxine remembers*
Napoli, Donna Jo. *The crossing*
Stevens, Janet. *Old bag of bones*

Indians of North America – Siksika

Goble, Paul. *The lost children*
Star boy
San Souci, Robert D. *The legend of Scarface*
Yolen, Jane. *Sky dogs*

Indians of North America – Sioux

Sheldon, Dyan. *Under the moon*

Indians of North America – Southwest

McDermott, Gerald. *Coyote*
Taylor, Harriet Peck. *Secrets of the stone*

Indians of North America – Suquamish

Seattle, Chief. *Brother eagle, sister sky*

Indians of North America – Taino

Jaffe, Nina. *The golden flower*

Indians of North America – Tewa

Clark, Ann Nolan. *In my mother's house*
Orona-Ramirez, Kristy. *Kiki's journey*

Indians of North America – Tlingit

Kimmel, Eric A. *The frog princess: a Tlingit legend from Alaska*
Sleator, William. *The angry moon*

Indians of North America – Tsimshian

Spalding, Andrea. *Solomon's tree*

Indians of North America – Wampanoag

Bartlett, Robert Merrill. *The story of Thanksgiving*
Bruchac, Joseph. *Squanto's journey*
Hennessy, B. G. *One little, two little, three little pilgrims*
Metaxas, Eric. *Squanto and the miracle of Thanksgiving*
Shore, Diane Z. *This is the feast*

Indians of North America – Windigos

Ross, Gayle. *The legend of the Windigo*

Indians of North America – Zapotec

Grossman, Patricia. *Saturday market*
Johnston, Tony. *The tale of Rabbit and Coyote*
Van Laan, Nancy. *La boda*

Indians of North America – Zuni

Pollock, Penny. *The turkey girl*
Rodanas, Kristina. *The dragonfly's tale*

Indians of South America

Knutson, Barbara. *Love and roast chicken*
Krebs, Laurie. *Up and down the Andes*
Reynolds, Jan. *Amazon*

Indians of South America – Karina

Maggi, María Elena. *The great canoe*

Indians of South America – Quechua

Van Laan, Nancy. *The magic bean tree*

Indians, American *see* Indians of Central America; Indians of North America; Indians of South America

Indifference *see* Behavior – indifference

Individuality *see* Character traits – individuality

Indonesian Archipelago *see* Foreign lands – South Sea Islands

Insects

Anastas, Margaret. *A hug for you*
Andreae, Giles. *Bustle in the bushes*
Beall, Pamela Conon. *Wee Sing if you're happy and you know it*
Berger, Melvin. *Buzz! a book about insects*
Biedrzycki, David. *Ace Lacewing, Bug Detective*
Bonwill, Ann. *Bug and Bear*
Carter, David A. *Chanukah bugs*
Easter bugs
How many bugs in a box?
Peekaboo bugs
Cyrus, Kurt. *Big rig bugs*
Dennard, Deborah. *Bullfrog at Magnolia Circle*
Dodd, Emma. *I love bugs!*
Downing, Johnette. *There was an old lady who swallowed some bugs*
Durango, Julia. *Pest fest*
Edwards, Pamela Duncan. *Bravo, Livingstone Mouse!*
Florian, Douglas. *Insectlopedia*
Frost, Helen. *Step gently out*
Gerber, Carole. *Seeds, bees, butterflies, and more!*
Glaser, Linda. *Not a buzz to be found*
Gran, Julia. *Big bug surprise*
Green, Emily K. *Walkingsticks*
Hanson, Warren. *Bugtown Boogie*
Harris, Trudy. *Pattern bugs*
Harvey, Jayne. *Busy bugs*
Hector, Julian. *The gentleman bug*
Himmelman, John. *Noisy bug sing-along*
Hines, Anna Grossnickle. *Miss Emma's wild garden*
Holmes, Anita. *Insect detector*
Hopkins, Lee Bennett. *Nasty bugs*
Hunter, Anne. *What's in the meadow?*

Jenkins, Steve. *Animals in flight*
Joyce, William. *The Leaf Men and the brave good bugs*
Kirk, David. *Little Miss Spider at Sunny Patch School*
Miss Spider's ABC
Miss Spider's new car
Leslie, Amanda. *Alfie and Betty Bug*
Lewis, J. Patrick. *Face bug*
The little buggers
Lewison, Wendy Cheyette. *So many boots*
Lionni, Leo. *Inch by inch*
McDonald, Megan. *Beetle McGrady eats bugs!*
Insects are my life
Reptiles are my life
McElligott, Matthew. *Bean thirteen*
McKelvey, Douglas Kaine. *Locust pocus*
Markle, Sandra. *Creepy, crawly baby bugs*
Insects
Martin, Bill, Jr. *The little squeegy bug*
Morrow, Barbara Olenyik. *Mr. Mosquito put on his tuxedo*
Mortensen, Denise Dowling. *Bug Patrol*
Munro, Roxie. *Busy builders*
Murawski, Darlyne A. *Bug faces*
Murphy, Stuart J. *The best bug parade*
Bug dance
Newgarden, Mark. *Bow-Wow bugs a bug*
O'Connor, Jane. *Fancy Nancy: explorer extraordinaire!*
Oppenheim, Joanne. *Have you seen bugs?*
Palatini, Margie. *The perfect pet*
Parker, Nancy Winslow. *Bugs*
Paulsen, Gary. *Canoe days*
Perlman, Janet. *The delicious bug*
Peters, Lisa Westberg. *Sleepyhead bear*
Pichon, Liz. *The very ugly bug*
Pienkowski, Jan. *Pizza!*
Pin, Isabel. *The seed*
Pinczes, Elinor J. *A remainder of one*
Rockwell, Anne. *Bugs are insects*
Bumblebee, bumblebee, do you know me?
Ryder, Joanne. *My father's hands*
Sabuda, Robert. *The movable Mother Goose*
Salzano, Tammi. *One little blueberry*
Shields, Carol Diggory. *The bugliest bug*
Sill, Cathryn. *About insects*
Siminovich, Lorena. *I like bugs*
Siomades, Lorianne. *Katy did it!*
Stein, Peter. *Bugs galore*
Sturges, Philemon. *I love bugs*
What's that sound, Woolly Bear?
Van Woerkom, Dorothy. *Hidden messages*
Voake, Steve. *Insect detective*
Ward, Jennifer. *Over in the garden*
Williams, Suzanne. *Old MacDonald in the city*
Wood, Audrey. *When the root children wake up*

Insects – ants

Aesop. *The ant and the grasshopper*, ill. by Amy Lowry Poole
The ant and the grasshopper, ill. by Sara Rojo
Allen, Judy. *Are you an ant?*
Andreae, Giles. *The pop-up Rumble in the jungle*
Rumble in the jungle
Baker, Keith. *Just how long can a long string be?!*
Becker, Bonny. *An ant's day off*
Cannon, Janell. *Crickwing*
Dorros, Arthur. *Ant cities*
Emberley, Rebecca. *The ant and the grasshopper*
Gomel, Luc. *The ant, energetic worker*
Gray, Luli. *Ant and Grasshopper*
Hepworth, Catherine. *ANTics! an alphabetical anthology*
Hodge, Deborah. *Ants*
Hoose, Philip M. *Hey little ant*
Landström, Olof. *Boo and Baa in the woods*
Lass, Bonnie. *Who took the cookies from the cookie jar?*
Loewen, Nancy. *Tiny workers*
McDonald, Megan. *Ant and Honey Bee, what a pair!*
McElligott, Matthew. *The lion's share*
Martin, David. *All for pie, pie for all*
Nelson, Kristin L. *Busy ants*
Nickle, John. *The ant bully*
O'Malley, Kevin. *Little Buggy runs away*
Peet, Bill. *The ant and the elephant*
Philpot, Lorna. *Find Anthony Ant*
Prince, Joshua. *I saw an ant in a parking lot*
I saw an ant on the railroad track
Sayre, April Pulley. *Army ant parade*
Sneed, Brad. *Deputy Harvey and the ant cow caper*
Van Allsburg, Chris. *Two bad ants*
Wells, Rosemary. *McDuff saves the day*
Wolkstein, Diane. *Step by step*
Young, Ed. *Night visitors*

Insects – bees

Barton, Byron. *Buzz, buzz, buzz*
Bell, Cece. *Bee-Wigged*
Cecil, Randy. *Horsefly and Honeybee*
Cole, Joanna. *The magic school bus inside a beehive*
Flanagan, Alice K. *Learning about bees from Mr. Krebs*
Florian, Douglas. *Unbeelievables*
Formento, Alison. *These bees count!*
Frazier, Craig. *Bee and Bird*
Galvin, Laura Gates. *Bumblebee at Apple Tree Lane*
Gibbons, Gail. *The honey makers*
Gran, Julia. *Big bug surprise*
Green, Emily K. *Bumblebees*
Gugler, Laurel Dee. *There's a billy goat in the garden*
Heiligman, Deborah. *Honeybees*
Hodge, Deborah. *Bees*
Hopkinson, Deborah. *The humblebee hunter*
Huber, Raymond. *Flight of the honey bee*
Kessler, Cristina. *The best beekeeper of Lalibela*
Krebs, Laurie. *The beeman*, ill. by Valeria Cis
The beeman, ill. by Melissa Iwai
Loewen, Nancy. *Busy buzzers*
McDonald, Megan. *Ant and Honey Bee, what a pair!*
Morales, Melita. *Jam and honey*
Nargi, Lela. *The honeybee man*
Neye, Emily. *Honeybees*
Petty, Dini. *The queen, the bear and the bumblebee*
Polacco, Patricia. *In Enzo's splendid gardens*
Rockwell, Anne. *Bumblebee, bumblebee, do you know me?*
Honey in a hive
Roode, Daniel. *Little Bea and the snowy day*
Rotner, Shelley. *The buzz on bees*
Ruzzier, Sergio. *Bear and Bee*
Sayre, April Pulley. *The bumblebee queen*
If you should hear a honey guide
Smallman, Steve. *The very greedy bee*
Spinelli, Eileen. *Buzz*
Wong, Janet S. *Buzz*

Insects – beetles

Carle, Eric. *The very clumsy click beetle*
Fleming, Denise. *Beetle bop*
Luján, Jorge. *Stephen and the beetle*
Murphy, Kelly. *The boll weevil ball*
Tada, Satoshi. *Mr. Beetle*

Insects – butterflies, caterpillars

Aardema, Verna. *Who's in Rabbit's house?*
Allen, Judy. *Are you a butterfly?*
Arnosky, Jim. *Crinkleroot's guide to knowing butterflies and moths*
Aston, Dianna Hutts. *A butterfly is patient*
Barner, Bob. *Dinosaurs roar, butterflies soar!*
Barringer, William. *Gregory and Alexander*
Bruel, Robert O. *Bob and Otto*
Bunting, Eve. *Butterfly house*
Carle, Eric. *The very hungry caterpillar*
Collicott, Sharleen. *Toestomper and the bad butterflies*
Toestomper and the caterpillars
Coville, Bruce. *The prince of butterflies*
Davol, Marguerite W. *Why butterflies go by on silent wings*
Donaldson, Julia. *Where's my mom?*
Edwards, Pamela Duncan. *Clara Caterpillar*
Ehlert, Lois. *Waiting for wings*
Elwell, Peter. *Adios Oscar!*
Engle, Margarita. *Summer birds*
Fleming, Denise. *In the tall, tall grass*
Foley, Greg. *Don't worry Bear*
Frost, Helen. *Monarch and milkweed*
Gibbons, Gail. *Monarch butterfly*
Glaser, Linda. *Magnificent monarchs*
Goldman, Judy. *Uncle Monarch and the Day of the Dead*
Heap, Sue. *Four friends in the garden*
Himmelman, John. *A monarch butterfly's life*
Horwood, Annie. *Butterfly, butterfly what colors do you see?*
Jarrett, Clare. *Arabella Miller's tiny caterpillar*
Joosse, Barbara. *Ghost wings*
Kelly, Irene. *It's a butterfly's life*
Kleven, Elisa. *Glasswings*
Kotzwinkle, William. *Walter, the farting dog: rough weather ahead*
Lawrence, Michael. *The caterpillar that roared*
Lionni, Leo. *The alphabet tree*
McBratney, Sam. *The caterpillow fight*
Madison, Alan. *Velma Gratch and the way cool butterfly*
Magloff, Lisa. *Butterfly*
Maier, Inger. *Ben's flying flowers*
Markle, Sandra. *Butterfly tree*
Martin, Bill, Jr. *Ten little caterpillars*
Middleton, Charlotte. *Nibbles' garden*
Murphy, Mary. *Caterpillar's wish*
Neye, Emily. *Butterflies*
Ó Flatharta, Antoine. *Hurry and the monarch*
O'Connor, Jane. *Bonjour, butterfly*
Patent, Dorothy Hinshaw. *Fabulous fluttering tropical butterflies*
Pedersen, Janet. *Houdini the amazing caterpillar*
Polacco, Patricia. *The butterfly*
Prosek, James. *Bird, butterfly, eel*
Rockwell, Anne. *Becoming butterflies*
Runton, Andy. *Owly and Wormy: friends all aflutter!*
Ryder, Joanne. *Where butterflies grow*
Sandved, Kjell Bloch. *The butterfly alphabet*
Schubert, Ingrid. *There's always room for one more*
Sierra, Judy. *The beautiful butterfly*
Singer, Marilyn. *Caterpillars*
Sturges, Philemon. *What's that sound, Woolly Bear?*
Sundgaard, Arnold. *The lamb and the butterfly*
Swope, Sam. *Gotta go! Gotta go!*
Symes, Ruth. *Harriet dancing*
Taylor, Harriet Peck. *Coyote and the laughing butterflies*
Wallace, Nancy Elizabeth. *Fly, monarch! Fly!*
Willis, Jeanne. *Tadpole's promise*
Winer, Yvonne. *Butterflies fly*

Insects – cockroaches

Cannon, Janell. *Crickwing*
Covell, David. *Rat and Roach*
Rat and Roach rock on!
Deedy, Carmen Agra. *Martina the beautiful cockroach*
Moreton, Daniel. *La Cucaracha Martina*
O'Malley, Kevin. *Leo Cockroach . . . toy tester*
Schneider, Howie. *Wilky the White House cockroach*

Insects – crickets

Bunting, Eve. *Christmas cricket*
Carle, Eric. *The very quiet cricket*
Caudill, Rebecca. *A pocketful of cricket*
Green, Emily K. *Crickets*
Waring, Geoff. *Oscar and the cricket*
Wheeler, Lisa. *Old Cricket*

Insects – dragonflies

Breen, Steve. *Stick*
Miller, Heather Lynn. *This is your life cycle*
Rodanas, Kristina. *The dragonfly's tale*

Insects – fireflies

Carle, Eric. *The very lonely firefly*
Drachman, Eric. *Leo the lightning bug*
Loewen, Nancy. *Living lights*
Ochiltree, Dianne. *It's a firefly night*
Oppenheim, Shulamith Levey. *Fireflies for Nathan*
Pinczes, Elinor J. *My full moon is square*
Sturges, Philemon. *Ten flashing fireflies*
Thomas, Patricia. *Firefly mountain*

Insects – fleas

Cneut, Carll. *The amazing love story of Mr. Morf*
Downey, Lynn. *The flea's sneeze*
Hanson, Mary Elizabeth. *The old man and the flea*
Lish, Ted. *The three little puppies and the big bad flea*
Marcus, Kimberly. *Scritch-scratch a perfect match*
Rogers, Paul. *Tiny*
Steig, Jeanne. *Fleas!*
Weninger, Brigitte. *The elf's hat*
Wood, Audrey. *The napping house wakes up*

Insects – flies

Aardema, Verna. *Half-a-ball-of-kenki*
Aylesworth, Jim. *Old Black Fly*
Cecil, Randy. *Horsefly and Honeybee*
Cronin, Doreen. *Diary of a fly*
Gollub, Matthew. *The Jazz Fly*
Jazz Fly 2

Howitt, Mary Botham. *Mary Howitt's The spider and the fly*
Jorgensen, Gail. *Gotcha!*
Little old lady who swallowed a fly. *I know an old lady*
I know an old lady who swallowed a fly, ill. by Stephen Gulbis
I know an old lady who swallowed a fly, ill. by Glen Rounds
I know an old lady who swallowed a fly, ill. by Nadine Bernard Westcott
There was an old lady who swallowed a fly, ill. by Pam Adams
There was an old lady who swallowed a fly, ill. by Simms Taback
Long, Ethan. *Soup for one*
Lozoff, Bo. *The wonderful life of a fly who couldn't fly*
Mack, Jeff. *Frog and Fly*
Rosen, Michael. *Tiny little fly*
Schwartz, Amy. *A beautiful girl*
Sierra, Judy. *Thelonius Monster's sky-high fly pie*
Trapani, Iza. *Shoo fly!*

Insects – gnats

Peet, Bill. *The gnats of knotty pine*

Insects – grasshoppers

Aesop. *The ant and the grasshopper*, ill. by Amy Lowry Poole
The ant and the grasshopper, ill. by Sara Rojo
Allen, Judy. *Are you a grasshopper?*
Bosca, Francesca. *The three grasshoppers*
Emberley, Rebecca. *The ant and the grasshopper*
Gray, Luli. *Ant and Grasshopper*
Green, Emily K. *Grasshoppers*
Loewen, Nancy. *Hungry hoppers*
Wolkstein, Diane. *Step by step*

Insects – ladybugs

Allen, Judy. *Are you a ladybug?*
Berger, Joe. *Bridget Fidget and the most perfect pet!*
Bono, Mary. *Ugh! a bug*
Carle, Eric. *The grouchy ladybug*
Chrustowski, Rick. *Bright beetle*
Dahl, Michael. *Lots of ladybugs!*
Donaldson, Julia. *What the ladybug heard*
Finn, Isobel. *The very lazy ladybug*
Fox, Mem. *Yoo-hoo, Ladybug!*
Gibbons, Gail. *Ladybugs*
Llewellyn, Claire. *Ladybug*
Loewen, Nancy. *Spotted beetles*
O'Malley, Kevin. *Little Buggy*
Little Buggy runs away
Posada, Mia. *Ladybugs*
Primavera, Elise. *The house at the end of Ladybug Lane*
Stephens, J. Moria. *Persephone, the ladybug*
Thomas, Jan. *Can you make a scary face?*

Insects – lice

Caffey, Donna. *Yikes-lice!*
Shannon, David. *Bugs in my hair!*
Stier, Catherine. *Bugs in my hair?!*
Van Laan, Nancy. *Nit-pickin'*

Insects – lightning bugs *see* Insects – fireflies

Insects – mosquitoes

Aardema, Verna. *Why mosquitoes buzz in people's ears*
Gershator, Phillis. *Zzzng! zzzng! zzzng!*
Knudsen, Michelle. *Bugged!*
Morrow, Barbara Olenyik. *Mr. Mosquito put on his tuxedo*
Ross, Gayle. *The legend of the Windigo*
Sloat, Teri. *The thing that bothered Farmer Brown*
Uribe, Verónica. *Buzz buzz buzz*

Insects – moths

Arnosky, Jim. *Crinkleroot's guide to knowing butterflies and moths*
Evans, Cambria. *Martha Moth makes socks*
Himmelman, John. *A luna moth's life*
Loewen, Nancy. *Night fliers*
Sandved, Kjell Bloch. *The butterfly alphabet*
Sturges, Philemon. *What's that sound, Woolly Bear?*

Insects – termites

Laden, Nina. *Roberto, the insect architect*
Rouss, Sylvia A. *The littlest pair*

Interracial marriage *see* Marriage, interracial

Inventions

Barretta, Gene. *Neo Leo*
Now and Ben
Timeless Thomas
Beaty, Andrea. *Rosie Revere, engineer*
Fisher, Leonard Everett. *Gutenberg*
Fleming, Candace. *Papa's mechanical fish*
Geisert, Arthur. *Lights out*
Harper, Charise Mericle. *Imaginative inventions*
Hopkins, Lee Bennett. *Incredible inventions*
James, Simon. *Baby Brains and RoboMom*
Joyce, William. *Sleepy time Olie*
Kelly, David A. *Miracle mud*
Kulling, Monica. *All aboard! Elijah McCoy's steam engine*
McCully, Emily Arnold. *Marvelous Mattie*
Milgrim, David. *Young MacDonald*
Perry, Andrea. *Here's what you do when you can't find your shoe*
Polacco, Patricia. *The junkyard wonders*
Priceman, Marjorie. *Hot air*
Riddell, Chris. *Wendel's workshop*
Taylor, Barbara. *I wonder why zippers have teeth and other questions about inventions*
Varela, Barry. *Gizmo*

Islands

Blackstone, Stella. *An island in the sun*
Breen, Steve. *The secret of Santa's island*
Brown, Margaret Wise. *The little island*
Bunting, Eve. *Mouse island*
Burdett, Lois. *The tempest for kids*
Buzzeo, Toni. *The sea chest*
Demas, Corinne. *The disappearing island*
Field, Rachel Lyman. *Grace for an island meal*
Gay, Marie-Louise. *On my island*

Gibbons, Gail. *Surrounded by sea*
Godkin, Celia. *Wolf island*
Isadora, Rachel. *Caribbean dream*
Joseph, Lynn. *Coconut kind of day*
Kellogg, Steven. *The island of the skog*
McCloskey, Robert. *Time of wonder*
MacLachlan, Patricia. *Painting the wind*
McMillan, Bruce. *Days of the ducklings*
Martin, Jacqueline Briggs. *On Sand Island*
Meddaugh, Susan. *Harry on the rocks*
Moore, Inga. *Captain Cat*
Pfister, Marcus. *Milo and the mysterious island*
Rahaman, Vashanti. *O Christmas tree*
Rockwell, Anne. *Ferryboat ride!*
Rohmann, Eric. *The cinder-eyed cats*
Rumford, James. *The Island-below-the-star*
Schaefer, Lola M. *An island grows*
Stevenson, James. *The castaway*
Stiles, Martha Bennett. *Island magic*
Stojic, Manya. *Wet pebbles under our feet*
Williams, Garth. *Benjamin's treasure*
Wisdom, Jude. *Whatever Wanda wanted*

Jackets *see* Clothing – coats

Janitors *see* Careers – custodians, janitors

Jealousy *see* Emotions – envy, jealousy

Jesters *see* Clowns, jesters

Jewelry

Andersen, Hans Christian. *The princess and the pea*
Fruisen, Catherine Myler. *My mother's pearls*
Kassirer, Sue. *What's next, Nina?*
Kinch, Devon. *Pretty Penny makes ends meet*
Lamm, C. Drew. *Gauchada*
Recorvits, Helen. *Yoon and the jade bracelet*
Wyeth, Sharon Dennis. *The granddaughter necklace*

Jewish culture

Abraham, Michelle Shapiro. *My cousin Tamar lives in Israel*
Adler, David A. *The children's book of Jewish holidays*
Hiding from the Nazis
A picture book of Hanukkah
A picture book of Israel
A picture book of Jewish holidays
A picture book of Passover
The story of Hanukkah
Aleichem, Sholem. *Hanukah money*
Baum, Maxie. *I have a little dreidel*
Biers-Ariel, Matt. *Solomon and the trees*
Capucilli, Alyssa Satin. *Happy Hanukkah, Biscuit*
Chwast, Seymour. *The miracle of Hanukkah*
Cohen, Deborah Bodin. *Papa Jethro*
Cutler, Jane. *Guttersnipe*
Davis, Aubrey. *Bagels from Benny*
Kishka for Koppel
Dollinger, Renate. *The rabbi who flew*
Edwards, Michelle. *The Hanukkah trike*
Papa's latkes
Room for the baby
Elissa, Barbara. *The remarkable journey of Josh's kippah*
Emerman, Ellen. *Is it Shabbos yet?*
Just right: the story of a Jewish home
Fagan, Cary. *Oy, feh, so?*
Fishman, Cathy Goldberg. *On Hanukkah*
On Passover
On Purim
On Rosh Hashanah and Yom Kippur
On Shabbat
When Jackie and Hank met
Flanagan, Alice K. *Passover*
Gadot, A. S. *The first gift*
Geras, Adèle. *Rebecca's Passover*
Glaser, Linda. *Hannah's way*
Hoppy Passover!
Mrs. Greenberg's messy Hanukkah
Gold-Vukson, Marji E. *The colors of my Jewish Year*
Grandpa and me on Tu B'Shevat
Goldin, Barbara Diamond. *Cakes and miracles*
A mountain of blintzes
Night lights
Groner, Judyth Saypol. *My first Hebrew word book*
Hanft, Josh. *The miracles of Passover*
Hanukkah lights
Heller, Linda. *How Dalia put a big yellow comforter inside a tiny blue box*
Herman, Charlotte. *First rain*
Hest, Amy. *The Friday nights of Nana*
Hirsh, Marilyn. *Potato pancakes all around*
Howland, Naomi. *Latkes, latkes, good to eat*
The matzah man
Hyde, Heidi Smith. *Emanuel and the Hanukkah rescue*
Mendel's accordion
Jaffe, Nina. *In the month of Kislev*
Tales for the seventh day
The way meat loves salt
Jules, Jacqueline. *Picnic at Camp Shalom*
Kimmel, Eric A. *The Chanukkah guest*
Gershon's monster
Hanukkah bear
Hershel and the Hanukkah goblins
Joseph and the Sabbath fish
The magic dreidels
Zigazak!
Kimmelman, Leslie. *Dance, sing, remember*
Hanukkah lights, Hanukkah nights
Hooray! it's Passover!
The runaway latkes
The Shabbat puppy
Sound the shofar!
Korngold, Jamie S. *Sadie and the big mountain*
Sadie's sukkah breakfast
Kosofsky, Chaim. *Much, much better*
Kropf, Latifa Berry. *It's Hanukkah time!*
It's seder time!
It's Shofar time!
Krulik, Nancy E. *Is it Hanukkah yet?*

Kuskin, Karla. *A great miracle happened there*
Lehman-Wilzig, Tami. *Keeping the promise*
Nathan blows out the Hanukkah candles
Levine, Abby. *This is the matzah*
Libney, Varda. *What I like about Passover*
Lister, Clare. *My first Passover [board book]*
The little red hen. *The Little Red Hen and the Passover matzah*
Londner, Renee. *Stones for Grandpa*
McDonough, Yona Zeldis. *Hammerin' Hank*
Manushkin, Fran. *Hooray for Hanukkah!*
Latkes and applesauce
Miriam's cup
Marshall, Linda Elovitz. *Grandma Rose's magic*
The passover lamb
Medoff, Francine. *The mouse in the matzah factory*
Melmed, Laura Krauss. *Eight winter nights*
Moishe's miracle
Meltzer, Amy. *A mezuzah on the door*
The Shabbat Princess
Michelson, Richard. *Across the alley*
Too young for Yiddish
Miller, William. *Jenny and the peddler*
Morris, Ann. *Grandma Esther remembers*
Newman, Lesléa. *The eight nights of Chanukah*
Matzo ball moon
Runaway dreidel
A sweet Passover
Oberman, Sheldon. *The always prayer shawl*
Perlov, Betty Rosenberg. *Rifka takes a bow*
Podwal, Mark H. *The menorah story*
A sweet year
Polacco, Patricia. *The blessing cup*
The keeping quilt
Mrs. Katz and Tush
Someone for Mr. Sussman
Tikvah means hope
The trees of the dancing goats
Rael, Elsa Okon. *Rivka's first Thanksgiving*
Randall, Ronne. *The Hanukkah mice*
Rappaport, Doreen. *The secret seder*
Rosen, Michael J. *Chanukah lights everywhere*
Elijah's angel
Our eight nights of Hanukkah
Rosenberg, Madelyn. *Happy birthday, tree!*
The Schmutzy Family
Rosenfeld, Dina Herman. *Five alive*
Get well soon
Rothenberg, Joan Keller. *Inside-out grandma*
Matzah ball soup
Rouss, Sylvia A. *The littlest frog*
Sammy Spider's first day of school
Sammy Spider's first Passover
Sammy Spider's first Shabbat
Sammy Spider's first Shavuot
Sammy Spider's first Tu B'Shevat
Sammy Spider's first Yom Kippur
Russo, Marisabina. *I will come back for you*
Sasso, Sandy Eisenberg. *Butterflies under our hats*
Schaefer, Lola M. *Hanukkah*
Schnur, Steven. *The tie man's miracle*
Schnur, Susan. *Tashlich at Turtle Rock*
Schotter, Roni. *Hanukkah!*
Passover!
Passover magic
Purim play
Schubert, Leda. *The Princess of Borscht*
Schur, Maxine Rose. *Day of delight*
Schwartz, Howard. *Gathering sparks*
Shollar, Leah. *A thread of kindness*
Shulevitz, Uri. *The magician*
Shulimson, Sarene. *Lights out Shabbat*
Shulman, Goldie. *Way too much challah dough*
Silverman, Erica. *Gittel's hands*
The Hanukkah hop!
Simhaee, Rebeka. *Sara finds a mitzva*
Simon, Norma. *The story of Hanukkah*
The story of Passover
Simpson, Lesley. *The Purim surprise*
Sinykin, Sheri. *Zayde comes to live*
Smith, Dian G. *Hanukkah lights*
Snyder, Laurel. *Baxter, the pig who wanted to be kosher*
Good night, laila tov
Sper, Emily. *Hanukkah: a counting book in English, Hebrew, and Yiddish*
The Passover seder
Spinner, Stephanie. *It's a miracle*
Stampler, Ann Redisch. *The rooster prince of Breslov*
Shlemazel and the remarkable spoon of Pohost
The wooden sword
Stone, Tanya Lee. *D is for dreidel*
Strauss, Linda Leopold. *The Elijah door*
Stuchner, Joan Betty. *Can hens give milk?*
The Kugel Valley Klezmer Band
Sugarman, Brynn Olenberg. *Rebecca's journey home*
Sussman, Joni Kibort. *My first Yiddish word book*
Taback, Simms. *Kibitzers and fools*
Tarbescu, Edith. *Annushka's voyage*
The boy who stuck out his tongue
Ungar, Richard. *Rachel captures the moon*
Rachel's gift
Rachel's library
Ungerer, Tomi. *Otto: the autobiography of a teddy bear*
Vorst, Rochel Groner. *The sukkah that I built*
Waldman, Debby. *Room enough for Daisy*
A sack full of feathers
Wisniewski, David. *Golem*
Wiviott, Meg. *Benno and the night of broken glass*
Wohl, Lauren L. *Matzoh mouse*
Woodruff, Elvira. *The memory coat*
Yolen, Jane. *Naming Liberty*
Yorinks, Arthur. *The Miami giant*
Zalben, Jane Breskin. *Beni's first Chanukah*
Beni's first wedding
Pearl's eight days of Chanukah
Pearl's Passover
Zemach, Margot. *It could always be worse*
Zolkower, Edie Stoltz. *Too many cooks*
Zucker, Jonny. *Apples and honey*
Four special questions
It's party time

Jobs *see* Careers

Jokes *see* Riddles & jokes

Jumping rope *see* Sports – jumping rope

Jungle

Aardema, Verna. *Rabbit makes a monkey of lion*
Alborough, Jez. *Tall*
Andreae, Giles. *The pop-up Rumble in the jungle*
Rumble in the jungle
Ashman, Linda. *Starry safari*

Baker, Liza. *Dinosaur days*
Balouch, Kristen. *The little little girl with the big big voice*
Base, Graeme. *Jungle drums*
Bateman, Teresa. *The frog with the big mouth*
Beaton, Clare. *How loud is a lion?*
Behrens, Janice. *Let's find rain forest animals*
Berkes, Marianne. *Over in the jungle*
Bilgrami, Shaheen. *Jungle art show*
Bright, Paul. *Quiet!*
Broach, Elise. *Gumption!*
Burnard, Damon. *I spy in the jungle*
Butler, John. *Bedtime in the jungle*
Callery, Sean. *Hide and seek in the jungle*
Campoy, F. Isabel. *Rosa Raposa*
Cannon, Janell. *Verdi*
Carle, Eric. *"Slowly, slowly, slowly," said the sloth*
Cherry, Lynne. *The great kapok tree*
Costello, Emily. *Realm of the panther*
Derrick, Patricia. *Riley the rhinoceros*
Downing, Johnette. *Amazon alphabet*
Du Quette, Keith. *Little Monkey lost*
Edwards, Pamela Duncan. *Roar*
Ellery, Amanda. *If I were a jungle animal*
Elya, Susan Middleton. *No more, por favor*
Faulkner, Keith. *The giraffe who cock-a-doodle-doo'd*
Jumbled jungle
The tallest shortest longest greenest brownest animal in the jungle!
Frampton, David. *The whole night through*
Freeman, Mylo. *Potty*
Geoghegan, Adrienne. *All your own teeth*
Gibbons, Gail. *Nature's green umbrella*
Gibert, Bruno. *The king is naked!*
Gollub, Matthew. *Jazz Fly 2*
Greene, Rhonda Gowler. *Jamboree day*
Grupper, Jonathan. *Destination, rain forest*
Gutman, Anne. *Lisa in the jungle*
Hewitt, Sally. *Face to face safari*
Isadora, Rachel. *A South African night*
Jennings, Linda. *Hide and seek birthday treat*
Johanasen, Heather. *About the rain forest*
Johnson, Rebecca. *Tree frog hears a sound*
Krebs, Laurie. *We're roaming in the rainforest*
Kroll, Steven. *Jungle bullies*
Levinson, Nancy Smiler. *Rain forests*
McPhail, David. *Edward in the jungle*
Mahy, Margaret. *17 kings and 42 elephants*
Simply delicious!
Mangan, Anne. *The monkey who wanted the moon*
Mitchell, Susan K. *The rainforest grew all around*
Mitton, Tony. *The Jungle Run*
Newman, Jeff. *Reginald*
Parker, Victoria. *Bearum scarum*
Paterson, Brian. *Zigby camps out*
Zigby hunts for treasure
Peck, Jan. *Way up high in a tall green tree*
Pritchett, Dylan. *The first music*
Robinson, Michelle. *What to do if an elephant stands on your foot*
Rosen, Michael. *Tiny little fly*
Ryder, Joanne. *Jaguar in the rain forest*
Sage, Angie. *Monkeys in the jungle*
Schaefer, Carole Lexa. *Big Little Monkey*
Slack, Michael. *Monkey truck*
Steig, William. *The Zabajaba Jungle*
Sykes, Julie. *Wait for me, Little Tiger*
Tafuri, Nancy. *Junglewalk*
Teyssèdre, Fabienne. *Joseph wants to read*
Tierney, Fiona. *Lion's lunch?*
Van Allsburg, Chris. *Jumanji*
Ward, Helen. *The tin forest*
Warhola, James. *If you're happy and you know it: jungle edition*
West, Colin. *One day in the jungle*
Wildsmith, Brian. *Jungle party*
Willis, Jeanne. *The boy who lost his bellybutton*
Witte, Anna. *The parrot Tico Tango*

Kindness *see* Character traits – kindness

Kindness to animals *see* Character traits – kindness to animals

Kissing

Capucilli, Alyssa Satin. *What kind of kiss?*
Daly, Niki. *No more kisses for Bernard!*
Gibson, Amy. *Catching kisses*
Got, Yves. *Sam loves kisses*
Grimm, Jacob and Wilhelm. *The frog prince*
Hample, Stoo. *I will kiss you (lots and lots and lots!)*
Hest, Amy. *Kiss good night*
Katz, Karen. *Counting kisses*
McAllister, Angela. *Take a kiss to school*
McLeod, Heather. *Kiss me!*
Monari, Manuela. *Zero kisses for me!*
Murphy, Mary. *A kiss like this*
Oram, Hiawyn. *Kiss it better*
Plourde, Lynn. *Dad, aren't you glad?*
Robbins, Maria Polushkin. *Mother, Mother, I want another*
Root, Phyllis. *Kiss the cow*
Rosenthal, Amy Krouse. *Plant a kiss*
Saltzberg, Barney. *Baby animal kisses*
Cornelius P. Mud, are you ready for school?
Kisses
Stein, David Ezra. *Dinosaur kisses*
Tafuri, Nancy. *All kinds of kisses*
Tarpley, Todd. *How about a kiss for me?*
Trewin, Trudie. *I lost my kisses*
Verburg, Bonnie. *The kiss box*
Walsh, Joanna. *The biggest kiss*
Watts, Frances. *Kisses for Daddy*
Yolen, Jane. *Mama's kiss*

Kites

Alborough, Jez. *Super Duck*
Baumgart, Klaus. *Laura's secret*
Clark, Katie. *Seagull Sam*
Emmett, Jonathan. *Someone bigger*
Heide, Florence Parry. *Princess Hyacinth*
Hest, Amy. *Little chick*
Hillenbrand, Will. *Kite day*
Jagtenberg, Yvonne. *Jack's kite*

Jeffers, Oliver. *Stuck*
Jiang, Ji-li. *Red kite, blue kite*
Khan, Rukhsana. *King for a day*
Krensky, Stephen. *Ben Franklin and his first kite*
Lin, Grace. *Kite flying*
Mayer, Mercer. *Shibumi and the kitemaker*
Mitchell, Robin. *Windy*
Murphy, Stuart J. *Let's fly a kite*
Peet, Bill. *Merle the high flying squirrel*
Rey, Margret. *Curious George flies a kite*
Stafford, Liliana. *Just dragon*
Wiese, Kurt. *Fish in the air*
Williams, Laura E. *The best winds*
Wisdom, Jude. *Whatever Wanda wanted*
Wright, Cliff. *Bear and kite*
Yolen, Jane. *The emperor and the kite*

Knights

Adkins, Jan. *What if you met a knight?*
Baillie, Allan. *Dragonquest*
Banks, Kate. *Max's castle*
Baynton, Martin. *Jane and the dragon*
Davey, Owen. *Night Knight*
dePaola, Tomie. *The knight and the dragon*
Donaldson, Julia. *A gold star for Zog*
Gibbons, Gail. *Knights in shining armor*
Goodall, John S. *Creepy castle*
Grahame, Kenneth. *The reluctant dragon*
Kraegel, Kenneth. *King Arthur's very great grandson*
Matthies, Janna. *Peter, the knight with asthma*
Mayer, Mercer. *The bravest knight*
Mayhew, James. *The knight who took all day*
Melling, David. *Good knight sleep tight*
Nash, Ogden. *Custard the dragon and the wicked knight*
Neuschwander, Cindy. *Sir Cumference and all the king's tens*
Peet, Bill. *Cowardly Clyde*
How Droofus the dragon lost his head
Rogers, Gregory. *The boy, the bear, the baron, the bard*
Midsummer knight
Scarry, Huck. *Looking into the Middle Ages*
Smith, Linda. *Sir Cassie to the rescue*
Sperring, Mark. *The sunflower sword*
Steele, Philip. *A knight's city*
Thomas, Shelley Moore. *A cold winter's Good Knight*
A Good Knight's rest
Good night, Good Knight
Take care, Good Knight
Tucker, Kathy. *Do knights take naps?*
Wheeler, Lisa. *Boogie knights*
Wojtowycz, David. *Elephant Joe, Brave Knight!*

Lady birds *see* Insects – ladybugs

Lakes, ponds

Arnosky, Jim. *Beaver pond, moose pond*
Day, Alexandra. *Carl's summer vacation*
Falwell, Cathryn. *Pond babies*
Scoot!
Fleming, Denise. *In the small, small pond*
Folgueira, Rodrigo. *Ribbit!*
Franco, Betsy. *Pond circle*
George, Lindsay Barrett. *Around the pond*
Heinz, Brian J. *Butternut Hollow Pond*
Jordan, Sandra. *Frog hunt*
London, Jonathan. *Loon Lake*
Martin, Jacqueline Briggs. *On Sand Island*
Mitton, Tony. *Down by the cool of the pool*
Pfeffer, Wendy. *Mallard duck at Meadow View Pond*
Quattlebaum, Mary. *Jo MacDonald saw a pond*
Ritchie, Alison. *Duck says don't!*
Rockwell, Anne. *Ducklings and pollywogs*
Root, Phyllis. *Rattletrap car*
Rattletrap car [board book]
Schoenherr, John. *Rebel*
Schofield, Jennifer. *Animal babies in ponds and rivers*
Serafini, Frank. *Looking closely around the pond*
Sidman, Joyce. *Song of the water boatman*
Taylor, Harriet Peck. *Coyote and the laughing butterflies*
Thompson, Lauren. *Little Quack's new friend*
Van Leeuwen, Jean. *Touch the sky summer*
Waddell, Martin. *The pig in the pond*
Wallace, Nancy Elizabeth. *Pond walk*

Lambs *see* Animals – babies; Animals – sheep

Language

Alda, Arlene. *Did you say pears?*
Aliki. *Communication*
Hello! Good-bye!
Allen, Susan. *Read anything good lately?*
Ancona, George. *Handtalk zoo*
Arnold, Tedd. *More parts*
Ayres, Katherine. *Up, down, and around*
Azarian, Mary. *A gardener's alphabet*
Baker, Alan. *Little Rabbit's first word book*
Banks, Kate. *Max's castle*
Max's dragon
Max's words
Barretta, Gene. *Dear deer*
Barton, Byron. *Tools*
Basher, Simon. *ABC kids*
Beaton, Clare. *Zoë and her zebra*
Bergen, Lara Rice. *Blue's world of words*
Berkes, Marianne. *Animalogy*
Bertrand, Diane Gonzales. *The party for Papa Luis / La fiesta para Papa Luis*
Best, Cari. *Beatrice spells some lulus and learns to write a letter*
Bloch, Serge. *Butterflies in my stomach and other school hazards*
You are what you eat
Brennan-Nelson, Denise. *My grandma likes to say*
Brocket, Jane. *Ruby, violet, lime*
Brown, Marc. *Arthur's really helpful word book*
Bruno, Elsa Knight. *Punctuation celebration*
Carle, Eric. *My very first book of words*
Carlson, Nancy. *ABC, I like me!*
Carr, Jan. *Greedy apostrophe*

Cassie, Brian. *Say it again*
Chambers, Angela. *Follow that chicken!*
Charlip, Remy. *Handtalk birthday*
Charlip, Remy, et al. *Handtalk*
Cheng, Andrea. *Grandfather counts*
Cleary, Brian P. *A lime, a mime, a pool of slime*
Peanut butter and jellyfishes
Coffelt, Nancy. *Aunt Ant leaves through the leaves*
Big, bigger, biggest!
Cousins, Lucy. *Maisy's amazing big book of words*
Cox, Phil Roxbee. *Fox on a box*
Goose on the loose
Shark in the park
Curtis, Jamie Lee. *Big words for little people*
Dahl, Michael. *If you were an adjective*
Day, Alexandra. *Frank and Ernest*
Frank and Ernest on the road
Frank and Ernest play ball
DeFelice, Cynthia C. *Nelly May has her say*
de Las Casas, Dianne. *The Little "Read" Hen*
de Lestrade, Agnès. *Phileas's fortune*
Donohue, Moira Rose. *Alfie the apostrophe*
Du Quette, Keith. *They call me Woolly*
Falwell, Cathryn. *Word wizard*
Feiffer, Kate. *Henry, the dog with no tail*
Feldman, Eve B. *Billy & Milly, short and silly*
Ferris, Jeri Chase. *Noah Webster and his words*
Fleming, Denise. *Shout! Shout it out!*
Gibbons, Gail. *Weather words and what they mean*
Got, Yves. *Sam's big book of words*
Groner, Judyth Saypol. *My first Hebrew word book*
Guy, Ginger Foglesong. *¡Bravo!*
Gwynne, Fred. *A chocolate moose for dinner*
A little pigeon toad
Hall, Michael. *Cat tale*
Hambleton, Laura. *Monkey business: fun with idioms*
Harper, Jo. *I could eat you up!*
Harris, Trudy. *Pattern bugs*
Harshman, Terry Webb. *Does a sea cow say moo?*
Heelan, Jamee Riggio. *Can you hear a rainbow?*
Heidbreder, Robert. *Lickety-split*
Heling, Kathryn. *Mouse makes magic*
Mouse's hide-and-seek words
Heller, Ruth. *A cache of jewels and other collective nouns*
Fantastic! wow! and unreal!
Kites sail high
Many luscious lollipops
Merry-go-round
Mine, all mine
Henry, Jed. *I speak dinosaur*
Hiatt, Fred. *Baby talk*
Hill, Eric. *Spot's big book of words / El libro grande de las palabras de Spot*
Spot's first words
Hills, Tad. *Rocket's mighty words*
Hoban, Tana. *All about where*
Holub, Joan. *Little red writing*
Hunter, Tom. *Build it up and knock it down*
Hurd, Thacher. *Cat's pajamas*
Hyman, Trina Schart. *A little alphabet*
Inkpen, Mick. *Kipper's book of opposites*
Isadora, Rachel. *Yo, Jo!*
Jay, Alison. *Christmastime*
Jenkins, Emily. *Small medium large*
Jenkins, Steve. *Move!*
Jocelyn, Marthe. *Where do you look?*
Jonas, Ann. *Watch William walk*
Joyce, Susan. *ABC nature riddles*
Keller, Laurie. *Do unto otters*
Konnecke, Ole. *The big book of words and pictures*
Krauss, Ruth. *A hole is to dig*
Kubler, Annie. *My first signs*
Lawlor, Laurie. *Muddy as a duck puddle and other American similes*
Lee, Tae-Jun. *Waiting for Mama*
Leedy, Loreen. *Crazy like a fox*
There's a frog in my throat
Lewis, J. Patrick. *Big is big and little little*
Long, Ethan. *Up, tall and high*
MacDonald, Ross. *Achoo! Bang! Crash!*
McLean, Dirk. *Play mas'! a carnival ABC*
McPhail, David. *Pig Pig meets the lion*
May, Eleanor. *Albert's amazing snail*
Michelson, Richard. *Too young for Yiddish*
Milgrim, David. *My friend Lucky*
Millman, Isaac. *Moses goes to a concert*
Moses goes to school
Moses goes to the circus
Mora, Pat. *Yum! Mmmm! Que rico!*
Mortimer, Rachael. *Song for a princess*
Moses, Will. *Raining cats and dogs*
My first farm
My first word, touch and feel
Nathan, Emma. *What do you call a group of turkeys?*
O'Connor, Jane. *Fancy Nancy: aspiring artist*
Fancy Nancy: explorer extraordinaire!
Fancy Nancy: ooh la la! it's beauty day
Fancy Nancy and the fabulous fashion boutique
Fancy Nancy splendiferous Christmas
Fancy Nancy's collection of fancy words
Ogburn, Jacqueline K. *Little treasures*
O'Malley, Kevin. *Animal crackers fly the coop*
Parish, Herman. *Amelia Bedelia's first library card*
Amelia Bedelia's first vote
Parker, Marjorie Blain. *A paddling of ducks*
Parr, Todd. *Big and little*
Black and white
Paul, Alison. *The crow (a not so scary story)*
Paul, Ann Whitford. *Word builder*
Pearson, Tracey Campbell. *Elephant's story*
Perl, Erica S. *Chicken Butt's back!*
Pulver, Robin. *The case of the incapacitated capitals*
Happy endings
Nouns and verbs have a field day
Punctuation takes a vacation
Silent letters loud and clear
Rankin, Laura. *The handmade counting book*
Rappaport, Doreen. *Abe's honest words*
Martin's big words
Reinhart, Matthew. *Animal popposites*
Ringgold, Faith. *Cassie's word quilt*
Rockwell, Anne. *What we like*
Rosenthal, Amy Krouse. *Al Pha's bet*
Exclamation mark
I scream, ice cream!
Wumbers
Rovetch, Lissa. *Ook the book*
Rumford, James. *There's a monster in the alphabet*
Schaefer, Carole Lexa. *ABCers*
Schotter, Roni. *The boy who loved words*
Seeger, Laura Vaccaro. *One boy*
Walter was worried
Serfozo, Mary. *What's what?*
Shannon, David. *Oops! a diaper David book*
Showers, Paul. *How you talk*
Snicket, Lemony. *13 words*
Sper, Emily. *The Passover seder*

Stanley, Mandy. *At the pool*
First word book
In the park
Sussman, Joni Kibort. *My first Yiddish word book*
Tapahonso, Luci. *Navajo ABC*
Tobin, Jim. *Sue MacDonald had a book*
The very inappropriate word
Trice, Linda. *Kenya's word*
Truss, Lynne. *Eats, shoots and leaves*
Viorst, Judith. *The alphabet from Z to A*
Walker, Sally M. *The Vowel family*
Walton, Rick. *Just me and 6,000 rats*
Wells, Rosemary. *Letters and sounds*
Max's first word
Max's ride
Wimmer, Sonja. *The word collector*
Winnie-the-Pooh's A B C
Wise, William. *Zany zoo*
Wishinsky, Frieda. *What's up, bear?*
Wood, Audrey. *Elbert's bad word*

Language – sign language *see* Sign language

Languages, foreign *see* Foreign languages

Laundry

Docherty, Thomas. *Wash-a-bye Bear*
Feeney, Tatyana. *Small Bunny's blue blanket*
Ford, Bernette. *No more blanket for Lambkin!*
Freeman, Don. *A pocket for Corduroy*
Ormondroyd, Edward. *Theodore*
Weeks, Sarah. *Mrs. McNosh hangs up her wash*
Willems, Mo. *Knuffle Bunny*

Law *see* Careers – judges; Careers – lawyers; Careers – police officers; Crime

Laziness *see* Character traits – laziness

Legends *see* Folk & fairy tales

Letters, cards

Ada, Alma Flor. *Dear Peter Rabbit*
With love, Little Red Hen
Adoff, Arnold. *Love letters*
Alexander, Claire. *Back to front and upside down*
Anholt, Laurence. *Seven for a secret*
Augustin, Barbara. *Antonella and her Santa Claus*
Bauer, Marion Dane. *My mother is mine*
Chen, Yong. *A gift*
Christelow, Eileen. *The desperate dog writes again*
Letters from a desperate dog
Cole, Barbara Hancock. *Anna and Natalie*
Collins, Ross. *Dear Vampa*
Crimi, Carolyn. *Dear Tabby*
Danneberg, Julie. *First year letters*
Daywalt, Drew. *The day the crayons quit*
De Vries, Anke. *Raf*
Durant, Alan. *Dear tooth fairy*
Edwards, Pamela Duncan. *Dear Tooth Fairy*
Flanagan, Alice K. *Here comes Mr. Eventoff with the mail!*
Letter carriers
Gravett, Emily. *Meerkat mail*
Harley, Bill. *Dear Santa*
Heide, Iris van der. *A strange day*
Hobbie, Holly. *Toot and Puddle*
Hodgkinson, Leigh. *Boris and the snoozebox*
Husband, Amy. *Dear Teacher*
Inches, Alison. *Corduroy writes a letter*
Jackson, Alison. *Thea's tree*
James, Simon. *Dear Mr. Blueberry*
Keats, Ezra Jack. *A letter to Amy*
Kempter, Christa. *Dear Little Lamb*
Klingel, Cynthia Fitterer. *Postal workers*
Leedy, Loreen. *Messages in the mailbox*
Lester, Alison. *Ernie dances to the didgeridoo*
Lillegard, Dee. *Tortoise brings the mail*
McAnulty, Stacy. *Dear Santasaurus*
McClatchy, Lisa. *Dear Tyrannosaurus Rex*
McElroy, Lisa Tucker. *Love, Lizzie*
Major, Kevin. *Aunt Olga's Christmas postcards*
Moore, Marian. *Dear Cinderella*
Nolen, Jerdine. *Plantzilla goes to camp*
Olson, Mary. *Nice try, Tooth Fairy*
Orloff, Karen Kaufman. *I wanna new room*
Owen, Ann. *Delivering your mail*
Pak, Soyung. *Dear Juno*
Pattison, Darcy. *The journey of Oliver K. Woodman*
Searching for Oliver K. Woodman
Poydar, Nancy. *Mailbox magic*
Pulver, Robin. *Thank you, Miss Doover*
Puttock, Simon. *Yours truly, Louisa*
Raffi. *Like me and you*
Rand, Gloria. *A pen pal for Max*
Rau, Dana Meachen. *I'll make you a card*
Ray, Deborah Kogan. *Lily's garden*
Rockwell, Anne. *Valentine's Day*
Rylant, Cynthia. *If you'll be my Valentine*
Little Whistle's Christmas
Seuss, Dr. *On beyond zebra*
Sloat, Teri. *Pieces of Christmas*
Stanley, Diane. *Raising Sweetness*
Stanton, Melissa. *My pen pal, Santa*
Steffensmeier, Alexander. *Millie waits for the mail*
Stein, David Ezra. *Love, Mouserella*
Steptoe, Javaka. *The Jones family express*
Stevens, Janet. *Help me, Mr. Mutt!*
Stewart, Sarah. *The gardener*
The quiet place
Straaten, Harmen van. *For me?*
Sullivan, Sarah. *Dear Baby*
Taback, Simms. *I miss you every day*
Postcards from camp
Teague, Mark. *Dear Mrs. LaRue*
Detective LaRue
LaRue across America
LaRue for mayor
Tonatiuh, Duncan. *Dear Primo*
Wallace, Nancy Elizabeth. *Look! Look! Look!*
Look! Look! Look! at sculpture
Wells, Rosemary. *Bunny mail*
Weninger, Brigitte. *A letter to Santa Claus*
Wigersma, Tanneke. *Baby brother*
Wild, Margaret. *Thank you, Santa*
Zweibel, Alan. *Our tree named Steve*

Libraries *see also* Books, reading

Aliki. *How a book is made*
Bernheimer, Kate. *The lonely book*
Bertram, Debbie. *The best book to read*

Bottner, Barbara. *Miss Brooks loves books! (and I don't)*
Brown, Monica. *Waiting for the Biblioburro*
Bruss, Deborah. *Book! book! book!*
Bunting, Eve. *Our library*
Bush, Laura. *Read all about it!*
Buzzeo, Toni. *Inside the books*
No T. Rex in the library
Penelope Popper book doctor
Carnavas, Peter. *The children who loved books*
Casanova, Mary. *The day Dirk Yeller came to town*
Caseley, Judith. *Sophie and Sammy's library sleepover*
Chapman, Susan Margaret. *Too much noise in the library*
Child, Lauren. *But, excuse me, that is my book*
Cleminson, Katie. *Otto the book bear*
Cotten, Cynthia. *The book boat's in*
Cousins, Lucy. *Maisy goes to the library*
Daugherty, James Henry. *Andy and the lion*
Deedy, Carmen Agra. *Return of the library dragon*
de Las Casas, Dianne. *There's a dragon in the library*
dePaola, Tomie. *The knight and the dragon*
Ernst, Lisa Campbell. *Stella Louella's runaway book*
Flanagan, Alice K. *Librarians*
Ms. Davison, our librarian
Fosberry, Jennifer. *Isabella star of the story*
Fox, Kathleen. *The pirates of plagiarism*
Fraser, Mary Ann. *I.Q. goes to the library*
Freedman, Deborah. *The Story of Fish and Snail*
Freeman, Don. *Quiet! There's a canary in the library*
Garland, Michael. *Miss Smith and the haunted library*
Gibbons, Gail. *Check it out! the book about libraries*
The gingerbread boy. *The Library Gingerbread Man*
Gonzalez, Lucia. *The storyteller's candle / La velita de los cuentos*
Grambling, Lois G. *Can I bring Woolly to the library, Ms. Reeder?*
Greene, Rhonda Gowler. *No pirates allowed! said Library Lou*
Hest, Amy. *The babies are coming!*
Horn, Emily. *Excuse me — are you a witch?*
Houston, Gloria. *Miss Dorothy and her bookmobile*
Hubbell, Patricia. *Check it out! reading, finding, helping*
Ivey, Randall. *Jay and the bounty of books*
Johnson, Angela. *Lottie Paris and the best place*
Joyce, William. *The fantastic flying books of Mr. Morris Lessmore*
Kimmel, Eric A. *I took my frog to the library*
King, M. G. *Librarian on the roof!*
Kirk, Daniel. *Library mouse*
Library mouse: a friend's tale
Library mouse: a world to explore
Library mouse: home sweet home
Knudsen, Michelle. *Library lion*
Lakin, Patricia. *Clarence the copy cat*
Rainy day
Lies, Brian. *Bats at the library*
Lindbergh, Reeve. *Homer the library cat*
McDonald, Megan. *When the library lights go out*
McGee, Marni. *Winston the book wolf*
McQuinn, Anna. *Lola at the library*
Mahoney, Daniel J. *The Saturday escape*
Malaspina, Ann. *Finding Lincoln*
Mayr, Diane. *Littlebat's Halloween story*
Meng, Cece. *The wonderful thing about hiccups*
Middleton, Charlotte. *Nibbles*
Miller, Heather. *Librarian*
Miller, Pat. *We're going on a book hunt*
Miller, William. *Richard Wright and the library card*
Mora, Pat. *A library for Juana*
Tomás and the library lady
Morris, Carla. *The boy who was raised by librarians*
Morton, Carlene. *The library pages*
Munro, Roxie. *The inside-outside book of libraries*
Murphy, Mary. *Koala and the flower*
Myron, Vicki. *Dewey*
Naden, Corinne J. *Ron's big mission*
Numeroff, Laura Joffe. *The Jellybeans and the big book bonanza*
Parish, Herman. *Amelia Bedelia's first library card*
Pauli, Lorenz. *The fox in the library*
Polacco, Patricia. *Aunt Chip and the great Triple Creek dam affair*
Radabaugh, Melinda Beth. *Going to the library*
Rahaman, Vashanti. *Read for me, Mama*
Rosenstock, Barb. *Thomas Jefferson builds a library*
Roth, Susan L. *Hands around the library*
Ruurs, Margriet. *My librarian is a camel*
Sadler, Marilyn. *Alistair in outer space*
Schoenherr, Ian. *Read it, don't eat it!*
Shea, Bob. *Dinosaur vs. the library*
Shea, Kitty. *Out and about at the public library*
Shields, Gillian. *Library Lily*
Sierra, Judy. *Mind your manners, B. B. Wolf*
Wild about books
Slegers, Liesbet. *Kevin goes to the library*
Spinelli, Eileen. *The best story*
Stadler, Alexander. *Beverly Billingsly borrows a book*
Stewart, Sarah. *The library*
Stoeke, Janet Morgan. *It's library day*
Turner, Ann Warren. *Pumpkin cat*
Twohy, Mike. *Poindexter makes a friend*
Ungar, Richard. *Rachel's library*
Willis, Jeanne. *Delilah D. at the library*
Winter, Jeanette. *Biblioburro*
The librarian of Basra
Woodruff, Elvira. *Can you guess where we're going?*
Yoo, Taeeun. *The little red fish*

Light, lights

Bang, Molly. *My light*
Berger, Melvin. *Switch on, switch off*
Blechman, Nicholas. *Night light*
Crews, Donald. *Light*
Gal, Susan. *Night lights*
Graham, Joan Bransfield. *Flicker flash*
Hayes, Geoffrey. *The bunny's night-light*
Holderness, Jackie. *What is a shadow?*
McDonald, Megan. *When the library lights go out*
Rocco, John. *Blackout*
Rosenberg, Liz. *Eli's night-light*
Schnur, Steven. *Night lights*
Shulevitz, Uri. *Dusk*
Snicket, Lemony. *The dark*
Swanson, Susan Marie. *The house in the night*
Swinburne, Stephen R. *Guess whose shadow?*
Waring, Geoff. *Oscar and the moth*

Lighthouses

Brett, Jan. *Comet's nine lives*
Briggs, Kelly Paul. *Lighthouse lullaby*
Brown, Ruth. *Gracie the lighthouse cat*
Buzzeo, Toni. *Lighthouse Christmas*
The sea chest

Fearrington, Ann. *Who sees the lighthouse?*
Haas, Rick de. *Peter and the winter sleepers*
Krensky, Stephen. *Sisters of Scituate Light*
Lamb, Albert. *The abandoned lighthouse*
Lobel, Anita. *One lighthouse, one moon*
Perrow, Angeli. *Lighthouse dog to the rescue*
Stainton, Sue. *The lighthouse cat*
Swift, Hildegarde Hoyt. *The little red lighthouse and the great gray bridge*
Wells, Rosemary. *The island light*

Lightning bugs *see* Insects – fireflies

Little people

San Souci, Robert D. *Little Pierre*
Tom Thumb. *The adventures of Tom Thumb*
Tom Thumb

Littleness *see* Character traits – smallness

Lost *see* Behavior – lost

Lost & found possessions *see* Behavior – lost & found possessions

Loyalty *see* Character traits – loyalty

Luck *see* Character traits – luck

Lullabies

Asch, Frank. *Barnyard lullaby*
Bang, Molly. *Ten, nine, eight*
Blomgren, Jennifer. *Where do I sleep?*
Bradman, Tony. *Daddy's lullaby*
Cabrera, Jane. *Twinkle, twinkle, little star*
Canyon, Christopher. *John Denver's Ancient rhymes*
Davies, Jacqueline. *The night is singing*
Davis, Caroline. *My little rocking horse lullabies*
de Las Casas, Dianne. *Mama's bayou*
The drowsy hours
Fox, Mem. *Sleepy bears*
Frampton, David. *The whole night through*
Frazee, Marla. *Hush, little baby: a folk song with pictures*
Ginsburg, Mirra. *Asleep, asleep*
Guthrie, James. *Last song*
Henderson, Kathy. *Hush, baby, hush!*
Ho, Minfong. *Hush!*
Hughes, Langston. *Lullaby (for a Black mother)*
Hush, little baby
Hush songs
Jewel. *Sweet dreams*
That's what I'd do
Kirk, Daniel. *Hush, little alien*
Kono, Erin Eitter. *Hula lullaby*
Lewis, Rose A. *Sweet dreams*
London, Jonathan. *Fireflies, fireflies, light my way*
Lullaby moons and a silver spoon
McGhee, Alison. *In the hollow of your hand*
MacLachlan, Patricia. *Lala salama*
McMullan, Kate. *If you were my bunny*
Markell, Denis. *Hush, Little Monster*
Melmed, Laura Krauss. *Jumbo's lullaby*
Metaxas, Eric. *It's time to sleep, my love*
Millen, C. M. *Blue bowl down*
Mitchard, Jacquelyn. *Baby bat's lullaby*
Newman, Lesléa. *Daddy's song*
Noda, Takayo. *Song of the flowers*
Numeroff, Laura Joffe. *Nighty-night, Cooper*
Pienkowski, Jan. *Good night, a pop-up lullaby*
Pinkney, Brian. *Hush, little baby*
Pomerantz, Charlotte. *All asleep*
Prap, Lila. *Animal lullabies*
Root, Phyllis. *All for the newborn baby*
What Baby wants
Selig, Josh. *Red & Yellow's noisy night*
Snyder, Betsy E. *Sweet dreams lullaby*
Staub, Leslie. *Bless this house*
Thomas, Jan. *Let's sing a lullaby with the Brave Cowboy*
Thomson, Sarah L. *Around the neighborhood*
Titherington, Jeanne. *Baby's boat*
Van Laan, Nancy. *Sleep, sleep, sleep*
When winter comes: a lullaby
Walty, Margaret. *Rock-a-bye baby*
Withrow, Sarah. *Be a baby*
Yolen, Jane. *Sleep, black bear, sleep*

Lying *see* Behavior – lying

Machines

Ashburn, Boni. *Builder Goose*
Barton, Byron. *Machines at work*
Big noisy trucks and diggers
Blum, Mark. *Big trucks and diggers in 3-D*
Braun, Sebastien. *Digger and Tom!*
Burton, Virginia Lee. *Katy and the big snow*
Mike Mulligan and his steam shovel
Carter, Don. *Get to work, trucks!*
Clement, Nathan. *Job site*
Copeland, Cynthia L. *What are you waiting for?*
Dahl, Michael. *One big building*
Dotlich, Rebecca Kai. *What can a crane pick up?*
Fry, Jenny. *Building numbers*
Geisert, Arthur. *Hogwash*
Gordon, David. *The three little rigs*
Granowsky, Alvin. *Diggers and cranes*
Hennessy, B. G. *Road builders*
Hill, Eric. *Spot goes to the farm*
Hill, Lee Sullivan. *Earthmovers*
Hines, Anna Grossnickle. *I am a backhoe*
Hoban, Tana. *Construction zone*
Dig, drill, dump, fill
Horvath, James. *Dig, dogs, dig*
Hudson, Cheryl Willis. *Construction zone*
Kilby, Don. *At a construction site*
In the city
In the country
Light, Steve. *Diggers go*

Low, William. *Machines go to work*
Machines go to work in the city
Lund, Deb. *Monsters on machines*
MacDonald, Suse. *Elephants on board*
Meltzer, Lynn. *The construction crew*
Merriam, Eve. *Bam, bam, bam*
Murphy, Andy. *Out and about at the dairy farm*
My big book of trucks and diggers
Nakagawa, Chihiro. *Who made this cake?*
Niemann, Christoph. *That's how!*
Nikola-Lisa, W. *One hole in the road*
Novak, Matt. *The everything machine*
Olson-Brown, Ellen. *Hush little digger*
Pallotta, Jerry. *The construction alphabet book*
Patrick, Jean L. S. *If I had a snowplow*
Peterson, Cris. *Fantastic farm machines*
Pringle, Laurence P. *Jesse builds a road*
Rockwell, Anne. *Good morning, Digger*
Rogers, Hal. *Combines*
Milking machines
Plows
Sadler, Marilyn. *Alistair's time machine*
Sayres, Brianna Caplan. *Where do diggers sleep at night?*
Schubert, Leda. *Here comes Darrell*
Steggall, Susan. *The diggers are coming!*
Stevenson, James. *Sam the Zamboni man*
Sutton, Sally. *Demolition*
Varela, Barry. *Gizmo*
Vestergaard, Hope. *Digger, dozer, dumper*
Watson, Wendy. *Holly's Christmas eve*
Wood, Jakki. *A hole in the road*

Magic

Adler, David A. *A picture book of Harry Houdini*
Agee, Jon. *Milo's hat trick*
Andersen, Hans Christian. *The tinderbox,* ill. by Warwick Hutton
The tinderbox, ill. by Bagram Ibatoulline
The tinderbox, ill. by Barry Moser
The wild swans, ill. by Anne Yvonne Gilbert
The wild swans, ill. by Susan Jeffers
Anno, Mitsumasa. *Anno's hat tricks*
Araki, Mie. *The magic toolbox*
Aylesworth, Jim. *The full belly bowl*
Baeten, Lieve. *The clever little witch*
Base, Graeme. *The Jewel Fish of Karnak*
Jungle drums
Little elephants
Bateman, Teresa. *Hamster Camp*
Baumgart, Klaus. *Laura's Christmas star*
Laura's secret
Baynton, Martin. *Jane and the magician*
Begin, Mary Jane. *The sorcerer's apprentice*
Bemelmans, Ludwig. *Madeline's Christmas*
Berenstain, Stan and Jan. *The Berenstain bears and the sitter*
Bianco, Margery Williams. *The velveteen rabbit,* ill. by David Jorgensen
The velveteen rabbit, ill. by Thea Kliros
The velveteen rabbit, ill. by Komako Sakai
The velveteen rabbit, ill. by Gennady Spirin
The velveteen rabbit: or, How toys became real, ill. by Allen Atkinson
The velveteen rabbit: or, How toys became real, ill. by Steve Johnson
Black, Harley. *Amazing magic school*
Bloom, Becky. *Mice make trouble*
Bogan, Paulette. *Momma's magical purse*
Bottner, Barbara. *Pish and Posh*
Bower, Tamara. *The shipwrecked sailor*
Bridwell, Norman. *The witch grows up*
Briggs, Raymond. *The puddleman*
Brown, Marcia. *Once a mouse . . .*
Brown, Monica. *Chavela and the magic bubble*
Buehner, Caralyn. *Snowmen all year*
Burdett, Lois. *The tempest for kids*
Burningham, John. *The magic bed*
Calmenson, Stephanie. *The frog principal*
Carmody, Isobelle. *Magic night*
Cate, Annette LeBlanc. *The magic rabbit*
Chase, Mary. *The wicked, wicked ladies in the haunted house*
Cleminson, Katie. *Magic box*
Coats, Lucy. *Neil's numberless world*
Cole, Babette. *Prince Cinders*
Cole, Joanna. *Bony-legs*
The magic school bus and the science fair expedition
The magic school bus in the time of the dinosaurs
The magic school bus inside a beehive
The magic school bus lost in the solar system
The magic school bus on the ocean floor
Compestine, Ying Chang. *The runaway wok*
Corderoy, Tracey. *Monty and Milli*
Cullen, Catherine Ann. *The magical, mystical, marvelous coat*
David, Ryan. *The magic raincoat*
DeFelice, Cynthia C. *One potato, two potato*
Demi. *The magic pillow*
dePaola, Tomie. *Big Anthony and the magic ring*
Brava Strega Nona!
Merry Christmas, Strega Nona
Strega Nona
Strega Nona meets her match
Strega Nona's gift
Strega Nona's harvest
Strega Nona's magic lessons
de Varennes, Monique. *The jewel box ballerinas*
Diakité, Baba Wagué. *Mee-an and the magic serpent*
Dickson, Louise. *The vanishing cat*
Dodd, Emma. *Foxy*
Foxy in love
Meow said the cow
DuBurke, Randy. *The moon ring*
Egielski, Richard. *Three magic balls*
Elschner, Geraldine. *Max's magic seeds*
The firebird. *The firebird,* ill. by Demi
The firebird, ill. by Rachel Isadora
The tale of the firebird
Foley, Greg. *Willoughby and the lion*
Fox, Mem. *The magic hat*
Franson, Scott E. *Un-brella*
Galdone, Paul. *The magic porridge pot*
Garland, Michael. *King Puck*
Miss Smith and the haunted library
Miss Smith reads again!
Miss Smith's incredible storybook
Geras, Adèle. *Swan Lake*
Gravett, Emily. *Spells*
Grimm, Jacob and Wilhelm. *Rose Red and the bear prince*
Rumpelstiltskin, ill. by Paul Galdone
Rumpelstiltskin, ill. by David Shaw
Rumpelstiltskin, ill. by Paul O. Zelinsky
The six swans
Snow White, ill. by Melinda Copper
Snow White, ill. by Quentin Gréban

Snow White, ill. by Trina Schart Hyman
Snow White, ill. by Charles Santore
Snow White and the seven dwarfs, ill. by Wanda Gág
Snow White and the seven dwarfs, ill. by Laura Ljungkvist
The water of life
Grindley, Sally. *The sorcerer's apprentice*
Harrison, Troon. *The floating orchard*
Hautzig, Deborah. *Beauty and the beast*
Hayes, Joe. *Little Gold Star / Estrellita de oro*
Helmer, Marilyn. *Three tales of enchantment*
Hoban, Russell. *Rosie's magic horse*
Hong, Chen Jiang. *The magic horse of Han Gan*
Hooks, William H. *Moss gown*
Howland, Naomi. *Latkes, latkes, good to eat*
Hru, Dakari. *Joshua's Masai mask*
Jackson, Shirley. *9 magic wishes*
Jane, Pamela. *Milo and the greatest trick ever*
Jeffers, Susan. *The twelve days of Christmas*
Johnston, Tony. *The badger and the magic fan*
Jones, Ursula. *The witch's children*
Kako, Satoshi. *Little Daruma and little Daikoku*
Kann, Victoria. *Emeraldalicious*
Kellogg, Steven. *The Pied Piper's magic*
Kennedy, Kim. *Pirate Pete's giant adventure*
Kimmel, Eric A. *Anansi and the magic stick*
Joha makes a wish
The three cabritos
Kitamura, Satoshi. *Me and my cat?*
Knight, Hilary. *Hilary Knight's the owl and the pussy-cat*
Könnecke, Ole. *Anton can do magic*
Kroll, Steven. *The big bunny and the magic show*
Kushner, Donn. *Peter's pixie*
Lachner, Dorothea. *Meredith's mixed-up magic*
LaMarche, Jim. *Up*
Langdo, Bryan. *Tornado Slim and the magic cowboy hat*
Larson, Kirby. *The magic kerchief*
Lester, Helen. *The revenge of the magic chicken*
Lucas, David. *Nutmeg*
McCaughrean, Geraldine. *Grandma Chickenlegs*
McDermott, Gerald. *Tim O'Toole and the wee folk*
MacDonald, Margaret Read. *The great smelly, slobbery small-toothed dog*
McGaw, Wayne T. *T-boy of the bayou*
McNaughton, Janet. *Brave Jack and the unicorn*
McPhail, David. *Moony B. Finch, fastest draw in the West*
Water boy
Many, Paul. *The great pancake escape*
Martin, Bill, Jr. *The magic pumpkin*
Trick or treat?
Mayer, Marianna. *Beauty and the beast*
Meddaugh, Susan. *Cinderella's rat*
The witch's walking stick
Melmed, Laura Krauss. *Moishe's miracle*
Modarressi, Mitra. *Yard sale*
Mollel, Tololwa M. *Orphan boy*
Song bird
Morrissey, Dean. *The Christmas ship*
The wizard mouse
Newman, Marlene. *Myron's magic cow*
Nolen, Jerdine. *Harvey Potter's balloon farm*
Norac, Carl. *My mommy is magic*
Norwich, William D. *Molly and the magic dress*
Ogburn, Jacqueline K. *The magic nesting doll*
Palatini, Margie. *Gone with the wand*
Peet, Bill. *Countdown to Christmas*
Jethro and Joel were a troll
Pelletier, Andrew T. *The toy farmer*
Peters, Stephanie True. *Raggedy Ann and Andy and the magic potion*
Pfister, Marcus. *Milo and the magical stones*
Polacco, Patricia. *Gifts of the heart*
Luba and the wren
My ol' man
Prelutsky, Jack. *The wizard*
Sabuda, Robert. *Beauty and the beast: a pop-up book of the classic fairy tale*
Sanderson, Ruth. *The golden mare, the firebird, and the magic ring*
San Souci, Robert D. *Feathertop*
The hired hand
The red heels
The secret of the stones
The silver charm
The talking eggs
The white cat
Seeger, Pete. *Abiyoyo*
Abiyoyo returns
Shah, Idries. *The boy without a name*
Shepard, Aaron. *One-eye! Two-eyes! Three-eyes!*
Shireen, Nadia. *Hey, Presto!*
Shulevitz, Uri. *The magician*
Simmons, Steven J. *Alice and Greta*
Alice and Greta's color magic
Greta's revenge
Sokol, Edward. *Meet Stinky Magee*
Somers, Kevin. *Meaner than meanest*
Stainton, Sue. *The chocolate cat*
Steig, William. *The amazing bone*
Caleb and Kate
Gorky rises
Solomon the rusty nail
Sylvester and the magic pebble
Tiffky Doofky
Zeke Pippin
Steptoe, John. *The story of jumping mouse*
Stevenson, James. *Yuck!*
Stewig, John Warren. *Clever Gretchen*
Stimpson, Colin. *Jack and the baked beanstalk*
Taulbert, Clifton L. *Little Cliff and the porch people*
Teague, Mark. *One Halloween night*
Tegen, Katherine Brown. *Snowman magic*
Thomas, Shelley Moore. *Good night, Good Knight*
Thomas, Valerie. *Winnie's midnight dragon*
Thompson, Lauren. *The Christmas magic*
Thomson, Bill. *Chalk*
Tibo, Gilles. *The cowboy kid*
Tom Tit Tot. *Tom Tit Tot*
Tseng, Grace. *White tiger, blue serpent*
Tunnell, Michael O. *Halloween pie*
Vallverdu, Josep. *Aladdin and the magic lamp / Aldino y la lampara maravillosa*
Van Allsburg, Chris. *The garden of Abdul Gasazi*
Probuditi!
The widow's broom
Van Dusen, Chris. *King Hugo's huge ego*
Wallace, Karen. *Scarlette Beane*
Walsh, Ellen Stoll. *Mouse magic*
Pip's magic
Walters, Catherine. *The magical snowman*
Wiesner, David. *The loathsome dragon*
Tuesday
Willard, Nancy. *The flying bed*
Williams, Sam. *Snowy magic*

Wisniewski, David. *Elfwyn's saga*
Wood, Audrey. *The flying dragon room*
Yep, Laurence. *The shell woman and the king*
Yolen, Jane. *The firebird*
Yoo, Taeeun. *The little red fish*

Mail *see* Careers – postal workers; Letters, cards; Post office

Mail carriers *see* Careers – postal workers; Letters, cards

Manners *see* Etiquette

Maps

Beck, Andrea. *Elliot digs for treasure*
Chancellor, Deborah. *Maps and mapping*
Elliot, David. *Henry's map*
Hartman, Gail. *As the crow flies*
Keller, Laurie. *The scrambled states of America*
The scrambled states of America talent show
Leedy, Loreen. *Mapping Penny's world*
Murphy, Stuart J. *Treasure map*
National Geographic Society [U.S.]. *National Geographic our world*
Paterson, Brian. *Zigby hunts for treasure*
Piepmeier, Charlotte. *Lucy's journey to the wild west*
Schaap, Martine. *Mop's treasure hunt*
Shulevitz, Uri. *How I learned geography*
Singer, Marilyn. *On the same day in March*
Stroud, Bettye. *The patchwork path*
Tyler, Jenny. *Big Pig on a dig*
Walters, Virginia. *Are we there yet, Daddy?*

Mardi Gras

Lionni, Leo. *The greentail mouse*

Marionettes *see* Puppets

Markets *see* Stores

Marriage, interracial

Adoff, Arnold. *Black is brown is tan*
McGill, Alice. *Molly Bannaky*
Senisi, Ellen B. *For my family, love, Allie*

Marriages *see* Weddings

Masks

Choi, Yangsook. *Behind the mask*
Cohen, Miriam. *The real-skin rubber monster mask*
Emberley, Ed. *Glad monster, sad monster*
Hru, Dakari. *Joshua's Masai mask*
Spalding, Andrea. *Solomon's tree*

Math *see* Counting, numbers

Mazes

Kalz, Jill. *An a-maze-ing amusement park adventure*
An a-maze-ing farm adventure
An a-maze-ing school adventure
An a-maze-ing zoo adventure
Munro, Roxie. *Mazescapes*
Philpot, Lorna. *Find Anthony Ant*

Meanness *see* Character traits – meanness

Mechanical men *see* Robots

Medical technicians *see* Careers – emergency medical technicians

Memories, memory

Aliki. *Christmas tree memories*
Bloom, Suzanne. *Fox forgets*
Blumenthal, Deborah. *Aunt Claire's yellow beehive hair*
Bonwill, Ann. *The Frazzle family finds a way*
Bowen, Anne. *I loved you before you were born*
Brisson, Pat. *Star blanket*
Bunting, Eve. *The memory string*
Cheng, Andrea. *The lemon sisters*
Cooke, Trish. *The grandad tree*
Cruise, Robin. *Little Mama forgets*
Doray, Malika. *One more Wednesday*
Dunrea, Olivier. *Peedie*
Fitzpatrick, Marie-Louise. *You, me and the big blue sea*
Fleischman, Paul. *The matchbox diary*
Foreman, Michael. *Cat in the manger*
Garland, Michael. *Grandpa's tractor*
Gerdner, Linda. *Grandfather's story cloth / Yawg daim paj ntaub dab neeg*
Hanson, Regina. *A season for mangoes*
Hines, Anna Grossnickle. *When the goblins came knocking*
Hopkinson, Deborah. *Bluebird summer*
Johnson, Angela. *The Rolling Store*
Joosse, Barbara. *Ghost wings*
Krishnaswami, Uma. *Chachaji's cup*
Kurtz, Jane. *Faraway home*
Laden, Nina. *Once upon a memory*
Leedahl, Shelley A. *The bone talker*
Lindbergh, Reeve. *My little grandmother often forgets*
Lloyd, Jennifer. *The best thing about kindergarten*
Lucke, Deb. *Sneezenesia*
Lynn, Sarah. *Tip-tap pop*
Lyons, Kelly Starling. *Tea cakes for Tosh*
MacLachlan, Patricia. *Snowflakes fall*
Monk, Isabell. *Blackberry stew*
Morris, Ann. *Grandma Esther remembers*
Grandma Francisca remembers
Grandma Lai Goon remembers
Grandma Lois remembers
Grandma Maxine remembers
Nivola, Claire A. *Orani*
O'Brien, Anne Sibley. *A path of stars*
Parker, Marjorie Blain. *Jasper's day*
Perkins, Lynne Rae. *The broken cat*
Polacco, Patricia. *Betty Doll*
Mrs. Mack
Priceman, Marjorie. *My nine lives / by Clio*

Rochelle, Belinda. *Jewels*
Santucci, Barbara. *Anna's corn*
Schick, Eleanor. *Mama*
Seinfeld, Jerry. *Halloween*
Smith, Lane. *Grandpa Green*
Steig, William. *When everybody wore a hat*
Stewart, Joel. *Addis Berner Bear forgets*
Turner, Ann Warren. *Abe Lincoln remembers*
Warner, Sunny. *The moon quilt*
Woodruff, Elvira. *The memory coat*
Woodson, Jacqueline. *Sweet, sweet memory*
Wyeth, Sharon Dennis. *The granddaughter necklace*
Zagwÿn, Deborah Turney. *The winter gift*
Zalben, Jane Breskin. *Pearl's marigolds for grandpa*

Merry-go-rounds

Cecil, Randy. *Gator*
Clements, Andrew. *Workshop*
Crews, Donald. *Carousel*
Kleven, Elisa. *A carousel tale*
Murphy, Stuart J. *Animals on board*
Rosenberg, Liz. *The carousel*
Selick, Henry. *Moongirl*
Ward, Lindsay. *Please bring balloons*

Messy *see* Behavior – messy

Metamorphosis

Aston, Dianna Hutts. *A butterfly is patient*
Barringer, William. *Gregory and Alexander*
Bunting, Eve. *Butterfly house*
Carle, Eric. *The very hungry caterpillar*
Collicott, Sharleen. *Toestomper and the bad butterflies*
Edwards, Pamela Duncan. *Clara Caterpillar*
Foley, Greg. *Don't worry Bear*
Frost, Helen. *Monarch and milkweed*
Geras, Adèle. *Swan Lake*
Gibbons, Gail. *Monarch butterfly*
Jarrett, Clare. *Arabella Miller's tiny caterpillar*
Martin, Bill, Jr. *Ten little caterpillars*
Middleton, Charlotte. *Nibbles' garden*
Murphy, Mary. *Caterpillar's wish*
Pedersen, Janet. *Houdini the amazing caterpillar*
Rockwell, Anne. *Becoming butterflies*
Runton, Andy. *Owly and Wormy: friends all aflutter!*
Ryder, Joanne. *Where butterflies grow*
Sturges, Philemon. *What's that sound, Woolly Bear?*
Willis, Jeanne. *Tadpole's promise*

Middle Ages

Adkins, Jan. *What if you met a knight?*
Ashburn, Boni. *Over at the castle*
Dick Whittington and his cat. *Dick Whittington and his cat*, ill. by Marcia Brown
Dick Whittington and his cat, ill. by Mélisande Potter
Gibbons, Gail. *Knights in shining armor*
Hindley, Judy. *Princess Rosa's winter*
Hodges, Margaret. *Saint George and the dragon*
Kaufman, Jeanne. *Young Henry and the dragon*
Nikola-Lisa, W. *Magic in the margins*
Olofsson, Helena. *The little jester*
Scarry, Huck. *Looking into the Middle Ages*
Steig, William. *The toy brother*
Tucker, Kathy. *Do knights take naps?*
Yep, Laurence. *The man who tricked a ghost*

Migration

Berkes, Marianne. *Going home: the mystery of animal migration*
Berne, Jennifer. *Calvin can't fly*
Cowcher, Helen. *Desert elephants*
Frost, Helen. *Monarch and milkweed*
George, Jean Craighead. *Luck*
Gerber, Carole. *Little red bat*
Lamstein, Sarah Marwil. *Big night for salamanders*
Madison, Alan. *Velma Gratch and the way cool butterfly*
Markle, Sandra. *Butterfly tree*
Ó Flatharta, Antoine. *Hurry and the monarch*
Prosek, James. *Bird, butterfly, eel*
Sayre, April Pulley. *Here come the humpbacks!*
Home at last
Turtle, turtle, watch out!, ill. by Lee Christiansen
Turtle, turtle, watch out!, ill. by Annie Patterson
Swope, Sam. *Gotta go! Gotta go!*
Thornhill, Jan. *Is this Panama?*
Wild, Margaret. *Lucy Goosey*
Willis, Nancy Carol. *Red knot*
Winkelman, Barbara Gaines. *Sockeye's journey home*
Woodson, Jacqueline. *This is the rope*

Mimes *see* Clowns, jesters

Ministers *see* Careers – clergy

Minorities *see* Ethnic groups in the U.S.

Mirages *see* Optical illusions

Mirrors

Baker, Jeannie. *Mirror*
Cobb, Vicki. *I see myself*
Lee, Suzy. *Mirror*
Schindel, John. *What did they see?*

Misbehavior *see* Behavior – misbehavior

Missions

Politi, Leo. *Song of the swallows*
Ryan, Pam Muñoz. *Nacho and Lolita*

Mist *see* Weather – fog

Mistakes *see* Behavior – mistakes

Misunderstanding *see* Behavior – misunderstanding

Mittens *see* Clothing – gloves, mittens

Money

Adler, David A. *Money madness*
Axelrod, Amy. *Pigs will be pigs*
Bair, Sheila. *Isabel's car wash*

Berenstain, Stan and Jan. *The Berenstain bears' trouble with money*
Brown, Marc. *Arthur's TV trouble*
Caple, Kathy. *Worm gets a job*
Carlson, Nancy. *Start saving, Henry!*
Child, Lauren. *But I've used all my pocket change*
I really, really need actual ice skates
Curious George and the puppies
Finlay, Lizzie. *Little Croc's purse*
Garhan Attebury, Nancy. *Out and about at the bank*
Out and about at the United States Mint
Gill, Shelley. *The big buck adventure*
Glass, Julie. *A dollar for Penny*
Harris, Trudy. *Jenny found a penny*
Inkpen, Mick. *The great pet sale*
Jenkins, Emily. *Lemonade in winter*
Kinch, Devon. *Pretty Penny cleans up*
Pretty Penny makes ends meet
Leedy, Loreen. *Follow the money*
McCaughrean, Geraldine. *One bright Penny*
McMillan, Bruce. *Jelly beans for sale*
Maestro, Betsy. *Dollars and cents for Harriet*
Marks, Jennifer L. *Sorting money*
Medina, Meg. *Tía Isa wants a car*
Milway, Katie Smith. *One hen*
Mollel, Tololwa M. *My rows and piles of coins*
Murphy, Stuart J. *The penny pot*
Sluggers' car wash
O'Connor, Jane. *Fancy Nancy and the fabulous fashion boutique*
O'Neill, Alexis. *Estela's swap*
Perez, Monica. *Curious George saves his pennies*
Pistoia, Sara. *Money*
Reid, Margarette S. *Lots and lots of coins*
Skinner, Daphne. *Tightwad Tod*
Stewart, Sarah. *The money tree*
Tada, Joni Eareckson. *The incredible discovery of Lindsey Renee*
Thayer, Tanya. *Counting money*
Earning money
Saving money
Spending money
Viorst, Judith. *Alexander, who used to be rich last Sunday*
Warwick, Dionne. *Little Man*
Wells, Rosemary. *Bunny money*
Max's bunny business
Williams, Rozanne Lanczak. *The coin counting book*
Ziefert, Harriet. *You can't buy a dinosaur with a dime*

Monsters

Adler, David A. *Perimeter, area, and volume*
Alexander, Lloyd. *The house Gobbaleen*
Alexander, Sue. *Who goes out on Halloween?*
Apple, Margot. *Brave Martha*
Armstrong, Matthew S. *Jane and Mizmow*
Armstrong-Ellis, Carey. *Ten creepy monsters*
Arnold, Tedd. *Five ugly monsters*
Huggly gets dressed
Huggly takes a bath
Ashman, Linda. *The essential worldwide monster guide*
Austin, Mike. *Monsters love colors*
Baker, Ken. *Brave little monster*
Bang, Molly. *Wiley and the hairy man*
Bardhan-Quallen, Sudipta. *Hampire!*
Barton, Bethany. *This monster cannot wait!*
This monster needs a haircut
Bauer, Marion Dane. *I'm not afraid of Halloween!*
Baum, Louis. *The mouse who braved bedtime*
Beaty, Andrea. *Hush, Baby Ghostling*
Beck, Scott. *Happy birthday, Monster!*
Monster sleepover!
Bennett, Kelly. *Vampire baby*
Boxall, Ed. *Francis the scaredy cat*
Brandle, Bine. *Flusi, the sock monster*
Brennan, Herbie. *Frankenstella and the video store monster*
Brennan-Nelson, Denise. *He's been a monster all day!*
Bright, Rachel. *Love Monster*
The brothers gruesome
Brown, Lisa. *Vampire boy's good night*
Brown, Marc. *Arthur's first sleepover*
Bunting, Eve. *Scary, scary Halloween*
Burnell, Heather Ayris. *Bedtime monster / ¡A dormir, pequeño monstruo!*
Case, Chris. *Sophie and the next-door monsters*
Catrow, David. *Monster mash*
Clanton, Ben. *Mo's mustache*
Cohen, Caron Lee. *Broom, zoom!*
Cohen, Miriam. *Jim meets the thing*
Collins, Ross. *Dear Vampa*
Côté, Geneviève. *Mr. King's things*
Crow, Kristyn. *Bedtime at the swamp*
Zombelina
Crum, Shutta. *Who took my hairy toe?*
Cushman, Doug. *Halloween good night*
Cuyler, Margery. *Monster mess!*
David, Lawrence. *The land of the hungry armadillos*
Day, Trevor. *Youch! it bites!*
Dickinson, Rebecca. *Over in the Hollow*
DiPucchio, Kelly. *Zombie in love*
Diviny, Sean. *Halloween Motel*
Docherty, Thomas. *Big scary monster*
Dormer, Frank W. *Socksquatch*
Doyle, Malachy. *Hungry! Hungry! Hungry!*
Dunbar, Joyce. *The monster who ate darkness*
Dyer, Sarah. *Clementine and Mungo*
Monster day at work
Egielski, Richard. *The sleepless little vampire*
Elliott, David. *Hazel Nutt, mad scientist*
Emberley, Ed. *Ed Emberley's bye-bye, big bad bullybug!*
Glad monster, sad monster
Go away, big green monster!
Nighty night Little Green Monster
Emberley, Rebecca. *If you're a monster and you know it*
Ten little beasties
Emberley, Rebecca, et al. *There was an old monster*
Evans, Cambria. *Bone soup*
Faulkner, Keith. *The monster who loved books*
Flaherty, A. W. *The luck of the Loch Ness monster*
Funke, Cornelia. *The wildest brother*
Gaiman, Neil. *The dangerous alphabet*
Gall, Chris. *Substitute creacher*
Gerstein, Mordicai. *The absolutely awful alphabet*
Gibala-Broxholm, Scott. *Maddie's monster dad*
Goodall, John S. *Creepy castle*
Greene, Rhonda Gowler. *Eek! Creak! Snicker, sneak*
Gunnufson, Charlotte. *Halloween hustle*
Haber, Tiffany Strelitz. *The monster who lost his mean*
Hamilton, Libby. *The monstrous book of monsters*
Harper, Charise Mericle. *The Monster Show*
Hawkins, Colin. *Creepy castle*

Hazen, Barbara Shook. *Who is your favorite monster, mama?*
Heinz, Brian J. *The monsters' test*
Heller, Nicholas. *Ogres! ogres! ogres!*
Helmer, Marilyn. *Spooky riddles*
Hemingway, Edward. *Bump in the night*
Hicks, Barbara Jean. *Jitterbug jam*
Monsters don't eat broccoli
Horton, Joan. *Working mummies*
Hout, Mies van. *Friends*
Howe, James. *There's a monster under my bed*
Howie, Betsy. *The Block Mess Monster*
Hutchins, Pat. *It's my birthday!*
Silly Billy!
Three-star Billy
The very worst monster
Where's the baby?
Inkpen, Mick. *Kipper's monster*
Irving, John. *A sound like someone trying not to make a sound*
Jamison, Jocelyn. *Drac's night out*
Jane, Pamela. *Little goblins ten*
Monster countdown
Monster mischief
Kaplan, Bruce Eric. *Monsters eat whiny children*
Kasza, Keiko. *Grandpa Toad's last secret*
Kellogg, Steven. *The island of the skog*
The mysterious tadpole
Ketteman, Helen. *Goodnight, Little Monster*
Kimmel, Eric A. *The three cabritos*
Kleven, Elisa. *A monster in the house*
Koller, Jackie French. *No such thing*
Kraegel, Kenneth. *King Arthur's very great grandson*
Kutner, Merrily. *The Zombie Nite Cafe*
Layne, Steven L. *My brother Dan's delicious*
Lazar, Tara. *The Monstore*
Lesynski, Loris. *Night school*
Leuck, Laura. *Goodnight, baby monster*
My beastly brother
My monster mama loves me so
Levis, Caron. *Stuck with the Blooz*
Lia, Simone. *Red's great chase*
Lichtenheld, Tom. *Everything I know about monsters*
Lodge, Bernard. *How scary*
Lund, Deb. *Monsters on machines*
Lundgren, Mary Beth. *Seven scary monsters*
McAllister, Angela. *Trust me, Mom!*
Yuck! That's not a monster
McCarty, Peter. *Jeremy draws a monster*
The monster returns
McDonnell, Patrick. *The monsters' monster*
McElligott, Matthew. *Even monsters need haircuts*
MacHale, D. J. *The monster princess*
McKissack, Patricia C. *Precious and the Boo Hag*
Mahoney, Daniel J. *Monstergarten*
Markell, Denis. *Hush, Little Monster*
Martin, Bill, Jr. *A beasty story*
Mayer, Marianna. *Pegasus*
Mayer, Mercer. *The bravest knight*
Liza Lou and the Yeller Belly Swamp
There are monsters everywhere
There's a nightmare in my closet
Mayer, Pamela. *The scariest monster in the whole wide world*
Medearis, Angela Shelf. *Tailypo*
Metz, Lorijo. *Floridius Bloom and the planet of Gloom*
Milgrim, David. *Some monsters are different*
Miranda, Anne. *Monster math*
Moffatt, Judith. *Trick-or-treat faces*
Mollel, Tololwa M. *Song bird*
Monster, be good!
Montes, Marisa. *Los gatos black on Halloween*
Moodie, Fiona. *Noko and the night monster*
Moore, Lilian. *Beware, take care*
Mosel, Arlene. *The funny little woman*
Murphy, Jill. *All for one*
Mystery manor
Namioka, Lensey. *Hungriest boy in the world*
Neubecker, Robert. *Beasty bath*
Noll, Amanda. *I need my monster*
Norac, Carl. *Monster, don't eat me!*
Nordling, Lee. *The bramble*
Numberman, Neil. *Do not build a Frankenstein!*
Numeroff, Laura Joffe. *Laura Numeroff's 10-step guide to living with your monster*
O'Connor, George. *Sally and the Some-Thing*
O'Keefe, Susan Heyboer. *Hungry monster ABC*
One hungry monster
O'Malley, Kevin. *Velcome*
Pace, Anne Marie. *Vampirina ballerina*
Vampirina ballerina hosts a sleepover
Paraskevas, Betty. *Maggie and the Ferocious Beast, the big carrot*
Maggie and the Ferocious Beast, the big scare
Patricelli, Leslie. *The Patterson puppies and the midnight monster party*
Peck, Richard. *Monster night at Grandma's house*
Peet, Bill. *Cyrus the unsinkable sea serpent*
Pfister, Marcus. *Rainbow fish and the sea monsters' cave*
Pickering, Jimmy. *Skelly the skeleton girl*
Pienkowski, Jan. *Haunted house*
Pinkney, Brian. *Cosmo and the robot*
Polacco, Patricia. *Some birthday!*
Prelutsky, Jack. *The baby uggs are hatching*
Puttock, Simon. *The baby that roared*
Reasoner, Charles. *Peek-a-boo monsters*
Redeker, Kent. *Don't squish the sasquatch!*
Reiner, Carl. *Tell me a scary story — but not too scary!*
Rex, Michael. *Goodnight goon*
Riggio, Anita. *Beware the Brindlebeast*
Rosoff, Meg. *Jumpy Jack and Googily*
Ross, Gayle. *The legend of the Windigo*
Sage, James. *Mr. Beast*
San Souci, Robert D. *The Hobyahs*
Pedro and the monkey
Sauer, Tammi. *Mostly monsterly*
Schaefer, Lola M. *Frankie Stein*
Frankie Stein starts school
Scheffler, Axel. *The scary monster*
Schneider, Josh. *Bedtime monsters*
Schnitzlein, Danny. *The monster who ate my peas*
Schultz, Sam. *Monster mayhem*
Scrimger, Richard. *Princess Bun Bun*
Seeger, Pete. *Abiyoyo*
Seibold, J. Otto. *Vunce upon a time*
Selick, Henry. *Moongirl*
Sendak, Maurice. *Mommy?*
Seven little monsters
Where the wild things are
Shannon, Margaret. *Gullible's troubles*
Sierra, Judy. *The house that Drac built*
Monster Goose
Thelonius Monster's sky-high fly pie
'Twas the fright before Christmas
Wiley and the Hairy Man
Silverman, Erica. *The Halloween house*
Simon, Annette. *Robot zombie Frankenstein!*

Sís, Peter. *Ship ahoy!*
Slonim, David. *I loathe you*
Spinelli, Eileen. *Wanda's monster*
Stadler, John. *Wilson and Miss Lovely*
Stein, David Ezra. *Monster hug!*
Stein, Mathilde. *The child cruncher*
Monstersong
Stephens, Helen. *Ruby and the noisy hippo*
Stevenson, James. *"Could be worse!"*
Stewart, Joel. *Dexter Bexley and the big blue beastie*
Stower, Adam. *Two left feet*
Taylor, Sean. *When a monster is born*
Tegen, Katherine Brown. *Dracula and Frankenstein are friends*
Thach, James Otis. *A child's guide to common household monsters*
Thomas, Frances. *One day, Daddy*
Todd, Mark. *What will you be for Halloween?*
Tunnell, Michael O. *Halloween pie*
Turkle, Brinton. *Do not open*
Van Nutt, Julia. *The monster in the shadows*
Vere, Ed. *Bedtime for monsters*
Vestergaard, Hope. *What do you do when a monster says boo?*
Viorst, Judith. *My mama says there aren't any zombies, ghosts, vampires, creatures, demons, monsters, fiends, goblins, or things*
Waechter, Phillip. *Rosie and the nightmares*
Waldron, Jan L. *John Pig's Halloween*
Walsh, Melanie. *Monster, monster*
Walton, Rick. *Frankenstein*
Weston, Martha. *Tuck's haunted house*
Wheeler, Lisa. *Boogie knights*
Whitman, Candace. *Lines that wiggle*
Whybrow, Ian. *Good night, monster*
Willems, Mo. *Leonardo the terrible monster*
Wing, Natasha. *Go to bed, monster!*
Winters, Kay. *The teeny tiny ghost and the monster*
Yaccarino, Dan. *The lima bean monster*
Yep, Laurence. *The Khan's daughter*
Yolen, Jane. *Creepy monsters, sleepy monsters*
Romping monsters, stomping monsters
Zalben, Jane Breskin. *Saturday night at the Beastro*
Zemach, Harve. *The judge*

Months of the year *see* Days of the week, months of the year

Moon

Agee, Jon. *Dmitri the astronaut*
Aldrin, Buzz. *Reaching for the moon*
Anderson, Stephen Axel. *I know the moon*
Arden, Carolyn. *Goose moon*
Asch, Frank. *Happy birthday, moon!*
Moonbear
Mooncake
Moondance
Moongame
Bartram, Simon. *Man on the moon: a day in the life of Bob*
Berenstain, Stan and Jan. *The Berenstain bears on the moon*
Berger, Barbara. *Grandfather Twilight*
Branley, Franklyn M. *What the moon is like*
Brown, Margaret Wise. *Goodnight moon*
Goodnight moon ABC
Goodnight moon 123: a counting book
Goodnight moon 123: a counting book [board book]
Burleigh, Robert. *One giant leap*
Butler, M. Christina. *Mouse and the moon*
Cain, Sheridan. *By the light of the moon*
Carle, Eric. *Papa, please get the moon for me*
Carroll, James Christopher. *The boy and the moon*
Chambers, Roland. *Rooftop rocket party*
Chichester Clark, Emma. *Eliza and the moonchild*
Clark, Karen Henry. *Sweet moon baby*
Conrad, Donna. *See you soon, Moon*
Cooper, Floyd. *Max and the tag-along moon*
Côté, Geneviève. *With you always, Little Monday*
Crews, Nina. *I'll catch the moon*
Daly, Niki. *Why the sun and moon live in the sky*
Dayrell, Elphinstone. *Why the sun and the moon live in the sky*
Dillon, Jana. *Lucky O'Leprechaun in school*
DiTerlizzi, Tony. *Jimmy Zangwow's out-of-this-world, moon pie adventure*
DuBurke, Randy. *The moon ring*
Ehlert, Lois. *Moon rope / Un lazo a la luna*
Elschner, Geraldine. *Moonchild, star of the sea*
Emmett, Jonathan. *Bringing down the moon*
Fletcher, Ralph. *Hello, harvest moon*
Floca, Brian. *Moonshot*
Florian, Douglas. *Comets, stars, the moon, and Mars*
Foley, Greg. *Willoughby and the moon*
Gerstein, Mordicai. *How to bicycle to the moon to plant sunflowers*
Gillmor, Don. *Yuck, a love story*
Goldberg, Myla. *Catching the moon*
Gollub, Matthew. *Gobble, quack, moon*
Griffith, Helen V. *Moonlight*
Hargrove, Linda. *Wings across the moon*
Harley, Bill. *Bear's all-night party*
Heller, Nicholas. *Elwood and the witch*
Henkes, Kevin. *Kitten's first full moon*
Horacek, Petr. *When the moon smiled*
Hunter, Anne. *Possum's harvest moon*
Jeffers, Oliver. *The way back home*
Joyce, William. *The Man in the Moon*
The Sandman: the story of Sanderson Mansnoozie
Kherdian, David. *Come back, Moon*
King, Thomas. *Coyote sings to the moon*
Kirk, Daniel. *Moondogs*
Krilanovich, Nadia. *Moon child*
Lin, Grace. *Thanking the moon*
Lobel, Anita. *Lena's sleep sheep*
Lobel, Gillian. *Little Honey Bear and the smiley moon*
Loth, Sebastian. *Clementine*
McCarthy, Meghan. *The adventures of Patty and the big red bus*
McCarty, Peter. *Moon plane*
McDermott, Gerald. *Anansi the spider*
McNulty, Faith. *If you decide to go to the moon*
McReynolds, Linda. *Eight days gone*
Mangan, Anne. *The monkey who wanted the moon*
Martin, Ruth. *Moon dreams*
Mora, Pat. *The night the moon fell*
Morrissey, Dean. *The crimson comet*
Mortensen, Lori. *Cindy Moo*
Mother Goose. *Hey, diddle, diddle,* ill. by Linda Bronson
Hey, diddle, diddle, ill. by Heather Collins
Murray, Marjorie Dennis. *Little Wolf and the moon*
Nishimura, Kae. *Bunny Lune*
Oxenbury, Helen. *Tom and Pippo see the moon*
Pearce, Clemency. *Frangoline and the midnight dream*

Pollock, Penny. *When the moon is full*
Porter, Pamela. *Yellow moon, apple moon*
Preston, Tim. *Pumpkin moon*
Raschka, Chris. *Can't sleep*
Rex, Adam. *Moonday*
Robert, Na'ima B. *Ramadan Moon*
Robledo, Honorio. *Nico visits the moon*
Roper, Janice M. *Dancing on the moon*
Rowe, John A. *Moondog*
Rymond, Lynda Gene. *Oscar and the mooncats*
Scheer, Julian. *By the light of the captured moon*
Schertle, Alice. *Witch Hazel*
Selick, Henry. *Moongirl*
Shea, Pegi Deitz. *New moon*
Shulman, Lisa. *The moon might be milk*
Sleator, William. *The angry moon*
Smith, Linda. *When Moon fell down*
Speed, Toby. *Two cool cows*
Spinelli, Eileen. *Rise the moon*
Spurling, Margaret. *Bilby moon*
Stevenson, Robert Louis. *The moon*, ill. by Tracey Campbell Pearson
The moon, ill. by Denise Saldutti
Stoop, Naoko. *Red Knit Cap Girl*
Suen, Anastasia. *Man on the moon*
The sun, the moon, and the stars
Tafuri, Nancy. *What the sun sees / What the moon sees*
Tan, Amy. *The moon lady*
Tarpley, Natasha Anastasia. *Joe-Joe's first flight*
Taylor, Joanne. *Full moon rising*
Thurber, James. *Many moons*, ill. by Marc Simont
Many moons, ill. by Louis Slobodkin
Trimble, Marcia. *Moonbeams for Santa*
Udry, Janice May. *The moon jumpers*
Ungar, Richard. *Rachel captures the moon*
Ungerer, Tomi. *Moon man*
Vail, Rachel. *Over the moon*
Ward, Helen. *Little Moon Dog*
Wilcox, Brian. *Full moon*
Wolkstein, Diane. *The day Ocean came to visit*
Wood, Audrey. *Moonflute*
Yaccarino, Dan. *Zoom! Zoom! Zoom! I'm off to the moon!*
Zolotow, Charlotte. *The moon was the best*

Mopeds *see* Motorcycles

Morning

Brenner, Barbara A. *Good morning, garden*
Brown, Margaret Wise. *A child's good morning book*
Freedman, Claire. *One magical morning*
Gay, Marie-Louise. *Good morning Sam*
Gleeson, Libby. *Cuddle time*
Good morning
Hannert, Todd. *Morning dance*
Hayward, Linda. *The King's chorus*
Henkes, Kevin. *Shhhh*
Hirschi, Ron. *When morning comes*
Hoffman, Don. *Good morning, good night Billy and Abigail*
McGee, Marni. *Wake up, me!*
Mortensen, Denise Dowling. *Wake up engines*
Most, Bernard. *Cock-a-doodle-moo!*
Murguia, Bethanie Deeney. *Snippet the early riser*
Murphy, Stuart J. *Get up and go!*
O'Mara, Carmel. *Good morning*
Pedersen, Janet. *Millie wants to play*
Pilkey, Dav. *The paperboy*
Raffi. *Rise and shine*
Rosenberg, Liz. *Nobody*
Sedaka, Neil. *Waking up is hard to do*
Shulevitz, Uri. *Dawn*
Siddals, Mary McKenna. *Morning song*
Stevens, April. *Waking up Wendell*
Tafuri, Nancy. *Early morning in the barn*
Tresselt, Alvin R. *Wake up, farm!*
Votaw, Carol. *Good morning, little polar bear*
Weninger, Brigitte. *"Mom, wake up and play!"*
Wick, Walter. *Can you see what I see? dream machine*
Yi, Hu Yong. *Good morning China*
Zolotow, Charlotte. *Something is going to happen*

Mother Goose *see* Nursery rhymes

Motion picture producers *see* Careers – motion picture producers

Motorcycles

Blake, Quentin. *Mrs. Armitage*
Hill, Lee Sullivan. *Motorcycles*
Meadows, Michelle. *Traffic pups*
O'Malley, Kevin. *Once upon a cool motorcycle dude*
Whitehead, Kathy. *Looking for Uncle Louie on the Fourth of July*

Mountain climbing *see* Sports – mountain climbing

Mountain lions *see* Animals – cougars

Mountains

Geisert, Bonnie. *Mountain town*
George, Jean Craighead. *Cliff hanger*
Gill, Shelley. *Up on Denali*
Grupper, Jonathan. *Destination — Rocky Mountains*
Huneck, Stephen. *Sally goes to the mountains*
Johnson, D. B. *Henry climbs a mountain*
Kimmel, Eric A. *The two mountains*
Locker, Thomas. *Mountain dance*
McCarthy, Meghan. *The adventures of Patty and the big red bus*
Moss, Miriam. *This is the mountain*
Nagda, Anne Whitehead. *World above the clouds*
Ray, Mary Lyn. *Basket moon*
Schmidt, Karen Lee. *Carl's nose*
Silvano, Wendi. *Just one more*
Wells, Rosemary. *The bear went over the mountain*
Zoehfeld, Kathleen Weidner. *How mountains are made*

Moving

Aliki. *Best friends together again*
We are best friends
Asch, Frank. *Goodbye house*
Beake, Lesley. *Home now*
Berenstain, Stan and Jan. *The Berenstain bears' moving day*
Blackstone, Stella. *Cleo on the move*
Blades, Ann. *Too small*
Bond, Felicia. *Poinsettia and her family*

Bottner, Barbara. *Rosa's room*
Bowers, Tim. *A new home*
Bullard, Lisa. *Trick-or-treat on Milton Street*
Byun, You. *Dream friends*
Carle, Eric. *Friends*
Carlson, Nancy. *My best friend moved away*
Carlstrom, Nancy White. *I'm not moving, Mama!*
Crum, Shutta. *A family for Old Mill Farm*
Cumming, Hannah. *The red boat*
D'Amico, Carmela. *Ella, the elegant elephant*
Denise, Anika. *Bella and Stella come home*
Glaser, Linda. *Hannah's way*
Gleeson, Libby. *Clancy and Millie and the very fine house*
Half a world away
Grindley, Sally. *A new room for William*
Hallowell, George. *Wagons ho!*
Harrison, Troon. *Courage to fly*
Havill, Juanita. *Jamaica's blue marker*
Hobbie, Holly. *Everything but the horse*
Hume, Stephen Eaton. *Red moon follows truck*
Johnson, Amy Crane. *Mason moves away / Mason se muda*
Johnson, Angela. *The leaving morning*
Johnston, Tony. *The quilt story*
Sunsets of the West
Juster, Norton. *Neville*
Kalan, Robert. *Moving day*
Keats, Ezra Jack. *The trip*
Kleven, Elisa. *The friendship wish*
Lawlor, Laurie. *Old Crump*
Lears, Laurie. *Megan's birthday tree*
Lobel, Anita. *Nini here and there*
Lobel, Arnold. *Ming Lo moves the mountain*
Lorenz, Albert. *The exceptionally, extraordinarily ordinary first day of school*
Macomber, Debbie. *The yippy, yappy Yorkie in the green doggy sweater*
Meltzer, Amy. *A mezuzah on the door*
Michelin, Linda. *Zuzu's wishing cake*
Moss, Miriam. *I'll be your friend, Smudge*
A new house for Smudge
Moss, Peggy. *One of us*
Numberman, Neil. *Do not build a Frankenstein!*
Park, Frances. *Good-bye, 382 Shin Dang Dong*
Pennypacker, Sara. *Stuart's cape*
Pérez, Amada Irma. *My diary from here to there / Mi diario de aquí hasta allá*
Piepmeier, Charlotte. *Lucy's journey to the wild west*
Ritz, Karen. *Windows with birds*
Rogers, Fred. *Moving*
Rostoker-Gruber, Karen. *Bandit*
Sharmat, Marjorie Weinman. *Gila monsters meet you at the airport*
Shreeve, Elizabeth. *Oliver at the window*
Siegel, Mark. *Moving house*
Simpson, Lesley. *The Purim surprise*
Smith, Dana Kessimakis. *A brave spaceboy*
Smith, Joseph A. *Circus train*
Stephens, Helen. *Fleabag*
Stevenson, James. *No friends*
Stewart, Shannon. *Sea crow*
Van Leeuwen, Jean. *Going west*
Viorst, Judith. *Alexander, who's not (do you hear me? I mean it!) going to move*
Waber, Bernard. *Gina*
Ira says goodbye
Wagner, Anke. *Tim's big move!*
Wong, Janet S. *Homegrown house*
Yaccarino, Dan. *Lawn to lawn*
Oswald
Yolen, Jane. *Elsie's bird*
Zagwÿn, Deborah Turney. *The winter gift*

Multi-ethnic *see* Ethnic groups in the U.S.

Multiple births – triplets

Brunhoff, Jean de. *Babar and his children*
Horse, Harry. *Little Rabbit's new baby*
Jenkins, Emily. *Daffodil*
Daffodil, crocodile

Multiple births – twins

Aliki. *Jack and Jake*
Arnold, Tedd. *The twin princes*
Barber, Tiki. *Game day*
Barber, Tiki, et al. *By my brother's side*
Teammates
Brown, Marc. *Arthur babysits*
dePaola, Tomie. *Boss for a day*
Hide-and-seek all week
Marcos
Meet the Barkers
A new Barker in the house
Geist, Ken. *Who's who?*
Hutchins, Pat. *Which witch is which?*
James, Brian. *Supertwins and the sneaky, slimy book worms*
The Supertwins and tooth trouble
The Supertwins meet the bad dogs from space
Supertwins meet the dangerous dino-robots
Kirsch, Vincent X. *Natalie and Naughtily*
LaReau, Kara. *Rocko and Spanky have company*
Lewison, Wendy Cheyette. *Two is for twins*
McElmurry, Jill. *Mess pets*
Mahy, Margaret. *Down the dragon's tongue*
Neuschwander, Cindy. *Pastry school in Paris*
Norling, Beth. *Sister night and sister day*
Norris, Kathleen. *The holy twins*
Peete, Holly Robinson. *My brother Charlie*
Roberts, Bethany. *Double trouble Groundhog Day*
Rockwell, Anne. *Brendan and Belinda and the slam dunk!*
Ryder, Joanne. *A pair of polar bears*
Schaap, Martine. *Mop and the birthday picnic*
Mop's backyard concert
Mop's mountain adventure
Mop's treasure hunt
Simon, Norma. *How do I feel?*
Stanley, Diane. *Thanksgiving on Plymouth Plantation*
Tuck, Justin. *Home-field advantage*
Voake, Charlotte. *Hello twins*
Walters, Catherine. *Are you there, Baby Bear?*
Weiss, Ellen. *Playtime for twins*
Wisniewski, David. *The warrior and the wise man*
Yang, Belle. *Always come home to me*
Yum, Hyewon. *The twins' blanket*
Zehler, Antonia. *Two fine ladies*
Two fine ladies have a tiff

Mummies

Bunting, Eve. *Ballywhinney Girl*
Crimi, Carolyn. *Where's my mummy?*
Horton, Joan. *Working mummies*
Rex, Michael. *Runaway mummy*

Schachner, Judith Byron. *Skippyjon Jones in mummy trouble*
Yates, Philip. *Ten little mummies*

Muppets *see* Puppets

Museums

Aliki. *My visit to the dinosaurs*
Armstrong-Ellis, Carey. *Prudy's problem and how she solved it*
Berenstain, Stan and Jan. *The Berenstain bears and the missing dinosaur bone*
Bernheimer, Kate. *The girl in the castle inside the museum*
Bilgrami, Shaheen. *Amazing dinosaur discovery*
Bliss, Harry. *Bailey at the museum*
Bourgeois, Paulette. *Franklin's class trip*
Brett, Jan. *Mossy*
Brown, Laurie Krasny. *Visiting the art museum*
Browne, Anthony. *The shape game*
Brunhoff, Laurent de. *Babar's Museum of Art*
Cohen, Miriam. *Lost in the museum*
Cousins, Lucy. *Maisy goes to the museum*
Cressy, Judith. *Can you find it?*
Can you find it, too?
dePaola, Tomie. *Bill and Pete go down the Nile*
Friedland, Katy. *Art museum opposites*
Gall, Chris. *Revenge of the Dinotrux*
Geisert, Arthur. *Mystery*
Hartland, Jessie. *How the dinosaur got to the museum*
How the meteorite got to the museum
How the sphinx got to the museum
Hooper, Meredith. *Celebrity cat*
Dogs' Night
Hopkins, Lee Bennett. *Behind the museum door*
Hurd, Thacher. *Art dog*
Johansen, K. V. *Pippin and the bones*
Katz, Susan. *Mrs. Brown on exhibit*
Kellogg, Steven. *Prehistoric Pinkerton*
Kirk, Daniel. *Library mouse: a museum adventure*
Lehman, Barbara. *Museum trip*
Lionni, Leo. *Matthew's dream*
Lithgow, John. *Carnival of the animals*
Micawber
Lucas, David. *Christmas at the toy museum*
Magnier, Thierry. *Isabelle and the angel*
Mauner, Claudia. *Zoe Sophia in New York*
Mayhew, James. *Katie and the Mona Lisa*
Katie and the sunflowers
Katie meets the Impressionists
Metropolitan Museum of Art, NY. *Museum shapes*
Middleton, Julie. *Are the dinosaurs dead, Dad?*
Munro, Roxie. *The inside-outside book of Texas*
The inside-outside book of Washington, D.C.
Neubecker, Robert. *Linus the vegetarian T. rex*
Rogers, Gregory. *The hero of Little Street*
Rohmann, Eric. *Time flies*
Ruzzier, Sergio. *The room of wonders*
Shea, Kitty. *Out and about at the science center*
Smith, Marie. *S is for Smithsonian*
Stevenson, James. *The most amazing dinosaur*
Trenc, Milan. *Another night at the museum*
Tunnell, Michael O. *The joke's on George*
Van Nutt, Julia. *Pignapped!*
Verde, Susan. *The museum*
Wahl, Jan. *The field mouse and the dinosaur named Sue*
I met a dinosaur
Weitzman, Jacqueline Preiss. *You can't take a balloon into the Metropolitan Museum*
You can't take a balloon into the National Gallery
Wellington, Monica. *Squeaking of art, the mice go to the museum*
Wheatley, Nadia. *Luke's way of looking*
Whybrow, Ian. *Harry and the dinosaurs at the museum*
Zalben, Jane Breskin. *Mousterpiece*

Music

Acheson, Alison. *Grandpa's music*
Alexander, Cecil Frances. *All creatures great and small*
Alger, Leclaire Gowans. *Always room for one more*
Aliki. *Ah, music!*
All night, all day
Alley, R. W. *There once was a witch*
Ancona, George. *Mi música / My music*
Anderson, Peggy Perry. *Chuck's band*
Appelt, Kathi. *Bats around the clock*
Bats on parade
Asch, Frank. *Barnyard lullaby*
Austin, Patricia. *The cat who loved Mozart*
Autry, Gene. *Here comes Santa Claus*
Baer, Gene. *Thump thump rat-a-tat-tat*
Barnwell, Ysaye M. *We are one*
Bateman, Teresa. *Harp o' gold*
Traveling Tom and the leprechaun
Bates, Katharine Lee. *America the beautiful*, ill. by Chris Gall
America the beautiful, ill. by Wendell Minor
Bates, Katharine Lee. *America the beautiful: together we stand*
The bear
Berkner, Laurie. *The story of my feelings*
Berlin, Irving. *Easter parade*
God bless America
Bosca, Francesca. *The three grasshoppers*
Brett, Jan. *Berlioz the bear*
Brokering, Herbert F. *Earth and all stars*
Brown, Marc. *Play rhymes*
Burke, Bobby. *Daddy's little girl*
Burleigh, Robert. *Lookin' for Bird in the big city*
Butler, Geoff. *Ode to Newfoundland*
Cabrera, Jane. *If you're happy and you know it*
The wheels on the bus
Calmenson, Stephanie. *Jazzmatazz!*
Canyon, Christopher. *John Denver's Ancient rhymes*
John Denver's Sunshine on my shoulders
Carle, Eric. *I see a song*
Carter, David A. *If you're happy and you know it, clap your hands*
Old MacDonald had a farm: a pop-up book
Carter, Don. *Heaven's all-star jazz band*
Casterline, L. C. *The sounds of music*
Celenza, Anna Harwell. *Duke Ellington's Nutcracker Suite*
The farewell symphony
Chernaik, Judith. *Carnival of the animals: poems inspired by Saint-Saëns' music*
Christensen, Bonnie. *Woody Guthrie, poet of the people*
Collins, Billy. *Daddy's little boy*
Comden, Betty, et al. *Flying to Neverland with Peter Pan*
Costanza, Stephen. *Vivaldi and the invisible orchestra*

Crimi, Carolyn. *Rock 'n' roll Mole*
Crow, Kristyn. *Cool Daddy Rat*
Cummings, Phil. *Boom bah!*
Curtis, Gavin. *The bat boy and his violin*
Czekaj, Jef. *Hip and Hop, don't stop!*
Yes, yes, Yaul!
Daly, Niki. *Ruby sings the blues*
Davis, David. *Jazz cats*
Delacre, Lulu. *Arroz con leche*
Las Navidades
Demas, Corinne. *Nina's waltz*
Dillon, Leo. *Jazz on a Saturday night*
Donaldson, Julia. *Tabby McTat, the musical cat*
Dylan, Bob. *Blowin' in the wind*
Ehrhardt, Karen. *This jazz man*
Elliott, David. *Hazel Nutt, mad scientist*
Ellwand, David. *Ten in the bed*
Emberley, Rebecca. *The ant and the grasshopper*
Falconer, Ian. *Olivia forms a band*
The farmer in the dell. *The farmer in the dell,* ill. by John O'Brien
The farmer in the dell, ill. by Alexandra Wallner
Fine, Howard. *A piggie Christmas*
Fitzgerald, Ella. *A-tisket, a-tasket*
Fleming, Candace. *Gabriella's song*
Frazee, Marla. *Hush, little baby: a folk song with pictures*
A frog he would a-wooing go [folk-song]. *Frog went a-courting*
Genechten, Guido van. *The big woods orchestra*
Gollub, Matthew. *Gobble, quack, moon*
The Jazz Fly
Jazz Fly 2
Goode, Diane. *Diane Goode's book of silly stories and songs*
Gordon, Gus. *Herman and Rosie*
Greenberg, Jan. *Ballet for Martha*
Greenfield, Eloise. *I make music*
Grimm, Jacob and Wilhelm. *Hans my hedgehog*
Guthrie, Woody. *Bling blang*
My dolly
This land is your land
Hale, Sarah Josepha Buell. *Mary had a little lamb,* ill. by Tomie dePaola
Mary had a little lamb, ill. by Laura Huliska-Beith
Mary had a little lamb, ill. by Salley Mavor
Mary had a little lamb, photos by Bruce McMillan
Hallworth, Grace. *Sing me a story*
Harris, John. *Jingle bells: how the holiday classic came to be*
Helmer, Marilyn. *Three tuneful tales*
Here we go round the mulberry bush
High, Linda Oatman. *Cool Bopper's choppers*
Hoberman, Mary Ann. *Bill Grogan's goat*
Hodges, Margaret. *Silent night: the song and its story*
Hooper, Maureen Brett. *Silent night: a Christmas carol is born*
Hoose, Philip M. *Hey little ant*
Horowitz, Dave. *Soon, Baboon, soon*
House, Catherine. *A stork in a baobab tree*
Hurd, Thacher. *Mama don't allow*
Hush, little baby
Hush songs
Hyde, Heidi Smith. *Mendel's accordion*
Ingalls, Ann. *The little piano girl*
Isadora, Rachel. *Ben's trumpet*
Bring on that beat
Ivimey, John William. *The complete story of the three blind mice*
Three blind mice
Jenkins, Emily. *Plonk, plonk, plonk!*
Jennings, Patrick. *Bat and Rat*
Johnson, Angela. *Violet's music*
Johnson, James Weldon. *Lift every voice and sing*
Lift ev'ry voice and sing
Johnson, Paul Brett. *Little Bunny Foo Foo*
Judd, Naomi. *Naomi Judd's guardian angels*
Katz, Karen. *The babies on the bus*
Keats, Ezra Jack. *Apt. 3*
The little drummer boy
Kellogg, Steven. *Yankee Doodle*
Kimmel, Eric A. *The Erie Canal pirates*
The three cabritos
Kirk, Daniel. *Go!*
Knight, Hilary. *A firefly in a fir tree*
Kovalski, Maryann. *Take me out to the ball game*
The wheels on the bus
Kroll, Steven. *By the dawn's early light: the story of the Star Spangled Banner*
Krosoczka, Jarrett J. *Punk Farm*
Krull, Kathleen. *M is for music*
Langstaff, John M. *Oh, a-hunting we will go*
Lenski, Lois. *I like winter*
Lionni, Leo. *Frederick*
Geraldine, the music mouse
Lithgow, John. *Never play music right next to the zoo*
Liu, Jae Soo. *Yellow umbrella*
Lloyd-Jones, Sally. *Old MacNoah had an ark*
Long, Sylvia. *Deck the hall*
McCloskey, Robert. *Lentil*
McDermott, Gerald. *Musicians of the sun*
McGhee, Alison. *Song of middle C*
McGinley-Nally, Sharon. *The friendly beasts*
McMullan, Kate. *Rock-a-baby band*
McPhail, David. *Mole music*
Madison, Alan. *Pecorino's first concert*
Manders, John. *The really awful musicians*
Margolin, H. Ellen. *Goin' to Boston*
Marsalis, Wynton. *Squeak, rumble, whomp! Whomp! Whomp!*
Martin, Jacqueline Briggs. *Chicken joy on Redbean Road*
Mayer, Mercer. *The little drummer mouse*
Mayhew, James. *Ella Bella ballerina and Swan Lake*
Ella Bella ballerina and The Nutcracker
Ella Bella ballerina and The sleeping beauty
Medearis, Angela Shelf. *The singing man*
Michelson, Richard. *Across the alley*
Milgrim, David. *Young MacDonald*
Miller, J. Philip. *We all sing with the same voice*
Miller, William. *The piano*
Rent party jazz
Millman, Isaac. *Moses goes to a concert*
Mills, Judith Christine. *The painted chest*
Mitton, Tony. *Farmer Joe and the music show*
Moore, Mary-Alice. *The wheels on the school bus*
Mora, Pat. *A piñata in a pine tree*
Moss, Lloyd. *Our marching band*
Zin! zin! zin! A violin
Myers, Walter Dean. *The blues of Flats Brown*
Nelson, Steve. *Frosty the snowman*
Frosty the snowman [board book]
Nygaard, Elizabeth. *Snake alley band*
Old MacDonald had a farm. *Old MacDonald had a farm,* ill. by Holly Berry
Old MacDonald had a farm, ill. by Jane Cabrera
Old MacDonald had a farm, ill. by Carol Jones

Old MacDonald had a farm, ill. by Tracey Campbell Pearson
Old MacDonald had a farm, ill. by Glen Rounds
Old MacDonald had a farm, ill. by Prue Theobalds
Olson-Brown, Ellen. *Hush little digger*
Orgill, Roxane. *Skit-scat raggedy cat*
Palatini, Margie. *The cheese*
Paxton, Tom. *Going to the zoo*
Pete the cat: the wheels on the bus
Peterson, Jeanne Whitehouse. *My mama sings*
Pinkney, Andrea Davis. *Duke Ellington*
Pinkney, Brian. *Hush, little baby*
Pinkney, Gloria Jean. *Music from our Lord's holy heaven*
Price, Leontyne. *Aïda*
Pritchett, Dylan. *The first music*
Prokofiev, Sergei Sergeievitch. *Peter and the wolf*, ill. by Charles Mikolaycak
Peter and the wolf, ill. by Josef Palecek
Peter and the wolf, ill. by Chris Raschka
Peter and the wolf, ill. by Vladimir Vagin
Protopopescu, Orel. *Thelonious Mouse*
Raffi. *Baby beluga*
Down by the bay
Everything grows
Like me and you
One light, one sun
Rise and shine
Shake my sillies out
Wheels on the bus
Raposo, Joe. *Sing!*
Raschka, Chris. *Charlie Parker played be bop*
Hip Hop Dog
John Coltrane's giant steps
Ray, Mary Lyn. *Shaker boy*
Robbins, Ruth. *Baboushka and the three kings*
Rodanas, Kristina. *The little drummer boy*
Root, Phyllis. *Rosie's fiddle*
Roth, Susan L. *Do re mi*
Santa Claus is coming to town
Sauer, Tammi. *Bawk and roll*
Schaefer, Carole Lexa. *Two scarlet songbirds*
Schanzer, Rosalyn. *The Old Chisholm Trail*
Schneider, Christine M. *Saxophone Sam and his snazzy jazz band*
Schomp, Virginia. *If you were a . . . musician*
Schuch, Steve. *A symphony of whales*
Sciurba, Katie. *Oye, Celia!*
Sedaka, Marc. *Dinosaur pet*
Seeger, Pete. *The deaf musicians*
Seskin, Steve. *Don't laugh at me*
Shea, Pegi Deitz. *The boy and the spell*
Shulevitz, Uri. *So sleepy story*
Simple gifts
Sís, Peter. *Play, Mozart, play*
Sloat, Teri. *Hark! The aardvark angels sing*
Smith, Charles R. *I'll be there*
My gal
Smith, Will. *Just the two of us*
Snell, Gordon. *Twelve days, a Christmas countdown*
Sorel, Edward. *The Saturday kid*
Stadler, Alexander. *Beverly Billingsly takes a bow*
Staines, Bill. *All God's critters*
Steig, William. *Roland, the minstrel pig*
Zeke Pippin
Stevens, Jan Romero. *Twelve lizards leaping*
Stewart, Joel. *Addis Berner Bear forgets*
Stinson, Kathy. *The man with the violin*
Stohs, Anita. *An Easter alleluia*
Sweet, Melissa. *Fiddle-i-fee*
Tashiro, Chisato. *Five nice mice*
Thien, Madeleine. *The Chinese violin*
Thomas, Joyce Carol. *The gospel Cinderella*
Titcomb, Gordon. *The last train*
Trapani, Iza. *I'm a little teapot*
The itsy bitsy spider
Jingle bells
Shoo fly!
Turner, Barbara J. *Out and about at the orchestra*
The twelve days of Christmas. English folk song.
The twelve days of Christmas
The 12 days of Christmas
The twelve days of Christmas
Twelve days of Christmas
The twelve days of Christmas, ill. by Laurel Long
The twelve days of Christmas, ill. by Ilse Plume
The twelve days of Christmas, ill. by Jane Ray
The twelve days of Christmas, ill. by Gennady Spirin
The twelve days of Christmas, ill. by Vladimir Vagin
The twelve days of Christmas [board book]
Vainio, Pirkko. *The Christmas angel*
Velasquez, Eric. *Grandma's records*
Voake, Charlotte. *Tweedle - dee - dee*
Wallace, Nancy Elizabeth. *Apples, apples, apples*
Walter, Mildred Pitts. *Ty's one-man band*
Walty, Margaret. *Rock-a-bye baby*
Wangerin, Walter. *Angels and all children*
Ward, B. J. *Farty Marty*
Ward, Jennifer. *Over in the garden*
Watts, Leslie Elizabeth. *The Baabaasheep Quartet*
Weatherford, Carole Boston. *Before John was a jazz giant*
Jazz baby
Weeks, Sarah. *Catfish Kate and the sweet swamp band*
Crocodile smile
Woof
Wells, Rosemary. *Bingo*
Westcott, Nadine Bernard. *Skip to my Lou*
There's a hole in the bucket
What a morning!
Wheeler, Lisa. *Jazz baby*
Wheeler, Opal. *Sing in praise*
Sing Mother Goose
Whippo, Walt. *Little white duck*
Wilder, Laura Ingalls. *My little house songbook*
Williams, Suzanne. *The witch casts a spell*
Williams, Vera B. *Music, music for everyone*
Willis, Jeanne. *The wheels on the bus: a read-along sing-along trip to the zoo*
Winter, Jeanette. *Kali's song*
Once upon a time in Chicago
Winter, Jonah. *Dizzy*
Wolkstein, Diane. *The banza*
Yarrow, Peter. *Puff, the magic dragon*
Yolen, Jane. *Jane Yolen's Old MacDonald songbook*
Zelinsky, Paul O. *The wheels on the bus*
Ziefert, Harriet. *Animal music*

Musical instruments

Bunting, Eve. *Hey diddle diddle*
Casterline, L. C. *The sounds of music*
Cox, Judy. *My family plays music*
Cummings, Phil. *Boom bah!*
Day, Nancy Raines. *A is for alliguitar*

Geringer, Laura. *Boom boom go away!*
Horowitz, Dave. *Soon, Baboon, soon*
Lithgow, John. *Never play music right next to the zoo*
The remarkable Farkle McBride
Madison, Alan. *Pecorino's first concert*
Marsalis, Wynton. *Squeak, rumble, whomp! Whomp! Whomp!*
Newton, Jill. *Crash bang donkey!*
Prokofiev, Sergei Sergeievitch. *Peter and the wolf,* ill. by Charles Mikolaycak
Peter and the wolf, ill. by Josef Palecek
Peter and the wolf, ill. by Chris Raschka
Peter and the wolf, ill. by Vladimir Vagin
Shahan, Sherry. *The jazzy alphabet*
Sklansky, Amy E. *The duck who played the kazoo*
Thorpe, Kiki. *Time to cha-cha-cha!*
Uhlberg, Myron. *A storm called Katrina*

Musical instruments – accordions

Hyde, Heidi Smith. *Mendel's accordion*
Williams, Vera B. *Music, music for everyone*

Musical instruments – bagpipes

DeFelice, Cynthia C. *Cold feet*

Musical instruments – bands

Alexander, Kwame. *Acoustic Rooster and his barnyard band*
Anderson, Peggy Perry. *Chuck's band*
Appelt, Kathi. *Bats on parade*
Baer, Gene. *Thump thump rat-a-tat-tat*
Boynton, Sandra. *Christmas parade*
Brett, Jan. *Berlioz the bear*
Carter, Don. *Heaven's all-star jazz band*
Costello, David Hyde. *Little Pig joins the band*
Covell, David. *Rat and Roach rock on!*
Emberley, Rebecca. *The ant and the grasshopper*
Hurd, Thacher. *Mama don't allow*
Johnson, Angela. *Violet's music*
Kassirer, Sue. *Math fair blues*
London, Jonathan. *Froggy plays in the band*
McMullan, Kate. *Rock-a-baby band*
Moss, Lloyd. *Our marching band*
Nygaard, Elizabeth. *Snake alley band*
Orgill, Roxane. *If I only had a horn*
Raschka, Chris. *John Coltrane's giant steps*
Schaap, Martine. *Mop's backyard concert*
Stuchner, Joan Betty. *The Kugel Valley Klezmer Band*
Walter, Mildred Pitts. *Ty's one-man band*
Weeks, Sarah. *Catfish Kate and the sweet swamp band*
Winter, Jeanette. *Once upon a time in Chicago*
Ziefert, Harriet. *Animal music*

Musical instruments – banjos

Busse, Sarah Martin. *Banjo granny*
Pinfold, Levi. *The Django*
Wolkstein, Diane. *The banza*

Musical instruments – cellos

Garriel, Barbara S. *I know a shy fellow who swallowed a cello*

Musical instruments – drums

Base, Graeme. *Jungle drums*
Crow, Kristyn. *Skeleton cat*
Davol, Marguerite W. *The loudest, fastest, best drummer in Kansas*
Francis, Panama. *David gets his drum*
Gollub, Matthew. *The Jazz Fly*
Greenwood, Mark. *Drummer boy of John John*
Guidone, Thea. *Drum city*
Kay, Verla. *Civil War drummer boy*
Keats, Ezra Jack. *The little drummer boy*
Long, Loren. *Drummer boy*
Mayer, Mercer. *The little drummer mouse*
Patricelli, Leslie. *Be quiet, Mike!*
Pinkwater, Daniel. *Bongo Larry*
Protopopescu, Orel. *Two sticks*
Rodanas, Kristina. *The little drummer boy*
Vernick, Audrey. *Teach your buffalo to play drums*
Warwick, Dionne. *Little Man*

Musical instruments – Fiddles *see* Musical instruments – violins

Musical instruments – flutes

Gillard, Denise. *Music from the sky*
Lionni, Leo. *Geraldine, the music mouse*

Musical instruments – guitars

All night, all day
Kovalski, Maryann. *The wheels on the bus*
Myers, Walter Dean. *The blues of Flats Brown*

Musical instruments – harmonicas

Battle-Lavert, Gwendolyn. *The music in Derrick's heart*
Keats, Ezra Jack. *Apt. 3*
McCloskey, Robert. *Lentil*
Steig, William. *Zeke Pippin*

Musical instruments – harps

Edwards, Pamela Duncan. *The leprechaun's gold*

Musical instruments – lutes

Steig, William. *Roland, the minstrel pig*

Musical instruments – orchestras

Costanza, Stephen. *Vivaldi and the invisible orchestra*
Kuskin, Karla. *The Philharmonic gets dressed*
Millman, Isaac. *Moses goes to a concert*
Snicket, Lemony. *The composer is dead*
Tripp, Paul. *Tubby the tuba*
Turner, Barbara J. *Out and about at the orchestra*

Musical instruments – pianos

Alda, Arlene. *Lulu's piano lesson*
All night, all day
Austin, Patricia. *The cat who loved Mozart*
Ingalls, Ann. *The little piano girl*
McGhee, Alison. *Song of middle C*
Miller, William. *The piano*
Perkins, Lynne Rae. *The cardboard piano*
Pinkney, Andrea Davis. *Duke Ellington*
Reynolds, Marilynn. *The magnificent piano recital*

Musical instruments – saxophones

High, Linda Oatman. *Cool Bopper's choppers*
Kallok, Emma. *Gem*
Raschka, Chris. *Charlie Parker played be bop*

Musical instruments – trombones

Weeks, Sarah. *Woof*

Musical instruments – trumpets

Burleigh, Robert. *Lookin' for Bird in the big city*
Isadora, Rachel. *Ben's trumpet*
Orgill, Roxane. *If I only had a horn*
Stewart, Joel. *Addis Berner Bear forgets*

Musical instruments – tubas

Tripp, Paul. *Tubby the tuba*

Musical instruments – violins

Carle, Eric. *I see a song*
Curtis, Gavin. *The bat boy and his violin*
Kraus, Robert. *Mort the sport*
McPhail, David. *Mole music*
Moss, Lloyd. *Zin! zin! zin! A violin*
Otsuka, Yuzo. *Suho's white horse*
Root, Phyllis. *Rosie's fiddle*
Sorel, Edward. *The Saturday kid*
Stinson, Kathy. *The man with the violin*
Thien, Madeleine. *The Chinese violin*

Mystery stories

Berenstain, Stan and Jan. *The bear detectives*
The Berenstain bears and the messy room
The Berenstain bears and the missing dinosaur bone
The Berenstain bears and the missing honey
Boatfield, Jonny. *The twilight book*
Catusanu, Mircea. *The strange case of the missing sheep*
Christelow, Eileen. *Where's the big bad wolf?*
Geisert, Arthur. *Mystery*
Nursery crimes
Gibbons, Gail. *The missing maple syrup sap mystery*
Grambling, Lois G. *Miss Hildy's missing cape caper*
Hurd, Thacher. *Art dog*
Jonas, Ann. *The thirteenth clue*
Kellogg, Steven. *The mystery of the flying orange pumpkin*
The mystery of the magic green ball
The mystery of the missing red mitten
The mystery of the stolen blue paint
Lass, Bonnie. *Who took the cookies from the cookie jar?*
Leedy, Loreen. *Missing math*
McDonald, Megan. *The great pumpkin switch*
Marzollo, Jean. *I spy treasure hunt*
Mauner, Claudia. *Zoe Sophia in New York*
Nash, Scott. *Tuff Fluff*
Selznick, Brian. *The invention of Hugo Cabret*
Sneed, Brad. *Deputy Harvey and the ant cow caper*
Snicket, Lemony. *The composer is dead*
Thompson, Richard. *The follower*
Tryon, Leslie. *Albert's Halloween*
Van Nutt, Julia. *The mystery of Mineral Gorge*

Mythical creatures

Aardema, Verna. *Anansi finds a fool*
Ahlberg, Janet. *Jeremiah in the dark wood*
Ashman, Linda. *The essential worldwide monster guide*
Bartram, Simon. *Man on the moon: a day in the life of Bob*
Carmody, Isobelle. *Magic night*
Carroll, Lewis. *Jabberwocky*
Child, Lauren. *Beware of the storybook wolves*
Conover, Chris. *The lion's share*
Duddle, Jonny. *The pirate cruncher*
Esckelson, Laura. *The copper braid of Shannon O'Shea*
Fairies, trolls and goblins galore
The firebird. *The firebird*, ill. by Demi
The firebird, ill. by Rachel Isadora
The tale of the firebird
Fisher, Leonard Everett. *Cyclops*
Theseus and the Minotaur
Goble, Paul. *Iktomi and the coyote*
Graham, Bob. *Max*
Greenfield, Eloise. *I can draw a weeposaur and other dinosaurs*
Hayes, Sarah. *Lucy Anna and the Finders*
James, Brian. *The Supertwins meet the bad dogs from space*
Jane, Pamela. *Little goblins ten*
Johnston, Tony. *Bigfoot Cinderrrrrella*
Kohara, Kazuno. *Here comes Jack Frost*
Kraegel, Kenneth. *King Arthur's very great grandson*
Larios, Julie. *Imaginary menagerie*
McBratney, Sam. *Once there was a Hoodie*
Magoon, Scott. *The boy who cried bigfoot!*
Mayer, Mercer. *The bravest knight*
Mora, Pat. *Abuelos*
Peet, Bill. *Cyrus the unsinkable sea serpent*
No such things
The pinkish, purplish, bluish egg
Plourde, Lynn. *Wild child*
Winter waits
Reinhart, Matthew. *Fairies and magical creatures*
Gods and heroes
Richards, Jean. *The first Olympic games*
Sabuda, Robert. *The Blizzard's robe*
Shepard, Aaron. *The sea king's daughter*
Sierra, Judy. *'Twas the fright before Christmas*
Singer, Marilyn. *Creature carnival*
Slater, Dashka. *The sea serpent and me*
Spires, Ashley. *Larf*
Todd, Barbara. *The rainmaker*
Washington, Donna L. *A big, spooky house*
Wilbur, Helen L. *Z is for Zeus*
Williams, Suzanne. *The witch casts a spell*
Wisniewski, David. *Golem*
Wood, Audrey. *The Bunyans*
The Tickleoctopus
Yolen, Jane. *The firebird*
Pegasus, the flying horse
Wings

Mythical creatures – aliens *see* Aliens

Mythical creatures – elves

deGroat, Diane. *Lola the elf*
Grimm, Jacob and Wilhelm. *The elves and the shoemaker*, ill. by Kirill Chelushkin

The elves and the shoemaker, ill. by Paul Galdone
The elves and the shoemaker, ill. by Margaret Walty
The shoemaker and his elves
The shoemaker and the elves, ill. by Adrienne Adams
The shoemaker and the elves, ill. by Ilse Plume
Joyce, William. *The Leaf Men and the brave good bugs*
Kimmel, Eric A. *Rip Van Winkle's return*
Krensky, Stephen. *How Santa lost his job*
Light, Steve. *The Christmas giant*
Lowell, Susan. *The bootmaker and the elves*
Maconie, Robin. *Alice and her fabulous teeth*
May, Robert Lewis. *Rudolph the red-nosed reindeer*
Novak, Matt. *The last Christmas present*
Wahl, Jan. *Elf night*
Williams, Sam. *Angel's Christmas cookies*
Snowy magic

Mythical creatures – genies

Lucas, David. *Nutmeg*
Sunami, Kitoba. *How the fisherman tricked the genie*

Mythical creatures – gnomes

Henterly, Jamichael. *Good night, garden gnome*

Mythical creatures – goblins

Alexander, Lloyd. *The house Gobbaleen*
Alexander, Sue. *Who goes out on Halloween?*
Bunting, Eve. *Scary, scary Halloween*
dePaola, Tomie. *Jamie O'Rourke and the pooka*
Doyle, Malachy. *Hungry! Hungry! Hungry!*
Fox, Mem. *The goblin and the empty chair*
Kimmel, Eric A. *Hershel and the Hanukkah goblins*
McDonald, Megan. *The Hinky Pink*
Sendak, Maurice. *Outside over there*

Mythical creatures – leprechauns

Balian, Lorna. *Leprechauns never lie*
Bateman, Teresa. *Fiona's luck*
Leprechaun gold
The leprechaun under the bed
Traveling Tom and the leprechaun
Bunting, Eve. *That's what leprechauns do*
Callahan, Sean. *The leprechaun who lost his rainbow*
Shannon and the world's tallest leprechaun
Chase, Mary. *The wicked, wicked ladies in the haunted house*
Colandro, Lucille. *There was an old lady who swallowed a clover!*
dePaola, Tomie. *Jamie O'Rourke and the big potato*
Dillon, Jana. *Lucky O'Leprechaun comes to America*
Lucky O'Leprechaun in school
Edwards, Pamela Duncan. *The leprechaun's gold*
Krensky, Stephen. *Too many leprechauns*
Shute, Linda. *Clever Tom and the leprechaun*
Tegen, Katherine Brown. *The story of the leprechaun*
Tucker, Kathy. *The leprechaun in the basement*
Welling, Peter J. *Shawn O'Hisser, the last snake in Ireland*

Mythical creatures – lutins

Willey, Margaret. *Clever Beatrice and the best little pony*

Mythical creatures – mermaids, mermen

Andersen, Hans Christian. *The little mermaid*, ill. by Charlene Delage
The little mermaid, ill. by Michael Hague
The little mermaid, ill. by Rachel Isadora
Bateman, Teresa. *The merbaby*
Clibbon, Meg. *Imagine you're a mermaid!*
Fraser, Mary Ann. *Mermaid sister*
Hakala, Marjorie Rose. *Mermaid dance*
Lucas, David. *The skeleton pirate*
Minters, Frances. *Princess Fishtail*
Pitcher, Caroline. *Mariana and the merchild*
San Souci, Robert D. *Nicholas Pipe*
Sukey and the mermaid
Sperring, Mark. *Mermaid dreams*
Willis, Jeanne. *Do little mermaids wet their beds*

Mythical creatures – ogres

Cole, Brock. *Good enough to eat*
Heller, Nicholas. *Ogres! ogres! ogres!*
Juster, Norton. *The odious ogre*
Kimmelman, Leslie. *The three bully goats*
Prelutsky, Jack. *Awful Ogre running wild*
Awful Ogre's awful day
San Souci, Robert D. *Little Pierre*
The silver charm
Sierra, Judy. *Tasty baby belly buttons*
Willard, Nancy. *Shadow story*

Mythical creatures – Pegasus

Mayer, Marianna. *Pegasus*
Yolen, Jane. *Pegasus, the flying horse*

Mythical creatures – phoenix

Demi. *The girl who drew a phoenix*

Mythical creatures – pixies

Kushner, Donn. *Peter's pixie*

Mythical creatures – pooka spirit

dePaola, Tomie. *Jamie O'Rourke and the pooka*
McDermott, Gerald. *Daniel O'Rourke*

Mythical creatures – trolls

Aardema, Verna. *Bimwili and the Zimwi*
Asbjørnsen, P. C. *The three billy goats Gruff*, ill. by Stephen Carpenter
The three billy goats Gruff, ill. by Paul Galdone
The three billy goats Gruff, ill. by Glen Rounds
The three billy goats Gruff, ill. by Janet Stevens
Bolliger, Max. *The happy troll*
Brett, Jan. *Christmas trolls*
Hedgie's surprise
Home for Christmas
The trouble with trolls
Who's that knocking on Christmas eve?
Grimm, Jacob and Wilhelm. *The glass mountain*
Mayer, Mercer. *The bravest knight*
Minters, Frances. *Princess Fishtail*
Mortimer, Rachael. *The three Billy Goats Fluff*
Palatini, Margie. *The three silly billies*
Peet, Bill. *Jethro and Joel were a troll*
Polacco, Patricia. *Oh, look!*

Prelutsky, Jack. *Monday's troll*
Root, Phyllis. *Lucia and the light*
Salley, Coleen. *Who's that tripping over my bridge?*
Wolff, Patricia Rae. *The toll-bridge troll*
Yolen, Jane. *Sister Bear*
Youngquist, Cathrene Valente. *The three Billygoats Gruff and Mean Calypso Joe*

Mythical creatures – unicorns

Heidbreder, Robert. *I wished for a unicorn*
McNaughton, Janet. *Brave Jack and the unicorn*
Mayer, Marianna. *The unicorn and the lake*
Mitchell, Adrian. *Nobody rides the unicorn*
Nahas, Sylvaine. *Nicolo's unicorn*
Reed, Neil. *The midnight unicorn*
Shea, Bob. *Unicorn thinks he's pretty great*
Sheldon, Dyan. *Unicorn dreams*
Yolen, Jane. *Where have the unicorns gone?*

Mythical creatures – werewolves

Collins, Ross. *Dear Vampa*
Salley, Coleen. *Epossumondas plays possum*

Name calling *see* Behavior – name calling

Names

Bayer, Jane. *A my name is Alice*
Bryan, Ashley. *Turtle knows your name*
Bunting, Eve. *Girls A to Z*
Capucilli, Alyssa Satin. *Hello, Biscuit!*
Carter, Alden R. *Big brother Dustin*
Catalanotto, Peter. *Matthew A.B.C.*
Child, Lauren. *That pesky rat*
Choi, Yangsook. *The name jar*
dePaola, Tomie. *Tom*
Dunklee, Annika. *My name is Elizabeth!*
Du Quette, Keith. *They call me Woolly*
Foreman, George. *Let George do it!*
Gadot, A. S. *The first gift*
Henkes, Kevin. *Chrysanthemum*
Inkpen, Mick. *Nothing*
Katz, Karen. *Princess Baby*
Lester, Helen. *A porcupine named Fluffy*
Lester, J. D. *Mommy calls me Monkeypants*
MacLachlan, Patricia. *Three names*
McQuade, Jacqueline. *Big babies*
Monk, Isabell. *Hope*
Mosel, Arlene. *Tikki Tikki Tembo*
Most, Bernard. *A dinosaur named after me*
Murphy, Stuart J. *Write on, Carlos!*
Murray, Alison. *Little Mouse*
Norac, Carl. *Hello, sweetie pie*
Pringle, Laurence P. *Naming the cat*
Raschka, Chris. *New York is English, Chattanooga is Creek*
Recorvits, Helen. *My name is Yoon*
Reynolds, Marilynn. *The name of the child*
Root, Phyllis. *The name quilt*
Rubin, C. M. *Eleanor, Ellatony, Ellencake, and me*
Sadu, Itah. *Christopher changes his name*
Sanders, Marilyn. *What's your name?*
Sasso, Sandy Eisenberg. *In God's name*
Shah, Idries. *The boy without a name*
Sutton, Jane. *Don't call me Sidney*
Swanson, Susan Marie. *The first thing my mama told me*
Tom Tit Tot. *Tom Tit Tot*
Waber, Bernard. *A lion named Shirley Williamson*
Whybrow, Ian. *Harry and the bucketful of dinosaurs*
Williams, Karen Lynn. *My name is Sangoel*
Wolff, Ashley. *I call my grandma Nana*
I call my grandpa Papa

Napping *see* Sleep

Native Americans *see* Eskimos; Indians of Central America; Indians of North America; Indians of South America

Nature

Alarcón, Francisco X. *From the bellybutton of the moon and other summer poems / Del ombligo de la luna y otros poemas de verano*
Alexander, Cecil Frances. *All creatures great and small*
All things bright and beautiful, ill. by Ashley Bryan
All things bright and beautiful, ill. by Anna Vojtech
All things bright and beautiful, ill. by Bruce Whatley
Alexander, Sue. *One more time, Mama*
Aliki. *Quiet in the garden*
Appelt, Kathi. *My father's house*
Arnold, Katya. *Let's find it!*
Arnosky, Jim. *At this very moment*
Babies in the bayou
Come out, muskrats
Crinkleroot's guide to giving back to nature
Crinkleroot's guide to knowing animal habitats
Crinkleroot's guide to knowing the trees
Crinkleroot's guide to walking in wild places
Crinkleroot's 25 birds every child should know
Crinkleroot's 25 fish every child should know
Crinkleroot's 25 mammals every child should know
Crinkleroot's visit to Crinkle Cove
Dolphins on the sand
I see animals hiding
Little Burro
Parrotfish and sunken ships
Wild tracks!
Asch, Frank. *The earth and I*
Bash, Barbara. *Urban roosts*
Berenstain, Stan and Jan. *The Berenstain bears and the wild, wild honey*
Berger, Melvin. *Look out for turtles!*
Berk, Ari. *Nightsong*
Berne, Jennifer. *Manfish*
Bernhard, Durga. *Earth, sky, wet, dry*
Bevis, Mary. *Wolf song*
Biro, Maureen Boyd. *Walking with Maga*
Blaikie, Lynn. *Beyond the northern lights*

Bloxam, Frances. *Antlers forever!*
Bogart, Jo Ellen. *Big and small, room for all*
Brett, Jan. *Mossy*
Bruchac, Joseph. *The circle of thanks*
Bryan, Ashley. *Sing to the sun*
Bunting, Eve. *Anna's table*
Peepers
Burleigh, Robert. *If you spent a day with Thoreau at Walden pond*
Carlstrom, Nancy White. *What does the sky say?*
Chaikin, Miriam. *Don't step on the sky*
Cherry, Lynne. *A river ran wild*
Chrustowski, Rick. *Turtle crossing*
Cole, Henry. *On Meadowview Street*
Collins, Pat Lowery. *The deer watch*
Cooke, Trish. *The grandad tree*
Corr, Christopher. *Whole world*
Davies, Nicola. *Just ducks!*
Delacre, Lulu. *How far do you love me?*
DePalma, Mary Newell. *A grand old tree*
Doolittle, Bev. *Reading the wild*
Ericsson, Jennifer A. *Whoo goes there?*
Ernst, Lisa Campbell. *Wake up, it's Spring!*
Farrar, Sid. *The year comes round*
Ferri, Giuliano. *Little Tad grows up*
Fisher, Aileen Lucia. *Do rabbits have Christmas?*
The story goes on
Fitzsimmons, David. *Curious critters*
Fleming, Denise. *In the tall, tall grass*
Underground
Where once there was a wood
Fletcher, Ralph. *Hello, harvest moon*
Ford, Miela. *Sunflower*
Formento, Alison. *This tree counts!*
This tree, 1, 2, 3
Fox, Paula. *Traces*
Franco, Betsy. *Bees, snails, and peacock tails*
Frisch, Aaron. *The lonely pine*
Frost, Helen. *Step gently out*
Galbraith, Kathryn O. *Planting the wild garden*
Genechten, Guido van. *The big woods orchestra*
George, Jean Craighead. *Dear Rebecca, winter is here*
Everglades
George, Kristine O'Connell. *The great frog race and other poems*
George, Lindsay Barrett. *Around the pond*
In the garden: who's been here?
In the woods
George, William T. *Beaver at Long Pond*
Box turtle at Long Pond
Christmas at Long Pond
Geraghty, Paul. *Help me!*
Gerber, Carole. *Seeds, bees, butterflies, and more!*
Gershator, Phillis. *Listen, listen*
Gibbons, Gail. *Beavers*
Gill, Shelley. *The egg*
Giogas, Valarie. *In my backyard*
Giovanni, Nikki. *The sun is so quiet*
Glaser, Linda. *It's fall*
It's spring
It's summer
It's winter
Our big home
Gomi, Taro. *Everyone poops*
Grimes, Nikki. *A pocketful of poems*
Grupper, Jonathan. *Destination — Rocky Mountains*
Destination, rain forest
Guiberson, Brenda Z. *Into the sea*
Mud city

Hall, Zoe. *The apple pie tree*
Hammersmith, Craig. *Watch it grow*
Heinz, Brian J. *The wolves*
Hewitt, Sally. *All year round*
Woods and meadows
Himmelman, John. *A wood frog's life*
Hines, Anna Grossnickle. *Gramma's walk*
Pieces, a year in poems and quilts
Hirschi, Ron. *Our three bears*
Summer
Hiscock, Bruce. *Ookpik*
Hoban, Tana. *Look book*
Hodgkins, Fran. *Who's been here?*
Horacek, Petr. *Butterfly butterfly*
Howell, Will C. *I call it sky*
Huber, Raymond. *Flight of the honey bee*
Isadora, Rachel. *There was a tree*
Issa, Kobayashi. *Today and today*
Jackson, Ellen. *Earth Mother*
Jenkins, Martin. *Can we save the tiger?*
Jenkins, Steve. *How to clean a hippopotamus*
Just a second
Johnson, D. B. *Henry works*
Johnston, Tony. *The whole green world*
Jolivet, Joëlle. *Almost everything*
Jordan, Helene J. *How a seed grows*
Joyce, Susan. *ABC nature riddles*
Kajikawa, Kimiko. *Close to you*
Kato, Yukiko. *In the meadow*
Kimura, Yuichi. *One sunny day . . .*
Klingel, Cynthia Fitterer. *Deserts*
Forests
Knight, Hilary. *A firefly in a fir tree*
Kurtz, Kevin. *A day in the salt marsh*
Lamstein, Sarah Marwil. *Big night for salamanders*
Lawler, Janet. *A mother's song*
LeBox, Annette. *Wild bog tea*
Lewis, J. Patrick. *Earth and me, our family tree*
Earth and you, a closer view
Lewis, Kevin. *Not inside this house!*
Lewis, Rose A. *Sweet dreams*
Lindbergh, Reeve. *North country spring*
Lionni, Leo. *A busy year*
Locker, Thomas. *Water dance*
London, Jonathan. *Dream weaver*
Flamingo sunset
Honey Paw and Lightfoot
Little lost tiger
Little swan
Red wolf country
Loomis, Christine. *Across America, I love you*
Luenn, Nancy. *Squish!*
Lyon, George Ella. *Counting on the woods*
McCarthy, Mary. *A closer look*
McClure, Nikki. *Apple*
McDonnell, Patrick. *Me . . . Jane*
MacLachlan, Patricia. *Fiona loves the night*
McLeod, Elaine. *Lessons from Mother Earth*
McNamara, Margaret. *Fall leaf project*
Maestro, Betsy. *Why do leaves change color?*
Mannis, Celeste Davidson. *One leaf rides the wind*
Markle, Sandra. *Little lost bat*
Martin, Bill, Jr. *I love our Earth*
Martin, Jacqueline Briggs. *Snowflake Bentley*
Merriam, Eve. *Low song*
Messner, Kate. *Over and under the snow*
Miles, Victoria. *Old Mother Bear*
Miller, Debbie S. *A caribou journey*
Morlock, Lisa. *Track that scat!*

Murray, Martine. *A moose called Mouse*
Myers, Walter Dean. *The story of the three kingdoms*
Noda, Takayo. *Dear world*
O'Connor, Jane. *Fancy Nancy: explorer extraordinaire!*
Olaleye, Isaac. *In the Rainfield*
Oliver, Narelle. *Twilight hunt*
Page, Robin. *Sisters and brothers*
Pallotta, Jerry. *Dory story*
Pandell, Karen. *I love you sun, I love you moon*
Paolilli, Paul. *Silver seeds*
Paquette, Ammi-Joan. *The tiptoe guide to tracking fairies*
Paterson, Katherine. *Brother Sun, Sister Moon*
Peddle, Daniel. *Snow day*
Peters, Lisa Westberg. *The sun, the wind and the rain*
Water's way
Pfeffer, Wendy. *From tadpole to frog*
Life in a coral reef
Pfister, Marcus. *Hopper's treetop adventure*
Questions, questions
Pollard, Nik. *The tide*
Poppenhäger, Nicole. *Snow leopards*
Powell, Consie. *The first day of winter*
Poydar, Nancy. *Snip, snip . . . snow!*
Preller, James. *Cardinal and sunflower*
Raczka, Bob. *Spring things*
Rau, Dana Meachen. *Stroll by the sea*
Reynolds, Aaron. *Carnivores*
Robey, Katharine Crawford. *Where's the party?*
Root, Phyllis. *If you want to see a caribou*
Rotner, Shelley. *Every season*
Ruddell, Deborah. *A whiff of pine, a hint of skunk*
Ruurs, Margriet. *In my backyard*
When we go camping
Ryder, Joanne. *Chipmunk song*
Step into the night
The waterfall's gift
Where butterflies grow
White bear, ice bear
Rylant, Cynthia. *Snow*
The stars will still shine
San Souci, Robert D. *The birds of Killingworth*
Sayre, April Pulley. *Eat like a bear*
Honk, honk, goose!
Schaefer, Lola M. *This is the sunflower*
Schnur, Steven. *Spring thaw*
Schoenherr, John. *Bear*
Schwartz, Roslyn. *Tales from Parc la Fontaine*
Seeger, Laura Vaccaro. *Green*
Selsam, Millicent E. *How to be a nature detective*
Shannon, George. *White is for blueberry*
Shulevitz, Uri. *Snow*
Siddals, Mary McKenna. *I'll play with you*
Sidman, Joyce. *Butterfly eyes and other secrets of the meadow*
Song of the water boatman
Ubiquitous
Siebert, Diane. *Sierra*
Sill, Cathryn. *Wetlands*
Simmons, Jane. *Come along, Daisy!*
Singer, Marilyn. *Turtle in July*
Snyder, Betsy E. *Sweet dreams lullaby*
Stiles, Martha Bennett. *Island magic*
Suzuki, David. *Salmon forest*
Swamp, Jake. *Giving thanks*
Swanson, Susan Marie. *To be like the sun*
Swinburne, Stephen R. *Lots and lots of zebra stripes*
What color is nature?
Tafuri, Nancy. *What the sun sees / What the moon sees*
Thornhill, Jan. *Is this Panama?*
Tomecek, Steve. *Dirt*
von Olfers, Sibylle. *Mother Earth and her children*
Waboose, Jan Bourdeau. *Morning on the lake*
Wallace, Karen. *Scarlette Beane*
Walsh, Melanie. *Do donkeys dance?*
Do lions live on lily pads?
Walters, Catherine. *When will it be spring?*
Weiss, George. *What a wonderful world*
Wells, Rosemary. *Forest of dreams*
Weninger, Brigitte. *Precious water*
Winter, Jeanette. *The watcher*
Winters, Kay. *Tiger trail*
Wolf watch
Winton, Tim. *The deep*
Wolff, Ashley. *Baby Bear sees blue*
Wood, Audrey. *Blue sky*
The Bunyans
When the root children wake up
Wood, Douglas. *Grandad's prayers of the earth*
No one but you
The secret of saying thanks
Where the sunrise begins
Yee, Wong Herbert. *Tracks in the snow*
Yezerski, Thomas. *Meadowlands*
Yolen, Jane. *A mirror to nature*
Welcome to the icehouse
Ziefert, Harriet. *One red apple*
Zolotow, Charlotte. *Say it!*
When the wind stops

Naughty *see* Behavior – misbehavior

Needing someone *see* Behavior – needing someone

Negotiation *see* Activities – trading

Neighborhoods *see* Communities, neighborhoods

Netherlands *see* Foreign lands – Holland

Night

Adlerman, Daniel. *Africa calling*
Adoff, Arnold. *Daring Dog and Captain Cat*
Ahlberg, Janet. *Funnybones*
Alexander, Martha G. *We're in big trouble, Blackboard Bear*
You're a genius, Blackboard Bear
Aliki. *Overnight at Mary Bloom's*
Almond, David. *Kate, the cat and the moon*
Anholt, Laurence. *Jack and the dreamsack*
Appelt, Kathi. *Cowboy dreams*
Apperley, Dawn. *Blossom and Boo stay up late*
Good night, sleep tight, little bunnies
Apple, Margot. *Brave Martha*
Arnold, Tedd. *Huggly gets dressed*
Huggly takes a bath
Arnosky, Jim. *All night near the water*
Raccoons and ripe corn
Asch, Frank. *Moonbear*
Ashman, Linda. *How to make a night*

Aylesworth, Jim. *Two terrible frights*
Baker, Ken. *Brave little monster*
Ballard, Robin. *Tonight and tomorrow*
Bartoletti, Susan Campbell. *Naamah and the ark at night*
Bauer, Marion Dane. *The longest night*
Beames, Margaret. *Night cat*
Bean, Jonathan. *At night*
Beck, Andrea. *Elliot's noisy night*
Berenstain, Stan and Jan. *Bears in the night*
The Berenstain bears in the dark
Berk, Ari. *Nightsong*
Bernhard, Durga. *While you are sleeping: a lift-the-flap book of time around the world*
Birdseye, Tom. *Oh yeah!*
Blackall, Sophie. *Are you awake?*
Bond, Felicia. *Poinsettia and the firefighters*
Bourgeois, Paulette. *Franklin in the dark*
Bradbury, Ray. *Switch on the night*
Brown, Margaret Wise. *The fathers are coming home*
Brunelle, Nicholas. *Snow moon*
Buehner, Caralyn. *Snowmen at night*
Snowmen at night [board book]
Bunting, Eve. *Ghost's hour, spook's hour*
Burningham, John. *It's a secret!*
Butler, John. *Hush, little ones*
While you were sleeping
Butterworth, Nick. *One snowy night*
Carlson, Melody. *When the creepy things come out*
Carman, William. *What's that noise?*
Carroll, James Christopher. *The boy and the moon*
Casanova, Mary. *Utterly otterly night*
Cohen, Caron Lee. *Martin and the giant lions*
Conrad, Donna. *See you soon, Moon*
Crews, Donald. *Night at the fair*
Crews, Nina. *I'll catch the moon*
DaCosta, Barbara. *Nighttime Ninja*
Davies, Jacqueline. *The night is singing*
Davies, Nicola. *Bat loves the night*
White owl, barn owl
Deacon, Alexis. *While you are sleeping*
De Monfreid, Dorothee. *Dark night*
De Roo, Elena. *The rain train*
Doyen, Denise. *Once upon a twice*
The drowsy hours
Dunbar, Joyce. *The monster who ate darkness*
Duncan, Lois. *I walk at night*
Edwards, Michelle. *What's that noise?*
Edwards, Pamela Duncan. *Wake-up kisses*
While the world is sleeping
Emberley, Barbara. *Night's nice*
Faulkner, Keith. *A trick or a treat?*
Feiffer, Kate. *No go sleep!*
Fletcher, Ralph. *Hello, harvest moon*
Ford, Bernette. *First snow*
Fox, Mem. *Night noises*
Fraser, Mary Ann. *Where are the night animals?*
Gabriel, Ashala. *Night night toes*
Gal, Susan. *Night lights*
Gallo, Frank. *Night sounds*
George, William T. *Beaver at Long Pond*
Gibbons, Gail. *Bats*
Ginsburg, Mirra. *Asleep, asleep*
Goossens, Philippe. *Knock! Knock! Knock! Who's there?*
Graber, Janet. *Jacob and the polar bears*
Greenfield, Eloise. *Night on Neighborhood Street*
Grey, Mini. *Toys in space*
Hargrove, Linda. *Wings across the moon*
Harris, Peter. *The night pirates*
Harshman, Marc. *All the way to morning*
Hartland, Jessie. *Night shift*
Hertz, Grete Janus. *Olie's bedtime walk*
Hirschi, Ron. *When night comes*
Hissey, Jane. *Hoot*
Hoberman, Mary Ann. *I'm going to Grandma's*
Hoffman, Don. *Good morning, good night Billy and Abigail*
Hopgood, Tim. *Wow! said the owl*
Horacek, Petr. *When the moon smiled*
Hosta, Dar. *I love the night*
Howe, James. *There's a monster under my bed*
Isadora, Rachel. *A South African night*
Johnson, Angela. *Joshua's night whispers*
Johnson, D. B. *Henry's night*
Johnston, Tony. *Desert song*
Little Rabbit goes to sleep
Jukes, Mavis. *You're a bear*
Keats, Ezra Jack. *Dreams*
Kenah, Katharine. *The dream shop*
Kudlinski, Kathleen V. *The sunset switch*
Lesynski, Loris. *Night school*
Lindbergh, Reeve. *Midnight farm*
London, Jonathan. *Fireflies, fireflies, light my way*
The owl who became the moon
Lullaby moons and a silver spoon
McDonald, Megan. *Whoo-oo is it?*
McGinty, Alice B. *Ten little lambs*
MacLachlan, Patricia. *Fiona loves the night*
Martin, Bill, Jr. *Barn dance!*
Martin, Ruth. *Moon dreams*
Mayer, Mercer. *You're the scaredy cat*
Milusich, Janice. *Off go their engines, off go their lights*
Moodie, Fiona. *Noko and the night monster*
Mora, Pat. *Delicious hullabaloo / Pachanga deliciosa*
Morales, Yuyi. *Little night*
Morgan, Mary. *My good night book*
Munro, Roxie. *Desert days, desert nights*
Murphy, Stuart J. *It's about time!*
Murray, Martine. *A moose called Mouse*
Na, Il Sung. *A book of sleep*
Newman, Lesléa. *Cats, cats, cats*
Nobisso, Josephine. *The moon's lullaby*
Ochiltree, Dianne. *It's a firefly night*
Pearce, Clemency. *Frangoline and the midnight dream*
Peck, Richard. *Monster night at Grandma's house*
Pedersen, Judy. *When night time comes near*
Pendziwol, Jean E. *Once upon a northern night*
Peters, Lisa Westberg. *Frankie works the night shift*
Pilkey, Dav. *The Moonglow Roll-O-Rama*
A pocketful of stars
Posey, Lee. *Night rabbits*
Powell, Polly. *Just dessert*
Prater, John. *On top of the world*
Purmell, Ann. *Where wild babies sleep*
Raschka, Chris. *Can't sleep*
Rathmann, Peggy. *Good night, Gorilla*
Ray, Mary Lyn. *Stars*
Rice, Eve. *Goodnight, goodnight*
Riley, Linnea Asplind. *Mouse mess*
Rinker, Sherri Duskey. *Steam train, dream train*
Robbins, Beth. *Tom's afraid of the dark*
Rocco, John. *Blackout*
Rockwell, Anne. *Here comes the night*
Rodriguez, Bobbie. *Sarah's sleepover*
Rohmann, Eric. *The cinder-eyed cats*

Rosenberg, Liz. *Eli's night-light*
Ross, Michael Elsohn. *Earth cycles*
Roth, Susan L. *Night-time numbers*
Runton, Andy. *Owly and Wormy: bright lights and starry nights!*
Ryan, Cheli Durán. *Hildilid's night*
Ryder, Joanne. *Step into the night*
Rylant, Cynthia. *Night in the country*
Sanromán, Susana. *Señora Reganoña*
Saunders, Karen. *Baby Badger's wonderful night*
Schnur, Steven. *Night lights*
Serfozo, Mary. *Whooo's there?*
Shulevitz, Uri. *Dusk*
So sleepy story
Simmons, Jane. *Daisy's favorite things*
Singer, Marilyn. *Quiet night*
Sloat, Teri. *The thing that bothered Farmer Brown*
Snicket, Lemony. *The dark*
Somary, Wolfgang. *Night and the candlemaker*
Southwell, Jandelyn. *The little country town*
Spinelli, Eileen. *Night shift daddy*
Rise the moon
Sproule, Gail. *Singing the dark*
Srinivasan, Divya. *Little Owl's night*
Stevenson, Robert Louis. *The moon*
Stolz, Mary. *Storm in the night*
Sturges, Philemon. *Ten flashing fireflies*
Stutson, Caroline. *Cats' night out*
Swanson, Susan Marie. *The house in the night*
Tafuri, Nancy. *Do not disturb*
What the sun sees / What the moon sees
Teague, David. *Franklin's big dreams*
Thomas, Patricia. *Firefly mountain*
Red sled
Thomas, Shelley Moore. *Putting the world to sleep*
Thompson, Lauren. *Little Quack's bedtime*
Thompson, Richard. *The night walker*
Thornhill, Jan. *Wild in the city*
Tillman, Nancy. *On the night you were born*
Tomlinson, Jill. *The owl who was afraid of the dark*
Van Allsburg, Chris. *The polar express*
Waboose, Jan Bourdeau. *Firedancers*
SkySisters
Waddell, Martin. *The big big sea*
Can't you sleep, Little Bear?
Owl babies
Owl babies [board book]
Sleep tight, Little Bear
Walsh, Ellen Stoll. *Pip's magic*
Walter, Mildred Pitts. *Darkness*
Waring, Geoff. *Oscar and the moth*
Watt, Mélanie. *Scaredy Squirrel at night*
Weiss, Nicki. *Where does the brown bear go?*
Where does the brown bear go? [board book]
Wellington, Monica. *Night rabbits*
Weston, Carrie. *If a chicken stayed for supper*
Whatley, Bruce. *Captain Pajamas*
Whitehouse, Patricia. *What's awake? A B C*
What's awake? 1 2 3
Wiesner, David. *Tuesday*
Wild, Margaret. *Midnight babies*
Winnick, Karen B. *Sybil's night ride*
Wolf, Karina. *The Insomniacs*
Wood, Audrey. *Moonflute*
Yaccarino, Dan. *Good night, Mr. Night*
Yee, Wong Herbert. *Summer days and nights*
Yolen, Jane. *Owl moon*
Zolotow, Charlotte. *When the wind stops*

Nightmares *see also* Bedtime; Monsters; Mythical creatures – goblins; Night; Sleep

Durango, Julia. *Dream hop*
Johnson, Lindan Lee. *The dream jar*
Karas, G. Brian. *Bebe's bad dream*
Klise, Kate. *Little Rabbit and the Night Mare*
Stadler, Alexander. *Beverly Billingsly borrows a book*
Waechter, Phillip. *Rosie and the nightmares*

No text *see* Wordless

Noise, sounds

Allard, Harry. *Bumps in the night*
Allen, Jonathan. *The little rabbit who liked to say moo*
Anholt, Catherine. *Chimp and Zee's noisy book*
Arnold, Caroline. *Noisytime for zoo animals*
Arnold, Katya. *Meow!*
Arnold, Marsha Diane. *Roar of a snore*
Asch, Frank. *Barnyard lullaby*
Aylesworth, Jim. *Cock-a-doodle-doo, creak, pop-pop, moo*
Country crossing
Baddiel, Ivor. *Cock-a-doodle quack! Quack!*
Balouch, Kristen. *The little little girl with the big big voice*
Beaton, Clare. *How loud is a lion?*
Beaumont, Karen. *No sleep for the sheep!*
Beck, Andrea. *Elliot's noisy night*
Bee, William. *And the cars go . . .*
And the train goes . . .
Beeke, Tiphanie. *Roar like a lion!*
Berenstain, Stan and Jan. *Bears in the night*
Berkes, Marianne. *Marsh music*
Big noisy trucks and diggers
Bock, Lee. *Oh, crumps! / Ay, caramba!*
Bolam, Emily. *Animals talk*
Bond, Felicia. *Poinsettia and the firefighters*
Bond, Rebecca. *Bravo, Maurice!*
Bright, Paul. *Quiet!*
Brown, Margaret Wise. *Bunny's noisy book*
Bunny's noisy book [board book]
Bruins, David. *The call of the cowboy*
Bruss, Deborah. *Book! book! book!*
Burleigh, Robert. *Clang-clang! beep-beep!*
Butler, John. *Can you growl like a bear?*
Carle, Eric. *My very first book of sounds*
The very quiet cricket
Carluccio, Maria. *The sounds around town*
Carman, William. *What's that noise?*
Carter, David A. *Old MacDonald had a farm: a pop-up book*
Cazet, Denys. *Nothing at all*
Chapman, Susan Margaret. *Too much noise in the library*
Chukovskii, Kornei Ivanovich. *Good morning, chick*
Cleary, Beverly. *The hullabaloo ABC*
Colato Laínez, René. *Señor Pancho had a rancho*
Cousins, Lucy. *Maisy's noisy day*
Coy, John. *Vroomaloom zoom*
Craig, Lindsey. *Farmyard beat*
Crimi, Carolyn. *The Louds move in!*
Cumberbatch, Judy. *Can you hear the sea?*
Cummings, Phil. *Boom bah!*
Czekaj, Jef. *Oink-a-doodle-moo*
Dallas-Conte, Juliet. *Cock-a-moo-moo*
Daly, Niki. *Ruby sings the blues*
Davies, Jacqueline. *The night is singing*

Davis, Katie. *Who hoots?*
Davol, Marguerite W. *The loudest, fastest, best drummer in Kansas*
Why butterflies go by on silent wings
DiPucchio, Kelly. *Dinosnores*
DiTerlizzi, Angela. *Say what?*
Dodd, Emma. *Dog's noisy day*
Meow said the cow
Doepker, David. *Farm babies*
Donaldson, Julia. *What the ladybug heard*
Doyle, Malachy. *Too noisy!*
Edwards, Michelle. *What's that noise?*
Edwards, Pamela Duncan. *Slop goes the soup*
Faulkner, Keith. *Do you have my quack?*
Feiffer, Jules. *Bark, George*
Fernandes, Eugenie. *Busy little mouse*
Fleming, Candace. *When Agnes caws*
Fleming, Denise. *Barnyard banter*
The cow who clucked
Fox, Mem. *Night noises*
Freedman, Claire. *Hushabye Lily*
Fuge, Charles. *Yip! Snap! Yap!*
Galdone, Paul. *Cat goes fiddle-i-fee*
Gallo, Frank. *Bird calls*
Night sounds
Garcia, Emma. *Tap tap bang bang*
Gershator, Phillis. *Listen, listen*
Who's in the farmyard?
Gibson, Ginger Foglesong. *Tiptoe Joe*
Giglio, Judy. *The tapping tale*
Glass, Beth Raisner. *Noises at night*
Godwin, Laura. *What the baby hears*
Gorbachev, Valeri. *Shhh!*
Greene, Rhonda Gowler. *Barnyard song*
Guiberson, Brenda Z. *Frog song*
Gundersheimer, Karen. *Find cat, wear hat*
Hänel, Wolfram. *Little elephant's song*
Harper, Jessica. *Nora's room*
Harris, Robie H. *When lions roar*
Harshman, Marc. *All the way to morning*
Hays, Anna Jane. *The pup speaks up*
Heidbreder, Robert. *Noisy poems for a busy day*
Heo, Yumi. *One afternoon*
One Sunday morning
Himmelman, John. *Noisy bug sing-along*
Noisy frog sing-along
Hindley, Judy. *Does a cow say boo?*
Ho, Minfong. *Hush!*
Horacek, Petr. *Choo choo*
Look out, Suzy Goose
Hubbell, Patricia. *My first airplane ride*
Pots and pans
Hutchins, Pat. *Good-night owl*
Ten red apples
Inkpen, Mick. *Honk!*
Irving, John. *A sound like someone trying not to make a sound*
Isadora, Rachel. *Listen to the city*
Janowitz, Tama. *Hear that?*
Jenkins, Steve. *Slap, squeak, and scatter*
Johnson, Angela. *Joshua's night whispers*
Johnson, David. *Snow sounds*
Jonas, Ann. *Bird talk*
Krensky, Stephen. *Noah's bark*
Krilanovich, Nadia. *Chicken, chicken, duck!*
Lavis, Steve. *Cock-a-doodle-doo*
Lawrence, John. *This little chick*
Lawrence, Mary. *What's that sound?*
Lemniscates. *Silence*
Leonard, Marcia. *Animal talk*
Leslie, Amanda. *Do crocodiles moo?*
Lewison, Wendy Cheyette. *"Buzz," said the bee*
Light, Steve. *Trains go*
Lin, Grace. *Okie-dokie, Artichokie*
Lloyd-Jones, Sally. *Old MacNoah had an ark*
Lobb, Janice. *Color and noise! Let's play with toys!*
London, Jonathan. *A train goes clickety-clack*
A truck goes rattley-bumpa
Wiggle, waggle
Long, Kathy. *Christopher sat straight up in bed*
Lucke, Deb. *Sneezenesia*
Maccarone, Grace. *Oink! moo! how do you do?*
McCloskey, Robert. *Lentil*
McCue, Lisa. *Quiet Bunny*
MacDonald, Margaret Read. *The squeaky door*
McDonald, Megan. *Whoo-oo is it?*
MacDonald, Ross. *Achoo! Bang! Crash!*
McFarlane, Sheryl. *In the city*
On the farm
McGee, Marni. *The noisy farm*
McGovern, Ann. *Too much noise*
Macken, JoAnn Early. *Baby says "moo!"*
Mahy, Margaret. *Boom Baby boom, boom*
Maitland, Barbara. *Moo in the morning*
Mandel, Peter. *Zoo ah-choooo*
Marsalis, Wynton. *Squeak, rumble, whomp! Whomp! Whomp!*
Martin, Bill, Jr. *Polar bear, polar bear, what do you hear?*
Mason, Adrienne. *Lu and Clancy sound off*
Massini, Sarah. *Trixie ten*
Matheis, Mickie. *Bedtime for Boo*
Mayo, Margaret. *Choo choo clickety-clack*
Medearis, Angela Shelf. *Rum-a-tum-tum*
Meister, Cari. *Busy, busy city street*
Milgrim, David. *Why Benny barks*
Miranda, Anne. *Beep! beep!*
Mitton, Tony. *Flashing fire engines*
Moon, Nicola. *Tick-tock, drip-drop*
Mora, Pat. *Listen to the desert / Oye al desierto*
Moreton, Daniel. *La Cucaracha Martina*
Most, Bernard. *The cow that went oink*
Z-Z-Zoink!
Mozelle, Shirley. *The bear upstairs*
Munsch, Robert N. *Mortimer*
Murphy, Jill. *Peace at last*
Murphy, Mary. *Please be quiet!*
Murphy, Stuart J. *Percy listens up*
Murphy, Yannick. *Ahwooooooooo!*
Newton, Jill. *Crash bang donkey!*
Nobles, Kristen M. *Drive this book*
Nygaard, Elizabeth. *Snake alley band*
O'Neill, Alexis. *Loud Emily*
Palatini, Margie. *Boo-hoo moo*
Moo who?
Park, Linda Sue. *Yum! Yuck!*
Patricelli, Leslie. *Be quiet, Mike!*
Pearson, Debora. *Big city song*
Pearson, Tracey Campbell. *Bob*
Pedersen, Janet. *Millie wants to play*
Perkins, Lynne Rae. *Snow music*
Pfeffer, Wendy. *Dolphin talk*
Phillips, Mildred. *And the cow said, "moo"!*
Polacco, Patricia. *Mommies say shhh!*
Raschka, Chris. *Talk to me about the alphabet*
Rauss, Ron. *Can I just take a nap?*
Rozen, Anna. *The merchant of noises*
Schwartz, Corey Rosen. *Hop! Plop!*

Scruggs, Afi. *Jump rope magic*
Seeger, Laura Vaccaro. *I had a rooster*
Selig, Josh. *Red & Yellow's noisy night*
Serfozo, Mary. *Rain talk*
Seuss, Dr. *Gerald McBoing Boing*
Gerald McBoing Boing sound book
Shaw, Nancy. *Raccoon tune*
Showers, Paul. *Hear your heart*
The listening walk
Simmons, Jane. *Daisy says coo!*
Daisy says, "If you're happy and you know it"
Daisy, the little duck with big feet
Daisy's day out
Daisy's hide-and-seek
Go to sleep, Daisy
Quack, Daisy, quack!
Singer, Marilyn. *City lullaby*
Quiet night
Skolsky, Mindy Warshaw. *Hannah and the whistling tea kettle*
Slingsby, Janet. *Hush-a-bye babies*
Sloat, Teri. *Farmer Brown goes round and round*
The thing that bothered Farmer Brown
Southwell, Jandelyn. *The little country town*
Spence, Robert, III. *Clickety clack*
Spier, Peter. *Gobble, growl, grunt*
Spires, Elizabeth. *The big meow*
Stephens, Helen. *Ruby and the noisy hippo*
Stevens, April. *Waking up Wendell*
Stevenson, Harvey. *Big scary wolf*
Sturges, Philemon. *What's that sound, Woolly Bear?*
Tafuri, Nancy. *Do not disturb*
The donkey's Christmas song
Teckentrup, Britta. *Little Wolf's song*
Thompson, Richard. *The night walker*
Thomson, Pat. *The squeaky, creaky bed*
Tillman, Nancy. *Tumford's rude noises*
Tresselt, Alvin R. *Wake up, farm!*
Turner, Sandy. *Silent night*
Tyger, Rory. *Newton*
Underwood, Deborah. *The Christmas quiet book*
The loud book!
The quiet book
Verboven, Agnes. *Ducks like to swim*
Vernick, Audrey. *Teach your buffalo to play drums*
Waber, Bernard. *The mouse that snored*
Waddell, Martin. *Let's go home, Little Bear*
Squeak-a-lot
Wadsworth, Ginger. *One tiger growls*
Wallace, Joseph E. *Big and noisy Simon*
Walsh, Melanie. *Do monkeys tweet?*
Walter, Virginia. *"Hi, pizza man!"*
Walton, Rick. *Little dogs say "Rough!"*
Waring, Geoff. *Oscar and the bat*
Weaver, Tess. *Frederick Finch, loudmouth*
Weinstein, Ellen Slusky. *Everywhere the cow says "Moo!"*
West, Colin. *One day in the jungle*
West, Judy. *Have you got my purr?*
Wildsmith, Brian. *Goat's trail*
Williams, Carol Ann. *Booming Bella*
Wilson, Karma. *Who goes there?*
Winer, Yvonne. *Frogs sing songs*
Winnick, Karen B. *Barn sneeze*
Wolff, Ferida. *It is the wind*
Wong, Janet S. *Buzz*
Yoon, Salina. *Do cows meow?*
Do crocs kiss?
Young, Ruth. *Who says moo?*
Zolotow, Charlotte. *The poodle who barked at the wind*

Noise, sounds – snoring *see* Sleep – snoring

Nomads

Baasansuren, Bolormaa. *My little round house*

North Pole *see* Foreign lands – Arctic

Northern lights

Kalz, Jill. *Northern lights*
Merski, P. K. *Roaring, boring, Alice*
Sabuda, Robert. *The Blizzard's robe*
Taylor, Harriet Peck. *Ulaq and the northern lights*
Waboose, Jan Bourdeau. *SkySisters*

Noses *see* Anatomy – noses; Senses – smell

Numbers *see* Counting, numbers

Nursery rhymes

Ada, Alma Flor. *¡Muu, moo!*
Pio peep!
Ahlberg, Janet. *The jolly Christmas postman*
Anholt, Catherine. *Come back, Jack!*
Ashburn, Boni. *Builder Goose*
Aylesworth, Jim. *The completed hickory dickory dock*
Baker, Keith. *Potato Joe*
Beaton, Clare. *Clare Beaton's bedtime rhymes*
Clare Beaton's farmyard rhymes
Clare Beaton's nursery rhymes
Billin-Frye, Paige. *One, two, buckle my shoe*
Brown, Marc. *Finger rhymes*
Hand rhymes
Play rhymes
Bush, Timothy. *Teddy bear, teddy bear*
Butler, John. *Ten in the den*
Cabrera, Jane. *One, two, buckle my shoe*
Twinkle, twinkle, little star
Cauley, Lorinda Bryan. *Clap your hands*
Charlip, Remy. *Sleepytime rhyme*
Chichester Clark, Emma. *Little Miss Muffet counts to ten*
Chorao, Kay. *The baby's bedtime book*
Knock at the door and other baby action rhymes
Christelow, Eileen. *Five little monkeys jumping on the bed*
Conway, David. *The great nursery rhyme disaster*
Cummings, Troy. *The Eensy Weensy Spider freaks out! (big-time!)*
Dann, Penny. *Eensy weensy spider*
Davis, Caroline. *My little rowboat*
Delessert, Etienne. *A was an apple pie*
dePaola, Tomie. *Favorite nursery tales*
Tomie de Paola's Mother Goose
Domanska, Janina. *If all the seas were one sea*
Edwards, Pamela Duncan. *The neat line*
Egielski, Richard. *Itsy bitsy spider*
Fitzgerald, Joanne. *Yum! Yum!*
Fleming, Denise. *The everything book*
The everything book [board book]
Fox, Mem. *Good night, sleep tight*

Galdone, Paul. *Cat goes fiddle-i-fee*
Gliori, Debi. *What's the time, Mr. Wolf?*
Grey, Mini. *The adventures of the dish and the spoon*
Hague, Michael. *Teddy bear, teddy bear*
Hale, Sarah Josepha Buell. *Mary had a little lamb*, ill. by Tomie dePaola
Mary had a little lamb, ill. by Laura Huliska-Beith
Mary had a little lamb, ill. by Salley Mavor
Mary had a little lamb, photos by Bruce McMillan
Harrington, Tim. *This little piggy*
Harris, Trudy. *The clock struck one*
Twenty hungry piggies
The Helen Oxenbury nursery collection
Heller, Nicholas. *This little piggy*
Hennessy, B. G. *The missing tarts*
Hill, Susanna Leonard. *The house that Mack built*
Hillenbrand, Will. *Fiddle-i-fee*
Mother Goose picture puzzles
Hoberman, Mary Ann. *Mary had a little lamb*
Miss Mary Mack
Honey, Elizabeth. *The moon in the man*
Horowitz, Dave. *Humpty Dumpty climbs again*
The house that Jack built. *The house that Jack built*, ill. by Diana Mayo
The house that Jack built, ill. by Jeanette Winter
This is the house that Jack built
Ivimey, John William. *The complete story of the three blind mice*
Three blind mice
Jackson, Alison. *If the shoe fits*
Jay, Alison. *Red green blue*
Jonovitz, Marilyn. *Three little kittens*
Kirk, Daniel. *Jack and Jill*
Kroll, Virginia L. *Jaha and Jamil went down the hill*
Levinthal, David. *Who pushed Humpty Dumpty?*
McMullan, Kate. *Baby Goose*
Martin, Bill, Jr. *Fire! Fire! said Mrs. McGuire*
"Fire! Fire!" said Mrs. McGuire
Martin, Sarah Catherine. *Old Mother Hubbard*
Old Mother Hubbard and her wonderful dog
Metzger, Steve. *Detective Blue*
Miranda, Anne. *To market, to market*
Mitton, Tony. *Riddledy piggledy*
Montgomery, Michael G. *Over the candlestick*
Morgan, Mary. *Dragon pizzeria*
Mortensen, Lori. *Cindy Moo*
Mother Goose. *Arnold Lobel book of Mother Goose*
The baby's lap book
The cat and the fiddle
The Chinese Mother Goose rhymes
Hey, diddle, diddle, ill. by Linda Bronson
Hey, diddle, diddle, ill. by Heather Collins
Hickory, dickory, dock
Hickory dickory dock and other nursery rhymes
Humpty Dumpty
Humpty Dumpty and other rhymes
Ian Penney's book of nursery rhymes
Jack and Jill
James Marshall's Mother Goose
Little Boy Blue and other rhymes
Little Miss Muffet, ill. by Heather Collins
Little Miss Muffet, ill. by Tracey Campbell Pearson
Mother Goose, ill. by Scott Cook
Mother Goose, ill. by Michael Hague
Mother Goose, ill. by Tasha Tudor
Mother Goose numbers on the loose
Mother Goose remembers
My first real Mother Goose [board book]
1, 2, buckle my shoe
One, two, buckle my shoe [board book]
Pat-a-cake, ill. by Olga Ivanov
Pat-a-cake, ill. by Annie Kubler
Pat-a-cake [board book]
Pussycat, pussycat and other rhymes
Richard Scarry's best Mother Goose ever
Rock-a-bye baby [board book]
This little piggy [board book]
The three jovial huntsmen
The three little kittens
Wee Willie Winkie [board book]
Wee Willie Winkie and other rhymes
Wendy Watson's Mother Goose
Will Moses Mother Goose
O'Malley, Kevin. *Humpty Dumpty egg-splodes*
One, two, skip a few!
Palatini, Margie. *The web files*
Pearson, Tracey Campbell. *Diddle diddle dumpling*
Hector Protector [board book]
Petersham, Maud. *The rooster crows*
Pierce, Terry. *Counting your way*
Pinkney, Jerry. *Three little kittens*
Polacco, Patricia. *Babushka's Mother Goose*
Potter, Beatrix. *Appley Dapply's nursery rhymes*
Cecily Parsley's nursery rhymes
Ragged Bear's book of nursery rhymes
Sabuda, Robert. *The movable Mother Goose*
Schoenherr, Ian. *Cat and mouse*
Scieszka, Jon. *The book that Jack wrote*
Truckery rhymes
Sendak, Maurice. *Hector Protector, and As I went over the water*
Sierra, Judy. *Monster Goose*
Simple Simon. *The adventures of Simple Simon*
Siomades, Lorianne. *The itsy bitsy spider*
Three little kittens
Spirin, Gennady. *A apple pie*
Stanley, Diane. *The Giant and the beanstalk*
Stevens, Janet. *And the dish ran away with the spoon*
Taylor, Alice. *A child's treasury of Irish rhymes*
Taylor, Jane. *Twinkle, twinkle little star*, ill. by Heather Collins
Twinkle, twinkle, little star, ill. by Michael Hague
Twinkle, twinkle little star, ill. by Julia Noonan
Twinkle, twinkle, little star, ill. by Jerry Pinkney
Thomson, Sarah L. *Around the neighborhood*
Trapani, Iza. *Baa baa black sheep*
Baa baa black sheep [board book]
The itsy bitsy spider
Rufus and friends
Vail, Rachel. *Over the moon*
Voce, Louise. *Over in the meadow*
Watson, Wendy. *Thanksgiving at our house*
Wells, Rosemary. *Max and Ruby's treasure hunt*
Wheeler, Opal. *Sing Mother Goose*
Wright, Danielle. *Japanese nursery rhymes*
Wu, Faye-Lynn. *Chinese and English nursery rhymes*
Zalben, Jane Breskin. *Hey, Mama Goose*
Zemach, Margot. *Some from the moon, some from the sun*
Ziefert, Harriet. *Mother Goose manners*
Ode to Humpty Dumpty

Nursery school *see* School – nursery

Occupations *see* Careers

Oceans *see* Sea & seashore

Octopuses

Baker, Keith. *My octopus arms*
Cazet, Denys. *The octopus*
Lauber, Patricia. *An octopus is amazing*
Mayer, Mercer. *Octopus soup*
Nyeu, Tao. *Squid and Octopus*
Paterson, Brian. *Zigby dives in*
Pitcher, Caroline. *Nico's octopus*
Scieszka, Jon. *Cowboy and Octopus*
Srinivasan, Divya. *Octopus alone*
Yaccarino, Dan. *An octopus followed me home*
Oswald

Odors *see* Senses – smell

Oil

Berger, Melvin. *Oil spill!*
Rand, Gloria. *Prince William*

Old age

Agee, Jon. *The retired kid*
Alsenas, Linas. *Peanut*
Altes, Marta. *My grandpa*
Altman, Linda Jacobs. *Singing with Momma Lou*
Arnosky, Jim. *Grandfather Buffalo*
Arro, Lena. *By geezers and galoshes!*
Barbour, Karen. *Mr. Williams*
Best, Cari. *Are you going to be good?*
Biro, Maureen Boyd. *Walking with Maga*
Bley, Anette. *And what comes after a thousand?*
Briggs, Raymond. *Jim and the beanstalk*
Bunting, Eve. *Can you do this, Old Badger?*
Cheng, Andrea. *The lemon sisters*
Cruise, Robin. *Little Mama forgets*
dePaola, Tomie. *Nana Upstairs and Nana Downstairs*
Fox, Mem. *Wilfrid Gordon McDonald Partridge*
Grimm, Jacob and Wilhelm. *The Bremen town band*
The Bremen town musicians, ill. by Bill Dickson
The Bremen town musicians, ill. by Ilse Plume
The Bremen town musicians, ill. by Bernadette Watts
The Bremen town musicians, ill. by Lisbeth Zwerger
Musicians of Bremen
Musicians of Bremen / Los musicos de Bremner
Henson, Heather. *Grumpy Grandpa*
Huling, Jan. *Ol' Bloo's boogie-woogie band and blues ensemble*
Johnson, Angela. *When I am old with you*
Joyce, William. *The Leaf Men and the brave good bugs*
Leedahl, Shelley A. *The bone talker*
Lindbergh, Reeve. *My little grandmother often forgets*
Lyons, Kelly Starling. *Tea cakes for Tosh*
Martin, Bill, Jr. *Little granny quarterback*
Miller, William. *The piano*
Muth, Jon J. *Zen ties*
Nanji, Shenaaz. *An alien in my house*
Newman, Jeff. *The boys*
Peet, Bill. *Smokey*
Powell, Consie. *Old dog Cora and the Christmas tree*
Price, Kathy. *The Bourbon Street musicians*
Proimos, James. *Joe's wish*
Puttock, Simon. *A ladder to the stars*
Ramsden, Ashley. *Seven fathers*
Reynolds, Marilynn. *A present for Mrs. Kazinski*
Rubin, Adam. *Those darn squirrels!*
Those darn squirrels and the cat next door
Those darn squirrels fly south
Schachner, Judith Byron. *The Grannyman*
Shelby, Anne. *The man who lived in a hollow tree*
Smith, Lane. *Grandpa Green*
Stead, Philip C. *A sick day for Amos McGee*
Stevens, Janet. *Old bag of bones*
Stroud, Bettye. *Down home at Miss Dessa's*
Tafolla, Carmen. *Baby Coyote and the old woman / El coyotito y la viejita*
Uchida, Yoshiko. *The wise old woman*
Urdahl, Catherine. *Emma's question*
Vega, Denise. *Grandmother, have the angels come?*
Walker, Sally M. *Druscilla's Halloween*
Weigelt, Udo. *Old Beaver*
Wild, Margaret. *Old Pig*
Winter, Jeanette. *Henri's scissors*
Yolen, Jane. *Miz Berlin walks*
Zolotow, Charlotte. *I know a lady*

Opossums *see* Animals – possums

Optical illusions

Anno, Mitsumasa. *Anno's alphabet*
Anno's counting book
Anno's counting house
Anno's Italy
Anno's journey
Mallat, Kathy. *Just ducky*
Priceman, Marjorie. *It's me, Marva!*
Rosenthal, Amy Krouse. *Duck! Rabbit!*

Optimism *see* Character traits – optimism

Orderliness *see* Character traits – orderliness

Orphans

Beake, Lesley. *Home now*
Bemelmans, Ludwig. *Madeline*
Madeline and the bad hat
Madeline and the gypsies
Madeline in London
Madeline's Christmas
Madeline's rescue
Burnett, Frances Hodgson. *A little princess*, ill. by Barbara McClintock
A little princess, ill. by Graham Rust
Calhoun, Mary. *A shepherd's gift*

Crunk, Tony. *Big Mama*
Goble, Paul. *The lost children*
Godden, Rumer. *The story of Holly and Ivy*
Hershenhorn, Esther. *Fancy that*
Joosse, Barbara. *Nikolai, the only bear*
Kay, Verla. *Orphan train*
Kessler, Cristina. *Jubela*
Manna, Anthony L. *The orphan*
Marciano, John Bemelmans. *Madeline and the cats of Rome*
Madeline and the old house in Paris
Madeline at the White House
Martin, Jacqueline Briggs. *The water gift and the pig of the pig*
Mollel, Tololwa M. *Orphan boy*
Noyes, Deborah. *When I met the wolf girls*
Odone, Jamison. *Honey badgers*
Oelschlager, Vanita. *I came from the water*
Polacco, Patricia. *Welcome Comfort*
Pomerantz, Charlotte. *The mousery*
Prigger, Mary Skillings. *Aunt Minnie McGranahan*
Rylant, Cynthia. *The bird house*
San Souci, Robert D. *The secret of the stones*
Selznick, Brian. *The invention of Hugo Cabret*
Stanley, Diane. *Raising Sweetness*
Ungerer, Tomi. *The three robbers*
Vander Zee, Ruth. *Always with you*
Willard, Nancy. *Shadow story*
Yolen, Jane. *The girl in the golden bower*

Outer space *see* Space & space ships

Pageants *see* Theater

Painters *see* Activities – painting; Careers – artists

Panthers *see* Animals – leopards

Paper

Compestine, Ying Chang. *The story of paper*
Czernecki, Stefan. *Paper lanterns*
Gibbons, Gail. *Deadline!*
Paper, paper everywhere
Howell, Will C. *Zoo flakes ABC*
Jeffers, Oliver. *The great paper caper*
Kleven, Elisa. *The paper princess*
Kroll, Virginia L. *Pink paper swans*
Melmed, Laura Krauss. *Little Oh*
Moffatt, Judith. *Snow shapes*
Reynolds, Peter H. *I'm here*

Parades

Appelt, Kathi. *Bats on parade*
Baer, Gene. *Thump thump rat-a-tat-tat*
Black, Michael Ian. *A pig parade is a terrible idea*
Bond, Rebecca. *The great doughnut parade*
Boswell, Addie. *The rain stomper*
Boynton, Sandra. *Christmas parade*
Corey, Shana. *Milly and the Macy's Parade*
Crews, Donald. *Parade*
Crimi, Carolyn. *Pugs in a Bug*
DiPucchio, Kelly. *Crafty Chloe: dress-up mess-up*
Ets, Marie Hall. *In the forest*
Freschet, Gina. *Naty's parade*
Greenberg, Melanie Hope. *Mermaids on parade*
Greenfield, Eloise. *Easter parade*
Guidone, Thea. *Drum city*
Hoffman, Mary. *Princess Grace*
Jane, Pamela. *Milo and the fire engine parade*
Janice. *Little Bear marches in the St. Patrick's Day parade*
Johnson, Angela. *The day Ray got away*
Joosse, Barbara. *Dog parade*
Hooray Parade
Kroll, Steven. *Mary McLean and the St. Patrick's Day parade*
Lasky, Kathryn. *Fourth of July bear*
Lenski, Lois. *The Easter Rabbit's parade*
London, Jonathan. *Froggy plays in the band*
McKee, David. *Elmer's special day*
Mora, Pat. *The rainbow tulip*
Roosa, Karen. *Pippa at the parade*
Sebe, Masayuki. *100 animals on parade!*
Sweet, Melissa. *Balloons over Broadway*
Wardlaw, Lee. *Red, white, and boom!*
Whitehead, Kathy. *Looking for Uncle Louie on the Fourth of July*
Winthrop, Elizabeth. *Halloween hats*
Ziefert, Harriet. *Circus parade*
First Night

Parks

Becker, Shari. *Maxwell's mountain*
Black, Sonia. *Hanging out with Mom*
Browne, Anthony. *Voices in the park*
Cohen, Caron Lee. *Martin and the giant lions*
Cotten, Cynthia. *Rain play*
Curious George and the dump truck
Flanagan, Alice K. *Exploring parks with Ranger Dockett*
Godwin, Laura. *Central Park serenade*
Gorbachev, Valeri. *Chicken chickens*
Granowsky, Alvin. *At the park*
Heo, Yumi. *One Sunday morning*
High, Linda Oatman. *The girl on the high-diving horse*
Hill, Eric. *Spot goes to the park*
Ichikawa, Satomi. *La La Rose*
Jenkins, Emily. *Water in the park*
Jones, Ursula. *The witch's children*
Kann, Victoria. *Emeraldalicious*
McKissack, Patricia C. *Messy Bessey's family reunion*
McPhail, David. *Henry Bear's park*
Mahy, Margaret. *Down the dragon's tongue*
Merriam, Eve. *Where's that cat?*
Morozumi, Atsuko. *In the park*
Noble, Sheilagh. *More*
Pratt, Pierre. *Park*

Rosenstock, Barb. *The camping trip that changed America*
Ruelle, Karen Gray. *Bark park*
Schaefer, Carole Lexa. *ABCers*
Schwartz, Roslyn. *Tales from Parc la Fontaine*
Sharratt, Nick. *Shark in the park*
Singer, Marilyn. *Didi and Daddy on the Promenade*
Springstubb, Tricia. *Phoebe and Digger*
Sweeney, Joan. *Suzette and the puppy*
Weeks, Sarah. *Oh my gosh, Mrs. McNosh!*

Parks – amusement

Cecil, Randy. *Gator*
Cobb, Annie. *The long wait*
Frazee, Marla. *Roller coaster*
Gavril, David. *Penelope Nuthatch and the big surprise*
Hartt-Sussman, Heather. *Here comes Hortense!*
Horse, Harry. *Little rabbit lost*
Kalz, Jill. *An a-maze-ing amusement park adventure*
May, Eleanor. *Albert is not scared*
Rogalski, Mark. *Tickets to ride*
Ziefert, Harriet. *Fun Land fun!*

Parrots *see* Birds – parakeets, parrots

Participation

Brown, Marc. *Finger rhymes*
Cronin, Doreen. *Wiggle*
Cuyler, Margery. *We're going on a lion hunt*
Diakité, Baba Wagué. *The hatseller and the monkeys*
Ets, Marie Hall. *Just me*
Hoban, Tana. *Where is it?*
Hutchins, Pat. *Good-night owl*
McLean, Janet. *Let's go, baby-o!*
Rosen, Michael. *We're going on a bear hunt*
Rueda, Claudia. *Huff and puff*
Serafini, Frank. *Looking closely along the shore*
Seuss, Dr. *Gerald McBoing Boing sound book*
Shaw, Charles Green. *It looked like spilt milk*
Simmons, Jane. *Daisy says, "Here we go round the mulberry bush"*
Daisy says, "If you're happy and you know it"
Slobodkina, Esphyr. *Caps for sale*
Circus caps for sale
Smith, Kathryn. *Little Donkey's Christmas story*
Little Lamb's Christmas story
Spier, Peter. *Gobble, growl, grunt*
Trapani, Iza. *I'm a little teapot*
Tullet, Hervé. *The book with a hole*
Press here
Two little eyes and other action rhymes
Wells, Rosemary. *Max and Ruby's treasure hunt*
Ziefert, Harriet. *Wiggle like an octopus*

Parties

Adams, Adrienne. *The Christmas party*
A Halloween happening
Allard, Harry. *The Stupids have a ball*
Allen, Joy. *Princess Palooza*
Princess party
Anholt, Catherine. *Happy birthday, Chimp and Zee*
Asch, Frank. *Popcorn*
Asher, Sandy. *What a party!*
Ashman, Linda. *Maxwell's magic mix-up*
Avraham, Kate Aver. *What will you be, Sara Mee?*
Awdry, W. *Happy birthday, Thomas!*
Bailey, Linda. *Stanley's party*
Baker, Roberta. *Olive's pirate party*
Beck, Scott. *Happy birthday, Monster!*
Berenstain, Stan and Jan. *The Berenstain bears and the slumber party*
Berry, Lynne. *The curious demise of a contrary cat*
Bertrand, Diane Gonzales. *The party for Papa Luis / La fiesta para Papa Luis*
Best, Cari. *Are you going to be good?*
Birchall, Mark. *Rabbit's birthday surprise*
Blackstone, Stella. *Bear's birthday*
Block party today
Bluemle, Elizabeth. *How do you wokka-wokka?*
Bluthenthal, Diana Cain. *I'm not invited?*
Brown, Marc. *Arthur's birthday*
Brown, Tameka Fryer. *Around our way on Neighbors' Day*
Brownlee, Sophia Grace. *Tea time with Sophia Grace and Rosie*
Buehner, Caralyn. *Snowmen at Christmas*
Bunting, Eve. *Little Badger's just-about birthday*
Button, Lana. *Willow finds a way*
Cabrera, Jane. *One, two, buckle my shoe*
Carlstrom, Nancy White. *Happy birthday, Jesse Bear!*
Chambers, Roland. *Rooftop rocket party*
Chavarría-Cháirez, Becky. *Magda's piñata magic / Magda y la piñata mágica*
Chess, Victoria. *The costume party*
Chodos-Irvine, Margaret. *Ella Sarah gets dressed*
Clarke, Jane. *Trumpet*
Cohen, Miriam. *Tough Jim*
Cousins, Lucy. *Maisy dresses up*
Cox, Judy. *Happy birthday, Mrs. Millie!*
Cronin, Doreen. *Click, clack, boo!*
Dale, Penny. *Dinosaur zoom!*
Day, Alexandra. *Follow Carl!*
deGroat, Diane. *Happy birthday to you, you belong in a zoo*
Dooley, Norah. *Everybody brings noodles*
Du Bois, William Pène. *Bear party*
Dyckman, Ame. *Tea party rules*
Ehlert, Lois. *Boo to you!*
Elya, Susan Middleton. *F is for fiesta*
Ets, Marie Hall. *Nine days to Christmas*
Evans, Cambria. *Martha Moth makes socks*
Fliess, Sue. *A gluten-free birthday for me!*
Ford, Bernette. *No more bottles for Bunny!*
Foreman, George. *Let George do it!*
Freeman, Don. *Dandelion*
Freeman, Tor. *Hooray! I'm five today!*
Friedman, Laurie. *Ruby Valentine saves the day*
Gantos, Jack. *Rotten Ralph's rotten romance*
Granowsky, Alvin. *Can I help?*
Greene, Rhonda Gowler. *Jamboree day*
Hanson, Warren. *Bugtown Boogie*
Hardy, Sarah Frances. *Puzzled by pink*
Harley, Bill. *Bear's all-night party*
Harper, Charise Mericle. *When Randolph turned rotten*
Harper, Jessica. *I'm not going to chase the cat today*
Hennessy, B. G. *Corduroy's birthday*
Hest, Amy. *Mabel dancing*
Hill, Eric. *Spot goes to a party*
Holub, Joan. *The Halloween Queen*
Howe, James. *Houndsley and Catina and the birthday surprise*
Huget, Jennifer LaRue. *The best birthday party ever*
Hughes, Shirley. *Alfie and the birthday surprise*
Hunter, Anne. *Possum's harvest moon*

Hunter, Sally. *Humphrey's birthday*
Hutchins, Pat. *The surprise party*
Titch and Daisy
Which witch is which?
Idle, Molly. *Tea Rex*
Inkpen, Mick. *Kipper's birthday*
Jennings, Linda. *Hide and seek birthday treat*
Johnston, Tony. *Laugh-out-loud baby*
Jonas, Ann. *The thirteenth clue*
Jonell, Lynne. *It's my birthday, too!*
Kassirer, Sue. *What's next, Nina?*
Keats, Ezra Jack. *A letter to Amy*
Keller, Holly. *Brave Horace*
Henry's happy birthday
Ketteman, Helen. *Bubba the cowboy prince*
Khan, Rukhsana. *Big red lollipop*
Kirk, David. *Miss Spider's tea party*
Koda-Callan, Elizabeth. *The squiggly Wigglys*
Kono, Erin Eitter. *Caterina and the perfect party*
Kropf, Latifa Berry. *It's Hanukkah time!*
Landry, Leo. *Trick or treat*
Leedy, Loreen. *The dragon Halloween party*
Lester, Helen. *Happy birdday, Tacky!*
Levine, Gail Carson. *Betsy Red Hoodie*
Levitin, Sonia. *When Elephant goes to a party*
Lillegard, Dee. *The Big Bug Ball*
Lindgren, Astrid. *Pippi Longstocking's after-Christmas party*
Ljungkvist, Laura. *Toni's topsy-turvy telephone day*
Lodge, Jo. *Happy birthday, Moo Moo*
Lord, Cynthia. *Happy birthday, Hamster*
McClatchy, Lisa. *Dear Tyrannosaurus Rex*
McClure, Wendy. *The princess and the peanut allergy*
McCormack, Caren McNelly. *The fiesta dress*
McCourt, Lisa, et al. *Chicken soup for little souls: Della Splatnuk birthday girl*
McDonald, Megan. *Ant and Honey Bee, what a pair!*
McElligott, Matthew. *Backbeard and the birthday suit*
Machado, Ana Maria. *What a party!*
Mackintosh, David. *Marshall Armstrong is new to our school*
McLarey, Kristina Thermaenius. *When you take a pig to a party*
Martin, Bill, Jr. *Rock it, sock it, number line*
Miranda, Anne. *Alphabet fiesta*
Monster math
Modell, Frank. *Ice cream soup*
Mora, Pat. *Delicious hullabaloo / Pachanga deliciosa*
Marimba!
Morrow, Barbara Olenyik. *Mr. Mosquito put on his tuxedo*
Mother Goose. *Hickory, dickory, dock*
Munsch, Robert N. *Moira's birthday*
Murphy, Stuart J. *Too many kangaroo things to do!*
Murray, Marjorie Dennis. *Halloween night*
Nikola-Lisa, W. *Shake dem Halloween bones*
Novak, Matt. *No zombies allowed*
Numeroff, Laura Joffe. *If you give a pig a party*
Otis and Sydney and the best birthday ever
O'Connor, Jane. *Bonjour, butterfly*
Older, Effin. *My two grandmothers*
Park, Linda Sue. *Xander's panda party*
Passen, Lisa. *The incredible shrinking teacher*
Paul, Ann Whitford. *Mañana Iguana*
Paxton, Tom. *Engelbert the elephant*
Pfister, Marcus. *Happy birthday, Bertie!*
Just the way you are
Pinkwater, Daniel. *Bad bears and a bunny*
Polacco, Patricia. *Some birthday!*
Potter, Beatrix. *The sly old cat*
Pryor, Bonnie. *Amanda and April*
Radabaugh, Melinda Beth. *Sleeping over*
Rader, Laura. *Tea for me, tea for you*
Raschka, Chris. *New York is English, Chattanooga is Creek*
Reid, Barbara. *The party*
Rim, Sujean. *Birdie's big-girl dress*
Roberts, Bethany. *Birthday mice*
Rollings, Susan. *New shoes, red shoes*
Rose, Deborah Lee. *Birthday zoo*
Ross, Tony. *I want a party!*
Rubin, Adam. *Secret pizza party*
Rumford, James. *Nine animals and the well*
Rylant, Cynthia. *Little Whistle's dinner party*
Sage, Angie. *Molly and the birthday party*
Samuels, Barbara. *Happy birthday, Dolores*
Scanlon, Elizabeth Garton. *Happy birthday, Bunny!*
Schaefer, Carole Lexa. *The Bora-Bora dress*
Schertle, Alice. *Jeremy Bean's St. Patrick's Day*
Schotter, Roni. *Mama, I'll give you the world*
Sendak, Maurice. *Bumble-ardy*
Shaw, Natalie. *Olivia plans a tea party*
Shute, Linda. *Halloween party*
Silbaugh, Elizabeth. *Raggedy Ann's birthday party book*
Soto, Gary. *Chato and the party animals*
The old man and his door
Stadler, Alexander. *Beverly Billingsly takes the cake*
Starr, Meg. *Alicia's happy day*
Steptoe, Javaka. *The Jones family express*
Stickland, Paul. *Bears*
Stock, Catherine. *The birthday present*
Sturges, Philemon. *This little pirate*
Surplice, Holly. *Guinea pig party*
Tafuri, Nancy. *The barn party*
Tegen, Katherine Brown. *Dracula and Frankenstein are friends*
Thompson, Kay. *Kay Thompson's Eloise takes a bawth (sic)*
Trapani, Iza. *Haunted party*
Tryon, Leslie. *Albert's birthday*
Tudor, Tasha. *The doll's Christmas*
Uff, Caroline. *Happy birthday, Lulu*
Vincent, Gabrielle. *Merry Christmas, Ernest and Celestine*
Waldron, Jan L. *John Pig's Halloween*
Walker, Anna. *I love birthdays*
Wallace, John. *Tiny Rabbit goes to a birthday party*
Wallace, Nancy Elizabeth. *Tell-a-bunny*
Watt, Mélanie. *Scaredy Squirrel has a birthday party*
Weinert, Matthias. *No bath, no cake!*
Wells, Rosemary. *Bunny party*
Weninger, Brigitte. *Happy birthday, Davy*
Wheeler, Lisa. *Boogie knights*
Willard, Nancy. *The mouse, the cat and Grandmother's hat*
Wood, Audrey. *The Birthday Queen*
Yolen, Jane. *Come to the fairies' ball*
Piggins
Yolleck, Joan. *Paris in the spring with Picasso*
Zalben, Jane Breskin. *Baby shower*
Saturday night at the Beastro

Patience *see* Character traits – patience

Pen pals

Brownlow, Mike. *Mickey Moonbeam*
Kempter, Christa. *Dear Little Lamb*
Kostecki-Shaw, Jenny Sue. *Same, same but different*
Moore, Marian. *Dear Cinderella*
Murphy, Stuart J. *Polly's pen pal*
Rand, Gloria. *A pen pal for Max*
Smallcomb, Pam. *Earth to Clunk*

Perfectionism *see* Character traits – perfectionism

Perseverance *see* Character traits – perseverance

Persistence *see* Character traits – persistence

Petroglyphs

Barnett, Mac. *Oh no! Not again!*
Gerstein, Mordicai. *The first drawing*
Taylor, Harriet Peck. *Secrets of the stone*
Wiesner, David. *Mr. Wuffles!*

Petroleum *see* Oil

Pets

Abercrombie, Barbara. *Bad dog, Dodger*
Abley, Mark. *Ghost cat*
Adoff, Arnold. *Daring Dog and Captain Cat*
Agee, Jon. *My rhinoceros*
Ajmera, Maya. *Animal friends: a global celebration of children and their animals*
A kid's best friend
Alsenas, Linas. *Peanut*
Anderson, Brian. *The prince's new pet*
Asch, Frank. *The last puppy*
Ashman, Linda. *No dogs allowed*
Bachelet, Gilles. *My cat, the silliest cat in the world*
When the silliest cat was small
Bartoletti, Susan Campbell. *Nobody's nosier than a cat*
Bedford, David. *The way I love you*
Bennett, Kelly. *Not Norman*
Berenstain, Stan and Jan. *The Berenstain bears' trouble with pets*
Berenzy, Alix. *Sammy*
Berger, Joe. *Bridget Fidget and the most perfect pet!*
Best, Cari. *Ava and the real Lucille*
The best cat in the world
Bibbel, Mark. *Oh, Harry!*
Biedrzycki, David. *Me and my dragon*
Me and my dragon: scared of Halloween
Boelts, Maribeth. *Before you were mine*
Bowen, Anne. *I know an old teacher*
Scooter in the outside
Brett, Jan. *Annie and the wild animals*
The first dog
Brown, Marc. *Arthur's new puppy*
Arthur's new puppy [board book]
Arthur's pet business
Arthur's TV trouble
Brown, Margaret Wise. *The good little bad little pig*
Brown, Peter. *Children make terrible pets*
Brunhoff, Laurent de. *Babar and the Wully-Wully*
Bunting, Eve. *Emma's turtle*
Burleigh, Robert. *Good-bye, Sheepie*
Calhoun, Mary. *High-wire Henry*
Calmenson, Stephanie. *May I pet your dog?*
Cannon, A. E. *Sophie's fish*
Capucilli, Alyssa Satin. *Bathtime for Biscuit*
Biscuit wins a prize
Happy birthday, Biscuit!
Castillo, Lauren. *Melvin and the boy*
Chall, Marsha Wilson. *Pick a pup*
Chamberlain, Margaret. *Please don't tease Tootsie*
Chataway, Carol. *The perfect pet*
Chichester Clark, Emma. *Will and Squill*
Child, Lauren. *That pesky rat*
Clements, Andrew. *Dogku*
Dolores and the big fire
Slippers loves to run
Tara and Tiree, fearless friends
Cochran, Bill. *The forever dog*
Cohen, Miriam. *Jim's dog Muffins*, ill. by Ronald Himler
Jim's dog Muffins, ill. by Lillian Hoban
Cole, Babette. *Princess Smartypants*
Cole, Henry. *Trudy*
Collicott, Sharleen. *Toestomper and the bad butterflies*
Cowen-Fletcher, Jane. *Hello, puppy!*
Crisp, Marty. *Black and white*
Cuyler, Margery. *Guinea pigs add up*
Daly, Cathleen. *Prudence wants a pet*
Daly, Niki. *What's cooking, Jamela?*
Davidson, Ellen Dee. *Princess Justina Albertina*
Davis, Patricia Anne. *Brian's bird*
Day, Alexandra. *Special deliveries*
dePaola, Tomie. *Little Grunt and the big egg*
DiPucchio, Kelly. *Gilbert goldfish wants a pet*
Dodd, Emma. *I don't want a posh dog*
What pet to get?
Dodds, Dayle Ann. *Pet wash*
Teacher's pets
Doyle, Malachy. *Sleepy Pendoodle*
Dubosarsky, Ursula. *Rex*
Duke, Kate. *Ready for pumpkins*
Eaton, Jason Carter. *How to train a train*
Elschner, Geraldine. *Fritz's fish*
Elsdale, Bob. *Mac side up*
Falwell, Cathryn. *P.J. and Puppy*
Farish, Terry. *The cat who liked potato soup*
Feiffer, Kate. *Which puppy?*
Flanagan, Alice K. *Buying a pet from Ms. Chavez*
Fleming, Denise. *Buster*
Foster, John. *Pet poems*
Fraser, Mary Ann. *I.Q. gets fit*
I.Q. goes to school
I.Q. goes to the library
I.Q., it's time
Pet shop follies
Pet shop lullaby
Gay, Marie-Louise. *What are you doing, Sam?*
Gibbs, Edward. *I spy pets*
Giff, Patricia Reilly. *Good luck, Ronald Morgan*
Goldfinger, Jennifer P. *A fish named Spot*
My dog Lyle
Gorbachev, Valeri. *The best cat*
Gottfried, Maya. *Good dog*
Graham, Bob. *"Let's get a pup!" said Kate*
"The trouble with dogs," said Dad
Grambling, Lois G. *Big Dog*
Granowsky, Alvin. *At the park*

Graves, Keith. *Pet boy*
Greenaway, Theresa. *Centipedes and millipedes*
Gregory, Nan. *How Smudge came*
Griff. *Shark-mad Stanley*
Grimes, Nikki. *When Gorilla goes walking*
Hanson, Mary Elizabeth. *The old man and the flea*
Harper, Charise Mericle. *Henry's heart*
Harris, Robie H. *Goodbye, Mousie*
Harrison, Troon. *Aaron's awful allergies*
Harvey, Amanda. *Dog days*
Dog-eared
Dog gone
Harvey, Matthea. *Cecil the pet glacier*
Haughton, Chris. *Oh no, George!*
Hayles, Marsha. *A pet of a pet*
Hays, Anna Jane. *The pup speaks up*
Heide, Florence Parry. *A promise is a promise*
Heiligman, Deborah. *Fun dog, sun dog*
Helakoski, Leslie. *Doggone feet!*
Hest, Amy. *Charley's first night*
When Charley met Grampa
Hill, Frances. *The bug cemetery*
Hindley, Judy. *The best thing about a puppy*
Hogg, Gary. *Look what the cat dragged in!*
Howard, Arthur. *Hoodwinked*
Hughes, Ted. *My brother Bert*
Hull, Rod. *Mr. Betts and Mr. Potts*
Imai, Ayano. *Chester*
Inkpen, Deborah. *Harriet and the little fat fairy*
Inkpen, Mick. *The great pet sale*
Kipper and Roly
Jackson, Ellen. *Abe Lincoln loved animals*
Jagtenberg, Yvonne. *Jack's rabbit*
Jarka, Jeff. *Love that kitty!*
Love that puppy!
Javernick, Ellen. *The birthday pet*
Jeffers, Oliver. *This moose belongs to me*
Johnson, Angela. *The girl who wore snakes*
Julius
Johnson, Paul Brett. *Lost*
Jonell, Lynne. *I need a snake*
Joosse, Barbara. *Bad dog school*
Jordan, Sandra. *Mr. and Mrs. Portly and their little dog Snack*
Joyce, William. *Dinosaur Bob*
Juan, Ana. *The pet shop revolution*
Katz, Bobbi. *Nothing but a dog*
Katz, Susan. *Oh, Theodore!*
Keats, Ezra Jack. *Maggie and the pirate*
Pet show!
Kellogg, Steven. *Can I keep him?*
The mysterious tadpole
Kerby, Johanna. *Little pink pup*
Kimmel, Eric A. *I took my frog to the library*
Kroll, Steven. *Patches lost and found*
Kroll, Virginia L. *Really rabbits*
Kulka, Joe. *My crocodile does not bite*
Kwon, Yoon-duck. *My cat copies me*
Lachner, Dorothea. *Smoky's special Easter present*
Lee, Chinlun. *The very kind rich lady and her one hundred dogs*
Lee, Ho Baek. *While we were out*
Lee, Spike. *Please, puppy, please*
Let me call you sweetheart
Lewis, Kim. *A puppy for Annie*
Liersch, Anne. *Nell and Fluffy*
Lindgren, Barbro. *Sam's cookie*
Lupton, David. *Goodbye, Brecken*
Lyon, Tammie. *Olive and Snowflake*
McClure, Gillian. *Tom Finger*
McDonnell, Flora. *Sparky*
McGhee, Alison. *Always*
MacLachlan, Patricia. *Bittle*
McPhail, David. *Emma's pet*
Mader, C. Roger. *Lost cat*
Mayer, Mercer. *Too many dinosaurs*
Mazer, Anne. *The salamander room*
Miller, Virginia. *Be gentle!*
Monks, Lydia. *Aaaarrgghh! spider!*
Moran, Alex. *Come here, tiger*
Morozumi, Atsuko. *My friend gorilla*
Morrison, Cathy. *I want a pet!*
Mozelle, Shirley. *The pig is in the pantry, the cat is on the shelf*
Nelson, Robin. *Pet fish*
Pet frog
Pet guinea pig
Pet hamster
Pet hermit crab
Nelson-Schmidt, Michelle. *Cats, cats!*
Dogs, dogs!
Newberry, Clare Turlay. *April's kittens*
Barkis
Niemann, Christoph. *The pet dragon*
Noble, Trinka Hakes. *Jimmy's boa and the big splash birthday bash*
Numeroff, Laura Joffe. *Laura Numeroff's 10-step guide to living with your monster*
O'Connor, Jane. *The perfect puppy for me*
Ohi, Ruth. *Pants off first*
Owen, Ann. *Caring for your pet*
Palatini, Margie. *The perfect pet*
Panzieri, Lucia. *The kindhearted crocodile*
Partridge, Elizabeth. *Big Cat Pepper*
Perret, Delphine. *The Big Bad Wolf and me*
Pfeffer, Wendy. *What's it like to be a fish?*
Phillips, Betty Lou. *Emily goes wild*
Pitcher, Caroline. *Nico's octopus*
Plourde, Lynn. *Dino pets*
Dino pets go to school
Polacco, Patricia. *Ginger and Petunia*
Mrs. Katz and Tush
Postgate, Daniel. *The snagglegrollop*
Poydar, Nancy. *Fish school*
Prap, Lila. *Doggy whys*
Pringle, Laurence P. *Naming the cat*
Rand, Gloria. *Little Flower*
Rathmann, Peggy. *10 minutes till bedtime*
Reiser, Lynn. *Any kind of dog*
Rennert, Laura Joy. *Buying, training and caring for your dinosaur*
Reynolds, Marilynn. *A present for Mrs. Kazinski*
Rickards, Lynne. *Jacob O'Reilly wants a pet*
Ries, Lori. *Aggie and Ben*
Robbins, Jacqui. *The new girl . . . and me*
Roberton, Fiona. *The perfect present*
Wanted: the perfect pet
Roberts, Victoria. *The best pet ever*
Robertson, M. P. *Hieronymous Betts and his unusual pets*
Rockwell, Anne. *My pet hamster*
Rogers, Fred. *When a pet dies*
Rostoker-Gruber, Karen. *Ferret fun*
Rotner, Shelley. *Pick a pet*
Rouillard, Wendy. *Barnaby's bunny*
Sadler, Judy Ann. *Sandwiches for Duke*
Samuels, Barbara. *Dolores meets her match*
San Souci, Robert D. *The silver charm*

Sauer, Tammi. *Me want pet!*
Schmid, Paul. *A pet for Petunia*
Schneider, Howie. *Chewy Louie*
Schwartz, Amy. *Oscar*
Schwartz, Henry. *How I captured a dinosaur*
Scillian, Devin. *Memoirs of a hamster*
Seeber, Dorothea P. *A pup just for me . . . A boy just for me*
Sharmat, Marjorie Weinman. *I'm the best*
Shea, Kitty. *Out and about at the vet clinic*
Shields, Gillian. *Dogfish*
Siegel, Randy. *My snake Blake*
Sierra, Judy. *There's a zoo in room 22*
Simeon, Jean-Pierre. *This is a poem that heals fish*
Slonim, David. *Patch*
Smath, Jerry. *Sammy Salami*
Smith, Maggie. *Desser, the best ever cat*
Spurr, Elizabeth. *A pig named Perrier*
Staake, Bob. *The first pup*
Stanley, Mandy. *In the park*
Perfect pets
Stevenson, James. *Mr. Hacker*
Will you please feed our cat?
Stower, Adam. *Silly doggy*
Stuve-Bodeen, Stephanie. *A small brown dog with a wet pink nose*
Swaim, Jessica. *The hound from the pound*
Talbott, Hudson. *It's all about me-ow*
Teague, Mark. *Dear Mrs. LaRue*
LaRue for mayor
Thomas, Jane Resh. *Scaredy dog*
Thoms, Susan Collins. *Cesar takes a break*
Townsend, Michael. *Cute and cuter*
Trapani, Iza. *How much is that doggie in the window?*
Row, row, row your boat
Turner, Pamela S. *Hachiko*
Uff, Caroline. *Hello, Lulu*
Umansky, Kaye. *I don't like Gloria!*
Urbanovic, Jackie. *Duck and cover*
Duck at the door
Vaughan, Marcia Kapok. *Whistling Dixie*
Verdick, Elizabeth. *Tails are not for pulling*
Viorst, Judith. *The tenth good thing about Barney*
Wahman, Wendy. *Don't lick the dog*
Ward, Lynd. *The biggest bear*
Waring, Richard. *Alberto the dancing alligator*
Weigelt, Udo. *Super Guinea Pig to the rescue*
Wells, Rosemary. *Lucy comes to stay*
Weninger, Brigitte. *Miko wants a dog*
Wheeler, Lisa. *The pet project*
Wilhelm, Hans. *I'll always love you*
Willems, Mo. *The pigeon wants a puppy!*
Williams, Sue. *Let's go visiting*
Wing, Natasha. *How to raise a dinosaur*
Winstead, Rosie. *Ruby and Bubbles*
Wolf, Jake. *Daddy, could I have an elephant?*
Yaccarino, Dan. *The birthday fish*
New pet
An octopus followed me home
Oswald
Zalben, Jane Breskin. *Baby shower*
Ziefert, Harriet. *Murphy meets the treadmill*
Zimmerman, Andrea Griffing. *My dog Toby*
Zolotow, Charlotte. *The old dog*
The poodle who barked at the wind

Physicians *see* Careers – doctors

Picture puzzles

Alarcón, Francisco X. *Iguanas in the snow and other winter poems / Iguanas en la nieve y otros poemas de invierno*
Animal I spy
Animal 123
Anno, Mitsumasa. *Anno's alphabet*
Anno's counting book
Anno's counting house
Anno's Italy
Anno's journey
Barber, Patti. *First number book*
Behrens, Janice. *Let's find rain forest animals*
Berner, Rotraut Susanne. *In the town all year 'round*
Bùi, Tak. *Spot the difference*
Carter, David A. *Blue 2*
One red dot
600 black spots
Whoo? Whoo?
Who's under that hat?
Yellow square
Cauley, Lorinda Bryan. *What do you know!*
Chedru, Delphine. *Spot it!*
Spot it again!
Cleary, Brian P. *Peanut butter and jellyfishes*
Cressy, Judith. *Can you find it?*
Can you find it, too?
Dahl, Michael. *Downhill fun*
Eggs and legs
Footprints in the snow
From the garden
Hands down
One big building
Davis, Kate. *Barnyard babies*
Ehlert, Lois. *In my world*
Ellwand, David. *Alfred's camera*
Alfred's party
Falken, Linda. *Can you find it?*
Faulkner, Keith. *A trick or a treat?*
Fox, Mem. *Yoo-hoo, Ladybug!*
Gannij, Joan. *Elusive moose*
Garland, Michael. *Americana adventure*
Christmas City
The great Easter egg hunt
Super snow day seek and find
Geisert, Arthur. *Mystery*
Gukova, Julia. *All mixed-up!*
Hale, Bruce. *Santa on the loose!*
Handford, Martin. *Find Waldo now*
The great Waldo search
Where's Waldo?
Herzog, Brad. *I spy with my little eye: baseball*
Hillenbrand, Will. *Mother Goose picture puzzles*
Jay, Alison. *Christmastime*
Red green blue
Jenkins, Steve. *I see a kookaburra*
Kamm, Katja. *Invisible*
Khing, T. T. *Where is the cake?*
Where is the cake now?
Kidslabel. *Spot 7: school*
Spot 7: Christmas
Ljungkvist, Laura. *Follow the line*
Follow the line through the house
Follow the line to school
MacDonald, Suse. *Look whooo's counting*
McGrath, Barbara Barbieri. *Kellogg's froot loops color fun book*
McMillan, Bruce. *Mouse views*

Marino, Gianna. *One too many*
Marzollo, Jean. *I spy*
I spy A to Z
I spy Christmas
I spy extreme challenger!
I spy fantasy
I spy gold challenger!
I spy little animals
I spy little book
I spy little bunnies
I spy little Christmas
I spy little letters
I spy little numbers
I spy little wheels
I spy, mystery
I spy school days
I spy spooky night
I spy super challenger!
I spy treasure hunt
I spy ultimate challenger!
I spy, year-round challenger!
Micklethwait, Lucy. *In the picture*
Moseley, Keith. *Where's the dinosaur?*
Munro, Roxie. *Amazement Park*
Circus
Ecomazes
Mazescapes
Mazeways
Nickle, John. *Alphabet explosion!*
Oliver, Narelle. *Twilight hunt*
Onishi, Satoru. *Who's hiding*
Pamintuan, Macky. *Twelve haunted rooms of Halloween*
Philpot, Lorna. *Find Anthony Ant*
Raczka, Bob. *Fall mixed up*
Ringgold, Faith. *Cassie's word quilt*
Rotner, Shelley. *Parts*
Schwartz, David M. *If you hopped like a frog*
Seeger, Laura Vaccaro. *The hidden alphabet*
Serafini, Frank. *Looking closely along the shore*
Staake, Bob. *Look! A book!*
Look! Another book!
Stevenson, Emma. *Hide-and-seek science*
Tildes, Phyllis Limbacher. *Animals in camouflage*
Toft, Kim Michelle. *Neptune's nursery*
One less fish
Trapani, Iza. *Rufus and friends*
Turner, Ann Warren. *Angel hide and seek*
Wegerif, Gay. *Up close*
Weitzman, Jacqueline Preiss. *You can't take a balloon into the National Gallery*
Whybrow, Ian. *Faraway farm*
Wick, Walter. *Can you see what I see? cool collections*
Can you see what I see? dream machine
Can you see what I see? once upon a time
Can you see what I see? out of this world
Can you see what I see? picture puzzles to search and solve
Can you see what I see? Seymour and the juice box boat
Can you see what I see? Seymour makes new friends
Can you see what I see? the night before Christmas
Can you see what I see? toyland express
Can you see what I see? treasure ship
Wiesmüller, Dieter. *In the blink of an eye*
Ziefert, Harriet. *Messy Bessie*

Pilgrims

Behrens, June. *The feast of Thanksgiving*
Bruchac, Joseph. *Squanto's journey*
Bunting, Eve. *How many days to America?*
Dalgliesh, Alice. *The Thanksgiving story*
George, Jean Craighead. *The first Thanksgiving*
Gibbons, Gail. *Thanksgiving Day*
Greene, Rhonda Gowler. *The very first Thanksgiving Day*
Hennessy, B. G. *One little, two little, three little pilgrims*
Kroll, Steven. *One tough turkey*
Metaxas, Eric. *Squanto and the miracle of Thanksgiving*
Peacock, Carol Antoinette. *Pilgrim cat*
Van Leeuwen, Jean. *Across the wide dark sea*

Pioneer life *see* U.S. history – frontier & pioneer life

Pirates

Ahlberg, Janet. *It was a dark and stormy night*
Andreae, Giles. *Captain Flinn and the pirate dinosaurs*
Captain Flinn and the pirate dinosaurs: missing treasure!
Arro, Lena. *By geezers and galoshes!*
Baker, Roberta. *Olive's pirate party*
Bardhan-Quallen, Sudipta. *Pirate princess*
Brown, Calef. *Pirateria*
Bunting, Eve. *Little Badger, terror of the seven seas*
Pirate boy
Burningham, John. *Come away from the water, Shirley*
Clibbon, Meg. *Imagine you're a pirate!*
Crimi, Carolyn. *Henry and the Buccaneer Bunnies*
Henry and the Crazed Chicken Pirates
Day, Jan. *The pirate, Pink*
Pirate Pink and treasures of the reef
Demas, Corinne. *Pirates go to school*
DiCamillo, Kate. *Louise*
Duddle, Jonny. *The pirate cruncher*
The pirates next door
Florian, Douglas. *Shiver me timbers!*
Fox, Kathleen. *The pirates of plagiarism*
Fox, Mem. *Tough Boris*
Freedman, Claire. *Pirates love underpants*
Funke, Cornelia. *Pirate girl*
Gaiman, Neil. *The dangerous alphabet*
Greene, Rhonda Gowler. *No pirates allowed! said Library Lou*
Grossmann-Hensel, Katharina. *Papa is a pirate*
Harley, Bill. *Dirty Joe, the pirate*
Harris, Peter. *The night pirates*
Helquist, Brett. *Roger, the jolly pirate*
Horowitz, Dave. *Twenty-six pirates*
Kay, Julia. *Gulliver Snip*
Keats, Ezra Jack. *Maggie and the pirate*
Kennedy, Kim. *Pirate Pete's giant adventure*
Kimmel, Eric A. *The Erie Canal pirates*
Robin Hook, pirate hunter!
Kladstrup, Kristin. *The gingerbread pirates*
Kramer, Andrew. *Pajama pirates*
Krosoczka, Jarrett J. *Bubble bath pirates*
Krupinski, Loretta. *Pirate treasure*
Lamm, C. Drew. *Pirates*
Lasky, Kathryn. *Pirate Bob*

Leuck, Laura. *I love my pirate papa*
Lichtenheld, Tom. *Everything I know about pirates*
Little old lady who swallowed a fly. *There was an old pirate who swallowed a fish*
Long, Melinda. *How I became a pirate*
Pirates don't change diapers
Lucas, David. *The skeleton pirate*
McCully, Emily Arnold. *The pirate queen*
McElligott, Matthew. *Backbeard and the birthday suit*
McFarland, Lyn Rossiter. *The pirate's parrot*
McNaughton, Colin. *Captain Abdul's little treasure*
Captain Abdul's pirate school
McNeil, Florence. *Sail away*
McPhail, David. *Edward and the pirates*
Marzollo, Jean. *I spy treasure hunt*
O'Malley, Kevin. *Captain Raptor and the space pirates*
Peck, Jan. *Pirate treasure hunt!*
Preller, James. *A pirate's guide to first grade*
A pirate's guide to recess
Priest, Robert H. *The pirate's eye*
Quattlebaum, Mary. *Pirate vs. pirate*
Reynolds, Aaron. *Pirates vs. cowboys*
Richardson, Bill. *Sally Dog Little*
Rosenthal, Marc. *Archie and the pirates*
Rubin, Susan Goldman. *Jean Laffite*
Schotter, Roni. *Captain Bob sets sail*
Siy, Alexandra. *One tractor*
Smith, Danna. *Pirate nap*
Sobel, June. *Shiver me letters*
Spires, Ashley. *Small Saul*
Sturges, Philemon. *This little pirate*
Thomson, Sarah L. *Pirates, ho!*
Tucker, Kathy. *Do pirates take baths?*
Weinert, Matthias. *No bath, no cake!*
Wolfe, Myra. *Charlotte Jane battles bedtime*

Planes *see* Airplanes, airports

Planets

Barner, Bob. *Stars, stars, stars*
Barrett, Judi. *Cloudy with a chance of meatballs 3*
Branley, Franklyn M. *The planets in our solar system*
Florian, Douglas. *Comets, stars, the moon, and Mars*
Gibbons, Gail. *The planets*
McNamara, Margaret. *The three little aliens and the big bad robot*
Metzger, Steve. *Pluto visits Earth!*
O'Brien, Patrick. *You are the first kid on Mars*
Pinkney, Brian. *Cosmo and the robot*
Rau, Dana Meachen. *Mars*
Theodorou, Rod. *Across the solar system*
Weitekamp, Margaret A. *Pluto's secret*
Wethered, Peggy. *Touchdown Mars!*
Yaccarino, Dan. *First day on a strange new planet*
New pet
Yorinks, Arthur. *Company's going*

Plants

Agran, Rick. *Pumpkin shivaree*
Aliki. *Corn is maize*
My visit to the aquarium
Arnold, Katya. *Let's find it!*
Azarian, Mary. *A gardener's alphabet*
Baker, Jeannie. *The hidden forest*
The story of rosy dock
Bang, Molly. *Living sunlight*
Ocean sunlight
Bardill, Linard. *The great golden thing*
Bash, Barbara. *Desert giant*
Berenstain, Stan and Jan. *The Berenstain bears and the prize pumpkin*
The Berenstain bears' that stump must go!
Bernhard, Durga. *Earth, sky, wet, dry*
Braun, Eric. *Trust me, Jack's beanstalk stinks*
Bruce, Lisa. *Fran's flower*
Butterworth, Nick. *Jasper's beanstalk*
Cannon, Janell. *Little Yau*
Carle, Eric. *The tiny seed*
Cash, Megan Montague. *What makes the seasons?*
Cave, Kathryn. *One child, one seed*
Cotten, Cynthia. *At the edge of the woods*
Day, Trevor. *Youch! it bites!*
Duke, Kate. *Ready for pumpkins*
Ehlert, Lois. *Leaf man*
Five little pumpkins, ill. by Ben Mantle
Five little pumpkins, ill. by Dan Yaccarino
Flanagan, Alice K. *Soil*
Fleischman, Paul. *Weslandia*
Fleming, Denise. *Where once there was a wood*
Ford, Miela. *Sunflower*
Gerber, Carole. *Seeds, bees, butterflies, and more!*
Gibbons, Gail. *The berry book*
From seed to plant
Nature's green umbrella
The vegetables we eat
Ginsburg, Mirra. *Mushroom in the rain*
Goodman, Emily. *Plant secrets*
Gourley, Robbin. *First garden*
Grey, Mini. *The very smart pea and the princess-to-be*
Grigsby, Susan. *In the garden with Dr. Carver*
Guiberson, Brenda Z. *Cactus hotel*
Hall, Zoe. *It's pumpkin time!*
Hammersmith, Craig. *Watch it grow*
Hayward, Linda. *What homework?*
Helmore, Jim. *Oh no, monster tomato!*
Henkes, Kevin. *So happy!*
Himmelman, John. *A dandelion's life*
Mouse in a meadow
Hines, Anna Grossnickle. *Miss Emma's wild garden*
Hobbie, Holly. *Toot and Puddle: wish you were here*
Honey, Elizabeth. *That's not a daffodil!*
Horn, Sandra Ann. *The dandelion wish*
Hubbell, Will. *Pumpkin Jack*
Hutchins, Pat. *Titch*
Inches, Alison. *Corduroy's garden*
Jack and the beanstalk. *Jack and the beanstalk*, ill. by Aljoscha Blau
Jack and the beanstalk, ill. by Steve Cox
Jack and the beanstalk, ill. by Nina Crews
Jack and the beanstalk, ill. by Julek Heller
Jack and the beanstalk, ill. by John Howe
Jack and the beanstalk, ill. by Steven Kellogg
Jack and the beanstalk, ill. by Albert Lorenz
Jack and the beanstalk, ill. by Niamh Sharkey
Jack and the beanstalk, ill. by Gennady Spirin
Jack and the beanstalk, ill. by Matt Tavares
Jacques and de beanstalk
Jackson, Alison. *Thea's tree*
Johnston, Tony. *Big red apple*
Keats, Ezra Jack. *Clementina's cactus*
Ketteman, Helen. *Waynetta and the cornstalk*
Kim, Sue. *How does a seed grow?*
Kimmel, Eric A. *Pumpkinhead*
Klingel, Cynthia Fitterer. *Forests*
Oceans

Kottke, Jan. *From seed to pumpkin*
Kranking, Kathy. *The ocean is . . .*
Krauss, Ruth. *The carrot seed*
Kudlinski, Kathleen V. *What do roots do?*
The little red hen. *The little red hen*
The little red hen: an old fable
Lobb, Janice. *Dig and sow! How do plants grow?*
Loki. *Jake Greenthumb*
Maass, Robert. *Garden*
McDonald, Megan. *The great pumpkin switch*
McGrath, Barbara Barbieri. *The little green witch*
McKy, Katie. *Pumpkin town!*
Mair, Samia J. *The perfect gift*
Martin, Bill, Jr. *Rock it, sock it, number line*
Marzollo, Jean. *Sun song*
Meddaugh, Susan. *Just Teenie*
Micucci, Charles. *The life and times of corn*
Mitchell, Susan K. *The rainforest grew all around*
Nolen, Jerdine. *Plantzilla goes to camp*
Osborne, Mary Pope. *Kate and the beanstalk*
Parkinson, Kathy. *The enormous turnip*
Peterson, Cris. *Seed soil sun*
Poole, Amy Lowry. *The pea blossom*
Posada, Mia. *Dandelions, stars in the grass*
Pulver, Robin. *Nobody's mother is in second grade*
Reiser, Lynn. *Earthdance*
Rey, H. A. *Elizabite*
Robbins, Ken. *Autumn leaves*
Seeds
Rockwell, Anne. *One bean*
Rubel, Nicole. *No more vegetables!*
Sage, James. *Farmer Smart's fat cat*
Santucci, Barbara. *Anna's corn*
Sasso, Sandy Eisenberg. *Naamah, Noah's wife*
Schaefer, Lola M. *This is the sunflower*
Schertle, Alice. *Witch Hazel*
Serafini, Frank. *Looking closely inside the garden*
Shields, Carol Diggory. *Martian rock*
Speed, Toby. *Brave potatoes*
Spilsbury, Louise. *Carrots*
Peas
Stihler, Chérie B. *The giant cabbage turnip*
Stimpson, Colin. *Jack and the baked beanstalk*
Tolstoy, Aleksey Nikolayevich. *The enormous turnip*
The gigantic turnip
Vagin, Vladimir. *The enormous carrot*
Van Rynbach, Iris. *Five little pumpkins*
Wallace, Karen. *Scarlette Beane*
Wallace, Nancy Elizabeth. *Paperwhite*
Pumpkin day
Weeks, Sarah. *Mrs. McNosh and the great big squash*
Wheeler, Lisa. *Jam and jelly by Holly and Nellie*
Wortche, Allison. *Rosie Sprout's time to shine*
Yacowitz, Caryn. *Pumpkin fiesta*
Yolen, Jane. *Welcome to the sea of sand*
Zoehfeld, Kathleen Weidner. *What's alive?*

Plays *see* Theater

Pockets *see* Clothing

Poetry

Ada, Alma Flor. *Gathering the sun*
Adoff, Arnold. *In for winter, out for spring*
Love letters
Street music
Touch the poem
Adoff, Jaime. *Small fry*
Agee, Jon. *Orangutan tongs*
Alarcón, Francisco X. *From the bellybutton of the moon and other summer poems / Del ombligo de la luna y otros poemas de verano*
Iguanas in the snow and other winter poems / Iguanas en la nieve y otros poemas de invierno
Alexander, Cecil Frances. *All things bright and beautiful*, ill. by Anna Vojtech
All things bright and beautiful, ill. by Bruce Whatley
Alexander, Elizabeth. *Praise song for the day*
Alger, Leclaire Gowans. *All in the morning early*
Altman, Susan. *Followers of the north star*
Amazing graces
Andreae, Giles. *Bustle in the bushes*
Cock-a-doodle-doo!
Dinosaurs galore!
Angelou, Maya. *Amazing peace*
My painted house, my friendly chicken, and me
Appelt, Kathi. *My father's house*
Archer, Peggy. *From dawn to dreams*
Name that dog!
Argueta, Jorge. *Arroz con leche / Rice pudding*
Guacamole
Sopa de frijoles: un poema para cocinar / Bean soup: a cooking poem
Tamalitos
Trees are hanging from the sky
Ashley Bryan's ABC of African American poetry
Ashman, Linda. *The essential worldwide monster guide*
Aylesworth, Jim. *The burger and the hot dog*
Bagert, Brod. *Giant children*
Shout!
Baird, Audrey B. *A cold snap!*
Storm coming!
Bates, Katharine Lee. *America the beautiful*, ill. by Chris Gall
America the beautiful, ill. by Wendell Minor
Bates, Katharine Lee. *America the beautiful: together we stand*
Becker, Helaine. *Mama likes to mambo*
Belle, Jennifer. *Animal stackers*
The best part of me
Big, bad, and a little bit scary
Bless the beasts
Bolden, Tonya. *Rock of ages*
Boling, Katherine. *New year be coming!*
Booth, Philip E. *Crossing*
Borden, Louise. *America is . . .*
Brooks, Gwendolyn. *Bronzeville boys and girls*
Brown, Margaret Wise. *The friendly book*
Give yourself to the rain
The Golden sleepy book
Love songs of the little bear
Nibble, nibble
Browning, Robert. *The pied piper of Hamelin*
Bruchac, Joseph. *The circle of thanks*
Thirteen moons on turtle's back
Bruno, Elsa Knight. *Punctuation celebration*
Bryan, Ashley. *Sing to the sun*
Bryant, Jen. *A river of words*
Bunting, Eve. *Anna's table*
Sing a song of piglets
Who was born this special day?
Burleigh, Robert. *Goal*
Bush, Timothy. *Ferocious girls, steamroller boys, and other poems in between*

Calmenson, Stephanie. *Good for you!*
Welcome, baby!
Cameron, Eileen. *Canyon*
Carabine, Sue. *A firefighter's night before Christmas*
Carlstrom, Nancy White. *Before you were born*
Thanksgiving Day at our house
What does the sky say?
Who said boo?
Carroll, Lewis. *Jabberwocky*
Carryl, Charles E. *The camel's lament*
Cendrars, Blaise. *Shadow*
Chaikin, Miriam. *Don't step on the sky*
Chernaik, Judith. *Carnival of the animals: poems inspired by Saint-Saëns' music*
A child's calendar
Chorao, Kay. *The baby's bedtime book*
Christelow, Eileen. *Five little monkeys jumping on the bed*
Christmas presents
Clavel, Bernard. *Castle of books*
Clements, Andrew. *Dogku*
Cline-Ransome, Lesa. *Quilt alphabet*
Clinton, Catherine. *Phillis's big test*
Come and play
Coombs, Kate. *Water sings blue*
Cooper, Floyd. *Coming home: from the life of Langston Hughes*
Crawley, Dave. *Cat poems*
Creech, Sharon. *Who's that baby?*
Cuetara, Mittie. *Baby business*
Cutlip, Kimbra L. *Firefighter's night before Christmas*
Danneberg, Julie. *Cowboy Slim*
Dawes, Kwame Senu Neville. *I saw your face*
Delacre, Lulu. *Arroz con leche*
Las Navidades
Dotlich, Rebecca Kai. *A family like yours*
In the spin of things
What is science?
Downes, Belinda. *Baby days*
The drowsy hours
Eastwick, Ivy O. *Some folks like cats, and other poems*
Elliott, David. *In the sea*
In the wild
Emberley, Barbara. *Drummer Hoff*
Night's nice
One wide river to cross
Esbaum, Jill. *Stanza*
Fairies, trolls and goblins galore
Farber, Norma. *How the hibernators came to Bethlehem*
Farrar, Sid. *The year comes round*
Field, Eugene. *Wynken, Blynken, and Nod*
Wynken, Blynken and Nod
Field, Rachel Lyman. *Grace for an island meal*
Figley, Marty Rhodes. *Emily and Carlo*
Fischer, Scott M. *Twinkle*
The fish is me
Fisher, Aileen Lucia. *Do rabbits have Christmas?*
The story goes on
Fitch, Sheree. *No two snowflakes*
Fletcher, Ralph. *Grandpa never lies*
Florian, Douglas. *Bow wow meow meow, it's rhyming cats and dogs*
Comets, stars, the moon, and Mars
Dinothesaurus
Handsprings
Insectlopedia
Lizards, frogs, and polliwogs
Poem runs
Poetrees
Shiver me timbers!
Summersaults
Unbeelievables
Zoo's who
For laughing out louder
Forman, Ruth. *Young Cornrows callin out the moon*
Foster, John. *Pet poems*
Fox, Paula. *Traces*
Frampton, David. *Mr. Ferlinghetti's poem*
My beastie book of ABC
Franco, Betsy. *Bees, snails, and peacock tails*
A curious collection of cats
A dazzling display of dogs
Frank, John. *A chill in the air*
How to catch a fish
Frasier, Debra. *On the day you were born*
Frost, Helen. *Step gently out*
Frost, Robert. *Stopping by woods on a snowy evening*
George, Kristine O'Connell. *Emma dilemma*
The great frog race and other poems
Little Dog and Duncan
Old Elm speaks
Gerber, Carole. *Seeds, bees, butterflies, and more!*
Gilchrist, Jan Spivey. *My America*
Gilman, Rita Golden. *Rice is life*
Giovanni, Nikki. *The sun is so quiet*
Glaser, Linda. *Emma's poem*
Godwin, Laura. *Barnyard prayers*
Gollub, Matthew. *Cool melons — turn to frogs*
Gottfried, Maya. *Good dog*
Our farm
Grady, Cynthia. *I lay my stitches down*
Graham, Joan Bransfield. *Flicker flash*
Splish splash
Grahame, Kenneth. *The reluctant dragon*
A grand celebration
Greenberg, David. *Don't forget your etiquette!*
Greenfield, Eloise. *Angels*
Big friend, little friend
Brothers and sisters
Daydreamers
The friendly four
I can draw a weeposaur and other dinosaurs
I make music
In the land of words
My doll, Keshia
Nathaniel talking
Night on Neighborhood Street
Grimes, Nikki. *Danitra Brown, class clown*
A pocketful of poems
Shoe magic
Voices of Christmas
When Daddy prays
When Gorilla goes walking
Grossman, Bill. *Timothy Tunny swallowed a bunny*
Guthrie, James. *Last song*
Gutman, Dan. *Casey back at bat*
Hague, Michael. *Animal friends: a collection of poems for children*
Hanukkah lights
Harness, Cheryl. *Papa's Christmas gift*
Harrison, David L. *The alligator in the closet and other poems around the house*
Farmer's garden
Heidbreder, Robert. *Noisy poems for a busy day*
The Helen Oxenbury nursery collection
Hines, Anna Grossnickle. *Pieces, a year in poems and quilts*

Honey, Elizabeth. *The moon in the man*
Hooper, Patricia. *Where do you sleep, little one?*
Hopkins, Lee Bennett. *All God's children*
Alphathoughts
April, bubbles, chocolate
Behind the museum door
City I love
Good books, good times
Good rhymes, good times
Incredible inventions
Merrily comes our harvest in
Nasty bugs
Ragged shadows
School supplies
Yummy! eating through a day
Hort, Lenny. *Tie your socks and clap your feet*
Horton, Joan. *Hippopotamus stew*
Hot potato
Howitt, Mary Botham. *Mary Howitt's The spider and the fly*
Hubbell, Patricia. *Black earth, gold sun*
Boo! Halloween poems and limericks
Bouncing time
City kids
Earthmates
Hudson, Cheryl Willis. *Bright eyes, brown skin*
Hudson, Wade. *Pass it on*
Hughes, Langston. *Carol of the brown king*
I, too, am America
Lullaby (for a Black mother)
My people
The Negro speaks of rivers
The sweet and sour animal book
Hughes, Shirley. *Olly and me*
Hundal, Nancy. *Camping*
I invited a dragon to dinner
Imagine that! poems of never-was
In daddy's arms I am tall
Issa, Kobayashi. *Today and today*
Iyengar, Malathi Michelle. *Tan to tamarind*
Jensen, Dana. *A meal of the stars*
Johnson, Angela. *Daddy calls me man*
Johnson, James Weldon. *The Creation*
Johnston, Tony. *The barn owls*
My Mexico / México mío
Joseph, Lynn. *Coconut kind of day*
Katz, Bobbi. *Once around the sun*
Katz, Susan. *Mrs. Brown on exhibit*
Oh, Theodore!
Kay, Verla. *Broken Feather*
Kennedy, Jimmy. *The teddy bears' picnic,* ill. by Michael Hague
The teddy bears' picnic, ill. by Prue Theobalds
Knight, Hilary. *Hilary Knight's the owl and the pussy-cat*
Krauss, Ruth. *Bears*
Kumin, Maxine. *Mites to astodons*
Kuskin, Karla. *Toots the cat*
Larios, Julie. *Imaginary menagerie*
Yellow elephant
Lear, Edward. *The owl and the pussycat,* ill. by Jan Brett
The owl and the pussycat, ill. by Paul Galdone
The owl and the pussycat, ill. by Anne Mortimer
The Quangle Wangle's hat
LeBox, Annette. *Salmon Creek*
Lee, Dennis. *Bubblegum delicious*
Lenski, Lois. *I like winter*
Now it's fall
Lesser, Carolyn. *What a wonderful day to be a cow*
Let there be light
Let's count the raindrops
Levine, Gail Carson. *Forgive me, I meant to do it*
Lewis, J. Patrick. *The bookworm's feast*
Doodle dandies
Face bug
Good mousekeeping
A hippopotamusn't
The little buggers
Long was the winter road they traveled
Riddle-icious
World Rat Day
Lillegard, Dee. *Go! poetry in motion: poems*
Hello school!
Wake up house!
Lin, Grace. *Robert's snowflakes*
Livingston, Myra Cohn. *Abraham Lincoln: a man for all the people*
Calendar
Celebrations
Keep on singing
Locker, Thomas. *Mountain dance*
Water dance
London, Jonathan. *Sun dance, water dance*
Longfellow, Henry Wadsworth. *Hiawatha*
Paul Revere's ride
Paul Revere's ride: the landlord's tale
Love to mamá
Luján, Jorge. *Beyond my hand*
Colors! / ¡Colores!
Lullaby moons and a silver spoon
Lyon, George Ella. *Book*
Counting on the woods
MacDonald, Suse. *Edward Lear's A was once an apple pie*
McGhee, Alison. *Only a witch can fly*
McGough, Roger. *What on earth can it be?*
MacLachlan, Patricia. *Cat talk*
Snowflakes fall
Maguire, John. *People*
Mak, Kam. *My Chinatown*
Mannis, Celeste Davidson. *One leaf rides the wind*
Maples in the mist
Marshall, James. *Pocketful of nonsense*
Marzollo, Jean. *I love you*
Mathers, Petra. *A cake for Herbie*
Mayo, Margaret. *Wiggle waggle fun*
Medina, Tony. *DeShawn days*
Melmed, Laura Krauss. *The first song ever sung*
This first Thanksgiving
Merriam, Eve. *Bam, bam, bam*
Blackberry ink
Halloween ABC
Micklos, John. *Daddy poems*
Mommy poems
Montenegro, Laura Nyman. *A bird about to sing*
Moore, Clement Clarke. *A creature was stirring*
The night before Christmas
The night before Christmas, ill. by Jan Brett
The night before Christmas, ill. by Tomie dePaola
The night before Christmas, ill. by Mary Engelbreit
The night before Christmas, ill. by Holly Hobbie
The night before Christmas, ill. by Rachel Isadora
The night before Christmas, ill. by Raquel Jaramillo
The night before Christmas, ill. by Anita Lobel
The night before Christmas, ill. by James Marshall
The night before Christmas, ill. by Will Moses

The night before Christmas, ill. by Ted Rand
The night before Christmas, ill. by Ruth Sanderson
The night before Christmas, ill. by Gennady Spirin
The night before Christmas, ill. by Tasha Tudor
The night before Christmas, ill. by Richard Jesse Watson
The night before Christmas, ill. by Wendy Watson
The night before Christmas, ill. by Bruce Whatley
The night before Christmas, ill. by Lisbeth Zwerger
The night before Christmas: a pop-up
The teddy bears' night before Christmas
'Twas the night before Christmas, ill. by Matt Tavares
'Twas the night before Christmas, ill. by Christopher Wormell
Moore, Lilian. *Beware, take care*
Mora, Pat. *Confetti*
Delicious hullabaloo / Pachanga deliciosa
The desert is my mother / El desierto es mi madre
Listen to the desert / Oye al desierto
This big sky
Yum! Mmmm! Que rico!
Moss, Jenny Jackson. *Cajun night after Christmas*
Mother Goose. *Arnold Lobel book of Mother Goose*
Mozelle, Shirley. *The kitchen talks*
Murphy, Elspeth Campbell. *Happy Easter, God*
Murphy, Sally. *Pearl verses the world*
Myers, Tim. *Basho and the fox*
Myers, Walter Dean. *Brown angels*
Harlem
Nash, Ogden. *The adventures of Isabel*, ill. by James Marshall
The adventures of Isabel, ill. by Bridget Starr Taylor
Custard the dragon and the wicked knight
Nicholls, Judith. *Someone I like*
Nidey, Kelli. *When autumn falls*
Nikola-Lisa, W. *Bein' with you this way*
Noda, Takayo. *Dear world*
Northey, Lawrence. *I'm a hop hop hoppity frog*
Numeroff, Laura Joffe. *Sometimes I wonder if poodles like noodles*
Nye, Naomi Shihab. *Come with me*
O'Connor, Jane. *Fancy Nancy: poet extraordinaire!*
O'Keefe, Susan Heyboer. *One hungry monster*
Olaleye, Isaac. *The distant talking drum*
Oppenheim, Joanne. *Have you seen trees?*
Otten, Charlotte F. *January rides the wind*
Otto, Carolyn. *Dinosaur chase*
The palm of my heart
Paolilli, Paul. *Silver seeds*
Pearson, Debora. *Leo's tree*
Pearson, Susan. *Slugs in love*
Perdorno, Willie. *Visiting Langston*
Perry, Andrea. *Here's what you do when you can't find your shoe*
Peters, Lisa Westberg. *Volcano wakes up!*
Pickering, Jimmy. *It's fall*
It's winter
Plourde, Lynn. *Pigs in the mud in the middle of the rud*
A pocketful of stars
Poems for the very young
Pollock, Penny. *When the moon is full*
Pomerantz, Charlotte. *All asleep*
Powell, Consie. *Amazing apples*
Prelutsky, Jack. *Awful Ogre running wild*
Awful Ogre's awful day
The baby uggs are hatching
Behold the bold umbrellaphant and other poems
Beneath a blue umbrella
Circus
The frogs wore red suspenders
Good sports
Halloween countdown
It's snowing! It's snowing!
Me I am!
Monday's troll
The pack rat's day and other poems
The queen of Eene
Rainy rainy Saturday
The Random House book of poetry for children
Read-aloud rhymes for the very young
Ride a purple pelican
The snopp on the sidewalk and other poems
Stardines swim high across the sky
There's no place like school
Tyrannosaurus was a beast
What a day it was at school!
Quattlebaum, Mary. *Winter friends*
Raczka, Bob. *Guyku*
Ray, Mary Lyn. *Mud*
Regan, Dian Curtis. *Barnyard slam*
Rhyme time around the day
Richards, Beah E. *Keep climbing, girls*
Richards, Laura Elizabeth Howe. *Jiggle joggle jee*
Rosales, Melodye Benson. *'Twas the night b'fore Christmas*
Rose, Deborah Lee. *The twelve days of kindergarten*
Rosen, Michael. *How the animals got their colors*
Rovetch, Lissa. *Ook the book*
Ruddell, Deborah. *Today at the Bluebird Cafe*
A whiff of pine, a hint of skunk
Ryan, Pam Muñoz. *The flag we love*
Ryder, Joanne. *Mouse tail moon*
Step into the night
Toad by the road
Rylant, Cynthia. *Baby face: a book of love for baby*
Sandburg, Carl. *From daybreak to good night*
Sayre, April Pulley. *The shape of Betts Meadow*
Scanlon, Elizabeth Garton. *A sock is a pocket for your toes*
Schertle, Alice. *Advice for a frog and other poems*
Button up!
How now, brown cow?
I am the cat
We
Schnur, Steven. *Autumn*
Spring
Summer
Winter
Schwartz, David M. *Where else in the wild?*
Where in the wild
Seabrooke, Brenda. *'Twas the day before Christmas*
Shakespeare, William. *To sleep, perchance to dream*
Shange, Ntozake. *Coretta Scott*
Ellington was not a street
Freedom's a-callin me
Shannon, George. *Busy in the garden*
Frog legs
Spring: a haiku story
Shields, Carol Diggory. *The bugliest bug*
Lunch money and other poems about school
Shore, Diane Z. *This is the feast*
Sidman, Joyce. *Butterfly eyes and other secrets of the meadow*
Meow ruff
Red sings from treetops

Song of the water boatman
Ubiquitous
Siebert, Diane. *Heartland*
Mojave
Sierra
Silvano, Wendi. *What does the wind say?*
Simeon, Jean-Pierre. *This is a poem that heals fish*
Simon, Francesca. *Toddler time*
Singer, Marilyn. *The company of crows*
Creature carnival
Every day's a dog's day
First food fight this fall and other school poems
A stick is an excellent thing
Turtle in July
Sklansky, Amy E. *Out of this world*
Sleigh bells and snowflakes
Smith, William Jay. *Around my room*
Snyder, Betsy E. *I haiku you*
Spinelli, Eileen. *Polar bear, arctic hare*
Summerbath, winterbath
Stevenson, Robert Louis. *Block city*, ill. by Daniel Kirk
Block city, ill. by Ashley Wolff
A child's garden of verses, ill. by Cooper Edens
A child's garden of verses, ill. by Diane Goode
A child's garden of verses, ill. by Jessie Willcox Smith
A child's garden of verses, ill. by Tasha Tudor
The little land
The moon, ill. by Tracey Campbell Pearson
The moon, ill. by Denise Saldutti
Where go the boats?
The sun, the moon, and the stars
Swann, Brian. *The house with no door*
Thayer, Ernest Lawrence. *Casey at the bat*
Casey at the bat: a ballad of the Republic, sung in the year 1888, ill. by Christopher Bing
Casey at the bat: a ballad of the Republic, sung in the year 1888, ill. by Patricia Polacco
This place I know
Thomas, Joyce Carol. *The blacker the berry*
Brown honey in broomwheat tea
Cherish me
Crowning glory
Gingerbread days
Troupe, Quincy. *Little Stevie Wonder*
Turner, Ann Warren. *The Christmas house*
In the heart
Secrets from the dollhouse
Udry, Janice May. *A tree is nice*
Unobagha, Uzoamaka Chinyelu. *Off to the sweet shores of Africa and other talking drum rhymes*
Up the hill and down
Uslander, Arlene. *That's what grandparents are for*
Vestergaard, Hope. *Digger, dozer, dumper*
Viorst, Judith. *The alphabet from Z to A*
Walker, Rob D. *Mama says*
Wardlaw, Lee. *Won Ton*
Watson, Wendy. *Hurray for the Fourth of July*
A Valentine for you
Weinstock, Robert. *Food hates you, too, and other poems*
Weisburd, Stefi. *Barefoot: poems for naked feet*
Weiss, George. *What a wonderful world*
Wells, Rosemary. *Carry me!*
Westcott, Nadine Bernard. *The lady with the alligator purse*
Wharnsby-Ali, Dawud. *A picnic of poems in Allah's green garden*
Wheeler, Lisa. *Wool gathering*
Whitehead, Jenny. *Lunch box mail and other poems*
Whiteley, Opal Stanley. *Only Opal*
Wick, Walter. *Can you see what I see? the night before Christmas*
Wilbur, Richard. *The disappearing alphabet*
Willard, Nancy. *The Moon and Riddles Diner and the Sunnyside Café*
Pish posh, said Hieronymous Bosch
A visit to William Blake's inn
Wilson, Anna. *Over in the grasslands*
Winnick, Karen B. *A year goes round*
Wise, William. *Dinosaurs forever*
Wong, Janet S. *Homegrown house*
Wood, Audrey. *Silly Sally [board book]*
Worth, Valerie. *Pug and other animal poems*
Xinran, Xue. *Motherbridge of love*
Yolen, Jane. *An egret's day*
A mirror to nature
The three bears holiday rhyme book
Welcome to the sea of sand
Ziefert, Harriet. *A bunny is funny*
Hanukkah haiku
Zolotow, Charlotte. *Some things go together*

Poltergeists *see* Ghosts

Ponds *see* Lakes, ponds

Ponies *see* Animals – horses, ponies

Poor *see* Homeless; Poverty

Pop-up books *see* Format, unusual – toy & movable books

Porpoises *see* Animals – dolphins

Post office

Ahlberg, Janet. *The jolly Christmas postman*
The jolly pocket postman
The jolly postman
Bergel, Colin. *Mail by the pail*
Carter, Don. *Send it!*
Gibbons, Gail. *The post office book*
Gliori, Debi. *Penguin post*
Horning, Sandra. *The giant hug*
Lendroth, Susan. *Calico Dorsey*
Rylant, Cynthia. *Mr. Griggs' work*
Schneider, Howie. *Fast 'n Snappy*
Scott, Ann Herbert. *Hi!*
Shea, Kitty. *Out and about at the post office*

Potty training *see* Toilet training

Pourquoi tales *see* Folk & fairy tales – pourquoi tales

Poverty

Andersen, Hans Christian. *The little match girl*, ill. by Rachel Isadora
The little match girl, ill. by Blair Lent
The little match girl, ill. by Jerry Pinkney
The little matchstick girl
Bartoletti, Susan Campbell. *The Christmas promise*
Boelts, Maribeth. *Happy like soccer*
Buitrago, Jairo. *Jimmy the greatest*
Burnett, Frances Hodgson. *A little princess*
Cutler, Jane. *Guttersnipe*
Fullerton, Alma. *A good trade*
Grimm, Jacob and Wilhelm. *Doctor All-Knowing*
Lipp, Frederick. *Running shoes*
Littlesugar, Amy. *Tree of hope*
Mahy, Margaret. *Down the back of the chair*
Mills, Lauren A. *The rag coat*
Milway, Katie Smith. *One hen*
Park, Frances. *The royal bee*
Quattlebaum, Mary. *The shine man*
Sawyer, Ruth. *Journey cake, ho!*
Shulevitz, Uri. *How I learned geography*
Thomas, Jane Resh. *Lights on the river*
Toscano, Charles. *Papa's pastries*
Vainio, Pirkko. *The Christmas angel*
Wilde, Oscar. *The happy prince*
Williams, Karen Lynn. *Beatrice's dream*
Woodson, Jacqueline. *Each kindness*
Ziefert, Harriet. *When I first came to this land*

Pow-wows

Bouchard, Dave. *The song within my heart*

Power failures

Rodriguez, Bobbie. *Sarah's sleepover*

Practicality *see* Character traits – practicality

Prairie wolves *see* Animals – coyotes

Prayers *see* Religion

Preachers *see* Careers – clergy

Pregnancy *see* Birth

Prehistoric man *see* Cave dwellers

Prehistory

Aliki. *Digging up dinosaurs*
Dinosaur bones
Dinosaurs are different
My visit to the dinosaurs
Andersen, Hans Christian. *The dinosaur's new clothes*
Arnold, Caroline. *Giant shark*
Barton, Byron. *Bones, bones, dinosaur bones*
Dinosaurs, dinosaurs
Berenstain, Stan and Jan. *The Berenstain bears and the missing dinosaur bone*
Berger, Melvin. *Why did the dinosaurs disappear?*
Bilgrami, Shaheen. *Amazing dinosaur discovery*
Brown, Laurie Krasny. *Dinosaurs alive and well*
Dinosaurs divorce
Dinosaurs to the rescue
Dinosaurs travel
When dinosaurs die
Brown, Marc. *Dinosaurs, beware!*
Carrick, Carol. *Patrick's dinosaurs*
Patrick's dinosaurs on the Internet
What happened to Patrick's dinosaurs?
Cole, Joanna. *The magic school bus in the time of the dinosaurs*
Curious George and the dinosaur
Dolenz, Micky. *Gakky Two-Feet*
Donnelly, Liza. *Dinosaurs' Halloween*
Florian, Douglas. *Dinothesaurus*
Gerstein, Mordicai. *The first drawing*
Gibbons, Gail. *Dinosaurs!*
Prehistoric animals
Harrison, Carol. *Dinosaurs everywhere!*
Hartmann, Wendy. *The dinosaurs are back and it's all your fault, Edward!*
Hennessy, B. G. *Busy Dinah Dinosaur*
The dinosaur who lived in my backyard
Meet Dinah Dinosaur
Jenkins, Steve. *Prehistoric actual size*
Joyce, William. *Dinosaur Bob*
Kellogg, Steven. *Prehistoric Pinkerton*
McCully, Emily Arnold. *The secret cave*
McMullan, Kate. *I'm bad!*
Most, Bernard. *A dinosaur named after me*
Dinosaur questions
How big were the dinosaurs?
If the dinosaurs came back
Whatever happened to the dinosaurs?
O'Brien, Patrick. *Sabertooth*
Otto, Carolyn. *Dinosaur chase*
Patkau, Karen. *Creatures*
Pfister, Marcus. *Dazzle the dinosaur*
Pulver, Robin. *Mrs. Toggle and the dinosaur*
Roth, Susan L. *Great big guinea pigs*
Sabuda, Robert. *Encyclopedia prehistorica: dinosaurs*
Encyclopedia prehistorica: mega-beasts
Encyclopedia prehistorica: sharks and other seamonsters
Schwartz, Henry. *How I captured a dinosaur*
Shields, Carol Diggory. *Saturday night at the dinosaur stomp*
Sís, Peter. *Dinosaur!*
Stevenson, James. *The most amazing dinosaur*
Stickland, Paul. *Dinosaur roar!*
Dinosaur stomp!
Ten terrible dinosaurs
Tankard, Jeremy. *Me hungry!*
Wahl, Jan. *The field mouse and the dinosaur named Sue*
I met a dinosaur

Prejudice

Amado, Elisa. *Tricycle*
Asim, Jabari. *Fifty cents and a dream*
Bandy, Michael S. *White water*
Barbour, Karen. *Mr. Williams*
Bauer, Marion Dane. *Harriet Tubman*
Birtha, Becky. *Grandmama's pride*
Boedoe, Geefwee. *Arrowville*
Brown, Ken. *What's the time, Grandma Wolf?*

Bunting, Eve. *Walking to school*
Carlson, Nancy. *Loudmouth George and the new neighbors*
Coles, Robert. *The story of Ruby Bridges*
Cooper, Floyd. *Willie and the All-Stars*
Couric, Katie. *The brand new kid*
Crowe, Chris. *Just as good*
Crowther, Kitty. *Jack and Jim*
Dray, Philip. *Yours for justice, Ida B. Wells*
Edwards, Pamela Duncan. *The bus ride that changed history*
Eversole, Robyn. *East Dragon, West Dragon*
Farris, Christine King. *March on!*
My brother Martin
Fishman, Cathy Goldberg. *When Jackie and Hank met*
Fries, Claudia. *A pig is moving in*
Giovanni, Nikki. *Rosa*
Gruska, Denise. *The only boy in ballet class*
Haskins, Jim. *Delivering justice*
Hoffman, Eric. *Play Lady / La Señora Juguetona*
Hughes, Shirley. *The Christmas Eve ghost*
Hume, Lachie. *Clancy the courageous cow*
Issa, Kai Jackson. *Howard Thurman's Great Hope*
King, Martin Luther, III. *My daddy, Dr. Martin Luther King, Jr.*
King, Martin Luther, Jr. *I have a dream*
Kittinger, Jo S. *Rosa's bus*
Klingel, Cynthia Fitterer. *Rosa Parks*
Kochan, Vera. *What if your best friend were blue?*
Krensky, Stephen. *Play ball, Jackie!*
Lester, Julius. *Let's talk about race*
Levy, Debbie. *We shall overcome*
Lorbiecki, Marybeth. *Jackie's bat*
McCourt, Lisa, et al. *Chicken soup for little souls: Della Splatnuk birthday girl*
McCully, Emily Arnold. *Wonder horse*
McKissack, Patricia C. *Goin' someplace special*
Malaspina, Ann. *Finding Lincoln*
Martins, Isabel Minhós. *My neighbor is a dog*
Mason, Margaret H. *These hands*
Medearis, Michael. *Daisy and the doll*
Michelson, Richard. *Across the alley*
Busing Brewster
Twice as good
Miller, William. *The bus ride*
Mitchell, Margaree King. *Susie Mae*
When Grandmama sings
Morris, Ann. *Grandma Lois remembers*
Myers, Walter Dean. *Muhammad Ali: the people's champion*
Naden, Corinne J. *Ron's big mission*
Nelson, Kadir. *Nelson Mandela*
Newton, Vanessa. *Let freedom sing*
Pfister, Marcus. *Milo and the mysterious island*
Pinkney, Andrea Davis. *Boycott blues*
Sit-in
Polacco, Patricia. *Mr. Lincoln's way*
Rahaman, Vashanti. *Divali rose*
Ramsey, Calvin Alexander. *Ruth and the Green Book*
Rappaport, Doreen. *The school is not white!*
Reynolds, Aaron. *Back of the bus*
Ringgold, Faith. *If a bus could talk*
Rosen, Michael. *This is our house*
Ruzzier, Sergio. *Bear and Bee*
Ryan, Pam Muñoz. *When Marian sang*
Sauer, Tammi. *Nugget and Fang*
Say, Allen. *The favorite daughter*
Schroeder, Alan. *Minty*
Shange, Ntozake. *Coretta Scott*
Whitewash
Shelton, Paula Young. *Child of the civil rights movement*
Shore, Diane Z. *This is the dream*
Sidjanski, Brigitte. *Little Chicken and Little Duck*
Skead, Robert. *Something to prove*
Slade, Suzanne. *Climbing Lincoln's steps*
Smalls, Irene. *Don't say ain't*
Tarpley, Natasha Anastasia. *Joe-Joe's first flight*
Tavares, Matt. *Henry Aaron's dream*
Tutu, Archbishop Desmond. *Desmond and the very mean word*
Ungerer, Tomi. *Flix*
Van Allsburg, Chris. *The widow's broom*
Vernick, Audrey. *She loved baseball*
Watkins, Angela Farris. *My Uncle Martin's words for America*
Weatherford, Carole Boston. *The Beatitudes*
Champions on the bench
Freedom on the menu
Wells, Rosemary. *Yoko*
Wiles, Debbie. *Freedom summer*
Woodson, Jacqueline. *The other side*
Yin. *Coolies*

Preschool *see* School – nursery

Pride *see* Character traits – pride

Priests *see* Careers – clergy

Problem solving

Aesop. *The crow and the pitcher*
Alexander, Martha G. *I'll protect you from the jungle beasts*
We're in big trouble, Blackboard Bear
Amann, Jürg. *Ten birds*
Armstrong-Ellis, Carey. *Prudy's problem and how she solved it*
Arnosky, Jim. *Mud time and more*
Asch, Frank. *Mr. Maxwell's mouse*
Berry, Lynne. *What floats in a moat?*
Brown, Jeff. *Flat Stanley*, ill. by Scott Nash
Flat Stanley, ill. by Tomi Ungerer
Butterworth, Nick. *Jingle bells*
Carlson, Nancy. *Harriet and the garden*
Chivers, Natalie. *Rhino's great big itch!*
Cole, Babette. *Princess Smartypants*
dePaola, Tomie. *Charlie needs a cloak*
Dierssen, Andreas. *The old red tractor*
Einhorn, Edward. *A very improbable story*
Gardella, Tricia. *Blackberry booties*
George, Lindsay Barrett. *In the garden: who's been here?*
In the woods
Grambling, Lois G. *Can I bring Woolly to the library, Ms. Reeder?*
Grindley, Sally. *Who is it?*
Harvey, Damian. *Just the thing!*
Hester, Denia Lewis. *Grandma Lena's big ol' turnip*
Johnson, Paul Brett. *Mr. Persnickety and Cat Lady*
Jonas, Ann. *Holes and peeks*
Joyce, William. *Big time Olie*
Keats, Ezra Jack. *Goggles*
Whistle for Willie

Knudsen, Michelle. *Bugged!*
Maccarone, Grace. *Miss Lina's ballerinas*
McCloskey, Robert. *Lentil*
McCully, Emily Arnold. *Marvelous Mattie*
McKee, David. *Elmer and the hippos*
Mamada, Mineko. *Which is round? which is bigger?*
Marino, Gianna. *Too tall houses*
Masini, Beatrice. *A brave little princess*
Mayer, Mercer. *Just big enough*
What do you do with a kangaroo?
Murguia, Bethanie Deeney. *Snippet the early riser*
Murphy, Stuart J. *The best vacation ever*
Treasure map
Nakagawa, Rieko. *Guri and Gura*
Olaleye, Isaac. *Bitter bananas*
Oxley, Jennifer. *The chicken problem*
Parenteau, Shirley. *Bears on chairs*
Parkinson, Kathy. *The enormous turnip*
Payne, Emmy. *Katy no-pocket*
Peck, Jan. *Giant peach yodel!*
Pett, Mark. *The boy and the airplane*
Poydar, Nancy. *The perfectly horrible Halloween*
Pulver, Robin. *Saturday is Dadurday*
Rice, Eve. *Peter's pockets*
Rock, Brian. *The deductive detective*
Root, Phyllis. *Rattletrap car*
Rattletrap car [board book]
Salat, Cristina. *Peanut's emergency*
SanAngelo, Ryan. *Eddie spaghetti*
Schmid, Paul. *Hugs from Pearl*
Perfectly Percy
Seuss, Dr. *Did I ever tell you how lucky you are?*
Hunches in bunches
Shannon, George. *Turkey Tot*
Souhami, Jessica. *The little, little house*
Spinelli, Eileen. *Wanda's monster*
Stevenson, James. *Quick! Turn the page!*
Tauss, Marc. *Superhero*
Titus, Eve. *Anatole and the cat*
Tolstoy, Aleksey Nikolayevich. *The enormous turnip*
The gigantic turnip
Uhlberg, Myron. *Mad Dog McGraw*
Vagin, Vladimir. *The enormous carrot*
Van Kampen, Vlasta. *It couldn't be worse*
Wallen, Ila. *The moon in my room*
Weeks, Sarah. *Ella, of course!*
Wells, Rosemary. *Hands off, Harry!*
Williams, Karen Lynn. *Painted dreams*
Yolen, Jane. *Piggins*
Young, Cybèle. *Ten birds*
Zemach, Margot. *It could always be worse*
Ziefert, Harriet. *You can't buy a dinosaur with a dime*

Progress

Burton, Virginia Lee. *The little house*
Peet, Bill. *Countdown to Christmas*
Farewell to Shady Glade
The wump world

Promptness, tardiness *see* Behavior – promptness, tardiness

Pumas *see* Animals – cougars

Punctuality *see* Behavior – promptness, tardiness

Puppets

Findlay, Lisa. *What's in Oscar's trashcan?*
Fitzpatrick, Marie-Louise. *Lizzy and Skunk*
Joosse, Barbara. *Hooray Parade*
Keats, Ezra Jack. *Louie*
McDonald, Megan. *When the library lights go out*
Potter, Giselle. *The year I didn't go to school*
Smith, Lane. *Pinocchio, the boy*
Sweet, Melissa. *Balloons over Broadway*
Trimble, Marcia. *Peppy's shadow*
Weiss, George. *What a wonderful world*
Who took the cookie?

Purses *see* Clothing – handbags, purses

Puzzles *see also* Picture puzzles; Rebuses; Riddles & jokes

Base, Graeme. *The Jewel Fish of Karnak*
Boatfield, Jonny. *The twilight book*
Capucilli, Karen. *The jelly bean fun book*
Fisher, Valorie. *How high can a dinosaur count?*
Maidment, Stella. *Cowboy puzzles*
Philpot, Lorna. *Find Anthony Ant*
Simmons, Jane. *Splish splash Daisy*
Waber, Bernard. *Do you see a mouse?*

Questioning *see* Character traits – questioning

Quicksand *see* Sand

Quilts

Bateson-Hill, Margaret. *Shota and the star quilt*
Bourgeois, Paulette. *Oma's quilt*
Brown, Margaret Wise. *Bunny's noisy book*
Bunny's noisy book [board book]
Cline-Ransome, Lesa. *Quilt alphabet*
Quilt counting
Downes, Belinda. *Baby days*
Dwyer, Mindy. *Quilt of dreams*
Flournoy, Valerie. *The patchwork quilt*
Gerdner, Linda. *Grandfather's story cloth / Yawg daim paj ntaub dab neeg*
Gibbons, Gail. *The quilting bee*
Guback, Georgia. *Luka's quilt*
Hines, Anna Grossnickle. *Pieces, a year in poems and quilts*
Hoberman, Mary Ann. *I'm going to Grandma's*
Hopkinson, Deborah. *Sweet Clara and the freedom quilt*
Howard, Ellen. *The log cabin quilt*
Johnston, Tony. *The quilt story*
That summer
Jonas, Ann. *The quilt*

Leedahl, Shelley A. *The bone talker*
Lowell, Susan. *The elephant quilt!*
McKissack, Patricia C. *Stitchin' and pullin'*
Moss, P. Buckley. *Reuben and the quilt*
Paschkis, Julie. *Mooshka*
Paul, Ann Whitford. *Eight hands round*
The seasons sewn
Polacco, Patricia. *The keeping quilt*
Ransom, Candice F. *The promise quilt*
Ringgold, Faith. *Cassie's word quilt*
Tar Beach
Root, Phyllis. *The name quilt*
Stroud, Bettye. *The patchwork path*
Torres, Leyla. *Liliana's grandmothers*
Van Leeuwen, Jean. *Papa and the pioneer quilt*
von Olfers, Sibylle. *Mother Earth and her children*
Wallace, Nancy Elizabeth. *The kindness quilt*
Warner, Sunny. *The moon quilt*
Woodson, Jacqueline. *Show way*
Yorinks, Arthur. *Quack!*
Zagwÿn, Deborah Turney. *The pumpkin blanket*

Rabbis *see* Careers – clergy

Race relations *see* Prejudice

Racially mixed *see* Ethnic groups in the U.S.

Radios

Barasch, Lynne. *Radio rescue*
Dorros, Arthur. *Radio Man / Don Radio*
Schneider, Christine M. *Saxophone Sam and his snazzy jazz band*

Railroads *see* Trains

Rain forest *see* Jungle

Rangers *see* Careers – park rangers

Reading *see* Books, reading

Rebuses

Capucilli, Alyssa Satin. *Inside a zoo in the city*
Edwards, Pamela Duncan. *Jack and Jill's treehouse*
Gilman, Rita Golden. *Mole in a hole*
The house that Jack built. *The house that Jack built*
Lewis, J. Patrick. *The fantastic 5 and 10¢ store*
Marzollo, Jean. *I love you*
I see a star
Mitter, Matt. *Once upon a rhyme*
Neitzel, Shirley. *The bag I'm taking to Grandma's*
The dress I'll wear to the party
The house I'll build for the wrens
I'm not feeling well today
I'm taking a trip on my train
We're making breakfast for mother
Who will I be?
Rau, Dana Meachen. *Flying*
Riding
Rolling
Sierra, Judy. *We love our school!*

Religion

Addasi, Maha. *Time to pray*
Adler, David A. *A picture book of Hanukkah*
A picture book of Israel
The story of Hanukkah
Aesop. *Androcles and the lion*
Ajmera, Maya. *Faith*
Aleichem, Sholem. *Hanukah money*
Alexander, Cecil Frances. *All creatures great and small*
All things bright and beautiful, ill. by Ashley Bryan
All things bright and beautiful, ill. by Anna Vojtech
All things bright and beautiful, ill. by Bruce Whatley
Aliki. *Mummies made in Egypt*
All night, all day
Amazing graces
Ammon, Richard. *An Amish Christmas*
Appelt, Kathi. *My father's house*
Baring-Gould, S. *Now the day is over*
Bartoletti, Susan Campbell. *Naamah and the ark at night*
Barton, Bob. *Paul Gallico's The small miracle*
Baylor, Byrd. *The way to start a day*
Bea, Holly. *Bless your heart*
My spiritual alphabet book
Bedard, Michael. *The wolf of Gubbio*
Bergren, Lisa Tawn. *God gave us Easter*
How big is God?
Bernier-Grand, Carmen T. *Our Lady of Guadalupe*
Bible. New Testament. *The Lord's prayer*
Bible. New Testament. Corinthians 1st, XIII. *Love is*
Bible. New Testament. Gospels. *Easter: from the King James Bible*
Bible. Old Testament. Ecclesiastes. *To every thing there is a season*
To everything there is a season
Bible. Old Testament. Genesis. *Genesis*
The Genesis of it all
Bible. Old Testament. Psalms. *I will rejoice*
The Lord is my shepherd
Psalms for young children
The twenty-third Psalm
Bible. Old Testament. Ruth. *Ruth and Naomi*
Bless the beasts
Bolden, Tonya. *Rock of ages*
Boling, Ruth L. *Come worship with me*
Borchard, Therese Johnson. *Taste and see the goodness of the Lord*
Boroson, Martin. *Becoming me*
Brokering, Herbert F. *Earth and all stars*
Brooks, Jeremy. *Let there be peace*
Buck, Nola. *A Christmas goodnight*

Bullard, Lisa. *Rashad's Ramadan and Eid al-Fitr*
Carlson, Lori Marie. *Hurray for Three Kings' Day*
Carlson, Melody. *The Easterville miracle*
Carlstrom, Nancy White. *Does God know how to tie shoes?*
What does the sky say?
A children's treasury of prayers
Cohen, Deborah Bodin. *Papa Jethro*
The seventh day
Davis, Aubrey. *Bagels from Benny*
Demi. *Joan of Arc*
dePaola, Tomie. *The clown of God*
The Lady of Guadalupe
The legend of Old Befana
Let the whole earth sing praise
The night of Las Posadas
Patrick
The song of Francis
Downey, Lynn. *This is the earth that God made*
Dungy, Tony. *You can do it!*
Egielski, Richard. *St. Francis and the wolf*
Emerman, Ellen. *Is it Shabbos yet?*
Farber, Norma. *How the hibernators came to Bethlehem*
Field, Rachel Lyman. *Grace for an island meal*
Prayer for a child
Filleul, Liz. *Tumbler*
Fisher, Leonard Everett. *The seven days of creation*
Fishman, Cathy Goldberg. *On Hanukkah*
On Passover
On Rosh Hashanah and Yom Kippur
On Shabbat
Fitch, Florence Mary. *A book about God*
Foreman, Michael. *Cat in the manger*
Gadot, A. S. *The first gift*
Tower of Babel
Ghazi, Suhaib Hamid. *Ramadan*
Gibfried, Diane. *Brother Juniper*
Gilani-Williams, Fawzia. *Nabeel's new pants*
Godwin, Laura. *Barnyard prayers*
Gold, August. *Does God hear my prayer?*
Gold-Vukson, Marji E. *The colors of my Jewish Year*
Grandpa and me on Tu B'Shevat
Goldin, Barbara Diamond. *A mountain of blintzes*
Goodings, Christina. *Creation story*
Lost sheep story
Grimes, Nikki. *At break of day*
When Daddy prays
Hanukkah lights
Hennessy, B. G. *The first night*
Hest, Amy. *The Friday nights of Nana*
Hirsh, Marilyn. *Potato pancakes all around*
Hoffman, Mary. *Miracles*
Parables, stories Jesus told
Hopkins, Lee Bennett. *All God's children*
How much does God love me?
Howard, Ellen. *The log cabin church*
Hughes, Shirley. *The Christmas Eve ghost*
I imagine angels
I've seen the promised land
Jaffe, Nina. *Tales for the seventh day*
Jalali, Reza. *Moon watchers*
Jeffs, Stephanie. *Jenny*
Josh
Johnson, Grace. *The candle in the window*
Johnson, James Weldon. *The Creation*
Jordan, Deloris. *Baby blessings*
Jules, Jacqueline. *Abraham's search for God*
Benjamin and the silver goblet
Kassirer, Sue. *Joseph and his coat of many colors*
Katz, Karen. *My first Ramadan*
Kimmel, Eric A. *The Chanukkah guest*
Gershon's monster
Hershel and the Hanukkah goblins
Joseph and the Sabbath fish
The lady in the blue cloak
Kimmelman, Leslie. *Dance, sing, remember*
Hanukkah lights, Hanukkah nights
Hooray! it's Passover!
The runaway latkes
The Shabbat puppy
Sound the shofar!
Kittinger, Jo S. *The house on Dirty-Third Street*
Krishnaswami, Uma. *Holi*
Kropf, Latifa Berry. *It's Hanukkah time!*
It's seder time!
It's Shofar time!
Krulik, Nancy E. *Is it Hanukkah yet?*
Kushner, Lawrence. *Because Nothing Looks Like God*
Kuskin, Karla. *A great miracle happened there*
Langton, Jane. *Saint Francis and the wolf*
Lehman-Wilzig, Tami. *Keeping the promise*
LeSourd, Nancy. *Christy, Christmastime at Cutter Gap*
Lester, Julius. *What a truly cool world*
Why heaven is far away
Let it shine
Let there be light
Lewis, Jacqueline Janette. *You are so wonderful*
Libney, Varda. *What I like about Passover*
Lindbergh, Reeve. *The circle of days*
On morning wings
Lister, Clare. *My first Passover [board book]*
Lundy, Charlotte. *Thank you, Esther*
Thank you, Ruth and Naomi
Maccarone, Grace. *A child's good night prayer*
McGee, Marni. *The colt and the king*
McGowan, Michael. *Sunday is for God*
Mackall, Dandi Daley. *The story of the Easter robin*
Madonna. *Yakov and the seven thieves*
Manushkin, Fran. *Hooray for Hanukkah!*
Latkes and applesauce
Miriam's cup
Martin, Bill, Jr. *Adam, Adam, what do you see?*
Marzollo, Jean. *Miriam and her brother Moses*
Mayer, Marianna. *Perseus*
Medina, Tony. *Christmas makes me think*
Moorman, Margaret. *Light the lights!*
Mora, Pat. *The beautiful lady*
The song of Francis and the animals
Moser, Barry. *Psalm 23*
Murphy, Elspeth Campbell. *Happy Easter, God*
Myra, Harold Lawrence. *Thanksgiving: what makes it special?*
Nelson, Kadir. *He's got the whole world in His hands*
Nelson, Marilyn. *Snook alone*
Nelson, Vaunda Micheaux. *Who will I be, Lord?*
Nettleton, Pamela Hill. *Martin Luther King, Jr*
Newman, Lesléa. *Matzo ball moon*
Noah, build your boat
Nobisso, Josephine. *The weight of a Mass*
Norris, Kathleen. *The holy twins*
O'Keefe, Susan Heyboer. *Good night, God bless*
Park, Linda Sue. *The third gift*
Paterson, Katherine. *Brother Sun, Sister Moon*
The light of the world
Pienkowski, Jan. *Easter*

Pinkney, Gloria Jean. *Music from our Lord's holy heaven*
Piper, Sophie. *I can say a prayer*
Podwal, Mark H. *The menorah story*
A sweet year
Polacco, Patricia. *Chicken Sunday*
Poole, Josephine. *Joan of Arc*
Ransom, Candice F. *Mother Teresa*
Ray, Mary Lyn. *Shaker boy*
Rock, Lois. *A child's book of graces*
God bless me, God bless you
I wonder why?
Learning about prayer
The Lord's prayer
Rosen, Michael J. *Chanukah lights everywhere*
Rosenfeld, Dina Herman. *How in the world does bread come from the earth?*
Rothenberg, Joan Keller. *Inside-out grandma*
Rouss, Sylvia A. *Sammy Spider's first Passover*
Sammy Spider's first Shabbat
Sammy Spider's first Shavuot
Sammy Spider's first Yom Kippur
Rylant, Cynthia. *Bless us all*
Give me grace
Sabuda, Robert. *St. Valentine*
San Souci, Robert D. *Little gold star*
Santangelo, Colony Elliott. *Brother Wolf of Gubbio*
Sasso, Sandy Eisenberg. *Cain and Abel*
For heaven's sake
God's paintbrush
In God's name
Schaefer, Lola M. *Hanukkah*
Schlessinger, Laura. *Dr. Laura Schlessinger's Where's God?*
Schotter, Roni. *Hanukkah!*
Passover!
Passover magic
Purim play
Schur, Maxine Rose. *Day of delight*
Schwartz, Howard. *Gathering sparks*
Shollar, Leah. *A thread of kindness*
Shulevitz, Uri. *The magician*
Shulimson, Sarene. *Lights out Shabbat*
Silverman, Erica. *Gittel's hands*
Simon, Norma. *The story of Hanukkah*
The story of Passover
Sinykin, Sheri. *Zayde comes to live*
Slate, Joseph. *Who is coming to our house?*
Slegers, Liesbet. *The child in the manger*
Sper, Emily. *Hanukkah: a counting book in English, Hebrew, and Yiddish*
The Passover seder
Stevens, Jan Romero. *Twelve lizards leaping*
Stiegemeyer, Julie. *Under the baobab tree*
Stohs, Anita. *An Easter alleluia*
Strauss, Linda Leopold. *The Elijah door*
Swain, Gwenyth. *I wonder as I wander*
Swamp, Jake. *Giving thanks*
Tada, Joni Eareckson. *The incredible discovery of Lindsey Renee*
Tarbescu, Edith. *Annushka's voyage*
Taylor, Shirley. *The cross in the egg*
Thomas, Joan G. *If Jesus came to my house*
Thomas, Joyce Carol. *Shouting*
Thompson, Lauren. *Love one another*
Thong, Roseanne. *Fly free!*
Tompert, Ann. *The pied piper of Peru*
Saint Nicholas
Saint Patrick
Trist, Glenda. *A child's book of prayers*
Tulloch, Shirley. *Who made me?*
Turner, Ann Warren. *Angel hide and seek*
Shaker hearts
Tutu, Archbishop Desmond. *God's dream*
Ungar, Richard. *Rachel's gift*
Van Leeuwen, Jean. *Across the wide dark sea*
Vidrine, Beverly Barras. *Easter Day alphabet*
Vischer, Phil. *Sidney and Norman*
Volkmer, Jane Anne. *Song of Chirimia / La Musica de la Chirimia*
Vorst, Rochel Groner. *The sukkah that I built*
Walker, Rob D. *Mama says*
Wangerin, Walter. *Angels and all children*
Water come down
Warren, Rick. *The Lord's prayer*
Weatherford, Carole Boston. *The Beatitudes*
Wedeven, Carol. *The Easter cave*
Wells, Rosemary. *The miraculous tale of the two Maries*
What a morning!
Wheeler, Opal. *Sing in praise*
Wildsmith, Brian. *The Easter story*
Joseph
Mary
Wilson, Karma. *Mortimer's first garden*
Winthrop, Elizabeth. *He is risen*
Wohl, Lauren L. *Matzoh mouse*
Wojciechowski, Susan. *The Christmas miracle of Jonathan Toomey*
Wood, Douglas. *Old Turtle*
Wood, Nancy C. *Mr. and Mrs. God in the creation kitchen*
Young, Ed. *What about me?*
Zacharias, Ravi. *The merchant and the thief*
Zalben, Jane Breskin. *Pearl's eight days of Chanukah*
Ziefert, Harriet. *First He made the sun*

Religion – Daniel

Auld, Mary. *Daniel in the lions' den*
Goldsboro, Bobby. *Jonah and the whale; and, Daniel in the lion's den*
Hartman, Bob. *Dinner in the lions' den*
McCarthy, Michael. *The story of Daniel in the lions' den*
Marzollo, Jean. *Daniel in the lion's den*

Religion – David

Auld, Mary. *David and Goliath*
Fisher, Leonard Everett. *David and Goliath*
Goldsboro, Bobby. *Noah and the ark; and, David and Goliath*

Religion – Hinduism

Gardeski, Christina Mia. *Diwali*
Pandya, Meenal. *Here comes Diwali*
Rahaman, Vashanti. *Divali rose*
Verma, Jatinder Nath. *The story of Divaali*

Religion – Islam

Addasi, Maha. *The white nights of Ramadan*
Cunnane, Kelly. *Deep in the Sahara*
Ghazi, Suhaib Hamid. *Ramadan*
Katz, Karen. *My first Ramadan*
Khan, Hena. *The night of the moon*
Mair, Samia J. *The perfect gift*

Mobin-Uddin, Asma. *The best Eid ever*
A party in Ramadan
Robert, Na'ima B. *Ramadan Moon*
Wharnsby-Ali, Dawud. *A picnic of poems in Allah's green garden*
Whitman, Sylvia. *Under the Ramadan moon*

Religion – Jonah

Auld, Mary. *The story of Jonah*
Bible. Old Testament. Jonah. *The Book of Jonah*
Goldsboro, Bobby. *Jonah and the whale; and, Daniel in the lion's den*
Spinelli, Eileen. *Jonah's whale*

Religion – Moses

Auld, Mary. *Exodus from Egypt*
Hodges, Margaret. *Moses*
Marzollo, Jean. *Miriam and her brother Moses*
Topek, Susan Remick. *Ten good rules*

Religion – Nativity

Bible. New Testament. Gospels. *Bethlehem*
The Christmas story: from the Gospel according to St. Luke from the King James Bible
The story of Christmas
Blaich, Ute. *The star*
Brebeuf, Jean de. *The Huron carol*
Brown, Margaret Wise. *A child is born*
Christmas in the barn
Bryan, Ashley. *Who built the stable?*
Bunting, Eve. *We were there*
Who was born this special day?
Byrd, Robert. *Saint Francis and the Christmas donkey*
Calhoun, Mary. *A shepherd's gift*
Chaconas, Dori. *Christmas mouseling*
Chorao, Kay. *The Christmas story*
Clements, Andrew. *Bright Christmas*
Cooney, Barbara. *The story of Christmas*
Cotten, Cynthia. *This is the stable*
Crawford, Sheryl Ann. *The baby who changed the world*
Crisp, Marty. *The most precious gift*
Crossley-Holland, Kevin. *How many miles to Bethlehem?*
Damjan, Mischa. *The little seahorse and the Christmas pearl*
dePaola, Tomie. *The birds of Bethlehem*
The story of the three wise kings
Dowley, Tim. *The shepherds' tale*
The wise men's tale
Gliori, Debi. *What can I give him?*
Greene, Rhonda Gowler. *The stable where Jesus was born*
Grimes, Nikki. *Voices of Christmas*
Hartman, Bob. *Granny Mae's Christmas play*
Hayles, Marsha. *The feathered crown*
Hickman, Martha Whitmore. *A baby born in Bethlehem*
Hoffman, Mary. *Three wise women*
Hogrogian, Nonny. *The first Christmas*
Hooks, William H. *The legend of the Christmas rose*
Horn, Sandra Ann. *Babushka*
Hughes, Langston. *Carol of the brown king*
Joslin, Mary. *On that Christmas night*
Keats, Ezra Jack. *The little drummer boy*
Ketcham, Sallie. *The Christmas bird*
Lewandowski, Frrich. *It's Christmas again*
Lewis, J. Patrick. *Long was the winter road they traveled*
Lloyd-Jones, Sally. *Song of the stars*
Lucado, Max. *Jacob's gift*
Maccarone, Grace. *A child was born*
McCaughrean, Geraldine. *Father and son*
MacDonald, Maryann. *The Christmas cat*
McGinley-Nally, Sharon. *The friendly beasts*
Mackall, Dandi Daley. *Off to Bethlehem!*
Mayer, Mercer. *The little drummer mouse*
Mayper, Monica. *Come and see*
Milligan, Bryce. *Brigid's cloak*
Morpurgo, Michael. *On angel wings*
Nazoa, Aquiles. *A small Nativity*
Nikola-Lisa, W. *Hallelujah!*
To hear the angels sing
Oppenheim, Joanne. *The Christmas witch*
Pasquali, Elena. *Ituku's Christmas journey*
Pfister, Marcus. *The Christmas star*
Rodanas, Kristina. *The little drummer boy*
Root, Phyllis. *All for the newborn baby*
Ryan, Pam Muñoz. *There was no snow on Christmas Eve*
Sahagun, Bernardino de. *Spirit child*
Schmid, Eleonore. *Hare's Christmas gift*
Slate, Joseph. *What star is this?*
Smith, Kathryn. *Little Donkey's Christmas story*
Little Lamb's Christmas story
Spang, Günter. *The ox and the Donkey*
Speirs, John. *The little boy's Christmas gift*
Spirin, Gennady. *We three kings*
Summers, Susan. *The fourth wise man*
Tafuri, Nancy. *The donkey's Christmas song*
Tazewell, Charles. *The littlest angel*, ill. by Deborah Lanino
The littlest angel, ill. by Paul Micich
The littlest angel, ill. by Rebecca Thornburgh
They followed a bright star
Thompson, Lauren. *One starry night*
Thury, Frederick. *The last straw*
Tolan, Stephanie S. *Bartholomew's blessing*
Walburg, Lori. *The legend of the candy cane*
Wangerin, Walter. *Probity Jones and the Fear Not Angel*
Wildsmith, Brian. *A Christmas story*
Wilson, Karma. *Mortimer's Christmas manger*
Winthrop, Elizabeth. *A child is born: the Christmas story*

Religion – Noah

Auld, Mary. *Noah's ark*
Cousins, Lucy. *Noah's ark*
Noah's ark [board book]
Cullen, Lynn. *Little Scraggly Hair*
Eitzen, Ruth. *Tara's flight*
Emberley, Barbara. *One wide river to cross*
Goldsboro, Bobby. *Noah and the ark; and, David and Goliath*
Goodhart, Pippa. *Noah makes a boat*
Greene, Rhonda Gowler. *Noah and the mighty ark*
Harker, Lesley. *Annie's ark*
Jonas, Ann. *Aardvarks, disembark!*
Krensky, Stephen. *Noah's bark*
Lloyd-Jones, Sally. *Old MacNoah had an ark*
Lunge-Larsen, Lise. *Noah's mittens*
McCarthy, Michael. *The story of Noah and the ark*
Mitton, Tony. *All afloat on Noah's boat!*
Paley, Joan. *One more river*

Philip, Neil. *Noah and the devil*
Pinkney, Jerry. *Noah's ark*
Rouss, Sylvia A. *The littlest pair*
Santore, Charles. *A stowaway on Noah's Ark*
Sasso, Sandy Eisenberg. *Naamah, Noah's wife*
Shapiro, Zachary. *We're all in the same boat*
Singer, Isaac Bashevis. *Why Noah chose the dove*
Spier, Peter. *Noah's ark*
Stewig, John Warren. *The animals watched*
Sting [Musician]. *Rock steady*
Tebbs, Victoria. *Noah's Ark story*
Walton, Rick. *Noah's square dance*
Wilson, Anne. *Noah's ark*

Remembering *see* Memories, memory

Repetitive stories *see* Cumulative tales

Reptiles

Arnosky, Jim. *Slither and crawl*
Fitzsimmons, David. *Curious critters*
Florian, Douglas. *Lizards, frogs, and polliwogs*
Green, Jen. *Reptiles*
Hood, Susan. *Spike, the mixed-up monster*
MacDonald, Margaret Read. *Give up, Gecko!*
McDonald, Megan. *Reptiles are my life*
Sill, Cathryn. *About amphibians*

Reptiles – alligators, crocodiles

Aliki. *Use your head, dear*
Beard, Alex. *Crocodile's tears*
Becker, Bonny. *The Christmas crocodile*
Bergman, Mara. *Snip snap!*
Bromley, Nick. *Open very carefully*
Brown, Jo. *Where's my mommy?*
Bynum, Janie. *Kiki's blankie*
Cecil, Randy. *Gator*
Chen, Chih-Yuan. *Guji Guji*
Chichester Clark, Emma. *Melrose and Croc*
Christelow, Eileen. *Five little monkeys sitting in a tree*
Five little monkeys wash the car
Jerome camps out
Cousins, Lucy. *Maisy, Charley, and the wobbly tooth*
Maisy cleans up
Maisy goes shopping
Dahl, Roald. *The enormous crocodile*
dePaola, Tomie. *Bill and Pete*
Bill and Pete go down the Nile
Bill and Pete to the rescue
Derrick, David G., Jr. *I'm the scariest thing in the jungle!*
Donnio, Sylviane. *I'd really like to eat a child*
Emberley, Rebecca. *The crocodile and the scorpion*
Federspiel, Jurg. *Alligator Mike*
Finlay, Lizzie. *Little Croc's purse*
Fleming, Candace. *Gator gumbo*
Freedman, Claire. *Where's your smile, crocodile?*
Gibbons, Gail. *Alligators and crocodiles*
Gomi, Taro. *The crocodile and the dentist*
Gordon, Gus. *Herman and Rosie*
Gralley, Jean. *Very boring alligator*
Gravett, Emily. *The odd egg*
Greenberg, David. *Crocs!*
Heos, Bridget. *What to expect when you're expecting hatchlings*
Hill, Eric. *Spot's baby sister*
Hovland, Henrik. *John Jensen feels different*
Huggins, Peter. *Trosclair and the alligator*
Hurd, Thacher. *Mama don't allow*
Jewell, Nancy. *Alligator wedding*
Kasza, Keiko. *My lucky birthday*
Ketteman, Helen. *The three little gators*
Kimmelman, Leslie. *How do I love you?*
Kipling, Rudyard. *How the elephant got his trunk*
Kleven, Elisa. *A carousel tale*
Ernst
The puddle pail
The wishing ball
Klingel, Cynthia Fitterer. *Crocodiles*
Kulka, Joe. *My crocodile does not bite*
Lakin, Patricia. *Camping day*
Rainy day
Lehrhaupt, Adam. *Warning: do not open this book!*
Lionni, Leo. *Cornelius*
An extraordinary egg
Llewellyn, Claire. *Crocodile*
Lodge, Jo. *Happy Snappy!*
Malkin, Michele. *Pinky's sweet tooth*
Marcellino, Fred. *I, crocodile*
Mayer, Mercer. *There's an alligator under my bed*
Montanari, Eva. *The crocodile's true colors*
Morris, Jennifer E. *May I please have a cookie?*
Moss, Jenny Jackson. *Cajun night after Christmas*
Noonan, Diana. *The crocodile*
Olson, Mary. *An alligator ate my brother*
Palatini, Margie. *No biting, Louise*
Panzieri, Lucia. *The kindhearted crocodile*
Paye, Won-Ldy. *Mrs. Chicken and the hungry crocodile*
Pizzoli, Greg. *The watermelon seed*
Polhemus, Coleman. *The crocodile blues*
Postgate, Daniel. *The richest crocodile in the world*
Protopopescu, Orel. *Two sticks*
Rayner, Catherine. *Solomon Crocodile*
Rowe, John A. *I want a hug*
Rylant, Cynthia. *Alligator boy*
Schmid, Paul. *Oliver and his alligator*
Schneider, Howie. *Fast 'n Snappy*
Schubert, Ingrid. *There's a crocodile under my bed!*
Sedaka, Neil. *Waking up is hard to do*
Sendak, Maurice. *Alligators all around*
Shipton, Jonathan. *No biting, horrible crocodile!*
Sierra, Judy. *Counting crocodiles*
The gift of the crocodile
Stevenson, James. *Monty*
No need for Monty
Taylor, Sean. *Crocodiles are the best animals of all*
Tourville, Amanda Doering. *A crocodile grows up*
Urbanovic, Jackie. *Duck and cover*
Vaughan, Marcia Kapok. *Snap!*
Vrombaut, An. *Clarabella's teeth*
Waber, Bernard. *Funny, funny Lyle*
Lovable Lyle
Lyle and the birthday party
Lyle at Christmas
Lyle at the office
Lyle finds his mother
Lyle, Lyle Crocodile
Lyle walks the dogs
Walsh, Ellen Stoll. *For Pete's sake*
Waring, Richard. *Alberto the dancing alligator*
Wells, Rosemary. *Hands off, Harry!*
Whitehouse, Patricia. *Alligator*
Whybrow, Ian. *Hello! Is this grandma?*
Willis, Jeanne. *The boy who lost his bellybutton*

Reptiles – chameleons

Benevelli, Alberto. *The colors of the chameleon*
Carle, Eric. *The mixed-up chameleon*
Cowley, Joy. *Chameleon, chameleon*
Dubosarsky, Ursula. *Rex*
Gravett, Emily. *Blue chameleon*
Long, Ethan. *Chamelia*
Na, Il Sung. *Hide and seek*
Perlman, Janet. *The delicious bug*
Phinn, Gervase. *Who am I?*
Watt, Mélanie. *Leon the chameleon*

Reptiles – iguanas

Alarcón, Francisco X. *Iguanas in the snow and other winter poems / Iguanas en la nieve y otros poemas de invierno*
Escoffier, Michaël. *Brief thief*
Johnston, Tony. *The iguana brothers, a perfect day*
Paul, Ann Whitford. *Count on Culebra*
Mañana Iguana
Robbins, Jacqui. *The new girl . . . and me*
Senisi, Ellen B. *All kinds of friends, even green*
Thoms, Susan Collins. *Cesar takes a break*

Reptiles – lizards

Carle, Eric. *The mixed-up chameleon*
Cummings, Pat. *Ananse and the lizard*
Leedy, Loreen. *The great graph contest*
Lionni, Leo. *A color of his own*
Mora, Pat. *Delicious hullabaloo / Pachanga deliciosa*
Murphy, Stuart J. *Leaping lizards*
Shannon, George. *Lizard's home*
Lizard's song
Strete, Craig Kee. *They thought they saw him*
Wiesner, David. *Art and Max*
Wood, Audrey. *Jubal's wish*

Reptiles – salamanders

Hood, Susan. *Spike, the mixed-up monster*
Lamstein, Sarah Marwil. *Big night for salamanders*
Mazer, Anne. *The salamander room*
Walsh, Ellen Stoll. *Pip's magic*

Reptiles – snakes

Aardema, Verna. *What's so funny, Ketu?*
Anaya, Rudolfo A. *Roadrunner's dance*
Arnosky, Jim. *Coyote raid in Cactus Canyon*
Crinkleroot's visit to Crinkle Cove
Rattlesnake dance
Aruego, José. *The last laugh*
Bower, Tamara. *The shipwrecked sailor*
Buckley, Richard. *The greedy python*
Burell, Sarah. *Diamond Jim Dandy and the sheriff*
Cannon, Janell. *Verdi*
Cheng, Christopher. *Python*
Davol, Marguerite W. *The snake's tales*
Diakité, Baba Wagué. *Mee-an and the magic serpent*
Gibbons, Gail. *Snakes*
Hayes, Joe. *The gum-chewing rattler*
Jarman, Julia. *Class Two at the zoo*
Johnson, Angela. *The girl who wore snakes*
Jonell, Lynne. *I need a snake*
Keller, Holly. *Help!*
Kimmel, Eric A. *Little Britches and the rattlers*
Kimura, Ken. *999 frogs wake up*
Kipling, Rudyard. *Rikki-tikki-tavi*, ill. by Lambert Davis
Rikki-tikki-tavi, ill. by Jerry Pinkney
Krensky, Stephen. *Mother's Day surprise*
Lauber, Patricia. *Snakes are hunters*
Lester, Julius. *Why heaven is far away*
McKee, David. *Elmer and Snake*
McPhail, David. *Sylvie and True*
Mason, Adrienne. *Snakes*
Noble, Trinka Hakes. *The day Jimmy's boa ate the wash*
Jimmy's boa and the big splash birthday bash
Jimmy's boa bounces back
Nygaard, Elizabeth. *Snake alley band*
Olaleye, Isaac. *Lake of the Big Snake*
Patent, Dorothy Hinshaw. *Slinky, scaly, slithery snakes*
Paul, Ann Whitford. *Count on Culebra*
Pilkey, Dav. *A friend for Dragon*
Pringle, Laurence P. *Snakes*
Shannon, George. *Lizard's home*
Siegel, Randy. *My snake Blake*
Stroud, Bettye. *Dance y'all*
Tseng, Grace. *White tiger, blue serpent*
Ungerer, Tomi. *Crictor*
Walsh, Ellen Stoll. *Mouse count*
Welling, Peter J. *Shawn O'Hisser, the last snake in Ireland*
Wildsmith, Brian. *Jungle party*
Yoon, Salina. *Opposnakes*

Reptiles – turtles, tortoises

Aesop. *The hare and the tortoise*, ill. by Paul Galdone
The hare and the tortoise, ill. by Carol Jones
The hare and the tortoise, ill. by Helen Ward
The hare and the tortoise / La liebre y la tortuga
The race
Road signs
The tortoise and the hare, ill. by Jerry Pinkney
The tortoise and the hare, ill. by Sara Rojo
The tortoise and the hare: an Aesop fable
Arnosky, Jim. *Turtle in the sea*
Bauer, Marion Dane. *Frog's best friend*
A mama for Owen
Berger, Melvin. *Look out for turtles!*
Bourgeois, Paulette. *Franklin and Harriet*
Franklin and the thunderstorm
Franklin in the dark
Franklin rides a bike
Franklin says "I love you"
Franklin's baby sister
Franklin's Christmas gift
Franklin's class trip
Franklin's new friend
Franklin's secret club
Brett, Jan. *Mossy*
Bryan, Ashley. *Turtle knows your name*
Buckley, Richard. *The foolish tortoise*
Bunting, Eve. *Emma's turtle*
Casin, Sheridan. *Little Turtle and the song of the sea*
Castillo, Lauren. *Melvin and the boy*
Chrustowski, Rick. *Turtle crossing*
Crowe, Carole. *Turtle girl*
Cyrus, Kurt. *The voyage of turtle Rex*
Czekaj, Jef. *Hip and Hop, don't stop!*
Yes, yes, Yaul!
Davies, Nicola. *One tiny turtle*
DeSpain, Pleasant. *The dancing turtle*

Downard, Barry. *The Race of the Century*
Falwell, Cathryn. *Scoot!*
Turtle splash!
Fleming, Candace. *Sunny Boy!*
George, Lucy M. *Back to school Tortoise*
George, Margaret. *Lucille lost*
George, William T. *Box turtle at Long Pond*
Gorbachev, Valeri. *Heron and Turtle*
Red red red
Turtle's penguin day
Whose hat is it?
Guiberson, Brenda Z. *Into the sea*
Himmelman, John. *Tudley didn't know*
Horn, Peter. *The best father of all*
When I grow up . . .
Horvath, David. *Just like Bossy Bear*
Jacobs, Francine. *Lonesome George, the giant tortoise*
Javernick, Ellen. *The birthday pet*
Jennings, Sharon. *Franklin forgives*
Franklin goes to the hospital
Franklin makes a deal
Franklin wants a badge
Franklin's Thanksgiving
Johnson, Rebecca. *Sea turtle's clever plan*
Joyce, William. *Bently and egg*
Kimmel, Eric A. *Anansi goes fishing*
Anansi's party time
Korman, Susan. *Box turtle at Silver Pond Lane*
Lillegard, Dee. *Tortoise brings the mail*
Loth, Sebastian. *Remembering Crystal*
Lowell, Susan. *The tortoise and the jackrabbit*
Luthardt, Kevin. *You're weird!*
McDermott, Gerald. *Jabutí the tortoise*
Marlow, Layn. *Hurry up and slow down*
Marshall, James. *Eugene*
Yummers too
Martin, Francesca. *Clever Tortoise*
Mollel, Tololwa M. *Ananse's feast*
The flying tortoise
Morrison, Toni. *The tortoise or the hare*
Ó Flatharta, Antoine. *Hurry and the monarch*
Oldland, Nicholas. *Making the moose out of life*
O'Malley, Kevin. *The great race*
Paul, Ann Whitford. *Tortuga in trouble*
Ross, Gayle. *How Turtle's back was cracked*
Rumford, James. *Tiger and turtle*
San Souci, Daniel. *The rabbit and the dragon king*
Sayre, April Pulley. *Turtle, turtle, watch out!*, ill. by Lee Christiansen
Turtle, turtle, watch out!, ill. by Annie Patterson
Swinburne, Stephen R. *Turtle tide*
Tingle, Tim. *When Turtle grew feathers*
Van Woerkom, Dorothy. *Harry and Shelburt*
Williams, Barbara. *Albert's gift for grandmother*
Winter, Jeanette. *Mama: a true story, in which a baby hippo loses his mama during a tsunami, but finds a new home*
Zagwÿn, Deborah Turney. *Turtle spring*

Resourcefulness *see* Behavior – resourcefulness

Responsibility *see* Character traits – responsibility

Rest *see* Sleep

Restaurants

Anderson, Peggy Perry. *Out to lunch*
Ashman, Linda. *No dogs allowed*
Dorros, Arthur. *When the pigs took over*
Downey, Lynn. *Matilda's humdinger*
Florence, Tyler. *Tyler makes spaghetti!*
Isadora, Rachel. *Happy belly, happy smile*
Krause, Ute. *Oscar and the very hungry dragon*
Kutner, Merrily. *The Zombie Nite Cafe*
Lewin, Ted. *Big Jimmy's Kum Kau Chinese take out*
Lin, Grace. *Dim sum for everyone*
London, Jonathan. *Froggy eats out*
Odanaka, Barbara. *A crazy day at the Critter Café*
Park, Frances. *The Have a Good Day Cafe*
Pearson, Tracey Campbell. *Where does Joe go?*
Perry, Robert. *Down at the Seaweed Café*
Polacco, Patricia. *In Enzo's splendid gardens*
Radabaugh, Melinda Beth. *Going to a restaurant*
Rockwell, Anne. *Truck stop*
Stowell, Penelope. *The greatest potatoes*
Waber, Bernard. *Fast food! gulp! gulp!*
Weatherford, Carole Boston. *Freedom on the menu*
Wellington, Monica. *Pizza at Sally's*
Whelan, Gloria. *The boy who wanted to cook*
Willard, Nancy. *The Moon and Riddles Diner and the Sunnyside Café*
Yee, Wong Herbert. *Hamburger Heaven*

Rhyming text

Aardema, Verna. *Bringing the rain to Kapiti Plain*
The riddle of the drum
ABC school riddles
Ada, Alma Flor. *The Christmas tree / El arbol de Navidad*
Adams, Diane. *I can do it myself!*
I want to help!
Adler, Victoria. *All of baby nose to toes*
Adlerman, Daniel. *Africa calling*
Adoff, Arnold. *Black is brown is tan*
Aesop. *Androcles and the lion: and other Aesop fables*
The race
Ahlberg, Allan. *Hooray for bread*
Ahlberg, Janet. *Each peach pear plum*
The jolly Christmas postman
The jolly pocket postman
The jolly postman
Peek-a-boo!
Alborough, Jez. *Captain Duck*
Duck in the truck
Duck's key where can it be?
Fix-it Duck
Hit the ball Duck
Ice cream bear
It's the bear
Six little chicks
Tall
Where's my teddy?
Alda, Arlene. *Here a face, there a face*
Sheep, sheep, sheep, help me fall asleep
Alexander, Kwame. *Acoustic Rooster and his barnyard band*
Alexander, Sue. *Who goes out on Halloween?*
Aliki. *Push button*
Allen, Joy. *Princess Palooza*
Princess party
Allen, Kathryn Madeline. *A kiss means I love you*
Allen, Pamela. *Who sank the boat?*
Anastas, Margaret. *A hug for you*

Mommy's best kisses
Anderson, Lena. *The hedgehog, the pig, and their little friend*
Anderson, Peggy Perry. *Chuck's band*
Chuck's truck
Out to lunch
Anderson, Stephen Axel. *I know the moon*
Andreae, Giles. *Giraffes can't dance*
I love my daddy
I love my mommy
Pants
The pop-up Rumble in the jungle
Rumble in the jungle
There's a house inside my mommy
Andrews, Sylvia. *Dancing in my bones*
Andrews-Goebel, Nancy. *The pot that Juan built*
Anholt, Catherine. *Happy birthday, Chimp and Zee*
What makes me happy?
Appelt, Kathi. *The Alley Cat's Meow*
Bats around the clock
Bats on parade
Brand-new baby blues
Cowboy dreams
Incredible me!
Merry Christmas, merry crow
Oh my baby, little one
Rain dance
Apperley, Dawn. *Good night, sleep tight, little bunnies*
Santa Claus will come tonight
Arena, Jennifer. *100 snowmen*
Armstrong-Ellis, Carey. *Ten creepy monsters*
Arnold, Marsha Diane. *Roar of a snore*
Arnold, Tedd. *Dirty Gert*
Five ugly monsters
Green Wilma
Green Wilma, frog in space
More parts
Parts
Arnosky, Jim. *Gobble it up!*
I'm a turkey!
A manatee morning
Arquette, Kerry. *What did you do today?*
Artell, Mike. *Petite Rouge*
Ashburn, Boni. *The fort that Jack built*
Over at the castle
Ashman, Linda. *Babies on the go*
Babies on the go [board book]
Castles, caves, and honeycombs
Creaky old house
How to make a night
Just another morning
M is for mischief
Mama's day
Maxwell's magic mix-up
Samantha on a roll
Starry safari
Stella, unleashed
To the beach!
When I was king
Asim, Jabari. *Daddy goes to work*
Aylesworth, Jim. *Cock-a-doodle-doo, creak, pop-pop, moo*
The folks in the valley
Little Bitty Mousie
My sister's rusty bike
Old Black Fly
One crow
Ayres, Katherine. *Up, down, and around*
Backx, Patsy. *Skippy and Jack*
Baer, Edith. *This is the way we go to school*
Baicker, Karen. *Pea pod babies*
You can do it too!
Bailey, Linda. *Goodnight, sweet pig*
Bailey, Mary Bryant. *Jeoffry's Christmas*
Baillie, Marilyn. *Nose to toes*
Baker, Keith. *Just how long can a long string be?!*
My octopus arms
No two alike
1-2-3 peas
Baker, Liza. *I love you because you're you*
Bang, Molly. *Ten, nine, eight*
Banks, Kate. *City cat*
Barack, Marcy. *Season song*
Baranski, Joan Sullivan. *Round is a pancake*
Bardhan-Quallen, Sudipta. *Chicks run wild*
Pirate princess
Barner, Bob. *Bears! bears! bears!*
Dinosaur bones
Penguins, penguins, everywhere!
Stars, stars, stars
Barnes, Brynne. *Colors of me*
Barnett, Mac. *Guess again!*
Barracca, Debra. *Maxi, the hero*
Maxi, the star
A taxi dog Christmas
Barracca, Sal. *The adventures of taxi dog*
Barrett, Judi. *Which witch is which?*
Bartoletti, Susan Campbell. *Nobody's nosier than a cat*
Bateman, Donna M. *Deep in the swamp*
Bateman, Teresa. *April foolishness*
Farm flu
Hamster Camp
Hunting the daddyosaurus
A plump and perky turkey
The princesses have a ball
Bauer, Marion Dane. *Halloween forest*
In like a lion out like a lamb
My mother is mine
One brown bunny
Thank you for me!
Baylor, Byrd. *The desert is theirs*
Everybody needs a rock
Bea, Holly. *Bless your heart*
My spiritual alphabet book
Beaton, Clare. *Daisy gets dressed*
Beaty, Andrea. *Hide and sheep*
Iggy Peck, architect
Rosie Revere, engineer
Beaumont, Karen. *Dini Dinosaur*
Doggone dogs!
Duck, duck, goose!
I ain't gonna paint no more!
Move over, Rover
No sleep for the sheep!
Shoe-la-la!
Who ate all the cookie dough?
Becker, Bonny. *Tickly prickly*
Bell, Babs. *Sputter, sputter, sput!*
Bemelmans, Ludwig. *Madeline*
Madeline and the bad hat
Madeline and the gypsies
Madeline in London
Madeline's Christmas
Madeline's rescue
Bennett, Artie. *The butt book*
Bentley, Dawn. *Fuzzy bear*
Fuzzy Bear's potty book

Bently, Peter. *The great sheep shenanigans*
Berenstain, Stan and Jan. *The bear detectives*
The Berenstain bears and the missing dinosaur bone
The Berenstain bears and the spooky old tree
The Berenstain bears' Christmas tree
The Berenstain bears' that stump must go!
He bear, she bear
Bergman, Mara. *Yum yum! What fun!*
Berkes, Marianne. *Marsh music*
Over in a river
Over in Australia
Over in the Arctic
Over in the forest
Over in the jungle
Bernhard, Durga. *In the fiddle is a song*
Berry, Lynne. *Duck dunks*
Duck skates
Duck tents
Ducking for apples
Bertram, Debbie. *The best book to read*
The best place to read
The best time to read
Bible. Old Testament. Psalms. *I will rejoice*
Billin-Frye, Paige. *One, two, buckle my shoe*
Billstrom, Dianne. *You can't go to school naked!*
Black, Sonia. *Hanging out with Mom*
Blackstone, Stella. *Alligator alphabet*
Bear at home
Bear at work
Bear in sunshine
Bear's birthday
Bear's busy family
Cleo and Caspar
Cleo in the snow
Cleo on the move
Cleo the cat
Cleo's alphabet book
Cleo's color book
Cleo's counting book
Come here, Cleo
How big is a pig?
I dreamt I was a dinosaur
An island in the sun
Octopus opposites
Secret seahorse
Secret seahorse [board book]
Ship shapes
Blaikie, Lynn. *Beyond the northern lights*
Blake, Quentin. *Fantastic Daisy Artichoke*
Blechman, Nicholas. *Night light*
Blegvad, Lenore. *First friends*
Blomgren, Jennifer. *Where do I sleep?*
Bluemle, Elizabeth. *Dogs on the bed*
Boedoe, Geefwee. *Arrowville*
Bolam, Emily. *I go potty*
Bonnett-Rampersaud, Louise. *How do you sleep?*
Never ask a bear
Bono, Mary. *Ugh! a bug*
Bowen, Anne. *I know an old teacher*
Bowie, C. W. *Busy fingers*
Busy toes
Boynton, Sandra. *Christmas parade*
Yay, you!
Bradby, Marie. *Once upon a farm*
Braeuner, Shellie. *The great dog wash*
Bramsen, Carin. *Hey, duck!*
Brennan, Eileen. *Bad Astrid*
Brennan, Linda Crotta. *Marshmallow kisses*
Brennan-Nelson, Denise. *He's been a monster all day!*
My grandma likes to say
Brenner, Barbara A. *Good morning, garden*
Brenner, Emily. *On the first day of grade school*
Bridwell, Norman. *Clifford's neighborhood*
Briere-Haquet, Alice. *Zebedee's balloon*
Briggs, Kelly Paul. *Lighthouse lullaby*
Bronson, Linda. *The circus alphabet*
The brothers gruesome
Brown, Calef. *Boy wonders*
Pirateria
Tippintown
Brown, Ken. *What's the time, Grandma Wolf?*
Brown, Margaret Wise. *Another important book*
A child is born
Christmas in the barn
My world of color
Sailor boy jig
Sleepy ABC, ill. by Karen Katz
Sleepy ABC, ill. by Esphyr Slobodkina
Where have you been?
Brown, Tameka Fryer. *Around our way on Neighbors' Day*
My cold plum lemon pie bluesy mood
Brownlow, Mike. *The big white book with almost nothing in it*
Way out West — with a baby!
Bruce, Lisa. *Engines, engines*
Bruchac, Joseph. *My father is taller than a tree*
Bruel, Nick. *A Bad Kitty Christmas*
Bryan, Ashley. *Beat the story-drum, pum-pum*
Can't scare me!
The cat's purr
Who built the stable?
Bryan, Sean. *A bear and his boy*
Buchanan, Sue. *Mud Pie Annie*
Buck, Nola. *A Christmas goodnight*
Buckley, Richard. *The foolish tortoise*
The greedy python
Buehner, Caralyn. *Snowmen all year*
Snowmen at Christmas
Snowmen at night
Snowmen at night [board book]
Would I ever lie to you?
Bunting, Eve. *The baby shower*
The bones of Fred McFee
Butterfly house
Flower garden
Happy birthday, dear duck
Have you seen my new blue socks?
Hey diddle diddle
The pumpkin fair
Scary, scary Halloween
Sunflower house
Burdett, Lois. *Hamlet for kids*
A midsummer night's dream for kids
Romeo and Juliet for kids
The tempest for kids
Burleigh, Robert. *Clang-clang! beep-beep!*
Hit the road, Jack
I love going through this book
Messenger, messenger
Bus-a-saurus bop
Butler, John. *Can you growl like a bear?*
Hush, little ones
Buxton, Jane. *The littlest llama*
Buzzeo, Toni. *Inside the books*
Caffey, Donna. *Yikes-lice!*

Cain, Janan. *The way I feel*
Calmenson, Stephanie. *Birthday at the Panda Palace*
Jazzmatazz!
Late for school!
Oopsy, teacher!
Cameron, C. C. *One for me, one for you*
Capucilli, Alyssa Satin. *Bear hugs*
Inside a zoo in the city
Mrs. McTats and her houseful of cats
What kind of kiss?
Carlson, Melody. *The Easterville miracle*
Farmer Brown's field trip
When the creepy things come out
Carlstrom, Nancy White. *Better not get wet, Jesse Bear*
Guess who's coming, Jesse Bear
Happy birthday, Jesse Bear!
How do you say it today, Jesse Bear?
It's about time, Jesse Bear
It's your first day of school, Annie Claire
Let's count it out, Jesse Bear
What a scare, Jesse Bear!
Where is Christmas, Jesse Bear?
Carney, Margaret. *Where does a tiger-heron spend the night?*
Carr, Jan. *Dappled apples*
Splish, splash, spring
Carter, David A. *Flapdoodle dinosaurs*
Carter, Don. *Old MacDonald drives a tractor*
Cartwright, Reg. *What we do*
Casanova, Mary. *One-dog canoe*
One-dog sleigh
Cash, Megan Montague. *I saw the sea and the sea saw me*
Casteel, Seth. *Underwater dogs*
Caswell, Deanna. *Train trip*
Cazet, Denys. *Nothing at all*
Chaconas, Dori. *Don't slam the door!*
Hurry down to Derry Fair
On a wintry morning
Virginnie's hat
When cows come home for Christmas
Chall, Marsha Wilson. *One pup's up*
Chamberlain, Margaret. *Please don't tease Tootsie*
Chapman, Nancy Kapp. *Doggie dreams*
Charlip, Remy. *Baby hearts and baby flowers*
"Mother, mother I feel sick"
Sleepytime rhyme
Chernesky, Felicia Sanzari. *Pick a circle, gather squares*
Chetkowski, Emily. *Pumpkin smile*
Chichester Clark, Emma. *Little Miss Muffet counts to ten*
Chitwood, Suzanne Tanner. *Wake up, big barn!*
Chorao, Kay. *Knock at the door and other baby action rhymes*
Christelow, Eileen. *Five little monkeys reading in bed*
Five little monkeys sitting in a tree
Five little monkeys wash the car
Christian, Cheryl. *Witches*
Churchill, Vicki. *Sometimes I like to curl up in a ball*
Clarke, Jane. *Dancing with the Dinosaurs*
Stuck in the mud
Clayton, Dallas. *An awesome book!*
An awesome book of love!
Cleary, Beverly. *The hullabaloo ABC*
Cleary, Brian P. *Eight wild nights*
A lime, a mime, a pool of slime
Peanut butter and jellyfishes
Clements, Andrew. *The handiest things in the world*
Clifton, Lucille. *Everett Anderson's goodbye*
One of the problems of Everett Anderson
Cline-Ransome, Lesa. *Quilt alphabet*
Quilt counting
Cocca-Leffler, Maryann. *Jungle Halloween*
Let it rain
Colandro, Lucille. *There was a cold lady who swallowed some snow!*
There was an old lady who swallowed a clover!
There was an old lady who swallowed some books!
Colborn, Mary Palenick. *Rainy day slug*
Collins, Suzanne. *When Charlie McButton lost power*
Conover, Chris. *The Christmas bears*
Corderoy, Tracey. *Hubble bubble, Granny trouble*
Cordsen, Carol Foskett. *Market day*
The milkman
Corey, Shana. *Boats!*
Cote, Nancy. *Jackson's blanket*
Cotten, Cynthia. *At the edge of the woods*
Rain play
Couric, Katie. *The brand new kid*
Cousins, Lucy. *Hooray for fish!*
Peck, peck, peck
Cowley, Joy. *Mrs. Wishy-Washy's Christmas*
Cox, Judy. *Snow day for Mouse*
Cox, Phil Roxbee. *Fox on a box*
Goose on the loose
Shark in the park
Coyle, Carmela LaVigna. *Do princesses have best friends forever?*
Do super heroes have teddy bears?
Craig, Lindsey. *Dancing feet!*
Farmyard beat
Crandall, Court. *Hugville*
Crawford, Laura. *In arctic waters*
Crimi, Carolyn. *Principal Fred won't go to bed*
Pugs in a Bug
Crisp, Marty. *Totally polar*
Crocker, Nancy. *Betty Lou Blue*
Cronin, Doreen. *Bounce*
Click, clack, splish, splash
Stretch
Wiggle
Crow, Kristyn. *Bedtime at the swamp*
Cool Daddy Rat
The middle-child blues
Skeleton cat
Zombelina
Crowley, Ned. *Nanook and Pryce*
Cruise, Robin. *Only you*
Crum, Shutta. *All on a sleepy night*
The bravest of the brave
A family for Old Mill Farm
Cullen, Catherine Ann. *The magical, mystical, marvelous coat*
Thirsty baby
Cummings, Pat. *Angel baby*
Clean your room, Harvey Moon!
My aunt came back
Curtis, Jamie Lee. *Big words for little people*
I'm gonna like me
Is there really a human race?
It's hard to be five
My brave year of firsts
My mommy hung the moon
Today I feel silly and other moods that make my day
Where do balloons go?
Cushman, Doug. *Christmas Eve good night*

Halloween good night
Cusimano, Maryann K. *You are my I love you*
You are my wish
You are my wonders
Cuyler, Margery. *Guinea pigs add up*
The little dump truck
Monster mess!
Princess Bess gets dressed
Skeleton for dinner
Cyrus, Kurt. *Big rig bugs*
Tadpole Rex
The voyage of turtle Rex
Dahl, Michael. *Goodnight baseball*
Daniels, Teri. *Just enough*
Davenier, Christine. *It's raining, it's pouring*
Davick, Linda. *I love you, nose! I love you, toes!*
Davidson, Rebecca Piatt. *All the world's a stage*
Davies, Jacqueline. *The night is singing*
Davies, Sarah. *Happy to be girls*
Davis, David. *Jazz cats*
Day, Nancy Raines. *A is for alliguitar*
Deady, Kathleen W. *All year long*
It's time!
Dealey, Erin. *Goldie Locks has chicken pox*
Degman, Lori. *1 zany zoo*
de Las Casas, Dianne. *Mama's bayou*
Demarest, Chris L. *Firefighters A to Z*
Hotshots!
Demas, Corinne. *Pirates go to school*
Dempsey, Kristy. *Mini racer*
Denise, Anika. *Pigs love potatoes*
DePalma, Mary Newell. *Bow-wow wiggle-waggle*
dePaola, Tomie. *Get dressed, Santa!*
De Regniers, Beatrice Schenk. *May I bring a friend?*
Dewdney, Anna. *Grumpy Gloria*
Llama Llama and the bully goat
Llama Llama home with Mama
Llama Llama mad at Mama
Llama Llama misses Mama
Llama, Llama red pajama
Llama Llama time to share
Nobunny's perfect
Roly Poly pangolin
Dickinson, Rebecca. *Over in the Hollow*
Diesen, Deborah. *The barefooted, bad-tempered baby brigade*
The pout-pout fish
The pout-pout fish in the big-big dark
Dionne, Wanda. *Little Thumb*
DiPucchio, Kelly. *Alfred Zector, book collector*
Dinosnores
DiTerlizzi, Angela. *Say what?*
DiTerlizzi, Tony. *G is for one gzonk!*
Diviny, Sean. *Halloween Motel*
Dixon, Ann. *Winter is . . .*
Dobbins, Jan. *Driving my tractor*
Docherty, Helen. *The Snatchabook*
Docherty, Thomas. *Wash-a-bye Bear*
Dodd, Emma. *Best bear*
I don't want a cool cat!
I don't want a posh dog
I love bugs!
Just like you
No matter what
Dodd, Lynley. *A dragon in a wagon*
Find me a tiger
Dodds, Dayle Ann. *Hello, sun!*
Pet wash
The prince won't go to bed
Where's Pup?
Dominguez, Angela. *Maria had a little llama/Maria tenia una llama pequena*
Donahue, Shari Faden. *The zebra-striped whale with the polka-dot tail*
Donaldson, Julia. *Charlie Cook's favorite book*
The fish who cried wolf
A gold star for Zog
The Highway Rat
One mole digging a hole
Room on the broom
Stick Man
Tabby McTat, the musical cat
Tyrannosaurus Drip
What the ladybug heard
Where's my mom?
Doner, Kim. *On a road in Africa*
Doodler, Todd H. *The zoo I drew*
Dorfman, Craig. *I knew you could!*
Dotlich, Rebecca Kai. *What can a crane pick up?*
What is round?
What is square?
Doughty, Rebecca. *Oh no! Time to go!*
Downey, Lynn. *The flea's sneeze*
This is the earth that God made
Downs, Mike. *You see a circus, I see —*
Doyle, Charlotte Lackner. *The bouncing, dancing, galloping ABC*
Doyle, Malachy. *Get happy*
Storm cats
Dragonwagon, Crescent. *All the awake animals are almost asleep*
Druce, Arden. *Halloween night*
Drummond, Allan. *Casey Jones*
Dubosarsky, Ursula. *The terrible plop*
Duddle, Jonny. *The pirate cruncher*
The pirates next door
Dunbar, Joyce. *Shoe baby*
Duncan, Lois. *I walk at night*
Song of the circus
Dunn, Todd. *We go together*
Durango, Julia. *Cha-cha chimps*
Go-go gorillas
Duval, Kathy. *Take me to your BBQ*
Edens, Cooper. *The Animal Mall*
Edwards, David. *The pen that Pa built*
Edwards, Pamela Duncan. *The grumpy morning*
Roar
Wake-up kisses
Warthogs in the kitchen
Warthogs paint
While the world is sleeping
Ehlert, Lois. *Boo to you!*
Feathers for lunch
Fish eyes
Lots of spots
Market day
Nuts to you!
Oodles of animals
Top cat
Waiting for wings
Ehrhardt, Karen. *This jazz man*
Elffers, Joost. *Do you love me?*
Elliott, David. *And here's to you!*
One little chicken
Ellwand, David. *Cinderlily*
Elya, Susan Middleton. *Adiós, tricycle*
Bebé goes shopping
Bebé goes to the beach

Cowboy Jose
Eight animals bake a cake
Eight animals on the town
F is for fiesta
Fire! ¡Fuego! Brave bomberos
No more, por favor
Oh no, gotta go #2
Rubia and the three osos
Tooth on the loose
A year full of holidays
Emberley, Ed. *The wing on a flea*
Emberley, Rebecca. *Mice on ice*
Emmett, Jonathan. *Someone bigger*
Engelbreit, Mary. *Mary Engelbreit's A merry little Christmas*
Ericsson, Jennifer A. *She did it!*
Ernst, Lisa Campbell. *Round like a ball!*
This is the van that Dad cleaned
Esbaum, Jill. *Estelle takes a bath*
Stanza
Eschbacher, Roger. *Nonsense! He yelled*
Road trip
Estefan, Gloria. *Noelle's treasure tale*
Evans, Lezlie. *The bunnies' picnic*
The bunnies' trip
Can you count ten toes?
Who loves the little lamb?
Evans, Nate. *Bang! Boom! Roar!*
Fallon, Jimmy. *Snowball fight!*
Falwell, Cathryn. *Christmas for 10*
Feast for ten
Gobble gobble
Mystery vine
Rainbow Stew
Scoot!
Shape capers
Turtle splash!
Fearrington, Ann. *Who sees the lighthouse?*
Feldman, Eve B. *Billy & Milly, short and silly*
Fernandes, Eugenie. *Big week for little mouse*
Busy little mouse
Kitten's spring
Kitten's winter
Ferreri, Della Ross. *How will I ever sleep in this bed?*
Ficocelli, Elizabeth. *Kid tea*
Fischer,.Scott M. *Jump!*
Fisher, Aileen Lucia. *Know what I saw?*
You don't look like your mother
Fisher, Doris. *My even day*
One odd day
Fitzpatrick, Marie-Louise. *I'm a tiger, too!*
Five little pumpkins, ill. by Ben Mantle
Five little pumpkins, ill. by Dan Yaccarino
Fleming, Candace. *Seven hungry babies*
Who invited you?
Fleming, Denise. *Barnyard banter*
Beetle bop
The first day of winter
In the small, small pond
Underground
Fliess, Sue. *A gluten-free birthday for me!*
Shoes for me!
Florian, Douglas. *A pig is big*
Flynn, Kitson. *Carrot in my pocket*
Foreman, Jack. *Say hello*
Fox, Lee. *Ella Kazoo will not brush her hair*
Fox, Mem. *Boo to a goose*
Good night, sleep tight
Hello, baby!
Let's count goats!
The magic hat
Shoes from grandpa
Sleepy bears
Ten little fingers and ten little toes
Time for bed
Two little monkeys
Where is the green sheep?
Where the giant sleeps
Yoo-hoo, Ladybug!
Zoo-looking
Frampton, David. *The whole night through*
Franco, Betsy. *Double play!*
Frazier, Craig. *Lots of dots*
Frederick, Heather Vogel. *Babyberry pie*
Hide and squeak
Fredrickson, Lane. *Watch your tongue, Cecily Beasley*
Freedman, Claire. *Dinosaurs love underpants*
One magical day
One magical morning
Pirates love underpants
Snuggle up, sleepy ones
Freymann, Saxton. *Dr. Pompo's nose*
One lonely seahorse
Friedman, Laurie. *Ruby Valentine saves the day*
Thanksgiving rules
Fuge, Charles. *Astonishing animal ABC*
I know a rhino
Fyleman, Rose. *Mice*
Gaiman, Neil. *Crazy hair*
The dangerous alphabet
Galbraith, Kathryn O. *Boo, bunny!*
Gall, Chris. *Substitute creacher*
Gannij, Joan. *Hidden hippo*
Garland, Michael. *Christmas City*
The great Easter egg hunt
Hooray José!
Last night at the zoo
Garriel, Barbara S. *I know a shy fellow who swallowed a cello*
Geist, Ken. *Who's who?*
George, Kristine O'Connell. *Up!*
Geras, Adèle. *Sleep tight, Ginger Kitten*
Gerber, Carole. *Spring blossoms*
Geringer, Laura. *Boom boom go away!*
Gershator, Phillis. *Listen, listen*
Moo, moo, brown cow! Have you any milk?
Summer is summer
Time for a hug
When it starts to snow
Who's awake in springtime?
Who's in the farmyard?
Who's in the forest?
Ghigna, Charles. *I see winter*
Gibson, Amy. *Split! Splat!*
Gilman, Rita Golden. *Mole in a hole*
The gingerbread boy. *The gingerbread boy*
The Gingerbread Man loose in the school
The Gingerbread Man loose on the fire truck
Whiff, sniff, nibble and chew
Ginkel, Anne. *I've got an elephant*
Giogas, Valarie. *In my backyard*
Glass, Beth Raisner. *Blue-ribbon dad*
Noises at night
Glass, Julie. *A dollar for Penny*
Gliori, Debi. *No matter what*
Polar Bolero
Stormy weather
What can I give him?

Where did that baby come from?
Godwin, Laura. *Central Park serenade*
Little white dog
One moon, two cats
This is the firefighter
What the baby hears
Goembel, Ponder. *Animal fair*
Gold-Vukson, Marji E. *Grandpa and me on Tu B'Shevat*
Gollub, Matthew. *The Jazz Fly*
Jazz Fly 2
Ten oni drummers
Good, Merle, et al. *Dan's pants*
Gow, Nancy. *Ten big toes and a prince's nose*
Graham Barber, Lynda. *Spy hops and belly flops*
Graham-Yooll, Liz. *Timothy Tib*
Gralley, Jean. *Very boring alligator*
Gravdahl, John. *Curious catwalk*
Graves, Keith. *Pet boy*
Gravett, Emily. *Monkey and me*
Gray, Rita. *The wild little horse*
Greenberg, David. *Crocs!*
Skunks
Greene, Rhonda Gowler. *At grandma's*
Barnyard song
Daddy is a cozy hug
Eek! Creak! Snicker, sneak
Jamboree day
Mommy is a soft, warm kiss
No pirates allowed! said Library Lou
The stable where Jesus was born
The very first Thanksgiving Day
Greenfield, Eloise. *Water, water*
Griffith, Helen V. *Moonlight*
Grossman, Bill. *My little sister ate one hare*
My little sister hugged an ape
Grossman, Virginia. *Ten little rabbits*
Guarino, Deborah. *Is your mama a llama?*
Guenther, James. *Turnagain, Ptarmigan, where did you go?*
Guidone, Thea. *Drum city*
Gulbis, Stephen. *Cowgirl Rosie and her five baby bison*
Gundersheimer, Karen. *Find cat, wear hat*
Gunnufson, Charlotte. *Halloween hustle*
Haber, Tiffany Strelitz. *The monster who lost his mean*
Ollie and Claire
Hächler, Bruno. *What does my teddy bear do all night?*
Hager, Sarah. *Dancing Matilda*
Hague, Kathleen. *Alphabears*
Calendarbears
Ten little bears
Hall, Algy Craig. *Dino bites!*
Hall, Marcellus. *Everyone sleeps*
Hall, Michael. *Cat tale*
My heart is like a zoo
Halls, Kelly Milner. *Dinosaur parade*
Hamburg, Jennifer. *A moose that says mooooooooo*
Hamilton, K. R. *This is the ocean*
Hamilton, Kersten. *Police officers on patrol*
Red truck
Hamilton, Richard. *Let's take over the kindergarten*
Polly's picnic
Hample, Stoo. *I will kiss you (lots and lots and lots!)*
Hamsa, Bobbie. *Fast-draw Freddie*
Hanson, Warren. *Bugtown Boogie*
Harby, Melanie. *All aboard for Dreamland!*
Hargrove, Linda. *Wings across the moon*
Harley, Bill. *Dirty Joe, the pirate*
Harper, Charise Mericle. *There was a bold lady who wanted a star*
Harper, Jessica. *I'm not going to chase the cat today*
Lizzy's do's and don'ts
Lizzy's ups and downs
Nora's room
Harris, Trudy. *Jenny found a penny*
100 days of school
Pattern bugs
Pattern fish
Twenty hungry piggies
Harrison, David L. *Piggy Wiglet*
Harshman, Marc. *Red are the apples*
Harshman, Terry Webb. *Does a sea cow say moo?*
Hart, Caryl. *The princess and the peas*
Harvey, Jayne. *Busy bugs*
Hatch, Elizabeth. *Halloween night*
Hawkins, Colin. *One, two, guess who?*
Hayles, Marsha. *Bunion Burt*
The feathered crown
He saves the day
Pajamas anytime
Hays, Anna Jane. *Kindergarten countdown*
Hegg, Tom. *Peef and his best friend*
Heidbreder, Robert. *Black and bittern was night*
I wished for a unicorn
A sea-wishing day
Heiligman, Deborah. *Cool dog, school dog*
Snow dog, go dog
Heinz, Brian J. *The monsters' test*
Red Fox at McCloskey's farm
Helakoski, Leslie. *Doggone feet!*
Heling, Kathryn. *Mouse's hide-and-seek words*
Heller, Ruth. *A cache of jewels and other collective nouns*
Color, color, color, color
Fantastic! wow! and unreal!
Kites sail high
Many luscious lollipops
Merry-go-round
Mine, all mine
The reason for a flower
Henderson, Kathy. *Baby knows best*
Henkes, Kevin. *Oh!*
Hennessy, B. G. *The missing tarts*
Hicks, Barbara Jean. *I like black and white*
Monsters don't eat broccoli
Hill, Isabel. *Building stories*
Hill, Susanna Leonard. *The house that Mack built*
Hindley, Judy. *Baby talk*
Do like a duck does
Eyes, nose, fingers and toes
Sleepy places
Hines, Anna Grossnickle. *When the goblins came knocking*
Hoban, Tana. *Where is it?*
Hoberman, Mary Ann. *All kinds of families*
And to think that we thought that we'd never be friends
A house is a house for me
I like old clothes
I'm going to Grandma's
The looking book
Mrs. O'Leary's cow
One of each
Right outside my window
The seven silly eaters

The two sillies
Hoffman, Don. *A counting book with Billy and Abigail*
Good morning, good night Billy and Abigail
Holub, Joan. *Apple countdown*
The Halloween Queen
The pizza that we made
Scat cats
Turkeys never gobble
Hood, Susan. *Just say boo!*
Look! I can read!
Hooks, William H. *A dozen dizzy dogs*
Hop a little, jump a little!
Horowitz, Dave. *Humpty Dumpty climbs again*
A monkey among us
Soon, Baboon, soon
Twenty-six pirates
Twenty-six princesses
The ugly pumpkin
Horsbrugh, Wilma. *The train to Glasgow*
Horton, Joan. *Math attack!*
Working mummies
Horvath, James. *Dig, dogs, dig*
Hosford, Kate. *Big birthday*
Big bouffant
Houran, Lori Haskins. *Dig those dinosaurs*
I will keep you safe and sound
Howard, Reginald. *The big, big wall*
Howland, Naomi. *Princess says goodnight*
Hru, Dakari. *Tickle, tickle*
Hubbard, Patricia. *My crayons talk*
Trick or treat countdown
Hubbell, Patricia. *Airplanes: soaring! diving! turning!*
Boats: speeding! sailing! cruising!
Cars: rushing! honking! zooming!
Check it out! reading, finding, helping
Firefighters!
Horses: trotting! prancing! racing!
Hurray for spring!
My first airplane ride
Police
Pots and pans
Rabbit moon
Sea, sand, me!
Shaggy dogs, waggy dogs
Sidewalk trip
Snow happy!
Teacher!
Trains: steaming! pulling! huffing!
Wrapping paper romp
Huck, Charlotte S. *A creepy countdown*
Hudes, Quiara Alegría. *Welcome to my neighborhood!*
Hudson, Cheryl Willis. *My friend Maya loves to dance*
Hueston, M. P. *The all-American jump and jive jig*
Hughes, Shirley. *Out and about*
Rhymes for Annie Rose
Hughes, Ted. *My brother Bert*
Hull, Rod. *Mr. Betts and Mr. Potts*
Hulme, Joy N. *Easter babies*
Hunter, Jana Novotny. *Little ones do*
When Daddy's truck picks me up
Hurd, Thacher. *Bad frogs*
Cat's pajamas
Hutchins, Hazel. *Beneath the bridge*
Hutchins, Pat. *Bumpety bump*
Ten red apples
Which witch is which?
The wind blew
Imbody, Amy. *Snug as a bug?*
Inches, Alison. *The stuffed animals get ready for bed*
Ipcizade, Catherine. *'Twas the Day before Zoo Day*
Irwin, Michael. *Bears in my bed*
Isadora, Rachel. *Bring on that beat*
Not just tutus
Isop, Laurie. *How do you hug a porcupine?*
Jack and the beanstalk. *Jacques and de beanstalk*
Jackson, Alison. *The ballad of Valentine*
I know an old lady who swallowed a pie
If the shoe fits
Jackson, Ellen. *The seven seas*
Jacobs, Paul DuBois. *Fire drill*
Jane, Pamela. *Monster countdown*
Monster mischief
Janovitz, Marilyn. *Play baby play!*
We love school!
Jarman, Julia. *Class Two at the zoo*
Two shy pandas
Jarrett, Clare. *Arabella Miller's tiny caterpillar*
Jay, Alison. *Red green blue*
Jennings, Linda. *Hide and seek birthday treat*
Jewel. *Sweet dreams*
Jewell, Nancy. *Alligator wedding*
Jocelyn, Marthe. *Ones and twos*
Johnson, Gillian. *My sister Gracie*
Johnston, Tony. *Chicken in the kitchen*
Desert dog
Off to kindergarten
The whole green world
Jones, Sylvie. *Who's in the tub?*
Joosse, Barbara. *Hooray Parade*
Jordan, Mary Ellen. *Lazy Daisy, cranky Frankie*
Jorgensen, Gail. *Crocodile beat*
Jorgensen, Richard. *Reading with Dad*
Joyce, Susan. *ABC nature riddles*
Joyce, William. *Rolie Polie Olie*
Sleepy time Olie
Jukes, Mavis. *You're a bear*
Kalan, Robert. *Moving day*
Karas, G. Brian. *Skidamarink*
Katz, Alan. *Don't say that word!*
Katz, Karen. *Ten tiny babies*
Twelve hats for Lena
Kaufman, Jeanne. *Young Henry and the dragon*
Kavanagh, Peter. *I love my mama*
Kay, Julia. *Gulliver Snip*
Kay, Verla. *Civil War drummer boy*
Covered wagons, bumpy trails
Gold fever
Hornbooks and inkwells
Iron horses
Orphan train
Whatever happened to the Pony Express?
Keillor, Garrison. *Daddy's girl*
Keller, Laurie. *Grandpa Gazillion's number yard*
Kelley, Marty. *The rules*
Summer stinks
Winter woes
Kelly, Luke. *Blanket and bear, a remarkable pair*
Kelly, Mij. *Achoo!*
A bed of your own!
Friendly Day
One more sheep
Where's my darling daughter?
Kerner, Susan. *Always by my side*
Kerr, Judith. *One night in the zoo*
Ketteman, Helen. *Goodnight, Little Monster*

If Beaver had a fever
Khalsa, Dayal Kaur. *Green cat*
Killion, Bette. *Just think!*
Kimmel, Eric A. *The Erie Canal pirates*
Kimmelman, Leslie. *Everybody bonjours!*
How do I love you?
Round the turkey
Kindermans, Martine. *You and me*
Kinerk, Robert. *Clorinda*
Clorinda plays baseball!
Clorinda takes flight
Timothy Cox will not change his socks
King, Stephen Michael. *Emily loves to bounce*
Kirk, Daniel. *Bus stop, bus go*
Honk honk! Beep beep!
Keisha Ann can!
Moondogs
Snow family
Trash trucks!
Kirk, David. *Little bird, Biddle bird*
Little bunny, Biddle bunny
Little Miss Spider
Little Miss Spider at Sunny Patch School
Little pig, Biddle pig
Miss Spider's ABC
Miss Spider's new car
Miss Spider's tea party
Kleven, Elisa. *Cozy light, cozy night*
Sun bread
Kneen, Maggie. *The Christmas surprise*
Koda-Callan, Elizabeth. *The squiggly Wigglys*
Kohuth, Jane. *Duck sock hop*
Koller, Jackie French. *Bouncing on the bed*
One monkey too many
Kono, Erin Eitter. *Hula lullaby*
Kramer, Andrew. *Pajama pirates*
Kranking, Kathy. *The ocean is . . .*
Krasnesky, Thad. *That cat can't stay*
Kraus, Robert. *Mouse in love*
Whose mouse are you?
Krauss, Ruth. *Goodnight, goodnight, sleepyhead*
Krebs, Laurie. *The beeman*, ill. by Valeria Cis
The beeman, ill. by Melissa Iwai
Off we go to Mexico
Up and down the Andes
We're roaming in the rainforest
We're sailing down the Nile
We're sailing to Galapagos
Krensky, Stephen. *I know a lot!*
Krieb, Mr. *We're off to find the witch's house*
Kroll, Virginia L. *Boy, you're amazing!*
Everybody has a teddy
Girl, you're amazing!
On the way to kindergarten
Uno, dos, tres, posada!
Kumin, Maxine. *Oh, Harry!*
Kurtz, Jane. *Rain romp*
Kurtz, Kevin. *A day in the salt marsh*
Kuskin, Karla. *A boy had a mother who bought him a hat*
Green as a bean
So, what's it like to be a cat?
Under my hood I have a hat
Kutner, Merrily. *Z is for zombie*
The Zombie Nite Cafe
Laden, Nina. *Clowns on vacation*
Peek-a-who?
Lass, Bonnie. *Who took the cookies from the cookie jar?*
Latifah, Queen. *Queen of the scene*
Lawler, Janet. *A father's song*
A mother's song
Snowzilla
Tyrannoclaus
Lawrence, Jennifer B. *Sad doggy*
Lawrence, John. *This little chick*
Lazo, Caroline. *Someday when my cat can talk*
Leedy, Loreen. *The dragon Halloween party*
The dragon Thanksgiving feast
Le Guin, Ursula K. *Cat dreams*
Lendroth, Susan. *Ocean wide, ocean deep*
Lessac, Frané. *Island Counting 123*
Lester, Alison. *Noni the pony*
Lester, J. D. *Mommy calls me Monkeypants*
Lesynski, Loris. *Rocksy*
Leuck, Laura. *Goodnight, baby monster*
I love my pirate papa
My beastly brother
My monster mama loves me so
One witch
Levenson, George. *Pumpkin circle*
Levine, Abby. *Daddies give you horsey rides*
This is the matzah
This is the pumpkin
This is the turkey
Levine, Arthur A. *Monday is one day*
Lewin, Betsy. *Where is Tippy Toes?*
Lewis, J. Patrick. *Arithme-tickle*
Big is big and little little
Earth and me, our family tree
Earth and you, a closer view
The fantastic 5 and 10¢ store
The house of Boo
Kindergarten cat
Riddle-lightful
Tulip at the bat
What's looking at you, kid?
Lewis, Jacqueline Janette. *You are so wonderful*
Lewis, Kevin. *Chugga-chugga choo-choo*
Dinosaur dinosaur
The lot at the end of my block
Not inside this house!
The runaway pumpkin
Lewis, Rose A. *Sweet dreams*
Lewison, Wendy Cheyette. *"Buzz," said the bee*
Going to sleep on the farm
Mud
So many boots
Two is for twins
Lies, Brian. *Bats at the ballgame*
Bats at the beach
Bats at the library
Lillegard, Dee. *Balloons, balloons, balloons*
The Big Bug Ball
Lindbergh, Reeve. *The awful aardvarks go to school*
The awful aardvarks shop for school
The hippie grandmother
Homer the library cat
Johnny Appleseed
Nobody owns the sky
North country spring
On morning wings
Our nest
Lithgow, John. *Carnival of the animals*
I'm a manatee
Mahalia Mouse goes to college
Marsupial Sue
Micawber
The remarkable Farkle McBride

Little old lady who swallowed a fly. *I know an old lady*
There was an old lady who swallowed a fly
There was an old monkey who swallowed a frog
Litwin, Eric. *Pete the cat: rocking in my school shoes*
Pete the cat saves Christmas
Livingston, Irene. *Finklehopper Frog*
Finklehopper Frog cheers
Ljungkvist, Laura. *Follow the line through the house*
Lloyd-Jones, Sally. *Time to say goodnight*
Lobel, Arnold. *The frogs and toads all sang*
Odd owls and stout pigs
On Market Street
Loehr, Patrick. *Mucumber McGee and the lunch lady's liver*
London, Jonathan. *Fireflies, fireflies, light my way*
I'm a truck driver
Park beat
A plane goes ka-zoom!
A train goes clickety-clack
A truck goes rattley-bumpa
What do you love?
What do you love? [board book]
Who bop
Long, Ethan. *Soup for one*
Long, Steffanie. *Such a silly baby!*
Longstreth, Galen Goodwin. *Yes, let's*
Loomis, Christine. *Astro Bunnies*
Cowboy bunnies
Scuba bunnies
Loth, Sebastian. *Zelda the Varigoose*
Low, Alice. *Aunt Lucy went to buy a hat*
Lubner, Susan. *Ruthie Bon Bair, do not go to bed with wringing wet hair!*
Lukasewich, Lori. *The night fire*
Lund, Deb. *All aboard the dinotrain*
Dinosailors
Dinosoaring
Monsters on machines
Lundgren, Mary Beth. *Seven scary monsters*
Lyon, George Ella. *Mama is a miner*
Planes fly!
Sleepsong
Trucks roll!
McArthur, Meher. *An ABC of what art can be*
McBratney, Sam. *The caterpillow fight*
McCall, Francis X. *A huge hog is a big pig*
Maccarone, Grace. *Cars! Cars! Cars!*
A child was born
Miss Lina's ballerinas
Miss Lina's ballerinas and the prince
Miss Lina's ballerinas and the wicked wish
Oink! moo! how do you do?
McCarthy, Michael. *The story of Daniel in the lions' den*
The story of Noah and the ark
MacDonald, Amy. *Cousin Ruth's tooth*
Quentin Fenton Herter three
Rachel Fister's blister
McDonald, Megan. *It's picture day today!*
McDonald, Rae A. *A fishing surprise*
MacDonald, Suse. *Elephants on board*
McDonnell, Patrick. *Art*
McEvoy, Anne. *Betsy B. Little*
McGee, Marni. *Sleepy me*
Wake up, me!
McGinley, Phyllis. *The year without a Santa Claus*
McGinty, Alice B. *Ten little lambs*
Thank you, world
McGough, Roger. *What on earth can it be?*
McGrath, Barbara Barbieri. *Kellogg's froot loops color fun book*
Kellogg's froot loops counting fun book
Teddy bear counting
McHenry, E. B. *Poodlena*
Mack, Jeff. *Hush little polar bear*
The things I can do
Mackall, Dandi Daley. *Off to Bethlehem!*
McKelvey, Douglas Kaine. *Locust pocus*
Macken, JoAnn Early. *Baby says "moo!"*
Waiting out the storm
McKissack, Patricia C. *Messy Bessey and the birthday overnight*
Messy Bessey's closet
Messy Bessey's holidays
McLaren, Chesley. *Zat cat!*
McLean, Janet. *Let's go, baby-o!*
MacLennan, Cathy. *Chicky Chicky Chook Chook*
McMillan, Bruce. *Puffins climb, penguins rhyme*
McMullan, Kate. *Rock-a-baby band*
McNaughton, Colin. *Not last night but the night before*
We're off to look for aliens
When I grow up
Maconie, Robin. *Alice and her fabulous teeth*
McPhail, David. *Pigs ahoy*
Pigs aplenty, pigs galore!
Those can-do pigs
McReynolds, Linda. *Eight days gone*
Maguire, Gregory. *Crabby Cratchitt*
Mahy, Margaret. *Bubble trouble*
The Christmas tree tangle
Down the back of the chair
The man from the land of Fandango
17 kings and 42 elephants
A summery Saturday morning
Mallat, Kathy. *Papa pride*
Maloney, Peter. *Belly button boy*
Mandel, Peter. *Jackhammer Sam*
Say hey
Manning, Maurie J. *The aunts go marching*
Many, Paul. *The great pancake escape*
Marciano, John Bemelmans. *Madeline and the cats of Rome*
Madeline and the old house in Paris
Madeline says merci
Marcus, Kimberly. *Scritch-scratch a perfect match*
Margalith, Joan. *The babies are landing*
Mariconda, Barbara. *Sort it out!*
Markell, Denis. *Hush, Little Monster*
Markes, Julie. *Shhhhh! Everybody's sleeping*
Thanks for Thanksgiving
Marshak, S. *The Month-Brothers*
Martin, Bill, Jr. *Adam, Adam, what do you see?*
Baby bear, baby bear, what do you see?
Barn dance!
Brown bear, brown bear, what do you see?
Chicka chicka boom boom
Chicka chicka boom boom [board book]
Here are my hands
Kitty Cat, Kitty Cat, are you going to school?
Kitty Cat, Kitty Cat, are you going to sleep?
Kitty Cat, Kitty Cat, are you waking up?
Listen to the rain
Little granny quarterback
Maestro plays
The magic pumpkin
Polar bear, polar bear, what do you hear?

Ten little caterpillars
The turning of the year
Martin, David. *Hanukkah lights*
Let's have a tree party!
Peep and Ducky
We've all got bellybuttons
Martin, Emily Winfield. *Dream animals*
Marzollo, Jean. *Do you know new?*
I spy
I spy Christmas
I spy extreme challenger!
I spy fantasy
I spy gold challenger!
I spy little animals
I spy little book
I spy little bunnies
I spy little Christmas
I spy little letters
I spy little numbers
I spy little wheels
I spy, mystery
I spy school days
I spy spooky night
I spy super challenger!
I spy treasure hunt
I spy ultimate challenger!
I spy, year-round challenger!
Mama, Mama
Papa, Papa
Pierre the penguin
Pretend you're a cat
Sun song
Ten cats have hats
Thanksgiving cats
Valentine cats
Matheson, Christie. *Tap the magic tree*
Mathews, Judith. *Nathaniel Willy, scared silly*
May, Robert Lewis. *Rudolph the red-nosed reindeer*
Mayer, Lynne. *Newton and me*
Maynard, Bill. *Santa's time off*
Mayo, Margaret. *Dig dig digging*
Emergency!
Stomp, dinosaur, stomp!
Wiggle waggle fun
Mazer, Norma Fox. *Has anyone seen my Emily Greene?*
Mazzola, Frank. *Counting is for the birds*
Meade, Holly. *If I never forever endeavor*
A place to sleep
Meadows, Michelle. *Hibernation station*
Itsy-bitsy baby mouse
Piggies in pajamas
Piggies in the kitchen
Pilot pups
Medearis, Angela Shelf. *Dancing with the Indians*
The ghost of Sifty-Sifty Sam
Rum-a-tum-tum
Meister, Cari. *Busy, busy city street*
Melmed, Laura Krauss. *Capital! Washington D.C. from A to Z*
Eight winter nights
Fright night flight
A hug goes around
I love you as much . . .
Jumbo's lullaby
Meltzer, Lynn. *The construction crew*
Melvin, Alice. *Counting birds*
Merberg, Julie. *In the garden with Van Gogh*
A magical day with Matisse
Merriam, Eve. *Low song*
Where's that cat?
Merski, P. K. *Roaring, boring, Alice*
Merz, Jennifer J. *Playground day*
Meyers, Susan. *Bear in the air*
Everywhere babies
Kittens! Kittens! Kittens!
Puppies! Puppies! Puppies!
Rock-a-bye room
This is the way a baby rides
Michelson, Richard. *Oh no, not ghosts!*
Ten times better
Milgrim, David. *Cows can't fly*
Here in space
How you got so smart
Why Benny barks
Millard, Glenda. *And red galoshes*
Isabella's garden
Millen, C. M. *Blue bowl down*
Miller, J. Philip. *We all sing with the same voice*
Miller, Pat. *We're going on a book hunt*
Miller, Ruth. *The bear on the bed*
I went to the farm
Milord, Susan. *If I could*
Milusich, Janice. *Off go their engines, off go their lights*
Minor, Florence. *If you were a penguin*
Minor, Wendell. *Christmas tree!*
My farm friends
Minters, Frances. *Cinder-Elly*
Princess Fishtail
Sleepless Beauty
Too big, too small, just right
Miranda, Anne. *Beep! beep!*
Monster math
Mitter, Matt. *ABC: alphabet rhymes*
Once upon a rhyme
1, 2, 3, counting rhymes
Mitton, Tony. *All afloat on Noah's boat!*
Cool cars
Dinosaurumpus
Down by the cool of the pool
Farmer Joe and the music show
Flashing fire engines
The Jungle Run
Playful little penguins
A very curious bear
Mizzoni, Chris. *Clancy with the puck*
Modarressi, Mitra. *Owlet's first flight*
Stay awake, Sally
Modesitt, Jeanne. *Oh, what a beautiful day!*
Moffatt, Judith. *The pumpkin man*
Trick-or-treat faces
Monks, Lydia. *The cat barked?*
Montes, Marisa. *Egg-napped!*
Los gatos black on Halloween
Moore, Elaine. *Roly-poly puppies*
Moore, Raina. *How do you say good night?*
Mora, Pat. *Marimba!*
One, two, three / Uno, dos, tres
Morales, Melita. *Jam and honey*
Moreillon, Judi. *Ready and waiting for you*
Morgan, Mary. *My good night book*
Morgan, Michaela. *Brave, brave mouse*
Morris, Ann. *Shoes, shoes, shoes*
Morrison, Cathy. *I want a pet!*
Morrison, Toni. *Peeny butter fudge*
Morrow, Barbara Olenyik. *Mr. Mosquito put on his tuxedo*

Morrow, Tara Jaye. *Mommy loves her baby; Daddy loves his baby*
Wake up engines
Mortensen, Denise Dowling. *Bug Patrol*
Wake up engines
Mortensen, Lori. *Cindy Moo*
Morton-Shaw, Christine. *Wake up, sleepy bear!*
Moss, Lloyd. *Our marching band*
Zin! zin! zin! A violin
Moss, Miriam. *Bare bear*
Mother Goose. *Hickory, dickory, dock*
Humpty Dumpty
1, 2, buckle my shoe
Pat-a-cake
Moulton, Mark Kimball. *Reindeer Christmas*
Muecke, Anne. *The dinosaurs' night before Christmas*
Muir, Leslie. *The little bitty bakery*
Munro, Roxie. *Circus*
Murphy, Stuart J. *Animals on board*
The best vacation ever
Circus shapes
Elevator magic
Every buddy counts
Get up and go!
Rabbit's pajama party
Same old horse
Murray, Alison. *One two that's my shoe!*
Murray, Marjorie Dennis. *Halloween night*
Myers, Tim. *Looking for Luna*
Neitzel, Shirley. *The bag I'm taking to Grandma's*
The dress I'll wear to the party
The house I'll build for the wrens
I'm not feeling well today
I'm taking a trip on my train
The jacket I wear in the snow
We're making breakfast for mother
Who will I be?
Neubecker, Robert. *Beasty bath*
What little boys are made of
Winter is for snow
Nevius, Carol. *Baseball hour*
Building with Dad
Karate hour
Soccer hour
Newbery, Linda. *Posy*
Newcome, Zita. *Pop-up toddlerobics*
Newman, Lesléa. *Cats, cats, cats*
Daddy's song
Dogs, dogs, dogs
Just like Mama
Pigs, pigs, pigs
Runaway dreidel
Skunk's spring surprise
Nichol, Barbara. *Trunks all aboard*
Niemann, Christoph. *Subway*
Nikola-Lisa, W. *Shake dem Halloween bones*
Summer sun risin'
To hear the angels sing
Noonan, Julia. *Bath day*
Breakfast time
Mouse by mouse
Norman, Kim. *I know a wee piggy*
If it's snowy and you know it, clap your paws!
Ten on the sled
North, Sherry. *Because I am your daddy*
Because you are my baby
Northey, Lawrence. *I'm a hop hop hoppity frog*
Novak, Matt. *Flip flop bop*
The Pillow War
A wish for you
Numeroff, Laura Joffe. *Chimps don't wear glasses*
When sheep sleep
Ochiltree, Dianne. *It's a firefly night*
Pillow pup
O'Connor, Jane. *Ready, set, skip!*
Odanaka, Barbara. *A crazy day at the Critter Café*
Smash! Mash! Crash! There goes the trash!
Oelschlager, Vanita. *Made in China*
O'Hair, Margaret. *My kitten*
My pup
Star baby
Sweet baby feet
Ohi, Ruth. *Me and my brother*
Me and my sister
O'Keefe, Susan Heyboer. *Baby day*
Good night, God bless
Hungry monster ABC
Love me, love you
Olson, David J. *The thunderstruck stork*
Olson-Brown, Ellen. *Ooh la la polka-dot boots*
One, two, skip a few!
Oppenheim, Joanne. *Have you seen bugs?*
Ormerod, Jan. *If you're happy and you know it!*
Ms. MacDonald has a class
Orozco, Jose-Luis. *Pancho Claus*
Over in the meadow
Owen, Karen. *I could be, you could be*
Owens, Mary Beth. *Panda whispers*
Oxenbury, Helen. *Pig tale*
Pacilio, V. J. *Ling Cho and his three friends*
Pallotta, Jerry. *A giraffe did one*
Pamintuan, Macky. *Twelve haunted rooms of Halloween*
Paquette, Ammi-Joan. *Ghost in the house*
Parenteau, Shirley. *Bears in beds*
Bears on chairs
Park, Linda Sue. *Bee-bim bop!*
What does Bunny see?
Xander's panda party
Parker, Marjorie Blain. *Your kind of mommy*
Parker, Victoria. *Bearum scarum*
Partridge, Elizabeth. *Big Cat Pepper*
Moon glowing
Patrick, Jean L. S. *If I had a snowplow*
Patten, Brian. *The big snuggle-up*
Paul, Ann Whitford. *Everything to spend the night . . . from A to Z*
If animals kissed goodnight
Paulsen, Gary. *Worksong*
Pearce, Clemency. *Frangoline and the midnight dream*
Pearson, Debora. *Big city song*
Pearson, Susan. *Hooray for feet!*
Pearson, Tracey Campbell. *Where does Joe go?*
Peck, Jan. *Way up high in a tall green tree*
Peddicord, Jane Ann. *That special little baby*
Peet, Bill. *Ella*
Hubert's hair-raising adventures
Huge Harold
Kermit the hermit
The kweeks of Kookatumdee
The luckiest one of all
No such things
The pinkish, purplish, bluish egg
Randy's dandy lions
Smokey
Zella, Zack, and Zodiac
Pelham, David. *Sam's pizza*
Sam's sandwich

Pendziwol, Jean E. *No dragons for tea*
The tale of Sir Dragon
A treasure at sea for dragon and me
Penn, Audrey. *A bedtime kiss for Chester Raccoon*
Perl, Erica S. *Ninety-three in my family*
Perlman, Willa. *Good night, world*
Perrin, Martine. *Cock-a-doodle who?*
Perry, Andrea. *The Bicklebys' birdbath*
Perry, Robert. *Down at the Seaweed Café*
Peters, Lisa Westberg. *October smiled back*
Sleepyhead bear
Pfister, Marcus. *Questions, questions*
Phillips, Christopher. *Ceci Ann's day of why*
Pickering, Jimmy. *It's fall*
Pilkey, Dav. *The Moonglow Roll-O-Rama*
'Twas the night before Thanksgiving
Pinczes, Elinor J. *Inchworm and a half*
My full moon is square
A remainder of one
Pinder, Eric. *If all the animals came inside*
Piven, Hanoch. *The perfect purple feather*
Plourde, Lynn. *Dino pets*
Dino pets go to school
Grandpappy snippy snappies
Spring's sprung
Wild child
Winter waits
Pollard, Nik. *The river*
Pomerantz, Charlotte. *Flap your wings and try*
Here comes Henny
The mousery
The piggy in the puddle
Poppy Bear
Porter, Pamela. *Yellow moon, apple moon*
Posada, Mia. *Ladybugs*
Robins
Postgate, Daniel. *Smelly Bill*
Smelly Bill: love stinks
Poydar, Nancy. *Rhyme time Valentine*
Prap, Lila. *Animal lullabies*
Daddies
Prelutsky, Jack. *The mean old mean hyena*
The terrible tiger
Wild witches' ball
The wizard
Price, Hope Lynne. *These hands*
Prince, April Jones. *What do wheels do all day?*
Prince, Joshua. *I saw an ant in a parking lot*
I saw an ant on the railroad track
Prochovnic, Dawn Babb. *The big blue bowl*
Hip hip hooray! It's Family Day!
Protopopescu, Orel. *Two sticks*
Pumphrey, Jerome. *Creepy things are scaring me*
Pym, Tasha. *Have you ever seen a sneep?*
Quattlebaum, Mary. *Jo MacDonald hiked in the woods*
Raczka, Bob. *Art is . . .*
Fall mixed up
Snowy, blowy winter
Spring things
Summer wonders
Who loves the fall?
Rader, Laura. *Tea for me, tea for you*
Radzinski, Kandy. *Where to sleep*
Randall, Ronne. *The Hanukkah mice*
Ransom, Candice F. *Tractor day*
Raschka, Chris. *Hip Hop Dog*
Little black crow
Rash, Andy. *Agent A to Agent Z*
Rasmussen, Halfdan. *The ladder*
Rau, Dana Meachen. *Chilly Charlie*
Clown around
I'll make you a card
Rubber duck
Shoo crow, shoo!
Rauss, Ron. *Can I just take a nap?*
Ray, Karen. *Sleep song*
Reasoner, Charles. *Peek-a-boo monsters*
Redding, Sue. *Up above and down below*
Redmond, E. S. *The Unruly Queen*
Reeves, Howard W. *There was an old witch*
Regan, Dana. *Monkey see, monkey do*
Reid, Barbara. *The party*
Reidy, Jean. *All through my town*
Light up the night
Too pickley!
Too purpley!
Reiser, Lynn. *My baby and me*
Reiss, Mike. *The boy who wouldn't share*
How Murray saved Christmas
Late for school
Santa claustrophobia
Reitman, Andrea. *Mouse in the house*
Rex, Michael. *Dunk skunk*
Goodnight goon
Rey, H. A. *Elizabite*
Reynolds, Aaron. *Snowbots*
Richardson, Bill. *But if they do*
Rickards, Lynne. *Jacob O'Reilly wants a pet*
Rinker, Sherri Duskey. *Steam train, dream train*
Ritchie, Alison. *Me and my dad!*
Me and my mom!
Rives. *If I were a polar bear*
Robbins, Ruth. *Baboushka and the three kings*
Roberts, Bethany. *Birthday mice*
Christmas mice
Easter mice
Fourth of July mice
Valentine mice!
Robertson, Patrisha Grainger. *Cirque du Soleil*
Robinson, Tim. *Tobias, the quig, and the rumplenut tree*
Rock, Lois. *God bless me, God bless you*
I wish tonight
I wonder why?
Roemer, Heidi Bee. *What kind of seeds are these?*
Rogers, Paul. *Ruby's dinnertime*
Ruby's potty
What will the weather be like today?
Rollings, Susan. *New shoes, red shoes*
Roode, Daniel. *Little Bea and the snowy day*
Roosa, Karen. *Beach day*
Pippa at the parade
Root, Phyllis. *Creak! said the bed*
Flip, flap, fly!
One duck stuck
One duck stuck [board book]
Rattletrap car
Rattletrap car [board book]
Ten sleepy sheep
Rose, Deborah Lee. *All the seasons of the year*
Birthday zoo
Someone's sleepy
The spelling bee before recess
Rosen, Michael J. *Avalanche*
Rosenberg, Liz. *Eli's night-light*
Rosenfeld, Dina Herman. *How in the world does bread come from the earth?*

Rosenthal, Amy Krouse. *It's not fair!*
Rosenthal, Betsy R. *Which shoes would you choose?*
Ross, Michael Elsohn. *Mama's milk*
Play with me
Rossetti-Shustak, Bernadette. *I love you through and through*
Roth, Carol. *All aboard to work — choo-choo!*
The little school bus
Will you still love me?
Roth, Ruby. *V is for vegan*
Roth, Susan L. *Night-time numbers*
Rothstein, Gloria. *Sheep asleep*
Rotner, Shelley. *Citybook*
Parts
Rubin, C. M. *Eleanor, Ellatony, Ellencake, and me*
Rubinger, Ami. *Dog number 1 dog number 10*
I dream of an elephant
Ryan, Pam Muñoz. *Armadillos sleep in dugouts*
The crayon counting book
Hello, Ocean!
Hello ocean / Hola mar
Mud is cake
There was no snow on Christmas Eve
Ryder, Joanne. *Bear of my heart*
Big bear ball
Chipmunk song
Dance by the light of the moon
Each living thing
A fawn in the grass
Won't you be my hugaroo?
Rylant, Cynthia. *All in a day*
Alligator boy
Bear day
Bless us all
Bunny bungalow
Give me grace
If you'll be my Valentine
Puppies and piggies
The stars will still shine
Sabuda, Robert. *Winter in white*
Sage, Angie. *Monkeys in the jungle*
Salas, Laura Purdie. *A leaf can be . . .*
Saltzberg, Barney. *All around the seasons*
I love cats
I love dogs
Kisses
Sanfield, Steve. *Snow*
Sanger, Amy Wilson. *First book of sushi*
San Souci, Robert D. *Cinderella Skeleton*
The Hobyahs
Santoro, Scott. *Which way to witch school?*
Sartell, Debra. *Time for bed, Baby Ted*
Saul, Carol P. *Barn cat*
Sava, Donna Lynn. *Teddy bear dreams*
Savage, Stephen. *Ten orange pumpkins*
Sayles, Elizabeth. *The goldfish yawned*
Sayre, April Pulley. *Go, go, grapes!*
Hush, little puppy
If you're hoppy
It's my city
Let's go nuts! seeds we eat
Rah, rah, radishes!
Trout, trout, trout
Vulture view
Sayres, Brianna Caplan. *Where do diggers sleep at night?*
Scanlon, Elizabeth Garton. *Happy birthday, Bunny!*
A sock is a pocket for your toes
Think big!
Schaefer, Lola M. *An island grows*
Loose tooth
This is the sunflower
Toolbox twins
Schafer, Milton. *That crazy Barb'ra*
Schertle, Alice. *Little Blue Truck*
Little Blue Truck leads the way
The skeleton in the closet
Schindel, John. *Busy penguins*
Schneider, Christine M. *Picky Mrs. Pickle*
Saxophone Sam and his snazzy jazz band
Schnitzlein, Danny. *The monster who ate my peas*
Schnur, Steven. *Night lights*
Schoenherr, Ian. *Cat and mouse*
Don't spill the beans!
Read it, don't eat it!
Schotter, Roni. *All about grandmas*
Doo-Wop Pop
When the Wizzy Foot goes walking
Schroeder, Lisa. *Baby can't sleep*
Schubert, Leda. *Feeding the sheep*
Schulman, Janet. *10 Easter egg hunters*
10 trick-or-treaters
10 Valentine friends
Schumaker, Ward. *Dance!*
Schwartz, Amy. *Lucy can't sleep*
Schwartz, Corey Rosen. *The three ninja pigs*
Scillian, Devin. *Brewster the rooster*
The scrubbly-bubbly car wash
Scruggs, Afi. *Jump rope magic*
Seeber, Dorothea P. *A pup just for me . . . A boy just for me*
Seibold, J. Otto. *Penguin dreams*
Sendak, Maurice. *Bumble-ardy*
Pierre
Seven little monsters
Sendelbach, Brian. *The underpants zoo*
Sensel, Joni. *Bears barge in*
Serfozo, Mary. *There's a square*
Who wants one?
Whooo's there?
Seuling, Barbara. *Spring song*
Seuss, Dr. *And to think that I saw it on Mulberry Street*
The butter battle book
Did I ever tell you how lucky you are?
Gerald McBoing Boing
Gerald McBoing Boing sound book
Happy birthday to you!
Horton hatches the egg
Horton hears a Who!
How the Grinch stole Christmas
Hunches in bunches
I can lick 30 tigers today and other stories
I had trouble getting to Solla Sollew
If I ran the circus
If I ran the zoo
The king's stilts
McElligot's pool
On beyond zebra
Scrambled eggs super!
The Sneetches, and other stories
Thidwick, the big-hearted moose
Seven spunky monkeys
Shahan, Sherry. *The jazzy alphabet*
Shannon, George. *Who put the cookies in the cookie jar?*
Shannon, Terry Miller. *Tub toys*
Sharratt, Nick. *The foggy, foggy forest*
Shark in the park

What's in the witch's kitchen?
Shaskan, Stephen. *A dog is a dog*
Shaw, Nancy. *Raccoon tune*
Sheep blast off!
Sheep in a jeep
Sheep in a shop
Sheep on a ship
Sheep out to eat
Sheep take a hike
Sheep trick or treat
Shea, Bob. *Race you to bed*
Shea, Pegi Deitz. *I see me!*
Shea, Susan A. *Do you know which one will grow?*
Sheehan, Monica. *Love is you and me*
Shields, Carol Diggory. *Day by day a week goes round*
Martian rock
Month by month a year goes round
Saturday night at the dinosaur stomp
Wombat walkabout
Shields, Gillian. *When the world was waiting for you*
Shindler, Ramon. *Found alphabet*
Shore, Diane Z. *Look both ways*
This is the dream
Shulevitz, Uri. *Rain rain rivers*
Shulman, Lisa. *Over in the meadow at the big ballet*
Shulman, Mark. *Gorilla Garage*
Shute, Linda. *Halloween party*
Siddals, Mary McKenna. *Compost stew*
Millions of snowflakes
Tell me a season
Siebert, Diane. *Cave*
Plane song
Train song
Truck song
Sierra, Judy. *Ballyhoo Bay*
Born to read
The house that Drac built
The secret science project that almost ate school
Sleepy little alphabet
Suppose you meet a dinosaur
Thelonius Monster's sky-high fly pie
There's a zoo in room 22
'Twas the fright before Christmas
We love our school!
Wild about books
Wild about you!
Zoozical
Silvano, Wendi. *What does the wind say?*
Silverman, Erica. *Follow the leader*
The Halloween house
The Hanukkah hop!
There was a wee woman . . .
Silverstein, Shel. *A giraffe and a half*
The giving tree
Simmons, Jane. *Daisy's favorite things*
Simon, Francesca. *Calling all toddlers*
Singer, Marilyn. *Boo hoo boo-boo*
The boy who cried alien
City lullaby
Fred's bed
I'm your bus
Let's build a clubhouse
Shoe bop!
Solomon sneezes
What is your dog doing?
Siomades, Lorianne. *Cuckoo can't find you*
Kangaroo and cricket
A place to bloom
Siy, Alexandra. *One tractor*
Skalak, Barbara Anne. *Waddle, waddle, quack, quack, quack*
Slack, Michael. *Elecopter*
Monkey truck
Slate, Joseph. *The great big wagon that rang*
I want to be free
Miss Bindergarten celebrates the last day of kindergarten
Miss Bindergarten celebrates the 100th day of kindergarten
Miss Bindergarten has a wild day in kindergarten
Miss Bindergarten stays home from kindergarten
Miss Bindergarten takes a field trip with kindergarten
What star is this?
Who is coming to our house?
Slater, Dashka. *Baby shoes*
Slater, Teddy. *Smooch your pooch*
Sloat, Teri. *Farmer Brown goes round and round*
Farmer Brown shears his sheep
Patty's pumpkin patch
Pieces of Christmas
There was an old lady who swallowed a trout
The thing that bothered Farmer Brown
This is the house that was tidy and neat
Slonim, David. *I loathe you*
Small, David. *George Washington's cows*
Smallman, Steve. *Dragon stew*
My dad!
Smalls, Irene. *My Pop Pop and me*
Smalls-Hector, Irene. *Kevin and his dad*
Smee, Nicola. *What's the matter, Bunny Blue?*
Smith, Charles R. *Dance with me*
I am the world
Smith, Danna. *Pirate nap*
Smith, Jada Pinkett. *Girls hold up this world*
Smith, Linda. *Mrs. Biddlebox*
When Moon fell down
Smith, Maggie. *One naked baby*
Pigs in pajamas
Smith, Mavis. *'Twas the day after Thanksgiving*
Smith, Stu. *The bubble gum kid*
Snell, Gordon. *'Twas the day after Christmas*
Snyder, Betsy E. *Sweet dreams lullaby*
Snyder, Laurel. *Good night, laila tov*
Sobel, June. *The goodnight train*
Shiver me letters
Souders, Taryn. *Whole-y cow!*
Soule, Jean Conder. *Never tease a weasel*
Southwell, Jandelyn. *The little country town*
Speed, Toby. *Two cool cows*
Spence, Robert, III. *Clickety clack*
Sperring, Mark. *The fairytale cake*
The shape of my heart
Spier, Peter. *Noah's ark*
Spinelli, Eileen. *City angel*
Do you have a cat?
Do you have a dog?
Here comes the year
Hug a bug
I know it's autumn
The perfect Christmas
Rise the moon
A safe place called home
Silly Tilly
Together at Christmas
What do angels wear?
When Mama comes home tonight
When no one is watching

When Papa comes home tonight
Spinelli, Jerry. *I can be anything!*
Spohn, Kate. *Snow play*
The wet dry book
Spurr, Elizabeth. *In the garden*
Two bears beneath the stairs
Staake, Bob. *The donut chef*
Look! A book!
Look! Another book!
Steggall, Susan. *The diggers are coming!*
Stein, Mathilde. *Monstersong*
Stein, Peter. *Bugs galore*
Cars galore
Stern, Ellen. *I saw a bullfrog*
Stewart, Sarah. *The library*
Stickland, Paul. *Bears*
Dinosaur roar!
Dinosaur stomp!
Ten terrible dinosaurs
Stiegemeyer, Julie. *Gobble gobble crash!*
Seven little bunnies
Sting [Musician]. *Rock steady*
Stockdale, Susan. *Bring on the birds*
Fabulous Fishes
Stoeke, Janet Morgan. *The bus stop*
It's library day
Stohs, Anita. *An Easter alleluia*
Stone, Tanya Lee. *D is for dreidel*
Sturges, Philemon. *How do you make a baby smile?*
I love bugs
I love school
I love tools!
I love trains
I love trucks!
Ten flashing fireflies
This little pirate
Waggers
Sturgis, Brenda Reeves. *10 turkeys in the road*
Stutson, Caroline. *By the light of the Halloween moon*
Cats' night out
Cowpokes
Night train
Prairie primer A to Z
Suen, Anastasia. *Baby born*
Baby born [board book]
Delivery
Raise the roof
Red light, green light
Road work ahead
Subway
Window music
Surplice, Holly. *Guinea pig party*
Swaim, Jessica. *The hound from the pound*
Swenson, Jamie A. *Boom! Boom! Boom!*
Szekeres, Cyndy. *Cyndy Szekeres' learn to count, funny bunnies*
Toby's please and thank you
Taback, Simms. *I miss you every day*
Tafolla, Carmen. *Fiesta babies*
Tafuri, Nancy. *Snowy flowy blowy*
Tang, Greg. *Math appeal*
Math fables
Math fables too
Tarpley, Todd. *How about a kiss for me?*
Ten tiny toes
Taxali, Gary. *This is silly!*
Taylor, Sean. *Crocodiles are the best animals of all*
Taylor-Butler, Christine. *Lamb's Easter surprise*
Tellis, Annabel. *If my dad were a dog*
Temple, Charles A. *Train*
Thach, James Otis. *A child's guide to common household monsters*
Thomas, Jan. *Here comes the big, mean dust bunny!*
Rhyming dust bunnies
Thomas, Patricia. *Red sled*
Thomas, Shelley Moore. *Putting the world to sleep*
Thompson, Lauren. *Chew, chew, gulp!*
Hop, hop, jump!
How many cats?
Leap back home to me
Thompson, Richard. *The follower*
Thomson, Sarah L. *Pirates, ho!*
Thong, Roseanne. *Gai see*
Round is a tortilla
Tummy girl
Thorpe, Kiki. *Lots of bots*
The three little pigs. *The three little pigs and the big bad wolf*
Tillman, Nancy. *The crown on your head*
The spirit of Christmas
Tumford the terrible
Tumford's rude noises
Wherever you are
Tobin, Jim. *Sue MacDonald had a book*
Todd, Mark. *Monster trucks*
What will you be for Halloween?
Toft, Kim Michelle. *Neptune's nursery*
One less fish
Trapani, Iza. *Row, row, row your boat*
What am I?
Trent, Shanda. *Farmers' market day*
Trimble, Marcia. *Moonbeams for Santa*
Trumbauer, Lisa. *The great reindeer rebellion*
Tryon, Leslie. *Albert's Christmas*
Albert's play
Tucker, Kathy. *Do cowboys ride bikes?*
Do knights take naps?
Do pirates take baths?
Tucker, Lindy. *Porkelia*
Turner, Ann Warren. *Angel hide and seek*
Shaker hearts
Two little eyes and other action rhymes
Tyler, Michael. *The skin you live in*
Ulmer, Wendy. *A isn't for fox*
Vamos, Samantha R. *Alphabet trucks*
Van Buren, David. *I love you as big as the world*
Van Dusen, Chris. *The circus ship*
Down to the sea with Mr. Magee
King Hugo's huge ego
Learning to ski with Mr. Magee
Randy Riley's really big hit
Van Laan, Nancy. *Little baby Bobby*
Little Fish lost
Mama rocks, Papa sings
Nit-pickin'
Possum come a-knocking
So say the little monkeys
This is the hat
A tree for me
Van Rynbach, Iris. *Five little pumpkins*
Varela, Barry. *Gizmo*
Vasilovich, Guy. *The 13 nights of Halloween*
Vaughan, Marcia Kapok. *We're going on a ghost hunt*
Verde, Susan. *The museum*
Verdick, Elizabeth. *Peep leap*
Vestergaard, Hope. *Hillside lullaby*
Potty animals
What do you do when a monster says boo?

Viau, Nancy. *Storm song*
von Olfers, Sibylle. *Mother Earth and her children*
Votaw, Carol. *Waking up down under*
Vozar, David. *Yo, hungry wolf!*
Waber, Bernard. *Fast food! gulp! gulp!*
Gina
The mouse that snored
Wahl, Jan. *Elf night*
I met a dinosaur
Wahman, Joe. *Snowboy 1, 2, 3*
Waite, Judy. *Mouse, look out!*
Waldron, Jan L. *Angel Pig and the hidden Christmas*
John Pig's Halloween
Walker, Anna. *I love birthdays*
I love my dad
I love my mom
Wallace, Nancy Elizabeth. *Rabbit's bedtime*
Wallen, Ila. *The moon in my room*
Walsh, Joanna. *The biggest kiss*
The perfect hug
Walters, Virginia. *Are we there yet, Daddy?*
Walton, Rick. *Baby's first year!*
The bear came over to my house
Bunny school
Frankenstein
How can you dance?
Little dogs say "Rough!"
Noah's square dance
So many bunnies
Ward, B. J. *Farty Marty*
Ward, Jennifer. *Over in the garden*
Somewhere in the ocean
Way up in the Arctic
Wardlaw, Lee. *The chair where bear sits*
Red, white, and boom!
Wargin, Kathy-jo. *Scare a bear*
Warnes, Tim. *Daddy hug*
Watson, Clyde. *Applebet*
Wax, Wendy. *A very mice Christmas*
Weatherford, Carole Boston. *Jazz baby*
Weeks, Sarah. *Be mine, be mine, sweet valentine*
Bite me, I'm a book
Bite me, I'm a shape
Bunny fun
I'm a pig
Mrs. McNosh and the great big squash
My somebody special
Oh my gosh, Mrs. McNosh!
Overboard!
Woof
Weigel, Jeff. *Atomic Ace (he's just my dad)*
Weiss, Nicki. *The world turns round and round*
Welch, Willy. *Dancing with Daddy*
Grumpy Bunnies
Wells, Rosemary. *Clean-up time*
First tomato
Love waves
Moss pillows
My kindergarten
Noisy Nora
Read to your bunny
Red boots
Shy Charles
Weninger, Brigitte. *The elf's hat*
Westcott, Nadine Bernard. *Peanut butter and jelly*
What will we do with the baby-o?
Wheeler, Lisa. *Boogie knights*
Castaway cats
Dino-basketball
Dino-football
Dino-hockey
Dino-soccer
Dino-wrestling
Jazz baby
Mammoths on the move
The pet project
Sixteen cows
White, Alexina B. *Frisky brisky hippity hop*
White, Becky. *Betsy Ross*
White, Kathryn. *Ruby's school walk*
Whitman, Candace. *Lines that wiggle*
Whittaker, Nicola. *Feet*
Hair
Whybrow, Ian. *Faraway farm*
Wick, Walter. *Can you see what I see? cool collections*
Can you see what I see? dream machine
Can you see what I see? once upon a time
Can you see what I see? out of this world
Can you see what I see? picture puzzles to search and solve
Can you see what I see? Seymour and the juice box boat
Can you see what I see? Seymour makes new friends
Can you see what I see? treasure ship
Wickberg, Susan. *Hey Mr. Choo-Choo, where are you going?*
Wilcox, Leah. *Waking Beauty*
Wild, Margaret. *Itsy-bitsy babies*
Willard, Nancy. *The mouse, the cat and Grandmother's hat*
Willey, Margaret. *Thanksgiving with me*
Williams, Brenda. *Home for a tiger, home for a bear*
Williams, Linda. *Horse in the pigpen*
Williams, Rozanne Lanczak. *The coin counting book*
Williams, Sam. *That's love*
Williams, Sue. *Dinnertime*
I went walking
I went walking [board book]
Let's go visiting
Williams, Suzanne. *Old MacDonald in the city*
Ten naughty little monkeys
Willis, Jeanne. *Do little mermaids wet their beds*
Hippospotamus
I'm sure I saw a dinosaur
Susan laughs
Wilner, Isabel. *A garden alphabet*
Wilson, Karma. *Animal strike at the zoo, it's true!*
Bear says thanks
Bear stays up for Christmas
Bear's loose tooth
The cow loves cookies
Dinos in the snow!
Hogwash!
Horseplay
How to bake an American pie
Mama always comes home
Mama, why?
Moose tracks!
Princess me
Sakes alive!
Sleepyhead
Whopper cake
Wilson, Sarah. *Friends and pals and brothers, too*
Love and kisses
Wing, Natasha. *The night before the night before Christmas*
Winters, Kay. *Wolf watch*
Winthrop, Elizabeth. *Halloween hats*

Shoes
Sledding
Witte, Anna. *The parrot Tico Tango*
Wojtusik, Elizabeth. *Kitty up!*
Wolf, Sallie. *Truck stuck*
Wolff, Ashley. *I call my grandma Nana*
I call my grandpa Papa
When Lucy goes out walking
Wolff, Ferida. *On Halloween night*
Wong, Janet S. *Grump*
Hide and seek
Wood, Audrey. *A dog needs a bone*
The napping house
The napping house wakes up
Piggy Pie Po
Silly Sally
Ten little fish
Wright, Cliff. *Bear and ball*
Bear and kite
Wright, Maureen. *Earth Day, birthday!*
Sleep, Big Bear, sleep!
Sneeze, Big Bear, sneeze
Wright, Michael. *Jake goes peanuts*
Jake starts school
Jake stays awake
Yaccarino, Dan. *Five little ducks*
Zoom! Zoom! Zoom! I'm off to the moon!
Yankovic, Al. *My new teacher and me!*
When I grow up
Yates, Philip. *Ten little mummies*
Yee, Wong Herbert. *Big black bear*
Detective Small in the amazing banana caper
Eek! There's a mouse in the house
Fireman Small
Fireman Small, fire down below
Fireman Small to the rescue
Mrs. Brown went to town
The Officers' Ball
A small Christmas
Summer days and nights
Tracks in the snow
Who likes rain?
Yektai, Niki. *Bears in pairs*
Hi bears, bye bears
Yolen, Jane. *Baby Bear's big dreams*
Baby Bear's books
Baby Bear's chairs
Beneath the ghost moon
Come to the fairies' ball
Creepy monsters, sleepy monsters
Dimity Duck
Harvest home
How do dinosaurs clean their rooms?
How do dinosaurs count to ten?
How do dinosaurs eat their food?
How do dinosaurs get well soon?
How do dinosaurs go to school?
How do dinosaurs learn their colors?
How do dinosaurs play with their friends?
How do dinosaurs say good night?
How do dinosaurs say Happy Chanukah?
How do dinosaurs say I love you?
How do dinosaurs say I'm mad?
How do dinosaurs say Merry Christmas?
Hush, little horsie
Mama's kiss
My father knows the names of things
Not all princesses dress in pink
Off we go!
Romping monsters, stomping monsters
Waking dragons
Where have the unicorns gone?
Young, Ruth. *Golden Bear*
Zalben, Jane Breskin. *Hey, Mama Goose*
Saturday night at the Beastro
Zemach, Harve. *The judge*
Ziefert, Harriet. *Animal music*
Beach party!
Clara Ann Cookie
Clara Ann Cookie go to bed!
Families have together
First He made the sun
First Night
From Kalamazoo to Timbuktu!
Hats off for the Fourth of July!
I swapped my dog
Messy Bessie
Rockheads
Toes have wiggles, kids have giggles
Train song
What do ducks dream?
What is part this, part that?
Wiggle like an octopus
William and the dragon
Zolotow, Charlotte. *Summer is . . .*
Zuffi, Stefano. *Art 123*

Riddles & jokes

Aardema, Verna. *Ji-nongo-nongo means riddles*
ABC school riddles
Agee, Jon. *Mr. Putney's quacking dog*
Anno, Mitsumasa. *Anno's math games*
Anno's math games II
Anno's math games III
Burns, Diane L., et al *Backyard beasties*
deGroat, Diane. *April Fool! watch out at school!*
Downs, Mike. *Pig giggles and rabbit rhymes*
Druce, Arden. *Halloween night*
Fisher, Doris. *Happy birthday to whooo?*
Granfield, Linda. *What am I?*
Grimm, Jacob and Wilhelm. *Rumpelstiltskin*, ill. by Paul Galdone
Rumpelstiltskin, ill. by David Shaw
Rumpelstiltskin, ill. by Paul O. Zelinsky
Grindley, Sally. *Who is it?*
Helmer, Marilyn. *Critter riddles*
Funtime riddles
Recess riddles
Spooky riddles
Yucky riddles
Yummy riddles
Hoffman, Mary. *Clever Katya*
Holub, Joan. *Geogra-fleas*
Joyce, Susan. *ABC nature riddles*
Krull, Kathleen. *Lincoln tells a joke*
Lewis, J. Patrick. *Arithme-tickle*
Riddle-icious
Riddle-lightful
Lobb, Janice. *Splish! Splosh! Why do we wash?*
McKee, David. *Elmer and Snake*
McNamara, Margaret. *The apple orchard riddle*
Marzollo, Jean. *I spy Christmas*
I spy extreme challenger!
I spy fantasy
I spy gold challenger!
I spy, mystery
I spy school days

I spy spooky night
I spy super challenger!
I spy treasure hunt
I spy ultimate challenger!
I spy, year-round challenger!
Medearis, Angela Shelf. *The freedom riddle*
Mitton, Tony. *Riddledy piggledy*
Modell, Frank. *Look out, it's April Fools' Day*
Potter, Beatrix. *The tale of Squirrel Nutkin*
Regan, Dian Curtis. *How do you know it's Halloween?*
Schultz, Sam. *Animal antics: the beast jokes ever*
Monster mayhem
Sidman, Joyce. *Butterfly eyes and other secrets of the meadow*
Sloat, Teri. *Rib-ticklers*
Swann, Brian. *The house with no door*
Thompson, Lauren. *One riddle, one answer*
Warrick, Karen Clemens. *If I had a tail*
Who needs that nose?
Wick, Walter. *Can you see what I see? treasure ship*
Wolff, Patricia Rae. *The toll-bridge troll*
Wright, Maureen. *Barnyard fun*
Young, Ruth. *Who says moo?*
Ziefert, Harriet. *What is part this, part that?*

Right & left *see* Concepts – left & right

Riots *see* Violence, nonviolence

Rivers

Ashforth, Camilla. *Willow on the river*
Atwell, Debby. *River*
Berkes, Marianne. *Over in a river*
Cameron, Eileen. *Canyon*
Cherry, Lynne. *A river ran wild*
Crampton, Gertrude. *Scuffy the tugboat*
Downing, Johnette. *Amazon alphabet*
Drawson, Blair. *All along the river*
George, Jean Craighead. *Everglades*
Harrison, David L. *Rivers*
Holling, Holling C. *Paddle-to-the-sea*
Hooper, Meredith. *River story*
Kellogg, Steven. *Mike Fink*
Kurtz, Jane. *River friendly, river wild*
LaMarche, Jim. *The raft*
Lewin, Ted. *Amazon boy*
Locker, Thomas. *Where the river begins*
London, Jonathan. *White water*
Miller, Debbie S. *River of life*
Pfeffer, Wendy. *The big flood*
Pollard, Nik. *The river*
Reynolds, Jan. *Amazon*
Sanders, Scott R. *Crawdad Creek*
Schofield, Jennifer. *Animal babies in ponds and rivers*
Walsh, Ellen Stoll. *Dot and Jabber and the mystery of the missing stream*

Roads

Hennessy, B. G. *Road builders*
Kilby, Don. *On the road*
Krishnaswami, Uma. *Out of the way! Out of the way!*
Lyon, George Ella. *Who came down that road?*
Morris, Dewi. *Sandy's street*
Nikola-Lisa, W. *One hole in the road*
Plourde, Lynn. *Pigs in the mud in the middle of the rud*
Pringle, Laurence P. *Jesse builds a road*
Skultety, Nancy. *From here to there*
Suen, Anastasia. *Road work ahead*
Sutton, Sally. *Roadwork*

Robbers *see* Crime

Robots

Barnett, Mac. *Oh no!*
Burks, James. *Beep and Bah*
Cushman, Doug. *Space cat*
Duddle, Jonny. *The king of space*
Dyckman, Ame. *Boy + Bot*
Gall, Chris. *Awesome Dawson*
Gritton, Steve. *The trouble with sisters and robots*
James, Brian. *Supertwins meet the dangerous dino-robots*
James, Simon. *Baby Brains and RoboMom*
Johnson, Stephen T. *My little blue robot*
Joyce, William. *Rolie Polie Olie*
Sleepy time Olie
Snowie Rolie
Kuszyk, R. Nicholas. *R Robot saves lunch*
Lester, Helen. *Wodney Wat's wobot*
Lucas, David. *The robot and the bluebird*
McCall, Bruce. *Marveltown*
McNamara, Margaret. *The three little aliens and the big bad robot*
Marshall, Edward. *Space case*
Novak, Matt. *The Robobots*
Pinkney, Brian. *Cosmo and the robot*
Reynolds, Aaron. *Snowbots*
Riddell, Chris. *Wendel's workshop*
Schwab, Eva. *Robert and the Robot*
Scieszka, Jon. *Robot Zot!*
Selznick, Brian. *The invention of Hugo Cabret*
Simon, Annette. *Robot zombie Frankenstein!*
Tauss, Marc. *Superhero*
Taylor, Sean. *Robomop*
Thorpe, Kiki. *Lots of bots*
Van Camp, Katie. *CookieBot!*
Van Dusen, Chris. *Randy Riley's really big hit*
Whybrow, Ian. *Sammy and the robots*
Yaccarino, Dan. *Doug unplugged*
If I had a robot

Rockets *see* Space & space ships

Rocking chairs *see* Furniture – chairs

Rocks

Aston, Dianna Hutts. *A rock is lively*
Baylor, Byrd. *Everybody needs a rock*
Bertrand, Lynne. *Granite baby*
Christian, Peggy. *If you find a rock*
Cole, Joanna. *The magic school bus inside the earth*
Flanagan, Alice K. *Rocks*
Goble, Paul. *Iktomi and the boulder*
Hurst, Carol Otis. *Rocks in his head*
Lesynski, Loris. *Rocksy*
McGuirk, Leslie. *If rocks could sing*
Pellant, Chris. *The best book of fossils, rocks, and minerals*

Polacco, Patricia. *My ol' man*
Stuve-Bodeen, Stephanie. *Elizabeti's doll*
Walker, Alice. *Finding the green stone*
Wallace, Nancy Elizabeth. *Rocks! rocks! rocks!*

Rodeos

Elya, Susan Middleton. *Cowboy Jose*
Gibbons, Gail. *Yippee-yay!*
Harper, Jo. *Ollie Jolly, rodeo clown*
Janni, Rebecca. *Every cowgirl loves a rodeo*
Munro, Roxie. *Rodeo*
Murphy, Stuart J. *Rodeo time*

Roosters *see* Birds – chickens

Royalty

Aardema, Verna. *The riddle of the drum*
Brunhoff, Laurent de. *Babar's USA*
Carle, Eric. *Walter the baker*
Climo, Shirley. *The Egyptian Cinderella*
The Korean Cinderella
Delessert, Etienne. *The seven dwarfs*
De Regniers, Beatrice Schenk. *May I bring a friend?*
Fisher, Leonard Everett. *Theseus and the Minotaur*
Fleischman, Paul. *Glass slipper, gold sandal*
Geras, Adèle. *The nutcracker*
Grimm, Jacob and Wilhelm *The goose girl*
Hans my hedgehog
Rumpelstiltskin, ill. by Paul Galdone
Rumpelstiltskin, ill. by David Shaw
Rumpelstiltskin, ill. by Paul O. Zelinsky
The water of life
Hague, Michael. *The nutcracker*
Helmer, Marilyn. *Three royal tales*
Hoffmann, E. T. A. *The nutcracker*, ill. by Renée Graef
The nutcracker, ill. by Alison Jay
The nutcracker, ill. by Peter Malone
The nutcracker, ill. by Maurice Sendak
The nutcracker, ill. by Lisbeth Zwerger
The Nutcracker and the Mouse King
The nutcracker ballet
Lee, Jeanne M. *Toad is the uncle of heaven*
Lin, Grace. *The red thread*
Marlowe, Pete. *One Arabian morning*
Martin, Bill, Jr. *Rock it, sock it, number line*
Mayer, Marianna. *Baba Yaga and Vasilisa the Brave*
Neuschwander, Cindy. *Sir Cumference and all the king's tens*
O'Malley, Kevin. *Once upon a royal superbaby*
Oppel, Kenneth. *The king's taster*
Price, Leontyne. *Aïda*
Rappaport, Doreen. *The new king*
San Souci, Robert D. *The white cat*
Seuss, Dr. *Bartholomew and the Oobleck*
Shulevitz, Uri. *One Monday morning*
Steig, William. *Roland, the minstrel pig*
Thomas, Shelley Moore. *Good night, Good Knight*
Wiesner, David. *The loathsome dragon*
Williams, Brenda. *The real princess*
Winthrop, Elizabeth. *Vasilissa the beautiful*
Wisniewski, David. *The warrior and the wise man*

Royalty – emperors

Aesop. *The ant and the grasshopper*
Andersen, Hans Christian. *The dinosaur's new clothes*
The emperor's new clothes, ill. by Angela Barrett
The emperor's new clothes, ill. by Virginia Lee Burton
The emperor's new clothes, ill. by Robert Byrd
The emperor's new clothes, ill. by Serena Curmi
The emperor's new clothes, ill. by Charlene DeLage
The emperor's new clothes, ill. by Jack Delano
The emperor's new clothes, ill. by Anne Rockwell
The emperor's new clothes, ill. by Janet Stevens
The emperor's new clothes, ill. by Eve Tharlet
The emperor's new clothes: a tale set in China
The nightingale, ill. by Nancy Ekholm Burkert
The nightingale, ill. by Pirkko Vainio
The nightingale, ill. by Lisbeth Zwerger
Bauld, Jane Scoggins. *Journey of the third seed*
Demi. *The empty pot*
Lasky, Kathryn. *The emperor's old clothes*
Marcellino, Fred. *I, crocodile*
Mayer, Mercer. *Shibumi and the kitemaker*
Perlman, Janet. *The Emperor Penguin's new clothes*
Shulevitz, Uri. *What is a wise bird like you doing in a silly tale like this?*
Wade, Mary Dodson. *No year of the cat*
Wang, Gabrielle. *The race for the Chinese zodiac*
Yolen, Jane. *The emperor and the kite*
Young, Ed. *Cat and Rat*

Royalty – khans

Yep, Laurence. *The Khan's daughter*

Royalty – kings

Balouch, Kristen. *The king and the three thieves*
Baranski, Joan Sullivan. *Round is a pancake*
Barnett, Mac. *Mustache!*
Biers-Ariel, Matt. *Solomon and the trees*
Black, Birdie. *Just right for Christmas*
Bosca, Francesca. *The apple king*
Brunhoff, Jean de. *Babar the king*
Babar the king [facsimile ed.]
Burdett, Lois. *Macbeth for kids*
Catchpool, Michael. *The cloud spinner*
Deedy, Carmen Agra. *The yellow star*
Diakité, Baba Wagué. *The magic gourd*
Dieterlé, Nathalie. *I am the king!*
Eisner, Will. *Sundiata*
Evans, Richard Paul. *The spyglass*
Farley, Carol J. *The king's secret*
Fisher, Jeff. *The hair scare*
Gershator, Phillis. *Only one cowry*
Gibert, Bruno. *The king is naked!*
Grimm, Jacob and Wilhelm *Iron John*, ill. by Trina Schart Hyman
Iron John, ill. by Winslow Pels
Hawthorne, Nathaniel. *King Midas and the golden touch*
Huling, Jan. *Puss in cowboy boots*
Krudop, Walter Lyon. *The man who caught fish*
Lepp, Bil. *The King of Little Things*
Lewis, Jill. *Don't read this book!*
MacDonald, Margaret Read. *Little Rooster's diamond button*
Mahy, Margaret. *17 kings and 42 elephants*
Manders, John. *The really awful musicians*
Martin, Rafe. *The Shark God*
Mayer, Marianna. *The prince and the pauper*

Medearis, Angela Shelf. *Too much talk*
Mitchell, Adrian. *Nobody rides the unicorn*
Miura, Taro. *The tiny king*
Myller, Rolf. *How big is a foot?*
Nobisso, Josephine. *The weight of a Mass*
Oberman, Sheldon. *The wisdom bird*
Ørdal, Stina Langlo. *Princess Aasta*
Osborne, Mary Pope. *The brave little seamstress*
Peet, Bill. *How Droofus the dragon lost his head*
Perrault, Charles. *Puss in boots,* ill. by Marcia Brown
Puss in boots, ill. by Lorinda Bryan Cauley
Puss in boots, ill. by Paul Galdone
Puss in boots, ill. by Steve Light
Puss in boots, ill. by Giuliano Lunelli
Puss in boots, ill. by Fred Marcellino
Puss in boots, ill. by Fred Marcellino
Puss in boots, ill. by Bernhard Oberdieck
Puss in boots, ill. by Jerry Pinkney
Puss in boots, ill. by Alain Vaës
Pfister, Marcus. *How Leo learned to be king*
Pienkowski, Jan. *Pizza!*
Pullman, Philip. *Puss in boots: the adventures of that most enterprising feline*
Rosenthal, Amy Krouse. *Al Pha's bet*
St. George, Judith. *Zarafa*
San Souci, Robert D. *A weave of words*
Sawyer, Ruth. *The remarkable Christmas of the cobbler's sons*
Seuss, Dr. *The king's stilts*
Sierra, Judy. *The beautiful butterfly*
Singleton, Debbie. *The king who wouldn't sleep*
Souhami, Jessica. *Rama and the demon king*
Steptoe, John. *Mufaro's beautiful daughters*
Stewig, John Warren. *King Midas*
Tchana, Katrin. *Sense Pass King*
Tom Thumb. *The adventures of Tom Thumb*
Van Dusen, Chris. *King Hugo's huge ego*
Ward, Helen. *The king of the birds*
Wilde, Oscar. *The happy prince*
Wisniewski, David. *Sundiata: lion king of Mali*
Wood, Audrey. *King Bidgood's in the bathtub*
Yep, Laurence. *The shell woman and the king*
Yolen, Jane. *King Long Shanks*

Royalty – pharaohs

Base, Graeme. *The Jewel Fish of Karnak*
Sabuda, Robert. *Tutankhamen's gift*

Royalty – princes

Allchin, Rosalind. *The frog princess*
Anderson, Brian. *The prince's new pet*
Arnold, Tedd. *The twin princes*
Burdett, Lois. *Hamlet for kids*
Cinderella
Climo, Shirley. *The Persian Cinderella*
Coburn, Jewell Reinhart. *Angkat Jouanah*
Cole, Babette. *Prince Cinders*
Daly, Jude. *Fair, brown and trembling*
Debecker, Benoît. *The naughty prince*
Demas, Corinne. *The magic apple*
Dodd, Emma. *Cinderelephant*
Dodds, Dayle Ann. *The prince won't go to bed*
The firebird. *The firebird,* ill. by Demi
The firebird, ill. by Rachel Isadora
The tale of the firebird
Geras, Adèle. *Sleeping beauty*
Swan Lake
Gow, Nancy. *Ten big toes and a prince's nose*
Grimm, Jacob and Wilhelm. *The frog prince,* ill. by Anne Yvonne Gilbert
The frog prince, ill. by Todd Ouren
Iron John, ill. by Trina Schart Hyman
Iron John, ill. by Winslow Pels
Rapunzel, ill. by Sarah Gibb
Rapunzel, ill. by Trina Schart Hyman
Rapunzel, ill. by Rachel Isadora
Rapunzel, ill. by Joma
Rapunzel, ill. by Kris Waldherr
Rapunzel, ill. by Paul O. Zelinsky
Rapunzel: a fairy tale
Rose Red and the bear prince
Sleeping Beauty
The sleeping beauty
Helmer, Marilyn. *Three prince charming tales*
Jackson, Ellen. *Cinder Edna*
Kimmel, Eric A. *The three princes*
Lattimore, Deborah Nourse. *Cinderhazel*
Lester, Helen. *Princess Penelope's parrot*
Lunge-Larsen, Lise. *The race of the Birkebeiners*
McCaughrean, Geraldine. *Beauty and the beast*
McLeod, Heather. *Kiss me!*
Manna, Anthony L. *The orphan*
Martin, Rafe. *The storytelling princess*
Milligan, Bryce. *The prince of Ireland and the three magic stallions*
Minters, Frances. *Cinder-Elly*
Osborne, Mary Pope. *Sleeping Bobby*
Perrault, Charles *Cinderella,* ill. by Nicoletta Ceccoli
Cinderella, ill. by Susan Jeffers
Cinderella, ill. by Loek Koopmans
Cinderella, ill. by James Marshall
Cinderella, ill. by Barbara McClintock
Cinderella / Cenicienta
Cinderella: a pop-up fairy tale
Cinderella: or, the little glass slipper
Piumini, Roberto. *Doctor Me Di Cin*
Roberts, Lynn. *Cinderella, an Art Deco love story*
Sanderson, Ruth. *Cinderella*
The enchanted wood
Papa Gatto
San Souci, Robert D. *Cinderella Skeleton*
Scieszka, Jon. *The frog prince, continued*
Shepard, Aaron. *One-eye! Two-eyes! Three-eyes!*
Souhami, Jessica. *Rama and the demon king*
Stampler, Ann Redisch. *The rooster prince of Breslov*
Stanley, Fay. *The last princess*
Verma, Jatinder Nath. *The story of Divaali*
Wells, Rosemary. *The little lame prince*
Wilson, Tony. *The princess and the packet of frozen peas*
Yolen, Jane. *The firebird*
Wings

Royalty – princesses

Allchin, Rosalind. *The frog princess*
Allen, Joy. *Princess Palooza*
Princess party
Alley, Zoe B. *There's a princess in the palace*
Andersen, Hans Christian. *The princess and the pea,* ill. by Emily Bolam
The princess and the pea, ill. by Charlene Delage
The princess and the pea, ill. by Dorothée Duntze

The princess and the pea, ill. by Maja Dusíková
The princess and the pea, ill. by Paul Galdone
The princess and the pea, ill. by Rachel Isadora
The princess and the pea, ill. by Bernhard Oberdieck
The princess and the pea, ill. by Janet Stevens
The princess and the pea, ill. by Alain Vaës
The princess and the pea in miniature
Andrews, Julie. *The very fairy princess*
The very fairy princess: here comes the flower girl!
The very fairy princess follows her heart
The very fairy princess sparkles in the snow
Auch, Mary Jane. *The princess and the pizza*
Bar-el, Dan. *Such a prince*
Bardhan-Quallen, Sudipta. *Pirate princess*
Bateman, Teresa. *The princesses have a ball*
Bonning, Tony. *Snog the frog*
Calvert, Pam. *Princess Peepers*
Princess Peepers picks a pet
Coh, Smiljana. *Princesses on the run*
Cole, Babette. *Princess Smartypants*
Coyle, Carmela LaVigna. *Do princesses have best friends forever?*
Do princesses really kiss frogs?
Cuyler, Margery. *Princess Bess gets dressed*
Davidson, Ellen Dee. *Princess Justina Albertina*
DeFelice, Cynthia C. *The real, true Dulcie Campbell*
Donaldson, Julia. *A gold star for Zog*
Edwards, Pamela Duncan. *Princess Pigtoria and the pea*
Emmett, Jonathan. *The princess and the pig*
Falconer, Ian. *Olivia and the fairy princesses*
Ferguson, Sarah. *Tea for Ruby*
Fleming, Candace. *Clever Jack takes the cake*
Funke, Cornelia. *Princess Pigsty*
Gardner, Carol. *Princess Zelda and the frog*
Goodhart, Pippa. *Arthur's tractor*
Gow, Nancy. *Ten big toes and a prince's nose*
Grambling, Lois G. *The witch who wanted to be a princess*
Grey, Mini. *The very smart pea and the princess-to-be*
Grimm, Jacob and Wilhelm. *The frog prince*, ill. by Anne Yvonne Gilbert
The frog prince, ill. by Todd Ouren
The golden goose
Sleeping Beauty
The sleeping beauty
Twelve dancing princesses
The twelve dancing princesses, ill. by Lucy Corvino
The twelve dancing princesses, ill. by Kinuko Y. Craft
The twelve dancing princesses, ill. by Rachel Isadora
The twelve dancing princesses, ill. by Gerald McDermott
The twelve dancing princesses, ill. by Jane Ray
The twelve dancing princesses, ill. by Suçie Stevenson
The twelve princesses
Hale, Bruce. *Snoring Beauty*
Hart, Caryl. *The princess and the peas*
Heide, Florence Parry. *Princess Hyacinth*
Hindley, Judy. *Princess Rosa's winter*
Hoffman, Mary. *Princess Grace*
Holabird, Katharine. *Angelina at the palace*
Horowitz, Dave. *Twenty-six princesses*
Howland, Naomi. *Princess says goodnight*
Huck, Charlotte S. *Princess Furball*
Joosse, Barbara. *Lovabye dragon*
Katz, Karen. *Princess Baby*
Princess Baby, night-night
Keller, Emily Snowell. *Sleeping Bunny*
Kimmel, Eric A. *The frog princess: a Tlingit legend from Alaska*
The three princes
Kleven, Elisa. *The paper princess*
LaRochelle, David. *The end*
Lee, Y. J. *The little moon princess*
Lendler, Ian. *An undone fairy tale*
Lester, Helen. *Princess Penelope's parrot*
Levert, Mireille. *The princess who had almost everything*
Lewison, Wendy Cheyette. *The princess and the potty*
Lum, Kate. *Princesses are not perfect*
Princesses are not quitters!
McCourt, Lisa. *Good night, Princess Pruney Toes*
McDonald, Megan. *The Hinky Pink*
MacHale, D. J. *The monster princess*
Mack, Todd. *Princess Penelope*
McKinlay, Meg. *No bears*
McNaughton, Janet. *Brave Jack and the unicorn*
Martin, Rafe. *The storytelling princess*
Masini, Beatrice. *A brave little princess*
Mayer, Mercer. *Shibumi and the kitemaker*
Melling, David. *Good knight sleep tight*
Metzger, Steve. *Will Princess Isabel ever say please?*
Milne, A. A. *The magic hill*
Milord, Susan. *Willa the wonderful*
Moore, Marian. *Dear Cinderella*
Mortimer, Rachael. *Song for a princess*
Murray, Alison. *Princess Penelope and the runaway kitten*
Numeroff, Laura Joffe. *Ponyella*
O'Malley, Kevin. *Once upon a cool motorcycle dude*
Ørdal, Stina Langlo. *Princess Aasta*
Orr, Wendy. *The princess and her panther*
Osborne, Mary Pope. *Sleeping Bobby*
Perlman, Janet. *The penguin and the pea*
Priceman, Marjorie. *Princess Picky*
Ray, Jane. *The apple-pip princess*
Ringgold, Faith. *The invisible princesses*
Ross, Tony. *I don't want to go to the hospital!*
I want a party!
I want my light on!
I want my tooth
I want to do it myself!
I want to win!
I want two birthdays!
Sauer, Tammi. *Princess in training*
Scieszka, Jon. *The frog prince, continued*
Scrimger, Richard. *Princess Bun Bun*
Shannon, Margaret. *The red wolf*
Shepard, Aaron. *The princess mouse*
Shields, Carol Diggory. *I am really a princess*
Spinelli, Eileen. *Princess Pig*
Stanley, Fay. *The last princess*
Strauss, Linda Leopold. *The princess gown*
Thompson, Lauren. *One riddle, one answer*
Thurber, James. *Many moons*, ill. by Marc Simont
Many moons, ill. by Louis Slobodkin
Underwood, Deborah. *Part-time princess*
Williams, Brenda. *The real princess*
Wilson, Karma. *Princess me*
Wilson, Tony. *The princess and the packet of frozen peas*
Yolen, Jane. *Not all princesses dress in pink*

Royalty – queens

Buehner, Caralyn. *The queen of style*
Burdett, Lois. *Macbeth for kids*
Cullen, Lynn. *Moi and Marie Antoinette*
Ellis, Sarah. *The queen's feet*
Engelbreit, Mary. *Queen of the class*
Falconer, Ian. *Olivia and the fairy princesses*
Foreman, Michael. *Oh! if only . . .*
Hennessy, B. G. *The missing tarts*
McGrory, Anik. *Mouton's impossible dream*
Masini, Beatrice. *A brave little princess*
Moore, Inga. *Captain Cat*
Nobisso, Josephine. *The weight of a Mass*
Oberman, Sheldon. *The wisdom bird*
Osborne, Mary Pope. *The brave little seamstress*
Paterson, John. *Blueberries for the queen*
Paxton, Tom. *Engelbert the elephant*
San Souci, Robert D. *A weave of words*
Wadham, Tim. *The queen of France*

Royalty – rajahs

Demi. *One grain of rice*

Royalty – sultans

Farmer, Nancy. *Clever Ali*
Lottridge, Celia Barker. *The little rooster and the diamond button*

Royalty – tsars

Gorbachev, Valeri. *The fool of the world and the flying ship: a Ukrainian folk tale*
Hoffman, Mary. *Clever Katya*
Ogburn, Jacqueline K. *The magic nesting doll*
Ransome, Arthur. *The fool of the world and the flying ship*
Sanderson, Ruth. *The golden mare, the firebird, and the magic ring*
San Souci, Robert D. *Peter and the blue witch baby*

Rummage sales *see* Garage sales, rummage sales

Running *see* Activities – running; Sports – racing

Running away *see* Behavior – running away

Safety

Berenstain, Stan and Jan. *The Berenstain bears learn about strangers*
Brill, Marlene Targ. *Margaret Knight, girl inventor*
Brown, Marc. *Dinosaurs, beware!*
Calmenson, Stephanie. *May I pet your dog?*
Cuyler, Margery. *Please play safe!*
Stop drop and roll
Ethan, Eric. *Helicopters*
Gordon, Sharon. *Bruises*
Hassett, John. *The nine lives of Dudley Dog*
Houran, Lori Haskins. *I will keep you safe and sound*
Jacobs, Paul DuBois. *Fire drill*
Kaczman, James. *A bird and his worm*
Kevi. *Don't talk to strangers*
Kurtz, Jane. *Do kangaroos wear seat belts?*
Lindgren, Barbro. *Sam's lamp*
Mayo, Margaret. *Emergency!*
Miller, Edward. *Fireboy to the rescue!*
Murphy, Stuart J. *Freda is found*
Pendziwol, Jean E. *No dragons for tea*
A treasure at sea for dragon and me
Pfister, Marcus. *Hang on, Hopper!*
Proimos, James. *The best bike ride ever*
Rex, Michael. *My fire engine*
Roche, Denis. *Little Pig is capable*
Salat, Cristina. *Peanut's emergency*
Shore, Diane Z. *Look both ways*
Spelman, Cornelia Maude. *Your body belongs to you*
Spinelli, Eileen. *A safe place called home*
Trottier, Maxine. *A safe place*

Sailors *see also* Careers – military

Ahlberg, Allan. *The baby in the hat*
Brown, Margaret Wise. *Sailor boy jig*
Calhoun, Mary. *Henry the sailor cat*
Crews, Donald. *Sail away*
Flanagan, Alice K. *Riding the ferry with Captain Cruz*
Friedman, Ina R. *How my parents learned to eat*
Joosse, Barbara. *Old Robert and the sea-silly cats*
Lendroth, Susan. *Ocean wide, ocean deep*
Lenski, Lois. *The little sailboat*
Lund, Deb. *Dinosailors*
Maass, Robert. *Tugboats*
Manning, Mick. *What a Viking!*
Meister, Cari. *Follow the drinking gourd: an Underground Railroad story*
Moore, Inga. *Captain Cat*
O'Neill, Alexis. *Loud Emily*
Rand, Gloria. *Sailing home*
Rosenthal, Eileen. *Bobo the sailor man!*
Shulevitz, Uri. *When I wore my sailor suit*
Van Allsburg, Chris. *The wreck of the Zephyr*
Waddell, Martin. *Sailor Bear*
Winter, Jeanette. *Follow the drinking gourd*
Zeman, Ludmila. *Sindbad*

Sand *see also* Sea & seashore – beaches

Inkpen, Mick. *Sandcastle*
Nolan, Dennis. *Sea of dreams*
Robertson, M. P. *The sandcastle*
Roddie, Shen. *Sandbear*
Yee, Brenda Shannon. *Sand castle*

Sandcastles *see* Sand

Santa Claus

Agee, Jon. *Little Santa*
Allen, Jonathan. *"I'm not Santa!"*
Alsenas, Linas. *Mrs. Claus takes a vacation*

Anderson, Derek. *How the Easter Bunny saved Christmas*
Apperley, Dawn. *Santa Claus will come tonight*
Arnold, Katya. *The adventures of Snowwoman*
Augustin, Barbara. *Antonella and her Santa Claus*
Autry, Gene. *Here comes Santa Claus*
Bailey, Mary Bryant. *Jeoffry's Christmas*
Barrett, Judi. *Santa from Cincinnati*
Bedford, David. *I've seen Santa!*
Biedrzycki, David. *Santa retires*
Breen, Steve. *The secret of Santa's island*
Brett, Jan. *The wild Christmas reindeer*
Briggs, Raymond. *Father Christmas*
Brown, Marc. *Arthur's Christmas*
Burgess, Mark. *Where teddy bears come from*
Burningham, John. *Harvey Slumfenburger's Christmas present*
Butler, M. Christina. *One special Christmas*
Catalano, Dominic. *Santa and the three bears*
Conover, Chris. *The Christmas bears*
Conrad, Pam. *The Tub People's Christmas*
Currey, Anna. *Truffle's Christmas*
David, Lawrence. *Peter Claus and the naughty list*
Demi. *The legend of Saint Nicholas*
dePaola, Tomie. *Get dressed, Santa!*
Donaldson, Julia. *Stick Man*
Dunrea, Olivier. *Merry Christmas, Ollie!*
Duquennoy, Jacques. *North Pole, South Pole*
Duval, Kathy. *The Three Bears' Christmas*
Emmett, Jonathan. *The Santa trap*
Evert, Lori. *The Christmas wish*
Faulkner, Keith. *Charlie Chimp's Christmas*
Frazee, Marla. *Santa Claus*
Gammell, Stephen. *Wake up, bear . . . It's Christmas!*
Hale, Bruce. *Santa on the loose!*
Harley, Bill. *Dear Santa*
Harry, Rebecca. *Snow Bunny's Christmas wish*
Hassett, Ann. *The finest Christmas tree*
High, Linda Oatman. *The last chimney of Christmas eve*
Hill, Eric. *Spot's magical Christmas*
Holmquist, Delano. *SantaSaurus*
Hurd, Thacher. *Santa Mouse and the ratdeer*
Jeffers, Susan. *The twelve days of Christmas*
Johnson, Crockett. *Harold at the North Pole*
Johnston, Tony. *A Kenya Christmas*
Joyce, William. *Santa calls*
Keane, Michael. *The night Santa got lost*
Kelley, True. *The dog who saved Santa*
Kellogg, Steven. *Santa Claus is comin' to town*
Krensky, Stephen. *How Santa got his job*
How Santa lost his job
Kroll, Steven. *Santa's crash-bang Christmas*
Lawler, Janet. *Tyrannoclaus*
Lee, Quinlan B. *Crazy Christmas chaos*
Lee, Stan. *Stan Lee's superhero Christmas*
Lester, Helen. *Tacky's Christmas*
Litwin, Eric. *Pete the cat saves Christmas*
McAnulty, Stacy. *Dear Santasaurus*
McCaughrean, Geraldine. *How the reindeer got their antlers*
McGinley, Phyllis. *The year without a Santa Claus*
McGuirk, Leslie. *Ho, ho, ho, Tucker!*
McPhail, David. *Santa's book of names*
Martin, Ruth. *Santa's on his way*
May, Robert Lewis. *Rudolph the red-nosed reindeer*
Maynard, Bill. *Santa's time off*
Milgrim, David. *Santa Duck*
Santa Duck and his merry helpers
Modugno, Maria. *Santa Claus and the three bears*
Moore, Clement Clarke. *A creature was stirring*
The night before Christmas
The night before Christmas, ill. by Jan Brett
The night before Christmas, ill. by Tomie dePaola
The night before Christmas, ill. by Mary Engelbreit
The night before Christmas, ill. by Holly Hobbie
The night before Christmas, ill. by Rachel Isadora
The night before Christmas, ill. by Raquel Jaramillo
The night before Christmas, ill. by Anita Lobel
The night before Christmas, ill. by James Marshall
The night before Christmas, ill. by Will Moses
The night before Christmas, ill. by Ted Rand
The night before Christmas, ill. by Ruth Sanderson
The night before Christmas, ill. by Gennady Spirin
The night before Christmas, ill. by Tasha Tudor
The night before Christmas, ill. by Richard Jesse Watson
The night before Christmas, ill. by Wendy Watson
The night before Christmas, ill. by Bruce Whatley
The night before Christmas, ill. by Lisbeth Zwerger
The night before Christmas: a pop-up
The teddy bears' night before Christmas
'Twas the night before Christmas, ill. by Matt Tavares
'Twas the night before Christmas, ill. by Christopher Wormell
Morrissey, Dean. *The Christmas ship*
Moss, Jenny Jackson. *Cajun night after Christmas*
Novak, Matt. *The last Christmas present*
Orozco, Jose-Luis. *Pancho Claus*
Paxton, Tom. *The story of Santa Claus*
Pearson, Tracey Campbell. *Where does Joe go?*
Peet, Bill. *Countdown to Christmas*
Pfister, Marcus. *Wake up, Santa Claus!*
Polacco, Patricia. *Gifts of the heart*
Welcome Comfort
Primavera, Elise. *Auntie Claus*
Auntie Claus and the key to Christmas
Pulver, Robin. *Christmas for a kitten*
Christmas kitten, home at last
Rawlinson, Julia. *Fletcher and the snowflake Christmas*
Rees, Douglas. *Jeannette Claus saves Christmas*
Reiss, Mike. *How Murray saved Christmas*
Santa claustrophobia
Rosales, Melodye Benson. *'Twas the night b'fore Christmas*
Rosenberg, Liz. *On Christmas eve*
Rylant, Cynthia. *Little Whistle's Christmas*
Sanders, Rob. *Cowboy Christmas*
Santa Claus is coming to town
Santa's little library of Christmas stories
Scotton, Rob. *Russell's Christmas magic*
Sharkey, Niamh. *Santasaurus*
Silvano, Wendi. *Turkey Claus*
Sloat, Teri. *Pieces of Christmas*
Smith, Cynthia Leitich. *Santa knows*
Solheim, James. *Santa's secrets revealed*
Stainton, Sue. *Santa's snow cat*
Stanton, Melissa. *My pen pal, Santa*
Stoeke, Janet Morgan. *Minerva Louise on Christmas Eve*
Sykes, Julie. *Careful, Santa*
Hurry, Santa!
Taylor, Jane. *Twinkle, twinkle little star*
Thompson, Lauren. *The Christmas magic*
Mouse's first Christmas

Mouse's first Christmas [board book]
Tompert, Ann. *Saint Nicholas*
Trimble, Marcia. *Moonbeams for Santa*
Trumbauer, Lisa. *The great reindeer rebellion*
Tryon, Leslie. *Albert's Christmas*
Turner, Sandy. *Silent night*
Van Allsburg, Chris. *The polar express*
Wallace, Ivy. *Pookie believes in Santa Claus*
Watson, Wendy. *Holly's Christmas eve*
Weinberg, Larry. *The Forgetful Bears help Santa*
Wells, Rosemary. *McDuff's new friend*
Max's Christmas
Weninger, Brigitte. *A letter to Santa Claus*
Wick, Walter. *Can you see what I see? the night before Christmas*
Wilder, Laura Ingalls. *Santa comes to little house*
Wilhelm, Hans. *Schnitzel's first Christmas*
Willey, Margaret. *Clever Beatrice Christmas*
Wolff, Patricia Rae. *A new, improved Santa*
Wood, Audrey. *The Christmas adventure of Space Elf Sam*
Yee, Wong Herbert. *A small Christmas*
Yin. *Dear Santa, please come to the 19th floor*
Yorinks, Arthur. *Christmas in July*

Saving things *see* Behavior – saving things

Scarecrows

Brown, Ken. *The scarecrow's hat*
Cazet, Denys. *Nothing at all*
Martin, Bill, Jr. *Barn dance!*
Patten, Brian. *The big snuggle-up*
Rau, Dana Meachen. *Shoo crow, shoo!*
Rylant, Cynthia. *Scarecrow*
San Souci, Robert D. *Feathertop*
Schertle, Alice. *Witch Hazel*
Williams, Linda. *The little old lady who was not afraid of anything*

School

Adams, Diane. *I want to help!*
Ajmera, Maya. *Back to school*
Alexander, Claire. *Back to front and upside down*
Aliki. *Marianthe's story one: painted words; Marianthe's story two: spoken memories*
A play's the thing
Allard, Harry. *Miss Nelson is back*
Miss Nelson is missing!
Alter, Anna. *Abigail spells*
Disappearing Desmond
Ancona, George. *It's our garden*
Anderson, Laurie Halse. *The hair of Zoe Fleefenbacher goes to school*
Andreae, Giles. *Captain Flinn and the pirate dinosaurs*
Captain Flinn and the pirate dinosaurs: missing treasure!
Andrews, Julie. *The very fairy princess follows her heart*
The very fairy princess sparkles in the snow
Arnold, Tedd. *Green Wilma*
Asim, Jabari. *Fifty cents and a dream*
Aston, Dianna Hutts. *Not so tall for six*
Baer, Edith. *This is the way we go to school*
Ballard, Robin. *My day, your day*
Barnett, Mac. *Billy Twitters and his big blue whale problem*
Bateman, Teresa. *The Bully Blockers Club*
Beaty, Andrea. *Artist Ted*
Firefighter Ted
Bercaw, Edna Coe. *Halmoni's day*
Berenstain, Stan and Jan. *The Berenstain bears' report card trouble*
The Berenstain bears' trouble at school
Berenzy, Alix. *Sammy*
Bergman, Mara. *Lively Elizabeth!*
Best, Cari. *Beatrice spells some lulus and learns to write a letter*
Bliss, Harry. *Bailey*
Bloom, Suzanne. *Piggy Monday*
Bond, Felicia. *The Halloween play*
Borden, Louise. *The day Eddie met the author*
The lost-and-found tooth
Bottner, Barbara. *Miss Brooks loves books! (and I don't)*
Bowen, Anne. *The great math tattle battle*
I know an old teacher
Bracken, Beth. *The little bully*
Too shy for show-and-tell
Brennan-Nelson, Denise. *Willow*
Brenner, Emily. *On the first day of grade school*
Bridges, Shirin Yim. *Ruby's wish*
Brisson, Pat. *I remember Miss Perry*
Bromley, Anne C. *The lunch thief*
Brown, Marc. *Arthur and the true Francine*
Arthur goes to school
Arthur turns green
Arthur's teacher moves in
Arthur's teacher trouble
Arthur's underwear
Arthur's Valentine
The true Francine
Bunting, Eve. *My special day at third street school*
Walking to school
Burnard, Damon. *Dave's haircut*
Burnett, Frances Hodgson. *A little princess*, ill. by Barbara McClintock
A little princess, ill. by Graham Rust
Burningham, John. *John Patrick Norman McHennessy — the boy who was always late*
Bus-a-saurus bop
Bush, Laura. *Read all about it!*
Button, Lana. *Willow's whispers*
Calmenson, Stephanie. *The frog principal*
Ollie's school day
The principal's new clothes
The teeny tiny teacher
Campbell, Bebe Moore. *I get so hungry*
Capucilli, Alyssa Satin. *Biscuit goes to school*
Biscuit loves school
Carlson, Nancy. *Henry and the bully*
Henry and the Valentine surprise
Henry's amazing imagination!
Henry's 100 days of kindergarten
Hooray for Grandparent's Day!
I don't like to read!
Sit still!
Think big!
Carrick, Carol. *Patrick's dinosaurs on the Internet*
Caseley, Judith. *Bully*
Cash, Rosanne. *Penelope Jane*
Catalanotto, Peter. *Matthew A.B.C.*
The secret lunch special
Caudill, Rebecca. *A pocketful of cricket*
Cazet, Denys. *A fish in his pocket*
Never poke a squid

Chall, Marsha Wilson. *Bonaparte*
Chapra, Mimi. *Amelia's show-and-tell fiesta / Amelia y la fiesta de "muestra y cuenta"*
Child, Lauren. *Say cheese!*
Choi, Yangsook. *The name jar*
Choldenko, Gennifer. *A giant crush*
How to make friends with a giant
Louder, Lili
Clements, Andrew. *Slippers at School*
Cocca-Leffler, Maryann. *Mr. Tanen's ties rule!*
Princess K.I.M. and the lie that grew
Princess Kim and too much truth
Theo's mood
Cohen, Miriam. *Bee my Valentine!*
Best friends
Don't eat too much turkey!
First grade takes a test, ill. by Ronald Himler
First grade takes a test, ill. by Lillian Hoban
It's George!
Jim meets the thing
No good in art
The real-skin rubber monster mask
See you in second grade!
Starring first grade
Tough Jim
When will I read?
Cole, Barbara Hancock. *Anna and Natalie*
Cole, Joanna. *The magic school bus explores the senses*
Coles, Robert. *The story of Ruby Bridges*
Compestine, Ying Chang. *The story of paper*
Conway, David. *Errol and his extraordinary nose*
Cook, Lisa Broadie. *Peanut butter and homework sandwiches*
Cooper, Ilene. *Jake's best thumb*
Corey, Shana. *First graders from Mars: Nergal and the Great Space Race*
First graders from Mars: Tera, star student
Couric, Katie. *The brand new kid*
Cox, Judy. *Carmen learns English*
Happy birthday, Mrs. Millie!
Creech, Sharon. *A fine, fine school*
Crews, Donald. *School bus*
School bus [board book]
Curious George goes to school
Curtis, Andrea. *What's for lunch?*
Cusimano, Maryann K. *You are my wonders*
Cutbill, Andy. *First week at cow school*
Cuyler, Margery. *Bullies never win*
Guinea pigs add up
Hooray for Reading Day!
I repeat, don't cheat!
Kindness is cooler, Mrs. Ruler
100th day worries
Stop drop and roll
We're going on a lion hunt
Dakos, Kalli. *Our principal promised to kiss a pig*
Daly, Niki. *Once upon a time*
D'Amico, Carmela. *Ella sets the stage*
Daniels, Teri. *Math man*
Danneberg, Julie. *The big test*
First year letters
Last day blues
Deedy, Carmen Agra. *Return of the library dragon*
Degen, Bruce. *I gotta draw*
deGroat, Diane. *Ants in your pants, worms in your plants!*
April Fool! watch out at school!
Jingle bells, homework smells
Liar, liar, pants on fire
No more pencils, no more books, no more teacher's dirty looks!
Roses are pink, your feet really stink
Trick or treat, smell my feet
Demas, Corinne. *Pirates go to school*
dePaola, Tomie. *The art lesson*
Bill and Pete
Bill and Pete go down the Nile
Hide-and-seek all week
Derby, Sally. *Whoosh went the wind!*
DeRubertis, Barbara. *Alexander Anteater's amazing act*
Bobby Baboon's banana be-bop
Dilly Dog's dizzy dancing
Dewdney, Anna. *Llama Llama and the bully goat*
Diesen, Deborah. *Picture day perfection*
Dillon, Jana. *Lucky O'Leprechaun in school*
DiPucchio, Kelly. *Grace for president*
Dodds, Dayle Ann. *Teacher's pets*
Dominguez, Angela. *Maria had a little llama/Maria tenia una llama pequena*
Donaldson, Julia. *A gold star for Zog*
Donovan, Gail. *The copycat fish*
A fishy story
Hidden treasures
Lost at sea
Dorros, Arthur. *The fungus that ate my school*
Drummond, Ree. *Charlie goes to school*
Dubosarsky, Ursula. *Rex*
Duke, Kate. *Ready for pumpkins*
Edwards, Pamela Duncan. *Gigi and Lulu's gigantic fight*
Ms. Bitsy Bat's kindergarten
Elkin, Mark. *Samuel's baby*
Elliott, Laura Malone. *Thanksgiving Day thanks*
Elschner, Geraldine. *Max's magic seeds*
Elvgren, Jennifer Riesmeyer. *Josias, hold the book*
Ely, Lesley. *Looking after Louis*
Emberley, Rebecca. *My school / Mi escuela*
Engelbreit, Mary. *Queen of the class*
Esham, Barbara. *Last to finish*
Everitt, Betsy. *Mean soup*
Falconer, Ian. *Olivia saves the circus*
Fergus, Maureen. *The day my mom came to kindergarten*
Finchler, Judy. *Congratulations, Miss Malarkey!*
Miss Malarkey leaves no reader behind
Miss Malarkey won't be in today
Testing Miss Malarkey
Fine, Edith Hope. *Water, weed, and wait*
Flanagan, Alice K. *Learning is fun with Mrs. Perez*
Riding the school bus with Mrs. Kramer
Teachers
Fontes, Justine Korman. *Signs of spring*
Formento, Alison. *This tree counts!*
This tree, 1, 2, 3
Franco, Betsy. *Double play!*
Fraser, Mary Ann. *I.Q. gets fit*
I.Q. goes to school
I.Q. goes to the library
I.Q., it's time
French, Simon. *Guess the baby*
Friedman, Darlene. *Star of the Week: a story of love, adoption, and brownies with sprinkles*
Gall, Chris. *Substitute creacher*
Gantos, Jack. *Not so Rotten Ralph*
Rotten Ralph's show and tell
Garden, Nancy. *Molly's family*
Garland, Michael. *Miss Smith reads again!*

Miss Smith's incredible storybook
Gerstein, Mordicai. *Minifred goes to school*
Giff, Patricia Reilly. *Today was a terrible day*
Giles, Almira Astudillo. *Willie wins*
The gingerbread boy. *The Gingerbread Man loose in the school*
Glaser, Linda. *Hannah's way*
Gorbachev, Valeri. *Turtle's penguin day*
Gran, Julia. *Big bug surprise*
Gregory, Nan. *Amber waiting*
Grigsby, Susan. *First peas to the table*
In the garden with Dr. Carver
Grimes, Nikki. *Danitra Brown, class clown*
Griswell, Kim T. *Rufus goes to school*
Gundersheimer, Karen. *Find cat, wear hat*
Gutman, Anne. *Gaspard and Lisa, friends forever*
Lisa in the jungle
Guy, Ginger Foglesong. *My school / Mi escuela*
Hader, Berta Hoerner. *The mighty hunter*
Hale, Bruce. *Clark the Shark*
Hale, Sarah Josepha Buell. *Mary had a little lamb*, ill. by Tomie dePaola
Mary had a little lamb, ill. by Laura Huliska-Beith
Mary had a little lamb, ill. by Salley Mavor
Mary had a little lamb, photos by Bruce McMillan
Hamilton, Richard. *Let's take over the kindergarten*
Hanlon, Abby. *Ralph tells a story*
Harley, Bill. *Lost and found*
Harper, Jamie. *Miss Mingo and the fire drill*
Harper, Jessica. *Lizzy's ups and downs*
Hassett, John. *The three silly girls Grubb*
Havill, Juanita. *Jamaica and the substitute teacher*
Jamaica is thankful
Hayes, Sarah. *Dog day*
Hays, Anna Jane. *Ready, set, preschool!*
Hayward, Linda. *A day in the life of a teacher*
What homework?
Heck, Ed. *Monkey lost*
Heelan, Jamee Riggio. *Can you hear a rainbow?*
Heiligman, Deborah. *Cool dog, school dog*
Helakoski, Leslie. *The smushy bus*
Helmer, Marilyn. *Recess riddles*
Henkes, Kevin. *Chrysanthemum*
El gran día de Lily / Lilly's big day
Lilly's purple plastic purse
Hilton, Perez. *The boy with pink hair*
Hoban, Russell. *Bread and jam for Frances*
Hodge, Deborah. *Lily and the mixed-up letters*
Hoffman, Mary. *Amazing Grace*
Princess Grace
Holabird, Katharine. *Angelina and Alice*
Holub, Joan. *Groundhog weather school*
Little red writing
Twinkle, star of the week
Hopkins, Lee Bennett. *School supplies*
Horn, Emily. *Excuse me — are you a witch?*
Horton, Joan. *Math attack!*
Howe, James. *The day the teacher went bananas*
Hubbell, Patricia. *Teacher!*
Hughes, Shirley. *Bobbo goes to school*
Hurwitz, Johanna. *Mighty Monty*
Husband, Amy. *Dear Teacher*
Hutchins, Pat. *Three-star Billy*
Isadora, Rachel. *Bea at ballet*
Isherwood, Shirley. *Flora the frog*
Iyengar, Malathi Michelle. *Romina's rangoli*
Jacobs, Paul DuBois. *Fire drill*
James, Brian. *Supertwins and the sneaky, slimy book worms*
Janovitz, Marilyn. *We love school!*
Jocelyn, Marthe. *Hannah's Collections*
Johnson, Doug. *Substitute teacher plans*
Joosse, Barbara. *Bad dog school*
Jules, Jacqueline. *Duck for Turkey Day*
Kalz, Jill. *An a-maze-ing school adventure*
Kann, Victoria. *Purplicious*
Katz, Alan. *Don't say that word!*
Kay, Verla. *Hornbooks and inkwells*
Keller, Holly. *That's mine, Horace*
Kelley, True. *Blabber Mouse*
Kent, Allegra. *Ballerina swan*
Kidslabel. *Spot 7: school*
Kirk, Daniel. *Keisha Ann can!*
Kleven, Elisa. *The apple doll*
Klise, Kate. *Little Rabbit and the Night Mare*
Knudsen, Michelle. *Argus*
Koster, Gloria. *The peanut-free cafe*
Krensky, Stephen. *Big bad wolves at school*
My teacher's secret life
Kroll, Steven. *Patches lost and found*
Will you be my valentine?
Kroll, Virginia L. *Ryan respects*
Krosoczka, Jarrett J. *Max for president*
Lakin, Patricia. *Snow day!*
Lambert, Martha Lewis. *I won't get lost*
Laminack, Lester L. *Jake's 100th day of school*
Lamstein, Sarah Marwil. *I like your buttons!*
Langley, Karen. *Shine*
Langreuter, Jutta. *Little Bear and the big fight*
Lasky, Kathryn. *Science fair bunnies*
Show and tell bunnies
Lauture, Denizé. *Running the road to ABC*
Layne, Steven L. *T is for teachers*
Lears, Laurie. *Becky the brave*
Leedy, Loreen. *Fraction action*
Messages in the mailbox
Mission — addition
Lefebvre, Jason. *Too much glue*
Lehman, Barbara. *The secret box*
LeSourd, Nancy. *Christy, Christmastime at Cutter Gap*
Lester, Helen. *Hooway for Wodney Wat*
Score one for the sloths
Tackylocks and the three bears
Three cheers for Tacky
Wodney Wat's wobot
Lesynski, Loris. *Night school*
Lewis, J. Patrick. *Kindergarten cat*
Lewis, Kim. *My friend Harry*
Lillegard, Dee. *Hello school!*
Lin, Grace. *Lissy's friends*
Lindbergh, Reeve. *The awful aardvarks go to school*
Lipp, Frederick. *Running shoes*
Lithgow, John. *Mahalia Mouse goes to college*
Littlesugar, Amy. *Freedom school, yes!*
Litwin, Eric. *Pete the cat: rocking in my school shoes*
Ljungkvist, Laura. *Follow the line to school*
Lloyd, Jennifer. *The best thing about kindergarten*
Loehr, Patrick. *Mucumber McGee and the lunch lady's liver*
Loewen, Nancy. *The last day of kindergarten*
London, Jonathan. *Froggy's first kiss*
Ludwig, Trudy. *The invisible boy*
Lundy, Charlotte. *Thank you, Esther*
Lyon, George Ella. *The pirate of kindergarten*
McAllister, Angela. *Take a kiss to school*
McBratney, Sam. *I'm sorry*
McCain, Becky R. *Nobody knew what to do*

McCourt, Lisa. *Chicken soup for little souls: The Goodness Gorillas*
Chicken soup for little souls: The new kid and the cookie thief
It's time for school, Stinky Face
McCully, Emily Arnold. *School*
McDonald, Megan. *Beetle McGrady eats bugs!*
Insects are my life
It's picture day today!
Reptiles are my life
McGinty, Alice B. *Eliza's kindergarten pet*
Mackintosh, David. *The Frank show*
Marshall Armstrong is new to our school
McKissack, Robert L. *Try your best*
MacLachlan, Patricia. *Three names*
McMillan, Bruce. *Mouse views*
McNaughton, Colin. *Captain Abdul's pirate school*
Once upon an ordinary school day
When I grow up
Madison, Alan. *Velma Gratch and the way cool butterfly*
Malaspina, Ann. *Yasmin's hammer*
Marciano, John Bemelmans. *Madeline and the old house in Paris*
Marshall, James. *The Cut-Ups crack up*
The Cut-Ups cut loose
Martin, Ann M. *Rachel Parker, kindergarten show-off*
Marx, Trish. *Kindergarten day USA and China*
Marzollo, Jean. *I spy school days*
Medearis, Michael. *Daisy and the doll*
Menchin, Scott. *Harry goes to dog school*
Michelson, Richard. *Busing Brewster*
Milgrim, David. *Eddie gets ready for school*
Miller, Edward. *Fireboy to the rescue!*
Miller, Margaret. *Now I'm big*
Mills, Claudia. *Ziggy's blue-ribbon day*
Milord, Susan. *Happy 100th day!*
Willa the wonderful
Mitchell, Margaree King. *Susie Mae*
Montanari, Eva. *The crocodile's true colors*
Moon, Nicola. *Something special*
Moore, Julianne. *Freckleface Strawberry and the dodgeball bully*
Moore, Mary-Alice. *The wheels on the school bus*
Moore-Mallinos, Jennifer. *My brother is autistic*
Mora, Pat. *The rainbow tulip*
Mortenson, Greg. *Listen to the wind*
Morton, Carlene. *The library pages*
Moses, Will. *Mary and her little lamb*
Moss, Marissa. *Regina's big mistake*
Moss, Miriam. *Wibble wobble*
Moss, Peggy. *One of us*
Munsch, Robert N. *Get out of bed!*
Mmm, cookies!
Show-and-tell
Stephanie's ponytail
Thomas' snowsuit
We share everything!
Murphy, Stuart J. *Get up and go!*
100 days of cool
The penny pot
Neitzel, Shirley. *I'm not feeling well today*
Neuschwander, Cindy. *Amanda Bean's amazing dream*
Nevius, Carol. *Building with Dad*
Nez, John. *One smart Cookie*
Norac, Carl. *Hello, sweetie pie*
Numeroff, Laura Joffe. *If you take a mouse to school*
O'Connor, Jane. *Fancy Nancy: poet extraordinaire!*
Ohi, Ruth. *Chicken, Pig, Cow and the class pet*
O'Malley, Kevin. *Straight to the pole*
O'Neill, Alexis. *The Recess Queen*
Ormerod, Jan. *Molly and her dad*
Ms. MacDonald has a class
Palacios, Argentina. *A Christmas surprise for Chabelita*
Palatini, Margie. *Bedhead*
Parish, Herman. *Amelia Bedelia's first valentine*
Amelia Bedelia's first vote
Park, Frances. *The royal bee*
Passen, Lisa. *Attack of the 50-foot teacher*
The incredible shrinking teacher
Pattou, Edith. *Mrs. Spitzer's garden*, ill. by Tricia Tusa
Mrs. Spitzer's garden, ill. by Tricia Tusa
Perl, Erica S. *Dotty*
Pete the cat: the wheels on the bus
Petrillo, Genevieve. *Keep your ear on the ball*
Pinkwater, Daniel. *Yo-yo man*
Plourde, Lynn. *Book Fair Day*
Dino pets go to school
Pajama day
School picture day
Polacco, Patricia. *The art of Miss Chew*
The junkyard wonders
The lemonade club
Mr. Lincoln's way
Thank you, Mr. Falker
Welcome Comfort
Pomeranc, Marion Hess. *The can-do Thanksgiving*
Portis, Antoinette. *Kindergarten diary*
Porto, Tony. *Blue aliens*
Get red
Poydar, Nancy. *The bad-news report card*
The biggest test in the universe
Busy Bea
No fair science fair
The perfectly horrible Halloween
Rhyme time Valentine
Snip, snip . . . snow!
Zip, zip . . . homework
Preller, James. *A pirate's guide to recess*
Prelutsky, Jack. *There's no place like school*
What a day it was at school!
Priceman, Marjorie. *Emeline at the circus*
Primavera, Elise. *Louise the big cheese and the back-to-school smarty-pants*
Pringle, Laurence P. *One room school*
Pulver, Robin. *Author day for room 3T*
Axle Annie
Axle Annie and the speed grump
The case of the incapacitated capitals
Happy endings
Mrs. Toggle and the dinosaur
Mrs. Toggle's beautiful blue shoe
Mrs. Toggle's zipper
Never say boo!
Nobody's mother is in second grade
Nouns and verbs have a field day
Punctuation takes a vacation
Silent letters loud and clear
Thank you, Miss Doover
Puttock, Simon. *Miss Fox*
Rania, Queen, consort of Abdullah II, King of Jordan. *The sandwich swap*
Rankin, Laura. *Ruthie and the (not so) teeny tiny lie*
Ransome, James. *My teacher*
Rappaport, Doreen. *The school is not white!*

Rathmann, Peggy. *Officer Buckle and Gloria*
Ruby the copycat
Rawlinson, Julia. *Mule school*
Recorvits, Helen. *Yoon and the jade bracelet*
Reed, Lynn Rowe. *Basil's birds*
Color chaos!
Reid, Barbara. *Perfect snow*
Reiser, Lynn. *Earthdance*
Reynolds, Aaron. *Superhero School*
Reynolds, Peter H. *Sky color*
Rickert, Janet Elizabeth. *Russ and the almost perfect day*
Robb, Diane Burton. *The alphabet war*
Robberecht, Thierry. *Sam tells stories*
Robbins, Jacqui. *The new girl . . . and me*
Two of a kind
Roche, Denis. *The best class picture ever*
Mim, gym, and June
Rockwell, Anne. *Becoming butterflies*
Career day
Father's Day
Halloween Day
Mother's Day
100 school days
St. Patrick's Day
Show and tell day
Thanksgiving Day
Valentine's Day
Rogers, Jacqueline. *Kindergarten ABC*
Tiptoe into kindergarten
Rose, Deborah Lee. *The spelling bee before recess*
The twelve days of kindergarten
The twelve days of springtime
Rosen, Michael. *Totally wonderful Miss Plumberry*
Roth, Carol. *The little school bus*
Rouillard, Wendy. *Barnaby's bunny*
Rumford, James. *Rain school*
Russo, Marisabina. *A very big bunny*
Ruurs, Margriet. *My school in the rain forest*
Ryder, Joanne. *Panda kindergarten*
Rylant, Cynthia. *The ticky-tacky doll*
Sadler, Marilyn. *Alistair's time machine*
Saltzberg, Barney. *Cornelius P. Mud, are you ready for school?*
Crazy hair day
Star of the week
Santoro, Scott. *Which way to witch school?*
Sauer, Tammi. *Mostly monsterly*
Say, Allen. *The favorite daughter*
Schachner, Judith Byron. *Skippyjon Jones class action*
Schaefer, Carole Lexa. *Kids like us*
Schafer, Milton. *That crazy Barb'ra*
Schertle, Alice. *Jeremy Bean's St. Patrick's Day*
Schmid, Paul. *Hugs from Pearl*
Schomp, Virginia. *If you were a . . . teacher*
Schreck, Karen Halvorsen. *Lucy's family tree*
Schrock, Jan West. *Give a goat*
Schwartz, Amy. *Oscar*
Things I learned in second grade
Scieszka, Jon. *Baloney, Henry P.*
Scotton, Rob. *Love, Splat*
Splat the cat: on with the show
Senisi, Ellen B. *All kinds of friends, even green*
Just kids
Shannon, David. *David goes to school*
Shaw, Hannah. *School for bandits*
Shea, Bob. *Big plans*
Sheldon, Dyan. *Unicorn dreams*
Shields, Carol Diggory. *Lunch money and other poems about school*
Shipton, Jonathan. *No biting, horrible crocodile!*
Shreeve, Elizabeth. *Oliver at the window*
Sierra, Judy. *The secret science project that almost ate school*
There's a zoo in room 22
Simms, Laura. *Rotten teeth*
Simon, Norma. *All families are special*
Singer, Marilyn. *First food fight this fall and other school poems*
I'm your bus
Slate, Joseph. *Miss Bindergarten celebrates the last day of kindergarten*
Miss Bindergarten celebrates the 100th day of kindergarten
Miss Bindergarten has a wild day in kindergarten
Miss Bindergarten stays home from kindergarten
Miss Bindergarten takes a field trip with kindergarten
Smallcomb, Pam. *Earth to Clunk*
Smalls, Irene. *Don't say ain't*
Spinelli, Eileen. *Miss Fox's class gets it wrong*
Miss Fox's class goes green
Miss Fox's class shapes up
Peace Week in Miss Fox's class
Spirin, Gennady. *Philipok*
Stadler, Alexander. *Beverly Billingsly takes a bow*
Stadler, John. *Wilson and Miss Lovely*
Stein, Janet. *This little bunny can bake*
Steptoe, John. *Creativity*
Stevens, Janet. *The little red pen*
Stier, Catherine. *Bugs in my hair?!*
Stoeke, Janet Morgan. *The bus stop*
It's library day
Minerva Louise at school
Surat, Michele Maria. *Angel child, dragon child*
Swann, Rick. *Our school garden!*
Tavares, Matt. *Becoming Babe Ruth*
Teague, Mark. *The lost and found*
The secret shortcut
Teyssèdre, Fabienne. *Joseph wants to read*
Thoms, Susan Collins. *Cesar takes a break*
Tobin, Jim. *The very inappropriate word*
Tryon, Leslie. *Albert's alphabet*
Patsy says
Udry, Janice May. *What Mary Jo shared*
Underwood, Deborah. *A balloon for Isabel*
Urdahl, Catherine. *Polka-dot fixes kindergarten*
Vail, Rachel. *Flabbersmashed about you*
Waber, Bernard. *Evie and Margie*
Wagner, Anke. *Tim's big move!*
Wallace, Nancy Elizabeth. *Ready, set, 100th day!*
Recycle every day!
The Valentine Express
Walton, Rick. *Bunny school*
Welch, Willy. *Grumpy Bunnies*
Wells, Rosemary. *First tomato*
Hands off, Harry!
Letters and sounds
McDuff goes to school
Miracle melts down
My kindergarten
Otto runs for President
Otto se presenta para presidente / Otto runs for President
Yoko
Yoko writes her name
Yoko's show-and-tell

Weston, Carrie. *The new bear at school*
White, Kathryn. *Ruby's school walk*
Whitehead, Jenny. *Lunch box mail and other poems*
Whiting, Sue. *The firefighters*
Wiesner, David. *Sector 7*
Williams, Karen Lynn. *Beatrice's dream*
Wing, Natasha. *Jalapeño bagels*
Winter, Jeanette. *Nasreen's secret school*
Winters, Kari-Lynn. *Gift days*
Winters, Kay. *The bears go to school*
The teeny tiny ghost and the monster
Wolff, Nancy. *It's time for school with Tallulah*
Wolff, Patricia Rae. *The toll-bridge troll*
Wood, Douglas. *What teachers can't do*
Woodson, Jacqueline. *Each kindness*
Wortche, Allison. *Rosie Sprout's time to shine*
Wright, Betty Ren. *The blizzard*
Yaccarino, Dan. *First day on a strange new planet*
Yankovic, Al. *When I grow up*
Yashima, Taro. *Crow boy*
Yolen, Jane. *How do dinosaurs go to school?*
Zemach, Kaethe. *Ms. McCaw learns to draw*
Ziefert, Harriet. *Buzzy had a little lamb*
Messy Bessie
Zimmett, Debbie. *Eddie enough*

School – field trips

Alberti, Theresa Jarosz. *Out and about at the planetarium*
Allard, Harry. *Miss Nelson has a field day*
Beaty, Andrea. *Iggy Peck, architect*
Bemelmans, Ludwig. *Madeline*
Bertram, Debbie. *The best book to read*
Bliss, Harry. *Bailey at the museum*
Bourgeois, Paulette. *Franklin's class trip*
Bunting, Eve. *One green apple*
Caseley, Judith. *Field Day Friday*
Cohen, Miriam. *Lost in the museum*
Cole, Joanna. *The magic school bus and the electric field trip*
The magic school bus and the science fair expedition
The magic school bus at the waterworks
The magic school bus in the time of the dinosaurs
The magic school bus inside a beehive
The magic school bus inside a hurricane
The magic school bus inside the human body
The magic school bus lost in the solar system
The magic school bus on the ocean floor
Cox, Judy. *Pick a pumpkin, Mrs. Millie!*
Cuyler, Margery. *That's good! That's bad! In Washington, D.C.*
Deady, Kathleen W. *Out and about at the zoo*
Dubois, Muriel L. *Out and about at the fire station*
Ericsson, Jennifer A. *Out and about at the bakery*
Formento, Alison. *These bees count!*
These seas count!
Garland, Michael. *Miss Smith and the haunted library*
The gingerbread boy. *The Gingerbread Man loose on the fire truck*
Harper, Jamie. *Miss Mingo weathers the storm*
Holub, Joan. *Apple countdown*
Pumpkin countdown
Jarman, Julia. *Class Two at the zoo*
Katz, Susan. *Mrs. Brown on exhibit*
Lithgow, John. *Carnival of the animals*
McNamara, Margaret. *The apple orchard riddle*
Mayr, Diane. *Out and about at the apple orchard*
Millman, Isaac. *Moses goes to a concert*
Murphy, Andy. *Out and about at the dairy farm*
Murphy, Stuart J. *Freda is found*
Noble, Trinka Hakes. *The day Jimmy's boa ate the wash*
Parish, Herman. *Amelia Bedelia's first field trip*
Plourde, Lynn. *Field trip day*
Poydar, Nancy. *Fish school*
Rechner, Amy. *Out and about at the aquarium*
Scotton, Rob. *Splat and the cool school trip*
Shea, Kitty. *Out and about at the post office*
Out and about at the science center
Out and about at the supermarket
Out and about at the vet clinic
Slate, Joseph. *Miss Bindergarten takes a field trip with kindergarten*
Spinelli, Eileen. *Miss Fox's class earns a field trip*
Watson, Richard Jesse. *The boy who went ape*
Williams, Carol Ann. *Booming Bella*

School – first day

Ahlberg, Janet. *Starting school*
Amado, Elisa. *What are you doing?*
Andrews, Julie. *Dumpy at school*
Anholt, Laurence. *Billy and the big new school*
Argueta, Jorge. *Moony Luna / Luna, Lunita Lunera*
Audet, Martine. *Martin on the moon*
Berenstain, Stan and Jan. *The Berenstain bears go to school*
Black, Harley. *Amazing magic school*
Blake, Stephanie. *I don't want to go to school!*
Bloch, Serge. *Butterflies in my stomach and other school hazards*
Bloom, Suzanne. *The bus for us*
Nuestro autobús / The bus for us
Borden, Louise. *Off to first grade*
Brillhart, Julie. *Molly rides the school bus*
Buzzeo, Toni. *Adventure Annie goes to kindergarten*
Carlson, Nancy. *First grade, here I come!*
Look out kindergarten, here I come!
Carlstrom, Nancy White. *It's your first day of school, Annie Claire*
Cazet, Denys. *Never spit on your shoes*
Chast, Roz. *Marco goes to school*
Child, Lauren. *I am too absolutely small for school*
Cocca-Leffler, Maryann. *Jack's talent*
Cohen, Miriam. *Will I have a friend?*, ill. by Ronald Himler
Will I have a friend?, ill. by Lillian Hoban
Colandro, Lucille. *There was an old lady who swallowed some books!*
Corey, Shana. *First graders from Mars: Horus's horrible day*
Cork, Barbara Taylor. *Sam starts school*
D'Amico, Carmela. *Ella, the elegant elephant*
Danneberg, Julie. *First day jitters*
Davis, Katie. *Kindergarten rocks!*
deGroat, Diane. *Brand-new pencils, brand-new books*
dePaola, Tomie. *Meet the Barkers*
Dewdney, Anna. *Llama Llama misses Mama*
Dodd, Emma. *Foxy*
Edwards, Becky. *My first day at nursery school*
Edwards, Pamela Duncan. *Dinosaur starts school*
Falwell, Cathryn. *David's drawing*
Ferguson, Sarah. *Emily's first day of school*
Forward, Toby. *What did you do today?*
Gantos, Jack. *Back to school for Rotten Ralph*
George, Lucy M. *Back to school Tortoise*

Goodman, Joan Elizabeth. *Bernard goes to school*
Gorbachev, Valeri. *Chicken chickens go to school*
Grandits, John. *Ten rules you absolutely must not break if you want to survive the school bus*
Greenfield, Eloise. *Me and Neesie*
Grindley, Sally. *It's my school*
Grogan, John. *Marley goes to school*
Hale, Nathan. *Yellowbelly and Plum go to school*
Harper, Jamie. *Miss Mingo and the first day of school*
Harper, Jessica. *A place called Kindergarten*
Harris, Robie H. *I am not going to school today*
Hartt-Sussman, Heather. *Noni is nervous*
Hays, Anna Jane. *Kindergarten countdown*
Henkes, Kevin. *Jessica*
Wemberly worried
Hennessy, B. G. *Mr. Ouchy's first day*
Hest, Amy. *Off to school, Baby Duck*
Hill, Eric. *Spot goes to school*
Jagtenberg, Yvonne. *Jack the wolf*
Janni, Rebecca. *Every cowgirl goes to school*
Johnston, Tony. *Off to kindergarten*
Kaufmann, Nancy. *Bye, Bye*
Kirk, David. *Little Miss Spider at Sunny Patch School*
Kroll, Virginia L. *On the way to kindergarten*
Langreuter, Jutta. *Little Bear goes to kindergarten*
Lasky, Kathryn. *Lunch bunnies*
Léonard, Marie. *Tibili, the little boy who didn't want to go to school*
Lester, Mike. *A is for salad*
Levitin, Sonia. *When Kangaroo goes to school*
London, Jonathan. *Froggy goes to school*
Lorenz, Albert. *The exceptionally, extraordinarily ordinary first day of school*
McCarty, Peter. *Henry in love*
McGhee, Alison. *Countdown to kindergarten*
McGinty, Alice B. *Eliza's kindergarten surprise*
McQuade, Jacqueline. *At preschool with Teddy Bear*
Mahoney, Daniel J. *Monstergarten*
Marshall, James. *Eugene*
Martin, Bill, Jr. *Kitty Cat, Kitty Cat, are you going to school?*
Millman, Isaac. *Moses goes to school*
Milord, Susan. *Happy school year!*
Mitchard, Jacquelyn. *Ready, set, school!*
Montanari, Eva. *A very full morning*
Moreillon, Judi. *Ready and waiting for you*
Morrow, Tara Jaye. *Panda goes to school*
Neubecker, Robert. *Wow! School!*
Novak, Matt. *Jazzbo goes to school*
Onyefulu, Ifeoma. *Deron goes to nursery school*
Ormerod, Jan. *When an elephant comes to school*
Pak, Soyung. *Sumi's first day of school ever*
Parish, Herman. *Amelia Bedelia's first day of school*
Parr, Todd. *Otto goes to school*
Pennypacker, Sara. *Stuart's cape*
Pérez, L. King. *First day in grapes*
Plourde, Lynn. *You're wearing that to school?!*
Poydar, Nancy. *First day, hooray!*
Preller, James. *A pirate's guide to first grade*
Quackenbush, Robert M. *First grade jitters*
Radabaugh, Melinda Beth. *Going to school*
Rankin, Joan. *First day*
Recorvits, Helen. *My name is Yoon*
Robbins, Beth. *Tom's first day at school*
Rockwell, Anne. *First day of school*
Welcome to kindergarten
Rodman, Mary Ann. *First grade stinks!*
Rosenberry, Vera. *Vera's first day of school*
Rouss, Sylvia A. *Sammy Spider's first day of school*
Rubel, Nicole. *Ham and Pickles*
Rusackas, Francesca. *I love you all day long*
Schaefer, Lola M. *Frankie Stein starts school*
Schmid, Paul. *Oliver and his alligator*
Schwartz, Amy. *Annabelle Swift, kindergartner*
Scotton, Rob. *Splat the cat*
Sierra, Judy. *We love our school!*
Slate, Joseph. *Miss Bindergarten gets ready for kindergarten*
Smalls-Hector, Irene. *Beginning school*
Stampler, Ann Redisch. *Go home, Mrs. Beekman!*
Stevenson, James. *That dreadful day*
Stewart, Amber. *Puddle's new school*
Stuve-Bodeen, Stephanie. *Elizabeti's school*
Tanner, Suzy-Jane. *Tinyflock Nursery School*
Taulbert, Clifton L. *Little Cliff's first day of school*
Uegaki, Chieri. *Suki's kimono*
Veldkamp, Tjibbe. *The school trip*
Vernick, Audrey. *Is your buffalo ready for kindergarten?*
Wells, Rosemary. *Emily's first 100 days of school*
How many? How much?
Timothy goes to school
Whybrow, Ian. *Harry and the dinosaurs go to school*
Wild, Margaret. *Tom goes to kindergarten*
Winget, Susan. *Tucker's four-carrot school day*
Winters, Kay. *This school year will be the best!*
Wright, Michael. *Jake starts school*
Yamashita, Haruo. *Seven little mice go to school*
Yankovic, Al. *My new teacher and me!*
Yum, Hyewon. *Mom, it's my first day of kindergarten!*

School – nursery

Alexander, Claire. *Lucy and the bully*
Bottner, Barbara. *An annoying ABC*
Brandt, Amy. *Benjamin comes back / Benjamin regresa*
When Katie was our teacher / Cuando Katie era nuestra maestra
Chodos-Irvine, Margaret. *Best best friends*
Codell, Esme Raji. *It's time for preschool!*
Cole, Joanna. *When Mommy and Daddy go to work*
Cousins, Lucy. *Maisy goes to preschool*
Day, Alexandra. *Carl goes to daycare*
Edvall, Lilian. *The rabbit who longed for home*
Edwards, Becky. *My first day at nursery school*
Elliott, David. *Hunter's best friend at school*
Gary, Meredith. *Sometimes you get what you want*
Golan, Avirama. *Little Naomi, Little Chick*
Henkes, Kevin. *Wemberly worried*
Hughes, Shirley. *Alfie and the big boys*
Korngold, Jamie S. *Sadie and the big mountain*
Kroll, Virginia L. *Everybody has a teddy*
Larsen, Andrew. *Bella and the bunny*
McQuade, Jacqueline. *At preschool with Teddy Bear*
Murkoff, Heidi Eisenberg. *What to expect at preschool*
Onyefulu, Ifeoma. *Deron goes to nursery school*
Rankin, Joan. *First day*
Rockwell, Anne. *My preschool*
President's Day
Rogers, Fred. *Going to day care*
Schaefer, Carole Lexa. *Someone says*
Schwartz, Amy. *The boys teams*
Senisi, Ellen B. *Hurray for pre-K!*
Sierra, Judy. *Preschool to the rescue*
Sturges, Philemon. *I love school*
Tanner, Suzy-Jane. *Tinyflock Nursery School*

Weeks, Sarah. *My somebody special*
Willems, Mo. *Knuffle Bunny too*

School teachers *see* Careers – teachers

Science

Adler, David A. *Redwoods are the tallest trees in the world*
Things that float and things that don't
Alberti, Theresa Jarosz. *Out and about at the planetarium*
Aliki. *Corn is maize*
Digging up dinosaurs
Dinosaurs are different
Fossils tell of long ago
The long lost coelacanth and other living fossils
My feet
My hands
My visit to the dinosaurs
A weed is a flower
Wild and woolly mammoths
Allen, Judy. *Are you a butterfly?*
Are you a grasshopper?
Are you a ladybug?
Are you a snail?
Are you an ant?
Allen, Pamela. *Who sank the boat?*
Anderson, Stephen Axel. *I know the moon*
Arnold, Caroline. *Too hot? too cold?*
Arnosky, Jim. *All about deer*
Crinkleroot's guide to knowing butterflies and moths
Dolphins on the sand
Gobble it up!
Asch, Frank. *The sun is my favorite star*
Atkins, Jeannine. *Mary Anning and the sea dragon*
Baby animals
Bang, Molly. *Living sunlight*
My light
Ocean sunlight
Barner, Bob. *Stars, stars, stars*
Barnett, Mac. *Oh no!*
Berenstain, Stan and Jan. *The Berenstain bears' science fair*
Berger, Melvin. *Brrr! a book about polar animals*
Buzz! a book about insects
Dive! a book of deep sea creatures
Early humans
Germs make me sick!
How do airplanes fly?
How's the weather?
Look out for turtles!
Oil spill!
Spinning spiders
Switch on, switch off
Why I sneeze, shiver, hiccup, and yawn
Berne, Jennifer. *Manfish*
Berry, Lynne. *What floats in a moat?*
Boothroyd, Jennifer. *What is a gas?*
Branley, Franklyn M. *Air is all around you*
Comets
Down comes the rain
Earthquakes
Eclipse
Flash, crash, rumble, and roll
Floating in space
Gravity is a mystery
Light and darkness
The planets in our solar system
Rain and hail
The sky is full of stars
Snow is falling
The sun, our nearest star
Sunshine makes the seasons
Tornado alert
Volcanoes, ill. by Megan Lloyd
Volcanoes, ill. by Marc Simont
What makes a magnet?
What makes day and night
What the moon is like
Brighton, Catherine. *Galileo's treasure box*
Brown, Don. *Rare treasure*
Carrick, Carol. *Patrick's dinosaurs*
Cash, Megan Montague. *What makes the seasons?*
Cassino, Mark, with Jon Nelson. *The story of snow*
Cobb, Vicki. *I fall down*
I get wet
I see myself
Open your eyes
Cole, Joanna. *How you were born*
The magic school bus and the climate challenge
The magic school bus and the science fair expedition
The magic school bus in the time of the dinosaurs
The magic school bus inside a beehive
The magic school bus inside a hurricane
The magic school bus inside the earth
The magic school bus inside the human body
The magic school bus lost in the solar system
The magic school bus on the ocean floor
My puppy is born
Davies, Jacqueline. *The boy who drew birds*
Dennard, Deborah. *Lemur landing*
Diffily, Deborah. *Jurassic shark*
Dorros, Arthur. *Ant cities*
The fungus that ate my school
Dotlich, Rebecca Kai. *What is science?*
Drummond, Allan. *Energy island*
Edwards, Wallace. *The extinct files*
Egan, Tim. *The experiments of Doctor Vermin*
Ferri, Giuliano. *Little Tad grows up*
Flanagan, Alice K. *Rocks*
Sunshine
Water
Weather
Wind
Gibbons, Gail. *Dinosaur discoveries*
Exploring the deep, dark sea
From seed to plant
Galaxies, galaxies!
Monarch butterfly
Prehistoric animals
Sharks
Soaring with the wind
Sun up, sun down
Glaser, Linda. *Magnificent monarchs*
Goldin, Augusta. *Ducks don't get wet*
Greenstein, Elaine. *The goose man*
Greenwood, Rosie. *I wonder why volcanoes blow their tops*
Harrison, David L. *Caves*
Earthquakes
Heller, Ruth. *Chickens aren't the only ones*
Hickling, Meg. *Boys, girls and body science*
Hirst, Robin. *My place in space*
Hiscock, Bruce. *Ookpik*
Hodge, Deborah. *Ants*
Bees

Eagles
Salmon
Holderness, Jackie. *What is a shadow?*
Hollenbeck, Kathleen M. *Islands of ice*
Hopkinson, Deborah. *The humblebee hunter*
Hort, Lenny. *Did dinosaurs eat pizza?*
Jenkins, Priscilla Belz. *A nest full of eggs*
Jenkins, Steve. *How to clean a hippopotamus*
Jolivet, Joëlle. *Almost everything*
Zoo-ology
Jordan, Helene J. *How a seed grows*
Kalz, Jill. *Northern lights*
Karas, G. Brian. *Atlantic*
Kleven, Elisa. *Glasswings*
Klingel, Cynthia Fitterer. *Deserts*
Knudsen, Michelle. *Argus*
Bugged!
A moldy mystery
Krebs, Laurie. *The beeman*, ill. by Valeria Cis
The beeman, ill. by Melissa Iwai
Kudlinski, Kathleen V. *Boy, were we wrong about dinosaurs!*
Boy, were we wrong about the solar system!
Lasky, Kathryn. *Science fair bunnies*
Lauber, Patricia. *Be a friend to trees*
Snakes are hunters
Who eats what?
Lehn, Barbara. *What is a scientist?*
Lobb, Janice. *Color and noise! Let's play with toys!*
Counting sheep! How do we sleep?
Dig and sow! How do plants grow?
Listen and see! What's on TV?
Locker, Thomas. *Sky tree*
Loewen, Nancy. *Busy buzzers*
Lunde, Darrin. *Hello, bumblebee bat*
Lyon, George Ella. *All the water in the world*
McCurry, Kristen. *Safari babies*
McMillan, Bruce. *Counting wildflowers*
McNamara, Margaret. *How many seeds in a pumpkin?*
McQuade, Jacqueline. *Small babies*
Maestro, Betsy. *How do apples grow?*
Why do leaves change color?
Manning, Mick. *Snap!*
Markle, Sandra. *Creepy, crawly baby bugs*
Sneaky, spinning, baby spiders
Mason, Adrienne. *Lu and Clancy sound off*
Snakes
Mayer, Lynne. *Newton and me*
Morrison, Gordon. *A drop of water*
Nagda, Anne Whitehead. *World above the clouds*
Offill, Jenny. *11 experiments that failed*
Parker, Michael. *You are a star!*
Parker, Nancy Winslow. *Bugs*
Patkau, Karen. *Creatures*
Peters, Lisa Westberg. *The sun, the wind and the rain*
Water's way
Pettenati, Jeanne K. *Galileo's journal, 1609–1610*
Pfeffer, Wendy. *From tadpole to frog*
Wiggling worms at work
Pfister, Marcus. *Ava's poppy*
Pipe, Jim. *What makes it swing?*
Polacco, Patricia. *Meteor!*
Posada, Mia. *Dandelions, stars in the grass*
Guess what is growing inside this egg
Poydar, Nancy. *No fair science fair*
Pringle, Laurence P. *Crows*
Snakes
Raab, Brigitte. *Where does pepper come from?*
Rau, Dana Meachen. *Mars*
Reynolds, Aaron. *Carnivores*
Rockwell, Anne. *Clouds*
One bean
What's so bad about gasoline?
Rotter, Charles. *Seals*
Walruses
Ryan, Pam Muñoz. *How do you raise a raisin?*
Ryder, Joanne. *Rainbow wings*
Where butterflies grow
Sabuda, Robert. *Encyclopedia prehistorica: mega-beasts*
Encyclopedia prehistorica: sharks and other seamonsters
Sadler, Marilyn. *Alistair's time machine*
St. Pierre, Stephanie. *Cheetahs*
Jaguars
Leopards
Lynx
Siberian tigers
Sayre, April Pulley. *Army ant parade*
Dig, wait, listen
The hungry hummingbird
Schaefer, Lola M. *Lifetime*
Schanzer, Rosalyn. *How Ben Franklin stole the lightning*
Schwartz, David M. *If you hopped like a frog*
Seuling, Barbara. *Flick a switch*
From head to toe
Shea, Kitty. *Out and about at the science center*
Showers, Paul. *A drop of blood*
Ears are for hearing
Hear your heart
Look at your eyes
Sleep is for everyone
Where does the garbage go?
Sierra, Judy. *The secret science project that almost ate school*
Sill, Cathryn. *Wetlands*
Sklansky, Amy E. *Where do chicks come from?*
Steig, William. *The toy brother*
Sykes, Julie. *Little Rocket's special star*
Tagholm, Sally. *The frog*
Tang, Greg. *Math fables too*
Toft, Kim Michelle. *Neptune's nursery*
Tomecek, Steve. *Dirt*
Tresselt, Alvin R. *Rain drop splash*
Van Woerkom, Dorothy. *Hidden messages*
Vern, Alex. *Where do frogs come from?*
Verstraete, Larry. *S is for scientists*
Voake, Steve. *Insect detective*
Wallace, Nancy Elizabeth. *Pond walk*
Rocks! rocks! rocks!
Wells, Robert E. *Did a dinosaur drink this water?*
Why do elephants need the sun?
Yolen, Jane. *Welcome to the icehouse*
Zoehfeld, Kathleen Weidner. *How mountains are made*
Secrets of the garden
What lives in a shell?
What's alive?

Scorpions

Emberley, Rebecca. *The crocodile and the scorpion*

Scuba diving *see* Sports – skin diving

Sea & seashore

Ahlberg, Allan. *The baby in the hat*
Aliki. *Those summers*
Arnold, Caroline. *Giant shark*
Arnosky, Jim. *Parrotfish and sunken ships*
Turtle in the sea
Asch, Frank. *Sand cake*
Ashforth, Camilla. *Willow by the sea*
Axelrod, Amy. *Pigs on a blanket*
Bailey, Linda. *Stanley at sea*
Baker, Jeannie. *The hidden forest*
Bang, Molly. *Ocean sunlight*
Yellow ball
Barclay, Jane. *Going on a journey to the sea*
Belton, Robyn. *Herbert*
Berger, Melvin. *Dive! a book of deep sea creatures*
Oil spill!
Berkes, Marianne. *Seashells by the seashore*
Berne, Jennifer. *Manfish*
Biro, Maureen Boyd. *Walking with Maga*
Blackstone, Stella. *An island in the sun*
Secret seahorse
Secret seahorse [board book]
Bouler, Olivia. *Olivia's birds*
Brenner, Barbara A. *One small place by the sea*
Brown, Marc. *D. W. all wet*
Brown, Margaret Wise. *Sneakers, the seaside cat*
Buckingham, Matt. *Bright Stanley*
Bunting, Eve. *Ducky*
Burdett, Lois. *Twelfth night for kids*
Burnard, Damon. *I spy in the ocean*
Burningham, John. *Come away from the water, Shirley*
Butterworth, Chris. *Sea horse*
Buzzeo, Toni. *The sea chest*
Calhoun, Mary. *Henry the sailor cat*
Carle, Eric. *A house for Hermit Crab*
10 little rubber ducks
Casin, Sheridan. *Little Turtle and the song of the sea*
Chin, Jason. *Coral reefs*
Coffey, Maria. *A cat adrift*
Cohen, Miriam. *See you in second grade!*
Cole, Joanna. *The magic school bus on the ocean floor*
Coombs, Kate. *Water sings blue*
Cottle, Joan. *Miles away from home*
Cousins, Lucy. *Hooray for fish!*
Maisy goes on vacation
Cowell, Cressida. *Hiccup the seasick Viking*
Cumberbatch, Judy. *Can you hear the sea?*
Dahl, Michael. *One giant splash*
Starry arms
Daly, Niki. *Why the sun and moon live in the sky*
Davies, Jacqueline. *The house takes a vacation*
Davies, Nicola. *Oceans and seas*
One tiny turtle
Day, Jan. *The pirate, Pink*
Pirate Pink and treasures of the reef
Demas, Corinne. *The boy who was generous with salt*
DiCamillo, Kate. *Louise*
Dickson, Louise. *The vanishing cat*
Domanska, Janina. *If all the seas were one sea*
Dunning, Joan. *Seabird in the forest*
Ehrlich, H. M. *Gotcha, Louie!*
Louie's goose
Elliott, David. *In the sea*
Engels-Fietzek, Petra. *Sophie and the seagull*
Field, Eugene. *Wynken, Blynken, and Nod*
Wynken, Blynken and Nod
Fisher, Leonard Everett. *Sky, sea, the jetty, and me*
Fitzpatrick, Marie-Louise. *You, me and the big blue sea*
Ford, Christine. *Ocean's child*
Formento, Alison. *These seas count!*
Frasier, Debra. *Out of the ocean*
Freymann, Saxton. *One lonely seahorse*
Galloway, Ruth. *Fidgety fish*
Gay, Marie-Louise. *Stella, star of the sea*
Geist, Ken. *The three little fish and the big bad shark*
Gibbons, Gail. *Coral reefs*
Exploring the deep, dark sea
Gibbs, Edward. *I spy under the sea*
Goudey, Alice E. *Houses from the sea*
Grassby, Donna. *A seaside alphabet*
Guiberson, Brenda Z. *Into the sea*
Gutman, Anne. *Gaspard at the seashore*
Hamilton, K. R. *This is the ocean*
Harris, Trudy. *Pattern fish*
Harshman, Terry Webb. *Does a sea cow say moo?*
Hayashi, Leslie Ann. *Fables from the sea*
Heidbreder, Robert. *A sea-wishing day*
Hines, Anna Grossnickle. *Gramma's walk*
Hodgkins, Fran. *Between the tides*
Horowitz, Ruth. *Crab moon*
Hort, Lenny. *We're going on a treasure hunt*
Hunter, Anne. *What's in the tide pool?*
Inkpen, Mick. *Sandcastle*
Jackson, Ellen. *The seven seas*
Johnson, Angela. *Joshua by the sea*
Karas, G. Brian. *Atlantic*
Klingel, Cynthia Fitterer. *Oceans*
Kranking, Kathy. *The ocean is . . .*
Kudlinski, Kathleen V. *The seaside switch*
Kuskin, Karla. *I am me*
Lawler, Janet. *Ocean counting*
Lawlor, Laurie. *Rachel Carson and her book that changed the world*
Lionni, Leo. *Swimmy*
Loomis, Christine. *Scuba bunnies*
McCarthy, Meghan. *The adventures of Patty and the big red bus*
McCarty, Peter. *Hondo and Fabian*
McCloskey, Robert. *One morning in Maine*
Time of wonder
McCurry, Kristen. *Ocean babies*
MacDonald, Margaret Read. *Surf war!*
McDonald, Megan. *Is this a house for Hermit Crab?*
McNaughton, Colin. *Oomph!*
Mahy, Margaret. *A summery Saturday morning*
Mason, Janeen I. *Ocean commotion*
Munsch, Robert N. *A promise is a promise*
Nelson, Robert Lyn. *Ocean friends*
Neubecker, Robert. *Wow! Ocean!*
Nivola, Claire A. *Life in the ocean*
Nolan, Dennis. *Sea of dreams*
O'Connor, George. *Ker-splash!*
Pallotta, Jerry. *Dory story*
Ocean counting: odd numbers
Peet, Bill. *Cyrus the unsinkable sea serpent*
Kermit the hermit
Perrin, Martine. *Look who's there!*
Peters, Lisa Westberg. *The sun, the wind and the rain*
Pfeffer, Wendy. *Life in a coral reef*
Pfister, Marcus. *Milo and the mysterious island*
Rainbow fish ABC
Rainbow fish and the sea monsters' cave
Pollard, Nik. *The tide*
Raff, Courtney Granet. *Giant of the sea*

Rand, Gloria. *Sailing home*
Reiser, Lynn. *Little clam*
Riddell, Chris. *Platypus*
Rockwell, Anne. *Ferryboat ride!*
Roop, Peter. *Down east in the ocean*
Rose, Deborah Lee. *Into the A, B, sea*
Ocean babies
Rylant, Cynthia. *The whales*
Sabuda, Robert. *Encyclopedia prehistorica: sharks and other seamonsters*
St. Pierre, Stephanie. *What the sea saw*
San Souci, Daniel. *The rabbit and the dragon king*
San Souci, Robert D. *Brave Margaret*
Nicholas Pipe
Santoro, Lucio. *Wild oceans*
Sarcone-Roach, Julia. *Subway story*
Schwarz, Viviane. *Shark and Lobster's amazing undersea adventure*
Serafini, Frank. *Looking closely along the shore*
Seven, John. *The ocean story*
Shepard, Aaron. *The sea king's daughter*
Sherry, Kevin. *I'm the best artist in the ocean*
I'm the biggest thing in the ocean
Simmons, Jane. *Ebb and Flo and the greedy gulls*
Sís, Peter. *An ocean world*
Ship ahoy!
Slate, Jenny. *Marcel the shell with shoes on*
Sperring, Mark. *Mermaid dreams*
Stevenson, James. *July*
Which one is Whitney?
Stevenson, Robert Louis. *Block city*, ill. by Daniel Kirk
Block city, ill. by Ashley Wolff
Stone, Lynn M. *Getting around*
Life of the kelp forest
Strauss, Susan. *When woman became the sea*
Sutherland, Marc. *MacMurtrey's wall*
Taylor, Eleanor. *Beep, beep, let's go!*
Titherington, Jeanne. *Baby's boat*
Toft, Kim Michelle. *Neptune's nursery*
Tokuda, Wendy. *Humphrey the lost whale*
Townsend, Emily Rose. *Seals*
Tresselt, Alvin R. *Hide and seek fog*
Tucker, Kathy. *Do pirates take baths?*
Turkle, Brinton. *Do not open*
Van Dusen, Chris. *Down to the sea with Mr. Magee*
Viva, Frank. *A long way away*
Waddell, Martin. *The big big sea*
Sailor Bear
Ward, Helen. *Old shell, new shell*
Ward, Jennifer. *Somewhere in the ocean*
Williams, Garth. *Benjamin's treasure*
Winkelman, Barbara Gaines. *Puffer's surprise*
Winton, Tim. *The deep*
Wolkstein, Diane. *The day Ocean came to visit*
Wood, Audrey. *The deep blue sea*
Yaccarino, Dan. *The fantastic undersea life of Jacques Cousteau*
Yee, Brenda Shannon. *Sand castle*
Yoon, Salina. *Penguin on vacation*
Zeman, Ludmila. *Sindbad*
Ziefert, Harriet. *Beach party!*
Wiggle like an octopus
Zoehfeld, Kathleen Weidner. *What lives in a shell?*

Sea & seashore – beaches

Ashman, Linda. *To the beach!*
Beardshaw, Rosalind. *Grandma's beach*
Berry, Lynne. *Duck dunks*
Breen, Steve. *The secret of Santa's island*
Briant, Ed. *A day at the beach*
Cash, Megan Montague. *I saw the sea and the sea saw me*
Clements, Andrew. *Because your daddy loves you*
Cooper, Elisha. *Beach*
Docherty, Thomas. *To the beach*
Elya, Susan Middleton. *Bebé goes to the beach*
Estefan, Gloria. *Noelle's treasure tale*
Frazee, Marla. *A couple of boys have the best week ever*
Greenberg, Melanie Hope. *Mermaids on parade*
Grey, Mini. *Traction Man and the beach odyssey*
Hill, Eric. *Spot goes to the beach*
Hubbell, Patricia. *Sea, sand, me!*
Huneck, Stephen. *Sally goes to the beach*
Inkpen, Mick. *Kipper's sunny day*
Johnson, Crockett. *Magic beach*
Keller, Holly. *Miranda's beach day*
Konagaya, Kiyomi. *Beach feet*
Lee, Suzy. *Wave*
Lies, Brian. *Bats at the beach*
Mathers, Petra. *Lottie's new beach towel*
Monroe, Chris. *Monkey with a tool belt and the seaside shenanigans*
Moore, Jodi. *When a dragon moves in*
Murphy, Patti Beling. *Elinor and Violet*
Naylor, Phyllis Reynolds. *Please do feed the bears*
Oxenbury, Helen. *Tom and Pippo on the beach*
Pendziwol, Jean E. *A treasure at sea for dragon and me*
Perry, Robert. *Down at the Seaweed Café*
Rau, Dana Meachen. *Stroll by the sea*
Robertson, M. P. *The sandcastle*
Rockwell, Anne. *At the beach*
Roosa, Karen. *Beach day*
Rotner, Shelley. *Senses at the seashore*
Ryan, Pam Muñoz. *Hello, Ocean!*
Hello ocean / Hola mar
Sierra, Judy. *Ballyhoo Bay*
Sís, Peter. *Beach ball*
Soman, David. *Ladybug Girl at the beach*
Stevenson, James. *The worst person in the world at Crab Beach*
Stojic, Manya. *Wet pebbles under our feet*
Thaler, Mike. *Pig Little*
Wallace, Nancy Elizabeth. *Shells! Shells! Shells!*
Walsh, Ellen Stoll. *Hamsters to the rescue*
Watt, Mélanie. *Scaredy Squirrel at the beach*
Waugh, Peter. *The great cannon beach mouse caper*
Weninger, Brigitte. *Miko goes on vacation*
Wiesner, David. *Flotsam*
Williams, Karen Lynn. *A beach tail*
Willis, Jeanne. *I'm sure I saw a dinosaur*
Yektai, Niki. *Bears at the beach*
Yoon, Salina. *At the beach*
Ziefert, Harriet. *Mighty Max*

Sea serpents *see* Monsters; Mythical creatures

Seahorses *see* Fish – seahorses

Seashore *see* Sand; Sea & seashore – beaches

Seasons

Adler, David A. *It's time to sleep, it's time to dream*

Adoff, Arnold. *In for winter, out for spring*
Alexander, Cecil Frances. *All things bright and beautiful*
Ammon, Richard. *An Amish year*
Anholt, Catherine. *Sun, snow, stars, sky*
Anno, Mitsumasa. *Anno's counting book*
Arnosky, Jim. *Outdoors on foot*
Austin, Heather. *Visiting Aunt Sylvia's*
Banks, Kate. *The great blue house*
Barack, Marcy. *Season song*
Berger, Carin. *Forever friends*
Berner, Rotraut Susanne. *In the town all year 'round*
Birnbaum, Abe. *Green eyes*
Blexbolex. *Seasons*
Branley, Franklyn M. *Sunshine makes the seasons*
Brown, Kerry. *Tupag the dreamer*
Brown, Margaret Wise. *The little island*
Love songs of the little bear
Browne, Anthony. *Voices in the park*
Bruchac, Joseph. *Thirteen moons on turtle's back*
Brunhoff, Laurent de. *Meet Babar and his family*
Burrowes, Adjoa J. *Grandma's purple flowers*
Carle, Eric. *The tiny seed*
Carlstrom, Nancy White. *How does the wind walk?*
Cash, Megan Montague. *What makes the seasons?*
Cooper, Elisha. *Farm*
Dahl, Michael. *From the garden*
Deady, Kathleen W. *All year long*
Edwards, Richard. *Copy me, Copycub*
Ehlert, Lois. *Red leaf, yellow leaf*
Ewart, Claire. *The giant*
Farrar, Sid. *The year comes round*
Fisher, Valorie. *Everything I need to know before I'm five*
Fleming, Denise. *In the small, small pond*
Frisch, Aaron. *The lonely pine*
Geisert, Bonnie. *Mountain town*
George, Jean Craighead. *Dear Rebecca, winter is here*
Look to the north
George, Kristine O'Connell. *Old Elm speaks*
Gershator, Phillis. *Listen, listen*
Gibbons, Gail. *Farming*
The reasons for seasons
The seasons of Arnold's apple tree
Glaser, Linda. *Hello, squirrels!*
Gomi, Taro. *Spring is here*
Gray, Luli. *Ant and Grasshopper*
Greene, Rhonda Gowler. *Daddy is a cozy hug*
Mommy is a soft, warm kiss
Greenstein, Elaine. *As big as you*
Guenther, James. *Turnagain, Ptarmigan, where did you go?*
Hall, Donald. *Ox-cart man*
Hall, Zoe. *The apple pie tree*
Henkes, Kevin. *Old Bear*
Hewitt, Sally. *All year round*
Woods and meadows
Hines, Anna Grossnickle. *Pieces, a year in poems and quilts*
Hoberman, Mary Ann. *Right outside my window*
Howell, Will C. *I call it sky*
Hubery, Julia. *A friend for all seasons*
Hunter, Anne. *Possum's harvest moon*
Issa, Kobayashi. *Today and today*
Johnson, Amy Crane. *Cinnamon and the April shower / Canela y el aguacero de abril*
Karas, G. Brian. *The village garage*
Katz, Bobbi. *Once around the sun*
Kespert, Deborah. *Rain and shine*
Kinsey-Warnock, Natalie. *From dawn till dusk*
Kirk, David. *Little bunny, Biddle bunny*
Kleven, Elisa. *Cozy light, cozy night*
Krauss, Ruth. *The growing story*
Lasky, Kathryn. *Mommy's hands*
Lesser, Carolyn. *What a wonderful day to be a cow*
Lin, Grace. *Our seasons*
Lionni, Leo. *A busy year*
Lister, Mary. *The Winter King and the Summer Queen*
Livingston, Myra Cohn. *Calendar*
Lobel, Arnold. *Frog and Toad all year*
Locker, Thomas. *Sky tree*
London, Jonathan. *Park beat*
McClure, Nikki. *Apple*
McGhee, Alison. *Making a friend*
Marshak, S. *The Month-Brothers*
Martin, Bill, Jr. *I love our Earth*
The turning of the year
Marzollo, Jean. *Once upon a springtime*
Matheson, Christie. *Tap the magic tree*
Messinger, Carla. *When the shadbush blooms*
Millard, Glenda. *Isabella's garden*
Murphy, Mary. *Here comes spring, and summer and fall and winter*
Näslund, Gorel Kristina. *Our apple tree*
Nikola-Lisa, W. *The year with Grandma Moses*
Oppenheim, Joanne. *Have you seen trees?*
Paul, Ann Whitford. *The seasons sewn*
Pfister, Marcus. *Ava's poppy*
Pollock, Penny. *When the moon is full*
Provensen, Alice. *A book of seasons*
The year at Maple Hill Farm
Raczka, Bob. *Guyku*
Rau, Dana Meachen. *In the yard*
Rockwell, Anne. *Ducklings and pollywogs*
First comes spring
Rose, Deborah Lee. *All the seasons of the year*
Rosenberry, Vera. *Run, jump, whiz, splash*
Ross, Michael Elsohn. *Earth cycles*
Rotner, Shelley. *Every season*
Ryder, Joanne. *Toad by the road*
Saltzberg, Barney. *All around the seasons*
Sayre, April Pulley. *Eat like a bear*
Schertle, Alice. *Very hairy bear*
Schubert, Leda. *Here comes Darrell*
Schulman, Janet. *A bunny for all seasons*
Seven, John. *A year with friends*
Shields, Carol Diggory. *Month by month a year goes round*
Siddals, Mary McKenna. *Tell me a season*
Sidman, Joyce. *Red sings from treetops*
Spinelli, Eileen. *Summerbath, winterbath*
Stead, Philip C. *Bear has a story to tell*
Stein, David Ezra. *Leaves*
Stewart, Sarah. *The money tree*
Tafuri, Nancy. *Snowy flowy blowy*
Takabayashi, Mari. *I live in Brooklyn*
Taylor, Theodore. *Hello, Arctic!*
Thong, Roseanne. *Gai see*
Train, Mary. *Time for the fair*
Trapani, Iza. *The bear went over the mountain*
Trimble, Marcia. *Flower Green*
Udry, Janice May. *A tree is nice*
Verdet, Andre. *All about time*
Wells, Rosemary. *Night sounds, morning colors*
Whitehouse, Patricia. *Seasons ABC*
Seasons 1 2 3
Wick, Walter. *Can you see what I see? cool collections*
Willems, Mo. *City dog, country frog*

Wilson, Sarah. *Friends and pals and brothers, too*
Wright, Joanna. *Bunnies on ice*
Yolen, Jane. *Welcome to the icehouse*
Zagwÿn, Deborah Turney. *Turtle spring*

Seasons – fall

Aesop. *The ant and the grasshopper*, ill. by Amy Lowry Poole
The ant and the grasshopper, ill. by Sara Rojo
Arnosky, Jim. *Every autumn comes the bear*
Berger, Carin. *The little yellow leaf*
Brenner, Tom. *And then comes Halloween*
Bunting, Eve. *Peepers*
The pumpkin fair
Burg, Ann. *Autumn walk*
Carr, Jan. *Dappled apples*
Chernesky, Felicia Sanzari. *Pick a circle, gather squares*
Emmett, Jonathan. *Leaf trouble*
Frank, John. *A chill in the air*
Freeman, Don. *One more acorn*
George, Lindsay Barrett. *In the woods*
Gerritsen, Paula. *Nuts*
Gibbons, Gail. *The pumpkin book*
Glaser, Linda. *It's fall*
Goldstone, Bruce. *Awesome autumn*
Hall, Zoe. *Fall leaves fall*
Harshman, Marc. *Red are the apples*
Hawk, Fran. *Count down to fall*
Hills, Tad. *Duck and Goose find a pumpkin*
Hirschi, Ron. *Fall*
Hoban, Julia. *Amy loves the wind*
Hopkins, Lee Bennett. *Merrily comes our harvest in*
Iwamura, Kazuo. *Hooray for fall!*
Jackson, Ellen. *The autumn equinox*
November
October
September
Jocelyn, Marthe. *Ready for autumn*
Koller, Jackie French. *Nickommoh!*
Lee, Huy Voun. *In the leaves*
Lenski, Lois. *Now it's fall*
Lipson, Eden Ross. *Applesauce season*
Maass, Robert. *A is for autumn*
When autumn comes
McCarty, Peter. *Fall ball*
McNamara, Margaret. *Fall leaf project*
Maestro, Betsy. *Why do leaves change color?*
Nidey, Kelli. *When autumn falls*
Pickering, Jimmy. *It's fall*
Plourde, Lynn. *Wild child*
Potter, Beatrix. *The tale of Squirrel Nutkin*
Raczka, Bob. *Fall mixed up*
Who loves the fall?
Rawlinson, Julia. *Fletcher and the falling leaves*
Robbins, Ken. *Autumn leaves*
Pumpkins
Rylant, Cynthia. *In November*
Schnur, Steven. *Autumn*
Schweninger, Ann. *Autumn days*
Shapiro, Jody Fickes. *Up, up, up! It's apple-picking time*
Slegers, Liesbet. *Fall leaves*
Spetter, Jung-Hee. *Lily and Trooper's fall*
Spinelli, Eileen. *I know it's autumn*
Now it is summer
Tafuri, Nancy. *The busy little squirrel*
Thayer, Tanya. *Fall*
Thompson, Lauren. *Mouse's first fall*
Tresselt, Alvin R. *Autumn harvest*
Van Allsburg, Chris. *The stranger*
Watson, Wendy. *Bedtime bunnies*
Whitehouse, Patricia. *Fall*
Wright, Maureen. *Sneeze, Big Bear, sneeze*
Ziefert, Harriet. *By the light of the harvest moon*
Zoehfeld, Kathleen Weidner. *Apples, apples*
Zolotow, Charlotte. *Say it!*

Seasons – spring

Arden, Carolyn. *Goose moon*
Bauer, Marion Dane. *In like a lion out like a lamb*
Beck, Andrea. *Elliot gets stuck*
Berenstain, Stan and Jan. *The Berenstain bears and the real Easter eggs*
Bourgeois, Paulette. *Franklin's baby sister*
Capucilli, Alyssa Satin. *Katy Duck is a caterpillar*
Carr, Jan. *Splish, splash, spring*
Chaconas, Dori. *Looking for Easter*
Chall, Marsha Wilson. *Sugarbush spring*
Cocca-Leffler, Maryann. *Let it rain*
De colores / Bright with colors
Ernst, Lisa Campbell. *Wake up, it's Spring!*
Esbaum, Jill. *Everything spring*
Fernandes, Eugenie. *Kitten's spring*
Florian, Douglas. *Handsprings*
Fogliano, Julie. *And then it's spring*
Fontes, Justine Korman. *Signs of spring*
Gerber, Carole. *Spring blossoms*
Gershator, Phillis. *Who's awake in springtime?*
Glaser, Linda. *It's spring*
Hillenbrand, Will. *Spring is here*
Hirschi, Ron. *Spring*
Hubbell, Patricia. *Hurray for spring!*
Hulme, Joy N. *Easter babies*
Hunter, Anne. *Possum and the peeper*
Iwamura, Kazuo. *Hooray for spring!*
Jackson, Ellen. *April*
March
May
The spring equinox
Jocelyn, Marthe. *Ready for spring*
Johnson, Crockett. *Will spring be early or will spring be late?*
Kimura, Ken. *999 frogs wake up*
Kinsey-Warnock, Natalie. *When spring comes*
Krauss, Ruth. *The happy day*
Lamstein, Sarah Marwil. *Big night for salamanders*
Lindbergh, Reeve. *North country spring*
Maass, Robert. *When spring comes*
Mansfield, Howard. *Hogwood steps out*
Miller, Edna. *Mousekin's Easter basket*
Minarik, Else Holmelund. *It's spring!*
Na, Il Sung. *Snow rabbit, spring rabbit*
Newman, Lesléa. *Skunk's spring surprise*
Peters, Lisa Westberg. *Cold little duck, duck, duck*
Pfister, Marcus. *Hopper*
Hopper hunts for spring
Pitcher, Caroline. *Are you spring?*
Plourde, Lynn. *Spring's sprung*
Poppy Bear
Raczka, Bob. *Spring things*
Rawlinson, Julia. *Fletcher and the springtime blossoms*
Ray, Mary Lyn. *Mud*
Rockwell, Anne. *My spring robin*
Rose, Deborah Lee. *The twelve days of springtime*
Schnur, Steven. *Spring*

Spring thaw
Schulman, Janet. *Countdown to spring*
Seuling, Barbara. *Spring song*
Shannon, George. *Spring: a haiku story*
Spetter, Jung-Hee. *Lily and Trooper's spring*
Thayer, Tanya. *Spring*
Thompson, Lauren. *Mouse's first spring*
Voake, Charlotte. *Tweedle - dee - dee*
von Olfers, Sibylle. *Mother Earth and her children*
Wallace, Nancy Elizabeth. *Paperwhite*
Walters, Catherine. *When will it be spring?*
Wells, Rosemary. *Forest of dreams*
Max's chocolate chicken
Whitehouse, Patricia. *Spring*
Wilde, Oscar. *The selfish giant*, ill. by S. Saelig Gallagher
The selfish giant, ill. by Fabian Negrin
The selfish giant, ill. by Lisbeth Zwerger
Wood, Audrey. *When the root children wake up*
Yee, Wong Herbert. *Who likes rain?*

Seasons – summer

Alarcón, Francisco X. *From the bellybutton of the moon and other summer poems / Del ombligo de la luna y otros poemas de verano*
Aliki. *Those summers*
Berenstain, Stan and Jan. *The Berenstain bears go to camp*
Brennan, Linda Crotta. *Marshmallow kisses*
Broach, Elise. *Wet dog!*
Bunting, Eve. *Sunflower house*
Crews, Nina. *One hot summer day*
Crisp, Marty. *Totally polar*
Day, Alexandra. *Carl's summer vacation*
English, Karen. *Hot day on Abbott Avenue*
Florian, Douglas. *Summersaults*
Frampton, David. *Mr. Ferlinghetti's poem*
Franco, Betsy. *Summer beat*
Freedman, Claire. *One magical day*
George, Lindsay Barrett. *Around the pond*
Gershator, Phillis. *Summer is summer*
Glaser, Linda. *It's summer*
Godwin, Laura. *Central Park serenade*
Greenberg, Melanie Hope. *Mermaids on parade*
Hakala, Marjorie Rose. *Mermaid dance*
Hayes, Karel. *The summer visitors*
Henkes, Kevin. *Grandpa and Bo*
Hesse, Karen. *Come on, rain*
Hirschi, Ron. *Summer*
Hughes, Susan. *Earth to Audrey*
Inkpen, Mick. *Hissss!*
Iwamura, Kazuo. *Hooray for summer!*
Jackson, Ellen. *August*
July
June
The summer solstice
Jocelyn, Marthe. *Ready for summer*
Kelley, Marty. *Summer stinks*
Korda, Lerryn. *It's vacation time*
Layton, Neal. *Hot, hot, hot*
Lewis, Kim. *One summer day*
Lister, Mary. *The Winter King and the Summer Queen*
London, Jonathan. *Sun dance, water dance*
Maass, Robert. *When summer comes*
McCloskey, Robert. *Time of wonder*
McClure, Nikki. *Mama, is it summer yet?*
Mahy, Margaret. *A summery Saturday morning*
Novak, Matt. *Flip flop bop*
Paulsen, Gary. *Canoe days*
Payne, Nina. *Summertime waltz*
Perry, Elizabeth. *Think cool thoughts*
Polacco, Patricia. *Mrs. Mack*
Posey, Lee. *Night rabbits*
Poydar, Nancy. *Cool Ali*
Raczka, Bob. *Summer wonders*
Scanlon, Elizabeth Garton. *All the world*
Scheer, Julian. *By the light of the captured moon*
Schnur, Steven. *Summer*
Spetter, Jung-Hee. *Lily and Trooper's summer*
Spinelli, Eileen. *Now it is summer*
Stevenson, James. *July*
Stroud, Bettye. *Down home at Miss Dessa's*
Thayer, Tanya. *Summer*
Thomas, Patricia. *Firefly mountain*
Van Leeuwen, Jean. *Touch the sky summer*
Weisburd, Stefi. *Barefoot: poems for naked feet*
Whitehouse, Patricia. *Summer*
Woodson, Jacqueline. *The other side*
Yee, Wong Herbert. *Summer days and nights*
Yolen, Jane. *Before the storm*
Zagwÿn, Deborah Turney. *The sea house*
Zolotow, Charlotte. *Summer is . . .*

Seasons – winter

Aesop. *The ant and the grasshopper*, ill. by Amy Lowry Poole
The ant and the grasshopper, ill. by Sara Rojo
Alarcón, Francisco X. *Iguanas in the snow and other winter poems / Iguanas en la nieve y otros poemas de invierno*
Arnosky, Jim. *Every autumn comes the bear*
Asch, Frank. *Good night, Baby Bear*
Mooncake
Baird, Audrey B. *A cold snap!*
Baker, Keith. *No two alike*
Bauer, Marion Dane. *The longest night*
Bean, Jonathan. *Big snow*
Berger, Carin. *A perfect day*
Berry, Lynne. *Duck skates*
Blackaby, Susan. *Brownie Groundhog and the February Fox*
Brownie Groundhog and the wintry surprise
Blades, Ann. *Mary of mile 18*
Blumenthal, Deborah. *Ice palace*
Brett, Jan. *The three snow bears*
Brunelle, Nicholas. *Snow moon*
Burton, Virginia Lee. *Katy and the big snow*
Butler, M. Christina. *One winter's day*
The smiley snowman
Snow friends
Caple, Kathy. *Hillary to the rescue*
Carlstrom, Nancy White. *Mama, will it snow tonight?*
The snow speaks
Carr, Jan. *Frozen noses*
Carrick, Carol. *The polar bears are hungry*
Casanova, Mary. *Utterly otterly night*
Cassino, Mark, with Jon Nelson. *The story of snow*
Chaconas, Dori. *On a wintry morning*
Chessa, Francesca. *Holly's red boots*
Child, Lauren. *Snow is my favorite and my best*
Christelow, Eileen. *The five-dog night*
Cooper, Elisha. *Bear dreams*
Cote, Nancy. *It feels like snow*
Cotten, Cynthia. *Snow ponies*
Crews, Nina. *Snowball*

Wallace, Nancy Elizabeth. *Snow [board book]*
Walters, Catherine. *The magical snowman*
When will it be spring?
Ward, Lindsay. *When Blue met Egg*
Watanabe, Shigeo. *Ice cream is falling!*
Watts, Bernadette. *The smallest snowflake*
Wellington, Monica. *Bunny's first snowflake*
Wells, Rosemary. *Forest of dreams*
Whitehouse, Patricia. *Winter*
Whybrow, Ian. *Bella gets her skates on*
Harry and the snow king
Wilson, Karma. *Dinos in the snow!*
Winget, Susan. *Sam the Snowman*
Wolff, Ashley. *Baby Bear counts one*
Wright, Maureen. *Sleep, Big Bear, sleep!*
Yamashita, Haruo. *Seven little mice have fun on the ice*
Yee, Wong Herbert. *Tracks in the snow*
Yolen, Jane. *Sleep, black bear, sleep*

Secrets *see* Behavior – secrets

Seeds

Alda, Arlene. *Morning glory Monday*
Anno, Mitsumasa. *Anno's magic seeds*
Aston, Dianna Hutts. *A seed is sleepy*
Bauld, Jane Scoggins. *Journey of the third seed*
Blackstone, Stella. *What's this?*
Buchanan, Jane. *Seed magic*
Carle, Eric. *The tiny seed*
Cave, Kathryn. *One child, one seed*
Christensen, Bonnie. *Plant a little seed*
Edwards, Nancy. *Glenna's seeds*
Galbraith, Kathryn O. *Planting the wild garden*
Geisert, Arthur. *The giant seed*
Gibbons, Gail. *From seed to plant*
Hall, Zoe. *The surprise garden*
Henkes, Kevin. *So happy!*
Himmelman, John. *A dandelion's life*
Honey, Elizabeth. *That's not a daffodil!*
Hubbell, Will. *Pumpkin Jack*
Jordan, Helene J. *How a seed grows*
Karon, Jan. *The trellis and the seed*
Kim, Sue. *How does a seed grow?*
Kottke, Jan. *From seed to pumpkin*
MacKay, Elly. *If you hold a seed*
Macken, JoAnn Early. *Flip, float, fly*
Middleton, Charlotte. *Nibbles*
Pak, Soyung. *A place to grow*
Pallotta, Jerry. *Who will plant a tree?*
Peterson, Cris. *Seed soil sun*
Pin, Isabel. *The seed*
Pizzoli, Greg. *The watermelon seed*
Ramirez, Melissa Bourbon. *The flight of the sunflower*
Robbins, Ken. *Seeds*
Rockwell, Anne. *One bean*
Roemer, Heidi Bee. *What kind of seeds are these?*
Santucci, Barbara. *Anna's corn*
Sasso, Sandy Eisenberg. *Naamah, Noah's wife*
Schaefer, Lola M. *This is the sunflower*
Swanson, Susan Marie. *To be like the sun*
Wallace, Nancy Elizabeth. *Planting seeds*
Seeds! Seeds! Seeds!
Walsh, Ellen Stoll. *Dot and Jabber and the great acorn mystery*
Wheeler, Eliza. *Miss Maple's seeds*

Seeing *see* Anatomy – eyes; Glasses; Disabilities – blindness; Senses – sight

Seeing eye dogs *see* Animals – service animals

Seeking better things *see* Behavior – seeking better things

Self-concept

Ackerman, Karen. *Bean's big day*
Adams, Diane. *I can do it myself!*
Adoff, Jaime. *Small fry*
Alexander, Claire. *Small Florence*
Aliki. *All by myself!*
Andrews, Julie. *Simeon's gift*
The very fairy princess
Appelt, Kathi. *Incredible me!*
Backker, Vera de. *Coco the koala*
Bansch, Helga. *Odd bird out*
Bar-el, Dan. *Not your typical dragon*
Barbero, Maria. *The bravest mouse*
Barnes, Brynne. *Colors of me*
Barnes, Laura T. *Ernest and the big itch*
Teeny tiny Ernest
Barnwell, Ysaye M. *No mirrors in my Nana's house*
Baryshnikov, Mikhail. *Because . . .*
Bea, Holly. *My spiritual alphabet book*
Bell, Cece. *Bee-Wigged*
Belton, Sandra. *Pictures for Miss Josie*
Bishop, Brett. *Clayton's path*
Blume, Judy. *The one in the middle is a green kangaroo*
Bonwill, Ann. *Naughty toes*
Borden, Louise. *A. Lincoln and me*
Boyce, Katie. *Hector the hermit crab*
Brennan, Eileen. *Dirtball Pete*
Brown, Lisa. *How to be*
Brown, Peter. *Mr. Tiger goes wild*
Browne, Anthony. *Willy the wimp*
Buchanan, Sue. *Mud Pie Annie*
Budnitz, Paul. *The hole in the middle*
Buehner, Caralyn. *Superdog, the heart of a hero*
Buitrago, Jairo. *Jimmy the greatest*
Bunting, Eve. *One green apple*
Carle, Eric. *The mixed-up chameleon*
Carlson, Nancy. *ABC, I like me!*
I like me
Think big!
Castle, Caroline. *For every child*
Catalanotto, Peter. *Matthew A.B.C.*
Cazet, Denys. *Will you read to me?*
Chen, Chih-Yuan. *The featherless chicken*
Cheng, Andrea. *Anna the bookbinder*
Chetkowski, Emily. *Pumpkin smile*
Clanton, Ben. *Mo's mustache*
Cocca-Leffler, Maryann. *Jack's talent*
Princess K.I.M. and the lie that grew
Cochran, Bill. *My parents are divorced, my elbows have nicknames, and other facts about me*
Cohen, Miriam. *No good in art*
Compestine, Ying Chang. *Crouching tiger*
Conway, David. *Errol and his extraordinary nose*
Corey, Shana. *First graders from Mars: Nergal and the Great Space Race*
First graders from Mars: The problem with Pelly
Cote, Nancy. *It's all about me!*

Milgrim, David. *How you got so smart*
Mills, Claudia. *Ziggy's blue-ribbon day*
Milway, Katie Smith. *Cappuccina goes to town*
Minarik, Else Holmelund. *Am I beautiful?*
Monks, Lydia. *The cat barked?*
Monnier, Miriam. *Just right*
Moore, Julianne. *Freckleface Strawberry*
Moss, Marissa. *Regina's big mistake*
Mueller, Doris L. *Small One's adventure*
Munsch, Robert N. *Makeup mess*
Murguia, Bethanie Deeney. *Zoe gets ready*
Murphy, Jill. *A piece of cake*
Nelson, Vaunda Micheaux. *Who will I be, Lord?*
Neubecker, Robert. *Courage of the blue boy*
Newman, Lesléa. *Miss Tutu's star*
Nishimura, Kae. *Dinah*
Nolan, Lucy A. *Jack Quack*
Nordling, Lee. *The bramble*
Obama, Barack. *Of thee I sing*
O'Connor, Jane. *Fancy Nancy*
Fancy Nancy: ooh la la! it's beauty day
Fancy Nancy and the posh puppy
Nancy la elegante / Fancy Nancy
Ready, set, skip!
Odone, Jamison. *Mole had everything*
Oram, Hiawyn. *Just Dog*
The wrong overcoat
Otoshi, Kathryn. *Zero*
Owen, Karen. *I could be, you could be*
Parr, Todd. *The okay book*
The thankful book
Peet, Bill. *Pamela Camel*
Pelley, Kathleen T. *Raj the bookstore tiger*
Peters, Bernadette. *Stella is a star!*
Pett, Mark. *The girl who never made mistakes*
Petty, Dini. *The queen, the bear and the bumblebee*
Pfister, Marcus. *Just the way you are*
Phinn, Gervase. *Who am I?*
Pinkney, Sandra L. *I am Latino*
Polacco, Patricia. *The art of Miss Chew*
The junkyard wonders
Prelutsky, Jack. *Me I am!*
Raschka, Chris. *Arlene sardine*
Waffle
Reynolds, Peter H. *The dot*
Ish
My very big little world
Richards, Beah E. *Keep climbing, girls*
Richardson, John. *Grunt*
Robinson, Fiona. *Whale shines*
Rosenthal, Amy Krouse. *Exclamation mark*
The OK book
One smart cookie: bite-size lessons for the school years and beyond
Rossetti-Shustak, Bernadette. *I love you through and through*
Rotner, Shelley. *What can you do?*
Rubin, C. M. *Eleanor, Ellatony, Ellencake, and me*
Russo, Marisabina. *A very big bunny*
Saltzberg, Barney. *Star of the week*
Scanlon, Elizabeth Garton. *Noodle and Lou*
Schneider, Christine M. *Picky Mrs. Pickle*
Schoonmaker, Elizabeth. *Square cat*
Schotter, Roni. *The boy who loved words*
Doo-Wop Pop
Schreck, Karen Halvorsen. *Lucy's family tree*
Schwartz, Amy. *Dee Dee and me*
Starring Miss Darlene
Schwarz, Viviane. *The adventures of a nose*
Seuss, Dr. *Oh, the places you'll go!*
Sharmat, Marjorie Weinman. *I'm terrific*
The 329th friend
Shea, Bob. *New socks*
Unicorn thinks he's pretty great
Shields, Carol Diggory. *I am really a princess*
Shipton, Jonathan. *What if?*
Shireen, Nadia. *Good little wolf*
Simon, Norma. *All kinds of children*
Why am I different?
Smallcomb, Pam. *I'm not*
Smith, Jada Pinkett. *Girls hold up this world*
Smith, Lane. *Pinocchio, the boy*
Spinelli, Eileen. *Princess Pig*
When no one is watching
Stein, David Ezra. *Pouch!*
Stewart, Amber. *Little by little*
Stone, Tanya Lee. *Who says women can't be doctors?*
Swanson, Susan Marie. *The first thing my mama told me*
Terry, Michael. *Rhino's horns*
Thompson, Kay. *Kay Thompson's Eloise's what I absolutely love love love*
Thompson, Lauren. *Wee little chick*
Tillman, Nancy. *The crown on your head*
Timmers, Leo. *Crow*
Turner, Sandy. *Otto's trunk*
Tyler, Michael. *The skin you live in*
Urdahl, Catherine. *Polka-dot fixes kindergarten*
Vail, Rachel. *Piggy Bunny*
Van Dusen, Chris. *King Hugo's huge ego*
van Lieshout, Maria. *Peep!*
Waddell, Martin. *Bee frog*
Waldron, Kevin. *Mr. Peek and the misunderstanding at the zoo*
Weeks, Sarah. *I'm a pig*
Weigelt, Udo. *Old Beaver*
Wells, Rosemary. *The gulps*
Wiesner, David. *Art and Max*
Willems, Mo. *Edwina, the dinosaur who didn't know she was extinct*
Williams, Carol Ann. *Booming Bella*
Wilson, Gina. *Ignis*
Winthrop, Elizabeth. *Squashed in the middle*
Wolff, Patricia Rae. *A new, improved Santa*
Wong, Benedict Norbert. *Lo and behold*
Lo and behold, good enough to eat
Wormell, Christopher. *Henry and the fox*
Wright, Joanna. *Bunnies on ice*
Yaccarino, Dan. *Unlovable*
Yerkes, Jennifer. *A funny little bird*
Ziefert, Harriet. *Squarehead*

Self-esteem *see* Self-concept

Self-image *see* Self-concept

Self-reliance *see* Character traits – confidence

Selfishness *see* Character traits – selfishness

Senses

Apperley, Dawn. *Don't wake the baby*
Blackstone, Stella. *Bear's busy family*

Cash, Megan Montague. *I saw the sea and the sea saw me*
Ciboul, Adele. *The five senses*
Cole, Joanna. *The magic school bus explores the senses*
Crummel, Susan Stevens. *Sherlock Bones and the missing cheese*
Goodman, Susan E. *It's a dog's life*
Hartley, Karen. *The sixth sense and other special senses*
Henderson, Kathy. *Look at you!*
Jenkins, Steve. *What do you do with a tail like this?*
Lears, Laurie. *Ian's walk*
Leigh, Heather. *Hey little baby!*
McMillan, Bruce. *Sense suspense*
Miller, Margaret. *My five senses*
Murphy, Mary. *You smell and taste and feel and see and hear*
Raschka, Chris. *Five for a little one*
Reiser, Lynn. *My cat Tuna*
My dog Truffle
Rosenfeld, Dina Herman. *Five alive*
Rotner, Shelley. *Senses at the seashore*
Senses in the city
Ryan, Pam Muñoz. *Hello, Ocean!*
Hello ocean / Hola mar
Seuss, Dr. *Gerald McBoing Boing*
Shannon, David. *David smells*
Sweeney, Joan. *Me and my senses*
Trapani, Iza. *The bear went over the mountain*
Wells, Rosemary. *Night sounds, morning colors*
Wood, Douglas. *No one but you*
Ziefert, Harriet. *You can't taste a pickle with your ear*

Senses – hearing

Aliki. *My five senses*
Ancona, George. *Handtalk zoo*
Charlip, Remy. *Handtalk birthday*
Charlip, Remy, et al. *Handtalk*
Hartley, Karen, et al. *Hearing in living things*
Millman, Isaac. *Moses goes to school*
Murphy, Stuart J. *Percy listens up*
Nelson, Robin. *Hearing*
Showers, Paul. *Ears are for hearing*
The listening walk
Soto, Gary. *The old man and his door*
Winnie-the-Pooh's A B C

Senses – sight

Aliki. *My five senses*
Brown, Marc. *Arthur's eyes*
Cobb, Vicki. *Open your eyes*
Gordon, Sharon. *Seeing*
Hartley, Karen. *Seeing in living things*
Keats, Ezra Jack. *Apt. 3*
Lyon, George Ella. *The pirate of kindergarten*
McCarthy, Mary. *A closer look*
Martin, Bill, Jr. *Knots on a counting rope*
Nelson, Robin. *Seeing*
Serafini, Frank. *Looking closely along the shore*
Shannon, George. *White is for blueberry*
Showers, Paul. *Look at your eyes*
Smith, Lane. *Glasses . . . who needs 'em?*
Young, Ed. *Seven blind mice*

Senses – smell

Aliki. *My five senses*
Allen, Jonathan. *Mucky moose*
Gordon, Sharon. *Smelling*
Hartley, Karen. *Smelling in living things*
Kajikawa, Kimiko. *Yoshi's feast*
Keller, Holly. *Nosy Rosie*
Kinerk, Robert. *Timothy Cox will not change his socks*
Nelson, Robin. *Smelling*
Palatini, Margie. *Gorgonzola*
Posthuma, Sieb. *Benny*
Southwell, Jandelyn. *The little country town*
Ward, B. J. *Farty Marty*

Senses – taste

Aliki. *My five senses*
Bonsignore, Joan. *Stick out your tongue*
Hartley, Karen. *Tasting in living things*
Nelson, Robin. *Tasting*

Senses – touch

Adoff, Arnold. *Touch the poem*
Aliki. *My five senses*
Becker, Bonny. *Tickly prickly*
Carle, Eric. *My very first book of touch*
Cottin, Menena. *The black book of colors*
Hartley, Karen. *Touching in living things*
Nelson, Robin. *Touching*
Sherman, Joanne. *Because it's my body*

Sex instruction

Allan, Nicholas. *Where Willy went*
Brown, Laurie Krasny. *What's the big secret?*
Collard, Sneed B. *Making animal babies*
Harris, Robie H. *What's in there?*
Saltz, Gail. *Amazing you*

Sex roles *see* Gender roles

Shadows

Asch, Frank. *Bear shadow*
Cendrars, Blaise. *Shadow*
Chorao, Kay. *Shadow night*
DiFiori, Lawrence. *Jackie and the Shadow Snatcher*
Freeman, Don. *Gregory's Shadow*
Hoban, Tana. *Shadows and reflections*
Hodgkinson, Leigh. *Boris and the wrong shadow*
Holderness, Jackie. *What is a shadow?*
Leathers, Philippa. *The black rabbit*
Lee, Suzy. *Shadow*
Lewin, Betsy. *Groundhog day*
MacDonald, Amy. *Quentin Fenton Herter three*
Pallotta, Jerry. *Who will see their shadows this year?*
Swinburne, Stephen R. *Guess whose shadow?*
Tompert, Ann. *Nothing sticks like a shadow*
Van Nutt, Julia. *The monster in the shadows*
Walter, Mildred Pitts. *Darkness*
Waring, Geoff. *Oscar and the moth*
Welling, Peter J. *Andrew McGroundhog and his shady shadow*
Willard, Nancy. *Shadow story*

Shaped books *see* Format, unusual

Sharing *see* Behavior – sharing

Shells *see* Sea & seashore

Ships *see* Boats, ships

Shopping

Agee, Jon. *Nothing*
Ahlberg, Allan. *The shopping expedition*
Baker, Jeannie. *Mirror*
Birchall, Mark. *Hen goes shopping*
Birdseye, Tom. *Soap! Soap! Don't forget the soap!*
Bulion, Leslie. *Fatuma's new cloth*
Burningham, John. *The shopping basket*
Chen, Chih-Yuan. *On my way to buy eggs*
Christelow, Eileen. *Five little monkeys go shopping*
Cocca-Leffler, Maryann. *Bus route to Boston*
Cousins, Lucy. *Maisy goes shopping*
Daly, Niki. *Next stop — Zanzibar Road!*
Not so fast Songololo
Darbyshire, Kristen. *Put it on the list!*
Day, Alexandra. *Carl goes shopping*
Dewdney, Anna. *Llama Llama mad at Mama*
Dodds, Dayle Ann. *The Kettles get new clothes*
Edens, Cooper. *The Animal Mall*
Elya, Susan Middleton. *Bebé goes shopping*
Flanagan, Alice K. *A busy day at Mr. Kang's grocery store*
Florence, Tyler. *Tyler makes pancakes!*
Gill, Shelley. *The big buck adventure*
Glass, Eleri. *The red shoes*
Grossman, Patricia. *Saturday market*
Hutchins, Pat. *Don't forget the bacon!*
Ichikawa, Satomi. *My father's shop*
Johnson, Marion. *Caillou, new shoes*
Kaplan, Michael B. *Betty Bunny wants everything*
Korchek, Lori. *Adventures of Cow, too*
Lindbergh, Reeve. *The awful aardvarks shop for school*
Lobel, Arnold. *On Market Street*
London, Jonathan. *Ali, child of the desert*
Long, Kathy. *The runaway shopping cart*
McAllister, Angela. *Trust me, Mom!*
Martin, David. *Five little piggies*
Melvin, Alice. *The high street*
Munsch, Robert N. *Something good*
Where is Gah-Ning?
Murphy, Stuart J. *Just enough carrots*
Oxenbury, Helen. *Tom and Pippo go shopping*
Potter, Beatrix. *The tale of Little Pig Robinson*
Pratt, Pierre. *Shopping*
Puttock, Simon. *Goat and Donkey in strawberry sunglasses*
Rader, Laura. *Santa's new suit*
Rockwell, Anne. *At the supermarket*
Russo, Marisabina. *Mama talks too much*
Rylant, Cynthia. *Brownie and Pearl see the sights*
Seibold, J. Otto. *Lost sloth*
Shaw, Nancy. *Sheep in a shop*
Sierra, Judy. *Suppose you meet a dinosaur*
Singer, Marilyn. *Shoe bop!*
Stevens, April. *Edwin speaks up*
Thayer, Tanya. *Spending money*
Trent, Shanda. *Farmers' market day*
Verdick, Elizabeth. *On-the-go time*
Wells, Rosemary. *Max's bunny business*
Shopping
Wood, Don. *Merry Christmas, big hungry bear*

Shops *see* Stores

Shows *see* Theater

Shyness *see* Character traits – shyness

Siam *see* Foreign lands – Thailand

Sibling rivalry

Alexander, Martha G. *Nobody asked me if I wanted a baby sister*
When the new baby comes, I'm moving out
Alter, Anna. *Estelle and Lucy*
Bedford, David. *Ella's games*
Berenstain, Stan and Jan. *The Berenstain bears and the double dare*
The Berenstain bears get in a fight
Blume, Judy. *The Pain and The Great One*
Blumenthal, Deborah. *Don't let the peas touch!*
Bond, Felicia. *Poinsettia and her family*
Bourgeois, Paulette. *Franklin and Harriet*
Bradman, Tony. *The perfect baby*
Broach, Elise. *What the no-good baby is good for*
Brown, Marc. *D. W. all wet*
Bunting, Eve. *Baby can*
Capucilli, Alyssa Satin. *Katy Duck, big sister*
Carlson, Nancy. *Harriet and Walt*
Cinderella
Climo, Shirley. *The Egyptian Cinderella*
The Korean Cinderella
The Persian Cinderella
Coburn, Jewell Reinhart. *Angkat*
Jouanah
Cole, Joanna. *The new baby at your house*
Cote, Nancy. *It's all about me!*
Daly, Jude. *Fair, brown and trembling*
Davies, Gill. *Wilbur waited*
deGroat, Diane. *Mother, you're the best! (but Sister, you're a pest!)*
Dempsey, Sheena. *Bye-bye baby brother!*
Dewan, Ted. *Crispin and the 3 little piglets*
Duke, Kate. *The tale of Pip and Squeak*
Gay, Marie-Louise. *Caramba and Henry*
Geras, Adèle. *Sleeping beauty*
Grimm, Jacob and Wilhelm. *The water of life*
Hall, Algy Craig. *Fine as we are*
Hänel, Wolfram. *Little elephant runs away*
Hazen, Barbara Shook. *Who is your favorite monster, mama?*
Henkes, Kevin. *Julius, the baby of the world*
Hoban, Russell. *A baby sister for Frances*
Holabird, Katharine. *Angelina's baby sister*
Hurwitz, Johanna. *Russell's secret*
Hutchins, Pat. *The very worst monster*
Itaya, Satoshi. *Buttons and Bo*
Jonell, Lynne. *It's my birthday, too!*
Joosse, Barbara. *I love you the purplest*
Joyce, William. *Santa calls*
Kassirer, Sue. *Joseph and his coat of many colors*
Keller, Holly. *Geraldine first*
Geraldine's baby brother
Koller, Jackie French. *Baby for sale*
Kroll, Steven. *The squirrels' Thanksgiving*
Lindgren, Barbro. *Benny and the binky*
Lobel, Gillian. *Too small for honey cake*

Lowell, Susan. *Cindy Ellen*
McCully, Emily Arnold. *New baby*
Manna, Anthony L. *The orphan*
Michels-Gualtieri, Akaela S. *I was born to be a sister*
Minters, Frances. *Cinder-Elly*
Montanari, Eva. *Tiff, Taff, and Lulu*
Murphy, Stuart J. *Give me half!*
Oelschlager, Vanita. *Made in China*
Orlean, Susan. *Lazy little loafers*
Palatini, Margie. *Goldie is mad*
Good as Goldie
Pelham, David. *Sam's pizza*
Perrault, Charles *Cinderella*, ill. by Nicoletta Ceccoli
Cinderella, ill. by Susan Jeffers
Cinderella, ill. by Loek Koopmans
Cinderella, ill. by James Marshall
Cinderella, ill. by Barbara McClintock
Cinderella / Cenicienta
Cinderella: a pop-up fairy tale
Cinderella: or, the little glass slipper
Plourde, Lynn. *Spring's sprung*
Polacco, Patricia. *My rotten redheaded older brother*
Pryor, Bonnie. *Amanda and April*
The porcupine mouse
Raschka, Chris. *The blushful hippopotamus*
Reynolds, Peter H. *The best kid in the world*
Richardson, John. *Grunt*
Robberecht, Thierry. *Back into Mommy's tummy*
Roberts, Lynn. *Cinderella, an Art Deco love story*
Rogers, Fred. *The new baby*
Rosenberry, Vera. *Vera's baby sister*
Russo, Marisabina. *The big brown box*
Samuels, Barbara. *Faye and Dolores*
What's so great about Cindy Snappleby?
Sanderson, Ruth. *Cinderella*
San Souci, Robert D. *Cinderella Skeleton*
Little gold star
Schwartz, Amy. *Annabelle Swift, kindergartner*
Scott, Ann Herbert. *On mother's lap*
On mother's lap [board book]
Scrimger, Richard. *Eugene's story*
Shields, Carol Diggory. *I wish my brother was a dog*
Skinner, Daphne. *Henry keeps score*
Steig, William. *The toy brother*
Steptoe, John. *Baby says*
Stevenson, James. *That's exactly the way it wasn't*
Worse than Willy!
Sullivan, Sarah. *Once upon a baby brother*
Viorst, Judith. *I'll fix Anthony*
Waddell, Martin. *Sam Vole and his brothers*
Wahl, Jan. *Mabel ran away with the toys*
Weeks, Sarah. *Sophie Peterman tells the truth!*
Wells, Rosemary. *Max counts his chickens*
Max's bedtime
Max's breakfast
Max's chocolate chicken
Peabody
Stanley and Rhoda
Wolff, Ashley. *Stella and Roy go camping*
Wynne-Jones, Tim. *The boat in the tree*
Yep, Laurence. *Dragon prince*
Yezerski, Thomas. *Queen of the world*
Young, Ed. *My Mei Mei*
Zolotow, Charlotte. *If it weren't for you*

Siblings *see* Family life – brothers; Family life – brothers & sisters; Family life – sisters; Family life – stepfamilies

Sickness *see* Health & fitness; Illness

Sight *see* Anatomy – eyes; Glasses; Disabilities – blindness; Senses – sight

Sign language

Acredolo, Linda P. *My first baby signs*
Browne, Anthony. *Little Beauty*
Domney, Alexis. *Splish, splat!*
Heller, Lora. *Sign language ABC*
Kubler, Annie. *My first signs*
McCully, Emily Arnold. *My heart glow*
Millman, Isaac. *Moses goes to a concert*
Prochovnic, Dawn Babb. *The big blue bowl*
Hip hip hooray! It's Family Day!
Uhlberg, Myron. *The printer*
Waller, Curt. *Baby's first signs*
More baby's first signs
Winnie-the-Pooh's A B C

Signs

Ashman, Linda. *No dogs allowed*
Slawson, Michele Benoit. *Signs for sale*
van Lieshout, Maria. *Backseat A-B-see*
Wells, Rosemary. *Yoko finds her way*

Singers *see* Careers – opera singers; Careers – singers

Sioux Indians *see* Indians of North America – Cheyenne (Sioux); Indians of North America – Dakota (Sioux); Indians of North America – Sioux

Sisters *see* Family life – brothers & sisters; Family life – sisters; Sibling rivalry

Skating *see* Sports – ice skating; Sports – hockey; Sports – roller skating

Sky

Belting, Natalia Maree. *The sun is a golden earring*
Berger, Barbara. *Thunder Bunny*
Branley, Franklyn M. *Comets*
The sky is full of stars
Cabrera, Jane. *Twinkle, twinkle, little star*
Carle, Eric. *Little cloud*
Little cloud [board book]
Carlstrom, Nancy White. *What does the sky say?*
Dayrell, Elphinstone. *Why the sun and the moon live in the sky*
Gerson, Mary-Joan. *Why the sky is far away*
Hopkinson, Deborah. *Maria's comet*
Luján, Jorge. *Sky blue accident / Accidente celeste*
Otto, Carolyn. *That sky, that rain*
Oughton, Jerrie. *How the stars fell into the sky*
Parker, Michael. *You are a star!*
Ray, Mary Lyn. *Stars*
Reynolds, Peter H. *Sky color*
Sabuda, Robert. *The Blizzard's robe*
Shaw, Charles Green. *It looked like spilt milk*

Taylor, Harriet Peck. *Ulaq and the northern lights*
Taylor, Jane. *Twinkle, twinkle little star,* ill. by Heather Collins
Twinkle, twinkle, little star, ill. by Michael Hague
Twinkle, twinkle little star, ill. by Julia Noonan
Twinkle, twinkle, little star, ill. by Jerry Pinkney
Waboose, Jan Bourdeau. *SkySisters*
Wilson, Karma. *Mama, why?*
Wood, Audrey. *Blue sky*

Slavery

Altman, Linda Jacobs. *The legend of Freedom Hill*
Armand, Glenda. *Love twelve miles long*
Asim, Jabari. *Fifty cents and a dream*
Bauer, Marion Dane. *Harriet Tubman*
Broyles, Anne. *Priscilla and the hollyhocks*
Carbone, Elisa. *Night running*
Cline-Ransome, Lesa. *Light in the darkness*
Words set me free
Cole, Henry. *Unspoken*
Edwards, Pamela Duncan. *Barefoot: escape on the Underground Railroad*
Evans, Shane W. *Underground: finding the light to freedom*
Fradin, Dennis. *The price of freedom*
Grady, Cynthia. *I lay my stitches down*
Grifalconi, Ann. *Ain't nobody a stranger to me*
The village that vanished
Hill, Laban Carrick. *Dave the potter*
Hopkinson, Deborah. *Sweet Clara and the freedom quilt*
Johnson, D. B. *Henry climbs a mountain*
Johnson, Dolores. *Now let me fly*
Johnson, James Weldon. *Lift every voice and sing*
Lift ev'ry voice and sing
Johnston, Tony. *The wagon*
Levine, Ellen. *Henry's freedom box*
Levy, Debbie. *We shall overcome*
Lilly, Melinda. *From slavery to freedom*
Lyons, Kelly Starling. *Ellen's broom*
Hope's gift
McGhee, Alison. *In the hollow of your hand*
McGill, Alice. *Molly Bannaky*
Way up and over everything
Medearis, Angela Shelf. *The freedom riddle*
Meister, Cari. *Follow the drinking gourd: an Underground Railroad story*
Nelson, Vaunda Micheaux. *Almost to freedom*
Nolen, Jerdine. *Big Jabe*
Pinkney, Andrea Davis. *Dear Benjamin Banneker*
Sojourner Truth's step-stomp stride
Rappaport, Doreen. *Freedom river*
Freedom ship
Raven, Margot Theis. *Night boat to freedom*
Riggio, Anita. *Secret signs*
Ringgold, Faith. *The invisible princesses*
Rochelle, Belinda. *Jewels*
Sanders, Nancy. *D is for drinking gourd*
Sanders, Scott R. *A place called Freedom*
Schroeder, Alan. *Minty*
Shange, Ntozake. *Freedom's a-callin me*
Siegelson, Kim L. *In the time of the drums*
Slate, Joseph. *I want to be free*
Smalls-Hector, Irene. *Jenny Reen and the Jack Muh Lantern*
Smith, Charles R. *Brick by brick*
Stroud, Bettye. *The leaving*
The patchwork path
Tate, Don. *It jes' happened*
Turner, Glennette Tilley. *An apple for Harriet Tubman*
Uchida, Yoshiko. *The bracelet*
Walker, Sally M. *Freedom song*
Weatherford, Carole Boston. *The Beatitudes*
Juneteenth jamboree
Moses: when Harriet Tubman led her people to freedom
Winter, Jeanette. *Follow the drinking gourd*
Woodson, Jacqueline. *Show way*
Wright, Courtni Crump. *Journey to freedom*
Jumping the broom

Sleep

Alexander, Martha G. *I'll protect you from the jungle beasts*
Andersen, Hans Christian. *The princess and the pea,* ill. by Emily Bolam
The princess and the pea, ill. by Charlene Delage
The princess and the pea, ill. by Dorothée Duntze
The princess and the pea, ill. by Maja Dusíková
The princess and the pea, ill. by Paul Galdone
The princess and the pea, ill. by Rachel Isadora
The princess and the pea, ill. by Bernhard Oberdieck
The princess and the pea, ill. by Janet Stevens
The princess and the pea, ill. by Alain Vaës
The princess and the pea in miniature
Apperley, Dawn. *Don't wake the baby*
Arnold, Caroline. *Sleepytime for zoo animals*
Arnold, Tedd. *Five ugly monsters*
Asch, Frank. *Good night, Baby Bear*
Baker, Roberta. *Olive's first sleepover*
Banks, Kate. *Close your eyes*
Batten, Mary. *Please don't wake the animals*
Bauer, Marion Dane. *Sleep, little one, sleep*
Bean, Jonathan. *At night*
Bergman, Mara. *Musical beds*
Oliver who would not sleep!
Blomgren, Jennifer. *Where do I sleep?*
Bonnett-Rampersaud, Louise. *How do you sleep?*
Branford, Henrietta. *Little Pig Figwort can't get to sleep*
Braun, Sebastien. *Back to bed, Ed!*
Brown, Margaret Wise. *The Golden sleepy book*
Sheep don't count sheep
Sleepy ABC, ill. by Karen Katz
Sleepy ABC, ill. by Esphyr Slobodkina
Butler, John. *Hush, little ones*
While you were sleeping
Camp, Lindsay. *The biggest bed in the world*
Capucilli, Alyssa Satin. *Little spotted cat*
Carman, William. *What's that noise?*
Caseley, Judith. *Sophie and Sammy's library sleepover*
Catusanu, Mircea. *The strange case of the missing sheep*
Child, Lauren. *My dream bed*
Cleland, Jo. *Getting your zzzzs*
Clements, Andrew. *Naptime for Slippers*
Collard, Sneed B. *Animals asleep*
Dahl, Michael. *Nap time for Kitty*
Deacon, Alexis. *While you are sleeping*
Demers, Dominique. *Every single night*
De Vries, Maggie. *How sleep found Tabitha*
Downey, Lynn. *The flea's sneeze*
The drowsy hours
Dunrea, Olivier. *Gideon*
Durango, Julia. *Dream hop*

Edwards, Richard. *Good night, Copycub*
Ehrlich, Fred. *Does a baboon sleep in a bed?*
Enersen, Adele. *When my baby dreams*
Fernandes, Eugenie. *Sleepy little mouse*
Field, Eugene. *Wynken, Blynken, and Nod*
Wynken, Blynken and Nod
Fletcher, Ralph. *The Sandman*
Fox, Mem. *Night noises*
Sleepy bears
Where the giant sleeps
Frampton, David. *The whole night through*
Freedman, Claire. *Snuggle up, sleepy ones*
Gamble, Isobel. *Who's that?*
Geras, Adèle. *Sleep tight, Ginger Kitten*
Gorbachev, Valeri. *Shhh!*
Grey, Mini. *The very smart pea and the princess-to-be*
Grimm, Jacob and Wilhelm. *Sleeping Beauty*
The sleeping beauty
Guy, Ginger Foglesong. *Siesta*
Hall, Marcellus. *Everyone sleeps*
Harshman, Marc. *All the way to morning*
Henkes, Kevin. *Shhhh*
Henry, Jed. *Good night, Mouse!*
Hertz, Grete Janus. *Olie's bedtime walk*
Hest, Amy. *Charley's first night*
Hill, Susanna Leonard. *Can't sleep without sheep*
Hindley, Judy. *Sleepy places*
Hooper, Patricia. *Where do you sleep, little one?*
Hurd, Thacher. *Sleepy Cadillac*
Hutchins, Pat. *Good-night owl*
Inkpen, Mick. *Kipper*
Jenkins, Steve. *Time to sleep*
Johnson, D. B. *Henry's night*
Johnston, Tony. *Little Rabbit goes to sleep*
Jonovitz, Marilyn. *Maybe, my baby*
Joosse, Barbara. *A houseful of Christmas*
Joyce, William. *The Sandman: the story of Sanderson Mansnoozie*
Kajikawa, Kimiko. *Sweet dreams: how animals sleep*
Kanevsky, Polly. *Sleepy boy*
Keats, Ezra Jack. *Dreams*
Kimmel, Eric A. *Rip Van Winkle's return*
Kraus, Robert. *Milton the early riser*
Lewis, Kim. *Good night, Harry*
Hooray for Harry
Lewison, Wendy Cheyette. *Going to sleep on the farm*
Lobb, Janice. *Counting sheep! How do we sleep?*
Logue, Mary. *Sleep like a tiger*
Long, Ethan. *One drowsy dragon*
McGhee, Alison. *In the hollow of your hand*
McGinty, Alice B. *Ten little lambs*
McMullan, Kate. *Papa's song*
McQuinn, Anna. *The sleep sheep*
Markes, Julie. *Shhhhh! Everybody's sleeping*
Meade, Holly. *A place to sleep*
Meadows, Michelle. *Hibernation station*
Metaxas, Eric. *It's time to sleep, my love*
Moon, Nicola. *Tick-tock, drip-drop*
Mortimer, Anne. *Bunny's Easter egg*
Most, Bernard. *Z-Z-Zoink!*
Munsch, Robert N. *Get out of bed!*
Murguia, Bethanie Deeney. *Snippet the early riser*
Murphy, Jill. *Peace at last*
Na, Il Sung. *A book of sleep*
Nobisso, Josephine. *The moon's lullaby*
The yawn
Noullet, Georgette. *Bed hog*
Novak, Matt. *The Pillow War*
Osborne, Mary Pope. *Sleeping Bobby*
Perlman, Janet. *The penguin and the pea*
Peters, Lisa Westberg. *Sleepyhead bear*
Pfister, Marcus. *Good night, little rainbow fish*
Purmell, Ann. *Where wild babies sleep*
Radzinski, Kandy. *Where to sleep*
Rauss, Ron. *Can I just take a nap?*
Robbins, Maria Polushkin. *Mother, Mother, I want another*
Root, Phyllis. *Creak! said the bed*
Ten sleepy sheep
Roth, Carol. *Little Bunny's sleepless night*
Roth, Judith L. *Goodnight, dragons*
Schubert, Leda. *Winnie all day long*
Schwartz, Amy. *Lucy can't sleep*
Scotton, Rob. *Russell the sheep*
Showers, Paul. *Sleep is for everyone*
Shulevitz, Uri. *So sleepy story*
Simmons, Jane. *The dreamtime fairies*
Go to sleep, Daisy
Slingsby, Janet. *Hush-a-bye babies*
Sloat, Teri. *The thing that bothered Farmer Brown*
Somary, Wolfgang. *Night and the candlemaker*
Stevenson, James. *We can't sleep*
Tafuri, Nancy. *Where we sleep*
Tucker, Kathy. *Do knights take naps?*
Uribe, Verónica. *Buzz buzz buzz*
Van Laan, Nancy. *Sleep, sleep, sleep*
Waber, Bernard. *Ira sleeps over*
Waddell, Martin. *Can't you sleep, Little Bear?*
Sleep tight, Little Bear
Walton, Rick. *So many bunnies*
Watt, Mélanie. *Scaredy Squirrel at night*
Weiss, Nicki. *Where does the brown bear go?*
Where does the brown bear go? [board book]
Whatley, Bruce. *Captain Pajamas*
Wolf, Karina. *The Insomniacs*
Wolff, Ferida. *It is the wind*
Wong, Janet S. *Grump*
Wood, Audrey. *It's Duffy time!*
Moonflute
The napping house
The napping house wakes up
Wright, Michael. *Jake stays awake*
Ziefert, Harriet. *Mommy, I want to sleep in your bed!*
What do ducks dream?
Zolotow, Charlotte. *The sleepy book*
Sleepy book

Sleep – snoring

Arnold, Marsha Diane. *Roar of a snore*
DiPucchio, Kelly. *Dinosnores*
Long, Kathy. *Christopher sat straight up in bed*
Long, Melinda. *When Papa snores*
Ohora, Zachariah. *Stop snoring, Bernard!*
Waber, Bernard. *The mouse that snored*

Sleepovers

Beck, Scott. *Monster sleepover!*
Becker, Bonny. *A bedtime for Bear*
Berenstain, Stan and Jan. *The Berenstain bears and the slumber party*
Brown, Marc. *Arthur's first sleepover*
Clarke, Jane. *Dippy's sleepover*
Ellis, Sarah. *Ben over night*
Giglio, Judy. *The tapping tale*
Greene, Rhonda Gowler. *At grandma's*

Harper, Charise Mericle. *When Randolph turned rotten*
Hill, Eric. *Spot sleeps over*
Jackson, Isaac. *Somebody's new pajamas*
Jennings, Sharon. *Franklin wants a badge*
Joosse, Barbara. *Sleepover at Gramma's house*
Leijten, Aileen. *Hugging hour!*
Long, Kathy. *Christopher sat straight up in bed*
McKissack, Patricia C. *Messy Bessey and the birthday overnight*
Mitchard, Jacquelyn. *Ready, set, school!*
Murphy, Stuart J. *Rabbit's pajama party*
Pace, Anne Marie. *Vampirina ballerina hosts a sleepover*
Pearce, Philippa. *Amy's three best things*
Pinkwater, Daniel. *Sleepover Larry*
Radabaugh, Melinda Beth. *Sleeping over*
Regan, Dian Curtis. *The Snow Blew Inn*
Robberecht, Thierry. *Sam's new friend*
Rodriguez, Bobbie. *Sarah's sleepover*
Smith, Maggie. *Pigs in pajamas*
Tyler, Anne. *Timothy Tugbottom says no!*
Vulliamy, Clara. *Small*
Waber, Bernard. *Bearsie Bear and the surprise sleepover party*
Winthrop, Elizabeth. *Squashed in the middle*

Sleight-of-hand *see* Magic

Smallness *see* Character traits – smallness

Smell *see* Anatomy – noses; Senses – smell

Smiles, smiling *see* Anatomy – faces

Snoring *see* Noise, sounds; Sleep – snoring

Snow *see* Weather – blizzards; Weather – snow

Snow plows *see* Machines

Snowmen

Arena, Jennifer. *100 snowmen*
Arnold, Katya. *The adventures of Snowwoman*
Briggs, Raymond. *The snowman*
The snowman [a lift-the-flap board book]
The snowman storybook
Buehner, Caralyn. *Snowmen all year*
Snowmen at Christmas
Snowmen at night
Snowmen at night [board book]
Butler, M. Christina. *The smiley snowman*
Carlson, Nancy. *Snowden*
Colandro, Lucille. *There was a cold lady who swallowed some snow!*
Cuyler, Margery. *The biggest, best snowman*
Doodler, Todd H. *Bear in long underwear*
Ehlert, Lois. *Snowballs*
Fleming, Denise. *The first day of winter*
Garland, Michael. *Christmas magic*
Gilmore, Rachna. *Making grizzle grow*
Hoban, Julia. *Amy loves the snow*
Joyce, William. *Snowie Rolie*
Kellogg, Steven. *The mystery of the missing red mitten*
Kirk, Daniel. *Snow family*
LaReau, Kara. *Snowbaby could not sleep*
Lawler, Janet. *Snowzilla*
McDaniels, Preston. *A perfect snowman*
McGhee, Alison. *Making a friend*
Mahoney, Daniel J. *A really good snowman*
Marlow, Layn. *You make me smile*
Miller, Edna. *Mousekin's frosty friend*
Moser, Lisa. *Perfect soup*
Nelson, Steve. *Frosty the snowman*
Frosty the snowman [board book]
Peddle, Daniel. *Snow day*
Pittman, Helena Clare. *The snowman's path*
Reid, Barbara. *Perfect snow*
Schaefer, Carole Lexa. *Snow pumpkin*
Scheffler, Axel. *The snowy day*
Tegen, Katherine Brown. *Snowman magic*
Wahman, Joe. *Snowboy 1, 2, 3*
Walters, Catherine. *The magical snowman*
Whybrow, Ian. *Harry and the snow king*
Wish, change, friend
Winget, Susan. *Sam the Snowman*
Wright, Maureen. *Sneezy the snowman*

Society Islands *see* Foreign lands – South Sea Islands

Soldiers *see* Careers – military

Soldiers, toy *see* Toys – soldiers

Solitude *see* Behavior – solitude

Songs

Alexander, Cecil Frances. *All creatures great and small*
All things bright and beautiful, ill. by Ashley Bryan
All things bright and beautiful, ill. by Anna Vojtech
All things bright and beautiful, ill. by Bruce Whatley
Alger, Leclaire Gowans. *All in the morning early*
All night, all day
Allen, Nancy Kelly. *"Happy Birthday"*
Alley, R. W. *There once was a witch*
Anderson, Derek. *Over the river*
Arnosky, Jim. *Gobble it up!*
I'm a turkey!
Ashburn, Boni. *Over at the castle*
Autry, Gene. *Here comes Santa Claus*
Aylesworth, Jim. *Our Abe Lincoln*
Baker, Ken. *Old MacDonald had a dragon*
Baring-Gould, S. *Now the day is over*
Barnwell, Ysaye M. *We are one*
Bateman, Donna M. *Out on the prairie*
Bates, Ivan. *Five little ducks*
Bates, Katharine Lee. *America the beautiful,* ill. by Chris Gall
America the beautiful, ill. by Wendell Minor
Bates, Katharine Lee. *America the beautiful: together we stand*
Baum, Maxie. *I have a little dreidel*

Beall, Pamela Conon. *Wee Sing if you're happy and you know it*
The bear
Berkes, Marianne. *Over in a river*
Berlin, Irving. *Easter parade*
  God bless America
Bonwill, Ann. *The Frazzle family finds a way*
Brebeuf, Jean de. *The Huron carol*
Brokering, Herbert F. *Earth and all stars*
Brown, Marc. *Play rhymes*
Burke, Bobby. *Daddy's little girl*
Busse, Sarah Martin. *Banjo granny*
Butler, Geoff. *Ode to Newfoundland*
Butler, John. *Bedtime in the jungle*
Cabrera, Jane. *Here we go round the mulberry bush*
  If you're happy and you know it
  Twinkle, twinkle, little star
  The wheels on the bus
Canyon, Christopher. *John Denver's Sunshine on my shoulders*
Carle, Eric. *Today is Monday*
Carter, David A. *If you're happy and you know it, clap your hands*
  Old MacDonald had a farm: a pop-up book
Catrow, David. *Monster mash*
Child, Lydia Maria. *Over the river and through the wood*
  Over the river and through the wood: the New England boy's song about Thanksgiving Day
Cleland, Jo. *Getting your zzzzs*
Cohan, George M. *You're a grand old flag*
Colato Laínez, René. *Señor Pancho had a rancho*
Collins, Billy. *Daddy's little boy*
Comden, Betty. *What's new at the zoo?*
Comden, Betty, et al. *Flying to Neverland with Peter Pan*
Conahan, Carolyn. *The twelve days of Christmas dogs*
Corr, Christopher. *Whole world*
Creech, Sharon. *Who's that baby?*
Crum, Shutta. *My mountain song*
Dale, Penny. *The boy on the bus*
Dann, Penny. *Eensy weensy spider*
Davenier, Christine. *It's raining, it's pouring*
De colores / Bright with colors
Dealey, Erin. *Deck the walls!*
Delacre, Lulu. *Arroz con leche*
  Las Navidades
Demas, Corinne. *Nina's waltz*
Dominguez, Angela. *Maria had a little llama/Maria tenia una llama pequena*
Downes, Belinda. *Baby days*
Downing, Johnette. *Down in Louisiana*
  There was an old lady who swallowed some bugs
  Today is Monday in Louisiana
Durango, Julia. *Angels watching over me*
Dylan, Bob. *Blowin' in the wind*
  Man gave names to all the animals
Egielski, Richard. *Itsy bitsy spider*, ill. by Richard Egielski
  Itsy bitsy spider, ill. by Richard Egielski
Ehrhardt, Karen. *This jazz man*
Ellwand, David. *Ten in the bed*
Emberley, Barbara. *One wide river to cross*
Emberley, Rebecca. *If you're a monster and you know it*
Emberley, Rebecca, et al. *There was an old monster*
Emmett, Jonathan. *She'll be coming 'round the mountain*
The farmer in the dell. *The farmer in the dell*, ill. by John O'Brien
  The farmer in the dell, ill. by Alexandra Wallner
Fine, Howard. *A piggie Christmas*
Fitzgerald, Ella. *A-tisket, a-tasket*
Fleming, Candace. *Gabriella's song*
The fox went out on a chilly night
A frog he would a-wooing go [folk-song]. *Frog went a-courtin'*
  Frog went a-courting
  Froggie went a courting
  Froggy went a-courtin'
Gershator, Phillis. *This is the day!*
Go tell Aunt Rhody
Goembel, Ponder. *Animal fair*
Goode, Diane. *Diane Goode's book of silly stories and songs*
Guthrie, Woody. *Bling blang*
  My dolly
  This land is your land
Hallworth, Grace. *Sing me a story*
Harburg, E. Y. *Over the rainbow*
Harris, John. *Jingle bells: how the holiday classic came to be*
Here we go round the mulberry bush
Hoberman, Mary Ann. *Bill Grogan's goat*
  Mary had a little lamb
Hodges, Margaret. *Silent night: the song and its story*
Hooper, Maureen Brett. *Silent night: a Christmas carol is born*
Hoose, Philip M. *Hey little ant*
House, Catherine. *A stork in a baobab tree*
Hush songs
Isadora, Rachel. *Old Mikamba had a farm*
  There was a tree
Ivimey, John William. *The complete story of the three blind mice*
  Three blind mice
Jackson, Jill. *Let there be peace on earth*
Jewel. *Sweet dreams*
Joel, Billy. *New York state of mind*
Johnson, James Weldon. *Lift every voice and sing*
  Lift ev'ry voice and sing
Johnson, Paul Brett. *Little Bunny Foo Foo*
  On top of spaghetti
Jonas, Ann. *Bird talk*
Judd, Naomi. *Naomi Judd's guardian angels*
Katz, Karen. *The babies on the bus*
Keats, Ezra Jack. *The little drummer boy*
Kellogg, Steven. *Give the dog a bone*
  A-hunting we will go!
  I was born about 10,000 years ago
  Santa Claus is comin' to town
  Yankee Doodle
Kennedy, Jimmy. *The teddy bears' picnic*
Key, Francis Scott. *The Star Spangled Banner*
  The Star-Spangled Banner
Kirk, Daniel. *Go!*
Knick knack paddy whack
Knight, Hilary. *A firefly in a fir tree*
Kovalski, Maryann. *The wheels on the bus*
Kroll, Steven. *By the dawn's early light: the story of the Star Spangled Banner*
Krosoczka, Jarrett J. *Punk Farm on tour*
Langstaff, John M. *Oh, a-hunting we will go*
  Over in the meadow
Lenski, Lois. *I like winter*
Let it shine
Let me call you sweetheart
Levy, Debbie. *We shall overcome*
Lithgow, John. *I got two dogs*
  Marsupial Sue

Never play music right next to the zoo
Little old lady who swallowed a fly. *I know an old lady*
I know an old lady who swallowed a fly, ill. by Stephen Gulbis
I know an old lady who swallowed a fly, ill. by Glen Rounds
I know an old lady who swallowed a fly, ill. by Nadine Bernard Westcott
There was an old lady who swallowed a fly, ill. by Pam Adams
There was an old lady who swallowed a fly, ill. by Simms Taback
There was an old monkey who swallowed a frog
There was an old pirate who swallowed a fish
Lloyd-Jones, Sally. *Old MacNoah had an ark*
Long, Ethan. *The croaky pokey!*
Long, Sylvia. *Deck the hall*
McCutcheon, John. *Happy adoption day!*
MacDonald, Margaret Read. *A hen, a chick, and a string guitar*
McGinley-Nally, Sharon. *The friendly beasts*
Margolin, H. Ellen. *Goin' to Boston*
Marley, Cedella. *Every little thing*
One love
Mayo, Margaret. *Wiggle waggle fun*
Meister, Cari. *Follow the drinking gourd: an Underground Railroad story*
Melmed, Laura Krauss. *The first song ever sung*
Milgrim, David. *Young MacDonald*
Miller, J. Philip. *We all sing with the same voice*
Mitchell, Susan K. *The rainforest grew all around*
Mohr, Joseph. *Silent night*
Moore, Mary-Alice. *The wheels on the school bus*
Mora, Pat. *A piñata in a pine tree*
Moses, Will. *Silent night*
Moss, Marissa. *Knick knack paddywack*
Munsch, Robert N. *Mortimer*
Nelson, Kadir. *He's got the whole world in His hands*
Nelson, Steve. *Frosty the snowman*
Frosty the snowman [board book]
Newman, Lesléa. *The eight nights of Chanukah*
Newton, Vanessa. *Let freedom sing*
Norman, Kim. *If it's snowy and you know it, clap your paws!*
Norworth, Jack. *Take me out to the ball game*
Take me out to the ballgame
Old MacDonald had a farm. *Old MacDonald*
Old MacDonald had a farm, ill. by Holly Berry
Old MacDonald had a farm, ill. by Jane Cabrera
Old MacDonald had a farm, ill. by Carol Jones
Old MacDonald had a farm, ill. by Tracey Campbell Pearson
Old MacDonald had a farm, ill. by Glen Rounds
Old MacDonald had a farm, ill. by Jessica Souhami
Old MacDonald had a farm, ill. by Prue Theobalds
Ormerod, Jan. *Ms. MacDonald has a class*
Over in the meadow
Palatini, Margie. *The cheese*
Three French hens
Paley, Joan. *One more river*
Paxton, Tom. *Going to the zoo*
Peek, Merle. *Mary wore her red dress and Henry wore his green sneakers*
Roll over!
Penner, Fred. *The cat came back*
Pete the cat: the wheels on the bus
Pinkney, Gloria Jean. *Music from our Lord's holy heaven*
Quattlebaum, Mary. *Jo MacDonald had a garden*
Jo MacDonald hiked in the woods
Jo MacDonald saw a pond
Raffi. *Baby beluga*
Down by the bay
Everything grows
Like me and you
One light, one sun
Rise and shine
Shake my sillies out
Wheels on the bus
Raposo, Joe. *Sing!*
Ray, Mary Lyn. *Shaker boy*
Robbins, Ruth. *Baboushka and the three kings*
Robinson, Fiona. *What animals really like*
Rodanas, Kristina. *The little drummer boy*
Rodgers, Richard. *My favorite things*
Roslonek, Steve. *The shape song swingalong*
Rox, John. *I want a hippopotamus for Christmas*
Rueda, Claudia. *Let's play in the forest while the wolf is not around*
Ryder, Joanne. *Dance by the light of the moon*
Santa Claus is coming to town
Schanzer, Rosalyn. *The Old Chisholm Trail*
Sedaka, Neil. *Waking up is hard to do*
Seeger, Laura Vaccaro. *I had a rooster*
Seskin, Steve. *A chance to shine*
Don't laugh at me
Shannon, George. *Lizard's song*
Shepard, Aaron. *The princess mouse*
Simmons, Jane. *Daisy says, "Here we go round the mulberry bush"*
Daisy says, "If you're happy and you know it"
Simple gifts
Sloat, Teri. *Hark! The aardvark angels sing*
Smith, Charles R. *I'll be there*
My gal
Smith, Will. *Just the two of us*
Snell, Gordon. *Twelve days, a Christmas countdown*
Spirin, Gennady. *We three kings*
Stadler, John. *Take me out to the ball game: a pop-up book*
Staines, Bill. *All God's critters*
Stevens, Jan Romero. *Twelve lizards leaping*
Stohs, Anita. *An Easter alleluia*
Swain, Gwenyth. *I wonder as I wander*
Sweet, Melissa. *Fiddle-i-fee*
Taylor, Jane. *Twinkle, twinkle little star*, ill. by Heather Collins
Twinkle, twinkle, little star, ill. by Michael Hague
Twinkle, twinkle little star, ill. by Julia Noonan
Twinkle, twinkle, little star, ill. by Jerry Pinkney
This little light of mine
Titcomb, Gordon. *The last train*
Tobin, Jim. *Sue MacDonald had a book*
Tompert, Ann. *A carol for Christmas*
Trapani, Iza. *The bear went over the mountain*
Here we go 'round the mulberry bush
How much is that doggie in the window?
I'm a little teapot
The itsy bitsy spider
Jingle bells
Shoo fly!
The twelve days of Christmas. English folk song. *The twelve days of Christmas*

The 12 days of Christmas
The twelve days of Christmas
Twelve days of Christmas
The twelve days of Christmas, ill. by Laurel Long
The twelve days of Christmas, ill. by Ilse Plume
The twelve days of Christmas, ill. by Jane Ray
The twelve days of Christmas, ill. by Gennady Spirin
The twelve days of Christmas, ill. by Vladimir Vagin
The twelve days of Christmas [board book]
Vasilovich, Guy. *The 13 nights of Halloween*
Vetter, Jennifer Riggs. *Down by the station*
Voake, Charlotte. *Tweedle - dee - dee*
Wallace, Nancy Elizabeth. *Apples, apples, apples*
Ward, Jennifer. *Over in the garden*
Warhola, James. *If you're happy and you know it: jungle edition*
Washington, Ned. *When you wish upon a star*
We wish you a merry Christmas
Weeks, Sarah. *Crocodile smile*
Weiss, George. *What a wonderful world*
Welch, Willy. *Playing right field*
Wells, Rosemary. *The bear went over the mountain*
Bingo
The itsy-bitsy spider
Westcott, Nadine Bernard. *Skip to my Lou*
There's a hole in the bucket
What a morning!
What will we do with the baby-o?
Wheeler, Opal. *Sing in praise*
Sing Mother Goose
Whippo, Walt. *Little white duck*
Wilder, Laura Ingalls. *My little house songbook*
Williams, Suzanne. *The witch casts a spell*
Willis, Jeanne. *The wheels on the bus: a read-along sing-along trip to the zoo*
Winans, CeCe, et al. *Colorful world*
Wood, Audrey. *Birdsong*
When the root children wake up
Yaccarino, Dan. *Five little ducks*
Yarrow, Peter. *Day is done*
Let's sing together!
Puff, the magic dragon
Yolen, Jane. *Jane Yolen's Old MacDonald songbook*
Zane, Alexander. *The wheels on the race car*
Zelinsky, Paul O. *The wheels on the bus*
Zemach, Margot. *Some from the moon, some from the sun*
Ziefert, Harriet. *Knick-knack paddywhack*
When I first came to this land

Sorcerers *see* Wizards

Sounds *see* Noise, sounds

South Pole *see* Foreign lands – Antarctic

Space & space ships

Agee, Jon. *Dmitri the astronaut*
Aldrin, Buzz. *Look to the stars*
Reaching for the moon
Alexander, Martha G. *You're a genius, Blackboard Bear*
Anderson, Derek. *Romeo and Lou blast off*
Arnold, Tedd. *Green Wilma, frog in space*
Aston, Dianna Hutts. *The moon over Star*
Austin, Mike. *Countdown with Milo*
Axelrod, Amy. *They'll believe me when I'm gone*
Barton, Byron. *I want to be an astronaut*
Bartram, Simon. *Bob's best-ever friend*
Man on the moon: a day in the life of Bob
Berenstain, Stan and Jan. *The Berenstain bears on the moon*
Branley, Franklyn M. *Floating in space*
The International Space Station
The planets in our solar system
Brett, Jan. *Hedgie blasts off!*
Brownlow, Mike. *Mickey Moonbeam*
Burleigh, Robert. *One giant leap*
Carrick, Carol. *Patrick's dinosaurs on the Internet*
Chambers, Roland. *Rooftop rocket party*
Cole, Joanna. *The magic school bus lost in the solar system*
Collicutt, Paul. *This rocket*
Corey, Shana. *First graders from Mars: Horus's horrible day*
First graders from Mars: Nergal and the Great Space Race
First graders from Mars: Tera, star student
First graders from Mars: The problem with Pelly
Cushman, Doug. *Space cat*
Dahl, Michael. *On the launch pad*
Debecker, Benoît. *The naughty prince*
Dillon, Jana. *Lucky O'Leprechaun in school*
DiTerlizzi, Tony. *Jimmy Zangwow's out-of-this-world, moon pie adventure*
Duddle, Jonny. *The king of space*
Elliott, David. *Hazel Nutt, Alien Hunter*
Fischer, Scott M. *Twinkle*
Floca, Brian. *Moonshot*
Gall, Chris. *There's nothing to do on Mars*
Gibbons, Gail. *Galaxies, galaxies!*
Hartland, Jessie. *How the meteorite got to the museum*
Hirst, Robin. *My place in space*
Holland, Simon. *Space*
Hurd, Thacher. *Moo Cow Kaboom!*
Jeffers, Oliver. *The way back home*
Kelly, Mark. *Mousetronaut*
Mousetronaut goes to Mars
Kirk, Daniel. *Moondogs*
Kudlinski, Kathleen V. *Boy, were we wrong about the solar system!*
Landry, Leo. *Space boy*
Lauber, Patricia. *You're aboard spaceship Earth*
Leedy, Loreen. *Postcards from Pluto*
Logan, Bob. *Rocket town*
Loomis, Christine. *Astro Bunnies*
McCarthy, Meghan. *The adventures of Patty and the big red bus*
McNamara, Margaret. *The three little aliens and the big bad robot*
McNaughton, Colin. *Here come the aliens!*
McNulty, Faith. *If you decide to go to the moon*
McPhail, David. *Tinker and Tom and the Star Baby*
McReynolds, Linda. *Eight days gone*
Marshall, Edward. *Space case*
Marshall, James. *Merry Christmas, space case*
Mayo, Margaret. *Zoom, rocket, zoom!*
Metzger, Steve. *Pluto visits Earth!*
Milgrim, David. *Another day in the Milky Way*
Morrissey, Dean. *The crimson comet*
Moss, Marissa. *Knick knack paddywack*
O'Brien, Patrick. *You are the first kid on Mars*

O'Malley, Kevin. *Captain Raptor and the moon mystery*
Captain Raptor and the space pirates
Oxenbury, Helen. *Tom and Pippo see the moon*
Pallotta, Jerry. *Twizzlers percentages book*
Peet, Bill. *The wump world*
Petty, Dini. *The queen, the bear and the bumblebee*
Pinkney, Brian. *Cosmo and the robot*
Rau, Dana Meachen. *Neil Armstrong*
Reidy, Jean. *Light up the night*
Rey, H. A. *Curious George gets a medal*
Rockwell, Anne. *Space vehicles*
Rowe, John A. *Moondog*
Sadler, Marilyn. *Alistair in outer space*
Alistair's time machine
Schachner, Judith Byron. *Skippyjon Jones, lost in spice*
Schomp, Virginia. *If you were an . . . astronaut*
Schories, Pat. *Jack and the night visitors*
Scieszka, Jon. *Baloney, Henry P.*
Robot Zot!
Shaw, Nancy. *Sheep blast off!*
Shields, Carol Diggory. *Martian rock*
Sís, Peter. *Starry messenger*
Sklansky, Amy E. *Out of this world*
Smallcomb, Pam. *Earth to Clunk*
Suen, Anastasia. *Man on the moon*
Theodorou, Rod. *Across the solar system*
Thomas, Frances. *One day, Daddy*
Ungerer, Tomi. *Moon man*
Van Allsburg, Chris. *Zathura*
Van Camp, Katie. *Harry and Horsie*
Viva, Frank. *A long way away*
Wakeman, Daniel. *Ben's bunny trouble*
Wallace, Nancy Elizabeth. *Stars! Stars! Stars!*
Weitekamp, Margaret A. *Pluto's secret*
Wells, Robert E. *What's so special about planet Earth?*
Wethered, Peggy. *Touchdown Mars!*
Wick, Walter. *Can you see what I see? out of this world*
Wiesner, David. *Mr. Wuffles!*
Wood, Audrey. *The Christmas adventure of Space Elf Sam*
Yaccarino, Dan. *First day on a strange new planet*
New pet
Zoom! Zoom! Zoom! I'm off to the moon!
Yolen, Jane. *Moon ball*
Yorinks, Arthur. *Company's coming*
Company's going
Quack!
Young, Ned. *Zoomer's out-of-this-world Christmas*

Spectacles *see* Glasses

Speech *see* Disabilities – stuttering; Language

Spelunking *see* Caves

Spiders

Aardema, Verna. *Anansi does the impossible!*
Anansi finds a fool
The vingananee and the tree toad
Berger, Melvin. *Spinning spiders*
Bodkin, Odds. *The Christmas cobwebs*
Carle, Eric. *The very busy spider*
Cronin, Doreen. *Diary of a spider*
Cummings, Troy. *The Eensy Weensy Spider freaks out! (big-time!)*
Dann, Penny. *Eensy weensy spider*
Dewey, Jennifer Owings. *Once I knew a spider*
Dodd, Emma. *I love bugs!*
Egielski, Richard. *Itsy bitsy spider*
Gibbons, Gail. *Spiders*
Himmelman, John. *A house spider's life*
Howitt, Mary Botham. *Mary Howitt's The spider and the fly*
Keens-Douglas, Richardo. *Anancy and the haunted house*
Ketteman, Helen. *Armadilly chili*
Kimmel, Eric A. *Anansi and the magic stick*
Anansi and the moss-covered rock
Anansi and the talking melon
Anansi goes fishing
Anansi's party time
Kirk, David. *Little Miss Spider*
Little Miss Spider at Sunny Patch School
Miss Spider's ABC
Miss Spider's new car
Miss Spider's tea party
Lasky, Kathryn. *Show and tell bunnies*
Lewis, J. Patrick. *The little buggers*
London, Jonathan. *Dream weaver*
McDermott, Gerald. *Anansi the spider*
Markle, Sandra. *Sneaky, spinning, baby spiders*
Mollel, Tololwa M. *Ananse's feast*
Monks, Lydia. *Aaaarrgghh! spider!*
Mother Goose. *Little Miss Muffet*
Murawski, Darlyne A. *Bug faces*
Musgrove, Margaret. *The spider weaver*
Noble, Trinka Hakes. *A Christmas spider's miracle*
Oppenheim, Joanne. *Have you seen bugs?*
Pienkowski, Jan. *Pizza!*
Rouss, Sylvia A. *Sammy Spider's first day of school*
Sammy Spider's first Passover
Sammy Spider's first Shabbat
Sammy Spider's first Tu B'Shevat
Sammy Spider's first Yom Kippur
Shields, Carol Diggory. *The bugliest bug*
Siomades, Lorianne. *The itsy bitsy spider*
Spinelli, Eileen. *Sophie's masterpiece*
Temple, Frances. *Tiger soup*
Trapani, Iza. *The itsy bitsy spider*
Wells, Rosemary. *The itsy-bitsy spider*
Williams, Brenda. *Home for a tiger, home for a bear*

Split page books *see* Format, unusual

Spooks *see* Ghosts; Mythical creatures – goblins

Sports

Adler, David A. *Joe Louis*
Axelrod, Amy. *Pigs on the ball*
Berenstain, Stan and Jan. *The Berenstain bears go out for the team*
The Berenstain bears' report card trouble
Blumenthal, Deborah. *Ice palace*
Brown, Don. *Bright path*
Carr, Jan. *Frozen noses*
Clayton, Elaine. *A blue ribbon for Sugar*
Deans, Karen. *Playing to win*
Hammerle, Susa. *Let's try horseback riding*
Hayden, Kate. *Horse show*
Lehn, Barbara. *What is an athlete?*

Lester, Helen. *Tacky and the Winter Games*
London, Jonathan. *White water*
McKissack, Robert L. *Try your best*
Mills, Claudia. *Ziggy's blue-ribbon day*
Mochizuki, Ken. *Be water, my friend*
Pendziwol, Jean E. *A treasure at sea for dragon and me*
Prelutsky, Jack. *Good sports*
Reiser, Lynn. *Play ball with me!*
Rex, Michael. *Dunk skunk*
Schomp, Virginia. *If you were a . . . ballplayer*
Stauffacher, Sue. *Nothing but trouble*
Ziefert, Harriet. *Murphy jumps a hurdle*

Sports - archery

Fisher, Leonard Everett. *William Tell*
San Souci, Robert D. *Robin Hood and the golden arrow*

Sports - baseball

Abbott, Bud. *Who's on first?*
Abrahams, Peter. *Quacky baseball*
Adler, David A. *Campy*
Satchel Paige
Alborough, Jez. *Hit the ball Duck*
Bildner, Phil. *Shoeless Joe and Black Betsy*
The shot heard 'round the world
Burleigh, Robert. *Home run*
Stealing home
Cooper, Elisha. *Ballpark*
Cooper, Floyd. *Willie and the All-Stars*
Cristaldi, Kathryn. *Baseball ballerina*
Baseball ballerina strikes out
Crowe, Chris. *Just as good*
Curtis, Gavin. *The bat boy and his violin*
Dahl, Michael. *Goodnight baseball*
Day, Alexandra. *Frank and Ernest play ball*
deGroat, Diane. *Homer*
Egan, Tim. *Roasted peanuts*
Ellery, Amanda. *If I were a jungle animal*
Elster, Jean Alicia. *Just call me Joe Joe*
Fauchald, Nick. *Batter up!*
Nice hit!
Fishman, Cathy Goldberg. *When Jackie and Hank met*
Florian, Douglas. *Poem runs*
Golenbock, Peter. *ABCs of baseball*
Hank Aaron
Gutman, Dan. *Casey back at bat*
Hernandez, Keith. *First-base hero*
Herzog, Brad. *I spy with my little eye: baseball*
Hopkinson, Deborah. *Girl wonder*
Hubbard, Crystal. *Catching the moon: the story of a young girl's baseball dream*
Isadora, Rachel. *Luke goes to bat*
Nick plays baseball
Jordan, Deloris. *Michael's golden rules*
Keane, Dave. *Daddy adventure day*
Kelly, David A. *Miracle mud*
Kinerk, Robert. *Clorinda plays baseball!*
Kovalski, Maryann. *Take me out to the ball game*
Kraus, Robert. *Mort the sport*
Krensky, Stephen. *Play ball, Jackie!*
Leonetti, Mike. *Swinging for the fences*
Lester, Helen. *Batter up Wombat*
Lewis, J. Patrick. *Tulip at the bat*
Lies, Brian. *Bats at the ballgame*
Lorbiecki, Marybeth. *Jackie's bat*
McCully, Emily Arnold. *Mouse practice*
McDonough, Yona Zeldis. *Hammerin' Hank*
Mackall, Dandi Daley. *A girl named Dan*
Madison, Alan. *Pecorino plays ball*
Madonna. *Mr. Peabody's apples*
Mammano, Julie. *Rhinos who play baseball*
Mandel, Peter. *Say hey*
Mara, Wil. *Jackie Robinson*
Mellage, Nanette. *Coming home*
Meshon, Aaron. *Take me out to the Yakyu*
Michelson, Richard. *Across the alley*
Mochizuki, Ken. *Baseball saved us*
Nevius, Carol. *Baseball hour*
Newman, Jeff. *The boys*
Norworth, Jack. *Take me out to the ball game*
Take me out to the ballgame
Pallotta, Jerry. *F is for Fenway*
Paxton, Tom. *The jungle baseball game*
Rappaport, Doreen. *Dirt on their skirts*
Robinson, Sharon. *Testing the ice*
Rodriguez, Alex. *Out of the ballpark*
Skead, Robert. *Something to prove*
Soto, Gary. *Lucky Luis*
Spradlin, Michael P. *Baseball from A to Z*
Stadler, John. *Take me out to the ball game: a pop-up book*
Tavares, Matt. *Becoming Babe Ruth*
Henry Aaron's dream
Mudball
Oliver's game
There goes Ted Williams
Zachary's ball
Thayer, Ernest Lawrence. *Casey at the bat*
Casey at the bat: a ballad of the Republic, sung in the year 1888, ill. by Christopher Bing
Casey at the bat: a ballad of the Republic, sung in the year 1888, ill. by Patricia Polacco
Uhlberg, Myron. *Dad, Jackie, and me*
Van Dusen, Chris. *Randy Riley's really big hit*
Van Nutt, Julia. *Skyrockets and snickerdoodles*
Vernick, Audrey. *Brothers at bat*
She loved baseball
Waber, Bernard. *Gina*
Weatherford, Carole Boston. *Champions on the bench*
Welch, Willy. *Playing right field*
Wheeler, Lisa. *Dino-baseball*
Wise, Bill. *Silent star*
Yolen, Jane. *All star!*
Moon ball
Zagwÿn, Deborah Turney. *Apple batter*

Sports - basketball

Bateman, Teresa. *The princesses have a ball*
Codell, Esmé Raji. *The basket ball*
Fauchald, Nick. *Jump ball!*
Garland, Michael. *Hooray José!*
Jordan, Deloris. *Dream big*
Salt in his shoes
Martin, Bill, Jr. *Swish!*
Meunier, Brian. *Bravo, Tavo!*
Paul, Chris. *Long shot*
Rockwell, Anne. *Brendan and Belinda and the slam dunk!*
Wheeler, Lisa. *Dino-basketball*

Sports – bicycling

Aylesworth, Jim. *My sister's rusty bike*
Beardshaw, Rosalind. *Grandpa's surprise*
Berry, Lynne. *Ducking for apples*
Best, Cari. *Sally Jean, the Bicycle Queen*
Blackstone, Stella. *Bear on a bike*
Bourgeois, Paulette. *Franklin rides a bike*
Braver, Vanita. *Madison and the two wheeler*
Brown, Marc. *D. W. rides again!*
Burleigh, Robert. *Messenger, messenger*
Crews, Donald. *Bicycle race*
Davies, Matt. *Ben rides on*
Eckart, Edana. *I can ride a bike*
Edwards, Michelle. *The Hanukkah trike*
Elya, Susan Middleton. *Adiós, tricycle*
Eriksson, Eva. *A crash course for Molly*
Gerstein, Mordicai. *How to bicycle to the moon to plant sunflowers*
Goldin, David. *Go-Go-Go!*
Hillenbrand, Will. *Off we go! a Bear and Mole story*
Janni, Rebecca. *Every cowgirl loves a rodeo*
London, Jonathan. *Froggy rides a bike*
Let's go, Froggy!
Mollel, Tololwa M. *My rows and piles of coins*
Montanari, Eva. *Dino bikes*
Olaleye, Isaac. *Bikes for rent!*
Proimos, James. *The best bike ride ever*
Ransome, James. *New red bike!*
Raschka, Chris. *Everyone can learn to ride a bicycle*
Rey, H. A. *Curious George rides a bike*
Say, Allen. *The bicycle man*
Shannon, David. *Duck on a bike*
Spinelli, Eileen. *A big boy now*
Tessler, Manya. *Yuki's ride home*
Tutu, Archbishop Desmond. *Desmond and the very mean word*
Viva, Frank. *Along a long road*
Wormell, Christopher. *Blue Rabbit and the runaway wheel*

Sports – bowling

Durand, Hallie. *Mitchell goes bowling*
Eckart, Edana. *I can bowl*

Sports – boxing

Adler, David A. *Joe Louis*
Buitrago, Jairo. *Jimmy the greatest*
Lewin, Ted. *At Gleason's gym*
Myers, Walter Dean. *Muhammad Ali: the people's champion*
Olshan, Matthew. *The mighty Lalouche*
Peña, Matt de la. *A nation's hope*
Winter, Jonah. *Muhammad Ali: champion of the world*

Sports – camping *see* Camps, camping

Sports – fishing

Aruego, José. *Splash!*
Banks, Kate. *That's Papa's way*
Bootman, Colin. *Fish for the Grand Lady*
Carney, Margaret. *The biggest fish in the lake*
Cook, Bernadine. *The little fish that got away*
Creech, Sharon. *Fishing in the air*
Cronin, Doreen. *Click, clack, splish, splash*
Crowley, Ned. *Nanook and Pryce*
Emmons, Chip. *Sammy wakes his dad*
Farish, Terry. *The cat who liked potato soup*
Frank, John. *How to catch a fish*
Gentle, Victor. *Killer sharks, killer people*
George, William T. *Fishing at Long Pond*
Gibbons, Gail. *Surrounded by sea*
Gréban, Quentin. *Nestor*
Henson, Heather. *Grumpy Grandpa*
Joosse, Barbara. *I love you the purplest*
Krudop, Walter Lyon. *The man who caught fish*
London, Jonathan. *Where the big fish are*
Luenn, Nancy. *Nessa's fish*
McDonald, Rae A. *A fishing surprise*
McKissack, Patricia C. *A million fish . . . more or less*
Martin, David. *Piggy and Dad go fishing*
Mayer, Mercer. *A boy, a dog, a frog and a friend*
A boy, a dog and a frog
Ness, Evaline. *Sam, Bangs, and moonshine*
Oppel, Kenneth. *Peg and the whale*
Partridge, Elizabeth. *Oranges on Golden Mountain*
Paterson, Brian. *Zigby dives in*
Potter, Beatrix. *The tale of Mr. Jeremy Fisher*, ill. by David Jorgensen
The tale of Mr. Jeremy Fisher, ill. by Beatrix Potter
Quigley, Mary. *Granddad's fishing buddy*
Rey, Margret. *Curious George flies a kite*
Roth, Roger. *Fishing for Methuselah*
San Souci, Robert D. *Six foolish fishermen*
Say, Allen. *A river dream*
Selick, Henry. *Moongirl*
Shannon, David. *Jangles*
Stevenson, Robert Louis. *The moon*
Williams, Garth. *Benjamin's treasure*
Yamashita, Haruo. *Seven little mice have fun on the ice*
Young, Judy. *H is for hook*

Sports – football

Barber, Tiki. *Game day*
Barber, Tiki, et al. *By my brother's side*
Teammates
Bildner, Phil. *The greatest game ever played*
Turkey Bowl
Fauchald, Nick. *Touchdown!*
Gruska, Denise. *The only boy in ballet class*
McCarty, Peter. *Fall ball*
Manning, Peyton. *Family huddle*
Martin, Bill, Jr. *Little granny quarterback*
Ransome, James. *Gunner, football hero*
Reynolds, Aaron. *Buffalo wings*
Wheeler, Lisa. *Dino-football*

Sports – golf

Fauchald, Nick. *Tee off!*
Michelson, Richard. *Twice as good*

Sports – gymnastics

Brown, Marc. *D. W. flips!*
Lasky, Kathryn. *Tumble bunnies*
Newcome, Zita. *Pop-up toddlerobics*
Roche, Denis. *Mim, gym, and June*
Taylor, Sean. *Boing!*

Sports – hiking

Coyle, Carmela LaVigna. *Do princesses really kiss frogs?*
Curious George goes hiking
Harper, Jamie. *Miss Mingo weathers the storm*
Johnson, D. B. *Henry hikes to Fitchburg*
Katschke, Judy. *Take a hike, Snoopy*
Korngold, Jamie S. *Sadie and the big mountain*
Shaw, Nancy. *Sheep take a hike*

Sports – hockey

Bailey, Linda. *The farm team*
Carter, Anne Laurel. *The F team*
Fauchald, Nick. *Face off!*
Leonetti, Mike. *Gretzky's game*
Mizzoni, Chris. *Clancy with the puck*
Napier, Matt. *Z is for zamboni*
Polacco, Patricia. *Rotten Richie and the ultimate dare*
Shaw, Mary. *Brady Brady and the big mistake*
Brady Brady and the great rink
Brady Brady and the runaway goalie
Brady Brady and the Twirlin' Torpedo
Stevenson, James. *Sam the Zamboni man*
Sylvester, Kevin. *Splinters*
Wheeler, Lisa. *Dino-hockey*

Sports – hunting

Cuyler, Margery. *We're going on a lion hunt*
Freedman, Claire. *Follow that bear if you dare!*
Hader, Berta Hoerner. *The mighty hunter*
Judes, Marie-Odile. *Max, the stubborn little wolf*
Kellogg, Steven. *Tallyho, Pinkerton!*
Kroll, Steven. *One tough turkey*
Langstaff, John M. *Oh, a-hunting we will go*
Lowry, Lois. *Crow call*
Miller, Pat. *We're going on a book hunt*
Peet, Bill. *Buford the little bighorn*
The gnats of knotty pine
Rohmer, Harriet, et al. *The invisible hunters*
Rosen, Michael. *We're going on a bear hunt*
Tankard, Jeremy. *Me hungry!*
Winter, Jeanette. *Kali's song*

Sports – ice skating

Bailey, Linda. *The best figure skater in the whole wide world*
Berger, Carin. *A perfect day*
Berry, Lynne. *Duck skates*
Bunge, Daniela. *The scarves*
Carlson, Nancy. *Snowden*
Child, Lauren. *I really, really need actual ice skates*
Emberley, Rebecca. *Mice on ice*
Holabird, Katharine. *Angelina ice skates*
Isadora, Rachel. *Sophie skates*
Karas, G. Brian. *Skidamarink*
Keller, Holly. *Pearl's new skates*
Medearis, Angela Shelf. *Poppa's itchy Christmas*
Spinelli, Eileen. *Callie Cat, ice skater*
Stevenson, James. *Sam the Zamboni man*
Whybrow, Ian. *Bella gets her skates on*
Wright, Joanna. *Bunnies on ice*
Yamaguchi, Kristi. *Dream big, little pig!*
It's a big world, little pig!

Sports – jumping rope

English, Karen. *Hot day on Abbott Avenue*

Sports – karate

Hellman, Gary. *The karate way*
Mayer, Mercer. *There are monsters everywhere*
Nevius, Carol. *Karate hour*
Rockwell, Anne. *Chip and the karate kick*
Schwartz, Corey Rosen. *The three ninja pigs*

Sports – martial arts

DaCosta, Barbara. *Nighttime Ninja*
Latimer, Alex. *The boy who cried ninja*
Schwartz, Corey Rosen. *The three ninja pigs*

Sports – mountain climbing

Becker, Shari. *Maxwell's mountain*
George, Jean Craighead. *Cliff hanger*

Sports – Olympics

Hennessy, B. G. *Olympics!*
Herzog, Brad. *G is for gold medal*
Jamieson, Victoria. *Olympig!*
Jordan, Deloris. *Dream big*
Lang, Heather. *Queen of the track*
Malaspina, Ann. *Touch the sky*
Richards, Jean. *The first Olympic games*
Yoo, Paula. *Sixteen years in sixteen seconds*

Sports – racing

Adams, Adrienne. *The great Valentine's Day balloon race*
Aesop. *The hare and the tortoise*, ill. by Paul Galdone
The hare and the tortoise, ill. by Carol Jones
The hare and the tortoise, ill. by Helen Ward
The hare and the tortoise / La liebre y la tortuga
The race
Road signs
The tortoise and the hare, ill. by Jerry Pinkney
The tortoise and the hare, ill. by Sara Rojo
The tortoise and the hare: an Aesop fable
Anderson, Peggy Perry. *We go in a circle*
Berenstain, Stan and Jan. *The Berenstain bears and the big road race*
Blake, Robert J. *Painter and Ugly*
Caseley, Judith. *Field Day Friday*
Clement, Nathan. *Speed*
Crews, Donald. *Bicycle race*
Dahl, Michael. *One checkered flag*
Dempsey, Kristy. *Mini racer*
Downard, Barry. *The Race of the Century*
Goldin, David. *Go-Go-Go!*
Golding, Theresa Martin. *Abby's asthma and the big race*
Herzog, Brad. *R is for race*
Kolar, Bob. *Racer dogs*
Lewin, Ted. *Horse song*
Libby, Barbara. *I rode the red horse*
London, Jonathan. *Sled dogs run*
Lord, Cynthia. *Hot rod Hamster*
Lowell, Susan. *The tortoise and the jackrabbit*
Lynn, Sarah. *1-2-3 va-va-vroom!*
McCarthy, Meghan. *The incredible life of Balto*
Seabiscuit

McMullan, Kate. *I'm fast*
Miranda, Anne. *Vroom, chugga, vroom-vroom*
Mitton, Tony. *The Jungle Run*
Mora, Pat. *The race of toad and deer*
Morrison, Toni. *The tortoise or the hare*
Nelson, Kristin L. *Monster trucks*
O'Malley, Kevin. *The great race*
Rex, Michael. *My race car*
Seibert, Patricia. *Mush!*
Tingle, Tim. *When Turtle grew feathers*
Todd, Mark. *Start your engines*
Trollinger, Patsi B. *Perfect timing*
Van Woerkom, Dorothy. *Harry and Shelburt*
Zane, Alexander. *The wheels on the race car*

Sports – roller skating

Ashman, Linda. *Samantha on a roll*
Pilkey, Dav. *The Moonglow Roll-O-Rama*
Saltzberg, Barney. *Hip, hip, hooray day!*

Sports – sailing

Beck, Andrea. *Elliot's shipwreck*
Blackstone, Stella. *An island in the sun*
Crews, Donald. *Sail away*
Haas, Rick de. *Peter and the seal*
Heidbreder, Robert. *A sea-wishing day*
Lund, Deb. *Dinosailors*
McNeil, Florence. *Sail away*
Schubert, Ingrid. *There's always room for one more*
Uhlberg, Myron. *Lemuel, the fool*
Van Dusen, Chris. *Down to the sea with Mr. Magee*
van Lieshout, Maria. *Hopper and Wilson*

Sports – skateboarding

Brimner, Larry Dane. *Cat on wheels*
Carlson, Nancy. *Arnie and the skateboard gang*
Howard, Arthur. *Cosmo zooms*

Sports – skiing

Berger, Carin. *A perfect day*
Calhoun, Mary. *Cross-country cat*
Dahl, Michael. *Downhill fun*
Huneck, Stephen. *Sally's snow adventure*
Peet, Bill. *Buford the little bighorn*
Van Dusen, Chris. *Learning to ski with Mr. Magee*

Sports – skin diving

Baker, Jeannie. *The hidden forest*
Loomis, Christine. *Scuba bunnies*

Sports – sledding

Blake, Robert J. *Painter and Ugly*
Casanova, Mary. *One-dog sleigh*
Chaconas, Dori. *On a wintry morning*
Curious George goes sledding
Day, Alexandra. *Carl's snowy afternoon*
Fearnley, Jan. *A perfect day for it*
Harper, Lee. *Snow! Snow! Snow!*
Judge, Lita. *Red sled*
Kortepeter, Paul. *Oliver's red toboggan*
London, Jonathan. *Sled dogs run*
McCarthy, Meghan. *The incredible life of Balto*
Norman, Kim. *Ten on the sled*
Rule, Rebecca. *The iciest, diciest, scariest sled ride ever!*
Seibert, Patricia. *Mush!*
Smee, Nicola. *Jingle-jingle*
Thomas, Patricia. *Red sled*
Winthrop, Elizabeth. *Sledding*

Sports – soccer

Aesop. *Bat's big game*
Boelts, Maribeth. *Happy like soccer*
Brown, Monica. *Pelé, king of soccer / Pelé, el rey del fútbol*
Browne, Anthony. *Willy the wizard*
Burleigh, Robert. *Goal*
Capucilli, Alyssa Satin. *My first soccer game*
Cline-Ransome, Lesa. *Young Pelé*
Diehl, David. *Goal! my soccer book*
Eckart, Edana. *I can play soccer*
Elliott, Laura Malone. *Hunter and Stripe and the soccer showdown*
Fauchald, Nick. *Score!*
Finchler, Judy. *You're a good sport, Miss Malarkey*
Flanagan, Alice K. *Coach John and his soccer team*
Fox, Diane. *Tyson the terrible*
Hamm, Mia. *Winners never quit*
Javaherbin, Mina. *Goal!*
Klingel, Cynthia Fitterer. *Soccer*
Kolar, Bob. *Big kicks*
Lester, Helen. *Hurty feelings*
London, Jonathan. *Froggy plays soccer*
McNaughton, Colin. *Preston's goal!*
Mammano, Julie. *Rhinos who play soccer*
Murphy, Stuart J. *Game time*
Nevius, Carol. *Soccer hour*
Pelé. *For the love of soccer!*
Rockwell, Anne. *Morgan plays soccer*
Rodriguez, Edel. *Sergio saves the game!*
Saltzberg, Barney. *Soccer mom from outer space*
Shahan, Sherry. *That's not how you play soccer, Daddy*
Sís, Peter. *Madlenka, soccer star*
Vyner, Tim. *World team*
Watson, Jesse Joshua. *Hope for Haiti*
Weninger, Brigitte. *Davy, soccer star!*
Wheeler, Lisa. *Dino-soccer*

Sports – Special Olympics

Pulver, Robin. *Way to go, Alex!*

Sports – surfing

Dempsey, Kristy. *Surfer chick*
Mammano, Julie. *Rhinos who surf*
Minters, Frances. *Princess Fishtail*
Sattler, Jennifer. *Pig kahuna*

Sports – swimming

Barclay, Jane. *Going on a journey to the sea*
Cooper, Susan. *Frog*
Cousins, Lucy. *Maisy learns to swim*
Maisy's pool
Eckart, Edana. *I can swim*
Fuge, Charles. *Swim, Little Wombat, swim!*
Ginsburg, Mirra. *The chick and the duckling*
Gutman, Anne. *Gaspard at the seashore*
Harper, Jamie. *Me too!*
Hest, Amy. *Make the team, Baby Duck*

Kliphuis, Christine. *Robbie and Ronnie*
Koch, Ed. *Eddie's little sister makes a splash*
Lin, Grace. *Olvina swims*
London, Jonathan. *Froggy learns to swim*
Lucke, Deb. *The boy who wouldn't swim*
Newman, Jeff. *Reginald*
Pfister, Marcus. *Hang on, Hopper!*
Reiser, Lynn. *Two dogs swimming*
Rice, Eve. *Swim!*
Riley, Linda Capus. *Elephants swim*
Rockwell, Anne. *Katie Catz makes a splash*
Rodriguez, Edel. *Sergio makes a splash*
Rylant, Cynthia. *Brownie and Pearl take a dip*
Schuurmans, Hilde. *Sydney won't swim*
Schwartz, Roslyn. *The mole sisters and the rainy day*
Scotton, Rob. *Splish, splash, Splat!*
Stanley, Mandy. *At the pool*
Stewart, Amber. *Little by little*
Volkmann, Roy. *Curious kittens*
Waddell, Martin. *The pig in the pond*
Ward, Nick. *Come on Baby Duck*
Watanabe, Shigeo. *Let's go swimming*
Webster, Christine. *Otter everywhere*
Weninger, Brigitte. *Miko goes on vacation*
Weston, Martha. *Tuck in the pool*
Wilson, Karma. *Don't be afraid, Little Pip*
Winton, Tim. *The deep*

Sports – T-ball

London, Jonathan. *Froggy plays T-ball*

Sports – Tae Kwon Do

Pinkney, Brian. *Jojo's flying side kick*

Sports – tennis

McG, Shane. *Tennis, anyone?*

Sports – volleyball

Fauchald, Nick. *Bump! set! spike!*

Sports – wrestling

Boelts, Maribeth. *Big Daddy, frog wrestler*
Morales, Yuyi. *Nino wrestles the world*
Wheeler, Lisa. *Dino-wrestling*

Sportsmanship

Elliott, Laura Malone. *Hunter and Stripe and the soccer showdown*
Finchler, Judy. *You're a good sport, Miss Malarkey*
Flanagan, Alice K. *Coach John and his soccer team*
Hamm, Mia. *Winners never quit*
Janni, Rebecca. *Every cowgirl loves a rodeo*
Jordan, Deloris. *Michael's golden rules*
Krosoczka, Jarrett J. *Max for president*
Lasky, Kathryn. *Tumble bunnies*
Robberecht, Thierry. *Sam is not a loser*
Rockwell, Anne. *Brendan and Belinda and the slam dunk!*
Rose, Deborah Lee. *The spelling bee before recess*

Squid

Nyeu, Tao. *Squid and Octopus*
Sherry, Kevin. *I'm the best artist in the ocean*
I'm the biggest thing in the ocean
Viva, Frank. *A long way away*

Stage *see* Theater

Stars

Barner, Bob. *Stars, stars, stars*
Baumgart, Klaus. *Laura's Christmas star*
Laura's secret
Laura's star
Benjamin, A. H. *Mouse, mole and the falling star*
Branley, Franklyn M. *The sky is full of stars*
Cabrera, Jane. *Twinkle, twinkle, little star*
Elschner, Geraldine. *Moonchild, star of the sea*
Fancher, Lou. *Star climbing*
Fischer, Scott M. *Twinkle*
Florian, Douglas. *Comets, stars, the moon, and Mars*
Gerber, Carole. *Annie Jump Cannon, astronomer*
Gibbons, Gail. *Stargazers*
Goble, Paul. *The lost children*
Grimm, Jacob and Wilhelm. *The star child*
Hansen, Felicity. *The first bear*
Hest, Amy. *Little chick*
Hoffman, Mary. *Three wise women*
Holub, Joan. *Twinkle, star of the week*
Horacek, Petr. *Suzy Goose and the Christmas star*
When the moon smiled
Langley, Karen. *Shine*
Lee, Y. J. *The little moon princess*
Lyon, George Ella. *My friend, the starfinder*
Mackall, Dandi Daley. *Seeing stars*
Marzollo, Jean. *I see a star*
Little Bear, you're a star!
Meister, Cari. *Follow the drinking gourd: an Underground Railroad story*
Mitton, Jacqueline. *Zoo in the sky*
Nelson, S. D. *The Star People*
Norman, Geoffrey. *Stars above us*
Oughton, Jerrie. *How the stars fell into the sky*
Parker, Michael. *You are a star!*
Pettenati, Jeanne K. *Galileo's journal, 1609–1610*
Pfister, Marcus. *The Christmas star*
Puttock, Simon. *A ladder to the stars*
Ray, Mary Lyn. *Stars*
Reynolds, Peter H. *Sydney's star*
Sís, Peter. *Starry messenger*
The sun, the moon, and the stars
Sykes, Julie. *Little Rocket's special star*
Taylor, Jane. *Twinkle, twinkle little star,* ill. by Heather Collins
Twinkle, twinkle, little star, ill. by Michael Hague
Twinkle, twinkle little star, ill. by Julia Noonan
Twinkle, twinkle, little star, ill. by Jerry PinkneyTazewell, Charles. *The littlest angel,* ill. by Deborah Lanino
The littlest angel, ill. by Paul Micich
The littlest angel, ill. by Rebecca Thornburgh
They followed a bright star
Tomecek, Steve. *Stars*
Wallace, Nancy Elizabeth. *Stars! Stars! Stars!*
Washington, Ned. *When you wish upon a star*
Wilson-Max, Ken. *Max's starry night*
Winter, Jeanette. *Follow the drinking gourd*

Stealing *see* Behavior – stealing; Crime

Steam shovels *see* Machines

Steamrollers *see* Machines

Step families *see* Divorce; Family life – stepfamilies

Stepchildren *see* Divorce; Family life – stepfamilies

Stepparents *see* Divorce; Family life – stepfamilies

Stones *see* Rocks

Stores

Agee, Jon. *Nothing*
Alakija, Polly. *Catch that goat!*
Averbeck, Jim. *The market bowl*
Berger, Joe. *My special one and only*
Bond, Michael. *Paddington Bear and the Christmas surprise*
Brown, Calef. *Pirateria*
Carling, Amelia Lau. *Mama and Papa have a store*
Corey, Shana. *Milly and the Macy's Parade*
Curious George visits a toy store
Daly, Niki. *Next stop — Zanzibar Road!*
Day, Alexandra. *Carl goes shopping*
Dematons, Charlotte. *Let's go*
DiSalvo, DyAnne. *Grandpa's corner store*
Egan, Tim. *The pink refrigerator*
Ehlert, Lois. *Market day*
Elya, Susan Middleton. *Bebé goes shopping*
Flanagan, Alice K. *A busy day at Mr. Kang's grocery store*
  Buying a pet from Ms. Chavez
Florence, Tyler. *Tyler makes pancakes!*
Fraser, Mary Ann. *Pet shop follies*
  Pet shop lullaby
Freeman, Don. *Corduroy*
Gibbons, Gail. *Department store*
Gomi, Taro. *I lost my dad*
Johnson, Angela. *The Rolling Store*
Juan, Ana. *The pet shop revolution*
Kirsch, Vincent X. *Natalie and Naughtily*
Korchek, Lori. *Adventures of Cow, too*
Krull, Kathleen. *Supermarket*
Lazar, Tara. *The Monstore*
Lewin, Ted. *Big Jimmy's Kum Kau Chinese take out*
  How much?
  Market!
Lewis, J. Patrick. *The fantastic 5 and 10¢ store*
Lobel, Arnold. *On Market Street*
Loupy, Christophe. *Don't worry, Wags*
Masters, Anthony. *Ricky's rat gang*
Meddaugh, Susan. *The witches' supermarket*
Melvin, Alice. *The high street*
Miranda, Anne. *To market, to market*
Modarressi, Mitra. *Yard sale*
Munsch, Robert N. *Something good*
Murphy, Stuart J. *Just enough carrots*
  Mall mania
Naylor, Phyllis Reynolds. *Sweet strawberries*
O'Neill, Alexis. *Estela's swap*
Parks, Carmen. *Farmers market*
Pelley, Kathleen T. *Raj the bookstore tiger*
Pienkowski, Jan. *Bel and Bub and the black hole*
Polacco, Patricia. *Something about Hensley's*
Potter, Beatrix. *Ginger and Pickles*
Rockwell, Anne. *At the supermarket*
Rylant, Cynthia. *Little Whistle*
  Little Whistle's Christmas
  Little Whistle's dinner party
  Little Whistle's medicine
Schaefer, Lola M. *Supermarket*
Schwartz, Joanne. *Our corner grocery store*
Seibold, J. Otto. *Lost sloth*
Shea, Kitty. *Out and about at the supermarket*
Sierra, Judy. *Suppose you meet a dinosaur*
Skolsky, Mindy Warshaw. *Hannah and the whistling tea kettle*
Thong, Roseanne. *Gai see*
Trent, Shanda. *Farmers' market day*
Wellington, Monica. *Apple farmer Annie*
Wells, Rosemary. *Max's dragon shirt*
Williams, Karen Lynn. *Tap-tap*
Yin. *Brothers*
Young, Ed. *Donkey trouble*

Stories in rhyme *see* Rhyming text

Strangers *see* Behavior – talking to strangers

Streams *see* Rivers

Streets *see* Roads

String

Baker, Keith. *Just how long can a long string be?!*
Boyle, Bob. *Hugo and the really, really, really long string*
Fleischman, Paul. *Lost!*
Geisert, Arthur. *The giant ball of string*

Stubbornness *see* Character traits – stubbornness

Submarines *see* Boats, ships

Sullivan Islands *see* Foreign lands – South Sea Islands

Sun

Aesop. *The contest between the Sun and the Wind*
Alda, Arlene. *Hurry Granny Annie*
Asch, Frank. *The sun is my favorite star*
Bang, Molly. *Living sunlight*
  My light
  Ocean sunlight
Baylor, Byrd. *The way to start a day*
Branley, Franklyn M. *Eclipse*
  The planets in our solar system
  The sun, our nearest star
  Sunshine makes the seasons
Canyon, Christopher. *John Denver's Sunshine on my shoulders*
Daly, Niki. *Why the sun and moon live in the sky*

Dayrell, Elphinstone. *Why the sun and the moon live in the sky*
Ellwand, David. *Midas Mouse*
Flanagan, Alice K. *Sunshine*
Gibbons, Gail. *Sun up, sun down*
Goudey, Alice E. *The day we saw the sun come up*
Hines, Anna Grossnickle. *What can you do in the sun?*
Kaner, Etta. *Who likes the sun?*
Kleven, Elisa. *Sun bread*
Lobel, Anita. *Hello, day!*
London, Jonathan. *Like butter on pancakes*
McDermott, Gerald. *Musicians of the sun*
Marzollo, Jean. *Sun song*
Nelson, Robin. *A sunny day*
Peet, Bill. *Cock-a-doodle Dudley*
Peterson, Cris. *Seed soil sun*
Polacco, Patricia. *I can hear the sun*
Root, Phyllis. *Lucia and the light*
San Souci, Robert D. *Peter and the blue witch baby*
Sherman, Pat. *The sun's daughter*
Shulevitz, Uri. *Dawn*
Slate, Joseph. *Story time for Little Porcupine*
The sun, the moon, and the stars
Tafuri, Nancy. *What the sun sees / What the moon sees*
Theodorou, Rod. *Across the solar system*
Tresselt, Alvin R. *Sun up*
Wells, Robert E. *Why do elephants need the sun?*
Wolkstein, Diane. *The day Ocean came to visit*
Wood, Douglas. *Where the sunrise begins*

Superstition

Hassett, John. *Father Sun, Mother Moon*
McNaughton, Colin. *Don't step on the crack!*
Rumford, James. *Don't touch my hat!*
Soto, Gary. *Lucky Luis*
Sutton, Jane. *The trouble with cauliflower*

Swamps

Appelt, Kathi. *Where, where is Swamp Bear?*
Arnosky, Jim. *Raccoon on his own*
Wild and swampy
Bateman, Donna M. *Deep in the swamp*
Berkes, Marianne. *Marsh music*
Chaconas, Dori. *Virginnie's hat*
Crow, Kristyn. *Bedtime at the swamp*
Dennard, Deborah. *Bullfrog at Magnolia Circle*
Downing, Johnette. *Down in Louisiana*
Doyen, Denise. *Once upon a twice*
Fleming, Candace. *Who invited you?*
Huggins, Peter. *Trosclair and the alligator*
Jewell, Nancy. *Alligator wedding*
LeBox, Annette. *Wild bog tea*
Root, Phyllis. *Big belching bog*
Salley, Coleen. *Epossumondas plays possum*
San Souci, Robert D. *Little Pierre*
Thomas, Joyce Carol. *The gospel Cinderella*
Vaughan, Marcia Kapok. *Whistling Dixie*
Weeks, Sarah. *Catfish Kate and the sweet swamp band*
Yolen, Jane. *Welcome to the river of grass*

Swapping *see* Activities – trading

Symbiosis

Stone, Lynn M. *Partners*

Talking to strangers *see* Behavior – talking to strangers

Tall tales

Aliki. *The story of Johnny Appleseed*
Anderson, Laurie Halse. *The big cheese of Third Street*
Andreasen, Dan. *The giant of Seville*
Aylesworth, Jim. *My sister's rusty bike*
Balcziak, Bill. *John Henry*
Paul Bunyan
Pecos Bill
Bateman, Teresa. *Paul Bunyan vs. Hals Halson*
Bertrand, Lynne. *Granite baby*
Codell, Esme Raji. *Seed by seed*
Cole, Brock. *Buttons*
Crunk, Tony. *Railroad John and the Red Rock run*
Davol, Marguerite W. *The loudest, fastest, best drummer in Kansas*
Derby, Sally. *Whoosh went the wind!*
Drummond, Allan. *Casey Jones*
Gorbachev, Valeri. *Where is the apple pie?*
Graves, Keith. *Uncle Blubbafink's seriously ridiculous stories*
Greathouse, Carol. *The dinosaur tamer*
Griffin, Kitty. *The foot-stomping adventures of Clementine Sweet*
Hayes, Joe. *The gum-chewing rattler*
Holt, Kimberly Willis. *The adventures of Granny Clearwater and Little Critter*
Isaacs, Anne. *Dust Devil*
Pancakes for supper!
Swamp Angel
Johnston, Tony. *Levi Strauss gets a bright idea*
Keats, Ezra Jack. *John Henry*
Kellogg, Steven. *I was born about 10,000 years ago*
Johnny Appleseed: a tall tale
Mike Fink
Paul Bunyan: a tall tale
Pecos Bill
Sally Ann Thunder Ann Whirlwind Crockett
Kimmel, Eric A. *The Erie Canal pirates*
The great Texas hamster drive
Koren, Edward. *Very hairy Harry*
Lester, Julius. *John Henry*
Lindbergh, Reeve. *Johnny Appleseed*
Luckhurst, Matt. *Paul Bunyan and Babe the Blue Ox*
McGill, Alice. *Sure as sunrise*
McKissack, Patricia C. *A million fish . . . more or less*
Madison, Alan. *The littlest grape stomper*
Miller, Bobbi. *Davy Crockett gets hitched*
Miss Sally Ann and the panther
Mora, Pat. *Doña Flor*
Nolen, Jerdine. *Big Jabe*
Harvey Potter's balloon farm
Thunder Rose
Oppel, Kenneth. *Peg and the whale*

Pinkney, Andrea Davis. *Peggony-Po*
Root, Phyllis. *Kiss the cow*
Paula Bunyan
Rosie's fiddle
Roth, Roger. *Fishing for Methuselah*
Roth, Susan L. *The biggest frog in Australia*
Rubel, Nicole. *A cowboy named Ernestine*
Schanzer, Rosalyn. *How Ben Franklin stole the lightning*
Schnitzler, Pattie L. *Widdermaker*
Shannon, David. *Jangles*
Shepard, Aaron. *Master man*
Shulevitz, Uri. *What is a wise bird like you doing in a silly tale like this?*
Sís, Peter. *A small tall tale from the far Far North*
Smith, Cynthia Leitich. *Holler Loudly*
Smith, Janice Lee. *Jess and the stinky cowboys*
Swain, Gwenyth. *Johnny Appleseed*
White, Linda Arms. *Comes a wind*
Willey, Margaret. *Clever Beatrice, an Upper Peninsula conte*
Williams, Suzanne. *Library Lil*
Wilson, Karma. *Whopper cake*
Wood, Audrey. *The Bunyans*
Wooldridge, Connie Nordhielm. *The legend of Strap Buckner*
Wright, Catherine. *Steamboat Annie and the thousand-pound catfish*
Yolen, Jane. *Johnny Appleseed: the legend and the truth*

Tardiness *see* Behavior – promptness, tardiness

Taxis

Agee, Jon. *The other side of town*
Barracca, Debra. *A taxi dog Christmas*
Barracca, Sal. *The adventures of taxi dog*
Milusich, Janice. *Off go their engines, off go their lights*

Teasing *see* Behavior – bullying, teasing

Teddy bears *see* Toys – bears

Teeth

Bate, Lucy. *Little rabbit's loose tooth*
Beeler, Selby B. *Throw your tooth on the roof*
Bennett, Kelly. *Vampire baby*
Borden, Louise. *The lost-and-found tooth*
Bouchard, Dave. *Fairy*
Bowen, Anne. *Tooth Fairy's first night*
Brockenbrough, Martha. *The Dinosaur Tooth Fairy*
Brown, Heather. *Chomp!*
Brown, Marc. *Arthur's tooth*
Chandra, Deborah. *George Washington's teeth*
Chetkowski, Emily. *Pumpkin smile*
Colato Laínez, René. *The Tooth Fairy meets El Ratón Pérez*
Cousins, Lucy. *Maisy, Charley, and the wobbly tooth*
Curious George goes to the dentist
Davis, Katie. *Mabel the Tooth Fairy and how she got her job*
Diakité, Penda. *I lost my tooth in Africa*
Durant, Alan. *Dear tooth fairy*
Edwards, Pamela Duncan. *Dear Tooth Fairy*
Elya, Susan Middleton. *Tooth on the loose*
Flanagan, Alice K. *Dr. Kanner, dentist with a smile*
Gomi, Taro. *The crocodile and the dentist*
Graham, Bob. *April and Esme, tooth fairies*
Grambling, Lois G. *This whole Tooth Fairy thing's nothing but a big rip-off!*
High, Linda Oatman. *Cool Bopper's choppers*
Hood, Susan. *The Tooth Mouse*
James, Brian. *The Supertwins and tooth trouble*
Jay, Betsy. *Jane vs. the Tooth Fairy*
Kann, Victoria. *Silverlicious*
Kaye, Marilyn. *The real tooth fairy*
Keller, Laurie. *Open wide*
McCloskey, Robert. *One morning in Maine*
MacDonald, Amy. *Cousin Ruth's tooth*
Maconie, Robin. *Alice and her fabulous teeth*
McPhail, David. *The bear's toothache*
Miles, Elizabeth J. *Mouths and teeth*
Miller, Edward. *The tooth book*
Moss, Miriam. *Wibble wobble*
Munsch, Robert N. *Andrew's loose tooth*
Murkoff, Heidi Eisenberg. *What to expect when you go to the dentist*
O'Brien, Patrick. *Megatooth*
Olson, Mary. *Nice try, Tooth Fairy*
Palatini, Margie. *Gone with the wand*
No biting, Louise
Paxton, Tom. *The story of the Tooth Fairy*
Rockwell, Harlow. *My dentist*
Rosenberry, Vera. *Vera goes to the dentist*
Ross, Tony. *I want my tooth*
Schaefer, Lola M. *Dental office*
Loose tooth
Simms, Laura. *Rotten teeth*
Sís, Peter. *Madlenka*
Swanson, Diane. *The dentist and you*
Vrombaut, An. *Clarabella's teeth*
Wilson, Karma. *Bear's loose tooth*

Telephone

Raschka, Chris. *Ring! Yo?*
Whybrow, Ian. *Hello! Is this grandma?*

Television

Barracca, Debra. *Maxi, the star*
Berenstain, Stan and Jan. *The Berenstain bears and too much TV*
Bergen, Lara Rice. *Blue's world of words*
Brown, Marc. *The bionic bunny show*
Lobb, Janice. *Listen and see! What's on TV?*
McCarty, Peter. *Chloe*
McPhail, David. *Fix-it*
Nickle, John. *TV Rex*
Polacco, Patricia. *Aunt Chip and the great Triple Creek dam affair*
Proimos, James. *Todd's TV*
Weigelt, Udo. *Super Guinea Pig to the rescue*

Telling stories *see* Activities – storytelling

Telling time *see* Clocks, watches; Time

Temper tantrums *see* Emotions – anger

Texas

Adler, David A. *A picture book of Sam Houston*
Borgo, Lacy. *Big Mama's baby*
Burell, Sarah. *Diamond Jim Dandy and the sheriff*
Fern, Tracey E. *Buffalo music*
Ketteman, Helen. *The three little gators*
Waynetta and the cornstalk
Kimmel, Eric A. *The great Texas hamster drive*
Jack and the giant barbecue
The lady in the blue cloak
Little Britches and the rattlers
The three cabritos
King, M. G. *Librarian on the roof!*
Munro, Roxie. *The inside-outside book of Texas*

Textless *see* Wordless

Theater

Ackerman, Karen. *Bean's big day*
Agee, Jon. *Milo's hat trick*
Aliki. *A play's the thing*
Avi. *Silent movie*
Beeke, Jemma. *The Rickety Barn show*
Behrens, June. *The feast of Thanksgiving*
Berenstain, Stan and Jan. *The Berenstain bears get stage fright*
Bond, Felicia. *The Halloween play*
Brown, Don. *Mack made movies*
Brown, Marc. *Arthur's Thanksgiving*
Calhoun, Mary. *Henry the Christmas cat*
Cohen, Miriam. *Starring first grade*
Comden, Betty, et al. *Flying to Neverland with Peter Pan*
Conway, David. *Errol and his extraordinary nose*
Crimi, Carolyn. *Rock 'n' roll Mole*
Cronin, Doreen. *Dooby dooby moo*
Curious George goes to a movie
D'Amico, Carmela. *Ella sets the stage*
Davidson, Rebecca Piatt. *All the world's a stage*
deGroat, Diane. *Liar, liar, pants on fire*
DePalma, Mary Newell. *The Nutcracker doll*
dePaola, Tomie. *The night of Las Posadas*
DeRubertis, Barbara. *Alexander Anteater's amazing act*
Dunrea, Olivier. *Appearing tonight! Mary Heather Elizabeth Livingstone*
Edwards, Pamela Duncan. *Bravo, Livingstone Mouse!*
Engelbreit, Mary. *Queen of the class*
Fox, Mem. *Wombat divine*
Francis, Pauline. *Sam stars at Shakespeare's Globe*
A frog he would a-wooing go [folk-song]. *Frog went a-courting*
Geras, Adèle. *Little ballet star*
Hartman, Bob. *Granny Mae's Christmas play*
Hoffman, Mary. *Amazing Grace*
Holabird, Katharine. *Angelina ice skates*
Angelina on stage
Hopkins, Lee Bennett. *Full moon and star*
Isadora, Rachel. *Lili on stage*
Isherwood, Shirley. *Flora the frog*
Ives, Penny. *Celestine, drama queen*
Jane, Pamela. *Milo and the greatest trick ever*
Keller, Laurie. *The scrambled states of America talent show*
Kontis, Alethea. *AlphaOops!*
Krensky, Stephen. *Shooting for the moon*
LaChanze. *Little diva*
Langley, Karen. *Shine*
Latimer, Alex. *Penguin's hidden talent*
Lawson, Julie. *Arizona Charlie and the Klondike Kid*
Lester, Helen. *Tackylocks and the three bears*
Lithgow, John. *Marsupial Sue presents "The Runaway Pancake"*
Littlesugar, Amy. *Tree of hope*
Long, Ethan. *The Wing Wing brothers math spectacular!*
McCully, Emily Arnold. *My real family*
McDonald, Megan. *Penguin and Little Blue*
McLean, Dirk. *Curtain up!*
McNaughton, Colin. *When I grow up*
Marshall, James. *Swine lake*
Mills, Elaine. *Marinetta at the ballet*
Ormerod, Jan. *Ms. MacDonald has a class*
Paraskevas, Betty. *Marvin, the tap-dancing horse*
Perlov, Betty Rosenberg. *Rifka takes a bow*
Potter, Giselle. *The year I didn't go to school*
Primavera, Elise. *Louise, the big cheese*
Rockwell, Anne. *President's Day*
Thanksgiving Day
Ruzzier, Sergio. *Amandina*
Say, Allen. *Kamishibai man*
Scanlon, Elizabeth Garton. *Think big!*
Schotter, Roni. *Purim play*
Schwartz, Amy. *Starring Miss Darlene*
Scotton, Rob. *Splat the cat: on with the show*
Sierra, Judy. *Zoozical*
Spinelli, Eileen. *Six hogs on a scooter*
Stadler, Alexander. *Beverly Billingsly takes a bow*
Trimble, Marcia. *Peppy's shadow*
Tryon, Leslie. *Albert's play*
Vail, Rachel. *Over the moon*
Waber, Bernard. *Evie and Margie*
Waterton, Betty. *A bumblebee sweater*
Whippo, Walt. *Little white duck*
Ziefert, Harriet. *Lights on Broadway*

Thieves *see* Crime

Thumb sucking

Cooper, Ilene. *Jake's best thumb*
Dionne, Wanda. *Little Thumb*
Primavera, Elise. *Thumb love*

Thunder *see* Weather – lightning, thunder; Weather – storms

Time

Adler, David A. *Time zones*
Ancona, George. *Handtalk zoo*
Appelt, Kathi. *Bats around the clock*
Axelrod, Amy. *Pigs on a blanket*
Aylesworth, Jim. *The completed hickory dickory dock*
Baker, Keith. *Hickory dickory dock*
Barnett, Mac. *Oh no! Not again!*
Becker, Bonny. *Just a minute*
Bernhard, Durga. *While you are sleeping: a lift-the-flap book of time around the world*
Blackstone, Stella. *Bear takes a trip*
Brown, Ken. *What's the time, Grandma Wolf?*
Carle, Eric. *The grouchy ladybug*
Carlstrom, Nancy White. *It's about time, Jesse Bear*

Charlip, Remy. *Why I will never ever ever ever have enough time to read this book*
Cousins, Lucy. *Maisy's first clock*
Fraser, Mary Ann. *I.Q., it's time*
Gibbons, Gail. *Clocks and how they go*
Gliori, Debi. *What's the time, Mr. Wolf?*
Gregory, Nan. *Amber waiting*
Handford, Martin. *Find Waldo now*
Where's Waldo now?
Harper, Dan. *Telling time with Big Mama Cat*
Harris, Trudy. *The clock struck one*
Hennessy, B. G. *Mr. Ouchy's first day*
Hutchins, Hazel. *A second is a hiccup*
Hutchins, Pat. *Clocks and more clocks*
Jenkins, Steve. *Just a second*
McCaughrean, Geraldine. *My grandmother's clock*
McMillan, Bruce. *Time to . . .*
Murphy, Stuart J. *Game time*
Get up and go!
It's about time!
Rodeo time
Older, Jules. *Telling time*
Omololu, Cynthia Jaynes. *When it's six o'clock in San Francisco*
Pilegard, Virginia Walton. *The warlord's alarm*
Plourde, Lynn. *Winter waits*
Richards, Kitty. *It's about time, Max!*
Rohmann, Eric. *Time flies*
Rosa-Mendoza, Gladys. *What time is it? / Qué hora es?*
Sadler, Marilyn. *Alistair's time machine*
Schuett, Stacey. *Somewhere in the world right now*
Scott, Janine. *Time to tell*
Singer, Marilyn. *Nine o'clock lullaby*
Skinner, Daphne. *All aboard!*
Stanley, Diane. *Joining the Boston Tea Party*
Sweeney, Joan. *Me counting time*
Verdet, Andre. *All about time*
Vyner, Tim. *World team*
Wood, Audrey. *It's Duffy time!*

Tin soldiers *see* Toys – soldiers

Toads *see* Frogs & toads

Toilet training

Amant, Kathleen. *On your potty, Little Rabbit*
Bentley, Dawn. *Fuzzy Bear's potty book*
Bolam, Emily. *I go potty*
Cole, Joanna. *My big boy potty*
My big girl potty
Elya, Susan Middleton. *Oh no, gotta go #2*
Falwell, Cathryn. *P.J. and Puppy*
Ford, Bernette. *No more diapers for Ducky!*
Freeman, Mylo. *Potty*
Gomi, Taro. *Everyone poops*
Hochman, David. *The potty train*
Jadoul, Emile. *All by myself!*
Katz, Karen. *A potty for me!*
Lewison, Wendy Cheyette. *The princess and the potty*
Lindgren, Barbro. *Sam's potty*
Manushkin, Fran. *Big girl panties*
Miller, Virginia. *On your potty!*
Morgan, Richard. *Zoo poo*
My potty book for boys
My potty book for girls
O'Connell, Rebecca. *Danny is done with diapers*
Oud, Pauline. *Ian's new potty*
Patricelli, Leslie. *Potty*
Piggy and Bear in their underwear
Richmond, Marianne. *Big girls go potty*
Rogers, Fred. *Going to the potty*
Rogers, Paul. *Ruby's potty*
Scheffler, Axel. *The little puddle*
Sears, William, M.D., et al. *You can go to the potty*
Shea, Bob. *Dinosaur vs. the potty*
Vestergaard, Hope. *Potty animals*
Wax, Wendy. *Even firefighters go to the potty*
Willems, Mo. *Time to pee*

Toilets

Harper, Charise Mericle. *Flush!*

Tongue twisters

Agee, Jon. *Orangutan tongs*
Cleary, Brian P. *Six sheep sip thick shakes and other tricky tongue twisters*
Mahy, Margaret. *Simply delicious!*
Pomerantz, Charlotte. *The piggy in the puddle*
Rovetch, Lissa. *Ook the book*

Tools

Araki, Mie. *The magic toolbox*
Barton, Byron. *Tools*
Carle, Eric. *My very first book of tools*
Clements, Andrew. *Workshop*
Connor, Leslie. *Miss Bridie chose a shovel*
Garcia, Emma. *Tap tap bang bang*
Garland, Sarah. *Eddie's toolbox and how to make and mend things*
Gibbons, Gail. *The art box*
Tool book
Lord, Janet. *Albert the fix-it man*
Mandel, Peter. *Jackhammer Sam*
Meltzer, Lynn. *The construction crew*
Miller, Margaret. *Who uses this?*
Miura, Taro. *Tools*
Monroe, Chris. *Monkey with a tool belt and the seaside shenanigans*
Morris, Ann. *Tools*
Neitzel, Shirley. *The house I'll build for the wrens*
Schaefer, Lola M. *Toolbox twins*
Singer, Marilyn. *Let's build a clubhouse*
Sturges, Philemon. *I love tools!*

Tooth fairy *see* Fairies; Teeth

Tortoises *see* Reptiles – turtles, tortoises

Towns *see* Cities, towns

Toy & movable books *see* Format, unusual – toy & movable books

Toys

Adlerman, Daniel. *Africa calling*
Amant, Kathleen. *Little Rabbit gets messy*
On your potty, Little Rabbit
Ayres, Katherine. *Matthew's truck*

Bardhan-Quallen, Sudipta. *The Mine-o-saur*
Beaumont, Karen. *Where's my t-r-u-c-k?*
Beck, Andrea. *Elliot bakes a cake*
Elliot digs for treasure
Elliot gets stuck
Elliot's bath
Elliot's Christmas surprise
Elliot's noisy night
Elliot's shipwreck
Bell, Cece. *Sock Monkey boogie-woogie*
Sock Monkey goes to Hollywood
Sock Monkey rides again
Berger, Joe. *My special one and only*
Bianco, Margery Williams. *The velveteen rabbit*, ill. by David Jorgensen
The velveteen rabbit, ill. by Thea Kliros
The velveteen rabbit, ill. by Komako Sakai
The velveteen rabbit, ill. by Gennady Spirin
The velveteen rabbit: or, How toys became real, ill. by Allen Atkinson
The velveteen rabbit: or, How toys became real, ill. by Steve Johnson
Birchall, Mark. *Rabbit's birthday surprise*
Rabbit's wooly sweater
Bourgeois, Paulette. *Franklin and Harriet*
Franklin's class trip
Brisson, Pat. *Hobbledy-clop*
Brown, Alan James. *Love-a-Duck*
Browne, Anthony. *Gorilla*
Bunting, Eve. *Ducky*
Butterworth, Nick. *Albert the bear*
Cabrera, Jane. *Ten in the bed*
Cader, Lisa Lebowitz. *When I wear my crown*
When I wear my tiara
Capucilli, Alyssa Satin. *Biscuit visits the pumpkin patch*
Carle, Eric. *10 little rubber ducks*
Carlson, Nancy. *Start saving, Henry!*
Chichester Clark, Emma. *I love you, Blue Kangaroo!*
Where are you, Blue Kangaroo?
Conrad, Pam. *The Tub People*
The Tub People's Christmas
Cooper, Helen. *Tatty-Ratty*
Cowell, Cressida. *Emily Brown and the Thing*
That rabbit belongs to Emily Brown
Crampton, Gertrude. *Scuffy the tugboat*
Crews, Nina. *Below*
Sky-high Guy
Crum, Shutta. *Mine!*
Curious George visits a toy store
Daly, Niki. *Old Bob's brown bear*
Deacon, Alexis. *While you are sleeping*
Denise, Anika. *Bella and Stella come home*
De Sève, Randall. *Mi barco / Toy boat*
Toy boat
De Vries, Anke. *Raf*
De Vries, Maggie. *How sleep found Tabitha*
Dewan, Ted. *Baby gets the zapper*
Dierssen, Andreas. *The old red tractor*
Donaldson, Julia. *One Ted falls out of bed*
Dunbar, Polly. *Penguin*
Pingüino / penguin
Dunrea, Olivier. *Gideon & Otto*
Egielski, Richard. *Slim and Jim*
Ehrlich, H. M. *Louie's goose*
Emberley, Rebecca. *My toys / Mi juguetes*
Ernst, Lisa Campbell. *The letters are lost!*
Falconer, Ian. *Olivia — and the missing toy*
Fearnley, Jan. *Milo Armadillo*
Feiffer, Jules. *I lost my bear*
Ferreri, Della Ross. *How will I ever sleep in this bed?*
Ford, Bernette. *No more blanket for Lambkin!*
Fox, Christyan. *What color is that, PiggyWiggy?*
Fox, Mem. *Tell me about your day today*
Frazee, Marla. *Santa Claus*
Freedman, Claire. *Night-night, Emily*
Gall, Chris. *Awesome Dawson*
Gershator, Phillis. *Moo, moo, brown cow! Have you any milk?*
Gravett, Emily. *Monkey and me*
Grey, Mini. *Toys in space*
Traction Man and the beach odyssey
Traction Man is here
Traction Man meets Turbodog
Hayes, Sarah. *Lucy Anna and the Finders*
Heck, Ed. *Monkey lost*
Henderson, Kathy. *Baby knows best*
Herman, R. A. *Gomer and Little Gomer*
Hindley, Judy. *Rosy's visitors*
Hissey, Jane. *Hoot*
Old Bear
Old Bear [board book]
Hoffman, Eric. *No fair to tigers / No es justo para los tigres*
Hoffmann, E. T. A. *The nutcracker*
Holmes, Janet A. *Have you seen Duck?*
Hoppe, Paul. *The woods*
Hughes, Shirley. *Bobbo goes to school*
Hutchins, Pat. *Tidy Titch*
Ichikawa, Satomi. *Come fly with me*
I am Pangoo the penguin
La La Rose
My little train
Inches, Alison. *The stuffed animals get ready for bed*
Inkpen, Mick. *Kipper's snowy day*
Kipper's toybox
Nothing
Thing
Inns, Christopher. *Next! please*
Jesset, Aurore. *Loopy*
Jocelyn, Marthe. *A day with Nellie*
Jonas, Ann. *Now we can go*
Joyce, William. *The Leaf Men and the brave good bugs*
Kastner, Jill. *Merry Christmas, Princess Dinosaur*
Princess Dinosaur
Kennedy, Marge M. *The book of boo!*
Kenney, Sean. *Cool cars and trucks*
Cool castles
Cool city
Cool creations in 35 pieces
Kirk, Daniel. *Honk honk! Beep beep!*
Kirsch, Vincent X. *Two little boys from Toolittle Toys*
Korchek, Lori. *Adventures of Cow, too*
Kruusval, Catarina. *Franny's friends*
Lane, Adam J. B. *Stop thief!*
LaReau, Kara. *Rocko and Spanky have company*
Lewis, Kim. *Good night, Harry*
Here we go Harry
Hooray for Harry
My friend Harry
Lewis, Paeony. *No more cookies!*
Lindgren, Barbro. *Sam's car*
Lionni, Leo. *Alexander and the wind-up mouse*
Lobb, Janice. *Color and noise! Let's play with toys!*
London, Jonathan. *My big rig*
Long, Loren. *Drummer boy*
Lucas, David. *Christmas at the toy museum*
Luthardt, Kevin. *Mine*

Lynn, Sarah. *1-2-3 va-va-vroom!*
McAllister, Angela. *The little blue rabbit*
Mama and Little Joe
McCully, Emily Arnold. *The Christmas gift*
McDonnell, Flora. *I love boats*
McDonnell, Patrick. *Me . . . Jane*
McNeil, Florence. *Sail away*
McPhail, David. *Bella loves Bunny*
The puddle
Marks, Jennifer L. *Sorting toys*
Marshall, James. *The Cut-Ups*
Marzollo, Jean. *I spy little wheels*
Masurel, Claire. *Christmas is coming*
Too big!
Meadows, Michelle. *Pilot pups*
Mills, Elaine. *Marinetta at the ballet*
Milne, A. A. *Eeyore loses a tail*
Tigger tales
Moore, Clement Clarke. *The teddy bears' night before Christmas*
Morrissey, Dean. *The Christmas ship*
Nash, Sarah. *Purrfect!*
Nash, Scott. *Tuff Fluff*
Newman, Lesléa. *A fire engine for Ruthie*
Ohi, Ruth. *Chicken, Pig, Cow and the class pet*
Chicken, Pig, Cow horse around
O'Malley, Kevin. *Leo Cockroach . . . toy tester*
Oppenheim, Shulamith Levey. *I love you, Bunny Rabbit*
Ormerod, Jan. *Miss Mouse's day*
Oxenbury, Helen. *Tom and Pippo go shopping*
Tom and Pippo in the garden
Tom and Pippo on the beach
Tom and Pippo see the moon
Patricelli, Leslie. *Binky*
Pelletier, Andrew T. *The amazing adventures of Bathman!*
The toy farmer
Perez, Monica. *Curious George saves his pennies*
Pett, Mark. *The boy and the airplane*
Phillipps, J. C. *Monkey Ono*
Pinkney, Andrea Davis. *Peggony-Po*
Pinkwater, Daniel. *Yo-yo man*
Polacco, Patricia. *Bun Bun Button*
Potter, Beatrix. *The tale of two bad mice*
Prater, John. *On top of the world*
Priest, Robert H. *The old pirate of Central Park*
Rau, Dana Meachen. *Rubber duck*
Ray, Mary Lyn. *All aboard*
Reiser, Lynn. *Any kind of dog*
Roberts, Bethany. *Cookie angel*
Rose, Deborah Lee. *Birthday zoo*
Rosenthal, Eileen. *Bobo the sailor man!*
I must have Bobo!
I'll save you Bobo!
Rylant, Cynthia. *Little Whistle*
Little Whistle's Christmas
Little Whistle's dinner party
Little Whistle's medicine
Samuels, Barbara. *The trucker*
Schertle, Alice. *Goodnight, Hattie, my dearie, my dove*
Schmid, Paul. *A pet for Petunia*
Schotter, Roni. *Room for Rabbit*
Schwartz, Amy. *Oscar*
Seuss, Dr. *The king's stilts*
Shannon, David. *Demasiados juguetes / too many toys*
Too many toys
Shannon, Terry Miller. *Tub toys*
Sif, Birgitta. *Oliver*
Simmons, Jane. *The dreamtime fairies*
Slonim, David. *Oh, Ducky*
Smith, Maggie. *Dear Daisy, get well soon*
Paisley
Soto, Gary. *My little car / Mi carrito*
Springstubb, Tricia. *Phoebe and Digger*
Stevenson, Robert Louis. *Block city*, ill. by Daniel Kirk
Block city, ill. by Ashley Wolff
Stickland, Paul. *Bears*
Tada, Joni Eareckson. *Forever friends*
Taylor, Sean. *The world champion of staying awake*
Thurber, James. *The great Quillow*
Van Camp, Katie. *CookieBot!*
Harry and Horsie
Van Leeuwen, Jean. *The strange adventures of Blue Dog*
Vulliamy, Clara. *Ellen and Penguin and the new baby*
Small
Waddell, Martin. *Rosie's babies*
Tom Rabbit
Wagner, Anke. *Tim's big move!*
Weber, Linda Kay. *Louie Larkey and the bad dream patrol*
Weiss, Nicki. *Where does the brown bear go?*
Where does the brown bear go? [board book]
Wells, Rosemary. *Bunny party*
Max's bedtime
Max's birthday
Max's toys
Weninger, Brigitte. *Double birthday*
Miko goes on vacation
What's the matter, Davy?
Whybrow, Ian. *Harry and the bucketful of dinosaurs*
Harry and the dinosaurs at the museum
Harry and the dinosaurs go to school
Harry and the dinosaurs say "Raahh"
Sammy and the robots
Wick, Walter. *Can you see what I see? toyland express*
Willems, Mo. *Knuffle Bunny*
Knuffle Bunny free
Knuffle Bunny too
Williams, Karen Lynn. *Galimoto*
Wilson, Karma. *Princess me*
Wisniewski, David. *Sumo Mouse*
Yorinks, Arthur. *Harry and Lulu*
Ziefert, Harriet. *Bunny's lessons*
Buzzy had a little lamb
Lucy rescued

Toys – balloons

Augustin, Barbara. *Antonella and her Santa Claus*
Baker, Alan. *Brown Rabbit's shape book*
Briere-Haquet, Alice. *Zebedee's balloon*
Curtis, Jamie Lee. *Where do balloons go?*
De Sève, Randall. *Mathilda and the orange balloon*
Faulkner, Keith. *Pop! went another balloon!*
Gorbachev, Valeri. *Molly who flew away*
Johnson, Angela. *The day Ray got away*
Kotzwinkle, William. *Walter, the farting dog: trouble at the yard sale*
Lillegard, Dee. *Balloons, balloons, balloons*
Munsch, Robert N. *Where is Gah-Ning?*
Nolen, Jerdine. *Harvey Potter's balloon farm*
Polacco, Patricia. *Bun Bun Button*
Rau, Dana Meachen. *Lots of balloons*
Robledo, Honorio. *Nico visits the moon*
Scheffler, Axel. *The big balloon*

Schmid, Paul. *Perfectly Percy*
Smith, Danna. *Balloon trees*
Sweet, Melissa. *Balloons over Broadway*
Taylor, Alastair. *Swollobog*
Ward, Lindsay. *Please bring balloons*
Weitzman, Jacqueline Preiss. *You can't take a balloon into the Metropolitan Museum*
You can't take a balloon into the National Gallery

Toys – balls

Bang, Molly. *Yellow ball*
Cronin, Doreen. *Bounce*
Egielski, Richard. *Three magic balls*
George, Lindsay Barrett. *Maggie's ball*
Hills, Tad. *Duck and Goose*
Kellogg, Steven. *The mystery of the magic green ball*
Lindgren, Barbro. *Sam's ball*
Raschka, Chris. *A ball for Daisy*
Schmid, Paul. *Peanut and Fifi have a ball*
Schubert, Leda. *Winnie plays ball*
Seeger, Laura Vaccaro. *What if?*
Stevens, Janet. *The great fuzz frenzy*
Sullivan, Mary. *Ball*
Tafuri, Nancy. *The ball bounced*
Wright, Cliff. *Bear and ball*

Toys – bears

Alborough, Jez. *My friend bear*
Where's my teddy?
Alexander, Martha G. *I'll protect you from the jungle beasts*
Allison, Catherine. *Brown paper bear*
Ashforth, Camilla. *Willow at Christmas*
Willow by the sea
Willow on the river
Aylesworth, Jim. *Teddy bear tears*
Bart, Kathleen. *Town Teddy and Country Bear go global*
Beck, Ian. *Home before dark*
Teddy's snowy day
Bond, Michael. *Paddington Bear goes to the hospital*
Paddington Bear in the garden
Burgess, Mark. *Where teddy bears come from*
Bush, Timothy. *Teddy bear, teddy bear*
Butterworth, Nick. *Albert the bear*
Carmichael, Clay. *Lonesome bear*
Cousins, Lucy. *Maisy's bedtime*
Coyle, Carmela Lavigna. *Do super heroes have teddy bears?*
Crimi, Carolyn. *Principal Fred won't go to bed*
Cusimano, Maryann K. *You are my I love you*
Daly, Niki. *Old Bob's brown bear*
Dewan, Ted. *One true bear*
Docherty, Thomas. *Wash-a-bye Bear*
Dodd, Emma. *Best bear*
Donaldson, Julia. *One Ted falls out of bed*
Doremus, Gaetan. *Bear despair*
Ellwand, David. *Ten in the bed*
Feiffer, Jules. *I lost my bear*
Fox, Christyan. *What shape is that, PiggyWiggy?*
Freedman, Claire. *Night-night, Emily*
Freeman, Don. *Beady Bear*
Corduroy
Corduroy's busy street and Corduroy goes to the doctor
A pocket for Corduroy
Gauch, Patricia Lee. *Bravo, Tanya*
Dance, Tanya
Gretz, Susanna. *Teddy bears cure a cold*
Guy, Ginger Foglesong. *Siesta*
Hächler, Bruno. *What does my teddy bear do all night?*
Hague, Kathleen. *Alphabears*
Numbears
Hague, Michael. *Teddy bear, teddy bear*
Hale, Nathan. *Yellowbelly and Plum go to school*
Hansen, Felicity. *The first bear*
Harris, Trudy. *Up bear, down bear*
Hegg, Tom. *Peef and his best friend*
Hennessy, B. G. *Corduroy at the zoo*
Corduroy's birthday
Corduroy's Christmas
Corduroy's Easter
Corduroy's Halloween
Hissey, Jane. *Old Bear*
Old Bear [board book]
Ichikawa, Satomi. *The first bear in Africa!*
Inches, Alison. *Corduroy writes a letter*
Corduroy's garden
Corduroy's hike
James, J. Alison. *The bears' Christmas surprise*
Johnston, Tony. *My best friend Bear*
Kelly, Luke. *Blanket and bear, a remarkable pair*
Kennedy, Jimmy. *The teddy bears' picnic*, ill. by Alexandra Day
The teddy bears' picnic, ill. by Michael Hague
The teddy bears' picnic, ill. by Prue Theobalds
Kennedy, Marge M. *The book of boo!*
Kroll, Virginia L. *Everybody has a teddy*
Lewis, Kim. *First snow*
Lindgren, Barbro. *Sam's teddy bear*
McCue, Lisa. *Corduroy's best Halloween ever!*
McFarland, Lyn Rossiter. *The pirate's parrot*
McGinness, Suzanne. *My bear Griz*
McGrath, Barbara Barbieri. *Teddy bear counting*
Mack, Jeff. *Hush little polar bear*
McKee, David. *Elmer and the lost teddy*
McPhail, David. *Ben loves Bear*
The teddy bear
McQuade, Jacqueline. *At preschool with Teddy Bear*
At the petting zoo with Teddy Bear
Christmas with Teddy Bear
Good times with Teddy Bear
Maitland, Barbara. *My bear and me*
Meserve, Jessica. *Bedtime without Arthur*
Meyers, Susan. *Bear in the air*
Milne, A. A. *Eeyore loses a tail*
Tigger tales
Moore, Clement Clarke. *The teddy bears' night before Christmas*
Murphy, Mary. *Some things change*
Naylor, Phyllis Reynolds. *Please do feed the bears*
Novak, Matt. *Jazzbo and Googy*
Ormondroyd, Edward. *Theodore*
Reynolds, Adrian. *Pete and Polo's farmyard adventure*
Root, Phyllis. *Contrary bear*
Rosen, Michael. *Red Ted and the lost things*
Sava, Donna Lynn. *Teddy bear dreams*
Schertle, Alice. *The adventures of old Bo Bear*
Schneider, Christine M. *I'm bored!*
Seeger, Laura Vaccaro. *Dog and Bear: three to get ready*
Dog and Bear: two friends, three stories
Dog and Bear: two's company
Simon, Charnan. *Messy Molly*
Smee, Nicola. *No bed without Ted*
Stadler, John. *Catilda*

Stead, Philip C. *Jonathan and the big blue boat*
Stephens, Helen. *The big adventure of the Smalls*
Tibo, Gilles. *The grand journey of Mr. Man*
Tildes, Phyllis Limbacher. *Billy's big-boy bed*
Tyger, Rory. *Newton*
Ungerer, Tomi. *Otto: the autobiography of a teddy bear*
Van Laan, Nancy. *Little baby Bobby*
Waber, Bernard. *Ira sleeps over*
Waddell, Martin. *Night night Cuddly Bear*
Sailor Bear
Small Bear lost
When the teddy bears came
Weber, Linda Kay. *Louie Larkey and the bad dream patrol*
Weninger, Brigitte. *Good-bye, Daddy!*
Wickstrom, Sylvie. *I love you, Mister Bear*
Wilson, Karma. *Sleepyhead*
Wishinsky, Frieda. *What's up, bear?*
Wright, Dare. *A gift from the lonely doll*
The lonely doll
Yektai, Niki. *Hi bears, bye bears*
Young, Ruth. *Golden Bear*
Yum, Hyewon. *Last night*
Ziefert, Harriet. *Clara Ann Cookie go to bed!*

Toys – blocks

Banks, Kate. *Max's castle*
Hutchins, Pat. *Changes, changes*

Toys – dolls

Beck, Andrea. *Elliot's emergency*
Bertrand, Diane Gonzales. *The last doll / La última muñeca*
Browne, Anthony. *Silly Billy*
Godden, Rumer. *The story of Holly and Ivy*
Greenfield, Eloise. *My doll, Keshia*
Grey, Mini. *Toys in space*
Guthrie, Woody. *My dolly*
Hall, Patricia. *Hooray for reading!*
Hobbie, Holly. *Fanny*
Fanny and Annabelle
Keller, Holly. *Geraldine's blanket*
Kroll, Steven. *The hand-me-down doll*
Lasky, Kathryn. *Sophie and Rose*
McClintock, Barbara. *Dahlia*
McKissack, Patricia C. *The all-I'll-ever-want Christmas doll*
Nettie Jo's friends
McPhail, David. *Emma in charge*
Mayer, Marianna. *Baba Yaga and Vasilisa the Brave*
Medearis, Michael. *Daisy and the doll*
Milgrim, David. *Time to get up, time to go*
Mills, Elaine. *Marinetta at the ballet*
Montanari, Eva. *My first . . .*
Nelson, Vaunda Micheaux. *Almost to freedom*
Newsome, Jill. *Dream dancer*
Norling, Beth. *The stone baby*
O'Connor, Jane. *Fancy Nancy: fanciest doll in the universe*
Ogburn, Jacqueline K. *The magic nesting doll*
Oram, Hiawyn. *Baba Yaga and the wise doll*
Ormerod, Jan. *Miss Mouse takes off*
Parot, Annelore. *Kimonos*
Pattison, Darcy. *The journey of Oliver K. Woodman*
Searching for Oliver K. Woodman
Peters, Stephanie True. *Raggedy Ann and Andy and the magic potion*
Pilgrim, Elza. *The china doll*
Polacco, Patricia. *Babushka's doll*
Betty Doll
Randall, Alison L. *The wheat doll*
Ransom, Candice F. *The Christmas dolls*
Russo, Marisabina. *The trouble with baby*
Santiago, Esmeralda. *A doll for Navidades*
Silbaugh, Elizabeth. *Raggedy Ann's birthday party book*
Steig, William. *Yellow and pink*
Stuve-Bodeen, Stephanie. *Elizabeti's doll*
Tada, Joni Eareckson. *Forever friends*
Tudor, Tasha. *The doll's Christmas*
Turner, Ann Warren. *Secrets from the dollhouse*
Wells, Rosemary. *Peabody*
Yoko's show-and-tell
Winthrop, Elizabeth. *Vasilissa the beautiful*
Wright, Dare. *A gift from the lonely doll*
The lonely doll
Zolotow, Charlotte. *William's doll*

Toys – rocking horses

Sokol, Edward. *Meet Stinky Magee*

Toys – soldiers

Andersen, Hans Christian. *The steadfast tin soldier*, ill. by Jen Corace
The steadfast tin soldier, ill. by Charlene Delage
The steadfast tin soldier, ill. by Paul Galdone
The steadfast tin soldier, ill. by Rachel Isadora
The steadfast tin soldier, ill. by P. J. Lynch
The steadfast tin soldier, ill. by Fred Marcellino
Rylant, Cynthia. *Little Whistle's medicine*

Toys – teddy bears *see* Toys – bears

Toys – tin soldiers *see* Toys – soldiers

Toys – trains

Lewis, Kevin. *Chugga-chugga choo-choo*
Mallat, Kathy. *Trouble on the tracks*
Richards, Laura Elizabeth Howe. *Jiggle joggle jee*

Toys – wagons

Dodd, Lynley. *A dragon in a wagon*
Lindgren, Barbro. *Sam's wagon*
Liwska, Renata. *Red wagon*
Powell, Alma. *My little wagon [board book]*
Pullen, Zachary. *Friday my Radio Flyer flew*

Tractors

Alborough, Jez. *The gobble gobble moooooo tractor book*
Big noisy trucks and diggers
Blum, Mark. *Big trucks and diggers in 3-D*
Carter, Don. *Old MacDonald drives a tractor*
Dierssen, Andreas. *The old red tractor*
Dobbins, Jan. *Driving my tractor*
Garland, Michael. *Grandpa's tractor*
Goodhart, Pippa. *Arthur's tractor*
Kilby, Don. *In the country*
Lewis, Kim. *One summer day*
Long, Loren. *Otis*

Otis and the puppy
Otis and the tornado
An Otis Christmas
Lund, Deb. *Monsters on machines*
Mayo, Margaret. *Dig dig digging*
Meng, Cece. *Tough chicks*
Nelson, Kristin L. *Farm tractors*
Pallotta, Jerry. *The construction alphabet book*
Peterson, Cris. *Fantastic farm machines*
Ransom, Candice F. *Tractor day*
Schubert, Leda. *Here comes Darrell*
Siy, Alexandra. *One tractor*
Stille, Darlene R. *Tractors*
van Lieshout, Elle. *The wish*

Traffic, traffic signs

Aesop. *Road signs*
Bell, Babs. *The bridge is up!*
Liu, Julia. *Gus, the dinosaur bus*
Meister, Cari. *Busy, busy city street*
Pearson, Debora. *Alphabeep*
Robbins, Ken. *Trucks, giants of the highway*
Schertle, Alice. *Little Blue Truck leads the way*
Suen, Anastasia. *Red light, green light*

Train engineers *see* Careers – railroad engineers

Trains

Awdry, W. *Happy birthday, Thomas!*
Aylesworth, Jim. *Country crossing*
Barton, Byron. *Trains*
Barton, Chris. *Shark vs. train*
Bee, William. *And the train goes . . .*
Blechman, Nicholas. *Night light*
Booth, Philip E. *Crossing*
C is for caboose
Caswell, Deanna. *Train trip*
Chall, Marsha Wilson. *Prairie train*
Cohen, Deborah Bodin. *Engineer Ari and the Rosh Hashana ride*
Collicutt, Paul. *This train*
Cooper, Elisha. *Train*
Crews, Donald. *Freight train*
Inside freight train
Shortcut
Crunk, Tony. *Railroad John and the Red Rock run*
Curious George takes a train
Dale, Penny. *Dinosaur rescue!*
De Roo, Elena. *The rain train*
Dorfman, Craig. *I knew you could!*
Drummond, Allan. *Casey Jones*
Eaton, Jason Carter. *How to train a train*
Emberley, Ed. *Ed Emberley's drawing book of trucks and trains*
Floca, Brian. *Locomotive*
Gibbons, Gail. *Trains*
Goble, Paul. *Death of the iron horse*
Gurney, John Steven. *Dinosaur train*
Harby, Melanie. *All aboard for Dreamland!*
High, Linda Oatman. *Tenth Avenue cowboy*
Highet, Alistair. *The yellow train*
Hill, Lee Sullivan. *Trains*
Hoberman, Mary Ann. *Bill Grogan's goat*
Horacek, Petr. *Choo choo*
Horsbrugh, Wilma. *The train to Glasgow*
Hubbell, Patricia. *Trains: steaming! pulling! huffing!*
Ichikawa, Satomi. *My little train*
Johnson, Angela. *I dream of trains*
Kay, Verla. *Iron horses*
Orphan train
Kelly, Mij. *William and the night train*
Kimmel, Eric A. *Stormy's hat*
Kulling, Monica. *All aboard! Elijah McCoy's steam engine*
Lakin, Patricia. *Subway sonata*
Lehman, Barbara. *Trainstop*
Lenski, Lois. *The little train*
Light, Steve. *Trains go*
London, Jonathan. *The owl who became the moon*
A train goes clickety-clack
Lund, Deb. *All aboard the dinotrain*
Macaulay, David. *Black and white*
McCully, Emily Arnold. *An outlaw Thanksgiving*
McMullan, Kate. *I'm fast*
McNamara, Margaret. *The whistle on the train*
McPhail, David. *Moony B. Finch, fastest draw in the West*
Mahy, Margaret. *Mister Whistler*
Maltbie, P. I. *Claude Monet: the painter who stopped the trains*
Miller, Heather Lynn. *Subway ride*
Moser, Lisa. *Railroad Hank*
Moss, Marissa. *True heart*
Neitzel, Shirley. *I'm taking a trip on my train*
Niemann, Christoph. *Subway*
Nobisso, Josephine. *John Blair and the great Hinckley fire*
Oram, Hiawyn. *Going to Grandpa's*
Peet, Bill. *The caboose who got loose*
Smokey
Pinkney, Gloria Jean. *The Sunday outing*
Piper, Watty. *The little engine that could,* ill. by George Hauman
The little engine that could, ill. by Loren Long
Prince, Joshua. *I saw an ant on the railroad track*
Ray, Mary Lyn. *All aboard*
Rex, Michael. *My freight train*
Rinker, Sherri Duskey. *Steam train, dream train*
Rockwell, Anne. *Trains*
Whoo! whoo! goes the train
Rogers, Hal. *Trains*
Roth, Carol. *All aboard to work — choo-choo!*
Rylant, Cynthia. *Silver packages*
Sarcone-Roach, Julia. *Subway story*
Siebert, Diane. *Train song*
Sís, Peter. *Train of states*
Skinner, Daphne. *All aboard!*
Smith, Joseph A. *Circus train*
Sobel, June. *The goodnight train*
Spence, Robert, III. *Clickety clack*
Steele, Philip. *Trains: the slide-out, see-through story of world-famous trains and railroads*
Steggall, Susan. *Rattle and rap*
Stevenson, James. *All aboard!*
Sturges, Philemon. *I love trains*
Stutson, Caroline. *Night train*
Suen, Anastasia. *Subway*
Window music
Temple, Charles A. *Train*
Thomas, Joyce Carol. *In the land of milk and honey*
Titcomb, Gordon. *The last train*
Tunnell, Michael O. *Mailing May*
Van Allsburg, Chris. *The polar express*
Voake, Charlotte. *Here comes the train*

Wickberg, Susan. *Hey Mr. Choo-Choo, where are you going?*
Wormell, Christopher. *Puff, puff, chugga-chugga*
Yin. *Coolies*
Ziefert, Harriet. *Train song*
Zimmerman, Andrea Griffing. *Train man*
Zullo, Germano. *Line 135*

Trains, toy *see* Toys – trains

Transportation

Baer, Edith. *This is the way we go to school*
Barton, Byron. *Airport*
Bell, Babs. *The bridge is up!*
Calmenson, Stephanie. *Late for school!*
Chancellor, Deborah. *Traveling on land*
Collicutt, Paul. *This train*
Cousins, Lucy. *Maisy's book of things that go*
Stop and go, Maisy
Crews, Donald. *School bus*
School bus [board book]
Truck
Dale, Penny. *Dinosaur zoom!*
Davis, Caroline. *My little rowboat*
Demarest, Chris L. *All aboard! a traveling alphabet*
Lindbergh
Durango, Julia. *Go-go gorillas*
Fecher, Sarah. *On the move*
Flanagan, Alice K. *Riding the ferry with Captain Cruz*
Riding the school bus with Mrs. Kramer
Freymann, Saxton. *Fast food*
Gibbons, Gail. *New road!*
Hill, Lee Sullivan. *Trains*
Kirk, Daniel. *Go!*
Kittinger, Jo S. *Rosa's bus*
Levinson, Riki. *I go with my family to Grandma's*
Lillegard, Dee. *Go! poetry in motion: poems*
London, Jonathan. *My big rig*
Lord, Janet. *Here comes Grandma!*
Maass, Robert. *Tugboats*
McCourt, Lisa. *I miss you, Stinky Face*
MacDonald, Suse. *Elephants on board*
Mayo, Margaret. *Choo choo clickety-clack*
Miller, Heather Lynn. *Subway ride*
Miranda, Anne. *Vroom, chugga, vroom-vroom*
Mitton, Tony. *Cool cars*
Morris, Ann. *On the go*
Mortensen, Denise Dowling. *Wake up engines*
Munro, Roxie. *Go! go! go!*
Nobles, Kristen M. *Drive this book*
Old MacDonald had a farm. *Old MacDonald had a farm*
Rau, Dana Meachen. *Riding*
Ways to go
Ringgold, Faith. *If a bus could talk*
Robbins, Ken. *Trucks, giants of the highway*
Rockwell, Anne. *Ferryboat ride!*
Planes
Things that go
Trains
Rogers, Hal. *Airplanes*
Buses
Cars
Trains
Rotner, Shelley. *Boats afloat*
Rylant, Cynthia. *Silver packages*
Schomp, Virginia. *If you were a . . . pilot*
Spinelli, Eileen. *Six hogs on a scooter*
Stanley, Mandy. *On the move*
Steggall, Susan. *Rattle and rap*
Red car, red bus
Stevenson, James. *No need for Monty*
Stickland, Paul. *Truck jam*
Stille, Darlene R. *Police cars*
Tractors
Suen, Anastasia. *Delivery*
Red light, green light
Subway
Temple, Charles A. *Train*
Timmers, Leo. *Bang*
Tunnell, Michael O. *Mailing May*
Vetter, Jennifer Riggs. *Down by the station*
Walker, Sally M. *Druscilla's Halloween*
Wellington, Monica. *Truck driver Tom*
Willems, Mo. *The pigeon loves things that go!*
Ziefert, Harriet. *From Kalamazoo to Timbuktu!*

Trees

Ada, Alma Flor. *The Christmas tree / El arbol de Navidad*
Adler, David A. *Redwoods are the tallest trees in the world*
Alexander, Sue. *Behold the trees*
Aliki. *Christmas tree memories*
Altman, Linda Jacobs. *Amelia's road*
Andersen, Hans Christian. *The fir tree*, ill. by Diane Goode
The fir tree, ill. by Bernadette Watts
Arnold, Tedd. *Dirty Gert*
Arnosky, Jim. *Crinkleroot's guide to knowing the trees*
Aston, Dianna Hutts. *An orange in January*
Atwood, Margaret. *Up in the tree*
Bailey, Mary Bryant. *Jeoffry's Christmas*
Baumgart, Klaus. *Laura's Christmas star*
Berenstain, Stan and Jan. *The Berenstain bears and the spooky old tree*
The Berenstain bears' Christmas tree
The Berenstain bears' that stump must go!
Berger, Carin. *The little yellow leaf*
Bond, Rebecca. *A city Christmas tree*
Bosca, Francesca. *The apple king*
Brallier, Jess M. *Tess's tree*
Brown, Margaret Wise. *The little fir tree*
Brown, Ruth. *The old tree*
Bunting, Eve. *Night tree*
Carney, Margaret. *At Grandpa's sugar bush*
Cherry, Lynne. *The great kapok tree*
Child, Lauren. *What planet are you from Clarice Bean?*
Chin, Jason. *Redwoods*
Codell, Esme Raji. *Seed by seed*
Cole, Henry. *The littlest evergreen*
Conrad, Pam. *The Tub People's Christmas*
Cooke, Trish. *The grandad tree*
Demas, Corinne. *Two Christmas mice*
DePalma, Mary Newell. *A grand old tree*
dePaola, Tomie. *The family Christmas tree book*
Devernay, Laetitia. *The conductor*
Donaldson, Julia. *Stick Man*
Dunrea, Olivier. *A Christmas tree for Pyn*
Ehlert, Lois. *Red leaf, yellow leaf*
Emmett, Jonathan. *Leaf trouble*
Flanagan, Alice K. *The Zieglers and their apple orchard*

Florian, Douglas. *Poetrees*
Foggo, Cheryl. *Dear baobab*
Formento, Alison. *This tree counts!*
This tree, 1, 2, 3
Frisch, Aaron. *The lonely pine*
Galbraith, Kathryn O. *Arbor Day square*
Geisert, Arthur. *Nursery crimes*
George, Kristine O'Connell. *Old Elm speaks*
George, William T. *Christmas at Long Pond*
Gerber, Carole. *Spring blossoms*
Winter trees
Gibbons, Gail. *The missing maple syrup sap mystery*
The seasons of Arnold's apple tree
Tell me, tree
Gold-Vukson, Marji E. *Grandpa and me on Tu B'Shevat*
Hall, Zoe. *The apple pie tree*
Fall leaves fall
Harrison, Troon. *The floating orchard*
Hassett, Ann. *The finest Christmas tree*
Helmer, Marilyn. *One splendid tree*
Hines, Gary. *A Christmas tree in the White House*
Holub, Joan. *Apple countdown*
Hopkins, H. Joseph. *The tree lady*
Houston, Gloria. *The year of the perfect Christmas tree*
Hubery, Julia. *A friend for all seasons*
Ichikawa, Satomi. *What the little fir tree wore to the Christmas party*
Jeffers, Oliver. *The great paper caper*
Stuck
Johnson, Jen Cullerton. *Seeds of change*
Johnston, Tony. *Big red apple*
Keister, Douglas. *Fernando's gift / El regalo de Fernando*
Kellogg, Steven. *Johnny Appleseed: a tall tale*
Kessler, Cristina. *My great-grandmother's gourd*
Kooser, Ted. *House held up by trees*
Krishnaswami, Uma. *Out of the way! Out of the way!*
Krupinski, Loretta. *Christmas in the city*
Landa, Norbert. *Little Bear and the wishing tree*
Larsen, Andrew. *In the tree house*
Lauber, Patricia. *Be a friend to trees*
Lears, Laurie. *Megan's birthday tree*
Light, Steve. *The Christmas giant*
Lindbergh, Reeve. *Johnny Appleseed*
Lionni, Leo. *A busy year*
Llewellyn, Claire. *Tree*
Locker, Thomas. *Sky tree*
London, Jonathan. *The sugaring-off party*
McClure, Nikki. *Apple*
MacKay, Elly. *If you hold a seed*
McPhail, David. *The family tree*
Henry Bear's Christmas
The Searcher and Old Tree
Maestro, Betsy. *How do apples grow?*
Why do leaves change color?
Mahy, Margaret. *The Christmas tree tangle*
Martin, Bill, Jr. *Chicka chicka boom boom*
Chicka chicka boom boom [board book]
Martin, David. *Let's have a tree party!*
Matheson, Christie. *Tap the magic tree*
Matteson, George. *The Christmas tugboat*
Mayr, Diane. *Out and about at the apple orchard*
Miller, Debbie S. *Are trees alive?*
Minor, Wendell. *Christmas tree!*
Moss, Miriam. *This is the tree*
Muldrow, Diane. *We planted a tree*
Munsch, Robert N. *Up, up, down!*
Napoli, Donna Jo. *Mama Miti*
Näslund, Gorel Kristina. *Our apple tree*
Nivola, Claire A. *Planting the trees of Kenya*
Obed, Ellen Bryan. *Who would like a Christmas tree?*
Oldland, Nicholas. *Big bear hug*
Oppenheim, Joanne. *Have you seen trees?*
Pallotta, Jerry. *Who will plant a tree?*
Pearson, Debora. *Leo's tree*
Peet, Bill. *Merle the high flying squirrel*
Perez, Monica. *Curious George plants a tree*
Pfister, Marcus. *Hopper's treetop adventure*
Pittman, Helena Clare. *The angel tree*
Powell, Consie. *Amazing apples*
Old dog Cora and the Christmas tree
Purmell, Ann. *Christmas tree farm*
Maple syrup season
Rawlinson, Julia. *Fletcher and the falling leaves*
Ray, Jane. *The apple-pip princess*
Ray, Mary Lyn. *Christmas farm*
Reed-Jones, Carol. *The tree in the ancient forest*
Reid, Barbara. *Picture a tree*
Reiser, Lynn. *Christmas counting*
Robbins, Ken. *Apples*
Autumn leaves
Robinson, Tim. *Tobias, the quig, and the rumplenut tree*
Rodman, Mary Ann. *A tree for Emmy*
Romain, Trevor. *Jemma's journey*
Rosenberg, Madelyn. *Happy birthday, tree!*
Rouss, Sylvia A. *Sammy Spider's first Tu B'Shevat*
Salas, Laura Purdie. *A leaf can be . . .*
Sayre, April Pulley. *Trout are made of trees*
Schotter, Roni. *In the piney woods*
Shelby, Anne. *The man who lived in a hollow tree*
Silverstein, Shel. *The giving tree*
Smith, Danna. *Balloon trees*
Smith, Linda. *The inside tree*
Spalding, Andrea. *Solomon's tree*
Speirs, John. *The little boy's Christmas gift*
Spilsbury, Louise. *Oranges*
Stein, David Ezra. *Leaves*
Stewart, Sarah. *The money tree*
Stiegemeyer, Julie. *Under the baobab tree*
Stoeke, Janet Morgan. *The Loopy Coop hens: letting go*
Swain, Gwenyth. *Johnny Appleseed*
Thompson, Lauren. *The apple pie that Papa baked*
Tolman, Marije. *The tree house*
Torres, Melissa A. *The great Christmas tree celebration*
Tresselt, Alvin R. *The gift of the tree*
Udry, Janice May. *A tree is nice*
Van Laan, Nancy. *A tree for me*
Van Leeuwen, Jean. *Nothing here but trees*
Walsh, Ellen Stoll. *Dot and Jabber and the great acorn mystery*
Ward, Helen. *The tin forest*
Welch, Willy. *Dancing with Daddy*
Weninger, Brigitte. *Little apple*
Williams, Sam. *Angel's Christmas cookies*
Winter, Jeanette. *The Christmas tree ship*
Wangari's trees of peace
Yolen, Jane. *Johnny Appleseed: the legend and the truth*
Zagwÿn, Deborah Turney. *Apple batter*
Ziefert, Harriet. *One red apple*
Zoehfeld, Kathleen Weidner. *Apples, apples*
Zolotow, Charlotte. *The beautiful Christmas tree*
Zweibel, Alan. *Our tree named Steve*

Trickery *see* Behavior – trickery

Tricks *see* Magic

Triplets *see* Multiple births – triplets

Trolls

McNiff, Dawn. *Mommy's little monster*

Trucks

Alborough, Jez. *Duck in the truck*
Anderson, Peggy Perry. *Chuck's truck*
Andrews, Julie. *Dumpy at school*
Dumpy the dump truck
Dumpy to the rescue!
Dumpy's apple shop
Armstrong, Jennifer. *Magnus at the fire*
Ashburn, Boni. *Builder Goose*
Ayres, Katherine. *Matthew's truck*
Barton, Byron. *Trucks*
Beaumont, Karen. *Where's my t-r-u-c-k?*
Big noisy trucks and diggers
Biggs, Brian. *123 beep beep beep!*
Bingham, Caroline. *Big book of rescue vehicles*
Blechman, Nicholas. *Night light*
Blum, Mark. *Big trucks and diggers in 3-D*
Braun, Sebastien. *Digger and Tom!*
Carr, Jan. *Big Truck and Little Truck*
Carter, Don. *Get to work, trucks!*
Clement, Nathan. *Drive*
Coffelt, Nancy. *Pug in a truck*
Crews, Donald. *Truck*
Crowther, Robert. *Amazing pop-up trucks*
Curious George and the dump truck
Curious George and the dump truck
Cuyler, Margery. *The little dump truck*
Cyrus, Kurt. *Big rig bugs*
Dale, Penny. *Dinosaur dig!*
Day, Alexandra. *Frank and Ernest on the road*
Emberley, Ed. *Ed Emberley's drawing book of trucks and trains*
Emergency!
Evans, Nate. *Bang! Boom! Roar!*
Floca, Brian. *Five trucks*
Gall, Chris. *Dinotrux*
Revenge of the Dinotrux
Garcia, Emma. *Tip tip dig dig*
Gergely, Tibor. *The great big fire engine book*
Gibbons, Gail. *Emergency!*
Trucks
The gingerbread boy. *The Gingerbread Man loose on the fire truck*
Goodwin-Sturges, Judy Sue. *Construction Kitties*
Gordon, David. *The three little rigs*
The ugly truckling
Hamilton, Kersten. *Red truck*
Hines, Anna Grossnickle. *I am a backhoe*
Horvath, James. *Dig, dogs, dig*
Houston, Gloria. *Miss Dorothy and her bookmobile*
Hundal, Nancy. *Number 21*
Hunter, Jana Novotny. *When Daddy's truck picks me up*
Imershein, Betsy. *Trucks*
Jane, Pamela. *Milo and the fire engine parade*
Kenney, Sean. *Cool cars and trucks*
Kilby, Don. *At a construction site*
In the city
In the country
On the road
Kirk, Daniel. *Trash trucks!*
Lee, Mark. *20 big trucks in the middle of the street*
Levine, Michelle. *Ambulances*
Light, Steve. *Diggers go*
London, Jonathan. *My big rig*
A truck goes rattley-bumpa
Low, William. *Machines go to work in the city*
Lyon, George Ella. *Trucks roll!*
Maass, Robert. *Little trucks with big jobs*
MacDonald, Suse. *Elephants on board*
McMullan, Kate. *I stink!*
I'm dirty!
Mayo, Margaret. *Dig dig digging*
Emergency!
Meister, Cari. *Busy, busy city street*
Milusich, Janice. *Off go their engines, off go their lights*
Miranda, Anne. *Beep! beep!*
Mitchell, Joyce Slayton. *Tractor-trailer trucker*
Mitton, Tony. *Flashing fire engines*
Moore, Patrick. *The mighty street sweeper*
My big book of trucks and diggers
Nelson, Kristin L. *Monster trucks*
Newman, Lesléa. *A fire engine for Ruthie*
Niemann, Christoph. *That's how!*
Nobles, Kristen M. *Drive this book*
Odanaka, Barbara. *Smash! Mash! Crash! There goes the trash!*
Olson-Brown, Ellen. *Hush little digger*
Pallotta, Jerry. *The construction alphabet book*
Patrick, Jean L. S. *If I had a snowplow*
Pearson, Debora. *Alphabeep*
Rex, Michael. *My fire engine*
Rinker, Sherri Duskey. *Goodnight, goodnight, construction site*
Robbins, Ken. *Trucks, giants of the highway*
Roberts, Cynthia. *Tow trucks*
Rockwell, Anne. *At the firehouse*
Fire engines
Good morning, Digger
Truck stop
Trucks
Samuels, Barbara. *The trucker*
Santoro, Scott. *Isaac the Ice Cream Truck*
Sayres, Brianna Caplan. *Where do diggers sleep at night?*
Schertle, Alice. *Little Blue Truck*
Little Blue Truck leads the way
Schomp, Virginia. *If you were a . . . truck driver*
Schubert, Leda. *Here comes Darrell*
Scieszka, Jon. *Melvin might?*
Smash! Crash!
Truckery rhymes
Siebert, Diane. *Truck song*
Sís, Peter. *Fire truck*
Trucks, trucks, trucks
Skultety, Nancy. *From here to there*
Steggall, Susan. *The diggers are coming!*
Stickland, Paul. *Truck jam*
Stille, Darlene R. *Police cars*
Stoeke, Janet Morgan. *Minerva Louise and the red truck*
Sturges, Philemon. *I love trucks!*
Suen, Anastasia. *Red light, green light*
Sutton, Sally. *Demolition*
Roadwork
Timmers, Leo. *Who is driving?*
Todd, Mark. *Monster trucks*

Vamos, Samantha R. *Alphabet trucks*
Vestergaard, Hope. *Digger, dozer, dumper*
Wellington, Monica. *Truck driver Tom*
Williams, Karen Lynn. *Tap-tap*
Wolf, Sallie. *Truck stuck*
Wood, Audrey. *Alphabet rescue*

Tsunamis

Bauer, Marion Dane. *A mama for Owen*
Hodges, Margaret. *The wave*
Kajikawa, Kimiko. *Tsunami!*
Kroll, Virginia L. *Selvakumar knew better*
Lucas, David. *Whale*
Ohi, Ruth. *Kenta and the big wave*
Winter, Jeanette. *Mama: a true story, in which a baby hippo loses his mama during a tsunami, but finds a new home*

TV *see* Television

Twilight

Berger, Barbara. *Grandfather Twilight*
Shulevitz, Uri. *Dusk*
Udry, Janice May. *The moon jumpers*

Twins *see* Multiple births – twins

U.S. history

Adler, David A. *Heroes for civil rights*
A picture book of Abraham Lincoln
A picture book of Benjamin Franklin
A picture book of Cesar Chavez
A picture book of Dolley and James Madison
A picture book of Eleanor Roosevelt
A picture book of George Washington
A picture book of Harry Houdini
A picture book of John and Abigail Adams
A picture book of John F. Kennedy
A picture book of John Hancock
A picture book of Martin Luther King, Jr
A picture book of Sam Houston
A picture book of Samuel Adams
A picture book of Thomas Jefferson
Aldrin, Buzz. *Look to the stars*
Reaching for the moon
Alexander, Elizabeth. *Praise song for the day*
Aliki. *The many lives of Benjamin Franklin*
The story of William Penn
A weed is a flower
Allegra, Mike. *Sarah gives thanks*
Allen, Kathy. *The U.S. Constitution*
Altman, Susan. *Followers of the north star*
Andersen, Hans Christian. *The tinderbox*
Anderson, Laurie Halse. *Thank you, Sarah*
Angleberger, Tom. *Crankee Doodle*
Appelt, Kathi. *Miss Lady Bird's wildflowers*
Armand, Glenda. *Love twelve miles long*
Armentrout, David. *John Muir*
Aston, Dianna Hutts. *The moon over Star*
Atwell, Debby. *Pearl*
Aulaire, Ingri Mortenson d'. *Abraham Lincoln*
Aylesworth, Jim. *Our Abe Lincoln*
Bandy, Michael S. *White water*
Barbour, Karen. *Mr. Williams*
Barretta, Gene. *Now and Ben*
Bartlett, Robert Merrill. *The story of Thanksgiving*
Bartoletti, Susan Campbell. *The Christmas promise*
The flag maker
Bates, Katharine Lee. *America the beautiful*, ill. by Chris Gall
America the beautiful, ill. by Wendell Minor
Bates, Katharine Lee. *America the beautiful: together we stand*
Battle-Lavert, Gwendolyn. *Papa's mark*
Bauer, Marion Dane. *Harriet Tubman*
Berlin, Irving. *God bless America*
Bildner, Phil. *The greatest game ever played*
The hallelujah flight
Shoeless Joe and Black Betsy
Binns, Tristan Boyer. *The Liberty Bell*
Birtha, Becky. *Grandmama's pride*
Lucky beans
Borden, Louise. *A. Lincoln and me*
America is . . .
Brill, Marlene Targ. *Bronco Charlie and the Pony Express*
Margaret Knight, girl inventor
Brown, Don. *Henry and the cannons*
Teedie
A voice from the wilderness
A wizard from the start
Brown, Monica. *Side by side / Lado a lado*
Brown, Tami Lewis. *Soar, Elinor!*
Broyles, Anne. *Priscilla and the hollyhocks*
Bruchac, Joseph. *Squanto's journey*
Brunhoff, Laurent de. *Babar's USA*
Bryant, Jen. *Abe's fish*
A splash of red
Bunting, Eve. *The blue and the gray*
The cart that carried Martin
A picnic in October
Burleigh, Robert. *If you spent a day with Thoreau at Walden pond*
One giant leap
Stealing home
Carbone, Elisa. *Heroes of the surf*
Night running
Chaconas, Dori. *Pennies in a jar*
Chandra, Deborah. *George Washington's teeth*
Cherry, Lynne. *A river ran wild*
Christensen, Bonnie. *Woody Guthrie, poet of the people*
Cline-Ransome, Lesa. *Light in the darkness*
Words set me free
Clinton, Catherine. *Phillis's big test*
When Harriet met Sojourner
Cohan, George M. *You're a grand old flag*
Cole, Barbara Hancock. *Anna and Natalie*
Cole, Henry. *Unspoken*
Collins, Suzanne. *Year of the jungle*
Cooney, Barbara. *Eleanor*
Cooper, Floyd. *Willie and the All-Stars*
Corey, Shana. *Here come the Girl Scouts!*

You forgot your skirt, Amelia Bloomer
Cotten, Cynthia. *Abbie in stitches*
The book boat's in
Dalgliesh, Alice. *The Thanksgiving story*
Davies, Jacqueline. *Tricking the Tallyman*
Demarest, Chris L. *Lindbergh*
Demas, Corinne. *Hurricane!*
dePaola, Tomie. *An early American Christmas*
My first Thanksgiving
Dray, Philip. *Yours for justice, Ida B. Wells*
Drummond, Allan. *Liberty*
Dunlap, Julie. *Louisa May and Mr. Thoreau's flute*
Edwards, David. *The pen that Pa built*
Edwards, Pamela Duncan. *Barefoot: escape on the Underground Railroad*
Boston Tea Party
The bus ride that changed history
Esbaum, Jill. *To the big top*
Evans, Shane W. *Underground: finding the light to freedom*
We march
Falken, Linda. *Can you find it?*
Farris, Christine King. *March on!*
My brother Martin
Ferris, Jeri Chase. *Noah Webster and his words*
Figley, Marty Rhodes. *The schoolchildren's blizzard*
Fisher, Leonard Everett. *Stars and stripes: our national flag*
Fisher, Mary M. *Rosita's bridge*
Fishman, Cathy Goldberg. *When Jackie and Hank met*
FitzGerald, Dawn. *Vinnie and Abraham*
Fleischman, Paul. *The matchbox diary*
Fleming, Candace. *Imogene's last stand*
Floca, Brian. *Lightship*
Locomotive
Moonshot
Fradin, Dennis. *The price of freedom*
Garland, Michael. *Americana adventure*
The President and Mom's apple pie
George, Jean Craighead. *The first Thanksgiving*
Gibbons, Gail. *Apples*
Gilchrist, Jan Spivey. *My America*
Giovanni, Nikki. *Lincoln and Douglass*
Rosa
Glaser, Linda. *Emma's poem*
Hannah's way
Gourley, Robbin. *First garden*
Grady, Cynthia. *I lay my stitches down*
Green, Stephanie. *Betsy Ross and the silver thimble*
Greene, Rhonda Gowler. *The very first Thanksgiving Day*
Greenfield, Eloise. *Easter parade*
Grifalconi, Ann. *Ain't nobody a stranger to me*
Griffin, Kitty. *The ride*
Grigsby, Susan. *First peas to the table*
In the garden with Dr. Carver
Grimes, Nikki. *Barack Obama*
Hall, Donald. *Lucy's Christmas*
Harness, Cheryl. *Mary Walker wears the pants*
Our colonial year
Harvey, Jeanne Walker. *My hands sing the blues*
Haskins, Jim. *Delivering justice*
Haugen, Brenda. *Thanksgiving*
Hearne, Betsy Gould. *Seven brave women*
Heinz, Brian J. *Nathan of yesteryear and Michael of today*
Helmer, Marilyn. *One splendid tree*
High, Linda Oatman. *The girl on the high-diving horse*
Tenth Avenue cowboy
Hilliard, Richard. *Godspeed, John Glenn*
Hines, Gary. *A Christmas tree in the White House*
Holbrook, Stewart. *America's Ethan Allen*
Hopkinson, Deborah. *Abe Lincoln crosses a creek*
Annie and Helen
Keep on!
Knit your bit
Howard, Elizabeth Fitzgerald. *Virgie goes to school with us boys*
Howard, Ginger. *William's house*
Hubbard, Crystal. *Catching the moon: the story of a young girl's baseball dream*
Hueston, M. P. *The all-American jump and jive jig*
Hurst, Carol Otis. *Rocks in his head*
Issa, Kai Jackson. *Howard Thurman's Great Hope*
I've seen the promised land
Jackson, Ellen. *Abe Lincoln loved animals*
Johnson, Angela. *A sweet smell of roses*
Wind flyers
Johnson, D. B. *Henry builds a cabin*
Henry hikes to Fitchburg
Johnson, Dolores. *Now let me fly*
Johnston, Tony. *The wagon*
Judge, Lita. *Pennies for elephants*
Jurmain, Suzanne Tripp. *Worst of friends*
Kalman, Maira. *Looking at Lincoln*
Kay, Verla. *Broken Feather*
Civil War drummer boy
Covered wagons, bumpy trails
Iron horses
Orphan train
Keller, Laurie. *The scrambled states of America*
The scrambled states of America talent show
Kellogg, Steven. *Mike Fink*
Yankee Doodle
Kerley, Barbara. *What to do about Alice?*
Key, Francis Scott. *The Star Spangled Banner*
The Star-Spangled Banner
King, Martin Luther, III. *My daddy, Dr. Martin Luther King, Jr.*
King, Martin Luther, Jr. *I have a dream*
Kinsey-Warnock, Natalie. *Nora's ark*
Kittinger, Jo S. *Rosa's bus*
Klingel, Cynthia Fitterer. *Paul Revere's ride*
Rosa Parks
Krensky, Stephen. *Hanukkah at Valley Forge*
A man for all seasons
Shooting for the moon
Sisters of Scituate Light
Kroll, Steven. *By the dawn's early light: the story of the Star Spangled Banner*
Lewis and Clark
Oh, what a Thanksgiving!
Krull, Kathleen. *Hillary Rodham Clinton*
Lincoln tells a joke
Pocahontas: princess of the New World
Kurtz, Jane. *River friendly, river wild*
Lang, Heather. *Queen of the track*
Lawlor, Laurie. *Old Crump*
Lee, Milly. *Earthquake*
Nim and the war effort
Lee-Tai, Amy. *A place where sunflowers grow / Sabaku ni saita himawari*
Lendroth, Susan. *Calico Dorsey*
Ocean wide, ocean deep
Levine, Ellen. *Henry's freedom box*

Levinson, Riki. *Watch the stars come out*
Lilly, Melinda. *From slavery to freedom*
Littlesugar, Amy. *Tree of hope*
Livingston, Myra Cohn. *Abraham Lincoln: a man for all the people*
Keep on singing
Longfellow, Henry Wadsworth. *Paul Revere's ride*
Paul Revere's ride: the landlord's tale
Loomis, Christine. *Across America, I love you*
Lowell, Susan. *The elephant quilt!*
Lyon, George Ella. *Cecil's story*
Lyons, Kelly Starling. *Ellen's broom*
Hope's gift
One million men and me
McCain, Meghan. *My dad, John McCain*
McCully, Emily Arnold. *My heart glow*
An outlaw Thanksgiving
McGill, Alice. *Molly Bannaky*
Mackall, Dandi Daley. *A girl named Dan*
McKissack, Patricia C. *The all-I'll-ever-want Christmas doll*
Goin' someplace special
Ol' Clip-Clop
Stitchin' and pullin'
McNamara, Margaret. *George Washington's birthday*
McReynolds, Linda. *Eight days gone*
Maestro, Betsy. *The story of the Statue of Liberty*
Malaspina, Ann. *Finding Lincoln*
Phillis sings out freedom
Touch the sky
Manning, Maurie J. *Laundry day*
Mara, Wil. *Amelia Earhart*
Marciano, John Bemelmans. *Madeline at the White House*
Markel, Michelle. *Brave girl*
Martin, Bill, Jr. *I pledge allegiance*
Martin, Jacqueline Briggs. *Snowflake Bentley*
Marzollo, Jean. *The little plant doctor*
Medearis, Angela Shelf. *The freedom riddle*
Meister, Cari. *Follow the drinking gourd: an Underground Railroad story*
Messinger, Carla. *When the shadbush blooms*
Metaxas, Eric. *Squanto and the miracle of Thanksgiving*
Michelson, Richard. *Busing Brewster*
Twice as good
Miller, Bobbi. *Davy Crockett gets hitched*
Miller, William. *The bus ride*
Rent party jazz
Minor, Wendell. *How big could your pumpkin grow?*
Yankee Doodle America
Mitchell, Margaree King. *Granddaddy's gift*
When Grandmama sings
Mochizuki, Ken. *Baseball saved us*
Moses, Will. *Mary and her little lamb*
Moss, Marissa. *Sky high*
Munro, Roxie. *The inside-outside book of Texas*
Myers, Walter Dean. *Muhammad Ali: the people's champion*
Young Martin's promise
Naden, Corinne J. *Ron's big mission*
Nelson, S. D. *Quiet hero*
Nettleton, Pamela Hill. *Abraham Lincoln*
Benjamin Franklin
George Washington
Martin Luther King, Jr
Pocahontas
Sally Ride
Neubecker, Robert. *Wow! America!*
Newton, Vanessa. *Let freedom sing*
Noguchi, Rick. *Flowers from Mariko*
Nolan, Janet. *The firehouse light*
Obama, Barack. *Change has come*
Of thee I sing
Ochiltree, Dianne. *Molly, by golly!*
Orgill, Roxane. *If I only had a horn*
Our children can soar
Parker, Robert Andrew. *Piano starts here*
Paterson, John. *Blueberries for the queen*
Peacock, Carol Antoinette. *Pilgrim cat*
Petersham, Maud. *An American ABC*
Peterson, Jeanne Whitehouse. *Don't forget Winona*
Pfeffer, Wendy. *The big flood*
Piepmeier, Charlotte. *Lucy's journey to the wild west*
Pinkney, Andrea Davis. *Boycott blues*
Dear Benjamin Banneker
Martin and Mahalia
Sit-in
Sojourner Truth's step-stomp stride
Plourde, Lynn. *Margaret Chase Smith*
Poffenberger, Nancy M. *September 11, 2001*
Preus, Margi. *The Peace Bell*
Pringle, Laurence P. *One room school*
Pryor, Bonnie. *The house on Maple Street*
Quattlebaum, Mary. *The shine man*
Ramsey, Calvin Alexander. *Belle, the last mule at Gee's Bend*
Ruth and the Green Book
Rand, Gloria. *Baby in a basket*
Ransom, Candice F. *The promise quilt*
Rappaport, Doreen. *Abe's honest words*
Eleanor, quiet no more
Freedom river
Freedom ship
Helen's big world
Jack's path of courage
Lady Liberty
Martin's big words
To dare mighty things
We are the many
Raschka, Chris. *New York is English, Chattanooga is Creek*
Raven, Margot Theis. *Night boat to freedom*
Ray, Mary Lyn. *Shaker boy*
Reynolds, Aaron. *Back of the bus*
Riggio, Anita. *Secret signs*
Ringgold, Faith. *Dinner at Aunt Connie's house*
Henry Ossawa Tanner
If a bus could talk
My dream of Martin Luther King
Rochelle, Belinda. *Jewels*
Rockliff, Mara. *Me and Momma and Big John*
My heart will not sit down
Rockwell, Anne. *Big George*
Romain, Trevor. *Jemma's journey*
Rosenstock, Barb. *The camping trip that changed America*
Thomas Jefferson builds a library
Rubin, Susan Goldman. *Jean Laffite*
Ryan, Pam Muñoz. *Amelia and Eleanor go for a ride*
The flag we love
When Marian sang
St. George, Judith. *So you want to be president?*
Sanders, Nancy. *D is for drinking gourd*
Santella, Andrew. *George Washington*
Schaefer, Lola M. *The Wright brothers*
Schanzer, Rosalyn. *How Ben Franklin stole the lightning*

The Old Chisholm Trail
Schneider, Howie. *Fast 'n Snappy*
Schroeder, Alan. *Baby Flo*
Minty
Sexton, Colleen A. *Let's meet Martin Luther King, Jr*
Shange, Ntozake. *Coretta Scott*
Freedom's a-callin me
Shelton, Paula Young. *Child of the civil rights movement*
Shore, Diane Z. *This is the dream*
Siebert, Diane. *Heartland*
Sís, Peter. *Train of states*
Skead, Robert. *Something to prove*
Slade, Suzanne. *Climbing Lincoln's steps*
The house that George built
Slate, Joseph. *The great big wagon that rang*
Small, David. *George Washington's cows*
Smalls-Hector, Irene. *Jenny Reen and the Jack Muh Lantern*
Smith, Charles R. *Brick by brick*
Smith, David J. *If America were a village*
Smith, Lane. *Abe Lincoln's dream*
John, Paul, George and Ben
Smith, Marie. *N is for our nation's capital*
S is for Smithsonian
Smucker, Anna Egan. *Golden delicious*
Spier, Peter. *We the people*
Stanley, Diane. *Joining the Boston Tea Party*
Thanksgiving on Plymouth Plantation
Stanley, Fay. *The last princess*
Stauffacher, Sue. *Nothing but trouble*
Stevenson, Harvey. *Looking at liberty*
Stewart, Sarah. *The gardener*
Stone, Tanya Lee. *Elizabeth leads the way*
Who says women can't be doctors?
Suen, Anastasia. *Man on the moon*
Swain, Gwenyth. *I wonder as I wander*
Riding to Washington
Tate, Don. *It jes' happened*
Tavares, Matt. *Henry Aaron's dream*
There goes Ted Williams
Thermes, Jennifer. *Sam Bennett's new shoes*
This place I know
Thomas, Joyce Carol. *In the land of milk and honey*
Thomas, Mark. *Clothes in Colonial America*
Fun and games in Colonial America
Work in Colonial America
Thomson, Sarah L. *Stars and stripes*
What Lincoln said
Tunnell, Michael O. *Mailing May*
Turkle, Brinton. *Thy friend, Obadiah*
Turner, Ann Warren. *Abe Lincoln remembers*
Shaker hearts
When Mr. Jefferson came to Philadelphia
Turner, Glennette Tilley. *An apple for Harriet Tubman*
Uchida, Yoshiko. *The bracelet*
Van Allsburg, Chris. *Queen of the falls*
Van Leeuwen, Jean. *Across the wide dark sea*
Van Steenwyk, Elizabeth. *First dog Fala*
Vernick, Audrey. *Brothers at bat*
She loved baseball
Vila, Laura. *Building Manhattan*
Waldman, Neil. *They came from the Bronx*
Walker, Sally M. *Freedom song*
Wallner, Alexandra. *Betsy Ross*
Susan B. Anthony
Warren, Sarah. *Dolores Huerta*
Washington, Donna L. *The story of Kwanzaa*
Watkins, Angela Farris. *My Uncle Martin's big heart*
My Uncle Martin's words for America
Watson, Renée. *Harlem's little blackbird*
Weatherford, Carole Boston. *The Beatitudes*
Before John was a jazz giant
Champions on the bench
Freedom on the menu
I, Matthew Henson
Juneteenth jamboree
Moses: when Harriet Tubman led her people to freedom
Weber, Elka. *The Yankee at the seder*
Wells, Rosemary. *The house in the mail*
Whitaker, Suzanne George. *The daring Miss Quimby*
White, Becky. *Betsy Ross*
Wilson, Karma. *How to bake an American pie*
Winnick, Karen B. *Sybil's night ride*
Winter, Jeanette. *The Christmas tree ship*
Follow the drinking gourd
Winter, Jonah. *Barack*
Muhammad Ali: champion of the world
Winters, Kay. *Abe Lincoln, the boy who loved books*
Wise, Bill. *Silent star*
Woodruff, Elvira. *Small beauties*
Woodson, Jacqueline. *Coming on home soon*
Show way
This is the rope
Wooldridge, Connie Nordhielm. *When Esther Morris headed west*
Wright, Courtni Crump. *Journey to freedom*
Jumping the broom
Yaccarino, Dan. *All the way to America*
Yamasaki, Katie. *Fish for Jimmy*
Yin. *Brothers*
Coolies
Yolen, Jane. *Letting Swift River go*
My brothers' flying machine
My Uncle Emily
Naming Liberty

U.S. history – frontier & pioneer life

Aliki. *The story of Johnny Appleseed*
Altman, Linda Jacobs. *The legend of Freedom Hill*
Amsden, Janet. *Grizzly Pete and the ghosts*
Aston, Claire. *Wild West*
Balcziak, Bill. *Paul Bunyan*
Pecos Bill
Bateman, Teresa. *Paul Bunyan vs. Hals Halson*
Browning, Diane. *Signed, Abiah Rose*
Brownlow, Mike. *Way out West — with a baby!*
Burell, Sarah. *Diamond Jim Dandy and the sheriff*
Casanova, Mary. *The day Dirk Yeller came to town*
Clement-Davies, David. *Spirit*
Codell, Esme Raji. *Seed by seed*
Crummel, Susan Stevens. *Ten-Gallon Bart and the Wild West Show*
Crunk, Tony. *Railroad John and the Red Rock run*
Davis, David. *Fandango stew*
Davis, Kenneth C. *Don't know much about the pioneers*
Emmett, Jonathan. *She'll be coming 'round the mountain*
Erdrich, Louise. *The range eternal*
Frank, John. *The toughest cowboy, Or, How the Wild West was tamed*
Galbraith, Kathryn O. *Arbor Day square*
Gibbons, Gail. *Yippee-yay!*

Glass, Andrew. *Bewildered for three days*
Griffin, Kitty. *Cowboy Sam and those confounded secrets*
Hallowell, George. *Wagons ho!*
Helldorfer, M. C. *Hog music*
Holt, Kimberly Willis. *The adventures of Granny Clearwater and Little Critter*
Holub, Joan. *Cinderdog and the wicked stepcat*
Hopkins, Jackie Mims. *The gold miner's daughter*
Howard, Ellen. *The log cabin Christmas*
The log cabin church
The log cabin quilt
Isaacs, Anne. *Dust Devil*
Swamp Angel
Jakes, John. *Susanna of the Alamo*
Johnston, Tony. *The cowboy and the black-eyed pea*
Levi Strauss gets a bright idea
Sunsets of the West
Kay, Verla. *Gold fever*
Hornbooks and inkwells
Whatever happened to the Pony Express?
Kellogg, Steven. *Johnny Appleseed: a tall tale*
Paul Bunyan: a tall tale
Pecos Bill
Sally Ann Thunder Ann Whirlwind Crockett
Kimmel, Eric A. *The great Texas hamster drive*
Little Red Hot
Kinsey-Warnock, Natalie. *The bear that heard crying*
Lawson, Robert. *They were strong and good*
Levitin, Sonia. *Boom town*
Nine for California
Lindbergh, Reeve. *Johnny Appleseed*
Lowell, Susan. *The bootmaker and the elves*
Cindy Ellen
Dusty Locks and the three bears
Luckhurst, Matt. *Paul Bunyan and Babe the Blue Ox*
MacLachlan, Patricia. *Nora's chicks*
Mara, Wil. *Laura Ingalls Wilder*
Miller, Bobbi. *Miss Sally Ann and the panther*
Napoli, Donna Jo. *The crossing*
Nolen, Jerdine. *Thunder Rose*
Paul, Ann Whitford. *The seasons sewn*
Randall, Alison L. *The wheat doll*
Reynolds, Aaron. *Pirates vs. cowboys*
Reynolds, Marilynn. *The new land*
The prairie fire
Root, Phyllis. *Paula Bunyan*
Rounds, Glen. *Cowboys*
Sod houses on the Great Plains
Rumford, James. *Don't touch my hat!*
Sanders, Scott R. *A place called Freedom*
Warm as wool
Schnitzler, Pattie L. *Widdermaker*
Smith, Janice Lee. *Jess and the stinky cowboys*
Sneed, Brad. *Deputy Harvey and the ant cow caper*
Sorensen, Henri. *New Hope*
Spradlin, Michael P. *Off like the wind!*
Stein, David Ezra. *Cowboy Ned and Andy*
Ned's new friend
Strand, Keith. *Grandfather's Christmas tree*
Stutson, Caroline. *Prairie primer A to Z*
Swain, Gwenyth. *Johnny Appleseed*
Turner, Ann Warren. *Dakota dugout*
Van Leeuwen, Jean. *Going west*
Nothing here but trees
Papa and the pioneer quilt
Van Steenwyk, Elizabeth. *Prairie Christmas*
Van Woerkom, Dorothy. *Becky and the bear*
Whiteley, Opal Stanley. *Only Opal*
Wilder, Laura Ingalls. *Going to town*
My little house songbook
Santa comes to little house
Winter, Jeanette. *Cowboy Charlie*
Wood, Audrey. *The Bunyans*
Wright, Courtni Crump. *Wagon train*
Yolen, Jane. *Elsie's bird*
Johnny Appleseed: the legend and the truth
Yorinks, Arthur. *Whitefish Will rides again*

Umbrellas

Bridges, Shirin Yim. *The Umbrella Queen*
Franson, Scott E. *Un-brella*
Liu, Jae Soo. *Yellow umbrella*
Na, Il Sung. *The thingamabob*
Sáenz, Benjamin Alire. *Grandma Fina and her wonderful umbrellas / La abuelita Fina y sus sombrillas maravillosas*
Schubert, Ingrid. *The umbrella*
Todd, Barbara. *The rainmaker*
Weeks, Sarah. *Ella, of course!*
Yashima, Taro. *Umbrella*

Uncles *see* Family life – aunts, uncles

Unhappiness *see* Emotions – happiness; Emotions – sadness

UNICEF

Castle, Caroline. *For every child*

Unnoticed, unseen *see* Behavior – unnoticed, unseen

Unusual format *see* Format, unusual

Vanity *see* Character traits – vanity

Vikings

Cowell, Cressida. *Hiccup the seasick Viking*
Manning, Mick. *What a Viking!*
Schachner, Judith Byron. *Yo, Vikings*
Smallman, Steve. *Dragon stew*

Violence, nonviolence

Adler, David A. *A picture book of Martin Luther King, Jr*
Brown, Monica. *Side by side / Lado a lado*
Bunting, Eve. *The cart that carried Martin*
Smoky night

Dylan, Bob. *Blowin' in the wind*
Evans, Shane W. *We march*
Farris, Christine King. *March on!*
My brother Martin
Halperin, Wendy Anderson. *Peace*
Jackson, Jill. *Let there be peace on earth*
Katz, Karen. *Can you say peace?*
King, Martin Luther, III. *My daddy, Dr. Martin Luther King, Jr.*
King, Martin Luther, Jr. *I have a dream*
Kittinger, Jo S. *Rosa's bus*
Leaf, Munro. *The story of Ferdinand the bull*
Levy, Debbie. *We shall overcome*
McGinty, Alice B. *Gandhi*
Nelson, Kadir. *Nelson Mandela*
Nettleton, Pamela Hill. *Martin Luther King, Jr*
Peet, Bill. *The pinkish, purplish, bluish egg*
Pinkney, Andrea Davis. *Martin and Mahalia*
Ramsey, Calvin Alexander. *Belle, the last mule at Gee's Bend*
Ringgold, Faith. *My dream of Martin Luther King*
Roth, Susan L. *Hands around the library*
Thompson, Lauren. *The forgiveness garden*
Watkins, Angela Farris. *My Uncle Martin's big heart*
My Uncle Martin's words for America

Volcanoes

Branley, Franklyn M. *Volcanoes*, ill. by Megan Lloyd
Volcanoes, ill. by Marc Simont
Geisert, Arthur. *The giant seed*
Greenwood, Rosie. *I wonder why volcanoes blow their tops*
Grifalconi, Ann. *The village of round and square houses*
Kimmel, Eric A. *The two mountains*
Peters, Lisa Westberg. *Volcano wakes up!*
Schaefer, Lola M. *An island grows*

Wagons *see* Toys – wagons

Waiters *see* Careers – waiters, waitresses

Waitresses *see* Careers – waiters, waitresses

War

Bartoletti, Susan Campbell. *The flag maker*
Biden, Jill. *Don't forget, God bless our troops*
Brown, Don. *Henry and the cannons*
Brunhoff, Laurent de. *Babar's battle*
Bunting, Eve. *The blue and the gray*
Gleam and Glow
One candle
So far from the sea
The wall
Chaconas, Dori. *Pennies in a jar*
Coerr, Eleanor. *Sadako*
Collins, Suzanne. *Year of the jungle*
Deedy, Carmen Agra. *The yellow star*
Demi. *Joan of Arc*
Dennis, Major Brian. *Nubs*
Fleming, Candace. *Boxes for Katje*
Fullerton, Alma. *A good trade*
Garland, Sherry. *The lotus seed*
Goble, Paul. *Death of the iron horse*
Greenfield, Eloise. *Easter parade*
Harness, Cheryl. *Mary Walker wears the pants*
Hearne, Betsy Gould. *Seven brave women*
Heide, Florence Parry. *Sami and the time of the troubles*
Helmer, Marilyn. *One splendid tree*
Holbrook, Stewart. *America's Ethan Allen*
Hopkinson, Deborah. *Knit your bit*
Johnson, Angela. *Wind flyers*
Keefer, Janice Kulyk. *Anna's goat*
Klingel, Cynthia Fitterer. *Paul Revere's ride*
Lee, Milly. *Nim and the war effort*
Lee-Tai, Amy. *A place where sunflowers grow / Sabaku ni saita himawari*
Littlesugar, Amy. *Lisette's angel*
Longfellow, Henry Wadsworth. *Paul Revere's ride*
Paul Revere's ride: the landlord's tale
Lyon, George Ella. *Cecil's story*
McCain, Meghan. *My dad, John McCain*
McElroy, Lisa Tucker. *Love, Lizzie*
Mckee, David. *Six men*
McPhail, David. *No!*
McQuinn, Anna. *My friend Jamal*
Mochizuki, Ken. *Baseball saved us*
Moss, Marissa. *Sky high*
Nadel, Carolina. *Daddy's home*
Oberman, Sheldon. *By the Hanukkah light*
O'Brien, Anne Sibley. *A path of stars*
Paterson, John. *Blueberries for the queen*
Pin, Isabel. *The seed*
Poffenberger, Nancy M. *September 11, 2001*
Polacco, Patricia. *The butterfly*
Poole, Josephine. *Joan of Arc*
Preus, Margi. *The Peace Bell*
Pringle, Laurence P. *One room school*
Radunsky, Vladimir. *Manneken pis*
Rappaport, Doreen. *Freedom ship*
The secret seder
Raven, Margot Theis. *Mercedes and the chocolate pilot*
Rumford, James. *Silent music*
Russo, Marisabina. *I will come back for you*
Sandman, Rochel. *Perfect porridge*
Santella, Andrew. *George Washington*
Seuss, Dr. *The butter battle book*
Shea, Pegi Deitz. *The whispering cloth*
Tibo, Gilles. *The grand journey of Mr. Man*
Turner, Ann Warren. *When Mr. Jefferson came to Philadelphia*
Ungerer, Tomi. *Otto: the autobiography of a teddy bear*
Vander Zee, Ruth. *Always with you*
Wade, Mary Dodson. *Cinco de Mayo*
Weber, Elka. *The Yankee at the seder*
Wells, Rosemary. *The language of doves*
Winnick, Karen B. *Sybil's night ride*
Winter, Jeanette. *The librarian of Basra*
Woodson, Jacqueline. *Coming on home soon*
Yamasaki, Katie. *Fish for Jimmy*

Yolen, Jane. *All those secrets of the world*
Youme. *Mali under the night sky*
Zhang, Song Nan. *The ballad of Mulan*
Ziefert, Harriet. *A new coat for Anna*

Washing machines *see* Machines

Watches *see* Clocks, watches

Water

Atwell, Debby. *River*
Base, Graeme. *The water hole*
Cobb, Vicki. *I get wet*
Cole, Joanna. *The magic school bus at the waterworks*
Cullen, Catherine Ann. *Thirsty baby*
Doyle, Malachy. *Splash, Joshua, splash!*
Flanagan, Alice K. *Water*
Graham, Joan Bransfield. *Splish splash*
Greenfield, Eloise. *Water, water*
Grobler, Piet. *Hey, frog!*
Hamilton, K. R. *This is the ocean*
Jenkins, Emily. *Water in the park*
Johnson, Neil. *The falling raindrop*
Kalz, Jill. *Water*
Kerley, Barbara. *A cool drink of water*
Kessler, Cristina. *My great-grandmother's gourd*
Lobb, Janice. *Splish! Splosh! Why do we wash?*
Locker, Thomas. *Water dance*
Lucado, Max. *All you ever need*
Lyon, George Ella. *All the water in the world*
MacDonald, Margaret Read. *Give up, Gecko!*
McDonnell, Flora. *Splash!*
McGhee, Alison. *Making a friend*
McPhail, David. *Water boy*
Morrison, Gordon. *A drop of water*
Peters, Lisa Westberg. *Water's way*
Riley, Linda Capus. *Elephants swim*
Ryder, Joanne. *The waterfall's gift*
Seim, Donna Marie. *Where is Simon, Sandy?*
Seuling, Barbara. *Drip! drop!*
Seven, John. *The ocean story*
Strauss, Rochelle. *One well*
Trenc, Milan. *Another night at the museum*
Verboven, Agnes. *Ducks like to swim*
Wells, Robert E. *Did a dinosaur drink this water?*
Weninger, Brigitte. *Precious water*
Yolen, Jane. *Letting Swift River go*
A mirror to nature

Weapons

Emberley, Barbara. *Drummer Hoff*
Könnecke, Ole. *Anton and the battle*
Krensky, Stephen. *Shooting for the moon*

Weather

Anholt, Catherine. *Sun, snow, stars, sky*
Baird, Audrey B. *A cold snap!*
Barrett, Judi. *Cloudy with a chance of meatballs*
Cloudy with a chance of meatballs 3
Pickles to Pittsburgh
Bauer, Marion Dane. *If frogs made the weather*
Berger, Melvin. *How's the weather?*
Blackstone, Stella. *Bear in sunshine*
Branley, Franklyn M. *Down comes the rain*
Rain and hail
Brown, Margaret Wise. *The little island*
Canyon, Christopher. *John Denver's Sunshine on my shoulders*
Carlstrom, Nancy White. *What does the sky say?*
Chambers, Catherine. *Heat wave*
Cole, Joanna. *The magic school bus and the climate challenge*
Cousins, Lucy. *Maisy's wonderful weather book*
Crews, Donald. *Cloudy day/sunny day*
Denega, Danielle. *Rain or shine*
DeWitt, Lyndia. *What will the weather be?*
Dodds, Dayle Ann. *Hello, sun!*
Flanagan, Alice K. *Weather*
Gibbons, Gail. *Weather words and what they mean*
Guiberson, Brenda Z. *Earth*
Harper, Jamie. *Miss Mingo weathers the storm*
Hill, Eric. *Spot looks at weather*
Hines, Anna Grossnickle. *What can you do in the sun?*
Holub, Joan. *Groundhog weather school*
Howell, Will C. *I call it sky*
Inkpen, Mick. *Kipper's book of weather*
Jackson, Ellen. *April*
August
December
February
January
July
June
March
May
November
October
September
Kespert, Deborah. *Rain and shine*
Krupinski, Loretta. *Pirate treasure*
Let's count the raindrops
Livinson, Nancy Smiler. *North Pole, South Pole*
Locker, Thomas. *Water dance*
McCloskey, Robert. *Time of wonder*
MacLennan, Cathy. *Chicky Chicky Chook Chook*
Marshak, S. *The Month-Brothers*
Michaels, Pat. *W is for wind*
Nelson, Robin. *A sunny day*
O'Mara, Carmel. *Sunny day*
Peters, Lisa Westberg. *The sun, the wind and the rain*
Water's way
Rogers, Paul. *What will the weather be like today?*
Ryan, Pam Muñoz. *There was no snow on Christmas Eve*
Schmidt, Karen Lee. *Carl's nose*
Singer, Marilyn. *On the same day in March*
Spinelli, Eileen. *Heat wave*
Stevenson, James. *Heat wave at Mud Flat*
Tresselt, Alvin R. *Sun up*
Vigna, Judith. *Boot weather*
Zolotow, Charlotte. *The storm book*

Weather – blizzards

Crummel, Susan Stevens. *Ten-Gallon Bart beats the heat*
Figley, Marty Rhodes. *The schoolchildren's blizzard*
Friedman, Laurie. *Ruby Valentine saves the day*
Haas, Rick de. *Peter and the winter sleepers*
Hill, Susanna Leonard. *April Fool, Phyllis!*
Hobbie, Holly. *Toot and Puddle, I'll be home for Christmas*
Hurst, Carol Otis. *Terrible storm*

Joosse, Barbara. *A houseful of Christmas*
Regan, Dian Curtis. *The Snow Blew Inn*
Spinelli, Eileen. *Coming through the blizzard*
Wright, Betty Ren. *The blizzard*

Weather – clouds

Arqués, Isabel M. *Ken's cloud*
Carle, Eric. *Little cloud*
Little cloud [board book]
Catchpool, Michael. *The cloud spinner*
dePaola, Tomie. *The cloud book*
Hoshino, Felicia. *Sora and the cloud*
Lichtenheld, Tom. *Cloudette*
Locker, Thomas. *Cloud dance*
Morrison, Toni. *Little Cloud and Lady Wind*
Nelson, Robin. *A cloudy day*
Niemann, Christoph. *The police cloud*
Rockwell, Anne. *Clouds*
Shaw, Charles Green. *It looked like spilt milk*
Wiesner, David. *Sector 7*

Weather – cold

Aillaud, Cindy Lou. *Recess at 20 below*
Chambers, Catherine. *Big freeze*
Powell, Consie. *The first day of winter*
Spinelli, Eileen. *Cold snap*
Together at Christmas

Weather – droughts

Aardema, Verna. *Bringing the rain to Kapiti Plain*
Conway, David. *Lila and the secret of rain*
Faundez, Anne. *The day the rains fell*
Hamilton, Virginia. *Drylongso*
Kamkwamba, William. *The boy who harnessed the wind*
Kessler, Cristina. *My great-grandmother's gourd*
Lind, Michael. *Bluebonnet girl*
Marino, Gianna. *Meet me at the moon*
Meunier, Brian. *Bravo, Tavo!*
Peterson, Jeanne Whitehouse. *Don't forget Winona*
Rappaport, Doreen. *The long-haired girl*
Ray, Jane. *The apple-pip princess*

Weather – floods

Arenson, Roberta. *Manu and the talking fish*
Auld, Mary. *Noah's ark*
Cousins, Lucy. *Noah's ark*
Noah's ark [board book]
Cullen, Lynn. *Little Scraggly Hair*
Eitzen, Ruth. *Tara's flight*
Emberley, Barbara. *One wide river to cross*
Goble, Paul. *Remaking the earth*
Goldsboro, Bobby. *Noah and the ark; and, David and Goliath*
Goodhart, Pippa. *Noah makes a boat*
Harker, Lesley. *Annie's ark*
Harrison, Troon. *The floating orchard*
Jonas, Ann. *Aardvarks, disembark!*
Kinsey-Warnock, Natalie. *Nora's ark*
Krensky, Stephen. *Noah's bark*
Kurtz, Jane. *River friendly, river wild*
Lloyd-Jones, Sally. *Old MacNoah had an ark*
Lyon, George Ella. *Come a tide*
McCarthy, Michael. *The story of Noah and the ark*
MacDonald, Alan. *Wilfred to the rescue*
Maggi, María Elena. *The great canoe*
Oelschlager, Vanita. *I came from the water*
Paley, Joan. *One more river*
Pfeffer, Wendy. *The big flood*
Pinkney, Jerry. *Noah's ark*
Rosen, Michael J. *The dog who walked with God*
Schneider, Josh. *You'll be sorry*
Shapiro, Zachary. *We're all in the same boat*
Singer, Isaac Bashevis. *Why Noah chose the dove*
Spier, Peter. *Noah's ark*
Stewart, Paul. *Rabbit's wish*
Stewig, John Warren. *The animals watched*
Sting [Musician]. *Rock steady*
Tebbs, Victoria. *Noah's Ark story*
Uhlberg, Myron. *A storm called Katrina*
Villa, Alvaro F. *Flood*
Walton, Rick. *Noah's square dance*
Wilson, Anne. *Noah's ark*
Woelfle, Gretchen. *Katje the windmill cat*

Weather – fog

McDonnell, Patrick. *Just like Heaven*
May, Robert Lewis. *Rudolph the red-nosed reindeer*
Tresselt, Alvin R. *Hide and seek fog*
Trotter, Deborah W. *How do you know?*

Weather – hurricanes

Berne, Jennifer. *Calvin can't fly*
Cole, Joanna. *The magic school bus inside a hurricane*
Demas, Corinne. *Hurricane!*
Gibbons, Gail. *Hurricanes!*
Lakin, Patricia. *Hurricane!*
Larson, Kirby. *Two Bobbies*
London, Jonathan. *Hurricane!*
Paterson, Diane. *Hurricane wolf*
Uhlberg, Myron. *A storm called Katrina*
Watson, Renée. *A place where hurricanes happen*
Zelch, Patti R. *Ready, set . . . wait!*

Weather – lightning, thunder

Bauer, Marion Dane. *Dinosaur thunder*
Bourgeois, Paulette. *Franklin and the thunderstorm*
Branley, Franklyn M. *Flash, crash, rumble, and roll*
Bryan, Ashley. *The story of lightning and thunder*
Cotten, Cynthia. *Rain play*
Crum, Shutta. *Thunder-Boomer!*
Flanagan, Alice K. *Thunder and lightning*
Geisert, Arthur. *Thunderstorm*
Gorbachev, Valeri. *Catty Jane who hated the rain*
Dragon is coming!
Griessman, Annette. *Like a hundred drums*
Hines, Anna Grossnickle. *Rumble thumble boom!*
Hobbie, Holly. *Toot and Puddle, you are my sunshine*
Hutchins, Hazel. *One dark night*
McPhail, David. *Weezer changes the world*
Mortensen, Denise Dowling. *Ohio thunder*
Polacco, Patricia. *Thunder cake*
Ray, Mary Lyn. *Boom!*
Shepard, Aaron. *Master man*
Swenson, Jamie A. *Boom! Boom! Boom!*

Weather – mist *see* Weather – fog

Weather – rain

Aardema, Verna. *Bringing the rain to Kapiti Plain*
Appelt, Kathi. *Rain dance*

Arnosky, Jim. *Rabbits and raindrops*
Arqués, Isabel M. *Ken's cloud*
Ashman, Linda. *Rain!*
Auld, Mary. *Noah's ark*
Baird, Audrey B. *Storm coming!*
Base, Graeme. *The water hole*
Beaumont, Karen. *Move over, Rover*
Bentley, Dawn. *Fuzzy bear*
Boswell, Addie. *The rain stomper*
Branley, Franklyn M. *Down comes the rain*
Rain and hail
Bridges, Margaret Park. *I love the rain*
Burningham, John. *Mr. Gumpy's motor car*
Carle, Eric. *Little cloud*
Little cloud [board book]
Cocca-Leffler, Maryann. *Let it rain*
Colborn, Mary Palenick. *Rainy day slug*
Conway, David. *Lila and the secret of rain*
Cotten, Cynthia. *Rain play*
Cousins, Lucy. *Noah's ark*
Noah's ark [board book]
Crews, Nina. *You are here*
Crimi, Carolyn. *Tessa's tip-tapping toes*
Cullen, Lynn. *Little Scraggly Hair*
Dawavendewa, Gerald. *The butterfly dance*
De Roo, Elena. *The rain train*
Docherty, Thomas. *To the beach*
Edwards, Pamela Duncan. *Warthogs paint*
Emberley, Barbara. *One wide river to cross*
Feiffer, Kate. *My side of the car*
Flanagan, Alice K. *Rain*
Freeman, Don. *Dandelion*
Gammell, Stephen. *Mudkin*
Gibson, Amy. *Split! Splat!*
Ginsburg, Mirra. *Mushroom in the rain*
Goodhart, Pippa. *Noah makes a boat*
Gorbachev, Valeri. *Catty Jane who hated the rain*
Nicky and the rainy day
One rainy day
Gutman, Anne. *Gaspard and Lisa's rainy day*
Hafner, Marylin. *Molly and Emmett's camping adventure*
Harker, Lesley. *Annie's ark*
Harrison, Troon. *The floating orchard*
Herman, Charlotte. *First rain*
Hesse, Karen. *Come on, rain*
Hines, Anna Grossnickle. *What can you do in the rain?*
Hoban, Julia. *Amy loves the rain*
Inkpen, Mick. *Kipper's rainy day*
Splosh!
Johanasen, Heather. *About the rain forest*
Johnson, Angela. *Rain feet*
Johnson, D. B. *Henry works*
Johnson, Neil. *The falling raindrop*
Jonas, Ann. *Aardvarks, disembark!*
Jones, Elizabeth. *Sunshine and Storm*
Kalan, Robert. *Rain*
Kaner, Etta. *Who likes the rain?*
Keats, Ezra Jack. *A letter to Amy*
Krensky, Stephen. *Noah's bark*
Kurtz, Jane. *Rain romp*
Lakin, Patricia. *Rainy day*
Lee, Jeanne M. *Toad is the uncle of heaven*
Lehman, Barbara. *Rainstorm*
Lewison, Wendy Cheyette. *So many boots*
Lichtenheld, Tom. *Cloudette*
Liu, Jae Soo. *Yellow umbrella*
London, Jonathan. *Puddles*
What the animals were waiting for
McCarthy, Michael. *The story of Noah and the ark*
Macken, JoAnn Early. *Waiting out the storm*
McPhail, David. *The puddle*
Maggi, María Elena. *The great canoe*
Manning, Maurie J. *The aunts go marching*
Martin, Bill, Jr. *Listen to the rain*
Millard, Glenda. *And red galoshes*
Mitchell, Marianne. *Gullywasher gulch*
Munsch, Robert N. *Mud puddle*
Nelson, Robin. *A rainy day*
Olaleye, Isaac. *In the Rainfield*
O'Mara, Carmel. *Rainy day*
Otto, Carolyn. *That sky, that rain*
Paley, Joan. *One more river*
Parker, Mary Jessie. *The deep, deep puddle*
Pinkney, Jerry. *Noah's ark*
Pinkwater, Daniel. *Rainy morning*
Plourde, Lynn. *Pigs in the mud in the middle of the rud*
Prelutsky, Jack. *Rainy rainy Saturday*
Raschka, Chris. *John Coltrane's giant steps*
Ray, Mary Lyn. *Red rubber boot day*
Rumford, James. *Rain school*
Salzano, Tammi. *One rainy day*
Scheer, Julian. *Rain makes applesauce*
Schwartz, Roslyn. *The mole sisters and the rainy day*
Serfozo, Mary. *Rain talk*
Shannon, David. *The rain came down*
Shannon, George. *April showers*
Shapiro, Zachary. *We're all in the same boat*
Sheth, Kashmira. *Monsoon afternoon*
Shulevitz, Uri. *Rain rain rivers*
Singer, Isaac Bashevis. *Why Noah chose the dove*
Spalding, Andrea. *It's raining, it's pouring*
Spetter, Jung-Hee. *Lily and Trooper's winter*
Spier, Peter. *Noah's ark*
Peter Spier's rain
Stevenson, James. *Heat wave at Mud Flat*
Stewart, Melissa. *When rain falls*
Stewig, John Warren. *The animals watched*
Sting [Musician]. *Rock steady*
Stock, Catherine. *Gugu's house*
Stojic, Manya. *Rain*
Sykes, Julie. *Smudge*
Tebbs, Victoria. *Noah's Ark story*
Todd, Barbara. *The rainmaker*
Tresselt, Alvin R. *Rain drop splash*
Verboven, Agnes. *Ducks like to swim*
Vincent, Gabrielle. *Ernest and Celestine's picnic*
Walton, Rick. *Noah's square dance*
Wilson, Anne. *Noah's ark*
Yashima, Taro. *Umbrella*
Yee, Wong Herbert. *Who likes rain?*
Zolotow, Charlotte. *The quarreling book*
The storm book

Weather – rainbows

Asch, Frank. *Skyfire*
Auld, Mary. *Noah's ark*
Barry, Frances. *Duckie's rainbow*
Callahan, Sean. *The leprechaun who lost his rainbow*
Cousins, Lucy. *Noah's ark*
Noah's ark [board book]
Cullen, Lynn. *Little Scraggly Hair*
Goodhart, Pippa. *Noah makes a boat*
Harburg, E. Y. *Over the rainbow*

Hines, Anna Grossnickle. *What can you do in the sun?*
Krupp, E. C. *The rainbow and you*
Lyon, George Ella. *My friend, the starfinder*
Paley, Joan. *One more river*
Pinkney, Jerry. *Noah's ark*
Pinkney, Sandra L. *A rainbow all around me*
Shannon, David. *The rain came down*
Singer, Isaac Bashevis. *Why Noah chose the dove*
Sting [Musician]. *Rock steady*
Walsh, Melanie. *Ned's rainbow*
Wilson, Anne. *Noah's ark*
Zolotow, Charlotte. *The storm book*

Weather – sandstorms

London, Jonathan. *Ali, child of the desert*

Weather – snow

Aillaud, Cindy Lou. *Recess at 20 below*
Alarcón, Francisco X. *Iguanas in the snow and other winter poems / Iguanas en la nieve y otros poemas de invierno*
Alborough, Jez. *Ice cream bear*
Andrews, Julie. *The very fairy princess sparkles in the snow*
Arqués, Isabel M. *Ken's cloud*
Bahr, Mary. *My brother loved snowflakes*
Bean, Jonathan. *Big snow*
Beck, Ian. *Teddy's snowy day*
Berger, Carin. *A perfect day*
Berry, Lynne. *Duck skates*
Bildner, Phil. *Turkey Bowl*
Blackstone, Stella. *Cleo in the snow*
Bradby, Marie. *The longest wait*
Branley, Franklyn M. *Snow is falling*
Brett, Jan. *The three snow bears*
Bruchac, James. *Rabbit's snow dance*
Brunelle, Nicholas. *Snow moon*
Burton, Virginia Lee. *Katy and the big snow*
Butler, M. Christina. *Snow friends*
Butterworth, Nick. *One snowy night*
Bynum, Janie. *Altoona up north*
Carle, Eric. *Dream snow*
Carlstrom, Nancy White. *Mama, will it snow tonight?*
The snow speaks
Casanova, Mary. *One-dog sleigh*
Cassino, Mark, with Jon Nelson. *The story of snow*
Chessa, Francesca. *Holly's red boots*
Child, Lauren. *Snow is my favorite and my best*
Colandro, Lucille. *There was a cold lady who swallowed some snow!*
Cole, Henry. *Trudy*
Cote, Nancy. *It feels like snow*
Cotten, Cynthia. *Snow ponies*
Cox, Judy. *Snow day for Mouse*
Crews, Nina. *Snowball*
Crisp, Marty. *Totally polar*
Croll, Carolyn. *The little snowgirl*
Curious George in the snow
Cuyler, Margery. *The biggest, best snowman*
da Costa, Deborah. *Snow in Jerusalem*
Dahl, Michael. *Footprints in the snow*
Day, Alexandra. *Carl's snowy afternoon*
deGroat, Diane. *Jingle bells, homework smells*
Denslow, Sharon Phillips. *In the snow*
DePrisco, Dorothea. *Snowbear's winter day*
Dooley, Norah. *Everybody serves soup*
Dunrea, Olivier. *It's snowing*
Emmett, Jonathan. *Diamond in the snow*
Fallon, Jimmy. *Snowball fight!*
Fearnley, Jan. *A perfect day for it*
Fitch, Sheree. *No two snowflakes*
Flanagan, Alice K. *Snow*
Fleischman, Paul. *Lost!*
Fleming, Denise. *The first day of winter*
Ford, Bernette. *First snow*
Gammell, Stephen. *Is that you, winter?*
Garland, Michael. *Super snow day seek and find*
Gay, Marie-Louise. *Stella, queen of the snow*
George, Jean Craighead. *Snow bear*
Gershator, Phillis. *When it starts to snow*
Gibbons, Gail. *It's snowing!*
Gliori, Debi. *The snow lambs*
Gorbachev, Valeri. *Me too!*
Gore, Leonid. *Danny's first snow*
Hächler, Bruno. *Anna's wish*
Hader, Berta Hoerner. *The big snow*
Halpern, Julie. *Toby and the snowflakes*
Harper, Lee. *Snow! Snow! Snow!*
Hawcock, Claire. *Mine, all mine!*
Heiligman, Deborah. *Snow dog, go dog*
Helquist, Brett. *Bedtime for Bear*
Henkes, Kevin. *Oh!*
Hest, Amy. *Charley's first night*
The reader
When Charley met Grampa
Hines, Anna Grossnickle. *What can you do in the snow?*
Hoban, Julia. *Amy loves the snow*
Hobbie, Holly. *Toot and Puddle: let it snow*
Toot and Puddle, I'll be home for Christmas
Hubbell, Patricia. *Snow happy!*
Huneck, Stephen. *Sally's snow adventure*
Inkpen, Mick. *Kipper's snowy day*
Iwamura, Kazuo. *Hooray for snow!*
Jennings, Linda. *Little puppy lost*
Joosse, Barbara. *Snow day!*
Joyce, William. *Snowie Rolie*
Katz, Karen. *Baby loves winter!*
Keats, Ezra Jack. *The snowy day*
The snowy day [board book]
Keller, Holly. *Geraldine's big snow*
Kneen, Maggie. *The Christmas surprise*
Krauss, Ruth. *The happy day*
Kroll, Virginia L. *Good citizen Sarah*
Lachner, Dorothea. *The gift from Saint Nicholas*
Lakin, Patricia. *Snow day!*
Laminack, Lester L. *Snow day!*
Landry, Leo. *The snow ghosts*
Lasky, Kathryn. *Lucille's snowsuit*
Lewis, Kim. *First snow*
Lin, Grace. *Robert's snowflakes*
London, Jonathan. *Froggy gets dressed*
Long, Loren. *An Otis Christmas*
McCully, Emily Arnold. *First snow*
An outlaw Thanksgiving
McGuirk, Leslie. *Tucker flips!*
McKee, David. *Elmer in the snow*
MacLachlan, Patricia. *Snowflakes fall*
McQuade, Jacqueline. *Snow babies*
Mahoney, Daniel J. *A really good snowman*
Marlow, Layn. *You make me smile*
Martin, Jacqueline Briggs. *Snowflake Bentley*
Marzollo, Jean. *Snow angel*
Mercer, Lynn. *Schubert's snowflakes*

Meschenmoser, Sebastian. *Waiting for winter*
Messner, Kate. *Over and under the snow*
Munsch, Robert N. *Thomas' snowsuit*
Murphy, Yannick. *Baby Polar*
Nelson, Robin. *A snowy day*
Neubecker, Robert. *Winter is for snow*
Norman, Kim. *If it's snowy and you know it, clap your paws!*
O'Malley, Kevin. *Straight to the pole*
Paradis, Susan. *Snow princess*
Patten, Brian. *The big snuggle-up*
Peddle, Daniel. *Snow day*
Pendziwol, Jean E. *Once upon a northern night*
Perkins, Lynne Rae. *Snow music*
Petersen, David. *Snowy Valentine*
Pfister, Marcus. *Penguin Pete and Little Tim*
Snow puppy
Pickering, Jimmy. *It's winter*
Poydar, Nancy. *Snip, snip . . . snow!*
Pulver, Robin. *Axle Annie*
Raczka, Bob. *Snowy, blowy winter*
Raschka, Chris. *John Coltrane's giant steps*
Reid, Barbara. *Perfect snow*
Reynolds, Aaron. *Snowbots*
Rockwell, Anne. *The first snowfall*
Roode, Daniel. *Little Bea and the snowy day*
Root, Phyllis. *Grandmother Winter*
Rosen, Michael J. *Avalanche*
Rosenberg, Liz. *On Christmas eve*
Rylant, Cynthia. *Snow*
Sabuda, Robert. *Winter's tale*
Sakai, Komako. *The snow day*
Sanfield, Steve. *Snow*
Schaefer, Carole Lexa. *Snow pumpkin*
Scheffler, Axel. *The snowy day*
Schoenherr, Ian. *Pip and Squeak*
Shulevitz, Uri. *Snow*
Siddals, Mary McKenna. *Millions of snowflakes*
Simmons, Jane. *Little Fern's first winter*
Soman, David. *Ladybug Girl and the big snow*
Spetter, Jung-Hee. *Lily and Trooper's winter*
Spinelli, Eileen. *Cold snap*
Spohn, Kate. *Snow play*
Stafford, Liliana. *The snow bear*
Steffensmeier, Alexander. *Millie in the snow*
Steig, William. *Brave Irene*
Stewart, Melissa. *Under the snow*
Stojic, Manya. *Snow*
Tegen, Katherine Brown. *Snowman magic*
Thomas, Peggy. *Snow dance*
Thompson, Lauren. *Mouse's first snow*
Tresselt, Alvin R. *White snow, bright snow*
Van Laan, Nancy. *Moose tales*
Waddell, Martin. *Snow bears*
Wahman, Joe. *Snowboy 1, 2, 3*
Wallace, Nancy Elizabeth. *Snow*
Snow [board book]
Ward, Lindsay. *When Blue met Egg*
Watanabe, Shigeo. *Ice cream is falling!*
Watts, Bernadette. *The smallest snowflake*
Weller, Frances Ward. *The angel of Mill Street*
Wellington, Monica. *Bunny's first snowflake*
Wells, Rosemary. *Red boots*
Whybrow, Ian. *Harry and the snow king*
Williams, Sam. *Snowy magic*
Wilson, Karma. *Dinos in the snow!*
Winget, Susan. *Sam the Snowman*
Young, Ned. *Zoomer's summer snowstorm*
Zolotow, Charlotte. *Something is going to happen*

Weather – storms

Anholt, Catherine. *Chimp and Zee and the big storm*
Asare, Meshack. *Sosu's call*
Baird, Audrey B. *Storm coming!*
Belton, Robyn. *Herbert*
Berger, Barbara. *Thunder Bunny*
Boswell, Addie. *The rain stomper*
Bourgeois, Paulette. *Franklin and the thunderstorm*
Bradby, Marie. *The longest wait*
Branley, Franklyn M. *Tornado alert*
Bright, Paul. *The bears in the bed and the great big storm*
Brown, Alan James. *Hoot and Holler*
Bryan, Ashley. *The story of lightning and thunder*
Burdett, Lois. *The tempest for kids*
Crews, Donald. *Sail away*
Crum, Shutta. *Thunder-Boomer!*
D'Amico, Carmela. *Ella sets sail*
Davol, Marguerite W. *Why butterflies go by on silent wings*
Doyle, Malachy. *Storm cats*
Emmett, Jonathan. *This way, Ruby!*
Fisher, Leonard Everett. *Sky, sea, the jetty, and me*
Flanagan, Alice K. *Thunder and lightning*
Geisert, Arthur. *Thunderstorm*
George, Jean Craighead. *Cliff hanger*
Gerritsen, Paula. *Nuts*
Gliori, Debi. *Mr. Bear to the rescue*
The snow lambs
Griessman, Annette. *Like a hundred drums*
Harvey, Brett. *My prairie Christmas*
Haughton, Emma. *Rainy day*
Hines, Anna Grossnickle. *Rumble thumble boom!*
Hobbie, Holly. *Toot and Puddle, I'll be home for Christmas*
Toot and Puddle, you are my sunshine
Hutchins, Hazel. *One dark night*
Iwamura, Kazuo. *Hooray for summer!*
Jennings, Sharon. *Bearcub and Mama*
Johnson, Amy Crane. *Cinnamon and the April shower / Canela y el aguacero de abril*
Keats, Ezra Jack. *Clementina's cactus*
Kimura, Yuichi. *One stormy night . . .*
Klise, Kate. *Grammy Lamby and the secret handshake*
Krensky, Stephen. *Milo and the really big bunny*
Kuiper, Nannie. *Bravo, brave beavers*
Landström, Olof. *Boo and Baa get wet*
Leeson, Christine. *Molly and the storm*
McBratney, Sam. *Just you and me*
Macken, JoAnn Early. *Waiting out the storm*
McPhail, David. *The Searcher and Old Tree*
Miller, William. *A house by the river*
Mortensen, Denise Dowling. *Ohio thunder*
Murphy, Yannick. *Baby Polar*
Perrow, Angeli. *Lighthouse dog to the rescue*
Polacco, Patricia. *Thunder cake*
Quackenbush, Robert M. *Batbaby*
Randall, Alison L. *The wheat doll*
Reynolds, Peter H. *Sydney's star*
Root, Phyllis. *Creak! said the bed*
Rosenberg, Liz. *On Christmas eve*
Sadler, Judy Ann. *Sandwiches for Duke*
Sampson, Michael R. *Caddie, the golf dog*
Seeger, Laura Vaccaro. *Walter was worried*
Sidman, Joyce. *Meow ruff*
Stainton, Sue. *The lighthouse cat*
Steig, William. *Brave Irene*
Stolz, Mary. *Storm in the night*

Sutherland, Marc. *MacMurtrey's wall*
Swenson, Jamie A. *Boom! Boom! Boom!*
Tafuri, Nancy. *The big storm*
Will you be my friend?
Trapani, Iza. *Row, row, row your boat*
Van Allsburg, Chris. *The wreck of the Zephyr*
Van Nutt, Julia. *Pumpkins from the sky?*
Viau, Nancy. *Storm song*
Wellington, Monica. *Night rabbits*
Wiesner, David. *Hurricane*
Williams, Garth. *Benjamin's treasure*
Yolen, Jane. *Before the storm*
Young, Ed. *The lost horse*

Weather – thunder *see* Weather – lightning, thunder

Weather – tornadoes

Arnold, Marsha Diane. *The bravest of us all*
Chambers, Catherine. *Tornado*
Fisher, Carolyn. *A twisted tale*
Gibbons, Gail. *Tornadoes!*
Griffin, Kitty. *The foot-stomping adventures of Clementine Sweet*
Lester, Helen. *Batter up Wombat*
Long, Loren. *Otis and the tornado*
Lyon, George Ella. *One lucky girl*
Prigger, Mary Skillings. *Aunt Minnie and the twister*
Sloat, Teri. *Farmer Brown goes round and round*

Weather – wind

Aesop. *The contest between the Sun and the Wind*
Asch, Frank. *Like a windy day*
Bauer, Marion Dane. *The longest night*
Birdsall, Jeanne. *Flora's very windy day*
Carlstrom, Nancy White. *How does the wind walk?*
Day, Nancy Raines. *On a windy night*
Derby, Sally. *Whoosh went the wind!*
DiPucchio, Kelly. *What's the magic word?*
Drummond, Allan. *Energy island*
Ehlert, Lois. *Leaf man*
Ets, Marie Hall. *Gilberto and the wind*
Flanagan, Alice K. *Wind*
Hamilton, Virginia. *Drylongso*
Hines, Anna Grossnickle. *What can you do in the wind?*
Hoban, Julia. *Amy loves the wind*
Huntington, Amy. *One Monday*
Hutchins, Pat. *The wind blew*
Kaner, Etta. *Who likes the wind?*
Keats, Ezra Jack. *A letter to Amy*
McKee, David. *Elmer and the wind*
Elmer takes off
McMillan, Bruce. *How the ladies stopped the wind*
Manceau, Edouard. *Windblown*
Martin, Bill, Jr. *Old devil wind*
Mitchell, Robin. *Windy*
Moore, Lilian. *While you were chasing a hat*
Morrison, Toni. *Little Cloud and Lady Wind*
Nelson, Robin. *A windy day*
Olaleye, Isaac. *In the Rainfield*
Poydar, Nancy. *Rhyme time Valentine*
Ramirez, Melissa Bourbon. *The flight of the sunflower*
Roberts, Bethany. *The wind's garden*
Salzano, Tammi. *One windy day*
Thompson, Lauren. *Mouse's first spring*
White, Linda Arms. *Comes a wind*
Wright, Maureen. *Sneeze, Big Bear, sneeze*
Zolotow, Charlotte. *When the wind stops*

Weather reporters *see* Careers – meteorologists

Weddings

Ammon, Richard. *An Amish wedding*
Andrews, Julie. *The very fairy princess: here comes the flower girl!*
Balian, Lorna. *A sweetheart for Valentine*
Barasch, Lynne. *The reluctant flower girl*
Bottner, Barbara. *Flower girl*
Brannen, Sarah S. *Uncle Bobby's wedding*
Broach, Elise. *Wet dog!*
Brown, Marc. *D. W. thinks big [board book]*
Bunting, Eve. *My mom's wedding*
Crunk, Tony. *Railroad John and the Red Rock run*
English, Karen. *Nadia's hands*
Finchler, Judy. *Congratulations, Miss Malarkey!*
Friedman, Laurie. *A style all her own*
A frog he would a-wooing go [folk-song]. *Frog went a-courting*
Froggie went a courting
Froggy went a-courtin'
Furgang, Kathy. *Flower girl*
Gantos, Jack. *Wedding bells for Rotten Ralph*
Grimm, Jacob and Wilhelm *The goose girl*
Rumpelstiltskin, ill. by Paul Galdone
Rumpelstiltskin, ill. by David Shaw
Rumpelstiltskin, ill. by Paul O. Zelinsky
Snow White and the seven dwarfs
Hartt-Sussman, Heather. *Nana's getting married*
Henkes, Kevin. *El gran día de Lily / Lilly's big day*
Lilly's big day
Holabird, Katharine. *Angelina and the royal wedding*
Jaffe, Nina. *The way meat loves salt*
Jewell, Nancy. *Alligator wedding*
Johnson, Angela. *The wedding*
Johnston, Tony. *The cowboy and the black-eyed pea*
LaTeef, Nelda. *The hunter and the ebony tree*
Lloyd-Jones, Sally. *How to get married by me, the bride*
Look, Lenore. *Uncle Peter's amazing Chinese wedding*
Lyons, Kelly Starling. *Ellen's broom*
Marshall, Janet Perry. *A honey of a day*
Masini, Beatrice. *Here comes the bride*
Mathers, Petra. *Dodo gets married*
Morris, Ann. *Weddings*
Munsch, Robert N. *Ribbon rescue*
Newman, Lesléa. *Donovan's big day*
Nobisso, Josephine. *The weight of a Mass*
Pilkey, Dav. *The Silly Gooses*
Polacco, Patricia. *Someone for Mr. Sussman*
Rylant, Cynthia. *The bookshop dog*
Sierra, Judy. *The beautiful butterfly*
Soto, Gary. *Snapshots from the wedding*
Stadler, John. *The cats of Mrs. Calamari*
Stanley, Mandy. *Lettice the flower girl*
Summers, Kate. *Milly's wedding*
Van Laan, Nancy. *La boda*
Wright, Courtni Crump. *Jumping the broom*
Yep, Laurence. *The Khan's daughter*
Yorinks, Arthur. *Company's going*
Young, Ed. *Mouse match*
Zalben, Jane Breskin. *Beni's first wedding*
Ziefert, Harriet. *Grandma's wedding album*

Weekdays *see* Days of the week, months of the year

West *see* U.S. history – frontier & pioneer life

Wheelchairs *see* Disabilities – physical disabilities

Wheels

Berenstain, Stan and Jan. *Bears on wheels*
Pearson, Debora. *Sophie's wheels*
Prince, April Jones. *What do wheels do all day?*
Rotner, Shelley. *Wheels around*

Whistles

Egielski, Richard. *Three magic balls*
Schaefer, Carole Lexa. *The little French whistle*

Willfulness *see* Character traits – willfulness

Wisdom *see* Character traits – wisdom

Wishing *see* Behavior – wishing

Witches

Adams, Adrienne. *A Halloween happening*
A woggle of witches
Alexander, Sue. *Who goes out on Halloween?*
Alley, R. W. *There once was a witch*
Andersen, Hans Christian. *The tinderbox*, ill. by Warwick Hutton
The tinderbox, ill. by Barry Moser
Baeten, Lieve. *The clever little witch*
The curious little witch
Happy birthday, Little Witch!
Balian, Lorna. *Humbug witch*
Barrett, Judi. *Which witch is which?*
Bateson-Hill, Margaret. *Masha and the firebird*
Berry, Lynne. *The curious demise of a contrary cat*
Bridwell, Norman. *The witch grows up*
The witch next door
Brokamp, Elizabeth. *The picky little witch*
Brown, Lisa. *Vampire boy's good night*
Christian, Cheryl. *Witches*
Cohen, Caron Lee. *Broom, zoom!*
Cole, Joanna. *Bony-legs*
Coppinger, Tom. *Curse in reverse*
Corderoy, Tracey. *Hubble bubble, Granny trouble*
Cuyler, Margery. *Skeleton for dinner*
Davis, Katie. *Scared stiff*
de Las Casas, Dianne. *The house that Witchy built*
dePaola, Tomie. *Big Anthony, his story*
Brava Strega Nona!
Merry Christmas, Strega Nona
Strega Nona
Strega Nona meets her match
Strega Nona takes a vacation
Strega Nona's gift
Strega Nona's harvest
Strega Nona's magic lessons
Desmoinaux, Christel. *"Hallo-what?"*
Donaldson, Julia. *Room on the broom*
Five little pumpkins, ill. by Ben Mantle
Five little pumpkins, ill. by Dan Yaccarino
Grambling, Lois G. *The witch who wanted to be a princess*
Grimm, Jacob and Wilhelm. *Hansel and Gretel*, ill. by Jen Corace
Hansel and Gretel, ill. by Rachel Isadora
Hansel and Gretel (1980), ill. by Susan Jeffers
Hansel and Gretel (2011), ill. by Susan Jeffers
Hansel and Gretel, ill. by Jane Ray
Hansel and Gretel, ill. by Claudia Wolf
Hansel and Gretel, ill. by Paul O. Zelinsky
Hansel and Gretel, ill. by Lisbeth Zwerger
Hansel and Gretel / Hansel y Gretel
Hansel and Gretel: a retelling from the original tale by the Brothers Grimm
Jorinda and Jorindel
Rapunzel, ill. by Sarah Gibb
Rapunzel, ill. by Trina Schart Hyman
Rapunzel, ill. by Rachel Isadora
Rapunzel, ill. by Joma
Rapunzel, ill. by Kris Waldherr
Rapunzel, ill. by Paul O. Zelinsky
Rapunzel: a fairy tale
The sleeping beauty
Snow White, ill. by Melinda Copper
Snow White, ill. by Quentin Gréban
Snow White, ill. by Trina Schart Hyman
Snow White and the seven dwarfs
Gukova, Julia. *All mixed-up!*
Halloweena
Heinz, Brian J. *The monsters' test*
Heller, Nicholas. *Elwood and the witch*
Horn, Emily. *Excuse me — are you a witch?*
Howard, Arthur. *Hoodwinked*
Johnston, Tony. *Go track a yak*
The vanishing pumpkin
Jones, Ursula. *The witch's children*
Kellogg, Steven. *The Christmas witch*
Kitamura, Satoshi. *Me and my cat?*
Kohara, Kazuno. *Ghosts in the house!*
Lachner, Dorothea. *Meredith's mixed-up magic*
Lattimore, Deborah Nourse. *Cinderhazel*
Leedy, Loreen. *2 x 2 = boo!*
Lester, Helen. *Me first*
Leuck, Laura. *One witch*
Little old lady who swallowed a fly. *I know an old lady*
Lucas, David. *Cake girl*
McCaughrean, Geraldine. *Grandma Chickenlegs*
McGhee, Alison. *A very brave witch*
McGrath, Barbara Barbieri. *The little green witch*
Manning, Jane. *Cat nights*
Marshall, James. *Hansel and Gretel*
Mayer, Marianna. *Baba Yaga and Vasilisa the Brave*
Meddaugh, Susan. *The witches' supermarket*
The witch's walking stick
Melmed, Laura Krauss. *Fright night flight*
Minters, Frances. *Sleepless Beauty*
Moerbeek, Kees. *The diary of Hansel and Gretel*
Mystery manor
Nash, Ogden. *The adventures of Isabel*, ill. by James Marshall
The adventures of Isabel, ill. by Bridget Starr Taylor
Novak, Matt. *No zombies allowed*
Oppenheim, Joanne. *The Christmas witch*
Oram, Hiawyn. *Baba Yaga and the wise doll*

Palatini, Margie. *Piggie pie*
Zoom Broom
Peet, Bill. *Big bad Bruce*
The Whingdingdilly
Prelutsky, Jack. *Monday's troll*
Wild witches' ball
Reeves, Howard W. *There was an old witch*
Rex, Michael. *Brooms are for flying*
Ross, Eileen. *The Halloween showdown*
San Souci, Robert D. *Feathertop*
Peter and the blue witch baby
The red heels
Santoro, Scott. *Which way to witch school?*
Scieszka, Jon. *The frog prince, continued*
Shannon, George. *A very witchy spelling bee*
Sharratt, Nick. *What's in the witch's kitchen?*
Shute, Linda. *Halloween party*
Silverman, Erica. *The Halloween house*
Simmons, Steven J. *Alice and Greta*
Alice and Greta's color magic
Greta's revenge
Somers, Kevin. *Meaner than meanest*
Steig, William. *Caleb and Kate*
Wizzil
Stevenson, James. *Emma*
Fried feathers for Thanksgiving
Happy Valentine's Day, Emma!
Yuck!
Tatcheva, Eva. *Witch Zelda's birthday cake*
Thomas, Valerie. *Winnie the witch*
Winnie's midnight dragon
Thompson, Richard. *The follower*
Tunnell, Michael O. *Halloween pie*
Van Allsburg, Chris. *The widow's broom*
Wahl, Jan. *Little Johnny Buttermilk*
Walker, Sally M. *Druscilla's Halloween*
Walton, Rick. *Pig, pigger, piggest*
Weil, Lisl. *The candy egg bunny*
Williams, Suzanne. *The witch casts a spell*
Winthrop, Elizabeth. *Vasilissa the beautiful*
Wolff, Ferida. *On Halloween night*
Wood, Audrey. *Heckedy Peg*
Yolen, Jane. *The flying witch*
The girl in the golden bower
Ziefert, Harriet. *Two little witches*

Wizards

Brunhoff, Laurent de. *Babar and the succotash bird*
Clibbon, Meg. *Imagine you're a wizard!*
Fox, Mem. *The magic hat*
Morrissey, Dean. *The wizard mouse*
Prelutsky, Jack. *The wizard*
Robertson, M. P. *The dragon snatcher*
Seder, Rufus Butler. *The Wizard of Oz*
Tom Thumb. *The adventures of Tom Thumb*
Walsh, Ellen Stoll. *Mouse magic*
Yolen, Jane. *The firebird*

Woodchucks *see* Animals – groundhogs

Woods *see* Forest, woods

Word games *see* Language

Wordless

Aliki. *Tabby*
Andreasen, Dan. *The treasure bath*
Anno, Mitsumasa. *Anno's Britain*
Anno's counting book
Anno's counting house
Anno's Italy
Anno's journey
Anno's U.S.A.
Arnosky, Jim. *Mouse letters*
Mouse numbers and letters
Mouse writing
Mud time and more
Baker, Jeannie. *Mirror*
Window
Bang, Molly. *The grey lady and the strawberry snatcher*
Becker, Aaron. *Journey*
Boyd, Lizi. *Inside outside*
Briggs, Raymond. *Father Christmas*
The snowman
Carle, Eric. *Do you want to be my friend?*
I see a song
Ceelen, Vicky. *Baby! baby!*
Cole, Henry. *Unspoken*
Cosentino, Ralph. *The marvelous misadventures of — Fun-Boy*
Crews, Donald. *Truck*
Day, Alexandra. *Carl goes shopping*
Carl's snowy afternoon
Follow Carl!
Good dog, Carl
dePaola, Tomie. *Pancakes for breakfast*
Desrosiers, Sylvie. *Hocus Pocus*
Hocus Pocus takes the train
Devernay, Laetitia. *The conductor*
Doremus, Gaetan. *Bear despair*
Dornbusch, Erica. *Finding Kate's shoes*
Dudley, Rebecca. *Hank finds an egg*
Dupasquier, Philippe. *1 2 3, follow me!*
Emberley, Ed. *Ed Emberley's big green drawing book*
Faller, Regis. *The adventures of Polo*
Polo
Polo and Lily
Polo and the dragon
Polo and the magician!
Fleischman, Paul. *Sidewalk circus*
Franson, Scott E. *Un-brella*
Frazier, Craig. *Bee and Bird*
Geisert, Arthur. *The giant seed*
Hogwash
Ice
Oops
Goodall, John S. *Creepy castle*
Shrewbettina's birthday
Gordon, Domenica More. *Archie*
Hoban, Tana. *Black on white*
Circles, triangles, and squares
Colors everywhere
Dig, drill, dump, fill
Exactly the opposite
Is it larger? Is it smaller?
Is it red? Is it yellow? Is it blue?
Is it rough? Is it smooth? Is it shiny?
Just look
Look book
Look! Look! Look!
More, fewer, less
Shadows and reflections

Shapes, shapes, shapes
So many circles, so many squares
Spirals, curves, fanshapes and lines
What is that?
Who are they?
Hogrogian, Nonny. *Cool cat*
Hutchins, Pat. *Changes, changes*
Idle, Molly. *Flora and the flamingo*
Jay, Alison. *Welcome to the zoo*
Kamm, Katja. *Invisible*
Keats, Ezra Jack. *Clementina's cactus*
Kitten for a day
Khing, T. T. *Where is the cake?*
Where is the cake now?
Lee, Suzy. *Mirror*
Wave
Lehman, Barbara. *Museum trip*
Rainstorm
The red book
The secret box
Trainstop
Liu, Jae Soo. *Yellow umbrella*
McCully, Emily Arnold. *The Christmas gift*
First snow
Four hungry kittens
New baby
Picnic
McDonnell, Patrick. *South*
Mayer, Mercer. *A boy, a dog, a frog and a friend*
A boy, a dog and a frog
Frog goes to dinner
Frog on his own
Frog, where are you?
Octopus soup
One frog too many
Newgarden, Mark. *Bow-Wow bugs a bug*
Newman, Jeff. *The boys*
Nickle, John. *Alphabet explosion!*
Nolan, Dennis. *Sea of dreams*
Ommen, Sylvia van. *The surprise*
Peddle, Daniel. *Snow day*
Pett, Mark. *The boy and the airplane*
Pinkney, Jerry. *The lion and the mouse*
Polhemus, Coleman. *The crocodile blues*
Raschka, Chris. *A ball for Daisy*
Daisy gets lost
Riphagen, Loes. *Animals home alone*
Rockhill, Dennis. *Polar slumber / Sueño polar*
Rodriguez, Béatrice. *The chicken thief*
Fox and hen together
Rogers, Gregory. *The boy, the bear, the baron, the bard*
The hero of Little Street
Midsummer knight
Rohmann, Eric. *Time flies*
Runton, Andy. *Owly and Wormy: bright lights and starry nights!*
Owly and Wormy: friends all aflutter!
Savage, Stephen. *Where's Walrus?*
Schories, Pat. *Jack and the night visitors*
Jack wants a snack
When Jack goes out
Schubert, Ingrid. *The umbrella*
Sís, Peter. *Dinosaur!*
An ocean world
Ship ahoy!
Sneed, Brad. *Picture a letter*
Spier, Peter. *Noah's ark*
Peter Spier's rain
Staake, Bob. *Bluebird*
Stevenson, James. *Grandpa's great city tour*
Tafuri, Nancy. *Do not disturb*
Early morning in the barn
Junglewalk
Rabbit's morning
Tanaka, Shinsuke. *Wings*
Thomson, Bill. *Chalk*
Fossil
Tolman, Marije. *The tree house*
Turkle, Brinton. *Deep in the forest*
Varon, Sara. *Chicken and Cat*
Chicken and Cat clean up
Villa, Alvaro F. *Flood*
Wakeman, Daniel. *Ben's bunny trouble*
Weitzman, Jacqueline Preiss. *You can't take a balloon into the Metropolitan Museum*
You can't take a balloon into the National Gallery
Wiesner, David. *Free fall*
Mr. Wuffles!
Sector 7
Wilson, April. *April Wilson's magpie magic*
Yum, Hyewon. *Last night*

Working *see* Activities – working; Careers

World

Ajmera, Maya. *Faith*
Ajmera, Maya, et al. *Healthy kids*
Our grandparents
What we wear
Amnesty International. *We are all born free*
Bart, Kathleen. *Town Teddy and Country Bear go global*
Branley, Franklyn M. *The planets in our solar system*
Brooks, Jeremy. *Let there be peace*
Brunhoff, Laurent de. *Babar's world tour*
Buzzeo, Toni. *Inside the books*
Caldicott, Chris. *World food alphabet*
Carney-Nunes, Charisse. *I dream for you a world*
Come and play
Corr, Christopher. *Whole world*
Curtis, Andrea. *What's for lunch?*
Delacre, Lulu. *How far do you love me?*
Frank, John. *How to catch a fish*
Halperin, Wendy Anderson. *Peace*
Here we go round the mulberry bush
Jackson, Ellen. *Earth Mother*
Jackson, Jill. *Let there be peace on earth*
Katz, Karen. *Can you say peace?*
Kerley, Barbara. *One world, one day*
The world is waiting for you
You and me together
Laroche, Giles. *If you lived here*
Lewin, Ted. *How much?*
Ljungkvist, Laura. *Follow the line around the world*
McGinty, Alice B. *Thank you, world*
Miller, Heather Lynn. *Subway ride*
Mora, Pat. *Join hands!*
Ogburn, Jacqueline K. *Little treasures*
Omololu, Cynthia Jaynes. *When it's six o'clock in San Francisco*
Peet, Bill. *Chester the worldly pig*
Perlman, Willa. *Good night, world*
Pow, Tom. *Who is the world for?*
Reynolds, Jan. *Celebrate!*
Ruurs, Margriet. *My librarian is a camel*
My school in the rain forest

Rylant, Cynthia. *The stars will still shine*
Scanlon, Elizabeth Garton. *All the world*
Schertle, Alice. *We*
Schubert, Ingrid. *The umbrella*
Schuett, Stacey. *Somewhere in the world right now*
Singer, Marilyn. *On the same day in March*
Sirett, Dawn. *Love your world*
Smith, Charles R. *I am the world*
Smith, David J. *This child, every child*
Spier, Peter. *People*
Valdivia, Paloma. *Up above and down below*
Walker, Rob D. *Mama says*
Weiss, Nicki. *The world turns round and round*
Willis, Jeanne. *Gorilla! Gorilla!*

Worrying *see* Behavior – worrying

Wrecking machines *see* Machines

Writers *see* Careers – writers; Children as authors

Writing letters *see* Letters, cards

Zodiac

Casey, Dawn. *The great race: the story of the Chinese zodiac*
Chin, Oliver. *The year of the tiger*
Demi. *The dragon's tale and other animal fables of the Chinese zodiac*
Orgel, Doris. *The cat's tale*
Van Woerkom, Dorothy. *The rat, the ox and the zodiac*
Wade, Mary Dodson. *No year of the cat*
Wang, Gabrielle. *The race for the Chinese zodiac*
Young, Ed. *Cat and Rat*

Zoos

Aliki. *My visit to the zoo*
Ancona, George. *Handtalk zoo*
Arnold, Caroline. *Mealtime for zoo animals*
Mother and baby zoo animals
Noisytime for zoo animals
Playtime for zoo animals
Sleepytime for zoo animals
Splashtime for zoo animals
Baby animals at the zoo
Barton, Byron. *Zoo animals*
Bleiman, Andrew. *ABC zooborns!*
Browne, Anthony. *Gorilla*
Little Beauty
Campbell, Rod. *Dear zoo*
Capucilli, Alyssa Satin. *Inside a zoo in the city*
Carle, Eric. *1, 2, 3 to the zoo*
Carrick, Carol. *Patrick's dinosaurs*
Child, Lauren. *But I've used all my pocket change*
Comden, Betty. *What's new at the zoo?*
Curious George visits the zoo
Cuyler, Margery. *That's good! That's bad!*
Deady, Kathleen W. *Out and about at the zoo*
Degman, Lori. *1 zany zoo*
Denim, Sue. *The Dumb Bunnies go to the zoo*
De Vicq de Cumptich, Roberto. *Bembo's zoo*
Doodler, Todd H. *The zoo I drew*
Dyer, Heather. *Tina and the penguin*
Dyer, Sarah. *Batty*
Elliott, George. *The boy who loved bananas*
Ellis, Andy. *When Lulu went to the zoo*
Feiffer, Kate. *My side of the car*
Fox, Mem. *Zoo-looking*
Garland, Michael. *Last night at the zoo*
Gershator, Phillis. *Zoo day, olé!*
Gibbons, Gail. *Zoo*
Goodman, Susan E. *What do you do — at the zoo?*
Hall, Michael. *My heart is like a zoo*
Hamburg, Jennifer. *A moose that says mooooooooo*
Harris, Robie H. *Who's in my family?*
Hart, Christopher. *Merwin, master of disguise*
Hatkoff, Isabella, et al. *Knut*
Heap, Sue. *Danny's drawing book*
Heder, Thyra. *Fraidyzoo*
Hennessy, B. G. *Corduroy at the zoo*
Hoban, Tana. *A children's zoo*
Hogg, Gary. *Beautiful Buehla and the zany zoo makeover*
Howe, James. *The day the teacher went bananas*
Hubbell, Patricia. *Bouncing time*
Ichikawa, Satomi. *I am Pangoo the penguin*
Ipcizade, Catherine. *'Twas the Day before Zoo Day*
Jarman, Julia. *Class Two at the zoo*
Jay, Alison. *Welcome to the zoo*
Judge, Lita. *Pennies for elephants*
Kalz, Jill. *An a-maze-ing zoo adventure*
Kerr, Judith. *One night in the zoo*
Ketteman, Helen. *If Beaver had a fever*
Kurtz, Jane. *Do kangaroos wear seat belts?*
Lithgow, John. *Never play music right next to the zoo*
McQuade, Jacqueline. *At the petting zoo with Teddy Bear*
Mandel, Peter. *Zoo ah-choooo*
Martin, Bill, Jr. *Polar bear, polar bear, what do you hear?*
Mead, Alice. *Billy and Emma*
Metzger, Steve. *The dancing clock*
Mora, Pat. *Marimba!*
Morgan, Richard. *Zoo poo*
Morozumi, Atsuko. *My friend gorilla*
Morris, Richard. *Bye-bye, baby!*
Morrison, Cathy. *I want a pet!*
Munari, Bruno. *Bruno Munari's zoo*
Munsch, Robert N. *Alligator baby*
Napoli, Donna Jo. *Bobby the bold*
Ohora, Zachariah. *Stop snoring, Bernard!*
Ormerod, Jan. *When we went to the zoo*
Park, Linda Sue. *Xander's panda party*
Paxton, Tom. *Going to the zoo*
Pfister, Marcus. *Charlie at the zoo*
Phillips, Betty Lou. *Emily goes wild*
Pichon, Liz. *Penguins*
Pilkey, Dav. *The Dumb Bunnies go to the zoo*
Pinkwater, Daniel. *Bad bears go visiting*
Bad bears in the big city
Irving and Muktuk

Rathmann, Peggy. *Good night, Gorilla*
Rex, Adam. *Pssst!*
Rey, H. A. *Curious George takes a job*
Rice, Eve. *Sam who never forgets*
Richardson, Justin. *And Tango makes three*
Rose, Deborah Lee. *Birthday zoo*
Ryder, Joanne. *Little panda*
A pair of polar bears
Sauer, Tammi. *Oh, nuts!*
Scotton, Rob. *Splat and the cool school trip*
Sendelbach, Brian. *The underpants zoo*
Seuss, Dr. *If I ran the zoo*
Sierra, Judy. *Wild about books*
Wild about you!
Zoozical
Slade, Suzanne. *What's new at the zoo? an animal adding adventure*
Smith, Marie. *Z is for zookeeper*
Stead, Philip C. *A sick day for Amos McGee*
Waber, Bernard. *A lion named Shirley Williamson*
Waldman, Neil. *They came from the Bronx*
Waldron, Kevin. *Mr. Peek and the misunderstanding at the zoo*
Whitehouse, Patricia. *Alligator*
Elephants
Flamingo
Hippopotamus
Ostrich
Sea lion
Tiger
Willis, Jeanne. *The wheels on the bus: a read-along sing-along trip to the zoo*
Wilson, Karma. *Animal strike at the zoo, it's true!*
Wise, William. *Zany zoo*
Ziefert, Harriet. *You and me: we're opposites*

Bibliographic Guide

Arranged alphabetically by author's name in boldface (or by title, if author is unknown), each entry includes title, illustrator, publisher, publication date, and subjects. Joint authors appear as short entries, with the main author name (in parentheses after the title) citing where the complete entry will be found. Where only an author and title are given, complete information is listed under the title as the main entry.

Aardema, Verna. *Anansi does the impossible! an Ashanti tale* ill. by Lisa Desimini. Atheneum, 1997. ISBN 978-0-689-81092-3 Subj: Folk & fairy tales. Foreign lands – Africa. Spiders.

Anansi finds a fool: an Ashanti tale ill. by Bryna Waldman. Dial, 1992. ISBN 978-0-8037-1165-5 Subj: Behavior – trickery. Folk & fairy tales. Mythical creatures. Spiders.

Bimwili and the Zimwi ill. by Susan Meddaugh. Dial, 1985. ISBN 978-0-8037-0213-4 Subj: Folk & fairy tales. Foreign lands – Africa. Foreign lands – Zanzibar. Mythical creatures – trolls.

Borreguita and the coyote ill. by Petra Mathers. Knopf, 1991. ISBN 978-0-679-90921-7 Subj: Animals – coyotes. Animals – sheep. Behavior – trickery. Folk & fairy tales. Foreign lands – Mexico.

Bringing the rain to Kapiti Plain: a Nandi tale ill. by Beatriz A. Vidal. Dial, 1981. ISBN 978-0-8037-0807-5 Subj: Cumulative tales. Folk & fairy tales. Foreign lands – Africa. Rhyming text. Weather – droughts. Weather – rain.

Half-a-ball-of-kenki: an Ashanti tale ill. by Diane Stanley Zuromskis. Warne, 1979. ISBN 978-0-7232-6158-2 Subj: Animals – leopards. Folk & fairy tales. Foreign lands – Africa. Insects – flies.

Jackal's flying lesson: a Khoikhoi tale ill. by Dale Gottlieb. Knopf, 1995. ISBN 978-0-679-95813-0 Subj: Activities – flying. Animals – jackals. Behavior – trickery. Birds. Folk & fairy tales. Foreign lands – Africa. Foreign lands – Namibia.

Ji-nongo-nongo means riddles ill. by Jerry Pinkney. Four Winds, 1978. ISBN 978-0-590-07474-2 Subj: Folk & fairy tales. Foreign lands – Africa. Riddles & jokes.

Koi and the kola nuts ill. by Joe Cepeda. Atheneum, 1999. ISBN 978-0-689-81760-1 Subj: Character traits – kindness to animals. Folk & fairy tales. Foreign lands – Liberia.

The lonely lioness and the ostrich chicks: a Masai tale ill. by Yumi Heo. Owen, 1992. ISBN 978-0-679-96934-1 Subj: Animals – lions. Animals – mongooses. Behavior – needing someone. Birds – ostriches. Emotions – loneliness. Folk & fairy tales. Foreign lands – Africa.

Misoso ill. by Reynold Ruffins. Knopf, 1994. ISBN 978-0-679-93430-1 Subj: Folk & fairy tales. Foreign lands – Africa.

Oh, Kojo! How could you! an Ashanti tale ill. by Marc Brown. Dial, 1984. ISBN 978-0-8037-0007-9 Subj: Folk & fairy tales. Foreign lands – Africa. Humorous stories.

Pedro and the padre ill. by Friso Henstra. Dial, 1991. ISBN 978-0-8037-0523-4 Subj: Character traits – honesty. Folk & fairy tales. Foreign lands – Mexico.

Princess Gorilla and a new kind of water ill. by Victoria Chess. Dial, 1988. ISBN 978-0-8037-0413-8 Subj: Animals. Animals – gorillas. Folk & fairy tales. Foreign lands – Africa.

Rabbit makes a monkey of lion ill. by Jerry Pinkney. Dial, 1988. ISBN 978-0-8037-0298-1 Subj: Animals. Behavior – trickery. Foreign lands – Africa. Jungle.

The riddle of the drum: a tale from Tizapan, Mexico ill. by Tony Chen. Four Winds, 1978. ISBN 978-0-590-07489-6 Subj: Cumulative tales. Folk & fairy tales. Foreign lands – Mexico. Rhyming text. Royalty.

Sebgugugu the glutton: a Bantu tale from Rwanda ill. by Nancy L. Clouse. Eerdmans, 1993. ISBN 978-0-8028-5073-7 Subj: Behavior – greed. Character traits – foolishness. Folk & fairy tales. Foreign lands – Africa. Foreign lands – Rwanda.

Traveling to Tondo: a tale of the Nkundo of Zaire ill. by Will Hillenbrand. Knopf, 1991. ISBN 978-0-679-90081-8 Subj: Activities – traveling. Animals. Folk & fairy tales. Foreign lands – Congo (Democratic Republic). Foreign lands – Zaire.

The vingananee and the tree toad ill. by Ellen Weiss. Warne, 1983. ISBN 978-0-7232-6217-6 Subj: Animals. Folk & fairy tales. Foreign lands – Africa. Foreign lands – Liberia. Spiders.

What's so funny, Ketu? a Nuer tale ill. by Marc Brown. Dial, 1982. ISBN 978-0-8037-9370-5 Subj: Animals. Behavior – secrets. Foreign lands – Africa. Foreign lands – Sudan. Humorous stories. Reptiles – snakes.

Who's in Rabbit's house? ill. by Leo Dillon and Diane Dillon. Dial, 1977. ISBN 978-0-8037-9551-8 Subj: Animals. Folk & fairy tales. Foreign lands – Africa. Humorous stories. Insects – butterflies, caterpillars.

Why mosquitoes buzz in people's ears: a West African tale ill. by Leo Dillon and Diane Dillon. Dial, 1975. ISBN 978-0-8037-6087-5 Subj: Animals. Caldecott award books. Folk & fairy tales. Foreign lands – Africa. Insects – mosquitoes.

Abbott, Bud. *Who's on first?* by Bud Abbott and Lou Costello ill. by John Martz. Quirk, 2013. ISBN 978-1-59474-590-4 Subj: Animals – bears. Animals – rabbits. Humorous stories. Sports – baseball.

ABC school riddles comp. by Susan Joyce; ill. by Freddie Levin. Peel Productions, 2001. ISBN 978-0-939217-54-0 Subj: ABC books. Rhyming text. Riddles & jokes.

Abeele, Veronique van den. *Still my Grandma* ill. by Claude K. Dubois. Eerdmans, 2007. ISBN 978-0-8028-5323-3 Subj: Family life – grandmothers. Illness – Alzheimer's.

Aber, Linda Williams. *Carrie measures up!* ill. by Joy Allen. Kane/Miller, 2001. ISBN 978-1-57565-100-2 Subj: Activities – knitting. Concepts – measurement. Family life – grandmothers.

Abercrombie, Barbara. *Bad dog, Dodger* ill. by Adam Gustavson. McElderry, 2002. ISBN 978-0-689-83782-1 Subj: Animals – babies. Animals – dogs. Pets.

The show-and-tell lion ill. by Lynne Cravath. Simon & Schuster, 2006. ISBN 978-0-689-86408-7 Subj: Behavior – lying. Character traits – honesty. Imagination.

Abley, Mark. *Ghost cat* ill. by Karen Reczuch. Douglas & McIntyre, 2001. ISBN 978-0-88899-433-2 Subj: Animals – cats. Death. Emotions – loneliness. Emotions – sadness. Pets.

Abouraya, Karen Leggett. *Hands around the library: protecting Egypt's treasured books* (Roth, Susan L.)

Abraham, Michelle Shapiro. *My cousin Tamar lives in Israel* ill. by Ann Koffsky. URJ Press, 2007. ISBN 978-0-8074-0989-3 Subj: Foreign lands – Israel. Jewish culture.

Abrahams, Peter. *Quacky baseball* ill. by Frank Morrison. HarperCollins, 2011. ISBN 978-0-06-122978-7 Subj: Birds – ducks. Sports – baseball.

Abrams, Douglas Carlton. *Desmond and the very mean word: a story of forgiveness* (Tutu, Archbishop Desmond)

Abrams, Douglas Carlton . *God's dream* (Tutu, Archbishop Desmond)

Abrams, Pam. *Now I eat my ABC's* ill. by Bruce Wolf. Scholastic, 2004. ISBN 978-0-439-64942-1 Subj: ABC books. Food. Format, unusual – board books.

Abramson, Jill. *Ready or not, here comes Scout* by Jill Abramson and Jane O'Connor ill. by Deborah Melmon. Viking, 2012. ISBN 978-0-670-01441-5 Subj: Animals – dogs. Behavior – misbehavior.

Acheson, Alison. *Grandpa's music: a story about Alzheimer's* ill. by Bill Farnsworth. Whitman, 2009. ISBN 978-0-8075-3052-8 Subj: Family life – grandfathers. Illness – Alzheimer's. Music.

Ackerman, Karen. *Bean's big day* ill. by Paul Mombourquette. Kids Can, 2004. ISBN 978-1-55337-444-2 Subj: Careers – actors. Cities, towns. Self-concept. Theater.

By the dawn's early light ill. by Catherine Stock. Atheneum, 1994. ISBN 978-0-689-31788-0 Subj: Activities – working. Ethnic groups in the U.S. – African Americans. Family life – grandmothers. Family life – mothers.

Song and dance man ill. by Stephen Gammell. Knopf, 1988. ISBN 978-0-394-99330-0 Subj: Activities – dancing. Caldecott award books. Family life – grandfathers.

Acredolo, Linda P. *My first baby signs* by Linda P. Acredolo and Susan Goodwyn; photos by Penny Gentieu. HarperCollins, 2002. ISBN 978-0-06-009074-6 Subj: Communication. Format, unusual – board books. Disabilities – deafness. Sign language.

Ada, Alma Flor. *The Christmas tree / El arbol de Navidad* ill. by Terry Ybáñez. Hyperion, 1997. ISBN

978-0-7868-0151-0 Subj: Cumulative tales. Foreign languages. Holidays – Christmas. Rhyming text. Trees.

Dear Peter Rabbit ill. by Leslie Tryon. Atheneum, 1994. ISBN 978-0-689-31850-4 Subj: Animals. Folk & fairy tales. Letters, cards.

Friend frog ill. by Lori Lohstoeter. Harcourt, 2000. ISBN 978-0-15-201522-0 Subj: Animals – mice. Friendship. Frogs & toads.

Gathering the sun: an alphabet in Spanish and English ill. by Simon Silva. Lothrop, 1997. ISBN 978-0-688-13904-9 Subj: ABC books. Foreign languages. Poetry.

The gold coin ill. by Neil Waldman. Macmillan, 1991. ISBN 978-0-689-31633-3 Subj: Behavior – stealing. Circular tales. Crime. Cumulative tales. Foreign lands – Central America.

I love Saturdays y domingos ill. by Elivia Savadier. Atheneum, 2002. ISBN 978-0-689-31819-1 Subj: Ethnic groups in the U.S. – Mexican Americans. Family life – grandparents. Foreign languages.

¡Muu, moo! rimas de animales = animal nursery rhymes by Alma Flor Ada and F. Isabel Campoy ill. by Viví Escrivá. HarperCollins, 2010. ISBN 978-0-06-134613-2 Subj: Foreign languages. Nursery rhymes.

Pio peep! by Alma Flor Ada and F. Isabel Campoy ill. by Viví Escrivá. English adaptations by Alice Schertle. HarperCollins, 2003. ISBN 978-0-688-16020-3 Subj: Foreign languages. Nursery rhymes.

The rooster who went to his uncle's wedding ill. by Kathleen Kuchera. Atheneum, 1993. ISBN 978-0-399-22412-6 Subj: Birds – chickens. Cumulative tales. Folk & fairy tales. Foreign lands.

With love, Little Red Hen ill. by Leslie Tryon. Atheneum, 2001. ISBN 978-0-689-82581-1 Subj: Ethnic groups in the U.S. – Cuban Americans. Letters, cards.

Adams, Adrienne. *The Christmas party* ill. by author. Scribners, 1978. ISBN 978-0-684-15930-0 Subj: Animals – rabbits. Holidays – Christmas. Parties.

The Easter egg artists ill. by author. Scribners, 1976. ISBN 978-0-684-14652-2 Subj: Activities – painting. Activities – vacationing. Animals – rabbits. Holidays – Easter.

The great Valentine's Day balloon race ill. by author. Scribners, 1980. ISBN 978-0-684-16640-7 Subj: Activities – ballooning. Animals – rabbits. Careers – artists. Holidays – Valentine's Day. Sports – racing.

A Halloween happening ill. by author. Scribners, 1981. ISBN 978-0-684-17166-1 Subj: Holidays – Halloween. Parties. Witches.

A woggle of witches ill. by author. Scribners, 1971. ISBN 978-0-684-12506-0 Subj: Holidays – Halloween. Witches.

Adams, Diane. *I can do it myself!* ill. by Nancy Hayashi. Peachtree, 2009. ISBN 978-1-56145-471-6 Subj: Bedtime. Rhyming text. Self-concept.

I want to help! ill. by Nancy Hayashi. Peachtree, 2012. ISBN 978-1-56145-630-7 Subj: Character traits – helpfulness. Rhyming text. School.

Adams, Eric J. *On the day his daddy left* by Eric J. Adams and Kathleen Adams ill. by Layne Johnson. Whitman, 2000. ISBN 978-0-8075-6072-3 Subj: Divorce. Family life.

Adams, Kathleen. *On the day his daddy left* (Adams, Eric J.)

Adams, Sarah. *Dave and Violet* ill. by author. Frances Lincoln, 2011. ISBN 978-1-84780-052-7 Subj: Character traits – shyness. Dragons. Friendship.

Gary and Ray ill. by author. Frances Lincoln, 2010. ISBN 978-1-84507-955-0 Subj: Animals – gorillas. Birds. Friendship.

Addasi, Maha. *Time to pray* ill. by Ned Gannon. Boyds Mills, 2010. ISBN 978-1-59078-611-6 Subj: Family life – grandmothers. Foreign lands – Middle East. Foreign languages. Religion.

The white nights of Ramadan ill. by Ned Gannon. Boyds Mills, 2008. ISBN 978-1-59078-523-2 Subj: Holidays – Ramadan. Religion – Islam.

Addy, Sharon Hart. *Lucky Jake* ill. by Wade Zahares. Houghton, 2007. ISBN 978-0-618-47286-4 Subj: Animals – pigs. Careers – miners. Character traits – luck.

When wishes were horses ill. by Brad Sneed. Houghton, 2002. ISBN 978-0-618-13166-2 Subj: Animals – horses, ponies. Behavior – wishing.

Adkins, Jan. *What if you met a knight?* ill. by author. Macmillan, 2006. ISBN 978-1-59643-148-5 Subj: Knights. Middle Ages.

Adler, David A. *Campy: the story of Roy Campanella* ill. by Gordon C. James. Penguin, 2007. ISBN 978-0-670-06041-2 Subj: Ethnic groups in the U.S. – African Americans. Disabilities – physical disabilities. Sports – baseball.

The children's book of Jewish holidays ill. by David Sears. Mesorah, 1987. ISBN 978-0-89906-810-7 Subj: Holidays. Jewish culture.

Fun with Roman numerals ill. by Edward Miller. Holiday, 2008. ISBN 978-0-8234-2060-5 Subj: Counting, numbers.

Helen Keller ill. by John Wallner. Holiday, 2003. ISBN 978-0-8234-1606-6 Subj: Character traits – persistence. Disabilities – blindness. Disabilities – deafness.

Heroes for civil rights ill. by Bill Farnsworth. Holiday, 2008. ISBN 978-0-8234-2008-7 Subj: Ethnic groups in the U.S. – African Americans. U.S. history.

Hiding from the Nazis ill. by Karen Ritz. Holiday, 1997. ISBN 978-0-8234-1288-4 Subj: Behavior – hiding. Family life. Holocaust. Jewish culture.

It's time to sleep, it's time to dream ill. by Kay Chorao. Holiday, 2009. ISBN 978-0-8234-1924-1 Subj: Bedtime. Family life. Seasons.

Joe Louis: America's fighter ill. by Terry Widener. Harcourt, 2005. ISBN 978-0-15-216480-5 Subj: Ethnic groups in the U.S. – African Americans. Sports. Sports – boxing.

A little at a time ill. by Paul Tong. Holiday House, 2010. ISBN 978-0-8234-1739-1 Subj: Character traits – questioning. Family life – grandfathers.

Millions, billions, and trillions: understanding big numbers ill. by Edward Miller. Holiday House, 2013. ISBN 978-0-8234-2403-0 Subj: Counting, numbers.

Money madness ill. by Edward Miller. Holiday, 2009. ISBN 978-0-8234-1474-1 Subj: Counting, numbers. Money.

Perimeter, area, and volume: a monster book of dimensions ill. by Edward Miller. Holiday House, 2012. ISBN 978-0-8234-2290-6 Subj: Concepts. Concepts – measurement. Monsters.

A picture book of Abraham Lincoln ill. by John Wallner and Alexandra Wallner. Holiday, 1989. ISBN 978-0-8234-0731-6 Subj: U.S. history.

A picture book of Amelia Earhart ill. by Jeff Fisher. Holiday, 1998. ISBN 978-0-8234-1315-7 Subj: Careers – airplane pilots.

A picture book of Benjamin Franklin ill. by John Wallner and Alexandra Wallner. Holiday, 1990. ISBN 978-0-8234-0792-7 Subj: U.S. history.

A picture book of Cesar Chavez by David A. Adler and Michael S. Adler ill. by Marie Olofsdotter. Holiday House, 2010. ISBN 978-0-8234-2202-9 Subj: Behavior – seeking better things. Careers – migrant workers. Ethnic groups in the U.S. – Mexican Americans. Farms. U.S. history.

A picture book of Dolley and James Madison by David A. Adler and Michael S. Adler ill. by Ronald Himler. Holiday, 2009. ISBN 978-0-8234-2009-4 Subj: U.S. history.

A picture book of Eleanor Roosevelt ill. by Robert Casilla. Holiday, 1991. ISBN 978-0-8234-0856-6 Subj: U.S. history.

A picture book of George Washington ill. by John Wallner and Alexandra Wallner. Holiday, 1989. ISBN 978-0-8234-0732-3 Subj: U.S. history.

A picture book of Hanukkah ill. by Linda Heller. Holiday, 1982. ISBN 978-0-8234-0458-2 Subj: Holidays – Hanukkah. Jewish culture. Religion.

A picture book of Harry Houdini by David A. Adler and Michael S. Adler ill. by Matt Collins. Holiday, 2009. ISBN 978-0-8234-2059-9 Subj: Careers – magicians. Magic. U.S. history.

A picture book of Israel ill. with photos. Holiday, 1984. ISBN 978-0-8234-0513-8 Subj: Foreign lands – Israel. Jewish culture. Religion.

A picture book of Jewish holidays ill. by Linda Heller. Holiday, 1981. ISBN 978-0-8234-0396-7 Subj: Holidays. Holidays – Hanukkah. Holidays – Passover. Jewish culture.

A picture book of John and Abigail Adams by David A. Adler and Michael S. Adler ill. by Ronald Himler. Holiday House, 2010. ISBN 978-0-8234-2007-0 Subj: U.S. history.

A picture book of John F. Kennedy ill. by Robert Casilla. Holiday, 1991. ISBN 978-0-8234-0884-9 Subj: U.S. history.

A picture book of John Hancock ill. by Ronald Himler. Holiday House, 2007. ISBN 978-0-8234-2005-6 Subj: U.S. history.

A picture book of Martin Luther King, Jr ill. by Robert Casilla. Holiday, 1989. ISBN 978-0-8234-0770-5 Subj: Ethnic groups in the U.S. – African Americans. U.S. history. Violence, nonviolence.

A picture book of Passover ill. by Linda Heller. Holiday, 1982. ISBN 978-0-8234-0439-1 Subj: Holidays – Passover. Jewish culture.

A picture book of Sam Houston by David A. Adler and Michael S. Adler ill. by Matt Collins. Holiday House, 2012. ISBN 978-0-8234-2369-9 Subj: Texas. U.S. history.

A picture book of Samuel Adams by David A. Adler and Michael S. Adler ill. by Ronald Himler. Holiday House, 2005. ISBN 978-0-8234-1846-6 Subj: U.S. history.

A picture book of Thomas Jefferson ill. by John Wallner and Alexandra Wallner. Holiday, 1990. ISBN 978-0-8234-0791-0 Subj: U.S. history.

Redwoods are the tallest trees in the world ill. by Kazue Mizumura. Crowell, 1978. ISBN 978-0-690-01368-9 Subj: Forest, woods. Science. Trees.

Satchel Paige: don't look back ill. by Terry Widener. Harcourt, 2007. ISBN 978-0-15-205585-1 Subj: Ethnic groups in the U.S. – African Americans. Sports – baseball.

The story of Hanukkah ill. by Jill Weber. Holiday House, 2011. ISBN 978-0-8234-2295-1 Subj: Holidays – Hanukkah. Jewish culture. Religion.

Things that float and things that don't ill. by Anna Raff. Holiday House, 2013. ISBN 978-0-8234-2862-5 Subj: Character traits – curiosity. Concepts. Science.

Time zones ill. by Edward Miller. Holiday House, 2010. ISBN 978-0-8234-2201-2 Subj: Time.

Adler, Michael S. *A picture book of Cesar Chavez* (Adler, David A.)

A picture book of Dolley and James Madison (Adler, David A.)

A picture book of Harry Houdini (Adler, David A.)

A picture book of John and Abigail Adams (Adler, David A.)

A picture book of Sam Houston (Adler, David A.)

A picture book of Samuel Adams (Adler, David A.)

Adler, Victoria. *All of baby nose to toes* ill. by Hiroe Nakata. Dial, 2009. ISBN 978-0-8037-3217-9 Subj: Babies. Rhyming text.

Baby, come away ill. by David Walker. Farrar, 2011. ISBN 978-0-374-30480-5 Subj: Animals. Babies.

Adlerman, Daniel. *Africa calling: nightime falling* ill. by Kimberly Adlerman. Whispering Coyote, 1996. ISBN 978-1-879085-98-5 Subj: Animals. Dreams. Foreign lands – Africa. Imagination. Night. Rhyming text. Toys.

Adoff, Arnold. *Black is brown is tan* ill. by Emily Arnold McCully. HarperCollins, 2002. ISBN 978-0-06-028777-1 Subj: Family life. Marriage, interracial. Rhyming text.

Daring Dog and Captain Cat ill. by Joe Cepeda. Simon & Schuster, 2001. ISBN 978-0-689-82599-6 Subj: Animals – cats. Animals – dogs. Night. Pets.

In for winter, out for spring ill. by Jerry Pinkney. Harcourt, 1991. ISBN 978-0-15-238637-5 Subj: Ethnic groups in the U.S. – African Americans. Family life. Poetry. Seasons.

Love letters ill. by Lisa Desimini. Blue Sky, 1997. ISBN 978-0-590-48478-7 Subj: Emotions – love. Letters, cards. Poetry.

Street music: city poems ill. by Karen Barbour. HarperCollins, 1994. ISBN 978-0-06-021523-1 Subj: Cities, towns. Poetry.

Touch the poem ill. by Bill Creevy. Scholastic, 1996. ISBN 978-0-590-47970-7 Subj: Poetry. Senses – touch.

Adoff, Jaime. *Small fry* ill. by Mike Reed. Dutton, 2008. ISBN 978-0-525-46935-3 Subj: Behavior – growing up. Character traits – smallness. Poetry. Self-concept.

Aesop. *Aesop's fables* retold by Beverley Naidoo; ill. by Piet Grobler. Frances Lincoln, 2011. ISBN 978-1-84780-007-7 Subj: Folk & fairy tales. Foreign lands – Africa.

Aesop's fables sel. by Michael Hague; ill. by selector. Holt, 1985. ISBN 978-0-03-002038-4 Subj: Folk & fairy tales.

Aesop's fables sel. by Heidi Holder; ill. by selector. Viking, 1981. ISBN 978-0-670-10643-1 Subj: Folk & fairy tales.

Aesop's fables by John Cech; ill. by Martin Jarrie. Sterling, 2009. ISBN 978-1-4027-5298-8 Subj: Folk & fairy tales.

Aesop's fables ill. by Jerry Pinkney. SeaStar, 2000. ISBN 978-1-58717-003-4 Subj: Folk & fairy tales.

Aesop's fables retold by Fiona Waters; ill. by Fulvio Testa. Trafalgar Square, 2011. ISBN 978-1-84939-049-1 Subj: Folk & fairy tales.

Androcles and the lion retold by Dennis Nolan; ill. by reteller. Harcourt, 1997. ISBN 978-0-15-203355-2 Subj: Animals – lions. Character traits – helpfulness. Character traits – kindness to animals. Folk & fairy tales. Foreign lands – Italy.

Androcles and the lion adapt. by Janet Stevens; ill. by adapter. Holiday, 1989. ISBN 978-0-8234-0768-2 Subj: Animals – lions. Character traits – helpfulness. Character traits – kindness to animals. Folk & fairy tales. Foreign lands – Italy. Religion.

Androcles and the lion: and other Aesop fables adapt. by Tom Paxton; ill. by Robert Rayevsky. Morrow, 1991. ISBN 978-0-688-09683-0 Subj: Animals – lions. Character traits – helpfulness. Character traits – kindness to animals. Folk & fairy tales. Foreign lands – Italy. Rhyming text.

Animal fables from Aesop adapt. by Barbara McClintock; ill. by adapter. Godine, 2000. ISBN 978-1-56792-144-1 Subj: Animals. Folk & fairy tales.

Anno's Aesop: a book of fables by Aesop and Mr. Fox adapt. by Mitsumasa Anno; ill. by adapter. Watts, 1989. ISBN 978-0-531-08374-1 Subj: Animals – foxes. Folk & fairy tales.

The ant and the grasshopper retold by Amy Lowry Poole; ill. by reteller. Holiday, 2000. ISBN 978-0-8234-1477-2 Subj: Activities – working. Folk & fairy tales. Foreign lands – China. Insects – ants. Insects – grasshoppers. Royalty – emperors. Seasons – fall. Seasons – winter.

The ant and the grasshopper retold by Mark White; ill. by Sara Rojo. Picture Window, 2004. ISBN 978-1-4048-0217-9 Subj: Activities – working. Folk & fairy tales. Insects – ants. Insects – grasshoppers. Seasons – fall. Seasons – winter.

Bat's big game retold by Margaret Read MacDonald; ill. by Eugenia Nobati. Whitman, 2008. ISBN 978-0-8075-0587-8 Subj: Animals. Animals – bats. Birds. Folk & fairy tales. Sports – soccer.

Belling the cat retold by Eric Blair; ill. by Diane Silverman. Picture Window, 2004. ISBN 978-1-4048-0321-3 Subj: Animals – cats. Animals – mice. Folk & fairy tales.

Belling the cat and other Aesop fables by Tom Paxton; ill. by Robert Rayevsky. Morrow, 1990. ISBN 978-0-688-08159-1 Subj: Animals. Folk & fairy tales.

The best of Aesop's fables retold by Margaret Clark; ill. by Charlotte Voake. Little, 1990. ISBN 978-0-316-14499-5 Subj: Folk & fairy tales.

The boy who cried wolf retold by Eric Blair; ill. by Diane Silverman. Picture Window, 2004. ISBN 978-1-4048-0319-0 Subj: Animals – wolves. Behavior – lying. Behavior – trickery. Folk & fairy tales.

The contest between the Sun and the Wind: an Aesop's fable retold by Heather Forest; ill. by Susan Gaber. August House, 2008. ISBN 978-0-87483-832-9 Subj: Contests. Folk & fairy tales. Sun. Weather – wind.

The country mouse and the city mouse retold by Eric Blair; ill. by Diane Silverman. Picture Window, 2004. ISBN 978-1-4048-0318-3 Subj: Animals – mice. Cities, towns. Country. Folk & fairy tales.

The crow and the pitcher retold by Eric Blair; ill. by Diane Silverman. Picture Window, 2004. ISBN 978-1-4048-0322-0 Subj: Birds – crows. Character traits – cleverness. Folk & fairy tales. Problem solving.

Doctor Coyote: a Native American Aesop's fables by John Bierhorst; ill. by Wendy Watson. Macmillan, 1987. ISBN 978-0-02-709780-1 Subj: Animals. Animals – coyotes. Folk & fairy tales. Indians of North America – Aztec.

The dog and the wolf retold by Eric Blair; ill. by Diane Silverman. Picture Window, 2004. ISBN 978-1-4048-0323-7 Subj: Animals – dogs. Animals – wolves. Character traits – freedom. Folk & fairy tales.

The donkey in the lion's skin sel. by Eric Blair; ill. by Diane Silverman. Picture Window, 2004. ISBN 978-1-4048-0320-6 Subj: Animals. Animals – donkeys. Animals – foxes. Behavior – trickery. Clothing. Disguises.

Fables from Aesop adapt. by Tom Lynch; ill. by adapter. Viking, 2000. ISBN 978-0-670-88948-8 Subj: Folk & fairy tales.

Feed me! an Aesop fable by William H. Hooks; ill. by Doug Cushman. G. Stevens, 1996. ISBN 978-0-8368-1616-7 Subj: Birds. Folk & fairy tales.

The fox and the grapes retold by Mark White; ill. by Sara Rojo. Picture Window, 2004. ISBN 978-1-4048-0218-6 Subj: Animals – foxes. Folk & fairy tales. Food.

Fox tails: four fables from Aesop ill. by Amy Lowry. Holiday House, 2012. ISBN 978-0-8234-2400-9 Subj: Animals. Animals – foxes. Behavior – trickery. Folk & fairy tales.

The goose that laid the golden egg retold by Mark White; ill. by Sara Rojo. Picture Window, 2004. ISBN 978-1-4048-0219-3 Subj: Behavior – greed. Birds – geese. Careers – farmers. Eggs. Folk & fairy tales.

The hare and the tortoise ill. by Paul Galdone. Whittlesey House, 1962. Subj: Animals – rabbits. Folk & fairy tales. Reptiles – turtles, tortoises. Sports – racing.

The hare and the tortoise retold by Carol Jones; ill. by reteller. Houghton, 1996. ISBN 978-0-395-81368-3 Subj: Animals – rabbits. Folk & fairy tales. Format, unusual – toy & movable books. Reptiles – turtles, tortoises. Sports – racing.

The hare and the tortoise retold by Helen Ward; ill. by reteller. Millbrook, 1999. ISBN 978-0-7613-1318-2 Subj: Animals – rabbits. Folk & fairy tales. Reptiles – turtles, tortoises. Sports – racing.

The hare and the tortoise / La liebre y la tortuga adapt. by Maria Eulalia Valeri; ill. by Max. Chronicle, 2006. ISBN 978-0-8118-5057-5 Subj: Animals – rabbits. Folk & fairy tales. Foreign languages. Reptiles – turtles, tortoises. Sports – racing.

The lion and the mouse by Gail Herman; ill. by Lisa McCue. Random House, 1998. ISBN 978-0-679-98674-4 Subj: Animals – lions. Animals – mice. Character traits – helpfulness. Folk & fairy tales.

The lion and the mouse retold by Mark White; ill. by Sara Rojo. Picture Window, 2004. ISBN 978-1-4048-0216-2 Subj: Animals – lions. Animals – mice. Character traits – helpfulness. Character traits – kindness. Folk & fairy tales.

The lion and the mouse sel. by Bernadette Watts; ill. by selector. NorthSouth, 2000. ISBN 978-0-7358-1221-5 Subj: Animals – lions. Animals – mice. Character traits – helpfulness. Folk & fairy tales.

The lion and the mouse and other Aesop fables retold by Doris Orgel; ill. by Bert Kitchen. DK, 2000. ISBN 978-0-7894-2665-9 Subj: Animals. Folk & fairy tales.

Milly and Tilly: the story of a town mouse and a country mouse by Kate Summers; ill. by Maggie Kneen. Dutton, 1997. ISBN 978-0-525-45801-2 Subj: Animals – mice. Cities, towns. Country. Folk & fairy tales.

Mouse and lion retold by Rand Burkert; ill. by Nancy Ekholm Burkert. Scholastic, 2011. ISBN 978-0-545-10147-9 Subj: Animals – lions. Animals – mice. Character traits – helpfulness. Character traits – kindness. Folk & fairy tales.

The race by Caroline Repchuk; ill. by Alison Jay. Chronicle, 2002. ISBN 978-0-8118-3500-8 Subj: Animals – rabbits. Folk & fairy tales. Reptiles – turtles, tortoises. Rhyming text. Sports – racing.

Road signs: a harey race with a tortoise by Margery Cuyler; ill. by Steve Haskamp. Winslow, 2000. ISBN 978-1-890817-23-7 Subj: Animals. Animals – rabbits. Folk & fairy tales. Reptiles – turtles, tortoises. Sports – racing. Traffic, traffic signs.

Smog, the city dog by Adria Meserve; ill. by author. Chronicle, 2002. ISBN 978-0-8118-3551-0 Subj: Animals – dogs. Behavior – sharing. Folk & fairy tales.

Three Aesop fox fables ill. by Paul Galdone. Seabury Pr., 1971. ISBN 978-0-395-28810-8 Subj: Animals – foxes. Behavior – trickery. Character traits – flattery. Folk & fairy tales.

The tortoise and the hare retold by Jerry Pinkney; ill. by reteller. Little, Brown, 2013. ISBN 978-0-316-18356-7 Subj: Animals – rabbits. Folk & fairy tales. Reptiles – turtles, tortoises. Sports – racing.

The tortoise and the hare retold by Mark White; ill. by Sara Rojo. Picture Window, 2004. ISBN 978-1-4048-0215-5 Subj: Animals – rabbits. Folk & fairy tales. Reptiles – turtles, tortoises. Sports – racing.

The tortoise and the hare: an Aesop fable adapt. by Janet Stevens; ill. by adapter. Holiday, 1984. ISBN 978-0-8234-0510-7 Subj: Animals – rabbits. Folk & fairy tales. Reptiles – turtles, tortoises. Sports – racing.

The town mouse and the country mouse ill. by Lorinda Bryan Cauley. Putnam, 1984. ISBN 978-0-399-21123-2 Subj: Animals – mice. Cities, towns. Country. Folk & fairy tales.

The town mouse and the country mouse adapt. by Janet Stevens; ill. by adapter. Holiday, 1987. ISBN 978-0-8234-0633-3 Subj: Animals – mice. Cities, towns. Country. Folk & fairy tales.

The town mouse and the country mouse: an Aesop fable retold by Helen Ward; ill. by reteller. Candlewick, 2012. ISBN 978-0-7636-6098-7 Subj: Animals – mice. Cities, towns. Country. Folk & fairy tales.

The town mouse and the country mouse: an Aesop fable retold by Bernadette Watts; ill. by reteller. NorthSouth, 1998. ISBN 978-1-55858-988-9 Subj: Animals – mice. Cities, towns. Country. Folk & fairy tales.

Town mouse, country mouse retold by Jan Brett; ill. by reteller. Putnam, 1994. ISBN 978-0-399-22622-9 Subj: Animals – cats. Animals – mice. Birds – owls. Cities, towns. Country. Folk & fairy tales.

Town mouse, country mouse retold by Carol Jones; ill. by reteller. Houghton, 1995. ISBN 978-0-395-71129-3 Subj: Animals – mice. Cities, towns. Country. Folk & fairy tales.

The wolf in sheep's clothing retold by Mark White; ill. by Sara Rojo. Picture Window, 2004. ISBN 978-1-4048-0220-9 Subj: Animals – sheep. Animals – wolves. Behavior – trickery. Clothing. Disguises. Folk & fairy tales.

Agee, Jon. *Dmitri the astronaut* ill. by author. HarperCollins, 1996. ISBN 978-0-06-205075-5 Subj: Animals. Careers – astronauts. Moon. Space & space ships.

The incredible painting of Felix Clousseau ill. by author. Farrar, 1988. ISBN 978-0-374-33633-2 Subj: Activities – painting. Art. Imagination.

Little Santa ill. by author. Dial, 2013. ISBN 978-0-8037-3906-2 Subj: Foreign lands – Arctic. Holidays – Christmas. Santa Claus.

Milo's hat trick ill. by author. Hyperion, 2001. ISBN 978-0-7868-0902-8 Subj: Animals – bears. Careers – magicians. Magic. Theater.

Mr. Putney's quacking dog ill. by author. Scholastic, 2010. ISBN 978-0-545-16203-6 Subj: Animals. Games. Riddles & jokes.

My rhinoceros ill. by author. Scholastic, 2011. ISBN 978-0-545-29441-6 Subj: Animals – rhinoceros. Crime. Pets.

Nothing ill. by author. Hyperion, 2007. ISBN 978-0-7868-3694-9 Subj: Humorous stories. Shopping. Stores.

Orangutan tongs: poems to tangle your tongue ill. by author. Hyperion, 2009. ISBN 978-1-4231-0315-8 Subj: Poetry. Tongue twisters.

The other side of town ill. by author. Scholastic, 2012. ISBN 978-0-545-16204-3 Subj: Aliens. Taxis.

The retired kid ill. by author. Hyperion, 2008. ISBN 978-1-4231-0314-1 Subj: Humorous stories. Old age.

Terrific ill. by author. Hyperion, 2005. ISBN 978-0-7868-5184-3 Subj: Behavior – bad day. Behavior – dissatisfaction. Birds – parakeets, parrots.

Z goes home ill. by author. Hyperion, 2003. ISBN 978-0-7868-1987-4 Subj: ABC books.

Agran, Rick. *Pumpkin shivaree* ill. by Sara Anderson. Handprint, 2003. ISBN 978-1-59354-006-7 Subj: Holidays – Halloween. Plants.

Ahlberg, Allan. *The adventures of Bert* by Allan Ahlberg and Raymond Briggs ill. by Raymond Briggs. Farrar, 2001. ISBN 978-0-374-30092-0 Subj: Humorous stories.

The baby in the hat ill. by André Amstutz. Candlewick, 2008. ISBN 978-0-7636-3958-7 Subj: Foreign lands – England. Sailors. Sea & seashore.

The baby's catalogue (Ahlberg, Janet)

A bit more Bert by Allan Ahlberg and Raymond Briggs ill. by Raymond Briggs. Farrar, 2002. ISBN 978-0-374-32489-6 Subj: Humorous stories.

Each peach pear plum: an "I spy" story (Ahlberg, Janet)

Funnybones (Ahlberg, Janet)

The Goldilocks variations: or Who's been snopperink in my woodootog? ill. by Jessica Ahlberg. Candlewick, 2012. ISBN 978-0-7636-6268-4 Subj: Folk & fairy tales. Format, unusual – toy & movable books. Humorous stories.

Half a pig ill. by Jessica Ahlberg. Candlewick, 2004. ISBN 978-0-7636-2373-9 Subj: Animals – pigs. Humorous stories.

Hooray for bread ill. by Bruce Ingman. Candlewick, 2013. ISBN 978-0-7636-6311-7 Subj: Activities – baking, cooking. Food. Rhyming text.

It was a dark and stormy night (Ahlberg, Janet)

Jeremiah in the dark wood (Ahlberg, Janet)

The jolly Christmas postman (Ahlberg, Janet)

The jolly pocket postman (Ahlberg, Janet)

The jolly postman (Ahlberg, Janet)

Peek-a-boo! (Ahlberg, Janet)

The pencil ill. by Bruce Ingman. Candlewick, 2008. ISBN 978-0-7636-3894-8 Subj: Activities – drawing. Emotions – loneliness. Imagination.

Playmates (Ahlberg, Janet)

Previously ill. by Bruce Ingman. Candlewick, 2007. ISBN 978-0-7636-3542-8 Subj: Folk & fairy tales.

The runaway dinner ill. by Bruce Ingman. Candlewick, 2006. ISBN 978-0-7636-3142-0 Subj: Behavior – running away. Food.

The shopping expedition ill. by André Amstutz. Candlewick, 2005. ISBN 978-0-7636-2586-3 Subj: Imagination. Shopping.

The snail house ill. by Gillian Tyler. Candlewick, 2000. ISBN 978-0-7636-0711-1 Subj: Activities – storytelling. Animals – snails. Concepts – size. Family life – grandmothers.

Starting school (Ahlberg, Janet)

Ahlberg, Janet. *The baby's catalogue* by Janet Ahlberg and Allan Ahlberg ill. by authors. Little, 1983. ISBN 978-0-316-02037-4 Subj: Babies. Family life.

Each peach pear plum: an "I spy" story by Janet Ahlberg and Allan Ahlberg ill. by authors. Viking, 1978. ISBN 978-0-670-28705-5 Subj: Games. Rhyming text.

Funnybones by Janet Ahlberg and Allan Ahlberg ill. by authors. Greenwillow, 1981. ISBN 978-0-688-84238-3 Subj: Activities – playing. Anatomy – skeletons. Ghosts. Night.

It was a dark and stormy night by Janet Ahlberg and Allan Ahlberg ill. by authors. Viking, 1993. ISBN 978-0-670-84620-7 Subj: Activities – storytelling. Character traits – cleverness. Crime. Pirates.

Jeremiah in the dark wood by Janet Ahlberg and Allan Ahlberg ill. by authors. Viking, 1987. ISBN 978-0-670-40637-1 Subj: Behavior – stealing. Forest, woods. Mythical creatures.

The jolly Christmas postman by Janet Ahlberg and Allan Ahlberg ill. by authors. Little, 1991. ISBN 978-0-316-02033-6 Subj: Careers – postal workers. Format, unusual. Holidays – Christmas. Nursery rhymes. Post office. Rhyming text.

The jolly pocket postman by Janet Ahlberg and Allan Ahlberg ill. by authors. Little, 1995. ISBN 978-0-316-60202-0 Subj: Careers – postal workers. Format, unusual – toy & movable books. Post office. Rhyming text.

The jolly postman by Janet Ahlberg and Allan Ahlberg ill. by authors. Little, 1986. ISBN 978-0-316-02036-7 Subj: Careers – postal workers. Format, unusual – toy & movable books. Post office. Rhyming text.

Peek-a-boo! by Janet Ahlberg and Allan Ahlberg ill. by authors. Viking, 1981. ISBN 978-0-670-54598-8 Subj: Babies. Family life. Format, unusual – toy & movable books. Games. Rhyming text.

Playmates by Janet Ahlberg and Allan Ahlberg ill. by authors. Viking, 1985. ISBN 978-0-670-55988-6 Subj: Activities – playing. Format, unusual – toy & movable books.

Starting school by Janet Ahlberg and Allan Ahlberg ill. by authors. Viking, 1988. ISBN 978-0-670-82175-4 Subj: School – first day.

Ahmed, Said Salah. *The lion's share / Qayb Libaax: a Somali folktale* ill. by Kelly Dupre. Minnesota Humanities Commission, 2006. ISBN 978-1-931016-12-4 Subj: Behavior – greed. Folk & fairy tales. Foreign lands – Somalia. Foreign languages.

Aigner-Clark, Julie. *Language nursery* ill. by Nadeem Zaidi. Hyperion, 2001. ISBN 978-0-7868-0810-6 Subj: Foreign languages. Format, unusual – board books.

You are the best medicine ill. by Jana Christy. HarperCollins, 2010. ISBN 978-0-06-195644-7 Subj: Emotions – love. Family life – mothers. Illness – cancer.

Aillaud, Cindy Lou. *Recess at 20 below* photos by author. Alaska Northwest, 2005. ISBN 978-0-88540-609-8 Subj: Alaska. Weather – cold. Weather – snow.

Ainslie, Tamsin. *I can say please* ill. by author. Kane/Miller, 2011. ISBN 978-1-61067-037-1 Subj: Etiquette.

I can say thank you ill. by author. Kane/Miller, 2011. ISBN 978-1-61067-038-8 Subj: Etiquette.

Ainsworth, Kimberly. *Hootenanny! a festive counting book* ill. by Jo Brown. Simon & Schuster, 2011. ISBN 978-1-4424-2273-5 Subj: Birds – owls. Counting, numbers.

Ajmera, Maya. *Animal friends: a global celebration of children and their animals* by Maya Ajmera and John D. Ivanko ill. with photos. Charlesbridge, 2002. ISBN 978-1-57091-502-4 Subj: Animals. Format, unusual – board books. Pets.

Back to school by Maya Ajmera and John D. Ivanko ill. with photos. Charlesbridge, 2001. ISBN 978-1-57091-383-9 Subj: Foreign lands. School.

Come out and play by Maya Ajmera and John D. Ivanko ill. with photos. Charlesbridge, 2001. ISBN 978-1-57091-385-3 Subj: Activities – playing. Foreign lands.

Faith by Maya Ajmera and Cynthia Pon ill. with photos. Charlesbridge, 2009. ISBN 978-1-58089-177-6 Subj: Religion. World.

A kid's best friend by Maya Ajmera and Alex Fisher ill. with photos. Charlesbridge, 2002. ISBN 978-1-57091-513-0 Subj: Animals – dogs. Pets.

To be a kid by Maya Ajmera and John D. Ivanko ill. with photos. Charlesbridge, 1999. ISBN 978-0-88106-841-2 Subj: Activities. Family life. Foreign lands.

Ajmera, Maya, et al. *Healthy kids.* Charlesbridge, 2013. ISBN 978-1-58089-436-4 Subj: Health & fitness. World.

Our grandparents: a global album. Charlesbridge, 2010. ISBN 978-1-57091-458-4 Subj: Family life – grandparents. World.

What we wear: dressing up around the world. Charlesbridge, 2012. ISBN 978-1-58089-416-6 Subj: Clothing. World.

Akin, Sara Laux. *Three scoops and a fig* ill. by Susan Kathleen Hartung. Peachtree, 2010. ISBN 978-1-56145-522-5 Subj: Ethnic groups in the U.S. – Italian Americans. Family life. Food.

Alakija, Polly. *Catch that goat!* ill. by author. Barefoot, 2002. ISBN 978-1-84148-908-7 Subj: Animals – goats. Counting, numbers. Foreign lands – Africa. Stores.

Alalou, Ali. *The butter man* (Alalou, Elizabeth)

Alalou, Elizabeth. *The butter man* by Elizabeth Alalou and Ali Alalou ill. by Julie Klear Essakalli. Charlesbridge, 2008. ISBN 978-1-58089-127-1 Subj: Food. Foreign lands – Morocco.

Alarcón, Francisco X. *From the bellybutton of the moon and other summer poems / Del ombligo de la luna y otros poemas de verano* ill. by Maya Christina Gonzalez. Children's Press, 1998. ISBN 978-0-89239-153-0 Subj: Foreign lands – Mexico. Foreign languages. Nature. Poetry. Seasons – summer.

Iguanas in the snow and other winter poems / Iguanas en la nieve y otros poemas de invierno ill. by Maya Christina Gonzalez. Children's Press, 2001. ISBN 978-0-89239-168-4 Subj: Foreign languages. Picture puzzles. Poetry. Reptiles – iguanas. Seasons – winter. Weather – snow.

Alberti, Theresa Jarosz. *Out and about at the planetarium* ill. by Becky Shipe. Picture Window, 2004. ISBN 978-1-4048-0299-5 Subj: Astronomy. School – field trips. Science.

Vietnam ABCs: a book about the people and places of Vietnam ill. by Natascha Alex Blanks. Picture Window, 2007. ISBN 978-1-4048-2251-1 Subj: ABC books. Foreign lands – Vietnam.

Alborough, Jez. *Captain Duck* ill. by author. HarperCollins, 2003. ISBN 978-0-06-052123-3 Subj: Animals. Birds – ducks. Boats, ships. Rhyming text.

Duck in the truck ill. by author. HarperCollins, 2000. ISBN 978-0-06-028685-9 Subj: Animals. Birds – ducks. Rhyming text. Trucks.

Duck's key where can it be? ill. by author. Kane/Miller, 2005. ISBN 978-1-929132-72-0 Subj: Behavior – lost & found possessions. Birds – ducks. Format, unusual – toy & movable books. Rhyming text.

Fix-it Duck ill. by author. HarperCollins, 2002. ISBN 978-0-06-000699-0 Subj: Animals. Birds – ducks. Rhyming text.

The gobble gobble moooooo tractor book ill. by author. Kane/Miller, 2010. ISBN 978-1-935279-66-2 Subj: Animals – sheep. Farms. Tractors.

Hit the ball Duck ill. by author. Kane/Miller, 2006. ISBN 978-1-929132-96-6 Subj: Birds – ducks. Rhyming text. Sports – baseball.

Hug ill. by author. Candlewick, 2000. ISBN 978-0-7636-1287-0 Subj: Animals. Animals – chimpanzees. Behavior – lost. Behavior – needing someone. Family life – mothers.

Ice cream bear ill. by author. Candlewick, 1997. ISBN 978-0-7636-0293-2 Subj: Animals – bears. Dreams. Food. Rhyming text. Weather – snow.

It's the bear ill. by author. Candlewick, 1994. ISBN 978-1-56402-486-2 Subj: Activities – picnicking. Animals – bears. Behavior – stealing. Emotions – fear. Family life – mothers. Food. Rhyming text.

My friend bear ill. by author. Candlewick, 1998. ISBN 978-0-7636-0583-4 Subj: Animals – bears. Emotions – loneliness. Friendship. Toys – bears.

Six little chicks ill. by author. Barron's, 2013. ISBN 978-1-43800-181-4 Subj: Animals – foxes. Birds – chickens. Rhyming text.

Super Duck ill. by author. Kane/Miller, 2009. ISBN 978-1-933605-89-0 Subj: Animals. Birds – ducks. Kites.

Tall ill. by author. Candlewick, 2005. ISBN 978-0-7636-2784-3 Subj: Animals. Animals – monkeys. Character traits – smallness. Concepts – size. Format, unusual – board books. Jungle. Rhyming text.

Watch out! Big Bro's coming! ill. by author. Candlewick, 1997. ISBN 978-0-7636-0130-0 Subj: Animals. Animals – mice. Concepts – size. Emotions – fear. Family life – brothers & sisters.

Where's my teddy? ill. by author. Candlewick, 1992. ISBN 978-1-56402-048-2 Subj: Animals – bears. Forest, woods. Rhyming text. Toys – bears.

Yes ill. by author. Candlewick, 2006. ISBN 978-0-7636-3183-3 Subj: Animals – chimpanzees. Bedtime. Behavior – fighting, arguing.

Alcott, Louisa May. *Little women* retold by Janet Allison Brown; ill. by Dinah Dryhurst. Viking, 2001. ISBN 978-0-670-89912-8 Subj: Family life – sisters.

An old-fashioned Thanksgiving ill. by James Bernardin. HarperCollins, 2005. ISBN 978-0-06-000451-4 Subj: Family life. Family life – grandmothers. Food. Holidays – Thanksgiving.

Alda, Arlene. *Arlene Alda's ABC* photos by author. Tricycle, 1993. ISBN 978-1-883672-01-0 Subj: ABC books.

Arlene Alda's 1 2 3: what do you see? photos by author. Tricycle, 1998. ISBN 978-1-883672-71-3 Subj: Counting, numbers.

Did you say pears? photos by author. Tundra, 2006. ISBN 978-0-88776-739-5 Subj: Language.

Except the color grey. Tundra, 2011. ISBN 978-1-77049-284-4 Subj: Concepts – color.

Hello, good-bye ill. by author. Tundra, 2009. ISBN 978-0-88776-900-9 Subj: Concepts – opposites.

Here a face, there a face photos by author. Tundra, 2008. ISBN 978-0-88776-845-3 Subj: Anatomy – faces. Rhyming text.

Hurry Granny Annie ill. by Eve Aldridge. Tricycle, 1999. ISBN 978-1-883672-72-0 Subj: Behavior – hurrying. Family life – grandmothers. Sun.

Iris has a virus ill. by Lisa Desimini. Tundra, 2008. ISBN 978-0-88776-844-6 Subj: Family life. Illness.

Lulu's piano lesson ill. by Lisa Desimini. Tundra, 2010. ISBN 978-0-88776-930-6 Subj: Activities – playing. Character traits – completing things. Musical instruments – pianos.

Morning glory Monday ill. by Maryann Kovalski. Tundra, 2003. ISBN 978-0-88776-620-6 Subj: Communities, neighborhoods. Ethnic groups in the U.S. – Italian Americans. Family life – mothers. Flowers. Seeds.

Sheep, sheep, sheep, help me fall asleep photos by author. Delacorte, 1992. ISBN 978-0-385-30791-8 Subj: Animals. Animals – sheep. Bedtime. Rhyming text.

Aldrin, Buzz. *Look to the stars* ill. by Wendell Minor. Putnam, 2009. ISBN 978-0-399-24721-7 Subj: Careers – astronauts. Space & space ships. U.S. history.

Reaching for the moon ill. by Wendell Minor. HarperCollins, 2005. ISBN 978-0-06-055446-0 Subj: Careers – astronauts. Moon. Space & space ships. U.S. history.

Aleichem, Sholem. *Hanukah money* ill. by Uri Shulevitz. Greenwillow, 1978. ISBN 978-0-688-84120-1 Subj: Folk & fairy tales. Foreign lands. Holidays – Hanukkah. Jewish culture. Religion.

Alexander, Cecil Frances. *All creatures great and small* ill. by Naoko Stoop. Sterling, 2012. ISBN 978-1-4027-8581-8 Subj: Animals. Creation. Format, unusual – board books. Music. Nature. Religion. Songs.

All things bright and beautiful ill. by Ashley Bryan. Simon & Schuster, 2010. ISBN 978-1-4169-8939-4 Subj: Creation. Nature. Religion. Songs.

All things bright and beautiful ill. by Anna Vojtech. NorthSouth, 2004. ISBN 978-0-7358-1892-7 Subj: Creation. Nature. Religion. Songs.

All things bright and beautiful ill. by Bruce Whatley. HarperCollins, 2001. ISBN 978-0-06-026618-9 Subj: Creation. Nature. Religion. Songs.

Alexander, Claire. *Back to front and upside down* ill. by author. Eerdmans, 2012. ISBN 978-0-8028-5414-8 Subj: Animals. Animals – dogs. Disabilities – dyslexia. Letters, cards. School.

Lucy and the bully ill. by author. Whitman, 2008. ISBN 978-0-8075-4786-1 Subj: Animals. Behavior – bullying, teasing. School – nursery.

Small Florence: piggy pop star! ill. by author. Whitman, 2010. ISBN 978-0-8075-7455-3 Subj: Animals – pigs. Behavior – bullying, teasing. Character traits – confidence. Family life – sisters. Self-concept.

Alexander, Elizabeth. *Praise song for the day: a poem for Barack Obama's presidential inauguration* ill. by David Diaz. HarperCollins, 2012. ISBN 978-0-06-192663-1 Subj: Ethnic groups in the U.S. – African Americans. Poetry. U.S. history.

Alexander, Jessica. *Look both ways: a cautionary tale* (Shore, Diane Z.)

This is the dream (Shore, Diane Z.)

Alexander, Kwame. *Acoustic Rooster and his barnyard band* ill. by Tim Bowers. Sleeping Bear, 2011. ISBN 978-1-58536-688-0 Subj: Birds – chickens. Careers – musicians. Contests. Musical instruments – bands. Rhyming text.

Alexander, Lloyd. *Fortune tellers* ill. by Trina Schart Hyman. Dutton, 1992. ISBN 978-0-525-44849-5 Subj: Careers – fortune tellers. Cumulative tales. Foreign lands – Africa. Foreign lands – Cameroon.

The house Gobbaleen ill. by Diane Goode. Dutton, 1995. ISBN 978-0-525-45289-8 Subj: Animals – cats. Behavior – trickery. Character traits – foolishness. Character traits – luck. Monsters. Mythical creatures – goblins.

How the cat swallowed thunder ill. by Judith Byron Schachner. Dutton, 2000. ISBN 978-0-525-46449-5 Subj: Animals – cats. Behavior – misbehavior. Folk & fairy tales – pourquoi tales.

Alexander, Martha G. *And my mean old mother will be sorry, Blackboard Bear* ill. by author. Candlewick, 2000. ISBN 978-0-7636-0668-8 Subj: Animals – bears. Behavior – running away. Emotions – anger. Imagination – imaginary friends.

Blackboard Bear ill. by author. 2nd ed. Candlewick, 1999. ISBN 978-0-7636-0667-1 Subj: Activities – playing. Animals – bears. Concepts – size. Imagination – imaginary friends.

I sure am glad to see you, Blackboard Bear ill. by author. Dial, 1976. ISBN 978-0-7636-0669-5 Subj: Animals – bears. Behavior – bullying, teasing. Imagination – imaginary friends.

I'll never share you, Blackboard Bear ill. by author. Candlewick, 2003. ISBN 978-0-7636-1590-1 Subj: Activities – drawing. Animals – bears. Behavior – sharing.

I'll protect you from the jungle beasts ill. by author. Dial, 1973. ISBN 978-0-8037-4309-0 Subj: Emotions – fear. Imagination – imaginary friends. Problem solving. Sleep. Toys – bears.

Max and the dumb flower picture by Martha G. Alexander and James Rumford ill. by Martha G. Alexander. Charlesbridge, 2009. ISBN 978-1-58089-156-1 Subj: Activities – drawing. Art. Character traits – individuality. Holidays – Mother's Day.

Nobody asked me if I wanted a baby sister ill. by author. Dial, 1971. ISBN 978-0-8037-6402-6 Subj: Babies. Emotions – envy, jealousy. Family life – new sibling. Family life – sisters. Sibling rivalry.

We're in big trouble, Blackboard Bear ill. by author. Dial, 1980. ISBN 978-0-8037-9742-0 Subj: Animals – bears. Behavior – misbehavior. Imagination – imaginary friends. Night. Problem solving.

When the new baby comes, I'm moving out ill. by author. Dial, 1979. ISBN 978-0-8037-9558-7 Subj: Animals – babies. Emotions – envy, jealousy. Family life – new sibling. Sibling rivalry.

You're a genius, Blackboard Bear ill. by author. Candlewick, 1995. ISBN 978-1-56402-238-7 Subj: Animals – bears. Dreams. Imagination – imaginary friends. Night. Space & space ships.

Alexander, Sue. *Behold the trees* ill. by Leonid Gore. Scholastic, 2001. ISBN 978-0-590-76211-3 Subj: Ecology. Foreign lands – Israel. Trees.

One more time, Mama ill. by David Soman. Marshall Cavendish, 1999. ISBN 978-0-7614-5051-1 Subj: Birth. Family life – mothers. Nature.

Who goes out on Halloween? ill. by G. Brian Karas. Bantam, 1990. ISBN 978-0-553-05891-8 Subj: Holidays – Halloween. Monsters. Mythical creatures – goblins. Rhyming text. Witches.

Alexander, Van. *A-tisket, a-tasket* (Fitzgerald, Ella)

Alger, Leclaire Gowans. *All in the morning early* ill. by Evaline Ness. Holt, 1963. Subj: Caldecott award honor books. Folk & fairy tales. Foreign lands – Scotland. Poetry. Songs.

Always room for one more ill. by Nonny Hogrogian. Holt, 1965. ISBN 978-0-8050-0331-4 Subj: Caldecott award books. Cumulative tales. Folk & fairy tales. Foreign lands – Scotland. Homes, houses. Music.

Aliki. *Ah, music!* ill. by author. HarperCollins, 2003. ISBN 978-0-06-028727-6 Subj: Music.

All by myself! ill. by author. HarperCollins, 2000. ISBN 978-0-06-028930-0 Subj: Activities. Character traits – confidence. Character traits – individuality. Self-concept.

At Mary Bloom's ill. by author. Greenwillow, 1976. ISBN 978-0-688-84048-8 Subj: Animals – babies. Animals – mice.

Best friends together again ill. by author. Greenwillow, 1995. ISBN 978-0-688-13754-0 Subj: Friendship. Moving.

Christmas tree memories ill. by author. HarperCollins, 1991. ISBN 978-0-06-020008-4 Subj: Family life. Holidays – Christmas. Memories, memory. Trees.

Communication ill. by author. Greenwillow, 1993. ISBN 978-0-688-11248-6 Subj: Activities – writing. Language.

Corn is maize: the gift of the Indians ill. by author. Crowell, 1976. ISBN 978-0-690-00976-7 Subj: Gardens, gardening. Indians of North America. Plants. Science.

Digging up dinosaurs ill. by author. Rev. ed. Crowell, 1988. ISBN 978-0-690-04716-5 Subj: Activities – digging. Dinosaurs. Humorous stories. Prehistory. Science.

Dinosaur bones ill. by author. HarperCollins, 1988. ISBN 978-0-690-04550-5 Subj: Dinosaurs. Prehistory.

Dinosaurs are different ill. by author. Crowell, 1985. ISBN 978-0-690-04458-4 Subj: Dinosaurs. Prehistory. Science.

Feelings ill. by author. Greenwillow, 1984. ISBN 978-0-688-03832-8 Subj: Emotions. Friendship.

Fossils tell of long ago ill. by author. Rev. ed. Crowell, 1990. ISBN 978-0-690-31379-6 Subj: Dinosaurs. Fossils. Science.

Hello! Good-bye! ill. by author. Greenwillow, 1996. ISBN 978-0-688-14334-3 Subj: Language.

How a book is made ill. by author. HarperCollins, 1986. ISBN 978-0-690-04498-0 Subj: Books, reading. Libraries.

I'm growing! ill. by author. HarperCollins, 1992. ISBN 978-0-06-020245-3 Subj: Behavior – growing up.

Jack and Jake ill. by author. Greenwillow, 1986. ISBN 978-0-688-06100-5 Subj: Behavior – mistakes. Character traits – individuality. Family life. Multiple births – twins.

The long lost coelacanth and other living fossils ill. by author. Crowell, 1973. ISBN 978-0-690-50478-1 Subj: Fish. Fossils. Science.

Manners ill. by author. Greenwillow, 1990. ISBN 978-0-688-09199-6 Subj: Etiquette.

The many lives of Benjamin Franklin ill. by author. Simon & Schuster, 1988. ISBN 978-0-671-66119-9 Subj: U.S. history.

Marianthe's story one: painted words; Marianthe's story two: spoken memories ill. by author. Greenwillow, 1998. ISBN 978-0-688-15662-6 Subj: Family life. Foreign lands. Format, unusual. School.

Milk from cow to carton ill. by author. HarperCollins, 1992. ISBN 978-0-06-020435-8 Subj: Animals – bulls, cows. Careers – farmers. Food.

Mummies made in Egypt ill. by author. Crowell, 1979. ISBN 978-0-690-03859-0 Subj: Death. Foreign lands – Egypt. Religion.

My feet ill. by author. HarperCollins, 1990. ISBN 978-0-690-04815-5 Subj: Anatomy – feet. Science.

My five senses ill. by author. Rev. ed. HarperCollins, 1989. ISBN 978-0-690-04794-3 Subj: Senses – hearing. Senses – sight. Senses – smell. Senses – taste. Senses – touch.

My hands ill. by author. Rev. ed. HarperCollins, 1992. ISBN 978-0-06-445096-6 Subj: Anatomy – hands. Science.

My visit to the aquarium ill. by author. HarperCollins, 1993. ISBN 978-0-06-021459-3 Subj: Animals. Aquariums. Fish. Plants.

My visit to the dinosaurs ill. by author. Rev. ed. Crowell, 1985. ISBN 978-0-690-04423-2 Subj: Dinosaurs. Museums. Prehistory. Science.

My visit to the zoo ill. by author. HarperCollins, 1997. ISBN 978-0-06-024943-4 Subj: Animals. Animals – endangered animals. Birds. Ecology. Zoos.

Overnight at Mary Bloom's ill. by author. Greenwillow, 1987. ISBN 978-0-688-06765-6 Subj: Activities. Activities – playing. Friendship. Night.

A play's the thing ill. by author. HarperCollins, 2005. ISBN 978-0-06-074356-7 Subj: Character traits – cooperation. School. Theater.

Push button ill. by author. HarperCollins, 2010. ISBN 978-0-06-167308-5 Subj: Activities – playing. Rhyming text.

Quiet in the garden ill. by author. Greenwillow, 2009. ISBN 978-0-06-155207-6 Subj: Gardens, gardening. Nature.

The story of Johnny Appleseed ill. by author. Simon & Schuster, 1988. Reprint. Originally published: Englewood Cliffs, N.J.: Prentice-Hall, ©1963. ISBN 978-0-671-66298-1 Subj: Character traits – generosity. Gardens, gardening. Tall tales. U.S. history – frontier & pioneer life.

The story of William Penn ill. by author. Simon & Schuster, 1994. ISBN 978-0-671-88558-8 Subj: Character traits – kindness. U.S. history.

Tabby ill. by author. HarperCollins, 1995. ISBN 978-0-06-024916-8 Subj: Animals – cats. Ethnic groups in the U.S. – Hispanic Americans. Wordless.

Those summers ill. by author. HarperCollins, 1996. ISBN 978-0-06-024938-0 Subj: Family life. Sea & seashore. Seasons – summer.

Three gold pieces: a Greek folk tale ill. by author. Pantheon, 1967. ISBN 978-0-394-91737-5 Subj: Character traits – luck. Folk & fairy tales. Foreign lands – Greece.

The twelve months ill. by adapter. Greenwillow, 1978. ISBN 978-0-688-84164-5 Subj: Behavior –

dissatisfaction. Character traits – optimism. Folk & fairy tales. Foreign lands – Greece.

The two of them ill. by author. Greenwillow, 1979. ISBN 978-0-688-84225-3 Subj: Character traits – helpfulness. Character traits – loyalty. Family life – grandfathers.

Use your head, dear ill. by author. Greenwillow, 1983. ISBN 978-0-688-01812-2 Subj: Behavior – forgetfulness. Birthdays. Reptiles – alligators, crocodiles.

We are best friends ill. by author. Greenwillow, 1982. ISBN 978-0-688-00823-9 Subj: Emotions – anger. Emotions – loneliness. Friendship. Moving.

A weed is a flower: the life of George Washington Carver ill. by author. Simon & Schuster, 1988. ISBN 978-0-671-66118-2 Subj: Character traits – perseverance. Ethnic groups in the U.S. – African Americans. Science. U.S. history.

Welcome, little baby ill. by author. Greenwillow, 1987. ISBN 978-0-688-06811-0 Subj: Babies. Family life.

Wild and woolly mammoths ill. by author. HarperCollins, 1996. ISBN 978-0-06-026277-8 Subj: Animals. Science.

Alko, Selina. *B is for Brooklyn* ill. by author. Holt, 2012. ISBN 978-0-8050-9213-4 Subj: ABC books. Cities, towns. Communities, neighborhoods.

Daddy Christmas and Hanukkah Mama ill. by author. Knopf, 2012. ISBN 978-0-375-86093-5 Subj: Family life – parents. Holidays – Christmas. Holidays – Hanukkah.

Every-day dress-up ill. by author. Random House, 2011. ISBN 978-0-375-86092-8 Subj: Activities – playing. Clothing. Imagination.

I'm your peanut butter big brother ill. by author. Knopf, 2009. ISBN 978-0-375-85627-3 Subj: Babies. Ethnic groups in the U.S. Family life – brothers.

All night, all day: a child's first book of African-American spirituals sel. by Ashley Bryan; ill. by Ashley Bryan. Macmillan, 1991. ISBN 978-0-689-31662-3 Subj: Ethnic groups in the U.S. – African Americans. Music. Musical instruments – guitars. Musical instruments – pianos. Religion. Songs.

Allan, Nicholas. *Where Willy went* ill. by author. Knopf, 2005. ISBN 978-0-375-93030-0 Subj: Sex instruction.

Allard, Harry. *Bumps in the night* ill. by James Marshall. Doubleday, 1979. ISBN 978-0-385-12943-5 Subj: Animals. Ghosts. Noise, sounds.

Miss Nelson has a field day ill. by James Marshall. Houghton, 1985. ISBN 978-0-395-36690-5 Subj: Behavior – secrets. Humorous stories. School – field trips.

Miss Nelson is back by Harry Allard and James Marshall ill. by James Marshall. Houghton, 1982. ISBN 978-0-395-32956-6 Subj: Behavior – misbehavior. Careers – teachers. Humorous stories. School.

Miss Nelson is missing! by Harry Allard and James Marshall ill. by James Marshall. Houghton, 1977. ISBN 978-0-395-25296-3 Subj: Behavior – misbehavior. Careers – teachers. Humorous stories. School.

Starlight goes to town ill. by George Booth. Farrar, 2008. ISBN 978-0-374-37187-6 Subj: Behavior – wishing. Birds – chickens. Humorous stories.

The Stupids die ill. by James Marshall. Houghton, 1981. ISBN 978-0-395-30347-4 Subj: Behavior – misunderstanding. Humorous stories.

The Stupids have a ball by Harry Allard and James Marshall ill. by James Marshall. Houghton, 1978. ISBN 978-0-395-26497-3 Subj: Family life. Humorous stories. Parties.

The Stupids step out ill. by James Marshall. Houghton, 1974. ISBN 978-0-395-18513-1 Subj: Activities. Family life. Humorous stories.

The Stupids take off by Harry Allard and James Marshall ill. by James Marshall. Houghton, 1989. ISBN 978-0-395-50068-2 Subj: Activities – flying. Family life. Humorous stories.

Allchin, Rosalind. *The frog princess* ill. by author. Kids Can, 2001. ISBN 978-1-55337-000-0 Subj: Frogs & toads. Royalty – princes. Royalty – princesses.

Allegra, Mike. *Sarah gives thanks: how Thanksgiving became a national holiday* ill. by David C. Gardner. Whitman, 2012. ISBN 978-0-8075-7239-9 Subj: Holidays – Thanksgiving. U.S. history.

Allen, Debbie. *Brothers of the knight* ill. by Kadir Nelson. Dial, 1999. ISBN 978-0-8037-2488-4 Subj: Activities – dancing. Family life – brothers. Folk & fairy tales. Foreign lands – Germany.

Dancing in the wings ill. by Kadir Nelson. Dial, 2000. ISBN 978-0-8037-2501-0 Subj: Activities – dancing. Ballet. Ethnic groups in the U.S. – African Americans.

Allen, Elanna. *Itsy Mitsy runs away* ill. by author. Atheneum, 2011. ISBN 978-1-4424-0671-1 Subj: Bedtime. Behavior – running away. Family life – fathers.

Allen, Jonathan. *Don't copy me!* ill. by author. Boxer Books, 2012. ISBN 978-1-907967-20-7 Subj: Behavior – imitation. Birds – puffins. Birds – seagulls.

"I'm not cute!" ill. by author. Hyperion, 2006. ISBN 978-0-7868-3720-5 Subj: Animals. Birds – owls. Character traits – appearance.

I'm not reading! ill. by author. Boxer Books , 2013. ISBN 978-1-907967-44-3 Subj: Animals. Birds – chickens. Birds – owls. Books, reading.

"I'm not Santa!" ill. by author. Hyperion, 2008. ISBN 978-1-4231-1300-3 Subj: Animals – rabbits. Birds – owls. Holidays – Christmas. Santa Claus.

"I'm not scared!" ill. by author. Hyperion, 2007. ISBN 978-0-7868-3722-9 Subj: Birds – owls. Emotions – fear.

The little rabbit who liked to say moo ill. by author. Boxer, 2008. ISBN 978-1-905417-78-0 Subj: Animals. Animals – rabbits. Noise, sounds.

Mucky moose ill. by author. Macmillan, 1991. ISBN 978-0-02-700251-5 Subj: Animals – moose. Animals – wolves. Character traits – cleanliness. Senses – smell.

Allen, Joy. *Princess Palooza* ill. by author. Penguin, 2011. ISBN 978-0-399-25455-0 Subj: Activities – playing. Imagination. Parties. Rhyming text. Royalty – princesses.

Princess party ill. by author. Putnam, 2009. ISBN 978-0-399-25259-4 Subj: Parties. Rhyming text. Royalty – princesses.

Allen, Judy. *Are you a butterfly?* by Judy Allen and Tudor Humphries ill. by Tudor Humphries. Kingfisher, 2000. ISBN 978-0-7534-5240-0 Subj: Insects – butterflies, caterpillars. Science.

Are you a grasshopper? by Judy Allen and Tudor Humphries ill. by Tudor Humphries. Kingfisher, 2002. ISBN 978-0-7534-5366-7 Subj: Insects – grasshoppers. Science.

Are you a ladybug? by Judy Allen and Tudor Humphries ill. by Tudor Humphries. Kingfisher, 2000. ISBN 978-0-7534-5241-7 Subj: Insects – ladybugs. Science.

Are you a snail? by Judy Allen and Tudor Humphries ill. by Tudor Humphries. Kingfisher, 2000. ISBN 978-0-7534-5242-4 Subj: Animals – snails. Science.

Are you an ant? by Judy Allen and Tudor Humphries ill. by Tudor Humphries. Kingfisher, 2002. ISBN 978-0-7534-5365-0 Subj: Insects – ants. Science.

Whales and dolphins ill. by Mike Bostock. Kingfisher, 2008. ISBN 978-0-7534-6225-6 Subj: Animals – dolphins. Animals – whales. Format, unusual – toy & movable books.

Allen, Kathryn Madeline. *A kiss means I love you* photos by Eric Futran. Whitman, 2012. ISBN 978-0-8075-4186-9 Subj: Communication. Emotions. Rhyming text.

Allen, Kathy. *The U.S. Constitution.* Capstone, 2006. ISBN 978-0-7368-9594-1 Subj: U.S. history.

Allen, Nancy Kelly. *"Happy Birthday": the story of the world's most popular song* ill. by Gary Undercuffler. Pelican, 2010. ISBN 978-1-58980-675-7 Subj: Birthdays. Songs.

Allen, Pamela. *Who sank the boat?* ill. by author. Coward, 1983. ISBN 978-0-698-20576-5 Subj: Animals. Boats, ships. Rhyming text. Science.

Allen, Susan. *Read anything good lately?* by Susan Allen and Jane Lindaman ill. by Vicky Enright. Millbrook, 2003. ISBN 978-0-7613-2322-8 Subj: ABC books. Books, reading. Language.

Used any numbers lately? by Susan Allen and Jane Lindaman ill. by Vicky Enright. Lerner, 2008. ISBN 978-0-8225-8658-6 Subj: ABC books. Counting, numbers.

Alley, R. W. *There once was a witch* ill. by author. HarperCollins, 2003. ISBN 978-0-06-000795-9 Subj: Format, unusual – board books. Holidays – Halloween. Music. Songs. Witches.

Alley, Zoe B. *There's a princess in the palace* ill. by R. W. Alley. Roaring Brook, 2010. ISBN 978-1-59643-471-4 Subj: Folk & fairy tales. Royalty – princesses.

There's a wolf at the door ill. by R. W. Alley. Roaring Brook, 2008. ISBN 978-1-59643-275-8 Subj: Animals – wolves. Folk & fairy tales.

Allison, Catherine. *Brown paper bear* ill. by Neil Reed. Scholastic, 2004. ISBN 978-0-439-63900-2 Subj: Toys – bears.

Almond, David. *Kate, the cat and the moon* ill. by Stephen Lambert. Random House, 2005. ISBN 978-0-385-90929-7 Subj: Animals – cats. Imagination. Night.

Alphin, Elaine Marie. *Dinosaur hunter* ill. by Don Bolognese. HarperCollins, 2003. ISBN 978-0-06-028304-9 Subj: Dinosaurs. Fossils.

Alrawi, Karim. *The girl who lost her smile* ill. by Czernecki, Stefan. Winslow, 2000. ISBN 978-1-890817-17-6 Subj: Emotions. Foreign lands – Iraq.

Alsdurf, Phyllis. *It's milking time* ill. by Steve Johnson. Random House, 2012. ISBN 978-0-375-86911-2 Subj: Animals – bulls, cows. Farms.

Alsenas, Linas. *Mrs. Claus takes a vacation* ill. by author. Scholastic, 2006. ISBN 978-0-439-77978-4 Subj: Activities – traveling. Activities – vacationing. Holidays – Christmas. Santa Claus.

Peanut ill. by author. Scholastic, 2007. ISBN 978-0-439-77980-7 Subj: Animals – camels. Animals – elephants. Circus. Old age. Pets.

Alter, Anna. *Abigail spells* ill. by author. Knopf, 2009. ISBN 978-0-375-85617-4 Subj: Animals – bears. Birds – chickens. Contests. Friendship. School.

Disappearing Desmond ill. by author. Random House, 2010. ISBN 978-0-375-86684-5 Subj: Animals. Behavior – hiding. Character traits – shyness. School.

Estelle and Lucy ill. by author. Greenwillow, 2001. ISBN 978-0-688-17883-3 Subj: Animals – cats. Animals – mice. Concepts – size. Family life – sisters. Sibling rivalry.

A photo for Greta ill. by author. Random House, 2011. ISBN 978-0-375-85618-1 Subj: Careers – photographers. Family life – fathers.

What can you do with an old red shoe? a green activity book about re-use ill. by author. Holt, 2009. ISBN 978-0-8050-8290-6 Subj: Activities – making things. Behavior – seeking better things. Ecology.

Altes, Marta. *My grandpa* ill. by author. Abrams, 2013. ISBN 978-1-4197-0588-5 Subj: Animals – bears. Family life – grandfathers. Old age.

Altman, Alexandra Jessup. *Waiting for Benjamin: a story about autism* ill. by Susan Keeter. Whitman, 2008. ISBN 978-0-8075-7364-8 Subj: Emotions – embarrassment. Family life – brothers. Disabilities – autism.

Altman, Linda Jacobs. *Amelia's road* ill. by Enrique O. Sánchez. Lee & Low, 1993. ISBN 978-1-880000-04-5 Subj: Activities – working. Behavior – seeking better things. Careers – migrant workers. Family life. Homes, houses. Trees.

The legend of Freedom Hill ill. by Cornelius Van Wright and Ying-Hwa Hu. Lee & Low, 2000. ISBN 978-1-58430-003-8 Subj: Ethnic groups in the U.S. – African Americans. Slavery. U.S. history – frontier & pioneer life.

Singing with Momma Lou ill. by author. Lee & Low, 2002. ISBN 978-1-58430-040-3 Subj: Ethnic groups in the U.S. – African Americans. Family life – grandmothers. Illness – Alzheimer's. Old age.

Altman, Susan. *Followers of the north star: rhymes about African American heroes, heroines, and historical times* by Susan Altman and Susan Lechner ill. by Byron Wooden. Children's Press, 1993. ISBN 978-0-516-05151-2 Subj: Ethnic groups in the U.S. – African Americans. Poetry. U.S. history.

Alvarez, Julia. *The secret footprints* ill. by Fabian Negrin. Knopf, 2000. ISBN 978-0-679-99309-4 Subj: Folk & fairy tales. Foreign lands – Dominican Republic. Indians of Central America – Taino.

Amado, Elisa. *Tricycle* ill. by Alfonso Ruano. Groundwood, 2007. ISBN 978-0-88899-614-5 Subj: Behavior – stealing. Friendship. Prejudice.

What are you doing? ill. by Manuel Monroy. Groundwood, 2011. ISBN 978-1-55498-070-3 Subj: Books, reading. Foreign lands – Mexico. School – first day.

Amann, Jürg. *Ten birds* ill. by Helga Gebert. NorthSouth, 2012. ISBN 978-0-7358-4100-0 Subj: Birds. Counting, numbers. Problem solving.

Amant, Kathleen. *Little Rabbit gets messy* ill. by author. Clavis, 2008. ISBN 978-1-60537-017-0 Subj: Animals – rabbits. Behavior – messy. Toys.

On your potty, Little Rabbit ill. by author. Clavis, 2008. ISBN 978-1-60537-015-6 Subj: Animals – rabbits. Toilet training. Toys.

Amato, Mary. *The chicken of the family* ill. by Delphine Durand. Putnam, 2008. ISBN 978-0-399-24196-3 Subj: Behavior – bullying, teasing. Birds – chickens. Family life – sisters. Farms.

Amazing graces: prayers and poems for children comp. by June Cotner; ill. by Jan Palmer. HarperCollins, 2001. ISBN 978-0-688-15567-4 Subj: Poetry. Religion.

Amenta, Charles A., III. *Russell's world: a story for kids about autism* ill. by Monika Pollak; photos by author. Magination, 2011. ISBN 978-1-4338-0975-0 Subj: Disabilities – autism.

American babies. Charlesbridge, 2010. ISBN 978-1-58089-280-3 Subj: Babies. Format, unusual – board books.

American Museum of Natural History. *Spot the animals: a lift-the-flap book of colors* ill. by Steve Jenkins. Sterling, 2012. ISBN 978-1-4027-7723-3 Subj: Animals. Format, unusual – toy & movable books.

Ammon, Richard. *An Amish Christmas* ill. by Pamela Patrick. Atheneum, 1996. ISBN 978-0-689-80377-2 Subj: Ethnic groups in the U.S. – Amish. Holidays – Christmas. Religion.

Amish horses ill. by Pamela Patrick. Atheneum, 2001. ISBN 978-0-689-82623-8 Subj: Animals – horses, ponies. Ethnic groups in the U.S. – Amish. Farms.

An Amish wedding ill. by Pamela Patrick. Atheneum, 1998. ISBN 978-0-689-81677-2 Subj: Ethnic groups in the U.S. – Amish. Weddings.

An Amish year ill. by Pamela Patrick. Atheneum, 2000. ISBN 978-0-689-82622-1 Subj: Ethnic groups in the U.S. – Amish. Seasons.

Amnesty International. *We are all born free: the Universal Declaration of Human Rights in pictures* ill.

with photos. Frances Lincoln, 2008. ISBN 978-1-84507-650-4 Subj: Character traits – freedom. World.

Amsden, Janet. *Grizzly Pete and the ghosts* ill. by John Beder. Annick, 2002. ISBN 978-1-55037-719-4 Subj: Careers – miners. Ghosts. U.S. history – frontier & pioneer life.

Amusing moments in the wild: animals and their friends ill. with photos. Moonstone, 2001. ISBN 978-0-9707768-3-9 Subj: Animals.

Anastas, Margaret. *A hug for you* ill. by Susan Winter. HarperCollins, 2005. ISBN 978-0-06-623614-8 Subj: Animals. Birds – ducks. Emotions – love. Family life – parents. Friendship. Insects. Rhyming text.

Mommy's best kisses ill. by Susan Winter. HarperCollins, 2003. ISBN 978-0-06-623606-3 Subj: Animals. Emotions – love. Family life – mothers. Rhyming text.

Anaya, Rudolfo A. *Farolitos for Abuelo* ill. by Edward Gonzales. Hyperion, 1998. ISBN 978-0-7868-2186-0 Subj: Death. Ethnic groups in the U.S. – Mexican Americans. Family life – grandfathers. Holidays – Christmas.

Roadrunner's dance ill. by David Diaz. Hyperion, 2000. ISBN 978-0-7868-2209-6 Subj: Animals. Behavior – bullying, teasing. Birds – roadrunners. Creation. Desert. Reptiles – snakes.

Ancona, George. *Barrio: José's neighborhood* ill. by author. Harcourt, 1998. ISBN 978-0-15-201049-2 Subj: Communities, neighborhoods. Ethnic groups in the U.S. – Hispanic Americans.

Handtalk zoo by George Ancona and Mary Beth Ancona; photos by author. Macmillan, 1989. ISBN 978-0-02-700801-2 Subj: Animals. Communication. Disabilities – deafness. Language. Senses – hearing. Time. Zoos.

It's our garden: from seeds to harvest in a school garden photos by author. Candlewick, 2013. ISBN 978-0-7636-5392-7 Subj: Gardens, gardening. School.

Mi música / My music photos by author. Scholastic, 2005. ISBN 978-0-516-25295-7 Subj: Ethnic groups in the U.S. – Hispanic Americans. Foreign languages. Music.

Mis abuelos / My grandparents photos by author. Scholastic, 2005. ISBN 978-0-516-25294-0 Subj: Ethnic groups in the U.S. – Hispanic Americans. Family life – grandparents. Foreign languages.

Mis comidas / My foods photos by author. Scholastic, 2005. ISBN 978-0-516-25292-6 Subj: Ethnic groups in the U.S. – Hispanic Americans. Food. Foreign languages.

Mis fiestas / My celebrations photos by author. Scholastic, 2005. ISBN 978-0-516-25290-2 Subj: Ethnic groups in the U.S. – Hispanic Americans. Foreign languages. Holidays.

Mis juegos / My games photos by author. Scholastic, 2005. ISBN 978-0-516-25293-3 Subj: Ethnic groups in the U.S. – Hispanic Americans. Foreign languages. Games.

Mis quehaceres / My chores photos by author. Scholastic, 2005. ISBN 978-0-516-25291-9 Subj: Activities – working. Character traits – helpfulness. Ethnic groups in the U.S. – Hispanic Americans. Foreign languages.

Ancona, Mary Beth. *Handtalk zoo* (Ancona, George)

Andersen, Hans Christian. *The dinosaur's new clothes* by Diane Goode; ill. by Diane Goode. Blue Sky, 1999. ISBN 978-0-590-38360-8 Subj: Character traits – pride. Character traits – vanity. Clothing. Dinosaurs. Folk & fairy tales. Imagination. Prehistory. Royalty – emperors.

The emperor's new clothes ill. by Angela Barrett. Candlewick, 1997. ISBN 978-0-7636-0119-5 Subj: Character traits – pride. Character traits – vanity. Clothing. Folk & fairy tales. Imagination. Royalty – emperors.

The emperor's new clothes ill. by Virginia Lee Burton. Houghton, 2004, 1949. ISBN 978-0-618-34420-8 Subj: Character traits – pride. Character traits – vanity. Clothing. Folk & fairy tales. Humorous stories. Imagination. Royalty – emperors.

The emperor's new clothes retold by Riki Levinson; ill. by Robert Byrd. Dutton, 1991. ISBN 978-0-525-44611-8 Subj: Animals. Character traits – pride. Character traits – vanity. Clothing. Folk & fairy tales. Humorous stories. Imagination. Royalty – emperors.

The emperor's new clothes retold by Louise John; ill. by Serena Curmi. Evans Brothers, 2011. ISBN 978-0-237-53895-8 Subj: Character traits – pride. Character traits – vanity. Clothing. Folk & fairy tales. Humorous stories. Imagination. Royalty – emperors.

The emperor's new clothes adapt. by Susan Blackaby; ill. by Charlene DeLage. Picture Window, 2004. ISBN 978-1-4048-0224-7 Subj: Character traits – pride. Character traits – vanity. Clothing. Folk & fairy tales. Humorous stories. Imagination. Royalty – emperors.

The emperor's new clothes adapt. by Jean Van Leeuwen; ill. by Jack Delano and Irene Delano. Random House, 1971. ISBN 978-0-394-82105-4 Subj: Character traits – pride. Character traits – vanity. Clothing. Folk & fairy tales. Humorous stories. Imagination. Royalty – emperors.

The emperor's new clothes ill. by Anne Rockwell. Crowell, 1982. ISBN 978-0-690-04149-1 Subj:

Character traits – pride. Character traits – vanity. Clothing. Folk & fairy tales. Humorous stories. Imagination. Royalty – emperors.

The emperor's new clothes adapt. by Janet Stevens; ill. by adapter. Holiday, 1985. ISBN 978-0-8234-0566-4 Subj: Character traits – pride. Character traits – vanity. Clothing. Folk & fairy tales. Humorous stories. Imagination. Royalty – emperors.

The emperor's new clothes adapt. by Eve Tharlet; ill. by adapter. NorthSouth, 2000. ISBN 978-0-7358-1341-0 Subj: Character traits – pride. Character traits – vanity. Clothing. Folk & fairy tales. Foreign lands – China. Humorous stories. Royalty – emperors.

The emperor's new clothes: a tale set in China retold by Demi; ill. by reteller. McElderry, 2000. ISBN 978-0-689-83068-6 Subj: Character traits – pride. Character traits – vanity. Clothing. Folk & fairy tales. Foreign lands – China. Humorous stories. Royalty – emperors.

The fir tree adapt. by Diane Goode; ill. by adapter. Random House, 1988. ISBN 978-0-394-81941-9 Subj: Folk & fairy tales. Holidays – Christmas. Trees.

The fir tree adapt. by Bernadette Watts; ill. by adapter. NorthSouth, 1990. ISBN 978-1-55858-093-0 Subj: Folk & fairy tales. Holidays – Christmas. Trees.

It's perfectly true! adapt. by Janet Stevens; ill. by adapter. Holiday, 1987. ISBN 978-0-8234-0672-2 Subj: Behavior – gossip. Character traits – vanity. Death. Folk & fairy tales.

The little match girl ill. by Rachel Isadora. Putnam, 1987. ISBN 978-0-399-21336-6 Subj: Death. Folk & fairy tales. Holidays – New Year's. Homeless. Poverty.

The little match girl ill. by Blair Lent. Houghton, 1968. ISBN 978-1-56397-470-0 Subj: Death. Folk & fairy tales. Holidays – New Year's. Homeless. Poverty.

The little match girl ill. by Jerry Pinkney. Fogelman, 1999. ISBN 978-0-8037-2314-6 Subj: Death. Folk & fairy tales. Holidays – New Year's. Homeless. Poverty.

The little matchstick girl ill. by Debbie Lavreys. Clavis, 2008. ISBN 978-1-60537-008-8 Subj: Death. Folk & fairy tales. Holidays – New Year's. Homeless. Poverty.

The little mermaid adapt. by Susan Blackaby; ill. by Charlene Delage. Picture Window, 2004. ISBN 978-1-4048-0221-6 Subj: Folk & fairy tales. Mythical creatures – mermaids, mermen.

The little mermaid ill. by Michael Hague. Holt, 1993. ISBN 978-0-8050-1010-7 Subj: Folk & fairy tales. Mythical creatures – mermaids, mermen.

The little mermaid retold by Rachel Isadora; ill. by reteller. Putnam, 1998. ISBN 978-0-399-22813-1 Subj: Folk & fairy tales. Mythical creatures – mermaids, mermen.

The nightingale ill. by Nancy Ekholm Burkert. HarperCollins, 1965. Subj: Birds – nightingales. Character traits – freedom. Folk & fairy tales. Foreign lands – China. Royalty – emperors.

The nightingale adapt. by Pirkko Vainio; ill. by adapter. NorthSouth, 2011. ISBN 978-0-7358-4029-4 Subj: Birds – nightingales. Character traits – freedom. Folk & fairy tales. Foreign lands – China. Royalty – emperors.

The nightingale ill. by Lisbeth Zwerger. NorthSouth, 1999. ISBN 978-0-7358-1118-8 Subj: Birds – nightingales. Character traits – freedom. Folk & fairy tales. Foreign lands – China. Royalty – emperors.

The princess and the pea retold by Harriet Ziefert; ill. by Emily Bolam. Viking, 1996. ISBN 978-0-670-86054-8 Subj: Folk & fairy tales. Royalty – princesses. Sleep.

The princess and the pea adapt. by Susan Blackaby; ill. by Charlene Delage. Picture Window, 2004. ISBN 978-1-4048-0223-0 Subj: Folk & fairy tales. Royalty – princesses. Sleep.

The princess and the pea ill. by Dorothée Duntze. Holt, 1985. ISBN 978-0-8050-0170-9 Subj: Folk & fairy tales. Royalty – princesses. Sleep.

The princess and the pea ill. by Maja Dusíková. Floris, 2012. ISBN 978-0-86315-857-5 Subj: Folk & fairy tales. Royalty – princesses. Sleep.

The princess and the pea ill. by Paul Galdone. Seabury Pr., 1978. ISBN 978-0-8164-3202-8 Subj: Folk & fairy tales. Royalty – princesses. Sleep.

The princess and the pea ill. by Rachel Isadora. Penguin, 2007. ISBN 978-0-399-24611-1 Subj: Folk & fairy tales. Foreign lands – Africa. Royalty – princesses. Sleep.

The princess and the pea retold by John Cech; ill. by Bernhard Oberdieck. Sterling, 2007. ISBN 978-1-4027-3065-8 Subj: Folk & fairy tales. Royalty – princesses. Sleep.

The princess and the pea adapt. by Janet Stevens; ill. by adapter. Holiday, 1982. ISBN 978-0-8234-0442-1 Subj: Folk & fairy tales. Royalty – princesses. Sleep.

The princess and the pea by Alain Vaës; ill. by Alain Vaës. Little, 2001. ISBN 978-0-316-89633-7 Subj: Behavior – greed. Folk & fairy tales. Humorous stories. Jewelry. Royalty – princesses. Sleep.

The princess and the pea in miniature: after the fairy tale by Hans Christian Andersen adapt. by Lauren Child photos by Polly Borland. Hyperion, 2006. ISBN 978-0-7868-3886-8 Subj: Folk & fairy tales. Royalty – princesses. Sleep.

The snow queen ill. by Angela Barrett. Candlewick, 1993. ISBN 978-1-56402-215-8 Subj: Character traits – bravery. Emotions – love. Folk & fairy tales.

The snow queen sel. & ed. by Neil Philip; ill. by Sally Holmes. Lothrop, 1989. ISBN 978-0-688-09048-7 Subj: Character traits – bravery. Emotions – love. Folk & fairy tales.

The snow queen adapt. by Amy Ehrlich; ill. by Susan Jeffers. Dial, 1982. ISBN 978-0-8037-8029-3 Subj: Character traits – bravery. Emotions – love. Folk & fairy tales.

The snow queen: a retelling of the fairy tale ill. by Bagram Ibatoulline. HarperCollins, 2013. ISBN 978-0-06-220950-4 Subj: Character traits – bravery. Emotions – love. Folk & fairy tales.

The steadfast tin soldier retold by Cynthia Rylant; ill. by Jen Corace. Abrams, 2013. ISBN 978-1-4197-0432-1 Subj: Folk & fairy tales. Toys – soldiers.

The steadfast tin soldier adapt. by Susan Blackaby; ill. by Charlene Delage. Picture Window, 2004. ISBN 978-1-4048-0226-1 Subj: Folk & fairy tales. Toys – soldiers.

The steadfast tin soldier ill. by Paul Galdone. Houghton, 1979. ISBN 978-0-395-28964-8 Subj: Folk & fairy tales. Toys – soldiers.

The steadfast tin soldier retold by Rachel Isadora; ill. by reteller. Putnam, 1996. ISBN 978-0-399-22676-2 Subj: Folk & fairy tales. Toys – soldiers.

The steadfast tin soldier ill. by P. J. Lynch. Harcourt, 1992. ISBN 978-0-15-200599-3 Subj: Folk & fairy tales. Toys – soldiers.

The steadfast tin soldier retold by Tor Seidler; ill. by Fred Marcellino. HarperCollins, 1992. ISBN 978-0-06-205001-4 Subj: Folk & fairy tales. Toys – soldiers.

The swineherd ill. by Lisbeth Zwerger. Morrow, 1982. ISBN 978-0-688-00930-4 Subj: Character traits – cleverness. Character traits – selfishness. Folk & fairy tales.

Sylvia Long's Thumbelina by Sylvia Long; ill. by author. Chronicle, 2010. ISBN 978-0-8118-5522-8 Subj: Character traits – smallness. Folk & fairy tales.

Thumbelina adapt. by Susan Blackaby; ill. by Charlene Delage. Picture Window, 2004. ISBN 978-1-4048-0225-4 Subj: Character traits – smallness. Folk & fairy tales.

Thumbelina ill. by Demi. Putnam, 1987. ISBN 978-0-396-09241-4 Subj: Character traits – smallness. Folk & fairy tales.

Thumbelina ill. by Arlene Graston. Delacorte, 1997. ISBN 978-0-385-32251-5 Subj: Character traits – smallness. Folk & fairy tales.

Thumbelina retold by Brian Alderson; ill. by Bagram Ibatoulline. Candlewick, 2009. ISBN 978-0-7636-2079-0 Subj: Character traits – smallness. Folk & fairy tales.

Thumbelina retold by Amy Ehrlich; ill. by Susan Jeffers. Dial, 1979. ISBN 978-0-8037-8815-2 Subj: Character traits – smallness. Folk & fairy tales.

Thumbelina retold by Lauren A. Mills; ill. by reteller. Little, Brown, 2005. ISBN 978-0-316-57359-7 Subj: Character traits – smallness. Folk & fairy tales.

Thumbeline ill. by Lisbeth Zwerger. Picture Book Studio, 1985. ISBN 978-0-88708-006-7 Subj: Character traits – smallness. Folk & fairy tales.

The tinderbox ill. by Warwick Hutton. Macmillan, 1988. ISBN 978-0-689-50458-7 Subj: Folk & fairy tales. Magic. Witches.

The tinderbox retold by Stephen Mitchell; ill. by Bagram Ibatoulline. Candlewick, 2007. ISBN 978-0-7636-2078-3 Subj: Careers – military. Folk & fairy tales. Magic.

The tinderbox ill. by Barry Moser. Little, 1990. ISBN 978-0-316-03938-3 Subj: Folk & fairy tales. Magic. U.S. history. Witches.

The ugly duckling ill. by Adrienne Adams. Scribners, 1965. Subj: Birds – ducks. Birds – swans. Character traits – appearance. Character traits – being different. Folk & fairy tales.

The ugly duckling adapt. by Sebastien Braun; ill. by adapter. Boxer, 2010. ISBN 978-1-907152-04-7 Subj: Birds – ducks. Birds – swans. Character traits – appearance. Character traits – being different. Folk & fairy tales.

The ugly duckling ill. by Lorinda Bryan Cauley. Harcourt, 1979. ISBN 978-0-15-292435-5 Subj: Birds – ducks. Birds – swans. Character traits – appearance. Character traits – being different. Folk & fairy tales.

The ugly duckling adapt. by Susan Blackaby; ill. by Charlene Delage. Picture Window, 2004. ISBN 978-1-4048-0222-3 Subj: Birds – ducks. Birds – swans. Character traits – appearance. Character traits – being different. Folk & fairy tales.

The ugly duckling ill. by Robert Ingpen. Minedition, 2005. ISBN 978-0-698-40010-8 Subj: Birds – ducks. Birds – swans. Character traits – appearance. Character traits – being different. Folk & fairy tales.

The ugly duckling retold by Rachel Isadora; ill. by reteller. Putnam, 2009. ISBN 978-0-399-25029-3 Subj: Birds – ducks. Birds – swans. Character traits – appearance. Character traits – being different. Folk & fairy tales. Foreign lands – Africa.

The ugly duckling ill. by Steve Johnson and Lou Fancher. Candlewick, 2008. ISBN 978-0-7636-2159-9 Subj: Birds – ducks. Birds – swans. Character traits – appearance. Character traits – being different. Folk & fairy tales.

The ugly duckling adapt. by Jerry Pinkney; ill. by adapter. Morrow, 1999. ISBN 978-0-688-15933-7 Subj: Birds – ducks. Birds – swans. Caldecott award honor books. Character traits – appearance. Character traits – being different. Folk & fairy tales.

The ugly duckling retold by Kevin Crossley-Holland; ill. by Meilo So. Knopf, 2001. ISBN 978-0-375-91319-8 Subj: Birds – ducks. Birds – swans. Character traits – appearance. Character traits – being different. Folk & fairy tales.

The ugly duckling ill. by Pirkko Vainio. NorthSouth, 2009. ISBN 978-0-7358-2226-9 Subj: Birds – ducks. Birds – swans. Character traits – appearance. Character traits – being different. Folk & fairy tales.

The ugly duckling retold by Bernadette Watts; ill. by reteller. NorthSouth, 2000. Subj: Birds – ducks. Birds – swans. Character traits – appearance. Character traits – being different. Folk & fairy tales.

The ugly duckling ill. by Roberta Wilson. Odyssey, 2010. ISBN 978-0-917665-86-8 Subj: Birds – ducks. Birds – swans. Character traits – appearance. Character traits – being different. Folk & fairy tales.

The wild swans ill. by Anne Yvonne Gilbert. Barefoot, 2005. ISBN 978-1-84148-164-7 Subj: Birds – swans. Folk & fairy tales. Magic.

The wild swans retold by Amy Ehrlich; ill. by Susan Jeffers. Dial, 1981. ISBN 978-0-8037-9391-0 Subj: Birds – swans. Folk & fairy tales. Magic.

The woman with the eggs adapt. by Jan Wahl; ill. by Ray Cruz. Crown, 1974. ISBN 978-0-517-51587-7 Subj: Behavior – greed. Eggs. Folk & fairy tales.

Anderson, Brian. *The prince's new pet* ill. by author. Roaring Brook, 2011. ISBN 978-1-59643-357-1 Subj: Concepts – color. Pets. Royalty – princes.

Anderson, Christine. *Bedtime!* ill. by Steven Salerno. Penguin, 2005. ISBN 978-0-399-24004-1 Subj: Bedtime.

Anderson, Derek. *Gladys goes out to lunch* ill. by author. Simon & Schuster, 2005. ISBN 978-0-689-85688-4 Subj: Animals – gorillas. Food.

How the Easter Bunny saved Christmas ill. by author. Simon & Schuster, 2006. ISBN 978-0-689-87634-9 Subj: Animals – rabbits. Character traits – helpfulness. Holidays – Christmas. Santa Claus.

Over the river: a turkey's tale ill. by author. Simon & Schuster, 2005. ISBN 978-0-689-87635-6 Subj: Birds – turkeys. Holidays – Thanksgiving. Songs.

Romeo and Lou blast off ill. by author. Simon & Schuster, 2007. ISBN 978-1-4169-3784-5 Subj: Animals – polar bears. Birds – penguins. Friendship. Space & space ships.

Story county: here we come! ill. by author. Scholastic, 2011. ISBN 978-0-545-16844-1 Subj: Animals. Farms.

Anderson, Hans Christian. *The penguin and the pea* (Perlman, Janet)

Anderson, Laurie Halse. *The big cheese of Third Street* ill. by David Gordon. Simon & Schuster, 2002. ISBN 978-0-689-82464-7 Subj: Behavior – bullying, teasing. Character traits – persistence. Concepts – size. Tall tales.

The hair of Zoe Fleefenbacher goes to school ill. by Ard Hoyt. Simon & Schuster, 2009. ISBN 978-0-689-85809-3 Subj: Behavior – misbehavior. Careers – teachers. Hair. Humorous stories. School.

No time for Mother's Day ill. by Dorothy Donohue. Whitman, 1999. ISBN 978-0-8075-4955-1 Subj: Family life – mothers. Gifts. Holidays – Mother's Day.

Thank you, Sarah: the woman who saved Thanksgiving ill. by Matt Faulkner. Simon & Schuster, 2002. ISBN 978-0-689-84787-5 Subj: Holidays – Thanksgiving. U.S. history.

Turkey pox ill. by Dorothy Donohue. Whitman, 1996. ISBN 978-0-8075-8127-8 Subj: Family life. Family life – grandmothers. Holidays – Thanksgiving. Illness – chicken pox.

Anderson, Lena. *The hedgehog, the pig, and their little friend* ill. by author. Farrar, 2007. ISBN 978-91-29-66742-4 Subj: Animals – hedgehogs. Animals – pigs. Behavior – lost. Rhyming text.

Anderson, M. T. *Strange Mr. Satie* ill. by Petra Mathers. Viking, 2003. ISBN 978-0-670-03637-0 Subj: Careers – composers. Foreign lands – France.

Anderson, Peggy Perry. *Chuck's band* ill. by author. Houghton, 2008. ISBN 978-0-618-96506-9 Subj: Animals. Farms. Music. Musical instruments – bands. Rhyming text.

Chuck's truck ill. by author. Houghton, 2006. ISBN 978-0-618-66836-6 Subj: Animals. Rhyming text. Trucks.

Joe on the go ill. by author. Houghton, 2007. ISBN 978-0-618-77331-2 Subj: Activities – playing. Family life – grandmothers. Frogs & toads.

Out to lunch ill. by author. Houghton, 1998. ISBN 978-0-395-89826-0 Subj: Behavior – misbehavior. Etiquette. Family life. Frogs & toads. Restaurants. Rhyming text.

Time for bed, the babysitter said ill. by author. Houghton, 1987. ISBN 978-0-395-41851-2 Subj: Activities – babysitting. Bedtime. Frogs & toads.

To the tub ill. by author. Houghton, 1996. ISBN 978-0-395-77614-8 Subj: Activities – bathing. Family life – fathers. Frogs & toads.

We go in a circle ill. by author. Houghton, 2004. ISBN 978-0-618-44756-5 Subj: Animals – horses, ponies. Disabilities. Sports – racing.

Anderson, Stephen Axel. *I know the moon* ill. by Greg Couch. Philomel, 2001. ISBN 978-0-399-23425-5 Subj: Animals. Emotions. Moon. Rhyming text. Science.

Andreae, Giles. *Bustle in the bushes* ill. by David Wojtowycz. Tiger Tales, 2012. ISBN 978-1-58925-109-0 Subj: Insects. Poetry.

Captain Flinn and the pirate dinosaurs ill. by Russell Ayto. Simon & Schuster, 2005. ISBN 978-1-4169-0713-8 Subj: Dinosaurs. Imagination. Pirates. School.

Captain Flinn and the pirate dinosaurs: missing treasure! ill. by Russell Ayto. Simon & Schuster, 2008. ISBN 978-1-4169-6745-3 Subj: Dinosaurs. Imagination. Pirates. School.

Cock-a-doodle-doo! ill. by David Wojtowycz. Tiger Tales, 2002. ISBN 978-1-58925-020-8 Subj: Animals. Poetry.

Dinosaurs galore! ill. by David Wojtowycz. Tiger Tales, 2005. ISBN 978-1-58925-044-4 Subj: Dinosaurs. Poetry.

Giraffes can't dance ill. by Guy Parker-Rees. Orchard, 2001. ISBN 978-0-439-28719-7 Subj: Activities – dancing. Animals – giraffes. Character traits – individuality. Rhyming text.

I love my daddy ill. by Emma Dodd. Hyperion, 2012. ISBN 978-1-4231-4328-4 Subj: Family life – fathers. Rhyming text.

I love my mommy ill. by Emma Dodd. Hyperion/ Disney, 2011. ISBN 978-1-4231-4327-7 Subj: Family life – mothers. Rhyming text.

Pants by Giles Andreae and Nick Sharratt ill. by Nick Sharratt. Fickling, 2003. ISBN 978-0-385-75014-1 Subj: Clothing – pants. Humorous stories. Rhyming text.

The pop-up Rumble in the jungle ill. by David Wojtowycz. Tiger Tales, 2001. ISBN 978-1-58925-658-3 Subj: Animals. Format, unusual – toy & movable books. Insects – ants. Jungle. Rhyming text.

Rumble in the jungle ill. by David Wojtowycz. Little Tiger, 1997. ISBN 978-1-888444-08-7 Subj: Animals. Insects – ants. Jungle. Rhyming text.

There's a house inside my mommy ill. by Vanessa Cabban. Whitman, 2002. ISBN 978-0-8075-7853-7 Subj: Babies. Birth. Family life – brothers. Family life – mothers. Rhyming text.

Andreasen, Dan. *The giant of Seville: a "tall" tale based on a true story* ill. by author. Abrams, 2007. ISBN 978-0-8109-0988-5 Subj: Character traits – kindness. Circus. Giants. Tall tales.

Saturday with Daddy ill. by author. Holt, 2013. ISBN 978-0-8050-8687-4 Subj: Animals – elephants. Day. Family life – fathers.

The treasure bath ill. by author. Holt, 2009. ISBN 978-0-8050-8686-7 Subj: Activities – bathing. Imagination. Wordless.

Andres, Kristina. *Elephant in the bathtub* ill. by author. NorthSouth, 2010. ISBN 978-0-7358-2291-7 Subj: Activities – bathing. Animals – elephants.

Good Little Wolf ill. by author. NorthSouth, 2008. ISBN 978-0-7358-2210-8 Subj: Animals – wolves. Behavior.

Andrews, Julie. *Dumpy at school* by Julie Andrews and Emma Walton Hamilton ill. by Tony Walton. Hyperion, 2000. ISBN 978-0-7868-0610-2 Subj: School – first day. Trucks.

Dumpy the dump truck by Julie Andrews and Emma Walton Hamilton ill. by Tony Walton. Hyperion, 2000. ISBN 978-0-7868-2523-3 Subj: Family life – grandfathers. Farms. Trucks.

Dumpy to the rescue! by Julie Andrews and Emma Walton Hamilton ill. by Tony Walton. HarperCollins, 2004. ISBN 978-0-06-052690-0 Subj: Animals – goats. Behavior – lost & found possessions. Family life. Trucks.

Dumpy's apple shop by Julie Andrews and Emma Walton Hamilton ill. by Tony Walton. HarperCollins, 2004. ISBN 978-0-06-052693-1 Subj: Food. Trucks.

Simeon's gift by Julie Andrews and Emma Walton Hamilton ill. by Gennady Spirin. HarperCollins, 2003. ISBN 978-0-06-008915-3 Subj: Careers – musicians. Self-concept.

The very fairy princess by Julie Andrews and Emma Walton Hamilton ill. by Christine Davenier. Little, Brown, 2010. ISBN 978-0-316-04050-1 Subj: Royalty – princesses. Self-concept.

The very fairy princess: here comes the flower girl! by Julie Andrews and Emma Walton Hamilton ill. by Christine Davenier. Little, Brown, 2012. ISBN 978-0-316-18561-5 Subj: Royalty – princesses. Weddings.

The very fairy princess follows her heart by Julie Andrews and Emma Walton Hamilton ill. by Christine Davenier. Little, Brown, 2013. ISBN 978-0-316-18559-2 Subj: Holidays – Valentine's Day. Royalty – princesses. School.

The very fairy princess sparkles in the snow by Julie Andrews and Emma Walton Hamilton ill. by Christine Davenier. Little, Brown, 2013. ISBN 978-0-316-21963-1 Subj: Activities – singing. Royalty – princesses. School. Weather – snow.

Andrews, Sylvia. *Dancing in my bones* ill. by Ellen Mueller. HarperCollins, 2001. ISBN 978-0-694-01316-6 Subj: Activities – dancing. Anatomy. Rhyming text.

Andrews-Goebel, Nancy. *The pot that Juan built* ill. by David Diaz. Lee & Low, 2002. ISBN 978-1-58430-038-0 Subj: Art. Careers – potters. Rhyming text.

Angelou, Maya. *Amazing peace: a Christmas poem* ill. by Steve Johnson and Lou Fancher. Random House, 2008. ISBN 978-0-375-84150-7 Subj: Holidays – Christmas. Poetry.

Angelina of Italy ill. by Lizzy Rockwell. Random House, 2004. ISBN 978-0-375-92832-1 Subj: Food. Foreign lands – Italy.

Kofi and his magic photos by Margaret Courtney-Clarke. Potter, 1996. ISBN 978-0-375-92566-5 Subj: Foreign lands – Ghana.

My painted house, my friendly chicken, and me photos by Margaret Courtney-Clarke. Random House, 2003. ISBN 978-0-375-92567-2 Subj: Art. Foreign lands – South Africa. Homes, houses. Poetry.

Angleberger, Tom. *Crankee Doodle* ill. by Cece Bell. Clarion, 2013. ISBN 978-0-547-81854-2 Subj: Animals – horses, ponies. Behavior – fighting, arguing. Humorous stories. U.S. history.

Anglund, Joan Walsh. *The brave cowboy* ill. by author. McMeel, 1959. ISBN 978-0-7407-0649-3 Subj: Activities – playing. Character traits – bravery. Cowboys, cowgirls. Games. Imagination.

Christmas is a time of giving ill. by author. Harcourt, 1961. ISBN 978-0-15-217863-5 Subj: Character traits – generosity. Holidays – Christmas.

The cowboy's Christmas ill. by author. Atheneum, 1972. ISBN 978-0-689-30301-2 Subj: Animals – bears. Cowboys, cowgirls. Holidays – Christmas. Imagination – imaginary friends.

A friend is someone who likes you ill. by author. Harcourt, 1958. ISBN 978-0-15-229678-0 Subj: Friendship.

Anholt, Catherine. *Chimp and Zee and the big storm* by Catherine Anholt and Laurence Anholt ill. by authors. Fogelman, 2002. ISBN 978-0-8037-2700-7 Subj: Animals – chimpanzees. Behavior – lost. Weather – storms.

Chimp and Zee's noisy book by Catherine Anholt and Laurence Anholt ill. by authors. Fogelman, 2002. ISBN 978-0-8037-2772-4 Subj: Animals. Animals – chimpanzees. Format, unusual – board books. Noise, sounds.

Come back, Jack! by Catherine Anholt and Laurence Anholt ill. by authors. Candlewick, 1994. ISBN 978-1-56402-313-1 Subj: Behavior – boredom. Books, reading. Nursery rhymes.

Happy birthday, Chimp and Zee by Catherine Anholt and Laurence Anholt ill. by authors. Frances Lincoln, 2006. ISBN 978-1-84507-507-1 Subj: Animals – chimpanzees. Birthdays. Parties. Rhyming text.

Monkey around with Chimp and Zee [board book] by Catherine Anholt and Laurence Anholt ill. by authors. Fogelman, 2002. ISBN 978-0-8037-2773-1 Subj: Animals – chimpanzees. Format, unusual – board books.

Sun, snow, stars, sky by Catherine Anholt and Laurence Anholt ill. by authors. Viking, 1995. ISBN 978-0-670-86196-5 Subj: Seasons. Weather.

What makes me happy? by Catherine Anholt and Laurence Anholt ill. by authors. Candlewick, 1995. ISBN 978-1-56402-482-4 Subj: Babies. Emotions. Rhyming text.

Anholt, Laurence. *Billy and the big new school* ill. by Catherine Anholt. Whitman, 1999. ISBN 978-0-8075-0743-8 Subj: Behavior – growing up. Birds. School – first day.

Chimp and Zee and the big storm (Anholt, Catherine)

Chimp and Zee's noisy book (Anholt, Catherine)

Come back, Jack! (Anholt, Catherine)

Happy birthday, Chimp and Zee (Anholt, Catherine)

Jack and the dreamsack ill. by Ross Collins. Bloomsbury, 2003. ISBN 978-1-58234-786-8 Subj: Dreams. Night.

Monkey around with Chimp and Zee [board book] (Anholt, Catherine)

Seven for a secret ill. by James Coplestone. Frances Lincoln, 2006. ISBN 978-1-84507-300-8 Subj: Death. Emotions – love. Family life – grandfathers. Letters, cards.

Sophie and the new baby ill. by Catherine Anholt. Whitman, 2000. ISBN 978-0-8075-7550-5 Subj: Babies. Birth. Family life – new sibling.

Sun, snow, stars, sky (Anholt, Catherine)

What makes me happy? (Anholt, Catherine)

Animal I spy: what can you spot? ill. by Kate Sheppard. Kingfisher, 2010. ISBN 978-0-7534-6395-6 Subj: Animals. Format, unusual – board books. Picture puzzles.

Animal 123: one to ten and back again ill. by Kate Sheppard. Kingfisher, 2010. ISBN 978-0-7534-6394-9 Subj: Animals. Counting, numbers. Format, unusual – board books. Picture puzzles.

Anno, Mitsumasa. *Anno's alphabet: an adventure in imagination* ill. by author. Crowell, 1975. ISBN 978-0-690-00546-2 Subj: ABC books. Imagination. Optical illusions. Picture puzzles.

Anno's Britain ill. by author. Philomel, 1982. ISBN 978-0-399-20861-4 Subj: Foreign lands – England. Games. Imagination. Wordless.

Anno's counting book ill. by author. Crowell, 1975. ISBN 978-0-690-01288-0 Subj: Counting, numbers. Imagination. Optical illusions. Picture puzzles. Seasons. Wordless.

Anno's counting house ill. by author. Philomel, 1982. ISBN 978-0-399-20896-6 Subj: Counting, numbers. Games. Imagination. Optical illusions. Picture puzzles. Wordless.

Anno's hat tricks ill. by author. Putnam, 1985. ISBN 978-0-399-21212-3 Subj: Counting, numbers. Magic.

Anno's Italy ill. by author. Collins-World, 1980. ISBN 978-0-529-05560-6 Subj: Foreign lands – Italy. Games. Imagination. Optical illusions. Picture puzzles. Wordless.

Anno's journey ill. by author. Putnam, 1981. ISBN 978-0-529-05419-7 Subj: Games. Imagination. Optical illusions. Picture puzzles. Wordless.

Anno's magic seeds ill. by author. Philomel, 1995. ISBN 978-0-399-22538-3 Subj: Counting, numbers. Gardens, gardening. Seeds.

Anno's math games ill. by author. Philomel, 1987. ISBN 978-0-399-21151-5 Subj: Concepts. Counting, numbers. Riddles & jokes.

Anno's math games II ill. by author. Putnam, 1989. ISBN 978-0-399-21615-2 Subj: Concepts. Counting, numbers. Riddles & jokes.

Anno's math games III ill. by author. Putnam, 1991. ISBN 978-0-399-22274-0 Subj: Concepts. Counting, numbers. Riddles & jokes.

Anno's U.S.A. ill. by author. Philomel, 1983. ISBN 978-0-399-20974-1 Subj: Games. Imagination. Wordless.

Annunziata, Jane. *Shy spaghetti and excited eggs: a kid's menu of feelings* (Nemiroff, Marc A.)

Aoki, Elaine M. *The White Swan express* (Okimoto, Jean Davies)

Appelt, Kathi. *The Alley Cat's Meow* ill. by Jon Goodell. Harcourt, 2002. ISBN 978-0-15-201980-8 Subj: Activities – dancing. Animals – cats. Rhyming text.

Bats around the clock ill. by Melissa Sweet. HarperCollins, 2000. ISBN 978-0-688-16470-6 Subj: Activities – dancing. Animals – bats. Clocks, watches. Music. Rhyming text. Time.

Bats on parade ill. by Melissa Sweet. Morrow, 1999. ISBN 978-0-688-15666-4 Subj: Animals – bats. Counting, numbers. Music. Musical instruments – bands. Parades. Rhyming text.

Brand-new baby blues ill. by Kelly Murphy. HarperCollins, 2010. ISBN 978-0-06-053233-8 Subj: Babies. Family life – new sibling. Rhyming text.

Cowboy dreams ill. by Barry Root. HarperCollins, 1999. ISBN 978-0-06-027764-2 Subj: Bedtime. Cowboys, cowgirls. Dreams. Night. Rhyming text.

Elephants aloft ill. by Keith Baker. Harcourt, 1993. ISBN 978-0-15-225384-4 Subj: Activities – ballooning. Animals – elephants. Foreign lands – Africa. Foreign lands – India.

Incredible me! ill. by G. Brian Karas. HarperCollins, 2003. ISBN 978-0-06-028623-1 Subj: Character traits – individuality. Rhyming text. Self-concept.

Merry Christmas, merry crow ill. by Jon Goodell. Harcourt, 2005. ISBN 978-0-15-202651-6 Subj: Birds – crows. Holidays – Christmas. Rhyming text.

Miss Lady Bird's wildflowers: how a first lady changed America ill. by Joy Fisher Hein. HarperCollins, 2005. ISBN 978-0-06-001108-6 Subj: Ecology. Flowers. U.S. history.

My father's house ill. by Raúl Colón. Penguin, 2007. ISBN 978-0-670-03669-1 Subj: Nature. Poetry. Religion.

Oh my baby, little one ill. by Jane Dyer. Harcourt, 2000. ISBN 978-0-15-200041-7 Subj: Emotions – love. Family life – mothers. Rhyming text.

Rain dance ill. by Emilie Chollat. HarperCollins, 2001. ISBN 978-0-694-01291-6 Subj: Counting, numbers. Rhyming text. Weather – rain.

Where, where is Swamp Bear? ill. by Megan Halsey. HarperCollins, 2002. ISBN 978-0-688-17103-2 Subj: Animals – bears. Family life – grandfathers. Swamps.

Apperley, Dawn. *Blossom and Boo: a story about best friends* ill. by author. Little, 2000. ISBN 978-0-316-04963-4 Subj: Animals – bears. Animals – rabbits. Friendship.

Blossom and Boo stay up late: a story about bedtime ill. by author. Little, 2002. ISBN 978-0-316-05312-9 Subj: Animals – bears. Animals – rabbits. Bedtime. Night.

Don't wake the baby ill. by author. Bloomsbury, 2001. ISBN 978-0-7475-5003-7 Subj: Animals –

squirrels. Babies. Family life – new sibling. Humorous stories. Senses. Sleep.

Flip and Flop ill. by author. Orchard, 2001. ISBN 978-0-439-28892-7 Subj: Activities – playing. Birds – penguins. Family life – brothers.

Good night, sleep tight, little bunnies ill. by author. Scholastic, 2002. ISBN 978-0-439-22525-0 Subj: Animals. Bedtime. Birds. Night. Rhyming text.

Santa Claus will come tonight ill. by author. Scholastic, 2002. ISBN 978-0-439-40449-5 Subj: Animals. Holidays – Christmas. Rhyming text. Santa Claus.

Apple, Margot. *Brave Martha* ill. by author. Houghton, 1999. ISBN 978-0-395-59422-3 Subj: Animals – cats. Bedtime. Emotions – fear. Monsters. Night.

Arabian Nights. *The tale of Ali Baba and the forty thieves: a story from the Arabian nights* retold by Eric A. Kimmel; ill. by Will Hillenbrand. Holiday, 1996. ISBN 978-0-8234-1258-7 Subj: Behavior – stealing. Folk & fairy tales. Foreign lands – Middle East.

Araki, Mie. *The magic toolbox: starring Fred and Lulu* ill. by author. Chronicle, 2003. ISBN 978-0-8118-3564-0 Subj: Animals – rabbits. Animals – rhinoceros. Magic. Tools.

Aralan, Haydé. *Milton* ill. by author. Chronicle, 2000. ISBN 978-0-8118-2762-1 Subj: Animals – cats.

Milton's Christmas ill. by author. Chronicle, 2000. ISBN 978-0-8118-2842-0 Subj: Animals – cats. Behavior – misbehavior. Holidays – Christmas.

Archambault, John. *Chicka chicka boom boom* (Martin, Bill, Jr.)

Chicka chicka boom boom [board book] (Martin, Bill, Jr.)

Here are my hands (Martin, Bill, Jr.)

Knots on a counting rope (Martin, Bill, Jr.)

Listen to the rain (Martin, Bill, Jr.)

The magic pumpkin (Martin, Bill, Jr.)

Archer, Peggy. *From dawn to dreams: poems for busy babies* ill. by Hanako Wakiyama. Candlewick, 2007. ISBN 978-0-7636-2467-5 Subj: Babies. Poetry.

Name that dog! puppy poems from a to z ill. by Stephanie Buscema. Penguin, 2010. ISBN 978-0-8037-3322-0 Subj: ABC books. Animals – dogs. Poetry.

Turkey surprise ill. by Thor Wickstrom. Penguin, 2005. ISBN 978-0-8037-2969-8 Subj: Birds – turkeys. Family life – brothers & sisters. Holidays – Thanksgiving.

Arden, Carolyn. *Goose moon* ill. by Jim Postier. Boyds Mills, 2004. ISBN 978-0-613-79879-2 Subj: Moon. Seasons – spring.

Arena, Jennifer. *100 snowmen* ill. by Stephen Gilpin. Amazon/Two Lions, 2013. ISBN 978-1-4778-4703-9 Subj: Counting, numbers. Rhyming text. Snowmen.

Arenson, Roberta. *Manu and the talking fish* ill. by author. Barefoot, 2000. ISBN 978-1-84148-032-9 Subj: Fish. Folk & fairy tales. Foreign lands – India. Weather – floods.

Argueta, Jorge. *Arroz con leche / Rice pudding: un poema para cocinar / a cooking poem* ill. by Fernando Vilela. Groundwood, 2010. ISBN 978-0-88899-981-8 Subj: Activities – baking, cooking. Food. Foreign languages. Poetry.

Guacamole: un poema para cocinar / a cooking poem ill. by Margarita Sada. Groundwood, 2012. ISBN 978-1-55498-133-5 Subj: Activities – baking, cooking. Food. Foreign languages. Poetry.

Moony Luna / Luna, Lunita Lunera ill. by Elizabeth Gomez. Children's Book Press, 2005. ISBN 978-0-89239-205-6 Subj: Foreign languages. School – first day.

Sopa de frijoles: un poema para cocinar / Bean soup: a cooking poem ill. by Rafael Yockteng. Groundwood, 2009. ISBN 978-0-88899-881-1 Subj: Activities – baking, cooking. Food. Foreign languages. Poetry.

Tamalitos: un poema para cocinar / a cooking poem ill. by Domi. Groundwood, 2013. ISBN 978-1-55498-300-1 Subj: Activities – baking, cooking. Food. Foreign languages. Poetry.

Trees are hanging from the sky ill. by Rafael Yockteng. Groundwood, 2003. ISBN 978-0-88899-509-4 Subj: Dreams. Foreign lands – El Salvador. Poetry.

Armand, Glenda. *Love twelve miles long* ill. by Colin Bootman. Lee & Low, 2011. ISBN 978-1-60060-245-0 Subj: Ethnic groups in the U.S. – African Americans. Family life – mothers. Slavery. U.S. history.

Armentrout, David. *John Muir* by David Armentrout and Patricia Armentrout ill. with photos. Rourke, 2002. ISBN 978-1-58952-055-4 Subj: Ecology. U.S. history.

Armentrout, Patricia. *John Muir* (Armentrout, David)

Armstrong, Jennifer. *Magnus at the fire* ill. by Owen Smith. Simon & Schuster, 2005. ISBN 978-0-689-83922-1 Subj: Animals – horses, ponies. Careers – firefighters. Trucks.

Once upon a banana ill. by David Small. Simon & Schuster, 2006. ISBN 978-0-689-84251-1 Subj: Food. Humorous stories.

Armstrong, Matthew S. *Jane and Mizmow* ill. by author. HarperCollins, 2011. ISBN 978-0-06-117719-4 Subj: Friendship. Monsters.

Armstrong-Ellis, Carey. *Prudy's problem and how she solved it* ill. by author. Abrams, 2002. ISBN 978-0-8109-0569-6 Subj: Behavior – collecting things. Humorous stories. Museums. Problem solving.

Ten creepy monsters ill. by author. Abrams, 2012. ISBN 978-1-4197-0433-8 Subj: Counting, numbers. Monsters. Rhyming text.

Arnold, Caroline. *Australian animals* ill. with photos. HarperCollins, 2000. ISBN 978-0-688-16767-7 Subj: Animals. Foreign lands – Australia.

Giant shark: megalodon, prehistoric super predator ill. by Laurie Caple. Clarion, 2000. ISBN 978-0-395-91419-9 Subj: Fish – sharks. Prehistory. Sea & seashore.

Mealtime for zoo animals photos by Richard Hewett. Carolrhoda, 1999. ISBN 978-1-57505-389-9 Subj: Animals. Food. Zoos.

Mother and baby zoo animals photos by Richard Hewett. Carolrhoda, 1999. ISBN 978-1-57505-285-4 Subj: Animals. Animals – babies. Zoos.

Noisytime for zoo animals photos by Richard Hewett. Carolrhoda, 1999. ISBN 978-1-57505-289-2 Subj: Animals. Noise, sounds. Zoos.

A penguin's world ill. by author. Picture Window, 2006. ISBN 978-1-4048-1323-6 Subj: Birds – penguins.

A platypus' world ill. by author. Picture Window, 2008. ISBN 978-1-4048-3985-4 Subj: Animals – platypuses. Foreign lands – Australia.

Playtime for zoo animals photos by Richard Hewett. Carolrhoda, 1999. ISBN 978-1-57505-287-8 Subj: Activities – playing. Animals. Zoos.

Sleepytime for zoo animals photos by Richard Hewett. Carolrhoda, 1999. ISBN 978-1-57505-290-8 Subj: Animals. Sleep. Zoos.

Splashtime for zoo animals photos by Richard Hewett. Carolrhoda, 1999. ISBN 978-1-57505-288-5 Subj: Activities – playing. Animals. Zoos.

Too hot? too cold? keeping body temperature just right ill. by Annie Patterson. Charlesbridge, 2013. ISBN 978-1-58089-276-6 Subj: Concepts – cold & heat. Science.

A warmer world: from polar bears to butterflies, how climate change affects wildlife ill. by Jamie Hogan. Charlesbridge, 2012. ISBN 978-1-58089-266-7 Subj: Ecology.

A wombat's world ill. by author. Picture Window, 2008. ISBN 978-1-4048-3986-1 Subj: Animals – wombats. Foreign lands – Australia.

Arnold, Katya, reteller. *The adventures of Snowwoman* ill. by reteller. Based on a story by V. Suteev. Holiday, 1998. ISBN 978-0-8234-1390-4 Subj: Animals. Holidays – Christmas. Santa Claus. Snowmen.

Elephants can paint, too! photos by author. Simon & Schuster, 2005. ISBN 978-0-689-86985-3 Subj: Activities – painting. Animals – elephants. Foreign lands – Thailand.

Let's find it! my first nature guide ill. by author. Holiday, 2002. ISBN 978-0-8234-1539-7 Subj: Animals. Nature. Plants.

Meow! ill. by reteller. Based on a story by V. Suteev. Holiday, 1998. ISBN 978-0-8234-1361-4 Subj: Animals. Animals – cats. Animals – dogs. Noise, sounds.

That apple is mine! ill. by reteller. Based on a story by V. Suteev. Holiday, 2000. ISBN 978-0-8234-1629-5 Subj: Behavior – sharing. Folk & fairy tales. Foreign lands – Russia.

Arnold, Marsha Diane. *The bravest of us all* ill. by Brad Sneed. Dial, 2000. ISBN 978-0-8037-2409-9 Subj: Character traits – bravery. Emotions – fear. Family life – sisters. Weather – tornadoes.

Metro cat ill. by Jack E. Davis. Golden, 2001. ISBN 978-0-307-10213-3 Subj: Animals – cats. Foreign lands – France.

Roar of a snore ill. by Pierre Pratt. Penguin, 2006. ISBN 978-0-8037-2936-0 Subj: Bedtime. Noise, sounds. Rhyming text. Sleep – snoring.

Arnold, Tedd. *Dirty Gert* ill. by author. Holiday House, 2013. ISBN 978-0-8234-2404-7 Subj: Humorous stories. Rhyming text. Trees.

Five ugly monsters ill. by author. Scholastic, 1995. ISBN 978-0-590-22226-6 Subj: Counting, numbers. Monsters. Rhyming text. Sleep.

Green Wilma ill. by author. Dial, 1993. ISBN 978-0-8037-1314-7 Subj: Character traits – being different. Dreams. Frogs & toads. Rhyming text. School.

Green Wilma, frog in space ill. by author. Dial, 2009. ISBN 978-0-8037-2698-7 Subj: Aliens. Frogs & toads. Rhyming text. Space & space ships.

Huggly gets dressed ill. by author. Scholastic, 1997. ISBN 978-0-590-11759-3 Subj: Clothing. Monsters. Night.

Huggly takes a bath ill. by author. Scholastic, 1998. ISBN 978-0-590-91820-6 Subj: Behavior – misbehavior. Monsters. Night.

More parts ill. by author. Dial, 2001. ISBN 978-0-8037-1417-5 Subj: Anatomy. Language. Rhyming text.

No jumping on the bed! ill. by author. Dial, 1987. ISBN 978-0-8037-0038-3 Subj: Bedtime. Behavior – misbehavior. Dreams. Furniture – beds. Imagination.

No more water in the tub! ill. by author. Dial, 1995. ISBN 978-0-8037-1583-7 Subj: Activities – bathing. Cumulative tales. Imagination.

Parts ill. by author. Dial, 1997. ISBN 978-0-8037-2041-1 Subj: Anatomy. Rhyming text.

The twin princes ill. by author. Penguin, 2007. ISBN 978-0-8037-2696-3 Subj: Birds – chickens. Contests. Multiple births – twins. Royalty – princes.

Arnosky, Jim. *All about deer* ill. by author. Scholastic, 1996. ISBN 978-0-590-46792-6 Subj: Animals – deer. Science.

All about frogs ill. by author. Scholastic, 2002. ISBN 978-0-590-48164-9 Subj: Frogs & toads.

All about manatees ill. by author. Scholastic, 2008. ISBN 978-0-439-90361-5 Subj: Animals – manatees.

All about turkeys ill. by author. Scholastic, 1998. ISBN 978-0-590-48147-2 Subj: Birds – turkeys.

All night near the water ill. by author. Putnam, 1994. ISBN 978-0-399-22629-8 Subj: Birds – ducks. Night.

Armadillo's orange ill. by author. Putnam, 2003. ISBN 978-0-399-23412-5 Subj: Animals – armadillos. Behavior – lost. Friendship. Homes, houses.

At this very moment ill. by author. Penguin, 2011. ISBN 978-0-525-42252-5 Subj: Animals. Nature.

Babies in the bayou ill. by author. Penguin, 2007. ISBN 978-0-399-22653-3 Subj: Animals. Babies. Nature.

Beaver pond, moose pond ill. by author. National Geographic, 2000. ISBN 978-0-7922-7692-0 Subj: Animals – beavers. Animals – moose. Lakes, ponds.

Come out, muskrats ill. by author. Lothrop, 1989. ISBN 978-0-688-05458-8 Subj: Animals – muskrats. Nature.

Coyote raid in Cactus Canyon ill. by author. Penguin, 2005. ISBN 978-0-399-23413-2 Subj: Animals – coyotes. Desert. Reptiles – snakes.

Crinkleroot's guide to giving back to nature ill. by author. Putnam, 2012. ISBN 978-0-399-25520-5 Subj: Ecology. Nature.

Crinkleroot's guide to knowing animal habitats ill. by author. Simon & Schuster, 1997. ISBN 978-0-689-80583-7 Subj: Animals. Nature.

Crinkleroot's guide to knowing butterflies and moths ill. by author. Simon & Schuster, 1996. ISBN 978-0-689-80587-5 Subj: Insects – butterflies, caterpillars. Insects – moths. Science.

Crinkleroot's guide to knowing the trees ill. by author. Macmillan, 1992. ISBN 978-0-02-705855-0 Subj: Forest, woods. Nature. Trees.

Crinkleroot's guide to walking in wild places ill. by author. Bradbury, 1990. ISBN 978-0-02-705842-0 Subj: Activities – walking. Nature.

Crinkleroot's 25 birds every child should know ill. by author. Bradbury, 1993. ISBN 978-0-02-705859-8 Subj: Birds. Nature.

Crinkleroot's 25 fish every child should know ill. by author. Bradbury, 1993. ISBN 978-0-02-705844-4 Subj: Fish. Nature.

Crinkleroot's 25 mammals every child should know ill. by author. Bradbury, 1994. ISBN 978-0-02-705845-1 Subj: Animals. Nature.

Crinkleroot's visit to Crinkle Cove ill. by author. Simon & Schuster, 1998. ISBN 978-0-689-81602-4 Subj: Ecology. Nature. Reptiles – snakes.

Deer at the brook ill. by author. Lothrop, 1986. ISBN 978-0-688-04100-7 Subj: Animals – deer.

Dolphins on the sand ill. by author. Putnam, 2008. ISBN 978-0-399-24606-7 Subj: Animals – dolphins. Nature. Science.

Every autumn comes the bear ill. by author. Putnam, 1993. ISBN 978-0-399-22508-6 Subj: Animals. Animals – bears. Hibernation. Seasons – fall. Seasons – winter.

Gobble it up! a fun song about eating! ill. by author. Scholastic, 2008. ISBN 978-0-439-90362-2 Subj: Animals. Food. Rhyming text. Science. Songs.

Grandfather Buffalo ill. by author. Penguin, 2006. ISBN 978-0-399-24169-7 Subj: Animals – buffaloes. Old age.

I see animals hiding ill. by author. Scholastic, 1995. ISBN 978-0-590-48143-4 Subj: Animals. Behavior – hiding. Nature.

I'm a turkey! ill. by author. Scholastic, 2009. ISBN 978-0-439-90364-6 Subj: Birds – turkeys. Rhyming text. Songs.

Little Burro ill. by author. Putnam, 2013. ISBN 978-0-399-25519-9 Subj: Animals – donkeys. Nature.

A manatee morning ill. by author. Simon & Schuster, 2000. ISBN 978-0-689-81604-8 Subj: Animals – manatees. Rhyming text.

Mouse letters: a very first alphabet book ill. by author. Clarion, 1999. ISBN 978-0-03-955538-2 Subj: ABC books. Animals – mice. Wordless.

Mouse numbers and letters ill. by author. Harcourt, 1982. ISBN 978-0-15-256022-5 Subj: ABC books. Animals – mice. Counting, numbers. Wordless.

Mouse writing ill. by author. Harcourt, 1983. ISBN 978-0-15-256028-7 Subj: ABC books. Activities – writing. Animals – mice. Birds. Wordless.

Mud time and more: Nathaniel stories ill. by author. Addison-Wesley, 1979. ISBN 978-0-201-00173-0 Subj: Problem solving. Wordless.

Outdoors on foot ill. by author. Coward, 1978. ISBN 978-0-698-30684-4 Subj: Activities – walking. Humorous stories. Seasons.

Parrotfish and sunken ships: exploring a tropical reef ill. by author. HarperCollins, 2007. ISBN 978-0-688-17123-0 Subj: Boats, ships. Nature. Sea & seashore.

Rabbits and raindrops ill. by author. Putnam, 1997. ISBN 978-0-399-22635-9 Subj: Animals – rabbits. Weather – rain.

Raccoon on his own ill. by author. Putnam, 2001. ISBN 978-0-399-22756-1 Subj: Animals – raccoons. Character traits – curiosity. Swamps.

Raccoons and ripe corn ill. by author. Lothrop, 1987. ISBN 978-0-688-05456-4 Subj: Animals – raccoons. Farms. Food. Night.

Rattlesnake dance ill. by author. Putnam, 2000. ISBN 978-0-399-22755-4 Subj: Activities – dancing. Reptiles – snakes.

Slither and crawl: eye to eye with reptiles ill. by author. Sterling, 2009. ISBN 978-1-4027-3986-6 Subj: Reptiles.

Slow down for manatees ill. by author. Penguin, 2010. ISBN 978-0-399-24170-3 Subj: Animals – manatees. Character traits – kindness to animals.

Turtle in the sea ill. by author. Putnam, 2002. ISBN 978-0-399-22757-8 Subj: Reptiles – turtles, tortoises. Sea & seashore.

Watching foxes ill. by author. Lothrop, 1985. ISBN 978-0-688-04260-8 Subj: Activities – playing. Animals – foxes.

Wild and swampy ill. by author. HarperCollins, 2000. ISBN 978-0-688-17120-9 Subj: Animals. Format, unusual – toy & movable books. Swamps.

Wild tracks! a guide to nature's footprints ill. by author. Sterling, 2008. ISBN 978-1-4027-3985-9 Subj: Animals. Nature.

Arqués, Isabel M. *Ken's cloud* ill. by Angela Pelaez. NorthSouth, 2001. ISBN 978-0-7358-1526-1 Subj: Behavior – boredom. Weather – clouds. Weather – rain. Weather – snow.

Arquette, Kerry. *What did you do today?* ill. by Nancy Hayashi. Harcourt, 2002. ISBN 978-0-15-201414-8 Subj: Activities. Animals. Rhyming text.

Arrigan, Mary. *Mario's angels: a story about the artist Giotto* ill. by Gillian McClure. Frances Lincoln, 2006. ISBN 978-1-84507-404-3 Subj: Angels. Art. Careers – artists.

Arro, Lena. *By geezers and galoshes!* ill. by Catarina Kruusval. R&S Books, 2001. ISBN 978-91-29-65348-9 Subj: Boats, ships. Family life – aunts, uncles. Old age. Pirates.

Artell, Mike. *Jacques and de beanstalk* (Jack and the beanstalk)

Petite Rouge: a Cajun Red Riding Hood ill. by Jim Harris. Dial, 2003. ISBN 978-0-8037-2514-0 Subj: Animals. Folk & fairy tales. Rhyming text.

Artzybasheff, Boris. *Seven Simeons* ill. by author. Viking, 1937. Subj: Caldecott award honor books.

Aruego, Ariane *see* Dewey, Ariane

Aruego, José. *The last laugh* by José Aruego and Ariane Dewey ill. by authors. Penguin, 2006. ISBN 978-0-8037-3093-9 Subj: Behavior – bullying, teasing. Birds – ducks. Reptiles – snakes.

Splash! by José Aruego and Ariane Dewey ill. by authors. Harcourt, 2001. ISBN 978-0-15-216256-6 Subj: Animals – bears. Character traits – clumsiness. Sports – fishing.

We hide, you seek by José Aruego and Ariane Dewey ill. by authors. Greenwillow, 1979. ISBN 978-0-688-84201-7 Subj: Animals. Behavior – hiding. Foreign lands – Africa. Games.

Weird friends: unlikely allies in the animal kingdom by José Aruego and Ariane Dewey ill. by authors. Harcourt, 2002. ISBN 978-0-15-202128-3 Subj: Animals. Behavior – needing someone. Fish.

Asare, Meshack. *Sosu's call* ill. by author. Kane/Miller, 2002. ISBN 978-1-929132-21-8 Subj: Animals – dogs. Character traits – bravery. Disabilities. Foreign lands – Africa. Weather – storms.

Asbjørnsen, P. C. *The three billy goats Gruff* retold by Stephen Carpenter; ill. by reteller. HarperCollins, 1998. ISBN 978-0-694-01033-2 Subj: Animals – goats. Character traits – cleverness. Folk & fairy tales. Mythical creatures – trolls.

The three billy goats Gruff ill. by Paul Galdone. Seabury Pr., 1973. ISBN 978-0-8164-3080-2 Subj: Animals – goats. Character traits – cleverness. Cumulative tales. Folk & fairy tales. Mythical creatures – trolls.

The three billy goats Gruff retold by Glen Rounds; ill. by reteller. Holiday, 1993. ISBN 978-0-8234-1015-6 Subj: Animals – goats. Character traits – cleverness. Cumulative tales. Folk & fairy tales. Mythical creatures – trolls.

The three billy goats Gruff adapt. by Janet Stevens; ill. by adapter. Harcourt, 1987. ISBN 978-0-15-286396-8 Subj: Animals – goats. Character traits – cleverness. Cumulative tales. Folk & fairy tales. Mythical creatures – trolls.

The three Billygoats Gruff and Mean Calypso Joe (Youngquist, Cathrene Valente)

Who's that tripping over my bridge? (Salley, Coleen)

Asch, Devin. *Baby Duck's new friend* (Asch, Frank)

Like a windy day (Asch, Frank)

Asch, Frank. *Baby Bird's first nest* ill. by author. Harcourt, 1999. ISBN 978-0-15-201726-2 Subj: Animals – babies. Birds. Character traits – helpfulness. Frogs & toads.

Baby Duck's new friend by Frank Asch and Devin Asch ill. by authors. Harcourt, 2001. ISBN 978-0-15-202257-0 Subj: Birds – ducks. Character traits – confidence.

Barnyard lullaby ill. by author. Simon & Schuster, 1998. ISBN 978-0-689-81363-4 Subj: Animals. Careers – farmers. Lullabies. Music. Noise, sounds.

Bear shadow ill. by author. Prentice-Hall, 1985. ISBN 978-0-13-071580-7 Subj: Animals – bears. Shadows.

Bear's bargain ill. by author. Prentice-Hall, 1985. ISBN 978-0-13-071606-4 Subj: Animals – bears. Birds. Emotions – envy, jealousy.

The Daily Comet: boy saves Earth from giant octopus! ill. by Devin Asch. Kids Can, 2010. ISBN 978-1-55453-281-0 Subj: Activities – writing. Humorous stories.

The earth and I ill. by author. Gulliver, 1994. ISBN 978-0-15-200443-9 Subj: Earth. Nature.

Good night, Baby Bear ill. by author. Harcourt, 1998. ISBN 978-0-15-200836-9 Subj: Animals – bears. Bedtime. Family life. Seasons – winter. Sleep.

Goodbye house ill. by author. Prentice-Hall, 1986. ISBN 978-0-13-360272-2 Subj: Animals – bears. Family life. Moving.

Happy birthday, Big Bad Wolf ill. by author. Kids Can, 2011. ISBN 978-1-55337-368-1 Subj: Animals – pigs. Animals – wolves. Birthdays.

Happy birthday, moon! ill. by author. Prentice-Hall, 1982. ISBN 978-0-13-383687-5 Subj: Animals – bears. Birthdays. Moon.

Here comes the cat (Vagin, Vladimir)

Just like daddy ill. by author. Prentice-Hall, 1981. ISBN 978-0-13-514042-0 Subj: Animals – bears. Behavior – imitation. Family life – fathers.

The last puppy ill. by author. Prentice-Hall, 1980. ISBN 978-0-13-524058-8 Subj: Animals – dogs. Pets.

Like a windy day by Frank Asch and Devin Asch ill. by authors. Harcourt, 2002. ISBN 978-0-15-216376-1 Subj: Activities. Weather – wind.

Monsieur Saguette and his baguette ill. by author. Kids Can, 2004. ISBN 978-1-55337-461-9 Subj: Character traits – helpfulness. Food.

Moonbear ill. by author. Simon & Schuster, 1993. ISBN 978-0-671-86743-0 Subj: Animals – bears. Birds. Food. Moon. Night.

Moonbear's books ill. by author. Simon & Schuster, 1993. ISBN 978-0-671-86744-7 Subj: Animals – bears. Books, reading. Format, unusual – board books.

Moonbear's canoe ill. by author. Simon & Schuster, 1993. ISBN 978-0-671-86745-4 Subj: Animals – bears. Canoes & canoeing. Format, unusual – board books.

Moonbear's dream ill. by author. Simon & Schuster, 1999. ISBN 978-0-689-82244-5 Subj: Animals. Animals – bears. Behavior – misbehavior. Birds. Dreams.

Moonbear's friend ill. by author. Simon & Schuster, 1993. ISBN 978-0-671-86746-1 Subj: Animals – bears. Friendship.

Moonbear's pet ill. by author. Simon & Schuster, 1997. ISBN 978-0-689-80794-7 Subj: Animals – bears. Birds. Fish. Friendship. Frogs & toads.

Mooncake ill. by author. Prentice-Hall, 1983. ISBN 978-0-13-601013-5 Subj: Animals – bears. Birds. Moon. Seasons – winter.

Moondance ill. by author. Scholastic, 1993. ISBN 978-0-590-45487-2 Subj: Activities – dancing. Animals – bears. Moon.

Moongame ill. by author. Prentice-Hall, 1984. ISBN 978-0-13-600503-2 Subj: Activities – dancing. Animals – bears. Behavior – hiding. Moon.

Mr. Maxwell's mouse ill. by Devin Asch. Kids Can, 2004. ISBN 978-1-55337-486-2 Subj: Animals – cats. Animals – mice. Problem solving.

Mrs. Marlowe's mice ill. by Devin Asch. Kids Can, 2007. ISBN 978-1-55453-022-9 Subj: Animals – cats. Animals – mice. Behavior – secrets.

Popcorn ill. by author. Parents' Magazine Pr., 1979. ISBN 978-0-8193-1002-6 Subj: Animals – bears. Food. Holidays – Halloween. Parties.

Sand cake ill. by author. Parents' Magazine Pr., 1979. ISBN 978-0-8193-0986-0 Subj: Activities – picnicking. Animals – bears. Humorous stories. Sea & seashore.

Skyfire ill. by author. Simon & Schuster, 1988. ISBN 978-0-671-66692-7 Subj: Animals – bears. Weather – rainbows.

The sun is my favorite star ill. by author. Harcourt, 2000. ISBN 978-0-15-202127-6 Subj: Astronomy. Science. Sun.

Ziggy Piggy and the three little pigs ill. by author. Kids Can, 1998. ISBN 978-1-55074-515-3 Subj: Animals – pigs. Animals – wolves. Character traits – cleverness. Folk & fairy tales.

Ashburn, Boni. *Builder Goose: it's construction rhyme time!* ill. by Sergio De Giorgi. Sterling, 2012. ISBN 978-1-4027-7118-7 Subj: Careers – construction workers. Machines. Nursery rhymes. Trucks.

The fort that Jack built ill. by Brett Helquist. Abrams, 2013. ISBN 978-1-41970-795-7 Subj: Activities – playing. Family life. Imagination. Rhyming text.

I had a favorite dress ill. by Julia Denos. Abrams, 2011. ISBN 978-1-4197-0016-3 Subj: Activities – sewing. Clothing – dresses.

Over at the castle ill. by Kelly Murphy. Abrams, 2010. ISBN 978-0-8109-8414-1 Subj: Castles. Counting, numbers. Dragons. Middle Ages. Rhyming text. Songs.

Asher, Sandy. *Here comes Gosling!* ill. by Keith Graves. Philomel, 2009. ISBN 978-0-399-25085-9 Subj: Activities – picnicking. Animals. Babies. Birds – geese. Frogs & toads.

Stella's dancing days ill. by Kathryn Brown. Harcourt, 2001. ISBN 978-0-15-201613-5 Subj: Activities – dancing. Animals – cats.

Too many frogs! ill. by Keith Graves. Penguin, 2005. ISBN 978-0-399-23978-6 Subj: Animals – rabbits. Behavior – solitude. Frogs & toads.

What a party! ill. by Keith Graves. Penguin, 2007. ISBN 978-0-399-24496-4 Subj: Birthdays. Family life – grandfathers. Frogs & toads. Parties.

Ashforth, Camilla. *Willow at Christmas* ill. by author. Candlewick, 2002. ISBN 978-0-7636-1850-6 Subj: Farms. Holidays – Christmas. Toys – bears.

Willow by the sea ill. by author. Candlewick, 2002. ISBN 978-0-7636-1401-0 Subj: Animals. Sea & seashore. Toys – bears.

Willow on the river ill. by author. Candlewick, 2002. ISBN 978-0-7636-1088-3 Subj: Activities – picnicking. Rivers. Toys – bears.

Ashley Bryan's ABC of African American poetry ill. by Ashley Bryan. Atheneum, 1997. ISBN 978-0-689-81209-5 Subj: ABC books. Ethnic groups in the U.S. – African Americans. Poetry.

Ashman, Linda. *Babies on the go* ill. by Jane Dyer. Harcourt, 2003. ISBN 978-0-15-201894-8 Subj: Animals – babies. Rhyming text.

Babies on the go [board book] ill. by Jane Dyer. Harcourt, 2007. ISBN 978-0-15-205886-9 Subj: Animals – babies. Format, unusual – board books. Rhyming text.

Castles, caves, and honeycombs ill. by Lauren Stringer. Harcourt, 2001. ISBN 978-0-15-202211-2 Subj: Animals. Homes, houses. Rhyming text.

Creaky old house: a topsy-turvy tale of a real fixer-upper ill. by Michael Chesworth. Sterling, 2009. ISBN 978-1-4027-4461-7 Subj: Family life. Homes, houses. Rhyming text.

Desmond and the naughtybugs ill. by Anik McCrory. Penguin, 2006. ISBN 978-0-525-47203-2 Subj: Behavior – misbehavior.

The essential worldwide monster guide ill. by David Small. Simon & Schuster, 2003. ISBN 978-0-689-82640-5 Subj: Monsters. Mythical creatures. Poetry.

How to make a night ill. by Tricia Tusa. HarperCollins, 2004. ISBN 978-0-06-029014-6 Subj: Bedtime. Night. Rhyming text.

Just another morning ill. by Claudio Muñoz. HarperCollins, 2004. ISBN 978-0-06-029054-2 Subj: Day. Imagination. Rhyming text.

M is for mischief: an A to Z of naughty children ill. by Nancy Carpenter. Dutton, 2008. ISBN 978-0-525-47564-4 Subj: ABC books. Behavior – misbehavior. Rhyming text.

Mama's day ill. by Jan Ormerod. Simon & Schuster, 2006. ISBN 978-0-689-83475-2 Subj: Babies. Family life – mothers. Rhyming text.

Maxwell's magic mix-up ill. by Regan Dunnick. Simon & Schuster, 2001. ISBN 978-0-689-83178-2 Subj: Birthdays. Careers – magicians. Parties. Rhyming text.

No dogs allowed ill. by Kristin Sorra. Sterling, 2011. ISBN 978-1-4027-5837-9 Subj: Pets. Restaurants. Signs & signboards.

Rain! ill. by Christian Robinson. Harcourt, 2013. ISBN 978-0-547-73395-1 Subj: Activities – playing. Weather – rain.

Samantha on a roll ill. by Christine Davenier. Farrar, 2011. ISBN 978-0-374-36399-4 Subj: Rhyming text. Sports – roller skating.

Starry safari ill. by Jeff Mack. Harcourt, 2005. ISBN 978-0-15-204766-5 Subj: Bedtime. Jungle. Rhyming text.

Stella, unleashed: notes from the doghouse ill. by Paul Meisel. Sterling, 2008. ISBN 978-1-4027-3987-3 Subj: Animals – dogs. Family life. Rhyming text.

The tale of Wagmore Gently ill. by John Bendall-Brunello. Dutton, 2002. ISBN 978-0-525-46916-2 Subj: Anatomy – tails. Animals – dogs.

To the beach! ill. by Nadine Bernard Westcott. Harcourt, 2005. ISBN 978-0-15-216490-4 Subj: Behavior – forgetfulness. Family life. Humorous stories. Rhyming text. Sea & seashore – beaches.

What could be better than this ill. by Linda S. Wingerter. Penguin, 2006. ISBN 978-0-525-46954-4 Subj: Emotions – love. Family life – parents.

When I was king ill. by David McPhail. HarperCollins, 2008. ISBN 978-0-06-029051-1 Subj: Babies. Family life – new sibling. Rhyming text.

Asim, Jabari. *Daddy goes to work* ill. by Aaron Boyd. Little, Brown, 2006. ISBN 978-0-316-73575-9 Subj: Activities – working. Ethnic groups in the U.S. – African Americans. Family life – fathers. Rhyming text.

Fifty cents and a dream: young Booker T. Washington ill. by Bryan Collier. Little, Brown, 2012. ISBN 978-0-316-08657-8 Subj: Behavior – seeking better things. Books, reading. Character traits – perseverance. Ethnic groups in the U.S. – African Americans. Prejudice. School. Slavery.

Aska, Warabe. *Tapicero tap tap* ill. by author. Tundra, 2006. ISBN 978-0-88776-760-9 Subj: Activities – storytelling. Character traits – ambition. Family life – grandfathers. Foreign lands – Spain.

Askani, Tanja. *A friend like you* ill. by author. Scholastic, 2009. ISBN 978-0-545-05851-3 Subj: Animals. Friendship.

Asper-Smith, Sarah. *I would tuck you in* ill. by Mitchell Watley. Sasquatch, 2012. ISBN 978-1-57061-844-4 Subj: Animals – babies. Bedtime.

Aston, Claire. *Wild West* ill. by Mark Stacey. Barron's, 2001. ISBN 978-0-7641-5312-9 Subj: U.S. history – frontier & pioneer life.

Aston, Dianna Hutts. *A butterfly is patient* ill. by Sylvia Long. Chronicle, 2011. ISBN 978-0-8118-6479-4 Subj: Insects – butterflies, caterpillars. Metamorphosis.

An egg is quiet ill. by Sylvia Long. Chronicle, 2006. ISBN 978-0-8118-4428-4 Subj: Eggs.

Loony Little ill. by Kelly Murphy. Candlewick, 2003. ISBN 978-0-7636-1682-3 Subj: Animals. Behavior – gossip. Birds – loons. Cumulative tales. Foreign lands – Arctic.

Mama Outside, Mama Inside ill. by Susan Gaber. Holt, 2006. ISBN 978-0-8050-7716-2 Subj: Babies. Birds. Birth. Family life – mothers.

The moon over Star ill. by Jerry Pinkney. Dial, 2008. ISBN 978-0-8037-3107-3 Subj: Ethnic groups in the U.S. – African Americans. Space & space ships. U.S. history.

Not so tall for six ill. by Frank W. Dormer. Charlesbridge, 2008. ISBN 978-1-57091-705-9 Subj: Behavior – bullying, teasing. Character traits – kindness. Character traits – smallness. School.

An orange in January ill. by Julie Maren. Penguin, 2007. ISBN 978-0-8037-3146-2 Subj: Food. Trees.

A rock is lively ill. by Sylvia Long. Chronicle, 2012. ISBN 978-1-4521-0645-8 Subj: Rocks.

A seed is sleepy ill. by Sylvia Long. Chronicle, 2007. ISBN 978-0-8118-5520-4 Subj: Seeds.

Atkins, Jeannine. *Mary Anning and the sea dragon* ill. by Michael Dooling. Farrar, 1999. ISBN 978-0-374-34840-3 Subj: Careers – paleontologists. Dinosaurs. Dragons. Foreign lands – England. Fossils. Science.

Robin's home ill. by Candace Whitman. Farrar, 2001. ISBN 978-0-374-36337-6 Subj: Behavior – growing up. Birds – robins.

Atwell, Debby. *Barn* ill. by author. Houghton, 1996. ISBN 978-0-395-78568-3 Subj: Barns.

Pearl ill. by author. Houghton, 2001. ISBN 978-0-395-88416-4 Subj: Family life. U.S. history.

River ill. by author. Houghton, 1999. ISBN 978-0-395-93546-0 Subj: Ecology. Rivers. Water.

The Thanksgiving door ill. by author. Houghton, 2003. ISBN 978-0-618-24036-4 Subj: Holidays – Thanksgiving. Immigrants.

Atwood, Margaret. *Up in the tree* ill. by author. Groundwood, 2006. ISBN 978-0-88899-729-6 Subj: Trees.

Auch, Herm. *Beauty and the beaks: a turkey's cautionary tale* (Auch, Mary Jane)

Chickerella (Auch, Mary Jane)

The plot chickens (Auch, Mary Jane)

Poultrygeist (Auch, Mary Jane)

The princess and the pizza (Auch, Mary Jane)

Souperchicken (Auch, Mary Jane)

Auch, Mary Jane. *Bantam of the opera* ill. by author. Holiday, 1997. ISBN 978-0-8234-1312-6 Subj: Activities – singing. Birds – chickens. Humorous stories.

Beauty and the beaks: a turkey's cautionary tale by Mary Jane Auch and Herm Auch ill. by authors. Holiday House, 2007. ISBN 978-0-8234-1990-6 Subj: Behavior – boasting. Birds – chickens. Birds – turkeys. Holidays – Thanksgiving.

Chickerella by Mary Jane Auch and Herm Auch ill. by authors. Holiday House, 2005. ISBN

978-0-8234-1804-6 Subj: Birds – chickens. Folk & fairy tales. Humorous stories.

The Easter egg farm ill. by author. Holiday, 1992. ISBN 978-0-8234-0917-4 Subj: Birds – chickens. Eggs. Holidays – Easter.

Eggs mark the spot ill. by author. Holiday, 1996. ISBN 978-0-8234-1242-6 Subj: Art. Birds – chickens. Crime. Eggs.

Hen lake ill. by author. Holiday, 1995. ISBN 978-0-8234-1188-7 Subj: Activities – dancing. Ballet. Birds – chickens. Birds – peacocks, peahens.

The nutquacker ill. by author. Holiday, 1999. ISBN 978-0-8234-1524-3 Subj: Animals. Birds – ducks. Farms. Holidays – Christmas.

Peeping Beauty ill. by author. Holiday, 1993. ISBN 978-0-8234-1001-9 Subj: Activities – dancing. Animals – foxes. Ballet. Birds – chickens.

The plot chickens by Mary Jane Auch and Herm Auch ill. by authors. Holiday House, 2009. ISBN 978-0-8234-2087-2 Subj: Activities – writing. Birds – chickens. Books, reading. Humorous stories.

Poultrygeist by Mary Jane Auch and Herm Auch ill. by authors. Holiday, 2003. ISBN 978-0-8234-1756-8 Subj: Animals. Behavior. Birds – chickens. Ghosts. Holidays – Halloween.

The princess and the pizza by Mary Jane Auch and Herm Auch ill. by Herm Auch. Holiday, 2002. ISBN 978-0-8234-1683-7 Subj: Activities – baking, cooking. Folk & fairy tales. Food. Humorous stories. Royalty – princesses.

Souperchicken by Mary Jane Auch and Herm Auch ill. by authors. Holiday, 2003. ISBN 978-0-8234-1704-9 Subj: Animals. Birds – chickens. Books, reading.

Audet, Martine. *Martin on the moon* ill. by Luc Melanson. Owlkids, 2012. ISBN 978-1-926973-16-6 Subj: Imagination. School – first day.

Auerbach, Annie. *Splat the cat: on with the show* (Scotton, Rob)

Augustin, Barbara. *Antonella and her Santa Claus* ill. by Gerhard Lahr. Kane/Miller, 2001. ISBN 978-1-929132-13-3 Subj: Letters, cards. Santa Claus. Toys – balloons.

Aulaire, Edgar Parin d'. *Abraham Lincoln* (Aulaire, Ingri Mortenson d')

Aulaire, Ingri Mortenson d'. *Abraham Lincoln* by Ingri Mortenson d' Aulaire and Edgar Parin d' Aulaire ill. by Ingri d' Aulaire and Edgar Parin d' Aulaire. Rev. ed. Doubleday, 1957. ISBN 978-0-385-07674-6 Subj: Caldecott award books. U.S. history.

Auld, Mary. *Daniel in the lions' den* ill. by Diana Mayo. Simon & Schuster, 1999. ISBN 978-0-531-14514-2 Subj: Animals – lions. Religion – Daniel.

David and Goliath ill. by Diana Mayo. Watts, 2000. ISBN 978-0-531-14522-7 Subj: Foreign lands – Israel. Giants. Religion – David.

Exodus from Egypt ill. by Diana Mayo. Watts, 2000. ISBN 978-0-531-14585-2 Subj: Foreign lands – Egypt. Religion – Moses.

My aunt and uncle ill. with photos. G. Stevens, 2004. ISBN 978-0-8368-3923-4 Subj: Family life. Family life – aunts, uncles.

My brother ill. with photos. G. Stevens, 2004. ISBN 978-0-8368-3924-1 Subj: Family life. Family life – brothers.

My dad ill. with photos. G. Stevens, 2004. ISBN 978-0-8368-3925-8 Subj: Family life. Family life – fathers.

My grandparents ill. with photos. G. Stevens, 2004. ISBN 978-0-8368-3926-5 Subj: Family life. Family life – grandparents.

My mom ill. with photos. G. Stevens, 2004. ISBN 978-0-8368-3927-2 Subj: Family life. Family life – mothers.

My sister ill. with photos. G. Stevens, 2004. ISBN 978-0-8368-3928-9 Subj: Family life. Family life – sisters.

Noah's ark ill. by Diana Mayo. Watts, 2000. ISBN 978-0-531-14523-4 Subj: Animals. Boats, ships. Religion – Noah. Weather – floods. Weather – rain. Weather – rainbows.

The story of Jonah ill. by Diana Mayo. Watts, 1999. ISBN 978-0-531-14517-3 Subj: Animals – whales. Religion – Jonah.

Austin, Heather. *Visiting Aunt Sylvia's: a Maine adventure* ill. by author. Down East, 2002. ISBN 978-0-89272-523-6 Subj: Family life – aunts, uncles. Seasons.

Austin, Margot. *A friend for Growl Bear* ill. by David McPhail. HarperCollins, 1999. ISBN 978-0-06-027802-1 Subj: Animals. Animals – bears. Behavior – needing someone.

Austin, Mike. *Countdown with Milo* ill. by author. Blue Apple, 2012. ISBN 978-1-60905-208-9 Subj: Animals – cats. Animals – mice. Counting, numbers. Format, unusual – board books. Space & space ships.

Monsters love colors ill. by author. HarperCollins, 2013. ISBN 978-0-06-212594-1 Subj: Concepts – color. Monsters.

Austin, Patricia. *The cat who loved Mozart* ill. by Henri Sorensen. Holiday, 2001. ISBN 978-0-8234-

1535-9 Subj: Animals – cats. Music. Musical instruments – pianos.

Autry, Gene. *Here comes Santa Claus* by Gene Autry and Oakley Haldeman ill. by Bruce Whatley. Words & music by Gene Autry & Oakley Haldeman. HarperCollins, 2002. ISBN 978-0-06-028269-1 Subj: Animals – dogs. Holidays – Christmas. Music. Santa Claus. Songs.

Averbeck, Jim. *Except if* ill. by author. Simon & Schuster, 2011. ISBN 978-1-4169-9544-9 Subj: Animals. Eggs.

In a blue room ill. by Tricia Tusa. Harcourt, 2008. ISBN 978-0-15-205992-7 Subj: Bedtime. Concepts – color.

The market bowl ill. by author. Charlesbridge, 2013. ISBN 978-1-58089-368-8 Subj: Activities – baking, cooking. Food. Foreign lands – Cameroon. Stores.

Oh no, Little Dragon! ill. by author. Atheneum, 2012. ISBN 978-1-4169-9545-6 Subj: Activities – bathing. Dragons. Family life – mothers.

Avi. *Silent movie* ill. by C. B. Mordan. Atheneum, 2003. ISBN 978-0-689-84145-3 Subj: Immigrants. Theater.

Avraham, Kate Aver. *What will you be, Sara Mee?* ill. by Anne Sibley O'Brien. Charlesbridge, 2010. ISBN 978-1-58089-210-0 Subj: Birthdays. Ethnic groups in the U.S. – Korean Americans. Family life. Parties.

Awdry, W. *Happy birthday, Thomas!* ill. by Owain Bell. Based on The Railway Series. Random House, 2003. ISBN 978-0-679-90809-8 Subj: Birthdays. Parties. Trains.

Axelrod, Amy. *Pigs in the corner: fun with math and dance* ill. by Sharon McGinley-Nally. Simon & Schuster, 2001. ISBN 978-0-689-82470-8 Subj: Activities – dancing. Animals – pigs.

Pigs in the pantry: fun with math and cooking ill. by Sharon McGinley-Nally. Simon & Schuster, 1997. ISBN 978-0-689-80665-0 Subj: Activities – baking, cooking. Animals – pigs. Counting, numbers. Food.

Pigs on a blanket ill. by Sharon McGinley-Nally. Simon & Schuster, 1996. ISBN 978-0-689-80505-9 Subj: Animals – pigs. Behavior – promptness, tardiness. Clocks, watches. Sea & seashore. Time.

Pigs on the ball: fun with math and sports ill. by Sharon McGinley-Nally. Simon & Schuster, 1998. ISBN 978-0-689-81565-2 Subj: Animals – pigs. Concepts – shape. Counting, numbers. Family life. Sports.

Pigs on the move: fun with math and travel ill. by Sharon McGinley-Nally. Simon & Schuster, 1999. ISBN 978-0-689-81070-1 Subj: Activities – traveling. Animals – pigs. Concepts – distance. Concepts – measurement. Holidays – Christmas.

Pigs will be pigs ill. by Sharon McGinley-Nally. Four Winds, 1994. ISBN 978-0-02-765415-8 Subj: Animals – pigs. Family life. Food. Money.

They'll believe me when I'm gone ill. by Jack E. Davis. Dutton, 2003. ISBN 978-0-525-46660-4 Subj: Family life. Humorous stories. Space & space ships.

Aylesworth, Jim. *The burger and the hot dog* ill. by Stephen Gammell. Atheneum, 2001. ISBN 978-0-689-83897-2 Subj: Food. Poetry.

Cock-a-doodle-doo, creak, pop-pop, moo ill. by Brad Sneed. Holiday House, 2012. ISBN 978-0-8234-2356-9 Subj: Animals. Farms. Noise, sounds. Rhyming text.

The completed hickory dickory dock ill. by Eileen Christelow. Macmillan, 1990. ISBN 978-0-689-31606-7 Subj: Animals – mice. Clocks, watches. Counting, numbers. Nursery rhymes. Time.

Country crossing ill. by Ted Rand. Macmillan, 1991. ISBN 978-0-689-31580-0 Subj: Noise, sounds. Trains.

The folks in the valley ill. by Stefano Vitale. HarperCollins, 1992. ISBN 978-0-06-021929-1 Subj: ABC books. Rhyming text.

The full belly bowl ill. by Wendy Anderson Halperin. Atheneum, 1998. ISBN 978-0-689-81033-6 Subj: Folk & fairy tales. Magic.

Little Bitty Mousie ill. by Michael Hague. Walker, 2007. ISBN 978-0-8027-9637-0 Subj: ABC books. Animals – mice. Rhyming text.

The mitten ill. by Barbara McClintock. Scholastic, 2009. ISBN 978-0-439-92544-0 Subj: Animals. Behavior – lost & found possessions. Folk & fairy tales. Foreign lands – Ukraine.

Mother Halverson's new cat ill. by Toni Goffe. Macmillan, 1989. ISBN 978-0-689-31465-0 Subj: Animals – cats. Character traits – practicality.

My sister's rusty bike ill. by Richard Hull. Atheneum, 1996. ISBN 978-0-689-31798-9 Subj: Activities – traveling. Rhyming text. Sports – bicycling. Tall tales.

Old Black Fly ill. by Stephen Gammell. Holt, 1992. ISBN 978-0-8050-1401-3 Subj: ABC books. Insects – flies. Rhyming text.

One crow: a counting rhyme ill. by Ruth Young. HarperCollins, 1988. ISBN 978-0-397-32175-9 Subj: Animals. Counting, numbers. Farms. Rhyming text.

Our Abe Lincoln ill. by Barbara McClintock. Scholastic, 2009. ISBN 978-0-439-92548-8 Subj: Songs. U.S. history.

Teddy bear tears ill. by Jo Ellen McAllister Stammen. Atheneum, 1997. ISBN 978-0-689-31776-7 Subj: Bedtime. Emotions – fear. Toys – bears.

Two terrible frights ill. by Eileen Christelow. Atheneum, 1987. ISBN 978-0-689-31327-1 Subj: Animals – mice. Emotions – fear. Night.

Ayres, Katherine. *Matthew's truck* ill. by Hideko Takahashi. Candlewick, 2005. ISBN 978-0-7636-2269-5 Subj: Activities – playing. Toys. Trucks.

Up, down, and around ill. by Nadine Bernard Westcott. Candlewick, 2007. ISBN 978-0-7636-2378-4 Subj: Gardens, gardening. Language. Rhyming text.

Azarian, Mary. *A gardener's alphabet* ill. by author. Houghton, 2000. ISBN 978-0-618-03380-5 Subj: ABC books. Gardens, gardening. Language. Plants.

Azore, Barbara. *Wanda and the frogs* ill. by Georgia Graham. Tundra, 2007. ISBN 978-0-88776-761-6 Subj: Frogs & toads. Humorous stories.

Wanda and the wild hair ill. by Georgia Graham. Tundra, 2005. ISBN 978-0-88776-717-3 Subj: Animals. Character traits – individuality. Cumulative tales. Hair.

Baasansuren, Bolormaa. *My little round house* by Bolormaa Baasansuren and Helen Mixter ill. by Bolormaa Baasansuren. Groundwood, 2009. ISBN 978-0-88899-934-4 Subj: Foreign lands – Mongolia. Nomads.

Baby animals ill. with photos. DK, 2003. ISBN 978-0-7894-9750-5 Subj: Animals – babies. Format, unusual – toy & movable books. Science.

Baby animals at the zoo. Kingfisher, 2012. ISBN 978-0-7534-6690-2 Subj: Animals – babies. Format, unusual – board books. Zoos.

Babypants, Caspar. *Augie to zebra: an alphabet book!* ill. by Kate Endle. Sasquatch, 2012. ISBN 978-1-57061-750-8 Subj: ABC books. Animals.

Bachelet, Gilles. *My cat, the silliest cat in the world* ill. by author. Abrams, 2006. ISBN 978-0-8109-4913-3 Subj: Animals – elephants. Humorous stories. Pets.

When the silliest cat was small ill. by author. Abrams, 2007. ISBN 978-0-8109-9415-7 Subj: Animals – elephants. Humorous stories. Pets.

Back, Rachel Tzvia. *The perfect purple feather* (Piven, Hanoch)

Backker, Vera de. *Coco the koala* ill. by author. G. Stevens, 2000. ISBN 978-0-8368-2729-3 Subj: Animals – koalas. Self-concept.

Backx, Patsy. *Josie and Mr. Fernandez* ill. by author. G. Stevens, 2002. ISBN 978-0-8368-3079-8 Subj: Animals – dogs. Behavior – sharing. Food.

Skippy and Jack ill. by author. G. Stevens, 2002. ISBN 978-0-8368-3080-4 Subj: Activities – dancing. Animals – dogs. Rhyming text.

Baddiel, Ivor. *Cock-a-doodle quack! Quack!* by Ivor Baddiel and Sophie Jubb ill. by Ailie Busby. Random House, 2007. ISBN 978-0-385-75104-9 Subj: Animals. Animals – babies. Birds – chickens. Farms. Noise, sounds.

Badescu, Ramona. *Big Rabbit's bad mood* ill. by Delphine Durand. Chronicle, 2009. ISBN 978-0-8118-6666-8 Subj: Animals. Animals – rabbits. Behavior – bad day. Birthdays.

Pomelo begins to grow ill. by Benjamin Chaud. Enchanted Lion, 2011. ISBN 978-1-59270-111-7 Subj: Animals – elephants. Behavior – growing up.

Pomelo's opposites ill. by Benjamin Chaud. Enchanted Lion, 2013. ISBN 978-1-59270-132-2 Subj: Animals – elephants. Concepts – opposites.

Bae, Hyun-Joo. *New clothes for New Year's day* ill. by author. Kane/Miller, 2007. ISBN 978-1-933605-29-6 Subj: Clothing. Foreign lands – Korea. Holidays – New Year's.

Baehr, Patricia. *Boo Cow* ill. by Margot Apple. Charlesbridge, 2010. ISBN 978-1-58089-108-0 Subj: Animals – bulls, cows. Birds – chickens. Ghosts.

Baek, Matthew J. *Be gentle with the dog, dear* ill. by author. Dial, 2008. ISBN 978-0-8037-3250-6 Subj: Animals – dogs. Babies. Behavior – misbehavior. Character traits – kindness to animals.

Panda and polar bear ill. by author. Dial, 2009. ISBN 978-0-8037-3359-6 Subj: Animals – pandas. Animals – polar bears. Character traits – being different.

Baer, Edith. *This is the way we go to school* ill. by Steve Björkman. Scholastic, 1990. ISBN 978-0-590-43161-3 Subj: Rhyming text. School. Transportation.

Baer, Gene. *Thump thump rat-a-tat-tat* ill. by Lois Ehlert. HarperCollins, 1989. ISBN 978-0-06-

020362-7 Subj: Music. Musical instruments – bands. Parades.

Baeten, Lieve. *The clever little witch* ill. by Wietse Fossey. NorthSouth, 2012. ISBN 978-0-7358-4079-9 Subj: Format, unusual. Magic. Witches.

The curious little witch. NorthSouth, 2010. ISBN 978-0-7358-2305-1 Subj: Format, unusual. Witches.

Happy birthday, Little Witch! ill. by author. NorthSouth, 2011. ISBN 978-0-7358-4043-0 Subj: Animals – cats. Behavior – lost. Birthdays. Format, unusual – toy & movable books. Witches.

Bagert, Brod. *Giant children* ill. by Tedd Arnold. Dial, 2002. ISBN 978-0-8037-2556-0 Subj: Poetry.

Shout! little poems that roar ill. by Sachiko Yoshikawa. Penguin, 2007. ISBN 978-0-8037-2972-8 Subj: Poetry.

Baguley, Elizabeth. *A long way from home* ill. by Jane Chapman. Tiger Tales, 2008. ISBN 978-1-58925-074-1 Subj: Animals – rabbits. Bedtime. Behavior – dissatisfaction.

Meggie moon ill. by Gregoire Mabire. Good Books, 2005. ISBN 978-1-56148-474-4 Subj: Activities – playing. Gender roles. Imagination.

Bahr, Mary. *My brother loved snowflakes* ill. by Laura Jacobsen. Boyds Mills, 2002. ISBN 978-1-56397-689-6 Subj: Careers – meteorologists. Careers – photographers. Weather – snow.

Baicker, Karen. *Pea pod babies* ill. by Sam Williams. Handprint, 2003. ISBN 978-1-59354-003-6 Subj: Babies. Character traits – individuality. Gardens, gardening. Rhyming text.

You can do it too! ill. by Ken Wilson-Max. Handprint, 2005. ISBN 978-1-59354-080-7 Subj: Ethnic groups in the U.S. – African Americans. Family life – brothers & sisters. Rhyming text.

Bailey, Linda. *The best figure skater in the whole wide world* ill. by Alan Daniel and Lea Daniel. Kids Can, 2001. ISBN 978-1-55074-879-6 Subj: Sports – ice skating.

The farm team ill. by Bill Slavin. Kids Can, 2006. ISBN 978-1-55337-850-1 Subj: Animals. Behavior – cheating. Character traits – bravery. Farms. Sports – hockey.

Goodnight, sweet pig ill. by Josée Masse. Kids Can, 2006. ISBN 978-1-55337-844-0 Subj: Animals – pigs. Bedtime. Counting, numbers. Rhyming text.

Stanley at sea ill. by Bill Slavin. Kids Can, 2008. ISBN 978-1-55453-193-6 Subj: Activities – traveling. Animals – dogs. Sea & seashore.

Stanley's beauty contest ill. by Bill Slavin. Kids Can, 2009. ISBN 978-1-55453-318-3 Subj: Animals – dogs. Contests.

Stanley's little sister ill. by Bill Slavin. Kids Can, 2010. ISBN 978-1-55453-487-6 Subj: Animals – cats. Animals – dogs. Friendship.

Stanley's party ill. by Bill Slavin. Kids Can, 2003. ISBN 978-1-55337-382-7 Subj: Animals – dogs. Parties.

Stanley's wild ride ill. by Bill Slavin. Kids Can, 2006. ISBN 978-1-55337-960-7 Subj: Animals – dogs. Behavior – running away.

Toads on toast ill. by Colin Jack. Kids Can, 2012. ISBN 978-1-55453-662-7 Subj: Activities – baking, cooking. Animals – foxes. Food. Frogs & toads.

Bailey, Mary Bryant. *Jeoffry's Christmas* ill. by Elizabeth Sayles. Farrar, 2002. ISBN 978-0-374-33676-9 Subj: Animals – cats. Holidays – Christmas. Rhyming text. Santa Claus. Trees.

Baillie, Allan. *Dragonquest* ill. by Wayne Harris. Candlewick, 2013. ISBN 978-0-7636-6617-0 Subj: Activities – traveling. Dragons. Knights.

Baillie, Marilyn. *Nose to toes* ill. by Marisol Sarrazin. Boyds Mills, 2001. ISBN 978-1-56397-319-2 Subj: Activities – playing. Animals. Imagination. Rhyming text.

Small wonders: baby animals in the wild ill. by Romi Caron. Maple Tree, 2006. ISBN 978-1-987066-72-0 Subj: Animals – babies.

Bair, Sheila. *Isabel's car wash* ill. by Judy Stead. Whitman, 2008. ISBN 978-0-8075-3652-0 Subj: Activities – working. Automobiles. Counting, numbers. Money.

Baird, Audrey B. *A cold snap! frosty poems* ill. by Patrick O'Brien. Wordsong, 2002. ISBN 978-1-56397-633-9 Subj: Poetry. Seasons – winter. Weather.

Storm coming! ill. by Patrick O'Brien. Wordsong, 2001. ISBN 978-1-56397-887-6 Subj: Poetry. Weather – rain. Weather – storms.

Baker, Alan. *Black and White Rabbit's ABC* ill. by author. Kingfisher, 1994. ISBN 978-1-85697-851-4 Subj: ABC books. Activities – painting. Animals – rabbits. Cumulative tales.

Brown Rabbit's shape book ill. by author. Kingfisher, 1994. ISBN 978-1-85697-950-4 Subj: Animals – rabbits. Concepts – shape. Toys – balloons.

Gray Rabbit's one, two, three ill. by author. Kingfisher, 1994. ISBN 978-1-85697-952-8 Subj: Animals. Animals – rabbits. Counting, numbers.

Little Rabbit's first number book ill. by author. Kingfisher, 1998. ISBN 978-0-7534-5167-0 Subj: Animals – rabbits. Counting, numbers.

Little Rabbit's first word book ill. by author. Kingfisher, 1996. ISBN 978-0-7534-5020-8 Subj: Animals – rabbits. Language.

White Rabbit's color book ill. by author. Kingfisher, 1994. ISBN 978-1-85697-953-5 Subj: Activities – painting. Animals – rabbits. Concepts – color.

Baker, Jeannie. *The hidden forest* ill. by author. Greenwillow, 2000. ISBN 978-0-688-15760-9 Subj: Foreign lands – Tasmania. Plants. Sea & seashore. Sports – skin diving.

Mirror ill. by author. Candlewick, 2010. ISBN 978-0-7636-4848-0 Subj: Foreign lands – Australia. Foreign lands – Morocco. Format, unusual – toy & movable books. Mirrors. Shopping. Wordless.

The story of rosy dock ill. by author. Greenwillow, 1995. ISBN 978-0-688-11493-0 Subj: Ecology. Foreign lands – Australia. Plants.

Where the forest meets the sea ill. by author. Greenwillow, 1988. ISBN 978-0-688-06364-1 Subj: Ecology. Foreign lands – Australia. Forest, woods.

Window ill. by author. Greenwillow, 1991. ISBN 978-0-688-08918-4 Subj: Ecology. Foreign lands – Australia. Wordless.

Baker, Keith. *Hickory dickory dock* ill. by author. Harcourt, 2007. ISBN 978-0-15-205818-0 Subj: Animals – mice. Clocks, watches. Time.

Just how long can a long string be?! ill. by author. Scholastic, 2009. ISBN 978-0-545-08661-5 Subj: Birds. Insects – ants. Rhyming text. String.

LMNO peas ill. by author. Simon & Schuster, 2010. ISBN 978-1-4169-9141-0 Subj: ABC books. Careers. Food.

My octopus arms ill. by author. Simon & Schuster, 2013. ISBN 978-1-4424-5843-7 Subj: Anatomy. Octopuses. Rhyming text.

No two alike ill. by author. Simon & Schuster, 2011. ISBN 978-1-4424-1742-7 Subj: Birds. Character traits – individuality. Rhyming text. Seasons – winter.

1-2-3 peas ill. by author. Simon & Schuster, 2012. ISBN 978-1-4424-4551-2 Subj: Counting, numbers. Food. Rhyming text.

Potato Joe ill. by author. Harcourt, 2008. ISBN 978-0-15-206230-9 Subj: Counting, numbers. Nursery rhymes.

Baker, Ken. *Brave little monster* ill. by Geoffrey Hayes. HarperCollins, 2001. ISBN 978-0-06-028699-6 Subj: Bedtime. Emotions – fear. Monsters. Night.

Old MacDonald had a dragon ill. by Christopher Santoro. Amazon, 2012. ISBN 978-0-7614-6175-3 Subj: Animals. Careers – farmers. Cumulative tales. Dragons. Farms. Songs.

Baker, Leslie A. *You bad dog!* ill. by author. Dutton, 2003. ISBN 978-0-525-47127-1 Subj: Activities – playing. Animals – dogs. Behavior – misbehavior.

Baker, Liza. *Dinosaur days* color by Sharon Matsumoto; ill. by Andy Chiang. HarperCollins, 2003. ISBN 978-0-06-000541-2 Subj: Activities – drawing. Dinosaurs. Jungle.

I love you because you're you ill. by David McPhail. Scholastic, 2001. ISBN 978-0-439-20638-9 Subj: Animals – foxes. Emotions – love. Family life – mothers. Rhyming text.

Baker, Olaf. *Where the buffaloes begin* ill. by Stephen Gammell. Warne, 1981. ISBN 978-0-670-82760-2 Subj: Animals – buffaloes. Caldecott award honor books. Folk & fairy tales. Indians of North America.

Baker, Roberta. *No ordinary Olive* ill. by Debbie Tilley. Little, 2002. ISBN 978-0-316-07336-3 Subj: Character traits – individuality. Family life – daughters. Family life – parents. Imagination.

Olive's first sleepover ill. by Debbie Tilley. Little, Brown, 2007. ISBN 978-0-316-73418-9 Subj: Bedtime. Emotions – fear. Friendship. Sleep.

Olive's pirate party ill. by Debbie Tilley. Little, Brown, 2005. ISBN 978-0-316-16792-5 Subj: Birthdays. Family life – aunts, uncles. Parties. Pirates.

Balcziak, Bill. *John Henry* ill. by Drew Rose. Compass Point, 2003. ISBN 978-0-7565-0457-1 Subj: Character traits – perseverance. Character traits – pride. Ethnic groups in the U.S. – African Americans. Folk & fairy tales. Tall tales.

Paul Bunyan ill. by Patrick Girouard. Compass Point, 2003. ISBN 978-0-7565-0459-5 Subj: Animals – oxen. Careers – lumberjacks. Tall tales. U.S. history – frontier & pioneer life.

Pecos Bill ill. by Roberta Collier-Morales. Compass Point, 2003. ISBN 978-0-7565-0460-1 Subj: Cowboys, cowgirls. Tall tales. U.S. history – frontier & pioneer life.

Balducci, Rita. *Little Bear's timeless tales* ill. by Amy Flynn. Reader's Digest, 2003. ISBN 978-0-7944-0215-0 Subj: Folk & fairy tales.

Balian, Lorna. *Bah! Humbug?* ill. by author. Abingdon, 1977. ISBN 978-0-687-02345-5 Subj: Holidays – Christmas.

Humbug rabbit ill. by author. Abingdon, 1974. ISBN 978-1-932065-40-4 Subj: Animals – rabbits. Eggs. Family life – grandmothers. Holidays – Easter.

Humbug witch ill. by author. Abingdon, 1965. ISBN 978-1-881772-24-8 Subj: Holidays – Halloween. Witches.

Leprechauns never lie ill. by author. Abingdon, 1980. ISBN 978-0-687-21371-9 Subj: Animals – cats. Folk & fairy tales. Foreign lands – Ireland. Humorous stories. Mythical creatures – leprechauns.

Mother's Mother's Day ill. by author. Abingdon, 1982. ISBN 978-0-685-57645-8 Subj: Animals – mice. Family life – mothers. Holidays – Mother's Day.

Sometimes it's turkey ill. by author. Abingdon, 1973. ISBN 978-0-687-39074-8 Subj: Birds – turkeys. Holidays – Thanksgiving.

A sweetheart for Valentine ill. by author. Abingdon, 1987. ISBN 978-0-687-40771-2 Subj: Giants. Holidays – Valentine's Day. Weddings.

Ballard, Robin. *I used to be the baby* ill. by author. Greenwillow, 2002. ISBN 978-0-06-029586-8 Subj: Babies. Family life – brothers.

My day, your day ill. by author. Greenwillow, 2001. ISBN 978-0-688-17796-6 Subj: Activities – working. Day. Family life – parents. School.

Tonight and tomorrow ill. by author. Greenwillow, 2000. ISBN 978-0-688-16790-5 Subj: Bedtime. Night.

Balouch, Kristen, reteller. *The king and the three thieves* ill. by reteller. Viking, 2000. ISBN 978-0-670-88059-1 Subj: Crime. Folk & fairy tales. Foreign lands – Iran. Royalty – kings.

The little little girl with the big big voice ill. by author. Simon & Schuster, 2011. ISBN 978-1-4424-0808-1 Subj: Character traits – smallness. Jungle. Noise, sounds.

Mystery bottle ill. by author. Hyperion, 2006. ISBN 978-0-7868-0999-8 Subj: Family life – grandfathers. Foreign lands – Iran.

Bandy, Michael S. *White water* by Michael S. Bandy and Eric Stein ill. by Shadra Strickland. Candlewick, 2011. ISBN 978-0-7636-3678-4 Subj: Ethnic groups in the U.S. – African Americans. Prejudice. U.S. history.

Bang, Molly. *All of me! a book of thanks* ill. by author. Scholastic, 2009. ISBN 978-0-545-04424-0 Subj: Anatomy.

Dawn ill. by author. Morrow, 1983. ISBN 978-0-688-02404-8 Subj: Activities – weaving. Behavior – secrets. Birds – cranes. Character traits – curiosity. Folk & fairy tales. Foreign lands – Japan.

Goose ill. by author. Blue Sky, 1996. ISBN 978-0-590-89005-2 Subj: Activities – flying. Animals – groundhogs. Birds – geese.

The grey lady and the strawberry snatcher ill. by author. Four Winds, 1980. ISBN 978-0-590-07547-3 Subj: Caldecott award honor books. Imagination. Wordless.

In my heart ill. by author. Little, Brown, 2006. ISBN 978-0-316-79617-0 Subj: Emotions – love. Family life.

Living sunlight: how plants bring the earth to life by Molly Bang and Penny Chrisholm ill. by Molly Bang. Scholastic, 2009. ISBN 978-0-545-04422-6 Subj: Plants. Science. Sun.

My light ill. by author. Scholastic, 2004. ISBN 978-0-439-48961-4 Subj: Light, lights. Science. Sun.

Ocean sunlight: how tiny plants feed the seas by Molly Bang and Penny Chisholm ill. by Molly Bang. Scholastic, 2012. ISBN 978-0-545-27322-0 Subj: Plants. Science. Sea & seashore. Sun.

The paper crane ill. by author. Greenwillow, 1985. ISBN 978-0-688-04109-0 Subj: Birds – cranes. Character traits – kindness. Folk & fairy tales.

Ten, nine, eight ill. by author. Greenwillow, 1983. ISBN 978-0-688-00907-6 Subj: Bedtime. Caldecott award honor books. Counting, numbers. Ethnic groups in the U.S. – African Americans. Lullabies. Rhyming text.

When Sophie gets angry — really, really angry . . . ill. by author. Blue Sky, 1999. ISBN 978-0-590-18979-8 Subj: Caldecott award honor books. Emotions – anger. Family life – sisters.

Wiley and the hairy man ill. by adapter. Macmillan, 1976. ISBN 978-0-02-708370-5 Subj: Character traits – cleverness. Ethnic groups in the U.S. – African Americans. Folk & fairy tales. Monsters.

Yellow ball ill. by author. Morrow, 1991. ISBN 978-0-688-06315-3 Subj: Activities – playing. Sea & seashore. Toys – balls.

Banks, Kate. *The bear in the book* ill. by Georg Hallensleben. Farrar, 2012. ISBN 978-0-374-30591-8 Subj: Animals – bears. Bedtime. Books, reading. Family life – mothers. Hibernation.

City cat ill. by Lauren Castillo. Farrar, 2013. ISBN 978-0-374-31321-0 Subj: Activities – traveling. Animals – cats. Foreign lands – Europe. Rhyming text.

Close your eyes ill. by Georg Hallensleben. Farrar, 2002. ISBN 978-0-374-31382-1 Subj: Animals – tigers. Dreams. Family life – mothers. Sleep.

The eraserheads ill. by Boris Kulikov. Farrar, 2010. ISBN 978-0-374-39920-7 Subj: Activities – drawing. Activities – writing. Imagination.

Fox ill. by Georg Hallensleben. Farrar, 2007. ISBN 978-0-374-39967-2 Subj: Animals – foxes. Behavior – growing up.

The great blue house ill. by Georg Hallensleben. Farrar, 2005. ISBN 978-0-374-32769-9 Subj: Homes, houses. Seasons.

Mama's coming home ill. by Tomasz Bogacki. Farrar, 2003. ISBN 978-0-374-34747-5 Subj: Activities – working. Family life. Family life – mothers. Gender roles.

Max's castle ill. by Boris Kulikov. Farrar, 2011. ISBN 978-0-374-39919-1 Subj: Family life – brothers. Imagination. Knights. Language. Toys – blocks.

Max's dragon ill. by Boris Kulikov. Farrar, 2008. ISBN 978-0-374-39921-4 Subj: Activities – playing. Dragons. Imagination. Language.

Max's words ill. by Boris Kulikov. Farrar, 2006. ISBN 978-0-374-39949-8 Subj: Activities – storytelling. Behavior – collecting things. Language.

The night worker ill. by Georg Hallensleben. Farrar, 2000. ISBN 978-0-374-35520-3 Subj: Activities – working. Careers – construction workers. Family life – fathers.

That's Papa's way ill. by Lauren Castillo. Farrar, 2009. ISBN 978-0-374-37445-7 Subj: Character traits – individuality. Family life – fathers. Sports – fishing.

This baby ill. by Gabi Swiatkowska. Farrar, 2011. ISBN 978-0-374-37514-0 Subj: Babies. Family life – new sibling.

What's coming for Christmas? ill. by Georg Hallensleben. Farrar, 2009. ISBN 978-0-374-39948-1 Subj: Animals. Farms. Holidays – Christmas.

Banks, Merry. *N is for Navidad* (Elya, Susan Middleton)

Bannerman, Helen. *Sam and the tigers: a new telling of Little Black Sambo* (Lester, Julius)

The story of Little Babaji ill. by Fred Marcellino. HarperCollins, 1996. ISBN 978-0-06-205065-6 Subj: Animals – tigers. Character traits – cleverness. Family life. Foreign lands – India.

The story of Little Black Sambo ill. by author. Applewood, 1996. ISBN 978-1-55709-414-8 Subj: Animals – tigers. Character traits – cleverness. Family life. Foreign lands – India.

The story of Little Black Sambo ill. by author. HarperCollins, 1990. ISBN 978-0-397-30006-8 Subj: Animals – tigers. Character traits – cleverness. Family life. Foreign lands – India.

The story of Little Black Sambo ill. by Christopher Bing. Handprint, 2003. ISBN 978-1-929766-55-0 Subj: Animals – tigers. Character traits – cleverness. Family life. Foreign lands – India.

Bansch, Helga. *Brava, Mimi!* ill. by author. NorthSouth, 2010. ISBN 978-0-7358-2322-8 Subj: Activities – dancing. Animals – mice. Ballet.

Odd bird out ill. by author. Gecko, 2011. ISBN 978-1-8774-6708-0 Subj: Birds – ravens. Character traits – being different. Self-concept.

Bar-el, Dan. *Not your typical dragon* ill. by Tim Bowers. Viking, 2013. ISBN 978-0-670-01402-6 Subj: Character traits – being different. Character traits – individuality. Dragons. Self-concept.

Such a prince ill. by John Manders. Houghton, 2007. ISBN 978-0-618-71468-1 Subj: Fairies. Folk & fairy tales. Royalty – princesses.

Barack, Marcy. *Season song* ill. by Thierry Courtin. HarperCollins, 2002. ISBN 978-0-694-01567-2 Subj: Format, unusual – board books. Rhyming text. Seasons.

Baranski, Joan Sullivan. *Round is a pancake* ill. by Yu-Mei Han. Dutton, 2001. ISBN 978-0-525-46173-9 Subj: Concepts – shape. Food. Rhyming text. Royalty – kings.

Barasch, Lynne. *First come the zebra* ill. by author. Lee & Low, 2009. ISBN 978-1-60060-365-5 Subj: Animals. Behavior – fighting, arguing. Character traits – cooperation. Foreign lands – Kenya.

Hiromi's hands ill. by author. Lee & Low, 2007. ISBN 978-1-58430-275-9 Subj: Careers – chefs, cooks. Ethnic groups in the U.S. – Japanese Americans. Food.

Radio rescue ill. by author. Farrar, 2000. ISBN 978-0-374-36166-2 Subj: Activities. Radios.

The reluctant flower girl ill. by author. HarperCollins, 2001. ISBN 978-0-06-028810-5 Subj: Family life – sisters. Friendship. Weddings.

Barber, Patti. *First number book* ill. by Mandy Stanley. Kingfisher, 2001. ISBN 978-0-7534-5338-4 Subj: Counting, numbers. Picture puzzles.

Barber, Ronde. *Game day* (Barber, Tiki)

Barber, Tiki. *Game day* by Tiki Barber and Ronde Barber ill. by Barry Root. Simon & Schuster, 2005. ISBN 978-1-4169-0093-1 Subj: Ethnic groups in the U.S. – African Americans. Family life – brothers. Multiple births – twins. Sports – football.

Barber, Tiki, et al. *By my brother's side* ill. by Barry Root. Simon & Schuster, 2004. ISBN 978-0-689-86559-6 Subj: Ethnic groups in the U.S. – African Americans. Family life – brothers. Multiple births – twins. Sports – football.

Teammates ill. by Barry Root. Simon & Schuster, 2006. ISBN 978-1-4169-2489-0 Subj: Character traits – perseverance. Ethnic groups in the U.S. – African Americans. Family life – brothers. Multiple births – twins. Sports – football.

Barbero, Maria. *The bravest mouse* ill. by author. NorthSouth, 2002. ISBN 978-0-7358-1709-8 Subj: Animals – cats. Animals – mice. Character traits – bravery. Self-concept.

Barbour, Karen. *Little Nino's pizzeria* ill. by author. Harcourt, 1987. ISBN 978-0-15-247650-2 Subj: Family life. Food.

Mr. Williams ill. by author. Holt, 2005. ISBN 978-0-8050-6773-6 Subj: Careers – farmers. Ethnic groups in the U.S. – African Americans. Farms. Old age. Prejudice. U.S. history.

Barclay, Eric. *Hiding Phil* ill. by author. Scholastic, 2013. ISBN 978-0-545-46477-2 Subj: Animals – elephants. Behavior – hiding things. Family life – brothers & sisters.

I can see just fine ill. by author. Abrams, 2013. ISBN 978-1-4197-0801-5 Subj: Anatomy – eyes. Careers – opticians, optometrists. Glasses.

Barclay, Jane. *Going on a journey to the sea* ill. by Elizabeth Mikau. Lobster, 2002. ISBN 978-1-894222-34-1 Subj: Activities – playing. Sea & seashore. Sports – swimming.

Bardhan-Quallen, Sudipta. *Chicks run wild* ill. by Ward Jenkins. Simon & Schuster, 2011. ISBN 978-1-4424-0673-5 Subj: Bedtime. Behavior – misbehavior. Birds – chickens. Family life – mothers. Rhyming text.

Flying eagle ill. by Deborah Kogan Ray. Charlesbridge, 2009. ISBN 978-1-57091-671-7 Subj: Birds – eagles. Foreign lands – Tanzania.

Hampire! ill. by Howard Fine. HarperCollins, 2011. ISBN 978-0-06-114239-0 Subj: Animals – pigs. Birds – ducks. Food. Humorous stories. Monsters.

The Mine-o-saur ill. by David Clark. Penguin, 2007. ISBN 978-0-399-24642-5 Subj: Behavior – greed. Behavior – sharing. Dinosaurs. Friendship. Toys.

Pirate princess ill. by Jill McElmurry. HarperCollins, 2012. ISBN 978-0-06-114242-0 Subj: Pirates. Rhyming text. Royalty – princesses.

Bardill, Linard. *The great golden thing* ill. by Miriam Monnier. NorthSouth, 2002. ISBN 978-0-7358-1594-0 Subj: Animals – bears. Animals – rabbits. Careers – magicians. Flowers. Plants.

Baring-Gould, S. *Now the day is over* ill. by Preston McDaniels. Morehouse, 2001. ISBN 978-0-8192-1868-1 Subj: Bedtime. Religion. Songs.

Barner, Bob. *Animal baths* ill. by author. Chronicle, 2011. ISBN 978-1-4521-0056-2 Subj: Activities – bathing. Animals.

Bears! bears! bears! ill. by author. Chronicle, 2010. ISBN 978-0-8118-7057-3 Subj: Animals – bears. Rhyming text.

The Day of the Dead / El Día de los Muertos ill. by author. Holiday House, 2010. ISBN 978-0-8234-2214-2 Subj: Foreign languages. Holidays – Day of the Dead.

Dinosaur bones ill. by author. Chronicle, 2001. ISBN 978-0-8118-3158-1 Subj: Careers – paleontologists. Dinosaurs. Fossils. Rhyming text.

Dinosaurs roar, butterflies soar! ill. by author. Chronicle, 2009. ISBN 978-0-8118-5663-8 Subj: Dinosaurs. Fossils. Insects – butterflies, caterpillars.

Penguins, penguins, everywhere! ill. by author. Chronicle, 2007. ISBN 978-0-8118-5664-5 Subj: Birds – penguins. Rhyming text.

Stars, stars, stars ill. by author. Chronicle, 2002. ISBN 978-0-8118-3159-8 Subj: Astronomy. Planets. Rhyming text. Science. Stars.

Barnes, Brynne. *Colors of me* ill. by Annika M. Nelson. Sleeping Bear, 2011. ISBN 978-1-58536-541-8 Subj: Concepts – color. Rhyming text. Self-concept.

Barnes, Laura T. *Ernest and the big itch* ill. by Carol A. Camburn. Barnsyard, 2002. ISBN 978-0-9674681-2-9 Subj: Animals – donkeys. Birds. Friendship. Self-concept.

Ernest's special Christmas ill. by Carol A. Camburn. Barnsyard, 2003. ISBN 978-0-9674681-3-6 Subj: Animals. Animals – donkeys. Character traits – helpfulness. Friendship.

Teeny tiny Ernest ill. by Carol A. Camburn. Barnsyard, 2000. ISBN 978-0-9674681-1-2 Subj: Animals – donkeys. Concepts – size. Self-concept.

Twist and Ernest ill. by Carol A. Camburn. Barnsyard, 1999. ISBN 978-0-9674681-0-5 Subj: Animals – donkeys. Animals – horses, ponies. Friendship.

Barnett, Mac. *Battle Bunny* (Scieszka, Jon)

Billy Twitters and his big blue whale problem ill. by Adam Rex. Hyperion, 2009. ISBN 978-0-7868-4958-1 Subj: Animals – whales. Behavior – misbehavior. Family life. School.

Chloe and the lion ill. by Adam Rex. Hyperion, 2012. ISBN 978-1-4231-1334-8 Subj: Activities – writing. Books, reading.

Count the monkeys ill. by Kevin Cornell. Disney/Hyperion, 2013. ISBN 978-1-4231-6065-6 Subj: Animals. Animals – monkeys. Counting, numbers.

Extra yarn ill. by Jon Klassen. HarperCollins, 2012. ISBN 978-0-06-195338-5 Subj: Activities – knitting. Caldecott award honor books. Concepts – color. Humorous stories. Imagination.

Guess again! ill. by Adam Rex. Simon & Schuster, 2009. ISBN 978-1-4169-5566-5 Subj: Format, unusual. Games. Rhyming text.

Mustache! ill. by Kevin Cornell. Hyperion/Disney, 2011. ISBN 978-1-4231-1671-4 Subj: Anatomy. Character traits – appearance. Character traits – vanity. Royalty – kings.

Oh no! (or how my science project destroyed the world) ill. by Dan Santat. Hyperion/Disney, 2010. ISBN 978-1-4231-2312-5 Subj: Humorous stories. Robots. Science.

Oh no! Not again! (or how I built a time machine to save history) (or at least my history grade) ill. by Dan Santat. Hyperion, 2012. ISBN 978-1-4231-4912-5 Subj: Activities – traveling. Humorous stories. Petroglyphs. Time.

Barnwell, Ysaye M. *No mirrors in my Nana's house* ill. by Synthia Saint James. Harcourt, 1999. ISBN 978-0-15-201825-2 Subj: Ethnic groups in the U.S. – African Americans. Family life – grandmothers. Self-concept.

We are one ill. by Brian Pinkney. Harcourt, 2008. ISBN 978-0-15-205735-0 Subj: Music. Songs.

Barracca, Debra. *The adventures of taxi dog* (Barracca, Sal)

Maxi, the hero by Debra Barracca and Sal Barracca ill. by Mark Buehner. Dial, 1991. ISBN 978-0-8037-0940-9 Subj: Animals – dogs. Cities, towns. Crime. Rhyming text.

Maxi, the star by Debra Barracca and Sal Barracca ill. by Alan Ayers. Dial, 1993. ISBN 978-0-8037-1349-9 Subj: Activities – traveling. Animals – dogs. Rhyming text. Television.

A taxi dog Christmas by Debra Barracca and Sal Barracca ill. by Alan Ayers. Dial, 1994. ISBN 978-0-8037-1368-0 Subj: Animals – dogs. Cities, towns. Holidays – Christmas. Rhyming text. Taxis.

Barracca, Sal. *The adventures of taxi dog* by Sal Barracca and Debra Barracca ill. by Mark Buehner. Dial, 1990. ISBN 978-0-8037-0672-9 Subj: Animals – dogs. Cities, towns. Rhyming text. Taxis.

Maxi, the hero (Barracca, Debra)

Maxi, the star (Barracca, Debra)

A taxi dog Christmas (Barracca, Debra)

Barrett, Judi. *Animals should definitely not act like people* ill. by Ron Barrett. Atheneum, 1980. ISBN 978-0-689-30768-3 Subj: Animals. Behavior – imitation.

Animals should definitely not wear clothing ill. by Ron Barrett. Atheneum, 1970. ISBN 978-0-689-20592-7 Subj: Animals. Behavior – imitation. Clothing.

Cloudy with a chance of meatballs ill. by Ron Barrett. Atheneum, 1978. ISBN 978-0-689-30647-1 Subj: Family life – grandfathers. Food. Imagination. Weather.

Cloudy with a chance of meatballs 3: Planet of the pies ill. by Isidre Monés. Atheneum, 2013. ISBN 978-1-4424-9027-7 Subj: Careers – astronauts. Family life – grandfathers. Food. Planets. Weather.

The marshmallow incident ill. by Ron Barrett. Scholastic, 2009. ISBN 978-0-545-04653-4 Subj: Concepts – left & right. Food. Humorous stories.

Never take a shark to the dentist and other things not to do ill. by John Nickle. Atheneum, 2008. ISBN 978-1-4169-0724-4 Subj: Animals. Humorous stories.

Pickles to Pittsburgh: the sequel to Cloudy with a chance of meatballs ill. by Ron Barrett. Atheneum, 1997. ISBN 978-0-689-80104-4 Subj: Family life – grandparents. Food. Weather.

Santa from Cincinnati ill. by Kevin Hawkes. Atheneum, 2012. ISBN 978-1-4424-2993-2 Subj: Holidays – Christmas. Santa Claus.

Which witch is which? ill. by Sharleen Collicott. Atheneum, 2001. ISBN 978-0-689-82940-6 Subj: Rhyming text. Witches.

Barrett, Mary Brigid. *Shoebox Sam* ill. by Frank Morrison. Zonderkidz, 2011. ISBN 978-0-310-71549-8 Subj: Careers – shoemakers. Character traits – generosity. Character traits – kindness. Clothing – shoes. Ethnic groups in the U.S. – African Americans. Homeless.

Barretta, Gene. *Dear deer: a book of homophones* ill. by author. Holt, 2007. ISBN 978-0-8050-8104-6 Subj: Animals. Language.

Neo Leo: the ageless ideas of Leonardo da Vinci ill. by author. Holt, 2009. ISBN 978-0-8050-8703-1 Subj: Careers – inventors. Inventions.

Now and Ben: the modern inventions of Benjamin Franklin ill. by author. Holt, 2006. ISBN 978-0-8050-7917-3 Subj: Careers – inventors. Inventions. U.S. history.

Timeless Thomas: how Thomas Edison changed our lives ill. by author. Holt, 2012. ISBN 978-0-8050-9108-3 Subj: Careers – inventors. Inventions.

Barringer, William. *Gregory and Alexander* ill. by Kim LaFave. Orca, 2003. ISBN 978-1-55143-252-6 Subj: Animals – mice. Friendship. Insects – butterflies, caterpillars. Metamorphosis.

Barron, Rex. *Fed up! a feast of frazzled foods* ill. by author. Putnam, 2000. ISBN 978-0-399-23450-7 Subj: ABC books. Food.

Barron, T. A. *Where is Grandpa?* ill. by Chris Soentpiet. Philomel, 2000. ISBN 978-0-399-23037-0 Subj: Death. Emotions – grief. Family life – grandfathers.

Barry, Frances. *Duckie's ducklings: a one-to-ten counting book* ill. by author. Candlewick, 2005. ISBN 978-0-7636-2514-6 Subj: Birds – ducks. Counting, numbers.

Duckie's rainbow ill. by author. Candlewick, 2003. ISBN 978-0-7636-2066-0 Subj: Birds – ducks. Concepts – color. Format, unusual – toy & movable books. Weather – rainbows.

Let's look at dinosaurs: a flip-the-flap book ill. by author. Candlewick, 2011. ISBN 978-0-7636-5354-5 Subj: Dinosaurs. Format, unusual – toy & movable books.

Let's save the animals: a flip-the-flap book ill. by author. Candlewick, 2010. ISBN 978-0-7636-4501-4 Subj: Animals – endangered animals. Format, unusual – toy & movable books.

Barry, Holly M. *Helen Keller's best friend Belle* ill. by Jennifer Thermes. Whitman, 2013. ISBN 978-0-8075-3198-3 Subj: Animals – dogs. Disabilities – blindness. Disabilities – deafness.

Bart, Kathleen. *Town Teddy and Country Bear go global* ill. by author. Reverie, 2011. ISBN 978-1-932485-60-8 Subj: Activities – traveling. Toys – bears. World.

Bartlett, Robert Merrill. *The story of Thanksgiving* ill. by Sally Wern Comport. HarperCollins, 2001. ISBN 978-0-06-028779-5 Subj: Holidays – Thanksgiving. Indians of North America – Wampanoag. U.S. history.

Bartoletti, Susan Campbell. *The Christmas promise* ill. by David Christiana. Blue Sky, 2001. ISBN 978-0-590-98451-5 Subj: Family life – daughters. Family life – fathers. Holidays – Christmas. Homeless. Poverty. U.S. history.

The flag maker ill. by Claire A. Nivola. Houghton, 2004. ISBN 978-0-618-26757-6 Subj: Flags. U.S. history. War.

Naamah and the ark at night ill. by Holly Meade. Candlewick, 2011. ISBN 978-0-7636-4242-6 Subj: Animals. Boats, ships. Night. Religion.

Nobody's diggier than a dog ill. by Beppe Giacobbe. Hyperion, 2005. ISBN 978-0-7868-1824-2 Subj: Animals – dogs.

Nobody's nosier than a cat ill. by Beppe Giacobbe. Hyperion, 2003. ISBN 978-0-7868-1614-9 Subj: Animals – cats. Pets. Rhyming text.

Barton, Bethany. *This monster cannot wait!* ill. by author. Dial, 2013. ISBN 978-0-8037-3779-2 Subj: Character traits – patience. Monsters.

This monster needs a haircut ill. by author. Dial, 2012. ISBN 978-0-8037-3733-4 Subj: Hair. Monsters.

Barton, Bob. *Paul Gallico's The small miracle* by Bob Barton and Paul Gallico ill. by Carolyn Croll. Holt, 2003. ISBN 978-0-8050-6745-3 Subj: Animals – donkeys. Foreign lands – Italy. Religion.

Barton, Byron. *Airplanes* ill. by author. Crowell, 1986. ISBN 978-0-690-04532-1 Subj: Airplanes, airports.

Airport ill. by author. Crowell, 1982. ISBN 978-0-690-04169-9 Subj: Airplanes, airports. Careers – airplane pilots. Transportation.

Boats ill. by author. Crowell, 1986. ISBN 978-0-690-04563-5 Subj: Boats, ships.

Bones, bones, dinosaur bones ill. by author. HarperCollins, 1990. ISBN 978-0-690-04827-8 Subj: Dinosaurs. Prehistory.

Building a house ill. by author. Greenwillow, 1981. ISBN 978-0-688-84291-8 Subj: Homes, houses.

Buzz, buzz, buzz ill. by author. Macmillan, 1973. ISBN 978-0-02-708450-4 Subj: Cumulative tales. Insects – bees.

Dinosaurs, dinosaurs ill. by author. HarperCollins, 1989. ISBN 978-0-690-04768-4 Subj: Dinosaurs. Prehistory.

I want to be an astronaut ill. by author. Crowell, 1988. ISBN 978-0-690-04744-8 Subj: Careers – astronauts. Character traits – ambition. Space & space ships.

Machines at work ill. by author. HarperCollins, 1987. ISBN 978-0-690-04573-4 Subj: Activities – working. Machines.

My car ill. by author. Greenwillow, 2001. ISBN 978-0-06-029625-4 Subj: Automobiles.

Tools ill. by author. HarperCollins, 1995. ISBN 978-0-694-00623-6 Subj: Language. Tools.

Trains ill. by author. Crowell, 1986. ISBN 978-0-690-04534-5 Subj: Trains.

Trucks ill. by author. Crowell, 1986. ISBN 978-0-690-04530-7 Subj: Trucks.

The wee little woman ill. by author. HarperCollins, 1995. ISBN 978-0-06-023388-4 Subj: Animals – cats. Behavior – running away. Behavior – stealing.

Zoo animals ill. by author. HarperCollins, 1995. ISBN 978-0-694-00620-5 Subj: Animals. Zoos.

Barton, Chris. *Shark vs. train* ill. by Tom Lichtenheld. Little, Brown, 2010. ISBN 978-0-316-00762-7 Subj: Contests. Fish – sharks. Trains.

Bartone, Elisa. *Peppe the lamplighter* ill. by Ted Lewin. Lothrop, 1993. ISBN 978-0-688-10269-2 Subj: Caldecott award honor books. Cities, towns. Ethnic groups in the U.S. – Italian Americans. Family life – brothers & sisters. Family life – fathers.

Bartram, Simon. *Bob's best-ever friend* ill. by author. Candlewick, 2009. ISBN 978-0-7636-4425-3 Subj: Aliens. Careers – astronauts. Space & space ships.

Man on the moon: a day in the life of Bob ill. by author. Candlewick, 2002. ISBN 978-0-7636-1897-1 Subj: Careers – astronauts. Moon. Mythical creatures. Space & space ships.

Baryshnikov, Mikhail. *Because . . .* by Mikhail Baryshnikov and Vladimir Radunsky ill. by Vladimir Radunsky. Simon & Schuster, 2007. ISBN 978-0-689-87582-3 Subj: Activities – dancing. Character traits – being different. Emotions – embarrassment. Family life – grandmothers. Self-concept.

Base, Graeme. *Animalia* ill. by author. Abrams, 1987. ISBN 978-0-8109-1868-9 Subj: ABC books. Animals.

The Jewel Fish of Karnak ill. by author. Abrams, 2011. ISBN 978-1-4197-0086-6 Subj: Crime. Foreign lands – Egypt. Magic. Puzzles. Royalty – pharaohs.

Jungle drums ill. by author. Abrams, 2004. ISBN 978-0-8109-5044-3 Subj: Animals. Animals – warthogs. Behavior – wishing. Foreign lands – Africa. Jungle. Magic. Musical instruments – drums.

The legend of the Golden Snail. Abrams, 2010. ISBN 978-0-8109-8965-8 Subj: Animals – snails. Boats, ships. Imagination.

Little elephants ill. by author. Abrams, 2012. ISBN 978-1-4197-0463-5 Subj: Animals – elephants. Character traits – smallness. Farms. Magic.

The water hole ill. by author. Abrams, 2001. ISBN 978-0-8109-4568-5 Subj: Animals. Counting, numbers. Water. Weather – rain.

Bash, Barbara. *Desert giant: the world of the Saguaro cactus* ill. by author. Little, 1988. ISBN 978-0-316-08301-0 Subj: Desert. Plants.

Urban roosts ill. by author. Little, 1990. ISBN 978-0-316-08306-5 Subj: Birds. Cities, towns. Nature.

Basher, Simon. *ABC kids* ill. by author. Kingfisher, 2011. ISBN 978-0-7534-6495-3 Subj: ABC books. Language.

Go! Go! Bobo: shapes ill. by author. Kingfisher, 2011. ISBN 978-0-7534-6494-6 Subj: Concepts – shape. Format, unusual – board books.

Bashevis, Isaac *see* Singer, Isaac Bashevis

Baskin, Leonard. *Hosie's alphabet* ill. by author. Words by Hosea, Tobias & Lisa Baskin. Viking, 1972. ISBN 978-0-670-37958-3 Subj: ABC books. Caldecott award honor books. Children as authors.

Bassède, Francine. *A day with the Bellyflops* ill. by author. Orchard, 2000. ISBN 978-0-531-33242-9 Subj: Animals – pigs. Family life – brothers & sisters. Family life – mothers.

Bastianich, Lidia. *Nonna tell me a story: Lidia's Christmas kitchen* ill. by Laura Logan. Running Press, 2010. ISBN 978-0-7624-3692-7 Subj: Activities – baking, cooking. Ethnic groups in the U.S. – Italian Americans. Family life – grandmothers. Food. Holidays – Christmas.

Nonna's birthday surprise ill. by Renée Graef. Running Press, 2013. ISBN 978-0-7624-4655-1 Subj: Activities – baking, cooking. Birthdays. Ethnic groups in the U.S. – Italian Americans. Family life – grandmothers. Food.

Bastin, Marjolein. *Christmas with Vera* ill. by author. NorthSouth, 2011. ISBN 978-0-7358-4044-7 Subj: Activities – making things. Animals – mice. Holidays – Christmas.

Bataille, Marion. *ABC3D* ill. by author. Roaring Brook, 2008. ISBN 978-1-59643-425-7 Subj: ABC books. Format, unusual – toy & movable books.

Bate, Lucy. *Little rabbit's loose tooth* ill. by Diane deGroat. Crown, 1975. ISBN 978-0-517-52240-0 Subj: Animals – rabbits. Fairies. Teeth.

Bateman, Donna M. *Deep in the swamp* ill. by Brian Lies. Charlesbridge, 2007. ISBN 978-1-57091-596-3 Subj: Counting, numbers. Ecology. Rhyming text. Swamps.

Out on the prairie ill. by Susan Swan. Charlesbridge, 2012. ISBN 978-1-58089-377-0 Subj: Animals. Ecology. Songs.

Bateman, Teresa. *April foolishness* ill. by Nadine Bernard Westcott. Whitman, 2004. ISBN 978-0-8075-0404-8 Subj: Family life – grandparents. Farms. Holidays – April Fools' Day. Rhyming text.

The Bully Blockers Club ill. by Jackie Urbanovic. Whitman, 2004. ISBN 978-0-8075-0918-0 Subj: Behavior – bullying, teasing. Clubs, gangs. School.

Farm flu ill. by Nadine Bernard Westcott. Whitman, 2001. ISBN 978-0-8075-2274-5 Subj: Animals. Farms. Illness – influenza. Rhyming text.

Fiona's luck ill. by Kelly Murphy. Charlesbridge, 2007. ISBN 978-1-57091-651-9 Subj: Character traits – luck. Foreign lands – Ireland. Mythical creatures – leprechauns.

The frog with the big mouth ill. by Will Terry. Whitman, 2008. ISBN 978-0-8075-2621-7 Subj: Animals. Foreign lands – South America. Frogs & toads. Jungle.

Gus, the pilgrim turkey ill. by Ellen Joy Sasaki. Whitman, 2008. ISBN 978-0-8075-1266-1 Subj: Activities – traveling. Birds – turkeys. Holidays – Thanksgiving.

Hamster Camp: how Harry got fit ill. by Nancy Cote. Whitman, 2005. ISBN 978-0-8075-3139-6 Subj: Animals – hamsters. Camps, camping. Health & fitness – exercise. Magic. Rhyming text.

Harp o' gold ill. by Jill Weber. Holiday, 2001. ISBN 978-0-8234-1523-6 Subj: Folk & fairy tales. Music.

Hunting the daddyosaurus ill. by Benrei Huang. Whitman, 2002. ISBN 978-0-8075-1433-7 Subj: Dinosaurs. Family life – brothers. Family life – fathers. Rhyming text.

Keeper of soles ill. by Yayo. Holiday House, 2006. ISBN 978-0-8234-1734-6 Subj: Behavior – trickery. Careers – shoemakers. Clothing – shoes. Death.

Leprechaun gold ill. by Rosanne Litzinger. Holiday, 1998. ISBN 978-0-8234-1344-7 Subj: Folk & fairy tales. Mythical creatures – leprechauns.

The leprechaun under the bed ill. by Paul Meisel. Holiday House, 2012. ISBN 978-0-8234-2221-0 Subj: Friendship. Mythical creatures – leprechauns.

The merbaby ill. by Patience Brewster. Holiday, 2001. ISBN 978-0-8234-1531-1 Subj: Careers – fishermen. Family life – brothers. Mythical creatures – mermaids, mermen.

Paul Bunyan vs. Hals Halson: the giant lumberjack challenge! ill. by C. B. Canga. Whitman, 2011. ISBN 978-0-8075-6367-0 Subj: Careers – lumberjacks. Contests. Tall tales. U.S. history – frontier & pioneer life.

A plump and perky turkey ill. by Jeff Shelly. Marshall Cavendish, 2004. ISBN 978-0-7714-5188-1 Subj: Birds – turkeys. Holidays – Thanksgiving. Rhyming text.

The princesses have a ball ill. by Lynne Cravath. Whitman, 2002. ISBN 978-0-8075-6626-8 Subj: Folk & fairy tales. Rhyming text. Royalty – princesses. Sports – basketball.

Traveling Tom and the leprechaun ill. by Mélisande Potter. Holiday House, 2007. ISBN 978-0-8234-1976-0 Subj: Folk & fairy tales. Foreign lands – Ireland. Music. Mythical creatures – leprechauns.

Bates, Ivan. *All by myself* ill. by author. HarperCollins, 2000. ISBN 978-0-06-028585-2 Subj: Animals. Animals – elephants. Character traits – individuality.

Five little ducks ill. by adapter. Scholastic, 2006. ISBN 978-0-439-74693-9 Subj: Birds – ducks. Counting, numbers. Songs.

Bates, Katharine Lee. *America the beautiful* ill. by Chris Gall. Little, 2004. ISBN 978-0-316-73743-2 Subj: Music. Poetry. Songs. U.S. history.

America the beautiful ill. by Wendell Minor. Putnam, 2003. ISBN 978-0-399-23885-7 Subj: Music. Poetry. Songs. U.S. history.

America the beautiful: together we stand ill. by Bryan Collier et al. Scholastic, 2013. ISBN 978-0-545-49207-2 Subj: Music. Poetry. Songs. U.S. history.

Bateson-Hill, Margaret. *Masha and the firebird* by Margaret Bateson-Hill and Anne Wilson ill. by Anne Wilson. Zero to Ten, 2000. ISBN 978-1-84089-134-8 Subj: Eggs. Folk & fairy tales. Foreign lands – Russia. Witches.

Shota and the star quilt Lakota text by Philomine Lakota; ill. by Christine Fowler. Zero to Ten, 2001, 1998. ISBN 978-1-84089-021-1 Subj: Indians of North America – Lakota (Sioux). Quilts.

Batt, Tanya Robyn. *The faerie's gift* ill. by Nicoletta Ceccoli. Barefoot, 2003. ISBN 978-1-84148-998-8 Subj: Activities – working. Fairies. Folk & fairy tales.

Batten, Mary. *Please don't wake the animals: a book about sleep* ill. by Higgins Bond. Peachtree, 2008. ISBN 978-1-56145-393-1 Subj: Animals. Sleep.

Who has a belly button? ill. by Higgins Bond. Peachtree, 2004. ISBN 978-1-56145-235-4 Subj: Anatomy – navels. Animals. Birth.

Battersby, Katherine. *Brave Squish Rabbit* ill. by author. Viking, 2012. ISBN 978-0-670-01268-8 Subj: Animals – rabbits. Character traits – bravery. Character traits – smallness. Emotions – fear.

Squish Rabbit ill. by author. Penguin, 2011. ISBN 978-0-670-01267-1 Subj: Animals – rabbits. Character traits – smallness. Emotions – loneliness. Friendship.

Battle-Lavert, Gwendolyn. *The music in Derrick's heart* ill. by Colin Bootman. Holiday, 2000. ISBN 978-0-8234-1353-9 Subj: Careers – musicians. Ethnic groups in the U.S. – African Americans. Musical instruments – harmonicas.

Papa's mark ill. by Colin Bootman. Holiday, 2003. ISBN 978-0-8234-1650-9 Subj: Activities – writing. Books, reading. Ethnic groups in the U.S. – African Americans. Family life – fathers. U.S. history.

The shaking bag ill. by Aminah Brenda Lynn Robinson. Whitman, 2000. ISBN 978-0-8075-7328-0 Subj: Birds – ravens. Character traits – generosity. Ethnic groups in the U.S. – African Americans.

Battut, Eric. *The fox and the hen* ill. by author. Boxer, 2010. ISBN 978-1-907152-02-3 Subj: Animals. Animals – foxes. Birds – chickens. Eggs. Farms.

Little Mouse's big secret ill. by author. Sterling, 2011. ISBN 978-1-4027-7462-1 Subj: Animals. Animals – mice. Behavior – secrets. Behavior – sharing.

The little pea ill. by author. Skyhorse/Sky Pony, 2011. ISBN 978-1-61608-482-0 Subj: Character traits – individuality.

Bauer, Marion Dane. *Christmas lights* ill. by Susan Mitchell. Simon & Schuster, 2006. ISBN 978-0-689-86942-6 Subj: Format, unusual – toy & movable books. Holidays – Christmas.

The cutest critter ill. by Stan Tekiela. Adventure, 2010. ISBN 978-1-59193-253-6 Subj: Animals – babies.

Dinosaur thunder ill. by Margaret Chodos-Irvine. Scholastic, 2012. ISBN 978-0-590-45296-0 Subj: Dinosaurs. Emotions – fear. Weather – lightning, thunder.

Frog's best friend ill. by Diane Dawson Hearn. Holiday, 2002. ISBN 978-0-8234-1501-4 Subj: Animals. Friendship. Frogs & toads. Reptiles – turtles, tortoises.

Grandmother's song ill. by Pamela Rossi. Simon & Schuster, 2000. ISBN 978-0-689-82272-8 Subj: Babies. Birth. Family life – grandmothers. Family life – mothers.

Halloween forest ill. by John Shelley. Holiday House, 2012. ISBN 978-0-8234-2324-8 Subj: Emotions – fear. Forest, woods. Holidays – Halloween. Rhyming text.

Harriet Tubman ill. by Tammie Lyon. Scholastic, 2010. ISBN 978-0-545-23257-9 Subj: Ethnic groups in the U.S. – African Americans. Prejudice. Slavery. U.S. history.

If frogs made the weather ill. by Dorothy Donohue. Holiday House, 2005. ISBN 978-0-8234-1622-6 Subj: Animals. Weather.

If you had a nose like an elephant's trunk ill. by Susan Winter. Holiday, 2001. ISBN 978-0-8234-1589-2 Subj: Anatomy. Animals.

If you were born a kitten ill. by Jo Ellen McAllister Stammen. Simon & Schuster, 1997. ISBN 978-0-689-80111-2 Subj: Animals. Animals – babies.

I'm not afraid of Halloween! a pop-up and flap book ill. by Rusty Fletcher. Simon & Schuster, 2006. ISBN 978-0-689-85050-9 Subj: Format, unusual – toy & movable books. Holidays – Halloween. Monsters.

In like a lion out like a lamb ill. by Emily Arnold McCully. Holiday House, 2011. ISBN 978-0-8234-2238-8 Subj: Rhyming text. Seasons – spring.

Jason's bears ill. by Kevin Hawkes. Hyperion, 2000. ISBN 978-0-7868-2303-1 Subj: Animals – bears. Emotions – fear. Family life – brothers.

The longest night ill. by Ted Lewin. Holiday, 2009. ISBN 978-0-8234-2054-4 Subj: Animals. Birds. Night. Seasons – winter. Weather – wind.

A mama for Owen ill. by John Butler. Simon & Schuster, 2007. ISBN 978-0-689-85787-4 Subj: Animals – hippopotamuses. Behavior – lost. Family life – mothers. Reptiles – turtles, tortoises. Tsunamis.

My mother is mine ill. by Peter Elwell. Simon & Schuster, 2001. ISBN 978-0-689-82267-4 Subj: Animals. Family life – mothers. Holidays – Mother's Day. Letters, cards. Rhyming text.

One brown bunny ill. by Ivan Bates. Scholastic, 2009. ISBN 978-0-439-68010-3 Subj: Animals – rabbits. Concepts – color. Counting, numbers. Rhyming text.

Sleep, little one, sleep ill. by author. Simon & Schuster, 1999. ISBN 978-0-689-82250-6 Subj: Animals. Bedtime. Family life – fathers. Sleep.

Thank you for me! ill. by Kristina Stephenson. Simon & Schuster, 2010. ISBN 978-0-689-85788-1 Subj: Anatomy. Rhyming text.

Toes, ears, and nose! a lift-the-flap book ill. by Karen Katz. Simon & Schuster, 2003. ISBN 978-0-689-84712-7 Subj: Anatomy. Format, unusual – toy & movable books.

Uh-oh! a lift-the-flap story ill. by Valeria Petrone. Simon & Schuster, 2002. ISBN 978-0-689-84711-0 Subj: Accidents. Format, unusual – toy & movable books.

Why do kittens purr? ill. by Henry Cole. Simon & Schuster, 2003. ISBN 978-0-689-84179-8 Subj: Animals. Behavior.

Bauer, Sepp. *The Christmas rose* ill. by Else Wenz-Vieetor. Charlesbridge, 2008. ISBN 978-1-58089-232-2 Subj: Activities – traveling. Foreign lands – Germany. Holidays – Christmas. Illness.

Bauld, Jane Scoggins. *Journey of the third seed* ill. by Cynthia G. Darr. Eakin, 2000. ISBN 978-1-57168-428-8 Subj: Foreign lands – Japan. Gardens, gardening. Royalty – emperors. Seeds.

Baum, Louis. *The mouse who braved bedtime* ill. by Susan Hellard. Bloomsbury, 2006. ISBN 978-1-58234-691-5 Subj: Animals – mice. Bedtime. Emotions – fear. Monsters.

Baum, Maxie. *I have a little dreidel* ill. by Julie Paschkis. Scholastic, 2006. ISBN 978-0-439-64997-1 Subj: Food. Holidays – Hanukkah. Jewish culture. Songs.

Baumgart, Klaus. *Laura's Christmas star* ill. by author. Little Tiger, 1999. ISBN 978-1-888444-59-9 Subj: Holidays – Christmas. Magic. Stars. Trees.

Laura's secret English text by Judy Waite; ill. by author. Tiger Tales, 2003. ISBN 978-1-58925-031-4 Subj: Behavior – wishing. Family life – brothers & sisters. Kites. Magic. Stars.

Laura's star ill. by author. Tiger Tales, 2002. ISBN 978-1-58925-374-2 Subj: Friendship. Stars.

Bayer, Jane. *A my name is Alice* ill. by Steven Kellogg. Dial, 1984. ISBN 978-0-8037-0124-3 Subj: ABC books. Animals. Names.

Baylor, Byrd. *The desert is theirs* ill. by Peter Parnall. Scribners, 1975. ISBN 978-0-684-14266-1 Subj: Caldecott award honor books. Desert. Ecology. Folk & fairy tales. Indians of North America – Papago. Rhyming text.

Everybody needs a rock ill. by Peter Parnall. Scribners, 1974. ISBN 978-0-684-13899-2 Subj: Rhyming text. Rocks.

Hawk, I'm your brother ill. by Peter Parnall. Scribners, 1976. ISBN 978-0-684-14571-6 Subj: Birds – hawks. Caldecott award honor books. Character traits – freedom. Indians of North America.

The way to start a day ill. by Peter Parnall. Aladdin, 1986, ©1978. ISBN 978-0-684-15651-4 Subj: Caldecott award honor books. Folk & fairy tales. Foreign lands. Religion. Sun.

When clay sings ill. by Tom Bahti. Scribners, 1972. ISBN 978-0-684-12807-8 Subj: Art. Caldecott award honor books. Indians of North America.

Baynton, Martin. *Jane and the dragon* ill. by author. Candlewick, 2007. ISBN 978-0-7636-3570-1 Subj: Clowns, jesters. Dragons. Knights.

Jane and the magician ill. by author. Candlewick, 2007. ISBN 978-0-7636-3571-8 Subj: Careers – magicians. Dragons. Magic.

Bea, Holly. *Bless your heart* ill. by Kim Howard. Kramer, 2001. ISBN 978-0-915811-94-6 Subj: Bedtime. Religion. Rhyming text.

My spiritual alphabet book ill. by Kim Howard. Kramer, 2000. ISBN 978-0-915811-83-0 Subj: ABC books. Religion. Rhyming text. Self-concept.

Beake, Lesley. *Home now* ill. by Karin Littlewood. Charlesbridge, 2007. ISBN 978-1-58089-162-2 Subj: Animals – elephants. Family life – aunts, uncles. Foreign lands – Africa. Illness – AIDS. Moving. Orphans.

Beall, Pamela Conon. *Wee Sing if you're happy and you know it* by Pamela Conon Beall and Susan Hagen Nipp ill. by Hala Wittwer. Price Stern Sloan, 2002. ISBN 978-0-8431-7759-6 Subj: Format, unusual – board books. Insects. Songs.

Beames, Margaret. *Night cat* ill. by Sue Hitchcock. Scholastic, 2003. ISBN 978-0-439-38576-3 Subj: Animals. Animals – cats. Gardens, gardening. Night.

Bean, Jonathan. *At night* ill. by author. Farrar, 2007. ISBN 978-0-374-30446-1 Subj: Bedtime. Night. Sleep.

Big snow ill. by author. Farrar, 2013. ISBN 978-0-374-30696-0 Subj: Seasons – winter. Weather – snow.

Building our house ill. by author. Farrar, 2013. ISBN 978-0-374-38023-6 Subj: Careers – construction workers. Family life. Homes, houses.

The bear: an American folk song ill. by Kenneth J. Spengler. Mondo, 2002. ISBN 978-1-59034-190-2 Subj: Animals – bears. Birds – eagles. Camps, camping. Music. Songs.

Beard, Alex. *Crocodile's tears* ill. by author. Abrams, 2012. ISBN 978-1-4197-0008-8 Subj: Animals – endangered animals. Ecology. Foreign lands – Africa. Reptiles – alligators, crocodiles.

Beardshaw, Rosalind. *Grandma's beach* ill. by author. Bloomsbury, 2004. ISBN 978-1-58234-935-0 Subj: Family life – grandmothers. Sea & seashore – beaches.

Grandpa's surprise ill. by author. Bloomsbury, 2004. ISBN 978-1-58234-934-3 Subj: Family life – grandfathers. Foreign lands – England. Sports – bicycling.

Beaton, Clare. *At home / A la maison* ill. by author. Barron's, 2001. ISBN 978-0-7641-1693-3 Subj: Foreign languages. Homes, houses.

Clare Beaton's action rhymes ill. by author. Barefoot, 2010. ISBN 978-1-84686-473-5 Subj: Format, unusual – board books. Games.

Clare Beaton's bedtime rhymes ill. by author. Barefoot, 2012. ISBN 978-1-84686-737-8 Subj: Animals. Bedtime. Format, unusual – board books. Nursery rhymes.

Clare Beaton's farmyard rhymes ill. by author. Barefoot, 2012. ISBN 978-1-84686-736-1 Subj: Animals. Farms. Format, unusual – board books. Nursery rhymes.

Clare Beaton's nursery rhymes ill. by author. Barefoot, 2010. ISBN 978-1-84686-472-8 Subj: Format, unusual – board books. Nursery rhymes.

Daisy gets dressed ill. by author. Barefoot, 2005. ISBN 978-1-84148-794-6 Subj: Clothing. Concepts – patterns. Rhyming text.

How loud is a lion? ill. by author. Barefoot, 2002. ISBN 978-1-84148-896-7 Subj: Animals. Jungle. Noise, sounds.

One moose, twenty mice ill. by author. Barefoot, 1999. ISBN 978-1-902283-37-1 Subj: Animals. Animals – cats. Counting, numbers.

One moose, twenty mice [board book] ill. by author. Barefoot, 1999. ISBN 978-1-84148-285-9 Subj: Animals. Animals – cats. Counting, numbers. Format, unusual – board books.

Zoë and her zebra ill. by author. Barefoot, 1999. ISBN 978-1-902283-75-3 Subj: ABC books. Language.

Beaty, Andrea. *Artist Ted* ill. by Pascal Lemaître. Simon & Schuster, 2012. ISBN 978-1-4169-5374-6 Subj: Animals – bears. Careers – artists. Imagination. School.

Doctor Ted ill. by Pascal Lemaître. Simon & Schuster, 2008. ISBN 978-1-4169-2820-1 Subj: Animals – bears. Careers – doctors. Imagination.

Firefighter Ted ill. by Pascal Lemaître. Simon & Schuster, 2009. ISBN 978-1-4169-2821-8 Subj: Animals – bears. Careers – firefighters. Imagination. School.

Hide and sheep ill. by Bill Mayer. Simon & Schuster, 2011. ISBN 978-1-4169-2544-6 Subj: Animals – sheep. Counting, numbers. Rhyming text.

Hush, Baby Ghostling ill. by Pascal Lemaître. Simon & Schuster, 2009. ISBN 978-1-4169-2545-3 Subj: Bedtime. Emotions – fear. Family life – mothers. Ghosts. Monsters.

Iggy Peck, architect ill. by David Roberts. Abrams, 2007. ISBN 978-0-8109-1106-2 Subj: Buildings. Careers – architects. Rhyming text. School – field trips.

Rosie Revere, engineer ill. by David Roberts. Abrams, 2013. ISBN 978-1-4197-0845-9 Subj: Careers – engineers. Character traits – perseverance. Inventions. Rhyming text.

When giants come to play ill. by Kevin Hawkes. Abrams, 2006. ISBN 978-0-8109-5759-6 Subj: Activities – playing. Giants.

Beaty, Daniel. *Knock knock: my dad's dream for me* ill. by Bryan Collier. Little, Brown, 2013. ISBN 978-0-316-20917-5 Subj: Behavior – growing up. Emotions – sadness. Ethnic groups in the U.S. – African Americans. Family life – fathers. Family life – single-parent families.

Beaumont, Karen. *Dini Dinosaur* ill. by Daniel Roode. Greenwillow, 2012. ISBN 978-0-06-207299-3 Subj: Activities – bathing. Bedtime. Clothing. Dinosaurs. Rhyming text.

Doggone dogs! ill. by David Catrow. Dial, 2008. ISBN 978-0-8037-3157-8 Subj: Animals – dogs. Counting, numbers. Rhyming text.

Duck, duck, goose! a coyote's on the loose! ill. by José Aruego and Ariane Dewey. HarperCollins, 2004. ISBN 978-0-06-050804-3 Subj: Animals. Animals – coyotes. Farms. Rhyming text.

I ain't gonna paint no more! ill. by David Catrow. Harcourt, 2005. ISBN 978-0-15-202488-8 Subj: Activities – painting. Rhyming text.

Move over, Rover ill. by Jane Dyer. Harcourt, 2006. ISBN 978-0-15-201979-2 Subj: Animals – dogs. Behavior – sharing. Rhyming text. Weather – rain.

No sleep for the sheep! ill. by Jackie Urbanovic. Houghton, 2011. ISBN 978-0-15-204969-0 Subj: Animals. Animals – sheep. Bedtime. Farms. Noise, sounds. Rhyming text.

Shoe-la-la! ill. by LeUyen Pham. Scholastic, 2011. ISBN 978-0-545-06705-8 Subj: Character traits – appearance. Clothing – shoes. Rhyming text.

Where's my t-r-u-c-k? ill. by David Catrow. Penguin, 2011. ISBN 978-0-8037-3222-3 Subj: Animals – dogs. Behavior – lost & found possessions. Toys. Trucks.

Who ate all the cookie dough? ill. by Eugene Yelchin. Holt, 2008. ISBN 978-0-8050-8267-8 Subj: Animals. Animals – kangaroos. Behavior – lost & found possessions. Rhyming text.

Beautiful moments in the wild: animals and their colors ill. with photos. Moonstone, 2002. ISBN 978-0-9707768-7-7 Subj: Animals. Concepts – color.

Beaver steals fire: a Salish Coyote story ill. by Sam Sandoval. Univ. of Nebraska, 2005. ISBN 978-0-8032-4323-1 Subj: Animals. Animals – coyotes. Behavior – stealing. Behavior – trickery. Fire. Folk & fairy tales. Indians of North America.

Bechtold, Lisze. *Edna's tale* ill. by author. Houghton, 2001. ISBN 978-0-618-09164-5 Subj: Anatomy – tails. Animals – cats.

Sally and the purple socks ill. by author. Philomel, 2008. ISBN 978-0-399-24734-7 Subj: Birds – ducks. Clothing – socks. Concepts – size.

Beck, Andrea. *Elliot bakes a cake* ill. by author. Kids Can, 1999. ISBN 978-1-55074-443-9 Subj: Activities – baking, cooking. Animals. Animals – moose. Birthdays. Toys.

Elliot digs for treasure ill. by author. Kids Can, 2001. ISBN 978-1-55074-806-2 Subj: Animals. Animals – moose. Behavior – hiding things. Gardens, gardening. Maps. Toys.

Elliot gets stuck ill. by author. Kids Can, 2002. ISBN 978-1-55337-014-7 Subj: Animals. Animals – moose. Seasons – spring. Toys.

Elliot's bath ill. by author. Kids Can, 2001. ISBN 978-1-55074-802-4 Subj: Activities – bathing. Animals. Animals – moose. Toys.

Elliot's Christmas surprise ill. by author. Kids Can, 2003. ISBN 978-1-55337-474-9 Subj: Animals. Animals – moose. Friendship. Gifts. Holidays – Christmas. Toys.

Elliot's emergency ill. by author. Kids Can, 1998. ISBN 978-1-55074-441-5 Subj: Activities – sewing. Animals. Animals – moose. Friendship. Toys – dolls.

Elliot's great big lift-the-flap book ill. by author. Kids Can, 2003. ISBN 978-1-55337-373-5 Subj: Animals – moose. Concepts – color. Concepts – shape. Counting, numbers. Format, unusual – toy & movable books.

Elliot's noisy night ill. by author. Kids Can, 2002. ISBN 978-1-55337-011-6 Subj: Animals – moose. Bedtime. Night. Noise, sounds. Toys.

Elliot's shipwreck ill. by author. Kids Can, 2000. ISBN 978-1-55074-698-3 Subj: Activities – playing. Animals. Animals – moose. Boats, ships. Friendship. Sports – sailing. Toys.

Beck, Ian. *Home before dark* ill. by author. Scholastic, 2001. ISBN 978-0-439-17522-7 Subj: Behavior – lost. Toys – bears.

Teddy's snowy day ill. by author. Scholastic, 2002. ISBN 978-0-439-17520-3 Subj: Behavior – lost. Toys – bears. Weather – snow.

Beck, Scott. *Happy birthday, Monster!* ill. by author. Abrams, 2007. ISBN 978-0-8109-9363-1 Subj: Birthdays. Dragons. Monsters. Parties.

Monster sleepover! ill. by author. Abrams, 2009. ISBN 978-0-8109-4059-8 Subj: Monsters. Sleepovers.

A mud pie for mother ill. by author. Dutton, 2003. ISBN 978-0-525-47040-3 Subj: Animals – pigs. Birthdays. Character traits – generosity. Family life – mothers. Gifts.

Pepito the brave ill. by author. Dutton, 2001. ISBN 978-0-525-46524-9 Subj: Birds. Character traits – bravery. Emotions – fear.

Becker, Aaron. *Journey* ill. by author. Candlewick, 2013. ISBN 978-0-7636-6053-6 Subj: Activities – drawing. Activities – traveling. Caldecott award honor books. Imagination. Wordless.

Becker, Bonny. *An ant's day off* ill. by Nina Laden. Simon & Schuster, 2003. ISBN 978-0-689-82274-2 Subj: Animals. Insects – ants.

A bedtime for Bear ill. by Kady MacDonald Denton. Candlewick, 2010. ISBN 978-0-7636-4101-6 Subj: Animals – bears. Animals – mice. Bedtime. Friendship. Sleepovers.

A birthday for Bear ill. by Kady MacDonald Denton. Candlewick, 2009. ISBN 978-0-7636-3746-0 Subj: Animals – bears. Animals – mice. Birthdays. Friendship.

The Christmas crocodile ill. by David Small. Simon & Schuster, 1997. ISBN 978-0-689-81503-4 Subj: Behavior – mistakes. Holidays – Christmas. Reptiles – alligators, crocodiles.

Just a minute ill. by Jack E. Davis. Simon & Schuster, 2003. ISBN 978-0-689-83374-8 Subj: Time.

The sniffles for Bear ill. by Kady MacDonald Denton. Candlewick, 2011. ISBN 978-0-7636-4756-8 Subj: Animals – bears. Animals – mice. Friendship. Illness – cold (disease).

Tickly prickly ill. by Shari Halpern. HarperCollins, 1999. ISBN 978-0-694-01239-8 Subj: Animals. Rhyming text. Senses – touch.

A visitor for Bear ill. by Kady MacDonald Denton. Candlewick, 2008. ISBN 978-0-7636-2807-9 Subj: Animals – bears. Animals – mice. Friendship.

Becker, Helaine. *Mama likes to mambo* ill. by John Beder. Stoddart, 2001. ISBN 978-0-7737-3316-9 Subj: Animals. Foreign lands – Canada. Poetry.

Becker, John Leonard. *Seven little rabbits* ill. by Barbara Cooney. Walker, 1973. ISBN 978-0-8027-6130-9 Subj: Animals – rabbits. Counting, numbers.

Becker, Shari. *Maxwell's mountain* ill. by Nicole Wong. Charlesbridge, 2006. ISBN 978-1-58089-047-2 Subj: Imagination. Parks. Sports – mountain climbing.

Becker, Suzy. *Manny's cows: the Niagara Falls tale* ill. by author. HarperCollins, 2006. ISBN 978-0-06-054152-1 Subj: Activities – vacationing. Animals – bulls, cows.

Bedard, Michael. *The wolf of Gubbio* ill. by Murray Kimber. Stoddart, 2000. ISBN 978-0-7737-3250-6 Subj: Animals – wolves. Folk & fairy tales. Religion.

Bedford, David. *Big bears can!* ill. by Gaby Hansen. Tiger Tales, 2001. ISBN 978-1-58925-006-2 Subj: Animals – bears. Concepts – size. Family life – brothers.

Ella's games ill. by Peter Kavanagh. Barron's, 2002. ISBN 978-0-7641-5583-3 Subj: Animals – mice. Family life – brothers & sisters. Sibling rivalry.

I've seen Santa! ill. by Tim Warnes. Tiger Tales, 2006. ISBN 978-1-58925-058-1 Subj: Animals – bears. Holidays – Christmas. Santa Claus.

Little Otter's big journey ill. by Susan Winter. Good Books, 2006. ISBN 978-1-56148-548-2 Subj: Animals – otters. Behavior – lost. Family life – mothers.

Mole's in love ill. by Rosalind Beardshaw. Tiger Tales, 2009. ISBN 978-1-58925-084-0 Subj: Animals – moles. Behavior – mistakes. Emotions – love. Glasses.

Shaggy Dog and the terrible itch ill. by Gwyneth Williamson. Barron's, 2001. ISBN 978-0-7641-5391-4 Subj: Activities – bathing. Animals – dogs. Illness.

Touch the sky, my little bear by David Bedford and Jane Chapman ill. by Jane Chapman. Handprint, 2001. ISBN 978-1-929766-20-8 Subj: Animals – polar bears. Behavior – growing up. Family life – mothers.

The way I love you ill. by Ann James. Simon & Schuster, 2005. ISBN 978-0-689-87625-7 Subj: Animals – dogs. Emotions – love. Pets.

Bee, William. *And the cars go . . .* ill. by author. Candlewick, 2013. ISBN 978-0-7636-6580-7 Subj: Automobiles. Noise, sounds.

And the train goes . . . ill. by author. Candlewick, 2007. ISBN 978-0-7636-3248-9 Subj: Birds – parakeets, parrots. Noise, sounds. Trains.

Whatever ill. by author. Candlewick, 2005. ISBN 978-0-7636-2886-4 Subj: Animals – tigers. Behavior – indifference. Family life – fathers.

Beeke, Jemma. *The Rickety Barn show* ill. by Lynne Chapman. Doubleday, 2001. ISBN 978-0-385-32795-4 Subj: Animals. Farms. Theater.

Beeke, Tiphanie. *Roar like a lion!* ill. by author. Gullane, 2001. ISBN 978-1-86233-143-3 Subj: Animals. Animals – endangered animals. Communication. Noise, sounds.

Beeler, Selby B. *How many Elephants?* ill. by Barney Saltzberg. Candlewick, 2004. ISBN 978-0-7636-1583-3 Subj: Animals – elephants. Counting, numbers. Format, unusual – toy & movable books.

Throw your tooth on the roof: tooth traditions from around the world ill. by G. Brian Karas. Houghton, 1998. ISBN 978-0-395-89108-7 Subj: Folk & fairy tales. Teeth.

Begin, Mary Jane. *The sorcerer's apprentice* ill. by author. Little, Brown, 2005. ISBN 978-0-316-73611-4 Subj: Folk & fairy tales. Magic.

Behrens, Janice. *Let's find rain forest animals: up, down, around* ill. with photos. Scholastic, 2007. ISBN 978-0-531-14874-7 Subj: Animals. Format, unusual. Games. Jungle. Picture puzzles.

Behrens, June. *The feast of Thanksgiving* ill. by Anne Siberell. Children's Press, 1974. ISBN 978-0-516-08725-2 Subj: Holidays – Thanksgiving. Pilgrims. Theater.

Beil, Karen Magnuson. *Jack's house* ill. by Mike Wohnoutka. Holiday House, 2008. ISBN 978-0-8234-1913-5 Subj: Animals – dogs. Careers – construction workers. Cumulative tales. Homes, houses.

Bell, Babs. *The bridge is up!* ill. by Rob Hefferan. HarperCollins, 2004. ISBN 978-0-06-053794-4 Subj: Automobiles. Bridges. Cumulative tales. Traffic, traffic signs. Transportation.

Sputter, sputter, sput! ill. by Bob Staake. HarperCollins, 2008. ISBN 978-0-06-056222-9 Subj: Automobiles. Rhyming text.

Bell, Cece. *Bee-Wigged* ill. by author. Candlewick, 2008. ISBN 978-0-7636-3614-2 Subj: Character traits – appearance. Disguises. Friendship. Humorous stories. Insects – bees. Self-concept.

Itty Bitty ill. by author. Candlewick, 2009. ISBN 978-0-7636-3616-6 Subj: Animals – dogs. Character traits – smallness.

Sock Monkey boogie-woogie: a friend is made ill. by author. Candlewick, 2004. ISBN 978-0-7636-2392-0 Subj: Activities – dancing. Animals – monkeys. Careers – actors. Toys.

Sock Monkey goes to Hollywood: a star is bathed ill. by author. Candlewick, 2003. ISBN 978-0-7636-1962-6 Subj: Animals – monkeys. Careers – actors. Character traits – cleanliness. Toys.

Sock Monkey rides again ill. by author. Candlewick, 2007. ISBN 978-0-7636-3089-8 Subj: Animals – monkeys. Careers – actors. Cowboys, cowgirls. Toys.

Belle, Jennifer. *Animal stackers* ill. by David McPhail. Hyperion, 2005. ISBN 978-0-7868-1834-1 Subj: ABC books. Animals. Poetry.

Belloni, Giulia. *Anything is possible* ill. by Marco Trevisan. OwlKids, 2013. ISBN 978-1-926973-91-3 Subj: Animals – sheep. Animals – wolves. Character traits – cooperation. Character traits – perseverance. Friendship.

Belting, Natalia Maree. *The sun is a golden earring* ill. by Bernarda Bryson. Holt, 1962. Subj: Caldecott award honor books. Folk & fairy tales. Sky.

Belton, Robyn. *Herbert: the true story of a brave sea dog* ill. by author. Candlewick, 2010. ISBN 978-0-7636-4741-4 Subj: Animals – dogs. Sea & seashore. Weather – storms.

Belton, Sandra. *Pictures for Miss Josie* ill. by Benny Andrews. Greenwillow, 2003. ISBN 978-0-688-17481-1 Subj: Careers – artists. Ethnic groups in the U.S. – African Americans. Friendship. Self-concept.

Bemelmans, Ludwig. *Madeline* ill. by author. Viking, 1939. Subj: Caldecott award honor books.

Foreign lands – France. Hospitals. Orphans. Rhyming text. School – field trips.

Madeline and the bad hat ill. by author. Viking, 1956. Subj: Behavior – animals, dislike of. Behavior – misbehavior. Foreign lands – France. Orphans. Rhyming text.

Madeline and the gypsies ill. by author. Viking, 1959. ISBN 978-0-670-44682-7 Subj: Behavior – lost. Foreign lands – France. Gypsies. Orphans. Rhyming text.

Madeline in London ill. by author. Viking, 1978, ©1961. ISBN 978-0-14-050199-5 Subj: Animals – horses, ponies. Birthdays. Foreign lands – England. Orphans. Rhyming text.

Madeline's Christmas ill. by author. Viking, 1985. ISBN 978-0-670-80666-9 Subj: Foreign lands – France. Holidays – Christmas. Illness. Magic. Orphans. Rhyming text.

Madeline's rescue ill. by author. Viking, 1978, ©1953. ISBN 978-0-14-050207-7 Subj: Animals – dogs. Caldecott award books. Foreign lands – France. Orphans. Rhyming text.

Bendall-Brunello, Tiziana. *I wish I could read! a story about making friends* ill. by John Bendall-Brunello. Amicus, 2011. ISBN 978-1-60992-109-5 Subj: Animals – pigs. Books, reading. Friendship.

Benevelli, Alberto. *The colors of the chameleon* ill. by Loretta Serofilloi. G. Stevens, 2002. ISBN 978-0-8368-3042-2 Subj: Animals. Concepts – color. Reptiles – chameleons.

Benjamin, A. H. *Mouse, mole and the falling star* ill. by John Bendall-Brunello. Dutton, 2002. ISBN 978-0-525-46880-6 Subj: Animals – mice. Animals – moles. Behavior – sharing. Friendship. Stars.

Bennett, Artie. *The butt book* ill. by Mike Lester. Bloomsbury, 2010. ISBN 978-1-59990-311-8 Subj: Anatomy. Rhyming text.

Bennett, Barbara. *Lion's precious gift* ill. by Amanda Hall. Barron's, 2002. ISBN 978-0-7641-5533-8 Subj: Animals – lions. Babies.

Bennett, Howard J. *Harry goes to the hospital: a story for children about what it's like to be in the hospital* ill. by M. S. Weber. Magination, 2008. ISBN 978-1-4338-0319-2 Subj: Hospitals. Illness.

Bennett, Jill. *Teeny tiny* ill. by Tomie dePaola. Putnam, 1986. ISBN 978-0-399-21293-2 Subj: Folk & fairy tales. Foreign lands – England. Ghosts.

Bennett, Kelly. *Dad and Pop: an ode to fathers and stepfathers* ill. by Paul Meisel. Candlewick, 2010. ISBN 978-0-7636-3379-0 Subj: Family life – fathers. Family life – stepfamilies.

Not Norman ill. by Noah Jones. Candlewick, 2005. ISBN 978-0-7636-2384-5 Subj: Ethnic groups in the U.S. – African Americans. Fish. Friendship. Pets.

Vampire baby ill. by Paul Meisel. Candlewick, 2013. ISBN 978-0-7636-4691-2 Subj: Babies. Family life – brothers & sisters. Monsters. Teeth.

Your daddy was just like you ill. by David Walker. Penguin, 2010. ISBN 978-0-399-25258-7 Subj: Behavior. Family life – fathers.

Benson, Kathleen. *Count your way through Afghanistan* (Haskins, Jim)

Count your way through Brazil (Haskins, Jim)

Count your way through Iran (Haskins, Jim)

Bentley, Dawn. *Busy little beaver* ill. by Beth Stover. Soundprints, 2003. ISBN 978-1-59249-011-0 Subj: Animals – beavers. Family life.

Fuzzy bear: a getting dressed book ill. by Krisztina Nagy. Piggy Toes, 1998. Subj: Animals – bears. Clothing. Format, unusual – toy & movable books. Rhyming text. Weather – rain.

Fuzzy Bear's potty book ill. by Krisztina Nagy. Piggy Toes, 2001. ISBN 978-1-58117-161-7 Subj: Animals – bears. Behavior – growing up. Format, unusual – toy & movable books. Rhyming text. Toilet training.

Welcome back, Puffin ill. by Beth Stover. Soundprints, 2003. ISBN 978-1-59249-009-7 Subj: Birds – puffins. Family life.

Bently, Peter. *The great sheep shenanigans* ill. by Mei Matsuoka. Andersen, 2012. ISBN 978-0-7613-8990-3 Subj: Animals – sheep. Animals – wolves. Behavior – trickery. Rhyming text.

King Jack and the dragon ill. by Helen Oxenbury. Penguin, 2011. ISBN 978-0-8037-3698-6 Subj: Activities – playing. Emotions – fear. Imagination.

Benzwie, Teresa. *Numbers on the move: 1 2 3 dance and count with me* ill. by Mark Weber. Temple Univ., 2011. ISBN 978-1-4399-0342-1 Subj: Activities – dancing. Counting, numbers.

Bercaw, Edna Coe. *Halmoni's day* ill. by Robert Hunt. Dial, 2000. ISBN 978-0-8037-2445-7 Subj: Ethnic groups in the U.S. – Korean Americans. Family life – grandmothers. School.

Berenstain, Jan. *The Berenstain bears trim the tree* by Jan Berenstain and Michael Berenstain ill. by authors. HarperCollins, 2007. ISBN 978-0-06-057417-8 Subj: Animals – bears. Format, unusual – toy & movable books. Holidays – Christmas.

Berenstain, Michael. *The Berenstain bears trim the tree* (Berenstain, Jan)

Berenstain, Stan and Jan. *The bear detectives: the case of the missing pumpkin* ill. by Stan Berenstain and Jan Berenstain. Random House, 1975. ISBN 978-0-394-93127-2 Subj: Animals – bears. Careers – detectives. Mystery stories. Rhyming text.

Bears in the night ill. by Stan Berenstain and Jan Berenstain. Random House, 1971. ISBN 978-0-394-92286-7 Subj: Animals – bears. Bedtime. Night. Noise, sounds.

Bears on wheels ill. by Stan Berenstain and Jan Berenstain. Random House, 1969. ISBN 978-0-394-90967-7 Subj: Animals – bears. Counting, numbers. Wheels.

The Berenstain bears and mama's new job ill. by Stan Berenstain and Jan Berenstain. Random House, 1984. ISBN 978-0-394-96881-0 Subj: Animals – bears. Careers.

The Berenstain bears and the bad dream ill. by Stan Berenstain and Jan Berenstain. Random House, 1988. ISBN 978-0-394-97341-8 Subj: Animals – bears. Dreams.

The Berenstain bears and the bad habit ill. by Stan Berenstain and Jan Berenstain. Random House, 1987. ISBN 978-0-394-97340-1 Subj: Animals – bears.

The Berenstain bears and the big road race ill. by Stan Berenstain and Jan Berenstain. Random House, 1987. ISBN 978-0-394-99134-4 Subj: Animals – bears. Sports – racing.

The Berenstain bears and the double dare ill. by Stan Berenstain and Jan Berenstain. Random House, 1988. ISBN 978-0-394-99748-3 Subj: Animals – bears. Sibling rivalry.

The Berenstain bears and the ghost of the forest ill. by Stan Berenstain and Jan Berenstain. Random House, 1988. ISBN 978-0-394-90565-5 Subj: Animals – bears. Forest, woods. Ghosts.

The Berenstain bears and the messy room ill. by Stan Berenstain and Jan Berenstain. Random House, 1983. ISBN 978-0-394-95639-8 Subj: Animals – bears. Mystery stories.

The Berenstain bears and the missing dinosaur bone ill. by Stan Berenstain and Jan Berenstain. Random House, 1980. ISBN 978-0-394-94447-0 Subj: Animals – bears. Museums. Mystery stories. Prehistory. Rhyming text.

The Berenstain bears and the missing honey ill. by Stan Berenstain and Jan Berenstain. Random House, 1987. ISBN 978-0-394-99133-7 Subj: Animals – bears. Mystery stories.

The Berenstain bears and the prize pumpkin ill. by Stan Berenstain and Jan Berenstain. Random House, 1990. ISBN 978-0-679-90847-0 Subj: Animals – bears. Holidays – Thanksgiving. Plants.

The Berenstain bears and the real Easter eggs ill. by Stan Berenstain and Jan Berenstain. Random House, 2002. ISBN 978-0-375-91133-0 Subj: Animals – bears. Eggs. Holidays – Easter. Seasons – spring.

The Berenstain bears and the sitter ill. by Stan Berenstain and Jan Berenstain. Random House, 1981. ISBN 978-0-394-94837-9 Subj: Activities – babysitting. Animals – bears. Magic.

The Berenstain bears and the slumber party ill. by Stan Berenstain and Jan Berenstain. McKay, 1990. ISBN 978-0-679-90419-9 Subj: Animals – bears. Bedtime. Parties. Sleepovers.

The Berenstain bears and the spooky old tree ill. by Stan Berenstain and Jan Berenstain. Random House, 1978. ISBN 978-0-394-93910-0 Subj: Animals – bears. Rhyming text. Trees.

The Berenstain bears and the trouble with friends ill. by Stan Berenstain and Jan Berenstain. Random House, 1987. ISBN 978-0-394-97339-5 Subj: Animals – bears. Friendship.

The Berenstain bears and the truth ill. by Stan Berenstain and Jan Berenstain. Random House, 1983. ISBN 978-0-394-95640-4 Subj: Animals – bears. Behavior – lying. Behavior – misbehavior. Family life.

The Berenstain bears and the week at grandma's ill. by Stan Berenstain and Jan Berenstain. Random House, 1986. ISBN 978-0-394-97335-7 Subj: Animals – bears. Family life – grandmothers.

The Berenstain bears and the wild, wild honey ill. by Stan Berenstain and Jan Berenstain. Random House, 1983. ISBN 978-0-394-85924-8 Subj: Animals – bears. Nature.

The Berenstain bears and too much birthday ill. by Stan Berenstain and Jan Berenstain. Random House, 1986. ISBN 978-0-394-97332-6 Subj: Animals – bears. Birthdays.

The Berenstain bears and too much junk food ill. by Stan Berenstain and Jan Berenstain. Random House, 1985. ISBN 978-0-394-97217-6 Subj: Animals – bears. Food.

The Berenstain bears and too much TV ill. by Stan Berenstain and Jan Berenstain. Random House, 1984. ISBN 978-0-394-96570-3 Subj: Animals – bears. Family life. Television.

The Berenstain bears and too much vacation ill. by Stan Berenstain and Jan Berenstain. Random House, 1989. ISBN 978-0-394-93014-5 Subj: Activities – vacationing. Animals – bears.

The Berenstain bears blaze a trail ill. by Stan Berenstain and Jan Berenstain. Random House, 1987. ISBN 978-0-394-99132-0 Subj: Animals – bears.

The Berenstain bears' Christmas tree ill. by Stan Berenstain and Jan Berenstain. Random House, 1980. ISBN 978-0-394-94566-8 Subj: Animals – bears. Family life. Holidays – Christmas. Rhyming text. Trees.

The Berenstain bears' counting book ill. by Stan Berenstain and Jan Berenstain. Random House, 1976. ISBN 978-0-394-83246-3 Subj: Animals – bears. Counting, numbers.

The Berenstain bears don't pollute anymore ill. by Stan Berenstain and Jan Berenstain. Random House, 1991. ISBN 978-0-679-92351-0 Subj: Animals – bears. Ecology.

The Berenstain bears forget their manners ill. by Stan Berenstain and Jan Berenstain. Random House, 1985. ISBN 978-0-394-97333-3 Subj: Animals – bears. Etiquette. Family life.

The Berenstain bears get in a fight ill. by Stan Berenstain and Jan Berenstain. Random House, 1982. ISBN 978-0-394-95132-4 Subj: Animals – bears. Behavior – bad day. Sibling rivalry.

The Berenstain bears get stage fright ill. by Stan Berenstain and Jan Berenstain. Random House, 1986. ISBN 978-0-394-97337-1 Subj: Animals – bears. Emotions – fear. Theater.

The Berenstain bears get the gimmies ill. by Stan Berenstain and Jan Berenstain. Random House, 1988. ISBN 978-0-394-90566-2 Subj: Animals – bears. Behavior – greed.

The Berenstain bears go out for the team ill. by Stan Berenstain and Jan Berenstain. Random House, 1987. ISBN 978-0-394-97338-8 Subj: Animals – bears. Sports.

The Berenstain bears go to camp ill. by Stan Berenstain and Jan Berenstain. Random House, 1982. ISBN 978-0-394-95131-7 Subj: Animals – bears. Camps, camping. Seasons – summer.

The Berenstain bears go to school ill. by Stan Berenstain and Jan Berenstain. Random House, 1978. ISBN 978-0-394-93736-6 Subj: Animals – bears. School – first day.

The Berenstain bears go to the doctor ill. by Stan Berenstain and Jan Berenstain. Random House, 1981. ISBN 978-0-394-94835-5 Subj: Animals – bears. Careers – doctors.

The Berenstain bears in the dark ill. by Stan Berenstain and Jan Berenstain. Random House, 1982. Subj: Animals – bears. Family life. Imagination. Night.

The Berenstain bears learn about strangers ill. by Stan Berenstain and Jan Berenstain. Random House, 1985. ISBN 978-0-394-87334-3 Subj: Animals – bears. Behavior – talking to strangers. Emotions – fear. Family life. Safety.

The Berenstain bears meet Santa Bear ill. by Stan Berenstain and Jan Berenstain. Random House, 1988. ISBN 978-0-394-89797-4 Subj: Animals – bears. Holidays – Christmas.

The Berenstain bears' moving day ill. by Stan Berenstain and Jan Berenstain. Random House, 1981. Subj: Animals – bears. Family life. Friendship. Moving.

The Berenstain bears no girls allowed ill. by Stan Berenstain and Jan Berenstain. Random House, 1986. ISBN 978-0-394-97331-9 Subj: Animals – bears. Clubs, gangs. Family life – brothers & sisters.

The Berenstain bears on the moon ill. by Stan Berenstain and Jan Berenstain. Random House, 1985. ISBN 978-0-394-97180-3 Subj: Animals – bears. Animals – dogs. Moon. Space & space ships.

The Berenstain bears ready, set, go! ill. by Stan Berenstain and Jan Berenstain. Random House, 1988. ISBN 978-0-394-90564-8 Subj: Animals – bears.

The Berenstain bears' report card trouble ill. by Stan Berenstain and Jan Berenstain. Random House, 2000. ISBN 978-0-375-91127-9 Subj: Animals – bears. Family life. School. Sports.

The Berenstain bears' science fair ill. by Stan Berenstain and Jan Berenstain. Random House, 1977. Subj: Animals – bears. Science.

The Berenstain bears' that stump must go! ill. by Stan Berenstain and Jan Berenstain. Random House, 2000. ISBN 978-0-679-98963-9 Subj: Animals – bears. Plants. Rhyming text. Trees.

The Berenstain bears trick or treat ill. by Stan Berenstain and Jan Berenstain. Random House, 1989. ISBN 978-0-679-90091-7 Subj: Animals – bears. Holidays – Halloween.

The Berenstain bears' trouble at school ill. by Stan Berenstain and Jan Berenstain. Random House, 1987. ISBN 978-0-394-97336-4 Subj: Animals – bears. Behavior. School.

The Berenstain bears' trouble with money ill. by Stan Berenstain and Jan Berenstain. Random House, 1983. Subj: Animals – bears. Money.

The Berenstain bears' trouble with pets ill. by Stan Berenstain and Jan Berenstain. Random House, 1990. ISBN 978-0-679-90848-7 Subj: Animals – bears. Pets.

The Berenstain bears visit the dentist ill. by Stan Berenstain and Jan Berenstain. Random House, 1981. Subj: Animals – bears. Careers – dentists.

The Berenstains' B book ill. by Stan Berenstain and Jan Berenstain. Random House, 1971. Subj: ABC books. Animals – bears.

He bear, she bear ill. by Stan Berenstain and Jan Berenstain. Random House, 1974. Subj: Animals – bears. Rhyming text.

Inside outside upside down ill. by Stan Berenstain and Jan Berenstain. Random House, 1968. Subj: Animals – bears. Concepts.

Old hat, new hat ill. by Stan Berenstain and Jan Berenstain. Random House, 1970. Subj: Animals – bears. Concepts – shape. Concepts – size.

Berenzy, Alix. *Sammy: the classroom guinea pig* ill. by author. Holt, 2005. ISBN 978-0-8050-4024-1 Subj: Animals – guinea pigs. Pets. School.

Berg, Charles Ramírez. *The gift of the poinsettia / El regalo de la flor de nochebuena* (Mora, Pat)

Bergel, Colin. *Mail by the pail* ill. by Mark Koenig. Wayne State Univ, 2000. ISBN 978-0-8143-2890-3 Subj: Birthdays. Boats, ships. Family life – fathers. Post office.

Bergen, Lara Rice. *Blue's world of words* ill. by Victoria Miller. Simon & Schuster, 2002. ISBN 978-0-689-84741-7 Subj: Animals – dogs. Dictionaries. Language. Television.

Berger, Barbara. *All the way to Lhasa* ill. by author. Philomel, 2002. ISBN 978-0-399-23387-6 Subj: Animals – yaks. Folk & fairy tales. Foreign lands – Tibet.

Angels on a pin ill. by author. Philomel, 2000. ISBN 978-0-399-23247-3 Subj: Cities, towns. Concepts – size.

Grandfather Twilight ill. by author. Putnam, 1986. ISBN 978-0-399-20996-3 Subj: Folk & fairy tales. Moon. Twilight.

Thunder Bunny ill. by author. Penguin, 2007. ISBN 978-0-399-22035-7 Subj: Animals – rabbits. Sky. Weather – storms.

Berger, Carin. *Forever friends* ill. by author. HarperCollins, 2010. ISBN 978-0-06-191528-4 Subj: Animals – rabbits. Birds. Friendship. Seasons.

The little yellow leaf ill. by author. Greenwillow, 2008. ISBN 978-0-06-145223-9 Subj: Seasons – fall. Trees.

OK go ill. by author. HarperCollins, 2009. ISBN 978-0-06-157666-9 Subj: Ecology.

A perfect day ill. by author. Greenwillow, 2012. ISBN 978-0-06-201580-8 Subj: Activities – playing. Day. Seasons – winter. Sports – ice skating. Sports – skiing. Weather – snow.

Berger, Gilda. *How do airplanes fly?* (Berger, Melvin)

How's the weather? (Berger, Melvin)

Why did the dinosaurs disappear? the great dinosaur mystery (Berger, Melvin)

Berger, Joe. *Bridget Fidget and the most perfect pet!* ill. by author. Dial, 2009. ISBN 978-0-8037-3405-0 Subj: Insects – ladybugs. Pets.

My special one and only ill. by author. Dial, 2012. ISBN 978-0-8037-3410-4 Subj: Animals – cats. Behavior – lost & found possessions. Stores. Toys.

Berger, Lou. *Dream dog* ill. by David Catrow. Random House, 2013. ISBN 978-0-375-86655-5 Subj: Animals – dogs. Family life – fathers. Illness – allergies. Imagination.

Berger, Melvin. *Brrr! a book about polar animals* ill. with photos. Scholastic, 2000. ISBN 978-0-439-20165-0 Subj: Animals. Foreign lands – Arctic. Science.

Buzz! a book about insects ill. with photos. Scholastic, 2000. ISBN 978-0-439-08748-3 Subj: Insects. Science.

Dive! a book of deep sea creatures ill. with photos. Scholastic, 2000. ISBN 978-0-439-08747-6 Subj: Animals. Boats, ships. Fish. Science. Sea & seashore.

Early humans: a pop-up book ill. by Michael Welply. Putnam, 1988. ISBN 978-0-399-21476-9 Subj: Format, unusual – toy & movable books. Science.

Germs make me sick! ill. by Marylin Hafner. Crowell, 1985. ISBN 978-0-690-04429-4 Subj: Illness. Science.

How do airplanes fly? by Melvin Berger and Gilda Berger ill. by Paul Babb. Ideals, 1996. ISBN 978-1-57102-058-1 Subj: Activities – flying. Airplanes, airports. Science.

How's the weather? by Melvin Berger and Gilda Berger ill. by John Emil Cymerman. Ideals, 1996. ISBN 978-0-8249-8641-4 Subj: Science. Weather.

Look out for turtles! ill. by Megan Lloyd. HarperCollins, 1992. ISBN 978-0-06-022540-7 Subj: Nature. Reptiles – turtles, tortoises. Science.

Oil spill! ill. by Paul Mirocha. HarperCollins, 1994. ISBN 978-0-06-022912-2 Subj: Ecology. Oil. Science. Sea & seashore.

Spinning spiders ill. by S. D. Schindler. HarperCollins, 2003. ISBN 978-0-06-028697-2 Subj: Science. Spiders.

Switch on, switch off ill. by Carolyn Croll. HarperCollins, 1992. ISBN 978-0-690-04786-8 Subj: Light, lights. Science.

Why did the dinosaurs disappear? the great dinosaur mystery by Melvin Berger and Gilda Berger ill. by Susan Harrison. Ideals, 1995. ISBN 978-1-57102-033-8 Subj: Dinosaurs. Prehistory.

Why I sneeze, shiver, hiccup, and yawn ill. by Paul Meisel. rev. ed. HarperCollins, 2000. ISBN 978-0-06-028143-4 Subj: Hiccups. Illness – allergies. Illness – asthma. Science.

Berger, Samantha. *Crankenstein* ill. by Dan Santat. Little, Brown, 2013. ISBN 978-0-316-12656-4 Subj: Activities – playing. Behavior – dissatisfaction. Emotions.

Martha doesn't say sorry ill. by Bruce Whatley. Little, Brown, 2009. ISBN 978-0-316-06682-2 Subj: Animals – otters. Character traits – stubbornness.

Martha doesn't share! ill. by Bruce Whatley. Little, Brown, 2010. ISBN 978-0-316-07367-7 Subj: Animals – otters. Behavior – sharing.

Bergman, Mara. *Lively Elizabeth! what happens when you push* ill. by Cassia Thomas. Whitman, 2010. ISBN 978-0-8075-4702-1 Subj: Activities – playing. Behavior – carelessness. School.

Musical beds ill. by Marjolein Pottie. McElderry, 2002. ISBN 978-0-689-84463-8 Subj: Bedtime. Family life. Sleep.

Oliver who would not sleep! ill. by Nick Naland. Scholastic, 2007. ISBN 978-0-439-92826-7 Subj: Bedtime. Imagination. Sleep.

Snip snap! what's that? ill. by Nick Maland. HarperCollins, 2005. ISBN 978-0-06-077754-8 Subj: Emotions – fear. Family life – brothers & sisters. Reptiles – alligators, crocodiles.

Yum yum! What fun! ill. by Nick Maland. Greenwillow, 2009. ISBN 978-0-06-168860-7 Subj: Animals. Food. Rhyming text.

Bergman, Tamar. *Where is?* ill. by Rutu Modan. Houghton, 2002. ISBN 978-0-618-09539-1 Subj: Animals – cats. Family life – grandparents. Family life – mothers.

Bergren, Lisa Tawn. *God gave us Easter* ill. by Laura J. Bryant. WaterBrook, 2013. ISBN 978-0-307-73072-5 Subj: Animals – polar bears. Holidays – Easter. Religion.

How big is God? ill. by Laura J. Bryant. HarperCollins, 2008. ISBN 978-0-06-113174-5 Subj: Religion.

Bergstein, Rita M. *Your own big bed* ill. by Susan Kathleen Hartung. Viking, 2008. ISBN 978-0-670-06079-5 Subj: Animals. Behavior – growing up. Furniture – beds.

Berk, Ari. *Nightsong* ill. by Loren Long. Simon & Schuster, 2012. ISBN 978-1-4169-7886-2 Subj: Animals – bats. Behavior – growing up. Nature. Night.

Berkeley, Jon. *Chopsticks* ill. by author. Random House, 2005. ISBN 978-0-375-83309-0 Subj: Activities – flying. Animals – mice. Dragons. Foreign lands – China.

Berkes, Marianne. *Animalogy: animal analogies* ill. by Cathy Morrison. Sylvan Dell, 2011. ISBN 978-1-60718-127-9 Subj: Animals. Language.

Going home: the mystery of animal migration ill. by Jennifer DiRubbio. Dawn, 2010. ISBN 978-1-58469-126-6 Subj: Animals. Migration.

Marsh music ill. by Robert Noreika. Millbrook, 2000. ISBN 978-0-7613-1850-7 Subj: Animals. Birds. Frogs & toads. Noise, sounds. Rhyming text. Swamps.

Over in a river: flowing out to the sea ill. by Jill Dubin. Dawn, 2013. ISBN 978-1-58469-330-7 Subj: Animals. Counting, numbers. Rhyming text. Rivers. Songs.

Over in Australia: amazing animals down under ill. by Jill Dubin. Dawn, 2011. ISBN 978-1-58469-135-8 Subj: Counting, numbers. Foreign lands – Australia. Rhyming text.

Over in the Arctic: where the cold winds blow ill. by Jill Dubin. Dawn, 2008. ISBN 978-1-58469-109-9 Subj: Animals. Counting, numbers. Foreign lands – Arctic. Rhyming text.

Over in the forest: come and take a peek ill. by Jill Dubin. Dawn, 2012. ISBN 978-1-58469-162-4 Subj: Animals. Counting, numbers. Forest, woods. Rhyming text.

Over in the jungle: a rainforest rhyme ill. by Jeanette Canyon. Dawn, 2007. ISBN 978-1-58469-091-7 Subj: Animals. Counting, numbers. Jungle. Rhyming text.

Seashells by the seashore ill. by Robert Noreika. Dawn, 2002. ISBN 978-1-58469-035-1 Subj: Counting, numbers. Sea & seashore.

Berkner, Laurie. *The story of my feelings* ill. by Caroline Jayne Church. Scholastic, 2007. ISBN 978-0-439-42915-3 Subj: Emotions. Music.

Berlin, Irving. *Easter parade* ill. by Lisa McCue. HarperCollins, 2003. ISBN 978-0-06-029126-6 Subj: Animals – rabbits. Holidays – Easter. Music. Songs.

God bless America ill. by Lynn Munsinger. HarperCollins, 2002. ISBN 978-0-06-009789-9 Subj: Music. Songs. U.S. history.

Bernadette *see* Watts, Bernadette

Berne, Jennifer. *Calvin can't fly: the story of a bookworm birdie* ill. by Keith Bendis. Sterling, 2010. ISBN 978-1-4027-7323-5 Subj: Activities – flying. Birds. Books, reading. Migration. Weather – hurricanes.

Manfish: a story of Jacques Cousteau ill. by Eric Puybaret. Chronicle, 2008. ISBN 978-0-8118-6063-5 Subj: Careers. Nature. Science. Sea & seashore.

On a beam of light: a story of Albert Einstein ill. by Vladimir Radunsky. Chronicle, 2013. ISBN 978-0-8118-7235-5 Subj: Careers – scientists. Character traits – individuality.

Berner, Rotraut Susanne. *In the town all year 'round* ill. by author. Chronicle, 2008. ISBN 978-0-8118-6474-9 Subj: Cities, towns. Picture puzzles. Seasons.

Bernhard, Durga. *Earth, sky, wet, dry: a book of nature opposites* ill. by author. Orchard, 2000. ISBN 978-0-531-33213-9 Subj: Animals. Concepts – opposites. Nature. Plants.

In the fiddle is a song: a lift-the-flap book of hidden potential ill. by author. Chronicle, 2006. ISBN 978-0-8118-4951-7 Subj: Format, unusual – toy & movable books. Rhyming text.

To and fro, fast and slow ill. by author. Walker, 2001. ISBN 978-0-8027-8783-5 Subj: Cities, towns. Concepts – opposites. Country. Divorce. Family life.

While you are sleeping: a lift-the-flap book of time around the world ill. by author. Charlesbridge, 2011. ISBN 978-1-57091-473-7 Subj: Day. Format, unusual – toy & movable books. Night. Time.

Bernheimer, Kate. *The girl in the castle inside the museum* ill. by Nicoletta Ceccoli. Random House, 2008. ISBN 978-0-375-83606-0 Subj: Castles. Emotions – loneliness. Museums.

The girl who wouldn't brush her hair ill. by Jake Parker. Random House, 2013. ISBN 978-0-375-86878-8 Subj: Animals – mice. Character traits – cleanliness. Hair. Hygiene.

The lonely book ill. by Chris Sheban. Random House, 2012. ISBN 978-0-375-86226-7 Subj: Books, reading. Emotions – loneliness. Libraries.

Bernier-Grand, Carmen T. *Our Lady of Guadalupe* ill. by Tonya Engel. Marshall Cavendish, 2012. ISBN 978-0-7614-6135-7 Subj: Foreign lands – Mexico. Religion.

Berry, Lynne. *The curious demise of a contrary cat* ill. by Luke LaMarca. Simon & Schuster, 2006. ISBN 978-1-4169-0211-9 Subj: Animals – cats. Parties. Witches.

Duck dunks ill. by Hiroe Nakata. Holt, 2008. ISBN 978-0-8050-8128-2 Subj: Birds – ducks. Counting, numbers. Rhyming text. Sea & seashore – beaches.

Duck skates ill. by Hiroe Nakata. Holt, 2005. ISBN 978-0-8050-7219-8 Subj: Birds – ducks. Rhyming text. Seasons – winter. Sports – ice skating. Weather – snow.

Duck tents ill. by Nakata Hiroe. Holt, 2009. ISBN 978-0-8050-8696-6 Subj: Birds – ducks. Camps, camping. Rhyming text.

Ducking for apples ill. by Hiroe Nakata. Holt, 2010. ISBN 978-0-8050-8935-6 Subj: Birds – ducks. Food. Rhyming text. Sports – bicycling.

What floats in a moat? ill. by Matthew Cordell. Simon & Schuster, 2013. ISBN 978-1-4169-9763-4 Subj: Animals – goats. Birds – chickens. Castles. Concepts. Problem solving. Science.

Berry, Matt. *Up on Daddy's shoulders* ill. by Lucy Corvino. Scholastic, 2006. ISBN 978-0-439-67045-6 Subj: Concepts – perspective. Family life – fathers.

Bertram, Debbie. *The best book to read* by Debbie Bertram and Susan Bloom ill. by Michael Garland. Random House, 2008. ISBN 978-0-375-84702-8 Subj: Books, reading. Libraries. Rhyming text. School – field trips.

The best place to read by Debbie Bertram and Susan Bloom ill. by Michael Garland. Random House, 2003. ISBN 978-0-375-92293-0 Subj: Books, reading. Family life – mothers. Furniture – chairs. Rhyming text.

The best time to read by Debbie Bertram and Susan Bloom ill. by Michael Garland. Random House, 2005. ISBN 978-0-375-93025-6 Subj: Books, reading. Rhyming text.

Bertrand, Diane Gonzales. *Family / familia* ill. by Pauline Rodriguez Howard. Piñata, 1999. ISBN 978-1-55885-269-3 Subj: Ethnic groups in the U.S. – Mexican Americans. Family life. Foreign languages.

The last doll / La última muñeca ill. by Anthony Accardo. Piñata, 2000. ISBN 978-1-55885-290-7 Subj: Birthdays. Ethnic groups in the U.S. – Mexican Americans. Foreign languages. Toys – dolls.

The party for Papa Luis / La fiesta para Papa Luis ill. by Alejandro Galindo. Arte Publico/Piñata, 2010. ISBN 978-1-55885-532-8 Subj: Birthdays. Cumulative tales. Ethnic groups in the U.S. – Mexican Americans. Language. Parties.

Sofía and the purple dress / Sofía y el vestido morado ill. by Lisa Fields. Arte Publico/Pinata, 2012. ISBN 978-1-55885-701-8 Subj: Clothing – dresses. Ethnic groups in the U.S. – Mexican Americans.

Family life. Food. Foreign languages. Health & fitness – exercise.

Uncle Chente's picnic / El picnic de Tío Chente ill. by Pauline Rodriguez Howard. Piñata, 2001. ISBN 978-1-55885-337-9 Subj: Activities – picnicking. Ethnic groups in the U.S. – Mexican Americans. Family life – aunts, uncles. Foreign languages. Holidays – Fourth of July.

Bertrand, Lynne. *Granite baby* ill. by Kevin Hawkes. Farrar, 2005. ISBN 978-0-374-32761-3 Subj: Babies. Giants. Rocks. Tall tales.

Best, Cari. *Are you going to be good?* ill. by G. Brian Karas. Farrar, 2005. ISBN 978-0-374-30394-5 Subj: Etiquette. Old age. Parties.

Ava and the real Lucille ill. by Madeline Valentine. Farrar, 2012. ISBN 978-0-374-39903-0 Subj: Birds – parakeets, parrots. Contests. Family life – sisters. Pets.

Beatrice spells some lulus and learns to write a letter ill. by Giselle Potter. Farrar, 2013. ISBN 978-0-374-39904-7 Subj: Activities – writing. Family life – grandmothers. Language. School.

Easy as pie ill. by Melissa Sweet. Farrar, 2010. ISBN 978-0-374-39929-0 Subj: Activities – baking, cooking. Food.

Sally Jean, the Bicycle Queen ill. by Christine Davenier. Farrar, 2006. ISBN 978-0-374-36386-4 Subj: Behavior – growing up. Character traits – perseverance. Sports – bicycling.

Three cheers for Catherine the Great! ill. by Giselle Potter. DK, 1999. ISBN 978-0-7894-2622-2 Subj: Birthdays. Family life – grandmothers. Gifts.

What's so bad about being an only child? ill. by Sophie Blackall. Farrar, 2007. ISBN 978-0-374-39943-6 Subj: Family life – only child.

When Catherine the Great and I were eight! ill. by Giselle Potter. Farrar, 2003. ISBN 978-0-374-39954-2 Subj: Activities – traveling. Automobiles. Communities, neighborhoods. Concepts – cold & heat. Ethnic groups in the U.S. – Russian Americans. Family life – grandmothers.

When we go walking ill. by Kyrsten Brooker. Amazon/Two Lions, 2013. ISBN 978-1-4778-1648-6 Subj: Activities – walking. Behavior – collecting things. Family life.

The best cat in the world ill. by Ronald Himler. Eerdmans, 2004. ISBN 978-0-8028-5252-6 Subj: Animals – cats. Death. Emotions – grief. Pets.

The best part of me: children talk about their bodies in pictures and words photos by Wendy Ewald. Little, 2002. ISBN 978-0-316-70306-2 Subj: Anatomy. Children as authors. Poetry.

Bevis, Mary. *Wolf song* ill. by Consie Powell. Raven, 2007. ISBN 978-0-9794202-0-7 Subj: Animals – wolves. Family life – aunts, uncles. Nature.

Bianco, Margery Williams. *The velveteen rabbit* ill. by David Jorgensen. Knopf, 1985. ISBN 978-0-394-87711-2 Subj: Animals – rabbits. Emotions – love. Folk & fairy tales. Magic. Toys.

The velveteen rabbit retold by Thea Kliros; ill. by Thea Kliros. HarperCollins, 2003. ISBN 978-0-06-052746-4 Subj: Animals – rabbits. Emotions – love. Folk & fairy tales. Magic. Toys.

The velveteen rabbit retold by Komako Sakai; ill. by Komako Sakai. Enchanted Lion, 2012. ISBN 978-1-59270-128-5 Subj: Animals – rabbits. Emotions – love. Folk & fairy tales. Magic. Toys.

The velveteen rabbit ill. by Gennady Spirin. Marshall Cavendish, 2011. ISBN 978-0-7614-5848-7 Subj: Animals – rabbits. Emotions – love. Folk & fairy tales. Magic. Toys.

The velveteen rabbit: or, How toys became real ill. by Allen Atkinson. Knopf, 1983. ISBN 978-0-394-53221-9 Subj: Animals – rabbits. Emotions – love. Folk & fairy tales. Magic. Toys.

The velveteen rabbit: or, How toys became real adapt. by Lou Fancher; ill. by Steve Johnson and Lou Fancher. Atheneum, 2002. ISBN 978-0-689-84134-7 Subj: Animals – rabbits. Emotions – love. Folk & fairy tales. Magic. Toys.

Bibbel, Mark. *Oh, Harry!* ill. by Sarah Massini. Holt, 2003. ISBN 978-0-8050-6851-1 Subj: Animals – cats. Furniture – beds. Pets.

Bibbons, Faye. *The day the picture man came* ill. by Sherry Meidell. Boyds Mills, 2003. ISBN 978-1-56397-161-7 Subj: Careers – photographers. Farms.

Bible. New Testament. *The Lord's prayer* ill. by Tim Ladwig. Eerdmans, 1999. ISBN 978-0-8028-5180-2 Subj: Ethnic groups in the U.S. – African Americans. Religion.

Bible. New Testament. Corinthians 1st, XIII. *Love is* adapt. by Wendy Anderson Halperin; ill. by adapter. Simon & Schuster, 2001. ISBN 978-0-689-82980-2 Subj: Emotions – love. Religion.

Bible. New Testament. Gospels. *Bethlehem: from the authorized version of the King James Bible* ed. by Fiona French; ill. by Fiona French. HarperCollins, 2001. ISBN 978-0-06-029623-0 Subj: Holidays – Christmas. Religion – Nativity.

The Christmas story: from the Gospel according to St. Luke from the King James Bible ill. by James Bernardin. HarperCollins, 2002. ISBN 978-0-06-028883-9 Subj: Holidays – Christmas. Religion – Nativity.

Easter: from the King James Bible ill. by Fiona French. HarperCollins, 2002. ISBN 978-0-06-623929-3 Subj: Holidays – Easter. Religion.

The story of Christmas ill. by Pamela Dalton. Chronicle, 2011. ISBN 978-1-4521-0470-6 Subj: Holidays – Christmas. Religion – Nativity.

Bible. Old Testament. Ecclesiastes. *To every thing there is a season* ill. by Leo Dillon and Diane Dillon. Blue Sky, 1998. ISBN 978-0-590-47887-8 Subj: Religion.

To everything there is a season ill. by Jude Daly. Eerdmans, 2006. ISBN 978-0-8028-5286-1 Subj: Religion.

Bible. Old Testament. Genesis. *Genesis* ill. by Ed Young. Geringer, 1997. ISBN 978-0-06-025356-1 Subj: Creation. Religion.

The Genesis of it all retold by Luci Shaw; ill. by Huai-Kuang Miao. Paraclete, 2006. ISBN 978-1-55725-480-1 Subj: Creation. Religion.

Bible. Old Testament. Jonah. *The Book of Jonah* adapt. by Peter Spier; ill. by adapter. Doubleday, 1985. ISBN 978-0-385-19335-1 Subj: Animals – whales. Religion – Jonah.

Bible. Old Testament. Psalms. *I will rejoice: celebrating Psalm 118* ill. by Amy Bates. Zondervan, 2007. ISBN 978-0-310-71117-9 Subj: Religion. Rhyming text.

The Lord is my shepherd ill. by Regolo Ricci. Tundra, 2007. ISBN 978-0-88776-776-0 Subj: Religion.

Psalms for young children ill. by Arno. Eerdmans, 2008. ISBN 978-0-8028-5322-6 Subj: Religion.

The twenty-third Psalm: from the King James Bible ill. by Michael Hague. Holt, 1997. ISBN 978-0-8050-3820-0 Subj: Religion.

Bible. Old Testament. Ruth. *Ruth and Naomi: a Bible story* retold by Jean Marzollo; ill. by reteller. Little, Brown, 2005. ISBN 978-0-316-74139-2 Subj: Religion.

Biden, Jill. *Don't forget, God bless our troops* ill. by Raúl Colón. Simon & Schuster, 2012. ISBN 978-1-4424-5735-5 Subj: Careers – military. Character traits – bravery. Family life. War.

Biedrzycki, David. *Ace Lacewing, Bug Detective: the big swat* ill. by author. Charlesbridge, 2010. ISBN 978-1-57091-747-9 Subj: Careers – detectives. Crime. Insects.

Me and my dragon ill. by author. Charlesbridge, 2011. ISBN 978-1-58089-278-0 Subj: Dragons. Pets.

Me and my dragon: scared of Halloween ill. by author. Charlesbridge, 2013. ISBN 978-1-58089-658-0 Subj: Clothing – costumes. Dragons. Holidays – Halloween. Pets.

Santa retires ill. by author. Charlesbridge, 2012. ISBN 978-1-58925-640-8 Subj: Holidays – Christmas. Santa Claus.

Bierhorst, John. *Doctor Coyote: a Native American Aesop's fables* (Aesop)

Biers-Ariel, Matt. *Solomon and the trees* ill. by Esti Silverberg-Kiss. UAHC Pr., 2001. ISBN 978-0-8074-0749-3 Subj: Foreign lands – Israel. Holidays. Jewish culture. Royalty – kings.

Big, bad, and a little bit scary: poems that bite back comp. by Wade Zahares; ill. by Wade Zahares. Viking, 2001. ISBN 978-0-670-03513-7 Subj: Animals. Poetry.

Big noisy trucks and diggers ill. with photos. Chronicle, 2001. ISBN 978-0-8118-3173-4 Subj: Careers – construction workers. Format, unusual – toy & movable books. Machines. Noise, sounds. Tractors. Trucks.

Biggs, Brian. *123 beep beep beep! a counting book* ill. by author. HarperCollins, 2013. ISBN 978-0-06-195812-0 Subj: Automobiles. Counting, numbers. Format, unusual – board books. Trucks.

Stop! go! a book of opposites ill. by author. HarperCollins, 2013. ISBN 978-0-06-195813-7 Subj: Concepts – opposites. Format, unusual – board books.

Bildner, Phil. *The greatest game ever played: a football story* ill. by Zachary Pullen. Penguin, 2006. ISBN 978-0-399-24171-0 Subj: Family life – fathers. Sports – football. U.S. history.

The hallelujah flight ill. by John Holyfield. Penguin, 2010. ISBN 978-0-399-24789-7 Subj: Activities – flying. Careers – airplane pilots. Ethnic groups in the U.S. – African Americans. U.S. history.

Shoeless Joe and Black Betsy ill. by C. F. Payne. Simon & Schuster, 2002. ISBN 978-0-689-82913-0 Subj: Sports – baseball. U.S. history.

The shot heard 'round the world ill. by C. F. Payne. Simon & Schuster, 2005. ISBN 978-0-689-86273-1 Subj: Sports – baseball.

Turkey Bowl ill. by C. F. Payne. Simon & Schuster, 2008. ISBN 978-0-689-87896-1 Subj: Family life. Holidays – Thanksgiving. Sports – football. Weather – snow.

Bileck, Marvin. *Rain makes applesauce* (Scheer, Julian)

Bilgrami, Shaheen. *Amazing dinosaur discovery: a magic skeleton* ill. by Mike Phillips and Phil Garner. Dinosaurs & skeletons ill. by Treve Tamblin.

Sterling, 2002. ISBN 978-0-8069-8591-6 Subj: Anatomy. Animals. Dinosaurs. Format, unusual – toy & movable books. Museums. Prehistory.

Farmyard painting party ill. by Patrick Girouard. Sterling, 2002. ISBN 978-1-4027-0205-1 Subj: Activities – painting. Animals. Concepts – color. Farms. Format, unusual – toy & movable books.

Incredible animal discovery ill. by Mike Phillips and Phil Garner. Animals & skeletons ill. by Chris Shields. Sterling, 2002. ISBN 978-0-8069-8593-0 Subj: Anatomy. Animals. Format, unusual – toy & movable books.

Jungle art show ill. by Patrick Girouard. Sterling, 2002. ISBN 978-1-4027-0206-8 Subj: Activities – painting. Animals. Art. Concepts – color. Format, unusual – toy & movable books. Jungle.

Billin-Frye, Paige. *One, two, buckle my shoe* ill. by author. Child's World, 2009. ISBN 978-1-60253-303-5 Subj: Counting, numbers. Nursery rhymes. Rhyming text.

Billingsley, Franny. *Big bad bunny* ill. by G. Brian Karas. Atheneum, 2008. ISBN 978-1-4169-0601-8 Subj: Animals – mice. Behavior – lost. Clothing – costumes. Family life. Imagination.

Billstrom, Dianne. *You can't go to school naked!* ill. by Don Kilpatrick, III. Putnam, 2008. ISBN 978-0-399-24738-5 Subj: Character traits – appearance. Clothing. Rhyming text.

Bingham, Caroline. *Big book of rescue vehicles* ill. with photos. DK, 2000. ISBN 978-0-7894-5454-6 Subj: Careers – firefighters. Careers – lifeguards. Trucks.

DK big book of airplanes ill. with photos. DK, 2001. ISBN 978-0-7894-6521-4 Subj: Airplanes, airports.

Bingham, Kelly. *Z is for Moose* ill. by Paul O. Zelinsky. Greenwillow, 2012. ISBN 978-0-06-079984-7 Subj: ABC books. Animals – moose. Animals – zebras. Humorous stories.

Binns, Tristan Boyer. *The Liberty Bell* ill. with photos. Heinemann, 2001. ISBN 978-1-58810-119-8 Subj: U.S. history.

Birchall, Mark. *Hen goes shopping* ill. by author. Dial, 2002. ISBN 978-0-8037-2690-1 Subj: Birds – chickens. Format, unusual – toy & movable books. Shopping.

Rabbit's birthday surprise ill. by author. Carolrhoda, 2002. ISBN 978-0-87614-910-2 Subj: Animals – rabbits. Behavior – lost & found possessions. Parties. Toys.

Rabbit's wooly sweater ill. by author. Carolrhoda, 2001. ISBN 978-1-57505-465-0 Subj: Animals – rabbits. Behavior. Clothing – sweaters. Toys.

Bird, Betsy. *Giant dance party* ill. by Brandon Dorman. Greenwillow, 2013. ISBN 978-0-06-196083-3 Subj: Activities – dancing. Emotions – fear. Giants.

Birdsall, Jeanne. *Flora's very windy day* ill. by Matt Phelan. Clarion, 2010. ISBN 978-0-618-98676-7 Subj: Family life – brothers & sisters. Weather – wind.

Lucky and Squash ill. by Jane Dyer. HarperCollins, 2012. ISBN 978-0-06-083150-9 Subj: Animals – dogs. Character traits – cleverness. Friendship.

Birdseye, Tom. *Look out, Jack! The giant is back* ill. by Will Hillenbrand. Holiday, 2001. ISBN 978-0-8234-1450-5 Subj: Folk & fairy tales. Giants.

Oh yeah! ill. by Ethan Long. Holiday, 2003. ISBN 978-0-8234-1649-3 Subj: Camps, camping. Character traits – bravery. Night.

Soap! Soap! Don't forget the soap! an Appalachian folktale ill. by Andrew Glass. Holiday, 1993. ISBN 978-0-8234-1005-7 Subj: Behavior – forgetfulness. Cumulative tales. Folk & fairy tales. Shopping.

Birnbaum, Abe. *Green eyes* ill. by author. Golden, 2001. ISBN 978-0-307-20203-1 Subj: Animals – cats. Caldecott award honor books. Seasons.

Biro, Maureen Boyd. *Walking with Maga* ill. by Joyce Wheeler. All About Kids, 2002. ISBN 978-0-9700863-4-1 Subj: Family life – grandmothers. Nature. Old age. Sea & seashore.

Birtha, Becky. *Grandmama's pride* ill. by Colin Bootman. Whitman, 2005. ISBN 978-0-8075-3028-3 Subj: Ethnic groups in the U.S. – African Americans. Family life. Prejudice. U.S. history.

Lucky beans ill. by Nicole Tadgell. Whitman, 2010. ISBN 978-0-8075-4782-3 Subj: Character traits – cleverness. Contests. Counting, numbers. Ethnic groups in the U.S. – African Americans. U.S. history.

Bishop, Brett. *Clayton's path* by Brett Bishop and Laura Olson ill. by Mona Eagle. Apogee, 2001. ISBN 978-0-9700035-3-9 Subj: Animals – mules. Disabilities – ADD. Self-concept.

Bishop, Claire Huchet. *The five Chinese brothers* by Claire Huchet Bishop and Kurt Wiese ill. by Kurt Wiese. Coward, 1938. ISBN 978-0-698-20044-9 Subj: Character traits – cleverness. Family life. Folk & fairy tales. Foreign lands – China.

Blabey, Aaron. *Pearl Barley and Charlie Parsley* ill. by author. Front Street, 2008. ISBN 978-1-59078-596-6 Subj: Character traits – individuality. Friendship.

Black, Birdie. *Just right for Christmas* ill. by Rosalind Beardshaw. Candlewick, 2012. ISBN 978-0-7636-6174-8 Subj: Family life – fathers. Gifts. Holidays – Christmas. Royalty – kings.

Black, Harley. *Amazing magic school* ill. by Dana Regan. Sterling, 2000. ISBN 978-0-8069-1553-1 Subj: Animals. Art. Concepts – color. Format, unusual – toy & movable books. Magic. School – first day.

Magic art class ill. by author. Sterling, 2000. ISBN 978-0-8069-0600-3 Subj: Activities – painting. Concepts – color. Format, unusual – toy & movable books.

Black, Michael Ian. *I'm bored* ill. by Debbie Ridpath Ohi. Simon & Schuster, 2012. ISBN 978-1-4424-1403-7 Subj: Behavior – boredom. Food. Imagination.

A pig parade is a terrible idea ill. by Kevin Hawkes. Simon & Schuster, 2010. ISBN 978-1-4169-7922-7 Subj: Animals – pigs. Humorous stories. Parades.

The purple kangaroo ill. by Peter Brown. Simon & Schuster, 2010. ISBN 978-1-4169-5771-3 Subj: Animals – monkeys. Humorous stories. Imagination.

Black, Sonia. *Hanging out with Mom* ill. by George Ford. Scholastic, 2000. ISBN 978-0-590-86636-1 Subj: Family life – mothers. Parks. Rhyming text.

Blackaby, Susan. *Brownie Groundhog and the February Fox* ill. by Carmen Segovia. Sterling, 2011. ISBN 978-1-4027-4336-8 Subj: Animals – foxes. Animals – groundhogs. Behavior – trickery. Friendship. Holidays – Groundhog Day. Seasons – winter.

Brownie Groundhog and the wintry surprise ill. by Carmen Segovia. Sterling, 2013. ISBN 978-1-4027-9836-8 Subj: Animals. Animals. Animals – groundhogs. Friendship. Seasons – winter.

Rembrandt's hat ill. by Mary Newell DePalma. Houghton, 2002. ISBN 978-0-618-11452-8 Subj: Animals – bears. Behavior – lost & found possessions. Clothing – hats.

Blackall, Sophie. *Are you awake?* ill. by author. Holt, 2011. ISBN 978-0-8050-7858-9 Subj: Bedtime. Character traits – questioning. Family life – mothers. Night.

Blackford, Harriet. *Elephant's story* ill. by Manya Stojic. Sterling, 2008. ISBN 978-1-905417-75-9 Subj: Animals – elephants. Animals – endangered animals. Foreign lands – Africa.

Tiger's story ill. by Manya Stojic. Sterling, 2007. ISBN 978-1-905417-39-1 Subj: Animals – tigers. Behavior – growing up.

Blackstone, Stella. *Alligator alphabet* ill. by Stephanie Bauer. Barefoot, 2005. ISBN 978-1-84148-494-5 Subj: ABC books. Animals. Rhyming text.

Bear at home ill. by Debbie Harter. Barefoot, 2001. ISBN 978-1-84148-436-5 Subj: Animals – bears. Homes, houses. Rhyming text.

Bear at work ill. by Debbie Harter. Barefoot, 2008. ISBN 978-1-84686-110-9 Subj: Animals – bears. Careers. Careers – postal workers. Rhyming text.

Bear in a square ill. by Debbie Harter. Barefoot, 1998. ISBN 978-1-84148-120-3 Subj: Animals – bears. Concepts – shape. Concepts – size. Counting, numbers.

Bear in sunshine ill. by Debbie Harter. Barefoot, 2001. ISBN 978-1-84148-321-4 Subj: Animals – bears. Rhyming text. Weather.

Bear on a bike ill. by Debbie Harter. Barefoot, 1999. ISBN 978-1-84148-121-0 Subj: Animals – bears. Ethnic groups in the U.S. – African Americans. Sports – bicycling.

Bear takes a trip ill. by Debbie Harter. Barefoot, 2012. ISBN 978-1-84686-756-9 Subj: Activities – traveling. Animals – bears. Clocks, watches. Time.

Bear's birthday ill. by Debbie Harter. Barefoot, 2011. ISBN 978-1-84686-515-2 Subj: Animals – bears. Birthdays. Counting, numbers. Parties. Rhyming text.

Bear's busy family ill. by Debbie Harter. Barefoot, 1999. ISBN 978-1-84148-391-7 Subj: Animals – bears. Concepts – color. Rhyming text. Senses.

Cleo and Caspar ill. by Caroline Mockford. Barefoot, 2001. ISBN 978-1-84148-440-2 Subj: Animals – cats. Animals – dogs. Friendship. Rhyming text.

Cleo in the snow ill. by Caroline Mockford. Barefoot, 2002. ISBN 978-1-84148-951-3 Subj: Animals – cats. Animals – dogs. Friendship. Rhyming text. Weather – snow.

Cleo on the move ill. by Caroline Mockford. Barefoot, 2002. ISBN 978-1-84148-898-1 Subj: Animals – cats. Animals – dogs. Friendship. Moving. Rhyming text.

Cleo the cat ill. by Caroline Mockford. Barefoot, 2000. ISBN 978-1-84148-259-0 Subj: Animals – cats. Friendship. Rhyming text.

Cleo's alphabet book ill. by Caroline Mockford. Barefoot, 2003. ISBN 978-1-84148-008-4 Subj: ABC books. Animals – cats. Rhyming text.

Cleo's color book ill. by Caroline Mockford. Barefoot, 2006. ISBN 978-1-905236-30-5 Subj: Animals – cats. Concepts – color. Rhyming text.

Cleo's counting book ill. by Caroline Mockford. Barefoot, 2003. ISBN 978-1-84148-207-1 Subj: Animals – cats. Counting, numbers. Rhyming text.

Come here, Cleo ill. by Caroline Mockford. Barefoot, 2001. ISBN 978-1-84148-329-0 Subj: Animals – cats. Rhyming text.

How big is a pig? ill. by Clare Beaton. Barefoot, 2000. ISBN 978-1-84148-077-0 Subj: Activities – storytelling. Animals. Farms. Rhyming text.

I dreamt I was a dinosaur ill. by Clare Beaton. Barefoot, 2005. ISBN 978-1-84148-238-5 Subj: Dinosaurs. Dreams. Rhyming text.

An island in the sun ill. by Nicoletta Ceccoli. Barefoot, 2002. ISBN 978-1-84148-193-7 Subj: Animals – dogs. Cumulative tales. Islands. Rhyming text. Sea & seashore. Sports – sailing.

Making minestrone ill. by Nan Brooks. Barefoot, 2000. ISBN 978-1-84148-211-8 Subj: Activities – baking, cooking. Food.

Octopus opposites ill. by Stephanie Bauer. Barefoot, 2010. ISBN 978-1-84686-328-8 Subj: Animals. Concepts – opposites. Rhyming text.

Secret seahorse ill. by Clare Beaton. Barefoot, 2004. ISBN 978-1-84148-704-5 Subj: Animals. Fish. Fish – seahorses. Foreign lands – South Sea Islands. Rhyming text. Sea & seashore.

Secret seahorse [board book] ill. by Clare Beaton. Barefoot, 2005. ISBN 978-1-905236-15-2 Subj: Animals. Fish. Fish – seahorses. Foreign lands – South Sea Islands. Format, unusual – board books. Rhyming text. Sea & seashore.

Ship shapes ill. by Siobhan Bell. Barefoot, 2006. ISBN 978-1-905236-34-3 Subj: Boats, ships. Concepts – shape. Rhyming text.

What's this? ill. by Caroline Mockford. Barefoot, 2000. ISBN 978-1-84148-018-3 Subj: Flowers. Gardens, gardening. Seeds.

You and me ill. by Giovanni Manna. Barefoot, 2000. ISBN 978-1-84148-263-7 Subj: Activities. Concepts – opposites.

Blackwood, Freya. *Ivy loves to give* ill. by author. Scholastic, 2010. ISBN 978-0-545-23467-2 Subj: Character traits – generosity. Gifts.

Blades, Ann. *Mary of mile 18* ill. by author. Tundra, 2001. ISBN 978-0-88776-581-0 Subj: Animals – dogs. Animals – wolves. Character traits – perseverance. Farms. Foreign lands – Canada. Seasons – winter.

Too small ill. by author. Douglas & McIntyre, 2000. ISBN 978-0-88899-400-4 Subj: Concepts – size. Family life. Foreign lands – Canada. Moving.

Blaich, Ute. *The star* ill. by Julie Wintz-Litty. NorthSouth, 2001. ISBN 978-0-7358-1510-0 Subj: Animals. Birds – owls. Character traits – kindness. Holidays – Christmas. Religion – Nativity.

Blaikie, Lynn. *Beyond the northern lights* ill. by author. Fitzhenry & Whiteside, 2006. ISBN 978-1-55041-123-2 Subj: Foreign lands – Arctic. Nature. Rhyming text.

Blake, Quentin. *Fantastic Daisy Artichoke* ill. by author. Red Fox, 2001. ISBN 978-0-09-940006-6 Subj: Animals. Friendship. Rhyming text.

Mrs. Armitage: queen of the road ill. by author. Peachtree, 2003. ISBN 978-1-56145-287-3 Subj: Animals – dogs. Automobiles. Family life – aunts, uncles. Motorcycles.

Blake, Robert J. *Fledgling* ill. by author. Philomel, 2000. ISBN 978-0-399-23321-0 Subj: Activities – flying. Birds – kestrels. Cities, towns.

Little devils ill. by author. Philomel, 2009. ISBN 978-0-399-24322-6 Subj: Animals – Tasmanian devils. Behavior – lost. Family life – mothers.

Painter and Ugly ill. by author. Penguin, 2011. ISBN 978-0-399-24323-3 Subj: Alaska. Animals – dogs. Friendship. Sports – racing. Sports – sledding.

Blake, Stephanie. *I don't want to go to school!* ill. by author. Random House, 2009. ISBN 978-0-375-85688-4 Subj: Animals – rabbits. Emotions – fear. School – first day.

Blankenship, Lee Ann. *Mr. Tuggle's troubles* ill. by Karen Dugan. Boyds Mills, 2005. ISBN 978-1-59078-196-8 Subj: Behavior – lost & found possessions. Behavior – messy. Character traits – orderliness. Clothing.

Blechman, Nicholas. *Night light* ill. by author. Scholastic, 2013. ISBN 978-0-545-46263-1 Subj: Airplanes, airports. Automobiles. Counting, numbers. Format, unusual. Light, lights. Rhyming text. Trains. Trucks.

Blegvad, Lenore. *First friends* ill. by Erik Blebgad. HarperCollins, 2000. ISBN 978-0-694-01273-2 Subj: Behavior – sharing. Friendship. Rhyming text.

Bleiman, Andrew. *ABC zooborns!* by Andrew Bleiman and Chris Eastland. Simon & Schuster, 2012. ISBN 978-1-4424-4371-6 Subj: ABC books. Animals. Zoos.

Bless the beasts: children's prayers and poems about animals ill. by Kris Waldherr. SeaStar, 2002. ISBN 978-1-58717-176-5 Subj: Animals. Poetry. Religion.

Blessing, Charlotte. *New old shoes* ill. by Gary R. Phillips. Pleasant St, 2009. ISBN 978-0-9792035-

6-5 Subj: Clothing – shoes. Foreign lands – Africa.

Blexbolex. *Seasons* ill. by author. Enchanted Lion, 2010. ISBN 978-1-59270-095-0 Subj: Seasons.

Bley, Anette. *And what comes after a thousand?* ill. by author. Kane/Miller, 2007. ISBN 978-1-933605-27-2 Subj: Death. Emotions – grief. Old age.

A friend ill. by author. Kane/Miller, 2009. ISBN 978-1-935279-00-6 Subj: Friendship.

Bliss, Harry. *Bailey* ill. by author. Scholastic, 2011. ISBN 978-0-545-23344-6 Subj: Animals – dogs. School.

Bailey at the museum ill. by author. Scholastic, 2012. ISBN 978-0-545-23345-3 Subj: Animals – dogs. Museums. School – field trips.

Bloch, Serge. *Butterflies in my stomach and other school hazards* ill. by author. Sterling, 2008. ISBN 978-1-4027-4158-6 Subj: Humorous stories. Language. School – first day.

You are what you eat: and other mealtime hazards ill. by author. Sterling, 2010. ISBN 978-1-4027-7130-9 Subj: Food. Humorous stories. Language.

Block party today ill. by Stéphanie Roth. Knopf, 2004. ISBN 978-0-375-92216-9 Subj: Communities, neighborhoods. Friendship. Parties.

Blomgren, Jennifer. *Where do I sleep?* ill. by Andrea Gabriel. Sasquatch, 2001. ISBN 978-1-57061-258-9 Subj: Animals – babies. Lullabies. Rhyming text. Sleep.

Blood, Charles L. *The goat in the rug* by Charles L. Blood and Martin A. Link ill. by Nancy Winslow Parker. Parents' Magazine Pr., 1976. ISBN 978-0-8193-0828-3 Subj: Activities – weaving. Animals – goats. Indians of North America – Navajo.

Bloom, Becky. *Crackers* ill. by Pascal Biet. Orchard, 2001. ISBN 978-0-531-30326-9 Subj: Activities – working. Animals – cats. Animals – mice. Character traits – kindness.

Mice make trouble ill. by Pascal Biet. Orchard, 2000. ISBN 978-0-531-33253-5 Subj: Activities – drawing. Animals – mice. Magic.

Bloom, Susan. *The best book to read* (Bertram, Debbie)

The best place to read (Bertram, Debbie)

The best time to read (Bertram, Debbie)

Bloom, Suzanne. *The bus for us* ill. by author. Boyds Mills, 2001. ISBN 978-1-56397-932-3 Subj: School – first day.

Feeding friendsies ill. by author. Boyds Mills, 2011. ISBN 978-1-59078-529-4 Subj: Food. Imagination.

Fox forgets ill. by author. Boyds Mills, 2013. ISBN 978-1-59078-996-4 Subj: Animals – bears. Animals – foxes. Behavior – forgetfulness. Birds – geese. Memories, memory.

A mighty fine time machine ill. by author. Boyds Mills, 2009. ISBN 978-1-59078-527-0 Subj: Activities – playing. Animals. Imagination.

No place for a pig ill. by author. Boyds Mills, 2003. ISBN 978-1-59078-047-3 Subj: Animals – pigs. Cities, towns. Homes, houses.

Nuestro autobús / The bus for us ill. by author. Boyds Mills, 2008. ISBN 978-1-59078-629-1 Subj: Foreign languages. School – first day.

Oh! What a surprise! ill. by author. Boyds Mills, 2012. ISBN 978-1-59078-892-9 Subj: Animals – bears. Animals – foxes. Birds – geese. Gifts.

Piggy Monday ill. by author. Whitman, 2001. ISBN 978-0-8075-6529-2 Subj: Animals – pigs. Etiquette. School.

A splendid friend, indeed ill. by author. Boyds Mills, 2005. ISBN 978-1-59078-286-6 Subj: Animals – polar bears. Birds – geese. Friendship.

What about Bear? ill. by author. Boyds Mills, 2010. ISBN 978-1-59078-528-7 Subj: Activities – playing. Animals – bears. Animals – foxes. Birds – geese. Friendship.

Blossom tales ill. by Sarah Dillard. Moon Mt, 2002. ISBN 978-0-9677929-8-9 Subj: Flowers. Folk & fairy tales. Foreign lands.

Bloxam, Frances. *Antlers forever!* ill. by Jim Sollers. Down East, 2001. ISBN 978-0-89272-512-0 Subj: Animals – moose. Nature.

Blue, Rose. *Ron's big mission* (Naden, Corinne J.)

Bluemle, Elizabeth. *Dogs on the bed* ill. by Anne Wilsdorf. Candlewick, 2008. ISBN 978-0-7636-2608-2 Subj: Animals – dogs. Bedtime. Furniture – beds. Rhyming text.

How do you wokka-wokka? ill. by Randy Cecil. Candlewick, 2009. ISBN 978-0-7636-3228-1 Subj: Activities – dancing. Communities, neighborhoods. Parties.

My father the dog ill. by Randy Cecil. Candlewick, 2006. ISBN 978-0-7636-2222-0 Subj: Animals – dogs. Family life – fathers.

Blum, Mark. *Big trucks and diggers in 3-D* ill. by author. Chronicle, 2001. ISBN 978-0-8118-3172-7 Subj: Format, unusual – toy & movable books. Machines. Tractors. Trucks.

Blume, Judy. *The one in the middle is a green kangaroo* ill. by Irene Trivas. Macmillan, 1991. ISBN 978-0-02-711055-5 Subj: Family life. Self-concept.

The Pain and The Great One ill. by Irene Trivas. McGraw-Hill, 1974. ISBN 978-0-02-711100-2 Subj: Family life. Sibling rivalry.

Blumenthal, Deborah. *Aunt Claire's yellow beehive hair* ill. by Mary GrandPré. Dial, 2001. ISBN 978-0-8037-2509-6 Subj: Behavior – collecting things. Family life. Memories, memory.

The blue house dog ill. by Adam Gustavson. Peachtree, 2010. ISBN 978-1-56145-537-9 Subj: Animals – dogs. Death. Emotions – grief.

Charlie hits it big ill. by Denise Brunkus. HarperCollins, 2008. ISBN 978-0-06-056353-0 Subj: Animals – guinea pigs. Careers – actors.

Don't let the peas touch! ill. by Timothy Basil Ering. Scholastic, 2004. ISBN 978-0-439-29732-5 Subj: Family life – sisters. Sibling rivalry.

Ice palace ill. by Ted Rand. Clarion, 2003. ISBN 978-0-618-15960-4 Subj: Fairs, festivals. Seasons – winter. Sports.

Bluthenthal, Diana Cain. *I'm not invited?* ill. by author. Atheneum, 2003. ISBN 978-0-689-84141-5 Subj: Emotions. Friendship. Parties.

Boase, Susan. *Lucky boy* ill. by author. Houghton, 2002. ISBN 978-0-618-13175-4 Subj: Animals – dogs. Behavior – needing someone. Emotions – grief.

Boatfield, Jonny. *The twilight book* ill. by author. Bloomsbury, 2000. ISBN 978-0-7475-5083-9 Subj: Books, reading. Games. Mystery stories. Puzzles.

Bober, Suzanne. *In the garden with Van Gogh* (Merberg, Julie)

A magical day with Matisse (Merberg, Julie)

Bock, Lee. *Oh, crumps! / Ay, caramba!* ill. by Morgan Midgett. Raven Tree, 2003. ISBN 978-0-9720192-4-8 Subj: Animals. Careers – farmers. Farms. Foreign languages. Noise, sounds.

Bodkin, Odds. *The Christmas cobwebs* ill. by Terry Widener. Harcourt, 2001. ISBN 978-0-15-201459-9 Subj: Ethnic groups in the U.S. – German Americans. Family life. Holidays – Christmas. Spiders.

The crane wife ill. by Gennady Spirin. Harcourt, 1998. ISBN 978-0-15-201407-0 Subj: Activities – weaving. Birds – cranes. Character traits – kindness to animals. Folk & fairy tales. Foreign lands – Japan.

Boedoe, Geefwee. *Arrowville* ill. by author. Geringer, 2004. ISBN 978-0-06-055599-3 Subj: Prejudice. Rhyming text.

Boelts, Maribeth. *Before you were mine* ill. by David Walker. Penguin, 2007. ISBN 978-0-399-24526-8 Subj: Animals – dogs. Pets.

Big Daddy, frog wrestler ill. by Benrei Huang. Whitman, 2000. ISBN 978-0-8075-0717-9 Subj: Family life – fathers. Frogs & toads. Sports – wrestling.

Happy like soccer ill. by Lauren Castillo. Candlewick, 2012. ISBN 978-0-7636-4616-5 Subj: Behavior – resourcefulness. Communities, neighborhoods. Ethnic groups in the U.S. – African Americans. Family life – aunts, uncles. Poverty. Sports – soccer.

Looking for Sleepy ill. by Bernadette Pons. Whitman, 2004. ISBN 978-0-8075-0447-5 Subj: Animals – bears. Bedtime. Family life – fathers. Family life – sons.

Sweet dreams, Little Bunny! ill. by Kathy Parkinson. Whitman, 2010. ISBN 978-0-8075-4589-8 Subj: Animals – rabbits. Bedtime. Format, unusual – board books.

Those shoes ill. by Noah Jones. Candlewick, 2007. ISBN 978-0-7636-2499-6 Subj: Character traits – appearance. Clothing – shoes. Ethnic groups in the U.S. – African Americans.

You're a brother, Little Bunny! ill. by Kathy Parkinson. Whitman, 2001. ISBN 978-0-8075-9446-9 Subj: Animals – rabbits. Babies. Family life – brothers. Family life – brothers & sisters. Family life – new sibling.

Bogacki, Tomasz. *Circus girl* ill. by author. Farrar, 2001. ISBN 978-0-374-31291-6 Subj: Character traits – helpfulness. Circus. Friendship.

My first garden ill. by author. Farrar, 2000. ISBN 978-0-374-32518-3 Subj: Gardens, gardening.

Bogan, Paulette. *Goodnight Lulu* ill. by author. Bloomsbury, 2003. ISBN 978-1-58234-803-2 Subj: Bedtime. Birds – chickens. Family life – mothers.

Lulu the big little chick ill. by author. Bloomsbury, 2009. ISBN 978-1-59990-343-9 Subj: Behavior – running away. Birds – chickens. Character traits – smallness. Concepts – size. Family life – mothers.

Momma's magical purse ill. by author. Bloomsbury, 2004. ISBN 978-1-58234-842-1 Subj: Animals – cats. Animals – dogs. Clothing – handbags, purses. Family life – mothers. Magic.

Spike in the city ill. by author. Putnam, 2000. ISBN 978-0-399-23442-2 Subj: Animals – dogs. Behavior – lost & found possessions. Cities, towns.

Bogart, Jo Ellen. *Big and small, room for all* ill. by Gillian Newland. Tundra, 2009. ISBN 978-0-88776-891-0 Subj: Concepts – size. Nature.

Bogue, Gary. *There's an opossum in my backyard* ill. by Chuck Todd. Heyday Books, 2007. ISBN 978-1-59714-059-1 Subj: Animals – babies. Animals – possums.

Bolam, Emily. *Animals talk* ill. by author. ME Media/Tiger Tales, 2010. ISBN 978-1-58925-855-6 Subj: Animals. Format, unusual – board books. Noise, sounds.

I go potty ill. by author. Scholastic, 2010. ISBN 978-0-531-25233-8 Subj: Format, unusual – board books. Rhyming text. Toilet training.

Bolden, Tonya. *Rock of ages: a tribute to the Black church* ill. by R. Gregory Christie. Knopf, 2001. ISBN 978-0-679-99485-5 Subj: Ethnic groups in the U.S. – African Americans. Poetry. Religion.

Boldt, Claudia. *Odd dog* ill. by author. North-South, 2012. ISBN 978-0-7358-4068-3 Subj: Animals – dogs. Behavior – sharing. Food. Friendship.

Boldt, Mike. *123 versus ABC* ill. by author. HarperCollins, 2013. ISBN 978-0-06-210299-7 Subj: ABC books. Counting, numbers. Humorous stories.

Boling, Katherine. *New year be coming! a Gullah year* ill. by Daniel Minter. Whitman, 2002. ISBN 978-0-8075-5590-3 Subj: Days of the week, months of the year. Poetry.

Boling, Ruth L. *Come worship with me* ill. by Tracey Dahle Carrier. Geneva, 2001. ISBN 978-0-664-50045-0 Subj: Days of the week, months of the year. Religion.

Bolliger, Max. *The happy troll* ill. by Peter Sís. Holt, 2005. ISBN 978-0-8050-6982-2 Subj: Activities – singing. Behavior – greed. Mythical creatures – trolls.

Bollinger, Peter. *Algernon Graeves is scary enough* ill. by author. HarperCollins, 2005. ISBN 978-0-06-052269-8 Subj: Clothing – costumes. Holidays – Halloween.

Bond, Felicia. *Big hugs, little hugs* ill. by author. Penguin, 2012. ISBN 978-0-399-25614-1 Subj: Animals. Hugging.

The Halloween play ill. by author. HarperCollins, 1999. ISBN 978-0-06-028684-2 Subj: Animals – mice. Holidays – Halloween. School. Theater.

Poinsettia and her family ill. by author. HarperCollins, 1981. ISBN 978-0-690-04145-3 Subj: Animals – pigs. Behavior. Family life. Moving. Sibling rivalry.

Poinsettia and the firefighters ill. by author. Crowell, 1984. ISBN 978-0-690-04400-3 Subj: Animals – pigs. Bedtime. Night. Noise, sounds.

Bond, Michael. *Paddington Bear* ill. by R. W. Alley. HarperCollins, 1998. ISBN 978-0-06-027854-0 Subj: Animals – bears.

Paddington Bear and the Busy Bee Carnival ill. by R. W. Alley. HarperCollins, 1998. ISBN 978-0-06-027765-9 Subj: Animals – bears. Contests. Fairs, festivals.

Paddington Bear and the Christmas surprise ill. by R. W. Alley. HarperCollins, 1997. ISBN 978-0-694-00897-1 Subj: Animals – bears. Careers. Holidays – Christmas. Stores.

Paddington Bear goes to the hospital by Michael Bond and Karen Jankel ill. by R. W. Alley. HarperCollins, 2001. ISBN 978-0-694-01563-4 Subj: Accidents. Hospitals. Toys – bears.

Paddington Bear in the garden ill. by R. W. Alley. HarperCollins, 2002. ISBN 978-0-06-029696-4 Subj: Gardens, gardening. Toys – bears.

Bond, Rebecca. *Bravo, Maurice!* ill. by author. Little, 2000. ISBN 978-0-316-10545-3 Subj: Careers. Family life. Noise, sounds.

A city Christmas tree ill. by author. Little, Brown, 2005. ISBN 978-0-316-53731-5 Subj: Holidays – Christmas. Trees.

The great doughnut parade ill. by author. Houghton, 2007. ISBN 978-0-618-77705-1 Subj: Cumulative tales. Food. Parades.

Bonnett-Rampersaud, Louise. *Bubble and Squeak* ill. by Susan Banta. Marshall Cavendish, 2006. ISBN 978-0-7614-5310-9 Subj: Animals – mice. Bedtime. Emotions – fear. Family life – brothers & sisters.

How do you sleep? ill. by Kristin Kest. Marshall Cavendish, 2005. ISBN 978-0-7614-5231-7 Subj: Animals. Rhyming text. Sleep.

Never ask a bear ill. by Doris Barrette. HarperCollins, 2009. ISBN 978-0-06-112876-9 Subj: Animals – bears. Rhyming text.

Polly Hopper's pouch ill. by Lina Chesak-Librace. Dutton, 2001. ISBN 978-0-525-46525-6 Subj: Animals – kangaroos. Character traits – curiosity. Foreign lands – Australia.

Bonning, Tony. *Fox tale soup* ill. by Sally Hobson. Simon & Schuster, 2002. ISBN 978-0-689-84900-8 Subj: Animals – foxes. Character traits – cleverness. Farms. Folk & fairy tales. Food.

Snog the frog ill. by Rosalind Beardshaw. Barron's, 2005. ISBN 978-0-7641-5824-7 Subj: Frogs & toads. Royalty – princesses.

Bono, Mary. *Ugh! a bug* ill. by author. Walker, 2002. ISBN 978-0-8027-8800-9 Subj: Insects – ladybugs. Rhyming text.

Bonsignore, Joan. *Stick out your tongue: fantastic facts, features, and functions of animal and human tongues* ill. by John Ward. Peachtree, 2001. ISBN 978-1-56145-230-9 Subj: Anatomy – tongues. Senses – taste.

Bonwill, Ann. *Bug and Bear: a story of true friendship* ill. by Layn Marlow. Marshall Cavendish, 2011. ISBN 978-0-7614-5902-6 Subj: Animals – bears. Friendship. Insects.

The Frazzle family finds a way ill. by Stephen Gammell. Holiday House, 2013. ISBN 978-0-8234-2405-4 Subj: Activities – singing. Behavior – forgetfulness. Family life. Memories, memory. Songs.

I am not a copycat! ill. by Simon Rickerty. Simon & Schuster, 2013. ISBN 978-1-4424-8053-7 Subj: Animals – hippopotamuses. Behavior – imitation. Birds. Friendship.

Naughty toes ill. by Teresa Murfin. Tiger Tales, 2011. ISBN 978-1-58925-103-8 Subj: Activities – dancing. Ballet. Family life – sisters. Self-concept.

The book of Pooh: Biglet adapt. by Marge Kennedy; photos by John E. Barrett. Based on the screenplay by Andy Yerkes. Disney, 2002. ISBN 978-0-7868-3363-4 Subj: Animals – pigs. Concepts – size. Dreams.

Booth, Philip E. *Crossing* ill. by Bagram Ibatoulline. Candlewick, 2001. ISBN 978-0-7636-1420-1 Subj: Poetry. Trains.

Boothroyd, Jennifer. *What is a gas?* ill. with photos. Lerner, 2007. ISBN 978-0-8225-6818-6 Subj: Science.

Bootman, Colin. *Fish for the Grand Lady* ill. by author. Holiday House, 2006. ISBN 978-0-8234-1898-5 Subj: Family life – grandmothers. Foreign lands – Trinidad. Sports – fishing.

Borchard, Therese Johnson. *Taste and see the goodness of the Lord* ill. by Phyllis V. Saroff. Paulist Pr., 2000. ISBN 978-0-8091-6665-7 Subj: Religion.

Borden, Louise. *A. Lincoln and me* ill. by Ted Lewin. Scholastic, 2000. ISBN 978-0-590-45714-9 Subj: Birthdays. Self-concept. U.S. history.

America is . . . ill. by Stacey Schuett. McElderry, 2002. ISBN 978-0-689-83900-9 Subj: Poetry. U.S. history.

Big brothers don't take naps ill. by Emma Dodd. Simon & Schuster, 2011. ISBN 978-1-4169-5503-0 Subj: Family life – brothers. Family life – new sibling.

The day Eddie met the author ill. by Adam Gustavson. McElderry, 2001. ISBN 978-0-689-83405-9 Subj: Books, reading. Careers – writers. School.

The lost-and-found tooth ill. by Adam Gustavson. Simon & Schuster, 2008. ISBN 978-1-4169-1814-1 Subj: School. Teeth.

Off to first grade ill. by Joan Rankin. Simon & Schuster, 2008. ISBN 978-0-689-87395-9 Subj: Behavior – worrying. School – first day.

Thanksgiving is . . . ill. by Steve Björkman. Scholastic, 1997. ISBN 978-0-590-33128-9 Subj: Holidays – Thanksgiving.

Borgo, Lacy. *Big Mama's baby* ill. by Nancy Cote. Boyds Mills, 2007. ISBN 978-1-59078-187-6 Subj: Animals – bulls, cows. Family life – grandmothers. Texas.

Boroson, Martin. *Becoming me: a story of creation* ill. by Chris Gilvan-Cartwright. Skylight Paths, 2000. ISBN 978-1-893361-11-9 Subj: Creation. Religion.

Bosca, Francesca. *The apple king* ill. by Giuliano Ferri. NorthSouth, 2001. ISBN 978-0-7358-1397-7 Subj: Animals. Behavior – sharing. Royalty – kings. Trees.

The three grasshoppers ill. by Giuliano Ferri. Purple Bear, 2006. ISBN 978-1-933327-13-6 Subj: Friendship. Insects – grasshoppers. Music.

Boswell, Addie. *The rain stomper* ill. by Eric Velasquez. Marshall Cavendish, 2008. ISBN 978-0-7614-5393-2 Subj: Ethnic groups in the U.S. – African Americans. Parades. Weather – rain. Weather – storms.

Bottner, Barbara. *An annoying ABC* ill. by Michael Emberley. Random House, 2011. ISBN 978-0-375-86708-8 Subj: ABC books. Behavior – misbehavior. School – nursery.

Bootsie Barker bites ill. by Peggy Rathmann. Putnam, 1992. ISBN 978-0-399-22125-5 Subj: Activities – playing. Behavior – bullying, teasing.

Flower girl ill. by Laura Grier. Marshall Cavendish, 2012. ISBN 978-0-7614-6119-7 Subj: Family life – aunts, uncles. Weddings.

Miss Brooks loves books! (and I don't) ill. by Michael Emberley. Random House, 2010. ISBN 978-0-375-84682-3 Subj: Books, reading. Libraries. School.

Pish and Posh by Barbara Bottner and Gerald Kruglik ill. by Barbara Bottner. Tegen, 2004. ISBN 978-0-06-051417-4 Subj: Behavior – lost & found possessions. Fairies. Magic.

Raymond and Nelda ill. by Nancy Hayashi. Peachtree, 2007. ISBN 978-1-56145-394-8 Subj: Animals – rabbits. Animals – squirrels. Careers – postal workers. Friendship.

Rosa's room ill. by Beth Spiegel. Peachtree, 2004. ISBN 978-1-56145-302-3 Subj: Family life – mothers. Friendship. Furniture – beds. Moving.

Wallace's lists by Barbara Bottner and Gerald Kruglik ill. by Olof Landström. Tegen, 2004. ISBN 978-0-06-000225-1 Subj: Animals – mice. Character traits – orderliness. Friendship.

Bouchard, Dave. *Fairy* ill. by Dean Griffiths. Orca, 2001. ISBN 978-1-55143-212-0 Subj: Fairies. Teeth.

Nokum is my teacher ill. by Allen Sapp. Fitzhenry & Whiteside, 2007. ISBN 978-0-88995-367-3 Subj: Family life – grandmothers. Foreign languages. Indians of North America – Cree.

The song within my heart ill. by Allen Sapp. Raincoast, 2002. ISBN 978-1-55192-559-2 Subj: Activities – storytelling. Indians of North America. Pow-wows.

Boudreau, Hélène. *I dare you not to yawn* ill. by Serge Bloch. Candlewick, 2013. ISBN 978-0-7636-5070-4 Subj: Bedtime.

Bouler, Olivia. *Olivia's birds: saving the Gulf* ill. by author. Sterling, 2011. ISBN 978-1-4027-8665-5 Subj: Birds. Behavior – resourcefulness. Character traits – generosity. Character traits – helpfulness. Sea & seashore.

Bourgeois, Paulette. *Fire fighters* ill. by Kim LaFave. Kids Can, 1998. ISBN 978-1-55074-438-5 Subj: Careers – firefighters. Communities, neighborhoods. Fire.

Franklin and Harriet ill. by Brenda Clark. Scholastic, 2001. ISBN 978-0-439-26424-2 Subj: Animals. Character traits – helpfulness. Family life – brothers & sisters. Reptiles – turtles, tortoises. Sibling rivalry. Toys.

Franklin and the thunderstorm ill. by Brenda Clark. Scholastic, 1998. ISBN 978-0-590-02635-2 Subj: Animals. Emotions – fear. Reptiles – turtles, tortoises. Weather – lightning, thunder. Weather – storms.

Franklin in the dark ill. by Brenda Clark. Kids Can, 1986. ISBN 978-0-919964-93-8 Subj: Emotions – fear. Night. Reptiles – turtles, tortoises.

Franklin rides a bike ill. by Brenda Clark. Kids Can, 1997. ISBN 978-1-55074-414-9 Subj: Animals. Reptiles – turtles, tortoises. Sports – bicycling.

Franklin says "I love you" ill. by Brenda Clark. Scholastic, 2002. ISBN 978-1-55337-035-2 Subj: Behavior – worrying. Birthdays. Family life – mothers. Gifts. Reptiles – turtles, tortoises.

Franklin's baby sister ill. by Brenda Clark. Scholastic, 2000. ISBN 978-1-55074-794-2 Subj: Babies. Family life – brothers & sisters. Reptiles – turtles, tortoises. Seasons – spring.

Franklin's Christmas gift ill. by Brenda Clark. Kids Can, 1998. ISBN 978-1-55074-466-8 Subj: Gifts. Holidays – Christmas. Reptiles – turtles, tortoises.

Franklin's class trip by Paulette Bourgeois and Sharon Jennings ill. by Brenda Clark. Scholastic, 1999. ISBN 978-0-590-13002-8 Subj: Animals. Dinosaurs. Museums. Reptiles – turtles, tortoises. School – field trips. Toys.

Franklin's new friend ill. by Brenda Clark. Scholastic, 1997. ISBN 978-0-590-02592-8 Subj: Animals – moose. Friendship. Reptiles – turtles, tortoises.

Franklin's secret club ill. by Brenda Clark. Kids Can, 1998. ISBN 978-0-590-13000-4 Subj: Animals. Clubs, gangs. Friendship. Reptiles – turtles, tortoises.

Garbage collectors ill. by Kim LaFave. Kids Can, 1998. ISBN 978-1-55074-440-8 Subj: Careers – sanitation workers. Communities, neighborhoods.

Oma's quilt ill. by Stéphane Jorisch. Kids Can, 2001. ISBN 978-1-55074-777-5 Subj: Family life – grandmothers. Quilts.

Police officers ill. by Kim LaFave. Kids Can, 1999. ISBN 978-1-55074-502-3 Subj: Careers – police officers. Communities, neighborhoods.

Postal workers ill. by Kim LaFave. Kids Can, 1998. ISBN 978-1-55074-504-7 Subj: Birthdays. Careers – postal workers. Communities, neighborhoods.

Bourguignon, Laurence. *Heart in the pocket* ill. by Valérie d'Heur. Eerdmans, 2008. ISBN 978-0-8028-5343-1 Subj: Animals – babies. Animals – kangaroos. Family life – mothers.

Boutignon, Beatrice. *Not all animals are blue: a big book of little differences* ill. by author. Kane/Miller, 2009. ISBN 978-1-933605-96-8 Subj: Animals. Character traits – individuality. Concepts.

Bowen, Anne. *Christmas is coming* ill. by Tomasz Bogacki. Lerner, 2007. ISBN 978-1-57505-934-1 Subj: Holidays – Christmas.

The great math tattle battle ill. by Jaime Zollars. Whitman, 2006. ISBN 978-0-8075-3163-1 Subj: Behavior – gossip. Counting, numbers. School.

I know an old teacher ill. by Stephen Gammell. Carolrhoda, 2008. ISBN 978-0-8225-7984-7 Subj: Careers – teachers. Cumulative tales. Pets. Rhyming text. School.

I loved you before you were born ill. by Greg Shed. HarperCollins, 2001. ISBN 978-0-06-028721-4 Subj: Babies. Family life – grandmothers. Memories, memory.

Scooter in the outside ill. by Abby Carter. Holiday House, 2012. ISBN 978-0-8234-2326-2 Subj: Animals – dogs. Character traits – responsibility. Pets.

Tooth Fairy's first night ill. by Jon Berkeley. Carolrhoda, 2005. ISBN 978-1-57505-753-8 Subj: Fairies. Teeth.

When you visit Grandma and Grandpa ill. by Tomasz Bogacki. Lerner, 2004. ISBN 978-1-57505-610-4 Subj: Babies. Family life – brothers & sisters. Family life – grandparents.

Bower, Gary. *Ivy's icicle* ill. by Jan Bower. Tyndale, 2002. ISBN 978-0-8423-7417-0 Subj: Behavior – forgiving. Family life – brothers & sisters. Family life – grandmothers.

Bower, Tamara. *The shipwrecked sailor: an Egyptian tale with hieroglyphs* ill. by author. Atheneum, 2000. ISBN 978-0-689-83046-4 Subj: Folk & fairy tales. Foreign lands – Egypt. Hieroglyphics. Magic. Reptiles – snakes.

Bowers, Tim. *A new home* ill. by author. Harcourt, 2002. ISBN 978-0-15-216564-2 Subj: Animals – squirrels. Friendship. Moving.

Bowie, C. W. *Busy fingers* ill. by Fred Willingham. Whispering Coyote, 2003. ISBN 978-1-58089-036-6 Subj: Anatomy – hands. Rhyming text.

Busy toes ill. by Fred Willingham. Whispering Coyote, 1998. ISBN 978-1-879085-72-5 Subj: Activities. Anatomy – toes. Rhyming text.

Bowles, Paula. *Scary Mary* ill. by author. Tiger Tales, 2012. ISBN 978-1-58925-110-6 Subj: Behavior – bullying, teasing. Birds – chickens. Emotions – loneliness.

Bowman, Patty. *The amazing Hamweenie* ill. by author. Philomel, 2012. ISBN 978-0-399-25688-2 Subj: Animals – cats. Imagination.

Boxall, Ed. *Francis the scaredy cat* ill. by author. Candlewick, 2002. ISBN 978-0-7636-1767-7 Subj: Animals – cats. Emotions – fear. Monsters.

Boyce, Katie. *Hector the hermit crab* ill. by author. Bloomsbury, 2003. ISBN 978-1-58234-800-1 Subj: Character traits – confidence. Crustaceans – crabs. Friendship. Self-concept.

Boyd, Lizi. *I love Daddy* ill. by author. Candlewick, 2004. ISBN 978-0-7636-2217-6 Subj: Activities. Family life – fathers. Family life – sons. Frogs & toads.

I love Mommy ill. by author. Candlewick, 2004. ISBN 978-0-7636-2216-9 Subj: Activities. Family life – mothers. Family life – sons. Frogs & toads.

Inside outside ill. by author. Chronicle, 2013. ISBN 978-1-4521-0644-1 Subj: Activities – playing. Concepts. Format, unusual. Wordless.

Boyden, Linda. *The blue roses* ill. by Amy Córdova. Lee & Low, 2002. ISBN 978-1-58430-037-3 Subj: Death. Emotions. Family life – grandfathers. Gardens, gardening. Indians of North America.

Boyer, Cécile. *Woof meow tweet-tweet* ill. by author. Seven Footer, 2011. ISBN 978-1-934734-60-5 Subj: Animals – cats. Animals – dogs. Birds.

Boyle, Bob. *Hugo and the really, really, really long string* ill. by author. Random House, 2010. ISBN 978-0-375-83423-3 Subj: Animals. String.

Boynton, Sandra. *Christmas parade* ill. by author. Simon & Schuster, 2012. ISBN 978-1-4424-6813-9 Subj: Animals. Holidays – Christmas. Musical instruments – bands. Parades. Rhyming text.

Yay, you! moving out, moving up, moving on ill. by author. Simon & Schuster, 2001. ISBN 978-0-689-84283-2 Subj: Character traits – individuality. Rhyming text.

Bracken, Beth. *The little bully* ill. by Jennifer A. Bell. Picture Window, 2012. ISBN 978-1-4048-6795-6 Subj: Animals. Behavior – bullying, teasing. Friendship. School.

Too shy for show-and-tell ill. by Jennifer A. Bell. Picture Window, 2011. ISBN 978-1-4048-6654-6 Subj: Animals – giraffes. Character traits – shyness. School.

Bradbury, Ray. *Switch on the night* ill. by Leo Dillon and Diane Dillon. Knopf, 2000, 1993. ISBN 978-0-375-80608-7 Subj: Emotions – fear. Friendship. Night.

Bradby, Marie. *The longest wait* ill. by Peter Catalanotto. Orchard, 1998. ISBN 978-0-531-08721-3 Subj: Careers – postal workers. Weather – snow. Weather – storms.

Momma, where are you from? ill. by Chris Soentpiet. Orchard, 2000. ISBN 978-0-531-33105-7 Subj: Cities, towns. Ethnic groups in the U.S. – African Americans. Family life – mothers.

More than anything else ill. by Chris Soentpiet. Orchard, 1995. ISBN 978-0-531-08764-0 Subj: Behavior – seeking better things. Books, reading. Ethnic groups in the U.S. – African Americans.

Once upon a farm ill. by Ted Rand. Orchard, 2002. ISBN 978-0-439-31766-5 Subj: Ethnic groups in the U.S. – African Americans. Farms. Rhyming text.

Bradford, Karleen. *You can't rush a cat* by Karleen Bradford and Leslie Elizabeth Watts ill. by Leslie Elizabeth Watts. Orca, 2004. ISBN 978-1-

55143-247-2 Subj: Animals – cats. Family life – grandfathers.

Bradford, Wade. *Why do I have to make my bed?* ill. by Johanna van der Sterre. Tricycle, 2011. ISBN 978-1-58246-327-8 Subj: Character traits – cleanliness. Family life – mothers.

Bradley, Kimberly Brubaker. *Ballerino Nate* ill. by R. W. Alley. Penguin, 2006. ISBN 978-0-8037-2954-4 Subj: Activities – dancing. Animals – dogs. Ballet. Character traits – being different.

Favorite things ill. by Laura Huliska-Beith. Dial, 2003. ISBN 978-0-8037-2597-3 Subj: Bedtime. Day. Family life – mothers. Imagination.

The perfect pony ill. by Shelagh McNicholas. Penguin, 2007. ISBN 978-0-8037-2851-6 Subj: Animals – horses, ponies.

Pop! a book about bubbles photos by Margaret Miller. HarperCollins, 2001. ISBN 978-0-06-028701-6 Subj: Bubbles.

Bradman, Tony. *Daddy's lullaby* ill. by Jason Cockcroft. McElderry, 2002. ISBN 978-0-689-84295-5 Subj: Family life – fathers. Lullabies.

The perfect baby ill. by Holly Swain. Egmont, 2010. ISBN 978-1-4052-2755-1 Subj: Family life – new sibling. Sibling rivalry.

Braeuner, Shellie. *The great dog wash* ill. by Robert Neubecker. Simon & Schuster, 2009. ISBN 978-1-4169-7116-0 Subj: Animals – dogs. Character traits – cleanliness. Rhyming text.

Braithwaite, Jill. *Police cars* ill. by author. Lerner, 2004. ISBN 978-0-8225-0770-3 Subj: Automobiles. Careers – police officers.

Brallier, Jess M. *Tess's tree* ill. by Peter H. Reynolds. HarperCollins, 2010. ISBN 978-0-06-168752-5 Subj: Trees.

Brami, Elisbeth. *Mommy time* by Elisbeth Brami and Anne-Sophie Tschiegg ill. by Anne-Sophie Tschiegg. Kane/Miller, 2002. ISBN 978-1-929132-22-5 Subj: Family life – mothers. Imagination.

Bramsen, Carin. *Hey, duck!* ill. by author. Random House, 2013. ISBN 978-0-375-86990-7 Subj: Animals – cats. Birds – ducks. Friendship. Rhyming text.

Brandenberg, Alexa. *Ballerina flying* ill. by author. HarperCollins, 2002. ISBN 978-0-06-029550-9 Subj: Activities – dancing. Ballet.

Brandenberg, Aliki *see* Aliki

Brandle, Bine. *Flusi, the sock monster* ill. by author. Kane/Miller, 2004. ISBN 978-1-929132-69-0 Subj: Behavior – lost & found possessions. Clothing – socks. Monsters.

Brandt, Amy. *Benjamin comes back / Benjamin regresa* ill. by Janice Lee Porter. Redleaf, 2000. ISBN 978-1-884834-79-0 Subj: Family life – mothers. Foreign languages. School – nursery.

When Katie was our teacher / Cuando Katie era nuestra maestra ill. by Janice Lee Porter. Redleaf, 2000. ISBN 978-1-884834-78-3 Subj: Careers – teachers. Foreign languages. School – nursery.

Branford, Henrietta. *Little Pig Figwort can't get to sleep* ill. by Claudio Muñoz. Clarion, 2000. ISBN 978-0-618-15968-0 Subj: Animals – pigs. Bedtime. Sleep.

Branley, Franklyn M. *Air is all around you* ill. by Holly Keller. Rev. ed. Crowell, 1986. ISBN 978-0-690-04503-1 Subj: Science.

Comets ill. by Giulio Maestro. Crowell, 1984. Subj: Science. Sky.

Down comes the rain ill. by James Graham Hale. HarperCollins, 1997. ISBN 978-0-06-025338-7 Subj: Science. Weather. Weather – rain.

Earthquakes ill. by Richard Rosenblum. HarperCollins, 1990. ISBN 978-0-690-04663-2 Subj: Earth. Science.

Eclipse: darkness in daytime ill. by Donald Crews. Rev. ed. HarperCollins, 1988. ISBN 978-0-690-04619-9 Subj: Science. Sun.

Flash, crash, rumble, and roll ill. by Barbara Emberley and Ed Emberley. Rev. ed. Crowell, 1985. ISBN 978-0-690-04425-6 Subj: Science. Weather – lightning, thunder.

Floating in space ill. by True Kelley. HarperCollins, 1998. ISBN 978-0-06-025433-9 Subj: Careers – astronauts. Science. Space & space ships.

Gravity is a mystery ill. by Don Madden. Rev. ed. Crowell, 1986. ISBN 978-0-690-04527-7 Subj: Science.

The International Space Station ill. by True Kelley. HarperCollins, 2000. ISBN 978-0-06-028703-0 Subj: Space & space ships.

Light and darkness ill. by Stacey Schuett. Rev. ed. HarperCollins, 1998. ISBN 978-0-06-027295-1 Subj: Science.

The planets in our solar system ill. by Don Madden. Crowell, 1981. ISBN 978-0-690-04026-5 Subj: Planets. Science. Space & space ships. Sun. World.

Rain and hail ill. by Harriett Barton. Rev. ed. Crowell, 1983. ISBN 978-0-690-04353-2 Subj: Science. Weather. Weather – rain.

The sky is full of stars ill. by Felicia Bond. Crowell, 1981. ISBN 978-0-690-04123-1 Subj: Science. Sky. Stars.

Snow is falling ill. by Holly Keller. Rev. ed. Crowell, 1986. ISBN 978-0-690-04548-2 Subj: Science. Weather – snow.

The sun, our nearest star ill. by Edward Miller. Rev. & newly ill. ed. HarperCollins, 2002. ISBN 978-0-06-028535-7 Subj: Earth. Science. Sun.

Sunshine makes the seasons ill. by Giulio Maestro. Rev. ed. Crowell, 1985. ISBN 978-0-690-04482-9 Subj: Science. Seasons. Sun.

Tornado alert ill. by Giulio Maestro. Crowell, 1988. ISBN 978-0-690-04688-5 Subj: Science. Weather – storms.

Volcanoes ill. by Megan Lloyd. HarperCollins, 2008. ISBN 978-0-06-028011-6 Subj: Science. Volcanoes.

Volcanoes ill. by Marc Simont. Crowell, 1985. ISBN 978-0-690-04431-7 Subj: Science. Volcanoes.

What makes a magnet? ill. by True Kelley. HarperCollins, 1996. ISBN 978-0-06-026442-0 Subj: Science.

What makes day and night ill. by Arthur Dorros. Rev. ed. Crowell, 1986. ISBN 978-0-690-04524-6 Subj: Earth. Science.

What the moon is like ill. by True Kelley. Rev. ed. Crowell, 1986. ISBN 978-0-690-04512-3 Subj: Moon. Science.

Brannen, Sarah S. *Uncle Bobby's wedding* ill. by author. Putnam, 2008. ISBN 978-0-399-24712-5 Subj: Family life – aunts, uncles. Homosexuality. Weddings.

Braun, Eric. *Trust me, Jack's beanstalk stinks: the story of Jack and the beanstalk as told by the giant* ill. by Cristian Bernardini. Picture Window, 2011. ISBN 978-1-4048-6675-1 Subj: Folk & fairy tales. Giants. Humorous stories. Plants.

Braun, Sebastien. *Back to bed, Ed!* ill. by author. Peachtree, 2010. ISBN 978-1-56145-518-8 Subj: Animals – mice. Bedtime. Sleep.

Digger and Tom! ill. by author. HarperCollins, 2013. ISBN 978-0-06-207752-3 Subj: Character traits – cooperation. Character traits – persistence. Machines. Trucks.

I love my daddy ill. by author. HarperCollins, 2004. ISBN 978-0-06-054311-2 Subj: Animals – bears. Day. Family life – fathers. Family life – sons.

I love my mommy ill. by author. HarperCollins, 2004. ISBN 978-0-06-054310-5 Subj: Animals – squirrels. Family life – mothers.

Toot and Pop! ill. by author. HarperCollins, 2012. ISBN 978-0-06-207750-9 Subj: Behavior – boasting. Boats, ships. Character traits – smallness. Character traits – vanity.

Who's hiding? ill. by author. Candlewick, 2013. ISBN 978-0-7636-5932-5 Subj: Behavior – hiding. Format, unusual – toy & movable books. Gardens, gardening.

Braver, Vanita. *Madison and the two wheeler* ill. by Carl DiRocco. Star Bright, 2007. ISBN 978-1-59572-110-5 Subj: Character traits – perseverance. Sports – bicycling.

Braybrooks, Ann. *Plenty of pockets* ill. by Scott Menchin. Harcourt, 2000. ISBN 978-0-15-202173-3 Subj: Character traits – orderliness. Clothing – pockets.

Breathed, Berkeley. *Edwurd Fudwupper fibbed big: explained by Fannie Fudwupper* ill. by author. Little, 2000. ISBN 978-0-316-10675-7 Subj: Aliens. Character traits – honesty. Family life – brothers & sisters.

Mars needs moms! ill. by author. Penguin, 2007. ISBN 978-0-399-24736-1 Subj: Aliens. Family life – mothers.

Brebeuf, Jean de. *The Huron carol* English lyrics by Jesse Edgar Middleton; ill. by Ian Wallace. Groundwood, 2006. ISBN 978-0-88899-711-1 Subj: Foreign lands – Canada. Holidays – Christmas. Religion – Nativity. Songs.

Breen, Steve. *Pug and Doug* ill. by author. Dial, 2013. ISBN 978-0-8037-3521-7 Subj: Animals – dogs. Behavior – misunderstanding. Birthdays. Friendship.

The secret of Santa's island ill. by author. Dial, 2009. ISBN 978-0-8037-3126-4 Subj: Activities – vacationing. Holidays – Christmas. Islands. Santa Claus. Sea & seashore – beaches.

Stick ill. by author. Penguin, 2007. ISBN 978-0-8037-3124-0 Subj: Frogs & toads. Insects – dragonflies.

Violet the pilot ill. by author. Dial, 2008. ISBN 978-0-8037-3125-7 Subj: Activities – flying. Behavior – resourcefulness. Careers – airplane pilots. Character traits – individuality.

Brennan, Eileen. *Bad Astrid* ill. by Regan Dunnick. Random House, 2013. ISBN 978-0-375-85580-1 Subj: Animals – dogs. Behavior – bullying, teasing. Rhyming text.

Dirtball Pete ill. by author. Random House, 2010. ISBN 978-0-375-83425-7 Subj: Behavior – messy. Character traits – cleanliness. Hygiene. Self-concept.

Brennan, Herbie. *Frankenstella and the video store monster* ill. by Cathy Gale. Bloomsbury, 2002. ISBN 978-1-58234-752-3 Subj: Monsters.

Brennan, Linda Crotta. *Marshmallow kisses* ill. by Mari Takabayashi. Houghton, 2000. ISBN 978-0-395-73872-6 Subj: Rhyming text. Seasons – summer.

Brennan, Rosemarie. *Willow* (Brennan-Nelson, Denise)

Brennan-Nelson, Denise. *Grady the goose* ill. by Michael Glenn Monroe. Sleeping Bear, 2006. ISBN 978-1-58536-282-0 Subj: Behavior – lost. Birds – geese.

He's been a monster all day! ill. by Cyd Moore. Sleeping Bear, 2013. ISBN 978-1-58536-827-3 Subj: Behavior – misbehavior. Monsters. Rhyming text.

J is for jack-o-lantern: a halloween alphabet ill. by Donald Wu. Sleeping Bear, 2009. ISBN 978-1-58536-443-5 Subj: ABC books. Holidays – Halloween.

My grandma likes to say ill. by Jane Monroe Donovan. Sleeping Bear, 2007. ISBN 978-1-58536-284-4 Subj: Language. Rhyming text.

Willow by Denise Brennan-Nelson and Rosemarie Brennan ill. by Cyd Moore. Sleeping Bear, 2008. ISBN 978-1-58536-342-1 Subj: Art. Careers – teachers. Imagination. School.

Brenner, Barbara A. *Beef stew* ill. by Catherine Siracusa. Random House, 2004, ©1990. ISBN 978-0-394-95046-4 Subj: Family life – grandmothers. Food. Friendship.

Good morning, garden ill. by Denise Ortakales. NorthWord, 2004. ISBN 978-1-55971-888-2 Subj: Gardens, gardening. Morning. Rhyming text.

One small place by the sea ill. by Thomas Leonard. HarperCollins, 2004. ISBN 978-0-688-17183-4 Subj: Animals. Ecology. Sea & seashore.

What the elephant told ill. by Akemi Gutierrez. Holt, 2003. ISBN 978-0-8050-6442-1 Subj: Animals – babies. Animals – elephants. Babies.

Brenner, Emily. *On the first day of grade school* ill. by Bruce Whatley. HarperCollins, 2004. ISBN 978-0-06-051041-1 Subj: Animals. Careers – teachers. Cumulative tales. Rhyming text. School.

Brenner, Tom. *And then comes Halloween* ill. by Holly Meade. Candlewick, 2009. ISBN 978-0-7636-3659-3 Subj: Holidays – Halloween. Seasons – fall.

Brett, Jan. *Annie and the wild animals* ill. by author. Houghton, 1985. ISBN 978-0-395-37800-7 Subj: Animals. Animals – cats. Emotions – loneliness. Pets.

Armadillo rodeo ill. by author. Putnam, 1995. ISBN 978-0-399-22803-2 Subj: Animals. Animals – armadillos. Behavior – mistakes. Family life.

Berlioz the bear ill. by author. Putnam, 1991. ISBN 978-0-399-22248-1 Subj: Animals. Animals – bears. Cumulative tales. Music. Musical instruments – bands.

Christmas trolls ill. by author. Putnam, 1993. ISBN 978-0-399-22507-9 Subj: Animals – hedgehogs. Behavior – sharing. Behavior – stealing. Holidays – Christmas. Mythical creatures – trolls.

Comet's nine lives ill. by author. Putnam, 1996. ISBN 978-0-399-22931-2 Subj: Animals – cats. Animals – dogs. Behavior – carelessness. Lighthouses.

Daisy comes home ill. by author. Putnam, 2002. ISBN 978-0-399-23618-1 Subj: Behavior – lost. Birds – chickens. Foreign lands – China.

The Easter egg ill. by author. Penguin, 2010. ISBN 978-0-399-25238-9 Subj: Animals – rabbits. Contests. Eggs. Holidays – Easter.

The first dog ill. by author. Harcourt, 1988. ISBN 978-0-15-227650-8 Subj: Animals – dogs. Animals – wolves. Art. Caves. Pets.

Fritz and the beautiful horses ill. by author. Houghton, 1981. ISBN 978-0-395-30850-9 Subj: Animals – horses, ponies. Behavior – wishing. Character traits – cleverness. Folk & fairy tales.

The hat ill. by author. Putnam, 1997. ISBN 978-0-399-23101-8 Subj: Animals. Animals – hedgehogs. Clothing.

Hedgie blasts off! ill. by author. Penguin, 2006. ISBN 978-0-399-24621-0 Subj: Animals – hedgehogs. Careers – astronauts. Careers – custodians, janitors. Space & space ships.

Hedgie's surprise ill. by author. Putnam, 2000. ISBN 978-0-399-23477-4 Subj: Animals – hedgehogs. Birds – chickens. Character traits – cleverness. Eggs. Food. Mythical creatures – trolls.

Home for Christmas ill. by author. Penguin, 2011. ISBN 978-0-399-25653-0 Subj: Behavior – running away. Character traits – helpfulness. Holidays – Christmas. Mythical creatures – trolls.

Honey, honey — lion! a story from Africa ill. by author. Penguin, 2005. ISBN 978-0-399-24463-6 Subj: Animals – badgers. Behavior – greed. Birds. Foreign lands – Africa.

The mitten ill. by author. Putnam, 1990. ISBN 978-0-399-23109-4 Subj: Behavior – lost & found possessions. Folk & fairy tales. Foreign lands – Ukraine. Format, unusual – board books.

Mossy ill. by author. Putnam, 2012. ISBN 978-0-399-25782-7 Subj: Character traits – kindness to animals. Ecology. Gardens, gardening. Museums. Nature. Reptiles – turtles, tortoises.

The three little dassies ill. by author. Penguin, 2010. ISBN 978-0-399-25499-4 Subj: Animals. Birds – eagles. Desert. Folk & fairy tales. Foreign lands – Africa. Homes, houses.

The three snow bears ill. by author. Penguin, 2007. ISBN 978-0-399-24792-7 Subj: Animals – polar bears. Folk & fairy tales. Foreign lands – Arctic. Seasons – winter. Weather – snow.

The trouble with trolls ill. by author. Putnam, 1992. ISBN 978-0-399-22336-5 Subj: Animals – dogs. Character traits – cleverness. Clothing. Mythical creatures – trolls.

Who's that knocking on Christmas eve? ill. by author. Putnam, 2002. ISBN 978-0-399-23873-4 Subj: Foreign lands – Norway. Holidays – Christmas. Mythical creatures – trolls.

The wild Christmas reindeer ill. by author. Putnam, 1990. ISBN 978-0-399-22192-7 Subj: Animals – reindeer. Holidays – Christmas. Santa Claus.

Brett, Jessica. *Animals on the go* ill. by Richard Cowdrey. Harcourt, 2000. ISBN 978-0-15-202584-7 Subj: Animals.

Brewer, Dan. *Silver seeds* (Paolilli, Paul)

Brewer, Paul. *Lincoln tells a joke: how laughter saved the president (and the country)* (Krull, Kathleen)

Breznak, Irene. *Sneezy Louise* ill. by Janet Pedersen. Random House, 2009. ISBN 978-0-375-85169-8 Subj: Behavior – bad day. Etiquette. Illness – cold (disease).

Brian, Janeen. *Where does Thursday go?* ill. by Stephen Michael King. Clarion, 2001. ISBN 978-0-618-21264-4 Subj: Animals – bears. Birds. Days of the week, months of the year.

Briant, Ed. *A day at the beach* ill. by author. HarperCollins, 2005. ISBN 978-0-06-079982-3 Subj: Animals – pandas. Family life – fathers. Sea & seashore – beaches.

Seven stories ill. by author. Macmillan, 2005. ISBN 978-1-59643-056-3 Subj: Books, reading. Folk & fairy tales.

Bridge, Chris. *Andrew's story: a book about a boy who beat cancer* photos by author. Lerner, 2002. ISBN 978-0-8225-2587-5 Subj: Health & fitness. Illness – cancer.

Bridges, Margaret Park. *Am I big or little?* ill. by Tracy Dockray. SeaStar, 2000. ISBN 978-1-58717-020-1 Subj: Concepts – size. Family life – mothers.

Edna elephant ill. by Janie Bynum. Candlewick, 2002. ISBN 978-0-7636-1555-0 Subj: Activities. Animals – elephants.

I love the rain ill. by Christine Davenier. Chronicle, 2005. ISBN 978-1-58717-208-3 Subj: Weather – rain.

Bridges, Shirin Yim. *Mary Wrightly, so politely* ill. by Maria Monescillo. Harcourt, 2013. ISBN 978-0-547-34248-1 Subj: Behavior – unnoticed, unseen. Character traits – assertiveness. Etiquette. Family life. Gifts.

Ruby's wish ill. by Sophie Blackall. Chronicle, 2002. ISBN 978-0-8118-3490-2 Subj: Foreign lands – China. Gender roles. School.

The Umbrella Queen ill. by Taeeun Yoo. Greenwillow, 2008. ISBN 978-0-06-075040-4 Subj: Activities – painting. Character traits – individuality. Foreign lands – Thailand. Umbrellas.

Bridwell, Norman. *Clifford counts bubbles* ill. by author. Scholastic, 1992. ISBN 978-0-590-45872-6 Subj: Animals – dogs. Bubbles. Counting, numbers.

Clifford goes to Hollywood ill. by author. Scholastic, 1981. ISBN 978-0-606-03090-8 Subj: Animals – dogs. Character traits – loyalty.

Clifford the champion ill. by author. Scholastic, 2009. ISBN 978-0-545-10146-2 Subj: Animals – dogs. Contests.

Clifford's ABC ill. by author. Scholastic, 1984. ISBN 978-0-590-48694-1 Subj: ABC books. Animals – dogs.

Clifford's good deeds ill. by author. Four Winds, 1975. ISBN 978-0-590-07439-1 Subj: Animals – dogs. Automobiles. Behavior – mistakes. Careers – firefighters. Character traits – helpfulness.

Clifford's Halloween ill. by author. Four Winds, 1967. ISBN 978-0-590-66159-1 Subj: Animals – dogs. Holidays – Halloween.

Clifford's neighborhood ill. by Carolyn Bracken and Ken Edwards. Scholastic, 2002. ISBN 978-0-439-33242-2 Subj: Animals – dogs. Format, unusual – toy & movable books. Rhyming text.

Glow-in-the-dark Halloween ill. by Thompson Bros. Scholastic, 2001. ISBN 978-0-439-30566-2 Subj: Animals – dogs. Format, unusual. Holidays – Halloween.

The witch grows up ill. by author. Scholastic, 1980. ISBN 978-0-590-30045-2 Subj: Humorous stories. Magic. Witches.

The witch next door ill. by author. Four Winds, 1966. ISBN 978-0-590-40433-4 Subj: Witches.

Briere-Haquet, Alice. *Zebedee's balloon* ill. by Olivier Philipponneau. Auzou, 2011. ISBN 978-2-733819-42-5 Subj: Behavior – lost & found possessions. Rhyming text. Toys – balloons.

Briggs, Kelly Paul. *Lighthouse lullaby* ill. by author. Down East, 2000. ISBN 978-0-89272-486-4 Subj: Bedtime. Lighthouses. Rhyming text.

Briggs, Raymond. *The adventures of Bert* (Ahlberg, Allan)

A bit more Bert (Ahlberg, Allan)

Father Christmas ill. by author. Random House, 1997. ISBN 978-0-679-88776-8 Subj: Holidays – Christmas. Santa Claus. Wordless.

Jim and the beanstalk ill. by author. Coward, 1970. ISBN 978-0-698-11577-4 Subj: Folk & fairy tales. Giants. Humorous stories. Old age.

The puddleman ill. by author. Red Fox, 2006. ISBN 978-0-09-945642-1 Subj: Activities – walking. Family life – grandfathers. Magic.

The snowman ill. by author. Random House, 1978. ISBN 978-0-394-93973-5 Subj: Friendship. Snowmen. Wordless.

The snowman [a lift-the-flap board book] ill. by author. Random House, 1998. ISBN 978-0-679-88896-3 Subj: Concepts – color. Counting, numbers. Format, unusual – toy & movable books. Snowmen.

The snowman storybook ill. by author. Random House, 1997. ISBN 978-0-679-98343-9 Subj: Snowmen.

Bright, Paul. *The bears in the bed and the great big storm* ill. by Jane Chapman. Good Books, 2008. ISBN 978-1-56148-636-6 Subj: Animals – bears. Bedtime. Emotions – fear. Weather – storms.

Grumpy Badger's Christmas ill. by Jane Chapman. Good Books, 2009. ISBN 978-1-56148-673-1 Subj: Animals – badgers. Hibernation. Holidays – Christmas.

Quiet! ill. by Guy Parker-Rees. Scholastic, 2003. ISBN 978-0-439-54512-9 Subj: Animals. Animals – lions. Jungle. Noise, sounds.

Bright, Rachel. *Love Monster* ill. by author. Farrar, 2013. ISBN 978-0-374-34646-1 Subj: Emotions – love. Monsters.

Bright, Robert. *Georgie* ill. by author. Doubleday, 1944. ISBN 978-0-385-07307-3 Subj: Family life. Farms. Ghosts.

Georgie's Christmas carol ill. by author. Doubleday, 1975. ISBN 978-0-385-02410-5 Subj: Ghosts. Holidays – Christmas.

Georgie's Halloween ill. by author. Doubleday, 1958. Subj: Ghosts. Holidays – Halloween.

Brighton, Catherine. *Galileo's treasure box* ill. by author. Walker, 2001. ISBN 978-0-8027-8768-2 Subj: Science.

Brill, Marlene Targ. *Bronco Charlie and the Pony Express* ill. by Craig Orback. Carolrhoda, 2004. ISBN 978-1-57505-587-9 Subj: Animals – horses, ponies. Careers – postal workers. U.S. history.

Margaret Knight, girl inventor ill. by Joanne Friar. Millbrook, 2001. ISBN 978-0-7613-1756-2 Subj: Activities – weaving. Careers – inventors. Children as inventors. Safety. U.S. history.

Brillhart, Julie. *Molly rides the school bus* ill. by author. Whitman, 2002. ISBN 978-0-8075-5210-0 Subj: Buses. School – first day.

Brimner, Larry Dane. *The big, beautiful, brown box* ill. by Christine Tripp. Children's Press, 2001. ISBN 978-0-516-22160-1 Subj: Activities – playing. Character traits – cooperation.

Cat on wheels ill. by Mary Peterson. Boyds Mills, 2000. ISBN 978-1-56397-747-3 Subj: Animals – cats. Behavior – carelessness. Imagination. Sports – skateboarding.

The littlest wolf ill. by José Aruego and Ariane Dewey. HarperCollins, 2002. ISBN 978-0-06-029040-5 Subj: Animals – wolves. Behavior – growing up.

Trick or treat, Old Armadillo ill. by Dominic Catalano. Boyds Mills, 2010. ISBN 978-1-59078-758-8 Subj: Animals – armadillos. Foreign languages. Holidays – Halloween.

Brion, David. *Space vehicles* (Rockwell, Anne)

Brisson, Pat. *Hobbledy-clop* ill. by Maxie Chambliss. Boyds Mills, 2003. ISBN 978-1-56397-888-3 Subj: Animals. Cumulative tales. Family life – grandmothers. Toys.

I remember Miss Perry ill. by Stéphane Jorisch. Penguin, 2006. ISBN 978-0-8037-2981-0 Subj: Careers – teachers. Death. Emotions – grief. School.

Melissa Parkington's beautiful, beautiful hair ill. by Suzanne Bloom. Boyds Mills, 2006. ISBN 978-1-59078-409-9 Subj: Character traits – appearance. Character traits – generosity. Hair.

Sometimes we were brave ill. by France Brassard. Boyds Mills, 2010. ISBN 978-1-59078-586-7 Subj: Careers – military. Emotions. Family life. Family life – mothers.

Star blanket ill. by Erica Magnus. Boyds Mills, 2003. ISBN 978-1-56397-889-0 Subj: Bedtime. Family life – fathers. Memories, memory.

Broach, Elise. *Gumption!* ill. by Richard Egielski. Simon & Schuster, 2010. ISBN 978-1-4169-1628-4 Subj: Animals. Family life – aunts, uncles. Jungle.

Wet dog! ill. by David Catrow. Penguin, 2005. ISBN 978-0-8037-2809-7 Subj: Animals – dogs. Seasons – summer. Weddings.

What the no-good baby is good for ill. by Abby Carter. Penguin, 2005. ISBN 978-0-399-23877-2 Subj: Babies. Family life – brothers & sisters. Family life – new sibling. Sibling rivalry.

When dinosaurs came with everything ill. by David Small. Simon & Schuster, 2007. ISBN 978-0-689-86922-8 Subj: Dinosaurs. Humorous stories.

Brockenbrough, Martha. *The Dinosaur Tooth Fairy* ill. by Israel Sanchez. Scholastic, 2013. ISBN 978-0-545-24466-4 Subj: Dinosaurs. Fairies. Teeth.

Brocket, Jane. *Circles, stars, and squares: looking for shapes* photos by author. Millbrook, 2012. ISBN 978-0-7613-4611-1 Subj: Concepts – shape.

Ruby, violet, lime: looking for color photos by author. Millbrook, 2011. ISBN 978-0-7613-4612-8 Subj: Concepts – color. Language.

Spotty, stripy, swirly: what are patterns? ill. by author. Millbrook, 2012. ISBN 978-0-7613-4613-5 Subj: Concepts – patterns.

Brokamp, Elizabeth. *The picky little witch* ill. by Marsha Riti. Pelican, 2011. ISBN 978-1-58980-882-9 Subj: Food. Holidays – Halloween. Witches.

Brokering, Herbert F. *Earth and all stars: hymns and songs for young and old* ill. by author. Augsburg Fortress, 2003. ISBN 978-0-8006-5929-5 Subj: Music. Religion. Songs.

Bromley, Anne C. *The lunch thief* ill. by Robert Casilla. Tilbury House, 2010. ISBN 978-0-88448-311-3 Subj: Behavior – stealing. Character traits – kindness. Homeless. School.

Bromley, Nick. *Open very carefully: a book with bite* ill. by Nicola O'Byrne. Candlewick, 2013. ISBN 978-0-7636-6163-2 Subj: Birds – ducks. Books, reading. Folk & fairy tales. Reptiles – alligators, crocodiles.

Bronson, Linda. *The circus alphabet* ill. by author. Holt, 2001. ISBN 978-0-8050-6294-6 Subj: ABC books. Circus. Rhyming text.

Brooks, Alan. *Frogs jump* ill. by Steven Kellogg. Scholastic, 1996. ISBN 978-0-590-45528-2 Subj: Animals. Counting, numbers.

Brooks, Erik. *Polar opposites* ill. by author. Marshall Cavendish, 2010. ISBN 978-0-7614-5685-8 Subj: Animals – polar bears. Birds – penguins. Character traits – individuality. Concepts – opposites. Foreign lands – Antarctic. Foreign lands – Arctic.

The practically perfect pajamas ill. by author. Winslow, 2000. ISBN 978-1-890817-22-0 Subj: Animals – polar bears. Behavior – bullying, teasing. Clothing – pajamas.

Slow days, fast friends ill. by author. Whitman, 2005. ISBN 978-0-8075-7437-9 Subj: Animals. Friendship.

Brooks, Gwendolyn. *Bronzeville boys and girls* ill. by Faith Ringgold. HarperCollins, 2007. ISBN 978-0-06-029505-9 Subj: Ethnic groups in the U.S. – African Americans. Poetry.

Brooks, Jeremy. *Let there be peace: prayers from around the world* ill. by Jude Daly. Frances Lincoln, 2009. ISBN 978-1-84507-530-9 Subj: Character traits – cooperation. Religion. World.

Brooks, Nigel. *Country mouse cottage: how we lived one hundred years ago* by Nigel Brooks and Abigail Homer ill. by authors. Walker, 2000. ISBN 978-0-8027-8752-1 Subj: Animals – mice. Country. Foreign lands – England.

Town mouse house: how we lived one hundred years ago by Nigel Brooks and Abigail Homer ill. by authors. Walker, 2000. ISBN 978-0-8027-8732-3 Subj: Animals – mice. Cities, towns. Foreign lands – England.

Brooks, Ron. *Fox* (Wild, Margaret)

The brothers gruesome ill. by Drahos Zak. Houghton, 2000. ISBN 978-0-618-00515-4 Subj: Behavior – greed. Monsters. Rhyming text.

Brown, Alan James. *Hoot and Holler* ill. by Rimantas Rolia. Knopf, 2001. ISBN 978-0-375-91417-1 Subj: Birds – owls. Emotions. Friendship. Weather – storms.

Love-a-Duck ill. by Francesca Chessa. Holiday House, 2010. ISBN 978-0-8234-2263-0 Subj: Activities – bathing. Behavior – lost & found possessions. Birds – ducks. Toys.

Brown, Calef. *Boy wonders* ill. by author. Simon & Schuster, 2011. ISBN 978-1-4169-7877-0 Subj: Character traits – questioning. Rhyming text.

Pirateria: the wonderful plunderful pirate emporium ill. by author. Atheneum, 2012. ISBN 978-1-4169-7878-7 Subj: Pirates. Rhyming text. Stores.

Tippintown ill. by author. Houghton, 2003. ISBN 978-0-618-14972-8 Subj: Imagination. Rhyming text.

Brown, Don. *Bright path: young Jim Thorpe* ill. by author. Macmillan, 2006. ISBN 978-1-59643-041-9 Subj: Indians of North America. Sports.

Henry and the cannons: an extraordinary true story of the American Revolution ill. by author. Roaring Brook, 2013. ISBN 978-1-59643-266-6 Subj: U.S. history. War.

Mack made movies ill. by author. Roaring Brook, 2003. ISBN 978-0-7613-2504-8 Subj: Careers – motion picture producers. Theater.

Odd boy out: young Albert Einstein ill. by author. Houghton, 2004. ISBN 978-0-618-49298-5 Subj: Behavior – misunderstanding. Careers – scientists. Character traits – individuality.

One giant leap: the story of Neil Armstrong ill. by author. Houghton, 1998. ISBN 978-0-395-88401-0 Subj: Careers – astronauts.

Rare treasure: Mary Anning and her remarkable discoveries ill. by author. Houghton, 1999. ISBN 978-0-395-92286-6 Subj: Careers – paleontologists. Foreign lands – England. Fossils. Gender roles. Science.

Ruth Law thrills a nation ill. by author. Ticknor & Fields, 1993. ISBN 978-0-395-66404-9 Subj: Airplanes, airports. Careers – airplane pilots.

Teedie: the story of young Teddy Roosevelt ill. by author. Houghton, 2009. ISBN 978-0-618-17999-2 Subj: Character traits – perseverance. U.S. history.

Uncommon traveler: Mary Kingsley in Africa ill. by author. Houghton, 2000. ISBN 978-0-618-00273-3 Subj: Careers – explorers. Foreign lands – Africa. Foreign lands – England.

A voice from the wilderness: the story of Anna Howard ill. by author. Houghton, 2001. ISBN 978-0-618-08362-6 Subj: U.S. history.

A wizard from the start: the incredible boyhood and amazing inventions of Thomas Edison ill. by author. Harcourt, 2010. ISBN 978-0-547-19487-5 Subj: Careers – inventors. U.S. history.

Brown, Heather. *Chomp!* ill. by author. Accord, 2012. ISBN 978-1-44941016-2 Subj: Anatomy – mouths. Animals. Format, unusual – toy & movable books. Teeth.

Brown, James. *Farm* ill. by author. Candlewick, 2013. ISBN 978-0-7636-5931-8 Subj: Animals. Farms. Format, unusual – board books.

Brown, Jeff. *Flat Stanley* ill. by Scott Nash. HarperCollins, 2006. ISBN 978-0-06-112904-9 Subj: Character traits – appearance. Family life. Humorous stories. Problem solving.

Flat Stanley ill. by Tomi Ungerer. HarperCollins, 1961. ISBN 978-0-06-020681-9 Subj: Character traits – appearance. Family life. Humorous stories. Problem solving.

Brown, Jo. *Hoppity skip Little Chick* ill. by author. Tiger Tales, 2005. ISBN 978-1-58925-045-1 Subj: Activities – playing. Birds – chickens.

Where's my mommy? ill. by author. Tiger Tales, 2002. ISBN 978-1-58295-019-2 Subj: Animals. Birds – chickens. Family life – mothers. Reptiles – alligators, crocodiles.

Brown, Ken. *The scarecrow's hat* ill. by author. Peachtree, 2001. ISBN 978-1-56145-240-8 Subj: Birds – chickens. Books, reading. Clothing – hats. Scarecrows.

What's the time, Grandma Wolf? ill. by author. Peachtree, 2001. ISBN 978-1-56145-250-7 Subj: Animals. Animals – wolves. Family life – grandmothers. Prejudice. Rhyming text. Time.

Brown, Kerry. *Tupag the dreamer* ill. by Linda Saport. Marshall Cavendish, 2001. ISBN 978-0-7614-5076-4 Subj: Creation. Eskimos. Foreign lands – Arctic. Seasons.

Brown, Laurie Krasny. *The bionic bunny show* (Brown, Marc)

Dinosaurs alive and well by Laurie Krasny Brown and Marc Brown ill. by authors. Little, 1990. ISBN 978-0-316-10998-7 Subj: Dinosaurs. Health & fitness. Prehistory.

Dinosaurs divorce by Laurie Krasny Brown and Marc Brown ill. by Marc Brown. Atlantic Monthly, 1986. ISBN 978-0-87113-089-1 Subj: Dinosaurs. Divorce. Prehistory.

Dinosaurs to the rescue by Laurie Krasny Brown and Marc Brown ill. by Marc Brown. Little, 1992. ISBN 978-0-316-11087-7 Subj: Dinosaurs. Ecology. Prehistory.

Dinosaurs travel by Laurie Krasny Brown and Marc Brown ill. by Marc Brown. Little, 1988. ISBN 978-0-316-11076-1 Subj: Activities – traveling. Dinosaurs. Prehistory.

How to be a friend: a guide to making friends and keeping them by Laurie Krasny Brown and Marc Brown ill. by Marc Brown. Little, 1998. ISBN 978-0-316-10913-0 Subj: Dinosaurs. Friendship.

Visiting the art museum by Laurie Krasny Brown and Marc Brown ill. by authors. Dutton, 1986. ISBN 978-0-525-44233-2 Subj: Art. Museums.

What's the big secret? talking about sex with girls and boys by Laurie Krasny Brown and Marc Brown ill. by Marc Brown. Little, 1997. ISBN 978-0-316-10915-4 Subj: Anatomy. Family life. Sex instruction.

When dinosaurs die: a guide to understanding death by Laurie Krasny Brown and Marc Brown ill. by Marc Brown. Little, 1996. ISBN 978-0-316-10917-8 Subj: Death. Dinosaurs. Emotions. Family life. Prehistory.

Brown, Lisa. *How to be* ill. by author. HarperCollins, 2006. ISBN 978-0-06-054636-6 Subj: Animals. Behavior – imitation. Imagination. Self-concept.

Vampire boy's good night ill. by author. HarperCollins, 2010. ISBN 978-0-06-114011-2 Subj: Holidays – Halloween. Monsters. Witches.

Brown, Marc. *Arthur and the true Francine* ill. by author. Little, 1996. ISBN 978-0-316-11136-2 Subj: Animals. Behavior – lying. School.

Arthur babysits ill. by author. Little, 1992. ISBN 978-0-316-11293-2 Subj: Activities – babysitting. Animals – aardvarks. Multiple births – twins.

Arthur goes to camp ill. by author. Little, 1982. ISBN 978-0-316-11218-5 Subj: Animals. Camps, camping.

Arthur goes to school ill. by author. Random House, 1995. ISBN 978-0-679-86734-0 Subj: Animals – aardvarks. Format, unusual – board books. Format, unusual – toy & movable books. School.

Arthur lost and found ill. by author. Little, 1998. ISBN 978-0-316-10912-3 Subj: Animals – aardvarks. Behavior – lost. Buses. Careers – bus drivers.

Arthur meets the president ill. by author. Little, 1991. ISBN 978-0-316-11265-9 Subj: Activities – traveling. Animals – aardvarks. Family life – sisters.

Arthur tricks the tooth fairy ill. by author. Random House, 1997. ISBN 978-0-679-98464-1 Subj: Animals – aardvarks. Behavior – trickery. Fairies. Family life – brothers & sisters.

Arthur turns green ill. by author. Little, Brown, 2011. ISBN 978-0-316-12924-4 Subj: Animals – aardvarks. Ecology. Family life – brothers & sisters. School.

Arthur writes a story ill. by author. Little, 1996. ISBN 978-0-316-10916-1 Subj: Activities – writing. Animals – aardvarks.

Arthur's animal adventure ill. by author. Random House, 2002. ISBN 978-0-375-80699-5 Subj: ABC books. Animals. Animals – aardvarks. Foreign lands – Australia. Format, unusual – board books.

Arthur's April fool ill. by author. Little, 1983. ISBN 978-0-316-11196-6 Subj: Animals. Holidays – April Fools' Day.

Arthur's baby ill. by author. Little, 1987. ISBN 978-0-316-11123-2 Subj: Animals – aardvarks. Babies. Family life – new sibling.

Arthur's birthday ill. by author. Little, 1989. ISBN 978-0-316-11073-0 Subj: Animals – aardvarks. Birthdays. Friendship. Parties.

Arthur's chicken pox ill. by author. Little, 1994. ISBN 978-0-316-11384-7 Subj: Animals – aardvarks. Circus. Family life. Illness – chicken pox.

Arthur's Christmas ill. by author. Little, 1984. ISBN 978-0-316-11180-5 Subj: Animals. Gifts. Holidays – Christmas. Santa Claus.

Arthur's computer disaster ill. by author. Little, 1997. ISBN 978-0-316-11016-7 Subj: Animals – aardvarks. Behavior – misbehavior. Computers.

Arthur's eyes ill. by author. Little, 1979. ISBN 978-0-316-11063-1 Subj: Animals. Glasses. Senses – sight.

Arthur's family vacation ill. by author. Little, 1993. ISBN 978-0-316-11312-0 Subj: Activities – vacationing. Animals – aardvarks. Family life.

Arthur's first sleepover ill. by author. Little, 1994. ISBN 978-0-316-11445-5 Subj: Animals – aardvarks. Behavior – misbehavior. Camps, camping. Family life – brothers & sisters. Monsters. Sleepovers.

Arthur's Halloween ill. by author. Little, 1982. ISBN 978-0-316-11116-4 Subj: Animals. Holidays – Halloween.

Arthur's neighborhood ill. by author. Random House, 1996. ISBN 978-0-679-86737-1 Subj: Animals – aardvarks. Communities, neighborhoods. Format, unusual – toy & movable books.

Arthur's new puppy ill. by author. Little, 1993. ISBN 978-0-316-11355-7 Subj: Animals – aardvarks. Animals – dogs. Pets.

Arthur's new puppy [board book] ill. by author. 1st board book ed. Little, 1997. ISBN 978-0-316-11133-1 Subj: Animals – aardvarks. Animals – dogs. Format, unusual – board books. Pets.

Arthur's nose ill. by author. Little, 1976. ISBN 978-0-316-11884-2 Subj: Anatomy – noses. Animals – aardvarks.

Arthur's perfect Christmas ill. by author. Little, 2000. ISBN 978-0-316-11968-9 Subj: Animals. Animals – aardvarks. Holidays – Christmas.

Arthur's pet business ill. by author. Little, 1990. ISBN 978-0-316-11262-8 Subj: Animals – aardvarks. Animals – dogs. Pets.

Arthur's really helpful word book ill. by author. Random House, 1997. ISBN 978-0-679-98735-2 Subj: Animals – aardvarks. Books, reading. Language.

Arthur's spookiest Halloween ill. by author. Random House, 2003. ISBN 978-0-375-81004-6 Subj: Animals – aardvarks. Format, unusual – toy & movable books. Holidays – Halloween.

Arthur's teacher moves in ill. by author. Little, 2000. ISBN 978-0-316-11979-5 Subj: Animals. Animals – aardvarks. Careers – teachers. School.

Arthur's teacher trouble ill. by author. Little, 1986. ISBN 978-0-87113-091-4 Subj: Animals. School.

Arthur's Thanksgiving ill. by author. Little, 1983. ISBN 978-0-316-11060-0 Subj: Animals. Holidays – Thanksgiving. Theater.

Arthur's tooth ill. by author. Little, 1985. ISBN 978-0-87113-006-8 Subj: Animals. Teeth.

Arthur's TV trouble ill. by author. Little, 1995. ISBN 978-0-316-10919-2 Subj: Animals – aardvarks. Money. Pets.

Arthur's underwear ill. by author. Little, 1999. ISBN 978-0-316-11012-9 Subj: Animals. Animals – aardvarks. Behavior – worrying. Clothing. Emotions – embarrassment. School.

Arthur's Valentine ill. by author. Little, 1980. ISBN 978-0-316-11062-4 Subj: Animals. Holidays – Valentine's Day. School.

The bionic bunny show by Marc Brown and Laurie Krasny Brown ill. by Marc Brown. Little, 1984. ISBN 978-0-316-11120-1 Subj: Animals. Animals – rabbits. Television.

D. W. all wet ill. by author. Little, 1988. ISBN 978-0-316-11077-8 Subj: Animals – anteaters. Sea & seashore. Sibling rivalry.

D. W. flips! ill. by author. Little, 1987. ISBN 978-0-316-11239-0 Subj: Animals – anteaters. Sports – gymnastics.

D. W., go to your room! ill. by author. Little, 1999. ISBN 978-0-316-10905-5 Subj: Animals – aardvarks. Character traits – meanness. Family life – sisters.

D. W. rides again! ill. by author. Little, 1998. ISBN 978-0-316-11128-7 Subj: Animals – aardvarks. Family life – brothers & sisters. Sports – bicycling.

D. W., the picky eater ill. by author. Little, 1995. ISBN 978-0-316-10957-4 Subj: Animals – aardvarks. Family life. Food.

D. W. thinks big [board book] ill. by author. Little, 1998. ISBN 978-0-316-11112-6 Subj: Accidents. Animals – aardvarks. Family life – brothers & sisters. Format, unusual – board books. Weddings.

D. W.'s library card ill. by author. Little, 2001. ISBN 978-0-316-11013-6 Subj: Animals – aardvarks. Books, reading. Family life – brothers & sisters.

D. W.'s lost blankie ill. by author. Little, 1998. ISBN 978-0-316-10914-7 Subj: Animals – aardvarks. Behavior – lost & found possessions. Family life.

Dinosaurs alive and well (Brown, Laurie Krasny)

Dinosaurs, beware! a safety guide by Marc Brown and Stephen Krensky ill. by authors. Little, 1982. ISBN 978-0-316-11228-4 Subj: Dinosaurs. Prehistory. Safety.

Dinosaurs divorce (Brown, Laurie Krasny)

Dinosaurs to the rescue (Brown, Laurie Krasny)

Dinosaurs travel (Brown, Laurie Krasny)

Finger rhymes ill. by author. Dutton, 1980. ISBN 978-0-525-29732-1 Subj: Games. Nursery rhymes. Participation.

Glasses for D. W. ill. by author. Random House, 1995. ISBN 978-0-679-98043-8 Subj: Animals – aardvarks. Family life – brothers & sisters. Glasses.

Hand rhymes ill. by selector. Dutton, 1985. ISBN 978-0-525-44201-1 Subj: Games. Nursery rhymes.

How to be a friend: a guide to making friends and keeping them (Brown, Laurie Krasny)

Perfect pigs: an introduction to manners by Marc Brown and Stephen Krensky ill. by authors. Little, 1983. ISBN 978-0-316-11079-2 Subj: Animals – pigs. Etiquette.

Play rhymes ill. by author. Dutton, 1987. ISBN 978-0-525-44336-0 Subj: Games. Music. Nursery rhymes. Songs.

The true Francine ill. by author. Little, 1987. ISBN 978-0-316-11212-3 Subj: Animals – aardvarks. Behavior. Friendship. School.

Visiting the art museum (Brown, Laurie Krasny)

What's the big secret? talking about sex with girls and boys (Brown, Laurie Krasny)

When dinosaurs die: a guide to understanding death (Brown, Laurie Krasny)

Brown, Marcia, adapt. *Once a mouse . . .* ill. by adapter. Scribners, 1961. ISBN 978-0-684-12662-3 Subj: Animals. Caldecott award books. Character traits – vanity. Concepts – size. Folk & fairy tales. Foreign lands – India. Magic.

Stone soup ill. by author. Scribners, 1947. ISBN 978-0-684-92296-6 Subj: Caldecott award honor books. Careers – military. Character traits – cleverness. Folk & fairy tales. Food. Foreign lands – Russia.

Brown, Margaret Wise. *Another important book* ill. by Chris Raschka. HarperCollins, 1999. ISBN 978-0-06-026283-9 Subj: Behavior – growing up. Rhyming text.

Bunny's noisy book ill. by Lisa McCue. Hyperion, 2000. ISBN 978-0-7868-2428-1 Subj: Animals – rabbits. Careers – seamstresses. Noise, sounds. Quilts.

Bunny's noisy book [board book] ill. by Lisa McCue. Hyperion, 2001. ISBN 978-0-7868-0744-4 Subj: Animals – rabbits. Careers – seamstresses. Format, unusual – board books. Noise, sounds. Quilts.

A child is born ill. by Floyd Cooper. Hyperion, 2000. ISBN 978-0-7868-2564-6 Subj: Holidays – Christmas. Religion – Nativity. Rhyming text.

A child's good morning book ill. by Karen Katz. HarperCollins, 2009. ISBN 978-0-06-128864-7 Subj: Animals. Morning.

Christmas in the barn ill. by Diane Goode. HarperCollins, 2004. ISBN 978-0-06-052635-1 Subj: Farms. Holidays – Christmas. Religion – Nativity. Rhyming text.

The dirty little boy ill. by Steven Salerno. Winslow, 2001. ISBN 978-1-890817-52-7 Subj: Activities – bathing. Animals. Character traits – cleanliness.

The fathers are coming home ill. by Stephen Savage. Simon & Schuster, 2010. ISBN 978-0-689-83345-8 Subj: Animals. Family life – fathers. Night.

The fierce yellow pumpkin ill. by Richard Egielski. HarperCollins, 2003. ISBN 978-0-06-024481-1 Subj: Behavior – wishing. Holidays – Halloween.

The friendly book ill. by Garth Williams. Random House, 2003. ISBN 978-0-307-10643-8 Subj: Animals. Poetry.

Give yourself to the rain ill. by Teri Weidner. McElderry, 2002. ISBN 978-0-689-83344-1 Subj: Poetry.

The golden egg book ill. by Leonard Weisgard. Simon & Schuster, 1947. ISBN 978-0-685-05367-6 Subj: Animals – rabbits. Birds – ducks. Eggs. Holidays – Easter.

The Golden sleepy book ill. by Garth Williams. Random House, 2004. ISBN 978-0-375-92779-9 Subj: Animals. Poetry. Sleep.

The good little bad little pig ill. by Dan Yaccarino. Hyperion, 2002. ISBN 978-0-7868-2514-1 Subj: Animals – pigs. Pets.

Goodnight moon ill. by Clement Hurd. HarperCollins, 1934. ISBN 978-0-590-73302-1 Subj: Animals – rabbits. Bedtime. Moon.

Goodnight moon ABC: an alphabet book ill. by Clement Hurd. HarperCollins, 2010. ISBN 978-0-06-189484-8 Subj: ABC books. Animals – rabbits. Bedtime. Moon.

Goodnight moon 123: a counting book ill. by Clement Hurd. HarperCollins, 2007. ISBN 978-0-06-112593-5 Subj: Animals – rabbits. Bedtime. Counting, numbers. Moon.

Goodnight moon 123: a counting book [board book] ill. by Clement Hurd. HarperCollins, 2008. ISBN 978-0-06-166755-8 Subj: Animals – rabbits. Bedtime. Counting, numbers. Format, unusual – board books. Moon.

The little fir tree ill. by Jim LaMarche. HarperCollins, 2005. ISBN 978-0-06-028190-8 Subj: Holidays – Christmas. Trees.

The little island ill. by Leonard Weisgard. Doubleday, 1946. Subj: Caldecott award books. Islands. Seasons. Weather.

Love songs of the little bear ill. by Susan Jeffers. Hyperion, 2001. ISBN 978-0-7868-2445-8 Subj: Animals – bears. Poetry. Seasons.

My world ill. by Clement Hurd. HarperCollins, 2002. ISBN 978-0-694-00862-9 Subj: Animals – rabbits. Family life.

My world of color ill. by Loretta Krupinski. Hyperion, 2002. ISBN 978-0-7868-2519-6 Subj: Concepts – color. Rhyming text.

Nibble, nibble ill. by Wendell Minor. HarperCollins, 2007. ISBN 978-0-06-059208-0 Subj: Poetry.

Robin's room ill. by Steve Johnson and Lou Fancher. Hyperion, 2002. ISBN 978-0-7868-2516-5 Subj: Character traits – being different. Family life. Homes, houses.

The runaway bunny ill. by Clement Hurd. HarperCollins, 1972, ©1942. ISBN 978-0-06-020766-3 Subj: Animals – rabbits. Behavior – running away. Family life – mothers. Holidays – Easter.

The runaway bunny [board book] ill. by Clement Hurd. HarperCollins, 2001. ISBN 978-0-694-01671-6 Subj: Animals – rabbits. Behavior – running away. Family life – mothers. Format, unusual – board books.

Sailor boy jig ill. by Dan Andreasen. McElderry, 2002. ISBN 978-0-689-83348-9 Subj: Activities – dancing. Animals – dogs. Concepts. Rhyming text. Sailors.

Sheep don't count sheep ill. by Benrei Huang. McElderry, 2003. ISBN 978-0-689-83346-5 Subj: Animals – sheep. Sleep.

Sleepy ABC ill. by Karen Katz. HarperCollins, 2010. ISBN 978-0-06-128863-0 Subj: ABC books. Bedtime. Rhyming text. Sleep.

Sleepy ABC ill. by Esphyr Slobodkina. HarperCollins, 1994. ISBN 978-0-06-024285-5 Subj: ABC books. Bedtime. Rhyming text. Sleep.

Sneakers, the seaside cat ill. by Anne Mortimer. HarperCollins, 2003. ISBN 978-0-06-028693-4 Subj: Animals – cats. Behavior – misbehavior. Sea & seashore.

Wheel on the chimney by Margaret Wise Brown and Tibor Gergely ill. by Tibor Gergely. Lippincott, 1954. ISBN 978-0-397-30296-3 Subj: Birds – storks. Caldecott award honor books. Character traits – luck. Foreign lands – Hungary.

Where have you been? ill. by Leo Dillon and Diane Dillon. HarperCollins, 2004. ISBN 978-0-06-028379-7 Subj: Animals. Rhyming text.

Brown, Monica. *Chavela and the magic bubble* ill. by Magaly Morales. Clarion, 2010. ISBN 978-0-547-24197-5 Subj: Ethnic groups in the U.S. – Mexican Americans. Family life – grandmothers. Magic.

My name is Gabito / Me llamo Gabito: the life of Gabriel García Márquez / la vida de Gabriel García Márquez ill. by Raul Cólon. Northland, 2007. ISBN 978-0-87358-934-5 Subj: Activities – writing. Careers – writers. Foreign lands – Colombia. Foreign languages.

Pelé, king of soccer / Pelé, el rey del fútbol ill. by Rudy Gutierrez. HarperCollins, 2009. ISBN 978-0-06-122779-0 Subj: Foreign lands – Brazil. Foreign languages. Sports – soccer.

Side by side / Lado a lado: the story of Dolores Huerta and Cesar Chavez / la historia de Dolores Huerta y Cesar Chavez ill. by Joe Cepeda. HarperCollins, 2010. ISBN 978-0-06-122781-3 Subj: Ethnic groups in the U.S. – Mexican Americans. Foreign languages. U.S. history. Violence, nonviolence.

Waiting for the Biblioburro ill. by John Parra. Tricycle, 2011. ISBN 978-1-58246-353-7 Subj: Animals – donkeys. Books, reading. Foreign lands – Colombia. Libraries.

Brown, Peter. *Children make terrible pets* ill. by author. Little, Brown, 2010. ISBN 978-0-316-01548-6 Subj: Animals – bears. Humorous stories. Pets.

Chowder ill. by author. Little, Brown, 2006. ISBN 978-0-316-01180-8 Subj: Animals – dogs. Character traits – being different.

The curious garden ill. by author. Little, Brown, 2009. ISBN 978-0-316-01547-9 Subj: Cities, towns. Ecology. Gardens, gardening.

Mr. Tiger goes wild ill. by author. Little, Brown, 2013. ISBN 978-0-316-20063-9 Subj: Animals – tigers. Behavior – boredom. Character traits – individuality. Self-concept.

You will be my friend! ill. by author. Little, Brown, 2011. ISBN 978-0-316-07030-0 Subj: Animals – bears. Friendship.

Brown, Ruth. *A dark, dark tale* ill. by author. Dial, 1981. ISBN 978-0-8037-1673-5 Subj: Cumulative tales. Foreign lands – England.

Gracie the lighthouse cat ill. by author. Andersen, 2011. ISBN 978-0-7613-7454-1 Subj: Animals – cats. Behavior – lost. Lighthouses.

Holly, the true story of a cat ill. by author. Holt, 2000. ISBN 978-0-8050-6500-8 Subj: Animals – cats. Holidays – Christmas.

Monkey's friends ill. by author. Kane/Miller, 2012. ISBN 978-1-61067-045-6 Subj: Animals. Animals – monkeys. Format, unusual – toy & movable books.

The old tree: an environmental fable ill. by author. Candlewick, 2007. ISBN 978-0-7636-3461-2 Subj: Ecology. Format, unusual – toy & movable books. Trees.

The tale of two mice: a cat-and-mouse tale ill. by author. Candlewick, 2008. ISBN 978-0-7636-4015-6 Subj: Animals – cats. Animals – mice. Format, unusual.

Brown, Stephanie Gwyn. *Bang! Boom! Roar! a busy crew of dinosaurs* (Evans, Nate)

Brown, Susan Taylor. *Oliver's must-do list* ill. by Mary Sullivan. Boyds Mills, 2005. ISBN 978-1-59078-198-2 Subj: Activities – playing. Animals – rhinoceros. Family life – mothers.

Brown, Tameka Fryer. *Around our way on Neighbors' Day* ill. by Charlotte Riley-Webb. Abrams, 2010. ISBN 978-0-8109-8971-9 Subj: Cities, towns. Communities, neighborhoods. Parties. Rhyming text.

My cold plum lemon pie bluesy mood ill. by Shane W. Evans. Viking, 2013. ISBN 978-0-670-01285-5 Subj: Concepts – color. Emotions. Ethnic groups in the U.S. – African Americans. Rhyming text.

Brown, Tami Lewis. *Soar, Elinor!* ill. by François Roca. Farrar, 2010. ISBN 978-0-374-37115-9 Subj: Activities – flying. Careers – airplane pilots. Gender roles. U.S. history.

Browne, Anthony. *Animal fair* ill. by author. Candlewick, 2002. ISBN 978-0-7636-1831-5 Subj: Animals. Animals – monkeys. Fairs, festivals. Format, unusual – toy & movable books.

Gorilla ill. by author. Candlewick, 2002, 1983. ISBN 978-0-7636-1813-1 Subj: Animals – gorillas. Birthdays. Family life – fathers. Imagination. Toys. Zoos.

How do you feel? ill. by author. Candlewick, 2012. ISBN 978-0-7636-5862-5 Subj: Animals – chimpanzees. Emotions.

I like books ill. by author. Knopf, 1989. ISBN 978-0-394-84186-1 Subj: Animals – chimpanzees. Books, reading.

I like books [board book] ill. by author. Candlewick, 2004. ISBN 978-0-7636-2162-9 Subj: Animals – chimpanzees. Books, reading. Format, unusual – board books.

Little Beauty ill. by author. Candlewick, 2008. ISBN 978-0-7636-3959-4 Subj: Animals – cats. Animals – gorillas. Sign language. Zoos.

Me and you ill. by author. Farrar, 2010. ISBN 978-0-374-34908-0 Subj: Animals – bears. Behavior – lost. Cities, towns. Folk & fairy tales.

My brother ill. by author. Farrar, 2007. ISBN 978-0-374-35120-5 Subj: Family life – brothers & sisters.

My dad ill. by author. DK, 2000. ISBN 978-0-7894-2681-9 Subj: Family life – fathers.

My mom ill. by author. Farrar, 2005. ISBN 978-0-374-35098-7 Subj: Family life – mothers.

One gorilla: a counting book ill. by author. Candlewick, 2013. ISBN 978-0-7636-6352-0 Subj: Animals – chimpanzees. Animals – gorillas. Animals

– lemurs. Animals – monkeys. Animals – orangutans. Counting, numbers.

The shape game ill. by author. Farrar, 2003. ISBN 978-0-374-36764-0 Subj: Art. Careers – writers. Careers – illustrators. Foreign lands – Great Britain. Museums.

Silly Billy ill. by author. Candlewick, 2006. ISBN 978-0-7636-3124-6 Subj: Behavior – worrying. Family life – grandmothers. Toys – dolls.

Voices in the park ill. by author. DK, 1998. ISBN 978-0-7894-2522-5 Subj: Animals – dogs. Animals – gorillas. Parks. Seasons.

Willy and Hugh ill. by author. Knopf, 1991. ISBN 978-0-679-91446-4 Subj: Animals – chimpanzees. Animals – gorillas. Friendship.

Willy the champ ill. by author. Knopf, 1986. ISBN 978-0-394-97907-6 Subj: Animals – chimpanzees. Animals – gorillas. Behavior – bullying, teasing.

Willy the dreamer ill. by author. Candlewick, 1998. ISBN 978-0-7636-0378-6 Subj: Animals – chimpanzees. Dreams.

Willy the wimp ill. by author. Knopf, 1985. ISBN 978-0-394-97061-5 Subj: Animals – chimpanzees. Animals – gorillas. Self-concept.

Willy the wizard ill. by author. Knopf, 1995. ISBN 978-0-679-97644-8 Subj: Animals – chimpanzees. Clothing – shoes. Sports – soccer.

Willy's pictures ill. by author. Candlewick, 2000. ISBN 978-0-7636-0962-7 Subj: Animals – chimpanzees. Art. Careers – artists.

Browne, Eileen. *Handa's hen* ill. by author. Candlewick, 2011. ISBN 978-0-7636-5361-3 Subj: Animals. Birds – chickens. Counting, numbers. Foreign lands – Kenya.

Browning, Diane. *Signed, Abiah Rose* ill. by author. Tricycle, 2010. ISBN 978-1-58246-311-7 Subj: Careers – artists. Gender roles. U.S. history – frontier & pioneer life.

Browning, Kurt. *T is for tutu: a ballet alphabet* (Rodriguez, Sonia)

Browning, Robert. *The pied piper of Hamelin* adapt. by Mercer Mayer; ill. by Mercer Mayer. Adapt. of the poem The pied piper of Hamelin by Robert Browning. Macmillan, 1987. ISBN 978-0-02-765361-8 Subj: Animals – rats. Behavior – trickery. Folk & fairy tales. Foreign lands – Germany.

The pied piper of Hamelin retold by Robert Holden; ill. by Drahos Zak. Houghton, 1998. ISBN 978-0-395-89918-2 Subj: Animals – rats. Behavior – trickery. Folk & fairy tales. Foreign lands – Germany. Poetry.

Brownlee, Sophia Grace. *Tea time with Sophia Grace and Rosie* by Sophia Grace Brownlee and Rosie McClelland ill. by Shelagh McNicholas. Scholastic, 2013. ISBN 978-0-545-50214-6 Subj: Family life – cousins. Friendship. Parties.

Brownlow, Mike. *The big white book with almost nothing in it* ill. by author. Ragged Bears, 2001. ISBN 978-1-929927-24-1 Subj: Format, unusual – toy & movable books. Rhyming text.

Mickey Moonbeam ill. by author. Bloomsbury, 2006. ISBN 978-1-58234-704-2 Subj: Concepts – size. Pen pals. Space & space ships.

Way out West — with a baby! ill. by author. Ragged Bears, 2000. ISBN 978-1-929927-04-3 Subj: Babies. Cowboys, cowgirls. Rhyming text. U.S. history – frontier & pioneer life.

Broyles, Anne. *Priscilla and the hollyhocks* ill. by Anna Alter. Charlesbridge, 2008. ISBN 978-1-57091-675-5 Subj: Ethnic groups in the U.S. – African Americans. Slavery. U.S. history.

Shy Mama's Halloween ill. by Leane Morin. Tilbury, 2000. ISBN 978-0-88448-218-5 Subj: Ethnic groups in the U.S. – Russian Americans. Family life. Holidays – Halloween. Immigrants.

Bruce, Lisa. *Engines, engines* by Lisa Bruce and Stephen Waterhouse ill. by Stephen Waterhouse. Bloomsbury, 2000. ISBN 978-0-7475-5013-6 Subj: Counting, numbers. Foreign lands – India. Rhyming text.

Fran's flower ill. by Rosalind Beardshaw. HarperCollins, 2000. ISBN 978-0-06-028621-7 Subj: Flowers. Gardens, gardening. Plants.

Fran's friend ill. by Rosalind Beardshaw. Bloomsbury, 2003. ISBN 978-1-58234-777-6 Subj: Animals – dogs. Friendship. Gifts.

Bruchac, James. *How Chipmunk got his stripes: a tale of bragging and teasing* (Bruchac, Joseph)

Rabbit's snow dance: a traditional Iroquois story by James Bruchac and Joseph Bruchac ill. by Jeff Newman. Dial, 2012. ISBN 978-0-8037-3270-4 Subj: Animals – rabbits. Folk & fairy tales – pourquoi tales. Indians of North America – Iroquois. Weather – snow.

Bruchac, Joseph. *Buffalo song* ill. by Bill Farnsworth. Lee & Low, 2008. ISBN 978-1-58430-280-3 Subj: Animals – buffaloes. Indians of North America.

The circle of thanks: Native American poems and songs of Thanksgiving ill. by Murv Jacob. BridgeWater, 1996. ISBN 978-0-8167-4012-3 Subj: Folk & fairy tales. Indians of North America. Nature. Poetry.

Crazy horse's vision ill. by S. D. Nelson. Lee & Low, 2000. ISBN 978-1-880000-94-6 Subj: Indians of North America – Lakota (Sioux).

The great ball game: a Muskogee story ill. by Susan L. Roth. Dial, 1994. ISBN 978-0-8037-1540-0 Subj: Animals. Behavior – fighting, arguing. Birds. Folk & fairy tales. Indians of North America – Creek. Indians of North America – Muskogee.

How Chipmunk got his stripes: a tale of bragging and teasing by Joseph Bruchac and James Bruchac ill. by José Aruego and Ariane Dewey. Dial, 2001. ISBN 978-0-8037-2404-4 Subj: Animals – chipmunks. Folk & fairy tales – pourquoi tales. Indians of North America.

Many nations: an alphabet of Native America ill. by Robert F. Goetzl. BridgeWater, 1997. ISBN 978-0-8167-4389-6 Subj: ABC books. Indians of North America.

My father is taller than a tree ill. by Wendy Anderson Halperin. Penguin, 2010. ISBN 978-0-8037-3173-8 Subj: Family life – fathers. Rhyming text.

Rabbit's snow dance: a traditional Iroquois story (Bruchac, James)

Squanto's journey ill. by Greg Shed. Silver Whistle, 2000. ISBN 978-0-15-201817-7 Subj: Holidays – Thanksgiving. Indians of North America – Wampanoag. Pilgrims. U.S. history.

Thirteen moons on turtle's back by Joseph Bruchac and Jonathan London ill. by Thomas Locker. Putnam, 1992. ISBN 978-0-399-22141-5 Subj: Folk & fairy tales. Indians of North America. Poetry. Seasons.

Bruel, Nick. *Bad Kitty* ill. by author. Macmillan, 2005. ISBN 978-1-59643-069-3 Subj: ABC books. Animals – cats. Behavior – misbehavior. Food.

A Bad Kitty Christmas ill. by author. Roaring Brook, 2011. ISBN 978-1-59643-668-8 Subj: Animals – cats. Behavior – misbehavior. Holidays – Christmas. Rhyming text.

Poor puppy ill. by author. Macmillan, 2007. ISBN 978-1-59643-270-3 Subj: ABC books. Animals – cats. Animals – dogs. Counting, numbers.

Bruel, Robert O. *Bob and Otto* ill. by Nick Bruel. Macmillan, 2007. ISBN 978-1-59643-203-1 Subj: Animals – worms. Friendship. Insects – butterflies, caterpillars.

Bruins, David. *The call of the cowboy* ill. by Hilary Leung. Kids Can, 2011. ISBN 978-1-55453-748-8 Subj: Animals – bears. Cowboys, cowgirls. Friendship. Noise, sounds.

Brumbeau, Jeff. *Miss Hunnicutt's hat* ill. by Gail de Marcken. Orchard, 2003. ISBN 978-0-439-31895-2 Subj: Character traits – individuality. Clothing – hats.

Brun-Cosme, Nadine. *Big Wolf and Little Wolf* ill. by Olivier Tallec. Enchanted Lion, 2009. ISBN 978-1-59270-084-4 Subj: Animals – wolves. Emotions – loneliness. Friendship.

Big Wolf and Little Wolf, such a beautiful orange! ill. by Olivier Tallec. Enchanted Lion, 2011. ISBN 978-1-59270-106-3 Subj: Animals – wolves. Behavior – worrying. Friendship.

Brunelle, Nicholas. *Snow moon* ill. by author. Penguin, 2005. ISBN 978-0-670-06024-5 Subj: Bedtime. Birds – owls. Night. Seasons – winter. Weather – snow.

Brunhoff, Jean de. *Babar and Father Christmas* ill. by author. Random House, 1940. ISBN 978-0-394-89265-8 Subj: Animals – elephants. Holidays – Christmas.

Babar and his children ill. by author. Random House, 1938. ISBN 978-0-394-90577-8 Subj: Animals – elephants. Multiple births – triplets.

Babar the king ill. by author. Random House, 1935. ISBN 978-0-394-90580-8 Subj: Animals – elephants. Royalty – kings.

Babar the king [facsimile ed.] ill. by author. Random House, 1986. ISBN 978-0-394-88245-1 Subj: Animals – elephants. Royalty – kings.

The story of Babar, the little elephant ill. by author. Random House, 1984, ©1933. ISBN 978-0-394-86823-3 Subj: Animals – elephants. Behavior – running away. Foreign lands – France.

The travels of Babar ill. by author. Random House, 1934, 1961. ISBN 978-0-394-90576-1 Subj: Activities – traveling. Animals – elephants.

Brunhoff, Laurent de. *B is for Babar: an alphabet book* ill. by author. Abrams, 2012. ISBN 978-1-4197-0298-3 Subj: ABC books. Animals – elephants. Format, unusual – board books.

Babar and the ghost ill. by author. Abrams, 1981. ISBN 978-0-8109-4398-8 Subj: Animals – elephants. Castles. Ghosts.

Babar and the ghost [easy-to-read ed.] ill. by author. Random House, 1986. ISBN 978-0-394-97908-3 Subj: Animals – elephants. Ghosts.

Babar and the succotash bird ill. by author. Abrams, 2000. ISBN 978-0-8109-5700-8 Subj: Animals – elephants. Birds. Wizards.

Babar and the Wully-Wully ill. by author. Abrams, 1975. ISBN 978-0-8109-4397-1 Subj: Animals – elephants. Pets.

Babar's ABC ill. by author. Abrams, 1983. ISBN 978-0-8109-5705-3 Subj: ABC books. Animals – elephants.

Babar's battle ill. by author. Random House, 1992. ISBN 978-0-679-91068-8 Subj: Animals – elephants. Animals – rhinoceros. War.

Babar's birthday surprise ill. by author. Random House, 1970. ISBN 978-0-394-90591-4 Subj: Animals – elephants. Birthdays.

Babar's little girl ill. by author. Abrams, 1987. ISBN 978-0-8109-5703-9 Subj: Animals – elephants. Behavior – carelessness. Behavior – lost. Character traits – kindness to animals.

Babar's Museum of Art: (closed Mondays) ill. by author. Abrams, 2003. ISBN 978-0-8109-4597-5 Subj: Animals – elephants. Art. Museums.

Babar's USA ill. by author. Abrams, 2008. ISBN 978-0-8109-7096-0 Subj: Activities – traveling. Animals – elephants. Royalty. U.S. history.

Babar's world tour ill. by author. Abrams, 2005. ISBN 978-0-8109-5780-0 Subj: Activities – traveling. Animals – elephants. World.

Meet Babar and his family ill. by author. Abrams, 2002. ISBN 978-0-8109-0555-9 Subj: Animals – elephants. Family life. Seasons.

Bruno, Elsa Knight. *Punctuation celebration* ill. by Jenny Whitehead. Holt, 2009. ISBN 978-0-8050-7973-9 Subj: Language. Poetry.

Bruss, Deborah. *Book! book! book!* ill. by Tiphanie Beeke. Scholastic, 2001. ISBN 978-0-439-13525-2 Subj: Animals. Books, reading. Libraries. Noise, sounds.

Brutschy, Jennifer. *Just one more story* ill. by Cat Bowman Smith. Orchard, 2001. ISBN 978-0-531-33296-2 Subj: Activities – storytelling. Activities – traveling. Family life – fathers.

Bruzzone, Catherine. *Puppy finds a friend / Cachorrito encuentra un amigo* ill. by John Bendall-Brunello. Barron's, 2000. ISBN 978-0-7641-5283-2 Subj: Activities – playing. Animals – babies. Animals – dogs. Foreign languages. Friendship.

Puppy finds a friend / Le petit chien se trouve un ami ill. by John Bendall-Brunello. Barron's, 2000. ISBN 978-0-7641-5285-6 Subj: Activities – playing. Animals – babies. Animals – dogs. Foreign languages. Friendship.

Bryan, Ashley, adapt. *Beat the story-drum, pum-pum* ill. by adapter. Atheneum, 1980. ISBN 978-0-689-30769-0 Subj: Cumulative tales. Folk & fairy tales. Foreign lands – Africa. Rhyming text.

Beautiful blackbird ill. by author. Atheneum, 2003. ISBN 978-0-689-84731-8 Subj: Birds – blackbirds. Folk & fairy tales. Foreign lands – Zambia.

Can't scare me! ill. by author. Atheneum, 2013. ISBN 978-1-4424-7657-8 Subj: Character traits – curiosity. Family life – grandmothers. Foreign lands – Caribbean Islands. Giants. Rhyming text.

The cat's purr ill. by author. Atheneum, 1985. ISBN 978-0-689-31086-7 Subj: Animals – cats. Animals – rats. Folk & fairy tales. Rhyming text.

Sing to the sun ill. by author. HarperCollins, 1992. ISBN 978-0-06-020833-2 Subj: Foreign lands – Caribbean Islands. Nature. Poetry.

The story of lightning and thunder ill. by author. Atheneum, 1993. ISBN 978-0-689-31836-8 Subj: Folk & fairy tales. Foreign lands – Africa. Weather – lightning, thunder. Weather – storms.

Turtle knows your name ill. by author. Macmillan, 1989. ISBN 978-0-689-31578-7 Subj: Family life – grandmothers. Folk & fairy tales. Names. Reptiles – turtles, tortoises.

Who built the stable? a Nativity poem ill. by author. Atheneum, 2012. ISBN 978-1-4424-0934-7 Subj: Religion – Nativity. Rhyming text.

Bryan, Sean. *A bear and his boy* ill. by Tom Murphy. Arcade, 2007. ISBN 978-1-55970-838-8 Subj: Animals – bears. Rhyming text.

Bryant, Jen. *Abe's fish: a boyhood tale of Abraham Lincoln* ill. by Amy Bates. Sterling, 2009. ISBN 978-1-4027-6252-9 Subj: Behavior – sharing. Character traits – freedom. U.S. history.

A river of words: the story of William Carlos Williams ill. by Melissa Sweet. Eerdmans, 2008. ISBN 978-0-8028-5302-8 Subj: Caldecott award honor books. Poetry.

A splash of red: the life and art of Horace Pippin ill. by Melissa Sweet. Knopf, 2013. ISBN 978-0-375-86712-5 Subj: Art. Careers – artists. Character traits – perseverance. Ethnic groups in the U.S. – African Americans. U.S. history.

Bryant, Megan E. *Alphasaurus* ill. by Luciana Navarro Powell. Chronicle, 2012. ISBN 978-1-4521-0748-6 Subj: ABC books. Dinosaurs. Format, unusual – board books.

Colorasaurus ill. by Luciana Navarro Powell. Chronicle, 2012. ISBN 978-1-4521-0814-8 Subj: Concepts – color. Dinosaurs. Format, unusual – board books.

Countasaurus ill. by Luciana Navarro Powell. Chronicle, 2012. ISBN 978-1-4521-0747-9 Subj: Counting, numbers. Dinosaurs. Format, unusual – board books.

Shapeasaurus ill. by Luciana Navarro Powell. Chronicle, 2012. ISBN 978-1-4521-0815-5 Subj: Concepts – shape. Dinosaurs. Format, unusual – board books.

Bryne, Gayle. *Sometimes it's grandmas and grandpas, not mommies and daddies* ill. by Mary Haverfield. Abbeville, 2009. ISBN 978-0-7892-1028-9 Subj: Family life – grandparents.

Buchanan, Jane. *Seed magic* ill. by Charlotte Riley-Webb. Peachtree, 2012. ISBN 978-1-56145-622-2 Subj: Birds. Cities, towns. Ethnic groups in the U.S. – African Americans. Disabilities – physical disabilities. Seeds.

Buchanan, Sue. *Mud Pie Annie: God's recipe for doing your best* by Sue Buchanan and Dana Shafer ill. by Joy Allen. Zondervan, 2001. ISBN 978-0-613-71694-9 Subj: Character traits – cleverness. Rhyming text. Self-concept.

Buck, Nola. *A Christmas goodnight* ill. by Sarah Jane Wright. HarperCollins, 2011. ISBN 978-0-06-166491-5 Subj: Holidays – Christmas. Religion. Rhyming text.

Buckingham, Matt. *Bright Stanley* ill. by author. Tiger Tales, 2006. ISBN 978-1-58925-059-8 Subj: Behavior – lost. Fish. Friendship. Sea & seashore.

Buckley, Carol. *Tarra and Bella: the elephant and dog who became best friends* ill. with photos. Putnam, 2009. ISBN 978-0-399-25443-7 Subj: Animals – dogs. Animals – elephants.

Buckley, Michael. *Kel Gilligan's daredevil stunt show* ill. by Dan Santat. Abrams, 2012. ISBN 978-1-4197-0379-9 Subj: Character traits – bravery. Humorous stories.

Buckley, Richard. *The foolish tortoise* ill. by Eric Carle. Picture Book Studio, 1985. ISBN 978-0-88708-002-9 Subj: Behavior – seeking better things. Folk & fairy tales. Reptiles – turtles, tortoises. Rhyming text.

The greedy python ill. by Eric Carle. Picture Book Studio, 1985. ISBN 978-0-88708-001-2 Subj: Behavior – greed. Folk & fairy tales. Reptiles – snakes. Rhyming text.

Budnitz, Paul. *The hole in the middle* ill. by Aya Kakeda. Hyperion/Disney, 2011. ISBN 978-1-4231-3761-0 Subj: Format, unusual. Friendship. Self-concept.

Buehner, Caralyn. *The queen of style* ill. by Mark Buehner. Dial, 2008. ISBN 978-0-8037-2878-3 Subj: Beauty shops. Behavior – boredom. Royalty – queens.

Snowmen all year ill. by Mark Buehner. Penguin, 2010. ISBN 978-0-8037-3383-1 Subj: Magic. Rhyming text. Snowmen.

Snowmen at Christmas ill. by Mark Buehner. Penguin, 2005. ISBN 978-0-8037-2995-7 Subj: Gifts. Holidays – Christmas. Parties. Rhyming text. Snowmen.

Snowmen at night ill. by Mark Buehner. Fogelman, 2002. ISBN 978-0-8037-2550-8 Subj: Night. Rhyming text. Snowmen.

Snowmen at night [board book] ill. by Mark Buehner. Dial, 2004. ISBN 978-0-8037-3041-0 Subj: Format, unusual – board books. Night. Rhyming text. Snowmen.

Superdog, the heart of a hero ill. by Mark Buehner. HarperCollins, 2004. ISBN 978-0-06-623621-6 Subj: Animals – dogs. Concepts – size. Self-concept.

Would I ever lie to you? ill. by Jack E. Davis. Penguin, 2007. ISBN 978-0-8037-2793-9 Subj: Behavior – bullying, teasing. Behavior – lying. Family life – cousins. Rhyming text.

Bùi, Tak. *Spot the difference* ill. by author. Tundra, 2012. ISBN 978-1-77049-279-0 Subj: Picture puzzles.

Buitrago, Jairo. *Jimmy the greatest* ill. by Rafael Yockteng. Groundwood, 2012. ISBN 978-1-55498-178-6 Subj: Books, reading. Cities, towns. Poverty. Self-concept. Sports – boxing.

Bulion, Leslie. *Fatuma's new cloth* ill. by Nicole Tadgell. Moon Mt, 2002. ISBN 978-0-9677929-7-2 Subj: Family life – mothers. Foreign lands – Africa. Shopping.

Bullard, Lisa. *Marco's Cinco de Mayo* ill. by Holli Conger. Millbrook, 2012. ISBN 978-0-7613-5082-8 Subj: Foreign lands – Mexico. Holidays – Cinco de Mayo.

Rashad's Ramadan and Eid al-Fitr ill. by Holli Conger. Millbrook, 2012. ISBN 978-0-7613-5079-8 Subj: Holidays. Holidays – Ramadan. Religion.

Trick-or-treat on Milton Street ill. by Joni Oeltjenbruns. Carolrhoda, 2001. ISBN 978-1-57505-158-1 Subj: Family life – stepfamilies. Holidays – Halloween. Moving.

Bunge, Daniela. *Cherry time* ill. by author. Minedition, 2007. ISBN 978-0-698-40057-3 Subj: Animals – dogs. Character traits – shyness. Friendship.

The scarves ill. by author. Minedition, 2006. ISBN 978-0-698-40045-0 Subj: Activities – knitting. Clothing – scarves. Family life – grandparents. Sports – ice skating.

Bunting, Eve. *Anna's table* ill. by Taia Morley. NorthWord, 2003. ISBN 978-1-55971-841-7 Subj: Behavior – collecting things. Nature. Poetry.

Baby can ill. by Maxie Chambliss. Boyds Mills, 2007. ISBN 978-1-59078-322-1 Subj: Babies. Emotions – love. Family life – new sibling. Sibling rivalry.

The baby shower ill. by Judy Love. Charlesbridge, 2007. ISBN 978-1-58089-139-4 Subj: Animals – babies. Animals – bulls, cows. Gifts. Rhyming text.

Ballywhinney Girl ill. by Emily Arnold McCully. Clarion, 2012. ISBN 978-0-547-55843-1 Subj: Foreign lands – Ireland. Mummies.

Big Bear's big boat ill. by Nancy Carpenter. Clarion, 2013. ISBN 978-0-618-58537-3 Subj: Animals – bears. Boats, ships.

The blue and the gray ill. by Ned Bittinger. Scholastic, 1996. ISBN 978-0-590-60197-9 Subj: Ethnic groups in the U.S. – African Americans. Friendship. U.S. history. War.

The bones of Fred McFee ill. by Kurt Cyrus. Harcourt, 2002. ISBN 978-0-15-202004-0 Subj: Anatomy – skeletons. Holidays – Halloween. Rhyming text.

Butterfly house ill. by Greg Shed. Scholastic, 1999. ISBN 978-0-590-84884-8 Subj: Family life – grandfathers. Insects – butterflies, caterpillars. Metamorphosis. Rhyming text.

Can you do this, Old Badger? ill. by LeUyen Pham. Harcourt, 1999. ISBN 978-0-15-201654-8 Subj: Animals – badgers. Old age.

The cart that carried Martin ill. by Don Tate. Charlesbridge, 2013. ISBN 978-1-58089-387-9 Subj: Ethnic groups in the U.S. – African Americans. U.S. history. Violence, nonviolence.

Christmas cricket ill. by Timothy Bush. Clarion, 2002. ISBN 978-0-618-06554-7 Subj: Holidays – Christmas. Insects – crickets.

The days of summer ill. by William Low. Harcourt, 2001. ISBN 978-0-15-201840-5 Subj: Divorce. Family life – grandparents. Family life – sisters.

A day's work ill. by Ronald Himler. Clarion, 1994. ISBN 978-0-395-67321-8 Subj: Activities – working. Character traits – honesty. Ethnic groups in the U.S. – Mexican Americans. Family life – grandfathers. Gardens, gardening.

December ill. by David Diaz. Harcourt, 1997. ISBN 978-0-15-201434-6 Subj: Character traits – helpfulness. Holidays – Christmas. Homeless.

Ducky ill. by David Wisniewski. Clarion, 1997. ISBN 978-0-395-75185-5 Subj: Activities – traveling. Sea & seashore. Toys.

Emma's turtle ill. by Marsha Winborn. Boyds Mills, 2007. ISBN 978-1-59078-350-4 Subj: Behavior – running away. Pets. Reptiles – turtles, tortoises.

Finn McCool and the great fish ill. by Zachary Pullen. Sleeping Bear, 2010. ISBN 978-1-58536-366-7 Subj: Fish. Folk & fairy tales. Foreign lands – Ireland. Giants.

Flower garden ill. by Kathryn Hewitt. Harcourt, 1994. ISBN 978-0-15-228776-4 Subj: Birthdays. Family life – mothers. Flowers. Gardens, gardening. Rhyming text.

Fly away home ill. by Ronald Himler. Houghton, 1991. ISBN 978-0-395-55962-8 Subj: Airplanes, airports. Family life – fathers. Homeless.

Ghost's hour, spook's hour ill. by author. Clarion, 1987. ISBN 978-0-89919-484-4 Subj: Animals – dogs. Emotions – fear. Family life. Night.

Girls A to Z ill. by Suzanne Bloom. Boyds Mills, 2002. ISBN 978-1-56397-147-1 Subj: Careers. Names.

Gleam and Glow ill. by Peter Sylvada. Harcourt, 2001. ISBN 978-0-15-202596-0 Subj: Fish. Foreign lands – Bosnia-Herzegovina. War.

Going home ill. by David Diaz. HarperCollins, 1996. ISBN 978-0-06-026296-9 Subj: Ethnic groups in the U.S. – Mexican Americans. Family life. Foreign lands – Mexico. Holidays – Christmas.

Happy birthday, dear duck ill. by Jan Brett. Clarion, 1988. ISBN 978-0-89919-541-4 Subj: Animals. Birds – ducks. Birthdays. Rhyming text.

Have you seen my new blue socks? ill. by Sergio Ruzzier. Clarion, 2013. ISBN 978-0-547-75267-9 Subj: Animals. Behavior – lost & found possessions. Birds – ducks. Clothing – socks. Rhyming text.

Hey diddle diddle ill. by Mary Ann Fraser. Boyds Mills, 2011. ISBN 978-1-59078-768-7 Subj: Animals. Musical instruments. Rhyming text.

How many days to America? a Thanksgiving story ill. by Beth Peck. Clarion, 1988. ISBN 978-0-89919-521-6 Subj: Character traits – freedom. Holidays – Thanksgiving. Pilgrims.

Hurry! Hurry! ill. by Jeff Mack. Harcourt, 2007. ISBN 978-0-15-205410-6 Subj: Animals. Birds – chickens. Farms.

Jin Woo ill. by Chris Soentpiet. Clarion, 2001. ISBN 978-0-395-93872-0 Subj: Adoption. Ethnic groups in the U.S. – Korean Americans. Family life – brothers.

Little Badger, terror of the seven seas ill. by LeUyen Pham. Harcourt, 2001. ISBN 978-0-15-202395-9 Subj: Animals – badgers. Imagination. Pirates.

Little Badger's just-about birthday ill. by LeUyen Pham. Harcourt, 2002. ISBN 978-0-15-202609-7 Subj: Animals. Animals – badgers. Birthdays. Parties.

The memory string ill. by Ted Rand. Clarion, 2000. ISBN 978-0-395-86146-2 Subj: Emotions – grief. Family life – stepfamilies. Memories, memory.

The Mother's Day mice ill. by Jan Brett. Clarion, 1986. ISBN 978-0-89919-387-8 Subj: Animals – mice. Holidays – Mother's Day.

Mouse island ill. by Dominic Catalano. Boyds Mills, 2008. ISBN 978-1-59078-447-1 Subj: Animals – cats. Animals – mice. Friendship. Islands.

My dog Jack is fat ill. by Michael Rex. Marshall Cavendish, 2011. ISBN 978-0-7614-5809-8 Subj: Animals – dogs. Health & fitness.

My mom's wedding ill. by Lisa Papp. Sleeping Bear, 2006. ISBN 978-1-58536-288-2 Subj: Divorce. Family life – mothers. Weddings.

My red balloon ill. by Kay Life. Boyds Mills, 2005. ISBN 978-1-59078-263-7 Subj: Careers – military. Family life – fathers.

My special day at third street school ill. by Suzanne Bloom. Boyds Mills, 2004. ISBN 978-0-613-79887-7 Subj: Careers – writers. School.

Night tree ill. by Ted Rand. Harcourt, 1991. ISBN 978-0-15-257425-3 Subj: Animals. Character traits – kindness to animals. Family life. Holidays – Christmas. Trees.

One candle ill. by Wendy Popp. Cotler, 2002. ISBN 978-0-06-028116-8 Subj: Holidays – Hanukkah. War.

One green apple ill. by Ted Lewin. Houghton, 2006. ISBN 978-0-618-43477-0 Subj: Ethnic groups in the U.S. – Arab Americans. Food. Immigrants. School – field trips. Self-concept.

Our library ill. by Maggie Smith. Clarion, 2008. ISBN 978-0-618-49458-3 Subj: Animals. Animals – raccoons. Books, reading. Character traits – cooperation. Libraries.

Peepers ill. by James Ransome. Harcourt, 2000. ISBN 978-0-15-260297-0 Subj: Activities – traveling. Nature. Seasons – fall.

A perfect Father's Day ill. by Susan Meddaugh. Houghton, 1991. ISBN 978-0-395-52590-6 Subj: Family life – fathers. Holidays – Father's Day.

A picnic in October ill. by Nancy Carpenter. Harcourt, 1999. ISBN 978-0-15-201656-2 Subj: Activities – picnicking. Birthdays. Emotions – embarrassment. Ethnic groups in the U.S. – Italian Americans. Family life – grandmothers. Immigrants. U.S. history.

Pirate boy ill. by Julie Fortenberry. Holiday House, 2011. ISBN 978-0-8234-2321-7 Subj: Family life – mothers. Imagination. Pirates.

The pumpkin fair ill. by Eileen Christelow. Clarion, 1997. ISBN 978-0-395-70060-0 Subj: Fairs, festivals. Rhyming text. Seasons – fall.

Riding the tiger ill. by David Frampton. Clarion, 2001. ISBN 978-0-395-79731-0 Subj: Animals – tigers. Cities, towns. Clubs, gangs.

Rudi's pond ill. by Ronald Himler. Clarion, 1999. ISBN 978-0-395-89067-7 Subj: Death. Emotions – grief. Friendship.

St. Patrick's Day in the morning ill. by Jan Brett. Houghton, 1980. ISBN 978-0-395-29098-9 Subj: Holidays – St. Patrick's Day.

Scary, scary Halloween ill. by Jan Brett. Houghton, 1986. ISBN 978-0-89919-414-1 Subj: Holidays – Halloween. Monsters. Mythical creatures – goblins. Rhyming text.

Sing a song of piglets: a calendar in verse ill. by Emily Arnold McCully. Clarion, 2002. ISBN 978-0-618-01137-7 Subj: Animals – babies. Animals – pigs. Days of the week, months of the year. Poetry.

Smoky night ill. by David Diaz. Harcourt, 1994. ISBN 978-0-15-269954-3 Subj: Caldecott award books. Cities, towns. Communities, neighborhoods. Emotions – anger. Ethnic groups in the U.S. Violence, nonviolence.

So far from the sea ill. by Chris Soentpiet. Clarion, 1998. ISBN 978-0-395-72095-0 Subj: Ethnic groups in the U.S. – Japanese Americans. Family life – grandfathers. War.

Sunflower house ill. by Kathryn Hewitt. Harcourt, 1996. ISBN 978-0-15-200483-5 Subj: Flowers. Gardens, gardening. Rhyming text. Seasons – summer.

Swan in love ill. by Jo Ellen McAllister Stammen. Atheneum, 2000. ISBN 978-0-689-82080-9 Subj: Animals. Birds – swans. Boats, ships. Emotions – love.

That's what leprechauns do ill. by Emily Arnold McCully. Houghton, 2006. ISBN 978-0-618-35410-8 Subj: Mythical creatures – leprechauns.

A turkey for Thanksgiving ill. by Diane deGroat. Ticknor & Fields, 1991. ISBN 978-0-89919-793-7 Subj: Animals – moose. Birds – turkeys. Holidays – Thanksgiving.

Tweak tweak ill. by Sergio Ruzzier. Clarion, 2011. ISBN 978-0-618-99851-7 Subj: Animals – elephants. Character traits – curiosity. Family life – mothers.

The Valentine bears ill. by Jan Brett. Seabury Pr., 1983. ISBN 978-0-89919-138-6 Subj: Animals – bears. Holidays – Valentine's Day.

Walking to school ill. by Michael Dooling. Clarion, 2008. ISBN 978-0-618-26144-4 Subj: Foreign lands – Ireland. Prejudice. School.

The wall ill. by Ronald Himler. Clarion, 1990. ISBN 978-0-395-51588-4 Subj: Careers – military. Family life. War.

We were there: a Nativity story ill. by Wendell Minor. Clarion, 2001. ISBN 978-0-395-82265-4 Subj: Animals. Holidays – Christmas. Religion – Nativity.

The Wednesday surprise ill. by Donald Garrick. Ticknor & Fields, 1989. ISBN 978-0-89919-721-0 Subj: Birthdays. Books, reading. Family life. Family life – grandmothers.

Who was born this special day? by Eve Bunting and Leonid Gore ill. by Leonid Gore. Atheneum,

2001. ISBN 978-0-689-82302-2 Subj: Holidays – Christmas. Poetry. Religion – Nativity.

Will it be a baby brother? ill. by Beth Spiegel. Boyds Mills, 2010. ISBN 978-1-59078-439-6 Subj: Babies. Family life – new sibling.

You were loved before you were born ill. by Karen Barbour. Scholastic, 2008. ISBN 978-0-439-04061-7 Subj: Emotions – love. Family life.

Burdett, Lois. *Hamlet for kids* intro. by Kenneth Branagh ill. by children. Firefly, 2000. ISBN 978-1-55209-522-5 Subj: Children as authors. Children as illustrators. Crime. Foreign lands – Denmark. Rhyming text. Royalty – princes.

Macbeth for kids ill. by children. Black Moss, 1996. ISBN 978-0-88753-287-0 Subj: Behavior – fighting, arguing. Children as authors. Children as illustrators. Crime. Foreign lands – Scotland. Royalty – kings. Royalty – queens.

A midsummer night's dream for kids ill. by children. Firefly, 1997. ISBN 978-1-55209-130-2 Subj: Children as authors. Children as illustrators. Dreams. Rhyming text.

Romeo and Juliet for kids ill. by children. Firefly, 1998. ISBN 978-1-55209-244-6 Subj: Behavior – fighting, arguing. Children as authors. Children as illustrators. Emotions – love. Family life. Rhyming text.

The tempest for kids ill. by children. Firefly, 1999. ISBN 978-1-55209-355-9 Subj: Children as authors. Children as illustrators. Emotions. Islands. Magic. Rhyming text. Weather – storms.

Twelfth night for kids ill. by children. Firefly, 1997. ISBN 978-0-88753-233-7 Subj: Behavior – mistakes. Behavior – trickery. Boats, ships. Character traits. Children as authors. Children as illustrators. Sea & seashore.

Burell, Sarah. *Diamond Jim Dandy and the sheriff* ill. by Bryan Langdo. Sterling, 2010. ISBN 978-1-4027-5737-2 Subj: Babies. Reptiles – snakes. Texas. U.S. history – frontier & pioneer life.

Burg, Ann. *Autumn walk* ill. by Kelly Asbury. HarperCollins, 2003. ISBN 978-0-06-009741-7 Subj: Format, unusual – board books. Seasons – fall.

Burg, Sarah Emmanuelle. *Do you still love me?* ill. by author. NorthSouth, 2010. ISBN 978-0-7358-2293-1 Subj: Behavior – fighting, arguing. Behavior – worrying. Family life – parents.

One more egg ill. by author. NorthSouth, 2006. ISBN 978-0-7358-2001-2 Subj: Animals – rabbits. Birds – chickens. Eggs. Farms. Holidays – Easter.

Burgess, Mark. *Where teddy bears come from* ill. by Russell Ayto. Peachtree, 2009. ISBN 978-1-56145-487-7 Subj: Animals – wolves. Books, reading. Holidays – Christmas. Santa Claus. Toys – bears.

Burke, Bobby. *Daddy's little girl* by Bobby Burke and Horace Gerlach ill. by Maggie Kneen. Words & music by Bobby Burke & Horace Gerlach. HarperCollins, 2004. ISBN 978-0-06-028722-1 Subj: Animals – rabbits. Family life – daughters. Family life – fathers. Music. Songs.

Burks, James. *Beep and Bah* ill. by author. Carolrhoda, 2012. ISBN 978-0-7613-6567-9 Subj: Animals – goats. Behavior – lost & found possessions. Clothing – socks. Robots.

Burleigh, Robert. *Clang-clang! beep-beep! listen to the city* ill. by Beppe Giacobbe. Simon & Schuster, 2009. ISBN 978-1-4169-4052-4 Subj: Cities, towns. Noise, sounds. Rhyming text.

Goal ill. by Stephen T. Johnson. Harcourt, 2001. ISBN 978-0-15-201789-7 Subj: Poetry. Sports – soccer.

Good-bye, Sheepie ill. by Peter Catalanotto. Marshall Cavendish, 2010. ISBN 978-0-7614-5598-1 Subj: Animals – dogs. Death. Family life – fathers. Pets.

Hit the road, Jack ill. by Ross MacDonald. Abrams, 2012. ISBN 978-1-4197-0399-7 Subj: Activities – traveling. Animals – rabbits. Rhyming text.

Home run: the story of Babe Ruth ill. by Mike Wimmer. Silver Whistle, 1998. ISBN 978-0-15-200970-0 Subj: Sports – baseball.

I love going through this book ill. by Dan Yaccarino. Cotler, 2001. ISBN 978-0-06-028806-8 Subj: Books, reading. Rhyming text.

If you spent a day with Thoreau at Walden pond ill. by Wendell Minor. Holt, 2012. ISBN 978-0-8050-9137-3 Subj: Activities – writing. Nature. U.S. history.

Langston's train ride ill. by Leonard Jenkins. Orchard, 2004. ISBN 978-0-439-35239-0 Subj: Careers – poets. Ethnic groups in the U.S. – African Americans.

Lookin' for Bird in the big city ill. by Marek Los. Harcourt, 2000. ISBN 978-0-15-202031-6 Subj: Careers – musicians. Cities, towns. Ethnic groups in the U.S. – African Americans. Music. Musical instruments – trumpets.

Messenger, messenger ill. by Barry Root. Atheneum, 2000. ISBN 978-0-689-82103-5 Subj: Careers – messengers. Cities, towns. Rhyming text. Sports – bicycling.

One giant leap ill. by Mike Wimmer. Philomel, 2009. ISBN 978-0-399-23883-3 Subj: Careers – astronauts. Moon. Space & space ships. U.S. history.

Stealing home: Jackie Robinson against the odds ill. by Mike Wimmer. Simon & Schuster, 2007. ISBN 978-0-689-86276-2 Subj: Ethnic groups in the

U.S. – African Americans. Sports – baseball. U.S. history.

Burnard, Damon. *Dave's haircut* ill. by author. Dutton, 2003. ISBN 978-0-525-46967-4 Subj: Careers – barbers. Hair. School.

I spy in the jungle ill. by Julia Cairns. Chronicle, 2001. ISBN 978-0-8118-2987-8 Subj: Animals. Format, unusual – board books. Games. Jungle.

I spy in the ocean ill. by Julia Cairns. Chronicle, 2001. ISBN 978-0-8118-2988-5 Subj: ABC books. Animals. Format, unusual – board books. Sea & seashore.

Burnell, Heather Ayris. *Bedtime monster / ¡A dormir, pequeño monstruo!* ill. by Bonnie Adamson. Raven Tree, 2010. ISBN 978-1-932748-80-2 Subj: Bedtime. Emotions – anger. Foreign languages. Monsters.

Burnett, Frances Hodgson. *A little princess* adapt. by Barbara McClintock; ill. by Barbara McClintock. HarperCollins, 2000. ISBN 978-0-06-029010-8 Subj: Foreign lands – England. Orphans. Poverty. School.

A little princess retold by Janet Allison Brown; ill. by Graham Rust. Viking, 2001. ISBN 978-0-670-89913-5 Subj: Foreign lands – England. Orphans. School.

A little princess retold by Janet Allison Brown; ill. by Graham Rust. Viking, 2001. ISBN 978-0-670-89913-5 Subj: Foreign lands – England. Orphans. School.

The secret garden retold by Janet Allison Brown; ill. by Graham Rus. Viking, 2001. ISBN 978-0-670-89911-1 Subj: Foreign lands – England. Gardens, gardening. Disabilities – physical disabilities.

Burningham, John. *Come away from the water, Shirley* ill. by author. Crowell, 1977. ISBN 978-0-690-01361-0 Subj: Imagination. Pirates. Sea & seashore.

Edwardo: the horriblest boy in the whole world ill. by author. Random House, 2007. ISBN 978-0-375-84053-1 Subj: Behavior – misbehavior.

First steps: letters, numbers, colors, opposites ill. by author. Candlewick, 1994. ISBN 978-1-56402-205-9 Subj: ABC books. Concepts. Concepts – color. Concepts – opposites. Counting, numbers.

Harvey Slumfenburger's Christmas present ill. by author. Candlewick, 1993. ISBN 978-1-56402-246-2 Subj: Character traits – helpfulness. Holidays – Christmas. Santa Claus.

It's a secret! ill. by author. Candlewick, 2009. ISBN 978-0-7636-4275-4 Subj: Activities – dancing. Animals – cats. Night.

John Patrick Norman McHennessy — the boy who was always late ill. by author. Crown, 1987. ISBN 978-0-517-56805-7 Subj: Behavior – promptness, tardiness. Imagination. School.

The magic bed ill. by author. Knopf, 2003. ISBN 978-0-375-92423-1 Subj: Dreams. Furniture – beds. Magic.

Mr. Gumpy's motor car ill. by author. Macmillan, 1975, 1973. ISBN 978-0-02-716200-4 Subj: Automobiles. Weather – rain.

Mr. Gumpy's outing ill. by author. Macmillan, 1971. ISBN 978-0-03-086613-5 Subj: Animals. Behavior – fighting, arguing. Boats, ships. Cumulative tales.

The shopping basket ill. by author. Candlewick, 1996. ISBN 978-1-56402-688-0 Subj: Animals. Character traits – cleverness. Humorous stories. Shopping.

There's going to be a baby ill. by Helen Oxenbury. Candlewick, 2010. ISBN 978-0-7636-4907-4 Subj: Babies. Family life – new sibling.

Tug-of-war ill. by author. Candlewick, 2013. ISBN 978-0-7636-6575-3 Subj: Animals – elephants. Animals – hippopotamuses. Animals – rabbits. Behavior – bullying, teasing. Behavior – trickery. Games.

Burns, Diane L., et al *Backyard beasties* ill. by Brian Gable. Carolrhoda, 2004. ISBN 978-1-57505-646-3 Subj: Animals. Riddles & jokes.

Burrowes, Adjoa J. *Grandma's purple flowers* ill. by author. Lee & Low, 2000. ISBN 978-1-880000-73-1 Subj: Death. Emotions. Family life – grandmothers. Seasons.

Burton, Virginia Lee. *Katy and the big snow* ill. by author. Houghton, 1943. ISBN 978-0-606-03726-6 Subj: Cities, towns. Cumulative tales. Machines. Seasons – winter. Weather – snow.

The little house ill. by author. Houghton, 1939. ISBN 978-0-606-01531-8 Subj: Caldecott award books. Cities, towns. Country. Ecology. Homes, houses. Progress.

Mike Mulligan and his steam shovel ill. by author. Houghton, 1967. ISBN 978-0-395-16961-2 Subj: Activities – working. Machines.

Bus-a-saurus bop ill. by David Clark. Bloomsbury, 2003. ISBN 978-1-58234-850-6 Subj: Buses. Rhyming text. School.

Bush, Jenna. *Read all about it!* (Bush, Laura)

Bush, Laura. *Read all about it!* by Laura Bush and Jenna Bush ill. by Denise Brunkus. HarperCollins, 2008. ISBN 978-0-06-156075-0 Subj: Books, reading. Libraries. School.

Bush, Timothy. *Ferocious girls, steamroller boys, and other poems in between* ill. by author. Orchard, 2000. ISBN 978-0-531-33250-4 Subj: Poetry.

Teddy bear, teddy bear ill. by author. Greenwillow, 2005. ISBN 978-0-06-057836-7 Subj: Activities. Behavior – lost. Nursery rhymes. Toys – bears.

Bushey, Jeanne. *The polar bear's gift* ill. by Vladyana Krykorka. Red Deer, 2000. ISBN 978-0-88995-220-1 Subj: Animals – polar bears. Character traits – helpfulness. Foreign lands – Canada. Friendship. Indians of North America – Inuit.

Busse, Sarah Martin. *Banjo granny* by Sarah Martin Busse and Jacqueline Briggs Martin ill. by Barry Root. Houghton, 2006. ISBN 978-0-618-33603-6 Subj: Family life – grandmothers. Musical instruments – banjos. Songs.

Bustos, Eduardo. *Going ape!* ill. by Lucho Rodriguez. Tundra, 2012. ISBN 978-1-77049-282-0 Subj: Animals – baboons. Animals – chimpanzees. Animals – gorillas. Animals – monkeys. Animals – orangutans.

Butler, Dori Hillestad. *F is for firefighting* ill. by Joan Waites. Pelican, 2007. ISBN 978-1-58980-420-3 Subj: ABC books. Careers – firefighters.

My grandpa had a stroke ill. by Nicole Wong. Magination, 2007. ISBN 978-1-59147-806-5 Subj: Family life – grandfathers. Illness.

Butler, Geoff. *Ode to Newfoundland* ill. by author. Tundra, 2003. ISBN 978-0-88776-631-2 Subj: Foreign lands – Canada. Music. Songs.

Butler, John. *Bedtime in the jungle* ill. by author. Peachtree, 2009. ISBN 978-1-56145-486-0 Subj: Animals. Bedtime. Counting, numbers. Jungle. Songs.

Can you growl like a bear? ill. by author. Peachtree, 2007. ISBN 978-1-56145-396-2 Subj: Animals. Bedtime. Noise, sounds. Rhyming text.

Hush, little ones ill. by author. Peachtree, 2003. ISBN 978-1-56145-269-9 Subj: Animals – babies. Night. Rhyming text. Sleep.

Pi-shu, the little panda ill. by author. Peachtree, 2001. ISBN 978-1-56145-242-2 Subj: Animals – babies. Animals – endangered animals. Animals – pandas.

Ten in the den ill. by author. Peachtree, 2005. ISBN 978-1-56145-344-3 Subj: Animals. Counting, numbers. Nursery rhymes.

Ten in the meadow ill. by author. Peachtree, 2006. ISBN 978-1-56145-372-6 Subj: Activities – playing. Animals. Behavior – hiding. Games.

While you were sleeping ill. by author. Peachtree, 1999. ISBN 978-1-56145-211-8 Subj: Animals. Bedtime. Counting, numbers. Night. Sleep.

Whose baby am I? ill. by author. Viking, 2001. ISBN 978-0-670-89683-7 Subj: Animals – babies.

Butler, Kristi T. *Rip's secret spot* ill. by Joe Cepeda. Harcourt, 2000. ISBN 978-0-15-202640-0 Subj: Animals – dogs. Behavior – lost & found possessions.

Butler, M. Christina. *Mouse and the moon* ill. by Tina Macnaughton. Good Books, 2012. ISBN 978-1-56148-747-9 Subj: Animals. Animals – mice. Friendship. Moon.

One snowy night ill. by Tina Macnaughton. Good Books, 2004. ISBN 978-1-56148-452-2 Subj: Animals. Character traits – generosity. Clothing – hats. Format, unusual – toy & movable books. Gifts. Holidays – Christmas.

One special Christmas ill. by Tina Macnaughton. Tiger Tales, 2013. ISBN 978-1-58925-145-8 Subj: Animals. Animals – hedgehogs. Gifts. Holidays – Christmas. Santa Claus.

One winter's day ill. by Tina Macnaughton. Good Books, 2006. ISBN 978-1-56148-532-1 Subj: Animals. Animals – hedgehogs. Character traits – kindness. Seasons – winter.

The smiley snowman ill. by Tina Macnaughton. Good Books, 2010. ISBN 978-1-56148-696-0 Subj: Animals. Seasons – winter. Snowmen.

Snow friends ill. by Tina Macnaughton. Good Books, 2005. ISBN 978-1-56148-485-0 Subj: Animals – bears. Friendship. Seasons – winter. Weather – snow.

The special blankie ill. by Tina Macnaughton. Good Books, 2010. ISBN 978-1-56148-682-3 Subj: Activities – babysitting. Animals – hedgehogs. Behavior – lost & found possessions.

Butterfield, Moira. *Magic world of learning* created by Jay Young; ill. by Sian Tucker. Sterling, 2001. ISBN 978-0-8069-5587-2 Subj: Format, unusual – toy & movable books. Games.

Butterworth, Chris. *How did that get in my lunchbox? the story of food* ill. by Lucia Gaggiotti. Candlewick, 2011. ISBN 978-0-7636-5005-6 Subj: Food. Health & fitness.

Sea horse: the shyest fish in the sea ill. by John Lawrence. Candlewick, 2006. ISBN 978-0-7636-2989-2 Subj: Fish – seahorses. Sea & seashore.

See what a seal can do ill. by Kate Nelms. Candlewick, 2013. ISBN 978-0-7636-6574-6 Subj: Animals – seals.

Butterworth, Nick. *Albert the bear* ill. by author. HarperCollins, 2002. ISBN 978-0-06-053688-6 Subj: Friendship. Toys. Toys – bears.

Jasper's beanstalk by Nick Butterworth and Mick Inkpen ill. by Mick Inkpen. Bradbury, 1993. ISBN

978-0-02-716231-8 Subj: Animals – cats. Behavior – dissatisfaction. Days of the week, months of the year. Plants.

Jingle bells ill. by author. Orchard, 1998. ISBN 978-0-531-30124-1 Subj: Animals – cats. Animals – mice. Holidays – Christmas. Problem solving.

My dad is awesome ill. by author. Candlewick, 1992. ISBN 978-1-56402-033-8 Subj: Behavior – boasting. Family life – fathers. Holidays – Father's Day.

One snowy night ill. by author. Little, 1990. ISBN 978-0-316-11918-4 Subj: Animals. Character traits – kindness to animals. Night. Weather – snow.

Button, Lana. *Willow finds a way* ill. by Tania Howells. Kids Can, 2013. ISBN 978-1-55453-842-3 Subj: Behavior – bullying, teasing. Character traits – assertiveness. Friendship. Parties.

Willow's whispers ill. by Tania Howells. Kids Can, 2010. ISBN 978-1-55453-280-3 Subj: Behavior – resourcefulness. Character traits – shyness. School.

Buxton, Jane. *The littlest llama* ill. by Jenny Cooper. Sterling, 2008. ISBN 978-1-4027-5277-3 Subj: Activities – playing. Animals – llamas. Foreign lands – South America. Rhyming text.

Buzzeo, Toni. *Adventure Annie goes to kindergarten* ill. by Amy Wummer. Penguin, 2010. ISBN 978-0-8037-3358-9 Subj: School – first day.

Adventure Annie goes to work ill. by Amy Wummer. Dial, 2009. ISBN 978-0-8037-3233-9 Subj: Behavior – lost. Careers. Family life – mothers.

Inside the books: readers and libraries around the world ill. by Jude Daly. Upstart, 2012. ISBN 978-1-60213-058-6 Subj: Books, reading. Libraries. Rhyming text. World.

Just like my Papa ill. by Mike Wohnoutka. Disney/Hyperion, 2013. ISBN 978-1-4231-4263-8 Subj: Animals – babies. Animals – lions. Family life – fathers. Foreign lands – Africa.

Lighthouse Christmas ill. by Nancy Carpenter. Penguin, 2011. ISBN 978-0-8037-3053-3 Subj: Airplanes, airports. Family life – brothers & sisters. Holidays – Christmas. Lighthouses.

No T. Rex in the library ill. by Sachiko Yoshikawa. Simon & Schuster, 2010. ISBN 978-1-4169-3927-6 Subj: Behavior – misbehavior. Dinosaurs. Libraries.

One cool friend ill. by David Small. Dial, 2012. ISBN 978-0-8037-3413-5 Subj: Aquariums. Birds – penguins. Caldecott award honor books. Friendship. Humorous stories.

Penelope Popper book doctor ill. by Jana Christy. Upstart, 2011. ISBN 978-1-60213-054-8 Subj: Books, reading. Libraries.

The sea chest ill. by Mary GrandPré. Dial, 2002. ISBN 978-0-8037-2703-8 Subj: Islands. Lighthouses. Sea & seashore.

Stay close to Mama ill. by Mike Wohnoutka. Hyperion, 2012. ISBN 978-1-4231-3482-4 Subj: Animals – babies. Animals – giraffes. Family life – mothers. Foreign lands – Africa.

Bynum, Janie. *Altoona up north* ill. by author. Harcourt, 2001. ISBN 978-0-15-202313-3 Subj: Animals – baboons. Concepts – cold & heat. Family life – aunts, uncles. Weather – snow.

Kiki's blankie ill. by author. Sterling, 2009. ISBN 978-1-4027-5910-9 Subj: Animals – monkeys. Behavior – lost & found possessions. Character traits – bravery. Reptiles – alligators, crocodiles.

Nutmeg and Barley: a budding friendship ill. by author. Candlewick, 2006. ISBN 978-0-7636-2382-1 Subj: Animals – mice. Animals – squirrels. Friendship.

Otis ill. by author. Harcourt, 2000. ISBN 978-0-15-202153-5 Subj: Animals – pigs. Character traits – cleanliness. Character traits – individuality. Friendship. Frogs & toads.

Byrd, Robert. *Saint Francis and the Christmas donkey* ill. by author. Dutton, 2000. ISBN 978-0-525-46480-8 Subj: Animals – donkeys. Holidays – Christmas. Religion – Nativity.

Byun, You. *Dream friends* ill. by author. Penguin/Nancy Paulsen, 2013. ISBN 978-0-399-25739-1 Subj: Dreams. Emotions – loneliness. Friendship. Imagination – imaginary friends. Moving.

C is for caboose: riding the rails from A to Z. Chronicle, 2007. ISBN 978-0-8118-5643-0 Subj: ABC books. Trains.

Cabatingan, Erin. *A is for Musk Ox* ill. by Matthew Myers. Roaring Brook, 2012. ISBN 978-1-59643-676-3 Subj: ABC books. Animals. Animals – muskoxen. Animals – zebras.

Musk Ox counts ill. by Matthew Myers. Roaring Brook, 2013. ISBN 978-1-59643-798-2 Subj: Animals. Animals – muskoxen. Animals – zebras. Counting, numbers.

Cabrera, Jane. *Bear's good night* ill. by author. Candlewick, 2002. ISBN 978-0-7636-1796-7 Subj: Animals – bears. Bedtime. Format, unusual – toy & movable books.

Here we go round the mulberry bush ill. by author. Holiday House, 2010. ISBN 978-0-8234-2288-3 Subj: Animals – dogs. Songs.

If you're happy and you know it ill. by author. Holiday House, 2005. ISBN 978-0-8234-1881-7 Subj: Animals. Emotions – happiness. Music. Songs.

Kitty's cuddles ill. by author. Holiday House, 2007. ISBN 978-0-8234-2066-7 Subj: Animals – cats. Hugging.

The lonesome polar bear ill. by author. Random House, 2002. ISBN 978-0-375-82410-4 Subj: Animals – polar bears. Behavior – needing someone. Friendship.

Mommy, carry me please! ill. by author. Holiday House, 2006. ISBN 978-0-8234-1935-7 Subj: Animals – babies. Family life – mothers.

Monkey's play time ill. by author. Candlewick, 2002. ISBN 978-0-7636-1795-0 Subj: Activities – playing. Animals. Animals – monkeys. Format, unusual – board books.

Old MacDonald had a farm (Old MacDonald had a farm)

One, two, buckle my shoe ill. by author. Holiday, 2009. ISBN 978-0-8234-2230-2 Subj: Birthdays. Counting, numbers. Nursery rhymes. Parties.

Ten in the bed ill. by author. Holiday House, 2006. ISBN 978-0-8234-2027-8 Subj: Bedtime. Counting, numbers. Toys.

Twinkle, twinkle, little star ill. by author. Holiday House, 2012. ISBN 978-0-8234-2519-8 Subj: Animals. Lullabies. Nursery rhymes. Sky. Songs. Stars.

The wheels on the bus ill. by author. Holiday House, 2011. ISBN 978-0-8234-2350-7 Subj: Buses. Foreign lands – Africa. Music. Songs.

Cader, Lisa Lebowitz. *When I wear my crown* ill. by Laura Huliska-Beith. Chronicle, 2002. ISBN 978-0-8118-3484-1 Subj: Activities – playing. Imagination. Toys.

When I wear my tiara ill. by Laura Huliska-Beith. Chronicle, 2002. ISBN 978-0-8118-3485-8 Subj: Activities – playing. Imagination. Toys.

Cadow, Kenneth M. *Alfie runs away* ill. by Lauren Castillo. Farrar, 2010. ISBN 978-0-374-30202-3 Subj: Behavior – running away. Family life – mothers.

Caffey, Donna. *Yikes-lice!* ill. by Patrick Girouard. Whitman, 1998. ISBN 978-0-8075-9374-5 Subj: Family life. Insects – lice. Rhyming text.

Cain, Janan. *The way I feel* ill. by author. Parenting Pr., 2000. ISBN 978-1-884734-71-7 Subj: Emotions. Rhyming text.

Cain, Sheridan. *By the light of the moon* ill. by Gaby Hansen. Tiger Tales, 2007. ISBN 978-1-58925-062-8 Subj: Animals – mice. Bedtime. Moon.

Calcagnino, Steve. *The body book* (Rotner, Shelley)

Caldicott, Chris. *World food alphabet* ill. with photos. Frances Lincoln, 2013. ISBN 978-1-84780-284-2 Subj: ABC books. Food. World.

Calhoun, Mary. *Blue-ribbon Henry* ill. by Erick Ingraham. Morrow, 1998. ISBN 978-0-688-14675-7 Subj: Animals – cats. Character traits – helpfulness. Fairs, festivals.

Cross-country cat ill. by Erick Ingraham. Morrow, 1979. ISBN 978-0-688-32186-4 Subj: Animals – cats. Character traits – cleverness. Sports – skiing.

Henry the Christmas cat ill. by Erick Ingraham. HarperCollins, 2002. ISBN 978-0-688-16561-1 Subj: Animals – cats. Animals – sheep. Holidays – Christmas. Theater.

Henry the sailor cat ill. by Erick Ingraham. Morrow, 1994. ISBN 978-0-688-10841-0 Subj: Animals – cats. Boats, ships. Sailors. Sea & seashore.

High-wire Henry ill. by Erick Ingraham. Morrow, 1991. ISBN 978-0-688-08984-9 Subj: Animals – cats. Animals – dogs. Emotions – envy, jealousy. Pets.

Hot-air Henry ill. by Erick Ingraham. Morrow, 1981. ISBN 978-0-688-00502-3 Subj: Activities – ballooning. Animals – cats.

A shepherd's gift ill. by Raúl Colón. HarperCollins, 2001. ISBN 978-0-688-15177-5 Subj: Careers – shepherds. Gifts. Holidays – Christmas. Orphans. Religion – Nativity.

Callahan, Sean. *The leprechaun who lost his rainbow* ill. by Nancy Cote. Whitman, 2009. ISBN 978-0-8075-4454-9 Subj: Family life – grandfathers. Holidays – St. Patrick's Day. Mythical creatures – leprechauns. Weather – rainbows.

Shannon and the world's tallest leprechaun ill. by Kathleen Kemly. Whitman, 2008. ISBN 978-0-8075-7326-6 Subj: Activities – dancing. Behavior – wishing. Concepts – size. Contests. Holidays – St. Patrick's Day. Mythical creatures – leprechauns.

A wild Father's Day ill. by Daniel Howarth. Whitman, 2009. ISBN 978-0-8075-2293-6 Subj: Animals. Holidays – Father's Day. Imagination.

Callan, Lyndall. *Dirt on their skirts* (Rappaport, Doreen)

Callery, Sean. *Hide and seek in the jungle* ill. by Rebecca Robinson. Kingfisher, 2010. ISBN 978-0-7534-6392-5 Subj: Animals. Format, unusual – board books. Jungle.

Calmenson, Stephanie. *Birthday at the Panda Palace* ill. by Doug Cushman. HarperCollins, 2007. ISBN 978-0-06-052663-4 Subj: Animals. Animals – mice. Animals – pandas. Birthdays. Gifts. Rhyming text.

The frog principal ill. by Denise Brunkus. Scholastic, 2001. ISBN 978-0-590-37070-7 Subj: Careers – school principals. Frogs & toads. Magic. School.

Good for you! toddler rhymes for toddler times ill. by Melissa Sweet. HarperCollins, 2001. ISBN 978-0-688-17737-9 Subj: Babies. Poetry.

Jazzmatazz! ill. by Bruce Degen. HarperCollins, 2008. ISBN 978-0-06-077289-5 Subj: Animals. Music. Rhyming text.

Late for school! ill. by Sachiko Yoshikawa. Carolrhoda, 2008. ISBN 978-1-57505-935-8 Subj: Behavior – promptness, tardiness. Careers – teachers. Rhyming text. Transportation.

May I pet your dog? the how-to guide for kids meeting dogs (and dogs meeting kids) ill. by Jan Ormerod. Houghton, 2007. ISBN 978-0-618-51034-4 Subj: Animals – dogs. Friendship. Pets. Safety.

Ollie's school day: a yes-and-no book ill. by Abby Carter. Holiday House, 2012. ISBN 978-0-8234-2377-4 Subj: Character traits – questioning. Day. School.

Oopsy, teacher! ill. by Sachiko Yoshikawa. Carolrhoda, 2012. ISBN 978-0-7613-5894-7 Subj: Behavior – lost & found possessions. Careers – teachers. Humorous stories. Rhyming text.

Perfect puppy ill. by Thomas Yezerski. Clarion, 2001. ISBN 978-0-618-01139-1 Subj: Animals – babies. Animals – dogs. Emotions – love.

The principal's new clothes ill. by Denise Brunkus. Scholastic, 1989. ISBN 978-0-590-41822-5 Subj: Careers – school principals. Careers – tailors. Character traits – pride. Character traits – vanity. Clothing. Folk & fairy tales. School.

The teeny tiny teacher ill. by Denis Roche. Scholastic, 1998. ISBN 978-0-590-37123-0 Subj: Careers – teachers. Folk & fairy tales. Ghosts. School.

Welcome, baby! ill. by Melissa Sweet. HarperCollins, 2002. ISBN 978-0-06-000492-7 Subj: Babies. Poetry.

Calvert, Pam. *Princess Peepers* ill. by Tuesday Mourning. Marshall Cavendish, 2008. ISBN 978-0-7614-5437-3 Subj: Behavior – bullying, teasing. Glasses. Royalty – princesses.

Princess Peepers picks a pet ill. by Tuesday Mourning. Marshall Cavendish, 2011. ISBN 978-0-7614-5815-9 Subj: Contests. Dragons. Glasses. Royalty – princesses.

Cameron, C. C. *One for me, one for you* ill. by Grace Lin. Roaring Brook, 2003. ISBN 978-0-7613-2807-0 Subj: Behavior – sharing. Counting, numbers. Rhyming text.

Cameron, Eileen. *Canyon* photos by Michael Collier. Mikaya, 2002. ISBN 978-1-931414-03-6 Subj: Canyons. Earth. Poetry. Rivers.

Camp, Lindsay. *The biggest bed in the world* ill. by Jonathan Langley. HarperCollins, 2000. ISBN 978-0-06-028687-3 Subj: Bedtime. Family life. Furniture – beds. Sleep.

Campbell, Ann-Jeanette. *Queenie Farmer had fifteen daughters* ill. by Holly Meade. Silver Whistle, 2002. ISBN 978-0-15-201933-4 Subj: Family life – daughters. Family life – mothers.

Campbell, Bebe Moore. *I get so hungry* ill. by Amy Bates. Putnam, 2008. ISBN 978-0-399-24311-0 Subj: Ethnic groups in the U.S. – African Americans. Health & fitness. School.

Campbell, K. G. *Lester's dreadful sweaters* ill. by K. G. Campbell. Kids Can, 2012. ISBN 978-1-55453-770-9 Subj: Activities – knitting. Circus. Clothing – sweaters. Clowns, jesters. Family life – cousins.

Campbell, Rod. *Dear zoo* ill. by author. Four Winds, 1984. ISBN 978-0-02-716440-4 Subj: Animals. Format, unusual – toy & movable books. Zoos.

Campoy, F. Isabel. *¡Muu, moo! rimas de animales = animal nursery rhymes* (Ada, Alma Flor)

Pio peep! (Ada, Alma Flor)

Rosa Raposa ill. by José Aruego and Ariane Dewey. Harcourt, 2002. ISBN 978-0-15-202161-0 Subj: Animals – foxes. Animals – jaguars. Behavior – trickery. Foreign lands – South America. Jungle.

Cannon, A. E. *Sophie's fish* ill. by Lee White. Viking, 2012. ISBN 978-0-670-01291-6 Subj: Behavior – worrying. Fish. Pets.

Cannon, Janell. *Crickwing* ill. by author. Harcourt, 2000. ISBN 978-0-15-201790-3 Subj: Character traits – helpfulness. Insects – ants. Insects – cockroaches.

Little Yau ill. by author. Harcourt, 2002. ISBN 978-0-15-201791-0 Subj: Disguises. Illness. Plants.

Stellaluna ill. by author. Harcourt, 1993. ISBN 978-0-15-280217-2 Subj: Animals – bats. Birds. Character traits – being different. Family life – mothers. Friendship.

Stellaluna: a pop-up book and mobile: a pop-up book and mobile ill. by author. Harcourt, 1997. ISBN 978-0-15-201530-5 Subj: Animals – bats. Birds. Character traits – being different. Family life – mothers. Format, unusual – toy & movable books. Friendship.

Verdi ill. by author. Harcourt, 1997. ISBN 978-0-15-201028-7 Subj: Behavior – growing up. Jungle. Reptiles – snakes.

Cantrell, Charlie. *A friend for Einstein: the smallest stallion* by Charlie Cantrell and Rachel Wagner. Hyperion/Disney, 2011. ISBN 978-1-4231-4563-9 Subj: Animals – horses, ponies. Character traits – smallness.

Canyon, Christopher, adapt. *John Denver's Ancient rhymes: a dolphin lullaby* ill. by adapter. Dawn, 2004. ISBN 978-1-58469-064-1 Subj: Animals – dolphins. Lullabies. Music.

John Denver's Sunshine on my shoulders ill. by adapter. Dawn, 2003. ISBN 978-0-613-68518-4 Subj: Music. Songs. Sun. Weather.

Caple, Kathy. *Hillary to the rescue* ill. by author. Carolrhoda, 2000. ISBN 978-1-57505-420-9 Subj: Animals – cats. Seasons – winter.

Worm gets a job ill. by author. Candlewick, 2004. ISBN 978-0-7636-1694-6 Subj: Activities – painting. Animals. Animals – worms. Contests. Money.

Capucilli, Alyssa Satin. *Bathtime for Biscuit* ill. by Pat Schories. HarperCollins, 1998. ISBN 978-0-06-027938-7 Subj: Activities – bathing. Animals – dogs. Pets.

Bear hugs ill. by Jim Ishi. Golden, 2000. ISBN 978-0-307-26113-7 Subj: Animals – bears. Emotions – love. Family life. Rhyming text.

Biscuit ill. by Pat Schories. HarperCollins, 1996. ISBN 978-0-06-026198-6 Subj: Animals – dogs. Bedtime.

Biscuit finds a friend ill. by Pat Schories. HarperCollins, 1997. ISBN 978-0-06-027413-9 Subj: Animals – dogs. Birds – ducks. Friendship.

Biscuit gives a gift ill. by Pat Schories. HarperCollins, 2004. ISBN 978-0-06-009467-6 Subj: Animals – dogs. Format, unusual – board books. Holidays.

Biscuit goes to school ill. by Pat Schories. HarperCollins, 2002. ISBN 978-0-06-028683-5 Subj: Animals – dogs. School.

Biscuit loves school ill. by Pat Schories. HarperCollins, 2003. ISBN 978-0-06-009454-6 Subj: Animals – dogs. Format, unusual – toy & movable books. School.

Biscuit visits the pumpkin patch ill. by Pat Schories. HarperCollins, 2004. ISBN 978-0-06-009466-9 Subj: Activities – bathing. Animals. Animals – moose. Toys.

Biscuit wants to play ill. by Pat Schories. HarperCollins, 2001. ISBN 978-0-06-028070-3 Subj: Activities – playing. Animals – babies. Animals – cats. Animals – dogs.

Biscuit wins a prize ill. by Pat Schories. HarperCollins, 2004. ISBN 978-0-06-009457-7 Subj: Animals – dogs. Pets.

Biscuit's big friend ill. by Pat Schories. HarperCollins, 2003. ISBN 978-0-06-029168-6 Subj: Animals – dogs. Friendship.

Biscuit's new trick ill. by Pat Schories. HarperCollins, 2000. ISBN 978-0-06-028068-0 Subj: Animals – babies. Animals – dogs.

Biscuit's picnic ill. by Pat Schories. HarperCollins, 1998. ISBN 978-0-06-028072-7 Subj: Activities – picnicking. Animals – dogs.

Biscuit's Valentine's Day ill. by Pat Schories. HarperCollins, 2001. ISBN 978-0-694-01222-0 Subj: Animals – babies. Animals – dogs. Format, unusual – toy & movable books. Holidays – Valentine's Day.

Happy birthday, Biscuit! ill. by Pat Schories. HarperCollins, 1999. ISBN 978-0-06-028361-2 Subj: Animals – cats. Animals – dogs. Birthdays. Pets.

Happy Hanukkah, Biscuit ill. by Pat Schories. HarperCollins, 2002. ISBN 978-0-694-01525-2 Subj: Animals – dogs. Format, unusual – toy & movable books. Gifts. Holidays – Hanukkah. Jewish culture.

Hello, Biscuit! ill. by Pat Schories. HarperCollins, 1998. ISBN 978-0-06-028071-0 Subj: Animals – dogs. Names.

Inside a zoo in the city ill. by Tedd Arnold. Scholastic, 2000. ISBN 978-0-590-99715-7 Subj: Animals. Cumulative tales. Rebuses. Rhyming text. Zoos.

Katy Duck ill. by Henry Cole. Simon & Schuster, 2007. ISBN 978-1-4169-1901-8 Subj: Activities – dancing. Birds – ducks. Emotions – fear. Format, unusual – board books.

Katy Duck, big sister ill. by Henry Cole. Simon & Schuster, 2007. ISBN 978-1-4169-4209-2 Subj: Activities – dancing. Birds – ducks. Family life – brothers & sisters. Format, unusual – board books. Sibling rivalry.

Katy Duck is a caterpillar ill. by Henry Cole. Simon & Schuster, 2009. ISBN 978-1-4169-6061-4 Subj: Activities – dancing. Birds – ducks. Seasons – spring.

Little spotted cat ill. by Dan Andreasen. Penguin, 2005. ISBN 978-0-8037-2692-5 Subj: Activities – playing. Animals – cats. Sleep.

Merry Christmas, from Biscuit ill. by Pat Schories. HarperCollins, 2001. ISBN 978-0-694-01522-1 Subj: Animals – dogs. Holidays – Christmas.

Mrs. McTats and her houseful of cats ill. by Joan Rankin. McElderry, 2001. ISBN 978-0-689-83185-0 Subj: ABC books. Animals – cats. Counting, numbers. Rhyming text.

My first ballet class photos by Leyah Jensen. Simon & Schuster, 2011. ISBN 978-1-4424-0895-1 Subj: Ballet. Format, unusual – toy & movable books.

My first soccer game: a book with foldout pages photos by Leyah Jensen. Simon & Schuster, 2011. ISBN 978-1-4424-2747-1 Subj: Format, unusual. Sports – soccer.

Only my dad and me ill. by Tiphanie Beeke. HarperCollins, 2003. ISBN 978-0-694-52584-3 Subj: Animals – rabbits. Family life – fathers. Format, unusual – toy & movable books.

Only my mom and me ill. by Tiphanie Beeke. HarperCollins, 2003. ISBN 978-0-694-52585-0 Subj: Animals – cats. Family life – mothers. Format, unusual – toy & movable books.

What kind of kiss? ill. by Hiroe Nakata. HarperCollins, 2002. ISBN 978-0-694-01573-3 Subj: Animals – bears. Family life – mothers. Kissing. Rhyming text.

Capucilli, Karen. *The jelly bean fun book* ill. with photos. Simon & Schuster, 2001. ISBN 978-0-689-84071-5 Subj: Food. Puzzles.

Caraballo, Samuel. *My big sister / Mi hermana mayor* ill. by Thelma Muraida. Arte Publico, 2012. ISBN 978-1-55885-750-6 Subj: Character traits – kindness. Ethnic groups in the U.S. – Hispanic Americans. Family life – brothers & sisters. Foreign languages.

Carabine, Sue. *A firefighter's night before Christmas* ill. by Shauna Mooney Kawasaki. Gibbs Smith, 2003. ISBN 978-1-58685-269-6 Subj: Careers – firefighters. Holidays – Christmas. Poetry.

Carbone, Elisa. *Heroes of the surf: a rescue story based on true* ill. by Nancy Carpenter. Viking, 2012. ISBN 978-0-670-06312-3 Subj: Boats, ships. U.S. history.

Night running: how James escaped with the help of his faithful dog ill. by E. B. Lewis. Knopf, 2008. ISBN 978-0-375-82247-6 Subj: Animals – dogs. Ethnic groups in the U.S. – African Americans. Slavery. U.S. history.

Carle, Eric. *The artist who painted a blue horse* ill. by author. Penguin, 2011. ISBN 978-0-399-25713-1 Subj: Activities – painting. Animals. Art. Careers – artists. Concepts – color.

Do you want to be my friend? ill. by author. Crowell, 1971. ISBN 978-0-690-24276-8 Subj: Animals – mice. Friendship. Wordless.

Does a kangaroo have a mother, too? ill. by author. HarperCollins, 2000. ISBN 978-0-06-028767-2 Subj: Animals. Family life – mothers.

Draw me a star ill. by author. Philomel, 1992. ISBN 978-0-399-21877-4 Subj: Activities – drawing. Circular tales.

Dream snow ill. by author. Philomel, 2000. ISBN 978-0-399-23579-5 Subj: Farms. Format, unusual – toy & movable books. Holidays – Christmas. Weather – snow.

Friends ill. by author. Philomel, 2013. ISBN 978-0-399-16533-7 Subj: Activities – traveling. Friendship. Moving.

From head to toe ill. by author. HarperCollins, 1997. ISBN 978-0-06-023516-1 Subj: Activities. Anatomy. Animals. Format, unusual – board books.

The grouchy ladybug ill. by author. Crowell, 1977. ISBN 978-0-690-01392-4 Subj: Behavior. Insects – ladybugs. Time.

Have you seen my cat? ill. by author. Watts, 1973. ISBN 978-0-531-02552-9 Subj: Animals – cats. Behavior – lost.

Hello, red fox ill. by author. Simon & Schuster, 1998. ISBN 978-0-689-81775-5 Subj: Animals. Art. Birthdays. Concepts – color. Frogs & toads. Holidays.

A house for Hermit Crab ill. by author. Simon & Schuster, 2004. ISBN 978-0-689-87064-4 Subj: Crustaceans – crabs. Homes, houses. Sea & seashore.

I see a song ill. by author. Crowell, 1973. ISBN 978-0-690-43307-4 Subj: Music. Musical instruments – violins. Wordless.

Little cloud ill. by author. Philomel, 1996. ISBN 978-0-399-23034-9 Subj: Concepts – shape. Imagination. Sky. Weather – clouds. Weather – rain.

Little cloud [board book] ill. by author. 1st board book ed. Philomel, 1998. ISBN 978-0-399-23191-9 Subj: Concepts – shape. Format, unusual – board books. Imagination. Sky. Weather – clouds. Weather – rain.

The mixed-up chameleon ill. by author. Rev. ed. Crowell, 1984. ISBN 978-0-690-00924-8 Subj: Character traits – being different. Concepts – color. Reptiles – chameleons. Reptiles – lizards. Self-concept.

My apron: a story from my childhood ill. by author. Philomel, 1994. ISBN 978-0-399-22824-7 Subj: Careers – plasterers. Clothing – aprons. Family life – aunts, uncles.

My very first book of colors ill. by author. HarperCollins, 1985. ISBN 978-0-694-00011-1 Subj: Concepts – color. Format, unusual.

My very first book of food ill. by author. Crowell, 1986. ISBN 978-0-694-00130-9 Subj: Food. Format, unusual – toy & movable books.

My very first book of growth ill. by author. Crowell, 1986. ISBN 978-0-694-00094-4 Subj: Behavior – growing up. Format, unusual.

My very first book of heads and tails ill. by author. Crowell, 1986. ISBN 978-0-694-00128-6 Subj: Anatomy. Format, unusual – toy & movable books.

My very first book of homes ill. by author. Crowell, 1986. ISBN 978-0-694-00092-0 Subj: Format, unusual. Homes, houses.

My very first book of motion ill. by author. Crowell, 1986. ISBN 978-0-694-00093-7 Subj: Concepts. Format, unusual.

My very first book of numbers ill. by author. HarperCollins, 1985. ISBN 978-0-694-00012-8 Subj: Counting, numbers. Format, unusual.

My very first book of shapes ill. by author. HarperCollins, 1985. ISBN 978-0-694-00013-5 Subj: Concepts – shape. Format, unusual.

My very first book of sounds ill. by author. Crowell, 1986. ISBN 978-0-694-00131-6 Subj: Format, unusual – toy & movable books. Noise, sounds.

My very first book of tools ill. by author. Crowell, 1986. ISBN 978-0-694-00129-3 Subj: Format, unusual – toy & movable books. Tools.

My very first book of touch ill. by author. Crowell, 1986. ISBN 978-0-694-00095-1 Subj: Format, unusual. Senses – touch.

My very first book of words ill. by author. HarperCollins, 1985. ISBN 978-0-694-00014-2 Subj: Format, unusual. Language.

1, 2, 3 to the zoo: a counting book ill. by author. Philomel, 1996. ISBN 978-0-399-23013-4 Subj: Animals. Counting, numbers. Zoos.

Pancakes, pancakes ill. by author. Knopf, 1970. ISBN 978-0-394-90490-0 Subj: Cumulative tales. Food.

Papa, please get the moon for me ill. by author. Alphabet Pr., 1986. ISBN 978-0-88708-026-5 Subj: Format, unusual – toy & movable books. Moon.

The rooster who set out to see the world ill. by author. Simon & Schuster, 1991. ISBN 978-0-88708-178-1 Subj: Activities – traveling. Birds – chickens. Counting, numbers.

Rooster's off to see the world ill. by author. Picture Book Studio, 1987. ISBN 978-0-88708-042-5 Subj: Activities – traveling. Birds – chickens. Counting, numbers.

The secret birthday message ill. by author. Crowell, 1972. ISBN 978-0-690-72348-9 Subj: Birthdays. Format, unusual – toy & movable books.

"Slowly, slowly, slowly," said the sloth ill. by author. Philomel, 2002. ISBN 978-0-399-23954-0 Subj: Animals. Animals – sloths. Jungle.

10 little rubber ducks ill. by author. HarperCollins, 2005. ISBN 978-0-06-074076-4 Subj: Animals. Birds – ducks. Counting, numbers. Format, unusual. Sea & seashore. Toys.

The tiny seed ill. by author. Rev. ed. Picture Book Studio, 1987. ISBN 978-0-88708-015-9 Subj: Plants. Seasons. Seeds.

Today is Monday ill. by author. Philomel, 1993. ISBN 978-0-399-21966-5 Subj: Animals. Days of the week, months of the year. Food. Songs.

The very busy spider ill. by author. Philomel, 1985. ISBN 978-0-399-21166-9 Subj: Animals. Spiders.

The very clumsy click beetle ill. by author. Philomel, 1999. ISBN 978-0-399-23201-5 Subj: Character traits – perseverance. Insects – beetles.

The very hungry caterpillar ill. by author. Collins-World, 1979. ISBN 978-0-529-00776-6 Subj: Days of the week, months of the year. Format, unusual. Insects – butterflies, caterpillars. Metamorphosis.

The very lonely firefly ill. by author. Philomel, 1995. ISBN 978-0-399-22774-5 Subj: Format, unusual – toy & movable books. Insects – fireflies.

The very quiet cricket ill. by author. Putnam, 1990. ISBN 978-0-399-21885-9 Subj: Format, unusual. Insects – crickets. Noise, sounds.

Walter the baker ill. by author. Simon & Schuster, 1995. ISBN 978-0-689-80078-8 Subj: Activities – working. Careers – bakers. Food. Royalty.

Watch out! A giant! ill. by author. Collins-World, 1978. ISBN 978-0-529-05456-2 Subj: Format, unusual – toy & movable books. Giants.

Carlin, Deborah. *What's love?* (Rotner, Shelley)

Carlin, Patricia. *Alfie is not afraid* ill. by author. Hyperion/Disney, 2012. ISBN 978-1-4231-4537-0 Subj: Animals – dogs. Camps, camping. Emotions – fear.

Carling, Amelia Lau. *Mama and Papa have a store* ill. by author. Groundwood, 2003. ISBN 978-0-88899-538-4 Subj: Family life. Foreign lands – Guatemala. Immigrants. Stores.

Carlson, Lori Marie. *Hurray for Three Kings' Day* ill. by Ed Martinez. Morrow, 1998. ISBN 978-0-688-16240-5 Subj: Ethnic groups in the U.S. – Hispanic Americans. Holidays. Religion.

Carlson, Melody. *The day the circus came to town* ill. by Ned Butterfield. Crossway, 2000. ISBN 978-1-58134-158-4 Subj: Circus.

The Easterville miracle ill. by Susan Reagan. Broadman & Holman, 2004. ISBN 978-0-8054-2680-9 Subj: Holidays – Easter. Religion. Rhyming text.

Farmer Brown's field trip ill. by Steve Björkman. Crossway, 2000. ISBN 978-1-58134-142-3 Subj: Careers – farmers. Glasses. Rhyming text.

Forever friends (Tada, Joni Eareckson)

When the creepy things come out ill. by Susan Reagan. Broadman & Holman, 2003. ISBN 978-0-8054-2687-8 Subj: Emotions – fear. Holidays – Halloween. Night. Rhyming text.

Carlson, Nancy. *ABC, I like me!* ill. by author. Viking, 1997. ISBN 978-0-670-87458-3 Subj: ABC books. Language. Self-concept.

Arnie and the skateboard gang ill. by author. Viking, 1995. ISBN 978-0-670-85722-7 Subj: Animals. Animals – cats. Character traits – bravery. Character traits – foolishness. Sports – skateboarding.

First grade, here I come! ill. by author. Penguin, 2006. ISBN 978-0-670-06127-3 Subj: Animals – mice. School – first day.

Get up and go! ill. by author. Penguin, 2006. ISBN 978-0-670-05981-2 Subj: Animals. Animals – pigs. Health & fitness – exercise.

Harriet and George's Christmas treat ill. by author. Carolrhoda, 2001. ISBN 978-1-57505-506-0 Subj: Animals – dogs. Animals – rabbits. Food. Holidays – Christmas.

Harriet and the garden ill. by author. Carolrhoda, 1982. ISBN 978-0-87614-184-7 Subj: Animals – dogs. Problem solving.

Harriet and the roller coaster ill. by author. Carolrhoda, 1982. ISBN 978-0-87614-183-0 Subj: Animals – dogs. Character traits – bravery.

Harriet and Walt ill. by author. Carolrhoda, 1982. ISBN 978-0-87614-185-4 Subj: Animals – dogs. Sibling rivalry.

Harriet's Halloween candy ill. by author. Carolrhoda, 1982. ISBN 978-0-87614-182-3 Subj: Animals – dogs. Behavior – greed.

Henry and the bully ill. by author. Penguin, 2010. ISBN 978-0-670-01148-3 Subj: Animals. Animals – mice. Behavior – bullying, teasing. School.

Henry and the Valentine surprise ill. by author. Viking, 2008. ISBN 978-0-670-06267-6 Subj: Animals – mice. Careers – teachers. Holidays – Valentine's Day. School.

Henry's amazing imagination! ill. by author. Viking, 2008. ISBN 978-0-670-06296-6 Subj: Activities – storytelling. Activities – writing. Imagination. School.

Henry's 100 days of kindergarten ill. by author. Penguin, 2005. ISBN 978-0-670-05977-5 Subj: Animals – mice. Counting, numbers. School.

Hooray for Grandparent's Day! ill. by author. Viking, 2000. ISBN 978-0-670-88876-4 Subj: Family life – grandparents. Friendship. School.

How about a hug? ill. by author. Viking, 2001. ISBN 978-0-670-03506-9 Subj: Animals. Animals – pigs.

I don't like to read! ill. by author. Penguin, 2007. ISBN 978-0-670-06191-4 Subj: Animals – mice. Books, reading. School.

I like me ill. by author. Viking, 1988. ISBN 978-0-670-82062-7 Subj: Character traits – individuality. Self-concept.

It's going to be perfect ill. by author. Viking, 1998. ISBN 978-0-670-87802-4 Subj: Dreams. Family life.

Look out kindergarten, here I come! ill. by author. Viking, 1999. ISBN 978-0-670-88378-3 Subj: Activities. Animals – mice. School – first day.

Louanne Pig in the mysterious Valentine ill. by author. Carolrhoda, 1985. ISBN 978-0-87614-282-0 Subj: Animals – pigs. Holidays – Valentine's Day.

Loudmouth George and the cornet ill. by author. Carolrhoda, 1983. ISBN 978-0-87614-214-1 Subj: Animals – rabbits. Behavior – boasting.

Loudmouth George and the fishing trip ill. by author. Carolrhoda, 1983. ISBN 978-0-87614-213-4 Subj: Animals – rabbits. Behavior – boasting.

Loudmouth George and the new neighbors ill. by author. Carolrhoda, 1983. ISBN 978-0-87614-216-5 Subj: Animals – rabbits. Behavior – boasting. Prejudice.

Loudmouth George and the sixth-grade bully ill. by author. Carolrhoda, 1983. ISBN 978-0-87614-217-2 Subj: Animals – rabbits. Behavior – boasting. Behavior – bullying, teasing. Behavior – stealing.

Loudmouth George earns his allowance ill. by author. Carolrhoda, 2007. ISBN 978-0-8225-6550-4 Subj: Animals – rabbits. Behavior – misbehavior. Character traits – willfulness.

My best friend moved away ill. by author. Viking, 2001. ISBN 978-0-670-89498-7 Subj: Friendship. Moving.

My family is forever ill. by author. Viking, 2004. ISBN 978-0-670-03650-9 Subj: Adoption. Ethnic groups in the U.S. – Asian Americans. Family life.

Sit still! ill. by author. Viking, 1996. ISBN 978-0-670-85721-0 Subj: Behavior – fidgeting. School.

Smile a lot! ill. by author. Carolrhoda, 2002. ISBN 978-0-87614-869-3 Subj: Character traits – optimism. Frogs & toads.

Snowden ill. by author. Viking, 1997. ISBN 978-0-670-88078-2 Subj: Friendship. Snowmen. Sports – ice skating.

Start saving, Henry! ill. by author. Viking, 2009. ISBN 978-0-670-01147-6 Subj: Animals – mice. Behavior – saving things. Money. Toys.

There's a big, beautiful world out there! ill. by author. Viking, 2002. ISBN 978-0-670-03580-9 Subj: Emotions – fear.

Think big! ill. by author. Carolrhoda, 2005. ISBN 978-1-57505-622-7 Subj: Character traits – appearance. Character traits – smallness. Concepts – size. Frogs & toads. School. Self-concept.

Think happy! ill. by author. Carolrhoda, 2009. ISBN 978-0-8225-8940-2 Subj: Animals. Emotions – happiness. Frogs & toads.

Carlstrom, Nancy White. *Before you were born* ill. by Linda Saport. Eerdmans, 2002. ISBN 978-0-8028-5185-7 Subj: Babies. Birth. Family life. Family life – parents. Poetry.

Better not get wet, Jesse Bear ill. by Bruce Degen. Macmillan, 1988. ISBN 978-0-02-717280-5 Subj: Animals – bears. Rhyming text.

Does God know how to tie shoes? ill. by Lori McElrath-Eslick. Eerdmans, 1993. ISBN 978-0-8028-5074-4 Subj: Religion.

Guess who's coming, Jesse Bear ill. by Bruce Degen. Simon & Schuster, 1998. ISBN 978-0-689-80702-2 Subj: Animals – bears. Family life – cousins. Rhyming text.

Happy birthday, Jesse Bear! ill. by Bruce Degen. Macmillan, 1994. ISBN 978-0-02-717277-5 Subj: Animals – bears. Birthdays. Parties. Rhyming text.

How do you say it today, Jesse Bear? ill. by Bruce Degen. Macmillan, 1992. ISBN 978-0-02-717276-8 Subj: Animals – bears. Days of the week, months of the year. Rhyming text.

How does the wind walk? ill. by Deborah Kogan Ray. Macmillan, 1993. ISBN 978-0-02-717275-1 Subj: Seasons. Weather – wind.

I'm not moving, Mama! ill. by Thor Wickstrom. Macmillan, 1990. ISBN 978-0-02-717286-7 Subj: Animals – mice. Moving.

It's about time, Jesse Bear ill. by Bruce Degen. Macmillan, 1990. ISBN 978-0-02-717351-2 Subj: Animals – bears. Rhyming text. Time.

It's your first day of school, Annie Claire ill. by Margie Moore. Abrams, 2009. ISBN 978-0-8109-4057-4 Subj: Animals – dogs. Behavior – worrying. Family life – mothers. Rhyming text. School – first day.

Jesse Bear, what will you wear? ill. by Bruce Degen. Macmillan, 1986. ISBN 978-0-02-717350-5 Subj: Animals – bears. Clothing. Family life.

Let's count it out, Jesse Bear ill. by Bruce Degen. Simon & Schuster, 1996. ISBN 978-0-689-80478-6 Subj: Animals – bears. Counting, numbers. Rhyming text.

Mama, will it snow tonight? ill. by Paul Tong. Boyds Mills, 2009. ISBN 978-1-59078-562-1 Subj: Animals – foxes. Animals – rabbits. Family life – mothers. Seasons – winter. Weather – snow.

The snow speaks ill. by Jane Dyer. Little, 1992. ISBN 978-0-316-12861-2 Subj: Country. Seasons – winter. Weather – snow.

Thanksgiving Day at our house ill. by R. W. Alley. Simon & Schuster, 1999. ISBN 978-0-689-80360-4 Subj: Family life. Holidays – Thanksgiving. Poetry.

The way to Wyatt's house ill. by Mary Morgan. Walker, 2000. ISBN 978-0-8027-8742-2 Subj: Animals. Farms. Friendship.

What a scare, Jesse Bear! ill. by Bruce Degen. Simon & Schuster, 1999. ISBN 978-0-689-81961-2 Subj: Animals – bears. Holidays – Halloween. Rhyming text.

What does the sky say? ill. by Tim Ladwig. Eerdmans, 2001. ISBN 978-0-8028-5208-3 Subj: Nature. Poetry. Religion. Sky. Weather.

Where is Christmas, Jesse Bear? ill. by Bruce Degen. Simon & Schuster, 2000. ISBN 978-0-689-81962-9 Subj: Animals – bears. Holidays – Christmas. Rhyming text.

Who said boo? Halloween poems for the very young ill. by R. W. Alley. Simon & Schuster, 1995. ISBN 978-0-689-80308-6 Subj: Holidays – Halloween. Poetry.

Carluccio, Maria. *I'm 3! Look what I can do* ill. by author. Holt, 2010. ISBN 978-0-8050-8313-2 Subj: Behavior – growing up.

The sounds around town ill. by author. Barefoot, 2008. ISBN 978-1-905236-28-2 Subj: Activities. Day. Noise, sounds.

Carman, William. *What's that noise?* ill. by author. Random House, 2002. ISBN 978-0-375-91052-4 Subj: Emotions – fear. Imagination. Night. Noise, sounds. Sleep.

Carmichael, Clay. *Lonesome bear* ill. by author. NorthSouth, 2001. ISBN 978-1-55858-968-1 Subj: Behavior – lost & found possessions. Toys – bears.

Carmody, Isobelle. *Magic night* ill. by Declan Lee. Random House, 2007. ISBN 978-0-375-83918-4 Subj: Animals – cats. Magic. Mythical creatures.

Carnavas, Peter. *The children who loved books* ill. by author. Kane/Miller, 2013. ISBN 978-1-61067-145-3 Subj: Books, reading. Libraries.

Carnesi, Monica. *Little dog lost: the true story of a brave dog named Baltic* ill. by author. Penguin, 2012. ISBN 978-0-399-25666-0 Subj: Animals – dogs. Foreign lands – Poland.

Carney, Margaret. *At Grandpa's sugar bush* ill. by Janet Wilson. Kids Can, 1998. ISBN 978-1-55074-341-8 Subj: Careers – farmers. Food. Foreign lands – Canada. Trees.

The biggest fish in the lake ill. by Janet Wilson. Kids Can, 2001. ISBN 978-1-55074-720-1 Subj: Family life – grandfathers. Sports – fishing.

Where does a tiger-heron spend the night? ill. by Mélanie Watt. Kids Can, 2002. ISBN 978-1-55337-022-2 Subj: Birds. Format, unusual – toy & movable books. Rhyming text.

Carney, Mary Lou. *The yippy, yappy Yorkie in the green doggy sweater* (Macomber, Debbie)

Carney-Nunes, Charisse. *I dream for you a world: a covenant for our children* ill. by Ann Marie Williams. Brand Nu Words, 2007. ISBN 978-0-9748142-3-0 Subj: World.

Carr, Jan. *Big Truck and Little Truck* ill. by Ivan Bates. Scholastic, 2000. ISBN 978-0-439-07177-2 Subj: Farms. Trucks.

Dappled apples ill. by Dorothy Donohue. Holiday, 2001. ISBN 978-0-8234-1583-0 Subj: Rhyming text. Seasons – fall.

Frozen noses ill. by Dorothy Donohue. Holiday, 1999. ISBN 978-0-8234-1462-8 Subj: Activities. Friendship. Seasons – winter. Sports.

Greedy apostrophe: a cautionary tale ill. by Ethan Long. Holiday House, 2007. ISBN 978-0-8234-2006-3 Subj: Behavior – greed. Language.

Splish, splash, spring ill. by Dorothy Donohue. Holiday, 2001. ISBN 978-0-8234-1578-6 Subj: Rhyming text. Seasons – spring.

Sweet hearts ill. by Dorothy Donohue. Holiday, 2003. ISBN 978-0-8234-1732-2 Subj: Animals – pandas. Holidays – Valentine's Day.

Carrer, Chiara. *Otto Carrotto* ill. by author. Eerdmans, 2011. ISBN 978-0-8028-5393-6 Subj: Animals – rabbits. Character traits – individuality. Food.

Carrick, Carol. *Big old bones: a dinosaur tale* ill. by Donald Carrick. Houghton, 1992. ISBN 978-0-395-61582-9 Subj: Dinosaurs.

Patrick's dinosaurs ill. by Donald Carrick. Houghton, 1983. ISBN 978-0-89919-189-8 Subj: Animals. Dinosaurs. Imagination. Prehistory. Science. Zoos.

Patrick's dinosaurs on the Internet ill. by David Milgrim. Clarion, 1999. ISBN 978-0-395-50949-4 Subj: Computers. Dinosaurs. Imagination. Prehistory. School. Space & space ships.

The polar bears are hungry ill. by Paul Carrick. Clarion, 2002. ISBN 978-0-618-15962-8 Subj: Animals – bears. Animals – polar bears. Seasons – winter.

Valentine ill. by Paddy Bouma. Clarion, 1995. ISBN 978-0-395-66554-1 Subj: Animals – sheep. Family life – grandmothers. Family life – mothers. Holidays – Valentine's Day.

What happened to Patrick's dinosaurs? ill. by Donald Carrick. Houghton, 1986. ISBN 978-0-89919-406-6 Subj: Dinosaurs. Imagination. Prehistory.

Carroll, James Christopher. *The boy and the moon* ill. by author. Sleeping Bear, 2010. ISBN 978-1-58536-521-0 Subj: Moon. Night.

Carroll, Lewis. *Jabberwocky* ill. by Christopher Myers. Hyperion, 2007. ISBN 978-1-4231-0372-1 Subj: Humorous stories. Mythical creatures. Poetry.

Carryl, Charles E. *The camel's lament* ill. by Charles Santore. Random House, 2004. ISBN 978-0-375-91426-3 Subj: Animals. Animals – camels. Poetry.

Cartaya, Pablo. *Tina Cocolina: queen of the cupcakes* by Pablo Cartaya and Martin Howard ill. by Kirsten Richards. Random House, 2010. ISBN 978-0-375-85891-8 Subj: Activities – baking, cooking. Character traits – individuality. Contests. Food.

Carter, Alden R. *Big brother Dustin* photos by Dan Young. Whitman, 1998. ISBN 978-0-8075-0715-5 Subj: Babies. Disabilities – Down syndrome. Family life – brothers & sisters. Names.

I'm tougher than asthma! by Alden R. Carter and Siri M. Carter; photos by Dan Young. Whitman, 1996. ISBN 978-0-8075-3474-8 Subj: Illness – asthma.

I'm tougher than diabetes! photos by Carol Shadis Carter. Whitman, 2001. ISBN 978-0-8075-1572-3 Subj: Illness – diabetes.

Seeing things my way photos by Carol S. Carter. Whitman, 1998. ISBN 978-0-8075-7296-2 Subj: Disabilities. Illness.

Carter, Anne Laurel. *Circus play* ill. by Joanne Fitzgerald. Orca, 2002. ISBN 978-1-55143-225-0 Subj: Circus. Imagination.

The F team ill. by Rose Cowles. Orca, 2003. ISBN 978-1-55143-241-0 Subj: Behavior – bullying, teasing. Character traits – perseverance. Sports – hockey.

My home bay ill. by Alan Daniel and Lea Daniel. Red Deer, 2004. ISBN 978-0-88995-284-3 Subj: Foreign lands – Canada. Friendship.

Under a prairie sky ill. by Alan Daniel and Lea Daniel. Orca, 2002. ISBN 978-1-55143-226-7 Subj: Careers – police officers. Foreign lands – Canada.

Carter, David A. *Blue 2: a pop-up book for children of all ages* ill. by author. Simon & Schuster, 2007. ISBN 978-1-4169-1781-6 Subj: Format, unusual – toy & movable books. Picture puzzles.

Chanukah bugs: a pop-up celebration ill. by author. Simon & Schuster, 2002. ISBN 978-0-689-81860-8 Subj: Format, unusual – toy & movable books. Holidays – Hanukkah. Insects.

Easter bugs: a springtime pop-up ill. by author. Simon & Schuster, 2001. ISBN 978-0-689-81862-2 Subj: Eggs. Format, unusual – toy & movable books. Holidays – Easter. Insects.

Flapdoodle dinosaurs: a colorful pop-up book ill. by author. Simon & Schuster, 2001. ISBN 978-0-689-84643-4 Subj: Dinosaurs. Format, unusual – toy & movable books. Rhyming text.

How many bugs in a box? ill. by author. Simon & Schuster, 1988. ISBN 978-0-671-64965-4 Subj: Format, unusual – toy & movable books. Insects.

If you're happy and you know it, clap your hands ill. by author. Scholastic, 1997. ISBN 978-0-590-93828-0 Subj: Emotions. Format, unusual. Music. Songs.

In a dark, dark wood: an old tale with a new twist ill. by author. Simon & Schuster, 2002. ISBN 978-0-689-85280-0 Subj: Format, unusual – toy & movable books. Ghosts. Homes, houses.

Old MacDonald had a farm: a pop-up book ill. by author. Scholastic, 2001. ISBN 978-0-439-26468-6 Subj: Animals. Careers – farmers. Cumulative tales. Farms. Format, unusual – toy & movable books. Music. Noise, sounds. Songs.

One red dot: a pop-up book for children of all ages ill. by author. Simon & Schuster, 2005. ISBN 978-0-689-87769-8 Subj: Counting, numbers. Format, unusual – toy & movable books. Picture puzzles.

Peekaboo bugs: a hide-and-seek book ill. by author. Simon & Schuster, 2002. ISBN 978-0-689-85035-6 Subj: Format, unusual – toy & movable books. Games. Insects.

600 black spots: a pop-up book for children of all ages ill. by author. Simon & Schuster, 2007. ISBN 978-1-4169-4092-0 Subj: Format, unusual – toy & movable books. Picture puzzles.

Whoo? Whoo? ill. by author. Simon & Schuster, 2007. ISBN 978-1-4169-3816-3 Subj: Animals. Character traits – questioning. Format, unusual – toy & movable books. Games. Picture puzzles.

Who's under that hat? ill. by author. Text by Sarah Weeks. Harcourt, 2005. ISBN 978-0-15-205467-0 Subj: Clothing. Format, unusual – toy & movable books. Picture puzzles.

Yellow square: a pop-up book for children of all ages ill. by author. Simon & Schuster, 2008. ISBN 978-1-4169-4093-7 Subj: Format, unusual – toy & movable books. Picture puzzles.

Carter, Don. *Get to work, trucks!* ill. by author. Roaring Brook, 2002. ISBN 978-0-7613-2518-5 Subj: Machines. Trucks.

Heaven's all-star jazz band ill. by author. Knopf, 2002. ISBN 978-0-375-91571-0 Subj: Careers – musicians. Ethnic groups in the U.S. – African Americans. Family life – grandfathers. Music. Musical instruments – bands.

Old MacDonald drives a tractor ill. by author. Macmillan, 2007. ISBN 978-1-59643-023-5 Subj: Careers – farmers. Farms. Rhyming text. Tractors.

Send it! ill. by author. Roaring Brook, 2003. ISBN 978-0-7613-2573-4 Subj: Careers – postal workers. Post office.

Carter, Siri M. *I'm tougher than asthma!* (Carter, Alden R.)

Cartier, Wesley. *Marco's run* ill. by Reynold Ruffins. Harcourt, 2001. ISBN 978-0-15-216243-6 Subj: Activities – running. Concepts – speed. Imagination.

Cartwright, Reg. *What we do* ill. by author. Holt, 2005. ISBN 978-0-8050-7671-4 Subj: Animals. Rhyming text.

Casalis, Anna. *Dinosaurs [board book]* ill. by Franco Tempesta. Simon & Schuster, 2001. ISBN 978-0-689-85130-8 Subj: Dinosaurs. Format, unusual – board books.

Casanova, Mary. *The day Dirk Yeller came to town* ill. by Ard Hoyt. Farrar, 2011. ISBN 978-0-374-31742-3 Subj: Books, reading. Crime. Libraries. U.S. history – frontier & pioneer life.

The hunter ill. by Ed Young. Atheneum, 2000. ISBN 978-0-689-82906-2 Subj: Folk & fairy tales. Foreign lands – China.

One-dog canoe ill. by Ard Hoyt. Kroupa, 2003. ISBN 978-0-374-35638-5 Subj: Animals. Canoes & canoeing. Rhyming text.

One-dog sleigh ill. by Ard Hoyt. Farrar, 2013. ISBN 978-0-374-35639-2 Subj: Animals. Rhyming text. Sports – sledding. Weather – snow.

Some cat! ill. by Ard Hoyt. Farrar, 2012. ISBN 978-0-374-37123-4 Subj: Animals – cats. Animals – dogs.

Some dog! ill. by Ard Hoyt. Farrar, 2007. ISBN 978-0-347-37133-3 Subj: Animals – dogs.

Utterly otterly day ill. by Ard Hoyt. Simon & Schuster, 2008. ISBN 978-1-4169-0868-5 Subj: Animals – otters. Behavior – needing someone. Family life.

Utterly otterly night ill. by Ard Hoyt. Simon & Schuster, 2011. ISBN 978-1-4169-7562-5 Subj: Animals – otters. Night. Seasons – winter.

Case, Chris. *Sophie and the next-door monsters* ill. by author. Walker, 2008. ISBN 978-0-8027-9756-8 Subj: Emotions – fear. Friendship. Monsters.

Caseley, Judith. *Bully* ill. by author. Greenwillow, 2001. ISBN 978-0-688-17868-0 Subj: Behavior – bullying, teasing. School.

Field Day Friday ill. by author. Greenwillow, 2000. ISBN 978-0-688-16762-2 Subj: Friendship. School – field trips. Sports – racing.

In style with Grandma Antoinette ill. by author. Tanglewood, 2005. ISBN 978-0-9749303-4-3 Subj: Beauty shops. Family life – grandmothers.

On the town ill. by author. Greenwillow, 2002. ISBN 978-0-06-029585-1 Subj: Communities, neighborhoods.

Sophie and Sammy's library sleepover ill. by author. Greenwillow, 1993. ISBN 978-0-688-10616-4 Subj: Books, reading. Family life – brothers & sisters. Libraries. Sleep.

Witch mama ill. by author. Greenwillow, 1996. ISBN 978-0-688-14458-6 Subj: Family life. Holidays – Halloween.

Casey, Dawn. *The great race: the story of the Chinese zodiac* ill. by Anne Wilson. Barefoot, 2006. ISBN 978-1-905236-77-0 Subj: Animals. Folk & fairy tales. Zodiac.

Casey, Patricia. *One day at Wood Green Animal Shelter* ill. by author. Candlewick, 2001. ISBN 978-0-7636-1210-8 Subj: Animals.

Casey, Tina. *The runaway Valentine* ill. by Theresa Smythe. Whitman, 2001. ISBN 978-0-8075-7178-1 Subj: Holidays – Valentine's Day.

Cash, Megan Montague. *Bow-Wow bugs a bug* (Newgarden, Mark)

Bow-Wow orders lunch (Newgarden, Mark)

I saw the sea and the sea saw me ill. by author. Viking, 2001. ISBN 978-0-670-89966-1 Subj: Animals. Rhyming text. Sea & seashore – beaches. Senses.

What makes the seasons? ill. by author. Viking, 2003. ISBN 978-0-670-03598-4 Subj: Animals – cats. Ethnic groups in the U.S. – African Americans. Plants. Science. Seasons.

Cash, Rosanne. *Penelope Jane: a fairy's tale* ill. by G. Brian Karas. Cotler, 2000. ISBN 978-0-06-027544-0 Subj: Fairies. Fire. School.

Casin, Sheridan. *Little Turtle and the song of the sea* ill. by Norma Burgin. Crocodile, 2000. ISBN 978-1-56656-355-0 Subj: Reptiles – turtles, tortoises. Sea & seashore.

Cassie, Brian. *Say it again* ill. by David Mooney. Charlesbridge, 2000. ISBN 978-0-88106-341-7 Subj: Animals. Language.

Cassino, Mark, with Jon Nelson. *The story of snow: the science of winter's wonder* ill. by Nora Aoyagi. Chronicle, 2009. ISBN 978-0-8118-6866-2 Subj: Science. Seasons – winter. Weather – snow.

Castaneda, Omar S. *Abuela's weave* ill. by Enrique O. Sánchez. Lee & Low, 1993. ISBN 978-1-880000-00-7 Subj: Activities – weaving. Fairs, festivals. Family life – grandmothers. Foreign lands – Guatemala.

Casteel, Seth. *Underwater dogs: kids edition* photos by author. Little, Brown, 2013. ISBN 978-0-316-25558-5 Subj: Activities – photographing. Animals – dogs. Rhyming text.

Castellucci, Cecil. *Grandma's gloves* ill. by Julia Denos. Candlewick, 2010. ISBN 978-0-7636-3168-0 Subj: Death. Family life – grandmothers. Gardens, gardening.

Casterline, L. C. *The sounds of music* ill. by Lane Yerkes. G. Stevens, 2004. ISBN 978-0-8368-4100-8 Subj: Music. Musical instruments.

Castillo, Lauren. *Melvin and the boy* ill. by author. Holt, 2011. ISBN 978-0-8050-8929-5 Subj: Pets. Reptiles – turtles, tortoises.

Castle, Caroline. *For every child: the UN Convention on the Rights of the Child in words and pictures.* Fogelman/UNICEF, 2001. ISBN 978-0-8037-2650-5 Subj: UNICEF. Self-concept.

Naughty! by Caroline Castle and Sam Childs ill. by Sam Childs. Knopf, 2001. ISBN 978-0-375-91359-4 Subj: Activities – playing. Animals – babies. Animals – hippopotamuses. Animals – zebras. Bedtime. Humorous stories.

Caswell, Deanna. *Train trip* ill. by Dan Andreasen. Hyperion/Disney, 2011. ISBN 978-1-4231-1837-4 Subj: Rhyming text. Trains.

Catalano, Dominic. *Mr. Bassett plays* ill. by author. Boyds Mills, 2003. ISBN 978-1-59078-007-7 Subj: Animals – dogs. Friendship.

Santa and the three bears ill. by author. Boyds Mills, 2000. ISBN 978-1-56397-864-7 Subj: Animals – bears. Holidays – Christmas. Santa Claus.

Catalanotto, Peter. *Emily's art* ill. by author. Atheneum, 2001. ISBN 978-0-689-83831-6 Subj: Careers – artists. Contests.

Ivan the terrier ill. by author. Simon & Schuster, 2007. ISBN 978-1-4169-1247-7 Subj: Animals – dogs. Behavior – misbehavior. Folk & fairy tales.

Kitten red, yellow, blue ill. by author. Simon & Schuster, 2005. ISBN 978-0-689-86562-6 Subj: Animals – cats. Careers. Concepts – color.

Matthew A.B.C. ill. by author. Atheneum, 2002. ISBN 978-0-689-84582-6 Subj: ABC books. Names. School. Self-concept.

Question Boy meets Little Miss Know-It-All ill. by author. Atheneum, 2012. ISBN 978-1-4424-0670-4 Subj: Character traits – curiosity. Character traits – questioning.

The secret lunch special by Peter Catalanotto and Pamela Schembri ill. by Peter Catalanotto. Holt, 2006. ISBN 978-0-8050-7838-1 Subj: Food. Friendship. School.

Catchpool, Michael. *The cloud spinner* ill. by Alison Jay. Knopf, 2012. ISBN 978-0-375-87011-8 Subj: Clothing. Ecology. Royalty – kings. Weather – clouds.

Cate, Annette LeBlanc. *The magic rabbit* ill. by author. Candlewick, 2007. ISBN 978-0-7636-2672-3 Subj: Animals – rabbits. Behavior – lost & found possessions. Careers – magicians. Magic.

Catrow, David. *Monster mash* ill. by author. Scholastic, 2012. ISBN 978-0-545-21479-7 Subj: Activities – dancing. Monsters. Songs.

Catusanu, Mircea. *The strange case of the missing sheep* ill. by author. Viking, 2009. ISBN 978-0-670-01131-5 Subj: Animals – dogs. Animals – sheep. Animals – wolves. Mystery stories. Sleep.

Caudill, Rebecca. *A pocketful of cricket* ill. by Evaline Ness. Holt, 1964. Subj: Behavior – sharing. Caldecott award honor books. Farms. Insects – crickets. School.

Cauley, Lorinda Bryan. *Clap your hands* ill. by author. Putnam, 1992. ISBN 978-0-399-22118-7 Subj: Activities. Activities – playing. Games. Nursery rhymes.

What do you know! ill. by author. Putnam, 2001. ISBN 978-0-399-23573-3 Subj: Picture puzzles.

Cave, Kathryn. *The boy who became an eagle* ill. by Nick Maland. DK, 2000. ISBN 978-0-7894-2666-6 Subj: Activities – flying. Fairs, festivals.

Henry's song ill. by Sue Hendra. Eerdmans, 2000. ISBN 978-0-8028-5198-7 Subj: Activities – singing. Animals. Character traits – individuality.

One child, one seed: a South African counting book photos by Gisèle Wulfsohn. Holt, 2003. ISBN 978-0-8050-7204-4 Subj: Counting, numbers. Foreign lands – South Africa. Plants. Seeds.

You've got dragons ill. by Nick Maland. Peachtree, 2003. ISBN 978-1-56145-284-2 Subj: Dragons. Emotions – fear.

Cazet, Denys. *December 24th* ill. by author. Bradbury, 1986. ISBN 978-0-02-717950-7 Subj: Animals – rabbits. Birthdays. Family life – grandfathers. Holidays.

Elvis the rooster almost goes to heaven ill. by author. HarperCollins, 2003. ISBN 978-0-06-000501-6 Subj: Birds – chickens. Humorous stories.

A fish in his pocket ill. by author. Watts, 1987. ISBN 978-0-531-08313-0 Subj: Birthdays. Character traits – kindness. Death. School.

Never poke a squid ill. by author. Orchard, 2000. ISBN 978-0-531-33279-5 Subj: Animals. Friendship. Holidays – Halloween. School.

Never spit on your shoes ill. by author. Orchard, 1990. ISBN 978-0-531-08447-2 Subj: Animals. Animals – cats. School – first day.

Nothing at all ill. by author. Orchard, 1994. ISBN 978-0-531-08672-8 Subj: Animals. Cumulative tales. Farms. Noise, sounds. Rhyming text. Scarecrows.

The octopus ill. by author. HarperCollins, 2005. ISBN 978-0-06-051089-3 Subj: Activities – storytelling. Animals – dogs. Family life – grandparents. Illness – chicken pox. Octopuses.

The perfect pumpkin pie ill. by author. Simon & Schuster, 2005. ISBN 978-0-689-86467-4 Subj: Activities – baking, cooking. Food. Ghosts. Holidays – Halloween.

Will you read to me? ill. by author. Simon & Schuster, 2007. ISBN 978-1-4169-0935-4 Subj: Animals – pigs. Books, reading. Self-concept.

Cech, John. *Aesop's fables* (Aesop)

Cecil, Randy. *Gator* ill. by author. Candlewick, 2007. ISBN 978-0-7636-2952-6 Subj: Merry-go-rounds. Parks – amusement. Reptiles – alligators, crocodiles.

Horsefly and Honeybee ill. by author. Holt, 2012. ISBN 978-0-8050-9300-1 Subj: Character traits – cooperation. Frogs & toads. Insects – bees. Insects – flies.

Cecka, Melanie. *Violet comes to stay* ill. by Emily Arnold McCully. Penguin, 2006. ISBN 978-0-670-06073-3 Subj: Animals – cats. Behavior – misbehavior. Homes, houses.

Violet goes to the country ill. by Emily Arnold McCully. Penguin, 2007. ISBN 978-0-670-06181-5 Subj: Animals – cats. Character traits – curiosity. Country.

Ceelen, Vicky. *Baby! baby!* photos by author. Random House, 2008. ISBN 978-0-375-84207-8 Subj: Animals. Babies. Wordless.

Celenza, Anna Harwell. *Duke Ellington's Nutcracker Suite* ill. by Don Tate. Charlesbridge, 2011. ISBN 978-1-57091-700-4 Subj: Careers – musicians. Ethnic groups in the U.S. – African Americans. Music.

The farewell symphony ill. by JoAnn E. Kitchel. Talewinds, 2000. ISBN 978-1-57091-406-5 Subj: Careers – composers. Music.

Cendrars, Blaise. *Shadow* ill. by Marcia Brown. Scribners, 1982. ISBN 978-0-684-17226-2 Subj: Caldecott award books. Folk & fairy tales. Foreign lands – Africa. Poetry. Shadows.

Chacon, Michelle Netten. *How the Indians bought the farm* (Strete, Craig Kee)

Chaconas, Dori. *Christmas mouseling* ill. by Susan Kathleen Hartung. Penguin, 2005. ISBN 978-0-670-05984-3 Subj: Animals – babies. Animals – mice. Family life – mothers. Holidays – Christmas. Religion – Nativity.

Dancing with Katya ill. by Constance R. Bergum. Peachtree, 2006. ISBN 978-1-56145-376-4 Subj: Activities – dancing. Ballet. Family life – brothers & sisters. Illness – poliomyelitis.

Don't slam the door! ill. by Will Hillenbrand. Candlewick, 2010. ISBN 978-0-7636-3709-5 Subj: Animals. Cumulative tales. Humorous stories. Rhyming text.

Dori the contrary hen ill. by Marsha Gray Carrington. Carolrhoda, 2007. ISBN 978-1-57505-749-1 Subj: Birds – chickens. Character traits – stubbornness. Farms.

Hurry down to Derry Fair ill. by Gillian Tyler. Candlewick, 2011. ISBN 978-0-7636-3208-3 Subj: Fairs, festivals. Family life. Rhyming text.

Looking for Easter ill. by Margie Moore. Whitman, 2008. ISBN 978-0-8075-4749-6 Subj: Animals. Animals – rabbits. Behavior – sharing. Holidays – Easter. Seasons – spring.

On a wintry morning ill. by Stephen T. Johnson. Viking, 2000. ISBN 978-0-670-89245-7 Subj: Family life – fathers. Rhyming text. Seasons – winter. Sports – sledding.

Pennies in a jar ill. by Ted Lewin. Peachtree, 2007. ISBN 978-1-56145-422-8 Subj: Emotions – fear. U.S. history. War.

Virginnie's hat ill. by Holly Meade. Candlewick, 2007. ISBN 978-0-7636-2397-5 Subj: Clothing – hats. Rhyming text. Swamps.

When cows come home for Christmas ill. by Lynne Chapman. Whitman, 2005. ISBN 978-0-8075-8877-2 Subj: Animals – bulls, cows. Holidays – Christmas. Rhyming text.

Chae, In Seon. *How do you count a dozen ducklings?* ill. by Seung Ha Rew. Whitman, 2006. ISBN 978-0-8075-1718-5 Subj: Birds – ducks. Counting, numbers.

Chaikin, Miriam. *Don't step on the sky: a handful of haiku* ill. by Hiroe Nakata. Holt, 2002. ISBN 978-0-8050-6474-2 Subj: Nature. Poetry.

Chall, Marsha Wilson. *Bonaparte* ill. by Wendy Anderson Halperin. DK, 2000. ISBN 978-0-7894-2617-8 Subj: Animals – dogs. Foreign lands – France. School.

Happy Birthday, America! ill. by Guy Porfirio. Lothrop, 2000. ISBN 978-0-688-13052-7 Subj: Family life. Holidays – Fourth of July.

One pup's up ill. by Henry Cole. Simon & Schuster, 2010. ISBN 978-1-4169-7960-9 Subj: Animals – dogs. Counting, numbers. Rhyming text.

Pick a pup ill. by Jed Henry. Simon & Schuster, 2011. ISBN 978-1-4169-7961-6 Subj: Animals – dogs. Character traits – kindness to animals. Pets.

Prairie train ill. by John Thompson. HarperCollins, 2003. ISBN 978-0-688-13434-1 Subj: Cities, towns. Country. Family life – grandmothers. Trains.

Sugarbush spring ill. by Jim Daly. Lothrop, 2000. ISBN 978-0-688-14908-6 Subj: Family life. Food. Seasons – spring.

Chamberlain, Margaret. *Please don't tease Tootsie* ill. by author. Dutton, 2008. ISBN 978-0-525-47982-6 Subj: Behavior – misbehavior. Character traits – kindness to animals. Pets. Rhyming text.

Chamberlin, Mary. *Mama Panya's pancakes: a village tale from Kenya* by Mary Chamberlin and Rich Chamberlin ill. by Julia Cairns. Barefoot, 2005. ISBN 978-1-84148-139-5 Subj: Character traits – generosity. Food. Foreign lands – Kenya.

Chamberlin, Rich. *Mama Panya's pancakes: a village tale from Kenya* (Chamberlin, Mary)

Chamberlin-Calamar, Pat. *Alaska's twelve days of summer* ill. by Shannon Cartwright. Sasquatch, 2003. ISBN 978-1-57061-341-8 Subj: Alaska. Animals. Counting, numbers.

Chambers, Angela. *Follow that chicken!* ill. by Simone Abel. Sterling, 2000. ISBN 978-0-8069-0310-1 Subj: Birds – chickens. Concepts – opposites. Format, unusual – board books. Format, unusual – toy & movable books. Language.

How now, cow? ill. by Simone Abel. Sterling, 2000. ISBN 978-0-8069-0275-3 Subj: Animals – bulls, cows. Format, unusual – board books. Format, unusual – toy & movable books.

Chambers, Catherine. *Big freeze* ill. with photos. Heinemann, 2002. ISBN 978-1-58810-658-2 Subj: Weather – cold.

Heat wave ill. with photos. Heinemann, 2002. ISBN 978-1-58810-657-5 Subj: Concepts – cold & heat. Weather.

Tornado ill. with photos. Heinemann, 2002. ISBN 978-1-58810-652-0 Subj: Weather – tornadoes.

Chambers, Roland. *Rooftop rocket party* ill. by author. Roaring Brook, 2003. ISBN 978-0-7613-2744-8 Subj: Careers – scientists. Moon. Parties. Space & space ships.

Chan, Arlene. *Awakening the dragon: the dragon boat festival* ill. by Song Nan Zhang. Tundra, 2004. ISBN 978-0-88776-656-5 Subj: Boats, ships. Fairs, festivals. Foreign lands – China.

Chan, Chin-Yi. *Good luck horse* ill. by Plao Chan. Whittlesey House, 1943. Subj: Animals – horses, ponies. Caldecott award honor books.

Chancellor, Deborah. *Holidays!* ill. with photos. DK, 2000. ISBN 978-0-7894-5710-3 Subj: Holidays.

Maps and mapping ill. with photos. Kingfisher, 2004. ISBN 978-0-7534-5759-7 Subj: Careers – cartographers. Maps.

Traveling on land ill. with photos. Two-Can, 2001. ISBN 978-0-915741-80-9 Subj: Activities – traveling. Transportation.

Chandra, Deborah. *George Washington's teeth* ill. by Brock Cole. Farrar, 2003. ISBN 978-0-374-32534-3 Subj: Teeth. U.S. history.

Chapman, Jane. *I'm not sleepy!* ill. by author. Good Books, 2012. ISBN 978-1-56148-765-3 Subj: Bedtime. Birds – owls. Family life – grandmothers.

Is it Christmas yet? ill. by author. Tiger Tales, 2013. ISBN 978-1-58925-149-6 Subj: Animals – bears. Holidays – Christmas.

Touch the sky, my little bear (Bedford, David)

Very special friends ill. by author. Good Books, 2012. ISBN 978-1-56148-748-6 Subj: Animals. Animals – mice. Friendship.

Chapman, Nancy Kapp. *Doggie dreams* ill. by Lee Chapman. Putnam, 2000. ISBN 978-0-399-23443-9 Subj: Animals – dogs. Dreams. Rhyming text.

Chapman, Susan Margaret. *Too much noise in the library* ill. by Abby Carter. Upstart, 2010. ISBN 978-1-60213-026-5 Subj: Libraries. Noise, sounds.

Chapra, Mimi. *Amelia's show-and-tell fiesta / Amelia y la fiesta de "muestra y cuenta"* ill. by Martha Avilés. HarperCollins, 2004. ISBN 978-0-06-050256-0 Subj: Ethnic groups in the U.S. – Cuban Americans. Foreign languages. School.

Sparky's bark / El ladrido de Sparky ill. by Viví Escrivá. HarperCollins, 2006. ISBN 978-0-06-053172-0 Subj: Activities – vacationing. Animals – dogs. Ethnic groups in the U.S. – Hispanic Americans. Foreign languages.

Charest, Emily MacLachlan. *Before you came* (MacLachlan, Patricia)

Bittle (MacLachlan, Patricia)

Cat talk (MacLachlan, Patricia)

Fiona loves the night (MacLachlan, Patricia)

Painting the wind (MacLachlan, Patricia)

Charles, Veronika Martenova. *The birdman* ill. by Annouchka Gravel Galouchko. Tundra, 2006. ISBN 978-0-88776-740-1 Subj: Birds. Careers – tailors. Emotions – grief. Foreign lands – India.

The maiden of the mist ill. by author. Stoddart, 2001. ISBN 978-0-7737-3297-1 Subj: Folk & fairy tales. Indians of North America – Seneca.

Charlip, Remy. *Baby hearts and baby flowers* ill. by author. Greenwillow, 2002. ISBN 978-0-06-029591-2 Subj: Babies. Bedtime. Rhyming text.

Handtalk birthday: a number and story book in sign language photos by George Ancona. Four Winds, 1987. ISBN 978-0-02-718080-0 Subj: Birthdays. Disabilities – deafness. Language. Senses – hearing.

"Mother, mother I feel sick" by Remy Charlip and Burton Supree ill. by Remy Charlip. Parents' Magazine Pr, 1966. ISBN 978-1-58246-043-7 Subj: Careers – doctors. Humorous stories. Illness. Rhyming text.

A perfect day ill. by author. HarperCollins, 2007. ISBN 978-0-06-051972-8 Subj: Day. Family life.

Sleepytime rhyme ill. by author. Greenwillow, 1999. ISBN 978-0-688-16272-6 Subj: Babies. Family life – mothers. Nursery rhymes. Rhyming text.

Why I will never ever ever ever have enough time to read this book ill. by Jon J. Muth. Tricycle, 2000. ISBN 978-1-58246-018-5 Subj: Books, reading. Day. Time.

Charlip, Remy, et al. *Handtalk: an ABC of finger spelling and sign language* ill. by George Ancona. Parents' Magazine Pr., 1974. ISBN 978-0-8193-0706-4 Subj: ABC books. Communication. Disabilities – deafness. Language. Senses – hearing.

Chase, Mary. *The wicked, wicked ladies in the haunted house* ill. by Peter Sís. Knopf, 2003. ISBN 978-0-375-92572-6 Subj: Ghosts. Magic. Mythical creatures – leprechauns.

Chast, Roz. *Marco goes to school* ill. by author. Simon & Schuster, 2012. ISBN 978-1-4424-5307-4 Subj: Birds. Friendship. School – first day.

Chataway, Carol. *The perfect pet* ill. by Greg Holfeld. Kids Can, 2001. ISBN 978-1-55337-178-6 Subj: Animals – pigs. Pets.

Chaucer, Geoffrey. *Chanticleer and the fox* adapt. by Barbara Cooney; ill. by Barbara Cooney. Adapt. of the "Nun's priest's tale" from the Canterbury tales. Crowell, 1958. ISBN 978-0-690-18562-1 Subj: Animals – foxes. Birds – chickens. Caldecott award books. Character traits – flattery. Farms. Folk & fairy tales.

Chaud, Benjamin. *The bear's song* ill. by author. Chronicle, 2013. ISBN 978-1-4521-1424-8 Subj: Animals – bears. Behavior – lost. Cities, towns. Family life – fathers. Foreign lands – France.

Chavarría-Cháirez, Becky. *Magda's piñata magic / Magda y la piñata mágica* ill. by Anne Vega. Piñata, 2001. ISBN 978-1-55885-320-1 Subj: Birthdays. Family life – brothers & sisters. Foreign languages. Parties.

Magda's tortillas / Las tortillas de Magada ill. by Anne Vega. Piñata, 2000. ISBN 978-1-55885-286-0 Subj: Activities – baking, cooking. Birthdays. Concepts – shape. Food. Foreign languages.

Chedru, Delphine. *Spot it! find the hidden creatures* ill. by author. Abrams, 2009. ISBN 978-0-8109-0632-7 Subj: Animals. Picture puzzles.

Spot it again! ill. by author. Abrams, 2011. ISBN 978-0-8109-9736-3 Subj: Format, unusual. Picture puzzles.

Chen, Chih-Yuan. *The best Christmas ever* ill. by author. Heryin, 2005. ISBN 978-0-9762056-2-3 Subj: Animals – bears. Gifts. Holidays – Christmas.

The featherless chicken ill. by author. Heryin, 2006. ISBN 978-0-9762056-9-2 Subj: Birds – chickens. Character traits – appearance. Character traits – being different. Self-concept.

Guji Guji ill. by author. Kane/Miller, 2004. ISBN 978-1-929132-67-6 Subj: Birds – ducks. Reptiles – alligators, crocodiles.

On my way to buy eggs ill. by author. Kane/Miller, 2003. ISBN 978-1-929132-49-2 Subj: Food. Foreign lands – Taiwan. Imagination. Shopping.

Chen, Kerstin. *Lord of the cranes* ill. by Jian Jiang Chen. NorthSouth, 2000. ISBN 978-0-7358-1193-5 Subj: Birds – cranes. Folk & fairy tales. Foreign lands – China.

Chen, Yong. *A gift* ill. by author. Boyds Mills, 2009. ISBN 978-1-59078-610-9 Subj: Ethnic groups in the U.S. – Chinese Americans. Foreign languages. Holidays – Chinese New Year. Letters, cards.

Cheng, Andrea. *Anna the bookbinder* ill. by Ted Rand. Walker, 2003. ISBN 978-0-8027-8831-3 Subj: Books, reading. Careers – bookbinders. Family life. Family life – fathers. Self-concept.

Grandfather counts ill. by Ange Zhang. Lee & Low, 2000. ISBN 978-1-58430-010-6 Subj: Communication. Ethnic groups in the U.S. – Chinese Americans. Family life – grandfathers. Language.

The lemon sisters ill. by Tatjana Mai-Wyss. Penguin, 2006. ISBN 978-0-399-24023-2 Subj: Birthdays. Family life – brothers & sisters. Memories, memory. Old age.

Cheng, Christopher. *Python* ill. by Mark Jackson. Candlewick, 2013. ISBN 978-0-7636-6396-4 Subj: Foreign lands – Australia. Reptiles – snakes.

Chernaik, Judith, editor. *Carnival of the animals: poems inspired by Saint-Saëns' music* ill. by Satoshi Kitamura. Candlewick, 2006. ISBN 978-0-7636-2960-1 Subj: Animals. Music. Poetry.

Chernesky, Felicia Sanzari. *Pick a circle, gather squares: a fall harvest of shapes* ill. by Susan Swan. Whitman, 2013. ISBN 978-0-8075-6538-4 Subj: Concepts – shape. Farms. Rhyming text. Seasons – fall.

Cherry, Lynne. *The great kapok tree: a tale of the Amazon rain forest* ill. by author. Harcourt, 1990. ISBN 978-0-15-200520-7 Subj: Animals. Ecology. Foreign lands – Brazil. Jungle. Trees.

How Groundhog's garden grew ill. by author. Blue Sky, 2003. ISBN 978-0-439-32371-0 Subj: Animals – groundhogs. Animals – squirrels. Food. Gardens, gardening.

A river ran wild ill. by author. Harcourt, 1992. ISBN 978-0-15-200542-9 Subj: Ecology. Nature. Rivers. U.S. history.

Cheshire, Marc. *Here comes Eloise!* by Marc Cheshire and Kay Thompson ill. by Carolyn Bracken. Based on Kay Thompson's Eloise & the art of Hilary Knight. Simon & Schuster, 2005. ISBN 978-0-689-87154-2 Subj: Format, unusual – toy & movable books. Hotels.

Love and kisses, Eloise ill. by Ted Enik. Based on Kay Thompson's Eloise & the art of Hilary Knight. Simon & Schuster, 2005. ISBN 978-0-689-87156-6 Subj: Emotions – love. Holidays – Valentine's Day.

Merry Christmas, Eloise! a lift-the-flap book ill. by Carolyn Bracken. Simon & Schuster, 2006. ISBN 978-0-689-87155-9 Subj: Format, unusual – toy & movable books. Holidays – Christmas.

Chess, Victoria. *The costume party* ill. by author. Kane/Miller, 2005. ISBN 978-1-929132-87-4 Subj: Animals – dogs. Clothing – costumes. Parties.

Chessa, Francesca. *Holly's red boots* ill. by author. Holiday, 2008. ISBN 978-0-8234-2158-9 Subj: Behavior – lost & found possessions. Clothing – boots. Seasons – winter. Weather – snow.

The mysterious package ill. by author. Bloomsbury, 2007. ISBN 978-1-59990-028-5 Subj: Family life – brothers & sisters. Imagination.

Chester, Jonathan. *Busy penguins* (Schindel, John)

Chetkowski, Emily. *Pumpkin smile* ill. by Dawn Peterson. Seven Coin, 2001. ISBN 978-0-9700974-2-2 Subj: Holidays – Halloween. Rhyming text. Self-concept. Teeth.

Chichester Clark, Emma. *Eliza and the moonchild* ill. by author. Trafalgar, 2008. ISBN 978-1-84270-577-3 Subj: Concepts – color. Moon.

Follow the leader! ill. by author. McElderry, 2003. ISBN 978-0-689-84296-2 Subj: Animals. Animals – tigers. Games.

Goldilocks and the three bears (The three bears)

I love you, Blue Kangaroo! ill. by author. Doubleday, 1999. ISBN 978-0-385-32638-4 Subj: Behavior – needing someone. Toys.

Little Miss Muffet counts to ten ill. by author. Andersen, 2010. ISBN 978-1-84270-955-9 Subj: Animals. Counting, numbers. Nursery rhymes. Rhyming text.

Melrose and Croc: a Christmas to remember ill. by author. Walker, 2006. ISBN 978-0-8027-9597-7 Subj: Animals – dogs. Emotions – loneliness. Friendship. Holidays – Christmas. Reptiles – alligators, crocodiles.

Piper ill. by author. Eerdmans, 2007. ISBN 978-0-902853-14-1 Subj: Animals – dogs. Behavior – running away. Character traits – kindness to animals.

Where are you, Blue Kangaroo? ill. by author. Random House, 2001. ISBN 978-0-385-32797-8 Subj: Animals – kangaroos. Toys.

Will and Squill ill. by author. Carolrhoda, 2006. ISBN 978-1-57505-936-5 Subj: Animals – cats. Animals – squirrels. Babies. Friendship. Pets.

Chicken Little. *Chicken Little* ill. by Sally Hobson. Simon & Schuster, 1994. ISBN 978-0-671-89548-8 Subj: Animals. Behavior – gossip. Behavior – trickery. Birds – chickens. Cumulative tales. Folk & fairy tales.

Henny Penny retold by Harriet Ziefert; ill. by Emily Bolam. Viking, 1997. ISBN 978-0-670-86810-0 Subj: Animals. Behavior – gossip. Behavior – trickery. Birds – chickens. Cumulative tales. Folk & fairy tales.

Henny Penny ill. by Paul Galdone. Seabury Pr., 1968. Subj: Animals. Behavior – gossip. Behavior – trickery. Birds – chickens. Cumulative tales. Folk & fairy tales.

Henny Penny retold by Vivian French; ill. by Sophie Windham. Bloomsbury, 2006. ISBN 978-1-58234-706-6 Subj: Animals. Behavior – gossip. Behavior – trickery. Birds – chickens. Cumulative tales. Folk & fairy tales.

Henny-Penny retold by Jane Wattenberg; ill. by reteller. Scholastic, 2000. ISBN 978-0-439-07817-7 Subj: Animals. Behavior – gossip. Behavior – trickery. Birds – chickens. Cumulative tales. Folk & fairy tales.

The sky is falling by Betty Miles; ill. by Cynthia Fisher. Simon & Schuster, 1998. ISBN 978-0-689-81790-8 Subj: Animals. Behavior – gossip. Behavior – trickery. Birds – chickens. Cumulative tales. Folk & fairy tales.

Child, Lauren. *Beware of the storybook wolves* ill. by author. Scholastic, 2001. ISBN 978-0-439-20500-9 Subj: Animals – wolves. Folk & fairy tales. Mythical creatures.

But, excuse me, that is my book ill. by author. Penguin, 2005. ISBN 978-0-8037-3096-0 Subj: Books, reading. Family life – brothers & sisters. Libraries.

But I've used all my pocket change ill. by author. Dial, 2012. ISBN 978-0-8037-3728-0 Subj: Behavior – saving things. Character traits – generosity. Family life – brothers & sisters. Money. Zoos.

Charlie and Lola's numbers ill. by author. Candlewick, 2007. ISBN 978-0-7636-3534-3 Subj: Counting, numbers. Family life – brothers & sisters. Format, unusual – board books.

Charlie and Lola's opposites ill. by author. Candlewick, 2007. ISBN 978-0-7636-3535-0 Subj: Concepts – opposites. Family life – brothers & sisters. Format, unusual – board books.

Clarice Bean, guess who's babysitting? ill. by author. Candlewick, 2001. ISBN 978-0-7636-1373-0 Subj: Activities – babysitting. Careers – firefighters. Family life – aunts, uncles.

Clarice Bean, that's me ill. by author. Candlewick, 1999. ISBN 978-0-7636-0961-0 Subj: Family life.

I am not sleepy and I will not go to bed ill. by author. Candlewick, 2001. ISBN 978-0-7636-1570-3 Subj: Animals. Bedtime.

I am too absolutely small for school ill. by author. Candlewick, 2004. ISBN 978-0-7636-2403-3 Subj: Family life – brothers & sisters. School – first day.

I completely know about guinea pigs ill. by author. Dial, 2008. ISBN 978-0-8037-3295-7 Subj: Animals – guinea pigs. Behavior – lost & found possessions. Family life – brothers & sisters.

I really, really need actual ice skates ill. by author. Penguin, 2010. ISBN 978-0-8037-3451-7 Subj: Family life – brothers & sisters. Money. Sports – ice skating.

I will never not ever eat a tomato ill. by author. Candlewick, 2000. ISBN 978-0-7636-1188-0 Subj: Family life – brothers & sisters. Food. Imagination.

I will never not ever eat a tomato [pop-up] ill. by author. Candlewick, 2007. ISBN 978-0-7636-3708-8 Subj: Family life – brothers & sisters. Food. Format, unusual – toy & movable books.

Maude: the not-so-noticeable Shrimpton ill. by Trisha Krauss. Candlewick, 2013. ISBN 978-0-7636-6515-9 Subj: Animals – tigers. Character traits – being different. Character traits – shyness. Family life.

My best, best friend ill. by author and Tiger Aspect Productions. Penguin, 2011. ISBN 978-0-8037-3586-6 Subj: Family life – brothers & sisters. Friendship.

My dream bed ill. by author. Scholastic, 2002. ISBN 978-0-439-30912-7 Subj: Format, unusual – toy & movable books. Furniture – beds. Sleep.

Say cheese! ill. by author. Penguin, 2007. ISBN 978-0-8037-3095-3 Subj: Character traits – cleanliness. Family life – brothers & sisters. School.

Snow is my favorite and my best ill. by author. Penguin, 2006. ISBN 978-0-8037-3174-5 Subj: Family life – brothers & sisters. Seasons – winter. Weather – snow.

That pesky rat ill. by author. Candlewick, 2002. ISBN 978-0-7636-1873-5 Subj: Animals – rats. Names. Pets.

What planet are you from Clarice Bean? ill. by author. Candlewick, 2002. ISBN 978-0-7636-1696-0 Subj: Ecology. Family life. Humorous stories. Trees.

Who wants to be a poodle: I don't ill. by author. Candlewick, 2009. ISBN 978-0-7636-4610-3 Subj: Animals – dogs. Behavior – dissatisfaction. Character traits – individuality.

Who's afraid of the big bad book? ill. by author. Hyperion, 2003. ISBN 978-0-7868-0926-4 Subj: Books, reading. Folk & fairy tales.

Child, Lydia Maria. *Over the river and through the wood* ill. by Brinton Turkle. First pub. in 1844 as The boy's Thanksgiving Day in the 2d vol. of the author's Flowers for children. Coward, 1974. ISBN 978-0-698-30553-3 Subj: Family life – grandparents. Farms. Holidays – Thanksgiving. Songs.

Over the river and through the wood: the New England boy's song about Thanksgiving Day ill. by Matt Tavares. Candlewick, 2011. ISBN 978-0-7636-2790-4 Subj: Family life – grandparents. Farms. Holidays – Thanksgiving. Songs.

A children's treasury of prayers ill. by Linda Bleck. Sterling, 2006. ISBN 978-1-4027-2982-9 Subj: Religion.

A child's calendar ill. by Trina Schart Hyman. Holiday, 1999. ISBN 978-0-8234-1445-1 Subj: Caldecott award honor books. Calendars. Days of the week, months of the year. Poetry.

Childs, Sam. *Naughty!* (Castle, Caroline)

Chin, Jason. *Coral reefs* ill. by author. Roaring Brook, 2011. ISBN 978-1-59643-563-6 Subj: Books, reading. Ecology. Imagination. Sea & seashore.

Redwoods ill. by author. Roaring Brook, 2009. ISBN 978-1-59643-430-1 Subj: Imagination. Trees.

Chin, Joel. *The falling raindrop* (Johnson, Neil)

Chin, Oliver. *The year of the tiger: tales from the Chinese zodiac* ill. by Justin Roth. Immedium, 2010. ISBN 978-1-59702-020-6 Subj: Animals. Animals – tigers. Zodiac.

Chin-Lee, Cynthia. *A is for Asia* ill. by Yumi Heo. Orchard, 1997. ISBN 978-0-531-33011-1 Subj: ABC books. Foreign lands – Asia.

Chinn, Karen. *Sam and the lucky money* ill. by Cornelius Van Wright and Ying-Hwa Hu. Lee & Low, 1995. ISBN 978-1-880000-13-7 Subj: Character traits – generosity. Ethnic groups in the U.S. – Chinese Americans. Holidays – Chinese New Year. Homeless.

Chisholm, Penny. *Ocean sunlight: how tiny plants feed the seas* (Bang, Molly)

Chitwood, Suzanne Tanner. *Wake up, big barn!* ill. by author. Scholastic, 2002. ISBN 978-0-439-26627-7 Subj: Animals. Farms. Rhyming text.

Chivers, Natalie. *Rhino's great big itch!* ill. by author. Good Books, 2010. ISBN 978-1-56148-684-7 Subj: Animals. Animals – rhinoceros. Birds. Problem solving.

Chocolate, Deborah. *El barrio* ill. by David Diaz. Holt, 2009. ISBN 978-0-8050-7457-4 Subj: Cities, towns. Communities, neighborhoods. Ethnic groups in the U.S. – Hispanic Americans.

Kente colors ill. by John Ward. Walker, 1996. ISBN 978-0-8027-8389-9 Subj: Clothing. Concepts – color. Foreign lands – Africa. Holidays – Kwanzaa.

Kwanzaa ill. by Melodye Benson Rosales. Children's Press, 1990. ISBN 978-0-516-03991-6 Subj: Ethnic groups in the U.S. – African Americans. Family life. Holidays – Kwanzaa.

Chodos-Irvine, Margaret. *Best best friends* ill. by author. Harcourt, 2006. ISBN 978-0-15-205694-0 Subj: Birthdays. Friendship. School – nursery.

Ella Sarah gets dressed ill. by author. Harcourt, 2003. ISBN 978-0-15-216413-3 Subj: Caldecott award honor books. Character traits – individuality. Clothing. Family life. Friendship. Parties.

Choi, Sook Nyul. *Halmoni and the picnic* ill. by Karen Dugan. Houghton, 1993. ISBN 978-0-395-61626-0 Subj: Ethnic groups in the U.S. – Korean Americans. Family life – grandmothers.

Choi, Yangsook. *Behind the mask* ill. by author. Farrar, 2006. ISBN 978-0-374-30522-2 Subj: Ethnic groups in the U.S. – Korean Americans. Family life – grandfathers. Holidays – Halloween. Masks.

The name jar ill. by author. Knopf, 2001. ISBN 978-0-375-90613-8 Subj: Ethnic groups in the U.S. – Korean Americans. Names. School.

Choldenko, Gennifer. *A giant crush* ill. by Melissa Sweet. Penguin, 2011. ISBN 978-0-399-24352-3 Subj: Character traits – shyness. Holidays – Valentine's Day. School.

How to make friends with a giant ill. by Amy Walrod. Penguin, 2006. ISBN 978-0-399-23779-9 Subj: Character traits – appearance. Concepts – size. Friendship. School.

Louder, Lili ill. by S. D. Schindler. Penguin, 2007. ISBN 978-0-399-24252-6 Subj: Behavior – bossy. Character traits – shyness. Friendship. School.

Chorao, Kay, compiler. *The baby's bedtime book* ill. by compiler. Dutton, 1984. ISBN 978-0-525-44149-6 Subj: Nursery rhymes. Poetry.

Bad boy, good boy ill. by author. Abrams, 2013. ISBN 978-1-4197-0520-5 Subj: Animals – dogs. Behavior – misbehavior.

The Christmas story ill. by adapter. Holiday, 1996. ISBN 978-0-8234-1251-8 Subj: Holidays – Christmas. Religion – Nativity.

Knock at the door and other baby action rhymes ill. by author. Dutton, 1999. ISBN 978-0-525-45969-9 Subj: Animals – cats. Babies. Nursery rhymes. Rhyming text.

Pig and Crow ill. by author. Holt, 2000. ISBN 978-0-8050-5863-5 Subj: Activities – trading. Animals – pigs. Behavior. Birds – crows.

Shadow night ill. by author. Dutton, 2001. ISBN 978-0-525-46685-7 Subj: Emotions – fear. Family life. Shadows.

Chou, Yih-Fen. *Mimi loves to mimic* ill. by Chih-Yuan Chen. Heryin, 2010. ISBN 978-0-9787550-8-9 Subj: Behavior – imitation. Character traits – curiosity.

Mimi says no ill. by Chih-Yuan Chen. Heryin, 2010. ISBN 978-0-9787550-7-2 Subj: Character traits – assertiveness. Character traits – stubbornness.

Choung, Euh-hee. *Minji's Salon* ill. by author. Kane/Miller, 2008. ISBN 978-1-933605-67-8 Subj: Beauty shops. Ethnic groups in the U.S. – Korean Americans. Imagination.

Chrisholm, Penny. *Living sunlight: how plants bring the earth to life* (Bang, Molly)

Christelow, Eileen. *The desperate dog writes again* ill. by author. Clarion, 2010. ISBN 978-0-547-24205-7 Subj: Activities – writing. Animals – dogs. Humorous stories. Letters, cards.

Don't wake up Mama! another five little monkeys story ill. by author. Clarion, 1992. ISBN 978-0-395-60176-1 Subj: Activities – baking, cooking. Animals – monkeys. Birthdays. Family life – mothers. Food.

The five-dog night ill. by author. Clarion, 1993. ISBN 978-0-395-62399-2 Subj: Animals – dogs. Seasons – winter.

Five little monkeys go shopping ill. by author. Houghton, 2007. ISBN 978-0-618-82161-7 Subj: Animals – monkeys. Counting, numbers. Shopping.

Five little monkeys jumping on the bed ill. by author. Houghton, 1991. ISBN 978-0-395-55701-3 Subj: Animals – monkeys. Bedtime. Behavior – misbehavior. Counting, numbers. Nursery rhymes. Poetry.

Five little monkeys reading in bed ill. by author. Clarion, 2011. ISBN 978-0-547-38610-2 Subj: Animals – monkeys. Bedtime. Books, reading. Rhyming text.

Five little monkeys sitting in a tree ill. by author. Houghton, 1991. ISBN 978-0-395-54434-1 Subj: Activities – picnicking. Animals – monkeys. Behavior – misbehavior. Counting, numbers. Reptiles – alligators, crocodiles. Rhyming text.

Five little monkeys trick-or-treat ill. by author. Clarion, 2013. ISBN 978-0-547-85893-7 Subj: Activities – babysitting. Animals – monkeys. Behavior

– trickery. Clothing – costumes. Holidays – Halloween.

Five little monkeys wash the car ill. by author. Clarion, 2000. ISBN 978-0-395-92566-9 Subj: Animals – monkeys. Automobiles. Reptiles – alligators, crocodiles. Rhyming text.

Five little monkeys with nothing to do ill. by author. Clarion, 1996. ISBN 978-0-395-75830-4 Subj: Animals – monkeys. Behavior – boredom. Family life.

The great pig escape ill. by author. Clarion, 1994. ISBN 978-0-395-66973-0 Subj: Animals – pigs. Behavior – running away. Careers – farmers.

The great pig search ill. by author. Clarion, 2001. ISBN 978-0-618-04910-3 Subj: Animals – pigs. Behavior – running away.

Jerome camps out ill. by author. Clarion, 1998. ISBN 978-0-395-75831-1 Subj: Behavior – bullying, teasing. Camps, camping. Reptiles – alligators, crocodiles.

Letters from a desperate dog ill. by author. Houghton, 2006. ISBN 978-0-618-51003-0 Subj: Activities – writing. Animals – dogs. Behavior – misbehavior. Careers – artists. Humorous stories. Letters, cards.

Not until Christmas, Walter! ill. by author. Clarion, 1997. ISBN 978-0-395-82273-9 Subj: Animals – dogs. Holidays – Christmas.

What do authors do? ill. by author. Clarion, 1995. ISBN 978-0-395-71124-8 Subj: Careers – artists. Careers – writers.

Where's the big bad wolf? ill. by author. Clarion, 2002. ISBN 978-0-618-18194-0 Subj: Animals. Animals – wolves. Careers – detectives. Humorous stories. Mystery stories.

Christensen, Bonnie. *Plant a little seed* ill. by author. Roaring Brook, 2012. ISBN 978-1-59643-550-6 Subj: Communities, neighborhoods. Gardens, gardening. Seeds.

Woody Guthrie, poet of the people ill. by author. Knopf, 2001. ISBN 978-0-375-91113-2 Subj: Careers – musicians. Music. U.S. history.

Christian, Cheryl. *Witches* ill. by Wish Williams. Star Bright, 2011. ISBN 978-1-59572-283-6 Subj: Holidays – Halloween. Rhyming text. Witches.

Christian, Mary Blount. *If not for the calico cat* ill. by Sebastià Serra. Penguin, 2007. ISBN 978-0-525-47779-2 Subj: Animals – cats. Boats, ships. Character traits – luck. Foreign lands – Japan.

Christian, Peggy. *If you find a rock* photos by Barbara Hirsch Lember. Harcourt, 2000. ISBN 978-0-15-239339-7 Subj: Rocks.

Christmas presents: holiday poetry sel. by Lee Bennett Hopkins; ill. by Melanie W. Hall. HarperCollins, 2004. ISBN 978-0-06-008055-6 Subj: Holidays – Christmas. Poetry.

Chrustowski, Rick. *Bright beetle* ill. by author. Holt, 2000. ISBN 978-0-8050-6058-4 Subj: Insects – ladybugs.

Hop frog ill. by author. Holt, 2003. ISBN 978-0-8050-6688-3 Subj: Frogs & toads.

Turtle crossing ill. by author. Holt, 2006. ISBN 978-0-8050-7498-7 Subj: Nature. Reptiles – turtles, tortoises.

Chukovskii, Kornei Ivanovich. *Good morning, chick* adapt. by Mirra Ginsburg; ill. by Byron Barton. Greenwillow, 1980. ISBN 978-0-688-84284-0 Subj: Birds – chickens. Noise, sounds.

Chung, Hyechong. *K is for Korea* ill. by Prodeepta Das. Frances Lincoln, 2008. ISBN 978-1-84507-789-1 Subj: ABC books. Foreign lands – Korea.

Church, Caroline Jayne. *Digby takes charge* ill. by author. Simon & Schuster, 2007. ISBN 978-1-4169-3441-7 Subj: Animals – dogs. Animals – sheep. Behavior – misbehavior. Character traits – kindness to animals. Farms.

Little Apple Goat ill. by author. Eerdmans, 2007. ISBN 978-0-8028-5320-2 Subj: Animals – goats. Food.

One more hug for Madison ill. by author. Scholastic, 2010. ISBN 978-0-545-16179-4 Subj: Animals – mice. Bedtime. Family life – mothers. Hugging.

One smart goose ill. by author. Scholastic, 2005. ISBN 978-0-439-68765-2 Subj: Animals – foxes. Behavior – bullying, teasing. Birds – geese. Character traits – cleanliness. Farms.

Ping Pong Pig ill. by author. Holiday House, 2008. ISBN 978-0-8234-2176-3 Subj: Activities – flying. Animals – pigs. Farms.

Ruff! and the wonderfully amazing busy day ill. by author. HarperCollins, 2013. ISBN 978-0-06-201498-6 Subj: Animals – dogs. Animals – mice. Birds – ducks. Character traits – kindness. Friendship.

Churchill, Vicki. *Sometimes I like to curl up in a ball* ill. by Charles Fuge. Sterling, 2001. ISBN 978-0-8069-7943-4 Subj: Animals – wombats. Rhyming text.

Chwast, Seymour. *Get dressed!* ill. by author. Abrams, 2012. ISBN 978-1-4197-0107-8 Subj: Clothing. Format, unusual – board books. Format, unusual – toy & movable books. Imagination.

Harry, I need you! ill. by author. Houghton, 2002. ISBN 978-0-618-17917-6 Subj: Animals – babies. Animals – cats. Imagination.

The miracle of Hanukkah ill. by author. Blue Apple, 2006. ISBN 978-1-59354-157-6 Subj: Holidays – Hanukkah. Jewish culture.

Ciboul, Adele. *The five senses* ill. by Clementine Collinet and Benoit Debecker, et al. Firefly, 2006. ISBN 978-1-55407-007-7 Subj: Format, unusual – toy & movable books. Senses.

Cinderella ill. by Kinuko Y. Craft. SeaStar, 2000. ISBN 978-1-58717-005-8 Subj: Family life – stepfamilies. Folk & fairy tales. Royalty – princes. Sibling rivalry.

Claflin, Willy. *The uglified ducky: a Maynard Moose tale* ill. by James Stimson. August House, 2008. ISBN 978-0-87483-858-9 Subj: Alaska. Animals – moose. Birds – ducks. Character traits – appearance. Character traits – being different. Folk & fairy tales.

Clanton, Ben. *Mo's mustache* ill. by author. Tundra, 2013. ISBN 978-1-77049-538-8 Subj: Behavior – imitation. Character traits – individuality. Monsters. Self-concept.

Vote for me! ill. by author. Kids Can, 2012. ISBN 978-1-55453-822-5 Subj: Animals – donkeys. Animals – elephants. Behavior – fighting, arguing. Behavior – name calling. Character traits – ambition.

Clark, Ann Nolan. *In my mother's house* ill. by Velino Herrera. Viking, 1941. Subj: Caldecott award honor books. Family life. Indians of North America – Tewa.

Clark, Karen Henry. *Sweet moon baby: an adoption tale* ill. by Patrice Barton. Random House, 2010. ISBN 978-0-375-85709-6 Subj: Adoption. Foreign lands – China. Moon.

Clark, Katie. *Seagull Sam* ill. by Amy Huntington. Down East, 2007. ISBN 978-0-89272-715-5 Subj: Birds – seagulls. Character traits – smallness. Family life – brothers & sisters. Kites.

Clark, Leslie Ann. *Peepsqueak!* ill. by author. HarperCollins, 2012. ISBN 978-0-06-207801-8 Subj: Activities – flying. Animals. Animals – babies. Birds – chickens. Farms.

Clark, Mary Higgins. *Ghost ship: a Cape Cod story* ill. by Wendell Minor. Simon & Schuster, 2007. ISBN 978-1-4169-3514-8 Subj: Boats, ships. Ghosts.

Clarke, Ginjer L. *Platypus!* ill. by Paul Mirocha. Random House, 2004. ISBN 978-0-375-92417-0 Subj: Animals – platypuses.

Sharks! ill. by Steven James Petruccio. Grosset, 2001. ISBN 978-0-448-42588-7 Subj: Fish – sharks.

Clarke, Jane. *The best of both nests* ill. by Anne Kennedy. Whitman, 2007. ISBN 978-0-8075-0668-4 Subj: Behavior – worrying. Birds – storks. Divorce.

Dancing with the Dinosaurs ill. by Lee Wildish. Charlesbridge, 2012. ISBN 978-1-936140-67-1 Subj: Activities – dancing. Dinosaurs. Rhyming text.

Dippy's sleepover ill. by Mary McQuillan. Barron's, 2006. ISBN 978-0-7641-3425-8 Subj: Behavior – bedwetting. Dinosaurs. Sleepovers.

Gilbert the hero ill. by Charles Fuge. Sterling, 2011. ISBN 978-1-4027-8040-0 Subj: Activities – playing. Family life – brothers. Fish – sharks.

Stuck in the mud ill. by Garry Parsons. Walker, 2008. ISBN 978-0-8027-9758-2 Subj: Birds – chickens. Character traits – helpfulness. Cumulative tales. Farms. Rhyming text.

Trumpet: the little elephant with a big temper ill. by Charles Fuge. Simon & Schuster, 2010. ISBN 978-1-4169-0482-3 Subj: Animals – elephants. Birthdays. Emotions – anger. Parties.

Clavel, Bernard. *Castle of books* ill. by Yan Nascimbene. Chronicle, 2001. ISBN 978-0-8118-3501-5 Subj: Castles. Family life. Poetry.

Clayton, Dallas. *An awesome book!* ill. by author. HarperCollins, 2012. ISBN 978-0-06-211468-6 Subj: Imagination. Rhyming text.

An awesome book of love! ill. by author. HarperCollins, 2013. ISBN 978-0-06-211666-6 Subj: Emotions – love. Rhyming text.

Clayton, Elaine. *A blue ribbon for Sugar* ill. by author. Macmillan, 2006. ISBN 978-1-59643-157-7 Subj: Animals – horses, ponies. Contests. Sports.

Cleary, Beverly. *The hullabaloo ABC* ill. by Ted Rand. Rev. ed. Morrow, 1998. ISBN 978-0-688-15183-6 Subj: ABC books. Farms. Noise, sounds. Rhyming text.

Cleary, Brian P. *Eight wild nights: a family Hanukkah tale* ill. by David Udovic. Lerner, 2006. ISBN 978-1-58013-152-0 Subj: Holidays – Hanukkah. Rhyming text.

A lime, a mime, a pool of slime: more about nouns ill. by Brian Gable. Lerner, 2006. ISBN 978-1-57505-937-2 Subj: Language. Rhyming text.

Peanut butter and jellyfishes: a very silly alphabet book ill. by Betsy E. Snyder. Lerner, 2007. ISBN 978-0-8225-6188-0 Subj: ABC books. Language. Picture puzzles. Rhyming text.

Six sheep sip thick shakes and other tricky tongue twisters ill. by Steve Mack. Millbrook, 2011. ISBN 978-1-58013-585-6 Subj: Tongue twisters.

Cleland, Jo. *Getting your zzzzs.* Rourke, 2012. ISBN 978-1-61810-085-6 Subj: Health & fitness. Sleep. Songs.

Clement, Nathan. *Drive* ill. by author. Front Street, 2008. ISBN 978-1-59078-517-1 Subj: Careers – truck drivers. Trucks.

Job site ill. by author. Boyds Mills, 2011. ISBN 978-1-59078-769-4 Subj: Careers – construction workers. Machines.

Speed ill. by author. Boyds Mills, 2013. ISBN 978-1-59078-937-7 Subj: Careers – race car drivers. Sports – racing.

Clement-Davies, David. *Spirit: stallion of the Cimarron* ill. by William Maughan. Dutton, 2002. ISBN 978-0-525-46735-9 Subj: Animals – horses, ponies. Indians of North America. U.S. history – frontier & pioneer life.

Clements, Andrew. *Because your daddy loves you* ill. by R. W. Alley. Houghton, 2005. ISBN 978-0-618-00361-7 Subj: Emotions – love. Family life – fathers. Sea & seashore – beaches.

Because your mommy loves you ill. by R. W. Alley. Clarion, 2012. ISBN 978-0-547-25522-4 Subj: Camps, camping. Emotions – love. Family life – mothers.

Big Al and Shrimpy ill. by Yoshi. Simon & Schuster, 2002. ISBN 978-0-689-84247-4 Subj: Concepts – size. Fish. Friendship.

Brave Norman ill. by Ellen Beier. Simon & Schuster, 2001. ISBN 978-0-689-82914-7 Subj: Animals – dogs. Disabilities – blindness.

Bright Christmas: an angel remembers ill. by Kate Kiesler. Clarion, 1996. ISBN 978-0-395-72096-7 Subj: Angels. Holidays – Christmas. Religion – Nativity.

Circus family dog ill. by Sue Truesdell. Clarion, 2000. ISBN 978-0-395-78648-2 Subj: Animals – dogs. Circus.

Dogku ill. by Tim Bowers. Simon & Schuster, 2007. ISBN 978-0-689-85823-9 Subj: Animals – dogs. Pets. Poetry.

Dolores and the big fire ill. by Ellen Beier. Simon & Schuster, 2002. ISBN 978-0-689-82916-1 Subj: Animals – cats. Pets.

The handiest things in the world photos by Raquel Jaramillo. Simon & Schuster, 2010. ISBN 978-1-4169-6166-6 Subj: Anatomy – hands. Rhyming text.

A million dots ill. by Mike Reed. Simon & Schuster, 2006. ISBN 978-0-689-85824-6 Subj: Counting, numbers.

Naptime for Slippers ill. by Janie Bynum. Penguin, 2005. ISBN 978-0-525-47287-2 Subj: Animals – dogs. Sleep.

Slippers at home ill. by Janie Bynum. Dutton, 2004. ISBN 978-0-525-47138-7 Subj: Animals – babies. Animals – dogs. Homes, houses.

Slippers at School ill. by Janie Bynum. Penguin, 2005. ISBN 978-0-525-47189-9 Subj: Animals – dogs. School.

Slippers loves to run ill. by Janie Bynum. Penguin, 2006. ISBN 978-0-525-47648-1 Subj: Animals – dogs. Family life. Hugging. Pets.

Tara and Tiree, fearless friends ill. by Ellen Beier. Simon & Schuster, 2002. ISBN 978-0-689-82917-8 Subj: Animals – dogs. Foreign lands – Canada. Pets.

Workshop ill. by David Wisniewski. Clarion, 1998. ISBN 978-0-395-85579-9 Subj: Merry-go-rounds. Tools.

Clemesha, David. *My dog Toby* (Zimmerman, Andrea Griffing)

Trashy town (Zimmerman, Andrea Griffing)

Cleminson, Katie. *Magic box: a magical story* ill. by author. Hyperion, 2009. ISBN 978-1-4231-2109-1 Subj: Animals – polar bears. Behavior – wishing. Birthdays. Magic.

Otto the book bear ill. by author. Hyperion, 2012. ISBN 978-1-4231-4562-2 Subj: Animals – bears. Books, reading. Libraries.

Clibbon, Lucy. *Imagine you're a fairy!* (Clibbon, Meg)

Imagine you're a mermaid! (Clibbon, Meg)

Imagine you're a pirate! (Clibbon, Meg)

Imagine you're a wizard! (Clibbon, Meg)

Clibbon, Meg. *Imagine you're a fairy!* by Meg Clibbon and Lucy Clibbon ill. by Lucy Clibbon. Annick, 2002. ISBN 978-1-55037-743-9 Subj: Fairies. Imagination.

Imagine you're a mermaid! by Meg Clibbon and Lucy Clibbon ill. by Lucy Clibbon. Annick, 2002. ISBN 978-1-55037-791-0 Subj: Imagination. Mythical creatures – mermaids, mermen.

Imagine you're a pirate! by Meg Clibbon and Lucy Clibbon ill. by Lucy Clibbon. Annick, 2002. ISBN 978-1-55037-741-5 Subj: Imagination. Pirates.

Imagine you're a wizard! by Meg Clibbon and Lucy Clibbon ill. by Lucy Clibbon. Annick, 2002. ISBN 978-1-55037-793-4 Subj: Imagination. Wizards.

Clifton, Lucille. *Everett Anderson's goodbye* ill. by Ann Grifalconi. Holt, 1983, 1988. ISBN 978-0-8050-0800-5 Subj: Death. Emotions – grief. Emotions – love. Ethnic groups in the U.S. – African Americans. Family life. Rhyming text.

One of the problems of Everett Anderson ill. by Ann Grifalconi. Holt, 2001. ISBN 978-0-8050-5201-5 Subj: Child abuse. Ethnic groups in the U.S. – African Americans. Rhyming text.

Three wishes ill. by Michael Hays. Doubleday, 1992. ISBN 978-0-385-30497-9 Subj: Behavior – wishing. Ethnic groups in the U.S. – African Americans. Friendship.

Clifton-Brown, Holly. *Annie Hoot and the knitting extravaganza* ill. by author. Andersen, 2010. ISBN 978-0-7613-6444-3 Subj: Activities – knitting. Activities – traveling. Birds – owls.

Climo, Shirley. *The Egyptian Cinderella* ill. by Ruth Heller. HarperCollins, 1989. ISBN 978-0-690-04824-7 Subj: Family life – stepfamilies. Folk & fairy tales. Foreign lands – Egypt. Royalty. Sibling rivalry.

The Irish Cinderlad ill. by Loretta Krupinski. HarperCollins, 1996. ISBN 978-0-06-024397-5 Subj: Animals – bulls, cows. Folk & fairy tales. Foreign lands – Ireland.

The Korean Cinderella ill. by Ruth Heller. HarperCollins, 1993. ISBN 978-0-06-020433-4 Subj: Family life – stepfamilies. Folk & fairy tales. Foreign lands – Korea. Royalty. Sibling rivalry.

The Persian Cinderella ill. by Robert Florczak. HarperCollins, 1999. ISBN 978-0-06-026765-0 Subj: Fairies. Family life – stepfamilies. Folk & fairy tales. Foreign lands – Persia. Royalty – princes. Sibling rivalry.

Tuko and the birds: a tale from the Philippines ill. by Francisco X. Mora. Holt, 2008. ISBN 978-0-8050-6559-6 Subj: Birds. Folk & fairy tales. Foreign lands – Philippines.

Cline-Ransome, Lesa. *Light in the darkness: a story about how slaves learned in secret* ill. by James Ransome. Disney/Jump at the Sun, 2013. ISBN 978-1-4231-3495-4 Subj: Books, reading. Ethnic groups in the U.S. – African Americans. Slavery. U.S. history.

Quilt alphabet ill. by James Ransome. Holiday, 2001. ISBN 978-0-8234-1453-6 Subj: ABC books. Country. Poetry. Quilts. Rhyming text.

Quilt counting ill. by James Ransome. SeaStar, 2002. ISBN 978-1-58717-178-9 Subj: Counting, numbers. Country. Quilts. Rhyming text.

Words set me free: the story of young Frederick Douglass ill. by James Ransome. Simon & Schuster, 2012. ISBN 978-1-4169-5903-8 Subj: Activities – writing. Books, reading. Ethnic groups in the U.S. – African Americans. Slavery. U.S. history.

Young Pelé: soccer's first star ill. by James Ransome. Random House, 2007. ISBN 978-0-375-83599-5 Subj: Foreign lands – Brazil. Sports – soccer.

Clinton, Catherine. *Phillis's big test* ill. by Sean Qualls. Houghton, 2008. ISBN 978-0-618-73739-0 Subj: Activities – writing. Careers – writers. Ethnic groups in the U.S. – African Americans. Poetry. U.S. history.

When Harriet met Sojourner ill. by Shane W. Evans. HarperCollins, 2007. ISBN 978-0-06-050425-0 Subj: Ethnic groups in the U.S. – African Americans. U.S. history.

Cneut, Carll. *The amazing love story of Mr. Morf* ill. by author. Clarion, 2003. ISBN 978-0-618-33170-3 Subj: Animals. Animals – dogs. Circus. Friendship. Insects – fleas.

Coat, Janik. *Hippopposites* ill. by author. Abrams, 2012. ISBN 978-1-4197-0151-1 Subj: Animals – hippopotamuses. Concepts – opposites.

Coats, Lucy. *Neil's numberless world* ill. by Neal Layton. DK, 2000. ISBN 978-0-7894-6354-8 Subj: Birthdays. Clocks, watches. Counting, numbers. Magic.

Cobb, Abigail Jane. *Meet my grandmother. She's a children's book author* (McElroy, Lisa Tucker)

Cobb, Annie. *The long wait* ill. by Liza Woodruff. Kane, 2000. ISBN 978-1-57565-094-4 Subj: Counting, numbers. Parks – amusement.

Cobb, Rebecca. *Missing Mommy: a book about bereavement* ill. by author. Holt, 2013. ISBN 978-0-8050-9507-4 Subj: Death. Emotions – grief. Emotions – sadness. Family life – mothers.

Cobb, Vicki. *I fall down* ill. by Julia Gorton. HarperCollins, 2004. ISBN 978-0-688-17843-7 Subj: Concepts – weight. Science.

I get wet ill. by Julia Gorton. HarperCollins, 2002. ISBN 978-0-688-17839-0 Subj: Science. Water.

I see myself ill. by Julia Gorton. HarperCollins, 2002. ISBN 978-0-688-17837-6 Subj: Mirrors. Science.

Open your eyes ill. by Cynthia C. Lewis. Millbrook, 2002. ISBN 978-0-7613-1705-0 Subj: Anatomy – eyes. Science. Senses – sight.

Coburn, Jewell Reinhart. *Angkat: the Cambodian Cinderella* ill. by Eddie Flotte. Shen's, 1998. ISBN 978-1-885008-09-1 Subj: Family life – stepfamilies. Folk & fairy tales. Foreign lands – Cambodia. Royalty – princes. Sibling rivalry.

Jouanah: a Hmong Cinderella ill. by Anne Sibley O'Brien. Adapt. by Jewell Reinhart Coburn and Tzexa Cherta Lee. Shen's, 1996. ISBN 978-1-885008-01-5 Subj: Family life – stepfamilies. Folk & fairy tales. Foreign lands. Royalty – princes. Sibling rivalry.

Cocca-Leffler, Maryann. *Bravery soup* ill. by author. Whitman, 2002. ISBN 978-0-8075-0870-1 Subj: Animals – bears. Animals – foxes. Animals – raccoons. Emotions – fear.

Bus route to Boston ill. by author. Boyds Mills, 2000. ISBN 978-1-56397-723-7 Subj: Activities – traveling. Buses. Cities, towns. Shopping.

Jack's talent ill. by author. Farrar, 2007. ISBN 978-0-374-33681-3 Subj: Behavior – worrying. School – first day. Self-concept.

Jungle Halloween ill. by author. Whitman, 2000. ISBN 978-0-8075-4056-5 Subj: Animals. Holidays – Halloween. Rhyming text.

Let it rain ill. by author. Scholastic, 2013. ISBN 978-0-545-45343-1 Subj: Activities. Rhyming text. Seasons – spring. Weather – rain.

Mr. Tanen's ties rule! ill. by author. Whitman, 2005. ISBN 978-0-8075-5308-4 Subj: Careers – school principals. Clothing – neckties. School.

Princess K.I.M. and the lie that grew ill. by author. Whitman, 2009. ISBN 978-0-8075-4178-4 Subj: Behavior – lying. Character traits – honesty. School. Self-concept.

Princess Kim and too much truth ill. by author. Whitman, 2011. ISBN 978-0-8075-6618-3 Subj: Character traits – honesty. School.

Rain brings frogs: a little book of hope ill. by author. HarperCollins, 2011. ISBN 978-0-06-196106-9 Subj: Character traits – optimism. Hope.

Theo's mood ill. by author. Whitman, 2013. ISBN 978-0-8075-7778-3 Subj: Babies. Emotions. Family life – new sibling. School.

Time to say bye-bye ill. by author. Viking, 2012. ISBN 978-0-670-01309-8 Subj: Activities. Babies. Bedtime. Day.

A vacation for Pooch ill. by author. Holt, 2013. ISBN 978-0-8050-9106-9 Subj: Activities – vacationing. Animals – dogs. Family life – grandfathers. Farms.

Cochran, Bill. *The forever dog* ill. by Dan Andreasen. HarperCollins, 2007. ISBN 978-0-06-053939-9 Subj: Animals – dogs. Death. Emotions – grief. Pets.

My parents are divorced, my elbows have nicknames, and other facts about me ill. by Steve Björkman. HarperCollins, 2009. ISBN 978-0-06-053942-9 Subj: Character traits – individuality. Divorce. Self-concept.

Cocovini, Abby. *What's inside your tummy, Mommy?* ill. by author. Holt, 2008. ISBN 978-0-8050-8760-4 Subj: Babies. Birth. Family life – mothers.

Codell, Esme Raji. *It's time for preschool!* ill. by Sue Ramá. Greenwillow, 2012. ISBN 978-0-06-145518-6 Subj: School – nursery.

Seed by seed: the legend and legacy of Johnny "Appleseed" Chapman ill. by Lynne Rae Perkins. Greenwillow, 2012. ISBN 978-0-06-145515-5 Subj: Activities – traveling. Gardens, gardening. Tall tales. Trees. U.S. history – frontier & pioneer life.

The basket ball ill. by Jennifer Plecas. Abrams, 2011. ISBN 978-1-4197-0007-1 Subj: Gender roles. Sports – basketball.

Coerr, Eleanor. *Circus day in Japan* ill. by author. Tuttle, 2010. ISBN 978-4-8053-1059-5 Subj: Circus. Foreign lands – Japan. Foreign languages.

Sadako ill. by Ed Young. Putnam, 1993. ISBN 978-0-399-21771-5 Subj: Birds – cranes. Death. Foreign lands – Japan. Illness. War.

Coffelt, Nancy. *Aunt Ant leaves through the leaves: a story with homophones and homonyms* ill. by author. Holiday House, 2012. ISBN 978-0-8234-2353-8 Subj: Activities – baking, cooking. Animals. Character traits – helpfulness. Language.

Big, bigger, biggest! ill. by author. Holt, 2009. ISBN 978-0-8050-8089-6 Subj: Animals. Language.

Catch that baby! ill. by Scott Nash. Simon & Schuster, 2011. ISBN 978-1-4169-9148-9 Subj: Activities – bathing. Babies. Humorous stories.

Fred stays with me! ill. by Tricia Tusa. Little, Brown, 2007. ISBN 978-0-316-88269-9 Subj: Animals – dogs. Divorce. Family life.

Pug in a truck ill. by author. Houghton, 2006. ISBN 978-0-618-56319-7 Subj: Animals – dogs. Careers – truck drivers. Trucks.

Coffey, Maria. *A cat adrift* ill. by Eugenie Fernandes. Annick, 2002. ISBN 978-1-55037-727-9 Subj: Animals – cats. Animals – rats. Sea & seashore.

Coh, Smiljana. *Princesses on the run* ill. by author. Running Press, 2013. ISBN 978-0-7624-4612-4 Subj: Behavior – boredom. Behavior – running away. Royalty – princesses.

Cohan, George M. *You're a grand old flag* ill. by Warren Kimble. Walker, 2007. ISBN 978-0-8027-9575-5 Subj: Flags. Songs. U.S. history.

Cohen, Caron Lee. *Broom, zoom!* ill. by Sergio Ruzzier. Simon & Schuster, 2010. ISBN 978-1-4169-9113-7 Subj: Character traits – cooperation. Character traits – cleanliness. Friendship. Monsters. Witches.

Digger Pig and the turnip ill. by Christopher Denise. Harcourt, 2000. ISBN 978-0-15-202524-3 Subj: Animals. Behavior – sharing. Character traits – laziness. Cumulative tales. Folk & fairy tales.

Happy to you! ill. by Rosanne Litzinger. Clarion, 2001. ISBN 978-0-689-82421-0 Subj: Babies. Emotions – happiness. Family life – mothers.

Martin and the giant lions ill. by Elizabeth Sayles. Clarion, 2002. ISBN 978-0-618-04908-0 Subj: Animals – lions. Dreams. Imagination. Night. Parks.

The mud pony: a traditional Skidi Pawnee tale ill. by Shonto Begay. Scholastic, 1988. ISBN 978-0-590-41525-5 Subj: Animals – horses, ponies. Folk & fairy tales. Indians of North America – Pawnee.

Cohen, Daniel. *Apatosaurus* ill. with photos. Bridgestone, 2001. ISBN 978-0-7368-0616-9 Subj: Dinosaurs. Fossils.

Pteranodon ill. with photos. Bridgestone, 2001. ISBN 978-0-7368-0612-1 Subj: Dinosaurs. Fossils.

Stegosaurus ill. with photos. Bridgestone, 2001. ISBN 978-0-7368-0618-3 Subj: Dinosaurs. Fossils.

Triceratops ill. with photos. Bridgestone, 2001. ISBN 978-0-7368-0619-0 Subj: Dinosaurs. Fossils.

Tyrannosaurus rex ill. with photos. Bridgestone, 2001. ISBN 978-0-7368-0620-6 Subj: Dinosaurs. Fossils.

Velociraptor ill. with photos. Bridgestone, 2001. ISBN 978-0-7368-0621-3 Subj: Dinosaurs. Fossils.

Cohen, Deborah Bodin. *Engineer Ari and the Rosh Hashana ride* ill. by Shahar Kober. Lerner, 2008. ISBN 978-0-8225-8648-7 Subj: Behavior – boasting. Foreign lands – Israel. Holidays – Rosh Hashanah. Trains.

Papa Jethro ill. by author. Kar-Ben, 2007. ISBN 978-1-58013-250-3 Subj: Family life – grandfathers. Jewish culture. Religion.

The seventh day ill. by Melanie W. Hall. Kar-Ben, 2005. ISBN 978-0-929371-24-5 Subj: Creation. Religion.

Cohen, Miriam. *Bee my Valentine!* ill. by Lillian Hoban. Greenwillow, 1978. ISBN 978-0-688-84129-4 Subj: Holidays – Valentine's Day. School.

Best friends ill. by Lillian Hoban. Aladdin, 1989, ©1971. ISBN 978-0-689-71334-7 Subj: Friendship. School.

Don't eat too much turkey! ill. by Lillian Hoban. Greenwillow, 1987. ISBN 978-0-688-07142-4 Subj: Behavior – sharing. School.

First grade takes a test ill. by Ronald Himler. Star Bright, 2006. ISBN 978-1-59572-054-2 Subj: Friendship. School.

First grade takes a test ill. by Lillian Hoban. Greenwillow, 1980. ISBN 978-0-688-84265-9 Subj: Friendship. School.

It's George! ill. by Lillian Hoban. Greenwillow, 1988. ISBN 978-0-688-06813-4 Subj: Character traits – being different. School.

Jim meets the thing ill. by Lillian Hoban. Greenwillow, 1981. ISBN 978-0-688-00617-4 Subj: Behavior – growing up. Emotions – fear. Monsters. School.

Jim's dog Muffins ill. by Ronald Himler. Star Bright, 2008. ISBN 978-1-59572-099-3 Subj: Animals – dogs. Death. Emotions – grief. Pets.

Jim's dog Muffins ill. by Lillian Hoban. Greenwillow, 1984. ISBN 978-0-688-02565-6 Subj: Animals – dogs. Death. Emotions – grief. Pets.

Lost in the museum ill. by Lillian Hoban. Greenwillow, 1979. ISBN 978-0-688-84187-4 Subj: Behavior – lost. Museums. School – field trips.

No good in art ill. by Lillian Hoban. Greenwillow, 1980. ISBN 978-0-688-80234-9 Subj: Art. School. Self-concept.

The real-skin rubber monster mask ill. by Lillian Hoban. Greenwillow, 1990. ISBN 978-0-688-09123-1 Subj: Emotions – fear. Holidays – Halloween. Masks. School.

See you in second grade! ill. by Lillian Hoban. Greenwillow, 1989. ISBN 978-0-688-07139-4 Subj: Friendship. School. Sea & seashore.

Starring first grade ill. by Lillian Hoban. Greenwillow, 1985. ISBN 978-0-688-04030-7 Subj: Behavior – misbehavior. School. Theater.

Tough Jim ill. by Lillian Hoban. Macmillan, 1974. ISBN 978-0-02-722760-4 Subj: Behavior – bullying, teasing. Parties. School.

When will I read? ill. by Lillian Hoban. Greenwillow, 1977. ISBN 978-0-688-84073-0 Subj: Books, reading. School.

Will I have a friend? ill. by Ronald Himler. Star Bright, 2009. ISBN 978-1-59572-069-6 Subj: Ethnic groups in the U.S. Friendship. School – first day.

Will I have a friend? ill. by Lillian Hoban. Macmillan, 1967. ISBN 978-0-689-71333-0 Subj: Ethnic groups in the U.S. Friendship. School – first day.

Cohen, Peter Zachary. *Boris's glasses* ill. by Olof Landström. Farrar, 2003. ISBN 978-91-29-65942-9 Subj: Animals. Animals – hamsters. Glasses.

Cohn, Diana. *Dream carver* ill. by Amy Córdova. Chronicle, 2002. ISBN 978-0-8118-1244-3 Subj: Animals. Art. Careers – woodcarvers. Foreign lands – Mexico.

Cohn, Scotti. *One wolf howls* ill. by Susan Detwiler. Sylvan Dell, 2009. ISBN 978-1-934359-92-1 Subj: Animals – wolves. Counting, numbers. Days of the week, months of the year.

Colandro, Lucille. *There was a cold lady who swallowed some snow!* ill. by Jared Lee. Scholastic, 2003. ISBN 978-0-439-47109-1 Subj: Cumulative tales. Rhyming text. Snowmen. Weather – snow.

There was an old lady who swallowed a clover! ill. by Jared Lee. Scholastic, 2012. ISBN 978-0-545-35222-2 Subj: Cumulative tales. Holidays – St. Patrick's Day. Mythical creatures – leprechauns. Rhyming text.

There was an old lady who swallowed some books! ill. by Jared Lee. Scholastic, 2012. ISBN 978-0-545-40287-3 Subj: Books, reading. Cumulative tales. Rhyming text. School – first day.

Colato Laínez, René. *My shoes and I* ill. by Fabricio Vanden Broeck. Boyds Mills, 2010. ISBN 978-1-59078-385-6 Subj: Clothing – shoes. Family life – fathers. Foreign lands – El Salvador. Immigrants.

Playing lotería / El juego de la lotería ill. by Jill Arena. Luna Rising, 2005. ISBN 978-0-87358-881-2 Subj: Fairs, festivals. Family life – grandmothers. Foreign lands – Mexico. Foreign languages.

Señor Pancho had a rancho ill. by Elwood H. Smith. Holiday House, 2013. ISBN 978-0-8234-2632-4 Subj: Animals. Farms. Foreign languages. Noise, sounds. Songs.

The Tooth Fairy meets El Ratón Pérez ill. by Tom Lintern. Tricycle, 2010. ISBN 978-1-58246-296-7 Subj: Ethnic groups in the U.S. – Mexican Americans. Fairies. Teeth.

Colborn, Mary Palenick. *Rainy day slug* ill. by Lorie Ann Grover. Sasquatch, 2000. ISBN 978-1-57061-238-1 Subj: Animals – slugs. Rhyming text. Weather – rain.

Cole, Babette. *Lady Lupin's book of etiquette* ill. by author. Peachtree, 2001. ISBN 978-1-56145-257-6 Subj: Animals – babies. Animals – dogs. Etiquette.

Prince Cinders ill. by author. Putnam, 1988. ISBN 978-0-399-21502-5 Subj: Folk & fairy tales. Magic. Royalty – princes.

Princess Smartypants ill. by author. Putnam, 1987. ISBN 978-0-399-21409-7 Subj: Pets. Problem solving. Royalty – princesses.

Truelove ill. by author. Dial, 2002. ISBN 978-0-8037-2717-5 Subj: Animals – dogs. Babies. Emotions – love. Humorous stories.

Cole, Barbara Hancock. *Anna and Natalie* ill. by Ronald Himler. Star Bright, 2007. ISBN 978-1-59572-105-1 Subj: Animals – dogs. Contests. Disabilities – blindness. Letters, cards. School. U.S. history.

Cole, Brock. *Buttons* ill. by author. Farrar, 2000. ISBN 978-0-374-31001-1 Subj: Clothing. Family life – daughters. Family life – fathers. Humorous stories. Tall tales.

Good enough to eat ill. by author. Farrar, 2007. ISBN 978-0-374-32737-8 Subj: Character traits – cleverness. Homeless. Mythical creatures – ogres.

Larky Mavis ill. by author. Farrar, 2001. ISBN 978-0-374-34365-1 Subj: Angels. Babies.

The money we'll save ill. by author. Farrar, 2011. ISBN 978-0-374-35011-6 Subj: Birds – turkeys. Family life. Holidays – Christmas.

Cole, Henry. *The littlest evergreen* ill. by author. HarperCollins, 2011. ISBN 978-0-06-114519-0 Subj: Ecology. Holidays – Christmas. Trees.

On Meadowview Street ill. by author. HarperCollins, 2007. ISBN 978-0-06-056481-0 Subj: Cities, towns. Ecology. Nature.

Trudy ill. by author. Greenwillow, 2009. ISBN 978-0-06-154267-1 Subj: Animals – goats. Pets. Weather – snow.

Unspoken: a story from the Underground Railroad ill. by author. Scholastic, 2012. ISBN 978-0-545-39997-5 Subj: Ethnic groups in the U.S. – African Americans. Slavery. U.S. history. Wordless.

Cole, Joanna. *Bony-legs* ill. by Dirk Zimmer. Four Winds, 1983. ISBN 978-0-590-07882-5 Subj: Folk & fairy tales. Foreign lands – Russia. Magic. Witches.

Bully trouble ill. by Marylin Hafner. Random House, 2003. ISBN 978-0-394-94949-9 Subj: Behavior – bullying, teasing.

How I was adopted: Samantha's story ill. by Maxie Chambliss. Morrow, 1995. ISBN 978-0-688-11930-0 Subj: Adoption. Family life.

How you were born photos by Margaret Miller. Rev. and expanded ed. Morrow, 1993. ISBN 978-0-688-12059-7 Subj: Babies. Birth. Family life. Science.

I'm a big brother ill. by Maxie Chambliss. Morrow, 1997. ISBN 978-0-688-14507-1 Subj: Babies. Family life – brothers.

I'm a big sister ill. by Maxie Chambliss. Morrow, 1997. ISBN 978-0-688-14509-5 Subj: Babies. Family life – sisters.

I'm a big sister ill. by Rosalinda Kightley. HarperCollins, 2010. ISBN 978-0-06-190062-4 Subj: Family life – new sibling. Family life – sisters.

The magic school bus and the climate challenge ill. by Bruce Degen. Scholastic, 2010. ISBN 978-0-590-10826-3 Subj: Ecology. Science. Weather.

The magic school bus and the electric field trip ill. by Bruce Degen. Scholastic, 1997. ISBN 978-0-590-44682-2 Subj: Careers – electricians. School – field trips.

The magic school bus and the science fair expedition ill. by Bruce Degen. Scholastic, 2006. ISBN 978-0-590-10824-9 Subj: Buses. Careers – teachers. Magic. School – field trips. Science.

The magic school bus at the waterworks ill. by Bruce Degen. Scholastic, 1986. ISBN 978-0-590-40361-0 Subj: School – field trips. Water.

The magic school bus explores the senses ill. by Bruce Degen. Scholastic, 1999. ISBN 978-0-590-44697-6 Subj: School. Senses.

The magic school bus in the time of the dinosaurs ill. by Bruce Degen. Scholastic, 1994. ISBN 978-0-590-44688-4 Subj: Buses. Careers – teachers. Dinosaurs. Magic. Prehistory. School – field trips. Science.

The magic school bus inside a beehive ill. by Bruce Degen. Scholastic, 1990. ISBN 978-0-590-44684-6 Subj: Buses. Careers – teachers. Insects – bees. Magic. School – field trips. Science.

The magic school bus inside a hurricane ill. by Bruce Degen. Scholastic, 1995. ISBN 978-0-590-44686-0 Subj: School – field trips. Science. Weather – hurricanes.

The magic school bus inside the earth ill. by Bruce Degen. Scholastic, 1987. ISBN 978-0-590-40759-5 Subj: Careers – geologists. Earth. Rocks. Science.

The magic school bus inside the human body ill. by Bruce Degen. Scholastic, 1989. ISBN 978-0-590-41426-5 Subj: Anatomy. School – field trips. Science.

The magic school bus lost in the solar system ill. by Bruce Degen. Scholastic, 1990. ISBN 978-0-590-41428-9 Subj: Buses. Careers – teachers. Magic. School – field trips. Science. Space & space ships.

The magic school bus on the ocean floor ill. by Bruce Degen. Scholastic, 1992. ISBN 978-0-590-41430-2 Subj: Buses. Careers – teachers. Magic. School – field trips. Science. Sea & seashore.

My big boy potty ill. by Maxie Chambliss. HarperCollins, 2000. ISBN 978-0-688-17042-4 Subj: Behavior – growing up. Toilet training.

My big girl potty ill. by Maxie Chambliss. HarperCollins, 2000. ISBN 978-0-688-17041-7 Subj: Behavior – growing up. Toilet training.

My friend the doctor ill. by Maxie Chambliss. HarperCollins, 2005. ISBN 978-0-06-050500-4 Subj: Careers – doctors. Health & fitness.

My new kitten photos by Margaret Miller. Morrow, 1995. ISBN 978-0-688-12902-6 Subj: Animals – cats. Friendship.

My puppy is born photos by Margaret Miller. Morrow, 1991. ISBN 978-0-688-09771-4 Subj: Animals – dogs. Birth. Science.

The new baby at your house photos by Hella Hammid. Morrow, 1998. ISBN 978-0-688-05807-4 Subj: Babies. Emotions – envy, jealousy. Family life – new sibling. Sibling rivalry.

Sharing is fun ill. by Maxie Chambliss. HarperCollins, 2004. ISBN 978-0-06-050499-1 Subj: Activities – playing. Behavior – sharing. Format, unusual – board books.

When Mommy and Daddy go to work ill. by Maxie Chambliss. HarperCollins, 2001. ISBN 978-0-688-17044-8 Subj: Family life – parents. School – nursery.

When you were inside mommy ill. by Maxie Chambliss. HarperCollins, 2001. ISBN 978-0-688-17043-1 Subj: Babies. Birth. Family life – mothers.

Cole, Kenneth, Dr. *No bad news* photos by John Ruebartsch. Whitman, 2001. ISBN 978-0-8075-4743-4 Subj: Careers – barbers. Cities, towns. Communities, neighborhoods. Ethnic groups in the U.S. – African Americans.

Coles, Robert. *The story of Ruby Bridges* ill. by George Ford. Scholastic, 1995. ISBN 978-0-590-43967-1 Subj: Character traits – bravery. Ethnic groups in the U.S. – African Americans. Prejudice. School.

Collard, Sneed B. *Animals asleep* ill. by Anik McGrory. Houghton, 2004. ISBN 978-0-618-27697-4 Subj: Animals. Sleep.

Beaks! ill. by Robin Brickman. Charlesbridge, 2002. ISBN 978-1-57091-387-7 Subj: Anatomy. Birds.

Leaving home ill. by Joan Dunning. Houghton, 2002. ISBN 978-0-618-11454-2 Subj: Animals – babies. Behavior. Behavior – growing up.

Making animal babies ill. by Steve Jenkins. Houghton, 2000. ISBN 978-0-395-95317-4 Subj: Animals. Sex instruction.

A platypus, probably ill. by Andrew Plant. Charlesbridge, 2005. ISBN 978-1-57091-583-3 Subj: Animals – platypuses.

Collet, Géraldine. *All by myself!* ill. by Coralie Saudo. OwlKids, 2011. ISBN 978-1-926973-12-8 Subj: Behavior – worrying. Birds – chickens. Family life – mothers.

Collicott, Sharleen. *Mildred and Sam* ill. by author. Geringer, 2003. ISBN 978-0-06-026682-0 Subj: Animals – mice. Babies. Family life. Homes, houses.

Toestomper and the bad butterflies ill. by author. Houghton, 2003. ISBN 978-0-618-14092-3 Subj: Behavior. Insects – butterflies, caterpillars. Metamorphosis. Pets.

Toestomper and the caterpillars ill. by author. Houghton, 1999. ISBN 978-0-395-91168-6 Subj: Animals. Behavior – bullying, teasing. Character traits – kindness to animals. Clubs, gangs. Insects – butterflies, caterpillars.

Collicutt, Paul. *This car* ill. by author. Farrar, 2002. ISBN 978-0-374-39965-8 Subj: Automobiles.

This rocket ill. by author. Farrar, 2005. ISBN 978-0-374-37484-6 Subj: Space & space ships.

This train ill. by author. Farrar, 1999. ISBN 978-0-374-37493-8 Subj: Trains. Transportation.

Collier, Bryan. *Uptown* ill. by author. Holt, 2000. ISBN 978-0-8050-5721-8 Subj: Cities, towns. Ethnic groups in the U.S. – African Americans.

Collington, Peter. *Clever cat* ill. by author. Random House, 2000. ISBN 978-0-375-90477-6 Subj: Animals – cats. Character traits – cleverness. Character traits – individuality. Humorous stories.

Collins, Billy. *Daddy's little boy* ill. by Maggie Kneen. HarperCollins, 2004. ISBN 978-0-06-029003-0 Subj: Animals – bears. Family life – fathers. Family life – sons. Music. Songs.

Collins, Pat Lowery. *The deer watch* ill. by David Slonim. Candlewick, 2013. ISBN 978-0-7636-4890-9 Subj: Animals – deer. Family life – fathers. Forest, woods. Nature.

I am a dancer ill. by Mark Graham. Lerner, 2008. ISBN 978-0-8225-6369-3 Subj: Activities – dancing.

Collins, Ross. *Alvie eats soup* ill. by author. Scholastic, 2002. ISBN 978-0-439-27265-0 Subj: Family life – grandmothers. Food.

Dear Vampa ill. by author. HarperCollins, 2009. ISBN 978-0-06-135534-9 Subj: Humorous stories. Letters, cards. Monsters. Mythical creatures – werewolves.

Doodleday ill. by author. Whitman, 2011. ISBN 978-0-8075-1683-6 Subj: Activities – drawing. Behavior – misbehavior. Family life – mothers.

Collins, Sheila Hebert. *'T Pousette et 't Poulette: a Cajun Hansel and Gretel* ill. by Patrick Soper. Pelican, 2001. ISBN 978-1-56554-764-3 Subj: Ethnic groups in the U.S. – Cajuns. Folk & fairy tales.

Collins, Suzanne. *When Charlie McButton lost power* ill. by Mike Lester. Penguin, 2005. ISBN 978-0-399-24000-3 Subj: Computers. Family life – brothers & sisters. Rhyming text.

Year of the jungle ill. by James Proimos. Scholastic, 2013. ISBN 978-0-545-42516-2 Subj: Careers – military. Emotions – fear. Family life – fathers. U.S. history. War.

Combs, Kathy. *Cowboy Sam and those confounded secrets* (Griffin, Kitty)

The foot-stomping adventures of Clementine Sweet (Griffin, Kitty)

Comden, Betty. *What's new at the zoo?* by Betty Comden and Adolph Green ill. by Travis Foster. Blue Apple, 2011. ISBN 978-1-60905-088-7 Subj: Animals. Format, unusual – toy & movable books. Songs. Zoos.

Comden, Betty, et al. *Flying to Neverland with Peter Pan: a lyrical journey with songs from the Broadway musical* ill. by Amy Bates. Blue Apple, 2012. ISBN 978-1-60905-249-2 Subj: Activities – flying. Imagination. Music. Songs. Theater.

Come and play: children of our world having fun. Bloomsbury, 2008. ISBN 978-1-59990-245-6 Subj: Activities – playing. Poetry. World.

Compestine, Ying Chang. *Boy dumplings* ill. by James Yamasaki. Holiday, 2009. ISBN 978-0-8234-1955-5 Subj: Activities – baking, cooking. Food. Foreign lands – China. Ghosts.

Crouching tiger ill. by Yan Nascimbene. Candlewick, 2011. ISBN 978-0-7636-4642-4 Subj: Ethnic groups in the U.S. – Chinese Americans. Family life – grandfathers. Holidays – Chinese New Year. Self-concept.

D is for dragon dance ill. by YongSheng Xuan. Holiday House, 2006. ISBN 978-0-8234-1887-9 Subj: ABC books. Foreign lands – China. Holidays – Chinese New Year.

The real story of stone soup ill. by Stéphane Jorisch. Penguin, 2007. ISBN 978-0-525-47493-7 Subj: Character traits – cleverness. Folk & fairy tales. Food. Foreign lands – China.

The runaway rice cake ill. by Tungwai Chau. Simon & Schuster, 2001. ISBN 978-0-689-82972-7 Subj: Character traits – generosity. Food. Foreign lands – China. Holidays – Chinese New Year.

The runaway wok: a Chinese New Year tale ill. by Sebastià Serra. Penguin, 2011. ISBN 978-0-525-42068-2 Subj: Activities – baking, cooking. Foreign lands – China. Holidays – Chinese New Year. Magic.

The story of chopsticks ill. by YongSheng Xuan. Holiday, 2001. ISBN 978-0-8234-1526-7 Subj: Food. Foreign lands – China.

The story of noodles ill. by YongSheng Xuan. Holiday, 2002. ISBN 978-0-8234-1600-4 Subj: Activities – baking, cooking. Food. Foreign lands – China.

The story of paper ill. by YongSheng Xuan. Holiday, 2003. ISBN 978-0-8234-1705-6 Subj: Foreign lands – China. Paper. School.

Compos, Tito. *Muffler man / El hombre mofle* ill. by Lamberto Alvarez and Beto Alvarez. Piñata, 2001. ISBN 978-1-55885-318-8 Subj: Art. Ethnic groups in the U.S. – Mexican Americans. Family life – fathers. Family life – sons. Foreign languages.

Compton, Joanne. *Ashpet: an Appalachian tale* ill. by Kenn Compton. Holiday, 1994. ISBN 978-0-8234-1106-1 Subj: Character traits – kindness. Folk & fairy tales.

Conahan, Carolyn. *The big wish* ill. by author. Chronicle, 2011. ISBN 978-0-8118-7040-5 Subj: Character traits – cooperation. Behavior – wishing. Contests.

The twelve days of Christmas dogs ill. by author. Penguin, 2005. ISBN 978-0-525-47486-9 Subj: Animals – dogs. Holidays – Christmas. Songs.

Connor, Leslie. *Miss Bridie chose a shovel* ill. by Mary Azarian. Houghton, 2004. ISBN 978-0-618-30564-3 Subj: Ethnic groups in the U.S. – Irish Americans. Immigrants. Tools.

Conover, Chris. *The Christmas bears* ill. by author. Farrar, 2008. ISBN 978-0-374-33275-4 Subj: Animals – bears. Holidays – Christmas. Rhyming text. Santa Claus.

The lion's share ill. by author. Farrar, 2000. ISBN 978-0-374-34532-7 Subj: Activities – flying. Animals. Animals – lions. Books, reading. Mythical creatures.

Conrad, Donna. *See you soon, Moon* ill. by Don Carter. Random House, 2001. ISBN 978-0-375-90656-5 Subj: Activities – traveling. Family life – grandmothers. Moon. Night.

Conrad, Pam. *The Tub People* ill. by Richard Egielski. HarperCollins, 1989. ISBN 978-0-06-021341-1 Subj: Activities – bathing. Toys.

The Tub People's Christmas ill. by Richard Egielski. Geringer, 1999. ISBN 978-0-06-026029-3 Subj: Holidays – Christmas. Santa Claus. Toys. Trees.

Consentino, Ralph. *The story of Honk-Honk-Ashoo and Swella-Bow-Wow* ill. by author. Penguin, 2005. ISBN 978-0-670-05997-3 Subj: Animals – dogs. Friendship.

Conway, David. *Errol and his extraordinary nose* ill. by Roberta Angaramo. Holiday House, 2010. ISBN 978-0-8234-2262-3 Subj: Anatomy – noses. Animals – elephants. School. Self-concept. Theater.

The great fairy tale disaster ill. by Melanie Williamson. Tiger Tales, 2012. ISBN 978-1-58925-111-3 Subj: Animals – wolves. Folk & fairy tales. Humorous stories.

The great nursery rhyme disaster ill. by Melanie Williamson. Tiger Tales, 2009. ISBN 978-1-58925-080-2 Subj: Humorous stories. Nursery rhymes.

Lila and the secret of rain ill. by Jude Daly. Frances Lincoln, 2008. ISBN 978-1-84507-407-4 Subj: Foreign lands – Kenya. Weather – droughts. Weather – rain.

The most important gift of all ill. by Karin Littlewood. School Specialty/Gingham Dog, 2006. ISBN 978-0-7696-4618-3 Subj: Animals. Emotions – love. Family life – new sibling. Foreign lands – Africa. Gifts.

Cook, Bernadine. *The little fish that got away* ill. by Crockett Johnson. HarperCollins, 2005. ISBN 978-0-06-055714-0 Subj: Fish. Sports – fishing.

Cook, Julia. *The "D" word: divorce* ill. by Phillip W. Rodgers. National Center for Youth Issues, 2011. ISBN 978-1-931636-76-6 Subj: Divorce.

Cook, Lisa Broadie. *Peanut butter and homework sandwiches* ill. by Jack E. Davis. Penguin, 2011. ISBN 978-0-399-24533-6 Subj: Careers – teachers. Homework. School.

Cooke, Trish. *The grandad tree* ill. by Sharon Wilson. Candlewick, 2000. ISBN 978-0-7636-0815-6 Subj: Death. Emotions – grief. Family life – grandfathers. Memories, memory. Nature. Trees.

So much ill. by Helen Oxenbury. Candlewick, 1994. ISBN 978-1-56402-344-5 Subj: Babies. Birthdays. Cumulative tales. Family life.

Coombs, Kate. *Hans my hedgehog: a tale from the Brothers Grimm* (Grimm, Jacob and Wilhelm)

The secret-keeper ill. by Heather Solomon. Simon & Schuster, 2006. ISBN 978-0-689-83963-4 Subj: Behavior – secrets.

Water sings blue ill. by Meilo So. Chronicle, 2012. ISBN 978-0-8118-7284-3 Subj: Poetry. Sea & seashore.

Cooney, Barbara. *Eleanor* ill. by author. Viking, 1996. ISBN 978-0-670-86159-0 Subj: Family life. U.S. history.

Miss Ramphius ill. by author. Viking, 1982. ISBN 978-0-670-47958-0 Subj: Activities – traveling. Flowers.

The story of Christmas ill. by Loretta Krupinski. HarperCollins, 1995. ISBN 978-0-06-023434-8

Subj: Holidays. Holidays – Christmas. Religion – Nativity.

Cooper, Elisha. *Ballpark* ill. by author. Greenwillow, 1998. ISBN 978-0-688-15755-5 Subj: Sports – baseball.

Beach ill. by author. Scholastic, 2006. ISBN 978-0-439-68785-0 Subj: Sea & seashore – beaches.

Bear dreams ill. by author. HarperCollins, 2006. ISBN 978-0-06-087428-5 Subj: Animals – bears. Hibernation. Seasons – winter.

Beaver is lost ill. by author. Random House, 2010. ISBN 978-0-375-85765-2 Subj: Animals – beavers. Behavior – lost.

Building ill. by author. Greenwillow, 1999. ISBN 978-0-688-16494-2 Subj: Buildings. Careers – architects.

Farm ill. by author. Scholastic, 2010. ISBN 978-0-545-07075-1 Subj: Farms. Seasons.

A good night walk ill. by author. Scholastic, 2005. ISBN 978-0-439-68783-6 Subj: Activities – walking. Communities, neighborhoods.

Homer ill. by author. Greenwillow, 2012. ISBN 978-0-06-201248-7 Subj: Animals – dogs.

Ice cream ill. by author. Greenwillow, 2002. ISBN 978-0-06-001424-7 Subj: Food.

Magic thinks big ill. by author. Greenwillow, 2004. ISBN 978-0-06-058165-7 Subj: Animals – cats. Behavior – indecision.

Train ill. by author. Scholastic, 2013. ISBN 978-0-545-38495-7 Subj: Activities – traveling. Trains.

Cooper, Floyd. *Coming home: from the life of Langston Hughes* ill. by author. Philomel, 1994. ISBN 978-0-399-22682-3 Subj: Ethnic groups in the U.S. – African Americans. Family life. Poetry.

Max and the tag-along moon ill. by author. Philomel, 2013. ISBN 978-0-399-23342-5 Subj: Ethnic groups in the U.S. – African Americans. Family life – grandfathers. Moon.

Willie and the All-Stars ill. by author. Philomel, 2008. ISBN 978-0-399-23340-1 Subj: Ethnic groups in the U.S. – African Americans. Prejudice. Sports – baseball. U.S. history.

Cooper, Helen. *Delicious! a pumpkin soup story* ill. by author. Farrar, 2007. ISBN 978-0-374-31756-0 Subj: Activities – baking, cooking. Animals. Animals – cats. Animals – squirrels. Birds – ducks. Friendship.

Dog biscuit ill. by author. Farrar, 2009. ISBN 978-0-374-31812-3 Subj: Animals – dogs. Behavior – worrying. Food. Humorous stories.

A pipkin of pepper ill. by author. Farrar, 2005. ISBN 978-0-374-35953-9 Subj: Activities – baking, cooking. Animals. Animals – cats. Animals – squirrels. Birds – ducks. Friendship.

Tatty-Ratty ill. by author. Farrar, 2002. ISBN 978-0-374-37386-3 Subj: Animals – rabbits. Behavior – lost & found possessions. Imagination. Toys.

Cooper, Ilene. *The golden rule* ill. by Gabi Swiatkowska. Abrams, 2007. ISBN 978-0-8109-0960-1 Subj: Behavior.

Jake's best thumb ill. by Claudio Muñoz. Dutton, 2008. ISBN 978-0-525-47788-4 Subj: Behavior – bullying, teasing. School. Thumb sucking.

Cooper, Susan. *Frog* ill. by Jane Browne. McElderry, 2002. ISBN 978-0-689-84302-0 Subj: Frogs & toads. Sports – swimming.

Copeland, Cynthia L. *What are you waiting for?* ill. by Mike Gordon. Millbrook, 2003. ISBN 978-0-7613-2804-9 Subj: Careers – construction workers. Machines.

Coppinger, Tom. *Curse in reverse* ill. by Dirk Zimmer. Atheneum, 2003. ISBN 978-0-689-83096-9 Subj: Folk & fairy tales. Witches.

Cora, Cat. *A suitcase surprise for Mommy* ill. by Joy Allen. Penguin, 2011. ISBN 978-0-8037-3332-9 Subj: Activities – traveling. Emotions – sadness. Family life – mothers.

Cordell, Matthew. *Another brother* ill. by author. Feiwel & Friends, 2012. ISBN 978-0-312-64324-9 Subj: Animals – sheep. Behavior – imitation. Family life – brothers.

Trouble gum ill. by author. Feiwel & Friends, 2009. ISBN 978-0-312-38774-7 Subj: Animals – pigs. Behavior – boredom. Behavior – misbehavior. Family life – brothers.

Corderoy, Tracey. *Hubble bubble, Granny trouble* ill. by Joe Berger. Candlewick, 2012. ISBN 978-0-7636-5904-2 Subj: Character traits – individuality. Family life – grandmothers. Rhyming text. Witches.

I want my mommy! ill. by Alison Edgson. Tiger Tales, 2013. ISBN 978-1-58925-130-4 Subj: Animals – mice. Family life – grandmothers.

The little white owl ill. by Jane Chapman. Good Books, 2010. ISBN 978-1-56148-693-9 Subj: Birds – owls. Character traits – being different. Friendship.

Monty and Milli: the totally amazing magic trick ill. by Tim Warnes. Good Books, 2012. ISBN 978-1-56148-742-4 Subj: Animals – mice. Family life – brothers & sisters. Magic.

Cordsen, Carol Foskett. *Market day* ill. by Douglas B. Jones. Dutton, 2008. ISBN 978-0-525-47883-6

Subj: Animals – bulls, cows. Behavior – forgetfulness. Careers – farmers. Farms. Rhyming text.

The milkman ill. by Douglas B. Jones. Penguin, 2005. ISBN 978-0-525-47208-7 Subj: Activities – working. Careers. Food. Rhyming text.

Corey, Dorothy. *You go away* ill. by Lisa Fox. Whitman, 2010. ISBN 978-0-8075-9440-7 Subj: Behavior – worrying. Family life.

Corey, Shana. *Ballerina bear* ill. by Pamela Paparone. Random House, 2002. ISBN 978-0-375-91416-4 Subj: Activities – dancing. Animals – bears. Ballet. Character traits – confidence.

Boats! ill. by Mike Reed. Random House, 2003. ISBN 978-0-375-90221-5 Subj: Boats, ships. Rhyming text.

First graders from Mars: Horus's horrible day ill. by Mark Teague. Scholastic, 2001. ISBN 978-0-439-26220-0 Subj: Aliens. Behavior – bad day. Humorous stories. School – first day. Space & space ships.

First graders from Mars: Nergal and the Great Space Race ill. by Mark Teague. Scholastic, 2002. ISBN 978-0-439-26633-8 Subj: Aliens. Health & fitness. Humorous stories. School. Self-concept. Space & space ships.

First graders from Mars: Tera, star student ill. by Mark Teague. Scholastic, 2002. ISBN 978-0-439-26634-5 Subj: Aliens. Behavior. Humorous stories. School. Space & space ships.

First graders from Mars: The problem with Pelly ill. by Mark Teague. Scholastic, 2002. ISBN 978-0-439-26632-1 Subj: Aliens. Character traits – individuality. Humorous stories. Self-concept. Space & space ships.

Here come the Girl Scouts! the amazing all-true story of Juliette "Daisy" Gordon Low and her great adventure ill. by Hadley Hooper. Scholastic, 2012. ISBN 978-0-545-34278-0 Subj: Clubs, gangs. U.S. history.

Milly and the Macy's Parade ill. by Brett Helquist. Scholastic, 2002. ISBN 978-0-439-29754-7 Subj: Cities, towns. Holidays – Christmas. Holidays – Thanksgiving. Immigrants. Parades. Stores.

You forgot your skirt, Amelia Bloomer ill. by Chesley McLaren. Scholastic, 2000. ISBN 978-0-439-07819-1 Subj: Clothing. Gender roles. U.S. history.

Cork, Barbara Taylor. *Katie goes to the hospital* ill. by Siobhan Dodds. McGraw-Hill, 2002. ISBN 978-1-57768-986-7 Subj: Hospitals. Illness.

Sam starts school ill. by Nicola Smee. McGraw-Hill, 2002. ISBN 978-1-57768-989-8 Subj: School – first day.

Corpi, Lucha. *Where fireflies dance / Ahí, donde bailan las luciérnagas* ill. by Mira Reisberg. Children's Book Press, 1997. ISBN 978-0-89239-145-5 Subj: Careers – writers. Family life. Family life – brothers & sisters. Foreign lands – Mexico. Foreign languages.

Corr, Christopher. *Whole world* ill. by author. Barefoot, 2007. ISBN 978-1-84686-043-0 Subj: Ecology. Nature. Songs. World.

Cort, Ben. *Pigs can't fly!* ill. by author. Barron's, 2002. ISBN 978-0-7641-5532-1 Subj: Animals – pigs. Behavior – imitation. Emotions – loneliness.

Cosentino, Ralph. *The marvelous misadventures of — Fun-Boy* ill. by author. Penguin, 2006. ISBN 978-0-670-05961-4 Subj: Humorous stories. Imagination. Wordless.

Costanza, Stephen. *Vivaldi and the invisible orchestra* ill. by author. Holt, 2012. ISBN 978-0-8050-7801-5 Subj: Careers – composers. Foreign lands – Italy. Imagination. Music. Musical instruments – orchestras.

Coste, Marion. *Finding Joy* ill. by Yong Chen. Boyds Mills, 2006. ISBN 978-1-59078-192-0 Subj: Adoption. Family life. Foreign lands – China.

Costello, David Hyde. *I can help* ill. by author. Farrar, 2010. ISBN 978-0-374-33526-7 Subj: Animals. Birds – ducks. Character traits – helpfulness.

Little Pig joins the band ill. by author. Charlesbridge, 2011. ISBN 978-1-58089-264-3 Subj: Animals – pigs. Careers – conductors (music). Character traits – smallness. Musical instruments – bands.

Costello, Emily. *Realm of the panther* ill. by Wes Siegrist. Soundprints, 2000. ISBN 978-1-56899-847-3 Subj: Animals – babies. Animals – cougars. Jungle.

Costello, Lou. *Who's on first?* (Abbott, Bud)

Côté, Geneviève. *Me and you* ill. by author. Kids Can, 2009. ISBN 978-1-55453-446-3 Subj: Animals – pigs. Animals – rabbits. Character traits – being different. Character traits – individuality.

Mr. King's things ill. by author. Kids Can, 2012. ISBN 978-1-55453-700-6 Subj: Behavior – collecting things. Ecology. Monsters.

What elephant? ill. by author. Kids Can, 2006. ISBN 978-1-55337-875-4 Subj: Animals – elephants.

With you always, Little Monday ill. by author. Harcourt, 2007. ISBN 978-0-15-205997-2 Subj: Animals. Animals – rabbits. Behavior – lost. Family life – mothers. Moon.

Without you ill. by author. Kids Can, 2011. ISBN 978-1-55453-620-7 Subj: Animals – pigs. Animals – rabbits. Behavior – fighting, arguing. Friendship.

Cote, Nancy. *It feels like snow* ill. by author. Boyds Mills, 2003. ISBN 978-1-59078-054-1 Subj: Behavior – sharing. Seasons – winter. Weather – snow.

It's all about me! ill. by author. Penguin, 2005. ISBN 978-0-399-24280-9 Subj: Family life – new sibling. Self-concept. Sibling rivalry.

Jackson's blanket ill. by author. Putnam, 2008. ISBN 978-0-399-24694-4 Subj: Behavior – growing up. Rhyming text.

Cotten, Cynthia. *Abbie in stitches* ill. by Beth Peck. Farrar, 2006. ISBN 978-0-374-30004-3 Subj: Activities – sewing. U.S. history.

At the edge of the woods ill. by Reg Cartwright. Holt, 2002. ISBN 978-0-8050-6354-7 Subj: Animals. Counting, numbers. Forest, woods. Plants. Rhyming text.

The book boat's in ill. by Frané Lessac. Holiday House, 2013. ISBN 978-0-8234-2521-1 Subj: Boats, ships. Books, reading. Libraries. U.S. history.

Rain play ill. by Javaka Steptoe. Holt, 2008. ISBN 978-0-8050-6795-8 Subj: Activities – playing. Parks. Rhyming text. Weather – lightning, thunder. Weather – rain.

Snow ponies ill. by Jason Cockcroft. Holt, 2001. ISBN 978-0-8050-6063-8 Subj: Animals – horses, ponies. Seasons – winter. Weather – snow.

This is the stable ill. by Delana Bettoli. Holt, 2006. ISBN 978-0-8050-7556-4 Subj: Religion – Nativity.

Cottin, Menena. *The black book of colors* ill. by Rosana Faria. Groundwood, 2008. ISBN 978-0-88899-873-6 Subj: Concepts – color. Disabilities – blindness. Senses – touch.

Cottle, Joan. *Miles away from home* ill. by author. Harcourt, 2001. ISBN 978-0-15-202212-9 Subj: Activities – vacationing. Animals – dogs. Behavior – misunderstanding. Sea & seashore.

Couric, Katie. *The brand new kid* ill. by Marjorie Priceman. Doubleday, 2000. ISBN 978-0-385-50030-2 Subj: Behavior – bullying, teasing. Ethnic groups in the U.S. – Hungarian Americans. Prejudice. Rhyming text. School.

Court, Rob. *Color.* Child's World, 2003. ISBN 978-1-56766-069-2 Subj: Art. Concepts – color.

Cousins, Lucy. *Count with Maisy* ill. by author. Candlewick, 1999. ISBN 978-0-7636-0234-5 Subj: Animals – mice. Counting, numbers. Format, unusual – board books.

Doctor Maisy ill. by author. Candlewick, 2001. ISBN 978-0-7636-1612-0 Subj: Activities – playing. Animals. Animals – mice. Birds.

Ha ha, Maisy! ill. by author. Candlewick, 2005. ISBN 978-0-7636-2633-4 Subj: Animals – mice. Format, unusual – toy & movable books.

Happy birthday, Maisy ill. by author. Candlewick, 1998. ISBN 978-0-7636-0577-3 Subj: Animals. Animals – mice. Birthdays. Format, unusual – toy & movable books.

Happy Easter, Maisy! ill. by author. Candlewick, 2007. ISBN 978-0-7636-3230-4 Subj: Animals – mice. Format, unusual – board books. Holidays – Easter.

Hooray for fish! ill. by author. Candlewick, 2005. ISBN 978-0-7636-2741-6 Subj: Family life – mothers. Fish. Rhyming text. Sea & seashore.

I'm the best ill. by author. Candlewick, 2010. ISBN 978-0-7636-4684-4 Subj: Animals. Animals – dogs. Behavior – boasting. Character traits – pride. Character traits – vanity. Friendship.

Maisy at the fair ill. by author. Candlewick, 2001. ISBN 978-0-7636-1500-0 Subj: Animals. Animals – mice. Fairs, festivals.

Maisy at the farm ill. by author. Candlewick, 1998. ISBN 978-0-7636-0576-6 Subj: Animals – mice. Farms. Format, unusual – toy & movable books.

Maisy big, Maisy small ill. by author. Candlewick, 2007. ISBN 978-0-7636-3406-3 Subj: Animals – mice. Concepts – opposites.

Maisy, Charley, and the wobbly tooth ill. by author. Candlewick, 2006. ISBN 978-0-7636-2904-5 Subj: Animals. Animals – mice. Careers – dentists. Reptiles – alligators, crocodiles. Teeth.

Maisy cleans up ill. by author. Candlewick, 2002. ISBN 978-0-7636-1711-0 Subj: Animals – mice. Friendship. Reptiles – alligators, crocodiles.

Maisy dresses up ill. by author. Candlewick, 1999. ISBN 978-0-7636-0885-9 Subj: Animals. Animals – mice. Clothing – costumes. Parties.

Maisy goes on vacation ill. by author. Candlewick, 2010. ISBN 978-0-7636-4752-0 Subj: Activities – vacationing. Animals – mice. Sea & seashore.

Maisy goes shopping ill. by author. Candlewick, 2001. ISBN 978-0-7636-1501-7 Subj: Animals – mice. Reptiles – alligators, crocodiles. Shopping.

Maisy goes to preschool ill. by author. Candlewick, 2009. ISBN 978-0-7636-4254-9 Subj: Animals – mice. School – nursery.

Maisy goes to the hospital ill. by author. Candlewick, 2007. ISBN 978-0-7636-3377-6 Subj: Animals – mice. Hospitals.

Maisy goes to the library ill. by author. Candlewick, 2005. ISBN 978-0-7636-2669-3 Subj: Animals – mice. Books, reading. Libraries.

Maisy goes to the museum ill. by author. Candlewick, 2008. ISBN 978-0-7636-3838-2 Subj: Animals – mice. Museums.

Maisy learns to swim ill. by author. Candlewick, 2013. ISBN 978-0-7636-6480-0 Subj: Animals – mice. Sports – swimming.

Maisy makes gingerbread ill. by author. Candlewick, 1999. ISBN 978-0-7636-0887-3 Subj: Activities – baking, cooking. Animals – mice. Food.

Maisy makes lemonade ill. by author. Candlewick, 2002. ISBN 978-0-7636-1728-8 Subj: Animals – elephants. Animals – mice. Behavior – sharing. Character traits – helpfulness.

Maisy's amazing big book of learning ill. by author. Candlewick, 2011. ISBN 978-0-7636-5481-8 Subj: Animals. Animals – mice. Concepts. Format, unusual – toy & movable books.

Maisy's amazing big book of words ill. by author. Candlewick, 2007. ISBN 978-0-7636-0794-4 Subj: Animals – mice. Format, unusual – toy & movable books. Language.

Maisy's bedtime ill. by author. Candlewick, 1999. ISBN 978-0-7636-0884-2 Subj: Animals. Animals – mice. Bedtime. Dreams. Toys – bears.

Maisy's book of things that go ill. by author. Candlewick, 2010. ISBN 978-0-7636-4614-1 Subj: Animals. Animals – mice. Format, unusual – toy & movable books. Transportation.

Maisy's colors ill. by author. Candlewick, 1997. ISBN 978-0-7636-0159-1 Subj: Animals – mice. Concepts – color.

Maisy's farm ill. by author. Candlewick, 2001. ISBN 978-0-7636-1294-8 Subj: Animals. Animals – mice. Farms. Format, unusual – toy & movable books.

Maisy's first clock ill. by author. Candlewick, 2002. ISBN 978-0-7636-1788-2 Subj: Animals – mice. Format, unusual – toy & movable books. Time.

Maisy's Halloween ill. by author. Candlewick, 2004. ISBN 978-0-7636-2579-5 Subj: Animals. Animals – mice. Format, unusual – board books. Holidays – Halloween.

Maisy's morning on the farm ill. by author. Candlewick, 2001. ISBN 978-0-7636-1610-6 Subj: Animals. Animals – mice. Farms.

Maisy's noisy day ill. by author. Candlewick, 2002. ISBN 978-0-7636-1917-6 Subj: Animals. Animals – mice. Format, unusual – board books. Noise, sounds.

Maisy's pirate treasure hunt ill. by author. Candlewick, 2004. ISBN 978-0-7636-2469-9 Subj: Animals – mice. Format, unusual – toy & movable books.

Maisy's pool ill. by author. Candlewick, 1999. ISBN 978-0-7636-0886-6 Subj: Animals. Animals – mice. Sports – swimming.

Maisy's rainbow dream ill. by author. Candlewick, 2003. ISBN 978-0-7636-2195-7 Subj: Animals – mice. Concepts – color. Dreams.

Maisy's twinkly, crinkly counting book ill. by author. Candlewick, 2004. ISBN 978-0-7636-2273-2 Subj: Animals – mice. Counting, numbers. Format, unusual – toy & movable books.

Maisy's wonderful weather book ill. by author. Candlewick, 2006. ISBN 978-0-7636-2987-8 Subj: Animals – mice. Format, unusual – toy & movable books. Weather.

More fun with Maisy! ill. by author. Candlewick, 2005. ISBN 978-0-7636-2632-7 Subj: Animals – mice. Format, unusual – toy & movable books.

Noah's ark ill. by author. Candlewick, 1993. ISBN 978-1-56402-213-4 Subj: Animals. Boats, ships. Religion – Noah. Weather – floods. Weather – rain. Weather – rainbows.

Noah's ark [board book] ill. by author. Candlewick, 2004. ISBN 978-0-7636-2446-0 Subj: Animals. Boats, ships. Format, unusual – board books. Religion – Noah. Weather – floods. Weather – rain. Weather – rainbows.

Peck, peck, peck ill. by author. Candlewick, 2013. ISBN 978-0-7636-6621-7 Subj: Birds – woodpeckers. Family life – fathers. Rhyming text.

Stop and go, Maisy ill. by author. Candlewick, 2005. ISBN 978-0-7636-2668-6 Subj: Animals – mice. Format, unusual – toy & movable books. Transportation.

Sweet dreams, Maisy ill. by author. Candlewick, 2005. ISBN 978-0-7636-2874-1 Subj: Animals – mice. Bedtime.

With love from Maisy ill. by author. Candlewick, 2005. ISBN 978-0-7636-2513-9 Subj: Animals – mice. Format, unusual – toy & movable books. Gifts.

Covell, David. *Rat and Roach: friends to the end* ill. by author. Viking, 2012. ISBN 978-0-670-01409-5 Subj: Animals – rats. Friendship. Insects – cockroaches.

Rat and Roach rock on! ill. by author. Viking, 2013. ISBN 978-0-670-01410-1 Subj: Animals – rats. Character traits – compromising. Emotions – fear. Friendship. Insects – cockroaches. Musical instruments – bands.

Coville, Bruce. *The prince of butterflies* ill. by John Clapp. Harcourt, 2002. ISBN 978-0-15-201454-4 Subj: Animals – endangered animals. Insects – butterflies, caterpillars.

Cowan, Charlotte. *Katie caught a cold* ill. by Katy Bratun. Hippocratic, 2008. ISBN 978-0-9753516-3-5 Subj: Animals. Animals – bears. Illness – cold (disease).

Peeper has a fever ill. by Susan Banta. Hippocratic, 2008. ISBN 978-0-9753516-2-8 Subj: Animals. Frogs & toads. Illness.

Sadie's sore throat ill. by Katy Bratun. Hippocratic, 2008. ISBN 978-0-9753516-4-2 Subj: Animals. Animals – giraffes. Illness.

Cowcher, Helen. *Desert elephants* ill. by author. Farrar, 2011. ISBN 978-0-374-31774-4 Subj: Animals – elephants. Character traits – cooperation. Character traits – kindness to animals. Foreign lands – Mali. Migration.

Cowell, Cressida. *Emily Brown and the Thing* ill. by Neal Layton. IPG/Hodder & Stoughton, 2012. ISBN 978-1-84616-694-5 Subj: Animals – rabbits. Bedtime. Toys.

Hiccup the seasick Viking ill. by author. Orchard, 2000. ISBN 978-0-531-30278-1 Subj: Character traits – bravery. Emotions – fear. Illness. Sea & seashore. Vikings.

That rabbit belongs to Emily Brown ill. by Neal Layton. Hyperion, 2007. ISBN 978-1-4231-0645-6 Subj: Animals – rabbits. Toys.

What shall we do with the Boo-Hoo Baby? ill. by author. Scholastic, 2003. ISBN 978-0-439-44266-4 Subj: Animals. Babies. Behavior. Emotions.

Cowen-Fletcher, Jane. *Hello, puppy!* ill. by author. Candlewick, 2010. ISBN 978-0-7636-4303-4 Subj: Animals – babies. Animals – dogs. Pets.

Mama zooms ill. by author. Scholastic, 1993. ISBN 978-0-590-45774-3 Subj: Family life – mothers. Disabilities – physical disabilities.

Cowley, Joy. *Chameleon, chameleon* photos by Nic Bishop. Scholastic, 2005. ISBN 978-0-439-66653-4 Subj: Reptiles – chameleons.

Gracias, the Thanksgiving turkey ill. by Joe Cepeda. Scholastic, 1996. ISBN 978-0-590-46976-0 Subj: Birds – turkeys. Careers – truck drivers. Ethnic groups in the U.S. – Puerto Rican Americans. Family life – fathers. Holidays – Thanksgiving.

Mrs. Goodstory ill. by Erica Dornbusch. Boyds Mills, 2001. ISBN 978-1-56397-774-9 Subj: Books, reading. Imagination.

Mrs. Wishy-Washy's Christmas ill. by Elizabeth Fuller. Penguin, 2005. ISBN 978-0-399-24344-8 Subj: Animals. Farms. Holidays – Christmas. Rhyming text.

Where horses run free ill. by Layne Johnson. Boyds Mills, 2003. ISBN 978-1-59078-062-6 Subj: Animals – horses, ponies. Cowboys, cowgirls.

Cox, Judy. *Carmen learns English* ill. by Angela Dominguez. Holiday House, 2010. ISBN 978-0-8234-2174-9 Subj: Ethnic groups in the U.S. – Mexican Americans. Family life – sisters. Foreign languages. School.

Cinco de Mouse-o! ill. by Jeffrey Ebbeler. Holiday House, 2010. ISBN 978-0-8234-2194-7 Subj: Animals – mice. Holidays – Cinco de Mayo.

Go to sleep, Groundhog ill. by Paul Meisel. Holiday, 2004. ISBN 978-0-8234-1645-5 Subj: Animals – groundhogs. Hibernation. Holidays – Groundhog Day.

Happy birthday, Mrs. Millie! ill. by Joe Mathieu. Marshall Cavendish, 2012. ISBN 978-0-7614-6126-5 Subj: Birthdays. Careers – teachers. Humorous stories. Parties. School.

Haunted house, haunted Mouse ill. by Jeffrey Ebbeler. Holiday House, 2011. ISBN 978-0-8234-2315-6 Subj: Animals – mice. Holidays – Halloween.

My family plays music ill. by Elbrite Brown. Holiday, 2003. ISBN 978-0-8234-1591-5 Subj: Careers – musicians. Family life. Musical instruments.

One is a feast for Mouse: a Thanksgiving tale ill. by Jeffrey Ebbeler. Holiday, 2008. ISBN 978-0-8234-1977-7 Subj: Animals – cats. Animals – mice. Behavior – greed. Holidays – Thanksgiving.

Pick a pumpkin, Mrs. Millie! ill. by Joe Mathieu. Marshall Cavendish, 2009. ISBN 978-0-7614-5573-8 Subj: Careers – teachers. Humorous stories. School – field trips.

Snow day for Mouse ill. by Jeffrey Ebbeler. Holiday House, 2012. ISBN 978-0-8234-2408-5 Subj: Animals – mice. Rhyming text. Weather – snow.

Cox, Phil Roxbee. *Fox on a box* ill. by Stephen Cartwright. Scholastic, 2004. ISBN 978-0-7945-0443-4 Subj: Animals – foxes. Format, unusual – toy & movable books. Language. Rhyming text.

Goose on the loose ill. by Stephen Cartwright. Scholastic, 2001. ISBN 978-0-613-75091-2 Subj: Birds – geese. Format, unusual – toy & movable books. Language. Rhyming text.

Shark in the park ill. by Stephen Cartwright. Scholastic, 2002. ISBN 978-0-439-52876-4 Subj: Fish – sharks. Format, unusual – toy & movable books. Language. Rhyming text.

Coxe, Molly. *Bunny and the beast* ill. by Pamela Silin-Palmer. Random House, 2001. ISBN 978-0-375-80468-7 Subj: Animals. Folk & fairy tales. Foreign lands – France.

Coy, John. *Two old potatoes and me* ill. by Carolyn Fisher. Knopf, 2003. ISBN 978-0-375-92180-3 Subj: Divorce. Family life – daughters. Family life – fathers. Food.

Vroomaloom zoom ill. by Joe Cepeda. Crown, 2000. ISBN 978-0-517-80010-2 Subj: Activities – traveling. Automobiles. Bedtime. Imagination. Noise, sounds.

Coyle, Carmela LaVigna. *Do princesses have best friends forever?* ill. by Mike Gordon and Carl Gordon. Taylor Trade, 2010. ISBN 978-1-58979-542-6 Subj: Friendship. Rhyming text. Royalty – princesses.

Do princesses really kiss frogs? ill. by Mike Gordon and Carl Gordon. Rising Moon, 2005. ISBN 978-0-87358-880-5 Subj: Character traits – questioning. Family life – fathers. Royalty – princesses. Sports – hiking.

Do super heroes have teddy bears? ill. by Mike Gordon. Taylor Trade, 2012. ISBN 978-1-58979-693-5 Subj: Character traits – questioning. Imagination. Rhyming text. Toys – bears.

Craig, Lindsey. *Dancing feet!* ill. by Marc Brown. Random House, 2010. ISBN 978-0-375-86181-9 Subj: Activities – dancing. Animals. Rhyming text.

Farmyard beat ill. by Marc Brown. Random House, 2011. ISBN 978-0-375-86455-1 Subj: Animals. Bedtime. Farms. Noise, sounds. Rhyming text.

Crampton, Gertrude. *Scuffy the tugboat* ill. by Tibor Gergely. Random House, 2003. ISBN 978-0-307-10547-9 Subj: Activities – traveling. Boats, ships. Rivers. Toys.

Crandall, Court. *Hugville* ill. by Joe Murray. Random House, 2005. ISBN 978-0-375-82418-0 Subj: Hugging. Rhyming text.

Crane, Carol. *D is for dancing dragon: a China alphabet* ill. by Zong-Zhou Wang. Sleeping Bear, 2006. ISBN 978-1-58536-273-8 Subj: ABC books. Foreign lands – China.

Crawford, Laura. *In arctic waters* ill. by Ben Hodson. Random House, 2007. ISBN 978-0-9768823-4-3 Subj: Animals. Foreign lands – Arctic. Rhyming text.

Crawford, Sheryl Ann. *The baby who changed the world* ill. by Sonya Wilson. Faith Kids, 2000. ISBN 978-0-7814-3431-7 Subj: Animals. Animals – donkeys. Religion – Nativity.

Crawley, Dave. *Cat poems* ill. by Tamara Petrosino. Boyds Mills, 2005. ISBN 978-1-59078-287-3 Subj: Animals – cats. Poetry.

Creech, Sharon. *A fine, fine school* ill. by Harry Bliss. HarperCollins, 2001. ISBN 978-0-06-027737-6 Subj: Careers – school principals. School.

Fishing in the air ill. by Chris Raschka. HarperCollins, 2000. ISBN 978-0-06-028112-0 Subj: Family life – fathers. Family life – sons. Imagination. Sports – fishing.

Who's that baby? new-baby songs ill. by David Diaz. HarperCollins, 2005. ISBN 978-0-06-052940-6 Subj: Babies. Poetry. Songs.

Cressy, Judith. *Can you find it?* ill. with paintings. Abrams, 2002. ISBN 978-0-8109-3279-1 Subj: Art. Museums. Picture puzzles.

Can you find it, too? ill. with paintings. Abrams, 2004. ISBN 978-0-8109-5046-7 Subj: Art. Museums. Picture puzzles.

Crews, Donald. *Bicycle race* ill. by author. Greenwillow, 1985. ISBN 978-0-688-05172-3 Subj: Counting, numbers. Sports – bicycling. Sports – racing.

Carousel ill. by author. Greenwillow, 1982. ISBN 978-0-688-00909-0 Subj: Merry-go-rounds.

Cloudy day/sunny day ill. by author. Harcourt, 1999. ISBN 978-0-15-201997-6 Subj: Activities – playing. Ethnic groups in the U.S. – African Americans. Weather.

Flying ill. by author. Greenwillow, 1986. ISBN 978-0-688-04319-3 Subj: Activities – flying. Airplanes, airports.

Freight train ill. by author. Greenwillow, 1978. ISBN 978-0-688-80165-6 Subj: Caldecott award honor books. Trains.

Harbor ill. by author. Greenwillow, 1982. ISBN 978-0-688-00862-8 Subj: Boats, ships.

Inside freight train ill. by author. HarperCollins, 2001. ISBN 978-0-688-17087-5 Subj: Format, unusual – toy & movable books. Trains.

Light ill. by author. Greenwillow, 1981. ISBN 978-0-688-00310-4 Subj: Concepts. Light, lights.

Night at the fair ill. by author. Greenwillow, 1998. ISBN 978-0-688-11484-8 Subj: Fairs, festivals. Night.

Parade ill. by author. Greenwillow, 1983. ISBN 978-0-688-01996-9 Subj: Cities, towns. Parades.

Sail away ill. by author. Greenwillow, 1995. ISBN 978-0-688-11054-3 Subj: Boats, ships. Family life. Sailors. Sports – sailing. Weather – storms.

School bus ill. by author. Greenwillow, 1984. ISBN 978-0-688-02808-4 Subj: Buses. School. Transportation.

School bus [board book] ill. by author. Greenwillow, 2002. ISBN 978-0-694-01690-7 Subj: Buses. Format, unusual – board books. School. Transportation.

Shortcut ill. by author. Greenwillow, 1992. ISBN 978-0-688-06436-5 Subj: Ethnic groups in the U.S. – African Americans. Trains.

Ten black dots ill. by author. Rev. ed. Greenwillow, 1986. ISBN 978-0-688-06068-8 Subj: Concepts – shape. Counting, numbers.

Truck ill. by author. Greenwillow, 1980. ISBN 978-0-688-84244-4 Subj: Caldecott award honor books. Transportation. Trucks. Wordless.

We read: A to Z ill. by author. Harper & Row, 1967. ISBN 978-0-688-03844-1 Subj: ABC books. Concepts.

Crews, Nina. *Below* photos by author. Holt, 2006. ISBN 978-0-8050-7728-5 Subj: Activities – playing. Imagination. Toys.

A ghost story ill. by author. Greenwillow, 2001. ISBN 978-0-688-17674-7 Subj: Ethnic groups in the U.S. – African Americans. Family life. Family life – aunts, uncles. Ghosts.

A high, low, near, far, loud, quiet story ill. by author. Greenwillow, 1999. ISBN 978-0-688-16795-0 Subj: Activities. Concepts – opposites. Family life – brothers & sisters.

I'll catch the moon ill. by author. Greenwillow, 1996. ISBN 978-0-688-14135-6 Subj: Imagination. Moon. Night.

One hot summer day ill. by author. Greenwillow, 1995. ISBN 978-0-688-13394-8 Subj: Cities, towns. Ethnic groups in the U.S. – African Americans. Seasons – summer.

Sky-high Guy ill. by author. Holt, 2010. ISBN 978-0-8050-8764-2 Subj: Activities – playing. Family life – brothers. Toys.

Snowball ill. by author. Greenwillow, 1997. ISBN 978-0-688-14929-1 Subj: Activities – playing. Seasons – winter. Weather – snow.

You are here ill. by author. Greenwillow, 1998. ISBN 978-0-688-15753-1 Subj: Ethnic groups in the U.S. – African Americans. Family life. Imagination. Weather – rain.

Crimi, Carolyn. *Dear Tabby* ill. by David Roberts. HarperCollins, 2011. ISBN 978-0-06-114245-1 Subj: Activities – writing. Animals. Animals – cats. Letters, cards.

Don't need friends ill. by Lynn Munsinger. Doubleday, 1999. ISBN 978-0-385-32643-8 Subj: Animals. Animals – dogs. Animals – rats. Behavior – needing someone. Friendship.

Henry and the Buccaneer Bunnies ill. by John Manders. Candlewick, 2005. ISBN 978-0-7636-2449-1 Subj: Animals – rabbits. Books, reading. Pirates.

Henry and the Crazed Chicken Pirates ill. by John Manders. Candlewick, 2009. ISBN 978-0-7636-3601-2 Subj: Activities – writing. Animals – rabbits. Birds – chickens. Books, reading. Pirates.

The Louds move in! ill. by Regan Dunnick. Marshall Cavendish, 2006. ISBN 978-0-7614-5221-8 Subj: Humorous stories. Noise, sounds.

Principal Fred won't go to bed ill. by Donald Wu. Marshall Cavendish, 2010. ISBN 978-0-7614-5709-1 Subj: Bedtime. Behavior – lost & found possessions. Careers – school principals. Rhyming text. Toys – bears.

Pugs in a Bug ill. by Stephanie Buscema. Dial, 2012. ISBN 978-0-8037-3320-6 Subj: Animals – dogs. Automobiles. Counting, numbers. Parades. Rhyming text.

Rock 'n' roll Mole ill. by Lynn Munsinger. Penguin, 2011. ISBN 978-0-8037-3166-0 Subj: Animals – moles. Emotions – fear. Music. Theater.

Tessa's tip-tapping toes ill. by Marsha Gray Carrington. Scholastic, 2002. ISBN 978-0-439-31768-9 Subj: Activities – dancing. Activities – singing. Animals – cats. Animals – mice. Weather – rain.

Where's my mummy? ill. by John Manders. Candlewick, 2008. ISBN 978-0-7636-3196-3 Subj: Bedtime. Emotions – fear. Family life – mothers. Mummies.

Crisp, Marty. *Black and white* ill. by Sherry Neidigh. Rising Moon, 2000. ISBN 978-0-87358-756-3 Subj: Animals. Animals – dogs. Farms. Pets.

The most precious gift: a story of the Nativity ill. by Floyd Cooper. Penguin, 2006. ISBN 978-0-399-24296-0 Subj: Animals – dogs. Religion – Nativity.

Totally polar ill. by Viv Eisner. Rising Moon, 2001. ISBN 978-0-87358-789-1 Subj: Humorous stories. Imagination. Rhyming text. Seasons – summer. Weather – snow.

Cristaldi, Kathryn. *Baseball ballerina* ill. by Abby Carter. Random House, 2003. ISBN 978-0-679-91734-2 Subj: Activities – dancing. Ballet. Gender roles. Sports – baseball.

Baseball ballerina strikes out ill. by Abby Carter. Random House, 2000. ISBN 978-0-679-99132-8 Subj: Activities – dancing. Ballet. Behavior – bullying, teasing. Sports – baseball.

Crocker, Nancy. *Betty Lou Blue* ill. by Boris Kulikov. Penguin, 2006. ISBN 978-0-8037-2937-7 Subj: Anatomy – feet. Behavior – bullying, teasing. Character traits – appearance. Rhyming text.

Croll, Carolyn. *The little snowgirl* ill. by author. Putnam, 1989. ISBN 978-0-399-21691-6 Subj: Folk & fairy tales. Foreign lands – Russia. Holidays – Christmas. Weather – snow.

Cronin, Doreen. *Bounce* ill. by Scott Menchin. Simon & Schuster, 2007. ISBN 978-1-4169-1627-7 Subj: Activities – jumping. Activities – playing. Animals – dogs. Rhyming text. Toys – balls.

Click, clack, boo! a tricky treat ill. by Betsy Lewin. Atheneum, 2013. ISBN 978-1-4424-6553-4 Subj: Animals. Farms. Holidays – Halloween. Parties.

Click, clack, moo ill. by Betsy Lewin. Simon & Schuster, 2000. ISBN 978-0-689-83213-0 Subj: Activities – writing. Animals – bulls, cows. Behavior – dissatisfaction. Birds. Caldecott award honor books. Careers – farmers. Farms.

Click, clack, quackity-quack: an alphabetical adventure ill. by Betsy Lewin. Simon & Schuster, 2005. ISBN 978-0-689-87715-5 Subj: ABC books. Activities – picnicking. Activities – writing. Animals. Birds – ducks. Farms.

Click, clack, splish, splash: a counting adventure ill. by Betsy Lewin. Simon & Schuster, 2006. ISBN 978-0-689-87716-2 Subj: Animals. Counting, numbers. Farms. Rhyming text. Sports – fishing.

Diary of a fly ill. by Harry Bliss. HarperCollins, 2007. ISBN 978-0-06-000156-8 Subj: Activities – writing. Insects – flies.

Diary of a spider ill. by Harry Bliss. HarperCollins, 2005. ISBN 978-0-06-000154-4 Subj: Activities – writing. Spiders.

Diary of a worm ill. by Harry Bliss. Cotler, 2003. ISBN 978-0-06-000151-3 Subj: Activities – writing. Animals – worms.

Dooby dooby moo ill. by Betsy Lewin. Simon & Schuster, 2006. ISBN 978-0-689-84507-9 Subj: Animals. Careers – farmers. Farms. Theater.

Duck for President ill. by Betsy Lewin. Simon & Schuster, 2004. ISBN 978-0-689-86377-6 Subj: Animals. Birds – ducks. Character traits – ambition. Farms. Humorous stories.

Giggle, giggle, quack ill. by Betsy Lewin. Simon & Schuster, 2002. ISBN 978-0-689-84506-2 Subj: Animals. Birds – ducks. Farms.

M.O.M. (Mom Operating Manual) ill. by Laura Cornell. Simon & Schuster, 2011. ISBN 978-1-4169-6150-5 Subj: Family life – mothers. Humorous stories.

Rescue bunnies ill. by Scott Menchin. HarperCollins, 2010. ISBN 978-0-06-112871-4 Subj: Animals – giraffes. Animals – rabbits.

Stretch ill. by Scott Menchin. Atheneum, 2009. ISBN 978-1-4169-5341-8 Subj: Animals – dogs. Health & fitness – exercise. Rhyming text.

Thump, quack, moo: a whacky adventure ill. by Betsy Lewin. Atheneum, 2008. ISBN 978-1-4169-1630-7 Subj: Animals. Birds – ducks. Careers – farmers. Farms.

Wiggle ill. by Scott Menchin. Atheneum, 2005. ISBN 978-0-689-86375-2 Subj: Activities. Animals – dogs. Participation. Rhyming text.

Crosby, Jeff. *Wiener Wolf* ill. by author. Hyperion/Disney, 2011. ISBN 978-1-4231-3983-6 Subj: Animals – dogs. Animals – wolves. Behavior – dissatisfaction.

Crossley-Holland, Kevin. *How many miles to Bethlehem?* ill. by Peter Malone. Scholastic, 2004. ISBN 978-0-439-67642-7 Subj: Holidays – Christmas. Religion – Nativity.

Crow, Kristyn. *Bedtime at the swamp* ill. by Macky Pamintuan. HarperCollins, 2008. ISBN 978-0-06-083951-2 Subj: Bedtime. Monsters. Rhyming text. Swamps.

Cool Daddy Rat ill. by Mike Lester. Putnam, 2008. ISBN 978-0-399-24375-2 Subj: Animals – rats. Music. Rhyming text.

The middle-child blues ill. by David Catrow. Putnam, 2009. ISBN 978-0-399-24735-4 Subj: Activities – singing. Family life – brothers & sisters. Rhyming text.

Skeleton cat ill. by Dan Drall. Scholastic, 2012. ISBN 978-0-545-15385-0 Subj: Anatomy – skeletons. Animals – cats. Musical instruments – drums. Rhyming text.

Zombelina ill. by Molly Idle. Walker, 2013. ISBN 978-0-8027-2803-6 Subj: Ballet. Careers – dancers. Monsters. Rhyming text.

Crowe, Carole. *Turtle girl* ill. by Jim Postier. Boyds Mills, 2008. ISBN 978-1-59078-262-0 Subj: Death. Ecology. Family life – grandmothers. Reptiles – turtles, tortoises.

Crowe, Chris. *Just as good: how Larry Doby changed America's game* ill. by Mike Benny. Candlewick, 2012. ISBN 978-0-7636-5026-1 Subj: Ethnic groups in the U.S. – African Americans. Prejudice. Sports – baseball.

Crowley, Ned. *Nanook and Pryce: gone fishing* ill. by Larry Day. HarperCollins, 2009. ISBN 978-0-06-133641-6 Subj: Activities – traveling. Foreign lands – Arctic. Rhyming text. Sports – fishing.

Crowther, Kitty. *Jack and Jim* ill. by author. Hyperion, 2000. ISBN 978-0-7868-2527-1 Subj: Birds. Friendship. Prejudice.

Crowther, Robert. *Amazing pop-up trucks* ill. by author. Candlewick, 2011. ISBN 978-0-7636-5587-7 Subj: Format, unusual – toy & movable books. Trucks.

Colors ill. by author. Candlewick, 2001. ISBN 978-0-7636-1404-1 Subj: Concepts – color. Format, unusual – toy & movable books.

Opposites ill. by author. Candlewick, 2005. ISBN 978-0-7636-2783-6 Subj: Concepts – opposites. Format, unusual – toy & movable books.

Shapes ill. by author. Candlewick, 2002. ISBN 978-0-7636-1889-6 Subj: Concepts – shape. Format, unusual – toy & movable books.

Cruickshank, Margrit. *We're going to feed the ducks* ill. by Rosie Reeve. G. Stevens, 2004. ISBN 978-0-8368-4027-8 Subj: Animals. Birds. Birds – ducks. Food.

Cruikshank, Beth. *Farley follows his nose* (Johnston, Lynn)

Cruise, Robin. *Bartleby speaks!* ill. by Kevin Hawkes. Farrar, 2009. ISBN 978-0-374-30514-7 Subj: Activities – talking. Behavior – growing up. Communication.

Little Mama forgets ill. by Stacey Dressen-McQueen. Farrar, 2006. ISBN 978-0-374-34613-3 Subj: Behavior – forgetfulness. Ethnic groups in the U.S. – Mexican Americans. Family life – grandmothers. Memories, memory. Old age.

Only you ill. by Margaret Chodos-Irvine. Harcourt, 2007. ISBN 978-0-15-216604-5 Subj: Emotions – love. Family life. Rhyming text.

Crum, Shutta. *All on a sleepy night* ill. by Sylvie Daigneault. Stoddart, 2001. ISBN 978-0-7737-3315-2 Subj: Bedtime. Family life – grandparents. Rhyming text.

The bravest of the brave ill. by Tim Bowers. Knopf, 2005. ISBN 978-0-375-92637-2 Subj: Animals. Animals – skunks. Character traits – bravery. Counting, numbers. Emotions – fear. Forest, woods. Rhyming text.

Dozens of cousins ill. by David Catrow. Clarion, 2013. ISBN 978-0-618-15874-4 Subj: Activities – picnicking. Activities – playing. Family life. Family life – cousins.

A family for Old Mill Farm ill. by Niki Daly. Houghton, 2007. ISBN 978-0-618-42846-5 Subj: Animals. Homes, houses. Moving. Rhyming text.

Fox and Fluff ill. by John Bendall-Brunello. Whitman, 2002. ISBN 978-0-8075-2544-9 Subj: Animals – foxes. Birds – chickens. Family life – fathers.

Mine! ill. by Patrice Barton. Random House, 2011. ISBN 978-0-375-86711-8 Subj: Babies. Behavior – sharing. Toys.

My mountain song ill. by Ted Rand. Clarion, 2004. ISBN 978-0-618-15970-3 Subj: Family life – cousins. Family life – grandparents. Farms. Songs.

Thunder-Boomer! ill. by Carol Thompson. Clarion, 2009. ISBN 978-0-618-61865-1 Subj: Animals – cats. Farms. Weather – lightning, thunder. Weather – storms.

Who took my hairy toe? ill. by Katya Krénina. Whitman, 2001. ISBN 978-0-8075-5972-7 Subj: Anatomy – toes. Folk & fairy tales. Holidays – Halloween. Monsters.

Crummel, Susan Stevens. *And the dish ran away with the spoon* (Stevens, Janet)

Cook-a-doodle-doo! (Stevens, Janet)

Find a cow now! (Stevens, Janet)

The great fuzz frenzy (Stevens, Janet)

Help me, Mr. Mutt! expert answers for dogs with people problems (Stevens, Janet)

The little red pen (Stevens, Janet)

My big dog (Stevens, Janet)

Sherlock Bones and the missing cheese ill. by Dorothy Donohue. Amazon, 2012. ISBN 978-0-7614-6186-9 Subj: Animals – dogs. Careers – detectives. Crime. Senses.

Ten-Gallon Bart ill. by Dorothy Donohue. Marshall Cavendish, 2006. ISBN 978-0-7614-5246-1 Subj: Animals – dogs. Animals – goats. Careers – sheriffs.

Ten-Gallon Bart and the Wild West Show ill. by Dorothy Donohue. Marshall Cavendish, 2008. ISBN 978-0-7614-5391-8 Subj: Animals – dogs. U.S. history – frontier & pioneer life.

Ten-Gallon Bart beats the heat ill. by Dorothy Donohue. Marshall Cavendish, 2010. ISBN 978-0-7614-5634-6 Subj: Alaska. Animals – dogs. Weather – blizzards.

Tumbleweed stew ill. by Janet Stevens. Harcourt, 2000. ISBN 978-0-15-202628-8 Subj: Animals – rabbits. Behavior – trickery.

Crumpacker, Bunny. *Alexander's pretending day* ill. by Dan Andreasen. Penguin, 2005. ISBN 978-0-525-46936-0 Subj: Character traits – questioning. Family life – mothers. Imagination.

Crunk, Tony. *Big Mama* ill. by Margot Apple. Farrar, 2000. ISBN 978-0-374-30688-5 Subj: Family life – grandmothers. Orphans.

Grandpa's overalls ill. by Scott Nash. Orchard, 2001. ISBN 978-0-531-33321-1 Subj: Animals – dogs. Careers – farmers. Clothing – pants. Family life – grandfathers. Farms.

Railroad John and the Red Rock run ill. by Michael Austin. Peachtree, 2006. ISBN 978-1-56145-363-4 Subj: Tall tales. Trains. U.S. history – frontier & pioneer life. Weddings.

Cuetara, Mittie. *Baby business* ill. by author. Dutton, 2003. ISBN 978-0-525-47026-7 Subj: Babies. Poetry.

Cullen, Catherine Ann. *The magical, mystical, marvelous coat* ill. by David Christiana. Little, 2001. ISBN 978-0-316-16334-7 Subj: Clothing. Magic. Rhyming text.

Thirsty baby ill. by David McPhail. Little, 2003. ISBN 978-0-316-16357-6 Subj: Babies. Folk & fairy tales. Rhyming text. Water.

Cullen, Lynn. *Little Scraggly Hair: a dog on Noah's Ark* ill. by Jacqueline Rogers. Holiday, 2003. ISBN 978-0-8234-1772-8 Subj: Anatomy – noses. Animals. Animals – dogs. Boats, ships. Religion – Noah. Weather – floods. Weather – rain. Weather – rainbows.

The mightiest heart ill. by Laurel Long. Dial, 1998. ISBN 978-0-8037-2293-4 Subj: Animals – dogs. Character traits – loyalty. Folk & fairy tales. Foreign lands – Wales.

Moi and Marie Antoinette ill. by Amy Young. Bloomsbury, 2006. ISBN 978-1-58234-958-9 Subj: Animals – dogs. Royalty – queens.

Cumberbatch, Judy. *Can you hear the sea?* ill. by Ken Wilson-Max. Bloomsbury, 2006. ISBN 978-1-58234-703-5 Subj: Family life – grandfathers. Foreign lands – Ghana. Noise, sounds. Sea & seashore.

Cumming, Hannah. *The red boat* ill. by author. Child's Play, 2012. ISBN 978-1-84643-493-8 Subj: Boats, ships. Character traits – confidence. Emotions – loneliness. Imagination. Moving.

Cummings, E. E. *Fairy tales* ill. by Meilo So. Liveright, 2004. ISBN 978-0-87140-658-3 Subj: Folk & fairy tales.

Cummings, Pat. *Ananse and the lizard* ill. by author. Holt, 2002. ISBN 978-0-8050-6476-6 Subj: Animals. Folk & fairy tales – pourquoi tales. Foreign lands – Ghana. Reptiles – lizards.

Angel baby ill. by author. Lothrop, 2000. ISBN 978-0-688-14822-5 Subj: Babies. Ethnic groups in the U.S. – African Americans. Family life – brothers & sisters. Rhyming text.

Clean your room, Harvey Moon! ill. by author. Bradbury, 1991. ISBN 978-0-02-725511-9 Subj: Character traits – cleanliness. Ethnic groups in the U.S. – African Americans. Rhyming text.

My aunt came back ill. by author. HarperCollins, 1998. ISBN 978-0-694-01059-2 Subj: Activities – traveling. Ethnic groups in the U.S. – African Americans. Family life – aunts, uncles. Rhyming text.

Cummings, Phil. *Boom bah!* ill. by Nina Rycroft. Kane/Miller, 2010. ISBN 978-1-935279-22-8 Subj: Animals. Music. Musical instruments. Noise, sounds.

Cummings, Troy. *The Eensy Weensy Spider freaks out! (big-time!)* ill. by author. Random House, 2010. ISBN 978-0-375-86582-4 Subj: Nursery rhymes. Self-concept. Spiders.

Cummins, Julie. *Country kid, city kid* ill. by Ted Rand. Holt, 2002. ISBN 978-0-8050-6467-4 Subj: Camps, camping. Cities, towns. Country. Farms.

Cumpiano, Ina. *Quinito, day and night / Quinito, dia y noche* ill. by José Ramírez. Children's Press, 2008. ISBN 978-0-89239-226-1 Subj: Concepts – opposites. Ethnic groups in the U.S. – Hispanic Americans. Family life. Foreign languages.

Quinito's neighborhood / El vecindario de Quinito ill. by Jose Ramirez. Children's Book Press, 2005. ISBN 978-0-89239-209-4 Subj: Communities, neighborhoods. Ethnic groups in the U.S. – Hispanic Americans. Foreign languages.

Cunnane, Kelly. *Chirchir is singing* ill. by Jude Daly. Random House, 2011. ISBN 978-0-375-86198-7 Subj: Activities – singing. Character traits – helpfulness. Family life. Foreign lands – Kenya.

Deep in the Sahara ill. by Hoda Hadadi. Random House, 2013. ISBN 978-0-375-87034-7 Subj: Clothing. Foreign lands – Mauritania. Religion – Islam.

For you are a Kenyan child ill. by Ana Juan. Simon & Schuster, 2006. ISBN 978-0-689-86194-9 Subj: Foreign lands – Kenya.

Curious George and the dinosaur ed. by Margret Rey and Alan J. Shalleck. Houghton, 1989. ISBN 978-0-395-51942-4 Subj: Animals – monkeys. Dinosaurs. Prehistory.

Curious George and the dump truck ill. from the Curious George film series. Houghton, 1984. ISBN 978-0-395-36635-6 Subj: Animals – monkeys. Character traits – curiosity. Trucks.

Curious George and the dump truck ill. in the style of H. A. Rey by Vipah Interactive. The 1984 ed. of this title has a different story line. Houghton, 1999. ISBN 978-0-395-97832-0 Subj: Animals – monkeys. Birds – ducks. Parks. Trucks.

Curious George and the hot air balloon ill. in the style of H. A. Rey by Vipah Interactive. Houghton, 1998. ISBN 978-0-395-92338-2 Subj: Activities – ballooning. Animals – monkeys. Behavior.

Curious George and the pizza ill. from the Curious George film series. Houghton, 1985. ISBN 978-0-395-39039-9 Subj: Animals – monkeys. Character traits – curiosity. Food.

Curious George and the puppies ill. in the style of H. A. Rey by Vipah Interactive. Houghton, 1998. ISBN 978-0-395-92334-4 Subj: Animals – dogs.

Animals – monkeys. Behavior – misbehavior. Money.

Curious George at the fire station ill. from the Curious George film series. Houghton, 1985. ISBN 978-0-395-39037-5 Subj: Animals – monkeys. Careers – firefighters. Character traits – curiosity.

Curious George goes camping ill. in the style of H. A. Rey by Vipah Interactive. Houghton, 1999. ISBN 978-0-395-97831-3 Subj: Animals – monkeys. Camps, camping.

Curious George goes hiking ill. from the Curious George film series. Houghton, 1985. ISBN 978-0-395-39038-2 Subj: Animals – monkeys. Character traits – curiosity. Sports – hiking.

Curious George goes sledding ill. from the Curious George film series. Houghton, 1984. ISBN 978-0-395-36637-0 Subj: Animals – monkeys. Character traits – curiosity. Sports – sledding.

Curious George goes to a chocolate factory. Based on the original character by Margret and H. A. Rey; ill. in the style of H. A. Rey by Vipah Interactive. Houghton, 1998. ISBN 978-0-395-91216-4 Subj: Animals – monkeys. Behavior – misbehavior. Food.

Curious George goes to a movie. Based on the original character by Margret and H. A. Rey: ill. in the style of H. A. Rey by Vipah Interactive. Houghton, 1998. ISBN 978-0-395-91901-9 Subj: Animals – monkeys. Behavior – misbehavior. Theater.

Curious George goes to an ice cream shop ed. by Margret Rey and Alan J. Shalleck. Houghton, 1989. ISBN 978-0-395-51943-1 Subj: Animals – monkeys. Food.

Curious George goes to school ed. by Margret Rey and Alan J. Shalleck. Houghton, 1989. ISBN 978-0-395-51944-8 Subj: Animals – monkeys. School.

Curious George goes to the aquarium ill. from the Curious George film series. Houghton, 1984. ISBN 978-0-395-36634-9 Subj: Animals – monkeys. Aquariums. Character traits – curiosity. Fish.

Curious George goes to the circus ill. from the Curious George film series. Houghton, 1984. ISBN 978-0-395-36636-3 Subj: Animals – monkeys. Character traits – curiosity. Circus.

Curious George goes to the dentist ed. by Margret Rey and Alan J. Shalleck. Houghton, 1989. ISBN 978-0-395-51941-7 Subj: Animals – monkeys. Careers – dentists. Teeth.

Curious George in the big city ill. in the style of H. A. Rey by Martha Weston. Houghton, 2001. ISBN 978-0-618-15252-0 Subj: Animals – monkeys. Character traits – curiosity. Cities, towns.

Curious George in the snow: based on the original character by Margret and H. A. Rey ill. in the style of H. A. Rey by Vipah Interactive. Houghton, 1998. ISBN 978-0-395-91902-6 Subj: Animals – monkeys. Behavior – misbehavior. Weather – snow.

Curious George makes pancakes ill. in the style of H. A. Rey by Vipah Interactive. Houghton, 1998. ISBN 978-0-395-92337-5 Subj: Animals – monkeys. Food. Hospitals.

Curious George takes a train ill. in the style of H. A. Rey by Martha Weston. Houghton, 2002. ISBN 978-0-618-06566-0 Subj: Animals – monkeys. Character traits – curiosity. Trains.

Curious George visits a toy store ill. in the style of H. A. Rey by Martha Weston. Houghton, 2002. ISBN 978-0-618-06398-7 Subj: Animals – monkeys. Character traits – curiosity. Stores. Toys.

Curious George visits the zoo ill. from the Curious George film series. Houghton, 1985. ISBN 978-0-395-39036-8 Subj: Animals – monkeys. Character traits – curiosity. Zoos.

Curious George's 1 to 10 and back again ill. by H. A. Rey. Houghton, 2001. ISBN 978-0-618-12074-1 Subj: Animals – monkeys. Counting, numbers. Format, unusual – board books.

Curlee, Lynn. *Skyscraper* ill. by author. Simon & Schuster, 2007. ISBN 978-0-689-84489-8 Subj: Buildings. Cities, towns.

Currey, Anna. *Truffle's Christmas* ill. by author. Orchard, 2000. ISBN 978-0-531-30289-7 Subj: Animals – mice. Holidays – Christmas. Santa Claus.

Curtis, Andrea. *What's for lunch? how schoolchildren eat around the world* ill. by Sophie Casson. Red Deer, 2012. ISBN 978-0-88995-482-3 Subj: Food. School. World.

Curtis, Gavin. *The bat boy and his violin* ill. by E. B. Lewis. Simon & Schuster, 1998. ISBN 978-0-689-80099-3 Subj: Ethnic groups in the U.S. – African Americans. Music. Musical instruments – violins. Sports – baseball.

Curtis, Jamie Lee. *Big words for little people* ill. by Laura Cornell. HarperCollins, 2008. ISBN 978-0-06-112760-1 Subj: Language. Rhyming text. Self-concept.

I'm gonna like me ill. by Laura Cornell. Cotler, 2002. ISBN 978-0-06-028762-7 Subj: Behavior. Rhyming text. Self-concept.

Is there really a human race? ill. by Laura Cornell. HarperCollins, 2006. ISBN 978-0-06-075346-7 Subj: Character traits – curiosity. Rhyming text.

It's hard to be five: learning how to work my control panel ill. by Laura Cornell. Cotler, 2004. ISBN 978-0-06-008096-9 Subj: Behavior – growing up. Rhyming text.

My brave year of firsts: tries, sighs, and high fives ill. by Laura Cornell. HarperCollins, 2012. ISBN 978-0-06-144155-4 Subj: Behavior – growing up. Character traits – bravery. Character traits – confidence. Character traits – perseverance. Rhyming text.

My mommy hung the moon: a love story ill. by Laura Cornell. HarperCollins, 2010. ISBN 978-0-06-029016-0 Subj: Family life – mothers. Rhyming text.

Tell me again about the night I was born ill. by Laura Cornell. HarperCollins, 1996. ISBN 978-0-06-024529-0 Subj: Adoption. Babies. Family life.

Today I feel silly and other moods that make my day ill. by Laura Cornell. HarperCollins, 1998. ISBN 978-0-06-024561-0 Subj: Emotions. Family life. Format, unusual – toy & movable books. Rhyming text.

When I was little: a four-year-old's memoir of her youth ill. by Laura Cornell. HarperCollins, 1993. ISBN 978-0-06-021079-3 Subj: Babies. Behavior – growing up.

Where do balloons go? ill. by Laura Cornell. HarperCollins, 2000. ISBN 978-0-06-027981-3 Subj: Rhyming text. Toys – balloons.

Curtis, Jennifer Keats. *Seahorses* ill. by Chad Wallace. Holt, 2012. ISBN 978-0-8050-9239-4 Subj: Fish – seahorses.

Cushman, Doug. *Christmas Eve good night* ill. by author. Holt, 2011. ISBN 978-0-8050-6603-6 Subj: Bedtime. Holidays – Christmas. Rhyming text.

Halloween good night ill. by author. Holt, 2010. ISBN 978-0-8050-8928-8 Subj: Bedtime. Holidays – Halloween. Monsters. Rhyming text.

Space cat ill. by author. HarperCollins, 2004. ISBN 978-0-06-008966-5 Subj: Animals – cats. Robots. Space & space ships.

Cusimano, Maryann K. *You are my I love you* ill. by Satomi Ichikawa. Philomel, 2001. ISBN 978-0-399-23392-0 Subj: Family life – parents. Rhyming text. Toys – bears.

You are my wish ill. by Satomi Ichikawa. Penguin, 2010. ISBN 978-0-399-24752-1 Subj: Animals – bears. Family life – grandparents. Rhyming text.

You are my wonders ill. by Satomi Ichikawa. Philomel, 2012. ISBN 978-0-399-25293-8 Subj: Animals. Careers – teachers. Rhyming text. School.

Cutbill, Andy. *The cow that laid an egg* ill. by Russell Ayto. HarperCollins, 2008. ISBN 978-0-06-137295-7 Subj: Animals – bulls, cows. Eggs. Humorous stories.

First week at cow school ill. by Russell Ayto. HarperCollins, 2012. ISBN 978-0-00-727338-6 Subj: Animals – bulls, cows. Humorous stories. School.

Cutler, Jane. *Guttersnipe* ill. by Emily Arnold McCully. Farrar, 2009. ISBN 978-0-374-32813-9 Subj: Character traits – perseverance. Character traits – responsibility. Foreign lands – Canada. Immigrants. Jewish culture. Poverty.

Cutlip, Kimbra L. *Firefighter's night before Christmas* ill. by James Rice. Pelican, 2002. ISBN 978-1-58980-054-0 Subj: Careers – firefighters. Holidays – Christmas. Poetry.

Cuyler, Margery. *The biggest, best snowman* ill. by Will Hillenbrand. Scholastic, 1998. ISBN 978-0-590-13922-9 Subj: Animals. Concepts – size. Seasons – winter. Snowmen. Weather – snow.

Bullies never win ill. by Arthur Howard. Simon & Schuster, 2009. ISBN 978-0-689-86187-1 Subj: Behavior – bullying, teasing. Behavior – worrying. Friendship. School. Self-concept.

The bumpy little pumpkin ill. by Will Hillenbrand. Scholastic, 2005. ISBN 978-0-439-52835-1 Subj: Family life – brothers & sisters. Holidays – Halloween.

Groundhog stays up late ill. by Jean Cassels. Walker, 2005. ISBN 978-0-8027-8939-6 Subj: Animals – groundhogs. Hibernation. Holidays – Groundhog Day.

Guinea pigs add up ill. by Tracey Campbell Pearson. Walker, 2010. ISBN 978-0-8027-9795-7 Subj: Animals – guinea pigs. Counting, numbers. Pets. Rhyming text. School.

Hooray for Reading Day! ill. by Arthur Howard. Simon & Schuster, 2008. ISBN 978-0-689-86188-8 Subj: Behavior – worrying. Books, reading. School.

I repeat, don't cheat! ill. by Arthur Howard. Simon & Schuster, 2010. ISBN 978-1-4169-7167-2 Subj: Behavior – cheating. Behavior – lying. Character traits – honesty. Friendship. School.

Kindness is cooler, Mrs. Ruler ill. by Sachiko Yohikawa. Simon & Schuster, 2007. ISBN 978-0-689-87344-7 Subj: Careers – teachers. Character traits – kindness. School.

The little dump truck ill. by Bob Kolar. Holt, 2009. ISBN 978-0-8050-8281-4 Subj: Rhyming text. Trucks.

Monster mess! ill. by S. D. Schindler. Simon & Schuster, 2008. ISBN 978-0-689-86405-6 Subj: Behavior – messy. Character traits – cleanliness. Monsters. Rhyming text.

100th day worries ill. by Arthur Howard. Simon & Schuster, 2000. ISBN 978-0-689-82979-6 Subj: Counting, numbers. School.

Please play safe! Penguin's guide to playground safety ill. by Will Hillenbrand. Scholastic, 2006. ISBN 978-0-439-52832-0 Subj: Activities – playing. Birds – penguins. Safety.

Princess Bess gets dressed ill. by Heather Maione. Simon & Schuster, 2009. ISBN 978-1-4169-3833-0 Subj: Clothing. Rhyming text. Royalty – princesses.

Road signs: a harey race with a tortoise (Aesop)

Skeleton for dinner ill. by Will Terry. Whitman, 2013. ISBN 978-0-8075-7398-3 Subj: Anatomy – skeletons. Behavior – misunderstanding. Rhyming text. Witches.

Skeleton hiccups ill. by S. D. Schindler. Simon & Schuster, 2002. ISBN 978-0-689-84770-7 Subj: Anatomy – skeletons. Ghosts. Hiccups.

Stop drop and roll ill. by Arthur Howard. Simon & Schuster, 2001. ISBN 978-0-689-84355-6 Subj: Behavior – worrying. Emotions – fear. Fire. Safety. School.

That's good! That's bad! ill. by David Catrow. Holt, 1991. ISBN 978-0-8050-1535-5 Subj: Animals. Zoos.

That's good! That's bad! In Washington, D.C. ill. by Michael Garland. Holt, 2007. ISBN 978-0-8050-7727-8 Subj: Geography. School – field trips.

We're going on a lion hunt ill. by Joe Mathieu. Marshall Cavendish, 2008. ISBN 978-0-7614-5454-0 Subj: Animals – lions. Games. Participation. School. Sports – hunting.

Cyrus, Kurt. *Big rig bugs* ill. by author. Walker, 2010. ISBN 978-0-8027-8674-6 Subj: Insects. Rhyming text. Trucks.

Tadpole Rex ill. by author. Harcourt, 2008. ISBN 978-0-15-205990-3 Subj: Dinosaurs. Frogs & toads. Rhyming text.

The voyage of turtle Rex ill. by author. Harcourt, 2011. ISBN 978-0-547-42924-3 Subj: Dinosaurs. Reptiles – turtles, tortoises. Rhyming text.

Czech, Jan M. *An American face* ill. by Frances Clancy. Child & Family Pr., 2000. ISBN 978-0-87868-718-3 Subj: Adoption. Ethnic groups in the U.S. – Korean Americans.

Czekaj, Jef. *A call for a new alphabet* ill. by author. Charlesbridge, 2011. ISBN 978-1-58089-228-5 Subj: ABC books. Humorous stories.

Cat secrets ill. by author. HarperCollins, 2011. ISBN 978-0-06-192088-2 Subj: Animals – cats. Humorous stories.

Hip and Hop, don't stop! ill. by author. Hyperion/Disney, 2010. ISBN 978-1-4231-1664-6 Subj: Animals – rabbits. Contests. Music. Reptiles – turtles, tortoises.

Oink-a-doodle-moo ill. by author. HarperCollins, 2012. ISBN 978-0-06-206011-2 Subj: Animals. Circular tales. Farms. Noise, sounds.

Yes, yes, Yaul! a Hip and Hop book ill. by author. Hyperion/Disney, 2012. ISBN 978-1-4231-4682-7 Subj: Animals – porcupines. Animals – rabbits. Behavior. Music. Reptiles – turtles, tortoises.

Czernecki, Stefan. *Huevos rancheros* ill. by author. Crocodile, 2002. ISBN 978-1-56656-428-1 Subj: Animals – coyotes. Birds – chickens. Character traits – cleverness.

Paper lanterns ill. by author. Talewinds, 2000. ISBN 978-1-57091-410-2 Subj: Character traits – persistence. Foreign lands – China. Paper.

DaCosta, Barbara. *Nighttime Ninja* ill. by Ed Young. Little, Brown, 2012. ISBN 978-0-316-20384-5 Subj: Bedtime. Ethnic groups in the U.S. – Japanese Americans. Family life – mothers. Imagination. Night. Sports – martial arts.

da Costa, Deborah. *Hanukkah moon* ill. by Gosia Mosz. Kar-Ben, 2007. ISBN 978-1-58013-244-2 Subj: Ethnic groups in the U.S. – Mexican Americans. Family life. Holidays – Hanukkah. Holidays – Rosh Kodesh.

Snow in Jerusalem ill. by Cornelius Van Wright and Ying-Hwa Hu. Whitman, 2001. ISBN 978-0-8075-7521-5 Subj: Animals – cats. Foreign lands – Israel. Weather – snow.

Daddo, Andrew. *Goodnight, me* ill. by Emma Quay. Bloomsbury, 2007. ISBN 978-1-59990-153-4 Subj: Animals – orangutans. Bedtime.

Dahl, Michael. *Bear says "thank you"* ill. by Oriol Vidal. Picture Window, 2012. ISBN 978-1-4048-6786-4 Subj: Animals – bears. Etiquette. Family life – mothers. Format, unusual – board books.

Downhill fun ill. by Todd Ouren. Picture Window, 2004. ISBN 978-1-4048-0579-8 Subj: Counting, numbers. Picture puzzles. Seasons – winter. Sports – skiing.

Eggs and legs ill. by Todd Ouren. Picture Window, 2005. ISBN 978-1-4048-0945-1 Subj: Counting, numbers. Eggs. Picture puzzles.

Footprints in the snow ill. by Todd Ouren. Picture Window, 2004. ISBN 978-1-4048-0946-8 Subj: Counting, numbers. Picture puzzles. Seasons – winter. Weather – snow.

From the garden ill. by Todd Ouren. Picture Window, 2004. ISBN 978-1-4048-0578-1 Subj: Counting, numbers. Food. Gardens, gardening. Picture puzzles. Seasons.

Goodnight baseball ill. by Christina Forshay. Capstone, 2013. ISBN 978-1-62370-000-3 Subj: Bedtime. Family life – fathers. Rhyming text. Sports – baseball.

Hands down ill. by Todd Ouren. Picture Window, 2004. ISBN 978-1-4048-0948-2 Subj: Counting, numbers. Picture puzzles.

Hippo says "excuse me." ill. by Oriol Vidal. Picture Window, 2012. ISBN 978-1-4048-6787-1 Subj: Animals. Animals – hippopotamuses. Etiquette. Format, unusual – board books.

If you were an adjective ill. by Sara Gray. Picture Window, 2006. ISBN 978-1-4048-1356-4 Subj: Language.

Lots of ladybugs! ill. by Todd Ouren. Picture Window, 2005. ISBN 978-1-4048-0944-4 Subj: Counting, numbers. Insects – ladybugs.

Nap time for Kitty ill. by Oriol Vidal. Capstone, 2011. ISBN 978-1-4048-5216-7 Subj: Animals – cats. Format, unusual – board books. Sleep.

On the launch pad ill. by Todd Ouren. Picture Window, 2004. ISBN 978-1-4048-0581-1 Subj: Counting, numbers. Space & space ships.

One big building ill. by Todd Ouren. Picture Window, 2004. ISBN 978-1-4048-0580-4 Subj: Counting, numbers. Machines. Picture puzzles.

One checkered flag ill. by Todd Ouren. Picture Window, 2004. ISBN 978-1-4048-0576-7 Subj: Automobiles. Counting, numbers. Sports – racing.

One giant splash ill. by Todd Ouren. Picture Window, 2004. ISBN 978-1-4048-0577-4 Subj: Animals. Counting, numbers. Fish. Sea & seashore.

Pie for piglets ill. by Todd Ouren. Picture Window, 2005. ISBN 978-1-4048-0943-7 Subj: Animals – pigs. Counting, numbers.

Starry arms ill. by Todd Ouren. Picture Window, 2004. ISBN 978-1-4048-0947-5 Subj: Animals. Counting, numbers. Sea & seashore.

Dahl, Roald. *The enormous crocodile* ill. by Quentin Blake. Knopf, 1978. ISBN 978-0-394-93594-2 Subj: Animals. Reptiles – alligators, crocodiles.

The giraffe and the pelly and me ill. by Quentin Blake. Farrar, 1985. ISBN 978-0-374-32602-9 Subj: Activities – working. Animals. Careers – window cleaners. Crime.

Dahlie, Elizabeth. *Bernelly and Harriet: the country mouse and the city mouse* ill. by author. Little, 2002. ISBN 978-0-316-60811-4 Subj: Animals – mice. Cities, towns. Country. Family life – cousins. Folk & fairy tales.

Dakos, Kalli. *Our principal promised to kiss a pig* by Kalli Dakos and Alicia DesMarteau ill. by Carl DiRocco. Whitman, 2004. ISBN 978-0-8075-6629-9 Subj: Animals – pigs. Books, reading. Careers – school principals. School.

Dale, Penny. *The boy on the bus* ill. by author. Candlewick, 2007. ISBN 978-0-7636-3381-3 Subj: Animals. Buses. Songs.

Dinosaur dig! ill. by author. Candlewick, 2011. ISBN 978-0-7636-5871-7 Subj: Careers – construction workers. Counting, numbers. Dinosaurs. Trucks.

Dinosaur rescue! ill. by author. Candlewick, 2013. ISBN 978-0-7636-6829-7 Subj: Dinosaurs. Trains.

Dinosaur zoom! ill. by author. Candlewick, 2012. ISBN 978-0-7636-6448-0 Subj: Automobiles. Birthdays. Dinosaurs. Parties. Transportation.

Dalgleish, Sharon. *Working dogs* ill. with photos. Chelsea, 2005. ISBN 978-0-7910-8275-1 Subj: Animals – dogs. Animals – service animals. Farms.

Dalgliesh, Alice. *The Thanksgiving story* ill. by Helen Moore Sewell. Scribners, 1987, ©1954. ISBN 978-0-684-18999-4 Subj: Caldecott award honor books. Holidays – Thanksgiving. Pilgrims. U.S. history.

Dallas-Conte, Juliet. *Cock-a-moo-moo* ill. by Alison Bartlett. Little, 2001. ISBN 978-0-316-60505-2 Subj: Animals. Birds – chickens. Farms. Noise, sounds.

Daly, Catherine. *Whiskers* ill. by Thomas Leonard. Golden, 2000. ISBN 978-0-307-46214-5 Subj: Animals. Hair.

Daly, Cathleen. *Prudence wants a pet* ill. by Stephen Michael King. Roaring Brook, 2011. ISBN 978-1-59643-468-4 Subj: Character traits – persistence. Imagination. Pets.

Daly, Jude. *Fair, brown and trembling: an Irish Cinderella story* ill. by author. Farrar, 2000. ISBN 978-0-374-32247-2 Subj: Family life – stepfamilies. Folk & fairy tales. Foreign lands – Ireland. Royalty – princes. Sibling rivalry.

Daly, Niki. *The dinosaurs are back and it's all your fault, Edward!* (Hartmann, Wendy)

Happy birthday, Jamela! ill. by author. Farrar, 2006. ISBN 978-0-374-32842-9 Subj: Birthdays. Clothing – shoes. Foreign lands – South Africa.

The herd boy ill. by author. Eerdmans, 2012. ISBN 978-0-8028-5417-9 Subj: Careers – shepherds. Character traits – ambition. Foreign lands – South Africa. Hope.

Jamela's dress ill. by author. Farrar, 1999. ISBN 978-0-374-33667-7 Subj: Clothing – dresses. Foreign lands – South Africa.

Next stop — Zanzibar Road! ill. by author. Clarion, 2012. ISBN 978-0-547-68852-7 Subj: Animals. Animals – elephants. Foreign lands – Africa. Shopping. Stores.

No more kisses for Bernard! ill. by author. Frances Lincoln, 2012. ISBN 978-1-84780-105-0 Subj: Family life – aunts, uncles. Kissing.

Not so fast Songololo ill. by author. Atheneum, 1986. ISBN 978-0-689-50367-2 Subj: Cities, towns. Family life – grandmothers. Foreign lands – Africa. Foreign lands – South Africa. Shopping.

Old Bob's brown bear ill. by author. Farrar, 2002. ISBN 978-0-374-35612-5 Subj: Family life – grandfathers. Toys. Toys – bears.

Once upon a time ill. by author. Farrar, 2003. ISBN 978-0-374-35633-0 Subj: Books, reading. Foreign lands – South Africa. Friendship. School.

Pretty Salma: a Little Red Riding Hood story from Africa ill. by author. Houghton, 2007. ISBN 978-0-618-72345-4 Subj: Animals – dogs. Behavior – trickery. Folk & fairy tales. Foreign lands – Africa.

Ruby sings the blues ill. by author. Bloomsbury, 2005. ISBN 978-1-58234-995-4 Subj: Activities – singing. Music. Noise, sounds.

A song for Jamela ill. by author. Frances Lincoln, 2010. ISBN 978-1-84507-871-3 Subj: Beauty shops. Foreign lands – South Africa.

Welcome to Zanzibar Road ill. by author. Houghton, 2006. ISBN 978-0-618-64926-6 Subj: Animals. Animals – elephants. Birds – chickens. Emotions – loneliness. Foreign lands – Africa. Homes, houses.

What's cooking, Jamela? ill. by author. Farrar, 2001. ISBN 978-0-374-35602-6 Subj: Birds – chickens. Emotions. Foreign lands – South Africa. Holidays – Christmas. Pets.

Why the sun and moon live in the sky ill. by author. Lothrop, 1995. ISBN 978-0-688-13332-0 Subj: Folk & fairy tales. Foreign lands – Nigeria. Moon. Sea & seashore. Sun.

D'Amico, Carmela. *Ella sets sail* by Carmela D'Amico and Steven D'Amico ill. by Steven D'Amico. Scholastic, 2008. ISBN 978-0-439-83155-0 Subj: Animals – elephants. Character traits – luck. Fairs, festivals. Weather – storms.

Ella sets the stage by Carmela D'Amico and Steven D'Amico ill. by Steven D'Amico. Scholastic, 2006. ISBN 978-0-439-83152-9 Subj: Animals – elephants. Character traits – shyness. School. Theater.

Ella takes the cake by Carmela D'Amico and Steven D'Amico ill. by Steven D'Amico. Scholastic, 2005. ISBN 978-0-439-62794-8 Subj: Animals – elephants. Character traits – helpfulness.

Ella, the elegant elephant by Carmela D'Amico and Steven D'Amico ill. by Steven D'Amico. Scholastic, 2004. ISBN 978-0-439-62792-4 Subj: Animals – elephants. Behavior – bullying, teasing. Clothing – hats. Moving. School – first day.

Suki and Mirabella by Carmela D'Amico and Steven D'Amico ill. by Steven D'Amico. Dial, 2013. ISBN 978-0-8037-3740-2 Subj: Animals – rabbits. Behavior – bossy. Family life – cousins.

Suki the very loud bunny by Carmela D'Amico and Steven D'Amico ill. by Steven D'Amico. Penguin, 2011. ISBN 978-0-525-42230-3 Subj: Animals – rabbits. Behavior – lost.

D'Amico, Steven. *Ella sets sail* (D'Amico, Carmela)

Ella sets the stage (D'Amico, Carmela)

Ella takes the cake (D'Amico, Carmela)

Ella, the elegant elephant (D'Amico, Carmela)

Suki and Mirabella (D'Amico, Carmela)

Suki the very loud bunny (D'Amico, Carmela)

Damjan, Mischa. *The little seahorse and the Christmas pearl* ill. by Alexander Reichstein. NorthSouth, 2001. ISBN 978-0-7358-1506-3 Subj: Fish – seahorses. Holidays – Christmas. Religion – Nativity.

Daniels, Teri. *G-Rex* ill. by Tracey Campbell Pearson. Orchard, 2000. ISBN 978-0-531-33243-6 Subj: Dinosaurs. Family life – brothers.

Just enough ill. by Harley Jessup. Viking, 2000. ISBN 978-0-670-88873-3 Subj: Rhyming text. Self-concept.

Math man ill. by Timothy Bush. Orchard, 2001. ISBN 978-0-439-29308-2 Subj: Counting, numbers. School.

Dann, Penny. *Eensy weensy spider* ill. by author. Barron's, 2003. ISBN 978-0-7641-5662-5 Subj: Format, unusual – board books. Games. Nursery rhymes. Songs. Spiders.

Danneberg, Julie. *The big test* ill. by Judy Love. Charlesbridge, 2011. ISBN 978-1-58089-360-2 Subj: Emotions – fear. School.

Cowboy Slim ill. by Margot Apple. Charlesbridge, 2006. ISBN 978-1-58089-045-8 Subj: Activities – writing. Cowboys, cowgirls. Poetry. Self-concept.

First day jitters ill. by Judy Love. Charlesbridge, 2000. ISBN 978-1-58089-054-0 Subj: Careers – teachers. School – first day.

First year letters ill. by Judy Love. Charlesbridge, 2003. ISBN 978-1-58089-084-7 Subj: Careers – teachers. Letters, cards. School.

Last day blues ill. by Judy Love. Charlesbridge, 2006. ISBN 978-1-58089-046-5 Subj: Careers – teachers. Gifts. School.

Danticat, Edwidge. *Eight days: a story of Haiti* ill. by Alix Delinois. Scholastic, 2010. ISBN 978-0-545-27849-2 Subj: Character traits – bravery. Earthquakes. Foreign lands – Haiti.

D'Antonio, Nancy. *Our baby from China* ill. by author. Whitman, 1997. ISBN 978-0-8075-6162-1 Subj: Adoption. Ethnic groups in the U.S. – Chinese Americans. Family life. Foreign lands – China.

Darbyshire, Kristen. *Put it on the list!* ill. by author. Dutton, 2009. ISBN 978-0-525-47906-2 Subj: Activities – writing. Birds – chickens. Family life. Shopping.

D'Arc, Karen Scourby. *My grandmother is a singing Yaya* ill. by Diane Palmisciano. Orchard, 2001. ISBN 978-0-531-33323-5 Subj: Activities – singing. Ethnic groups in the U.S. – Greek Americans. Family life – grandmothers.

Darrow, Sharon. *Old Thunder and Miss Raney* ill. by Kathryn Brown. DK, 2000. ISBN 978-0-7894-2619-2 Subj: Animals – horses, ponies. Contests. Fairs, festivals. Food.

Yafi's family: an Ethiopian boy's journey of love, loss, and adoption (Pettitt, Linda)

Daugherty, James Henry. *Andy and the lion* ill. by author. Viking, 1938. ISBN 978-0-670-12433-6 Subj: Animals – lions. Caldecott award honor books. Character traits – kindness to animals. Humorous stories. Libraries.

D'Aulaire, Edgar Parin *see* Aulaire, Edgar Parin d'

D'Aulaire, Ingri Mortenson *see* Aulaire, Ingri Mortenson d'

Davenier, Christine. *It's raining, it's pouring* ill. by author. Imagine, 2012. ISBN 978-1-936140-77-0 Subj: Games. Rhyming text. Songs.

Davey, Owen. *Night Knight* ill. by author. Candlewick, 2012. ISBN 978-0-7636-5838-0 Subj: Bedtime. Imagination. Knights.

Davick, Linda. *I love you, nose! I love you, toes!* ill. by author. Simon & Schuster, 2013. ISBN 978-1-4424-6037-9 Subj: Anatomy. Rhyming text.

David, Lawrence. *Full moon* (Wilcox, Brian)

The land of the hungry armadillos ill. by Frédérique Bertrand. Doubleday, 2000. ISBN 978-0-385-32698-8 Subj: Animals – armadillos. Behavior – greed. Family life – brothers & sisters. Monsters.

Peter Claus and the naughty list ill. by Delphine Durand. Doubleday, 2001. ISBN 978-0-385-32654-4 Subj: Behavior. Holidays – Christmas. Santa Claus.

Superhero Max ill. by Tara Calahan King. Doubleday, 2002. ISBN 978-0-385-32746-6 Subj: Clothing – costumes. Holidays – Halloween.

David, Ryan. *The magic raincoat* ill. by Sibylla Benatova. Boyds Mills, 2007. ISBN 978-1-932425-68-0 Subj: Clothing – coats. Magic.

Davidson, Ellen Dee. *Princess Justina Albertina: a cautionary tale* ill. by Michael Chesworth. Charlesbridge, 2007. ISBN 978-1-57091-652-6 Subj: Character traits – selfishness. Character traits – willfulness. Pets. Royalty – princesses.

Davidson, Rebecca Piatt. *All the world's a stage* ill. by Anita Lobel. Greenwillow, 2003. ISBN 978-0-06-029627-8 Subj: Careers – writers. Cumulative tales. Rhyming text. Theater.

Davies, Gill. *Can't, don't, won't* by Gill Davies and Rachael O'Neill ill. by Rachael O'Neill. Sterling, 2001. ISBN 978-0-8069-7841-3 Subj: Behavior – misbehavior. Behavior – running away. Birds – penguins. Character traits – laziness.

Tiny's big wish by Gill Davies and Rachael O'Neill ill. by Rachael O'Neill. Sterling, 2001. ISBN 978-0-8069-7839-0 Subj: Animals – elephants. Behavior – growing up.

Wilbur waited by Gill Davies and Rachael O'Neill ill. by Rachael O'Neill. Sterling, 2001. ISBN 978-0-8069-7843-7 Subj: Animals – tigers. Babies. Family life – brothers & sisters. Family life – new sibling. Sibling rivalry.

Davies, Jacqueline. *The boy who drew birds: a story of John James Audubon* ill. by Melissa Sweet. Houghton, 2004. ISBN 978-0-618-24343-3 Subj: Birds. Careers – artists. Careers – ornithologists. Science.

The house takes a vacation ill. by Lee White. Marshall Cavendish, 2007. ISBN 978-0-7314-5331-4 Subj: Activities – vacationing. Homes, houses. Sea & seashore.

The night is singing ill. by Kyrsten Brooker. Penguin, 2006. ISBN 978-0-8037-3004-5 Subj: Bedtime. Country. Lullabies. Night. Noise, sounds. Rhyming text.

Tricking the Tallyman ill. by S. D. Schindler. Knopf, 2009. ISBN 978-0-375-83909-2 Subj: Counting, numbers. U.S. history.

Davies, Matt. *Ben rides on* ill. by author. Roaring Brook, 2013. ISBN 978-1-59643-794-4 Subj: Behavior – bullying, teasing. Crime. Sports – bicycling.

Davies, Nicola. *Bat loves the night* ill. by Sarah Fox-Davies. Candlewick, 2001. ISBN 978-0-7636-1202-3 Subj: Animals – bats. Night.

Dolphin baby! ill. by Brita Granström. Candlewick, 2012. ISBN 978-0-7636-5548-8 Subj: Animals – babies. Animals – dolphins.

Ice bear: in the steps of the polar bear ill. by Gary Blythe. Candlewick, 2005. ISBN 978-0-7636-2759-1 Subj: Animals – polar bears.

Just ducks! ill. by Salvatore Rubbino. Candlewick, 2012. ISBN 978-0-7636-5936-3 Subj: Birds – ducks. Nature.

Oceans and seas ill. with photos. Kingfisher, 2004. ISBN 978-0-7534-5758-0 Subj: Ecology. Sea & seashore.

One tiny turtle ill. by Jane Chapman. Candlewick, 2001. ISBN 978-0-7636-1549-9 Subj: Reptiles – turtles, tortoises. Sea & seashore.

White owl, barn owl ill. by Michael Foreman. Candlewick, 2007. ISBN 978-0-7636-3364-6 Subj: Birds – owls. Family life – grandfathers. Night.

Davies, Sarah. *Happy to be girls* ill. by Jenny Mattheson. Penguin, 2005. ISBN 978-0-399-23983-0 Subj: Rhyming text. Self-concept.

Davies, Stephen. *Don't spill the milk!* ill. by Christopher Corr. Andersen, 2013. ISBN 978-1-46772-028-1 Subj: Character traits – responsibility. Emotions – love. Foreign lands – Africa.

Davis, Anne. *No dogs allowed!* ill. by author. HarperCollins, 2011. ISBN 978-0-06-075353-5 Subj: Animals – cats. Animals – dogs. Character traits – kindness to animals. Friendship.

Davis, Aubrey. *Bagels from Benny* ill. by Dusan Petricic. Kids Can, 2003. ISBN 978-1-55337-417-6 Subj: Family life – grandfathers. Folk & fairy tales. Food. Foreign lands – Spain. Jewish culture. Religion.

A hen for Izzy Pippik ill. by Marie Lafrance. Kids Can, 2012. ISBN 978-1-55453-243-8 Subj: Behavior – lost & found possessions. Birds – chickens. Character traits – perseverance. Folk & fairy tales.

Kishka for Koppel ill. by Sheldon Cohen. Orca, 2011. ISBN 978-1-55469-299-6 Subj: Behavior – wishing. Character traits – foolishness. Folk & fairy tales. Jewish culture.

Davis, Caroline. *My little rocking horse lullabies* ill. by author. Simon & Schuster, 2002. ISBN 978-0-689-84687-8 Subj: Format, unusual – board books. Lullabies.

My little rowboat ill. by author. Simon & Schuster, 2002. ISBN 978-0-689-84686-1 Subj: Format, unusual – board books. Nursery rhymes. Transportation.

Davis, David. *Fandango stew* ill. by Ben Galbraith. Sterling, 2011. ISBN 978-1-4027-6527-8 Subj: Behavior – trickery. Character traits – cleverness. Folk & fairy tales. Food. U.S. history – frontier & pioneer life.

Jazz cats ill. by Chuck Galey. Pelican, 2001. ISBN 978-1-56554-859-6 Subj: Animals – cats. Music. Rhyming text.

Davis, Jacky. *The amazing adventures of Bumblebee Boy* (Soman, David)

Ladybug Girl (Soman, David)

Ladybug Girl and Bingo (Soman, David)

Ladybug Girl and Bumblebee Boy (Soman, David)

Ladybug Girl and the big snow (Soman, David)

Ladybug Girl and the Bug Squad (Soman, David)

Ladybug Girl at the beach (Soman, David)

Davis, Jerry. *Little Chicken's big day* by Jerry Davis and Katie Davis ill. by Katie Davis. Simon & Schuster, 2011. ISBN 978-1-4424-1401-3 Subj: Behavior – lost. Birds – chickens. Family life – mothers.

Davis, Jill. *Orangutans are ticklish: fun facts from an animal photographer* photos by Steve Grubman. Random House, 2010. ISBN 978-0-375-85886-4 Subj: Activities – photographing. Animals. Careers – photographers.

Davis, Kate. *Barnyard babies* ill. by C. D. Hullinger. Innovative KIDS, 2001. ISBN 978-1-58476-061-0 Subj: Animals – babies. Format, unusual – toy & movable books. Picture puzzles.

Davis, Katie. *Kindergarten rocks!* ill. by author. Harcourt, 2005. ISBN 978-0-15-204932-4 Subj: Emotions – fear. School – first day.

Little Chicken's big day (Davis, Jerry)

Mabel the Tooth Fairy and how she got her job ill. by author. Harcourt, 2003. ISBN 978-0-15-216307-5 Subj: Careers – dentists. Fairies. Humorous stories. Teeth.

Scared stiff ill. by author. Harcourt, 2001. ISBN 978-0-15-202305-8 Subj: Emotions – fear. Witches.

Who hoots? ill. by author. Harcourt, 2002. ISBN 978-0-15-216616-8 Subj: Animals. Noise, sounds.

Davis, Kenneth C. *Don't know much about the pioneers* ill. by Renée Williams-Andriani. HarperCollins, 2003. ISBN 978-0-06-028618-7 Subj: Activities – traveling. U.S. history – frontier & pioneer life.

Davis, Lee. *Feeding time* photos by author. DK, 2001. ISBN 978-0-7894-7358-5 Subj: Animals. Food.

Davis, Nancy. *A garden of opposites* ill. by author. Random House, 2009. ISBN 978-0-375-85666-2 Subj: Concepts – opposites. Format, unusual – toy & movable books. Gardens, gardening.

Davis, Patricia Anne. *Brian's bird* ill. by Layne Johnson. Whitman, 2000. ISBN 978-0-8075-0881-7 Subj: Birds – parakeets, parrots. Family life – brothers. Disabilities – blindness. Pets.

Davol, Marguerite W. *The loudest, fastest, best drummer in Kansas* ill. by Cat Bowman Smith. Orchard, 2000. ISBN 978-0-531-33191-0 Subj: Musical instruments – drums. Noise, sounds. Tall tales.

The snake's tales ill. by Yumi Heo. Orchard, 2002. ISBN 978-0-439-31769-6 Subj: Activities – storytelling. Reptiles – snakes.

Why butterflies go by on silent wings ill. by Rob Roth. Orchard, 2001. ISBN 978-0-531-33322-8 Subj: Insects – butterflies, caterpillars. Noise, sounds. Weather – storms.

Dawavendewa, Gerald. *The butterfly dance* ill. by author. Abbeville, 2001. ISBN 978-0-7892-0161-4 Subj: Activities – dancing. Indians of North America – Hopi. Weather – rain.

Dawes, Kwame Senu Neville. *I saw your face* ill. by Tom Feelings. Penguin, 2005. ISBN 978-0-8037-1894-4 Subj: Art. Ethnic groups in the U.S. – African Americans. Foreign lands – Africa. Poetry.

Day, Alexandra. *Carl goes shopping* ill. by author. Farrar, 1989. ISBN 978-0-374-31110-0 Subj: Animals – dogs. Shopping. Stores. Wordless.

Carl goes to daycare ill. by author. Farrar, 1993. ISBN 978-0-374-31093-6 Subj: Activities – playing. Animals – dogs. School – nursery.

Carl's birthday ill. by author. Farrar, 1995. ISBN 978-0-374-31144-5 Subj: Activities – babysitting. Animals – dogs. Behavior – misbehavior. Birthdays.

Carl's sleepy afternoon ill. by author. Farrar, 2005. ISBN 978-0-374-31088-2 Subj: Activities. Animals – dogs.

Carl's snowy afternoon ill. by author. Farrar, 2009. ISBN 978-0-374-31086-8 Subj: Animals – dogs. Sports – sledding. Weather – snow. Wordless.

Carl's summer vacation ill. by author. Farrar, 2008. ISBN 978-0-374-31085-1 Subj: Activities – vacationing. Animals – dogs. Lakes, ponds. Seasons – summer.

The fairy dogfather ill. by author. Laughing Elephant/Green Tiger, 2012. ISBN 978-1-59583-455-3 Subj: Animals – dogs. Humorous stories.

Follow Carl! ill. by author. Farrar, 1998. ISBN 978-0-374-34380-4 Subj: Activities – babysitting. Activities – playing. Animals – dogs. Parties. Wordless.

Frank and Ernest ill. by author. Scholastic, 1988. ISBN 978-0-590-41557-6 Subj: Animals – bears. Animals – elephants. Character traits – helpfulness. Language.

Frank and Ernest on the road ill. by author. Scholastic, 1994. ISBN 978-0-590-45048-5 Subj: Animals – bears. Animals – elephants. Careers – truck drivers. Language. Trucks.

Frank and Ernest play ball ill. by author. Scholastic, 1990. ISBN 978-0-590-42548-3 Subj: Animals – bears. Animals – elephants. Dictionaries. Language. Sports – baseball.

Good dog, Carl ill. by author. Green Tiger, 1985. ISBN 978-0-88138-062-0 Subj: Activities – babysitting. Animals – dogs. Wordless.

Special deliveries by Alexandra Day and Cooper Edens ill. by Alexandra Day. HarperCollins, 2001. ISBN 978-0-06-205152-3 Subj: Animals. Careers – postal workers. Pets.

Day, Jan. *The pirate, Pink* ill. by Janeen I. Mason. Pelican, 2001. ISBN 978-1-56554-879-4 Subj: Family life – daughters. Family life – fathers. Pirates. Sea & seashore.

Pirate Pink and treasures of the reef ill. by Janeen I. Mason. Pelican, 2003. ISBN 978-1-58980-086-1 Subj: Family life – daughters. Family life – fathers. Pirates. Sea & seashore.

Day, Marie. *Edward the "crazy man"* ill. by author. Annick, 2002. ISBN 978-1-55037-721-7 Subj: Friendship. Homeless. Illness – mental illness.

Day, Nancy Raines. *A is for alliguitar: musical alphabeasts* ill. by Herb Leonhard. Pelican, 2012. ISBN 978-1-4556-1557-5 Subj: ABC books. Musical instruments. Rhyming text.

A kitten's year ill. by Anne Mortimer. HarperCollins, 2000. ISBN 978-0-06-027231-9 Subj: Animals – cats. Days of the week, months of the year.

The lion's whiskers: an Ethiopian folktale ill. by Ann Grifalconi. Scholastic, 1995. ISBN 978-0-590-45803-0 Subj: Animals – lions. Family life – stepfamilies. Folk & fairy tales. Foreign lands – Ethiopia.

On a windy night ill. by George Bates. Abrams, 2010. ISBN 978-0-8109-3900-4 Subj: Emotions – fear. Holidays – Halloween. Weather – wind.

Day, Trevor. *Youch! it bites! real-life monsters up close* ill. with photos. Simon & Schuster, 2000. ISBN 978-0-689-83416-5 Subj: Animals. Format, unusual – toy & movable books. Monsters. Plants.

Dayrell, Elphinstone. *Why the sun and the moon live in the sky: an African folktale* ill. by Blair Lent. Houghton, 1968. Subj: Caldecott award honor books. Folk & fairy tales. Foreign lands – Africa. Moon. Sky. Sun.

Daywalt, Drew. *The day the crayons quit* ill. by Oliver Jeffers. Philomel, 2013. ISBN 978-0-399-25537-3 Subj: Behavior – dissatisfaction. Concepts – color. Letters, cards.

Deacon, Alexis. *Cheese belongs to you!* ill. by Viviane Schwarz. Candlewick, 2013. ISBN 978-0-7636-6608-8 Subj: Animals – rats. Behavior – sharing. Character traits – selfishness. Cumulative tales. Food.

A place to call home ill. by Viviane Schwarz. Candlewick, 2011. ISBN 978-0-7636-5360-6 Subj: Activities – traveling. Animals – hamsters. Homes, houses.

Slow Loris ill. by author. Kane/Miller, 2002. ISBN 978-1-929132-27-0 Subj: Animals. Animals – lorises.

While you are sleeping ill. by author. Farrar, 2006. ISBN 978-0-374-38330-5 Subj: Holidays – Christmas. Night. Sleep. Toys.

Deady, Kathleen W. *All year long* ill. by Linda Bronson. Carolrhoda, 2004. ISBN 978-1-57505-537-4 Subj: Rhyming text. Seasons.

It's time! ill. by Jill Newton. HarperCollins, 2002. ISBN 978-0-694-01565-8 Subj: Animals. Animals – babies. Animals – dogs. Farms. Rhyming text.

Out and about at the zoo ill. by Anne McMullen. Picture Window, 2003. ISBN 978-1-4048-0041-0 Subj: Animals. School – field trips. Zoos.

Dealey, Erin. *Deck the walls! a wacky Christmas carol* ill. by Nick Ward. Sleeping Bear, 2013. ISBN 978-1-58536-857-0 Subj: Food. Holidays – Christmas. Songs.

Goldie Locks has chicken pox ill. by Hanako Wakiyama. Atheneum, 2002. ISBN 978-0-689-82981-9 Subj: Family life – brothers & sisters. Illness – chicken pox. Rhyming text.

Dean, James. *Valentine's Day is cool* ill. by author. HarperCollins, 2013. ISBN 978-0-06-219865-5 Subj: Animals – cats. Holidays – Valentine's Day.

De Anda, Diane. *Dancing Miranda / Baila, Miranda, baila* ill. by Lamberto Alvarez. Piñata, 2001. ISBN 978-1-55885-323-2 Subj: Activities – dancing. Ethnic groups in the U.S. – Hispanic Americans. Family life – daughters. Family life – mothers. Foreign languages. Disabilities – physical disabilities. Illness – poliomyelitis.

A day without sugar / Un dia sin azucar ill. by Janet Montecalvo. Arte Publico/Pinata, 2012. ISBN 978-1-55885-702-5 Subj: Ethnic groups in the U.S. – Hispanic Americans. Family life – aunts, uncles. Food. Foreign languages. Health & fitness. Illness – diabetes.

The patchwork garden / pedacitos de huerto ill. by Oksana Kemarskaya. Arte Publico, 2013. ISBN 978-1-55885-763-6 Subj: Communities, neighborhoods. Family life – grandmothers. Foreign languages. Gardens, gardening.

Deans, Karen. *Playing to win: the story of Althea Gibson* ill. by Elbrite Brown. Holiday House, 2007. ISBN 978-0-8234-1926-5 Subj: Ethnic groups in the U.S. – African Americans. Sports.

DeBear, Kirsten. *Be quiet, Marina!* photos by Laura Dwight. Star Bright, 2001. ISBN 978-1-887734-79-0 Subj: Activities – playing. Friendship. Disabilities – cerebral palsy. Disabilities – Down syndrome.

Debecker, Benoît. *The naughty prince* ill. by author. Abrams, 2001. ISBN 978-0-8109-4304-9 Subj: Behavior – misbehavior. Character traits – meanness. Frogs & toads. Royalty – princes. Space & space ships.

De Beer, Hans. *Little Polar Bear and the big balloon* ill. by author. NorthSouth, 2002. ISBN 978-0-7358-1533-9 Subj: Activities – ballooning. Activities – flying. Animals – polar bears. Birds – puffins.

Little Polar Bear and the submarine ill. by author. NorthSouth, 2011. ISBN 978-0-7358-4030-0 Subj: Animals – polar bears. Boats, ships.

Little Polar Bear and the whales ill. by author. NorthSouth, 2009. ISBN 978-0-7358-2209-2 Subj: Animals – polar bears. Animals – whales. Foreign lands – Arctic.

Oh no, Ono! ill. by author. NorthSouth, 2004. ISBN 978-0-7358-1938-2 Subj: Animals – dogs. Character traits – curiosity. Farms. Humorous stories.

De Brunhoff, Jean *see* Brunhoff, Jean de

De Brunhoff, Laurent *see* Brunhoff, Laurent de

De colores / Bright with colors ill. by David Diaz. Marshall Cavendish, 2008. ISBN 978-0-7614-5431-1 Subj: Foreign languages. Seasons – spring. Songs.

Dee, Ruby. *Two ways to count to ten: a Liberian folktale* ill. by Susan Meddaugh. Holt, 1988. ISBN 978-0-8050-0407-6 Subj: Character traits – cleverness. Folk & fairy tales. Foreign lands – Africa.

Deedy, Carmen Agra. *Martina the beautiful cockroach: a Cuban folktale* ill. by Michael Austin. Peachtree, 2007. ISBN 978-1-56145-399-3 Subj: Animals – mice. Folk & fairy tales. Foreign lands – Cuba. Insects – cockroaches.

Return of the library dragon ill. by Michael P. White. Peachtree, 2012. ISBN 978-1-56145-621-5 Subj: Books, reading. Careers – librarians. Dragons. Libraries. School.

The yellow star: the legend of King Christian X of Denmark ill. by Henri Sorensen. Peachtree, 2000. ISBN 978-1-56145-208-8 Subj: Character traits – bravery. Foreign lands – Denmark. Royalty – kings. War.

Deegan, Kim. *My first book of numbers* ill. by author. Bloomsbury, 2002. ISBN 978-1-58234-755-4 Subj: Counting, numbers. Format, unusual – board books.

My first book of opposites ill. by author. Bloomsbury, 2002. ISBN 978-1-58234-756-1 Subj: Concepts – opposites. Format, unusual – board books.

DeFelice, Cynthia C. *Cold feet* ill. by Robert Andrew Parker. DK, 2000. ISBN 978-0-7894-2636-9 Subj: Behavior – trickery. Careers – musicians. Clothing – boots. Musical instruments – bagpipes.

Nelly May has her say ill. by Henry Cole. Farrar, 2013. ISBN 978-0-374-39899-6 Subj: Folk & fairy tales. Foreign lands – England. Humorous stories. Language.

One potato, two potato ill. by Andrea U'Ren. Farrar, 2006. ISBN 978-0-374-35640-8 Subj: Food. Humorous stories. Magic.

The real, true Dulcie Campbell ill. by R. W. Alley. Farrar, 2002. ISBN 978-0-374-36220-1 Subj: Books, reading. Family life. Royalty – princesses.

Degen, Bruce. *I gotta draw* ill. by author. HarperCollins, 2012. ISBN 978-0-06-028417-6 Subj: Activities – drawing. Animals – dogs. Art. School.

Degman, Lori. *1 zany zoo* ill. by Colin Jack. Simon & Schuster, 2010. ISBN 978-1-4169-8990-5 Subj: Counting, numbers. Rhyming text. Zoos.

deGroat, Diane. *Ants in your pants, worms in your plants! (Gilbert goes green)* ill. by author. HarperCollins, 2011. ISBN 978-0-06-176511-7 Subj: Animals – possums. Ecology. Holidays – Earth Day. School.

April Fool! watch out at school! ill. by author. HarperCollins, 2009. ISBN 978-0-06-143042-8 Subj: Holidays – April Fools' Day. Riddles & jokes. School.

Brand-new pencils, brand-new books ill. by author. HarperCollins, 2005. ISBN 978-0-06-072615-7 Subj: Animals – possums. School – first day.

Good night, sleep tight, don't let the bedbugs bite ill. by author. SeaStar, 2002. ISBN 978-1-58717-129-1 Subj: Animals – possums. Camps, camping. Ghosts.

Happy birthday to you, you belong in a zoo ill. by author. Morrow, 1999. ISBN 978-0-688-16545-1 Subj: Animals. Birthdays. Friendship. Gifts. Parties.

Homer by Diane deGroat and Shelley Rotner ill. by Diane deGroat. Scholastic, 2012. ISBN 978-0-545-33272-9 Subj: Animals – dogs. Dreams. Sports – baseball.

Jingle bells, homework smells ill. by author. HarperCollins, 2000. ISBN 978-0-688-17544-3 Subj: Animals. Animals – possums. Holidays – Christmas. Homework. School. Weather – snow.

Last one in is a rotten egg! ill. by author. HarperCollins, 2007. ISBN 978-0-06-089294-4 Subj: Animals – possums. Behavior – bossy. Behavior – sharing. Family life – cousins. Holidays – Easter.

Liar, liar, pants on fire ill. by author. SeaStar, 2003. ISBN 978-1-58717-215-1 Subj: Animals – possums. Behavior – lying. Character traits – honesty. School. Self-concept. Theater.

Lola the elf ill. by author. Night Sky, 2002. ISBN 978-1-59014-081-9 Subj: Animals – possums. Character traits – helpfulness. Format, unusual – toy & movable books. Holidays – Christmas. Mythical creatures – elves.

Mother, you're the best! (but Sister, you're a pest!) ill. by author. HarperCollins, 2008. ISBN 978-0-06-123899-4 Subj: Animals – possums. Character traits – helpfulness. Family life – brothers & sisters. Holidays – Mother's Day. Sibling rivalry.

No more pencils, no more books, no more teacher's dirty looks! ill. by author. HarperCollins, 2006. ISBN 978-0-06-079114-8 Subj: Careers – teachers. Friendship. School.

Roses are pink, your feet really stink ill. by author. Morrow, 1996. ISBN 978-0-688-13605-5 Subj: Animals. Behavior – misbehavior. Holidays – Valentine's Day. School.

Trick or treat, smell my feet ill. by author. Morrow, 1998. ISBN 978-0-688-15767-8 Subj: Animals. Clothing – costumes. Family life – brothers & sisters. Holidays – Halloween. School.

Delacre, Lulu. *Arroz con leche: popular songs and rhymes from Latin America* ill. by author. Scholastic, 1989. ISBN 978-0-590-42442-4 Subj: Foreign languages. Games. Music. Poetry. Songs.

How far do you love me? ill. by author. Lee & Low, 2013. ISBN 978-1-60060-882-7 Subj: Emotions – love. Nature. World.

Las Navidades: popular Christmas songs from Latin America ill. by selector. Scholastic, 1990. ISBN 978-0-590-43548-2 Subj: Foreign languages. Holidays – Christmas. Music. Poetry. Songs.

de Las Casas, Dianne. *Blue frog: the legend of chocolate* ill. by Holly Stone-Barker. Pelican, 2011. ISBN 978-1-4556-1459-2 Subj: Folk & fairy tales. Food. Foreign lands – Mexico. Indians of North America – Aztec.

The house that Witchy built ill. by Holly Stone-Barker. Pelican, 2011. ISBN 978-1-58980-965-9 Subj: Cumulative tales. Holidays – Halloween. Witches.

The Little "Read" Hen ill. by Holly Stone-Barker. Pelican, 2013. ISBN 978-1-4556-1702-9 Subj: Activities – writing. Animals. Birds – chickens. Folk & fairy tales. Language.

Mama's bayou ill. by Holly Stone-Barker. Pelican, 2010. ISBN 978-1-58980-787-7 Subj: Family life – mothers. Lullabies. Rhyming text.

There's a dragon in the library ill. by Marita Gentry. Pelican, 2011. ISBN 978-1-58980-844-7 Subj: Books, reading. Dragons. Libraries.

Delessert, Etienne. *A was an apple pie: an English nursery rhyme* ill. by author. Creative Editions, 2005. ISBN 978-1-56846-196-0 Subj: ABC books. Nursery rhymes.

Alert! ill. by author. Houghton, 2007. ISBN 978-0-618-73474-0 Subj: Animals – moles. Behavior – collecting things. Crime.

Full color ill. by author. Creative Editions, 2008. ISBN 978-1-56846-206-6 Subj: Concepts – color.

Hungry for numbers ill. by author. Creative Editions, 2006. ISBN 978-1-56846-198-4 Subj: Counting, numbers. Food.

The seven dwarfs ill. by author. Creative Editions, 2001. ISBN 978-0-439-27863-8 Subj: Dwarfs, midgets. Folk & fairy tales. Foreign lands – Germany. Forest, woods. Royalty.

de Lestrade, Agnès. *Phileas's fortune: a story about self-expression* ill. by Valeria Docampo. Magination, 2010. ISBN 978-1-4338-0790-9 Subj: Communication. Language.

Demarest, Chris L. *All aboard! a traveling alphabet* ill. by Bill Mayer. Simon & Schuster, 2008. ISBN 978-0-689-85249-7 Subj: ABC books. Transportation.

Alpha Bravo Charlie: the military alphabet ill. by author. Simon & Schuster, 2005. ISBN 978-0-689-86928-0 Subj: ABC books. Careers – military.

Firefighters A to Z ill. by author. McElderry, 2000. ISBN 978-0-689-83798-2 Subj: ABC books. Careers – firefighters. Fire. Rhyming text.

Hotshots! ill. by author. McElderry, 2003. ISBN 978-0-689-84816-2 Subj: Careers – firefighters. Fire. Forest, woods. Rhyming text.

Lindbergh ill. by author. Crown, 1993. ISBN 978-0-517-58719-5 Subj: Activities – flying. Airplanes, airports. Transportation. U.S. history.

Smokejumpers one to ten ill. by author. McElderry, 2002. ISBN 978-0-689-84120-0 Subj: Activities – flying. Careers – firefighters. Counting, numbers. Forest, woods.

Demas, Corinne. *Always in trouble* ill. by Noah Jones. Scholastic, 2009. ISBN 978-0-545-02453-2 Subj: Animals – dogs. Behavior – misbehavior. Humorous stories.

The boy who was generous with salt ill. by Michael Hays. Marshall Cavendish, 2002. ISBN 978-0-7614-5099-3 Subj: Birthdays. Careers – chefs, cooks. Careers – fishermen. Sea & seashore.

The disappearing island ill. by Ted Lewin. Simon & Schuster, 2000. ISBN 978-0-689-80539-4 Subj: Birthdays. Boats, ships. Family life – grandmothers. Islands.

Halloween surprise ill. by R. W. Alley. Walker, 2011. ISBN 978-0-8027-8612-8 Subj: Clothing – costumes. Holidays – Halloween.

Here comes trouble! ill. by Noah Jones. Scholastic, 2013. ISBN 978-0-545-35906-1 Subj: Animals – cats. Animals – dogs. Friendship.

Hurricane! ill. by Lenice Strohmeier. Marshall Cavendish, 2000. ISBN 978-0-7614-5052-8 Subj: U.S. history. Weather – hurricanes.

The magic apple ill. by Alexi Natchev. Golden, 2001. ISBN 978-0-307-46334-0 Subj: Character traits – generosity. Family life – sisters. Folk & fairy tales. Royalty – princes.

Nina's waltz ill. by Deborah Lanino. Orchard, 2000. ISBN 978-0-531-33281-8 Subj: Contests. Family life – fathers. Music. Songs.

Pirates go to school ill. by John Manders. Scholastic, 2011. ISBN 978-0-545-20629-7 Subj: Pirates. Rhyming text. School.

Two Christmas mice ill. by Stéphanie Roth. Holiday House, 2005. ISBN 978-0-8234-1785-8 Subj: Animals – mice. Holidays – Christmas. Trees.

Valentine surprise ill. by R. W. Alley. Walker, 2008. ISBN 978-0-8027-9664-6 Subj: Activities – making things. Concepts – shape. Days of the week, months of the year. Holidays – Valentine's Day.

Dematons, Charlotte. *Let's go* ill. by author. Front Street, 2001. ISBN 978-1-886910-65-2 Subj: Imagination. Stores.

Demers, Dominique. *Every single night* ill. by Nicolas Debon. Groundwood, 2006. ISBN 978-0-88899-699-2 Subj: Animals. Bedtime. Family life – fathers. Sleep.

Old Thomas and the little fairy English text by Sheila Fischman; ill. by Stéphane Poulin. Dominique & Friends, 2000. ISBN 978-1-894363-45-7 Subj: Animals – dogs. Careers – fishermen. Emotions – anger. Fairies.

Demi. *The boy who painted dragons* ill. by author. Simon & Schuster, 2007. ISBN 978-1-4169-2469-2 Subj: Activities – painting. Careers – artists. Character traits – bravery. Dragons. Emotions – fear.

The dragon's tale and other animal fables of the Chinese zodiac ill. by reteller. Holt, 1996. ISBN 978-0-8050-3446-2 Subj: Dragons. Folk & fairy tales. Foreign lands – China. Zodiac.

The empty pot ill. by author. Holt, 1990. ISBN 978-0-8050-1217-0 Subj: Character traits – honesty. Folk & fairy tales. Foreign lands – China. Gardens, gardening. Royalty – emperors.

The girl who drew a phoenix ill. by author. Simon & Schuster, 2008. ISBN 978-1-4169-5347-0 Subj: Activities – drawing. Foreign lands – China. Mythical creatures – phoenix.

The greatest treasure ill. by author. Scholastic, 1998. ISBN 978-0-590-31339-1 Subj: Folk & fairy tales. Foreign lands – China.

Joan of Arc ill. by author. Marshall Cavendish, 2011. ISBN 978-0-7614-5953-8 Subj: Foreign lands – France. Religion. War.

The legend of Saint Nicholas ill. by author. McElderry, 2003. ISBN 978-0-689-84681-6 Subj: Holidays – Christmas. Santa Claus.

The magic pillow ill. by author. Simon & Schuster, 2008. ISBN 978-1-4169-2470-8 Subj: Dreams. Foreign lands – China. Magic.

One grain of rice: a mathematical folktale ill. by author. Scholastic, 1997. ISBN 978-0-590-93998-0 Subj: Character traits – cleverness. Character traits – selfishness. Counting, numbers. Folk & fairy tales. Royalty – rajahs.

De Monfreid, Dorothee. *Dark night* ill. by author. Random House, 2009. ISBN 978-0-375-85687-7 Subj: Animals. Emotions – fear. Night.

Dempsey, Kristy. *Mini racer* ill. by Bridget Strevens-Marzo. Bloomsbury, 2010. ISBN 978-1-59990-170-1 Subj: Animals. Rhyming text. Sports – racing.

Surfer chick ill. by author. Abrams, 2012. ISBN 978-1-4197-0188-7 Subj: Birds – chickens. Character traits – confidence. Character traits – perseverance. Sports – surfing.

Dempsey, Sheena. *Bye-bye baby brother!* ill. by author. Candlewick, 2013. ISBN 978-0-7636-6241-7 Subj: Babies. Family life – brothers. Family life – new sibling. Sibling rivalry.

Denchfield, Nick. *Charlie Chick* ill. by Ant Parker. Harcourt, 2007. ISBN 978-0-15-206013-8 Subj: Birds – chickens. Format, unusual – toy & movable books.

Denega, Danielle. *Numbers* ill. by Donald Grant. Scholastic, 2001. ISBN 978-0-439-29728-8 Subj: Counting, numbers. Format, unusual – toy & movable books.

Rain or shine ill. by Pierre-Marie Valat. Scholastic, 2001. ISBN 978-0-439-29730-1 Subj: Format, unusual – toy & movable books. Weather.

Denim, Sue. *The Dumb Bunnies* ill. by Dav Pilkey. Blue Sky, 1994. ISBN 978-0-590-47798-7 Subj: Animals – rabbits. Family life.

The Dumb Bunnies' Easter ill. by Dav Pilkey. Blue Sky, 1995. ISBN 978-0-590-20241-1 Subj: Animals – rabbits. Family life. Holidays – Christmas. Holidays – Easter.

The Dumb Bunnies go to the zoo ill. by Dav Pilkey. Blue Sky, 1997. ISBN 978-0-590-84735-3 Subj: Animals. Animals – rabbits. Family life. Zoos.

Make way for Dumb Bunnies ill. by Dav Pilkey. Blue Sky, 1996. ISBN 978-0-590-58286-5 Subj: Activities. Animals – rabbits. Family life.

Denise, Anika. *Bella and Stella come home* ill. by Christopher Denise. Penguin, 2010. ISBN 978-0-399-24243-4 Subj: Moving. Toys.

Pigs love potatoes ill. by Christopher Denise. Penguin, 2007. ISBN 978-0-399-24036-2 Subj: Activities – baking, cooking. Animals – pigs. Counting, numbers. Food. Rhyming text.

Dennard, Deborah. *Bullfrog at Magnolia Circle* ill. by Kristin Kest. Soundprints, 2002. ISBN 978-1-931465-04-5 Subj: Animals. Frogs & toads. Insects. Swamps.

Hedgehog haven ill. by Robert Hynes. Soundprints, 2001. ISBN 978-1-56899-987-6 Subj: Animals – hedgehogs. Country. Ecology. Foreign lands – England. Format, unusual.

Koala country ill. by James McKinnon. Soundprints, 2000. ISBN 978-1-56899-887-9 Subj: Animals. Animals – koalas. Foreign lands – Australia. Forest, woods.

Lemur landing ill. by Kristin Kest. Soundprints, 2001. ISBN 978-1-56899-978-4 Subj: Animals

– lemurs. Foreign lands – Madagascar. Forest, woods. Science.

Dennis, Major Brian. *Nubs: the true story of a mutt, a marine and a miracle* by Major Brian Dennis and Kirby Larson. Little, Brown, 2009. ISBN 978-0-316-05318-1 Subj: Animals – dogs. Careers – military. Character traits – kindness to animals. Foreign lands – Iraq. War.

DeNoble, Augustine. *Brother Joseph* ill. by Judith Brown. Ignatius, 2000. ISBN 978-1-883937-40-9 Subj: Careers – artists. Careers – clergy.

Denslow, Sharon Phillips. *In the snow* ill. by Nancy Tafuri. HarperCollins, 2005. ISBN 978-0-06-059684-2 Subj: Animals. Seasons – winter. Weather – snow.

DePalma, Mary Newell. *Bow-wow wiggle-waggle* ill. by author. Eerdmans, 2012. ISBN 978-0-8028-5408-7 Subj: Animals – dogs. Rhyming text.

A grand old tree ill. by author. Scholastic, 2005. ISBN 978-0-439-62334-6 Subj: Ecology. Nature. Trees.

The Nutcracker doll ill. by author. Scholastic, 2007. ISBN 978-0-439-80242-0 Subj: Activities – dancing. Ballet. Holidays – Christmas. Theater.

The perfect gift ill. by author. Scholastic, 2010. ISBN 978-0-545-15402-2 Subj: Animals. Birds – parakeets, parrots. Books, reading. Family life – grandmothers. Gifts.

The strange egg ill. by author. Houghton, 2001. ISBN 978-0-618-09507-0 Subj: Animals – monkeys. Birds. Eggs. Friendship.

Uh-oh! ill. by author. Eerdmans, 2011. ISBN 978-0-8028-5372-1 Subj: Behavior – misbehavior. Dinosaurs.

dePaola, Tomie. *Angels, angels everywhere* ill. by author. Penguin, 2005. ISBN 978-0-399-24370-7 Subj: Angels.

The art lesson ill. by author. Putnam, 1989. ISBN 978-0-399-21688-6 Subj: Art. Family life. School.

The baby sister ill. by author. Putnam, 1996. ISBN 978-0-399-22908-4 Subj: Babies. Family life – grandmothers. Family life – new sibling. Family life – sisters.

Baby's first Christmas ill. by author. Putnam, 1988. ISBN 978-0-399-21591-9 Subj: Babies. Holidays – Christmas.

Big Anthony and the magic ring ill. by author. Harcourt, 1979. ISBN 978-0-15-207124-0 Subj: Character traits – appearance. Magic.

Big Anthony, his story ill. by author. Putnam, 1998. ISBN 978-0-399-23189-6 Subj: Folk & fairy tales. Foreign lands – Italy. Witches.

Bill and Pete ill. by author. Putnam, 1978. ISBN 978-0-399-20646-7 Subj: Birds – plovers. Foreign lands – Africa. Humorous stories. Reptiles – alligators, crocodiles. School.

Bill and Pete go down the Nile ill. by author. Putnam, 1987. ISBN 978-0-399-21395-3 Subj: Behavior – stealing. Birds – plovers. Foreign lands – Egypt. Museums. Reptiles – alligators, crocodiles. School.

Bill and Pete to the rescue ill. by author. Putnam, 1998. ISBN 978-0-399-23208-4 Subj: Animals. Birds – plovers. Reptiles – alligators, crocodiles.

The birds of Bethlehem ill. by author. Penguin, 2012. ISBN 978-0-399-25780-3 Subj: Birds. Religion – Nativity.

Boss for a day ill. by author. Grosset, 2002. ISBN 978-0-448-42618-1 Subj: Activities – working. Animals – dogs. Behavior – bossy. Family life – brothers & sisters. Multiple births – twins.

Brava Strega Nona! a heartwarming pop-up book ill. by author. Putnam, 2008. ISBN 978-0-399-24453-7 Subj: Foreign languages. Format, unusual – toy & movable books. Magic. Witches.

Charlie needs a cloak ill. by author. Prentice-Hall, 1973. ISBN 978-0-13-128355-8 Subj: Animals – mice. Animals – sheep. Clothing – coats. Problem solving.

The cloud book ill. by author. Holiday, 1975. ISBN 978-0-8234-0531-2 Subj: Weather – clouds.

The clown of God: an old story ill. by author. Harcourt, 1978. ISBN 978-0-15-219175-7 Subj: Foreign lands – Italy. Holidays – Christmas. Religion.

An early American Christmas ill. by author. Holiday, 1987. ISBN 978-0-8234-0617-3 Subj: Holidays – Christmas. U.S. history.

The family Christmas tree book ill. by author. Holiday, 1980. ISBN 978-0-8234-0416-2 Subj: Family life. Holidays – Christmas. Trees.

Favorite nursery tales ill. by adapter. Putnam, 1986. ISBN 978-0-399-21319-9 Subj: Folk & fairy tales. Nursery rhymes.

Fin M'Coul: the giant of Knockmany Hill ill. by author. Holiday, 1981. ISBN 978-0-8234-0384-4 Subj: Folk & fairy tales. Foreign lands – Ireland. Giants.

Get dressed, Santa! ill. by author. Grosset, 1996. ISBN 978-0-448-41258-0 Subj: Format, unusual – board books. Holidays – Christmas. Rhyming text. Santa Claus.

Hide-and-seek all week ill. by author. Grosset, 2001. ISBN 978-0-448-42545-0 Subj: Animals – dogs. Games. Multiple births – twins. School.

Jamie O'Rourke and the big potato ill. by author. Putnam, 1992. ISBN 978-0-399-22257-3 Subj:

Character traits – laziness. Folk & fairy tales. Foreign lands – Ireland. Mythical creatures – leprechauns.

Jamie O'Rourke and the pooka ill. by author. Putnam, 2000. ISBN 978-0-399-23467-5 Subj: Character traits – laziness. Foreign lands – Ireland. Mythical creatures – goblins. Mythical creatures – pooka spirit.

Jingle, the Christmas clown ill. by author. Putnam, 1992. ISBN 978-0-399-22338-9 Subj: Animals. Circus. Clowns, jesters. Foreign lands – Italy. Holidays – Christmas.

The knight and the dragon ill. by author. Putnam, 1980. ISBN 978-0-606-03327-5 Subj: Dragons. Knights. Libraries.

The Lady of Guadalupe ill. by author. Holiday, 1980. ISBN 978-0-8234-0373-8 Subj: Foreign lands – Mexico. Religion.

The legend of Old Befana ill. by author. Harcourt, 1980. ISBN 978-0-15-243816-6 Subj: Folk & fairy tales. Foreign lands – Italy. Religion.

The legend of the bluebonnet ill. by author. Putnam, 1983. ISBN 978-0-399-20937-6 Subj: Flowers. Folk & fairy tales. Indians of North America – Comanche.

The legend of the Indian paintbrush ill. by author. Putnam, 1987. ISBN 978-0-399-21534-6 Subj: Activities – painting. Flowers. Folk & fairy tales. Indians of North America – Great Plains.

Let the whole earth sing praise ill. by author. Penguin, 2011. ISBN 978-0-399-25478-9 Subj: Creation. Religion.

Little Grunt and the big egg: a prehistoric fairy tale ill. by author. Penguin, 2006. ISBN 978-0-399-24529-9 Subj: Dinosaurs. Folk & fairy tales. Pets.

Marcos: red, yellow, blue ill. by author. Putnam, 2003. ISBN 978-0-399-24010-2 Subj: Concepts – color. Family life – brothers & sisters. Foreign languages. Format, unusual – board books. Multiple births – twins.

Meet the Barkers: Morgan and Moffat go to school ill. by author. Putnam, 2001. ISBN 978-0-399-23708-9 Subj: Animals – dogs. Family life – brothers & sisters. Multiple births – twins. School – first day.

Merry Christmas, Strega Nona ill. by author. Harcourt, 1986. ISBN 978-0-15-253183-6 Subj: Foreign lands – Italy. Holidays – Christmas. Humorous stories. Magic. Witches.

My first Thanksgiving ill. by author. Putnam, 1992. ISBN 978-0-399-22327-3 Subj: Friendship. Holidays – Thanksgiving. U.S. history.

My mother is so smart ill. by author. Penguin, 2010. ISBN 978-0-399-25442-0 Subj: Family life – mothers.

Nana Upstairs and Nana Downstairs ill. by author. Putnam, 1998. ISBN 978-0-399-23108-7 Subj: Death. Emotions – grief. Family life – grandmothers. Family life – great-grandparents. Old age.

A new Barker in the house ill. by author. Putnam, 2002. ISBN 978-0-399-23865-9 Subj: Adoption. Animals – dogs. Ethnic groups in the U.S. – Hispanic Americans. Family life – brothers & sisters. Multiple births – twins.

The night of Las Posadas ill. by author. Putnam, 1999. ISBN 978-0-399-23400-2 Subj: Holidays – Christmas. Religion. Theater.

Now one foot, now the other ill. by author. Putnam, 1981. ISBN 978-0-399-20774-7 Subj: Family life – grandfathers. Illness.

Oliver Button is a sissy ill. by author. Harcourt, 1979. ISBN 978-0-15-257852-7 Subj: Activities – dancing. Ballet. Character traits – individuality.

Pancakes for breakfast ill. by author. Harcourt, 1978. ISBN 978-0-15-259455-8 Subj: Activities – baking, cooking. Food. Wordless.

Patrick: patron saint of Ireland ill. by author. Holiday, 1992. ISBN 978-0-8234-0924-2 Subj: Foreign lands – Ireland. Religion.

The popcorn book ill. by author. Holiday, 1978. ISBN 978-0-8234-0314-1 Subj: Activities – baking, cooking. Food.

The quicksand book ill. by author. Holiday, 1977. ISBN 978-0-8234-0291-5 Subj: Behavior – carelessness.

The song of Francis ill. by author. Putnam, 2009. ISBN 978-0-399-25210-5 Subj: Activities – singing. Birds. Religion.

The story of the three wise kings ill. by author. Putnam, 1983. ISBN 978-0-399-20998-7 Subj: Holidays – Christmas. Religion – Nativity.

Strega Nona: an old tale ill. by author. Prentice-Hall, 1975. ISBN 978-0-13-851600-0 Subj: Behavior – forgetfulness. Caldecott award honor books. Humorous stories. Magic. Witches.

Strega Nona meets her match ill. by author. Putnam, 1993. ISBN 978-0-399-22421-8 Subj: Folk & fairy tales. Humorous stories. Magic. Witches.

Strega Nona takes a vacation ill. by author. Putnam, 2000. ISBN 978-0-399-23562-7 Subj: Activities – vacationing. Bubbles. Witches.

Strega Nona's gift ill. by author. Penguin, 2011. ISBN 978-0-399-25649-3 Subj: Holidays. Magic. Witches.

Strega Nona's harvest ill. by author. Putnam, 2009. ISBN 978-0-399-25291-4 Subj: Gardens, gardening. Humorous stories. Magic. Witches.

Strega Nona's magic lessons ill. by author. Harcourt, 1982. ISBN 978-0-15-281785-5 Subj: Behavior – carelessness. Humorous stories. Magic. Witches.

Tom ill. by author. Putnam, 1993. ISBN 978-0-399-22417-1 Subj: Family life – grandfathers. Friendship. Names.

Tomie de Paola's Mother Goose by Tomie dePaola and Mother Goose ill. by selector. Putnam, 1985. ISBN 978-0-399-21258-1 Subj: Nursery rhymes.

Tony's bread ill. by author. Putnam, 1989. ISBN 978-0-399-21693-0 Subj: Careers – bakers. Folk & fairy tales. Food. Foreign lands – Italy.

DePrisco, Dorothea. *Snowbear's winter day* ill. by Dagmar Fehlau. Piggy Toes, 2002. ISBN 978-1-58117-133-4 Subj: Activities – playing. Animals. Animals – bears. Forest, woods. Format, unusual – toy & movable books. Seasons – winter. Weather – snow.

What will I become? ill. by Annie Lunsford. Piggy Toes, 2002. ISBN 978-1-58117-160-0 Subj: Animals – babies. Format, unusual – toy & movable books.

Who lives here? ill. by Annie Lunsford. Piggy Toes, 2002. ISBN 978-1-58117-159-4 Subj: Animals. Format, unusual – toy & movable books. Homes, houses.

Derby, Sally. *No mush today* ill. by Nicole Tadgell. Lee & Low, 2008. ISBN 978-1-60060-238-2 Subj: Ethnic groups in the U.S. – African Americans. Family life – grandmothers. Family life – new sibling.

Two fools and a horse ill. by Robert Rayevsky. Marshall Cavendish, 2002. ISBN 978-0-7614-5119-8 Subj: Behavior – lost & found possessions. Careers – peddlers. Crime.

Whoosh went the wind! ill. by Vincent Nguyen. Marshall Cavendish, 2006. ISBN 978-0-7614-5309-3 Subj: School. Tall tales. Weather – wind.

De Regniers, Beatrice Schenk. *May I bring a friend?* ill. by Beni Montresor. Atheneum, 1964. ISBN 978-0-689-20615-3 Subj: Animals. Caldecott award books. Friendship. Humorous stories. Rhyming text. Royalty.

What did you put in your pocket? ill. by Michael Grejniec. HarperCollins, 2003. ISBN 978-0-06-029029-0 Subj: Animals. Clothing. Cumulative tales. Days of the week, months of the year. Food.

De Roo, Elena. *The rain train* ill. by Brian Lovelock. Candlewick, 2011. ISBN 978-0-7636-5313-2 Subj: Night. Trains. Weather – rain.

Derrick, David G., Jr. *I'm the scariest thing in the jungle!* ill. by author. Immedium, 2013. ISBN 978-1-59702087-9 Subj: Animals – tigers. Emotions – fear. Reptiles – alligators, crocodiles.

Derrick, Patricia. *Riley the rhinoceros* ill. by J.-P. Loppo Martinez. KSB Promotions, 2007. ISBN 978-1-933818-15-3 Subj: Animals. Animals – rhinoceros. Jungle.

DeRubertis, Barbara. *Alexander Anteater's amazing act* ill. by R. W. Alley. Kane, 2010. ISBN 978-1-57565-304-4 Subj: ABC books. Animals – anteaters. School. Theater.

Bobby Baboon's banana be-bop ill. by R. W. Alley. Kane, 2010. ISBN 978-1-57565-305-1 Subj: ABC books. Animals – baboons. Counting, numbers. School.

Corky Cub's crazy caps ill. by R. W. Alley. Kane, 2010. ISBN 978-1-57565-306-8 Subj: Animals – bears. Clothing – hats. Friendship.

Dilly Dog's dizzy dancing ill. by R. W. Alley. Kane, 2010. ISBN 978-1-57565-307-5 Subj: ABC books. Activities – dancing. Animals – dogs. School.

Lulu's lemonade ill. by Paige Billin-Frye. Kane, 2000. ISBN 978-1-57565-093-7 Subj: Activities – baking, cooking. Concepts – measurement. Food.

De Sève, Randall. *Mathilda and the orange balloon* ill. by Jen Corace. HarperCollins, 2010. ISBN 978-0-06-172685-9 Subj: Animals – sheep. Self-concept. Toys – balloons.

Mi barco / Toy boat ill. by Loren Long. Juventud, 2007. ISBN 978-84-26-13657-2 Subj: Behavior – lost & found possessions. Foreign languages. Toys.

Toy boat ill. by Loren Long. Penguin, 2007. ISBN 978-0-399-24374-5 Subj: Behavior – lost & found possessions. Toys.

Desimini, Lisa. *Dot the Firedog* ill. by author. Blue Sky, 2001. ISBN 978-0-439-23322-4 Subj: Animals – dogs. Careers – firefighters.

DesMarteau, Alicia. *Our principal promised to kiss a pig* (Dakos, Kalli)

Desmoinaux, Christel. *"Hallo-what?"* ill. by author. McElderry, 2003. ISBN 978-0-689-84795-0 Subj: Holidays – Halloween. Witches.

Mrs. Hen's big surprise ill. by author. McElderry, 2000. ISBN 978-0-689-83403-5 Subj: Animals. Birds – chickens. Dinosaurs. Eggs.

Desmond, Jenni. *Red cat blue cat* ill. by author. Blue Apple, 2012. ISBN 978-1-60905-248-5 Subj: Animals – cats. Behavior – fighting, arguing. Emotions – envy, jealousy. Self-concept.

DeSpain, Pleasant. *The dancing turtle: a folktale from Brazil* ill. by David Boston. August House, 1998.

ISBN 978-0-87483-502-1 Subj: Behavior – trickery. Folk & fairy tales. Foreign lands – Brazil. Reptiles – turtles, tortoises.

Desrosiers, Sylvie. *Hocus Pocus* by Sylvie Desrosiers and Rémy Simard. Kids Can, 2011. ISBN 978-1-55453-577-4 Subj: Animals – dogs. Animals – rabbits. Character traits – cleverness. Wordless.

Hocus Pocus takes the train ill. by Rémy Simard. Kids Can, 2013. ISBN 978-1-55453-956-7 Subj: Animals – rabbits. Behavior – lost & found possessions. Careers – magicians. Format, unusual – graphic novels. Wordless.

de Varennes, Monique. *The jewel box ballerinas* ill. by Ana Juan. Random House, 2007. ISBN 978-0-375-83605-3 Subj: Friendship. Magic.

Devernay, Laetitia. *The conductor* ill. by author. Chronicle, 2011. ISBN 978-1-4521-0491-1 Subj: Careers – conductors (music). Imagination. Trees. Wordless.

De Vicq de Cumptich, Roberto. *Bembo's zoo* ill. by author. Holt, 2000. ISBN 978-0-8050-6382-0 Subj: ABC books. Animals. Zoos.

Devine, Monica. *Carry me, Mama* ill. by Pauline Paquin. Stoddart, 2001. ISBN 978-0-7737-3317-6 Subj: Activities – walking. Behavior – growing up. Family life.

Devlin, Harry. *Cranberry autumn* (Devlin, Wende)

Cranberry Christmas (Devlin, Wende)

Cranberry Easter (Devlin, Wende)

Cranberry Valentine (Devlin, Wende)

Devlin, Harry . *Cranberry Thanksgiving* (Devlin, Wende)

Devlin, Jane. *Hattie the bad* ill. by Joe Berger. Penguin, 2010. ISBN 978-0-8037-3447-0 Subj: Behavior – misbehavior.

Devlin, Wende. *Cranberry autumn* by Wende Devlin and Harry Devlin ill. by Harry Devlin. Four Winds, 1993. ISBN 978-0-02-729936-6 Subj: Character traits – helpfulness. Family life – grandmothers. Garage sales, rummage sales.

Cranberry Christmas by Wende Devlin and Harry Devlin ill. by authors. Parents' Magazine Pr., 1976. ISBN 978-0-8193-0845-0 Subj: Behavior – sharing. Character traits – helpfulness. Holidays – Christmas.

Cranberry Easter by Wende Devlin and Harry Devlin ill. by Harry Devlin. Four Winds, 1990. ISBN 978-0-02-729935-9 Subj: Behavior – worrying. Holidays – Easter.

Cranberry Halloween ill. by Harry Devlin. Four Winds, 1982. ISBN 978-0-590-07854-2 Subj: Behavior – stealing. Holidays – Halloween.

Cranberry Thanksgiving by Wende Devlin and Harry Devlin ill. by Harry Devlin. Parents' Magazine Pr., 1971. ISBN 978-0-8193-0499-5 Subj: Holidays – Thanksgiving.

Cranberry Valentine by Wende Devlin and Harry Devlin ill. by authors. Four Winds, 1986. ISBN 978-0-02-729200-8 Subj: Character traits – shyness. Holidays – Valentine's Day.

DeVorkin, David. *Pluto's secret: an icy world's tale of discovery* (Weitekamp, Margaret A.)

De Vries, Anke. *Raf* ill. by Charlotte Dematons. Boyds Mills, 2009. ISBN 978-1-59078-749-6 Subj: Animals – giraffes. Behavior – lost & found possessions. Foreign lands – Africa. Letters, cards. Toys.

De Vries, Maggie. *How sleep found Tabitha* ill. by Sheena Lott. Orca, 2002. ISBN 978-1-55143-193-2 Subj: Bedtime. Imagination. Sleep. Toys.

Dewan, Ted. *Baby gets the zapper* ill. by author. Random House, 2002. ISBN 978-0-385-74618-2 Subj: Activities – playing. Babies. Imagination. Toys.

Crispin and the 3 little piglets ill. by author. Doubleday, 2003. ISBN 978-0-385-74633-5 Subj: Animals – pigs. Babies. Family life – brothers & sisters. Family life – new sibling. Sibling rivalry.

Crispin, the pig who had it all ill. by author. Doubleday, 2000. ISBN 978-0-385-32540-0 Subj: Activities – playing. Animals – pigs. Holidays – Christmas.

One true bear ill. by author. Walker, 2009. ISBN 978-0-8027-8495-7 Subj: Careers – military. Character traits – kindness. Toys – bears.

Dewdney, Anna. *Grumpy Gloria* ill. by author. Penguin, 2006. ISBN 978-0-670-06123-5 Subj: Animals – dogs. Emotions. Rhyming text.

Llama Llama and the bully goat ill. by author. Viking, 2013. ISBN 978-0-670-01395-1 Subj: Animals – goats. Animals – llamas. Behavior – bullying, teasing. Rhyming text. School.

Llama Llama home with Mama ill. by author. Penguin, 2011. ISBN 978-0-670-01232-9 Subj: Animals – llamas. Family life – mothers. Illness. Rhyming text.

Llama Llama mad at Mama ill. by author. Penguin, 2007. ISBN 978-0-670-06240-9 Subj: Animals – llamas. Emotions – anger. Family life – mothers. Rhyming text. Shopping.

Llama Llama misses Mama ill. by author. Viking, 2009. ISBN 978-0-670-06198-3 Subj: Animals –

llamas. Emotions. Family life – mothers. Rhyming text. School – first day.

Llama, Llama red pajama ill. by author. Penguin, 2005. ISBN 978-0-670-05983-6 Subj: Animals – llamas. Bedtime. Family life – mothers. Rhyming text.

Llama Llama time to share ill. by author. Viking, 2012. ISBN 978-0-670-01233-6 Subj: Animals – llamas. Behavior – sharing. Rhyming text.

Nobunny's perfect ill. by author. Viking, 2008. ISBN 978-0-670-06288-1 Subj: Animals – rabbits. Behavior – misbehavior. Etiquette. Rhyming text.

Roly Poly pangolin ill. by author. Penguin, 2010. ISBN 978-0-670-01160-5 Subj: Animals – anteaters. Animals – endangered animals. Emotions – fear. Friendship. Rhyming text.

Dewey, Ariane. *The last laugh* (Aruego, José)

Splash! (Aruego, José)

We hide, you seek (Aruego, José)

Weird friends: unlikely allies in the animal kingdom (Aruego, José)

Dewey, Jennifer Owings. *Once I knew a spider* ill. by Jean Cassels. Walker, 2002. ISBN 978-0-8027-8700-2 Subj: Family life. Seasons – winter. Spiders.

DeWitt, Lyndia. *What will the weather be?* ill. by Carolyn Croll. HarperCollins, 1991. ISBN 978-0-06-021597-2 Subj: Weather.

Diakité, Baba Wagué. *The hatseller and the monkeys: a West African folktale* ill. by author. Scholastic, 1999. ISBN 978-0-590-96069-4 Subj: Animals – monkeys. Careers – peddlers. Clothing – hats. Folk & fairy tales. Foreign lands – Africa. Participation.

The hunterman and the crocodiles ill. by author. Scholastic, 1997. ISBN 978-0-590-89828-7 Subj: Behavior – lying. Folk & fairy tales. Foreign lands – Africa.

The magic gourd ill. by author. Scholastic, 2003. ISBN 978-0-439-43960-2 Subj: Animals – rabbits. Behavior – greed. Folk & fairy tales. Foreign lands – Mali. Royalty – kings.

Mee-an and the magic serpent: a folktale from Mali ill. by author. Groundwood, 2007. ISBN 978-0-88899-719-7 Subj: Folk & fairy tales. Foreign lands – Mali. Magic. Reptiles – snakes.

Diakité, Penda. *I lost my tooth in Africa* ill. by Baba Wagué Diakité. Scholastic, 2006. ISBN 978-0-439-66226-0 Subj: Birds – chickens. Foreign lands – Mali. Teeth.

Díaz, Katacha. *Badger at Sandy Ridge Road* ill. by Kristin Kest. Soundprints, 2005. ISBN 978-1-59249-420-0 Subj: Animals. Animals – badgers.

Carolina's gift ill. by Gredna Landolt. Soundprints, 2002. ISBN 978-1-56899-695-0 Subj: Birthdays. Family life – grandmothers. Foreign lands – Peru. Gifts.

DiCamillo, Kate. *Great joy* ill. by Bagram Ibatoulline. Candlewick, 2007. ISBN 978-0-7636-2920-5 Subj: Animals – monkeys. Character traits – helpfulness. Emotions. Holidays – Christmas. Homeless.

Louise: the adventures of a chicken ill. by Harry Bliss. HarperCollins, 2008. ISBN 978-0-06-075554-6 Subj: Birds – chickens. Pirates. Sea & seashore.

Dick Whittington and his cat. *Dick Whittington and his cat* retold by Marcia Brown; ill. by reteller. Scribners, 1950. Subj: Activities – trading. Animals – cats. Caldecott award honor books. Folk & fairy tales. Foreign lands – England. Middle Ages.

Dick Whittington and his cat retold by Margaret Hodges; ill. by Mélisande Potter. Holiday House, 2006. ISBN 978-0-8234-1987-6 Subj: Animals – cats. Folk & fairy tales. Foreign lands – England. Middle Ages.

Dickens, Charles. *The animals' Christmas carol* (Smath, Jerry)

Dickinson, Rebecca. *Over in the Hollow* ill. by Stephan Britt. Chronicle, 2009. ISBN 978-0-8118-5035-3 Subj: Counting, numbers. Holidays – Halloween. Monsters. Rhyming text.

Dickson, Louise. *The vanishing cat* ill. by Pat Cupples. Kids Can, 2001. ISBN 978-1-55337-026-0 Subj: Activities – traveling. Animals – cats. Animals – dogs. Boats, ships. Careers – detectives. Magic. Sea & seashore.

Dicmas, Courtney. *Harold finds a voice* ill. by author. Child's Play, 2013. ISBN 978-1-84643-550-8 Subj: Behavior – imitation. Birds – parakeets, parrots. Character traits – individuality. Foreign lands – France.

Diehl, David. *Goal! my soccer book* ill. by author. Sterling, 2008. ISBN 978-1-60059-241-6 Subj: Format, unusual – board books. Sports – soccer.

Dierssen, Andreas. *The old red tractor* ill. by Daniel Sohr. NorthSouth, 2006. ISBN 978-0-7358-2088-3 Subj: Emotions – envy, jealousy. Problem solving. Toys. Tractors.

Timid Timmy ill. by Felix Scheinberger. NorthSouth, 2003. ISBN 978-0-7358-1812-5 Subj: Animals – rabbits. Character traits – bravery. Character traits – honesty.

Timmy's new friend ill. by Felix Scheinberger. NorthSouth, 2004. ISBN 978-0-7358-1921-4 Subj: Animals – bears. Animals – rabbits. Behavior – forgiving. Friendship.

Diesen, Deborah. *The barefooted, bad-tempered baby brigade* ill. by Tracy Dockray. Tricycle, 2010. ISBN 978-1-58246-274-5 Subj: Babies. Humorous stories. Rhyming text.

Picture day perfection ill. by Dan Santat. Abrams, 2013. ISBN 978-1-4197-0844-2 Subj: Activities – photographing. Behavior – messy. School.

The pout-pout fish ill. by Dan Hanna. Farrar, 2008. ISBN 978-0-374-36096-2 Subj: Emotions – sadness. Fish. Friendship. Rhyming text.

The pout-pout fish in the big-big dark ill. by Dan Hanna. Farrar, 2010. ISBN 978-0-374-30798-1 Subj: Behavior – lost & found possessions. Emotions – fear. Fish. Rhyming text.

Dieterlé, Nathalie. *I am the king!* ill. by author. Orchard, 2001. ISBN 978-0-531-30324-5 Subj: Animals – rabbits. Behavior – misbehavior. Family life. Royalty – kings.

Diffily, Deborah. *Jurassic shark* ill. by Karen Carr. HarperCollins, 2004. ISBN 978-0-06-008250-5 Subj: Fish – sharks. Fossils. Science.

DiFiori, Lawrence. *Jackie and the Shadow Snatcher* ill. by author. Random House, 2006. ISBN 978-0-375-97515-8 Subj: Behavior – lost & found possessions. Crime. Shadows.

Diggs, Taye. *Chocolate me!* ill. by Shane W. Evans. Feiwel & Friends, 2011. ISBN 978-0-312-60326-7 Subj: Behavior – bullying, teasing. Character traits – individuality. Ethnic groups in the U.S. – African Americans. Family life – mothers. Self-concept.

Dijkstra, Lida. *Cute* ill. by Marije Tolman. Boyds Mills, 2007. ISBN 978-1-59078-505-8 Subj: Animals – rabbits. Self-concept.

Dijs, Carla. *Mommy, what if —?* ill. by author. Simon & Schuster, 2002. ISBN 978-0-689-84692-2 Subj: Animals. Animals – elephants. Family life – mothers. Format, unusual – toy & movable books.

Dillon, Diane. *Jazz on a Saturday night* (Dillon, Leo)

Dillon, Jana. *Lucky O'Leprechaun comes to America* ill. by author. Pelican, 2000. ISBN 978-1-56554-816-9 Subj: Ethnic groups in the U.S. – Irish Americans. Family life – aunts, uncles. Humorous stories. Mythical creatures – leprechauns.

Lucky O'Leprechaun in school ill. by author. Pelican, 2003. ISBN 978-1-58980-035-9 Subj: Moon. Mythical creatures – leprechauns. School. Space & space ships.

Dillon, Leo. *Jazz on a Saturday night* by Leo Dillon and Diane Dillon ill. by authors. Scholastic, 2007. ISBN 978-0-590-47893-9 Subj: Careers – musicians. Music.

Dineen, Jacqueline. *Lions* ill. with photos. Smart Apple Media, 2004. ISBN 978-1-58340-230-6 Subj: Animals – lions.

Dionne, Wanda. *Little Thumb* ill. by Jana Dillon. Pelican, 2000. ISBN 978-1-56554-754-4 Subj: Rhyming text. Thumb sucking.

Diouf, Sylviane A,. *Bintou's braids* ill. by Shane W. Evans. Chronicle, 2001. ISBN 978-0-8118-2514-6 Subj: Foreign lands – Africa. Hair.

DiPucchio, Kelly. *Alfred Zector, book collector* ill. by Macky Pamintuan. HarperCollins, 2010. ISBN 978-0-06-000581-8 Subj: Behavior – collecting things. Books, reading. Rhyming text.

Crafty Chloe ill. by Heather Ross. Simon & Schuster, 2012. ISBN 978-1-4424-2123-3 Subj: Activities – making things. Birthdays. Gifts.

Crafty Chloe: dress-up mess-up ill. by Heather Ross. Simon & Schuster, 2013. ISBN 978-1-4424-2124-0 Subj: Activities – making things. Clothing – costumes. Friendship. Parades.

Dinosnores ill. by Ponder Goembel. HarperCollins, 2005. ISBN 978-0-06-051578-2 Subj: Dinosaurs. Noise, sounds. Rhyming text. Sleep – snoring.

Gilbert goldfish wants a pet ill. by Bob Shea. Penguin, 2011. ISBN 978-0-8037-3394-7 Subj: Fish. Pets.

Grace for president ill. by LeUyen Pham. Hyperion, 2008. ISBN 978-0-7868-3919-3 Subj: Behavior – seeking better things. Careers. Character traits – ambition. Gender roles. School.

The sandwich swap (Rania, Queen, consort of Abdullah II, King of Jordan)

What's the magic word? ill. by Marsha Winborn. HarperCollins, 2005. ISBN 978-0-06-000579-5 Subj: Animals. Birds. Weather – wind.

Zombie in love ill. by Scott Campbell. Simon & Schuster, 2011. ISBN 978-1-4424-0270-6 Subj: Emotions – loneliness. Humorous stories. Monsters.

DiSalvo, DyAnne. *A castle on Viola Street* ill. by author. HarperCollins, 2001. ISBN 978-0-688-17691-4 Subj: Character traits – generosity. Homes, houses.

Grandpa's corner store ill. by author. HarperCollins, 2000. ISBN 978-0-688-16717-2 Subj: Communities, neighborhoods. Family life – grandfathers. Stores.

Ditchfield, Christin. *Cowlick!* ill. by Rosalind Beardshaw. Random House, 2007. ISBN 978-0-375-83540-7 Subj: Animals – bulls, cows. Character traits – appearance. Hair. Humorous stories.

DiTerlizzi, Angela. *Say what?* ill. by Joey Chou. Simon & Schuster, 2011. ISBN 978-1-4169-8694-2 Subj: Animals. Noise, sounds. Rhyming text.

DiTerlizzi, Tony. *G is for one gzonk! an alpha-number-bet book* ill. by author. Simon & Schuster, 2006. ISBN 978-0-689-85290-9 Subj: ABC books. Counting, numbers. Rhyming text.

Jimmy Zangwow's out-of-this-world, moon pie adventure ill. by author. Simon & Schuster, 2000. ISBN 978-0-689-82215-5 Subj: Food. Imagination. Moon. Space & space ships.

Ted ill. by author. Simon & Schuster, 2001. ISBN 978-0-689-83235-2 Subj: Family life – fathers. Imagination – imaginary friends.

Divakaruni, Chitra Banerjee. *Grandma and the great gourd: a Bengali folktale* ill. by Susy Pilgrim Waters. Roaring Brook, 2013. ISBN 978-1-59643-378-6 Subj: Behavior – resourcefulness. Behavior – trickery. Family life – grandmothers. Folk & fairy tales. Foreign lands – India.

Diviny, Sean. *Halloween Motel* ill. by Joe Rocco. HarperCollins, 2000. ISBN 978-0-06-028816-7 Subj: Ghosts. Holidays – Halloween. Hotels. Monsters. Rhyming text.

Dixon, Amy Jackson. *Cajun night after Christmas* (Moss, Jenny Jackson)

Dixon, Ann. *Waiting for Noël* ill. by Mark Graham. Eerdmans, 2000. ISBN 978-0-8028-5192-5 Subj: Babies. Birth. Birthdays. Family life. Holidays – Christmas.

Winter is . . . ill. by Mindy Dwyer. Alaska Northwest, 2002. ISBN 978-0-88240-543-8 Subj: Family life – brothers & sisters. Rhyming text. Seasons – winter.

Dobbins, Jan. *Driving my tractor* ill. by David Sim. Barefoot, 2009. ISBN 978-1-84686-358-5 Subj: Animals. Counting, numbers. Rhyming text. Tractors.

Docherty, Helen. *The Snatchabook* ill. by author. Sourcebooks/Jabberwocky, 2013. ISBN 978-1-4022-9082-4 Subj: Animals. Bedtime. Books, reading. Crime. Forest, woods. Rhyming text.

Docherty, Thomas. *Big scary monster* ill. by author. Candlewick, 2010. ISBN 978-0-7636-4787-2 Subj: Behavior – bullying, teasing. Concepts – size. Monsters.

To the beach ill. by author. Candlewick, 2009. ISBN 978-0-7636-4429-1 Subj: Activities – traveling. Imagination. Sea & seashore – beaches. Weather – rain.

Wash-a-bye Bear ill. by author. Candlewick, 2013. ISBN 978-0-7636-6486-2 Subj: Laundry. Rhyming text. Toys – bears.

Dockray, Tracy. *The lost and found pony* ill. by author. Feiwel & Friends, 2011. ISBN 978-0-312-59259-2 Subj: Animals – horses, ponies. Character traits – kindness to animals. Circus.

Dodd, Emma. *Best bear* ill. by author. Good Books, 2008. ISBN 978-1-56148-638-0 Subj: Bedtime. Rhyming text. Toys – bears.

Cinderelephant ill. by author. Scholastic, 2013. ISBN 978-0-545-53285-3 Subj: Animals – elephants. Folk & fairy tales. Royalty – princes.

Dog's ABC ill. by author. Dutton, 2000. ISBN 978-0-525-46837-0 Subj: ABC books. Animals – dogs.

Dog's colorful day ill. by author. Dutton, 2001. ISBN 978-0-525-46528-7 Subj: Animals – dogs. Concepts – color. Counting, numbers.

Dog's noisy day ill. by author. Dutton, 2003. ISBN 978-0-525-47015-1 Subj: Animals. Animals – dogs. Farms. Noise, sounds.

Forever ill. by author. Candlewick, 2013. ISBN 978-0-7636-7132-7 Subj: Animals – polar bears. Emotions – love. Family life – mothers.

Foxy ill. by author. HarperCollins, 2012. ISBN 978-0-06-201419-1 Subj: Animals – foxes. Behavior – mistakes. Behavior – worrying. Magic. School – first day.

Foxy in love ill. by author. HarperCollins, 2013. ISBN 978-0-06-201422-1 Subj: Animals – foxes. Emotions – love. Holidays – Valentine's Day. Magic.

I am small ill. by author. Scholastic, 2011. ISBN 978-0-545-35370-0 Subj: Birds – penguins. Character traits – smallness. Family life.

I don't want a cool cat! ill. by author. Little, Brown, 2010. ISBN 978-0-316-03674-0 Subj: Animals – cats. Rhyming text.

I don't want a posh dog ill. by author. Little, Brown, 2009. ISBN 978-0-316-03390-9 Subj: Animals – dogs. Character traits – assertiveness. Pets. Rhyming text.

I love bugs! ill. by author. Holiday House, 2010. ISBN 978-0-8234-2280-7 Subj: Insects. Rhyming text. Spiders.

Just like you ill. by author. Dutton, 2008. ISBN 978-0-525-47933-8 Subj: Animals – bears. Family life – fathers. Rhyming text.

Meow said the cow ill. by author. Scholastic, 2011. ISBN 978-0-545-31861-7 Subj: Animals. Farms. Magic. Noise, sounds.

No matter what ill. by author. Dutton, 2008. ISBN 978-0-525-47932-1 Subj: Animals – elephants. Emotions – love. Family life – mothers. Rhyming text.

What pet to get? ill. by author. Scholastic, 2008. ISBN 978-0-545-03570-5 Subj: Family life. Imagination. Pets.

Dodd, Lynley. *A dragon in a wagon* ill. by author. G. Stevens, 2000. ISBN 978-0-8368-2687-6 Subj: Animals – dogs. Imagination. Rhyming text. Toys – wagons.

Find me a tiger ill. by author. G. Stevens, 2001. ISBN 978-0-8368-2781-1 Subj: Animals. Behavior – hiding. Rhyming text.

Dodds, Dayle Ann. *Hello, sun!* ill. by Sachiko Yoshikawa. Penguin, 2005. ISBN 978-0-8037-2895-0 Subj: Clothing. Rhyming text. Weather.

The Kettles get new clothes ill. by Jill McElmurry. Candlewick, 2002. ISBN 978-0-7636-1091-3 Subj: Animals – dogs. Clothing. Shopping.

Pet wash ill. by Tor Freeman. Candlewick, 2001. ISBN 978-0-7636-0989-4 Subj: Activities – bathing. Animals. Pets. Rhyming text.

The prince won't go to bed ill. by Kyrsten Brooker. Farrar, 2007. ISBN 978-0-374-36108-2 Subj: Bedtime. Behavior – misbehavior. Rhyming text. Royalty – princes.

Teacher's pets ill. by Marylin Hafner. Candlewick, 2006. ISBN 978-0-7636-2252-7 Subj: Careers – teachers. Pets. School.

Where's Pup? ill. by Pierre Pratt. Dial, 2003. ISBN 978-0-8037-2744-1 Subj: Animals – dogs. Circus. Clowns, jesters. Format, unusual – toy & movable books. Rhyming text.

Dodgson, Charles Lutwidge *see* Carroll, Lewis

Doepker, David. *Animal babies* ill. with photos. Sterling, 2004. ISBN 978-1-4027-1717-8 Subj: Animals – babies. Format, unusual – board books.

Farm babies ill. with photos. Sterling, 2004. ISBN 978-1-4027-1714-7 Subj: Animals – babies. Farms. Format, unusual – board books. Noise, sounds.

Doerrfeld, Cori. *Penny loves pink* ill. by author. Little, Brown, 2011. ISBN 978-0-316-05458-4 Subj: Babies. Concepts – color. Family life – brothers & sisters. Family life – new sibling.

Dolenz, Micky. *Gakky Two-Feet* ill. by David Clark. Penguin, 2006. ISBN 978-0-399-24468-1 Subj: Behavior – bullying, teasing. Character traits – individuality. Prehistory.

Dollinger, Renate. *The rabbi who flew* ill. by author. Booksmythe, 2001. ISBN 978-0-945585-20-6 Subj: Activities – flying. Careers – clergy. Careers – shoemakers. Jewish culture.

Domanska, Janina. *If all the seas were one sea* ill. by author. Macmillan, 1971. ISBN 978-0-02-732540-9 Subj: Caldecott award honor books. Nursery rhymes. Sea & seashore.

Domeniconi, David. *M is for masterpiece: an art alphabet* ill. by Will Bullas. Sleeping Bear, 2006. ISBN 978-1-58536-276-9 Subj: ABC books. Art.

Dominguez, Angela. *Let's go, Hugo!* ill. by author. Dial, 2013. ISBN 978-0-8037-3864-5 Subj: Activities – flying. Birds. Emotions – fear. Foreign lands – France.

Maria had a little llama/Maria tenia una llama pequena ill. by author. Holt, 2013. ISBN 978-0-8050-9333-9 Subj: Animals – llamas. Foreign lands – Peru. Foreign languages. Rhyming text. School. Songs.

Domney, Alexis. *Splish, splat!* ill. by Alice Crawford. Second Story, 2011. ISBN 978-1-897187-88-3 Subj: Careers – artists. Disabilities – deafness. Sign language.

Donahue, Shari Faden. *The zebra-striped whale with the polka-dot tail* ill. by author. Arimax, 2001. ISBN 978-0-9634287-3-8 Subj: Animals. Imagination. Rhyming text.

Donaldson, Julia. *Charlie Cook's favorite book* ill. by Axel Scheffler. Penguin, 2006. ISBN 978-0-8037-3142-4 Subj: Books, reading. Rhyming text.

The fish who cried wolf ill. by Axel Scheffler. Scholastic, 2008. ISBN 978-0-439-92825-0 Subj: Activities – storytelling. Fish. Imagination. Rhyming text.

A gold star for Zog ill. by Axel Scheffler. Scholastic, 2012. ISBN 978-0-545-41724-2 Subj: Dragons. Knights. Rhyming text. Royalty – princesses. School.

The Highway Rat ill. by Axel Scheffler. Scholastic, 2013. ISBN 978-0-545-47758-1 Subj: Animals – rats. Crime. Rhyming text.

One mole digging a hole ill. by Nick Sharratt. Macmillan UK, 2010. ISBN 978-0-230-70647-7 Subj: Counting, numbers. Gardens, gardening. Rhyming text.

One Ted falls out of bed ill. by Anna Currey. Holt, 2006. ISBN 978-0-8050-7787-2 Subj: Bedtime. Counting, numbers. Toys. Toys – bears.

Room on the broom ill. by Axel Scheffler. Dial, 2001. ISBN 978-0-8037-2657-4 Subj: Animals. Behavior – lost & found possessions. Dragons. Rhyming text. Witches.

Stick Man ill. by Axel Scheffler. Scholastic, 2009. ISBN 978-0-545-15761-2 Subj: Holidays – Christmas. Rhyming text. Santa Claus. Trees.

Tabby McTat, the musical cat ill. by Axel Scheffler. Scholastic, 2012. ISBN 978-0-545-45168-0 Subj: Animals – cats. Music. Rhyming text.

Tyrannosaurus Drip ill. by David Roberts. Feiwel & Friends, 2008. ISBN 978-0-312-37747-2 Subj: Dinosaurs. Humorous stories. Rhyming text. Self-concept.

What the ladybug heard ill. by Lydia Monks. Holt, 2010. ISBN 978-0-8050-9028-4 Subj: Animals. Farms. Insects – ladybugs. Noise, sounds. Rhyming text.

Where's my mom? ill. by Axel Scheffler. Dial, 2008. ISBN 978-0-8037-3228-5 Subj: Animals. Animals – monkeys. Family life – mothers. Insects – butterflies, caterpillars. Rhyming text.

Doner, Kim. *On a road in Africa* ill. by author. Tricycle, 2008. ISBN 978-1-58246-230-1 Subj: Animals. Foreign lands – Kenya. Rhyming text.

Donnelly, Jennifer. *Humble pie* ill. by Stephen Gammell. Atheneum, 2002. ISBN 978-0-689-84435-5 Subj: Behavior. Behavior – greed. Folk & fairy tales. Food.

Donnelly, Liza. *Dinosaurs' Halloween* ill. by author. Scholastic, 1987. ISBN 978-0-590-41025-0 Subj: Cities, towns. Dinosaurs. Holidays – Halloween. Prehistory.

Donnio, Sylviane. *I'd really like to eat a child* ill. by Dorothée de Monfreid. Random House, 2007. ISBN 978-0-375-83761-6 Subj: Food. Reptiles – alligators, crocodiles.

Donofrio, Beverly. *Mary and the mouse, the mouse and Mary* ill. by Barbara McClintock. Random House, 2007. ISBN 978-0-375-83609-1 Subj: Animals – mice. Friendship.

Donohue, Dorothy. *Veggie soup* ill. by author. Winslow, 2000. ISBN 978-1-890817-21-3 Subj: Activities – baking, cooking. Animals. Animals – rabbits. Food. Friendship.

Donohue, Moira Rose. *Alfie the apostrophe* ill. by JoAnn Adinolfi. Whitman, 2006. ISBN 978-0-8075-0255-6 Subj: Language.

Donovan, Gail. *The copycat fish* ill. by David Austin Clar. Night Sky, 2001. ISBN 978-1-59014-018-5 Subj: Fish. Format, unusual. School.

A fishy story ill. by David Austin Clar. Night Sky, 2001. ISBN 978-1-59014-019-2 Subj: Character traits – honesty. Fish. Format, unusual. School.

Hidden treasures ill. by David Austin Clar. Night Sky, 2001. ISBN 978-1-59014-021-5 Subj: Fish. School.

Lost at sea ill. by David Austin Clar. Night Sky, 2001. ISBN 978-1-59014-020-8 Subj: Behavior – lost. Fish. Format, unusual. School.

Donovan, Sandy. *Bob the Alien discovers the Dewey Decimal System* ill. by Martin Haake. Picture Window, 2010. ISBN 978-1-4048-5757-5 Subj: Aliens. Books, reading.

Bored Bella learns about fiction and nonfiction ill. by Leeza Hernandez. Picture Window, 2010. ISBN 978-1-4048-5758-2 Subj: Behavior – boredom. Books, reading.

Karl and Carolina uncover the parts of a book ill. by Michael Mullan. Picture Window, 2010. ISBN 978-1-4048-5760-5 Subj: Books, reading.

Pingpong Perry experiences how a book is made ill. by James Christoph. Picture Window, 2010. ISBN 978-1-4048-5759-9 Subj: Books, reading.

Doodler, Todd H. *Bear in long underwear* ill. by author. Blue Apple, 2011. ISBN 978-1-60905-100-6 Subj: Animals – bears. Seasons – winter. Snowmen.

The zoo I drew ill. by author. Random House, 2009. ISBN 978-0-375-85201-5 Subj: ABC books. Rhyming text. Zoos.

Dooley, Norah. *Everybody brings noodles* ill. by Peter J. Thornton. Carolrhoda, 2002. ISBN 978-0-87614-455-8 Subj: Communities, neighborhoods. Ethnic groups in the U.S. Food. Foreign lands. Parties.

Everybody cooks rice ill. by Peter J. Thornton. Carolrhoda, 1991. ISBN 978-0-87614-412-1 Subj: Ethnic groups in the U.S. Family life. Food.

Everybody serves soup ill. by Peter J. Thornton. Carolrhoda, 2000. ISBN 978-1-57505-422-3 Subj: Activities – baking, cooking. Ethnic groups in the U.S. Food. Gifts. Weather – snow.

Dooley, Virginia. *Tubes in my ears: my trip to the hospital* ill. by Miriam Katin. Mondo, 1996. ISBN 978-1-57255-118-3 Subj: Hospitals. Illness.

Doolittle, Bev. *Reading the wild* ill. by Elise Maclay. Greenwich Workshop, 2001. ISBN 978-0-86713-061-4 Subj: Animals. Birds. Nature.

Doray, Malika. *One more Wednesday* ill. by author. Greenwillow, 2001. ISBN 978-0-06-029590-5 Subj: Animals. Death. Emotions – grief. Family life – grandmothers. Memories, memory.

Doremus, Gaetan. *Bear despair* ill. by author. Enchanted Lion, 2012. ISBN 978-1-59270-125-4 Subj: Animals. Animals – bears. Toys – bears. Wordless.

Dorfman, Craig. *I knew you could!* ill. by Christina Ong. Platt, 2003. ISBN 978-0-448-43148-2 Subj: Rhyming text. Self-concept. Trains.

Dormer, Frank W. *The obstinate pen* ill. by author. Holt, 2012. ISBN 978-0-8050-9295-0 Subj: Activities – drawing. Activities – writing. Character traits – stubbornness.

Socksquatch ill. by author. Holt, 2010. ISBN 978-0-8050-8952-3 Subj: Clothing – socks. Monsters.

Dornbusch, Erica. *Finding Kate's shoes* ill. by author. Firefly, 2001. ISBN 978-1-55037-671-5 Subj: Behavior – lost & found possessions. Clothing – shoes. Family life – mothers. Imagination. Wordless.

Dorros, Alex. *Número uno* by Alex Dorros and Arthur Dorros ill. by Susan Guevara. Abrams, 2007. ISBN 978-0-8109-5764-0 Subj: Behavior – fighting, arguing. Character traits – cooperation. Contests. Foreign languages. Humorous stories.

Dorros, Arthur. *Abuela* ill. by Elisa Kleven. Dutton, 1991. ISBN 978-0-525-44750-4 Subj: Activities – flying. Cities, towns. Ethnic groups in the U.S. Family life – grandmothers. Foreign languages.

Ant cities ill. by author. Crowell, 1987. ISBN 978-0-690-04570-3 Subj: Insects – ants. Science.

City chicken ill. by Henry Cole. HarperCollins, 2003. ISBN 978-0-06-028483-1 Subj: Animals. Birds – chickens. Cities, towns. Country. Humorous stories.

The fungus that ate my school ill. by David Catrow. Scholastic, 2000. ISBN 978-0-590-47704-8 Subj: School. Science.

Julio's magic ill. by Ann Grifalconi. HarperCollins, 2005. ISBN 978-0-06-029005-4 Subj: Activities – wood carving. Careers – woodcarvers. Contests. Foreign lands – Mexico. Friendship.

Mama and me ill. by Rudy Gutierrez. HarperCollins, 2011. ISBN 978-0-06-058160-2 Subj: Ethnic groups in the U.S. – Hispanic Americans. Family life – mothers. Foreign languages.

Número uno (Dorros, Alex)

Papa and me ill. by Rudy Gutierrez. HarperCollins, 2008. ISBN 978-0-06-058156-5 Subj: Ethnic groups in the U.S. – Hispanic Americans. Family life – fathers. Family life – sons. Foreign languages.

Radio Man / Don Radio: a story in English and Spanish. Text in English and Spanish. HarperCollins, 1993. ISBN 978-0-06-021548-4 Subj: Careers – migrant workers. Communication. Ethnic groups in the U.S. – Mexican Americans. Farms. Foreign languages. Radios.

Tonight is carnaval ill. with photos. Dutton, 1991. ISBN 978-0-525-44641-5 Subj: Fairs, festivals. Farms. Foreign lands – Peru.

When the pigs took over ill. by Diane Greenseid. Dutton, 2002. ISBN 978-0-525-42030-9 Subj: Animals – pigs. Animals – snails. Ethnic groups in the U.S. – Mexican Americans. Humorous stories. Restaurants.

Dotlich, Rebecca Kai. *A family like yours* ill. by Tammie Lyon. Boyds Mills, 2002. ISBN 978-1-56397-916-3 Subj: Family life. Poetry.

In the spin of things ill. by Karen Dugan. Boyds Mills, 2003. ISBN 978-1-56397-145-7 Subj: Concepts – motion. Poetry.

Mama loves ill. by Kathryn Brown. HarperCollins, 2004. ISBN 978-0-06-029408-3 Subj: Animals – pigs. Family life – mothers.

Papa loves ill. by Kathryn Brown. HarperCollins, 2003. ISBN 978-0-06-029406-9 Subj: Animals – pigs. Family life – fathers.

What can a crane pick up? ill. by Mike Lowery. Knopf, 2012. ISBN 978-0-375-86726-2 Subj: Machines. Rhyming text.

What is a triangle? photos by Maria Ferrari. HarperCollins, 2000. ISBN 978-0-694-01392-0 Subj: Concepts – shape.

What is round? photos by Maria Ferrari. HarperCollins, 1999. ISBN 978-0-694-01208-4 Subj: Concepts – shape. Rhyming text.

What is science? ill. by Sachiko Yoshikawa. Holt, 2006. ISBN 978-0-8050-7394-2 Subj: Poetry. Science.

What is square? photos by Maria Ferrari. HarperCollins, 1999. ISBN 978-0-694-01207-7 Subj: Concepts – shape. Rhyming text.

Doughty, Rebecca. *Oh no! Time to go! a book of goodbyes* ill. by author. Random House, 2009. ISBN 978-0-375-84981-7 Subj: Emotions. Family life. Rhyming text.

Douglas, Ann. *Before you were born* ill. by Eugenie Fernandes. Firefly, 2000. ISBN 978-1-894379-01-4 Subj: Babies. Birth. Family life. Family life – mothers.

Douglas, Erin. *Get that pest!* ill. by Wong Herbert Yee. Harcourt, 2000. ISBN 978-0-15-202548-9 Subj: Careers – farmers. Crime. Eggs. Farms.

Douglas, Richardo Keens *see* Keens-Douglas, Richardo

Dowley, Tim. *The shepherds' tale* by Tim Dowley and Peter Wyart ill. by Martin Pierce. Kregel, 2002. ISBN 978-0-8254-7257-2 Subj: Format, unusual –

toy & movable books. Holidays – Christmas. Religion – Nativity.

The wise men's tale by Tim Dowley and Peter Wyart ill. by Martin Pierce. Kregel, 2002. ISBN 978-0-8254-7256-5 Subj: Format, unusual – toy & movable books. Holidays – Christmas. Religion – Nativity.

Downard, Barry, reteller. *The Race of the Century* ill. by reteller. Simon & Schuster, 2008. ISBN 978-1-4169-2509-5 Subj: Animals – rabbits. Humorous stories. Reptiles – turtles, tortoises. Sports – racing.

Downes, Belinda. *Baby days: a quilt of rhymes and pictures* ill. by author. Candlewick, 2006. ISBN 978-0-7636-2786-7 Subj: Babies. Poetry. Quilts. Songs.

Downey, Lisa. *The pirates of plagiarism* (Fox, Kathleen)

Downey, Lynn. *The flea's sneeze* ill. by Karla Firehammer. Holt, 2000. ISBN 978-0-8050-6103-1 Subj: Animals. Farms. Insects – fleas. Rhyming text. Sleep.

Matilda's humdinger ill. by Tim Bowers. Random House, 2006. ISBN 978-0-375-92403-3 Subj: Activities – storytelling. Animals. Animals – cats. Careers – waiters, waitresses. Restaurants.

The tattletale ill. by Pamela Paparone. Holt, 2006. ISBN 978-0-8050-7152-8 Subj: Animals – pigs. Behavior – gossip. Family life – brothers & sisters.

This is the earth that God made ill. by Benrei Huang. Augsburg Fortress, 2000. ISBN 978-0-8066-3960-4 Subj: Creation. Cumulative tales. Religion. Rhyming text.

Downie, Mary Alice. *A pioneer ABC* ill. by Mary Jane Gerber. Tundra, 2005. ISBN 978-0-88776-688-6 Subj: ABC books. Foreign lands – Canada.

Downing, Johnette. *Amazon alphabet* ill. by author. Pelican, 2011. ISBN 978-1-58980-879-9 Subj: ABC books. Foreign lands – South America. Jungle. Rivers.

Down in Louisiana: traditional song ill. by Deborah Ousley Kadair. Pelican, 2007. ISBN 978-1-58980-451-7 Subj: Animals. Counting, numbers. Songs. Swamps.

There was an old lady who swallowed some bugs ill. by adapter. Pelican, 2010. ISBN 978-1-58980-858-4 Subj: Cumulative tales. Folk & fairy tales. Frogs & toads. Insects. Songs.

Today is Monday in Louisiana ill. by Deborah Ousley Kadair. Pelican, 2006. ISBN 978-1-58980-406-7 Subj: Days of the week, months of the year. Food. Songs.

Downing, Julie. *No hugs till Saturday* ill. by author. Clarion, 2008. ISBN 978-0-618-91078-6 Subj: Days of the week, months of the year. Dragons. Family life. Hugging.

Downs, Mike. *Pig giggles and rabbit rhymes* ill. by David Sheldon. Chronicle, 2002. ISBN 978-0-8118-3114-7 Subj: Animals. Humorous stories. Riddles & jokes.

You see a circus, I see — ill. by Anik McGrory. Charlesbridge, 2005. ISBN 978-1-58089-097-7 Subj: Circus. Family life. Rhyming text.

Dowson, Nick. *Tigress* ill. by Jane Chapman. Candlewick, 2004. ISBN 978-0-7636-2325-8 Subj: Animals – babies. Animals – tigers. Behavior – growing up. Family life – mothers.

Tracks of a panda ill. by Yu Rong. Candlewick, 2007. ISBN 978-0-7636-3146-8 Subj: Animals – pandas.

Doyen, Denise. *Once upon a twice* ill. by Barry Moser. Random House, 2009. ISBN 978-0-375-85612-9 Subj: Animals – mice. Character traits – bravery. Night. Swamps.

Doyle, Charlotte Lackner. *The bouncing, dancing, galloping ABC* ill. by Julia Gorton. Penguin, 2006. ISBN 978-0-399-23778-2 Subj: ABC books. Activities – playing. Rhyming text.

Doyle, Malachy. *Baby see, baby do!* ill. by Britta Teckentrup. Putnam, 2002. ISBN 978-0-399-23728-7 Subj: Animals – babies. Babies. Format, unusual – toy & movable books.

Cow ill. by Angelo Rinaldi. McElderry, 2002. ISBN 978-0-689-84462-1 Subj: Animals – bulls, cows. Farms.

Get happy ill. by Caroline Uff. Walker, 2011. ISBN 978-0-8027-2271-3 Subj: Behavior. Emotions – happiness. Rhyming text.

Horse ill. by Angelo Rinaldi. Simon & Schuster, 2008. ISBN 978-1-4169-2467-8 Subj: Animals – horses, ponies. Farms.

Hungry! Hungry! Hungry! ill. by Paul Hess. Peachtree, 2000. ISBN 978-1-56145-241-5 Subj: Food. Monsters. Mythical creatures – goblins.

Sleepy Pendoodle ill. by Julie Vivas. Candlewick, 2002. ISBN 978-0-7636-1561-1 Subj: Animals – dogs. Pets.

Splash, Joshua, splash! ill. by Ken Wilson-Max. Bloomsbury, 2004. ISBN 978-1-58234-837-7 Subj: Family life – grandmothers. Water.

Storm cats ill. by Stuart Trotter. McElderry, 2002. ISBN 978-0-689-84464-5 Subj: Animals – cats. Friendship. Rhyming text. Weather – storms.

Too noisy! ill. by Ed Vere. Candlewick, 2012. ISBN 978-0-7636-6226-4 Subj: Behavior – lost. Behavior – solitude. Family life. Noise, sounds.

Well, a crocodile can! ill. by Britta Teckentrup. Millbrook, 2000. ISBN 978-0-7613-1032-7 Subj: Activities. Animals. Behavior. Format, unusual – toy & movable books.

Drachman, Eric. *Leo the lightning bug* ill. by James Muscarello. Kidwick, 2001. ISBN 978-0-9703809-0-6 Subj: Insects – fireflies. Self-concept.

Dragonwagon, Crescent. *All the awake animals are almost asleep* ill. by David McPhail. Little, Brown, 2012. ISBN 978-0-316-07045-4 Subj: ABC books. Animals. Bedtime. Rhyming text.

Drawson, Blair. *All along the river* ill. by author. Douglas & McIntyre, 2003. ISBN 978-0-88899-546-9 Subj: Canoes & canoeing. Family life – grandfathers. Imagination. Rivers.

Dray, Philip. *Yours for justice, Ida B. Wells: the daring life of a crusading journalist* ill. by Stephen Alcorn. Peachtree, 2008. ISBN 978-1-56145-417-4 Subj: Careers – journalists. Ethnic groups in the U.S. – African Americans. Gender roles. Prejudice. U.S. history.

Drehsen, Britta. *Flip-o-storic* ill. by Sara Ball. Abbeville, 2011. ISBN 978-0-7892-1099-9 Subj: Dinosaurs. Format, unusual – toy & movable books.

Drescher, Henrik. *Hubert the Pudge: a vegetarian tale* ill. by author. Candlewick, 2006. ISBN 978-0-7636-1992-3 Subj: Food. Health & fitness.

The drowsy hours: poems for bedtime sel. by Susan Pearson; ill. by Peter Malone. HarperCollins, 2002. ISBN 978-0-06-029421-2 Subj: Bedtime. Lullabies. Night. Poetry. Sleep.

Druce, Arden. *Halloween night* ill. by David Wenzel. Rising Moon, 2001. ISBN 978-0-87358-797-6 Subj: Holidays – Halloween. Rhyming text. Riddles & jokes.

Drummond, Allan. *Casey Jones* ill. by author. Farrar, 2001. ISBN 978-0-374-31175-9 Subj: Careers – engineers. Rhyming text. Tall tales. Trains.

Energy island: how one community harnessed the wind and changed their world ill. by author. Farrar, 2011. ISBN 978-0-374-32184-0 Subj: Foreign lands – Denmark. Science. Weather – wind.

Liberty ill. by author. Farrar, 2002. ISBN 978-0-374-34385-9 Subj: Character traits – freedom. U.S. history.

Tin Lizzie ill. by author. Farrar, 2008. ISBN 978-0-374-32000-3 Subj: Automobiles. Family life – grandfathers.

Drummond, Ree. *Charlie goes to school* ill. by Diane deGroat. HarperCollins, 2013. ISBN 978-0-06-221920-6 Subj: Animals. Animals – dogs. School.

Charlie the ranch dog ill. by Diane deGroat. HarperCollins, 2011. ISBN 978-0-06-199655-9 Subj: Animals – dogs. Careers – ranchers.

Duble, Kathleen Benner. *Pilot mom* ill. by Alan Marks. Charlesbridge, 2003. ISBN 978-1-57091-555-0 Subj: Careers – airplane pilots. Careers – military. Family life – daughters. Family life – mothers.

Dubois, Muriel L. *Out and about at the fire station* ill. by Anne McMullen. Picture Window, 2003. ISBN 978-1-4048-0039-7 Subj: Careers – firefighters. Fire. School – field trips.

Du Bois, William Pène. *Bear party* ill. by author. Viking, 1951. ISBN 978-0-14-050793-5 Subj: Animals. Animals – koalas. Caldecott award honor books. Emotions – anger. Parties.

Lion ill. by author. Viking, 1957. ISBN 978-0-670-42950-9 Subj: Animals – lions. Caldecott award honor books.

Dubosarsky, Ursula. *Rex* ill. by David Mackintosh. Macmillan, 2006. ISBN 978-1-59643-186-7 Subj: Activities – writing. Imagination. Pets. Reptiles – chameleons. School.

The terrible plop ill. by Andrew Joyner. Farrar, 2009. ISBN 978-0-374-37428-0 Subj: Animals – rabbits. Behavior – mistakes. Emotions – fear. Rhyming text.

Dubuc, Marianne. *Animal masquerade* ill. by author. Kids Can, 2012. ISBN 978-1-55453-782-2 Subj: Animals. Fairs, festivals.

DuBurke, Randy. *The moon ring* ill. by author. Chronicle, 2002. ISBN 978-0-8118-3487-2 Subj: Ethnic groups in the U.S. – African Americans. Family life – grandmothers. Magic. Moon.

Duckling ed. by Nicola Deschamps; photos by Jane Burton. DK, 2002. ISBN 978-0-7894-7856-6 Subj: Birds – ducks. Counting, numbers. Format, unusual – board books.

Duddle, Jonny. *The king of space: soon the whole universe will know my name!* ill. by author. Candlewick, 2013. ISBN 978-0-7636-6435-0 Subj: Robots. Space & space ships.

The pirate cruncher ill. by author. Candlewick, 2010. ISBN 978-0-7636-4876-3 Subj: Mythical creatures. Pirates. Rhyming text.

The pirates next door: starring the Jolley-Rogers ill. by author. Candlewick, 2012. ISBN 978-0-7636-5842-7 Subj: Pirates. Rhyming text.

Dudley, Rebecca. *Hank finds an egg* ill. by author. Peter Pauper, 2013. ISBN 978-1-4413-1158-0 Subj: Animals. Birds – hummingbirds. Character traits – kindness. Character traits – persistence. Eggs. Wordless.

Duffield, Katy. *Farmer McPeepers and his missing milk cows* ill. by Steve Gray. Rising Moon, 2003. ISBN 978-0-87358-825-6 Subj: Animals – bulls, cows. Careers – farmers. Farms. Glasses. Humorous stories.

Dugan, Joanne. *ABC NYC: a book about seeing New York City* photos by author. Abrams, 2005. ISBN 978-0-8109-5854-8 Subj: ABC books. Cities, towns.

Duke, Kate. *One guinea pig is not enough* ill. by author. Dutton, 1998. ISBN 978-0-525-45918-7 Subj: Activities – playing. Animals – guinea pigs. Counting, numbers.

Ready for pumpkins ill. by author. Knopf, 2012. ISBN 978-0-375-87068-2 Subj: Animals – guinea pigs. Gardens, gardening. Pets. Plants. School.

The tale of Pip and Squeak ill. by author. Penguin, 2007. ISBN 978-0-525-47777-8 Subj: Animals – mice. Family life – brothers & sisters. Sibling rivalry.

Twenty is too many ill. by author. Dutton, 2000. ISBN 978-0-525-42026-2 Subj: Animals – guinea pigs. Boats, ships. Counting, numbers.

Duke, Shirley Smith. *No bows!* ill. by Jenny Mattheson. Peachtree, 2006. ISBN 978-1-56145-356-6 Subj: Character traits – appearance. Character traits – individuality.

Dumont, Jean-François. *The chickens build a wall* ill. by author. Eerdmans, 2013. ISBN 978-0-8028-5422-3 Subj: Animals – hedgehogs. Birds – chickens. Character traits – being different.

Dunbar, Joyce. *The monster who ate darkness* ill. by Jimmy Liao. Candlewick, 2008. ISBN 978-0-7636-3859-7 Subj: Bedtime. Emotions – fear. Monsters. Night.

Shoe baby ill. by Polly Dunbar. Candlewick, 2005. ISBN 978-0-7636-2779-9 Subj: Activities – traveling. Babies. Clothing – shoes. Rhyming text.

The very small ill. by Debi Gliori. Harcourt, 2000. ISBN 978-0-15-202346-1 Subj: Animals – bears. Behavior – lost. Behavior – sharing. Concepts – size.

Where's my sock? ill. by Sanja Rescek. Scholastic, 2006. ISBN 978-0-439-74831-5 Subj: Behavior – lost & found possessions. Clothing – socks.

Dunbar, Polly. *Arthur's dream boat* ill. by author. Candlewick, 2012. ISBN 978-0-7636-5867-0 Subj: Boats, ships. Character traits – appearance. Dreams.

Dog Blue ill. by author. Candlewick, 2004. ISBN 978-0-7636-2476-7 Subj: Animals – dogs. Concepts – color. Imagination.

Flyaway Katie ill. by author. Candlewick, 2004. ISBN 978-0-7636-2366-1 Subj: Concepts – color. Emotions. Imagination.

Happy Hector ill. by author. Candlewick, 2008. ISBN 978-0-7636-4110-8 Subj: Animals – pigs. Behavior – sharing. Friendship.

Hello Tilly ill. by author. Candlewick, 2008. ISBN 978-0-7636-4109-2 Subj: Animals. Friendship.

Penguin ill. by author. Candlewick, 2007. ISBN 978-0-7636-3404-9 Subj: Birds – penguins. Toys.

Pingüino / penguin ill. by author. Serres, 2008. ISBN 978-84-79-01859-7 Subj: Birds – penguins. Foreign languages. Toys.

Pretty Pru ill. by author. Candlewick, 2009. ISBN 978-0-7636-4272-3 Subj: Animals. Character traits – appearance. Clothing – handbags, purses. Friendship.

Where's Tumpty? ill. by author. Candlewick, 2009. ISBN 978-0-7636-4273-0 Subj: Activities – playing. Animals. Animals – elephants. Behavior – hiding. Friendship.

Duncan, Alice Faye. *Honey baby sugar child* ill. by Susan Keeter. Simon & Schuster, 2005. ISBN 978-0-689-84678-6 Subj: Emotions – love. Ethnic groups in the U.S. – African Americans. Family life – mothers.

Duncan, Lois. *I walk at night* ill. by Steve Johnson and Lou Fancher. Viking, 2000. ISBN 978-0-670-87513-9 Subj: Activities – walking. Animals – cats. Night. Rhyming text.

Song of the circus ill. by Meg Cundiff. Philomel, 2002. ISBN 978-0-399-23397-5 Subj: Animals – tigers. Character traits – bravery. Circus. Rhyming text.

Dungy, Tony. *You can do it!* ill. by Amy Bates. Simon & Schuster, 2008. ISBN 978-1-4169-5461-3 Subj: Behavior – growing up. Careers – dentists. Character traits – ambition. Ethnic groups in the U.S. – African Americans. Family life. Religion.

Dunklee, Annika. *My name is Elizabeth!* ill. by Matthew Forsythe. Kids Can, 2011. ISBN 978-1-55453-560-6 Subj: Character traits – assertiveness. Names.

Dunlap, Julie. *Louisa May and Mr. Thoreau's flute* by Julie Dunlap and Marybeth Lorbiecki ill. by Mary Azarian. Dial, 2002. ISBN 978-0-8037-2470-9 Subj: Careers – writers. U.S. history.

Dunn, Todd. *We go together* ill. by Miki Sakamoto. Sterling, 2007. ISBN 978-1-4027-3260-7 Subj: Concepts. Rhyming text.

Dunnick, Regan. *Sweet dreams, Douglas* ill. by author. Junior League of Houston, 2002. ISBN 978-0-9632421-3-6 Subj: Animals. Animals – dogs. Bedtime. Dreams. Imagination.

Dunning, Joan. *Seabird in the forest: the mystery of the marbled murrelet.* Boyds Mills, 2011. ISBN 978-1-59078-715-1 Subj: Birds. Sea & seashore.

Dunrea, Olivier. *Appearing tonight! Mary Heather Elizabeth Livingstone* ill. by author. Farrar, 2000. ISBN 978-0-374-30455-3 Subj: Careers – actors. Theater.

Bear Noel ill. by author. Farrar, 2000. ISBN 978-0-374-40001-9 Subj: Animals. Animals – bears. Cumulative tales. Holidays – Christmas.

A Christmas tree for Pyn ill. by author. Penguin, 2011. ISBN 978-0-399-24506-0 Subj: Family life – fathers. Gifts. Holidays – Christmas. Trees.

Gideon ill. by author. Houghton Mifflin, 2012. ISBN 978-0-618-43661-3 Subj: Activities – playing. Birds – geese. Farms. Sleep.

Gideon & Otto ill. by author. Houghton Mifflin, 2012. ISBN 978-0-618-43662-0 Subj: Behavior – lost & found possessions. Birds – geese. Toys.

Gossie's busy day: a first tab book ill. by author. Houghton, 2007. ISBN 978-0-618-82148-8 Subj: Birds – geese. Format, unusual – toy & movable books.

It's snowing ill. by author. Farrar, 2002. ISBN 978-0-374-39992-4 Subj: Babies. Family life – mothers. Weather – snow.

Jasper & Joop ill. by author. Houghton Mifflin, 2013. ISBN 978-0-547-86762-5 Subj: Behavior – messy. Birds – geese. Character traits – cleanliness. Friendship.

Little cub ill. by author. Philomel, 2012. ISBN 978-0-399-24235-9 Subj: Animals – babies. Animals – bears. Emotions – fear. Emotions – loneliness.

Merry Christmas, Ollie! ill. by author. Houghton, 2008. ISBN 978-0-618-53242-1 Subj: Birds – geese. Holidays – Christmas. Santa Claus.

Old Bear and his cub ill. by author. Penguin, 2010. ISBN 978-0-399-24507-7 Subj: Animals – bears. Emotions – love. Family life – fathers.

Ollie ill. by author. Houghton, 2003. ISBN 978-0-618-33928-0 Subj: Birds – geese. Character traits – patience. Eggs. Family life – new sibling.

Ollie the stomper ill. by author. Houghton, 2003. ISBN 978-0-618-33930-3 Subj: Birds – geese. Clothing – boots.

Ollie's Easter eggs [board book] ill. by author. Harcourt, 2013. ISBN 978-0-547-85918-7 Subj: Behavior – hiding things. Birds – geese. Eggs. Format, unusual – board books. Holidays – Easter.

Ollie's Easter eggs ill. by author. Houghton Mifflin, 2010. ISBN 978-0-618-53243-8 Subj: Behavior – hiding things. Birds – geese. Eggs. Holidays – Easter.

Ollie's Halloween ill. by author. Harcourt, 2010. ISBN 978-0-618-53241-4 Subj: Birds – geese. Holidays – Halloween.

Peedie ill. by author. Houghton, 2004. ISBN 978-0-618-35652-2 Subj: Birds – geese. Clothing – hats. Memories, memory.

Dupasquier, Philippe. *1 2 3, follow me!* ill. by author. Candlewick, 2002. ISBN 978-0-7636-1797-4 Subj: Animals. Counting, numbers. Format, unusual – board books. Wordless.

Dupre, Kelly. *The raven's gift* ill. by author. Houghton, 2001. ISBN 978-0-618-01171-1 Subj: Activities – traveling. Birds – ravens. Foreign lands – Greenland.

Duquennoy, Jacques. *North Pole, South Pole* ill. by author. Raincoast, 2000. ISBN 978-1-55192-411-3 Subj: Birds – penguins. Foreign lands – Antarctic. Foreign lands – Arctic. Holidays – Christmas. Santa Claus.

Du Quette, Keith. *Little Monkey lost* ill. by author. Penguin, 2007. ISBN 978-0-399-24294-6 Subj: Animals – monkeys. Behavior – lost. Jungle.

They call me Woolly: what animal names can tell us ill. by author. Putnam, 2002. ISBN 978-0-399-23445-3 Subj: Animals. Language. Names.

Durand, Hallie. *Mitchell goes bowling* ill. by Tony Fucile. Candlewick, 2013. ISBN 978-0-7636-6049-9 Subj: Family life – fathers. Sports – bowling.

Mitchell's license ill. by Tony Fucile. Candlewick, 2011. ISBN 978-0-7636-4496-3 Subj: Activities – playing. Bedtime. Family life – fathers.

Durango, Julia. *Angels watching over me* ill. by Elisa Kleven. Simon & Schuster, 2007. ISBN 978-0-689-86252-6 Subj: Angels. Songs.

Cha-cha chimps ill. by Eleanor Taylor. Simon & Schuster, 2006. ISBN 978-0-689-86456-8 Subj: Activities – dancing. Animals – chimpanzees. Counting, numbers. Rhyming text.

Dream hop ill. by Jared Lee. Simon & Schuster, 2005. ISBN 978-0-689-87163-4 Subj: Bedtime. Dreams. Nightmares. Sleep.

Go-go gorillas ill. by Eleanor Taylor. Simon & Schuster, 2010. ISBN 978-1-4169-3779-1 Subj: Animals – gorillas. Rhyming text. Transportation.

Pest fest ill. by Kurt Cyrus. Simon & Schuster, 2007. ISBN 978-0-689-85569-6 Subj: Contests. Insects.

Yum! Yuck! a foldout book of people sounds (Park, Linda Sue)

Durant, Alan. *Big Bad Bunny* ill. by Guy Parker-Rees. Dutton, 2001. ISBN 978-0-525-46667-3 Subj: Animals – rabbits. Behavior – misbehavior. Crime.

Brown Bear gets in shape ill. by Annabel Hudson. Kingfisher, 2004. ISBN 978-0-7534-5797-9 Subj: Animals – bears. Animals – chimpanzees. Animals – rabbits.

Burger boy ill. by Mei Matsuoka. Houghton, 2006. ISBN 978-0-618-71466-7 Subj: Food. Humorous stories.

Dear tooth fairy ill. by Vanessa Cabban. Candlewick, 2003. ISBN 978-0-7636-2175-9 Subj: Fairies. Format, unusual – toy & movable books. Letters, cards. Teeth.

A dinosaur called Tiny ill. by Jo Simpson. HarperCollins, 2008. ISBN 978-0-06-136633-8 Subj: Character traits – smallness. Concepts – size. Dinosaurs.

I love you, little monkey ill. by Katharine McEwen. Simon & Schuster, 2007. ISBN 978-1-4169-2481-4 Subj: Animals – monkeys. Emotions – love.

Dutton, Sandra. *Dear Miss Perfect: a beast's guide to proper behavior* ill. by author. Houghton, 2007. ISBN 978-0-618-67717-7 Subj: Animals. Behavior. Etiquette.

Duval, Kathy. *Take me to your BBQ* ill. by Adam McCauley. Disney/Hyperion, 2013. ISBN 978-1-4231-2255-5 Subj: Activities – dancing. Aliens. Food. Rhyming text.

The Three Bears' Christmas ill. by Paul Meisel. Holiday House, 2005. ISBN 978-0-8234-1871-8 Subj: Animals – bears. Holidays – Christmas. Santa Claus.

The Three Bears' Halloween ill. by Paul Meisel. Holiday House, 2007. ISBN 978-0-8234-2032-2 Subj: Animals – bears. Holidays – Halloween.

Duvall, Deborah L. *The opossum's tale: a grandmother story* ill. by Murv Jacob. Univ. of New Mexico, 2005. ISBN 978-0-8263-3694-1 Subj: Anatomy – tails. Animals – possums. Folk & fairy tales. Indians of North America – Cherokee.

Duvoisin, Roger Antoine. *Petunia* ill. by author. 50th anniversary ed. Knopf, 1977. ISBN 978-0-394-90865-6 Subj: Animals. Birds – geese. Books, reading. Character traits – pride. Farms. Friendship. Humorous stories.

Dwyer, Mindy. *Quilt of dreams* ill. by author. Alaska Northwest, 2000. ISBN 978-0-88240-522-3 Subj: Family life – grandmothers. Family life – mothers. Quilts.

Dyckman, Ame. *Boy + Bot* ill. by Dan Yaccarino. Knopf, 2012. ISBN 978-0-375-86756-9 Subj: Friendship. Robots.

Tea party rules ill. by K. G. Campbell. Viking, 2013. ISBN 978-0-670-78501-8 Subj: Animals – bears. Etiquette. Parties.

Dyer, Heather. *Tina and the penguin* ill. by Mireille Levert. Kids Can, 2002. ISBN 978-1-55074-947-2 Subj: Behavior – running away. Birds – penguins. Foreign lands – Antarctic. Zoos.

Dyer, Jane. *Little Brown Bear and the bundle of joy* ill. by author. Little, Brown, 2005. ISBN 978-0-316-17469-5 Subj: Animals – bears. Babies. Family life – new sibling.

Dyer, Sarah. *Batty* ill. by author. Frances Lincoln, 2011. ISBN 978-1-84780-084-8 Subj: Animals – bats. Character traits – being different. Zoos.

Clementine and Mungo ill. by author. Bloomsbury, 2004. ISBN 978-1-58234-883-4 Subj: Animals. Family life – brothers & sisters. Monsters.

Monster day at work ill. by author. Frances Lincoln, 2010. ISBN 978-1-84780-069-5 Subj: Family life – fathers. Monsters.

Dylan, Bob. *Blowin' in the wind* ill. by Jon J Muth. Sterling, 2011. ISBN 978-1-4027-8002-8 Subj: Music. Songs. Violence, nonviolence.

Man gave names to all the animals ill. by Jim Arnosky. Sterling, 2010. ISBN 978-1-4027-6858-3 Subj: Animals. Songs.

Eachus, Jennifer. *I'm sorry* (McBratney, Sam)

Earnhardt, Donna W. *Being Frank* ill. by Andrea Castellani. Flashlight, 2012. ISBN 978-1-93626-119-2 Subj: Character traits – honesty. Character traits – kindness. Family life – grandfathers.

Eastland, Chris. *ABC zooborns!* (Bleiman, Andrew)

Eastman, P. D. *The alphabet book* ill. by author. Random House, 2000. ISBN 978-0-375-80603-2 Subj: ABC books.

Eastwick, Ivy O. *Some folks like cats, and other poems* comp. by Walter B. Barbe; ill. by Mary Kurnick Maass. Boyds Mills, 2002. ISBN 978-1-56397-450-2 Subj: Poetry.

Eaton, Jason Carter. *The day my runny nose ran away* ill. by Ethan Long. Dutton, 2002. ISBN 978-0-525-47013-7 Subj: Anatomy – noses. Behavior – running away.

How to train a train ill. by John Rocco. Candlewick, 2013. ISBN 978-0-7636-6307-0 Subj: Pets. Trains.

Eaton, Maxwell. *Best buds* ill. by author. Random House, 2006. ISBN 978-0-375-93803-0 Subj: Animals – pigs. Food. Friendship.

The mystery ill. by author. Knopf, 2008. ISBN 978-0-375-83807-1 Subj: Activities – painting. Animals – pigs. Friendship.

Superheroes ill. by author. Random House, 2007. ISBN 978-0-375-83805-7 Subj: Activities – playing. Animals – pigs. Friendship.

Two dumb ducks ill. by author. Random House, 2010. ISBN 978-0-375-84576-5 Subj: Behavior – bullying, teasing. Behavior – name calling. Birds – ducks. Birds – seagulls.

Eckart, Edana. *I can bowl* ill. with photos. Children's Press, 2002. ISBN 978-0-516-23972-9 Subj: Family life – fathers. Sports – bowling.

I can play soccer ill. with photos. Children's Press, 2002. ISBN 978-0-516-23969-9 Subj: Sports – soccer.

I can ride a bike ill. with photos. Children's Press, 2002. ISBN 978-0-516-23967-5 Subj: Sports – bicycling.

I can swim ill. with photos. Children's Press, 2002. ISBN 978-0-516-23970-5 Subj: Family life – mothers. Sports – swimming.

Eclare, Melanie. *A handful of sunshine* ill. with photos. Ragged Bears, 2000. ISBN 978-1-929927-14-2 Subj: Flowers. Gardens, gardening.

A harvest of color: growing a vegetable garden ill. with photos. Ragged Bears, 2002. ISBN 978-1-929927-31-9 Subj: Communities, neighborhoods. Food. Gardens, gardening.

Edens, Cooper. *The Animal Mall* by Cooper Edens and Daniel Lane ill. by Edward Miller. Dial, 2000. ISBN 978-0-8037-1984-2 Subj: Animals. Rhyming text. Shopping.

Special deliveries (Day, Alexandra)

Edgemon, Darcie. *Seamore, the very forgetful porpoise* ill. by J. Otto Seibold. HarperCollins, 2008. ISBN 978-0-06-085075-3 Subj: Animals – dolphins. Behavior – forgetfulness. Behavior – lost & found possessions. Friendship.

Edgett, Ken. *Touchdown Mars! an ABC adventure* (Wethered, Peggy)

Edvall, Lilian. *The rabbit who longed for home* ill. by Anna-Clara Tidholm. R&S Books, 2001. ISBN 978-91-29-65391-5 Subj: Animals – rabbits. Emotions. School – nursery.

Edwards, Becky. *My first day at nursery school* ill. by Anthony Flintoft. Bloomsbury, 2002. ISBN 978-1-58234-761-5 Subj: Emotions. School – first day. School – nursery.

Edwards, David. *The pen that Pa built* ill. by Ashley Wolff. Ten Speed, 2007. ISBN 978-1-58246-153-3 Subj: Animals – sheep. Cumulative tales. Farms. Rhyming text. U.S. history.

Edwards, Michelle. *The Hanukkah trike* ill. by Kathryn Mitter. Whitman, 2010. ISBN 978-0-8075-3126-6 Subj: Holidays – Hanukkah. Jewish culture. Sports – bicycling.

Papa's latkes ill. by Stacey Schuett. Candlewick, 2004. ISBN 978-0-7636-0779-1 Subj: Emotions – grief. Family life – fathers. Family life – single-parent families. Holidays – Hanukkah. Jewish culture.

Room for the baby ill. by Jana Christy. Random House, 2012. ISBN 978-0-375-87090-3 Subj: Activities – sewing. Holidays – Hanukkah. Jewish culture.

What's that noise? by Michelle Edwards and Phyllis Root ill. by Paul Meisel. Candlewick, 2002. ISBN 978-0-7636-1350-1 Subj: Emotions – fear. Family life – brothers. Night. Noise, sounds.

Edwards, Nancy. *Glenna's seeds* ill. by Sarah K. Hoctor. Child & Family Pr., 2001. ISBN 978-0-87868-788-6 Subj: Character traits – kindness. Communities, neighborhoods. Ethnic groups in the U.S. Seeds.

Edwards, Nicola. *Goodnight Baxter* ill. by author. Running Press, 2004. ISBN 978-0-7624-1725-4 Subj: Animals – babies. Animals – dogs. Bedtime. Emotions – love. Friendship.

Edwards, Pamela Duncan. *Barefoot: escape on the Underground Railroad* ill. by Henry Cole. HarperCollins, 1997. ISBN 978-0-06-027137-4 Subj: Behavior – running away. Ethnic groups in the U.S. – African Americans. Slavery. U.S. history.

Boston Tea Party ill. by Henry Cole. Putnam, 2001. ISBN 978-0-399-23357-9 Subj: U.S. history.

Bravo, Livingstone Mouse! ill. by Henry Cole. Hyperion, 2000. ISBN 978-0-7868-0307-1 Subj: Activities – dancing. Animals. Animals – mice. Insects. Theater.

The bus ride that changed history: the story of Rosa Parks ill. by Danny Shanahan. Houghton, 2005. ISBN 978-0-618-44911-8 Subj: Ethnic groups in the U.S. – African Americans. Prejudice. U.S. history.

Clara Caterpillar ill. by Henry Cole. HarperCollins, 2001. ISBN 978-0-06-028996-6 Subj: Insects – butterflies, caterpillars. Metamorphosis.

Dear Tooth Fairy ill. by Marie-Louise Fitzpatrick. Tegen, 2003. ISBN 978-0-06-623973-6 Subj: Fairies. Letters, cards. Teeth.

Dinosaur starts school ill. by Deborah Allwright. Whitman, 2009. ISBN 978-0-8075-1600-3 Subj: Behavior – worrying. Dinosaurs. School – first day.

Gigi and Lulu's gigantic fight ill. by Henry Cole. Tegen, 2004. ISBN 978-0-06-050753-4 Subj: Behavior – fighting, arguing. Friendship. School. Self-concept.

The grumpy morning ill. by Darcia Labrosse. Hyperion, 1998. ISBN 978-0-7868-2279-9 Subj: Animals. Behavior – promptness, tardiness. Farms. Rhyming text.

Honk! ill. by Henry Cole. Hyperion, 1998. ISBN 978-0-7868-2384-0 Subj: Activities – dancing. Ballet. Birds – swans.

Jack and Jill's treehouse ill. by Henry Cole. HarperCollins, 2008. ISBN 978-0-06-009077-7 Subj: Buildings. Cumulative tales. Homes, houses. Rebuses.

The leprechaun's gold ill. by Henry Cole. Tegen, 2004. ISBN 978-0-06-623975-0 Subj: Behavior – greed. Careers – harpists. Foreign lands – Ireland. Musical instruments – harps. Mythical creatures – leprechauns.

McGillycuddy could ill. by Sue Porter. Tegen, 2005. ISBN 978-0-06-029001-6 Subj: Animals. Animals – kangaroos. Farms.

The mixed-up rooster ill. by Megan Lloyd. HarperCollins, 2006. ISBN 978-0-06-028999-7 Subj: Birds – chickens. Character traits – being different.

Ms. Bitsy Bat's kindergarten ill. by Henry Cole. Hyperion, 2005. ISBN 978-0-7868-0669-0 Subj: Animals. Animals – bats. Careers – teachers. School.

Muldoon ill. by Henry Cole. Hyperion, 2002. ISBN 978-0-7868-2305-5 Subj: Animals – dogs. Humorous stories.

The neat line: scribbling through Mother Goose ill. by Diana Cain Bluthenthal. HarperCollins, 2005. ISBN 978-0-06-623971-2 Subj: Activities – drawing. Books, reading. Nursery rhymes.

The old house ill. by Henry Cole. Penguin, 2007. ISBN 978-0-525-47796-9 Subj: Friendship. Homes, houses.

Princess Pigtoria and the pea ill. by Henry Cole. Scholastic, 2010. ISBN 978-0-545-15625-7 Subj: Animals – pigs. Folk & fairy tales. Humorous stories. Royalty – princesses.

Roar ill. by Henry Cole. HarperCollins, 2000. ISBN 978-0-06-028385-8 Subj: Animals. Animals – lions. Counting, numbers. Jungle. Rhyming text.

Rosie's roses ill. by Henry Cole. HarperCollins, 2003. ISBN 978-0-06-028998-0 Subj: Birthdays. Family life – aunts, uncles. Flowers – roses. Gifts.

Rude mule ill. by Barbara Nascimbeni. Holt, 2002. ISBN 978-0-8050-7007-1 Subj: Animals – mules. Behavior. Etiquette.

Slop goes the soup ill. by Henry Cole. Hyperion, 2001. ISBN 978-0-7868-2411-3 Subj: Animals – warthogs. Character traits – clumsiness. Noise, sounds.

Some smug slug ill. by Henry Cole. HarperCollins, 1996. ISBN 978-0-06-024792-8 Subj: Animals. Animals – slugs.

Wake-up kisses ill. by Henry Cole. HarperCollins, 2002. ISBN 978-0-06-623977-4 Subj: Animals – babies. Night. Rhyming text.

Warthogs in a box ill. by Henry Cole. Disney, 2002. ISBN 978-0-7868-0894-6 Subj: Animals – warthogs. Format, unusual – board books. Friendship.

Warthogs in the kitchen: a sloppy counting book ill. by Henry Cole. Hyperion, 1998. ISBN 978-0-7868-2351-2 Subj: Activities – baking, cooking. Animals – warthogs. Counting, numbers. Rhyming text.

Warthogs paint ill. by Henry Cole. Hyperion, 2001. ISBN 978-0-7868-2412-0 Subj: Activities – painting. Animals – warthogs. Concepts – color. Rhyming text. Weather – rain.

While the world is sleeping ill. by Daniel Kirk. Scholastic, 2010. ISBN 978-0-545-01756-5 Subj: Animals. Bedtime. Birds – owls. Night. Rhyming text.

The worrywarts ill. by Henry Cole. HarperCollins, 1999. ISBN 978-0-06-028150-2 Subj: Activities – walking. Animals. Behavior – worrying.

The Wright brothers ill. by Henry Cole. Hyperion, 2003. ISBN 978-0-7868-2682-7 Subj: Activities – flying. Airplanes, airports. Careers – airplane pilots. Cumulative tales.

Edwards, Richard. *Always Copycub* ill. by Susan Winter. HarperCollins, 2001. ISBN 978-0-06-029691-9 Subj: Animals – bears. Behavior – lost. Games.

Copy me, Copycub ill. by Susan Winter. HarperCollins, 1999. ISBN 978-0-06-028571-5 Subj: Animals – bears. Family life – mothers. Seasons.

Good night, Copycub ill. by Susan Winter. HarperCollins, 2004. ISBN 978-0-06-056671-5 Subj: Animals. Animals – bears. Bedtime. Sleep.

Edwards, Wallace. *The extinct files: my science project* ill. by author. Kids Can, 2006. ISBN 978-1-55337-971-3 Subj: Dinosaurs. Humorous stories. Science.

Edwardson, Debby Dahl. *Whale snow* ill. by Annie Patterson. Talewinds, 2003. ISBN 978-1-57091-393-8 Subj: Animals – whales. Eskimos. Indians of North America – Inuit.

Eeckhout, Emmanuelle. *There's no such thing as ghosts!* ill. by author. Kane/Miller, 2008. ISBN 978-1-933605-91-3 Subj: Ghosts.

Egan, Kate. *Kate and Nate are running late!* ill. by Dan Yaccarino. Feiwel & Friends, 2012. ISBN 978-1-250-00080-4 Subj: Behavior – hurrying. Behavior – promptness, tardiness. Family life – single-parent families.

Egan, Tim. *Dodsworth in London* ill. by author. Houghton, 2009. ISBN 978-0-547-13816-9 Subj: Activities – traveling. Animals. Birds – ducks. Foreign lands – England.

Dodsworth in New York ill. by author. Houghton, 2007. ISBN 978-0-618-77708-2 Subj: Activities – traveling. Animals. Behavior – hiding. Birds – ducks. Humorous stories.

Dodsworth in Paris ill. by author. Houghton, 2008. ISBN 978-0-618-98062-8 Subj: Activities – traveling. Animals. Birds – ducks. Foreign lands – France.

Dodsworth in Rome ill. by author. Harcourt, 2011. ISBN 978-0-547-39006-2 Subj: Activities – traveling. Animals. Birds – ducks. Foreign lands – Italy.

The experiments of Doctor Vermin ill. by author. Houghton, 2002. ISBN 978-0-618-13224-9 Subj: Animals – pigs. Animals – wolves. Careers – chefs, cooks. Emotions – fear. Holidays – Halloween. Science.

A mile from Ellington Station ill. by author. Houghton, 2001. ISBN 978-0-618-00393-8 Subj: Animals – bears. Animals – dogs. Emotions – envy, jealousy.

The pink refrigerator ill. by author. Houghton, 2007. ISBN 978-0-618-63154-4 Subj: Animals. Character traits – laziness. Stores.

Roasted peanuts ill. by author. Houghton, 2006. ISBN 978-0-618-33718-7 Subj: Animals – cats. Animals – horses, ponies. Friendship. Sports – baseball.

Serious farm ill. by author. Houghton, 2003. ISBN 978-0-618-22694-8 Subj: Animals. Careers – farmers. Farms.

The trial of Cardigan Jones ill. by author. Houghton, 2004. ISBN 978-0-618-40237-3 Subj: Animals. Animals – moose. Crime. Food.

Egielski, Richard. *Itsy bitsy spider* ill. by author. Atheneum, 2012. ISBN 978-1-4169-9895-2 Subj: Character traits – persistence. Format, unusual – toy & moveable books. Nursery rhymes. Songs. Spiders.

St. Francis and the wolf ill. by author. HarperCollins, 2005. ISBN 978-0-06-623870-8 Subj: Animals – wolves. Foreign lands – Italy. Religion.

The sleepless little vampire ill. by author. Scholastic, 2011. ISBN 978-0-545-14597-8 Subj: Bedtime. Cumulative tales. Monsters.

Slim and Jim ill. by author. HarperCollins, 2002. ISBN 978-0-06-028353-7 Subj: Animals – cats. Animals – mice. Animals – rats. Toys.

Three magic balls ill. by author. HarperCollins, 2000. ISBN 978-0-06-026033-0 Subj: Activities – whistling. Magic. Toys – balls. Whistles.

Ehlert, Lois. *Boo to you!* ill. by author. Simon & Schuster, 2009. ISBN 978-1-4169-8625-6 Subj: Animals – cats. Animals – mice. Parties. Rhyming text.

Circus ill. by author. HarperCollins, 1992. ISBN 978-0-06-020253-8 Subj: Circus.

Color farm ill. by author. HarperCollins, 1990. ISBN 978-0-397-32441-5 Subj: Concepts – color. Concepts – shape. Format, unusual.

Color zoo ill. by author. HarperCollins, 1990. ISBN 978-0-397-32260-2 Subj: Caldecott award honor books. Concepts – color. Concepts – shape. Format, unusual.

Cuckoo, a Mexican folktale / Cucú: un cuento folklórico mexicano ill. by author. Harcourt, 1997. ISBN 978-0-15-200274-9 Subj: Birds. Birds – cuckoos. Character traits – bravery. Fire. Folk & fairy tales. Foreign lands – Mexico. Foreign languages. Indians of Central America – Maya.

Eating the alphabet ill. by author. Harcourt, 1996. ISBN 978-0-15-201036-2 Subj: ABC books. Food.

Feathers for lunch ill. by author. Harcourt, 1990. ISBN 978-0-15-230550-5 Subj: Animals – cats. Birds. Rhyming text.

Fish eyes: a book you can count on ill. by author. Harcourt, 1990. ISBN 978-0-15-201618-0 Subj: Concepts – color. Counting, numbers. Fish. Rhyming text.

Growing vegetable soup ill. by author. Harcourt, 1987. ISBN 978-0-15-232575-6 Subj: Food. Gardens, gardening.

Hands ill. by author. Harcourt, 1997. ISBN 978-0-15-201506-0 Subj: Activities – making things.

Anatomy – hands. Family life. Format, unusual – toy & movable books.

In my world ill. by author. Harcourt, 2002. ISBN 978-0-15-216269-6 Subj: Concepts. Format, unusual. Picture puzzles.

Leaf man ill. by author. Harcourt, 2005. ISBN 978-0-15-205304-8 Subj: Format, unusual. Plants. Weather – wind.

Lots of spots ill. by author. Simon & Schuster, 2010. ISBN 978-1-4424-0289-8 Subj: Animals. Disguises. Rhyming text.

Market day ill. by author. Harcourt, 2000. ISBN 978-0-15-202158-0 Subj: Farms. Rhyming text. Stores.

Mole's hill: a woodland tale ill. by author. Harcourt, 1994. ISBN 978-0-15-255116-2 Subj: Animals – foxes. Animals – moles. Folk & fairy tales. Indians of North America – Seneca.

Moon rope / Un lazo a la luna ill. by adapter. Harcourt, 1992. ISBN 978-0-15-255343-2 Subj: Animals – foxes. Animals – moles. Folk & fairy tales. Foreign lands – Peru. Foreign languages. Moon.

Nuts to you! ill. by author. Harcourt, 1993. ISBN 978-0-15-257647-9 Subj: Animals – squirrels. Rhyming text.

Oodles of animals ill. by author. Harcourt, 2008. ISBN 978-0-15-206274-3 Subj: Animals. Character traits – individuality. Rhyming text.

Planting a rainbow ill. by author. Harcourt, 1988. ISBN 978-0-15-262609-9 Subj: Flowers. Gardens, gardening.

Red leaf, yellow leaf ill. by author. Harcourt, 1991. ISBN 978-0-15-266197-7 Subj: Seasons. Trees.

Rrralph ill. by author. Simon & Schuster, 2011. ISBN 978-1-4424-1305-4 Subj: Animals – dogs. Humorous stories.

Snowballs ill. by author. Harcourt, 1995. ISBN 978-0-15-200074-5 Subj: Seasons – winter. Snowmen.

Top cat ill. by author. Harcourt, 1998. ISBN 978-0-15-201739-2 Subj: Animals – cats. Behavior – sharing. Rhyming text.

Wag a tail ill. by author. Harcourt, 2007. ISBN 978-0-15-205843-2 Subj: Animals – dogs.

Waiting for wings ill. by author. Harcourt, 2001. ISBN 978-0-15-202608-0 Subj: Format, unusual – toy & movable books. Insects – butterflies, caterpillars. Rhyming text.

Ehrhardt, Karen. *This jazz man* ill. by R. G. Roth. Harcourt, 2006. ISBN 978-0-15-205307-9 Subj: Ethnic groups in the U.S. – African Americans. Music. Rhyming text. Songs.

Ehrlich, Amy. *Baby Dragon* ill. by Will Hillenbrand. Candlewick, 2008. ISBN 978-0-7636-2840-6 Subj: Character traits – patience. Dragons. Family life – mothers.

Ehrlich, Fred. *A bunny is funny* (Ziefert, Harriet)

Does a baboon sleep in a bed? ill. by Emily Bolam. Blue Apple, 2006. ISBN 978-1-59354-142-2 Subj: Animals. Sleep.

Does a camel cook? ill. by Emily Bolam. Blue Apple, 2007. ISBN 978-1-59354-588-8 Subj: Animals. Food.

Does a chimp wear clothes? ill. by Emily Bolam. Blue Apple, 2005. ISBN 978-1-59354-110-1 Subj: Animals. Clothing.

Does a duck have a daddy? ill. by Emily Bolam. Blue Apple, 2004. ISBN 978-1-59354-032-6 Subj: Animals. Family life – fathers.

Does a giraffe drive? ill. by Emily Bolam. Blue Apple, 2007. ISBN 978-1-59354-614-4 Subj: Animals. Concepts – motion.

Does a mouse have a mommy? ill. by Emily Bolam. Blue Apple, 2004. ISBN 978-1-59354-034-0 Subj: Animals. Family life – mothers.

Does a seal smile? ill. by Emily Bolam. Blue Apple, 2006. ISBN 978-1-59354-168-2 Subj: Anatomy – faces. Animals. Communication.

Does an elephant take a bath? ill. by Emily Bolam. Blue Apple, 2005. ISBN 978-1-59354-111-8 Subj: Activities – bathing. Animals. Character traits – cleanliness.

Ehrlich, H. M. *Gotcha, Louie!* ill. by Emily Bolam. Houghton, 2002. ISBN 978-0-618-19549-7 Subj: Activities – playing. Family life – mothers. Sea & seashore.

Louie's goose ill. by Emily Bolam. Houghton, 2000. ISBN 978-0-618-03023-1 Subj: Sea & seashore. Toys.

Eichenberg, Fritz. *Ape in cape* ill. by author. Harcourt, 1952. ISBN 978-0-15-203722-2 Subj: ABC books. Caldecott award honor books.

Eilenberg, Max. *Cowboy Kid* ill. by Sue Heap. Candlewick, 2000. ISBN 978-0-7636-1058-6 Subj: Bedtime. Family life – fathers.

Squeak's good idea ill. by Patrick Benson. Candlewick, 2001. ISBN 978-0-7636-1591-8 Subj: Activities – picnicking. Animals – elephants.

Einhorn, Edward. *A very improbable story* ill. by Adam Gustavson. Charlesbridge, 2008. ISBN 978-1-57091-871-1 Subj: Animals – cats. Concepts. Games. Problem solving.

Eisner, Will. *Sundiata* ill. by author. NBM, 2003. ISBN 978-1-56163-332-6 Subj: Disabilities. Folk &

fairy tales. Foreign lands – Africa. Foreign lands – Mali. Royalty – kings.

Eitzen, Ruth. *Tara's flight* ill. by Allan Eitzen. Boyds Mills, 2008. ISBN 978-1-59078-563-8 Subj: Birds – pigeons. Religion – Noah. Weather – floods.

Elffers, Joost. *Baby food* (Freymann, Saxton)

Do you love me? ill. by author. HarperCollins, 2008. ISBN 978-0-06-166799-2 Subj: Emotions – love. Rhyming text.

Dog food (Freymann, Saxton)

Dr. Pompo's nose (Freymann, Saxton)

Fast food (Freymann, Saxton)

Food for thought: the complete book of concepts for growing minds (Freymann, Saxton)

Food play (Freymann, Saxton)

How are you peeling? foods with moods (Freymann, Saxton)

One lonely seahorse (Freymann, Saxton)

Elissa, Barbara. *The remarkable journey of Josh's kippah* ill. by Farida Zaman. Lerner/Kar-Ben, 2010. ISBN 978-0-8225-9911-1 Subj: Activities – traveling. Jewish culture.

Elkin, Mark. *Samuel's baby* ill. by Amy Wummer. Tricycle, 2010. ISBN 978-1-58246-301-8 Subj: Babies. Family life – new sibling. School.

Ellery, Amanda. *If I had a dragon* ill. by Tom Ellery. Simon & Schuster, 2006. ISBN 978-1-4169-0924-8 Subj: Activities – playing. Dragons. Family life – brothers & sisters. Imagination.

If I were a jungle animal ill. by Tom Ellery. Simon & Schuster, 2009. ISBN 978-1-4169-3778-4 Subj: Animals. Imagination. Jungle. Sports – baseball.

Elliot, David. *Henry's map* ill. by author. Philomel, 2013. ISBN 978-0-399-16072-1 Subj: Animals – pigs. Character traits – orderliness. Farms. Maps.

Elliott, David. *And here's to you!* ill. by Randy Cecil. Candlewick, 2004. ISBN 978-0-7636-1427-0 Subj: Animals. Birds. Rhyming text.

Finn throws a fit! ill. by Timothy Basil Ering. Candlewick, 2009. ISBN 978-0-7636-2356-2 Subj: Behavior – misbehavior. Emotions – anger.

Hazel Nutt, Alien Hunter ill. by True Kelley. Holiday, 2004. ISBN 978-0-8234-1843-5 Subj: Humorous stories. Space & space ships.

Hazel Nutt, mad scientist ill. by True Kelley. Holiday, 2003. ISBN 978-0-8234-1711-7 Subj: Careers – scientists. Humorous stories. Monsters. Music.

Hunter's best friend at school ill. by Lynn Munsinger. HarperCollins, 2002. ISBN 978-0-06-000231-2 Subj: Animals – raccoons. Behavior. Friendship. School – nursery.

In the sea ill. by Holly Meade. Candlewick, 2012. ISBN 978-0-7636-4498-7 Subj: Animals. Poetry. Sea & seashore.

In the wild ill. by Holly Meade. Candlewick, 2010. ISBN 978-0-7636-4497-0 Subj: Animals. Poetry.

Knitty Kitty ill. by Christopher Denise. Candlewick, 2008. ISBN 978-0-7636-3169-7 Subj: Activities – knitting. Animals – cats. Family life.

On the farm ill. by Holly Meade. Candlewick, 2008. ISBN 978-0-7636-3322-6 Subj: Farms.

One little chicken: a counting book ill. by Ethan Long. Holiday House, 2007. ISBN 978-0-8234-1983-8 Subj: Activities – dancing. Birds – chickens. Counting, numbers. Rhyming text.

Elliott, George. *The boy who loved bananas* ill. by Andrej Krystoforski. Kids Can, 2005. ISBN 978-1-55337-744-3 Subj: Animals – monkeys. Behavior – imitation. Food. Humorous stories. Zoos.

Elliott, Laura Malone. *Hunter and Stripe and the soccer showdown* ill. by Lynn Munsinger. HarperCollins, 2005. ISBN 978-0-06-052759-4 Subj: Animals – raccoons. Friendship. Sports – soccer. Sportsmanship.

Hunter's big sister ill. by Lynn Munsinger. HarperCollins, 2007. ISBN 978-0-06-000233-6 Subj: Animals – raccoons. Family life – brothers & sisters.

A string of hearts ill. by Lynn Munsinger. HarperCollins, 2010. ISBN 978-0-06-000085-1 Subj: Animals. Friendship. Holidays – Valentine's Day.

Thanksgiving Day thanks ill. by Lynn Munsinger. HarperCollins, 2013. ISBN 978-0-06-000236-7 Subj: Animals. Holidays – Thanksgiving. School.

Elliott, Rebecca. *Just because* ill. by author. Lion, 2011. ISBN 978-0-7459-6267-2 Subj: Family life – brothers & sisters. Disabilities – physical disabilities.

Ellis, Andy. *When Lulu went to the zoo* ill. by author. Andersen, 2010. ISBN 978-0-7613-5499-4 Subj: Zoos.

Ellis, Sarah. *Ben over night* ill. by Kim LaFave. Fitzhenry & Whiteside, 2005. ISBN 978-1-55041-807-1 Subj: Emotions – fear. Sleepovers.

Big Ben ill. by Kim Lafave. Fitzhenry & Whiteside, 2001. ISBN 978-1-55041-679-4 Subj: Family life – brothers & sisters.

The queen's feet ill. by Dusan Petricic. Red Deer, 2006. ISBN 978-0-88995-320-8 Subj: Anatomy – feet. Royalty – queens.

Salmon forest (Suzuki, David)

Ellis, Veronica Freeman. *Afro-Bets, first book about Africa* ill. by George Ford. Just Us, 1989. ISBN 978-0-940975-12-5 Subj: Foreign lands – Africa.

Ellwand, David. *Alfred's camera: a collection of picture puzzles* ill. by author. Dutton, 1998. ISBN 978-0-525-45978-1 Subj: Animals – dogs. Behavior – lost & found possessions. Picture puzzles.

Alfred's party ill. by author. Dutton, 2000. ISBN 978-0-525-46385-6 Subj: Animals – dogs. Behavior – lost & found possessions. Birthdays. Picture puzzles.

Cinderlily libretto by Christine Tagg; ill. by author. Candlewick, 2003. ISBN 978-0-7636-2328-9 Subj: Ballet. Flowers. Folk & fairy tales. Foreign lands – France. Rhyming text.

Midas Mouse photos by author. Lothrop, 2000. ISBN 978-0-688-16745-5 Subj: Animals – mice. Behavior – wishing. Sun.

Ten in the bed photos by author. Handprint, 2000. ISBN 978-1-929766-49-9 Subj: Counting, numbers. Format, unusual – board books. Music. Songs. Toys – bears.

Elschner, Geraldine. *Fritz's fish* ill. by Daniela Bunge. Penguin, 2006. ISBN 978-0-698-40028-3 Subj: Fish. Pets.

Mark's messy room ill. by Alexandra Junge. Minedition, 2006. ISBN 978-0-698-40047-4 Subj: Animals – cats. Behavior – messy. Character traits – cleanliness.

Max's magic seeds ill. by Jean-Pierre Corderoch. Penguin, 2007. ISBN 978-0-698-40059-7 Subj: Behavior – boredom. Flowers. Magic. School.

Moonchild, star of the sea ill. by Lieselotte Schwarz. NorthSouth, 2002. ISBN 978-0-7358-1665-7 Subj: Earth. Moon. Stars.

Pashmina the little Christmas goat ill. by Angela Kehlenbeck. Penguin, 2006. ISBN 978-0-698-40046-7 Subj: Animals – goats. Holidays – Christmas.

Elsdale, Bob. *Mac side up* ill. by author. Dutton, 2000. ISBN 978-0-525-46467-9 Subj: Animals – cats. Animals – ferrets. Humorous stories. Pets.

Elster, Jean Alicia. *Just call me Joe Joe* ill. by Nicole Tadgell. Judson Pr., 2001. ISBN 978-0-8170-1398-1 Subj: Ethnic groups in the U.S. – African Americans. Self-concept. Sports – baseball.

Elvgren, Jennifer Riesmeyer. *Josias, hold the book* ill. by Nicole Tadgell. Boyds Mills, 2006. ISBN 978-1-59078-318-4 Subj: Family life. Food. Foreign lands – Haiti. Gardens, gardening. School.

Elwell, Peter. *Adios Oscar! a butterfly fable* ill. by author. Scholastic, 2009. ISBN 978-0-545-07159-8 Subj: Insects – butterflies, caterpillars.

Ely, Lesley. *Looking after Louis* ill. by Polly Dunbar. Whitman, 2004. ISBN 978-0-8075-4746-5 Subj: Disabilities – autism. School.

Elya, Susan Middleton. *Adiós, tricycle* ill. by Elisabeth Schlossberg. Putnam, 2009. ISBN 978-0-399-24522-0 Subj: Animals – pigs. Ethnic groups in the U.S. – Hispanic Americans. Foreign languages. Garage sales, rummage sales. Rhyming text. Sports – bicycling.

Bebé goes shopping ill. by Steven Salerno. Harcourt, 2006. ISBN 978-0-15-205426-7 Subj: Babies. Foreign languages. Rhyming text. Shopping. Stores.

Bebé goes to the beach ill. by Steven Salerno. Harcourt, 2008. ISBN 978-0-15-206000-8 Subj: Babies. Foreign languages. Rhyming text. Sea & seashore – beaches.

Cowboy Jose ill. by Tim Raglin. Penguin, 2005. ISBN 978-0-399-23570-2 Subj: Cowboys, cowgirls. Foreign languages. Rhyming text. Rodeos.

Eight animals bake a cake ill. by Lee Chapman. Putnam, 2002. ISBN 978-0-399-23468-2 Subj: Activities – baking, cooking. Animals. Foreign languages. Rhyming text.

Eight animals on the town ill. by Lee Chapman. Putnam, 2000. ISBN 978-0-399-23437-8 Subj: Animals. Counting, numbers. Foreign languages. Rhyming text.

F is for fiesta ill. by G. Brian Karas. Penguin, 2006. ISBN 978-0-399-24225-0 Subj: ABC books. Birthdays. Foreign languages. Parties. Rhyming text.

Fairy trails: a story told in English and Spanish ill. by Mercedes McDonald. Bloomsbury, 2005. ISBN 978-1-58234-927-5 Subj: Books, reading. Foreign languages.

Fire! ¡Fuego! Brave bomberos ill. by Dan Santat. Bloomsbury, 2012. ISBN 978-1-59990-461-0 Subj: Careers – firefighters. Fire. Foreign languages. Rhyming text.

N is for Navidad by Susan Middleton Elya and Merry Banks ill. by Joe Cepeda. Chronicle, 2007. ISBN 978-0-8118-5205-0 Subj: ABC books. Family life. Foreign lands – Mexico. Foreign languages. Holidays – Christmas.

No more, por favor ill. by David Walker. Penguin, 2010. ISBN 978-0-399-24766-8 Subj: Animals. Family life – parents. Food. Foreign languages. Jungle. Rhyming text.

Oh no, gotta go #2 ill. by Lynne Avril. Penguin, 2007. ISBN 978-0-399-24308-0 Subj: Activities – picnicking. Foreign languages. Rhyming text. Toilet training.

Rubia and the three osos ill. by Melissa Sweet. Hyperion/Disney, 2010. ISBN 978-1-4231-1252-5 Subj: Animals – bears. Folk & fairy tales. Foreign languages. Rhyming text.

Say hola to Spanish ill. by Loretta Lopez. Lee & Low, 1996. ISBN 978-1-880000-29-8 Subj: Foreign languages.

Sophie's trophy ill. by Viviana Garofoli. Penguin, 2006. ISBN 978-0-399-24199-4 Subj: Activities – singing. Family life – brothers & sisters. Foreign languages. Frogs & toads. Self-concept.

Tooth on the loose ill. by Jenny Mattheson. Putnam, 2008. ISBN 978-0-399-24459-9 Subj: Ethnic groups in the U.S. – Hispanic Americans. Foreign languages. Gifts. Rhyming text. Teeth.

A year full of holidays ill. by Diana Cain Bluthenthal. Penguin, 2010. ISBN 978-0-399-23733-1 Subj: Days of the week, months of the year. Holidays. Rhyming text.

Emberley, Barbara. *Drummer Hoff* ill. by Ed Emberley. Adapt. from a folk verse. Prentice-Hall, 1967. ISBN 978-0-13-220822-2 Subj: Caldecott award books. Careers – military. Cumulative tales. Poetry. Weapons.

Night's nice ill. by Ed Emberley. Little, Brown, 2008. ISBN 978-0-316-06623-5 Subj: Night. Poetry.

One wide river to cross ill. by Ed Emberley. Adapt. of the American folk song. Prentice-Hall, 1966. ISBN 978-0-316-23445-0 Subj: Animals. Caldecott award honor books. Folk & fairy tales. Poetry. Religion – Noah. Songs. Weather – floods. Weather – rain.

Emberley, Ed. *Chicken Little* (Emberley, Rebecca)

Ed Emberley's big green drawing book ill. by author. Little, 1979. ISBN 978-0-316-23595-2 Subj: Art. Wordless.

Ed Emberley's big orange drawing book ill. by author. Little, 1980. ISBN 978-0-316-23418-4 Subj: Art.

Ed Emberley's big purple drawing book ill. by author. Little, 1981. ISBN 978-0-316-23422-1 Subj: Art.

Ed Emberley's bye-bye, big bad bullybug! ill. by author. Little, Brown, 2007. ISBN 978-0-316-01762-6 Subj: Behavior – bullying, teasing. Format, unusual – toy & movable books. Monsters.

Ed Emberley's drawing book: make a world ill. by author. Little, 1972. ISBN 978-0-316-23598-3 Subj: Art.

Ed Emberley's drawing book of trucks and trains ill. by author. Little, 2002. ISBN 978-0-316-23898-4 Subj: Activities – drawing. Trains. Trucks.

Ed Emberley's fingerprint drawing book ill. by author. Little, 2000. ISBN 978-0-316-23638-6 Subj: Activities – drawing. Anatomy – hands.

Glad monster, sad monster: a book about feelings ill. by author. Little, 1997. ISBN 978-0-316-57395-5 Subj: Emotions. Format, unusual – toy & movable books. Masks. Monsters.

Go away, big green monster! ill. by author. Little, 1992. ISBN 978-0-316-23653-9 Subj: Bedtime. Emotions – fear. Format, unusual – toy & movable books. Monsters.

If you're a monster and you know it (Emberley, Rebecca)

Nighty night Little Green Monster ill. by author. Little, Brown, 2013. ISBN 978-0-316-21041-6 Subj: Bedtime. Format, unusual – toy & movable books. Monsters.

The red hen by Ed Emberley and Rebecca Emberley ill. by Ed Emberley. Roaring Brook, 2010. ISBN 978-1-59643-492-9 Subj: Activities – baking, cooking. Animals. Behavior – sharing. Birds – chickens. Character traits – helpfulness. Cumulative tales. Folk & fairy tales.

Ten little beasties (Emberley, Rebecca)

Thanks, Mom! ill. by author. Little, 2003. ISBN 978-0-316-24022-2 Subj: Animals. Animals – mice. Circus. Family life – mothers. Food.

Where's my sweetie pie? ill. by author. Little, Brown, 2010. ISBN 978-0-316-01891-3 Subj: Animals. Format, unusual – board books. Format, unusual – toy & movable books.

The wing on a flea ill. by author. Little, 2001. ISBN 978-0-316-23487-0 Subj: Concepts – shape. Rhyming text.

Emberley, Rebecca. *The ant and the grasshopper* ill. by Ed Emberley. Roaring Brook, 2012. ISBN 978-1-59643-493-6 Subj: Activities – working. Insects – ants. Insects – grasshoppers. Music. Musical instruments – bands.

Chicken Little by Rebecca Emberley and Ed Emberley ill. by authors. Roaring Brook, 2009. ISBN 978-1-59643-464-6 Subj: Animals. Behavior – gossip. Behavior – trickery. Birds – chickens. Cumulative tales. Folk & fairy tales.

The crocodile and the scorpion ill. by Ed Emberley. Roaring Brook, 2013. ISBN 978-1-59643-494-3 Subj: Behavior – trickery. Folk & fairy tales. Reptiles – alligators, crocodiles. Scorpions.

If you're a monster and you know it by Rebecca Emberley and Ed Emberley ill. by Rebecca Emberley. Scholastic, 2010. ISBN 978-0-545-21829-0 Subj: Emotions – happiness. Monsters. Songs.

Mice on ice ill. by Ed Emberley. Holiday House, 2012. ISBN 978-0-8234-2576-1 Subj: Animals – cats. Animals – mice. Rhyming text. Sports – ice skating.

My animals / Mis animales ill. by author. Little, 2002. ISBN 978-0-316-17343-8 Subj: Animals.

Foreign languages. Format, unusual – board books.

My big book of Spanish words ill. by author. Little, Brown, 2008. ISBN 978-0-316-11803-3 Subj: Foreign languages.

My city / Mi cuidad ill. by author. Little, 2005. ISBN 978-0-316-00051-2 Subj: Cities, towns. Foreign languages. Format, unusual – board books.

My clothes / Mi ropa ill. by author. Little, 2002. ISBN 978-0-316-17454-1 Subj: Clothing. Foreign languages. Format, unusual – board books.

My colors / Mis colores ill. by author. Little, 2000. ISBN 978-0-316-23347-7 Subj: Concepts – color. Foreign languages. Format, unusual – board books.

My food / Mi comida ill. by author. Little, 2002. ISBN 978-0-316-17718-4 Subj: Food. Foreign languages. Format, unusual – board books.

My garden / Mi jardin ill. by author. Little, 2005. ISBN 978-0-316-00049-9 Subj: Foreign languages. Format, unusual – board books. Gardens, gardening.

My house / Mi casa ill. by author. Little, 1990. ISBN 978-0-316-23637-9 Subj: Foreign languages. Format, unusual – board books. Homes, houses.

My numbers / Mis números ill. by author. Little, 2000. ISBN 978-0-316-23350-7 Subj: Counting, numbers. Foreign languages. Format, unusual – board books.

My opposites / Mis opuestos ill. by author. Little, 2000. ISBN 978-0-316-23345-3 Subj: Concepts – opposites. Foreign languages. Format, unusual – board books.

My room / Mi cuarto ill. by author. Little, 2005. ISBN 978-0-316-00052-9 Subj: Foreign languages. Format, unusual – board books. Homes, houses.

My school / Mi escuela ill. by author. Little, 2005. ISBN 978-0-316-00050-5 Subj: Foreign languages. Format, unusual – board books. School.

My shapes / Mis formas ill. by author. Little, 2000. ISBN 978-0-316-23355-2 Subj: Concepts – shape. Foreign languages. Format, unusual – board books.

My toys / Mi juguetes ill. by author. Little, 2002. ISBN 978-0-316-17494-7 Subj: Foreign languages. Format, unusual – board books. Toys.

The red hen (Emberley, Ed)

Ten little beasties by Rebecca Emberley and Ed Emberley ill. by authors. Roaring Brook, 2011. ISBN 978-1-59643-627-5 Subj: Counting, numbers. Monsters.

Three cool kids ill. by author. Little, 1995. ISBN 978-0-316-23666-9 Subj: Animals – goats. Animals – rats. Cities, towns. Folk & fairy tales.

Emberley, Rebecca, et al. *There was an old monster* ill. by author and Ed Emberley. Scholastic, 2009. ISBN 978-0-545-10145-5 Subj: Cumulative tales. Monsters. Songs.

Emergency! ed. by Nicola Deschamps; photos by Richard Leeney, et al. DK, 2001. ISBN 978-0-7894-7414-8 Subj: Careers – firefighters. Fire. Format, unusual – board books. Trucks.

Emerman, Ellen. *Is it Shabbos yet?* ill. by Tova Leff. Hachai, 2001. ISBN 978-1-929628-02-5 Subj: Holidays. Jewish culture. Religion.

Just right: the story of a Jewish home ill. by Sarah Kranz. Hachai, 1999. ISBN 978-0-922613-91-5 Subj: Family life. Homes, houses. Jewish culture.

Emmett, Jonathan. *The best gift of all* ill. by Vanessa Cabban. Candlewick, 2008. ISBN 978-0-7636-3860-3 Subj: Animals. Animals – moles. Friendship. Gifts. Illness – cold (disease).

Bringing down the moon ill. by Vanessa Cabban. Candlewick, 2001. ISBN 978-0-7636-1577-2 Subj: Animals. Animals – moles. Moon.

Diamond in the snow ill. by Vanessa Cabban. Candlewick, 2007. ISBN 978-0-7636-3117-8 Subj: Animals – moles. Seasons – winter. Weather – snow.

I love you always and forever ill. by Daniel Howarth. Scholastic, 2007. ISBN 978-0-439-91654-7 Subj: Animals – mice. Behavior – growing up. Emotions – love.

Leaf trouble ill. by Caroline Jayne Church. Scholastic, 2009. ISBN 978-0-545-16070-4 Subj: Animals – squirrels. Seasons – fall. Trees.

No place like home ill. by Vanessa Cabban. Candlewick, 2005. ISBN 978-0-7636-2554-2 Subj: Animals. Animals – moles. Homes, houses.

The princess and the pig ill. by Poly Bernatene. Walker, 2011. ISBN 978-0-8027-2334-5 Subj: Animals – pigs. Royalty – princesses.

Ruby in her own time ill. by Rebecca Harry. Scholastic, 2004. ISBN 978-0-439-57915-5 Subj: Birds – ducks. Character traits – smallness.

The Santa trap ill. by Poly Bernatene. Peachtree, 2012. ISBN 978-1-56145-670-3 Subj: Behavior – misbehavior. Holidays – Christmas. Santa Claus.

She'll be coming 'round the mountain ill. by Deborah Allwright. Simon & Schuster, 2007. ISBN 978-1-4169-3652-7 Subj: Songs. U.S. history – frontier & pioneer life.

Someone bigger ill. by Adrian Reynolds. Clarion, 2004. ISBN 978-0-618-44397-0 Subj: Concepts – size. Kites. Rhyming text.

This way, Ruby! ill. by Rebecca Harry. Scholastic, 2007. ISBN 978-0-439-87992-7 Subj: Behavior – lost. Birds – ducks. Character traits – smallness. Weather – storms.

Emmons, Chip. *Sammy wakes his dad* ill. by Shirley Venit Anger. Star Bright, 2002. ISBN 978-1-887734-87-5 Subj: Family life – fathers. Disabilities – physical disabilities. Sports – fishing.

Empson, Jo. *Rabbityness* ill. by author. Child's Play, 2012. ISBN 978-1-84643-492-1 Subj: Animals – rabbits. Behavior – lost. Character traits – being different.

Enderle, Dotti. *The Library Gingerbread Man* (The gingerbread boy)

Enderle, Judith Ross. *Smile, Principessa!* by Judith Ross Enderle and Stephanie Jacob Gordon ill. by Serena Curmi. Simon & Schuster, 2007. ISBN 978-1-4169-1004-6 Subj: Emotions – envy, jealousy. Family life – new sibling.

Enersen, Adele. *When my baby dreams* ill. by author. HarperCollins, 2012. ISBN 978-0-06-207175-0 Subj: Babies. Dreams. Sleep.

Engelbreit, Mary. *Mary Engelbreit's A merry little Christmas: celebrate from a to z* ill. by author. HarperCollins, 2006. ISBN 978-0-06-074159-4 Subj: ABC books. Animals – mice. Holidays – Christmas. Rhyming text.

Queen of Christmas ill. by author. HarperCollins, 2003. ISBN 978-0-06-008176-8 Subj: Gifts. Holidays – Christmas.

Queen of Halloween ill. by author. HarperCollins, 2008. ISBN 978-0-06-008190-4 Subj: Emotions – fear. Holidays – Halloween.

Queen of the class ill. by author. HarperCollins, 2004. ISBN 978-0-06-008179-9 Subj: Royalty – queens. School. Theater.

Engels-Fietzek, Petra. *Sophie and the seagull* ill. by Julia Ginsbach. G. Stevens, 2002. ISBN 978-0-8368-3174-0 Subj: Birds – seagulls. Friendship. Sea & seashore.

Engle, Margarita. *Summer birds: the butterflies of Maria Merian* ill. by Julie Paschkis. Holt, 2010. ISBN 978-0-8050-8937-0 Subj: Activities – painting. Art. Insects – butterflies, caterpillars.

English, Karen. *The baby on the way* ill. by Sean Qualls. Farrar, 2005. ISBN 978-0-374-37361-0 Subj: Babies. Ethnic groups in the U.S. – African Americans. Family life – grandmothers.

Hot day on Abbott Avenue ill. by Javaka Steptoe. Clarion, 2004. ISBN 978-0-395-98527-4 Subj: Ethnic groups in the U.S. – African Americans. Friendship. Seasons – summer. Sports – jumping rope.

Nadia's hands ill. by Jonathan Weiner. Boyds Mills, 1999. ISBN 978-1-56397-667-4 Subj: Ethnic groups in the U.S. – Pakistani Americans. Family life. Self-concept. Weddings.

Speak English for us, Marisol ill. by Enrique O. Sánchez. Whitman, 2000. ISBN 978-0-8075-7554-3 Subj: Ethnic groups in the U.S. – Hispanic Americans. Foreign languages.

Erdrich, Liselotte. *Bears make rock soup and other stories* ill. by Lisa Fifield. Children's Book Press, 2002. ISBN 978-0-89239-172-1 Subj: Animals. Indians of North America – Great Plains.

Erdrich, Louise. *The range eternal* ill. by Steve Johnson and Lou Fancher. Hyperion, 2002. ISBN 978-0-7868-0220-3 Subj: Activities – baking, cooking. U.S. history – frontier & pioneer life.

Ericsson, Jennifer A. *Home to me, home to you* ill. by Ashley Wolff. Little, Brown, 2005. ISBN 978-0-316-60922-7 Subj: Activities – working. Careers. Family life – mothers.

Out and about at the bakery ill. by Anne McMullen. Picture Window, 2003. ISBN 978-1-4048-0037-3 Subj: Activities – baking, cooking. Careers – bakers. School – field trips.

A piece of chalk ill. by Michelle Shapiro. Macmillan, 2007. ISBN 978-1-59643-057-0 Subj: Activities – drawing. Concepts – color.

She did it! ill. by Nadine Bernard Westcott. Farrar, 2002. ISBN 978-0-374-36776-3 Subj: Behavior – messy. Family life – sisters. Rhyming text.

Whoo goes there? ill. by Bert Kitchen. Roaring Brook, 2009. ISBN 978-1-59643-371-7 Subj: Animals. Birds – owls. Nature.

Eriksson, Eva. *A crash course for Molly* ill. by author. Farrar, 2005. ISBN 978-91-29-66156-9 Subj: Animals. Family life – grandmothers. Sports – bicycling.

Erlbruch, Wolf. *The big question* by Wolf Erlbruch and Michael Reynolds ill. by Wolf Erlbruch. Europa, 2005. ISBN 978-1-933372-03-7 Subj: Character traits – questioning. Self-concept.

Ernst, Lisa Campbell. *The gingerbread girl* (The gingerbread boy)

The Gingerbread Girl goes animal crackers ill. by author. Penguin, 2011. ISBN 978-0-525-42259-4 Subj: Animals – foxes. Behavior – running away. Cumulative tales. Food.

Goldilocks returns ill. by author. Simon & Schuster, 2000. ISBN 978-0-689-82537-8 Subj: Animals – bears. Folk & fairy tales. Humorous stories.

The letters are lost! ill. by author. Viking, 1996. ISBN 978-0-670-86336-5 Subj: ABC books. Toys.

Little Red Riding Hood: a newfangled prairie tale ill. by author. Simon & Schuster, 1995. ISBN 978-0-689-80145-7 Subj: Activities – baking, cooking. Animals – wolves. Behavior – talking to strangers. Family life – grandmothers. Folk & fairy tales.

Round like a ball! ill. by author. Blue Apple, 2008. ISBN 978-1-934706-01-5 Subj: Earth. Rhyming text.

Stella Louella's runaway book ill. by author. Simon & Schuster, 1998. ISBN 978-0-689-81883-7 Subj: Behavior – lost & found possessions. Careers – librarians. Cumulative tales. Libraries.

Sylvia Jean, drama queen ill. by author. Penguin, 2005. ISBN 978-0-525-46962-9 Subj: Animals – pigs. Clothing – costumes. Self-concept.

Sylvia Jean, scout supreme ill. by author. Penguin, 2010. ISBN 978-0-525-47873-7 Subj: Animals – pigs. Character traits – helpfulness. Clubs, gangs. Disguises.

This is the van that Dad cleaned ill. by author. Simon & Schuster, 2005. ISBN 978-0-689-86190-1 Subj: Automobiles. Character traits – cleanliness. Family life – fathers. Rhyming text.

Wake up, it's Spring! ill. by author. HarperCollins, 2004. ISBN 978-0-06-008986-3 Subj: Animals. Nature. Seasons – spring.

Esbaum, Jill. *Estelle takes a bath* ill. by Mary Newell DePalma. Holt, 2006. ISBN 978-0-8050-7741-4 Subj: Activities – bathing. Animals – mice. Rhyming text.

Everything spring. National Geographic, 2010. ISBN 978-1-4263-0607-5 Subj: Seasons – spring.

Stanza ill. by Jack E. Davis. Harcourt, 2009. ISBN 978-0-15-205998-9 Subj: Activities – writing. Animals – dogs. Behavior – misbehavior. Contests. Poetry. Rhyming text. Self-concept.

To the big top ill. by David Gordon. Farrar, 2008. ISBN 978-0-374-39934-4 Subj: Character traits – helpfulness. Circus. Friendship. U.S. history.

Tom's tweet ill. by Dan Santat. Random House, 2011. ISBN 978-0-375-85171-1 Subj: Animals – cats. Birds. Emotions – loneliness. Friendship.

Eschbacher, Roger. *Nonsense! He yelled* ill. by Adrian Johnson. Dial, 2002. ISBN 978-0-8037-2582-9 Subj: ABC books. Rhyming text.

Road trip ill. by Thor Wickstrom. Penguin, 2006. ISBN 978-0-8037-2927-8 Subj: Activities – traveling. Family life. Rhyming text.

Esckelson, Laura. *The copper braid of Shannon O'Shea* ill. by Pam Newton. Dutton, 2003. ISBN 978-0-525-46138-8 Subj: Foreign lands – Ireland. Hair. Mythical creatures.

Escoffier, Michael. *Rabbit and the Not-So-Big-Bad Wolf* ill. by Kris DiGiacomo. Holiday House, 2013. ISBN 978-0-8234-2813-7 Subj: Animals – rabbits. Animals – wolves.

Brief thief ill. by Kris DiGiacomo. Enchanted Lion, 2013. ISBN 978-1-59270-131-5 Subj: Clothing – underwear. Crime. Reptiles – iguanas.

Me first! ill. by Kris DiGiacomo. Enchanted Lion, 2013. ISBN 978-1-59270-136-0 Subj: Behavior – bossy. Birds – ducks. Family life – brothers & sisters.

Esham, Barbara. *Last to finish: a story about the smartest boy in math class* ill. by Mike Gordon. Mainstream, 2008. ISBN 978-1-60336-456-0 Subj: Character traits – confidence. Counting, numbers. School.

Estefan, Gloria. *Noelle's treasure tale: a new magically mysterious adventure* ill. by Michael Garland. HarperCollins, 2006. ISBN 978-0-06-112614-7 Subj: Animals – dogs. Rhyming text. Sea & seashore – beaches.

Ethan, Eric. *Helicopters* ill. with photos. G. Stevens, 2002. ISBN 978-0-8368-3046-0 Subj: Character traits – helpfulness. Helicopters. Safety.

Ets, Marie Hall. *Gilberto and the wind* ill. by author. Viking, 1978, ©1963. ISBN 978-0-670-34025-5 Subj: Ethnic groups in the U.S. – Mexican Americans. Weather – wind.

In the forest ill. by author. Viking, 1944. ISBN 978-0-670-39687-0 Subj: Activities – picnicking. Animals. Caldecott award honor books. Forest, woods. Imagination. Parades.

Just me ill. by author. Viking, 1978, ©1965. ISBN 978-0-670-41109-2 Subj: Animals. Caldecott award honor books. Participation.

Mister Penny ill. by author. Viking, 1935. Subj: Animals. Caldecott award honor books. Farms.

Mr. Penny's race horse ill. by author. Viking, 1956. Subj: Animals – horses, ponies. Caldecott award honor books. Fairs, festivals. Farms.

Mr. T. W. Anthony Woo ill. by author. Viking, 1951. Subj: Animals – cats. Animals – dogs. Animals – mice. Caldecott award honor books.

Nine days to Christmas ill. by author. Viking, 1959. ISBN 978-0-670-51350-5 Subj: Caldecott award books. Ethnic groups in the U.S. – Mexican Americans. Foreign lands – Mexico. Holidays – Christmas. Parties.

Play with me ill. by author. Viking, 1955. ISBN 978-0-670-55977-0 Subj: Activities – playing. Animals. Behavior. Caldecott award honor books.

Eure, Wesley. *A fish out of water.* Designed and ill. by Meredith College Art Department. Pelican, 2000. ISBN 978-1-56554-850-3 Subj: Animals. Birds. Character traits – compromising. Emotions – love. Fish.

Evans, Cambria. *Bone soup* ill. by author. Houghton, 2008. ISBN 978-0-618-80908-0 Subj: Folk & fairy tales. Food. Ghosts. Monsters.

Martha Moth makes socks ill. by author. Houghton, 2006. ISBN 978-0-618-55745-5 Subj: Birthdays. Clothing – socks. Gifts. Insects – moths. Parties.

Evans, Kristina. *What's special about me, Mama?* ill. by Javaka Steptoe. Hyperion/Disney, 2011. ISBN 978-0-7868-5274-1 Subj: Character traits – individuality. Emotions – love. Ethnic groups in the U.S. – African Americans. Family life – mothers. Self-concept.

Evans, Lezlie. *The bunnies' picnic* ill. by Kay Chorao. Hyperion, 2007. ISBN 978-0-7868-1612-5 Subj: Activities – baking, cooking. Activities – picnicking. Animals – rabbits. Food. Rhyming text.

The bunnies' trip ill. by Kay Chorao. Hyperion, 2008. ISBN 978-0-7868-1898-3 Subj: Activities – traveling. Animals – rabbits. Rhyming text.

Can you count ten toes? count to 10 in 10 different languages ill. by Denis Roche. Houghton, 1999. ISBN 978-0-395-90499-2 Subj: Counting, numbers. Foreign languages. Rhyming text.

Can you greet the whole wide world? twelve common phrases in twelve different languages ill. by Denis Roche. Houghton, 2006. ISBN 978-0-618-56327-2 Subj: Foreign languages.

Who loves the little lamb? ill. by David McPhail. Hyperion/Disney, 2010. ISBN 978-1-4231-1659-2 Subj: Animals – babies. Emotions – love. Family life – mothers. Rhyming text.

Evans, Nate. *Bang! Boom! Roar! a busy crew of dinosaurs* by Nate Evans and Stephanie Gwyn Brown ill. by Christopher Santoro. HarperCollins, 2012. ISBN 978-0-06-087960-0 Subj: ABC books. Careers – construction workers. Dinosaurs. Rhyming text. Trucks.

The Jellybeans and the big art adventure (Numeroff, Laura Joffe)

The Jellybeans and the big book bonanza (Numeroff, Laura Joffe)

The Jellybeans and the big camp kickoff (Numeroff, Laura Joffe)

The Jellybeans and the big dance (Numeroff, Laura Joffe)

Ponyella (Numeroff, Laura Joffe)

Sherman Crunchley (Numeroff, Laura Joffe)

Evans, Richard Paul. *The light of Christmas* ill. by Daniel Craig. Simon & Schuster, 2002. ISBN 978-0-689-83468-4 Subj: Character traits – kindness. Holidays – Christmas.

The spyglass ill. by Jonathan Linton. Simon & Schuster, 2001. ISBN 978-0-689-83466-0 Subj: Character traits – ambition. Royalty – kings.

The tower ill. by Jonathan Linton. Simon & Schuster, 2001. ISBN 978-0-689-83467-7 Subj: Character traits – pride. Character traits – vanity.

Evans, Shane W. *Underground: finding the light to freedom* ill. by Shane W. Evans. Roaring Brook, 2011. ISBN 978-1-59643-538-4 Subj: Character traits – freedom. Ethnic groups in the U.S. – African Americans. Slavery. U.S. history.

We march ill. by Shane W. Evans. Roaring Brook, 2012. ISBN 978-1-59643-539-1 Subj: Ethnic groups in the U.S. – African Americans. U.S. history. Violence, nonviolence.

Everitt, Betsy. *Mean soup* ill. by author. Harcourt, 1992. ISBN 978-0-15-253146-1 Subj: Activities – baking, cooking. Behavior – bad day. Emotions – anger. Food. School.

Eversole, Robyn. *East Dragon, West Dragon* ill. by Scott Campbell. Atheneum, 2012. ISBN 978-0-689-85828-4 Subj: Dragons. Prejudice.

Evert, Lori. *The Christmas wish* photos by Per Breiehagen. Random House, 2013. ISBN 978-0-375-97173-0 Subj: Activities – traveling. Animals. Holidays – Christmas. Santa Claus.

Ewart, Claire. *The giant* ill. by author. Walker, 2003. ISBN 978-0-8027-8837-5 Subj: Emotions – grief. Family life – fathers. Farms. Seasons.

Fackelmayer, Regina. *The gifts* ill. by Christa Unzner. NorthSouth, 2009. ISBN 978-0-7358-2265-8 Subj: Character traits – helpfulness. Character traits – kindness. Holidays – Christmas.

Fagan, Cary. *Ella May and the wishing stone* ill. by Geneviève Côté. Tundra, 2011. ISBN 978-1-77049-225-7 Subj: Behavior – wishing. Friendship.

Mr. Zinger's hat ill. by Dusan Petricic. Tundra, 2012. ISBN 978-1-77049-253-0 Subj: Activities – storytelling. Careers – writers. Circular tales. Clothing – hats. Imagination.

Oy, feh, so? ill. by Gary Clement. Groundwood, 2013. ISBN 978-1-55498-148-9 Subj: Family life – aunts, uncles. Jewish culture.

Faglia, Matteo. *Happy birthday, I'm 1* ill. by Luana Rinaldo. Kane/Miller, 2001. ISBN 978-1-929132-07-2 Subj: Animals – rabbits. Birthdays. Food. Format, unusual – board books.

Happy birthday, I'm 2 ill. by Silvia Vignale. Kane/Miller, 2001. ISBN 978-1-929132-08-9 Subj: Animals – dogs. Birthdays. Food. Format, unusual – board books.

Happy birthday, I'm 3 ill. by Sophie Fatus. Kane/Miller, 2001. ISBN 978-1-929132-09-6 Subj: Animals – cats. Birthdays. Food. Format, unusual – board books.

Happy birthday, I'm 4 ill. by Antonella Abbatiello. Kane/Miller, 2001. ISBN 978-1-929132-10-2 Subj: Animals – bears. Birthdays. Food. Format, unusual – board books.

Fairies, trolls and goblins galore comp. by Dilys Evans; ill. by Jacqueline Rogers. Simon & Schuster, 2000. ISBN 978-0-689-82352-7 Subj: Fairies. Mythical creatures. Poetry.

Falconer, Ian. *Olivia* ill. by author. Atheneum, 2000. ISBN 978-0-689-82953-6 Subj: Activities. Animals – pigs. Behavior. Caldecott award honor books.

Olivia and the fairy princesses ill. by author. Atheneum, 2012. ISBN 978-1-4424-5027-1 Subj: Animals – pigs. Character traits – individuality. Royalty – princesses. Royalty – queens. Self-concept.

Olivia — and the missing toy ill. by author. Atheneum, 2003. ISBN 978-0-689-85291-6 Subj: Animals – pigs. Behavior – lost & found possessions. Format, unusual – board books. Toys.

Olivia counts ill. by author. Atheneum, 2002. ISBN 978-0-689-85087-5 Subj: Animals – babies. Animals – pigs. Counting, numbers. Format, unusual – board books.

Olivia forms a band ill. by author. Simon & Schuster, 2006. ISBN 978-1-4169-2454-8 Subj: Animals – pigs. Music.

Olivia goes to Venice ill. by author. Simon & Schuster, 2010. ISBN 978-1-4169-9674-3 Subj: Activities – vacationing. Animals – pigs. Foreign lands – Italy.

Olivia saves the circus ill. by author. Atheneum, 2001. ISBN 978-0-689-82954-3 Subj: Animals – pigs. Circus. School.

Olivia's opposites ill. by author. Atheneum, 2002. ISBN 978-0-689-85088-2 Subj: Animals – babies. Animals – pigs. Behavior. Concepts – opposites. Format, unusual – board books.

Falken, Linda. *Can you find it?* Abrams, 2010. ISBN 978-0-8109-8890-3 Subj: Art. Picture puzzles. U.S. history.

Falkenstern, Lisa. *A dragon moves in* ill. by author. Marshall Cavendish, 2011. ISBN 978-0-7614-5947-7 Subj: Animals – hedgehogs. Animals – rabbits. Dragons. Homes, houses.

Faller, Regis. *The adventures of Polo* ill. by author. Macmillan, 2006. ISBN 978-1-59643-160-7 Subj: Activities – traveling. Animals – dogs. Imagination. Wordless.

Polo: the runaway book ill. by author. Macmillan, 2007. ISBN 978-1-59643-189-8 Subj: Activities – traveling. Animals – dogs. Imagination. Wordless.

Polo and Lily ill. by author. Roaring Brook, 2009. ISBN 978-1-59643-496-7 Subj: Animals – dogs. Animals – rabbits. Friendship. Wordless.

Polo and the dragon ill. by author. Roaring Brook, 2009. ISBN 978-1-59643-498-1 Subj: Animals – dogs. Dragons. Imagination. Wordless.

Polo and the magician! ill. by author. Roaring Brook, 2009. ISBN 978-1-59643-497-4 Subj: Activities – traveling. Animals – dogs. Careers – magicians. Circus. Wordless.

Fallon, Jimmy. *Snowball fight!* ill. by Adam Stower. Penguin, 2005. ISBN 978-0-525-47456-2 Subj: Rhyming text. Weather – snow.

Falwell, Cathryn. *Christmas for 10* ill. by author. Clarion, 1998. ISBN 978-0-395-85581-2 Subj: Counting, numbers. Ethnic groups in the U.S. – African Americans. Holidays – Christmas. Rhyming text.

David's drawing ill. by author. Lee & Low, 2001. ISBN 978-1-58430-031-1 Subj: Activities – drawing. Ethnic groups in the U.S. – African Americans. Friendship. School – first day.

Feast for ten ill. by author. Clarion, 1993. ISBN 978-0-395-62037-3 Subj: Activities – baking, cooking. Counting, numbers. Ethnic groups in the U.S. – African Americans. Family life. Rhyming text.

Gobble gobble ill. by author. Dawn, 2011. ISBN 978-158469-148-8; Subj: Birds – turkeys. Rhyming text.

Mystery vine: a pumpkin surprise ill. by author. HarperCollins, 2009. ISBN 978-0-06-177198-9 Subj: Food. Gardens, gardening. Rhyming text.

P.J. and Puppy ill. by author. Clarion, 1997. ISBN 978-0-395-56918-4 Subj: Animals – dogs. Family life – mothers. Pets. Toilet training.

Pond babies ill. by author. Down East, 2011. ISBN 978-0-89272-920-3 Subj: Animals – babies. Lakes, ponds.

Rainbow Stew ill. by author. Lee & Low, 2013. ISBN 978-1-60060-847-6 Subj: Activities – baking, cooking. Family life – grandfathers. Food. Rhyming text.

Scoot! ill. by author. Greenwillow, 2008. ISBN 978-0-06-128882-1 Subj: Lakes, ponds. Reptiles – turtles, tortoises. Rhyming text.

Shape capers ill. by author. HarperCollins, 2007. ISBN 978-0-06-123700-3 Subj: Concepts – shape. Rhyming text.

Turtle splash! ill. by author. Greenwillow, 2001. ISBN 978-0-06-029463-2 Subj: Counting, numbers. Reptiles – turtles, tortoises. Rhyming text.

We have a baby ill. by author. Clarion, 1993. ISBN 978-0-395-62038-0 Subj: Babies. Family life.

Word wizard ill. by author. Clarion, 1998. ISBN 978-0-395-85580-5 Subj: Imagination. Language.

Fancher, Lou. *Star climbing* ill. by Steve Johnson. HarperCollins, 2006. ISBN 978-0-06-073902-7 Subj: Bedtime. Imagination. Stars.

Farber, Norma. *How the hibernators came to Bethlehem* ill. by Barbara Cooney. Walker, 2006. ISBN 978-0-8027-9610-3 Subj: Animals. Holidays – Christmas. Poetry. Religion.

Fardell, John. *Jeremiah Jellyfish flies high!* ill. by author. IPG/Andersen, 2012. ISBN 978-1-84939-147-4 Subj: Activities – flying. Airplanes, airports. Animals.

Farish, Terry. *The cat who liked potato soup* ill. by Barry Root. Candlewick, 2003. ISBN 978-0-7636-0834-7 Subj: Animals – cats. Food. Friendship. Pets. Sports – fishing.

Farley, Brianne. *Ike's incredible ink* ill. by author. Candlewick, 2013. ISBN 978-0-7636-6296-7 Subj: Activities – writing.

Farley, Carol J. *The king's secret* ill. by Robert Jew. HarperCollins, 2001. ISBN 978-0-688-12777-0 Subj: ABC books. Behavior – secrets. Foreign lands – Korea. Foreign languages. Royalty – kings.

Farmer, Bonnie. *Isaac's dreamcatcher* ill. by Anouk Perusse-Bell. Lobster, 2001. ISBN 978-1-894222-46-4 Subj: Dreams. Emotions – fear. Indians of North America.

The farmer in the dell. *The farmer in the dell* ill. by John O'Brien. Boyds Mills, 2000. ISBN 978-1-56397-775-6 Subj: Careers – farmers. Farms. Games. Music. Songs.

The farmer in the dell ill. by Alexandra Wallner. Holiday, 1998. ISBN 978-0-8234-1382-9 Subj: Careers – farmers. Farms. Games. Music. Songs.

Farmer, Nancy. *Clever Ali* ill. by Gail de Marcken. Scholastic, 2006. ISBN 978-0-439-37014-1 Subj: Birds – pigeons. Family life – fathers. Foreign lands – Egypt. Royalty – sultans.

Farrar, Sid. *The year comes round: haiku through the seasons* ill. by Ilse Plume. Whitman, 2012. ISBN 978-0-8075-8129-2 Subj: Nature. Poetry. Seasons.

Farris, Christine King. *March on! the day my brother Martin changed the world* ill. by London Ladd. Scholastic, 2008. ISBN 978-0-545-03537-8 Subj: Ethnic groups in the U.S. – African Americans. Prejudice. U.S. history. Violence, nonviolence.

My brother Martin: a sister remembers growing up with the Rev. Dr. Martin Luther King ill. by Chris Soentpiet. Simon & Schuster, 2003. ISBN 978-0-689-84387-7 Subj: Ethnic groups in the U.S. – African Americans. Family life – brothers & sisters. Prejudice. U.S. history. Violence, nonviolence.

Fauchald, Nick. *Batter up! you can play softball* ill. by Ronnie Rooney. Picture Window, 2006. ISBN 978-1-4048-1152-2 Subj: Sports – baseball.

Bump! set! spike! you can play volleyball ill. by Ronnie Rooney. Picture Window, 2006. ISBN 978-1-4048-1153-9 Subj: Sports – volleyball.

Face off! you can play hockey ill. by Ronnie Rooney. Picture Window, 2006. ISBN 978-1-4048-1154-6 Subj: Sports – hockey.

Jump ball! you can play basketball ill. by Bill Dickson. Picture Window, 2004. ISBN 978-1-4048-0261-2 Subj: Sports – basketball.

Nice hit! you can play baseball ill. by Bill Dickson. Picture Window, 2004. ISBN 978-1-4048-0259-9 Subj: Sports – baseball.

Score! you can play soccer ill. by Bill Dickson. Picture Window, 2004. ISBN 978-1-4048-0262-9 Subj: Sports – soccer.

Tee off! you can play golf ill. by Ronnie Rooney. Picture Window, 2006. ISBN 978-1-4048-1155-3 Subj: Sports – golf.

Touchdown! you can play football ill. by Bill Dickson. Picture Window, 2004. ISBN 978-1-4048-0260-5 Subj: Sports – football.

Faulkenberry, Lauren. *What do animals do on the weekend?* ill. by author. Novello, 2002. ISBN 978-0-9708972-4-4 Subj: ABC books. Activities. Animals.

Faulkner, Keith. *Charlie Chimp's Christmas* ill. by Jonathan Lambert. Barron's, 2002. ISBN 978-0-7641-5556-7 Subj: Animals – chimpanzees. Format, unusual – toy & movable books. Holidays – Christmas. Santa Claus.

Do you have my quack? ill. by Rob Hefferan. Scholastic, 2001. ISBN 978-0-439-24085-7 Subj: Animals. Birds – ducks. Farms. Format, unusual – toy & movable books. Noise, sounds.

The giraffe who cock-a-doodle-doo'd ill. by Jonathan Lambert. Dial, 2002. ISBN 978-0-8037-2739-7 Subj: Animals. Format, unusual – toy & movable books. Jungle.

Jumbled jungle ill. by Jonathan Lambert. Scholastic, 2001. ISBN 978-0-439-30903-5 Subj: Animals. Format, unusual – toy & movable books. Jungle.

The monster who loved books ill. by Jonathan Lambert. Orchard, 2002. ISBN 978-0-439-34099-1 Subj: Books, reading. Format, unusual – toy & movable books. Monsters.

Pop! went another balloon! ill. by Rory Tyger. Dutton, 2002. ISBN 978-0-525-47122-6 Subj: Counting, numbers. Format, unusual – toy & movable books. Toys – balloons.

Rexerella ill. by Graham Kennedy. Paper engineering by Jonathan Lambert. Simon & Schuster, 2002. ISBN 978-0-689-85355-5 Subj: Dinosaurs. Format, unusual – toy & movable books.

The scared little bear ill. by Jonathan Lambert. 1st American Ed. Scholastic, 2000. ISBN 978-0-531-30267-5 Subj: Bedtime. Emotions – fear. Format, unusual – toy & movable books.

The tallest shortest longest greenest brownest animal in the jungle! ill. by Rory Tyger. Dutton, 2002. ISBN 978-0-525-46868-4 Subj: Animals. Format, unusual – toy & movable books. Friendship. Jungle.

A trick or a treat? ill. by Manhar Chauhan. Dutton, 2001. ISBN 978-0-525-46765-6 Subj: Format, unusual – toy & movable books. Holidays – Halloween. Night. Picture puzzles.

Faundez, Anne. *The day the rains fell* ill. by Karin Littlewood. IPG/Tamarind, 2010. ISBN 978-1-84853-015-7 Subj: Foreign lands – Africa. Weather – droughts.

Fearnley, Jan. *Arthur and the meanies* ill. by author. Egmont UK, 2011. ISBN 978-1-4052-5380-2 Subj: Animals. Animals – elephants. Behavior – bullying, teasing. Friendship.

Just like you ill. by author. Candlewick, 2001. ISBN 978-0-7636-1322-8 Subj: Animals – babies. Animals – mice. Bedtime. Family life – parents.

Martha in the middle ill. by author. Candlewick, 2008. ISBN 978-0-7636-3800-9 Subj: Animals – mice. Behavior – running away. Family life – brothers & sisters. Frogs & toads.

Milo Armadillo ill. by author. Candlewick, 2009. ISBN 978-0-7636-4575-5 Subj: Animals – armadillos. Family life – grandmothers. Toys.

Mr. Wolf and the three bears ill. by author. Harcourt, 2002. ISBN 978-0-15-216423-2 Subj: Activities – baking, cooking. Animals – bears. Animals – wolves. Birthdays.

Mr. Wolf's pancakes ill. by author. Tiger Tales, 2001. ISBN 978-1-888444-76-6 Subj: Activities – baking, cooking. Animals – wolves. Food.

A perfect day for it ill. by author. Harcourt, 2002. ISBN 978-0-15-216634-2 Subj: Animals. Animals – bears. Friendship. Sports – sledding. Weather – snow.

The search for the perfect child ill. by author. Candlewick, 2006. ISBN 978-0-7636-3231-1 Subj: Animals – dogs. Behavior. Character traits – perfectionism.

A special something ill. by author. Hyperion, 2000. ISBN 978-0-7868-0589-1 Subj: Babies. Birth. Family life. Family life – new sibling. Imagination.

Watch out! ill. by author. Candlewick, 2004. ISBN 978-0-7636-2318-0 Subj: Animals – mice. Behavior. Family life – mothers.

Fearrington, Ann. *Who sees the lighthouse?* ill. by Giles Laroche. Putnam, 2002. ISBN 978-0-399-23703-4 Subj: Counting, numbers. Lighthouses. Rhyming text.

Fecher, Sarah. *On the move* by Sarah Fecher and Deborah Kespert ill. by Gaëtan Evrard. Story by Belinda Webster; computer Ill. by Jon Stuart. Two-Can, 2000. ISBN 978-1-58728-605-6 Subj: Transportation.

Federspiel, Jurg. *Alligator Mike* ill. by Petra Rappo. NorthSouth, 2007. ISBN 978-0-7358-2124-8 Subj: Character traits – kindness to animals. Reptiles – alligators, crocodiles.

Feelings, Muriel. *Jambo means hello: Swahili alphabet book* ill. by Tom Feelings. Dial, 1974. ISBN 978-0-8037-4346-5 Subj: ABC books. Caldecott award honor books. Foreign lands – Africa. Foreign languages.

Moja means one: Swahili counting book ill. by Tom Feelings. Dial, 1972. ISBN 978-0-8037-5711-0 Subj: Caldecott award honor books. Counting, numbers. Foreign lands – Africa. Foreign languages.

Feeney, Tatyana. *Little Owl's orange scarf* ill. by author. Knopf, 2013. ISBN 978-0-449-81411-6 Subj: Behavior – lost & found possessions. Birds – owls. Clothing – scarves. Family life – mothers.

Small Bunny's blue blanket ill. by author. Knopf, 2012. ISBN 978-0-375-87087-3 Subj: Animals – rabbits. Laundry.

Feiffer, Jules. *Bark, George* ill. by author. HarperCollins, 1999. ISBN 978-0-06-205185-1 Subj: Animals – dogs. Humorous stories. Noise, sounds.

The daddy mountain ill. by author. Hyperion, 2004. ISBN 978-0-7868-0912-7 Subj: Family life – daughters. Family life – fathers.

I lost my bear ill. by author. Morrow, 1998. ISBN 978-0-688-15148-5 Subj: Behavior – lost & found possessions. Family life. Toys. Toys – bears.

Feiffer, Kate. *But I wanted a baby brother!* ill. by Diane Goode. Simon & Schuster, 2010. ISBN 978-1-4169-3941-2 Subj: Babies. Family life – brothers & sisters.

Double pink ill. by Bruce Ingman. Simon & Schuster, 2005. ISBN 978-0-689-87190-0 Subj: Concepts – color.

Henry, the dog with no tail ill. by Jules Feiffer. Simon & Schuster, 2007. ISBN 978-1-4169-1614-7 Subj: Anatomy – tails. Animals – dogs. Language. Self-concept.

My mom is trying to ruin my life ill. by Diane Goode. Simon & Schuster, 2009. ISBN 978-1-4169-4100-2 Subj: Emotions – embarrassment. Family life – parents. Humorous stories.

My side of the car ill. by Jules Feiffer. Candlewick, 2011. ISBN 978-0-7636-4405-5 Subj: Family life – fathers. Weather – rain. Zoos.

No go sleep! ill. by Jules Feiffer. Simon & Schuster, 2012. ISBN 978-1-4424-1683-3 Subj: Babies. Bedtime. Family life. Night.

President Pennybaker ill. by Diane Goode. Simon & Schuster, 2008. ISBN 978-1-4169-1354-2 Subj: Animals – dogs. Behavior – seeking better things. Character traits – ambition.

Which puppy? ill. by Jules Feiffer. Simon & Schuster, 2009. ISBN 978-1-4169-9147-2 Subj: Animals. Animals – dogs. Ethnic groups in the U.S. – African Americans. Family life. Pets.

Feldman, Eve B. *Billy & Milly, short and silly* ill. by Tuesday Mourning. Putnam, 2009. ISBN 978-0-399-24651-7 Subj: Language. Rhyming text.

Feldman, Thea. *Who you callin' chicken?* photos by Stephen Green-Armytage. Abrams, 2003. ISBN 978-0-8109-4593-7 Subj: Birds – chickens.

Felix, Monique. *The rumor* ill. by author. Creative Education, 2011. ISBN 978-1-56846-219-6 Subj: Animals. Animals – wolves. Behavior – gossip. Communication.

Fenton, Joe. *Boo!* ill. by author. Simon & Schuster, 2010. ISBN 978-1-4169-7936-4 Subj: Disguises. Ghosts.

Ferber, Brenda A. *The yuckiest, stinkiest, best Valentine ever* ill. by Tedd Arnold. Dial, 2012. ISBN 978-0-8037-3505-7 Subj: Emotions – love. Holidays – Valentine's Day. Humorous stories.

Fergus, Maureen. *The day my mom came to kindergarten* ill. by Mike Lowery. Kids Can, 2013. ISBN 978-1-55453-698-6 Subj: Behavior – misbehavior. Family life – mothers. School.

Ferguson, Sarah. *Ballerina Rosie* ill. by Diane Goode. Simon & Schuster, 2012. ISBN 978-1-4424-3066-2 Subj: Ballet. Careers – dancers. Self-concept.

Emily's first day of school ill. by Ian Cunliffe. Sterling, 2010. ISBN 978-1-4027-7392-1 Subj: School – first day.

Tea for Ruby ill. by Robin Preiss-Glasser. Simon & Schuster, 2008. ISBN 978-1-4169-5419-4 Subj: Etiquette. Royalty – princesses.

Fern, Tracey E. *Buffalo music* ill. by Lauren Castillo. Clarion, 2008. ISBN 978-0-618-72341-6 Subj: Animals – buffaloes. Texas.

Fernandes, Eugenie. *Big week for little mouse* ill. by Kim Fernandes. Kids Can, 2004. ISBN 978-1-55337-665-1 Subj: Animals – mice. Birthdays. Concepts – opposites. Days of the week, months of the year. Rhyming text.

Busy little mouse ill. by Kim Fernandes; photos by Pat Lacroix. Kids Can, 2002. ISBN 978-1-55074-776-8 Subj: Animals. Animals – mice. Farms. Noise, sounds. Rhyming text.

Kitten's spring ill. by author. Kids Can, 2010. ISBN 978-1-55453-340-4 Subj: Animals – babies. Animals – cats. Farms. Rhyming text. Seasons – spring.

Kitten's winter ill. by author. Kids Can, 2011. ISBN 978-1-55453-343-5 Subj: Animals. Animals – cats. Rhyming text. Seasons – winter.

Sleepy little mouse ill. by Kim Fernandes. Kids Can, 2000. ISBN 978-1-55074-701-0 Subj: Animals – mice. Behavior. Emotions. Sleep.

Ferreri, Della Ross. *How will I ever sleep in this bed?* ill. by Capucine Mazille. Sterling, 2005. ISBN 978-1-4027-1492-4 Subj: Bedtime. Furniture – beds. Rhyming text. Toys.

Ferri, Giuliano. *Little Tad grows up* ill. by author. Penguin, 2007. ISBN 978-0-698-40060-3 Subj: Behavior – growing up. Frogs & toads. Nature. Science.

Ferris, Jeri Chase. *Noah Webster and his words* ill. by Vincent X. Kirsch. Houghton Mifflin, 2012. ISBN 978-0-547-39055-0 Subj: Careers – teachers. Dictionaries. Language. U.S. history.

Feutl, Rita. *Room enough for Daisy* (Waldman, Debby)

Ficocelli, Elizabeth. *Kid tea* ill. by Glin Dibley. Marshall Cavendish, 2007. ISBN 978-0-7614-5333-

8 Subj: Activities – bathing. Concepts – color. Days of the week, months of the year. Rhyming text.

Field, Eugene. *Wynken, Blynken and Nod* ill. by Johanna Westerman. NorthSouth, 1995. ISBN 978-1-55858-423-5 Subj: Poetry. Sea & seashore. Sleep.

Wynken, Blynken, and Nod: a Dutch lullaby ill. by Giselle Potter. Random House, 2008. ISBN 978-0-375-84196-5 Subj: Poetry. Sea & seashore. Sleep.

Field, Rachel Lyman. *Grace for an island meal* ill. by Cynthia Jabar. Farrar, 2006. ISBN 978-0-374-32759-0 Subj: Islands. Poetry. Religion.

Prayer for a child ill. by Elizabeth Orton Jones. Macmillan, 1944. ISBN 978-0-02-735190-3 Subj: Caldecott award books. Religion.

Fielding, Beth. *Animal eyes.* EarlyLight, 2011. ISBN 978-0-9797455-5-3 Subj: Anatomy – eyes. Animals.

Animal tails. EarlyLight, 2011. ISBN 978-0-9797455-8-4 Subj: Anatomy – tails. Animals.

Fierstein, Harvey. *The sissy duckling* ill. by Henry Cole. Simon & Schuster, 2002. ISBN 978-0-689-83566-7 Subj: Birds – ducks. Gender roles. Self-concept.

Figley, Marty Rhodes. *Emily and Carlo* ill. by Catherine Stock. Charlesbridge, 2012. ISBN 978-1-58089-274-2 Subj: Animals – dogs. Poetry.

The schoolchildren's blizzard ill. by Shelly O. Haas. Carolrhoda, 2004. ISBN 978-1-57505-586-2 Subj: Careers – teachers. Family life – sisters. U.S. history. Weather – blizzards.

Filleul, Liz. *Tumbler* ill. by Susan Field. Augsburg Fortress, 2001. ISBN 978-0-8066-4268-0 Subj: Careers – acrobats. Religion.

Finch, Mary. *The little red hen* (The little red hen)

Finchler, Judy. *Congratulations, Miss Malarkey!* by Judy Finchler and Kevin O'Malley ill. by Kevin O'Malley. Walker, 2009. ISBN 978-0-8027-9835-0 Subj: Careers – teachers. School. Weddings.

Miss Malarkey leaves no reader behind by Judy Finchler and Kevin O'Malley ill. by Kevin O'Malley. Walker, 2006. ISBN 978-0-8027-8084-3 Subj: Books, reading. Careers – teachers. School.

Miss Malarkey won't be in today ill. by Kevin O'Malley. Walker, 2000. ISBN 978-0-8027-8653-1 Subj: Careers – teachers. Illness. School.

Testing Miss Malarkey ill. by Kevin O'Malley. Walker, 2000. ISBN 978-0-8027-8739-2 Subj: Careers – teachers. School.

You're a good sport, Miss Malarkey ill. by Kevin O'Malley. Walker, 2002. ISBN 978-0-8027-8816-0 Subj: Careers – coaches. Careers – teachers. Sports – soccer. Sportsmanship.

Findlay, Lisa. *What's in Oscar's trashcan?* ill. by Joe Ewers. Random House, 2002. ISBN 978-0-375-81580-5 Subj: Behavior – lost & found possessions. Format, unusual – toy & movable books. Puppets.

Fine, Edith Hope. *Water, weed, and wait* by Edith Hope Fine and Angela Demos Halpin ill. by Colleen M. Madden. Tricycle, 2010. ISBN 978-1-58246-320-9 Subj: Gardens, gardening. School.

Fine, Howard. *A piggie Christmas* ill. by author. Hyperion, 2000. ISBN 978-0-7868-2505-9 Subj: Animals – pigs. Holidays – Christmas. Music. Songs.

Finlay, Lizzie. *Little Croc's purse* ill. by author. Eerdmans, 2011. ISBN 978-0-8028-5392-9 Subj: Behavior – bullying, teasing. Character traits – honesty. Clothing – handbags, purses. Money. Reptiles – alligators, crocodiles.

Finn, Isobel. *The very lazy ladybug* ill. by Jack Tickle. Tiger Tales, 2001. ISBN 978-1-58925-007-9 Subj: Activities – flying. Animals. Character traits – laziness. Insects – ladybugs.

The firebird. *The firebird* retold by Demi; ill. by reteller. Holt, 1994. ISBN 978-0-8050-3244-4 Subj: Ballet. Behavior – stealing. Folk & fairy tales. Foreign lands – Russia. Magic. Mythical creatures. Royalty – princes.

The firebird adapt. by Rachel Isadora; ill. by adapter. Putnam, 1994. ISBN 978-0-399-22510-9 Subj: Ballet. Behavior – stealing. Folk & fairy tales. Foreign lands – Russia. Magic. Mythical creatures. Royalty – princes.

The tale of the firebird ill. by Gennady Spirin. Philomel, 2002. ISBN 978-0-399-23584-9 Subj: Ballet. Behavior – stealing. Folk & fairy tales. Foreign lands – Russia. Magic. Mythical creatures. Royalty – princes.

Firmin, Josie. *My week* ill. by author. Candlewick, 2001. ISBN 978-0-7636-1548-2 Subj: Days of the week, months of the year. Format, unusual – toy & movable books.

Fischer, Scott M. *Jump!* ill. by author. Simon & Schuster, 2010. ISBN 978-1-4169-7884-8 Subj: Activities – jumping. Animals. Rhyming text.

Twinkle ill. by author. Simon & Schuster, 2007. ISBN 978-1-4169-3980-1 Subj: Format, unusual – toy & movable books. Poetry. Space & space ships. Stars.

The fish is me sel. by Neil Philip; ill. by Claire Henley. Clarion, 2002. ISBN 978-0-618-15939-0 Subj: Activities – bathing. Poetry.

Fisher, Aileen Lucia. *Do rabbits have Christmas?* ill. by Sarah Fox-Davies. Holt, 2007. ISBN 978-0-8050-7491-8 Subj: Animals. Holidays – Christmas. Nature. Poetry. Seasons – winter.

Know what I saw? ill. by Deborah Durland DeSaix. Macmillan, 2005. ISBN 978-1-59643-055-6 Subj: Animals. Counting, numbers. Rhyming text.

The story goes on ill. by Mique Moriuchi. Macmillan, 2005. ISBN 978-1-59643-037-2 Subj: Nature. Poetry.

You don't look like your mother ill. by Lilith Jones. Mondo, 2002. ISBN 978-1-58653-856-9 Subj: Animals – babies. Birds – robins. Rhyming text.

Fisher, Alex. *A kid's best friend* (Ajmera, Maya)

Fisher, Carolyn. *A twisted tale* ill. by author. Knopf, 2002. ISBN 978-0-375-91540-6 Subj: Animals. Farms. Humorous stories. Weather – tornadoes.

Fisher, Doris. *Happy birthday to whooo? a baby animal riddle book* ill. by Lisa Downey. Sylvan Dell, 2006. ISBN 978-0-9768823-1-2 Subj: Animals – babies. Riddles & jokes.

My even day by Doris Fisher and Dani Sneed ill. by Karen Lee. Sylvan Dell, 2007. ISBN 978-0-9777423-3-2 Subj: Counting, numbers. Rhyming text.

One odd day by Doris Fisher and Dani Sneed ill. by Karen Lee. Sylvan Dell, 2006. ISBN 978-0-9768823-3-6 Subj: Counting, numbers. Rhyming text.

Fisher, Jeff. *The hair scare* ill. by author. Bloomsbury, 2005. ISBN 978-1-58234-672-4 Subj: Hair. Royalty – kings.

Fisher, Leonard Everett. *Cyclops* ill. by author. Holiday, 1991. ISBN 978-0-8234-0891-7 Subj: Folk & fairy tales. Mythical creatures.

David and Goliath ill. by adapter. Holiday, 1993. ISBN 978-0-8234-0997-6 Subj: Foreign lands – Israel. Giants. Religion – David.

Gutenberg ill. by author. Macmillan, 1993. ISBN 978-0-02-735238-2 Subj: Careers – printers. Communication. Inventions.

The seven days of creation ill. by author. Adapt. from the Bible. Holiday, 1981. ISBN 978-0-8234-0398-1 Subj: Creation. Religion.

Sky, sea, the jetty, and me ill. by author. Marshall Cavendish, 2001. ISBN 978-0-7614-5082-5 Subj: Sea & seashore. Weather – storms.

Stars and stripes: our national flag ill. by author. Holiday, 1993. ISBN 978-0-8234-1053-8 Subj: U.S. history.

Theseus and the Minotaur ill. by author. Holiday, 1988. ISBN 978-0-8234-0703-3 Subj: Folk & fairy tales. Mythical creatures. Royalty.

William Tell ill. by author. Farrar, 1996. ISBN 978-0-374-38436-4 Subj: Folk & fairy tales. Foreign lands – Switzerland. Sports – archery.

Fisher, Mary M. *Rosita's bridge* ill. by Barbara Mathews Whitehead. Maverick, 2001. ISBN 978-1-893271-18-0 Subj: Careers – singers. Ethnic groups in the U.S. – Mexican Americans. U.S. history.

Fisher, Valorie. *Ellsworth's extraordinary electric ears and other amazing alphabet anecdotes* ill. with photos. Atheneum, 2003. ISBN 978-0-689-85030-1 Subj: ABC books.

Everything I need to know before I'm five ill. by author. Random House, 2011. ISBN 978-0-375-86865-8 Subj: Concepts. Counting, numbers. Seasons.

How high can a dinosaur count? and other math mysteries ill. by author. Random House, 2006. ISBN 978-0-375-83608-4 Subj: Counting, numbers. Puzzles.

My big brother ill. with photos. Atheneum, 2002. ISBN 978-0-689-84327-3 Subj: Family life – brothers.

Fishman, Anna Schnur. *Tashlich at Turtle Rock* (Schnur, Susan)

Fishman, Cathy Goldberg. *On Hanukkah* ill. by Melanie W. Hall. Atheneum, 1998. ISBN 978-0-689-80643-8 Subj: Holidays – Hanukkah. Jewish culture. Religion.

On Passover ill. by Melanie W. Hall. Atheneum, 1997. ISBN 978-0-689-80528-8 Subj: Holidays – Passover. Jewish culture. Religion.

On Purim ill. by Melanie W. Hall. Atheneum, 2000. ISBN 978-0-689-82392-3 Subj: Family life. Holidays – Purim. Jewish culture.

On Rosh Hashanah and Yom Kippur ill. by Melanie W. Hall. Atheneum, 1997. ISBN 978-0-689-80526-4 Subj: Holidays – Rosh Hashanah. Holidays – Yom Kippur. Jewish culture. Religion.

On Shabbat ill. by Melanie W. Hall. Atheneum, 2001. ISBN 978-0-689-83894-1 Subj: Family life. Holidays. Jewish culture. Religion.

When Jackie and Hank met ill. by Mark Elliott. Amazon Children's, 2012. ISBN 978-0-7614-6140-1 Subj: Ethnic groups in the U.S. – African Americans. Jewish culture. Prejudice. Sports – baseball. U.S. history.

Fitch, Florence Mary. *A book about God* ill. by Henri Sorensen. Lothrop, 1999. ISBN 978-0-688-16129-3 Subj: Religion.

Fitch, Sheree. *No two snowflakes* ill. by Janet Wilson. Orca, 2001. ISBN 978-1-55143-206-9 Subj: Poetry. Weather – snow.

Fitz-Gibbon, Sally. *On Uncle John's farm* ill. by Brian Deines. Fitzhenry & Whiteside, 2005. ISBN 978-1-55041-691-6 Subj: Careers – farmers. Farms.

Two shoes, blue shoes, new shoes! ill. by Farida Zaman. Fitzhenry & Whiteside, 2003. ISBN 978-1-55041-729-6 Subj: Activities. Clothing – shoes.

FitzGerald, Dawn. *Vinnie and Abraham* ill. by Catherine Stock. Charlesbridge, 2007. ISBN 978-1-57091-658-8 Subj: Art. U.S. history.

Fitzgerald, Ella. *A-tisket, a-tasket* by Ella Fitzgerald and Van Alexander ill. by Ora Eitan. Philomel, 2003. ISBN 978-0-399-23206-0 Subj: Behavior – lost & found possessions. Music. Songs.

Fitzgerald, Joanne. *This is me and where I am* ill. by author. Fitzhenry & Whiteside, 2004. ISBN 978-1-55041-819-4 Subj: Cities, towns. Homes, houses.

Yum! Yum! delicious nursery rhymes ill. by author. Fitzhenry & Whiteside, 2007. ISBN 978-1-55041-888-0 Subj: Animals. Food. Nursery rhymes.

Fitzpatrick, Marie-Louise. *I'm a tiger, too!* ill. by author. Roaring Brook, 2002. ISBN 978-0-7613-2410-2 Subj: Activities – playing. Animals. Imagination. Rhyming text.

Lizzy and Skunk ill. by author. DK, 2000. ISBN 978-0-7894-6163-6 Subj: Behavior – lost. Emotions – fear. Puppets.

You, me and the big blue sea ill. by author. Roaring Brook, 2002. ISBN 978-0-7613-2806-3 Subj: Activities – traveling. Boats, ships. Family life – mothers. Memories, memory. Sea & seashore.

Fitzsimmons, David. *Curious critters* photos by author. Wild Iris, 2011. ISBN 978-1-936607-69-3 Subj: Animals. Frogs & toads. Nature. Reptiles.

Five little pumpkins ill. by Ben Mantle. Tiger Tales, 2010. ISBN 978-1-58925-856-3 Subj: Counting, numbers. Format, unusual – board books. Holidays – Halloween. Plants. Rhyming text. Witches.

Five little pumpkins ill. by Dan Yaccarino. HarperCollins, 1998. ISBN 978-0-694-01177-3 Subj: Counting, numbers. Format, unusual – board books. Holidays – Halloween. Plants. Rhyming text. Witches.

Flack, Marjorie. *Ask Mr. Bear* ill. by author. Macmillan, 1932. ISBN 978-0-02-735390-7 Subj: Animals. Animals – bears. Birthdays. Emotions – love. Family life – mothers.

The story about Ping by Marjorie Flack and Kurt Wiese ill. by Kurt Wiese. Viking, 1933. Subj: Behavior – misbehavior. Birds – ducks. Foreign lands – China.

Flaherty, A. W. *The luck of the Loch Ness monster: a tale of picky eating* ill. by Scott Magoon. Houghton, 2007. ISBN 978-0-618-55644-1 Subj: Food. Monsters.

Flanagan, Alice K. *Ask Nurse Pfaff, she'll help you!* photos by Christine Osinski. Children's Press, 1997. ISBN 978-0-516-20495-6 Subj: Careers – nurses. Hospitals.

A busy day at Mr. Kang's grocery store photos by Christine Osinski. Children's Press, 1996. ISBN 978-0-516-20047-7 Subj: Careers – storekeepers. Communities, neighborhoods. Ethnic groups in the U.S. – Korean Americans. Shopping. Stores.

Buying a pet from Ms. Chavez photos by Romie Flanagan. Children's Press, 1998. ISBN 978-0-516-20773-5 Subj: Careers – storekeepers. Communities, neighborhoods. Pets. Stores.

Call Mr. Vasquez, he'll fix it! photos by Christine Osinski. Children's Press, 1996. ISBN 978-0-516-20045-3 Subj: Careers – custodians, janitors. Careers – handymen. Homes, houses.

Chinese New Year ill. by Svetlana Zhurkina. Compass Point, 2004. ISBN 978-0-7565-0479-3 Subj: Ethnic groups in the U.S. – Chinese Americans. Fairs, festivals. Holidays – Chinese New Year.

Choosing eyeglasses with Mrs. Koutris photos by Romie Flanagan. Children's Press, 1998. ISBN 978-0-516-20775-9 Subj: Careers – opticians, optometrists. Careers – storekeepers. Glasses.

Christmas ill. by Viki Woodworth. Compass Point, 2002. ISBN 978-0-7565-0085-6 Subj: Holidays – Christmas.

Cinco de Mayo ill. by Patrick Girouard. Compass Point, 2004. ISBN 978-0-7565-0480-9 Subj: Ethnic groups in the U.S. – Mexican Americans. Foreign lands – Mexico. Holidays – Cinco de Mayo.

Coach John and his soccer team photos by Christine Osinski. Children's Press, 1998. ISBN 978-0-516-20777-3 Subj: Careers – coaches. Communities, neighborhoods. Sports – soccer. Sportsmanship.

A day in court with Mrs. Trinh photos by Christine Osinski. Children's Press, 1997. ISBN 978-0-516-20008-8 Subj: Careers – lawyers. Crime.

Dr. Friedman helps animals photos by Christine Osinski. Children's Press, 1999. ISBN 978-0-516-21138-1 Subj: Animals. Careers – veterinarians.

Dr. Kanner, dentist with a smile photos by Christine Osinski. Children's Press, 1997. ISBN 978-0-516-20493-2 Subj: Careers – dentists. Teeth.

Exploring parks with Ranger Dockett photos by Christine Osinski. Children's Press, 1997. ISBN 978-0-516-20496-3 Subj: Careers – park rangers. Parks.

Farmers ill. with photos. Compass Point, 2003. ISBN 978-0-7565-0305-5 Subj: Careers – farmers. Farms.

Flying an agricultural plane with Mr. Miller photos by Romie Flanagan. Children's Press, 1999. ISBN 978-0-516-21132-9 Subj: Airplanes, airports. Careers – airplane pilots. Farms.

Halloween ill. by Patrick Girouard. Compass Point, 2002. ISBN 978-0-7565-0086-3 Subj: Holidays – Halloween.

Here comes Mr. Eventoff with the mail! photos by Christine Osinski. Children's Press, 1998. ISBN 978-0-516-20776-6 Subj: Careers – postal workers. Communities, neighborhoods. Letters, cards.

Learning about bees from Mr. Krebs photos by Christine Osinski. Children's Press, 1999. ISBN 978-0-516-21136-7 Subj: Careers – beekeepers. Insects – bees.

Learning is fun with Mrs. Perez photos by Romie Flanagan. Children's Press, 1998. ISBN 978-0-516-20774-2 Subj: Careers – teachers. Foreign languages. School.

Letter carriers ill. with photos. Compass Point, 2000. ISBN 978-0-7565-0010-8 Subj: Careers – postal workers. Communities, neighborhoods. Letters, cards.

Librarians ill. with photos. Compass Point, 2001. ISBN 978-0-7565-0063-4 Subj: Books, reading. Careers – librarians. Libraries.

Mayors ill. with photos. Compass Point, 2001. ISBN 978-0-7565-0064-1 Subj: Careers – mayors. Cities, towns. Communities, neighborhoods.

Mr. Paul and Mr. Luecke build communities photos by Romie Flanagan. Children's Press, 1999. ISBN 978-0-516-21131-2 Subj: Careers – construction workers. Homes, houses.

Mr. Santizo's tasty treats! photos by Romie Flanagan. Children's Press, 1998. ISBN 978-0-516-20771-1 Subj: Careers – bakers. Ethnic groups in the U.S. – Guatemalan Americans.

Mr. Yee fixes cars photos by Romie Flanagan. Children's Press, 1998. ISBN 978-0-516-20772-8 Subj: Automobiles. Careers – mechanics.

Mrs. Scott's beautiful art photos by Romie Flanagan. Children's Press, 1999. ISBN 978-0-516-21135-0 Subj: Careers – artists. Indians of North America – Cherokee.

Ms. Davison, our librarian photos by Christine Osinski. Children's Press, 1996. ISBN 978-0-516-20009-5 Subj: Books, reading. Careers – librarians. Communities, neighborhoods. Libraries.

Ms. Murphy fights fires photos by Christine Osinski. Children's Press, 1997. ISBN 978-0-516-20494-9 Subj: Careers – firefighters. Communities, neighborhoods. Fire.

Officer Brown keeps neighborhoods safe photos by Christine Osinski. Children's Press, 1998. ISBN 978-0-516-20780-3 Subj: Careers – police officers. Communities, neighborhoods. Crime.

Passover ill. by Ann Koffsky. Compass Point, 2004. ISBN 978-0-7565-0481-6 Subj: Holidays – Passover. Jewish culture.

Police officers ill. with photos. Compass Point, 2000. ISBN 978-0-7565-0011-5 Subj: Careers – police officers. Communities, neighborhoods. Crime.

Rain ill. with photos. Child's World, 2003. ISBN 978-1-56766-452-2 Subj: Weather – rain.

Raising cows on the Koebels' farm photos by Romie Flanagan. Children's Press, 1999. ISBN 978-0-516-21133-6 Subj: Animals – bulls, cows. Careers – farmers. Farms.

Riding the ferry with Captain Cruz photos by Christine Osinski. Children's Press, 1996. ISBN 978-0-516-20046-0 Subj: Boats, ships. Sailors. Transportation.

Riding the school bus with Mrs. Kramer photos by Christine Osinski. Children's Press, 1998. ISBN 978-0-516-20779-7 Subj: Careers – bus drivers. Communities, neighborhoods. School. Transportation.

Rocks ill. with photos. Compass Point, 2001. ISBN 978-0-7565-0033-7 Subj: Earth. Rocks. Science.

Snow ill. with photos. Child's World, 2003. ISBN 978-1-56766-453-9 Subj: Weather – snow.

Soil ill. with photos. Compass Point, 2001. ISBN 978-0-7565-0035-1 Subj: Animals. Earth. Ecology. Plants.

Sunshine ill. with photos. Child's World, 2003. ISBN 978-1-56766-454-6 Subj: Science. Sun.

Teachers ill. with photos. Compass Point, 2001. ISBN 978-0-7565-0066-5 Subj: Careers – teachers. School.

Thanksgiving ill. by Kathie Kelleher. Compass Point, 2002. ISBN 978-0-7565-0087-0 Subj: Holidays – Thanksgiving.

Thunder and lightning ill. with photos. Child's World, 2003. ISBN 978-1-56766-451-5 Subj: Weather – lightning, thunder. Weather – storms.

Valentine's Day ill. by Shelly Dieterichs. Compass Point, 2002. ISBN 978-0-7565-0088-7 Subj: Holidays – Valentine's Day.

A visit to the Gravesens' farm photos by Christine Osinski. Children's Press, 1998. ISBN 978-0-516-20778-0 Subj: Careers – farmers. Communities, neighborhoods. Family life. Farms.

Water ill. with photos. Compass Point, 2001. ISBN 978-0-7565-0038-2 Subj: Earth. Science. Water.

Weather ill. with photos. Compass Point, 2001. ISBN 978-0-7565-0039-9 Subj: Science. Weather.

The Wilsons, a house-painting team photos by Christine Osinski. Children's Press, 1996. ISBN 978-0-516-20216-7 Subj: Activities – painting. Careers – artists. Homes, houses.

Wind ill. with photos. Child's World, 2003. ISBN 978-1-56766-455-3 Subj: Science. Weather – wind.

The Zieglers and their apple orchard photos by Romie Flanagan. Children's Press, 1999. ISBN 978-0-516-21134-3 Subj: Careers – farmers. Farms. Food. Trees.

Flattinger, Hubert. *Stormy night* ill. by Nathalie Duroussy. NorthSouth, 2002. ISBN 978-0-7358-1667-1 Subj: Bedtime. Emotions – fear. Family life – mothers.

Fleischer-Camp, Dean. *Marcel the shell with shoes on: things about me* (Slate, Jenny)

Fleischman, Paul. *Glass slipper, gold sandal: a worldwide Cinderella* ill. by Julie Paschkis. Holt, 2007. ISBN 978-0-8050-7953-1 Subj: Folk & fairy tales. Foreign lands. Royalty.

Lost! a story in string ill. by C. B. Mordan. Holt, 2000. ISBN 978-0-8050-5583-2 Subj: Behavior – lost. String. Weather – snow.

The matchbox diary ill. by Bagram Ibatoulline. Candlewick, 2013. ISBN 978-0-7636-4601-1 Subj: Behavior – collecting things. Ethnic groups in the U.S. – Italian Americans. Family life – great-grandparents. Immigrants. Memories, memory. U.S. history.

Sidewalk circus ill. by Kevin Hawkes. Candlewick, 2004. ISBN 978-0-7636-1107-1 Subj: Circus. Cities, towns. Wordless.

Weslandia ill. by Kevin Hawkes. Candlewick, 1999. ISBN 978-0-7636-0006-8 Subj: Gardens, gardening. Plants.

Fleming, Candace. *Boxes for Katje* ill. by Stacey Dressen-McQueen. Farrar, 2003. ISBN 978-0-374-30922-0 Subj: Character traits – generosity. Foreign lands – Holland. War.

Clever Jack takes the cake ill. by G. Brian Karas. Random House, 2010. ISBN 978-0-375-84979-4 Subj: Activities – storytelling. Birthdays. Folk & fairy tales. Food. Royalty – princesses.

Gabriella's song ill. by Giselle Potter. Atheneum, 1997. ISBN 978-0-689-80973-6 Subj: Foreign lands – Italy. Music. Songs.

Gator gumbo ill. by Sally Anne Lambert. Farrar, 2004. ISBN 978-0-374-38050-2 Subj: Animals. Food. Reptiles – alligators, crocodiles.

Imogene's last stand ill. by Nancy Carpenter. Random House, 2009. ISBN 978-0-375-83607-7 Subj: Character traits – assertiveness. Self-concept. U.S. history.

Muncha! Muncha! Muncha! ill. by G. Brian Karas. Atheneum, 2002. ISBN 978-0-689-83152-2 Subj: Animals – rabbits. Gardens, gardening.

Oh, no! ill. by Eric Rohmann. Random House, 2012. ISBN 978-0-375-84271-9 Subj: Animals. Cumulative tales.

Papa's mechanical fish ill. by Boris Kulikov. Farrar, 2013. ISBN 978-0-374-39908-5 Subj: Boats, ships. Careers – inventors. Family life. Inventions.

Seven hungry babies ill. by Eugene Yelchin. Simon & Schuster, 2010. ISBN 978-1-4169-5402-6 Subj: Babies. Birds. Counting, numbers. Rhyming text.

Sunny Boy! the life and times of a tortoise ill. by Anne Wilsdorf. Farrar, 2005. ISBN 978-0-374-37297-2 Subj: Reptiles – turtles, tortoises.

Tippy-tippy-tippy, hide! ill. by G. Brian Karas. Simon & Schuster, 2007. ISBN 978-0-689-87479-6 Subj: Animals – rabbits. Behavior – hiding.

When Agnes caws ill. by Giselle Potter. Atheneum, 1999. ISBN 978-0-689-81471-6 Subj: Birds. Foreign lands – Himalayas. Noise, sounds.

Who invited you? ill. by George Booth. Atheneum, 2001. ISBN 978-0-689-83153-9 Subj: Animals. Counting, numbers. Rhyming text. Swamps.

Fleming, Denise. *Alphabet under construction* ill. by author. Holt, 2002. ISBN 978-0-8050-6848-1 Subj: ABC books. Activities – making things. Animals – mice.

Barnyard banter ill. by author. Holt, 1994. ISBN 978-0-8050-1957-5 Subj: Animals. Farms. Noise, sounds. Rhyming text.

Beetle bop ill. by author. Harcourt, 2007. ISBN 978-0-15-205936-1 Subj: Insects – beetles. Rhyming text.

Buster ill. by author. Holt, 2003. ISBN 978-0-8050-6279-3 Subj: Animals – cats. Animals – dogs. Behavior – running away. Emotions – envy, jealousy. Pets.

Buster goes to Cowboy Camp ill. by author. Holt, 2008. ISBN 978-0-8050-7892-3 Subj: Animals – dogs. Camps, camping. Cowboys, cowgirls.

Count! ill. by author. Holt, 1992. ISBN 978-0-8050-1595-9 Subj: Animals. Counting, numbers.

The cow who clucked ill. by author. Holt, 2006. ISBN 978-0-8050-7365-2 Subj: Animals. Animals – bulls, cows. Noise, sounds.

The everything book ill. by author. Holt, 2000. ISBN 978-0-8050-6292-2 Subj: Concepts. Nursery rhymes.

The everything book [board book] ill. by author. Holt, 2004. ISBN 978-0-8050-7709-4 Subj: Concepts. Format, unusual – board books. Nursery rhymes.

The first day of winter ill. by author. Holt, 2005. ISBN 978-0-8050-7384-3 Subj: Counting, numbers. Rhyming text. Seasons – winter. Snowmen. Weather – snow.

In the small, small pond ill. by author. Holt, 1993. ISBN 978-0-8050-2264-3 Subj: Animals. Caldecott award honor books. Frogs & toads. Lakes, ponds. Rhyming text. Seasons.

In the tall, tall grass ill. by author. Holt, 1991. ISBN 978-0-8050-1635-2 Subj: Insects – butterflies, caterpillars. Nature.

Lunch ill. by author. Holt, 1992. ISBN 978-0-8050-1636-9 Subj: Animals – mice. Concepts – color. Food.

Mama cat has three kittens ill. by author. Holt, 1998. ISBN 978-0-8050-5745-4 Subj: Animals – babies. Animals – cats. Character traits – being different. Family life – brothers & sisters.

Shout! Shout it out! ill. by author. Holt, 2011. ISBN 978-0-8050-9237-0 Subj: ABC books. Animals – mice. Counting, numbers. Language.

Sleepy, oh so sleepy ill. by author. Holt, 2010. ISBN 978-0-8050-8126-8 Subj: Animals. Bedtime. Family life – mothers.

Time to sleep ill. by author. Holt, 1997. ISBN 978-0-8050-3762-3 Subj: Animals – bears. Hibernation. Seasons – winter.

Underground ill. by author. Simon & Schuster, 2012. ISBN 978-1-4424-5882-6 Subj: Animals. Nature. Rhyming text.

Where once there was a wood ill. by author. Holt, 1996. ISBN 978-0-8050-3761-6 Subj: Animals. Nature. Plants.

Flesher, Vivienne. *Alfred's nose* photos by author. HarperCollins, 2008. ISBN 978-0-06-084313-7 Subj: Anatomy – noses. Animals – dogs. Clothing – costumes. Self-concept.

Fletcher, Ashlee. *My dog, my cat* ill. by author. Tanglewood, 2011. ISBN 978-1-933718-22-4 Subj: Animals – cats. Animals – dogs.

Fletcher, Ralph. *The circus surprise* ill. by Vladimir Vagin. Clarion, 2001. ISBN 978-0-395-98029-3 Subj: Behavior – lost. Circus. Clowns, jesters.

Grandpa never lies ill. by Harvey Stevenson. Clarion, 2000. ISBN 978-0-395-79770-9 Subj: Death. Emotions – grief. Family life – grandfathers. Family life – grandmothers. Poetry.

Hello, harvest moon ill. by Kate Kiesler. Clarion, 2003. ISBN 978-0-618-16451-6 Subj: Moon. Nature. Night.

The Sandman ill. by Richard Cowdrey. Holt, 2008. ISBN 978-0-8050-7726-1 Subj: Dragons. Sleep.

Fliess, Sue. *A gluten-free birthday for me!* ill. by Jennifer Morris. Whitman, 2013. ISBN 978-0-8075-2955-3 Subj: Birthdays. Food. Illness – allergies. Parties. Rhyming text.

Shoes for me! ill. by Michael Laughead. Marshall Cavendish, 2011. ISBN 978-0-7614-5825-8 Subj: Animals – hippopotamuses. Clothing – shoes. Rhyming text.

Floca, Brian. *Five trucks* ill. by author. DK, 1999. ISBN 978-0-7894-2561-4 Subj: Airplanes, airports. Trucks.

Lightship ill. by author. Simon & Schuster, 2007. ISBN 978-1-4169-2436-4 Subj: Boats, ships. U.S. history.

Locomotive ill. by author. Atheneum, 2013. ISBN 978-1-4169-9415-2 Subj: Caldecott award books. Trains. U.S. history.

Moonshot: the flight of Apollo 11 ill. by author. Atheneum, 2009. ISBN 978-1-4169-5046-2 Subj: Careers – astronauts. Moon. Space & space ships. U.S. history.

Florence, Tyler. *Tyler makes pancakes!* ill. by Craig Frazier. HarperCollins, 2012. ISBN 978-0-06-204752-6 Subj: Activities – baking, cooking. Food. Shopping. Stores.

Tyler makes spaghetti! ill. by Craig Frazier. HarperCollins, 2013. ISBN 978-0-06-204756-4 Subj: Activities – baking, cooking. Food. Restaurants.

Florian, Douglas. *Bow wow meow meow, it's rhyming cats and dogs* ill. by author. Harcourt, 2003. ISBN 978-0-15-216395-2 Subj: Animals – cats. Animals – dogs. Poetry.

Comets, stars, the moon, and Mars: space poems and paintings ill. by author. Harcourt, 2007. ISBN 978-0-15-205372-7 Subj: Moon. Planets. Poetry. Stars.

Dinothesaurus: prehistoric poems and paintings ill. by author. Atheneum, 2009. ISBN 978-1-4169-7978-4 Subj: Dinosaurs. Poetry. Prehistory.

Handsprings ill. by author. HarperCollins, 2006. ISBN 978-0-06-009281-8 Subj: Poetry. Seasons – spring.

Insectlopedia ill. by author. Harcourt, 1998. ISBN 978-0-15-201306-6 Subj: Insects. Poetry.

Lizards, frogs, and polliwogs ill. by author. Harcourt, 2001. ISBN 978-0-15-202591-5 Subj: Amphibians. Frogs & toads. Poetry. Reptiles.

A pig is big ill. by author. Greenwillow, 2000. ISBN 978-0-688-17126-1 Subj: Concepts – size. Rhyming text.

Poem runs: baseball poems and paintings ill. by author. Harcourt, 2012. ISBN 978-0-547-68838-1 Subj: Poetry. Sports – baseball.

Poetrees ill. by author. Simon & Schuster, 2010. ISBN 978-1-4169-8672-0 Subj: Poetry. Trees.

Shiver me timbers! pirate poems & paintings ill. by Robert Neubecker. Simon & Schuster, 2012. ISBN 978-1-4424-1321-4 Subj: Pirates. Poetry.

Summersaults ill. by author. Greenwillow, 2002. ISBN 978-0-06-029268-3 Subj: Poetry. Seasons – summer.

Unbeelievables: honeybee poems and paintings ill. by author. Simon & Schuster, 2012. ISBN 978-1-4424-2652-8 Subj: Insects – bees. Poetry.

Zoo's who: poems and paintings ill. by author. Harcourt, 2005. ISBN 978-0-15-204639-2 Subj: Animals. Poetry.

Flournoy, Valerie. *The patchwork quilt* ill. by Jerry Pinkney. Dial, 1985. ISBN 978-0-8037-0098-7 Subj: Ethnic groups in the U.S. – African Americans. Family life – grandmothers. Quilts.

Floyd, Madeleine. *Cold paws, warm heart* ill. by author. Candlewick, 2005. ISBN 978-0-7636-2761-4 Subj: Animals – polar bears. Concepts – cold & heat. Emotions – loneliness. Friendship.

Flynn, Kitson. *Carrot in my pocket* ill. by Denise Ortakales. Moon Mt, 2001. ISBN 978-0-9677929-6-5 Subj: Animals. Behavior – lost & found possessions. Farms. Rhyming text.

Foggo, Cheryl. *Dear baobab* ill. by Qin Leng. Second Story, 2011. ISBN 978-1-897187-91-3 Subj: Adoption. Emotions – loneliness. Family life. Family life – aunts, uncles. Foreign lands – Africa. Trees.

Fogliano, Julie. *And then it's spring* ill. by Erin E. Stead. Roaring Brook, 2012. ISBN 978-1-59643-624-4 Subj: Gardens, gardening. Seasons – spring.

If you want to see a whale ill. by Erin E. Stead. Roaring Brook, 2013. ISBN 978-1-59643-731-9 Subj: Animals – whales. Character traits – patience. Imagination.

Foley, Greg. *Don't worry Bear* ill. by author. Viking, 2008. ISBN 978-0-670-06245-4 Subj: Animals. Animals – bears. Behavior – worrying. Insects – butterflies, caterpillars. Metamorphosis.

Good luck Bear ill. by author. Viking, 2009. ISBN 978-0-670-06258-4 Subj: Animals. Animals – bears. Character traits – luck.

I miss you Mouse ill. by author. Penguin, 2010. ISBN 978-0-670-01238-1 Subj: Animals – bears. Animals – mice. Format, unusual – toy & movable books. Friendship.

Make a wish Bear ill. by author. Viking, 2012. ISBN 978-0-670-01239-8 Subj: Animals – bears. Behavior – wishing. Friendship.

Purple Little Bird ill. by author. HarperCollins, 2011. ISBN 978-0-06-200828-2 Subj: Animals. Birds. Concepts – color. Homes, houses.

Thank you, Bear ill. by author. Penguin, 2007. ISBN 978-0-670-06165-5 Subj: Animals. Animals – bears. Animals – mice. Friendship. Gifts.

Willoughby and the lion ill. by author. HarperCollins, 2009. ISBN 978-0-06-154750-8 Subj: Animals – lions. Behavior – wishing. Friendship. Magic.

Willoughby and the moon ill. by author. HarperCollins, 2010. ISBN 978-0-06-154753-9 Subj: Animals – snails. Emotions – fear. Moon.

Folgueira, Rodrigo. *Ribbit!* ill. by Poly Bernatene. Knopf, 2013. ISBN 978-0-307-98146-2 Subj: Animals – pigs. Behavior – needing someone. Friendship. Frogs & toads. Lakes, ponds.

Fontes, Justine Korman. *Black meets White* ill. by Geoff Waring. Candlewick, 2005. ISBN 978-0-7636-1933-6 Subj: Concepts – color. Format, unusual – toy & movable books.

Signs of spring ill. by Rob Hefferan. Mondo, 2002. ISBN 978-1-59034-180-3 Subj: Animals – mice. School. Seasons – spring.

For laughing out louder: more poems to tickle your funnybone sel. by Jack Prelutsky; ill. by Marjorie Priceman. Knopf, 1995. ISBN 978-0-679-87063-0 Subj: Poetry.

Ford, Bernette. *Ballet Kitty* ill. by Sam Williams. Boxer, 2007. ISBN 978-1-905417-56-8 Subj: Animals – cats. Ballet.

Bright eyes, brown skin (Hudson, Cheryl Willis)

First snow ill. by Sebastien Braun. Holiday House,, 2005. ISBN 978-0-8234-1937-1 Subj: Animals – rabbits. Night. Seasons – winter. Weather – snow.

No more biting for Billy Goat! ill. by Sam Williams. Boxer Books, 2013. ISBN 978-1-907967-31-3 Subj: Animals – goats. Behavior – misbehavior.

No more blanket for Lambkin! ill. by Sam Williams. Boxer, 2009. ISBN 978-1-906250-28-7 Subj: Animals – sheep. Birds – ducks. Friendship. Laundry. Toys.

No more bottles for Bunny! ill. by Sam Williams. Boxer, 2007. ISBN 978-1-905417-34-6 Subj: Animals – rabbits. Behavior – growing up. Parties.

No more diapers for Ducky! ill. by Sam Williams. Sterling, 2007. ISBN 978-1-905417-38-4 Subj: Birds – ducks. Format, unusual – board books. Toilet training.

No more pacifier for Piggy! ill. by Sam Williams. Sterling, 2008. ISBN 978-1-905417-89-6 Subj: Animals – pigs. Babies. Behavior – growing up.

Ford, Christine. *Ocean's child* by Christine Ford and Trish Holland ill. by David Diaz. Golden, 2009. ISBN 978-0-375-84752-3 Subj: Animals. Bedtime. Canoes & canoeing. Family life – mothers. Foreign lands – Arctic. Indians of North America – Inuit. Sea & seashore.

Ford, Gilbert. *Flying lessons* ill. by author. Hyperion/Disney, 2010. ISBN 978-1-4231-1997-5 Subj: Airplanes, airports. Birds – doves. Character traits – being different.

Ford, Juwanda G. *K is for Kwanzaa: a Kwanzaa alphabet book* ill. by Ken Wilson-Max. Scholastic, 1997. ISBN 978-0-590-92200-5 Subj: ABC books. Ethnic groups in the U.S. – African Americans. Holidays – Kwanzaa.

Together for Kwanzaa ill. by Shelly Hehenberger. Random House, 2000. ISBN 978-0-375-90329-8 Subj: Ethnic groups in the U.S. – African Americans. Family life – brothers & sisters. Holidays – Kwanzaa.

Ford, Lauren. *The ageless story* ill. by author. Dodd, 1939. Subj: Caldecott award honor books.

Ford, Miela. *Follow the leader* photos by author. Greenwillow, 1996. ISBN 978-0-688-14655-9 Subj: Activities – playing. Animals – polar bears.

Mom and me ill. by author. Greenwillow, 1998. ISBN 978-0-688-15890-3 Subj: Activities – playing. Animals – polar bears. Family life – mothers. Foreign lands – Arctic.

Sunflower ill. by Sally Noll. Greenwillow, 1995. ISBN 978-0-688-13302-3 Subj: Flowers. Gardens, gardening. Nature. Plants.

Fore, S. J. *Read to Tiger* ill. by R. W. Alley. Penguin, 2010. ISBN 978-0-670-01140-7 Subj: Animals – tigers. Books, reading.

Tiger can't sleep ill. by R. W. Alley. Penguin, 2006. ISBN 978-0-670-06078-8 Subj: Animals – tigers. Bedtime. Emotions – fear.

Foreman, George. *Let George do it!* by George Foreman and Fran Manushkin ill. by Whitney Martin. Simon & Schuster, 2005. ISBN 978-0-689-87807-7 Subj: Birthdays. Family life. Humorous stories. Names. Parties.

Foreman, Jack. *Say hello* ill. by Michael Foreman. Candlewick, 2008. ISBN 978-0-7636-3657-9 Subj: Animals – dogs. Emotions – loneliness. Rhyming text.

Foreman, Michael. *Cat in the manger* ill. by author. Holt, 2001. ISBN 978-0-8050-6677-7 Subj: Animals – cats. Holidays – Christmas. Memories, memory. Religion.

Fortunately, unfortunately ill. by author. Andersen, 2011. ISBN 978-0-7613-7460-2 Subj: Activities – traveling. Behavior – resourcefulness.

Friends ill. by author. Andersen, 2012. ISBN 978-1-46770317-8 Subj: Animals – cats. Fish. Friendship.

The littlest dinosaur ill. by author. Walker, 2008. ISBN 978-0-8027-9759-9 Subj: Character traits – bravery. Character traits – smallness. Dinosaurs. Friendship.

Mia's story: a sketchbook of hopes and dreams ill. by author. Candlewick, 2006. ISBN 978-0-7636-3063-8 Subj: Animals – dogs. Flowers. Foreign lands – Chile.

Oh! if only . . . ill. by author. Andersen, 2013. ISBN 978-1-46771-213-2 Subj: Animals – dogs. Emotions – embarrassment. Royalty – queens.

Forest, Heather, reteller. *Stone soup* ill. by Susan Gaber. August House, 1998. ISBN 978-0-87483-498-7 Subj: Behavior – sharing. Character traits – cleverness. Folk & fairy tales. Food.

Forler, Nan. *Bird child* ill. by François Thisdale. Tundra, 2009. ISBN 978-0-88776-894-1 Subj: Activities – flying. Behavior – bullying, teasing. Self-concept.

Forman, Ruth. *Young Cornrows callin out the moon: poem* ill. by Cbabi Bayoc. Children's Book Press, 2007. ISBN 978-0-89239-218-6 Subj: Communities, neighborhoods. Ethnic groups in the U.S. – African Americans. Poetry.

Formento, Alison. *These bees count!* ill. by Sarah Snow. Whitman, 2012. ISBN 978-0-8075-7868-1 Subj: Counting, numbers. Insects – bees. School – field trips.

These seas count! ill. by Sarah Snow. Whitman, 2013. ISBN 978-0-8075-7871-1 Subj: Counting, numbers. Ecology. School – field trips. Sea & seashore.

This tree counts! ill. by Sarah Snow. Whitman, 2010. ISBN 978-0-8075-7890-2 Subj: Counting, numbers. Nature. School. Trees.

This tree, 1, 2, 3 ill. by Sarah Snow. Whitman, 2011. ISBN 978-0-8075-7891-9 Subj: Counting, numbers. Format, unusual – board books. Nature. School. Trees.

Forss, Sarah. *Alphasaurs and other prehistoric types* (Werner, Sharon)

Forward, Toby. *Ben's Christmas carol* ill. by Ruth Brown. Dutton, 1996. ISBN 978-0-525-45593-6 Subj: Animals – mice. Behavior – greed. Behavior – sharing. Holidays – Christmas.

What did you do today? ill. by Carol Thompson. Clarion, 2004. ISBN 978-0-618-49586-3 Subj: School – first day.

Fosberry, Jennifer. *Isabella: girl on the go* ill. by Mike Litwin. Sourcebooks/Jabberwocky, 2012. ISBN 978-1-4022-6648-5 Subj: Activities – playing. Imagination.

Isabella star of the story ill. by Mike Litwin. Sourcebooks/Jabberwocky, 2013. ISBN 978-1-4022-7936-2 Subj: Books, reading. Imagination. Libraries.

Foster, John. *Pet poems* ill. by Korky Paul. Oxford Univ. Pr., 2000. ISBN 978-0-19-276191-0 Subj: Animals. Pets. Poetry.

Fox, Christyan. *Astronaut PiggyWiggy* by Christyan Fox and Diane Fox ill. by Christyan Fox. Handprint, 2002. ISBN 978-1-929766-41-3 Subj: Animals – pigs. Careers – astronauts. Imagination.

Count to ten, PiggyWiggy! by Christyan Fox and Diane Fox ill. by Christyan Fox. Handprint, 2001. ISBN 978-1-929766-18-5 Subj: Activities – baking, cooking. Animals – pigs. Counting, numbers. Food. Format, unusual – board books.

Fire fighter PiggyWiggy by Christyan Fox and Diane Fox ill. by Christyan Fox. Handprint, 2001. ISBN 978-1-929766-16-1 Subj: Animals – pigs. Careers – firefighters. Imagination.

Tyson the terrible (Fox, Diane)

What color is that, PiggyWiggy? by Christyan Fox and Diane Fox ill. by Christyan Fox. Handprint, 2001. ISBN 978-1-929766-17-8 Subj: Animals – pigs. Clowns, jesters. Concepts – color. Format, unusual – board books. Toys.

What shape is that, PiggyWiggy? by Christyan Fox and Diane Fox ill. by Christyan Fox. Handprint, 2002. ISBN 978-1-929766-44-4 Subj: Animals – pigs. Format, unusual – board books. Toys – bears.

Fox, Diane. *Astronaut PiggyWiggy* (Fox, Christyan)

Count to ten, PiggyWiggy! (Fox, Christyan)

Fire fighter PiggyWiggy (Fox, Christyan)

Tyson the terrible by Diane Fox and Christyan Fox ill. by authors. Bloomsbury, 2007. ISBN 978-1-58234-734-9 Subj: Dinosaurs. Emotions – fear. Format, unusual – toy & movable books. Friendship. Sports – soccer.

What color is that, PiggyWiggy? (Fox, Christyan)

What shape is that, PiggyWiggy? (Fox, Christyan)

Fox, Kathleen. *The pirates of plagiarism* by Kathleen Fox and Lisa Downey ill. by Lisa Downey. Upstart, 2010. ISBN 978-1-60213-053-1 Subj: Behavior – cheating. Books, reading. Libraries. Pirates.

Fox, Lee. *Ella Kazoo will not brush her hair* ill. by Jennifer Plecas. Walker, 2010. ISBN 978-0-8027-8836-8 Subj: Hair. Hygiene. Rhyming text.

Fox, Mem. *Boo to a goose* ill. by David Miller. Dial, 1998. ISBN 978-0-8037-2274-3 Subj: Birds – geese. Rhyming text.

The goblin and the empty chair ill. by Leo Dillon. Simon & Schuster, 2009. ISBN 978-1-4169-8585-3 Subj: Character traits – appearance. Emotions – loneliness. Mythical creatures – goblins. Self-concept.

Good night, sleep tight ill. by Judy Horacek. Scholastic, 2013. ISBN 978-0-545-53370-6 Subj: Activities – babysitting. Bedtime. Nursery rhymes. Rhyming text.

Harriet, you'll drive me wild ill. by Marla Frazee. Harcourt, 2000. ISBN 978-0-15-201977-8 Subj: Character traits – clumsiness. Emotions – anger. Family life – mothers.

Hattie and the fox ill. by Patricia Mullins. Bradbury, 1987. ISBN 978-0-02-735470-6 Subj: Animals. Birds – chickens. Cumulative tales. Farms.

Hello, baby! ill. by Steve Jenkins. Simon & Schuster, 2009. ISBN 978-1-4169-8513-6 Subj: Animals. Babies. Rhyming text.

Hunwick's egg ill. by Pamela Lofts. Harcourt, 2005. ISBN 978-0-15-216318-1 Subj: Animals – bandicoots. Eggs. Friendship.

Koala Lou ill. by Pamela Lofts. Harcourt, 1989. ISBN 978-0-15-200502-3 Subj: Animals – koalas. Emotions – love. Family life – mothers.

Let's count goats! ill. by Jan Thomas. Simon & Schuster, 2010. ISBN 978-1-4424-0598-1 Subj: Animals – goats. Counting, numbers. Rhyming text.

The magic hat ill. by Tricia Tusa. Harcourt, 2002. ISBN 978-0-15-201025-6 Subj: Magic. Rhyming text. Wizards.

Night noises ill. by Terry Denton. Harcourt, 1989. ISBN 978-0-15-200543-6 Subj: Animals – dogs. Birthdays. Night. Noise, sounds. Sleep.

A particular cow ill. by Terry Denton. Harcourt, 2006. ISBN 978-0-15-200250-3 Subj: Animals – bulls, cows. Humorous stories.

Possum magic ill. by Julie Vivas. Abingdon, 1987. ISBN 978-0-687-31732-5 Subj: Activities – traveling. Animals – possums. Behavior – wishing. Food. Foreign lands – Australia.

Shoes from grandpa ill. by Patricia Mullins. Watts, 1990. ISBN 978-0-531-08448-9 Subj: Behavior – growing up. Clothing. Cumulative tales. Family life – grandfathers. Rhyming text.

Sleepy bears ill. by Kerry Argent. Harcourt, 1999. ISBN 978-0-15-202016-3 Subj: Animals – bears. Lullabies. Rhyming text. Sleep.

Sophie ill. by Aminah Brenda Lynn Robinson. Harcourt, 1994. ISBN 978-0-15-277160-7 Subj: Birth. Death. Emotions – love. Family life – grandfathers.

Tell me about your day today ill. by Lauren Stringer. Simon & Schuster, 2012. ISBN 978-1-4169-9006-2 Subj: Bedtime. Imagination. Toys.

Ten little fingers and ten little toes ill. by Helen Oxenbury. Harcourt, 2008. ISBN 978-0-15-206057-2 Subj: Anatomy – hands. Anatomy – toes. Babies. Rhyming text.

Time for bed ill. by Jane Dyer. Harcourt, 1993. ISBN 978-0-15-288183-2 Subj: Animals. Bedtime. Family life. Rhyming text.

Tough Boris ill. by Kathryn Brown. Harcourt, 1994. ISBN 978-0-15-289612-6 Subj: Birds – parakeets, parrots. Pirates.

Two little monkeys ill. by Jill Barton. Simon & Schuster, 2012. ISBN 978-1-4169-8687-4 Subj: Animals – leopards. Animals – monkeys. Rhyming text.

Where is the green sheep? ill. by Judy Horacek. Harcourt, 2004. ISBN 978-0-15-204907-2 Subj: Animals – sheep. Rhyming text.

Where the giant sleeps ill. by Vladimir Radunsky. Harcourt, 2007. ISBN 978-0-15-205785-5 Subj: Bedtime. Rhyming text. Sleep.

Wilfrid Gordon McDonald Partridge ill. by Julie Vivas. Kane/Miller, 1985. ISBN 978-0-916291-04-4 Subj: Behavior – forgetfulness. Old age.

Wombat divine ill. by Kerry Argent. Harcourt, 1996. ISBN 978-0-15-201416-2 Subj: Animals. Animals – wombats. Holidays – Christmas. Theater.

Yoo-hoo, Ladybug! ill. by Laura Ljungkvist. Simon & Schuster, 2013. ISBN 978-1-4424-3400-4 Subj: Insects – ladybugs. Picture puzzles. Rhyming text.

Zoo-looking ill. by Candace Whitman. Mondo, 1996. ISBN 978-1-57255-010-0 Subj: Animals. Rhyming text. Zoos.

Fox, Paula. *Traces* ill. by Karla Kuskin. Front Street, 2008. ISBN 978-1-932425-43-7 Subj: Nature. Poetry.

The fox went out on a chilly night ill. by Peter Spier. Doubleday, 1961. ISBN 978-0-385-00231-8 Subj: Animals – foxes. Caldecott award honor books. Folk & fairy tales. Songs.

Fradin, Dennis. *The price of freedom: how one town stood up to slavery* by Dennis Fradin and Judith Bloom Fradin ill. by Eric Velasquez. Walker, 2013. ISBN 978-0-8027-2166-2 Subj: Character traits – assertiveness. Character traits – bravery. Ethnic groups in the U.S. – African Americans. Slavery. U.S. history.

Fradin, Judith Bloom. *The price of freedom: how one town stood up to slavery* (Fradin, Dennis)

Fraggalosch, Audrey. *Great grizzly wilderness* ill. by Donald G. Eberhart. Soundprints, 2000. ISBN 978-1-56899-838-1 Subj: Animals – bears. Family life.

Grizzly bear family ill. by Donald G. Eberhart. Soundprints, 2003. ISBN 978-1-59249-048-6 Subj: Animals – bears. Behavior – growing up. Family life – mothers. Hibernation.

Trails above the tree line ill. by Higgins Bond. Soundprints, 2002. ISBN 978-1-56899-941-8 Subj: Animals – babies. Animals – sheep. Family life – mothers.

Frame, Jeron Ashford. *Yesterday I had the blues* ill. by Donald G. Eberhart. Tricycle, 2003. ISBN 978-1-58246-084-0 Subj: Emotions. Ethnic groups in the U.S. – African Americans. Family life.

Frampton, David. *Mr. Ferlinghetti's poem* ill. by author. Eerdmans, 2006. ISBN 978-0-8028-5290-8 Subj: Careers – firefighters. Poetry. Seasons – summer.

My beastie book of ABC ill. by author. HarperCollins, 2002. ISBN 978-0-06-028823-5 Subj: ABC books. Animals. Poetry.

The whole night through ill. by author. HarperCollins, 2002. ISBN 978-0-06-028826-6 Subj: Animals – leopards. Jungle. Lullabies. Rhyming text. Sleep.

Franceschelli, Christopher. *Alphablock* ill. by Peskimo. Abrams, 2013. ISBN 978-1-4197-0936-4 Subj: ABC books. Format, unusual – toy & movable books.

(Oliver) ill. by Gaby Kooijman et al. Lemniscaat, 2011. ISBN 978-1-9359-5401-9 Subj: Birds – chickens. Eggs. Format, unusual.

Francis, Lee DeCora. *Kunu's basket: a story from Indian Island* ill. by Susan Drucker. Tilbury, 2012. ISBN 978-0-88448-330-4 Subj: Activities – weaving. Character traits – perseverance. Family life – grandfathers. Indians of North America.

Francis, Panama. *David gets his drum* by Panama Francis and Bob Reiser ill. by Eric Velasquez. Marshall Cavendish, 2002. ISBN 978-0-7614-5088-7 Subj: Careers – musicians. Family life. Musical instruments – drums.

Francis, Pauline. *Sam stars at Shakespeare's Globe* ill. by Jane Tattersfield. Frances Lincoln, 2006. ISBN 978-1-84507-406-7 Subj: Careers – actors. Foreign lands – England. Theater.

Franco, Betsy. *Bees, snails, and peacock tails: patterns and shapes--naturally* ill. by Steve Jenkins. Simon & Schuster, 2008. ISBN 978-1-4169-0386-4 Subj: Concepts – shape. Nature. Poetry.

Birdsongs ill. by Steve Jenkins. Simon & Schuster, 2007. ISBN 978-0-689-87777-3 Subj: Birds. Counting, numbers.

A curious collection of cats: concrete poems ill. by Michael Wertz. Tricycle, 2009. ISBN 978-1-58246-248-6 Subj: Animals – cats. Poetry.

A dazzling display of dogs: concrete poems ill. by Michael Wertz. Tricycle, 2011. ISBN 978-1-58246-343-8 Subj: Animals – dogs. Poetry.

Double play! monkeying around with addition ill. by Doug Cushman. Tricycle, 2011. ISBN 978-1-58246-384-1 Subj: Animals – monkeys. Counting, numbers. Rhyming text. School.

Pond circle ill. by Stefano Vitale. Simon & Schuster, 2009. ISBN 978-1-4169-4021-0 Subj: Animals. Ecology. Lakes, ponds.

Summer beat ill. by Charlotte Middleton. Simon & Schuster, 2007. ISBN 978-1-4169-1237-8 Subj: Activities. Seasons – summer.

Why the frog has big eyes ill. by Joung Un Kim. Harcourt, 2000. ISBN 978-0-15-202536-6 Subj: Folk & fairy tales. Frogs & toads.

Frank, John. *A chill in the air: nature poems for fall and winter* ill. by Mike Reed. Simon & Schuster, 2003. ISBN 978-0-689-83923-8 Subj: Poetry. Seasons – fall. Seasons – winter.

How to catch a fish ill. by Peter Sylvada. Macmillan, 2007. ISBN 978-1-59643-163-8 Subj: Foreign lands. Poetry. Sports – fishing. World.

The toughest cowboy, Or, How the Wild West was tamed ill. by Zachary Pullen. Simon & Schuster, 2004. ISBN 978-0-689-83462-2 Subj: Animals – dogs. Cowboys, cowgirls. Humorous stories. U.S. history – frontier & pioneer life.

Frankel, Erin. *Dare!* ill. by Paula Heaphy. Free Spirit, 2012. ISBN 978-1-57542-399-9 Subj: Behavior – bullying, teasing. Emotions – fear. Self-concept.

Tough! ill. by Paula Heaphy. Free Spirit, 2012. ISBN 978-1-57542-400-2 Subj: Behavior – bullying, teasing. Friendship. Self-concept.

Weird! ill. by Paula Heaphy. Free Spirit, 2012. ISBN 978-1-57542-398-2 Subj: Behavior – bullying, teasing. Character traits – individuality. Self-concept.

Franson, Scott E. *Un-brella* ill. by author. Macmillan, 2007. ISBN 978-1-59643-179-9 Subj: Magic. Umbrellas. Wordless.

Frantz, Jennifer. *Totem poles* ill. by Allan Eitzen. Grosset, 2001. ISBN 978-0-448-42476-7 Subj: Indians of North America – Haida.

Fraser, Mary Ann. *Heebie-Jeebie Jamboree* ill. by author. Boyds Mills, 2011. ISBN 978-1-59078-857-8 Subj: Fairs, festivals. Family life – brothers & sisters. Holidays – Halloween.

How animal babies stay safe ill. by author. HarperCollins, 2002. ISBN 978-0-06-028804-4 Subj: Animals – babies. Family life – parents.

I.Q. gets fit ill. by author. Walker, 2007. ISBN 978-0-8027-9558-8 Subj: Animals – mice. Health & fitness. Pets. School.

I.Q. goes to school ill. by author. Walker, 2002. ISBN 978-0-8027-8813-9 Subj: Animals – mice. Pets. School.

I.Q. goes to the library ill. by author. Walker, 2003. ISBN 978-0-8027-8877-1 Subj: Animals – mice. Libraries. Pets. School.

I.Q., it's time ill. by author. Walker, 2005. ISBN 978-0-8027-8978-5 Subj: Animals – mice. Clocks, watches. Pets. School. Time.

Mermaid sister ill. by author. Bloomsbury, 2008. ISBN 978-0-8027-9746-9 Subj: Family life – sisters. Mythical creatures – mermaids, mermen.

Pet shop follies ill. by author. Boyds Mills, 2010. ISBN 978-1-59078-619-2 Subj: Character traits – cooperation. Pets. Stores.

Pet shop lullaby ill. by author. Boyds Mills, 2009. ISBN 978-1-59078-618-5 Subj: Animals – hamsters. Bedtime. Pets. Stores.

Where are the night animals? ill. by author. HarperCollins, 1999. ISBN 978-0-06-027718-5 Subj: Animals. Night.

Frasier, Debra. *A birthday cake is no ordinary cake* ill. by author. Harcourt, 2006. ISBN 978-0-15-205742-8 Subj: Birthdays. Calendars.

A fabulous fair alphabet ill. by author. Simon & Schuster, 2010. ISBN 978-1-4169-9817-4 Subj: ABC books. Fairs, festivals.

On the day you were born ill. by author. Harcourt, 1991. ISBN 978-0-15-257995-1 Subj: Babies. Birth. Poetry.

Out of the ocean ill. by author. Harcourt, 1998. ISBN 978-0-15-258849-6 Subj: Family life – mothers. Sea & seashore.

Spike: ugliest dog in the universe ill. by author. Simon & Schuster, 2013. ISBN 978-1-4424-1452-5 Subj: Animals – dogs. Character traits – bravery. Contests.

Fraustino, Lisa Rowe. *The hickory chair* ill. by Benny Andrews. Scholastic, 2000. ISBN 978-0-590-52248-9 Subj: Death. Family life – grandmothers. Disabilities – blindness.

Frazee, Marla. *Boot and Shoe* ill. by author. Simon & Schuster, 2012. ISBN 978-1-4424-2247-6 Subj: Animals – dogs. Animals – squirrels. Friendship.

The boss baby ill. by author. Simon & Schuster, 2010. ISBN 978-1-4424-0167-9 Subj: Babies. Behavior – bossy.

A couple of boys have the best week ever ill. by author. Harcourt, 2008. ISBN 978-0-15-206020-6 Subj: Activities – vacationing. Caldecott award honor books. Family life – grandparents. Humorous stories. Sea & seashore – beaches.

Hush, little baby: a folk song with pictures ill. by author. Harcourt, 2007. ISBN 978-0-15-205887-6 Subj: Babies. Character traits – generosity. Cumulative tales. Format, unusual – board books. Lullabies. Music.

Roller coaster ill. by author. Harcourt, 2003. ISBN 978-0-15-204554-8 Subj: Emotions – fear. Parks – amusement.

Santa Claus: the world's number one toy expert ill. by author. Harcourt, 2005. ISBN 978-0-15-204970-6 Subj: Gifts. Holidays – Christmas. Santa Claus. Toys.

Walk on! a guide for babies of all ages ill. by author. Harcourt, 2006. ISBN 978-0-15-205573-8 Subj: Activities – walking. Babies. Behavior – growing up. Self-concept.

Frazier, Craig. *Bee and Bird* ill. by author. Roaring Brook, 2011. ISBN 978-1-59643-660-2 Subj: Birds. Insects – bees. Wordless.

Lots of dots ill. by author. Chronicle, 2010. ISBN 978-0-8118-7715-2 Subj: Concepts – shape. Rhyming text.

Frederick, Heather Vogel. *Babyberry pie* ill. by Amy Schwartz. Harcourt, 2010. ISBN 978-0-15-205927-9 Subj: Babies. Bedtime. Rhyming text.

Hide and squeak. Simon & Schuster, 2011. ISBN 978-0-689-85570-2 Subj: Animals – mice. Bedtime. Family life – fathers. Rhyming text.

Fredericks, Anthony D. *In one tidepool: crabs, snails, and salty tails* ill. by Jennifer DiRubbio. Dawn, 2002. ISBN 978-1-58469-039-9 Subj: Animals. Birds – geese. Forest, woods. Seasons – winter.

Fredrickson, Lane. *Watch your tongue, Cecily Beasley* ill. by Jon Davis. Sterling, 2012. ISBN 978-1-4027-7089-0 Subj: Behavior – misbehavior. Birds. Etiquette. Rhyming text.

Freedman, Claire. *Dinosaurs love underpants* ill. by Ben Cort. Simon & Schuster, 2010. ISBN 978-1-4169-8938-7 Subj: Clothing – underwear. Dinosaurs. Rhyming text.

Follow that bear if you dare! ill. by Alison Edgson. Good Books, 2008. ISBN 978-1-56148-588-8 Subj: Animals – bears. Animals – rabbits. Sports – hunting.

Hushabye Lily ill. by John Bendall-Brunello. Orchard, 2003. ISBN 978-0-439-47106-0 Subj: Animals – rabbits. Bedtime. Noise, sounds.

Night-night, Emily ill. by Jane Massey. Tiger Tales, 2003. ISBN 978-1-58925-032-1 Subj: Bedtime. Behavior – lost & found possessions. Toys. Toys – bears.

One magical day ill. by Tina Macnaughton. Good Books, 2007. ISBN 978-1-56148-567-3 Subj: Animals. Day. Rhyming text. Seasons – summer.

One magical morning ill. by Louise Ho. Good Books, 2005. ISBN 978-1-56148-472-0 Subj: Animals. Animals – bears. Family life – mothers. Morning. Rhyming text.

Pirates love underpants ill. by Ben Cort. Aladdin, 2013. ISBN 978-1-4424-8512-9 Subj: Clothing – underwear. Pirates. Rhyming text.

Snuggle up, sleepy ones ill. by Tina Macnaughton. Good Books, 2005. ISBN 978-1-56148-475-1 Subj: Animals. Bedtime. Rhyming text. Sleep.

Where's your smile, crocodile? ill. by Sean Julian. Peachtree, 2001. ISBN 978-1-56145-251-4 Subj: Animals. Emotions. Reptiles – alligators, crocodiles.

Freedman, Deborah. *Blue chicken* ill. by author. Penguin, 2011. ISBN 978-0-670-01293-0 Subj: Activities – painting. Birds – chickens. Careers – artists. Character traits – helpfulness. Concepts – color.

Scribble ill. by author. Random House, 2007. ISBN 978-0-375-83966-5 Subj: Activities – drawing. Family life – brothers & sisters. Imagination.

The Story of Fish and Snail ill. by author. Viking, 2013. ISBN 978-0-670-78489-9 Subj: Activities – storytelling. Animals – snails. Books, reading. Fish. Libraries.

Freeman, Don. *Beady Bear* ill. by author. Viking, 1954. ISBN 978-0-670-15056-4 Subj: Behavior – running away. Toys – bears.

Bearymore ill. by author. Viking, 1976. ISBN 978-0-670-15174-5 Subj: Animals – bears. Circus. Hibernation.

Corduroy ill. by author. Viking, 1968. ISBN 978-0-670-24133-0 Subj: Clothing. Emotions – love. Ethnic groups in the U.S. – African Americans. Stores. Toys – bears.

Corduroy's busy street and Corduroy goes to the doctor ill. by author. Live Oak Media, 1989. ISBN

978-0-87499-133-8 Subj: Careers – doctors. Communities, neighborhoods. Format, unusual – board books. Toys – bears.

Dandelion ill. by author. Viking, 1964. ISBN 978-0-670-25532-0 Subj: Animals – lions. Character traits – appearance. Parties. Weather – rain.

Earl the squirrel ill. by author. Penguin, 2005. ISBN 978-0-670-06019-1 Subj: Animals – squirrels.

Gregory's Shadow ill. by author. Viking, 2000. ISBN 978-0-670-89328-7 Subj: Animals – groundhogs. Holidays – Groundhog Day. Shadows.

One more acorn by Don Freeman and Roy Freeman ill. by Don Freeman and Jody Wheeler. Penguin, 2010. ISBN 978-0-670-01083-7 Subj: Animals – squirrels. Seasons – fall.

A pocket for Corduroy ill. by author. Viking, 1978. ISBN 978-0-670-56172-8 Subj: Clothing. Ethnic groups in the U.S. – African Americans. Laundry. Toys – bears.

Quiet! There's a canary in the library ill. by author. Golden Gate, 1969. ISBN 978-0-516-08737-5 Subj: Birds – canaries. Emotions – embarrassment. Imagination. Libraries.

Freeman, Mylo. *Potty* ill. by author. Tricycle, 2002. ISBN 978-1-58246-070-3 Subj: Animals. Behavior – growing up. Jungle. Toilet training.

Freeman, Roy. *One more acorn* (Freeman, Don)

Freeman, Tor. *Hooray! I'm five today!* ill. by author. Candlewick, 2004. ISBN 978-0-7636-2452-1 Subj: Animals. Birthdays. Parties.

Olive and the bad mood ill. by author. Candlewick, 2013. ISBN 978-0-7636-6657-6 Subj: Animals – cats. Behavior – bad day. Behavior – sharing. Friendship.

Olive and the big secret ill. by author. Candlewick, 2012. ISBN 978-0-7636-6149-6 Subj: Animals. Animals – cats. Behavior – secrets.

French, Jackie. *Christmas wombat* ill. by Bruce Whatley. Harcourt, 2012. ISBN 978-0-547-86872-1 Subj: Animals – wombats. Holidays – Christmas.

Diary of a baby wombat ill. by Bruce Whatley. Clarion, 2010. ISBN 978-0-547-43005-8 Subj: Activities – writing. Animals – babies. Animals – wombats.

Diary of a wombat ill. by Bruce Whatley. Clarion, 2003. ISBN 978-0-618-38136-4 Subj: Animals – wombats.

Josephine wants to dance ill. by Bruce Whatley. Abrams, 2007. ISBN 978-0-8109-9431-7 Subj: Activities – dancing. Animals – kangaroos. Ballet. Foreign lands – Australia.

Pete the sheep-sheep ill. by Bruce Whatley. Houghton, 2005. ISBN 978-0-618-56862-8 Subj: Animals – dogs. Animals – sheep. Humorous stories.

French, Simon. *Guess the baby* ill. by Donna Rawlins. Clarion, 2002. ISBN 978-0-618-25989-2 Subj: Babies. School.

French, Vivian. *Growing frogs* ill. by Alison Bartlett. Candlewick, 2000. ISBN 978-0-7636-0317-5 Subj: Animals – babies. Frogs & toads.

A present for mom ill. by Dana Kubick. Candlewick, 2002. ISBN 978-0-7636-1587-1 Subj: Animals – cats. Gifts. Holidays – Mother's Day.

Yucky worms ill. by Jessica Ahlberg. Candlewick, 2010. ISBN 978-0-7636-4446-8 Subj: Animals – worms. Family life – grandmothers. Gardens, gardening.

Freschet, Gina. *Beto and the bone dance* ill. by author. Farrar, 2001. ISBN 978-0-374-31720-1 Subj: Ethnic groups in the U.S. – Mexican Americans. Holidays – Day of the Dead.

Naty's parade ill. by author. Farrar, 2000. ISBN 978-0-374-35500-5 Subj: Behavior – lost. Holidays. Parades.

Freymann, Saxton. *Baby food* by Saxton Freymann and Joost Elffers ill. by Saxton Freymann. Scholastic, 2006. ISBN 978-0-439-11021-1 Subj: Animals – babies. Food. Format, unusual – board books.

Dog food by Saxton Freymann and Joost Elffers ill. by Saxton Freymann. Scholastic, 2006. ISBN 978-0-439-11020-4 Subj: Animals – dogs. Food. Format, unusual – board books.

Dr. Pompo's nose by Saxton Freymann and Joost Elffers ill. by authors. Scholastic, 2000. ISBN 978-0-439-11013-6 Subj: Anatomy – noses. Rhyming text.

Fast food by Saxton Freymann and Joost Elffers ill. by Saxton Freymann. Scholastic, 2006. ISBN 978-0-439-11019-8 Subj: Food. Transportation.

Food for thought: the complete book of concepts for growing minds by Saxton Freymann and Joost Elffers ill. by Saxton Freymann. Scholastic, 2005. ISBN 978-0-439-11018-1 Subj: ABC books. Concepts – color. Concepts – opposites. Concepts – shape. Counting, numbers. Food. Format, unusual – board books.

Food play by Saxton Freymann and Joost Elffers ill. by Saxton Freymann. Chronicle, 2006. ISBN 978-0-8118-5705-5 Subj: Food.

How are you peeling? foods with moods by Saxton Freymann and Joost Elffers ill. by Saxton Freymann. Scholastic, 2004. ISBN 978-0-439-59841-5 Subj: Emotions. Food.

One lonely seahorse by Saxton Freymann and Joost Elffers ill. by authors. Scholastic, 2000. ISBN 978-0-439-11014-3 Subj: Counting, numbers. Fish –

seahorses. Friendship. Rhyming text. Sea & seashore.

Friday, Mary Ellen. *It's a bad day* ill. by Glin Dibley. Rising Moon, 2006. ISBN 978-0-87358-904-8 Subj: Behavior – bad day. Character traits – luck.

Friedlaender, Linda K. *Look! Look! Look!* (Wallace, Nancy Elizabeth)

Friedland, Katy. *Art museum opposites* by Katy Friedland and Marla K. Shoemaker. Temple Univ., 2010. ISBN 978-1-4399-0523-4 Subj: Art. Concepts – opposites. Museums.

Friedman, Caitlin. *How do you feed a hungry giant? a munch-and-sip pop-up book* ill. by Shaw Nielsen. Workman, 2011. ISBN 978-0-7611-5752-6 Subj: Food. Format, unusual – toy & movable books. Giants.

Friedman, Darlene. *Star of the Week: a story of love, adoption, and brownies with sprinkles* ill. by Roger Roth. HarperCollins, 2009. ISBN 978-0-06-114136-2 Subj: Adoption. Ethnic groups in the U.S. – Chinese Americans. School.

Friedman, Ina R. *How my parents learned to eat* ill. by Allen Say. Houghton, 1984. ISBN 978-0-395-35379-0 Subj: Family life. Sailors.

Friedman, Laurie. *Love, Ruby Valentine* ill. by Lynne Cravath. Carolrhoda, 2006. ISBN 978-1-57505-899-3 Subj: Gifts. Holidays – Valentine's Day.

Ruby Valentine saves the day ill. by Lynne Avril. Carolrhoda, 2010. ISBN 978-0-7613-4213-7 Subj: Holidays – Valentine's Day. Parties. Rhyming text. Weather – blizzards.

A style all her own ill. by Sharon Watts. Lerner, 2005. ISBN 978-1-57505-599-2 Subj: Character traits – individuality. Clothing – dresses. Weddings.

Thanksgiving rules ill. by Teresa Murfin. Carolrhoda, 2009. ISBN 978-0-8225-7983-0 Subj: Holidays – Thanksgiving. Rhyming text.

Friedman, Mel. *Kitten castle* by Mel Friedman and Ellen Weiss ill. by Lynn Adams. Kane, 2001. ISBN 978-1-57565-103-3 Subj: Animals – babies. Animals – cats. Concepts – shape.

Friedrich, Molly. *You're not my real mother!* ill. by Christy Hale. Little, Brown, 2004. ISBN 978-0-316-60553-3 Subj: Adoption. Family life. Self-concept.

Friedrich, Otto. *The Easter bunny that overslept* (Friedrich, Priscilla)

Friedrich, Priscilla. *The Easter bunny that overslept* by Priscilla Friedrich and Otto Friedrich ill. by Adrienne Adams. Lothrop, 1957. ISBN 978-0-688-01541-1 Subj: Holidays – Easter.

Friend, Catherine. *Eddie the raccoon* ill. by Wong Herbert Yee. Candlewick, 2004. ISBN 978-0-7636-2334-0 Subj: Activities. Animals – raccoons.

Funny Ruby ill. by Rachel Merriman. Candlewick, 2000. ISBN 978-0-7636-1066-1 Subj: Activities. Animals – sheep.

The perfect nest ill. by John Manders. Candlewick, 2007. ISBN 978-0-7636-2430-9 Subj: Animals – cats. Behavior – trickery. Birds. Eggs. Farms.

Fries, Claudia. *A pig is moving in* ill. by author. Orchard, 2000. ISBN 978-0-531-33307-5 Subj: Animals. Communities, neighborhoods. Homes, houses. Prejudice.

Frisch, Aaron. *The lonely pine* ill. by Etienne Delessert. Creative Editions, 2011. ISBN 978-1-56846-214-1 Subj: Nature. Seasons. Trees.

Frith, Margaret. *Frida Kahlo: the artist who painted herself* ill. by Tomie dePaola. Grosset, 2003. ISBN 978-0-448-43239-7 Subj: Careers – artists. Foreign lands – Mexico.

Fritts, Mary Bahr. *If Nathan were here* ill. by Karen Jerome. Eerdmans, 2000. ISBN 978-0-8028-5187-1 Subj: Death. Emotions – grief. Friendship.

A frog he would a-wooing go [folk-song]. *Frog went a-courtin'* retold by John M. Langstaff; ill. by Feodor Rojankovsky. Harcourt, 1955. ISBN 978-0-15-230214-6 Subj: Animals. Caldecott award books. Frogs & toads. Songs.

Frog went a-courting: a musical play in six acts retold by Dominic Catalano; ill. by reteller. Boyds Mills, 1998. ISBN 978-1-56397-637-7 Subj: Animals. Frogs & toads. Music. Songs. Theater. Weddings.

Froggie went a courting adapt. by Marjorie Priceman; ill. by adapter. Little, 1999. ISBN 978-0-316-71227-9 Subj: Animals. Frogs & toads. Songs. Weddings.

Froggy went a-courtin' adapt. by Gillian Tyler; ill. by adapter. Candlewick, 2005. ISBN 978-0-7636-2306-7 Subj: Animals. Frogs & toads. Songs. Weddings.

Fromental, Jean-Luc. *365 penguins* by Jean-Luc Fromental and Joëlle Jolivet ill. by authors. Abrams, 2006. ISBN 978-0-8109-4460-2 Subj: Birds – penguins. Counting, numbers. Holidays – New Year's.

Frost, Helen. *Monarch and milkweed* ill. by Leonid Gore. Atheneum, 2008. ISBN 978-1-4169-0085-6 Subj: Insects – butterflies, caterpillars. Metamorphosis. Migration.

Step gently out ill. by Rick Lieder. Candlewick, 2012. ISBN 978-0-7636-5601-0 Subj: Insects. Nature. Poetry.

Frost, Robert. *Stopping by woods on a snowy evening* ill. by Susan Jeffers. Dutton, 1978. ISBN 978-0-525-40115-5 Subj: Forest, woods. Poetry. Seasons – winter.

Fruisen, Catherine Myler. *My mother's pearls* ill. by author. Star Bright, 2005. ISBN 978-1-59572-005-4 Subj: Family life – daughters. Family life – mothers. Jewelry.

Fry, Jenny. *Building numbers* ill. by Jacqueline East. Barron's, 2002. ISBN 978-0-7641-5499-7 Subj: Counting, numbers. Machines.

Fry, Stella. *Grandpa's garden* ill. by Sheila Moxley. Barefoot, 2012. ISBN 978-1-84686-053-9 Subj: Family life – grandfathers. Gardens, gardening.

Fucile, Tony. *Let's do nothing!* ill. by author. Candlewick, 2009. ISBN 978-0-7636-3440-7 Subj: Activities – playing.

Fuge, Charles. *Astonishing animal ABC* ill. by author. Sterling, 2011. ISBN 978-1-4027-8645-7 Subj: ABC books. Animals. Rhyming text.

I know a rhino ill. by author. Sterling, 2002. ISBN 978-1-4027-0137-5 Subj: Activities – playing. Animals. Imagination. Rhyming text.

Swim, Little Wombat, swim! ill. by author. Sterling, 2005. ISBN 978-1-4027-2375-9 Subj: Animals – platypuses. Animals – wombats. Friendship. Sports – swimming.

Three little dinosaurs ill. by author. Sterling, 2012. ISBN 978-1-4027-9645-6 Subj: Activities – flying. Dinosaurs.

Where to, Little Wombat? ill. by author. Sterling, 2006. ISBN 978-1-4027-3698-8 Subj: Animals – wombats. Format, unusual – board books. Homes, houses.

Yip! Snap! Yap! ill. by author. Tricycle, 2001. ISBN 978-1-58246-046-8 Subj: Animals – dogs. Noise, sounds.

Fuller, Sandy F. *The Blues go birding across America* (Malnor, Carol L.)

My cat, coon cat ill. by Jeannie Brett. Islandport, 2011. ISBN 978-1-934031-32-2 Subj: Animals – cats.

Fullerton, Alma. *A good trade* ill. by Karen Patkau. Pajama Press, 2012. ISBN 978-0-9869495-9-3 Subj: Clothing – shoes. Foreign lands – Uganda. Poverty. War.

Funke, Cornelia. *Pirate girl* ill. by Kerstin Meyer. Scholastic, 2005. ISBN 978-0-439-71672-7 Subj: Pirates.

Princess Pigsty ill. by Kerstin Meyer. Scholastic, 2007. ISBN 978-0-439-98855-1 Subj: Behavior – misbehavior. Character traits – cleanliness. Royalty – princesses. Self-concept.

The wildest brother ill. by Kerstin Meyer. Scholastic, 2006. ISBN 978-0-439-82862-8 Subj: Emotions – fear. Family life – brothers & sisters. Monsters.

Furgang, Kathy. *Flower girl* ill. by Harley Jessup. Viking, 2002. ISBN 978-0-670-88950-1 Subj: Weddings.

Furrow, Elena. *Ready to dream* (Napoli, Donna Jo)

Furrow, Eva. *Bobby the bold* (Napoli, Donna Jo)

Furstinger, Nancy. *Maggie's second chance: a gentle dog's rescue* ill. by Joe Hyatt. Gryphon, 2011. ISBN 978-0-940719-11-8 Subj: Animals – dogs. Character traits – kindness to animals.

Fyleman, Rose. *Mice* ill. by Lois Ehlert. Simon & Schuster, 2012. ISBN 978-1-4424-5684-6 Subj: Animals – mice. Rhyming text.

Gabriel, Ashala. *Night night toes* ill. by Sue Porter. Simon & Schuster, 2002. ISBN 978-0-689-85089-9 Subj: Animals – bears. Bedtime. Format, unusual – toy & movable books. Night.

Gadot, A. S. *The first gift* ill. by Marie Lafrance. Lerner, 2006. ISBN 978-1-58013-146-9 Subj: Jewish culture. Names. Religion.

Tower of Babel ill. by Cecilia Rebora. Lerner/Kar-Ben, 2010. ISBN 978-0-8225-9917-3 Subj: Religion.

Gág, Wanda. *Millions of cats* ill. by author. Coward, 1928. ISBN 978-0-698-20091-3 Subj: Animals – cats. Character traits – practicality. Cumulative tales.

Gaiman, Neil. *Chu's day* ill. by Adam Rex. HarperCollins, 2013. ISBN 978-0-06-201781-9 Subj: Animals – pandas. Illness.

Crazy hair ill. by Dave McKean. HarperCollins, 2009. ISBN 978-0-06-057908-1 Subj: Character traits – appearance. Hair. Humorous stories. Rhyming text.

The dangerous alphabet ill. by Gris Grimly. HarperCollins, 2008. ISBN 978-0-06-078333-4 Subj: ABC books. Emotions – fear. Monsters. Pirates. Rhyming text.

Instructions ill. by Charles Vess. HarperCollins, 2010. ISBN 978-0-06-196030-7 Subj: Activities – traveling. Self-concept.

Gainer, Cindy. *I'm like you, you're like me: a book about understanding and appreciating each other* ill. by Miki Sakamoto. Free Spirit, 2011. ISBN 978-1-57542-383-8 Subj: Character traits – cooperation. Character traits – individuality. Character traits – kindness.

Gal, Susan. *Day by day* ill. by author. Knopf., 2012. ISBN 978-0-375-86959-4 Subj: Animals – pigs. Communities, neighborhoods. Family life.

Night lights ill. by author. Knopf, 2009. ISBN 978-0-375-85862-8 Subj: Bedtime. Family life – mothers. Light, lights. Night.

Please take me for a walk ill. by author. Random House, 2010. ISBN 978-0-375-85863-5 Subj: Animals – dogs.

Galbraith, Kathryn O. *Arbor Day square* ill. by Cyd Moore. Peachtree, 2010. ISBN 978-1-56145-517-1 Subj: Family life – fathers. Holidays. Trees. U.S. history – frontier & pioneer life.

Boo, bunny! ill. by Jeff Mack. Harcourt, 2008. ISBN 978-0-15-216246-7 Subj: Animals – rabbits. Emotions – fear. Holidays – Halloween. Rhyming text.

Planting the wild garden ill. by Wendy Anderson Halperin. Peachtree, 2011. ISBN 978-1-56145-563-8 Subj: Nature. Seeds.

Galdone, Joanna. *The tailypo: a ghost story* ill. by Paul Galdone. Seabury Pr., 1977. ISBN 978-0-8164-3191-5 Subj: Ghosts.

Galdone, Paul, adapt. *Cat goes fiddle-i-fee* ill. by adapter. Clarion, 1985. ISBN 978-0-89919-336-6 Subj: Animals. Cumulative tales. Farms. Noise, sounds. Nursery rhymes.

The magic porridge pot ill. by author. Seabury Pr., 1976. ISBN 978-0-8164-3173-1 Subj: Behavior – forgetfulness. Behavior – sharing. Folk & fairy tales. Food. Magic.

The teeny-tiny woman: a ghost story ill. by adapter. Clarion, 1984. ISBN 978-0-89919-270-3 Subj: Emotions. Folk & fairy tales. Ghosts.

What's in fox's sack? ill. by author. Houghton, 1982. ISBN 978-0-89919-062-4 Subj: Character traits – cleverness. Folk & fairy tales.

Galindo, Mary Sue. *Icy watermelon / Sandía fría* ill. by Pauline Rodriguez Howard. Piñata, 2001. ISBN 978-1-55885-306-5 Subj: Ethnic groups in the U.S. – Mexican Americans. Family life – grandparents. Foreign languages.

Galko, Francine. *Cave animals* ill. with photos. Heinemann, 2003. ISBN 978-1-4034-0176-2 Subj: Animals. Caves. Ecology.

Gall, Chris. *Awesome Dawson* ill. by author. Little, Brown, 2013. ISBN 978-0-316-21330-1 Subj: Behavior – collecting things. Careers – inventors. Ecology. Robots. Toys.

Dinotrux ill. by author. Little, Brown, 2009. ISBN 978-0-316-02777-9 Subj: Dinosaurs. Trucks.

Revenge of the Dinotrux ill. by author. Little, Brown, 2012. ISBN 978-0-316-13288-6 Subj: Behavior – misbehavior. Books, reading. Dinosaurs. Museums. Trucks.

Substitute creacher ill. by author. Little, Brown, 2011. ISBN 978-0-316-08915-9 Subj: Careers – teachers. Monsters. Rhyming text. School.

There's nothing to do on Mars ill. by author. Little, Brown, 2008. ISBN 978-0-316-16684-3 Subj: Behavior – boredom. Space & space ships.

Gallico, Paul. *Paul Gallico's The small miracle* (Barton, Bob)

Gallo, Frank. *Bird calls* ill. by Lori Lohstoeter. Sounds recorded by Michael DiGiorgio. Innovative KIDS, 2001. ISBN 978-1-58476-064-1 Subj: Birds. Format, unusual – toy & movable books. Noise, sounds.

Night sounds ill. by Lori Lohstoeter. Sounds recorded by Michael DiGiorgio. Innovative KIDS, 2001. ISBN 978-1-58476-065-8 Subj: Animals. Format, unusual – toy & movable books. Night. Noise, sounds.

Galloway, Ruth. *Clumsy crab* ill. by author. Tiger Tales, 2005. ISBN 978-1-58925-050-5 Subj: Crustaceans – crabs. Self-concept.

Fidgety fish ill. by author. Tiger Tales, 2001. ISBN 978-1-58925-012-3 Subj: Caves. Fish. Sea & seashore.

Galvin, Laura Gates. *Bumblebee at Apple Tree Lane* ill. by Kristin Kest. Soundprints, 2000. ISBN 978-1-56899-820-6 Subj: Insects – bees.

River Otter at Autumn Lane ill. by Christopher Leeper. Soundprints, 2002. ISBN 978-1-931465-62-5 Subj: Animals – otters. Behavior – growing up. Family life.

Gamble, Isobel. *Who's that?* by Isobel Gamble and Tim Warnes ill. by Tim Warnes. Barron's, 2001. ISBN 978-0-7641-5335-8 Subj: Animals. Bedtime.

Format, unusual – toy & movable books. Homes, houses. Sleep.

Gammell, Stephen. *How about going for a ride* ill. by author. Harcourt, 2001. ISBN 978-0-15-202682-0 Subj: Activities – traveling. Automobiles. Family life – brothers & sisters.

Is that you, winter? ill. by author. Silver Whistle, 1997. ISBN 978-0-15-201415-5 Subj: Behavior – bad day. Seasons – winter. Weather – snow.

Mudkin ill. by author. Carolrhoda, 2011. ISBN 978-0-7613-5790-2 Subj: Activities – playing. Imagination. Weather – rain.

Wake up, bear . . . It's Christmas! ill. by author. Morrow, 1990. ISBN 978-0-688-09934-3 Subj: Animals – bears. Hibernation. Holidays – Christmas. Santa Claus.

Gannij, Joan. *Elusive moose* ill. by Clare Beaton. Barefoot, 2006. ISBN 978-1-905236-75-6 Subj: Animals – moose. Picture puzzles.

Hidden hippo ill. by Clare Beaton. Barefoot, 2008. ISBN 978-1-84686-170-3 Subj: Animals. Foreign lands – Africa. Rhyming text.

Gantos, Jack. *Back to school for Rotten Ralph* ill. by Nicole Rubel. HarperCollins, 1998. ISBN 978-0-06-027532-7 Subj: Animals – cats. Character traits – selfishness. Emotions – envy, jealousy. Emotions – fear. Friendship. School – first day.

Happy birthday, Rotten Ralph ill. by Nicole Rubel. Houghton, 1990. ISBN 978-0-395-53766-4 Subj: Animals – cats. Behavior – misbehavior. Birthdays.

The nine lives of Rotten Ralph ill. by Nicole Rubel. Houghton, 2009. ISBN 978-0-618-80046-9 Subj: Animals – cats. Behavior – misbehavior.

Not so Rotten Ralph ill. by Nicole Rubel. Houghton, 1994. ISBN 978-0-395-62302-2 Subj: Animals – cats. Behavior – misbehavior. School.

Rotten Ralph ill. by Nicole Rubel. Houghton, 1976. ISBN 978-0-395-24276-6 Subj: Animals – cats. Behavior – misbehavior.

Rotten Ralph's rotten Christmas ill. by Nicole Rubel. Houghton, 1984. ISBN 978-0-395-35380-6 Subj: Animals – cats. Character traits – meanness. Emotions – envy, jealousy. Holidays – Christmas.

Rotten Ralph's rotten romance ill. by Nicole Rubel. Houghton, 1997. ISBN 978-0-395-73978-5 Subj: Animals – cats. Behavior – misbehavior. Holidays – Valentine's Day. Parties.

Rotten Ralph's show and tell ill. by Nicole Rubel. Houghton, 1989. ISBN 978-0-395-44312-5 Subj: Animals – cats. Character traits – meanness. School.

Rotten Ralph's trick or treat ill. by Nicole Rubel. Houghton, 1986. ISBN 978-0-395-38943-0 Subj: Animals – cats. Character traits – meanness. Holidays – Halloween.

Wedding bells for Rotten Ralph ill. by Nicole Rubel. HarperCollins, 1999. ISBN 978-0-06-027534-1 Subj: Animals – cats. Behavior – misbehavior. Weddings.

Worse than Rotten Ralph ill. by Nicole Rubel. Houghton, 1978. ISBN 978-0-395-28106-2 Subj: Animals – cats. Behavior – misbehavior. Character traits – meanness.

García, Cheo. *Pick a pet* (Rotner, Shelley)

Garcia, Emma. *Tap tap bang bang* ill. by author. Boxer, 2010. ISBN 978-1-907152-00-9 Subj: Noise, sounds. Tools.

Tip tip dig dig ill. by author. Boxer, 2007. ISBN 978-1-905417-59-9 Subj: Trucks.

Gardella, Tricia. *Blackberry booties* ill. by Glo Coalson. Orchard, 2000. ISBN 978-0-531-33184-2 Subj: Activities – trading. Gifts. Problem solving.

Garden, Nancy. *Molly's family* ill. by Sharon Wooding. Farrar, 2004. ISBN 978-0-374-35002-4 Subj: Adoption. Behavior – bullying, teasing. Family life – mothers. School.

Gardeski, Christina Mia. *Diwali* ill. with photos. Children's Press, 2001. ISBN 978-0-516-22372-8 Subj: Foreign lands – India. Holidays – Divali. Religion – Hinduism.

Gardiner, Lindsey. *Good night, Poppy and Max* ill. by author. Little, 2002. ISBN 978-0-316-60122-1 Subj: Animals – dogs. Bedtime. Counting, numbers. Format, unusual – board books.

Here come Poppy and Max ill. by author. Little, 2000. ISBN 978-0-316-60346-1 Subj: Activities – playing. Animals – dogs. Imagination.

If you're happy and you know it! (Ormerod, Jan)

When Poppy and Max grow up ill. by author. Little, 2001. ISBN 978-0-316-60342-3 Subj: Activities – playing. Animals – dogs. Careers. Imagination.

Gardner, Carol. *Princess Zelda and the frog* photos by Shane Young. Feiwel & Friends, 2011. ISBN 978-0-312-60325-0 Subj: Animals – dogs. Frogs & toads. Royalty – princesses.

Gardner, Sally. *Mama, don't go out tonight* ill. by author. Bloomsbury, 2002. ISBN 978-1-58234-790-5 Subj: Activities – babysitting. Family life – mothers. Imagination.

Garelli, Cristina. *Farm friends clean up* ill. by Francesca Chessa. Crown, 2000. ISBN 978-0-517-80082-9 Subj: Animals. Character traits – cleanliness. Farms. Hygiene.

Garhan Attebury, Nancy. *Out and about at city hall* ill. by Zachary Trover. Picture Window, 2006. ISBN 978-1-4048-1146-1 Subj: Cities, towns.

Out and about at the bank ill. by Zachary Trover. Picture Window, 2006. ISBN 978-1-4048-1147-8 Subj: Money.

Out and about at the hospital ill. by Zachary Trover. Picture Window, 2006. ISBN 978-1-4048-1148-5 Subj: Hospitals. Illness.

Out and about at the United States Mint ill. by Zachary Trover. Picture Window, 2006. ISBN 978-1-4048-1151-5 Subj: Money.

Garland, Michael. *Americana adventure: a look again book* ill. by author. Dutton, 2008. ISBN 978-0-525-47945-1 Subj: Family life – aunts, uncles. Picture puzzles. U.S. history.

Christmas City ill. by author. Dutton, 2002. ISBN 978-0-525-46904-9 Subj: Holidays – Christmas. Picture puzzles. Rhyming text.

Christmas magic ill. by author. Dutton, 2001. ISBN 978-0-525-46797-7 Subj: Holidays – Christmas. Snowmen.

Grandpa's tractor ill. by author. Boyds Mills, 2011. ISBN 978-1-59078-762-5 Subj: Family life – grandfathers. Farms. Memories, memory. Tractors.

The great Easter egg hunt ill. by author. Penguin, 2005. ISBN 978-0-525-47357-2 Subj: Holidays – Easter. Picture puzzles. Rhyming text.

Hooray José! ill. by author. Marshall Cavendish, 2007. ISBN 978-0-7614-5345-1 Subj: Animals – mice. Character traits – perseverance. Concepts – size. Rhyming text. Sports – basketball.

How many mice? ill. by author. Penguin, 2007. ISBN 978-0-525-47833-1 Subj: Animals – mice. Counting, numbers.

Icarus Swinebuckle ill. by author. Whitman, 2000. ISBN 978-0-8075-3495-3 Subj: Activities – flying. Animals – pigs.

King Puck ill. by author. HarperCollins, 2007. ISBN 978-0-06-084809-5 Subj: Animals – goats. Books, reading. Fairies. Foreign lands – Ireland. Magic.

Last night at the zoo ill. by author. Boyds Mills, 2001. ISBN 978-1-56397-759-6 Subj: Animals. Behavior – running away. Rhyming text. Zoos.

Miss Smith and the haunted library ill. by author. Dutton, 2009. ISBN 978-0-525-42139-9 Subj: Books, reading. Careers – teachers. Libraries. Magic. School – field trips.

Miss Smith reads again! ill. by author. Penguin, 2006. ISBN 978-0-525-47722-8 Subj: Books, reading. Careers – teachers. Dinosaurs. Magic. School.

Miss Smith's incredible storybook ill. by author. Dutton, 2003. ISBN 978-0-525-47133-2 Subj: Books, reading. Careers – teachers. Magic. School.

The President and Mom's apple pie ill. by author. Dutton, 2003. ISBN 978-0-525-46887-5 Subj: Food. U.S. history.

Super snow day seek and find ill. by author. Penguin, 2010. ISBN 978-0-525-42245-7 Subj: Family life – aunts, uncles. Picture puzzles. Weather – snow.

Garland, Sarah. *Eddie's toolbox and how to make and mend things* ill. by author. Frances Lincoln, 2011. ISBN 978-1-84780-053-4 Subj: Character traits – helpfulness. Communities, neighborhoods. Friendship. Tools.

Garland, Sherry. *The lotus seed* ill. by Tatsuro Kiuchi. Harcourt, 1993. ISBN 978-0-15-249465-0 Subj: Ethnic groups in the U.S. – Vietnamese Americans. Family life – grandmothers. Foreign lands – Vietnam. War.

My father's boat ill. by Ted Rand. Scholastic, 1998. ISBN 978-0-590-47867-0 Subj: Boats, ships. Careers – fishermen. Ethnic groups in the U.S. – Vietnamese Americans.

Garner, Alan. *Little red hen* (The little red hen)

Garriel, Barbara S. *I know a shy fellow who swallowed a cello* ill. by John O'Brien. Boyds Mills, 2004. ISBN 978-1-56397-962-0 Subj: Cumulative tales. Humorous stories. Musical instruments – cellos. Rhyming text.

Gary, Meredith. *Sometimes you get what you want* ill. by Lisa Brown. HarperCollins, 2008. ISBN 978-0-06-114015-0 Subj: Behavior. Family life – brothers & sisters. School – nursery.

Gassman, Julie. *Crabby pants* ill. by Richard Watson. Picture Window, 2010. ISBN 978-1-4048-6165-7 Subj: Behavior – misbehavior. Clothing – pants. Emotions – anger.

Gauch, Patricia Lee. *Bravo, Tanya* ill. by Satomi Ichikawa. Putnam, 1992. ISBN 978-0-399-22145-3 Subj: Activities – dancing. Ballet. Toys – bears.

Dance, Tanya ill. by Satomi Ichikawa. Putnam, 1989. ISBN 978-0-399-21521-6 Subj: Activities – dancing. Ballet. Behavior – imitation. Toys – bears.

Presenting Tanya, the Ugly Duckling ill. by Satomi Ichikawa. Philomel, 1999. ISBN 978-0-399-23200-8 Subj: Activities – dancing. Ballet. Self-concept.

Tanya and Emily in a dance for two ill. by Satomi Ichikawa. Philomel, 1994. ISBN 978-0-399-22688-5 Subj: Activities – dancing. Ballet. Friendship.

Gavril, David. *Penelope Nuthatch and the big surprise* ill. by author. Abrams, 2006. ISBN 978-0-8109-5762-6 Subj: Behavior – worrying. Birds. Parks – amusement.

Gay, Marie-Louise. *Caramba* ill. by author. Groundwood, 2005. ISBN 978-0-88899-667-1 Subj: Animals – cats. Imagination.

Caramba and Henry ill. by author. Groundwood, 2011. ISBN 978-1-55498-097-0 Subj: Animals – cats. Family life – brothers. Sibling rivalry.

Good morning Sam ill. by author. Douglas & McIntyre, 2003. ISBN 978-0-88899-528-5 Subj: Clothing. Family life – brothers & sisters. Humorous stories. Morning.

On my island ill. by author. Douglas & McIntyre, 2000. ISBN 978-0-88899-396-0 Subj: Animals. Behavior – boredom. Islands.

Read me a story, Stella ill. by author. Groundwood, 2013. ISBN 978-1-55498-216-5 Subj: Activities. Books, reading. Family life – brothers & sisters.

Roslyn Rutabaga and the biggest hole on earth! ill. by author. Groundwood, 2010. ISBN 978-0-88899-994-8 Subj: Activities – digging. Animals – rabbits. Family life – fathers.

Stella, fairy of the forest ill. by author. Douglas & McIntyre, 2002. ISBN 978-0-88899-448-6 Subj: Animals. Fairies. Family life – brothers & sisters. Forest, woods.

Stella, queen of the snow ill. by author. Douglas & McIntyre, 2000. ISBN 978-0-88899-404-2 Subj: Activities – playing. Family life – brothers & sisters. Weather – snow.

Stella, star of the sea ill. by author. Douglas & McIntyre, 1999. ISBN 978-0-88899-337-3 Subj: Family life – brothers & sisters. Sea & seashore.

What are you doing, Sam? ill. by author. Groundwood, 2006. ISBN 978-0-88899-734-0 Subj: Animals – dogs. Behavior – messy. Family life – brothers & sisters. Pets.

When Stella was very, very small ill. by author. Groundwood, 2009. ISBN 978-0-88899-906-1 Subj: Behavior – growing up. Character traits – smallness. Family life – brothers & sisters. Imagination.

Gay, Michel. *Zee is not scared* ill. by author. Clarion, 2004. ISBN 978-0-618-43931-7 Subj: Animals – zebras. Bedtime. Emotions – fear. Family life – parents.

Geisel, Theodor Seuss *see* Seuss, Dr.

Geisert, Arthur. *Country road ABC: an illustrated journey through America's farmland* ill. by author. Harcourt, 2010. ISBN 978-0-547-19469-1 Subj: ABC books. Farms.

Desert town (Geisert, Bonnie)

The giant ball of string ill. by author. Houghton, 2002. ISBN 978-0-618-13221-8 Subj: Animals – pigs. Behavior – lost & found possessions. Character traits – cooperation. String.

The giant seed ill. by author. Enchanted Lion, 2012. ISBN 978-1-59270-115-5 Subj: Animals – pigs. Behavior – resourcefulness. Seeds. Volcanoes. Wordless.

Hogwash ill. by author. Houghton, 2008. ISBN 978-0-618-77332-9 Subj: Activities – bathing. Animals – pigs. Character traits – cleanliness. Machines. Wordless.

Ice ill. by author. Enchanted Lion, 2011. ISBN 978-1-59270-098-1 Subj: Animals – pigs. Character traits – cleverness. Character traits – cooperation. Wordless.

Lights out ill. by author. Houghton, 2005. ISBN 978-0-618-47892-7 Subj: Animals – pigs. Bedtime. Character traits – cleverness. Emotions – fear. Inventions.

Mountain town (Geisert, Bonnie)

Mystery ill. by author. Houghton, 2003. ISBN 978-0-618-27293-8 Subj: Animals – pigs. Careers – detectives. Crime. Family life – grandfathers. Museums. Mystery stories. Picture puzzles.

Nursery crimes ill. by author. Houghton, 2001. ISBN 978-0-618-06487-8 Subj: Animals – pigs. Crime. Farms. Holidays – Thanksgiving. Mystery stories. Trees.

Oops ill. by author. Houghton, 2006. ISBN 978-0-618-60904-8 Subj: Animals – pigs. Wordless.

Pigaroons ill. by author. Houghton, 2004. ISBN 978-0-618-41058-3 Subj: Animals – pigs. Crime. Fairs, festivals.

Thunderstorm ill. by author. Enchanted Lion, 2013. ISBN 978-1-59270-133-9 Subj: Weather – lightning, thunder. Weather – storms.

Geisert, Bonnie. *Desert town* by Bonnie Geisert and Arthur Geisert ill. by Arthur Geisert. Houghton, 2001. ISBN 978-0-395-95387-7 Subj: Cities, towns. Desert.

Mountain town by Bonnie Geisert and Arthur Geisert ill. by Arthur Geisert. Houghton, 2000. ISBN 978-0-395-95390-7 Subj: Cities, towns. Mountains. Seasons.

Geist, Ken. *The three little fish and the big bad shark* ill. by Julia Gorton. Scholastic, 2007. ISBN 978-0-439-71962-9 Subj: Fish. Fish – sharks. Sea & seashore.

Who's who? ill. by Henry Cole. Feiwel & Friends, 2012. ISBN 978-0-312-64437-6 Subj: Animals. Multiple births – twins. Rhyming text.

Genechten, Guido van. *Because you are my friend* ill. by author. Clavis, 2011. ISBN 978-1-60537-095-8 Subj: Animals – polar bears. Family life – mothers. Friendship.

The big woods orchestra ill. by author. Clavis, 2012. ISBN 978-1-60537-113-9 Subj: Birds. Forest, woods. Music. Nature.

Flop-Ear ill. by author. Barron's, 2001. ISBN 978-0-7641-1762-6 Subj: Anatomy – ears. Animals – rabbits. Character traits – individuality.

Guess what? ill. by author. Clavis, 2012. ISBN 978-1-60537-116-0 Subj: Animals. Format, unusual – toy & movable books.

Guess where? ill. by author. Clavis, 2012. ISBN 978-1-60537-115-3 Subj: Animals. Format, unusual – toy & movable books.

Kai-Mook ill. by author. Clavis, 2011. ISBN 978-1-60537-096-5 Subj: Animals – babies. Animals – elephants.

No ghost under my bed ill. by author. Clavis, 2010. ISBN 978-1-60537-069-9 Subj: Bedtime. Birds – penguins. Emotions – fear.

Ricky and the squirrel ill. by author. Clavis, 2010. ISBN 978-1-60537-078-1 Subj: Animals – rabbits. Animals – squirrels. Death.

Ricky is brave ill. by author. Clavis, 2011. ISBN 978-1-60537-097-2 Subj: Animals – rabbits. Camps, camping. Character traits – bravery. Emotions – fear.

Gentieu, Penny. *Baby! Talk!* ill. by author. Crown, 1999. ISBN 978-0-517-80028-7 Subj: Activities. Babies.

Grow! babies! ill. by author. Crown, 2000. ISBN 978-0-517-80029-4 Subj: Babies. Behavior – growing up.

Gentle, Victor. *Baby sharks* by Victor Gentle and Janet Perry Marshall ill. with photos. G. Stevens, 2001. ISBN 978-0-8368-2824-5 Subj: Animals – babies. Fish – sharks.

Killer sharks, killer people by Victor Gentle and Janet Perry Marshall ill. with photos. G. Stevens, 2001. ISBN 978-0-8368-2826-9 Subj: Fish – sharks. Sports – fishing.

Orcas, killer whales by Victor Gentle and Janet Perry Marshall ill. with photos. G. Stevens, 2001. ISBN 978-0-8368-2883-2 Subj: Animals – whales.

Shark camouflage and armor by Victor Gentle and Janet Perry Marshall ill. with photos. G. Stevens, 2001. ISBN 978-0-8368-2827-6 Subj: Disguises. Fish – sharks.

Very big sharks by Victor Gentle and Janet Perry Marshall ill. with photos. G. Stevens, 2001. ISBN 978-0-8368-2828-3 Subj: Fish – sharks.

The world's strangest shark by Victor Gentle and Janet Perry Marshall ill. with photos. G. Stevens, 2001. ISBN 978-0-8368-2829-0 Subj: Fish – sharks.

Geoghegan, Adrienne. *All your own teeth* ill. by Cathy Gale. Dial, 2001. ISBN 978-0-8037-2655-0 Subj: Activities – painting. Animals. Jungle.

George, Bobby. *Montessori number work* by Bobby George and June George ill. by Alyssa Nassner. Abrams, 2012. ISBN 978-1-4197-0412-3 Subj: Counting, numbers. Format, unusual – board books.

George, Jean Craighead. *The buffalo are back* ill. by Wendell Minor. Penguin, 2010. ISBN 978-0-525-42215-0 Subj: Animals – buffaloes. Animals – endangered animals. Ecology.

Cliff hanger ill. by Wendell Minor. HarperCollins, 2002. ISBN 978-0-06-000261-9 Subj: Animals – dogs. Family life – fathers. Mountains. Sports – mountain climbing. Weather – storms.

Dear Rebecca, winter is here ill. by Loretta Krupinski. HarperCollins, 1993. ISBN 978-0-06-021140-0 Subj: Family life – grandmothers. Nature. Seasons. Seasons – winter.

The eagles are back ill. by Wendell Minor. Dial, 2013. ISBN 978-0-8037-3771-6 Subj: Animals – endangered animals. Birds – eagles. Ecology.

Everglades ill. by Wendell Minor. HarperCollins, 1995. ISBN 978-0-06-021229-2 Subj: Ecology. Nature. Rivers.

The first Thanksgiving ill. by Thomas Locker. Philomel, 1993. ISBN 978-0-399-21991-7 Subj: Holidays – Thanksgiving. Pilgrims. U.S. history.

Frightful's daughter ill. by Daniel San Souci. Dutton, 2002. ISBN 978-0-525-46907-0 Subj: Birds – falcons.

Frightful's daughter meets the Baron Weasel ill. by Daniel San Souci. Penguin, 2007. ISBN 978-0-525-47202-5 Subj: Animals – weasels. Birds – falcons.

The last polar bear ill. by Wendell Minor. HarperCollins, 2009. ISBN 978-0-06-124067-6 Subj: Animals – polar bears. Ecology. Foreign lands – Arctic.

Look to the north: a wolf pup diary ill. by Lucia Washburn. HarperCollins, 1997. ISBN 978-0-06-023640-3 Subj: Animals – babies. Animals – wolves. Behavior – growing up. Seasons.

Luck ill. by Wendell Minor. HarperCollins, 2006. ISBN 978-0-06-008201-7 Subj: Birds – cranes. Migration.

Morning, noon, and night ill. by Wendell Minor. HarperCollins, 1999. ISBN 978-0-06-023628-1 Subj: Activities. Animals. Day.

Nutik and Amaroq play ball ill. by Ted Rand. HarperCollins, 2001. ISBN 978-0-06-028166-3 Subj: Animals – wolves. Eskimos. Foreign lands – Arctic.

Nutik, the wolf pup ill. by Ted Rand. HarperCollins, 2001. ISBN 978-0-06-028164-9 Subj: Animals – wolves. Eskimos. Family life – brothers & sisters. Foreign lands – Arctic.

Snow bear ill. by Wendell Minor. Hyperion, 1999. ISBN 978-0-7868-0456-6 Subj: Activities – playing. Animals – polar bears. Eskimos. Foreign lands – Arctic. Weather – snow.

The wolves are back ill. by Wendell Minor. Dutton, 2008. ISBN 978-0-525-47947-5 Subj: Animals – endangered animals. Animals – wolves. Ecology.

George, June. *Montessori number work* (George, Bobby)

George, Kristine O'Connell. *Emma dilemma: big sister poems* ill. by Nancy Carpenter. Clarion, 2011. ISBN 978-0-618-42842-7 Subj: Family life – sisters. Poetry.

The great frog race and other poems ill. by Kate Kiesler. Clarion, 1997. ISBN 978-0-395-77607-0 Subj: Counting, numbers. Nature. Poetry.

Little Dog and Duncan ill. by June Otani. Clarion, 2002. ISBN 978-0-618-11758-1 Subj: Animals – dogs. Poetry.

Old Elm speaks ill. by Kate Kiesler. Clarion, 1998. ISBN 978-0-395-87611-4 Subj: Poetry. Seasons. Trees.

Up! ill. by Hiroe Nakata. Houghton, 2005. ISBN 978-0-618-06489-2 Subj: Concepts – up & down. Family life – fathers. Rhyming text.

George, Lindsay Barrett. *Around the pond: who's been here?* ill. by author. Greenwillow, 1996. ISBN 978-0-688-14377-0 Subj: Animals. Lakes, ponds. Nature. Seasons – summer.

Beaver at Long Pond (George, William T.)

In the garden: who's been here? ill. by author. HarperCollins, 2006. ISBN 978-0-06-078762-2 Subj: Animals. Gardens, gardening. Nature. Problem solving.

In the woods: who's been here? ill. by author. Greenwillow, 1995. ISBN 978-0-688-12319-2 Subj: Activities – walking. Animals. Forest, woods. Nature. Problem solving. Seasons – fall.

Maggie's ball ill. by author. HarperCollins, 2010. ISBN 978-0-06-172166-3 Subj: Animals – dogs. Behavior – lost & found possessions. Toys – balls.

My bunny and me ill. by author. Greenwillow, 2001. ISBN 978-0-688-16075-3 Subj: Animals – rabbits. Imagination.

The secret ill. by author. HarperCollins, 2005. ISBN 978-0-06-029600-1 Subj: Animals. Behavior – secrets. Emotions – love.

That pup! ill. by author. HarperCollins, 2011. ISBN 978-0-06-200413-0 Subj: Animals – dogs. Animals – squirrels.

George, Lucy M. *Back to school Tortoise* ill. by Merel Eyckerman. Whitman, 2011. ISBN 978-0-8075-0510-6 Subj: Behavior – worrying. Careers – teachers. Reptiles – turtles, tortoises. School – first day.

George, Margaret. *Lucille lost: a true adventure* by Margaret George and Christopher J. Murphy ill. by Debra Bandelin and Bob Dacey. Penguin, 2006. ISBN 978-0-670-06093-1 Subj: Behavior – lost & found possessions. Reptiles – turtles, tortoises.

George, William T. *Beaver at Long Pond* by William T. George and Lindsay Barrett George ill. by Lindsay Barrett George. Greenwillow, 1988. ISBN 978-0-688-07107-3 Subj: Animals – beavers. Nature. Night.

Box turtle at Long Pond ill. by Lindsay Barrett George. Greenwillow, 1989. ISBN 978-0-688-08185-0 Subj: Nature. Reptiles – turtles, tortoises.

Christmas at Long Pond ill. by Lindsay Barrett George. Greenwillow, 1992. ISBN 978-0-688-09215-3 Subj: Animals. Family life – fathers. Forest, woods. Holidays – Christmas. Nature. Seasons – winter. Trees.

Fishing at Long Pond ill. by Lindsay Barrett George. Greenwillow, 1991. ISBN 978-0-688-09402-7 Subj: Animals. Family life – grandfathers. Sports – fishing.

Geraghty, Paul. *Help me!* ill. by author. IPG/Andersen, 2012. ISBN 978-1-84939-027-9 Subj: Animals. Foreign lands – Africa. Nature.

The hoppameleon ill. by author. Barron's, 2001. ISBN 978-0-7641-5406-5 Subj: Animals. Friendship. Frogs & toads. Self-concept.

Gerardi, Jan. *The little recycler* ill. by author. Random House, 2013. ISBN 978-0-375-86172-7 Subj: Ecology. Format, unusual – board books.

Geras, Adèle. *The Cats of Cuckoo Square, Geejay the Hero* ill. by Tony Ross. Dell, 2003. ISBN 978-0-385-90082-9 Subj: Communities, neighborhoods. Illness – allergies.

Giselle ill. by Emma Chichester Clark. David & Charles, 2000. ISBN 978-1-86233-226-3 Subj: Activities – dancing. Ballet.

Little ballet star ill. by Shelagh McNicholas. Dial, 2008. ISBN 978-0-8037-3237-7 Subj: Ballet. Family life – aunts, uncles. Theater.

My wishes for you ill. by Cliff Wright. Simon & Schuster, 2002. ISBN 978-0-689-85333-3 Subj: Animals. Animals – rabbits. Behavior – wishing. Day. Family life – parents.

The nutcracker ill. by Emma Chichester Clark. David & Charles, 2000. ISBN 978-1-86233-236-2 Subj: Activities – dancing. Animals – mice. Ballet. Careers – toy makers. Folk & fairy tales. Holidays – Christmas. Imagination. Royalty.

Rebecca's Passover ill. by Sheila Moxley. Frances Lincoln, 2004. ISBN 978-1-84507-155-4 Subj: Holidays – Passover. Jewish culture.

Sleep tight, Ginger Kitten ill. by Catherine Walters. Dutton, 2001. ISBN 978-0-525-46771-7 Subj: Animals – cats. Rhyming text. Sleep.

Sleeping beauty ill. by Emma Chichester Clark. David & Charles, 2000. ISBN 978-1-86233-246-1 Subj: Activities – dancing. Ballet. Family life – stepfamilies. Folk & fairy tales. Royalty – princes. Sibling rivalry.

Swan Lake ill. by Emma Chichester Clark. David & Charles, 2000. ISBN 978-1-86233-231-7 Subj: Activities – dancing. Ballet. Birds – swans. Careers – magicians. Folk & fairy tales. Magic. Metamorphosis. Royalty – princes.

Time for ballet ill. by Shelagh McNicholas. Dial, 2004. ISBN 978-0-8037-2978-0 Subj: Activities – dancing. Ballet.

Gerber, Carole. *Annie Jump Cannon, astronomer* ill. by Christina Wald. Pelican, 2011. ISBN 978-1-58980-911-6 Subj: Careers – astronomers. Gender roles. Stars.

Little red bat ill. by Christina Wald. Sylvan Dell, 2010. ISBN 978-1-60718-069-2 Subj: Animals – bats. Hibernation. Migration.

Seeds, bees, butterflies, and more! poems for two voices ill. by Eugene Yelchin. Holt, 2013. ISBN 978-0-8050-9211-0 Subj: Insects. Nature. Plants. Poetry.

Spring blossoms ill. by Leslie Evans. Charlesbridge, 2013. ISBN 978-1-58089-412-8 Subj: Flowers. Rhyming text. Seasons – spring. Trees.

Winter trees ill. by Leslie Evans. Charlesbridge, 2008. ISBN 978-1-58089-168-4 Subj: Seasons – winter. Trees.

Gerdner, Linda. *Grandfather's story cloth / Yawg daim paj ntaub dab neeg* by Linda Gerdner and Sarah Langford ill. by Stuart Loughridge. Shen's, 2008. ISBN 978-1-885008-34-3 Subj: Ethnic groups in the U.S. – Hmong Americans. Family life – grandfathers. Illness – Alzheimer's. Memories, memory. Quilts.

Gergely, Tibor. *The great big fire engine book* ill. by author. 1st Random House ed. Golden, 2003. ISBN 978-0-307-90321-1 Subj: Careers – firefighters. Format, unusual – board books. Trucks.

Wheel on the chimney (Brown, Margaret Wise)

Geringer, Laura. *Boom boom go away!* ill. by Bagram Ibatoulline. Simon & Schuster, 2010. ISBN 978-0-689-85093-6 Subj: Bedtime. Musical instruments. Rhyming text.

Gerlach, Horace. *Daddy's little girl* (Burke, Bobby)

Germein, Katrina. *My dad thinks he's funny* ill. by Tom Jellett. Candlewick, 2013. ISBN 978-0-7636-6522-7 Subj: Family life – fathers.

Gerritsen, Paula. *Nuts* ill. by author. Boyds Mills, 2006. ISBN 978-1-932425-66-6 Subj: Animals – mice. Seasons – fall. Weather – storms.

Gershator, David. *Summer is summer* (Gershator, Phillis)

Gershator, Phillis. *Listen, listen* ill. by Alison Jay. Barefoot, 2007. ISBN 978-1-84686-084-3 Subj: Nature. Noise, sounds. Rhyming text. Seasons.

Moo, moo, brown cow! Have you any milk? ill. by Giselle Potter. Random House, 2011. ISBN 978-0-375-86744-6 Subj: Animals. Bedtime. Farms. Rhyming text. Toys.

Only one cowry: Dahomean tale ill. by David Soman. Orchard, 2000. ISBN 978-0-531-33288-7 Subj: Folk & fairy tales. Foreign lands – Africa. Royalty – kings.

Sky sweeper ill. by Holly Meade. Farrar, 2007. ISBN 978-0-374-37007-7 Subj: Activities – working. Foreign lands – Japan. Gardens, gardening. Self-concept.

Summer is summer by Phillis Gershator and David Gershator ill. by Sophie Blackall. Holt, 2006. ISBN 978-0-8050-7444-4 Subj: Rhyming text. Seasons – summer.

This is the day! ill. by Marjorie Priceman. Houghton, 2007. ISBN 978-0-618-49746-1 Subj: Babies. Days of the week, months of the year. Family life – mothers. Songs.

Time for a hug by Phillis Gershator and Mim Green ill. by David Walker. Sterling, 2012. ISBN 978-1-4027-7862-9 Subj: Animals – rabbits. Family life – mothers. Hugging. Rhyming text.

When it starts to snow ill. by Martin Matje. Holt, 1998. ISBN 978-0-8050-5404-0 Subj: Animals. Rhyming text. Seasons – winter. Weather – snow.

Who's awake in springtime? by Phillis Gershator and Mim Green ill. by Emilie Chollat. Holt, 2010. ISBN 978-0-8050-6390-5 Subj: Animals.

Bedtime. Cumulative tales. Rhyming text. Seasons – spring.

Who's in the farmyard? ill. by Jill McDonald. Barefoot, 2012. ISBN 978-1-84686-574-9 Subj: Animals. Farms. Noise, sounds. Rhyming text.

Who's in the forest? ill. by Jill McDonald. Barefoot, 2010. ISBN 978-1-84686-476-6 Subj: Animals. Forest, woods. Rhyming text.

Zoo day, olé! a counting book ill. by Santiago Cohen. Marshall Cavendish, 2009. ISBN 978-0-7614-5462-5 Subj: Counting, numbers. Foreign languages. Zoos.

Zzzng! zzzng! zzzng! a Yoruba tale ill. by Theresa Smith. Orchard, 1998. ISBN 978-0-531-08873-9 Subj: Folk & fairy tales. Foreign lands – Africa. Insects – mosquitoes.

Gerson, Mary-Joan. *Why the sky is far away* ill. by Carla Golembe. Little, 1992. ISBN 978-0-316-30852-6 Subj: Behavior – greed. Folk & fairy tales. Foreign lands – Nigeria. Sky.

Gerstein, Mordicai. *The absolutely awful alphabet* ill. by author. Harcourt, 1999. ISBN 978-0-15-201494-0 Subj: ABC books. Animals. Monsters.

A book ill. by author. Roaring Brook, 2009. ISBN 978-1-59643-251-2 Subj: Activities – writing. Books, reading. Imagination.

The first drawing ill. by author. Little, Brown, 2013. ISBN 978-0-316-20478-1 Subj: Activities – drawing. Imagination. Petroglyphs. Prehistory.

How to bicycle to the moon to plant sunflowers: a simple but brilliant plan in 24 easy steps ill. by author. Roaring Brook, 2013. ISBN 978-1-59643-512-4 Subj: Activities – traveling. Imagination. Moon. Sports – bicycling.

Leaving the nest ill. by author. Farrar, 2007. ISBN 978-0-374-34369-9 Subj: Animals. Behavior – growing up. Family life – mothers. Self-concept.

The man who walked between the towers ill. by author. Roaring Brook, 2003. ISBN 978-0-7613-2868-1 Subj: Activities. Caldecott award books. Careers – aerialists. Format, unusual – toy & movable books.

Minifred goes to school ill. by author. HarperCollins, 2009. ISBN 978-0-06-075889-9 Subj: Animals – cats. Behavior – misbehavior. Character traits – being different. School.

Gervais, Bernadette. *Out of sight* (Pittau, Francisco)

Geser, Gretchen. *One bright ring* ill. by author. Holt, 2013. ISBN 978-0-8050-9279-0 Subj: Behavior – lost & found possessions. Character traits – honesty. Cities, towns. Counting, numbers.

Ghazi, Suhaib Hamid. *Ramadan* ill. by Omar Rayyan. Holiday, 1996. ISBN 978-0-8234-1254-9 Subj: Holidays – Ramadan. Religion. Religion – Islam.

Ghigna, Charles. *I see winter* ill. by Ag Jatkowska. Picture Window, 2011. ISBN 978-1-4048-6588-4 Subj: Rhyming text. Seasons – winter.

Gibala-Broxholm, Scott. *Maddie's monster dad* ill. by author. Marshall Cavendish, 2011. ISBN 978-0-7614-5846-3 Subj: Activities – playing. Family life – fathers. Imagination. Monsters.

Gibbons, Gail. *Alligators and crocodiles* ill. by author. Holiday House, 2010. ISBN 978-0-8234-2234-0 Subj: Reptiles – alligators, crocodiles.

Apples ill. by author. Holiday, 2000. ISBN 978-0-8234-1497-0 Subj: Activities – baking, cooking. Food. U.S. history.

The art box ill. by author. Holiday, 1998. ISBN 978-0-8234-1386-7 Subj: Art. Careers – artists. Tools.

Bats ill. by author. Holiday, 1999. ISBN 978-0-8234-1457-4 Subj: Animals – bats. Behavior. Night.

Beavers ill. by author. Holiday House, 2013. ISBN 978-0-8234-2412-2 Subj: Animals – beavers. Nature.

The berry book ill. by author. Holiday, 2002. ISBN 978-0-8234-1697-4 Subj: Activities – baking, cooking. Food. Plants.

Boat book ill. by author. Holiday, 1983. ISBN 978-0-8234-0478-0 Subj: Boats, ships.

Cats ill. by author. Holiday, 1996. ISBN 978-0-8234-1253-2 Subj: Animals – cats.

Check it out! the book about libraries ill. by author. Harcourt, 1985. ISBN 978-0-15-216400-3 Subj: Libraries.

Clocks and how they go ill. by author. Crowell, 1979. ISBN 978-0-690-03974-0 Subj: Clocks, watches. Time.

Coral reefs ill. by author. Holiday House, 2007. ISBN 978-0-8234-2080-3 Subj: Ecology. Sea & seashore.

Corn ill. by author. Holiday, 2008. ISBN 978-0-8234-2169-5 Subj: Food. Gardens, gardening.

County fair ill. by author. Little, 1994. ISBN 978-0-316-30951-6 Subj: Country. Fairs, festivals.

Deadline! from news to newspaper ill. by author. HarperCollins, 1987. ISBN 978-0-690-04602-1 Subj: Activities – working. Paper.

Department store ill. by author. Crowell, 1984. ISBN 978-0-690-04367-9 Subj: Stores.

Dinosaur discoveries ill. by author. Holiday House, 2005. ISBN 978-0-8234-1971-5 Subj: Dinosaurs. Science.

Dinosaurs! ill. by author. Holiday, 2008. ISBN 978-0-8234-2143-5 Subj: Dinosaurs. Prehistory.

Dogs ill. by author. Holiday, 1996. ISBN 978-0-8234-1226-6 Subj: Animals – dogs.

Ducks ill. by author. Holiday, 2001. ISBN 978-0-8234-1567-0 Subj: Birds – ducks.

Easter ill. by author. Holiday, 1989. ISBN 978-0-8234-0737-8 Subj: Holidays – Easter.

Elephants of Africa ill. by author. Holiday House, 2008. ISBN 978-0-8234-2168-8 Subj: Animals – elephants. Foreign lands – Africa.

Emergency! ill. by author. Holiday, 1994. ISBN 978-0-8234-1128-3 Subj: Careers. Character traits – helpfulness. Trucks.

Exploring the deep, dark sea ill. by author. Little, 1999. ISBN 978-0-316-30945-5 Subj: Boats, ships. Ecology. Science. Sea & seashore.

Farming ill. by author. Holiday, 1988. ISBN 978-0-8234-0682-1 Subj: Careers. Farms. Seasons.

Fill it up! all about service stations ill. by author. Crowell, 1985. ISBN 978-0-690-04440-9 Subj: Automobiles. Careers.

Fire! Fire! ill. by author. Crowell, 1984. ISBN 978-0-690-04416-4 Subj: Careers – firefighters.

Flying ill. by author. Holiday, 1986. ISBN 978-0-8234-0599-2 Subj: Activities – ballooning. Activities – flying. Airplanes, airports.

Frogs ill. by author. Holiday, 1993. ISBN 978-0-8234-1052-1 Subj: Frogs & toads.

From seed to plant ill. by author. Holiday, 1991. ISBN 978-0-8234-0872-6 Subj: Plants. Science. Seeds.

Galaxies, galaxies! ill. by author. Holiday House, 2006. ISBN 978-0-8234-2002-5 Subj: Science. Space & space ships.

Giant pandas ill. by author. Holiday, 2002. ISBN 978-0-8234-1761-2 Subj: Animals – endangered animals. Animals – pandas. Foreign lands – China.

Gorillas ill. by author. Holiday House, 2011. ISBN 978-0-8234-2236-4 Subj: Animals – gorillas.

Grizzly bears ill. by author. Holiday, 2003. ISBN 978-0-8234-1793-3 Subj: Animals – bears. Animals – endangered animals.

Groundhog Day ill. by author. Holiday House, 2007. ISBN 978-0-8234-2003-2 Subj: Holidays – Groundhog Day.

Gulls — gulls — gulls ill. by author. Holiday, 1997. ISBN 978-0-8234-1323-2 Subj: Birds – seagulls.

Halloween ill. by author. Holiday, 1984. ISBN 978-0-8234-0524-4 Subj: Holidays – Halloween.

Halloween is . . . ill. by author. Holiday, 2002. ISBN 978-0-8234-1758-2 Subj: Holidays – Halloween.

Happy birthday! ill. by author. Holiday, 1986. ISBN 978-0-8234-0614-2 Subj: Birthdays.

The honey makers ill. by author. Morrow, 1997. ISBN 978-0-688-11387-2 Subj: Food. Insects – bees.

How a house is built ill. by author. Holiday, 1990. ISBN 978-0-8234-0841-2 Subj: Activities – making things. Homes, houses.

Hurricanes! ill. by author. Holiday, 2009. ISBN 978-0-8234-2233-3 Subj: Weather – hurricanes.

Ice cream: the full scoop ill. by author. Holiday House, 2006. ISBN 978-0-8234-2000-1 Subj: Food.

It's snowing! ill. by author. Holiday House, 2011. ISBN 978-0-8234-2237-1 Subj: Seasons – winter. Weather – snow.

Knights in shining armor ill. by author. Little, 1995. ISBN 978-0-316-30948-6 Subj: Knights. Middle Ages.

Ladybugs ill. by author. Holiday House, 2012. ISBN 978-0-8234-2368-2 Subj: Insects – ladybugs.

The milk makers ill. by author. Macmillan, 1985. ISBN 978-0-02-736640-2 Subj: Farms. Food.

The missing maple syrup sap mystery: or, How maple syrup is made ill. by author. Warne, 1979. ISBN 978-0-7232-6167-4 Subj: Activities. Food. Mystery stories. Trees.

Monarch butterfly ill. by author. Holiday, 1989. ISBN 978-0-8234-0773-6 Subj: Insects – butterflies, caterpillars. Metamorphosis. Science.

Nature's green umbrella: tropical rain forests ill. by author. Morrow, 1994. ISBN 978-0-688-12353-6 Subj: Animals. Ecology. Jungle. Plants.

New road! ill. by author. Crowell, 1983. ISBN 978-0-690-04343-3 Subj: Transportation.

Owls ill. by author. Holiday House, 2005. ISBN 978-0-8234-1880-0 Subj: Birds – owls.

Paper, paper everywhere ill. by author. Harcourt, 1983. ISBN 978-0-15-259488-6 Subj: Paper.

Penguins! ill. by author. Holiday, 1998. ISBN 978-0-8234-1388-1 Subj: Birds – penguins. Foreign lands – Antarctic.

Pigs ill. by author. Holiday, 1999. ISBN 978-0-8234-1441-3 Subj: Animals – pigs.

The planets ill. by author. Rev. ed. Holiday House, 2005. ISBN 978-0-8234-1957-9 Subj: Astronomy. Planets.

Playgrounds ill. by author. Holiday, 1985. ISBN 978-0-8234-0553-4 Subj: Activities – playing.

Polar bears ill. by author. Holiday, 2001. ISBN 978-0-8234-1593-9 Subj: Animals – polar bears.

The post office book: mail and how it moves ill. by author. Crowell, 1982. ISBN 978-0-690-04199-6 Subj: Careers – postal workers. Communication. Post office.

The pottery place ill. by author. Harcourt, 1987. ISBN 978-0-15-263265-6 Subj: Careers.

Prehistoric animals ill. by author. Holiday, 1988. ISBN 978-0-8234-0707-1 Subj: Animals. Prehistory. Science.

Puff — flash — bang! a book about signals ill. by author. Morrow, 1993. ISBN 978-0-688-07378-7 Subj: Communication.

The pumpkin book ill. by author. Holiday, 1999. ISBN 978-0-8234-1465-9 Subj: Gardens, gardening. Seasons – fall.

The quilting bee ill. by author. HarperCollins, 2004. ISBN 978-0-688-16398-3 Subj: Activities – sewing. Quilts.

The reasons for seasons ill. by author. Holiday, 1995. ISBN 978-0-8234-1174-0 Subj: Seasons.

Recycle! ill. by author. Little, 1992. ISBN 978-0-316-30971-4 Subj: Ecology.

Say woof! the day of a country veterinarian ill. by author. Macmillan, 1992. ISBN 978-0-02-736781-2 Subj: Animals. Careers – veterinarians. Illness.

The seasons of Arnold's apple tree ill. by author. Harcourt, 1988. ISBN 978-0-15-271246-4 Subj: Food. Seasons. Trees.

Sharks ill. by author. Holiday, 1992. ISBN 978-0-8234-0960-0 Subj: Fish – sharks. Science.

Snakes ill. by author. Holiday, 2008. ISBN 978-0-8234-2122-0 Subj: Reptiles – snakes.

Soaring with the wind: the bald eagle ill. by author. Morrow, 1998. ISBN 978-0-688-13731-1 Subj: Birds – eagles. Science.

Spiders ill. by author. Holiday, 1993. ISBN 978-0-8234-1006-4 Subj: Spiders.

Stargazers ill. by author. Holiday, 1992. ISBN 978-0-8234-0983-9 Subj: Astronomy. Stars.

Sun up, sun down ill. by author. Harcourt, 1983. ISBN 978-0-15-282781-6 Subj: Science. Sun.

Surrounded by sea ill. by author. Little, 1991. ISBN 978-0-316-30961-5 Subj: Careers – fishermen. Islands. Sports – fishing.

Tell me, tree ill. by author. Little, 2002. ISBN 978-0-316-30903-5 Subj: Trees.

Thanksgiving Day ill. by author. Holiday, 1983. ISBN 978-0-8234-0489-6 Subj: Holidays – Thanksgiving. Pilgrims.

The too-great bread bake book ill. by author. Warne, 1980. ISBN 978-0-7232-6182-7 Subj: Activities – baking, cooking.

Tool book ill. by author. Holiday, 1982. ISBN 978-0-8234-0444-5 Subj: Tools.

Tornadoes! ill. by author. Holiday, 2009. ISBN 978-0-8234-2216-6 Subj: Weather – tornadoes.

Trains ill. by author. Holiday, 1987. ISBN 978-0-8234-0640-1 Subj: Trains.

Trucks ill. by author. Crowell, 1981. ISBN 978-0-690-04119-4 Subj: Trucks.

Tunnels ill. by author. Holiday, 1984. ISBN 978-0-8234-0507-7 Subj: Activities – digging.

Up goes the skyscraper! ill. by author. Four Winds, 1986. ISBN 978-0-02-736780-5 Subj: Buildings. Cities, towns.

Valentine's Day ill. by author. Holiday, 1985. ISBN 978-0-8234-0572-5 Subj: Holidays – Valentine's Day.

Valentine's Day is — ill. by author. Holiday House, 2006. ISBN 978-0-8234-1852-7 Subj: Holidays – Valentine's Day.

The vegetables we eat ill. by author. Holiday House, 2007. ISBN 978-0-8234-2001-8 Subj: Food. Plants.

Weather words and what they mean ill. by author. Holiday, 1990. ISBN 978-0-8234-0805-4 Subj: Language. Weather.

Whales ill. by author. Holiday, 1991. ISBN 978-0-8234-0900-6 Subj: Animals – whales.

Yippee-yay! a book about cowboys and cowgirls ill. by author. Little, 1998. ISBN 978-0-316-30944-8 Subj: Animals – bulls, cows. Cowboys, cowgirls. Rodeos. U.S. history – frontier & pioneer life.

Zoo ill. by author. Crowell, 1987. ISBN 978-0-690-04633-5 Subj: Activities – working. Animals. Zoos.

Gibbs, Edward. *I spy on the farm* ill. by author. Candlewick, 2013. ISBN 978-0-7636-6431-2 Subj: Animals. Concepts – color. Farms. Format, unusual – toy & movable books.

I spy pets ill. by author. Candlewick, 2013. ISBN 978-0-7636-6622-4 Subj: Format, unusual – toy & movable books. Pets.

I spy under the sea ill. by author. Candlewick, 2012. ISBN 978-0-7636-5952-3 Subj: Animals. Counting, numbers. Format, unusual – toy & movable books. Sea & seashore.

I spy with my little eye ill. by author. Candlewick, 2011. ISBN 978-0-7636-5284-5 Subj: Animals.

Concepts – color. Format, unusual – toy & movable books.

Gibbs, Lynne. *Don't slurp your soup!* ill. by John Eastwood. McGraw-Hill, 2003. ISBN 978-1-57768-556-2 Subj: Etiquette.

Gibert, Bruno. *The king is naked!* ill. by author. Clarion, 2004. ISBN 978-0-618-41067-5 Subj: Animals. Animals – lions. Clothing. Jungle. Royalty – kings.

Gibfried, Diane. *Brother Juniper* ill. by Meilo So. Houghton, 2006. ISBN 978-0-618-54361-8 Subj: Character traits – generosity. Foreign lands – Italy. Religion.

Gibson, Amy. *Catching kisses* ill. by Maria van Lieshout. Feiwel & Friends, 2013. ISBN 978-0-312-37647-5 Subj: Kissing.

Split! Splat! ill. by Steve Björkman. Scholastic, 2012. ISBN 978-0-439-58753-2 Subj: Activities – playing. Animals – dogs. Rhyming text. Weather – rain.

Gibson, Ginger Foglesong. *Tiptoe Joe* ill. by Laura Rankin. Greenwillow, 2013. ISBN 978-0-06-177203-0 Subj: Animals. Animals – babies. Animals – bears. Noise, sounds.

Gibson, Karen Bush. *Child care workers* ill. with photos. Bridgestone, 2001. ISBN 978-0-7368-0622-0 Subj: Careers. Communities, neighborhoods.

Emergency medical technicians ill. with photos. Bridgestone, 2001. ISBN 978-0-7368-0623-7 Subj: Careers. Communities, neighborhoods.

Pharmacists ill. with photos. Bridgestone, 2001. ISBN 978-0-7368-0624-4 Subj: Careers – pharmacists. Communities, neighborhoods.

Truck drivers ill. with photos. Bridgestone, 2001. ISBN 978-0-7368-0625-1 Subj: Careers – truck drivers. Communities, neighborhoods.

Gifaldi, David. *Ben, king of the river* ill. by Layne Johnson. Whitman, 2001. ISBN 978-0-8075-0635-6 Subj: Camps, camping. Disabilities – mental Disabilities. Family life – brothers.

Giff, Patricia Reilly. *Good luck, Ronald Morgan* ill. by Susanna Natti. Viking, 1996. ISBN 978-0-670-86303-7 Subj: Animals – cats. Animals – dogs. Pets.

Today was a terrible day ill. by Susanna Natti. Viking, 1980. ISBN 978-0-670-81830-3 Subj: Behavior – bad day. School.

Giganti, Paul. *Each orange had eight slices* ill. by Donald Crews. Greenwillow, 1992. ISBN 978-0-688-10429-0 Subj: Counting, numbers.

How many blue birds flew away? a counting book with a difference ill. by Donald Crews. HarperCollins, 2005. ISBN 978-0-06-000763-8 Subj: Counting, numbers.

How many snails? a counting book ill. by Donald Crews. Greenwillow, 1988. ISBN 978-0-688-06370-2 Subj: Counting, numbers.

Giglio, Judy. *The tapping tale* ill. by Joe Cepeda. Harcourt, 2000. ISBN 978-0-15-202572-4 Subj: Animals – dogs. Noise, sounds. Sleepovers.

Gilani-Williams, Fawzia. *Nabeel's new pants: an Eid tale* ill. by Proiti Roy. Marshall Cavendish, 2010. ISBN 978-0-7614-5629-2 Subj: Clothing – pants. Family life. Foreign lands – Turkey. Holidays – Ramadan. Religion.

Gilbert, Jane. *Indescribably Arabella* ill. by author. Atheneum, 2003. ISBN 978-0-689-85321-0 Subj: Character traits – individuality.

Gilchrist, Jan Spivey. *My America* ill. by Ashley Bryan and Jan Spivey Gilchrist. HarperCollins, 2007. ISBN 978-0-06-079105-6 Subj: Poetry. U.S. history.

Giles, Almira Astudillo. *Willie wins* ill. by Carl Angel. Lee & Low, 2001. ISBN 978-1-58430-023-6 Subj: Ethnic groups in the U.S. – Filipino Americans. Family life – fathers. School.

Gill, Shelley. *The big buck adventure* by Shelley Gill and Deborah Tobola ill. by Grace Lin. Charlesbridge, 2000. ISBN 978-0-88106-294-6 Subj: Counting, numbers. Money. Shopping.

The egg ill. by Jo-Ellen Bosson. Charlesbridge, 2001. ISBN 978-1-57091-377-8 Subj: Eggs. Nature.

Up on Denali ill. by Shannon Cartwright. Sasquatch, 2006. ISBN 978-1-57061-366-1 Subj: Alaska. Mountains.

Gill-Brown, Vanessa. *Rufferella* ill. by Mandy Stanley. Scholastic, 2001. ISBN 978-0-439-25617-9 Subj: Animals – dogs. Behavior – imitation.

Gillard, Denise. *Music from the sky* ill. by Stephen Taylor. Douglas & McIntyre, 2001. ISBN 978-0-88899-311-3 Subj: Family life – grandfathers. Musical instruments – flutes.

Gillham, Bill. *How many sharks in the bath?* ill. by Christyan Fox. Frances Lincoln, 2005. ISBN 978-1-84507-288-9 Subj: Animals. Counting, numbers.

Gilliland, Judith Heide. *The day of Ahmed's secret* (Heide, Florence Parry)

Sami and the time of the troubles (Heide, Florence Parry)

Gillmor, Don. *Yuck, a love story* ill. by Marie-Louise Gay. Stoddart, 2000. ISBN 978-0-7737-3218-6 Subj: Birthdays. Friendship. Moon.

Gilman, Rita Golden. *Mole in a hole* ill. by Holly Hannon. Random House, 2003. ISBN 978-0-679-99037-6 Subj: Animals. Animals – moles. Rebuses. Rhyming text.

Rice is life ill. by Yangsook Choi. Holt, 2000. ISBN 978-0-8050-5719-5 Subj: Animals. Food. Foreign lands – Indonesia. Poetry.

Gilmore, Rachna. *Making grizzle grow* ill. by Leslie Elizabeth Watts. Fitzhenry & Whiteside, 2008. ISBN 978-1-55041-885-9 Subj: Emotions – anger. Family life – daughters. Family life – fathers. Imagination. Snowmen.

The gingerbread boy. *Can't catch me* by John Hassett and Ann Hassett ill. by authors. Houghton, 2006. ISBN 978-0-618-70490-3 Subj: Behavior – running away. Cumulative tales.

Gingerbread baby retold by Jan Brett; ill. by reteller. Putnam, 1999. ISBN 978-0-399-23444-6 Subj: Behavior – running away. Cumulative tales. Folk & fairy tales. Food. Format, unusual – toy & movable books.

The gingerbread boy retold by Harriet Ziefert; ill. by Emily Bolam. Viking, 1995. ISBN 978-0-670-86052-4 Subj: Behavior – running away. Cumulative tales. Folk & fairy tales.

The gingerbread boy retold by Richard Egielski; ill. by reteller. Geringer, 1997. ISBN 978-0-06-026031-6 Subj: Behavior – running away. Cumulative tales. Folk & fairy tales. Food.

The gingerbread boy ill. by Paul Galdone. Seabury Pr., 1975. ISBN 978-0-8164-3132-8 Subj: Behavior – running away. Cumulative tales. Folk & fairy tales. Food. Rhyming text.

The Gingerbread Cowboy ill. by Holly Berry. HarperCollins, 2006. ISBN 978-0-06-077863-7 Subj: Animals – coyotes. Behavior – running away. Cowboys, cowgirls. Cumulative tales. Folk & fairy tales. Food.

The gingerbread girl by Lisa Campbell Ernst; ill. by author. Penguin, 2006. ISBN 978-0-525-47667-2 Subj: Behavior – running away. Cumulative tales. Folk & fairy tales. Food.

The gingerbread man retold by Carol Jones; ill. by reteller. Houghton, 2002. ISBN 978-0-618-18822-2 Subj: Behavior – running away. Cumulative tales. Folk & fairy tales. Food.

The gingerbread man retold by Eric A. Kimmel; ill. by Megan Lloyd. Holiday, 1993. ISBN 978-0-8234-0824-5 Subj: Behavior – running away. Cumulative tales. Folk & fairy tales.

The gingerbread man retold by Jim Aylesworth; ill. by Barbara McClintock. Scholastic, 1998. ISBN 978-0-590-97219-2 Subj: Behavior – running away. Cumulative tales. Folk & fairy tales. Food.

The gingerbread man by Béatrice Rodriguez; ill. by author. NorthSouth, 2012. ISBN 978-0-7358-4086-7 Subj: Behavior – running away. Cumulative tales. Folk & fairy tales. Food.

The Gingerbread Man loose in the school by Laura Murray; ill. by Mike Lowery. Penguin, 2011. ISBN 978-0-399-25052-1 Subj: Behavior – running away. Cumulative tales. Folk & fairy tales. Food. Rhyming text. School.

The Gingerbread Man loose on the fire truck by Laura Murray; ill. by Mike Lowery. Putnam, 2013. ISBN 978-0-399-25779-7 Subj: Behavior – running away. Folk & fairy tales. Food. Rhyming text. School – field trips. Trucks.

The Library Gingerbread Man by Dotti Enderle; ill. by Colleen M. Madden. Upstart, 2010. ISBN 978-1-60213-048-7 Subj: Behavior – running away. Cumulative tales. Food. Libraries.

The pancake boy adapt. by Lorinda Bryan Cauley; ill. by adapter. Putnam, 1988. ISBN 978-0-399-21505-6 Subj: Behavior – running away. Cumulative tales. Folk & fairy tales. Food.

Señorita Gordita by Helen Ketteman; ill. by Will Terry. Whitman, 2012. ISBN 978-0-8075-7302-0 Subj: Behavior – running away. Cumulative tales. Folk & fairy tales. Food. Foreign languages.

Whiff, sniff, nibble and chew: the Gingerbread boy retold by Charlotte Pomerantz; ill. by Monica Incisa. Greenwillow, 1984. ISBN 978-0-688-02552-6 Subj: Behavior – running away. Cumulative tales. Folk & fairy tales. Rhyming text.

Ginkel, Anne. *I've got an elephant* ill. by Janie Bynum. Peachtree, 2006. ISBN 978-1-56145-373-3 Subj: Animals – elephants. Counting, numbers. Emotions – loneliness. Rhyming text.

Ginsburg, Mirra. *Across the stream* ill. by Nancy Tafuri. Greenwillow, 1982. ISBN 978-0-688-01206-9 Subj: Animals – foxes. Birds – chickens. Birds – ducks. Dreams.

Asleep, asleep ill. by Nancy Tafuri. Greenwillow, 1992. ISBN 978-0-688-09154-5 Subj: Bedtime. Lullabies. Night.

The chick and the duckling ill. by José Aruego and Ariane Dewey. Macmillan, 1972. ISBN 978-0-02-735940-4 Subj: Birds – chickens. Birds – ducks. Sports – swimming.

Clay boy ill. by Joseph A. Smith. Adapt. from a Russian folk tale. Greenwillow, 1997. ISBN 978-0-688-14410-4 Subj: Activities – making things. Folk & fairy tales. Foreign lands – Russia.

Mushroom in the rain ill. by José Aruego and Ariane Dewey. Macmillan, 1988, 1974. ISBN 978-0-

02-736241-1 Subj: Animals. Animals – foxes. Plants. Weather – rain.

Giogas, Valarie. *In my backyard* ill. by Katherine Zecca. Sylvan Dell, 2007. ISBN 978-0-9777423-1-8 Subj: Animals. Counting, numbers. Nature. Rhyming text.

Giovanni, Nikki. *Lincoln and Douglass: an American friendship* ill. by Bryan Collier. Holt, 2008. ISBN 978-0-8050-8264-7 Subj: Ethnic groups in the U.S. – African Americans. Friendship. U.S. history.

Rosa ill. by Bryan Collier. Holt, 2005. ISBN 978-0-8050-7106-1 Subj: Caldecott award honor books. Character traits – bravery. Ethnic groups in the U.S. – African Americans. Prejudice. U.S. history.

The sun is so quiet ill. by Ashley Bryan. Holt, 1996. ISBN 978-0-8050-4119-4 Subj: Ethnic groups in the U.S. – African Americans. Nature. Poetry.

Girnis, Margaret. *ABC for you and me* photos by Shirley Leaman Green. Whitman, 2000. ISBN 978-0-8075-0101-6 Subj: ABC books. Disabilities – Down syndrome.

1, 2, 3 for you and me photos by Shirley Leaman Green. Whitman, 2001. ISBN 978-0-8075-6107-2 Subj: Counting, numbers. Disabilities – Down syndrome.

Glaser, Byron. *Bonz, inside-out* by Byron Glaser and Sandra Higashi ill. by authors. Abrams, 2003. ISBN 978-0-8109-4599-9 Subj: Anatomy – skeletons.

Glaser, Jason. *Pinkeye* ill. with photos. Capstone, 2006. ISBN 978-0-7368-4292-1 Subj: Anatomy – eyes. Health & fitness. Illness.

Glaser, Linda. *Emma's poem: the voice of the Statue of Liberty* ill. by Claire A. Nivola. Houghton Mifflin, 2010. ISBN 978-0-547-17184-5 Subj: Poetry. U.S. history.

Garbage helps our garden grow: a compost story ill. by Shelley Rotner. Millbrook, 2010. ISBN 978-0-7613-4911-2 Subj: Ecology. Gardens, gardening.

Hannah's way ill. by Adam Gustavson. Lerner/Kar-Ben, 2012. ISBN 978-0-7613-5138-2 Subj: Friendship. Jewish culture. Moving. School. U.S. history.

Hello, squirrels! scampering through the seasons ill. by Gay W. Holland. Lerner, 2006. ISBN 978-0-7613-2887-2 Subj: Animals – squirrels. Seasons.

Hoppy Passover! ill. by Daniel Howarth. Whitman, 2011. ISBN 978-0-8075-3380-2 Subj: Animals – rabbits. Holidays – Passover. Jewish culture.

It's fall ill. by Susan Swan. Millbrook, 2001. ISBN 978-0-7613-1758-6 Subj: Nature. Seasons – fall.

It's spring ill. by Susan Swan. Millbrook, 2002. ISBN 978-0-7613-1760-9 Subj: Nature. Seasons – spring.

It's summer ill. by Susan Swan. Millbrook, 2003. ISBN 978-0-7613-1757-9 Subj: Nature. Seasons – summer.

It's winter ill. by Susan Swan. Millbrook, 2002. ISBN 978-0-7613-1759-3 Subj: Nature. Seasons – winter.

Magnificent monarchs ill. by Gay W. Holland. Millbrook, 2000. ISBN 978-0-7613-1700-5 Subj: Insects – butterflies, caterpillars. Science.

Mrs. Greenberg's messy Hanukkah ill. by Nancy Cote. Whitman, 2004. ISBN 978-0-8075-5297-1 Subj: Activities – baking, cooking. Character traits – orderliness. Food. Holidays – Hanukkah. Jewish culture.

Not a buzz to be found: insects in winter ill. by Jaime Zollars. Millbrook, 2011. ISBN 978-0-7613-5644-8 Subj: Insects. Seasons – winter.

Our big home ill. by Elisa Kleven. Millbrook, 2000. ISBN 978-0-7613-1650-3 Subj: Earth. Nature.

Glass, Andrew. *Bewildered for three days: as to why Daniel Boone never wore his coonskin cap* ill. by author. Holiday, 2000. ISBN 978-0-8234-1446-8 Subj: Animals – bears. Animals – raccoons. U.S. history – frontier & pioneer life.

The wondrous whirligig: the Wright Brothers' first flying machine ill. by author. Holiday, 2003. ISBN 978-0-8234-1717-9 Subj: Activities – flying. Careers – inventors. Helicopters.

Glass, Beth Raisner. *Blue-ribbon dad* ill. by Margie Moore. Abrams, 2011. ISBN 978-0-8109-9727-1 Subj: Animals – squirrels. Family life – fathers. Rhyming text.

Noises at night by Beth Raisner Glass and Susan Lubner ill. by Bruce Whatley. Abrams, 2005. ISBN 978-0-8109-5750-3 Subj: Bedtime. Noise, sounds. Rhyming text.

Glass, Eleri. *The red shoes* ill. by Ashley Spires. PGW, 2008. ISBN 978-1-894965-78-1 Subj: Character traits – appearance. Clothing – shoes. Shopping.

Glass, Julie. *A dollar for Penny* ill. by Joy Allen. Random House, 2000. ISBN 978-0-679-98973-8 Subj: Birthdays. Money. Rhyming text.

Glassman, Peter. *My dad's job* ill. by Timothy Bush. Simon & Schuster, 2003. ISBN 978-0-689-82890-4 Subj: Careers. Family life – fathers. Imagination.

Gleeson, Libby. *Clancy and Millie and the very fine house* ill. by Freya Blackwood. Little Hare, 2010. ISBN 978-1-921541-19-3 Subj: Friendship. Homes, houses. Imagination. Moving.

Cuddle time ill. by Julie Vivas. Candlewick, 2004. ISBN 978-0-7636-2320-3 Subj: Family life. Morning.

Half a world away ill. by Freya Blackwood. Scholastic, 2007. ISBN 978-0-439-88977-3 Subj: Friendship. Moving.

Glenn, Sharlee. *Just what Mama needs* ill. by Amiko Hirao. Harcourt, 2008. ISBN 978-0-15-205759-6 Subj: Days of the week, months of the year. Family life – mothers. Imagination.

Glicksman, Caroline. *Eric the math bear* ill. by author. Knopf, 2003. ISBN 978-0-375-92432-3 Subj: Animals – bears. Counting, numbers. Crime.

Gliori, Debi. *Can I have a hug?* ill. by author. Orchard, 2002. ISBN 978-0-439-27602-3 Subj: Animals – bears. Format, unusual – board books.

Flora's blanket ill. by author. Orchard, 2001. ISBN 978-0-531-30305-4 Subj: Animals – rabbits. Bedtime. Behavior – lost & found possessions.

Flora's surprise ill. by author. Orchard, 2003. ISBN 978-0-439-45590-9 Subj: Animals – rabbits. Gardens, gardening. Homes, houses.

Mr. Bear to the rescue ill. by author. Orchard, 2000. ISBN 978-0-531-30276-7 Subj: Animals. Animals – bears. Forest, woods. Homes, houses. Weather – storms.

Mr. Bear's new baby ill. by author. Orchard, 1999. ISBN 978-0-531-30152-4 Subj: Animals – bears. Babies. Family life.

No matter what ill. by author. Harcourt, 1999. ISBN 978-0-15-202061-3 Subj: Animals – foxes. Emotions – love. Family life. Rhyming text.

Penguin post ill. by author. Harcourt, 2001. ISBN 978-0-15-216765-3 Subj: Babies. Birds – penguins. Post office.

Polar Bolero ill. by author. Harcourt, 2001. ISBN 978-0-15-202436-9 Subj: Activities – dancing. Animals – polar bears. Bedtime. Rhyming text.

The scariest thing of all ill. by author. Walker, 2012. ISBN 978-0-8027-2391-8 Subj: Animals – rabbits. Character traits – bravery. Emotions – fear.

The snow lambs ill. by author. Scholastic, 1996. ISBN 978-0-590-20304-3 Subj: Animals – dogs. Animals – sheep. Weather – snow. Weather – storms.

Stormy weather ill. by author. Walker, 2009. ISBN 978-0-8027-9419-2 Subj: Animals – foxes. Bedtime. Family life – mothers. Rhyming text.

The trouble with dragons ill. by author. Walker, 2008. ISBN 978-0-8027-9789-6 Subj: Dragons. Ecology.

What can I give him? ill. by author. Holiday, 1998. ISBN 978-0-8234-1392-8 Subj: Gifts. Holidays – Christmas. Religion – Nativity. Rhyming text.

What's the time, Mr. Wolf? ill. by author. Walker, 2012. ISBN 978-0-8027-3432-7 Subj: Animals – pigs. Animals – wolves. Birthdays. Nursery rhymes. Time.

Where did that baby come from? ill. by author. Harcourt, 2005. ISBN 978-0-15-205373-4 Subj: Animals – tigers. Babies. Family life – new sibling. Rhyming text.

Go tell Aunt Rhody ill. by Aliki. Macmillan, 1974. ISBN 978-0-02-700410-6 Subj: Family life – aunts, uncles. Folk & fairy tales. Games. Songs.

Goble, Paul. *Adopted by the eagles: a Plains Indian story of friendship and treachery* ill. by author. Bradbury, 1994. ISBN 978-0-02-736575-7 Subj: Animals – horses, ponies. Birds – eagles. Folk & fairy tales. Indians of North America – Lakota (Sioux).

Beyond the ridge ill. by author. Bradbury, 1988. ISBN 978-0-02-736581-8 Subj: Death. Indians of North America – Great Plains.

Buffalo woman ill. by author. Bradbury, 1984. ISBN 978-0-02-737720-0 Subj: Folk & fairy tales. Indians of North America.

Crow chief: a Plains Indian story ill. by author. Orchard, 1992. ISBN 978-0-531-08547-9 Subj: Birds – crows. Folk & fairy tales. Indians of North America – Crow.

Death of the iron horse ill. by author. Bradbury, 1987. ISBN 978-0-02-737830-6 Subj: Indians of North America – Cheyenne (Sioux). Trains. War.

The dream wolf ill. by author. Rev. ed. of The friendly wolf. Bradbury, 1990. ISBN 978-0-02-736585-6 Subj: Folk & fairy tales. Indians of North America – Great Plains.

The gift of the sacred dog ill. by author. Bradbury, 1980. ISBN 978-0-87888-165-9 Subj: Animals – horses, ponies. Folk & fairy tales. Gifts. Indians of North America – Great Plains.

The girl who loved wild horses ill. by author. Dutton, 1978. ISBN 978-0-87888-121-5 Subj: Animals – horses, ponies. Caldecott award books. Indians of North America.

The great race of the birds and animals ill. by author. Bradbury, 1991. ISBN 978-0-689-71452-8 Subj: Animals. Birds. Creation. Folk & fairy tales. Indians of North America – Cheyenne (Sioux).

Her seven brothers ill. by author. Bradbury, 1988. ISBN 978-0-02-737960-0 Subj: Animals – buffaloes. Folk & fairy tales. Indians of North America – Cheyenne (Sioux).

Iktomi and the berries: a Plains Indian story ill. by author. Orchard, 1989. ISBN 978-0-531-08419-9

Subj: Folk & fairy tales. Indians of North America – Great Plains.

Iktomi and the boulder: a Plains Indian story ill. by author. Watts, 1988. ISBN 978-0-531-08360-4 Subj: Birthdays. Character traits – conceit. Folk & fairy tales. Indians of North America – Dakota (Sioux). Indians of North America – Great Plains. Rocks.

Iktomi and the buffalo skull: a Plains Indian story ill. by author. Orchard, 1991. ISBN 978-0-531-08511-0 Subj: Behavior – trickery. Character traits – conceit. Folk & fairy tales. Indians of North America – Great Plains.

Iktomi and the buzzard: a Plains Indian story ill. by author. Orchard, 1994. ISBN 978-0-531-08662-9 Subj: Behavior – trickery. Birds – buzzards. Folk & fairy tales. Indians of North America – Dakota (Sioux). Indians of North America – Great Plains.

Iktomi and the coyote: a Plains Indian story ill. by author. Orchard, 1998. ISBN 978-0-531-33108-8 Subj: Behavior – trickery. Folk & fairy tales. Indians of North America – Great Plains. Mythical creatures.

Iktomi and the ducks: a Plains Indian story ill. by author. Orchard, 1990. ISBN 978-0-531-08483-0 Subj: Animals – coyotes. Behavior – trickery. Birds – ducks. Folk & fairy tales. Indians of North America – Great Plains.

The legend of the White Buffalo Woman ill. by author. National Geographic, 1998. ISBN 978-0-7922-7074-4 Subj: Folk & fairy tales. Indians of North America – Lakota (Sioux).

The lost children: the boys who were neglected ill. by author. Bradbury, 1993. ISBN 978-0-02-736555-9 Subj: Character traits – meanness. Folk & fairy tales. Indians of North America – Blackfoot. Indians of North America – Siksika. Orphans. Stars.

Love flute ill. by author. Bradbury, 1992. ISBN 978-0-02-736261-9 Subj: Character traits – shyness. Emotions – love. Folk & fairy tales. Indians of North America – Dakota (Sioux).

Mystic horse ill. by author. HarperCollins, 2003. ISBN 978-0-06-029814-2 Subj: Animals – horses, ponies. Folk & fairy tales. Indians of North America – Great Plains. Indians of North America – Pawnee.

Remaking the earth: a creation story from the Great Plains of North America ill. by author. Orchard, 1996. ISBN 978-0-531-08874-6 Subj: Creation. Folk & fairy tales. Indians of North America – Great Plains. Weather – floods.

The return of the buffaloes: a Plains Indian story about famine and renewal of the earth ill. by author. National Geographic, 1996. ISBN 978-0-7922-2714-4 Subj: Animals – buffaloes. Folk & fairy tales. Food. Indians of North America – Lakota (Sioux). Indians of North America – Great Plains.

Star boy ill. by author. Bradbury, 1983. ISBN 978-0-02-722660-7 Subj: Activities – dancing. Character traits – appearance. Folk & fairy tales. Indians of North America – Siksika.

Godard, Alex. *Mama, across the sea* adapt. from the French by George Wen; ill. by author. Holt, 2000. ISBN 978-0-8050-6161-1 Subj: Behavior – needing someone. Family life – grandmothers. Family life – mothers. Foreign lands – Caribbean Islands.

Godden, Rumer. *The story of Holly and Ivy* ill. by Barbara Cooney. Penguin, 2006. ISBN 978-0-670-06219-5 Subj: Holidays – Christmas. Orphans. Toys – dolls.

Godkin, Celia. *Wolf island* ill. by author. Fitzhenry & Whiteside, 2006. ISBN 978-1-55455-007-4 Subj: Animals – wolves. Islands.

Godwin, Laura. *Barnyard prayers* ill. by Brian Selznick. Hyperion, 2000. ISBN 978-0-7868-0355-2 Subj: Animals. Poetry. Religion.

Central Park serenade ill. by Barry Root. HarperCollins, 2002. ISBN 978-0-06-025892-4 Subj: Cities, towns. Parks. Rhyming text. Seasons – summer.

Little white dog ill. by Dan Yaccarino. Hyperion, 1998. ISBN 978-0-7868-2256-0 Subj: Animals. Concepts – color. Concepts – shape. Imagination. Rhyming text.

One moon, two cats ill. by Yoko Tanaka. Simon & Schuster, 2011. ISBN 978-1-4424-1202-6 Subj: Animals – cats. Cities, towns. Farms. Rhyming text.

This is the firefighter ill. by Julian Hector. Hyperion, 2009. ISBN 978-1-4231-0800-9 Subj: Careers – firefighters. Rhyming text.

What the baby hears ill. by Mary Morgan. Hyperion, 2002. ISBN 978-0-7868-2484-7 Subj: Animals – babies. Family life – parents. Noise, sounds. Rhyming text.

Goecke, Michael P. *Diplodocus* ill. by author. Abdo, 2002. ISBN 978-1-57765-633-3 Subj: Dinosaurs.

Goembel, Ponder, adapt. *Animal fair* ill. by adapter. Marshall Cavendish, 2010. ISBN 978-0-7614-5642-1 Subj: Animals. Fairs, festivals. Rhyming text. Songs.

Going, K. L. *Dog in charge* ill. by Dan Santat. Dial, 2012. ISBN 978-0-8037-3479-1 Subj: Animals – cats. Animals – dogs. Behavior – misbehavior.

Golan, Avirama. *Little Naomi, Little Chick* ill. by Raaya Karas. Eerdmans, 2013. ISBN 978-0-8028-

5427-8 Subj: Birds – chickens. Farms. School – nursery.

Gold, August. *Does God hear my prayer?* ill. by Diane Hardy Waller. Skylight Paths, 2005. ISBN 978-1-59473-102-0 Subj: Religion.

Gold-Vukson, Marji E. *The colors of my Jewish Year* ill. by author. Kar-Ben, 1998. ISBN 978-1-58013-011-0 Subj: Concepts – color. Format, unusual – board books. Jewish culture. Religion.

Grandpa and me on Tu B'Shevat ill. by Leslie Evans. Kar-Ben, 2004. ISBN 978-1-58013-122-3 Subj: Cumulative tales. Family life – grandfathers. Holidays. Jewish culture. Religion. Rhyming text. Trees.

Goldberg, Myla. *Catching the moon* ill. by Chris Sheban. Scholastic, 2007. ISBN 978-0-439-57686-4 Subj: Moon.

Goldberg, Whoopi. *Whoopi's big book of manners* ill. by Olo. Hyperion, 2006. ISBN 978-0-7868-5295-6 Subj: Etiquette.

Goldfinger, Jennifer P. *A fish named Spot* ill. by author. Little, 2001. ISBN 978-0-316-32047-4 Subj: Fish. Pets.

My dog Lyle ill. by author. Houghton, 2007. ISBN 978-0-618-63983-0 Subj: Animals – dogs. Pets.

Goldhor, Susan Henne. *Franny B. Kranny, there's a bird in your hair* (Lerner, Harriet Goldhor)

Goldie, Sonia. *Ghosts* ill. by Marc Boutavant. Enchanted Lion, 2013. ISBN 978-1-59270-142-1 Subj: Ghosts.

Goldin, Augusta. *Ducks don't get wet* ill. by Leonard P. Kessler. Crowell, 1989. ISBN 978-0-690-04782-0 Subj: Birds – ducks. Science.

Goldin, Barbara Diamond. *Cakes and miracles: a Purim tale* ill. by Jaime Zollars. Marshall Cavendish, 2010. ISBN 978-0-7614-5701-5 Subj: Activities – baking, cooking. Disabilities – blindness. Holidays – Purim. Jewish culture.

A mountain of blintzes ill. by Anik McGrory. Harcourt, 2001. ISBN 978-0-15-201902-0 Subj: Food. Holidays – Shavuot. Jewish culture. Religion.

Night lights ill. by Laura Sucher. UAHC Pr., 2002. ISBN 978-0-8074-0803-2 Subj: Emotions – fear. Holidays – Sukkot. Jewish culture.

Goldin, David. *Go-Go-Go!* ill. by author. Abrams, 2000. ISBN 978-0-8109-4141-0 Subj: Animals. Sports – bicycling. Sports – racing.

Golding, Theresa Martin. *Abby's asthma and the big race* ill. by Margeaux Lucas. Whitman, 2009. ISBN 978-0-8075-0465-9 Subj: Activities – running. Illness – asthma. Sports – racing.

Memorial Day surprise ill. by Alexandra Artigas. Boyds Mills, 2004. ISBN 978-1-59078-048-0 Subj: Ethnic groups in the U.S. Family life – grandfathers. Holidays – Memorial Day.

Goldman, Judy. *Uncle Monarch and the Day of the Dead* ill. by Rene King Moreno. Boyds Mills, 2008. ISBN 978-1-59078-425-9 Subj: Death. Family life – aunts, uncles. Foreign lands – Mexico. Holidays – Day of the Dead. Insects – butterflies, caterpillars.

Goldsboro, Bobby. *Jonah and the whale; and, Daniel in the lion's den* ill. by Toni Donelow Stewart. New Canaan, 2003. ISBN 978-1-889658-28-5 Subj: Animals – lions. Animals – whales. Religion – Daniel. Religion – Jonah.

Noah and the ark; and, David and Goliath ill. by Toni Donelow Stewart. New Canaan, 2003. ISBN 978-1-889658-27-8 Subj: Animals – mice. Birds – ducks. Boats, ships. Foreign lands – Israel. Giants. Religion – David. Religion – Noah. Weather – floods.

Goldstone, Bruce. *Awesome autumn* ill. by author. Holt, 2012. ISBN 978-0-8050-9210-3 Subj: Seasons – fall.

Great estimations ill. with photos. Holt, 2006. ISBN 978-0-8050-7446-8 Subj: Concepts. Counting, numbers.

That's a possibility! a book about what might happen photos by author. Holt, 2013. ISBN 978-0-8050-8998-1 Subj: Concepts. Counting, numbers.

Golenbock, Peter. *ABCs of baseball* ill. by Dan Andreasen. Dial, 2012. ISBN 978-0-8037-3711-2 Subj: ABC books. Sports – baseball.

Hank Aaron ill. by Paul Lee. Harcourt, 2001. ISBN 978-0-15-202093-4 Subj: Character traits – bravery. Ethnic groups in the U.S. – African Americans. Sports – baseball.

Gollub, Matthew. *Cool melons — turn to frogs: the life and poems of Issa* ill. by Kazuko G. Stone. Lee & Low, 1998. ISBN 978-1-880000-71-7 Subj: Careers – poets. Foreign lands – Japan. Poetry.

Gobble, quack, moon ill. by Judy Love. Tortuga, 2002. ISBN 978-1-889910-20-8 Subj: Activities – dancing. Animals. Animals – bulls, cows. Moon. Music.

The Jazz Fly: starring the Jazz Bugs ill. by Karen Hanke. Tortuga, 2000. ISBN 978-1-889910-17-8 Subj: Animals. Insects – flies. Music. Musical instruments – drums. Rhyming text.

Jazz Fly 2: the jungle pachanga ill. by Karen Hanke. Tortuga, 2010. ISBN 978-1-889910-44-4 Subj:

Foreign languages. Insects – flies. Jungle. Music. Rhyming text.

Ten oni drummers ill. by Kazuko G. Stone. Lee & Low, 2000. ISBN 978-1-58430-011-3 Subj: Counting, numbers. Foreign lands – Japan. Foreign languages. Rhyming text.

Golson, Terry. *Tillie lays an egg* ill. by Ben Fink. Scholastic, 2009. ISBN 978-0-545-00537-1 Subj: Birds – chickens. Eggs. Farms.

Gomel, Luc. *The ant, energetic worker* photos by Rémy Amann, et al. Charlesbridge, 2001. ISBN 978-1-57091-451-5 Subj: Insects – ants.

Gomi, Taro. *The crocodile and the dentist* ill. by author. Millbrook, 1994. ISBN 978-1-56294-555-8 Subj: Careers – dentists. Reptiles – alligators, crocodiles. Teeth.

Everyone poops ill. by author. Kane/Miller, 1993. ISBN 978-0-916291-45-7 Subj: Nature. Toilet training.

I lost my dad ill. by author. Kane/Miller, 2001. ISBN 978-1-929132-04-1 Subj: Behavior – lost. Family life – fathers. Stores.

Spring is here ill. by author. Chronicle, 1989. ISBN 978-0-87701-626-7 Subj: Animals – bulls, cows. Seasons.

Gonyea, Mark. *A book about color* ill. by author. Holt, 2010. ISBN 978-0-8050-9055-0 Subj: Concepts – color.

The spooky box ill. by author. Holt, 2013. ISBN 978-0-8050-8813-7 Subj: Character traits – questioning. Emotions – fear. Format, unusual – toy & movable books.

Gonzalez, Lucia. *The storyteller's candle / La velita de los cuentos* ill. by Lulu Delacre. Children's Book Press, 2008. ISBN 978-0-89239-222-3 Subj: Activities – storytelling. Careers – librarians. Ethnic groups in the U.S. – Puerto Rican Americans. Foreign languages. Libraries.

Good, Merle, et al. *Dan's pants* ill. by Cheryl Benner. Good Books, 2000. ISBN 978-1-56148-307-5 Subj: Clothing – pants. Rhyming text.

Good morning ill. by Summer Durantz. Simon & Schuster, 2002. ISBN 978-0-689-85099-8 Subj: Format, unusual – board books. Morning.

Goodall, Jane. *The eagle and the wren* ill. by Alexander Reichstein. NorthSouth, 2000. ISBN 978-0-7358-1380-9 Subj: Birds. Character traits – cooperation. Folk & fairy tales.

Goodall, John S. *Creepy castle* ill. by author. Rev. jacket ed. McElderry, 1998. ISBN 978-0-689-82205-6 Subj: Animals – mice. Format, unusual. Knights. Monsters. Wordless.

Shrewbettina's birthday ill. by author. Rev. jacket ed. McElderry, 1998. ISBN 978-0-689-82206-3 Subj: Animals – shrews. Birthdays. Format, unusual. Wordless.

Goode, Diane. *Diane Goode's book of silly stories and songs* ill. by author. Dutton, 1992. ISBN 978-0-525-44967-6 Subj: Folk & fairy tales. Humorous stories. Music. Songs.

The dinosaur's new clothes (Andersen, Hans Christian)

Mama's perfect present ill. by author. Dutton, 1996. ISBN 978-0-525-45493-9 Subj: Animals – dogs. Birthdays. Family life – brothers & sisters. Family life – mothers. Foreign lands – France.

The most perfect spot ill. by author. HarperCollins, 2006. ISBN 978-0-06-072697-3 Subj: Activities – picnicking. Animals – dogs. Family life – mothers.

Tiger trouble ill. by author. Blue Sky, 2001. ISBN 978-0-439-20866-6 Subj: Animals – dogs. Animals – tigers. Cities, towns. Crime. Homes, houses.

Goodhart, Pippa. *Arthur's tractor: a fairy tale with mechanical parts* ill. by Colin Paine. Bloomsbury, 2003. ISBN 978-1-58234-847-6 Subj: Careers – farmers. Dragons. Humorous stories. Royalty – princesses. Tractors.

Little Nelly's big book ill. by Andy Rowland. Bloomsbury, 2012. ISBN 978-1-59990-779-6 Subj: Animals – elephants. Animals – mice. Books, reading. Concepts – size. Self-concept.

Noah makes a boat ill. by Bernard Lodge. Houghton, 1997. ISBN 978-0-395-86957-4 Subj: Animals. Boats, ships. Religion – Noah. Weather – floods. Weather – rain. Weather – rainbows.

Pudgy, a puppy to love ill. by Caroline Jayne Church. Scholastic, 2003. ISBN 978-0-439-45699-9 Subj: Animals – babies. Animals – dogs. Behavior – needing someone. Behavior – running away. Friendship.

Three little ghosties ill. by AnnaLaura Cantone. Bloomsbury, 2007. ISBN 978-1-58234-711-0 Subj: Ghosts.

You choose ill. by Nick Sharratt. Kane/Miller, 2012. ISBN 978-1-61067-076-0 Subj: Character traits – individuality. Character traits – questioning. Self-concept.

Goodings, Christina. *Creation story* ill. by Melanie Mitchell. Lion, 2010. ISBN 978-0-7459-6089-0 Subj: Creation. Religion.

Lost sheep story ill. by Melanie Mitchell. Lion, 2010. ISBN 978-0-7459-6087-6 Subj: Animals – sheep. Behavior – lost. Religion.

Goodings, Lennie. *When you grow up* ill. by Jenny Jones. Fogelman, 2001. ISBN 978-0-8037-2677-2 Subj: Animals – bears. Behavior – growing up. Careers. Family life – mothers.

Goodman, Emily. *Plant secrets* ill. by Phyllis Limbacher Tildes. Charlesbridge, 2009. ISBN 978-1-58089-204-9 Subj: Plants.

Goodman, Joan Elizabeth. *Ballet Bunnies* ill. by author. Marshall Cavendish, 2008. ISBN 978-0-7614-5392-5 Subj: Animals – rabbits. Ballet.

Bernard goes to school ill. by Dominic Catalano. Boyds Mills, 2001. ISBN 978-1-56397-958-3 Subj: Animals – elephants. School – first day.

Goodman, Susan E. *Chopsticks for my noodle soup: Eliza's life in Malaysia* photos by Michael Doolittle. Millbrook, 2000. ISBN 978-0-7613-1552-0 Subj: Family life. Foreign lands – Malaysia.

It's a dog's life ill. by David Slonim. Roaring Brook, 2012. ISBN 978-1-59643-448-6 Subj: Animals – dogs. Senses.

What do you do — at the zoo? ill. by Steve Pica. Millbrook, 2002. ISBN 978-0-7613-2755-4 Subj: Animals. Careers – zookeepers. Zoos.

Goodrich, Carter. *A creature was stirring: one boy's night before Christmas* (Moore, Clement Clarke)

Say hello to Zorro! ill. by author. Simon & Schuster, 2011. ISBN 978-1-4169-3893-4 Subj: Animals – dogs.

Zorro gets an outfit ill. by author. Simon & Schuster, 2012. ISBN 978-1-4424-3535-3 Subj: Animals – dogs. Clothing – costumes. Emotions – embarrassment.

Goodwin-Sturges, Judy Sue. *Construction Kitties* ill. by Shari Halpern. Holt, 2013. ISBN 978-0-8050-9105-2 Subj: Animals – cats. Careers – construction workers. Trucks.

Goodwyn, Susan. *My first baby signs* (Acredolo, Linda P.)

Goossens, Philippe. *Knock! Knock! Knock! Who's there?* ill. by author. NorthSouth, 2013. ISBN 978-0-7358-4122-2 Subj: Animals – bears. Emotions – fear. Friendship. Night.

Gorbachev, Valeri. *The best cat* ill. by author. Candlewick, 2010. ISBN 978-0-7636-3675-3 Subj: Animals – cats. Family life – brothers & sisters. Pets.

Big Little Elephant ill. by author. Harcourt, 2005. ISBN 978-0-15-205195-2 Subj: Activities – playing. Animals – elephants. Concepts – size. Emotions – loneliness. Friendship.

Catty Jane who hated the rain ill. by author. Boyds Mills, 2012. ISBN 978-1-59078-700-7 Subj: Animals – cats. Friendship. Weather – lightning, thunder. Weather – rain.

Catty Jane who loved to dance ill. by author. Boyds Mills, 2013. ISBN 978-1-59078-982-7 Subj: Activities – dancing. Animals – cats. Ballet. Friendship.

Chicken chickens ill. by author. NorthSouth, 2001. ISBN 978-0-7358-1542-1 Subj: Activities – playing. Animals. Birds – chickens. Character traits – confidence. Parks.

Chicken chickens go to school ill. by author. NorthSouth, 2003. ISBN 978-0-7358-1767-8 Subj: Animals. Birds – chickens. Character traits – shyness. Friendship. School – first day.

Christopher counting ill. by author. Philomel, 2008. ISBN 978-0-399-24629-6 Subj: Animals – rabbits. Counting, numbers.

Dragon is coming! ill. by author. Harcourt, 2009. ISBN 978-0-15-205196-9 Subj: Animals. Animals – mice. Behavior – gossip. Cumulative tales. Emotions – fear. Weather – lightning, thunder.

The fool of the world and the flying ship: a Ukrainian folk tale ill. by adapter. Star Bright, 1998. ISBN 978-1-887734-19-6 Subj: Activities – flying. Boats, ships. Character traits – cleverness. Folk & fairy tales. Foreign lands – Ukraine. Royalty – tsars.

Heron and Turtle ill. by author. Penguin, 2006. ISBN 978-0-399-24321-9 Subj: Birds – herons. Friendship. Reptiles – turtles, tortoises.

How to be friends with a dragon ill. by author. Whitman, 2012. ISBN 978-0-8075-3432-8 Subj: Dragons. Etiquette. Family life – brothers & sisters.

Me too! ill. by author. Holiday House, 2013. ISBN 978-0-8234-2744-4 Subj: Animals – bears. Animals – chipmunks. Friendship. Weather – snow.

The missing chick ill. by author. Candlewick, 2009. ISBN 978-0-7636-3676-0 Subj: Behavior – lost. Birds – chickens. Careers – firefighters. Careers – police officers.

Molly who flew away ill. by author. Philomel, 2009. ISBN 978-0-399-25211-2 Subj: Animals. Animals – mice. Fairs, festivals. Toys – balloons.

Nicky and the big, bad wolves ill. by author. NorthSouth, 1998. ISBN 978-1-55858-918-6 Subj: Animals – rabbits. Animals – wolves. Bedtime. Dreams. Emotions – fear.

Nicky and the fantastic birthday gift ill. by author. NorthSouth, 2000. ISBN 978-0-7358-1379-3 Subj: Animals – rabbits. Birthdays. Family life – mothers.

Nicky and the rainy day ill. by author. NorthSouth, 2002. ISBN 978-0-7358-1645-9 Subj: Animals – rabbits. Family life – brothers & sisters. Weather – rain.

One rainy day ill. by author. Philomel, 2002. ISBN 978-0-399-23628-0 Subj: Animals. Animals

– goats. Animals – pigs. Counting, numbers. Weather – rain.

Red red red ill. by author. Penguin, 2007. ISBN 978-0-399-24628-9 Subj: Animals. Character traits – curiosity. Concepts – color. Reptiles – turtles, tortoises.

Shhh! ill. by author. Penguin, 2011. ISBN 978-0-399-25429-1 Subj: Family life – brothers. Noise, sounds. Sleep.

That's what friends are for ill. by author. Penguin, 2005. ISBN 978-0-399-23966-3 Subj: Animals – goats. Animals – pigs. Friendship.

Turtle's penguin day ill. by author. Knopf, 2008. ISBN 978-0-375-84374-7 Subj: Birds – penguins. Imagination. Reptiles – turtles, tortoises. School.

What's the big idea, Molly? ill. by author. Penguin, 2010. ISBN 978-0-399-25428-4 Subj: Activities – writing. Animals. Animals – mice. Birthdays. Gifts.

When someone is afraid ill. by Kostya Gorbachev. Star Bright, 2005. ISBN 978-1-932065-99-2 Subj: Dreams. Emotions – fear.

Where is the apple pie? ill. by author. Philomel, 1999. ISBN 978-0-399-23385-2 Subj: Animals. Character traits – questioning. Circular tales. Tall tales.

Whose hat is it? ill. by author. HarperCollins, 2004. ISBN 978-0-06-053435-6 Subj: Animals. Behavior – lost & found possessions. Clothing – hats. Reptiles – turtles, tortoises.

Gordon, David. *The three little rigs* ill. by author. Geringer, 2005. ISBN 978-0-06-058119-0 Subj: Family life – brothers. Machines. Trucks.

The ugly truckling ill. by author. Geringer, 2004. ISBN 978-0-06-054601-4 Subj: Airplanes, airports. Family life – brothers & sisters. Self-concept. Trucks.

Gordon, Domenica More. *Archie* ill. by author. Bloomsbury, 2012. ISBN 978-1-59990-936-3 Subj: Activities – sewing. Animals – dogs. Clothing. Wordless.

Gordon, Gus. *Herman and Rosie* ill. by author. Roaring Brook, 2013. ISBN 978-1-59643-856-9 Subj: Animals – deer. Cities, towns. Emotions – loneliness. Friendship. Music. Reptiles – alligators, crocodiles.

Gordon, Sharon. *Asthma* ill. with photos. Children's Press, 2003. ISBN 978-0-516-22582-1 Subj: Health & fitness. Illness – asthma.

Bruises ill. with photos. Children's Press, 2002. ISBN 978-0-516-22568-5 Subj: Health & fitness. Safety.

Cuts and scrapes ill. with photos. Children's Press, 2002. ISBN 978-0-516-22566-1 Subj: Health & safety. Illness.

Pinkeye ill. with photos. Children's Press, 2003. ISBN 978-0-516-22583-8 Subj: Anatomy – eyes. Health & fitness. Illness.

Seeing ill. with photos. Children's Press, 2001. ISBN 978-0-516-22291-2 Subj: Anatomy – eyes. Health & fitness. Senses – sight.

Smelling ill. with photos. Children's Press, 2001. ISBN 978-0-516-22292-9 Subj: Anatomy – noses. Health & fitness. Senses – smell.

Gordon, Stephanie Jacob. *Smile, Principessa!* (Enderle, Judith Ross)

Gore, Leonid. *Danny's first snow* ill. by author. Simon & Schuster, 2007. ISBN 978-1-4169-1330-6 Subj: Animals – rabbits. Seasons – winter. Weather – snow.

Mommy, where are you? ill. by author. Atheneum, 2009. ISBN 978-1-4169-5505-4 Subj: Animals – mice. Family life – mothers. Format, unusual – toy & movable books.

When I grow up ill. by author. Scholastic, 2009. ISBN 978-0-545-08597-7 Subj: Behavior – growing up. Family life – fathers.

Who was born this special day? (Bunting, Eve)

The wonderful book ill. by author. Scholastic, 2010. ISBN 978-0-545-08598-4 Subj: Animals. Books, reading. Forest, woods.

Worms for lunch? ill. by author. Scholastic, 2011. ISBN 978-0-545-24338-4 Subj: Animals. Food. Format, unusual.

Gormley, Greg. *Dog in boots* ill. by Roberta Angaramo. Holiday House, 2011. ISBN 978-0-8234-2347-7 Subj: Animals – dogs. Clothing – shoes.

Goss, Gary. *Where does food come from?* (Rotner, Shelley)

Got, Yves. *Sam loves kisses* ill. by author. Chronicle, 2002. ISBN 978-0-8118-3505-3 Subj: Emotions. Format, unusual – board books. Kissing.

Sam's big book of words ill. by author. Chronicle, 2001. ISBN 978-0-8118-3088-1 Subj: Animals – rabbits. Dictionaries. Language.

Sam's little sister ill. by author. Chronicle, 2002. ISBN 978-0-8118-3504-6 Subj: Animals – rabbits. Family life – brothers & sisters. Format, unusual – board books.

Gottfried, Maya. *Good dog* ill. by Robert Rahway Zakanitch. Knopf, 2005. ISBN 978-0-375-93049-2 Subj: Animals – dogs. Pets. Poetry.

Last night I dreamed a circus ill. by Robert Rahway Zakanitch. Random House, 2003. ISBN 978-0-375-92388-3 Subj: Circus. Dreams.

Our farm: by the animals of Farm Sanctuary ill. by Robert Rahway Zakanitch. Random House, 2010. ISBN 978-0-375-86118-5 Subj: Animals. Character traits – kindness to animals. Farms. Poetry.

Goudey, Alice E. *The day we saw the sun come up* ill. by Adrienne Adams. Scribners, 1961. Subj: Caldecott award honor books. Family life. Sun.

Houses from the sea ill. by Adrienne Adams. Scribners, 1959. Subj: Caldecott award honor books. Sea & seashore.

Gourley, Robbin. *Bring me some apples and I'll make you a pie: a story about Edna Lewis* ill. by author. Clarion, 2009. ISBN 978-0-618-15836-2 Subj: Activities – baking, cooking. Ethnic groups in the U.S. – African Americans. Family life. Farms. Food.

First garden: the White House garden and how it grew ill. by author. Clarion, 2011. ISBN 978-0-547-48224-8 Subj: Food. Gardens, gardening. Plants. U.S. history.

Gow, Nancy. *Ten big toes and a prince's nose.* Sterling, 2010. ISBN 978-1-4027-6396-0 Subj: Anatomy – feet. Anatomy – noses. Rhyming text. Royalty – princes. Royalty – princesses. Self-concept.

Gower, Catherine. *Long-Long's new year: a story about the Chinese spring festival* ill. by He Zhihong. Periplus/Tuttle, 2005. ISBN 978-0-8048-3666-1 Subj: Family life – grandfathers. Holidays – Chinese New Year.

Graber, Janet. *Jacob and the polar bears* ill. by Sandra Salzillo-Shields. Moon Mt, 2002. ISBN 978-1-931659-00-0 Subj: Animals – polar bears. Clothing – pajamas. Humorous stories. Night.

Grady, Cynthia. *I lay my stitches down: poems of American slavery* ill. by Michele Wood. Eerdmans, 2012. ISBN 978-0-8028-5386-8 Subj: Character traits – freedom. Ethnic groups in the U.S. – African Americans. Poetry. Slavery. U.S. history.

Graham, Bob. *April and Esme, tooth fairies* ill. by author. Candlewick, 2010. ISBN 978-0-7636-4683-7 Subj: Fairies. Family life – sisters. Teeth.

A bus called Heaven ill. by author. Candlewick, 2012. ISBN 978-0-7636-5893-9 Subj: Character traits – cooperation. Buses. Communities, neighborhoods.

Dimity Dumpty: the story of Humpty's little sister ill. by author. Candlewick, 2007. ISBN 978-0-7636-3078-2 Subj: Character traits – shyness. Circus. Eggs. Family life – brothers & sisters.

How to heal a broken wing ill. by author. Candlewick, 2008. ISBN 978-0-7636-3903-7 Subj: Birds. Character traits – kindness to animals.

Jethro Byrd, fairy child ill. by author. Candlewick, 2002. ISBN 978-0-7636-1772-1 Subj: Activities – picnicking. Fairies.

"Let's get a pup!" said Kate ill. by author. Candlewick, 2001. ISBN 978-0-7636-1452-2 Subj: Animals – dogs. Family life. Pets.

Max ill. by author. Candlewick, 2000. ISBN 978-0-7636-1138-5 Subj: Activities – flying. Imagination. Mythical creatures.

Oscar's half birthday ill. by author. Candlewick, 2005. ISBN 978-0-7636-2699-0 Subj: Activities – picnicking. Birthdays. Ethnic groups in the U.S. Family life.

The silver button ill. by author. Candlewick, 2013. ISBN 978-0-7636-6437-4 Subj: Activities – walking. Babies. Cities, towns.

"The trouble with dogs," said Dad ill. by author. Candlewick, 2007. ISBN 978-0-7636-3316-5 Subj: Animals – dogs. Pets.

Graham, Elspeth. *Cloud tea monkeys* (Peet, Mal)

Graham, Joan Bransfield. *Flicker flash* ill. by Nancy Davis. Houghton, 1999. ISBN 978-0-395-90501-2 Subj: Light, lights. Poetry.

Splish splash ill. by Steven Scott. Houghton, 1994. ISBN 978-0-395-70128-7 Subj: Poetry. Water.

Graham, Tom. *Five little firefighters* ill. by author. Holt, 2008. ISBN 978-0-8050-8697-3 Subj: Careers – firefighters. Character traits – helpfulness.

Graham-Barber, Lynda. *Spy hops and belly flops* ill. by Brian Lies. Houghton, 2004. ISBN 978-0-618-22291-9 Subj: Animals. Behavior. Forest, woods. Rhyming text.

Graham-Yooll, Liz. *Timothy Tib* ill. by author. Ragged Bears, 2001. ISBN 978-1-929927-25-8 Subj: Animals – cats. Rhyming text.

Grahame, Kenneth. *The reluctant dragon* abridged by Inga Moore; ill. by Inga Moore. Candlewick, 2004. ISBN 978-0-7636-2199-5 Subj: Dragons. Knights. Poetry.

The wind in the willows retold by Janet Allison Brown; ill. by Joanne Moss. Viking, 2001. ISBN 978-0-670-89914-2 Subj: Animals. Animals – badgers. Animals – moles. Animals – rats. Foreign lands – England. Frogs & toads.

A wind in the willows Christmas ill. by Michael Hague. SeaStar, 2000. ISBN 978-1-58717-007-2 Subj: Animals. Animals – moles. Animals – rats. Holidays – Christmas. Homes, houses.

Gralley, Jean. *Very boring alligator* ill. by author. Holt, 2001. ISBN 978-0-8050-6328-8 Subj: Reptiles – alligators, crocodiles. Rhyming text.

Gramatky, Hardie. *Little Toot* ill. by author. Putnam, 1939. Subj: Boats, ships. Character traits – ambition.

Grambling, Lois G. *Big Dog* ill. by Andrew L. San Diego. Marshall Cavendish, 2001. ISBN 978-0-7614-5045-0 Subj: Animals – dogs. Dinosaurs. Pets.

Can I bring Woolly to the library, Ms. Reeder? ill. by Judy Love. Charlesbridge, 2012. ISBN 978-1-58089-281-0 Subj: Animals – woolly mammoths. Careers – librarians. Libraries. Problem solving.

Grandma tells a story ill. by Fred Willingham. Whispering Coyote, 2001. ISBN 978-1-58089-057-1 Subj: Babies. Birth. Family life – grandparents.

Here comes T. Rex Cottontail ill. by Jack E. Davis. HarperCollins, 2007. ISBN 978-0-06-053129-4 Subj: Animals – rabbits. Character traits – helpfulness. Dinosaurs. Eggs. Holidays – Easter.

Miss Hildy's missing cape caper ill. by Bridget Starr Taylor. Random House, 2000. ISBN 978-0-375-90196-6 Subj: Birds – flamingos. Holidays – Halloween. Mystery stories.

My mom is a firefighter ill. by Jane Manning. HarperCollins, 2007. ISBN 978-0-06-058640-9 Subj: Careers – firefighters. Family life – mothers.

T. Rex and the Mother's Day hug ill. by Jack E. Davis. HarperCollins, 2008. ISBN 978-0-06-053126-3 Subj: Dinosaurs. Holidays – Mother's Day. Hugging.

T. Rex trick-or-treats ill. by Jack E. Davis. HarperCollins, 2005. ISBN 978-0-06-050253-9 Subj: Dinosaurs. Holidays – Halloween.

This whole Tooth Fairy thing's nothing but a big rip-off! ill. by Thomas Payne. Marshall Cavendish, 2002. ISBN 978-0-7614-5104-4 Subj: Animals. Animals – hippopotamuses. Fairies. Teeth.

The witch who wanted to be a princess ill. by Judy Love. Whispering Coyote, 2002. ISBN 978-1-58089-062-5 Subj: Character traits – honesty. Folk & fairy tales. Royalty – princesses. Self-concept. Witches.

Gran, Julia. *Big bug surprise* ill. by author. Scholastic, 2007. ISBN 978-0-439-67609-0 Subj: Insects. Insects – bees. School.

A grand celebration: grandparents in poetry sel. by Carol G. Hittleman and Daniel R. Hittleman; ill. by Kay Life. Boyds Mills, 2002. ISBN 978-1-56397-901-9 Subj: Family life – grandparents. Poetry.

Grandits, John. *Ten rules you absolutely must not break if you want to survive the school bus* ill. by Michael Austin. Clarion, 2011. ISBN 978-0-618-78822-4 Subj: Buses. Emotions – fear. Family life – brothers. School – first day.

Granfield, Linda. *The legend of the panda* ill. by Song Nan Zhang. Tundra, 1998. ISBN 978-0-88776-421-9 Subj: Animals – pandas. Folk & fairy tales. Foreign lands – China.

What am I? ill. by Jennifer Herbert. Tundra, 2007. ISBN 978-0-88776-812-5 Subj: Riddles & jokes.

Graniczewski, Wojciech. *Found alphabet* (Shindler, Ramon)

Granowsky, Alvin. *At the park* ill. with photos & ill. Copper Beech, 2001. ISBN 978-0-7613-2167-5 Subj: Animals – dogs. Family life – fathers. Family life – sons. Parks. Pets.

Can I help? ill. by author. Copper Beech, 2001. ISBN 978-0-7613-2172-9 Subj: Activities – picnicking. Character traits – helpfulness. Parties.

Diggers and cranes ill. by author. Copper Beech, 2000. ISBN 978-0-7613-1222-2 Subj: Machines.

Dinosaurs ill. by author. Copper Beech, 2000. ISBN 978-0-7613-1217-8 Subj: Dinosaurs.

Granström, Brita. *Snap!* (Manning, Mick)

Woolly mammoth (Manning, Mick)

Grant, Brianna K. *We are girls who love to run / Somos chicas y a nosotras nos encanta correr* ill. by Nicholas A. Wright. Balanced Steps, 2008. ISBN 978-0-9798511-1-7 Subj: Activities – running. Foreign languages. Gender roles. Self-concept.

Grant, Joan. *Cat and Fish* ill. by Neil Curtis. Simply Read, 2005. ISBN 978-1-894965-14-9 Subj: Animals – cats. Fish. Friendship.

Grant, Rose Marie. *Andiamo, Weasel* ill. by Jon Goodell. Knopf, 2002. ISBN 978-0-375-90607-7 Subj: Animals – weasels. Animals – wolves. Birds – crows. Character traits – confidence. Foreign lands – Italy. Self-concept.

Grassby, Donna. *A seaside alphabet* ill. by Susan Tooke. Tundra, 2000. ISBN 978-0-88776-516-2 Subj: Foreign lands – Canada. Sea & seashore.

Gravdahl, John. *Curious catwalk* ill. by author. Propeller, 2003. ISBN 978-0-9678577-8-7 Subj: Animals – cats. Character traits – curiosity. Rhyming text.

Graves, Keith. *Chicken Big* ill. by author. Chronicle, 2010. ISBN 978-0-8118-7237-9 Subj: Birds – chickens. Character traits – being different. Concepts – size.

Loretta, ace Pinky Scout ill. by author. Scholastic, 2002. ISBN 978-0-439-36831-5 Subj: Self-concept.

Pet boy ill. by author. Chronicle, 2000. ISBN 978-0-8118-2672-3 Subj: Behavior – boredom. Character traits – responsibility. Pets. Rhyming text.

Uncle Blubbafink's seriously ridiculous stories ill. by author. Scholastic, 2001. ISBN 978-0-439-24083-3 Subj: Tall tales.

The unexpectedly bad hair of Barcelona Smith ill. by author. Penguin, 2006. ISBN 978-0-399-24273-1 Subj: Behavior – worrying. Hair.

Gravett, Emily. *Again!* ill. by author. Simon & Schuster, 2013. ISBN 978-1-4424-5231-2 Subj: Bedtime. Books, reading. Dragons.

Blue chameleon ill. by author. Simon & Schuster, 2011. ISBN 978-1-4424-1958-2 Subj: Concepts – color. Concepts – shape. Reptiles – chameleons.

Dogs ill. by author. Simon & Schuster, 2010. ISBN 978-1-4169-8703-1 Subj: Animals – dogs.

Meerkat mail ill. by author. Simon & Schuster, 2007. ISBN 978-1-416-93473-8 Subj: Activities – traveling. Animals – meerkats. Foreign lands – Africa. Format, unusual – toy & movable books. Letters, cards.

Monkey and me ill. by author. Simon & Schuster, 2008. ISBN 978-1-4169-5457-6 Subj: Activities – playing. Animals. Animals – monkeys. Rhyming text. Toys.

The odd egg ill. by author. Simon & Schuster, 2009. ISBN 978-1-4169-6872-6 Subj: Birds – ducks. Eggs. Reptiles – alligators, crocodiles.

Orange pear apple bear ill. by author. Simon & Schuster, 2007. ISBN 978-1-4169-3999-3 Subj: Animals – bears. Concepts – color. Concepts – shape.

The rabbit problem ill. by author. Simon & Schuster, 2010. ISBN 978-1-4424-1255-2 Subj: Animals – rabbits. Counting, numbers. Days of the week, months of the year. Format, unusual – toy & movable books.

Spells ill. by author. Simon & Schuster, 2009. ISBN 978-1-4169-8270-8 Subj: Books, reading. Format, unusual. Frogs & toads. Imagination. Magic.

Wolf won't bite! ill. by author. Simon & Schuster, 2012. ISBN 978-1-4424-2763-1 Subj: Animals – pigs. Animals – wolves. Circus.

Wolves ill. by author. Simon & Schuster, 2006. ISBN 978-1-4169-1491-4 Subj: Animals – rabbits. Animals – wolves. Humorous stories.

Gray, Kes. *Eat your peas* ill. by Nick Sharratt. DK, 2000. ISBN 978-0-7894-2667-3 Subj: Character traits – persistence. Family life – daughters. Family life – mothers. Food.

The "Get well soon" book ill. by Mary McQuillan. Millbrook, 2000. ISBN 978-0-7613-1922-1 Subj: Animals. Illness.

006 and a half ill. by Nick Sharratt. Abrams, 2007. ISBN 978-0-8109-1719-4 Subj: Behavior – secrets. Family life – daughters. Family life – mothers.

Gray, Luli. *Ant and Grasshopper* ill. by Giuliano Ferri. Simon & Schuster, 2011. ISBN 978-1-4169-5140-7 Subj: Activities – singing. Activities – working. Folk & fairy tales. Friendship. Insects – ants. Insects – grasshoppers. Seasons.

Gray, Nigel. *Time to play!* ill. by Bob Graham. Candlewick, 2008. ISBN 978-0-7636-4013-2 Subj: Activities – playing. Family life. Format, unusual – toy & movable books. Imagination.

Gray, Rita. *Nonna's porch* ill. by Terry Widener. Hyperion, 2004. ISBN 978-0-7868-1613-2 Subj: Country. Family life – grandmothers.

The wild little horse ill. by Ashley Wolff. Penguin, 2005. ISBN 978-0-525-47455-5 Subj: Animals – horses, ponies. Rhyming text.

Gray, Samantha. *Birds* by Samantha Gray and Sarah Walker ill. with photos. DK, 2002. ISBN 978-0-7894-8550-2 Subj: Birds.

Greathouse, Carol. *The dinosaur tamer* ill. by John Shroades. Dutton, 2009. ISBN 978-0-525-47866-9 Subj: Cowboys, cowgirls. Dinosaurs. Tall tales.

Gréban, Quentin. *Nestor* ill. by author. Mondo, 2001. ISBN 978-1-58653-855-2 Subj: Animals – babies. Animals – elephants. Animals – monkeys. Sports – fishing.

Green, Adolph. *What's new at the zoo?* (Comden, Betty)

Green, Alison. *The fox in the dark* ill. by Deborah Allwright. Tiger Tales, 2010. ISBN 978-1-58925-091-8 Subj: Animals. Emotions – fear.

Green, Dan. *Wild alphabet: an A to Zoo pop-up book* ill. by Mike Haines. Kingfisher, 2010. ISBN 978-0-7534-6472-4 Subj: ABC books. Animals. Format, unusual – toy & movable books.

Green, Emily K. *Bumblebees* ill. with photos. Scholastic, 2006. ISBN 978-0-531-17859-1 Subj: Insects – bees.

Crickets ill. with photos. Scholastic, 2006. ISBN 978-0-531-17861-4 Subj: Insects – crickets.

Grasshoppers ill. with photos. Scholastic, 2006. ISBN 978-0-531-17864-5 Subj: Insects – grasshoppers.

Walkingsticks ill. with photos. Scholastic, 2006. ISBN 978-0-531-17865-2 Subj: Insects.

Green, Jen. *Birds* ill. with photos. Copper Beech, 2000. ISBN 978-0-7613-1216-1 Subj: Birds.

Our new baby ill. by Christopher O'Neill. Copper Beech, 1998. ISBN 978-0-7613-0871-3 Subj: Babies. Family life – brothers & sisters.

Reptiles ill. with photos. Copper Beech, 2000. ISBN 978-0-7613-1214-7 Subj: Reptiles.

Green, Mim. *Time for a hug* (Gershator, Phillis)

Who's awake in springtime? (Gershator, Phillis)

Green, Stephanie. *Betsy Ross and the silver thimble* ill. by Diana Magnuson. Aladdin, 2002. ISBN 978-0-689-84967-1 Subj: Activities – sewing. Careers – tailors. Flags. U.S. history.

Not just another moose ill. by Andrea Wallace. Marshall Cavendish, 2000. ISBN 978-0-7614-5061-0 Subj: Animals – moose. Humorous stories. Self-concept.

Greenaway, Theresa. *Centipedes and millipedes* ill. by Dick Twinney and Stefan Chabluk; photos by Chris Fairclough. Raintree, 2000. ISBN 978-0-7398-1829-9 Subj: Crustaceans – centipedes, millipedes. Pets.

Greenberg, David. *Crocs!* ill. by Lynn Munsinger. Little, Brown, 2008. ISBN 978-0-316-07306-6 Subj: Humorous stories. Reptiles – alligators, crocodiles. Rhyming text.

Don't forget your etiquette! the essential guide to misbehavior ill. by Nadine Bernard Westcott. Farrar, 2006. ISBN 978-0-374-34990-5 Subj: Etiquette. Poetry.

Skunks ill. by Lynn Munsinger. Little, 2001. ISBN 978-0-316-32606-3 Subj: Animals – skunks. Rhyming text.

Greenberg, Jan. *Ballet for Martha: making Appalachian Spring* by Jan Greenberg and Sandra Jordan ill. by Brian Floca. Roaring Brook, 2010. ISBN 978-1-59643-338-0 Subj: Activities – dancing. Ballet. Music.

Greenberg, Melanie Hope. *Mermaids on parade* ill. by author. Putnam, 2008. ISBN 978-0-399-24708-8 Subj: Parades. Sea & seashore – beaches. Seasons – summer.

Greene, Carol. *Where is that cat?* ill. by Loretta Krupinski. Hyperion, 1999. ISBN 978-0-7868-2399-4 Subj: Animals – cats. Behavior – hiding.

Greene, Rhonda Gowler. *At grandma's* ill. by Karla Firehammer. Holt, 2003. ISBN 978-0-8050-6336-3 Subj: Family life – grandmothers. Rhyming text. Sleepovers.

Barnyard song ill. by Robert Bender. Atheneum, 1997. ISBN 978-0-689-80758-9 Subj: Animals. Farms. Illness. Noise, sounds. Rhyming text.

The beautiful world that God made ill. by Anne Wilson. Eerdmans, 2002. ISBN 978-0-8028-5213-7 Subj: Creation. Earth.

Daddy is a cozy hug ill. by Maggie Smith. Walker, 2010. ISBN 978-0-8027-9728-5 Subj: Family life – fathers. Rhyming text. Seasons.

Eek! Creak! Snicker, sneak ill. by Joseph A. Smith. Atheneum, 2002. ISBN 978-0-689-83047-1 Subj: Behavior – trickery. Emotions – fear. Monsters. Rhyming text.

Firebears: the rescue team ill. by Dan Andreasen. Holt, 2005. ISBN 978-0-8050-7010-1 Subj: Animals – bears. Careers – firefighters.

Jamboree day ill. by Jason Wolff. Orchard, 2001. ISBN 978-0-439-29310-5 Subj: Animals. Jungle. Parties. Rhyming text.

Mommy is a soft, warm kiss ill. by Maggie Smith. Walker, 2010. ISBN 978-0-8027-9729-2 Subj: Family life – mothers. Rhyming text. Seasons.

No pirates allowed! said Library Lou ill. by Brian Ajhar. Sleeping Bear, 2013. ISBN 978-1-58536-796-2 Subj: Books, reading. Careers – librarians. Libraries. Pirates. Rhyming text.

Noah and the mighty ark ill. by Santiago Cohen. Zondervan, 2007. ISBN 978-0-310-71097-4 Subj: Animals. Boats, ships. Religion – Noah.

The stable where Jesus was born ill. by Susan Gaber. Atheneum, 1999. ISBN 978-0-689-81258-3 Subj: Holidays – Christmas. Religion – Nativity. Rhyming text.

The very first Thanksgiving Day ill. by Susan Gaber. Atheneum, 2002. ISBN 978-0-689-83301-4 Subj: Holidays – Thanksgiving. Pilgrims. Rhyming text. U.S. history.

Greene, Sheppard M. *We all sing with the same voice* (Miller, J. Philip)

Greenfield, Eloise. *Angels* ill. by Jan Spivey Gilchrist. Jump at the Sun, 1998. ISBN 978-0-7868-0442-9 Subj: Angels. Ethnic groups in the U.S. – African Americans. Poetry.

Big friend, little friend ill. by Jan Spivey Gilchrist. Black Butterfly, 1991. ISBN 978-0-86316-204-6 Subj: Activities – playing. Ethnic groups in the U.S. – African Americans. Format, unusual – board books. Friendship. Poetry.

Brothers and sisters: family poems ill. by Jan Spivey Gilchrist. HarperCollins, 2009. ISBN 978-0-06-056284-7 Subj: Ethnic groups in the U.S. – African Americans. Family life – brothers & sisters. Poetry.

Daydreamers ill. by Tom Feelings. Dial, 1981. ISBN 978-0-8037-2134-0 Subj: Ethnic groups in the U.S. – African Americans. Poetry.

Easter parade ill. by Jan Spivey Gilchrist. Hyperion, 1997. ISBN 978-0-7868-0326-2 Subj: Ethnic groups in the U.S. – African Americans. Family life – cousins. Holidays – Easter. Parades. U.S. history. War.

First pink light ill. by Moneta Barnett. Crowell, 1976. ISBN 978-0-690-01087-9 Subj: Ethnic groups in the U.S. – African Americans. Family life – fathers.

The friendly four ill. by Jan Spivey Gilchrist. HarperCollins, 2006. ISBN 978-0-06-000760-7 Subj: Activities – playing. Imagination. Poetry.

Grandpa's face ill. by Floyd Cooper. Putnam, 1988. ISBN 978-0-399-21525-4 Subj: Character traits – appearance. Family life – grandfathers.

I can draw a weeposaur and other dinosaurs ill. by Jan Spivey Gilchrist. Greenwillow, 2001. ISBN 978-0-688-17635-8 Subj: Dinosaurs. Imagination. Mythical creatures. Poetry.

I make music ill. by Jan Spivey Gilchrist. Black Butterfly, 1991. ISBN 978-0-86316-205-3 Subj: Ethnic groups in the U.S. – African Americans. Family life. Format, unusual – board books. Music. Poetry.

In the land of words ill. by Jan Spivey Gilchrist. HarperCollins, 2004. ISBN 978-0-06-028994-2 Subj: Poetry.

Me and Neesie ill. by Jan Spivey Gilchrist. HarperCollins, 2005. ISBN 978-0-06-000702-7 Subj: Ethnic groups in the U.S. – African Americans. Family life. Imagination – imaginary friends. School – first day.

My doll, Keshia ill. by Jan Spivey Gilchrist. Black Butterfly, 1991. ISBN 978-0-86316-203-9 Subj: Activities – playing. Ethnic groups in the U.S. – African Americans. Format, unusual – board books. Poetry. Toys – dolls.

Nathaniel talking ill. by Jan Spivey Gilchrist. Black Butterfly, 1988. ISBN 978-0-86316-200-8 Subj: Ethnic groups in the U.S. – African Americans. Poetry.

Night on Neighborhood Street ill. by Jan Spivey Gilchrist. Dial, 1991. ISBN 978-0-8037-0778-8 Subj: Cities, towns. Communities, neighborhoods. Ethnic groups in the U.S. – African Americans. Night. Poetry.

Water, water ill. by Jan Spivey Gilchrist. HarperCollins, 1999. ISBN 978-0-694-01247-3 Subj: Ethnic groups in the U.S. – African Americans. Rhyming text. Water.

Greenfield, Howard. *Waking up is hard to do* (Sedaka, Neil)

Greenfield, Monica. *Waiting for Christmas* ill. by Jan Spivey Gilchrist. Scholastic, 1996. ISBN 978-0-590-52700-2 Subj: Ethnic groups in the U.S. – African Americans. Family life. Holidays – Christmas.

Greenstein, Elaine. *As big as you* ill. by author. Knopf, 2002. ISBN 978-0-375-91353-2 Subj: Babies. Behavior – growing up. Family life – mothers. Seasons.

Dreaming: a countdown to sleep ill. by author. Scholastic, 2000. ISBN 978-0-439-06302-9 Subj: Bedtime. Counting, numbers.

The goose man: the story of Konrad Lorenz ill. by author. Clarion, 2010. ISBN 978-0-547-08459-6 Subj: Birds – geese. Careers – scientists. Foreign lands – Austria. Science.

Greenwood, Mark. *Drummer boy of John John* ill. by Frané Lessac. Lee & Low, 2012. ISBN 978-1-60060-652-6 Subj: Fairs, festivals. Foreign lands – Trinidad. Musical instruments – drums.

Greenwood, Rosie. *I wonder why volcanoes blow their tops* ill. by author. Kingfisher, 2004. ISBN 978-0-7534-5751-1 Subj: Science. Volcanoes.

Gregorowski, Christopher. *Fly, eagle, fly! an African fable* ill. by Niki Daly. McElderry, 2000. ISBN 978-0-689-82398-5 Subj: Activities – flying. Birds – eagles. Folk & fairy tales. Foreign lands – Africa. Self-concept.

Gregory, Nan. *Amber waiting* ill. by Kady MacDonald Denton. Red Deer, 2003. ISBN 978-0-88995-258-4 Subj: Behavior – promptness, tardiness. School. Time.

How Smudge came ill. by Ron Lightburn. Walker, 1997. ISBN 978-0-88995-143-3 Subj: Animals – dogs. Character traits – loyalty. Disabilities – Down syndrome. Pets.

Pink ill. by author. Groundwood, 2007. ISBN 978-0-88899-781-4 Subj: Behavior – greed. Concepts – color. Family life.

Wild Girl and Gran ill. by Ron Lightburn. Red Deer, 2000. ISBN 978-0-88995-221-8 Subj: Death. Emotions – grief. Family life – grandmothers. Foreign lands – Canada. Friendship. Imagination.

Gretz, Susanna. *Rabbit food* ill. by author. Candlewick, 1999. ISBN 978-0-7636-0731-9 Subj: Animals – rabbits. Family life – aunts, uncles. Food.

Riley and Rose in the picture ill. by author. Candlewick, 2005. ISBN 978-0-7636-2681-5 Subj: Activities – drawing. Animals – cats. Animals – dogs. Behavior – fighting, arguing. Friendship.

Teddy bears cure a cold by Susanna Gretz and Alison Sage ill. by Susanna Gretz. Four Winds, 1985. ISBN 978-0-590-07949-5 Subj: Illness. Toys – bears.

Grey, Mini. *The adventures of the dish and the spoon* ill. by author. Random House, 2006. ISBN 978-0-375-93691-3 Subj: Crime. Humorous stories. Nursery rhymes.

Ginger bear ill. by author. Random House, 2007. ISBN 978-0-375-84253-5 Subj: Activities – baking, cooking. Emotions – loneliness. Food. Friendship.

Three by the sea ill. by author. Random House, 2011. ISBN 978-0-375-86784-2 Subj: Animals. Character traits – cooperation. Friendship.

Toys in space ill. by author. Knopf, 2013. ISBN 978-0-307-97812-7 Subj: Activities – storytelling. Night. Toys. Toys – dolls.

Traction Man and the beach odyssey ill. by author. Knopf, 2012. ISBN 978-0-375-86952-5 Subj: Sea & seashore – beaches. Toys.

Traction Man is here ill. by author. Knopf, 2005. ISBN 978-0-375-93191-8 Subj: Clothing – costumes. Family life. Toys.

Traction Man meets Turbodog ill. by author. Knopf, 2008. ISBN 978-0-375-85583-2 Subj: Behavior – lost & found possessions. Imagination. Toys.

The very smart pea and the princess-to-be ill. by author. Knopf, 2003. ISBN 978-0-375-92626-6 Subj: Folk & fairy tales. Plants. Royalty – princesses. Sleep.

Griessman, Annette. *The fire* ill. by Leonid Gore. Penguin, 2005. ISBN 978-0-399-24019-5 Subj: Ethnic groups in the U.S. – Hispanic Americans. Family life. Fire.

Like a hundred drums ill. by Julie Monks. Houghton, 2006. ISBN 978-0-618-55878-0 Subj: Animals. Family life – grandmothers. Weather – lightning, thunder. Weather – storms.

Grifalconi, Ann. *Ain't nobody a stranger to me* ill. by Jerry Pinkney. Hyperion, 2007. ISBN 978-0-7868-1857-0 Subj: Character traits – freedom. Ethnic groups in the U.S. – African Americans. Family life – grandfathers. Slavery. U.S. history.

Tiny's hat ill. by author. HarperCollins, 1999. ISBN 978-0-06-027655-3 Subj: Clothing – hats. Emotions – grief. Ethnic groups in the U.S. – African Americans. Family life – fathers.

The village of round and square houses ill. by author. Little, 1986. ISBN 978-0-316-32862-3 Subj: Caldecott award honor books. Folk & fairy tales. Foreign lands – Africa. Volcanoes.

The village that vanished ill. by Kadir Nelson. Dial, 2002. ISBN 978-0-8037-2623-9 Subj: Behavior – hiding. Ethnic groups in the U.S. – African Americans. Foreign lands – Africa. Slavery.

Griff. *Shark-mad Stanley* ill. by author. Hyperion, 2000. ISBN 978-0-7868-0594-5 Subj: Fish – sharks. Imagination. Pets.

Griffin, Kitty. *Cowboy Sam and those confounded secrets* by Kitty Griffin and Kathy Combs ill. by Mike Wohnoutka. Clarion, 2001. ISBN 978-0-618-08854-6 Subj: Behavior – secrets. Humorous stories. U.S. history – frontier & pioneer life.

The foot-stomping adventures of Clementine Sweet by Kitty Griffin and Kathy Combs ill. by Mike Wohnoutka. Clarion, 2004. ISBN 978-0-618-24746-2 Subj: Behavior. Humorous stories. Tall tales. Weather – tornadoes.

The ride: the legend of Betsy Dowdy ill. by Marjorie Priceman. Simon & Schuster, 2010. ISBN 978-1-4169-2816-4 Subj: Character traits – bravery. U.S. history.

Griffin, Molly Beth. *Loon baby* ill. by Anne Hunter. Houghton Mifflin, 2011. ISBN 978-0-547-25487-6 Subj: Behavior – worrying. Birds – loons.

Griffith, Helen V. *Moonlight* ill. by Laura Dronzek. HarperCollins, 2012. ISBN 978-0-06-203285-0 Subj: Animals – rabbits. Bedtime. Moon. Rhyming text.

Grigsby, Susan. *First peas to the table: how Thomas Jefferson inspired a school garden* ill. by Nicole Tadgell. Whitman, 2012. ISBN 978-0-8075-2452-7 Subj: Contests. Food. Gardens, gardening. School. U.S. history.

In the garden with Dr. Carver ill. by Nicole Tadgell. Whitman, 2010. ISBN 978-0-8075-3630-8 Subj: Ethnic groups in the U.S. – African Americans. Gardens, gardening. Plants. School. U.S. history.

Grimes, Nikki. *At break of day* ill. by Paul Morin. Eerdmans, 1995. ISBN 978-0-8028-5104-8 Subj: Creation. Religion.

Barack Obama: son of promise, child of hope ill. by Bryan Collier. Simon & Schuster, 2008. ISBN 978-1-4169-7144-3 Subj: Ethnic groups in the U.S. – African Americans. U.S. history.

Danitra Brown, class clown ill. by E. B. Lewis. HarperCollins, 2005. ISBN 978-0-688-17290-9 Subj: Ethnic groups in the U.S. – African Americans. Friendship. Poetry. School.

Minnie's new friend ill. by Peter Emslie and Darren Hunt. Western, 1992. ISBN 978-0-307-11524-9 Subj: Animals. Friendship.

A pocketful of poems ill. by Javaka Steptoe. Clarion, 2001. ISBN 978-0-395-93868-3 Subj: Cities, towns. Nature. Poetry.

Shoe magic ill. by Terry Widener. Orchard, 2000. ISBN 978-0-531-33286-3 Subj: Clothing – shoes. Poetry.

Voices of Christmas ill. by Eric Velasquez. Zondervan, 2009. ISBN 978-0-310-71192-6 Subj: Holidays – Christmas. Poetry. Religion – Nativity.

Welcome, Precious ill. by Bryan Collier. Scholastic, 2006. ISBN 978-0-439-55702-3 Subj: Babies. Ethnic groups in the U.S. – African Americans.

When Daddy prays ill. by Tim Ladwig. Eerdmans, 2002. ISBN 978-0-8028-5152-9 Subj: Ethnic groups in the U.S. – African Americans. Family life – fathers. Poetry. Religion.

When Gorilla goes walking ill. by Shane W. Evans. Scholastic, 2007. ISBN 978-0-439-31770-2 Subj: Animals – cats. Ethnic groups in the U.S. – African Americans. Friendship. Pets. Poetry.

Grimm, Edward. *The doorman* ill. by Ted Lewin. Orchard, 2000. ISBN 978-0-531-33280-1 Subj: Careers – doormen. Death. Emotions – grief. Homes, houses.

Grimm, Jacob and Wilhelm. *As luck would have it: from the Brothers Grimm* ill. by Daniel San Souci. August House, 2008. ISBN 978-0-87483-833-6 Subj: Animals – bears. Folk & fairy tales. Foreign lands – Germany. Humorous stories.

Battle of the beasts: a tale of epic proportions from the brothers Grimm retold by Diz Wallis; ill. by reteller. Ragged Bears, 2000. ISBN 978-1-929927-15-9 Subj: Animals. Behavior – fighting, arguing. Birds. Folk & fairy tales.

The brave little tailor retold by Olga Dugina; retold by Andrej Dugin; ill. by authors. Abrams, 2000. ISBN 978-0-8109-4113-7 Subj: Careers – tailors. Character traits – bravery. Folk & fairy tales. Foreign lands – Germany. Giants.

The brave little tailor retold by Eric Blair; ill. by David Shaw. Picture Window, 2004. ISBN 978-1-4048-0315-2 Subj: Careers – tailors. Character traits – bravery. Folk & fairy tales. Foreign lands – Germany. Giants.

The Bremen town band retold by Brian Wildsmith; ill. by reteller. Oxford Univ. Pr., 1999. ISBN 978-0-19-279034-7 Subj: Animals. Careers – musicians. Crime. Folk & fairy tales. Old age.

The Bremen town musicians retold by Eric Blair; ill. by Bill Dickson. Picture Window, 2004. ISBN 978-1-4048-0310-7 Subj: Animals. Careers – musicians. Crime. Folk & fairy tales. Old age.

The Bremen town musicians retold by Ilse Plume; ill. by reteller. Doubleday, 1980. ISBN 978-0-385-15162-7 Subj: Animals. Careers – musicians. Crime. Folk & fairy tales. Old age.

The Bremen town musicians ill. by Bernadette Watts. NorthSouth, 1992. ISBN 978-1-55858-148-7 Subj: Animals. Careers – musicians. Crime. Folk & fairy tales. Old age.

The Bremen town musicians ill. by Lisbeth Zwerger. Penguin, 2007. ISBN 978-0-698-40042-9 Subj: Animals. Careers – musicians. Crime. Folk & fairy tales. Old age.

Doctor All-Knowing: a folk tale from the Brothers Grimm retold by Doris Orgel; ill. by Alexandra Boiger. Atheneum, 2008. ISBN 978-1-4169-1246-0 Subj: Careers – doctors. Folk & fairy tales. Poverty.

The elves and the shoemaker retold by John Cech; ill. by Kirill Chelushkin. Sterling, 2007. ISBN 978-1-4027-3067-2 Subj: Careers – shoemakers. Character traits – helpfulness. Folk & fairy tales. Foreign lands – Germany. Mythical creatures – elves.

The elves and the shoemaker ill. by Paul Galdone. Clarion, 1984. ISBN 978-0-89919-226-0 Subj: Careers – shoemakers. Character traits – helpfulness. Folk & fairy tales. Foreign lands – Germany. Mythical creatures – elves.

The elves and the shoemaker ill. by Margaret Walty. Barefoot, 1998. ISBN 978-1-901223-69-9 Subj: Careers – shoemakers. Character traits – helpfulness. Folk & fairy tales. Foreign lands – Germany. Mythical creatures – elves.

The fisherman and his wife retold by Rosemary Wells; ill. by Eleanor Hubbard. Dial, 1998. ISBN 978-0-8037-1851-7 Subj: Animals – cats. Behavior – greed. Folk & fairy tales.

The fisherman and his wife retold by Rachel Isadora; ill. by reteller. Putnam, 2008. ISBN 978-0-399-24771-2 Subj: Behavior – greed. Folk & fairy tales. Foreign lands – Africa.

The fisherman and his wife retold by Eric Blair; ill. by Todd Ouren. Picture Window, 2004. ISBN 978-1-4048-0317-6 Subj: Behavior – greed. Folk & fairy tales.

The fisherman and the turtle adapt. by Eric A. Kimmel; ill. by Martha Avilés. Marshall Cavendish, 2008. ISBN 978-0-7614-5387-1 Subj: Behavior – greed. Folk & fairy tales. Foreign lands – Mexico.

The frog prince retold by Kathy-Jo Wargin; ill. by Anne Yvonne Gilbert. Mitten, 2007. ISBN 978-1-58726-279-1 Subj: Folk & fairy tales. Frogs & toads. Kissing. Royalty – princes. Royalty – princesses.

The frog prince retold by Eric Blair; ill. by Todd Ouren. Picture Window, 2004. ISBN 978-1-4048-0313-8 Subj: Folk & fairy tales. Frogs & toads. Royalty – princes. Royalty – princesses.

The glass mountain adapt. by Diane Wolkstein; ill. by Louisa Bauer. Morrow, 1999. ISBN 978-0-688-14848-5 Subj: Folk & fairy tales. Mythical creatures – trolls.

The golden goose retold by Dennis McDermott; ill. by reteller. Morrow, 2000. ISBN 978-0-688-11403-

9 Subj: Behavior – greed. Birds – geese. Character traits – kindness. Folk & fairy tales. Royalty – princesses.

The goose girl: a story from the Brothers Grimm retold by Eric A. Kimmel; ill. by Robert Sauber. Holiday, 1995. ISBN 978-0-8234-1074-3 Subj: Folk & fairy tales. Royalty. Weddings.

Hans my hedgehog: a tale from the Brothers Grimm by Kate Coombs; ill. by John Nickle. Atheneum, 2012. ISBN 978-1-4169-1533-1 Subj: Animals – hedgehogs. Folk & fairy tales. Foreign lands – Germany. Music. Royalty.

Hansel and Gretel retold by Cynthia Rylant; ill. by Jen Corace. Hyperion, 2008. ISBN 978-1-4231-1186-3 Subj: Behavior – lost. Folk & fairy tales. Forest, woods. Witches.

Hansel and Gretel retold by Rachel Isadora; ill. by reteller. Putnam, 2009. ISBN 978-0-399-25028-6 Subj: Behavior – lost. Folk & fairy tales. Foreign lands – Africa. Forest, woods. Witches.

Hansel and Gretel retold by Amy Ehrlich; ill. by Susan Jeffers. Penguin, 2011. ISBN 978-0-525-42221-1 Subj: Behavior – lost. Folk & fairy tales. Forest, woods. Witches.

Hansel and Gretel ill. by Susan Jeffers. Dial, 1980. ISBN 978-0-8037-3491-3 Subj: Behavior – lost. Folk & fairy tales. Forest, woods. Witches.

Hansel and Gretel retold by Jane Ray; ill. by reteller. Candlewick, 1997. ISBN 978-0-7636-0358-8 Subj: Behavior – lost. Folk & fairy tales. Forest, woods. Witches.

Hansel and Gretel retold by Eric Blair; ill. by Claudia Wolf. Picture Window, 2004. ISBN 978-1-4048-0316-9 Subj: Behavior – lost. Folk & fairy tales. Forest, woods. Witches.

Hansel and Gretel retold by Rika Lesser; ill. by Paul O. Zelinsky. Dodd, 1984. ISBN 978-0-396-08449-5 Subj: Behavior – lost. Caldecott award honor books. Folk & fairy tales. Forest, woods. Witches.

Hansel and Gretel ill. by Lisbeth Zwerger. Morrow, 1980. ISBN 978-0-688-32198-7 Subj: Behavior – lost. Folk & fairy tales. Forest, woods. Witches.

Hansel and Gretel / Hansel y Gretel adapt. by Elisabet Abeya; ill. by Cristina Losantos. Chronicle, 2005. ISBN 978-0-8118-4793-3 Subj: Behavior – lost. Folk & fairy tales. Foreign languages. Forest, woods. Witches.

Hansel and Gretel: a retelling from the original tale by the Brothers Grimm retold by Will Moses; ill. by reteller. Penguin, 2006. ISBN 978-0-399-24234-2 Subj: Behavior – lost. Folk & fairy tales. Forest, woods. Witches.

Iron John adapt. by Eric A. Kimmel; ill. by Trina Schart Hyman. Holiday, 1994. ISBN 978-0-8234-1073-6 Subj: Folk & fairy tales. Foreign lands – Germany. Royalty – kings. Royalty – princes.

Iron John retold by Marianna Mayer; ill. by Winslow Pels. Morrow, 1998. ISBN 978-0-688-11555-5 Subj: Folk & fairy tales. Foreign lands – Germany. Royalty – kings. Royalty – princes.

Jorinda and Jorindel retold by Bernadette Watts; ill. by reteller. NorthSouth, 2005. ISBN 978-0-7358-1987-0 Subj: Folk & fairy tales. Witches.

Little red cap ill. by Lisbeth Zwerger. Morrow, 1983. ISBN 978-0-688-01715-6 Subj: Animals – wolves. Behavior – talking to strangers. Folk & fairy tales.

Little Red Riding Hood retold by Lari Don; ill. by Célia Chauffrey. Barefoot, 2012. ISBN 978-1-84686-766-8 Subj: Animals – wolves. Behavior – talking to strangers. Folk & fairy tales.

Little Red Riding Hood retold by Margaret Hillert; ill. by Gwen Connelly. Follett, 1982. ISBN 978-0-695-41543-3 Subj: Animals – wolves. Behavior – talking to strangers. Folk & fairy tales.

Little Red Riding Hood retold by Trina Schart Hyman; ill. by reteller. Holiday, 1983. ISBN 978-0-8234-0470-4 Subj: Animals – wolves. Behavior – talking to strangers. Caldecott award honor books. Folk & fairy tales.

Little Red Riding Hood retold by Jerry Pinkney; ill. by reteller. Little, Brown, 2007. ISBN 978-0-316-01355-0 Subj: Animals – wolves. Behavior – talking to strangers. Folk & fairy tales.

Little Red Riding Hood adapt. by Gennady Spirin; ill. by adapter. Marshall Cavendish, 2010. ISBN 978-0-7614-5704-6 Subj: Animals – wolves. Behavior – talking to strangers. Folk & fairy tales.

Little Red Riding Hood ill. by Bernadette Watts. NorthSouth, 2009. ISBN 978-0-7358-2256-6 Subj: Animals – wolves. Behavior – talking to strangers. Folk & fairy tales.

Little Red Riding Hood retold by Andrea Wisnewski; ill. by reteller. Godine, 2007. ISBN 978-1-56792-303-2 Subj: Animals – wolves. Behavior – talking to strangers. Folk & fairy tales.

Musicians of Bremen retold by Niroot Puttapipat; ill. by reteller. Candlewick, 2005. ISBN 978-0-7636-2758-4 Subj: Animals. Careers – musicians. Crime. Folk & fairy tales. Old age.

Musicians of Bremen / Los musicos de Bremner: a bilingual book adapt. by Roser Ros; ill. by Pep Montserrat. Chronicle, 2005. ISBN 978-0-8118-4795-7 Subj: Animals. Careers – musicians. Crime. Folk & fairy tales. Foreign languages. Old age.

The rabbit's bride retold by Holly Meade; ill. by reteller. Marshall Cavendish, 2001. ISBN 978-0-7614-5081-8 Subj: Animals – rabbits. Character traits – cleverness. Folk & fairy tales. Foreign lands – Germany.

Rapunzel adapt. by Allison Sage; ill. by Sarah Gibb. Whitman, 2011. ISBN 978-0-8075-6804-0 Subj: Folk & fairy tales. Hair. Royalty – princes. Witches.

Rapunzel retold by Barbara Rogasky; ill. by Trina Schart Hyman. Holiday, 1982. ISBN 978-0-8234-0454-4 Subj: Folk & fairy tales. Hair. Royalty – princes. Witches.

Rapunzel retold by Rachel Isadora; ill. by reteller. Putnam, 2008. ISBN 978-0-399-24772-9 Subj: Folk & fairy tales. Foreign lands – Africa. Hair. Royalty – princes. Witches.

Rapunzel adapt. by Francesc Bofill; ill. by Joma. Chronicle, 2006. ISBN 978-0-8118-5059-9 Subj: Folk & fairy tales. Hair. Royalty – princes. Witches.

Rapunzel retold by Amy Ehrlich; ill. by Kris Waldherr. Dial, 1989. ISBN 978-0-8037-0655-2 Subj: Folk & fairy tales. Hair. Royalty – princes. Witches.

Rapunzel retold by Paul O. Zelinsky; ill. by reteller. Dutton, 1997. ISBN 978-0-525-45607-0 Subj: Caldecott award books. Folk & fairy tales. Hair. Royalty – princes. Witches.

Rapunzel: a fairy tale ill. by Maja Dusíková. NorthSouth, 1997. ISBN 978-1-55858-685-7 Subj: Folk & fairy tales. Hair. Royalty – princes. Witches.

Rose Red and the bear prince adapt. by Dan Andreasen; ill. by adapter. HarperCollins, 2000. ISBN 978-0-06-027967-7 Subj: Animals – bears. Dwarfs, midgets. Folk & fairy tales. Magic. Royalty – princes.

Rumpelstiltskin adapt. by Paul Galdone; ill. by adapter. Houghton, 1985. ISBN 978-0-89919-266-6 Subj: Folk & fairy tales. Magic. Riddles & jokes. Royalty. Weddings.

Rumpelstiltskin retold by Eric Blair; ill. by David Shaw. Picture Window, 2004. ISBN 978-1-4048-0311-4 Subj: Folk & fairy tales. Magic. Riddles & jokes. Royalty. Weddings.

Rumpelstiltskin adapt. by Paul O. Zelinsky; ill. by adapter. Dutton, 1986. ISBN 978-0-525-44265-3 Subj: Folk & fairy tales. Magic. Riddles & jokes. Royalty. Weddings.

Seven at one blow: a tale from the Brothers Grimm retold by Eric A. Kimmel; ill. by Megan Lloyd. Holiday, 1998. ISBN 978-0-8234-1383-6 Subj: Careers – tailors. Character traits – bravery. Folk & fairy tales. Foreign lands – Germany. Giants.

The shoemaker and his elves retold by Eric Blair; ill. by Bill Dickson. Picture Window, 2004. ISBN 978-1-4048-0314-5 Subj: Careers – shoemakers. Character traits – helpfulness. Folk & fairy tales. Foreign lands – Germany. Mythical creatures – elves.

The shoemaker and the elves ill. by Adrienne Adams. Macmillan, 1972. ISBN 978-0-684-12982-2 Subj: Careers – shoemakers. Character traits – helpfulness. Folk & fairy tales. Foreign lands – Germany. Mythical creatures – elves.

The shoemaker and the elves retold by Ilse Plume; ill. by reteller. Harcourt, 1991. ISBN 978-0-15-274050-4 Subj: Careers – shoemakers. Character traits – helpfulness. Folk & fairy tales. Foreign lands – Germany. Mythical creatures – elves.

The six swans retold by Robert D. San Souci; ill. by Daniel San Souci. Simon & Schuster, 1989. ISBN 978-0-671-65848-9 Subj: Birds – swans. Family life – brothers & sisters. Folk & fairy tales. Magic.

Sleeping Beauty ill. by Maja Dusíková. NorthSouth, 2012. ISBN 978-0-7358-4087-4 Subj: Fairies. Folk & fairy tales. Royalty – princes. Royalty – princesses. Sleep.

The sleeping beauty retold by Trina Schart Hyman; ill. by reteller. Little, 1977. ISBN 978-0-316-38702-6 Subj: Fairies. Folk & fairy tales. Royalty – princes. Royalty – princesses. Sleep. Witches.

Snow White retold by Melinda Copper; ill. by reteller. Penguin, 2005. ISBN 978-0-525-47474-6 Subj: Animals. Dwarfs, midgets. Emotions – envy, jealousy. Folk & fairy tales. Magic. Witches.

Snow White ill. by Quentin Gréban. NorthSouth, 2009. ISBN 978-0-7358-2257-3 Subj: Dwarfs, midgets. Emotions – envy, jealousy. Folk & fairy tales. Magic. Witches.

Snow White ill. by Trina Schart Hyman. Little, 1999, 1974. ISBN 978-0-316-35450-9 Subj: Dwarfs, midgets. Emotions – envy, jealousy. Folk & fairy tales. Magic. Witches.

Snow White ill. by Charles Santore. Sterling, 2010. ISBN 978-1-4027-7157-6 Subj: Dwarfs, midgets. Emotions – envy, jealousy. Folk & fairy tales. Magic.

Snow White and the seven dwarfs ill. by Wanda Gág. Coward, 1938. Subj: Caldecott award honor books. Dwarfs, midgets. Emotions – envy, jealousy. Folk & fairy tales. Magic. Weddings.

Snow White and the seven dwarfs retold by Laura Ljungkvist; ill. by reteller. Abrams, 2003. ISBN 978-0-8109-4241-7 Subj: Dwarfs, midgets. Emotions – envy, jealousy. Folk & fairy tales. Magic. Witches.

The star child adapt. by J. Alison James; ill. by Bernadette Watts. NorthSouth, 2010. ISBN 978-0-7358-2330-3 Subj: Behavior – sharing. Character traits – generosity. Folk & fairy tales. Stars.

The story of Little Red Riding Hood ill. by Christopher Bing. Chronicle, 2010. ISBN 978-0-8118-

6886-7 Subj: Animals – wolves. Behavior – talking to strangers. Folk & fairy tales.

The three spinning fairies retold by Lisa Campbell Ernst; ill. by reteller. Dutton, 2002. ISBN 978-0-525-46826-4 Subj: Character traits – laziness. Fairies. Folk & fairy tales. Foreign lands – Germany.

Twelve dancing princesses retold by Brigette Barrager; ill. by reteller. Chronicle, 2011. ISBN 978-0-8118-7696-4 Subj: Activities – dancing. Folk & fairy tales. Royalty – princesses.

The twelve dancing princesses retold by John Cech; ill. by Lucy Corvino. Sterling, 2009. ISBN 978-1-4027-4435-8 Subj: Activities – dancing. Folk & fairy tales. Royalty – princesses.

The twelve dancing princesses retold by Marianna Mayer; ill. by Kinuko Y. Craft. Morrow, 1989. ISBN 978-0-688-02026-2 Subj: Activities – dancing. Folk & fairy tales. Royalty – princesses.

The twelve dancing princesses ill. by Rachel Isadora. Penguin, 2007. ISBN 978-0-399-24744-6 Subj: Activities – dancing. Folk & fairy tales. Foreign lands – Africa. Royalty – princesses.

The twelve dancing princesses retold by Marianna Mayer; ill. by Gerald McDermott. Morrow, 1988. Subj: Activities – dancing. Folk & fairy tales. Royalty – princesses.

The twelve dancing princesses retold by Jane Ray; ill. by reteller. Dutton, 1996. ISBN 978-0-525-45595-0 Subj: Activities – dancing. Folk & fairy tales. Royalty – princesses.

The twelve dancing princesses retold by Suçie Stevenson; ill. by reteller. Yearling, 1995. ISBN 978-0-385-32167-9 Subj: Activities – dancing. Folk & fairy tales. Royalty – princesses.

The twelve princesses retold by Gordon Fitchett; ill. by reteller. Fogelman, 2000. ISBN 978-0-8037-2474-7 Subj: Activities – dancing. Birds – ducks. Folk & fairy tales. Royalty – princesses.

The water of life adapt. by Barbara Rogasky; ill. by Trina Schart Hyman. Holiday, 1986. ISBN 978-0-8234-0552-7 Subj: Character traits – pride. Folk & fairy tales. Magic. Royalty. Sibling rivalry.

Grindley, Sally. *Can we play too, Piglittle?* ill. by Andy Ellis. Barron's, 2000. ISBN 978-0-7641-1582-0 Subj: Activities – playing. Animals – pigs. Behavior – sharing. Character traits – selfishness.

The giant postman ill. by Wendy Smith. Kingfisher, 2000. ISBN 978-0-7534-5319-3 Subj: Careers – postal workers. Concepts – size. Friendship.

It's my school ill. by Margaret Chamberlain. Walker, 2006. ISBN 978-0-8027-8086-7 Subj: Family life – brothers & sisters. School – first day.

Little Elephant Thunderfoot ill. by John Butler. Peachtree, 1999. ISBN 978-1-56145-180-7 Subj: Animals – babies. Animals – elephants.

Mucky Duck ill. by Neal Layton. Bloomsbury, 2003. ISBN 978-1-58234-821-6 Subj: Activities. Birds – ducks. Character traits – cleanliness.

A new room for William ill. by Carol Thompson. Candlewick, 2000. ISBN 978-0-7636-1196-5 Subj: Divorce. Family life. Homes, houses. Moving.

Silly Goose and Dizzy Duck play hide-and-seek ill. by Adrian Reynolds. DK, 1999. ISBN 978-0-7894-4844-6 Subj: Animals – foxes. Birds – ducks. Birds – geese. Games.

The sorcerer's apprentice ill. by Thomas Taylor. Fogelman, 2002. ISBN 978-0-8037-2726-7 Subj: Folk & fairy tales. Magic.

The sulky vulture ill. by Michael Terry. Bloomsbury, 2003. ISBN 978-1-58234-794-3 Subj: Behavior – bad day. Behavior – dissatisfaction. Birds – vultures.

What are friends for? ill. by Penny Dann. Kingfisher, 1998. ISBN 978-0-7534-5108-3 Subj: Animals – bears. Animals – foxes. Friendship.

What will I do without you? ill. by Penny Dann. Kingfisher, 1999. ISBN 978-0-7534-5110-6 Subj: Animals – bears. Animals – foxes. Animals – squirrels. Friendship. Hibernation. Seasons – winter.

Where are my chicks? ill. by Jill Newton. Fogelman, 1999. ISBN 978-0-8037-2497-6 Subj: Animals. Behavior – lost. Birds – chickens. Counting, numbers.

Who is it? ill. by Rosalind Beardshaw. Peachtree, 2000. ISBN 978-1-56145-224-8 Subj: Folk & fairy tales. Problem solving. Riddles & jokes.

Grist, Julie. *Flying, just plane fun* ill. by author. Spoonbender, 2003. ISBN 978-0-9725750-0-3 Subj: Activities – flying. Airplanes, airports. Family life – grandfathers.

Griswell, Kim T. *Rufus goes to school* ill. by Valeri Gorbachev. Sterling, 2013. ISBN 978-1-4549-0416-8 Subj: Animals – pigs. Books, reading. Careers – school principals. School.

Gritton, Steve. *The trouble with sisters and robots* ill. by author. Whitman, 2009. ISBN 978-0-8075-8090-5 Subj: Family life – sisters. Robots.

Grobler, Piet. *Hey, frog!* ill. by author. Front Street, 2002. ISBN 978-1-886910-84-3 Subj: Animals. Behavior – greed. Frogs & toads. Water.

Grogan, John. *Bad dog, Marley!* ill. by Richard Cowdrey. HarperCollins, 2007. ISBN 978-0-06-117114-7 Subj: Animals – dogs. Behavior – misbehavior.

Marley goes to school ill. by Richard Cowdrey. HarperCollins, 2009. ISBN 978-0-06-156151-1 Subj: Animals – dogs. School – first day.

Trick or treat, Marley! ill. by Richard Cowdrey. HarperCollins, 2011. ISBN 978-0-06-185755-3 Subj: Animals – dogs. Holidays – Halloween.

A very Marley Christmas ill. by Richard Cowdrey. HarperCollins, 2008. ISBN 978-0-06-137292-6 Subj: Animals – dogs. Holidays – Christmas.

Groner, Judyth Saypol. *My first Hebrew word book* ill. by Pepi Marzel. Kar-Ben, 2005. ISBN 978-1-58013-126-1 Subj: Foreign languages. Jewish culture. Language.

Grossman, Bill. *My little sister ate one hare* ill. by Kevin Hawkes. Crown, 1996. ISBN 978-0-517-59601-2 Subj: Counting, numbers. Rhyming text.

My little sister hugged an ape ill. by Kevin Hawkes. Knopf, 2004. ISBN 978-0-517-80018-8 Subj: ABC books. Emotions. Family life – sisters. Rhyming text.

Timothy Tunny swallowed a bunny ill. by Kevin Hawkes. Geringer, 2000. ISBN 978-0-06-028758-0 Subj: Humorous stories. Poetry.

Grossman, Patricia. *Saturday market* by Patricia Grossman and Enrique O. Sánchez ill. by Enrique O. Sánchez. Lothrop, 1994. ISBN 978-0-688-12177-8 Subj: Foreign lands – Mexico. Indians of North America – Zapotec. Shopping.

Grossman, Virginia. *Ten little rabbits* ill. by Sylvia Long. Chronicle, 1991. ISBN 978-0-87701-552-9 Subj: Animals – rabbits. Counting, numbers. Indians of North America. Rhyming text.

Grossmann-Hensel, Katharina. *Papa is a pirate* ill. by author. NorthSouth, 2009. ISBN 978-0-7358-2237-5 Subj: Family life – fathers. Pirates.

Groundhog at Evergreen Road ill. by Higgins Bond. Soundprints, 2003. ISBN 978-1-59249-022-6 Subj: Animals – groundhogs. Behavior – growing up. Homes, houses.

Grover, Jan Zitz. *A home for Dakota* ill. by Nancy Lane. Gryphon, 2008. ISBN 978-0-940719-05-7 Subj: Animals – dogs. Character traits – kindness to animals.

Grupper, Jonathan. *Destination — Rocky Mountains* ill. with photos. National Geographic, 2001. ISBN 978-0-7922-7722-4 Subj: Animals. Ecology. Mountains. Nature.

Destination, rain forest ill. with photos. National Geographic, 1997. ISBN 978-0-7922-7018-8 Subj: Ecology. Jungle. Nature.

Gruska, Denise. *The only boy in ballet class* ill. by Amy Wummer. Gibbs Smith, 2007. ISBN 978-1-4236-0220-0 Subj: Activities – dancing. Ballet. Prejudice. Sports – football.

Guarino, Deborah. *Is your mama a llama?* ill. by Steven Kellogg. Scholastic, 1989. ISBN 978-0-590-41387-9 Subj: Animals. Animals – llamas. Rhyming text.

Guarnaccia, Steven. *The three little pigs: an architectural tale* ill. by author. Abrams, 2010. ISBN 978-0-8109-8941-2 Subj: Animals – pigs. Animals – wolves. Careers – architects. Character traits – cleverness. Folk & fairy tales.

Guback, Georgia. *Luka's quilt* ill. by author. Greenwillow, 1994. ISBN 978-0-688-12155-6 Subj: Family life – grandmothers. Hawaii. Quilts.

Gudeon, Adam. *Me and Meow* ill. by author. HarperCollins, 2011. ISBN 978-0-06-199821-8 Subj: Activities – playing. Animals – cats.

Guenther, James. *Turnagain, Ptarmigan, where did you go?* ill. by Shannon Cartwright. Sasquatch, 2000. ISBN 978-1-57061-237-4 Subj: Alaska. Birds – ptarmigans. Rhyming text. Seasons.

Guest, C. Z. *Tiny green thumbs* ill. by Loretta Krupinski. Hyperion, 2000. ISBN 978-0-7868-0516-7 Subj: Animals – mice. Animals – rabbits. Family life – grandmothers. Gardens, gardening.

Guest, Elissa Haden. *Harriet's had enough!* ill. by Paul Meisel. Candlewick, 2009. ISBN 978-0-7636-3454-4 Subj: Animals – raccoons. Character traits – orderliness. Family life.

Gugler, Laurel Dee. *There's a billy goat in the garden* ill. by Clare Beaton. Barefoot, 2003. ISBN 978-1-84148-089-3 Subj: Animals. Animals – goats. Folk & fairy tales. Foreign lands – Puerto Rico. Insects – bees.

Guiberson, Brenda Z. *Cactus hotel* ill. by Megan Lloyd. Holt, 1991. ISBN 978-0-8050-1333-7 Subj: Desert. Ecology. Plants.

Earth: feeling the heat ill. by Chad Wallace. Holt, 2010. ISBN 978-0-8050-7719-3 Subj: Earth. Ecology. Weather.

The emperor lays an egg ill. by Joan Paley. Holt, 2001. ISBN 978-0-8050-6204-5 Subj: Birds – penguins. Family life.

Frog song ill. by Gennady Spirin. Holt, 2013. ISBN 978-0-8050-9254-7 Subj: Frogs & toads. Noise, sounds.

Ice bears ill. by Ilya Spirin. Holt, 2008. ISBN 978-0-8050-7607-3 Subj: Animals – polar bears. Foreign lands – Arctic.

Into the sea ill. by Alix Berenzy. Holt, 1996. ISBN 978-0-8050-2263-6 Subj: Nature. Reptiles – turtles, tortoises. Sea & seashore.

Moon bear ill. by Ed Young. Holt, 2010. ISBN 978-0-8050-8977-6 Subj: Animals – bears. Animals – endangered animals.

Mud city: a flamingo story ill. by author. Holt, 2005. ISBN 978-0-8050-7177-1 Subj: Birds – flamingos. Nature.

Guidone, Thea. *Drum city* ill. by Vanessa Brantley Newton. Tricycle, 2010. ISBN 978-1-58246-308-7 Subj: Musical instruments – drums. Parades. Rhyming text.

Guion, Melissa. *Baby penguins everywhere!* ill. by author. Philomel, 2012. ISBN 978-0-399-25535-9 Subj: Animals – babies. Behavior – solitude. Birds – penguins.

Gukova, Julia. *All mixed-up!* ill. by author. North-South, 2000. ISBN 978-0-7358-1300-7 Subj: Format, unusual – toy & movable books. Picture puzzles. Witches.

Gulbis, Stephen. *Cowgirl Rosie and her five baby bison* ill. by author. Little, 2001. ISBN 978-0-316-64712-0 Subj: Animals – babies. Animals – buffaloes. Behavior – lost & found possessions. Cowboys, cowgirls. Rhyming text.

Gundersheimer, Karen. *Find cat, wear hat* ill. by author. Scholastic, 1995. ISBN 978-0-590-48061-1 Subj: Activities – playing. Format, unusual – board books. Noise, sounds. Rhyming text. School.

Gunnufson, Charlotte. *Halloween hustle* ill. by Kevan Atteberry. Amazon/Two Lions, 2013. ISBN 978-1-4778-1723-0 Subj: Activities – dancing. Anatomy – skeletons. Holidays – Halloween. Monsters. Rhyming text.

Gunzi, Christiane. *Colors* ill. by author. Two-Can, 2001. ISBN 978-1-58728-236-2 Subj: Concepts – color.

Numbers ill. by author. Two-Can, 2001. ISBN 978-1-58728-237-9 Subj: Counting, numbers.

Shapes ill. by author. Two-Can, 2001. ISBN 978-1-58728-238-6 Subj: Concepts – shape.

Sizes ill. by author. Two-Can, 2001. ISBN 978-1-58728-239-3 Subj: Concepts – size.

Gurney, John Steven. *Dinosaur train* ill. by author. HarperCollins, 2002. ISBN 978-0-06-029246-1 Subj: Bedtime. Dinosaurs. Trains.

Gutch, Michael. *Sticky, sticky, stuck!* ill. by Steve Björkman. HarperCollins, 2013. ISBN 978-0-06-199818-8 Subj: Computers. Cumulative tales. Family life.

Guthrie, James. *Last song* ill. by Eric Rohmann. Roaring Brook, 2010. ISBN 978-1-59643-508-7 Subj: Animals – squirrels. Bedtime. Lullabies. Poetry.

Guthrie, Woody. *Bling blang* ill. by Vladimir Radunsky. Candlewick, 2000. ISBN 978-0-7636-0769-2 Subj: Homes, houses. Music. Songs.

My dolly ill. by Vladimir Radunsky. Candlewick, 2001. ISBN 978-0-7636-0770-8 Subj: Music. Songs. Toys – dolls.

This land is your land ill. by Kathy Jakobsen. With a tribute by Pete Seeger. Little, 1998. ISBN 978-0-316-39215-0 Subj: Music. Songs.

Gutierrez, Akemi. *The mummy and other adventures of Sam and Alice* ill. by author. Houghton, 2005. ISBN 978-0-618-50761-0 Subj: Activities – playing. Family life – brothers & sisters.

Gutman, Anne. *Gaspard and Lisa, friends forever* by Anne Gutman and Georg Hallensleben ill. by Georg Hallensleben. Knopf, 2003. ISBN 978-0-375-82253-7 Subj: Animals – dogs. Friendship. School.

Gaspard and Lisa's Christmas surprise by Anne Gutman and Georg Hallensleben ill. by Georg Hallensleben. Knopf, 2002. ISBN 978-0-375-82229-2 Subj: Animals – dogs. Gifts. Holidays – Christmas.

Gaspard and Lisa's rainy day by Anne Gutman and Georg Hallensleben ill. by Georg Hallensleben. Knopf, 2003. ISBN 978-0-375-82252-0 Subj: Animals – dogs. Behavior – boredom. Behavior – misbehavior. Friendship. Weather – rain.

Gaspard at the seashore by Anne Gutman and Georg Hallensleben ill. by Georg Hallensleben. Knopf, 2002. ISBN 978-0-375-81118-0 Subj: Animals – dogs. Camps, camping. Sea & seashore. Sports – swimming.

Gaspard in the hospital by Anne Gutman and Georg Hallensleben ill. by Georg Hallensleben. Knopf, 2001. ISBN 978-0-375-81116-6 Subj: Animals – dogs. Hospitals.

Gaspard on vacation by Anne Gutman and Georg Hallensleben ill. by Georg Hallensleben. Knopf, 2001. ISBN 978-0-375-81115-9 Subj: Activities – vacationing. Animals – dogs. Boats, ships. Foreign lands – Italy.

Lisa in New York by Anne Gutman and Georg Hallensleben ill. by Georg Hallensleben. Knopf, 2002. ISBN 978-0-375-81119-7 Subj: Animals – dogs. Behavior – lost. Family life – aunts, uncles.

Lisa in the jungle by Anne Gutman and Georg Hallensleben ill. by Georg Hallensleben. Knopf, 2003. ISBN 978-0-375-82254-4 Subj: Animals – dogs. Character traits – honesty. Jungle. School.

Lisa's airplane trip by Anne Gutman and Georg Hallensleben ill. by Georg Hallensleben. Knopf, 2001. ISBN 978-0-375-81114-2 Subj: Activities – traveling. Airplanes, airports. Animals – dogs.

Lisa's baby sister by Anne Gutman and Georg Hallensleben ill. by Georg Hallensleben. Knopf, 2003. ISBN 978-0-375-82251-3 Subj: Animals – dogs. Babies. Behavior. Family life – new sibling. Family life – sisters.

Gutman, Dan. *Casey back at bat* ill. by Steve Johnson and Lou Fancher. HarperCollins, 2007. ISBN 978-0-06-056025-6 Subj: Poetry. Sports – baseball.

Guy, Ginger Foglesong. *¡Bravo!* ill. by Rene King Moreno. HarperCollins, 2010. ISBN 978-0-06-173180-8 Subj: Activities – playing. Foreign languages. Language.

Fiesta ill. by Rene King Moreno. Greenwillow, 1996. ISBN 978-0-688-14332-9 Subj: Counting, numbers. Fairs, festivals. Foreign lands – Mexico. Foreign languages.

My grandma / Mi abuelita ill. by Viví Escrivá. HarperCollins, 2007. ISBN 978-0-06-079098-1 Subj: Family life. Foreign languages.

My school / Mi escuela ill. by Viví Escrivá. HarperCollins, 2006. ISBN 978-0-06-079101-8 Subj: Foreign languages. School.

Perros! perros! dogs! dogs! a story in English and Spanish ill. by Sharon Glick. HarperCollins, 2006. ISBN 978-0-06-083574-3 Subj: Animals – dogs. Concepts – opposites. Foreign languages.

Siesta ill. by René King Moreno. HarperCollins, 2005. ISBN 978-0-06-056063-8 Subj: Family life – brothers & sisters. Foreign languages. Sleep. Toys – bears.

Gwynne, Fred. *A chocolate moose for dinner* ill. by author. Messner, 1981. ISBN 978-0-671-43706-0 Subj: Imagination. Language.

A little pigeon toad ill. by author. Simon & Schuster, 1988. ISBN 978-0-671-66659-0 Subj: Imagination. Language.

Haas, Irene. *Bess and Bella* ill. by author. Simon & Schuster, 2006. ISBN 978-1-4169-0013-9 Subj: Birds. Emotions – loneliness. Friendship.

Haas, Jessie. *Appaloosa zebra* ill. by Margot Apple. Greenwillow, 2002. ISBN 978-0-688-17881-9 Subj: ABC books. Animals – horses, ponies.

Hurry! ill. by Joseph A. Smith. Greenwillow, 2000. ISBN 978-0-688-16889-6 Subj: Careers – farmers. Family life – grandparents.

Haas, Rick de. *Peter and the seal* ill. by author. NorthSouth, 2012. ISBN 978-0-7358-4061-4 Subj: Animals – seals. Boats, ships. Sports – sailing.

Peter and the winter sleepers ill. by author. NorthSouth, 2011. ISBN 978-0-7358-4033-1 Subj: Animals. Lighthouses. Seasons – winter. Weather – blizzards.

Haber, Tiffany Strelitz. *The monster who lost his mean* ill. by Kirstie Edmunds. Holt, 2012. ISBN 978-0-8050-9375-9 Subj: Behavior – bullying, teasing. Monsters. Rhyming text. Self-concept.

Ollie and Claire ill. by Matthew Cordell. Philomel, 2013. ISBN 978-0-399-25603-5 Subj: Animals – dogs. Behavior – boredom. Friendship. Rhyming text.

Hächler, Bruno. *Anna's wish* ill. by Friederike Rave. NorthSouth, 2008. ISBN 978-0-7358-2207-8 Subj: Behavior – wishing. Holidays – Christmas. Weather – snow.

What does my teddy bear do all night? ill. by Birte Müller. Minedition, 2005. ISBN 978-0-698-40029-0 Subj: Bedtime. Rhyming text. Toys – bears.

Hacohen, Dean. *Tuck me in!* by Dean Hacohen and Sherry Scharschmidt ill. by Dean Hacohen. Candlewick, 2010. ISBN 978-0-7636-4728-5 Subj: Animals. Bedtime. Format, unusual – toy & movable books.

Hader, Berta Hoerner. *The big snow* by Berta Hoerner Hader and Elmer Hader ill. by authors. Macmillan, 1948. Subj: Caldecott award books. Weather – snow.

Cock-a-doodle doo: the story of a little red rooster by Berta Hoerner Hader and Elmer Hader ill. by authors. Macmillan, 1939. Subj: Birds – chickens. Birds – ducks. Caldecott award honor books. Farms.

The mighty hunter by Berta Hoerner Hader and Elmer Hader ill. by authors. Macmillan, 1943. Subj: Caldecott award honor books. Ecology. Indians of North America. School. Sports – hunting.

Hader, Elmer. *The big snow* (Hader, Berta Hoerner)

Cock-a-doodle doo: the story of a little red rooster (Hader, Berta Hoerner)

The mighty hunter (Hader, Berta Hoerner)

Hafner, Marylin. *Molly and Emmett's camping adventure* ill. by author. McGraw-Hill, 2001. ISBN 978-1-57768-894-5 Subj: Animals – cats. Camps, camping. Weather – rain.

Molly and Emmett's surprise garden ill. by author. McGraw-Hill, 2000. ISBN 978-1-57768-895-2 Subj: Animals – cats. Food. Gardens, gardening.

Hager, Sarah. *Dancing Matilda* ill. by Kelly Murphy. HarperCollins, 2005. ISBN 978-0-06-051453-2 Subj: Activities – dancing. Rhyming text.

Hague, Kathleen. *Alphabears: an ABC book* ill. by Michael Hague. Holt, 1984. Subj: ABC books. Rhyming text. Toys – bears.

Calendarbears: a book of months ill. by Michael Hague. Holt, 1997. ISBN 978-0-8050-3818-7 Subj: Animals – bears. Calendars. Days of the week, months of the year. Rhyming text.

Good night, fairies ill. by Michael Hague. SeaStar, 2002. ISBN 978-1-58717-134-5 Subj: Bedtime. Fairies. Family life – mothers.

Numbears: a counting book ill. by Michael Hague. Holt, 1986. ISBN 978-0-03-007194-2 Subj: Counting, numbers. Toys – bears.

Ten little bears: a counting rhyme ill. by Michael Hague. Morrow, 1999. ISBN 978-0-688-16383-9 Subj: Animals – bears. Counting, numbers. Rhyming text.

Hague, Michael, compiler. *Animal friends: a collection of poems for children* ill. by compiler. Holt, 2007. ISBN 978-0-8050-3817-0 Subj: Animals. Poetry.

The nutcracker text by Sarah L. Thomson; ill. by author. SeaStar, 2003. ISBN 978-1-58717-255-7 Subj: Activities – dancing. Animals – mice. Ballet. Careers – toy makers. Folk & fairy tales. Holidays – Christmas. Imagination. Royalty.

Teddy bear, teddy bear ill. by author. Morrow, 1993. ISBN 978-0-688-12085-6 Subj: Games. Nursery rhymes. Toys – bears.

Haines, Mike. *Countdown to bedtime* ill. by David Melling. Hyperion, 2001. ISBN 978-0-7868-0741-3 Subj: Animals – porcupines. Animals – raccoons. Bedtime. Format, unusual – toy & movable books.

Hakala, Marjorie Rose. *Mermaid dance* ill. by Mark Jones. Blue Apple, 2009. ISBN 978-1-934706-47-3 Subj: Mythical creatures – mermaids, mermen. Seasons – summer.

Haldeman, Oakley. *Here comes Santa Claus* (Autry, Gene)

Hale, Bruce. *Clark the Shark* ill. by Guy Francis. HarperCollins, 2013. ISBN 978-0-06-219226-4 Subj: Behavior – misbehavior. Fish – sharks. School.

Santa on the loose! ill. by David Garbot. HarperFestival, 2012. ISBN 978-0-06-202262-2 Subj: Holidays – Christmas. Picture puzzles. Santa Claus.

Snoring Beauty ill. by Howard Fine. Harcourt, 2008. ISBN 978-0-15-216314-3 Subj: Dragons. Folk & fairy tales. Humorous stories. Royalty – princesses.

Hale, Christy. *Dreaming up: a celebration of building* ill. by author. Lee & Low, 2012. ISBN 978-1-60060-651-9 Subj: Activities – playing. Art. Buildings.

Hale, Dean. *Scapegoat: the story of a goat named Oat and a chewed-up coat.* Bloomsbury, 2011. ISBN 978-1-59990-468-9 Subj: Animals – goats. Behavior – lying.

Hale, Nathan. *Yellowbelly and Plum go to school* ill. by author. Penguin, 2007. ISBN 978-0-399-24624-1 Subj: School – first day. Toys – bears.

Hale, Sarah Josepha Buell. *Mary had a little lamb* ill. by Tomie dePaola. Holiday, 1984. ISBN 978-0-8234-0509-1 Subj: Animals – sheep. Music. Nursery rhymes. School.

Mary had a little lamb ill. by Laura Huliska-Beith. Marshall Cavendish, 2011. ISBN 978-0-7614-5824-1 Subj: Animals – sheep. Music. Nursery rhymes. School.

Mary had a little lamb photos by Bruce McMillan. Scholastic, 1990. ISBN 978-0-590-43773-8 Subj: Animals – sheep. Music. Nursery rhymes. School.

Mary had a little lamb ill. by Salley Mavor. Orchard, 1995. ISBN 978-0-531-08725-1 Subj: Animals – sheep. Nursery rhymes. School.

Haley, Alex. *Young Martin's promise* (Myers, Walter Dean)

Haley, Amanda. *It's a baby's world* ill. by author. Little, 2001. ISBN 978-0-316-34596-5 Subj: Activities. Babies. Day.

Haley, Gail E. *A story, a story* ill. by author. Aladdin, 1988, ©1970. ISBN 978-0-689-71201-2 Subj: Caldecott award books. Folk & fairy tales. Foreign lands – Africa.

Two bad boys: a very old Cherokee tale ill. by author. Dutton, 1996. ISBN 978-0-525-45311-6 Subj: Activities – working. Creation. Indians of North America – Cherokee.

Halfmann, Janet. *Eggs 1, 2, 3: who will the babies be?* ill. by Betsy Thompson. Blue Apple, 2012. ISBN 978-1-60905-191-4 Subj: Animals – babies. Counting, numbers. Eggs. Format, unusual.

Hall, Algy Craig. *Dino bites!* ill. by author. Boxer Books, 2013. ISBN 978-1-907967-50-4 Subj: Concepts – size. Cumulative tales. Dinosaurs. Rhyming text.

Fine as we are ill. by author. Boxer, 2008. ISBN 978-1-905417-72-8 Subj: Family life – new sibling. Frogs & toads. Sibling rivalry.

Mammoth and me ill. by author. Sterling, 2012. ISBN 978-1-9079-6722-1 Subj: Animals – woolly mammoths. Friendship.

Hall, Donald. *Lucy's Christmas* ill. by Michael McCurdy. Harcourt, 1994. ISBN 978-0-15-276870-6 Subj: Activities – making things. Family life. Holidays – Christmas. U.S. history.

Ox-cart man ill. by Barbara Cooney. Viking, 1979. ISBN 978-0-670-53328-2 Subj: Activities – working. Caldecott award books. Farms. Seasons.

Hall, Kathy *see* McMullan, Kate

Hall, Marcellus. *Everyone sleeps* ill. by author. Penguin/Nancy Paulsen, 2013. ISBN 978-0-399-25793-3 Subj: Animals – dogs. Bedtime. Rhyming text. Sleep.

Hall, Margaret. *Corn* ill. with photos. Heinemann, 2003. ISBN 978-1-58810-617-9 Subj: Activities – baking, cooking. Farms. Food.

Peanuts ill. with photos. Heinemann, 2003. ISBN 978-1-58810-619-3 Subj: Activities – baking, cooking. Farms. Food.

Hall, Michael. *Cat tale* ill. by author. Greenwillow, 2012. ISBN 978-0-06-191516-1 Subj: Animals – cats. Language. Rhyming text.

My heart is like a zoo ill. by author. HarperCollins, 2010. ISBN 978-0-06-191510-9 Subj: Animals. Concepts – shape. Emotions. Rhyming text. Zoos.

Perfect square ill. by author. HarperCollins, 2011. ISBN 978-0-06-191513-0 Subj: Character traits – individuality. Concepts – shape. Emotions – happiness. Self-concept.

Hall, Mikele. *Mommy works, Daddy works* (Pedersen, Marika)

Hall, Patricia. *Hooray for reading!* ill. by Kathryn Mitter. Simon & Schuster, 2002. ISBN 978-0-689-85206-0 Subj: Books, reading. Toys – dolls.

Hall, Richard. *Humphrey the lost whale* (Tokuda, Wendy)

Hall, Zoe. *The apple pie tree* ill. by Shari Halpern. Scholastic, 1996. ISBN 978-0-590-62382-7 Subj: Food. Nature. Seasons. Trees.

Fall leaves fall ill. by Shari Halpern. Scholastic, 2000. ISBN 978-0-590-10079-3 Subj: Seasons – fall. Trees.

It's pumpkin time! ill. by Shari Halpern. Scholastic, 1994. ISBN 978-0-590-47833-5 Subj: Holidays – Halloween. Plants.

The surprise garden ill. by Shari Halpern. Blue Sky, 1998. ISBN 978-0-590-10075-5 Subj: Gardens, gardening. Seeds.

Hallensleben, Georg. *Gaspard and Lisa, friends forever* (Gutman, Anne)

Gaspard and Lisa's Christmas surprise (Gutman, Anne)

Gaspard and Lisa's rainy day (Gutman, Anne)

Gaspard at the seashore (Gutman, Anne)

Gaspard in the hospital (Gutman, Anne)

Gaspard on vacation (Gutman, Anne)

Lisa in New York (Gutman, Anne)

Lisa in the jungle (Gutman, Anne)

Lisa's airplane trip (Gutman, Anne)

Lisa's baby sister (Gutman, Anne)

Halloweena ill. by Victoria Roberts. Atheneum, 2002. ISBN 978-0-689-82825-6 Subj: Holidays – Halloween. Witches.

Hallowell, George. *Wagons ho!* by George Hallowell and Joan Holub ill. by Lynne Avril. Whitman, 2011. ISBN 978-0-8075-8612-9 Subj: Moving. U.S. history – frontier & pioneer life.

Halls, Kelly Milner. *Dinosaur parade: a spectacle of prehistoric proportions* ill. by Rick C. Spears. Sterling, 2008. ISBN 978-1-60059-267-6 Subj: Dinosaurs. Rhyming text.

I bought a baby chicken ill. by Karen Stormer Brooks. Boyds Mills, 2000. ISBN 978-1-56397-800-5 Subj: Animals – babies. Birds – chickens. Counting, numbers.

Hallworth, Grace. *Sing me a story* ill. by John Clementson. August House, 2002. ISBN 978-0-87483-672-1 Subj: Activities – dancing. Folk & fairy tales. Foreign lands – Caribbean Islands. Music. Songs.

Halperin, Wendy Anderson. *Peace* ill. by author. Atheneum, 2013. ISBN 978-068982552-1 Subj: Violence, nonviolence. World.

Halpern, Julie. *Toby and the snowflakes* ill. by Matthew Cordell. Houghton, 2004. ISBN 978-0-618-42004-9 Subj: Activities – playing. Emotions – loneliness. Friendship. Weather – snow.

Halpin, Angela Demos. *Water, weed, and wait* (Fine, Edith Hope)

Hambleton, Laura. *Monkey business: fun with idioms* by Laura Hambleton and Sedat Turhan ill. by Hervé Tullet. Milet, 2007. ISBN 978-1-84059-499-7 Subj: Language.

Hamburg, Jennifer. *A moose that says mooooooooooo* ill. by Sue Truesdell. Farrar, 2013. ISBN 978-0-374-35058-1 Subj: Animals. Imagination. Rhyming text. Zoos.

Hamilton, Arlene. *Only a cow* ill. by Dean Griffiths. Fitzhenry & Whiteside, 2006. ISBN 978-1-55041-871-2 Subj: Animals – bulls, cows. Animals – horses, ponies. Emotions – envy, jealousy. Fairs, festivals.

Hamilton, Emma Walton. *Dumpy at school* (Andrews, Julie)

Dumpy the dump truck (Andrews, Julie)

Dumpy to the rescue! (Andrews, Julie)

Dumpy's apple shop (Andrews, Julie)

Simeon's gift (Andrews, Julie)

The very fairy princess (Andrews, Julie)

The very fairy princess: here comes the flower girl! (Andrews, Julie)

The very fairy princess follows her heart (Andrews, Julie)

The very fairy princess sparkles in the snow (Andrews, Julie)

Hamilton, K. R. *This is the ocean* ill. by Lorianne Siomades. Boyds Mills, 2001. ISBN 978-1-56397-890-6 Subj: Rhyming text. Sea & seashore. Water.

Hamilton, Kersten. *Firefighters to the rescue!* ill. by Rich Davis. Penguin, 2005. ISBN 978-0-670-03503-8 Subj: Careers – firefighters.

Police officers on patrol ill. by R. W. Alley. Viking, 2009. ISBN 978-0-670-06315-4 Subj: Careers – police officers. Rhyming text.

Red truck ill. by Valeria Petrone. Viking, 2008. ISBN 978-0-670-06275-1 Subj: Character traits – helpfulness. Rhyming text. Trucks.

Hamilton, Libby. *The monstrous book of monsters* ill. by Jonny Duddle and Aleksei Bitskoff. Candlewick, 2011. ISBN 978-0-7636-5756-7 Subj: Format, unusual – toy & movable books. Monsters.

Hamilton, Martha. *The ghost catcher: a Bengali folktale* by Martha Hamilton and Mitch Weiss ill. by Kristen Balouch. August House, 2008. ISBN 978-0-87483-835-0 Subj: Careers – barbers. Character traits – generosity. Folk & fairy tales. Foreign lands – India. Ghosts.

The hidden feast: a folktale from the American South by Martha Hamilton and Mitch Weiss ill. by Don Tate. August House, 2006. ISBN 978-0-87483-758-2 Subj: Animals. Etiquette. Farms. Folk & fairy tales.

Priceless gifts: a folktale from Italy by Martha Hamilton and Mitch Weiss ill. by John Kanzler. August House, 2007. ISBN 978-0-87483-788-9 Subj: Animals – cats. Animals – rats. Folk & fairy tales. Foreign lands – Italy. Gifts.

Hamilton, Richard. *Let's take over the kindergarten* ill. by Sue Heap. Bloomsbury, 2007. ISBN 978-1-58234-707-3 Subj: Rhyming text. School.

Polly's picnic ill. by Sophy Williams. Bloomsbury, 2003. ISBN 978-1-58234-819-3 Subj: Activities – picnicking. Animals. Behavior – sharing. Rhyming text.

Hamilton, Virginia. *Drylongso* ill. by Jerry Pinkney. Harcourt, 1992. ISBN 978-0-15-224241-1 Subj: Ecology. Ethnic groups in the U.S. – African Americans. Farms. Weather – droughts. Weather – wind.

The girl who spun gold ill. by Leo Dillon and Diane Dillon. Blue Sky, 2000. ISBN 978-0-590-47378-1 Subj: Activities – weaving. Behavior – greed. Folk & fairy tales. Foreign lands – West Indies.

Jaguarundi ill. by Floyd Cooper. Blue Sky, 1995. ISBN 978-0-590-47366-8 Subj: Animals. Animals – endangered animals. Animals – jaguars. Behavior – seeking better things. Ecology.

Hamm, Mia. *Winners never quit* ill. by Carol Thompson. HarperCollins, 2004. ISBN 978-0-06-074051-1 Subj: Sports – soccer. Sportsmanship.

Hammerle, Susa. *Let's try horseback riding* ill. by Kyrima Trapp. NorthSouth, 2006. ISBN 978-0-7358-2093-7 Subj: Animals – horses, ponies. Sports.

Hammersmith, Craig. *Patterns* ill. with photos. Compass Point, 2003. ISBN 978-0-7565-0452-6 Subj: Concepts.

Watch it grow ill. with photos. Compass Point, 2002. ISBN 978-0-7565-0246-1 Subj: Nature. Plants.

What is a family? ill. with photos. Compass Point, 2003. ISBN 978-0-7565-0367-3 Subj: Family life.

Hammerstein, Oscar. *My favorite things* (Rodgers, Richard)

Hammill, Matt. *Sir Reginald's logbook* ill. by author. Kids Can, 2008. ISBN 978-1-55453-202-5 Subj: Humorous stories. Imagination.

Hample, Stoo. *I will kiss you (lots and lots and lots!)* ill. by author. Candlewick, 2005. ISBN 978-0-7636-2787-4 Subj: Animals – rabbits. Emotions – love. Family life – mothers. Kissing. Rhyming text.

Hamsa, Bobbie. *Fast-draw Freddie* ill. by Susan Miller. Rev. ed. Children's Press, 2000. ISBN 978-0-516-22153-3 Subj: Activities – drawing. Rhyming text.

Handford, Martin. *Find Waldo now* ill. by author. Little, 1994. ISBN 978-0-316-34232-2 Subj: Activities – traveling. Games. Picture puzzles. Time.

The great Waldo search ill. by author. Little, 1989. ISBN 978-0-316-34282-7 Subj: Activities – traveling. Games. Picture puzzles.

Where's Waldo? ill. by author. Candlewick, 1997. ISBN 978-0-7636-0310-6 Subj: Activities – traveling. Behavior – lost & found possessions. Foreign lands. Games. Picture puzzles.

Where's Waldo? In Hollywood ill. by author. Candlewick, 1993. ISBN 978-1-56402-294-3 Subj: Activities – traveling. Games.

Where's Waldo? The fantastic journey ill. by author. Candlewick, 1997. ISBN 978-0-7636-0309-0 Subj: Activities – traveling. Games. Imagination.

Where's Waldo? The wonder book ill. by author. Candlewick, 1997. ISBN 978-0-7636-0312-0 Subj: Activities – traveling. Behavior – lost & found possessions. Games.

Where's Waldo now? ill. by author. Candlewick, 1997. ISBN 978-0-7636-0308-3 Subj: Activities – traveling. Games. Time.

Handforth, Thomas. *Mei Li* ill. by author. Doubleday, 1938. ISBN 978-0-385-07401-8 Subj: Caldecott award books. Foreign lands – China. Holidays – Chinese New Year.

Hänel, Wolfram. *Little elephant runs away* ill. by Cristina Kadmon. NorthSouth, 2001. ISBN 978-0-7358-1444-8 Subj: Behavior – lost. Behavior – running away. Family life – brothers & sisters. Sibling rivalry.

Little elephant's song ill. by Cristina Kadmon. NorthSouth, 2000. ISBN 978-0-7358-1298-7 Subj: Animals – elephants. Behavior – growing up. Family life. Noise, sounds.

Hanft, Josh. *The miracles of Passover* ill. by Seymour Chwast. Blue Apple, 2007. ISBN 978-1-59354-600-7 Subj: Holidays – Passover. Jewish culture.

Hanlon, Abby. *Ralph tells a story* ill. by author. Amazon, 2012. ISBN 978-0-7614-6180-7 Subj: Activities – storytelling. Activities – writing. School. Self-concept.

Hannert, Todd. *Morning dance* ill. by author. Chronicle, 2001. ISBN 978-0-8118-2812-3 Subj: Activities – dancing. Morning.

Hansen, Felicity. *The first bear* ill. by Anthony Carnabuci. Barefoot, 2000. ISBN 978-1-84148-012-1 Subj: Animals – bears. Creation. Stars. Toys – bears.

Hansen, P. *My granny's purse.* Workman, 2003. ISBN 978-0-7611-2978-3 Subj: Clothing – handbags, purses. Family life – grandmothers. Format, unusual – toy & movable books.

Hanson, Mary Elizabeth. *The difference between babies and cookies* ill. by Debbie Tilley. Harcourt, 2002. ISBN 978-0-15-202406-2 Subj: Babies. Family life – new sibling. Family life – sisters.

The old man and the flea ill. by David Webber Merrell. Rising Moon, 2001. ISBN 978-0-87358-776-1 Subj: Insects – fleas. Pets.

Hanson, Regina. *A season for mangoes* ill. by Eric Velasquez. Clarion, 2004. ISBN 978-0-618-15972-7 Subj: Activities – storytelling. Death. Emotions – grief. Family life – grandmothers. Foreign lands – Jamaica. Memories, memory.

Hanson, Warren. *Bugtown Boogie* ill. by Steve Johnson and Lou Fancher. HarperCollins, 2008. ISBN 978-0-06-059937-9 Subj: Activities – dancing. Insects. Parties. Rhyming text.

It's Monday, Mrs. Jolly Bones! ill. by Tricia Tusa. Simon & Schuster, 2013. ISBN 978-1-4424-1229-3 Subj: Careers – housekeepers. Character traits – cleanliness. Days of the week, months of the year. Humorous stories.

Hanukkah lights sel. by Lee Bennett Hopkins; ill. by Melanie W. Hall. HarperCollins, 2004. ISBN 978-0-06-008052-5 Subj: Holidays – Hanukkah. Jewish culture. Poetry. Religion.

Hapka, Cathy. *Margret and H. A. Rey's Merry Christmas, Curious George.* Houghton, 2006. ISBN 978-0-618-69237-8 Subj: Animals – monkeys. Character traits – curiosity. Holidays – Christmas. Hospitals. Humorous stories.

Harburg, E. Y. *Over the rainbow* ill. by Eric Puybaret. Imagine, 2010. ISBN 978-1-936140-00-8 Subj: Songs. Weather – rainbows.

Harby, Melanie. *All aboard for Dreamland!* ill. by Geraldo Valério. Simon & Schuster, 2008. ISBN 978-1-4169-6127-7 Subj: Bedtime. Rhyming text. Trains.

Hardin, Melinda. *Hero dad* ill. by Bryan Langdo. Marshall Cavendish, 2010. ISBN 978-0-7614-5713-8 Subj: Careers – military. Family life – fathers.

Hardy, Sarah Frances. *Puzzled by pink* ill. by author. Viking, 2012. ISBN 978-0-670-01320-3 Subj: Birthdays. Character traits – individuality. Family life – sisters. Parties.

Hargrove, Linda. *Wings across the moon* ill. by Joung Un Kim. HarperCollins, 2001. ISBN 978-0-694-01280-0 Subj: Animals. Moon. Night. Rhyming text.

Harjo, Joy. *The good luck cat* ill. by Paul Lee. Harcourt, 2000. ISBN 978-0-15-232197-0 Subj: Animals – cats. Character traits – luck. Indians of North America.

Harker, Lesley. *Annie's ark* ill. by author. Scholastic, 2002. ISBN 978-0-439-36823-0 Subj: Animals. Boats, ships. Religion – Noah. Weather – floods. Weather – rain.

Harley, Bill. *Bear's all-night party* ill. by Melissa Ferreira. August House, 2001. ISBN 978-0-87483-572-4 Subj: Animals. Animals – bears. Moon. Parties.

Dear Santa: the letters of James B. Dobbins ill. by R. W. Alley. HarperCollins, 2005. ISBN 978-0-06-623779-4 Subj: Behavior. Holidays – Christmas. Letters, cards. Santa Claus.

Dirty Joe, the pirate: a true story ill. by Jack E. Davis. HarperCollins, 2008. ISBN 978-0-06-623780-0 Subj: Clothing. Family life – brothers & sisters. Pirates. Rhyming text.

Lost and found ill. by Adam Gustavson. Peachtree, 2012. ISBN 978-1-56145-628-4 Subj: Behavior – lost & found possessions. Careers – custodians, janitors. Clothing – hats. Family life – grandmothers. School.

Harline, Leigh. *When you wish upon a star* (Washington, Ned)

Harness, Cheryl. *Mary Walker wears the pants: the true story of the doctor, reformer, and civil war hero* ill. by Carlo Molinari. Whitman, 2013. ISBN 978-0-8075-4990-2 Subj: Careers – doctors. Character traits – assertiveness. Character traits – being different. Gender roles. U.S. history. War.

Our colonial year ill. by author. Simon & Schuster, 2005. ISBN 978-0-689-83479-0 Subj: Days of the week, months of the year. U.S. history.

Papa's Christmas gift: around the world on the night before Christmas ill. by author. Simon & Schuster, 1995. ISBN 978-0-689-80344-4 Subj: Holidays – Christmas. Poetry.

Harper, Anita. *It's not fair!* ill. by Mary McQuillan. Holiday House, 2007. ISBN 978-0-8234-2094-0 Subj: Animals – cats. Emotions – envy, jealousy. Family life – brothers & sisters. Family life – new sibling.

Harper, Charise Mericle. *Amy and Ivan* ill. by author. Ten Speed, 2006. ISBN 978-1-58246-134-2 Subj: Birds. Counting, numbers. Format, unusual – toy & movable books. Gifts.

The best birthday ever! by me (Lana Kittie) ill. by author. Hyperion/Disney, 2011. ISBN 978-1-4231-3776-4 Subj: Animals – cats. Birthdays. Etiquette. Imagination.

Cupcake: a journey to special ill. by author. Hyperion/Disney, 2010. ISBN 978-1-4231-1897-8 Subj: Character traits – appearance. Food. Friendship. Self-concept.

Flush! the scoop on poop throughout the ages ill. by author. Little, Brown, 2007. ISBN 978-0-316-01064-1 Subj: Health & fitness. Toilets.

Henry's heart ill. by author. Holt, 2011. ISBN 978-0-8050-8989-9 Subj: Anatomy. Animals – dogs. Emotions. Health & fitness. Pets.

Imaginative inventions ill. by author. Little, 2001. ISBN 978-0-316-34725-9 Subj: Inventions.

Mimi and Lulu: three sweet stories, one forever friendship ill. by author. HarperCollins, 2009. ISBN 978-0-06-175583-5 Subj: Activities – playing. Friendship.

The Monster Show ill. by author. Houghton, 2004. ISBN 978-0-618-38797-7 Subj: Monsters.

Pink me up ill. by author. Random House, 2010. ISBN 978-0-375-85607-5 Subj: Activities – picnicking. Animals – rabbits. Concepts – color. Family life – fathers.

There was a bold lady who wanted a star ill. by author. Little, 2002. ISBN 978-0-316-14673-9 Subj: Cumulative tales. Folk & fairy tales. Rhyming text.

The trouble with normal ill. by author. Houghton, 2003. ISBN 978-0-618-15626-9 Subj: Animals – squirrels. Homes, houses.

When I grow up ill. by author. Chronicle, 2001. ISBN 978-0-8118-2905-2 Subj: Behavior – growing up.

When Randolph turned rotten ill. by author. Random House, 2007. ISBN 978-0-375-84071-5 Subj: Animals – beavers. Birds – geese. Birthdays. Friendship. Parties. Self-concept. Sleepovers.

Harper, Dan. *Sit, Truman* ill. by Barry Moser and Cara Moser. Harcourt, 2001. ISBN 978-0-15-202616-5 Subj: Activities. Animals – dogs.

Telling time with Big Mama Cat ill. by Barry Moser and Cara Moser. Harcourt, 1998. ISBN 978-0-15-201738-5 Subj: Animals – cats. Clocks, watches. Format, unusual – toy & movable books. Time.

Harper, Jamie. *Don't grown-ups ever have fun?* ill. by author. Little, 2003. ISBN 978-0-316-14664-7 Subj: Behavior. Family life – parents.

Me too! ill. by author. Little, Brown, 2005. ISBN 978-0-316-60552-6 Subj: Behavior – imitation. Family life – brothers & sisters. Sports – swimming.

Miles to go ill. by author. Candlewick, 2010. ISBN 978-0-7636-3598-5 Subj: Automobiles. Imagination.

Miss Mingo and the fire drill ill. by author. Candlewick, 2009. ISBN 978-0-7636-3597-8 Subj: Animals. Birds – flamingos. Careers – firefighters. School.

Miss Mingo and the first day of school ill. by author. Candlewick, 2006. ISBN 978-0-7636-2410-1 Subj: Animals. Birds – flamingos. Careers – teachers. School – first day.

Miss Mingo weathers the storm ill. by author. Candlewick, 2012. ISBN 978-0-7636-4931-9 Subj: Animals. School – field trips. Sports – hiking. Weather.

Night night, Baby Bundt ill. by author. Candlewick, 2007. ISBN 978-0-7636-3239-7 Subj: Bedtime. Format, unusual – board books.

Splish splash, Baby Bundt ill. by author. Candlewick, 2007. ISBN 978-0-7636-3240-3 Subj: Activities – bathing. Format, unusual – board books.

Harper, Jessica. *I'm not going to chase the cat today* ill. by Lindsay Harper DuPont. HarperCollins, 2000. ISBN 978-0-688-17637-2 Subj: Animals – cats. Animals – dogs. Animals – mice. Parties. Rhyming text.

Lizzy's do's and don'ts ill. by Lindsay Harper DuPont. HarperCollins, 2002. ISBN 978-0-06-623861-6 Subj: Behavior. Family life – mothers. Rhyming text.

Lizzy's ups and downs ill. by Lindsay Harper DuPont. HarperCollins, 2004. ISBN 978-0-06-052064-9 Subj: Emotions. Family life – mothers. Rhyming text. School.

Nora's room ill. by Lindsay Harper DuPont. HarperCollins, 2001. ISBN 978-0-06-029137-2 Subj: Imagination. Noise, sounds. Rhyming text.

A place called Kindergarten ill. by G. Brian Karas. Penguin, 2006. ISBN 978-0-399-24226-7 Subj: Animals. Farms. School – first day.

Harper, Jo. *I could eat you up!* ill. by Kay Chorao. Holiday House, 2007. ISBN 978-0-8234-1733-9 Subj: Animals. Family life – parents. Language.

Ollie Jolly, rodeo clown ill. by Amy Meissner. WestWinds, 2002. ISBN 978-1-55868-552-9 Subj: Clowns, jesters. Cowboys, cowgirls. Rodeos.

Harper, Lee. *The Emperor's cool clothes* ill. by author. Marshall Cavendish, 2011. ISBN 978-0-7614-5948-4 Subj: Birds – penguins. Character traits – appearance. Character traits – vanity. Clothing. Folk & fairy tales. Humorous stories.

Snow! Snow! Snow! ill. by author. Simon & Schuster, 2009. ISBN 978-1-4169-8454-2 Subj: Animals – dogs. Family life – fathers. Sports – sledding. Weather – snow.

Harpham, Wendy Schlessel. *The hope tree* (Numeroff, Laura Joffe)

Harrington, Janice N. *Busy-busy Little Chick* ill. by Brian Pinkney. Farrar, 2013. ISBN 978-0-374-34746-8 Subj: Birds – chickens. Folk & fairy tales. Foreign lands – Africa. Homes, houses.

The chicken-chasing queen of Lamar County ill. by Shelley Jackson. Farrar, 2007. ISBN 978-0-374-31251-0 Subj: Birds – chickens. Ethnic groups in the U.S. – African Americans. Farms.

Roberto walks home ill. by Jody Wheeler. Viking, 2008. ISBN 978-0-670-06316-1 Subj: Emotions – anger. Ethnic groups in the U.S. – Hispanic Americans. Family life – brothers.

Harrington, Tim. *This little piggy* ill. by author. HarperCollins, 2013. ISBN 978-0-06-221808-7 Subj: Anatomy – toes. Counting, numbers. Nursery rhymes.

Harris, Joel Chandler. *Jump! the adventures of Brer Rabbit* adapt. by Van Dyke Parks and Malcolm Jones; ill. by Barry Moser. Harcourt, 1986. ISBN 978-0-15-241350-7 Subj: Animals. Folk & fairy tales.

Jump again! more adventures of Brer Rabbit adapt. by Van Dyke Parks; ill. by Barry Moser. Harcourt, 1987. ISBN 978-0-15-241352-1 Subj: Animals. Folk & fairy tales.

Harris, John. *A giraffe goes to Paris* (Holmes, Mary Tavener)

Jingle bells: how the holiday classic came to be ill. by Adam Gustavson. Peachtree, 2011. ISBN 978-1-56145-590-4 Subj: Music. Seasons – winter. Songs.

Harris, Peter. *The night pirates* ill. by Deborah Allwright. Scholastic, 2006. ISBN 978-0-439-79959-1 Subj: Bedtime. Night. Pirates.

Perfect Prudence ill. by Deborah Allwright. Gingham Dog, 2003. ISBN 978-1-57768-437-4 Subj: Character traits – perfectionism.

Harris, Robie H. *The day Leo said I hate you!* ill. by Molly Bang. Little, Brown, 2008. ISBN 978-0-316-06580-1 Subj: Behavior – fighting, arguing. Emotions – anger. Emotions – hate. Family life – mothers.

Don't forget to come back ill. by Harry Bliss. Candlewick, 2004. ISBN 978-0-7636-1782-0 Subj: Activities – babysitting. Behavior. Family life.

Go! Go! Maria! ill. by Michael Emberley. McElderry, 2003. ISBN 978-0-689-83258-1 Subj: Behavior – growing up. Family life.

Goodbye, Mousie ill. by Jan Ormerod. McElderry, 2001. ISBN 978-0-689-83217-8 Subj: Animals – mice. Death. Emotions – grief. Pets.

Hi, new baby ill. by Michael Emberley. Candlewick, 2000. ISBN 978-0-7636-0539-1 Subj: Babies. Family life – brothers & sisters. Family life – new sibling.

I am not going to school today ill. by Jan Ormerod. McElderry, 2001. ISBN 978-0-689-83913-9 Subj: School – first day.

I love messes! ill. by Nicole Hollander. Little, Brown, 2005. ISBN 978-0-316-10946-8 Subj: Behavior – messy. Character traits – cleanliness. Character traits – orderliness.

I'm all dressed! ill. by Nicole Hollander. Little, Brown, 2005. ISBN 978-0-316-10948-2 Subj: Character traits – individuality. Clothing.

Mail Harry to the moon! ill. by Michael Emberley. Little, Brown, 2008. ISBN 978-0-316-15376-8 Subj: Family life – brothers. Family life – new sibling. Imagination.

Maybe a bear ate it! ill. by Michael Emberley. Scholastic, 2007. ISBN 978-0-439-92961-5 Subj: Animals. Bedtime. Books, reading. Imagination.

What's in there? all about before you were born ill. by Nadine Bernard Westcott. Candlewick, 2013. ISBN 978-0-7636-3630-2 Subj: Babies. Birth. Family life – new sibling. Sex instruction.

When lions roar ill. by Chris Raschka. Scholastic, 2013. ISBN 978-0-545-11283-3 Subj: Emotions – fear. Noise, sounds.

Who has what? all about girls' bodies and boys' bodies ill. by Nadine Bernard Westcott. Candlewick, 2011. ISBN 978-0-7636-2931-1 Subj: Anatomy.

Who's in my family? all about our families ill. by Nadine Bernard Westcott. Candlewick, 2012. ISBN 978-0-7636-3631-9 Subj: Character traits – being different. Ethnic groups in the U.S. Family life. Zoos.

Harris, Teresa E. *Summer Jackson: grown up* ill. by A. G. Ford. HarperCollins, 2011. ISBN 978-0-06-185757-7 Subj: Behavior – growing up. Ethnic groups in the U.S. – African Americans. Family life.

Harris, Trudy. *The clock struck one: a time-telling tale* ill. by Carrie Hartman. Millbrook, 2009. ISBN 978-0-8225-9067-5 Subj: Animals. Nursery rhymes. Time.

Jenny found a penny ill. by John Hovell. Lerner, 2007. ISBN 978-0-8225-6725-7 Subj: Counting, numbers. Money. Rhyming text.

100 days of school ill. by Beth Griffis Johnson. Millbrook, 1999. ISBN 978-0-7613-1271-0 Subj: Counting, numbers. Rhyming text.

Pattern bugs ill. by Anne Canevari Green. Millbrook, 2001. ISBN 978-0-7613-2107-1 Subj: Concepts – patterns. Insects. Language. Rhyming text.

Pattern fish ill. by Anne Canevari Green. Millbrook, 2000. ISBN 978-0-7613-1712-8 Subj: Concepts – patterns. Fish. Rhyming text. Sea & seashore.

Say something, Perico ill. by Cecilia Rébora. Lerner/Kar-Ben, 2011. ISBN 978-0-7613-5231-0 Subj: Birds – parakeets, parrots. Foreign languages.

Tally cat keeps track ill. by Andrew N. Harris. Millbrook, 2010. ISBN 978-0-7613-4451-3 Subj: Animals – cats. Counting, numbers. Friendship.

Twenty hungry piggies ill. by Andrew N. Harris. Lerner, 2007. ISBN 978-0-8225-6370-9 Subj: Animals – pigs. Counting, numbers. Nursery rhymes. Rhyming text.

Up bear, down bear ill. by Ora Eitan. Houghton, 2001. ISBN 978-0-395-97767-5 Subj: Concepts – up & down. Format, unusual – board books. Toys – bears.

Harrison, Carol. *Dinosaurs everywhere!* ill. by Richard Courtney. Scholastic, 1998. ISBN 978-0-590-00089-5 Subj: Dinosaurs. Prehistory.

Harrison, David L. *The alligator in the closet and other poems around the house* ill. by Jane Kendall. Boyds Mills, 2003. ISBN 978-1-56397-994-1 Subj: Homes, houses. Poetry.

The book of giant stories ill. by Philippe Fix. Boyds Mills, 2001. ISBN 978-1-56397-976-7 Subj: Folk & fairy tales. Giants.

Caves ill. by Cheryl Nathan. Boyds Mills, 2001. ISBN 978-1-56397-915-6 Subj: Caves. Science.

Dylan, the eagle-hearted chicken ill. by Karen Stormer Brooks. Boyds Mills, 2002. ISBN 978-1-56397-982-8 Subj: Behavior – imitation. Birds – chickens. Birds – eagles.

Earthquakes ill. by Cheryl Nathan. Boyds Mills, 2004. ISBN 978-1-59078-243-9 Subj: Earthquakes. Science.

Farmer's garden ill. by Arden Johnson-Petrov. Boyds Mills, 2000. ISBN 978-1-56397-776-3 Subj: Animals – dogs. Gardens, gardening. Poetry.

A perfect home for a family ill. by Roberta Angaramo. Holiday House, 2013. ISBN 978-0-8234-2338-5 Subj: Animals. Animals – raccoons. Homes, houses.

Piggy Wiglet ill. by Karen Stormer Brooks. Boyds Mills, 2007. ISBN 978-1-59078-386-3 Subj: Animals – pigs. Behavior – running away. Rhyming text.

Rivers ill. by Cheryl Nathan. Boyds Mills, 2002. ISBN 978-1-56397-968-2 Subj: Rivers.

Harrison, Joanna. *Grizzly dad* ill. by author. Random House, 2009. ISBN 978-0-385-75173-5 Subj: Animals – bears. Behavior – bad day. Family life – fathers.

Harrison, Troon. *Aaron's awful allergies* ill. by Eugenie Fernandes. Kids Can, 1998. ISBN 978-1-55074-299-2 Subj: Illness – allergies. Pets.

Courage to fly ill. by Zhong-Yang Huang. Red Deer, 2002. ISBN 978-0-88995-273-7 Subj: Character traits – bravery. Cities, towns. Ethnic groups in the U.S. – African Americans. Friendship. Moving.

The floating orchard ill. by Miranda Jones. Tundra, 2000. ISBN 978-0-88776-439-4 Subj: Boats, ships. Magic. Trees. Weather – floods. Weather – rain.

Harry, Rebecca. *Snow Bunny's Christmas wish* ill. by author. Scholastic, 2013. ISBN 978-0-545-54103-9 Subj: Animals – rabbits. Character traits – kindness. Holidays – Christmas. Santa Claus.

Harshman, Marc. *All the way to morning* ill. by Felipe Dávalos. Marshall Cavendish, 1999. ISBN 978-0-7614-5042-9 Subj: Bedtime. Night. Noise, sounds. Sleep.

Only one neighborhood ill. by Barbara Garrison. Penguin, 2007. ISBN 978-0-525-47468-5 Subj: Communities, neighborhoods. Counting, numbers.

Red are the apples by Marc Harshman and Cheryl Ryan ill. by Wade Zahares. Gulliver, 2001. ISBN 978-0-15-201917-4 Subj: Concepts – color. Gardens, gardening. Rhyming text. Seasons – fall.

Harshman, Terry Webb. *Does a sea cow say moo?* ill. by George McClements. Bloomsbury, 2008. ISBN 978-1-58234-740-0 Subj: Language. Rhyming text. Sea & seashore.

Hart, Caryl. *The princess and the peas* ill. by Sarah Warburton. Candlewick, 2013. ISBN 978-0-7636-6532-6 Subj: Food. Rhyming text. Royalty – princesses.

Hart, Christopher. *Merwin, master of disguise* ill. by author. Watson-Guptill, 2002. ISBN 978-0-8230-3049-1 Subj: Animals – elephants. Humorous stories. Zoos.

Hartland, Jessie. *Bon appetit! the delicious life of Julia Child* ill. by author. Random House, 2012. ISBN 978-0-375-86944-0 Subj: Activities – baking, cooking. Careers – chefs, cooks. Food. Foreign lands – France.

How the dinosaur got to the museum ill. by author. Blue Apple, 2011. ISBN 978-1-60905-090-0 Subj: Careers – paleontologists. Dinosaurs. Museums.

How the meteorite got to the museum ill. by author. Blue Apple, 2013. ISBN 978-1-60905-252-2 Subj: Museums. Space & space ships.

How the sphinx got to the museum ill. by author. Blue Apple, 2010. ISBN 978-1-60905-032-0 Subj: Art. Foreign lands – Egypt. Museums.

Night shift ill. by author. Bloomsbury, 2007. ISBN 978-1-59990-025-4 Subj: Activities – working. Careers. Night.

Hartley, Karen. *Seeing in living things* by Karen Hartley and Chris Marco; photos by Philip Taylor. Heinemann, 2000. ISBN 978-1-57572-247-4 Subj: Anatomy – eyes. Senses – sight.

The sixth sense and other special senses by Karen Hartley and Chris Marco; photos by Philip Taylor. Heinemann, 2000. ISBN 978-1-57572-248-1 Subj: Animals. Senses.

Smelling in living things by Karen Hartley and Chris Marco; photos by Philip Taylor. Heinemann, 2000. ISBN 978-1-57572-249-8 Subj: Anatomy – noses. Senses – smell.

Tasting in living things by Karen Hartley and Chris Marco; photos by Philip Taylor. Heinemann, 2000. ISBN 978-1-57572-250-4 Subj: Anatomy – tongues. Senses – taste.

Touching in living things by Karen Hartley and Chris Marco; photos by Philip Taylor. Heinemann, 2000. ISBN 978-1-57572-251-1 Subj: Senses – touch.

Hartley, Karen, et al. *Hearing in living things* ill. with photos. Heinemann, 2000. ISBN 978-1-57572-246-7 Subj: Anatomy – ears. Senses – hearing.

Hartman, Bob. *Dinner in the lions' den* ill. by Tim Raglin. Penguin, 2007. ISBN 978-0-399-24674-6 Subj: Animals – lions. Religion – Daniel.

Granny Mae's Christmas play ill. by Lynne Cravath. Augsburg Fortress, 2001. ISBN 978-0-8066-4063-1 Subj: Family life. Family life – grandmothers. Holidays – Christmas. Religion – Nativity. Theater.

The wolf who cried boy ill. by Tim Raglin. Putnam, 2002. ISBN 978-0-399-23578-8 Subj: Animals – wolves. Food.

Hartman, Gail. *As the crow flies* ill. by Harvey Stevenson. Bradbury, 1991. ISBN 978-0-02-743005-9 Subj: Animals. Maps.

Hartmann, Wendy. *The dinosaurs are back and it's all your fault, Edward!* by Wendy Hartmann and Niki Daly ill. by Niki Daly. McElderry, 1997. ISBN

978-0-689-81152-4 Subj: Dinosaurs. Eggs. Family life – brothers. Prehistory.

Hartt-Sussman, Heather. *Here comes Hortense!* ill. by Georgia Graham. Tundra, 2012. ISBN 978-1-77049-221-9 Subj: Emotions – envy, jealousy. Family life – grandmothers. Parks – amusement.

Nana's getting married ill. by Georgia Graham. Tundra, 2010. ISBN 978-0-88776-911-5 Subj: Family life – grandmothers. Weddings.

Noni is nervous ill. by Geneviève Côté. Tundra, 2013. ISBN 978-1-77049-323-0 Subj: Behavior – worrying. School – first day.

Harvey, Amanda. *Dog days* ill. by author. Random House, 2003. ISBN 978-0-385-90860-3 Subj: Animals – cats. Animals – dogs. Pets.

Dog-eared ill. by author. Doubleday, 2002. ISBN 978-0-385-72911-6 Subj: Anatomy – ears. Animals – dogs. Pets. Self-concept.

Dog gone ill. by author. Random House, 2004. ISBN 978-0-385-90870-2 Subj: Animals – dogs. Pets.

Harvey, Brett. *My prairie Christmas* ill. by Deborah Kogan Ray. Holiday, 1990. ISBN 978-0-8234-0827-6 Subj: Holidays – Christmas. Weather – storms.

Harvey, Damian. *Just the thing!* ill. by Lynne Chapman. School Specialty/Gingham Dog, 2005. ISBN 978-0-7696-4300-7 Subj: Animals – gorillas. Problem solving.

Harvey, Jayne. *Busy bugs* ill. by Bernard Adnet. Grosset, 2003. ISBN 978-0-448-43234-2 Subj: Concepts – patterns. Counting, numbers. Insects. Rhyming text.

Harvey, Jeanne Walker. *My hands sing the blues: Romare Bearden's childhood journey* ill. by Elizabeth Zunon. Marshall Cavendish, 2011. ISBN 978-0-7614-5810-4 Subj: Art. Careers – artists. Ethnic groups in the U.S. – African Americans. U.S. history.

Harvey, Matthea. *Cecil the pet glacier* ill. by Giselle Potter. Random House, 2012. ISBN 978-0-375-86773-6 Subj: Behavior – lost & found possessions. Foreign lands – Norway. Pets.

Haseley, Dennis. *The invisible moose* ill. by Steven Kellogg. Penguin, 2006. ISBN 978-0-8037-2892-9 Subj: Animals – moose. Character traits – shyness.

A story for Bear ill. by Jim LaMarche. Harcourt, 2002. ISBN 978-0-15-200239-8 Subj: Animals – bears. Books, reading.

Twenty heartbeats ill. by Ed Young. Roaring Brook, 2008. ISBN 978-1-59643-238-3 Subj: Activities – painting. Animals – horses, ponies. Art. Careers – artists.

Haskins, Jim. *Count your way through Afghanistan* by Jim Haskins and Kathleen Benson ill. by Megan Moore. Lerner, 2006. ISBN 978-1-57505-880-1 Subj: Counting, numbers. Foreign lands – Afghanistan. Foreign languages.

Count your way through Africa ill. by Barbara Knutson. Carolrhoda, 1989. ISBN 978-0-87614-347-6 Subj: Counting, numbers. Foreign lands – Africa. Foreign languages.

Count your way through Brazil by Jim Haskins and Kathleen Benson ill. by Liz Brenner Dodson. Carolrhoda, 1996. ISBN 978-0-87614-873-0 Subj: Counting, numbers. Foreign lands – Brazil. Foreign languages.

Count your way through Canada ill. by Steve Michaels. Carolrhoda, 1989. ISBN 978-0-87614-350-6 Subj: Counting, numbers. Foreign lands – Canada.

Count your way through China ill. by Dennis Hockerman. Carolrhoda, 1987. ISBN 978-0-87614-302-5 Subj: Counting, numbers. Foreign lands – China. Foreign languages.

Count your way through France ill. by Andrea Shine. Carolrhoda, 1996. ISBN 978-0-87614-874-7 Subj: Counting, numbers. Foreign lands – France. Foreign languages.

Count your way through Germany ill. by Helen Byers. Carolrhoda, 1992. ISBN 978-0-87614-407-7 Subj: Counting, numbers. Foreign lands – Germany. Foreign languages.

Count your way through Greece ill. by Janice Lee Porter. Carolrhoda, 1996. ISBN 978-0-87614-875-4 Subj: Counting, numbers. Foreign lands – Greece. Foreign languages.

Count your way through India ill. by Liz Brenner Dodson. Carolrhoda, 1990. ISBN 978-0-87614-414-5 Subj: Counting, numbers. Foreign lands – India. Foreign languages.

Count your way through Iran by Jim Haskins and Kathleen Benson ill. by Farida Zaman. Lerner, 2006. ISBN 978-1-57505-881-8 Subj: Counting, numbers. Foreign lands – Iran. Foreign languages.

Count your way through Ireland ill. by Beth Wright. Carolrhoda, 1996. ISBN 978-0-87614-872-3 Subj: Counting, numbers. Foreign lands – Ireland.

Count your way through Israel ill. by Rick Hanson. Carolrhoda, 1990. ISBN 978-0-87614-415-2 Subj: Counting, numbers. Foreign lands – Israel. Foreign languages.

Count your way through Italy ill. by Beth Wright. Carolrhoda, 1990. ISBN 978-0-87614-406-0 Subj:

Counting, numbers. Foreign lands – Italy. Foreign languages.

Count your way through Japan ill. by Martin Skoro. Carolrhoda, 1987. ISBN 978-0-87614-301-8 Subj: Counting, numbers. Foreign lands – Japan. Foreign languages.

Count your way through Korea ill. by Dennis Hockerman. Carolrhoda, 1989. ISBN 978-0-87614-348-3 Subj: Counting, numbers. Foreign lands – Korea. Foreign languages.

Count your way through Mexico ill. by Helen Byers. Carolrhoda, 1989. ISBN 978-0-87614-349-0 Subj: Counting, numbers. Foreign lands – Mexico. Foreign languages.

Count your way through Russia ill. by Vera Mednikov. Carolrhoda, 1987. ISBN 978-0-87614-303-2 Subj: Counting, numbers. Foreign lands – Russia. Foreign languages.

Count your way through the Arab world ill. by Dana Gustafson. Carolrhoda, 1987. ISBN 978-0-87616-304-7 Subj: Counting, numbers. Foreign lands – Arabia. Foreign languages.

Delivering justice: W. W. Law and the fight for civil rights ill. by Benny Andrews. Candlewick, 2006. ISBN 978-0-7636-2592-4 Subj: Ethnic groups in the U.S. – African Americans. Prejudice. U.S. history.

Hasler, Eveline. *A tale of two brothers* ill. by Kathi Bhend. NorthSouth, 2006. ISBN 978-0-7358-2102-6 Subj: Character traits – kindness. Character traits – meanness. Family life – brothers & sisters. Folk & fairy tales. Foreign lands – Switzerland.

Hassett, Ann. *Can't catch me* (The gingerbread boy)

Father Sun, Mother Moon (Hassett, John)

The finest Christmas tree by Ann Hassett and John Hassett ill. by authors. Houghton, 2005. ISBN 978-0-618-50901-0 Subj: Holidays – Christmas. Santa Claus. Trees.

Mouse in the house (Hassett, John)

The nine lives of Dudley Dog (Hassett, John)

The three silly girls Grubb (Hassett, John)

Too many frogs! by Ann Hassett and John Hassett ill. by John Hassett. Harcourt, 2011. ISBN 978-0-547-36299-1 Subj: Activities – baking, cooking. Family life – grandmothers. Frogs & toads.

Hassett, John. *Can't catch me* (The gingerbread boy)

Father Sun, Mother Moon by John Hassett and Ann Hassett ill. by authors. Houghton, 2001. ISBN 978-0-395-97565-7 Subj: Concepts – color. Superstition.

The finest Christmas tree (Hassett, Ann)

Mouse in the house by John Hassett and Ann Hassett ill. by authors. Houghton, 2004. ISBN 978-0-618-35317-0 Subj: Animals. Character traits – orderliness. Family life – grandmothers.

The nine lives of Dudley Dog by John Hassett and Ann Hassett ill. by John Hassett. Houghton, 2008. ISBN 978-0-618-81153-3 Subj: Animals – cats. Animals – dogs. Safety.

The three silly girls Grubb by John Hassett and Ann Hassett ill. by authors. Houghton, 2002. ISBN 978-0-618-14183-8 Subj: Behavior – bullying, teasing. Folk & fairy tales. School.

Too many frogs! (Hassett, Ann)

Hatch, Elizabeth. *Halloween night* ill. by Jimmy Pickering. Random House, 2005. ISBN 978-0-385-90887-0 Subj: Cumulative tales. Holidays – Halloween. Rhyming text.

Hatkoff, Craig. *Good-bye tonsils* (Hatkoff, Juliana Lee)

Hatkoff, Craig, et al. *Leo the snow leopard: the true story of an amazing rescue.* Scholastic, 2010. ISBN 978-0-545-22927-2 Subj: Animals – endangered animals. Animals – leopards.

Looking for Miza: the true story of the mountain gorilla family who rescued one of their own photos by Peter Greste. Scholastic, 2008. ISBN 978-0-545-08540-3 Subj: Animals – endangered animals. Animals – gorillas. Behavior – lost. Foreign lands – Congo (Democratic Republic).

Winter's tail: how one little dolphin learned to swim again ill. with photos. Scholastic, 2009. ISBN 978-0-545-12335-8 Subj: Anatomy – tails. Animals – dolphins. Character traits – kindness to animals.

Hatkoff, Isabella, et al. *Knut: how one little polar bear captivated the world* ill. with photos. Scholastic, 2007. ISBN 978-0-545-04716-6 Subj: Animals – polar bears. Zoos.

Hatkoff, Juliana Lee. *Good-bye tonsils* by Juliana Lee Hatkoff and Craig Hatkoff ill. by Marilyn Mets. Viking, 2001. ISBN 978-0-670-89775-9 Subj: Hospitals. Illness – tonsillectomy.

Haugen, Brenda. *Thanksgiving* ill. by Todd Ouren. Picture Window, 2004. ISBN 978-1-4048-0191-2 Subj: Holidays – Thanksgiving. U.S. history.

Haughton, Chris. *Little Owl lost* ill. by author. Candlewick, 2010. ISBN 978-0-7636-5022-3 Subj: Behavior – lost. Birds – owls.

Oh no, George! ill. by author. Candlewick, 2012. ISBN 978-0-7636-5546-4 Subj: Animals – dogs. Behavior – misbehavior. Pets.

Haughton, Emma. *Rainy day* ill. by Angelo Rinaldi. Carolrhoda, 2000. ISBN 978-1-57505-452-0 Subj: Activities – walking. Divorce. Family life – fathers. Weather – storms.

Hausman, Gerald. *Coyote walks on two legs* ill. by Floyd Cooper. Philomel, 1993. ISBN 978-0-399-22018-0 Subj: Animals – coyotes. Behavior – greed. Behavior – trickery. Character traits – vanity. Folk & fairy tales. Indians of North America – Navajo.

Eagle boy ill. by Cara Moser and Barry Moser. HarperCollins, 1996. ISBN 978-0-06-021101-1 Subj: Birds – eagles. Folk & fairy tales. Indians of North America – Navajo.

Hautzig, Deborah. *Beauty and the beast* ill. by Kathy Mitchell. Random House, 1995. ISBN 978-0-679-95296-1 Subj: Character traits – loyalty. Emotions – love. Folk & fairy tales. Magic.

Havill, Juanita. *Call the horse lucky* ill. by Nancy Lane. Gryphon, 2010. ISBN 978-0-940719-10-1 Subj: Animals – horses, ponies. Character traits – kindness to animals.

Jamaica and Brianna ill. by Anne Sibley O'Brien. Houghton, 1993. ISBN 978-0-395-64489-8 Subj: Clothing – boots. Emotions – envy, jealousy. Ethnic groups in the U.S. – African Americans. Ethnic groups in the U.S. – Asian Americans. Friendship.

Jamaica and the substitute teacher ill. by Anne Sibley O'Brien. Houghton, 1999. ISBN 978-0-395-90503-6 Subj: Behavior – cheating. Behavior – misbehavior. Careers – teachers. Ethnic groups in the U.S. – African Americans. School. Self-concept.

Jamaica is thankful ill. by Anne Sibley O'Brien. Houghton, 2009. ISBN 978-0-618-98231-8 Subj: Animals – cats. Ethnic groups in the U.S. – African Americans. Family life – brothers & sisters. Illness – allergies. School.

Jamaica Tag-Along ill. by Anne Sibley O'Brien. Houghton, 1989. ISBN 978-0-395-49602-2 Subj: Activities – playing. Ethnic groups in the U.S. – African Americans. Family life – brothers & sisters. Friendship.

Jamaica's blue marker ill. by Anne Sibley O'Brien. Houghton, 1995. ISBN 978-0-395-72036-3 Subj: Emotions – sadness. Ethnic groups in the U.S. – African Americans. Moving.

Jamaica's find ill. by Anne Sibley O'Brien. Houghton, 1986. ISBN 978-0-395-39376-5 Subj: Behavior – lost & found possessions. Character traits – honesty. Ethnic groups in the U.S. – African Americans.

Just like a baby ill. by Christine Davenier. Chronicle, 2009. ISBN 978-0-8118-5026-1 Subj: Babies. Careers. Family life.

Hawcock, Claire. *Mine, all mine!* ill. by Chiara Pasqualotto. Boxer, 2009. ISBN 978-1-906250-76-8 Subj: Animals – squirrels. Behavior – sharing. Seasons – winter. Weather – snow.

Hawk, Fran. *Count down to fall* ill. by Sherry Neidigh. Sylvan Dell, 2009. ISBN 978-1-934359-94-5 Subj: Counting, numbers. Seasons – fall.

Hawkes, Kevin. *The wicked big toddlah* ill. by author. Random House, 2007. ISBN 978-0-375-82427-2 Subj: Babies. Giants. Humorous stories.

The wicked big toddlah goes to New York ill. by author. Random House, 2011. ISBN 978-0-375-86188-8 Subj: Activities – traveling. Babies. Behavior – lost. Giants. Humorous stories.

Hawkins, Colin. *Creepy castle* by Colin Hawkins and Jacqui Hawkins ill. by Jacqui Hawkins. Barron's, 2001. ISBN 978-0-7641-5438-6 Subj: Castles. Format, unusual – toy & movable books. Ghosts. Monsters.

Fairytale news by Colin Hawkins and Jacqui Hawkins ill. by Jacqui Hawkins. Candlewick, 2004. ISBN 978-0-7636-2166-7 Subj: Careers – journalists. Folk & fairy tales.

One, two, guess who? by Colin Hawkins and Jacqui Hawkins ill. by Jacqui Hawkins. Barron's, 2001. ISBN 978-0-7641-5341-9 Subj: Counting, numbers. Folk & fairy tales. Format, unusual – toy & movable books. Rhyming text.

Hawkins, Emily. *Little snow goose* ill. by Maggie Kneen. Dutton, 2009. ISBN 978-0-525-42166-5 Subj: Animals – foxes. Birds – geese. Character traits – responsibility. Friendship.

Hawkins, Jacqui. *Creepy castle* (Hawkins, Colin)

Fairytale news (Hawkins, Colin)

One, two, guess who? (Hawkins, Colin)

Hawthorne, Nathaniel. *King Midas and the golden touch* adapt. by Kathryn Hewitt; ill. by Kathryn Hewitt. Harcourt, 1987. ISBN 978-0-15-242800-6 Subj: Behavior – greed. Folk & fairy tales. Royalty – kings.

Hayashi, Leslie Ann. *Fables from the sea* ill. by Kathleen Wong Bishop. Univ. of Hawaii Pr., 2000. ISBN 978-0-8248-2224-8 Subj: Animals. Hawaii. Sea & seashore.

Hayden, Kate. *Horse show* ill. with photos. DK, 2001. ISBN 978-0-7894-7372-1 Subj: Animals – horses, ponies. Sports.

Hayes, Geoffrey. *The bunny's night-light: a glow-in-the-dark search* ill. by author. Random House, 2012. ISBN 978-0-375-86926-6 Subj: Animals – rabbits. Bedtime. Light, lights.

Patrick at the circus ill. by author. Hyperion, 2002. ISBN 978-0-7868-2595-0 Subj: Animals – bears. Circus. Clowns, jesters.

Hayes, Joe. *Don't say a word, Mamá/No digas nada, Mamá* ill. by Esau Andrade. Cinco Puntos, 2013. ISBN 978-1-935955-29-0 Subj: Character traits – generosity. Ethnic groups in the U.S. – Hispanic Americans. Family life – sisters. Foreign languages. Gardens, gardening.

The gum-chewing rattler ill. by Antonio Castro Lopez. Cinco Puntos, 2006. ISBN 978-0-938317-99-9 Subj: Reptiles – snakes. Tall tales.

Juan Verdades, the man who could not tell a lie ill. by Joseph Daniel Fiedler. Orchard, 2001. ISBN 978-0-439-29311-2 Subj: Behavior – lying. Folk & fairy tales. Foreign languages.

Little Gold Star / Estrellita de oro ill. by Gloria Osuna Perez and Lucia Angela Perez. Cinco Puntos, 2000. ISBN 978-0-938317-49-4 Subj: Birds – hawks. Folk & fairy tales. Foreign languages. Magic.

Hayes, Karel. *The summer visitors* ill. by author. Down East, 2011. ISBN 978-0-89272-918-0 Subj: Animals – bears. Seasons – summer.

The winter visitors ill. by author. Down East, 2007. ISBN 978-0-89272-750-6 Subj: Animals – bears. Seasons – winter.

Hayes, Sarah. *Dog day* ill. by Hannah Broadway. Farrar, 2008. ISBN 978-0-374-31810-9 Subj: Animals – dogs. Careers – teachers. School.

Lucy Anna and the Finders ill. by author. Candlewick, 2000. ISBN 978-0-7636-1200-9 Subj: Behavior – lost & found possessions. Behavior – resourcefulness. Mythical creatures. Toys.

Hayles, Marsha. *Bunion Burt* ill. by Jack E. Davis. Simon & Schuster, 2009. ISBN 978-1-4169-4132-3 Subj: Anatomy – feet. Clothing – shoes. Rhyming text.

The feathered crown ill. by Bernadette Pons. Holt, 2002. ISBN 978-0-8050-6421-6 Subj: Birds. Gifts. Holidays – Christmas. Religion – Nativity. Rhyming text.

He saves the day ill. by Lynne Cravath. Putnam, 2001. ISBN 978-0-399-23363-0 Subj: Activities. Imagination. Rhyming text.

Pajamas anytime ill. by Hiroe Nakata. Penguin, 2005. ISBN 978-0-399-23871-0 Subj: Clothing – pajamas. Days of the week, months of the year. Rhyming text.

A pet of a pet ill. by Scott Nash. Dial, 2001. ISBN 978-0-8037-2512-6 Subj: Animals. Farms. Pets. Self-concept.

Haynes, Max. *Grandma's gone to live in the stars* ill. by author. Whitman, 2000. ISBN 978-0-8075-3026-9 Subj: Death. Emotions – grief. Family life – grandmothers.

Hays, Anna Jane. *Kindergarten countdown* ill. by Linda Davick. Random House, 2007. ISBN 978-0-375-84252-8 Subj: Counting, numbers. Rhyming text. School – first day.

The pup speaks up ill. by Valeria Petrone. Random House, 2003. ISBN 978-0-375-91232-0 Subj: Animals. Animals – dogs. Noise, sounds. Pets.

Ready, set, preschool! ill. by True Kelley. Random House, 2005. ISBN 978-0-375-92519-1 Subj: Concepts. Games. School.

Hayward, Linda. *A day in the life of a builder* ill. with photos. DK, 2001. ISBN 978-0-7894-7364-6 Subj: Careers – construction workers. Homes, houses.

A day in the life of a dancer ill. with photos. DK, 2001. ISBN 978-0-7894-7370-7 Subj: Activities – dancing. Ballet. Careers – dancers.

A day in the life of a firefighter ill. with photos. DK, 2001. ISBN 978-0-613-35098-3 Subj: Careers – firefighters. Fire.

A day in the life of a teacher ill. with photos. DK, 2001. ISBN 978-0-7894-7368-4 Subj: Careers – teachers. School.

I am a book ill. by Carol Nicklaus. Lerner, 2005. ISBN 978-0-7613-1826-2 Subj: Books, reading.

The King's chorus ill. by Jennifer P. Goldfinger. Houghton, 2006. ISBN 978-0-618-51618-6 Subj: Animals. Birds – chickens. Farms. Morning.

Pepe and Papa ill. by Laura Huliska-Beith. Golden, 2001. ISBN 978-0-307-46114-8 Subj: Folk & fairy tales. Humorous stories.

What homework? ill. by Page Eastburn O'Rourke. Kane, 2002. ISBN 978-1-57565-116-3 Subj: Plants. School.

Hazen, Barbara Shook. *Katie's wish* ill. by Emily Arnold McCully. Dial, 2003. ISBN 978-0-8037-2478-5 Subj: Ethnic groups in the U.S. – Irish Americans. Family life – fathers. Family life – grandparents. Foreign lands – Ireland.

Who is your favorite monster, mama? ill. by Maryann Kovalski. Hyperion, 2006. ISBN 978-0-7868-1810-5 Subj: Family life. Monsters. Sibling rivalry.

Head, Judith. *Mud soup* ill. by Susan Guevara. Random House, 2003. ISBN 978-0-375-91087-6 Subj: Activities – baking, cooking. Ethnic groups in the U.S. – Mexican Americans. Food. Foreign languages.

Headley, Justina Chen. *The patch* ill. by Mitch Vane. Charlesbridge, 2006. ISBN 978-1-58089-049-6 Subj: Activities – dancing. Ballet. Glasses. Self-concept.

Heap, Sue. *Danny's drawing book* ill. by author. Candlewick, 2008. ISBN 978-0-7636-3654-8 Subj: Activities – drawing. Foreign lands – Africa. Imagination. Zoos.

Four friends in the garden ill. by author. Candlewick, 2004. ISBN 978-0-7636-2371-5 Subj: Animals – bears. Animals – rabbits. Animals – sheep. Friendship. Gardens, gardening. Insects – butterflies, caterpillars.

What shall we play? ill. by author. Candlewick, 2002. ISBN 978-0-7636-1685-4 Subj: Activities – playing. Imagination.

Hearne, Betsy Gould. *Seven brave women* ill. by Bethanne Andersen. Greenwillow, 1997. ISBN 978-0-688-14503-3 Subj: Character traits – bravery. Family life. Immigrants. U.S. history. War.

Heath, Amy. *Sofie's role* ill. by Sheila Hamanaka. Four Winds, 1992. ISBN 978-0-02-743505-4 Subj: Activities – baking, cooking. Careers – bakers. Ethnic groups in the U.S. – African Americans. Family life. Holidays – Christmas.

Heck, Ed. *Monkey lost* ill. by author. Simon & Schuster, 2005. ISBN 978-0-689-04633-9 Subj: Animals – monkeys. Behavior – lost. School. Toys.

Hector, Julian. *The gentleman bug* ill. by author. Simon & Schuster, 2010. ISBN 978-1-4169-9467-1 Subj: Books, reading. Insects. Self-concept.

Heder, Thyra. *Fraidyzoo* ill. by author. Abrams, 2013. ISBN 978-1-4197-0776-6 Subj: ABC books. Emotions – fear. Zoos.

Heelan, Jamee Riggio. *Can you hear a rainbow?* ill. by Nicola Simmonds. Peachtree, 2002. ISBN 978-1-56145-268-2 Subj: Communication. Disabilities – deafness. Language. School.

The making of my special hand, Madison's story ill. by Nicola Simmonds. Peachtree, 1998. ISBN 978-1-56145-186-9 Subj: Disabilities – physical disabilities.

Rolling along, the story of Taylor and his wheelchair ill. by Nicola Simmonds. Peachtree, 2000. ISBN 978-1-56145-219-4 Subj: Disabilities – cerebral palsy. Disabilities – physical disabilities.

Hegg, Tom. *Peef and his best friend* ill. by Warren Hanson. Waldman, 2001. ISBN 978-0-931674-49-5 Subj: Friendship. Rhyming text. Toys – bears.

Heidbreder, Robert. *Black and bittern was night* ill. by John Martz. Kids Can, 2013. ISBN 978-1-55453-302-2 Subj: Anatomy – skeletons. Holidays – Halloween. Rhyming text.

Drumheller dinosaur dance ill. by Bill Slavin. Kids Can, 2004. ISBN 978-1-55337-393-3 Subj: Activities – dancing. Dinosaurs.

I wished for a unicorn ill. by Kady MacDonald Denton. Kids Can, 2000. ISBN 978-1-55074-543-6 Subj: Activities – playing. Behavior – wishing. Imagination. Mythical creatures – unicorns. Rhyming text.

Lickety-split ill. by Dusan Petricic. Kids Can, 2007. ISBN 978-1-55337-710-8 Subj: Language.

Noisy poems for a busy day ill. by Lori Joy Smith. Kids Can, 2012. ISBN 978-1-55453-706-8 Subj: Activities. Day. Noise, sounds. Poetry.

A sea-wishing day ill. by Kady MacDonald Denton. Kids Can, 2007. ISBN 978-1-55337-707-8 Subj: Rhyming text. Sea & seashore. Sports – sailing.

Heide, Florence Parry. *Always listen to your mother* by Florence Parry Heide and Roxanne Heide Pierce ill. by Kyle M. Stone. Hyperion/Disney, 2010. ISBN 978-1-4231-1395-9 Subj: Character traits – cooperation. Behavior – misbehavior. Humorous stories.

The day of Ahmed's secret by Florence Parry Heide and Judith Heide Gilliland ill. by Ted Lewin. Lothrop, 1990. ISBN 978-0-688-08895-8 Subj: Activities – working. Activities – writing. Behavior – secrets. Foreign lands – Egypt.

The one and only Marigold ill. by Jill McElmurry. Random House, 2009. ISBN 978-0-375-84031-9 Subj: Animals – monkeys. Character traits – individuality. Friendship.

Princess Hyacinth: the surprising tale of a girl who floated ill. by Lane Smith. Random House, 2009. ISBN 978-0-375-84501-7 Subj: Activities – flying. Behavior – boredom. Kites. Royalty – princesses.

A promise is a promise ill. by Tony Auth. Candlewick, 2007. ISBN 978-0-7636-2285-5 Subj: Pets.

Sami and the time of the troubles by Florence Parry Heide and Judith Heide Gilliland ill. by Ted Lewin. Clarion, 1992. ISBN 978-0-395-55964-2 Subj: Family life. Foreign lands – Lebanon. War.

Some things are scary ill. by Jules Feiffer. Candlewick, 2000. ISBN 978-0-7636-1222-1 Subj: Emotions – fear.

Heide, Iris van der. *The red chalk* ill. by Marije Tolman. Boyds Mills, 2006. ISBN 978-1-932425-79-6

Subj: Activities – playing. Activities – trading. Behavior – boredom.

A strange day ill. by Marijke ten Cate. Boyds Mills, 2007. ISBN 978-1-932425-94-9 Subj: Character traits – helpfulness. Contests. Letters, cards.

Heiligman, Deborah. *Babies* ill. by Laura Freeman. National Geographic, 2002. ISBN 978-0-7922-8205-1 Subj: Babies. Behavior – growing up.

The boy who loved math: the improbable life of Paul Erdös ill. by LeUyen Pham. Roaring Brook, 2013. ISBN 978-1-59643-307-6 Subj: Careers – mathematicians. Character traits – individuality. Counting, numbers. Foreign lands – Hungary.

Cool dog, school dog ill. by Tim Bowers. Marshall Cavendish, 2009. ISBN 978-0-7614-5561-5 Subj: Animals – dogs. Rhyming text. School.

Fun dog, sun dog ill. by Tim Bowers. Marshall Cavendish, 2005. ISBN 978-0-7614-5162-4 Subj: Animals – dogs. Pets.

Honeybees ill. by Carla Golembe. National Geographic, 2002. ISBN 978-0-7922-6678-5 Subj: Insects – bees.

Snow dog, go dog ill. by Tim Bowers. Amazon/Two Lions, 2013. ISBN 978-1-4778-1724-7 Subj: Animals – dogs. Behavior – lost. Rhyming text. Weather – snow.

Heinz, Brian J. *Butternut Hollow Pond* ill. by Bob Marstall. Millbrook, 2000. ISBN 978-0-7613-0268-1 Subj: Animals. Ecology. Lakes, ponds.

The monsters' test ill. by Sal Murdocca. Millbrook, 1996. ISBN 978-0-7613-0095-3 Subj: Holidays – Halloween. Monsters. Rhyming text. Witches.

Nathan of yesteryear and Michael of today ill. by Joanne Friar. Lerner, 2006. ISBN 978-0-7613-2893-3 Subj: U.S. history.

Red Fox at McCloskey's farm ill. by Chris Sheban. Creative Editions, 2006. ISBN 978-1-56846-195-3 Subj: Animals – foxes. Farms. Rhyming text.

The wolves ill. by Bernie Fuchs. Dial, 1996. ISBN 978-0-8037-1736-7 Subj: Animals – endangered animals. Animals – wolves. Nature.

Helakoski, Leslie. *Big chickens* ill. by Henry Cole. Penguin, 2006. ISBN 978-0-525-47575-0 Subj: Animals – wolves. Birds – chickens. Emotions – fear. Farms.

Big chickens fly the coop ill. by Henry Cole. Dutton, 2008. ISBN 978-0-525-47915-4 Subj: Birds – chickens. Farms. Humorous stories.

Big chickens go to town ill. by Henry Cole. Penguin, 2010. ISBN 978-0-525-42162-7 Subj: Birds – chickens. Cities, towns. Emotions – fear.

Doggone feet! ill. by author. Boyds Mills, 2013. ISBN 978-1-59078-933-9 Subj: Animals – dogs. Family life. Pets. Rhyming text.

Fair cow ill. by author. Marshall Cavendish, 2010. ISBN 978-0-7614-5684-1 Subj: Animals – bulls, cows. Character traits – individuality. Fairs, festivals.

The smushy bus ill. by Sal Murdocca. Millbrook, 2002. ISBN 978-0-7613-1398-4 Subj: Buses. Careers – bus drivers. Counting, numbers. School.

Woolbur ill. by Lee Harper. HarperCollins, 2008. ISBN 978-0-06-084726-5 Subj: Animals – sheep. Behavior. Character traits – individuality.

The Helen Oxenbury nursery collection ill. by Helen Oxenbury. Knopf, 2004. ISBN 978-0-375-92992-2 Subj: Folk & fairy tales. Nursery rhymes. Poetry.

Heling, Kathryn. *Clothesline clues to jobs people do* by Kathryn Heling and Deborah Hembrook ill. by Andy Robert Davies. Charlesbridge, 2012. ISBN 978-1-58089-251-3 Subj: Careers. Clothing.

Mouse makes magic by Kathryn Heling and Deborah Hembrook ill. by Patrick Joseph. Random House, 2003. ISBN 978-0-375-92184-1 Subj: Animals – mice. Language.

Mouse's hide-and-seek words by Kathryn Heling and Deborah Hembrook ill. by Patrick Joseph. Random House, 2003. ISBN 978-0-375-92185-8 Subj: Animals – mice. Language. Rhyming text.

Helldorfer, M. C. *Hog music* ill. by S. D. Schindler. Viking, 2000. ISBN 978-0-670-87182-7 Subj: Activities – traveling. Family life – aunts, uncles. Gifts. U.S. history – frontier & pioneer life.

Heller, Linda. *How Dalia put a big yellow comforter inside a tiny blue box: and other wonders of tzedakah* ill. by Stacey Dressen-McQueen. Tricycle, 2011. ISBN 978-1-58246-378-0 Subj: Character traits – generosity. Family life – brothers & sisters. Jewish culture.

Heller, Lora. *Sign language ABC* ill. by author. Sterling, 2012. ISBN 978-1-4027-6392-2 Subj: ABC books. Sign language.

Heller, Nicholas. *Elwood and the witch* ill. by Joseph A. Smith. Greenwillow, 2000. ISBN 978-0-689-16946-5 Subj: Activities – flying. Animals – pigs. Moon. Witches.

Ogres! ogres! ogres! a feasting frenzy from A to Z ill. by Joseph A. Smith. Greenwillow, 1999. ISBN 978-0-688-16987-9 Subj: Food. Monsters. Mythical creatures – ogres.

This little piggy ill. by Sonja Lamut. Greenwillow, 1997. ISBN 978-0-688-15175-1 Subj: Bedtime. Family life – grandmothers. Nursery rhymes.

Heller, Ruth. *A cache of jewels and other collective nouns* ill. by author. Grosset, 1989. ISBN 978-0-448-19211-6 Subj: Language. Rhyming text.

Chickens aren't the only ones ill. by author. Grosset, 1981. ISBN 978-0-448-01872-0 Subj: Eggs. Science.

Color, color, color, color ill. by author. Putnam, 1995. ISBN 978-0-399-22815-5 Subj: Concepts – color. Rhyming text.

Fantastic! wow! and unreal! a book about interjections and conjunctions ill. by author. Grosset, 1998. ISBN 978-0-448-41862-9 Subj: Language. Rhyming text.

Kites sail high: a book about verbs ill. by author. Grosset, 1988. ISBN 978-0-448-10480-5 Subj: Language. Rhyming text.

Many luscious lollipops: a book about adjectives ill. by author. Sandcastle Books, 1992. ISBN 978-0-448-03151-4 Subj: Language. Rhyming text.

Merry-go-round ill. by author. Sandcastle Books, 1992. ISBN 978-0-448-40085-3 Subj: Language. Rhyming text.

Mine, all mine: a book about pronouns ill. by author. Grosset, 1997. ISBN 978-0-448-41606-9 Subj: Language. Rhyming text.

The reason for a flower ill. by author. Grosset, 1983. ISBN 978-0-448-14495-5 Subj: Flowers. Rhyming text.

Hellman, Gary. *The karate way* ill. by author. Doubleday, 2001. ISBN 978-0-385-32742-8 Subj: Self-concept. Sports – karate.

Hellums, Julia Pemberton. *Hold the anchovies!* (Rotner, Shelley)

Helmer, Diana Star. *The cat who came for tacos* ill. by Viví Escrivá. Whitman, 2003. ISBN 978-0-8075-5106-6 Subj: Animals – cats. Etiquette.

Helmer, Marilyn. *Critter riddles* ill. by Eric Parker. Kids Can, 2003. ISBN 978-1-55337-445-9 Subj: Humorous stories. Riddles & jokes.

Funtime riddles ill. by Jane Kurisu. Kids Can, 2004. ISBN 978-1-55337-579-1 Subj: Riddles & jokes.

One splendid tree ill. by Dianne Eastman. Kids Can, 2005. ISBN 978-1-55337-683-5 Subj: Family life. Holidays – Christmas. Trees. U.S. history. War.

Recess riddles ill. by Jane Kurisu. Kids Can, 2004. ISBN 978-1-55337-577-7 Subj: Riddles & jokes. School.

Spooky riddles ill. by Eric Parker. Kids Can, 2003. ISBN 978-1-55337-447-3 Subj: Monsters. Riddles & jokes.

Three barnyard tales ill. by Laura Watson. Kids Can, 2002. ISBN 978-1-55074-796-6 Subj: Animals. Birds. Folk & fairy tales.

Three cat and mouse tales ill. by Josée Masse. Kids Can, 2004. ISBN 978-1-55074-943-4 Subj: Animals – cats. Animals – mice. Folk & fairy tales.

Three prince charming tales ill. by Kasia Charko. Kids Can, 2000. ISBN 978-1-55074-761-4 Subj: Folk & fairy tales. Royalty – princes.

Three royal tales ill. by Dianna Bonder. Kids Can, 2003. ISBN 978-1-55074-939-7 Subj: Folk & fairy tales. Royalty.

Three tales of enchantment ill. by Kasia Charko. Kids Can, 2001. ISBN 978-1-55074-843-7 Subj: Folk & fairy tales. Magic.

Three tales of three ill. by Chris Jackson. Kids Can, 2000. ISBN 978-1-55074-759-1 Subj: Animals. Folk & fairy tales.

Three tales of trickery ill. by Noushin Pajouhesh. Kids Can, 2002. ISBN 978-1-55074-937-3 Subj: Behavior – trickery. Folk & fairy tales.

Three teeny tiny tales ill. by Veselina Tomova. Kids Can, 2001. ISBN 978-1-55074-841-3 Subj: Concepts – size. Folk & fairy tales.

Three tuneful tales ill. by Kasia Charko. Kids Can, 2003. ISBN 978-1-55074-941-0 Subj: Folk & fairy tales. Music.

Yucky riddles ill. by Eric Parker. Kids Can, 2003. ISBN 978-1-55337-448-0 Subj: Riddles & jokes.

Yummy riddles ill. by Eric Parker. Kids Can, 2003. ISBN 978-1-55337-446-6 Subj: Food. Riddles & jokes.

Helmore, Jim. *Oh no, monster tomato!* ill. by Karen Wall. Egmont UK, 2011. ISBN 978-1-4052-4741-2 Subj: Contests. Gardens, gardening. Plants.

Helquist, Brett. *Bedtime for Bear* ill. by author. HarperCollins, 2010. ISBN 978-0-06-050205-8 Subj: Animals – bears. Hibernation. Seasons – winter. Weather – snow.

Grumpy Goat ill. by author. HarperCollins, 2013. ISBN 978-0-06-113953-6 Subj: Animals – goats. Behavior – dissatisfaction. Farms. Friendship.

Roger, the jolly pirate ill. by author. HarperCollins, 2004. ISBN 978-0-06-623806-7 Subj: Humorous stories. Pirates.

Hembrook, Deborah. *Clothesline clues to jobs people do* (Heling, Kathryn)

Mouse makes magic (Heling, Kathryn)

Mouse's hide-and-seek words (Heling, Kathryn)

Hemingway, Edward. *Bad apple: a tale of friendship* ill. by author. Putnam, 2012. ISBN 978-

0-399-25191-7 Subj: Animals – worms. Food. Friendship.

Bump in the night ill. by author. Putnam, 2008. ISBN 978-0-399-24761-3 Subj: Bedtime. Monsters.

Henderson, Alicia Terry. *Call me black, call me beautiful* ill. by Jennifer C. Kindert. Royal Regal, 2002. ISBN 978-0-9719490-1-0 Subj: Character traits – individuality. Ethnic groups in the U.S. – African Americans. Self-concept.

Henderson, Kathy. *And the good brown earth* ill. by author. Candlewick, 2004. ISBN 978-0-7636-2301-2 Subj: Family life – grandmothers. Gardens, gardening.

Baby knows best ill. by Brita Granström. Little, 2001. ISBN 978-0-316-60580-9 Subj: Babies. Rhyming text. Toys.

Hush, baby, hush! lullabies from around the world ill. by Pam Smy. Frances Lincoln, 2011. ISBN 978-1-84507-967-3 Subj: Foreign languages. Lullabies.

Look at you! a baby body book ill. by Paul Howard. Candlewick, 2006. ISBN 978-0-7636-2745-4 Subj: Anatomy. Babies. Senses.

Hendra, Sue. *Barry, the fish with fingers* ill. by author. Random House, 2010. ISBN 978-0-375-85894-9 Subj: Anatomy – hands. Fish.

Henkes, Kevin. *Bailey goes camping* ill. by author. Greenwillow, 1985. ISBN 978-0-688-05702-2 Subj: Animals – rabbits. Camps, camping. Family life.

The biggest boy ill. by Nancy Tafuri. Greenwillow, 1995. ISBN 978-0-688-12830-2 Subj: Concepts – shape. Concepts – size.

Birds ill. by Laura Dronzek. Greenwillow, 2009. ISBN 978-0-06-136304-7 Subj: Birds. Concepts – color. Concepts – shape. Concepts – size.

Chester's way ill. by author. Greenwillow, 1988. ISBN 978-0-688-07608-5 Subj: Animals – mice. Behavior – bullying, teasing.

Chrysanthemum ill. by author. Greenwillow, 1991. ISBN 978-0-688-09700-4 Subj: Animals – mice. Names. School.

Circle dogs ill. by Dan Yaccarino. Greenwillow, 1998. ISBN 978-0-688-15447-9 Subj: Animals – dogs. Concepts – shape.

Good-bye, Curtis ill. by Marisabina Russo. Greenwillow, 1995. ISBN 978-0-688-12828-9 Subj: Careers – postal workers. Communities, neighborhoods.

A good day ill. by author. HarperCollins, 2007. ISBN 978-0-06-114019-8 Subj: Animals. Behavior – bad day.

El gran día de Lily / Lilly's big day ill. by author. Greenwillow, 2008. ISBN 978-0-06-136316-0 Subj: Animals – mice. Careers – teachers. Foreign languages. School. Weddings.

Grandpa and Bo ill. by author. Greenwillow, 1986. ISBN 978-0-688-04957-7 Subj: Family life – grandfathers. Seasons – summer.

Jessica ill. by author. Greenwillow, 1989. ISBN 978-0-688-07830-0 Subj: Friendship. Imagination – imaginary friends. School – first day.

Julius, the baby of the world ill. by author. Greenwillow, 1990. ISBN 978-0-688-08944-3 Subj: Animals – mice. Family life. Sibling rivalry.

Kitten's first full moon ill. by author. Greenwillow, 2004. ISBN 978-0-06-058829-8 Subj: Animals – babies. Animals – cats. Behavior – misunderstanding. Caldecott award books. Moon.

Lilly's big day ill. by author. HarperCollins, 2006. ISBN 978-0-06-074236-2 Subj: Animals – mice. Careers – teachers. Character traits – assertiveness. Emotions – anger. Weddings.

Lilly's chocolate heart ill. by author. HarperCollins, 2004. ISBN 978-0-06-056066-9 Subj: Animals – mice. Format, unusual – board books. Holidays – Valentine's Day.

Lilly's purple plastic purse ill. by author. Greenwillow, 1996. ISBN 978-0-688-12898-2 Subj: Animals – mice. Careers – teachers. Clothing – handbags, purses. Emotions – anger. School.

Little white rabbit ill. by author. HarperCollins, 2011. ISBN 978-0-06-200642-4 Subj: Animals – rabbits. Character traits – curiosity. Imagination.

My garden ill. by author. HarperCollins, 2010. ISBN 978-0-06-171517-4 Subj: Gardens, gardening. Imagination.

Oh! ill. by Laura Dronzek. Greenwillow, 1999. ISBN 978-0-688-17054-7 Subj: Activities – playing. Animals. Rhyming text. Seasons – winter. Weather – snow.

Old Bear ill. by author. Greenwillow, 2008. ISBN 978-0-06-155205-2 Subj: Animals – bears. Dreams. Hibernation. Seasons.

Owen ill. by author. Greenwillow, 1993. ISBN 978-0-688-11450-3 Subj: Animals – mice. Behavior – growing up. Caldecott award honor books.

Sheila Rae, the brave ill. by author. Greenwillow, 1987. ISBN 978-0-688-07156-1 Subj: Animals – mice. Behavior – lost. Character traits – bravery. Family life – sisters.

Sheila Rae's peppermint stick ill. by author. HarperCollins, 2001. ISBN 978-0-06-029451-9 Subj: Animals – mice. Behavior – sharing. Family life – sisters. Food. Format, unusual – board books.

Shhhh ill. by author. Greenwillow, 1989. ISBN 978-0-688-07986-4 Subj: Family life. Morning. Sleep.

So happy! ill. by Anita Lobel. HarperCollins, 2005. ISBN 978-0-06-056484-1 Subj: Animals – rabbits. Plants. Seeds.

A weekend with Wendell ill. by author. Greenwillow, 1986. ISBN 978-0-688-06326-9 Subj: Activities – playing. Animals – mice. Behavior – misbehavior. Character traits – selfishness.

Wemberly worried ill. by author. Greenwillow, 2000. ISBN 978-0-688-17028-8 Subj: Animals – mice. Behavior – worrying. School – first day. School – nursery.

Hennessy, B. G. *Because of you: a book of kindness* ill. by Hiroe Nakata. Candlewick, 2005. ISBN 978-0-7636-1926-8 Subj: Character traits – kindness.

The boy who cried wolf ill. by Boris Kulikov. Simon & Schuster, 2006. ISBN 978-0-689-87433-8 Subj: Animals – wolves. Behavior – lying. Behavior – trickery. Folk & fairy tales.

Busy Dinah Dinosaur ill. by Ana Martin Larrañaga. Candlewick, 2000. ISBN 978-0-7636-1140-8 Subj: Activities. Dinosaurs. Prehistory.

Corduroy at the zoo ill. by Lisa McCue. Based on the character by Don Freeman. Viking, 2000. ISBN 978-0-670-89288-4 Subj: Animals. Format, unusual – toy & movable books. Toys – bears. Zoos.

Corduroy's birthday ill. by Lisa McCue. Based on the character by Don Freeman. Viking, 1997. ISBN 978-0-670-87065-3 Subj: Birthdays. Format, unusual – toy & movable books. Parties. Toys – bears.

Corduroy's Christmas ill. by Lisa McCue. Based on the character by Don Freeman. Viking, 1992. ISBN 978-0-670-84477-7 Subj: Format, unusual – toy & movable books. Holidays – Christmas. Toys – bears.

Corduroy's Easter ill. by Lisa McCue. Based on the character by Don Freeman. Viking, 1998. ISBN 978-0-670-88101-7 Subj: Format, unusual – toy & movable books. Holidays – Easter. Toys – bears.

Corduroy's Halloween ill. by Lisa McCue. Based on the character by Don Freeman. Viking, 1995. ISBN 978-0-670-86193-4 Subj: Clothing – costumes. Format, unusual – toy & movable books. Holidays – Halloween. Toys – bears.

The dinosaur who lived in my backyard ill. by Susan Davis. Viking, 1988. ISBN 978-0-670-81685-9 Subj: Dinosaurs. Imagination. Prehistory.

The first night ill. by Lou Fancher and Steve Johnson. Viking, 1993. ISBN 978-0-670-83026-8 Subj: Holidays – Christmas. Religion.

Meet Dinah Dinosaur ill. by Ana Martin Larrañaga. Candlewick, 2000. ISBN 978-0-7636-1133-0 Subj: Dinosaurs. Prehistory.

The missing tarts ill. by Tracey Campbell Pearson. Viking, 1989. ISBN 978-0-670-82039-9 Subj: Behavior – stealing. Nursery rhymes. Rhyming text. Royalty – queens.

Mr. Ouchy's first day ill. by Paul Meisel. Penguin, 2006. ISBN 978-0-399-24248-9 Subj: Careers – teachers. Counting, numbers. School – first day. Time.

Olympics! ill. by Michael Chesworth. Viking, 1996. ISBN 978-0-670-86522-2 Subj: Sports – Olympics.

One little, two little, three little pilgrims ill. by Lynne Cravath. Viking, 1999. ISBN 978-0-670-87779-9 Subj: Counting, numbers. Indians of North America – Wampanoag. Pilgrims.

Road builders ill. by Simms Taback. Viking, 1994. ISBN 978-0-670-83390-0 Subj: Careers – construction workers. Machines. Roads.

Henrichs, Wendy. *I am Tama, lucky cat: a Japanese legend* ill. by Yoshiko Jaeggi. Peachtree, 2011. ISBN 978-1-56145-589-8 Subj: Animals – cats. Folk & fairy tales. Foreign lands – Japan.

When Anju loved being an elephant ill. by John Butler. Sleeping Bear, 2011. ISBN 978-1-58536-533-3 Subj: Animals – elephants. Character traits – kindness to animals. Circus. Foreign lands – Indonesia.

Henry, Jed. *Cheer up, Mouse!* ill. by author. Houghton Mifflin, 2013. ISBN 978-0-547-68107-8 Subj: Animals. Animals – mice. Emotions – sadness. Friendship. Hugging.

Good night, Mouse! ill. by author. Houghton Mifflin, 2013. ISBN 978-0-547-98156-7 Subj: Animals – mice. Bedtime. Friendship. Sleep.

I speak dinosaur ill. by author. Abrams, 2012. ISBN 978-1-4197-0233-4 Subj: Behavior – misbehavior. Dinosaurs. Etiquette. Language.

Henry, Rohan. *The gift box* ill. by author. Abrams, 2012. ISBN 978-1-4197-0167-2 Subj: Animals – dogs. Animals – elephants. Friendship.

Henry, Steve. *Nobody asked me!* ill. by author. HarperCollins, 2001. ISBN 978-0-688-17866-6 Subj: Animals – cats. Family life – brothers. Family life – new sibling.

Henson, Heather. *Grumpy Grandpa* ill. by Ross MacDonald. Atheneum, 2009. ISBN 978-1-4169-0811-1 Subj: Family life – grandfathers. Old age. Sports – fishing.

Henterly, Jamichael. *Good night, garden gnome* ill. by author. Dial, 2001. ISBN 978-0-8037-2531-7 Subj: Gardens, gardening. Mythical creatures – gnomes.

Heo, Yumi. *Father's rubber shoes* ill. by author. Orchard, 1995. ISBN 978-0-531-08723-7 Subj: Careers – storekeepers. Clothing – shoes. Ethnic groups in the U.S. – Korean Americans. Family life – fathers.

The green frogs ill. by author. Houghton, 1996. ISBN 978-0-395-68378-1 Subj: Behavior – misbehavior. Folk & fairy tales. Foreign lands – Korea. Frogs & toads.

Lady Hahn and her seven friends ill. by author. Holt, 2012. ISBN 978-0-8050-4127-9 Subj: Activities – sewing. Behavior – boasting. Behavior – fighting, arguing. Careers – seamstresses. Character traits – vanity. Foreign lands – Korea.

One afternoon ill. by author. Orchard, 1994. ISBN 978-0-531-08695-7 Subj: Cities, towns. Communities, neighborhoods. Family life – mothers. Noise, sounds.

One Sunday morning ill. by author. Orchard, 1999. ISBN 978-0-531-33156-9 Subj: Cities, towns. Family life – fathers. Noise, sounds. Parks.

Ten days and nine nights: an adoption story ill. by author. Random House, 2009. ISBN 978-0-375-84718-9 Subj: Adoption. Ethnic groups in the U.S. – Korean Americans. Family life.

Heos, Bridget. *Mustache baby* ill. by Joy Ang. Clarion, 2013. ISBN 978-0-547-77357-5 Subj: Babies. Behavior. Character traits – appearance. Self-concept.

What to expect when you're expecting hatchlings: a guide for crocodilian parents (and curious kids) ill. by Stéphane Jorisch. Millbrook, 2012. ISBN 978-0-7613-5860-2 Subj: Reptiles – alligators, crocodiles.

What to expect when you're expecting joeys: a guide for marsupial parents (and curious kids) ill. by Stéphane Jorisch. Millbrook, 2011. ISBN 978-0-7613-5859-6 Subj: Animals – babies. Animals – marsupials.

Hepworth, Catherine. *ANTics! an alphabetical anthology* ill. by author. Putnam, 1992. ISBN 978-0-399-21862-0 Subj: ABC books. Insects – ants.

Herbert, Gail. *Mattland* (Hutchins, Hazel)

Here we go round the mulberry bush ill. by Sophie Fatus. Barefoot, 2007. ISBN 978-1-84686-035-5 Subj: Music. Songs. World.

Herkert, Barbara. *Birds in your backyard* ill. by author. Dawn, 2001. ISBN 978-1-58469-026-9 Subj: Activities. Birds.

Herman, Charlotte. *First rain* ill. by Kathryn Mitter. Whitman, 2010. ISBN 978-0-8075-2453-4 Subj: Foreign lands – Israel. Jewish culture. Weather – rain.

The memory cupboard ill. by Ben F. Stahl. Whitman, 2003. ISBN 978-0-8075-5055-7 Subj: Family life. Family life – grandmothers. Holidays – Thanksgiving.

Herman, Gail. *The lion and the mouse* (Aesop)

Herman, R. A. *Gomer and Little Gomer* ill. by Steve Haskamp. Penguin, 2005. ISBN 978-0-525-47359-6 Subj: Animals – dogs. Toys.

Hernandez, Keith. *First-base hero* ill. by John Manders. Golden, 2002. ISBN 978-0-307-10626-1 Subj: Format, unusual – toy & movable books. Sports – baseball.

Hernandez, Leeza. *Dog gone!* ill. by author. Putnam, 2012. ISBN 978-0-399-25447-5 Subj: Animals – dogs. Behavior – lost & found possessions. Behavior – running away.

Herrera, Juan Felipe. *Grandma and Me at the flea / Los meros meros remateros* ill. by Anita de Lucio-Brock. Children's Book Press, 2002. ISBN 978-0-89239-171-4 Subj: Communities, neighborhoods. Ethnic groups in the U.S. – Mexican Americans. Family life – grandmothers. Foreign languages.

Hershenhorn, Esther. *Fancy that* ill. by Megan Lloyd. Holiday, 2003. ISBN 978-0-8234-1605-9 Subj: Careers – artists. Family life – brothers & sisters. Orphans.

Hertz, Grete Janus. *Olie's bedtime walk* ill. by Nynke Mare Talsma. Star Bright, 2002. ISBN 978-1-887734-90-5 Subj: Activities – walking. Activities – working. Night. Sleep.

Herzog, Brad. *G is for gold medal: an Olympics alphabet* ill. by Doug Bowles. Sleeping Bear, 2011. ISBN 978-1-58536-462-6 Subj: ABC books. Sports – Olympics.

I spy with my little eye: baseball ill. by David Milne. Sleeping Bear, 2011. ISBN 978-1-58536-496-1 Subj: Picture puzzles. Sports – baseball.

R is for race: a stock car alphabet ill. by Jane Gilltrap Bready. Sleeping Bear, 2006. ISBN 978-1-58536-272-1 Subj: ABC books. Automobiles. Sports – racing.

Hesse, Karen. *Come on, rain* ill. by Jon J. Muth. Scholastic, 1999. ISBN 978-0-590-33125-8 Subj: Activities – dancing. Ethnic groups in the U.S. – African Americans. Family life – daughters. Family life – mothers. Seasons – summer. Weather – rain.

Spuds ill. by Wendy Watson. Scholastic, 2008. ISBN 978-0-439-87993-4 Subj: Character traits – honesty. Country. Emotions – love. Family life. Food.

Hest, Amy. *The babies are coming!* ill. by Chloë Cheese. Crown, 1997. ISBN 978-0-517-70944-3 Subj: Activities – storytelling. Babies. Libraries.

Baby Duck and the bad eyeglasses ill. by Jill Barton. Candlewick, 1996. ISBN 978-1-56402-680-4 Subj: Birds – ducks. Family life – grandfathers. Glasses.

Baby Duck and the cozy blanket ill. by Jill Barton. Candlewick, 2002. ISBN 978-0-7636-1582-6 Subj: Birds – ducks. Format, unusual – board books.

Charley's first night ill. by Helen Oxenbury. Candlewick, 2012. ISBN 978-0-7636-4055-2 Subj: Animals – dogs. Character traits – kindness to animals. Pets. Sleep. Weather – snow.

The dog who belonged to no one ill. by Amy Bates. Abrams, 2008. ISBN 978-0-8109-9483-6 Subj: Animals – dogs. Emotions – loneliness.

The Friday nights of Nana ill. by Claire A. Nivola. Candlewick, 2001. ISBN 978-0-7636-0658-9 Subj: Family life – grandmothers. Jewish culture. Religion.

Guess who, Baby Duck ill. by Jill Barton. Candlewick, 2004. ISBN 978-0-7636-1981-7 Subj: Activities – photographing. Birds – ducks. Family life – grandfathers. Illness – cold (disease).

Kiss good night ill. by Anita Jeram. Candlewick, 2001. ISBN 978-0-7636-0780-7 Subj: Animals – bears. Bedtime. Family life – mothers. Kissing.

Little chick ill. by Anita Jeram. Candlewick, 2009. ISBN 978-0-7636-2890-1 Subj: Birds – chickens. Gardens, gardening. Kites. Stars.

Mabel dancing ill. by Christine Davenier. Candlewick, 2000. ISBN 978-0-7636-0746-3 Subj: Activities – dancing. Bedtime. Family life – parents. Parties.

Make the team, Baby Duck ill. by Jill Barton. Candlewick, 2002. ISBN 978-0-7636-1541-3 Subj: Birds – ducks. Character traits – confidence. Family life – grandfathers. Sports – swimming.

Nana's birthday party ill. by Amy Schwartz. Morrow, 1993. ISBN 978-0-688-07498-2 Subj: Birthdays. Careers – artists. Cities, towns. Family life – cousins. Family life – grandmothers.

Off to school, Baby Duck ill. by Jill Barton. Candlewick, 1999. ISBN 978-0-7636-0244-4 Subj: Babies. Birds – ducks. Emotions – fear. Family life – grandfathers. School – first day.

The purple coat ill. by Amy Schwartz. Four Winds, 1986. ISBN 978-0-02-743640-2 Subj: Careers – tailors. Clothing – coats. Concepts – color. Family life. Family life – grandfathers.

The reader ill. by Lauren Castillo. Amazon Children's, 2012. ISBN 978-0-7614-6184-5 Subj: Animals – dogs. Books, reading. Seasons – winter. Weather – snow.

When Charley met Grampa ill. by Helen Oxenbury. Candlewick, 2013. ISBN 978-0-7636-5314-9 Subj: Animals – dogs. Family life – grandfathers. Pets. Weather – snow.

When you meet a bear on Broadway ill. by Elivia Savadier. Farrar, 2009. ISBN 978-0-374-40015-6 Subj: Animals – bears. Behavior – lost. Cities, towns. Family life – mothers.

You can do it, Sam ill. by Anita Jeram. Candlewick, 2003. ISBN 978-0-7636-1934-3 Subj: Animals – bears. Character traits – confidence. Family life – mothers. Food.

You're the boss, Baby Duck ill. by Jill Barton. Candlewick, 1997. ISBN 978-1-56402-667-5 Subj: Babies. Birds – ducks. Emotions – envy, jealousy. Family life – brothers & sisters. Family life – grandfathers. Self-concept.

Hester, Denia Lewis. *Grandma Lena's big ol' turnip* ill. by Jackie Urbanovic. Whitman, 2005. ISBN 978-0-8075-3027-6 Subj: Character traits – cooperation. Cumulative tales. Ethnic groups in the U.S. – African Americans. Farms. Food. Problem solving.

Hewett, Joan. *A flamingo chick grows up* photos by Richard Hewett. Carolrhoda, 2001. ISBN 978-1-57505-164-2 Subj: Animals – babies. Behavior – growing up. Birds – flamingos.

A giraffe calf grows up photos by Richard Hewett. Carolrhoda, 2004. ISBN 978-1-57505-197-0 Subj: Animals – babies. Animals – giraffes. Behavior – growing up.

A harbor seal pup grows up photos by Richard Hewett. Carolrhoda, 2002. ISBN 978-1-57505-166-6 Subj: Animals – babies. Animals – seals. Behavior – growing up.

A kangaroo joey grows up photos by Richard Hewett. Carolrhoda, 2002. ISBN 978-1-57505-165-9 Subj: Animals – babies. Animals – kangaroos. Behavior – growing up.

A koala joey grows up photos by Richard Hewett. Carolrhoda, 2004. ISBN 978-1-57505-198-7 Subj: Animals – babies. Animals – koalas. Behavior – growing up.

A monkey baby grows up photos by Richard Hewett. Carolrhoda, 2004. ISBN 978-1-57505-199-4 Subj: Animals – babies. Animals – monkeys. Behavior – growing up.

A penguin chick grows up photos by Richard Hewett. Carolrhoda, 2004. ISBN 978-1-57505-200-7 Subj: Animals – babies. Behavior – growing up. Birds – penguins.

A tiger cub grows up photos by Richard Hewett. Carolrhoda, 2002. ISBN 978-1-57505-163-5 Subj: Animals – babies. Animals – tigers. Behavior – growing up.

Hewitt, Kathryn. *No dogs here!* ill. by author. Penguin, 2005. ISBN 978-0-525-47200-1 Subj: Animals – dogs. Days of the week, months of the year.

Hewitt, Sally. *All year round* ill. by Tony Kenyon and Mike Atkinson. Copper Beech, 2000. ISBN 978-0-7613-1208-6 Subj: Animals. Ecology. Nature. Seasons.

Animal homes story by Inga Phipps; ill. by Fiametta Dogi. Two-Can, 2000. ISBN 978-1-58728-600-1 Subj: Animals. Homes, houses.

Face to face safari ill. by Chris Gilvan-Cartwright. Abrams, 2003. ISBN 978-0-8109-4261-5 Subj: Animals. Format, unusual – toy & movable books. Jungle.

Woods and meadows ill. by Tony Kenyon and Mike Atkinson. Copper Beech, 2000. ISBN 978-0-7613-1207-9 Subj: Animals. Ecology. Forest, woods. Nature. Seasons.

Heyer, Marilee. *The weaving of a dream: a Chinese folktale* ill. by author. Viking, 1986. ISBN 978-0-670-80555-6 Subj: Activities – weaving. Folk & fairy tales. Foreign lands – China.

Heyward, Du Bose. *The country bunny and the little gold shoes* ill. by Marjorie Flack. Houghton, 1974, ©1939. ISBN 978-0-395-18557-5 Subj: Animals – rabbits. Character traits – kindness. Holidays – Easter.

Hiatt, Fred. *Baby talk* ill. by Mark Graham. McElderry, 1999. ISBN 978-0-689-82146-2 Subj: Babies. Family life – brothers. Language.

Hickling, Meg. *Boys, girls and body science* ill. by Kim LaFave. Harbour, 2002. ISBN 978-1-55017-236-2 Subj: Anatomy. Science.

Hickman, Martha Whitmore. *A baby born in Bethlehem* ill. by Giuliano Ferri. Whitman, 1999. ISBN 978-0-8075-5522-4 Subj: Holidays – Christmas. Religion – Nativity.

Hickman, Pamela. *It's moving day!* ill. by Geraldo Valério. Kids Can, 2008. ISBN 978-1-55453-074-8 Subj: Animals. Homes, houses.

Hickox, Rebecca. *The golden sandal* ill. by Will Hillenbrand. Holiday, 1998. ISBN 978-0-8234-1331-7 Subj: Clothing. Family life – stepfamilies. Folk & fairy tales. Foreign lands – Iraq.

Hicks, Barbara Jean. *I like black and white* ill. by Lila Prap. Tiger Tales, 2006. ISBN 978-1-58925-057-4 Subj: Concepts – color. Rhyming text.

Jitterbug jam: a monster tale ill. by Alexis Deacon. Farrar, 2005. ISBN 978-0-374-33685-1 Subj: Bedtime. Emotions – fear. Monsters.

Monsters don't eat broccoli ill. by Sue Hendra. Knopf, 2009. ISBN 978-0-375-85686-0 Subj: Food. Imagination. Monsters. Rhyming text.

The secret life of Walter Kitty ill. by Dan Santat. Random House, 2007. ISBN 978-0-375-83196-6 Subj: Animals – cats. Humorous stories.

Higashi, Sandra. *Bonz, inside-out* (Glaser, Byron)

Higgins, Ryan. *Wilfred* ill. by author. Dial, 2013. ISBN 978-0-8037-3732-7 Subj: Friendship. Giants. Hair.

High, Linda Oatman. *Cool Bopper's choppers* ill. by John O'Brien. Boyds Mills, 2007. ISBN 978-1-59078-379-5 Subj: Music. Musical instruments – saxophones. Teeth.

The girl on the high-diving horse ill. by Ted Lewin. Philomel, 2003. ISBN 978-0-399-23649-5 Subj: Animals – horses, ponies. Careers – photographers. Family life – fathers. Parks. U.S. history.

The last chimney of Christmas eve ill. by Kestutis Kasparavicius. Boyds Mills, 2001. ISBN 978-1-56397-804-3 Subj: Careers. Holidays – Christmas. Santa Claus.

Tenth Avenue cowboy ill. by Bill Farnsworth. Eerdmans, 2008. ISBN 978-0-8028-5330-1 Subj: Behavior – bullying, teasing. Cities, towns. Cowboys, cowgirls. Trains. U.S. history.

Under New York ill. by Robert Rayevsky. Holiday, 2001. ISBN 978-0-8234-1551-9 Subj: Cities, towns. Concepts – opposites.

Winter shoes for Shadow Horse ill. by Ted Lewin. Boyds Mills, 2001. ISBN 978-1-56397-472-4 Subj: Animals – horses, ponies. Careers – blacksmiths. Family life – fathers.

Highet, Alistair. *The yellow train* based on a story by Fred Bernard; ill. by François Roca. Creative Editions, 2000. ISBN 978-1-56846-128-1 Subj: Careers – engineers. Family life – grandfathers. Trains.

Hill, Elizabeth Starr. *Evan's corner* ill. by Sandra Speidel. Rev. ed. Viking, 1991. ISBN 978-0-670-82830-2 Subj: Character traits – helpfulness. Ethnic groups in the U.S. – African Americans. Family life.

Hill, Eric. *Spot at home* ill. by author. Putnam, 1991. ISBN 978-0-399-21774-6 Subj: Animals – dogs. Format, unusual – board books.

Spot at play ill. by author. Putnam, 1985. ISBN 978-0-399-21228-4 Subj: Activities – playing. Animals. Animals – dogs.

Spot at the fair ill. by author. Putnam, 1985. ISBN 978-0-399-21229-1 Subj: Animals. Animals – dogs. Fairs, festivals. Format, unusual – board books.

Spot bakes a cake ill. by author. Putnam, 1994. ISBN 978-0-399-22701-1 Subj: Activities – baking, cooking. Animals – dogs. Birthdays. Food. Format, unusual – toy & movable books.

Spot counts from 1 to 10 ill. by author. Putnam, 1989. ISBN 978-0-399-21672-5 Subj: Animals. Animals – dogs. Counting, numbers. Format, unusual – board books.

Spot goes to a party ill. by author. Putnam, 1992. ISBN 978-0-399-22409-6 Subj: Animals – dogs. Cowboys, cowgirls. Format, unusual – toy & movable books. Parties.

Spot goes to school ill. by author. Putnam, 1984. ISBN 978-0-399-21073-0 Subj: Animals – dogs. Format, unusual – toy & movable books. School – first day.

Spot goes to the beach ill. by author. Putnam, 1985. ISBN 978-0-399-21247-5 Subj: Activities – playing. Animals – dogs. Family life. Format, unusual – toy & movable books. Sea & seashore – beaches.

Spot goes to the circus ill. by author. Putnam, 1986. ISBN 978-0-399-21317-5 Subj: Animals – dogs. Circus. Format, unusual – board books.

Spot goes to the farm ill. by author. Putnam, 1987. ISBN 978-0-399-21434-9 Subj: Animals. Animals – dogs. Farms. Format, unusual – board books. Machines.

Spot goes to the park ill. by author. Putnam, 1991. ISBN 978-0-399-21833-0 Subj: Activities – playing. Animals – dogs. Format, unusual – toy & movable books. Parks.

Spot looks at colors ill. by author. Putnam, 1986. ISBN 978-0-399-21349-6 Subj: Animals – dogs. Concepts – color. Format, unusual – board books.

Spot looks at opposites ill. by author. Putnam, 1989. ISBN 978-0-399-21681-7 Subj: Animals – dogs. Concepts – opposites. Format, unusual – board books.

Spot looks at shapes ill. by author. Putnam, 1986. ISBN 978-0-399-21350-2 Subj: Animals – dogs. Concepts – shape. Format, unusual – board books.

Spot looks at weather ill. by author. Putnam, 1989. ISBN 978-0-399-21673-2 Subj: Animals – dogs. Format, unusual – board books. Weather.

Spot on the farm ill. by author. Putnam, 1985. ISBN 978-0-399-21230-7 Subj: Animals. Animals – dogs. Farms. Format, unusual – board books.

Spot sleeps over ill. by author. Putnam, 1990. ISBN 978-0-399-21815-6 Subj: Activities – playing. Animals – dogs. Format, unusual – toy & movable books. Friendship. Sleepovers.

Spot visits his grandparents ill. by author. Putnam, 1996. ISBN 978-0-399-23033-2 Subj: Animals – dogs. Family life – grandparents. Format, unusual – board books.

Spot's baby sister ill. by author. Putnam, 1989. ISBN 978-0-399-21640-4 Subj: Animals – dogs. Animals – hippopotamuses. Format, unusual – toy & movable books. Reptiles – alligators, crocodiles.

Spot's big book of words / El libro grande de las palabras de Spot ill. by author. Rev. ed. Putnam, 1989. ISBN 978-0-399-21689-3 Subj: Animals – dogs. Foreign languages. Language.

Spot's birthday party ill. by author. Putnam, 1982. ISBN 978-0-399-20903-1 Subj: Birthdays. Folk & fairy tales. Format, unusual – toy & movable books.

Spot's first Christmas ill. by author. Putnam, 1983. ISBN 978-0-399-20963-5 Subj: Animals – dogs. Format, unusual – toy & movable books. Holidays – Christmas.

Spot's first Easter ill. by author. Putnam, 1988. ISBN 978-0-399-21435-6 Subj: Animals – dogs. Eggs. Format, unusual – toy & movable books. Holidays – Easter.

Spot's first walk ill. by author. Putnam, 1981. ISBN 978-0-399-20838-6 Subj: Activities – walking. Animals – dogs. Format, unusual – toy & movable books.

Spot's first words ill. by author. Putnam, 1986. ISBN 978-0-399-21348-9 Subj: Animals – dogs. Format, unusual – board books. Language.

Spot's magical Christmas ill. by author. Putnam, 1995. ISBN 978-0-399-22912-1 Subj: Animals – dogs. Format, unusual – board books. Holidays – Christmas. Santa Claus.

Where's Spot? ill. by author. Putnam, 1980. ISBN 978-0-399-20758-7 Subj: Behavior – lost. Folk & fairy tales. Format, unusual – toy & movable books.

Hill, Frances. *The bug cemetery* ill. by Vera Rosenberry. Holt, 2002. ISBN 978-0-8050-6370-7 Subj: Death. Emotions – grief. Pets.

Hill, Isabel. *Building stories* photos by author. Star Bright, 2011. ISBN 978-1-59572-279-9 Subj: Buildings. Rhyming text.

Hill, Laban Carrick. *Dave the potter: artist, poet, slave* ill. by Bryan Collier. Little, Brown, 2010. ISBN 978-0-316-10731-0 Subj: Art. Caldecott award honor books. Careers – potters. Ethnic groups in the U.S. – African Americans. Slavery.

Hill, Lee Sullivan. *Earthmovers* ill. with photos. Lerner, 2003. ISBN 978-0-8225-0689-8 Subj: Careers – construction workers. Machines.

Homes keep us warm ill. with photos. Carolrhoda, 2001. ISBN 978-1-57505-430-8 Subj: Homes, houses.

Motorcycles ill. with photos. Lerner, 2004. ISBN 978-0-8225-0695-9 Subj: Motorcycles.

Trains photos by Howard Ande. Lerner, 2003. ISBN 978-0-8225-0692-8 Subj: Trains. Transportation.

Hill, Mary. *Let's make pizza* ill. with photos. Children's Press, 2002. ISBN 978-0-516-23959-0 Subj: Activities – baking, cooking. Food.

Let's make tacos ill. with photos. Children's Press, 2002. ISBN 978-0-516-23957-6 Subj: Activities – baking, cooking. Food.

Hill, Meggan. *Nico and Lola: kindness shared between a boy and a dog* photos by Susan M. Graunke. HarperCollins, 2010. ISBN 978-0-06-199043-4 Subj: Animals – dogs. Character traits – kindness to animals.

Hill, Ros. *Shamoo: a whale of a cow* ill. by author. Simon & Schuster, 2005. ISBN 978-0-689-04634-6 Subj: Animals – bulls, cows. Animals – whales.

Hill, Susanna Leonard. *April Fool, Phyllis!* ill. by Jeffrey Ebbeler. Holiday House, 2011. ISBN 978-0-8234-2270-8 Subj: Animals – groundhogs. Holidays – April Fools' Day. Weather – blizzards.

Can't sleep without sheep ill. by Mike Wohnoutka. Walker, 2010. ISBN 978-0-8027-2066-5 Subj: Animals. Animals – sheep. Bedtime. Counting, numbers. Sleep.

The house that Mack built ill. by Ken Wilson-Max. Simon & Schuster, 2002. ISBN 978-0-689-84813-1 Subj: Cumulative tales. Format, unusual – toy & movable books. Homes, houses. Nursery rhymes. Rhyming text.

Not yet, Rose ill. by Nicole Rutten. Eerdmans, 2009. ISBN 978-0-8028-5326-4 Subj: Animals – hamsters. Babies. Family life – new sibling.

Punxsutawney Phyllis ill. by Jeffrey Ebbeler. Holiday House, 2005. ISBN 978-0-8234-1872-5 Subj: Animals – groundhogs. Gender roles. Holidays – Groundhog Day.

Hillenbrand, Jane. *What a treasure!* ill. by Will Hillenbrand. Holiday House, 2006. ISBN 978-0-8234-1896-1 Subj: Animals – moles. Character traits – confidence. Character traits – pride.

Hillenbrand, Will. *Fiddle-i-fee* ill. by author. Harcourt, 2002. ISBN 978-0-15-201945-7 Subj: Animals. Babies. Cumulative tales. Farms. Nursery rhymes.

Kite day ill. by author. Holiday House, 2012. ISBN 978-0-8234-1603-5 Subj: Animals – bears. Animals – moles. Kites.

Louie! ill. by author. Philomel, 2009. ISBN 978-0-399-24707-1 Subj: Activities – drawing. Animals – pigs. Art.

Mother Goose picture puzzles ill. by author. Marshall Cavendish, 2011. ISBN 978-0-7614-5808-1 Subj: Nursery rhymes. Picture puzzles.

My book box ill. by author. Harcourt, 2006. ISBN 978-0-15-202029-3 Subj: Animals – elephants. Books, reading.

Off we go! a Bear and Mole story ill. by author. Holiday House, 2013. ISBN 978-0-8234-2520-4 Subj: Animals – bears. Animals – moles. Sports – bicycling.

Spring is here ill. by author. Holiday House, 2011. ISBN 978-0-8234-1602-8 Subj: Animals – bears. Animals – moles. Seasons – spring.

Hilliard, Richard. *Godspeed, John Glenn* ill. by author. Boyds Mills, 2006. ISBN 978-1-59078-384-9 Subj: Careers – astronauts. U.S. history.

Hills, Tad. *Duck and Goose* ill. by author. Random House, 2006. ISBN 978-0-375-93611-1 Subj: Birds – ducks. Birds – geese. Friendship. Toys – balls.

Duck and Goose find a pumpkin ill. by author. Random House, 2009. ISBN 978-0-375-85813-0 Subj: Birds – ducks. Birds – geese. Format, unusual – board books. Seasons – fall.

Duck and Goose, how are you feeling? ill. by author. Schwartz & Wade, 2009. ISBN 978-0-375-84629-8 Subj: Birds – ducks. Birds – geese. Emotions. Format, unusual – board books.

Duck and Goose, 1, 2, 3 ill. by author. Schwartz & Wade, 2008. ISBN 978-0-375-85621-1 Subj: Birds – ducks. Birds – geese. Counting, numbers. Format, unusual – board books.

Duck, Duck, Goose ill. by author. Random House, 2007. ISBN 978-0-375-84068-5 Subj: Birds – ducks. Birds – geese. Friendship.

How Rocket learned to read ill. by author. Random House, 2010. ISBN 978-0-375-85899-4 Subj: Animals – dogs. Birds. Books, reading.

Rocket writes a story ill. by author. Random House, 2012. ISBN 978-0-375-87086-6 Subj: Activities – writing. Animals – dogs. Birds. Birds – owls. Books, reading.

Rocket's mighty words ill. by author. Random House, 2013. ISBN 978-0-385-37233-6 Subj: Animals – dogs. Birds. Format, unusual – board books. Language.

What's up, Duck? a book of opposites ill. by author. Random House, 2008. ISBN 978-0-375-84738-7 Subj: Birds – ducks. Birds – geese. Concepts – opposites. Format, unusual – board books.

Hilton, Perez. *The boy with pink hair* ill. by Jen Hill. Penguin, 2011. ISBN 978-0-451-23420-9 Subj: Behavior – bullying, teasing. Character traits – being different. Hair. School. Self-concept.

Himmelman, John. *Chickens to the rescue* ill. by author. Holt, 2006. ISBN 978-0-8050-7951-7 Subj: Birds – chickens. Character traits – helpfulness. Farms.

Cows to the rescue ill. by author. Holt, 2011. ISBN 978-0-8050-9249-3 Subj: Animals – bulls, cows. Fairs, festivals. Farms. Humorous stories.

A dandelion's life ill. by author. Children's Press, 1998. ISBN 978-0-516-21177-0 Subj: Flowers. Plants. Seeds.

A house spider's life ill. by author. Children's Press, 1999. ISBN 978-0-516-21185-5 Subj: Spiders.

Katie and the puppy next door ill. by author. Holt, 2013. ISBN 978-0-8050-9484-8 Subj: Animals – dogs. Behavior – sharing.

Katie loves the kittens ill. by author. Holt, 2008. ISBN 978-0-8050-8682-9 Subj: Animals – cats. Animals – dogs. Character traits – patience. Friendship.

A luna moth's life ill. by author. Children's Press, 1998. ISBN 978-0-516-20821-3 Subj: Insects – moths.

A monarch butterfly's life ill. by author. Children's Press, 1999. ISBN 978-0-516-21147-3 Subj: Insects – butterflies, caterpillars.

Mouse in a meadow ill. by author. Charlesbridge, 2005. ISBN 978-1-57091-520-8 Subj: Animals. Ecology. Plants.

Noisy bug sing-along ill. by author. Dawn, 2013. ISBN 978-1-58469-192-1 Subj: Insects. Noise, sounds.

Noisy frog sing-along ill. by author. Dawn, 2013. ISBN 978-1-58469-339-0 Subj: Frogs & toads. Noise, sounds.

Pigs to the rescue ill. by author. Holt, 2010. ISBN 978-0-8050-8683-6 Subj: Animals – pigs. Character traits – helpfulness. Farms.

A pill bug's life ill. by author. Children's Press, 1999. ISBN 978-0-516-21165-7 Subj: Crustaceans.

10 little hot dogs ill. by author. Marshall Cavendish, 2010. ISBN 978-0-7614-5797-8 Subj: Animals – dogs. Counting, numbers.

Tudley didn't know ill. by author. Sylvan Dell, 2006. ISBN 978-0-9764943-6-2 Subj: Character traits – individuality. Friendship. Reptiles – turtles, tortoises.

A wood frog's life ill. by author. Children's Press, 1998. ISBN 978-0-516-21178-7 Subj: Forest, woods. Frogs & toads. Nature.

Hindley, Judy. *Baby talk* ill. by Brita Granström. Candlewick, 2006. ISBN 978-0-7636-2971-7 Subj: Activities – talking. Babies. Rhyming text.

The best thing about a puppy ill. by Patricia Casey. Candlewick, 1998. ISBN 978-0-7636-0596-4 Subj: Animals – babies. Animals – dogs. Pets.

Do like a duck does ill. by Ivan Bates. Candlewick, 2002. ISBN 978-0-7636-1668-7 Subj: Animals – foxes. Birds – ducks. Rhyming text.

Does a cow say boo? ill. by Brita Granström. Candlewick, 2002. ISBN 978-0-7636-1718-9 Subj: Animals. Farms. Noise, sounds.

Eyes, nose, fingers and toes ill. by Brita Granström. Candlewick, 1999. ISBN 978-0-7636-0440-0 Subj: Anatomy. Rhyming text.

Princess Rosa's winter ill. by Margaret Chamberlain. Kingfisher, 2005. ISBN 978-0-7534-5859-4 Subj: Middle Ages. Royalty – princesses. Seasons – winter.

Rosy's visitors ill. by Helen Craig. Candlewick, 2002. ISBN 978-0-7636-1769-1 Subj: Homes, houses. Imagination. Toys.

Sleepy places ill. by Tor Freeman. Candlewick, 2006. ISBN 978-0-7636-2983-0 Subj: Animals. Bedtime. Rhyming text. Sleep.

What's in baby's morning ill. by Jo Burroughes. Candlewick, 2004. ISBN 978-0-7636-2372-2 Subj: Activities. Babies. Family life.

Hines, Anna Grossnickle. *Big like me* ill. by author. Greenwillow, 1989. ISBN 978-0-688-08355-7 Subj: Babies. Behavior – growing up. Family life.

Daddy makes the best spaghetti ill. by author. Clarion, 1986. ISBN 978-0-89919-388-5 Subj: Family life. Family life – fathers. Gender roles.

Even if I spill my milk? ill. by author. Clarion, 1994. ISBN 978-0-395-65010-3 Subj: Character traits – questioning. Emotions. Family life.

Gramma's walk ill. by author. Greenwillow, 1993. ISBN 978-0-688-11481-7 Subj: Family life – grandmothers. Disabilities – physical disabilities. Imagination. Nature. Sea & seashore.

I am a backhoe ill. by author. Tricycle, 2010. ISBN 978-1-58246-306-3 Subj: Activities – playing. Imagination. Machines. Trucks.

I am a Tyrannosaurus ill. by author. Tricycle, 2011. ISBN 978-1-58246-413-8 Subj: Dinosaurs. Imagination.

Miss Emma's wild garden ill. by author. Greenwillow, 1997. ISBN 978-0-688-14693-1 Subj: Animals. Birds. Flowers. Gardens, gardening. Insects. Plants.

My grandma is coming to town ill. by Melissa Sweet. Candlewick, 2003. ISBN 978-0-7636-1237-5 Subj: Family life – grandmothers.

My own big bed ill. by Mary Watson. Greenwillow, 1998. ISBN 978-0-688-15600-8 Subj: Emotions – fear. Furniture – beds.

No, no Jack! ill. by Pierre Pratt. Dial, 2002. ISBN 978-0-8037-2612-3 Subj: Animals – dogs. Behavior – hiding things. Format, unusual – toy & movable books.

1, 2, buckle my shoe (Mother Goose)

Pieces, a year in poems and quilts ill. by author. Greenwillow, 2001. ISBN 978-0-688-16964-0 Subj: Nature. Poetry. Quilts. Seasons.

Rumble thumble boom! ill. by author. Greenwillow, 1992. ISBN 978-0-688-10912-7 Subj: Bedtime. Emotions – fear. Weather – lightning, thunder. Weather – storms.

The secret keeper ill. by author. Greenwillow, 1990. ISBN 978-0-688-08946-7 Subj: Behavior – secrets. Family life. Holidays – Christmas.

What can you do in the rain? ill. by Thea Kliros. Greenwillow, 1999. ISBN 978-0-688-16077-7 Subj: Activities. Format, unusual – board books. Weather – rain.

What can you do in the snow? ill. by Thea Kliros. Greenwillow, 1999. ISBN 978-0-688-16078-4 Subj: Activities. Format, unusual – board books. Weather – snow.

What can you do in the sun? ill. by Thea Kliros. Greenwillow, 1999. ISBN 978-0-688-16080-7 Subj: Activities. Format, unusual – board books. Sun. Weather. Weather – rainbows.

What can you do in the wind? ill. by Thea Kliros. Greenwillow, 1999. ISBN 978-0-688-16079-1 Subj: Activities. Format, unusual – board books. Games. Weather – wind.

What Joe saw ill. by author. Greenwillow, 1994. ISBN 978-0-688-13124-1 Subj: Behavior – promptness, tardiness. Character traits – individuality.

When the goblins came knocking ill. by author. Greenwillow, 1995. ISBN 978-0-688-13736-6 Subj: Holidays – Halloween. Memories, memory. Rhyming text.

When we married Gary ill. by author. Greenwillow, 1996. ISBN 978-0-688-14277-3 Subj: Emotions – love. Family life – stepfamilies.

Whose shoes? ill. by LeUyen Pham. Harcourt, 2001. ISBN 978-0-15-201773-6 Subj: Animals – mice. Clothing – shoes. Family life. Format, unusual – toy & movable books.

Hines, Gary. *A Christmas tree in the White House* ill. by Alexandra Wallner. Holt, 1998. ISBN 978-0-8050-5076-9 Subj: Ecology. Holidays – Christmas. Trees. U.S. history.

Hirschi, Ron. *Fall* photos by Thomas D. Mangelsen. Dutton, 1991. ISBN 978-0-525-65053-9 Subj: Animals. Seasons – fall.

Our three bears photos by Thomas D. Mangelsen. Boyds Mills, 2008. ISBN 978-1-59078-015-2 Subj: Animals – bears. Nature.

Spring photos by Thomas D. Mangelsen. Dutton, 1990. ISBN 978-0-525-65037-9 Subj: Animals. Seasons – spring.

Summer photos by Thomas D. Mangelsen. Dutton, 1991. ISBN 978-0-525-65054-6 Subj: Animals. Nature. Seasons – summer.

When morning comes photos by Thomas D. Mangelsen. Boyds Mills, 2000. ISBN 978-1-56397-767-1 Subj: Animals. Birds. Morning.

When night comes photos by Thomas D. Mangelsen. Boyds Mills, 2000. ISBN 978-1-56397-766-4 Subj: Animals. Birds. Night.

Winter photos by Thomas D. Mangelsen. Dutton, 1990. ISBN 978-0-525-65026-3 Subj: Animals. Seasons – winter.

Hirsh, Marilyn. *Potato pancakes all around: a Hanukkah tale* ill. by author. Bonim Books, 1978. ISBN 978-0-88482-762-7 Subj: Food. Holidays – Hanukkah. Jewish culture. Religion.

Hirst, Robin. *My place in space* by Robin Hirst and Sally Hirst ill. by Roland Harvey and Joe Levine. Watts, 1990. ISBN 978-0-531-08459-5 Subj: Astronomy. Buses. Science. Space & space ships.

Hirst, Sally. *My place in space* (Hirst, Robin)

Hiscock, Bruce. *Coyote and badger: desert hunters of the Southwest* ill. by author. Boyds Mills, 2001. ISBN 978-1-56397-848-7 Subj: Animals. Animals – badgers. Animals – coyotes. Character traits – cooperation. Desert.

Ookpik: the travels of a snowy owl ill. by author. Boyds Mills, 2008. ISBN 978-1-59078-461-7 Subj: Birds – owls. Nature. Science.

Hiskey, Iris. *The secret of the first one up* ill. by Renée Graef. NorthWord, 2003. ISBN 978-1-55971-867-7 Subj: Animals – groundhogs. Holidays – Groundhog Day.

Hissey, Jane. *Hoot* ill. by author. Random House, 1997. Subj: Bedtime. Birds – owls. Night. Toys.

Old Bear ill. by author. Philomel, 1986. ISBN 978-0-399-21401-1 Subj: Friendship. Toys. Toys – bears.

Old Bear [board book] ill. by author. 1st American board book ed. Philomel, 1997. ISBN 978-0-399-23205-3 Subj: Format, unusual – board books. Friendship. Toys. Toys – bears.

Ho, Minfong. *Brother Rabbit: a Cambodian tale* ill. by Jennifer Hewitson. Lothrop, 1997. ISBN 978-0-688-12553-0 Subj: Animals. Animals – rabbits. Folk & fairy tales. Foreign lands – Cambodia.

Hush! a Thai lullaby ill. by Holly Meade. Orchard, 1996. ISBN 978-0-531-08850-0 Subj: Animals. Caldecott award honor books. Family life – mothers. Foreign lands – Thailand. Lullabies. Noise, sounds.

Hoban, Julia. *Amy loves the rain* ill. by Lillian Hoban. HarperCollins, 1989. ISBN 978-0-06-022358-8 Subj: Family life. Weather – rain.

Amy loves the snow ill. by Lillian Hoban. HarperCollins, 1989. ISBN 978-0-06-022395-3 Subj: Family life. Snowmen. Weather – snow.

Amy loves the sun ill. by Lillian Hoban. HarperCollins, 1988. ISBN 978-0-06-022397-7 Subj: Family life. Flowers.

Amy loves the wind ill. by Lillian Hoban. HarperCollins, 1988. ISBN 978-0-06-022403-5 Subj: Seasons – fall. Weather – wind.

Hoban, Russell. *A baby sister for Frances* ill. by Lillian Hoban. HarperCollins, 1964. ISBN 978-0-06-022336-6 Subj: Animals – badgers. Behavior – running away. Emotions – envy, jealousy. Family life. Sibling rivalry.

A bargain for Frances ill. by Lillian Hoban. HarperCollins, 1992. ISBN 978-0-06-022330-4 Subj: Animals – badgers. Friendship.

Bedtime for Frances ill. by Garth Williams. HarperCollins, 1995. ISBN 978-0-06-022351-9 Subj: Animals – badgers. Bedtime. Emotions – fear.

Best friends for Frances ill. by Lillian Hoban. HarperCollins, 1994. ISBN 978-0-06-022328-1 Subj: Animals – badgers. Family life – brothers. Family life – sisters. Friendship.

A birthday for Frances ill. by Lillian Hoban. HarperCollins, 1995. ISBN 978-0-06-022339-7 Subj: Animals – badgers. Birthdays. Emotions – envy, jealousy.

Bread and jam for Frances ill. by Lillian Hoban. HarperCollins, 1993. ISBN 978-0-06-022360-1 Subj: Animals – badgers. Food. School.

Rosie's magic horse ill. by Quentin Blake. Candlewick, 2013. ISBN 978-0-7636-6400-8 Subj: Animals – horses, ponies. Dreams. Magic.

Hoban, Tana. *A B See!* photos by author. Greenwillow, 1982. ISBN 978-0-688-00833-8 Subj: ABC books.

All about where photos by author. Greenwillow, 1991. ISBN 978-0-688-09698-4 Subj: Concepts. Language.

Black on white photos by author. Greenwillow, 1993. ISBN 978-0-688-11918-8 Subj: Concepts. Wordless.

A children's zoo photos by author. Greenwillow, 1985. ISBN 978-0-688-05204-1 Subj: Animals. Birds. Zoos.

Circles, triangles, and squares photos by author. Macmillan, 1974. ISBN 978-0-02-744830-6 Subj: Concepts – shape. Wordless.

Colors everywhere photos by author. Greenwillow, 1994. ISBN 978-0-688-12763-3 Subj: Concepts – color. Wordless.

Construction zone photos by author. Greenwillow, 1997. ISBN 978-0-688-12285-0 Subj: Activities – making things. Machines.

Count and see photos by author. Macmillan, 1972. ISBN 978-0-02-744800-9 Subj: Counting, numbers.

Cubes, cones, cylinders and spheres photos by author. Greenwillow, 2000. ISBN 978-0-688-15326-7 Subj: Concepts – shape.

Dig, drill, dump, fill photos by author. Greenwillow, 1975. ISBN 978-0-688-84016-7 Subj: Activities – digging. Machines. Wordless.

Dots, spots, speckles, and stripes photos by author. Greenwillow, 1987. ISBN 978-0-688-06863-9 Subj: Concepts. Concepts – color. Concepts – shape.

Exactly the opposite photos by author. Greenwillow, 1990. ISBN 978-0-688-08862-0 Subj: Concepts – opposites. Wordless.

I read signs photos by author. Greenwillow, 1983. ISBN 978-0-688-02318-8 Subj: Books, reading. Communication.

I read symbols photos by author. Greenwillow, 1983. ISBN 978-0-688-02332-4 Subj: Books, reading. Communication.

I walk and read photos by author. Greenwillow, 1984. ISBN 978-0-688-02576-2 Subj: Activities – walking. Books, reading.

Is it larger? Is it smaller? photos by author. Greenwillow, 1985. ISBN 978-0-688-04028-4 Subj: Concepts – size. Wordless.

Is it red? Is it yellow? Is it blue? photos by author. Greenwillow, 1978. ISBN 978-0-688-84171-3 Subj: Cities, towns. Concepts – color. Concepts – shape. Concepts – size. Wordless.

Is it rough? Is it smooth? Is it shiny? photos by author. Greenwillow, 1984. ISBN 978-0-688-03824-3 Subj: Concepts. Wordless.

Just look photos by author. Greenwillow, 1996. ISBN 978-0-688-14041-0 Subj: Format, unusual – toy & movable books. Wordless.

Let's count photos by author. Greenwillow, 1999. ISBN 978-0-688-16009-8 Subj: Counting, numbers.

Look book photos by author. Greenwillow, 1997. ISBN 978-0-688-14972-7 Subj: Format, unusual – toy & movable books. Nature. Wordless.

Look! Look! Look! photos by author. Greenwillow, 1988. ISBN 978-0-688-07240-7 Subj: Concepts. Format, unusual. Wordless.

Look up, look down photos by author. Greenwillow, 1992. ISBN 978-0-688-10578-5 Subj: Concepts – up & down.

More, fewer, less photos by author. Greenwillow, 1998. ISBN 978-0-688-15694-7 Subj: Concepts. Counting, numbers. Wordless.

Of colors and things photos by author. Greenwillow, 1989. ISBN 978-0-688-07535-4 Subj: Concepts – color.

Over, under and through photos by author. Aladdin, 1987. ISBN 978-0-689-71111-4 Subj: Concepts.

Shadows and reflections photos by author. Greenwillow, 1990. ISBN 978-0-688-07090-8 Subj: Shadows. Wordless.

Shapes, shapes, shapes photos by author. Greenwillow, 1985. ISBN 978-0-688-05833-3 Subj: Concepts – shape. Wordless.

So many circles, so many squares photos by author. Greenwillow, 1998. ISBN 978-0-688-15166-9 Subj: Concepts – shape. Wordless.

Spirals, curves, fanshapes and lines photos by author. Greenwillow, 1992. ISBN 978-0-688-11229-5 Subj: Concepts – shape. Concepts – size. Wordless.

26 letters and 99 cents photos by author. Greenwillow, 1987. ISBN 978-0-688-06362-7 Subj: ABC books. Counting, numbers. Format, unusual.

What is that? photos by author. Greenwillow, 1994. ISBN 978-0-688-12920-0 Subj: Format, unusual – board books. Wordless.

Where is it? photos by author. Macmillan, 1974. ISBN 978-0-02-744070-6 Subj: Animals – rabbits. Participation. Rhyming text.

White on black photos by author. Greenwillow, 1993. ISBN 978-0-688-11919-5 Subj: Concepts. Format, unusual – board books.

Who are they? photos by author. Greenwillow, 1994. ISBN 978-0-688-12921-7 Subj: Animals. Format, unusual – board books. Wordless.

Hobbie, Holly. *Everything but the horse* ill. by author. Little, Brown, 2010. ISBN 978-0-316-07019-5 Subj: Animals – horses, ponies. Birthdays. Farms. Moving.

Fanny ill. by author. Little, Brown, 2008. ISBN 978-0-316-16687-4 Subj: Character traits – individuality. Toys – dolls.

Fanny and Annabelle ill. by author. Little, Brown, 2009. ISBN 978-0-316-16688-1 Subj: Activities – writing. Character traits – honesty. Toys – dolls.

Gem ill. by author. Little, Brown, 2012. ISBN 978-0-316-20334-0 Subj: Ecology. Frogs & toads.

Toot and Puddle ill. by author. Little, 1997. ISBN 978-0-316-36552-9 Subj: Activities – traveling. Animals – pigs. Friendship. Letters, cards.

Toot and Puddle: let it snow ill. by author. Little, Brown, 2007. ISBN 978-0-316-16686-7 Subj: Animals – pigs. Friendship. Gifts. Holidays – Christmas. Weather – snow.

Toot and Puddle: wish you were here ill. by author. Little, Brown, 2005. ISBN 978-0-316-36602-1 Subj: Activities – traveling. Animals – pigs. Friendship. Illness. Plants.

Toot and Puddle, a present for Toot ill. by author. Little, 1998. ISBN 978-0-316-36556-7 Subj: Animals – pigs. Birthdays. Gifts.

Toot and Puddle, I'll be home for Christmas ill. by author. Little, 2001. ISBN 978-0-316-36623-6 Subj: Activities – traveling. Animals – pigs. Holidays – Christmas. Weather – blizzards. Weather – snow. Weather – storms.

Toot and Puddle, Puddle's ABC ill. by author. Little, 2000. ISBN 978-0-316-36593-2 Subj: ABC books. Animals – pigs.

Toot and Puddle, top of the world ill. by author. Little, 2002. ISBN 978-0-316-36513-0 Subj: Activities – traveling. Animals – pigs. Foreign lands – France. Foreign lands – Nepal. Friendship.

Toot and Puddle, you are my sunshine ill. by author. Little, 1999. ISBN 978-0-316-36562-8 Subj: Animals – pigs. Emotions. Friendship. Weather – lightning, thunder. Weather – storms.

Hoberman, Mary Ann. *All kinds of families* ill. by Marc Boutavant. Little, Brown, 2009. ISBN 978-0-316-14633-3 Subj: Family life. Rhyming text.

And to think that we thought that we'd never be friends ill. by Kevin Hawkes. Crown, 1999. ISBN 978-0-517-80070-6 Subj: Family life – brothers & sisters. Friendship. Rhyming text.

Bill Grogan's goat ill. by Nadine Bernard Westcott. Little, 2002. ISBN 978-0-316-36232-0 Subj: Animals – goats. Music. Songs. Trains.

A house is a house for me ill. by Betty Fraser. Viking, 1978. ISBN 978-0-670-38016-9 Subj: Homes, houses. Rhyming text.

I like old clothes ill. by Patrice Barton. Knopf, 2012. ISBN 978-0-375-86951-8 Subj: Clothing. Rhyming text.

I'm going to Grandma's ill. by Tiphanie Beeke. Harcourt, 2007. ISBN 978-0-15-216592-5 Subj: Family life – grandparents. Night. Quilts. Rhyming text.

"It's simple," said Simon ill. by Meilo So. Knopf, 2001. ISBN 978-0-375-91201-6 Subj: Animals. Animals – tigers. Humorous stories.

The looking book ill. by Laura Huliska-Beith. Little, 2002. ISBN 978-0-316-36328-0 Subj: Animals – cats. Behavior – lost & found possessions. Counting, numbers. Rhyming text.

Mary had a little lamb ill. by Nadine Bernard Westcott. Little, 2003. ISBN 978-0-316-60687-5 Subj: Animals – sheep. Nursery rhymes. Songs.

Miss Mary Mack ill. by Nadine Bernard Westcott. Little, 1998. ISBN 978-0-316-93118-2 Subj: Animals – elephants. Nursery rhymes.

Mrs. O'Leary's cow ill. by Jenny Mattheson. Little, Brown, 2007. ISBN 978-0-316-14840-5 Subj: Animals – bulls, cows. Fire. Rhyming text.

One of each ill. by Marjorie Priceman. Little, 1997. ISBN 978-0-316-36731-8 Subj: Animals – dogs. Behavior – sharing. Friendship. Rhyming text.

Right outside my window ill. by Nicholas Wilton. Mondo, 2002. ISBN 978-1-59034-194-0 Subj: Rhyming text. Seasons.

The seven silly eaters ill. by Marla Frazee. Harcourt, 1997. ISBN 978-0-15-200096-7 Subj: Birthdays. Family life – brothers & sisters. Family life – mothers. Food. Rhyming text.

The two sillies ill. by Lynne Cravath. Harcourt, 2000. ISBN 978-0-15-202221-1 Subj: Animals – cats. Animals – mice. Rhyming text.

Hochman, David. *The potty train* by David Hochman and Ruth Kennison ill. by Derek Anderson. Simon & Schuster, 2008. ISBN 978-1-4169-2833-1 Subj: Toilet training.

Hodge, Deborah. *Ants* ill. by Julian Mulock. Kids Can, 2004. ISBN 978-1-55337-066-6 Subj: Insects – ants. Science.

Bees ill. by Julian Mulock. Kids Can, 2004. ISBN 978-1-55337-065-9 Subj: Insects – bees. Science.

Eagles ill. by Nancy Gray Ogle. Kids Can, 2000. ISBN 978-1-55074-715-7 Subj: Birds – eagles. Science.

Emma's story ill. by Song Nan Zhang. Tundra, 2003. ISBN 978-0-88776-632-9 Subj: Adoption. Family life. Foreign lands – Canada. Foreign lands – China. Self-concept.

Lily and the mixed-up letters ill. by France Brassard. Tundra, 2007. ISBN 978-0-88776-757-9 Subj: Books, reading. Character traits – perseverance. Disabilities – dyslexia. School. Self-concept.

Salmon ill. by Nancy Gray Ogle. Kids Can, 2002. ISBN 978-1-55074-961-8 Subj: Fish. Science.

Watch me grow! a down-to-earth look at growing food in the city photos by Brian Harris. Kids Can, 2011. ISBN 978-1-55453-618-4 Subj: Cities, towns. Gardens, gardening.

Hodge, Marie. *Are you sleepy yet, Petey?* ill. by Renée Graef. Sterling, 2005. ISBN 978-1-4027-1265-4 Subj: Animals – dogs. Bedtime.

Hodges, Margaret. *Moses* ill. by Barry Moser. Harcourt, 2006. ISBN 978-0-15-200946-5 Subj: Religion – Moses.

Saint George and the dragon ill. by Trina Schart Hyman. Little, 1984. ISBN 978-0-316-36789-9 Subj: Caldecott award books. Dragons. Folk & fairy tales. Foreign lands – England. Middle Ages.

Silent night: the song and its story ill. by Tim Ladwig. Eerdmans, 1997. ISBN 978-0-8028-5138-3 Subj: Family life. Holidays – Christmas. Music. Songs.

The wave ill. by Blair Lent. Houghton, 1964. ISBN 978-0-395-06817-5 Subj: Caldecott award honor books. Folk & fairy tales. Foreign lands – Japan. Tsunamis.

Hodgkins, Fran. *Between the tides* ill. by Jim Sollers. Down East, 2007. ISBN 978-0-89272-727-8 Subj: Sea & seashore.

The cat of Strawberry Hill: a true story ill. by Lesia Sochor. Down East, 2005. ISBN 978-0-89272-684-4 Subj: Animals – cats. Behavior – lost.

How people learned to fly ill. by True Kelley. HarperCollins, 2007. ISBN 978-0-06-029558-5 Subj: Activities – flying. Airplanes, airports.

Who's been here? a tale in tracks ill. by Karel Hayes. Down East, 2008. ISBN 978-0-89272-714-8 Subj: Animals. Nature.

Hodgkinson, Leigh. *Boris and the snoozebox* ill. by author. Tiger Tales, 2008. ISBN 978-1-58925-071-0 Subj: Activities – traveling. Animals – cats. Letters, cards.

Boris and the wrong shadow ill. by author. Tiger Tales, 2009. ISBN 978-1-58925-082-6 Subj: Animals – cats. Animals – mice. Shadows.

Goldilocks and just one bear ill. by author. Candlewick, 2012. ISBN 978-0-7636-6172-4 Subj: Animals – bears. Behavior – misbehavior. Cities, towns. Folk & fairy tales. Humorous stories.

Limelight Larry ill. by author. Tiger Tales, 2011. ISBN 978-1-58925-102-1 Subj: Animals. Behavior – boasting. Birds – peacocks, peahens.

Smile! ill. by author. HarperCollins, 2010. ISBN 978-0-06-185269-5 Subj: Anatomy – faces. Behavior – bad day. Behavior – lost & found possessions. Emotions. Family life.

Hodson, Sally. *Granny's clan: a tale of wild orcas* ill. by Ann Jones. Dawn, 2012. ISBN 978-1-58469-172-3 Subj: Animals – whales.

Hoe, Susan. *Which shoes would you choose?* ill. by Mircea Catusanu. Innovative KIDS, 2002. ISBN 978-1-58476-102-0 Subj: Clothing – shoes. Format, unusual – board books.

Hoffman, Don. *Billy is a big boy* ill. by Todd Dakins. Popcorn, 2000. ISBN 978-0-9702518-0-0 Subj: Behavior – growing up.

A counting book with Billy and Abigail ill. by Todd Dakins. Dalmation, 2004. ISBN 978-1-4037-0543-3 Subj: Counting, numbers. Format, unusual – board books. Rhyming text.

Good morning, good night Billy and Abigail ill. by Todd Dakins. Dalmation, 2004. ISBN 978-1-4037-0542-6 Subj: Family life. Format, unusual – board books. Morning. Night. Rhyming text.

Hoffman, Elizabeth Stokes. *Miss Renée's mice* ill. by Dawn Peterson. Down East, 2001. ISBN 978-0-89272-505-2 Subj: Animals – mice. Homes, houses.

Miss Renée's mice go to an exhibition ill. by Dawn Peterson. Down East, 2003. ISBN 978-0-89272-581-6 Subj: Animals – mice. Country. Fairs, festivals.

Hoffman, Eric. *No fair to tigers / No es justo para los tigres* ill. by Janice Lee Porter. Redleaf, 1999. ISBN 978-1-884834-62-2 Subj: Animals – tigers. Foreign languages. Disabilities – physical disabilities. Toys.

Play Lady / La Señora Juguetona ill. by Suzanne Tornquist. Redleaf, 1999. ISBN 978-1-884834-61-5 Subj: Crime. Foreign languages. Gardens, gardening. Prejudice.

Hoffman, Mary. *Amazing Grace* ill. by Caroline Binch. Dial, 1991. ISBN 978-0-8037-1040-5 Subj: Ethnic groups in the U.S. – African Americans. School. Self-concept. Theater.

Clever Katya ill. by Marie Cameron. Barefoot, 1998. ISBN 978-1-901223-64-4 Subj: Animals – horses, ponies. Folk & fairy tales. Foreign lands – Russia. Riddles & jokes. Royalty – tsars.

Grace at Christmas ill. by Cornelius Van Wright and Ying-Hwa Hu. Penguin, 2011. ISBN 978-0-8037-3577-4 Subj: Ethnic groups in the U.S. – African Americans. Family life. Holidays – Christmas.

Miracles: wonders Jesus worked ill. by Jackie Morris. Fogelman, 2001. ISBN 978-0-8037-2610-9 Subj: Religion.

Parables, stories Jesus told ill. by Jackie Morris. Fogelman, 2000. ISBN 978-0-8037-2560-7 Subj: Religion.

Princess Grace ill. by Cornelius Van Wright. Dial, 2008. ISBN 978-0-8037-3260-5 Subj: Ethnic groups in the U.S. – African Americans. Parades. Royalty – princesses. School.

Three wise women ill. by Lynne Russell. Fogelman, 1999. ISBN 978-0-8037-2466-2 Subj: Character traits – wisdom. Holidays – Christmas. Religion – Nativity. Stars.

Hoffmann, E. T. A. *The nutcracker* adapt. by Janet Schulman; ill. by Renée Graef. HarperCollins, 1999. ISBN 978-0-06-027814-4 Subj: Activities – dancing. Animals – mice. Ballet. Careers – toy makers. Folk & fairy tales. Holidays – Christmas. Imagination. Royalty.

The nutcracker by Alison Jay; ill. by author. Penguin, 2010. ISBN 978-0-8037-3285-8 Subj: Activities – dancing. Animals – mice. Ballet. Folk & fairy tales. Holidays – Christmas. Imagination. Royalty. Toys.

The nutcracker retold by Stephanie Spinner; ill. by Peter Malone. Knopf, 2008. ISBN 978-0-375-84464-5 Subj: Activities – dancing. Animals – mice. Ballet. Careers – toy makers. Folk & fairy tales. Holidays – Christmas. Imagination. Royalty.

The nutcracker ill. by Maurice Sendak. Crown, 1984. ISBN 978-0-517-55285-8 Subj: Activities – dancing. Animals – mice. Ballet. Careers – toy makers. Folk & fairy tales. Holidays – Christmas. Imagination. Royalty.

The nutcracker retold by Anthea Bell; ill. by Lisbeth Zwerger. Picture Book Studio, 1987. ISBN 978-0-88708-051-7 Subj: Activities – dancing. Animals – mice. Ballet. Careers – toy makers. Folk & fairy tales. Holidays – Christmas. Imagination. Royalty.

The Nutcracker and the Mouse King adapt. by Wren Maysen; ill. by Gail de Marcken. Scholastic, 2009. ISBN 978-0-545-03773-0 Subj: Activities – dancing. Animals – mice. Ballet. Careers – toy makers. Folk & fairy tales. Holidays – Christmas. Imagination. Royalty.

The nutcracker ballet retold by Vladimir Vasilévich Vagin; ill. by Vladimir Vagin. Scholastic, 1995. ISBN 978-0-590-47220-3 Subj: Activities – dancing. Animals – mice. Ballet. Careers – toy makers. Folk & fairy tales. Holidays – Christmas. Imagination. Royalty.

Hofmeyr, Dianne. *The star-bearer* ill. by Jude Daly. Farrar, 2001. ISBN 978-0-374-37181-4 Subj: Creation. Foreign lands – Egypt.

Hogg, Gary. *Beautiful Buehla and the zany zoo makeover* ill. by Victoria Chess. HarperCollins, 2006. ISBN 978-0-06-009420-1 Subj: Animals. Character traits – appearance. Zoos.

Look what the cat dragged in! ill. by Mike Wohnoutka. Penguin, 2005. ISBN 978-0-525-46984-1 Subj: Animals – cats. Character traits – laziness. Pets.

Hogrogian, Nonny. *The contest* ill. by author. Greenwillow, 1976. ISBN 978-0-688-84042-6 Subj: Caldecott award honor books. Crime. Folk & fairy tales. Foreign lands – Armenia.

Cool cat ill. by author. Roaring Brook, 2009. ISBN 978-1-59643-429-5 Subj: Activities – painting. Animals – cats. Art. Wordless.

The first Christmas ill. by author. Greenwillow, 1995. ISBN 978-0-688-13580-5 Subj: Holidays – Christmas. Religion – Nativity.

One fine day ill. by author. Macmillan, 1971. ISBN 978-0-606-01196-9 Subj: Animals – foxes. Caldecott award books. Cumulative tales.

The tiger of Turkestan ill. by author. Hampton Roads, 2002. ISBN 978-1-57174-308-4 Subj: Animals – tigers. Character traits – individuality.

Höjer, Dan. *Heart of mine* by Dan Höjer and Lotta Höjer ill. by authors. R&S Books, 2001. ISBN 978-91-29-65301-4 Subj: Adoption. Babies. Family life. Foreign lands.

Höjer, Lotta. *Heart of mine* (Höjer, Dan)

Holabird, Katharine. *Angelina and Alice* ill. by Helen Craig. Potter/Crown, 1987. ISBN 978-0-517-56074-7 Subj: Animals – mice. Friendship. School.

Angelina and Henry ill. by Helen Craig. Pleasant, 2002. ISBN 978-1-58485-523-1 Subj: Animals – mice. Behavior – lost. Camps, camping. Family life – aunts, uncles. Forest, woods.

Angelina and the princess ill. by Helen Craig. Crown, 1984. ISBN 978-0-517-55273-5 Subj: Activities – dancing. Animals – mice. Ballet.

Angelina and the royal wedding ill. by Helen Craig. Penguin, 2010. ISBN 978-0-670-01213-8 Subj: Animals – mice. Weddings.

Angelina at the fair ill. by Helen Craig. Crown, 1985. ISBN 978-0-517-55744-0 Subj: Animals – mice. Fairs, festivals. Friendship.

Angelina at the palace ill. by Helen Craig. Penguin, 2005. ISBN 978-0-670-06048-1 Subj: Animals – mice. Ballet. Royalty – princesses.

Angelina ballerina ill. by Helen Craig. 3rd ed. Pleasant, 2004. ISBN 978-1-58485-952-9 Subj: Activities – dancing. Animals – mice. Ballet.

Angelina dances ill. by Helen Craig. Random House, 1992. ISBN 978-0-679-83484-7 Subj: Activities – dancing. Animals – mice. Ballet. Format, unusual – board books.

Angelina ice skates ill. by Helen Craig. 2nd ed. Pleasant, 2001. ISBN 978-1-58485-146-2 Subj: Animals – mice. Holidays – New Year's. Sports – ice skating. Theater.

Angelina on stage ill. by Helen Craig. Crown, 1986. ISBN 978-0-517-56073-0 Subj: Activities – dancing. Animals – mice. Ballet. Theater.

Angelina, star of the show ill. by Helen Craig. Viking, 2008. ISBN 978-0-670-01108-7 Subj: Activities – dancing. Animals – mice. Behavior – misbehavior. Boats, ships. Family life – grandparents.

Angelina's baby sister ill. by Helen Craig. Pleasant, 2000. ISBN 978-1-58485-132-5 Subj: Animals – mice. Babies. Family life – new sibling. Family life – sisters. Sibling rivalry.

Angelina's ballet class ill. by Catherine Kanner. Based on the illustrations of Helen Craig. Pleasant, 2001. ISBN 978-0-613-49711-4 Subj: Activities – dancing. Animals – mice. Ballet.

Angelina's Christmas ill. by Helen Craig. Crown, 1986. ISBN 978-0-517-55823-2 Subj: Animals – mice. Careers – postal workers. Family life – cousins. Holidays – Christmas.

Angelina's Halloween ill. by Helen Craig. Pleasant, 2000. ISBN 978-1-58485-152-3 Subj: Animals – mice. Holidays – Halloween.

Christmas in Mouseland. Based on the illustrations of Helen Craig. Penguin, 2007. ISBN 978-0-448-44663-9 Subj: Activities – dancing. Animals – mice. Ballet. Holidays – Christmas.

Christmas with Angelina ill. by Helen Craig. Random House, 1992. ISBN 978-0-679-83485-4 Subj: Animals – mice. Holidays – Christmas.

Holbrook, Stewart. *America's Ethan Allen* ill. by Lynd Ward. Houghton, 1949. ISBN 978-0-395-24449-4 Subj: Caldecott award honor books. U.S. history. War.

Holderness, Jackie. *What is a shadow?* ill. by author. Copper Beech, 2002. ISBN 978-0-7613-2821-6 Subj: Light, lights. Science. Shadows.

Holland, Simon. *Space* ill. with photos. DK, 2001. ISBN 978-0-7894-8182-5 Subj: Astronomy. Space & space ships.

Holland, Trish. *Ocean's child* (Ford, Christine)

Hollenbeck, Kathleen M. *Islands of ice* ill. by John Paul Genzo. Soundprints, 2001. ISBN 978-1-56899-965-4 Subj: Animals – seals. Science.

Holling, Holling C. *Paddle-to-the-sea* ill. by author. Houghton, 1941. ISBN 978-0-395-15082-5 Subj: Caldecott award honor books. Foreign lands – Canada. Rivers.

Holm, Sharon Lane. *Zoe's hats* ill. by author. Boyds Mills, 2003. ISBN 978-1-59078-042-8 Subj: Clothing – hats. Concepts – color. Concepts – patterns.

Holmberg, Bo R. *A day with Dad* ill. by Eva Eriksson. Candlewick, 2008. ISBN 978-0-7636-3221-2 Subj: Divorce. Family life – fathers.

Holmes, Anita. *Can you find us?* ill. with photos. Benchmark, 2001. ISBN 978-0-7614-1108-6 Subj: Animals. Disguises.

Flowers and friends ill. with photos. Benchmark, 2001. ISBN 978-0-7614-1113-0 Subj: Flowers. Friendship. Gardens, gardening.

Insect detector ill. with photos. Benchmark, 2001. ISBN 978-0-7614-1110-9 Subj: Insects.

Where robins fly ill. with photos. Benchmark, 2001. ISBN 978-0-7614-1109-3 Subj: Birds – robins.

Who dug that hole? ill. with photos. Marshall Cavendish, 2001. ISBN 978-0-7614-1112-3 Subj: Animals. Homes, houses.

Holmes, Janet A. *Have you seen Duck?* ill. by Jonathan Bentley. Scholastic, 2011. ISBN 978-0-545-22488-8 Subj: Behavior – lost & found possessions. Birds – ducks. Toys.

Me and you ill. by Judith Rossell. NorthSouth, 2009. ISBN 978-0-7358-2250-4 Subj: Activities – playing. Animals – mice. Animals – rabbits. Friendship.

Holmes, Mary Tavener. *A giraffe goes to Paris* by Mary Tavener Holmes and John Harris ill. by Jon Cannell. Marshall Cavendish, 2010. ISBN 978-0-7614-5595-0 Subj: Activities – traveling. Animals – giraffes. Foreign lands – France.

Holmquist, Delano. *SantaSaurus* ill. by Chuck Galey. Pelican, 2002. ISBN 978-1-56554-933-3 Subj: Character traits – kindness. Dinosaurs. Holidays – Christmas. Santa Claus.

Holt, Kimberly Willis. *The adventures of Granny Clearwater and Little Critter* ill. by Laura Huliska-Beith. Holt, 2010. ISBN 978-0-8050-7899-2 Subj: Behavior – lost. Family life – grandmothers. Tall tales. U.S. history – frontier & pioneer life.

Skinny brown dog ill. by Donald Saaf. Holt, 2007. ISBN 978-0-8050-7587-8 Subj: Animals – dogs. Careers – bakers.

Waiting for Gregory ill. by Gabi Swiatkowska. Holt, 2006. ISBN 978-0-8050-7388-1 Subj: Babies. Birth. Family life – cousins.

Holt, Sharon. *Did my mother do that?* ill. by Brian Lovelock. Candlewick, 2010. ISBN 978-0-7636-4685-1 Subj: Animals – babies. Bedtime. Birth.

Holub, Joan. *Apple countdown* ill. by Jan Smith. Whitman, 2009. ISBN 978-0-8075-0398-0 Subj: Counting, numbers. Food. Rhyming text. School – field trips. Trees.

Cinderdog and the wicked stepcat ill. by author. Whitman, 2001. ISBN 978-0-8075-1178-7 Subj: Animals – cats. Animals – dogs. Cowboys, cowgirls. U.S. history – frontier & pioneer life.

Geogra-fleas ill. by Regan Dunnick. Whitman, 2004. ISBN 978-0-8075-2818-1 Subj: Geography. Riddles & jokes.

Groundhog weather school ill. by Kristin Sorra. Putnam, 2009. ISBN 978-0-399-24659-3 Subj: Animals – groundhogs. Holidays – Groundhog Day. School. Weather.

The Halloween Queen ill. by Theresa Smythe. Whitman, 2004. ISBN 978-0-8075-3138-9 Subj: Holidays – Halloween. Parties. Rhyming text.

Little red writing ill. by Melissa Sweet. Chronicle, 2013. ISBN 978-0-81187-869-2 Subj: Activities – writing. Humorous stories. Language. School.

The pizza that we made ill. by Lynne Cravath. Viking, 2001. ISBN 978-0-670-03520-5 Subj: Activities – baking, cooking. Food. Rhyming text.

Pumpkin countdown ill. by Jan Smith. Whitman, 2012. ISBN 978-0-8075-6660-2 Subj: Counting, numbers. Farms. Food. School – field trips.

Scat cats ill. by Rich Davis. Viking, 2001. ISBN 978-0-670-89279-2 Subj: Animals – cats. Rhyming text.

Turkeys never gobble ill. by Jennifer Beck Harris. HarperCollins, 2002. ISBN 978-0-06-008091-4 Subj: Animals. Etiquette. Format, unusual – board books. Holidays – Thanksgiving. Rhyming text.

Twinkle, star of the week ill. by Paul Nicholls. Whitman, 2010. ISBN 978-0-8075-8131-5 Subj: Behavior – wishing. School. Stars.

Vincent van Gogh: sunflowers and swirly stars ill. with art reproductions. Grosset, 2001. ISBN 978-0-448-42612-9 Subj: Art. Careers – artists.

Wagons ho! (Hallowell, George)

Why do cats meow? ill. by Anna DiVito. Dial, 2001. ISBN 978-0-8037-2503-4 Subj: Animals – cats. Character traits – questioning.

Why do dogs bark? ill. by Anna DiVito. Dial, 2001. ISBN 978-0-8037-2504-1 Subj: Animals – dogs. Character traits – questioning.

Zero the hero ill. by Tom Lichtenheld. Holt, 2012. ISBN 978-0-8050-9384-1 Subj: Counting, numbers. Humorous stories.

Homer, Abigail. *Country mouse cottage: how we lived one hundred years ago* (Brooks, Nigel)

Town mouse house: how we lived one hundred years ago (Brooks, Nigel)

Honey, Elizabeth. *The moon in the man* ill. by author. Allen & Unwin, 2002. ISBN 978-1-86508-455-8 Subj: Nursery rhymes. Poetry.

That's not a daffodil! ill. by author. IPG/Allen & Unwin, 2012. ISBN 978-1-7423-7248-8 Subj: Gardens, gardening. Imagination. Plants. Seeds.

Hong, Chen Jiang. *The magic horse of Han Gan* ill. by author. Enchanted Lion, 2006. ISBN 978-1-59270-063-9 Subj: Activities – painting. Animals – horses, ponies. Art. Careers – artists. Folk & fairy tales. Foreign lands – China. Magic.

Hood, Susan. *Just say boo!* ill. by Jed Henry. HarperCollins, 2012. ISBN 978-0-06-201029-2 Subj: Etiquette. Holidays – Halloween. Rhyming text.

Look! I can read! ill. by Amy Wummer. Grosset, 2000. ISBN 978-0-448-42282-4 Subj: Books, reading. Ethnic groups in the U.S. – African Americans. Rhyming text.

Meet Trouble ill. by Kristina Stephenson. Grosset, 2001. ISBN 978-0-448-42455-2 Subj: Animals – cats. Behavior – misbehavior.

Spike, the mixed-up monster ill. by Melissa Sweet. Simon & Schuster, 2012. ISBN 978-1-4424-0601-8 Subj: Animals. Foreign languages. Reptiles. Reptiles – salamanders.

The Tooth Mouse ill. by Janice Nadeau. Kids Can, 2012. ISBN 978-1-55453-565-1 Subj: Animals – mice. Character traits – bravery. Character traits – cleverness. Character traits – honesty. Teeth.

Hooks, Bell. *Be boy buzz* ill. by Chris Raschka. Hyperion, 2002. ISBN 978-0-7868-2633-9 Subj: Activities. Ethnic groups in the U.S. – African Americans. Gender roles.

Grump groan growl ill. by Chris Raschka. Hyperion, 2008. ISBN 978-0-7868-0816-8 Subj: Emotions – anger.

Happy to be nappy ill. by Chris Raschka. Hyperion, 1999. ISBN 978-0-7868-2377-2 Subj: Ethnic groups in the U.S. – African Americans. Hair.

Hooks, William H. *A dozen dizzy dogs* ill. by Gary Baseman. G. Stevens, 1997. ISBN 978-0-8368-1748-5 Subj: Animals – dogs. Counting, numbers. Rhyming text.

Feed me! an Aesop fable (Aesop)

The legend of the Christmas rose ill. by Richard Williams. HarperCollins, 1998. ISBN 978-0-06-027103-9 Subj: Family life – brothers & sisters. Flowers – roses. Foreign lands – Sweden. Holidays – Christmas. Religion – Nativity.

Moss gown ill. by Donald Carrick. Clarion, 1987. ISBN 978-0-89919-460-8 Subj: Family life – fathers. Folk & fairy tales. Magic.

Hooper, Maureen Brett. *Silent night: a Christmas carol is born* ill. by Kasi Kubiak. Boyds Mills, 2001. ISBN 978-1-56397-782-4 Subj: Holidays – Christmas. Music. Songs.

Hooper, Meredith. *Celebrity cat* ill. by Bee Willey. Frances Lincoln, 2006. ISBN 978-1-84507-290-2 Subj: Animals – cats. Art. Museums.

Dogs' Night ill. by Allan Curless and Mark Burgess. Millbrook, 2000. ISBN 978-0-7613-1824-8 Subj: Animals – dogs. Art. Museums.

River story ill. by Bee Willey. Candlewick, 2000. ISBN 978-0-7636-0792-0 Subj: Rivers.

Hooper, Patricia. *Where do you sleep, little one?* ill. by John Winch. Holiday, 2001. ISBN 978-0-8234-1668-4 Subj: Animals. Poetry. Sleep.

Hoose, Hannah. *Hey little ant* (Hoose, Philip M.)

Hoose, Philip M. *Hey little ant* by Philip M. Hoose and Hannah Hoose ill. by Debbie Tilley. Tricycle, 1998. ISBN 978-1-883672-54-6 Subj: Character traits – kindness to animals. Insects – ants. Music. Songs.

Hop a little, jump a little! ill. by Annie Kubler. Child's Play, 2010. ISBN 978-1-84643-341-2 Subj: Activities. Babies. Format, unusual – board books. Rhyming text.

Hopgood, Tim. *Wow! said the owl* ill. by author. Farrar, 2009. ISBN 978-0-374-38518-7 Subj: Birds – owls. Character traits – curiosity. Concepts – color. Day. Night.

Hopkins, H. Joseph. *The tree lady: the true story of how one tree-loving woman changed a city forever* ill. by Jill McElmurry. Simon & Schuster, 2013. ISBN 978-1-4424-1402-0 Subj: Character traits – persistence. Cities, towns. Gardens, gardening. Gender roles. Trees.

Hopkins, Jackie Mims. *The gold miner's daughter: a melodramatic fairytale* ill. by Jon Goodell. Peachtree, 2006. ISBN 978-1-56145-362-7 Subj: Folk & fairy tales. U.S. history – frontier & pioneer life.

Prairie chicken little ill. by Henry Cole. Peachtree, 2013. ISBN 978-1-56145-694-9 Subj: Animals – coyotes. Behavior – gossip. Birds – chickens. Cumulative tales. Folk & fairy tales.

Hopkins, Lee Bennett. *All God's children* ill. by Amanda Schaffer. Harcourt, 1998. ISBN 978-0-15-201499-5 Subj: Poetry. Religion.

Alphathoughts ill. by Marla Baggetta. Wordsong, 2003. ISBN 978-1-56397-979-8 Subj: ABC books. Poetry.

April, bubbles, chocolate: an ABC of poetry ill. by Barry Root. Simon & Schuster, 1994. ISBN 978-0-671-75911-7 Subj: ABC books. Poetry.

Behind the museum door ill. by Stacey Dressen-McQueen. Abrams, 2007. ISBN 978-0-8109-1204-5 Subj: Art. Museums. Poetry.

City I love ill. by Marcellus Hall. Abrams, 2009. ISBN 978-0-8109-8327-4 Subj: Cities, towns. Poetry.

Full moon and star ill. by Marcellus Hall. Abrams, 2011. ISBN 978-1-4197-0013-2 Subj: Activities – writing. Character traits – cooperation. Friendship. Theater.

Good books, good times ill. by Harvey Stevenson. HarperCollins, 1990. ISBN 978-0-06-022528-5 Subj: Books, reading. Poetry.

Good rhymes, good times ill. by Frané Lessac. HarperCollins, 1995. ISBN 978-0-06-023500-0 Subj: Poetry.

Incredible inventions ill. by Julia Sarcone-Roach. Greenwillow, 2009. ISBN 978-0-06-087245-8 Subj: Inventions. Poetry.

Merrily comes our harvest in ill. by Ben Shecter. Harcourt, 1978. ISBN 978-0-15-253179-9 Subj: Holidays – Thanksgiving. Poetry. Seasons – fall.

Nasty bugs: poems ill. by Will Terry. Dial, 2012. ISBN 978-0-8037-3716-7 Subj: Insects. Poetry.

Ragged shadows: poems of Halloween night ill. by Giles Laroche. Little, 1993. ISBN 978-0-316-37276-3 Subj: Holidays – Halloween. Poetry.

School supplies ill. by Renee Flower. Simon & Schuster, 1996. ISBN 978-0-671-51172-2 Subj: Poetry. School.

Yummy! eating through a day ill. by Renée Flower. Simon & Schuster, 2000. ISBN 978-0-689-81755-7 Subj: Food. Poetry.

Hopkinson, Deborah. *Abe Lincoln crosses a creek: a tall, thin tale (introducing his forgotten frontier friend)* ill. by John Hendrix. Random House, 2008. ISBN 978-0-375-83768-5 Subj: Character traits – bravery. Friendship. U.S. history.

Annie and Helen ill. by Raúl Colón. Random House, 2012. ISBN 978-0-375-85706-5 Subj: Careers – teachers. Disabilities – blindness. Disabilities – deafness. U.S. history.

Bluebird summer ill. by Bethanne Andersen. Greenwillow, 2001. ISBN 978-0-688-17399-9 Subj: Death. Emotions. Family life – grandfathers. Farms. Memories, memory.

Fannie in the kitchen ill. by Nancy Carpenter. Atheneum, 2001. ISBN 978-0-689-81965-0 Subj: Activities – baking, cooking.

Girl wonder ill. by Terry Widener. Atheneum, 2003. ISBN 978-0-689-83300-7 Subj: Sports – baseball.

The humblebee hunter: inspired by the life and experiments of Charles Darwin and his children ill. by Jen Corace. Hyperion, 2010. ISBN 978-1-4231-1356-0 Subj: Foreign lands – England. Insects – bees. Science.

Keep on! the story of Matthew Henson, co-discoverer of the North Pole ill. by Stephen Alcorn. Peachtree, 2009. ISBN 978-1-56145-473-0 Subj: Careers – explorers. Ethnic groups in the U.S. – African Americans. Foreign lands – Arctic. U.S. history.

Knit your bit: a World War I story ill. by Steven Guarnaccia. Putnam, 2013. ISBN 978-0-399-25241-9 Subj: Activities – knitting. Clothing. Gender roles. U.S. history. War.

Maria's comet ill. by Deborah Lanino. Atheneum, 1999. ISBN 978-0-689-81501-0 Subj: Careers – astronomers. Family life. Sky.

Sweet Clara and the freedom quilt ill. by author. Knopf, 1993. ISBN 978-0-679-92311-4 Subj: Activities – sewing. Behavior – seeking better things. Ethnic groups in the U.S. – African Americans. Quilts. Slavery.

Hoppe, Paul. *Hat* ill. by author. Bloomsbury, 2009. ISBN 978-1-59990-247-0 Subj: Behavior – lost & found possessions. Clothing – hats. Imagination.

The woods ill. by author. Chronicle, 2011. ISBN 978-0-8118-7547-9 Subj: Bedtime. Behavior – lost & found possessions. Character traits – bravery. Emotions – fear. Toys.

Horacek, Petr. *Animal opposites: a pop-up book* ill. by author. Candlewick, 2013. ISBN 978-0-7636-6776-4 Subj: Animals. Concepts – opposites. Format, unusual – toy & movable books.

Beep beep ill. by author. Candlewick, 2008. ISBN 978-0-7636-3482-7 Subj: Automobiles. Format, unusual – board books.

Butterfly butterfly: a book of colors ill. by author. Candlewick, 2007. ISBN 978-0-7636-3343-1 Subj: Concepts – color. Format, unusual. Nature.

Choo choo ill. by author. Candlewick, 2008. ISBN 978-0-7636-3477-3 Subj: Format, unusual – board books. Noise, sounds. Trains.

Flip's day ill. by author. Candlewick, 2002. ISBN 978-0-7636-1798-1 Subj: Birds – penguins. Format, unusual – toy & movable books.

Jonathan and Martha ill. by author. Phaidon, 2012. ISBN 978-0-7148-6351-1 Subj: Animals – worms. Behavior – fighting, arguing. Behavior – sharing. Format, unusual.

Look out, Suzy Goose ill. by author. Candlewick, 2008. ISBN 978-0-7636-3803-0 Subj: Animals. Behavior – solitude. Birds – geese. Character traits – individuality. Noise, sounds.

My elephant ill. by author. Candlewick, 2009. ISBN 978-0-7636-4566-3 Subj: Animals – elephants. Behavior – misbehavior. Family life – grandparents. Imagination.

One spotted giraffe ill. by author. Candlewick, 2012. ISBN 978-0-7636-6157-1 Subj: Animals. Counting, numbers. Format, unusual – toy & movable books.

Puffin Peter ill. by author. Candlewick, 2013. ISBN 978-0-7636-6572-2 Subj: Animals – whales. Behavior – lost. Birds – puffins. Friendship.

Silly Suzy Goose ill. by author. Candlewick, 2006. ISBN 978-0-7636-3040-9 Subj: Animals. Animals – lions. Birds – geese. Character traits – individuality. Self-concept.

Strawberries are red ill. by author. Candlewick, 2001. ISBN 978-0-7636-1461-4 Subj: Concepts – color. Food. Format, unusual – toy & movable books.

Suzy Goose and the Christmas star ill. by author. Candlewick, 2009. ISBN 978-0-7636-4487-1 Subj: Animals. Behavior – lost. Birds – geese. Holidays – Christmas. Stars.

What is black and white? ill. by author. Candlewick, 2001. ISBN 978-0-7636-1460-7 Subj: Concepts – color.

When the moon smiled ill. by author. Candlewick, 2004. ISBN 978-0-7636-2209-1 Subj: Animals. Counting, numbers. Moon. Night. Stars.

Horn, Emily. *Excuse me — are you a witch?* ill. by Pawel Pawlak. Whispering Coyote, 2003. ISBN 978-1-58089-093-9 Subj: Animals – cats. Libraries. School. Witches.

Horn, Peter. *The best father of all* ill. by Cristina Kadmon. NorthSouth, 2003. ISBN 978-0-7358-1680-0 Subj: Animals. Family life – fathers. Reptiles – turtles, tortoises.

When I grow up . . . ill. by Cristina Kadmon. NorthSouth, 1999. ISBN 978-0-7358-1149-2 Subj: Behavior – growing up. Family life – fathers. Reptiles – turtles, tortoises.

Horn, Sandra Ann. *Babushka* ill. by Sophie Fatus. Barefoot, 2002. ISBN 978-1-84148-353-5 Subj: Folk & fairy tales. Foreign lands – Russia. Holidays – Christmas. Religion – Nativity.

The dandelion wish ill. by Jason Cockcroft. DK, 2000. ISBN 978-0-7894-6326-5 Subj: Behavior – wishing. Fairs, festivals. Plants.

Horning, Sandra. *The giant hug* ill. by Valeri Gorbachev. Knopf, 2005. ISBN 978-0-375-92477-4 Subj: Animals – pigs. Careers – postal workers. Cumulative tales. Family life – grandmothers. Hugging. Post office.

Hornsey, Chris. *Why do I have to eat off the floor?* ill. by Gwen Perkins. Walker, 2007. ISBN 978-0-8027-9617-2 Subj: Animals – dogs. Character traits – questioning. Humorous stories.

Horowitz, Dave. *Buy my hats!* ill. by author. Penguin, 2010. ISBN 978-0-399-25275-4 Subj: Animals. Careers – salespeople. Clothing – hats. Friendship.

Chico the brave. Penguin, 2012. ISBN 978-0-399-25636-3 Subj: Animals – llamas. Birds – chickens. Character traits – bravery. Emotions – fear. Foreign lands – Peru.

Duck, duck, moose ill. by author. Putnam, 2009. ISBN 978-0-399-24782-8 Subj: Activities – traveling. Animals – moose. Birds – ducks.

Humpty Dumpty climbs again ill. by author. Putnam, 2008. ISBN 978-0-399-24773-6 Subj: Character traits – bravery. Eggs. Humorous stories. Nursery rhymes. Rhyming text.

A monkey among us ill. by author. HarperCollins, 2004. ISBN 978-0-06-054335-8 Subj: Animals – giraffes. Animals – hippopotamuses. Animals – monkeys. Rhyming text.

Soon, Baboon, soon ill. by author. Penguin, 2005. ISBN 978-0-399-24268-7 Subj: Animals. Animals – baboons. Character traits – patience. Music. Musical instruments. Rhyming text.

Twenty-six pirates ill. by author. Penguin/Nancy Paulsen, 2013. ISBN 978-0-399-25777-3 Subj: ABC books. Pirates. Rhyming text.

Twenty-six princesses ill. by author. Putnam, 2008. ISBN 978-0-399-24607-4 Subj: ABC books. Rhyming text. Royalty – princesses.

The ugly pumpkin ill. by author. Penguin, 2005. ISBN 978-0-399-24267-0 Subj: Food. Holidays – Halloween. Holidays – Thanksgiving. Rhyming text.

Horowitz, Ruth. *Crab moon* ill. by Kate Kiesler. Candlewick, 2000. ISBN 978-0-7636-0709-8 Subj: Animals. Crustaceans – crabs. Sea & seashore.

Horrocks, Anita. *Silas' seven grandparents* ill. by Helen Flook. Orca, 2010. ISBN 978-1-55143-561-9 Subj: Family life – grandparents. Family life – stepfamilies.

Horsbrugh, Wilma. *The train to Glasgow* ill. by Paul Cox. Clarion, 2004. ISBN 978-0-618-38143-2 Subj: Cumulative tales. Rhyming text. Trains.

Horse, Harry. *Little rabbit lost* ill. by author. Peachtree, 2002. ISBN 978-1-56145-273-6 Subj: Animals – rabbits. Behavior – lost. Parks – amusement.

Little Rabbit runaway ill. by author. Peachtree, 2005. ISBN 978-1-56145-343-6 Subj: Animals – rabbits. Behavior – running away.

Little Rabbit's new baby ill. by author. Peachtree, 2008. ISBN 978-1-56145-431-0 Subj: Animals – rabbits. Babies. Family life – new sibling. Multiple births – triplets.

Hort, Lenny. *Did dinosaurs eat pizza? mysteries science hasn't solved* ill. by John O'Brien. Holt, 2006. ISBN 978-0-8050-6757-6 Subj: Dinosaurs. Science.

Tie your socks and clap your feet ill. by Stephen Kroninger. Atheneum, 2000. ISBN 978-0-689-83195-9 Subj: Humorous stories. Poetry.

We're going on a treasure hunt photos by Tom Arma. Abrams, 2003. ISBN 978-0-8109-4654-5 Subj: Animals. Babies. Clothing – costumes. Games. Sea & seashore.

We're going on safari photos by Tom Arma. Abrams, 2002. ISBN 978-0-8109-0574-0 Subj: Animals. Babies. Clothing – costumes.

Horton, Joan. *Hippopotamus stew: and other silly animal poems* ill. by JoAnn Adinolfi. Holt, 2006. ISBN 978-0-8050-7350-8 Subj: Animals. Poetry.

Math attack! ill. by Kyrsten Brooker. Farrar, 2009. ISBN 978-0-374-34861-8 Subj: Behavior – worrying. Counting, numbers. Rhyming text. School.

Working mummies ill. by Drazen Kozjan. Farrar, 2012. ISBN 978-0-374-38524-8 Subj: Careers. Family life – mothers. Monsters. Mummies. Rhyming text.

Horvath, David. *Bossy bear* ill. by author. Hyperion, 2007. ISBN 978-1-4231-0336-3 Subj: Animals – bears. Behavior – bossy.

Just like Bossy Bear ill. by author. Hyperion, 2009. ISBN 978-1-4231-1097-2 Subj: Animals – bears. Behavior – bossy. Reptiles – turtles, tortoises.

Horvath, James. *Dig, dogs, dig: a construction tail* ill. by author. HarperCollins, 2013. ISBN 978-0-06-218964-6 Subj: Animals – dogs. Careers – construction workers. Machines. Rhyming text. Trucks.

Horwood, Annie. *Butterfly, butterfly what colors do you see?* ill. by author. Simon & Schuster, 2001. ISBN 978-0-689-84075-3 Subj: Concepts – color. Format, unusual – toy & movable books. Insects – butterflies, caterpillars.

Hosford, Kate. *Big birthday* ill. by Holly Clifton-Brown. Carolrhoda, 2012. ISBN 978-0-7613-5410-9 Subj: Behavior – dissatisfaction. Birthdays. Character traits – individuality. Rhyming text.

Big bouffant ill. by Holly Clifton-Brown. Carolrhoda, 2011. ISBN 978-0-7613-5409-3 Subj: Character traits – appearance. Character traits – individuality. Hair. Rhyming text.

Infinity and me ill. by Gabi Swiatkowska. Carolrhoda, 2012. ISBN 978-0-7613-6726-0 Subj: Character traits – smallness. Concepts – size. Counting, numbers.

Hoshino, Felicia. *Sora and the cloud* ill. by author. Immedium, 2012. ISBN 978-1-59702-027-5 Subj: Foreign languages. Imagination. Weather – clouds.

Hosta, Dar. *I love the night* ill. by author. Brown Dog, 2003. ISBN 978-0-9721967-0-3 Subj: Animals. Night.

Hot potato: mealtime rhymes sel. by Neil Philip; ill. by Claire Henley. Clarion, 2004. ISBN 978-0-618-31554-3 Subj: Food. Poetry.

Houblon, Marie. *A world of colors: seeing colors in a new way* ill. with photos. National Geographic, 2009. ISBN 978-1-4263-0556-6 Subj: Concepts – color.

Houran, Lori Haskins. *Dig those dinosaurs* ill. by Francisca Marquez. Whitman, 2013. ISBN 978-0-8075-1579-2 Subj: Careers – paleontologists. Dinosaurs. Fossils. Rhyming text.

I will keep you safe and sound ill. by Petra Brown. Scholastic, 2013. ISBN 978-0-545-19751-9 Subj: Animals – babies. Family life – parents. Rhyming text. Safety.

House, Catherine. *A stork in a baobab tree: an African twelve days of Christmas* ill. by Polly Alakija. Frances Lincoln, 2011. ISBN 978-1-84780-116-6 Subj: Cumulative tales. Foreign lands – Africa. Holidays – Christmas. Music. Songs.

The house that Jack built. *The house that Jack built* ill. by Diana Mayo. Barefoot, 2001. ISBN 978-1-84148-251-4 Subj: Cumulative tales. Nursery rhymes.

The house that Jack built retold by Jeanette Winter; ill. by reteller. Dial, 2000. ISBN 978-0-8037-2524-9 Subj: Cumulative tales. Nursery rhymes. Rebuses.

This is the house that Jack built ill. by Simms Taback. Putnam, 2002. ISBN 978-0-399-23488-0 Subj: Cumulative tales. Nursery rhymes.

Houston, Gloria. *Miss Dorothy and her bookmobile* ill. by Susan Condie Lamb. HarperCollins, 2011. ISBN 978-0-06-029155-6 Subj: Books, reading. Libraries. Trucks.

My Great-Aunt Arizona ill. by Susan Condie Lamb. HarperCollins, 1992. ISBN 978-0-06-022607-7 Subj: Careers – teachers. Family life – aunts, uncles.

The year of the perfect Christmas tree: an Appalachian story ill. by Barbara Cooney. Dial, 1988. ISBN 978-0-8037-0300-1 Subj: Family life. Holidays – Christmas. Trees.

Hout, Mies van. *Friends* ill. by Mies van Hout. Lemniscaat, 2013. ISBN 978-1-9359-5423-1 Subj: Friendship. Monsters.

Happy ill. by Mies van Hout. Lemniscaat, 2012. ISBN 978-1-935954-14-9 Subj: Emotions. Fish.

Hovland, Henrik. *John Jensen feels different* ill. by Torill Kove. Eerdmans, 2012. ISBN 978-0-8028-5399-8 Subj: Character traits – appearance. Character traits – individuality. Reptiles – alligators, crocodiles. Self-concept.

How much does God love me? ill. by Rory Tyger. Barron's, 2001. ISBN 978-0-7641-5405-8 Subj: Format, unusual – toy & movable books. Religion.

Howard, Arthur. *Cosmo zooms* ill. by author. Harcourt, 1999. ISBN 978-0-15-201788-0 Subj: Animals – dogs. Self-concept. Sports – skateboarding.

Hoodwinked ill. by author. Harcourt, 2001. ISBN 978-0-15-202656-1 Subj: Pets. Witches.

When I was five ill. by author. Harcourt, 1996. ISBN 978-0-15-200261-9 Subj: Behavior – growing up. Friendship.

Howard, Elizabeth Fitzgerald. *Aunt Flossie's hats (and crab cakes later)* ill. by James Ransome. Houghton, 1991. ISBN 978-0-395-54682-6 Subj: Clothing – hats. Ethnic groups in the U.S. – African Americans. Family life – aunts, uncles.

Chita's Christmas tree ill. by Floyd Cooper. Bradbury, 1989. ISBN 978-0-02-744621-0 Subj: Ethnic groups in the U.S. – African Americans. Holidays – Christmas.

Virgie goes to school with us boys ill. by E. B. Lewis. Simon & Schuster, 1999. ISBN 978-0-689-80076-4 Subj: Ethnic groups in the U.S. – African Americans. Gender roles. U.S. history.

Howard, Ellen. *The log cabin Christmas* ill. by Ronald Himler. Holiday, 2000. ISBN 978-0-8234-1381-2 Subj: Family life. Holidays – Christmas. U.S. history – frontier & pioneer life.

The log cabin church ill. by Ronald Himler. Holiday, 2002. ISBN 978-0-8234-1740-7 Subj: Family life. Religion. U.S. history – frontier & pioneer life.

The log cabin quilt ill. by Ronald Himler. Holiday, 1996. ISBN 978-0-8234-1247-1 Subj: Family life – grandmothers. Quilts. U.S. history – frontier & pioneer life.

Howard, Ginger. *William's house* ill. by Larry Day. Millbrook, 2001. ISBN 978-0-7613-1674-9 Subj: Homes, houses. U.S. history.

Howard, Martin. *Tina Cocolina: queen of the cupcakes* (Cartaya, Pablo)

Howard, Reginald. *The big, big wall* ill. by José Aruego and Ariane Dewey. Harcourt, 2000. ISBN 978-0-15-216504-8 Subj: Eggs. Friendship. Rhyming text.

Howe, James. *Brontorina* ill. by Randy Cecil. Candlewick, 2010. ISBN 978-0-7636-4437-6 Subj: Ballet. Concepts – size. Dinosaurs.

The day the teacher went bananas ill. by Lillian Hoban. Dutton, 1984. ISBN 978-0-525-44107-6 Subj: Animals – gorillas. School. Zoos.

Horace and Morris but mostly Dolores ill. by Amy Walrod. Atheneum, 1999. ISBN 978-0-689-31874-0 Subj: Animals – mice. Clubs, gangs. Friendship.

Horace and Morris join the chorus (but what about Dolores?) ill. by Amy Walrod. Atheneum, 2002. ISBN 978-0-689-83939-9 Subj: Activities – singing. Animals – mice. Character traits – persistence. Emotions – anger. Friendship.

Horace and Morris say cheese (which makes Dolores sneeze!) ill. by Amy Walrod. Atheneum, 2005. ISBN 978-0-689-83940-5 Subj: Animals – mice. Food. Illness – allergies.

Houndsley and Catina ill. by Marie-Louise Gay. Candlewick, 2006. ISBN 978-0-7636-2404-0 Subj: Activities – baking, cooking. Activities – writing. Animals – cats. Animals – dogs. Friendship.

Houndsley and Catina and the birthday surprise ill. by Marie-Louise Gay. Candlewick, 2006. ISBN 978-0-7636-2405-7 Subj: Animals – cats. Animals – dogs. Birthdays. Friendship. Parties.

I wish I were a butterfly ill. by Ed Young. Harcourt, 1987. ISBN 978-0-15-200470-5 Subj: Behavior – wishing. Emotions – envy, jealousy.

Otter and odder: a love story ill. by Chris Raschka. Candlewick, 2012. ISBN 978-0-7636-4174-0 Subj: Animals – otters. Character traits – being different. Emotions – love. Fish.

There's a dragon in my sleeping bag ill. by David S. Rose. Atheneum, 1994. ISBN 978-0-689-31873-3 Subj: Dragons. Family life – brothers. Imagination – imaginary friends.

There's a monster under my bed ill. by David S. Rose. Atheneum, 1986. ISBN 978-0-689-31178-9 Subj: Emotions – fear. Furniture – beds. Monsters. Night.

Howell, Will C. *I call it sky* ill. by John Ward. Walker, 1999. ISBN 978-0-8027-8678-4 Subj: Friendship. Nature. Seasons. Weather.

Zoo flakes ABC ill. by author. Walker, 2002. ISBN 978-0-8027-8826-9 Subj: ABC books. Activities – making things. Animals. Art. Paper.

Howie, Betsy. *The Block Mess Monster* ill. by C. B. Decker. Holt, 2008. ISBN 978-0-8050-7940-1 Subj: Character traits – cleanliness. Family life – mothers. Monsters.

Howitt, Mary Botham. *Mary Howitt's The spider and the fly* ill. by Tony DiTerlizzi. Simon & Schuster, 2002. ISBN 978-0-689-85289-3 Subj: Caldecott award honor books. Insects – flies. Poetry. Spiders.

Howland, Naomi. *ABCDrive!* ill. by author. Clarion, 1994. ISBN 978-0-395-66414-8 Subj: ABC books. Activities – traveling. Automobiles.

Latkes, latkes, good to eat: a Chanukah story ill. by author. Clarion, 1999. ISBN 978-0-395-89903-8 Subj: Folk & fairy tales. Foreign lands – Russia. Holidays – Hanukkah. Jewish culture. Magic.

The matzah man ill. by author. Clarion, 2002. ISBN 978-0-618-11750-5 Subj: Behavior – running away. Cumulative tales. Food. Holidays – Passover. Jewish culture.

Princess says goodnight ill. by David Small. HarperCollins, 2010. ISBN 978-0-06-145525-4 Subj: Bedtime. Rhyming text. Royalty – princesses.

Hru, Dakari. *Joshua's Masai mask* ill. by Anna Rich. Lee & Low, 1993. ISBN 978-1-880000-02-1 Subj: Behavior – wishing. Ethnic groups in the U.S. – African Americans. Magic. Masks.

Tickle, tickle ill. by Ken Wilson-Max. Roaring Brook, 2002. ISBN 978-0-7613-1537-7 Subj: Activities – playing. Babies. Family life – fathers. Games. Rhyming text.

Hruby, Emily. *Counting in the garden* ill. by Patrick Hruby. AMMO, 2011. ISBN 978-1-934429-70-9 Subj: Animals. Counting, numbers. Gardens, gardening.

Hubbard, Crystal. *Catching the moon: the story of a young girl's baseball dream* ill. by Randy DuBurke. Lee & Low, 2005. ISBN 978-1-58430-243-8 Subj: Character traits – perseverance. Ethnic groups in the U.S. – African Americans. Gender roles. Sports – baseball. U.S. history.

Hubbard, Patricia. *My crayons talk* ill. by G. Brian Karas. Holt, 1996. ISBN 978-0-8050-3529-2 Subj: Concepts – color. Rhyming text.

Trick or treat countdown ill. by Michael Letzig. Holiday, 1999. ISBN 978-0-8234-1367-6 Subj: Counting, numbers. Holidays – Halloween. Rhyming text.

Hubbard, Woodleigh Marx. *All that you are* ill. by author. Putnam, 2000. ISBN 978-0-399-23364-7 Subj: Character traits – optimism. Self-concept.

Whoa, jealousy ill. by Madeleine Houston. Putnam, 2002. ISBN 978-0-399-23435-4 Subj: Behavior. Emotions – envy, jealousy.

Hubbell, Patricia. *Airplanes: soaring! diving! turning!* ill. by Megan Halsey. Marshall Cavendish, 2008. ISBN 978-0-7614-5388-8 Subj: Airplanes, airports. Rhyming text.

Black earth, gold sun ill. by Mary Newell DePalma. Marshall Cavendish, 2001. ISBN 978-0-7614-5090-0 Subj: Gardens, gardening. Poetry.

Boats: speeding! sailing! cruising! ill. by Megan Halsey. Marshall Cavendish, 2009. ISBN 978-0-7614-5524-0 Subj: Boats, ships. Rhyming text.

Boo! Halloween poems and limericks ill. by Jeff Spackman. Marshall Cavendish, 1998. ISBN 978-0-7614-5023-8 Subj: Holidays – Halloween. Poetry.

Bouncing time ill. by Melissa Sweet. HarperCollins, 2000. ISBN 978-0-688-17376-0 Subj: Babies. Family life. Poetry. Zoos.

Cars: rushing! honking! zooming! ill. by Megan Halsey. Marshall Cavendish, 2006. ISBN 978-0-7614-5296-6 Subj: Automobiles. Rhyming text.

Check it out! reading, finding, helping ill. by Nancy Speir. Marshall Cavendish, 2011. ISBN 978-0-7614-5803-6 Subj: Books, reading. Libraries. Rhyming text.

City kids ill. by Teresa Flavin. Marshall Cavendish, 2001. ISBN 978-0-7614-5079-5 Subj: Cities, towns. Poetry.

Earthmates ill. by Jean Cassels. Marshall Cavendish, 2000. ISBN 978-0-7614-5062-7 Subj: Animals. Poetry.

Firefighters! speeding! spraying! saving! ill. by Viviana Garofoli. Marshall Cavendish, 2007. ISBN 978-0-7614-5337-6 Subj: Careers – firefighters. Rhyming text.

Horses: trotting! prancing! racing! ill. by Joe Mathieu. Marshall Cavendish, 2011. ISBN 978-0-7614-5949-1 Subj: Animals – horses, ponies. Rhyming text.

Hurray for spring! ill. by Taia Morley. NorthWord, 2005. ISBN 978-1-55971-913-1 Subj: Rhyming text. Seasons – spring.

My first airplane ride ill. by Nancy Speir. Marshall Cavendish, 2008. ISBN 978-0-7614-5436-6 Subj: Activities – traveling. Airplanes, airports. Noise, sounds. Rhyming text.

Police: hurrying! helping! saving! ill. by Viviana Garofoli. Marshall Cavendish, 2008. ISBN 978-

0-7614-5421-2 Subj: Careers – police officers. Rhyming text.

Pots and pans ill. by Diane deGroat. HarperCollins, 1998. ISBN 978-0-694-01072-1 Subj: Activities – playing. Format, unusual – board books. Noise, sounds. Rhyming text.

Rabbit moon ill. by Wendy Watson. Marshall Cavendish, 2002. ISBN 978-0-7614-5103-7 Subj: Animals – rabbits. Days of the week, months of the year. Holidays. Rhyming text.

Sea, sand, me! ill. by Lisa Campbell Ernst. HarperCollins, 2001. ISBN 978-0-688-17379-1 Subj: Family life – mothers. Rhyming text. Sea & seashore – beaches.

Shaggy dogs, waggy dogs ill. by Donald Wu. Marshall Cavendish, 2011. ISBN 978-0-7614-5957-6 Subj: Animals – dogs. Rhyming text.

Sidewalk trip ill. by Mari Takabayashi. HarperCollins, 1999. ISBN 978-0-694-01174-2 Subj: Activities – walking. Cities, towns. Communities, neighborhoods. Family life – mothers. Rhyming text.

Snow happy! ill. by Hiroe Nakata. Tricycle, 2010. ISBN 978-1-58246-329-2 Subj: Activities – playing. Rhyming text. Weather – snow.

Teacher! sharing, helping, caring ill. by Nancy Speir. Marshall Cavendish, 2009. ISBN 978-0-7614-5574-5 Subj: Careers – teachers. Rhyming text. School.

Trains: steaming! pulling! huffing! ill. by Megan Halsey and Sean Addy. Marshall Cavendish, 2005. ISBN 978-0-7614-5194-5 Subj: Rhyming text. Trains.

Wrapping paper romp ill. by Jennifer Plecas. HarperCollins, 1998. ISBN 978-0-694-01098-1 Subj: Animals – cats. Babies. Format, unusual – board books. Gifts. Holidays – Halloween. Rhyming text.

Hubbell, Will. *Pumpkin Jack* ill. by author. Whitman, 2000. ISBN 978-0-8075-6665-7 Subj: Holidays – Halloween. Plants. Seeds.

Huber, Raymond. *Flight of the honey bee* ill. by Brian Lovelock. Candlewick, 2013. ISBN 978-0-7636-6760-3 Subj: Insects – bees. Nature.

Hubery, Julia. *A friend for all seasons* ill. by Mei Matsuoka. Simon & Schuster, 2007. ISBN 978-1-4169-2685-6 Subj: Animals – raccoons. Seasons. Trees.

Huck, Charlotte S. *A creepy countdown* ill. by Joseph A. Smith. Greenwillow, 1998. ISBN 978-0-688-15461-5 Subj: Counting, numbers. Holidays – Halloween. Rhyming text.

Princess Furball ill. by Anita Lobel. Greenwillow, 1989. ISBN 978-0-688-07838-6 Subj: Character traits – cleverness. Folk & fairy tales. Royalty – princesses.

Hucke, Johannes. *Pip in the Grand Hotel* ill. by Daniel Muller. NorthSouth, 2009. ISBN 978-0-7358-2225-2 Subj: Animals – mice. Hotels.

Hudelhoff, Allen H. *Cats and kids* ill. by Anne Canevari Green. Millbrook, 2002. ISBN 978-0-7613-2668-7 Subj: Activities – playing. Animals – cats. Character traits – cooperation.

Hudes, Quiara Alegría. *Welcome to my neighborhood! a barrio ABC* ill. by Shino Arihara. Scholastic, 2010. ISBN 978-0-545-09424-5 Subj: ABC books. Communities, neighborhoods. Ethnic groups in the U.S. – Hispanic Americans. Foreign languages. Rhyming text.

Hudson, Cheryl Willis. *Bright eyes, brown skin* by Cheryl Willis Hudson and Bernette Ford ill. by George Ford. Just Us, 1990. ISBN 978-0-940975-10-1 Subj: Ethnic groups in the U.S. – African Americans. Poetry.

Construction zone photos by Richard Sobol. Candlewick, 2006. ISBN 978-0-7636-2684-6 Subj: Buildings. Careers – construction workers. Machines.

My friend Maya loves to dance ill. by Eric Velasquez. Abrams, 2010. ISBN 978-0-8109-8328-1 Subj: Activities – dancing. Ethnic groups in the U.S. – African Americans. Disabilities – physical disabilities. Rhyming text.

Hudson, Wade. *Pass it on: African-American poetry for children* ill. by Floyd Cooper. Scholastic, 1993. ISBN 978-0-590-45770-5 Subj: Ethnic groups in the U.S. – African Americans. Poetry.

Hueston, M. P. *The all-American jump and jive jig* ill. by Amanda Haley. Sterling, 2010. ISBN 978-1-4027-5143-1 Subj: Activities – dancing. Rhyming text. U.S. history.

Huget, Jennifer LaRue. *The beginner's guide to running away from home* ill. by Red Nose Studio. Schwartz & Wade, 2013. ISBN 978-0-375-86739-2 Subj: Behavior – running away. Family life. Family life – new sibling.

The best birthday party ever ill. by LeUyen Pham. Random House, 2011. ISBN 978-0-375-84763-9 Subj: Birthdays. Parties.

How to clean your room in 10 easy steps ill. by Edward Koren. Random House, 2010. ISBN 978-0-375-84410-2 Subj: Character traits – cleanliness. Humorous stories.

Thanks a lot, Emily Post! ill. by Alexandra Boiger. Random House, 2009. ISBN 978-0-375-83853-8 Subj: Behavior. Etiquette. Family life – mothers.

Huggins, Peter. *Trosclair and the alligator* ill. by Lindsey Gardiner. Star Bright, 2006. ISBN 978-1-932065-98-5 Subj: Reptiles – alligators, crocodiles. Swamps.

Hughes, Langston. *Carol of the brown king: nativity poems* ill. by Ashley Bryan. Atheneum, 1998. ISBN 978-0-689-81877-6 Subj: Ethnic groups in the U.S. – African Americans. Holidays – Christmas. Poetry. Religion – Nativity.

I, too, am America ill. by Bryan Collier. Simon & Schuster, 2012. ISBN 978-1-4424-2008-3 Subj: Ethnic groups in the U.S. – African Americans. Poetry.

Lullaby (for a Black mother) ill. by Sean Qualls. Harcourt, 2013. ISBN 978-0-547-36265-6 Subj: Ethnic groups in the U.S. – African Americans. Family life – mothers. Lullabies. Poetry.

My people ill. by Charles R. Smith. Atheneum, 2009. ISBN 978-1-4169-3540-7 Subj: Character traits – pride. Ethnic groups in the U.S. – African Americans. Poetry. Self-concept.

The Negro speaks of rivers ill. by E. B. Lewis. Disney/Jump at the Sun, 2009. ISBN 978-0-7868-1867-9 Subj: Ethnic groups in the U.S. – African Americans. Poetry.

The sweet and sour animal book ill. by Harlem School of the Arts students. Oxford Univ. Pr., 1994. ISBN 978-0-19-509185-4 Subj: ABC books. Animals. Art. Children as illustrators. Poetry.

Hughes, Sarah. *Let's play hopscotch* ill. with photos. Children's Press, 2000. ISBN 978-0-516-23112-9 Subj: Activities – playing. Games.

Let's play jacks ill. with photos. Children's Press, 2000. ISBN 978-0-516-23113-6 Subj: Activities – playing. Games.

Hughes, Shirley. *Alfie and the big boys* ill. by author. Random House, 2008. ISBN 978-0-370-32884-3 Subj: Foreign lands – England. School – nursery.

Alfie and the birthday surprise ill. by author. Lothrop, 1998. ISBN 978-0-688-15187-4 Subj: Animals – cats. Birthdays. Gifts. Parties.

Alfie gets in first ill. by author. Lothrop, 1982. ISBN 978-0-688-00849-9 Subj: Cumulative tales. Homes, houses.

Alfie's ABC ill. by author. Lothrop, 1998. ISBN 978-0-688-16126-2 Subj: ABC books. Family life – brothers & sisters.

Annie Rose is my little sister ill. by author. Candlewick, 2003. ISBN 978-0-7636-1959-6 Subj: Activities. Family life – brothers & sisters.

Bobbo goes to school ill. by author. Candlewick, 2013. ISBN 978-0-7636-6524-1 Subj: Behavior – lost & found possessions. School. Toys.

The Christmas Eve ghost ill. by author. Candlewick, 2010. ISBN 978-0-7636-4472-7 Subj: Holidays – Christmas. Prejudice. Religion.

Don't want to go! ill. by author. Candlewick, 2010. ISBN 978-0-7636-5091-9 Subj: Activities – babysitting. Emotions – anger. Emotions – fear.

Giving ill. by author. Candlewick, 1993. ISBN 978-1-56402-129-8 Subj: Character traits – generosity. Family life.

Olly and me ill. by author. Candlewick, 2004. ISBN 978-0-7636-2374-6 Subj: Babies. Family life. Family life – brothers & sisters. Poetry.

Olly and me 1-2-3 ill. by author. Candlewick, 2009. ISBN 978-0-7636-4016-3 Subj: Counting, numbers. Family life – brothers & sisters.

Out and about ill. by author. Lothrop, 1988. ISBN 978-0-688-07691-7 Subj: Family life. Foreign lands – England. Rhyming text.

Rhymes for Annie Rose ill. by author. Lothrop, 1995. ISBN 978-0-688-14220-9 Subj: Family life – brothers & sisters. Rhyming text.

Hughes, Susan. *Earth to Audrey* ill. by Stéphane Poulin. Kids Can, 2005. ISBN 978-1-55337-843-3 Subj: Character traits – individuality. Friendship. Imagination. Seasons – summer.

Hughes, Ted. *My brother Bert* ill. by Tracey Campbell Pearson. Farrar, 2009. ISBN 978-0-374-39982-5 Subj: Behavior – collecting things. Pets. Rhyming text.

Hughes, Vi. *Aziz, the story teller* ill. by Stefan Czernecki. Crocodile, 2001. ISBN 978-1-56656-456-4 Subj: Activities – storytelling. Family life – fathers.

Hulbert, Laura. *Who has these feet?* ill. by Erik Brooks. Holt, 2011. ISBN 978-0-8050-8907-3 Subj: Anatomy – feet. Animals.

Who has this tail? ill. by Erik Brooks. Holt, 2012. ISBN 978-0-8050-9429-9 Subj: Anatomy – tails. Animals.

Huling, Jan. *Ol' Bloo's boogie-woogie band and blues ensemble* ill. by Henri Sorensen. Peachtree, 2010. ISBN 978-1-56145-436-5 Subj: Animals. Careers – musicians. Crime. Folk & fairy tales. Old age.

Puss in cowboy boots ill. by Phil Huling. Simon & Schuster, 2002. ISBN 978-0-689-83119-5 Subj: Animals – cats. Character traits – cleverness. Clothing – boots. Folk & fairy tales. Foreign lands – France. Royalty – kings.

Hull, Rod. *Mr. Betts and Mr. Potts* ill. by Jo Davies. Barefoot, 2000. ISBN 978-1-84148-106-7 Subj: Animals. Careers – veterinarians. Illness. Pets. Rhyming text.

Hulme, Joy N. *Easter babies: a springtime counting book* ill. by Dan Andreasen. Sterling, 2010. ISBN 978-1-4027-6352-6 Subj: Animals – babies. Counting, numbers. Farms. Holidays – Easter. Rhyming text. Seasons – spring.

Hume, Lachie. *Clancy the courageous cow* ill. by author. HarperCollins, 2007. ISBN 978-0-06-117249-6 Subj: Animals – bulls, cows. Character traits – appearance. Character traits – individuality. Prejudice.

Hume, Stephen Eaton. *Red moon follows truck* ill. by Leslie Elizabeth Watts. Orca, 2001. ISBN 978-1-55143-218-2 Subj: Activities – traveling. Animals – dogs. Camps, camping. Foreign lands – Canada. Moving.

Humphries, Tudor. *Are you a butterfly?* (Allen, Judy)

Are you a grasshopper? (Allen, Judy)

Are you a ladybug? (Allen, Judy)

Are you a snail? (Allen, Judy)

Are you an ant? (Allen, Judy)

Hundal, Nancy. *Camping* ill. by Brian Deines. Fitzhenry & Whiteside, 2002. ISBN 978-1-55041-668-8 Subj: Activities – vacationing. Camps, camping. Family life. Poetry.

Number 21 ill. by Brian Deines. Fitzhenry & Whiteside, 2001. ISBN 978-1-55041-543-8 Subj: Family life – fathers. Trucks.

Twilight fairies ill. by Don Kilby. Fitzhenry & Whiteside, 2002. ISBN 978-1-55041-645-9 Subj: Fairies.

Huneck, Stephen. *Sally gets a job* ill. by author. Abrams, 2008. ISBN 978-0-8109-9493-5 Subj: Animals – dogs. Imagination.

Sally goes to the beach ill. by author. Abrams, 2000. ISBN 978-0-8109-4186-1 Subj: Animals – dogs. Sea & seashore – beaches.

Sally goes to the farm ill. by author. Abrams, 2002. ISBN 978-0-8109-4498-5 Subj: Animals. Animals – dogs. Farms.

Sally goes to the mountains ill. by author. Abrams, 2001. ISBN 978-0-8109-4485-5 Subj: Animals – dogs. Camps, camping. Mountains.

Sally's great balloon adventure ill. by author. Abrams, 2010. ISBN 978-0-8109-8331-1 Subj: Activities – ballooning. Animals – dogs.

Sally's snow adventure ill. by author. Abrams, 2006. ISBN 978-0-8109-7061-8 Subj: Animals – dogs. Behavior – lost. Seasons – winter. Sports – skiing. Weather – snow.

Hunt, Joyce. *Keep looking!* (Selsam, Millicent E.)

Hunter, Anne. *Possum and the peeper* ill. by author. Houghton, 1998. ISBN 978-0-395-84631-5 Subj: Animals. Animals – possums. Frogs & toads. Seasons – spring.

Possum's harvest moon ill. by author. Houghton, 1996. ISBN 978-0-395-73575-6 Subj: Animals. Animals – possums. Moon. Parties. Seasons.

What's in the meadow? ill. by author. Houghton, 2000. ISBN 978-0-618-01512-2 Subj: Animals. Birds. Insects.

What's in the tide pool? ill. by author. Houghton, 2000. ISBN 978-0-618-01510-8 Subj: Animals. Sea & seashore.

Hunter, Dette. *38 ways to entertain your babysitter* ill. by Stephen MacEachern. Annick, 2003. ISBN 978-1-55037-795-8 Subj: Activities – babysitting. Activities – baking, cooking. Activities – making things. Games.

38 ways to entertain your grandparents ill. by Deirdre Betteridge. Annick, 2002. ISBN 978-1-55037-749-1 Subj: Activities – baking, cooking. Activities – making things. Family life – grandparents. Games.

Hunter, Jana Novotny. *Little ones do* ill. by Sally Anne Lambert. Dutton, 2001. ISBN 978-0-525-46690-1 Subj: Dragons. Family life – parents. Rhyming text.

When Daddy's truck picks me up ill. by Carol Thompson. Whitman, 2006. ISBN 978-0-8075-8914-4 Subj: Family life – fathers. Rhyming text. Trucks.

Hunter, Sally. *Humphrey's bedtime* ill. by author. Holt, 2001. ISBN 978-0-8050-6903-7 Subj: Animals – elephants. Bedtime. Family life – brothers & sisters.

Humphrey's birthday ill. by author. Holt, 2003. ISBN 978-0-8050-7421-5 Subj: Animals – elephants. Birthdays. Parties.

Humphrey's Christmas ill. by author. Holt, 2002. ISBN 978-0-8050-7176-4 Subj: Animals – elephants. Family life – brothers & sisters. Holidays – Christmas.

Humphrey's corner ill. by author. Holt, 2001. ISBN 978-0-8050-6786-6 Subj: Activities – playing. Animals – elephants. Family life – mothers.

Hunter, Tom. *Build it up and knock it down* ill. by James Yang. HarperCollins, 2002. ISBN 978-0-694-01568-9 Subj: Concepts – opposites. Friendship. Language.

Huntington, Amy. *One Monday* ill. by author. Orchard, 2001. ISBN 978-0-439-29304-4 Subj: Farms. Weather – wind.

Hurd, Thacher. *Art dog* ill. by author. HarperCollins, 1996. ISBN 978-0-06-024425-5 Subj: Activities – painting. Animals – dogs. Art. Museums. Mystery stories.

Bad frogs ill. by author. Candlewick, 2009. ISBN 978-0-7636-3253-3 Subj: Behavior – misbehavior. Frogs & toads. Rhyming text.

Cat's pajamas ill. by author. HarperCollins, 2001. ISBN 978-0-694-01058-5 Subj: Animals – cats. Format, unusual – board books. Language. Rhyming text.

Little Mouse's big Valentine ill. by author. HarperCollins, 1990. ISBN 978-0-06-026193-1 Subj: Animals – mice. Holidays – Valentine's Day.

Mama don't allow ill. by author. HarperCollins, 1984. ISBN 978-0-06-022690-9 Subj: Animals – possums. Music. Musical instruments – bands. Reptiles – alligators, crocodiles.

Moo Cow Kaboom! ill. by author. HarperCollins, 2003. ISBN 978-0-06-050502-8 Subj: Animals – bulls, cows. Farms. Space & space ships.

Santa Mouse and the ratdeer ill. by author. HarperCollins, 1998. ISBN 978-0-06-027694-2 Subj: Accidents. Animals – mice. Behavior – bad day. Holidays – Christmas. Santa Claus.

Sleepy Cadillac: a bedtime drive ill. by author. HarperCollins, 2005. ISBN 978-0-06-073021-5 Subj: Automobiles. Bedtime. Sleep.

The weaver ill. by Elisa Kleven. Farrar, 2010. ISBN 978-0-374-38254-4 Subj: Activities – weaving. Dreams.

Zoom City ill. by author. HarperCollins, 1998. ISBN 978-0-694-01057-8 Subj: Automobiles. Cities, towns.

Hurst, Carol Otis. *Rocks in his head* ill. by James Stevenson. Greenwillow, 2001. ISBN 978-0-06-029404-5 Subj: Behavior – collecting things. Rocks. U.S. history.

Terrible storm ill. by S. D. Schindler. HarperCollins, 2007. ISBN 978-0-06-009001-2 Subj: Family life – grandfathers. Seasons – winter. Weather – blizzards.

Hurst, Margaret M. *Grannie and the Jumbie* ill. by author. HarperCollins, 2001. ISBN 978-0-06-623633-9 Subj: Folk & fairy tales. Foreign lands – Caribbean Islands.

Hurston, Zora Neale. *The six fools* adapt. by Joyce Carol Thomas; ill. by Ann Tanksley. HarperCollins, 2006. ISBN 978-0-06-000647-1 Subj: Character traits – foolishness. Ethnic groups in the U.S. – African Americans. Folk & fairy tales.

Hurwitz, Johanna. *Ethan out and about* ill. by Brian Floca. Candlewick, 2002. ISBN 978-0-7636-1098-2 Subj: Animals. Family life – fathers. Food.

Mighty Monty ill. by Anik McGrory. Candlewick, 2008. ISBN 978-0-7636-2977-9 Subj: Character traits – shyness. Illness – asthma. School.

Russell's secret ill. by Heather Maione. HarperCollins, 2001. ISBN 978-0-688-17575-7 Subj: Babies. Family life – brothers & sisters. Sibling rivalry.

Hurwitz, Laura. *Polar bear puzzle* (Lumry, Amanda)

Safari in South Africa (Lumry, Amanda)

Husband, Amy. *Dear Teacher* ill. by author. Sourcebooks, 2010. ISBN 978-1-4022-4268-7 Subj: Imagination. Letters, cards. School.

Hush, little baby ill. by Marla Frazee. Browndeer, 1999. ISBN 978-0-15-201429-2 Subj: Babies. Character traits – generosity. Cumulative tales. Lullabies. Music.

Hush songs: African American lullabies col., ed., & commentary by Joyce Carol Thomas; ill. by Brenda Joysmith. Jump at the Sun, 2000. ISBN 978-0-7868-2488-5 Subj: Ethnic groups in the U.S. – African Americans. Lullabies. Music. Songs.

Hutchins, Hazel. *Beneath the bridge* ill. by Ruth Ohi. Annick, 2004. ISBN 978-1-55037-859-7 Subj: Activities – traveling. Boats, ships. Dreams. Rhyming text.

I'd know you anywhere ill. by Ruth Ohi. Annick, 2002. ISBN 978-1-55037-747-7 Subj: Disguises. Family life – fathers.

Mattland by Hazel Hutchins and Gail Herbert ill. by Dusan Petricic. Annick, 2008. ISBN 978-1-55451-121-1 Subj: Character traits – cooperation. Friendship.

One dark night ill. by Susan Kathleen Hartung. Viking, 2001. ISBN 978-0-670-89246-4 Subj: Animals – babies. Animals – cats. Family life – grandparents. Weather – lightning, thunder. Weather – storms.

A second is a hiccup: a child's book of time ill. by Kady MacDonald Denton. Scholastic, 2007. ISBN 978-0-439-83106-2 Subj: Time.

The sidewalk rescue ill. by Ruth Ohi. Annick, 2004. ISBN 978-1-55037-831-3 Subj: Activities – drawing. Art.

Two so small ill. by Ruth Ohi. Firefly, 2000. ISBN 978-1-55037-651-7 Subj: Babies. Concepts – size. Format, unusual – toy & movable books. Giants.

Up dog ill. by Fanny. Annick, 2012. ISBN 978-155451-389-5 Subj: Animals – dogs. Format, unusual – board books.

Hutchins, Pat. *Barn dance!* ill. by author. HarperCollins, 2007. ISBN 978-0-06-089122-0 Subj: Activities – dancing. Animals. Farms.

Bumpety bump ill. by author. HarperCollins, 2006. ISBN 978-0-06-056000-3 Subj: Birds – chickens. Family life – grandfathers. Farms. Rhyming text.

Changes, changes ill. by author. Macmillan, 1971. ISBN 978-0-02-745870-1 Subj: Toys – blocks. Wordless.

Clocks and more clocks ill. by author. Macmillan, 1994. ISBN 978-0-02-745921-0 Subj: Clocks, watches. Humorous stories. Time.

Don't forget the bacon! ill. by author. Greenwillow, 1975. ISBN 978-0-688-84019-8 Subj: Behavior – forgetfulness. Cumulative tales. Food. Humorous stories. Shopping.

The doorbell rang ill. by author. Greenwillow, 1986. ISBN 978-0-688-05252-2 Subj: Behavior – sharing. Family life. Friendship.

Good-night Owl ill. by author. Macmillan, 1991. ISBN 978-0-689-71541-9 Subj: Birds – owls. Cumulative tales. Noise, sounds. Participation. Sleep.

Happy birthday, Sam ill. by author. Greenwillow, 1978. ISBN 978-0-688-84160-7 Subj: Birthdays. Family life – grandfathers.

It's my birthday! ill. by author. Greenwillow, 1999. ISBN 978-0-688-09664-9 Subj: Behavior – sharing. Birthdays. Family life. Gifts. Monsters.

Little pink pig ill. by author. Greenwillow, 1994. ISBN 978-0-688-12015-3 Subj: Animals. Animals – pigs. Bedtime. Behavior – promptness, tardiness.

My best friend ill. by author. Greenwillow, 1993. ISBN 978-0-688-11486-2 Subj: Ethnic groups in the U.S. – African Americans. Friendship.

1 hunter ill. by author. Greenwillow, 1982. ISBN 978-0-688-00615-0 Subj: Animals. Counting, numbers.

Rosie's walk ill. by author. Macmillan, 1968. ISBN 978-0-02-745850-3 Subj: Animals – foxes. Birds – chickens. Farms. Humorous stories.

Rosie's walk [board book] ill. by author. 1st Little Simon board book ed. Simon & Schuster, 1998. ISBN 978-0-689-82231-5 Subj: Animals. Animals – foxes. Birds – chickens. Farms. Format, unusual – board books.

Shrinking mouse ill. by author. Greenwillow, 1997. ISBN 978-0-688-13962-9 Subj: Animals. Concepts – perspective. Concepts – size.

Silly Billy! ill. by author. Greenwillow, 1992. ISBN 978-0-688-10818-2 Subj: Family life – brothers & sisters. Monsters.

The surprise party ill. by author. Macmillan, 1986, 1969. ISBN 978-0-02-745930-2 Subj: Animals. Behavior – gossip. Parties.

Ten red apples ill. by author. Greenwillow, 2000. ISBN 978-0-688-16798-1 Subj: Animals. Counting, numbers. Food. Noise, sounds. Rhyming text.

Three-star Billy ill. by author. Greenwillow, 1994. ISBN 978-0-688-13079-4 Subj: Behavior – misbehavior. Monsters. School.

Tidy Titch ill. by author. Greenwillow, 1991. ISBN 978-0-688-09964-0 Subj: Behavior. Family life. Toys.

Titch ill. by author. Macmillan, 1971. Subj: Concepts – size. Cumulative tales. Family life. Plants.

Titch and Daisy ill. by author. Greenwillow, 1996. ISBN 978-0-688-13960-5 Subj: Behavior – hiding. Character traits – shyness. Friendship. Parties.

The very worst monster ill. by author. Greenwillow, 1985. ISBN 978-0-688-04011-6 Subj: Monsters. Sibling rivalry.

What game shall we play? ill. by author. Greenwillow, 1990. ISBN 978-0-688-09197-2 Subj: Animals. Games.

Where's the baby? ill. by author. Greenwillow, 1988. ISBN 978-0-688-05934-7 Subj: Babies. Behavior – lost. Behavior – misbehavior. Character traits – cleanliness. Monsters.

Which witch is which? ill. by author. Greenwillow, 1989. ISBN 978-0-688-06358-0 Subj: Games. Holidays – Halloween. Multiple births – twins. Parties. Rhyming text.

The wind blew ill. by author. Macmillan, 1974. ISBN 978-0-02-745910-4 Subj: Rhyming text. Weather – wind.

You'll soon grow into them, Titch ill. by author. Greenwillow, 1983. ISBN 978-0-688-01771-2 Subj: Clothing. Family life.

Hyde, Heidi Smith. *Emanuel and the Hanukkah rescue* ill. by Jamel Akib. Lerner/Kar-Ben, 2012. ISBN 978-0-7613-6625-6 Subj: Boats, ships. Holidays – Hanukkah. Jewish culture.

Mendel's accordion ill. by Johanna van der Sterre. Lerner, 2007. ISBN 978-1-58013-212-1 Subj: Immigrants. Jewish culture. Music. Musical instruments – accordions.

Hyde, Margaret E. *Matisse for kids.* Penguin, 2004. ISBN 978-1-58980-204-9 Subj: Art. Careers – artists. Format, unusual – board books.

Van Gogh for kids. Penguin, 2004. ISBN 978-1-58980-207-0 Subj: Art. Careers – artists. Format, unusual – board books.

Hyman, Trina Schart. *A little alphabet* ill. by author. SeaStar, 2000. Originally pub. Little, Brown, ©1980. ISBN 978-1-58717-008-9 Subj: ABC books. Language.

I imagine angels ed. by William Lach. Atheneum, 2000. ISBN 978-0-689-84080-7 Subj: Angels. Art. Religion.

I invited a dragon to dinner ill. by Chris L. Demarest. Philomel, 2002. ISBN 978-0-399-23567-2 Subj: Humorous stories. Poetry.

Ichikawa, Satomi. *Come fly with me* ill. by author. Philomel, 2008. ISBN 978-0-399-24679-1 Subj: Activities – flying. Airplanes, airports. Animals – dogs. Foreign lands – France. Imagination. Toys.

The first bear in Africa! ill. by author. Philomel, 2001. ISBN 978-0-399-23485-9 Subj: Behavior – lost & found possessions. Foreign lands – Africa. Toys – bears.

I am Pangoo the penguin ill. by author. Penguin, 2006. ISBN 978-0-399-23313-5 Subj: Behavior – running away. Birds – penguins. Toys. Zoos.

La La Rose ill. by author. Philomel, 2004. ISBN 978-0-399-24029-4 Subj: Animals – rabbits. Behavior – lost. Foreign lands – France. Parks. Toys.

My father's shop ill. by author. Kane/Miller, 2006. ISBN 978-1-929132-99-7 Subj: Family life – fathers. Foreign lands – Morocco. Shopping.

My little train ill. by author. Penguin, 2010. ISBN 978-0-399-25453-6 Subj: Animals. Imagination. Toys. Trains.

What the little fir tree wore to the Christmas party ill. by author. Philomel, 2001. ISBN 978-0-399-23746-1 Subj: Holidays – Christmas. Trees.

Idle, Molly. *Flora and the flamingo* ill. by author. Chronicle, 2013. ISBN 978-1-4521-1006-6 Subj: Activities – dancing. Birds – flamingos. Caldecott award honor books. Format, unusual – toy & movable books. Friendship. Wordless.

Tea Rex ill. by author. Viking, 2013. ISBN 978-0-670-01430-9 Subj: Dinosaurs. Etiquette. Parties.

Iijima, Geneva Cobb. *The way we do it in Japan* ill. by Paige Billin-Frye. Whitman, 2002. ISBN 978-0-8075-7822-3 Subj: Family life – parents. Foreign lands – Japan. Foreign languages.

Imagine that! poems of never-was sel. by Jack Prelutsky; ill. by Kevin Hawkes. Knopf, 1998. ISBN 978-0-679-98206-7 Subj: Imagination. Poetry.

Imai, Ayano. *Chester* ill. by author. Minedition, 2007. ISBN 978-0-698-40062-7 Subj: Animals – dogs. Behavior – running away. Pets.

The 108th sheep ill. by author. Tiger Tales, 2007. ISBN 978-1-58925-063-5 Subj: Animals – sheep. Bedtime. Counting, numbers.

Imbody, Amy. *Snug as a bug?* ill. by Mike Gordon. Zondervan, 2001. ISBN 978-0-310-70063-0 Subj: Bedtime. Rhyming text.

Imershein, Betsy. *Trucks* photos by author. Simon & Schuster, 2000. ISBN 978-0-689-82887-4 Subj: Format, unusual – board books. Trucks.

In daddy's arms I am tall ill. by Javaka Steptoe. Lee & Low, 1997. ISBN 978-1-880000-31-1 Subj: Ethnic groups in the U.S. – African Americans. Family life – fathers. Poetry.

Inches, Alison. *Corduroy writes a letter* ill. by Allan Eitzen. Based on the character created by Don Freeman. Viking, 2002. ISBN 978-0-670-03548-9 Subj: Activities – writing. Letters, cards. Toys – bears.

Corduroy's garden ill. by Allan Eitzen. Based on the character created by Don Freeman. Viking, 2002. ISBN 978-0-670-03547-2 Subj: Gardens, gardening. Plants. Toys – bears.

Corduroy's hike ill. by Allan Eitzen. Based on the character created by Don Freeman. Viking, 2001. ISBN 978-0-670-88945-7 Subj: Activities – walking. Behavior – lost. Toys – bears.

The stuffed animals get ready for bed ill. by Bryan Langdo. Harcourt, 2006. ISBN 978-0-15-216466-9 Subj: Bedtime. Rhyming text. Toys.

Ingalls, Ann. *The little piano girl: the story of Mary Lou Williams, jazz legend* by Ann Ingalls and Maryann Macdonald ill. by Giselle Potter. Houghton Mifflin, 2010. ISBN 978-0-618-95974-7 Subj: Careers – musicians. Ethnic groups in the U.S. – African Americans. Music. Musical instruments – pianos.

Inkpen, Deborah. *Harriet and the little fat fairy* ill. by author. Barron's, 2002. ISBN 978-0-7641-5562-8 Subj: Animals – hamsters. Fairies. Holidays – Christmas. Pets.

Inkpen, Mick. *The great pet sale* ill. by author. Orchard, 1999. ISBN 978-0-531-30130-2 Subj: Animals. Money. Pets.

Hissss! ill. by author. Harcourt, 2000. ISBN 978-0-15-202415-4 Subj: Animals – dogs. Seasons – summer.

Honk! ill. by author. Harcourt, 1998. ISBN 978-0-15-202284-6 Subj: Animals – dogs. Birds – geese. Noise, sounds.

Jasper's beanstalk (Butterworth, Nick)

Kipper ill. by author. Little, 1992. ISBN 978-0-316-41883-6 Subj: Animals – dogs. Behavior – imitation. Sleep.

Kipper and Roly ill. by author. Harcourt, 2001. ISBN 978-0-15-216344-0 Subj: Animals – dogs. Animals – hamsters. Animals – pigs. Birthdays. Gifts. Pets.

Kipper's A to Z ill. by author. Harcourt, 2000. ISBN 978-0-15-202594-6 Subj: ABC books. Animals. Animals – dogs. Animals – pigs.

Kipper's birthday ill. by author. Harcourt, 1993. ISBN 978-0-15-200503-0 Subj: Animals – dogs. Behavior – mistakes. Birthdays. Parties.

Kipper's book of colors ill. by author. Harcourt, 1995. ISBN 978-0-15-200647-1 Subj: Animals – dogs. Concepts – color.

Kipper's book of numbers ill. by author. Harcourt, 1995. ISBN 978-0-15-200646-4 Subj: Animals. Animals – dogs. Counting, numbers.

Kipper's book of opposites ill. by author. Harcourt, 1995. ISBN 978-0-15-200668-6 Subj: Animals – dogs. Concepts – opposites. Language.

Kipper's book of weather ill. by author. Harcourt, 1995. ISBN 978-0-15-200644-0 Subj: Animals – dogs. Weather.

Kipper's Christmas eve ill. by author. Harcourt, 1999. ISBN 978-0-15-202660-8 Subj: Animals – dogs. Format, unusual – toy & movable books. Friendship. Holidays – Christmas.

Kipper's monster ill. by author. Harcourt, 2002. ISBN 978-0-15-216614-4 Subj: Animals – dogs. Camps, camping. Monsters.

Kipper's rainy day ill. by Stuart Trotter. Based on the books by Mick Inkpen. Harcourt, 2001. ISBN 978-0-15-216351-8 Subj: Animals – dogs. Format, unusual – toy & movable books. Weather – rain.

Kipper's snowy day ill. by author. Harcourt, 1996. ISBN 978-0-15-201362-2 Subj: Activities – playing. Animals – dogs. Friendship. Toys. Weather – snow.

Kipper's sunny day ill. by Stuart Trotter. Based on the books by Mick Inkpen. Harcourt, 2002. ISBN 978-0-15-216357-0 Subj: Animals – dogs. Format, unusual – toy & movable books. Sea & seashore – beaches.

Kipper's toybox ill. by author. Harcourt, 1992. ISBN 978-0-15-200501-6 Subj: Animals – dogs. Animals – mice. Counting, numbers. Toys.

Meow! ill. by author. Harcourt, 2000. ISBN 978-0-15-202666-0 Subj: Animals. Animals – cats. Animals – dogs.

Nothing ill. by author. Orchard, 1998. ISBN 978-0-531-30076-3 Subj: Names. Self-concept. Toys.

Picnic ill. by author. Harcourt, 2001. ISBN 978-0-15-216319-8 Subj: Activities – picnicking. Animals. Animals – dogs.

Sandcastle ill. by author. Harcourt, 1998. ISBN 978-0-15-202296-9 Subj: Sand. Sea & seashore.

Splosh! ill. by author. Harcourt, 1998. ISBN 978-0-15-202299-0 Subj: Animals. Animals – dogs. Weather – rain.

Swing! ill. by author. Harcourt, 2000. ISBN 978-0-15-202672-1 Subj: Activities – playing. Animals – dogs. Friendship.

Thing ill. by author. Harcourt, 2001. ISBN 978-0-15-216326-6 Subj: Animals – dogs. Bubbles. Toys.

Wibbly Pig can make a tent ill. by author. Golden, 1995. ISBN 978-0-307-16628-9 Subj: Activities – making things. Activities – playing. Animals – pigs. Camps, camping. Format, unusual – board books.

Wibbly Pig is upset ill. by author. Golden, 1995. ISBN 978-0-307-16629-6 Subj: Animals – pigs. Emotions. Format, unusual – board books.

Wibbly Pig likes bananas ill. by author. Golden, 1995. ISBN 978-0-307-16630-2 Subj: Animals – pigs. Food. Format, unusual – board books.

Wibbly Pig opens his presents ill. by author. Golden, 1995. ISBN 978-0-307-16627-2 Subj: Animals – pigs. Format, unusual – board books. Gifts.

Inns, Christopher. *Next! please* ill. by author. Tricycle, 2001. ISBN 978-1-58246-038-3 Subj: Illness. Toys.

Intrater, Roberta Grobel. *Peek-a-boo!* ill. by author. Scholastic, 1997. ISBN 978-0-590-05896-4 Subj: Babies. Family life. Format, unusual – board books. Games.

Smile! ill. by author. Scholastic, 1997. ISBN 978-0-590-05899-5 Subj: Babies. Family life. Format, unusual – board books.

Intriago, Patricia. *Dot* ill. by author. Farrar, 2011. ISBN 978-0-374-31835-2 Subj: Concepts – opposites.

Ipcizade, Catherine. *'Twas the Day before Zoo Day* ill. by Ben Hodson. Sylvan Dell, 2008. ISBN 978-1-934359-08-2 Subj: Animals. Rhyming text. Zoos.

Irving, John. *A sound like someone trying not to make a sound* ill. by Tatjana Hauptmann. Random House, 2004. ISBN 978-0-385-90910-5 Subj: Animals – mice. Bedtime. Family life – fathers. Monsters. Noise, sounds.

Irving, Washington. *The legend of Sleepy Hollow* retold by Diane Wolkstein; ill. by R. W. Alley. Morrow, 1987. ISBN 978-0-688-06533-1 Subj: Folk & fairy tales. Ghosts. Holidays – Halloween. Humorous stories.

The legend of Sleepy Hollow retold by Robert D. San Souci; ill. by Daniel San Souci. Doubleday, 1986. ISBN 978-0-385-23397-2 Subj: Folk & fairy tales. Holidays – Halloween.

Irwin, Michael. *Bears in my bed* ill. by author. Bennett, 2000. ISBN 978-0-8069-7535-1 Subj: Animals – bears. Imagination. Rhyming text.

Isaacs, Anne. *Dust Devil* ill. by Paul O. Zelinsky. Random House, 2010. ISBN 978-0-375-86722-4 Subj: Animals – horses, ponies. Tall tales. U.S. history – frontier & pioneer life.

Pancakes for supper! ill. by Mark Teague. Scholastic, 2006. ISBN 978-0-439-64483-9 Subj: Animals. Character traits – cleverness. Food. Tall tales.

Swamp Angel ill. by Paul O. Zelinsky. Dutton, 1994. ISBN 978-0-525-45271-3 Subj: Caldecott award honor books. Tall tales. U.S. history – frontier & pioneer life.

Isadora, Rachel. *ABC pop!* ill. by author. Viking, 1999. ISBN 978-0-670-88329-5 Subj: ABC books. Art.

At the crossroads ill. by author. Greenwillow, 1991. ISBN 978-0-688-05271-3 Subj: Emotions. Family life. Foreign lands – South Africa.

Bea at ballet ill. by author. Penguin, 2012. ISBN 978-0-399-25409-3 Subj: Ballet. School.

Ben's trumpet ill. by author. Greenwillow, 1979. ISBN 978-0-688-80194-6 Subj: Caldecott award honor books. Ethnic groups in the U.S. – African Americans. Music. Musical instruments – trumpets.

Bring on that beat ill. by author. Putnam, 2001. ISBN 978-0-399-23232-9 Subj: Ethnic groups in the U.S. – African Americans. Music. Rhyming text.

Caribbean dream ill. by author. Putnam, 1998. ISBN 978-0-399-23230-5 Subj: Dreams. Foreign lands – Caribbean Islands. Islands.

Happy belly, happy smile ill. by author. Harcourt, 2009. ISBN 978-0-15-206546-1 Subj: Ethnic groups in the U.S. – Chinese Americans. Family life – grandfathers. Food. Restaurants.

Lili at ballet ill. by author. Putnam, 1993. ISBN 978-0-399-22423-2 Subj: Activities – dancing. Ballet.

Lili on stage ill. by author. Putnam, 1995. ISBN 978-0-399-22637-3 Subj: Activities – dancing. Ballet. Careers – dancers. Theater.

Listen to the city ill. by author. Putnam, 2000. ISBN 978-0-399-23047-9 Subj: Cities, towns. Noise, sounds.

Luke goes to bat ill. by author. Penguin, 2005. ISBN 978-0-399-23604-4 Subj: Character traits – perseverance. Ethnic groups in the U.S. – African Americans. Family life – grandmothers. Sports – baseball.

Nick plays baseball ill. by author. Putnam, 2001. ISBN 978-0-399-23231-2 Subj: Sports – baseball.

Not just tutus ill. by author. Putnam, 2003. ISBN 978-0-399-23603-7 Subj: Activities – dancing. Ballet. Rhyming text.

Old Mikamba had a farm ill. by author. Penguin/Nancy Paulsen, 2013. ISBN 978-0-399-25740-7 Subj: Animals. Cumulative tales. Farms. Foreign lands – Africa. Songs.

123 pop! ill. by author. Viking, 2000. ISBN 978-0-670-88859-7 Subj: Counting, numbers.

Over the green hills ill. by author. Greenwillow, 1992. ISBN 978-0-688-10510-5 Subj: Activities – traveling. Communities, neighborhoods. Family life – grandmothers. Foreign lands – South Africa.

Peekaboo bedtime ill. by author. Putnam, 2008. ISBN 978-0-399-24384-4 Subj: Bedtime. Ethnic groups in the U.S. – African Americans. Games.

Peekaboo morning ill. by author. Putnam, 2002. ISBN 978-0-399-23602-0 Subj: Ethnic groups in the U.S. – African Americans. Games.

Peekaboo morning [board book] ill. by author. Putnam, 2008. ISBN 978-0-399-25153-5 Subj: Activities. Babies. Ethnic groups in the U.S. – African Americans. Format, unusual – board books. Games.

Say hello! ill. by author. Penguin, 2010. ISBN 978-0-399-25230-3 Subj: Cities, towns. Communities, neighborhoods. Foreign languages.

Sophie skates ill. by author. Putnam, 1999. ISBN 978-0-399-23046-2 Subj: Sports – ice skating.

A South African night ill. by author. Greenwillow, 1998. ISBN 978-0-688-11390-2 Subj: Animals. Foreign lands – Africa. Foreign lands – South Africa. Jungle. Night.

There was a tree ill. by author. Penguin, 2012. ISBN 978-0-399-25741-4 Subj: Cumulative tales. Foreign lands – Africa. Nature. Songs.

Twelve days of Christmas (The twelve days of Christmas. English folk song)

Uh-oh! ill. by author. Harcourt, 2008. ISBN 978-0-15-205765-7 Subj: Behavior – misbehavior. Ethnic groups in the U.S. – African Americans.

What a family! ill. by author. Penguin, 2006. ISBN 978-0-399-24254-0 Subj: Family life.

Yo, Jo! ill. by author. Harcourt, 2007. ISBN 978-0-15-205783-1 Subj: Communities, neighborhoods. Ethnic groups in the U.S. – African

Americans. Family life – brothers & sisters. Family life – grandfathers. Language.

Isherwood, Shirley. *Flora the frog* ill. by Anna C. Leplar. Peachtree, 2000. ISBN 978-1-56145-223-1 Subj: Frogs & toads. School. Theater.

Isol. *Petit, the monster* ill. by author. Groundwood, 2010. ISBN 978-0-88899-947-4 Subj: Behavior – misbehavior.

Isop, Laurie. *How do you hug a porcupine?* ill. by Gwen Millward. Simon & Schuster, 2011. ISBN 978-1-4424-1291-0 Subj: Animals. Hugging. Rhyming text.

Issa, Kai Jackson. *Howard Thurman's Great Hope* ill. by Arthur L. Dawson. Lee & Low, 2008. ISBN 978-1-60060-249-8 Subj: Ethnic groups in the U.S. – African Americans. Prejudice. U.S. history.

Issa, Kobayashi. *Today and today* ill. by G. Brian Karas. Scholastic, 2007. ISBN 978-0-439-59078-5 Subj: Foreign lands – Japan. Nature. Poetry. Seasons.

Itaya, Satoshi. *Buttons and Bo* ill. by author. NorthSouth, 2004. ISBN 978-0-7358-1883-5 Subj: Animals – bears. Behavior – lost. Family life – brothers. Forest, woods. Sibling rivalry.

Ivanko, John D. *Animal friends: a global celebration of children and their animals* (Ajmera, Maya)

Back to school (Ajmera, Maya)

Come out and play (Ajmera, Maya)

To be a kid (Ajmera, Maya)

I've seen the promised land ill. by Leonard Jenkins. HarperCollins, 2004. ISBN 978-0-06-027704-8 Subj: Careers – clergy. Ethnic groups in the U.S. – African Americans. Religion. U.S. history.

Ives, Penny. *Celestine, drama queen* ill. by author. Scholastic, 2009. ISBN 978-0-545-08149-8 Subj: Birds – ducks. Emotions – fear. Theater.

Rabbit pie ill. by author. Penguin, 2006. ISBN 978-0-670-05951-5 Subj: Animals – rabbits. Bedtime.

Ivey, Randall. *Jay and the bounty of books* ill. by Chuck Galey. Pelican, 2007. ISBN 978-1-58980-372-5 Subj: Books, reading. Giants. Libraries.

Ivimey, John William. *The complete story of the three blind mice* ill. by Paul Galdone. Clarion, 1987. ISBN 978-0-89919-481-3 Subj: Animals – mice. Music. Nursery rhymes. Songs.

Three blind mice ill. by Victoria Chess. Little, 1990. ISBN 978-0-316-13867-3 Subj: Animals – mice. Music. Nursery rhymes. Songs.

Iwai, Melissa. *Soup day* ill. by author. Holt, 2010. ISBN 978-0-8050-9004-8 Subj: Activities – baking, cooking. Family life – mothers. Food.

Iwamura, Kazuo. *Bedtime in the forest* ill. by author. NorthSouth, 2010. ISBN 978-0-7358-2310-5 Subj: Animals – squirrels. Bedtime. Birds – owls.

Hooray for fall! ill. by author. NorthSouth, 2009. ISBN 978-0-7358-2252-8 Subj: Animals – squirrels. Seasons – fall.

Hooray for snow! ill. by author. NorthSouth, 2009. ISBN 978-0-7358-2219-1 Subj: Animals – squirrels. Birds. Seasons – winter. Weather – snow.

Hooray for spring! ill. by author. NorthSouth, 2009. ISBN 978-0-7358-2228-3 Subj: Animals – squirrels. Seasons – spring.

Hooray for summer! ill. by author. NorthSouth, 2010. ISBN 978-0-7358-2285-6 Subj: Animals – squirrels. Seasons – summer. Weather – storms.

Iyengar, Malathi Michelle. *Romina's rangoli* ill. by Jennifer Wanardi. Shen's, 2007. ISBN 978-1-885008-32-9 Subj: Character traits – individuality. Ethnic groups in the U.S. – East Indian Americans. Ethnic groups in the U.S. – Mexican Americans. School.

Tan to tamarind: poems about the color brown ill. by Jamel Akib. Children's Book Press, 2009. ISBN 978-0-89239-227-8 Subj: Anatomy – skin. Concepts – color. Poetry.

Jack and the beanstalk. *Jack and the beanstalk* retold by Anthea Bell; ill. by Aljoscha Blau. NorthSouth, 2000. ISBN 978-0-7358-1375-5 Subj: Folk & fairy tales. Foreign lands – England. Giants. Plants.

Jack and the beanstalk retold by Maggie Moore; ill. by Steve Cox. Picture Window, 2003. ISBN 978-1-4048-0059-5 Subj: Folk & fairy tales. Giants. Plants.

Jack and the beanstalk retold by Nina Crews; ill. by reteller. Holt, 2011. ISBN 978-0-8050-8765-9 Subj: Cities, towns. Folk & fairy tales. Giants. Plants.

Jack and the beanstalk ill. by Julek Heller. Doubleday, 1992. ISBN 978-0-385-30693-5 Subj: Folk & fairy tales. Giants. Plants.

Jack and the beanstalk retold by John Howe; ill. by reteller. Little, 1989. ISBN 978-0-316-37579-5 Subj: Folk & fairy tales. Giants. Plants.

Jack and the beanstalk retold by Steven Kellogg; ill. by reteller. Morrow, 1991. ISBN 978-0-688-10251-7 Subj: Folk & fairy tales. Giants. Plants.

Jack and the beanstalk retold by Albert Lorenz; ill. by reteller. Abrams, 2002. ISBN 978-0-8109-1160-4 Subj: Folk & fairy tales. Giants. Plants.

Jack and the beanstalk retold by Richard Walker; ill. by Niamh Sharkey. Barefoot, 1999. ISBN 978-1-902283-13-5 Subj: Folk & fairy tales. Giants. Plants.

Jack and the beanstalk retold by Ann Keay Beneduce; ill. by Gennady Spirin. Philomel, 1999. ISBN 978-0-399-23118-6 Subj: Folk & fairy tales. Giants. Plants.

Jack and the beanstalk retold by E. Nesbit; ill. by Matt Tavares. Candlewick, 2006. ISBN 978-0-7636-2124-7 Subj: Folk & fairy tales. Giants. Plants.

Jacques and de beanstalk by Mike Artell; ill. by Jim Harris. Penguin, 2010. ISBN 978-0-8037-2816-5 Subj: Folk & fairy tales. Giants. Plants. Rhyming text.

Jackson, Aimee. *Ocean babies* (McCurry, Kristen)

Safari babies (McCurry, Kristen)

Jackson, Alison. *The ballad of Valentine* ill. by Tricia Tusa. Dutton, 2002. ISBN 978-0-525-46720-5 Subj: Holidays – Valentine's Day. Rhyming text.

I know an old lady who swallowed a pie ill. by Judith Byron Schachner. Dutton, 1997. ISBN 978-0-525-45645-2 Subj: Cumulative tales. Folk & fairy tales. Food. Holidays – Thanksgiving. Humorous stories. Rhyming text.

If the shoe fits ill. by Karla Firehammer. Holt, 2001. ISBN 978-0-8050-6466-7 Subj: Homes, houses. Nursery rhymes. Rhyming text.

Thea's tree ill. by Janet Pedersen. Dutton, 2008. ISBN 978-0-525-47443-2 Subj: Folk & fairy tales. Letters, cards. Plants.

Jackson, Byron. *The saggy baggy elephant* (Jackson, Kathryn)

Jackson, Chris. *The Gaggle sisters river tour* ill. by author. Lobster, 2002. ISBN 978-1-894222-58-7 Subj: Birds – geese. Character traits – pride. Family life – sisters.

Jackson, Ellen. *Abe Lincoln loved animals* ill. by Doris Ettlinger. Whitman, 2008. ISBN 978-0-8075-0123-8 Subj: Character traits – kindness to animals. Pets. U.S. history.

April ill. by Kay Life. Charlesbridge, 2002. ISBN 978-0-88106-908-2 Subj: Days of the week, months of the year. Holidays. Seasons – spring. Weather.

August ill. by Pat DeWitt and Robin DeWitt. Charlesbridge, 2002. ISBN 978-0-88106-921-1 Subj: Days of the week, months of the year. Holidays. Seasons – summer. Weather.

The autumn equinox ill. by Jan Davey Ellis. Millbrook, 2000. ISBN 978-0-7613-1354-0 Subj: Fairs, festivals. Holidays. Seasons – fall.

Cinder Edna ill. by Kevin O'Malley. Lothrop, 1994. ISBN 978-0-688-12323-9 Subj: Folk & fairy tales. Royalty – princes.

December ill. by Pat DeWitt and Robin DeWitt. Charlesbridge, 2002. ISBN 978-0-88106-958-7 Subj: Days of the week, months of the year. Holidays. Seasons – winter. Weather.

Earth Mother ill. by Leo Dillon and Diane Dillon. Walker, 2005. ISBN 978-0-8027-8993-8 Subj: Ecology. Nature. World.

February ill. by Pat DeWitt and Robin DeWitt. Charlesbridge, 2002. ISBN 978-0-88106-996-9 Subj: Days of the week, months of the year. Holidays. Seasons – winter. Weather.

January ill. by Pat DeWitt and Robin DeWitt. Charlesbridge, 2002. ISBN 978-0-88106-995-2 Subj: Days of the week, months of the year. Holidays. Seasons – winter. Weather.

July ill. by Pat DeWitt and Robin DeWitt. Charlesbridge, 2002. ISBN 978-0-88106-920-4 Subj: Days of the week, months of the year. Holidays. Seasons – summer. Weather.

June ill. by Kay Life. Charlesbridge, 2002. ISBN 978-0-88106-919-8 Subj: Days of the week, months of the year. Holidays. Seasons – summer. Weather.

March ill. by Kay Life. Charlesbridge, 2002. ISBN 978-0-88106-905-1 Subj: Days of the week, months of the year. Holidays. Seasons – spring. Weather.

May ill. by Kay Life. Charlesbridge, 2002. ISBN 978-0-88106-918-1 Subj: Days of the week, months of the year. Holidays. Seasons – spring. Weather.

November ill. by Pat DeWitt and Robin DeWitt. Charlesbridge, 2002. ISBN 978-0-88106-927-3 Subj: Days of the week, months of the year. Holidays. Seasons – fall. Weather.

October ill. by Pat DeWitt and Robin DeWitt. Charlesbridge, 2002. ISBN 978-0-88106-923-5 Subj: Days of the week, months of the year. Holidays. Seasons – fall. Weather.

September ill. by Pat DeWitt and Robin DeWitt. Charlesbridge, 2002. ISBN 978-0-88106-922-8

Subj: Days of the week, months of the year. Holidays. Seasons – fall. Weather.

The seven seas ill. by Bill Slavin and Esperança Melo. Eerdmans, 2011. ISBN 978-0-8028-5341-7 Subj: Animals – rabbits. Concepts – color. Geography. Imagination. Rhyming text. Sea & seashore.

Sometimes bad things happen photos by Shelley Rotner. Millbrook, 2002. ISBN 978-0-7613-2810-0 Subj: Behavior – bad day. Character traits – helpfulness. Emotions. Emotions – happiness.

The spring equinox ill. by Jan Davey Ellis. Millbrook, 2002. ISBN 978-0-7613-1955-9 Subj: Holidays. Seasons – spring.

The summer solstice ill. by Jan Davey Ellis. Millbrook, 2001. ISBN 978-0-7613-1623-7 Subj: Holidays. Seasons – summer.

The winter solstice ill. by Jan Davey Ellis. Millbrook, 1994. ISBN 978-1-56294-400-1 Subj: Holidays. Seasons – winter.

Jackson, Emma. *A home for Dixie: the true story of a rescued puppy* photos by Bob Carey. Collins, 2008. ISBN 978-0-06-144962-8 Subj: Animals – dogs. Character traits – kindness to animals.

Jackson, Isaac. *Somebody's new pajamas* ill. by David Soman. Dial, 1996. ISBN 978-0-8037-1549-3 Subj: Clothing – pajamas. Ethnic groups in the U.S. – African Americans. Family life. Friendship. Sleepovers.

Jackson, Jill. *Let there be peace on earth: and let it begin with me* by Jill Jackson and Sy Miller ill. by David Diaz. Tricycle, 2009. ISBN 978-1-58246-285-1 Subj: Character traits – cooperation. Songs. Violence, nonviolence. World.

Jackson, Kathryn. *The golden circus book* ill. by Alice Provensen and Martin Provensen. Random House, 2005. ISBN 978-0-375-83215-4 Subj: Circus. Format, unusual – board books.

Pantaloon ill. by Steven Salerno. Random House, 2010. ISBN 978-0-375-85624-2 Subj: Activities – baking, cooking. Animals – dogs. Careers – bakers. Character traits – helpfulness.

The saggy baggy elephant by Kathryn Jackson and Byron Jackson ill. by Tenggren. Golden, 2003. ISBN 978-0-375-92590-0 Subj: Animals – elephants. Behavior – worrying.

Jackson, Shelley. *Mimi's Dada Catifesto* ill. by author. Clarion, 2010. ISBN 978-0-547-12681-4 Subj: Animals – cats. Art.

Jackson, Shirley. *9 magic wishes* ill. by Miles Hyman. Farrar, 2001. ISBN 978-0-374-35525-8 Subj: Behavior – wishing. Magic.

Jacobs, Francine. *Lonesome George, the giant tortoise* ill. by Jean Cassels. Walker, 2003. ISBN 978-0-8027-8865-8 Subj: Animals – endangered animals. Foreign lands – Galapagos Islands. Reptiles – turtles, tortoises.

Jacobs, Joseph. *King of the cats: a ghost story* adapt. by Paul Galdone; ill. by Paul Galdone. Houghton, 1980. ISBN 978-0-395-29030-9 Subj: Animals – cats. Folk & fairy tales. Ghosts.

The three sillies adapt. by Steven Kellogg; ill. by Steven Kellogg. Candlewick, 1999. ISBN 978-0-7636-0811-8 Subj: Animals. Animals – pigs. Character traits – foolishness. Folk & fairy tales.

Jacobs, Julie. *My heart is a magic house* ill. by Bernadette Pons. Whitman, 2007. ISBN 978-0-8075-5335-0 Subj: Behavior – worrying. Emotions – love. Family life – new sibling.

Jacobs, Paul DuBois. *Abiyoyo returns* (Seeger, Pete)

The deaf musicians (Seeger, Pete)

Fire drill by Paul DuBois Jacobs and Jennifer Swender ill. by Huy Voun Lee. Holt, 2010. ISBN 978-0-8050-8953-0 Subj: Fire. Rhyming text. Safety. School.

Some friends to feed: the story of Stone Soup (Seeger, Pete)

Jadoul, Emile. *All by myself!* ill. by author. Eerdmans, 2012. ISBN 978-0-8028-5411-7 Subj: Behavior – growing up. Birds – penguins. Family life. Toilet training.

Good night, Chickie ill. by author. Eerdmans, 2011. ISBN 978-0-8028-5378-3 Subj: Bedtime. Behavior – worrying. Birds – chickens. Family life – mothers.

Jaffe, Nina. *The golden flower: a Taino myth from Puerto Rico* ill. by Enrique O. Sánchez. Simon & Schuster, 1996. ISBN 978-0-02-747585-2 Subj: Creation. Folk & fairy tales. Foreign lands – Puerto Rico. Indians of North America – Taino.

In the month of Kislev: a story for Hanukkah ill. by Louise August. Viking, 1992. ISBN 978-0-670-82863-0 Subj: Folk & fairy tales. Holidays – Hanukkah. Jewish culture.

Tales for the seventh day ill. by Kelly Stribling Sutherland. Scholastic, 2000. ISBN 978-0-590-12054-8 Subj: Folk & fairy tales. Jewish culture. Religion.

The way meat loves salt: a Cinderella tale from the Jewish tradition ill. by Louise August. Holt, 1998. ISBN 978-0-8050-4384-6 Subj: Emotions – love. Family life – fathers. Folk & fairy tales. Foreign lands – Europe. Jewish culture. Weddings.

Jagtenberg, Yvonne. *Jack the wolf* ill. by author. Roaring Brook, 2002. ISBN 978-0-7613-2855-

1 Subj: Animals – wolves. Humorous stories. School – first day. Self-concept.

Jack's kite ill. by author. Roaring Brook, 2004. ISBN 978-0-7613-2940-4 Subj: Camps, camping. Kites.

Jack's rabbit ill. by author. Roaring Brook, 2003. ISBN 978-0-7613-2916-9 Subj: Activities – drawing. Animals – rabbits. Behavior – running away. Pets.

Jahn-Clough, Lisa. *Alicia's best friends* ill. by author. Houghton, 2003. ISBN 978-0-618-23951-1 Subj: Friendship.

Felicity and Cordelia: a tale of two bunnies ill. by author. Farrar, 2011. ISBN 978-0-374-32300-4 Subj: Activities – ballooning. Activities – traveling. Animals – rabbits. Friendship.

Little dog ill. by author. Houghton, 2006. ISBN 978-0-618-57405-6 Subj: Animals – dogs. Careers – artists.

Missing Molly ill. by author. Houghton, 2000. ISBN 978-0-618-00980-0 Subj: Behavior – hiding. Friendship. Games.

On the hill ill. by author. Houghton, 2004. ISBN 978-0-618-40741-5 Subj: Animals. Emotions – loneliness. Homes, houses.

Simon and Molly plus Hester ill. by author. Houghton, 2001. ISBN 978-0-618-08220-9 Subj: Friendship.

Jakes, John. *Susanna of the Alamo* ill. by Paul Bacon. Harcourt, 1986. ISBN 978-0-15-200595-5 Subj: Character traits – bravery. U.S. history – frontier & pioneer life.

Jalali, Reza. *Moon watchers: Shirin's Ramadan miracle* ill. by Anne Sibley O'Brien. Tilbury House, 2010. ISBN 978-0-88448-321-2 Subj: Family life – brothers & sisters. Holidays – Ramadan. Religion.

James, Betsy. *Tadpoles* ill. by author. Dutton, 1999. ISBN 978-0-525-46197-5 Subj: Animals – babies. Behavior. Frogs & toads.

James, Brian. *Supertwins and the sneaky, slimy book worms* ill. by Chris L. Demarest. Scholastic, 2004. ISBN 978-0-613-72181-3 Subj: Animals – worms. Family life – brothers & sisters. Multiple births – twins. School.

The Supertwins and tooth trouble ill. by Chris L. Demarest. Scholastic, 2003. ISBN 978-0-439-46624-0 Subj: Crime. Fairies. Family life – brothers & sisters. Multiple births – twins. Teeth.

The Supertwins meet the bad dogs from space ill. by Chris L. Demarest. Scholastic, 2003. ISBN 978-0-439-46623-3 Subj: Animals – dogs. Family life – brothers & sisters. Multiple births – twins. Mythical creatures.

Supertwins meet the dangerous dino-robots ill. by Chris L. Demarest. Scholastic, 2003. ISBN 978-0-439-46625-7 Subj: Careers – scientists. Dinosaurs. Family life – brothers & sisters. Multiple births – twins. Robots.

James, J. Alison, adapt. *The bears' Christmas surprise* ill. by Angela Kehlenbeck. NorthSouth, 2000. ISBN 978-0-7358-1364-9 Subj: Emotions – loneliness. Holidays – Christmas. Toys – bears.

James, Simon. *Baby Brains and RoboMom* ill. by author. Candlewick, 2008. ISBN 978-0-7636-3463-6 Subj: Babies. Humorous stories. Inventions. Robots.

The birdwatchers ill. by author. Candlewick, 2002. ISBN 978-0-7636-1676-2 Subj: Birds. Family life – grandfathers.

Dear Mr. Blueberry ill. by author. Macmillan, 1991. ISBN 978-0-689-50529-4 Subj: Animals – whales. Careers – teachers. Imagination. Letters, cards.

George flies south ill. by author. Candlewick, 2011. ISBN 978-0-7636-5724-6 Subj: Activities – flying. Behavior – growing up. Birds.

Little One Step ill. by author. Candlewick, 2003. ISBN 978-0-7636-2070-7 Subj: Birds – ducks. Family life – brothers. Games.

Nurse Clementine ill. by author. Candlewick, 2013. ISBN 978-0-7636-6382-7 Subj: Careers – nurses. Family life.

Jamieson, Victoria. *Olympig! the triumphant story of an underdog* ill. by author. Dial, 2012. ISBN 978-0-8037-3536-1 Subj: Animals. Animals – pigs. Self-concept. Sports – Olympics.

Jamison, Jocelyn. *Drac's night out* ill. by Bill Basso. Price Stern Sloan, 2001. ISBN 978-0-8431-4393-5 Subj: Monsters.

Jane, Pamela. *Little goblins ten* ill. by Jane Manning. HarperCollins, 2011. ISBN 978-0-06-176798-2 Subj: Counting, numbers. Holidays – Halloween. Monsters. Mythical creatures.

Milo and the fire engine parade ill. by Meredith Johnson. Mondo, 2002. ISBN 978-1-59034-192-6 Subj: Animals – dogs. Careers – firefighters. Parades. Trucks.

Milo and the greatest trick ever ill. by Meredith Johnson. Mondo, 2002. ISBN 978-1-59034-187-2 Subj: Animals – cats. Magic. Theater.

Monster countdown ill. by Nick Zarin-Ackerman. Mondo, 2001. ISBN 978-1-58653-857-6 Subj: Counting, numbers. Monsters. Rhyming text.

Monster mischief ill. by Vera Rosenberry. Atheneum, 2001. ISBN 978-0-689-80471-7 Subj: Holidays – Halloween. Monsters. Rhyming text.

Janice. *Little Bear marches in the St. Patrick's Day parade* ill. by Mariana. Lothrop, 1967. Subj: Animals – bears. Holidays – St. Patrick's Day. Parades.

Little Bear's Christmas ill. by Mariana. Lothrop, 1964. ISBN 978-0-688-51076-3 Subj: Animals – bears. Character traits – generosity. Hibernation. Holidays – Christmas.

Little Bear's Thanksgiving ill. by Mariana. Lothrop, 1967. ISBN 978-0-688-51078-7 Subj: Animals – bears. Holidays – Thanksgiving.

Janisch, Heinz. *The merry pranks of Till Eulenspiegel* ill. by Lisbeth Zwerger. NorthSouth, 2001. ISBN 978-1-55858-806-6 Subj: Behavior – trickery. Folk & fairy tales. Foreign lands – Germany.

Jankel, Karen. *Paddington Bear goes to the hospital* (Bond, Michael)

Janni, Rebecca. *Every cowgirl goes to school* ill. by Lynne Avril. Dial, 2013. ISBN 978-0-8037-3937-6 Subj: Cowboys, cowgirls. Friendship. School – first day.

Every cowgirl loves a rodeo. Dial, 2012. ISBN 978-0-8037-3734-1 Subj: Cowboys, cowgirls. Fairs, festivals. Rodeos. Sports – bicycling. Sportsmanship.

Every cowgirl needs a horse ill. by Lynne Avril. Penguin, 2010. ISBN 978-0-525-42164-1 Subj: Birthdays. Cowboys, cowgirls. Imagination.

Every cowgirl needs dancing boots ill. by Lynne Avril. Penguin, 2011. ISBN 978-0-525-42341-6 Subj: Activities – dancing. Character traits – compromising. Cowboys, cowgirls. Emotions – loneliness. Friendship.

Janovitz, Marilyn. *A, B, see!* ill. by author. Chronicle, 2005. ISBN 978-0-8118-4673-8 Subj: ABC books. Animals. Format, unusual – toy & movable books.

Baby, Baby, Baby! ill. by author. Sourcebooks, 2010. ISBN 978-1-4022-4414-8 Subj: Babies. Format, unusual – board books.

Play baby play! ill. by author. Sourcebooks, 2012. ISBN 978-1-4022-6224-1 Subj: Activities – playing. Babies. Rhyming text.

We love school! ill. by author. NorthSouth, 2007. ISBN 978-0-7358-2112-5 Subj: Animals – cats. Rhyming text. School.

Janowitz, Tama. *Hear that?* ill. by Tracy Dockray. SeaStar, 2001. ISBN 978-1-58717-075-1 Subj: Family life – mothers. Noise, sounds.

Jarka, Jeff. *Love that kitty! the story of a boy who wanted to be a cat* ill. by author. Holt, 2010. ISBN 978-0-8050-9053-6 Subj: Animals – cats. Family life. Imagination. Pets.

Love that puppy! the story of a boy who wanted to be a dog ill. by author. Holt, 2009. ISBN 978-0-8050-8741-3 Subj: Animals – dogs. Family life. Imagination. Pets.

Jarman, Julia. *Class Two at the zoo* ill. by Lynne Chapman. Carolrhoda, 2007. ISBN 978-0-8225-7132-2 Subj: Reptiles – snakes. Rhyming text. School – field trips. Zoos.

Two shy pandas ill. by Susan Varley. Andersen, 2013. ISBN 978-1-46771-141-8 Subj: Animals – pandas. Character traits – shyness. Rhyming text.

Jarrett, Clare. *Arabella Miller's tiny caterpillar* ill. by author. Candlewick, 2008. ISBN 978-0-7636-3660-9 Subj: Insects – butterflies, caterpillars. Metamorphosis. Rhyming text.

The best picnic ever ill. by author. Candlewick, 2004. ISBN 978-0-7636-2370-8 Subj: Activities – picnicking. Activities – playing. Animals.

Jaspersohn, William. *The two brothers* ill. by Michael A. Donato. Vermont Folklife Center, 2000. ISBN 978-0-916718-16-9 Subj: Ethnic groups in the U.S. – German Americans. Family life – brothers. Farms. Immigrants.

Javaherbin, Mina. *Goal!* ill. by A. G. Ford. Candlewick, 2010. ISBN 978-0-7636-4571-7 Subj: Behavior – bullying, teasing. Foreign lands – South Africa. Friendship. Sports – soccer.

The secret message ill. by Bruce Whatley. Hyperion/Disney, 2010. ISBN 978-1-4231-1044-6 Subj: Birds – parakeets, parrots. Folk & fairy tales. Foreign lands – Iran.

Javernick, Ellen. *The birthday pet* ill. by Kevin O'Malley. Marshall Cavendish, 2009. ISBN 978-0-7614-5522-6 Subj: Pets. Reptiles – turtles, tortoises.

What if everybody did that? ill. by Colleen M. Madden. Marshall Cavendish, 2010. ISBN 978-0-7614-5686-5 Subj: Behavior. Character traits.

Jay, Alison. *Christmastime* ill. by author. Dial, 2012. ISBN 978-0-8037-3804-1 Subj: Holidays – Christmas. Language. Picture puzzles.

The nutcracker (Hoffmann, E. T. A)

1 2 3: a child's first counting book ill. by author. Penguin, 2007. ISBN 978-0-525-47836-2 Subj: Counting, numbers. Dreams. Folk & fairy tales.

Red green blue: a first book of colors ill. by author. Penguin, 2010. ISBN 978-0-525-42303-4 Subj:

Concepts – color. Nursery rhymes. Picture puzzles. Rhyming text.

Welcome to the zoo ill. by author. Dial, 2008. ISBN 978-0-8037-3177-6 Subj: Animals. Wordless. Zoos.

Jay, Betsy. *Jane vs. the Tooth Fairy* ill. by Lori Osiecki. Rising Moon, 2000. ISBN 978-0-87358-739-6 Subj: Fairies. Teeth.

Jeffers, Oliver. *The great paper caper* ill. by author. Philomel, 2009. ISBN 978-0-399-25097-2 Subj: Activities – making things. Animals. Animals – bears. Ecology. Paper. Trees.

The heart and the bottle ill. by author. Penguin, 2010. ISBN 978-0-399-25452-9 Subj: Death. Emotions – grief. Emotions – loneliness.

The Hueys in The new sweater ill. by author. Philomel, 2012. ISBN 978-0-399-25767-4 Subj: Character traits – individuality. Clothing – sweaters. Self-concept.

The incredible book eating boy ill. by author. Penguin, 2007. ISBN 978-0-399-24749-1 Subj: Books, reading. Food.

Lost and found ill. by author. Penguin, 2006. ISBN 978-0-399-24503-9 Subj: Behavior – lost. Birds – penguins. Emotions – loneliness. Foreign lands – Antarctic. Friendship.

Stuck ill. by author. Penguin, 2011. ISBN 978-0-399-25737-7 Subj: Humorous stories. Kites. Trees.

This moose belongs to me ill. by author. Philomel, 2012. ISBN 978-0-399-16103-2 Subj: Animals – moose. Pets.

Up and down. Penguin, 2010. ISBN 978-0-399-25545-8 Subj: Activities – flying. Birds – penguins. Friendship.

The way back home ill. by author. Philomel, 2008. ISBN 978-0-399-25074-3 Subj: Aliens. Character traits – helpfulness. Friendship. Moon. Space & space ships.

Jeffers, Susan. *Forest of dreams* (Wells, Rosemary)

My Chincoteague pony ill. by author. Hyperion, 2008. ISBN 978-1-4231-0023-2 Subj: Animals – horses, ponies.

The twelve days of Christmas ill. by author. HarperCollins, 2013. ISBN 978-0-06-206615-2 Subj: Gifts. Holidays – Christmas. Magic. Santa Claus.

Jeffs, Stephanie. *Jenny: coming to terms with the death of a sibling* ill. by Jacqui Thomas. Abingdon, 2006. ISBN 978-0-687-49709-6 Subj: Death. Emotions – grief. Family life – brothers & sisters. Illness. Religion.

Josh: coming to terms with the death of a friend ill. by Jacqui Thomas. Abingdon, 2006. ISBN 978-0-687-49719-5 Subj: Death. Emotions – grief. Friendship. Religion.

Jenkins, Emily. *Daffodil* ill. by Tomasz Bogacki. Farrar, 2004. ISBN 978-0-374-31676-1 Subj: Character traits – individuality. Clothing – dresses. Family life – sisters. Multiple births – triplets.

Daffodil, crocodile ill. by Tomasz Bogacki. Farrar, 2007. ISBN 978-0-374-39944-3 Subj: Character traits – individuality. Family life – sisters. Imagination. Multiple births – triplets.

Five creatures ill. by Tomasz Bogacki. Farrar, 2001. ISBN 978-0-374-32341-7 Subj: Animals – cats. Family life.

Lemonade in winter: a book about two kids counting money ill. by G. Brian Karas. Random House, 2012. ISBN 978-0-375-85883-3 Subj: Counting, numbers. Family life – brothers & sisters. Money. Seasons – winter.

Love you when you whine ill. by Sergio Ruzzier. Farrar, 2006. ISBN 978-0-374-34652-2 Subj: Animals – cats. Behavior – misbehavior. Emotions – love. Family life – mothers.

Num, num, num! a Bea and Haha book ill. by Tomasz Bogacki. Farrar, 2006. ISBN 978-0-374-30583-3 Subj: Animals – ferrets. Animals – hippopotamuses. Format, unusual – board books. Friendship.

Plonk, plonk, plonk! a Bea and Haha book ill. by Tomasz Bogacki. Farrar, 2006. ISBN 978-0-374-30585-7 Subj: Animals – ferrets. Animals – hippopotamuses. Format, unusual – board books. Friendship. Music.

Skunkdog ill. by Pierre Pratt. Farrar, 2008. ISBN 978-0-374-37009-1 Subj: Animals – dogs. Animals – skunks. Friendship.

Small medium large ill. by Tomasz Bogacki. Star Bright, 2011. ISBN 978-1-59572-278-2 Subj: Concepts – size. Language.

That new animal ill. by Pierre Pratt. Farrar, 2005. ISBN 978-0-374-37443-3 Subj: Animals – dogs. Babies.

Up, up, up! a Bea and Haha book ill. by Tomasz Bogacki. Farrar, 2006. ISBN 978-0-374-30584-0 Subj: Animals – ferrets. Animals – hippopotamuses. Character traits – helpfulness. Format, unusual – board books. Friendship.

Water in the park: a book about water and the times of the day ill. by Stephanie Graegin. Random House, 2013. ISBN 978-0-375-87002-6 Subj: Day. Parks. Water.

What happens on Wednesdays ill. by Lauren Castillo. Farrar, 2007. ISBN 978-0-374-38303-9 Subj: Day. Family life.

Jenkins, Martin. *Can we save the tiger?* ill. by Vicky White. Candlewick, 2011. ISBN 978-0-7636-4909-8 Subj: Animals – endangered animals. Nature.

Jenkins, Priscilla Belz. *Falcons nest on skyscrapers* ill. by Megan Lloyd. HarperCollins, 1996. ISBN 978-0-06-021105-9 Subj: Animals – endangered animals. Birds – falcons. Cities, towns.

A nest full of eggs ill. by Lizzy Rockwell. HarperCollins, 1995. ISBN 978-0-06-023442-3 Subj: Birds – robins. Eggs. Science.

Jenkins, Steve. *Actual size* ill. by author. Houghton, 2004. ISBN 978-0-618-37594-3 Subj: Anatomy. Animals. Concepts – size.

Almost gone: the world's rarest animals ill. by author. HarperCollins, 2006. ISBN 978-0-06-053600-8 Subj: Animals – endangered animals.

Animals in flight by Steve Jenkins and Robin Page ill. by Steve Jenkins. Houghton, 2001. ISBN 978-0-618-12351-3 Subj: Activities – flying. Animals. Birds. Dinosaurs. Insects.

Animals upside down: a pull, pop, lift and learn book! by Steve Jenkins and Robin Page ill. by Steve Jenkins. Houghton Mifflin, 2013. ISBN 978-0-547-34127-9 Subj: Animals. Format, unusual – toy & movable books.

Big and little ill. by author. Houghton, 1996. ISBN 978-0-395-72664-8 Subj: Animals. Concepts – size.

Biggest, strongest, fastest ill. by author. Ticknor & Fields, 1995. ISBN 978-0-395-69701-6 Subj: Animals. Concepts.

Dogs and cats ill. by author. Houghton, 2007. ISBN 978-0-618-50767-2 Subj: Animals – cats. Animals – dogs. Format, unusual.

Hottest, coldest, highest, deepest ill. by author. Houghton, 1998. ISBN 978-0-395-89999-1 Subj: Earth. Geography.

How many ways can you catch a fly? (Page, Robin)

How to clean a hippopotamus: a look at unusual animal partnerships by Steve Jenkins and Robin Page ill. by Steve Jenkins. Houghton Mifflin, 2010. ISBN 978-0-547-24515-7 Subj: Animals. Nature. Science.

I see a kookaburra by Steve Jenkins and Robin Page ill. by Steve Jenkins. Houghton, 2005. ISBN 978-0-618-50764-1 Subj: Animals. Ecology. Picture puzzles.

Just a second: a different way to look at time ill. by author. Houghton Mifflin, 2011. ISBN 978-0-618-70896-3 Subj: Nature. Time.

Living color ill. by author. Houghton, 2007. ISBN 978-0-618-70897-0 Subj: Animals. Concepts – color.

Move! by Steve Jenkins and Robin Page ill. by Steve Jenkins. Houghton, 2006. ISBN 978-0-618-64637-1 Subj: Animals. Concepts – motion. Language.

My first day: what animals do on day one by Steve Jenkins and Robin Page ill. by Steve Jenkins. Houghton Mifflin, 2013. ISBN 978-0-547-73851-2 Subj: Animals – babies.

Never smile at a monkey: and 17 other important things to remember ill. by author. Houghton, 2009. ISBN 978-0-618-96620-2 Subj: Animals.

Perros y gatos / dogs and cats ill. by author. Juventud, 2008. ISBN 978-84-26-13669-5 Subj: Animals – cats. Animals – dogs. Foreign languages. Format, unusual.

Prehistoric actual size ill. by author. Houghton, 2005. ISBN 978-0-618-53578-1 Subj: Anatomy. Animals. Concepts – size. Prehistory.

Sisters and brothers: sibling relationships in the animal world (Page, Robin)

Slap, squeak, and scatter ill. by author. Houghton, 2001. ISBN 978-0-618-03376-8 Subj: Animals. Communication. Noise, sounds.

Time for a bath by Steve Jenkins and Robin Page ill. by Steve Jenkins. Houghton Mifflin, 2011. ISBN 978-0-547-25037-3 Subj: Activities – bathing. Animals.

Time to eat by Steve Jenkins and Robin Page ill. by Steve Jenkins. Houghton Mifflin, 2011. ISBN 978-0-547-25032-8 Subj: Animals. Food.

Time to sleep by Steve Jenkins and Robin Page ill. by Steve Jenkins. Houghton Mifflin, 2011. ISBN 978-0-547-25040-3 Subj: Animals. Sleep.

What do you do when something wants to eat you? ill. by author. Houghton, 1997. ISBN 978-0-395-82514-3 Subj: Animals.

What do you do with a tail like this? ill. by author. Houghton, 2003. ISBN 978-0-618-25628-0 Subj: Anatomy. Animals. Caldecott award honor books. Games. Senses.

Jenks, Deneen. *Flowers from Mariko* (Noguchi, Rick)

Jennewein, Lenore. *Chick-o-Saurus Rex* ill. by Daniel Jennewein. Simon & Schuster, 2013. ISBN 978-1-4424-5186-5 Subj: Animals. Behavior – bullying, teasing. Birds – chickens. Character traits – bravery. Dinosaurs.

Jennings, Linda. *Hide and seek birthday treat* ill. by Joanne Partis. Barron's, 2001. ISBN 978-0-7641-5336-5 Subj: Animals. Animals – leopards. Behavior – hiding. Birthdays. Games. Jungle. Parties. Rhyming text.

Little puppy lost ill. by Alison Edgson. Good Books, 2008. ISBN 978-1-56148-635-9 Subj: Animals – dogs. Behavior – lost. Weather – snow.

Jennings, Patrick. *Bat and Rat* ill. by Matthew Cordell. Abrams, 2012. ISBN 978-1-4197-0160-3 Subj: Animals – bats. Animals – rats. Friendship. Music.

Jennings, Sharon. *Bearcub and Mama* ill. by Mélanie Watt. Kids Can, 2005. ISBN 978-1-55337-566-1 Subj: Animals – bears. Family life – mothers. Family life – sons. Weather – storms.

C'mere, boy! ill. by Ashley Spires. Kids Can, 2010. ISBN 978-1-55453-440-1 Subj: Animals – dogs. Humorous stories.

Franklin forgives ill. by Celéste Gagnon et al. Based on the Franklin books by Paulette Bourgeois & Brenda Clark. Kids Can, 2004. ISBN 978-0-439-62159-5 Subj: Animals. Behavior – forgiving. Reptiles – turtles, tortoises.

Franklin goes to the hospital ill. by Brenda Clark. Based on the Franklin books by Paulette Bourgeois & Brenda Clark. Kids Can, 2000. ISBN 978-1-55074-732-4 Subj: Hospitals. Illness. Reptiles – turtles, tortoises.

Franklin makes a deal ill. by Sean Jeffrey et al. Based on the Franklin books by Paulette Bourgeois & Brenda Clark. Kids Can, 2003. ISBN 978-1-55337-469-5 Subj: Activities – trading. Animals. Reptiles – turtles, tortoises.

Franklin wants a badge ill. by Sean Jeffrey et al. Based on the Franklin books by Paulette Bourgeois & Brenda Clark. Kids Can, 2003. ISBN 978-1-55337-467-1 Subj: Animals. Friendship. Reptiles – turtles, tortoises. Sleepovers.

Franklin's class trip (Bourgeois, Paulette)

Franklin's Thanksgiving ill. by Brenda Clark. Based on the Franklin books by Paulette Bourgeois & Brenda Clark. Scholastic, 2001. ISBN 978-1-55074-798-0 Subj: Family life – grandparents. Holidays – Thanksgiving. Reptiles – turtles, tortoises.

The happily ever afternoon ill. by Ron Lightburn. Annick, 2006. ISBN 978-1-55037-945-7 Subj: Imagination.

No monsters here ill. by Ruth Ohi. Fitzhenry & Whiteside, 2004. ISBN 978-1-55041-787-6 Subj: Bedtime. Emotions – fear. Family life – fathers.

Priscilla and Rosy ill. by Linda Hendry. Fitzhenry & Whiteside, 2001. ISBN 978-1-55041-676-3 Subj: Animals – rats. Character traits – loyalty. Friendship.

Priscilla's paw de deux ill. by Linda Hendry. Fitzhenry & Whiteside, 2002. ISBN 978-1-55041-718-0 Subj: Activities – dancing. Animals – cats. Animals – rats. Ballet. Character traits – cooperation. Emotions – fear.

Jensen, Dana. *A meal of the stars: poems up and down* ill. by Tricia Tusa. Houghton Mifflin, 2012. ISBN 978-0-547-39007-9 Subj: Poetry.

Jeppson, Ann-Sofie. *Here comes Pontus* ill. by Catarina Kruusval. R&S Books, 2000. ISBN 978-91-29-64561-3 Subj: Animals – horses, ponies. Farms.

You're growing up, Pontus ill. by Catarina Kruusval. Farrar, 2001. ISBN 978-91-29-65393-9 Subj: Animals – horses, ponies. Behavior – growing up.

Jeram, Anita. *I love my little storybook* ill. by author. Candlewick, 2002. ISBN 978-0-7636-1698-4 Subj: Animals – rabbits. Books, reading. Imagination.

Jessell, Tim. *Falcon* ill. by author. Random House, 2012. ISBN 978-0-375-86866-5 Subj: Activities – flying. Birds – falcons. Imagination.

Jesset, Aurore. *Loopy* ill. by Barbara Korthues. NorthSouth, 2008. ISBN 978-0-7358-2175-0 Subj: Behavior – lost & found possessions. Toys.

Jewel. *Sweet dreams* ill. by Amy Bates. Simon & Schuster, 2013. ISBN 978-1-4424-8931-8 Subj: Bedtime. Lullabies. Rhyming text. Songs.

That's what I'd do ill. by Amy Bates. Simon & Schuster, 2012. ISBN 978-1-4424-5813-0 Subj: Bedtime. Family life – mothers. Lullabies.

Jewell, Nancy. *Alligator wedding* ill. by J. Rutland. Holt, 2010. ISBN 978-0-8050-6819-1 Subj: Reptiles – alligators, crocodiles. Rhyming text. Swamps. Weddings.

Jeyaveeran, Ruth. *The road to Mumbai* ill. by author. Houghton, 2004. ISBN 978-0-618-43419-0 Subj: Animals – monkeys. Foreign lands – India. Imagination.

Jiang, Ji-li. *The magical Monkey King, mischief in heaven* ill. by Hui Hui Su-Kennedy. HarperCollins, 2002. ISBN 978-0-06-029544-8 Subj: Animals – monkeys. Folk & fairy tales. Foreign lands – China.

Red kite, blue kite ill. by Greg Ruth. Disney/Hyperion, 2013. ISBN 978-1-4231-2753-6 Subj: Family life – fathers. Foreign lands – China. Kites.

Jiménez, Francisco. *The Christmas gift / El regalo de Navidad* ill. by Claire B. Cotts. Houghton, 2000. ISBN 978-0-395-92869-1 Subj: Character traits – kindness. Ethnic groups in the U.S. – Mexican Americans. Foreign languages. Holidays – Christmas. Immigrants.

Jobling, Curtis. *Frankenstein's cat* ill. by author. Simon & Schuster, 2001. ISBN 978-0-689-84695-3

Subj: Animals – cats. Animals – dogs. Humorous stories.

Jocelyn, Marthe. *ABC x 3: english, espanol, francais* ill. by Tom Slaughter. Tundra, 2005. ISBN 978-0-88776-707-4 Subj: ABC books. Foreign languages.

A day with Nellie ill. by author. Tundra, 2002. ISBN 978-0-88776-600-8 Subj: Activities – playing. Toys.

Eats ill. by Tom Slaughter. Tundra, 2007. ISBN 978-0-88776-820-0 Subj: Animals. Food.

Hannah and the seven dresses ill. by author. Dutton, 1999. ISBN 978-0-525-46113-5 Subj: Birthdays. Clothing – dresses.

Hannah's Collections ill. by author. Dutton, 2000. ISBN 978-0-525-46442-6 Subj: Behavior – collecting things. School.

Mayfly ill. by author. Tundra, 2004. ISBN 978-0-88776-676-3 Subj: Activities – vacationing. Cities, towns. Country. Homes, houses.

Ones and twos by Marthe Jocelyn and Nell Jocelyn ill. by Marthe Jocelyn. Tundra, 2011. ISBN 978-1-77049-220-2 Subj: Counting, numbers. Friendship. Rhyming text.

Ready for autumn ill. by author. Tundra, 2008. ISBN 978-0-88776-861-3 Subj: Clothing. Format, unusual – board books. Seasons – fall.

Ready for spring ill. by author. Tundra, 2008. ISBN 978-0-88776-849-1 Subj: Clothing. Format, unusual – board books. Seasons – spring.

Ready for summer ill. by author. Tundra, 2008. ISBN 978-0-88776-860-6 Subj: Clothing. Format, unusual – board books. Seasons – summer.

Ready for winter ill. by author. Tundra, 2008. ISBN 978-0-88776-848-4 Subj: Clothing. Format, unusual – board books. Seasons – winter.

Same same ill. by Tom Slaughter. Tundra, 2009. ISBN 978-0-88776-885-9 Subj: Concepts.

Where do you look? by Marthe Jocelyn and Nell Jocelyn ill. by Marthe Jocelyn. Tundra, 2013. ISBN 978-1-77049-376-6 Subj: Language.

Jocelyn, Nell. *Ones and twos* (Jocelyn, Marthe)

Where do you look? (Jocelyn, Marthe)

Joel, Billy. *New York state of mind* ill. by Izak. Scholastic, 2005. ISBN 978-0-439-55382-7 Subj: Cities, towns. Songs.

Johanasen, Heather. *About the rain forest* by Heather Johanasen and Sindy McKay ill. with photos. Treasure Bay, 2000. ISBN 978-1-891327-23-0 Subj: Ecology. Jungle. Weather – rain.

Johansen, Hanna. *The duck and the owl* ill. by Kathi Bhend. Godine, 2005. ISBN 978-1-56792-285-1 Subj: Birds – ducks. Birds – owls. Friendship.

Johansen, K. V. *Pippin and Pudding* ill. by Bernice Lum. Kids Can, 2001. ISBN 978-1-55074-631-0 Subj: Animals – cats. Animals – dogs. Friendship.

Pippin and the bones ill. by Bernice Lum. Kids Can, 2000. ISBN 978-1-55074-629-7 Subj: Anatomy – skeletons. Fossils. Museums.

Pippin takes a bath ill. by Bernice Lum. Kids Can, 1999. ISBN 978-1-55074-627-3 Subj: Activities – bathing. Animals – dogs.

Johnson, Amy Crane. *Cinnamon and the April shower / Canela y el aguacero de abril* ill. by Robb Mommaerts. Raven Tree, 2003. ISBN 978-0-9720192-2-4 Subj: Animals. Birds – ravens. Foreign languages. Forest, woods. Seasons. Weather – storms.

Mason moves away / Mason se muda ill. by Robb Mommaerts. Raven Tree, 2004. ISBN 978-0-9720192-3-1 Subj: Animals – beavers. Birds – ravens. Ecology. Foreign languages. Moving.

Johnson, Angela. *Daddy calls me man* ill. by Rhonda Mitchell. Orchard, 1997. ISBN 978-0-531-33042-5 Subj: Careers – artists. Ethnic groups in the U.S. – African Americans. Family life. Poetry.

The day Ray got away ill. by Luke LaMarca. Simon & Schuster, 2010. ISBN 978-0-689-87375-1 Subj: Behavior – running away. Parades. Toys – balloons.

Do like Kyla ill. by James Ransome. Watts, 1990. ISBN 978-0-531-08452-6 Subj: Ethnic groups in the U.S. – African Americans. Family life – brothers & sisters.

Down the winding road ill. by Shane W. Evans. DK, 2000. ISBN 978-0-7894-2596-6 Subj: Country. Ethnic groups in the U.S. – African Americans. Family life. Friendship.

The girl who wore snakes ill. by James Ransome. Orchard, 1993. ISBN 978-0-531-08641-4 Subj: Animals. Ethnic groups in the U.S. – African Americans. Family life – aunts, uncles. Pets. Reptiles – snakes.

I dream of trains ill. by Loren Long. Simon & Schuster, 2003. ISBN 978-0-689-82609-2 Subj: Activities – working. Dreams. Family life – fathers. Trains.

Joshua by the sea ill. by Rhonda Mitchell. Orchard, 1994. ISBN 978-0-531-06846-5 Subj: Ethnic groups in the U.S. – African Americans. Format, unusual – board books. Sea & seashore.

Joshua's night whispers ill. by Rhonda Mitchell. Orchard, 1994. ISBN 978-0-531-06847-2 Subj: Ethnic groups in the U.S. – African Americans. Family life – fathers. Format, unusual – board books. Night. Noise, sounds.

Julius ill. by Dav Pilkey. Orchard, 1993. ISBN 978-0-531-08615-5 Subj: Animals – pigs. Ethnic groups in the U.S. – African Americans. Family life – grandfathers. Pets.

The leaving morning ill. by David Soman. Orchard, 1992. ISBN 978-0-531-08592-9 Subj: Emotions. Ethnic groups in the U.S. – African Americans. Family life. Moving.

Lily Brown's paintings ill. by E. B. Lewis. Scholastic, 2007. ISBN 978-0-439-78225-8 Subj: Activities – painting. Ethnic groups in the U.S. – African Americans. Imagination.

Lottie Paris and the best place ill. by Scott M. Fischer. Simon & Schuster, 2013. ISBN 978-0-689-87378-2 Subj: Books, reading. Ethnic groups in the U.S. – African Americans. Friendship. Libraries.

Lottie Paris lives here ill. by Scott M. Fischer. Simon & Schuster, 2011. ISBN 978-0-689-87377-5 Subj: Activities. Behavior. Day. Ethnic groups in the U.S. – African Americans. Family life – fathers. Imagination.

One of three ill. by David Soman. Watts, 1991. ISBN 978-0-531-08555-4 Subj: Ethnic groups in the U.S. – African Americans. Family life – sisters.

Rain feet ill. by Rhonda Mitchell. Orchard, 1994. ISBN 978-0-531-06849-6 Subj: Ethnic groups in the U.S. – African Americans. Format, unusual – board books. Weather – rain.

The Rolling Store ill. by Peter Catalanotto. Orchard, 1997. ISBN 978-0-531-33015-9 Subj: Careers – peddlers. Ethnic groups in the U.S. – African Americans. Family life – grandfathers. Memories, memory. Stores.

Shoes like Miss Alice's ill. by Ken Page. Orchard, 1995. ISBN 978-0-531-08664-3 Subj: Activities – babysitting. Clothing – shoes. Ethnic groups in the U.S. – African Americans.

A sweet smell of roses ill. by Eric Velasquez. Simon & Schuster, 2005. ISBN 978-0-689-83252-9 Subj: Ethnic groups in the U.S. – African Americans. Family life – sisters. U.S. history.

Tell me a story, mama ill. by David Soman. Watts, 1989. ISBN 978-0-531-08394-9 Subj: Family life – mothers.

Those building men ill. by Mike Benny. Blue Sky, 1999. ISBN 978-0-590-66521-6 Subj: Activities – making things. Careers – construction workers.

Violet's music ill. by Laura Huliska-Beith. Dial, 2004. ISBN 978-0-8037-2740-3 Subj: Careers – musicians. Music. Musical instruments – bands.

The wedding ill. by David Soman. Orchard, 1999. ISBN 978-0-531-33139-2 Subj: Ethnic groups in the U.S. – African Americans. Family life – sisters. Weddings.

When I am old with you ill. by David Soman. Watts, 1990. ISBN 978-0-531-08484-7 Subj: Ethnic groups in the U.S. – African Americans. Family life – grandfathers. Old age.

Wind flyers ill. by Loren Long. Simon & Schuster, 2007. ISBN 978-0-689-84879-7 Subj: Activities – flying. Careers – airplane pilots. Ethnic groups in the U.S. – African Americans. U.S. history. War.

Johnson, Crockett. *Harold and the purple crayon* ill. by author. HarperCollins, 1955. ISBN 978-0-06-022936-8 Subj: Art. Humorous stories. Imagination.

Harold at the North Pole: a Christmas journey with the purple crayon ill. by author. HarperCollins, 1958. ISBN 978-0-06-028074-1 Subj: Holidays – Christmas. Humorous stories. Imagination. Santa Claus.

Magic beach ill. by author. Boyds Mills, 2005. ISBN 978-1-932425-27-7 Subj: Imagination. Sea & seashore – beaches.

A picture for Harold's room ill. by author. HarperCollins, 1960. ISBN 978-0-06-023006-7 Subj: Art. Humorous stories. Imagination.

Will spring be early or will spring be late? ill. by author. Crowell, 1959. ISBN 978-0-690-89423-3 Subj: Animals – groundhogs. Holidays – Groundhog Day. Seasons – spring.

Johnson, D. B. *Eddie's kingdom* ill. by author. Houghton, 2005. ISBN 978-0-618-56299-2 Subj: Activities – drawing. Behavior – fighting, arguing. Communities, neighborhoods. Homes, houses.

Four legs bad, two legs good! ill. by author. Houghton, 2007. ISBN 978-0-618-80909-7 Subj: Animals. Character traits – laziness. Farms.

Henry builds a cabin ill. by author. Houghton, 2002. ISBN 978-0-618-13201-0 Subj: Animals – bears. Homes, houses. U.S. history.

Henry climbs a mountain ill. by author. Houghton, 2003. ISBN 978-0-618-26902-0 Subj: Animals – bears. Character traits – being different. Imagination. Mountains. Slavery.

Henry hikes to Fitchburg ill. by author. Houghton, 2000. ISBN 978-0-395-96867-3 Subj: Activities – walking. Sports – hiking. U.S. history.

Henry works ill. by author. Houghton, 2004. ISBN 978-0-618-42003-2 Subj: Activities – walking. Activities – working. Activities – writing. Animals – bears. Nature. Weather – rain.

Henry's night by D. B. Johnson and Linda Michelin ill. by D. B. Johnson. Houghton, 2009.

ISBN 978-0-547-05663-0 Subj: Animals – bears. Bedtime. Night. Sleep.

Magritte's marvelous hat ill. by D. B. Johnson. Houghton Mifflin, 2012. ISBN 978-0-547-55864-6 Subj: Animals – dogs. Art. Careers – artists. Clothing – hats. Foreign lands – France.

Palazzo inverso ill. by author. Harcourt, 2010. ISBN 978-0-15-23999-6 Subj: Art. Buildings. Careers – artists. Format, unusual.

Johnson, David. *Snow sounds: an onomatopoeic story* ill. by author. Houghton, 2006. ISBN 978-0-618-47310-6 Subj: Holidays – Christmas. Noise, sounds.

Johnson, Dinah. *Black magic* ill. by R. Gregory Christie. Holt, 2010. ISBN 978-0-8050-7833-6 Subj: Ethnic groups in the U.S. – African Americans. Self-concept.

Quinnie Blue ill. by James Ransome. Holt, 2000. ISBN 978-0-8050-4378-5 Subj: Ethnic groups in the U.S. – African Americans. Family life – grandmothers.

Johnson, Dolores. *Now let me fly: the story of a slave family* ill. by author. Macmillan, 1993. ISBN 978-0-02-747699-6 Subj: Ethnic groups in the U.S. – African Americans. Slavery. U.S. history.

Johnson, Doug. *Substitute teacher plans* ill. by Tammy Smith. Holt, 2002. ISBN 978-0-8050-6520-6 Subj: Activities. Careers – teachers. Humorous stories. School.

Johnson, G. Francis. *Has anybody lost a glove?* ill. by Dimitrea Tokunbo. Boyds Mills, 2004. ISBN 978-1-59078-041-1 Subj: Behavior – lost & found possessions. Clothing – gloves, mittens. Communities, neighborhoods.

Johnson, Gillian. *My sister Gracie* ill. by author. Tundra, 2000. ISBN 978-0-88776-514-8 Subj: Animals – dogs. Family life – brothers & sisters. Rhyming text.

Johnson, Grace. *The candle in the window* ill. by Mark Elliott. Fleming H. Revell, 2003. ISBN 978-0-8007-1815-2 Subj: Careers – shoemakers. Character traits – kindness. Foreign lands – Germany. Holidays – Christmas. Religion.

Johnson, James Weldon. *The Creation* ill. by James Ransome. Holiday, 1994. ISBN 978-0-8234-1069-9 Subj: Creation. Ethnic groups in the U.S. – African Americans. Poetry. Religion.

Lift every voice and sing ill. by Bryan Collier. HarperCollins, 2007. ISBN 978-0-06-054147-7 Subj: Ethnic groups in the U.S. – African Americans. Music. Slavery. Songs.

Lift ev'ry voice and sing ill. by Jan Spivey Gilchrist. Scholastic, 1995. ISBN 978-0-590-46982-1 Subj: Ethnic groups in the U.S. – African Americans. Music. Slavery. Songs.

Johnson, Jen Cullerton. *Seeds of change: planting a path to peace* ill. by Sonia Lynn Sadler. Lee & Low, 2010. ISBN 978-1-60060-367-9 Subj: Character traits – responsibility. Ecology. Foreign lands – Kenya. Trees.

Johnson, Lindan Lee. *The dream jar* ill. by Serena Curmi. Houghton, 2005. ISBN 978-0-618-17698-4 Subj: Bedtime. Dreams. Family life – brothers & sisters. Nightmares.

Johnson, Marion. *Caillou, new shoes* adapt. by Éric Sévigny; ill. by CINAR Animation. Chouette, 2002. ISBN 978-2-89450-327-0 Subj: Behavior – growing up. Clothing – shoes. Family life – mothers. Shopping.

Johnson, Neil. *The falling raindrop* by Neil Johnson and Joel Chin ill. by authors. Tricycle, 2010. ISBN 978-1-58246-312-4 Subj: Behavior – worrying. Water. Weather – rain.

Johnson, Paul Brett. *Bearhide and crow* ill. by author. Holiday, 2000. ISBN 978-0-8234-1470-3 Subj: Activities – trading. Behavior – greed. Birds – crows. Humorous stories.

The cow who wouldn't come down ill. by author. Orchard, 1993. ISBN 978-0-531-08631-5 Subj: Activities – flying. Animals – bulls, cows. Farms.

The goose who went off in a huff ill. by author. Orchard, 2001. ISBN 978-0-439-40842-4 Subj: Animals – babies. Animals – elephants. Birds – geese. Family life – mothers. Humorous stories.

Jack outwits the giants ill. by author. McElderry, 2002. ISBN 978-0-689-83902-3 Subj: Behavior – trickery. Folk & fairy tales. Giants.

Little Bunny Foo Foo: told and sung by the Good Fairy ill. by author. Scholastic, 2004. ISBN 978-0-439-37301-2 Subj: Animals – rabbits. Behavior – misbehavior. Fairies. Humorous stories. Music. Songs.

Lost ill. by Celeste Lewis. Orchard, 1996. ISBN 978-0-531-08851-7 Subj: Animals – dogs. Behavior – lost. Camps, camping. Desert. Pets.

Mr. Persnickety and Cat Lady ill. by author. Orchard, 2000. ISBN 978-0-531-33283-2 Subj: Animals – cats. Animals – mice. Communities, neighborhoods. Problem solving.

Old Dry Fry ill. by author. Scholastic, 1999. ISBN 978-0-590-37658-7 Subj: Careers – clergy. Folk & fairy tales.

On top of spaghetti lyrics by Tom Glazer; ill. by author. Scholastic, 2006. ISBN 978-0-439-74944-2 Subj: Animals. Food. Songs.

The pig who ran a red light ill. by author. Orchard, 1999. ISBN 978-0-531-33136-1 Subj: Activities. Animals – pigs. Behavior.

Johnson, Rebecca. *The proud pelican's secret* photos by Steve Parish. Gareth Stevens, 2005. ISBN 978-0-8368-5974-4 Subj: Birds – pelicans. Character traits – appearance. Character traits – pride.

Sea turtle's clever plan photos by Steve Parish. Gareth Stevens, 2005. ISBN 978-0-8368-5975-1 Subj: Character traits – cleverness. Reptiles – turtles, tortoises.

Tree frog hears a sound photos by Steve Parish. Gareth Stevens, 2005. ISBN 978-0-8368-5976-8 Subj: Frogs & toads. Jungle.

Johnson, Stephen T. *Alphabet city* ill. by author. Viking, 1995. ISBN 978-0-670-85631-2 Subj: ABC books. Caldecott award honor books. Cities, towns. Concepts.

City by numbers ill. by author. Viking, 1998. ISBN 978-0-670-87251-0 Subj: Counting, numbers.

My little blue robot ill. by author. Harcourt, 2002. ISBN 978-0-15-216524-6 Subj: Activities – making things. Format, unusual – toy & movable books. Robots.

Johnson, Suzanne C. *Fribbity ribbit* ill. by Debbie Tilley. Knopf, 2001. ISBN 978-0-375-91199-6 Subj: Family life. Frogs & toads. Humorous stories.

Johnson-Davies, Denys. *Goha, the wise fool* ill. by Hany el Saed Ahmed and Hag Hamdy Mohamed Fattouh. Penguin, 2005. ISBN 978-0-399-24222-9 Subj: Character traits – cleverness. Character traits – foolishness. Folk & fairy tales. Foreign lands – Middle East.

Johnston, Lynn. *Farley follows his nose* by Lynn Johnston and Beth Cruikshank ill. by Lynn Johnston. Bowen Press, 2009. ISBN 978-0-06-170234-1 Subj: Animals – dogs. Behavior – lost. Behavior – running away.

Johnston, Tony. *The badger and the magic fan* ill. by Tomie dePaola. Putnam, 1990. ISBN 978-0-399-21945-0 Subj: Anatomy – noses. Animals – badgers. Behavior – trickery. Folk & fairy tales. Foreign lands – Japan. Magic.

The barn owls ill. by Deborah Kogan Ray. Charlesbridge, 2000. ISBN 978-0-88106-981-5 Subj: Barns. Birds – owls. Poetry.

Big red apple ill. by Judith Hoffman Corwin. Scholastic, 1999. ISBN 978-0-439-09860-1 Subj: Circular tales. Plants. Trees.

Bigfoot Cinderrrrrella ill. by James Warhola. Putnam, 1998. ISBN 978-0-399-23021-9 Subj: Folk & fairy tales. Forest, woods. Mythical creatures.

The cat with seven names ill. by Christine Davenier. Charlesbridge, 2013. ISBN 978-1-58089-381-7 Subj: Animals – cats. Communities, neighborhoods. Emotions – loneliness.

Chicken in the kitchen ill. by Eleanor Taylor. Simon & Schuster, 2005. ISBN 978-0-689-85641-9 Subj: Birds – chickens. Rhyming text.

The cowboy and the black-eyed pea ill. by Warren Ludwig. Putnam, 1992. ISBN 978-0-399-22330-3 Subj: Cowboys, cowgirls. Folk & fairy tales. U.S. history – frontier & pioneer life. Weddings.

Day of the Dead ill. by Jeanette Winter. Harcourt, 1997. ISBN 978-0-15-222863-7 Subj: Foreign lands – Mexico. Holidays – Day of the Dead.

Desert dog ill. by Robert Weatherford. Sierra Club, 2001. ISBN 978-0-87156-979-0 Subj: Animals – dogs. Animals – goats. Desert. Rhyming text.

Desert song ill. by Ed Young. Sierra Club, 2000. ISBN 978-0-87156-491-7 Subj: Animals. Desert. Night.

Farmer Mack measures his pig ill. by Megan Lloyd. HarperCollins, 1986. ISBN 978-0-06-023018-0 Subj: Animals – pigs. Behavior – boasting. Farms.

The ghost of Nicholas Greebe ill. by S. D. Schindler. Dial, 1996. ISBN 978-0-8037-1649-0 Subj: Anatomy – skeletons. Animals – dogs. Ghosts.

Go track a yak ill. by Tim Raglin. Simon & Schuster, 2003. ISBN 978-0-689-83789-0 Subj: Animals – yaks. Family life – parents. Folk & fairy tales. Humorous stories. Witches.

The iguana brothers, a perfect day ill. by Mark Teague. Blue Sky, 1995. ISBN 978-0-590-47468-9 Subj: Family life – brothers. Foreign lands – Mexico. Reptiles – iguanas.

A Kenya Christmas ill. by Leonard Jenkins. Holiday, 2003. ISBN 978-0-8234-1623-3 Subj: Family life – aunts, uncles. Foreign lands – Kenya. Holidays – Christmas. Santa Claus.

Laugh-out-loud baby ill. by Stephen Gammell. Simon & Schuster, 2012. ISBN 978-1-4424-1380-1 Subj: Babies. Family life. Parties.

Levi Strauss gets a bright idea: a fairly fabricated story of a pair of pants ill. by Stacy Innerst. Harcourt, 2011. ISBN 978-0-15-206145-6 Subj: Activities – sewing. Clothing – pants. Tall tales. U.S. history – frontier & pioneer life.

Little Rabbit goes to sleep ill. by Harvey Stevenson. HarperCollins, 1994. ISBN 978-0-06-021241-4 Subj: Animals – rabbits. Bedtime. Emotions – fear. Family life – grandfathers. Night. Sleep.

My abuelita ill. by Yuyi Morales. Harcourt, 2009. ISBN 978-0-15-216330-3 Subj: Activities – storytelling. Ethnic groups in the U.S. – Mexican

Americans. Family life – grandmothers. Foreign languages.

My best friend Bear ill. by Joy Allen. Rising Moon, 2001. ISBN 978-0-87358-775-4 Subj: Activities – sewing. Family life – mothers. Toys – bears.

My Mexico / México mío ill. by F. John Sierra. Putnam, 1996. ISBN 978-0-399-22275-7 Subj: Foreign lands – Mexico. Foreign languages. Poetry.

Noel ill. by Cheng-Khee Chee. Carolrhoda, 2005. ISBN 978-1-57505-752-1 Subj: Holidays – Christmas.

Off to kindergarten ill. by Melissa Sweet. Houghton, 2007. ISBN 978-0-439-73090-7 Subj: Rhyming text. School – first day.

P is for piñata: a Mexico alphabet ill. by John Parra. Sleeping Bear, 2008. ISBN 978-1-58536-144-1 Subj: ABC books. Foreign lands – Mexico.

The quilt story ill. by Tomie dePaola. Putnam, 1984. ISBN 978-0-399-21009-9 Subj: Family life. Moving. Quilts.

Soup bone ill. by Margot Tomes. Harcourt, 1990. ISBN 978-0-15-277255-0 Subj: Anatomy – skeletons. Friendship. Holidays – Halloween.

Sunsets of the West ill. by Ted Lewin. Putnam, 2002. ISBN 978-0-399-22659-5 Subj: Family life. Moving. U.S. history – frontier & pioneer life.

The tale of Rabbit and Coyote ill. by Tomie dePaola. Putnam, 1994. ISBN 978-0-399-22258-0 Subj: Animals – coyotes. Animals – rabbits. Folk & fairy tales. Foreign lands – Mexico. Indians of North America – Zapotec.

That summer ill. by Barry Moser. Harcourt, 2002. ISBN 978-0-15-201585-5 Subj: Death. Emotions – grief. Family life. Family life – brothers. Quilts.

The vanishing pumpkin ill. by Tomie dePaola. Putnam, 1983. ISBN 978-0-399-20991-8 Subj: Holidays – Halloween. Witches.

The wagon ill. by James Ransome. Tambourine, 1996. ISBN 978-0-688-13537-9 Subj: Ethnic groups in the U.S. – African Americans. Slavery. U.S. history.

The whole green world ill. by Elisa Kleven. Farrar, 2005. ISBN 978-0-374-38400-5 Subj: Ecology. Nature. Rhyming text.

Jolivet, Joëlle. *Almost everything* ill. by author. Macmillan, 2005. ISBN 978-1-59643-090-7 Subj: Nature. Science.

365 penguins (Fromental, Jean-Luc)

Zoo-ology ill. by author. Roaring Brook, 2003. ISBN 978-0-7613-2780-6 Subj: Animals. Science.

Jonas, Ann. *Aardvarks, disembark!* ill. by author. Greenwillow, 1990. ISBN 978-0-688-07207-0 Subj: ABC books. Animals. Animals – endangered animals. Boats, ships. Religion – Noah. Weather – floods. Weather – rain.

Bird talk ill. by author. Greenwillow, 1999. ISBN 978-0-688-14173-8 Subj: Birds. Noise, sounds. Songs.

Color dance ill. by author. Greenwillow, 1989. ISBN 978-0-688-05990-3 Subj: Activities – dancing. Concepts – color.

Holes and peeks ill. by author. Greenwillow, 1984. ISBN 978-0-688-02538-0 Subj: Emotions – fear. Problem solving.

Now we can go ill. by author. Greenwillow, 1986. ISBN 978-0-688-04803-7 Subj: Toys.

The quilt ill. by author. Greenwillow, 1984. ISBN 978-0-688-03826-7 Subj: Bedtime. Dreams. Quilts.

Reflections ill. by author. Greenwillow, 1987. ISBN 978-0-688-06141-8 Subj: Concepts. Format, unusual.

Round trip ill. by author. Greenwillow, 1983. ISBN 978-0-688-01781-1 Subj: Activities – traveling. Cities, towns.

Splash! ill. by author. Greenwillow, 1995. ISBN 978-0-688-11052-9 Subj: Animals. Counting, numbers. Ethnic groups in the U.S. – African Americans. Fish.

The thirteenth clue ill. by author. Greenwillow, 1992. ISBN 978-0-688-09742-4 Subj: Birthdays. Format, unusual. Mystery stories. Parties.

The trek ill. by author. Greenwillow, 1985. ISBN 978-0-688-04799-3 Subj: Activities – walking. Animals. Games. Imagination.

Two bear cubs ill. by author. Greenwillow, 1982. ISBN 978-0-688-01408-7 Subj: Animals – bears. Behavior – lost. Family life – mothers.

Watch William walk ill. by author. Greenwillow, 1997. ISBN 978-0-688-14175-2 Subj: Activities – walking. Animals – dogs. Birds – ducks. Language.

When you were a baby ill. by author. Greenwillow, 1982. ISBN 978-0-688-00864-2 Subj: Activities. Behavior – growing up.

Where can it be? ill. by author. Greenwillow, 1986. ISBN 978-0-688-05246-1 Subj: Behavior – lost & found possessions. Format, unusual – toy & movable books.

Jonathan, Langley. *Missing* ill. by author. Marshall Cavendish, 2000. ISBN 978-0-7614-5078-8 Subj: Animals – cats. Behavior – lost.

Jonell, Lynne. *Bravemole* ill. by author. Putnam, 2002. ISBN 978-0-399-23962-5 Subj: Behavior – needing someone. Family life – mothers.

I need a snake ill. by Petra Mathers. Putnam, 1998. ISBN 978-0-399-23176-6 Subj: Family life – mothers. Pets. Reptiles – snakes.

It's my birthday, too! ill. by Petra Mathers. Putnam, 1999. ISBN 978-0-399-23323-4 Subj: Animals – dogs. Birthdays. Family life – brothers. Parties. Sibling rivalry.

Mom pie ill. by Petra Mathers. Putnam, 2001. ISBN 978-0-399-23422-4 Subj: Behavior – needing someone. Family life – mothers.

When Mommy was mad ill. by Petra Mathers. Putnam, 2002. ISBN 978-0-399-23433-0 Subj: Emotions – anger. Family life – mothers.

Jones, Christianne. *Lacey Walker, nonstop talker* ill. by Richard Watson. Picture Window, 2012. ISBN 978-1-4048-6796-3 Subj: Activities – talking. Birds – owls. Etiquette.

Jones, Elizabeth. *Sunshine and Storm* ill. by James Coplestone. Ragged Bears, 2001. ISBN 978-1-929927-27-2 Subj: Animals – cats. Animals – dogs. Emotions – anger. Friendship. Weather – rain.

Jones, Sylvie. *Who's in the tub?* ill. by Pascale Constantin. Blue Apple, 2007. ISBN 978-1-59354-612-0 Subj: Activities – bathing. Animals. Imagination. Rhyming text.

Jones, Ursula. *The witch's children* ill. by Russell Ayto. Holt, 2003. ISBN 978-0-8050-7205-1 Subj: Magic. Parks. Witches.

Jonovitz, Marilyn. *Good morning, Little Fox* ill. by author. NorthSouth, 2001. ISBN 978-0-7358-1441-7 Subj: Animals – foxes. Family life – fathers. Family life – sons. Food.

Maybe, my baby ill. by author. NorthSouth, 2003. ISBN 978-0-7358-1763-0 Subj: Animals – babies. Family life – parents. Sleep.

Three little kittens ill. by author. NorthSouth, 2002. ISBN 978-0-7358-1643-5 Subj: Animals – cats. Behavior – lost & found possessions. Clothing – gloves, mittens. Nursery rhymes.

Joosse, Barbara. *Bad dog school* ill. by Jennifer Plecas. Clarion, 2004. ISBN 978-0-618-13331-4 Subj: Animals – dogs. Pets. School.

Dog parade ill. by Eugene Yelchin. Harcourt, 2011. ISBN 978-0-15-206690-1 Subj: Animals – dogs. Clothing – costumes. Parades.

Friends (mostly) ill. by Tomaso Milian. HarperCollins, 2010. ISBN 978-0-06-088221-1 Subj: Friendship.

Ghost wings ill. by Giselle Potter. Chronicle, 2001. ISBN 978-0-8118-2164-3 Subj: Death. Family life – grandmothers. Foreign lands – Mexico. Holidays – Day of the Dead. Insects – butterflies, caterpillars. Memories, memory.

Grandma calls me Beautiful ill. by Barbara Lavallee. Chronicle, 2008. ISBN 978-0-8118-5815-1 Subj: Activities – storytelling. Emotions – love. Family life – grandmothers. Hawaii. Self-concept.

Higgledy-piggledy chicks ill. by Rick Chrustowski. HarperCollins, 2010. ISBN 978-0-06-075042-8 Subj: Animals – babies. Birds – chickens. Farms.

Hooray Parade ill. by Hyewon Yum. Viking, 2013. ISBN 978-0-670-01334-0 Subj: Family life – grandmothers. Parades. Puppets. Rhyming text.

A houseful of Christmas ill. by Betsy Lewin. Holt, 2001. ISBN 978-0-8050-6391-2 Subj: Family life. Family life – grandmothers. Holidays – Christmas. Sleep. Weather – blizzards.

I love you the purplest ill. by Mary Whyte. Chronicle, 1996. ISBN 978-0-8118-0718-0 Subj: Family life – brothers. Family life – mothers. Sibling rivalry. Sports – fishing.

Lovabye dragon ill. by Randy Cecil. Candlewick, 2012. ISBN 978-0-7636-5408-5 Subj: Bedtime. Dragons. Emotions – loneliness. Friendship. Royalty – princesses.

Love is a good thing to feel ill. by Jennifer Plecas. Philomel, 2008. ISBN 978-0-399-25168-9 Subj: Emotions – love.

Mama, do you love me? ill. by Barbara Lavallee. Chronicle, 1991. ISBN 978-0-87701-759-2 Subj: Emotions – love. Eskimos. Family life – mothers.

Nikolai, the only bear ill. by Renata Liwska. Penguin, 2005. ISBN 978-0-399-23884-0 Subj: Adoption. Animals – bears. Foreign lands – Russia. Orphans.

Nugget and Darling ill. by Sue Truesdell. Clarion, 1997. ISBN 978-0-395-64571-0 Subj: Animals – cats. Animals – dogs. Character traits – kindness to animals. Emotions – envy, jealousy.

Old Robert and the sea-silly cats ill. by Jan Jutte. Philomel, 2012. ISBN 978-0-399-25430-7 Subj: Activities – playing. Animals – cats. Sailors.

Papa do you love me? ill. by Barbara Lavallee. Chronicle, 2005. ISBN 978-0-8118-4265-5 Subj: Emotions – love. Family life – fathers. Foreign lands – Africa.

Please is a good word to say ill. by Jennifer Plecas. Penguin, 2007. ISBN 978-0-399-24217-5 Subj: Behavior – misbehavior. Etiquette.

Roawr! ill. by Jan Jutte. Philomel, 2009. ISBN 978-0-399-24777-4 Subj: Animals – bears. Bedtime. Imagination.

Sleepover at Gramma's house ill. by Jan Jutte. Penguin, 2010. ISBN 978-0-399-25261-7 Subj: Activities – playing. Animals – elephants. Family life – grandmothers. Sleepovers.

Snow day! ill. by Jennifer Plecas. Clarion, 1995. ISBN 978-0-395-66588-6 Subj: Family life. Weather – snow.

Wind-wild dog ill. by Kate Kiesler. Holt, 2006. ISBN 978-0-8050-7053-8 Subj: Alaska. Animals – dogs.

Jordan, Deloris. *Baby blessings: a prayer for the day you are born* ill. by James Ransome. Simon & Schuster, 2010. ISBN 978-1-4169-5362-3 Subj: Emotions – love. Ethnic groups in the U.S. – African Americans. Family life – parents. Religion.

Dream big: Michael Jordan and the pursuit of Olympic gold ill. by Barry Root. Simon & Schuster, 2012. ISBN 978-1-4424-1269-9 Subj: Character traits – perseverance. Ethnic groups in the U.S. – African Americans. Sports – basketball. Sports – Olympics.

Michael's golden rules by Deloris Jordan and Roslyn M. Jordan; intro. by Michael Jordan; ill. by Kadir Nelson. Simon & Schuster, 2007. ISBN 978-0-689-87016-3 Subj: Character traits – persistence. Ethnic groups in the U.S. – African Americans. Family life – aunts, uncles. Sports – baseball. Sportsmanship.

Salt in his shoes: Michael Jordan in pursuit of a dream by Deloris Jordan and Roslyn M. Jordan ill. by Kadir Nelson. Simon & Schuster, 2000. ISBN 978-0-689-83371-7 Subj: Careers. Concepts – size. Family life. Sports – basketball.

Jordan, Helene J. *How a seed grows* ill. by Loretta Krupinski. Rev. ed. HarperCollins, 1992. ISBN 978-0-06-020185-2 Subj: Gardens, gardening. Nature. Science. Seeds.

Jordan, Mary Ellen. *Lazy Daisy, cranky Frankie* ill. by Andrew Weldon. Whitman, 2013. ISBN 978-0-8075-4400-6 Subj: Animals. Character traits – laziness. Farms. Humorous stories. Rhyming text.

Jordan, Roslyn M. *Michael's golden rules* (Jordan, Deloris)

Salt in his shoes: Michael Jordan in pursuit of a dream (Jordan, Deloris)

Jordan, Sandra. *Ballet for Martha: making Appalachian Spring* (Greenberg, Jan)

Frog hunt photos by author. Roaring Brook, 2002. ISBN 978-0-7613-2652-6 Subj: Animals. Frogs & toads. Lakes, ponds.

Mr. and Mrs. Portly and their little dog Snack ill. by Christine Davenier. Farrar, 2009. ISBN 978-0-374-35089-5 Subj: Animals – dogs. Art. Character traits – bravery. Crime. Pets.

Jorgensen, Gail. *Crocodile beat* ill. by Patricia Mullins. Bradbury, 1989. ISBN 978-0-02-748010-8 Subj: Animals. Rhyming text.

Gotcha! ill. by Kerry Argent. Scholastic, 1997. ISBN 978-0-590-96208-7 Subj: Animals. Animals – bears. Birthdays. Insects – flies.

Jorgensen, Richard. *Reading with Dad* ill. by Warren Hanson. Waldman, 2000. ISBN 978-0-931674-41-9 Subj: Behavior – growing up. Books, reading. Family life – fathers. Rhyming text.

Joseph, Lynn. *Coconut kind of day* ill. by Sandra Speidel. Lothrop, 1992. ISBN 978-0-688-09120-0 Subj: Foreign lands – Trinidad. Islands. Poetry.

Fly, Bessie, fly ill. by Yvonne Buchanan. Simon & Schuster, 1998. ISBN 978-0-689-81339-9 Subj: Airplanes, airports. Careers – airplane pilots. Ethnic groups in the U.S. – African Americans.

An island Christmas ill. by Catherine Stock. Clarion, 1992. ISBN 978-0-395-58761-4 Subj: Foreign lands – Trinidad. Holidays – Christmas.

Joslin, Mary. *On that Christmas night* ill. by Helen Cann. Good Books, 2005. ISBN 978-1-56148-494-2 Subj: Holidays – Christmas. Religion – Nativity.

The shore beyond ill. by Alison Jay. Good Books, 2000. ISBN 978-1-56148-316-7 Subj: Activities – traveling. Behavior – growing up. Self-concept.

Joubert, Beverly. *African animal alphabet* by Beverly Joubert and Dereck Joubert; photos by author. National Geographic, 2011. ISBN 978-1-4263-0781-2 Subj: ABC books. Animals. Foreign lands – Africa.

Joubert, Dereck. *African animal alphabet* (Joubert, Beverly)

Joyce, Susan. *ABC nature riddles* ill. by Doug DuBosque. Peel Productions, 2000. ISBN 978-0-939217-53-3 Subj: ABC books. Language. Nature. Rhyming text. Riddles & jokes.

Joyce, William. *Bently and egg* ill. by author. HarperCollins, 1992. ISBN 978-0-06-020386-3 Subj: Birds – ducks. Character traits – helpfulness. Eggs. Frogs & toads. Reptiles – turtles, tortoises.

Big time Olie ill. by author. Geringer, 2002. ISBN 978-0-06-008811-8 Subj: Behavior – growing up. Concepts – size. Family life. Problem solving.

A day with Wilbur Robinson ill. by author. HarperCollins, 2006. ISBN 978-0-06-089098-8 Subj: Family life.

Dinosaur Bob: and his adventures with the family Lazardo ill. by author. Expanded ed. HarperCollins, 1995. ISBN 978-0-06-021075-5 Subj: Activities – vacationing. Dinosaurs. Family life. Pets. Prehistory.

The fantastic flying books of Mr. Morris Lessmore ill. by author. Atheneum, 2012. ISBN 978-1-4424-5702-7 Subj: Activities – flying. Books, reading. Libraries.

George shrinks ill. by author. HarperCollins, 1985. ISBN 978-0-06-023071-5 Subj: Activities – babysitting. Concepts – size. Family life.

The Leaf Men and the brave good bugs ill. by author. HarperCollins, 1996. ISBN 978-0-06-027238-8 Subj: Character traits – helpfulness. Gardens, gardening. Insects. Mythical creatures – elves. Old age. Toys.

The Man in the Moon ill. by author. Simon & Schuster, 2011. ISBN 978-1-4424-3041-9 Subj: Imagination. Moon.

Rolie Polie Olie ill. by author. Geringer, 1999. ISBN 978-0-06-027164-0 Subj: Concepts – shape. Rhyming text. Robots.

The Sandman: the story of Sanderson Mansnoozie ill. by author. Atheneum, 2012. ISBN 978-1-4424-3042-6 Subj: Bedtime. Dreams. Moon. Sleep.

Santa calls ill. by author. HarperCollins, 1993. ISBN 978-0-06-021134-9 Subj: Activities – flying. Family life – brothers & sisters. Friendship. Santa Claus. Sibling rivalry.

Sleepy time Olie ill. by author. Geringer, 2001. ISBN 978-0-06-029614-8 Subj: Bedtime. Inventions. Rhyming text. Robots.

Snowie Rolie ill. by author. Geringer, 2000. ISBN 978-0-06-029286-7 Subj: Robots. Snowmen. Weather – snow.

Juan, Ana. *The pet shop revolution* ill. by author. Scholastic, 2011. ISBN 978-0-545-12810-0 Subj: Animals. Character traits – kindness to animals. Pets. Stores.

Jubb, Sophie. *Cock-a-doodle quack! Quack!* (Baddiel, Ivor)

Judd, Naomi. *Naomi Judd's guardian angels* ill. by Dan Andreasen. HarperCollins, 2000. ISBN 978-0-06-027208-1 Subj: Angels. Family life – great-grandparents. Music. Songs.

Judes, Marie-Odile. *Max, the stubborn little wolf* ill. by Martine Bourre. HarperCollins, 2001. ISBN 978-0-06-029417-5 Subj: Animals – wolves. Careers. Family life – fathers. Sports – hunting.

Judge, Lita. *How big were dinosaurs?* ill. by author. Roaring Brook, 2013. ISBN 978-1-59643-719-7 Subj: Concepts – size. Dinosaurs.

Pennies for elephants ill. by author. Hyperion, 2009. ISBN 978-1-4231-1390-4 Subj: Animals – elephants. U.S. history. Zoos.

Red hat ill. by author. Atheneum, 2013. ISBN 978-1-4424-4232-0 Subj: Animals. Clothing – hats. Forest, woods.

Red sled ill. by author. Simon & Schuster, 2011. ISBN 978-1-4424-2007-6 Subj: Animals. Seasons – winter. Sports – sledding.

Jukes, Mavis. *You're a bear* ill. by Steve Johnson and Lou Fancher. Knopf, 2003. ISBN 978-0-375-90267-3 Subj: Animals – bears. Imagination. Night. Rhyming text.

Jules, Jacqueline. *Abraham's search for God* ill. by Natascia Ugliano. Kar-Ben, 2007. ISBN 978-1-58013-243-5 Subj: Religion.

Benjamin and the silver goblet ill. by Natascia Ugliano. Lerner, 2009. ISBN 978-0-8225-8757-6 Subj: Religion.

Duck for Turkey Day ill. by Kathryn Mitter. Whitman, 2009. ISBN 978-0-8075-1734-5 Subj: Ethnic groups in the U.S. – Vietnamese Americans. Holidays – Thanksgiving. School.

No English ill. by Amy Huntington. Mitten, 2007. ISBN 978-1-58726-474-0 Subj: Character traits – kindness. Emotions – loneliness. Friendship. Immigrants.

Picnic at Camp Shalom ill. by Deborah Melmon. Lerner/Kar-Ben, 2011. ISBN 978-0-7613-6661-4 Subj: Camps, camping. Friendship. Jewish culture.

Julian, Alison. *Brave as a bunny can be* ill. by author. Waldman, 2001. ISBN 978-0-931674-46-4 Subj: Animals – rabbits. Character traits – bravery. Emotions – fear. Family life.

Jurmain, Suzanne Tripp. *Worst of friends: Thomas Jefferson, John Adams, and the true story of an American feud* ill. by Larry Day. Penguin, 2011. ISBN 978-0-525-47903-1 Subj: Friendship. U.S. history.

Just like father ill. by John Huxtable. Based on the books by Hans de Beer. Sterling, 2003. ISBN 978-1-4027-1289-0 Subj: Animals – polar bears. Family life – fathers. Format, unusual – board books.

Juster, Norton. *The hello, goodbye window* ill. by Chris Raschka. Hyperion, 2005. ISBN 978-0-7868-0914-1 Subj: Caldecott award books. Family life – grandparents.

Neville ill. by G. Brian Karas. Random House, 2011. ISBN 978-0-375-86765-1 Subj: Behavior – resourcefulness. Emotions – loneliness. Moving.

The odious ogre ill. by Jules Feiffer. Scholastic, 2010. ISBN 978-0-545-16202-9 Subj: Character traits – kindness. Mythical creatures – ogres.

Sourpuss and sweetie pie ill. by Chris Raschka. Scholastic, 2008. ISBN 978-0-439-92943-1 Subj:

Behavior – misbehavior. Emotions – love. Family life – grandparents.

Kabakov, Vladimir. *R is for Russia* photos by Prodeepta Das. Frances Lincoln, 2011. ISBN 978-1-84780-102-9 Subj: ABC books. Foreign lands – Russia.

Kaczman, James. *A bird and his worm* ill. by author. Houghton, 2002. ISBN 978-0-618-09460-8 Subj: Activities – traveling. Animals – worms. Behavior – talking to strangers. Birds. Character traits – being different. Safety.

Kahng, Kim. *The loathsome dragon* (Wiesner, David)

Kaiser, Ruth. *The smiley book of colors* ill. by author. Random House, 2012. ISBN 978-0-375-86983-9 Subj: Concepts – color. Emotions – happiness.

Kajikawa, Kimiko. *Close to you: how animals bond* ill. by author. Holt, 2008. ISBN 978-0-8050-8123-7 Subj: Animals – babies. Nature.

Sweet dreams: how animals sleep ill. by author. Holt, 1999. ISBN 978-0-8050-5890-1 Subj: Animals. Sleep.

Tsunami! ill. by Ed Young. Philomel, 2009. ISBN 978-0-399-25006-4 Subj: Character traits – wisdom. Folk & fairy tales. Foreign lands – Japan. Tsunamis.

Yoshi's feast ill. by Yumi Heo. DK, 2000. ISBN 978-0-7894-2607-9 Subj: Activities – dancing. Folk & fairy tales. Foreign lands – Japan. Friendship. Senses – smell.

Kako, Satoshi. *Little Daruma and little Daikoku* ill. by author. Tuttle, 2003. ISBN 978-0-8048-3351-6 Subj: Character traits – cooperation. Foreign lands – Japan. Friendship. Magic.

Little Daruma and little Kaminari ill. by author. Tuttle, 2002. ISBN 978-0-8048-3348-6 Subj: Behavior – lost & found possessions. Foreign lands – Japan. Friendship.

Kalan, Robert. *Blue sea* ill. by Donald Crews. Greenwillow, 1979. ISBN 978-0-688-84184-3 Subj: Concepts – size. Fish.

Jump, frog, jump! ill. by Byron Barton. Greenwillow, 1981. ISBN 978-0-688-84271-0 Subj: Cumulative tales. Frogs & toads.

Moving day ill. by Yossi Abolafia. Greenwillow, 1996. ISBN 978-0-688-13949-0 Subj: Crustaceans – crabs. Cumulative tales. Moving. Rhyming text.

Rain ill. by Donald Crews. Greenwillow, 1978. ISBN 978-0-688-84139-3 Subj: Weather – rain.

Kallok, Emma. *Gem* ill. by Joel Bower. Tricycle, 2001. ISBN 978-1-58246-027-7 Subj: Babies. Birth. Children as authors. Ethnic groups in the U.S. Family life – new sibling. Musical instruments – saxophones.

Kalman, Maira. *Looking at Lincoln* ill. by author. Penguin, 2012. ISBN 978-0-399-24039-3 Subj: U.S. history.

What Pete ate from A-Z ill. by author. Putnam, 2001. ISBN 978-0-399-23362-3 Subj: ABC books. Animals – dogs.

Kalz, Jill. *An a-maze-ing amusement park adventure* ill. by Mattia Cerato. Capstone, 2010. ISBN 978-1-4048-6023-0 Subj: Mazes. Parks – amusement.

An a-maze-ing farm adventure ill. by Mattia Cerato. Picture Window, 2010. ISBN 978-1-4048-6038-4 Subj: Farms. Mazes.

An a-maze-ing school adventure ill. by Mattia Cerato. Picture Window, 2010. ISBN 978-1-4048-6039-1 Subj: Mazes. School.

An a-maze-ing zoo adventure ill. by Mattia Cerato. Picture Window, 2010. ISBN 978-1-4048-6024-7 Subj: Mazes. Zoos.

Fruits ill. with photos. Smart Apple Media, 2003. ISBN 978-1-58340-299-3 Subj: Food. Health & fitness.

Northern lights ill. with photos. Creative Editions, 2004. ISBN 978-1-58341-326-5 Subj: Northern lights. Science.

Water ill. with photos. Smart Apple Media, 2003. ISBN 978-1-58340-302-0 Subj: Water.

Kamine, Jane. *Mommy's hands* (Lasky, Kathryn)

Kamish, Daniel. *Diggy Dan* by Daniel Kamish and David Kamish ill. by Daniel Kamish. Random House, 2001. ISBN 978-0-375-90576-6 Subj: Character traits – cleanliness. Character traits – orderliness. Children as illustrators. Imagination.

Kamish, David. *Diggy Dan* (Kamish, Daniel)

Kamkwamba, William. *The boy who harnessed the wind* by William Kamkwamba and Bryan Mealer ill. by Elizabeth Zunon. Dial, 2012. ISBN 978-0-8037-3511-8 Subj: Behavior – resourcefulness. Foreign lands – Malawi. Weather – droughts.

Kamm, Katja. *Invisible* ill. by author. NorthSouth, 2006. ISBN 978-0-7358-2052-4 Subj: Art. Picture puzzles. Wordless.

Kaner, Etta. *And the winner is . . .: amazing animal athletes* ill. by David Anderson. Kids Can, 2013. ISBN 978-1-55453-904-8 Subj: Animals. Contests.

Who likes the rain? ill. by Marie Lafrance. Kids Can, 2007. ISBN 978-1-55337-841-9 Subj: Format, unusual – toy & movable books. Weather – rain.

Who likes the sun? ill. by Marie Lafrance. Kids Can, 2007. ISBN 978-1-55337-840-2 Subj: Format, unusual – toy & movable books. Sun.

Who likes the wind? ill. by Marie Lafrance. Kids Can, 2006. ISBN 978-1-55337-839-6 Subj: Format, unusual – toy & movable books. Weather – wind.

Kanevsky, Polly. *Sleepy boy* ill. by Stephanie Anderson. Simon & Schuster, 2006. ISBN 978-0-689-86735-4 Subj: Animals – lions. Bedtime. Family life – fathers. Sleep.

Kangas, Juli. *The surprise visitor* ill. by author. Penguin, 2005. ISBN 978-0-8037-2989-6 Subj: Animals. Animals – mice. Eggs.

Kann, Elizabeth. *Pinkalicious* (Kann, Victoria)

Purplicious (Kann, Victoria)

Kann, Victoria. *Emeraldalicious* ill. by author. HarperCollins, 2013. ISBN 978-0-06-178126-1 Subj: Ecology. Gardens, gardening. Magic. Parks.

Pinkalicious by Victoria Kann and Elizabeth Kann ill. by Victoria Kann. HarperCollins, 2006. ISBN 978-0-06-077639-8 Subj: Concepts – color. Food.

Purplicious by Victoria Kann and Elizabeth Kann ill. by Victoria Kann. HarperCollins, 2007. ISBN 978-0-06-124405-6 Subj: Character traits – individuality. Concepts – color. School.

Silverlicious ill. by author. HarperCollins, 2011. ISBN 978-0-06-178123-0 Subj: Fairies. Family life – brothers & sisters. Teeth.

Kanninen, Barbara. *A story with pictures* ill. by Lynn Rowe Reed. Holiday House, 2007. ISBN 978-0-8234-2049-0 Subj: Books, reading. Careers – writers. Careers – illustrators. Imagination.

Kaplan, Bruce Eric. *Monsters eat whiny children* ill. by author. Simon & Schuster, 2010. ISBN 978-1-4169-8689-8 Subj: Behavior – misbehavior. Family life – brothers & sisters. Monsters.

Kaplan, Michael B. *Betty Bunny didn't do it* ill. by Stéphane Jorisch. Dial, 2013. ISBN 978-0-8037-3858-4 Subj: Animals – rabbits. Behavior – lying. Character traits – honesty. Family life.

Betty Bunny loves chocolate cake ill. by Stéphane Jorisch. Penguin, 2011. ISBN 978-0-8037-3407-4 Subj: Animals – rabbits. Character traits – patience. Food.

Betty Bunny wants everything ill. by Stéphane Jorisch. Dial, 2012. ISBN 978-0-8037-3408-1 Subj: Animals – rabbits. Behavior – greed. Emotions – anger. Family life. Shopping.

Karas, G. Brian. *Atlantic* ill. by author. Putnam, 2002. ISBN 978-0-399-23632-7 Subj: Science. Sea & seashore.

Bebe's bad dream ill. by author. Greenwillow, 2000. ISBN 978-0-688-16183-5 Subj: Aliens. Family life – brothers & sisters. Nightmares.

On Earth ill. by author. Penguin, 2005. ISBN 978-0-399-24025-6 Subj: Earth.

Skidamarink ill. by author. HarperCollins, 2002. ISBN 978-0-694-01595-5 Subj: Animals – polar bears. Birds – penguins. Emotions – love. Format, unusual – toy & movable books. Rhyming text. Sports – ice skating.

The village garage ill. by author. Holt, 2010. ISBN 978-0-8050-8716-1 Subj: Careers. Cities, towns. Seasons.

Karon, Jan. *The trellis and the seed* ill. by Robert Gantt Steele. Viking, 2003. ISBN 978-0-670-89289-1 Subj: Behavior – growing up. Flowers. Seeds.

Kasbarian, Lucine, reteller. *The greedy sparrow: an Armenian tale* ill. by Maria Zaikina. Marshall Cavendish, 2011. ISBN 978-0-7614-5821-2 Subj: Behavior – greed. Behavior – trickery. Birds – sparrows. Folk & fairy tales.

Kasparavicius, Kestutis. *The bear family's world tour Christmas* ill. by author. Abrams, 2002. ISBN 978-0-8109-0573-3 Subj: Activities – traveling. Animals – bears. Holidays – Christmas.

Kassirer, Sue. *Joseph and his coat of many colors* ill. by Danuta Jarecka. Simon & Schuster, 1997. ISBN 978-0-689-81227-9 Subj: Clothing – coats. Religion. Sibling rivalry.

Math fair blues ill. by Jerry Smath. Kane, 2001. ISBN 978-0-613-39339-3 Subj: Concepts – shape. Counting, numbers. Fairs, festivals. Musical instruments – bands.

What's next, Nina? ill. by Page Eastburn O'Rourke. Kane, 2001. ISBN 978-1-57565-106-4 Subj: Concepts – patterns. Family life – sisters. Jewelry. Parties.

Kastner, Jill. *Merry Christmas, Princess Dinosaur* ill. by author. Greenwillow, 2002. ISBN 978-0-06-000472-9 Subj: Dinosaurs. Holidays – Christmas. Toys.

Princess Dinosaur ill. by author. Greenwillow, 2001. ISBN 978-0-688-17046-2 Subj: Animals – dogs. Dinosaurs. Toys.

Kasza, Keiko. *Badger's fancy meal* ill. by author. Penguin, 2007. ISBN 978-0-399-24603-6 Subj: Animals – badgers. Food.

The dog who cried wolf ill. by author. Penguin, 2005. ISBN 978-0-399-24247-2 Subj: Animals – dogs. Animals – wolves. Self-concept.

Don't laugh, Joe ill. by author. Putnam, 1997. ISBN 978-0-399-23036-3 Subj: Animals – bears. Animals – possums. Behavior.

Dorothy and Mikey ill. by author. Putnam, 2000. ISBN 978-0-399-23356-2 Subj: Activities – playing. Animals – hippopotamuses. Friendship.

Grandpa Toad's last secret ill. by author. Putnam, 1995. ISBN 978-0-399-22610-6 Subj: Family life – grandfathers. Frogs & toads. Monsters.

The mightiest ill. by author. Putnam, 2001. ISBN 978-0-399-23586-3 Subj: Animals – bears. Animals – elephants. Animals – lions. Giants.

A mother for Choco ill. by author. Putnam, 1992. ISBN 978-0-399-21841-5 Subj: Adoption. Animals. Birds. Emotions – love. Family life – mothers.

My lucky birthday ill. by author. Penguin, 2013. ISBN 978-0-399-25763-6 Subj: Animals – pigs. Behavior – trickery. Birthdays. Reptiles – alligators, crocodiles.

Ready for anything ill. by author. Putnam, 2009. ISBN 978-0-399-25235-8 Subj: Activities – picnicking. Animals – raccoons. Behavior – worrying. Birds – ducks. Character traits – kindness.

Silly Goose's big story ill. by author. Putnam, 2012. ISBN 978-0-399-25542-7 Subj: Activities – storytelling. Animals. Birds – geese. Friendship.

The wolf's chicken stew ill. by author. Putnam, 1987. ISBN 978-0-399-21400-4 Subj: Animals – wolves. Birds – chickens. Character traits – generosity. Food.

Kato, Yukiko. *In the meadow* ill. by Komako Sakai. Enchanted Lion, 2011. ISBN 978-1-59270-108-7 Subj: Behavior – lost. Nature.

Katschke, Judy. *Take a hike, Snoopy* ill. by Nick LoBianco and Peter LoBianco. Simon & Schuster, 2002. ISBN 978-0-689-84938-1 Subj: Animals – dogs. Birds. Camps, camping. Sports – hiking.

Katz, Alan. *Don't say that word!* ill. by David Catrow. Simon & Schuster, 2007. ISBN 978-0-689-86971-6 Subj: Etiquette. Humorous stories. Rhyming text. School.

Katz, Bobbi. *Nothing but a dog* ill. by Jane Manning. Penguin, 2010. ISBN 978-0-525-47858-4 Subj: Animals – dogs. Pets.

Once around the sun ill. by LeUyen Pham. Harcourt, 2006. ISBN 978-0-15-216397-6 Subj: Days of the week, months of the year. Poetry. Seasons.

Katz, Jon. *Lenore finds a friend: a true story from Bedlam Farm* ill. by author. Holt, 2012. ISBN 978-0-8050-9220-2 Subj: Animals – dogs. Farms. Friendship.

Meet the dogs of Bedlam Farm photos by author. Holt, 2011. ISBN 978-0-8050-9219-6 Subj: Animals – dogs. Farms.

Katz, Karen. *The babies on the bus* ill. by author. Holt, 2011. ISBN 978-0-8050-9011-6 Subj: Babies. Buses. Music. Songs.

Baby loves winter! ill. by author. Simon & Schuster, 2013. ISBN 978-1-4424-5213-8 Subj: Babies. Format, unusual – board books. Seasons – winter. Weather – snow.

Can you say peace? ill. by author. Holt, 2006. ISBN 978-0-8050-7893-0 Subj: Foreign languages. Violence, nonviolence. World.

The colors of us ill. by author. Holt, 1999. ISBN 978-0-8050-5864-2 Subj: Character traits – individuality. Concepts – color. Ethnic groups in the U.S.

Counting kisses ill. by author. McElderry, 2001. ISBN 978-0-689-83470-7 Subj: Counting, numbers. Kissing.

Daddy hugs 1 2 3 ill. by author. Simon & Schuster, 2005. ISBN 978-0-689-87771-1 Subj: Emotions – love. Family life – fathers. Hugging.

Mommy hugs ill. by author. Simon & Schuster, 2006. ISBN 978-0-689-87772-8 Subj: Family life – mothers. Hugging.

My first Ramadan ill. by author. Holt, 2007. ISBN 978-0-8050-7894-7 Subj: Holidays – Ramadan. Religion. Religion – Islam.

Now I'm big ill. by author. Simon & Schuster, 2013. ISBN 978-1-4169-3547-6 Subj: Babies. Behavior – growing up.

Over the moon ill. by author. Holt, 1997. ISBN 978-0-8050-5013-4 Subj: Adoption. Babies.

A potty for me! a lift-the-flap instruction manual ill. by author. Simon & Schuster, 2005. ISBN 978-0-689-87423-9 Subj: Format, unusual – toy & movable books. Toilet training.

Princess Baby ill. by author. Random House, 2008. ISBN 978-0-375-84119-4 Subj: Babies. Names. Royalty – princesses.

Princess Baby, night-night ill. by author. Random House, 2009. ISBN 978-0-375-84462-1 Subj: Babies. Bedtime. Royalty – princesses.

Ten tiny babies ill. by author. Simon & Schuster, 2008. ISBN 978-1-4169-3546-9 Subj: Babies. Counting, numbers. Rhyming text.

Ten tiny tickles ill. by author. Simon & Schuster, 2005. ISBN 978-0-689-85976-2 Subj: Babies. Counting, numbers.

Twelve hats for Lena ill. by author. McElderry, 2002. ISBN 978-0-689-84873-5 Subj: Clothing – hats. Days of the week, months of the year. Rhyming text.

Where is baby's mommy? ill. by author. Simon & Schuster, 2000. ISBN 978-0-689-83561-2 Subj: Babies. Family life – mothers. Format, unusual – toy & movable books. Games.

Katz, Susan. *Mrs. Brown on exhibit* ill. by R. W. Alley. Simon & Schuster, 2002. ISBN 978-0-689-82970-3 Subj: Museums. Poetry. School – field trips.

Oh, Theodore! guinea pig poems ill. by Stacey Schuett. Houghton, 2007. ISBN 978-0-618-70222-0 Subj: Animals – guinea pigs. Pets. Poetry.

When the shadbush blooms (Messinger, Carla)

Katz, Susan B. *ABC, baby me!* ill. by Alicia Padrón. Random House, 2010. ISBN 978-0-375-86679-1 Subj: ABC books. Babies. Format, unusual – board books.

Katzler, Eva. *Florentine and Pig* ill. by Jess Mikhail. Bloomsbury, 2012. ISBN 978-1-59990-847-2 Subj: Activities – baking, cooking. Activities – picnicking. Animals – pigs. Friendship.

Katzman, Nicole. *Nathan blows out the Hanukkah candles* (Lehman-Wilzig, Tami)

Kaufman, Jeanne. *Young Henry and the dragon* ill. by Daria Tessler. Shenanigan, 2011. ISBN 978-1-934860-11-3 Subj: Dragons. Fire. Middle Ages. Rhyming text.

Kaufmann, Nancy. *Bye, Bye* ill. by Jung-Hee Spetter. Front Street, 2003. ISBN 978-1-886910-95-9 Subj: Animals. Animals – pigs. Family life – fathers. School – first day.

Kavanagh, Peter. *I love my mama* ill. by Jane Chapman. Simon & Schuster, 2003. ISBN 978-0-689-85691-4 Subj: Activities. Animals – elephants. Day. Family life – mothers. Rhyming text.

Kawata, Ken. *Animal tails* ill. by Masayuki Yabuuchi. Kane/Miller, 2001. ISBN 978-1-929132-05-8 Subj: Anatomy – tails. Animals.

Kay, Julia. *Gulliver Snip* ill. by author. Holt, 2008. ISBN 978-0-8050-7992-0 Subj: Activities – bathing. Imagination. Pirates. Rhyming text.

Kay, Verla. *Broken Feather* ill. by Stephen Alcorn. Putnam, 2002. ISBN 978-0-399-23550-4 Subj: Indians of North America – Nez Perce. Poetry. U.S. history.

Civil War drummer boy ill. by Larry Day. Putnam, 2012. ISBN 978-0-399-23992-2 Subj: Musical instruments – drums. Rhyming text. U.S. history.

Covered wagons, bumpy trails ill. by S. D. Schindler. Putnam, 2000. ISBN 978-0-399-22928-2 Subj: Activities – traveling. Homes, houses. Rhyming text. U.S. history.

Gold fever ill. by S. D. Schindler. Putnam, 1999. ISBN 978-0-399-23027-1 Subj: Careers – miners. Rhyming text. U.S. history – frontier & pioneer life.

Hornbooks and inkwells ill. by S. D. Schindler. Penguin, 2011. ISBN 978-0-399-23870-3 Subj: Rhyming text. School. U.S. history – frontier & pioneer life.

Iron horses ill. by Michael McCurdy. Putnam, 1999. ISBN 978-0-399-23119-3 Subj: Rhyming text. Trains. U.S. history.

Orphan train ill. by Ken Stark. Putnam, 2003. ISBN 978-0-399-23613-6 Subj: Family life – brothers & sisters. Orphans. Rhyming text. Trains. U.S. history.

Whatever happened to the Pony Express? ill. by Kimberly Bulcken Root and Barry Root. Penguin, 2010. ISBN 978-0-399-24483-4 Subj: Animals – horses, ponies. Careers – postal workers. Rhyming text. U.S. history – frontier & pioneer life.

Kaye, Marilyn. *The real tooth fairy* ill. by Helen Cogancherry. Harcourt, 1990. ISBN 978-0-15-265780-2 Subj: Fairies. Teeth.

Keane, Dave. *Daddy adventure day* ill. by Sue Ramá. Penguin, 2011. ISBN 978-0-399-24627-2 Subj: Family life – fathers. Sports – baseball.

Sloppy Joe ill. by Denise Brunkus. HarperCollins, 2009. ISBN 978-0-06-171020-9 Subj: Behavior – messy. Character traits – cleanliness. Character traits – individuality. Family life. Illness.

Keane, Michael. *The night Santa got lost: how NORAD saved Christmas* ill. by Michael Garland. Regnery Pub., 2012. ISBN 978-1-5969-8810-1 Subj: Behavior – lost. Careers – military. Holidays – Christmas. Santa Claus.

Keats, Ezra Jack. *Apt. 3* ill. by author. Macmillan, 1971. ISBN 978-0-689-71059-9 Subj: Cities, towns. Disabilities – blindness. Ethnic groups in the U.S. – African Americans. Family life. Music. Musical instruments – harmonicas. Senses – sight.

Clementina's cactus ill. by author. Viking, 1999. ISBN 978-0-670-88545-9 Subj: Desert. Plants. Weather – storms. Wordless.

Dreams ill. by author. Macmillan, 1974. ISBN 978-0-02-749610-9 Subj: Dreams. Ethnic groups in the U.S. – African Americans. Imagination. Night. Sleep.

Goggles ill. by author. Macmillan, 1969. ISBN 978-0-02-749590-4 Subj: Behavior – bullying, teasing. Caldecott award honor books. Cities, towns. Ethnic groups in the U.S. – African Americans. Problem solving.

Hi, cat! ill. by author. Viking, 1999. ISBN 978-0-670-88546-6 Subj: Animals – cats. Cities, towns. Ethnic groups in the U.S. – African Americans.

Jennie's hat ill. by author. HarperCollins, 1966. ISBN 978-0-06-023114-9 Subj: Behavior – dissatisfaction. Character traits – kindness to animals. Clothing – hats.

John Henry ill. by author. HarperCollins, 1965. ISBN 978-0-394-99052-1 Subj: Character traits – perseverance. Character traits – pride. Ethnic groups in the U.S. – African Americans. Folk & fairy tales. Tall tales.

Kitten for a day ill. by author. Watts, 1974. ISBN 978-0-531-02714-1 Subj: Animals – cats. Animals – dogs. Wordless.

A letter to Amy ill. by author. HarperCollins, 1968. ISBN 978-0-06-023109-5 Subj: Ethnic groups in the U.S. – African Americans. Friendship. Letters, cards. Parties. Weather – rain. Weather – wind.

The little drummer boy ill. by author. Words & music by Katherine Davis, Henry Onorati & Harry Simeonne. Aladdin, 1987, ©1968. ISBN 978-0-689-71158-9 Subj: Gifts. Holidays – Christmas. Music. Musical instruments – drums. Religion – Nativity. Songs.

Louie ill. by author. Greenwillow, 1975. ISBN 978-0-688-84002-0 Subj: Character traits – shyness. Ethnic groups in the U.S. – African Americans. Puppets.

Louie's search ill. by author. Four Winds, 1989, ©1980. ISBN 978-0-689-71354-5 Subj: Behavior – needing someone. Family life.

Maggie and the pirate ill. by author. Four Winds, 1979. ISBN 978-0-590-07602-9 Subj: Death. Pets. Pirates.

My dog is lost! ill. by author. Viking, 1999. ISBN 978-0-670-88550-3 Subj: Animals – dogs. Behavior – lost. Careers – police officers. Ethnic groups in the U.S. Ethnic groups in the U.S. – Puerto Rican Americans. Foreign languages.

One red sun: a counting book ill. by author. Viking, 1999. ISBN 978-0-670-88478-0 Subj: Counting, numbers. Format, unusual – board books.

Pet show! ill. by author. Puffin, 2001, ©1972. ISBN 978-0-670-03504-5 Subj: Animals. Cities, towns. Communities, neighborhoods. Ethnic groups in the U.S. – African Americans. Pets.

Peter's chair ill. by author. HarperCollins, 1967. ISBN 978-0-06-023112-5 Subj: Babies. Behavior – sharing. Ethnic groups in the U.S. – African Americans. Family life – new sibling. Friendship. Furniture – chairs. Self-concept.

The snowy day ill. by author. Viking, 1962. Subj: Activities – playing. Caldecott award books. Ethnic groups in the U.S. – African Americans. Seasons – winter. Weather – snow.

The snowy day [board book] ill. by author. Viking, 1996. ISBN 978-0-670-86733-2 Subj: Activities – playing. Caldecott award books. Ethnic groups in the U.S. – African Americans. Format, unusual – board books. Seasons – winter. Weather – snow.

The trip ill. by author. Greenwillow, 1978. ISBN 978-0-688-84123-2 Subj: Emotions – loneliness. Ethnic groups in the U.S. – African Americans. Holidays – Halloween. Imagination. Moving.

Whistle for Willie ill. by author. Viking, 1964. Subj: Activities – whistling. Animals – dogs. Ethnic groups in the U.S. – African Americans. Problem solving. Self-concept.

Keefer, Janice Kulyk. *Anna's goat* ill. by Janet Wilson. Orca, 2000. ISBN 978-1-55143-153-6 Subj: Animals – goats. Family life – sisters. Foreign lands – Europe. War.

Keeler, Patricia A. *A huge hog is a big pig* (McCall, Francis X.)

Keens-Douglas, Richardo. *Anancy and the haunted house* ill. by Stéphane Jorisch. Annick, 2002. ISBN 978-1-55037-737-8 Subj: Folk & fairy tales. Holidays – Halloween. Homes, houses. Spiders.

Keep, Linda Lowery. *Day of the Dead* ill. by Barbara Knutson. Carolrhoda, 2004. ISBN 978-0-87614-914-0 Subj: Foreign lands – Mexico. Holidays – Day of the Dead.

Keillor, Garrison. *Daddy's girl* ill. by Robin Preiss-Glasser. Hyperion, 2005. ISBN 978-0-7868-1986-7 Subj: Family life – fathers. Rhyming text.

Keister, Douglas. *Fernando's gift / El regalo de Fernando* ill. with photos. Sierra Club, 1995. ISBN 978-0-87156-414-6 Subj: Ecology. Family life. Foreign lands – Costa Rica. Foreign languages. Forest, woods. Gifts. Trees.

To grandmother's house: a visit to old-town Beijing photos by author. Gibbs Smith, 2008. ISBN 978-1-4236-0283-5 Subj: Family life – grandmothers. Foreign lands – China. Homes, houses.

Keller, Emily Snowell. *Sleeping Bunny* ill. by author. Random House, 2003. ISBN 978-0-375-

91541-3 Subj: Animals. Animals – rabbits. Folk & fairy tales. Royalty – princesses.

Keller, Holly. *Brave Horace* ill. by author. Greenwillow, 1998. ISBN 978-0-688-15408-0 Subj: Animals – leopards. Character traits – bravery. Emotions – fear. Parties.

Cecil's garden ill. by author. Greenwillow, 2002. ISBN 978-0-06-029594-3 Subj: Animals. Animals – rabbits. Behavior – fighting, arguing.

Geraldine and Mrs. Duffy ill. by author. Greenwillow, 2000. ISBN 978-0-688-16888-9 Subj: Activities – babysitting. Animals – pigs. Family life – brothers & sisters.

Geraldine first ill. by author. Greenwillow, 1996. ISBN 978-0-688-14150-9 Subj: Animals – pigs. Family life. Sibling rivalry.

Geraldine's baby brother ill. by author. Greenwillow, 1994. ISBN 978-0-688-12006-1 Subj: Animals – pigs. Babies. Emotions – envy, jealousy. Family life – new sibling. Sibling rivalry.

Geraldine's big snow ill. by author. Greenwillow, 1988. ISBN 978-0-688-07514-9 Subj: Animals – pigs. Weather – snow.

Geraldine's blanket ill. by author. Greenwillow, 1984. ISBN 978-0-688-02540-3 Subj: Animals – pigs. Family life. Toys – dolls.

Help! a story of friendship ill. by author. HarperCollins, 2007. ISBN 978-0-06-123913-7 Subj: Animals. Animals – mice. Behavior – resourcefulness. Emotions – fear. Friendship. Reptiles – snakes.

Henry's Fourth of July ill. by author. Greenwillow, 1985. ISBN 978-0-688-04013-0 Subj: Activities – picnicking. Animals – possums. Holidays – Fourth of July.

Henry's happy birthday ill. by author. Greenwillow, 1990. ISBN 978-0-688-09451-5 Subj: Animals – possums. Birthdays. Parties.

Horace ill. by author. Greenwillow, 1991. ISBN 978-0-688-09832-2 Subj: Adoption. Animals – leopards. Character traits – being different. Self-concept.

Jacob's tree ill. by author. Greenwillow, 1999. ISBN 978-0-688-15996-2 Subj: Animals – bears. Behavior – growing up. Concepts – size. Family life.

Merry Christmas, Geraldine ill. by author. Greenwillow, 1997. ISBN 978-0-688-14501-9 Subj: Animals – pigs. Character traits – stubbornness. Holidays – Christmas.

Miranda's beach day ill. by author. HarperCollins, 2009. ISBN 978-0-06-158298-1 Subj: Family life – mothers. Sea & seashore – beaches.

Nosy Rosie ill. by author. HarperCollins, 2006. ISBN 978-0-06-078758-5 Subj: Animals – foxes. Behavior – bullying, teasing. Character traits – helpfulness. Senses – smell.

Pearl's new skates ill. by author. HarperCollins, 2005. ISBN 978-0-06-056281-6 Subj: Animals – rabbits. Character traits – persistence. Sports – ice skating.

Sophie's window ill. by author. HarperCollins, 2005. ISBN 978-0-06-056283-0 Subj: Animals – dogs. Birds – pigeons. Emotions – fear. Friendship.

That's mine, Horace ill. by author. Greenwillow, 2000. ISBN 978-0-688-17159-9 Subj: Animals. Behavior. Character traits – honesty. School.

Keller, John G. *The rubber-legged ducky* ill. by Henry Cole. Harcourt, 2008. ISBN 978-0-15-205289-8 Subj: Animals – foxes. Birds – ducks. Character traits – being different. Character traits – individuality.

Keller, Laurie. *Arnie the doughnut* ill. by author. Holt, 2003. ISBN 978-0-8050-6283-0 Subj: Food. Humorous stories.

Do unto otters: a book about manners ill. by author. Holt, 2007. ISBN 978-0-8050-7996-8 Subj: Animals. Behavior. Etiquette. Language.

Grandpa Gazillion's number yard ill. by author. Holt, 2005. ISBN 978-0-8050-6282-3 Subj: Counting, numbers. Humorous stories. Rhyming text.

Open wide: tooth school inside ill. by author. Holt, 2000. ISBN 978-0-8050-6192-5 Subj: Careers – dentists. Health & fitness. Teeth.

The scrambled states of America ill. by author. Holt, 1998. ISBN 978-0-8050-5802-4 Subj: Geography. Maps. U.S. history.

The scrambled states of America talent show ill. by author. Holt, 2008. ISBN 978-0-8050-7997-5 Subj: Geography. Maps. Theater. U.S. history.

Kelley, Ellen A. *My life as a chicken* ill. by Michael Slack. Harcourt, 2007. ISBN 978-0-15-205306-2 Subj: Birds – chickens. Humorous stories.

Kelley, Marty. *The rules* ill. by author. Zino, 2000. ISBN 978-1-55933-284-2 Subj: Behavior. Rhyming text.

Summer stinks ill. by author. Zino, 2001. ISBN 978-1-55933-291-0 Subj: ABC books. Rhyming text. Seasons – summer.

Twelve terrible things ill. by author. Tricycle, 2008. ISBN 978-1-58246-229-5 Subj: Humorous stories.

Winter woes ill. by author. Zino, 2005. ISBN 978-1-55933-306-1 Subj: Behavior – worrying. Rhyming text. Seasons – winter.

Kelley, True. *Blabber Mouse* ill. by author. Dutton, 2001. ISBN 978-0-525-46742-7 Subj: Animals – mice. Behavior – secrets. School.

Claude Monet ill. by author. Grosset, 2001. ISBN 978-0-448-42613-6 Subj: Activities – painting. Careers – artists. Foreign lands – France.

The dog who saved Santa ill. by author. Holiday, 2008. ISBN 978-0-8234-2120-6 Subj: Animals – dogs. Holidays – Christmas. Santa Claus.

I've got chicken pox ill. by author. Dutton, 1994. ISBN 978-0-525-45185-3 Subj: Illness – chicken pox.

Kellogg, Steven. *Aster Aardvark's alphabet adventures* ill. by author. Morrow, 1987. ISBN 978-0-688-07257-5 Subj: ABC books. Animals. Animals – aardvarks. Birds.

A beasty story (Martin, Bill, Jr.)

Best friends ill. by author. Dial, 1986. ISBN 978-0-8037-0101-4 Subj: Animals – dogs. Emotions – envy, jealousy. Friendship.

Can I keep him? ill. by author. Dial, 1971. ISBN 978-0-8037-0989-8 Subj: Family life. Pets.

Chicken Little ill. by author. Morrow, 1985. ISBN 978-0-688-05691-9 Subj: Animals. Behavior – trickery. Birds – chickens. Folk & fairy tales.

The Christmas witch ill. by author. Dial, 1992. ISBN 978-0-8037-1269-0 Subj: Holidays – Christmas. Witches.

Give the dog a bone ill. by author. SeaStar, 2000. ISBN 978-1-58717-002-7 Subj: Animals – dogs. Counting, numbers. Songs.

A-hunting we will go! ill. by author. Morrow, 1998. ISBN 978-0-688-14945-1 Subj: Bedtime. Songs.

I was born about 10,000 years ago: a tall tale ill. by author. Morrow, 1996. ISBN 978-0-688-13412-9 Subj: Folk & fairy tales. Songs. Tall tales.

The island of the skog ill. by author. Dial, 1973. ISBN 978-0-8037-3840-9 Subj: Animals – mice. Boats, ships. Islands. Monsters.

Johnny Appleseed: a tall tale ill. by author. Morrow, 1988. ISBN 978-0-688-06418-1 Subj: Activities – traveling. Gardens, gardening. Tall tales. Trees. U.S. history – frontier & pioneer life.

Mike Fink: a tall tale ill. by author. Morrow, 1992. ISBN 978-0-688-07004-5 Subj: Boats, ships. Rivers. Tall tales. U.S. history.

The mysterious tadpole ill. by author. Dial, 1977. ISBN 978-0-8037-6246-6 Subj: Frogs & toads. Monsters. Pets.

The mystery of the flying orange pumpkin ill. by author. Dial, 1980. ISBN 978-0-8037-6116-2 Subj: Holidays – Halloween. Mystery stories.

The mystery of the magic green ball ill. by author. Dial, 1978. ISBN 978-0-8037-6215-2 Subj: Behavior – lost & found possessions. Gypsies. Mystery stories. Toys – balls.

The mystery of the missing red mitten ill. by author. Dial, 2000. ISBN 978-0-8037-2566-9 Subj: Behavior – lost & found possessions. Clothing – gloves, mittens. Mystery stories. Snowmen.

The mystery of the stolen blue paint ill. by author. Dial, 1982. ISBN 978-0-8037-5659-5 Subj: Mystery stories.

Paul Bunyan: a tall tale ill. by reteller. Morrow, 1984. ISBN 978-0-688-03850-2 Subj: Animals – oxen. Careers – lumberjacks. Tall tales. U.S. history – frontier & pioneer life.

Pecos Bill ill. by reteller. Morrow, 1986. ISBN 978-0-688-05872-2 Subj: Cowboys, cowgirls. Tall tales. U.S. history – frontier & pioneer life.

A penguin pup for Pinkerton ill. by author. Dial, 2001. ISBN 978-0-8037-2536-2 Subj: Animals – dogs. Birds – penguins. Eggs.

The Pied Piper's magic ill. by author. Dial, 2009. ISBN 978-0-8037-2818-9 Subj: Animals – rats. Folk & fairy tales. Magic.

Pinkerton, behave! ill. by author. Dial, 1979. ISBN 978-0-8037-6575-7 Subj: Animals – dogs.

Prehistoric Pinkerton ill. by author. Dial, 1987. ISBN 978-0-8037-0323-0 Subj: Animals – dogs. Behavior – misbehavior. Dinosaurs. Museums. Prehistory.

Ralph's secret weapon ill. by author. Dial, 1983. ISBN 978-0-8037-7087-4 Subj: Activities – vacationing. Imagination.

A rose for Pinkerton ill. by author. Dial, 1981. ISBN 978-0-8037-7503-9 Subj: Animals – cats. Animals – dogs. Behavior – imitation.

Sally Ann Thunder Ann Whirlwind Crockett ill. by author. Morrow, 1995. ISBN 978-0-688-14043-4 Subj: Tall tales. U.S. history – frontier & pioneer life.

Santa Claus is comin' to town lyrics by Haven Gillespi; ill. by author. HarperCollins, 2004. ISBN 978-0-06-623849-4 Subj: Holidays – Christmas. Santa Claus. Songs.

Tallyho, Pinkerton! ill. by author. Dial, 1982. ISBN 978-0-8037-8743-8 Subj: Animals – cats. Animals – dogs. Sports – hunting.

Yankee Doodle ill. by author. Four Winds, 1980, ©1976. ISBN 978-0-590-07782-8 Subj: Music. Songs. U.S. history.

Kelly, David A. *Miracle mud: Lena Blackburne and the secret mud that changed baseball* ill. by Oliver Dominguez. Millbrook, 2013. ISBN 978-0-7613-

8092-4 Subj: Careers – inventors. Inventions. Sports – baseball.

Kelly, Irene. *Even an octopus needs a home* ill. by author. Holiday House, 2011. ISBN 978-0-8234-2235-7 Subj: Animals. Homes, houses.

Even an ostrich needs a nest: where birds begin ill. by author. Holiday, 2009. ISBN 978-0-8234-2102-2 Subj: Birds. Homes, houses.

It's a butterfly's life ill. by author. Holiday House, 2007. ISBN 978-0-8234-1860-2 Subj: Insects – butterflies, caterpillars.

Kelly, Luke. *Blanket and bear, a remarkable pair* ill. by Yoko Tanaka. Putnam, 2013. ISBN 978-0-399-25681-3 Subj: Behavior – growing up. Behavior – lost & found possessions. Rhyming text. Toys – bears.

Kelly, Mark. *Mousetronaut: based on a (partially) true story* ill. by C. F. Payne. Simon & Schuster, 2012. ISBN 978-1-4424-5824-6 Subj: Animals – mice. Careers – astronauts. Character traits – bravery. Space & space ships.

Mousetronaut goes to Mars ill. by C. F. Payne. Simon & Schuster, 2013. ISBN 978-1-4424-8426-9 Subj: Animals – mice. Careers – astronauts. Space & space ships.

Kelly, Mij. *Achoo! good manners can be contagious!* ill. by Mary McQuillan. Barron's, 2009. ISBN 978-0-7641-6969-4 Subj: Animals. Behavior. Etiquette. Health & fitness. Hygiene. Rhyming text.

A bed of your own! ill. by Mary McQuillan. Barron's, 2011. ISBN 978-0-7641-4768-5 Subj: Animals. Bedtime. Farms. Rhyming text.

Friendly Day ill. by Charles Fuge. Barron's, 2013. ISBN 978-1-43800-345-0 Subj: Animals. Character traits – kindness. Rhyming text.

One more sheep ill. by Russell Ayto. Peachtree, 2006. ISBN 978-1-56145-378-8 Subj: Animals – sheep. Animals – wolves. Behavior – trickery. Rhyming text.

Where's my darling daughter? ill. by Katharine McEwen. Good Books, 2006. ISBN 978-1-56148-537-6 Subj: Animals. Behavior – lost. Farms. Rhyming text.

William and the night train ill. by Alison Jay. Farrar, 2001. ISBN 978-0-374-38437-1 Subj: Activities – traveling. Bedtime. Trains.

Kelly, Sheila M. *The A.D.D. book for kids* (Rotner, Shelley)

Feeling thankful (Rotner, Shelley)

I'm adopted! (Rotner, Shelley)

Lots of grandparents (Rotner, Shelley)

Lots of moms (Rotner, Shelley)

Shades of people (Rotner, Shelley)

What can you do? (Rotner, Shelley)

Kempter, Christa. *Dear Little Lamb* ill. by Frauke Weldin. NorthSouth, 2006. ISBN 978-0-7358-2086-9 Subj: Activities – writing. Animals – sheep. Animals – wolves. Letters, cards. Pen pals.

Wally and Mae ill. by Frauke Weldin. NorthSouth, 2008. ISBN 978-0-7358-2208-5 Subj: Animals – bears. Animals – rabbits. Character traits – cleanliness.

When Mama can't sleep ill. by Natascha Rosenberg. NorthSouth, 2011. ISBN 978-0-7358-4015-7 Subj: Bedtime. Behavior – worrying. Family life. Family life – mothers.

Kenah, Katharine. *The dream shop* ill. by Peter Catalanotto. HarperCollins, 2002. ISBN 978-0-688-17901-4 Subj: Dreams. Night.

Predator attack! ill. with photos. McGraw-Hill, 2004. ISBN 978-0-7696-3176-9 Subj: Animals.

Kennedy, Cindy. *The star of Christmas* ill. by Dennis Bredow. Zondervan, 2002. ISBN 978-0-310-70504-8 Subj: Foreign lands – England. Holidays – Christmas.

Kennedy, Jimmy. *The teddy bears' picnic* ill. by Alexandra Day. Green Tiger, 1983. ISBN 978-0-88138-010-1 Subj: Activities – picnicking. Toys – bears.

The teddy bears' picnic ill. by Michael Hague. Holt, 1992. ISBN 978-0-8050-1008-4 Subj: Activities – picnicking. Poetry. Songs. Toys – bears.

The teddy bears' picnic ill. by Prue Theobalds. HarperCollins, 1987. ISBN 978-0-87226-153-2 Subj: Activities – picnicking. Poetry. Toys – bears.

Kennedy, Kim. *Hee-Haw-Dini and the Great Zambini* ill. by Doug Kennedy. Abrams, 2009. ISBN 978-0-8109-7025-0 Subj: Animals – donkeys. Animals – mice. Careers – magicians. Character traits – persistence.

Pirate Pete's giant adventure ill. by Doug Kennedy. Abrams, 2006. ISBN 978-0-8109-5965-1 Subj: Birds – parakeets, parrots. Giants. Magic. Pirates.

Kennedy, Marge M. *The book of boo!* by Marge M. Kennedy and Mitchell Kriegman; photos by John E. Barrett. Disney, 2002. ISBN 978-0-7868-3364-1 Subj: Animals. Toys. Toys – bears.

Kenney, Sean. *Cool cars and trucks* ill. with photos. Holt, 2009. ISBN 978-0-8050-8761-1 Subj: Automobiles. Toys. Trucks.

Cool castles ill. with photos. Holt, 2012. ISBN 978-0-8050-9539-5 Subj: Castles. Toys.

Cool city photos by John E. Barrett. Holt, 2011. ISBN 978-0-8050-8762-8 Subj: Cities, towns. Toys.

Cool creations in 35 pieces ill. with photos. Holt, 2013. ISBN 978-0-8050-9692-7 Subj: Imagination. Toys.

Kennison, Ruth. *The potty train* (Hochman, David)

Kensington, Mary Jane. *Dear Cinderella* (Moore, Marian)

Kent, Allegra. *Ballerina swan* ill. by Emily Arnold McCully. Holiday House, 2012. ISBN 978-0-8234-2373-6 Subj: Ballet. Birds – swans. School.

Kenyon, Tony. *Hyacinth Hop has the hic-hops* ill. by author. Ragged Bears, 2000. ISBN 978-1-929927-06-7 Subj: Animals – rabbits. Hiccups.

Kepes, Juliet. *Five little monkeys* ill. by author. Houghton, 1952. Subj: Animals. Animals – monkeys. Caldecott award honor books.

Kerby, Johanna. *Little pink pup* photos by author. Penguin, 2010. ISBN 978-0-399-25435-2 Subj: Animals – dogs. Animals – pigs. Pets.

Kerby, Mona. *Owney, the mail-pouch pooch* ill. by Lynne Barasch. Farrar, 2008. ISBN 978-0-374-35685-9 Subj: Activities – traveling. Animals – dogs. Careers – postal workers.

Kerley, Barbara. *A cool drink of water* ill. by author. National Geographic, 2002. ISBN 978-0-7922-6723-2 Subj: Water.

One world, one day ill. with photos. National Geographic, 2009. ISBN 978-1-4263-0460-6 Subj: Day. World.

What to do about Alice? how Alice Roosevelt broke the rules, charmed the world, and drove her father Teddy crazy! ill. by Edwin Fotheringham. Scholastic, 2008. ISBN 978-0-439-92231-9 Subj: Behavior – misbehavior. Character traits – confidence. U.S. history.

The world is waiting for you ill. with photos. National Geographic, 2013. ISBN 978-1-4263-1114-7 Subj: Activities. Behavior – growing up. Careers. World.

You and me together: moms, dads, and kids around the world ill. with photos. National Geographic, 2005. ISBN 978-0-7922-8298-3 Subj: Family life – parents. World.

Kern, Noris. *I love you with all my heart* ill. by author. Chronicle, 1998. ISBN 978-0-8118-2031-8 Subj: Animals – polar bears. Emotions – love. Family life – mothers.

Kerner, Susan. *Always by my side* ill. by Ian P. Benfold Haywood. Star Bright, 2013. ISBN 978-1-59572-336-9 Subj: Death. Emotions – grief. Emotions – sadness. Family life. Rhyming text.

Kerr, Judith. *One night in the zoo* ill. by author. Kane/Miller, 2010. ISBN 978-1-935279-37-2 Subj: Counting, numbers. Rhyming text. Zoos.

Kespert, Deborah. *On the move* (Fecher, Sarah)

Rain and shine ill. by Fran Jordan. Two-Can, 2000. ISBN 978-1-58728-609-4 Subj: Careers – meteorologists. Seasons. Weather.

Kessler, Cristina. *The best beekeeper of Lalibela: a tale from Africa* ill. by Leonard Jenkins. Holiday House, 2006. ISBN 978-0-8234-1858-9 Subj: Careers – beekeepers. Character traits – perseverance. Foreign lands – Ethiopia. Gender roles. Insects – bees.

Jubela ill. by Jo Ellen McAllister Stammen. Simon & Schuster, 2001. ISBN 978-0-689-81895-0 Subj: Animals – babies. Animals – rhinoceros. Foreign lands – Africa. Orphans.

My great-grandmother's gourd ill. by Walter Lyon Krudop. Orchard, 2000. ISBN 978-0-531-33284-9 Subj: Family life – grandmothers. Foreign lands – Sudan. Trees. Water. Weather – droughts.

Ketcham, Sallie. *The Christmas bird* ill. by Stacey Schuett. Augsburg Fortress, 2000. ISBN 978-0-8066-3871-3 Subj: Birds – robins. Folk & fairy tales. Foreign lands – England. Holidays – Christmas. Religion – Nativity.

Ketteman, Helen. *Armadillo tattletale* ill. by Keith Graves. Scholastic, 2000. ISBN 978-0-590-99723-2 Subj: Animals – armadillos. Behavior – gossip.

Armadilly chili ill. by Will Terry. Whitman, 2004. ISBN 978-0-8075-0457-4 Subj: Animals – armadillos. Behavior – sharing. Birds – bluebirds. Character traits – laziness. Food. Friendship. Frogs & toads. Spiders.

Bubba the cowboy prince: a fractured Texas tale ill. by James Warhola. Scholastic, 1997. ISBN 978-0-590-25506-6 Subj: Animals – bulls, cows. Cowboys, cowgirls. Folk & fairy tales. Humorous stories. Parties.

Goodnight, Little Monster ill. by Bonnie Leick. Marshall Cavendish, 2010. ISBN 978-0-7614-5683-4 Subj: Bedtime. Monsters. Rhyming text.

If Beaver had a fever ill. by Kevin O'Malley. Marshall Cavendish, 2011. ISBN 978-0-7614-5951-4 Subj: Animals – bears. Careers – doctors. Family life – mothers. Illness. Rhyming text. Zoos.

Señorita Gordita (The gingerbread boy)

The three little gators ill. by Will Terry. Whitman, 2009. ISBN 978-0-8075-7824-7 Subj: Folk & fairy tales. Homes, houses. Reptiles – alligators, crocodiles. Texas.

Waynetta and the cornstalk: a Texas fairy tale ill. by Diane Greenseid. Whitman, 2007. ISBN 978-

0-8075-8687-7 Subj: Folk & fairy tales. Giants. Plants. Texas.

Kevi. *Don't talk to strangers* ill. by JibJab Media. Scholastic, 2003. ISBN 978-0-439-31385-8 Subj: Behavior – talking to strangers. Safety.

Key, Francis Scott. *The Star Spangled Banner* ill. by Dana Regan. Random House, 2002. ISBN 978-0-375-91596-3 Subj: Songs. U.S. history.

The Star-Spangled Banner ill. by Peter Spier. Doubleday, 1973. ISBN 978-0-385-07746-0 Subj: Songs. U.S. history.

Khalsa, Dayal Kaur. *Green cat* ill. by author. Tundra, 2002. ISBN 978-0-88776-586-5 Subj: Animals – cats. Rhyming text.

Khan, Hena. *The night of the moon: a Muslim holiday story* ill. by Julie Paschkis. Chronicle, 2008. ISBN 978-0-8118-6062-8 Subj: Ethnic groups in the U.S. – Lebanese Americans. Holidays – Ramadan. Religion – Islam.

Khan, Rukhsana. *Big red lollipop* ill. by Sophie Blackall. Penguin, 2010. ISBN 978-0-670-06287-4 Subj: Birthdays. Ethnic groups in the U.S. – Pakistani Americans. Family life – sisters. Parties.

King for a day ill. by Christiane Krömer. Lee & Low, 2013. ISBN 978-1-60060-659-5 Subj: Contests. Fairs, festivals. Foreign lands – Pakistan. Disabilities – physical disabilities. Kites.

Kherdian, David. *Come back, Moon* ill. by Nonny Hogrogian. Simon & Schuster, 2013. ISBN 978-1-4424-5887-1 Subj: Animals. Animals – bears. Forest, woods. Moon.

Khing, T. T. *Where is the cake?* ill. by T. T. Khing. Abrams, 2007. ISBN 978-0-8109-1798-9 Subj: Animals. Behavior – stealing. Food. Picture puzzles. Wordless.

Where is the cake now? ill. by T. T. Khing. Abrams, 2009. ISBN 978-0-8109-8926-9 Subj: Animals. Behavior – stealing. Food. Picture puzzles. Wordless.

Kidslabel. *Spot 7: Christmas* ill. with photos. Chronicle, 2006. ISBN 978-0-8118-5323-1 Subj: Holidays – Christmas. Picture puzzles.

Spot 7: school ill. with photos. Chronicle, 2006. ISBN 978-0-8118-5324-8 Subj: Picture puzzles. School.

Kilaka, John. *True friends: a tale from Tanzania* ill. by author. Groundwood, 2006. ISBN 978-0-88899-698-5 Subj: Animals – elephants. Animals – rats. Folk & fairy tales. Foreign lands – Tanzania. Friendship.

Kilby, Don. *At a construction site* ill. by author. Kids Can, 2003. ISBN 978-1-55337-378-0 Subj: Careers – construction workers. Machines. Trucks.

In the city ill. by author. Kids Can, 2004. ISBN 978-1-55337-471-8 Subj: Cities, towns. Machines. Trucks.

In the country ill. by author. Kids Can, 2004. ISBN 978-1-55337-472-5 Subj: Country. Machines. Tractors. Trucks.

On the road ill. by author. Kids Can, 2003. ISBN 978-1-55337-379-7 Subj: Roads. Trucks.

Killen, Nicola. *Not me!* ill. by author. Egmont, 2010. ISBN 978-1-4052-4829-7 Subj: Behavior – messy. Character traits – responsibility.

Killion, Bette. *Just think!* ill. by Linda Bronson. HarperCollins, 2001. ISBN 978-0-694-01315-9 Subj: Concepts. Family life – mothers. Rhyming text.

Kilodavis, Cheryl. *My princess boy* ill. by Suzanne DeSimone. Simon & Schuster, 2010. ISBN 978-1-4424-2988-8 Subj: Behavior – bullying, teasing. Character traits – being different. Character traits – individuality. Gender roles.

Kim, Sue. *How does a seed grow?* ill. by Tilde. Simon & Schuster, 2010. ISBN 978-1-4169-9435-0 Subj: Format, unusual – board books. Plants. Seeds.

Kimmel, Elizabeth Cody. *Glamsters* ill. by Jackie Urbanovic. Hyperion, 2008. ISBN 978-1-4231-1148-1 Subj: Animals – hamsters. Self-concept.

My penguin Osbert ill. by H. B. Lewis. Candlewick, 2004. ISBN 978-0-7636-1699-1 Subj: Birds – penguins. Gifts. Holidays – Christmas. Humorous stories.

My penguin Osbert in love ill. by H. B. Lewis. Candlewick, 2009. ISBN 978-0-7636-3032-4 Subj: Birds – penguins. Emotions – love. Foreign lands – Antarctic. Helicopters.

Kimmel, Eric A. *Anansi and the magic stick* ill. by Janet Stevens. Holiday, 2001. ISBN 978-0-8234-1443-7 Subj: Animals – hyenas. Folk & fairy tales. Foreign lands – Africa. Magic. Spiders.

Anansi and the moss-covered rock ill. by Janet Stevens. Holiday, 1990. ISBN 978-0-8234-0689-0 Subj: Animals. Behavior – trickery. Folk & fairy tales. Spiders.

Anansi and the talking melon ill. by Janet Stevens. Holiday, 1994. ISBN 978-0-8234-1104-7 Subj: Animals. Animals – elephants. Behavior – trickery. Folk & fairy tales. Foreign lands – Africa. Spiders.

Anansi goes fishing ill. by Janet Stevens. Holiday, 1992. ISBN 978-0-8234-0918-1 Subj: Behavior – trickery. Folk & fairy tales. Foreign lands – Africa. Reptiles – turtles, tortoises. Spiders.

Anansi's party time ill. by Janet Stevens. Holiday, 2008. ISBN 978-0-8234-1922-7 Subj: Behavior – trickery. Folk & fairy tales. Foreign lands – Africa. Reptiles – turtles, tortoises. Spiders.

The birds' gift: a Ukrainian Easter story ill. by Katya Krenina. Holiday, 1999. ISBN 978-0-8234-1384-3 Subj: Birds. Character traits – kindness to animals. Eggs. Folk & fairy tales. Foreign lands – Ukraine. Holidays – Easter.

The Chanukkah guest ill. by Giyora Karmi. Holiday, 1990. ISBN 978-0-8234-0788-0 Subj: Holidays – Hanukkah. Jewish culture. Religion.

Easy work! an old tale ill. by Andrew Glass. Holiday, 1998. ISBN 978-0-8234-1349-2 Subj: Folk & fairy tales. Foreign lands – Norway.

The Erie Canal pirates ill. by Andrew Glass. Holiday, 2002. ISBN 978-0-8234-1657-8 Subj: Boats, ships. Folk & fairy tales. Music. Pirates. Rhyming text. Tall tales.

The frog princess: a Tlingit legend from Alaska ill. by Rosanne Litzinger. Holiday House, 2006. ISBN 978-0-8234-1618-9 Subj: Folk & fairy tales. Frogs & toads. Indians of North America – Tlingit. Royalty – princesses.

Gershon's monster: a story for the Jewish New Year ill. by Jon J. Muth. Scholastic, 2000. ISBN 978-0-439-10839-3 Subj: Folk & fairy tales. Holidays – Rosh Hashanah. Jewish culture. Religion.

The great Texas hamster drive ill. by Bruce Whatley. Marshall Cavendish, 2007. ISBN 978-0-7614-5357-4 Subj: Animals – hamsters. Tall tales. Texas. U.S. history – frontier & pioneer life.

Hanukkah bear ill. by Mike Wohnoutka. Holiday House, 2013. ISBN 978-0-8234-2855-7 Subj: Animals – bears. Food. Holidays – Hanukkah. Jewish culture.

Hershel and the Hanukkah goblins ill. by Trina Schart Hyman. Holiday, 1989. ISBN 978-0-8234-0769-9 Subj: Caldecott award honor books. Holidays – Hanukkah. Jewish culture. Mythical creatures – goblins. Religion.

I took my frog to the library ill. by Blanche Sims. Viking, 1990. ISBN 978-0-670-82418-2 Subj: Animals. Libraries. Pets.

Jack and the giant barbecue ill. by John Manders. Amazon Children's, 2012. ISBN 978-0-7614-6128-9 Subj: Activities – baking, cooking. Food. Giants. Texas.

Joha makes a wish: a Middle Eastern tale ill. by Omar Rayyan. Marshall Cavendish, 2010. ISBN 978-0-7614-5599-8 Subj: Behavior – wishing. Foreign lands – Middle East. Magic.

Joseph and the Sabbath fish ill. by Martina Peluso. Lerner/Kar-Ben, 2011. ISBN 978-0-7613-5908-1 Subj: Folk & fairy tales. Jewish culture. Religion.

The lady in the blue cloak: legends from the Texas missions ill. by Susan Guevara. Holiday House, 2006. ISBN 978-0-8234-1738-4 Subj: Religion. Texas.

Little Britches and the rattlers ill. by Vincent Nguyen. Marshall Cavendish, 2008. ISBN 978-0-7614-5432-8 Subj: Cowboys, cowgirls. Reptiles – snakes. Texas.

Little Red Hot ill. by Laura Huliska-Beith. Amazon/Two Lions, 2013. ISBN 978-1-4778-1638-7 Subj: Animals – wolves. Folk & fairy tales. Food. U.S. history – frontier & pioneer life.

The magic dreidels ill. by Katya Krénina. Holiday, 1996. ISBN 978-0-8234-1256-3 Subj: Folk & fairy tales. Holidays – Hanukkah. Jewish culture.

Medio Pollito: a Spanish tale ill. by Valeria Docampo. Marshall Cavendish, 2010. ISBN 978-0-7614-5705-3 Subj: Birds – chickens. Folk & fairy tales. Foreign lands – Spain.

The mysterious guests: a Sukkot story ill. by Katya Krenina. Holiday, 2008. ISBN 978-0-8234-1893-0 Subj: Character traits – selfishness. Holidays – Sukkot.

Pumpkinhead ill. by Steve Haskamp. Winslow, 2001. ISBN 978-1-890817-33-6 Subj: Activities – traveling. Anatomy – heads. Animals – squirrels. Plants.

Rip Van Winkle's return ill. by Leonard Everett Fisher. Farrar, 2007. ISBN 978-0-374-36308-6 Subj: Behavior – lost. Folk & fairy tales. Mythical creatures – elves. Sleep.

Robin Hook, pirate hunter! ill. by Michael Dooling. Scholastic, 2001. ISBN 978-0-590-68199-5 Subj: Pirates.

The runaway tortilla ill. by Randy Cecil. Winslow, 2000. ISBN 978-1-890817-18-3 Subj: Behavior – running away. Cumulative tales. Folk & fairy tales.

Stormy's hat: just right for a railroad man ill. by Andrea U'Ren. Farrar, 2008. ISBN 978-0-374-37262-0 Subj: Activities – sewing. Careers – railroad engineers. Clothing – hats. Trains.

The three cabritos ill. by Stephen Gilpin. Marshall Cavendish, 2007. ISBN 978-0-7614-5343-7 Subj: Animals – goats. Character traits – cleverness. Folk & fairy tales. Magic. Monsters. Music. Texas.

The three little tamales ill. by Valeria Docampo. Marshall Cavendish, 2009. ISBN 978-0-7614-5519-6 Subj: Animals – wolves. Behavior – running away. Folk & fairy tales. Food.

The three princes ill. by Leonard Everett Fisher. Holiday, 1994. ISBN 978-0-8234-1115-3 Subj: Folk & fairy tales. Foreign lands – Arabia. Royalty – princes. Royalty – princesses.

The two mountains: an Aztec legend ill. by Leonard Everett Fisher. Holiday, 2000. ISBN 978-0-8234-

1504-5 Subj: Folk & fairy tales. Foreign lands – Mexico. Indians of North America – Aztec. Mountains. Volcanoes.

Zigazak! ill. by Jon Goodell. Doubleday, 2001. ISBN 978-0-385-32652-0 Subj: Careers – clergy. Holidays – Hanukkah. Jewish culture.

Kimmel, Haven. *Orville, a dog story* ill. by Robert Andrew Parker. Clarion, 2003. ISBN 978-0-618-15955-0 Subj: Animals – dogs. Emotions. Farms.

Kimmelman, Leslie. *Dance, sing, remember* ill. by Ora Eitan. HarperCollins, 2000. ISBN 978-0-06-027726-0 Subj: Holidays. Jewish culture. Religion.

Everybody bonjours! ill. by Sarah McMenemy. Knopf, 2008. ISBN 978-0-375-84443-0 Subj: Foreign lands – France. Foreign languages. Rhyming text.

Hanukkah lights, Hanukkah nights ill. by John Himmelman. HarperCollins, 1992. ISBN 978-0-06-020369-6 Subj: Family life. Holidays – Hanukkah. Jewish culture. Religion.

Hooray! it's Passover! ill. by John Himmelman. HarperCollins, 1996. ISBN 978-0-06-024674-7 Subj: Family life. Holidays – Passover. Jewish culture. Religion.

How do I love you? ill. by Lisa McCue. HarperCollins, 2005. ISBN 978-0-06-001200-7 Subj: Counting, numbers. Emotions – love. Family life. Reptiles – alligators, crocodiles. Rhyming text.

The Little Red Hen and the Passover matzah (The little red hen)

Round the turkey ill. by Nancy Cote. Whitman, 2002. ISBN 978-0-8075-7131-6 Subj: Family life. Holidays – Thanksgiving. Rhyming text.

The runaway latkes ill. by Paul Yalowitz. Whitman, 2000. ISBN 978-0-8075-7176-7 Subj: Behavior – running away. Holidays – Hanukkah. Jewish culture. Religion.

The Shabbat puppy ill. by Jaime Zollars. Marshall Cavendish, 2012. ISBN 978-0-7614-6145-6 Subj: Activities – walking. Animals – dogs. Family life – grandfathers. Jewish culture. Religion.

Sound the shofar! a story for Rosh Hashanah and Yom Kippur ill. by John Himmelman. HarperCollins, 1998. ISBN 978-0-06-027498-6 Subj: Family life – aunts, uncles. Holidays – Rosh Hashanah. Holidays – Yom Kippur. Jewish culture. Religion.

The three bully goats ill. by Will Terry. Whitman, 2011. ISBN 978-0-8075-7900-8 Subj: Animals – babies. Animals – goats. Behavior – bullying, teasing. Mythical creatures – ogres.

Kimura, Ken. *999 frogs wake up* ill. by Yasunari Murakami. NorthSouth, 2013. ISBN 978-0-7358-4108-6 Subj: Frogs & toads. Reptiles – snakes. Seasons – spring.

999 tadpoles ill. by Yasunari Murakami. NorthSouth, 2011. ISBN 978-0-7358-4013-3 Subj: Birds – hawks. Frogs & toads.

Kimura, Yuichi. *One stormy night . . .* ill. by Hiroshi Abe. Kodansha, 2003. ISBN 978-4-7700-2970-6 Subj: Animals – goats. Animals – wolves. Emotions – fear. Foreign lands – Japan. Friendship. Weather – storms.

One sunny day . . . ill. by Hiroshi Abe. Kodansha, 2003. ISBN 978-4-7700-2971-3 Subj: Animals – goats. Animals – wolves. Emotions – fear. Foreign lands – Japan. Friendship. Nature.

Kinch, Devon. *Pretty Penny cleans up* ill. by author. Random House, 2012. ISBN 978-0-375-86736-1 Subj: Animals – dogs. Money.

Pretty Penny makes ends meet ill. by author. Random House, 2013. ISBN 978-0-375-86737-8 Subj: Character traits – helpfulness. Counting, numbers. Jewelry. Money.

Kindermans, Martine. *You and me* by Martine Kindermans and Sasha Quinton ill. by Martine Kindermans. Penguin, 2006. ISBN 978-0-399-24471-1 Subj: Birds – geese. Emotions – love. Family life – mothers. Rhyming text.

Kinerk, Robert. *Clorinda* ill. by Steven Kellogg. Simon & Schuster, 2003. ISBN 978-0-689-86449-0 Subj: Activities – dancing. Animals – bulls, cows. Ballet. Character traits – perseverance. Rhyming text.

Clorinda plays baseball! ill. by Steven Kellogg. Simon & Schuster, 2012. ISBN 978-0-689-86865-8 Subj: Animals – bulls, cows. Character traits – helpfulness. Friendship. Rhyming text. Sports – baseball.

Clorinda takes flight ill. by Steven Kellogg. Simon & Schuster, 2007. ISBN 978-0-689-86864-1 Subj: Activities – flying. Animals. Animals – bulls, cows. Character traits – perseverance. Rhyming text.

Timothy Cox will not change his socks ill. by Stephen Gammell. Simon & Schuster, 2005. ISBN 978-0-689-87181-8 Subj: Animals – dogs. Character traits – perseverance. Clothing – socks. Rhyming text. Senses – smell.

King, Dedie. *I see the sun in Afghanistan* ill. by Judith Inglese. Satya House, 2011. ISBN 978-0-9818720-8-7 Subj: Family life. Foreign lands – Afghanistan. Foreign languages.

I see the sun in Russia ill. by Judith Inglese. Satya, 2012. ISBN 978-1-93587-408-9 Subj: Family life. Foreign lands – Russia. Foreign languages.

King, M. G. *Librarian on the roof! a true story* ill. by Stephen Gilpin. Whitman, 2010. ISBN 978-0-8075-4512-6 Subj: Careers – librarians. Libraries. Texas.

King, Martin Luther, III. *My daddy, Dr. Martin Luther King, Jr.* ill. by A. G. Ford. Amistad, 2013. ISBN 978-0-06-028075-8 Subj: Ethnic groups in the U.S. – African Americans. Family life – fathers. Prejudice. U.S. history. Violence, nonviolence.

King, Martin Luther, Jr. *I have a dream* ill. by Kadir Nelson. Random House, 2012. ISBN 978-0-375-85887-1 Subj: Dreams. Ethnic groups in the U.S. – African Americans. Prejudice. U.S. history. Violence, nonviolence.

King, Stephen Michael. *Emily loves to bounce* ill. by author. Philomel, 2003. ISBN 978-0-399-23886-4 Subj: Activities – jumping. Activities – playing. Rhyming text.

Mutt dog! ill. by author. Harcourt, 2005. ISBN 978-0-15-205561-5 Subj: Animals – dogs. Homeless.

You: a story of love and friendship ill. by author. HarperCollins, 2011. ISBN 978-0-06-206014-3 Subj: Animals – dogs. Birds. Friendship.

King, Thomas. *Coyote sings to the moon* ill. by Johnny Wales. WestWinds, 2001. ISBN 978-1-55868-642-7 Subj: Animals. Animals – coyotes. Creation. Folk & fairy tales. Moon.

Kinkade, Sheila. *My family* photos by Elaine Little. Charlesbridge, 2006. ISBN 978-1-57091-662-5 Subj: Family life. Foreign lands.

Kinney, Jessica. *The pig scramble* ill. by Sarah S. Brannen. Islandport, 2011. ISBN 978-1-934031-61-2 Subj: Animals – pigs. Contests. Fairs, festivals.

Kinsey, Helen. *The bear that heard crying* (Kinsey-Warnock, Natalie)

Kinsey-Warnock, Natalie. *The bear that heard crying* by Natalie Kinsey-Warnock and Helen Kinsey ill. by Ted Rand. Cobblehill, 1993. ISBN 978-0-525-65103-1 Subj: Animals – bears. Behavior – lost. U.S. history – frontier & pioneer life.

A Christmas like Helen's ill. by Mary Azarian. Houghton, 2004. ISBN 978-0-618-23137-9 Subj: Family life. Farms. Holidays – Christmas.

A farm of her own ill. by Kathleen Kolb. Dutton, 2001. ISBN 978-0-525-46507-2 Subj: Family life – aunts, uncles. Family life – cousins. Farms.

From dawn till dusk ill. by Mary Azarian. Houghton, 2002. ISBN 978-0-618-18655-6 Subj: Family life. Farms. Seasons.

Nora's ark ill. by Emily Arnold McCully. HarperCollins, 2005. ISBN 978-0-06-029517-2 Subj: Family life – grandparents. Farms. U.S. history. Weather – floods.

When spring comes ill. by Stacey Schuett. Dutton, 1993. ISBN 978-0-525-45008-5 Subj: Family life – fathers. Farms. Seasons – spring.

Kipling, Rudyard. *The beginning of the armadillos* ill. by Lorinda Bryan Cauley. Harcourt, 1985. ISBN 978-0-15-206380-1 Subj: Animals – armadillos.

The elephant's child ill. by Lorinda Bryan Cauley. Harcourt, 1983. ISBN 978-0-15-225385-1 Subj: Animals. Animals – elephants. Character traits – curiosity. Foreign lands – Africa.

How the camel got his hump ill. by Lisbeth Zwerger. NorthSouth, 2001. ISBN 978-0-7358-1483-7 Subj: Animals. Animals – camels. Behavior – misbehavior. Folk & fairy tales – pourquoi tales. Foreign lands – Africa.

How the elephant got his trunk retold by Jean Richards; ill. by Norman Gorbaty. Holt, 2003. ISBN 978-0-8050-6699-9 Subj: Anatomy – noses. Animals. Animals – elephants. Character traits – curiosity. Folk & fairy tales – pourquoi tales. Foreign lands – Africa. Reptiles – alligators, crocodiles.

How the leopard got his spots ill. by Lori Lohstoeter. Picture Book Studio, 1989. ISBN 978-0-88708-112-5 Subj: Animals – leopards. Folk & fairy tales – pourquoi tales.

Rikki-tikki-tavi ill. by Lambert Davis. Harcourt, 1992. ISBN 978-0-15-267015-3 Subj: Animals – mongooses. Character traits – bravery. Character traits – cleverness. Foreign lands – India. Reptiles – snakes.

Rikki-tikki-tavi adapt. by Jerry Pinkney; ill. by Jerry Pinkney. Morrow, 1997. ISBN 978-0-688-14321-3 Subj: Animals – mongooses. Character traits – bravery. Character traits – cleverness. Foreign lands – India. Reptiles – snakes.

Kirby, Pamela F. *What bluebirds do* ill. with photos. Boyds Mills, 2009. ISBN 978-1-59078-614-7 Subj: Birds – bluebirds.

Kirk, Daniel. *Bigger* ill. by author. Putnam, 1998. ISBN 978-0-399-23127-8 Subj: Behavior – growing up. Concepts – size. Self-concept.

Bus stop, bus go ill. by author. Putnam, 2001. ISBN 978-0-399-23333-3 Subj: Animals – hamsters. Buses. Rhyming text.

Go! ill. by author. Hyperion, 2001. ISBN 978-0-7868-0305-7 Subj: Music. Songs. Transportation.

Honk honk! Beep beep! ill. by author. Hyperion/Disney, 2010. ISBN 978-1-4231-2486-3 Subj: Activities – traveling. Automobiles. Imagination. Rhyming text. Toys.

Hush, little alien ill. by author. Hyperion, 1999. ISBN 978-0-7868-2469-4 Subj: Aliens. Bedtime. Lullabies.

Jack and Jill ill. by author. Putnam, 2003. ISBN 978-0-399-23553-5 Subj: Behavior – wishing. Humorous stories. Nursery rhymes.

Keisha Ann can! ill. by author. Putnam, 2008. ISBN 978-0-399-24179-6 Subj: Character traits – pride. Ethnic groups in the U.S. – African Americans. Rhyming text. School.

Library mouse ill. by author. Abrams, 2007. ISBN 978-0-8109-9346-4 Subj: Activities – writing. Animals – mice. Books, reading. Careers – writers. Character traits – shyness. Libraries.

Library mouse: a friend's tale ill. by author. Abrams, 2009. ISBN 978-0-8109-8927-6 Subj: Activities – writing. Animals – mice. Books, reading. Careers – writers. Character traits – shyness. Libraries.

Library mouse: a museum adventure ill. by author. Abrams, 2012. ISBN 978-1-4197-0173-3 Subj: Activities – writing. Animals – cats. Animals – mice. Art. Careers – artists. Careers – explorers. Museums.

Library mouse: a world to explore ill. by author. Abrams, 2010. ISBN 978-0-8109-8968-9 Subj: Animals – mice. Careers – explorers. Character traits – bravery. Emotions – fear. Friendship. Libraries.

Library mouse: home sweet home ill. by author. Abrams, 2013. ISBN 978-1-4197-0544-1 Subj: Animals – mice. Books, reading. Buildings. Homes, houses. Libraries.

Moondogs ill. by author. Putnam, 1999. ISBN 978-0-399-23128-5 Subj: Animals – dogs. Moon. Rhyming text. Space & space ships.

Snow family ill. by author. Hyperion, 2000. ISBN 978-0-7868-2244-7 Subj: Family life – parents. Rhyming text. Snowmen.

Ten things I love about you ill. by author. Penguin/ Nancy Paulsen, 2012. ISBN 978-0-399-25288-4 Subj: Activities – writing. Animals – pigs. Animals – rabbits. Friendship.

Trash trucks! ill. by author. Putnam, 1997. ISBN 978-0-399-22927-5 Subj: Careers – sanitation workers. Rhyming text. Trucks.

Kirk, David. *Little bird, Biddle bird* ill. by author. Scholastic, 2001. ISBN 978-0-439-26092-3 Subj: Birds. Food. Rhyming text. Self-concept.

Little bunny, Biddle bunny ill. by author. Scholastic, 2002. ISBN 978-0-439-33819-6 Subj: Animals – rabbits. Rhyming text. Seasons.

Little Miss Spider ill. by author. Scholastic, 1999. ISBN 978-0-439-08389-8 Subj: Emotions – love. Family life – mothers. Rhyming text. Spiders.

Little Miss Spider at Sunny Patch School ill. by author. Scholastic, 2000. ISBN 978-0-439-08727-8 Subj: Insects. Rhyming text. School – first day. Spiders.

Little pig, Biddle pig ill. by author. Scholastic, 2001. ISBN 978-0-439-30575-4 Subj: Animals – pigs. Character traits – cleanliness. Rhyming text.

Miss Spider's ABC ill. by author. Scholastic, 1998. ISBN 978-0-590-28279-6 Subj: ABC books. Birthdays. Insects. Rhyming text. Spiders.

Miss Spider's new car ill. by author. Scholastic, 1997. ISBN 978-0-590-30713-0 Subj: Automobiles. Insects. Rhyming text. Spiders.

Miss Spider's tea party ill. by author. Scholastic, 1994. ISBN 978-0-590-47724-6 Subj: Emotions – fear. Parties. Rhyming text. Spiders.

Oh So Tiny bunny ill. by author. Feiwel & Friends, 2013. ISBN 978-1-250-01688-1 Subj: Animals – babies. Animals – rabbits. Character traits – smallness. Dreams.

Kirk, Katie. *Eli, no!* ill. by author. Abrams, 2011. ISBN 978-0-8109-8964-1 Subj: Animals – dogs. Behavior – misbehavior.

Kirsch, Vincent X. *Forsythia and me* ill. by author. Farrar, 2011. ISBN 978-0-374-32438-4 Subj: Behavior – sharing. Character traits – helpfulness. Friendship.

Freddie and Gingersnap ill. by author. Hyperion/ Disney, 2013. ISBN 978-1-4231-5958-2 Subj: Dinosaurs. Dragons. Friendship.

Natalie and Naughtily ill. by author. Bloomsbury, 2008. ISBN 978-1-59990-269-2 Subj: Character traits – helpfulness. Family life – sisters. Multiple births – twins. Stores.

Two little boys from Toolittle Toys ill. by author. Bloomsbury, 2010. ISBN 978-1-59990-428-3 Subj: Family life – brothers. Toys.

Kirwan, Wednesday. *Minerva the monster* ill. by author. Sterling, 2008. ISBN 978-1-4027-5718-1 Subj: Animals – dogs. Family life.

Nobody notices Minerva ill. by author. Sterling, 2007. ISBN 978-1-4027-4728-1 Subj: Animals – dogs. Behavior – misbehavior. Family life.

Kitamura, Satoshi. *Comic adventures of Boots* ill. by author. Farrar, 2002. ISBN 978-0-374-31455-2 Subj: Animals – cats.

Me and my cat? ill. by author. Farrar, 2000. ISBN 978-0-374-34906-6 Subj: Animals – cats. Magic. Witches.

Pablo the artist ill. by author. Farrar, 2006. ISBN 978-0-374-35687-3 Subj: Animals – elephants. Art. Careers – artists. Friendship.

Kittinger, Jo S. *The house on Dirty-Third Street* ill. by Thomas Gonzalez. Peachtree, 2012. ISBN 978-1-56145-619-2 Subj: Communities, neighborhoods. Homes, houses. Hope. Religion.

Rosa's bus: the ride to civil rights ill. by Steven Walker. Calkins Creek, 2010. ISBN 978-1-59078-722-9 Subj: Ethnic groups in the U.S. – African Americans. Prejudice. Transportation. U.S. history. Violence, nonviolence.

Kladstrup, Kristin. *The gingerbread pirates* ill. by Matt Tavares. Candlewick, 2009. ISBN 978-0-7636-3223-6 Subj: Food. Holidays – Christmas. Pirates.

Klassen, Jon. *I want my hat back* ill. by author. Candlewick, 2011. ISBN 978-0-7636-5598-3 Subj: Animals – bears. Behavior – lost & found possessions. Clothing – hats.

This is not my hat ill. by author. Candlewick, 2012. ISBN 978-0-7636-5599-0 Subj: Caldecott award books. Clothing – hats. Crime. Fish. Humorous stories.

Klausmeier, Jesse. *Open this little book* ill. by Suzy Lee. Chronicle, 2013. ISBN 978-0-8118-6783-2 Subj: Animals. Books, reading. Character traits – cooperation. Concepts – color. Format, unusual – toy & movable books. Giants.

Klein, Tali. *Hop! Plop!* (Schwartz, Corey Rosen)

Kleven, Elisa. *The apple doll* ill. by author. Farrar, 2007. ISBN 978-0-374-30380-8 Subj: Activities – making things. Food. School.

A carousel tale ill. by author. Tricycle, 2009. ISBN 978-1-58246-239-4 Subj: Anatomy – tails. Art. Merry-go-rounds. Reptiles – alligators, crocodiles.

Cozy light, cozy night ill. by author. Creston, 2013. ISBN 978-1-939547-02-6 Subj: Rhyming text. Seasons.

The dancing deer and the foolish hunter ill. by author. Dutton, 2002. ISBN 978-0-525-46832-5 Subj: Activities – dancing. Animals – deer. Birds. Ecology. Forest, woods.

Ernst ill. by author. Tricycle, 2002. ISBN 978-1-58246-053-6 Subj: Birthdays. Reptiles – alligators, crocodiles.

The friendship wish ill. by author. Penguin, 2011. ISBN 978-0-525-42374-4 Subj: Angels. Animals – dogs. Emotions – loneliness. Friendship. Moving.

Glasswings: a butterfly's story ill. by author. Dial, 2013. ISBN 978-0-8037-3742-6 Subj: Behavior – lost. Cities, towns. Ecology. Insects – butterflies, caterpillars. Science.

A monster in the house ill. by author. Dutton, 1998. ISBN 978-0-525-45973-6 Subj: Babies. Family life – brothers. Monsters.

The paper princess ill. by author. Dutton, 1994. ISBN 978-0-525-45231-7 Subj: Activities – drawing. Activities – flying. Paper. Royalty – princesses.

The puddle pail ill. by author. Dutton, 1997. ISBN 978-0-525-45803-6 Subj: Behavior – collecting things. Family life – brothers. Reptiles – alligators, crocodiles.

Sun bread ill. by author. Dutton, 2001. ISBN 978-0-525-46674-1 Subj: Animals. Careers – bakers. Food. Rhyming text. Sun.

Welcome home, Mouse ill. by author. Tricycle, 2010. ISBN 978-1-58246-277-6 Subj: Animals – elephants. Animals – mice. Character traits – clumsiness. Friendship. Homes, houses.

The wishing ball ill. by author. Farrar, 2006. ISBN 978-0-374-38449-4 Subj: Animals – cats. Behavior – wishing. Birds – crows. Reptiles – alligators, crocodiles.

Kleven, Sandy. *The right touch: a read aloud story to help prevent child sexual abuse* ill. by Jody Bergsma. Illumination, 1997. ISBN 978-0-935699-10-4 Subj: Child abuse. Family life.

Kling, Kevin. *Big little brother* ill. by Chris Monroe. Borealis, 2011. ISBN 978-0-87351-844-4 Subj: Behavior – bullying, teasing. Family life – brothers.

Klingel, Cynthia Fitterer. *Crocodiles* by Cynthia Fitterer Klingel and Robert B. Noyed ill. with photos. Child's World, 2002. ISBN 978-1-56766-942-8 Subj: Reptiles – alligators, crocodiles.

Dancers by Cynthia Fitterer Klingel and Robert B. Noyed ill. with photos. Child's World, 2002. ISBN 978-1-56766-939-8 Subj: Activities – dancing. Careers – dancers.

Deserts by Cynthia Fitterer Klingel and Robert B. Noyed ill. with photos. Child's World, 2001. ISBN 978-1-56766-972-5 Subj: Animals. Desert. Nature. Science.

Farmers by Cynthia Fitterer Klingel and Robert B. Noyed ill. with photos. Child's World, 2002. ISBN 978-1-56766-940-4 Subj: Careers – farmers. Farms.

Firefighters by Cynthia Fitterer Klingel and Robert B. Noyed ill. with photos. Child's World, 2002. ISBN 978-1-56766-938-1 Subj: Careers – firefighters. Fire.

Forests by Cynthia Fitterer Klingel and Robert B. Noyed ill. with photos. Child's World, 2002. ISBN

978-1-56766-973-2 Subj: Animals. Forest, woods. Nature. Plants.

Grizzly bears by Cynthia Fitterer Klingel and Robert B. Noyed ill. with photos. Child's World, 2002. ISBN 978-1-56766-943-5 Subj: Animals – bears.

Halloween by Cynthia Fitterer Klingel and Robert B. Noyed ill. with photos. Child's World, 2002. ISBN 978-1-56766-955-8 Subj: Holidays – Halloween.

Manatees by Cynthia Fitterer Klingel and Robert B. Noyed ill. with photos. Child's World, 2002. ISBN 978-1-56766-944-2 Subj: Animals – manatees.

Oceans by Cynthia Fitterer Klingel and Robert B. Noyed ill. with photos. Child's World, 2002. ISBN 978-1-56766-974-9 Subj: Animals. Plants. Sea & seashore.

Paul Revere's ride by Cynthia Fitterer Klingel and Robert B. Noyed ill. with photos. Child's World, 2002. ISBN 978-1-56766-960-2 Subj: U.S. history. War.

Postal workers by Cynthia Fitterer Klingel and Robert B. Noyed ill. with photos. Child's World, 2002. ISBN 978-1-56766-941-1 Subj: Careers – postal workers. Letters, cards.

Rosa Parks by Cynthia Fitterer Klingel and Robert B. Noyed ill. with photos. Child's World, 2002. ISBN 978-1-56766-951-0 Subj: Ethnic groups in the U.S. – African Americans. Prejudice. U.S. history.

Soccer by Cynthia Fitterer Klingel and Robert B. Noyed ill. with photos. Child's World, 2001. ISBN 978-1-56766-805-6 Subj: Sports – soccer.

Thanksgiving by Cynthia Fitterer Klingel and Robert B. Noyed ill. with photos. Child's World, 2003. ISBN 978-1-56766-956-5 Subj: Holidays – Thanksgiving.

Timber wolves by Cynthia Fitterer Klingel and Robert B. Noyed ill. with photos. Child's World, 2002. ISBN 978-1-56766-945-9 Subj: Animals – wolves.

Underground by Cynthia Fitterer Klingel and Robert B. Noyed ill. with photos. Child's World, 2002. ISBN 978-1-56766-975-6 Subj: Ecology.

Klinting, Lars. *What do you want?* ill. by author. Groundwood, 2006. ISBN 978-0-88899-636-7 Subj: Behavior – wishing.

Kliphuis, Christine. *Robbie and Ronnie* ill. by Charlotte Dematons. NorthSouth, 2002. ISBN 978-0-7358-1627-5 Subj: Behavior – bullying, teasing. Concepts – size. Friendship. Sports – swimming.

Klise, Kate. *Grammy Lamby and the secret handshake* ill. by M. Sarah Klise. Holt, 2012. ISBN 978-0-8050-9313-1 Subj: Animals – sheep. Character traits – helpfulness. Family life – grandmothers. Weather – storms.

Imagine Harry ill. by M. Sarah Klise. Harcourt, 2007. ISBN 978-0-15-205704-6 Subj: Animals – rabbits. Imagination – imaginary friends.

Little Rabbit and the Meanest Mother on Earth ill. by M. Sarah Klise. Harcourt, 2010. ISBN 978-0-15-206201-9 Subj: Animals – rabbits. Behavior – messy. Circus. Family life – mothers.

Little Rabbit and the Night Mare ill. by M. Sarah Klise. Harcourt, 2008. ISBN 978-0-15-205717-6 Subj: Animals – rabbits. Behavior – worrying. Emotions – fear. Nightmares. School.

Stand straight, Ella Kate: the true story of a real giant ill. by M. Sarah Klise. Penguin, 2010. ISBN 978-0-8037-3404-3 Subj: Character traits – being different. Concepts – size. Giants.

Why do you cry? not a sob story ill. by M. Sarah Klise. Holt, 2006. ISBN 978-0-8050-7319-5 Subj: Animals. Animals – rabbits. Emotions.

Kloske, Geoffrey. *Once upon a time, the end (asleep in 60 seconds)* ill. by Barry Blitt. Simon & Schuster, 2005. ISBN 978-0-689-86619-7 Subj: Bedtime. Books, reading. Folk & fairy tales.

Knapp, Ruthie. *Who stole Mona Lisa?* ill. by Jill McElmurry. Bloomsbury, 2010. ISBN 978-1-59990-058-2 Subj: Activities – painting. Art. Crime.

Kneen, Maggie. *Chocolate moose* ill. by author. Penguin, 2011. ISBN 978-0-525-42202-0 Subj: Activities – baking, cooking. Animals – mice. Animals – moose. Careers – bakers.

The Christmas surprise ill. by author. Chronicle, 2001. ISBN 978-0-8118-3210-6 Subj: Animals – pigs. Holidays – Christmas. Rhyming text. Weather – snow.

Knick knack paddy whack ill. by Christiane Engel. Barefoot, 2008. ISBN 978-1-84686-144-4 Subj: Activities – making things. Counting, numbers. Cumulative tales. Songs.

Knight, Hilary. *A firefly in a fir tree* ill. by author. Tegen, 2004. ISBN 978-0-06-000992-2 Subj: Animals – mice. Holidays – Christmas. Music. Nature. Songs.

Hilary Knight's the owl and the pussy-cat by Hilary Knight and Edward Lear ill. by Hilary Knight. Based on The owl and the pussy-cat by Edward Lear. Macmillan, 1983. ISBN 978-0-02-750900-7 Subj: Imagination. Magic. Poetry.

Knight, Margy Burns. *Africa is not a country* by Margy Burns Knight and Mark Melnicove ill. by Anne Sibley O'Brien. Millbrook, 2000. ISBN 978-0-7613-1266-6 Subj: Foreign lands – Africa.

Talking walls ill. by Anne Sibley O'Brien. Tilbury, 1992. ISBN 978-0-88448-102-7 Subj: Foreign lands.

Knister. *Sophie's dance* ill. by Mandy Schlunt. Minedition, 2007. ISBN 978-0-698-40056-6 Subj: Activities – dancing. Family life – grandmothers.

Knowlton, Laurie Lazzaro. *Why cowgirls are such sweet talkers* ill. by James Rice. Pelican, 2000. ISBN 978-1-56554-698-1 Subj: Behavior. Cowboys, cowgirls.

Knudsen, Michelle. *Argus* ill. by Andréa Wesson. Candlewick, 2011. ISBN 978-0-7636-3790-3 Subj: Birds – chickens. Dragons. School. Science.

Big Mean Mike ill. by Scott Magoon. Candlewick, 2012. ISBN 978-0-7636-4990-6 Subj: Animals – dogs. Animals – rabbits. Character traits – kindness to animals. Self-concept.

Bugged! ill. by Blanche Sims. Kane, 2008. ISBN 978-1-57565-259-7 Subj: Insects – mosquitoes. Problem solving. Science.

Library lion ill. by Kevin Hawkes. Candlewick, 2006. ISBN 978-0-7636-2262-6 Subj: Animals – lions. Character traits – helpfulness. Libraries.

A moldy mystery ill. by Barry Gott. Kane, 2006. ISBN 978-1-57565-167-5 Subj: Family life – brothers & sisters. Science.

Knutson, Barbara. *Love and roast chicken* ill. by author. Lerner, 2004. ISBN 978-1-57505-657-9 Subj: Animals – guinea pigs. Behavior – trickery. Folk & fairy tales. Foreign lands – South America. Indians of South America.

Koch, Ed. *Eddie's little sister makes a splash* by Ed Koch and Pat Koch ill. by James Warhola. Penguin, 2007. ISBN 978-0-399-24310-3 Subj: Activities – vacationing. Family life – brothers & sisters. Sports – swimming.

Koch, Pat. *Eddie's little sister makes a splash* (Koch, Ed)

Kochan, Vera. *What if your best friend were blue?* ill. by Viviana Garofoli. Marshall Cavendish, 2011. ISBN 978-0-7614-5897-5 Subj: Character traits – appearance. Character traits – being different. Friendship. Prejudice.

Koda-Callan, Elizabeth. *The squiggly Wigglys* ill. by author. Workman, 2003. ISBN 978-0-7611-2821-2 Subj: Family life. Food. Format, unusual – toy & movable books. Parties. Rhyming text.

Kohara, Kazuno. *Ghosts in the house!* ill. by author. Roaring Brook, 2008. ISBN 978-1-59643-427-1 Subj: Ghosts. Homes, houses. Witches.

Here comes Jack Frost ill. by author. Roaring Brook, 2009. ISBN 978-1-59643-442-2 Subj: Emotions – loneliness. Mythical creatures. Seasons – winter.

Kohuth, Jane. *Duck sock hop* ill. by Jane Porter. Dial, 2012. ISBN 978-0-8037-3712-9 Subj: Activities – dancing. Birds – ducks. Clothing – socks. Rhyming text.

Kolanovic, Dubravka. *Everyone needs a friend* ill. by author. Price Stern Sloan, 2010. ISBN 978-0-8431-9918-5 Subj: Animals – mice. Animals – wolves. Emotions – loneliness. Friendship.

Kolar, Bob. *Big kicks* ill. by author. Candlewick, 2008. ISBN 978-0-7636-3390-5 Subj: Animals – bears. Sports – soccer.

Racer dogs ill. by author. Dutton, 2003. ISBN 978-0-525-45939-2 Subj: Animals – dogs. Automobiles. Sports – racing.

Koller, Jackie French. *Baby for sale* ill. by Janet Pedersen. Marshall Cavendish, 2002. ISBN 978-0-7614-5106-8 Subj: Babies. Family life – brothers & sisters. Sibling rivalry.

Bouncing on the bed ill. by Anna Grossnickle Hines. Orchard, 1999. ISBN 978-0-531-33138-5 Subj: Activities. Rhyming text.

Nickommoh! a Thanksgiving celebration ill. by Marcia Sewall. Atheneum, 1999. ISBN 978-0-689-81094-7 Subj: Holidays – Thanksgiving. Indians of North America – Narragansett. Seasons – fall.

No such thing ill. by Betsy Lewin. Boyds Mills, 1997. ISBN 978-1-56397-490-8 Subj: Bedtime. Emotions – fear. Family life – mothers. Monsters.

One monkey too many ill. by Lynn Munsinger. Harcourt, 1999. ISBN 978-0-15-200006-6 Subj: Animals – monkeys. Counting, numbers. Rhyming text.

Konagaya, Kiyomi. *Beach feet* ill. by Masamitsu Saito. Enchanted Lion, 2012. ISBN 978-1-59270-121-6 Subj: Anatomy – feet. Sea & seashore – beaches.

Konnecke, Ole. *Anthony and the girls* ill. by author. Farrar, 2006. ISBN 978-0-374-30376-1 Subj: Activities – playing. Behavior – indifference. Emotions.

The big book of words and pictures ill. by author. Gecko, 2012. ISBN 978-1-87757-905-9 Subj: Format, unusual – board books. Language.

Anton and the battle ill. by author. Gecko, 2013. ISBN 978-1-87757-926-4 Subj: Animals – dogs. Behavior – fighting, arguing. Weapons.

Anton can do magic ill. by author. Gecko, 2011. ISBN 978-1-8774-6737-0 Subj: Clothing – hats. Humorous stories. Magic.

Kono, Erin Eitter. *Caterina and the perfect party* ill. by author. Dial, 2013. ISBN 978-0-8037-3902-4 Subj: Birds. Character traits – perfectionism. Parties.

Hula lullaby ill. by author. Little, Brown, 2005. ISBN 978-0-316-73591-9 Subj: Bedtime. Family life – mothers. Hawaii. Lullabies. Rhyming text.

Kontis, Alethea. *Alpha oops! The day Z went first* ill. by Bob Kolar. Candlewick, 2006. ISBN 978-0-7636-2728-7 Subj: ABC books.

AlphaOops! H is for Halloween ill. by Bob Kolar. Candlewick, 2010. ISBN 978-0-7636-3966-2 Subj: ABC books. Holidays – Halloween. Theater.

Kooser, Ted. *House held up by trees: not far from here, I have seen a house held up by the hands of trees, this is its story* ill. by Jon Klassen. Candlewick, 2012. ISBN 978-0-7636-5107-7 Subj: Homes, houses. Trees.

Kopelke, Lisa. *Excuse me!* ill. by author. Simon & Schuster, 2003. ISBN 978-0-689-85111-7 Subj: Behavior. Etiquette. Frogs & toads.

Koponen, Libby. *Mmm . . . let's eat!* ill. by Betsy Thompson. Blue Apple, 2013. ISBN 978-1-60905-292-8 Subj: Animals. Food. Format, unusual – toy & movable books.

Korchek, Lori. *Adventures of Cow, too* photos by Marshall Taylor. Ten Speed, 2007. ISBN 978-1-58246-189-2 Subj: Animals – bulls, cows. Shopping. Stores. Toys.

Korda, Lerryn. *Into the wild* ill. by author. Candlewick, 2010. ISBN 978-0-7636-4812-1 Subj: Animals. Camps, camping. Friendship.

It's vacation time ill. by author. Candlewick, 2010. ISBN 978-0-7636-4813-8 Subj: Activities – vacationing. Animals. Friendship. Seasons – summer.

Koren, Edward. *Very hairy Harry* ill. by author. Cotler, 2003. ISBN 978-0-06-050908-8 Subj: Careers – barbers. Hair. Tall tales.

Korman, Susan. *Box turtle at Silver Pond Lane* ill. by Stephen Marchesi. Soundprints, 2000. ISBN 978-1-56899-860-2 Subj: Reptiles – turtles, tortoises.

Kornell, Max. *Bear with me* ill. by author. Penguin, 2011. ISBN 978-0-399-25257-0 Subj: Animals – bears. Behavior – dissatisfaction. Family life.

Korngold, Jamie S. *Sadie and the big mountain* ill. by Julie Fortenberry. Lerner Kar-Ben, 2012. ISBN 978-0-7613-6492-4 Subj: Holidays – Shavuot. Jewish culture. School – nursery. Sports – hiking.

Sadie's sukkah breakfast ill. by Julie Fortenberry. Lerner/Kar-Ben, 2011. ISBN 978-0-7613-5647-9 Subj: Holidays – Sukkot. Jewish culture.

Kortepeter, Paul. *Oliver's red toboggan* ill. by Susan Wheeler. Penguin, 2006. ISBN 978-0-525-47752-5 Subj: Animals – rabbits. Behavior – fighting, arguing. Behavior – sharing. Family life – brothers & sisters. Sports – sledding.

Kosofsky, Chaim. *Much, much better* ill. by Jessica Schiffman. Hachai, 2006. ISBN 978-1-929628-22-3 Subj: Family life. Folk & fairy tales. Foreign lands – Iraq. Jewish culture.

Kostecki-Shaw, Jenny Sue. *My travelin' eye* ill. by author. Holt, 2008. ISBN 978-0-8050-8169-5 Subj: Anatomy – eyes. Character traits – individuality. Health & fitness.

Same, same but different ill. by author. Holt, 2011. ISBN 978-0-8050-8946-2 Subj: Foreign lands – India. Friendship. Pen pals.

Koster, Gloria. *The peanut-free cafe* ill. by Maryann Cocca-Leffler. Whitman, 2006. ISBN 978-0-8075-6386-1 Subj: Food. Illness – allergies. School.

Kottke, Jan. *From seed to pumpkin* ill. by author. Children's Press, 2000. ISBN 978-0-516-23309-3 Subj: Plants. Seeds.

Kotzwinkle, William. *Walter, the farting dog* by William Kotzwinkle and Glenn Murray ill. by Audrey Colman. Frog, Ltd, 2001. ISBN 978-1-58394-053-2 Subj: Animals – dogs.

Walter, the farting dog: rough weather ahead by William Kotzwinkle and Glenn Murray ill. by Audrey Colman. Dutton, 2005. ISBN 978-0-525-47218-6 Subj: Activities – flying. Animals – dogs. Insects – butterflies, caterpillars.

Walter, the farting dog: trouble at the yard sale by William Kotzwinkle and Glenn Murray ill. by Audrey Colman. Dutton, 2004. ISBN 978-0-525-47217-9 Subj: Animals – dogs. Clowns, jesters. Crime. Garage sales, rummage sales. Toys – balloons.

Kovacs, Deborah. *Katie Copley* ill. by Jared T. Williams. Godine, 2007. ISBN 978-1-56792-332-2 Subj: Animals – dogs. Animals – service animals. Behavior – lost & found possessions. Hotels.

Kovalski, Maryann. *Omar's Halloween* ill. by author. Fitzhenry & Whiteside, 2006. ISBN 978-1-55041-559-9 Subj: Clothing – costumes. Holidays – Halloween.

Take me out to the ball game ill. by author. Fitzhenry & Whiteside, 2004. ISBN 978-1-55041-897-2 Subj: Family life – grandmothers. Music. Sports – baseball.

The wheels on the bus ill. by author. Little, 1987. ISBN 978-0-316-50256-6 Subj: Buses. Family life – grandmothers. Music. Musical instruments – guitars. Songs.

Kozielski, Dolores. *On Halloween night* (Wolff, Ferida)

Kraegel, Kenneth. *King Arthur's very great grandson* ill. by author. Candlewick, 2012. ISBN 978-0-7636-5311-8 Subj: Dragons. Friendship. Knights. Monsters. Mythical creatures.

Krall, Dan. *The great lollipop caper* ill. by author. Simon & Schuster, 2013. ISBN 978-1-4424-4460-7 Subj: Crime. Food. Humorous stories.

Kramer, Andrew. *Pajama pirates* ill. by Leslie Lammle. HarperCollins, 2010. ISBN 978-0-06-125194-8 Subj: Bedtime. Pirates. Rhyming text.

Kranking, Kathy. *The ocean is . . .* photos by Norbert Wu. Holt, 2003. ISBN 978-0-8050-7097-2 Subj: Animals. Plants. Rhyming text. Sea & seashore.

Krasnesky, Thad. *That cat can't stay* ill. by David Parkins. Flashlight, 2010. ISBN 978-0-9799746-5-6 Subj: Animals – cats. Rhyming text.

Kraus, Robert. *Another mouse to feed* ill. by José Aruego and Ariane Dewey. Simon & Schuster, 1989. ISBN 978-0-671-66522-7 Subj: Animals – mice. Family life.

Come out and play, little mouse ill. by José Aruego and Ariane Dewey. Delmar, 1991. ISBN 978-0-8273-4504-1 Subj: Activities – playing. Animals – cats. Animals – mice. Behavior – trickery.

Leo the late bloomer ill. by José Aruego. Simon & Schuster, 1987. ISBN 978-0-671-96078-0 Subj: Animals – tigers. Behavior – growing up.

Little Louie the baby bloomer ill. by José Aruego and Ariane Dewey. HarperCollins, 1998. ISBN 978-0-06-026294-5 Subj: Animals – tigers. Family life – brothers.

Milton the early riser ill. by José Aruego and Ariane Dewey. Simon & Schuster, 1987. ISBN 978-0-671-66272-1 Subj: Animals – pandas. Sleep.

Mort the sport ill. by John Himmelman. Orchard, 2000. ISBN 978-0-531-33247-4 Subj: Games. Musical instruments – violins. Sports – baseball.

Mouse in love ill. by Ariane Dewey and José Aruego. Orchard, 2000. ISBN 978-0-531-33297-9 Subj: Animals – mice. Communities, neighborhoods. Emotions – love. Rhyming text.

Where are you going, little mouse? ill. by José Aruego and Ariane Dewey. Greenwillow, 1986. ISBN 978-0-688-04295-0 Subj: Animals – mice. Behavior – running away. Behavior – seeking better things.

Whose mouse are you? ill. by José Aruego. Aladdin, 1986. ISBN 978-0-02-751190-1 Subj: Animals – mice. Rhyming text.

Krause, Ute. *Oscar and the very hungry dragon* ill. by author. NorthSouth, 2010. ISBN 978-0-7358-2306-8 Subj: Activities – baking, cooking. Behavior – trickery. Character traits – cleverness. Dragons. Restaurants.

Krauss, Ruth. *And I love you* ill. by Steven Kellogg. Scholastic, 2010. ISBN 978-0-439-02459-4 Subj: Animals – cats. Emotions – love. Family life.

Bears ill. by Maurice Sendak. HarperCollins, 2005. ISBN 978-0-06-075716-8 Subj: Animals – bears. Poetry.

The carrot seed ill. by Crockett Johnson. Scholastic, 1974, ©1945. ISBN 978-0-06-023351-8 Subj: Character traits – optimism. Gardens, gardening. Plants. Self-concept.

Goodnight, goodnight, sleepyhead ill. by Jane Dyer. HarperCollins, 2004. ISBN 978-0-06-028895-2 Subj: Bedtime. Rhyming text.

The growing story ill. by Helen Oxenbury. HarperCollins, 2007. ISBN 978-0-06-024716-4 Subj: Animals – babies. Behavior – growing up. Seasons.

The happy day ill. by Marc Simont. HarperCollins, 1949. ISBN 978-0-06-023396-9 Subj: Caldecott award honor books. Hibernation. Seasons – spring. Seasons – winter. Weather – snow.

A hole is to dig: a first book of first definitions ill. by Maurice Sendak. HarperCollins, 1952. ISBN 978-0-06-023406-5 Subj: Activities – digging. Language.

A very special house ill. by Maurice Sendak. HarperCollins, 1953. ISBN 978-0-06-023456-0 Subj: Caldecott award honor books. Homes, houses. Imagination.

You're just what I need ill. by Julia Noonan. HarperCollins, 1998. ISBN 978-0-06-027515-0 Subj: Emotions. Family life – mothers. Games.

Krebs, Laurie. *The beeman* ill. by Valeria Cis. Barefoot, 2008. ISBN 978-1-84686-146-8 Subj: Careers – beekeepers. Family life – grandfathers. Insects – bees. Rhyming text. Science.

The beeman ill. by Melissa Iwai. National Geographic, 2002. ISBN 978-0-7922-7224-3 Subj: Careers – beekeepers. Family life – grandfathers. Insects – bees. Rhyming text. Science.

Off we go to Mexico: an adventure in the sun ill. by Christopher Corr. Barefoot, 2006. ISBN 978-1-905236-40-4 Subj: Activities – traveling. Foreign lands – Mexico. Foreign languages. Rhyming text.

Up and down the Andes: a Peruvian festival tale ill. by Aurelia Fronty. Barefoot, 2008. ISBN 978-1-84686-203-8 Subj: Foreign lands – Peru. Indians of South America. Rhyming text.

We all went on safari ill. by Julia Cairns. Barefoot, 2003. ISBN 978-1-84148-478-5 Subj: Counting, numbers. Foreign lands – Tanzania. Foreign languages.

We're riding on a caravan: an adventure on the Silk Road ill. by Helen Cann. Barefoot, 2005. ISBN 978-1-84148-343-6 Subj: Activities – traveling. Foreign lands – China.

We're roaming in the rainforest: an Amazon adventure ill. by Anne Wilson. Barefoot, 2010. ISBN 978-1-84686-331-8 Subj: Animals. Jungle. Rhyming text.

We're sailing down the Nile: a journey through Egypt ill. by Anne Wilson. Barefoot, 2007. ISBN 978-1-84686-040-9 Subj: Activities – traveling. Foreign lands – Egypt. Rhyming text.

We're sailing to Galapagos: a week in the Pacific ill. by Grazia Restelli. Barefoot, 2005. ISBN 978-1-84148-902-5 Subj: Activities – traveling. Animals. Foreign lands – Galapagos Islands. Rhyming text.

Kreisler, Ken. *Everybody works* (Rotner, Shelley)

Krensky, Stephen. *Ben Franklin and his first kite* ill. by Bert Dodson. Aladdin, 2002. ISBN 978-0-689-84985-5 Subj: Careers – inventors. Careers – scientists. Kites.

Big bad wolves at school ill. by Brad Sneed. Simon & Schuster, 2007. ISBN 978-0-689-38799-9 Subj: Animals – wolves. School.

The crimson comet (Morrissey, Dean)

Dinosaurs, beware! a safety guide (Brown, Marc)

Hanukkah at Valley Forge ill. by Greg Harlin. Penguin, 2006. ISBN 978-0-525-47738-9 Subj: Holidays – Hanukkah. U.S. history.

How Santa got his job ill. by S. D. Schindler. Simon & Schuster, 1998. ISBN 978-0-689-80697-1 Subj: Careers. Holidays – Christmas. Santa Claus.

How Santa lost his job ill. by S. D. Schindler. Simon & Schuster, 2001. ISBN 978-0-689-83173-7 Subj: Careers. Holidays – Christmas. Mythical creatures – elves. Santa Claus.

I know a lot! ill. by Sara Gillingham. Abrams, 2013. ISBN 978-1-4197-0938-8 Subj: Character traits – confidence. Concepts – opposites. Ethnic groups in the U.S. – African Americans. Format, unusual – board books. Rhyming text.

A man for all seasons: the life of George Washington Carver ill. by Wil Clay. Collins, 2008. ISBN 978-0-06-027885-4 Subj: Careers – scientists. Ethnic groups in the U.S. – African Americans. U.S. history.

Milo and the really big bunny ill. by Melissa Suber. Simon & Schuster, 2006. ISBN 978-0-689-87345-4 Subj: Animals – rabbits. Character traits – appearance. Holidays – Easter. Weather – storms.

Mother's Day surprise ill. by Kathi Ember. Marshall Cavendish, 2010. ISBN 978-0-7614-5633-9 Subj: Animals. Gifts. Holidays – Mother's Day. Reptiles – snakes.

My teacher's secret life ill. by JoAnn Adinolfi. Simon & Schuster, 1996. ISBN 978-0-689-80271-3 Subj: Careers – teachers. Communities, neighborhoods. School.

Noah's bark ill. by Rogé. Carolrhoda, 2010. ISBN 978-0-8225-7645-7 Subj: Animals. Boats, ships. Noise, sounds. Religion – Noah. Weather – floods. Weather – rain.

Perfect pigs: an introduction to manners (Brown, Marc)

Play ball, Jackie! ill. by Joe Morse. Millbrook, 2011. ISBN 978-0-8225-9030-9 Subj: Ethnic groups in the U.S. – African Americans. Prejudice. Sports – baseball.

Shooting for the moon ill. by Bernie Fuchs. Kroupa, 2001. ISBN 978-0-374-36843-2 Subj: Theater. U.S. history. Weapons.

Sisters of Scituate Light ill. by Stacey Schuett. Dutton, 2008. ISBN 978-0-525-47792-1 Subj: Character traits – bravery. Family life – sisters. Lighthouses. U.S. history.

Spark the firefighter ill. by Amanda Haley. Dutton, 2008. ISBN 978-0-525-47887-4 Subj: Careers – firefighters. Dragons. Emotions – fear.

Too many leprechauns: or how that pot o' gold got to the end of the rainbow ill. by Dan Andreasen. Simon & Schuster, 2007. ISBN 978-0-689-85112-4 Subj: Folk & fairy tales. Foreign lands – Ireland. Mythical creatures – leprechauns.

What a mess! ill. by Joe Mathieu. Random House, 2001. ISBN 978-0-375-90220-8 Subj: Character traits – cleanliness.

The youngest fairy godmother ever ill. by Diana Cain Bluthenthal. Simon & Schuster, 2000. ISBN 978-0-689-82011-3 Subj: Behavior – wishing. Fairies.

Krieb, Mr. *We're off to find the witch's house* ill. by R. W. Alley. Penguin, 2005. ISBN 978-0-525-47003-8 Subj: Holidays – Halloween. Rhyming text.

Kriegman, Mitchell. *The book of boo!* (Kennedy, Marge M.)

Krilanovich, Nadia. *Chicken, chicken, duck!* ill. by author. Tricycle, 2011. ISBN 978-1-58246-385-8 Subj: Animals. Birds. Farms. Games. Noise, sounds.

Moon child ill. by Elizabeth Sayles. Tricycle, 2010. ISBN 978-1-58246-325-4 Subj: Animals. Bedtime. Moon.

Krishnaswami, Uma. *Bringing Asha home* ill. by Jamel Akib. Lee & Low, 2006. ISBN 978-1-58430-

259-9 Subj: Adoption. Babies. Ethnic groups in the U.S. – East Indian Americans. Family life.

Chachaji's cup ill. by Soumya Sitaraman. Children's Book Press, 2003. ISBN 978-0-89239-178-3 Subj: Ethnic groups in the U.S. – East Indian Americans. Family life – aunts, uncles. Memories, memory.

The happiest tree: a yoga story ill. by Ruth Jeyaveeran. Lee & Low, 2005. ISBN 978-1-58430-237-7 Subj: Ethnic groups in the U.S. – East Indian Americans. Health & fitness. Self-concept.

Holi ill. with photos. Children's Press, 2003. ISBN 978-0-516-22863-1 Subj: Fairs, festivals. Religion.

Out of the way! Out of the way! ill. by Uma Krishnaswamy. Groundwood, 2012. ISBN 978-1-55498-130-4 Subj: Roads. Trees.

Remembering Grandpa ill. by Layne Johnson. Boyds Mills, 2007. ISBN 978-1-59078-424-2 Subj: Animals – rabbits. Death. Emotions – grief. Family life – grandparents.

Kroll, Steven. *The big bunny and the Easter eggs* ill. by Janet Stevens. Holiday, 1982. ISBN 978-0-8234-0436-0 Subj: Animals – rabbits. Holidays – Easter. Illness.

The big bunny and the magic show ill. by Janet Stevens. Holiday, 1986. ISBN 978-0-8234-0589-3 Subj: Animals – rabbits. Holidays – Easter. Magic.

By the dawn's early light: the story of the Star Spangled Banner ill. by Dan Andreasen. Scholastic, 1994. ISBN 978-0-590-45054-6 Subj: Music. Songs. U.S. history.

The hand-me-down doll ill. by Dan Andreasen. Marshall Cavendish, 2012. ISBN 978-0-7614-6124-1 Subj: Emotions – loneliness. Toys – dolls.

The Hanukkah mice ill. by Michelle Shapiro. Marshall Cavendish, 2008. ISBN 978-0-7614-5428-1 Subj: Animals – mice. Holidays – Hanukkah.

Happy Father's Day ill. by Marylin Hafner. Holiday, 1987. ISBN 978-0-523-40671-8 Subj: Family life – fathers. Holidays – Father's Day.

Happy Mother's Day ill. by Marylin Hafner. Holiday, 1985. ISBN 978-0-8234-0504-6 Subj: Family life. Holidays – Mother's Day.

It's April Fools' Day! ill. by Jeni Bassett. Holiday, 1990. ISBN 978-0-8234-0747-7 Subj: Animals – cats. Behavior – bullying, teasing. Holidays – April Fools' Day.

It's Groundhog Day! ill. by Jeni Bassett. Holiday, 1987. ISBN 978-0-8234-0643-2 Subj: Activities – picnicking. Animals. Holidays – Groundhog Day.

Jungle bullies ill. by Vincent Nguyen. Marshall Cavendish, 2006. ISBN 978-0-7614-5297-3 Subj: Animals. Behavior – bullying, teasing. Behavior – sharing. Jungle.

Lewis and Clark: explorers of the American West ill. by Richard Williams. Holiday, 1994. ISBN 978-0-8234-1034-7 Subj: Careers – explorers. U.S. history.

Mary McLean and the St. Patrick's Day parade ill. by Michael Dooling. Scholastic, 1991. ISBN 978-0-590-43701-1 Subj: Cities, towns. Ethnic groups in the U.S. – Irish Americans. Holidays – St. Patrick's Day. Parades.

Oh, Tucker! ill. by Scott Nash. Candlewick, 1998. ISBN 978-0-7636-0429-5 Subj: Animals – dogs. Character traits – clumsiness.

Oh, what a Thanksgiving! ill. by S. D. Schindler. Scholastic, 1988. ISBN 978-0-590-40613-0 Subj: Holidays – Thanksgiving. Imagination. U.S. history.

One tough turkey: a Thanksgiving story ill. by John Wallner. Holiday, 1982. ISBN 978-0-8234-0457-5 Subj: Birds – turkeys. Holidays – Thanksgiving. Pilgrims. Sports – hunting.

Patches: an art story ill. by Barry Gott. Winslow, 2001. ISBN 978-1-890817-53-4 Subj: Activities – drawing. Animals – guinea pigs. Behavior – lost & found possessions. Children as authors. Children as illustrators.

Patches lost and found ill. by Barry Gott. Marshall Cavendish, 2005. ISBN 978-0-7614-5217-1 Subj: Activities – drawing. Animals – guinea pigs. Behavior – lost & found possessions. Pets. School.

Pooch on the loose: a Christmas adventure ill. by Michael Garland. Marshall Cavendish, 2005. ISBN 978-0-7614-5239-3 Subj: Animals – dogs. Behavior – lost. Holidays – Christmas.

Santa's crash-bang Christmas ill. by Tomie dePaola. Holiday, 1977. ISBN 978-0-8234-0302-8 Subj: Holidays – Christmas. Santa Claus.

The squirrels' Thanksgiving ill. by Jeni Bassett. Holiday, 1991. ISBN 978-0-8234-0823-8 Subj: Animals – squirrels. Family life. Holidays – Thanksgiving. Sibling rivalry.

Stuff! reduce, reuse, recycle ill. by Steve Cox. Marshall Cavendish, 2009. ISBN 978-0-7614-5570-7 Subj: Animals – pack rats. Behavior – collecting things. Ecology. Garage sales, rummage sales.

Super-dragon ill. by Douglas Holgate. Marshall Cavendish, 2011. ISBN 978-0-7614-5819-7 Subj: Activities – flying. Contests. Dragons.

That makes me mad ill. by Christine Davenier. SeaStar, 2002. ISBN 978-1-58717-184-0 Subj: Behavior. Emotions – anger. Family life – mothers.

The Tyrannosaurus game ill. by S. D. Schindler. Marshall Cavendish, 2010. ISBN 978-0-7614-5603-2 Subj: Activities – storytelling. Dinosaurs. Games. Imagination.

Will you be my valentine? ill. by Lillian Hoban. Holiday, 1993. ISBN 978-0-8234-0925-9 Subj: Activities – making things. Behavior – indifference. Holidays – Valentine's Day. School.

Kroll, Virginia L. *Africa brothers and sisters* ill. by Vanessa French. Four Winds, 1993. ISBN 978-0-02-751166-6 Subj: Ethnic groups in the U.S. – African Americans. Family life – fathers. Foreign lands – Africa.

Boy, you're amazing! ill. by Sachiko Yoshikawa. Whitman, 2004. ISBN 978-0-8075-0868-8 Subj: Activities. Rhyming text. Self-concept.

Can you dance, Dalila? ill. by Nancy Carpenter. Simon & Schuster, 1996. ISBN 978-0-689-80551-6 Subj: Activities – dancing. Ballet. Ethnic groups in the U.S. – African Americans.

Cristina keeps a promise ill. by Enrique O. Sánchez. Whitman, 2006. ISBN 978-0-8075-1350-7 Subj: Behavior. Character traits – responsibility.

Equal shmequal: a math adventure ill. by Philomena O'Neill. Charlesbridge, 2005. ISBN 978-1-57091-891-9 Subj: Counting, numbers.

Everybody has a teddy ill. by Sophie Allsopp. Sterling, 2007. ISBN 978-1-4027-3580-6 Subj: Rhyming text. School – nursery. Toys – bears.

Faraway drums ill. by Floyd Cooper. Little, 1998. ISBN 978-0-316-50449-2 Subj: Cities, towns. Ethnic groups in the U.S. – African Americans. Family life – sisters. Foreign lands – Africa. Imagination.

Forgiving a friend ill. by Paige Billin-Frye. Whitman, 2005. ISBN 978-0-8075-0618-9 Subj: Behavior – forgiving. Friendship.

Girl, you're amazing! ill. by Mélisande Potter. Whitman, 2001. ISBN 978-0-8075-2930-0 Subj: Gender roles. Rhyming text.

Good citizen Sarah ill. by Nancy Cote. Whitman, 2007. ISBN 978-0-8075-2992-8 Subj: Behavior. Character traits – helpfulness. Weather – snow.

Good neighbor Nicholas ill. by Nancy Cote. Whitman, 2006. ISBN 978-0-8075-2998-0 Subj: Behavior. Character traits – kindness.

Hands! ill. by Cathryn Falwell. Boyds Mills, 1997. ISBN 978-1-56397-051-1 Subj: Anatomy – hands.

Honest Ashley ill. by Nancy Cote. Whitman, 2006. ISBN 978-0-8075-3371-0 Subj: Character traits – honesty. Homework.

Jaha and Jamil went down the hill: an African Mother Goose ill. by Katherine Roundtree. Charlesbridge, 1995. ISBN 978-0-88106-867-2 Subj: Foreign lands – Africa. Nursery rhymes.

Jason takes responsibility ill. by Nancy Cote. Whitman, 2005. ISBN 978-0-8075-2537-1 Subj: Birthdays. Character traits – responsibility. Family life – grandmothers.

Makayla cares about others ill. by Nancy Cote. Whitman, 2007. ISBN 978-0-8075-4945-2 Subj: Character traits – helpfulness. Emotions – fear.

Masai and I ill. by Nancy Carpenter. Four Winds, 1992. ISBN 978-0-02-751165-9 Subj: Ethnic groups in the U.S. – African Americans. Family life. Foreign lands – Africa.

On the way to kindergarten ill. by Elisabeth Schlossberg. Penguin, 2006. ISBN 978-0-399-24168-0 Subj: Animals – bears. Behavior – growing up. Rhyming text. School – first day.

Pink paper swans ill. by Nancy L. Clouse. Eerdmans, 1994. ISBN 978-0-8028-5081-2 Subj: Ethnic groups in the U.S. – Japanese Americans. Illness. Paper.

Really rabbits ill. by Philomena O'Neill. Charlesbridge, 2006. ISBN 978-1-57091-897-1 Subj: Animals – rabbits. Character traits – cleanliness. Pets.

Ryan respects ill. by Paige Billin-Frye. Whitman, 2006. ISBN 978-0-8075-6946-7 Subj: Behavior – bullying, teasing. School.

Selvakumar knew better ill. by Xiaojun Li. Shen's, 2006. ISBN 978-1-885008-29-9 Subj: Animals – dogs. Foreign lands – India. Tsunamis.

The Thanksgiving bowl ill. by Philomena O'Neill. Pelican, 2007. ISBN 978-1-58980-365-7 Subj: Family life – grandmothers. Holidays – Thanksgiving.

Uno, dos, tres, posada! let's celebrate Christmas ill. by Loretta Lopez. Penguin, 2006. ISBN 978-0-670-05923-2 Subj: Counting, numbers. Ethnic groups in the U.S. – Hispanic Americans. Holidays – Christmas. Rhyming text.

Kromhout, Rindert. *Little Donkey and the babysitter* ill. by Annemarie van Haeringen. NorthSouth, 2006. ISBN 978-0-7358-2057-9 Subj: Activities – babysitting. Animals – donkeys. Birds – chickens.

Little Donkey and the birthday present ill. by Annemarie van Haeringen. NorthSouth, 2007. ISBN 978-0-7358-2132-3 Subj: Animals – donkeys. Animals – yaks. Birthdays. Character traits – generosity. Gifts.

Kropf, Latifa Berry. *It's Hanukkah time!* photos by Tod Cohen. Kar-Ben, 2004. ISBN 978-1-58013-120-9 Subj: Family life – grandparents. Holidays – Hanukkah. Jewish culture. Parties. Religion.

It's seder time! photos by Tod Cohen. Kar-Ben, 2004. ISBN 978-1-58013-092-9 Subj: Holidays – Passover. Holidays – Seder. Jewish culture. Religion.

It's Shofar time! ill. by Tod Cohen. Kar-Ben, 2006. ISBN 978-1-58013-158-2 Subj: Holidays – Rosh Hashanah. Jewish culture. Religion.

Krosoczka, Jarrett J. *Annie was warned* ill. by author. Knopf, 2003. ISBN 978-0-375-91567-3 Subj: Holidays – Halloween. Homes, houses.

Baghead ill. by author. Dragonfly Books, 2004. ISBN 978-0-375-91566-6 Subj: Hair. Humorous stories.

Bubble bath pirates ill. by author. Viking, 2003. ISBN 978-0-670-03599-1 Subj: Activities – bathing. Family life – mothers. Pirates.

Giddy up, Cowgirl ill. by author. Penguin, 2006. ISBN 978-0-670-06050-4 Subj: Character traits – helpfulness. Family life – daughters. Family life – mothers.

Good night, Monkey Boy ill. by author. Knopf, 2001. ISBN 978-0-375-91121-7 Subj: Bedtime. Family life – mothers. Family life – sons.

Max for president ill. by author. Knopf, 2004. ISBN 978-0-375-92428-6 Subj: Friendship. School. Sportsmanship.

My buddy, Slug ill. by author. Random House, 2006. ISBN 978-0-375-83342-7 Subj: Animals – slugs. Emotions. Friendship.

Ollie the purple elephant ill. by author. Random House, 2011. ISBN 978-0-375-86654-8 Subj: Activities – dancing. Animals – cats. Animals – elephants. Circus. Family life.

Punk Farm ill. by author. Random House, 2005. ISBN 978-0-375-92429-3 Subj: Animals. Farms. Music.

Punk Farm on tour ill. by author. Random House, 2007. ISBN 978-0-375-83343-4 Subj: Animals. Farms. Songs.

Krudop, Walter Lyon. *The man who caught fish* ill. by author. Farrar, 2000. ISBN 978-0-374-34786-4 Subj: Behavior – greed. Folk & fairy tales. Foreign lands – Thailand. Royalty – kings. Sports – fishing.

Kruglik, Gerald. *Pish and Posh* (Bottner, Barbara)

Wallace's lists (Bottner, Barbara)

Krulik, Nancy E. *Is it Hanukkah yet?* ill. by DyAnne DiSalvo. Random House, 2003. ISBN 978-0-375-90286-4 Subj: Holidays – Hanukkah. Jewish culture. Religion.

Krull, Kathleen. *Big wig* ill. by Peter Malone. Scholastic, 2011. ISBN 978-0-439-67640-3 Subj: Hair.

The boy on Fairfield Street: how Ted Geisel grew up to become Dr. Seuss ill. by Steve Johnson and Lou Fancher. Decorative ill. by Dr. Seuss. Random House, 2004. ISBN 978-0-375-92298-5 Subj: Books, reading. Careers – writers. Careers – illustrators.

Hillary Rodham Clinton: dreams taking flight ill. by Amy Bates. Simon & Schuster, 2008. ISBN 978-1-4169-7129-0 Subj: Character traits – persistence. Gender roles. U.S. history.

Lincoln tells a joke: how laughter saved the president (and the country) by Kathleen Krull and Paul Brewer ill. by Stacy Innerst. Harcourt, 2010. ISBN 978-0-15-206639-0 Subj: Riddles & jokes. U.S. history.

M is for music ill. by Stacy Innerst. Harcourt, 2003. ISBN 978-0-15-201438-4 Subj: ABC books. Music.

Pocahontas: princess of the New World ill. by David Diaz. Walker, 2007. ISBN 978-0-8027-9555-7 Subj: Indians of North America – Powhatan. U.S. history.

Supermarket ill. by Melanie Hope Greenberg. Holiday, 2001. ISBN 978-0-8234-1546-5 Subj: Food. Stores.

Krupinski, Loretta. *Christmas in the city* ill. by author. Hyperion, 2002. ISBN 978-0-7868-2652-0 Subj: Animals – mice. Cities, towns. Holidays – Christmas. Trees.

Pirate treasure ill. by author. Penguin, 2006. ISBN 978-0-525-47579-8 Subj: Animals – mice. Farms. Pirates. Weather.

Krupp, E. C. *The rainbow and you* ill. by Robin Rector Krupp. HarperCollins, 2000. ISBN 978-0-688-15602-2 Subj: Weather – rainbows.

Kruusval, Catarina. *Franny's friends* ill. by author. Farrar, 2008. ISBN 978-91-29-66836-0 Subj: Activities – picnicking. Behavior – lost & found possessions. Imagination. Toys.

Krykorka, Ian. *Carl, the Christmas carp* ill. by Vladyana Krykorka. Orca, 2006. ISBN 978-1-55143-329-5 Subj: Fish. Foreign lands – Czechoslovakia. Holidays – Christmas.

Kubler, Annie. *My first signs* ill. by author. Child's Play, 2005. ISBN 978-1-904550-39-6 Subj: Language. Sign language.

Kudlinski, Kathleen V. *Boy, were we wrong about dinosaurs!* ill. by S. D. Schindler. Penguin, 2005. ISBN 978-0-525-46978-0 Subj: Dinosaurs. Science.

Boy, were we wrong about the solar system! ill. by John Rocco. Dutton, 2008. ISBN 978-0-525-46979-7 Subj: Science. Space & space ships.

The seaside switch ill. by Lindy Burnett. NorthWord, 2007. ISBN 978-1-55971-964-3 Subj: Ecology. Sea & seashore.

The sunset switch ill. by Lindy Burnett. NorthWord, 2005. ISBN 978-1-55971-916-2 Subj: Animals. Night.

What do roots do? ill. by David Schuppert. NorthWord, 2005. ISBN 978-1-55971-896-7 Subj: Plants.

Kuiper, Nannie. *Bailey the bear cub* ill. by Jeska Verstegen. NorthSouth, 2002. ISBN 978-0-7358-1625-1 Subj: Animals – babies. Animals – bears. Behavior – growing up. Family life – mothers.

Bravo, brave beavers ill. by Jeska Verstegen. NorthSouth, 2004. ISBN 978-0-7358-1916-0 Subj: Animals – beavers. Character traits – cooperation. Family life. Weather – storms.

Kuklin, Susan. *Families* photos by author. Hyperion, 2006. ISBN 978-0-7868-0822-9 Subj: Emotions – love. Family life.

Kulka, Joe. *My crocodile does not bite* ill. by author. Carolrhoda, 2013. ISBN 978-0-7613-8937-8 Subj: Behavior – boasting. Contests. Pets. Reptiles – alligators, crocodiles.

Wolf's coming ill. by author. Carolrhoda, 2007. ISBN 978-1-57505-930-3 Subj: Animals – wolves. Birthdays.

Kulling, Monica. *All aboard! Elijah McCoy's steam engine* ill. by Bill Slavin. Tundra, 2010. ISBN 978-0-88776-945-0 Subj: Careers – inventors. Ethnic groups in the U.S. – African Americans. Inventions. Trains.

Kumin, Maxine. *Mites to astodons: a book of animal poems* ill. by Pamela Zagarenski. Houghton, 2006. ISBN 978-0-618-50753-5 Subj: Animals. Poetry.

Oh, Harry! ill. by Barry Moser. Roaring Brook, 2011. ISBN 978-1-59643-439-4 Subj: Animals – horses, ponies. Behavior – misbehavior. Rhyming text.

What color is Caesar? ill. by Alison Friend. Candlewick, 2010. ISBN 978-0-7636-3432-2 Subj: Animals – dogs. Concepts – color. Self-concept.

Kunhardt, Katharine. *Let's count the puppies* photos by author. HarperCollins, 2004. ISBN 978-0-06-054337-2 Subj: Animals – babies. Animals – dogs. Counting, numbers.

Kurtz, Jane. *Do kangaroos wear seat belts?* ill. by Jane Manning. Penguin, 2005. ISBN 978-0-525-47358-9 Subj: Animals. Safety. Zoos.

Faraway home ill. by E. B. Lewis. Harcourt, 2000. ISBN 978-0-15-200036-3 Subj: Ethnic groups in the U.S. – African Americans. Family life – fathers. Foreign lands – Ethiopia. Memories, memory.

In the small, small night ill. by Rachel Isadora. HarperCollins, 2005. ISBN 978-0-06-623813-5 Subj: Activities – storytelling. Bedtime. Character traits – perseverance. Family life – brothers & sisters. Folk & fairy tales. Foreign lands – Ghana. Immigrants.

Rain romp: stomping away a grouchy day ill. by Dyanna Wolcott. Greenwillow, 2002. ISBN 978-0-06-029806-7 Subj: Behavior. Family life – parents. Rhyming text. Weather – rain.

River friendly, river wild ill. by Neil Brennan. Simon & Schuster, 2000. ISBN 978-0-689-82049-6 Subj: Family life. Rivers. U.S. history. Weather – floods.

Kurtz, Kevin. *A day in the salt marsh* ill. by Consie Powell. Sylvan Dell, 2007. ISBN 978-0-9768823-5-0 Subj: Ecology. Nature. Rhyming text.

Kushner, Donn. *Peter's pixie* ill. by Sylvie Daigneault. Tundra, 2003. ISBN 978-0-88776-603-9 Subj: Family life – brothers. Family life – new sibling. Magic. Mythical creatures – pixies.

Kushner, Karen. *Because Nothing Looks Like God* (Kushner, Lawrence)

Kushner, Lawrence. *Because Nothing Looks Like God* by Lawrence Kushner and Karen Kushner ill. by Dawn Majewski. Jewish Lights, 2000. ISBN 978-1-58023-092-6 Subj: Religion.

Kushner, Tony. *Brundibar* ill. by Maurice Sendak. Hyperion, 2003. ISBN 978-0-7868-0904-2 Subj: Activities – singing. Behavior – bullying, teasing. Family life – brothers & sisters.

Kuskin, Karla. *A boy had a mother who bought him a hat* ill. by Kevin Hawkes. HarperCollins, 2010. ISBN 978-0-06-075330-6 Subj: Family life – mothers. Rhyming text.

A great miracle happened there: a Chanukah story ill. by Robert Andrew Parker. Willa Perlman Books, 1993. ISBN 978-0-06-023618-2 Subj: Family life. Holidays – Hanukkah. Jewish culture. Religion.

Green as a bean ill. by Melissa Iwai. HarperCollins, 2007. ISBN 978-0-06-075334-4 Subj: Character traits – questioning. Rhyming text.

I am me ill. by Dyanna Wolcott. Simon & Schuster, 2000. ISBN 978-0-689-81473-0 Subj: Character traits – individuality. Family life. Sea & seashore.

The Philharmonic gets dressed ill. by Marc Simont. HarperCollins, 1982. ISBN 978-0-06-023622-9 Subj: Clothing. Musical instruments – orchestras.

So, what's it like to be a cat? ill. by Betsy Lewin. Simon & Schuster, 2005. ISBN 978-0-689-84733-2 Subj: Animals – cats. Rhyming text.

Toots the cat ill. by Lisze Bechtold. Holt, 2005. ISBN 978-0-8050-6841-2 Subj: Animals – cats. Poetry.

Under my hood I have a hat ill. by Fumi Kosaka. Geringer, 2004. ISBN 978-0-06-057243-3 Subj: Clothing. Rhyming text. Seasons – winter.

Kusugak, Michael. *A promise is a promise* (Munsch, Robert N.)

Kuszyk, R. Nicholas. *R Robot saves lunch* ill. by author. Putnam, 2009. ISBN 978-0-399-24757-6 Subj: Humorous stories. Robots.

Kutner, Merrily. *Z is for zombie* ill. by John Manders. Whitman, 1999. ISBN 978-0-8075-9490-2 Subj: ABC books. Holidays – Halloween. Rhyming text.

The Zombie Nite Cafe ill. by Ethan Long. Holiday House, 2007. ISBN 978-0-8234-1963-0 Subj: Monsters. Restaurants. Rhyming text.

Kvasnosky, Laura McGee. *Really truly Bingo* ill. by author. Candlewick, 2008. ISBN 978-0-7636-3210-6 Subj: Activities – playing. Animals – dogs. Behavior – boredom. Imagination – imaginary friends.

Kwon, Yoon-duck. *My cat copies me* ill. by author. Kane/Miller, 2007. ISBN 978-1-933605-26-5 Subj: Animals – cats. Imagination. Pets.

LaChanze. *Little diva* ill. by Brian Pinkney. Feiwel & Friends, 2010. ISBN 978-0-312-37010-7 Subj: Careers – actors. Family life – mothers. Theater.

Lachenmeyer, Nathaniel. *The origami master* ill. by Aki Sogabe. Whitman, 2008. ISBN 978-0-8075-6134-8 Subj: Activities – making things. Birds. Foreign lands – Japan.

Lachner, Dorothea. *Danny, the angry lion* ill. by Gusti. NorthSouth, 2000. ISBN 978-0-7358-1387-8 Subj: Emotions – anger.

The gift from Saint Nicholas ill. by Maja Dusíková. NorthSouth, 1995. ISBN 978-1-55858-457-0 Subj: Holidays – Christmas. Weather – snow.

Meredith's mixed-up magic ill. by Christa Unzner. NorthSouth, 2000. ISBN 978-0-7358-1190-4 Subj: Magic. Witches.

Smoky's special Easter present ill. by Christa Unzner. NorthSouth, 1996. ISBN 978-1-55858-574-4 Subj: Activities. Animals – rabbits. Holidays – Easter. Pets.

Lachtman, Ofelia Dumas. *Pepita takes time / Pepita, siempre tarde* Spanish by Alejandra Balestra; ill. by Alex Pardo DeLange. Piñata, 2001. ISBN 978-1-55885-304-1 Subj: Behavior – promptness, tardiness. Ethnic groups in the U.S. – Hispanic Americans. Foreign languages.

Lackner, Michelle Myers. *Toil in the soil* ill. by Daniel Powers. Millbrook, 2001. ISBN 978-0-7613-1807-1 Subj: Animals – worms.

Lacombe, Benjamin. *Cherry and Olive* ill. by author. Walker, 2007. ISBN 978-0-8027-9707-0 Subj: Animals – dogs. Behavior – bullying, teasing. Emotions – loneliness.

Lacome, Julie. *Ruthie's big old coat* ill. by author. Candlewick, 2000. ISBN 978-0-7636-0969-6 Subj: Activities – playing. Animals – rabbits. Clothing – coats.

Laden, Nina. *Bad dog* ill. by author. Walker, 2000. ISBN 978-0-8027-8748-4 Subj: Animals – dogs. Behavior – misbehavior. Humorous stories.

Clowns on vacation ill. by author. Walker, 2002. ISBN 978-0-8027-8781-1 Subj: Activities – vacationing. Clowns, jesters. Rhyming text.

Once upon a memory ill. by Renata Liwska. Little, Brown, 2013. ISBN 978-0-316-20816-1 Subj: Behavior – growing up. Character traits – questioning. Memories, memory.

Peek-a-who? ill. by author. Chronicle, 2000. ISBN 978-0-8118-2602-0 Subj: Format, unusual – board books. Rhyming text.

Roberto, the insect architect ill. by author. Chronicle, 2000. ISBN 978-0-8118-2465-1 Subj: Careers – architects. Insects – termites.

Laird, Elizabeth. *A book of promises* ill. by Michael Frith. DK, 2000. ISBN 978-0-7894-2547-8 Subj: Emotions – love. Family life.

Lairla, Sergio. *Abel and the wolf* ill. by Alessandra Roberti. NorthSouth, 2004. ISBN 978-0-7358-1903-0 Subj: Animals – wolves. Emotions. Forest, woods. Friendship.

Lakin, Patricia. *Camping day* ill. by Scott Nash. Dial, 2009. ISBN 978-0-8037-3309-1 Subj: Camps, camping. Friendship. Reptiles – alligators, crocodiles.

Clarence the copy cat ill. by John Manders. Doubleday, 2002. ISBN 978-0-385-32747-3 Subj: Animals – cats. Animals – mice. Libraries.

Fat chance Thanksgiving ill. by Stacey Schuett. Whitman, 2001. ISBN 978-0-8075-2288-2 Subj: Books, reading. Communities, neighborhoods. Holidays – Thanksgiving. Homes, houses.

Hurricane! ill. by Vanessa Lubach. Millbrook, 2000. ISBN 978-0-7613-1616-9 Subj: Family life – fathers. Weather – hurricanes.

Rainy day ill. by Scott Nash. Penguin, 2007. ISBN 978-0-8037-3092-2 Subj: Activities – playing. Behavior – boredom. Books, reading. Libraries. Reptiles – alligators, crocodiles. Weather – rain.

Snow day! ill. by Scott Nash. Dial, 2002. ISBN 978-0-8037-2642-0 Subj: School. Weather – snow.

Subway sonata ill. by Heather Maione. Millbrook, 2001. ISBN 978-0-7613-1464-6 Subj: Careers – artists. Cities, towns. Trains.

Lallemand, Orianne. *The wolf who wanted to change his color* ill. by Eleonore Thuillier. Auzou, 2012. ISBN 978-2-7338-1945-6 Subj: Animals – wolves. Concepts – color. Self-concept.

LaMarche, Jim. *Lost and found: three dog stories* ill. by author. Chronicle, 2009. ISBN 978-0-8118-6401-5 Subj: Animals – dogs. Behavior – lost. Behavior – lost & found possessions.

The raft ill. by author. HarperCollins, 2000. ISBN 978-0-688-13978-0 Subj: Animals. Boats, ships. Family life – grandmothers. Rivers.

Up ill. by author. Chronicle, 2006. ISBN 978-0-8118-4445-1 Subj: Careers – fishermen. Character traits – smallness. Family life – brothers & sisters. Magic. Self-concept.

Lamb, Albert. *The abandoned lighthouse* ill. by David McPhail. Roaring Brook, 2011. ISBN 978-1-59643-525-4 Subj: Animals – bears. Boats, ships. Lighthouses.

Sam's winter hat ill. by David McPhail. Scholastic, 2006. ISBN 978-0-439-79304-9 Subj: Animals – bears. Behavior – lost & found possessions. Clothing – hats.

Tell me the day backwards ill. by David McPhail. Candlewick, 2011. ISBN 978-0-7636-5055-1 Subj: Animals – bears. Bedtime. Day. Family life – mothers.

Lamb, Rosy. *Paul meets Bernadette* ill. by author. Candlewick, 2013. ISBN 978-0-7636-6130-4 Subj: Character traits – curiosity. Fish. Imagination.

Lambert, Martha Lewis. *I won't get lost* ill. by Kate Duke. HarperCollins, 2003. ISBN 978-0-06-028961-4 Subj: Behavior – lost. Dragons. School.

Why do you love me? (Schlessinger, Laura)

Laminack, Lester L. *Jake's 100th day of school* ill. by Judy Love. Peachtree, 2006. ISBN 978-1-56145-355-9 Subj: Counting, numbers. School.

Saturdays and teacakes ill. by Chris Soentpiet. Peachtree, 2004. ISBN 978-1-56145-303-0 Subj: Activities – baking, cooking. Character traits – helpfulness. Family life – grandmothers.

Snow day! ill. by Adam Gustavson. Peachtree, 2007. ISBN 978-1-56145-418-1 Subj: Careers – teachers. Seasons – winter. Weather – snow.

Three hens and a peacock ill. by Henry Cole. Peachtree, 2011. ISBN 978-1-56145-564-5 Subj: Behavior – dissatisfaction. Birds – chickens. Birds – peacocks, peahens. Farms.

Lamm, C. Drew. *Gauchada* ill. by Fabian Negrin. Knopf, 2001. ISBN 978-0-375-91267-2 Subj: Foreign lands – Argentina. Jewelry.

Pirates ill. by Stacey Schuett. Hyperion, 2001. ISBN 978-0-7868-0392-7 Subj: Books, reading. Emotions – fear. Family life – brothers & sisters. Pirates.

Lamstein, Sarah Marwil. *Big night for salamanders* ill. by Carol Benioff. Boyds Mills, 2010. ISBN 978-1-932425-98-7 Subj: Character traits – kindness to animals. Ecology. Migration. Nature. Reptiles – salamanders. Seasons – spring.

I like your buttons! ill. by Nancy Cote. Whitman, 1999. ISBN 978-0-8075-3510-3 Subj: Character traits – kindness. School.

Landa, Norbert. *The great monster hunt* ill. by Tim Warnes. Good Books, 2010. ISBN 978-1-56148-681-6 Subj: Animals. Emotions – fear. Imagination.

Little Bear and the wishing tree ill. by Simon Mendez. Good Books, 2007. ISBN 978-1-56148-566-6 Subj: Animals – bears. Behavior – sharing. Behavior – wishing. Emotions – anger. Family life – brothers & sisters. Trees.

Landman, Tanya. *Mary's penny* ill. by Richard Holland. Candlewick, 2010. ISBN 978-0-7636-4768-1 Subj: Farms. Gender roles.

Landolf, Diane Wright. *What a good big brother!* ill. by Steve Johnson. Random House, 2009. ISBN 978-0-375-84258-0 Subj: Babies. Family life – brothers & sisters.

Landry, Leo. *Eat your peas, Ivy Louise!* ill. by author. Houghton, 2005. ISBN 978-0-618-44886-9 Subj: Circus. Food. Imagination.

The snow ghosts ill. by author. Houghton, 2003. ISBN 978-0-618-19655-5 Subj: Ghosts. Weather – snow.

Space boy ill. by author. Houghton, 2007. ISBN 978-0-618-60568-2 Subj: Bedtime. Space & space ships.

Trick or treat ill. by author. Houghton Mifflin, 2012. ISBN 978-0-547-24969-8 Subj: Clothing – costumes. Ghosts. Holidays – Halloween. Parties.

Landström, Lena. *Boo and Baa get wet* (Landström, Olof)

Boo and Baa have company by Lena Landström and Olof Landström ill. by Olof Landström. Farrar, 2006. ISBN 978-91-29-66546-8 Subj: Animals – sheep. Humorous stories.

Boo and Baa in the woods (Landström, Olof)

A hippo's tale ill. by author. Farrar, 2007. ISBN 978-91-29-66603-8 Subj: Activities – bathing. Animals – hippopotamuses. Animals – monkeys. Foreign lands – Africa.

The little hippos' adventure ill. by author. Farrar, 2002. ISBN 978-91-29-65500-1 Subj: Animals – hippopotamuses.

Landström, Olof. *Boo and Baa get wet* by Olof Landström and Lena Landström ill. by authors. Farrar, 2000. ISBN 978-91-29-64752-5 Subj: Animals – sheep. Humorous stories. Weather – storms.

Boo and Baa have company (Landström, Lena)

Boo and Baa in the woods by Olof Landström and Lena Landström ill. by authors. Farrar, 2000. ISBN 978-91-29-64754-9 Subj: Activities – picnicking. Animals – sheep. Forest, woods. Humorous stories. Insects – ants.

Lane, Adam J. B. *Stop thief!* ill. by author. Roaring Brook, 2012. ISBN 978-1-59643-693-0 Subj: Behavior – growing up. Crime. Toys.

Lane, Daniel. *The Animal Mall* (Edens, Cooper)

Lang, Aubrey. *The adventures of Baby Bear* photos by Wayne Lynch. Fitzhenry & Whiteside, 2001. ISBN 978-1-55041-670-1 Subj: Animals – babies. Animals – bears.

Baby elephant photos by Wayne Lynch. Fitzhenry & Whiteside, 2002. ISBN 978-1-55041-715-9 Subj: Animals – babies. Animals – elephants.

Baby fox photos by Wayne Lynch. Fitzhenry & Whiteside, 2002. ISBN 978-1-55041-688-6 Subj: Animals – babies. Animals – foxes.

Baby lion photos by Wayne Lynch. Fitzhenry & Whiteside, 2002. ISBN 978-1-55041-711-1 Subj: Animals – babies. Animals – lions.

Baby mountain sheep photos by Wayne Lynch. Fitzhenry & Whiteside, 2008. ISBN 978-1-55455-042-5 Subj: Animals – sheep.

Baby penguin photos by Wayne Lynch. Fitzhenry & Whiteside, 2001. ISBN 978-1-55041-675-6 Subj: Animals – babies. Birds – penguins.

Lang, Glenna. *Looking out for Sarah* ill. by author. Talewinds, 2001. ISBN 978-0-88106-647-0 Subj: Animals – dogs. Animals – service animals. Disabilities – blindness.

Lang, Heather. *Queen of the track: Alice Coachman, Olympic high-jump champion* ill. by Floyd Cooper. Boyds Mills, 2012. ISBN 978-1-59078-850-9 Subj: Ethnic groups in the U.S. – African Americans. Sports – Olympics. U.S. history.

Langdo, Bryan. *The dog who loved the good life* ill. by author. Holt, 2001. ISBN 978-0-8050-6494-0 Subj: Animals – dogs.

Tornado Slim and the magic cowboy hat ill. by author. Marshall Cavendish, 2011. ISBN 978-0-7614-5962-0 Subj: Clothing – hats. Cowboys, cowgirls. Magic.

Lange, Willem. *John and Tom* ill. by Bert Dodson. Vermont Folklife Center, 2001. ISBN 978-0-916718-17-6 Subj: Accidents. Animals – horses, ponies. Careers – lumberjacks.

Langen, Annette. *I won't comb my hair!* ill. by Frauke Bahr. NorthSouth, 2010. ISBN 978-0-7358-2315-0 Subj: Character traits – appearance. Character traits – stubbornness. Hair.

Langford, Sarah. *Grandfather's story cloth / Yawg daim paj ntaub dab neeg* (Gerdner, Linda)

Langley, Jonathan. *Shine* (Langley, Karen)

Langley, Karen. *Shine* by Karen Langley and Jonathan Langley ill. by Jonathan Langley. Marshall Cavendish, 2002. ISBN 978-0-7614-5127-3 Subj: Family life – fathers. Holidays – Christmas. School. Stars. Theater.

Langreuter, Jutta. *Little Bear and the big fight* by Jutta Langreuter and Vera Sobat ill. by Vera Sobat. Millbrook, 1998. ISBN 978-0-7613-0403-6 Subj: Animals – bears. Behavior – misbehavior. Emotions – anger. Friendship. School.

Little Bear brushes his teeth by Jutta Langreuter and Vera Sobat ill. by Vera Sobat. Millbrook, 1997. ISBN 978-0-7613-0190-5 Subj: Animals – bears. Family life. Hygiene.

Little Bear goes to kindergarten by Jutta Langreuter and Vera Sobat ill. by Vera Sobat. Millbrook, 1997. ISBN 978-0-7613-0191-2 Subj: Animals – bears. Friendship. School – first day.

Little Bear won't go to bed ill. by Vera Sobat. Millbrook, 2000. ISBN 978-0-7613-1872-9 Subj: Animals – bears. Bedtime.

Langsen, Richard C. *When someone in the family drinks too much* ill. by Nicole Rubel. Dial, 1996. ISBN 978-0-8037-1687-2 Subj: Animals – bears. Family life. Illness – alcoholism.

Langstaff, John M. *Oh, a-hunting we will go* ill. by Nancy Winslow Parker. Atheneum, 1974. ISBN 978-0-689-50007-7 Subj: Folk & fairy tales. Music. Songs. Sports – hunting.

Over in the meadow ill. by Feodor Rojankovsky. Includes Over in the meadow (for voice and piano) by Marshall Woodbridge. Harcourt, 1957. ISBN 978-0-15-258854-0 Subj: Animals. Counting, numbers. Folk & fairy tales. Songs.

Langton, Jane. *Saint Francis and the wolf* ill. by Ilse Plume. Godine, 2007. ISBN 978-1-56792-320-9 Subj: Animals – wolves. Folk & fairy tales. Religion.

Lansky, Vicki. *It's not your fault, KoKo Bear: a read-together book for parents and young children during divorce* ill. by Jane Prince. Book Peddlers, 1998. ISBN 978-0-916773-46-5 Subj: Animals – bears. Divorce. Family life.

LaReau, Kara. *Mr. Prickles: a quill-fated love story* ill. by Scott Magoon. Roaring Brook, 2011. ISBN 978-1-59643-483-7 Subj: Animals – porcupines. Emotions – loneliness. Friendship.

Otto: the boy who loved cars ill. by Scott Magoon. Roaring Brook, 2011. ISBN 978-1-59643-484-4 Subj: Automobiles. Humorous stories.

Rocko and Spanky have company ill. by Jenna LaReau. Harcourt, 2006. ISBN 978-0-15-216618-2 Subj: Animals – monkeys. Multiple births – twins. Toys.

Snowbaby could not sleep ill. by Jim Ishikawa. Little, Brown, 2005. ISBN 978-0-316-60703-2 Subj: Bedtime. Emotions – loneliness. Snowmen.

Ugly fish ill. by Scott Magoon. Harcourt, 2006. ISBN 978-0-15-205082-5 Subj: Behavior – bullying, teasing. Behavior – sharing. Character traits – appearance. Emotions – loneliness. Fish.

Larios, Julie. *Imaginary menagerie: a book of curious creatures* ill. by Julie Paschkis. Harcourt, 2008. ISBN 978-0-15-206325-2 Subj: Mythical creatures. Poetry.

Yellow elephant: a bright bestiary ill. by Julie Paschkis. Harcourt, 2006. ISBN 978-0-15-205422-9 Subj: Animals. Concepts – color. Poetry.

Laroche, Giles. *If you lived here: houses of the world* ill. by author. Harcourt, 2011. ISBN 978-0-547-23892-0 Subj: Homes, houses. World.

LaRochelle, David. *The end* ill. by Richard Egielski. Scholastic, 2007. ISBN 978-0-439-64011-4 Subj: Folk & fairy tales. Humorous stories. Royalty – princesses.

The haunted hamburger and other ghostly stories ill. by Paul Meisel. Penguin, 2011. ISBN 978-0-525-42272-3 Subj: Activities – storytelling. Bedtime. Family life – brothers & sisters. Ghosts.

How Martha saved her parents from green beans ill. by Mark Fearing. Dial, 2013. ISBN 978-0-8037-3766-2 Subj: Family life. Food. Humorous stories.

It's a tiger ill. by Jeremy Tankard. Chronicle, 2012. ISBN 978-0-8118-6925-6 Subj: Activities – storytelling. Animals. Animals – tigers. Imagination.

Moo! ill. by Mike Wohnoutka. Walker, 2013. ISBN 978-0-8027-3409-9 Subj: Animals – bulls, cows. Automobiles. Behavior – misbehavior.

1+1=5: and other unlikely additions ill. by Brenda Sexton. Sterling, 2010. ISBN 978-1-4027-5995-6 Subj: Counting, numbers. Imagination.

Larsen, Andrew. *Bella and the bunny* ill. by Kate Endle. Kids Can, 2007. ISBN 978-1-55337-970-6 Subj: Animals – rabbits. Clothing – sweaters. School – nursery.

The imaginary garden ill. by Irene Luxbacher. Kids Can, 2009. ISBN 978-1-55453-279-7 Subj: Activities – painting. Art. Gardens, gardening. Imagination.

In the tree house ill. by Dusan Petricic. Kids Can, 2013. ISBN 978-1-55453-635-1 Subj: Family life – brothers. Homes, houses. Trees.

Larson, Bonnie. *When animals were people / Cuando los animales eran personas* ill. by Modesto Rivera Lemus. Clear Light, 2002. ISBN 978-1-57416-051-2 Subj: Animals. Folk & fairy tales – pourquoi tales. Foreign lands – Mexico. Foreign languages. Indians of North America – Huichol.

Larson, Kirby. *The magic kerchief* ill. by Rosanne Litzinger. Holiday, 2000. ISBN 978-0-8234-1473-4 Subj: Clothing. Folk & fairy tales. Magic.

Nubs: the true story of a mutt, a marine and a miracle (Dennis, Major Brian)

Two Bobbies: a true story of Hurricane Katrina, friendship, and survival by Kirby Larson and Mary Nethery ill. by Jean Cassels. Walker, 2008. ISBN 978-0-8027-9754-4 Subj: Animals – cats. Animals – dogs. Weather – hurricanes.

Laschütza, Susanne. *Nat the bat* ill. by author. G. Stevens, 2003. ISBN 978-0-8368-3573-1 Subj: Animals – bats. Animals – dogs.

Lasky, Kathryn. *Baby love* ill. by Jennifer Plecas. Candlewick, 2001. ISBN 978-1-56402-679-8 Subj: Babies.

The emperor's old clothes ill. by David Catrow. Harcourt, 1999. ISBN 978-0-15-200384-5 Subj: Careers – farmers. Clothing. Folk & fairy tales. Humorous stories. Royalty – emperors.

Fourth of July bear ill. by Helen Cogancherry. Morrow, 1991. ISBN 978-0-688-08288-8 Subj: Animals – bears. Friendship. Holidays – Fourth of July. Parades.

Lucille camps in ill. by Marylin Hafner. Knopf, 2003. ISBN 978-0-517-80042-3 Subj: Animals – pigs. Camps, camping. Family life.

Lucille's snowsuit ill. by Marylin Hafner. Crown, 2000. ISBN 978-0-517-80038-6 Subj: Animals – pigs. Clothing. Family life – brothers & sisters. Weather – snow.

Lunch bunnies ill. by Marylin Hafner. Little, 1996. ISBN 978-0-316-51525-2 Subj: Animals – rabbits. Behavior – worrying. School – first day.

Mommy's hands by Kathryn Lasky and Jane Kamine ill. by Darcia Labrosse. Hyperion, 2002. ISBN 978-0-7868-2225-6 Subj: Anatomy – hands. Family life – mothers. Seasons.

Pirate Bob ill. by David Clark. Charlesbridge, 2006. ISBN 978-1-57091-595-6 Subj: Behavior – greed. Pirates.

Science fair bunnies ill. by Marylin Hafner. Candlewick, 2000. ISBN 978-0-7636-0729-6 Subj: Animals – rabbits. Fairs, festivals. School. Science.

Show and tell bunnies ill. by Marylin Hafner. Candlewick, 1998. ISBN 978-0-7636-0396-0 Subj: Animals – rabbits. School. Spiders.

Sophie and Rose ill. by Wendy Anderson Halperin. Candlewick, 1998. ISBN 978-0-7636-0459-2 Subj: Family life. Toys – dolls.

Starring Lucille ill. by Marylin Hafner. Crown, 2001. ISBN 978-0-517-80039-3 Subj: Activities – dancing. Animals – pigs. Ballet. Birthdays. Family life – brothers & sisters.

Tumble bunnies ill. by Marylin Hafner. Candlewick, 2005. ISBN 978-0-7636-2265-7 Subj: Animals – rabbits. Sports – gymnastics. Sportsmanship.

Lass, Bonnie. *Who took the cookies from the cookie jar?* by Bonnie Lass and Philemon Sturges ill. by Ashley Wolff. Little, 2000. ISBN 978-0-316-82016-5 Subj: Animals. Food. Insects – ants. Mystery stories. Rhyming text.

LaTeef, Nelda. *The hunter and the ebony tree* ill. by author. Moon Mt, 2002. ISBN 978-0-9677929-9-6 Subj: Folk & fairy tales. Foreign lands – Africa. Weddings.

Latifah, Queen. *Queen of the scene* ill. by Frank Morrison. HarperCollins, 2006. ISBN 978-0-06-077857-6 Subj: Character traits – confidence. Ethnic groups in the U.S. – African Americans. Rhyming text. Self-concept.

Latimer, Alex. *The boy who cried ninja* ill. by author. Peachtree, 2011. ISBN 978-0-56145-579-9 Subj: Behavior – lying. Character traits – honesty. Sports – martial arts.

Lion vs Rabbit ill. by author. Peachtree, 2013. ISBN 978-1-56145-709-0 Subj: Animals. Animals – lions. Animals – rabbits. Behavior – bullying, teasing. Behavior – trickery. Foreign lands – Africa.

Penguin's hidden talent ill. by author. Peachtree, 2012. ISBN 978-1-56145-629-1 Subj: Animals. Behavior – resourcefulness. Birds – penguins. Character traits – assertiveness. Theater.

Latter, Jill. *Mama Hen's big day* ill. by author. NorthSouth, 2013. ISBN 978-0-7358-4109-3 Subj: Birds – chickens. Eggs.

Lattimore, Deborah Nourse. *Cinderhazel: the Cinderella of Halloween* ill. by author. Scholastic, 1997. ISBN 978-0-590-20232-9 Subj: Character traits – cleanliness. Royalty – princes. Witches.

Lauber, Patricia. *Be a friend to trees* ill. by Holly Keller. HarperCollins, 1994. ISBN 978-0-06-021529-3 Subj: Ecology. Science. Trees.

An octopus is amazing ill. by Holly Keller. Crowell, 1990. ISBN 978-0-690-04862-9 Subj: Octopuses.

Snakes are hunters ill. by Holly Keller. HarperCollins, 1988. ISBN 978-0-690-04630-4 Subj: Reptiles – snakes. Science.

What you never knew about tubs, toilets and showers ill. by John Manders. Simon & Schuster, 2001. ISBN 978-0-689-82420-3 Subj: Activities – bathing. Character traits – cleanliness.

Who eats what? ill. by Holly Keller. HarperCollins, 1995. ISBN 978-0-06-022982-5 Subj: Ecology. Food. Science.

You're aboard spaceship Earth ill. by Holly Keller. HarperCollins, 1996. ISBN 978-0-06-024408-8 Subj: Earth. Space & space ships.

Lauture, Denizé. *Running the road to ABC* ill. by Reynold Ruffins. Simon & Schuster, 1996. ISBN 978-0-689-80507-3 Subj: ABC books. Foreign lands – Haiti. School.

Laverde, Arlene. *Alaska's three pigs* ill. by Mindy Dwyer. Sasquatch, 2000. ISBN 978-1-57061-229-9 Subj: Alaska. Animals – pigs. Folk & fairy tales. Homes, houses.

Lavis, Steve. *Cock-a-doodle-doo: a farmyard counting book* ill. by author. Dutton, 1997. ISBN 978-0-525-67542-6 Subj: Animals. Counting, numbers. Noise, sounds.

Jump! ill. by author. Lodestar, 1998. ISBN 978-0-525-67578-5 Subj: Activities. Animals. Behavior – imitation. Birds.

On the farm ill. by author. Ragged Bears, 2001. ISBN 978-1-929927-23-4 Subj: Animals. Farms. Format, unusual – toy & movable books.

Law, Diane. *Come out and play: count around the world in five languages* ill. by author. NorthSouth,

2006. ISBN 978-0-7358-2060-9 Subj: Counting, numbers. Foreign languages.

Lawler, Janet. *A father's song* ill. by Lucy Corvino. Sterling, 2006. ISBN 978-1-4027-2501-2 Subj: Activities – playing. Emotions – love. Family life – fathers. Rhyming text.

A mother's song ill. by Kathleen Kemly. Sterling, 2010. ISBN 978-1-4027-6968-9 Subj: Family life – mothers. Nature. Rhyming text.

Ocean counting ill. with photos. National Geographic, 2013. ISBN 978-1-4263-1116-1 Subj: Animals. Counting, numbers. Sea & seashore.

Snowzilla ill. by Amanda Haley. Amazon, 2012. ISBN 978-0-7614-6188-3 Subj: Rhyming text. Snowmen.

Tyrannoclaus ill. by John Shroades. HarperCollins, 2009. ISBN 978-0-06-117054-6 Subj: Dinosaurs. Holidays – Christmas. Rhyming text. Santa Claus.

Lawlor, Laurie. *Muddy as a duck puddle and other American similes* ill. by Ethan Long. Holiday House, 2010. ISBN 978-0-8234-2229-6 Subj: ABC books. Language.

Old Crump ill. by John Winch. Holiday, 2002. ISBN 978-0-8234-1608-0 Subj: Activities – traveling. Animals – oxen. Desert. Moving. U.S. history.

Rachel Carson and her book that changed the world ill. by Laura Beingessner. Holiday House, 2012. ISBN 978-0-8234-2370-5 Subj: Careers – scientists. Ecology. Gender roles. Sea & seashore.

Lawrence, Jennifer B. *Sad doggy* ill. by Timothy Basil Ering. Piggy Toes, 2001. ISBN 978-1-58117-066-5 Subj: Animals – dogs. Emotions – sadness. Format, unusual – toy & movable books. Rhyming text.

Lawrence, John. *This little chick* ill. by author. Candlewick, 2002. ISBN 978-0-7636-1716-5 Subj: Animals. Animals – babies. Birds – chickens. Noise, sounds. Rhyming text.

Lawrence, Mary. *What's that sound?* ill. by Lynn Adams. Kane, 2002. ISBN 978-1-57565-118-7 Subj: Country. Family life. Noise, sounds.

Lawrence, Michael. *Baby loves* ill. by Adrian Reynolds. DK, 1999. ISBN 978-0-7894-3410-4 Subj: Babies. Emotions – love. Format, unusual – board books.

The caterpillar that roared ill. by Alison Bartlett. DK, 2000. ISBN 978-0-7894-5618-2 Subj: Animals. Behavior – imitation. Insects – butterflies, caterpillars. Self-concept.

Lawson, Dorie McCullough. *Tex* photos by author. Trafalgar Square, 2011. ISBN 978-1-57076-501-8 Subj: Careers – ranchers. Cowboys, cowgirls. Dreams. Imagination.

Lawson, Janet. *Audrey and Barbara* ill. by author. Atheneum, 2002. ISBN 978-0-689-83896-5 Subj: Animals – cats. Imagination.

Lawson, Julie. *Arizona Charlie and the Klondike Kid* ill. by Kasia Charko. Orca, 2003. ISBN 978-1-55143-250-2 Subj: Cowboys, cowgirls. Crime. Foreign lands – Canada. Theater.

Lawson, Robert. *They were strong and good* ill. by author. Viking, 1940. ISBN 978-0-670-69949-0 Subj: Caldecott award books. Family life. U.S. history – frontier & pioneer life.

Layne, Deborah Dover. *T is for teachers: a school alphabet* (Layne, Steven L.)

Layne, Steven L. *Love the baby* ill. by Ard Hoyt. Pelican, 2007. ISBN 978-1-58980-392-3 Subj: Animals – rabbits. Babies. Emotions – envy, jealousy. Family life – new sibling.

My brother Dan's delicious ill. by Chuck Galey. Pelican, 2003. ISBN 978-1-58980-071-7 Subj: Emotions – fear. Family life – brothers. Monsters.

T is for teachers: a school alphabet by Steven L. Layne and Deborah Dover Layne ill. by Doris Ettlinger. Sleeping Bear, 2005. ISBN 978-1-58536-159-5 Subj: ABC books. Careers – teachers. School.

Layton, Neal. *Hot, hot, hot* ill. by author. Candlewick, 2004. ISBN 978-0-7636-2148-3 Subj: Animals. Behavior – resourcefulness. Seasons – summer.

Smile if you're human ill. by author. Dial, 1998. ISBN 978-0-8037-2381-8 Subj: Aliens. Animals. Animals – gorillas. Family life.

Lazar, Tara. *The Monstore* ill. by James Burks. Simon & Schuster, 2013. ISBN 978-1-4424-2017-5 Subj: Family life – brothers & sisters. Monsters. Stores.

Lazo, Caroline. *Someday when my cat can talk* ill. by Kyrsten Brooker. Random House, 2008. ISBN 978-0-375-83754-8 Subj: Activities – traveling. Animals – cats. Imagination. Rhyming text.

Leaf, Munro. *The story of Ferdinand the bull* ill. by Robert Lawson. Viking, 1936. Subj: Animals – bulls, cows. Character traits – individuality. Foreign lands – Spain. Violence, nonviolence.

Wee Gillis ill. by Robert Lawson. Puffin, 1985, ©1938. ISBN 978-0-14-050535-1 Subj: Caldecott award honor books. Foreign lands – Scotland.

Lear, Edward. *Hilary Knight's the owl and the pussycat* (Knight, Hilary)

The owl and the pussycat ill. by Jan Brett. Putnam, 1991. ISBN 978-0-399-21925-2 Subj: Animals – cats. Birds – owls. Poetry.

The owl and the pussycat ill. by Paul Galdone. Houghton, 1987. ISBN 978-0-89919-505-6 Subj: Animals – cats. Birds – owls. Poetry.

The owl and the pussycat ill. by Anne Mortimer. HarperCollins, 2006. ISBN 978-0-06-027229-6 Subj: Animals – cats. Birds – owls. Poetry.

The Quangle Wangle's hat ill. by Louise Voce. Candlewick, 2005. ISBN 978-0-7636-1289-4 Subj: Clothing – hats. Humorous stories. Poetry.

Lears, Laurie. *Becky the brave: a story about epilepsy* ill. by Gail Piazza. Whitman, 2002. ISBN 978-0-8075-0601-1 Subj: Character traits – bravery. Family life – sisters. Illness – epilepsy. School.

Ben has something to say: a story about stuttering ill. by Karen Ritz. Whitman, 2000. ISBN 978-0-8075-0633-2 Subj: Animals – dogs. Disabilities – stuttering. Emotions – fear.

Ian's walk: a story about autism ill. by Karen Ritz. Whitman, 1998. ISBN 978-0-8075-3480-9 Subj: Behavior – lost. Family life – brothers & sisters. Disabilities – autism. Senses.

Megan's birthday tree: a story about open adoption ill. by Bill Farnsworth. Whitman, 2005. ISBN 978-0-8075-5036-6 Subj: Adoption. Birthdays. Family life. Moving. Trees.

Nathan's wish: a story about cerebral palsy ill. by Stacey Schuett. Whitman, 2005. ISBN 978-0-8075-7101-9 Subj: Birds – owls. Disabilities – cerebral palsy.

Waiting for Mr. Goose ill. by Karen Ritz. Whitman, 1999. ISBN 978-0-8075-8628-0 Subj: Birds – geese. Character traits – kindness to animals. Disabilities.

Leathers, Philippa. *The black rabbit* ill. by author. Candlewick, 2013. ISBN 978-0-7636-5714-7 Subj: Animals – rabbits. Shadows.

LeBox, Annette. *Salmon Creek* ill. by Karen Reczuch. Douglas & McIntyre, 2002. ISBN 978-0-88899-458-5 Subj: Fish. Poetry.

Wild bog tea ill. by Harvey Chan. Douglas & McIntyre, 2001. ISBN 978-0-88899-406-6 Subj: Family life – grandfathers. Nature. Swamps.

Lechner, Susan. *Followers of the north star: rhymes about African American heroes, heroines, and historical times* (Altman, Susan)

Ledwon, Peter. *Midnight math twelve terrific math games* ill. by Marilyn Mets. Holiday, 2000. ISBN 978-0-8234-1530-4 Subj: Animals. Counting, numbers. Games.

Lee, Chinlun. *Good dog, Paw* ill. by author. Candlewick, 2004. ISBN 978-0-7636-2178-0 Subj: Animals. Animals – dogs. Careers – veterinarians. Emotions – love.

The very kind rich lady and her one hundred dogs ill. by author. Candlewick, 2001. ISBN 978-0-7636-1290-0 Subj: Animals – dogs. Pets.

Lee, Dennis. *Bubblegum delicious* ill. by David McPhail. HarperCollins, 2001. ISBN 978-0-06-623709-1 Subj: Foreign lands – Canada. Poetry.

Lee, Ho Baek. *While we were out* ill. by author. Kane/Miller, 2002. ISBN 978-1-929132-44-7 Subj: Activities. Animals – rabbits. Pets.

Lee, Huy Voun. *In the leaves* ill. by author. Holt, 2005. ISBN 978-0-8050-6764-4 Subj: Farms. Foreign languages. Seasons – fall.

1, 2, 3 go! ill. by author. Holt, 2000. ISBN 978-0-8050-6205-2 Subj: Counting, numbers. Foreign languages.

Lee, Jeanne M. *Silent lotus* ill. by author. Farrar, 1991. ISBN 978-0-374-36911-8 Subj: Activities – dancing. Foreign lands – Cambodia. Disabilities – deafness. Disabilities – physical disabilities.

The song of Mu Lan ill. by author. Front Street, 1995. ISBN 978-1-886910-00-3 Subj: Careers – military. Character traits – bravery. Folk & fairy tales. Foreign lands – China.

Toad is the uncle of heaven: a Vietnamese folk tale ill. by reteller. Holt, 1985. ISBN 978-0-03-004652-0 Subj: Animals. Folk & fairy tales. Frogs & toads. Royalty. Weather – rain.

Lee, Mark. *20 big trucks in the middle of the street* ill. by Kurt Cyrus. Candlewick, 2013. ISBN 978-0-7636-5809-0 Subj: Counting, numbers. Trucks.

Lee, Milly. *Earthquake* ill. by Yangsook Choi. Farrar, 2001. ISBN 978-0-374-39964-1 Subj: Earthquakes. Ethnic groups in the U.S. – Chinese Americans. U.S. history.

Landed ill. by Yangsook Choi. Farrar, 2006. ISBN 978-0-374-34314-9 Subj: Ethnic groups in the U.S. – Chinese Americans. Immigrants.

Nim and the war effort ill. by Yangsook Choi. Farrar, 1997. ISBN 978-0-374-22262-8 Subj: Ethnic groups in the U.S. – Chinese Americans. Family life. U.S. history. War.

Lee, Quinlan B. *Crazy Christmas chaos* ill. by Clive Scruton. HarperCollins, 2002. ISBN 978-0-694-01683-9 Subj: Holidays – Christmas. Santa Claus.

Lee, Spike. *Giant steps to change the world* by Spike Lee and Tonya Lewis Lee ill. by Sean Qualls. Simon & Schuster, 2011. ISBN 978-0-689-86815-3

Subj: Character traits. Character traits – perseverance. Self-concept.

Please, puppy, please by Spike Lee and Tonya Lewis Lee ill. by Kadir Nelson. Simon & Schuster, 2005. ISBN 978-0-689-86804-7 Subj: Animals – dogs. Ethnic groups in the U.S. – African Americans. Pets.

Lee, Stan. *Stan Lee's superhero Christmas* ill. by Tim Jessell. Tegen, 2004. ISBN 978-0-06-056560-2 Subj: Holidays – Christmas. Santa Claus.

Lee, Suzy. *Mirror* ill. by author. Seven Footer, 2010. ISBN 978-1-934734-39-1 Subj: Mirrors. Wordless.

Shadow ill. by author. Chronicle, 2010. ISBN 978-0-8118-7280-5 Subj: Imagination. Shadows.

Wave ill. by author. Chronicle, 2008. ISBN 978-0-8118-5924-0 Subj: Sea & seashore – beaches. Wordless.

Lee, Tae-Jun. *Waiting for Mama: a bilingual picture book* ill. by Dong-Seong Kim. NorthSouth, 2007. ISBN 978-0-7358-2143-9 Subj: Family life – mothers. Foreign lands – Korea. Language.

Lee, Tonya Lewis. *Giant steps to change the world* (Lee, Spike)

Please, puppy, please (Lee, Spike)

Lee, Y. J. *The little moon princess* ill. by author. HarperCollins, 2010. ISBN 978-0-06-154736-2 Subj: Birds – sparrows. Royalty – princesses. Stars.

Lee-Tai, Amy. *A place where sunflowers grow / Sabaku ni saita himawari* ill. by Felicia Hoshino. Children's Book Press, 2006. ISBN 978-0-89239-215-5 Subj: Art. Ethnic groups in the U.S. – Japanese Americans. Flowers. Foreign languages. U.S. history. War.

Leedahl, Shelley A. *The bone talker* ill. by Bill Slavin. Red Deer, 2000. ISBN 978-0-88995-214-0 Subj: Activities – sewing. Communities, neighborhoods. Family life – grandmothers. Memories, memory. Old age. Quilts.

Leedy, Loreen. *Crazy like a fox: a simile story* ill. by author. Holiday House, 2008. ISBN 978-0-8234-1719-3 Subj: Animals – foxes. Birthdays. Language.

The dragon Halloween party ill. by author. Holiday, 1986. ISBN 978-0-8234-0611-1 Subj: Dragons. Holidays – Halloween. Parties. Rhyming text.

The dragon Thanksgiving feast ill. by author. Holiday, 1990. ISBN 978-0-8234-0828-3 Subj: Dragons. Food. Holidays – Thanksgiving. Rhyming text.

The edible pyramid: good eating every day ill. by author. Rev. ed. Holiday House, 2007. ISBN 978-0-8234-2074-2 Subj: Food. Health & fitness.

Follow the money ill. by author. Holiday, 2002. ISBN 978-0-8234-1587-8 Subj: Money.

Fraction action ill. by author. Holiday, 1994. ISBN 978-0-8234-1109-2 Subj: Animals. Counting, numbers. School.

The Furry News ill. by author. Holiday, 1990. ISBN 978-0-8234-0793-4 Subj: Activities – writing. Animals. Careers – journalists. Communication. Communities, neighborhoods.

The great graph contest ill. by author. Holiday House, 2005. ISBN 978-0-8234-1710-0 Subj: Animals – snails. Contests. Counting, numbers. Frogs & toads. Reptiles – lizards.

The great trash bash ill. by author. Holiday, 1991. ISBN 978-0-8234-0869-6 Subj: Animals. Ecology.

It's probably Penny ill. by author. Holt, 2007. ISBN 978-0-8050-7389-8 Subj: Animals – dogs.

Jack and the hungry giant eat right with MyPlate ill. by author. Holiday House, 2013. ISBN 978-0-8234-2602-7 Subj: Food. Giants. Health & fitness.

Mapping Penny's world ill. by author. Holt, 2000. ISBN 978-0-8050-6178-9 Subj: Animals – dogs. Maps.

Messages in the mailbox ill. by author. Holiday, 1991. ISBN 978-0-8234-0889-4 Subj: Activities – writing. Letters, cards. School.

Missing math: a number mystery ill. by author. Marshall Cavendish, 2008. ISBN 978-0-7614-5385-7 Subj: Animals. Counting, numbers. Mystery stories.

Mission — addition ill. by author. Holiday, 1997. ISBN 978-0-8234-1307-2 Subj: Animals. Counting, numbers. School.

Postcards from Pluto ill. by author. Holiday, 1993. ISBN 978-0-8234-1000-2 Subj: Astronomy. Space & space ships.

Seeing symmetry ill. by author. Holiday House, 2012. ISBN 978-0-8234-2360-6 Subj: Concepts.

There's a frog in my throat: 312 animal sayings from the horse's mouth by Loreen Leedy and Pat Street ill. by Loreen Leedy. Winslow, 2001. ISBN 978-1-890817-24-4 Subj: Animals. Language.

2 x 2 = boo! a set of spooky multiplication stories ill. by author. Holiday, 1995. ISBN 978-0-8234-1190-0 Subj: Counting, numbers. Holidays – Halloween. Witches.

Leeson, Christine. *Molly and the storm* ill. by Gaby Hansen. Tiger Tales, 2003. ISBN 978-1-58925-027-7 Subj: Animals. Animals – mice. Friendship. Weather – storms.

Lefebvre, Jason. *Too much glue* ill. by Zac Retz. Flashlight, 2013. ISBN 978-1-936261-27-7 Subj: Art. School.

Le Guin, Ursula K. *Cat dreams* ill. by S. D. Schindler. Scholastic, 2009. ISBN 978-0-545-04216-1 Subj: Animals – cats. Dreams. Rhyming text.

Lehman, Barbara. *Museum trip* ill. by author. Houghton, 2006. ISBN 978-0-618-58125-2 Subj: Imagination. Museums. Wordless.

Rainstorm ill. by author. Houghton, 2007. ISBN 978-0-618-75639-1 Subj: Imagination. Weather – rain. Wordless.

The red book ill. by author. Houghton, 2004. ISBN 978-0-618-42858-8 Subj: Books, reading. Caldecott award honor books. Friendship. Wordless.

The secret box ill. by author. Houghton Mifflin, 2011. ISBN 978-0-547-23868-5 Subj: Behavior – secrets. Imagination. School. Wordless.

Trainstop ill. by author. Houghton, 2008. ISBN 978-0-618-75640-7 Subj: Character traits – helpfulness. Imagination. Trains. Wordless.

Lehman-Wilzig, Tami. *Keeping the promise: a Torah's journey* ill. by Craig Orback. Kar-Ben, 2004. ISBN 978-1-58013-117-9 Subj: Holocaust. Jewish culture. Religion.

Nathan blows out the Hanukkah candles by Tami Lehman-Wilzig and Nicole Katzman ill. by Jeremy Tugeau. Lerner/Kar-Ben, 2011. ISBN 978-0-7613-6657-7 Subj: Family life – brothers. Disabilities – autism. Holidays – Hanukkah. Jewish culture.

Lehn, Barbara. *What is a scientist?* photos by Carol Krauss. Millbrook, 1998. ISBN 978-0-7613-1272-7 Subj: Careers – scientists. Science.

What is a teacher? photos by Carol Krauss. Millbrook, 2000. ISBN 978-0-7613-1713-5 Subj: Careers – teachers.

What is an athlete? photos by Carol Krauss. Millbrook, 2002. ISBN 978-0-7613-2258-0 Subj: Sports.

Lehrhaupt, Adam. *Warning: do not open this book!* ill. by Matthew Forsythe. Simon & Schuster, 2013. ISBN 978-1-4424-3582-7 Subj: Animals – monkeys. Birds – toucans. Books, reading. Reptiles – alligators, crocodiles.

Leigh, Heather. *Hey little baby!* ill. by Geneviève Côté. Simon & Schuster, 2012. ISBN 978-1-4169-8979-0 Subj: Babies. Senses.

Leijten, Aileen. *Hugging hour!* ill. by author. Philomel, 2009. ISBN 978-0-399-24680-7 Subj: Behavior – worrying. Family life – grandmothers. Sleepovers.

Leiner, Katherine. *Mama does the mambo* ill. by Edel Rodriguez. Hyperion, 2001. ISBN 978-0-7868-0646-1 Subj: Activities – dancing. Emotions – grief. Foreign lands – Cuba.

Lemniscates. *Silence* ill. by author. Magination, 2012. ISBN 978-1-4338-1137-1 Subj: Behavior – solitude. Character traits – patience. Noise, sounds.

Lendler, Ian. *An undone fairy tale* ill. by Whitney Martin. Simon & Schuster, 2005. ISBN 978-0-689-86677-7 Subj: Folk & fairy tales. Food. Humorous stories. Royalty – princesses.

Lendroth, Susan. *Calico Dorsey: mail dog of the mining camps* ill. by Adam Gustavson. Tricycle, 2010. ISBN 978-1-58246-318-6 Subj: Animals – dogs. Careers – postal workers. Post office. U.S. history.

Ocean wide, ocean deep ill. by Raul Allen. Tricycle, 2008. ISBN 978-1-58246-232-5 Subj: Family life. Rhyming text. Sailors. U.S. history.

Le Neouanic, Lionel. *Little smudge* ill. by author. Boxer, 2006. ISBN 978-1-905417-22-3 Subj: Character traits – being different. Concepts – shape. Emotions – loneliness. Friendship.

L'Engle, Madeleine. *The other dog* ill. by Christine Davenier. SeaStar, 2001. ISBN 978-1-58717-041-6 Subj: Animals – dogs. Babies.

Lenski, Lois. *The Easter Rabbit's parade* ill. by author. Random House, 2004. ISBN 978-0-375-92748-5 Subj: Animals. Holidays – Easter. Parades.

I like winter ill. by author. Random House, 2000, ©1950. ISBN 978-0-375-91068-5 Subj: Music. Poetry. Seasons – winter. Songs.

The little airplane ill. by author. Random House, 2003, ©1938. ISBN 978-0-375-91079-1 Subj: Airplanes, airports. Careers – airplane pilots.

The little family ill. by author. Random House, 2002, ©1932. ISBN 978-0-375-91077-7 Subj: Family life.

The little fire engine ill. by author. Random House, 2000, ©1946. ISBN 978-0-375-82263-6 Subj: Careers – firefighters.

The little sailboat ill. by author. Random House, 2003. ISBN 978-0-375-91078-4 Subj: Animals – dogs. Boats, ships. Sailors.

The little train ill. by author. Random House, 2002, ©1940. ISBN 978-0-375-82264-3 Subj: Careers – railroad engineers. Trains.

Now it's fall ill. by author. Random House, 2000, ©1948. ISBN 978-0-375-91069-2 Subj: Poetry. Seasons – fall.

Papa Small ill. by author. Random House, 2004, ©1951. ISBN 978-0-375-92749-2 Subj: Family life. Family life – fathers.

Policeman Small ill. by author. Random House, 2001, ©1962. ISBN 978-0-375-91072-2 Subj: Careers – police officers. Cities, towns.

Lent, Blair. *Ruby and Fred* ill. by author. Holt, 2000. ISBN 978-0-8050-6117-8 Subj: Animals – cats. Animals – dogs. Birds.

Leodhas, Sorche Nic *see* Alger, Leclaire Gowans

Leonard, Marcia. *Animal talk* photos by Dorothy Handelman. HarperCollins, 2000. ISBN 978-0-694-01363-0 Subj: Animals. Noise, sounds.

Babies help out photos by Dorothy Handelman. HarperCollins, 2001. ISBN 978-0-694-01369-2 Subj: Babies.

Favorite colors photos by Dorothy Handelman. HarperCollins, 2001. ISBN 978-0-694-01370-8 Subj: Concepts – color.

Food is fun! photos by Dorothy Handelman. HarperCollins, 2000. ISBN 978-0-694-01366-1 Subj: Activities – baking, cooking. Food.

Peek-a-boo, baby! photos by Dorothy Handelman. HarperCollins, 2000. ISBN 978-0-694-01373-9 Subj: Babies. Games.

Léonard, Marie. *Tibili, the little boy who didn't want to go to school* ill. by Andrée Prigent. Kane/Miller, 2002. ISBN 978-1-929132-20-1 Subj: Animals. Books, reading. Foreign lands – Africa. School – first day.

Leonetti, Mike. *Gretzky's game* ill. by Greg Banning. Raincoast, 2006. ISBN 978-1-55192-851-7 Subj: Sports – hockey.

Swinging for the fences: Hank Aaron and me ill. by David Kim. Chronicle, 2008. ISBN 978-0-8118-5662-1 Subj: Character traits – patience. Sports – baseball.

Lepp, Bil. *The King of Little Things* ill. by David Wenzel. Peachtree, 2013. ISBN 978-1-56145-708-3 Subj: Behavior – greed. Character traits – smallness. Concepts – size. Royalty – kings.

Lerch. *Swim! swim!* ill. by author. Scholastic, 2010. ISBN 978-0-545-09419-1 Subj: Emotions – loneliness. Fish. Friendship.

Lerman, Josh. *How to raise Mom and Dad: instructions from someone who figured it out* ill. by Greg Clarke. Dutton, 2009. ISBN 978-0-525-47870-6 Subj: Family life – parents. Humorous stories.

Lerner, Harriet Goldhor. *Franny B. Kranny, there's a bird in your hair* by Harriet Goldhor Lerner and Susan Henne Goldhor ill. by Helen Oxenbury. HarperCollins, 2000. ISBN 978-0-06-024683-9 Subj: Birds. Family life. Hair.

LeSieg, Theo., *see* Seuss, Dr.

Leslie, Amanda. *Alfie and Betty Bug* ill. by author. Handprint, 2001. ISBN 978-1-929766-33-8 Subj: Animals. Animals – elephants. Format, unusual – toy & movable books. Insects.

Are chickens stripy? ill. by author. Handprint, 2000. ISBN 978-1-929766-09-3 Subj: Animals. Birds – chickens. Format, unusual – toy & movable books.

Do crocodiles moo? ill. by author. Handprint, 2000. ISBN 978-1-929766-08-6 Subj: Animals. Concepts – color. Format, unusual – toy & movable books. Noise, sounds.

Flappy, waggy, wiggly ill. by author. Dutton, 1999. ISBN 978-0-525-46182-1 Subj: Animals. Format, unusual – toy & movable books.

Who's that scratching at my door? ill. by author. Handprint, 2001. ISBN 978-1-929766-19-2 Subj: Activities – playing. Animals. Animals – dogs. Format, unusual – toy & movable books.

LeSourd, Nancy. *Christy, Christmastime at Cutter Gap* by Nancy LeSourd and Catherine Marshall ill. by Bill Farnsworth. Based on the novel by Catherine Marshall. Zondervan, 2003. ISBN 978-0-310-70571-0 Subj: Holidays – Christmas. Religion. School.

Lessac, Frané. *Island Counting 123* ill. by author. Candlewick, 2005. ISBN 978-0-7636-1960-2 Subj: Counting, numbers. Foreign lands – Caribbean Islands. Rhyming text.

Lesser, Carolyn. *What a wonderful day to be a cow* ill. by Melissa Bay Mathis. Knopf, 1995. ISBN 978-0-679-92430-2 Subj: Animals. Days of the week, months of the year. Farms. Poetry. Seasons.

Lester, Alison. *Ernie dances to the didgeridoo* ill. by author. Houghton, 2001. ISBN 978-0-618-10442-0 Subj: Australian aborigines. Foreign lands – Australia. Letters, cards.

Noni the pony ill. by author. Simon & Schuster, 2012. ISBN 978-1-4424-5959-5 Subj: Animals. Animals – horses, ponies. Farms. Rhyming text.

Running with the horses ill. by author. NorthSouth, 2011. ISBN 978-0-7358-4002-7 Subj: Animals – horses, ponies. Character traits – bravery. Character traits – loyalty. Foreign lands – Austria.

Sophie Scott goes south ill. by author. Houghton Mifflin, 2013. ISBN 978-054408895-5 Subj: Activities – traveling. Foreign lands – Antarctic.

Lester, Helen. *All for me and none for all* ill. by Lynn Munsinger. Houghton Mifflin, 2012. ISBN 978-

0-547-68834-3 Subj: Animals – pigs. Behavior – greed. Behavior – sharing.

Author: a true story ill. by author. Houghton, 1997. ISBN 978-0-395-82744-4 Subj: Careers – writers. Disabilities.

Batter up Wombat ill. by Lynn Munsinger. Houghton, 2006. ISBN 978-0-618-73784-0 Subj: Animals – wombats. Sports – baseball. Weather – tornadoes.

Happy birdday, Tacky! ill. by Lynn Munsinger. Houghton Mifflin, 2013. ISBN 978-0-547-91228-8 Subj: Birds – penguins. Birthdays. Parties.

Hooway for Wodney Wat ill. by Lynn Munsinger. Houghton, 1999. ISBN 978-0-395-92392-4 Subj: Animals. Animals – rats. Behavior – bullying, teasing. Disabilities. School.

Hurty feelings ill. by Lynn Munsinger. Houghton, 2004. ISBN 978-0-618-41082-8 Subj: Animals – elephants. Animals – hippopotamuses. Behavior. Emotions. Sports – soccer.

It wasn't my fault ill. by Lynn Munsinger. Houghton, 1985. ISBN 978-0-395-35629-6 Subj: Animals. Cumulative tales.

Listen, Buddy ill. by Lynn Munsinger. Houghton, 1995. ISBN 978-0-395-72361-6 Subj: Animals – rabbits.

Me first ill. by Lynn Munsinger. Houghton, 1992. ISBN 978-0-395-58706-5 Subj: Animals – pigs. Behavior. Character traits – selfishness. Witches.

A porcupine named Fluffy ill. by Lynn Munsinger. Houghton, 1986. ISBN 978-0-395-36895-4 Subj: Animals – porcupines. Names.

Princess Penelope's parrot ill. by Lynn Munsinger. Houghton, 1996. ISBN 978-0-395-78320-7 Subj: Birds – parakeets, parrots. Character traits – selfishness. Emotions – anger. Royalty – princes. Royalty – princesses.

The revenge of the magic chicken ill. by Lynn Munsinger. Houghton, 1990. ISBN 978-0-395-50929-6 Subj: Birds – chickens. Magic.

Score one for the sloths ill. by Lynn Munsinger. Houghton, 2001. ISBN 978-0-618-10857-2 Subj: Animals – pigs. Animals – sloths. Character traits – ambition. Character traits – laziness. School.

The sheep in wolf's clothing ill. by Lynn Munsinger. Houghton, 2007. ISBN 978-0-618-86844-5 Subj: Animals – sheep. Animals – wolves. Clothing. Disguises.

Something might happen ill. by Lynn Munsinger. Houghton, 2003. ISBN 978-0-618-25406-4 Subj: Animals – lemurs. Behavior – worrying. Emotions – fear. Family life – aunts, uncles.

Tacky and the Emperor ill. by Lynn Munsinger. Houghton, 2000. ISBN 978-0-395-98120-7 Subj: Birds – penguins. Clothing.

Tacky and the Winter Games ill. by Lynn Munsinger. Houghton, 2005. ISBN 978-0-618-55659-5 Subj: Birds – penguins. Seasons – winter. Sports.

Tacky goes to camp ill. by Lynn Munsinger. Houghton, 2009. ISBN 978-0-618-98812-9 Subj: Birds – penguins. Camps, camping.

Tacky in trouble ill. by Lynn Munsinger. Houghton, 1998. ISBN 978-0-395-86113-4 Subj: Animals – elephants. Behavior. Birds – penguins.

Tacky the penguin ill. by Lynn Munsinger. Houghton, 1988. ISBN 978-0-395-45536-4 Subj: Animals – wolves. Birds – penguins. Character traits – individuality.

Tackylocks and the three bears ill. by Lynn Munsinger. Houghton, 2002. ISBN 978-0-618-22490-6 Subj: Birds – penguins. School. Theater.

Tacky's Christmas ill. by Lynn Munsinger. Houghton Mifflin, 2010. ISBN 978-0-547-17208-8 Subj: Birds – penguins. Holidays – Christmas. Santa Claus.

Three cheers for Tacky ill. by Lynn Munsinger. Houghton, 1994. ISBN 978-0-395-66841-2 Subj: Birds – penguins. Character traits – individuality. Cheerleading. Friendship. School.

Wodney Wat's wobot ill. by Lynn Munsinger. Harcourt, 2011. ISBN 978-0-547-36756-9 Subj: Animals. Animals – rats. Behavior – bullying, teasing. Disabilities. Robots. School.

Lester, J. D. *Mommy calls me Monkeypants* ill. by Hiroe Nakata. Robin Corey, 2009. ISBN 978-0-375-84502-4 Subj: Babies. Format, unusual – board books. Names. Rhyming text.

Lester, Julius. *Ackamarackus: Julius Lester's sumptuously silly fantastically funny fables* ill. by Emilie Chollat. Scholastic, 2001. ISBN 978-0-590-48913-3 Subj: Animals. Folk & fairy tales.

Albidaro and the mischievous dream ill. by Jerry Pinkney. Fogelman, 2000. ISBN 978-0-8037-1987-3 Subj: Animals. Behavior. Dreams.

Black cowboy, wild horses ill. by Jerry Pinkney. Dial, 1998. ISBN 978-0-8037-1788-6 Subj: Animals – horses, ponies. Cowboys, cowgirls. Ethnic groups in the U.S. – African Americans.

The hungry ghosts ill. by Geraldo Valério. Dial, 2009. ISBN 978-0-8037-2513-3 Subj: Ghosts.

John Henry ill. by Jerry Pinkney. Dial, 1994. ISBN 978-0-8037-1607-0 Subj: Caldecott award honor books. Character traits – perseverance. Character traits – pride. Ethnic groups in the U.S. – African Americans. Folk & fairy tales. Tall tales.

Let's talk about race ill. by Karen Barbour. HarperCollins, 2005. ISBN 978-0-06-028598-2 Subj: Ethnic groups in the U.S. Prejudice.

Sam and the tigers: a new telling of Little Black Sambo by Julius Lester and Helen Bannerman ill. by Jerry Pinkney. Dial, 1996. ISBN 978-0-8037-2029-9 Subj: Animals – tigers. Character traits – cleverness. Clothing. Family life. Foreign lands – India. Humorous stories.

Shining ill. by Terea D. Shaffer. Silver Whistle, 2000. ISBN 978-0-15-200773-7 Subj: Disabilities. Foreign lands – Africa.

What a truly cool world ill. by Joe Cepeda. Scholastic, 1999. ISBN 978-0-590-86468-8 Subj: Angels. Creation. Ethnic groups in the U.S. – African Americans. Religion.

Why heaven is far away ill. by Joe Cepeda. Scholastic, 2002. ISBN 978-0-439-17871-6 Subj: Angels. Ethnic groups in the U.S. – African Americans. Folk & fairy tales – pourquoi tales. Religion. Reptiles – snakes.

Lester, Mike. *A is for salad* ill. by author. Putnam, 2000. ISBN 978-0-399-23388-3 Subj: ABC books. School – first day.

Lesynski, Loris. *Night school* ill. by author. Firefly, 2001. ISBN 978-1-55037-585-5 Subj: Bedtime. Monsters. Night. School.

Rocksy ill. by author. Annick, 2002. ISBN 978-1-55037-751-4 Subj: Behavior – wishing. Rhyming text. Rocks.

Let it shine: three favorite spirituals ill. by Ashley Bryan. Simon & Schuster, 2007. ISBN 978-0-689-84732-5 Subj: Religion. Songs.

Let me call you sweetheart ill. by Amanda Haley. HarperCollins, 2002. ISBN 978-0-694-01556-6 Subj: Animals – dogs. Holidays – Valentine's Day. Pets. Songs.

Let there be light: poems and prayers for repairing the world comp. by Jane Breskin Zalben; ill. by Jane Breskin Zalben. Dutton, 2002. ISBN 978-0-525-46995-7 Subj: Poetry. Religion.

Let's count the raindrops ill. by Fumi Kosaka. Viking, 2001. ISBN 978-0-670-89689-9 Subj: Poetry. Weather.

Leuck, Laura. *Goodnight, baby monster* ill. by Nigel McMullen. HarperCollins, 2002. ISBN 978-0-06-029152-5 Subj: Bedtime. Monsters. Rhyming text.

I love my pirate papa ill. by Kyle M. Stone. Harcourt, 2007. ISBN 978-0-15-205664-3 Subj: Family life – fathers. Pirates. Rhyming text.

My beastly brother ill. by Scott Nash. HarperCollins, 2003. ISBN 978-0-06-029548-6 Subj: Family life – brothers. Monsters. Rhyming text.

My monster mama loves me so ill. by Mark Buehner. Lothrop, 1999. ISBN 978-0-688-16867-4 Subj: Family life – mothers. Monsters. Rhyming text.

One witch ill. by S. D. Schindler. Walker, 2003. ISBN 978-0-8027-8860-3 Subj: Counting, numbers. Holidays – Halloween. Rhyming text. Witches.

Levenson, George. *Pumpkin circle: the story of a garden* photos by Shmuel Thaler. Tricycle, 1999. ISBN 978-1-58246-004-8 Subj: Gardens, gardening. Rhyming text.

Levert, Mireille. *Eddie Longpants* ill. by author. Groundwood, 2005. ISBN 978-0-88899-671-8 Subj: Behavior – bullying, teasing. Character traits – being different.

An island in the soup ill. by author. Douglas & McIntyre, 2001. ISBN 978-0-88899-403-5 Subj: Food. Imagination.

The princess who had almost everything ill. by Josée Masse. Tundra, 2008. ISBN 978-0-88776-887-3 Subj: Behavior – boredom. Imagination. Royalty – princesses.

Levine, Abby. *Daddies give you horsey rides* ill. by John Bendall-Brunello. Whitman, 2004. ISBN 978-0-8075-1429-0 Subj: Activities. Family life – fathers. Rhyming text.

Gretchen Groundhog, it's your day! ill. by Nancy Cote. Whitman, 1998. ISBN 978-0-8075-3058-0 Subj: Animals – groundhogs. Holidays – Groundhog Day.

This is the matzah ill. by Paige Billin-Frye. Whitman, 2005. ISBN 978-0-8075-7885-8 Subj: Holidays – Passover. Holidays – Seder. Jewish culture. Rhyming text.

This is the pumpkin ill. by Paige Billin-Frye. Whitman, 1997. ISBN 978-0-8075-7886-5 Subj: Cumulative tales. Holidays – Halloween. Rhyming text.

This is the turkey ill. by Paige Billin-Frye. Whitman, 2000. ISBN 978-0-8075-7888-9 Subj: Family life. Holidays – Thanksgiving. Rhyming text.

Levine, Arthur A. *Monday is one day* ill. by Julian Hector. Scholastic, 2011. ISBN 978-0-439-78924-0 Subj: Activities – working. Counting, numbers. Days of the week, months of the year. Family life. Rhyming text.

Levine, Deb. *Parker picks* ill. by Pedro Martin. Simon & Schuster, 2002. ISBN 978-0-689-83456-1 Subj: Anatomy – noses. Behavior.

Levine, Ellen. *Henry's freedom box* ill. by Kadir Nelson. Scholastic, 2007. ISBN 978-0-439-77733-9 Subj: Caldecott award honor books. Character traits – freedom. Ethnic groups in the U.S. – African Americans. Slavery. U.S. history.

Seababy: a little otter returns home ill. by Jon Van Zyle. Walker, 2012. ISBN 978-0-8027-9808-4 Subj: Animals – babies. Animals – otters. Aquariums. Behavior – lost.

Levine, Gail Carson. *Betsy Red Hoodie* ill. by Scott Nash. HarperCollins, 2010. ISBN 978-0-06-146870-4 Subj: Animals – sheep. Animals – wolves. Birthdays. Careers – shepherds. Family life – grandmothers. Folk & fairy tales. Parties.

Betsy who cried wolf ill. by Scott Nash. HarperCollins, 2002. ISBN 978-0-06-028764-1 Subj: Animals – sheep. Animals – wolves. Careers – shepherds.

Forgive me, I meant to do it: false apology poems ill. by Matthew Cordell. HarperCollins, 2012. ISBN 978-0-06-178725-6 Subj: Behavior. Folk & fairy tales. Poetry.

Levine, Joan. *Topsy-turvy bedtime* ill. by Tony Auth. Candlewick, 2008. ISBN 978-0-7636-3008-9 Subj: Bedtime.

Levine, Michelle. *Ambulances* ill. with photos. Lerner, 2004. ISBN 978-0-8225-0769-7 Subj: Careers – emergency medical technicians. Trucks.

Red foxes ill. with photos. Lerner, 2004. ISBN 978-0-8225-3774-8 Subj: Animals – foxes.

Levine, Sara. *Bone by bone: comparing animal skeletons* ill. by T. S. Spookytooth. Millbrook, 2013. ISBN 978-0-7613-8464-9 Subj: Anatomy – skeletons. Animals.

Levins, Sandra. *Do you sing Twinkle? a story about remarriage and new family* ill. by Bryan Langdo. Magination, 2009. ISBN 978-1-4338-0539-4 Subj: Divorce. Family life – stepfamilies.

Levinson, Nancy Smiler. *Death Valley* ill. by Diane Dawson Hearn. Holiday, 2001. ISBN 978-0-8234-1566-3 Subj: Desert. Ecology.

Rain forests ill. by Diane Dawson Hearn. Holiday, 2008. ISBN 978-0-8234-1899-2 Subj: Ecology. Jungle.

Levinson, Riki. *I go with my family to Grandma's* ill. by Diane Goode. Dutton, 1990. ISBN 978-0-525-44261-5 Subj: Activities – photographing. Family life. Family life – grandmothers. Transportation.

Watch the stars come out ill. by Diane Goode. Dutton, 1985. ISBN 978-0-525-44205-9 Subj: Family life. Family life – grandmothers. U.S. history.

Levinthal, David. *Who pushed Humpty Dumpty? and other notorious nursery tale mysteries* ill. by John Nickle. Random House, 2012. ISBN 978-0-375-84195-8 Subj: Careers – detectives. Folk & fairy tales. Nursery rhymes.

Levis, Caron. *Stuck with the Blooz* ill. by Jon Davis. Harcourt, 2012. ISBN 978-0-547-74560-2 Subj: Emotions – sadness. Monsters.

Levitin, Sonia. *Boom town* ill. by Cat Bowman Smith. Orchard, 1998. ISBN 978-0-531-33043-2 Subj: Careers – bakers. Careers – miners. Cities, towns. U.S. history – frontier & pioneer life.

Nine for California ill. by Cat Bowman Smith. Orchard, 1996. ISBN 978-0-531-08877-7 Subj: Activities – traveling. Family life. U.S. history – frontier & pioneer life.

When Elephant goes to a party ill. by Jeff Seaver. Rising Moon, 2001. ISBN 978-0-87358-751-8 Subj: Animals – elephants. Etiquette. Humorous stories. Parties.

When Kangaroo goes to school ill. by Jeff Seaver. Rising Moon, 2001. ISBN 978-0-87358-791-4 Subj: Animals – kangaroos. Etiquette. School – first day.

Levy, Debbie. *We shall overcome: the story of a song* ill. by Vanessa Brantley Newton. Disney/Jump at the Sun, 2013. ISBN 978-1-4231-1954-8 Subj: Ethnic groups in the U.S. – African Americans. Prejudice. Slavery. Songs. Violence, nonviolence.

Levy, Janice. *Celebrate! It's cinco de mayo! / Celebremos! Es el cinco de mayo!* ill. by Loretta Lopez. Whitman, 2007. ISBN 978-0-8075-1176-3 Subj: Foreign lands – Mexico. Foreign languages. Holidays – Cinco de Mayo.

Lewandowski, Frrich. *It's Christmas again* ill. by Kathryn H. Delisle. Ambassador, 2000. ISBN 978-1-929039-04-3 Subj: Animals. Holidays – Christmas. Religion – Nativity.

Lewin, Betsy. *Groundhog day* ill. by author. Scholastic, 2000. ISBN 978-0-439-10802-7 Subj: Animals – groundhogs. Holidays – Groundhog Day. Shadows.

Horse song: the Naadam of Mongolia (Lewin, Ted)

Thumpy Feet ill. by author. Holiday House, 2013. ISBN 978-0-8234-2901-1 Subj: Activities – playing. Animals – cats.

Where is Tippy Toes? ill. by author. Simon & Schuster, 2010. ISBN 978-1-4169-3808-8 Subj: Animals – cats. Format, unusual – toy & movable books. Rhyming text.

Lewin, Hugh. *Jafta* ill. by Lisa Kopper. Carolrhoda, 1983. ISBN 978-0-87614-207-3 Subj: Emotions. Family life. Foreign lands – Africa.

Jafta — the homecoming ill. by Lisa Kopper. Knopf, 1994. ISBN 978-0-679-84722-9 Subj: Emotions. Family life – fathers. Foreign lands – South Africa.

Jafta's father ill. by Lisa Kopper. Carolrhoda, 1983. ISBN 978-0-87614-209-7 Subj: Family life – fathers. Foreign lands – Africa.

Jafta's mother ill. by Lisa Kopper. Carolrhoda, 1983. ISBN 978-0-87614-208-0 Subj: Family life – mothers. Foreign lands – Africa.

Lewin, Ted. *Amazon boy* ill. by author. Macmillan, 1993. ISBN 978-0-02-757383-1 Subj: Birthdays. Boats, ships. Cities, towns. Ecology. Foreign lands – Brazil. Rivers.

At Gleason's gym ill. by author. Macmillan, 2007. ISBN 978-1-59643-231-4 Subj: Sports – boxing.

Big Jimmy's Kum Kau Chinese take out ill. by author. HarperCollins, 2002. ISBN 978-0-688-16027-2 Subj: Activities – baking, cooking. Family life – fathers. Family life – sons. Restaurants. Stores.

Fair! ill. by author. Lothrop, 1997. ISBN 978-0-688-12851-7 Subj: Country. Fairs, festivals.

Horse song: the Naadam of Mongolia by Ted Lewin and Betsy Lewin ill. by authors. Lee & Low, 2008. ISBN 978-1-58430-277-3 Subj: Animals – horses, ponies. Foreign lands – Mongolia. Sports – racing.

How much? visiting markets around the world ill. by author. HarperCollins, 2006. ISBN 978-0-688-17553-5 Subj: Stores. World.

Market! ill. by author. Lothrop, 1996. ISBN 978-0-688-12162-4 Subj: Foreign lands. Stores.

Lewis, Anne Margaret. *Fly blanky fly* ill. by Elisa Chevarri. HarperCollins, 2012. ISBN 978-0-06-199996-3 Subj: Bedtime. Imagination.

What am I? Christmas ill. by Tom Mills. Whitman, 2011. ISBN 978-0-8075-8958-8 Subj: Format, unusual – toy & movable books. Holidays – Christmas.

Lewis, J. Patrick. *Arithme-tickle* ill. by Frank Remkiewicz. Harcourt, 2002. ISBN 978-0-15-216418-8 Subj: Counting, numbers. Rhyming text. Riddles & jokes.

Big is big and little little: a book of contrasts ill. by Bob Barner. Holiday House, 2007. ISBN 978-0-8234-1909-8 Subj: Concepts – opposites. Language. Rhyming text.

The bookworm's feast ill. by John O'Brien. Dial, 1999. ISBN 978-0-8037-1693-3 Subj: Games. Humorous stories. Poetry.

Doodle dandies: poems that take shape ill. by Lisa Desimini. Atheneum, 1998. ISBN 978-0-689-81075-6 Subj: Poetry.

Earth and me, our family tree ill. by Christopher Canyon. Dawn, 2002. ISBN 978-1-58469-031-3 Subj: Animals. Earth. Nature. Rhyming text.

Earth and you, a closer view ill. by Christopher Canyon. Dawn, 2001. ISBN 978-1-58469-016-0 Subj: Earth. Ecology. Geography. Nature. Rhyming text.

Face bug ill. by Kelly Murphy; photos by Frederic B. Siskind. Boyds Mills, 2013. ISBN 978-1-59078-925-4 Subj: Insects. Poetry.

The fantastic 5 and 10¢ store: a rebus adventure ill. by Valorie Fisher. Random House, 2010. ISBN 978-0-375-85878-9 Subj: Rebuses. Rhyming text. Stores.

Good mousekeeping ill. by Lisa Desimini. Atheneum, 2001. ISBN 978-0-689-83161-4 Subj: Animals. Homes, houses. Poetry.

A hippopotamusn't ill. by Victoria Chess. Dial, 1990. ISBN 978-0-8037-0519-7 Subj: Animals. Poetry.

The house of Boo ill. by Katya Krénina. Atheneum, 1998. ISBN 978-0-689-80356-7 Subj: Ghosts. Holidays – Halloween. Rhyming text.

Kindergarten cat ill. by Ailie Busby. Random House, 2010. ISBN 978-0-375-84475-1 Subj: Animals – cats. Rhyming text. School.

The little buggers: insect and spider poems ill. by Victoria Chess. Dial, 1998. ISBN 978-0-8037-1770-1 Subj: Insects. Poetry. Spiders.

Long was the winter road they traveled: a tale of the nativity ill. by Drew Bairley. Dial, 1997. ISBN 978-0-8037-1815-9 Subj: Animals. Holidays – Christmas. Poetry. Religion – Nativity.

Riddle-icious ill. by Debbie Tilley. Knopf, 1996. ISBN 978-0-679-94011-1 Subj: Poetry. Riddles & jokes.

Riddle-lightful: oodles of little riddle-poems ill. by Debbie Tilley. Knopf, 1998. ISBN 978-0-679-98760-4 Subj: Rhyming text. Riddles & jokes.

Tulip at the bat ill. by Amiko Hirao. Little, Brown, 2007. ISBN 978-0-316-61280-7 Subj: Animals. Humorous stories. Rhyming text. Sports – baseball.

What's looking at you, kid? ill. by Renée Graef. Sleeping Bear, 2012. ISBN 978-1-58536-793-1 Subj: Animals. Rhyming text.

World Rat Day: poems about real holidays you've never heard of ill. by Anna Raff. Candlewick, 2013. ISBN 978-0-7636-5402-3 Subj: Holidays. Poetry.

Lewis, Jacqueline Janette. *You are so wonderful* ill. by Jeremy Tugeau. Augsburg Fortress, 2003. ISBN 978-0-8066-4553-7 Subj: Creation. Religion. Rhyming text. Self-concept.

Lewis, Jill. *Don't read this book!* ill. by Deborah Allwright. Tiger Tales, 2010. ISBN 978-1-58925-094-9 Subj: Folk & fairy tales. Royalty – kings.

Lewis, Kevin. *Chugga-chugga choo-choo* ill. by Daniel Kirk. Hyperion, 1999. ISBN 978-0-7868-2379-6 Subj: Rhyming text. Toys – trains.

Dinosaur dinosaur ill. by Daniel Kirk. Scholastic, 2006. ISBN 978-0-439-60371-3 Subj: Dinosaurs. Rhyming text.

The lot at the end of my block ill. by Reg Cartwright. Hyperion, 2001. ISBN 978-0-7868-2512-7 Subj: Buildings. Careers – construction workers. Cumulative tales. Rhyming text.

Not inside this house! ill. by David Ercolini. Scholastic, 2011. ISBN 978-0-439-43981-7 Subj: Animals. Character traits – curiosity. Humorous stories. Nature. Rhyming text.

The runaway pumpkin ill. by S. D. Schindler. Orchard, 2003. ISBN 978-0-439-43974-9 Subj: Holidays – Halloween. Rhyming text.

Lewis, Kim. *Emma's lamb* ill. by author. Four Winds, 1991. ISBN 978-0-02-758821-7 Subj: Animals – sheep. Behavior – needing someone. Farms.

First snow ill. by author. Candlewick, 1993. ISBN 978-1-56402-194-6 Subj: Animals – dogs. Animals – sheep. Behavior – lost & found possessions. Farms. Toys – bears. Weather – snow.

Floss ill. by author. Candlewick, 1992. ISBN 978-1-56402-010-9 Subj: Activities – playing. Activities – working. Animals – dogs.

Friends ill. by author. Candlewick, 1997. ISBN 978-0-7636-0346-5 Subj: Emotions – anger. Farms. Friendship.

Good night, Harry ill. by author. Candlewick, 2004. ISBN 978-0-7636-2206-0 Subj: Animals – elephants. Bedtime. Friendship. Sleep. Toys.

Here we go Harry ill. by author. Candlewick, 2005. ISBN 978-0-7636-2549-8 Subj: Activities – flying. Animals. Animals – elephants. Friendship. Toys.

Hooray for Harry ill. by author. Candlewick, 2006. ISBN 978-0-7636-2962-5 Subj: Animals – elephants. Behavior – lost & found possessions. Friendship. Sleep. Toys.

Just like Floss ill. by author. Candlewick, 1998. ISBN 978-0-7636-0684-8 Subj: Animals – babies. Animals – dogs. Farms.

Little Baa ill. by author. Candlewick, 2001. ISBN 978-0-7636-1447-8 Subj: Animals – babies. Animals – sheep. Farms.

Little calf ill. by author. Candlewick, 2000. ISBN 978-0-7636-0899-6 Subj: Animals – babies. Animals – bulls, cows. Farms.

Little lamb ill. by author. Candlewick, 2000. ISBN 978-0-7636-0900-9 Subj: Animals – babies. Animals – sheep. Farms.

Little puppy ill. by author. Candlewick, 2000. ISBN 978-0-7636-0901-6 Subj: Animals – babies. Animals – dogs. Farms.

My friend Harry ill. by author. Candlewick, 1995. ISBN 978-1-56402-617-0 Subj: Animals – elephants. School. Toys.

One summer day ill. by author. Candlewick, 1996. ISBN 978-1-56402-883-9 Subj: Activities – walking. Country. Seasons – summer. Tractors.

A puppy for Annie ill. by author. Candlewick, 2006. ISBN 978-0-7636-3200-7 Subj: Animals – dogs. Pets.

Seymour and Henry ill. by author. Candlewick, 2009. ISBN 978-0-7636-4243-3 Subj: Activities – playing. Behavior – hiding. Birds – ducks. Family life – mothers.

The shepherd boy ill. by author. Four Winds, 1990. ISBN 978-0-02-758581-0 Subj: Animals – sheep. Careers – shepherds.

Lewis, Paeony. *I'll always love you* ill. by Penny Ives. Tiger Tales, 2002. ISBN 978-0-613-52270-0 Subj: Animals – bears. Behavior – worrying. Family life – mothers.

No more cookies! ill. by Brita Granström. Scholastic, 2005. ISBN 978-0-439-68332-6 Subj: Food. Toys.

No more yawning! ill. by Brita Granström. Scholastic, 2008. ISBN 978-0-545-02957-5 Subj: Bedtime.

Lewis, Rob. *Friends* ill. by author. Holt, 2001. ISBN 978-0-8050-6691-3 Subj: Animals – rabbits. Communities, neighborhoods. Friendship.

Lewis, Rose A. *Every year on your birthday* ill. by Jane Dyer. Little, Brown, 2007. ISBN 978-0-316-52552-7 Subj: Adoption. Birthdays. Ethnic groups in the U.S. – Chinese Americans.

I love you like crazy cakes ill. by Jane Dyer. Little, 2002. ISBN 978-0-316-52576-3 Subj: Adoption. Babies. Family life. Foreign lands – China.

Orange Peel's pocket ill. by Grace Zong. Abrams, 2010. ISBN 978-0-8109-8394-6 Subj: Adoption. Clothing. Ethnic groups in the U.S. – Chinese Americans.

Sweet dreams ill. by Jen Corace. Abrams, 2012. ISBN 978-1-4197-0189-4 Subj: Bedtime. Lullabies. Nature. Rhyming text.

Lewis, Wendy A. *In Abby's hands* ill. by Marilyn Mets and Peter Ledwon. Red Deer, 2003. ISBN 978-0-88995-282-9 Subj: Animals – dogs. Character traits – confidence.

Lewison, Wendy Cheyette. *"Buzz," said the bee* ill. by Hans Wilhelm. Scholastic, 1992. ISBN 978-0-590-44185-8 Subj: Animals. Cumulative tales. Noise, sounds. Rhyming text.

Going to sleep on the farm ill. by Juan Wijngaard. Dial, 1992. ISBN 978-0-8037-1097-9 Subj: Animals. Bedtime. Cumulative tales. Farms. Rhyming text. Sleep.

Mud ill. by Maryann Cocca-Leffler. Random House, 2001. ISBN 978-0-679-80251-8 Subj: Activities – playing. Rhyming text.

The princess and the potty ill. by Rick Brown. Simon & Schuster, 1994. ISBN 978-0-671-87284-7 Subj: Behavior – growing up. Royalty – princesses. Toilet training.

So many boots ill. by Tony Griego. Scholastic, 2000. ISBN 978-0-439-09865-6 Subj: Clothing – boots. Insects. Rhyming text. Weather – rain.

Two is for twins ill. by Hiroe Nakata. Penguin, 2006. ISBN 978-0-670-06128-0 Subj: Counting, numbers. Multiple births – twins. Rhyming text.

Lia, Simone. *Red's great chase* ill. by author. Dutton, 2000. ISBN 978-0-525-46213-2 Subj: Activities – playing. Monsters.

Liao, Jimmy. *The sound of colors: a journey of the imagination* ill. by author. Little, Brown, 2005. ISBN 978-0-316-93992-8 Subj: Disabilities – blindness. Imagination.

Libby, Barbara. *I rode the red horse: Secretariat's Belmont race* ill. by author. Eclipse, 2003. ISBN 978-1-58150-096-7 Subj: Animals – horses, ponies. Sports – racing.

Libney, Varda. *What I like about Passover* ill. by author. Simon & Schuster, 2002. ISBN 978-0-689-84491-1 Subj: Format, unusual – board books. Holidays – Passover. Jewish culture. Religion.

Lichtenheld, Tom. *Bridget's beret* ill. by author. Holt, 2010. ISBN 978-0-8050-8775-8 Subj: Activities – drawing. Careers – artists. Clothing – hats. Self-concept.

Cloudette ill. by author. Holt, 2011. ISBN 978-0-8050-8776-5 Subj: Character traits – smallness. Concepts – size. Weather – clouds. Weather – rain.

E-mergency! by Tom Lichtenheld and Ezra Fields Meyer ill. by Tom Lichtenheld. Chronicle, 2011. ISBN 978-0-8118-7898-2 Subj: ABC books. Humorous stories.

Everything I know about monsters ill. by author. Simon & Schuster, 2002. ISBN 978-0-689-84381-5 Subj: Monsters.

Everything I know about pirates ill. by author. Simon & Schuster, 2000. ISBN 978-0-689-82625-2 Subj: Pirates.

What's with this room? ill. by author. Little, Brown, 2005. ISBN 978-0-316-59286-4 Subj: Behavior – messy. Character traits – cleanliness. Humorous stories.

Liebman, Daniel. *I want to be a builder* ill. with photos. Firefly, 2003. ISBN 978-1-55297-758-3 Subj: Careers – construction workers.

I want to be a cowboy ill. with photos. Firefly, 1999. ISBN 978-1-55209-447-1 Subj: Careers. Cowboys, cowgirls.

I want to be a doctor ill. with photos. Firefly, 2000. ISBN 978-1-55209-463-1 Subj: Careers – doctors.

I want to be a firefighter ill. with photos. Firefly, 1999. ISBN 978-1-55209-448-8 Subj: Careers – firefighters. Communities, neighborhoods. Fire.

I want to be a librarian ill. with photos. Firefly, 2001. ISBN 978-1-55297-691-3 Subj: Careers – librarians.

I want to be a mechanic ill. with photos. Firefly, 2003. ISBN 978-1-55297-695-1 Subj: Careers – mechanics.

I want to be a musician ill. with photos. Firefly, 2003. ISBN 978-1-55297-760-6 Subj: Careers – musicians.

I want to be a nurse ill. with photos. Firefly, 2001. ISBN 978-1-55209-568-3 Subj: Careers – nurses.

I want to be a police officer ill. with photos. Firefly, 2000. ISBN 978-1-55209-467-9 Subj: Careers – police officers. Communities, neighborhoods.

I want to be a teacher ill. with photos. Firefly, 2001. ISBN 978-1-55209-572-0 Subj: Careers – teachers.

I want to be a truck driver ill. with photos. Firefly, 2001. ISBN 978-1-55209-576-8 Subj: Careers – truck drivers.

I want to be a vet ill. with photos. Firefly, 2000. ISBN 978-1-55209-471-6 Subj: Careers – veterinarians.

I want to be a zookeeper ill. with photos. Firefly, 2003. ISBN 978-1-55297-699-9 Subj: Careers – zookeepers.

Liersch, Anne. *Nell and Fluffy* ill. by Christa Unzner. NorthSouth, 2001. ISBN 978-0-7358-1424-0 Subj: Animals – guinea pigs. Character traits – responsibility. Pets.

Lies, Brian. *Bats at the ballgame* ill. by author. Harcourt, 2010. ISBN 978-0-547-24970-4 Subj: Animals – bats. Rhyming text. Sports – baseball.

Bats at the beach ill. by author. Houghton, 2006. ISBN 978-0-618-55744-8 Subj: Activities – picnicking. Animals – bats. Rhyming text. Sea & seashore – beaches.

Bats at the library ill. by author. Houghton, 2008. ISBN 978-0-618-99923-1 Subj: Animals – bats. Books, reading. Libraries. Rhyming text.

Light, Steve. *The Christmas giant* ill. by author. Candlewick, 2010. ISBN 978-0-7636-4692-9 Subj: Friendship. Giants. Holidays – Christmas. Mythical creatures – elves. Trees.

Diggers go ill. by author. Chronicle, 2013. ISBN 978-1-4521-1864-2 Subj: Format, unusual – board books. Machines. Trucks.

The shoemaker extraordinaire ill. by author. Abrams, 2003. ISBN 978-0-8109-4236-3 Subj: Careers – shoemakers. Clothing – shoes. Folk & fairy tales. Giants.

Trains go ill. by author. Chronicle, 2012. ISBN 978-0-8118-7942-2 Subj: Format, unusual – board books. Noise, sounds. Trains.

Zephyr takes flight ill. by author. Candlewick, 2012. ISBN 978-0-7636-5695-9 Subj: Activities – flying. Imagination.

Lillegard, Dee. *Balloons, balloons, balloons* ill. by Bernadette Pons. Penguin, 2007. ISBN 978-0-525-45940-8 Subj: Animals – rabbits. Rhyming text. Toys – balloons.

The Big Bug Ball ill. by Rex Barron. Putnam, 1999. ISBN 978-0-399-23121-6 Subj: Activities – dancing. Parties. Rhyming text.

Go! poetry in motion: poems ill. by Valeri Gorbachev. Random House, 2006. ISBN 978-0-375-92387-6 Subj: Concepts – motion. Poetry. Transportation.

Hello school! ill. by Don Carter. Knopf, 2001. ISBN 978-0-375-91020-3 Subj: Poetry. School.

Tortoise brings the mail ill. by Jillian Lund. Dutton, 1997. ISBN 978-0-525-45156-3 Subj: Animals. Careers – postal workers. Letters, cards. Reptiles – turtles, tortoises.

Wake up house! rooms full of poems ill. by Don Carter. Knopf, 2000. ISBN 978-0-679-98351-4 Subj: Furniture. Homes, houses. Poetry.

Lilly, Melinda. *From slavery to freedom* ill. by Lori McElrath-Eslick. Rourke, 2003. ISBN 978-1-58952-363-0 Subj: Slavery. U.S. history.

Lin, Grace. *Dim sum for everyone* ill. by author. Knopf, 2001. ISBN 978-0-375-91082-1 Subj: Activities – baking, cooking. Ethnic groups in the U.S. – Chinese Americans. Food. Restaurants.

Fortune cookie fortunes ill. by author. Knopf, 2004. ISBN 978-0-375-91521-5 Subj: Character traits – luck. Ethnic groups in the U.S. – Chinese Americans. Food.

Kite flying ill. by author. Knopf, 2002. ISBN 978-0-375-91520-8 Subj: Kites.

Lissy's friends ill. by author. Penguin, 2007. ISBN 978-0-670-06072-6 Subj: Activities – making things. Character traits – shyness. Friendship. School.

Okie-dokie, Artichokie ill. by author. Viking, 2003. ISBN 978-0-670-03623-3 Subj: Animals – giraffes. Animals – monkeys. Friendship. Holidays – Christmas. Homes, houses. Noise, sounds.

Olvina flies ill. by author. Holt, 2003. ISBN 978-0-8050-6711-8 Subj: Activities – traveling. Airplanes, airports. Animals – pigs. Birds – chickens. Emotions – fear.

Olvina swims ill. by author. Holt, 2007. ISBN 978-0-8050-7661-5 Subj: Birds – chickens. Birds – penguins. Emotions – fear. Hawaii. Sports – swimming.

Our seasons by Grace Lin and Ranida T. McKneally ill. by Grace Lin. Charlesbridge, 2006. ISBN 978-1-57091-360-0 Subj: Seasons.

The red thread: an adoption fairy tale ill. by author. Whitman, 2007. ISBN 978-0-8075-6922-1 Subj: Adoption. Folk & fairy tales. Foreign lands – China. Royalty.

Robert's snowflakes: artists' snowflakes for cancer's cure. Comp. by Grace Lin & Robert Mercer. Penguin, 2005. ISBN 978-0-670-06044-3 Subj: Art. Illness – cancer. Poetry. Weather – snow.

Thanking the moon: celebrating the Mid-Autumn Moon Festival ill. by author. Random House, 2010. ISBN 978-0-375-86101-7 Subj: Ethnic groups in the U.S. – Chinese Americans. Fairs, festivals. Family life. Food. Holidays. Moon.

The ugly vegetables ill. by author. Charlesbridge, 1999. ISBN 978-0-88106-336-3 Subj: Ethnic groups in the U.S. – Chinese Americans. Flowers. Food. Gardens, gardening.

Linch, Tanya. *My duck* ill. by author. Scholastic, 2000. ISBN 978-0-439-20670-9 Subj: Activities – writing. Birds – ducks. Careers – teachers.

Lind, Michael. *Bluebonnet girl* ill. by Kate Kiesler. Holt, 2003. ISBN 978-0-8050-6573-2 Subj: Behavior – greed. Flowers. Folk & fairy tales. Indians of North America – Comanche. Weather – droughts.

Lindaman, Jane. *Read anything good lately?* (Allen, Susan)

Used any numbers lately? (Allen, Susan)

Zip it! ill. by Nancy Carlson. Carolrhoda, 2012. ISBN 978-0-7613-5592-2 Subj: Clothing. Family life – fathers. Humorous stories.

Lindbergh, Reeve. *The awful aardvarks go to school* ill. by Tracey Campbell Pearson. Viking, 1997. ISBN 978-0-670-85920-7 Subj: ABC books. Animals – aardvarks. Behavior – misbehavior. Rhyming text. School.

The awful aardvarks shop for school ill. by Tracey Campbell Pearson. Viking, 2000. ISBN 978-0-

670-88763-7 Subj: Animals – aardvarks. Behavior – misbehavior. Rhyming text. Shopping.

Bridget and the gray wolves ill. by Pija Lindenbaum. R&S Books, 2001. ISBN 978-91-29-65395-3 Subj: Animals – wolves. Behavior – lost. Emotions – fear.

The circle of days ill. by Cathie Felstead. Candlewick, 1998. ISBN 978-0-7636-0357-1 Subj: Creation. Religion.

The day the goose got loose ill. by Steven Kellogg. Dial, 1990. ISBN 978-0-8037-0409-1 Subj: Animals. Behavior – misbehavior. Birds – geese. Farms.

The hippie grandmother ill. by Abby Carter. Candlewick, 2002. ISBN 978-0-7636-0671-8 Subj: Family life – grandmothers. Rhyming text.

Homer the library cat ill. by Anne Wilsdorf. Candlewick, 2011. ISBN 978-0-7636-3448-3 Subj: Animals – cats. Libraries. Rhyming text.

Johnny Appleseed ill. by Kathy Jakobsen. Little, 1990. ISBN 978-0-316-52618-0 Subj: Activities – traveling. Gardens, gardening. Rhyming text. Tall tales. Trees. U.S. history – frontier & pioneer life.

Midnight farm ill. by Susan Jeffers. Dial, 1987. ISBN 978-0-8037-0333-9 Subj: Animals. Counting, numbers. Farms. Night.

My little grandmother often forgets ill. by Kathryn Brown. Candlewick, 2007. ISBN 978-0-7636-1989-3 Subj: Behavior – forgetfulness. Family life – grandmothers. Memories, memory. Old age.

Nobody owns the sky: the story of "brave Bessie" Coleman ill. by Pamela Paparone. Candlewick, 1996. ISBN 978-1-56402-533-3 Subj: Activities – flying. Airplanes, airports. Ethnic groups in the U.S. – African Americans. Rhyming text.

North country spring ill. by Liz Sivertson. Houghton, 1997. ISBN 978-0-395-82819-9 Subj: Animals. Nature. Rhyming text. Seasons – spring.

On morning wings ill. by Holly Meade. Candlewick, 2002. ISBN 978-0-7636-1106-4 Subj: Religion. Rhyming text.

Our nest ill. by Jill McElmurry. Candlewick, 2004. ISBN 978-0-7636-1286-3 Subj: Homes, houses. Rhyming text.

Lindenbaum, Pija. *Mini Mia and her darling uncle* ill. by author. R&S Books, 2007. ISBN 978-91-29-66734-9 Subj: Emotions – envy, jealousy. Family life – aunts, uncles.

Linders, Clara. *The very best door of all* by Clara Linders and Marijke ten Cate ill. by Marijke ten Cate. Front Street, 2001. ISBN 978-1-886910-64-5 Subj: Animals – badgers. Animals – porcupines. Birthdays. Friendship. Gifts.

Lindgren, Astrid. *Pippi Longstocking's after-Christmas party* ill. by Michael Chesworth. Viking, 1996. ISBN 978-0-679-86790-6 Subj: Character traits – assertiveness. Foreign lands – Sweden. Holidays – Christmas. Parties.

Lindgren, Barbro. *Benny and the binky* ill. by Olof Landström. Farrar, 2002. ISBN 978-91-29-65497-4 Subj: Animals – pigs. Babies. Sibling rivalry.

Benny's had enough ill. by Olof Landström. R&S Books, 1999. ISBN 978-91-29-64563-7 Subj: Animals – pigs. Behavior – running away. Family life – mothers.

Oink, oink, Benny ill. by Olof Landström. Farrar, 2008. ISBN 978-91-29-66855-1 Subj: Animals – pigs. Behavior – misbehavior. Family life – brothers.

Sam's ball ill. by Eva Eriksson. Morrow, 1983. ISBN 978-0-688-02359-1 Subj: Animals – cats. Toys – balls.

Sam's bath ill. by Eva Eriksson. Morrow, 1983. ISBN 978-0-688-02362-1 Subj: Activities – bathing. Animals – dogs.

Sam's car ill. by Eva Eriksson. Morrow, 1982. ISBN 978-0-688-01263-2 Subj: Behavior – sharing. Toys.

Sam's cookie ill. by Eva Eriksson. Morrow, 1982. ISBN 978-0-688-01267-0 Subj: Behavior – sharing. Pets.

Sam's lamp ill. by Eva Eriksson. Morrow, 1983. ISBN 978-0-688-02356-0 Subj: Safety.

Sam's potty ill. by Eva Eriksson. Morrow, 1986. ISBN 978-0-688-06603-1 Subj: Behavior – growing up. Toilet training.

Sam's teddy bear ill. by Eva Eriksson. Morrow, 1982. ISBN 978-0-688-01270-0 Subj: Toys – bears.

Sam's wagon ill. by Eva Eriksson. Morrow, 1986. ISBN 978-0-688-05803-6 Subj: Animals – dogs. Toys – wagons.

Lindsay, Jeanne Warren. *Do I have a daddy?* ill. by Jami Moffett. Morning Glory, 2000. ISBN 978-1-885356-62-8 Subj: Family life. Family life – fathers. Family life – mothers.

Ling, Nancy Tupper. *My sister, Alicia May* ill. by Shennen Bersani. Pleasant St, 2009. ISBN 978-0-9792035-9-6 Subj: Family life – sisters. Disabilities – Down syndrome.

Link, Martin A. *The goat in the rug* (Blood, Charles L.)

Lionni, Leo. *Alexander and the wind-up mouse* ill. by author. Pantheon, 1969. ISBN 978-0-394-90914-1 Subj: Animals – mice. Caldecott award honor books. Emotions – envy, jealousy. Friendship. Toys.

The alphabet tree ill. by author. Knopf, 2004. ISBN 978-0-394-91016-1 Subj: ABC books. Activities – writing. Insects – butterflies, caterpillars.

The biggest house in the world ill. by author. Pantheon, 1968. ISBN 978-0-394-90944-8 Subj: Animals. Behavior – greed.

A busy year ill. by author. Knopf, 1992. ISBN 978-0-679-92464-7 Subj: Animals – mice. Nature. Seasons. Trees.

A color of his own ill. by author. Delmar, 1990. ISBN 978-0-8273-4114-2 Subj: Character traits – individuality. Concepts – color. Reptiles – lizards.

Cornelius ill. by author. Pantheon, 1983. ISBN 978-0-394-95419-6 Subj: Character traits – being different. Reptiles – alligators, crocodiles.

An extraordinary egg ill. by author. Knopf, 1994. ISBN 978-0-679-95840-6 Subj: Eggs. Friendship. Frogs & toads. Reptiles – alligators, crocodiles.

Fish is fish ill. by author. Pantheon, 1970. ISBN 978-0-394-90440-5 Subj: Behavior – misunderstanding. Fish. Friendship. Frogs & toads.

Frederick ill. by author. Random House, 1973, ©1967. ISBN 978-0-394-82614-1 Subj: Animals – mice. Caldecott award honor books. Music.

Frederick's fables ill. by author. Pantheon, 1985. ISBN 978-0-394-87710-5 Subj: Animals.

Geraldine, the music mouse ill. by author. Pantheon, 1979. ISBN 978-0-394-94238-4 Subj: Animals – mice. Music. Musical instruments – flutes.

The greentail mouse ill. by author. Pantheon, 1973. ISBN 978-0-394-92678-0 Subj: Animals – mice. Mardi Gras.

Inch by inch ill. by author. Astor-Honor, 1960. ISBN 978-0-8392-3010-6 Subj: Birds. Caldecott award honor books. Concepts – measurement. Insects.

It's mine! a fable ill. by author. Knopf, 1986. ISBN 978-0-394-97000-4 Subj: Behavior – fighting, arguing. Frogs & toads.

Let's make rabbits ill. by author. Knopf, 1992. Originally published: New York: Pantheon Books, ©1982. ISBN 978-0-679-82640-8 Subj: Activities. Animals – rabbits. Art. Imagination.

Little blue and little yellow ill. by author. Mulberry, 1994. ISBN 978-0-688-13285-9 Subj: Concepts – color. Friendship.

Matthew's dream ill. by author. Knopf, 1991. ISBN 978-0-679-91075-6 Subj: Animals – mice. Careers – artists. Museums.

Mr. McMouse ill. by author. Knopf, 1992. ISBN 978-0-679-93890-3 Subj: Animals – mice. Friendship. Self-concept.

Nicolas, where have you been? ill. by author. Knopf, 1987. ISBN 978-0-394-98370-7 Subj: Animals – mice. Friendship.

Pezzettino ill. by author. Pantheon, 1975. ISBN 978-0-394-93156-2 Subj: Character traits – individuality. Concepts – shape. Self-concept.

Six crows ill. by author. Knopf, 1988. ISBN 978-0-394-99572-4 Subj: Birds – crows. Birds – owls. Farms.

Swimmy ill. by author. Random House, 1973, ©1963. ISBN 978-0-394-82620-2 Subj: Caldecott award honor books. Fish. Sea & seashore.

Theodore and the talking mushroom ill. by author. Pantheon, 1971. ISBN 978-0-394-82312-6 Subj: Animals – mice. Character traits – optimism.

Tico and the golden wings ill. by author. Knopf, 1975, ©1964. ISBN 978-0-394-83078-0 Subj: Birds. Character traits – generosity. Character traits – individuality. Character traits – questioning. Folk & fairy tales.

Tillie and the wall ill. by author. Knopf, 1989. ISBN 978-0-394-92155-6 Subj: Animals – mice. Behavior – seeking better things.

Lipkind, William. *Finders keepers* by William Lipkind and Nicolas Mordvinoff ill. by Nicolas Mordvinoff. Harcourt, 1951. ISBN 978-0-15-227529-7 Subj: Animals – dogs. Caldecott award books. Character traits – selfishness.

Lipp, Frederick. *The caged birds of Phnom Penh* ill. by Ronald Himler. Holiday, 2001. ISBN 978-0-8234-1534-2 Subj: Behavior – wishing. Birds. Foreign lands – Canada.

Running shoes ill. by Jason Gaillard. Charlesbridge, 2008. ISBN 978-1-58089-175-2 Subj: Clothing – shoes. Foreign lands – Cambodia. Poverty. School.

Lipson, Eden Ross. *Applesauce season* ill. by Mordicai Gerstein. Roaring Brook, 2009. ISBN 978-1-59643-216-1 Subj: Activities – baking, cooking. Food. Seasons – fall.

Lipton, Leonard. *Puff, the magic dragon* (Yarrow, Peter)

Lish, Ted. *The three little puppies and the big bad flea* ill. by Charles Jordan. Munchweiler, 2001. ISBN 978-0-7940-0001-1 Subj: Animals – dogs. Family life – mothers. Homes, houses. Insects – fleas.

Lister, Clare. *My first Passover [board book]* ill. with photos. DK, 2002. ISBN 978-0-7894-8452-9 Subj: Format, unusual – board books. Holidays – Passover. Jewish culture. Religion.

Lister, Mary. *The Winter King and the Summer Queen* ill. by Diana Mayo. Barefoot, 2002. ISBN

978-1-84148-357-3 Subj: Behavior – sharing. Seasons. Seasons – summer. Seasons – winter.

Lithgow, John. *Carnival of the animals* ill. by Boris Kulikov. Simon & Schuster, 2004. ISBN 978-0-689-86721-7 Subj: Animals. Imagination. Museums. Rhyming text. School – field trips.

I got two dogs ill. by Robert Neubecker. Simon & Schuster, 2008. ISBN 978-1-4169-5881-9 Subj: Animals – dogs. Songs.

I'm a manatee ill. by Ard Hoyt. Simon & Schuster, 2003. ISBN 978-0-689-85427-9 Subj: Animals – manatees. Imagination. Rhyming text.

Mahalia Mouse goes to college ill. by Igor Oleynikov. Simon & Schuster, 2007. ISBN 978-1-4169-2715-0 Subj: Animals – mice. Rhyming text. School.

Marsupial Sue ill. by Jack E. Davis. Simon & Schuster, 2001. ISBN 978-0-689-84394-5 Subj: Animals – kangaroos. Rhyming text. Self-concept. Songs.

Marsupial Sue presents "The Runaway Pancake" ill. by Jack E. Davis. Simon & Schuster, 2005. ISBN 978-0-689-87847-3 Subj: Animals – kangaroos. Theater.

Micawber ill. by C. F. Payne. Simon & Schuster, 2002. ISBN 978-0-689-83341-0 Subj: Animals – squirrels. Careers – artists. Museums. Rhyming text.

Never play music right next to the zoo ill. by Leeza Hernandez. Simon & Schuster, 2013. ISBN 978-1-4424-6743-9 Subj: Animals. Dreams. Music. Musical instruments. Songs. Zoos.

The remarkable Farkle McBride ill. by C. F. Payne. Simon & Schuster, 2000. ISBN 978-0-689-83340-3 Subj: Careers – conductors (music). Careers – musicians. Format, unusual – toy & movable books. Musical instruments. Rhyming text.

Little Bear's Valentine ill. by Heather Green. HarperCollins, 2003. ISBN 978-0-06-052244-5 Subj: Animals. Animals – bears. Family life – mothers. Holidays – Valentine's Day.

Little, Jean. *Pippin the Christmas pig* ill. by H. Werner Zimmermann. Scholastic, 2004. ISBN 978-0-439-65062-5 Subj: Animals. Animals – pigs. Gifts. Holidays – Christmas.

Little old lady who swallowed a fly. *I know an old lady* retold by G. Brian Karas; ill. by reteller. Scholastic, 1994. ISBN 978-0-590-46575-5 Subj: Cumulative tales. Folk & fairy tales. Foreign lands – England. Insects – flies. Rhyming text. Songs. Witches.

I know an old lady who swallowed a fly ill. by Stephen Gulbis. Scholastic, 2001. ISBN 978-0-439-24328-5 Subj: Cumulative tales. Folk & fairy tales. Foreign lands – England. Format, unusual – toy & movable books. Insects – flies. Songs.

I know an old lady who swallowed a fly retold by Glen Rounds; ill. by reteller. Holiday, 1990. ISBN 978-0-8234-0814-6 Subj: Cumulative tales. Folk & fairy tales. Foreign lands – England. Insects – flies. Songs.

I know an old lady who swallowed a fly retold by Nadine Bernard Westcott; ill. by reteller. Little, 1980. ISBN 978-0-316-93128-1 Subj: Cumulative tales. Folk & fairy tales. Foreign lands – England. Insects – flies. Songs.

There was an old lady who swallowed a fly ill. by Pam Adams. Child's Play, 1990. ISBN 978-0-85953-021-7 Subj: Cumulative tales. Folk & fairy tales. Foreign lands – Canada. Format, unusual – toy & movable books. Insects – flies. Songs.

There was an old lady who swallowed a fly retold by Simms Taback; ill. by reteller. Viking, 1997. ISBN 978-0-670-86939-8 Subj: Caldecott award honor books. Cumulative tales. Folk & fairy tales. Format, unusual. Insects – flies. Rhyming text. Songs.

There was an old monkey who swallowed a frog by Jennifer Ward; ill. by Steve Gray. Marshall Cavendish, 2010. ISBN 978-0-7614-5580-6 Subj: Animals. Cumulative tales. Folk & fairy tales. Frogs & toads. Rhyming text. Songs.

There was an old pirate who swallowed a fish by Jennifer Ward; ill. by Steve Gray. Amazon, 2012. ISBN 978-0-7614-6196-8 Subj: Cumulative tales. Fish. Pirates. Songs.

The little red hen. *The little red hen* ill. by Byron Barton. HarperCollins, 1993. ISBN 978-0-06-021676-4 Subj: Activities – baking, cooking. Animals. Behavior – sharing. Birds – chickens. Character traits – laziness. Cumulative tales. Farms. Folk & fairy tales.

The little red hen retold by Harriet Ziefert; ill. by Emily Bolam. Viking, 1995. ISBN 978-0-670-86050-0 Subj: Activities – baking, cooking. Animals. Behavior – sharing. Birds – chickens. Character traits – laziness. Cumulative tales. Farms. Folk & fairy tales.

The little red hen ill. by Paul Galdone. Seabury Pr., 1973. ISBN 978-0-8164-3099-4 Subj: Activities – baking, cooking. Animals. Behavior – sharing. Birds – chickens. Character traits – laziness. Cumulative tales. Farms. Folk & fairy tales.

Little red hen by Alan Garner; ill. by Norman Messenger. DK, 1997. ISBN 978-0-7894-1171-6 Subj: Activities – baking, cooking. Animals. Behavior – sharing. Birds – chickens. Character traits – laziness. Cumulative tales. Farms. Folk & fairy tales.

The little red hen retold by Jerry Pinkney; ill. by reteller. Penguin, 2006. ISBN 978-0-8037-2935-

3 Subj: Activities – baking, cooking. Animals. Behavior – sharing. Birds – chickens. Character traits – laziness. Cumulative tales. Farms. Folk & fairy tales.

The little red hen by Mary Finch; ill. by Kate Slater. Barefoot, 2013. ISBN 978-1-84686-575-6 Subj: Activities – baking, cooking. Animals. Behavior – sharing. Birds – chickens. Character traits – laziness. Cumulative tales. Farms. Folk & fairy tales. Plants.

The little red hen retold by John Escott; ill. by Annie West. Gingham Dog, 2003. ISBN 978-1-57768-492-3 Subj: Activities – baking, cooking. Animals. Behavior – sharing. Birds – chickens. Character traits – laziness. Cumulative tales. Farms. Folk & fairy tales.

The little red hen retold by Margot Zemach; ill. by reteller. Farrar, 1983. ISBN 978-0-374-34621-8 Subj: Activities – baking, cooking. Animals. Behavior – sharing. Birds – chickens. Character traits – laziness. Cumulative tales. Farms. Folk & fairy tales.

The little red hen: an old fable retold by Heather Forest; ill. by Susan Gaber. August House, 2006. ISBN 978-0-87483-795-7 Subj: Activities – baking, cooking. Animals. Behavior – sharing. Birds – chickens. Character traits – laziness. Cumulative tales. Folk & fairy tales. Plants.

The Little Red Hen and the Passover matzah by Leslie Kimmelman; ill. by Paul Meisel. Holiday House, 2010. ISBN 978-0-8234-1952-4 Subj: Activities – baking, cooking. Animals. Behavior – sharing. Birds – chickens. Character traits – laziness. Folk & fairy tales. Holidays – Passover. Jewish culture.

The Little Red Hen makes a pizza retold by Philemon Sturges; ill. by Amy Walrod. Dutton, 1999. ISBN 978-0-525-45953-8 Subj: Activities – baking, cooking. Animals. Behavior – sharing. Birds – chickens. Character traits – laziness. Cumulative tales. Farms. Folk & fairy tales.

Littlesugar, Amy. *Clown child* ill. by Kimberly Bulcken Root. Penguin, 2006. ISBN 978-0-399-23106-3 Subj: Circus. Clowns, jesters.

Freedom school, yes! ill. by Floyd Cooper. Philomel, 2001. ISBN 978-0-399-23006-6 Subj: Ethnic groups in the U.S. – African Americans. School.

Lisette's angel ill. by Max Ginsburg. Dial, 2002. ISBN 978-0-8037-2435-8 Subj: Careers – military. Foreign lands – France. War.

Tree of hope ill. by Floyd Cooper. Philomel, 1999. ISBN 978-0-399-23300-5 Subj: Careers – actors. Ethnic groups in the U.S. – African Americans. Poverty. Theater. U.S. history.

Litwin, Eric. *Pete the cat: I love my white shoes* ill. by James Dean. HarperCollins, 2010. ISBN 978-0-06-190622-0 Subj: Animals – cats. Clothing – shoes. Concepts – color.

Pete the cat: rocking in my school shoes ill. by James Dean. HarperCollins, 2011. ISBN 978-0-06-191024-1 Subj: Activities – singing. Animals – cats. Clothing – shoes. Rhyming text. School.

Pete the cat and his four groovy buttons ill. by James Dean. HarperCollins, 2012. ISBN 978-0-06-211058-9 Subj: Activities – singing. Animals – cats. Clothing. Counting, numbers.

Pete the cat saves Christmas ill. by James Dean. HarperCollins, 2012. ISBN 978-0-06-211062-6 Subj: Animals – cats. Holidays – Christmas. Rhyming text. Santa Claus.

Liu, Jae Soo. *Yellow umbrella* ill. by author. Kane/Miller, 2002. ISBN 978-1-929132-36-2 Subj: Concepts – color. Music. Umbrellas. Weather – rain. Wordless.

Liu, Julia. *Gus, the dinosaur bus* ill. by Bei Lynn. Houghton Mifflin, 2013. ISBN 978-0-547-90573-0 Subj: Buses. Dinosaurs. Traffic, traffic signs.

Livingston, Irene. *Finklehopper Frog* ill. by Brian Lies. Tricycle, 2003. ISBN 978-1-58246-075-8 Subj: Activities – running. Animals – rabbits. Character traits – individuality. Frogs & toads. Rhyming text.

Finklehopper Frog cheers ill. by Brian Lies. Ten Speed, 2005. ISBN 978-1-58246-138-0 Subj: Activities – picnicking. Animals – rabbits. Friendship. Frogs & toads. Rhyming text.

Livingston, Myra Cohn. *Abraham Lincoln: a man for all the people* ill. by Samuel Byrd. Holiday, 1993. ISBN 978-0-8234-1049-1 Subj: Poetry. U.S. history.

Calendar ill. by Will Hillenbrand. Holiday House, 2007. ISBN 978-0-8234-1725-4 Subj: Calendars. Days of the week, months of the year. Poetry. Seasons.

Celebrations ill. by Leonard Everett Fisher. Holiday, 1985. ISBN 978-0-8234-0550-3 Subj: Holidays. Poetry.

Keep on singing: a ballad of Marian Anderson ill. by Samuel Byrd. Holiday, 1994. ISBN 978-0-8234-1098-9 Subj: Ethnic groups in the U.S. – African Americans. Poetry. U.S. history.

Valentine poems ill. by Patience Brewster. Holiday, 1987. ISBN 978-0-8234-0587-9 Subj: Animals. Holidays – Valentine's Day.

Livingstone, Star. *Harley* ill. by Molly Bang. SeaStar, 2001. ISBN 978-1-58717-049-2 Subj: Animals – llamas. Animals – sheep.

Livinson, Nancy Smiler. *North Pole, South Pole* ill. by Diane Dawson Hearn. Holiday, 2002. ISBN

978-0-8234-1737-7 Subj: Animals. Foreign lands – Antarctic. Foreign lands – Arctic. Weather.

Liwska, Renata. *Little panda* ill. by author. Houghton, 2008. ISBN 978-0-618-96627-1 Subj: Animals – pandas. Family life – grandfathers.

Red wagon ill. by author. Penguin, 2011. ISBN 978-0-399-25237-2 Subj: Activities – playing. Animals. Animals – foxes. Imagination. Toys – wagons.

Ljungkvist, Laura. *Follow the line* ill. by author. Penguin, 2006. ISBN 978-0-670-06049-8 Subj: Counting, numbers. Imagination. Picture puzzles.

Follow the line around the world ill. by author. Viking, 2008. ISBN 978-0-670-06334-5 Subj: Animals. Geography. World.

Follow the line through the house ill. by author. Penguin, 2007. ISBN 978-0-670-06225-6 Subj: Homes, houses. Imagination. Picture puzzles. Rhyming text.

Follow the line to school ill. by author. Penguin, 2011. ISBN 978-0-670-01226-8 Subj: Picture puzzles. School.

Pepi sings a new song ill. by author. Simon & Schuster, 2010. ISBN 978-1-4169-9138-0 Subj: Activities – singing. Birds – parakeets, parrots. Foreign languages.

Toni's topsy-turvy telephone day ill. by author. Abrams, 2001. ISBN 978-0-8109-4486-2 Subj: Food. Humorous stories. Parties.

Llewellyn, Claire. *Crocodile* ill. by Simon Mendez. NorthWord, 2004. ISBN 978-1-55971-900-1 Subj: Animals – babies. Format, unusual. Reptiles – alligators, crocodiles.

Duck ill. by Simon Mendez. NorthWord, 2004. ISBN 978-1-55971-878-3 Subj: Animals – babies. Birds – ducks. Format, unusual.

Ladybug ill. by Simon Mendez. NorthWord, 2004. ISBN 978-1-55971-892-9 Subj: Format, unusual. Insects – ladybugs.

Tree ill. by Simon Mendez. NorthWord, 2004. ISBN 978-1-55971-879-0 Subj: Food. Format, unusual. Trees.

Lloyd, David. *Polly Molly Woof Woof* ill. by Charlotte Hard. Candlewick, 2000. ISBN 978-0-7636-0755-5 Subj: Animals – dogs. Emotions – happiness.

Lloyd, Jennifer. *The best thing about kindergarten* ill. by Qin Leng. Simply Read, 2013. ISBN 978-1-897476-82-6 Subj: Memories, memory. School.

Lloyd, Sam. *Chief Rhino to the rescue!* ill. by author. Holt, 2009. ISBN 978-0-8050-8821-2 Subj: Animals – rhinoceros. Careers – firefighters. Character traits – bravery.

Doctor Meow's big emergency ill. by author. Holt, 2008. ISBN 978-0-8050-8819-9 Subj: Animals – cats. Careers – doctors. Hospitals.

Mr. Pusskins: a love story ill. by author. Simon & Schuster, 2006. ISBN 978-1-4169-2517-0 Subj: Animals – cats. Behavior – running away.

Mr. Pusskins and Little Whiskers: another love story ill. by author. Atheneum, 2008. ISBN 978-1-4169-5796-6 Subj: Animals – cats.

Lloyd-Jones, Sally. *Being a pig is nice: a child's-eye view of manners* ill. by Dan Krall. Random House, 2009. ISBN 978-0-375-84187-3 Subj: Animals. Behavior. Etiquette.

How to be a baby — by me, the big sister ill. by Sue Heap. Random House, 2007. ISBN 978-0-375-83843-9 Subj: Babies. Family life – brothers & sisters.

How to get a job — by me, the boss ill. by Sue Heap. Random House, 2011. ISBN 978-0-375-86664-7 Subj: Careers.

How to get married by me, the bride ill. by Sue Heap. Random House, 2009. ISBN 978-0-375-84118-7 Subj: Weddings.

Just because you're mine ill. by Frank Endersby. HarperCollins, 2012. ISBN 978-0-06-201476-4 Subj: Animals – squirrels. Bedtime. Emotions – love. Family life.

Old MacNoah had an ark ill. by Jill Newton. HarperCollins, 2008. ISBN 978-0-06-055717-1 Subj: Animals. Boats, ships. Cumulative tales. Music. Noise, sounds. Religion – Noah. Songs. Weather – floods.

Song of the stars: a Christmas story ill. by Alison Jay. Zonderkidz, 2011. ISBN 978-0-310-72291-5 Subj: Holidays – Christmas. Religion – Nativity.

Time to say goodnight ill. by Jane Chapman. HarperCollins, 2006. ISBN 978-0-06-054328-0 Subj: Animals. Bedtime. Rhyming text.

The ultimate guide to grandmas and grandpas! ill. by Michael Emberley. HarperCollins, 2008. ISBN 978-0-06-075687-1 Subj: Animals. Family life – grandparents.

Lo, Ginnie. *Auntie Yang's great soybean picnic* ill. by Beth Lo. Lee & Low, 2012. ISBN 978-1-60060-442-3 Subj: Activities – picnicking. Ethnic groups in the U.S. – Chinese Americans. Family life. Family life – aunts, uncles. Food.

Lobb, Janice. *Color and noise! Let's play with toys!* ill. by Peter Utton and Ann Savage. Kingfisher, 2001. ISBN 978-0-7534-5362-9 Subj: Concepts – color. Noise, sounds. Science. Toys.

Counting sheep! How do we sleep? ill. by Peter Utton and Ann Savage. Kingfisher, 2001. ISBN 978-0-7534-5361-2 Subj: Science. Sleep.

Dig and sow! How do plants grow? ill. by Peter Utton and Ann Savage. Kingfisher, 2000. ISBN 978-0-7534-5245-5 Subj: Plants. Science.

Listen and see! What's on TV? ill. by Peter Utton and Ann Savage. Kingfisher, 2001. ISBN 978-0-7534-5336-0 Subj: Science. Television.

Splish! Splosh! Why do we wash? ill. by Peter Utton and Ann Savage. Kingfisher, 2000. ISBN 978-0-7534-5244-8 Subj: Activities – bathing. Character traits – cleanliness. Health & fitness. Riddles & jokes. Water.

Lobel, Anita. *Alison's zinnia* ill. by author. Greenwillow, 1990. ISBN 978-0-688-08866-8 Subj: ABC books. Flowers.

Animal antics: A to Z ill. by author. HarperCollins, 2005. ISBN 978-0-06-051815-8 Subj: ABC books. Animals. Circus.

Hello, day! ill. by author. Greenwillow, 2008. ISBN 978-0-06-078765-3 Subj: Animals. Day. Sun.

Lena's sleep sheep ill. by author. Knopf, 2013. ISBN 978-0-449-81025-5 Subj: Animals – sheep. Bedtime. Clothing – costumes. Moon.

Nini here and there ill. by author. HarperCollins, 2007. ISBN 978-0-06-078767-7 Subj: Animals – cats. Moving.

Nini lost and found ill. by author. Random House, 2010. ISBN 978-0-375-85880-2 Subj: Animals – cats. Behavior – lost & found possessions.

One lighthouse, one moon ill. by author. Greenwillow, 2000. ISBN 978-0-688-15540-7 Subj: Animals – cats. Counting, numbers. Days of the week, months of the year. Lighthouses.

Ten hungry rabbits: counting and color concepts ill. by author. Knopf, 2012. ISBN 978-0-375-86864-1 Subj: Animals – rabbits. Concepts – color. Counting, numbers. Food. Gardens, gardening.

Lobel, Arnold. *Days with Frog and Toad* ill. by author. HarperCollins, 1979. ISBN 978-0-06-023964-0 Subj: Friendship. Frogs & toads.

Fables ill. by author. HarperCollins, 1980. ISBN 978-0-06-023974-9 Subj: Animals. Caldecott award books.

Frog and Toad all year ill. by author. HarperCollins, 1976. ISBN 978-0-06-023951-0 Subj: Friendship. Frogs & toads. Seasons.

Frog and Toad are friends ill. by author. HarperCollins, 1970. ISBN 978-0-06-023958-9 Subj: Caldecott award honor books. Friendship. Frogs & toads.

The frog and toad pop-up book ill. by author. HarperCollins, 1986. ISBN 978-0-06-023986-2 Subj: Format, unusual – toy & movable books. Frogs & toads.

Frog and Toad together ill. by author. HarperCollins, 1971. ISBN 978-0-06-023959-6 Subj: Friendship. Frogs & toads.

The frogs and toads all sang ill. by author and Adrianne Lobel. HarperCollins, 2009. ISBN 978-0-06-180022-1 Subj: Frogs & toads. Rhyming text.

Ming Lo moves the mountain ill. by author. Greenwillow, 1982. ISBN 978-0-688-00611-2 Subj: Foreign lands – China. Moving.

Odd owls and stout pigs: a book of nonsense ill. by Adrianne Lobel. HarperCollins, 2009. ISBN 978-0-06-180054-2 Subj: Animals – pigs. Birds – owls. Rhyming text.

On Market Street ill. by Anita Lobel. Greenwillow, 1981. ISBN 978-0-688-84309-0 Subj: ABC books. Caldecott award honor books. Rhyming text. Shopping. Stores.

Lobel, Gillian. *Does anybody love me?* ill. by Rosalind Beardshaw. Good Books, 2002. ISBN 978-1-56148-368-6 Subj: Behavior – running away. Family life – grandfathers. Family life – parents. Self-concept.

Little Honey Bear and the smiley moon ill. by Tim Warnes. Good Books, 2006. ISBN 978-1-56148-533-8 Subj: Animals. Animals – bears. Behavior – lost. Family life – mothers. Moon. Seasons – winter.

Too small for honey cake ill. by Sebastien Braun. Harcourt, 2006. ISBN 978-0-15-206097-8 Subj: Animals – foxes. Babies. Family life. Sibling rivalry.

Locker, Thomas. *Cloud dance* ill. by author. Harcourt, 2000. ISBN 978-0-15-202231-0 Subj: Weather – clouds.

Mountain dance ill. by author. Harcourt, 2001. ISBN 978-0-15-202622-6 Subj: Mountains. Poetry.

Sky tree ill. by author and Candace Christiansen. HarperCollins, 1995. ISBN 978-0-06-024884-0 Subj: Science. Seasons. Trees.

Water dance ill. by author. Harcourt, 2002. ISBN 978-0-15-216396-9 Subj: Nature. Poetry. Water. Weather.

Where the river begins ill. by author. Dial, 1984. ISBN 978-0-89370-090-4 Subj: Family life – grandfathers. Rivers.

Lodge, Bernard. *How scary* ill. by author. Houghton, 2001. ISBN 978-0-618-11547-1 Subj: Counting, numbers. Monsters.

Shoe Shoe Baby ill. by Katherine Lodge. Random House, 2000. ISBN 978-0-375-81084-8 Subj: Clothing – shoes.

Lodge, Jo. *Happy birthday, Moo Moo* ill. by author. Little, 2001. ISBN 978-0-316-66644-2 Subj: Animals. Birthdays. Format, unusual – toy & movable books. Parties.

Happy Snappy! a Mr.Croc book about feelings ill. by author. IPG/Hodder, 2012. ISBN 978-0-3409-8879-4 Subj: Emotions. Format, unusual – board books. Format, unusual – toy & movable books. Reptiles – alligators, crocodiles.

Moo Moo goes to the city ill. by author. Little, 2002. ISBN 978-0-316-65582-8 Subj: Animals – bulls, cows. Cities, towns. Format, unusual – toy & movable books.

Loehr, Patrick. *Mucumber McGee and the lunch lady's liver* ill. by author. HarperCollins, 2008. ISBN 978-0-06-082330-6 Subj: Food. Humorous stories. Rhyming text. School.

Loewen, Nancy. *Busy buzzers* ill. by Brandon Reibeling. Picture Window, 2004. ISBN 978-1-4048-0143-1 Subj: Insects – bees. Science.

Hungry hoppers ill. by Brandon Reibeling. Picture Window, 2004. ISBN 978-1-4048-0146-2 Subj: Insects – grasshoppers.

The last day of kindergarten ill. by Sachiko Yoshikawa. Marshall Cavendish, 2011. ISBN 978-0-7614-5807-7 Subj: School.

Living lights ill. by Brandon Reibeling. Picture Window, 2004. ISBN 978-1-4048-0145-5 Subj: Insects – fireflies.

Night fliers ill. by Brandon Reibeling. Picture Window, 2004. ISBN 978-1-4048-0144-8 Subj: Insects – moths.

Spotted beetles ill. by Melissa Voda. Picture Window, 2004. ISBN 978-1-4048-0142-4 Subj: Insects – ladybugs.

Tiny workers ill. by Brandon Reibeling. Picture Window, 2004. ISBN 978-1-4048-0141-7 Subj: Insects – ants.

Logan, Bob. *Rocket town* ill. by author. Sourcebooks, 2011. ISBN 978-1-4022-4186-4 Subj: Format, unusual – board books. Space & space ships.

Logue, Mary. *Sleep like a tiger* ill. by Pamela Zagarenski. Houghton Mifflin, 2012. ISBN 978-0-547-64102-7 Subj: Animals. Bedtime. Caldecott award honor books. Sleep.

Lohans, Alison. *Waiting for the sun* ill. by Marilyn Mets and Peter Ledwon. Red Deer, 2002. ISBN 978-0-88995-240-9 Subj: Babies. Birth. Family life – new sibling.

Loki. *Jake Greenthumb* ill. by Jason Gaillard. Mondo, 2002. ISBN 978-1-59034-186-5 Subj: Character traits – helpfulness. Gardens, gardening. Plants.

Lomas Garza, Carmen. *In my family* ill. by author. Children's Book Press, 1996. ISBN 978-0-89239-138-7 Subj: Ethnic groups in the U.S. – Hispanic Americans. Family life. Foreign languages.

Londner, Renee. *Stones for Grandpa* ill. by Martha Avilés. Lerner/Kar-Ben, 2013. ISBN 978-0-7613-7495-4 Subj: Death. Family life – grandfathers. Jewish culture.

London, Jonathan. *Ali, child of the desert* ill. by Ted Lewin. Lothrop, 1997. ISBN 978-0-688-12561-5 Subj: Behavior – lost. Desert. Foreign lands – Morocco. Shopping. Weather – sandstorms.

Baby whale's journey ill. by Jon Van Zyle. Chronicle, 1999. ISBN 978-0-8118-2496-5 Subj: Animals – babies. Animals – whales.

Count the ways, Little Brown Bear ill. by Margie Moore. Dutton, 2002. ISBN 978-0-525-46097-8 Subj: Animals – bears. Counting, numbers. Emotions – love. Family life – mothers.

Crunch munch ill. by Michael Rex. Silver Whistle, 2001. ISBN 978-0-15-202603-5 Subj: Animals. Food.

Do your ABC's, Little Brown Bear ill. by Margie Moore. Penguin, 2005. ISBN 978-0-525-47360-2 Subj: ABC books. Animals – bears. Family life – fathers.

Dream weaver ill. by Rocco Baviera. Silver Whistle, 1997. ISBN 978-0-15-200944-1 Subj: Nature. Spiders.

Fireflies, fireflies, light my way ill. by Linda Messier. Viking, 1996. ISBN 978-0-670-85442-4 Subj: Animals. Indians of North America. Lullabies. Night. Rhyming text.

Flamingo sunset ill. by Kristina Rodanas. Marshall Cavendish, 2008. ISBN 978-0-7614-5384-9 Subj: Birds – flamingos. Nature.

Froggy eats out ill. by Frank Remkiewicz. Viking, 2001. ISBN 978-0-670-89686-8 Subj: Behavior – misbehavior. Family life – parents. Food. Frogs & toads. Restaurants.

Froggy gets dressed ill. by Frank Remkiewicz. Viking, 1992. ISBN 978-0-670-84249-0 Subj: Clothing. Frogs & toads. Hibernation. Seasons – winter. Weather – snow.

Froggy goes to bed ill. by Frank Remkiewicz. Viking, 2000. ISBN 978-0-670-88860-3 Subj: Bedtime. Frogs & toads.

Froggy goes to camp ill. by Frank Remkiewicz. Viking, 2008. ISBN 978-0-670-01098-1 Subj: Camps, camping. Frogs & toads.

Froggy goes to Hawaii ill. by Frank Remkiewicz. Penguin, 2011. ISBN 978-0-670-01221-3 Subj: Activities – traveling. Frogs & toads. Hawaii.

Froggy goes to school ill. by Frank Remkiewicz. Viking, 1996. ISBN 978-0-670-86726-4 Subj: Clothing. Dreams. Frogs & toads. School – first day.

Froggy goes to the doctor ill. by Frank Remkiewicz. Viking, 2002. ISBN 978-0-670-03578-6 Subj: Careers – doctors. Frogs & toads. Humorous stories.

Froggy learns to swim ill. by Frank Remkiewicz. Viking, 1995. ISBN 978-0-670-85551-3 Subj: Emotions – fear. Frogs & toads. Sports – swimming.

Froggy plays in the band ill. by Frank Remkiewicz. Viking, 2002. ISBN 978-0-670-03532-8 Subj: Animals. Contests. Frogs & toads. Musical instruments – bands. Parades.

Froggy plays soccer ill. by Frank Remkiewicz. Viking, 1999. ISBN 978-0-670-88257-1 Subj: Animals. Frogs & toads. Sports – soccer.

Froggy plays T-ball ill. by Frank Remkiewicz. Penguin, 2007. ISBN 978-0-670-06187-7 Subj: Frogs & toads. Sports – T-ball.

Froggy rides a bike ill. by Frank Remkiewicz. Penguin, 2006. ISBN 978-0-670-06099-3 Subj: Frogs & toads. Sports – bicycling.

Froggy's first Christmas ill. by Frank Remkiewicz. Viking, 2000. ISBN 978-0-670-89220-4 Subj: Animals. Frogs & toads. Holidays – Christmas.

Froggy's first kiss ill. by Frank Remkiewicz. Viking, 1998. ISBN 978-0-670-87064-6 Subj: Emotions – love. Frogs & toads. Holidays – Valentine's Day. School.

Froggy's Halloween ill. by Frank Remkiewicz. Viking, 1999. ISBN 978-0-670-88449-0 Subj: Clothing – costumes. Frogs & toads. Holidays – Halloween.

Gone again ptarmigan ill. by Jon Van Zyle. National Geographic, 2001. ISBN 978-0-7922-7561-9 Subj: Animals. Birds – ptarmigans. Ecology. Foreign lands – Arctic.

Here comes Doctor Hippo ill. by Gilles Eduar. Boyds Mills, 2012. ISBN 978-1-59078-851-6 Subj: Animals – hippopotamuses. Careers – doctors. Family life – mothers. Imagination.

Here comes firefighter Hippo ill. by Gilles Eduar. Boyds Mills, 2013. ISBN 978-1-59078-968-1 Subj: Animals – hippopotamuses. Careers – firefighters. Imagination.

Honey Paw and Lightfoot ill. by Jon Van Zyle. Chronicle, 1994. ISBN 978-0-8118-0533-9 Subj: Animals – bears. Nature.

Hurricane! ill. by Henri Sorensen. Lothrop, 1998. ISBN 978-0-688-12978-1 Subj: Family life. Foreign lands – Puerto Rico. Weather – hurricanes.

Ice Bear and Little Fox ill. by Daniel San Souci. Dutton, 1998. ISBN 978-0-525-45907-1 Subj: Animals – foxes. Animals – polar bears. Foreign lands – Arctic. Indians of North America – Inuit.

I'm a truck driver ill. by David Parkins. Holt, 2010. ISBN 978-0-8050-7989-0 Subj: Careers – truck drivers. Rhyming text.

Jackrabbit ill. by Deborah Kogan Ray. Crown, 1996. ISBN 978-0-517-59658-6 Subj: Animals – rabbits. Character traits – kindness to animals.

Let's go, Froggy! ill. by Frank Remkiewicz. Viking, 1994. ISBN 978-0-670-85055-6 Subj: Activities – picnicking. Behavior – lost & found possessions. Frogs & toads. Sports – bicycling.

Like butter on pancakes ill. by G. Brian Karas. Viking, 1995. ISBN 978-0-670-85130-0 Subj: Farms. Sun.

Little lost tiger ill. by Ilya Spirin. Amazon Children's, 2012. ISBN 978-0-7614-6130-2 Subj: Animals – tigers. Behavior – lost. Fire. Foreign lands – Russia. Nature.

Little penguin: the Emperor of Antarctica ill. by Julie Olson. Marshall Cavendish, 2011. ISBN 978-0-7614-5954-5 Subj: Animals – babies. Birds – penguins. Foreign lands – Antarctic.

Little swan ill. by Kristina Rodanas. Marshall Cavendish, 2009. ISBN 978-0-7614-5523-3 Subj: Birds – swans. Nature.

Loon Lake ill. by Susan Ford. Chronicle, 2001. ISBN 978-0-8118-2003-5 Subj: Animals. Birds – loons. Canoes & canoeing. Family life – fathers. Family life – sons. Lakes, ponds.

Moshi moshi ill. by Yoshi Miyake. Millbrook, 1998. ISBN 978-0-7613-0110-3 Subj: Activities – traveling. Family life – brothers. Foreign lands – Japan.

Mustang canyon ill. by Daniel San Souci. Dutton, 2000. ISBN 978-0-525-45596-7 Subj: Animals – horses, ponies. Canyons.

My big rig ill. by Viviana Garofoli. Marshall Cavendish, 2007. ISBN 978-0-7614-5346-8 Subj: Imagination. Toys. Transportation. Trucks.

The owl who became the moon ill. by Ted Rand. Dutton, 1993. ISBN 978-0-525-45054-2 Subj: Animals. Birds – owls. Night. Trains.

Panther, shadow of the swamp ill. by Paul Morin. Candlewick, 2000. ISBN 978-1-56402-623-1 Subj: Animals – cougars.

Park beat: rhyming through the seasons ill. by Woodleigh Marx Hubbard. HarperCollins, 2000. ISBN 978-0-688-13995-7 Subj: Rhyming text. Seasons.

A plane goes ka-zoom! ill. by Denis Roche. Holt, 2010. ISBN 978-0-8050-8970-7 Subj: Airplanes, airports. Rhyming text.

Puddles ill. by G. Brian Karas. Viking, 1997. ISBN 978-0-670-87218-3 Subj: Activities – playing. Clothing – boots. Weather – rain.

Red wolf country ill. by Daniel San Souci. Dutton, 1996. ISBN 978-0-525-45191-4 Subj: Animals – wolves. Nature.

Sled dogs run ill. by Jon Van Zyle. Walker, 2005. ISBN 978-0-8027-8958-7 Subj: Alaska. Animals – dogs. Sports – racing. Sports – sledding.

Snuggle wuggle ill. by Michael Rex. Silver Whistle, 2000. ISBN 978-0-15-202159-7 Subj: Animals – babies.

The sugaring-off party ill. by Gilles Pelletier. Dutton, 1995. ISBN 978-0-525-45187-7 Subj: Family life – grandmothers. Food. Foreign lands – Canada. Trees.

Sun dance, water dance ill. by Greg Couch. Dutton, 2001. ISBN 978-0-525-46682-6 Subj: Activities – playing. Poetry. Seasons – summer.

Thirteen moons on turtle's back (Bruchac, Joseph)

A train goes clickety-clack ill. by Denis Roche. Holt, 2007. ISBN 978-0-8050-7972-2 Subj: Noise, sounds. Rhyming text. Trains.

A truck goes rattley-bumpa ill. by Denis Roche. Holt, 2005. ISBN 978-0-8050-7233-4 Subj: Noise, sounds. Rhyming text. Trucks.

What do you love? ill. by Karen Lee Schmidt. Harcourt, 2000. ISBN 978-0-15-201919-8 Subj: Animals – dogs. Emotions – love. Family life – mothers. Rhyming text.

What do you love? [board book] ill. by Karen Lee Schmidt. Harcourt, 2004. ISBN 978-0-15-205054-2 Subj: Animals – dogs. Emotions – love. Family life – mothers. Format, unusual – board books. Rhyming text.

What the animals were waiting for ill. by Paul Morin. Scholastic, 2002. ISBN 978-0-439-33630-7 Subj: Animals. Foreign lands – Africa. Weather – rain.

Where the big fish are ill. by Adam Gustavson. Candlewick, 2001. ISBN 978-0-7636-0922-1 Subj: Boats, ships. Character traits – perseverance. Fish. Sports – fishing.

White water ill. by Jill Kastner. Viking, 2001. ISBN 978-0-670-89286-0 Subj: Rivers. Sports.

Who bop ill. by Henry Cole. HarperCollins, 2000. ISBN 978-0-06-027918-9 Subj: Activities – dancing. Animals. Rhyming text.

Wiggle, waggle ill. by Michael Rex. Harcourt, 1999. ISBN 978-0-15-201940-2 Subj: Activities – walking. Animals. Noise, sounds.

Long, Ethan. *Bird and Birdie in a fine day* ill. by author. Tricycle, 2010. ISBN 978-1-58246-321-6 Subj: Birds. Friendship.

The book that Zack wrote ill. by author. Blue Apple, 2011. ISBN 978-1-60905-060-3 Subj: Activities – writing. Books, reading. Cumulative tales. Format, unusual.

Chamelia ill. by author. Little, Brown, 2011. ISBN 978-0-316-08612-7 Subj: Character traits – appearance. Character traits – individuality. Clothing. Reptiles – chameleons.

The croaky pokey! ill. by author. Holiday House, 2011. ISBN 978-0-8234-2291-3 Subj: Frogs & toads. Songs.

My dad, my hero ill. by author. Sourcebooks, 2011. ISBN 978-1-4022-4239-7 Subj: Family life – fathers.

One drowsy dragon ill. by author. Scholastic, 2010. ISBN 978-0-545-16557-0 Subj: Counting, numbers. Dragons. Sleep.

Soup for one ill. by author. Running Press, 2012. ISBN 978-0-7624-4354-3 Subj: Counting, numbers. Food. Insects – flies. Rhyming text.

Up, tall and high ill. by author. Putnam, 2012. ISBN 978-0-399-25611-0 Subj: Birds. Concepts – size. Format, unusual – toy & movable books. Language.

The Wing Wing brothers carnival de math ill. by author. Holiday House, 2013. ISBN 978-0-8234-2604-1 Subj: Birds – ducks. Counting, numbers. Family life – brothers.

The Wing Wing brothers math spectacular! ill. by author. Holiday House, 2012. ISBN 978-0-8234-2320-0 Subj: Birds – ducks. Counting, numbers. Family life – brothers. Theater.

Long, Heather. *Max & Milo go to sleep!* ill. by Ethan Long. Simon & Schuster, 2013. ISBN 978-1-4424-5143-8 Subj: Animals – beavers. Bedtime. Family life – brothers.

Long, Kathy. *Christopher sat straight up in bed* ill. by Patricia Cantor. Eerdmans, 2013. ISBN 978-0-8028-5359-2 Subj: Bedtime. Family life – grandparents. Noise, sounds. Sleep – snoring. Sleepovers.

The runaway shopping cart ill. by Susan Estelle Kwas. Penguin, 2007. ISBN 978-0-525-47187-5 Subj: Behavior – running away. Cumulative tales. Shopping.

Long, Loren. *Drummer boy* ill. by author. Philomel, 2008. ISBN 978-0-399-25174-0 Subj: Behavior – lost. Careers – musicians. Holidays – Christmas. Musical instruments – drums. Toys.

Otis ill. by author. Philomel, 2009. ISBN 978-0-399-25248-8 Subj: Farms. Tractors.

Otis and the puppy ill. by author. Philomel, 2013. ISBN 978-0-399-25469-7 Subj: Animals – dogs. Behavior – lost & found possessions. Farms. Friendship. Tractors.

Otis and the tornado ill. by author. Penguin, 2011. ISBN 978-0-399-25477-2 Subj: Farms. Tractors. Weather – tornadoes.

An Otis Christmas ill. by author. Philomel, 2013. ISBN 978-0-399-16395-1 Subj: Animals – horses, ponies. Character traits – bravery. Farms. Holidays – Christmas. Tractors. Weather – snow.

Long, Melinda. *Hiccup snickup* ill. by Thor Wickstrom. Simon & Schuster, 2001. ISBN 978-0-689-82245-2 Subj: Family life. Hiccups.

How I became a pirate ill. by David Shannon. Harcourt, 2003. ISBN 978-0-15-201848-1 Subj: Imagination. Pirates.

Pirates don't change diapers ill. by David Shannon. Harcourt, 2007. ISBN 978-0-15-205353-6 Subj: Pirates.

When Papa snores ill. by Holly Meade. Simon & Schuster, 2000. ISBN 978-0-689-81943-8 Subj: Family life – grandparents. Sleep – snoring.

Long, Steffanie. *Such a silly baby!* by Steffanie Long and Richard Lorig ill. by Amanda Shepherd. Chronicle, 2008. ISBN 978-0-8118-5134-3 Subj: Animals. Babies. Humorous stories. Rhyming text.

Long, Sylvia. *Deck the hall* ill. by author. Chronicle, 2000. ISBN 978-0-8118-2821-5 Subj: Animals – rabbits. Foreign lands – England. Holidays – Christmas. Music. Songs.

Sylvia Long's Thumbelina (Andersen, Hans Christian)

Longfellow, Henry Wadsworth. *Hiawatha* ill. by Susan Jeffers. Dial, 1983. ISBN 978-0-8037-0014-7 Subj: Indians of North America – Iroquois. Poetry.

Paul Revere's ride ill. by Nancy Winslow Parker. Mulberry, 1993. ISBN 978-0-688-12387-1 Subj: Poetry. U.S. history. War.

Paul Revere's ride: the landlord's tale ill. by Charles Santore. HarperCollins, 2003. ISBN 978-0-688-16552-9 Subj: Poetry. U.S. history. War.

Longstreth, Galen Goodwin. *Yes, let's* ill. by Maris Wicks. Tanglewood, 2013. ISBN 978-1-933718-87-3 Subj: Activities – hiking. Activities – picnicking. Family life. Rhyming text.

Loo, Sanne te. *Ping-Li's kite* ill. by author. Front Street, 2002. ISBN 978-1-886910-75-1 Subj: Folk & fairy tales. Foreign lands – China.

Look at me! ill. by Rachel Fuller. Child's Play, 2010. ISBN 978-1-84643-278-1 Subj: Format, unusual – board books. Self-concept.

Look, Lenore. *Brush of the gods* ill. by Meilo So. Random House, 2013. ISBN 978-0-375-87001-9 Subj: Activities – painting. Art. Careers – artists. Foreign lands – China.

Henry's first-moon birthday ill. by Yumi Heo. Atheneum, 2001. ISBN 978-0-689-82294-0 Subj: Babies. Birthdays. Ethnic groups in the U.S. – Chinese Americans. Family life – brothers & sisters. Family life – grandmothers.

Love as strong as ginger ill. by Stephen T. Johnson. Atheneum, 1999. ISBN 978-0-689-81248-4 Subj: Activities – working. Ethnic groups in the U.S. – Chinese Americans. Family life – grandmothers.

Polka Dot Penguin Pottery ill. by Yumi Heo. Random House, 2011. ISBN 978-0-375-86332-5 Subj: Activities – writing. Ethnic groups in the U.S. – Chinese Americans. Family life – grandparents.

Uncle Peter's amazing Chinese wedding ill. by Yumi Heo. Simon & Schuster, 2006. ISBN 978-0-689-84458-4 Subj: Ethnic groups in the U.S. – Chinese Americans. Family life – aunts, uncles. Weddings.

Loomis, Christine. *Across America, I love you* ill. by Kate Kiesler. Hyperion, 2000. ISBN 978-0-7868-2314-7 Subj: Family life. Nature. U.S. history.

Astro Bunnies ill. by Ora Eitan. Putnam, 1998. ISBN 978-0-399-23175-9 Subj: Animals – rabbits. Rhyming text. Space & space ships.

The best Father's Day present ever ill. by Pamela Paparone. Penguin, 2007. ISBN 978-0-399-24253-3 Subj: Animals – snails. Family life – fathers. Holidays – Father's Day.

Cowboy bunnies ill. by Ora Eitan. Putnam, 1997. ISBN 978-0-399-22625-0 Subj: Activities – playing. Animals – rabbits. Country. Cowboys, cowgirls. Rhyming text.

Hattie hippo ill. by Robert Neubecker. Scholastic, 2006. ISBN 978-0-439-54340-8 Subj: Animals – hippopotamuses.

Scuba bunnies ill. by Ora Eitan. Putnam, 2004. ISBN 978-0-399-23465-1 Subj: Animals. Animals – rabbits. Rhyming text. Sea & seashore. Sports – skin diving.

López, Susana. *The best family in the world* ill. by Ulises Wensell. Kane/Miller, 2010. ISBN 978-1-935279-47-1 Subj: Adoption. Family life.

Lorbiecki, Marybeth. *Jackie's bat* ill. by Brian Pinkney. Simon & Schuster, 2006. ISBN 978-0-689-84102-6 Subj: Ethnic groups in the U.S. – African Americans. Prejudice. Sports – baseball.

Louisa May and Mr. Thoreau's flute (Dunlap, Julie)

Lord, Cynthia. *Happy birthday, Hamster* ill. by Derek Anderson. Scholastic, 2011. ISBN 978-0-545-25522-6 Subj: Animals – hamsters. Birthdays. Parties.

Hot rod Hamster ill. by Derek Anderson. Scholastic, 2010. ISBN 978-0-545-03530-9 Subj: Animals – dogs. Animals – hamsters. Animals – mice. Automobiles. Sports – racing.

Lord, Janet. *Albert the fix-it man* ill. by Julie Paschkis. Peachtree, 2008. ISBN 978-1-56145-433-4 Subj: Character traits – helpfulness. Communities, neighborhoods. Tools.

Here comes Grandma! ill. by Julie Paschkis. Holt, 2005. ISBN 978-0-8050-7666-0 Subj: Family life – grandmothers. Transportation.

Where is Catkin? ill. by Julie Paschkis. Peachtree, 2010. ISBN 978-1-56145-523-2 Subj: Animals – cats.

Lorenz, Albert. *The exceptionally, extraordinarily ordinary first day of school* ill. by author. Abrams, 2010. ISBN 978-0-8109-8960-3 Subj: Moving. School – first day.

Lorig, Richard. *Such a silly baby!* (Long, Steffanie)

Loth, Sebastian. *Clementine* ill. by author. NorthSouth, 2011. ISBN 978-0-7358-4009-6 Subj: Activities – traveling. Animals – snails. Concepts – shape. Format, unusual. Moon.

Remembering Crystal ill. by author. NorthSouth, 2010. ISBN 978-0-7358-2300-6 Subj: Birds – geese. Death. Reptiles – turtles, tortoises.

Zelda the Varigoose ill. by author. NorthSouth, 2012. ISBN 978-0-7358-4076-8 Subj: Birds – geese. Format, unusual. Imagination. Rhyming text.

Lottridge, Celia Barker. *Berta, a remarkable dog* ill. by Elsa Myotte. Groundwood, 2002. ISBN 978-0-88899-461-5 Subj: Adoption. Animals. Animals – dogs. Behavior – needing someone. Farms.

The little rooster and the diamond button ill. by Joanne Fitzgerald. Douglas & McIntyre, 2001. ISBN 978-0-88899-443-1 Subj: Birds – chickens. Clothing. Folk & fairy tales. Foreign lands – Hungary. Royalty – sultans.

One watermelon seed ill. by Karen Patkau. Fitzhenry & Whiteside, 2008. ISBN 978-1-55455-034-0 Subj: Concepts – color. Counting, numbers. Gardens, gardening.

Louie, Ai-Ling. *Yeh Shen: a Cinderella story from China* ill. by Ed Young. Putnam, 1990. ISBN 978-0-399-20900-0 Subj: Folk & fairy tales. Foreign lands – China.

Louie, Therese On. *Raymond's perfect present* ill. by Suling Wang. Lee & Low, 2002. ISBN 978-1-58430-055-7 Subj: Birds. Communities, neighborhoods. Ethnic groups in the U.S. – Chinese Americans. Flowers. Gifts. Illness.

Louis, Catherine. *Liu and the bird: a journey in Chinese calligraphy* ill. by author. NorthSouth, 2006. ISBN 978-0-7358-2050-0 Subj: Activities – traveling. Activities – writing. Foreign lands – China.

Louise, Tina. *When I grow up* ill. by Oliver Corwin. Abrams, 2007. ISBN 978-0-8109-3948-6 Subj: Animals. Behavior – growing up.

Loupy, Christophe. *Don't worry, Wags* ill. by Eve Tharlet. NorthSouth, 2003. ISBN 978-0-7358-1850-7 Subj: Animals – dogs. Behavior – lost. Behavior – worrying. Stores.

Wiggles ill. by Eve Tharlet. NorthSouth, 2005. ISBN 978-0-7358-1981-8 Subj: Animals – dogs. Character traits – curiosity. Farms.

Loux, Lynn C. *The day I could fly* ill. by Guy Porfirio. NorthWord, 2003. ISBN 978-1-55971-866-0 Subj: Activities – flying. Birds – crows. Imagination.

Love, Pamela. *A loon alone* ill. by Shannon Sycks. Down East, 2002. ISBN 978-0-89272-517-5 Subj: Behavior – hiding. Birds – loons.

A moose's morning ill. by Lesia Sochor. Down East, 2007. ISBN 978-0-89272-733-9 Subj: Animals – moose.

Love to mamá ed. by Pat Mora; ill. by Paula Barragán. Lee & Low, 2001. ISBN 978-1-58430-019-9 Subj: Family life – grandmothers. Family life – mothers. Foreign languages. Poetry.

Lovell, Patty. *Have fun, Molly Lou Melon* ill. by David Catrow. Putnam, 2012. ISBN 978-0-399-25406-2 Subj: Activities – making things. Family life – grandmothers. Friendship. Imagination.

Stand tall, Molly Lou Melon ill. by David Catrow. Putnam, 2001. ISBN 978-0-399-23416-3 Subj: Behavior – bullying, teasing. Family life – grandmothers. Self-concept.

Low, Alice. *Aunt Lucy went to buy a hat* ill. by Laura Huliska-Beith. HarperCollins, 2004. ISBN 978-0-06-008972-6 Subj: Behavior – lost & found possessions. Clothing – hats. Humorous stories. Rhyming text.

Low, Joseph. *Mice twice* ill. by author. Aladdin, 1986, ©1980. ISBN 978-0-689-71060-5 Subj: Animals – mice. Caldecott award honor books.

Low, William. *Machines go to work* ill. by author. Holt, 2009. ISBN 978-0-8050-8759-8 Subj: Format, unusual – toy & movable books. Machines.

Machines go to work in the city ill. by author. Holt, 2012. ISBN 978-0-8050-9050-5 Subj: Cities, towns. Format, unusual – toy & movable books. Machines. Trucks.

Lowell, Susan. *The bootmaker and the elves* ill. by Tom Curry. Orchard, 1997. ISBN 978-0-531-33044-9 Subj: Careers – shoemakers. Character traits – helpfulness. Clothing – boots. Cowboys, cowgirls. Folk & fairy tales. Humorous stories. Mythical creatures – elves. U.S. history – frontier & pioneer life.

Cindy Ellen: a wild western Cinderella ill. by Jane Manning. HarperCollins, 2000. ISBN 978-0-06-027447-4 Subj: Fairies. Family life – stepfamilies. Folk & fairy tales. Sibling rivalry. U.S. history – frontier & pioneer life.

Dusty Locks and the three bears ill. by Randy Cecil. Holt, 2001. ISBN 978-0-8050-5862-8 Subj: Animals – bears. U.S. history – frontier & pioneer life.

The elephant quilt! stitch by stitch to California! ill. by Stacey Dressen-McQueen. Farrar, 2008. ISBN 978-0-374-38223-0 Subj: Quilts. U.S. history.

Josefina javelina: a hairy tale ill. by Bruce MacPherson. Rising Moon, 2005. ISBN 978-0-87358-790-7 Subj: Animals – coyotes. Animals – pigs. Ballet.

Little Red Cowboy Hat ill. by Randy Cecil. Holt, 1997. ISBN 978-0-8050-3508-7 Subj: Animals – bulls, cows. Animals – wolves. Clothing – hats. Family life – grandmothers. Folk & fairy tales.

The three little javelinas ill. by Jim Harris. Northland, 1992. ISBN 978-0-87358-542-2 Subj: Animals – coyotes. Animals – pigs. Character traits – cleverness. Folk & fairy tales.

The tortoise and the jackrabbit ill. by Jim Harris. Northland, 1994. ISBN 978-0-87358-586-6 Subj: Animals. Animals – rabbits. Desert. Folk & fairy tales. Reptiles – turtles, tortoises. Sports – racing.

Lowry, Lois. *Crow call* ill. by Bagram Ibatoulline. Scholastic, 2009. ISBN 978-0-545-03035-9 Subj: Birds – crows. Family life – fathers. Sports – hunting.

Lozoff, Bo. *The wonderful life of a fly who couldn't fly* ill. by Beth Stover. Hampton Roads, 2002. ISBN 978-1-57174-286-5 Subj: Insects – flies. Self-concept.

Lubner, Susan. *Noises at night* (Glass, Beth Raisner)

Ruthie Bon Bair, do not go to bed with wringing wet hair! ill. by Bruce Whatley. Abrams, 2006. ISBN 978-0-8109-5470-0 Subj: Behavior – bad day. Hair. Humorous stories. Rhyming text.

Lucado, Max. *Alabaster's song: Christmas through the eyes of an angel* ill. by Michael Garland. Word Pub, 1996. ISBN 978-0-8499-1307-5 Subj: Activities – singing. Angels. Holidays – Christmas.

All you ever need ill. by Douglas Klauba. Crossway, 2000. ISBN 978-1-58134-134-8 Subj: Behavior. Character traits – generosity. Water.

Jacob's gift ill. by Robert Hunt. Tommy Nelson, 1998. ISBN 978-0-8499-5830-4 Subj: Careers – carpenters. Religion – Nativity.

Lucas, David. *Cake girl* ill. by author. Farrar, 2009. ISBN 978-0-374-39909-2 Subj: Birthdays. Emotions – loneliness. Friendship. Witches.

Christmas at the toy museum ill. by author. Candlewick, 2012. ISBN 978-0-7636-5868-7 Subj: Holidays – Christmas. Museums. Toys.

Halibut Jackson ill. by author. Knopf, 2004. ISBN 978-0-375-92690-7 Subj: Character traits – individuality. Character traits – shyness. Clothing.

Nutmeg ill. by author. Random House, 2006. ISBN 978-0-375-93519-0 Subj: Imagination. Magic. Mythical creatures – genies.

The robot and the bluebird ill. by author. Farrar, 2008. ISBN 978-0-374-36330-7 Subj: Birds – bluebirds. Character traits. Robots.

The skeleton pirate ill. by author. Candlewick, 2013. ISBN 978-0-7636-6107-6 Subj: Anatomy – skeletons. Animals – whales. Mythical creatures – mermaids, mermen. Pirates.

Something to do ill. by author. Philomel, 2009. ISBN 978-0-399-25247-1 Subj: Activities – drawing. Animals – bears. Imagination.

Whale ill. by author. Random House, 2007. ISBN 978-0-375-84338-9 Subj: Animals – whales. Tsunamis.

Luciani, Brigitte. *Those messy Hempels* ill. by Vanessa Hié. NorthSouth, 2004. ISBN 978-0-7358-1910-8 Subj: Behavior – lost & found possessions. Character traits – cleanliness. Food.

Lucke, Deb. *The boy who wouldn't swim* ill. by author. Clarion, 2008. ISBN 978-0-618-91484-5 Subj: Emotions – fear. Family life – brothers & sisters. Sports – swimming.

Sneezenesia ill. by author. Clarion, 2010. ISBN 978-0-547-33006-8 Subj: Anatomy – noses. Humorous stories. Memories, memory. Noise, sounds.

Luckhurst, Matt. *Paul Bunyan and Babe the Blue Ox: the great pancake adventure* ill. by author. Abrams, 2012. ISBN 978-1-4197-0420-8 Subj: Animals – oxen. Careers – lumberjacks. Food. Tall tales. U.S. history – frontier & pioneer life.

Ludwig, Trudy. *Better than you* ill. by Adam Gustavson. Random House, 2011. ISBN 978-1-58246-380-3 Subj: Behavior – boasting. Friendship. Self-concept.

The invisible boy ill. by Patrice Barton. Knopf, 2013. ISBN 978-1-58246-450-3 Subj: Activities

– drawing. Behavior – unnoticed, unseen. Emotions – loneliness. Friendship. School.

Luenn, Nancy. *A gift for Abuelita* ill. by Robert Chapman. Rising Moon, 1998. ISBN 978-0-87358-688-7 Subj: Death. Ethnic groups in the U.S. – Mexican Americans. Family life – grandmothers. Foreign languages. Holidays – Day of the Dead.

Mother earth ill. by Neil Waldman. Atheneum, 1992. ISBN 978-0-689-31668-5 Subj: Earth. Ecology.

Nessa's fish ill. by Neil Waldman. Atheneum, 1990. ISBN 978-0-689-31477-3 Subj: Eskimos. Family life – grandmothers. Indians of North America. Sports – fishing.

Nessa's story ill. by Neil Waldman. Atheneum, 1994. ISBN 978-0-689-31782-8 Subj: Eskimos. Family life – grandmothers. Foreign lands – Arctic. Imagination.

Otter play ill. by Anna Vojtech. Atheneum, 1998. ISBN 978-0-689-81126-5 Subj: Activities – playing. Animals – otters.

Squish! a wetland walk ill. by Ronald Himler. Atheneum, 1994. ISBN 978-0-689-31842-9 Subj: Activities – walking. Ecology. Nature.

Luján, Jorge. *Beyond my hand* ill. by Georgina Quintana. Groundwood, 2002. ISBN 978-0-88899-460-8 Subj: Poetry.

Colors! / ¡Colores! ill. by Piet Grobler. Groundwood, 2008. ISBN 978-0-88899-863-7 Subj: Concepts – color. Foreign languages. Poetry.

Sky blue accident / Accidente celeste ill. by Piet Grobler. Groundwood, 2007. ISBN 978-0-88899-805-7 Subj: Accidents. Foreign languages. Sky.

Stephen and the beetle ill. by Chiara Carrer. Groundwood, 2012. ISBN 978-1-55498-192-2 Subj: Character traits – kindness to animals. Insects – beetles.

Lukasewich, Lori. *The night fire* ill. by author. Stoddart, 2001. ISBN 978-0-7737-3296-4 Subj: Careers – firefighters. Rhyming text.

Lullaby moons and a silver spoon ill. by Brooke Dyer. Little, 2003. ISBN 978-0-316-17474-9 Subj: Lullabies. Night. Poetry.

Lum, Kate. *Princesses are not perfect* ill. by Susan Hellard. Bloomsbury, 2010. ISBN 978-1-59990-432-0 Subj: Royalty – princesses. Self-concept.

Princesses are not quitters! ill. by Susan Hellard. Bloomsbury, 2003. ISBN 978-1-58234-762-2 Subj: Activities – working. Royalty – princesses.

What! cried Granny ill. by Adrian Johnson. Dial, 1999. ISBN 978-0-8037-2382-5 Subj: Activities – making things. Bedtime. Family life – grandmothers. Furniture – beds.

Lumry, Amanda. *Polar bear puzzle* by Amanda Lumry and Laura Hurwitz. Eaglemont, 2007. ISBN 978-1-60040-004-9 Subj: Animals – polar bears. Ecology. Foreign lands – Canada.

Safari in South Africa by Amanda Lumry and Laura Hurwitz ill. by Sarah McIntyre. Eaglemont, 2003. ISBN 978-0-9662257-8-5 Subj: Animals. Ecology. Foreign lands – South Africa.

Lund, Deb. *All aboard the dinotrain* ill. by Howard Fine. Harcourt, 2006. ISBN 978-0-15-205237-9 Subj: Dinosaurs. Rhyming text. Trains.

Dinosailors ill. by Howard Fine. Harcourt, 2003. ISBN 978-0-15-204609-5 Subj: Dinosaurs. Rhyming text. Sailors. Sports – sailing.

Dinosoaring ill. by Howard Fine. Harcourt, 2012. ISBN 978-0-15-206016-9 Subj: Activities – flying. Airplanes, airports. Dinosaurs. Rhyming text.

Monsters on machines ill. by Robert Neubecker. Harcourt, 2008. ISBN 978-0-15-205365-9 Subj: Careers – construction workers. Machines. Monsters. Rhyming text. Tractors.

Tell me my story, Mama ill. by Hiroe Nakata. HarperCollins, 2004. ISBN 978-0-06-028877-8 Subj: Babies. Birth. Family life – parents.

Lunde, Darrin. *Hello, baby beluga* ill. by Patricia J. Wynne. Charlesbridge, 2011. ISBN 978-1-57091-739-4 Subj: Animals – whales.

Hello, bumblebee bat ill. by Patricia J. Wynne. Charlesbridge, 2007. ISBN 978-1-57091-374-7 Subj: Animals – bats. Animals – endangered animals. Science.

Meet the meerkat ill. by Patricia J. Wynne. Charlesbridge, 2007. ISBN 978-1-58089-110-3 Subj: Animals – meerkats.

Monkey colors ill. by Patricia J. Wynne. Charlesbridge, 2012. ISBN 978-1-57091-741-7 Subj: Animals – monkeys.

Lunde, Stein Erik. *My father's arms are a boat* ill. by Oyvind Torseter. Enchanted Lion, 2013. ISBN 978-1-59270-124-7 Subj: Death. Emotions – grief. Family life – fathers.

Lundgren, Mary Beth. *Seven scary monsters* ill. by Howard Fine. Clarion, 2003. ISBN 978-0-395-88913-8 Subj: Bedtime. Monsters. Rhyming text.

Lundy, Charlotte. *Thank you, Esther* ill. by Evelyn Diane Overcash. Bay Light, 2002. ISBN 978-0-9670280-4-0 Subj: Religion. School. Self-concept.

Thank you, Ruth and Naomi ill. by Miriam Sagasti. Bay Light, 2004. ISBN 978-0-9741817-0-7 Subj: Friendship. Religion.

Lunge-Larsen, Lise. *Noah's mittens: the story of felt* ill. by Matthew Trueman. Houghton, 2006. ISBN 978-0-618-32950-2 Subj: Animals – sheep. Clothing. Religion – Noah.

The race of the Birkebeiners ill. by Mary Azarian. Houghton, 2001. ISBN 978-0-618-10313-3 Subj: Folk & fairy tales. Foreign lands – Norway. Royalty – princes.

Lupton, David. *Goodbye, Brecken: a story about the death of a pet* ill. by author. Magination, 2013. ISBN 978-1-4338-1290-3 Subj: Animals – dogs. Death. Pets.

Lupton, Hugh. *Pirican Pic and Pirican Mor* ill. by Yumi Heo. Barefoot, 2003. ISBN 978-1-84148-070-1 Subj: Cumulative tales. Folk & fairy tales. Foreign lands – Scotland.

Luthardt, Kevin. *Flying* ill. by author. Peachtree, 2009. ISBN 978-1-56145-430-3 Subj: Character traits – questioning. Ethnic groups in the U.S. – African Americans. Family life – fathers.

Hats ill. by author. Whitman, 2004. ISBN 978-0-8075-3171-6 Subj: Clothing – hats. Friendship.

Mine ill. by author. Atheneum, 2001. ISBN 978-0-689-83237-6 Subj: Behavior – sharing. Family life – brothers. Toys.

You're weird! ill. by author. Penguin, 2005. ISBN 978-0-8037-2986-5 Subj: Animals – rabbits. Behavior – name calling. Friendship. Reptiles – turtles, tortoises.

Luxbacher, Irene. *Mattoo, let's play!* ill. by author. Kids Can, 2010. ISBN 978-1-55453-424-1 Subj: Animals – cats.

Lynn, Sarah. *1-2-3 va-va-vroom! a counting book* ill. by Daniel Griffo. Amazon, 2012. ISBN 978-0-7614-6162-3 Subj: Activities – playing. Automobiles. Counting, numbers. Imagination. Sports – racing. Toys.

Tip-tap pop ill. by Valeria Docampo. Marshall Cavendish, 2010. ISBN 978-0-7614-5712-1 Subj: Activities – dancing. Family life – grandfathers. Memories, memory.

Lyon, George Ella. *All the water in the world* ill. by Katherine Tillotson. Atheneum, 2011. ISBN 978-1-4169-7130-6 Subj: Science. Water.

Book ill. by Peter Catalanotto. DK, 1999. ISBN 978-0-7894-2560-7 Subj: Books, reading. Poetry.

Cecil's story ill. by Peter Catalanotto. Watts, 1991. ISBN 978-0-531-08512-7 Subj: Emotions – fear. Family life. Illness. U.S. history. War.

Come a tide ill. by Stephen Gammell. Watts, 1990. ISBN 978-0-531-08454-0 Subj: Family life. Weather – floods.

Counting on the woods photos by Ann W. Olson. DK, 1998. ISBN 978-0-7894-2480-8 Subj: Counting, numbers. Forest, woods. Nature. Poetry.

Mama is a miner ill. by Peter Catalanotto. Orchard, 1994. ISBN 978-0-531-08703-9 Subj: Activities – working. Careers – miners. Family life – mothers. Gender roles. Rhyming text.

Mother to tigers ill. by Peter Catalanotto. Atheneum, 2003. ISBN 978-0-689-84221-4 Subj: Animals. Careers – zookeepers.

My friend, the starfinder ill. by Stephen Gammell. Atheneum, 2008. ISBN 978-1-4169-2738-9 Subj: Activities – storytelling. Stars. Weather – rainbows.

No dessert forever! ill. by Peter Catalanotto. Simon & Schuster, 2006. ISBN 978-1-4169-0385-7 Subj: Behavior – fighting, arguing. Emotions – anger. Family life.

One lucky girl ill. by Irene Trivas. DK, 2000. ISBN 978-0-7894-2613-0 Subj: Family life. Homes, houses. Weather – tornadoes.

The pirate of kindergarten ill. by Lynne Avril. Simon & Schuster, 2010. ISBN 978-1-4169-5024-0 Subj: Anatomy – eyes. School. Senses – sight.

Planes fly! ill. by Mick Wiggins. Atheneum, 2013. ISBN 978-1-4424-5025-7 Subj: Airplanes, airports. Rhyming text.

Sleepsong ill. by Peter Catalanotto. Atheneum, 2009. ISBN 978-0-689-86973-0 Subj: Animals. Babies. Bedtime. Rhyming text.

Trucks roll! ill. by Craig Frazier. Simon & Schuster, 2007. ISBN 978-1-4169-2435-7 Subj: Rhyming text. Trucks.

Who came down that road? ill. by Peter Catalanotto. Orchard, 1992. ISBN 978-0-531-08587-5 Subj: Imagination. Roads.

You and me and home sweet home ill. by Stephanie Anderson. Atheneum, 2009. ISBN 978-0-689-87589-2 Subj: Communities, neighborhoods. Ethnic groups in the U.S. – African Americans. Homes, houses.

Lyon, Tammie. *Olive and Snowflake* ill. by author. Marshall Cavendish, 2011. ISBN 978-0-7614-5955-2 Subj: Animals – dogs. Behavior – worrying. Pets.

Lyons, Kelly Starling. *Ellen's broom* ill. by Daniel Minter. Putnam, 2012. ISBN 978-0-399-25003-3 Subj: Ethnic groups in the U.S. – African Americans. Slavery. U.S. history. Weddings.

Hope's gift ill. by Don Tate. Putnam, 2012. ISBN 978-0-399-16001-1 Subj: Character traits – freedom. Ethnic groups in the U.S. – African Americans. Slavery. U.S. history.

One million men and me ill. by Peter Ambush. Just Us, 2007. ISBN 978-1-933491-07-3 Subj: Ethnic groups in the U.S. – African Americans. U.S. history.

Tea cakes for Tosh ill. by E. B. Lewis. Putnam, 2012. ISBN 978-0-399-25213-6 Subj: Activities – baking, cooking. Ethnic groups in the U.S. – African Americans. Family life – grandmothers. Memories, memory. Old age.

Maass, Robert. *A is for autumn* photos by author. Holt, 2011. ISBN 978-0-8050-9093-2 Subj: ABC books. Seasons – fall.

Garbage ill. by author. Holt, 2000. ISBN 978-0-8050-5951-9 Subj: Careers – sanitation workers. Ecology.

Garden ill. by author. Holt, 1998. ISBN 978-0-8050-5477-4 Subj: Gardens, gardening. Plants.

Little trucks with big jobs photos by author. Holt, 2007. ISBN 978-0-8050-7748-3 Subj: Trucks.

Tugboats ill. by author. Holt, 1997. ISBN 978-0-8050-3116-4 Subj: Boats, ships. Sailors. Transportation.

When autumn comes photos by author. Holt, 1990. ISBN 978-0-8050-1259-0 Subj: Seasons – fall.

When spring comes photos by author. Holt, 1994. ISBN 978-0-8050-2085-4 Subj: Seasons – spring.

When summer comes photos by author. Holt, 1993. ISBN 978-0-8050-2087-8 Subj: Seasons – summer.

When winter comes photos by author. Holt, 1993. ISBN 978-0-8050-2086-1 Subj: Seasons – winter.

McAlister, Caroline. *Holy Molé! a folktale from Mexico* ill. by Stefan Czernecki. August House, 2007. ISBN 978-0-87483-775-9 Subj: Activities – baking, cooking. Folk & fairy tales. Food. Foreign lands – Mexico.

McAllister, Angela. *Found you, Little Wombat!* ill. by Charles Fuge. Sterling, 2004. ISBN 978-1-4027-1599-0 Subj: Animals – wombats. Behavior – lost.

Harry's box ill. by Jenny Jones. Bloomsbury, 2003. ISBN 978-1-58234-772-1 Subj: Activities – playing. Animals – dogs. Imagination.

The little blue rabbit ill. by Jason Cockcroft. Bloomsbury, 2003. ISBN 978-1-58234-834-6 Subj: Animals – rabbits. Behavior – needing someone. Emotions. Toys.

Little Mist ill. by Sarah Fox-Davies. Random House, 2011. ISBN 978-0-375-86788-0 Subj: Animals – babies. Animals – leopards.

Mama and Little Joe ill. by Terry Milne. Simon & Schuster, 2007. ISBN 978-1-4169-1631-4 Subj: Animals – kangaroos. Behavior – lost. Emotions – love. Toys.

My mom has x-ray vision ill. by Alex T. Smith. Tiger Tales, 2011. ISBN 978-1-58925-097-0 Subj: Family life – mothers. Humorous stories.

Night-night, little one ill. by Maggie Kneen. Random House, 2003. ISBN 978-0-385-90861-0 Subj: Animals – rabbits. Bedtime. Family life – mothers.

Take a kiss to school ill. by Susan Hellard. Bloomsbury, 2006. ISBN 978-1-58234-702-8 Subj: Animals – moles. Kissing. School.

Trust me, Mom! ill. by Ross Collins. Bloomsbury, 2005. ISBN 978-1-58234-955-8 Subj: Behavior – resourcefulness. Emotions – fear. Family life – mothers. Monsters. Shopping.

Yuck! That's not a monster ill. by Alison Edgson. Good Books, 2010. ISBN 978-1-56148-683-0 Subj: Character traits – being different. Character traits – individuality. Family life. Monsters.

McAnulty, Stacy. *Dear Santasaurus* ill. by Jef Kaminsky. Boyds Mills, 2013. ISBN 978-1-59078-876-9 Subj: Activities – writing. Behavior – misbehavior. Dinosaurs. Holidays – Christmas. Letters, cards. Santa Claus.

McArthur, Meher. *An ABC of what art can be* ill. by Esther Pearl Watson. Getty Museum, 2010. ISBN 978-0-89236-999-7 Subj: ABC books. Art. Rhyming text.

Macaulay, David. *Angelo* ill. by author. Houghton, 2002. ISBN 978-0-618-16826-2 Subj: Birds – pigeons. Character traits – kindness to animals. Friendship.

Black and white ill. by author. Houghton, 1990. ISBN 978-0-395-52151-9 Subj: Animals – bulls, cows. Caldecott award books. Family life. Trains.

Castle ill. by author. Houghton, 1977. ISBN 978-0-395-25784-5 Subj: Caldecott award honor books.

Cathedral ill. by author. Houghton, 1973. ISBN 978-0-395-17513-2 Subj: Caldecott award honor books.

McBratney, Sam. *The caterpillow fight* ill. by Jill Barton. Candlewick, 1996. ISBN 978-1-56402-804-4 Subj: Bedtime. Behavior – misbehavior. Insects – butterflies, caterpillars. Rhyming text.

The dark at the top of the stairs ill. by Ivan Bates. Candlewick, 1996. ISBN 978-1-56402-640-8 Subj: Animals – cats. Animals – mice. Bedtime. Character traits – curiosity. Emotions – fear.

Guess how much I love you ill. by Anita Jeram. Candlewick, 1995. ISBN 978-1-56402-473-2 Subj: Animals – rabbits. Bedtime. Emotions – love. Family life – fathers.

I'll always be your friend ill. by Kim Lewis. HarperCollins, 2001. ISBN 978-0-06-029485-4 Subj: Animals – foxes. Emotions – anger. Family life – mothers.

I'm sorry by Sam McBratney and Jennifer Eachus; ed. by Robert Warren; ill. by Jennifer Eachus. HarperCollins, 2000. ISBN 978-0-06-028686-6 Subj: Behavior – fighting, arguing. Emotions – anger. Friendship. School.

In the light of the moon and other bedtime stories ill. by Kady MacDonald Denton. Kingfisher, 2001. ISBN 978-0-7534-5224-0 Subj: Bedtime.

Just you and me ill. by Ivan Bates. Candlewick, 1998. ISBN 978-0-7636-0436-3 Subj: Animals. Birds – geese. Weather – storms.

Once there was a Hoodie ill. by Paul Hess. Putnam, 2001. ISBN 978-0-399-23581-8 Subj: Behavior – needing someone. Emotions – happiness. Mythical creatures.

There, there ill. by Ivan Bates. Candlewick, 2013. ISBN 978-0-7636-6702-3 Subj: Animals – bears. Emotions – love. Family life – fathers. Hugging.

Yes we can! ill. by Charles Fuge. HarperCollins, 2007. ISBN 978-0-06-121515-5 Subj: Animals – kangaroos. Behavior – bullying, teasing. Character traits – individuality. Friendship.

McBrier, Page. *Beatrice's goat* ill. by Lori Lohstoeter. Atheneum, 2001. ISBN 978-0-689-82460-9 Subj: Animals – goats. Foreign lands – Uganda.

McCain, Becky R. *Grandmother's dreamcatcher* ill. by Stacey Schuett. Whitman, 1998. ISBN 978-0-8075-3031-3 Subj: Activities – making things. Dreams. Family life – grandmothers. Indians of North America – Chippewa.

Nobody knew what to do: a story about bullying ill. by Todd Leonard. Whitman, 2001. ISBN 978-0-8075-5711-2 Subj: Behavior – bullying, teasing. School.

McCain, Meghan. *My dad, John McCain* ill. by Dan Andreasen. Aladdin, 2008. ISBN 978-1-4169-7528-1 Subj: Family life – fathers. U.S. history. War.

McCall, Bruce. *Marveltown* ill. by author. Farrar, 2008. ISBN 978-0-374-39925-2 Subj: Careers – inventors. Robots.

McCall, Francis X. *A huge hog is a big pig* by Francis X. McCall and Patricia A. Keeler ill. with photos. Greenwillow, 2002. ISBN 978-0-06-029766-4 Subj: Animals. Games. Rhyming text.

Maccarone, Grace. *Cars! Cars! Cars!* ill. by David A. Carter. Scholastic, 1995. ISBN 978-0-590-47572-3 Subj: Automobiles. Rhyming text.

A child was born ill. by Sam Williams. Scholastic, 2000. ISBN 978-0-439-18296-6 Subj: Holidays – Christmas. Religion – Nativity. Rhyming text.

A child's good night prayer ill. by Sam Williams. Scholastic, 2001. ISBN 978-0-439-23505-1 Subj: Bedtime. Religion.

Miss Lina's ballerinas ill. by Christine Davenier. Feiwel & Friends, 2010. ISBN 978-0-312-38243-8 Subj: Ballet. Counting, numbers. Problem solving. Rhyming text.

Miss Lina's ballerinas and the prince ill. by Christine Davenier. Feiwel & Friends, 2011. ISBN 978-0-312-64963-0 Subj: Activities – dancing. Ballet. Character traits – shyness. Rhyming text.

Miss Lina's ballerinas and the wicked wish ill. by Christine Davenier. Feiwel & Friends, 2012. ISBN 978-1-250-00580-9 Subj: Activities – dancing. Ballet. Rhyming text.

Oink! moo! how do you do? ill. by Hans Wilhelm. Scholastic, 1994. ISBN 978-0-590-48161-8 Subj: Animals. Careers – farmers. Farms. Noise, sounds. Rhyming text.

The three bears ABC: an alphabet book ill. by Hollie Hibbert. Whitman, 2013. ISBN 978-0-8075-7904-6 Subj: ABC books. Animals – bears. Folk & fairy tales.

McCarthy, Conor Clarke. *Just add one Chinese sister* (McMahon, Patricia)

McCarthy, Mary. *A closer look* ill. by author. HarperCollins, 2007. ISBN 978-0-06-124073-7 Subj: Concepts. Nature. Senses – sight.

McCarthy, Meghan. *The adventures of Patty and the big red bus* ill. by author. Knopf, 2005. ISBN 978-0-375-92939-7 Subj: Activities – traveling. Buses. Family life – sisters. Imagination. Moon. Mountains. Sea & seashore. Space & space ships.

Astronaut handbook ill. by author. Knopf, 2008. ISBN 978-0-375-84459-1 Subj: Careers – astronauts.

City hawk: the story of Pale Male ill. by author. Simon & Schuster, 2007. ISBN 978-1-4169-3359-5 Subj: Birds – hawks.

George upside down ill. by author. Viking, 2003. ISBN 978-0-670-03608-0 Subj: Behavior. Character traits – individuality.

The incredible life of Balto ill. by author. Random House, 2011. ISBN 978-0-375-84460-7 Subj: Alaska. Animals – dogs. Sports – racing. Sports – sledding.

Seabiscuit: the wonder horse ill. by author. Simon & Schuster, 2008. ISBN 978-1-4169-3360-1 Subj: Animals – horses, ponies. Sports – racing.

McCarthy, Michael. *The story of Daniel in the lions' den* ill. by Giuliano Ferri. Barefoot, 2005. ISBN 978-1-84148-209-5 Subj: Animals – lions. Religion – Daniel. Rhyming text.

The story of Noah and the ark ill. by Giuliano Ferri. Barefoot, 2001. ISBN 978-1-84148-361-0 Subj: Animals. Boats, ships. Religion – Noah. Rhyming text. Weather – floods. Weather – rain.

McCarty, Peter. *Baby steps* ill. by author. Holt, 2000. ISBN 978-0-8050-5953-3 Subj: Babies. Behavior – growing up.

Chloe ill. by author. HarperCollins, 2012. ISBN 978-0-06-114291-8 Subj: Animals – rabbits. Family life. Imagination. Television.

Fabian escapes ill. by author. Holt, 2007. ISBN 978-0-8050-7713-1 Subj: Animals – cats. Animals – dogs.

Fall ball ill. by author. Holt, 2013. ISBN 978-0-8050-9253-0 Subj: Seasons – fall. Sports – football.

Henry in love ill. by author. HarperCollins, 2010. ISBN 978-0-06-114288-8 Subj: Animals – cats. Animals – rabbits. Emotions – love. School – first day.

Hondo and Fabian ill. by author. Holt, 2002. ISBN 978-0-8050-6352-3 Subj: Animals – cats. Animals – dogs. Caldecott award honor books. Sea & seashore.

Jeremy draws a monster ill. by author. Holt, 2009. ISBN 978-0-8050-6934-1 Subj: Activities – drawing. Emotions – loneliness. Monsters.

Little bunny on the move ill. by author. Holt, 1999. ISBN 978-0-8050-4620-5 Subj: Activities – traveling. Animals. Animals – rabbits. Homes, houses.

The monster returns ill. by author. Holt, 2012. ISBN 978-0-8050-9030-7 Subj: Activities – drawing. Friendship. Monsters.

Moon plane ill. by author. Holt, 2006. ISBN 978-0-8050-7943-2 Subj: Activities – flying. Airplanes, airports. Imagination. Moon.

McCaughrean, Geraldine. *Beauty and the beast* ill. by Gary Blythe. Carolrhoda, 2000. ISBN 978-1-57505-491-9 Subj: Emotions – love. Folk & fairy tales. Foreign lands – France. Royalty – princes.

Father and son: a nativity story ill. by Fabian Negrin. Hyperion, 2006. ISBN 978-1-4231-0344-8 Subj: Family life – fathers. Holidays – Christmas. Religion – Nativity.

Grandma Chickenlegs ill. by Moira Kemp. Carolrhoda, 2000. ISBN 978-1-57505-415-5 Subj: Family life – stepfamilies. Folk & fairy tales. Foreign lands – Russia. Magic. Witches.

How the reindeer got their antlers ill. by Heather Holland. Holiday, 2000. ISBN 978-0-8234-1562-5 Subj: Animals – reindeer. Character traits – individuality. Character traits – pride. Holidays – Christmas. Santa Claus. Self-concept.

My grandmother's clock ill. by Stephen Lambert. Clarion, 2002. ISBN 978-0-618-21695-6 Subj: Clocks, watches. Family life – grandmothers. Time.

One bright Penny ill. by Paul Howard. Viking, 2002. ISBN 978-0-670-03588-5 Subj: Behavior – trickery. Family life – fathers. Money.

McClatchy, Lisa. *Dear Tyrannosaurus Rex* ill. by John Manders. Random House, 2010. ISBN 978-0-375-85608-2 Subj: Birthdays. Dinosaurs. Letters, cards. Parties.

McClelland, Rosie. *Tea time with Sophia Grace and Rosie* (Brownlee, Sophia Grace)

McClements, George. *Baron von Baddie and the ice ray incident* ill. by author. Harcourt, 2008. ISBN 978-0-15-206138-8 Subj: Behavior – misbehavior. Humorous stories.

Dinosaur Woods: can seven clever critters save their forest home? ill. by author. Simon & Schuster, 2009. ISBN 978-1-4169-8626-3 Subj: Animals. Dinosaurs. Ecology. Forest, woods.

Night of the Veggie Monster ill. by author. Bloomsbury, 2008. ISBN 978-1-59990-061-2 Subj: Behavior – misbehavior. Food.

Ridin' dinos with Buck Bronco ill. by author. Harcourt, 2007. ISBN 978-0-15-205989-7 Subj: Cowboys, cowgirls. Dinosaurs.

McClintock, Barbara. *Adele and Simon* ill. by author. Farrar, 2006. ISBN 978-0-374-38044-1 Subj: Behavior – lost & found possessions. Family life – brothers & sisters. Foreign lands – France.

Adele and Simon in America ill. by author. Farrar, 2008. ISBN 978-0-374-39924-5 Subj: Activities – traveling. Behavior – lost & found possessions. Family life – aunts, uncles. Family life – brothers & sisters.

Dahlia ill. by author. Farrar, 2002. ISBN 978-0-374-31678-5 Subj: Activities – playing. Family life – aunts, uncles. Toys – dolls.

Molly and the magic wishbone ill. by author. Farrar, 2000. ISBN 978-0-374-34999-8 Subj: Behavior – wishing. Fairies. Family life – brothers & sisters.

McCloskey, Robert. *Blueberries for Sal* ill. by author. Viking, 1948. ISBN 978-0-670-17591-8 Subj: Animals – bears. Behavior – lost. Caldecott award honor books. Family life. Food.

Lentil ill. by author. Viking, 1940. ISBN 978-0-670-42357-6 Subj: Music. Musical instruments – harmonicas. Noise, sounds. Problem solving.

Make way for ducklings ill. by author. Viking, 1941. ISBN 978-0-670-45149-4 Subj: Birds – ducks. Caldecott award books. Careers – police officers. Cities, towns.

One morning in Maine ill. by author. Viking, 1952. ISBN 978-0-670-52627-7 Subj: Caldecott award honor books. Family life. Sea & seashore. Teeth.

Time of wonder ill. by author. Viking, 1957. ISBN 978-0-670-71512-1 Subj: Caldecott award books. Islands. Sea & seashore. Seasons – summer. Weather.

McClure, Gillian. *Tom Finger* ill. by author. Bloomsbury, 2002. ISBN 978-1-58234-782-0 Subj: Animals – cats. Gifts. Pets.

McClure, Nikki. *Apple* ill. by author. Abrams, 2012. ISBN 978-1-4197-0378-2 Subj: Food. Nature. Seasons. Trees.

How to be a cat ill. by author. Abrams, 2013. ISBN 978-1-4197-0528-1 Subj: Animals – babies. Animals – cats.

Mama, is it summer yet? ill. by author. Abrams, 2010. ISBN 978-0-8109-8468-4 Subj: Character traits – questioning. Seasons – summer.

McClure, Wendy. *The princess and the peanut allergy* ill. by Tammie Lyon. Whitman, 2009. ISBN 978-0-8075-6623-7 Subj: Birthdays. Illness – allergies. Parties.

McCormack, Caren McNelly. *The fiesta dress: a quinceañera tale* ill. by Martha Avilés. Marshall Cavendish, 2009. ISBN 978-0-7614-5467-0 Subj: Birthdays. Clothing – dresses. Ethnic groups in the U.S. – Hispanic Americans. Family life – sisters. Parties.

McCormick, Wendy. *Daddy, will you miss me?* ill. by Jennifer Eachus. Simon & Schuster, 1999. ISBN 978-0-689-81898-1 Subj: Behavior – needing someone. Emotions – loneliness. Family life – fathers. Foreign lands – Africa.

The night you were born ill. by Sophy Williams. Peachtree, 2000. ISBN 978-1-56145-225-5 Subj: Babies. Family life – aunts, uncles. Family life – brothers & sisters. Family life – new sibling.

McCourt, Lisa, adapt. *Chicken soup for little souls: The best night out with Dad* ill. by Bert Dodson. Health Communications, 1997. ISBN 978-1-55874-508-7 Subj: Character traits – generosity. Circus. Family life – fathers.

Chicken soup for little souls: Della Splatnuk birthday girl ill. by Pat Grant Porter. Health Communications, 1999. ISBN 978-1-55874-600-8 Subj: Birthdays. Friendship. Parties. Prejudice.

Chicken soup for little souls: The Goodness Gorillas ill. by Pat Grant Porter. Health Communications, 1997. ISBN 978-1-55874-505-6 Subj: Character traits – kindness. Clubs, gangs. School.

Chicken soup for little souls: The never-forgotten doll ill. by Mary O'Keefe Young. Health Communications, 1997. ISBN 978-1-55874-507-0 Subj: Activities – babysitting. Behavior – lost & found possessions. Birthdays. Character traits – kindness. Gifts.

Chicken soup for little souls: The new kid and the cookie thief ill. by Mary O'Keefe Young. Health Communications, 1998. ISBN 978-1-55874-588-9 Subj: Character traits – shyness. Friendship. School.

Good night, Princess Pruney Toes ill. by Cyd Moore. BridgeWater, 2001. ISBN 978-0-8167-5205-8 Subj: Bedtime. Family life – daughters. Family life – fathers. Imagination. Royalty – princesses.

Happy Halloween, Stinky Face ill. by Cyd Moore. Scholastic, 2007. ISBN 978-0-439-77977-7 Subj: Family life – mothers. Holidays – Halloween. Imagination.

I love you, Stinky Face ill. by Cyd Moore. Troll, 1997. ISBN 978-0-8167-4392-6 Subj: Bedtime. Emotions – love. Family life – mothers. Imagination.

I miss you, Stinky Face ill. by Cyd Moore. BridgeWater, 1999. ISBN 978-0-8167-5647-6 Subj: Activities – traveling. Family life – mothers. Transportation.

It's time for school, Stinky Face ill. by Cyd Moore. BridgeWater, 2000. ISBN 978-0-8167-6961-2 Subj: Family life – mothers. Imagination. School.

Merry Christmas, Stinky Face ill. by Cyd Moore. Scholastic, 2003. ISBN 978-0-439-63577-6 Subj: Family life – mothers. Holidays – Christmas. Imagination.

McCue, Lisa. *Corduroy's best Halloween ever!* ill. by author. Based on the character by Don Freeman. Grosset, 2001. ISBN 978-0-448-42499-6 Subj: Clothing – costumes. Holidays – Halloween. Toys – bears.

Quiet Bunny ill. by author. Sterling, 2009. ISBN 978-1-4027-5719-8 Subj: Animals – rabbits. Character traits – individuality. Noise, sounds.

Quiet Bunny and Noisy Puppy ill. by author. Sterling, 2011. ISBN 978-1-4027-8559-7 Subj: Animals – dogs. Animals – rabbits. Friendship. Seasons – winter.

McCullough, Sharon Pierce. *Bunbun at bedtime* ill. by author. Barefoot, 2001. ISBN 978-1-84148-438-9 Subj: Animals – rabbits. Bedtime.

Bunbun, the middle one ill. by author. Barefoot, 2001. ISBN 978-1-84148-377-1 Subj: Animals – rabbits. Family life – brothers & sisters.

McCully, Emily Arnold. *The Christmas gift* ill. by author. HarperCollins, 1988. ISBN 978-0-06-024212-1 Subj: Animals – mice. Family life – grandfathers. Gifts. Holidays – Christmas. Toys. Wordless.

First snow ill. by author. HarperCollins, 1985. ISBN 978-0-06-623853-1 Subj: Activities – playing. Animals – mice. Seasons – winter. Weather – snow. Wordless.

Four hungry kittens ill. by author. Dial, 2001. ISBN 978-0-8037-2505-8 Subj: Animals – cats. Wordless.

Hurry! ill. by author. Harcourt, 2000. ISBN 978-0-15-201579-4 Subj: Animals – endangered animals. Behavior – hurrying.

Marvelous Mattie: how Margaret E. Knight became an inventor ill. by author. Farrar, 2006. ISBN 978-0-374-34810-6 Subj: Careers – scientists. Inventions. Problem solving.

Mirette and Bellini cross Niagara Falls ill. by author. Putnam, 2000. ISBN 978-0-399-23348-7 Subj: Careers – aerialists. Ethnic groups in the U.S. – French Americans. Immigrants.

Mirette on the high wire ill. by author. Putnam, 1992. ISBN 978-0-399-22130-9 Subj: Caldecott award books. Careers – aerialists. Emotions – fear. Foreign lands – France.

Monk camps out ill. by author. Scholastic, 2000. ISBN 978-0-439-09976-9 Subj: Animals – mice. Camps, camping. Family life.

Mouse practice ill. by author. Scholastic, 1999. ISBN 978-0-590-68220-6 Subj: Animals – mice. Character traits – persistence. Sports – baseball.

My heart glow: Alice Cogswell, Thomas Gallaudet, and the birth of American sign language ill. by author. Hyperion, 2008. ISBN 978-1-4231-0028-7 Subj: Disabilities – deafness. Sign language. U.S. history.

My real family ill. by author. Browndeer, 1994. ISBN 978-0-15-277698-5 Subj: Adoption. Animals – bears. Animals – sheep. Behavior – running away. Family life. Theater.

New baby ill. by author. HarperCollins, 1988. ISBN 978-0-06-024131-5 Subj: Animals – mice. Sibling rivalry. Wordless.

An outlaw Thanksgiving ill. by author. Dial, 1998. ISBN 978-0-8037-2198-2 Subj: Crime. Holidays – Thanksgiving. Trains. U.S. history. Weather – snow.

Picnic ill. by author. HarperCollins, 1984. ISBN 978-0-06-024099-8 Subj: Activities – picnicking. Animals – mice. Behavior – lost. Wordless.

The pirate queen ill. by author. Putnam, 1995. ISBN 978-0-399-22657-1 Subj: Boats, ships. Foreign lands – Ireland. Pirates.

Popcorn at the palace ill. by author. Browndeer, 1997. ISBN 978-0-15-277699-2 Subj: Family life – fathers. Food. Foreign lands – England.

School ill. by author. HarperCollins, 2005. ISBN 978-0-06-623856-2 Subj: Animals – mice. School.

The secret cave: discovering Lascaux ill. by author. Farrar, 2010. ISBN 978-0-374-36694-0 Subj: Art. Caves. Prehistory.

Wonder horse: the true story of the world's smartest horse ill. by author. Holt, 2010. ISBN 978-0-8050-8793-2 Subj: Animals – horses, ponies. Careers – veterinarians. Ethnic groups in the U.S. – African Americans. Prejudice.

McCurdy, Michael. *An Algonquian year: the year according to the full moon* ill. by author. Houghton, 2000. ISBN 978-0-618-00705-9 Subj: Days of the week, months of the year. Food. Indians of North America – Algonquin.

McCurry, Kristen. *Ocean babies* by Kristen McCurry and Aimee Jackson; photos by Anup Shah. NorthWord, 2004. ISBN 978-1-55971-898-1 Subj: Animals. Animals – babies. Format, unusual – board books. Sea & seashore.

Safari babies by Kristen McCurry and Aimee Jackson; photos by Anup Shah. NorthWord, 2004. ISBN 978-1-55971-899-8 Subj: Animals. Animals – babies. Format, unusual – board books. Science.

McCutcheon, John. *Happy adoption day!* ill. by Julie Paschkis. Little, 1996. ISBN 978-0-316-55455-8 Subj: Adoption. Family life. Songs.

McDaniels, Preston. *A perfect snowman* ill. by author. Simon & Schuster, 2007. ISBN 978-1-4169-1026-8 Subj: Behavior – sharing. Seasons – winter. Snowmen.

McDermott, Gerald. *Anansi the spider: a tale from the Ashanti* ill. by author. Holt, 1972. ISBN 978-0-03-080236-2 Subj: Caldecott award honor books. Folk & fairy tales. Foreign lands – Africa. Moon. Spiders.

Arrow to the sun: a Pueblo Indian tale ill. by author. Viking, 1974. ISBN 978-0-670-13369-7 Subj: Caldecott award books. Folk & fairy tales. Indians of North America – Pueblo.

Coyote: a trickster tale from the American Southwest ill. by author. Harcourt, 1994. ISBN 978-0-15-220724-3 Subj: Activities – flying. Animals –

coyotes. Birds – crows. Folk & fairy tales. Indians of North America – Southwest.

Daniel O'Rourke: an Irish tale ill. by author. Viking, 1986. ISBN 978-0-670-80924-0 Subj: Dreams. Folk & fairy tales. Foreign lands – Ireland. Mythical creatures – pooka spirit.

Jabutí the tortoise ill. by author. Harcourt, 2001. ISBN 978-0-15-200496-5 Subj: Behavior – trickery. Folk & fairy tales – pourquoi tales. Foreign lands – South America. Reptiles – turtles, tortoises.

Monkey: a trickster tale from India ill. by author. Harcourt, 2011. ISBN 978-0-15-216596-3 Subj: Animals – monkeys. Behavior – trickery. Character traits – cleverness. Folk & fairy tales. Foreign lands – India.

Musicians of the sun ill. by author. Simon & Schuster, 1997. ISBN 978-0-689-80706-0 Subj: Folk & fairy tales. Foreign lands – Mexico. Indians of North America – Aztec. Music. Sun.

Pig-Boy: a trickster tale from Hawai'i ill. by author. Harcourt, 2009. ISBN 978-0-15-216590-1 Subj: Animals – pigs. Behavior – trickery. Folk & fairy tales. Hawaii.

Raven: a trickster tale from the Pacific Northwest ill. by author. Harcourt, 1993. ISBN 978-0-15-265661-4 Subj: Behavior – trickery. Birds – ravens. Caldecott award honor books. Folk & fairy tales. Indians of North America.

Tim O'Toole and the wee folk ill. by author. Viking, 1990. ISBN 978-0-670-80393-4 Subj: Behavior – trickery. Cities, towns. Folk & fairy tales. Magic.

Zomo the rabbit ill. by author. Harcourt, 1992. ISBN 978-0-15-299967-4 Subj: Animals – rabbits. Behavior – trickery. Foreign lands – Africa.

MacDonald, Alan. *Beware of the bears!* ill. by Gwyneth Williamson. Little Tiger, 1998. ISBN 978-1-888444-28-5 Subj: Animals – bears. Character traits – orderliness.

The pig in a wig ill. by Paul Hess. Peachtree, 1999. ISBN 978-1-56145-197-5 Subj: Animals – pigs. Hair. Self-concept.

Wilfred to the rescue: stories from Brambly Hedge ill. by Lizzie Sanders. Simon & Schuster, 2006. ISBN 978-1-4169-0901-9 Subj: Animals. Animals – mice. Behavior – lost. Foreign lands – England. Weather – floods.

MacDonald, Amy. *Cousin Ruth's tooth* ill. by Marjorie Priceman. Houghton, 1996. ISBN 978-0-395-71253-5 Subj: Behavior – growing up. Behavior – lost & found possessions. Family life. Rhyming text. Teeth.

Please, Malese! a trickster tale from Haiti ill. by Emily Lisker. DK, 2001. ISBN 978-0-7894-2647-5 Subj: Behavior – trickery. Folk & fairy tales. Foreign lands – Haiti.

Quentin Fenton Herter three ill. by Giselle Potter. Farrar, 2002. ISBN 978-0-374-36170-9 Subj: Behavior. Behavior – misbehavior. Humorous stories. Rhyming text. Shadows.

Rachel Fister's blister ill. by Marjorie Priceman. Houghton, 1990. ISBN 978-0-395-52152-6 Subj: Illness. Rhyming text.

MacDonald, Elizabeth. *The wolf is coming!* ill. by Ken Brown. Dutton, 1998. ISBN 978-0-525-45952-1 Subj: Animals. Animals – rabbits. Animals – wolves. Cumulative tales.

MacDonald, Golden *see* Brown, Margaret Wise

MacDonald, Margaret Read. *Conejito: a folktale from Panama* ill. by Geraldo Valério. August House, 2006. ISBN 978-0-87483-779-7 Subj: Animals – rabbits. Behavior – trickery. Folk & fairy tales. Foreign lands – Panama. Foreign languages.

Fat cat ill. by Julie Paschkis. August House, 2001. ISBN 978-0-87483-616-5 Subj: Animals – cats. Animals – mice. Folk & fairy tales. Foreign lands – Denmark.

The girl who wore too much Thai text by Supaporn Vathanaprida; ill. by Yvonne Davis. August House, 1998. ISBN 978-0-87483-503-8 Subj: Character traits – vanity. Clothing. Folk & fairy tales. Foreign lands – Thailand.

Give up, Gecko! a folktale from Uganda ill. by Deborah Melmon. Amazon/Two Lions, 2013. ISBN 978-1-4778-1635-6 Subj: Animals. Character traits – perseverance. Folk & fairy tales. Foreign lands – Uganda. Reptiles. Water.

The great smelly, slobbery small-toothed dog ill. by Julie Paschkis. Random House, 2007. ISBN 978-0-87483-808-4 Subj: Animals – dogs. Character traits – appearance. Emotions – love. Folk & fairy tales. Magic.

A hen, a chick, and a string guitar ill. by Sophie Fatus. Barefoot, 2005. ISBN 978-1-84148-796-0 Subj: Animals. Counting, numbers. Cumulative tales. Folk & fairy tales. Songs.

How many donkeys? an Arabic counting tale by Margaret Read MacDonald and Nadia Jameel Taibah ill. by Carol Liddiment. Whitman, 2009. ISBN 978-0-8075-3424-3 Subj: Counting, numbers. Folk & fairy tales. Foreign lands – Saudi Arabia. Foreign languages.

Little Rooster's diamond button ill. by Will Terry. Whitman, 2007. ISBN 978-0-8075-4644-4 Subj: Behavior – greed. Birds – chickens. Clothing. Folk & fairy tales. Foreign lands – Hungary. Royalty – kings.

Mabela the clever ill. by Tim Coffey. Whitman, 2001. ISBN 978-0-8075-4902-5 Subj: Animals –

cats. Animals – mice. Folk & fairy tales. Foreign lands – Africa.

The old woman who lived in a vinegar bottle ill. by Nancy Dunaway Fowlkes. August House, 1995. ISBN 978-0-87483-415-4 Subj: Behavior – dissatisfaction. Folk & fairy tales. Foreign lands – England.

Pickin' peas ill. by Pat Cummings. HarperCollins, 1998. ISBN 978-0-06-027970-7 Subj: Animals – rabbits. Behavior – trickery. Ethnic groups in the U.S. – African Americans. Folk & fairy tales. Gardens, gardening.

Slop! a Welsh folktale ill. by Yvonne Davis. Fulcrum Kids, 1997. ISBN 978-1-55591-352-6 Subj: Character traits – kindness. Fairies. Folk & fairy tales. Foreign lands – Wales.

The squeaky door ill. by Mary Newell DePalma. HarperCollins, 2006. ISBN 978-0-06-028373-5 Subj: Animals. Bedtime. Cumulative tales. Emotions – fear. Family life – grandmothers. Folk & fairy tales. Noise, sounds.

Surf war! a folktale from the Marshall Islands ill. by Geraldo Valério. August House, 2009. ISBN 978-0-87483-889-3 Subj: Ecology. Folk & fairy tales. Foreign lands. Sea & seashore.

Teeny Weeny Bop ill. by Diane Greenseid. Whitman, 2006. ISBN 978-0-8075-7992-3 Subj: Cumulative tales. Folk & fairy tales.

Too many fairies: a Celtic tale ill. by Susan Mitchell. Marshall Cavendish, 2010. ISBN 978-0-7614-5604-9 Subj: Fairies. Folk & fairy tales.

Tuck-me-in tales ill. by Yvonne Davis. August House, 1996. ISBN 978-0-87483-461-1 Subj: Bedtime. Folk & fairy tales.

Tunjur! Tunjur! Tunjur! a Palestinian folktale ill. by Alik Arzoumanian. Marshall Cavendish, 2006. ISBN 978-0-7614-5225-6 Subj: Behavior – stealing. Folk & fairy tales. Foreign lands – Palestine.

MacDonald, Maryann. *The Christmas cat* ill. by Amy Bates. Dial, 2013. ISBN 978-0-8037-3498-2 Subj: Animals – cats. Religion – Nativity.

How to hug ill. by Jana Christy. Marshall Cavendish, 2011. ISBN 978-0-7614-5804-3 Subj: Hugging.

The little piano girl: the story of Mary Lou Williams, jazz legend (Ingalls, Ann)

The pink party ill. by Judy Stead. Marshall Cavendish, 2011. ISBN 978-0-7614-5814-2 Subj: Concepts – color. Emotions – envy, jealousy. Friendship.

McDonald, Megan. *Ant and Honey Bee, what a pair!* ill. by G. Brian Karas. Candlewick, 2005. ISBN 978-0-7636-1265-8 Subj: Clothing – costumes. Insects – ants. Insects – bees. Parties.

Beetle McGrady eats bugs! ill. by Jane Manning. HarperCollins, 2005. ISBN 978-0-06-001355-4 Subj: Character traits – bravery. Food. Insects. School.

The great pumpkin switch ill. by Ted Lewin. Watts, 1992. ISBN 978-0-531-08600-1 Subj: Family life – grandfathers. Mystery stories. Plants.

Hen hears gossip ill. by Joung Un Kim. Greenwillow, 2008. ISBN 978-0-06-113876-8 Subj: Animals. Behavior – gossip. Birds – chickens.

The Hinky Pink: an old tale ill. by Brian Floca. Atheneum, 2008. ISBN 978-0-689-87588-5 Subj: Activities – sewing. Clothing – dresses. Folk & fairy tales. Mythical creatures – goblins. Royalty – princesses.

Insects are my life ill. by Paul Brett Johnson. Orchard, 1995. ISBN 978-0-531-08724-4 Subj: Behavior – collecting things. Family life. Insects. School.

Is this a house for Hermit Crab? ill. by S. D. Schindler. Watts, 1990. ISBN 978-0-531-08455-7 Subj: Crustaceans – crabs. Sea & seashore.

It's picture day today! ill. by Katherine Tillotson. Atheneum, 2009. ISBN 978-1-4169-2434-0 Subj: Activities – making things. Art. Rhyming text. School.

Penguin and Little Blue ill. by Katherine Tillotson. Atheneum, 2003. ISBN 978-0-689-84415-7 Subj: Birds – penguins. Foreign lands – Antarctic. Theater.

Reptiles are my life ill. by Paul Brett Johnson. Orchard, 2001. ISBN 978-0-439-29306-8 Subj: Friendship. Insects. Reptiles. School.

When the library lights go out ill. by Katherine Tillotson. Simon & Schuster, 2005. ISBN 978-0-689-86170-3 Subj: Animals. Behavior – lost. Libraries. Light, lights. Puppets.

Whoo-oo is it? ill. by S. D. Schindler. Watts, 1992. ISBN 978-0-531-08574-5 Subj: Birds – owls. Night. Noise, sounds.

McDonald, Rae A. *A fishing surprise* ill. by Kathleen Kemly. NorthWord, 2007. ISBN 978-1-55971-977-3 Subj: Family life – brothers & sisters. Food. Rhyming text. Sports – fishing.

MacDonald, Ross. *Achoo! Bang! Crash!* ill. by author. Roaring Brook, 2003. ISBN 978-0-7613-2900-8 Subj: ABC books. Language. Noise, sounds.

Another perfect day ill. by author. Roaring Brook, 2002. ISBN 978-0-7613-2659-5 Subj: Dreams.

Bad baby ill. by author. Macmillan, 2005. ISBN 978-1-59643-064-8 Subj: Babies. Concepts – size. Family life – brothers & sisters. Family life – new sibling.

MacDonald, Suse. *Alphabatics* ill. by author. Bradbury, 1986. ISBN 978-0-02-761520-3 Subj: ABC books. Caldecott award honor books.

Circus opposites: an interactive extravaganza! ill. by author. Simon & Schuster, 2010. ISBN 978-1-4169-7154-2 Subj: Circus. Concepts – opposites. Format, unusual – toy & movable books.

Edward Lear's A was once an apple pie ill. by adapter. Scholastic, 2005. ISBN 978-0-439-66056-3 Subj: ABC books. Poetry.

Elephants on board ill. by author. Harcourt, 1999. ISBN 978-0-15-200951-9 Subj: Animals – elephants. Circus. Machines. Rhyming text. Transportation. Trucks.

Fish, swish! splash, dash! counting round and round ill. by author. Simon & Schuster, 2007. ISBN 978-1-4169-3605-3 Subj: Counting, numbers. Fish. Format, unusual.

Look whooo's counting ill. by author. Scholastic, 2000. ISBN 978-0-590-68320-3 Subj: Animals. Counting, numbers. Picture puzzles.

Shape by shape ill. by author. Simon & Schuster, 2009. ISBN 978-1-4169-7147-4 Subj: Concepts – shape. Dinosaurs. Format, unusual.

McDonnell, Christine. *Dog wants to play* ill. by Jeff Mack. Viking, 2009. ISBN 978-0-670-01126-1 Subj: Activities – playing. Animals. Animals – dogs.

Goyangi means cat ill. by Steve Johnson and Lou Fancher. Penguin, 2011. ISBN 978-0-670-01179-7 Subj: Adoption. Animals – cats. Behavior – lost & found possessions. Emotions – loneliness. Ethnic groups in the U.S. – Korean Americans.

McDonnell, Flora. *Flora McDonnell's ABC* ill. by author. Candlewick, 1997. ISBN 978-0-7636-0118-8 Subj: ABC books.

Giddy-up! Let's ride! ill. by author. Candlewick, 2002. ISBN 978-0-7636-1778-3 Subj: Animals. Animals – horses, ponies.

I love animals ill. by author. Candlewick, 1994. ISBN 978-1-56402-387-2 Subj: Animals. Character traits – kindness to animals. Farms.

I love boats ill. by author. Candlewick, 1995. ISBN 978-1-56402-539-5 Subj: Activities – bathing. Boats, ships. Toys.

Sparky ill. by author. Candlewick, 2004. ISBN 978-0-7636-2208-4 Subj: Animals – dogs. Pets.

Splash! ill. by author. Candlewick, 1999. ISBN 978-0-7636-0481-3 Subj: Animals. Animals – elephants. Water.

McDonnell, Patrick. *Art* ill. by author. Little, Brown, 2006. ISBN 978-0-316-11491-2 Subj: Activities – drawing. Art. Rhyming text.

The gift of nothing ill. by author. Little, Brown, 2005. ISBN 978-0-316-11488-2 Subj: Animals – cats. Animals – dogs. Friendship. Gifts.

Just like Heaven ill. by author. Little, Brown, 2006. ISBN 978-0-316-11493-6 Subj: Animals – cats. Animals – dogs. Weather – fog.

Me . . . Jane ill. by author. Little, Brown, 2011. ISBN 978-0-316-04546-9 Subj: Animals. Animals – chimpanzees. Caldecott award honor books. Careers – scientists. Nature. Toys.

The monsters' monster ill. by author. Little, Brown, 2012. ISBN 978-0-316-04547-6 Subj: Behavior – misbehavior. Monsters.

South ill. by author. Little, Brown, 2008. ISBN 978-0-316-00509-8 Subj: Animals – cats. Birds. Emotions – loneliness. Wordless.

Wag! ill. by author. Little, Brown, 2009. ISBN 978-0-316-04548-3 Subj: Anatomy – tails. Animals – cats. Animals – dogs.

McDonough, Yona Zeldis. *Hammerin' Hank: the life of Hank Greenberg* ill. by Malcah Zeldis. Walker, 2006. ISBN 978-0-8027-8997-6 Subj: Jewish culture. Sports – baseball.

McElligott, Matthew. *Backbeard and the birthday suit: the hairiest pirate who ever lived* ill. by author. Walker, 2006. ISBN 978-0-8027-8065-2 Subj: Birthdays. Character traits – cleanliness. Clothing. Hair. Parties. Pirates.

Bean thirteen ill. by author. Penguin, 2007. ISBN 978-0-399-24535-0 Subj: Counting, numbers. Insects.

Even aliens need snacks ill. by author. Walker, 2012. ISBN 978-0-8027-2398-7 Subj: Activities – baking, cooking. Aliens. Food.

Even monsters need haircuts ill. by author. Walker, 2010. ISBN 978-0-8027-8819-1 Subj: Careers – barbers. Monsters.

The lion's share ill. by author. Walker, 2009. ISBN 978-0-8027-9768-1 Subj: Animals – lions. Behavior – misbehavior. Counting, numbers. Etiquette. Insects – ants.

McElmurry, Jill. *I'm not a baby!* ill. by author. Random House, 2006. ISBN 978-0-375-93614-2 Subj: Babies. Behavior – growing up. Humorous stories.

Mad about plaid ill. by author. Morrow, 2000. ISBN 978-0-688-16952-7 Subj: Behavior – lost & found possessions. Clothing – handbags, purses. Concepts – patterns.

Mario makes a move ill. by author. Random House, 2012. ISBN 978-0-375-86854-2 Subj: Activities – dancing. Animals – squirrels.

Mess pets ill. by author. SeaStar, 2002. ISBN 978-1-58717-175-8 Subj: Character traits – cleanliness.

Character traits – orderliness. Family life – sisters. Health & fitness. Multiple births – twins.

McElroy, Lisa Tucker. *Love, Lizzie: letters to a military mom* ill. by Diane Paterson. Whitman, 2005. ISBN 978-0-8075-4777-9 Subj: Careers – military. Emotions – loneliness. Family life – mothers. Letters, cards. War.

Meet my grandmother. She's a children's book author by Lisa Tucker McElroy and Abigail Jane Cobb; photos by Joel Benjamin. Millbrook, 2001. ISBN 978-0-7613-1972-6 Subj: Activities – writing. Careers – writers. Family life – grandmothers.

McEvoy, Anne. *Betsy B. Little* ill. by Jacqueline Rogers. HarperCollins, 2009. ISBN 978-0-06-059337-7 Subj: Animals – giraffes. Ballet. Concepts – size. Rhyming text. Self-concept.

McFarland, Lyn Rossiter. *Mouse went out to get a snack* ill. by Jim McFarland. Farrar, 2005. ISBN 978-0-374-37672-7 Subj: Animals – mice. Counting, numbers. Food.

The pirate's parrot ill. by Jim McFarland. Tricycle, 2000. ISBN 978-1-58246-014-7 Subj: Behavior – fighting, arguing. Behavior – mistakes. Birds – parakeets, parrots. Pirates. Toys – bears.

Widget and the puppy ill. by Jim McFarland. Farrar, 2004. ISBN 978-0-374-38429-6 Subj: Animals – cats. Animals – dogs. Behavior – lost.

McFarlane, Sheryl. *In the city* ill. by Kim LaFave. Fitzhenry & Whiteside, 2004. ISBN 978-1-55041-812-5 Subj: Cities, towns. Format, unusual – board books. Noise, sounds.

On the farm ill. by Kim LaFave. Fitzhenry & Whiteside, 2004. ISBN 978-1-55041-814-9 Subj: Animals. Farms. Format, unusual – board books. Noise, sounds.

McG, Shane. *Tennis, anyone?* ill. by author. Carolrhoda, 2007. ISBN 978-0-8225-6901-5 Subj: Sports – tennis.

McGaw, Wayne T. *T-boy of the bayou* ill. by George Crespo. Carolrhoda, 2002. ISBN 978-0-87614-648-4 Subj: Birds – herons. Careers – fishermen. Crustaceans – shrimp. Fish. Magic.

McGee, Marni. *The colt and the king* ill. by John Winch. Holiday, 2002. ISBN 978-0-8234-1695-0 Subj: Animals – donkeys. Holidays. Religion.

The noisy farm ill. by Leonie Shearing. Bloomsbury, 2004. ISBN 978-1-58234-879-7 Subj: Animals. Day. Farms. Noise, sounds.

Sleepy me ill. by Sam Williams. Simon & Schuster, 2001. ISBN 978-0-689-82378-7 Subj: Bedtime. Family life – fathers. Rhyming text.

Wake up, me! ill. by Sam Williams. Simon & Schuster, 2002. ISBN 978-0-689-83163-8 Subj: Behavior. Family life – parents. Morning. Rhyming text.

Winston the book wolf ill. by Ian Beck. Walker, 2006. ISBN 978-0-8027-9569-4 Subj: Animals – wolves. Books, reading. Libraries.

McGhee, Alison. *Always* ill. by Pascal Lemaître. Simon & Schuster, 2009. ISBN 978-1-4169-7481-9 Subj: Animals – dogs. Character traits – loyalty. Pets.

Bye-bye, crib ill. by Ross MacDonald. Simon & Schuster, 2008. ISBN 978-1-4169-1621-5 Subj: Behavior – growing up. Furniture – beds.

The case of the missing donut ill. by Isabel Roxas. Dial, 2013. ISBN 978-0-8037-3925-3 Subj: Activities – playing. Food. Humorous stories.

Countdown to kindergarten ill. by Harry Bliss. Harcourt, 2002. ISBN 978-0-15-202516-8 Subj: Emotions – fear. School – first day.

In the hollow of your hand ill. by Michael Cummings. Houghton, 2000. ISBN 978-0-395-85755-7 Subj: Ethnic groups in the U.S. – African Americans. Lullabies. Slavery. Sleep.

Little boy ill. by Peter H. Reynolds. Atheneum, 2008. ISBN 978-1-4169-5872-7 Subj: Behavior – growing up. Family life – fathers.

Making a friend ill. by Marc Rosenthal. Simon & Schuster, 2011. ISBN 978-1-4169-8998-1 Subj: Friendship. Seasons. Snowmen. Water.

Only a witch can fly ill. by Taeeun Yoo. Feiwel & Friends, 2009. ISBN 978-0-312-37503-4 Subj: Activities – flying. Character traits – persistence. Holidays – Halloween. Poetry.

So many days ill. by Taeeun Yoo. Simon & Schuster, 2010. ISBN 978-1-4169-5857-4 Subj: Self-concept.

Someday ill. by Peter H. Reynolds. Simon & Schuster, 2006. ISBN 978-1-4169-2811-9 Subj: Behavior – growing up. Family life – mothers.

Song of middle C ill. by Scott Menchin. Candlewick, 2009. ISBN 978-0-7636-3013-3 Subj: Emotions – fear. Imagination. Music. Musical instruments – pianos.

A very brave witch ill. by Harry Bliss. Simon & Schuster, 2006. ISBN 978-0-689-86730-9 Subj: Character traits – bravery. Holidays – Halloween. Witches.

McGill, Alice. *Molly Bannaky* ill. by Chris Soentpiet. Houghton, 1999. ISBN 978-0-395-72287-9 Subj: Books, reading. Ethnic groups in the U.S. – African Americans. Farms. Immigrants. Marriage, interracial. Slavery. U.S. history.

Sure as sunrise: stories of Bruh Rabbit and his walkin' talkin' friends ill. by Don Tate. Houghton, 2004. ISBN 978-0-618-21196-8 Subj: Animals. Ethnic groups in the U.S. – African Americans. Folk & fairy tales. Tall tales.

Way up and over everything ill. by Jude Daly. Houghton, 2008. ISBN 978-0-618-38796-0 Subj: Activities – flying. Ethnic groups in the U.S. – African Americans. Folk & fairy tales. Slavery.

McGinley, Phyllis. *The year without a Santa Claus* ill. by John Manders. Marshall Cavendish, 2010. ISBN 978-0-7614-5799-2 Subj: Character traits – generosity. Gifts. Holidays – Christmas. Rhyming text. Santa Claus.

McGinley-Nally, Sharon. *The friendly beasts* ill. by author. Greenwillow, 2000. ISBN 978-0-688-17422-4 Subj: Animals. Holidays – Christmas. Music. Religion – Nativity. Songs.

McGinness, Suzanne. *My bear Griz* ill. by author. Frances Lincoln, 2011. ISBN 978-1-84780-113-5 Subj: Animals – bears. Toys – bears.

McGinty, Alice B. *Eliza's kindergarten pet* ill. by Nancy Speir. Marshall Cavendish, 2010. ISBN 978-0-7614-5702-2 Subj: Animals – guinea pigs. Behavior – lost & found possessions. Behavior – worrying. School.

Eliza's kindergarten surprise ill. by Nancy Speir. Marshall Cavendish, 2007. ISBN 978-0-7614-5351-2 Subj: Behavior – collecting things. Family life – mothers. School – first day.

Gandhi: a march to the sea ill. by Thomas Gonzalez. Amazon/Two Lions, 2013. ISBN 978-1-4778-1644-8 Subj: Behavior – seeking better things. Character traits – perseverance. Foreign lands – India. Violence, nonviolence.

Ten little lambs ill. by Melissa Sweet. Dial, 2002. ISBN 978-0-8037-2596-6 Subj: Animals – sheep. Counting, numbers. Night. Rhyming text. Sleep.

Thank you, world ill. by Wendy Anderson Halperin. Penguin, 2007. ISBN 978-0-8037-2705-2 Subj: Rhyming text. World.

McGough, Roger. *What on earth can it be?* ill. by Lydia Monks. Simon & Schuster, 2002. ISBN 978-0-689-85351-7 Subj: Humorous stories. Poetry. Rhyming text.

McGovern, Ann. *Too much noise* ill. by Simms Taback. Houghton, 1967. ISBN 978-0-590-02435-8 Subj: Humorous stories. Noise, sounds.

McGowan, Michael. *Sunday is for God* ill. by Steve Johnson and Lou Fancher. Random House, 2010. ISBN 978-0-375-84188-0 Subj: Days of the week, months of the year. Ethnic groups in the U.S. – African Americans. Family life. Religion.

McGrath, Barbara Barbieri. *Kellogg's froot loops color fun book* ill. by Frank Mazzola. HarperCollins, 2001. ISBN 978-0-694-01577-1 Subj: Concepts – color. Food. Format, unusual – board books. Picture puzzles. Rhyming text.

Kellogg's froot loops counting fun book ill. by Rob Bolster and Frank Mazzola, Jr. HarperCollins, 2000. ISBN 978-0-694-01506-1 Subj: Counting, numbers. Food. Rhyming text.

The little gray bunny ill. by Violet Kim. Charlesbridge, 2013. ISBN 978-1-58089-394-7 Subj: Animals. Animals – rabbits. Character traits – laziness. Farms. Holidays – Easter.

The little green witch ill. by Martha G. Alexander. Charlesbridge, 2005. ISBN 978-1-58089-042-7 Subj: Character traits – laziness. Plants. Witches.

Teddy bear counting ill. by Tim Nihoff. Charlesbridge, 2010. ISBN 978-1-58089-215-5 Subj: Concepts – color. Concepts – shape. Counting, numbers. Rhyming text. Toys – bears.

McGraw, Sheila. *Pussycats everywhere* ill. by author. Firefly, 2000. ISBN 978-1-55209-346-7 Subj: Animals – cats. Behavior – lost. Humorous stories.

McGrory, Anik. *Kidogo* ill. by author. Bloomsbury, 2005. ISBN 978-1-58234-974-9 Subj: Animals – elephants. Character traits – smallness. Concepts – size. Foreign lands – Africa.

Mouton's impossible dream ill. by author. Harcourt, 2000. ISBN 978-0-15-202195-5 Subj: Activities – ballooning. Animals – sheep. Behavior – wishing. Birds. Royalty – queens.

McGuinness-Kelly, Tracy-Lee. *Bad Cat puts on his top hat* ill. by author. Little, 2005. ISBN 978-0-316-60547-2 Subj: Animals – cats. Behavior – trickery.

McGuirk, Leslie. *Ho, ho, ho, Tucker!* ill. by author. Candlewick, 2005. ISBN 978-0-7636-2582-5 Subj: Animals – dogs. Holidays – Christmas. Santa Claus.

If rocks could sing: a discovered alphabet ill. by author. Tricycle, 2011. ISBN 978-1-58246-370-4 Subj: ABC books. Rocks.

Lucky Tucker ill. by author. Candlewick, 2008. ISBN 978-0-7636-3389-9 Subj: Animals – dogs. Character traits – luck. Holidays – St. Patrick's Day.

Snail boy ill. by author. Candlewick, 2003. ISBN 978-0-7636-1259-7 Subj: Animals – snails. Behavior – needing someone. Concepts – size.

Tucker flips! ill. by author. Dutton, 1999. ISBN 978-0-525-46259-0 Subj: Activities – playing. Animals – dogs. Weather – snow.

Tucker off his rocker ill. by author. Dutton, 2000. ISBN 978-0-525-46398-6 Subj: Activities. Animals – dogs.

Tucker over the top ill. by author. Dutton, 2000. ISBN 978-0-525-46465-5 Subj: Animals – dogs. Circus.

Tucker's spooky Halloween ill. by author. Candlewick, 2007. ISBN 978-0-7636-3181-9 Subj: Animals – dogs. Clothing – costumes. Holidays – Halloween.

Machado, Ana Maria. *What a party!* ill. by Helene Moreau. Groundwood, 2013. ISBN 978-1-55498-168-7 Subj: Birthdays. Communities, neighborhoods. Food. Parties.

Wolf wanted ill. by Laurent Cardon. Groundwood, 2010. ISBN 978-0-88899-880-4 Subj: Animals – wolves. Folk & fairy tales.

MacHale, D. J. *The monster princess* ill. by Alexandra Boiger. Simon & Schuster, 2010. ISBN 978-1-4169-4809-4 Subj: Monsters. Royalty – princesses. Self-concept.

McHenry, E. B. *Has anyone seen Winnie and Jean?* ill. by author. Bloomsbury, 2007. ISBN 978-1-58234-999-2 Subj: Animals – dogs. Behavior – lost. Behavior – running away.

Poodlena ill. by author. Bloomsbury, 2004. ISBN 978-1-58234-824-7 Subj: Activities – playing. Animals – dogs. Character traits – cleanliness. Rhyming text.

Mack, Jeff. *Ah ha!* ill. by author. Chronicle, 2013. ISBN 978-1-4521-1265-7 Subj: Cumulative tales. Frogs & toads.

Frog and Fly: six slurpy stories ill. by author. Philomel, 2012. ISBN 978-0-399-25617-2 Subj: Frogs & toads. Humorous stories. Insects – flies.

Good news, bad news ill. by author. Chronicle, 2012. ISBN 978-1-4521-0110-1 Subj: Activities – picnicking. Animals – mice. Animals – rabbits. Behavior – bad day. Character traits – optimism.

Hush little polar bear ill. by author. Roaring Brook, 2008. ISBN 978-1-59643-368-7 Subj: Bedtime. Dreams. Rhyming text. Toys – bears.

The things I can do ill. by author. Roaring Brook, 2013. ISBN 978-1-59643-675-6 Subj: Books, reading. Character traits – confidence. Rhyming text. Self-concept.

Mack, Todd. *Princess Penelope* ill. by Julia Gran. Scholastic, 2003. ISBN 978-0-439-22436-9 Subj: Family life – parents. Royalty – princesses.

Mackall, Dandi Daley. *A girl named Dan* ill. by Renée Graef. Sleeping Bear, 2008. ISBN 978-1-58536-351-3 Subj: Gender roles. Sports – baseball. U.S. history.

Off to Bethlehem! ill. by R. W. Alley. HarperCollins, 2002. ISBN 978-0-694-01505-4 Subj: Religion – Nativity. Rhyming text.

Seeing stars ill. by Claudine Gevry. Simon & Schuster, 2006. ISBN 978-1-4169-0361-1 Subj: Stars.

The story of the Easter robin ill. by Anna Vojtech. Zonderkidz, 2010. ISBN 978-0-310-71331-9 Subj: Birds – robins. Family life – grandmothers. Holidays – Easter. Religion.

There's a baby in there! ill. by Carlynn Whitt. Amazon, 2012. ISBN 978-0-7614-6191-3 Subj: Babies. Birth. Family life – new sibling.

MacKay, Elly. *If you hold a seed* ill. by author. Running Press, 2013. ISBN 978-0-7624-4721-3 Subj: Character traits – patience. Seeds. Trees.

McKay, Hilary. *Pirates ahoy!* ill. by Alex Ayliffe. McElderry, 2000. ISBN 978-0-689-83114-0 Subj: Activities – playing. Family life – cousins. Family life – grandmothers. Imagination.

McKay, Sindy. *About the rain forest* (Johanasen, Heather)

McKee, David. *Elmer* ill. by author. Lothrop, 1989. ISBN 978-0-688-09172-9 Subj: Animals – elephants. Character traits – being different.

Elmer again ill. by author. Lothrop, 1991. ISBN 978-0-688-11597-5 Subj: Animals – elephants. Behavior – boredom.

Elmer and Rose ill. by author. Andersen, 2010. ISBN 978-0-7613-5493-2 Subj: Animals – elephants. Character traits – being different. Character traits – individuality.

Elmer and Snake ill. by author. Andersen, 2013. ISBN 978-1-46772-033-5 Subj: Animals – elephants. Behavior – trickery. Reptiles – snakes. Riddles & jokes.

Elmer and Super El ill. by author. Andersen, 2012. ISBN 978-0-7613-8989-7 Subj: Activities – sewing. Animals. Animals – elephants. Clothing.

Elmer and the big bird ill. by author. Andersen, 2012. ISBN 978-1-46770319-2 Subj: Animals – elephants. Behavior – bullying, teasing. Birds. Character traits – cooperation.

Elmer and the hippos ill. by author. Andersen, 2010. ISBN 978-0-7613-6442-9 Subj: Animals – elephants. Animals – hippopotamuses. Character traits – cooperation. Problem solving.

Elmer and the kangaroo ill. by author. HarperCollins, 2000. ISBN 978-0-688-17951-9 Subj: Animals – elephants. Animals – kangaroos. Self-concept.

Elmer and the lost teddy ill. by author. Lothrop, 1999. ISBN 978-0-688-16912-1 Subj: Animals – elephants. Behavior – lost & found possessions. Toys – bears.

Elmer and the wind ill. by author. Lothrop, 1998. Subj: Activities – flying. Animals – elephants. Weather – wind.

Elmer and Wilbur ill. by author. Lothrop, 1996. ISBN 978-0-688-14934-5 Subj: Animals – elephants. Behavior – lost. Friendship.

Elmer in the snow ill. by author. Lothrop, 1995. ISBN 978-0-688-14596-5 Subj: Activities – playing. Animals – elephants. Friendship. Weather – snow.

Elmer takes off ill. by author. Lothrop, 1998. ISBN 978-0-688-15785-2 Subj: Activities – flying. Animals – elephants. Weather – wind.

Elmer's Christmas ill. by author. Lerner/Kar-Ben, 2011. ISBN 978-0-7613-8088-7 Subj: Animals – elephants. Holidays – Christmas.

Elmer's special day ill. by author. Andersen, 2009. ISBN 978-0-7613-5154-2 Subj: Animals. Animals – elephants. Parades.

Six men ill. by author. NorthSouth, 2011. ISBN 978-0-7358-4050-8 Subj: War.

McKelvey, Douglas Kaine. *Locust pocus* ill. by Richard Egielski. Philomel, 2001. ISBN 978-0-399-23452-1 Subj: Insects. Rhyming text.

Macken, JoAnn Early. *Baby says "moo!"* ill. by David Walker. Hyperion/Disney, 2011. ISBN 978-1-4231-3400-8 Subj: Babies. Noise, sounds. Rhyming text.

Flip, float, fly: seeds on the move ill. by Pamela Paparone. Holiday, 2008. ISBN 978-0-8234-2043-8 Subj: Seeds.

Waiting out the storm ill. by Susan Gaber. Candlewick, 2010. ISBN 978-0-7636-3378-3 Subj: Family life – mothers. Rhyming text. Weather – rain. Weather – storms.

McKenna, Sharon. *Good morning, sunshine: a grandpa story* ill. by author. Red Cygnet, 2007. ISBN 978-1-60108-003-5 Subj: Family life – grandfathers.

McKinlay, Meg. *No bears* ill. by Leila Rudge. Candlewick, 2012. ISBN 978-0-7636-5890-8 Subj: Activities – storytelling. Animals – bears. Royalty – princesses.

McKinlay, Penny. *Flabby Tabby* ill. by Britta Teckentrup. Frances Lincoln, 2006. ISBN 978-1-84507-090-8 Subj: Animals – cats. Health & fitness – exercise.

McKinley, Cindy. *One smile* ill. by Mary Gregg Byrne. Illumination, 2002. ISBN 978-0-935699-23-4 Subj: Character traits – kindness. Circular tales.

MacKinnon, Debbie. *Eye spy shapes* photos by Anthea Sieveking. Charlesbridge, 2000. ISBN 978-0-88106-135-2 Subj: Concepts – shape. Format, unusual.

Mackintosh, David. *The Frank show* ill. by author. Abrams, 2012. ISBN 978-1-4197-0393-5 Subj: Careers – military. Family life – grandfathers. School.

Marshall Armstrong is new to our school ill. by author. Abrams, 2011. ISBN 978-1-4197-0036-1 Subj: Birthdays. Character traits – individuality. Parties. School.

McKissack, Fredrick. *Messy Bessey* (McKissack, Patricia C.)

Messy Bessey / Ada, la desordenada (McKissack, Patricia C.)

Messy Bessey and the birthday overnight (McKissack, Patricia C.)

Messy Bessey's closet (McKissack, Patricia C.)

Messy Bessey's family reunion (McKissack, Patricia C.)

Messy Bessey's holidays (McKissack, Patricia C.)

McKissack, Patricia C. *The all-I'll-ever-want Christmas doll* ill. by Jerry Pinkney. Random House, 2007. ISBN 978-0-375-93759-0 Subj: Behavior – sharing. Family life – brothers & sisters. Holidays – Christmas. Toys – dolls. U.S. history.

Flossie and the fox ill. by Rachel Isadora. Dial, 1986. ISBN 978-0-8037-0251-6 Subj: Animals – foxes. Ethnic groups in the U.S. – African Americans.

Goin' someplace special ill. by Jerry Pinkney. Atheneum, 2001. ISBN 978-0-689-81885-1 Subj: Ethnic groups in the U.S. – African Americans. Prejudice. U.S. history.

The honest-to-goodness truth ill. by Giselle Potter. Atheneum, 2000. ISBN 978-0-689-82668-9 Subj: Behavior – lying. Character traits – honesty. Ethnic groups in the U.S. – African Americans.

Ma Dear's aprons ill. by Floyd Cooper. Atheneum, 1997. ISBN 978-0-689-81051-0 Subj: Careers – housekeepers. Clothing – aprons. Ethnic groups in the U.S. – African Americans.

Messy Bessey by Patricia C. McKissack and Fredrick McKissack ill. by Dana Regan. Children's Press, 1999. ISBN 978-0-516-21650-8 Subj: Behavior – messy. Character traits – cleanliness. Character traits – orderliness. Ethnic groups in the U.S. – African Americans.

Messy Bessey / Ada, la desordenada by Patricia C. McKissack and Fredrick McKissack ill. by Richard Hackney. Children's Press, 1988. ISBN 978-0-516-32083-0 Subj: Behavior – messy. Character traits – cleanliness. Ethnic groups in the U.S. – African Americans. Foreign languages.

Messy Bessey and the birthday overnight by Patricia C. McKissack and Fredrick McKissack ill. by Dana Regan. Children's Press, 1998. ISBN 978-0-516-20828-2 Subj: Birthdays. Character traits – cleanliness. Character traits – helpfulness. Friendship. Rhyming text. Sleepovers.

Messy Bessey's closet by Patricia C. McKissack and Fredrick McKissack ill. by Richard Hackney. Children's Press, 1989. ISBN 978-0-516-02091-4 Subj: Behavior – messy. Ethnic groups in the U.S. – African Americans. Rhyming text.

Messy Bessey's family reunion by Patricia C. McKissack and Fredrick McKissack ill. by Dana Regan. Children's Press, 2000. ISBN 978-0-516-20830-5 Subj: Character traits – cleanliness. Ethnic groups in the U.S. – African Americans. Family life. Parks.

Messy Bessey's holidays by Patricia C. McKissack and Fredrick McKissack ill. by Dana Regan. Children's Press, 1999. ISBN 978-0-516-20829-9 Subj: Activities – baking, cooking. Character traits – cleanliness. Ethnic groups in the U.S. – African Americans. Holidays – Christmas. Holidays – Hanukkah. Holidays – Kwanzaa. Rhyming text.

A million fish . . . more or less ill. by Dena Schutzer. Knopf, 1992. ISBN 978-0-679-90692-6 Subj: Folk & fairy tales. Sports – fishing. Tall tales.

Mirandy and Brother Wind ill. by Jerry Pinkney. Knopf, 1988. ISBN 978-0-394-88765-4 Subj: Activities – dancing. Caldecott award honor books. Ethnic groups in the U.S. – African Americans. Folk & fairy tales.

Nettie Jo's friends ill. by Scott Cook. Knopf, 1989. ISBN 978-0-394-99158-0 Subj: Clothing. Family life. Toys – dolls.

Ol' Clip-Clop: a ghost story ill. by Eric Velasquez. Holiday House, 2013. ISBN 978-0-8234-2265-4 Subj: Careers – lawyers. Character traits – meanness. Ghosts. U.S. history.

Precious and the Boo Hag by Patricia C. McKissack and Onawumi Jean Moss ill. by Kyrsten Brooker. Simon & Schuster, 2005. ISBN 978-0-689-85194-0 Subj: Character traits – bravery. Ethnic groups in the U.S. – African Americans. Illness. Monsters.

Stitchin' and pullin': a Gee's Bend quilt ill. by Cozbi A. Cabrera. Random House, 2008. ISBN 978-0-375-83163-8 Subj: Ethnic groups in the U.S. – African Americans. Family life. Quilts. U.S. history.

McKissack, Robert L. *Try your best* ill. by Joe Cepeda. Harcourt, 2004. ISBN 978-0-15-205089-4 Subj: Careers – teachers. School. Self-concept. Sports.

McKneally, Ranida T. *Our seasons* (Lin, Grace)

McKy, Katie. *Pumpkin town! (or, nothing is better and worse than pumpkins)* ill. by Pablo Bernasconi. Houghton, 2006. ISBN 978-0-618-60569-9 Subj: Family life – brothers & sisters. Plants.

MacLachlan, Patricia. *All the places to love* ill. by Mike Wimmer. HarperCollins, 1994. ISBN 978-0-06-021099-1 Subj: Babies. Birth. Country. Family life. Farms.

Before you came by Patricia MacLachlan and Emily MacLachlan Charest ill. by David Diaz. HarperCollins, 2011. ISBN 978-0-06-051234-7 Subj: Babies. Family life – mothers.

Bittle by Patricia MacLachlan and Emily MacLachlan Charest ill. by Dan Yaccarino. Cotler, 2004. ISBN 978-0-06-000962-5 Subj: Animals – cats. Animals – dogs. Babies. Pets.

Cat talk by Patricia MacLachlan and Emily MacLachlan Charest ill. by Barry Moser. Amistad, 2013. ISBN 978-0-06-027978-3 Subj: Animals – cats. Poetry.

Fiona loves the night by Patricia MacLachlan and Emily MacLachlan Charest ill. by Amanda Shepherd. HarperCollins, 2007. ISBN 978-0-06-057031-6 Subj: Nature. Night.

Lala salama: a Tanzanian lullaby ill. by Elizabeth Zunon. Candlewick, 2011. ISBN 978-0-7636-4747-6 Subj: Family life – mothers. Foreign lands – Tanzania. Lullabies.

Nora's chicks ill. by Kathryn Brown. Candlewick, 2013. ISBN 978-0-7636-4753-7 Subj: Birds – chickens. Emotions – loneliness. Friendship. Immigrants. U.S. history – frontier & pioneer life.

Painting the wind by Patricia MacLachlan and Emily MacLachlan Charest ill. by Katy Schneider. Cotler, 2003. ISBN 978-0-06-029799-2 Subj: Activities – painting. Careers – artists. Islands.

The sick day ill. by Jane Dyer. Random House, 2001. ISBN 978-0-385-90007-2 Subj: Family life – fathers. Illness.

Snowflakes fall ill. by Steven Kellogg. Random House, 2013. ISBN 978-0-385-37693-8 Subj: Character traits – hopefulness. Memories, memory. Poetry. Weather – snow.

Three names ill. by Alexander Pertzoff. HarperCollins, 1991. ISBN 978-0-06-024036-3 Subj: Animals – dogs. Family life – great-grandparents. Names. School.

Who loves me? ill. by Amanda Shepherd. Cotler, 2005. ISBN 978-0-06-027977-6 Subj: Animals – cats. Animals – dogs. Emotions – love. Family life.

You were the first ill. by Stephanie Graegin. Little, Brown, 2013. ISBN 978-0-316-18533-2 Subj: Babies. Family life.

Your moon, my moon: a grandmother's words to a faraway child ill. by Bryan Collier. Simon & Schuster, 2011. ISBN 978-1-4169-7950-0 Subj: Family life – grandmothers. Foreign lands – Africa.

McLaren, Chesley. *Zat cat! a haute couture tail* ill. by author. Scholastic, 2002. ISBN 978-0-439-27316-9 Subj: Animals – cats. Foreign lands – France. Rhyming text.

McLarey, Kristina Thermaenius. *When you take a pig to a party* by Kristina Thermaenius McLarey and Myra McLarey ill. by Marjory Wunsch. Orchard, 2000. ISBN 978-0-531-33257-3 Subj: Animals – pigs. Humorous stories. Parties.

McLarey, Myra. *When you take a pig to a party* (McLarey, Kristina Thermaenius)

McLean, Dirk. *Curtain up!* ill. by France Brassard. Tundra, 2010. ISBN 978-0-88776-899-6 Subj: Careers – actors. Theater.

Play mas'! a carnival ABC ill. by author. Tundra, 2000. ISBN 978-0-88776-486-8 Subj: ABC books. Fairs, festivals. Foreign lands – Caribbean Islands. Foreign languages. Language.

McLean, Janet. *Let's go, baby-o!* ill. by Andrew McLean. IPG/Allen & Unwin, 2012. ISBN 978-1-7423-7564-9 Subj: Activities – playing. Babies. Participation. Rhyming text.

MacLean, Kerry Lee. *Peaceful piggy meditation* ill. by author. Whitman, 2004. ISBN 978-0-8075-6380-9 Subj: Animals – pigs. Careers – artists. Careers – writers.

Maclear, Kyo. *Spork* ill. by Isabelle Arsenault. Kids Can, 2010. ISBN 978-1-55337-736-8 Subj: Character traits – being different. Character traits – individuality. Self-concept.

Virginia Wolf ill. by Isabelle Arsenault. Kids Can, 2012. ISBN 978-1-55453-649-8 Subj: Emotions. Family life – sisters.

McLellan, Stephanie Simpson. *The chicken cat* ill. by Sean Cassidy. Fitzhenry & Whiteside, 2000. ISBN 978-1-55041-531-5 Subj: Activities – flying. Animals – babies. Animals – cats. Birds – chickens. Ethnic groups in the U.S. – African Americans. Friendship.

MacLennan, Cathy. *Chicky Chicky Chook Chook* ill. by author. Sterling, 2007. ISBN 978-1-905417-40-7 Subj: Activities – playing. Animals. Rhyming text. Weather.

McLeod, Bob. *Super hero ABC* ill. by author. HarperCollins, 2006. ISBN 978-0-06-074514-1 Subj: ABC books.

McLeod, Elaine. *Lessons from Mother Earth* ill. by Colleen Wood. Douglas & McIntyre, 2002. ISBN 978-0-88899-312-0 Subj: Family life – grandmothers. Gardens, gardening. Indians of North America. Nature.

MacLeod, Elizabeth. *What did dinosaurs eat?* ill. by Gordon Sauvé. Kids Can, 2001. ISBN 978-1-55337-460-2 Subj: Dinosaurs.

McLeod, Heather. *Kiss me! (I'm a prince!)* ill. by Brooke Kerrigan. Fitzhenry & Whiteside, 2011. ISBN 978-1-55455-161-3 Subj: Folk & fairy tales. Frogs & toads. Kissing. Royalty – princes.

McLerran, Alice. *Roxaboxen* ill. by Barbara Cooney. Lothrop, 1991. ISBN 978-0-688-07593-4 Subj: Activities – playing. Desert. Imagination.

McLimans, David. *Gone wild* ill. by author. Walker, 2006. ISBN 978-0-8027-9563-2 Subj: ABC books. Animals – endangered animals. Caldecott award honor books.

McMahon, Patricia. *Just add one Chinese sister* by Patricia McMahon and Conor Clarke McCarthy ill. by Karen Jerome. Boyds Mills, 2005. ISBN 978-1-56397-989-7 Subj: Adoption. Ethnic groups in the U.S. – Chinese Americans.

McMillan, Bruce. *Counting wildflowers* ill. by author. Lothrop, 1986. ISBN 978-0-688-02860-2 Subj: Counting, numbers. Flowers. Science.

Days of the ducklings photos by author. Houghton, 2001. ISBN 978-0-618-04878-6 Subj: Birds – ducks. Ecology. Foreign lands – Iceland. Islands.

Dry or wet? photos by author. Lothrop, 1988. ISBN 978-0-688-07101-1 Subj: Concepts.

Eating fractions photos by author. Scholastic, 1991. ISBN 978-0-590-43770-7 Subj: Counting, numbers.

Fire engine shapes photos by author. Lothrop, 1988. ISBN 978-0-688-07843-0 Subj: Concepts – shape.

Growing colors photos by author. Lothrop, 1988. ISBN 978-0-688-07845-4 Subj: Concepts – color.

How the ladies stopped the wind ill. by Gunnella. Houghton, 2007. ISBN 978-0-618-77330-5 Subj: Behavior – resourcefulness. Foreign lands – Iceland. Weather – wind.

Jelly beans for sale photos by author. Scholastic, 1996. ISBN 978-0-590-86584-5 Subj: Counting, numbers. Money.

Mouse views: what the class pet saw ill. by author. Holiday, 1993. ISBN 978-0-8234-1008-8 Subj: Animals – mice. Picture puzzles. School.

Nights of the pufflings photos by author. Houghton, 1995. ISBN 978-0-395-70810-1 Subj: Birds – puffins. Character traits – kindness to animals. Foreign lands – Iceland.

One, two, one pair! photos by author. Scholastic, 1991. ISBN 978-0-590-43767-7 Subj: Concepts. Counting, numbers.

The problem with chickens ill. by Gunnella. Houghton, 2005. ISBN 978-0-618-58581-6 Subj: Behavior – resourcefulness. Birds – chickens. Character traits – cleverness. Foreign lands – Iceland.

Puffins climb, penguins rhyme photos by author. Harcourt, 1995. ISBN 978-0-15-200362-3 Subj: Birds – penguins. Birds – puffins. Rhyming text.

Sense suspense: a guessing game for the five senses photos by author. Scholastic, 1994. ISBN 978-0-590-47904-2 Subj: Concepts. Foreign lands – Caribbean Islands. Senses.

Time to . . . photos by author. Lothrop, 1989. ISBN 978-0-688-08856-9 Subj: Clocks, watches. Time.

McMullan, Kate. *Baby Goose* ill. by Pascal Lemaître. Hyperion, 2002. ISBN 978-0-7868-2380-2 Subj: Nursery rhymes.

Bulldog's big day ill. by Pascal Lemaître. Scholastic, 2011. ISBN 978-0-545-17155-7 Subj: Activities – baking, cooking. Animals – dogs. Careers. Careers – bakers.

I stink! ill. by Jim McMullan. Colter, 2002. ISBN 978-0-06-029849-4 Subj: Careers – sanitation workers. Trucks.

If you were my bunny ill. by David McPhail. Scholastic, 1996. ISBN 978-0-590-52749-1 Subj: Animals – babies. Babies. Bedtime. Family life – mothers. Lullabies.

I'm bad! ill. by Jim McMullan. HarperCollins, 2008. ISBN 978-0-06-122971-8 Subj: Dinosaurs. Prehistory.

I'm big! ill. by Jim McMullan. HarperCollins, 2010. ISBN 978-0-06-122974-9 Subj: Behavior – lost. Dinosaurs.

I'm dirty! ill. by Jim McMullan. HarperCollins, 2006. ISBN 978-0-06-009294-8 Subj: Careers – construction workers. Counting, numbers. Trucks.

I'm fast ill. by Jim McMullan. HarperCollins, 2012. ISBN 978-0-06-192085-1 Subj: Automobiles. Contests. Sports – racing. Trains.

Papa's song ill. by Jim McMullan. Farrar, 2000. ISBN 978-0-374-35732-0 Subj: Animals – bears. Babies. Family life – fathers. Sleep.

Rock-a-baby band ill. by Janie Bynum. Little, 2003. ISBN 978-0-316-60858-9 Subj: Babies. Music. Musical instruments – bands. Rhyming text.

Supercat ill. by Pascal Lemaître. Workman, 2002. ISBN 978-0-7611-2644-7 Subj: Animals. Animals – babies. Animals – cats. Format, unusual – board books.

Supercat to the rescue ill. by Pascal Lemaître. Workman, 2003. ISBN 978-0-7611-2734-5 Subj: Animals – cats. Animals – mice. Babies.

McNamara, Margaret. *The apple orchard riddle* ill. by G. Brian Karas. Schwartz & Wade, 2013. ISBN 978-0-375-84744-8 Subj: Food. Riddles & jokes. School – field trips.

Apples A to Z ill. by Jake Parker. Scholastic, 2012. ISBN 978-0-439-72808-9 Subj: ABC books. Animals. Food.

Fall leaf project ill. by Mike Gordon. Simon & Schuster, 2006. ISBN 978-1-4169-1538-6 Subj: Nature. Seasons – fall.

George Washington's birthday: a mostly true tale ill. by Barry Blitt. Random House, 2012. ISBN 978-0-375-84499-7 Subj: Birthdays. U.S. history.

How many seeds in a pumpkin? ill. by G. Brian Karas. Random House, 2007. ISBN 978-0-375-84014-2 Subj: Counting, numbers. Food. Science.

The three little aliens and the big bad robot ill. by Mark Fearing. Random House, 2011. ISBN 978-0-375-86689-0 Subj: Aliens. Humorous stories. Planets. Robots. Space & space ships.

The whistle on the train ill. by Richard Egielski. Hyperion, 2008. ISBN 978-0-7868-4890-4 Subj: Format, unusual – toy & movable books. Trains.

McNaughton, Colin. *Boo!* ill. by author. Harcourt, 1996. ISBN 978-0-15-200834-5 Subj: Animals – pigs. Disguises.

Captain Abdul's little treasure ill. by author. Candlewick, 2006. ISBN 978-0-7636-3045-4 Subj: Babies. Pirates.

Captain Abdul's pirate school ill. by author. Candlewick, 1994. ISBN 978-1-56402-429-9 Subj: Behavior – misbehavior. Pirates. School.

Don't step on the crack! ill. by author. Dial, 2001. ISBN 978-0-8037-2611-6 Subj: Superstition.

Here come the aliens! ill. by author. Candlewick, 1995. ISBN 978-1-56402-642-2 Subj: Aliens. Space & space ships.

Little boo! ill. by author. Harcourt, 2000. ISBN 978-0-15-202671-4 Subj: Animals – pigs.

Little goal! ill. by author. Harcourt, 2001. ISBN 978-0-15-202525-0 Subj: Animals – pigs.

Little oops! ill. by author. Harcourt, 2001. ISBN 978-0-15-202537-3 Subj: Animals – pigs.

Little suddenly! ill. by author. Harcourt, 2000. ISBN 978-0-15-202531-1 Subj: Animals – pigs.

Not last night but the night before ill. by Emma Chichester Clark. Candlewick, 2009. ISBN 978-

0-7636-4420-8 Subj: Birthdays. Books, reading. Imagination. Rhyming text.

Once upon an ordinary school day ill. by Satoshi Kitamura. Farrar, 2005. ISBN 978-0-374-35634-7 Subj: Careers – teachers. School.

Oomph! ill. by author. Harcourt, 2001. ISBN 978-0-15-216463-8 Subj: Animals – pigs. Animals – wolves. Emotions – love. Sea & seashore.

Oops! ill. by author. Harcourt, 1997. ISBN 978-0-15-201588-6 Subj: Animals – pigs. Animals – wolves. Character traits – cleverness.

Preston's goal! ill. by author. Harcourt, 1998. ISBN 978-0-15-201816-0 Subj: Animals – pigs. Animals – wolves. Character traits – clumsiness. Humorous stories. Sports – soccer.

Suddenly! ill. by author. Harcourt, 1995. ISBN 978-0-15-200308-1 Subj: Animals – pigs. Animals – wolves. Humorous stories.

We're off to look for aliens ill. by author. Candlewick, 2008. ISBN 978-0-7636-3636-4 Subj: Aliens. Rhyming text.

When I grow up ill. by author. Candlewick, 2005. ISBN 978-0-7636-2675-4 Subj: Careers. Rhyming text. School. Theater.

McNaughton, Janet. *Brave Jack and the unicorn* ill. by Susan Tooke. Tundra, 2005. ISBN 978-0-88776-677-0 Subj: Character traits – kindness. Folk & fairy tales. Foreign lands – Canada. Magic. Mythical creatures – unicorns. Royalty – princesses.

McNeil, Florence. *Sail away* ill. by David McPhail. Orca, 2000. ISBN 978-1-55143-147-5 Subj: Boats, ships. Imagination. Pirates. Sports – sailing. Toys.

McNiff, Dawn. *Mommy's little monster* ill. by Kate Willis-Crowley. Scholastic, 2013. ISBN 978-0-545-48057-4 Subj: Activities – babysitting. Family life – mothers. Trolls.

McNulty, Faith. *If you decide to go to the moon* ill. by Steven Kellogg. Scholastic, 2005. ISBN 978-0-590-48359-9 Subj: Moon. Space & space ships.

Macomber, Debbie. *The yippy, yappy Yorkie in the green doggy sweater* by Debbie Macomber and Mary Lou Carney ill. by Sally Anne Lambert. HarperCollins, 2012. ISBN 978-0-06-165096-3 Subj: Animals – dogs. Behavior – running away. Moving.

Maconie, Robin. *Alice and her fabulous teeth* ill. by Catherine Myler Fruisen. Cedco, 2000. ISBN 978-0-7683-2176-0 Subj: Dreams. Fairies. Mythical creatures – elves. Rhyming text. Teeth.

McPhail, David. *The bear's toothache* ill. by author. Puffin, 1978, ©1972. ISBN 978-0-14-050263-3 Subj: Animals – bears. Character traits – kindness to animals. Illness. Teeth.

Bella loves Bunny ill. by author. Abrams, 2013. ISBN 978-1-4197-0543-4 Subj: Animals – rabbits. Format, unusual – board books. Friendship. Toys.

Ben loves Bear ill. by author. Abrams, 2013. ISBN 978-1-4197-0386-7 Subj: Format, unusual – board books. Friendship. Toys – bears.

Big Brown Bear goes to town ill. by author. Harcourt, 2006. ISBN 978-1-4156-7142-9 Subj: Animals – bears. Animals – rats. Friendship.

Big Brown Bear's birthday surprise ill. by author. Harcourt, 2007. ISBN 978-0-15-206098-5 Subj: Animals – bears. Animals – rats. Birthdays. Friendship.

Big brown bear's up and down day ill. by author. Harcourt, 2003. ISBN 978-0-15-216407-2 Subj: Animals – bears. Animals – rats. Friendship.

Boy on the brink ill. by author. Holt, 2006. ISBN 978-0-8050-7618-9 Subj: Dreams. Imagination.

Budgie and Boo ill. by author. Abrams, 2009. ISBN 978-0-8109-8324-3 Subj: Animals – bears. Animals – rabbits. Friendship.

Drawing lessons from a bear ill. by author. Little, 2000. ISBN 978-0-316-56345-1 Subj: Activities – drawing. Animals – bears. Careers – artists.

Edward and the pirates ill. by author. Little, 1997. ISBN 978-0-316-56344-4 Subj: Books, reading. Imagination. Pirates.

Edward in the jungle ill. by author. Little, 2001. ISBN 978-0-316-56391-8 Subj: Animals. Imagination. Jungle.

Emma in charge ill. by author. Penguin, 2005. ISBN 978-0-525-47411-1 Subj: Activities – playing. Animals – bears. Imagination. Toys – dolls.

Emma's pet ill. by author. Dutton, 1987. ISBN 978-0-525-44210-3 Subj: Activities – vacationing. Animals – bears. Behavior – needing someone. Family life. Pets.

Emma's vacation ill. by author. Dutton, 1987. ISBN 978-0-525-44315-5 Subj: Activities – vacationing. Animals – bears. Family life.

The family tree ill. by author. Holt, 2012. ISBN 978-0-8050-9057-4 Subj: Ecology. Trees.

Farm morning ill. by author. Harcourt, 1985. ISBN 978-0-15-227299-9 Subj: Animals. Birds. Farms.

Fix-it ill. by author. Dutton, 1984. ISBN 978-0-525-44093-2 Subj: Books, reading. Television.

Henry Bear's Christmas ill. by author. Atheneum, 2001. ISBN 978-0-689-82198-1 Subj: Animals – bears. Animals – raccoons. Holidays – Christmas. Trees.

Henry Bear's park ill. by author. Atheneum, 2001. ISBN 978-0-689-83967-2 Subj: Activities – ballooning. Animals – bears. Family life – fathers. Parks.

Lost ill. by author. Little, 1990. ISBN 978-0-316-56329-1 Subj: Animals – bears. Behavior – lost.

Mole music ill. by author. Holt, 1999. ISBN 978-0-8050-2819-5 Subj: Animals – moles. Music. Musical instruments – violins.

Moony B. Finch, fastest draw in the West ill. by author. Artists & Writers Guild, 1994. ISBN 978-0-307-17554-0 Subj: Activities – drawing. Crime. Imagination. Magic. Trains.

No! ill. by author. Roaring Brook, 2009. ISBN 978-1-59643-288-8 Subj: Character traits. War.

Pig Pig and the magic photo album ill. by author. Dutton, 1986. ISBN 978-0-525-44238-7 Subj: Activities – photographing. Animals – pigs. Imagination.

Pig Pig gets a job ill. by author. Dutton, 1990. ISBN 978-0-525-44619-4 Subj: Activities – working. Animals – pigs. Careers.

Pig Pig goes to camp ill. by author. Dutton, 1983. ISBN 978-0-525-44064-2 Subj: Animals – pigs. Camps, camping.

Pig Pig grows up ill. by author. Dutton, 1980. ISBN 978-0-525-37027-7 Subj: Animals – pigs. Behavior – growing up.

Pig Pig meets the lion ill. by author. Charlesbridge, 2012. ISBN 978-1-58089-358-9 Subj: Animals – lions. Animals – pigs. Friendship. Language.

Pig Pig returns ill. by author. Charlesbridge, 2011. ISBN 978-1-58089-356-5 Subj: Activities – traveling. Animals – pigs. Behavior – worrying.

Pig Pig rides ill. by author. Dutton, 1982. ISBN 978-0-525-44024-6 Subj: Activities – playing. Animals – pigs. Imagination.

Pigs ahoy ill. by author. Dutton, 1995. ISBN 978-0-525-45334-5 Subj: Animals – pigs. Boats, ships. Rhyming text.

Pigs aplenty, pigs galore! ill. by author. Dutton, 1993. ISBN 978-0-525-45079-5 Subj: Animals – pigs. Food. Rhyming text.

The puddle ill. by author. Farrar, 1998. ISBN 978-0-374-36148-8 Subj: Animals. Toys. Weather – rain.

Santa's book of names ill. by author. Little, 1993. ISBN 978-0-316-56335-2 Subj: Books, reading. Character traits – helpfulness. Holidays – Christmas. Santa Claus.

The Searcher and Old Tree ill. by author. Charlesbridge, 2008. ISBN 978-1-58089-223-0 Subj: Animals – raccoons. Trees. Weather – storms.

Something special ill. by author. Little, 1988. ISBN 978-0-316-56324-6 Subj: Activities – painting. Animals – raccoons.

Sylvie and True ill. by author. Farrar, 2007. ISBN 978-0-374-37364-1 Subj: Animals – rabbits. Friendship. Reptiles – snakes.

The teddy bear ill. by author. Holt, 2002. ISBN 978-0-8050-6414-8 Subj: Behavior – lost & found possessions. Emotions – love. Homeless. Toys – bears.

Those can-do pigs ill. by author. Dutton, 1996. ISBN 978-0-525-45495-3 Subj: Activities. Animals – pigs. Rhyming text.

Tinker and Tom and the Star Baby ill. by author. Little, 1998. ISBN 978-0-316-56349-9 Subj: Aliens. Animals – bears. Imagination. Space & space ships.

Waddles ill. by author. Abrams, 2011. ISBN 978-0-8109-8415-8 Subj: Animals – raccoons. Birds – ducks. Friendship.

Water boy ill. by author. Abrams, 2007. ISBN 978-0-8109-1784-2 Subj: Emotions – fear. Magic. Water.

Weezer changes the world ill. by author. Simon & Schuster, 2009. ISBN 978-1-4169-9000-0 Subj: Animals – dogs. Behavior – seeking better things. Concepts – change. Weather – lightning, thunder.

McQuade, Jacqueline. *At preschool with Teddy Bear* ill. by author. Dial, 1999. ISBN 978-0-8037-2394-8 Subj: Family life – fathers. Format, unusual – board books. School – first day. School – nursery. Toys – bears.

At the petting zoo with Teddy Bear ill. by author. Dial, 1999. ISBN 978-0-8037-2395-5 Subj: Animals. Format, unusual – board books. Toys – bears. Zoos.

Big babies ill. by author. Sterling, 2000. ISBN 978-0-8069-7537-5 Subj: Animals. Animals – babies. Names.

Christmas with Teddy Bear ill. by author. Dial, 1996. ISBN 978-0-8037-2075-6 Subj: Holidays – Christmas. Toys – bears.

Farm babies ill. by author. Sterling, 2000. ISBN 978-0-8069-7539-9 Subj: Animals – babies. Farms.

Good times with Teddy Bear ill. by author. Dial, 1997. ISBN 978-0-8037-2076-3 Subj: Activities. Animals – cats. Family life. Toys – bears.

Small babies ill. by author. Sterling, 2000. ISBN 978-0-8069-7541-2 Subj: Animals. Animals – babies. Science.

Snow babies ill. by author. Sterling, 2000. ISBN 978-1-85602-366-5 Subj: Animals. Animals – babies. Foreign lands – Antarctic. Foreign lands – Arctic. Weather – snow.

McQuinn, Anna. *Lola at the library* ill. by Rosalind Beardshaw. Charlesbridge, 2006. ISBN 978-1-58089-113-4 Subj: Books, reading. Ethnic groups in the U.S. – African Americans. Libraries.

Lola loves stories ill. by Rosalind Beardshaw. Charlesbridge, 2010. ISBN 978-1-58089-258-2 Subj: Activities – playing. Activities – storytelling. Books, reading. Ethnic groups in the U.S. – African Americans. Imagination.

Lola reads to Leo ill. by Rosalind Beardshaw. Charlesbridge, 2012. ISBN 978-1-58089-403-6 Subj: Babies. Books, reading. Ethnic groups in the U.S. – African Americans. Family life – brothers & sisters. Family life – new sibling.

My friend Jamal ill. by author. Annick, 2008. ISBN 978-1-55451-123-5 Subj: Foreign lands – Somalia. Friendship. Immigrants. War.

My friend Mei Jing ill. by Ben Frey. Annick, 2009. ISBN 978-1-55451-153-2 Subj: Ethnic groups in the U.S. – African Americans. Ethnic groups in the U.S. – Chinese Americans. Friendship.

The sleep sheep ill. by Hannah Shaw. Scholastic, 2010. ISBN 978-0-545-23145-9 Subj: Animals – sheep. Bedtime. Counting, numbers. Sleep.

McReynolds, Linda. *Eight days gone* ill. by Ryan O'Rourke. Charlesbridge, 2012. ISBN 978-1-58089-364-0 Subj: Careers – astronauts. Moon. Rhyming text. Space & space ships. U.S. history.

Maddern, Eric. *Nail soup* ill. by Paul Hess. Frances Lincoln, 2007. ISBN 978-1-84507-479-1 Subj: Character traits – cleverness. Folk & fairy tales. Foreign lands – Sweden.

Mader, C. Roger. *Lost cat* ill. by author. Houghton Mifflin, 2013. ISBN 978-0-547-97458-3 Subj: Animals – cats. Behavior – lost. Clothing – shoes. Pets.

Madison, Alan. *The littlest grape stomper* ill. by Giselle Potter. Random House, 2007. ISBN 978-0-375-83675-6 Subj: Anatomy – toes. Food. Tall tales.

Pecorino plays ball ill. by AnnaLaura Cantone. Simon & Schuster, 2006. ISBN 978-0-689-86522-0 Subj: Humorous stories. Sports – baseball.

Pecorino's first concert ill. by AnnaLaura Cantone. Simon & Schuster, 2005. ISBN 978-0-689-85952-6 Subj: Humorous stories. Music. Musical instruments.

Velma Gratch and the way cool butterfly ill. by Kevin Hawkes. Random House, 2007. ISBN 978-0-375-83597-1 Subj: Insects – butterflies, caterpillars. Migration. School.

Madonna. *Mr. Peabody's apples* ill. by Loren Long Callaway. Viking, 2003. ISBN 978-0-670-05883-9 Subj: Behavior – gossip. Character traits – honesty. Food. Sports – baseball.

Yakov and the seven thieves ill. by Gennady Spirin. Callaway, 2004. ISBN 978-0-670-05887-7 Subj: Careers – shoemakers. Crime. Illness. Religion.

Madrigal, Antonio Hernandez. *Erandi's braids* ill. by Tomie dePaola. Putnam, 1999. ISBN 978-0-399-23212-1 Subj: Birthdays. Family life – mothers. Foreign lands – Mexico. Hair.

Maestro, Betsy. *Bats* ill. by Giulio Maestro. Scholastic, 1994. ISBN 978-0-590-46150-4 Subj: Animals – bats.

Coming to America ill. by Susannah Ryan. Scholastic, 1996. ISBN 978-0-590-44151-3 Subj: Ethnic groups in the U.S.

Dollars and cents for Harriet ill. by Giulio Maestro. Crown, 1988. ISBN 978-0-517-56958-0 Subj: Counting, numbers. Money.

How do apples grow? ill. by Giulio Maestro. HarperCollins, 1992. ISBN 978-0-06-020056-5 Subj: Food. Science. Trees.

The story of the Statue of Liberty by Betsy Maestro and Giulio Maestro ill. by Giulio Maestro. Lothrop, 1986. ISBN 978-0-688-05773-2 Subj: Art. U.S. history.

Why do leaves change color? ill. by Loretta Krupinski. HarperCollins, 1994. ISBN 978-0-06-022874-3 Subj: Nature. Science. Seasons – fall. Trees.

Maestro, Giulio. *The story of the Statue of Liberty* (Maestro, Betsy)

Maggi, María Elena. *The great canoe* ill. by Gloria Calderón. Douglas & McIntyre, 2001. ISBN 978-0-88899-444-8 Subj: Animals. Canoes & canoeing. Folk & fairy tales. Indians of South America – Karina. Weather – floods. Weather – rain.

Magloff, Lisa. *Bear* ill. by author. DK, 2003. ISBN 978-0-7566-0194-2 Subj: Animals – babies. Animals – bears. Behavior – growing up.

Butterfly ill. with photos. DK, 2003. ISBN 978-0-7566-0193-5 Subj: Animals – babies. Behavior – growing up. Insects – butterflies, caterpillars.

Duckling ill. with photos. DK, 2003. ISBN 978-0-7894-9628-7 Subj: Animals – babies. Behavior – growing up. Birds – ducks.

Elephant ill. with photos. DK, 2005. ISBN 978-0-7566-1155-2 Subj: Animals – babies. Animals – elephants. Behavior – growing up.

Frog ill. with photos. DK, 2003. ISBN 978-0-7894-9629-4 Subj: Animals – babies. Behavior – growing up. Frogs & toads.

Kitten ill. with photos. DK, 2005. ISBN 978-0-7566-1156-9 Subj: Animals – babies. Animals – cats. Behavior – growing up.

Penguin ill. with photos. DK, 2004. ISBN 978-0-7566-0263-5 Subj: Animals – babies. Behavior – growing up. Birds – penguins.

Rabbit ill. with photos. DK, 2004. ISBN 978-0-7566-0262-8 Subj: Animals – babies. Animals – rabbits. Behavior – growing up.

Magnier, Thierry. *Isabelle and the angel* ill. by Georg Hallensleben. Chronicle, 2000. ISBN 978-0-8118-2526-9 Subj: Angels. Animals – pigs. Careers – artists. Museums.

Magoon, Scott. *The boy who cried bigfoot!* ill. by author. Simon & Schuster, 2013. ISBN 978-1-4424-1257-6 Subj: Behavior – lying. Crime. Mythical creatures.

Hugo and Miles in I've painted everything! ill. by author. Houghton, 2007. ISBN 978-0-618-64638-8 Subj: Animals – dogs. Animals – elephants. Art. Foreign lands – France.

Maguire, Gregory. *Crabby Cratchitt* ill. by Andrew Glass. Clarion, 2000. ISBN 978-0-395-60485-4 Subj: Birds – chickens. Careers – farmers. Farms. Rhyming text.

Maguire, John. *People* ill. by Pauline Bewick. Collins, 2001. ISBN 978-1-903464-06-9 Subj: Character traits – individuality. Poetry.

Mahoney, Daniel J. *Monstergarten* ill. by Jef Kaminsky. Feiwel & Friends, 2013. ISBN 978-1-250-01441-2 Subj: Behavior – worrying. Monsters. School – first day.

The perfect clubhouse ill. by author. Clarion, 2004. ISBN 978-0-618-34672-1 Subj: Animals. Character traits – cooperation. Clubs, gangs. Friendship.

A really good snowman ill. by author. Houghton, 2005. ISBN 978-0-618-47554-4 Subj: Animals – bears. Character traits – helpfulness. Contests. Family life – brothers & sisters. Snowmen. Weather – snow.

The Saturday escape ill. by author. Clarion, 2002. ISBN 978-0-618-13326-0 Subj: Activities – storytelling. Animals. Behavior. Books, reading. Character traits – responsibility. Libraries.

Mahy, Margaret. *Boom Baby boom, boom* ill. by Patricia MacCarthy. Viking, 1997. ISBN 978-0-670-87314-2 Subj: Animals. Babies. Family life – mothers. Food. Noise, sounds.

Bubble trouble ill. by Polly Dunbar. Clarion, 2009. ISBN 978-0-547-07421-4 Subj: Bubbles. Humorous stories. Rhyming text.

The Christmas tree tangle ill. by Anthony Kerins. McElderry, 1994. ISBN 978-0-689-50616-1 Subj: Animals. Animals – cats. Cumulative tales. Holidays – Christmas. Rhyming text. Trees.

Down the back of the chair ill. by Polly Dunbar. Houghton, 2006. ISBN 978-0-618-69395-5 Subj: Behavior – lost & found possessions. Furniture – chairs. Poverty. Rhyming text.

Down the dragon's tongue ill. by Patricia MacCarthy. Orchard, 2000. ISBN 978-0-531-30272-9 Subj: Family life – fathers. Multiple births – twins. Parks.

The great white man-eating shark ill. by Jonathan Allen. Dial, 1990. ISBN 978-0-8037-0749-8 Subj: Behavior – trickery. Fish – sharks.

The green bath ill. by Steven Kellogg. Scholastic, 2013. ISBN 978-0-545-20667-9 Subj: Activities – bathing. Imagination.

The man from the land of Fandango ill. by Polly Dunbar. Clarion, 2012. ISBN 978-0-547-81988-4 Subj: Humorous stories. Imagination. Rhyming text.

Mister Whistler ill. by Gavin Bishop. Gecko, 2013. ISBN 978-1-87746-791-2 Subj: Activities – dancing. Activities – whistling. Behavior – lost & found possessions. Trains.

The rattlebang picnic ill. by Steven Kellogg. Dial, 1994. ISBN 978-0-8037-1319-2 Subj: Activities – picnicking. Automobiles. Family life.

The seven Chinese brothers ill. by Jean Tseng and Mou-Sien Tseng. Scholastic, 1990. ISBN 978-0-590-42055-6 Subj: Character traits – cleverness. Family life. Folk & fairy tales. Foreign lands – China.

17 kings and 42 elephants ill. by Patricia MacCarthy. Dial, 1987. ISBN 978-0-8037-0458-9 Subj: Animals. Jungle. Rhyming text. Royalty – kings.

Simply delicious! ill. by Jonathan Allen. Orchard, 1999. ISBN 978-0-531-33181-1 Subj: Animals. Food. Jungle. Tongue twisters.

A summery Saturday morning ill. by Selina Young. Viking, 1998. ISBN 978-0-670-87943-4 Subj: Animals. Birds – geese. Humorous stories. Rhyming text. Sea & seashore. Seasons – summer.

Maidment, Stella. *Cowboy puzzles* ill. by Daniela Dogliani. Amicus/QEB, 2012. ISBN 978-1-60992-271-9 Subj: Behavior – lost & found possessions. Cowboys, cowgirls. Puzzles.

Maier, Inger. *Ben's flying flowers* ill. by Maria Bogade. Magination, 2012. ISBN 978-1-4338-1133-3 Subj: Death. Emotions – grief. Emotions – sadness. Illness. Insects – butterflies, caterpillars.

Mair, Samia J. *The perfect gift* ill. by Craig Howarth. Kube, 2010. ISBN 978-0-86037-438-1 Subj:

Family life – brothers & sisters. Gifts. Holidays. Plants. Religion – Islam.

Maitland, Barbara. *Moo in the morning* ill. by Andrew Kulman. Farrar, 2000. ISBN 978-0-374-35038-3 Subj: Animals. Cities, towns. Farms. Noise, sounds.

My bear and me ill. by Lisa Flather. McElderry, 1999. ISBN 978-0-689-82085-4 Subj: Activities. Bedtime. Toys – bears.

Maizes, Sarah. *On my way to bed* ill. by Michael Paraskevas. Walker, 2013. ISBN 978-0-8027-2366-6 Subj: Bedtime. Imagination.

On my way to the bath ill. by Michael Paraskevas. Walker, 2012. ISBN 978-0-8027-2364-2 Subj: Activities – bathing. Imagination.

Major, Kevin. *Aunt Olga's Christmas postcards* ill. by Bruce Roberts. Groundwood, 2005. ISBN 978-0-88899-593-3 Subj: Behavior – collecting things. Family life – aunts, uncles. Holidays – Christmas. Letters, cards.

Eh to zed? ill. by Alan Daniel. Red Deer, 2002. ISBN 978-0-88995-272-0 Subj: ABC books. Foreign lands – Canada.

Mak, Kam. *My Chinatown* ill. by author. HarperCollins, 2002. ISBN 978-0-06-029191-4 Subj: Cities, towns. Ethnic groups in the U.S. – Chinese Americans. Immigrants. Poetry.

Makhijani, Pooja. *Mama's saris* ill. by Elena Gomez. Little, Brown, 2007. ISBN 978-0-316-01105-1 Subj: Clothing. Ethnic groups in the U.S. – East Indian Americans. Family life – daughters. Family life – mothers.

Malaspina, Ann. *Finding Lincoln* ill. by Colin Bootman. Whitman, 2009. ISBN 978-0-8075-2435-0 Subj: Ethnic groups in the U.S. – African Americans. Libraries. Prejudice. U.S. history.

Phillis sings out freedom: the story of George Washington and Phillis Wheatley ill. by Susan Keeter. Whitman, 2010. ISBN 978-0-8075-6545-2 Subj: Careers – poets. Ethnic groups in the U.S. – African Americans. U.S. history.

Touch the sky: Alice Coachman, Olympic high jumper ill. by Eric Velasquez. Whitman, 2012. ISBN 978-0-8075-8035-6 Subj: Character traits – perseverance. Ethnic groups in the U.S. – African Americans. Sports – Olympics. U.S. history.

Yasmin's hammer ill. by Doug Chayka. Lee & Low, 2010. ISBN 978-1-60060-359-4 Subj: Foreign lands – Bangladesh. School.

Malkin, Michele. *Pinky's sweet tooth* ill. by author. Dutton, 2003. ISBN 978-0-525-47088-5 Subj: Activities – baking, cooking. Reptiles – alligators, crocodiles.

Mallat, Kathy. *Just ducky* ill. by author. Walker, 2001. ISBN 978-0-8027-8824-5 Subj: Activities – playing. Birds – ducks. Friendship. Optical illusions.

Papa pride ill. by author. Walker, 2005. ISBN 978-0-8027-8964-8 Subj: Animals – wolves. Family life – fathers. Rhyming text.

Trouble on the tracks ill. by author. Walker, 2001. ISBN 978-0-8027-8773-6 Subj: Activities – playing. Animals – cats. Toys – trains.

Malnor, Carol L. *The Blues go birding across America* by Carol L. Malnor and Sandy F. Fuller ill. by Louise Schroeder. Dawn, 2010. ISBN 978-1-58469-124-2 Subj: Birds. Holidays – Fourth of July.

Maloney, Peter. *Belly button boy* by Peter Maloney and Felicia Zekauskas ill. by authors. Dial, 2000. ISBN 978-0-8037-2542-3 Subj: Anatomy – navels. Character traits – cleanliness. Rhyming text.

His mother's nose by Peter Maloney and Felicia Zekauskas ill. by authors. Dial, 2001. ISBN 978-0-8037-2545-4 Subj: Anatomy. Character traits – individuality. Family life. Self-concept.

One foot two feet: an exceptional counting book by Peter Maloney and Felicia Zekauskas ill. by authors. Penguin, 2011. ISBN 978-0-399-25446-8 Subj: Concepts. Counting, numbers.

Maltbie, P. I. *Claude Monet: the painter who stopped the trains* ill. by Joseph A. Smith. Abrams, 2010. ISBN 978-0-8109-8961-0 Subj: Art. Careers – artists. Trains.

Mamada, Mineko. *Which is round? which is bigger?* ill. by author. Kids Can, 2013. ISBN 978-1-55453-973-4 Subj: Character traits – questioning. Concepts. Problem solving.

Mammano, Julie. *Rhinos who play baseball* ill. by author. Chronicle, 2003. ISBN 978-0-8118-3605-0 Subj: Animals – rhinoceros. Sports – baseball.

Rhinos who play soccer ill. by author. Chronicle, 2001. ISBN 978-0-8118-2779-9 Subj: Animals – rhinoceros. Sports – soccer.

Rhinos who rescue ill. by author. Chronicle, 2007. ISBN 978-0-8118-5419-1 Subj: Animals – rhinoceros. Careers – firefighters.

Rhinos who surf ill. by author. Chronicle, 1996. ISBN 978-0-8118-1000-5 Subj: Animals – rhinoceros. Sports – surfing.

Manceau, Edouard. *Windblown* ill. by author. OwlKids, 2013. ISBN 978-1-926973-77-7 Subj: Animals. Concepts – shape. Imagination. Weather – wind.

Mandel, Peter. *Jackhammer Sam* ill. by David Catrow. Roaring Brook, 2011. ISBN 978-1-59643-

034-1 Subj: Careers – construction workers. Rhyming text. Tools.

Say hey: a song of Willie Mays ill. by Don Tate. Hyperion, 2000. ISBN 978-0-7868-2417-5 Subj: Ethnic groups in the U.S. – African Americans. Rhyming text. Sports – baseball.

Zoo ah-choooo ill. by Elwood H. Smith. Holiday House, 2012. ISBN 978-0-8234-2317-0 Subj: Illness – cold (disease). Noise, sounds. Zoos.

Mandell, Muriel, adapt. *A donkey reads: adapted from a Turkish folktale* ill. by André Letria. Star Bright, 2011. ISBN 978-1-59572-256-0 Subj: Animals – donkeys. Character traits – cleverness. Folk & fairy tales. Foreign lands – Turkey.

Manders, John. *The really awful musicians* ill. by author. Clarion, 2011. ISBN 978-0-547-32820-1 Subj: Careers – musicians. Music. Royalty – kings.

Mangan, Anne. *The monkey who wanted the moon* ill. by Catherine Walters. Crocodile, 2001. ISBN 978-1-56656-376-5 Subj: Animals – monkeys. Behavior – greed. Jungle. Moon.

Manna, Anthony L. *The orphan: a Cinderella story from Greece* by Anthony L. Manna and Soula Mitakidou ill. by Giselle Potter. Random House, 2011. ISBN 978-0-375-86691-3 Subj: Family life – stepfamilies. Folk & fairy tales. Foreign lands – Greece. Orphans. Royalty – princes. Sibling rivalry.

Manners mash-up: a goofy guide to good behavior ill. by Tedd Arnold et al. Penguin, 2011. ISBN 978-0-8037-3480-7 Subj: Etiquette.

Manning, Eli, et al. *Family huddle* (Manning, Peyton)

Manning, Jane. *Cat nights* ill. by author. HarperCollins, 2008. ISBN 978-0-06-113888-1 Subj: Animals – cats. Character traits – individuality. Witches.

Millie Fierce ill. by author. Philomel, 2012. ISBN 978-0-399-25642-4 Subj: Behavior – misbehavior. Self-concept.

My first baby games ill. by author. HarperCollins, 2001. ISBN 978-0-694-01435-4 Subj: Babies. Games.

Manning, Maurie J. *The aunts go marching* ill. by author. Boyds Mills, 2003. ISBN 978-1-59078-026-8 Subj: Counting, numbers. Cumulative tales. Family life – aunts, uncles. Rhyming text. Weather – rain.

Kitchen dance ill. by author. Clarion, 2008. ISBN 978-0-618-99110-5 Subj: Activities – dancing. Bedtime. Ethnic groups in the U.S. – Hispanic Americans. Family life.

Laundry day ill. by author. Clarion, 2012. ISBN 978-0-547-24196-8 Subj: Behavior – lost & found possessions. Communities, neighborhoods. U.S. history.

Manning, Mick. *Cock-a-doodle hooooooo!* ill. by Brita Granström. Good Books, 2007. ISBN 978-1-56148-568-0 Subj: Birds – chickens. Birds – owls. Character traits – helpfulness. Farms.

Dino-dinners ill. by Brita Granström. Holiday House, 2007. ISBN 978-0-8234-2089-6 Subj: Dinosaurs.

Snap! by Mick Manning and Brita Granström ill. by authors. Frances Lincoln, 2006. ISBN 978-1-84507-408-1 Subj: Food. Science.

Supermom ill. by Brita Granström. Whitman, 2001. ISBN 978-0-8075-7666-3 Subj: Animals. Family life – mothers.

What a Viking! ill. by Brita Granström. R&S Books, 2000. ISBN 978-91-29-64883-6 Subj: Foreign lands – Scandinavia. Sailors. Vikings.

Woolly mammoth by Mick Manning and Brita Granström ill. by Brita Granström. Frances Lincoln, 2009. ISBN 978-1-84507-860-7 Subj: Animals – woolly mammoths.

Manning, Peyton. *Family huddle* by Peyton Manning and Eli Manning, et al ill. by Jim Madsen. Scholastic, 2009. ISBN 978-0-545-15377-5 Subj: Family life. Sports – football.

Mannis, Celeste Davidson. *One leaf rides the wind* ill. by Susan Kathleen Hartung. Viking, 2002. ISBN 978-0-670-03525-0 Subj: Counting, numbers. Gardens, gardening. Nature. Poetry.

Mansfield, Howard. *Hogwood steps out: a good, good pig story* ill. by Barry Moser. Roaring Brook, 2008. ISBN 978-1-59643-269-7 Subj: Animals – pigs. Behavior – misbehavior. Farms. Seasons – spring.

Manson, Ainslie. *Ballerinas don't wear glasses* ill. by Dean Griffiths. Orca, 2000. ISBN 978-1-55143-176-5 Subj: Activities – dancing. Ballet. Family life – brothers & sisters. Self-concept.

Manuel, Lynn. *Camels always do* ill. by Kasia Charko. Orca, 2004. ISBN 978-1-55143-284-7 Subj: Animals – camels. Foreign lands – British Columbia.

The trouble with Tilly Trumble ill. by Diane Greenseid. Abrams, 2006. ISBN 978-0-8109-5972-9 Subj: Animals – dogs. Behavior – collecting things. Furniture – chairs.

Manushkin, Fran. *Big girl panties* ill. by Valeria Petrone. Random House, 2012. ISBN 978-0-307-93152-8 Subj: Toilet training.

Hooray for Hanukkah! ill. by author. Random House, 2001. ISBN 978-0-375-91043-2 Subj: Holidays – Hanukkah. Jewish culture. Religion.

How mama brought the spring ill. by Holly Berry. Dutton, 2008. ISBN 978-0-525-42027-9 Subj: Family life – grandmothers. Food. Foreign lands – Belarus. Seasons – winter.

Latkes and applesauce ill. by Robin Spowart. Scholastic, 1990. ISBN 978-0-590-42261-1 Subj: Holidays – Hanukkah. Jewish culture. Religion.

Let George do it! (Foreman, George)

Miriam's cup: a Passover story ill. by Bob Dacey. Scholastic, 1998. ISBN 978-0-590-67720-2 Subj: Holidays – Passover. Jewish culture. Religion.

The shivers in the fridge ill. by Paul O. Zelinsky. Penguin, 2006. ISBN 978-0-525-46943-8 Subj: Imagination.

Many, Paul. *Dad's bald head* ill. by Kevin O'Malley. Walker, 2007. ISBN 978-0-8027-9579-3 Subj: Family life – fathers. Hair.

The great pancake escape ill. by Scott Goto. Walker, 2002. ISBN 978-0-8027-8796-5 Subj: Activities – baking, cooking. Careers – magicians. Food. Magic. Rhyming text.

Manzano, Sonia. *A box full of kittens* ill. by Matt Phelan. Simon & Schuster, 2007. ISBN 978-0-689-83089-1 Subj: Animals – cats. Babies. Character traits – helpfulness. Ethnic groups in the U.S. – Puerto Rican Americans.

No dogs allowed ill. by Jon J. Muth. Atheneum, 2004. ISBN 978-0-689-83088-4 Subj: Activities – picnicking. Animals – dogs. Automobiles. Ethnic groups in the U.S. – Puerto Rican Americans. Family life.

Maples in the mist: children's poems from the Tang Dynasty ill. by Jean Tseng and Mou-Sien Tseng. Lothrop, 1996. ISBN 978-0-688-12044-3 Subj: Foreign lands – China. Poetry.

Mara, Wil. *Amelia Earhart* ill. with photos. Children's Press, 2002. ISBN 978-0-516-22522-7 Subj: Activities – flying. Careers – airplane pilots. U.S. history.

Jackie Robinson ill. with photos. Children's Press, 2002. ISBN 978-0-516-22520-3 Subj: Careers. Ethnic groups in the U.S. – African Americans. Sports – baseball.

Laura Ingalls Wilder ill. with photos. Children's Press, 2003. ISBN 978-0-516-22855-6 Subj: Careers – writers. U.S. history – frontier & pioneer life.

Marcellino, Fred. *I, crocodile* ill. by author. HarperCollins, 1999. ISBN 978-0-06-205199-8 Subj: Food. Foreign lands – Egypt. Foreign lands – France. Humorous stories. Reptiles – alligators, crocodiles. Royalty – emperors.

Marchon, Benoit. *Spoonful!* ill. by Soledad Bravi. Harcourt, 2013. ISBN 978-0-547-89313-6 Subj: Food. Format, unusual – board books.

Marciano, John Bemelmans. *Delilah* ill. by author. Viking, 2002. ISBN 978-0-670-03523-6 Subj: Animals – babies. Animals – sheep. Careers – farmers. Character traits – individuality. Farms. Friendship.

Madeline and the cats of Rome ill. by author. Viking, 2008. ISBN 978-0-670-06297-3 Subj: Animals – cats. Crime. Foreign lands – Italy. Orphans. Rhyming text.

Madeline and the old house in Paris ill. by author. Viking, 2013. ISBN 978-0-670-78485-1 Subj: Foreign lands – France. Ghosts. Orphans. Rhyming text. School.

Madeline at the White House ill. by author. Penguin, 2011. ISBN 978-0-670-01228-2 Subj: Holidays – Easter. Orphans. U.S. history.

Madeline says merci ill. by author. Viking, 2001. ISBN 978-0-670-03505-2 Subj: Etiquette. Rhyming text.

Marco, Chris. *Seeing in living things* (Hartley, Karen)

The sixth sense and other special senses (Hartley, Karen)

Smelling in living things (Hartley, Karen)

Tasting in living things (Hartley, Karen)

Touching in living things (Hartley, Karen)

Marcos, subcomandante. *The story of colors / La historia de los colores* ill. by Domitila Domínguez. Cinco Puntos, 1999. ISBN 978-0-938317-45-6 Subj: Concepts – color. Folk & fairy tales – pourquoi tales. Foreign lands – Mexico. Foreign languages. Indians of Central America – Maya.

Marcus, Kimberly. *Scritch-scratch a perfect match* ill. by Mike Lester. Penguin, 2011. ISBN 978-0-399-25004-0 Subj: Animals – dogs. Insects – fleas. Rhyming text.

Marcus, Leonard S. *Oscar: the big adventures of a little sock monkey* (Schwartz, Amy)

Margalith, Joan. *The babies are landing* ill. by Linda Bronson. Chronicle, 2000. ISBN 978-0-8118-2674-7 Subj: Babies. Rhyming text.

Margolin, H. Ellen. *Goin' to Boston* ill. by Emily Bolam. Handprint, 2002. ISBN 978-1-929766-45-1 Subj: Activities – traveling. Cumulative tales. Music. Songs.

Mariconda, Barbara. *Sort it out!* ill. by Sherry Rogers. Sylvan Dell, 2008. ISBN 978-1-934359-11-2 Subj: Animals – pack rats. Behavior – collecting things. Character traits – orderliness. Counting, numbers. Rhyming text.

Marin, Cheech. *Cheech and the spooky ghost bus* ill. by Orlando L. Ramirez. HarperCollins, 2009. ISBN 978-0-06-113211-7 Subj: Careers – bus drivers. Ghosts.

Marino, Gianna. *Meet me at the moon* ill. by author. Viking, 2012. ISBN 978-0-670-01313-5 Subj: Animals – elephants. Family life – mothers. Foreign lands – Africa. Weather – droughts.

One too many: a seek and find counting book ill. by author. Chronicle, 2010. ISBN 978-0-8118-6908-9 Subj: Animals. Counting, numbers. Picture puzzles.

Too tall houses ill. by author. Viking, 2012. ISBN 978-0-670-01314-2 Subj: Animals – rabbits. Birds – owls. Character traits – cooperation. Homes, houses. Problem solving.

Zoopa: an animal alphabet ill. by author. Chronicle, 2005. ISBN 978-0-8118-4789-6 Subj: ABC books. Animals. Food.

Markel, Michelle. *Brave girl: Clara and the Shirtwaist Makers' Strike of 1909* ill. by Melissa Sweet. HarperCollins, 2013. ISBN 978-0-06-180442-7 Subj: Activities – working. Behavior – seeking better things. Character traits – bravery. Clothing. U.S. history.

The fantastic jungles of Henri Rousseau ill. by Amanda Hall. Eerdmans, 2012. ISBN 978-0-8028-5364-6 Subj: Art. Careers – artists. Character traits – perseverance. Foreign lands – France.

Tyrannosaurus math ill. by Doug Cushman. Tricycle, 2009. ISBN 978-1-58246-282-0 Subj: Counting, numbers. Dinosaurs.

Markell, Denis. *Hush, Little Monster* ill. by Melissa Iwai. Simon & Schuster, 2012. ISBN 978-1-4424-4195-8 Subj: Family life – fathers. Lullabies. Monsters. Rhyming text.

Markes, Julie. *Good thing you're not an octopus!* ill. by Maggie Smith. HarperCollins, 2001. ISBN 978-0-06-028466-4 Subj: Activities. Animals. Self-concept.

Shhhhh! Everybody's sleeping ill. by David Parkins. HarperCollins, 2005. ISBN 978-0-06-053791-3 Subj: Bedtime. Rhyming text. Sleep.

Sidewalk ABC ill. by Jennifer Markes. HarperCollins, 2001. ISBN 978-0-694-01455-2 Subj: ABC books. Format, unusual – board books.

Sidewalk 1 2 3 ill. by Jennifer Markes. HarperCollins, 2001. ISBN 978-0-694-01500-9 Subj: Counting, numbers. Format, unusual – board books.

Thanks for Thanksgiving ill. by Doris Barrette. HarperCollins, 2004. ISBN 978-0-06-051097-8 Subj: Holidays – Thanksgiving. Rhyming text.

Markham, Beryl. *The good lion* ill. by Don Brown. Houghton, 2005. ISBN 978-0-618-56306-7 Subj: Animals – lions. Foreign lands – Africa.

Markle, Sandra. *Bats: biggest! littlest!* Boyds Mills, 2013. ISBN 978-1-59078-952-0 Subj: Animals – bats. Concepts – size.

Butterfly tree ill. by Leslie Wu. Peachtree, 2011. ISBN 978-1-56145-539-3 Subj: Insects – butterflies, caterpillars. Migration.

Creepy, crawly baby bugs ill. with photos. Walker, 1996. ISBN 978-0-8027-8444-5 Subj: Animals – babies. Insects. Science.

Family pack ill. by Alan Marks. Charlesbridge, 2011. ISBN 978-1-58089-217-9 Subj: Animals – endangered animals. Animals – wolves.

Finding home ill. by Alan Marks. Charlesbridge, 2008. ISBN 978-1-58089-122-6 Subj: Animals – koalas. Fire. Foreign lands – Australia.

Hip-pocket papa ill. by Alan Marks. Charlesbridge, 2010. ISBN 978-1-57091-708-0 Subj: Foreign lands – Australia. Frogs & toads.

How many baby pandas? ill. with photos. Walker, 2009. ISBN 978-0-8027-9783-4 Subj: Animals – pandas. Counting, numbers. Foreign lands – China.

Insects: biggest! littlest! photos by Simon Pollard. Boyds Mills, 2009. ISBN 978-1-59078-512-6 Subj: Insects.

Little lost bat ill. by Alan Marks. Charlesbridge, 2006. ISBN 978-1-57091-656-4 Subj: Animals – bats. Nature.

A mother's journey ill. by Alan Marks. Charlesbridge, 2005. ISBN 978-1-57091-621-2 Subj: Birds – penguins. Family life.

Sharks: biggest! littlest! ill. with photos. Boyds Mills, 2008. ISBN 978-1-59078-513-3 Subj: Concepts – size. Fish – sharks.

Sneaky, spinning, baby spiders ill. with photos. Walker, 2008. ISBN 978-0-8027-9697-4 Subj: Science. Spiders.

Waiting for ice ill. by Alan Marks. Charlesbridge, 2012. ISBN 978-1-58089-255-1 Subj: Animals – polar bears. Ecology.

Marks, Jennifer L. *Sorting by size* ill. with photos. Capstone, 2006. ISBN 978-0-7368-6740-5 Subj: Concepts – size.

Sorting money ill. with photos. Capstone, 2006. ISBN 978-0-7368-6738-2 Subj: Money.

Sorting toys ill. with photos. Capstone, 2006. ISBN 978-0-7368-6737-5 Subj: Toys.

Marley, Cedella, reteller. *Every little thing* ill. by Vanessa Brantley Newton. Chronicle, 2012. ISBN 978-1-4521-0697-7 Subj: Activities – playing. Birds. Day. Songs.

One love: based on the song by Bob Marley ill. by Vanessa Brantley Newton. Chronicle, 2011. ISBN 978-1-4521-0224-5 Subj: Emotions – love. Songs.

Marlow, Layn. *Hurry up and slow down* ill. by author. Holiday, 2009. ISBN 978-0-8234-2178-7 Subj: Animals – rabbits. Bedtime. Behavior – hurrying. Reptiles – turtles, tortoises.

You make me smile ill. by author. Holiday House, 2013. ISBN 978-0-8234-2922-6 Subj: Snowmen. Weather – snow.

Marlowe, Pete. *One Arabian morning* ill. by Charles Bell. Annick, 2000. ISBN 978-1-55037-659-3 Subj: Foreign lands. Imagination. Royalty.

Marlowe, Sara. *No ordinary apple: a story about eating mindfully* ill. by Philip Pascuzzo. Wisdom Publications, 2013. ISBN 978-1-61429-076-6 Subj: Behavior. Character traits – patience. Character traits – wisdom. Food.

Marsalis, Wynton. *Squeak, rumble, whomp! Whomp! Whomp! a sonic adventure* ill. by Paul Rogers. Candlewick, 2012. ISBN 978-0-7636-3991-4 Subj: Careers – musicians. Communities, neighborhoods. Ethnic groups in the U.S. – African Americans. Music. Musical instruments. Noise, sounds.

Marsh, T. J. *Somewhere in the ocean* (Ward, Jennifer)

Marshak, S. *The Month-Brothers: a Slavic tale* ill. by Diane Stanley. Morrow, 1983. ISBN 978-0-688-01510-7 Subj: Foreign lands – Czechoslovakia. Rhyming text. Seasons. Weather.

Marshall, Catherine. *Christy, Christmastime at Cutter Gap* (LeSourd, Nancy)

Marshall, Edward. *Space case* ill. by James Marshall. Dial, 1980. ISBN 978-0-8037-8007-1 Subj: Holidays – Halloween. Robots. Space & space ships.

Marshall, James. *The Cut-Ups* ill. by author. Viking, 1984. ISBN 978-0-670-25195-7 Subj: Behavior – misbehavior. Humorous stories. Toys.

The Cut-Ups at Camp Custer ill. by author. Viking, 1989. ISBN 978-0-670-82051-1 Subj: Behavior – misbehavior. Camps, camping. Humorous stories.

The Cut-Ups carry on ill. by author. Viking, 1990. ISBN 978-0-670-81645-3 Subj: Activities – dancing. Contests. Humorous stories.

The Cut-Ups crack up ill. by author. Viking, 1992. ISBN 978-0-670-84486-9 Subj: Automobiles. Behavior – misbehavior. Humorous stories. School.

The Cut-Ups cut loose ill. by author. Viking, 1987. ISBN 978-0-670-80740-6 Subj: Behavior – misbehavior. Friendship. Humorous stories. School.

Eugene ill. by author. Houghton, 2000. ISBN 978-0-618-07319-1 Subj: Animals. Careers – teachers. Format, unusual – board books. Reptiles – turtles, tortoises. School – first day.

George and Martha ill. by author. Houghton, 1972. ISBN 978-0-395-13732-1 Subj: Animals – hippopotamuses. Friendship.

George and Martha back in town ill. by author. Houghton, 1984. ISBN 978-0-395-35386-8 Subj: Animals – hippopotamuses. Behavior – misbehavior. Friendship.

George and Martha encore ill. by author. Houghton, 1973. ISBN 978-0-395-17512-5 Subj: Activities – dancing. Animals – hippopotamuses. Friendship.

George and Martha one fine day ill. by author. Houghton, 1978. ISBN 978-0-395-27154-4 Subj: Animals – hippopotamuses. Friendship.

George and Martha rise and shine ill. by author. Houghton, 1976. ISBN 978-0-395-24738-9 Subj: Animals – hippopotamuses. Friendship.

George and Martha 'round and 'round ill. by author. Houghton, 1988. ISBN 978-0-395-46763-3 Subj: Activities – vacationing. Animals – hippopotamuses. Friendship. Imagination.

George and Martha, tons of fun ill. by author. Houghton, 1980. ISBN 978-0-395-29524-3 Subj: Animals – hippopotamuses. Character traits – vanity.

Hansel and Gretel ill. by reteller. Dial, 1990. ISBN 978-0-8037-0828-0 Subj: Behavior – lost. Folk & fairy tales. Forest, woods. Witches.

Merry Christmas, space case ill. by author. Dial, 1986. ISBN 978-0-8037-0216-5 Subj: Holidays – Christmas. Space & space ships.

Miss Nelson is back (Allard, Harry)

Miss Nelson is missing! (Allard, Harry)

Pocketful of nonsense ill. by author. Artists & Writers Guild, 1993. ISBN 978-0-307-17552-6 Subj: Poetry.

Portly McSwine ill. by author. Houghton, 1979. ISBN 978-0-395-28003-4 Subj: Animals – pigs. Behavior – worrying.

Red Riding Hood ill. by reteller. Dial, 1987. ISBN 978-0-8037-0345-2 Subj: Animals – wolves. Behavior – talking to strangers. Folk & fairy tales.

The Stupids have a ball (Allard, Harry)

The Stupids take off (Allard, Harry)

Swine lake ill. by Maurice Sendak. HarperCollins, 1999. ISBN 978-0-06-205171-4 Subj: Activities – dancing. Animals – pigs. Animals – wolves. Ballet. Theater.

Wings: a tale of two chickens ill. by author. Viking, 1986. ISBN 978-0-670-80961-5 Subj: Animals – foxes. Birds – chickens. Books, reading.

Yummers! ill. by author. Houghton, 1973. ISBN 978-0-395-14757-3 Subj: Animals – pigs. Food. Illness.

Yummers too: the second course ill. by author. Houghton, 1986. ISBN 978-0-395-38990-4 Subj: Animals – pigs. Behavior – greed. Food. Reptiles – turtles, tortoises.

Marshall, Janet Perry. *Baby sharks* (Gentle, Victor)

A honey of a day ill. by author. Greenwillow, 2000. ISBN 978-0-688-16917-6 Subj: Animals. Flowers. Weddings.

Killer sharks, killer people (Gentle, Victor)

Orcas, killer whales (Gentle, Victor)

Shark camouflage and armor (Gentle, Victor)

Very big sharks (Gentle, Victor)

The world's strangest shark (Gentle, Victor)

Marshall, Linda Elovitz. *Grandma Rose's magic* ill. by Ag Jatkowska. Lerner/Kar-Ben, 2012. ISBN 978-0-7613-5215-0 Subj: Activities – sewing. Character traits – generosity. Family life – grandmothers. Jewish culture.

The passover lamb ill. by Tatjana Mai-Wyss. Random House, 2013. ISBN 978-0-307-93177-1 Subj: Animals – sheep. Character traits – questioning. Farms. Holidays – Passover. Holidays – Seder. Jewish culture.

Talia and the rude vegetables ill. by Francesca Assirelli. Lerner/Kar-Ben, 2011. ISBN 978-0-7613-5217-4 Subj: Food. Gardens, gardening. Holidays – Rosh Hashanah.

Martin, Ann M. *Rachel Parker, kindergarten show-off* ill. by Nancy Poydar. Holiday, 1992. ISBN 978-0-8234-0935-8 Subj: Character traits – conceit. Emotions – envy, jealousy. Ethnic groups in the U.S. – African Americans. Friendship. School.

Martin, Bernard H. *Chicken Chuck* (Martin, Bill, Jr.)

Martin, Bill, Jr. *Adam, Adam, what do you see?* by Bill Martin, Jr. and Michael R. Sampson ill. by Cathie Felstead. Tommy Nelson, 2000. ISBN 978-0-8499-7614-8 Subj: Religion. Rhyming text.

Baby bear, baby bear, what do you see? ill. by Eric Carle. Holt, 2007. ISBN 978-0-8050-8336-1 Subj: Animals. Animals – bears. Cumulative tales. Rhyming text.

Barn dance! ill. by Ted Rand. Holt, 1986. ISBN 978-0-8050-0089-4 Subj: Activities – dancing. Barns. Country. Dreams. Night. Rhyming text. Scarecrows.

A beasty story by Bill Martin, Jr. and Steven Kellogg ill. by Steven Kellogg. Harcourt, 1999. ISBN 978-0-15-201683-8 Subj: Animals – mice. Forest, woods. Monsters.

Brown bear, brown bear, what do you see? ill. by Eric Carle. Holt, 1992. ISBN 978-0-8050-1744-1 Subj: Animals – bears. Concepts – color. Cumulative tales. Rhyming text.

Chicka chicka boom boom by Bill Martin, Jr. and John Archambault ill. by Lois Ehlert. Simon & Schuster, 1989. ISBN 978-0-617-67949-3 Subj: ABC books. Rhyming text. Trees.

Chicka chicka boom boom [board book] by Bill Martin, Jr. and John Archambault ill. by Lois Ehlert. Simon & Schuster, 1993. ISBN 978-0-671-87893-1 Subj: ABC books. Format, unusual – board books. Rhyming text. Trees.

Chicken Chuck by Bill Martin, Jr. and Bernard H. Martin ill. by Steven Salerno. Winslow, 2000. ISBN 978-1-890817-31-2 Subj: Animals. Animals – horses, ponies. Birds – chickens. Character traits – individuality. Circus. Farms.

Fire! Fire! said Mrs. McGuire ill. by Richard Egielski. Harcourt, 1996. ISBN 978-0-15-227562-4 Subj: Birthdays. Careers – firefighters. Fire. Nursery rhymes.

"Fire! Fire!" said Mrs. McGuire ill. by Vladimir Radunsky. Harcourt, 2006. ISBN 978-0-15-205725-1 Subj: Birthdays. Careers – firefighters. Fire. Nursery rhymes.

Here are my hands by Bill Martin, Jr. and John Archambault ill. by Ted Rand. Holt, 1998. ISBN 978-0-8050-5911-3 Subj: Anatomy. Rhyming text.

I love our Earth by Bill Martin, Jr. and Michael R. Sampson ill. by Dan Lipow. Charlesbridge, 2006. ISBN 978-1-58089-106-6 Subj: Earth. Nature. Seasons.

I pledge allegiance commentary by Michael R. Sampson; ill. by Chris Raschka. Candlewick, 2002. ISBN 978-0-7636-2527-6 Subj: Format, unusual – board books. U.S. history.

Kitty Cat, Kitty Cat, are you going to school? by Bill Martin, Jr. and Michael R. Sampson ill. by Laura J. Bryant. Amazon/Two Lions, 2013. ISBN 978-1-4778-1722-3 Subj: Animals – cats. Rhyming text. School – first day.

Kitty Cat, Kitty Cat, are you going to sleep? by Bill Martin, Jr. and Michael R. Sampson ill. by Laura J. Bryant. Marshall Cavendish, 2011. ISBN 978-0-7614-5946-0 Subj: Animals – cats. Bedtime. Rhyming text.

Kitty Cat, Kitty Cat, are you waking up? by Bill Martin, Jr. and Michael R. Sampson ill. by Laura J. Bryant. Marshall Cavendish, 2008. ISBN 978-0-7614-5438-0 Subj: Animals – cats. Rhyming text.

Knots on a counting rope by Bill Martin, Jr. and John Archambault ill. by Ted Rand. Holt, 1987. ISBN 978-0-8050-0571-4 Subj: Character traits – bravery. Disabilities – blindness. Emotions – love. Family life – grandfathers. Indians of North America. Senses – sight.

Listen to the rain by Bill Martin, Jr. and John Archambault ill. by James R. Endicott. Holt, 1988. ISBN 978-0-8050-0682-7 Subj: Rhyming text. Weather – rain.

Little granny quarterback by Bill Martin, Jr. and Michael R. Sampson ill. by Michael Chesworth. Boyds Mills, 2001. ISBN 978-1-56397-930-9 Subj: Dreams. Family life – grandmothers. Old age. Rhyming text. Sports – football.

The little squeegy bug by Bill Martin, Jr. and Michael R. Sampson ill. by Pat Corrigan. Winslow, 2001. ISBN 978-1-890817-90-9 Subj: Insects.

Maestro plays ill. by Vladimir Radunsky. Holt, 1994. ISBN 978-0-8050-1746-5 Subj: Careers – musicians. Rhyming text.

The magic pumpkin by Bill Martin, Jr. and John Archambault ill. by Robert J. Lee. Holt, 1989. ISBN 978-0-8050-1134-0 Subj: Holidays – Halloween. Magic. Rhyming text.

Old devil wind ill. by Barry Root. Harcourt, 1993. ISBN 978-0-15-257768-1 Subj: Cumulative tales. Ghosts. Holidays – Halloween. Weather – wind.

Polar bear, polar bear, what do you hear? ill. by Eric Carle. Holt, 1991. ISBN 978-0-8050-1759-5 Subj: Animals. Noise, sounds. Rhyming text. Zoos.

Rock it, sock it, number line by Bill Martin, Jr. and Michael R. Sampson ill. by Heather Cahoon. Holt, 2001. ISBN 978-0-8050-6304-2 Subj: Counting, numbers. Food. Parties. Plants. Royalty.

Swish! by Bill Martin, Jr. and Michael R. Sampson ill. by Michael Chesworth. Holt, 1997. ISBN 978-0-8050-4498-0 Subj: Sports – basketball.

Ten little caterpillars ill. by Lois Ehlert. Simon & Schuster, 2011. ISBN 978-1-4424-3385-4 Subj: Counting, numbers. Insects – butterflies, caterpillars. Metamorphosis. Rhyming text.

Trick or treat? by Bill Martin, Jr. and Michael R. Sampson ill. by Paul Meisel. Simon & Schuster, 2002. ISBN 978-0-689-84968-8 Subj: Behavior – trickery. Food. Holidays – Halloween. Magic.

The turning of the year ill. by Greg Shed. Harcourt, 1998. ISBN 978-0-15-201085-0 Subj: Days of the week, months of the year. Rhyming text. Seasons.

Martin, David. *All for pie, pie for all* ill. by Valeri Gorbachev. Candlewick, 2006. ISBN 978-0-7636-2393-7 Subj: Activities – baking, cooking. Animals – cats. Animals – mice. Behavior – sharing. Food. Insects – ants.

Five little piggies ill. by Susan Meddaugh. Candlewick, 1998. ISBN 978-1-56402-918-8 Subj: Animals – pigs. Family life. Shopping.

Hanukkah lights ill. by Melissa Sweet. Candlewick, 2009. ISBN 978-0-7636-3029-4 Subj: Format, unusual – board books. Holidays – Hanukkah. Rhyming text.

Let's have a tree party! ill. by John Manders. Candlewick, 2012. ISBN 978-0-7636-3704-0 Subj: Animals. Forest, woods. Rhyming text. Trees.

Little Bunny and the magic Christmas tree ill. by Valeri Gorbachev. Candlewick, 2011. ISBN 978-0-7636-3693-7 Subj: Animals – rabbits. Character traits – smallness. Holidays – Christmas.

Monkey business ill. by Scott Nash. Candlewick, 2000. ISBN 978-0-7636-1178-1 Subj: Animals – monkeys. Birthdays. Family life – mothers.

Monkey trouble ill. by Scott Nash. Candlewick, 2000. ISBN 978-0-7636-1179-8 Subj: Animals – monkeys. Behavior – misbehavior.

Peep and Ducky ill. by David Walker. Candlewick, 2013. ISBN 978-0-7636-5039-1 Subj: Activities – playing. Birds – bluebirds. Birds – ducks. Friendship. Rhyming text.

Piggy and Dad ill. by Frank Remkiewicz. Candlewick, 2001. ISBN 978-0-7636-1326-6 Subj: Activities. Animals – pigs. Family life – fathers.

Piggy and Dad go fishing ill. by Frank Remkiewicz. Candlewick, 2005. ISBN 978-0-7636-2506-1 Subj: Animals – pigs. Animals – worms. Family life – fathers. Fish. Sports – fishing.

We've all got bellybuttons ill. by Randy Cecil. Candlewick, 2005. ISBN 978-0-7636-1775-2 Subj: Anatomy. Anatomy – navels. Animals. Rhyming text.

Martin, Emily Winfield. *Dream animals* ill. by author. Random House, 2013. ISBN 978-0-449-81080-4 Subj: Animals. Bedtime. Dreams. Rhyming text.

Martin, Francesca. *Clever Tortoise: a traditional African tale* ill. by author. Candlewick, 2000. ISBN 978-0-7636-0506-3 Subj: Animals. Folk & fairy tales. Foreign lands – Tanzania. Reptiles – turtles, tortoises.

Martín, Hugo C. *Pablo's Christmas* ill. by Lee Chapman. Sterling, 2006. ISBN 978-1-4027-2560-9 Subj: Activities – wood carving. Family life. Farms. Foreign lands – Mexico. Holidays – Christmas.

Martin, Jacqueline Briggs. *Banjo granny* (Busse, Sarah Martin)

Chicken joy on Redbean Road: a bayou country romp ill. by Melissa Sweet. Houghton, 2007. ISBN 978-0-618-50759-7 Subj: Activities – singing. Birds – chickens. Farms. Food. Illness. Music.

The chiru of High Tibet: a true story ill. by Linda S. Wingerter. Harcourt, 2010. ISBN 978-0-618-58130-6 Subj: Animals – endangered animals. Foreign lands – Tibet.

Farmer Will Allen and the growing table ill. by Eric-Shabazz Larkin. Readers to Eaters, 2013. ISBN 978-0-98366-153-5 Subj: Behavior – seeking better things. Cities, towns. Communities, neighborhoods. Ethnic groups in the U.S. – African Americans. Gardens, gardening.

On Sand Island ill. by David Johnson. Houghton, 2003. ISBN 978-0-618-23151-5 Subj: Activities – trading. Boats, ships. Family life. Islands. Lakes, ponds.

Snowflake Bentley ill. by Mary Azarian. Houghton, 1998. ISBN 978-0-395-86162-2 Subj: Caldecott award books. Careers – photographers. Careers – scientists. Nature. U.S. history. Weather – snow.

The water gift and the pig of the pig ill. by Linda S. Wingerter. Houghton, 2002. ISBN 978-0-618-07436-5 Subj: Animals – pigs. Family life – grandfathers. Orphans.

Martin, Rafe. *The language of birds* ill. by Susan Gaber. Putnam, 2000. ISBN 978-0-399-22925-1 Subj: Character traits – kindness to animals. Folk & fairy tales. Foreign lands – Russia.

The rough-face girl ill. by David Shannon. Putnam, 1992. ISBN 978-0-399-21859-0 Subj: Family life – sisters. Folk & fairy tales. Indians of North America – Algonquin.

The Shark God ill. by David Shannon. Scholastic, 2001. ISBN 978-0-590-39500-7 Subj: Character traits – kindness to animals. Fish – sharks. Folk & fairy tales. Hawaii. Royalty – kings.

The storytelling princess ill. by Kimberly Bulcken Root. Putnam, 2001. ISBN 978-0-399-22924-4 Subj: Activities – storytelling. Royalty – princes. Royalty – princesses.

Will's mammoth ill. by Stephen Gammell. Putnam, 1989. ISBN 978-0-399-21627-5 Subj: Animals. Imagination.

Martin, Ruth. *Moon dreams* ill. by Olivier Latyk. Candlewick, 2010. ISBN 978-0-7636-5012-4 Subj: Day. Dreams. Moon. Night.

Santa's on his way ill. by Sophy Williams. Candlewick, 2011. ISBN 978-0-7636-5555-6 Subj: Format, unusual – toy & movable books. Holidays – Christmas. Santa Claus.

Martin, Sarah Catherine. *Old Mother Hubbard* retold by Jane Cabrera; ill. by Jane Cabrera. Based on *The comic adventures of Old Mother Hubbard and her dog,* originally published in London, 1805, by John Harris. Holiday, 2001. ISBN 978-0-8234-1659-2 Subj: Animals – dogs. Nursery rhymes.

Old Mother Hubbard and her wonderful dog ill. by James Marshall. Farrar, 1991. ISBN 978-0-374-35621-7 Subj: Animals – dogs. Nursery rhymes.

Martin-James, Kathleen. *Soaring bald eagles* ill. with photos. Lerner, 2001. ISBN 978-0-8225-3636-9 Subj: Birds – eagles.

Martín Larrañaga, Ana. *Pepo and Lolo and the red apple* ill. by author. Candlewick, 2004. ISBN 978-0-7636-2036-3 Subj: Animals – pigs. Birds – chickens. Character traits – cooperation. Food.

Pepo and Lolo are friends ill. by author. Candlewick, 2004. ISBN 978-0-7636-1982-4 Subj: Animals – pigs. Birds – chickens. Friendship.

Woo! The not-so-scary Ghost ill. by author. Scholastic, 2000. ISBN 978-0-439-16958-5 Subj: Behavior – running away. Emotions – fear. Ghosts.

Martins, Isabel Minhós. *Little lamb, have you any wool?* ill. by Yara Kono. OwlKids, 2012. ISBN 978-1-926973-14-2 Subj: Activities – knitting. Animals – sheep. Behavior – sharing. Character traits – cooperation. Clothing. Friendship.

My neighbor is a dog ill. by Madalena Matoso. OwlKids, 2013. ISBN 978-1-926973-68-5 Subj: Animals. Animals – dogs. Character traits – being different. Prejudice.

Marx, Patricia. *Dot in Larryland: the big little book of an odd-sized friendship* ill. by Roz Chast. Bloomsbury, 2009. ISBN 978-1-59990-181-7 Subj: Character traits – smallness. Concepts – size. Emotions – loneliness. Friendship. Humorous stories.

Marx, Trish. *Kindergarten day USA and China: a flip-me-over book* photos by Ellen B. Senisi. Charlesbridge, 2010. ISBN 978-1-58089-219-3 Subj: Foreign lands – China. Format, unusual. School.

Marzollo, Jean. *Baby's alphabet* photos by Nancy Sheehan. Roaring Brook, 2002. ISBN 978-0-7613-2760-8 Subj: ABC books. Babies.

Daniel in the lion's den ill. by reteller. Little, 2003. ISBN 978-0-316-74132-3 Subj: Animals – lions. Religion – Daniel.

Do you know new? ill. by Mari Takabayashi. HarperCollins, 1997. ISBN 978-0-694-00870-4 Subj: Babies. Format, unusual – board books. Rhyming text.

Help me learn addition ill. by Chad Phillips. Holiday House, 2012. ISBN 978-0-8234-2398-9 Subj: Counting, numbers.

Help me learn numbers 0-20 photos by Chad Phillips. Holiday House, 2011. ISBN 978-0-8234-2334-7 Subj: Counting, numbers.

Help me learn subtraction ill. by Chad Phillips. Holiday House, 2012. ISBN 978-0-8234-2401-6 Subj: Counting, numbers.

I love you: a rebus poem ill. by Suse MacDonald. Scholastic, 2000. ISBN 978-0-590-37656-3 Subj: Concepts. Emotions – love. Poetry. Rebuses.

I see a star ill. by Suse MacDonald. Scholastic, 2002. ISBN 978-0-439-26616-1 Subj: Holidays – Christmas. Rebuses. Stars.

I spy: a book of picture riddles photos by Walter Wick. Scholastic, 1992. ISBN 978-0-590-45087-4 Subj: Picture puzzles. Rhyming text.

I spy A to Z: a book of picture riddles photos by Walter Wick. Scholastic, 2009. ISBN 978-0-545-10782-2 Subj: ABC books. Picture puzzles.

I spy Christmas: a book of picture riddles photos by Walter Wick. Scholastic, 1992. ISBN 978-0-590-45846-7 Subj: Holidays – Christmas. Picture puzzles. Rhyming text. Riddles & jokes.

I spy extreme challenger! a book of picture riddles photos by Walter Wick. Scholastic, 2000. ISBN 978-0-439-19900-1 Subj: Picture puzzles. Rhyming text. Riddles & jokes.

I spy fantasy: a book of picture riddles photos by Walter Wick. Scholastic, 1994. ISBN 978-0-590-46295-2 Subj: Imagination. Picture puzzles. Rhyming text. Riddles & jokes.

I spy gold challenger! a book of picture riddles photos by Walter Wick. Scholastic, 1998. ISBN 978-0-590-04296-3 Subj: Picture puzzles. Rhyming text. Riddles & jokes.

I spy little animals photos by Walter Wick. Scholastic, 1998. ISBN 978-0-590-11711-1 Subj: Animals. Format, unusual – board books. Picture puzzles. Rhyming text.

I spy little book photos by Walter Wick. Scholastic, 1997. ISBN 978-0-590-34129-5 Subj: Format, unusual – board books. Picture puzzles. Rhyming text.

I spy little bunnies photos by Walter Wick. Scholastic, 2001. ISBN 978-0-439-22158-0 Subj: Animals – rabbits. Picture puzzles. Rhyming text.

I spy little Christmas photos by Walter Wick. Scholastic, 1999. ISBN 978-0-439-08331-7 Subj: Holidays – Christmas. Picture puzzles. Rhyming text.

I spy little letters photos by Walter Wick. Scholastic, 2000. ISBN 978-0-439-11496-7 Subj: ABC books. Picture puzzles. Rhyming text.

I spy little numbers photos by Walter Wick. Scholastic, 1999. ISBN 978-0-590-68714-0 Subj: Counting, numbers. Picture puzzles. Rhyming text.

I spy little wheels photos by Walter Wick. Scholastic, 1998. ISBN 978-0-590-04706-7 Subj: Format, unusual – board books. Picture puzzles. Rhyming text. Toys.

I spy, mystery photos by Walter Wick. Scholastic, 1993. ISBN 978-0-590-46294-5 Subj: Picture puzzles. Rhyming text. Riddles & jokes.

I spy school days: a book of picture riddles photos by Walter Wick. Scholastic, 1995. ISBN 978-0-590-48135-9 Subj: Picture puzzles. Rhyming text. Riddles & jokes. School.

I spy spooky night: a book of picture riddles photos by Walter Wick. Scholastic, 1996. ISBN 978-0-590-48137-3 Subj: Ghosts. Holidays – Halloween. Picture puzzles. Rhyming text. Riddles & jokes.

I spy super challenger! a book of picture riddles photos by Walter Wick. Scholastic, 1997. ISBN 978-0-590-34128-8 Subj: Picture puzzles. Rhyming text. Riddles & jokes.

I spy treasure hunt: a book of picture riddles photos by Walter Wick. Scholastic, 2007. ISBN 978-0-439-02674-1 Subj: Mystery stories. Picture puzzles. Pirates. Rhyming text. Riddles & jokes.

I spy ultimate challenger! a book of picture riddles photos by Walter Wick. Scholastic, 2003. ISBN 978-0-439-45401-8 Subj: Picture puzzles. Rhyming text. Riddles & jokes.

I spy, year-round challenger! photos by Walter Wick. Scholastic, 2001. ISBN 978-0-439-31634-7 Subj: Days of the week, months of the year. Picture puzzles. Rhyming text. Riddles & jokes.

Little Bear, you're a star! A Greek myth about the constellations ill. by reteller. Little, Brown, 2005. ISBN 978-0-316-74135-4 Subj: Animals – bears. Stars.

The little plant doctor: a story about George Washington Carver ill. by Ken Wilson-Max. Holiday House, 2011. ISBN 978-0-8234-2325-5 Subj: Careers – scientists. Ethnic groups in the U.S. – African Americans. U.S. history.

Mama, Mama ill. by Laura Regan. HarperCollins, 1999. ISBN 978-0-694-01245-9 Subj: Animals. Family life – mothers. Format, unusual – board books. Rhyming text.

Miriam and her brother Moses ill. by reteller. Little, 2003. ISBN 978-0-316-74131-6 Subj: Religion. Religion – Moses.

Once upon a springtime ill. by Jacqueline Rogers. Scholastic, 1997. ISBN 978-0-590-46017-0 Subj: Animals – deer. Seasons.

Papa, Papa ill. by Simone Kaplan. HarperCollins, 2000. ISBN 978-0-694-01246-6 Subj: Animals. Family life – fathers. Format, unusual – board books. Rhyming text.

Pierre the penguin: a true story ill. by Laura Regan. Sleeping Bear, 2010. ISBN 978-1-58536-485-5 Subj: Birds – penguins. Character traits – kindness to animals. Rhyming text.

Pretend you're a cat ill. by Jerry Pinkney. Dial, 1990. ISBN 978-0-8037-0774-0 Subj: Animals. Behavior – imitation. Imagination. Rhyming text.

Snow angel ill. by Jacqueline Rogers. Scholastic, 1995. ISBN 978-0-590-48748-1 Subj: Angels. Behavior – lost. Weather – snow.

Sun song ill. by Laura Regan. HarperCollins, 1995. ISBN 978-0-06-020788-5 Subj: Animals. Plants. Rhyming text. Sun.

Ten cats have hats: a counting book ill. by David McPhail. Scholastic, 1994. ISBN 978-0-590-46968-5 Subj: Animals. Counting, numbers. Rhyming text.

Ten little Christmas presents ill. by author. Scholastic, 2008. ISBN 978-0-545-02791-5 Subj: Animals. Counting, numbers. Gifts. Holidays – Christmas.

Thanksgiving cats ill. by Hans Wilhelm. Scholastic, 1999. ISBN 978-0-590-03714-3 Subj: Animals – cats. Holidays – Thanksgiving. Rhyming text.

Valentine cats ill. by Hans Wilhelm. Scholastic, 1996. ISBN 978-0-590-47596-9 Subj: Animals – cats. Holidays – Valentine's Day. Rhyming text.

Masini, Beatrice. *A brave little princess* ill. by Octavia Monaco. Barefoot, 2000. ISBN 978-1-84148-267-5 Subj: Character traits – bravery. Concepts – patterns. Folk & fairy tales. Problem solving. Royalty – princesses. Royalty – queens.

Here comes the bride ill. by AnnaLaura Cantone. Tundra, 2010. ISBN 978-0-88776-898-9 Subj: Activities – sewing. Clothing – dresses. Weddings.

Mason, Adrienne. *Lu and Clancy sound off* ill. by Pat Cupples. Kids Can, 2002. ISBN 978-1-55337-058-1 Subj: Animals – dogs. Careers – detectives. Noise, sounds. Science.

Lu and Clancy's spy stuff ill. by Pat Cupples. Kids Can, 2000. ISBN 978-1-55074-693-8 Subj: Animals – dogs. Careers – detectives. Disguises.

Snakes ill. by Nancy Gray Ogle. Kids Can, 2005. ISBN 978-1-55337-627-9 Subj: Reptiles – snakes. Science.

Mason, Janeen I. *Ocean commotion: life on the reef* ill. by author. Pelican, 2010. ISBN 978-1-58980-783-9 Subj: Crustaceans – crabs. Sea & seashore.

Mason, Margaret H. *These hands* ill. by Floyd Cooper. Harcourt, 2011. ISBN 978-0-547-21566-2 Subj: Anatomy – hands. Ethnic groups in the U.S. – African Americans. Family life – grandfathers. Prejudice.

Massini, Sarah. *Trixie ten* ill. by author. Holt, 2013. ISBN 978-0-8050-9520-3 Subj: Behavior – running away. Family life – brothers & sisters. Noise, sounds.

Masters, Anthony. *Ricky's rat gang* ill. by Chris Fisher. Kingfisher, 2004. ISBN 978-0-7534-5800-6 Subj: Animals – mice. Behavior – bullying, teasing. Stores.

Masurel, Claire. *A cat and a dog* ill. by Bob Kolar. NorthSouth, 2001. ISBN 978-1-55858-950-6 Subj: Animals – cats. Animals – dogs. Behavior – fighting, arguing. Friendship.

Christmas is coming ill. by Marie H. Henry. Chronicle, 1998. ISBN 978-0-8118-2106-3 Subj: Behavior – sharing. Holidays – Christmas. Toys.

Domino ill. by David Walker. Candlewick, 2007. ISBN 978-0-7636-2862-8 Subj: Animals – dogs. Character traits – smallness.

Too big! ill. by Hanako Wakiyama. Chronicle, 1999. ISBN 978-0-8118-2090-5 Subj: Concepts – size. Dinosaurs. Toys.

Two homes ill. by Kady MacDonald Denton. Candlewick, 2001. ISBN 978-0-7636-0511-7 Subj: Divorce. Emotions – love. Family life – parents. Homes, houses.

Matheis, Mickie. *Bedtime for Boo* ill. by Bonnie Leick. Random House, 2012. ISBN 978-0-375-86991-4 Subj: Bedtime. Ghosts. Noise, sounds.

Mathers, Petra. *A cake for Herbie* ill. by author. Atheneum, 2000. ISBN 978-0-689-83017-4 Subj: Animals. Birds – ducks. Contests. Poetry.

Dodo gets married ill. by author. Atheneum, 2001. ISBN 978-0-689-83018-1 Subj: Birds – dodos. Weddings.

Herbie's secret Santa ill. by author. Atheneum, 2002. ISBN 978-0-689-83550-6 Subj: Birds. Careers – bakers. Character traits – honesty. Friendship. Holidays – Christmas.

Lottie's new beach towel ill. by author. Atheneum, 1998. ISBN 978-0-689-81606-2 Subj: Birds – chickens. Character traits – cleverness. Gifts. Sea & seashore – beaches.

Lottie's new friend ill. by author. Atheneum, 1999. ISBN 978-0-689-82014-4 Subj: Birds. Emotions – envy, jealousy. Friendship.

Matheson, Christie. *Tap the magic tree* ill. by author. Greenwillow, 2013. ISBN 978-0-06-227445-8 Subj: Activities. Rhyming text. Seasons. Trees.

Mathews, Judith, reteller. *Nathaniel Willy, scared silly* also retold by Fay Robinson; ill. by Alexi Natchev. Bradbury, 1994. ISBN 978-0-02-765285-7 Subj: Animals. Bedtime. Emotions – fear. Family life – grandmothers. Folk & fairy tales. Rhyming text.

Matsuoka, Mei. *Footprints in the snow* ill. by author. Holt, 2008. ISBN 978-0-8050-8792-5 Subj: Activities – writing. Animals – wolves. Friendship.

Matteson, George. *The Christmas tugboat: how the Rockefeller Center Christmas tree came to New York City* by George Matteson and Adele Ursone ill. by James Ransome. Clarion, 2012. ISBN 978-0-618-99215-7 Subj: Boats, ships. Family life. Holidays – Christmas. Trees.

Matthews, Tina. *Out of the egg* ill. by author. Houghton, 2007. ISBN 978-0-618-73741-3 Subj: Birds – chickens. Folk & fairy tales.

Matthies, Janna. *The goodbye cancer garden* ill. by Kristi Valiant. Whitman, 2011. ISBN 978-0-8075-2994-2 Subj: Family life – mothers. Gardens, gardening. Illness – cancer.

Peter, the knight with asthma ill. by Anthony Lewis. Whitman, 2009. ISBN 978-0-8075-6517-9 Subj: Illness – asthma. Knights.

Mauner, Claudia. *Zoe Sophia in New York: the mystery of the Pink Phoenix papers* by Claudia Mauner and Elisa Smalley ill. by Claudia Mauner. Chronicle, 2006. ISBN 978-0-8118-4877-0 Subj: Family life. Museums. Mystery stories.

Zoe Sophia's scrapbook by Claudia Mauner and Elisa Smalley ill. by Claudia Mauner. Chronicle, 2003. ISBN 978-0-8118-3606-7 Subj: Activities – traveling. Animals – dogs. Behavior – lost. Family life – aunts, uncles. Foreign lands – Italy.

Maurer, Tracy. *Growing flowers* ill. with photos. Rourke, 2001. ISBN 978-1-55916-251-7 Subj: Flowers. Gardens, gardening.

May, Eleanor. *Albert is not scared* ill. by Deborah Melmon. Kane, 2013. ISBN 978-1-57565-629-8 Subj: Animals – mice. Concepts – left & right. Concepts – up & down. Emotions – fear. Parks – amusement.

Albert's amazing snail ill. by Deborah Melmon. Kane, 2012. ISBN 978-1-57565-448-5 Subj: Animals – mice. Animals – snails. Character traits – patience. Concepts. Language.

The mousier the merrier ill. by Deborah Melmon. Kane, 2012. ISBN 978-1-57565-447-8 Subj: Animals – mice. Counting, numbers.

May, Kathy. *Molasses man* ill. by Felicia Marshall. Holiday, 2000. ISBN 978-0-8234-1438-3 Subj: Ethnic groups in the U.S. – African Americans. Family life. Family life – grandfathers.

May, Robert Lewis. *Rudolph the red-nosed reindeer* ill. by David Wenzel. Grosset, 2001. ISBN 978-0-448-42534-4 Subj: Anatomy – noses. Animals – reindeer. Holidays – Christmas. Mythical creatures – elves. Rhyming text. Santa Claus. Weather – fog.

Mayer, Lynne. *Newton and me* ill. by Sherry Rogers. Sylvan Dell, 2010. ISBN 978-1-60718-067-8 Subj: Rhyming text. Science.

Mayer, Marianna. *Baba Yaga and Vasilisa the Brave* ill. by Kinuko Y. Craft. Morrow, 1994. ISBN 978-0-688-08501-8 Subj: Folk & fairy tales. Foreign lands – Russia. Royalty. Toys – dolls. Witches.

Beauty and the beast ill. by Mercer Mayer. SeaStar, 2000. ISBN 978-1-58717-018-8 Subj: Animals. Character traits – appearance. Character traits – loyalty. Emotions – love. Folk & fairy tales. Magic.

One frog too many (Mayer, Mercer)

Pegasus ill. by Kinuko Y. Craft. Morrow, 1998. ISBN 978-0-688-13382-5 Subj: Folk & fairy tales. Foreign lands – Greece. Monsters. Mythical creatures – Pegasus.

Perseus ill. by Joel Spector. Fogelman, 2002. ISBN 978-0-8037-2619-2 Subj: Folk & fairy tales. Foreign lands – Greece. Religion.

The prince and the pauper ill. by Gary A. Lippincott. Dial, 1999. ISBN 978-0-8037-2099-2 Subj: Behavior – growing up. Behavior – misunderstanding. Character traits – individuality. Royalty – kings.

The unicorn and the lake ill. by Michael Hague. Dial, 1982. ISBN 978-0-8037-9338-5 Subj: Character traits – bravery. Mythical creatures – unicorns.

Mayer, Mercer. *A boy, a dog, a frog and a friend* ill. by author. Dial, 1971. ISBN 978-0-8037-0755-9 Subj: Animals – dogs. Friendship. Frogs & toads. Sports – fishing. Wordless.

A boy, a dog and a frog ill. by author. Dial, 1967. ISBN 978-0-8037-0767-2 Subj: Animals – dogs. Friendship. Frogs & toads. Sports – fishing. Wordless.

The bravest knight ill. by author. Penguin, 2007. ISBN 978-0-8037-3206-3 Subj: Imagination. Knights. Monsters. Mythical creatures. Mythical creatures – trolls.

Bun Bun's birthday ill. by author. Random House, 1996. ISBN 978-0-679-87368-6 Subj: Behavior – growing up. Behavior – misunderstanding. Birthdays.

Frog goes to dinner ill. by author. Dial, 1974. ISBN 978-0-8037-3381-7 Subj: Food. Frogs & toads. Wordless.

Frog on his own ill. by author. Dial, 1973. ISBN 978-0-8037-2695-6 Subj: Frogs & toads. Wordless.

Frog, where are you? ill. by author. Dial, 1969. ISBN 978-0-8037-2732-8 Subj: Friendship. Frogs & toads. Wordless.

Just big enough ill. by author. HarperCollins, 2004. ISBN 978-0-06-053964-1 Subj: Behavior – bullying, teasing. Behavior – growing up. Concepts – size. Family life – grandfathers. Problem solving.

Just for you ill. by author. Golden Pr., 1975. ISBN 978-0-307-12542-2 Subj: Character traits – helpfulness. Emotions – love. Family life – mothers.

Just me and my dad ill. by author. Golden Pr., 1977. ISBN 978-0-307-61839-9 Subj: Camps, camping. Family life – fathers.

The little drummer mouse: a Christmas story ill. by author. Penguin, 2006. ISBN 978-0-8037-3147-9 Subj: Animals – mice. Holidays – Christmas. Music. Musical instruments – drums. Religion – Nativity.

Liza Lou and the Yeller Belly Swamp ill. by author. Parents' Magazine Pr., 1976. ISBN 978-0-8193-0802-3 Subj: Character traits – bravery. Ethnic groups in the U.S. – African Americans. Monsters.

Octopus soup ill. by author. Marshall Cavendish, 2011. ISBN 978-0-7614-5812-8 Subj: Octopuses. Wordless.

One frog too many by Mercer Mayer and Marianna Mayer ill. by Mercer Mayer. Dial, 1975. ISBN 978-0-8037-4858-3 Subj: Emotions – envy, jealousy. Frogs & toads. Wordless.

Shibumi and the kitemaker ill. by author. Marshall Cavendish, 1999. ISBN 978-0-7614-5054-2 Subj: Family life – fathers. Foreign lands – Japan. Kites. Royalty – emperors. Royalty – princesses.

There are monsters everywhere ill. by author. Penguin, 2005. ISBN 978-0-8037-0621-7 Subj: Emotions – fear. Monsters. Sports – karate.

There's a nightmare in my closet ill. by author. Dial, 1990. ISBN 978-0-8037-0843-3 Subj: Bedtime. Emotions – fear. Monsters.

There's an alligator under my bed ill. by author. Dial, 1987. ISBN 978-0-8037-0375-9 Subj: Bedtime. Emotions – fear. Reptiles – alligators, crocodiles.

Too many dinosaurs ill. by author. Holiday House, 2011. ISBN 978-0-8234-2316-3 Subj: Dinosaurs. Pets.

What do you do with a kangaroo? ill. by author. Four Winds, 1973. ISBN 978-0-590-72851-5 Subj: Animals. Humorous stories. Problem solving.

You're the scaredy cat ill. by author. Parents' Magazine Pr., 1974. ISBN 978-0-8193-0763-7 Subj: Camps, camping. Emotions – fear. Night.

Mayer, Pamela. *The Grandma cure* ill. by John Nez. Penguin, 2005. ISBN 978-0-525-47559-0 Subj: Behavior – fighting, arguing. Family life – grandmothers. Illness – cold (disease).

The scariest monster in the whole wide world ill. by Lydia Monks. Putnam, 2001. ISBN 978-0-399-23459-0 Subj: Clothing – costumes. Family life – grandmothers. Holidays – Halloween. Monsters.

Mayhew, James. *Ella Bella ballerina and Swan Lake* ill. by author. Barron's, 2011. ISBN 978-0-7641-6407-1 Subj: Ballet. Music.

Ella Bella ballerina and The Nutcracker ill. by author. Barron's, 2012. ISBN 978-0-7641-6581-8 Subj: Activities – dancing. Ballet. Holidays – Christmas. Imagination. Music.

Ella Bella ballerina and The sleeping beauty ill. by author. Barron's, 2008. ISBN 978-0-7641-6118-6 Subj: Ballet. Music.

Katie and the Mona Lisa ill. by author. Orchard, 1999. ISBN 978-0-531-30177-7 Subj: Art. Careers – artists. Museums.

Katie and the sunflowers ill. by author. Orchard, 2001. ISBN 978-0-531-30325-2 Subj: Art. Family life – grandmothers. Imagination. Museums.

Katie meets the Impressionists ill. by author. Orchard, 1999. ISBN 978-0-531-30151-7 Subj: Art. Careers – artists. Museums.

The knight who took all day ill. by author. Scholastic, 2005. ISBN 978-0-439-74829-2 Subj: Dragons. Knights.

Where's my hug? ill. by Susan Hellard. Bloomsbury, 2008. ISBN 978-1-59990-225-8 Subj: Cumulative tales. Family life. Hugging.

Maynard, Bill. *Santa's time off* ill. by Tom Browning. Putnam, 1997. ISBN 978-0-399-23138-4 Subj: Activities – vacationing. Rhyming text. Santa Claus.

Mayo, Margaret. *Choo choo clickety-clack* ill. by Alex Ayliffe. Carolrhoda, 2005. ISBN 978-1-57505-819-1 Subj: Format, unusual – board books. Noise, sounds. Transportation.

Dig dig digging ill. by Alex Ayliffe. Holt, 2002. ISBN 978-0-8050-6840-5 Subj: Rhyming text. Tractors. Trucks.

Emergency! ill. by Alex Ayliffe. Carolrhoda, 2002. ISBN 978-0-87614-922-5 Subj: Careers – emergency medical technicians. Careers – firefighters. Rhyming text. Safety. Trucks.

Roar! ill. by Alex Ayliffe. Carolrhoda, 2007. ISBN 978-0-7613-9473-0 Subj: Animals.

Stomp, dinosaur, stomp! ill. by Alex Ayliffe. Walker, 2010. ISBN 978-0-8027-2195-2 Subj: Activities. Dinosaurs. Rhyming text.

Wiggle waggle fun ill. by 24 illustrators. Knopf, 2002. ISBN 978-0-375-91529-1 Subj: Poetry. Rhyming text. Songs.

Zoom, rocket, zoom! ill. by Alex Ayliffe. Walker, 2012. ISBN 978-0-8027-2790-9 Subj: Careers – astronauts. Space & space ships.

Mayper, Monica. *Come and see: a Christmas story* ill. by Stacey Schuett. HarperCollins, 1999. ISBN 978-0-06-023527-7 Subj: Holidays – Christmas. Religion – Nativity.

Mayr, Diane. *Littlebat's Halloween story* ill. by Gideon Kendall. Whitman, 2001. ISBN 978-0-8075-7629-8 Subj: Activities – storytelling. Animals – bats. Holidays – Halloween. Libraries.

Out and about at the apple orchard ill. by Anne McMullen. Picture Window, 2003. ISBN 978-1-4048-0036-6 Subj: Farms. Food. School – field trips. Trees.

Run, Turkey, run ill. by Laura Rader. Walker, 2007. ISBN 978-0-8027-9630-1 Subj: Behavior – hiding. Birds – turkeys. Holidays – Thanksgiving.

Mazer, Anne. *The salamander room* ill. by Steve Johnson. Knopf, 1991. ISBN 978-0-394-92945-3 Subj: Ecology. Imagination. Pets. Reptiles – salamanders.

Mazer, Norma Fox. *Has anyone seen my Emily Greene?* ill. by Christine Davenier. Candlewick, 2007. ISBN 978-0-7636-1384-6 Subj: Behavior – hiding. Family life – fathers. Rhyming text.

Mazzola, Frank. *Counting is for the birds* ill. by author. Charlesbridge, 1997. ISBN 978-0-88106-952-5 Subj: Birds. Counting, numbers. Rhyming text.

Mead, Alice. *Billy and Emma* ill. by Christy Hale. Farrar, 2000. ISBN 978-0-374-30705-9 Subj: Birds. Birds – macaws. Crime. Friendship. Zoos.

Meade, Holly. *If I never forever endeavor* ill. by author. Candlewick, 2011. ISBN 978-0-7636-4071-2 Subj: Activities – flying. Birds. Character traits – assertiveness. Character traits – bravery. Rhyming text.

Inside, inside, inside ill. by author. Marshall Cavendish, 2005. ISBN 978-0-7614-5125-9 Subj: Family life – brothers & sisters. Games.

John Willy and Freddy McGee ill. by author. Marshall Cavendish, 1998. ISBN 978-0-7614-5033-7 Subj: Animals – guinea pigs. Behavior – running away. Character traits – freedom.

John Willy and Freddy McGee [board book] ill. by author. Marshall Cavendish, 2007. ISBN 978-0-7614-5363-5 Subj: Animals – guinea pigs. Behavior – running away. Character traits – freedom. Format, unusual – board books.

A place to sleep ill. by author. Marshall Cavendish, 2001. ISBN 978-0-7614-5096-2 Subj: Animals. Bedtime. Rhyming text. Sleep.

Meadows, Michelle. *Hibernation station* ill. by Kurt Cyrus. Simon & Schuster, 2010. ISBN 978-1-4169-3788-3 Subj: Animals. Hibernation. Rhyming text. Sleep.

Itsy-bitsy baby mouse ill. by Matthew Cordell. Simon & Schuster, 2012. ISBN 978-1-4169-3786-9 Subj: Animals – mice. Behavior – lost. Rhyming text.

Piggies in pajamas ill. by Ard Hoyt. Simon & Schuster, 2013. ISBN 978-1-4169-4982-4 Subj: Animals – pigs. Bedtime. Rhyming text.

Piggies in the kitchen ill. by Ard Hoyt. Simon & Schuster, 2011. ISBN 978-1-4169-3787-6 Subj: Activities – baking, cooking. Animals – pigs. Rhyming text.

Pilot pups ill. by Dan Andreasen. Simon & Schuster, 2008. ISBN 978-1-4169-2484-5 Subj: Airplanes, airports. Animals – dogs. Careers – airplane pilots. Rhyming text. Toys.

Traffic pups ill. by Dan Andreasen. Simon & Schuster, 2011. ISBN 978-1-4169-2485-2 Subj: Animals – dogs. Careers – police officers. Motorcycles.

Mealer, Bryan. *The boy who harnessed the wind* (Kamkwamba, William)

Meddaugh, Susan. *The best place* ill. by author. Houghton, 1999. ISBN 978-0-395-97994-5 Subj: Animals. Animals – wolves. Behavior – dissatisfaction. Homes, houses.

Cinderella's rat ill. by author. Houghton, 1997. ISBN 978-0-395-86833-1 Subj: Animals – rats. Family life – brothers & sisters. Humorous stories. Magic.

Harry on the rocks ill. by author. Houghton, 2003. ISBN 978-0-618-27603-5 Subj: Boats, ships. Dragons. Eggs. Islands.

Hog-eye ill. by author. Houghton, 1995. ISBN 978-0-395-74276-1 Subj: Activities – baking, cooking. Animals – pigs. Animals – wolves. Books, reading.

Just Teenie ill. by author. Houghton, 2006. ISBN 978-0-618-68565-3 Subj: Character traits – appearance. Concepts – size. Plants.

Martha and Skits ill. by author. Houghton, 2000. ISBN 978-0-618-05776-4 Subj: Animals – dogs. Behavior – growing up.

Martha blah blah ill. by author. Houghton, 1996. ISBN 978-0-395-79755-6 Subj: Animals – dogs. Food.

Martha calling ill. by author. Houghton, 1994. ISBN 978-0-395-69825-9 Subj: Activities – vacationing. Animals – dogs.

Martha says it with flowers ill. by author. Houghton Mifflin, 2010. ISBN 978-0-547-21058-2 Subj:

Animals – dogs. Birthdays. Family life – grandmothers. Gifts.

Martha speaks ill. by author. Houghton, 1992. ISBN 978-0-395-63313-7 Subj: Animals – dogs.

Martha walks the dog ill. by author. Houghton, 1998. ISBN 978-0-395-90494-7 Subj: Animals – dogs. Behavior – bullying, teasing. Birds – parakeets, parrots.

Perfectly Martha ill. by author. Houghton, 2004. ISBN 978-0-618-37857-9 Subj: Animals – dogs. Careers – detectives.

Tree of birds ill. by author. Houghton, 1990. ISBN 978-0-395-53147-1 Subj: Birds. Character traits – kindness to animals.

The witches' supermarket ill. by author. Houghton, 1991. ISBN 978-0-395-57034-0 Subj: Animals – dogs. Holidays – Halloween. Stores. Witches.

The witch's walking stick ill. by author. Houghton, 2005. ISBN 978-0-618-52948-3 Subj: Behavior – wishing. Magic. Witches.

Medearis, Angela Shelf. *Annie's gifts* ill. by Anna Rich. Just Us, 1994. ISBN 978-0-940975-30-9 Subj: Ethnic groups in the U.S. – African Americans. Gifts. Self-concept.

Daisy and the doll (Medearis, Michael)

Dancing with the Indians ill. by Samuel Byrd. Holiday, 1991. ISBN 978-0-8234-0893-1 Subj: Activities – dancing. Ethnic groups in the U.S. – African Americans. Indians of North America – Seminole. Rhyming text.

The freedom riddle ill. by John Ward. Dutton, 1995. ISBN 978-0-525-67469-6 Subj: Ethnic groups in the U.S. – African Americans. Folk & fairy tales. Riddles & jokes. Slavery. U.S. history.

The ghost of Sifty-Sifty Sam ill. by Jacqueline Rogers. Scholastic, 1997. ISBN 978-0-590-48290-5 Subj: Careers – chefs, cooks. Ethnic groups in the U.S. – African Americans. Ghosts. Homes, houses. Rhyming text.

Poppa's itchy Christmas ill. by John Ward. Holiday, 1998. ISBN 978-0-8234-1298-3 Subj: Clothing. Holidays – Christmas. Sports – ice skating.

Poppa's new pants ill. by John Ward. Holiday, 1995. ISBN 978-0-8234-1155-9 Subj: Behavior – mistakes. Clothing. Clothing – pants. Ethnic groups in the U.S. – African Americans.

Rum-a-tum-tum ill. by James Ransome. Holiday, 1997. ISBN 978-0-8234-1143-6 Subj: Communities, neighborhoods. Ethnic groups in the U.S. – African Americans. Noise, sounds. Rhyming text.

Seven spools of thread: a Kwanzaa story ill. by Daniel Minter. Whitman, 2000. ISBN 978-0-8075-7315-0 Subj: Activities – weaving. Folk & fairy tales. Foreign lands – Ghana. Holidays – Kwanzaa.

The singing man: adapted from a West African folktale ill. by Terea D. Shaffer. Holiday, 1994. ISBN 978-0-8234-1103-0 Subj: Folk & fairy tales. Foreign lands – Nigeria. Music.

Tailypo: a newfangled tall tale ill. by Sterling Brown. Holiday, 1996. ISBN 978-0-8234-1249-5 Subj: Ethnic groups in the U.S. – African Americans. Folk & fairy tales. Monsters.

Too much talk ill. by Stefano Vitale. Candlewick, 1995. ISBN 978-1-56402-323-0 Subj: Cumulative tales. Folk & fairy tales. Foreign lands – Ghana. Royalty – kings.

Medearis, Michael. *Daisy and the doll* by Michael Medearis and Angela Shelf Medearis ill. by Larry Johnson. Vermont Folklife Center, 2000. ISBN 978-0-916718-15-2 Subj: Ethnic groups in the U.S. – African Americans. Prejudice. School. Self-concept. Toys – dolls.

Medina, Meg. *Tía Isa wants a car* ill. by Claudio Muñoz. Candlewick, 2011. ISBN 978-0-7636-4156-6 Subj: Automobiles. Behavior – resourcefulness. Ethnic groups in the U.S. – Hispanic Americans. Family life – aunts, uncles. Money.

Medina, Sarah. *Sad* ill. by Jo Brooker. Heinemann, 2007. ISBN 978-1-4034-9293-7 Subj: Emotions – sadness.

Medina, Tony. *Christmas makes me think* ill. by Chandra Cox. Lee & Low, 2001. ISBN 978-1-58430-024-3 Subj: Behavior – sharing. Ethnic groups in the U.S. – African Americans. Holidays – Christmas. Religion.

DeShawn days ill. by R. Gregory Christie. Lee & Low, 2001. ISBN 978-1-58430-022-9 Subj: Cities, towns. Ethnic groups in the U.S. – African Americans. Family life. Poetry.

Medoff, Francine. *The mouse in the matzah factory* ill. by Nicole in den Bosch. Kar-Ben, 2003. ISBN 978-1-58013-048-6 Subj: Animals – mice. Food. Jewish culture.

Meggs, Libby Phillips. *Go home! the true story of James the cat* ill. by author. Whitman, 2000. ISBN 978-0-8075-2975-1 Subj: Animals – cats. Behavior – needing someone. Homeless.

Meisel, Paul. *Zara's hats* ill. by author. Dutton, 2003. ISBN 978-0-525-45465-6 Subj: Behavior – resourcefulness. Clothing – hats. Family life – fathers.

Meister, Cari. *Busy, busy city street* ill. by Steven Guarnaccia. Viking, 2000. ISBN 978-0-670-88944-0 Subj: Automobiles. Cities, towns. Noise, sounds. Rhyming text. Traffic, traffic signs. Trucks.

Follow the drinking gourd: an Underground Railroad story ill. by Robert Squier. Picture Window, 2012. ISBN 978-1-4048-7375-9 Subj: Ethnic groups in the U.S. – African Americans. Sailors. Slavery. Songs. Stars. U.S. history.

Skinny and fats, best friends ill. by Steve Björkman. Holiday, 2002. ISBN 978-0-8234-1692-9 Subj: Activities – baking, cooking. Animals – pigs. Animals – rabbits. Friendship.

Melanson, Luc. *Topsy-Turvy Town* ill. by author. Tundra, 2010. ISBN 978-0-88776-920-7 Subj: Imagination.

Mellage, Nanette. *Coming home* ill. by Cornelius Van Wright and Ying-Hwa Hu. BridgeWater, 2001. ISBN 978-0-8167-7009-0 Subj: Careers. Ethnic groups in the U.S. – African Americans. Sports – baseball.

Melling, David. *Don't worry, Douglas!* ill. by author. Tiger Tales, 2011. ISBN 978-1-58925-106-9 Subj: Animals – bears. Character traits – helpfulness. Clothing – hats.

Good knight sleep tight ill. by author. Barron's, 2006. ISBN 978-0-7641-5878-0 Subj: Knights. Royalty – princesses.

Hugless Douglas ill. by author. Tiger Tales, 2010. ISBN 978-1-58925-098-7 Subj: Animals – bears. Hugging.

The Scallywags ill. by author. Barron's, 2006. ISBN 978-0-7641-5991-6 Subj: Animals – wolves. Etiquette. Humorous stories.

Melmed, Laura Krauss. *Capital! Washington D.C. from A to Z* ill. by Frané Lessac. HarperCollins, 2003. ISBN 978-0-688-17562-7 Subj: ABC books. Cities, towns. Rhyming text.

Eight winter nights: a family Hanukkah book ill. by Elisabeth Schlossberg. Chronicle, 2010. ISBN 978-0-8118-5552-5 Subj: Holidays – Hanukkah. Jewish culture. Rhyming text.

The first song ever sung ill. by Ed Young. Lothrop, 1993. ISBN 978-0-688-08231-4 Subj: Bedtime. Foreign lands – Japan. Poetry. Songs.

Fright night flight ill. by Henry Cole. HarperCollins, 2002. ISBN 978-0-06-029702-2 Subj: Holidays – Halloween. Rhyming text. Witches.

A hug goes around ill. by Betsy Lewin. HarperCollins, 2002. ISBN 978-0-688-14681-8 Subj: Day. Emotions. Family life. Rhyming text.

I love you as much . . . ill. by Henri Sorensen. 1st Tupelo board books ed. Tupelo, 1998. ISBN 978-0-688-15978-8 Subj: Animals. Family life – mothers. Format, unusual – board books. Rhyming text.

Jumbo's lullaby ill. by Henri Sorensen. Lothrop, 1999. ISBN 978-0-688-16996-1 Subj: Animals – elephants. Bedtime. Dreams. Foreign lands – Africa. Lullabies. Rhyming text.

Little Oh ill. by Jim LaMarche. Lothrop, 1997. ISBN 978-0-688-14209-4 Subj: Behavior – lost. Family life. Paper.

Moishe's miracle ill. by David Slonim. HarperCollins, 2000. ISBN 978-0-688-14683-2 Subj: Folk & fairy tales. Holidays – Hanukkah. Jewish culture. Magic.

New York, New York! the Big Apple from A to Z ill. by Frané Lessac. HarperCollins, 2005. ISBN 978-0-06-054876-6 Subj: ABC books. Cities, towns.

The rainbabies ill. by Jim LaMarche. Lothrop, 1992. ISBN 978-0-688-10756-7 Subj: Babies. Folk & fairy tales.

This first Thanksgiving ill. by Mark Buehner. HarperCollins, 2001. ISBN 978-0-688-14555-2 Subj: Counting, numbers. Holidays – Thanksgiving. Poetry.

Melnicove, Mark. *Africa is not a country* (Knight, Margy Burns)

Meltzer, Amy. *A mezuzah on the door* ill. by Janice Fried. Kar-Ben, 2007. ISBN 978-1-58013-249-7 Subj: Jewish culture. Moving.

The Shabbat Princess ill. by Martha Avilés. Lerner/Kar-Ben, 2011. ISBN 978-0-7613-5142-9 Subj: Family life. Jewish culture.

Meltzer, Lynn. *The construction crew* ill. by Carrie Eko-Burgess. Holt, 2011. ISBN 978-0-8050-8884-7 Subj: Careers – construction workers. Machines. Rhyming text. Tools.

Melvin, Alice. *Counting birds* ill. by author. Abrams, 2010. ISBN 978-1-85437-855-2 Subj: Birds. Counting, numbers. Rhyming text.

The high street ill. by author. Abrams, 2011. ISBN 978-1-85437-943-6 Subj: Cumulative tales. Shopping. Stores.

Menchin, Scott. *Harry goes to dog school* ill. by author. HarperCollins, 2012. ISBN 978-0-06-195801-4 Subj: Animals – dogs. Imagination. School.

Taking a bath with the dog and other things that make me happy ill. by author. Candlewick, 2007. ISBN 978-0-7636-2919-9 Subj: Character traits – questioning. Emotions – happiness.

What if everything had legs? ill. by author. Candlewick, 2011. ISBN 978-0-7636-4220-4 Subj: Anatomy. Character traits – questioning. Imagination.

Mendes, Valerie. *Look at me, Grandma!* ill. by Claire Fletcher. Scholastic, 2001. ISBN 978-0-

439-29654-0 Subj: Babies. Dreams. Family life – aunts, uncles. Family life – brothers & sisters. Family life – grandmothers. Family life – new sibling.

Meng, Cece. *Bedtime is canceled* ill. by Aurelie Neyret. Clarion, 2012. ISBN 978-0-547-63668-9 Subj: Bedtime.

I will not read this book ill. by Joy Ang. Clarion, 2011. ISBN 978-0-547-04971-7 Subj: Bedtime. Books, reading. Family life.

Tough chicks ill. by Melissa Suber. Clarion, 2009. ISBN 978-0-618-82415-1 Subj: Animals. Birds – chickens. Self-concept. Tractors.

The wonderful thing about hiccups ill. by Janet Pedersen. Houghton, 2007. ISBN 978-0-618-59544-0 Subj: Animals – hippopotamuses. Family life – brothers & sisters. Hiccups. Libraries.

Menotti, Andrea. *How many jelly beans? a giant book of giant numbers!* ill. by Yancey Labat. Chronicle, 2012. ISBN 978-1-4521-0206-1 Subj: Counting, numbers. Food. Format, unusual.

Merberg, Julie. *In the garden with Van Gogh* by Julie Merberg and Suzanne Bober. Chronicle, 2002. ISBN 978-0-8118-3415-5 Subj: Art. Careers – artists. Format, unusual – board books. Rhyming text.

A magical day with Matisse by Julie Merberg and Suzanne Bober. Chronicle, 2002. ISBN 978-0-8118-3414-8 Subj: Art. Careers – artists. Format, unusual – board books. Rhyming text.

Mercer, Lynn. *Schubert's snowflakes* ill. by author. Sagebrush, 2001. ISBN 978-0-9535413-6-2 Subj: Animals – polar bears. Weather – snow.

Meres, Jonathan. *The big bad rumor* ill. by Jacqueline East. Orchard, 2000. ISBN 978-0-531-30292-7 Subj: Animals. Behavior – gossip. Birds. Communication.

Merlin, Christophe. *Under the hood* ill. by author. Candlewick, 2011. ISBN 978-0-7636-5535-8 Subj: Animals – bears. Automobiles. Careers – mechanics. Format, unusual – toy & movable books.

Merriam, Eve. *Bam, bam, bam* ill. by Dan Yaccarino. Holt, 1995. ISBN 978-0-8050-3527-8 Subj: Buildings. Cities, towns. Machines. Poetry.

Blackberry ink ill. by Hans Wilhelm. Morrow, 1985. ISBN 978-0-688-04151-9 Subj: Poetry.

Halloween ABC ill. by Lane Smith. Macmillan, 1987. ISBN 978-0-02-766870-4 Subj: ABC books. Holidays – Halloween. Poetry.

Low song ill. by Pamela Paparone. McElderry, 2001. ISBN 978-0-689-82820-1 Subj: Nature. Rhyming text.

12 ways to get to 11 ill. by Bernie Karlin. Simon & Schuster, 1993. ISBN 978-0-671-75544-7 Subj: Counting, numbers.

Where's that cat? by Eve Merriam and Pamela Pollack ill. by Joanna Harrison. McElderry, 2000. ISBN 978-0-689-82904-8 Subj: Animals – cats. Parks. Rhyming text.

Merski, P. K. *Roaring, boring, Alice* ill. by Mark Weber. Skeezel, 2004. ISBN 978-0-9747217-0-5 Subj: Animals – mice. Foreign lands – Arctic. Northern lights. Rhyming text.

Merz, Jennifer J. *Playground day* ill. by author. Houghton, 2007. ISBN 978-0-618-81696-5 Subj: Activities – playing. Animals. Behavior – imitation. Imagination. Rhyming text.

Meschenmoser, Sebastian. *Waiting for winter* ill. by author. Kane/Miller, 2009. ISBN 978-1-935279-04-4 Subj: Animals. Weather – snow.

Meserve, Adria. *No room for Napoleon* ill. by author. Farrar, 2006. ISBN 978-0-374-35536-4 Subj: Animals – dogs. Behavior – sharing. Character traits – selfishness. Friendship. Homes, houses.

Smog, the city dog (Aesop)

Meserve, Jessica. *Bedtime without Arthur* ill. by author. Andersen, 2010. ISBN 978-0-7613-5497-0 Subj: Bedtime. Behavior – lost & found possessions. Emotions – fear. Family life – brothers & sisters. Toys – bears.

Small sister ill. by author. Houghton, 2007. ISBN 978-0-618-77658-0 Subj: Character traits – smallness. Family life – brothers & sisters. Self-concept.

Meshon, Aaron. *Take me out to the Yakyu* ill. by author. Atheneum, 2013. ISBN 978-1-4424-4177-4 Subj: Ethnic groups in the U.S. – Japanese Americans. Family life – grandfathers. Foreign lands – Japan. Foreign languages. Sports – baseball.

Messinger, Carla. *When the shadbush blooms* by Carla Messinger and Susan Katz ill. by David Kanietakeron Fadden. Ten Speed, 2007. ISBN 978-1-58246-192-2 Subj: Family life. Indians of North America – Lenape. Seasons. U.S. history.

Messner, Kate. *Over and under the snow* ill. by Christopher Silas Neal. Chronicle, 2011. ISBN 978-0-8118-6784-9 Subj: Animals. Hibernation. Nature. Seasons – winter. Weather – snow.

Metaxas, Eric. *It's time to sleep, my love* ill. by Nancy Tillman. Feiwel & Friends, 2008. ISBN 978-0-312-38371-8 Subj: Animals. Bedtime. Lullabies. Sleep.

Squanto and the miracle of Thanksgiving ill. by Shannon Stirnweis. Nelson, 1999. ISBN 978-0-

8499-5864-9 Subj: Holidays – Thanksgiving. Indians of North America – Wampanoag. Pilgrims. U.S. history.

Metropolitan Museum of Art, NY. *Museum shapes.* Little, Brown, 2005. ISBN 978-0-316-05698-4 Subj: Art. Concepts – shape. Museums.

Metz, Lorijo. *Floridius Bloom and the planet of Gloom* ill. by Matt Phelan. Penguin, 2007. ISBN 978-0-8037-3084-7 Subj: Behavior – greed. Friendship. Monsters.

Metzger, Steve. *The dancing clock* ill. by John Nez. Tiger Tales, 2011. ISBN 978-1-58925-100-7 Subj: Animals – monkeys. Clocks, watches. Zoos.

Detective Blue ill. by Tedd Arnold. Scholastic, 2011. ISBN 978-0-545-17286-8 Subj: Careers – detectives. Humorous stories. Nursery rhymes.

Pluto visits Earth! ill. by Jared Lee. Scholastic, 2012. ISBN 978-0-545-24934-8 Subj: Planets. Space & space ships.

Will Princess Isabel ever say please? ill. by Amanda Haley. Holiday House, 2012. ISBN 978-0-8234-2323-1 Subj: Etiquette. Royalty – princesses.

Meunier, Brian. *Bravo, Tavo!* ill. by Perky Edgerton. Penguin, 2007. ISBN 978-0-525-47478-4 Subj: Clothing – shoes. Foreign lands – Mexico. Sports – basketball. Weather – droughts.

Meyer, Ezra Fields. *E-mergency!* (Lichtenheld, Tom)

Meyers, Susan. *Bear in the air* ill. by Amy Bates. Abrams, 2010. ISBN 978-0-8109-8398-4 Subj: Behavior – lost & found possessions. Rhyming text. Toys – bears.

Everywhere babies ill. by Marla Frazee. Harcourt, 2004. ISBN 978-0-15-205315-4 Subj: Activities. Babies. Rhyming text.

Kittens! Kittens! Kittens! ill. by David Walker. Abrams, 2007. ISBN 978-0-8109-1218-2 Subj: Animals – cats. Rhyming text.

Puppies! Puppies! Puppies! ill. by David Walker. Abrams, 2005. ISBN 978-0-8109-5856-2 Subj: Animals – dogs. Rhyming text.

Rock-a-bye room ill. by Amy Bates. Abrams, 2013. ISBN 978-1-4197-0537-3 Subj: Babies. Bedtime. Rhyming text.

This is the way a baby rides ill. by Hiroe Nakata. Abrams, 2005. ISBN 978-0-8109-5763-3 Subj: Animals. Babies. Behavior – imitation. Rhyming text.

Michaels, Pat. *W is for wind: a weather alphabet* ill. by Melanie Rose. Sleeping Bear, 2005. ISBN 978-1-58536-237-0 Subj: ABC books. Weather.

Michelin, Linda. *Henry's night* (Johnson, D. B.)

Zuzu's wishing cake ill. by D. B. Johnson. Houghton, 2006. ISBN 978-0-618-64640-1 Subj: Activities – making things. Behavior – wishing. Food. Friendship. Moving.

Michels-Gualtieri, Akaela S. *I was born to be a sister* ill. by Marcy Ramsey. Platypus Media, 2001. ISBN 978-1-930775-03-9 Subj: Babies. Children as authors. Family life – brothers & sisters. Sibling rivalry.

Michelson, Richard. *Across the alley* ill. by E. B. Lewis. Penguin, 2006. ISBN 978-0-399-23970-0 Subj: Ethnic groups in the U.S. – African Americans. Friendship. Jewish culture. Music. Prejudice. Sports – baseball.

Busing Brewster ill. by R. G. Roth. Random House, 2010. ISBN 978-0-375-83334-2 Subj: Ethnic groups in the U.S. – African Americans. Prejudice. School. U.S. history.

Oh no, not ghosts! ill. by Adam McCauley. Harcourt, 2006. ISBN 978-0-15-205186-0 Subj: Emotions – fear. Family life – brothers & sisters. Rhyming text.

Ten times better ill. by author. Marshall Cavendish, 2001. ISBN 978-0-7614-5070-2 Subj: Animals. Counting, numbers. Format, unusual – toy & movable books. Rhyming text.

Too young for Yiddish ill. by Neil Waldman. Talewinds, 2002. ISBN 978-0-88106-118-5 Subj: Family life – grandfathers. Jewish culture. Language.

Twice as good: the story of William Powell and Clearview, the only golf course designed, built, and owned by an African American ill. by Eric Velasquez. Sleeping Bear, 2012. ISBN 978-1-58536-466-4 Subj: Ethnic groups in the U.S. – African Americans. Prejudice. Sports – golf. U.S. history.

Micklethwait, Lucy. *In the picture.* Frances Lincoln, 2010. ISBN 978-1-84507-636-8 Subj: Art. Picture puzzles.

Micklos, John. *Daddy poems* foreword by Jim Trelease; ill. by Robert Casilla. Boyds Mills, 2000. ISBN 978-1-56397-735-0 Subj: Family life – fathers. Poetry.

Mommy poems ill. by Lori McElrath-Eslick. Boyds Mills, 2001. ISBN 978-1-56397-849-4 Subj: Family life – mothers. Poetry.

Micucci, Charles. *The life and times of corn* ill. by author. Houghton, 2009. ISBN 978-0-618-50751-1 Subj: Food. Plants.

Middleton, Charlotte. *Nibbles: a green tale* ill. by author. Marshall Cavendish, 2010. ISBN 978-0-

7614-5791-6 Subj: Animals – guinea pigs. Ecology. Gardens, gardening. Libraries. Seeds.

Nibbles' garden: another green tale ill. by author. Marshall Cavendish, 2012. ISBN 978-0-7614-6134-0 Subj: Animals – guinea pigs. Gardens, gardening. Insects – butterflies, caterpillars. Metamorphosis.

Middleton, Julie. *Are the dinosaurs dead, Dad?* ill. by Russell Ayto. Peachtree, 2013. ISBN 978-1-56145-690-1 Subj: Dinosaurs. Family life – fathers. Museums.

Miles, Betty. *The sky is falling* (Chicken Little)

Miles, Elizabeth J. *Ears* ill. with photos. Heinemann, 2003. ISBN 978-1-4034-0014-7 Subj: Anatomy – ears. Animals.

Mouths and teeth ill. with photos. Heinemann, 2003. ISBN 978-1-4034-0018-5 Subj: Anatomy – mouths. Animals. Teeth.

Noses ill. with photos. Heinemann, 2003. ISBN 978-1-4034-0019-2 Subj: Anatomy – noses. Animals.

Wings, fins, and flippers ill. with photos. Heinemann, 2003. ISBN 978-1-4034-0023-9 Subj: Anatomy – fins. Anatomy – wings. Animals.

Miles, Victoria. *Old Mother Bear* ill. by Molly Bang. Chronicle, 2007. ISBN 978-0-8118-5033-9 Subj: Animals – bears. Foreign lands – Canada. Nature.

Milgrim, David. *Amelia makes a movie* ill. by author. Putnam, 2008. ISBN 978-0-399-24670-8 Subj: Careers – actors. Careers – motion picture producers. Family life – brothers & sisters.

Another day in the Milky Way ill. by author. Penguin, 2007. ISBN 978-0-399-24548-0 Subj: Dreams. Space & space ships.

Best baby ever ill. by author. Putnam, 2009. ISBN 978-0-399-25204-4 Subj: Babies. Family life – parents.

Cows can't fly ill. by author. Viking, 1998. ISBN 978-0-670-87475-0 Subj: Animals – bulls, cows. Imagination. Rhyming text.

Dog brain ill. by author. Viking, 1996. ISBN 978-0-670-86935-0 Subj: Animals – dogs. Behavior – misbehavior.

Eddie gets ready for school ill. by author. Scholastic, 2011. ISBN 978-0-545-27329-9 Subj: Character traits – assertiveness. Character traits – confidence. Humorous stories. School.

Here in space ill. by author. BridgeWater, 1997. ISBN 978-0-8167-4393-3 Subj: Earth. Rhyming text.

How you got so smart ill. by author. Penguin, 2010. ISBN 978-0-399-25260-0 Subj: Behavior – growing up. Rhyming text. Self-concept.

My friend Lucky ill. by author. Atheneum, 2002. ISBN 978-0-689-84253-5 Subj: Animals – dogs. Concepts – opposites. Language.

Santa Duck ill. by author. Putnam, 2008. ISBN 978-0-399-25018-7 Subj: Animals. Birds – ducks. Holidays – Christmas. Santa Claus.

Santa Duck and his merry helpers ill. by author. Penguin, 2010. ISBN 978-0-399-25473-4 Subj: Birds – ducks. Family life – brothers & sisters. Holidays – Christmas. Santa Claus.

Some monsters are different ill. by author. Holt, 2013. ISBN 978-0-8050-9519-7 Subj: Character traits – being different. Character traits – individuality. Monsters.

Time to get up, time to go ill. by author. Houghton, 2006. ISBN 978-0-618-51998-9 Subj: Activities – playing. Gender roles. Toys – dolls.

Why Benny barks ill. by author. Random House, 1994. ISBN 978-0-679-86157-7 Subj: Animals – dogs. Noise, sounds. Rhyming text.

Young MacDonald ill. by author. Penguin, 2006. ISBN 978-0-525-47570-5 Subj: Animals. Careers – inventors. Farms. Inventions. Music. Songs.

Milhous, Katherine. *The egg tree* ill. by author. Aladdin, 1992, ©1950. ISBN 978-0-689-71568-6 Subj: Caldecott award books. Eggs. Holidays – Easter.

Milich, Zoran. *The city ABC book* ill. by author. Kids Can, 2001. ISBN 978-1-55074-942-7 Subj: ABC books. Cities, towns.

City colors ill. by author. Kids Can, 2004. ISBN 978-1-55337-542-5 Subj: Cities, towns. Concepts – color.

City 1 2 3 ill. by author. Kids Can, 2005. ISBN 978-1-55337-540-1 Subj: Cities, towns. Counting, numbers.

City signs ill. by author. Kids Can, 2002. ISBN 978-1-55337-003-1 Subj: Cities, towns. Communication.

Millard, Glenda. *And red galoshes: a story about a rainy day* ill. by Jonathan Bentley. IPG/Little Hare, 2013. ISBN 978-1-921541-46-9 Subj: Clothing – boots. Rhyming text. Weather – rain.

Isabella's garden ill. by Rebecca Cool. Candlewick, 2012. ISBN 978-0-7636-6016-1 Subj: Cumulative tales. Gardens, gardening. Rhyming text. Seasons.

Millen, C. M. *Blue bowl down* ill. by Holly Meade. Candlewick, 2004. ISBN 978-0-7636-1817-9 Subj:

Activities – baking, cooking. Food. Lullabies. Rhyming text.

Miller, Bobbi. *Davy Crockett gets hitched* ill. by Megan Lloyd. Holiday, 2009. ISBN 978-0-8234-1837-4 Subj: Tall tales. U.S. history.

Miss Sally Ann and the panther ill. by Megan Lloyd. Holiday House, 2012. ISBN 978-0-8234-1833-6 Subj: Tall tales. U.S. history – frontier & pioneer life.

Miller, David. *Just like you and me* ill. by author. Dial, 1999. ISBN 978-0-8037-2586-7 Subj: Animals.

Miller, Debbie S. *Are trees alive?* ill. by Stacey Schuett. Walker, 2002. ISBN 978-0-8027-8801-6 Subj: Ecology. Forest, woods. Trees.

A caribou journey ill. by Jon Van Zyle. Little, 1994. ISBN 978-0-316-57380-1 Subj: Alaska. Animals – reindeer. Nature.

River of life ill. by Jon Van Zyle. Clarion, 2000. ISBN 978-0-395-96790-4 Subj: Alaska. Ecology. Rivers.

Woolly mammoth journey ill. by Jon Van Zyle. Little, 2001. ISBN 978-0-316-57212-5 Subj: Animals – woolly mammoths.

Miller, Edna. *Mousekin's Christmas eve* ill. by author. Prentice-Hall, 1965. ISBN 978-0-13-604454-3 Subj: Animals – mice. Holidays – Christmas.

Mousekin's Easter basket ill. by author. Prentice-Hall, 1987. ISBN 978-0-13-604141-2 Subj: Animals – mice. Holidays – Easter. Seasons – spring.

Mousekin's frosty friend ill. by author. Simon & Schuster, 1990. ISBN 978-0-671-70445-2 Subj: Animals – mice. Character traits – kindness to animals. Food. Snowmen.

Mousekin's golden house ill. by author. Prentice-Hall, 1964. ISBN 978-0-13-604232-7 Subj: Animals – mice. Hibernation. Holidays – Halloween. Seasons – winter.

Mousekin's Thanksgiving ill. by author. Prentice-Hall, 1985. ISBN 978-0-13-604299-0 Subj: Animals. Animals – mice. Forest, woods. Holidays – Thanksgiving.

Miller, Edward. *Fireboy to the rescue! a fire safety book* ill. by author. Holiday House, 2010. ISBN 978-0-8234-2222-7 Subj: Careers – firefighters. Safety. School.

The tooth book: a guide to healthy teeth and gums ill. by author. Holiday, 2008. ISBN 978-0-8234-2092-6 Subj: Health & fitness. Teeth.

Miller, Elizabeth I. *Just like home / Como en mi tierra* ill. by Mira Reisberg. Whitman, 1999. ISBN 978-0-8075-4068-8 Subj: Ethnic groups in the U.S. – Hispanic Americans. Foreign languages. Homes, houses. Immigrants.

Miller, Heather. *Cowboy* ill. by author. Heinemann, 2003. ISBN 978-1-4034-0366-7 Subj: Careers. Cowboys, cowgirls.

Librarian ill. with photos. Heinemann, 2003. ISBN 978-1-4034-0369-8 Subj: Careers – librarians. Libraries.

My chickens ill. by author. Children's Press, 2000. ISBN 978-0-516-23105-1 Subj: Birds – chickens. Farms.

My goats ill. by author. Children's Press, 2000. ISBN 978-0-516-23107-5 Subj: Animals – goats. Farms.

My horses ill. by author. Children's Press, 2000. ISBN 978-0-516-23108-2 Subj: Animals – horses, ponies. Farms.

My pigs ill. by author. Children's Press, 2000. ISBN 978-0-516-23109-9 Subj: Animals – pigs. Farms.

Zookeeper ill. with photos. Heinemann, 2003. ISBN 978-1-4034-0373-5 Subj: Careers – zookeepers.

Miller, Heather Lynn. *Subway ride* ill. by Sue Ramá. Charlesbridge, 2009. ISBN 978-1-58089-111-0 Subj: Trains. Transportation. World.

This is your life cycle ill. by Michael Chesworth. Clarion, 2008. ISBN 978-0-618-72485-7 Subj: Insects – dragonflies.

Miller, J. Philip. *We all sing with the same voice* by J. Philip Miller and Sheppard M. Greene ill. by Paul Meisel. HarperCollins, 2001. ISBN 978-0-06-027475-7 Subj: Ethnic groups in the U.S. Music. Rhyming text. Songs.

Miller, Margaret. *Baby faces* ill. by author. Simon & Schuster, 1998. ISBN 978-0-689-81911-7 Subj: Anatomy – faces. Babies. Format, unusual – board books.

Big and little ill. by author. Greenwillow, 1998. ISBN 978-0-688-14749-5 Subj: Concepts – opposites. Concepts – size.

Can you guess? ill. by author. Greenwillow, 1993. ISBN 978-0-688-11181-6 Subj: Character traits – questioning.

Guess who? photos by author. Simon & Schuster, 1996. ISBN 978-0-688-12784-8 Subj: Format, unusual – board books.

I love colors ill. by author. Simon & Schuster, 1999. ISBN 978-0-689-82356-5 Subj: Animals. Babies. Concepts – color. Family life. Format, unusual – board books.

My five senses photos by author. Simon & Schuster, 1994. ISBN 978-0-671-79168-1 Subj: Senses.

Now I'm big photos by author. Greenwillow, 1996. ISBN 978-0-688-14078-6 Subj: Babies. Concepts – size. School.

What's on my head? ill. by author. Simon & Schuster, 1998. ISBN 978-0-689-81912-4 Subj: Anatomy – heads. Clothing – hats. Format, unusual – board books.

Who uses this? photos by author. Greenwillow, 1990. ISBN 978-0-688-08279-6 Subj: Careers. Tools.

Whose hat? photos by author. Greenwillow, 1988. ISBN 978-0-688-06907-0 Subj: Careers. Clothing – hats.

Whose shoe? photos by author. Greenwillow, 1991. ISBN 978-0-688-10009-4 Subj: Clothing – shoes. Games.

Miller, Pat. *Squirrel's New Year's resolution* ill. by Kathi Ember. Whitman, 2010. ISBN 978-0-8075-7591-8 Subj: Animals. Animals – squirrels. Character traits – helpfulness. Holidays – New Year's.

Substitute Groundhog ill. by Kathi Ember. Whitman, 2006. ISBN 978-0-8075-7643-4 Subj: Animals. Animals – groundhogs. Holidays – Groundhog Day. Illness.

We're going on a book hunt ill. by Nadine Bernard Westcott. Upstart, 2008. ISBN 978-1-60213-034-0 Subj: Books, reading. Libraries. Rhyming text. Sports – hunting.

Miller, Pat Zietlow. *Sophie's squash* ill. by Anne Wilsdorf. Random House, 2013. ISBN 978-0-307-978-96-7 Subj: Food. Friendship. Gardens, gardening.

Miller, Ruth. *The bear on the bed* ill. by Bill Slavin. Kids Can, 2002. ISBN 978-1-55337-036-9 Subj: Animals – bears. Rhyming text.

I went to the farm ill. by Per-Henrik Gurth. Kids Can, 2000. ISBN 978-1-55074-705-8 Subj: Activities – playing. Animals. Farms. Rhyming text.

Miller, Sara Swan. *Cat in the bag* ill. by Benton Mahan. Children's Press, 2001. ISBN 978-0-516-22014-7 Subj: Activities – traveling. Animals – cats.

Miller, Sy. *Let there be peace on earth: and let it begin with me* (Jackson, Jill)

Miller, Virginia. *Be gentle!* ill. by author. Candlewick, 1997. ISBN 978-0-7636-0251-2 Subj: Animals – bears. Animals – cats. Pets.

I love you just the way you are ill. by author. Candlewick, 1998. ISBN 978-0-7636-0664-0 Subj: Animals – bears. Behavior – bad day.

In a minute! ill. by author. Candlewick, 2000. ISBN 978-0-7636-1270-2 Subj: Activities – playing. Animals – bears.

On your potty! ill. by author. Greenwillow, 1991. ISBN 978-0-688-10618-8 Subj: Animals – bears. Behavior – growing up. Etiquette. Toilet training.

Ten red apples ill. by author. Candlewick, 2002. ISBN 978-0-7636-1901-5 Subj: Animals – bears. Animals – cats. Counting, numbers. Food.

Miller, William. *The bus ride* ill. by John Ward. Intro. by Rosa Parks. Lee & Low, 1998. ISBN 978-1-880000-60-1 Subj: Ethnic groups in the U.S. – African Americans. Prejudice. U.S. history.

A house by the river ill. by Cornelius Van Wright and Ying-Hwa Hu. Lee & Low, 1997. ISBN 978-1-880000-48-9 Subj: Emotions – fear. Ethnic groups in the U.S. – African Americans. Family life – mothers. Homes, houses. Weather – storms.

Jenny and the peddler ill. by Rod Brown. Dial, 2000. ISBN 978-0-8037-2046-6 Subj: Careers – peddlers. Country. Ethnic groups in the U.S. – African Americans. Jewish culture.

The piano ill. by Susan Keeter. Lee & Low, 2000. ISBN 978-1-880000-98-4 Subj: Ethnic groups in the U.S. – African Americans. Music. Musical instruments – pianos. Old age.

Rent party jazz ill. by Charlotte Riley-Webb. Lee & Low, 2001. ISBN 978-1-58430-025-0 Subj: Ethnic groups in the U.S. – African Americans. Music. U.S. history.

Richard Wright and the library card ill. by R. Gregory Christie. Lee & Low, 1997. ISBN 978-1-880000-57-1 Subj: Books, reading. Ethnic groups in the U.S. – African Americans. Libraries.

Milligan, Bryce. *Brigid's cloak* ill. by Helen Cann. Eerdmans, 2002. ISBN 978-0-8028-5224-3 Subj: Clothing – coats. Folk & fairy tales. Foreign lands – Ireland. Religion – Nativity.

The prince of Ireland and the three magic stallions ill. by Preston McDaniels. Holiday, 2003. ISBN 978-0-8234-1573-1 Subj: Emotions – envy, jealousy. Folk & fairy tales. Foreign lands – Ireland. Royalty – princes.

Millman, Isaac. *Moses goes to a concert* ill. by author. Farrar, 1998. ISBN 978-0-374-35067-3 Subj: Communication. Disabilities – deafness. Language. Music. Musical instruments – orchestras. School – field trips. Sign language.

Moses goes to school ill. by author. Farrar, 2000. ISBN 978-0-374-35069-7 Subj: Disabilities – deafness. Language. School – first day. Senses – hearing.

Moses goes to the circus ill. by author. Farrar, 2003. ISBN 978-0-374-35064-2 Subj: Circus. Communication. Disabilities – deafness. Language.

Mills, Claudia. *Ziggy's blue-ribbon day* ill. by R. W. Alley. Farrar, 2005. ISBN 978-0-374-32352-3 Subj: Activities – drawing. School. Self-concept. Sports.

Mills, Elaine. *Marinetta at the ballet* ill. by author. Andersen, 2001. ISBN 978-1-59019-439-3 Subj: Ballet. Theater. Toys. Toys – dolls.

Mills, Judith Christine. *The painted chest* ill. by author. Key Porter Kids, 2000. ISBN 978-1-55263-015-0 Subj: Activities – dancing. Activities – playing. Activities – working. Music.

Mills, Lauren A. *The rag coat* ill. by author. Little, 1991. ISBN 978-0-316-57407-5 Subj: Behavior – sharing. Clothing. Friendship. Poverty.

Milne, A. A. *Eeyore loses a tail* ill. by Ernest H. Shepard. Dutton, 2001. ISBN 978-0-525-46703-8 Subj: Anatomy – tails. Toys. Toys – bears.

The magic hill ill. by Isabel Bodor Brown. Dutton, 2000. ISBN 978-0-525-46147-0 Subj: Flowers. Folk & fairy tales. Royalty – princesses.

Tigger tales ill. by Ernest H. Shepard. Dutton, 2002. ISBN 978-0-525-46941-4 Subj: Toys. Toys – bears.

Milord, Susan. *The ghost on the hearth* ill. by Lydia Dabcovich. Vermont Folklife Center, 2003. ISBN 978-0-916718-18-3 Subj: Farms. Foreign lands – Canada. Ghosts.

Happy 100th day! ill. by Mary Newell DePalma. Scholastic, 2011. ISBN 978-0-439-88281-1 Subj: Birthdays. Books, reading. Counting, numbers. School.

Happy school year! ill. by Mary Newell DePalma. Scholastic, 2008. ISBN 978-0-439-88280-4 Subj: Behavior – worrying. Emotions – fear. School – first day.

If I could: a mother's promise ill. by Christopher Denise. Candlewick, 2008. ISBN 978-0-7636-2348-7 Subj: Animals – raccoons. Emotions – love. Family life – mothers. Rhyming text.

Love that baby ill. by author. Houghton, 2005. ISBN 978-0-618-56323-4 Subj: Babies. Emotions – love.

Willa the wonderful ill. by author. Houghton, 2003. ISBN 978-0-618-27522-9 Subj: Animals – pigs. Fairies. Royalty – princesses. School.

Milusich, Janice. *Off go their engines, off go their lights* ill. by David Gordon. Dutton, 2008. ISBN 978-0-525-47940-6 Subj: Automobiles. Night. Rhyming text. Taxis. Trucks.

Milway, Katie Smith. *Cappuccina goes to town* ill. by Eugenie Fernandes. Kids Can, 2002. ISBN 978-1-55074-807-9 Subj: Animals – bulls, cows. Cities, towns. Farms. Self-concept.

The good garden: how one family went from hunger to having enough ill. by Sylvie Daigneault. Kids Can, 2010. ISBN 978-1-55453-488-3 Subj: Food. Foreign lands – Honduras. Gardens, gardening.

Mimi's village and how basic health care transformed it ill. by Eugenie Fernandes. Kids Can, 2012. ISBN 978-1-55453-722-8 Subj: Character traits – cleanliness. Foreign lands – Kenya. Health & fitness. Illness.

One hen: how one small loan made a big difference ill. by Eugenie Fernandes. Kids Can, 2008. ISBN 978-1-55453-028-1 Subj: Behavior – seeking better things. Birds – chickens. Foreign lands – Ghana. Money. Poverty.

Minarik, Else Holmelund. *Am I beautiful?* ill. by Yossi Abolafia. Greenwillow, 1992. ISBN 978-0-688-09912-1 Subj: Animals. Animals – hippopotamuses. Family life – mothers. Self-concept.

It's spring! ill. by Margaret Bloy Graham. Greenwillow, 1989. ISBN 978-0-688-07620-7 Subj: Animals – cats. Seasons – spring.

Little Bear's new friend ill. by Heather Green. HarperCollins, 2002. ISBN 978-0-06-623688-9 Subj: Animals – bears. Behavior – lost. Friendship.

Minor, Florence. *Christmas tree!* (Minor, Wendell)

If you were a penguin ill. by Wendell Minor. HarperCollins, 2009. ISBN 978-0-06-113097-7 Subj: Birds – penguins. Rhyming text.

Minor, Wendell. *Christmas tree!* by Wendell Minor and Florence Minor ill. by authors. HarperCollins, 2005. ISBN 978-0-06-056035-5 Subj: Holidays – Christmas. Rhyming text. Trees.

How big could your pumpkin grow? ill. by author. Penguin/Nancy Paulsen, 2013. ISBN 978-0-399-24684-5 Subj: Food. Imagination. U.S. history.

My farm friends ill. by author. Penguin, 2011. ISBN 978-0-399-24477-3 Subj: Animals. Farms. Rhyming text.

Pumpkin heads ill. by author. Blue Sky, 2000. ISBN 978-0-590-52105-5 Subj: Holidays – Halloween.

Yankee Doodle America: the spirit of 1776 from A to Z ill. by author. Penguin, 2006. ISBN 978-0-399-24003-4 Subj: ABC books. U.S. history.

Minshull, Evelyn White. *Eaglet's world* ill. by Andrea Gabriel. Whitman, 2002. ISBN 978-0-8075-8929-8 Subj: Activities – flying. Behavior – growing up. Birds – eagles.

Minters, Frances. *Cinder-Elly* ill. by G. Brian Karas. Viking, 1994. ISBN 978-0-670-84417-3 Subj: Folk & fairy tales. Rhyming text. Royalty – princes. Sibling rivalry.

Princess Fishtail ill. by G. Brian Karas. Viking, 2002. ISBN 978-0-670-03529-8 Subj: Humorous stories. Mythical creatures – mermaids, mermen. Mythical creatures – trolls. Rhyming text. Sports – surfing.

Sleepless Beauty ill. by G. Brian Karas. Viking, 1996. ISBN 978-0-670-87033-2 Subj: Folk & fairy tales. Rhyming text. Witches.

Too big, too small, just right ill. by Janie Bynum. Harcourt, 2001. ISBN 978-0-15-202157-3 Subj: Animals – rabbits. Concepts – opposites. Rhyming text.

Miranda, Anne. *Alphabet fiesta.* ill. by young children. Turtle, 2001. ISBN 978-1-890515-29-4 Subj: ABC books. Animals. Animals – zebras. Birthdays. Children as illustrators. Parties.

Beep! beep! ill. by David Murphy. Turtle, 1999. ISBN 978-1-890515-14-0 Subj: Automobiles. Imagination. Noise, sounds. Rhyming text. Trucks.

Monster math ill. by Polly Powell. Harcourt, 1999. ISBN 978-0-15-201835-1 Subj: Birthdays. Counting, numbers. Monsters. Parties. Rhyming text.

Pignic ill. by Rosekrans Hoffman. Boyds Mills, 1996. ISBN 978-1-56397-558-5 Subj: ABC books. Activities – picnicking. Animals – pigs.

To market, to market ill. by Janet Stevens. Harcourt, 1997. ISBN 978-0-15-200035-6 Subj: Animals. Animals – pigs. Nursery rhymes. Stores.

Vroom, chugga, vroom-vroom ill. by David Murphy. Turtle, 1998. ISBN 978-1-890515-07-2 Subj: Automobiles. Counting, numbers. Sports – racing. Transportation.

Mitakidou, Soula. *The orphan: a Cinderella story from Greece* (Manna, Anthony L.)

Mitchard, Jacquelyn. *Baby bat's lullaby* ill. by Julia Noonan. HarperCollins, 2004. ISBN 978-0-06-050761-9 Subj: Animals – bats. Bedtime. Family life – mothers. Lullabies.

Ready, set, school! ill. by Paul Ratz de Tagyos. HarperCollins, 2007. ISBN 978-0-06-050766-4 Subj: Animals – raccoons. Family life – parents. School – first day. Sleepovers.

Mitchell, Adrian. *Nobody rides the unicorn* ill. by Stephen Lambert. Scholastic, 2000. ISBN 978-0-439-11204-8 Subj: Mythical creatures – unicorns. Royalty – kings.

Mitchell, Brian Stokes. *Lights on Broadway: a theatrical tour from A to Z* (Ziefert, Harriet)

Mitchell, Joyce Slayton. *Tractor-trailer trucker: a powerful truck book* photos by Steven Borns. Tricycle, 2000. ISBN 978-1-58246-010-9 Subj: Careers – truck drivers. Trucks.

Mitchell, Lori. *Different just like me* ill. by author. Charlesbridge, 1999. ISBN 978-0-88106-975-4 Subj: Character traits – individuality. Family life – grandmothers.

Mitchell, Margaree King. *Granddaddy's gift* ill. by Larry Johnson. BridgeWater, 1996. ISBN 978-0-8167-4010-9 Subj: Character traits – bravery. Ethnic groups in the U.S. – African Americans. Family life – grandfathers. U.S. history.

Susie Mae ill. by Melodye Benson Rosales. Lothrop, 2000. ISBN 978-0-688-15222-2 Subj: Ethnic groups in the U.S. – African Americans. Prejudice. School.

Uncle Jed's barbershop ill. by James Ransome. Simon & Schuster, 1993. ISBN 978-0-671-76969-7 Subj: Careers – barbers. Character traits – perseverance. Ethnic groups in the U.S. – African Americans. Family life – aunts, uncles.

When Grandmama sings ill. by James Ransome. HarperCollins, 2012. ISBN 978-0-688-17563-4 Subj: Activities – singing. Ethnic groups in the U.S. – African Americans. Family life – grandmothers. Prejudice. U.S. history.

Mitchell, Marianne. *Gullywasher gulch* ill. by Normand Chartier. Boyds Mills, 2002. ISBN 978-1-56397-123-5 Subj: Character traits – generosity. Weather – rain.

Joe Cinders ill. by Bryan Langdo. Holt, 2002. ISBN 978-0-8050-6529-9 Subj: Clothing – boots. Cowboys, cowgirls. Folk & fairy tales.

Mitchell, Rhonda. *The talking cloth* ill. by author. Orchard, 1997. ISBN 978-0-531-33004-3 Subj: Ethnic groups in the U.S. – African Americans. Family life – aunts, uncles. Foreign lands – Africa.

Mitchell, Robin. *Windy* by Robin Mitchell and Judith Steedman; photos by Mia Cunningham. Simply Read, 2002. ISBN 978-0-9688768-2-4 Subj: Kites. Weather – wind.

Mitchell, Susan K. *The rainforest grew all around* ill. by Connie McLennan. Random House, 2007. ISBN 978-0-9768823-6-7 Subj: Animals. Jungle. Plants. Songs.

Mitter, Matt. *ABC: alphabet rhymes* ill. by Doug Cushman. G. Stevens, 2004. ISBN 978-0-8368-4095-7 Subj: ABC books. Animals. Rhyming text.

Once upon a rhyme ill. by Susan Banta. G. Stevens, 2004. ISBN 978-0-8368-4096-4 Subj: Animals. Humorous stories. Rebuses. Rhyming text.

1, 2, 3, counting rhymes ill. by Doug Cushman. G. Stevens, 2004. ISBN 978-0-8368-4094-0 Subj: Animals. Counting, numbers. Farms. Rhyming text.

Mitton, Jacqueline. *Zoo in the sky: a book of animal constellations* ill. by Christina Balit. Star maps by Wil Tirion. National Geographic, 1998. ISBN 978-0-7922-7069-0 Subj: Stars.

Mitton, Tony. *All afloat on Noah's boat!* ill. by Guy Parker-Rees. Scholastic, 2007. ISBN 978-0-439-87397-0 Subj: Animals. Boats, ships. Religion – Noah. Rhyming text.

Cool cars ill. by Ant Parker. Houghton, 2005. ISBN 978-0-7534-5802-0 Subj: Automobiles. Rhyming text. Transportation.

Dinosaurumpus ill. by Guy Parker-Rees. Orchard, 2003. ISBN 978-0-439-39514-4 Subj: Activities – dancing. Dinosaurs. Rhyming text.

Down by the cool of the pool ill. by Guy Parker-Rees. Orchard, 2002. ISBN 978-0-439-30915-8 Subj: Activities – dancing. Animals. Frogs & toads. Lakes, ponds. Rhyming text.

Farmer Joe and the music show ill. by Guy Parker-Rees. Scholastic, 2009. ISBN 978-0-545-12493-5 Subj: Animals. Farms. Music. Rhyming text.

Flashing fire engines by Tony Mitton and Ant Parker ill. by Ant Parker. Kingfisher, 1998. ISBN 978-0-7534-5104-5 Subj: Careers – firefighters. Noise, sounds. Rhyming text. Trucks.

The Jungle Run ill. by Guy Parker-Rees. Scholastic, 2012. ISBN 978-0-545-39256-3 Subj: Activities – running. Animals. Jungle. Rhyming text. Sports – racing.

Playful little penguins ill. by Guy Parker-Rees. Walker, 2007. ISBN 978-0-8027-9710-0 Subj: Animals – seals. Behavior – lost. Birds – penguins. Rhyming text.

Riddledy piggledy ill. by Paddy Mounter. Fickling, 2003. ISBN 978-0-385-75033-2 Subj: Nursery rhymes. Riddles & jokes.

Rumble, roar, dinosaur! more prehistoric poems with lift-the-flap surprises! ill. by Lynne Chapman. Kingfisher, 2010. ISBN 978-0-7534-1932-8 Subj: Dinosaurs. Format, unusual – toy & movable books.

A very curious bear ill. by Paul Howard. Random House, 2009. ISBN 978-0-375-85083-7 Subj: Animals – bears. Character traits – curiosity. Character traits – questioning. Rhyming text.

Miura, Taro. *The tiny king* ill. by author. Candlewick, 2013. ISBN 978-0-7636-6687-3 Subj: Character traits – smallness. Emotions – happiness. Royalty – kings.

Tools ill. by author. Chronicle, 2006. ISBN 978-0-8118-5519-8 Subj: Tools.

Mixter, Helen. *My little round house* (Baasansuren, Bolormaa)

Mizzoni, Chris. *Clancy with the puck* ill. by author. Raincoast, 2007. ISBN 978-1-55192-804-3 Subj: Rhyming text. Sports – hockey.

Mobin-Uddin, Asma. *The best Eid ever* ill. by Laura Jacobsen. Boyds Mills, 2007. ISBN 978-1-59078-431-0 Subj: Holidays. Religion – Islam.

A party in Ramadan ill. by Laura Jacobsen. Boyds Mills, 2009. ISBN 978-1-59078-604-8 Subj: Holidays – Ramadan. Religion – Islam.

Mochizuki, Ken. *Baseball saved us* ill. by Dom Lee. Lee & Low, 1993. ISBN 978-1-880000-01-4 Subj: Ethnic groups in the U.S. – Japanese Americans. Sports – baseball. U.S. history. War.

Be water, my friend: the early years of Bruce Lee ill. by Dom Lee. Lee & Low, 2006. ISBN 978-1-58430-265-0 Subj: Ethnic groups in the U.S. – Chinese Americans. Sports.

Modan, Rutu. *Maya makes a mess* ill. by author. TOON, 2012. ISBN 978-1-93517-917-7 Subj: Behavior – messy. Etiquette. Food. Format, unusual – graphic novels.

Modarressi, Mitra. *Owlet's first flight* ill. by author. Putnam, 2012. ISBN 978-0-399-25526-7 Subj: Activities – flying. Birds – owls. Emotions – fear. Rhyming text.

Stay awake, Sally ill. by author. Penguin, 2007. ISBN 978-0-399-24545-9 Subj: Animals – raccoons. Bedtime. Family life – parents. Rhyming text.

Taking care of Mama ill. by author. Penguin, 2010. ISBN 978-0-399-25216-7 Subj: Animals – raccoons. Family life – mothers. Illness.

Yard sale ill. by author. DK, 2000. ISBN 978-0-7894-2651-2 Subj: Communities, neighborhoods. Magic. Stores.

Modell, Frank. *Goodbye old year, hello new year* ill. by author. Greenwillow, 1984. ISBN 978-0-688-03939-4 Subj: Holidays – New Year's.

Ice cream soup ill. by author. Greenwillow, 1988. ISBN 978-0-688-07771-6 Subj: Birthdays. Parties.

Look out, it's April Fools' Day ill. by author. Greenwillow, 1985. ISBN 978-0-688-04017-8 Subj: Holidays – April Fools' Day. Riddles & jokes.

One zillion valentines ill. by author. Greenwillow, 1981. ISBN 978-0-688-00569-6 Subj: Character traits – practicality. Holidays – Valentine's Day.

Modesitt, Jeanne. *Little Bunny's Easter surprise* ill. by Robin Spowart. Simon & Schuster, 1999. ISBN 978-0-689-82491-3 Subj: Animals – rabbits. Behavior – hiding things. Holidays – Easter.

Little Mouse's happy birthday ill. by Robin Spowart. Boyds Mills, 2007. ISBN 978-1-59078-272-9 Subj: Animals – mice. Birthdays. Family life.

Oh, what a beautiful day! a counting book ill. by Robin Spowart. Boyds Mills, 2009. ISBN 978-1-56397-409-0 Subj: Animals. Counting, numbers. Day. Rhyming text.

Modugno, Maria. *Santa Claus and the three bears* ill. by Jane Dyer. HarperCollins, 2013. ISBN 978-0-06-170023-1 Subj: Animals – polar bears. Holidays – Christmas. Santa Claus.

Moerbeek, Kees. *The diary of Hansel and Gretel* ill. by author. Simon & Schuster, 2002. ISBN 978-0-689-84602-1 Subj: Behavior – lost. Folk & fairy tales. Forest, woods. Format, unusual – toy & movable books. Witches.

Moers, Hermann. *Rufus and Max* ill. by Philippe Goossens. NorthSouth, 2003. ISBN 978-0-7358-1798-2 Subj: Activities – playing. Animals – dogs. Imagination.

Moffatt, Judith. *The pumpkin man* ill. by author. Scholastic, 1998. ISBN 978-0-590-63865-4 Subj: Holidays – Halloween. Rhyming text.

Snow shapes ill. by author. Scholastic, 2000. ISBN 978-0-439-09858-8 Subj: Activities – making things. Art. Paper. Seasons – winter.

Trick-or-treat faces: a glowing book you can read in the dark! ill. by author. Scholastic, 2000. ISBN 978-0-439-18299-7 Subj: Format, unusual. Holidays – Halloween. Monsters. Rhyming text.

Mohammed, Khadra. *My name is Sangoel* (Williams, Karen Lynn)

Mohr, Joseph, verses. *Silent night* ill. by Susan Jeffers. Orig. title: Stille Nacht, heilige Nacht. Dutton, 1984. ISBN 978-0-525-44144-1 Subj: Holidays – Christmas. Songs.

Molk, Laurel. *Good job, Oliver!* ill. by author. Crown, 1999. ISBN 978-0-517-70976-4 Subj: Animals – rabbits. Gardens, gardening.

Mollel, Tololwa M. *Ananse's feast: an Ashanti tale* ill. by Andrew Glass. Clarion, 1997. ISBN 978-0-395-67402-4 Subj: Behavior – trickery. Country. Folk & fairy tales. Foreign lands – Ghana. Reptiles – turtles, tortoises. Spiders.

The flying tortoise: an Igbo tale ill. by Barbara Spurll. Oxford Univ. Pr., 1993. ISBN 978-0-395-68845-8 Subj: Behavior – greed. Behavior – trickery. Folk & fairy tales. Foreign lands – Nigeria. Reptiles – turtles, tortoises.

Kele's secret ill. by Catherine Stock. Dutton, 1997. ISBN 978-0-525-67500-6 Subj: Birds – chickens. Family life – grandparents. Foreign lands – Tanzania.

Kitoto the mighty ill. by Kristi Frost. Stoddart, 1998. ISBN 978-0-7737-3019-9 Subj: Animals – mice. Folk & fairy tales. Foreign lands – Africa.

My rows and piles of coins ill. by E. B. Lewis. Clarion, 1999. ISBN 978-0-395-75186-2 Subj: Foreign lands – Tanzania. Money. Sports – bicycling.

Orphan boy ill. by Paul Morin. Clarion, 1991. ISBN 978-0-89919-985-6 Subj: Folk & fairy tales. Foreign lands – Kenya. Magic. Orphans.

Rhinos for lunch and elephants for supper ill. by Barbara Spurll. Houghton, 1992. ISBN 978-0-395-60734-3 Subj: Animals. Cumulative tales. Emotions – fear. Foreign lands – Kenya.

Song bird ill. by Rosanne Litzinger. Clarion, 1999. ISBN 978-0-395-82908-0 Subj: Birds. Folk & fairy tales. Foreign lands – Tanzania. Magic. Monsters.

Subira subira ill. by Linda Saport. Clarion, 2000. ISBN 978-0-395-91809-8 Subj: Character traits – patience. Folk & fairy tales. Foreign lands – Tanzania.

To dinner, for dinner ill. by Synthia Saint James. Holiday, 2000. ISBN 978-0-8234-1527-4 Subj: Animals. Animals – leopards. Animals – rabbits. Foreign lands – Africa.

Monari, Manuela. *Zero kisses for me!* ill. by Virginie Soumagnac. Tundra, 2010. ISBN 978-1-77049-208-0 Subj: Animals – bears. Bedtime. Kissing.

Monk, Isabell. *Blackberry stew* ill. by Janice Lee Porter. Carolrhoda, 2005. ISBN 978-1-57505-605-0 Subj: Death. Emotions – grief. Emotions – sadness. Family life – grandfathers. Memories, memory.

Family ill. by Janice Lee Porter. Carolrhoda, 2001. ISBN 978-1-57505-485-8 Subj: Ethnic groups in the U.S. – African Americans. Family life. Food.

Hope ill. by Janice Lee Porter. Carolrhoda, 1999. ISBN 978-1-57505-230-4 Subj: Ethnic groups in the U.S. – African Americans. Family life – aunts, uncles. Names.

Monks, Lydia. *Aaaarrgghh! spider!* ill. by author. Houghton, 2004. ISBN 978-0-618-43250-9 Subj: Pets. Spiders.

The cat barked? ill. by author. Dial, 1999. ISBN 978-0-8037-2338-2 Subj: Animals – cats. Animals – dogs. Rhyming text. Self-concept.

Monnier, Miriam. *Just right* ill. by author. NorthSouth, 2001. ISBN 978-0-7358-1522-3 Subj: Behavior – growing up. Family life – mothers. Self-concept.

Monroe, Chris. *Cookie, the walker* ill. by author. Carolrhoda, 2013. ISBN 978-0-7613-5617-2 Subj:

Activities – walking. Animals – dogs. Character traits – being different.

Monkey with a tool belt and the seaside shenanigans ill. by author. Carolrhoda, 2011. ISBN 978-0-7613-5616-5 Subj: Animals – elephants. Animals – monkeys. Sea & seashore – beaches. Tools.

Sneaky sheep ill. by author. Carolrhoda, 2010. ISBN 978-0-7613-5615-8 Subj: Animals – dogs. Animals – sheep. Behavior – misbehavior.

Monson, A. M. *Wanted . . . best friend* ill. by Lynn Munsinger. Dial, 1997. ISBN 978-0-8037-1485-4 Subj: Animals – cats. Animals – mice. Friendship. Games.

Monster, be good! ill. by Natalie Marshall. Blue Apple, 2013. ISBN 978-1-60905-314-7 Subj: Behavior. Etiquette. Monsters.

Montanari, Donata. *Children around the world* ill. by author. Kids Can, 2001. ISBN 978-1-55337-064-2 Subj: Etiquette. Foreign lands.

Montanari, Eva. *The crocodile's true colors* ill. by author. Watson-Guptill, 2002. ISBN 978-0-8230-2435-3 Subj: Animals. Concepts. Foreign lands – Africa. Reptiles – alligators, crocodiles. School.

Dino bikes ill. by author. NorthSouth, 2004. ISBN 978-0-7358-1918-4 Subj: Behavior – bullying, teasing. Dinosaurs. Sports – bicycling.

My first . . . ill. by author. Houghton, 2007. ISBN 978-0-618-64644-9 Subj: Books, reading. Gifts. Toys – dolls.

Tiff, Taff, and Lulu ill. by author. Houghton, 2004. ISBN 978-0-618-40238-0 Subj: Family life – sisters. Sibling rivalry.

A very full morning ill. by author. Houghton, 2006. ISBN 978-0-618-56318-0 Subj: Animals – rabbits. Behavior – worrying. Careers – teachers. School – first day.

Montenegro, Laura Nyman. *A bird about to sing* ill. by author. Houghton, 2003. ISBN 978-0-618-18865-9 Subj: Character traits – shyness. Poetry.

Montes, Marisa. *Egg-napped!* ill. by Marsha Winborn. HarperCollins, 2002. ISBN 978-0-06-028951-5 Subj: Animals. Behavior – lost & found possessions. Birds – geese. Eggs. Rhyming text.

Juan Bobo goes to work: a Puerto Rican folktale ill. by Joe Cepeda. Morrow, 2000. ISBN 978-0-688-16234-4 Subj: Folk & fairy tales. Foreign lands – Puerto Rico.

Los gatos black on Halloween ill. by Yuyi Morales. Holt, 2006. ISBN 978-0-8050-7429-1 Subj: Animals – cats. Foreign languages. Holidays – Day of the Dead. Holidays – Halloween. Monsters. Rhyming text.

Montgomery, Michael G., compiler. *Over the candlestick: classic nursery rhymes and the real stories behind them* also comp. by Wayne Montgomery; ill. by Michael G. Montgomery. Peachtree, 2002. ISBN 978-1-56145-259-0 Subj: Nursery rhymes.

Montijo, Rhode. *The Halloween Kid* ill. by author. Simon & Schuster, 2010. ISBN 978-1-4169-3575-9 Subj: Cowboys, cowgirls. Holidays – Halloween.

Montserrat, Pep. *Ms. Rubinstein's beauty* ill. by author. Sterling, 2006. ISBN 978-1-4027-3063-4 Subj: Character traits – appearance. Character traits – individuality. Circus.

Moodie, Fiona. *Noko and the night monster* ill. by author. Marshall Cavendish, 2001. ISBN 978-0-7614-5093-1 Subj: Animals – aardvarks. Animals – porcupines. Emotions – fear. Monsters. Night.

Moon, Nicola. *Lucy's picture* ill. by Alex Ayliffe. Dial, 1995. ISBN 978-0-8037-1833-3 Subj: Activities – making things. Art. Disabilities – blindness. Family life – grandfathers.

Something special ill. by Alex Ayliffe. Peachtree, 1997. ISBN 978-1-56145-137-1 Subj: Babies. Family life – brothers & sisters. School.

Tick-tock, drip-drop ill. by Eleanor Taylor. Bloomsbury, 2004. ISBN 978-1-58234-944-2 Subj: Animals – moles. Animals – rabbits. Bedtime. Noise, sounds. Sleep.

Moore, Clement Clarke. *A creature was stirring: one boy's night before Christmas* by Clement Clarke Moore and Carter Goodrich ill. by Carter Goodrich. Simon & Schuster, 2006. ISBN 978-0-689-86399-8 Subj: Holidays – Christmas. Poetry. Santa Claus.

The night before Christmas ill. by Jan Brett. Putnam, 1998. ISBN 978-0-399-23190-2 Subj: Holidays – Christmas. Poetry. Santa Claus.

The night before Christmas ill. by Tomie dePaola. Holiday, 1980. ISBN 978-0-8234-0414-8 Subj: Holidays – Christmas. Poetry. Santa Claus.

The night before Christmas ill. by Mary Engelbreit. HarperCollins, 2002. ISBN 978-0-06-008161-4 Subj: Holidays – Christmas. Poetry. Santa Claus.

The night before Christmas ill. by Holly Hobbie. Little, Brown, 2013. ISBN 978-0-316-07018-8 Subj: Holidays – Christmas. Poetry. Santa Claus.

The night before Christmas retold by Rachel Isadora; ill. by reteller. Putnam, 2009. ISBN 978-0-399-25408-6 Subj: Animals – mice. Foreign lands – Africa. Holidays – Christmas. Poetry. Santa Claus.

The night before Christmas ill. by Raquel Jaramillo. Atheneum, 2001. ISBN 978-0-689-84053-1 Subj: Holidays – Christmas. Poetry. Santa Claus.

The night before Christmas ill. by Anita Lobel. Knopf, 1984. ISBN 978-0-394-96863-6 Subj: Holidays – Christmas. Poetry. Santa Claus.

The night before Christmas ill. by James Marshall. Scholastic, 1989. ISBN 978-0-590-33805-9 Subj: Holidays – Christmas. Poetry. Santa Claus.

The night before Christmas ill. by Will Moses. Penguin, 2006. ISBN 978-0-399-23745-4 Subj: Holidays – Christmas. Poetry. Santa Claus.

The night before Christmas ill. by Ted Rand. North-South, 1995. ISBN 978-1-55858-466-2 Subj: Holidays – Christmas. Poetry. Santa Claus.

The night before Christmas ill. by Ruth Sanderson. Little, 1997. ISBN 978-0-316-57963-6 Subj: Holidays – Christmas. Poetry. Santa Claus.

The night before Christmas ill. by Gennady Spirin. Marshall Cavendish, 2006. ISBN 978-0-7614-5298-0 Subj: Holidays – Christmas. Poetry. Santa Claus.

The night before Christmas ill. by Tasha Tudor. Little, 1999. ISBN 978-0-316-85579-2 Subj: Holidays – Christmas. Poetry. Santa Claus.

The night before Christmas comp. by Cooper Edens and Harold Darling ill. by various 19th- & 20th-century artists. A classic illustrated ed. Chronicle, 1998. ISBN 978-0-8118-1712-7 Subj: Holidays – Christmas. Poetry. Santa Claus.

The night before Christmas ill. by Richard Jesse Watson. HarperCollins, 2006. ISBN 978-0-06-075742-7 Subj: Holidays – Christmas. Poetry. Santa Claus.

The night before Christmas ill. by Wendy Watson. Houghton, 1990. ISBN 978-0-395-53624-7 Subj: Holidays – Christmas. Poetry. Santa Claus.

The night before Christmas ill. by Bruce Whatley. HarperCollins, 1999. ISBN 978-0-06-026609-7 Subj: Holidays – Christmas. Poetry. Santa Claus.

The night before Christmas ill. by Lisbeth Zwerger. Penguin, 2005. ISBN 978-0-698-40030-6 Subj: Holidays – Christmas. Poetry. Santa Claus.

The night before Christmas: a pop-up ill. by Robert Sabuda. Simon & Schuster, 2002. ISBN 978-0-689-83899-6 Subj: Format, unusual – toy & movable books. Holidays – Christmas. Poetry. Santa Claus.

The teddy bears' night before Christmas photos by Monica Stevenson. Scholastic, 1999. ISBN 978-0-590-03243-8 Subj: Holidays – Christmas. Poetry. Santa Claus. Toys. Toys – bears.

'Twas the night before Christmas ill. by Matt Tavares. Candlewick, 2002. ISBN 978-0-7636-1585-7 Subj: Holidays – Christmas. Poetry. Santa Claus.

'Twas the night before Christmas ill. by Christopher Wormell. Running Press, 2010. ISBN 978-0-7624-2717-8 Subj: Holidays – Christmas. Poetry. Santa Claus.

Moore, Elaine. *Roly-poly puppies* ill. by Jacqueline Rogers. Scholastic, 1996. ISBN 978-0-590-46665-3 Subj: Animals – dogs. Counting, numbers. Rhyming text.

Moore, Eva. *Lucky ducklings* ill. by Nancy Carpenter. Scholastic, 2013. ISBN 978-0-439-44861-1 Subj: Birds – ducks. Character traits – kindness to animals. Family life – mothers.

Moore, Genevieve. *Catherine's story* ill. by Karin Littlewood. Frances Lincoln, 2010. ISBN 978-1-84507-655-9 Subj: Family life – fathers. Family life – single-parent families. Disabilities – physical disabilities.

Moore, Inga. *Captain Cat* ill. by author. Candlewick, 2013. ISBN 978-0-7636-6151-9 Subj: Animals – cats. Animals – rats. Islands. Royalty – queens. Sailors.

A house in the woods ill. by author. Candlewick, 2011. ISBN 978-0-7636-5277-7 Subj: Animals. Homes, houses.

Moore, Jodi. *When a dragon moves in* ill. by Howard McWilliam. Flashlight, 2011. ISBN 978-0-979974-67-0 Subj: Dragons. Imagination. Sea & seashore – beaches.

Moore, Julianne. *Freckleface Strawberry* ill. by LeUyen Pham. Bloomsbury, 2007. ISBN 978-1-59990-107-7 Subj: Anatomy. Friendship. Self-concept.

Freckleface Strawberry and the dodgeball bully ill. by LeUyen Pham. Bloomsbury, 2009. ISBN 978-1-59990-316-3 Subj: Behavior – bullying, teasing. Games. School.

Freckleface Strawberry: best friends forever ill. by LeUyen Pham. Bloomsbury, 2011. ISBN 978-1-59990-551-8 Subj: Anatomy. Friendship. Gender roles.

Moore, Lilian. *Beware, take care: fun and spooky poems* ill. by Howard Fine. Holt, 2006. ISBN 978-0-8050-6917-4 Subj: Dragons. Emotions – fear. Ghosts. Monsters. Poetry.

While you were chasing a hat ill. by Rosanne Litzinger. HarperCollins, 2001. ISBN 978-0-694-01342-5 Subj: Clothing – hats. Family life – grandfathers. Weather – wind.

Moore, Liz. *Zizi and Tish* ill. by Liz Milkau. Orca, 2003. ISBN 978-1-55143-254-0 Subj: Emotions – envy, jealousy. Family life – sisters.

Moore, Maggie. *Little Red Riding Hood* ill. by Paula Knight. Picture Window, 2003. ISBN 978-1-4048-0064-9 Subj: Animals – wolves. Behavior – talking to strangers. Family life – grandmothers. Folk & fairy tales. Foreign lands – Germany.

The three little pigs (The three little pigs)

Moore, Marian. *Dear Cinderella* by Marian Moore and Mary Jane Kensington ill. by Julie Olson. Scholastic, 2012. ISBN 978-0-545-34220-9 Subj: Folk & fairy tales. Letters, cards. Pen pals. Royalty – princesses.

Moore, Mary-Alice. *The wheels on the school bus* ill. by Laura Huliska-Beith. HarperCollins, 2006. ISBN 978-0-06-059427-5 Subj: Buses. Music. School. Songs.

Moore, Patrick. *The mighty street sweeper* ill. by author. Holt, 2006. ISBN 978-0-8050-7789-6 Subj: Trucks.

Moore, Raina. *How do you say good night?* ill. by Robin Luebs. HarperCollins, 2008. ISBN 978-0-06-083163-9 Subj: Animals. Bedtime. Family life. Rhyming text.

Moore-Mallinos, Jennifer. *It's ok to be me! just like you, I can do almost anything!* ill. by Marta Fabrega. Barron's, 2007. ISBN 978-0-7641-3584-2 Subj: Disabilities – physical disabilities.

Mom has cancer! ill. by Marta Fàbrega. Barron's, 2008. ISBN 978-0-7641-4074-7 Subj: Family life – mothers. Illness – cancer.

My brother is autistic ill. by Marta Fàbrega. Barron's, 2008. ISBN 978-0-7641-4044-0 Subj: Emotions – embarrassment. Family life – brothers. Disabilities – autism. School.

When my parents forgot how to be friends ill. by Marta Fabrega. Barron's, 2005. ISBN 978-0-7641-3172-1 Subj: Divorce. Family life.

Moorman, Margaret. *Light the lights!* ill. by author. Scholastic, 1994. ISBN 978-0-590-47003-2 Subj: Family life. Holidays – Christmas. Holidays – Hanukkah. Religion.

Mora, Pat. *Abuelos* ill. by Amelia Lau Carling. Groundwood, 2008. ISBN 978-0-88899-716-6 Subj: Behavior. Ethnic groups in the U.S. – Hispanic Americans. Mythical creatures.

The bakery lady / La señora de la panadería ill. by Pablo Torrecilla. Piñata, 2001. ISBN 978-1-55885-343-0 Subj: Activities – baking, cooking. Ethnic groups in the U.S. – Mexican Americans. Food. Foreign languages. Holidays.

The beautiful lady: Our Lady of Guadalupe ill. by Steve Johnson and Lou Fancher. Knopf, 2012. ISBN 978-0-375-86838-2 Subj: Foreign lands – Mexico. Indians of North America – Aztec. Religion.

A birthday basket for Tía ill. by Cecily Lang. Macmillan, 1992. ISBN 978-0-02-767400-2 Subj: Animals – cats. Birthdays. Ethnic groups in the U.S. – Mexican Americans. Family life – aunts, uncles. Gifts.

Book fiesta! celebrate Children's Day/Book Day / Celebremos El día de los niños/El día de los libros: a bilingual picture book ill. by Rafael López. HarperCollins, 2009. ISBN 978-0-06-128877-7 Subj: Books, reading. Foreign languages. Holidays.

Confetti ill. by Enrique O. Sánchez. Lee & Low, 1996. ISBN 978-1-880000-25-0 Subj: Ethnic groups in the U.S. – Mexican Americans. Foreign languages. Poetry.

Delicious hullabaloo / Pachanga deliciosa ill. by Francisco X. Mora. Piñata, 1998. ISBN 978-1-55885-246-4 Subj: Animals. Desert. Foreign languages. Night. Parties. Poetry. Reptiles – lizards.

The desert is my mother / El desierto es mi madre ill. by Daniel Lechón. Piñata, 1994. ISBN 978-1-55885-121-4 Subj: Desert. Foreign languages. Poetry.

Doña Flor: a tall tale about a giant woman with a great big heart ill. by Raúl Colón. Random House, 2005. ISBN 978-0-679-98002-5 Subj: Animals – cougars. Giants. Tall tales.

The gift of the poinsettia / El regalo de la flor de nochebuena by Pat Mora and Charles Ramírez Berg ill. by Charles Ramírez Berg. Piñata, 1995. ISBN 978-1-55885-137-5 Subj: Foreign lands – Mexico. Foreign languages. Gifts. Holidays – Christmas.

Gracias / Thanks ill. by John Parra. Lee & Low, 2009. ISBN 978-1-60060-258-0 Subj: Character traits. Ethnic groups in the U.S. – Hispanic Americans. Foreign languages.

Here, kitty, kitty! / ¡Ven, gatita, ven! ill. by Maribel Suárez. HarperCollins, 2008. ISBN 978-0-06-085044-9 Subj: Animals – cats. Foreign languages.

Join hands! ill. by George Ancona. Charlesbridge, 2008. ISBN 978-1-58089-202-5 Subj: Activities. Friendship. World.

Let's eat! / A comer! ill. by Maribel Suárez. HarperCollins, 2008. ISBN 978-0-06-085038-8 Subj: Family life. Food. Foreign languages.

A library for Juana: the world of Sor Juana Inés ill. by Beatriz A. Vidal. Knopf, 2002. ISBN 978-0-375-80643-8 Subj: Books, reading. Careers – writers. Careers – nuns. Foreign lands – Mexico. Libraries.

Listen to the desert / Oye al desierto ill. by Francisco X. Mora. Clarion, 1994. ISBN 978-0-395-67292-1 Subj: Animals. Desert. Foreign languages. Noise, sounds. Poetry.

Marimba! animales from A to Z ill. by Doug Cushman. Houghton, 2006. ISBN 978-0-618-19453-7 Subj: ABC books. Animals. Foreign languages. Parties. Rhyming text. Zoos.

The night the moon fell: a Maya myth retold ill. by Domi. Douglas & McIntyre, 2000. ISBN 978-0-88899-398-4 Subj: Folk & fairy tales. Foreign lands – Mexico. Indians of Central America – Maya. Moon.

One, two, three / Uno, dos, tres ill. by Barbara Lavallee. Clarion, 1996. ISBN 978-0-395-67294-5 Subj: Birthdays. Counting, numbers. Foreign languages. Rhyming text.

Pablo's tree ill. by Cecily Lang. Macmillan, 1994. ISBN 978-0-02-767401-9 Subj: Adoption. Birthdays. Ethnic groups in the U.S. – Mexican Americans. Family life – grandfathers.

A piñata in a pine tree: a Latino twelve days of Christmas ill. by Magaly Morales. Clarion, 2009. ISBN 978-0-618-84198-1 Subj: Cumulative tales. Foreign lands – Latin America. Foreign languages. Holidays – Christmas. Music. Songs.

The race of toad and deer ill. by Maya Itzna Brooks. Orchard, 1995. ISBN 978-0-531-08777-0 Subj: Animals. Behavior – trickery. Folk & fairy tales. Foreign lands – Guatemala. Foreign languages. Sports – racing.

The rainbow tulip ill. by Elizabeth Sayles. Viking, 1999. ISBN 978-0-670-87291-6 Subj: Character traits – being different. Ethnic groups in the U.S. – Mexican Americans. Holidays – May Day. Parades. School.

The song of Francis and the animals ill. by David Frampton. Eerdmans, 2005. ISBN 978-0-8028-5253-3 Subj: Animals. Character traits – kindness to animals. Religion.

Sweet dreams / Dulces suenos ill. by Maribel Suárez. HarperCollins, 2008. ISBN 978-0-06-085041-8 Subj: Animals. Bedtime. Family life – grandmothers. Foreign languages.

This big sky ill. by Steve Jenkins. Scholastic, 1998. ISBN 978-0-590-37120-9 Subj: Animals. Desert. Poetry.

Tomás and the library lady ill. by Raúl Colón. Knopf, 1997. ISBN 978-0-679-90401-4 Subj: Books, reading. Careers – librarians. Careers – migrant workers. Ethnic groups in the U.S. – Mexican Americans. Libraries.

Yum! Mmmm! Que rico! Americas' sproutings ill. by Rafael López. Lee & Low, 2007. ISBN 978-1-58430-271-1 Subj: Food. Language. Poetry.

Morales, Melita. *Jam and honey* ill. by Laura J. Bryant. Tricycle, 2011. ISBN 978-1-58246-299-8 Subj: Insects – bees. Rhyming text.

Morales, Yuyi. *Just a minute: a trickster tale and counting book* ill. by author. Chronicle, 2003. ISBN 978-0-8118-3758-3 Subj: Behavior – trickery. Counting, numbers. Folk & fairy tales. Foreign lands – Mexico.

Just in case: a trickster tale and Spanish alphabet book ill. by author. Roaring Brook, 2008. ISBN 978-1-59643-329-8 Subj: ABC books. Anatomy – skeletons. Behavior – trickery. Birthdays. Folk & fairy tales. Foreign languages. Gifts.

Little night ill. by author. Macmillan, 2007. ISBN 978-1-59643-088-4 Subj: Bedtime. Night.

Nino wrestles the world ill. by author. Roaring Brook, 2013. ISBN 978-1-59643-604-6 Subj: Ethnic groups in the U.S. – Mexican Americans. Family life – brothers & sisters. Foreign languages. Sports – wrestling.

Moran, Alex. *Boots for Beth* ill. by Lisa Campbell Ernst. Harcourt, 2002. ISBN 978-0-15-216558-1 Subj: Animals. Animals – pigs. Clothing – boots.

Come here, tiger ill. by Lisa Campbell Ernst. Harcourt, 2001. ISBN 978-0-15-216218-4 Subj: Animals. Animals – cats. Pets.

Sam and Jack ill. by Tim Bowers. Harcourt, 2001. ISBN 978-0-15-216240-5 Subj: Animals – cats. Animals – mice. Friendship.

Morck, Irene. *Old bird* by Irene Morck and Muriel Wood ill. by Muriel Wood. Fitzhenry & Whiteside, 2003. ISBN 978-1-55041-695-4 Subj: Activities – working. Animals – horses, ponies. Friendship.

Mordvinoff, Nicolas. *Finders keepers* (Lipkind, William)

Moreillon, Judi. *Ready and waiting for you* ill. by Catherine Stock. Eerdmans, 2013. ISBN 978-0-8028-5355-4 Subj: Rhyming text. School – first day.

Moreton, Daniel, reteller. *La Cucaracha Martina: a Caribbean folktale* ill. by reteller. Turtle, 1997. ISBN 978-1-890515-03-4 Subj: Animals. Cities, towns. Folk & fairy tales. Foreign lands – Caribbean Islands. Foreign languages. Insects – cockroaches. Noise, sounds.

Morgan, Mary. *Dragon pizzeria* ill. by author. Knopf, 2008. ISBN 978-0-375-82309-1 Subj: Dragons. Folk & fairy tales. Food. Nursery rhymes.

My good night book ill. by author. Dutton, 2003. ISBN 978-0-525-46987-2 Subj: Bedtime. Format, unusual – toy & movable books. Night. Rhyming text.

Morgan, Michaela. *Brave, brave mouse* ill. by Michelle Cartlidge. Whitman, 2004. ISBN 978-0-8075-0869-5 Subj: Animals – mice. Character traits – bravery. Emotions – fear. Rhyming text.

Bunny wishes ill. by Caroline Jayne Church. Scholastic, 2007. ISBN 978-0-439-91812-1 Subj: Animals – mice. Animals – rabbits. Behavior – wishing. Friendship. Seasons – winter.

Dear bunny: a bunny love story ill. by Caroline Jayne Church. Scholastic, 2006. ISBN 978-0-439-74833-9 Subj: Activities – writing. Animals – mice. Animals – rabbits. Character traits – shyness. Emotions – love. Friendship.

Morgan, Richard. *Zoo poo* ill. by author. Barron's, 2004. ISBN 978-0-613-81357-0 Subj: Behavior – growing up. Toilet training. Zoos.

Morgan-Vanroyen, Mary. *Curious Rosie* ill. by author. Hyperion, 2000. ISBN 978-0-7868-0477-1 Subj: Animals – mice. Character traits – curiosity.

Gentle Rosie ill. by author. Hyperion, 1999. ISBN 978-0-7868-0474-0 Subj: Animals – mice. Behavior.

Patient Rosie ill. by author. Hyperion, 2000. ISBN 978-0-7868-0476-4 Subj: Animals – mice. Character traits – patience.

Sleep tight, little mouse ill. by author. Knopf, 2003. ISBN 978-0-375-92308-1 Subj: Animals – mice. Bedtime. Family life – mothers.

Wild Rosie ill. by author. Hyperion, 1999. ISBN 978-0-7868-0475-7 Subj: Activities – playing. Animals – mice. Behavior.

Morison, Toby. *Little Louie takes off* ill. by author. Walker, 2007. ISBN 978-0-8027-9645-5 Subj: Activities – flying. Birds – penguins. Emotions – loneliness.

Morlock, Lisa. *Track that scat!* ill. by Carrie Anne Bradshaw. Sleeping Bear, 2012. ISBN 978-1-58536-536-4 Subj: Animals. Nature.

Moroney, Trace. *When I'm feeling angry* ill. by author. School Specialty/Gingham Dog, 2006. ISBN 978-0-7696-4424-0 Subj: Animals – rabbits. Emotions – anger.

When I'm feeling happy ill. by author. School Specialty/Gingham Dog, 2006. ISBN 978-0-7696-4425-7 Subj: Animals – rabbits. Emotions – happiness.

When I'm feeling sad ill. by author. School Specialty/Gingham Dog, 2006. ISBN 978-0-7696-4426-4 Subj: Animals – rabbits. Emotions – sadness.

When I'm feeling scared ill. by author. School Specialty/Gingham Dog, 2006. ISBN 978-0-7696-4427-1 Subj: Animals – rabbits. Emotions – fear.

Morozumi, Atsuko. *Helping daddy* ill. by author. Knopf, 2000. ISBN 978-0-375-80593-6 Subj: Family life. Format, unusual – board books.

In the park ill. by author. Knopf, 2000. ISBN 978-0-375-80591-2 Subj: Format, unusual – board books. Parks.

My friend gorilla ill. by author. Farrar, 1998. ISBN 978-0-374-35458-9 Subj: Animals – gorillas. Foreign lands – Africa. Friendship. Pets. Zoos.

One gorilla ill. by author. Farrar, 1990. ISBN 978-0-374-35644-6 Subj: Animals. Animals – gorillas. Counting, numbers.

Playing ill. by author. Knopf, 2000. ISBN 978-0-375-80592-9 Subj: Activities – playing. Format, unusual – board books.

Time for bed ill. by author. Knopf, 2000. ISBN 978-0-375-80594-3 Subj: Bedtime. Format, unusual – board books.

Morpurgo, Michael. *On angel wings* ill. by Quentin Blake. Candlewick, 2007. ISBN 978-0-7636-3466-7 Subj: Angels. Holidays – Christmas. Religion – Nativity.

The silver swan ill. by Christian Birmingham. Fogelman, 2000. ISBN 978-0-8037-2543-0 Subj: Birds – swans. Seasons – winter.

Wombat goes walkabout ill. by Christian Birmingham. Candlewick, 2000. ISBN 978-0-7636-1168-2 Subj: Animals. Animals – wombats. Behavior – lost. Foreign lands – Australia.

Morris, Ann. *Bread, bread, bread* photos by Ken Heyman. Lothrop, 1989. ISBN 978-0-688-06335-1 Subj: Food.

Families ill. with photos. HarperCollins, 2000. ISBN 978-0-688-17199-5 Subj: Character traits – individuality. Family life.

Grandma Esther remembers photos by Peter Linenthal. Millbrook, 2002. ISBN 978-0-7613-2318-1 Subj: Family life – grandmothers. Holocaust. Jewish culture. Memories, memory.

Grandma Francisca remembers photos by Peter Linenthal. Millbrook, 2002. ISBN 978-0-7613-2315-0 Subj: Ethnic groups in the U.S. – Hispanic Americans. Family life – grandmothers. Memories, memory.

Grandma Lai Goon remembers photos by Peter Linenthal. Millbrook, 2002. ISBN 978-0-7613-2314-3 Subj: Ethnic groups in the U.S. – Chinese Americans. Family life – grandmothers. Foreign lands – China. Memories, memory.

Grandma Lois remembers photos by Peter Linenthal. Millbrook, 2002. ISBN 978-0-7613-2316-7 Subj: Ethnic groups in the U.S. – African Americans. Family life – grandmothers. Memories, memory. Prejudice.

Grandma Maxine remembers photos by Peter Linenthal. Millbrook, 2002. ISBN 978-0-7613-2317-4 Subj: Family life – grandmothers. Indians of North America – Shoshone. Memories, memory.

Hats, hats, hats photos by Ken Heyman. Lothrop, 1989. ISBN 978-0-688-06339-9 Subj: Clothing – hats.

Houses and homes photos by Ken Heyman. Lothrop, 1992. ISBN 978-0-688-10169-5 Subj: Foreign lands. Homes, houses.

Light the candle! Bang the drum! ill. by Peter Linenthal. Dutton, 1997. ISBN 978-0-525-45639-1 Subj: Holidays.

Loving photos by Ken Heyman. Lothrop, 1990. ISBN 978-0-688-06341-2 Subj: Emotions – love. Family life. Foreign lands.

The mommy book photos by Ken Heyman. Silver Pr., 1996. ISBN 978-0-382-24693-7 Subj: Family life – mothers.

On the go photos by Ken Heyman. Lothrop, 1990. ISBN 978-0-688-06337-5 Subj: Foreign lands. Transportation.

Play photos by Ken Heyman. Lothrop, 1998. ISBN 978-0-688-14553-8 Subj: Activities – playing. Foreign lands. Imagination.

Shoes, shoes, shoes photos by author. Lothrop, 1995. ISBN 978-0-688-13667-3 Subj: Clothing – shoes. Rhyming text.

Tools photos by Ken Heyman. Lothrop, 1992. ISBN 978-0-688-10171-8 Subj: Tools.

Weddings photos by Ken Heyman. Lothrop, 1995. ISBN 978-0-688-13273-6 Subj: Clothing. Weddings.

Work photos by Ken Heyman. Lothrop, 1998. ISBN 978-0-688-14867-6 Subj: Activities – working. Careers. Foreign lands.

Morris, Bob. *Crispin the Terrible* ill. by Dasha Ziborova. Callaway, 2000. ISBN 978-0-935112-44-3 Subj: Animals – cats. Imagination.

Morris, Carla. *The boy who was raised by librarians* ill. by Brad Sneed. Peachtree, 2007. ISBN 978-1-56145-391-7 Subj: Books, reading. Careers – librarians. Libraries.

Morris, Dewi. *Sandy's street* ill. by author. Little, 2001. ISBN 978-0-316-83609-8 Subj: Animals – cats. Format, unusual – toy & movable books. Roads.

Morris, Jackie. *I am Cat* ill. by author. Frances Lincoln, 2013. ISBN 978-1-84780-135-7 Subj: Animals – cats.

Morris, Jennifer E. *May I please have a cookie?* ill. by Jennifer Morris. Scholastic, 2005. ISBN 978-0-439-73819-4 Subj: Etiquette. Food. Reptiles – alligators, crocodiles.

Morris, Richard. *Bye-bye, baby!* ill. by Larry Day. Walker, 2009. ISBN 978-0-8027-9772-8 Subj: Babies. Family life – new sibling. Zoos.

Morrison, Cathy. *I want a pet!* ill. by author. Tiger Tales, 2012. ISBN 978-1-58925-113-7 Subj: Pets. Rhyming text. Zoos.

Morrison, Gordon. *A drop of water* ill. by author. Houghton, 2006. ISBN 978-0-618-58557-1 Subj: Science. Water.

Morrison, Slade. *Little Cloud and Lady Wind* (Morrison, Toni)

Peeny butter fudge (Morrison, Toni)

The tortoise or the hare (Morrison, Toni)

Morrison, Toni. *The book of mean people* ill. by Pascal Lemaître. Hyperion, 2002. ISBN 978-0-7868-2471-7 Subj: Behavior – bullying, teasing. Behavior – fighting, arguing. Character traits – meanness. Emotions – anger.

Little Cloud and Lady Wind by Toni Morrison and Slade Morrison ill. by Sean Qualls. Simon & Schuster, 2010. ISBN 978-1-4169-8523-5 Subj: Character traits – individuality. Weather – clouds. Weather – wind.

Peeny butter fudge by Toni Morrison and Slade Morrison ill. by Joe Cepeda. Simon & Schuster, 2009. ISBN 978-1-4169-8332-3 Subj: Activities – playing. Ethnic groups in the U.S. – African Americans. Family life – grandmothers. Food. Rhyming text.

The tortoise or the hare by Toni Morrison and Slade Morrison ill. by Joe Cepeda. Simon & Schuster, 2010. ISBN 978-1-4169-8334-7 Subj: Animals – rabbits. Folk & fairy tales. Reptiles – turtles, tortoises. Sports – racing.

Morrissey, Dean. *The Christmas ship* ill. by author. HarperCollins, 2000. ISBN 978-0-06-028576-0 Subj: Boats, ships. Gifts. Holidays – Christmas. Magic. Santa Claus. Toys.

The crimson comet by Dean Morrissey and Stephen Krensky ill. by Dean Morrissey. HarperCollins, 2006. ISBN 978-0-06-008070-9 Subj: Bedtime. Family life – brothers & sisters. Moon. Space & space ships.

The wizard mouse ill. by author. HarperCollins, 2011. ISBN 978-0-06-008066-2 Subj: Animals – mice. Magic. Wizards.

Morrow, Barbara Olenyik. *Mr. Mosquito put on his tuxedo* ill. by Ponder Goembel. Holiday, 2009. ISBN 978-0-8234-2072-8 Subj: Insects. Insects – mosquitoes. Parties. Rhyming text.

Morrow, Tara Jaye. *Mommy loves her baby; Daddy loves his baby* ill. by Tiphanie Beeke. HarperCollins, 2003. ISBN 978-0-06-029078-8 Subj: Animals. Babies. Emotions – love. Family life – parents. Format, unusual. Rhyming text.

Panda goes to school ill. by Aaron Boyd. Sterling, 2007. ISBN 978-1-4027-4313-9 Subj: Animals – pandas. Family life – mothers. School – first day.

Morstad, Julie. *How to* ill. by author. Simply Read, 2013. ISBN 978-1-897476-57-4 Subj: Activities – playing. Behavior. Character traits. Imagination.

Mortensen, Denise Dowling. *Bug Patrol* ill. by Cece Bell. Clarion, 2013. ISBN 978-0-618-79024-1 Subj: Careers – police officers. Insects. Rhyming text.

Ohio thunder ill. by Kate Kiesler. Houghton, 2006. ISBN 978-0-618-59542-6 Subj: Farms. Weather – lightning, thunder. Weather – storms.

Wake up engines ill. by Melissa Iwai. Houghton, 2007. ISBN 978-0-618-51736-7 Subj: Morning. Rhyming text. Transportation.

Mortensen, Lori. *Cindy Moo* ill. by Jeff Mack. HarperCollins, 2012. ISBN 978-0-06-204393-1 Subj: Animals – bulls, cows. Character traits – persistence. Moon. Nursery rhymes. Rhyming text.

Cowpoke Clyde and Dirty Dawg ill. by Michael Austin. Clarion, 2013. ISBN 978-0-547-23993-4 Subj: Activities – bathing. Animals – dogs. Cowboys, cowgirls.

Mortenson, Greg. *Listen to the wind: the story of Dr. Greg and three cups of tea* by Greg Mortenson and Susan L. Roth ill. by Susan L. Roth. Dial, 2009. ISBN 978-0-8037-3058-8 Subj: Behavior – seeking better things. Character traits – completing things. Character traits – perseverance. Foreign lands – Pakistan. Gender roles. School.

Mortimer, Anne. *Bunny's Easter egg* ill. by author. HarperCollins, 2010. ISBN 978-0-06-126664-2 Subj: Animals – rabbits. Eggs. Holidays – Easter. Sleep.

Pumpkin cat ill. by author. HarperCollins, 2011. ISBN 978-0-06-187485-7 Subj: Animals – cats. Animals – mice. Gardens, gardening. Holidays – Halloween.

Mortimer, Rachael. *Red Riding Hood and the sweet little wolf* ill. by Liz Pichon. Tiger Tales, 2013. ISBN 978-1-58925-117-5 Subj: Animals – wolves. Character traits – being different. Family life – grandmothers. Folk & fairy tales.

Song for a princess ill. by Maddy McClellan. Scholastic, 2010. ISBN 978-0-545-24835-8 Subj: Activities – storytelling. Birds. Communication. Emotions – loneliness. Language. Royalty – princesses.

The three Billy Goats Fluff ill. by Liz Pichon. Tiger Tales, 2011. ISBN 978-1-58925-101-4 Subj: Activities – knitting. Animals – goats. Mythical creatures – trolls.

Morton, Carlene. *The library pages* ill. by Valeria Docampo. Upstart, 2010. ISBN 978-1-60213-045-6 Subj: Holidays – April Fools' Day. Libraries. School.

Morton, Lone. *Hurry up, Molly / Apúrate, Molly* ill. by Gill Scriven. Barron's, 2000. ISBN 978-0-7641-5286-3 Subj: Bedtime. Family life – fathers. Foreign languages.

Hurry up, Molly / Dépêche-toi, Molly ill. by Gill Scriven. Barron's, 2000. ISBN 978-0-7641-5287-0 Subj: Bedtime. Family life – fathers. Foreign languages.

Morton-Shaw, Christine. *Wake up, sleepy bear!* by Christine Morton-Shaw and Greg Shaw ill. by John Butler. Penguin, 2006. ISBN 978-0-670-06175-4 Subj: Animals – babies. Rhyming text.

Mosel, Arlene. *The funny little woman* ill. by Blair Lent. Dutton, 1972. ISBN 978-0-525-30265-0 Subj: Caldecott award books. Foreign lands – Japan. Monsters.

Tikki Tikki Tembo ill. by Blair Lent. Holt, 1968. ISBN 978-0-8050-0662-9 Subj: Folk & fairy tales. Foreign lands – China. Names.

Moseley, Keith. *Where's the dinosaur?* ill. by author. Sterling, 2012. ISBN 978-1-4027-8894-9 Subj: Activities – ballooning. Counting, numbers. Dinosaurs. Family life – grandfathers. Picture puzzles.

Moser, Barry. *Psalm 23* ill. by author. Zondervan, 2008. ISBN 978-0-310-71085-1 Subj: Careers – shepherds. Foreign lands – Caribbean Islands. Religion.

Moser, Lisa. *Cowboy Boyd and Mighty Calliope* ill. by Sebastiaan Van Doninck. Random House, 2013. ISBN 978-0-375-87056-9 Subj: Animals – rhinoceros. Careers – ranchers. Cowboys, cowgirls.

Perfect soup ill. by Ben Mantle. Random House, 2010. ISBN 978-0-375-86014-0 Subj: Animals – mice. Cumulative tales. Food. Snowmen.

Railroad Hank ill. by Benji Davies. Random House, 2012. ISBN 978-0-375-86849-8 Subj: Careers – railroad engineers. Family life – grandmothers. Farms. Humorous stories. Trains.

Watermelon wishes ill. by Stacey Schuett. Houghton, 2006. ISBN 978-0-618-56433-0 Subj: Behavior – wishing. Family life – grandfathers. Food.

Moses, Will. *Mary and her little lamb: the true story of the famous nursery rhyme* ill. by author. Penguin, 2011. ISBN 978-0-399-25154-2 Subj: Animals – sheep. Farms. School. U.S. history.

Raining cats and dogs: a collection of irresistible idioms and illustrations to tickle the funny bones of young people ill. by author. Philomel, 2008. ISBN 978-0-399-24233-5 Subj: Language.

Silent night ill. by author. Philomel, 1997. ISBN 978-0-399-23100-1 Subj: Babies. Family life. Holidays – Christmas. Songs.

Moss, Jenny Jackson. *Cajun night after Christmas* by Jenny Jackson Moss and Amy Jackson Dixon ill. by James Rice. Pelican, 2000. ISBN 978-1-56554-779-7 Subj: Ethnic groups in the U.S. Holidays – Christmas. Poetry. Reptiles – alligators, crocodiles. Santa Claus.

Moss, Lloyd. *Our marching band* ill. by Diana Cain Bluthenthal. Putnam, 2001. ISBN 978-0-399-23335-7 Subj: Music. Musical instruments – bands. Rhyming text.

Zin! zin! zin! A violin ill. by Marjorie Priceman. Simon & Schuster, 1995. ISBN 978-0-671-88239-6 Subj: Caldecott award honor books. Counting, numbers. Music. Musical instruments – violins. Rhyming text.

Moss, Marissa. *Knick knack paddywack* ill. by author. Houghton, 1992. ISBN 978-0-395-54701-4 Subj: Activities – making things. Animals – dogs. Counting, numbers. Cumulative tales. Songs. Space & space ships.

Regina's big mistake ill. by author. Houghton, 1990. ISBN 978-0-395-55330-5 Subj: Activities – drawing. Art. Careers – artists. School. Self-concept.

Sky high: the true story of Maggie Gee ill. by Carl Angel. Tricycle, 2009. ISBN 978-1-58246-280-6 Subj: Careers – airplane pilots. Ethnic groups in the U.S. – Chinese Americans. Gender roles. U.S. history. War.

True heart ill. by C. F. Payne. Silver Whistle, 1999. ISBN 978-0-15-201344-8 Subj: Careers – engineers. Gender roles. Trains.

Moss, Miriam. *A babysitter for Billy Bear* ill. by Anna Currey. Dial, 2008. ISBN 978-0-8037-3269-8 Subj: Activities – babysitting. Animals – bears. Behavior – worrying.

Bad hare day ill. by Lynne Chapman. Bloomsbury, 2003. ISBN 978-1-58234-785-1 Subj: Animals. Animals – rabbits. Behavior – misbehavior. Family life – aunts, uncles. Hair.

Bare bear ill. by Mary McQuillan. Holiday House, 2005. ISBN 978-0-8234-1934-0 Subj: Animals – bears. Behavior – lost & found possessions. Clothing. Rhyming text.

I'll be your friend, Smudge ill. by Lynne Chapman. Gullane, 2001. ISBN 978-1-86233-207-2 Subj: Animals – mice. Birthdays. Friendship. Moving.

It's my turn, Smudge ill. by Lynne Chapman. Gullane, 2001. ISBN 978-1-86233-287-4 Subj: Animals – mice. Behavior – sharing.

Matty in a mess! ill. by Jane Simmons. Andersen, 2010. ISBN 978-1-84270-812-5 Subj: Animals – bears. Animals – cats. Behavior – messy. Character traits – cleanliness.

Matty takes off! ill. by Jane Simmons. Andersen, 2010. ISBN 978-1-84270-758-6 Subj: Activities – traveling. Animals – bears. Animals – cats. Behavior – lost & found possessions.

A new house for Smudge ill. by Lynne Chapman. Gullane, 2001. ISBN 978-1-86233-202-7 Subj: Animals – mice. Homes, houses. Moving.

Smudge's grumpy day ill. by Lynne Chapman. Gullane, 2001. ISBN 978-1-86233-282-9 Subj: Behavior – bad day. Behavior – running away. Emotions – anger.

The snow bear ill. by Maggie Kneen. Dutton, 2000. ISBN 978-0-525-46658-1 Subj: Activities – playing. Animals – polar bears. Behavior – lost. Family life – mothers. Foreign lands – Arctic.

This is the mountain ill. by Adrienne Kennaway. Frances Lincoln, 2011. ISBN 978-1-84507-984-0 Subj: Foreign lands – Africa. Mountains.

This is the oasis ill. by Adrienne Kennaway. Kane/Miller, 2005. ISBN 978-1-929132-76-8 Subj: Desert. Foreign lands – Africa.

This is the tree ill. by Adrienne Kennaway. Kane/Miller, 2000. ISBN 978-0-916291-98-3 Subj: Animals. Ecology. Foreign lands – Africa. Trees.

Wibble wobble ill. by Joanna Mockler. Tiger Tales, 2001. ISBN 978-1-58925-013-0 Subj: Behavior – lost & found possessions. School. Teeth.

Moss, Onawumi Jean. *Precious and the Boo Hag* (McKissack, Patricia C.)

Moss, P. Buckley. *Reuben and the quilt* ill. by author. Text by Merle Good. Good Books, 1999. ISBN 978-1-56148-234-4 Subj: Crime. Ethnic groups in the U.S. – Amish. Quilts.

Moss, Peggy. *One of us* ill. by Penny Weber. Tilbury House, 2010. ISBN 978-0-88448-322-9 Subj: Character traits – individuality. Friendship. Moving. School.

Say something ill. by Lea Lyon. Tilbury, 2004. ISBN 978-0-88448-261-1 Subj: Behavior – bullying, teasing.

Moss, Thylias. *I want to be* ill. by Jerry Pinkney. Dial, 1993. ISBN 978-0-8037-1287-4 Subj: Behavior – growing up. Ethnic groups in the U.S. – African Americans.

Most, Bernard. *ABC T-Rex* ill. by author. Harcourt, 2000. ISBN 978-0-15-202007-1 Subj: ABC books. Dinosaurs.

Cock-a-doodle-moo! ill. by author. Harcourt, 1996. ISBN 978-0-15-201252-6 Subj: Animals. Birds – chickens. Careers – farmers. Farms. Morning.

The cow that went oink ill. by author. Harcourt, 1990. ISBN 978-0-15-220195-1 Subj: Animals. Noise, sounds.

A dinosaur named after me ill. by author. Harcourt, 1991. ISBN 978-0-15-223494-2 Subj: Dinosaurs. Names. Prehistory.

Dinosaur questions ill. by author. Harcourt, 1995. ISBN 978-0-15-292885-8 Subj: Dinosaurs. Prehistory.

How big were the dinosaurs? ill. by author. Harcourt, 1994. ISBN 978-0-15-236800-5 Subj: Concepts – size. Dinosaurs. Prehistory.

If the dinosaurs came back ill. by author. Harcourt, 1995. ISBN 978-0-15-238020-5 Subj: Dinosaurs. Imagination. Prehistory.

A pair of protoceratops ill. by author. Harcourt, 1998. ISBN 978-0-15-201443-8 Subj: Activities. Dinosaurs.

A trio of triceratops ill. by author. Harcourt, 1998. ISBN 978-0-15-201448-3 Subj: Activities. Dinosaurs.

Whatever happened to the dinosaurs? ill. by author. Harcourt, 1995. ISBN 978-0-15-200378-4 Subj: Dinosaurs. Prehistory.

Z-Z-Zoink! ill. by author. Harcourt, 1999. ISBN 978-0-15-292845-2 Subj: Animals – pigs. Birds – owls. Noise, sounds. Sleep.

Mother Goose. *Arnold Lobel book of Mother Goose* ill. by Arnold Lobel. Knopf, 1997. ISBN 978-0-679-98736-9 Subj: Nursery rhymes. Poetry.

Baa baa black sheep (Trapani, Iza)

Baa baa black sheep [board book] (Trapani, Iza)

The baby's lap book ill. by Kay Chorao. Dutton, 1990. ISBN 978-0-525-44604-0 Subj: Nursery rhymes.

The cat and the fiddle: a treasury of nursery rhymes ill. by Jackie Morris. Frances Lincoln, 2011. ISBN 978-1-84507-987-4 Subj: Nursery rhymes.

The Chinese Mother Goose rhymes by Robert Wyndham; ill. by Ed Young. Sel. & ed. by Robert Wyndham. Putnam, 1982. ISBN 978-0-399-20866-9 Subj: Nursery rhymes.

Hey, diddle, diddle comp. by Linda Bronson; ill. by compiler. Holt, 2003. ISBN 978-0-8050-6754-5 Subj: Animals. Moon. Nursery rhymes.

Hey, diddle, diddle ill. by Heather Collins. Kids Can, 2003. ISBN 978-1-55337-078-9 Subj: Animals. Moon. Nursery rhymes.

Hickory, dickory, dock ill. by Heather Collins. Kids Can, 1997. ISBN 978-1-55074-408-8 Subj: Format, unusual – board books. Nursery rhymes.

Hickory, dickory, dock adapt. by Robin Muller; ill. by Suzanne Duranceau. Scholastic, 1994. ISBN 978-0-590-47278-4 Subj: Animals. Clocks, watches. Parties. Rhyming text.

Hickory dickory dock and other nursery rhymes ill. by Carol Jones. Houghton, 1992. ISBN 978-0-395-60834-0 Subj: Format, unusual. Nursery rhymes.

Humpty Dumpty ill. by Annie Kubler. Child's Play, 2010. ISBN 978-1-84643-339-9 Subj: Eggs. Format, unusual – board books. Nursery rhymes. Rhyming text.

Humpty Dumpty and other rhymes ed. by Iona Opie; ill. by Rosemary Wells. Candlewick, 1997. ISBN 978-0-7636-0353-3 Subj: Format, unusual – board books. Nursery rhymes.

Ian Penney's book of nursery rhymes ill. by Ian Penney. Abrams, 1994. ISBN 978-0-8109-3733-8 Subj: Nursery rhymes.

Jack and Jill ill. by Heather Collins. Kids Can, 2003. ISBN 978-1-55337-075-8 Subj: Format, unusual – board books. Nursery rhymes.

James Marshall's Mother Goose ill. by James Marshall. Farrar, 1979. ISBN 978-0-374-33653-0 Subj: Nursery rhymes.

Little Boy Blue and other rhymes ed. by Iona Opie; ill. by Rosemary Wells. Candlewick, 1997. ISBN 978-0-7636-0354-0 Subj: Format, unusual – board books. Nursery rhymes.

Little Miss Muffet ill. by Heather Collins. Kids Can, 2003. ISBN 978-1-55337-076-5 Subj: Format, unusual – board books. Nursery rhymes.

Little Miss Muffet adapt. by Tracey Campbell Pearson; ill. by adapter. Farrar, 2005. ISBN 978-0-374-30862-9 Subj: Format, unusual – board books. Nursery rhymes. Spiders.

Mother Goose sel. by Scott Cook; ill. by selector. Knopf, 1994. ISBN 978-0-679-90949-1 Subj: Nursery rhymes.

Mother Goose sel. by Michael Hague; ill. by selector. Holt, 1984. ISBN 978-0-03-070723-0 Subj: Nursery rhymes.

Mother Goose ill. by Tasha Tudor. Walck, 1944. Subj: Caldecott award honor books. Nursery rhymes.

Mother Goose numbers on the loose adapt. by Leo Dillon; adapt. by Diane Dillon; ill. by authors. Harcourt, 2007. ISBN 978-0-15-205676-6 Subj: Counting, numbers. Nursery rhymes.

Mother Goose remembers ill. by Clare Beaton. Barefoot, 2000. ISBN 978-1-84148-073-2 Subj: Nursery rhymes.

The movable Mother Goose (Sabuda, Robert)

My first real Mother Goose [board book] ill. by Blanche Fisher Wright. Scholastic, 2000. ISBN 978-0-439-14671-5 Subj: Format, unusual – board books. Nursery rhymes.

1, 2, buckle my shoe by Anna Grossnickle Hines; ill. by author. Harcourt, 2008. ISBN 978-0-15-206305-4 Subj: Counting, numbers. Nursery rhymes. Rhyming text.

One, two, buckle my shoe [board book] ill. by Heather Collins. Kids Can, 1997. ISBN 978-1-55074-410-1 Subj: Nursery rhymes.

Over the candlestick: classic nursery rhymes and the real stories behind them (Montgomery, Michael G.)

Pat-a-cake adapt. by R. A. Herman; ill. by Olga Ivanov and Aleksey Ivanov. Handprint, 2005. ISBN 978-1-59354-039-5 Subj: Activities – baking, cooking. Format, unusual – board books. Games. Nursery rhymes.

Pat-a-cake ill. by Annie Kubler. Child's Play, 2010. ISBN 978-1-84643-338-2 Subj: Activities – baking, cooking. Format, unusual – board books. Nursery rhymes. Rhyming text.

Pat-a-cake [board book] ill. by Heather Collins. Kids Can, 2003. ISBN 978-1-55337-077-2 Subj: Format, unusual – board books. Nursery rhymes.

Pussycat, pussycat and other rhymes ed. by Iona Opie; ill. by Rosemary Wells. Candlewick, 1997. ISBN 978-0-7636-0355-7 Subj: Format, unusual – board books. Nursery rhymes.

Richard Scarry's best Mother Goose ever ill. by Richard Scarry. Golden Pr., 1970. ISBN 978-0-307-15578-8 Subj: Nursery rhymes.

Rock-a-bye baby [board book] ill. by Heather Collins. Kids Can, 2000. ISBN 978-1-55074-572-6 Subj: Format, unusual – board books. Nursery rhymes.

This little piggy [board book] ill. by Heather Collins. Kids Can, 1997. ISBN 978-1-55074-404-0 Subj: Format, unusual – board books. Nursery rhymes.

The three jovial huntsmen ill. by Susan Jeffers. Bradbury, 1973. ISBN 978-0-87888-023-2 Subj: Caldecott award honor books. Nursery rhymes.

Three little kittens (Siomades, Lorianne)

The three little kittens ill. by Paul Galdone. Clarion, 1986. ISBN 978-0-89919-426-4 Subj: Animals – cats. Behavior – lost & found possessions. Clothing – gloves, mittens. Nursery rhymes.

Tomie de Paola's Mother Goose (dePaola, Tomie)

Wee Willie Winkie [board book] ill. by Heather Collins. Kids Can, 2000. ISBN 978-1-55074-568-9 Subj: Format, unusual – board books. Nursery rhymes.

Wee Willie Winkie and other rhymes ed. by Iona Opie; ill. by Rosemary Wells. Candlewick, 1997. ISBN 978-0-7636-0356-4 Subj: Format, unusual – board books. Nursery rhymes.

Wendy Watson's Mother Goose ill. by Wendy Watson. Lothrop, 1989. ISBN 978-0-688-05708-4 Subj: Nursery rhymes.

Will Moses Mother Goose ill. by Will Moses. Philomel, 2003. ISBN 978-0-399-23744-7 Subj: Nursery rhymes.

Mould, Wendy. *Ants in my pants* ill. by author. Clarion, 2001. ISBN 978-0-618-09640-4 Subj: Clothing. Humorous stories. Imagination.

Moulton, Mark Kimball. *Reindeer Christmas* ill. by Karen Hillard Good. Simon & Schuster, 2008. ISBN 978-1-4169-6108-6 Subj: Animals – reindeer. Holidays – Christmas. Rhyming text.

The very best pumpkin ill. by Karen Hillard Good. Simon & Schuster, 2010. ISBN 978-1-4169-8288-3 Subj: Farms. Friendship. Gardens, gardening.

Moundlic, Charlotte. *The scar* ill. by Olivier Tallec. Candlewick, 2011. ISBN 978-0-7636-5341-5 Subj: Death. Emotions – grief. Family life – mothers.

Moxley, Sheila. *ABCD an alphabet book of cats and dogs* ill. by author. Little, 2001. ISBN 978-0-316-59240-6 Subj: ABC books. Animals – cats. Animals – dogs.

Mozelle, Shirley. *The bear upstairs* ill. by Doug Cushman. Holt, 2005. ISBN 978-0-8050-6820-7 Subj: Activities – baking, cooking. Animals – bears. Noise, sounds.

The kitchen talks ill. by Petra Mathers. Holt, 2006. ISBN 978-0-8050-7143-6 Subj: Food. Homes, houses. Poetry.

The pig is in the pantry, the cat is on the shelf ill. by Jennifer Plecas. Clarion, 2000. ISBN 978-0-395-78627-7 Subj: Animals. Behavior – misbehavior. Farms. Homes, houses. Pets.

Mraz, David. *Little Goose* ill. by Margot Apple. Tricycle, 2009. ISBN 978-1-58246-190-8 Subj: Birds – geese. Family life – mothers.

Muecke, Anne. *The dinosaurs' night before Christmas* ill. by Nathan Hale. Chronicle, 2008. ISBN 978-0-8118-6322-3 Subj: Dinosaurs. Holidays – Christmas. Rhyming text.

Mueller, Dagmar H. *David's world: a picture book about living with autism* ill. by Verena Ballhaus. Skyhorse/Sky Pony, 2012. ISBN 978-1-61608-962-7 Subj: Disabilities – autism.

Mueller, Doris L. *Small One's adventure* ill. by Parker Fulton. All About Kids, 2003. ISBN 978-0-

9710278-1-7 Subj: Animals – elephants. Behavior – growing up. Concepts – size. Self-concept.

Muir, Leslie. *C.R. Mudgeon* ill. by Julian Hector. Simon & Schuster, 2012. ISBN 978-1-4169-7906-7 Subj: Animals – hedgehogs. Animals – squirrels. Friendship.

The little bitty bakery ill. by Betsy Lewin. Hyperion/Disney, 2011. ISBN 978-1-4231-1640-0 Subj: Activities – baking, cooking. Animals – elephants. Animals – mice. Birthdays. Rhyming text.

Muldrow, Diane. *We planted a tree* ill. by Bob Staake. Random House, 2010. ISBN 978-0-375-86432-2 Subj: Ecology. Trees.

Müller, Birte. *Finn cooks* ill. by author. NorthSouth, 2004. ISBN 978-0-7358-1936-8 Subj: Activities – baking, cooking. Family life – mothers. Food. Health & fitness.

I can dress myself! ill. by author. NorthSouth, 2007. ISBN 978-0-7358-2128-6 Subj: Animals – rabbits. Clothing.

Muller, Robin. *Badger's new house* ill. by author. Holt, 2002. ISBN 978-0-8050-6383-7 Subj: Animals – badgers. Animals – mice. Homes, houses.

The lucky old woman ill. by author. Kids Can, 1987. ISBN 978-0-921103-07-3 Subj: Folk & fairy tales.

Mullins, Patricia. *One horse waiting for me* ill. by author. Simon & Schuster, 1998. ISBN 978-0-689-81381-8 Subj: Animals – horses, ponies. Counting, numbers.

V for vanishing: an alphabet of endangered animals ill. by author. HarperCollins, 1994. ISBN 978-0-06-023557-4 Subj: ABC books. Animals – endangered animals.

Munari, Bruno. *ABC* ill. by author. Collins-World, 1960. Subj: ABC books.

Bruno Munari's zoo ill. by author. Collins-World, 1963. Subj: Animals. Birds. Zoos.

Munro, Roxie. *Amazement Park* ill. by author. Chronicle, 2005. ISBN 978-0-8118-4581-6 Subj: Picture puzzles.

Busy builders ill. by author. Marshall Cavendish, 2012. ISBN 978-0-7614-6105-0 Subj: Insects.

Circus ill. by author. Chronicle, 2006. ISBN 978-0-8118-5209-8 Subj: Circus. Format, unusual – toy & movable books. Picture puzzles. Rhyming text.

Desert days, desert nights ill. by author. Bright Sky, 2010. ISBN 978-1-933979-77-9 Subj: Day. Desert. Ecology. Night.

Ecomazes: twelve Earth adventures ill. by author. Sterling, 2010. ISBN 978-1-4027-6393-9 Subj: Earth. Ecology. Picture puzzles.

Go! go! go! with more than 70 flaps to uncover and discover ill. by author. Sterling, 2009. ISBN 978-1-4027-3773-2 Subj: Concepts – speed. Format, unusual – toy & movable books. Transportation.

Hatch! ill. by author. Marshall Cavendish, 2011. ISBN 978-0-7614-5882-1 Subj: Birds. Character traits – questioning. Eggs.

The inside-outside book of libraries ill. by author. Dutton, 1996. ISBN 978-0-525-45608-7 Subj: Libraries.

The inside-outside book of London ill. by author. Dutton, 1989. ISBN 978-0-525-44522-7 Subj: Cities, towns. Foreign lands – England.

The inside-outside book of New York City ill. by author. Dodd, 1985. ISBN 978-0-396-08513-3 Subj: Cities, towns.

The inside-outside book of Paris ill. by author. Dutton, 1992. ISBN 978-0-525-44863-1 Subj: Cities, towns. Foreign lands – France.

The inside-outside book of Texas ill. by author. SeaStar, 2001. ISBN 978-1-58717-050-8 Subj: Activities – traveling. Cities, towns. Country. Cowboys, cowgirls. Museums. Texas. U.S. history.

The inside-outside book of Washington, D.C. ill. by author. Dutton, 1987. ISBN 978-0-525-44298-1 Subj: Activities – traveling. Cities, towns. Museums.

Inside-outside dinosaurs ill. by author. Marshall Cavendish, 2009. ISBN 978-0-7614-5624-7 Subj: Dinosaurs.

Mazescapes ill. by author. SeaStar, 2001. ISBN 978-1-58717-060-7 Subj: Activities – traveling. Cities, towns. Country. Games. Mazes. Picture puzzles.

Mazeways: A to Z ill. by author. Sterling, 2007. ISBN 978-1-4027-3774-9 Subj: Picture puzzles.

Rodeo ill. by author. Bright Sky, 2007. ISBN 978-1-933979-03-8 Subj: Rodeos.

Munsch, Robert N. *Aaron's hair* ill. by Alan Daniel and Lea Daniel. Scholastic, 2000. ISBN 978-0-439-19258-3 Subj: Behavior – running away. Emotions. Hair.

Alligator baby ill. by Michael Martchenko. Scholastic, 1997. ISBN 978-0-590-21101-7 Subj: Animals. Babies. Family life – brothers & sisters. Family life – new sibling. Zoos.

Andrew's loose tooth ill. by Michael Martchenko. Scholastic, 1998. ISBN 978-0-590-21102-4 Subj: Behavior – growing up. Fairies. Teeth.

Angela's airplane ill. by Michael Martchenko. Firefly, 1988. ISBN 978-1-55037-027-0 Subj: Activities – flying. Airplanes, airports. Behavior – misbehavior.

David's father ill. by Michael Martchenko. Firefly, 1983. ISBN 978-0-920236-62-8 Subj: Character traits – kindness. Giants.

The fire station ill. by Michael Martchenko. Firefly, 1991. ISBN 978-1-55037-170-3 Subj: Careers – firefighters.

Get out of bed! ill. by Alan Daniel. Scholastic, 1998. ISBN 978-0-590-21103-1 Subj: School. Sleep.

I have to go! ill. by Michael Martchenko. Firefly, 1987. ISBN 978-0-920303-77-1 Subj: Behavior – growing up. Family life.

Love you forever ill. by Sheila McGraw. Firefly, 1994, 1986. ISBN 978-0-920668-36-8 Subj: Emotions – love. Family life – mothers. Foreign lands – Canada.

Makeup mess ill. by Michael Martchenko. Scholastic, 2001. ISBN 978-0-439-18771-8 Subj: Beauty shops. Character traits – appearance. Self-concept.

Mmm, cookies! ill. by Michael Martchenko. Scholastic, 2000. ISBN 978-0-590-89603-0 Subj: Behavior – trickery. Family life. Food. School.

Moira's birthday ill. by Michael Martchenko. Firefly, 1987. ISBN 978-0-920303-85-6 Subj: Behavior – misbehavior. Birthdays. Parties.

More pies ill. by Michael Martchenko. Cartwheel, 2002. ISBN 978-0-439-18773-2 Subj: Contests. Food.

Mortimer ill. by Michael Martchenko. Firefly, 1985. ISBN 978-0-920303-12-2 Subj: Bedtime. Noise, sounds. Songs.

Mud puddle ill. by author. Firefly, 1982. ISBN 978-0-920236-47-5 Subj: Activities – playing. Character traits – cleanliness. Foreign lands – Canada. Weather – rain.

The paper bag princess ill. by Michael Martchenko. Firefly, 1980. ISBN 978-0-920236-82-6 Subj: Character traits – appearance. Dragons.

Pigs ill. by Michael Martchenko. Firefly, 1989. ISBN 978-1-55037-039-3 Subj: Animals – pigs.

A promise is a promise by Robert N. Munsch and Michael Kusugak ill. by Vladyana Krykorka. Firefly, 1988. ISBN 978-1-55037-009-6 Subj: Eskimos. Folk & fairy tales. Foreign lands – Canada. Sea & seashore.

Purple, green and yellow ill. by Hélène Desputeaux. Firefly, 1992. ISBN 978-1-55037-255-7 Subj: Concepts – color.

Ribbon rescue ill. by Eugenie Fernandes. Scholastic, 1999. ISBN 978-0-590-89012-0 Subj: Character traits – generosity. Clothing – dresses. Weddings.

Show-and-tell ill. by Michael Martchenko. Firefly, 1991. ISBN 978-1-55037-195-6 Subj: School.

Something good ill. by Michael Martchenko. Firefly, 1990. ISBN 978-1-55037-099-7 Subj: Family life – fathers. Shopping. Stores.

Stephanie's ponytail ill. by Michael Martchenko. Firefly, 1996. ISBN 978-1-55037-485-8 Subj: Behavior – imitation. Character traits – appearance. Cumulative tales. Hair. School.

Thomas' snowsuit ill. by Michael Martchenko. Firefly, 1985. ISBN 978-0-920303-32-0 Subj: Careers – teachers. Clothing. Foreign lands – Canada. School. Seasons – winter. Weather – snow.

Up, up, down! ill. by Michael Martchenko. Scholastic, 2001. ISBN 978-0-439-18770-1 Subj: Activities. Trees.

Wait and see ill. by Michael Martchenko. Firefly, 1993. ISBN 978-1-55037-335-6 Subj: Behavior – wishing. Birthdays. Foreign lands – Canada. Friendship.

We share everything! ill. by Michael Martchenko. Scholastic, 1999. ISBN 978-0-590-89600-9 Subj: Behavior – sharing. School.

Where is Gah-Ning? ill. by Hélène Desputeaux. Annick, 1994. ISBN 978-1-55037-982-2 Subj: Family life – fathers. Foreign lands – Canada. Shopping. Toys – balloons.

Zoom ill. by Michael Martchenko. Cartwheel, 2003. ISBN 978-0-439-18774-9 Subj: Concepts – speed. Disabilities – physical disabilities.

Munson, Derek. *Enemy pie* ill. by Tara Calahan King. Chronicle, 2000. ISBN 978-0-8118-2778-2 Subj: Family life – fathers. Food. Friendship.

Muntean, Michaela. *Do not open this book!* ill. by Pascal Lemaître. Scholastic, 2006. ISBN 978-0-439-66037-2 Subj: Activities – writing. Animals – pigs. Books, reading. Humorous stories.

Murawski, Darlyne A. *Bug faces* ill. with photos. National Geographic, 2000. ISBN 978-0-7922-7557-2 Subj: Insects. Spiders.

Murguia, Bethanie Deeney. *Snippet the early riser* ill. by author. Knopf, 2013. ISBN 978-1-58246-460-2 Subj: Animals – snails. Family life. Morning. Problem solving. Sleep.

Zoe gets ready ill. by author. Scholastic, 2012. ISBN 978-0-545-34215-5 Subj: Character traits – appearance. Character traits – individuality. Clothing. Self-concept.

Zoe's room (no sisters allowed) ill. by author. Scholastic, 2013. ISBN 978-0-545-45781-1 Subj: Family life – sisters.

Murkoff, Heidi Eisenberg. *What to expect at a play date* ill. by Laura Rader. HarperCollins, 2001.

ISBN 978-0-694-01330-2 Subj: Activities – playing. Behavior. Friendship.

What to expect at preschool ill. by Laura Rader. HarperCollins, 2001. ISBN 978-0-694-01326-5 Subj: Activities. Friendship. School – nursery.

What to expect when the new baby comes home ill. by Laura Rader. HarperCollins, 2001. ISBN 978-0-694-01327-2 Subj: Babies. Family life – brothers & sisters. Family life – new sibling.

What to expect when you go to the dentist ill. by Laura Rader. HarperCollins, 2002. ISBN 978-0-694-01328-9 Subj: Careers – dentists. Health & fitness. Teeth.

What to expect when you go to the doctor ill. by Laura Rader. HarperCollins, 2000. ISBN 978-0-694-01324-1 Subj: Careers – doctors. Health & fitness.

Murphy, Andy. *Out and about at the dairy farm* ill. by Anne McMullen. Picture Window, 2003. ISBN 978-1-4048-0038-0 Subj: Animals – bulls, cows. Farms. Machines. School – field trips.

Murphy, Christopher J. *Lucille lost: a true adventure* (George, Margaret)

Murphy, Elspeth Campbell. *Happy Easter, God* ill. by Jim Lewis. Bethany Backyard, 2001. ISBN 978-0-7642-2386-0 Subj: Holidays – Easter. Poetry. Religion.

Murphy, Jill. *All for one* ill. by author. Candlewick, 1999. ISBN 978-0-7636-0785-2 Subj: Activities – playing. Friendship. Monsters.

Mr. Large in charge ill. by author. Candlewick, 2007. ISBN 978-0-7636-3504-6 Subj: Animals – elephants. Family life – fathers. Illness.

Peace at last ill. by author. Dial, 1980. ISBN 978-0-8037-6758-4 Subj: Animals – bears. Noise, sounds. Sleep.

A piece of cake ill. by author. Candlewick, 1997. ISBN 978-0-7636-0572-8 Subj: Animals – elephants. Food. Self-concept.

A quiet night in ill. by author. Candlewick, 1994. ISBN 978-1-56402-248-6 Subj: Animals – elephants. Bedtime. Family life.

Murphy, Jim. *Fergus and the Night-Demon: an Irish ghost story* ill. by John Manders. Houghton, 2006. ISBN 978-0-618-33955-6 Subj: Character traits – laziness. Emotions – fear. Foreign lands – Ireland. Ghosts.

Murphy, Kelly. *The boll weevil ball* ill. by author. Holt, 2002. ISBN 978-0-8050-6712-5 Subj: Activities – dancing. Concepts – size. Insects – beetles.

Murphy, Liz. *ABC doctor: staying healthy from A to Z* ill. by author. Blue Apple, 2007. ISBN 978-1-59354-593-2 Subj: ABC books. Careers – doctors. Health & fitness.

Murphy, Mary. *The Alphabet Keeper* ill. by author. Knopf, 2003. ISBN 978-0-375-92347-0 Subj: ABC books. Character traits – freedom.

Caterpillar's wish ill. by author. DK, 1999. ISBN 978-0-7894-2593-5 Subj: Behavior – wishing. Insects – butterflies, caterpillars. Metamorphosis.

Here comes spring, and summer and fall and winter ill. by author. DK, 1999. ISBN 978-0-7894-3484-5 Subj: Animals – dogs. Seasons.

How kind ill. by author. Candlewick, 2002. ISBN 978-0-7636-1732-5 Subj: Animals. Character traits – kindness. Circular tales. Farms.

I feel happy, and sad, and angry, and glad ill. by author. DK, 2000. ISBN 978-0-7894-2680-2 Subj: Animals – dogs. Emotions.

I like it when . . . ill. by author. Harcourt, 1997. ISBN 978-0-15-200039-4 Subj: Activities. Birds – penguins. Family life – parents.

I like it when . . . [board book] ill. by author. Harcourt, 1997. ISBN 978-0-15-205649-0 Subj: Activities. Birds – penguins. Family life – parents. Format, unusual – board books.

A kiss like this ill. by author. Candlewick, 2012. ISBN 978-0-7636-61823. Subj: Animals – babies. Format, unusual – toy & movable books. Kissing.

Koala and the flower ill. by author. Roaring Brook, 2002. ISBN 978-0-7613-2674-8 Subj: Animals. Animals – koalas. Character traits – curiosity. Character traits – questioning. Flowers. Libraries.

Panda Foo and the new friend ill. by author. Candlewick, 2007. ISBN 978-0-7636-3405-6 Subj: Activities – picnicking. Animals – pandas. Friendship.

Please be quiet! ill. by author. Houghton, 1999. ISBN 978-0-395-97113-0 Subj: Birds – penguins. Family life – mothers. Noise, sounds.

Quick Duck! ill. by author. Candlewick, 2013. ISBN 978-0-7636-6022-2 Subj: Birds – ducks. Concepts. Format, unusual – board books.

Slow snail ill. by author. Candlewick, 2013. ISBN 978-0-7636-6023-9 Subj: Animals – snails. Concepts. Format, unusual – board books.

Some things change ill. by author. Houghton, 2001. ISBN 978-0-618-00334-1 Subj: Activities. Birds – penguins. Concepts – change. Toys – bears.

You smell and taste and feel and see and hear ill. by author. DK, 1997. ISBN 978-0-7894-2471-6 Subj: Animals – dogs. Senses.

Murphy, Patti Beling. *Elinor and Violet* ill. by author. Little, 2003. ISBN 978-0-316-91034-7 Subj: Behavior – misbehavior. Birds – chickens. Family life – grandmothers. Friendship. Sea & seashore – beaches.

Murphy, Sally. *Pearl verses the world* ill. by Heather Potter. Candlewick, 2011. ISBN 978-0-7636-4821-3 Subj: Death. Emotions – grief. Emotions – loneliness. Family life – grandmothers. Poetry.

Murphy, Stuart J. *Animals on board* ill. by R. W. Alley. HarperCollins, 1998. ISBN 978-0-06-027443-6 Subj: Animals. Counting, numbers. Merry-go-rounds. Rhyming text.

Beep beep, vroom vroom! ill. by Chris L. Demarest. HarperCollins, 2000. ISBN 978-0-06-028017-8 Subj: Automobiles. Counting, numbers.

The best bug parade ill. by Holly Keller. HarperCollins, 1996. ISBN 978-0-06-025872-6 Subj: Counting, numbers. Insects.

The best vacation ever ill. by Nadine Bernard Westcott. HarperCollins, 1997. ISBN 978-0-06-026767-4 Subj: Activities – vacationing. Family life. Problem solving. Rhyming text.

Betcha! ill. by S. D. Schindler. HarperCollins, 1997. ISBN 978-0-06-026769-8 Subj: Counting, numbers. Friendship.

Bigger, better, best ill. by Marsha Winborn. HarperCollins, 2002. ISBN 978-0-06-028919-5 Subj: Concepts – measurement. Concepts – size.

Bug dance ill. by Christopher Santoro. HarperCollins, 2002. ISBN 978-0-06-446252-5 Subj: Counting, numbers. Insects.

Captain Invincible and the space shapes ill. by Rémy Simard. HarperCollins, 2001. ISBN 978-0-06-028023-9 Subj: Concepts – shape. Counting, numbers.

Circus shapes ill. by Edward Miller. HarperCollins, 1998. ISBN 978-0-06-027437-5 Subj: Circus. Concepts – shape. Rhyming text.

Dave's down-to-earth rock shop ill. by Cat Bowman Smith. HarperCollins, 2000. ISBN 978-0-06-028019-2 Subj: Counting, numbers.

Dinosaur deals ill. by Kevin O'Malley. HarperCollins, 2001. ISBN 978-0-06-028927-0 Subj: Activities – trading. Counting, numbers. Dinosaurs.

Earth Day — hooray! ill. by Renée Williams-Andriani. HarperCollins, 2004. ISBN 978-0-06-000127-8 Subj: Counting, numbers. Ecology. Holidays.

Elevator magic ill. by G. Brian Karas. HarperCollins, 1997. ISBN 978-0-06-446709-4 Subj: Counting, numbers. Elevators, escalators. Rhyming text.

Every buddy counts ill. by Fiona Dunbar. HarperCollins, 1997. ISBN 978-0-06-026773-5 Subj: Counting, numbers. Rhyming text.

A fair bear share ill. by John Speirs. HarperCollins, 1998. ISBN 978-0-06-446714-8 Subj: Activities – baking, cooking. Animals – bears. Counting, numbers. Food.

Freda is found ill. by Tim Jones. Charlesbridge, 2011. ISBN 978-1-58089-462-3 Subj: Animals. Behavior – lost. Safety. School – field trips.

Game time ill. by Cynthia Jabar. HarperCollins, 2000. ISBN 978-0-06-028025-3 Subj: Clocks, watches. Sports – soccer. Time.

Get up and go! ill. by Diane Greenseid. HarperCollins, 1996. ISBN 978-0-06-025882-5 Subj: Animals – dogs. Morning. Rhyming text. School. Time.

Give me half! ill. by G. Brian Karas. HarperCollins, 1996. ISBN 978-0-06-025874-0 Subj: Behavior – sharing. Counting, numbers. Friendship. Sibling rivalry.

The greatest gymnast of all ill. by Cynthia Jabar. HarperCollins, 1998. ISBN 978-0-06-027609-6 Subj: Concepts. Counting, numbers.

Henry the fourth ill. by Scott Nash. HarperCollins, 1999. ISBN 978-0-06-027611-9 Subj: Animals – dogs. Counting, numbers.

It's about time! ill. by John Speirs. HarperCollins, 2005. ISBN 978-0-06-055768-3 Subj: Clocks, watches. Day. Night. Time.

Jack the builder ill. by Michael Rex. HarperCollins, 2006. ISBN 978-0-06-055775-1 Subj: Counting, numbers. Imagination.

Just enough carrots ill. by Frank Remkiewicz. HarperCollins, 1997. ISBN 978-0-06-026779-7 Subj: Animals – rabbits. Counting, numbers. Food. Shopping. Stores.

Leaping lizards ill. by JoAnn Adinolfi. HarperCollins, 2005. ISBN 978-0-06-000130-8 Subj: Counting, numbers. Reptiles – lizards.

Left, right, Emma! ill. by Tim Jones. Charlesbridge, 2012. ISBN 978-1-58089-472-2 Subj: Concepts – left & right.

Let's fly a kite ill. by Brian Floca. HarperCollins, 2000. ISBN 978-0-06-028035-2 Subj: Behavior – sharing. Concepts. Kites.

Mall mania ill. by Renée Williams-Andriani. HarperCollins, 2006. ISBN 978-0-06-055776-8 Subj: Counting, numbers. Stores.

Missing mittens ill. by G. Brian Karas. HarperCollins, 2001. ISBN 978-0-06-028027-7 Subj: Concepts. Counting, numbers.

Monster musical chairs ill. by Scott Nash. HarperCollins, 2000. ISBN 978-0-06-028021-5 Subj: Counting, numbers. Games.

More or less ill. by David Wenzel. HarperCollins, 2005. ISBN 978-0-06-053165-2 Subj: Activities – picnicking. Counting, numbers. Games.

100 days of cool ill. by John Bendall-Brunello. HarperCollins, 2004. ISBN 978-0-06-000121-6 Subj: Counting, numbers. School.

A pair of socks ill. by Lois Ehlert. HarperCollins, 1996. ISBN 978-0-06-025880-1 Subj: Clothing – socks.

The penny pot ill. by Lynne Cravath. HarperCollins, 1998. ISBN 978-0-06-027607-2 Subj: Counting, numbers. Fairs, festivals. Money. School.

Pepper's journal ill. by Marsha Winborn. HarperCollins, 2000. ISBN 978-0-06-027619-5 Subj: Animals – babies. Animals – cats. Calendars.

Percy listens up ill. by Tim Jones. Charlesbridge, 2012. ISBN 978-1-58089-468-5 Subj: Noise, sounds. Senses – hearing.

Polly's pen pal ill. by Rémy Simard. HarperCollins, 2005. ISBN 978-0-06-053168-3 Subj: Concepts – measurement. Pen pals.

Probably pistachio ill. by Marsha Winborn. HarperCollins, 2001. ISBN 978-0-06-028029-1 Subj: Behavior – bad day. Concepts.

Rabbit's pajama party ill. by Frank Remkiewicz. HarperCollins, 1999. ISBN 978-0-06-027617-1 Subj: Animals – rabbits. Family life – mothers. Rhyming text. Sleepovers.

Ready, set, hop! ill. by John Buller. HarperCollins, 1996. ISBN 978-0-06-025878-8 Subj: Activities – jumping. Counting, numbers. Frogs & toads.

Rodeo time ill. by David Wenzel. HarperCollins, 2006. ISBN 978-0-06-055778-2 Subj: Rodeos. Time.

Same old horse ill. by Steve Björkman. HarperCollins, 2005. ISBN 978-0-06-055770-6 Subj: Animals – horses, ponies. Character traits – persistence. Counting, numbers. Rhyming text.

Seaweed soup ill. by Frank Remkiewicz. HarperCollins, 2001. ISBN 978-0-06-446736-0 Subj: Behavior – sharing. Counting, numbers. Food.

Sluggers' car wash ill. by Barney Saltzberg. HarperCollins, 2002. ISBN 978-0-06-028921-8 Subj: Activities – working. Counting, numbers. Money.

The sundae scoop ill. by Cynthia Jabar. HarperCollins, 2003. ISBN 978-0-06-028924-9 Subj: Counting, numbers.

Too many kangaroo things to do! ill. by Kevin O'Malley. HarperCollins, 1996. ISBN 978-0-06-025884-9 Subj: Animals – kangaroos. Birthdays. Counting, numbers. Parties.

Treasure map ill. by Tricia Tusa. HarperCollins, 2004. ISBN 978-0-06-028036-9 Subj: Clubs, gangs. Maps. Problem solving.

Write on, Carlos! ill. by Tim Jones. Charlesbridge, 2011. ISBN 978-1-58089-464-7 Subj: Activities – writing. Animals. Names.

Murphy, Yannick. *Ahwooooooooo!* ill. by Claudio Muñoz. Houghton, 2006. ISBN 978-0-618-11762-8 Subj: Animals – wolves. Family life – grandfathers. Noise, sounds.

Baby Polar ill. by Kristen Balouch. Clarion, 2009. ISBN 978-0-618-99850-0 Subj: Animals – polar bears. Family life – mothers. Weather – snow. Weather – storms.

Murray, Alison. *Apple pie ABC* ill. by author. Hyperion/Disney, 2011. ISBN 978-1-4231-3694-1 Subj: ABC books. Activities – baking, cooking. Animals – dogs.

Little Mouse ill. by author. Disney/Hyperion, 2013. ISBN 978-1-4231-4330-7 Subj: Bedtime. Family life – mothers. Names.

One two that's my shoe! ill. by author. Hyperion/Disney, 2012. ISBN 978-1-4231-4329-1 Subj: Animals – dogs. Counting, numbers. Rhyming text.

Princess Penelope and the runaway kitten ill. by author. Candlewick, 2013. ISBN 978-0-7636-6952-2 Subj: Animals – cats. Behavior – boredom. Royalty – princesses.

Murray, Andrew. *Have you seen Chester?* ill. by Nicola Slater. HarperCollins, 2003. ISBN 978-0-06-057187-0 Subj: Animals – cats. Animals – dogs. Behavior – fighting, arguing. Behavior – running away.

Murray, Glenn. *Walter, the farting dog* (Kotzwinkle, William)

Walter, the farting dog: rough weather ahead (Kotzwinkle, William)

Walter, the farting dog: trouble at the yard sale (Kotzwinkle, William)

Murray, Laura. *The Gingerbread Man loose in the school* (The gingerbread boy)

The Gingerbread Man loose on the fire truck (The gingerbread boy)

Murray, Marjorie Dennis. *Halloween night* ill. by Brandon Dorman. HarperCollins, 2008. ISBN 978-0-06-135186-0 Subj: Holidays – Halloween. Parties. Rhyming text.

Little Wolf and the moon ill. by Stacey Shuett. Marshall Cavendish, 2002. ISBN 978-0-7614-5100-6 Subj: Animals – babies. Animals – wolves. Moon.

Murray, Martine. *A moose called Mouse* ill. by author. Allen & Unwin, 2001. ISBN 978-1-86508-495-4 Subj: Animals – moose. Friendship. Games. Nature. Night.

Musgrove, Margaret. *Ashanti to Zulu* ill. by Leo Dillon and Diane Dillon. Dial, 1976. ISBN 978-0-8037-0358-2 Subj: ABC books. Caldecott award books. Foreign lands – Africa.

The spider weaver: a legend of kente cloth ill. by Julia Cairns. Blue Sky, 2001. ISBN 978-0-590-98787-5 Subj: Activities – weaving. Careers – weavers. Folk & fairy tales. Foreign lands – Ghana. Spiders.

Muth, Jon J., reteller. *Stone soup* ill. by reteller. Scholastic, 2003. ISBN 978-0-439-33909-4 Subj: Careers – clergy. Character traits – cleverness. Folk & fairy tales. Food. Foreign lands – China.

The three questions ill. by author. Scholastic, 2002. ISBN 978-0-439-19996-4 Subj: Animals. Behavior.

Zen ghosts ill. by author. Scholastic, 2010. ISBN 978-0-439-63430-4 Subj: Activities – storytelling. Animals – pandas. Family life – brothers & sisters. Ghosts. Holidays – Halloween.

Zen shorts ill. by author. Scholastic, 2005. ISBN 978-0-439-33911-7 Subj: Activities – storytelling. Animals – pandas. Caldecott award honor books. Family life – brothers & sisters. Folk & fairy tales.

Zen ties ill. by author. Scholastic, 2008. ISBN 978-0-439-63425-0 Subj: Animals – pandas. Character traits – helpfulness. Family life – brothers & sisters. Old age.

My big book of trucks and diggers. Chronicle, 2011. ISBN 978-0-8118-7892-0 Subj: Format, unusual – board books. Machines. Trucks.

My busy day photos by Steve Gorton, et al. DK, 2001. ISBN 978-0-7894-7407-0 Subj: Activities. Format, unusual.

My doctor's bag. DK, 2002. ISBN 978-0-7894-8520-5 Subj: Careers – doctors. Format, unusual.

My first farm ill. with photos. DK, 2002. ISBN 978-0-7894-8524-3 Subj: Farms. Format, unusual – board books. Language.

My first word, touch and feel ill. with photos. DK, 2001. ISBN 978-0-7894-7931-0 Subj: Format, unusual – board books. Language.

My new baby ill. by Rachel Fuller. Child's Play, 2010. ISBN 978-1-84643-276-7 Subj: Family life – new sibling. Format, unusual – board books.

My potty book for boys ill. with photos. DK, 2001. ISBN 978-0-7894-4889-7 Subj: Behavior – growing up. Toilet training.

My potty book for girls ill. with photos. DK, 2001. ISBN 978-0-7894-4845-3 Subj: Behavior – growing up. Toilet training.

Myer, Andy. *Delia's dull day: an incredibly boring story* ill. by author. Sleeping Bear, 2012. ISBN 978-1-58536-804-4 Subj: Behavior – boredom. Humorous stories.

Myers, Christopher. *Sparrows* ill. by author. Hyperion, 2001. ISBN 978-0-7868-2373-4 Subj: Birds. Birds – sparrows. Cities, towns. Ethnic groups in the U.S. – African Americans. Homeless.

Wings ill. by author. Scholastic, 2000. ISBN 978-0-590-03377-0 Subj: Activities – flying. Anatomy – wings. Character traits – being different.

Myers, Tim. *Basho and the fox* ill. by Oki S. Han. Marshall Cavendish, 2000. ISBN 978-0-7614-5068-9 Subj: Animals – foxes. Poetry.

Down at the Dino Wash Deluxe ill. by Macky Pamintuan. Sterling, 2013. ISBN 978-1-4027-7798-1 Subj: Activities – bathing. Character traits – cleanliness. Dinosaurs.

Looking for Luna ill. by Mike Reed. Marshall Cavendish, 2009. ISBN 978-0-7614-5564-6 Subj: Animals – cats. Behavior – lost & found possessions. Family life – fathers. Rhyming text.

Myers, Walter Dean. *The blues of Flats Brown* ill. by Nina Laden. Holiday, 2000. ISBN 978-0-8234-1480-2 Subj: Animals – dogs. Music. Musical instruments – guitars.

Brown angels ill. with photos. HarperCollins, 1993. ISBN 978-0-06-022918-4 Subj: Angels. Ethnic groups in the U.S. – African Americans. Poetry.

Harlem: a poem ill. by Christopher Myers. Scholastic, 1997. ISBN 978-0-590-54340-8 Subj: Caldecott award honor books. Careers – illustrators. Careers – writers. Cities, towns. Ethnic groups in the U.S. – African Americans. Poetry.

Looking for the easy life ill. by Lee Harper. HarperCollins, 2011. ISBN 978-0-06-054375-4 Subj: Animals – monkeys. Behavior – seeking better things.

Muhammad Ali: the people's champion ill. by Alix Delinois. HarperCollins, 2010. ISBN 978-0-06-029131-0 Subj: Ethnic groups in the U.S. – African Americans. Prejudice. Sports – boxing. U.S. history.

The story of the three kingdoms ill. by Ashley Bryan. HarperCollins, 1995. ISBN 978-0-06-024287-9 Subj: Animals. Nature.

Young Martin's promise by Walter Dean Myers and Alex Haley ill. by Barbara Higgins Bond. Alex Haley, general editor. Raintree, 1993. ISBN 978-0-8114-7210-4 Subj: Ethnic groups in the U.S. – African Americans. U.S. history.

Myller, Rolf. *How big is a foot?* ill. by author. Atheneum, 1962. ISBN 978-0-689-20298-8 Subj: Birthdays. Concepts – measurement. Humorous stories. Royalty – kings.

Myra, Harold Lawrence. *Thanksgiving: what makes it special?* ill. by Jane Kurisu. Nelson, 2002. ISBN 978-1-4003-0006-8 Subj: Holidays – Thanksgiving. Religion.

Myron, Vicki. *Dewey: there's a cat in the library!* by Vicki Myron and Bret Witter ill. by Steve James. Little, Brown, 2009. ISBN 978-0-316-06874-1 Subj: Animals – cats. Libraries.

Mystery manor ill. by Phil Wilson. Design by Willabel L. Tong; paper engineering by José R. Seminario. Piggy Toes, 2000. ISBN 978-1-58117-108-2 Subj: Animals – dogs. Format, unusual – toy & movable books. Ghosts. Monsters. Witches.

Na, Il Sung. *A book of sleep* ill. by author. Knopf, 2009. ISBN 978-0-375-86223-6 Subj: Animals. Birds – owls. Night. Sleep.

Hide and seek ill. by author. Knopf, 2012. ISBN 978-0-375-87078-1 Subj: Animals. Animals – elephants. Behavior – hiding. Games. Reptiles – chameleons.

Snow rabbit, spring rabbit: a book of changing seasons ill. by author. Random House, 2011. ISBN 978-0-375-86786-6 Subj: Animals. Animals – rabbits. Seasons – spring. Seasons – winter.

The thingamabob ill. by author. Random House, 2010. ISBN 978-0-375-86106-2 Subj: Animals – elephants. Imagination. Umbrellas.

Nadel, Carolina. *Daddy's home* ill. by author. Mookind, 2011. ISBN 978-0-9792761-4-9 Subj: Careers – military. Emotions – anger. Family life – fathers. War.

Naden, Corinne J. *Ron's big mission* by Corinne J. Naden and Rose Blue ill. by Don Tate. Dutton, 2009. ISBN 978-0-525-47849-2 Subj: Careers – astronauts. Ethnic groups in the U.S. – African Americans. Libraries. Prejudice. U.S. history.

Nadimi, Suzan. *The rich man and the parrot* ill. by Ande Cook. Whitman, 2007. ISBN 978-0-8075-5059-5 Subj: Behavior – trickery. Birds – parakeets, parrots. Character traits – freedom. Folk & fairy tales. Foreign lands – Persia.

Nagda, Anne Whitehead. *A home for panda* ill. by Jim Effler. Soundprints, 2003. ISBN 978-1-59249-045-5 Subj: Animals – pandas. Foreign lands – China. Homes, houses.

A tiger tale ill. by Paul Kratter. Soundprints, 2003. ISBN 978-1-59249-042-4 Subj: Animals – tigers. Foreign lands – Nepal.

World above the clouds ill. by Paul Kratter. Soundprints, 2000. ISBN 978-1-56899-878-7 Subj: Animals – leopards. Foreign lands – Himalayas. Mountains. Science.

Nagel, Karen. *Shapes that roll* ill. by Steve Wilson. Blue Apple, 2009. ISBN 978-1-934706-81-7 Subj: Concepts – shape.

Nahas, Sylvaine. *Nicolo's unicorn* ill. by Bimba Landmann. Watson-Guptill, 2001. ISBN 978-0-8230-5580-7 Subj: Dreams. Mythical creatures – unicorns.

Nakagawa, Chihiro. *Who made this cake?* ill. by Junji Koyose. Front Street, 2008. ISBN 978-1-59078-595-9 Subj: Activities – baking, cooking. Character traits – smallness. Machines.

Nakagawa, Rieko. *Guri and Gura* by Rieko Nakagawa and Yuriko Yamawaki ill. by Yuriko Yamawaki. Tuttle, 2002. ISBN 978-0-8048-3352-3 Subj: Activities – baking, cooking. Animals – mice. Behavior – sharing. Eggs. Food. Problem solving.

Guri and Gura's special gift by Rieko Nakagawa and Yuriko Yamawaki ill. by Yuriko Yamawaki. Tuttle, 2002. ISBN 978-0-8048-3357-8 Subj: Activities – baking, cooking. Animals – mice. Behavior – sharing. Food.

Nakamura, Katherine Riley. *Song of night* ill. by Linnea Asplind Riley. Blue Sky, 2002. ISBN 978-0-439-26678-9 Subj: Animals. Animals – babies. Bedtime.

Nakawaki, Hatsue. *Wait! wait!* ill. by Komako Sakai. Enchanted Lion, 2013. ISBN 978-1-59270-138-4 Subj: Animals. Family life – fathers.

Namioka, Lensey. *Hungriest boy in the world* ill. by Aki Sogabe. Holiday, 2001. ISBN 978-0-8234-1542-7 Subj: Food. Foreign lands – Japan. Monsters.

Nanji, Shenaaz. *An alien in my house* ill. by Chum McLeod. Second Story, 2003. ISBN 978-1-896764-77-1 Subj: Character traits – being different. Family life – grandfathers. Old age.

Treasure for lunch ill. by Yvonne Cathcart. Second Story, 2000. ISBN 978-1-896764-32-0 Subj: Behavior – sharing. Food.

Napier, Matt. *Z is for zamboni* ill. by Melanie Rose. Sleeping Bear, 2002. ISBN 978-1-58536-065-9 Subj: ABC books. Sports – hockey.

Napoli, Donna Jo. *Albert* ill. by Jim LaMarche. Harcourt, 2001. ISBN 978-0-15-201572-5 Subj: Birds. Homes, houses.

Bobby the bold by Donna Jo Napoli and Eva Furrow ill. by Ard Hoyt. Penguin, 2006. ISBN 978-0-8037-2990-2 Subj: Animals – bonobos. Animals – chimpanzees. Character traits – appearance. Character traits – being different. Hair. Zoos.

The crossing ill. by Jim Madsen. Simon & Schuster, 2011. ISBN 978-1-4169-9474-9 Subj: Indians of North America – Shoshone. U.S. history – frontier & pioneer life.

Flamingo dream ill. by Cathie Felstead. Greenwillow, 2002. ISBN 978-0-688-17863-5 Subj: Death. Emotions. Emotions – grief. Family life – fathers. Illness – cancer.

Mama Miti: Wangari Maathai and the trees of Kenya ill. by Kadir Nelson. Simon & Schuster, 2010. ISBN 978-1-4169-3505-6 Subj: Character traits – responsibility. Ecology. Foreign lands – Kenya. Trees.

Ready to dream by Donna Jo Napoli and Elena Furrow ill. by Bronwyn Bancroft. Bloomsbury, 2009. ISBN 978-1-59990-049-0 Subj: Art. Careers – artists. Dreams. Foreign lands – Australia.

Rocky, the cat who barks ill. by Tamara Petrosino. Dutton, 2002. ISBN 978-0-525-46544-7 Subj: Animals – cats. Animals – dogs. Friendship.

The wishing club: a story about fractions ill. by Anna Currey. Holt, 2007. ISBN 978-0-8050-7665-3 Subj: Behavior – wishing. Counting, numbers. Family life – brothers & sisters.

Narahashi, Keiko. *Two girls can!* ill. by author. McElderry, 2000. ISBN 978-0-689-82618-4 Subj: Friendship.

Nargi, Lela. *The honeybee man* ill. by Kyrsten Brooker. Random House, 2011. ISBN 978-0-375-84980-0 Subj: Careers – beekeepers. Insects – bees.

Nash, Ogden. *The adventures of Isabel* ill. by James Marshall. Little, 1991. ISBN 978-0-316-59874-3 Subj: Animals – bears. Character traits – bravery. Emotions – fear. Giants. Poetry. Witches.

The adventures of Isabel ill. by Bridget Starr Taylor. Sourcebooks/Jabberwocky, 2008. ISBN 978-1-4022-1027-3 Subj: Animals – bears. Character traits – bravery. Emotions – fear. Giants. Poetry. Witches.

Custard the dragon and the wicked knight ill. by Lynn Munsinger. Little, 1996. ISBN 978-0-316-59882-8 Subj: Character traits – bravery. Dragons. Knights. Poetry.

Nash, Sarah. *Purrfect!* ill. by Pamela Venus. Tamarind, 2010. ISBN 978-1-870516-86-0 Subj: Ethnic groups in the U.S. – African Americans. Toys.

Nash, Scott. *Tuff Fluff: the case of Duckie's missing brain* ill. by author. Candlewick, 2004. ISBN 978-0-7636-1882-7 Subj: Activities – storytelling. Careers – detectives. Mystery stories. Toys.

Näslund, Gorel Kristina. *Our apple tree* ill. by Kristina Digman. Macmillan, 2005. ISBN 978-1-59643-052-5 Subj: Food. Seasons. Trees.

Nathan, Emma. *What do you call a group of turkeys?* ill. with photos. Blackbirch, 2000. ISBN 978-1-56711-357-0 Subj: Birds. Birds – turkeys. Language.

National Geographic Society [U.S.]. *National Geographic our world: a child's first picture atlas* ill. with photos. National Geographic, 2000. ISBN 978-0-7922-7576-3 Subj: Geography. Maps.

Naylor, Phyllis Reynolds. *Keeping a Christmas secret* ill. by Lena Shiffman. Macmillan, 1993. ISBN 978-0-689-71760-4 Subj: Behavior – secrets. Gifts. Holidays – Christmas.

King of the playground ill. by Nola Langner Malone. Atheneum, 1991. ISBN 978-0-689-31558-9 Subj: Activities – playing. Behavior – bullying, teasing. Friendship.

Please do feed the bears ill. by Ana López-Escrivá. Atheneum, 2002. ISBN 978-0-689-82561-3 Subj: Activities – picnicking. Animals – bears. Sea & seashore – beaches. Toys – bears.

Sweet strawberries ill. by Rosalind Charney Kaye. Atheneum, 1999. ISBN 978-0-689-81338-2 Subj: Behavior. Food. Stores.

Nazoa, Aquiles. *A small Nativity* ill. by Ana Palmero Caceres. Groundwood, 2007. ISBN 978-0-88899-839-2 Subj: Foreign lands – Venezuela. Holidays – Christmas. Religion – Nativity.

Nedwidek, John. *Ducks don't wear socks* ill. by Lee White. Viking, 2008. ISBN 978-0-670-06136-5 Subj: Birds – ducks. Clothing. Humorous stories.

Neitzel, Shirley. *The bag I'm taking to Grandma's* ill. by Nancy Winslow Parker. Greenwillow, 1995. ISBN 978-0-688-12961-3 Subj: Activities – traveling. Cumulative tales. Rebuses. Rhyming text.

The dress I'll wear to the party ill. by Nancy Winslow Parker. Greenwillow, 1992. ISBN 978-0-688-09960-2 Subj: Clothing. Cumulative tales. Rebuses. Rhyming text.

The house I'll build for the wrens ill. by Nancy Winslow Parker. Greenwillow, 1997. ISBN 978-0-688-14974-1 Subj: Activities – making things. Birds. Cumulative tales. Homes, houses. Rebuses. Rhyming text. Tools.

I'm not feeling well today ill. by Nancy Winslow Parker. Greenwillow, 2001. ISBN 978-0-688-17381-4 Subj: Cumulative tales. Illness. Rebuses. Rhyming text. School.

I'm taking a trip on my train ill. by Nancy Winslow Parker. Greenwillow, 1999. ISBN 978-0-688-15834-7 Subj: Activities – playing. Cumulative tales. Imagination. Rebuses. Rhyming text. Trains.

The jacket I wear in the snow ill. by Nancy Winslow Parker. Greenwillow, 1989. ISBN 978-0-688-08030-3 Subj: Clothing. Cumulative tales. Rhyming text.

We're making breakfast for mother ill. by Nancy Winslow Parker. Greenwillow, 1997. ISBN 978-0-688-14576-7 Subj: Family life – mothers. Food. Rebuses. Rhyming text.

Who will I be? a Halloween rebus story ill. by Nancy Winslow Parker. HarperCollins, 2005. ISBN 978-0-06-056068-3 Subj: Clothing – costumes. Holidays – Halloween. Rebuses. Rhyming text.

Nelson, Kadir. *He's got the whole world in His hands* ill. by author. Penguin, 2005. ISBN 978-0-8037-2850-9 Subj: Religion. Songs.

Nelson Mandela ill. by author. HarperCollins, 2013. ISBN 978-0-06-178374-6 Subj: Foreign lands – South Africa. Prejudice. Violence, nonviolence.

Nelson, Kristin L. *Busy ants* ill. with photos. Lerner, 2004. ISBN 978-0-8225-3775-5 Subj: Insects – ants.

Clever raccoons ill. with photos. Lerner, 2001. ISBN 978-0-8225-3763-2 Subj: Animals – raccoons.

Farm tractors ill. with photos. Lerner, 2003. ISBN 978-0-8225-0690-4 Subj: Farms. Tractors.

Monster trucks photos by David Huntoon, et al. Lerner, 2003. ISBN 978-0-8225-0691-1 Subj: Sports – racing. Trucks.

Nelson, Marilyn. *Beautiful ballerina* ill. by Susan Kuklin. Scholastic, 2009. ISBN 978-0-545-08920-3 Subj: Ballet.

Ostrich and Lark ill. by Kuru Art Project. Boyds Mills, 2012. ISBN 978-1-59078-702-1 Subj: Birds – larks. Birds – ostriches. Foreign lands – Africa.

Snook alone ill. by Timothy Basil Ering. Candlewick, 2010. ISBN 978-0-7636-2667-9 Subj: Animals – dogs. Character traits – loyalty. Friendship. Religion.

Nelson, Robert Lyn. *Ocean friends* ill. by author. NorthWord, 2003. ISBN 978-1-55971-840-0 Subj: Animals. Animals – dolphins. Sea & seashore.

Nelson, Robin. *A cloudy day* ill. by author. Lerner, 2002. ISBN 978-0-8225-0172-5 Subj: Weather – clouds.

A day ill. by author. Lerner, 2002. ISBN 978-0-8225-0177-0 Subj: Day. Days of the week, months of the year.

Hearing ill. with photos. Lerner, 2002. ISBN 978-0-8225-1264-6 Subj: Anatomy – ears. Senses – hearing.

Months ill. with photos. Lerner, 2002. ISBN 978-0-8225-0179-4 Subj: Days of the week, months of the year.

Pet fish ill. with photos. Lerner, 2003. ISBN 978-0-8225-1267-7 Subj: Fish. Pets.

Pet frog ill. with photos. Lerner, 2003. ISBN 978-0-8225-1271-4 Subj: Frogs & toads. Pets.

Pet guinea pig ill. with photos. Lerner, 2003. ISBN 978-0-8225-1268-4 Subj: Animals – guinea pigs. Pets.

Pet hamster ill. with photos. Lerner, 2003. ISBN 978-0-8225-1269-1 Subj: Animals – hamsters. Pets.

Pet hermit crab ill. with photos. Lerner, 2003. ISBN 978-0-8225-1270-7 Subj: Crustaceans – crabs. Pets.

A rainy day ill. with photos. Lerner, 2002. ISBN 978-0-8225-0173-2 Subj: Weather – rain.

Seeing ill. with photos. Lerner, 2002. ISBN 978-0-8225-1262-2 Subj: Anatomy – eyes. Senses – sight.

Smelling ill. with photos. Lerner, 2002. ISBN 978-0-8225-1263-9 Subj: Anatomy – noses. Senses – smell.

A snowy day ill. with photos. Lerner, 2002. ISBN 978-0-8225-0175-6 Subj: Seasons – winter. Weather – snow.

Staying clean ill. with photos. Lerner, 2005. ISBN 978-0-8225-2638-4 Subj: Character traits – cleanliness. Health & fitness.

A sunny day ill. with photos. Lerner, 2002. ISBN 978-0-8225-0176-3 Subj: Sun. Weather.

Tasting ill. with photos. Lerner, 2002. ISBN 978-0-8225-1265-3 Subj: Anatomy – tongues. Senses – taste.

Touching ill. with photos. Lerner, 2002. ISBN 978-0-8225-1266-0 Subj: Senses – touch.

A week ill. with photos. Lerner, 2002. ISBN 978-0-8225-0178-7 Subj: Days of the week, months of the year.

A windy day ill. with photos. Lerner, 2001. ISBN 978-0-8225-0174-9 Subj: Weather – wind.

Nelson, S. D. *Gift horse: a Lakota story* ill. by author. Abrams, 1999. ISBN 978-0-8109-4127-4 Subj: Animals – horses, ponies. Behavior – growing up. Indians of North America – Dakota (Sioux).

Quiet hero: the Ira Hayes story ill. by author. Lee & Low, 2006. ISBN 978-1-58430-263-6 Subj: Careers – military. Indians of North America – Pima. U.S. history.

The Star People ill. by author. Abrams, 2003. ISBN 978-0-8109-4584-5 Subj: Family life – brothers & sisters. Family life – grandmothers. Fire. Indians of North America – Lakota. Stars.

Nelson, Steve. *Frosty the snowman* by Steve Nelson and Jack Rollins ill. by Wade Zahares. Imagine, 2013. ISBN 978-1-62354-012-8 Subj: Music. Seasons – winter. Snowmen. Songs.

Frosty the snowman [board book] by Steve Nelson and Jack Rollins ill. by Sam Williams. Scholastic, 2013. ISBN 978-0-545-45005-8 Subj: Format, unusual – board books. Music. Seasons – winter. Snowmen. Songs.

Nelson, Vaunda Micheaux. *Almost to freedom* ill. by Colin Bootman. Carolrhoda, 2003. ISBN 978-1-57505-342-4 Subj: Character traits – freedom. Ethnic groups in the U.S. – African Americans. Slavery. Toys – dolls.

Who will I be, Lord? ill. by Sean Qualls. Random House, 2009. ISBN 978-0-375-84342-6 Subj: Ethnic groups in the U.S. – African Americans. Religion. Self-concept.

Nelson-Schmidt, Michelle. *Cats, cats!* ill. by author. Kane/Miller, 2011. ISBN 978-1-61067-042-5 Subj: Animals – cats. Format, unusual. Pets.

Dogs, dogs! ill. by author. Kane/Miller, 2011. ISBN 978-1-61067-041-8 Subj: Animals – dogs. Format, unusual. Pets.

Nemiroff, Marc A. *Shy spaghetti and excited eggs: a kid's menu of feelings* by Marc A. Nemiroff and Jane Annunziata ill. by Christine Battuz. Magination, 2011. ISBN 978-1-4338-0956-9 Subj: Emotions.

Nesbitt, Kenn. *More bears!* ill. by Troy Cummings. Sourcebooks, 2010. ISBN 978-1-4022-3835-2 Subj: Animals – bears. Careers – writers. Humorous stories.

Ness, Evaline. *Sam, Bangs, and moonshine* ill. by author. Holt, 1966. ISBN 978-0-606-01326-0 Subj: Caldecott award books. Imagination. Sports – fishing.

Nethery, Mary. *Two Bobbies: a true story of Hurricane Katrina, friendship, and survival* (Larson, Kirby)

Nettleton, Pamela Hill. *Abraham Lincoln* ill. by Becky Shipe. Picture Window, 2004. ISBN 978-1-4048-0185-1 Subj: U.S. history.

Benjamin Franklin ill. by Jeff Yesh. Picture Window, 2004. ISBN 978-1-4048-0186-8 Subj: Careers – inventors. Careers – printers. Careers – scientists. U.S. history.

George Washington ill. by Jeff Yesh. Picture Window, 2004. ISBN 978-1-4048-0184-4 Subj: Careers. Careers – farmers. Careers – military. U.S. history.

Martin Luther King, Jr ill. by Garry Nichols. Picture Window, 2004. ISBN 978-1-4048-0188-2 Subj: Careers – clergy. Ethnic groups in the U.S. – African Americans. Religion. U.S. history. Violence, nonviolence.

Pocahontas ill. by Jeff Yesh. Picture Window, 2004. ISBN 978-1-4048-0187-5 Subj: Indians of North America – Powhatan. U.S. history.

Sally Ride ill. by Becky Shipe. Picture Window, 2004. ISBN 978-1-4048-0189-9 Subj: Careers – astronauts. U.S. history.

Neubecker, Robert. *Beasty bath* ill. by author. Scholastic, 2005. ISBN 978-0-439-64000-8 Subj: Activities – bathing. Imagination. Monsters. Rhyming text.

Courage of the blue boy ill. by author. Ten Speed, 2006. ISBN 978-1-58246-182-3 Subj: Activities – traveling. Animals – bulls, cows. Concepts – color. Self-concept.

Linus the vegetarian T. rex ill. by author. Simon & Schuster, 2013. ISBN 978-1-4169-8512-9 Subj: Dinosaurs. Food. Museums.

What little boys are made of ill. by author. HarperCollins, 2012. ISBN 978-0-06-202355-1 Subj: Activities – playing. Imagination. Rhyming text.

Winter is for snow ill. by author. Disney/Hyperion, 2013. ISBN 978-1-4231-7831-6 Subj: Family life – brothers & sisters. Rhyming text. Seasons – winter. Weather – snow.

Wow! America! ill. by author. Hyperion, 2006. ISBN 978-0-7868-3816-5 Subj: U.S. history.

Wow! City! ill. by author. Hyperion, 2004. ISBN 978-0-7868-0951-6 Subj: Cities, towns.

Wow! Ocean! ill. by author. Hyperion/Disney, 2011. ISBN 978-1-4231-3113-7 Subj: Sea & seashore.

Wow! School! ill. by author. Hyperion, 2007. ISBN 978-0-7868-3896-7 Subj: School – first day.

Neugebauer, Charise. *The real winner* ill. by Barbara Nascimbeni. NorthSouth, 2000. ISBN 978-0-7358-1253-6 Subj: Animals – hippopotamuses. Animals – raccoons. Contests.

Neuschwander, Cindy. *Amanda Bean's amazing dream* ill. by Liza Woodruff. Scholastic, 1998. ISBN 978-0-590-30012-4 Subj: Counting, numbers. Dreams. School.

Pastry school in Paris: an adventure in capacity ill. by Bryan Langdo. Holt, 2009. ISBN 978-0-8050-8314-9 Subj: Activities – baking, cooking. Concepts. Family life – brothers & sisters. Foreign lands – France. Multiple births – twins.

Sir Cumference and all the king's tens: a math adventure ill. by Wayne Geehan. Charlesbridge, 2009. ISBN 978-1-57091-727-1 Subj: Birthdays. Counting, numbers. Knights. Royalty.

Nevius, Carol. *Baseball hour* ill. by Bill Thomson. Marshall Cavendish, 2008. ISBN 978-0-7614-5380-2 Subj: Rhyming text. Sports – baseball.

Building with Dad ill. by Bill Thomson. Marshall Cavendish, 2006. ISBN 978-0-7614-5312-3 Subj: Careers – construction workers. Rhyming text. School.

Karate hour ill. by Bill Thomson. Marshall Cavendish, 2004. ISBN 978-0-7614-5169-3 Subj: Rhyming text. Sports – karate.

Soccer hour ill. by Bill Thomson. Marshall Cavendish, 2011. ISBN 978-0-7614-5689-6 Subj: Rhyming text. Sports – soccer.

Newberry, Clare Turlay. *April's kittens* ill. by author. HarperCollins, 1940. ISBN 978-0-06-024401-9 Subj: Animals – cats. Caldecott award honor books. Pets.

Barkis ill. by author. HarperCollins, 1938. Subj: Animals – dogs. Caldecott award honor books. Pets.

Marshmallow ill. by author. HarperCollins, 1942. Subj: Animals – cats. Animals – rabbits. Caldecott award honor books. Friendship.

Newbery, Linda. *Posy* ill. by Catherine Rayner. Atheneum, 2009. ISBN 978-1-4169-7112-2 Subj: Animals – cats. Rhyming text.

Newcome, Zita. *Pop-up toddlerobics* ill. by author. Candlewick, 2002. ISBN 978-0-7636-1838-4 Subj: Activities – playing. Health & fitness. Rhyming text. Sports – gymnastics.

Newgarden, Mark. *Bow-Wow bugs a bug* by Mark Newgarden and Megan Montague Cash ill. by authors. Harcourt, 2007. ISBN 978-0-15-205813-5 Subj: Animals – dogs. Insects. Wordless.

Bow-Wow orders lunch by Mark Newgarden and Megan Montague Cash ill. by authors. Harcourt, 2007. ISBN 978-0-15-205829-6 Subj: Animals – dogs. Food. Format, unusual – board books.

Newhouse, Maxwell. *The house that Max built* ill. by author. Tundra, 2008. ISBN 978-0-88776-774-6 Subj: Buildings. Careers – construction workers. Homes, houses.

Newman, Barbara Johansen. *Glamorous glasses* ill. by author. Boyds Mills, 2012. ISBN 978-1-59078-878-3 Subj: Character traits – appearance. Family life – cousins. Glasses.

Newman, Jeff. *The boys* ill. by author. Simon & Schuster, 2010. ISBN 978-1-4169-5012-7 Subj: Character traits – shyness. Days of the week, months of the year. Old age. Sports – baseball. Wordless.

Hippo! No, rhino! ill. by author. Little, Brown, 2006. ISBN 978-0-316-15573-1 Subj: Animals – rhinoceros. Humorous stories.

Reginald ill. by author. Doubleday, 2003. ISBN 978-0-385-74634-2 Subj: Animals. Animals – bulls, cows. Jungle. Sports – swimming.

Newman, Lesléa. *Cats, cats, cats* ill. by Erika Oller. Simon & Schuster, 2001. ISBN 978-0-689-83077-8 Subj: Animals – cats. Night. Rhyming text.

Daddy, Papa, and me ill. by Carol Thompson. Tricycle, 2009. ISBN 978-1-58246-262-2 Subj: Family life – fathers. Family life – same-sex parents. Format, unusual – board books. Homosexuality.

Daddy's song ill. by Karen Ritz. Holt, 2007. ISBN 978-0-8050-6975-4 Subj: Bedtime. Emotions – love. Family life – fathers. Lullabies. Rhyming text.

Dogs, dogs, dogs ill. by Erika Oller. Simon & Schuster, 2002. ISBN 978-0-698-84492-6 Subj: Activities. Animals – dogs. Counting, numbers. Rhyming text.

Donovan's big day ill. by Mike Dutton. Tricycle, 2011. ISBN 978-1-58246-332-2 Subj: Family life – mothers. Homosexuality. Weddings.

The eight nights of Chanukah ill. by Elivia Savadier. Abrams, 2005. ISBN 978-0-8109-5785-5 Subj: Holidays – Hanukkah. Jewish culture. Songs.

A fire engine for Ruthie ill. by Cyd Moore. Clarion, 2004. ISBN 978-0-618-15989-5 Subj: Activities – playing. Toys. Trucks.

Heather has two mommies ill. by Diana Souza. Alyson Wonderland, 2000. ISBN 978-1-55583-570-5 Subj: Family life – daughters. Family life – mothers. Family life – same-sex parents. Homosexuality.

Just like Mama ill. by Julia Gorton. Abrams, 2010. ISBN 978-0-8109-8393-9 Subj: Family life – mothers. Rhyming text.

Matzo ball moon ill. by Elaine Greenstein. Clarion, 1998. ISBN 978-0-395-71530-7 Subj: Family life – grandmothers. Food. Holidays – Passover. Jewish culture. Religion.

Miss Tutu's star ill. by Carey Armstrong-Ellis. Abrams, 2010. ISBN 978-0-8109-8396-0 Subj: Ballet. Emotions – fear. Self-concept.

Mommy, Mama, and Me ill. by Carol Thompson. Tricycle, 2009. ISBN 978-1-58246-263-9 Subj: Family life – mothers. Family life – same-sex parents. Format, unusual – board books. Homosexuality.

Pigs, pigs, pigs ill. by Erika Oller. Simon & Schuster, 2003. ISBN 978-0-689-84979-4 Subj: Animals – pigs. Careers – entertainers. Rhyming text.

Runaway dreidel ill. by Kyrsten Brooker. Holt, 2002. ISBN 978-0-8050-6237-3 Subj: Games. Holidays – Hanukkah. Jewish culture. Rhyming text.

Skunk's spring surprise ill. by Valeri Gorbachev. Harcourt, 2007. ISBN 978-0-15-205683-4 Subj: Animals. Animals – skunks. Friendship. Rhyming text. Seasons – spring.

A sweet Passover ill. by David Slonim. Abrams, 2012. ISBN 978-0-8109-9737-0 Subj: Activities – baking, cooking. Family life – grandfathers. Food. Holidays – Passover. Jewish culture.

Newman, Marjorie. *Just like me* ill. by Ken Wilson-Max. Walker, 2006. ISBN 978-0-8027-8080-5 Subj: Babies. Family life – brothers & sisters. Family life – new sibling.

Mole and the baby bird ill. by Patrick Benson. Bloomsbury, 2002. ISBN 978-1-58234-784-4 Subj: Animals – moles. Birds. Emotions – love.

Mole and the baby bird [board book] ill. by Patrick Benson. Bloomsbury, 2002. ISBN 978-1-58234-914-5 Subj: Animals – moles. Birds. Emotions – love. Format, unusual – board books.

Newman, Marlene. *Myron's magic cow* ill. by Jago. Barefoot, 2005. ISBN 978-1-84148-496-9 Subj: Animals – bulls, cows. Behavior – wishing. Folk & fairy tales. Magic.

Newman, Nanette. *What will you be, Grandma?* ill. by Emma Chichester Clark. Candlewick, 2012. ISBN 978-0-7636-6099-4 Subj: Family life – grandmothers. Imagination.

Newsome, Jill. *Dream dancer* ill. by Claudio Muñoz. HarperCollins, 2002. ISBN 978-0-06-000932-8 Subj: Activities – dancing. Ballet. Family life – grandmothers. Illness. Toys – dolls.

Newton, Jill. *Crash bang donkey!* ill. by author. Whitman, 2010. ISBN 978-0-8075-1330-9 Subj: Animals – donkeys. Farms. Musical instruments. Noise, sounds.

Newton, Vanessa. *Let freedom sing* ill. by Vanessa Brantley Newton. Blue Apple, 2009. ISBN 978-1-934706-90-9 Subj: Ethnic groups in the U.S. – African Americans. Prejudice. Songs. U.S. history.

Neye, Emily. *Butterflies* ill. by Ron Broda. Grosset, 2000. ISBN 978-0-448-42280-0 Subj: Insects – butterflies, caterpillars.

Honeybees ill. by Thomas Leonard. Golden, 2002. ISBN 978-0-307-46217-6 Subj: Insects – bees.

Nez, John. *One smart Cookie* ill. by author. Whitman, 2006. ISBN 978-0-8075-6099-0 Subj: Animals – dogs. Books, reading. Fire. School.

Nic Leodhas, Sorche *see* Alger, Leclaire Gowans

Nichol, Barbara. *Trunks all aboard* ill. by Sir William Cornelius Van Horne. Tundra, 2001. ISBN 978-0-88776-536-0 Subj: ABC books. Animals – elephants. Rhyming text.

Nicholls, Judith. *Billywise* ill. by Jason Cockcroft. Bloomsbury, 2002. ISBN 978-1-58234-778-3 Subj: Behavior – growing up. Birds – owls. Family life – mothers.

Someone I like: poems about people ill. by Giovanni Manna. Barefoot, 2000. ISBN 978-1-84148-004-6 Subj: Emotions. Family life. Friendship. Poetry.

Nichols, Grace. *Whoa, Baby, whoa!* ill. by Eleanor Taylor. Bloomsbury, 2012. ISBN 978-1-59990-742-0 Subj: Babies.

Nickle, John. *Alphabet explosion! Search and count from alien to zebra* ill. by author. Random House, 2006. ISBN 978-0-375-83598-8 Subj: ABC books. Counting, numbers. Picture puzzles. Wordless.

The ant bully ill. by author. Scholastic, 1999. ISBN 978-0-590-39591-5 Subj: Behavior – bullying, teasing. Concepts – size. Insects – ants.

TV Rex ill. by author. Scholastic, 2001. ISBN 978-0-439-12043-2 Subj: Emotions – grief. Family life – grandfathers. Imagination. Television.

Nidey, Kelli. *When autumn falls* ill. by Susan Swan. Whitman, 2004. ISBN 978-0-8075-0490-1 Subj: Poetry. Seasons – fall.

Niekerk, Clarabelle van. *Understanding Sam and Asperger syndrome* by Clarabelle van Niekerk and Liezl Venter ill. by Clarabelle van Niekerk. Skeezel, 2008. ISBN 978-0-9747217-1-2 Subj: Disabilities – autism.

Nielsen, Laura. *Mrs. Muddle's holidays* ill. by Thomas Yezerski. Farrar, 2008. ISBN 978-0-374-35094-9 Subj: Communities, neighborhoods. Holidays.

Niemann, Christoph. *The pet dragon: a story about adventure, friendship, and Chinese characters* ill. by author. Greenwillow, 2008. ISBN 978-0-06-157776-5 Subj: Activities – writing. Dragons. Foreign lands – China. Foreign languages. Pets.

The police cloud ill. by author. Random House, 2007. ISBN 978-0-375-83963-4 Subj: Careers – police officers. Weather – clouds.

Subway ill. by author. HarperCollins, 2010. ISBN 978-0-06-157779-6 Subj: Cities, towns. Family life – fathers. Rhyming text. Trains.

That's how! ill. by author. HarperCollins, 2011. ISBN 978-0-06-201963-9 Subj: Imagination. Machines. Trucks.

Nijssen, Elfi. *Laurie* ill. by Eline van Lindenhuizen. Clavis, 2010. ISBN 978-1-60537-072-9 Subj: Disabilities – deafness.

Nikola-Lisa, W. *Bein' with you this way* ill. by Michael Bryant. Lee & Low, 1994. ISBN 978-1-880000-05-2 Subj: Activities – playing. Ethnic groups in the U.S. Ethnic groups in the U.S. – African Americans. Friendship. Poetry.

Can you top that? ill. by Hector Viveros Lee. Lee & Low, 2000. ISBN 978-1-880000-99-1 Subj: Activities – drawing. Animals. Counting, numbers.

Hallelujah! a Christmas celebration ill. by Synthia Saint James. Atheneum, 1999. ISBN 978-0-689-81673-4 Subj: Ethnic groups in the U.S. – African Americans. Holidays – Christmas. Religion – Nativity.

Magic in the margins: a medieval tale of bookmaking ill. by Bonnie Christensen. Houghton, 2007. ISBN 978-0-618-49642-6 Subj: Animals – mice. Art. Books, reading. Middle Ages.

One hole in the road ill. by Dan Yaccarino. Holt, 1996. ISBN 978-0-8050-4285-6 Subj: Counting, numbers. Machines. Roads.

One, two, three Thanksgiving! ill. by Robin Kramer. Whitman, 1991. ISBN 978-0-8075-6109-6 Subj: Counting, numbers. Family life. Holidays – Thanksgiving.

Shake dem Halloween bones ill. by Mike Reed. Houghton, 1997. ISBN 978-0-395-73095-9 Subj: Holidays – Halloween. Parties. Rhyming text.

Summer sun risin' ill. by Don Tate. Lee & Low, 2002. ISBN 978-1-58430-034-2 Subj: Ethnic groups in the U.S. – African Americans. Family life. Farms. Rhyming text.

To hear the angels sing ill. by Jill Weber. Holiday, 2002. ISBN 978-0-8234-1627-1 Subj: Holidays – Christmas. Religion – Nativity. Rhyming text.

The year with Grandma Moses ill. by Grandma Moses. Holt, 2000. ISBN 978-0-8050-6243-4 Subj: Art. Careers – artists. Seasons.

Nimmo, Jenny. *Esmeralda and the children next door* ill. by Paul Howard. Houghton, 2000. ISBN 978-0-618-02902-0 Subj: Circus. Concepts – size. Friendship. Illness.

Something wonderful ill. by Debbie Boon. Harcourt, 2001. ISBN 978-0-15-216486-7 Subj: Birds – chickens. Character traits – being different.

Niner, Holly L. *I can't stop! a story about Tourette Syndrome* ill. by Meryl Treatner. Whitman, 2005. ISBN 978-0-8075-3620-9 Subj: Disabilities.

Mr. Worry ill. by Greg Swearingen. Whitman, 2004. ISBN 978-0-8075-5182-0 Subj: Behavior. Illness – mental illness.

Nipp, Susan Hagen. *Wee Sing if you're happy and you know it* (Beall, Pamela Conon)

Nishimura, Kae. *Bunny Lune* ill. by author. Houghton, 2007. ISBN 978-0-618-71606-7 Subj: Animals – rabbits. Moon.

Dinah ill. by author. Clarion, 2004. ISBN 978-0-618-33612-8 Subj: Animals – cats. Behavior – lost. Humorous stories. Self-concept.

Nishizuka, Koko. *The beckoning cat: based on a Japanese folktale* ill. by Rosanne Litzinger. Holiday, 2009. ISBN 978-0-8234-2051-3 Subj: Animals – cats. Character traits – luck. Folk & fairy tales. Foreign lands – Japan.

Nivola, Claire A. *The forest* ill. by author. Farrar, 2002. ISBN 978-0-374-32452-0 Subj: Animals – mice. Emotions – fear. Forest, woods.

Life in the ocean: the story of oceanographer Sylvia Earle ill. by author. Farrar, 2012. ISBN 978-0-374-38068-7 Subj: Careers – oceanographers. Ecology. Sea & seashore.

Orani: my father's village ill. by author. Farrar, 2011. ISBN 978-0-374-35657-6 Subj: Foreign lands – Italy. Memories, memory.

Planting the trees of Kenya: the story of Wangari Maathai ill. by author. Farrar, 2008. ISBN 978-0-374-39918-4 Subj: Ecology. Foreign lands – Kenya. Trees.

Noah, build your boat: Old Testament stories and pictures by kids ed. by Jeff Kunkel. Augsburg Fortress, 2002. ISBN 978-0-8066-4402-8 Subj: Children as authors. Children as illustrators. Religion.

Nobisso, Josephine. *Grandpa loved* ill. by Maureen Hyde. 2nd ed. Gingerbread House, 2000. ISBN 978-0-940112-01-8 Subj: Death. Emotions – grief. Emotions – love. Family life – grandfathers.

John Blair and the great Hinckley fire ill. by Ted Rose. Houghton, 2000. ISBN 978-0-618-01560-3 Subj: Character traits – bravery. Ethnic groups in the U.S. – African Americans. Fire. Trains.

The moon's lullaby ill. by Glo Coalson. Orchard, 2001. ISBN 978-0-439-29312-9 Subj: Activities. Bedtime. Night. Sleep.

The weight of a Mass ill. by Katalin Szegedi. Gingerbread House, 2002. ISBN 978-0-940112-09-4 Subj: Religion. Royalty – kings. Royalty – queens. Weddings.

The yawn ill. by Glo Coalson. Orchard, 2001. ISBN 978-0-531-33319-8 Subj: Sleep.

Noble, Sheilagh. *More* ill. by author. Zero to Ten, 2000. ISBN 978-1-84089-127-0 Subj: Animals – dogs. Family life – mothers. Parks.

Noble, Trinka Hakes. *A Christmas spider's miracle* ill. by Stephen Costanza. Sleeping Bear, 2011. ISBN 978-1-58536-602-6 Subj: Folk & fairy tales. Holidays – Christmas. Spiders.

The day Jimmy's boa ate the wash ill. by Steven Kellogg. Dial, 1980. ISBN 978-0-8037-1724-4 Subj: Activities. Humorous stories. Reptiles – snakes. School – field trips.

Jimmy's boa and the big splash birthday bash ill. by Steven Kellogg. Dial, 1989. ISBN 978-0-8037-0540-1 Subj: Birthdays. Humorous stories. Pets. Reptiles – snakes.

Jimmy's boa bounces back ill. by Steven Kellogg. Dial, 1984. ISBN 978-0-8037-0049-9 Subj: Humorous stories. Reptiles – snakes.

Nobles, Kristen M. *Drive this book* ill. by author. Chronicle, 2001. ISBN 978-0-8118-2861-1 Subj: Automobiles. Format, unusual – toy & movable books. Noise, sounds. Transportation. Trucks.

Noda, Takayo. *Dear world* ill. by author. Dial, 2002. ISBN 978-0-8037-2644-4 Subj: Nature. Poetry.

Song of the flowers ill. by author. Penguin, 2006. ISBN 978-0-8037-2934-6 Subj: Flowers. Lullabies.

Noguchi, Rick. *Flowers from Mariko* by Rick Noguchi and Deneen Jenks ill. by Michelle Reiko Kumata. Lee & Low, 2001. ISBN 978-1-58430-032-8 Subj: Ethnic groups in the U.S. – Japanese Americans. Gardens, gardening. U.S. history.

Nolan, Dennis. *Sea of dreams* ill. by author. Roaring Brook, 2011. ISBN 978-1-59643-470-7 Subj: Sand. Sea & seashore. Wordless.

Nolan, Janet. *A Father's Day thank you* ill. by Kathi Ember. Whitman, 2007. ISBN 978-0-8075-2291-2 Subj: Animals – bears. Art. Family life – fathers. Gifts. Holidays – Father's Day.

The firehouse light ill. by Marie Lafrance. Tricycle, 2010. ISBN 978-1-58246-298-1 Subj: Careers – firefighters. Fire. U.S. history.

The St. Patrick's Day shillelagh ill. by Ben F. Stahl. Whitman, 2002. ISBN 978-0-8075-7344-0 Subj: Activities – storytelling. Ethnic groups in the U.S. – Irish Americans. Foreign lands – Ireland. Holidays – St. Patrick's Day. Immigrants.

Nolan, Lucy A. *Jack Quack* ill. by Andréa Wesson. Marshall Cavendish, 2001. ISBN 978-0-7614-5091-7 Subj: Animals – babies. Birds – ducks. Self-concept.

Nolen, Jerdine. *Big Jabe* ill. by Kadir Nelson. Lothrop, 2000. ISBN 978-0-688-13663-5 Subj: Ethnic groups in the U.S. – African Americans. Slavery. Tall tales.

Harvey Potter's balloon farm ill. by Mark Buehner. Lothrop, 1994. ISBN 978-0-688-07888-1 Subj: Farms. Magic. Tall tales. Toys – balloons.

Hewitt Anderson's great big life ill. by Kadir Nelson. Simon & Schuster, 2005. ISBN 978-0-689-86866-5 Subj: Character traits – smallness. Concepts – size. Family life. Giants.

In my momma's kitchen ill. by Colin Bootman. Lothrop, 1999. ISBN 978-0-688-12761-9 Subj: Activities – baking, cooking. Family life. Homes, houses.

Pitching in for Eubie ill. by E. B. Lewis. HarperCollins, 2007. ISBN 978-0-06-056960-0 Subj: Character traits – helpfulness. Ethnic groups in the U.S. – African Americans. Family life.

Plantzilla goes to camp ill. by David Catrow. Simon & Schuster, 2005. ISBN 978-0-689-86803-0 Subj: Behavior – bullying, teasing. Camps, camping. Humorous stories. Letters, cards. Plants.

Raising dragons ill. by Elise Primavera. Silver Whistle, 1998. ISBN 978-0-15-201288-5 Subj: Careers. Dragons. Eggs. Farms. Friendship.

Thunder Rose ill. by Kadir Nelson. Harcourt, 2003. ISBN 978-0-15-216472-0 Subj: Ethnic groups in the U.S. – African Americans. Tall tales. U.S. history – frontier & pioneer life.

Noll, Amanda. *I need my monster* ill. by Howard McWilliam. Flashlight, 2009. ISBN 978-0-9799746-2-5 Subj: Bedtime. Monsters.

Noonan, Diana. *The crocodile* ill. with photos. Chelsea, 2003. ISBN 978-0-7910-6964-6 Subj: Animals – endangered animals. Reptiles – alligators, crocodiles.

Noonan, Julia. *Bath day* ill. by author. Scholastic, 2000. ISBN 978-0-439-11492-9 Subj: Activities – bathing. Animals – dogs. Rhyming text.

Breakfast time ill. by author. Scholastic, 2000. ISBN 978-0-439-11490-5 Subj: Animals – dogs. Food. Rhyming text.

Hare and Rabbit, friends forever ill. by author. Scholastic, 2000. ISBN 978-0-439-08753-7 Subj: Animals – rabbits. Character traits – cleanliness. Circus. Friendship.

Mouse by mouse ill. by author. Dutton, 2003. ISBN 978-0-525-46864-6 Subj: Animals – mice. Counting, numbers. Format, unusual – toy & movable books. Rhyming text.

Norac, Carl. *Hello, sweetie pie* ill. by Claude K. Dubois. Random House, 2000. ISBN 978-0-385-32733-6 Subj: Animals – hamsters. Names. School.

I love to cuddle ill. by Claude K. Dubois. Doubleday, 1999. ISBN 978-0-385-32646-9 Subj: Animals – hamsters. Emotions – loneliness. Format, unusual – board books.

I love you so much ill. by Claude K. Dubois. Doubleday, 1997. ISBN 978-0-385-32512-7 Subj: Animals – hamsters. Emotions – love. Family life.

Monster, don't eat me! ill. by Carll Cneut. Groundwood, 2007. ISBN 978-0-88899-800-2 Subj: Animals – pigs. Behavior – greed. Food. Monsters.

My daddy is a giant ill. by Ingrid Godon. Clarion, 2005. ISBN 978-0-618-44399-4 Subj: Concepts – size. Family life – fathers.

My mommy is magic ill. by Ingrid Godon. Houghton, 2007. ISBN 978-0-618-75766-4 Subj: Family life – mothers. Magic.

Nordling, Lee. *The bramble* ill. by Bruce Zick. Carolrhoda, 2013. ISBN 978-0-7613-5856-5 Subj: Format, unusual – graphic novels. Monsters. Self-concept.

Norling, Beth. *Sister night and sister day* ill. by author. Retelling of the Grimm's fairy tale Mother Holle. Allen & Unwin, 2000. ISBN 978-1-86448-863-0 Subj: Family life – sisters. Folk & fairy tales. Foreign lands – Germany. Multiple births – twins.

The stone baby ill. by author. Lothian, 2004. ISBN 978-0-7344-0353-7 Subj: Activities – traveling. Birds. Emotions. Toys – dolls.

Norman, Geoffrey. *Stars above us* ill. by E. B. Lewis. Putnam, 2009. ISBN 978-0-399-24724-8 Subj: Careers – military. Emotions – fear. Family life – fathers. Stars.

Norman, Kim. *I know a wee piggy* ill. by Henry Cole. Dial, 2012. ISBN 978-0-8037-3735-8 Subj: Animals – pigs. Concepts – color. Cumulative tales. Fairs, festivals. Rhyming text.

If it's snowy and you know it, clap your paws! ill. by Liza Woodruff. Sterling, 2013. ISBN 978-1-4549-0384-0 Subj: Animals. Rhyming text. Seasons – winter. Songs. Weather – snow.

Ten on the sled ill. by Liza Woodruff. Sterling, 2010. ISBN 978-1-4027-7076-0 Subj: Animals. Counting, numbers. Rhyming text. Seasons – winter. Sports – sledding.

Norris, Kathleen. *The holy twins: Benedict and Scholastica* ill. by Tomie dePaola. Putnam, 2001. ISBN 978-0-399-23424-8 Subj: Careers – clergy. Careers – nuns. Family life – brothers & sisters. Foreign lands – Italy. Multiple births – twins. Religion.

Norris, Leslie. *Albert and the angels* ill. by Mordicai Gerstein. Farrar, 2000. ISBN 978-0-374-30192-7 Subj: Angels. Animals – dogs. Behavior – lost & found possessions. Holidays – Christmas.

North, Sherry. *Because I am your daddy* ill. by Marcellus Hall. Abrams, 2010. ISBN 978-0-8109-8392-2 Subj: Family life – fathers. Rhyming text.

Because you are my baby ill. by Marcellus Hall. Abrams, 2008. ISBN 978-0-8109-9482-9 Subj: Babies. Emotions – love. Family life – mothers. Rhyming text.

Champ's story: dogs get cancer too! ill. by Kathleen Rietz. Sylvan Dell, 2010. ISBN 978-1-60718-077-7 Subj: Animals – dogs. Illness – cancer.

Northey, Lawrence. *I'm a hop hop hoppity frog* ill. by Julie Northey. Stoddart, 2002. ISBN 978-0-7737-3335-0 Subj: Frogs & toads. Poetry. Rhyming text.

Norwich, William D. *Molly and the magic dress* ill. by M. Scott Miller. Doubleday, 2002. ISBN 978-0-385-32745-9 Subj: Animals – cats. Clothing – dresses. Emotions – loneliness. Imagination. Magic.

Norworth, Jack. *Take me out to the ball game* ill. by Amiko Hirao. Imagine, 2011. ISBN 978-1-936140-26-8 Subj: Songs. Sports – baseball.

Take me out to the ballgame: the sensational baseball song ill. by Jim Burke. Little, Brown, 2006. ISBN 978-0-316-75819-2 Subj: Songs. Sports – baseball.

Noullet, Georgette. *Bed hog* ill. by David Slonim. Marshall Cavendish, 2011. ISBN 978-0-7614-5823-4 Subj: Animals – dogs. Sleep.

Novak, Matt. *The everything machine* ill. by author. Roaring Brook, 2009. ISBN 978-1-59643-268-4 Subj: Character traits – cleanliness. Humorous stories. Machines.

Flip flop bop ill. by author. Macmillan, 2005. ISBN 978-1-59643-049-5 Subj: Clothing – shoes. Rhyming text. Seasons – summer.

Jazzbo and Googy ill. by author. Hyperion, 2000. ISBN 978-0-7868-2340-6 Subj: Animals – bears. Animals – pigs. Friendship. Toys – bears.

Jazzbo goes to school ill. by author. Hyperion, 1999. ISBN 978-0-7868-2339-0 Subj: Animals – bears. School – first day.

The last Christmas present ill. by author. Orchard, 1993. ISBN 978-0-531-08645-2 Subj: Holidays – Christmas. Mythical creatures – elves. Santa Claus.

No zombies allowed ill. by author. Atheneum, 2001. ISBN 978-0-689-84130-9 Subj: Holidays – Halloween. Parties. Witches.

The Pillow War ill. by author. Orchard, 1998. ISBN 978-0-531-33048-7 Subj: Animals – dogs. Behavior – fighting, arguing. Family life – brothers & sisters. Rhyming text. Sleep.

The Robobots ill. by author. DK, 1999. ISBN 978-0-7894-2566-9 Subj: Communities, neighborhoods. Robots.

Too many bunnies ill. by author. Macmillan, 2005. ISBN 978-1-59643-038-9 Subj: Animals – rabbits. Format, unusual – toy & movable books.

A wish for you ill. by author. HarperCollins, 2010. ISBN 978-0-06-155202-1 Subj: Babies. Family life. Rhyming text.

Novesky, Amy. *Georgia in Hawaii: when Georgia O'Keeffe painted what she pleased* ill. by Yuyi Morales. Harcourt, 2012. ISBN 978-0-15-205420-5 Subj: Careers – artists. Character traits – assertiveness. Hawaii.

Noyed, Robert B. *Crocodiles* (Klingel, Cynthia Fitterer)

Dancers (Klingel, Cynthia Fitterer)

Deserts (Klingel, Cynthia Fitterer)

Farmers (Klingel, Cynthia Fitterer)

Firefighters (Klingel, Cynthia Fitterer)

Forests (Klingel, Cynthia Fitterer)

Grizzly bears (Klingel, Cynthia Fitterer)

Halloween (Klingel, Cynthia Fitterer)

Manatees (Klingel, Cynthia Fitterer)

Oceans (Klingel, Cynthia Fitterer)

Paul Revere's ride (Klingel, Cynthia Fitterer)

Postal workers (Klingel, Cynthia Fitterer)

Rosa Parks (Klingel, Cynthia Fitterer)

Soccer (Klingel, Cynthia Fitterer)

Thanksgiving (Klingel, Cynthia Fitterer)

Timber wolves (Klingel, Cynthia Fitterer)

Underground (Klingel, Cynthia Fitterer)

Noyes, Deborah. *When I met the wolf girls* ill. by August Hall. Houghton, 2007. ISBN 978-0-618-60567-5 Subj: Foreign lands – India. Orphans.

Numberman, Neil. *Do not build a Frankenstein!* ill. by author. HarperCollins, 2009. ISBN 978-0-06-156816-9 Subj: Humorous stories. Monsters. Moving.

Numeroff, Laura Joffe. *The Chicken sisters* ill. by Sharleen Collicott. Geringer, 1997. ISBN 978-0-06-026680-6 Subj: Animals. Birds – chickens. Family life – sisters. Farms.

Chimps don't wear glasses ill. by Joseph Mathieu. Simon & Schuster, 1995. ISBN 978-0-671-87007-2 Subj: Activities. Animals. Imagination. Rhyming text.

The hope tree by Laura Joffe Numeroff and Wendy Schlessel Harpham ill. by David McPhail. Simon & Schuster, 1999. ISBN 978-0-689-84526-0 Subj: Animals. Emotions. Family life – mothers. Illness – cancer.

If you give a cat a cupcake ill. by Felicia Bond. HarperCollins, 2008. ISBN 978-0-06-028324-7 Subj: Animals – cats. Character traits – kindness to animals. Circular tales.

If you give a dog a donut ill. by Felicia Bond. HarperCollins, 2011. ISBN 978-0-06-026683-7 Subj: Animals – dogs. Character traits – kindness to animals. Circular tales.

If you give a moose a muffin ill. by Felicia Bond. HarperCollins, 1991. ISBN 978-0-06-024406-4 Subj: Animals – moose. Character traits – kindness to animals. Circular tales.

If you give a mouse a cookie ill. by Felicia Bond. HarperCollins, 1985. ISBN 978-0-06-024587-0 Subj: Animals – mice. Behavior – imitation. Character traits – kindness to animals. Circular tales.

If you give a pig a pancake ill. by Felicia Bond. Geringer, 1998. ISBN 978-0-06-026687-5 Subj: Animals – pigs. Character traits – kindness to animals. Circular tales.

If you give a pig a party ill. by Felicia Bond. HarperCollins, 2005. ISBN 978-0-06-028327-8 Subj: Animals – pigs. Circular tales. Parties.

If you take a mouse to school ill. by Felicia Bond. Geringer, 2002. ISBN 978-0-06-028329-2 Subj: Animals – mice. School.

If you take a mouse to the movies ill. by Felicia Bond. Geringer, 2000. ISBN 978-0-06-027868-7 Subj: Activities. Animals – mice. Holidays – Christmas.

The Jellybeans and the big art adventure by Laura Joffe Numeroff and Nate Evans ill. by Lynn Munsinger. Abrams, 2012. ISBN 978-1-4197-0171-9 Subj: Activities – painting. Animals. Character traits – cooperation. Friendship.

The Jellybeans and the big book bonanza by Laura Joffe Numeroff and Nate Evans ill. by Lynn Munsinger. Abrams, 2010. ISBN 978-0-8109-8412-7 Subj: Animals. Books, reading. Friendship. Libraries.

The Jellybeans and the big camp kickoff by Laura Joffe Numeroff and Nate Evans ill. by Lynn Munsinger. Abrams, 2011. ISBN 978-0-8109-9765-3 Subj: Animals. Camps, camping. Character traits – cooperation. Friendship.

The Jellybeans and the big dance by Laura Joffe Numeroff and Nate Evans ill. by Lynn Munsinger.

Abrams, 2008. ISBN 978-0-8109-9352-5 Subj: Animals. Ballet. Character traits – cooperation.

Laura Numeroff's 10-step guide to living with your monster ill. by Nate Evans. Geringer, 2002. ISBN 978-0-06-623823-4 Subj: Humorous stories. Monsters. Pets.

Merry Christmas, Mouse! ill. by Felicia Bond. HarperCollins, 2007. ISBN 978-0-06-134499-2 Subj: Animals – mice. Counting, numbers. Holidays – Christmas.

Nighty-night, Cooper ill. by Lynn Munsinger. Houghton Mifflin, 2013. ISBN 978-0-547-40205-5 Subj: Animals – kangaroos. Bedtime. Family life – mothers. Lullabies.

Otis and Sydney and the best birthday ever ill. by Dan Andreasen. Abrams, 2010. ISBN 978-0-8109-8959-7 Subj: Animals – bears. Birthdays. Friendship. Parties.

Ponyella by Laura Joffe Numeroff and Nate Evans ill. by Lynn Munsinger. Hyperion/Disney, 2011. ISBN 978-1-4231-0259-5 Subj: Animals – horses, ponies. Fairies. Folk & fairy tales. Royalty – princesses.

Sherman Crunchley by Laura Joffe Numeroff and Nate Evans ill. by Tim Bowers. Dutton, 2003. ISBN 978-0-525-47130-1 Subj: Animals – dogs. Careers – police officers. Character traits – individuality. Clothing – hats.

Sometimes I wonder if poodles like noodles ill. by Tim Bowers. Simon & Schuster, 1999. ISBN 978-0-689-80563-9 Subj: Humorous stories. Poetry.

What brothers do best ill. by Lynn Munsinger. Chronicle, 2012. ISBN 978-1-4521-1073-8 Subj: Family life – brothers. Format, unusual – board books.

What brothers do best; What sisters do best ill. by Lynn Munsinger. Chronicle, 2009. ISBN 978-0-8118-6545-6 Subj: Character traits – helpfulness. Family life – brothers & sisters.

What daddies do best ill. by Lynn Munsinger. Simon & Schuster, 2002. ISBN 978-0-689-84466-9 Subj: Animals – foxes. Buildings. Cities, towns. Family life – fathers. Gender roles.

What grandmas do best; What grandpas do best ill. by Lynn Munsinger. Simon & Schuster, 2000. ISBN 978-0-689-80552-3 Subj: Animals. Family life – grandfathers. Family life – grandmothers. Format, unusual.

What mommies do best ill. by Lynn Munsinger. Simon & Schuster, 1998. ISBN 978-0-689-80577-6 Subj: Activities – picnicking. Animals – mice. Gender roles.

What puppies do best ill. by Lynn Munsinger. Chronicle, 2011. ISBN 978-0-8118-6601-9 Subj: Activities. Animals – babies. Animals – dogs.

When sheep sleep ill. by David McPhail. Abrams, 2006. ISBN 978-0-8109-5469-4 Subj: Animals. Animals – sheep. Bedtime. Counting, numbers. Rhyming text.

Why a disguise? ill. by David McPhail. Simon & Schuster, 1996. ISBN 978-0-671-87006-5 Subj: Character traits – appearance.

Would I trade my parents? ill. by James Bernardin. Abrams, 2009. ISBN 978-0-8109-0637-2 Subj: Family life – parents.

Nunes, Susan Miho. *The last dragon* ill. by Chris Soentpiet. Clarion, 1995. ISBN 978-0-395-67020-0 Subj: Dragons. Ethnic groups in the U.S. – Chinese Americans. Family life – aunts, uncles.

Nye, Naomi Shihab. *Come with me: poems for a journey* ill. by Dan Yaccarino. Greenwillow, 2000. ISBN 978-0-688-15947-4 Subj: Activities – traveling. Poetry.

Sitti's secrets ill. by Nancy Carpenter. Four Winds, 1994. ISBN 978-0-02-768460-5 Subj: Ethnic groups in the U.S. – Arab Americans. Family life – grandmothers. Foreign lands – Palestine. Foreign languages.

Nyeu, Tao. *Bunny days* ill. by author. Penguin, 2010. ISBN 978-0-8037-3330-5 Subj: Animals – babies. Animals – bears. Animals – rabbits.

Squid and Octopus: friends for always ill. by author. Dial, 2012. ISBN 978-0-8037-3565-1 Subj: Friendship. Octopuses. Squid.

Nygaard, Elizabeth. *Snake alley band* ill. by Betsy Lewin. Doubleday, 1998. ISBN 978-0-385-32323-9 Subj: Animals. Music. Musical instruments – bands. Noise, sounds. Reptiles – snakes.

Ó Flatharta, Antoine. *Hurry and the monarch* ill. by Meilo So. Knopf, 2005. ISBN 978-0-375-93003-4 Subj: Friendship. Insects – butterflies, caterpillars. Migration. Reptiles – turtles, tortoises.

Obama, Barack. *Change has come: an artist celebrates our American spirit* ill. by Kadir Nelson. Simon & Schuster, 2009. ISBN 978-1-4169-8955-4 Subj: Ethnic groups in the U.S. – African Americans. U.S. history.

Of thee I sing: a letter to my daughters ill. by Loren Long. Random House, 2010. ISBN 978-0-375-

83527-8 Subj: Character traits. Self-concept. U.S. history.

Obed, Ellen Bryan. *Who would like a Christmas tree?* ill. by Anne Hunter. Houghton, 2009. ISBN 978-0-547-04625-9 Subj: Days of the week, months of the year. Holidays – Christmas. Trees.

Oberman, Sheldon. *The always prayer shawl* ill. by Ted Lewin. Boyds Mills, 1994. ISBN 978-1-878093-22-6 Subj: Clothing. Family life – grandfathers. Immigrants. Jewish culture.

By the Hanukkah light ill. by Neil Waldman. Boyds Mills, 1997. ISBN 978-1-56397-658-2 Subj: Family life – grandfathers. Holidays – Hanukkah. Holocaust. War.

The wisdom bird: a tale of Solomon and Sheba ill. by Neil Waldman. Boyds Mills, 2000. ISBN 978-1-56397-816-6 Subj: Birds. Character traits – wisdom. Folk & fairy tales. Foreign lands – Africa. Foreign lands – Israel. Royalty – kings. Royalty – queens.

Oborne, Martine. *One beautiful baby* ill. by Ingrid Godon. Little, 2002. ISBN 978-0-316-06562-7 Subj: Babies.

O'Brien, Anne Sibley. *A path of stars* ill. by author. Charlesbridge, 2012. ISBN 978-1-57091-735-6 Subj: Character traits – perseverance. Death. Emotions – grief. Ethnic groups in the U.S. – Cambodian Americans. Family life – grandmothers. Memories, memory. War.

O'Brien, Patrick. *Captain Raptor and the space pirates* (O'Malley, Kevin)

Gigantic! how big were the dinosaurs? ill. by author. Holt, 1999. ISBN 978-0-8050-5738-6 Subj: Concepts – size. Dinosaurs.

Megatooth ill. by author. Holt, 2001. ISBN 978-0-8050-6214-4 Subj: Fish – sharks. Teeth.

Sabertooth ill. by author. Holt, 2008. ISBN 978-0-8050-7105-4 Subj: Animals – tigers. Dinosaurs. Prehistory.

You are the first kid on Mars ill. by author. Putnam, 2009. ISBN 978-0-399-24634-0 Subj: Planets. Space & space ships.

O'Callahan, Jay. *Raspberries!* ill. by Will Moses. Philomel, 2009. ISBN 978-0-399-25181-8 Subj: Careers – bakers. Character traits – kindness. Character traits – perseverance. Food.

Ochiltree, Dianne. *It's a firefly night* ill. by Betsy E. Snyder. Blue Apple, 2013. ISBN 978-1-60905-291-1 Subj: Family life – fathers. Insects – fireflies. Night. Rhyming text.

Molly, by golly! the legend of Molly Williams, America's first female firefighter ill. by Kathleen Kemly. Boyds Mills, 2012. ISBN 978-1-59078-721-2 Subj: Careers – chefs, cooks. Careers – firefighters. Ethnic groups in the U.S. – African Americans. Gender roles. U.S. history.

Pillow pup ill. by Mireille d' Allancé. McElderry, 2002. ISBN 978-0-689-83408-0 Subj: Activities – playing. Animals – dogs. Rhyming text.

O'Connell, Jennifer. *It's Halloween night!* ill. by Jennifer Morris. Scholastic, 2012. ISBN 978-0-545-40283-5 Subj: Clothing – costumes. Holidays – Halloween.

O'Connell, Rebecca. *Baby parade* ill. by Susie Poole. Whitman, 2013. ISBN 978-0-8075-0509-0 Subj: Babies. Family life.

Danny is done with diapers: a potty ABC ill. by Amanda Gulliver. Whitman, 2010. ISBN 978-0-8075-1466-5 Subj: ABC books. Toilet training.

O'Connor, George. *Ker-splash!* ill. by author. Simon & Schuster, 2005. ISBN 978-0-689-87682-0 Subj: Activities – playing. Behavior – bullying, teasing. Imagination. Sea & seashore.

Sally and the Some-Thing ill. by author. Macmillan, 2006. ISBN 978-1-59643-141-6 Subj: Friendship. Monsters.

Uncle Bigfoot ill. by author. Roaring Brook, 2008. ISBN 978-1-59643-271-0 Subj: Anatomy – feet. Character traits – being different. Family life – aunts, uncles. Giants.

O'Connor, Jane. *Bonjour, butterfly* ill. by Robin Preiss-Glasser. HarperCollins, 2008. ISBN 978-0-06-123588-7 Subj: Birthdays. Insects – butterflies, caterpillars. Parties.

Fancy Nancy ill. by Robin Preiss-Glasser. HarperCollins, 2006. ISBN 978-0-06-054209-2 Subj: Clothing. Family life. Self-concept.

Fancy Nancy: aspiring artist ill. by Robin Preiss-Glasser. HarperCollins, 2011. ISBN 978-0-06-191526-0 Subj: Activities – drawing. Art. Language.

Fancy Nancy: explorer extraordinaire! ill. by Robin Preiss-Glasser. HarperCollins, 2009. ISBN 978-0-06-168486-9 Subj: Birds. Clubs, gangs. Insects. Language. Nature.

Fancy Nancy: fanciest doll in the universe ill. by Robin Preiss-Glasser. HarperCollins, 2013. ISBN 978-0-06-170384-3 Subj: Behavior – misbehavior. Family life – sisters. Toys – dolls.

Fancy Nancy: ooh la la! it's beauty day ill. by Robin Preiss-Glasser. HarperCollins, 2010. ISBN 978-0-06-191525-3 Subj: Beauty shops. Birthdays. Language. Self-concept.

Fancy Nancy: poet extraordinaire! ill. by Robin Preiss-Glasser. HarperCollins, 2010. ISBN 978-0-06-189643-9 Subj: Activities – writing. Poetry. School.

Fancy Nancy and the fabulous fashion boutique ill. by Robin Preiss-Glasser. HarperCollins, 2010. ISBN 978-0-06-123592-4 Subj: Character traits – generosity. Family life – sisters. Language. Money.

Fancy Nancy and the posh puppy ill. by Robin Preiss-Glasser. HarperCollins, 2012. ISBN 978-0-06-221052-4 Subj: Animals – dogs. Character traits – appearance. Family life. Self-concept.

Fancy Nancy splendiferous Christmas ill. by Robin Preiss-Glasser. HarperCollins, 2009. ISBN 978-0-06-123590-0 Subj: Family life. Holidays – Christmas. Language.

Fancy Nancy's collection of fancy words: from accessories to zany ill. by Robin Preiss-Glasser. HarperCollins, 2008. ISBN 978-0-06-154923-6 Subj: ABC books. Language.

Nancy la elegante / Fancy Nancy ill. by Robin Preiss-Glasser. HarperCollins, 2008. ISBN 978-0-06-143528-7 Subj: Clothing. Family life. Foreign languages. Self-concept.

The perfect puppy for me ill. by Jessie Hartland. Viking, 2003. ISBN 978-0-670-03614-1 Subj: Animals – dogs. Pets.

Ready or not, here comes Scout (Abramson, Jill)

Ready, set, skip! ill. by Ann James. Penguin, 2007. ISBN 978-0-670-06216-4 Subj: Activities. Character traits – persistence. Rhyming text. Self-concept.

The snow globe family ill. by S. D. Schindler. Penguin, 2006. ISBN 978-0-399-24242-7 Subj: Family life.

O'Connor, Teddy. *A new brain for Igor* ill. by Bill Basso. Random House, 2003. ISBN 978-0-375-90626-8 Subj: Anatomy – brain. Careers – scientists.

Odanaka, Barbara. *A crazy day at the Critter Café* ill. by Lee White. Simon & Schuster, 2009. ISBN 978-1-4169-3914-6 Subj: Animals. Restaurants. Rhyming text.

Smash! Mash! Crash! There goes the trash! ill. by Will Hillenbrand. Simon & Schuster, 2006. ISBN 978-0-689-85160-5 Subj: Animals – pigs. Careers – sanitation workers. Rhyming text. Trucks.

Oddino, Licia. *Finn and the fairies* ill. by Alessandra Toni. Purple Bear, 2006. ISBN 978-1-933327-17-4 Subj: Careers – tailors. Fairies.

Odone, Jamison. *Honey badgers* ill. by author. Boyds Mills, 2007. ISBN 978-1-932425-51-2 Subj: Animals – badgers. Orphans.

Mole had everything ill. by author. Blue Apple, 2012. ISBN 978-1-60905-224-9 Subj: Animals – moles. Behavior – seeking better things. Character traits – orderliness. Self-concept.

Oelschlager, Vanita. *Bonyo Bonyo: the true story of a brave boy from Kenya* ill. by Kristin Blackwood. Vanita, 2010. ISBN 978-0-9819714-3-8 Subj: Careers – doctors. Foreign lands – Kenya.

I came from the water: one Haitian boy's incredible tale of survival ill. by Mike Blanc. Vanita, 2012. ISBN 978-0-9832904-4-5 Subj: Earthquakes. Foreign lands – Haiti. Illness. Orphans. Weather – floods.

Made in China: a story of adoption ill. by Kristin Blackwood. Vanita, 2008. ISBN 978-0-9800162-3-9 Subj: Adoption. Ethnic groups in the U.S. – Chinese Americans. Family life. Rhyming text. Sibling rivalry.

A tale of two daddies ill. by Kristin Blackwood. Vanita, 2010. ISBN 978-0-9819714-5-2 Subj: Family life – fathers. Homosexuality.

A tale of two mommies ill. by Mike Blanc. Vanita, 2011. ISBN 978-0-9826366-6-4 Subj: Family life – mothers. Homosexuality.

Ofanansky, Allison. *Harvest of light* ill. by Eliyahu Alpern. Lerner, 2008. ISBN 978-0-8225-7389-0 Subj: Food. Foreign lands – Israel. Holidays – Hanukkah.

Offill, Jenny. *11 experiments that failed* ill. by Nancy Carpenter. Random House, 2011. ISBN 978-0-375-84762-2 Subj: Careers – scientists. Character traits – questioning. Science.

17 things I'm not allowed to do anymore ill. by Nancy Carpenter. Random House, 2006. ISBN 978-0-375-83596-4 Subj: Behavior – misbehavior.

Ogburn, Jacqueline K. *The bake shop ghost* ill. by Marjorie Priceman. Houghton, 2005. ISBN 978-0-618-44557-8 Subj: Careers – bakers. Food. Ghosts.

Little treasures ill. by Chris Raschka. Houghton Mifflin, 2012. ISBN 978-0-547-42862-8 Subj: Foreign languages. Language. World.

The magic nesting doll ill. by Laurel Long. Dial, 2000. ISBN 978-0-8037-2414-3 Subj: Family life – grandmothers. Folk & fairy tales. Magic. Royalty – tsars. Toys – dolls.

Oh, Jiwon. *Cat and mouse* ill. by author. HarperCollins, 2003. ISBN 978-0-06-052744-0 Subj: Animals – cats. Animals – mice. Friendship.

O'Hair, Margaret. *My kitten* ill. by Tammie Lyon. Marshall Cavendish, 2011. ISBN 978-0-7614-5811-1 Subj: Animals – babies. Animals – cats. Rhyming text.

My pup ill. by Tammie Lyon. Marshall Cavendish, 2008. ISBN 978-0-7614-5389-5 Subj: Animals – dogs. Rhyming text.

Star baby ill. by Erin Eitter Kono. Houghton, 2005. ISBN 978-0-618-30668-8 Subj: Babies. Rhyming text.

Sweet baby feet ill. by Tracy Dockray. Farrar, 2012. ISBN 978-0-374-37348-1 Subj: Anatomy – feet. Babies. Rhyming text.

Ohi, Ruth. *And you can come too* ill. by author. Annick, 2005. ISBN 978-1-55037-905-1 Subj: Activities – playing. Behavior – running away. Family life.

Chicken, Pig, Cow and the class pet ill. by author. Annick, 2011. ISBN 978-1-55451-347-5 Subj: Animals – bulls, cows. Animals – hamsters. Animals – pigs. Birds – chickens. School. Toys.

Chicken, Pig, Cow horse around ill. by author. Annick, 2010. ISBN 978-1-55451-245-4 Subj: Animals – bulls, cows. Animals – horses, ponies. Animals – pigs. Birds – chickens. Toys.

Chicken, Pig, Cow's first fight ill. by author. Annick, 2012. ISBN 978-1-55451-371-0 Subj: Animals – bulls, cows. Animals – pigs. Behavior – fighting, arguing. Birds – chickens.

Clara and the Bossy ill. by author. Annick, 2006. ISBN 978-1-55037-943-3 Subj: Animals – guinea pigs. Behavior – bossy. Friendship.

The couch was a castle ill. by author. Annick, 2006. ISBN 978-1-55451-014-6 Subj: Animals – guinea pigs. Family life – brothers & sisters. Imagination.

Kenta and the big wave ill. by author. Annick, 2013. ISBN 978-1-55451-577-6 Subj: Behavior – lost & found possessions. Foreign lands – Japan. Tsunamis.

Me and my brother ill. by author. Annick, 2007. ISBN 978-1-55451-091-7 Subj: Family life – brothers & sisters. Rhyming text.

Me and my sister ill. by author. Annick, 2005. ISBN 978-1-55037-892-4 Subj: Family life – brothers & sisters. Rhyming text.

Pants off first ill. by author. Fitzhenry & Whiteside, 2001. ISBN 978-1-55041-667-1 Subj: Bedtime. Clothing. Family life – mothers. Format, unusual – board books. Pets.

A trip with Grandma ill. by author. Annick, 2007. ISBN 978-1-55451-072-6 Subj: Activities – traveling. Animals – guinea pigs. Behavior – worrying. Family life – brothers & sisters. Family life – grandmothers.

Ohmura, Tomoko. *The long, long line* ill. by author. OwlKids, 2013. ISBN 978-1-926973-92-0 Subj: Animals. Concepts – size. Counting, numbers.

OHora, Zachariah. *No fits, Nilson!* ill. by author. Dial, 2013. ISBN 978-0-8037-3852-2 Subj: Animals – gorillas. Emotions – anger.

Stop snoring, Bernard! ill. by author. Holt, 2011. ISBN 978-0-8050-9002-4 Subj: Animals – otters. Sleep – snoring. Zoos.

O'Keefe, Susan Heyboer. *Baby day* ill. by Robin Spowart. Boyds Mills, 2006. ISBN 978-1-59078-981-0 Subj: Activities – playing. Animals – bears. Babies. Family life. Rhyming text.

Good night, God bless ill. by Hideko Takahashi. Holt, 1999. ISBN 978-0-8050-6008-9 Subj: Bedtime. Religion. Rhyming text.

Hungry monster ABC ill. by Lynn Munsinger. Little, Brown, 2007. ISBN 978-0-316-15574-8 Subj: ABC books. Monsters. Rhyming text.

Love me, love you ill. by Robin Spowart. Boyds Mills, 2001. ISBN 978-1-56397-837-1 Subj: Animals – rabbits. Emotions – love. Family life – mothers. Rhyming text.

One hungry monster ill. by Lynn Munsinger. Little, 1989. ISBN 978-0-316-63385-7 Subj: Counting, numbers. Food. Monsters. Poetry.

Okimoto, Jean Davies. *The White Swan express* by Jean Davies Okimoto and Elaine M. Aoki ill. by Meilo So. Clarion, 2002. ISBN 978-0-618-16453-0 Subj: Adoption. Babies. Ethnic groups in the U.S. – Chinese Americans. Family life – parents. Foreign lands – China.

Olaleye, Isaac. *Bikes for rent!* ill. by Chris L. Demarest. Orchard, 2001. ISBN 978-0-531-33290-0 Subj: Foreign lands – Nigeria. Sports – bicycling.

Bitter bananas ill. by Ed Young. Caroline House, 1994. ISBN 978-1-56397-039-9 Subj: Animals – baboons. Character traits – cleverness. Food. Foreign lands – Africa. Foreign lands – Nigeria. Problem solving.

The distant talking drum ill. by Frané Lessac. Wordsong, 1995. ISBN 978-1-56397-095-5 Subj: Foreign lands – Nigeria. Poetry.

In the Rainfield: who is the greatest? ill. by Ann Grifalconi. Blue Sky, 2000. ISBN 978-0-590-48363-6 Subj: Contests. Folk & fairy tales. Foreign lands – Nigeria. Nature. Weather – rain. Weather – wind.

Lake of the Big Snake ill. by Claudia Shepard. Boyds Mills, 1998. ISBN 978-1-56397-096-2 Subj: Foreign lands – Africa. Forest, woods. Reptiles – snakes.

Old MacDonald had a farm. *Old MacDonald* retold by Rosemary Wells; ill. by reteller. Scholastic, 1998. ISBN 978-0-590-76985-3 Subj: Animals. Careers – farmers. Cumulative tales. Farms. Songs.

Old MacDonald had a farm ill. by Holly Berry. NorthSouth, 1994. ISBN 978-1-55858-282-8 Subj: Animals. Careers – farmers. Cumulative tales. Farms. Music. Songs.

Old MacDonald had a farm by Jane Cabrera; ill. by author. Holiday, 2008. ISBN 978-0-8234-2141-1 Subj: Animals. Careers – farmers. Cumulative tales. Farms. Music. Songs.

Old MacDonald had a farm ill. by Carol Jones. Houghton, 1989. ISBN 978-0-395-49212-3 Subj: Animals. Careers – farmers. Cumulative tales. Farms. Format, unusual. Music. Songs.

Old MacDonald had a farm ill. by Tracey Campbell Pearson. Dial, 1984. ISBN 978-0-8037-0070-3 Subj: Animals. Careers – farmers. Cumulative tales. Farms. Music. Songs.

Old MacDonald had a farm ill. by Glen Rounds. Holiday, 1989. ISBN 978-0-8234-0739-2 Subj: Animals. Careers – farmers. Cumulative tales. Farms. Music. Songs.

Old MacDonald had a farm retold by Jessica Souhami; designed by Paul McAlinden; ill. by reteller. Orchard, 1996. ISBN 978-0-531-09493-8 Subj: Animals. Careers – farmers. Cumulative tales. Farms. Format, unusual – toy & movable books. Songs. Transportation.

Old MacDonald had a farm ill. by Prue Theobalds. Peter Bedrick, 1991. ISBN 978-0-87226-452-6 Subj: Animals. Careers – farmers. Cumulative tales. Farms. Music. Songs.

The old woman and her pig. *The old woman and her pig* adapt. by Eric A. Kimmel; ill. by Giyora Karmi. Holiday, 1992. ISBN 978-0-8234-0970-9 Subj: Cumulative tales. Folk & fairy tales.

The old woman and her pig: an Appalachian folktale retold by Margaret Read MacDonald; ill. by John Kanzler. HarperCollins, 2007. ISBN 978-0-06-028090-1 Subj: Cumulative tales. Folk & fairy tales.

Older, Effin. *My two grandmothers* ill. by Nancy Hayashi. Harcourt, 2000. ISBN 978-0-15-200785-0 Subj: Family life – grandmothers. Holidays – Christmas. Holidays – Hanukkah. Parties.

Older, Jules. *Telling time: how to tell time on digital and analog clocks* ill. by Megan Halsey. Charlesbridge, 2000. ISBN 978-0-88106-396-7 Subj: Clocks, watches. Time.

Oldland, Nicholas. *Big bear hug* ill. by author. Kids Can, 2009. ISBN 978-1-55453-464-7 Subj: Animals – bears. Ecology. Hugging. Trees.

The busy beaver ill. by author. Kids Can, 2011. ISBN 978-1-55453-749-5 Subj: Animals – beavers. Behavior – carelessness.

Dinosaur countdown ill. by author. Kids Can, 2012. ISBN 978-1-55453-834-8 Subj: Counting, numbers. Dinosaurs.

Making the moose out of life ill. by author. Kids Can, 2010. ISBN 978-1-55453-580-4 Subj: Animals – moose. Friendship. Reptiles – turtles, tortoises.

Up the creek ill. by author. Kids Can, 2013. ISBN 978-1-894786-32-4 Subj: Animals. Canoes & canoeing.

O'Leary, Sara. *When you were small* ill. by Julie Morstad. Simply Read, 2006. ISBN 978-1-894965-36-1 Subj: Character traits – smallness. Concepts – size. Family life – fathers. Imagination.

Olfers, Sibylle Von. *When the root children wake up* (Wood, Audrey)

Oliver, Narelle. *Twilight hunt: a seek-and-find book* ill. by author. Star Bright, 2007. ISBN 978-1-59572-107-5 Subj: Behavior – hiding. Birds – owls. Disguises. Nature. Picture puzzles.

Oller, Erika. *The cabbage soup solution* ill. by author. Dutton, 2004. ISBN 978-0-525-47005-2 Subj: Animals – cats. Animals – rabbits. Farms. Food. Humorous stories.

Olofsson, Helena. *The little jester* ill. by author. R&S Books, 2002. ISBN 978-91-29-65499-8 Subj: Books, reading. Careers – clergy. Clowns, jesters. Foreign lands – France. Middle Ages.

Olsen, Sylvia. *Yetsa's sweater* ill. by Joan Larson. Sono Nis, 2006. ISBN 978-1-55039-155-8 Subj: Animals – sheep. Clothing – sweaters. Foreign lands – British Columbia. Indians of North America.

Olshan, Matthew. *The mighty Lalouche* ill. by Sophie Blackall. Random House, 2013. ISBN 978-0-375-86225-0 Subj: Careers – postal workers. Foreign lands – France. Sports – boxing.

Olson, David J. *The thunderstruck stork* ill. by Lynn Munsinger. Whitman, 2007. ISBN 978-0-8075-7910-7 Subj: Animals. Animals – babies. Birds – storks. Rhyming text.

Olson, Julie. *Tickle, tickle! itch, twitch!* ill. by author. Marshall Cavendish, 2010. ISBN 978-0-7614-5714-5 Subj: Animals – groundhogs. Animals – mice.

Olson, Laura. *Clayton's path* (Bishop, Brett)

Olson, Mary. *An alligator ate my brother* ill. by Tammie Lyon. Boyds Mills, 2000. ISBN 978-1-56397-803-6 Subj: Family life – brothers. Reptiles – alligators, crocodiles.

Nice try, Tooth Fairy ill. by Katherine Tillotson. Simon & Schuster, 2000. ISBN 978-0-689-82422-7 Subj: Fairies. Letters, cards. Teeth.

Olson, Nathan. *Animal patterns* ill. with photos. Capstone, 2006. ISBN 978-0-7368-6728-3 Subj: Animals. Concepts – patterns.

Olson-Brown, Ellen. *Hush little digger* ill. by Lee White. Ten Speed, 2006. ISBN 978-1-58246-160-1 Subj: Machines. Music. Trucks.

Ooh la la polka-dot boots ill. by Christiane Engel. Tricycle, 2010. ISBN 978-1-58246-287-5 Subj: Clothing – boots. Format, unusual. Rhyming text.

O'Malley, Kevin. *Animal crackers fly the coop* ill. by author. Walker, 2010. ISBN 978-0-8027-9837-4 Subj: Animals. Humorous stories. Language.

Bud ill. by author. Walker, 2000. ISBN 978-0-8027-8719-4 Subj: Animals – rhinoceros. Character traits – orderliness. Family life – grandfathers. Gardens, gardening.

Captain Raptor and the moon mystery ill. by Patrick O'Brien. Walker, 2005. ISBN 978-0-8027-8935-8 Subj: Aliens. Dinosaurs. Space & space ships.

Captain Raptor and the space pirates by Kevin O'Malley and Patrick O'Brien ill. by Patrick O'Brien. Walker, 2007. ISBN 978-0-8027-9571-7 Subj: Dinosaurs. Pirates. Space & space ships.

Congratulations, Miss Malarkey! (Finchler, Judy)

Gimme cracked corn and I will share ill. by author. Walker, 2007. ISBN 978-0-8027-9684-4 Subj: Birds – chickens. Humorous stories.

The great race ill. by author. Walker, 2011. ISBN 978-0-8027-2158-7 Subj: Animals – rabbits. Folk & fairy tales. Reptiles – turtles, tortoises. Sports – racing.

Humpty Dumpty egg-splodes ill. by author. Walker, 2001. ISBN 978-0-8027-8757-6 Subj: Character traits – meanness. Emotions – anger. Nursery rhymes.

Leo Cockroach . . . toy tester ill. by author. Walker, 1999. ISBN 978-0-8027-8690-6 Subj: Insects – cockroaches. Toys.

Little Buggy ill. by author. Harcourt, 2002. ISBN 978-0-15-216339-6 Subj: Activities – flying. Family life – fathers. Insects – ladybugs.

Little Buggy runs away ill. by author. Harcourt, 2003. ISBN 978-0-15-216550-5 Subj: Behavior – fighting, arguing. Behavior – running away. Family life – fathers. Insects – ants. Insects – ladybugs.

Miss Malarkey leaves no reader behind (Finchler, Judy)

Once upon a cool motorcycle dude ill. by author and Carol Heyer, et al. Walker, 2005. ISBN 978-0-8027-8949-5 Subj: Activities – writing. Giants. Motorcycles. Royalty – princesses.

Once upon a royal superbaby ill. by author and Carol Heyer. Walker, 2010. ISBN 978-0-8027-2164-8 Subj: Activities – writing. Babies. Royalty.

Roller coaster ill. by author. Lothrop, 1995. ISBN 978-0-688-13972-8 Subj: Fairs, festivals.

Straight to the pole ill. by author. Walker, 2003. ISBN 978-0-8027-8868-9 Subj: Imagination. School. Weather – snow.

Velcome ill. by author. Walker, 1997. ISBN 978-0-8027-8629-6 Subj: Activities – storytelling. Holidays – Halloween. Monsters.

O'Mara, Carmel. *Good morning* ill. by author. Harcourt, 2000. ISBN 978-0-15-202135-1 Subj: Activities. Animals – bears. Family life – parents. Morning.

Good night ill. by author. Harcourt, 2000. ISBN 978-0-15-202136-8 Subj: Activities. Animals – bears. Family life – parents.

Rainy day ill. by author. Harcourt, 2001. ISBN 978-0-15-201934-1 Subj: Activities – playing. Animals – bears. Animals – rabbits. Format, unusual – board books. Friendship. Weather – rain.

Sunny day ill. by author. Harcourt, 2001. ISBN 978-0-15-202066-8 Subj: Activities – playing. Animals – bears. Animals – rabbits. Format, unusual – board books. Weather.

Ommen, Sylvia van. *The surprise* ill. by author. Boyds Mills, 2007. ISBN 978-1-932425-85-7 Subj: Animals – giraffes. Animals – sheep. Gifts. Wordless.

Omololu, Cynthia Jaynes. *When it's six o'clock in San Francisco: a trip through time zones* ill. by Randy DuBurke. Clarion, 2009. ISBN 978-0-618-76827-1 Subj: Time. World.

One, two, skip a few! ill. by Roberta Arenson. Barefoot, 1998. ISBN 978-1-901223-99-6 Subj: Counting, numbers. Nursery rhymes. Rhyming text.

O'Neill, Alexis. *Estela's swap* ill. by Enrique O. Sánchez. Lee & Low, 2002. ISBN 978-1-58430-044-1 Subj: Activities – trading. Ethnic groups in the U.S. – Mexican Americans. Family life – fathers. Money. Stores.

Loud Emily ill. by Nancy Carpenter. Simon & Schuster, 1998. ISBN 978-0-689-81078-7 Subj: Animals – whales. Boats, ships. Noise, sounds. Sailors.

The Recess Queen ill. by Laura Huliska-Beith. Scholastic, 2002. ISBN 978-0-439-20637-2 Subj: Behavior – bullying, teasing. School.

O'Neill, Rachael. *Can't, don't, won't* (Davies, Gill)

Tiny's big wish (Davies, Gill)

Wilbur waited (Davies, Gill)

Onishi, Satoru. *Who's hiding* ill. by author. Kane/Miller, 2007. ISBN 978-1-933605-24-1 Subj: Animals. Disguises. Picture puzzles.

Onyefulu, Ifeoma. *An African Christmas* ill. with photos. Frances Lincoln, 2005. ISBN 978-1-84507-387-9 Subj: Foreign lands – Africa. Holidays – Christmas.

Deron goes to nursery school photos by author. Frances Lincoln, 2010. ISBN 978-1-84507-864-5 Subj: Foreign lands – Ghana. School – first day. School – nursery.

Grandma comes to stay photos by author. Frances Lincoln, 2010. ISBN 978-1-84507-865-7 Subj: Family life – grandmothers. Foreign lands – Ghana.

Ogbo: sharing life in an African village ill. by author. Gulliver, 1996. ISBN 978-0-15-200498-9 Subj: Foreign lands – Nigeria.

Omer's favorite place photos by author. Frances Lincoln, 2011. ISBN 978-1-84780-241-5 Subj: Activities – playing. Family life. Foreign lands – Ethiopia.

Saying goodbye ill. with photos. Millbrook, 2001. ISBN 978-0-7613-1965-8 Subj: Death. Emotions – grief. Foreign lands – Nigeria.

A triangle for Adaora ill. with photos. Dutton, 2000. ISBN 978-0-525-46382-5 Subj: Concepts – shape. Foreign lands – Africa.

Onyefulu, Obi. *Chinye* ill. by Evie Safarewicz. Viking, 1994. ISBN 978-0-670-85115-7 Subj: Folk & fairy tales. Foreign lands – Africa.

Oppel, Kenneth. *The king's taster* ill. by Steve Johnson and Lou Fancher. HarperCollins, 2009. ISBN 978-0-06-075372-6 Subj: Animals – dogs. Food. Royalty.

Peg and the whale ill. by Terry Widener. Simon & Schuster, 2000. ISBN 978-0-689-82423-4 Subj: Animals – whales. Boats, ships. Sports – fishing. Tall tales.

Oppenheim, Joanne. *The Christmas witch* ill. by Annie Mitra. G. Stevens, 1997. ISBN 978-0-8368-1697-6 Subj: Folk & fairy tales. Holidays – Christmas. Religion – Nativity. Witches.

Have you seen bugs? ill. by Ron Broda. Scholastic, 1997. ISBN 978-0-590-05963-3 Subj: Insects. Rhyming text. Spiders.

Have you seen trees? ill. by Jean Tseng and Mou-Sien Tseng. Scholastic, 1995. ISBN 978-0-590-46691-2 Subj: Poetry. Seasons. Trees.

Oppenheim, Shulamith Levey. *Ali and the magic stew* ill. by Winslow Pels. Boyds Mills, 2002. ISBN 978-1-56397-869-2 Subj: Careers – beggars. Family life – fathers. Foreign lands – Iran. Illness.

Fireflies for Nathan ill. by John Ward. Tambourine, 1994. ISBN 978-0-688-12148-8 Subj: Ethnic groups in the U.S. – African Americans. Family life – grandparents. Insects – fireflies.

I love you, Bunny Rabbit ill. by Cyd Moore. Boyds Mills, 1995. ISBN 978-1-56397-322-2 Subj: Emotions – love. Toys.

Oram, Hiawyn. *Baba Yaga and the wise doll* ill. by Ruth Brown. Dutton, 1998. ISBN 978-0-525-45947-7 Subj: Behavior – trickery. Folk & fairy tales. Foreign lands – Russia. Toys – dolls. Witches.

Badger's bad mood ill. by Susan Varley. Scholastic, 1998. ISBN 978-0-590-18920-0 Subj: Animals. Animals – badgers. Animals – moles. Behavior – bad day. Friendship.

Gerda the goose ill. by David Melling. Barron's, 2000. ISBN 978-0-7641-1484-7 Subj: Birds – geese.

Going to Grandpa's ill. by Frédéric Joos. Dutton, 2001. ISBN 978-0-525-46701-4 Subj: Animals – bears. Family life – grandfathers. Trains.

Just Dog ill. by Lisa Flather. Chronicle, 1998. ISBN 978-0-8118-2247-3 Subj: Animals – cats. Animals – dogs. Self-concept.

Kiss it better ill. by Frédéric Joos. Dutton, 2000. ISBN 978-0-525-46386-3 Subj: Animals – bears. Behavior – bad day. Emotions – love. Kissing.

My friend Fred ill. by Rosie Reeve. Tiger Tales, 2012. ISBN 978-1-58925-105-2 Subj: Animals – dogs. Behavior – sharing. Friendship.

The wrong overcoat ill. by Mark Birchall. Carolrhoda, 2000. ISBN 978-1-57505-453-7 Subj: Animals – chimpanzees. Character traits – individuality. Clothing – coats. Self-concept.

Ørdal, Stina Langlo. *Princess Aasta* ill. by author. Bloomsbury, 2002. ISBN 978-1-58234-783-7 Subj: Animals – bears. Animals – polar bears. Behavior – resourcefulness. Friendship. Royalty – kings. Royalty – princesses.

Orgel, Doris. *The cat's tale: why the years are named for animals* ill. by Meilo So. Roaring Brook, 2008. ISBN 978-1-59643-202-4 Subj: Animals. Folk & fairy tales. Foreign lands – China. Zodiac.

Orgill, Roxane. *If I only had a horn* ill. by Leonard Jenkins. Houghton, 1997. ISBN 978-0-395-75919-6 Subj: Careers – musicians. Ethnic groups in the U.S. – African Americans. Musical instruments – bands. Musical instruments – trumpets. U.S. history.

Skit-scat raggedy cat: Ella Fitzgerald ill. by Sean Qualls. Candlewick, 2010. ISBN 978-0-7636-1733-2 Subj: Careers – singers. Ethnic groups in the U.S. – African Americans. Music.

Orlean, Susan. *Lazy little loafers* ill. by G. Brian Karas. Abrams, 2008. ISBN 978-0-8109-7027-4 Subj: Babies. Humorous stories. Sibling rivalry.

Orloff, Karen Kaufman. *I wanna new room* ill. by David Catrow. Penguin, 2010. ISBN 978-0-399-25405-5 Subj: Behavior – sharing. Family life. Homes, houses. Letters, cards.

Ormerod, Jan. *If you're happy and you know it!* by Jan Ormerod and Lindsey Gardiner ill. by Lindsey Gardiner. Star Bright, 2003. ISBN 978-1-932065-07-7 Subj: Animals. Emotions – happiness. Rhyming text.

Maudie and Bear ill. by Freya Blackwood. Putnam, 2012. ISBN 978-0-399-25709-4 Subj: Animals – bears. Friendship.

Miss Mouse takes off ill. by author. HarperCollins, 2001. ISBN 978-0-688-17871-0 Subj: Activities – traveling. Airplanes, airports. Toys – dolls.

Miss Mouse's day ill. by author. HarperCollins, 2001. ISBN 978-0-688-16334-1 Subj: Activities – playing. Animals – mice. Toys.

Molly and her dad ill. by Carol Thompson. Roaring Brook, 2008. ISBN 978-1-59643-285-7 Subj: Family life – fathers. School.

Ms. MacDonald has a class ill. by author. Clarion, 1996. ISBN 978-0-395-77611-7 Subj: Animals. Cumulative tales. Farms. Rhyming text. School. Songs. Theater.

When an elephant comes to school ill. by author. Scholastic, 2005. ISBN 978-0-439-73967-2 Subj: Animals – elephants. School – first day.

When we went to the zoo ill. by author. Lothrop, 1991. ISBN 978-0-688-09879-7 Subj: Animals. Zoos.

Who's whose? ill. by author. Lothrop, 1998. ISBN 978-0-688-14679-5 Subj: Activities. Family life.

Ormondroyd, Edward. *Theodore* ill. by Juli Kangas. Dial, 2009. ISBN 978-0-8037-3163-9 Subj: Character traits – appearance. Character traits – kindness. Laundry. Toys – bears.

Orona-Ramirez, Kristy. *Kiki's journey* ill. by Jonathan Day. Children's Book Press, 2006. ISBN 978-0-89239-214-8 Subj: Activities – traveling. Family life. Indians of North America – Tewa.

Orozco, Jose-Luis. *Pancho Claus* ill. by Ashley Wolff. Dial, 2013. ISBN 978-0-8037-3756-3 Subj: Foreign languages. Holidays – Christmas. Rhyming text. Santa Claus.

Rin, rin, rin / do, re, mi: libro ilustrado en Español e Inglés / a picture book in Spanish and English ill. by David Diaz. Scholastic, 2005. ISBN 978-0-439-64941-4 Subj: Books, reading. Counting, numbers. Foreign languages.

Orr, Wendy. *The princess and her panther* ill. by Lauren Stringer. Simon & Schuster, 2010. ISBN 978-1-4169-9780-1 Subj: Animals – leopards. Camps, camping. Family life – sisters. Imagination. Royalty – princesses.

Osborne, Mary Pope. *The brave little seamstress* ill. by Giselle Potter. Atheneum, 2002. ISBN 978-0-689-84486-7 Subj: Careers – tailors. Character traits – bravery. Folk & fairy tales. Giants. Royalty – kings. Royalty – queens.

Happy birthday, America ill. by Peter Catalanotto. Roaring Brook, 2003. ISBN 978-0-7613-2761-5 Subj: Family life. Holidays – Fourth of July.

Kate and the beanstalk ill. by Giselle Potter. Atheneum, 2000. ISBN 978-0-689-82550-7 Subj: Folk & fairy tales. Giants. Plants.

New York's bravest ill. by Steve Johnson and Lou Fancher. Knopf, 2002. ISBN 978-0-375-92196-4 Subj: Careers – firefighters. Character traits – bravery. Cities, towns.

Sleeping Bobby ill. by Giselle Potter. Simon & Schuster, 2005. ISBN 978-0-689-87668-4 Subj: Folk & fairy tales. Royalty – princes. Royalty – princesses. Sleep.

Osofsky, Audrey. *Dreamcatcher* ill. by Ed Young. Watts, 1992. ISBN 978-0-531-08588-2 Subj: Babies. Dreams. Family life. Folk & fairy tales. Indians of North America – Ojibwa.

Otoshi, Kathryn. *One* ill. by author. Ko Kids, 2008. ISBN 978-0-9723946-4-2 Subj: Behavior – bullying, teasing. Character traits – bravery. Concepts – color. Counting, numbers. Emotions.

Zero ill. by author. KO Kids, 2010. ISBN 978-0-9723946-3-5 Subj: Character traits – cooperation. Counting, numbers. Self-concept.

Otsuka, Yuzo, reteller. *Suho's white horse: a Mongolian legend* ill. by Suekichi Akaba. R.I.C, 2007. ISBN 978-1-74126-021-2 Subj: Animals – horses, ponies. Emotions – love. Folk & fairy tales. Foreign lands – Mongolia. Musical instruments – violins.

Otten, Charlotte F. *January rides the wind: a book of months* ill. by Todd L. W. Doney. Lothrop, 1997. ISBN 978-0-688-12557-8 Subj: Days of the week, months of the year. Poetry.

Otto, Carolyn. *Dinosaur chase* ill. by Thacher Hurd. HarperCollins, 1991. ISBN 978-0-06-021614-6 Subj: Bedtime. Dinosaurs. Poetry. Prehistory.

Our puppies are growing ill. by Mary Morgan. HarperCollins, 1998. ISBN 978-0-06-027272-2 Subj: Animals – babies. Animals – dogs. Behavior – growing up.

That sky, that rain ill. by Megan Lloyd. HarperCollins, 1990. ISBN 978-0-690-04765-3 Subj:

Family life – grandfathers. Farms. Sky. Weather – rain.

What color is camouflage? ill. by Megan Lloyd. HarperCollins, 1996. ISBN 978-0-06-027099-5 Subj: Animals. Character traits – appearance.

Oud, Pauline. *Ian's new potty* ill. by author. Clavis, 2011. ISBN 978-1-60537-103-0 Subj: Behavior – growing up. Toilet training.

Oughton, Jerrie. *How the stars fell into the sky* ill. by Lisa Desimini. Houghton, 1992. ISBN 978-0-395-58798-0 Subj: Folk & fairy tales. Indians of North America – Navajo. Sky. Stars.

The magic weaver of rugs ill. by Lisa Desimini. Houghton, 1994. ISBN 978-0-395-66140-6 Subj: Activities – weaving. Folk & fairy tales. Indians of North America – Navajo.

Our children can soar: a celebration of Rosa, Barack, and the pioneers of change ill. by Cozbi A. Cabrera. Bloomsbury, 2009. ISBN 978-1-59990-418-4 Subj: Ethnic groups in the U.S. – African Americans. Hope. U.S. history.

Over in the meadow ill. by Ezra Jack Keats. Four Winds, 1971. Subj: Animals. Counting, numbers. Folk & fairy tales. Rhyming text. Songs.

Overend, Jenni. *Welcome with love* ill. by Julie Vivas. Kane/Miller, 2000. ISBN 978-0-916291-96-9 Subj: Babies. Birth. Family life.

Owen, Ann. *Caring for your pet* ill. by Eric Thomas. Picture Window, 2004. ISBN 978-1-4048-0087-8 Subj: Careers – veterinarians. Pets.

Delivering your mail ill. by Eric Thomas. Picture Window, 2004. ISBN 978-1-4048-0091-5 Subj: Careers – postal workers. Letters, cards.

Keeping you healthy ill. by Eric Thomas. Picture Window, 2004. ISBN 978-1-4048-0085-4 Subj: Careers – doctors. Health & fitness.

Keeping you safe ill. by Eric Thomas. Picture Window, 2003. ISBN 978-1-4048-0089-2 Subj: Careers – police officers.

Protecting your home ill. by Eric Thomas. Picture Window, 2004. ISBN 978-1-4048-0088-5 Subj: Careers – firefighters. Fire.

Taking your places ill. by Eric Thomas. Picture Window, 2004. ISBN 978-1-4048-0090-8 Subj: Buses. Careers – bus drivers. Communities, neighborhoods.

Owen, Karen. *I could be, you could be* ill. by Barroux. Barefoot, 2011. ISBN 978-1-84686-405-6 Subj: Rhyming text. Self-concept.

Owens, Mary Beth. *Panda whispers* ill. by author. Penguin, 2007. ISBN 978-0-525-47171-4 Subj: Animals. Bedtime. Dreams. Rhyming text.

Oxenbury, Helen. *It's my birthday* ill. by author. Candlewick, 1994. ISBN 978-1-56402-412-1 Subj: Activities – baking, cooking. Animals. Birthdays. Cumulative tales. Food.

Pig tale ill. by author. Simon & Schuster, 2005. ISBN 978-1-4169-0277-5 Subj: Animals – pigs. Behavior – greed. Rhyming text.

Tom and Pippo go shopping ill. by author. Macmillan, 1989. ISBN 978-0-689-71278-4 Subj: Animals – monkeys. Shopping. Toys.

Tom and Pippo in the garden ill. by author. Macmillan, 1989. ISBN 978-0-689-71275-3 Subj: Animals – monkeys. Gardens, gardening. Toys.

Tom and Pippo on the beach ill. by author. Candlewick, 1993. ISBN 978-1-56402-181-6 Subj: Animals – monkeys. Sea & seashore – beaches. Toys.

Tom and Pippo see the moon ill. by author. Macmillan, 1989. ISBN 978-0-689-71277-7 Subj: Animals – monkeys. Moon. Space & space ships. Toys.

Oxley, Jennifer. *The chicken problem* ill. by Billy Aronson. Random House, 2012. ISBN 978-0-375-86989-1 Subj: Animals – cats. Birds – chickens. Counting, numbers. Farms. Problem solving.

Oyibo, Papa. *Big brother, little sister* ill. by John Clementson. Barefoot, 2000. ISBN 978-1-84148-117-3 Subj: Animals – elephants. Animals – mice. Character traits – helpfulness. Friendship.

Pace, Anne Marie. *Vampirina ballerina* ill. by LeUyen Pham. Disney/Hyperion, 2012. ISBN 978-1-4231-5753-3 Subj: Ballet. Careers – dancers. Character traits – perseverance. Monsters.

Vampirina ballerina hosts a sleepover ill. by LeUyen Pham. Hyperion/Disney, 2013. ISBN 978-1-4231-7570-4 Subj: Ballet. Careers – dancers. Monsters. Sleepovers.

Pacilio, V. J. *Ling Cho and his three friends* ill. by Scott Cook. Farrar, 2000. ISBN 978-0-374-34545-7 Subj: Behavior – sharing. Foreign lands – China. Friendship. Rhyming text.

Packard, Edward. *Big numbers: and pictures that show just how big they are!* ill. by Sal Murdocca. Millbrook, 2000. ISBN 978-0-7613-1570-4 Subj: Concepts – size. Counting, numbers.

Page, Gail. *Bobo and the new neighbor* ill. by author. Bloomsbury, 2008. ISBN 978-1-59990-009-4 Subj: Animals – dogs. Humorous stories.

How to be a good cat ill. by author. Bloomsbury, 2011. ISBN 978-1-59990-474-0 Subj: Animals – cats. Animals – dogs.

Page, Robin. *Animals in flight* (Jenkins, Steve)

Animals upside down: a pull, pop, lift and learn book! (Jenkins, Steve)

How many ways can you catch a fly? by Robin Page and Steve Jenkins ill. by Steve Jenkins. Houghton, 2008. ISBN 978-0-618-96634-9 Subj: Animals.

How to clean a hippopotamus: a look at unusual animal partnerships (Jenkins, Steve)

I see a kookaburra (Jenkins, Steve)

Move! (Jenkins, Steve)

My first day: what animals do on day one (Jenkins, Steve)

Sisters and brothers: sibling relationships in the animal world by Robin Page and Steve Jenkins ill. by Steve Jenkins. Houghton, 2008. ISBN 978-0-618-37596-7 Subj: Animals. Nature.

Time for a bath (Jenkins, Steve)

Time to eat (Jenkins, Steve)

Time to sleep (Jenkins, Steve)

Pak, Soyung. *Dear Juno* ill. by Susan Kathleen Hartung. Viking, 1999. ISBN 978-0-670-88252-6 Subj: Ethnic groups in the U.S. – Korean Americans. Family life – grandmothers. Foreign languages. Letters, cards.

A place to grow ill. by Marcelino Truong. Scholastic, 2002. ISBN 978-0-439-13015-8 Subj: Ethnic groups in the U.S. – Korean Americans. Family life – fathers. Gardens, gardening. Immigrants. Seeds.

Sumi's first day of school ever ill. by Joung Un Kim. Viking, 2003. ISBN 978-0-670-03522-9 Subj: Ethnic groups in the U.S. – Korean Americans. School – first day.

Palacios, Argentina. *A Christmas surprise for Chabelita* ill. by Lori Lohstoeter. BridgeWater, 1993. ISBN 978-0-8167-3131-2 Subj: Family life – grandparents. Family life – mothers. Foreign lands – Panama. School.

Palatini, Margie. *Bad boys get cookie!* ill. by Henry Cole. HarperCollins, 2006. ISBN 978-0-06-074437-3 Subj: Animals – wolves. Food.

Bad boys get henpecked! ill. by Henry Cole. HarperCollins, 2009. ISBN 978-0-06-074433-5 Subj: Animals – wolves. Birds – chickens.

Bedhead ill. by Jack E. Davis. Simon & Schuster, 2000. ISBN 978-0-689-82397-8 Subj: Hair. School.

Boo-hoo moo ill. by Keith Graves. HarperCollins, 2009. ISBN 978-0-06-114375-5 Subj: Animals – bulls, cows. Humorous stories. Noise, sounds.

The cheese ill. by Steve Johnson and Lou Fancher. HarperCollins, 2007. ISBN 978-0-06-052630-6 Subj: Careers – farmers. Farms. Games. Music. Songs.

Ding dong ding dong ill. by Howard Fine. Hyperion, 1999. ISBN 978-0-7868-2367-3 Subj: Animals – gorillas. Careers – salespeople. Humorous stories.

Earthquack ill. by Barry Moser. Simon & Schuster, 2002. ISBN 978-0-689-84280-1 Subj: Animals. Birds – ducks. Earthquakes. Humorous stories.

Goldie and the three hares ill. by Jack E. Davis. HarperCollins, 2011. ISBN 978-0-06-125314-0 Subj: Animals – rabbits. Behavior – misbehavior.

Goldie is mad ill. by author. Hyperion, 2001. ISBN 978-0-7868-2490-8 Subj: Babies. Emotions – anger. Family life – brothers & sisters. Sibling rivalry.

Gone with the wand: a fairy's tale ill. by Brian Ajhar. Scholastic, 2009. ISBN 978-0-439-72768-6 Subj: Behavior – bad day. Fairies. Magic. Teeth.

Good as Goldie ill. by author. Hyperion, 2000. ISBN 978-0-7868-2435-9 Subj: Behavior – dissatisfaction. Family life – brothers & sisters. Sibling rivalry.

Gorgonzola: a very stinkysaurus ill. by Tim Bowers. HarperCollins, 2007. ISBN 978-0-06-073897-6 Subj: Birds. Dinosaurs. Hygiene. Senses – smell.

Hogg, Hogg, and Hog ill. by author. Simon & Schuster, 2011. ISBN 978-1-4424-0322-2 Subj: Animals – pigs. Character traits – ambition. Cities, towns.

Lousy rotten stinkin' grapes ill. by Barry Moser. Simon & Schuster, 2009. ISBN 978-0-689-80246-1 Subj: Animals – foxes. Folk & fairy tales. Food.

Moo who? ill. by Keith Graves. Tegen, 2004. ISBN 978-0-06-000106-3 Subj: Animals. Animals – bulls, cows. Noise, sounds.

Moosetache ill. by Henry Cole. Hyperion, 1997. ISBN 978-0-7868-2246-1 Subj: Animals – moose. Hair.

No biting, Louise ill. by Matthew Reinhart. HarperCollins, 2007. ISBN 978-0-06-052627-6 Subj: Reptiles – alligators, crocodiles. Teeth.

Oink? ill. by Henry Cole. Simon & Schuster, 2006. ISBN 978-0-689-86258-8 Subj: Animals – pigs. Farms. Humorous stories.

The perfect pet ill. by Bruce Whatley. HarperCollins, 2003. ISBN 978-0-06-000109-4 Subj: Character traits – persistence. Insects. Pets.

Piggie pie ill. by Howard Fine. Clarion, 1995. ISBN 978-0-395-71691-5 Subj: Animals – pigs. Animals – wolves. Character traits – appearance. Holidays – Halloween. Witches.

Shelly ill. by Guy Francis. Penguin, 2006. ISBN 978-0-525-47565-1 Subj: Behavior – bossy. Birds – chickens. Character traits – smallness.

Stuff ill. by Noah Jones. HarperCollins, 2011. ISBN 978-0-06-171921-9 Subj: Animals – rabbits. Behavior – collecting things. Friendship.

Three French hens ill. by Richard Egielski. Hyperion, 2005. ISBN 978-0-7868-5167-6 Subj: Animals – foxes. Birds – chickens. Foreign lands – France. Humorous stories. Songs.

The three silly billies ill. by Barry Moser. Simon & Schuster, 2005. ISBN 978-0-689-85862-8 Subj: Animals – goats. Books, reading. Humorous stories. Mythical creatures – trolls.

Tub-boo-boo ill. by Glin Dibley. Simon & Schuster, 2001. ISBN 978-0-689-82394-7 Subj: Activities – bathing. Family life. Family life – brothers.

The web files ill. by Richard Egielski. Hyperion, 2001. ISBN 978-0-7868-2366-6 Subj: Careers – detectives. Farms. Humorous stories. Nursery rhymes.

Zak's lunch ill. by Howard Fine. Clarion, 1998. ISBN 978-0-395-81674-5 Subj: Family life – mothers. Food. Imagination.

Zoom Broom ill. by Howard Fine. Hyperion, 1998. ISBN 978-0-7868-0322-4 Subj: Animals – foxes. Witches.

Paley, Joan, adapt. *One more river* ill. by adapter. Little, 2002. ISBN 978-0-316-60702-5 Subj: Animals. Boats, ships. Counting, numbers. Religion – Noah. Songs. Weather – floods. Weather – rain. Weather – rainbows.

Pallotta, Jerry. *The airplane alphabet book* by Jerry Pallotta and Fred Stillwell ill. by Rob Bolster. Charlesbridge, 1997. ISBN 978-0-88106-907-8 Subj: ABC books. Airplanes, airports.

The construction alphabet book ill. by Rob Bolster. Charlesbridge, 2006. ISBN 978-1-57091-437-9 Subj: ABC books. Machines. Tractors. Trucks.

The crayon counting book (Ryan, Pam Muñoz)

Dory story ill. by David Biedrzycki. Talewinds, 2000. ISBN 978-0-88106-075-1 Subj: Activities – bathing. Animals. Boats, ships. Fish. Imagination. Nature. Sea & seashore.

F is for Fenway: America's oldest major league ballpark ill. by John S. Dykes. Sleeping Bear, 2012. ISBN 978-1-58536-788-7 Subj: ABC books. Sports – baseball.

A giraffe did one ill. by Tatjana Mai-Wyss. Sleeping Bear, 2012. ISBN 978-1-58536-641-5 Subj: Animals. Behavior – misbehavior. Rhyming text.

The jet alphabet book ill. by Rob Bolster. Charlesbridge, 1999. ISBN 978-0-88106-916-7 Subj: ABC books. Airplanes, airports.

Ocean counting: odd numbers ill. by Shennen Bersani. Charlesbridge, 2005. ISBN 978-0-88106-151-2 Subj: Animals. Counting, numbers. Sea & seashore.

Twizzlers percentages book ill. by Rob Bolster. Scholastic, 2001. ISBN 978-0-439-25407-6 Subj: Aliens. Counting, numbers. Space & space ships.

Who will plant a tree? ill. by Thomas Leonard. Sleeping Bear, 2010. ISBN 978-1-58536-502-9 Subj: Seeds. Trees.

Who will see their shadows this year? ill. by David Biedrzycki. Scholastic, 2013. ISBN 978-0-545-47275-3 Subj: Animals. Animals – groundhogs. Holidays – Groundhog Day. Seasons – winter. Shadows.

The palm of my heart: poetry by African American children ed. by Davida Adedjouma; ill. by R. Gregory Christie. Lee & Low, 1996. ISBN 978-1-880000-41-0 Subj: Children as authors. Ethnic groups in the U.S. – African Americans. Poetry.

Pamintuan, Macky. *Twelve haunted rooms of Halloween* ill. by author. Sterling, 2011. ISBN 978-1-4027-7935-0 Subj: Animals – bears. Counting, numbers. Holidays – Halloween. Picture puzzles. Rhyming text.

Pandell, Karen. *I love you sun, I love you moon* ill. by Tomie dePaola. Putnam, 1994. ISBN 978-0-399-22628-1 Subj: Ecology. Nature.

Pandya, Meenal. *Here comes Diwali* recipes by Laxmi Jain; ill. by author. MeeRa, 2000. ISBN 978-0-9635539-3-5 Subj: Holidays. Holidays – Divali. Religion – Hinduism.

Pantone: colors ill. by Helen Dardik. Abrams, 2012. ISBN 978-1-4197-0180-1 Subj: Concepts – color. Format, unusual – board books.

Panzieri, Lucia. *The kindhearted crocodile* ill. by Anton Gionata Ferrari. Holiday House, 2013. ISBN 978-0-8234-2767-3 Subj: Behavior – hiding. Books, reading. Character traits – helpfulness. Pets. Reptiles – alligators, crocodiles.

Paola, Tomie de *see* dePaola, Tomie

Paolilli, Paul. *Silver seeds* by Paul Paolilli and Dan Brewer ill. by Steve Johnson and Lou Fancher.

Viking, 2001. ISBN 978-0-670-88941-9 Subj: Imagination. Nature. Poetry.

Papineau, Lucie. *Lulu's pajamas* ill. by Stéphane Jorisch. Kids Can, 2009. ISBN 978-1-55453-371-8 Subj: Animals – mice. Bedtime. Character traits – cleanliness. Clothing – pajamas.

Paquette, Ammi-Joan. *Ghost in the house* ill. by Adam Record. Candlewick, 2013. ISBN 978-0-7636-5529-7 Subj: Counting, numbers. Cumulative tales. Ghosts. Rhyming text.

The tiptoe guide to tracking fairies ill. by Christa Unzner. Tanglewood, 2009. ISBN 978-1-933718-20-0 Subj: Behavior – hiding. Fairies. Nature.

Paradis, Susan. *My Daddy* ill. by author. Front Street, 1998. ISBN 978-1-886910-30-0 Subj: Activities. Family life – fathers.

My mommy ill. by author. Front Street, 2002. ISBN 978-1-886910-73-7 Subj: Emotions – love. Family life – mothers.

Snow princess ill. by author. Boyds Mills, 2005. ISBN 978-1-932425-31-4 Subj: Family life – fathers. Imagination. Weather – snow.

Paraskevas, Betty. *Chocolate at the Four Seasons* ill. by Michael Paraskevas. Little, Brown, 2007. ISBN 978-0-306-01375-8 Subj: Animals – dogs. Character traits – shyness. Hotels.

Maggie and the Ferocious Beast, the big carrot ill. by Michael Paraskevas. Simon & Schuster, 2000. ISBN 978-0-689-82490-6 Subj: Activities – digging. Animals – mice. Animals – pigs. Animals – rabbits. Character traits – helpfulness. Gardens, gardening. Monsters.

Maggie and the Ferocious Beast, the big scare ill. by Michael Paraskevas. Simon & Schuster, 1999. ISBN 978-0-689-82489-0 Subj: Animals – mice. Animals – pigs. Emotions – fear. Monsters.

Marvin, the tap-dancing horse ill. by Michael Paraskevas. Simon & Schuster, 2001. ISBN 978-0-689-82153-0 Subj: Activities – dancing. Animals – horses, ponies. Fairs, festivals. Friendship. Theater.

Nibbles O'Hare ill. by Michael Paraskevas. Simon & Schuster, 2001. ISBN 978-0-689-82865-2 Subj: Animals – rabbits. Holidays – Easter.

Parenteau, Shirley. *Bears in beds* ill. by David Walker. Candlewick, 2012. ISBN 978-0-7636-5338-5 Subj: Animals – bears. Bedtime. Rhyming text.

Bears on chairs ill. by David Walker. Candlewick, 2009. ISBN 978-0-7636-3588-6 Subj: Animals – bears. Behavior – sharing. Furniture – chairs. Problem solving. Rhyming text.

One frog sang ill. by Cynthia Jabar. Candlewick, 2006. ISBN 978-0-7636-2394-4 Subj: Counting, numbers. Frogs & toads.

Parish, Herman. *Amelia Bedelia's first apple pie* ill. by Lynne Avril. HarperCollins, 2010. ISBN 978-0-06-196409-1 Subj: Activities – baking, cooking. Family life – grandparents. Humorous stories.

Amelia Bedelia's first day of school ill. by Lynne Avril. Greenwillow, 2009. ISBN 978-0-06-154455-2 Subj: Humorous stories. School – first day.

Amelia Bedelia's first field trip ill. by Lynne Avril. HarperCollins, 2011. ISBN 978-0-06-196413-8 Subj: Farms. Humorous stories. School – field trips.

Amelia Bedelia's first library card ill. by Lynne Avril. HarperCollins, 2013. ISBN 978-0-06-209512-1 Subj: Books, reading. Language. Libraries.

Amelia Bedelia's first valentine ill. by Lynne Avril. Greenwillow, 2009. ISBN 978-0-06-154458-3 Subj: Holidays – Valentine's Day. Humorous stories. School.

Amelia Bedelia's first vote ill. by Lynne Avril. HarperCollins, 2012. ISBN 978-0-06-209405-6 Subj: Behavior – seeking better things. Language. School.

Go west, Amelia Bedelia! ill. by Lynn Sweat. HarperCollins, 2011. ISBN 978-0-06-084361-8 Subj: Careers – ranchers. Family life – aunts, uncles. Humorous stories.

Park, Frances. *Good-bye, 382 Shin Dang Dong* ill. by Yangsook Choi. National Geographic, 2002. ISBN 978-0-7922-7985-3 Subj: Ethnic groups in the U.S. – Korean Americans. Foreign lands – Korea. Moving.

The Have a Good Day Cafe by Frances Park and Ginger Park ill. by Katherine Potter. Lee & Low, 2005. ISBN 978-1-58430-171-4 Subj: Ethnic groups in the U.S. – Korean Americans. Family life – grandmothers. Immigrants. Restaurants.

My freedom trip by Frances Park and Ginger Park ill. by Debra Reid Jenkins. Boyds Mills, 1998. ISBN 978-1-56397-468-7 Subj: Character traits – freedom. Foreign lands – Korea (North). Immigrants.

The royal bee by Frances Park and Ginger Park ill. by Christopher Zhong-Yuan Zhang. Boyds Mills, 2000. ISBN 978-1-56397-614-8 Subj: Contests. Foreign lands – Korea. Poverty. School.

Where on earth is my bagel? by Frances Park and Ginger Park ill. by Grace Lin. Lee & Low, 2001. ISBN 978-1-58430-033-5 Subj: Activities – baking, cooking. Food. Foreign lands – Korea. Imagination.

Park, Ginger. *The Have a Good Day Cafe* (Park, Frances)

My freedom trip (Park, Frances)

The royal bee (Park, Frances)

Where on earth is my bagel? (Park, Frances)

Park, Linda Sue. *Bee-bim bop!* ill. by Ho Baek Lee. Houghton, 2005. ISBN 978-0-618-26511-4 Subj: Activities – baking, cooking. Food. Foreign lands – Korea. Rhyming text.

The firekeeper's son ill. by Julie Downing. Clarion, 2003. ISBN 978-0-618-13337-6 Subj: Character traits – responsibility. Family life – fathers. Foreign lands – Korea.

The third gift ill. by Bagram Ibatoulline. Clarion, 2011. ISBN 978-0-547-20195-5 Subj: Family life – fathers. Holidays – Christmas. Religion.

What does Bunny see? s book of colors and flowers ill. by Maggie Smith. Houghton, 2005. ISBN 978-0-618-23485-1 Subj: Animals – rabbits. Concepts – color. Flowers. Gardens, gardening. Rhyming text.

Xander's panda party ill. by Matt Phelan. Houghton Mifflin, 2013. ISBN 978-0-547-55865-3 Subj: Animals. Animals – pandas. Parties. Rhyming text. Zoos.

Yum! Yuck! a foldout book of people sounds by Linda Sue Park and Julia Durango ill. by Sue Ramá. Charlesbridge, 2005. ISBN 978-1-57091-659-5 Subj: Foreign languages. Format, unusual – toy & movable books. Noise, sounds.

Parker, Ant. *Flashing fire engines* (Mitton, Tony)

Parker, Kim. *Counting in the garden* ill. by author. Scholastic, 2005. ISBN 978-0-439-69452-0 Subj: Animals. Counting, numbers. Gardens, gardening.

Parker, Marjorie Blain. *Colorful dreamer: the story of artist Henri Matisse* ill. by Holly Berry. Dial, 2012. ISBN 978-0-8037-3758-7 Subj: Activities – painting. Art. Careers – artists. Foreign lands – France.

Jasper's day ill. by Janet Wilson. Kids Can, 2002. ISBN 978-1-55074-957-1 Subj: Animals – dogs. Death. Emotions – grief. Memories, memory.

Mama's little duckling ill. by Mike Wohnoutka. Dutton, 2008. ISBN 978-0-525-47950-5 Subj: Behavior – growing up. Birds – ducks. Family life – mothers.

A paddling of ducks: animals in groups from A to Z ill. by Joseph Kelly. Kids Can, 2010. ISBN 978-1-55337-682-8 Subj: ABC books. Animals. Language.

When dads don't grow up ill. by R. W. Alley. Dial, 2012. ISBN 978-0-8037-3717-4 Subj: Behavior – growing up. Family life – fathers.

Your kind of mommy ill. by Cyd Moore. Penguin, 2007. ISBN 978-0-525-46989-6 Subj: Animals. Family life – mothers. Rhyming text.

Parker, Mary Jessie. *The deep, deep puddle* ill. by Deborah Zemke. Dial, 2013. ISBN 978-0-8037-3765-5 Subj: Counting, numbers. Weather – rain.

Parker, Michael. *You are a star!* ill. by Judith Rossell. Walker, 2012. ISBN 978-0-8027-2841-8 Subj: Astronomy. Science. Sky. Stars.

Parker, Nancy Winslow. *Bugs* by Nancy Winslow Parker and Joan Richards Wright ill. by Nancy Winslow Parker. Greenwillow, 1987. ISBN 978-0-688-06624-6 Subj: Insects. Science.

Parker, Robert Andrew. *Piano starts here: the young Art Tatum* ill. by author. Random House, 2008. ISBN 978-0-375-83965-8 Subj: Careers – musicians. Ethnic groups in the U.S. – African Americans. U.S. history.

Parker, Victoria. *Bearum scarum* ill. by Emily Bolam. Viking, 2002. ISBN 978-0-670-03546-5 Subj: Animals. Animals – bears. Counting, numbers. Jungle. Rhyming text.

Parkhurst, Carolyn. *Cooking with Henry and Elliebelly* ill. by Dan Yaccarino. Feiwel & Friends, 2010. ISBN 978-0-312-54848-3 Subj: Activities – baking, cooking. Family life – brothers & sisters. Imagination.

Parkinson, Curtis. *Emily's eighteen aunts* ill. by Andrea Wayne-von Königslöw. Stoddart, 2002. ISBN 978-0-7737-3336-7 Subj: Character traits – individuality. Family life – aunts, uncles. Humorous stories.

Parkinson, Kathy, adapt. *The enormous turnip* ill. by adapter. Whitman, 1985. ISBN 978-0-8075-2062-8 Subj: Behavior – sharing. Character traits – cooperation. Cumulative tales. Folk & fairy tales. Foreign lands – Russia. Plants. Problem solving.

Parks, Carmen. *Farmers market* ill. by Edward Martinez. Harcourt, 2002. ISBN 978-0-15-216680-9 Subj: Careers – farmers. Country. Family life – parents. Stores.

Parlato, Stephen. *The world that loved books* ill. by author. Simply Read, 2003. ISBN 978-1-894965-04-0 Subj: Books, reading. Imagination.

Parnell, Peter. *And Tango makes three* (Richardson, Justin)

Christian, the hugging lion (Richardson, Justin)

Parot, Annelore. *Kimonos* ill. by author. Chronicle, 2011. ISBN 978-1-4521-0493-5 Subj: Foreign lands – Japan. Format, unusual – toy & movable books. Toys – dolls.

Parr, Todd. *The best friends book* ill. by author. Little, 2000. ISBN 978-0-316-69201-4 Subj: Friendship.

Big and little ill. by author. Little, 2001. ISBN 978-0-316-69291-5 Subj: Concepts – size. Format, unusual – board books. Language.

Black and white ill. by author. Little, 2001. ISBN 978-0-316-69225-0 Subj: Concepts – color. Format, unusual – board books. Language.

The daddy book ill. by author. Little, 2002. ISBN 978-0-316-60799-5 Subj: Family life – fathers.

Do's and don'ts ill. by author. Little, 1999. ISBN 978-0-316-69213-7 Subj: Behavior. Etiquette.

The earth book ill. by author. Little, Brown, 2010. ISBN 978-0-316-04265-9 Subj: Earth. Ecology.

The feel good book ill. by author. Little, 2002. ISBN 978-0-316-07206-9 Subj: Emotions – happiness.

The feelings book ill. by author. Little, 2000. ISBN 978-0-316-69131-4 Subj: Emotions.

The grandma book ill. by author. Little, Brown, 2006. ISBN 978-0-316-05802-5 Subj: Family life – grandmothers.

The grandpa book ill. by author. Little, Brown, 2006. ISBN 978-0-316-05801-8 Subj: Family life – grandfathers.

The I Love You Book ill. by author. Little, Brown, 2009. ISBN 978-0-316-01985-9 Subj: Emotions – love.

The mommy book ill. by author. Little, 2002. ISBN 978-0-316-60827-5 Subj: Family life – mothers.

The okay book ill. by author. Little, 1999. ISBN 978-0-316-69220-5 Subj: Character traits – individuality. Self-concept.

Otto goes to school ill. by author. Little, Brown, 2005. ISBN 978-0-316-83533-6 Subj: Animals – dogs. School – first day.

Reading makes you feel good ill. by author. Little, Brown, 2005. ISBN 978-0-316-16004-9 Subj: Books, reading.

The thankful book ill. by author. Little, Brown, 2012. ISBN 978-0-316-18101-3 Subj: Character traits. Self-concept.

Things that make you feel good, things that make you feel bad ill. by author. Little, 1999. ISBN 978-0-316-69270-0 Subj: Emotions.

This is my hair ill. by author. Little, 1999. ISBN 978-0-316-69236-6 Subj: Hair.

Underwear do's and don'ts ill. by author. Little, 2000. ISBN 978-0-316-69151-2 Subj: Clothing. Humorous stories.

We belong together: a book about adoption and families ill. by author. Little, Brown, 2005. ISBN 978-0-316-01668-1 Subj: Adoption. Family life.

Partis, Joanne. *Stripe* ill. by author. Carolrhoda, 2000. ISBN 978-1-57505-450-6 Subj: Animals – babies. Animals – tigers. Behavior – misbehavior.

Stripe's naughty sister ill. by author. Carolrhoda, 2002. ISBN 978-0-87614-466-4 Subj: Animals – tigers. Family life – brothers & sisters.

Partridge, Elizabeth. *Big Cat Pepper* ill. by Lauren Castillo. Bloomsbury, 2009. ISBN 978-1-59990-024-7 Subj: Animals – cats. Death. Pets. Rhyming text.

Moon glowing ill. by Joan Paley. Dutton, 2002. ISBN 978-0-525-46873-8 Subj: Animals. Hibernation. Rhyming text. Seasons – winter.

Oranges on Golden Mountain ill. by Aki Sogabe. Dutton, 2001. ISBN 978-0-525-46453-2 Subj: Ethnic groups in the U.S. – Chinese Americans. Family life – aunts, uncles. Foreign lands – China. Immigrants. Sports – fishing.

Pig's eggs ill. by Martha Weston. Golden, 2000. ISBN 978-0-307-10232-4 Subj: Activities – painting. Animals – pigs. Birds – chickens. Eggs.

Paschkis, Julie. *Apple cake: a recipe for love* ill. by author. Harcourt, 2012. ISBN 978-0-547-80745-4 Subj: Activities – baking, cooking. Books, reading. Emotions – love.

Mooshka: a quilt story ill. by author. Peachtree, 2012. ISBN 978-1-56145-620-8 Subj: Activities – storytelling. Behavior – sharing. Family life – new sibling. Quilts.

Pasquali, Elena. *Ituku's Christmas journey* ill. by Dubravka Kolanovic. Good Books, 2005. ISBN 978-1-56148-495-9 Subj: Holidays – Christmas. Indians of North America – Inuit. Religion – Nativity.

Passen, Lisa. *Attack of the 50-foot teacher* ill. by author. Holt, 2000. ISBN 978-0-8050-6100-0 Subj: Aliens. Careers – teachers. Concepts – size. Holidays – Halloween. School.

The incredible shrinking teacher ill. by author. Holt, 2002. ISBN 978-0-8050-6452-0 Subj: Careers – teachers. Concepts – size. Humorous stories. Parties. School.

Patent, Dorothy Hinshaw. *Bold and bright, black-and-white animals* ill. by Kendahl Jan Jubb. Walker, 1998. ISBN 978-0-8027-8673-9 Subj: Animals. Concepts – color.

Fabulous fluttering tropical butterflies ill. by Kendahl Jan Jubb. Walker, 2003. ISBN 978-0-8027-8839-9 Subj: Insects – butterflies, caterpillars.

Slinky, scaly, slithery snakes ill. by Kendahl Jan Jubb. Walker, 2000. ISBN 978-0-8027-8744-6 Subj: Reptiles – snakes.

Paterson, Brian. *Zigby camps out* ill. by author. HarperCollins, 2002. ISBN 978-0-06-052921-5 Subj: Animals. Animals – meerkats. Animals – zebras. Birds – guinea fowl. Camps, camping. Jungle.

Zigby dives in ill. by author. HarperCollins, 2004. ISBN 978-0-06-053799-9 Subj: Animals – zebras. Octopuses. Sports – fishing.

Zigby hunts for treasure ill. by author. HarperCollins, 2003. ISBN 978-0-06-052922-2 Subj: Animals – meerkats. Animals – zebras. Canoes & canoeing. Jungle. Maps.

Paterson, Diane. *Hurricane wolf* ill. by author. Whitman, 2006. ISBN 978-0-8075-3438-0 Subj: Family life. Weather – hurricanes.

Paterson, John. *Blueberries for the queen* by John Paterson and Katherine Paterson ill. by Susan Jeffers. HarperCollins, 2004. ISBN 978-0-06-623943-9 Subj: Food. Royalty – queens. U.S. history. War.

Paterson, Katherine. *Blueberries for the queen* (Paterson, John)

Brother Sun, Sister Moon: Saint Francis of Assisi's canticle of the creatures ill. by Pamela Dalton. Chronicle, 2011. ISBN 978-0-8118-7734-3 Subj: Nature. Religion.

The light of the world: the life of Jesus for children ill. by François Roca. Scholastic, 2008. ISBN 978-0-545-01172-3 Subj: Religion.

The tale of the Mandarin ducks ill. by Leo Dillon and Diane Dillon. Dutton, 1990. ISBN 978-0-525-67283-8 Subj: Birds – ducks. Folk & fairy tales. Foreign lands – Japan.

Patkau, Karen. *Creatures: yesterday and today* ill. by author. Tundra, 2008. ISBN 978-0-88776-833-0 Subj: Animals. Prehistory. Science.

Patricelli, Leslie. *Baby happy, baby sad* ill. by author. Candlewick, 2008. ISBN 978-0-7636-3245-8 Subj: Babies. Emotions. Format, unusual – board books.

Be quiet, Mike! ill. by author. Candlewick, 2011. ISBN 978-0-7636-4477-2 Subj: Animals – monkeys. Musical instruments – drums. Noise, sounds.

Binky ill. by author. Candlewick, 2005. ISBN 978-0-7636-2364-7 Subj: Babies. Format, unusual – board books. Toys.

The birthday box ill. by author. Candlewick, 2007. ISBN 978-0-7636-2825-3 Subj: Birthdays. Imagination.

Blankie ill. by author. Candlewick, 2005. ISBN 978-0-7636-2363-0 Subj: Babies. Format, unusual – board books.

Fa la la ill. by author. Candlewick, 2012. ISBN 978-0-7636-3247-2 Subj: Babies. Format, unusual – board books. Holidays – Christmas.

Faster! Faster! ill. by author. Candlewick, 2012. ISBN 978-0-7636-5473-3 Subj: Animals. Concepts – speed. Family life – fathers. Imagination.

Higher! Higher! ill. by author. Candlewick, 2009. ISBN 978-0-7636-3241-0 Subj: Activities – swinging. Imagination.

No no, yes yes ill. by author. Candlewick, 2008. ISBN 978-0-7636-3244-1 Subj: Babies. Behavior. Format, unusual – board books.

The Patterson puppies and the midnight monster party ill. by author. Candlewick, 2010. ISBN 978-0-7636-3243-4 Subj: Animals – dogs. Bedtime. Emotions – fear. Monsters.

Potty ill. by author. Candlewick, 2010. ISBN 978-0-7636-4476-5 Subj: Toilet training.

Tubby ill. by author. Candlewick, 2010. ISBN 978-0-7636-4567-0 Subj: Activities – bathing. Activities – playing.

Patrick, Jean L. S. *If I had a snowplow* ill. by Karen Dugan. Boyds Mills, 2001. ISBN 978-1-56397-746-6 Subj: Family life – mothers. Machines. Rhyming text. Trucks.

Patschke, Steve. *The spooky book* ill. by Matthew McElligott. Walker, 1999. ISBN 978-0-8027-8693-7 Subj: Books, reading. Emotions – fear. Homes, houses.

Patten, Brian. *The big snuggle-up* ill. by Nicola Bayley. Kane/Miller, 2011. ISBN 978-1-61067-036-4 Subj: Animals. Behavior – sharing. Character traits – generosity. Rhyming text. Scarecrows. Weather – snow.

Patterson, Rebecca. *My no, no, no day!* ill. by author. Viking, 2012. ISBN 978-0-670-01405-7 Subj: Behavior – bad day. Behavior – misbehavior. Emotions.

Pattison, Darcy. *Desert baths* ill. by Kathleen Rietz. Sylvan Dell, 2012. ISBN 978-1-607185-25-3 Subj: Activities – bathing. Animals. Desert.

The journey of Oliver K. Woodman ill. by Joe Cepeda. Harcourt, 2003. ISBN 978-0-15-202329-4 Subj: Activities – traveling. Letters, cards. Toys – dolls.

Searching for Oliver K. Woodman ill. by Joe Cepeda. Harcourt, 2005. ISBN 978-0-15-205184-6 Subj: Activities – traveling. Letters, cards. Toys – dolls.

Pattou, Edith. *Mrs. Spitzer's garden* ill. by Tricia Tusa. Harcourt, 2001. ISBN 978-0-15-201978-5 Subj: Careers – teachers. Gardens, gardening. School.

Mrs. Spitzer's garden ill. by Tricia Tusa. Gift edition. Harcourt, 2007. ISBN 978-0-15-205802-9 Subj: Careers – teachers. Gardens, gardening. School.

Patz, Nancy. *Babies can't eat kimchee!* by Nancy Patz and Susan L. Roth ill. by authors. Bloomsbury, 2007. ISBN 978-1-59990-017-9 Subj: Babies. Behavior – growing up. Ethnic groups in the U.S. – Korean Americans. Family life – brothers & sisters. Family life – new sibling. Food.

Paul, Alison. *The crow (a not so scary story)* ill. by author. Houghton, 2007. ISBN 978-0-618-66380-4 Subj: Birds – crows. Emotions – fear. Language.

Paul, Ann Whitford. *Count on Culebra: go from 1 to 10 in Spanish* ill. by Ethan Long. Holiday, 2008. ISBN 978-0-8234-2124-4 Subj: Counting, numbers. Desert. Foreign languages. Reptiles – iguanas. Reptiles – snakes.

Eight hands round ill. by Jeanette Winter. HarperCollins, 1991. ISBN 978-0-06-024704-1 Subj: ABC books. Quilts.

Everything to spend the night . . . from A to Z ill. by Maggie Smith. DK, 1999. ISBN 978-0-7894-2511-9 Subj: ABC books. Bedtime. Family life – grandfathers. Rhyming text.

Fiesta fiasco ill. by Ethan Long. Holiday House, 2007. ISBN 978-0-8234-2037-7 Subj: Animals. Birthdays. Desert. Foreign languages. Gifts.

Hello toes! Hello feet! ill. by Nadine Bernard Westcott. DK, 1998. ISBN 978-0-7894-2481-5 Subj: Activities – playing. Anatomy – feet. Anatomy – toes. Animals – dogs. Clothing – shoes.

If animals kissed goodnight ill. by David Walker. Farrar, 2008. ISBN 978-0-374-38051-9 Subj: Animals. Bedtime. Rhyming text.

Mañana Iguana ill. by Ethan Long. Holiday House, 2004. ISBN 978-0-8234-1808-4 Subj: Character traits – laziness. Desert. Foreign languages. Parties. Reptiles – iguanas.

The seasons sewn ill. by Michael McCurdy. Browndeer, 1996. ISBN 978-0-15-276918-5 Subj: Activities – sewing. Quilts. Seasons. U.S. history – frontier & pioneer life.

Tortuga in trouble ill. by Ethan Long. Holiday, 2009. ISBN 978-0-8234-2180-0 Subj: Animals – coyotes. Desert. Family life – grandmothers. Folk & fairy tales. Foreign languages. Reptiles – turtles, tortoises.

Word builder ill. by Kurt Cyrus. Simon & Schuster, 2009. ISBN 978-1-4169-3981-8 Subj: Careers – construction workers. Language.

Paul, Chris. *Long shot: never too small to dream big* ill. by Frank Morrison. Simon & Schuster, 2009. ISBN 978-1-4169-5079-0 Subj: Character traits – persistence. Character traits – smallness. Ethnic groups in the U.S. – African Americans. Sports – basketball.

Paul, Korky. *Tiny* (Rogers, Paul)

Paul, Ruth. *Hedgehog's magic tricks* ill. by author. Candlewick, 2013. ISBN 978-0-7636-6385-8 Subj: Animals. Animals – hedgehogs. Careers – magicians. Friendship.

Pauli, Lorenz. *The fox in the library* ill. by Kathrin Scharer. NorthSouth, 2013. ISBN 978-0-7358-4150-5 Subj: Animals – foxes. Animals – mice. Behavior – trickery. Birds – chickens. Books, reading. Libraries.

Paulsen, Gary. *Canoe days* ill. by Ruth Wright Paulsen. Doubleday, 1999. ISBN 978-0-385-32524-0 Subj: Birds. Canoes & canoeing. Fish. Insects. Seasons – summer.

Worksong ill. by Ruth Wright Paulsen. Harcourt, 1997. ISBN 978-0-15-200980-9 Subj: Activities – working. Careers. Rhyming text.

Pavlova, Anna. *I dreamed I was a ballerina* ill. with art by Edgar Degas. Atheneum, 2001. ISBN 978-0-689-84676-2 Subj: Activities – dancing. Ballet. Careers – dancers. Character traits – ambition. Foreign lands – Russia.

Paxton, Tom. *Belling the cat and other Aesop fables* (Aesop)

Engelbert the elephant ill. by Steven Kellogg. Morrow, 1990. ISBN 978-0-688-08936-8 Subj: Activities – dancing. Animals – elephants. Etiquette. Parties. Royalty – queens.

Going to the zoo ill. by Karen Lee Schmidt. Morrow, 1996. ISBN 978-0-688-13801-1 Subj: Animals. Music. Songs. Zoos.

The jungle baseball game ill. by Karen Lee Schmidt. Morrow, 1999. ISBN 978-0-688-13980-3 Subj: Animals – hippopotamuses. Animals – monkeys. Sports – baseball.

The story of Santa Claus ill. by Michael Dooling. Morrow, 1995. ISBN 978-0-688-11365-0 Subj: Folk & fairy tales. Holidays – Christmas. Santa Claus.

The story of the Tooth Fairy ill. by Robert Sauber. Morrow, 1996. ISBN 978-0-688-12988-0 Subj: Fairies. Folk & fairy tales. Friendship. Teeth.

Paye, Won-Ldy. *Head, body, legs* retold by Won-Ldy Paye and Margaret H. Lippert; ill. by Julie Paschkis. Holt, 2002. ISBN 978-0-8050-6570-1 Subj: Character traits – cooperation. Folk & fairy tales. Foreign lands – Liberia.

Mrs. Chicken and the hungry crocodile retold by Won-Ldy Paye and Margaret H. Lippert; ill. by Julie Paschkis. Holt, 2003. ISBN 978-0-8050-7047-7 Subj: Birds – chickens. Folk & fairy tales. Foreign lands – Liberia. Reptiles – alligators, crocodiles.

Payne, Emmy. *Katy no-pocket* ill. by H. A. Rey. Houghton, 1944. ISBN 978-0-395-52141-0 Subj: Animals – kangaroos. Clothing – aprons. Clothing – pockets. Problem solving.

Payne, Nina. *Summertime waltz* ill. by Gabi Swiatkowska. Farrar, 2005. ISBN 978-0-374-37291-0 Subj: Seasons – summer.

Peaceful moments in the wild: animals and their homes ill. with photos. Moonstone, 2001. ISBN 978-0-9707768-1-5 Subj: Animals. Homes, houses.

Peacock, Carol Antoinette. *Mommy far, Mommy near* ill. by Shawn Costello Brownell. Whitman, 2000. ISBN 978-0-8075-5234-6 Subj: Adoption. Emotions. Ethnic groups in the U.S. – Chinese Americans. Family life – mothers.

Pilgrim cat ill. by Doris Ettlinger. Whitman, 2004. ISBN 978-0-8075-6532-2 Subj: Animals – cats. Boats, ships. Pilgrims. U.S. history.

Pearce, Clemency. *Frangoline and the midnight dream* ill. by Rebecca Elliott. Scholastic, 2011. ISBN 978-0-545-31426-8 Subj: Behavior – misbehavior. Moon. Night. Rhyming text.

Pearce, Philippa. *Amy's three best things* ill. by Helen Craig. Candlewick, 2013. ISBN 978-0-7636-6314-8 Subj: Family life – grandmothers. Imagination. Sleepovers.

Pearle, Ida. *A child's day: an alphabet of play* ill. by author. Harcourt, 2008. ISBN 978-0-15-206552-2 Subj: ABC books. Activities.

Pearson, Debora. *Alphabeep* ill. by Edward Miller. Holiday, 2003. ISBN 978-0-8234-1722-3 Subj: ABC books. Automobiles. Traffic, traffic signs. Trucks.

Big city song ill. by Lynn Rowe Reed. Holiday House, 2006. ISBN 978-0-8234-1988-3 Subj: Cities, towns. Noise, sounds. Rhyming text.

Leo's tree ill. by Nora Hilb. Annick, 2004. ISBN 978-1-55037-844-3 Subj: Behavior – growing up. Poetry. Trees.

Sophie's wheels ill. by Nora Hilb. Annick, 2006. ISBN 978-1-55451-038-2 Subj: Behavior – growing up. Wheels.

Pearson, Susan. *Hooray for feet!* ill. by Roxanna Baer-Block. Blue Apple, 2005. ISBN 978-1-59354-093-7 Subj: Anatomy – feet. Rhyming text.

How to teach a slug to read ill. by David Slonim. Marshall Cavendish, 2011. ISBN 978-0-7614-5805-0 Subj: Animals – slugs. Books, reading.

Slugs in love ill. by Kevin O'Malley. Marshall Cavendish, 2006. ISBN 978-0-7614-5311-6 Subj: Activities – writing. Animals – slugs. Character traits – shyness. Emotions – love. Poetry.

We're going on a ghost hunt ill. by S. D. Schindler. Amazon Children's, 2012. ISBN 978-0-7614-6307-8 Subj: Ghosts. Holidays – Halloween. Imagination.

Pearson, Tracey Campbell. *Bob* ill. by author. Farrar, 2002. ISBN 978-0-374-39957-3 Subj: Animals. Birds – chickens. Humorous stories. Noise, sounds.

Diddle diddle dumpling ill. by author. Farrar, 2005. ISBN 978-0-374-30861-2 Subj: Format, unusual – board books. Nursery rhymes.

Elephant's story ill. by author. Farrar, 2013. ISBN 978-0-374-39913-9 Subj: Animals. Animals – elephants. Books, reading. Language.

Hector Protector [board book] ill. by author. Farrar, 2004. ISBN 978-0-374-30860-5 Subj: Format, unusual – board books. Nursery rhymes.

The purple hat ill. by author. Farrar, 1997. ISBN 978-0-374-36153-2 Subj: Birds. Clothing – hats. Forest, woods.

Where does Joe go? ill. by author. Farrar, 1999. ISBN 978-0-374-38319-0 Subj: Restaurants. Rhyming text. Santa Claus. Seasons – winter.

Peck, Jan. *The giant carrot* ill. by Barry Root. Dial, 1998. ISBN 978-0-8037-1824-1 Subj: Behavior – sharing. Folk & fairy tales. Food. Foreign lands – Russia.

Giant peach yodel! ill. by Barry Root. Pelican, 2012. ISBN 978-1-58980-980-2 Subj: Character traits – cooperation. Cumulative tales. Folk & fairy tales. Food. Problem solving.

Pirate treasure hunt! ill. by Adrian Tans. Pelican, 2008. ISBN 978-1-58980-549-1 Subj: Imagination. Pirates.

Way up high in a tall green tree ill. by Valeria Petrone. Simon & Schuster, 2005. ISBN 978-1-4169-0071-9 Subj: Animals. Bedtime. Imagination. Jungle. Rhyming text.

Peck, Richard. *Monster night at Grandma's house* ill. by Don Freeman. Dial, 2003. ISBN 978-0-8037-2904-9 Subj: Bedtime. Emotions – fear. Family life – grandmothers. Monsters. Night.

Peddicord, Jane Ann. *That special little baby* ill. by Meilo So. Harcourt, 2007. ISBN 978-0-15-205430-4 Subj: Babies. Rhyming text.

Peddle, Daniel. *Snow day* ill. by author. Doubleday, 2000. ISBN 978-0-385-32693-3 Subj: Nature. Snowmen. Weather – snow. Wordless.

Pedersen, Janet. *Houdini the amazing caterpillar* ill. by author. Clarion, 2008. ISBN 978-0-618-89332-4 Subj: Insects – butterflies, caterpillars. Metamorphosis.

Millie wants to play ill. by author. Candlewick, 2004. ISBN 978-0-7636-1993-0 Subj: Animals – bulls, cows. Morning. Noise, sounds.

Pedersen, Judy. *When night time comes near* ill. by author. Viking, 2000. ISBN 978-0-670-88259-5 Subj: Bedtime. Communities, neighborhoods. Night.

Pedersen, Marika. *Mommy works, Daddy works* by Marika Pedersen and Mikele Hall ill. by Deirdre Betteridge. Annick, 2000. ISBN 978-1-55037-657-9 Subj: Activities – working. Family life – parents.

Peek, Merle, adapt. *Mary wore her red dress and Henry wore his green sneakers* ill. by adapter. Clarion, 1985. ISBN 978-0-89919-324-3 Subj: Animals. Animals – bears. Birthdays. Concepts – color. Songs.

Roll over! a counting song ill. by author. Houghton, 1981. ISBN 978-0-395-29438-3 Subj: Counting, numbers. Songs.

Peet, Bill. *The ant and the elephant* ill. by author. Little, 1972. ISBN 978-0-395-13734-5 Subj: Animals. Animals – elephants. Character traits – helpfulness. Character traits – selfishness. Cumulative tales. Insects – ants.

Big bad Bruce ill. by author. Houghton, 1977. ISBN 978-0-395-25150-8 Subj: Animals – bears. Behavior – bullying, teasing. Forest, woods. Humorous stories. Witches.

Bill Peet: an autobiography ill. by author. Houghton, 1989. ISBN 978-0-395-50932-6 Subj: Caldecott award honor books.

Buford the little bighorn ill. by author. Houghton, 1967. Subj: Animals – sheep. Character traits – individuality. Humorous stories. Sports – hunting. Sports – skiing.

The caboose who got loose ill. by author. Houghton, 1971. ISBN 978-0-395-12578-6 Subj: Behavior – dissatisfaction. Ecology. Trains.

Chester the worldly pig ill. by author. Houghton, 1965. Subj: Animals – pigs. Circus. Humorous stories. World.

Cock-a-doodle Dudley ill. by author. Houghton, 1990. ISBN 978-0-395-55331-2 Subj: Animals. Birds – chickens. Farms. Sun.

Countdown to Christmas ill. by author. Houghton, 1972. ISBN 978-0-87464-199-8 Subj: Holidays – Christmas. Humorous stories. Magic. Progress. Santa Claus.

Cowardly Clyde ill. by author. Houghton, 1979. ISBN 978-0-395-27802-4 Subj: Animals – horses, ponies. Character traits – bravery. Humorous stories. Knights.

Cyrus the unsinkable sea serpent ill. by author. Houghton, 1975. ISBN 978-0-395-20272-2 Subj: Character traits – helpfulness. Monsters. Mythical creatures. Sea & seashore.

Eli ill. by author. Houghton, 1978. ISBN 978-0-606-03378-7 Subj: Animals – lions. Birds – vultures. Friendship. Humorous stories.

Ella ill. by author. Houghton, 1964. ISBN 978-0-395-17577-4 Subj: Animals – elephants. Behavior – lost. Character traits – conceit. Circus. Rhyming text.

Encore for Eleanor ill. by author. Houghton, 1981. ISBN 978-0-395-29860-2 Subj: Animals – elephants. Art.

Farewell to Shady Glade ill. by author. Houghton, 1966. ISBN 978-0-395-18975-7 Subj: Animals. Ecology. Progress.

Fly, Homer, fly ill. by author. Houghton, 1969. Subj: Birds – pigeons. Cities, towns. Ecology.

The gnats of knotty pine ill. by author. Houghton, 1975. ISBN 978-0-395-21405-3 Subj: Animals. Ecology. Insects – gnats. Sports – hunting.

How Droofus the dragon lost his head ill. by author. Houghton, 1971. ISBN 978-0-395-15085-6 Subj: Dragons. Knights. Royalty – kings.

Hubert's hair-raising adventures ill. by author. Houghton, 1959. Subj: Animals – lions. Careers – barbers. Humorous stories. Rhyming text.

Huge Harold ill. by author. Houghton, 1961. ISBN 978-0-395-32923-8 Subj: Animals – rabbits. Character traits – kindness to animals. Concepts – size. Humorous stories. Rhyming text.

Jennifer and Josephine ill. by author. Houghton, 1967. ISBN 978-0-395-18225-3 Subj: Animals – cats. Automobiles. Humorous stories.

Jethro and Joel were a troll ill. by author. Houghton, 1987. ISBN 978-0-395-43081-1 Subj: Humorous stories. Magic. Mythical creatures – trolls.

Kermit the hermit ill. by author. Houghton, 1965. ISBN 978-0-395-15084-9 Subj: Behavior – greed. Crustaceans – crabs. Humorous stories. Rhyming text. Sea & seashore.

The kweeks of Kookatumdee ill. by author. Houghton, 1985. ISBN 978-0-395-37902-8 Subj: Activities – flying. Behavior – greed. Birds. Rhyming text.

The luckiest one of all ill. by author. Houghton, 1982. ISBN 978-0-395-31863-8 Subj: Behavior –

dissatisfaction. Emotions – envy, jealousy. Rhyming text.

Merle the high flying squirrel ill. by author. Houghton, 1974. ISBN 978-0-395-18452-3 Subj: Activities – flying. Animals – squirrels. Humorous stories. Kites. Trees.

No such things ill. by author. Houghton, 1983. ISBN 978-0-395-33888-9 Subj: Animals. Mythical creatures. Rhyming text.

Pamela Camel ill. by author. Houghton, 1984. ISBN 978-0-395-35975-4 Subj: Animals – camels. Behavior – running away. Self-concept.

The pinkish, purplish, bluish egg ill. by author. Houghton, 1963. ISBN 978-0-395-18472-1 Subj: Birds. Birds – doves. Eggs. Mythical creatures. Rhyming text. Violence, nonviolence.

Randy's dandy lions ill. by author. Houghton, 1964. ISBN 978-0-395-18507-0 Subj: Animals – lions. Circus. Humorous stories. Rhyming text.

Smokey ill. by author. Houghton, 1962. ISBN 978-0-395-15992-7 Subj: Old age. Rhyming text. Trains.

The spooky tail of Prewitt Peacock ill. by author. Houghton, 1973. ISBN 978-0-395-15494-6 Subj: Birds – peacocks, peahens. Character traits – being different. Character traits – individuality.

The Whingdingdilly ill. by author. Houghton, 1970. ISBN 978-0-395-24729-7 Subj: Animals – dogs. Behavior – dissatisfaction. Character traits – optimism. Witches.

The wump world ill. by author. Houghton, 1970. ISBN 978-0-395-19841-4 Subj: Ecology. Progress. Space & space ships.

Zella, Zack, and Zodiac ill. by author. Houghton, 1986. ISBN 978-0-395-40567-3 Subj: Animals – zebras. Behavior – needing someone. Birds – ostriches. Rhyming text.

Peet, Mal. *Cloud tea monkeys* by Mal Peet and Elspeth Graham ill. by Juan Wijngaard. Candlewick, 2010. ISBN 978-0-7636-4453-6 Subj: Animals – monkeys. Character traits – kindness to animals. Family life – mothers. Foreign lands – Himalayas. Illness.

Peete, Holly Robinson. *My brother Charlie* by Holly Robinson Peete and Ryan Elizabeth Peete ill. by Shane W. Evans. Scholastic, 2010. ISBN 978-0-545-09466-5 Subj: Ethnic groups in the U.S. – African Americans. Family life – brothers & sisters. Disabilities – autism. Multiple births – twins.

Peete, Ryan Elizabeth. *My brother Charlie* (Peete, Holly Robinson)

Pegram, Laura. *Daughter's Day blues* ill. by Cornelius Van Wright and Ying-Hwa Hu. Dial, 2000. ISBN 978-0-8037-1557-8 Subj: Ethnic groups in the U.S. – African Americans. Family life – brothers & sisters. Family life – grandmothers.

Pelé. *For the love of soccer!* ill. by Frank Morrison. Hyperion/Disney, 2010. ISBN 978-1-4231-1538-0 Subj: Sports – soccer.

Pelham, David. *A is for animals* ill. by author. Simon & Schuster, 1991. ISBN 978-0-671-72495-5 Subj: ABC books. Animals. Format, unusual – toy & movable books.

Crawlies creep ill. by author. Dutton, 1996. ISBN 978-0-525-45576-9 Subj: Animals. Format, unusual – toy & movable books.

Sam's pizza ill. by author. Dutton, 1996. ISBN 978-0-525-45594-3 Subj: Activities – baking, cooking. Family life – brothers & sisters. Food. Format, unusual – toy & movable books. Rhyming text. Sibling rivalry.

Sam's sandwich ill. by author. Dutton, 1991. ISBN 978-0-525-44751-1 Subj: Family life – brothers & sisters. Food. Format, unusual – toy & movable books. Rhyming text.

Pellant, Chris. *The best book of fossils, rocks, and minerals* ill. by author. Kingfisher, 2000. ISBN 978-0-7534-5274-5 Subj: Fossils. Rocks.

Pelletier, Andrew T. *The amazing adventures of Bathman!* ill. by Peter Elwell. Penguin, 2005. ISBN 978-0-525-47164-6 Subj: Activities – bathing. Toys.

The toy farmer ill. by Scott Nash. Penguin, 2007. ISBN 978-0-525-47649-8 Subj: Careers – farmers. Farms. Magic. Toys.

Pelletier, David. *The graphic alphabet* ill. by author. Orchard, 1996. ISBN 978-0-531-36001-9 Subj: ABC books. Caldecott award honor books. Concepts.

Pelley, Kathleen T. *Inventor McGregor* ill. by Michael Chesworth. Farrar, 2006. ISBN 978-0-374-33606-6 Subj: Careers – inventors. Family life.

Magnus Maximus, a marvelous measurer ill. by S. D. Schindler. Farrar, 2010. ISBN 978-0-374-34725-3 Subj: Concepts – measurement. Counting, numbers.

Raj the bookstore tiger ill. by Paige Keiser. Charlesbridge, 2011. ISBN 978-1-58089-230-8 Subj: Animals – cats. Self-concept. Stores.

Pelton, Mindy L. *When Dad's at sea* ill. by Robert Gantt Steele. Whitman, 2004. ISBN 978-0-8075-6339-7 Subj: Behavior – needing someone. Boats, ships. Careers – airplane pilots. Careers – military. Family life – fathers.

Peña, Matt de la. *A nation's hope: the story of boxing legend Joe Louis* ill. by Kadir Nelson. Penguin, 2011. ISBN 978-0-8037-3167-7 Subj: Ethnic groups in the U.S. – African Americans. Sports – boxing.

Pendziwol, Jean E. *No dragons for tea: fire safety for kids (and dragons)* ill. by Martine Gourbault. Kids Can, 1999. ISBN 978-1-55074-569-6 Subj: Dragons. Fire. Friendship. Rhyming text. Safety.

Once upon a northern night ill. by Isabelle Arsenault. Groundwood, 2013. ISBN 978-1-55498-138-0 Subj: Night. Seasons – winter. Weather – snow.

The red sash ill. by Nicolas Debon. Groundwood, 2005. ISBN 978-0-88899-589-6 Subj: Careers – fur traders. Foreign lands – Canada. Indians of North America – Metis.

The tale of Sir Dragon: dealing with bullies for kids (and dragons) ill. by Martine Gourbault. Kids Can, 2007. ISBN 978-1-55453-135-6 Subj: Behavior – bullying, teasing. Dragons. Rhyming text.

A treasure at sea for dragon and me ill. by Martine Gourbault. Kids Can, 2005. ISBN 978-1-55337-721-4 Subj: Dragons. Rhyming text. Safety. Sea & seashore – beaches. Sports.

Penn, Audrey. *A bedtime kiss for Chester Raccoon* ill. by Barbara L. Gibson. Tanglewood, 2011. ISBN 978-1-933718-52-1 Subj: Animals – raccoons. Bedtime. Emotions – fear. Format, unusual – board books. Rhyming text.

A color game for Chester Raccoon ill. by Barbara L. Gibson. Tanglewood, 2012. ISBN 978-1-933718-58-3 Subj: Animals – raccoons. Concepts – color. Format, unusual – board books.

Penner, Fred. *The cat came back* ill. by Renee Reichert. Macmillan, 2005. ISBN 978-1-59643-030-3 Subj: Animals – cats. Character traits – persistence. Songs.

Pennypacker, Sara. *Pierre in love* ill. by Petra Mathers. Scholastic, 2007. ISBN 978-0-439-51740-9 Subj: Animals – mice. Animals – rabbits. Ballet. Careers – fishermen. Emotions – love.

Stuart's cape ill. by Martin Matje. Orchard, 2002. ISBN 978-0-439-30180-0 Subj: Behavior – worrying. Imagination. Moving. School – first day.

Perdorno, Willie. *Visiting Langston* ill. by Bryan Collier. Holt, 2002. ISBN 978-0-8050-6744-6 Subj: Careers – poets. Ethnic groups in the U.S. – African Americans. Poetry.

Peretz, Isaac Loeb. *The magician* (Shulevitz, Uri)

Pérez, Amada Irma. *My diary from here to there / Mi diario de aquí hasta allá* ill. by Maya Christina Gonzalez. Children's Book Press, 2002. ISBN 978-0-89239-175-2 Subj: Ethnic groups in the U.S. – Mexican Americans. Family life. Foreign languages. Immigrants. Moving.

My very own room / Mi propio cuartito ill. by Maya Christina Gonzalez. Lee & Low, 2000. ISBN 978-0-89239-164-6 Subj: Ethnic groups in the U.S. – Mexican Americans. Family life. Foreign languages. Homes, houses.

Pérez, L. King. *First day in grapes* ill. by Robert Casilla. Lee & Low, 2002. ISBN 978-1-58430-045-8 Subj: Careers – migrant workers. Character traits – confidence. Ethnic groups in the U.S. – Mexican Americans. School – first day.

Perez, Monica. *Curious George plants a tree* ill. by Anna Grossnickle Hines. Houghton, 2009. ISBN 978-0-547-15087-1 Subj: Animals – monkeys. Ecology. Trees.

Curious George saves his pennies ill. by Mary O'Keefe Young. Houghton Mifflin, 2013. ISBN 978-0-547-63231-5 Subj: Animals – monkeys. Behavior – saving things. Money. Toys.

Pericoli, Matteo. *See the city* ill. by author. Knopf, 2004. ISBN 978-0-375-82469-2 Subj: Activities – drawing. Cities, towns. Format, unusual.

Tommaso and the missing line ill. by author. Knopf, 2008. ISBN 978-0-375-84102-6 Subj: Activities – drawing. Behavior – lost & found possessions. Foreign lands – Italy. Imagination.

The true story of Stellina ill. by author. Random House, 2006. ISBN 978-0-375-93273-1 Subj: Birds – finches. Character traits – kindness to animals.

Perkins, Lynne Rae. *The broken cat* ill. by author. Greenwillow, 2002. ISBN 978-0-06-029264-5 Subj: Animals – cats. Careers – veterinarians. Family life. Illness. Memories, memory.

The cardboard piano ill. by author. Greenwillow, 2008. ISBN 978-0-06-154265-7 Subj: Friendship. Musical instruments – pianos.

Home lovely ill. by author. Greenwillow, 1995. ISBN 978-0-688-13688-8 Subj: Family life. Gardens, gardening.

Pictures from our vacation ill. by author. HarperCollins, 2007. ISBN 978-0-06-085098-2 Subj: Activities – photographing. Activities – vacationing. Family life. Foreign lands – Canada.

Snow music ill. by author. Greenwillow, 2003. ISBN 978-0-06-623956-9 Subj: Animals – dogs. Behavior – lost & found possessions. Noise, sounds. Seasons – winter. Weather – snow.

Perl, Erica S. *Chicken Butt's back!* ill. by Henry Cole. Abrams, 2011. ISBN 978-0-8109-9729-5 Subj: Birds – chickens. Humorous stories. Language.

Dotty ill. by Julia Denos. Abrams, 2010. ISBN 978-0-8109-8962-7 Subj: Emotions – anger. Imagination – imaginary friends. School.

Ninety-three in my family ill. by Mike Lester. Abrams, 2006. ISBN 978-0-8109-5760-2 Subj: Counting, numbers. Family life. Rhyming text.

Perlman, Janet. *The delicious bug* ill. by author. Kids Can, 2009. ISBN 978-1-55337-996-6 Subj: Behavior – sharing. Insects. Reptiles – chameleons.

The Emperor Penguin's new clothes ill. by author. Viking, 1995. ISBN 978-0-670-85864-4 Subj: Birds – penguins. Character traits – pride. Character traits – vanity. Clothing. Folk & fairy tales. Imagination. Royalty – emperors.

The penguin and the pea by Janet Perlman and Hans Christian Anderson ill. by reteller. Kids Can, 2004. ISBN 978-1-55074-832-1 Subj: Birds – penguins. Folk & fairy tales. Royalty – princesses. Sleep.

Perlman, Willa. *Good night, world* ill. by Carolyn Fisher. Simon & Schuster, 2011. ISBN 978-1-4424-0197-4 Subj: Bedtime. Rhyming text. World.

Perlov, Betty Rosenberg. *Rifka takes a bow* ill. by Cosei Kawa. Lerner/Kar-Ben, 2013. ISBN 978-0-7613-8127-3 Subj: Jewish culture. Theater.

Perrault, Charles. *Cinderella* retold by Sarah L. Thomson; ill. by Nicoletta Ceccoli. Amazon Children's, 2012. ISBN 978-0-7614-6170-8 Subj: Family life – stepfamilies. Folk & fairy tales. Royalty – princes. Sibling rivalry.

Cinderella retold by Amy Ehrlich; ill. by Susan Jeffers. Dial, 1985. ISBN 978-0-8037-0206-6 Subj: Family life – stepfamilies. Folk & fairy tales. Royalty – princes. Sibling rivalry.

Cinderella ill. by Loek Koopmans. NorthSouth, 1999. ISBN 978-0-7358-1052-5 Subj: Family life – stepfamilies. Folk & fairy tales. Royalty – princes. Sibling rivalry.

Cinderella retold by Barbara McClintock; ill. by reteller. Scholastic, 2005. ISBN 978-0-439-56145-7 Subj: Family life – stepfamilies. Folk & fairy tales. Royalty – princes. Sibling rivalry.

Cinderella retold by Barbara Karlin; ill. by James Marshall. Little, 1989. ISBN 978-0-316-54654-6 Subj: Family life – stepfamilies. Folk & fairy tales. Royalty – princes. Sibling rivalry.

Cinderella / Cenicienta adapt. by Francesc Boada; ill. by Monse Fransoy. Chronicle, 2001. ISBN 978-0-8118-3084-3 Subj: Family life – stepfamilies. Folk & fairy tales. Foreign lands – France. Foreign languages. Royalty – princes. Sibling rivalry.

Cinderella: a pop-up fairy tale retold by Matthew Reinhart; ill. by reteller. Simon & Schuster, 2005. ISBN 978-1-4169-0501-1 Subj: Family life – stepfamilies. Folk & fairy tales. Format, unusual – toy & movable books. Royalty – princes. Sibling rivalry.

Cinderella: or, the little glass slipper ill. by Marcia Brown. Aladdin, 1988, ©1954. ISBN 978-0-689-71261-6 Subj: Caldecott award books. Family life – stepfamilies. Folk & fairy tales. Royalty – princes. Sibling rivalry.

Puss in boots ill. by Marcia Brown. Scribners, 1952. Subj: Animals – cats. Caldecott award honor books. Character traits – cleverness. Folk & fairy tales. Royalty – kings.

Puss in boots adapt. by Lorinda Bryan Cauley; ill. by adapter. Harcourt, 1986. ISBN 978-0-15-264227-3 Subj: Animals – cats. Character traits – cleverness. Folk & fairy tales. Royalty – kings.

Puss in boots ill. by Paul Galdone. Seabury Pr., 1976. ISBN 978-0-8164-3159-5 Subj: Animals – cats. Character traits – cleverness. Folk & fairy tales. Royalty – kings.

Puss in boots retold by Steve Light; ill. by reteller. Abrams, 2002. ISBN 978-0-8109-4368-1 Subj: Animals – cats. Character traits – cleverness. Clothing – boots. Folk & fairy tales. Royalty – kings.

Puss in boots retold by Kurt Baumann; ill. by Giuliano Lunelli. NorthSouth, 1999. ISBN 978-0-7358-1159-1 Subj: Animals – cats. Character traits – cleverness. Folk & fairy tales. Royalty – kings.

Puss in boots ill. by Fred Marcellino. Farrar, 1990. ISBN 978-0-374-36160-0 Subj: Animals – cats. Caldecott award honor books. Character traits – cleverness. Folk & fairy tales. Royalty – kings.

Puss in boots ill. by Fred Marcellino. Farrar, 1998. ISBN 978-0-374-46034-1 Subj: Animals – cats. Character traits – cleverness. Folk & fairy tales. Royalty – kings.

Puss in boots retold by John Cech; ill. by Bernhard Oberdieck. Sterling, 2010. ISBN 978-1-4027-4436-5 Subj: Animals – cats. Character traits – cleverness. Folk & fairy tales. Royalty – kings.

Puss in boots retold by Jerry Pinkney; ill. by reteller. Dial, 2012. ISBN 978-0-8037-1642-1 Subj: Animals – cats. Character traits – cleverness. Clothing – boots. Folk & fairy tales. Royalty – kings.

Puss in boots retold by Lincoln Kirstein; ill. by Alain Vaës. Little, 1992. ISBN 978-0-316-89506-4 Subj: Animals – cats. Character traits – cleverness. Folk & fairy tales. Royalty – kings.

Perret, Delphine. *The Big Bad Wolf and me* ill. by author. Sterling, 2006. ISBN 978-1-4027-3725-1 Subj: Animals – wolves. Pets.

The Big Bad Wolf goes on vacation ill. by author. Sterling, 2013. ISBN 978-1-4027-8633-4 Subj: Activities – vacationing. Animals – wolves. Family life – grandfathers.

Perrin, Martine. *Cock-a-doodle who?* ill. by author. Whitman, 2012. ISBN 978-0-8075-1107-7 Subj: Animals. Farms. Format, unusual. Rhyming text.

Look who's there! ill. by author. Whitman, 2011. ISBN 978-0-8075-7676-2 Subj: Animals. Format, unusual – toy & movable books. Sea & seashore.

Perrow, Angeli. *Lighthouse dog to the rescue* ill. by Emily Harris. Down East, 2000. ISBN 978-0-89272-487-1 Subj: Animals – dogs. Lighthouses. Weather – storms.

Many hands: a Penobscot Indian story ill. by Heather Austin. Down East, 2010. ISBN 978-0-89272-782-7 Subj: Activities – weaving. Family life – grandmothers. Indians of North America.

Sirius, the dog star ill. by Emily Harris. Down East, 2002. ISBN 978-0-89272-545-8 Subj: Animals – dogs. Behavior – resourcefulness. Boats, ships.

Perry, Andrea. *The Bicklebys' birdbath* ill. by Roberta Angaramo. Simon & Schuster, 2010. ISBN 978-1-4169-0624-7 Subj: Birds. Cumulative tales. Rhyming text.

Here's what you do when you can't find your shoe ill. by Alan Snow. Atheneum, 2003. ISBN 978-0-689-83067-9 Subj: Inventions. Poetry.

Perry, Elizabeth. *Think cool thoughts* ill. by Linda Bronson. Houghton, 2005. ISBN 978-0-618-23493-6 Subj: Ethnic groups in the U.S. – African Americans. Family life – aunts, uncles. Seasons – summer.

Perry, John. *The book that eats people* ill. by Mark Fearing. Tricycle, 2009. ISBN 978-1-58246-268-4 Subj: Books, reading.

Perry, Michael. *Daniel's ride* ill. by Lee Ballard. Free Will, 2001. ISBN 978-0-9701771-9-3 Subj: Automobiles. Family life – brothers.

Perry, Phyllis J. *Pandas' earthquake escape* ill. by Susan Detwiler. Sylvan Dell, 2010. ISBN 978-1-60718-071-5 Subj: Animals – pandas. Earthquakes. Foreign lands – China.

Perry, Robert. *Down at the Seaweed Café* ill. by Greta Guzek. Raincoast, 2002. ISBN 978-1-55192-473-1 Subj: Restaurants. Rhyming text. Sea & seashore – beaches.

Petach, Heidi. *Goldilocks and the three hares* ill. by author. Putnam, 1995. ISBN 978-0-399-22828-5 Subj: Animals – rabbits. Folk & fairy tales.

Wee three pigs ill. by author. Grosset, 2002. ISBN 978-0-448-42528-3 Subj: Animals – pigs. Holidays – Christmas. Homes, houses.

Pete the cat: the wheels on the bus ill. by Eric Litwin. HarperCollins, 2013. ISBN 978-0-06-219871-6 Subj: Animals – cats. Buses. Music. School. Songs.

Peters, Bernadette. *Stella is a star!* ill. by Liz Murphy. Blue Apple, 2010. ISBN 978-1-60905-008-5 Subj: Animals – dogs. Ballet. Disguises. Self-concept.

Peters, Lisa Westberg. *Cold little duck, duck, duck* ill. by Sam Williams. Greenwillow, 2000. ISBN 978-0-688-16179-8 Subj: Birds – ducks. Imagination. Seasons – spring.

Frankie works the night shift ill. by Jennifer Taylor. HarperCollins, 2010. ISBN 978-0-06-009095-1 Subj: Animals – cats. Counting, numbers. Night.

October smiled back ill. by Ed Young. Holt, 1996. ISBN 978-0-8050-1776-2 Subj: Days of the week, months of the year. Rhyming text.

Sleepyhead bear ill. by Ian Schoenherr. HarperCollins, 2006. ISBN 978-0-06-059675-0 Subj: Animals – bears. Insects. Rhyming text. Sleep.

The sun, the wind and the rain ill. by Ted Rand. Holt, 1988. ISBN 978-0-8050-0699-5 Subj: Nature. Science. Sea & seashore. Weather.

Volcano wakes up! ill. by Steve Jenkins. Holt, 2010. ISBN 978-0-8050-8287-6 Subj: Poetry. Volcanoes.

Water's way ill. by Ted Rand. Arcade, 1991. ISBN 978-1-55970-062-7 Subj: Nature. Science. Water. Weather.

Peters, Stephanie True. *Raggedy Ann and Andy and the magic potion* ill. by Reg Sandland. Adapt. by Stephanie True Peters from the stories by Johnny Gruelle. Simon & Schuster, 2001. ISBN 978-0-689-83180-5 Subj: Fairies. Magic. Toys – dolls.

Petersen, David. *Snowy Valentine* ill. by author. HarperCollins, 2011. ISBN 978-0-06-146378-5 Subj: Animals. Animals – rabbits. Holidays – Valentine's Day. Weather – snow.

Petersham, Maud. *An American ABC* by Maud Petersham and Miska Petersham ill. by authors. Macmillan, 1941. Subj: ABC books. Caldecott award honor books. U.S. history.

The rooster crows by Maud Petersham and Miska Petersham ill. by authors. Macmillan, 1945. ISBN 978-0-02-773100-2 Subj: Caldecott award books. Nursery rhymes.

Petersham, Miska. *An American ABC* (Petersham, Maud)

The rooster crows (Petersham, Maud)

Peterson, Cris. *Amazing grazing* photos by Alvis Upitis. Boyds Mills, 2002. ISBN 978-1-56397-942-2 Subj: Animals – bulls, cows. Careers – ranchers. Ecology.

Extra cheese, please! photos by Alvis Upitis. Boyds Mills, 1994. ISBN 978-1-56397-177-8 Subj: Animals – bulls, cows. Careers – farmers. Farms. Food.

Fantastic farm machines ill. by David R. Lundquist. Boyds Mills, 2006. ISBN 978-1-59078-271-2 Subj: Farms. Machines. Tractors.

Seed soil sun: Earth's recipe for food photos by David R. Lundquist. Boyds Mills, 2010. ISBN 978-1-59078-713-7 Subj: Gardens, gardening. Plants. Seeds. Sun.

Peterson, Jeanne Whitehouse. *Don't forget Winona* ill. by Kimberly Bulcken Root. Cotler, 2004. ISBN 978-0-06-027198-5 Subj: Family life. Family life – sisters. U.S. history. Weather – droughts.

My mama sings ill. by Sandra Speidel. HarperCollins, 1994. ISBN 978-0-06-023859-9 Subj: Activities – singing. Ethnic groups in the U.S. – African Americans. Family life – mothers. Music.

Peterson, Mary. *Piggies in the pumpkin patch* by Mary Peterson and Jennifer Rofé ill. by Mary Peterson. Charlesbridge, 2010. ISBN 978-1-57091-460-7 Subj: Animals – pigs. Farms.

Peterson, Melissa. *Hanna's Christmas* ill. by Melissa Iwai. HarperCollins, 2001. ISBN 978-0-694-01371-5 Subj: Ethnic groups in the U.S. – Swedish Americans. Format, unusual – board books. Holidays – Christmas.

Petrillo, Genevieve. *Keep your ear on the ball* ill. by Lea Lyon. Tilbury, 2007. ISBN 978-0-88448-296-3 Subj: Character traits – helpfulness. Games. Disabilities – blindness. School.

Pett, Mark. *The boy and the airplane* ill. by author. Simon & Schuster, 2013. ISBN 978-1-4424-5123-0 Subj: Airplanes, airports. Behavior – lost & found possessions. Gifts. Problem solving. Toys. Wordless.

The girl who never made mistakes by Mark Pett and Gary Rubinstein ill. by Mark Pett. Sourcebooks, 2011. ISBN 978-1-4022-5544-1 Subj: Behavior – worrying. Character traits – perfectionism. Self-concept.

Pettenati, Jeanne K. *Galileo's journal, 1609–1610* ill. by Paolo Rui. Charlesbridge, 2006. ISBN 978-1-57091-879-7 Subj: Astronomy. Careers – astronomers. Careers – scientists. Science. Stars.

Pettitt, Linda. *Yafi's family: an Ethiopian boy's journey of love, loss, and adoption* by Linda Pettitt and Sharon Darrow ill. by Jan Spivey Gilchrist. Amharic Kids, 2010. ISBN 978-0-9797481-4-1 Subj: Adoption. Foreign lands – Australia. Foreign lands – Ethiopia.

Petty, Dini. *The queen, the bear and the bumblebee* ill. by Rose Cowles. Beyond Words, 2000. ISBN 978-1-58270-036-6 Subj: Animals – bears. Behavior – wishing. Friendship. Insects – bees. Self-concept. Space & space ships.

Petz, Moritz. *Wish you were here* ill. by Quentin Gréban. NorthSouth, 2005. ISBN 978-0-7358-2005-0 Subj: Animals – hedgehogs. Animals – mice. Friendship.

Pfeffer, Wendy. *The big flood* ill. by Vanessa Lubach. Millbrook, 2001. ISBN 978-0-7613-1653-4 Subj: Farms. Rivers. U.S. history. Weather – floods.

Dolphin talk ill. by Helen Davie. HarperCollins, 2003. ISBN 978-0-06-028802-0 Subj: Animals – dolphins. Communication. Noise, sounds.

From tadpole to frog ill. by Holly Keller. HarperCollins, 1994. ISBN 978-0-06-023117-0 Subj: Frogs & toads. Nature. Science.

Life in a coral reef ill. by Steve Jenkins. Collins, 2009. ISBN 978-0-06-029553-0 Subj: Nature. Sea & seashore.

Mallard duck at Meadow View Pond ill. by Taylor Oughton. Soundprints, 2001. ISBN 978-1-56899-956-2 Subj: Animals – babies. Behavior – growing up. Birds – ducks. Family life. Lakes, ponds.

What's it like to be a fish? ill. by Holly Keller. HarperCollins, 1996. ISBN 978-0-06-024429-3 Subj: Fish. Pets.

Wiggling worms at work ill. by Steve Jenkins. HarperCollins, 2004. ISBN 978-0-06-028449-7 Subj: Animals – worms. Science.

Pfister, Marcus. *Animal ABC* ill. by author. NorthSouth, 2013. ISBN 978-0-7358-4136-9 Subj: ABC books. Animals.

Ava's poppy ill. by author. NorthSouth, 2012. ISBN 978-0-7358-4057-7 Subj: Flowers. Science. Seasons.

Bertie: just like daddy ill. by author. NorthSouth, 2009. ISBN 978-0-7358-2224-5 Subj: Animals – hippopotamuses. Behavior – imitation. Family life – fathers.

Bertie at bedtime ill. by author. NorthSouth, 2008. ISBN 978-0-7358-2194-1 Subj: Animals – hippopotamuses. Bedtime.

Charlie at the zoo ill. by author. NorthSouth, 2004. ISBN 978-0-7358-2144-6 Subj: Animals. Birds – ducks. Format, unusual. Zoos.

The Christmas star ill. by author. NorthSouth, 1993. ISBN 978-1-55858-204-0 Subj: Holidays – Christmas. Religion – Nativity. Stars.

Dazzle the dinosaur ill. by author. NorthSouth, 1994. ISBN 978-1-55858-338-2 Subj: Dinosaurs. Prehistory.

Good night, little rainbow fish ill. by author. NorthSouth, 2012. ISBN 978-0-7358-4082-9 Subj: Bedtime. Fish. Sleep.

Hang on, Hopper! ill. by Rosemary Lanning. NorthSouth, 1995. ISBN 978-1-55858-404-4 Subj: Animals – rabbits. Safety. Sports – swimming.

Happy birthday, Bertie! ill. by author. NorthSouth, 2010. ISBN 978-0-7358-2280-1 Subj: Animals – hippopotamuses. Birthdays. Parties.

The happy hedgehog ill. by author. NorthSouth, 2000. ISBN 978-0-7358-1165-2 Subj: Animals – hedgehogs. Family life – grandfathers.

Hopper ill. by author. NorthSouth, 1991. ISBN 978-1-55858-106-7 Subj: Animals – rabbits. Seasons – spring. Seasons – winter.

Hopper hunts for spring ill. by author. NorthSouth, 1992. ISBN 978-1-55858-139-5 Subj: Animals. Animals – rabbits. Frogs & toads. Seasons – spring.

Hopper's treetop adventure ill. by author. NorthSouth, 1997. ISBN 978-1-55858-681-9 Subj: Animals – rabbits. Animals – squirrels. Nature. Trees.

How Leo learned to be king ill. by author. NorthSouth, 1998. ISBN 978-1-55858-914-8 Subj: Animals. Animals – lions. Behavior. Royalty – kings.

Just the way you are ill. by author. NorthSouth, 2002. ISBN 978-0-7358-1615-2 Subj: Animals. Format, unusual – toy & movable books. Parties. Self-concept.

Make a wish, Honey Bear! ill. by author. NorthSouth, 1999. ISBN 978-0-7358-1244-4 Subj: Animals – bears. Behavior – wishing. Birthdays.

Milo and the magical stones ill. by author. NorthSouth, 1997. ISBN 978-1-55858-682-6 Subj: Animals – mice. Behavior. Format, unusual – toy & movable books. Magic.

Milo and the mysterious island ill. by author. NorthSouth, 2000. ISBN 978-0-7358-1352-6 Subj: Animals – mice. Islands. Prejudice. Sea & seashore.

Penguin Pete and Little Tim ill. by author. NorthSouth, 1994. ISBN 978-1-55858-302-3 Subj: Activities – walking. Birds – penguins. Family life – fathers. Weather – snow.

Questions, questions ill. by author. NorthSouth, 2011. ISBN 978-0-7358-4000-3 Subj: Animals – hippopotamuses. Character traits – questioning. Nature. Rhyming text.

The rainbow fish ill. by author. NorthSouth, 1992. ISBN 978-0-7358-1748-7 Subj: Behavior – sharing. Character traits – appearance. Emotions – loneliness. Fish.

Rainbow fish ABC ill. by author. NorthSouth, 2002. ISBN 978-0-7358-1714-2 Subj: ABC books. Fish. Sea & seashore.

Rainbow fish and the big blue whale ill. by author. NorthSouth, 1998. ISBN 978-0-7358-1010-5 Subj: Animals – whales. Behavior – fighting, arguing. Fish.

Rainbow fish and the sea monsters' cave ill. by author. NorthSouth, 2001. ISBN 978-0-7358-1537-7 Subj: Caves. Fish. Monsters. Sea & seashore.

Rainbow fish to the rescue! ill. by author. NorthSouth, 1995. ISBN 978-1-55858-487-7 Subj: Character traits – appearance. Emotions – fear. Fish. Fish – sharks. Friendship.

Snow puppy ill. by author. NorthSouth, 2011. ISBN 978-0-7358-4031-7 Subj: Animals – dogs. Behavior – lost. Weather – snow.

Wake up, Santa Claus! ill. by author. NorthSouth, 1996. ISBN 978-1-55858-606-2 Subj: Behavior – hurrying. Dreams. Holidays – Christmas. Santa Claus.

Where is my friend? ill. by author. Holt, 1986. ISBN 978-0-03-008033-3 Subj: Animals – porcupines. Format, unusual – board books. Friendship.

Pham, LeUyen. *All the things I love about you* ill. by author. HarperCollins, 2010. ISBN 978-0-06-199029-8 Subj: Emotions – love. Family life – mothers.

Big sister, little sister ill. by author. Hyperion, 2005. ISBN 978-0-7868-5182-9 Subj: Character traits – individuality. Family life – brothers & sisters.

Philip, Neil. *Noah and the devil* ill. by Isabelle Brent. Clarion, 2001. ISBN 978-0-618-11754-3 Subj: Boats, ships. Devil. Folk & fairy tales. Foreign lands – Romania. Religion – Noah.

Phillipps, J. C. *Monkey Ono* ill. by author. Viking, 2013. ISBN 978-0-670-78505-6 Subj: Animals – monkeys. Behavior – resourcefulness. Toys.

Phillips, Betty Lou. *Emily goes wild* ill. by Sharon Watts. Gibbs Smith, 2003. ISBN 978-1-58685-268-9 Subj: Animals – monkeys. Behavior – misbehavior. Pets. Zoos.

Phillips, Christopher. *Ceci Ann's day of why* ill. by Shino Arihara. Ten Speed, 2006. ISBN 978-1-58246-171-7 Subj: Character traits – questioning. Ethnic groups in the U.S. – African Americans. Rhyming text.

Phillips, Mildred. *And the cow said, "moo"!* ill. by Sonja Lamut. Greenwillow, 2000. ISBN 978-0-688-16803-2 Subj: Animals. Farms. Noise, sounds.

Philpot, Graham. *Find Anthony Ant* (Philpot, Lorna)

Where is Little Harry? ill. by author. Candlewick, 2001. ISBN 978-0-7636-1439-3 Subj: Animals – pigs. Behavior – hiding. Format, unusual – toy & movable books. Games.

Philpot, Lorna. *Find Anthony Ant* by Lorna Philpot and Graham Philpot ill. by Lorna Philpot. Sterling, 2006. ISBN 978-1-905417-10-0 Subj: Counting, numbers. Insects – ants. Mazes. Picture puzzles. Puzzles.

Phinn, Gervase. *Who am I?* ill. by Tony Ross. Andersen, 2012. ISBN 978-0-7613-8996-5 Subj: Character traits – individuality. Reptiles – chameleons. Self-concept.

Pia Toya: a Goshute Indian legend. Retold & Ill. by the children & teachers of Ibapah Elementary school. Univ. of Utah Pr., 2000. ISBN 978-0-87480-661-8 Subj: Animals – coyotes. Birds – hawks. Children as authors. Children as illustrators. Creation. Folk & fairy tales. Indians of North America – Goshute. Indians of North America – Great Basin.

Pichon, Liz. *Penguins* ill. by author. Scholastic, 2008. ISBN 978-0-545-02215-6 Subj: Activities – photographing. Birds – penguins. Zoos.

The three horrid little pigs ill. by author. Tiger Tales, 2008. ISBN 978-1-58925-077-2 Subj: Animals – pigs. Animals – wolves. Behavior – misbehavior. Humorous stories.

The very ugly bug ill. by author. Tiger Tales, 2005. ISBN 978-1-58925-048-2 Subj: Character traits – appearance. Insects.

Pickering, Jimmy. *It's fall* ill. by author. Smallfellow, 2002. ISBN 978-1-931290-15-9 Subj: Animals – dogs. Poetry. Rhyming text. Seasons – fall.

It's winter ill. by author. Smallfellow, 2002. ISBN 978-1-931290-16-6 Subj: Animals – dogs. Poetry. Seasons – winter. Weather – snow.

Skelly the skeleton girl ill. by author. Simon & Schuster, 2007. ISBN 978-1-4169-1192-0 Subj: Anatomy – skeletons. Animals – dogs. Monsters.

Pickthall, Marjorie L. C. *The worker in sandalwood: a Christmas Eve miracle* ill. by Frances Tyrrell. Dutton, 1994. ISBN 978-0-525-45332-1 Subj: Careers – carpenters. Foreign lands – Canada. Holidays – Christmas.

Pienkowski, Jan. *Bel and Bub and the baby bird* ill. by author. DK, 2000. ISBN 978-0-7894-6526-9 Subj: Angels. Birds.

Bel and Bub and the bad snowball ill. by author. DK, 2000. ISBN 978-0-7894-6529-0 Subj: Angels. Behavior – bullying, teasing. Emotions – anger.

Bel and Bub and the big brown box ill. by author. DK, 2000. ISBN 978-0-7894-6527-6 Subj: Angels. Behavior – sharing.

Bel and Bub and the black hole ill. by author. DK, 2000. ISBN 978-0-7894-6528-3 Subj: Angels. Character traits – bravery. Dragons. Friendship. Stores.

Easter ill. by author. Knopf, 1989. ISBN 978-0-394-82455-0 Subj: Holidays – Easter. Religion.

Good night, a pop-up lullaby ill. by author. Paper engineering by Helen Balmer & Martin Taylor. Candlewick, 1999. ISBN 978-0-7636-0763-0 Subj: Format, unusual – toy & movable books. Lullabies.

Haunted house ill. by Jane Walmsley. Dutton, 1979. ISBN 978-0-525-46802-8 Subj: Format, unusual – toy & movable books. Ghosts. Homes, houses. Monsters.

Pizza! ill. by author and David Walser. Paper engineering by Helen Balmer & Martin Taylor. Candlewick, 2001. ISBN 978-0-7636-1626-7 Subj: Animals. Food. Format, unusual – toy & movable books. Insects. Royalty – kings. Spiders.

Piepmeier, Charlotte. *Lucy's journey to the wild west* ill. by author. Azro, 2002. ISBN 978-1-929115-07-5 Subj: Activities – traveling. Animals – dogs. Geography. Maps. Moving. U.S. history.

Pierce, Roxanne Heide. *Always listen to your mother* (Heide, Florence Parry)

Pierce, Terry, editor. *Counting your way: number nursery rhymes* ill. by Andrea Petrlik Huseinovic. Picture Window, 2007. ISBN 978-1-4048-2346-4 Subj: Counting, numbers. Nursery rhymes.

Piernas-Davenport, Gail. *Shanté Keys and the New Year's peas* ill. by Marion Eldridge. Whitman, 2007. ISBN 978-0-8075-7330-3 Subj: Ethnic groups in the U.S. – African Americans. Family life. Food. Holidays – New Year's.

Piers, Helen. *Who's in my bed?* ill. by Dave Saunders. Marshall Cavendish, 1999. ISBN 978-0-7614-5046-7 Subj: Animals. Bedtime. Character traits – orderliness. Cumulative tales. Farms. Format, unusual – toy & movable books.

Piggy and Bear in their underwear ill. by Dara Goldman. Innovative KIDS, 2002. ISBN 978-1-58476-101-3 Subj: Behavior – growing up. Clothing – underwear. Format, unusual – toy & movable books. Toilet training.

Pilegard, Virginia Walton. *The warlord's alarm: a mathematical adventure* ill. by Nicolas Debon. Pelican, 2006. ISBN 978-1-58980-378-7 Subj: Clocks, watches. Foreign lands – China. Time.

The warlord's beads ill. by Nicolas Debon. Pelican, 2001. ISBN 978-1-56554-863-3 Subj: Counting, numbers. Foreign lands – China.

The warlord's puzzle ill. by Nicolas Debon. Pelican, 2000. ISBN 978-1-56554-495-6 Subj: Concepts – shape. Folk & fairy tales. Foreign lands – China.

Pilgrim, Elza. *The china doll* ill. by Carmen Segovia. Sterling, 2006. ISBN 978-1-4027-2223-3 Subj: Birthdays. Gifts. Toys – dolls.

Pilkey, Dav. *Dragon's fat cat* ill. by author. Orchard, 1992. ISBN 978-0-531-08582-0 Subj: Animals – cats. Dragons.

Dragon's merry Christmas ill. by author. Orchard, 1991. ISBN 978-0-531-08557-8 Subj: Character traits – generosity. Dragons. Holidays – Christmas.

The Dumb Bunnies ill. by author. Blue Sky, 2007, ©1994. ISBN 978-0-545-03938-3 Subj: Animals – rabbits. Character traits – foolishness. Family life. Humorous stories.

The Dumb Bunnies' Easter ill. by author. Blue Sky, 2009, ©1995. ISBN 978-0-545-03946-8 Subj: Animals – rabbits. Character traits – foolishness. Family life. Holidays – Christmas. Holidays – Easter. Humorous stories.

The Dumb Bunnies go to the zoo ill. by author. Blue Sky, 2009, ©1997. ISBN 978-0-545-03937-6 Subj: Animals – rabbits. Character traits – foolishness. Family life. Humorous stories. Zoos.

A friend for Dragon ill. by author. Orchard, 1991. ISBN 978-0-531-05934-0 Subj: Dragons. Emotions – loneliness. Friendship. Reptiles – snakes.

The Hallo-wiener ill. by author. Blue Sky, 1995. ISBN 978-0-590-41703-7 Subj: Animals – dogs. Family life. Holidays – Halloween.

Make way for Dumb Bunnies ill. by author. Blue Sky, 2007, ©1996. ISBN 978-0-545-03939-0 Subj: Activities. Animals – rabbits. Character traits – foolishness. Family life. Humorous stories.

The Moonglow Roll-O-Rama ill. by author. Orchard, 1995. ISBN 978-0-531-08726-8 Subj: Animals. Night. Rhyming text. Sports – roller skating.

The paperboy ill. by author. Orchard, 1996. ISBN 978-0-531-08856-2 Subj: Activities – working. Caldecott award honor books. Morning.

The Silly Gooses ill. by author. Blue Sky, 1997. ISBN 978-0-590-94733-6 Subj: Behavior. Birds – geese. Humorous stories. Weddings.

'Twas the night before Thanksgiving ill. by author. Watts, 1990. ISBN 978-0-531-08505-9 Subj: Birds – turkeys. Holidays – Thanksgiving. Rhyming text.

When cats dream ill. by author. Watts, 1992. ISBN 978-0-531-08597-4 Subj: Animals – cats. Art. Dreams.

Pin, Isabel. *The seed* ill. by author. NorthSouth, 2001. ISBN 978-0-7358-1408-0 Subj: Insects. Seeds. War.

Pinczes, Elinor J. *Inchworm and a half* ill. by Randall Enos. Houghton, 2001. ISBN 978-0-395-82849-6 Subj: Animals – worms. Concepts – measurement. Counting, numbers. Food. Gardens, gardening. Rhyming text.

My full moon is square ill. by Randall Enos. Houghton, 2002. ISBN 978-0-618-15489-0 Subj: Books, reading. Frogs & toads. Insects – fireflies. Rhyming text.

A remainder of one ill. by Bonnie MacKain. Houghton, 1995. ISBN 978-0-395-69455-8 Subj: Counting, numbers. Insects. Rhyming text.

Pinder, Eric. *If all the animals came inside* ill. by Marc Brown. Little, Brown, 2012. ISBN 978-0-316-09883-0 Subj: Animals. Imagination. Rhyming text.

Pinfold, Levi. *Black dog* ill. by author. Candlewick, 2012. ISBN 978-0-7636-6097-0 Subj: Animals – dogs. Concepts – size. Emotions – fear. Family life.

The Django ill. by author. Candlewick, 2010. ISBN 978-0-7636-4788-9 Subj: Behavior – misbehavior. Gypsies. Imagination – imaginary friends. Musical instruments – banjos.

Pinkney, Andrea Davis. *Alvin Ailey* ill. by Brian Pinkney. Hyperion, 1993. ISBN 978-1-56282-414-3 Subj: Activities – dancing. Careers – dancers. Ethnic groups in the U.S. – African Americans.

Bill Pickett, rodeo ridin' cowboy ill. by Brian Pinkney. Harcourt, 1996. ISBN 978-0-15-200100-1 Subj: Cowboys, cowgirls. Ethnic groups in the U.S. – African Americans.

Boycott blues: how Rosa Parks inspired a nation ill. by Brian Pinkney. Greenwillow, 2008. ISBN 978-0-06-082118-0 Subj: Ethnic groups in the U.S. – African Americans. Prejudice. U.S. history.

Dear Benjamin Banneker ill. by Brian Pinkney. Harcourt, 1994. ISBN 978-0-15-200417-0 Subj: Careers – astronomers. Ethnic groups in the U.S. – African Americans. Slavery. U.S. history.

Duke Ellington: the piano prince and his orchestra ill. by Brian Pinkney. Hyperion, 1998. ISBN 978-0-7868-2150-1 Subj: Caldecott award honor books. Careers – musicians. Ethnic groups in the U.S. – African Americans. Music. Musical instruments – pianos.

Martin and Mahalia: his words, her song ill. by Brian Pinkney. Little, Brown, 2013. ISBN 978-0-316-07013-3 Subj: Careers – singers. Ethnic groups in the U.S. – African Americans. U.S. history. Violence, nonviolence.

Mim's Christmas jam ill. by Brian Pinkney. Harcourt, 2001. ISBN 978-0-15-201918-1 Subj: Ethnic groups in the U.S. – African Americans. Family life. Food. Holidays – Christmas.

Peggony-Po: a whale of a tale ill. by Brian Pinkney. Hyperion, 2006. ISBN 978-0-7868-1958-4 Subj: Animals – whales. Tall tales. Toys.

Sit-in: how four friends stood up by sitting down ill. by Brian Pinkney. Little, Brown, 2010. ISBN 978-0-316-07016-4 Subj: Ethnic groups in the U.S. – African Americans. Prejudice. U.S. history.

Sojourner Truth's step-stomp stride ill. by Brian Pinkney. Jump at the Sun, 2009. ISBN 978-0-7868-0767-3 Subj: Character traits – freedom. Ethnic groups in the U.S. – African Americans. Slavery. U.S. history.

Pinkney, Brian. *The adventures of sparrowboy* ill. by author. Simon & Schuster, 1997. ISBN 978-0-689-81071-8 Subj: Activities – flying. Behavior – bullying, teasing. Communities, neighborhoods. Ethnic groups in the U.S. – African Americans. Humorous stories.

Cosmo and the robot ill. by author. Greenwillow, 2000. ISBN 978-0-688-15941-2 Subj: Monsters. Planets. Robots. Space & space ships.

Hush, little baby ill. by adapter. HarperCollins, 2006. ISBN 978-0-06-055994-6 Subj: Babies. Character traits – generosity. Cumulative tales. Lullabies. Music.

Jojo's flying side kick ill. by author. Simon & Schuster, 1995. ISBN 978-0-671-88111-5 Subj: Character traits – perseverance. Family life. Sports – Tae Kwon Do.

Pinkney, Gloria Jean. *Back home* ill. by Jerry Pinkney. Dial, 1992. ISBN 978-0-8037-1169-3 Subj: Ethnic groups in the U.S. – African Americans. Family life. Farms.

Music from our Lord's holy heaven ill. by Jerry Pinkney and Brian Pinkney, et al. HarperCollins, 2005. ISBN 978-0-06-000769-0 Subj: Music. Religion. Songs.

The Sunday outing ill. by Jerry Pinkney. Dial, 1994. ISBN 978-0-8037-1199-0 Subj: Activities – traveling. Ethnic groups in the U.S. – African Americans. Family life. Farms. Trains.

Pinkney, Jerry. *The lion and the mouse* ill. by author. Little, Brown, 2009. ISBN 978-0-316-01356-7 Subj: Animals – lions. Animals – mice. Caldecott award books. Character traits – helpfulness. Folk & fairy tales. Wordless.

Noah's ark ill. by author. SeaStar, 2002. ISBN 978-1-58717-202-1 Subj: Animals. Boats, ships. Caldecott award honor books. Religion – Noah. Weather – floods. Weather – rain. Weather – rainbows.

Three little kittens ill. by author. Penguin, 2010. ISBN 978-0-8037-3533-0 Subj: Animals – cats. Behavior – lost & found possessions. Clothing – gloves, mittens. Nursery rhymes.

Pinkney, Sandra L. *I am Latino: the beauty in me* photos by Myles C. Pinkney. Little, Brown, 2007. ISBN 978-0-316-16009-4 Subj: Ethnic groups in the U.S. – Hispanic Americans. Self-concept.

A rainbow all around me photos by Myles C. Pinkney. Scholastic, 2002. ISBN 978-0-439-30928-8 Subj: Anatomy – skin. Concepts – color. Ethnic groups in the U.S. Weather – rainbows.

Read and rise photos by Myles C. Pinkney. Foreword by Maya Angelou. Scholastic, 2006. ISBN 978-0-439-30929-5 Subj: Books, reading. Ethnic groups in the U.S. – African Americans.

Shades of black photos by Myles C. Pinkney. Scholastic, 2000. ISBN 978-0-439-14892-4 Subj: Ethnic groups in the U.S. – African Americans.

Pinkwater, Daniel. *At the Hotel Larry* ill. by Jill Pinkwater. Marshall Cavendish, 1997. ISBN 978-0-7614-5005-4 Subj: Animals – polar bears. Careers – lifeguards. Hotels. Humorous stories.

Bad bear detectives: an Irving and Muktuk story ill. by Jill Pinkwater. Houghton, 2006. ISBN 978-0-618-43125-0 Subj: Animals – polar bears. Behavior – stealing. Careers – detectives. Humorous stories.

Bad bears and a bunny ill. by Jill Pinkwater. Houghton, 2005. ISBN 978-0-618-33926-6 Subj: Animals – polar bears. Animals – rabbits. Behavior. Hotels. Humorous stories. Parties.

Bad bears go visiting ill. by Jill Pinkwater. Houghton, 2007. ISBN 978-0-618-43126-7 Subj: Animals – polar bears. Humorous stories. Zoos.

Bad bears in the big city ill. by Jill Pinkwater. Houghton, 2003. ISBN 978-0-618-25208-4 Subj: Animals – polar bears. Behavior – misbehavior. Cities, towns. Food. Humorous stories. Zoos.

Bear in love ill. by Will Hillenbrand. Candlewick, 2012. ISBN 978-0-7636-4569-4 Subj: Animals – bears. Animals – rabbits. Behavior – sharing. Food. Friendship.

Bear's Picture ill. by D. B. Johnson. Houghton, 2008. ISBN 978-0-618-75923-1 Subj: Animals – bears. Art. Careers – artists. Concepts – color.

Beautiful Yetta: the Yiddish chicken ill. by Jill Pinkwater. Feiwel & Friends, 2010. ISBN 978-0-312-55824-6 Subj: Behavior – lost. Birds – chickens. Birds – parakeets, parrots. Cities, towns. Foreign languages.

Bongo Larry ill. by Jill Pinkwater. Marshall Cavendish, 1998. ISBN 978-0-7614-5020-7 Subj: Animals – bears. Animals – polar bears. Careers – musicians. Humorous stories. Musical instruments – drums.

Dancing Larry ill. by Jill Pinkwater. Marshall Cavendish, 2006. ISBN 978-0-7614-5220-1 Subj: Activities – dancing. Animals – polar bears. Ballet. Humorous stories.

I am the dog ill. by Jack E. Davis. HarperCollins, 2010. ISBN 978-0-06-055505-4 Subj: Animals – dogs. Humorous stories.

Ice-cream Larry ill. by Jill Pinkwater. Marshall Cavendish, 1999. ISBN 978-0-7614-5043-6 Subj: Animals – polar bears. Behavior – misbehavior. Food. Humorous stories.

Irving and Muktuk ill. by Jill Pinkwater. Houghton, 2001. ISBN 978-0-618-09334-2 Subj: Animals – polar bears. Animals – rabbits. Behavior – misbehavior. Zoos.

The picture of Morty and Ray ill. by Jack E. Davis. HarperCollins, 2003. ISBN 978-0-06-623786-2 Subj: Activities – painting. Behavior – misbehavior. Humorous stories.

Rainy morning ill. by Jill Pinkwater. Atheneum, 1998. ISBN 978-0-689-81143-2 Subj: Animals. Character traits – kindness to animals. Circus. Food. Homes, houses. Weather – rain.

Sleepover Larry ill. by Jill Pinkwater. Marshall Cavendish, 2007. ISBN 978-0-7614-5314-7 Subj: Animals – polar bears. Humorous stories. Sleepovers.

Wolf Christmas ill. by Jill Pinkwater. Marshall Cavendish, 1998. ISBN 978-0-7614-5030-6 Subj: Animals – wolves. Holidays – Christmas.

Yo-yo man ill. by Jack E. Davis. HarperCollins, 2007. ISBN 978-0-06-055502-3 Subj: Behavior – bullying, teasing. School. Toys.

Young Larry ill. by Jill Pinkwater. Marshall Cavendish, 1997. ISBN 978-0-7614-5004-7 Subj: Animals – polar bears. Behavior – growing up. Careers – lifeguards. Family life – brothers. Family life – mothers. Foreign lands – Canada. Humorous stories.

Pinto, Sara. *Apples and oranges: going bananas with pairs* ill. by author. Bloomsbury, 2008. ISBN 978-1-59990-103-9 Subj: Concepts. Imagination.

Pipe, Jim. *Baby animals* ill. with photos. Stargazer, 2007. ISBN 978-1-59604-111-0 Subj: Animals – babies.

Dogs ill. with photos. Stargazer, 2007. ISBN 978-1-59604-113-4 Subj: Animals – dogs.

Farm animals ill. with photos. Stargazer, 2007. ISBN 978-1-59604-112-7 Subj: Animals. Farms.

Horses ill. with photos. Stargazer, 2007. ISBN 978-1-59604-114-1 Subj: Animals – horses, ponies.

What makes it swing? ill. by author. Copper Beech, 2002. ISBN 978-0-7613-2822-3 Subj: Concepts. Science.

Piper, Sophie. *I can say a prayer* ill. by Emily Bolam. IPG/Lion, 2011. ISBN 978-0-7459-6233-7 Subj: Religion.

Piper, Watty. *The little engine that could* ill. by George Hauman and Doris Hauman. Retold from *The pony engine,* by Mable C. Bragg. This version first pub. in 1955. 60th anniversary ed. Platt, 1990. ISBN 978-0-448-40041-9 Subj: Character traits – perseverance. Trains.

The little engine that could ill. by Loren Long. Penguin, 2005. ISBN 978-0-399-24467-4 Subj: Character traits – perseverance. Trains.

Pippin-Mathur, Courtney. *Maya was grumpy* ill. by author. Flashlight, 2013. ISBN 978-1-9362611-3-0 Subj: Behavior – bad day. Family life – grandmothers.

Pirner, Connie White. *Even little kids get diabetes* ill. by Nadine Bernard Westcott. Whitman, 1991. ISBN 978-0-8075-2158-8 Subj: Hospitals. Illness – diabetes.

Pistoia, Sara. *Counting* ill. by author. Child's World, 2003. ISBN 978-1-56766-114-9 Subj: Counting, numbers.

Money ill. by author. Child's World, 2003. ISBN 978-1-56766-116-3 Subj: Counting, numbers. Money.

Pitcher, Caroline. *Are you spring?* ill. by Cliff Wright. DK, 2000. ISBN 978-0-7894-5614-4 Subj: Animals. Animals – bears. Seasons – spring.

Mariana and the merchild: a folk tale from Chile ill. by Jackie Morris. Eerdmans, 2000. ISBN 978-0-8028-5204-5 Subj: Folk & fairy tales. Foreign lands – Chile. Mythical creatures – mermaids, mermen.

Nico's octopus ill. by Nilesh Mistry. Crocodile, 2003. ISBN 978-1-56656-483-0 Subj: Death. Octopuses. Pets.

Pittau, Francisco. *Out of sight* by Francisco Pittau and Bernadette Gervais ill. by authors. Chronicle, 2010. ISBN 978-0-8118-7712-1 Subj: Animals. Format, unusual – toy & movable books.

Pittman, Helena Clare. *The angel tree* ill. by Jo Ellen McAllister Stammen. Dial, 1998. ISBN 978-0-8037-1941-5 Subj: Angels. Communities, neighborhoods. Friendship. Holidays – Christmas. Trees.

The snowman's path ill. by Raúl Colón. Dial, 2000. ISBN 978-0-8037-2170-8 Subj: Friendship. Snowmen.

Pitzer, Susanna. *Not afraid of dogs* ill. by Larry Day. Walker, 2006. ISBN 978-0-8027-8067-6 Subj: Animals – dogs. Behavior – animals, dislike of. Emotions – fear.

Piumini, Roberto. *Doctor Me Di Cin* ill. by Piet Grobler. Front Street, 2001. ISBN 978-1-886910-67-6 Subj: Careers – doctors. Foreign lands – China. Royalty – princes.

Piven, Hanoch. *Let's make faces* ill. by author. Simon & Schuster, 2013. ISBN 978-1-4169-1532-4 Subj: Anatomy – faces. Art. Imagination.

The perfect purple feather by Hanoch Piven and Rachel Tzvia Back; photos by Adi Gilad. Silhouettes by Janet Stein; photos by Adi Gilad. Little, 2002. ISBN 978-0-316-76657-9 Subj: Animals. Feathers. Rhyming text.

Pizzoli, Greg. *The watermelon seed* ill. by author. Disney/Hyperion, 2013. ISBN 978-1-4231-7101-0 Subj: Behavior – worrying. Imagination. Reptiles – alligators, crocodiles. Seeds.

Platt, Cynthia. *A little bit of love* ill. by Hannah Whitty. Tiger Tales, 2011. ISBN 978-1-58925-095-6 Subj: Activities – baking, cooking. Animals – mice. Family life – mothers.

Player, Micah. *Chloe, instead* ill. by author. Chronicle, 2012. ISBN 978-0-8118-7865-4 Subj: Character traits – individuality. Family life – sisters.

Plecas, Jennifer. *Olive's perfect world: a friendship story* ill. by author. Philomel, 2013. ISBN 978-0-399-25287-7 Subj: Animals – cats. Emotions – sadness. Friendship.

Pretend ill. by author. Penguin, 2011. ISBN 978-0-399-23430-9 Subj: Family life – fathers. Imagination.

Plourde, Lynn. *Book Fair Day* ill. by Thor Wickstrom. Penguin, 2006. ISBN 978-0-525-47696-2 Subj: Books, reading. School.

Dad, aren't you glad? ill. by Amy Wummer. Penguin, 2005. ISBN 978-0-525-47362-6 Subj: Family life – fathers. Kissing.

Dino pets ill. by Gideon Kendall. Penguin, 2007. ISBN 978-0-525-47778-5 Subj: Dinosaurs. Pets. Rhyming text.

Dino pets go to school ill. by Gideon Kendall. Penguin, 2011. ISBN 978-0-525-42232-7 Subj: Dinosaurs. Pets. Rhyming text. School.

Field trip day ill. by Thor Wickstrom. Penguin, 2010. ISBN 978-0-525-47994-9 Subj: Farms. School – field trips.

Grandpappy snippy snappies ill. by Christopher Santoro. HarperCollins, 2009. ISBN 978-0-06-028050-5 Subj: Careers – farmers. Clothing. Humorous stories. Rhyming text.

Margaret Chase Smith: a woman for president ill. by David McPhail. Charlesbridge, 2008. ISBN 978-1-58089-234-6 Subj: Gender roles. U.S. history.

A mountain of mittens ill. by Mitch Vane. Charlesbridge, 2007. ISBN 978-1-57091-585-7 Subj: Behavior – lost & found possessions. Clothing – gloves, mittens. Seasons – winter.

Only cows allowed! ill. by Rebecca Harrison Reed. Down East, 2011. ISBN 978-0-89272-790-2 Subj: Animals. Animals – bulls, cows. Farms. Humorous stories.

Pajama day ill. by Thor Wickstrom. Penguin, 2005. ISBN 978-0-525-47355-8 Subj: Behavior – forgetfulness. Clothing – pajamas. School.

Pigs in the mud in the middle of the rud ill. by John Schoenherr. Blue Sky, 1997. ISBN 978-0-590-56863-0 Subj: Animals – pigs. Character traits – stubbornness. Humorous stories. Poetry. Roads. Weather – rain.

School picture day ill. by Thor Wickstrom. Dutton, 2002. ISBN 978-0-525-46886-8 Subj: Activities – photographing. School.

Spring's sprung ill. by Greg Couch. Simon & Schuster, 2002. ISBN 978-0-689-84229-0 Subj: Family life – sisters. Rhyming text. Seasons – spring. Sibling rivalry.

Wild child ill. by Greg Couch. Simon & Schuster, 1999. ISBN 978-0-689-81552-2 Subj: Bedtime. Mythical creatures. Rhyming text. Seasons – fall.

Winter waits ill. by Greg Couch. Simon & Schuster, 2001. ISBN 978-0-689-83268-0 Subj: Mythical creatures. Rhyming text. Seasons – winter. Time.

You're wearing that to school?! ill. by Sue Cornelison. Disney/Hyperion, 2013. ISBN 978-1-4231-5510-2 Subj: Animals – hippopotamuses. Animals – mice. Character traits – individuality. Clothing. School – first day.

A pocketful of stars: poems about the night ill. by Emma Shaw-Smith. Barefoot, 2000. ISBN 978-1-902283-84-5 Subj: Night. Poetry.

Podwal, Mark H. *The menorah story* ill. by author. Greenwillow, 1998. ISBN 978-0-688-15759-3 Subj: Holidays – Hanukkah. Jewish culture. Religion.

A sweet year ill. by author. Random House, 2003. ISBN 978-0-385-90869-6 Subj: Food. Holidays. Jewish culture. Religion.

Poems for the very young sel. by Michael Rosen; ill. by Bob Graham. Kingfisher, 2004. ISBN 978-0-7534-5816-7 Subj: Children as authors. Poetry.

Poffenberger, Nancy M. *September 11, 2001* ill. by the Lotspeich School students. Fun Pub, 2002. ISBN 978-0-938293-12-5 Subj: Cities, towns. Crime. U.S. history. War.

Polacco, Patricia. *Appelemando's dreams* ill. by author. Putnam, 1991. ISBN 978-0-399-21800-2 Subj: Dreams. Imagination.

The art of Miss Chew ill. by author. Putnam, 2012. ISBN 978-0-399-25703-2 Subj: Art. Careers – teachers. Character traits – individuality. Disabilities. School. Self-concept.

Aunt Chip and the great Triple Creek dam affair ill. by author. Philomel, 1996. ISBN 978-0-399-22943-5 Subj: Books, reading. Libraries. Television.

Babushka's doll ill. by author. Simon & Schuster, 1990. ISBN 978-0-671-68343-6 Subj: Toys – dolls.

Babushka's Mother Goose ill. by author. Philomel, 1995. ISBN 978-0-399-22747-9 Subj: Family life – grandmothers. Folk & fairy tales. Foreign lands – Russia. Nursery rhymes.

Betty Doll ill. by author. Philomel, 2001. ISBN 978-0-399-23638-9 Subj: Family life – mothers. Illness – cancer. Memories, memory. Toys – dolls.

The blessing cup ill. by author. Simon & Schuster, 2013. ISBN 978-1-4424-5047-9 Subj: Family life. Immigrants. Jewish culture.

Bun Bun Button ill. by author. Penguin, 2011. ISBN 978-0-399-25472-7 Subj: Behavior – lost & found possessions. Character traits – luck. Family life – grandmothers. Toys. Toys – balloons.

The butterfly ill. by author. Philomel, 2000. ISBN 978-0-399-23170-4 Subj: Behavior – hiding. Behavior – secrets. Character traits – freedom. Foreign lands – France. Insects – butterflies, caterpillars. War.

Chicken Sunday ill. by author. Putnam, 1992. ISBN 978-0-399-22133-0 Subj: Eggs. Ethnic groups in the U.S. – African Americans. Family life – grandmothers. Friendship. Holidays – Easter. Religion.

Emma Kate ill. by author. Penguin, 2005. ISBN 978-0-399-24452-0 Subj: Animals – elephants. Friendship. Imagination.

Gifts of the heart ill. by author. Penguin, 2013. ISBN 978-0-399-16094-3 Subj: Careers – housekeepers. Family life. Gifts. Holidays – Christmas. Magic. Santa Claus.

Ginger and Petunia ill. by author. Penguin, 2007. ISBN 978-0-399-24539-8 Subj: Animals – pigs. Pets.

I can hear the sun ill. by author. Philomel, 1996. ISBN 978-0-399-22520-8 Subj: Birds – geese. Character traits – being different. Ethnic groups in the U.S. – African Americans. Homeless. Sun.

In Enzo's splendid gardens ill. by author. Philomel, 1997. ISBN 978-0-399-23107-0 Subj: Accidents. Cumulative tales. Food. Humorous stories. Insects – bees. Restaurants.

In our mothers' house ill. by author. Philomel, 2009. ISBN 978-0-399-25076-7 Subj: Ethnic groups in the U.S. Family life – mothers. Family life – same-sex parents. Homosexuality.

The junkyard wonders ill. by author. Penguin, 2010. ISBN 978-0-399-25078-1 Subj: Careers – teachers. Disabilities. Inventions. School. Self-concept.

Just plain Fancy ill. by author. Bantam, 1990. ISBN 978-0-553-07062-0 Subj: Birds – peacocks, peahens. Eggs. Farms.

The keeping quilt ill. by author. Simon & Schuster, 1998. ISBN 978-0-689-82090-8 Subj: Immigrants. Jewish culture. Quilts.

The lemonade club ill. by author. Penguin, 2007. ISBN 978-0-399-24540-4 Subj: Careers – teachers. Illness – cancer. School.

Luba and the wren ill. by author. Philomel, 1999. ISBN 978-0-399-23168-1 Subj: Behavior – wishing. Birds – wrens. Folk & fairy tales. Foreign lands – Ukraine. Magic.

Meteor! ill. by author. Dodd, 1987. ISBN 978-0-396-08910-0 Subj: Country. Science.

Mommies say shhh! ill. by author. Penguin, 2005. ISBN 978-0-399-24341-7 Subj: Animals. Family life – mothers. Noise, sounds.

Mr. Lincoln's way ill. by author. Philomel, 2001. ISBN 978-0-399-23754-6 Subj: Behavior – bullying, teasing. Birds. Careers – school principals. Prejudice. School.

Mrs. Katz and Tush ill. by author. Bantam, 1992. ISBN 978-0-553-08122-0 Subj: Animals – cats. Ethnic groups in the U.S. – African Americans. Friendship. Jewish culture. Pets.

Mrs. Mack ill. by author. Philomel, 1998. ISBN 978-0-399-23167-4 Subj: Animals – horses, ponies. Memories, memory. Seasons – summer.

My ol' man ill. by author. Philomel, 1995. ISBN 978-0-399-22822-3 Subj: Family life – fathers. Imagination. Magic. Rocks.

My rotten redheaded older brother ill. by author. Simon & Schuster, 1994. ISBN 978-0-671-72751-2 Subj: Family life – brothers & sisters. Family life – grandparents. Sibling rivalry.

Oh, look! ill. by author. Philomel, 2004. ISBN 978-0-399-24223-6 Subj: Animals – goats. Fairs, festivals. Mythical creatures – trolls.

Picnic at Mudsock Meadow ill. by author. Putnam, 1992. ISBN 978-0-399-21811-8 Subj: Activities – picnicking. Holidays – Halloween.

Rechenka's eggs ill. by author. Putnam, 1988. ISBN 978-0-399-21501-8 Subj: Birds – geese. Eggs. Folk & fairy tales.

Rotten Richie and the ultimate dare ill. by author. Penguin, 2006. ISBN 978-0-399-24531-2 Subj: Ballet. Behavior – bullying, teasing. Contests. Family life – brothers & sisters. Sports – hockey.

Some birthday! ill. by author. Simon & Schuster, 1991. ISBN 978-0-671-72750-5 Subj: Birthdays. Family life – fathers. Monsters. Parties.

Someone for Mr. Sussman ill. by author. Philomel, 2008. ISBN 978-0-399-25075-0 Subj: Family life – grandmothers. Jewish culture. Weddings.

Something about Hensley's ill. by author. Penguin, 2006. ISBN 978-0-399-24538-1 Subj: Family life – single-parent families. Stores.

Thank you, Mr. Falker ill. by author. Philomel, 1998. ISBN 978-0-399-23166-7 Subj: Books, reading. Careers – teachers. Disabilities. School.

Thunder cake ill. by author. Putnam, 1990. ISBN 978-0-399-22231-3 Subj: Emotions – fear. Family life – grandmothers. Weather – lightning, thunder. Weather – storms.

Tikvah means hope ill. by author. Doubleday, 1994. ISBN 978-0-385-32059-7 Subj: Animals – cats. Fire. Holidays – Sukkot. Jewish culture.

The trees of the dancing goats ill. by author. Simon & Schuster, 1996. ISBN 978-0-689-80862-3 Subj: Ethnic groups in the U.S. – Russian Americans. Family life – grandparents. Holidays – Christmas. Holidays – Hanukkah. Jewish culture.

Welcome Comfort ill. by author. Philomel, 1999. ISBN 978-0-399-23169-8 Subj: Holidays – Christmas. Orphans. Santa Claus. School.

Polhemus, Coleman. *The crocodile blues* ill. by author. Candlewick, 2007. ISBN 978-0-7636-3543-5 Subj: Eggs. Reptiles – alligators, crocodiles. Wordless.

Politi, Leo. *Juanita* ill. by author. Scribners, 1948. Subj: Caldecott award honor books. Ethnic groups in the U.S. – Mexican Americans.

Pedro, the angel of Olvera Street ill. by author. Scribners, 1946. Subj: Caldecott award honor books. Ethnic groups in the U.S. – Mexican Americans. Holidays – Christmas.

Song of the swallows ill. by author. Scribners, 1949. ISBN 978-0-684-18831-7 Subj: Birds – swallows. Caldecott award books. Ethnic groups in the U.S. – Mexican Americans. Missions.

Pollack, Pamela. *Where's that cat?* (Merriam, Eve)

Pollard, Nik. *The river* ill. by author. Roaring Brook, 2003. ISBN 978-0-7613-2858-2 Subj: Rhyming text. Rivers.

The tide ill. by author. Roaring Brook, 2002. ISBN 978-0-7613-2467-6 Subj: Nature. Sea & seashore.

Pollock, Penny. *The turkey girl: a Zuni Cinderella story* ill. by Ed Young. Little, 1996. ISBN 978-0-316-71314-6 Subj: Birds – turkeys. Character traits – loyalty. Folk & fairy tales. Indians of North America – Zuni.

When the moon is full ill. by Mary Azarian. Little, 2001. ISBN 978-0-316-71317-7 Subj: Folk & fairy tales. Indians of North America. Moon. Poetry. Seasons.

Pomeranc, Marion Hess. *The American Wei* ill. by DyAnne DiSalvo. Whitman, 1998. ISBN 978-0-8075-0312-6 Subj: Ethnic groups in the U.S. – Chinese Americans. Fairies. Immigrants.

The can-do Thanksgiving ill. by Nancy Cote. Whitman, 1998. ISBN 978-0-8075-1054-4 Subj: Food. Holidays – Thanksgiving. School.

Pomerantz, Charlotte. *All asleep* ill. by Nancy Tafuri. Greenwillow, 1984. ISBN 978-0-688-03762-8 Subj: Bedtime. Lullabies. Poetry.

Flap your wings and try ill. by Nancy Tafuri. Greenwillow, 1989. ISBN 978-0-688-08020-4 Subj: Activities – flying. Birds. Rhyming text.

Here comes Henny ill. by Nancy Winslow Parker. Greenwillow, 1994. ISBN 978-0-688-12356-7 Subj: Birds – chickens. Rhyming text.

The mousery ill. by Kurt Cyrus. Harcourt, 2000. ISBN 978-0-15-202304-1 Subj: Animals – mice. Character traits – generosity. Orphans. Rhyming text.

One duck, another duck ill. by José Aruego and Ariane Dewey. Greenwillow, 1984. ISBN 978-0-688-03745-1 Subj: Birds – ducks. Counting, numbers.

The piggy in the puddle ill. by James Marshall. Macmillan, 1974. ISBN 978-0-02-774900-7 Subj: Animals – pigs. Rhyming text. Tongue twisters.

You're not my best friend anymore ill. by David Soman. Dial, 1998. ISBN 978-0-8037-1560-8 Subj: Birthdays. Friendship. Gifts.

Pomeroy, Diana. *One potato* ill. by author. Harcourt, 1996. ISBN 978-0-15-200300-5 Subj: Counting, numbers. Food.

Wildflower ABC ill. by author. Harcourt, 1997. ISBN 978-0-15-201041-6 Subj: ABC books. Activities. Flowers.

Pon, Cynthia. *Faith* (Ajmera, Maya)

Poole, Amy Lowry. *How the rooster got his crown* ill. by author. Holiday, 1999. ISBN 978-0-8234-1389-8 Subj: Birds – chickens. Creation. Folk & fairy tales – pourquoi tales. Foreign lands – China.

The pea blossom ill. by reteller. Based on the Hans Christian Andersen story: Five peas in a pod. Holiday House, 2005. ISBN 978-0-8234-1864-0 Subj: Folk & fairy tales. Foreign lands – China. Plants.

Poole, Josephine. *Joan of Arc* ill. by Angela Barrett. Knopf, 1998. ISBN 978-0-679-99041-3 Subj: Foreign lands – France. Religion. War.

Poppenhäger, Nicole. *Snow leopards* ill. by Ivan Gantschev. NorthSouth, 2006. ISBN 978-0-7358-2087-6 Subj: Animals – leopards. Nature.

Poppy Bear ill. by Catherine Deeter. Beyond Words, 2001. ISBN 978-1-58270-042-7 Subj: Animals – bears. Ecology. Gardens, gardening. Rhyming text. Seasons – spring.

Porter, Pamela. *Yellow moon, apple moon* ill. by Matt James. Groundwood, 2008. ISBN 978-0-88899-809-5 Subj: Bedtime. Moon. Rhyming text.

Porter, Sue. *Parsnip* ill. by author. DK, 1997. ISBN 978-0-7894-2470-9 Subj: Animals – babies. Animals – sheep. Format, unusual – toy & movable books. Seasons – winter.

Portis, Antoinette. *Kindergarten diary* ill. by author. HarperCollins, 2010. ISBN 978-0-06-145691-6 Subj: School.

No es una caja / not a box ill. by author. Barcelona, 2008. ISBN 978-84-96-95722-0 Subj: Activities – playing. Animals – rabbits. Foreign languages. Imagination.

Not a box ill. by author. HarperCollins, 2006. ISBN 978-0-06-112322-1 Subj: Activities – playing. Animals – rabbits. Imagination.

Not a stick ill. by author. HarperCollins, 2008. ISBN 978-0-06-112325-2 Subj: Activities – playing. Animals – pigs. Imagination.

A penguin story ill. by author. HarperCollins, 2009. ISBN 978-0-06-145688-6 Subj: Birds – penguins. Character traits – being different. Concepts – color.

Princess Super Kitty ill. by author. HarperCollins, 2011. ISBN 978-0-06-182725-9 Subj: Activities – playing. Imagination.

Portnoy, Mindy Avra. *A tale of two seders* ill. by Valeria Cis. Lerner/Kar-Ben, 2010. ISBN 978-0-8225-9907-4 Subj: Divorce. Family life. Holidays – Passover.

Where do people go when they die? ill. by Shelly O. Haas. Kar-Ben, 2004. ISBN 978-1-58013-081-3 Subj: Death. Family life.

Porto, Tony. *Blue aliens.* Conceived & designed by 3CD (Tony Porto, Mitch Rice, Glenn Deutsch). Little, 2003. ISBN 978-0-316-61359-0 Subj: Aliens. Concepts – color. School.

Get red. Conceived & designed by 3CD (Tony Porto, Mitch Rice, Glenn Deutsch). Little, 2002. ISBN 978-0-316-60940-1 Subj: Aliens. Concepts – color. School.

Posada, Mia. *Dandelions, stars in the grass* ill. by author. Carolrhoda, 2000. ISBN 978-1-57505-383-7 Subj: Flowers. Plants. Science.

Guess what is growing inside this egg ill. by author. Lerner, 2007. ISBN 978-0-8225-6192-7 Subj: Eggs. Science.

Ladybugs ill. by author. Carolrhoda, 2002. ISBN 978-0-87614-334-6 Subj: Insects – ladybugs. Rhyming text.

Robins ill. by author. Carolrhoda, 2004. ISBN 978-1-57505-615-9 Subj: Birds – robins. Rhyming text.

Posey, Lee. *Night rabbits* ill. by Michael G. Montgomery. Peachtree, 1999. ISBN 978-1-56145-164-7 Subj: Animals – rabbits. Family life – fathers. Homes, houses. Night. Seasons – summer.

Post, Peggy. *Emily's everyday manners* by Peggy Post and Cindy Post Senning ill. by Steve Björkman. HarperCollins, 2006. ISBN 978-0-06-076177-6 Subj: Etiquette.

Emily's out and about book (Senning, Cindy Post)

Postgate, Daniel. *The richest crocodile in the world* ill. by author. Collins, 2003. ISBN 978-0-00-710388-1 Subj: Friendship. Reptiles – alligators, crocodiles.

Smelly Bill ill. by author. NorthSouth, 2007. ISBN 978-0-7358-2135-4 Subj: Animals – dogs. Rhyming text.

Smelly Bill: love stinks ill. by author. Whitman, 2010. ISBN 978-0-8075-7464-5 Subj: Activities – bathing. Animals – dogs. Rhyming text.

The snagglegrollop ill. by Nick Price. Scholastic, 2009. ISBN 978-0-545-10470-8 Subj: Family life. Friendship. Imagination. Pets.

Posthuma, Sieb. *Benny* ill. by author. Kane/Miller, 2002. ISBN 978-1-929132-43-0 Subj: Animals – dogs. Family life – mothers. Illness – cold (disease). Senses – smell.

Potter, Alicia. *Mrs. Harkness and the panda* ill. by Melissa Sweet. Knopf, 2012. ISBN 978-0-375-84448-5 Subj: Animals – pandas. Character traits – perseverance. Foreign lands – China.

Potter, Beatrix. *Appley Dapply's nursery rhymes* ill. by author. Warne, 1917. ISBN 978-0-7232-0613-2 Subj: Animals. Nursery rhymes.

Cecily Parsley's nursery rhymes ill. by author. Warne, 1922. ISBN 978-0-7232-0614-9 Subj: Animals. Nursery rhymes.

The complete adventures of Peter Rabbit ill. by author. Warne, 1982. ISBN 978-0-7232-6165-0 Subj: Animals – rabbits. Behavior – misbehavior.

Ginger and Pickles ill. by author. First pub. in 1909. Warne, 1937. Subj: Animals. Stores.

More tales from Beatrix Potter ill. by author. Warne, 1987. ISBN 978-0-7232-3366-4 Subj: Animals.

Peter Rabbit's ABC ill. by author. Warne, 1999, ©1987. ISBN 978-0-7232-3423-4 Subj: ABC books. Animals.

Peter Rabbit's one two three ill. by author. Warne, 1999, ©1988. ISBN 978-0-7232-3424-1 Subj: Animals – rabbits. Counting, numbers.

The pie and the patty-pan ill. by author. First pub. in 1905. Warne, 1933. Subj: Animals – cats. Animals – dogs. Behavior – trickery.

Roly-Poly pudding ill. by author. First pub. in 1908. Warne, 1936. Subj: Animals – cats.

The sly old cat ill. by author. Warne, 1971. ISBN 978-0-7232-1420-5 Subj: Animals – cats. Animals – rats. Character traits – cleverness. Etiquette. Parties.

The story of fierce bad rabbit ill. by author. Warne, 1906. Subj: Animals – rabbits.

The story of Miss Moppet ill. by author. Warne, 1906. ISBN 978-0-7232-0612-5 Subj: Animals – cats. Behavior – trickery.

The tailor of Gloucester ill. by author. Warne, 1931. Subj: Animals – mice. Careers – tailors. Character traits – helpfulness.

The tale of Benjamin Bunny ill. by author. Warne, 1904. ISBN 978-0-7232-0595-1 Subj: Animals – rabbits. Behavior – misbehavior.

The tale of Jemima Puddle-Duck ill. by author. First pub. in 1910. Warne, 1936. Subj: Birds – ducks. Eggs.

The tale of Jemima Puddle-Duck and other farmyard tales: the tale of Mr. Jeremy Fisher; the tale of Mrs. Tiggy-Winkle; the tale of Pigling Bland ill. by author. Large format ed. Warne, 1987. ISBN 978-0-7232-3425-8 Subj: Animals. Birds.

The tale of Johnny Town-Mouse ill. by author. Warne, 1918. ISBN 978-0-7232-0604-0 Subj: Animals – mice.

The tale of Little Pig Robinson ill. by author. Warne, 1930. Subj: Animals – pigs. Behavior – talking to strangers. Boats, ships. Shopping.

The tale of Mr. Jeremy Fisher ill. by David Jorgensen. Picture Book Studio, 1989. ISBN 978-0-88708-094-4 Subj: Frogs & toads. Sports – fishing.

The tale of Mr. Jeremy Fisher ill. by author. Warne, 1934. ISBN 978-0-7232-6231-2 Subj: Frogs & toads. Sports – fishing.

The tale of Mr. Tod ill. by author. First pub. in 1911. Warne, 1939. Subj: Animals – badgers. Animals – foxes. Animals – rabbits.

The tale of Mrs. Tiggy-Winkle ill. by author. Warne, 1905. Subj: Animals – hedgehogs. Clothing.

The tale of Mrs. Tittlemouse ill. by author. Warne, 1910. ISBN 978-0-7232-6235-0 Subj: Animals – mice. Character traits – cleanliness.

The tale of Mrs. Tittlemouse and other mouse stories: the tale of Johnny Town-Mouse; the tale of two bad mice; the tailor of Gloucester ill. by author. Large format ed. Warne, 1985. ISBN 978-0-7232-3324-4 Subj: Animals – mice.

The tale of Peter Rabbit ill. by Margot Apple. Troll, 1979. ISBN 978-0-89375-124-1 Subj: Animals – rabbits. Behavior – misbehavior.

The tale of Peter Rabbit ill. by author. Warne, 1902. ISBN 978-0-7232-0592-0 Subj: Animals – rabbits. Behavior – misbehavior. Farms.

The tale of Peter Rabbit and other stories ill. by Allen Atkinson. Knopf, 1982. ISBN 978-0-394-52845-8 Subj: Animals.

The tale of Pigling Bland ill. by author. Warne, 1941, 1913. ISBN 978-0-7232-0606-4 Subj: Animals – pigs.

The tale of Squirrel Nutkin ill. by author. Warne, 1903. ISBN 978-0-7232-0593-7 Subj: Animals – squirrels. Birds – owls. Riddles & jokes. Seasons – fall.

The tale of the faithful dove ill. by Marie Angel. Warne, 1970. Subj: Birds – doves. Character traits – loyalty.

The tale of the Flopsy Bunnies ill. by author. Warne, 1909, 1937. ISBN 978-0-7232-0601-9 Subj: Animals – rabbits. Character traits – cleverness.

The tale of the Flopsy Bunnies ill. by Wendy Rasmussen. Child's World, 2009. ISBN 978-1-60253-297-7 Subj: Animals – rabbits. Character traits – cleverness.

The tale of Timmy Tiptoes ill. by author. Warne, 1911, 1939. ISBN 978-0-7232-0603-3 Subj: Animals – squirrels.

The tale of Tom Kitten ill. by author. Warne, 1907. ISBN 978-0-7232-0599-9 Subj: Animals – cats. Humorous stories.

The tale of Tuppeny ill. by Marie Angel. Warne, 1971. Subj: Animals – guinea pigs.

The tale of two bad mice ill. by author. Warne, 1904, 1934. Subj: Animals – mice. Behavior – misbehavior. Toys.

A treasury of Peter Rabbit and other stories ill. by author. Watts, 1978. Subj: Animals.

The two bad mice: pop-up book ill. by author. Warne, 1986. ISBN 978-0-7232-3360-2 Subj: Animals – mice. Behavior – misbehavior. Format, unusual – toy & movable books.

Where's Peter Rabbit? ill. by Colin Twinn. Warne, 1988. ISBN 978-0-7232-3519-4 Subj: Animals – rabbits. Behavior – misbehavior. Format, unusual.

Yours affectionately, Peter Rabbit: miniature letters ill. by author. Warne, 1984. ISBN 978-0-7232-3178-3 Subj: Animals. Communication.

Potter, Giselle. *The year I didn't go to school* ill. by author. Atheneum, 2002. ISBN 978-0-689-84730-1 Subj: Activities – traveling. Foreign lands – Italy. Puppets. Theater.

Pow, Tom. *Tell me one thing, Dad* ill. by Ian Andrew. Candlewick, 2004. ISBN 978-0-7636-2474-3 Subj: Bedtime. Emotions – love. Family life – daughters. Family life – fathers. Games.

Who is the world for? ill. by Robert Ingpen. Candlewick, 2000. ISBN 978-0-7636-1280-1 Subj: Animals. Family life – parents. World.

Powell, Alma. *America's promise* ill. by Marsha Winborn. HarperCollins, 2003. ISBN 978-0-06-052173-8 Subj: Clubs, gangs. Communities, neighborhoods.

My little wagon [board book] ill. by Marsha Winborn. HarperCollins, 2003. ISBN 978-0-06-052193-6 Subj: Activities – playing. Animals – bears. Format, unusual – board books. Toys – wagons.

Powell, Consie. *Amazing apples* ill. by author. Whitman, 2003. ISBN 978-0-8075-0399-7 Subj: Careers – farmers. Food. Poetry. Trees.

The first day of winter ill. by author. Whitman, 2005. ISBN 978-0-8075-2450-3 Subj: Nature. Seasons – winter. Weather – cold.

Old dog Cora and the Christmas tree ill. by author. Whitman, 1999. ISBN 978-0-8075-5968-0 Subj: Animals – dogs. Family life. Holidays – Christmas. Old age. Trees.

Powell, Polly. *Just dessert* ill. by author. Harcourt, 1996. ISBN 978-0-15-200383-8 Subj: Emotions – fear. Food. Imagination. Night.

Poydar, Nancy. *The bad-news report card* ill. by author. Holiday House, 2006. ISBN 978-0-8234-1992-0 Subj: Behavior – worrying. School.

The biggest test in the universe ill. by author. Holiday House, 2005. ISBN 978-0-8234-1944-9 Subj: Behavior – worrying. School.

Busy Bea ill. by author. McElderry, 1994. ISBN 978-0-689-50592-8 Subj: Behavior – lost & found possessions. Ethnic groups in the U.S. – African Americans. Family life – grandmothers. School.

Cool Ali ill. by author. McElderry, 1996. ISBN 978-0-689-80755-8 Subj: Activities – drawing. Cities, towns. Concepts – shape. Concepts – size. Seasons – summer.

First day, hooray! ill. by author. Holiday, 1999. ISBN 978-0-8234-1437-6 Subj: Careers – bus drivers. Careers – school principals. Careers – teachers. School – first day.

Fish school ill. by author. Holiday, 2009. ISBN 978-0-8234-2140-4 Subj: Aquariums. Fish. Pets. School – field trips.

Mailbox magic ill. by author. Holiday, 2000. ISBN 978-0-8234-1525-0 Subj: Character traits – patience. Letters, cards.

No fair science fair ill. by author. Holiday House, 2011. ISBN 978-0-8234-2269-2 Subj: Character traits – persistence. School. Science.

The perfectly horrible Halloween ill. by author. Holiday, 2001. ISBN 978-0-8234-1592-2 Subj: Clothing – costumes. Holidays – Halloween. Problem solving. School.

Rhyme time Valentine ill. by author. Holiday, 2003. ISBN 978-0-8234-1684-4 Subj: Ethnic groups in the U.S. – African Americans. Holidays – Valentine's Day. Rhyming text. School. Weather – wind.

Snip, snip . . . snow! ill. by author. Holiday, 1997. ISBN 978-0-8234-1328-7 Subj: Activities – playing. Nature. School. Seasons – winter. Weather – snow.

Zip, zip . . . homework ill. by author. Holiday, 2008. ISBN 978-0-8234-2090-2 Subj: Behavior – lying. Character traits – honesty. School.

Prager, Ellen J. *Earthquakes* ill. by Susan Greenstein. National Geographic, 2002. ISBN 978-0-7922-8202-0 Subj: Earthquakes.

Prap, Lila. *Animal lullabies* ill. by author. NorthSouth, 2006. ISBN 978-0-7358-2097-5 Subj: Animals. Lullabies. Rhyming text.

Animals speak ill. by author. NorthSouth, 2006. ISBN 978-0-7358-2058-6 Subj: Animals. Foreign languages.

Daddies ill. by author. NorthSouth, 2007. ISBN 978-0-7358-2140-8 Subj: Animals. Bedtime. Family life – fathers. Rhyming text.

Dinosaurs?! ill. by author. NorthSouth, 2010. ISBN 978-0-7358-2284-9 Subj: Dinosaurs.

Doggy whys ill. by author. NorthSouth, 2011. ISBN 978-0-7358-4014-0 Subj: Animals – cats. Animals – dogs. Pets.

Prater, John. *Hold tight!* ill. by author. Barron's, 2003. ISBN 978-0-7641-2304-7 Subj: Animals – bears. Family life – grandfathers.

On top of the world ill. by author. Mondo, 1998. ISBN 978-1-57255-649-2 Subj: Animals. Night. Toys.

Pratt, Pierre. *Car* ill. by author. Candlewick, 2001. ISBN 978-0-7636-1390-7 Subj: Animals. Animals – elephants. Animals – mice. Automobiles. Birds.

Home ill. by author. Candlewick, 2001. ISBN 978-0-7636-1389-1 Subj: Animals – elephants. Animals – mice. Format, unusual – board books. Friendship. Homes, houses.

I see . . . my mom / I see . . . my dad ill. by author. Annick, 2001. ISBN 978-1-55037-624-1 Subj: Anatomy. Family life – parents. Format, unusual.

I see . . . my sister / I see . . . my cat ill. by author. Annick, 2001. ISBN 978-1-55037-625-8 Subj: Anatomy. Animals – cats. Family life – parents. Format, unusual.

Park ill. by author. Candlewick, 2001. ISBN 978-0-7636-1391-4 Subj: Animals. Animals – elephants. Animals – mice. Format, unusual – board books. Parks.

Shopping ill. by author. Candlewick, 2001. ISBN 978-0-7636-1392-1 Subj: Animals – elephants. Animals – mice. Clothing – shoes. Format, unusual – board books. Shopping.

Preller, James. *Cardinal and sunflower* ill. by Huy Voun Lee. HarperCollins, 1998. ISBN 978-0-06-026223-5 Subj: Birds – cardinals. Flowers. Nature.

A pirate's guide to first grade ill. by Greg Ruth. Feiwel & Friends, 2010. ISBN 978-0-312-36928-6 Subj: Pirates. School – first day.

A pirate's guide to recess ill. by Greg Ruth. Feiwel & Friends, 2013. ISBN 978-1-250-00515-1 Subj: Pirates. School.

Prelutsky, Jack. *Awful Ogre running wild* ill. by Paul O. Zelinsky. Greenwillow, 2008. ISBN 978-0-06-623866-1 Subj: Mythical creatures – ogres. Poetry.

Awful Ogre's awful day ill. by Paul O. Zelinsky. Greenwillow, 2001. ISBN 978-0-688-07779-2 Subj: Mythical creatures – ogres. Poetry.

The baby uggs are hatching ill. by James Stevenson. Greenwillow, 1982. ISBN 978-0-688-00923-6 Subj: Humorous stories. Imagination. Monsters. Poetry.

Behold the bold umbrellaphant and other poems ill. by Carin Berger. HarperCollins, 2006. ISBN 978-0-06-054318-1 Subj: Animals. Imagination. Poetry.

Beneath a blue umbrella ill. by Garth Williams. Greenwillow, 1990. ISBN 978-0-688-06429-7 Subj: Animals. Poetry.

Circus ill. by Arnold Lobel. Macmillan, 1974. ISBN 978-0-02-775060-7 Subj: Circus. Poetry.

The frogs wore red suspenders ill. by Petra Mathers. Greenwillow, 2002. ISBN 978-0-688-16720-2 Subj: Poetry.

Good sports: rhymes about running, jumping, throwing, and more ill. by Chris Raschka. Random House, 2007. ISBN 978-0-375-83700-5 Subj: Poetry. Sports.

Halloween countdown ill. by Dan Yaccarino. HarperCollins, 2002. ISBN 978-0-06-000512-2 Subj: Counting, numbers. Format, unusual – board books. Ghosts. Holidays – Halloween. Poetry.

It's snowing! It's snowing! winter poems ill. by Yossi Abolafia. HarperCollins, 2006. ISBN 978-0-06-053715-9 Subj: Poetry. Seasons – winter.

Me I am! ill. by Christine Davenier. Farrar, 2007. ISBN 978-0-374-64902-9 Subj: Character traits – individuality. Poetry. Self-concept.

The mean old mean hyena ill. by Arnold Lobel. Greenwillow, 1978. ISBN 978-0-688-84163-8 Subj: Animals – hyenas. Character traits – meanness. Rhyming text.

Monday's troll ill. by Peter Sís. Greenwillow, 1996. ISBN 978-0-688-09644-1 Subj: Fairies. Mythical creatures – trolls. Poetry. Witches.

The pack rat's day and other poems ill. by Margaret Bloy Graham. Macmillan, 1974. ISBN 978-0-02-775050-8 Subj: Animals. Poetry.

The queen of Eene ill. by Victoria Chess. Greenwillow, 1978. ISBN 978-0-688-84144-7 Subj: Humorous stories. Poetry.

Rainy rainy Saturday ill. by Marylin Hafner. Greenwillow, 1980. ISBN 978-0-688-84252-9 Subj: Poetry. Weather – rain.

The Random House book of poetry for children ill. by Arnold Lobel. Random House, 1983. ISBN 978-0-394-95010-5 Subj: Humorous stories. Poetry.

Read-aloud rhymes for the very young ill. by Marc Brown. Knopf, 1986. ISBN 978-0-394-97218-3 Subj: Poetry.

Ride a purple pelican ill. by Garth Williams. Greenwillow, 1986. ISBN 978-0-688-04031-4 Subj: Imagination. Poetry.

The snopp on the sidewalk and other poems ill. by Byron Barton. Greenwillow, 1977. ISBN 978-0-688-84084-6 Subj: Humorous stories. Imagination. Poetry.

Stardines swim high across the sky: and other poems ill. by Carin Berger. Greenwillow, 2013. ISBN 978-0-06-201464-1 Subj: Animals. Imagination. Poetry.

The terrible tiger ill. by Arnold Lobel. Macmillan, 1970. ISBN 978-0-689-71300-2 Subj: Animals – tigers. Cumulative tales. Rhyming text.

There's no place like school ill. by Jane Manning. HarperCollins, 2010. ISBN 978-0-06-082338-2 Subj: Poetry. School.

Tyrannosaurus was a beast ill. by Arnold Lobel. Greenwillow, 1988. ISBN 978-0-688-06443-3 Subj: Dinosaurs. Poetry.

What a day it was at school! ill. by Doug Cushman. HarperCollins, 2006. ISBN 978-0-06-082335-1 Subj: Poetry. School.

Wild witches' ball ill. by Kelly Asbury. HarperCollins, 2004. ISBN 978-0-06-052972-7 Subj: Counting, numbers. Holidays – Halloween. Rhyming text. Witches.

The wizard ill. by Brandon Dorman. HarperCollins, 2007. ISBN 978-0-06-124076-8 Subj: Magic. Rhyming text. Wizards.

Preston, Tim. *Pumpkin moon* ill. by Simon Bartram. Dutton, 2001. ISBN 978-0-525-46713-7 Subj: Holidays – Halloween. Moon.

Preus, Margi. *The Peace Bell* ill. by Hideko Takahashi. Holt, 2008. ISBN 978-0-8050-7800-8 Subj: Family life – grandmothers. Foreign lands – Japan. Friendship. Holidays – New Year's. U.S. history. War.

Price, Hope Lynne. *These hands* ill. by Bryan Collier. Hyperion, 1999. ISBN 978-0-7868-2320-8 Subj: Anatomy – hands. Ethnic groups in the U.S. – African Americans. Family life – mothers. Rhyming text.

Price, Kathy. *The Bourbon Street musicians* ill. by Andrew Glass. Clarion, 2002. ISBN 978-0-618-04076-6 Subj: Animals. Careers – musicians. Crime. Folk & fairy tales. Old age.

Price, Leontyne. *Aïda* ill. by Leo Dillon and Diane Dillon. Retells the story of Giuseppe Verdi's opera. Harcourt, 1990. ISBN 978-0-15-200405-7 Subj: Emotions – love. Foreign lands – Egypt. Music. Royalty.

Price, Mara. *Grandma's chocolate / El chocolate de Abuelita* ill. by Lisa Fields. Arte Publico/Piñata, 2010. ISBN 978-1-55885-587-8 Subj: Ethnic groups in the U.S. – Mexican Americans. Family life – grandmothers. Foreign languages. Gifts. Indians of Central America – Maya.

Price, Mathew. *Dumbo* ill. by Atsuko Morozumi. Disney, 2000. ISBN 978-0-7868-3274-3 Subj: Animals – elephants. Circus.

Patch and the rabbits ill. by Emma Chichester Clark. Orchard, 2000. ISBN 978-0-531-30265-1 Subj: Animals – dogs. Animals – rabbits. Dreams. Format, unusual – toy & movable books.

Priceman, Marjorie. *Emeline at the circus* ill. by author. Knopf, 1999. ISBN 978-0-679-87685-4 Subj: Careers – teachers. Circus. School.

Hot air: the (mostly) true story of the first hot-air balloon ride ill. by author. Simon & Schuster, 2005. ISBN 978-0-689-82642-9 Subj: Activities – ballooning. Caldecott award honor books. Careers – inventors. Inventions.

How to make a cherry pie and see the U.S.A. ill. by author. Knopf, 2008. ISBN 978-0-375-81255-2 Subj: Activities – baking, cooking. Activities – traveling. Food.

How to make an apple pie and see the world ill. by author. Knopf, 1994. ISBN 978-0-679-93705-0 Subj: Activities – baking, cooking. Activities – traveling. Food.

It's me, Marva! ill. by author. Knopf, 2001. ISBN 978-0-679-98993-6 Subj: Careers – inventors. Concepts – color. Optical illusions.

My nine lives / by Clio ill. by author. Atheneum, 1998. ISBN 978-0-689-81135-7 Subj: Animals – cats. Memories, memory.

Princess Picky ill. by author. Roaring Brook, 2002. ISBN 978-0-7613-2418-8 Subj: Activities – flying. Character traits – stubbornness. Food. Royalty – princesses.

Priest, Robert H. *The old pirate of Central Park* ill. by author. Houghton, 1999. ISBN 978-0-395-90505-0 Subj: Activities – playing. Boats, ships. Toys.

The pirate's eye ill. by author. Houghton, 2005. ISBN 978-0-618-43990-4 Subj: Activities – drawing. Anatomy – eyes. Behavior – lost & found possessions. Character traits – generosity. Pirates.

Prigger, Mary Skillings. *Aunt Minnie and the twister* ill. by Betsy Lewin. Clarion, 2002. ISBN 978-0-618-11136-7 Subj: Family life – aunts, uncles. Farms. Homes, houses. Weather – tornadoes.

Aunt Minnie McGranahan ill. by Betsy Lewin. Clarion, 1999. ISBN 978-0-618-60488-3 Subj: Character traits – orderliness. Family life – aunts, uncles. Family life – brothers & sisters. Orphans.

Primavera, Elise. *Auntie Claus* ill. by author. Harcourt, 1999. ISBN 978-0-15-201909-9 Subj: Family life – aunts, uncles. Foreign lands – Arctic. Holidays – Christmas. Santa Claus.

Auntie Claus and the key to Christmas ill. by author. Harcourt, 2002. ISBN 978-0-15-202441-3 Subj: Family life – aunts, uncles. Foreign lands – Arctic. Holidays – Christmas. Santa Claus.

The house at the end of Ladybug Lane ill. by Valeria Docampo. Random House, 2012. ISBN 978-0-375-85584-9 Subj: Behavior – wishing. Character traits – cleanliness. Character traits – individuality. Insects – ladybugs.

Louise, the big cheese: divine diva ill. by Diane Goode. Simon & Schuster, 2009. ISBN 978-1-4169-7180-1 Subj: Friendship. Theater.

Louise the big cheese and the back-to-school smarty-pants ill. by Diane Goode. Simon & Schuster, 2011. ISBN 978-1-4424-0600-1 Subj: Careers – teachers. Character traits – ambition. School.

Louise the big cheese and the la-di-da shoes ill. by Diane Goode. Simon & Schuster, 2010. ISBN 978-1-4169-7181-8 Subj: Character traits – appearance. Character traits – vanity. Clothing – shoes.

Louise the big cheese and the Ooh-la-la Charm School ill. by Diane Goode. Simon & Schuster, 2012. ISBN 978-1-4424-0599-8 Subj: Character traits – ambition. Etiquette. Friendship.

Thumb love ill. by author. Random House, 2010. ISBN 978-0-375-84481-2 Subj: Humorous stories. Thumb sucking.

Prince, April Jones. *Twenty-one elephants and still standing* ill. by François Roca. Houghton, 2005. ISBN 978-0-618-44887-6 Subj: Animals – elephants. Bridges.

What do wheels do all day? ill. by Giles Laroche. Houghton, 2006. ISBN 978-0-618-56307-4 Subj: Rhyming text. Wheels.

Prince, Joshua. *I saw an ant in a parking lot* ill. by Macky Pamintuan. Sterling, 2007. ISBN 978-1-4027-3823-4 Subj: Humorous stories. Insects – ants. Rhyming text.

I saw an ant on the railroad track ill. by Macky Pamintuan. Sterling, 2006. ISBN 978-1-4027-2183-0 Subj: Humorous stories. Insects – ants. Rhyming text. Trains.

Pringle, Laurence P. *Bear hug* ill. by Kate Salley Palmer. Boyds Mills, 2003. ISBN 978-1-56397-876-0 Subj: Animals – bears. Camps, camping. Family life – fathers.

Crows ill. by Bob Marstall. Boyds Mills, 2002. ISBN 978-1-56397-899-9 Subj: Birds – crows. Science.

Everybody has a bellybutton ill. by Clare Wood. Boyds Mills, 1997. ISBN 978-1-56397-009-2 Subj: Anatomy – navels. Birth. Family life.

Jesse builds a road ill. by Leslie Holt Morrill. Macmillan, 1989. ISBN 978-0-02-775311-0 Subj: Imagination. Machines. Roads.

Naming the cat ill. by Katherine Potter. Walker, 1997. ISBN 978-0-8027-8622-7 Subj: Animals – cats. Names. Pets.

Octopus hug ill. by Kate Salley Palmer. Boyds Mills, 1993. ISBN 978-1-56397-034-4 Subj: Activities – playing. Family life.

One room school ill. by Barbara Garrison. Boyds Mills, 1998. ISBN 978-1-56397-583-7 Subj: School. U.S. history. War.

Snakes ill. by Meryl Henderson. Boyds Mills, 2004. ISBN 978-1-59078-003-9 Subj: Reptiles – snakes. Science.

Pritchett, Andy. *Stick!* ill. by author. Candlewick, 2013. ISBN 978-0-7636-6616-3 Subj: Activities – playing. Animals. Animals – dogs.

Pritchett, Dylan. *The first music* ill. by Erin Bennett Banks. August House, 2006. ISBN 978-0-87483-776-6 Subj: Foreign lands – Africa. Jungle. Music.

Prochovnic, Dawn Babb. *The big blue bowl: sign language for food* ill. by Stephanie Bauer. Abdo, 2009. ISBN 978-1-60270-668-2 Subj: Food. Rhyming text. Sign language.

Hip hip hooray! It's Family Day! sign language for family ill. by Stephanie Bauer. ABDO/Magic Wagon, 2012. ISBN 978-1-61641-837-3 Subj: Family life. Rhyming text. Sign language.

Proimos, James. *The best bike ride ever* ill. by Johanna Wright. Dial, 2012. ISBN 978-0-8037-3850-8 Subj: Accidents. Imagination. Safety. Sports – bicycling.

Joe's wish ill. by author. Harcourt, 1998. ISBN 978-0-15-201831-3 Subj: Behavior – wishing. Family life – grandfathers. Old age.

The loudness of Sam ill. by author. Harcourt, 1999. ISBN 978-0-15-202087-3 Subj: Cities, towns. Emotions. Family life – aunts, uncles.

Paulie Pastrami achieves world peace ill. by author. Little, Brown, 2009. ISBN 978-0-316-03292-6 Subj: Behavior – seeking better things. Behavior – sharing. Character traits – kindness. Food.

Todd's TV ill. by author. HarperCollins, 2010. ISBN 978-0-06-170985-2 Subj: Family life – parents. Television.

Prokofiev, Sergei Sergeievitch. *Peter and the wolf* ill. by Charles Mikolaycak. Viking, 1982. ISBN 978-0-670-54919-1 Subj: Animals – wolves. Character traits – cleverness. Folk & fairy tales. Foreign lands – Russia. Music. Musical instruments.

Peter and the wolf ill. by Josef Palecek. Picture Book Studio, 1987. ISBN 978-0-88708-049-4 Subj: Animals – wolves. Character traits – cleverness. Folk & fairy tales. Foreign lands – Russia. Music. Musical instruments.

Peter and the wolf retold by Chris Raschka; ill. by Chris Raschka. Simon & Schuster, 2008. ISBN 978-0-689-85652-5 Subj: Animals – wolves. Character traits – cleverness. Folk & fairy tales. Foreign lands – Russia. Music. Musical instruments.

Peter and the wolf retold by Vladimir Vagin; ill. by Vladimir Vagin. Scholastic, 2000. ISBN 978-0-590-38608-1 Subj: Animals – wolves. Character traits – cleverness. Folk & fairy tales. Foreign lands – Russia. Music. Musical instruments.

Prosek, James. *Bird, butterfly, eel* ill. by author. Simon & Schuster, 2009. ISBN 978-0-689-86829-0 Subj: Birds. Fish. Insects – butterflies, caterpillars. Migration.

Protopopescu, Orel. *Thelonious Mouse* ill. by Anne Wilsdorf. Farrar, 2011. ISBN 978-0-374-37447-1 Subj: Animals – cats. Animals – mice. Music.

Two sticks ill. by Anne Wilsdorf. Farrar, 2007. ISBN 978-0-374-38022-9 Subj: Musical instruments – drums. Reptiles – alligators, crocodiles. Rhyming text.

Provencher, Rose-Marie. *Mouse cleaning* ill. by Bernadette Pons. Holt, 2001. ISBN 978-0-8050-6240-3 Subj: Animals – mice. Behavior – messy. Character traits – cleanliness. Homes, houses.

Provensen, Alice. *A book of seasons* by Alice Provensen and Martin Provensen ill. by authors. Random House, 1976. ISBN 978-0-394-83242-5 Subj: Seasons.

The glorious flight: across the channel with Louis Blériot by Alice Provensen and Martin Provensen ill. by authors. Viking, 1983. ISBN 978-0-14-050729-4 Subj: Activities – flying. Airplanes, airports. Caldecott award books.

Klondike gold ill. by author. Simon & Schuster, 2005. ISBN 978-0-689-84885-8 Subj: Careers – miners. Foreign lands – Yukon Territory.

Town and country by Alice Provensen and Martin Provensen ill. by authors. Crown, 1984. ISBN 978-0-15-200182-7 Subj: Cities, towns. Country.

The year at Maple Hill Farm by Alice Provensen and Martin Provensen ill. by authors. Atheneum, 1978. ISBN 978-0-689-20494-4 Subj: Animals. Days of the week, months of the year. Farms. Seasons.

Provensen, Martin. *A book of seasons* (Provensen, Alice)

The glorious flight: across the channel with Louis Blériot (Provensen, Alice)

Town and country (Provensen, Alice)

The year at Maple Hill Farm (Provensen, Alice)

Pryor, Bonnie. *Amanda and April* ill. by Diane deGroat. Morrow, 1986. ISBN 978-0-688-05870-8 Subj: Animals – pigs. Family life – sisters. Parties. Sibling rivalry.

The dream jar ill. by Mark Graham. Morrow, 1996. ISBN 978-0-688-13062-6 Subj: Activities – working. Cities, towns. Ethnic groups in the U.S. – Russian Americans. Family life. Immigrants.

The house on Maple Street ill. by Beth Peck. Morrow, 1987. ISBN 978-0-688-06381-8 Subj: U.S. history.

Merry Christmas, Amanda and April ill. by Diane deGroat. Morrow, 1990. ISBN 978-0-688-07545-3 Subj: Animals – pigs. Family life – sisters. Holidays – Christmas.

The porcupine mouse ill. by Mary Jane Begin. Morrow, 1988. ISBN 978-0-688-07154-7 Subj: Animals – mice. Character traits – bravery. Emotions – fear. Sibling rivalry.

Pullen, Zachary. *Friday my Radio Flyer flew* ill. by author. Simon & Schuster, 2008. ISBN 978-1-4169-3983-2 Subj: Family life – fathers. Toys – wagons.

Pullman, Philip. *Puss in boots: the adventures of that most enterprising feline* ill. by Ian Beck. Knopf, 2000. ISBN 978-0-375-81354-2 Subj: Animals – cats. Character traits – cleverness. Folk & fairy tales. Foreign lands – France. Royalty – kings.

Pulver, Robin. *Alicia's tutu* ill. by Mark Graham. Dial, 1997. ISBN 978-0-8037-1933-0 Subj: Activities – dancing. Ballet. Behavior – wishing. Family life. Family life – grandmothers. Furniture – beds.

Author day for room 3T ill. by Chuck Richards. Houghton, 2005. ISBN 978-0-618-35406-1 Subj: Careers – writers. School.

Axle Annie ill. by Tedd Arnold. Dial, 1999. ISBN 978-0-8037-2096-1 Subj: Careers – bus drivers. School. Weather – snow.

Axle Annie and the speed grump ill. by Tedd Arnold. Penguin, 2005. ISBN 978-0-8037-2787-8 Subj: Accidents. Activities – driving. Careers – bus drivers. School.

The case of the incapacitated capitals ill. by Lynn Rowe Reed. Holiday House, 2012. ISBN 978-0-8234-2402-3 Subj: Activities – writing. Careers – teachers. Language. School.

Christmas for a kitten ill. by Layne Johnson. Whitman, 2003. ISBN 978-0-8075-1151-0 Subj: Animals – cats. Holidays – Christmas. Santa Claus.

Christmas kitten, home at last ill. by Layne Johnson. Whitman, 2010. ISBN 978-0-8075-1157-2 Subj: Animals – cats. Holidays – Christmas. Illness – allergies. Santa Claus.

Happy endings: a story about suffixes ill. by Lynn Rowe Reed. Holiday House, 2011. ISBN 978-0-8234-2296-8 Subj: Language. School.

Mrs. Toggle and the dinosaur ill. by R. W. Alley. Four Winds, 1991. ISBN 978-0-02-775452-0 Subj: Careers – teachers. Dinosaurs. Prehistory. School.

Mrs. Toggle's beautiful blue shoe ill. by R. W. Alley. Four Winds, 1991. ISBN 978-0-02-775456-8 Subj: Careers – teachers. Clothing – shoes. School.

Mrs. Toggle's zipper ill. by R. W. Alley. Four Winds, 1990. ISBN 978-0-02-775451-3 Subj: Careers – teachers. Clothing – coats. Humorous stories. School.

Never say boo! ill. by Deb Lucke. Holiday, 2009. ISBN 978-0-8234-2110-7 Subj: Character traits – being different. Ghosts. School.

Nobody's mother is in second grade ill. by G. Brian Karas. Dial, 1992. ISBN 978-0-8037-1211-9 Subj: Family life – mothers. Plants. School.

Nouns and verbs have a field day ill. by Lynn Rowe Reed. Holiday House, 2006. ISBN 978-0-8234-1982-1 Subj: Language. School.

Punctuation takes a vacation ill. by Lynn Rowe Reed. Holiday House, 2003. ISBN 978-0-8234-1687-5 Subj: Activities – vacationing. Language. School.

Saturday is Dadurday ill. by R. W. Alley. Walker, 2013. ISBN 978-0-8027-8691-3 Subj: Emotions – sadness. Family life – fathers. Problem solving.

Silent letters loud and clear ill. by Lynn Rowe Reed. Holiday, 2008. ISBN 978-0-8234-2127-5 Subj: Language. School.

Thank you, Miss Doover ill. by Stephanie Roth Sisson. Holiday House, 2010. ISBN 978-0-8234-2046-9 Subj: Activities – writing. Letters, cards. School.

Way to go, Alex! ill. by Elizabeth Wolf. Whitman, 1999. ISBN 978-0-8075-1583-9 Subj: Disabilities. Family life – brothers & sisters. Sports – Special Olympics.

Pumphrey, Jerome. *Creepy things are scaring me* ill. by Rosanne Litzinger. HarperCollins, 2003. ISBN 978-0-06-028963-8 Subj: Bedtime. Emotions – fear. Rhyming text.

Purcell, Rebecca. *Super Chicken* ill. by author. Scholastic, 2013. ISBN 978-0-545-45170-3 Subj: Activities – playing. Birds – chickens. Format, unusual – board books. Imagination.

Purmell, Ann. *Apple cider making days* ill. by Joanne Friar. Millbrook, 2002. ISBN 978-0-7613-2364-8 Subj: Careers – farmers. Family life – grandfathers. Farms. Food.

Christmas tree farm ill. by Jill Weber. Holiday House, 2006. ISBN 978-0-8234-1886-2 Subj: Activities – working. Careers – farmers. Farms. Holidays – Christmas. Trees.

Maple syrup season ill. by Jill Weber. Holiday, 2008. ISBN 978-0-8234-1891-6 Subj: Family life. Food. Trees.

Where wild babies sleep ill. by Lorianne Siomades. Boyds Mills, 2003. ISBN 978-1-59078-049-7 Subj: Animals – babies. Bedtime. Night. Sleep.

Puttock, Simon. *The baby that roared* ill. by Nadia Shireen. Candlewick, 2012. ISBN 978-0-7636-5903-5 Subj: Animals. Animals – deer. Babies. Monsters.

Big bad wolf is good ill. by Lynne Chapman. Sterling, 2002. ISBN 978-0-8069-0027-8 Subj: Animals. Animals – wolves. Behavior. Friendship.

Goat and Donkey in strawberry sunglasses ill. by Russell Julian. Good Books, 2007. ISBN 978-1-56148-572-7 Subj: Animals – donkeys. Animals – goats. Friendship. Shopping.

Goat and Donkey in the great outdoors ill. by Russell Julian. Good Books, 2007. ISBN 978-1-56148-573-4 Subj: Activities – vacationing. Animals – donkeys. Animals – goats. Friendship.

A ladder to the stars ill. by Alison Jay. Holt, 2001. ISBN 978-0-8050-6783-5 Subj: Activities – dancing. Behavior – wishing. Old age. Stars.

Little lost cowboy ill. by Caroline Jayne Church. Egmont, 2011. ISBN 978-1-60684-259-1 Subj: Animals – coyotes. Behavior – lost.

Miss Fox ill. by Holly Swain. Frances Lincoln, 2006. ISBN 978-1-84507-475-3 Subj: Animals – foxes. Animals – sheep. Careers – teachers. School.

Squeaky clean ill. by Mary McQuillan. Little, 2002. ISBN 978-0-316-78816-8 Subj: Activities – bathing. Animals – pigs. Hygiene.

A story for Hippo ill. by Alison Jay. Scholastic, 2001. ISBN 978-0-439-26219-4 Subj: Animals – hippopotamuses. Animals – monkeys. Death. Emotions – grief. Friendship.

Yours truly, Louisa ill. by Jo Kiddie. HarperCollins, 2009. ISBN 978-0-06-136634-5 Subj: Activities – writing. Animals – pigs. Character traits – cleanliness. Farms. Letters, cards.

Pym, Tasha. *Have you ever seen a sneep?* ill. by Joel Stewart. Farrar, 2009. ISBN 978-0-374-32868-9 Subj: Imagination. Rhyming text.

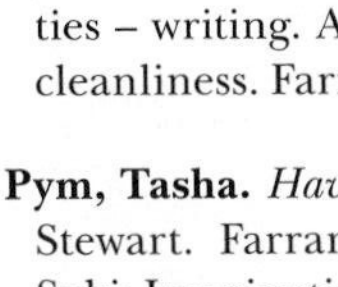

Quackenbush, Robert M. *Batbaby* ill. by author. Random House, 1997. ISBN 978-0-679-98541-9

Subj: Animals – bats. Animals – squirrels. Bedtime. Weather – storms.

First grade jitters ill. by Yan Nascimbene. HarperCollins, 2010. ISBN 978-0-06-077632-9 Subj: Behavior – worrying. School – first day.

Quattlebaum, Mary. *Jo MacDonald had a garden* ill. by Laura J. Bryant. Dawn, 2012. ISBN 978-1-58469-164-8 Subj: Ecology. Gardens, gardening. Songs.

Jo MacDonald hiked in the woods ill. by Laura J. Bryant. Dawn, 2013. ISBN 978-1-58469-334-5 Subj: Activities – hiking. Animals. Forest, woods. Rhyming text. Songs.

Jo MacDonald saw a pond ill. by Laura J. Bryant. Dawn, 2011. ISBN 978-1-58469-150-1 Subj: Lakes, ponds. Songs.

Pirate vs. pirate: the terrific tale of a big, blustery maritime match ill. by Alexandra Boiger. Hyperion/Disney, 2011. ISBN 978-1-4231-2201-2 Subj: Contests. Emotions – love. Pirates.

The shine man ill. by Tim Ladwig. Eerdmans, 2001. ISBN 978-0-8028-5181-9 Subj: Careers – shoe shiners. Character traits – generosity. Holidays – Christmas. Poverty. U.S. history.

Sparks fly high: the legend of Dancing Point ill. by Leonid Gore. Farrar, 2006. ISBN 978-0-374-34452-8 Subj: Activities – dancing. Character traits – pride. Contests. Devil. Folk & fairy tales.

Winter friends ill. by Hiroe Nakata. Random House, 2005. ISBN 978-0-385-90868-9 Subj: Behavior – lost & found possessions. Clothing – gloves, mittens. Friendship. Poetry. Seasons – winter.

Quigley, Mary. *Granddad's fishing buddy* ill. by Stéphane Jorisch. Penguin, 2007. ISBN 978-0-8037-2942-1 Subj: Birds – herons. Family life – grandfathers. Sports – fishing.

Quinton, Sasha. *You and me* (Kindermans, Martine)

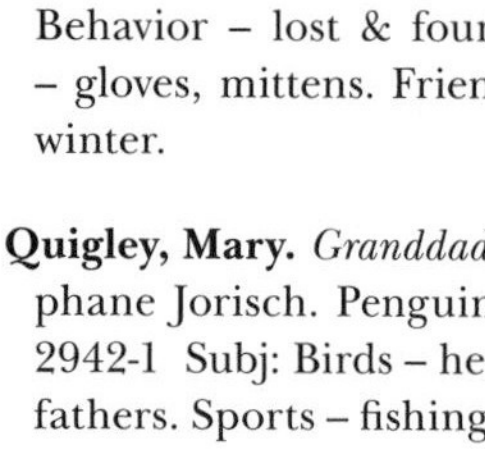

Raab, Brigitte. *Where does pepper come from? and other fun facts* ill. by Manuela Olten. NorthSouth, 2006. ISBN 978-0-7358-2070-8 Subj: Character traits – questioning. Science.

Raczka, Bob. *Art is . . .* ill. with photos. Millbrook, 2003. ISBN 978-0-7613-2874-2 Subj: Art. Rhyming text.

Fall mixed up ill. by Chad Cameron. Carolrhoda, 2011. ISBN 978-0-7613-4606-7 Subj: Picture puzzles. Rhyming text. Seasons – fall.

Guyku: a year of haiku for boys ill. by Peter H. Reynolds. Harcourt, 2010. ISBN 978-0-547-24003-9 Subj: Poetry. Seasons.

No one saw: ordinary things through the eyes of an artist ill. with famous 20th-century works of art. Millbrook, 2002. ISBN 978-0-7613-2370-9 Subj: Art. Careers – artists.

Snowy, blowy winter ill. by Judy Stead. Whitman, 2008. ISBN 978-0-8075-7526-0 Subj: Rhyming text. Seasons – winter. Weather – snow.

Spring things ill. by Judy Stead. Whitman, 2007. ISBN 978-0-8075-7596-3 Subj: Nature. Rhyming text. Seasons – spring.

Summer wonders ill. by Judy Stead. Whitman, 2009. ISBN 978-0-8075-7653-3 Subj: Rhyming text. Seasons – summer.

3-D ABC: a sculptural alphabet ill. with photos. Lerner, 2006. ISBN 978-0-7613-9456-3 Subj: ABC books.

Who loves the fall? ill. by Judy Stead. Whitman, 2007. ISBN 978-0-8075-9037-9 Subj: Rhyming text. Seasons – fall.

Radabaugh, Melinda Beth. *Getting a haircut* ill. with photos. Heinemann, 2003. ISBN 978-1-4034-0225-7 Subj: Careers – barbers. Hair.

Going to a restaurant ill. with photos. Heinemann, 2003. ISBN 978-1-4034-0226-4 Subj: Careers – chefs, cooks. Careers – waiters, waitresses. Food. Restaurants.

Going to school ill. with photos. Heinemann, 2003. ISBN 978-1-4034-0227-1 Subj: Careers – teachers. School – first day.

Going to the library ill. with photos. Heinemann, 2003. ISBN 978-1-4034-0230-1 Subj: Books, reading. Careers – librarians. Libraries.

Sleeping over ill. with photos. Heinemann, 2003. ISBN 978-1-4034-0231-8 Subj: Parties. Sleepovers.

Radcliffe, Theresa. *Bashi, elephant baby* ill. by John Butler. Viking, 1997. ISBN 978-0-670-87054-7 Subj: Animals – babies. Animals – elephants. Family life – mothers. Foreign lands – Africa.

Nanu, penguin chick ill. by John Butler. Viking, 2000. ISBN 978-0-670-88638-8 Subj: Birds – penguins. Foreign lands – Antarctic.

Rader, Laura. *Santa's new suit* ill. by author. HarperCollins, 2000. ISBN 978-0-06-028439-8 Subj:

Clothing – suits. Holidays – Christmas. Humorous stories. Shopping.

Tea for me, tea for you ill. by author. HarperCollins, 2003. ISBN 978-0-06-008634-3 Subj: Animals – pigs. Counting, numbers. Food. Parties. Rhyming text.

Radunsky, Vladimir. *Because . . .* (Baryshnikov, Mikhail)

Manneken pis ill. by author. Atheneum, 2002. ISBN 978-0-689-83193-5 Subj: Folk & fairy tales. Foreign lands – Belgium. War.

One: a nice story about an awful braggart ill. by author. Viking, 2003. ISBN 978-0-670-03564-9 Subj: Animals – armadillos. Character traits – pride. Character traits – vanity.

Ten: a wonderful story ill. by author. Viking, 2002. ISBN 978-0-670-03563-2 Subj: Animals – armadillos. Babies. Birth.

You? ill. by author. Harcourt, 2009. ISBN 978-0-15-205177-8 Subj: Animals – dogs. Emotions – loneliness.

Radzinski, Kandy. *Where to sleep* ill. by author. Sleeping Bear, 2009. ISBN 978-1-58536-436-7 Subj: Animals – cats. Rhyming text. Sleep.

Rael, Elsa Okon. *Rivka's first Thanksgiving* ill. by Maryann Kovalski. McElderry, 2001. ISBN 978-0-689-83901-6 Subj: Holidays – Thanksgiving. Immigrants. Jewish culture.

Raff, Courtney Granet. *Giant of the sea* ill. by Shawn Gould. Soundprints, 2002. ISBN 978-1-931465-71-7 Subj: Animals – whales. Family life – mothers. Sea & seashore.

Raffi. *Baby beluga* ill. by Ashley Wolff. Words & music by author. Crown, 1990. ISBN 978-0-517-57840-7 Subj: Animals – endangered animals. Animals – whales. Foreign lands – Arctic. Music. Songs.

Down by the bay ill. by Nadine Bernard Westcott. Words & music by author. Crown, 1987. ISBN 978-0-517-56644-2 Subj: Music. Songs.

Everything grows photos by Bruce McMillan. Words & music by author. Crown, 1989. ISBN 978-0-517-57275-7 Subj: Music. Songs.

Like me and you ill. by Lillian Hoban. Words & music by Raffi & Debi Pike. Crown, 1994. ISBN 978-0-517-59588-6 Subj: Foreign lands. Letters, cards. Music. Songs.

One light, one sun ill. by Eugenie Fernandes. Words & music by author. Crown, 1988. ISBN 978-0-517-56785-2 Subj: Family life. Music. Songs.

Rise and shine ill. by Eugenie Fernandes. Words & music by Raffi, & Bonnie & Bert Simpson. Crown, 1996. ISBN 978-0-517-70940-5 Subj: Morning. Music. Songs.

Shake my sillies out ill. by David Allender. Words & music by author. Crown, 1987. ISBN 978-0-517-56646-6 Subj: Music. Songs.

Wheels on the bus ill. by Sylvie Wickstrom. Words & music by author. Crown, 1988. ISBN 978-0-517-56784-5 Subj: Foreign lands – France. Music. Songs.

Ragged Bear's book of nursery rhymes sel. by Diz Wallis; ill. by Diz Wallis. Ragged Bears, 2001. ISBN 978-1-929927-36-4 Subj: Nursery rhymes.

Rahaman, Vashanti. *Divali rose* ill. by Jamel Akib. Boyds Mills, 2008. ISBN 978-1-59078-524-9 Subj: Character traits – honesty. Family life – grandfathers. Foreign lands – Trinidad. Holidays – Divali. Prejudice. Religion – Hinduism.

O Christmas tree ill. by Frané Lessac. Boyds Mills, 1996. ISBN 978-1-56397-237-9 Subj: Foreign lands – Caribbean Islands. Foreign lands – West Indies. Holidays – Christmas. Islands.

Read for me, Mama ill. by Lori McElrath-Eslick. Boyds Mills, 1997. ISBN 978-1-56397-313-0 Subj: Books, reading. Family life – mothers. Libraries.

Ramirez, Melissa Bourbon. *The flight of the sunflower* ill. by Nadine Takvorian. All About Kids, 2002. ISBN 978-0-9700863-0-3 Subj: Flowers. Seeds. Weather – wind.

Ramos, Jorge. *I'm just like my mom / Me parezco tanto a mi mamá; I'm just like my dad / Me parezco tanto a mi papá* ill. by Akemi Gutierrez. HarperCollins, 2008. ISBN 978-0-06-123968-7 Subj: Family life – parents. Format, unusual.

Ramos, Mario. *I am so handsome* ill. by author. Gecko, 2012. ISBN 978-1-87757-919-6 Subj: Animals – wolves. Character traits – pride. Character traits – vanity. Folk & fairy tales.

I am so strong ill. by author. Gecko, 2011. ISBN 978-0-9582-7877-5 Subj: Animals – wolves. Behavior – bullying, teasing. Dragons.

Ramsden, Ashley, reteller. *Seven fathers* ill. by Ed Young. Roaring Brook, 2011. ISBN 978-1-59643-544-5 Subj: Behavior – lost. Character traits – persistence. Folk & fairy tales. Old age.

Ramsey, Calvin Alexander. *Belle, the last mule at Gee's Bend: a civil rights story* by Calvin Alexander Ramsey and Bettye Stroud ill. by John Holyfield. Candlewick, 2011. ISBN 978-0-7636-4058-3 Subj: Animals – mules. Ethnic groups in the U.S. – African Americans. U.S. history. Violence, nonviolence.

Ruth and the Green Book ill. by Floyd Cooper. Carolrhoda, 2010. ISBN 978-0-7613-5255-6 Subj:

Activities – traveling. Ethnic groups in the U.S. – African Americans. Prejudice. U.S. history.

Rand, Betseygail. *Big Bunny* by Betseygail Rand and Colleen Rand ill. by C. S. W. Rand. Tricycle, 2011. ISBN 978-1-58246-376-6 Subj: Animals – rabbits. Behavior – running away. Concepts – size. Eggs. Holidays – Easter.

Rand, Colleen. *Big Bunny* (Rand, Betseygail)

Rand, Gloria. *Baby in a basket* ill. by Ted Rand. Cobblehill, 1997. ISBN 978-0-525-65233-5 Subj: Accidents. Alaska. Babies. Family life. U.S. history.

Little Flower ill. by R. W. Alley. Holt, 2002. ISBN 978-0-8050-6480-3 Subj: Accidents. Animals – pigs. Pets.

A pen pal for Max ill. by Ted Rand. Holt, 2005. ISBN 978-0-8050-7586-1 Subj: Foreign lands – Chile. Friendship. Letters, cards. Pen pals.

Prince William ill. by Ted Rand. Holt, 1992. ISBN 978-0-8050-1841-7 Subj: Alaska. Animals – mice. Ecology. Oil.

Sailing home ill. by Ted Rand. NorthSouth, 2001. ISBN 978-0-7358-1540-7 Subj: Boats, ships. Family life. Sailors. Sea & seashore.

Randall, Alison L. *The wheat doll* ill. by Bill Farnsworth. Peachtree, 2008. ISBN 978-1-56145-456-3 Subj: Behavior – lost & found possessions. Toys – dolls. U.S. history – frontier & pioneer life. Weather – storms.

Randall, Angel. *Snow angels* by Angel Randall and Chris Schoebinger ill. by Brandon Dorman. Shadow Mountain, 2011. ISBN 978-1-60641-046-2 Subj: Angels. Character traits – helpfulness.

Randall, Ronne. *The Hanukkah mice* ill. by Maggie Kneen. Chronicle, 2002. ISBN 978-0-8118-3623-4 Subj: Animals – mice. Holidays – Hanukkah. Jewish culture. Rhyming text.

Rania, Queen, consort of Abdullah II, King of Jordan. *The sandwich swap* by Rania, Queen, consort of Abdullah II, King of Jordan and Kelly DiPucchio ill. by Tricia Tusa. Hyperion/Disney, 2010. ISBN 978-1-4231-2484-9 Subj: Character traits – being different. Food. Friendship. School.

Rankin, Joan. *First day* ill. by author. McElderry, 2002. ISBN 978-0-689-84563-5 Subj: Animals. Animals – dogs. School – first day. School – nursery.

Wow! It's great being a duck ill. by author. McElderry, 1998. ISBN 978-0-689-81756-4 Subj: Animals – foxes. Birds – ducks.

You're somebody special, Walliwigs! ill. by author. McElderry, 1999. ISBN 978-0-689-82230-8 Subj: Animals. Birds – chickens. Birds – parakeets, parrots. Character traits – being different. Character traits – individuality. Emotions – love.

Rankin, Laura. *Fluffy and Baron* ill. by author. Penguin, 2006. ISBN 978-0-8037-2953-7 Subj: Animals – dogs. Birds – ducks. Friendship.

The handmade counting book ill. by author. Dial, 1998. ISBN 978-0-8037-2311-5 Subj: Counting, numbers. Disabilities – deafness. Language.

Ruthie and the (not so) teeny tiny lie ill. by author. Bloomsbury, 2007. ISBN 978-1-59990-010-0 Subj: Animals – foxes. Behavior – lying. Character traits – honesty. School.

Ransom, Candice F. *The Christmas dolls* ill. by Moira Fain. Walker, 1998. ISBN 978-0-8027-8661-6 Subj: Family life – mothers. Holidays – Christmas. Toys – dolls.

Mother Teresa ill. by Elaine Verstraete. Carolrhoda, 2001. ISBN 978-1-57505-441-4 Subj: Careers – nuns. Religion.

The promise quilt ill. by Ellen Beier. Walker, 1999. ISBN 978-0-8027-8695-1 Subj: Activities – making things. Activities – sewing. Quilts. U.S. history.

Tractor day ill. by Laura J. Bryant. Walker, 2007. ISBN 978-0-8027-8090-4 Subj: Farms. Rhyming text. Tractors.

Ransom, Jeanie Franz. *Don't squeal unless it's a big deal: a tale of tattletales* ill. by Jackie Urbanovic. Magination, 2006. ISBN 978-1-59147-239-1 Subj: Animals – pigs. Behavior – fighting, arguing. Behavior – gossip.

I don't want to talk about it ill. by Kathryn Kunz Finney. Magination, 2000. ISBN 978-1-55798-664-1 Subj: Divorce. Emotions – love. Family life – parents.

What do parents do? (. . . When you're not home) ill. by Cyd Moore. Peachtree, 2007. ISBN 978-1-56145-409-9 Subj: Family life – parents. Humorous stories.

Ransome, Arthur. *The fool of the world and the flying ship* ill. by Uri Shulevitz. Farrar, 1968. ISBN 978-0-374-32442-1 Subj: Activities – flying. Boats, ships. Caldecott award books. Character traits – cleverness. Folk & fairy tales. Foreign lands – Ukraine. Royalty – tsars.

Ransome, James. *Gunner, football hero* ill. by author. Holiday House, 2010. ISBN 978-0-8234-2053-7 Subj: Sports – football.

My teacher ill. by author. Dial, 2012. ISBN 978--08037-3259-9 Subj: Careers – teachers. School.

New red bike! ill. by author. Holiday House, 2011. ISBN 978-0-8234-2226-5 Subj: Behavior – sharing. Sports – bicycling.

Rao, Sandhya. *My mother's sari* ill. by Nina Sabnani. NorthSouth, 2006. ISBN 978-0-7358-2101-9 Subj: Clothing. Ethnic groups in the U.S. – East Indian Americans. Family life – daughters. Family life – mothers.

Raposo, Joe. *Sing!* ill. by Tom Lichtenheld. Holt, 2013. ISBN 978-0-8050-9071-0 Subj: Activities – singing. Music. Songs.

Rappaport, Doreen. *Abe's honest words: the life of Abraham Lincoln* ill. by Kadir Nelson. Hyperion, 2008. ISBN 978-1-4231-0408-7 Subj: Language. U.S. history.

Dirt on their skirts by Doreen Rappaport and Lyndall Callan ill. by E. B. Lewis. Dial, 2000. ISBN 978-0-8037-2042-8 Subj: Sports – baseball.

Eleanor, quiet no more: the life of Eleanor Roosevelt ill. by Gary Kelley. Hyperion, 2009. ISBN 978-0-7868-5141-6 Subj: Character traits – perseverance. Character traits – shyness. U.S. history.

Freedom river ill. by Bryan Collier. Hyperion, 2000. ISBN 978-0-7868-0350-7 Subj: Character traits – bravery. Character traits – freedom. Ethnic groups in the U.S. – African Americans. Slavery. U.S. history.

Freedom ship ill. by Curtis James. Hyperion, 2006. ISBN 978-0-7868-0645-4 Subj: Boats, ships. Character traits – freedom. Ethnic groups in the U.S. – African Americans. Slavery. U.S. history. War.

Helen's big world: the life of Helen Keller ill. by Matt Tavares. Disney/Hyperion, 2012. ISBN 978-0-7868-0890-8 Subj: Careers – teachers. Disabilities – blindness. Disabilities – deafness. U.S. history.

Jack's path of courage: the life of John F. Kennedy ill. by Matt Tavares. Hyperion/Disney, 2010. ISBN 978-1-4231-2272-2 Subj: Character traits – bravery. U.S. history.

Lady Liberty: a biography ill. by Matt Tavares. Candlewick, 2008. ISBN 978-0-7636-2530-6 Subj: Careers – sculptors. U.S. history.

The long-haired girl ill. by Ming-Yi Yang. Dial, 1995. ISBN 978-0-8037-1412-0 Subj: Behavior – secrets. Character traits – bravery. Folk & fairy tales. Foreign lands – China. Weather – droughts.

Martin's big words ill. by Bryan Collier. Hyperion, 2001. ISBN 978-0-7868-2591-2 Subj: Caldecott award honor books. Careers – clergy. Ethnic groups in the U.S. – African Americans. Language. U.S. history.

The new king ill. by E. B. Lewis. Dial, 1995. ISBN 978-0-8037-1461-8 Subj: Death. Emotions – grief. Family life – fathers. Folk & fairy tales. Foreign lands – Madagascar. Royalty.

The school is not white! a true story of the civil rights movement ill. by Curtis James. Hyperion, 2005. ISBN 978-0-7868-1838-9 Subj: Ethnic groups in the U.S. – African Americans. Prejudice. School.

The secret seder ill. by Emily Arnold McCully. Hyperion, 2005. ISBN 978-0-7868-0777-2 Subj: Character traits – bravery. Foreign lands – France. Holidays – Passover. Jewish culture. War.

To dare mighty things: the life of Theodore Roosevelt ill. by C. F. Payne. Hyperion/Disney, 2013. ISBN 978-1-4231-2488-7 Subj: Character traits – ambition. Character traits – perseverance. U.S. history.

We are the many ill. by Cornelius Van Wright and Ying-Hwa Hu. HarperCollins, 2002. ISBN 978-0-06-001139-0 Subj: Indians of North America. U.S. history.

Raschka, Chris. *Arlene sardine* ill. by author. Orchard, 1998. ISBN 978-0-531-33111-8 Subj: Fish. Food. Self-concept.

A ball for Daisy ill. by author. Random House, 2011. ISBN 978-0-375-85861-1 Subj: Animals – dogs. Caldecott award books. Toys – balls. Wordless.

The blushful hippopotamus ill. by author. Orchard, 1996. ISBN 978-0-531-08882-1 Subj: Animals – hippopotamuses. Emotions – embarrassment. Family life – brothers & sisters. Sibling rivalry.

Can't sleep ill. by author. Orchard, 1995. ISBN 978-0-531-08779-4 Subj: Animals – dogs. Bedtime. Emotions – fear. Moon. Night.

Charlie Parker played be bop ill. by author. Watts, 1992. ISBN 978-0-531-08599-8 Subj: Careers – musicians. Ethnic groups in the U.S. – African Americans. Music. Musical instruments – saxophones.

Daisy gets lost ill. by author. Random House, 2013. ISBN 978-0-449-81741-4 Subj: Animals – dogs. Behavior – lost. Emotions – fear. Wordless.

Everyone can learn to ride a bicycle ill. by author. Random House, 2013. ISBN 978-0-375-87007-1 Subj: Character traits – persistence. Family life – fathers. Sports – bicycling.

Five for a little one ill. by author. Simon & Schuster, 2006. ISBN 978-0-689-84599-4 Subj: Animals – rabbits. Counting, numbers. Senses.

Hip Hop Dog ill. by Vladimir Radunsky. HarperCollins, 2010. ISBN 978-0-06-123963-2 Subj: Animals – dogs. Music. Rhyming text.

John Coltrane's giant steps ill. by author. Atheneum, 2002. ISBN 978-0-689-84598-7 Subj: Animals – cats. Music. Musical instruments – bands. Weather – rain. Weather – snow.

Little black crow ill. by author. Simon & Schuster, 2010. ISBN 978-0-689-84601-4 Subj: Birds – crows. Character traits – questioning. Imagination. Rhyming text.

Moosey Moose ill. by author. Hyperion, 2000. ISBN 978-0-7868-0581-5 Subj: Animals. Animals – moose. Clothing – pants.

Mysterious Thelonious ill. by author. Orchard, 1997. ISBN 978-0-531-33057-9 Subj: Careers – musicians. Concepts – color. Ethnic groups in the U.S. – African Americans.

New York is English, Chattanooga is Creek ill. by author. Simon & Schuster, 2005. ISBN 978-0-689-84600-7 Subj: Cities, towns. Names. Parties. U.S. history.

The purple balloon ill. by author. Random House, 2007. ISBN 978-0-375-84146-0 Subj: Death. Emotions – grief. Illness.

Ring! Yo? ill. by author. DK, 2000. ISBN 978-0-7894-2614-7 Subj: Emotions. Friendship. Telephone.

Sluggy Slug ill. by author. Hyperion, 2000. ISBN 978-0-7868-0584-6 Subj: Animals – slugs.

Talk to me about the alphabet ill. by author. Holt, 2003. ISBN 978-0-8050-6782-8 Subj: ABC books. Noise, sounds.

Waffle ill. by author. Atheneum, 2001. ISBN 978-0-689-83838-5 Subj: Behavior – worrying. Character traits – bravery. Emotions – fear. Self-concept.

Whaley Whale ill. by author. Hyperion, 2000. ISBN 978-0-7868-0583-9 Subj: Animals – whales. Behavior – hiding.

Wormy Worm ill. by author. Hyperion, 2000. ISBN 978-0-7868-0582-2 Subj: Animals – worms.

Yo! Yes? ill. by author. Orchard, 1993. ISBN 978-0-531-08619-3 Subj: Caldecott award honor books. Emotions. Ethnic groups in the U.S. – African Americans. Friendship.

Rash, Andy. *Agent A to Agent Z* ill. by author. Scholastic, 2004. ISBN 978-0-439-36882-7 Subj: ABC books. Careers – detectives. Rhyming text.

Are you a horse? ill. by author. Scholastic, 2009. ISBN 978-0-439-72417-3 Subj: Animals. Cowboys, cowgirls.

Rasmussen, Halfdan. *The ladder* ill. by Pierre Pratt. Candlewick, 2006. ISBN 978-0-7636-2282-4 Subj: Format, unusual. Imagination. Rhyming text.

Rathmann, Peggy. *Good night, Gorilla* ill. by author. Putnam, 1994. ISBN 978-0-399-22445-4 Subj: Animals. Careers – zookeepers. Night. Zoos.

Officer Buckle and Gloria ill. by author. Putnam, 1995. ISBN 978-0-399-22616-8 Subj: Animals – dogs. Behavior – sharing. Caldecott award books. Careers – police officers. School.

Ruby the copycat ill. by author. Scholastic, 1991. ISBN 978-0-590-43747-9 Subj: Animals – cats. Behavior – imitation. School.

10 minutes till bedtime ill. by author. Putnam, 1998. ISBN 978-0-399-23103-2 Subj: Animals – hamsters. Bedtime. Pets.

Rau, Dana Meachen. *Chilly Charlie* ill. by Martin Lemelman. Children's Press, 2001. ISBN 978-0-516-22210-3 Subj: Concepts – cold & heat. Rhyming text.

Clown around ill. by Nate Evans. Compass Point, 2001. ISBN 978-0-7565-0074-0 Subj: Circus. Clowns, jesters. Rhyming text.

Dr. Seuss ill. with photos. Children's Press, 2003. ISBN 978-0-516-22593-7 Subj: Careers – writers. Careers – illustrators.

Explore in a cave photos by Romie Flanagan. Rourke, 2000. ISBN 978-1-57103-318-5 Subj: Caves.

Flying ill. with photos. Benchmark, 2006. ISBN 978-0-7614-2319-5 Subj: Activities – flying. Rebuses.

I'll make you a card ill. by Jan Bryan-Hunt. Compass Point, 2002. ISBN 978-0-7565-0172-3 Subj: Days of the week, months of the year. Holidays. Letters, cards. Rhyming text.

In the yard ill. by Elizabeth Wolf. Compass Point, 2001. ISBN 978-0-7565-0116-7 Subj: Character traits – helpfulness. Family life – parents. Seasons.

Lots of balloons ill. by Jayoung Cho. Compass Point, 2001. ISBN 978-0-7565-0117-4 Subj: Concepts – color. Toys – balloons.

Mars photos by author. Compass Point, 2002. ISBN 978-0-7565-0199-0 Subj: Planets. Science.

Neil Armstrong ill. with photos. Children's Press, 2003. ISBN 978-0-516-22592-0 Subj: Careers – astronauts. Space & space ships.

Rectangles ill. with photos. Marshall Cavendish, 2006. ISBN 978-0-7614-2282-2 Subj: Concepts – shape.

Riding ill. with photos. Benchmark, 2006. ISBN 978-0-7614-2317-1 Subj: Rebuses. Transportation.

Rolling ill. with photos. Benchmark, 2006. ISBN 978-0-7614-2314-0 Subj: Concepts – motion. Rebuses.

Rubber duck ill. by Patrick Girouard. Compass Point, 2002. ISBN 978-0-7565-0121-1 Subj: Rhyming text. Toys.

The secret code ill. by Bari Weissman. Children's Press, 1998. ISBN 978-0-516-20700-1 Subj: Books, reading. Disabilities – blindness.

Shoo crow, shoo! ill. by Mary Rojas. Compass Point, 2001. ISBN 978-0-7565-0072-6 Subj: Rhyming text. Scarecrows.

Stroll by the sea photos by author. Rourke, 2000. ISBN 978-1-57103-320-8 Subj: Nature. Sea & seashore – beaches.

Ways to go ill. by Jane Conteh-Morgan. Compass Point, 2001. ISBN 978-0-7565-0071-9 Subj: Transportation.

Rausch, Molly. *My cold went on vacation* ill. by Nora Krug. Penguin, 2011. ISBN 978-0-399-25474-1 Subj: Humorous stories. Illness – cold (disease).

Rauss, Ron. *Can I just take a nap?* ill. by Rob Shepperson. Simon & Schuster, 2012. ISBN 978-1-4424-3497-4 Subj: Noise, sounds. Rhyming text. Sleep.

Rave, Friederike. *Outfoxing the fox* ill. by author. NorthSouth, 2010. ISBN 978-0-7358-2295-5 Subj: Animals – foxes. Birds – chickens.

Raven, Margot Theis. *Mercedes and the chocolate pilot* ill. by Gijsbert van Frankenhuyzen. Sleeping Bear, 2002. ISBN 978-1-58536-069-7 Subj: Airplanes, airports. Careers – airplane pilots. Foreign lands – Germany. War.

Night boat to freedom ill. by E. B. Lewis. Farrar, 2006. ISBN 978-0-374-31266-4 Subj: Ethnic groups in the U.S. – African Americans. Slavery. U.S. history.

Ravishankar, Anushka. *Elephants never forget!* ill. by Christiane Pieper. Houghton, 2008. ISBN 978-81-86-21104-5 Subj: Animals – buffaloes. Animals – elephants.

Rawlinson, Julia. *Fletcher and the falling leaves* ill. by Tiphanie Beeke. HarperCollins, 2006. ISBN 978-0-06-113401-2 Subj: Animals – foxes. Seasons – fall. Trees.

Fletcher and the snowflake Christmas ill. by Tiphanie Beeke. HarperCollins, 2010. ISBN 978-0-06-199033-5 Subj: Animals – foxes. Friendship. Holidays – Christmas. Santa Claus. Seasons – winter.

Fletcher and the springtime blossoms ill. by Tiphanie Beeke. Greenwillow, 2009. ISBN 978-0-06-168855-3 Subj: Animals – foxes. Flowers. Seasons – spring.

Mule school ill. by Lynne Chapman. Good Books, 2008. ISBN 978-1-56148-597-0 Subj: Animals – mules. Character traits – being different. School.

A surprise for Rosie ill. by Tim Warnes. Tiger Tales, 2005. ISBN 978-1-58925-046-8 Subj: Activities – ballooning. Animals – rabbits.

Rawson, Katherine. *If you were a parrot* ill. by Sherry Rogers. Sylvan Dell, 2006. ISBN 978-0-9764943-9-3 Subj: Birds – parakeets, parrots.

Ray, Deborah Kogan. *Lily's garden* ill. by author. Roaring Brook, 2002. ISBN 978-0-7613-2653-3 Subj: Food. Gardens, gardening. Letters, cards.

Ray, Jane. *The apple-pip princess* ill. by author. Candlewick, 2008. ISBN 978-0-7636-3747-7 Subj: Folk & fairy tales. Food. Royalty – princesses. Trees. Weather – droughts.

The dollhouse fairy ill. by author. Candlewick, 2010. ISBN 978-0-7636-4411-6 Subj: Behavior – worrying. Fairies. Family life – fathers. Illness.

Ray, Karen. *Sleep song* ill. by Rhonda Mitchell. Orchard, 1995. ISBN 978-0-531-08728-2 Subj: Activities. Bedtime. Games. Rhyming text.

Ray, Mary Lyn. *All aboard* ill. by Amiko Hirao. Little, 2002. ISBN 978-0-316-73507-0 Subj: Animals – rabbits. Toys. Trains.

Basket moon ill. by Barbara Cooney. Little, 1999. ISBN 978-0-316-73521-6 Subj: Activities – making things. Careers. Family life – fathers. Mountains.

Boom! ill. by Steven Salerno. Disney/Hyperion, 2013. ISBN 978-1-4231-6238-4 Subj: Animals – dogs. Character traits – bravery. Emotions – fear. Weather – lightning, thunder.

Christmas farm ill. by Barry Root. Harcourt, 2008. ISBN 978-0-15-216290-0 Subj: Holidays – Christmas. Trees.

Mud ill. by Lauren Stringer. Harcourt, 1996. ISBN 978-0-15-256263-2 Subj: Poetry. Seasons – spring.

Red rubber boot day ill. by Lauren Stringer. Harcourt, 2000. ISBN 978-0-15-213756-4 Subj: Activities – playing. Clothing – boots. Weather – rain.

Shaker boy ill. by Jeanette Winter. Harcourt, 1994. ISBN 978-0-15-276921-5 Subj: Ethnic groups in the U.S. – Shakers. Music. Religion. Songs. U.S. history.

Stars ill. by Marla Frazee. Simon & Schuster, 2011. ISBN 978-1-4424-2249-1 Subj: Concepts – shape. Night. Sky. Stars.

Raye, Rebekah. *The very best bed* ill. by author. Tilbury, 2006. ISBN 978-0-88448-284-0 Subj: Animals. Animals – squirrels. Bedtime. Homes, houses.

Rayner, Catherine. *Abigail* ill. by author. Tiger Tales, 2013. ISBN 978-1-58925-147-2 Subj: Animals. Animals – giraffes. Counting, numbers.

Augustus and his smile ill. by author. Good Books, 2006. ISBN 978-1-56148-510-9 Subj: Anatomy – faces. Animals – tigers. Emotions – happiness.

The bear who shared ill. by author. Penguin, 2011. ISBN 978-0-8037-3576-7 Subj: Animals – bears. Animals – mice. Animals – raccoons. Behavior – sharing. Friendship.

Ernest, the moose who doesn't fit ill. by author. Farrar, 2010. ISBN 978-0-374-32217-5 Subj: Animals – moose. Behavior – resourcefulness. Concepts – size. Format, unusual – toy & movable books.

Solomon Crocodile ill. by author. Farrar, 2011. ISBN 978-0-374-38064-9 Subj: Activities – playing. Friendship. Reptiles – alligators, crocodiles.

Reagan, Jean. *How to babysit a grandpa* ill. by Lee Wildish. Knopf, 2012. ISBN 978-0-375-86713-2 Subj: Activities – babysitting. Family life – grandfathers.

Reasoner, Charles. *Animal babies!* ill. by author. Rourke, 2011. ISBN 978-1-61236-054-6 Subj: Animals – babies.

One blue fish: a colorful counting book ill. by author. Simon & Schuster, 2010. ISBN 978-1-4169-9672-9 Subj: Concepts – color. Counting, numbers. Format, unusual – toy & movable books.

Peek-a-boo monsters ill. by author and Marina LeRay. Capstone, 2013. ISBN 978-1-47952-170-8 Subj: Format, unusual – board books. Monsters. Rhyming text.

Rechner, Amy. *Out and about at the aquarium* ill. by Becky Shipe. Picture Window, 2004. ISBN 978-1-4048-0298-8 Subj: Animals. Aquariums. Fish. School – field trips.

Recorvits, Helen. *My name is Yoon* ill. by Gabi Swiatkowska. Farrar, 2003. ISBN 978-0-374-35114-4 Subj: Ethnic groups in the U.S. – Korean Americans. Immigrants. Names. School – first day.

Yoon and the Christmas mitten ill. by Gabi Swiatkowska. Farrar, 2006. ISBN 978-0-374-38688-7 Subj: Ethnic groups in the U.S. – Korean Americans. Holidays – Christmas. Immigrants.

Yoon and the jade bracelet ill. by Gabi Swiatkowska. Farrar, 2008. ISBN 978-0-374-38689-4 Subj: Behavior – bullying, teasing. Ethnic groups in the U.S. – Korean Americans. Jewelry. School.

Redding, Sue. *Up above and down below* ill. by author. Chronicle, 2006. ISBN 978-0-8118-4876-3 Subj: Concepts – up & down. Rhyming text.

Redeker, Kent. *Don't squish the sasquatch!* ill. by Bob Staake. Disney/Hyperion, 2012. ISBN 978-1-4231-5232-3 Subj: Buses. Humorous stories. Monsters.

Redmond, E. S. *The Unruly Queen* ill. by E. S. Redmond. Candlewick, 2012. ISBN 978-0-7636-3445-2 Subj: Behavior – misbehavior. Rhyming text.

Reed, Lynn Rowe. *Basil's birds* ill. by author. Marshall Cavendish, 2010. ISBN 978-0-7614-5627-8 Subj: Birds. Careers – custodians, janitors. School.

Color chaos! ill. by author. Holiday House, 2010. ISBN 978-0-8234-2257-9 Subj: Concepts – color. School.

Pedro, his perro, and the alphabet sombrero ill. by author. Hyperion, 1995. ISBN 978-0-7868-2058-0 Subj: ABC books. Animals – dogs. Birthdays. Clothing – hats. Foreign languages.

Please don't upset P.U. Zorilla! ill. by author. Random House, 2006. ISBN 978-0-375-93654-8 Subj: Animals – skunks. Careers.

Roscoe and the pelican rescue ill. by author. Holiday House, 2011. ISBN 978-0-8234-2352-1 Subj: Birds – pelicans. Character traits – kindness to animals. Ecology.

Thelonius Turkey lives! (on Felicia Ferguson's farm) ill. by author. Random House, 2005. ISBN 978-0-375-93126-0 Subj: Birds – turkeys. Farms. Holidays – Thanksgiving.

Reed, Neil. *The midnight unicorn* ill. by author. Sterling, 2006. ISBN 978-1-4027-3218-8 Subj: Imagination. Mythical creatures – unicorns.

Reed-Jones, Carol. *The tree in the ancient forest* ill. by Christopher Canyon. Dawn, 1995. ISBN 978-1-883220-32-7 Subj: Ecology. Forest, woods. Trees.

Rees, Douglas. *Jeannette Claus saves Christmas* ill. by Olivier Latyk. Simon & Schuster, 2010. ISBN 978-1-4169-2686-3 Subj: Behavior – resourcefulness. Holidays – Christmas. Illness. Santa Claus.

Reeves, Howard W. *There was an old witch* ill. by David Catrow. Hyperion, 1998. ISBN 978-0-7868-2387-1 Subj: Holidays – Halloween. Rhyming text. Witches.

Regan, Dana. *Monkey see, monkey do* ill. by author. Grosset, 2000. ISBN 978-0-448-42414-9 Subj: Animals – monkeys. Rhyming text.

Regan, Dian Curtis. *Barnyard slam* ill. by Paul Meisel. Holiday House, 2009. ISBN 978-0-8234-1907-4 Subj: Animals. Farms. Poetry.

How do you know it's Halloween? ill. by Fumi Kosaka. Simon & Schuster, 2002. ISBN 978-0-689-84570-3 Subj: Format, unusual – toy & movable books. Holidays – Halloween. Humorous stories. Riddles & jokes.

The Snow Blew Inn ill. by Doug Cushman. Holiday House, 2011. ISBN 978-0-8234-2351-4 Subj: Animals. Animals – cats. Sleepovers. Weather – blizzards.

Regan, Lara Jo. *What is Mr. Winkle?* photos by author. Random House, 2001. ISBN 978-0-375-

81554-6 Subj: Animals – dogs. Humorous stories.

A Winkle in time photos by Michael Regan. Random House, 2003. ISBN 978-0-375-92487-3 Subj: Activities. Animals – dogs.

Reibstein, Mark. *Wabi Sabi* ill. by Ed Young. Little, Brown, 2008. ISBN 978-0-316-11825-5 Subj: Activities – traveling. Animals. Animals – cats. Character traits – questioning.

Reich, Susanna. *Minette's feast: the delicious story of Julia Child and her cat* ill. by Amy Bates. Abrams, 2012. ISBN 978-1-4197-0177-1 Subj: Activities – baking, cooking. Animals – cats. Careers – chefs, cooks. Food. Foreign lands – France.

Reichert, Amy. *Take your mama to work today* ill. by Alexandra Boiger. Atheneum, 2012. ISBN 978-1-4169-7095-8 Subj: Activities – working. Careers. Family life – mothers. Humorous stories.

Reid, Barbara. *The party* ill. by author. Scholastic, 1999. ISBN 978-0-590-97801-9 Subj: Family life. Parties. Rhyming text.

Perfect snow ill. by author. Whitman, 2011. ISBN 978-0-8075-6492-9 Subj: Character traits – cooperation. School. Snowmen. Weather – snow.

Picture a tree ill. by author. Whitman, 2013. ISBN 978-0-8075-6526-1 Subj: Trees.

Reid, Margarette S. *Lots and lots of coins* ill. by True Kelley. Penguin, 2011. ISBN 978-0-525-47879-9 Subj: Behavior – collecting things. Counting, numbers. Money.

Reider, Katja. *The big little sneeze* ill. by Wolfgang Slawski. NorthSouth, 2002. ISBN 978-0-7358-1629-9 Subj: Animals. Animals – bears. Character traits – helpfulness. Illness.

Snail started it! by Katja Reider and Angela von Roehl ill. by Angela von Roehl. NorthSouth, 1999. ISBN 978-1-55858-707-6 Subj: Animals. Animals – snails. Behavior. Cumulative tales.

Reidy, Hannah. *All sorts of clothes* ill. by Emma Dodd. Picture Window, 2005. ISBN 978-1-4048-1063-1 Subj: Clothing.

Reidy, Jean. *All through my town* ill. by Leo Timmers. Bloomsbury, 2013. ISBN 978-1-59990-785-7 Subj: Animals – rabbits. Cities, towns. Rhyming text.

Light up the night ill. by Margaret Chodos-Irvine. Hyperion/Disney, 2011. ISBN 978-1-4231-2024-7 Subj: Bedtime. Cumulative tales. Imagination. Rhyming text. Space & space ships.

Time out for monsters! ill. by Robert Neubecker. Hyperion/Disney, 2012. ISBN 978-1-4231-3127-4 Subj: Activities – drawing. Behavior – misbehavior. Imagination.

Too pickley! ill. by Geneviève Leloup. Bloomsbury, 2010. ISBN 978-1-59990-309-5 Subj: Behavior. Food. Rhyming text.

Too purpley! ill. by Geneviève Leloup. Bloomsbury, 2010. ISBN 978-1-59990-307-1 Subj: Behavior – indecision. Character traits – appearance. Clothing. Rhyming text.

Reinen, Judy. *Bow wow* ill. with photos. Little, 2001. ISBN 978-0-316-83290-8 Subj: Activities. Animals – dogs.

Meow ill. with photos. Little, 2001. ISBN 978-0-316-83342-4 Subj: Activities. Animals – cats.

Reiner, Carl. *Tell me a scary story — but not too scary!* ill. by James Bennett. Little, 2003. ISBN 978-0-316-83329-5 Subj: Ghosts. Monsters.

Reinhart, Matthew. *Animal popposites* ill. by author. Simon & Schuster, 2002. ISBN 978-0-689-84423-2 Subj: Animals. Concepts – opposites. Format, unusual – toy & movable books. Language.

Encyclopedia prehistorica: dinosaurs (Sabuda, Robert)

Encyclopedia prehistorica: mega-beasts (Sabuda, Robert)

Encyclopedia prehistorica: sharks and other seamonsters (Sabuda, Robert)

Fairies and magical creatures by Matthew Reinhart and Robert Sabuda ill. by authors. Candlewick, 2008. ISBN 978-0-7636-3172-7 Subj: Fairies. Format, unusual – toy & movable books. Mythical creatures.

Gods and heroes by Matthew Reinhart and Robert Sabuda ill. by authors. Candlewick, 2010. ISBN 978-0-7636-3171-0 Subj: Format, unusual – toy & movable books. Mythical creatures.

Reisberg, Joanne A. *Zachary Zormer shape transformer: a math adventure* ill. by David Hohn. Charlesbridge, 2006. ISBN 978-1-57091-875-9 Subj: Concepts – shape. Counting, numbers.

Reiser, Bob. *David gets his drum* (Francis, Panama)

Reiser, Lynn. *Any kind of dog* ill. by author. Greenwillow, 1992. ISBN 978-0-688-10915-8 Subj: Animals – dogs. Family life – mothers. Imagination. Pets. Toys.

Christmas counting ill. by author. Greenwillow, 1992. ISBN 978-0-688-10677-5 Subj: Counting, numbers. Cumulative tales. Holidays – Christmas. Trees.

Earthdance ill. by author. Greenwillow, 1999. ISBN 978-0-688-16327-3 Subj: Earth. Plants. School.

Hardworking puppies ill. by author. Harcourt, 2006. ISBN 978-0-15-205404-5 Subj: Animals – dogs. Careers. Counting, numbers.

Little clam ill. by author. Greenwillow, 1998. ISBN 978-0-688-15909-2 Subj: Activities – storytelling. Animals. Bedtime. Sea & seashore.

My baby and me photos by Penny Gentieu. Knopf, 2008. ISBN 978-0-375-85205-3 Subj: Babies. Family life – brothers & sisters. Rhyming text.

My cat Tuna ill. by author. Greenwillow, 2001. ISBN 978-0-688-16874-2 Subj: Animals – cats. Format, unusual – toy & movable books. Senses.

My dog Truffle ill. by author. Greenwillow, 2001. ISBN 978-0-688-16875-9 Subj: Animals – dogs. Format, unusual – toy & movable books. Seasons – winter. Senses.

My way / A mi manera: a Margaret and Margarita story / un cuento de Margarita y Margaret ill. by author. HarperCollins, 2007. ISBN 978-0-06-084101-0 Subj: Foreign languages. Friendship.

Play ball with me! ill. by author. Random House, 2006. ISBN 978-0-375-83244-4 Subj: Format, unusual – toy & movable books. Sports.

The surprise family ill. by author. Greenwillow, 1994. ISBN 978-0-688-11672-9 Subj: Birds – chickens. Birds – ducks. Emotions – love.

Two dogs swimming ill. by author. HarperCollins, 2005. ISBN 978-0-06-008648-0 Subj: Animals – dogs. Sports – swimming.

Two mice in three fables ill. by author. Greenwillow, 1995. ISBN 978-0-688-13390-0 Subj: Animals – mice. Friendship.

Reiss, Mike. *The boy who wouldn't share* ill. by David Catrow. HarperCollins, 2008. ISBN 978-0-06-059132-8 Subj: Behavior – greed. Family life – brothers & sisters. Rhyming text.

How Murray saved Christmas ill. by David Catrow. Price Stern Sloan, 2000. ISBN 978-0-8431-7610-0 Subj: Holidays – Christmas. Rhyming text. Santa Claus.

Late for school ill. by Michael Austin. Peachtree, 2003. ISBN 978-1-56145-286-6 Subj: Behavior – promptness, tardiness. Cities, towns. Humorous stories. Rhyming text.

Merry un-Christmas ill. by David Catrow. HarperCollins, 2006. ISBN 978-0-06-059126-7 Subj: Holidays – Christmas. Humorous stories.

Santa claustrophobia ill. by David Catrow. Price Stern Sloan, 2002. ISBN 978-0-8431-7756-5 Subj: Activities – vacationing. Holidays. Holidays – Christmas. Humorous stories. Rhyming text. Santa Claus.

Reitman, Andrea. *Mouse in the house* ill. by Karen Bell. Paper engineering by Renée Jablow. Piggy Toes, 2001. ISBN 978-1-58117-156-3 Subj: Animals – mice. Format, unusual – toy & movable books. Rhyming text.

Rempt, Fiona. *Snail's birthday wish* ill. by Noelle Smit. Boxer, 2007. ISBN 978-1-905417-52-0 Subj: Animals. Animals – snails. Birthdays. Gifts.

Rennert, Laura Joy. *Buying, training and caring for your dinosaur* ill. by Marc Brown. Knopf, 2009. ISBN 978-0-375-83679-4 Subj: Dinosaurs. Humorous stories. Pets.

Repchuk, Caroline. *The race* (Aesop)

Rex, Adam. *Moonday* ill. by author. Disney/Hyperion, 2013. ISBN 978-1-4231-1920-3 Subj: Moon.

Pssst! ill. by author. Harcourt, 2007. ISBN 978-0-15-205817-3 Subj: Zoos.

Rex, Michael. *Brooms are for flying* ill. by author. Holt, 2000. ISBN 978-0-8050-6410-0 Subj: Holidays – Halloween. Witches.

Dunk skunk ill. by author. Penguin, 2005. ISBN 978-0-399-24281-6 Subj: Animals. Rhyming text. Sports.

Furious George goes bananas: a primate parody ill. by author. Penguin, 2010. ISBN 978-0-399-25433-8 Subj: Animals – gorillas. Humorous stories.

Goodnight goon: a petrifying parody ill. by author. Putnam, 2008. ISBN 978-0-399-24534-3 Subj: Bedtime. Humorous stories. Monsters. Rhyming text.

My fire engine ill. by author. Holt, 1999. ISBN 978-0-8050-5391-3 Subj: Careers – firefighters. Fire. Imagination. Safety. Trucks.

My freight train ill. by author. Holt, 2002. ISBN 978-0-8050-6682-1 Subj: Careers – railroad engineers. Trains.

My race car ill. by author. Holt, 2000. ISBN 978-0-8050-6101-7 Subj: Automobiles. Careers – race car drivers. Sports – racing.

The pie is cherry ill. by author. Holt, 2001. ISBN 978-0-8050-6717-0 Subj: Activities – baking, cooking. Food.

Runaway mummy: a petrifying parody ill. by author. Putnam, 2009. ISBN 978-0-399-25203-7 Subj: Behavior – running away. Family life – mothers. Mummies.

You can do anything, Daddy! ill. by author. Penguin, 2007. ISBN 978-0-399-24298-4 Subj: Bedtime. Family life – fathers. Humorous stories.

Rey, H. A. *Billy's picture* (Rey, Margret)

Cecily G and the nine monkeys ill. by author. Houghton, 1989, ©1942. ISBN 978-0-395-18430-

1 Subj: Animals – giraffes. Animals – monkeys. Humorous stories.

Curious George ill. by author. Houghton, 1941. Subj: Animals – monkeys. Careers – firefighters. Character traits – curiosity. Humorous stories.

Curious George gets a medal ill. by author. Houghton, 1957. Subj: Animals – monkeys. Character traits – curiosity. Humorous stories. Space & space ships.

Curious George goes to the hospital (Rey, Margret)

Curious George learns the alphabet ill. by author. Houghton, 1963. ISBN 978-0-395-16031-2 Subj: ABC books. Animals – monkeys. Character traits – curiosity.

Curious George rides a bike ill. by author. Houghton, 1952. ISBN 978-0-395-16964-3 Subj: Animals – monkeys. Character traits – curiosity. Circus. Humorous stories. Sports – bicycling.

Curious George takes a job ill. by author. Houghton, 1947. Subj: Animals – monkeys. Careers – window cleaners. Character traits – curiosity. Humorous stories. Zoos.

Elizabite: adventures of a carnivorous plant ill. by author. Houghton, 1999. ISBN 978-0-395-97702-6 Subj: Humorous stories. Plants. Rhyming text.

The original Curious George ill. by author. Printed from H. A. Rey's original watercolors. Houghton, 1998. ISBN 978-0-395-92272-9 Subj: Animals – monkeys. Careers – firefighters. Character traits – curiosity. Humorous stories.

Rey, Margret. *Billy's picture* by Margret Rey and H. A. Rey ill. by H. A. Rey. HarperCollins, 1948. Subj: Activities – drawing. Animals. Art. Humorous stories.

Curious George flies a kite ill. by H. A. Rey. Houghton, 1958. Subj: Animals – monkeys. Character traits – curiosity. Humorous stories. Kites. Sports – fishing.

Curious George goes to the hospital by Margret Rey and H. A. Rey ill. by H. A. Rey. In collaboration with the Children's Hospital Medical Center, Boston. Houghton, 1966. Subj: Animals – monkeys. Behavior – lost. Character traits – curiosity. Hospitals. Humorous stories.

Pretzel ill. by H. A. Rey. HarperCollins, 1941. Subj: Animals – dogs.

Spotty ill. by H. A. Rey. Houghton, 1997. ISBN 978-0-395-83736-8 Subj: Animals – rabbits. Character traits – being different.

Reyher, Rebecca. *My mother is the most beautiful woman in the world* ill. by Ruth S. Gannett. Lothrop, 1945. Subj: Caldecott award honor books. Family life – mothers.

Reynolds, Aaron. *Back of the bus* ill. by Floyd Cooper. Penguin, 2010. ISBN 978-0-399-25091-0 Subj: Character traits – bravery. Ethnic groups in the U.S. – African Americans. Prejudice. U.S. history.

Buffalo wings ill. by Paulette Bogan. Bloomsbury, 2007. ISBN 978-1-59990-062-9 Subj: Activities – baking, cooking. Animals. Birds – chickens. Food. Sports – football.

Carnivores ill. by Dan Santat. Chronicle, 2013. ISBN 978-0-8118-6690-3 Subj: Animals – lions. Animals – wolves. Ecology. Fish – sharks. Food. Nature. Science.

Chicks and salsa ill. by Paulette Bogan. Bloomsbury, 2005. ISBN 978-1-58234-972-5 Subj: Activities – baking, cooking. Birds – chickens. Farms. Food.

Creepy carrots! ill. by Peter Brown. Simon & Schuster, 2012. ISBN 978-1-4424-0297-3 Subj: Animals – rabbits. Caldecott award honor books. Emotions – fear. Food.

Metal man ill. by Paul Hoppe. Charlesbridge, 2008. ISBN 978-1-58089-150-9 Subj: Art. Ethnic groups in the U.S. – African Americans.

Pirates vs. cowboys ill. by David Barneda. Knopf, 2013. ISBN 978-0-375-85874-1 Subj: Communication. Cowboys, cowgirls. Pirates. U.S. history – frontier & pioneer life.

Snowbots ill. by David Barneda. Random House, 2010. ISBN 978-0-375-85873-4 Subj: Rhyming text. Robots. Weather – snow.

Superhero School ill. by Andy Rash. Bloomsbury, 2009. ISBN 978-1-59990-166-4 Subj: Counting, numbers. School.

Reynolds, Adrian. *Pete and Polo's farmyard adventure* ill. by author. Orchard, 2002. ISBN 978-0-439-30913-4 Subj: Birds – ducks. Counting, numbers. Family life – grandfathers. Farms. Toys – bears.

Reynolds, Jan. *Amazon* photos by author. Harcourt, 1993. ISBN 978-0-15-202832-9 Subj: Foreign lands – South America. Indians of South America. Rivers.

Celebrate! connections among cultures photos by author. Lee & Low, 2006. ISBN 978-1-58430-253-7 Subj: Fairs, festivals. Foreign lands. Holidays. World.

Down under photos by author. Harcourt, 1992. ISBN 978-0-15-224182-7 Subj: Foreign lands – Australia.

Far north photos by author. Harcourt, 1992. ISBN 978-0-15-227178-7 Subj: Foreign lands – Arctic. Foreign lands – Lapland. Foreign lands – Norway.

Himalaya photos by author. Harcourt, 1991. ISBN 978-0-15-234465-8 Subj: Foreign lands – Nepal.

Sahara photos by author. Harcourt, 1991. ISBN 978-0-15-269959-8 Subj: Desert. Foreign lands – Sahara Desert.

Reynolds, Marilynn. *The magnificent piano recital* ill. by Laura Fernandez and Rick Jacobson. Orca, 2001. ISBN 978-1-55143-180-2 Subj: Careers – teachers. Family life – mothers. Musical instruments – pianos.

The name of the child ill. by Don Kilby. Orca, 2002. ISBN 978-1-55143-221-2 Subj: Babies. Character traits – bravery. Emotions – fear. Foreign lands – Canada. Illness – influenza. Names.

The new land: a first year on the prairie ill. by Stephen McCallum. Orca, 1997. ISBN 978-1-55143-069-0 Subj: Family life. Farms. Immigrants. U.S. history – frontier & pioneer life.

The prairie fire ill. by Don Kilby. Orca, 1999. ISBN 978-1-55143-137-6 Subj: Farms. Fire. U.S. history – frontier & pioneer life.

A present for Mrs. Kazinski ill. by Lynn Smith-Ary. Orca, 2001. ISBN 978-1-55143-196-3 Subj: Animals – cats. Birthdays. Old age. Pets.

Reynolds, Michael. *The big question* (Erlbruch, Wolf)

Reynolds, Peter H. *The best kid in the world: a SugarLoaf book* ill. by author. Simon & Schuster, 2006. ISBN 978-0-689-87624-0 Subj: Emotions – envy, jealousy. Family life – brothers & sisters. Sibling rivalry.

The dot ill. by author. Candlewick, 2003. ISBN 978-0-7636-1961-9 Subj: Art. Character traits – confidence. Self-concept.

I'm here ill. by author. Simon & Schuster, 2011. ISBN 978-1-4169-9649-4 Subj: Airplanes, airports. Character traits – being different. Friendship. Disabilities – autism. Paper.

Ish ill. by author. Candlewick, 2004. ISBN 978-0-7636-2344-9 Subj: Art. Family life – brothers & sisters. Self-concept.

My very big little world: a SugarLoaf book ill. by author. Simon & Schuster, 2006. ISBN 978-0-689-87621-9 Subj: Family life. Self-concept.

Rose's garden ill. by author. Candlewick, 2009. ISBN 978-0-7636-4641-7 Subj: Cities, towns. Flowers. Gardens, gardening.

Sky color ill. by author. Candlewick, 2012. ISBN 978-0-7636-2345-6 Subj: Activities – painting. Careers – artists. Concepts – color. School. Sky.

The smallest gift of Christmas ill. by author. Candlewick, 2013. ISBN 978-0-7636-6103-8 Subj: Behavior – dissatisfaction. Behavior – wishing. Family life. Gifts. Holidays – Christmas.

Sydney's star ill. by author. Simon & Schuster, 2001. ISBN 978-0-689-83184-3 Subj: Animals – mice. Boats, ships. Careers – inventors. Contests. Stars. Weather – storms.

Rheingrover, Jean Sasso. *Veronica's first year* ill. by Kay Life. Whitman, 1996. ISBN 978-0-8075-8474-3 Subj: Babies. Disabilities – Down syndrome. Family life – new sibling. Family life – sisters.

Rhyme time around the day ill. by Carol Thompson. Oxford Univ. Pr., 2000. ISBN 978-0-19-276227-6 Subj: Activities. Poetry.

Ribke, Simone T. *The shapes we eat* ill. with photos. Children's Press, 2004. ISBN 978-0-516-24431-0 Subj: Concepts – shape. Counting, numbers. Food.

Rice, Eve. *At Grammy's house* ill. by Nancy Winslow Parker. Greenwillow, 1990. ISBN 978-0-688-08875-0 Subj: Family life – grandparents.

Benny bakes a cake ill. by author. Greenwillow, 1993. ISBN 978-0-688-11580-7 Subj: Activities – baking, cooking. Animals – dogs. Behavior – misbehavior. Birthdays.

Goodnight, goodnight ill. by author. Greenwillow, 1980. ISBN 978-0-688-84254-3 Subj: Bedtime. Night.

Peter's pockets ill. by Nancy Winslow Parker. Greenwillow, 1989. ISBN 978-0-688-07242-1 Subj: Clothing – pants. Clothing – pockets. Problem solving.

Sam who never forgets ill. by author. Greenwillow, 1977. ISBN 978-0-688-84088-4 Subj: Animals. Food. Zoos.

Swim! ill. by Marisabina Russo. Greenwillow, 1996. ISBN 978-0-688-14275-9 Subj: Family life – fathers. Sports – swimming.

Richard, Françoise. *On Cat Mountain* adapt. by Arthur A. Levine; ill. by Anne Buguet. Putnam, 1994. ISBN 978-0-399-22608-3 Subj: Animals – cats. Character traits – kindness. Folk & fairy tales. Foreign lands – Japan.

Richards, Beah E. *Keep climbing, girls* ill. by R. Gregory Christie. Simon & Schuster, 2006. ISBN 978-1-4169-0264-5 Subj: Ethnic groups in the U.S. – African Americans. Poetry. Self-concept.

Richards, Jean. *The first Olympic games: a gruesome Greek myth with a happy ending* ill. by Kat Thacker. Millbrook, 2000. ISBN 978-0-7613-1311-3 Subj: Mythical creatures. Sports – Olympics.

Richards, Kitty. *It's about time, Max!* ill. by Gioia Fiammenghi. Kane/Miller, 2000. ISBN 978-1-57565-088-3 Subj: Clocks, watches. Time.

Richards, Laura Elizabeth Howe. *Jiggle joggle jee* ill. by Sam Williams. Greenwillow, 2001. ISBN 978-0-688-17833-8 Subj: Babies. Poetry. Toys – trains.

Richardson, Bill. *But if they do* ill. by Marc Mongeau. Firefly, 2003. ISBN 978-1-55037-787-3 Subj: Bedtime. Humorous stories. Rhyming text.

Sally Dog Little ill. by Céline Malépart. Annick, 2003. ISBN 978-1-55037-759-0 Subj: Animals – dogs. Ghosts. Pirates.

Richardson, John. *Grunt* ill. by author. Clarion, 2001. ISBN 978-0-618-15974-1 Subj: Animals – pigs. Character traits – individuality. Family life. Self-concept. Sibling rivalry.

Richardson, Justin. *And Tango makes three* by Justin Richardson and Peter Parnell ill. by Henry Cole. Simon & Schuster, 2005. ISBN 978-0-689-87845-9 Subj: Birds – penguins. Family life – same-sex parents. Homosexuality. Zoos.

Christian, the hugging lion by Justin Richardson and Peter Parnell ill. by Amy Bates. Simon & Schuster, 2010. ISBN 978-1-4169-8662-1 Subj: Animals – lions. Foreign lands – England. Foreign lands – Kenya.

Richmond, Marianne. *Big girls go potty* ill. by author. Sourcebooks, 2012. ISBN 978-1-4022-6662-1 Subj: Toilet training.

I'm not tired yet! ill. by author. Sourcebooks/Jabberwocky, 2012. ISBN 978-1-4022-6878-6 Subj: Bedtime. Family life – mothers.

Oh, the things my mom will do . . . ill. by author. Sourcebooks/Jabberwocky, 2013. ISBN 978-1-4022-8233-1 Subj: Family life – mothers.

Rickards, Lynne. *Jacob O'Reilly wants a pet* ill. by Lee Wildish. Barron's, 2010. ISBN 978-0-7641-6311-1 Subj: Pets. Rhyming text.

Pink! ill. by Margaret Chamberlain. Scholastic, 2009. ISBN 978-0-545-08608-0 Subj: Behavior – bullying, teasing. Birds – penguins. Character traits – appearance. Character traits – being different. Concepts – color.

Rickert, Janet Elizabeth. *Russ and the almost perfect day* photos by Pete McGahan. Woodbine, 2000. ISBN 978-1-890627-18-8 Subj: Behavior – lost & found possessions. Disabilities – Down syndrome. Disabilities – mental disabilities. School.

Riddell, Chris. *Platypus* ill. by author. Harcourt, 2001. ISBN 978-0-15-216493-5 Subj: Animals – platypuses. Crustaceans – crabs. Sea & seashore.

Platypus and the lucky day ill. by author. Harcourt, 2002. ISBN 978-0-15-216723-3 Subj: Animals – platypuses. Behavior – bad day. Character traits – luck.

Wendel's workshop ill. by author. HarperCollins, 2010. ISBN 978-0-06-144930-7 Subj: Animals – mice. Character traits – cleanliness. Inventions. Robots.

Riddle, Tohby. *The singing hat* ill. by author. Farrar, 2001. ISBN 978-0-374-36934-7 Subj: Birds. Clothing – hats.

Riehle, Mary Ann McCabe. *A is for airplane: an aviation alphabet* ill. by David Craig. Sleeping Bear, 2009. ISBN 978-1-58536-358-2 Subj: ABC books. Airplanes, airports.

Ries, Lori. *Aggie and Ben: three stories* ill. by Frank W. Dormer. Charlesbridge, 2006. ISBN 978-1-57091-594-9 Subj: Animals – dogs. Pets.

Fix it, Sam ill. by Sue Ramá. Charlesbridge, 2007. ISBN 978-1-57091-598-7 Subj: Character traits – helpfulness. Family life – brothers & sisters.

Punk wig ill. by Erin Eitter Kono. Boyds Mills, 2008. ISBN 978-1-59078-486-0 Subj: Family life. Hair. Illness – cancer.

Riggio, Anita. *Beware the Brindlebeast* ill. by author. Caroline House, 1994. ISBN 978-1-56397-133-4 Subj: Folk & fairy tales. Foreign lands – England. Holidays – Halloween. Monsters.

Secret signs: along the Underground Railroad ill. by author. Boyds Mills, 1997. ISBN 978-1-56397-555-4 Subj: Behavior – secrets. Ethnic groups in the U.S. – African Americans. Slavery. U.S. history.

Riggs, Shannon. *Not in Room 204* ill. by Jaime Zollars. Whitman, 2007. ISBN 978-0-8075-5764-8 Subj: Child abuse. Emotions – fear. Family life.

Riley, Linda Capus. *Elephants swim* ill. by Steve Jenkins. Houghton, 1995. ISBN 978-0-395-73654-8 Subj: Animals. Sports – swimming. Water.

Riley, Linnea Asplind. *Mouse mess* ill. by author. Blue Sky, 1997. ISBN 978-0-590-10048-9 Subj: Animals – mice. Behavior – messy. Food. Night.

Rim, Sujean. *Birdie's big-girl dress* ill. by author. Little, Brown, 2011. ISBN 978-0-316-13287-9 Subj: Birthdays. Clothing – dresses. Parties.

Birdie's big-girl shoes ill. by author. Little, Brown, 2009. ISBN 978-0-316-04470-7 Subj: Activities – playing. Clothing – shoes.

Rinck, Maranke. *I feel a foot!* ill. by Martijn van der Linden. Boyds Mills, 2008. ISBN 978-1-59078-638-3 Subj: Animals. Imagination.

Ringgold, Faith. *Cassie's word quilt* ill. by author. Knopf, 2002. ISBN 978-0-375-91200-9 Subj: Ethnic groups in the U.S. – African Americans. Language. Picture puzzles. Quilts.

Dinner at Aunt Connie's house ill. by author. Hyperion, 1993. ISBN 978-1-56282-426-6 Subj: Art. Ethnic groups in the U.S. – African Americans. Family life. Food. U.S. history.

Henry Ossawa Tanner: his boyhood dream comes true ill. by author. Bunker Hill, 2011. ISBN 978-1-59373-092-5 Subj: Careers – artists. Ethnic groups in the U.S. – African Americans. U.S. history.

If a bus could talk ill. by author. Simon & Schuster, 1999. ISBN 978-0-689-81892-9 Subj: Ethnic groups in the U.S. – African Americans. Prejudice. Transportation. U.S. history.

The invisible princesses ill. by author. Crown, 1999. ISBN 978-0-517-80025-6 Subj: Ethnic groups in the U.S. – African Americans. Family life. Folk & fairy tales. Royalty – princesses. Slavery.

My dream of Martin Luther King ill. by author. Crown, 1995. ISBN 978-0-517-59977-8 Subj: Dreams. Ethnic groups in the U.S. – African Americans. U.S. history. Violence, nonviolence.

Tar Beach ill. by author. Crown, 1991. ISBN 978-0-517-58031-8 Subj: Activities – flying. Caldecott award honor books. Cities, towns. Dreams. Ethnic groups in the U.S. – African Americans. Quilts.

Rinker, Sherri Duskey. *Goodnight, goodnight, construction site* ill. by Tom Lichtenheld. Chronicle, 2011. ISBN 978-0-8118-7782-4 Subj: Bedtime. Trucks.

Steam train, dream train ill. by Tom Lichtenheld. Chronicle, 2013. ISBN 978-1-4521-0920-6 Subj: Animals. Night. Rhyming text. Trains.

Riphagen, Loes. *Animals home alone.* Seven Footer, 2011. ISBN 978-1-934734-55-1 Subj: Animals. Wordless.

Ritchie, Alison. *Duck says don't!* ill. by Hannah George. Good Books, 2012. ISBN 978-1-56148-745-5 Subj: Behavior – bossy. Birds – ducks. Birds – geese. Lakes, ponds.

Me and my dad! ill. by Alison Edgson. Good Books, 2007. ISBN 978-1-56148-565-9 Subj: Animals – bears. Emotions – love. Family life – fathers. Rhyming text.

Me and my mom! ill. by Alison Edgson. Good Books, 2009. ISBN 978-1-56148-657-1 Subj: Animals – bears. Emotions – love. Family life – mothers. Rhyming text.

What Bear likes best! ill. by Dubravka Kolanovic. Good Books, 2005. ISBN 978-1-56148-473-7 Subj: Activities – playing. Animals – bears. Friendship.

Ritz, Karen. *Windows with birds* ill. by author. Boyds Mills, 2010. ISBN 978-1-59078-656-7 Subj: Animals – cats. Friendship. Homes, houses. Moving.

Rives. *If I were a polar bear* ill. by author. Piggy Toes, 2001. ISBN 978-1-58117-046-7 Subj: Animals – polar bears. Foreign lands – Arctic. Format, unusual – toy & movable books. Rhyming text.

Robart, Rose. *The cake that Mack ate* ill. by Maryann Kovalski. Little, 1987. ISBN 978-0-87113-121-8 Subj: Cumulative tales. Farms. Food.

Robb, Diane Burton. *The alphabet war* ill. by Gail Piazza. Whitman, 2004. ISBN 978-0-8075-0302-7 Subj: Books, reading. Disabilities – dyslexia. School.

Robberecht, Thierry. *Back into Mommy's tummy* ill. by Philippe Goossens. Houghton, 2005. ISBN 978-0-618-58106-1 Subj: Babies. Emotions – envy, jealousy. Family life – mothers. Family life – new sibling. Sibling rivalry.

I can't do anything! ill. by Annick Masson. Magination, 2013. ISBN 978-1-4338-1309-2 Subj: Animals. Behavior – misbehavior. Etiquette. Family life.

Sam is never scared ill. by Philippe Goossens. Houghton, 2006. ISBN 978-0-618-73278-4 Subj: Emotions – fear.

Sam is not a loser ill. by Philippe Goossens. Clarion, 2008. ISBN 978-0-618-99210-2 Subj: Games. Sportsmanship.

Sam tells stories ill. by Philippe Goossens. Houghton, 2007. ISBN 978-0-618-73280-7 Subj: Activities – storytelling. Behavior – lying. Character traits – honesty. Friendship. School.

Sam's new friend ill. by Philippe Goossens. Clarion, 2008. ISBN 978-0-618-91448-7 Subj: Animals. Character traits – kindness. Friendship. Sleepovers.

Sarah's little ghosts ill. by Philippe Goossens. Houghton, 2007. ISBN 978-0-618-89210-5 Subj: Behavior – lying. Ghosts.

Stolen smile ill. by Philippe Goossens. Random House, 2002. ISBN 978-0-385-90850-4 Subj: Behavior – bullying, teasing. Emotions.

Robbins, Beth. *Tom, Ally, and the baby-sitter* ill. by Jon Stuart. DK, 2001. ISBN 978-0-7894-7426-1 Subj: Activities – babysitting. Animals – cats. Animals – rabbits. Emotions – fear.

Tom, Ally, and the new baby ill. by Jon Stuart. DK, 2001. ISBN 978-0-7894-7431-5 Subj: Animals – cats. Babies. Family life – brothers & sisters. Family life – new sibling.

Tom and Ally visit the doctor ill. by Jon Stuart. DK, 2001. ISBN 978-0-7894-7429-2 Subj: Animals –

cats. Careers – doctors. Emotions – fear. Family life – brothers & sisters.

Tom's afraid of the dark ill. by Jon Stuart. DK, 2001. ISBN 978-0-7894-7421-6 Subj: Animals – cats. Bedtime. Emotions – fear. Imagination. Night.

Tom's first day at school ill. by Jon Stuart. DK, 2001. ISBN 978-0-7894-7423-0 Subj: Animals. Animals – cats. School – first day.

Tom's new haircut ill. by Jon Stuart. DK, 2001. ISBN 978-0-7894-7425-4 Subj: Animals. Animals – cats. Careers – barbers. Emotions – fear. Hair.

Robbins, Jacqui. *The new girl . . . and me* ill. by Matt Phelan. Simon & Schuster, 2006. ISBN 978-0-689-86468-1 Subj: Ethnic groups in the U.S. – African Americans. Friendship. Pets. Reptiles – iguanas. School.

Two of a kind ill. by Matt Phelan. Atheneum, 2009. ISBN 978-1-4169-2437-1 Subj: Behavior – bullying, teasing. Character traits – individuality. Friendship. School.

Robbins, Ken. *Apples* photos by author. Atheneum, 2002. ISBN 978-0-689-83024-2 Subj: Activities – baking, cooking. Farms. Food. Trees.

Autumn leaves ill. by author. Scholastic, 1998. ISBN 978-0-590-29879-7 Subj: Plants. Seasons – fall. Trees.

Pumpkins photos by author. Macmillan, 2006. ISBN 978-1-59643-184-3 Subj: Gardens, gardening. Seasons – fall.

Seeds ill. by author. Atheneum, 2005. ISBN 978-0-689-85041-7 Subj: Plants. Seeds.

Trucks, giants of the highway photos by author. Atheneum, 1999. ISBN 978-0-689-82664-1 Subj: Traffic, traffic signs. Transportation. Trucks.

Robbins, Maria Polushkin. *Mother, Mother, I want another* ill. by Jon Goodell. Random House, 2005. ISBN 978-0-375-92588-7 Subj: Bedtime. Family life – mothers. Kissing. Sleep.

Robbins, Ruth. *Baboushka and the three kings* ill. by Nicolas Sidjakov. Adapt. from a Russian folk tale; verse by Edith R. Thomas; music by Mary Clement Sanks. Parnassus, 1960. ISBN 978-0-395-27672-3 Subj: Caldecott award books. Folk & fairy tales. Foreign lands – Russia. Holidays – Christmas. Music. Rhyming text. Songs.

Robert, Na'ima B. *Ramadan Moon* ill. by Shirin Adl. Frances Lincoln, 2009. ISBN 978-1-84507-922-2 Subj: Holidays – Ramadan. Moon. Religion – Islam.

Roberton, Fiona. *The perfect present* ill. by author. Putnam, 2012. ISBN 978-0-399-25773-5 Subj: Animals – dogs. Birds – ducks. Birthdays. Gifts. Pets.

Wanted: the perfect pet ill. by author. Penguin, 2010. ISBN 978-0-399-25461-1 Subj: Birds – ducks. Disguises. Pets.

Roberts, Bethany. *Birthday mice* ill. by Doug Cushman. Clarion, 2002. ISBN 978-0-618-07772-4 Subj: Animals. Animals – mice. Birthdays. Cowboys, cowgirls. Parties. Rhyming text.

Christmas mice ill. by Doug Cushman. Clarion, 2000. ISBN 978-0-395-91204-1 Subj: Animals – cats. Animals – mice. Holidays – Christmas. Rhyming text.

Cookie angel ill. by Vladimir Vagin. Holt, 2007. ISBN 978-0-8050-6974-7 Subj: Activities – baking, cooking. Angels. Holidays – Christmas. Toys.

Double trouble Groundhog Day ill. by Lorinda Bryan Cauley. Holt, 2008. ISBN 978-0-8050-8280-7 Subj: Animals – groundhogs. Character traits – cooperation. Family life – brothers & sisters. Holidays – Groundhog Day. Multiple births – twins.

Easter mice ill. by Doug Cushman. Clarion, 2003. ISBN 978-0-618-16455-4 Subj: Animals – mice. Eggs. Holidays – Easter. Rhyming text.

Fourth of July mice ill. by Doug Cushman. Clarion, 2004. ISBN 978-0-618-31367-9 Subj: Activities. Animals – mice. Holidays – Fourth of July. Rhyming text.

Gramps and the fire dragon ill. by Melissa Iwai. Clarion, 1997. ISBN 978-0-395-69849-5 Subj: Activities – storytelling. Bedtime. Family life – grandfathers. Fire. Imagination.

Rosie to the rescue ill. by Kay Chorao. Holt, 2003. ISBN 978-0-8050-6486-5 Subj: Animals – squirrels. Family life – aunts, uncles. Family life – parents. Imagination.

Valentine mice! ill. by Doug Cushman. Clarion, 1997. ISBN 978-0-395-77518-9 Subj: Animals. Animals – mice. Holidays – Valentine's Day. Rhyming text.

Waiting-for-Christmas stories ill. by Sarah Stapler. Clarion, 1994. ISBN 978-0-395-67324-9 Subj: Animals – rabbits. Bedtime. Holidays – Christmas.

Waiting-for-Papa stories ill. by Sarah Stapler. HarperCollins, 1990. ISBN 978-0-06-025051-5 Subj: Animals – rabbits. Family life – fathers.

Waiting-for-spring stories ill. by William Joyce. HarperCollins, 1984. ISBN 978-0-06-025062-1 Subj: Animals – rabbits. Seasons – winter.

The wind's garden ill. by Melanie Hope Greenberg. Holt, 2001. ISBN 978-0-8050-6367-7 Subj: Gardens, gardening. Weather – wind.

Roberts, Cynthia. *Tow trucks* ill. with photos. Child's World, 2007. ISBN 978-1-59296-836-7 Subj: Trucks.

Roberts, David. *Dirty Bertie* ill. by author. Abrams, 2003. ISBN 978-0-8109-4259-2 Subj: Behavior. Character traits – cleanliness.

Roberts, Lynn. *Cinderella, an Art Deco love story* ill. by David Roberts. Abrams, 2001. ISBN 978-0-8109-4168-7 Subj: Family life – stepfamilies. Folk & fairy tales. Royalty – princes. Sibling rivalry.

Rapunzel, a groovy fairy tale ill. by David Roberts. Abrams, 2003. ISBN 978-0-8109-4242-4 Subj: Character traits – meanness. Family life – aunts, uncles. Folk & fairy tales. Hair.

Roberts, Victoria. *The best pet ever* ill. by Deborah Allwright. Tiger Tales, 2010. ISBN 978-1-58925-089-5 Subj: Imagination. Pets.

Robertson, M. P. *The dragon snatcher* ill. by author. Penguin, 2005. ISBN 978-0-8037-3103-5 Subj: Dragons. Eggs. Wizards.

The egg ill. by author. Fogelman, 2001. ISBN 978-0-8037-2546-1 Subj: Behavior – needing someone. Dragons. Eggs.

Hieronymous Betts and his unusual pets ill. by author. Frances Lincoln, 2005. ISBN 978-1-84507-289-6 Subj: Family life – brothers & sisters. Pets.

The sandcastle ill. by author. Rising Moon, 2001. ISBN 978-0-87358-782-2 Subj: Behavior – wishing. Sand. Sea & seashore – beaches.

Robertson, Patrisha Grainger. *Cirque du Soleil* photos by Al Seib. Abrams, 2003. ISBN 978-0-8109-4515-9 Subj: Circus. Concepts – color. Rhyming text.

Robey, Katharine Crawford. *Where's the party?* ill. by Kate Endle. Charlesbridge, 2011. ISBN 978-1-58089-268-1 Subj: Birds. Nature.

Robins, Arthur. *The teeny tiny woman: a traditional tale* ill. by author. Candlewick, 1998. ISBN 978-0-7636-0444-8 Subj: Folk & fairy tales. Foreign lands – England. Ghosts.

Robinson, Bruce. *The obvious elephant* ill. by Sophie Windham. Bloomsbury, 2002. ISBN 978-1-58234-769-1 Subj: Animals – elephants. Humorous stories.

Robinson, Fiona. *Whale shines: an artistic tale* ill. by author. Abrams, 2013. ISBN 978-1-4197-0848-0 Subj: Animals – whales. Art. Careers – artists. Character traits – confidence. Self-concept.

What animals really like: a new song composed & conducted by Mr. Herbert Timberteeth ill. by author. Abrams, 2011. ISBN 978-0-8109-8976-4 Subj: Animals. Careers – composers. Careers – conductors (music). Humorous stories. Songs.

Robinson, Michelle. *Ding dong! Gorilla!* ill. by Leonie Lord. Peachtree, 2013. ISBN 978-1-56145-730-4 Subj: Animals – gorillas. Behavior – messy. Behavior – misbehavior.

What to do if an elephant stands on your foot ill. by Peter H. Reynolds. Dial, 2012. ISBN 978-0-8037-3398-5 Subj: Animals. Humorous stories. Jungle.

Robinson, Sharon. *Testing the ice: a true story about Jackie Robinson* ill. by Kadir Nelson. Scholastic, 2009. ISBN 978-0-545-05251-1 Subj: Character traits – bravery. Ethnic groups in the U.S. – African Americans. Family life – fathers. Sports – baseball.

Robinson, Sue. *I want to play* ill. by Andy Beckett. Barron's, 2002. ISBN 978-0-7641-5486-7 Subj: Animals – babies. Animals – cats. Family life – mothers. Friendship.

Robinson, Tim. *Tobias, the quig, and the rumplenut tree* ill. by author. Winslow, 2000. ISBN 978-1-890817-20-6 Subj: Birds. Ecology. Rhyming text. Trees.

Robledo, Honorio. *Nico visits the moon* ill. by author. Cinco Puntos, 2001. ISBN 978-0-938317-57-9 Subj: Animals – cats. Family life – parents. Moon. Toys – balloons.

Rocco, John. *Blackout* ill. by author. Hyperion/Disney, 2011. ISBN 978-1-4231-2190-9 Subj: Caldecott award honor books. Family life. Light, lights. Night.

Super Hair-o and the barber of doom ill. by author. Disney/Hyperion, 2013. ISBN 978-1-4231-2189-3 Subj: Careers – barbers. Hair.

Wolf! Wolf! ill. by author. Hyperion, 2007. ISBN 978-1-4231-0012-6 Subj: Animals – wolves. Behavior – lying. Behavior – trickery. Folk & fairy tales. Foreign lands – China.

Roche, Denis. *The best class picture ever* ill. by author. Scholastic, 2003. ISBN 978-0-439-26983-4 Subj: Activities – photographing. Careers – teachers. School.

Little Pig is capable ill. by author. Houghton, 2002. ISBN 978-0-395-91368-0 Subj: Animals – pigs. Animals – wolves. Behavior – worrying. Safety.

Mim, gym, and June ill. by author. Houghton, 2003. ISBN 978-0-618-15254-4 Subj: Behavior – bullying, teasing. Friendship. School. Sports – gymnastics.

Rochelle, Belinda. *Jewels* ill. by Cornelius Van Wright and Ying-Hwa Hu. Lodestar, 1998. ISBN 978-0-525-67502-0 Subj: Activities – storytelling. Ethnic groups in the U.S. – African Americans. Family life – great-grandparents. Memories, memory. Slavery. U.S. history.

Rock, Brian. *The deductive detective* ill. by Sherry Rogers. Sylvan Dell, 2013. ISBN 978-1-60718-613-

7 Subj: Animals. Birds – ducks. Crime. Problem solving.

With all my heart ill. by Samantha Chaffey. Tiger Tales, 2012. ISBN 978-1-58925-648-4 Subj: Animals – bears. Emotions – love. Family life – mothers.

Rock, Lois. *A child's book of graces* ill. by Alison Jay. Good Books, 2006. ISBN 978-1-56148-514-7 Subj: Religion.

God bless me, God bless you ill. by John Bendall-Brunello. Baker Books, 2001. ISBN 978-0-8010-4488-5 Subj: Bedtime. Religion. Rhyming text.

I wish tonight ill. by Anne Wilson. Good Books, 2000. ISBN 978-1-56148-315-0 Subj: Behavior – wishing. Dreams. Rhyming text.

I wonder why? ill. by Christopher Corr. Chronicle, 2001. ISBN 978-0-8118-3169-7 Subj: Religion. Rhyming text.

Learning about prayer ill. by Maureen Galvani. Little, 2003. ISBN 978-0-316-60557-1 Subj: Religion.

The Lord's prayer ill. by Debbie Lush. Paulist Pr., 1999. ISBN 978-0-8091-6679-4 Subj: Religion.

Now we have a baby ill. by Jane Massey. Good Books, 2004. ISBN 978-1-56148-451-5 Subj: Babies. Emotions – love. Family life. Family life – new sibling. Format, unusual – board books.

Rockhill, Dennis. *Polar slumber / Sueño polar* ill. by author. Raven Tree, 2004. ISBN 978-0-9724973-1-2 Subj: Animals – polar bears. Dreams. Wordless.

Rockliff, Mara. *Me and Momma and Big John* ill. by William Low. Candlewick, 2012. ISBN 978-0-7636-4359-1 Subj: Buildings. Careers. Character traits – persistence. Ethnic groups in the U.S. – African Americans. Family life – mothers. U.S. history.

My heart will not sit down ill. by Ann Tanksley. Knopf, 2012. ISBN 978-0-375-84569-7 Subj: Behavior – sharing. Character traits – generosity. Foreign lands – Cameroon. U.S. history.

Rocklin, Joanne. *This book is haunted* ill. by JoAnn Adinolfi. HarperCollins, 2001. ISBN 978-0-06-028457-2 Subj: Ghosts. Holidays – Halloween. Homes, houses.

Rockwell, Anne. *Apples and pumpkins* ill. by Lizzy Rockwell. Simon & Schuster, 2011. ISBN 978-1-4424-0350-5 Subj: Food. Holidays – Halloween.

At the beach ill. by Harlow Rockwell. Macmillan, 1987. ISBN 978-0-02-777940-0 Subj: Activities – playing. Sea & seashore – beaches.

At the firehouse ill. by author. HarperCollins, 2003. ISBN 978-0-06-029816-6 Subj: Careers – firefighters. Trucks.

At the supermarket ill. by author. Holt, 2010. ISBN 978-0-8050-7662-2 Subj: Shopping. Stores.

Backyard bear ill. by Megan Halsey. Walker, 2006. ISBN 978-0-8027-9573-1 Subj: Animals – bears. Communities, neighborhoods.

Becoming butterflies ill. by Megan Halsey. Walker, 2002. ISBN 978-0-8027-8798-9 Subj: Insects – butterflies, caterpillars. Metamorphosis. School.

Big George: how a shy boy became President Washington ill. by Matt Phelan. Houghton, 2009. ISBN 978-0-15-216583-3 Subj: Character traits – bravery. Character traits – shyness. U.S. history.

Boats ill. by author. Dutton, 1982. ISBN 978-0-525-44004-8 Subj: Animals – bears. Boats, ships.

The boy who wouldn't obey: a Mayan legend ill. by author. Greenwillow, 2000. ISBN 978-0-688-14881-2 Subj: Behavior – misbehavior. Folk & fairy tales. Indians of Central America – Maya.

Brendan and Belinda and the slam dunk! ill. by Paul Meisel. HarperCollins, 2007. ISBN 978-0-06-028443-5 Subj: Animals – pigs. Family life – brothers & sisters. Multiple births – twins. Sports – basketball. Sportsmanship.

Bugs are insects ill. by Steve Jenkins. HarperCollins, 2001. ISBN 978-0-06-028569-2 Subj: Insects.

Bumblebee, bumblebee, do you know me? a garden guessing game ill. by author. HarperCollins, 1999. ISBN 978-0-06-028212-7 Subj: Flowers. Insects. Insects – bees.

Career day ill. by Lizzy Rockwell. HarperCollins, 2000. ISBN 978-0-06-027566-2 Subj: Careers. School.

Cars ill. by author. Dutton, 1984. ISBN 978-0-525-44079-6 Subj: Automobiles.

Chip and the karate kick ill. by Paul Meisel. HarperCollins, 2004. ISBN 978-0-06-028446-6 Subj: Animals. Animals – rabbits. Character traits – patience. Sports – karate.

Clouds ill. by Frané Lessac. Collins, 2008. ISBN 978-0-06-445220-5 Subj: Science. Weather – clouds.

Ducklings and pollywogs ill. by Lizzy Rockwell. Macmillan, 1994. ISBN 978-0-02-777452-8 Subj: Family life – fathers. Lakes, ponds. Seasons.

Father's Day ill. by Lizzy Rockwell. HarperCollins, 2005. ISBN 978-0-06-051378-8 Subj: Activities – writing. Books, reading. Family life – fathers. Holidays – Father's Day. School.

Ferryboat ride! ill. by Maggie Smith. Crown, 1999. ISBN 978-0-517-70959-7 Subj: Boats, ships. Islands. Sea & seashore. Transportation.

Fire engines ill. by author. Dutton, 1986. ISBN 978-0-525-44259-2 Subj: Animals – dogs. Careers – firefighters. Trucks.

First comes spring ill. by author. Crowell, 1985. ISBN 978-0-690-04455-3 Subj: Animals – bears. Seasons.

First day of school ill. by Lizzy Rockwell. HarperCollins, 2011. ISBN 978-0-06-050191-4 Subj: School – first day.

The first snowfall by Anne Rockwell and Harlow Rockwell ill. by authors. Macmillan, 1987. ISBN 978-0-02-777770-3 Subj: Seasons – winter. Weather – snow.

Good morning, Digger ill. by Melanie Hope Greenberg. Penguin, 2005. ISBN 978-0-670-05959-1 Subj: Machines. Trucks.

Growing like me ill. by Holly Keller. Harcourt, 2001. ISBN 978-0-15-202202-0 Subj: Behavior – growing up.

Halloween Day ill. by Lizzy Rockwell. HarperCollins, 1997. ISBN 978-0-06-027568-6 Subj: Clothing – costumes. Holidays – Halloween. School.

Here comes the night ill. by author. Holt, 2006. ISBN 978-0-8050-7663-9 Subj: Bedtime. Night.

Honey in a hive ill. by S. D. Schindler. HarperCollins, 2005. ISBN 978-0-06-028567-8 Subj: Food. Insects – bees.

Katie Catz makes a splash ill. by Paul Meisel. HarperCollins, 2003. ISBN 978-0-06-028445-9 Subj: Animals. Animals – cats. Emotions – fear. Sports – swimming.

Little shark ill. by Megan Halsey. Walker, 2005. ISBN 978-0-8027-8955-6 Subj: Fish – sharks.

Long ago yesterday ill. by author. Greenwillow, 1999. ISBN 978-0-688-14411-1 Subj: Babies. Family life.

Morgan plays soccer ill. by Paul Meisel. HarperCollins, 2001. ISBN 978-0-06-028444-2 Subj: Animals. Animals – bears. Sports – soccer.

Mother's Day ill. by Lizzy Rockwell. HarperCollins, 2004. ISBN 978-0-06-051375-7 Subj: Holidays – Mother's Day. School.

My pet hamster ill. by Bernice Lum. HarperCollins, 2002. ISBN 978-0-06-028565-4 Subj: Animals – hamsters. Pets.

My preschool ill. by author. Holt, 2008. ISBN 978-0-8050-7955-5 Subj: School – nursery.

My spring robin ill. by Harlow Rockwell and Lizzy Rockwell. Macmillan, 1989. ISBN 978-0-02-777611-9 Subj: Birds – robins. Flowers. Seasons – spring.

No! No! No! ill. by author. Macmillan, 1995. ISBN 978-0-02-777782-6 Subj: Behavior – bad day. Family life.

Once upon a time this morning ill. by Suçie Stevenson. Greenwillow, 1997. ISBN 978-0-688-14707-5 Subj: Babies. Family life.

One bean ill. by Megan Halsey. Walker, 1998. ISBN 978-0-8027-8649-4 Subj: Plants. Science. Seeds.

100 school days ill. by Lizzy Rockwell. HarperCollins, 2002. ISBN 978-0-06-029145-7 Subj: Counting, numbers. School.

Our yard is full of birds ill. by Lizzy Rockwell. Macmillan, 1992. ISBN 978-0-02-777273-9 Subj: Birds.

Planes by Anne Rockwell and Harlow Rockwell ill. by authors. Dutton, 1985. ISBN 978-0-525-44159-5 Subj: Airplanes, airports. Transportation.

President's Day ill. by Lizzy Rockwell. HarperCollins, 2008. ISBN 978-0-06-050194-5 Subj: Holidays. School – nursery. Theater.

St. Patrick's Day ill. by Lizzy Rockwell. HarperCollins, 2010. ISBN 978-0-06-050197-6 Subj: Holidays – St. Patrick's Day. School.

Show and tell day ill. by Lizzy Rockwell. HarperCollins, 1997. ISBN 978-0-06-027301-9 Subj: Character traits – individuality. School.

Space vehicles by Anne Rockwell and David Brion ill. by authors. Dutton, 1994. ISBN 978-0-525-45270-6 Subj: Animals – cats. Space & space ships.

Thanksgiving Day ill. by Lizzy Rockwell. HarperCollins, 1999. ISBN 978-0-06-027795-6 Subj: Holidays – Thanksgiving. School. Theater.

Things that go ill. by author. Dutton, 1986. ISBN 978-0-525-44266-0 Subj: Transportation.

Trains ill. by author. Dutton, 1988. ISBN 978-0-525-44377-3 Subj: Trains. Transportation.

Truck stop ill. by Melissa Iwai. Viking, 2013. ISBN 978-0-670-06261-4 Subj: Restaurants. Trucks.

Trucks ill. by author. Dutton, 1984. ISBN 978-0-525-44147-2 Subj: Trucks.

Two blue jays ill. by Megan Halsey. Walker, 2003. ISBN 978-0-8027-8841-2 Subj: Birds – bluejays. Family life – parents.

Valentine's Day ill. by Lizzy Rockwell. HarperCollins, 2001. ISBN 978-0-06-028515-9 Subj: Holidays – Valentine's Day. Letters, cards. School.

Welcome to kindergarten ill. by author. Walker, 2001. ISBN 978-0-8027-8746-0 Subj: Emotions – fear. School – first day.

What we like ill. by author. Macmillan, 1992. ISBN 978-0-02-777274-6 Subj: Activities – making things. Concepts. Language.

What's so bad about gasoline? fossil fuels and what they do ill. by Paul Meisel. Collins, 2009. ISBN 978-0-06-157528-0 Subj: Earth. Ecology. Science.

Whoo! whoo! goes the train ill. by author and Vanessa van der Baan. HarperCollins, 2009. ISBN 978-0-06-056227-4 Subj: Activities – traveling. Trains.

Willy can count ill. by author. Little, 1989. ISBN 978-1-55970-013-9 Subj: Activities – walking. Counting, numbers. Country. Family life – mothers.

Rockwell, Harlow. *The first snowfall* (Rockwell, Anne)

My dentist ill. by author. Greenwillow, 1975. ISBN 978-0-688-84004-4 Subj: Careers – dentists. Teeth.

My doctor ill. by author. Macmillan, 1973. ISBN 978-0-02-777480-1 Subj: Careers – doctors. Health & fitness.

Planes (Rockwell, Anne)

Rockwell, Lizzy. *The busy body book* ill. by author. Crown, 2004. ISBN 978-0-375-92203-9 Subj: Health & fitness – exercise.

Hello baby! ill. by author. Crown, 1999. ISBN 978-0-517-80012-6 Subj: Babies. Birth. Family life – brothers & sisters. Family life – new sibling.

Rodanas, Kristina. *The dragonfly's tale* ill. by author. Houghton, 1992. ISBN 978-0-395-57003-6 Subj: Folk & fairy tales. Indians of North America – Zuni. Insects – dragonflies.

Follow the stars ill. by reteller. Little, 1998. ISBN 978-0-7614-5029-0 Subj: Creation. Folk & fairy tales. Indians of North America – Ojibwa.

The little drummer boy ill. by author. Words & music by Katherine Davis, Henry Onorati & Harry Simeonne. Clarion, 2001. ISBN 978-0-395-97015-7 Subj: Gifts. Holidays – Christmas. Music. Musical instruments – drums. Religion – Nativity. Songs.

Roddie, Shen. *Not now, Mrs. Wolf* ill. by Selina Young. DK, 2000. ISBN 978-0-7894-5613-7 Subj: Animals – babies. Animals – wolves. Birds – ducks. Family life – mothers.

Sandbear ill. by Jenny Jones. Bloomsbury, 2002. ISBN 978-1-58234-758-5 Subj: Animals – bears. Animals – rabbits. Friendship. Sand.

Toes are to tickle ill. by Kady MacDonald Denton. Tricycle, 1997. ISBN 978-1-883672-49-2 Subj: Activities – playing. Babies. Family life – brothers & sisters. Games.

Rodgers, Richard. *My favorite things* by Richard Rodgers and Oscar Hammerstein ill. by Renée Graef. HarperCollins, 2001. ISBN 978-0-06-029233-1 Subj: Songs.

Rodman, Mary Ann. *First grade stinks!* ill. by Beth Spiegel. Peachtree, 2006. ISBN 978-1-56145-377-1 Subj: Behavior – bad day. School – first day.

My best friend ill. by E. B. Lewis. Penguin, 2005. ISBN 978-0-670-05989-8 Subj: Activities – playing. Ethnic groups in the U.S. – African Americans. Friendship.

Surprise soup ill. by G. Brian Karas. Viking, 2009. ISBN 978-0-670-06274-4 Subj: Activities – baking, cooking. Animals – bears. Family life – brothers. Family life – new sibling. Food.

A tree for Emmy ill. by Tatjana Mai-Wyss. Peachtree, 2009. ISBN 978-1-56145-475-4 Subj: Birthdays. Trees.

Rodriguez, Alex. *Out of the ballpark* ill. by Frank Morrison. HarperCollins, 2007. ISBN 978-0-06-115194-1 Subj: Character traits – persistence. Sports – baseball.

Rodriguez, Béatrice. *The chicken thief* ill. by author. Enchanted Lion, 2010. ISBN 978-1-59270-092-9 Subj: Animals – foxes. Birds – chickens. Wordless.

Fox and hen together ill. by author. Enchanted Lion, 2011. ISBN 978-1-59270-109-4 Subj: Animals – foxes. Birds – chickens. Friendship. Wordless.

The gingerbread man (The gingerbread boy)

Rodriguez, Bobbie. *Sarah's sleepover* ill. by Mark Graham. Viking, 2000. ISBN 978-0-670-87750-8 Subj: Family life – cousins. Games. Disabilities – blindness. Night. Power failures. Sleepovers.

Rodriguez, Edel. *Sergio makes a splash* ill. by author. Little, Brown, 2008. ISBN 978-0-316-06616-7 Subj: Birds – penguins. Emotions – fear. Sports – swimming.

Sergio saves the game! ill. by author. Little, Brown, 2009. ISBN 978-0-316-06617-4 Subj: Birds – penguins. Character traits – clumsiness. Sports – soccer.

Rodríguez, Rachel Victoria. *Through Georgia's eyes* ill. by Julie Paschkis. Holt, 2006. ISBN 978-0-8050-7740-7 Subj: Art. Careers – artists.

Rodriguez, Sonia. *T is for tutu: a ballet alphabet* by Sonia Rodriguez and Kurt Browning ill. by Wilson Ong. Sleeping Bear, 2011. ISBN 978-1-58536-312-4 Subj: ABC books. Ballet.

Roe, Eileen. *With my brother / Con mi hermano* ill. by Robert Casilla. Bradbury, 1991. ISBN 978-0-02-777373-6 Subj: Ethnic groups in the U.S. – Mexican Americans. Family life – brothers. Foreign languages.

Roemer, Heidi Bee. *What kind of seeds are these?* ill. by Olena Kassian. NorthWord, 2006. ISBN 978-1-55971-955-1 Subj: Rhyming text. Seeds.

Rofé, Jennifer. *Piggies in the pumpkin patch* (Peterson, Mary)

Rogalski, Mark. *Tickets to ride: an alphabetic amusement* ill. by author. Running Press, 2006. ISBN 978-0-7624-2782-6 Subj: ABC books. Parks – amusement.

Rogers, Emma. *Ruby's dinnertime* (Rogers, Paul)

Ruby's potty (Rogers, Paul)

Rogers, Fred. *Adoption* photos by Jim Judkis. Putnam, 1994. ISBN 978-0-399-22432-4 Subj: Adoption. Emotions. Family life.

Divorce photos by Jim Judkis. Putnam, 1998. ISBN 978-0-399-22449-2 Subj: Divorce. Family life.

Extraordinary friends photos by Jim Judkis. Putnam, 2000. ISBN 978-0-399-23146-9 Subj: Disabilities. Friendship.

Going on an airplane photos by Jim Judkis. Putnam, 1989. ISBN 978-0-399-21635-0 Subj: Activities – traveling. Airplanes, airports.

Going to day care photos by Jim Judkis. Putnam, 1985. ISBN 978-0-399-21235-2 Subj: School – nursery.

Going to the doctor photos by Jim Judkis. Putnam, 1986. ISBN 978-0-399-21298-7 Subj: Careers – doctors.

Going to the hospital photos by Jim Judkis. Putnam, 1988. ISBN 978-0-399-21503-2 Subj: Hospitals. Illness.

Going to the potty photos by Jim Judkis. Putnam, 1986. ISBN 978-0-399-21296-3 Subj: Behavior – growing up. Toilet training.

If we were all the same ill. by Pat Sustendal. Random House, 1988. ISBN 978-0-394-98778-1 Subj: Character traits – individuality.

Making friends photos by Jim Judkis. Putnam, 1987. ISBN 978-0-399-21382-3 Subj: Activities – playing. Emotions. Friendship.

Moving photos by Jim Judkis. Putnam, 1987. ISBN 978-0-399-21383-0 Subj: Communities, neighborhoods. Emotions. Family life. Friendship. Moving.

The new baby photos by Jim Judkis. Putnam, 1985. ISBN 978-0-399-21236-9 Subj: Babies. Family life – new sibling. Sibling rivalry.

When a pet dies photos by Jim Judkis. Putnam, 1988. ISBN 978-0-399-21504-9 Subj: Death. Emotions – grief. Pets.

Rogers, Gregory. *The boy, the bear, the baron, the bard* ill. by author. Macmillan, 2004. ISBN 978-1-59643-009-9 Subj: Animals – bears. Foreign lands – England. Knights. Wordless.

The hero of Little Street ill. by author. Roaring Brook, 2012. ISBN 978-1-59643-729-6 Subj: Art. Foreign lands. Imagination. Museums. Wordless.

Midsummer knight ill. by author. Macmillan, 2007. ISBN 978-1-56943-183-6 Subj: Animals – bears. Foreign lands – England. Knights. Wordless.

Rogers, Hal. *Airplanes* ill. with photos. Child's World, 2001. ISBN 978-1-56766-962-6 Subj: Airplanes, airports. Transportation.

Buses ill. with photos. Child's World, 2001. ISBN 978-1-56766-963-3 Subj: Buses. Transportation.

Cars ill. with photos. Child's World, 2001. ISBN 978-1-56766-964-0 Subj: Automobiles. Transportation.

Combines ill. with photos. Child's World, 2001. ISBN 978-1-56766-754-7 Subj: Farms. Machines.

Milking machines ill. with photos. Child's World, 2001. ISBN 978-1-56766-753-0 Subj: Animals – bulls, cows. Farms. Machines.

Plows ill. with photos. Child's World, 2001. ISBN 978-1-56766-755-4 Subj: Farms. Machines.

Trains ill. with photos. Child's World, 2001. ISBN 978-1-56766-965-7 Subj: Trains. Transportation.

Rogers, Jacqueline. *Kindergarten ABC* ill. by author. Scholastic, 2002. ISBN 978-0-439-36837-7 Subj: ABC books. Books, reading. School.

Tiptoe into kindergarten ill. by author. Scholastic, 1999. ISBN 978-0-590-46653-0 Subj: Family life – brothers & sisters. School.

Rogers, Paul. *Ruby's dinnertime* by Paul Rogers and Emma Rogers ill. by Emma Rogers. Dutton, 2002. ISBN 978-0-525-46847-9 Subj: Animals – mice. Behavior – growing up. Family life. Food. Rhyming text.

Ruby's potty by Paul Rogers and Emma Rogers ill. by Emma Rogers. Dutton, 2001. ISBN 978-0-525-46816-5 Subj: Animals – mice. Behavior – growing up. Rhyming text. Toilet training.

Tiny by Paul Rogers and Korky Paul ill. by Korky Paul. Dutton, 2002. ISBN 978-1-929132-26-3 Subj: Insects – fleas.

What will the weather be like today? ill. by Kazuko. Greenwillow, 1990. ISBN 978-0-688-08951-1 Subj: Rhyming text. Weather.

Rohmann, Eric. *Bone dog* ill. by author. Roaring Brook, 2011. ISBN 978-1-59643-150-8 Subj: Anatomy – skeletons. Animals – dogs. Death. Holidays – Halloween.

The cinder-eyed cats ill. by author. Crown, 1997. ISBN 978-0-517-70897-2 Subj: Animals – cats. Bedtime. Boats, ships. Dreams. Islands. Night.

Clara and Asha ill. by author. Macmillan, 2005. ISBN 978-1-59643-031-0 Subj: Bedtime. Fish. Imagination – imaginary friends.

My friend Rabbit ill. by author. Roaring Brook, 2002. ISBN 978-0-7613-2420-1 Subj: Animals – mice. Animals – rabbits. Caldecott award books. Friendship.

Pumpkinhead ill. by author. Knopf, 2003. ISBN 978-0-375-92416-3 Subj: Activities – traveling. Character traits – being different. Character traits – individuality.

Time flies ill. by author. Crown, 1994. ISBN 978-0-517-59599-2 Subj: Birds. Caldecott award honor books. Dinosaurs. Museums. Time. Wordless.

Rohmer, Harriet. *Atariba and Niguayona: a story from the Taino people of Puerto Rico* ill. by Consuelo Mendez. Adapt. by Harriet Rohmer and Jesus Guerrero Rea. Children's Book Press, 1988. ISBN 978-0-89239-026-7 Subj: Character traits – kindness. Foreign lands – Puerto Rico. Illness.

How we came to the fifth world: a creation story from Ancient Mexico ill. by Graciela Carrillo. Adapt. by Harriet Rohmer and Mary Anchondo. Children's Book Press, 1988. ISBN 978-0-89239-024-3 Subj: Creation. Folk & fairy tales. Foreign lands – Mexico.

Mother scorpion country by Harriet Rohmer and Dorminster Wilson ill. by Virginia Stearns. Children's Book Press, 1987. ISBN 978-0-89239-032-8 Subj: Emotions – love. Folk & fairy tales. Foreign lands – Nicaragua.

Rohmer, Harriet, et al. *The invisible hunters* ill. by Joe Sam. Children's Book Press, 1987. ISBN 978-0-89239-031-1 Subj: Behavior – greed. Folk & fairy tales. Foreign lands – Nicaragua. Sports – hunting.

Rollings, Susan. *New shoes, red shoes* ill. by author. Orchard, 2000. ISBN 978-0-531-30268-2 Subj: Birthdays. Clothing – shoes. Parties. Rhyming text.

Rollins, Jack. *Frosty the snowman* (Nelson, Steve)

Frosty the snowman [board book] (Nelson, Steve)

Romain, Trevor. *Jemma's journey* ill. by Pat Lopez. Boyds Mills, 2002. ISBN 978-1-56397-937-8 Subj: Ethnic groups in the U.S. – African Americans. Family life – grandmothers. Trees. U.S. history.

Rong, Yu. *A lovely day for Amelia Goose* ill. by author. Candlewick, 2004. ISBN 978-0-7636-2309-8 Subj: Birds – geese. Day. Frogs & toads.

Roode, Daniel. *Little Bea and the snowy day* ill. by author. HarperCollins, 2011. ISBN 978-0-06-199395-4 Subj: Activities – playing. Insects – bees. Rhyming text. Weather – snow.

Roop, Connie. *Down east in the ocean: a Maine counting book* (Roop, Peter)

Let's celebrate Earth Day by Connie Roop and Peter Roop ill. by Gwen Connelly. Millbrook, 2001. ISBN 978-0-7613-1812-5 Subj: Ecology. Holidays – Earth Day.

Roop, Peter. *Down east in the ocean: a Maine counting book* by Peter Roop and Connie Roop ill. by Nicole Fazio. Down East, 2011. ISBN 978-0-89272-709-4 Subj: Counting, numbers. Sea & seashore.

Let's celebrate Earth Day (Roop, Connie)

Roosa, Karen. *Beach day* ill. by Maggie Smith. Clarion, 2001. ISBN 978-0-618-02923-5 Subj: Rhyming text. Sea & seashore – beaches.

Pippa at the parade ill. by Julie Fortenberry. Boyds Mills, 2009. ISBN 978-1-59078-567-6 Subj: Holidays – Fourth of July. Parades. Rhyming text.

Root, Barry. *Gumbrella* ill. by author. Putnam, 2002. ISBN 978-0-399-23347-0 Subj: Animals. Animals – elephants. Character traits – kindness to animals.

Root, Phyllis. *All for the newborn baby* ill. by Nicola Bayley. Candlewick, 2000. ISBN 978-0-7636-0093-8 Subj: Holidays – Christmas. Lullabies. Religion – Nativity.

Aunt Nancy and Cousin Lazybones ill. by David Parkins. Candlewick, 1998. ISBN 978-1-56402-425-1 Subj: Character traits – laziness. Family life – cousins.

Aunt Nancy and Old Man Trouble ill. by David Parkins. Candlewick, 1996. ISBN 978-1-56402-347-6 Subj: Behavior – trickery. Folk & fairy tales.

Big belching bog ill. by Betsy Bowen. Univ. of Minnesota, 2010. ISBN 978-0-8166-3359-3 Subj: Ecology. Swamps.

Big Momma makes the world ill. by Helen Oxenbury. Candlewick, 2002. ISBN 978-0-7636-1132-3 Subj: Creation.

Contrary bear ill. by Laura Cornell. HarperCollins, 1996. ISBN 978-0-06-025086-7 Subj: Behavior – mistakes. Family life – fathers. Toys – bears.

Creak! said the bed ill. by Regan Dunnick. Candlewick, 2010. ISBN 978-0-7636-2004-2 Subj: Cumulative tales. Family life. Furniture – beds. Rhyming text. Sleep. Weather – storms.

Flip, flap, fly! ill. by David Walker. Candlewick, 2009. ISBN 978-0-7636-3109-3 Subj: Animals – babies. Rhyming text.

Grandmother Winter ill. by Beth Krommes. Houghton, 1999. ISBN 978-0-395-88399-0 Subj: Birds – geese. Folk & fairy tales. Foreign lands – Germany. Seasons – winter. Weather – snow.

If you want to see a caribou ill. by Jim Meyer. Houghton, 2004. ISBN 978-0-618-39314-5 Subj: Animals – reindeer. Nature.

Kiss the cow ill. by Will Hillenbrand. Candlewick, 2000. ISBN 978-0-7636-0298-7 Subj: Animals – bulls, cows. Kissing. Tall tales.

Looking for a moose ill. by Randy Cecil. Candlewick, 2006. ISBN 978-0-7636-2005-9 Subj: Animals – moose. Games.

Lucia and the light ill. by Mary GrandPré. Candlewick, 2006. ISBN 978-0-7636-2296-1 Subj: Animals – cats. Mythical creatures – trolls. Seasons – winter. Sun.

Mrs. Potter's pig ill. by Russell Ayto. Candlewick, 1996. ISBN 978-1-56402-924-9 Subj: Animals – pigs. Babies. Character traits – cleanliness. Character traits – orderliness.

The name quilt ill. by Margot Apple. Farrar, 2003. ISBN 978-0-374-35484-8 Subj: Family life – grandmothers. Names. Quilts.

Oliver finds his way ill. by Christopher Denise. Candlewick, 2002. ISBN 978-0-7636-1383-9 Subj: Animals – babies. Animals – bears. Behavior – lost. Family life – parents.

One duck stuck ill. by Jane Chapman. Candlewick, 1998. ISBN 978-0-7636-1566-6 Subj: Animals. Birds – ducks. Counting, numbers. Rhyming text.

One duck stuck [board book] ill. by Jane Chapman. Candlewick, 1998. ISBN 978-0-7636-1104-0 Subj: Animals. Birds – ducks. Counting, numbers. Format, unusual – board books. Rhyming text.

Paula Bunyan ill. by Kevin O'Malley. Farrar, 2009. ISBN 978-0-374-35759-7 Subj: Tall tales. U.S. history – frontier & pioneer life.

Rattletrap car ill. by Jill Barton. Candlewick, 2001. ISBN 978-0-7636-0919-1 Subj: Automobiles. Family life. Humorous stories. Lakes, ponds. Problem solving. Rhyming text.

Rattletrap car [board book] ill. by Jill Barton. Candlewick, 2001. ISBN 978-0-7636-2007-3 Subj: Automobiles. Family life. Format, unusual – board books. Humorous stories. Lakes, ponds. Problem solving. Rhyming text.

Rosie's fiddle ill. by Kevin O'Malley. Lothrop, 1997. ISBN 978-0-688-12853-1 Subj: Contests. Devil. Music. Musical instruments – violins. Tall tales.

Scrawny cat ill. by Alison Friend. Candlewick, 2011. ISBN 978-0-7636-4164-1 Subj: Animals – cats. Behavior – lost. Emotions – loneliness.

Ten sleepy sheep ill. by Susan Gaber. Candlewick, 2004. ISBN 978-0-7636-1545-1 Subj: Animals – sheep. Bedtime. Rhyming text. Sleep.

Toot toot zoom! ill. by Matthew Cordell. Candlewick, 2009. ISBN 978-0-7636-3452-0 Subj: Animals. Animals – foxes. Automobiles. Friendship.

What Baby wants ill. by Jill Barton. Candlewick, 1998. ISBN 978-0-7636-0207-9 Subj: Babies. Family life. Farms. Lullabies.

What's that noise? (Edwards, Michelle)

Roper, Janice M. *Dancing on the moon* ill. by Lauren Grimm. SIDS Ed. Services, 2001. ISBN 978-0-9641218-6-7 Subj: Babies. Death. Dreams. Emotions – envy, jealousy. Emotions – grief. Family life – brothers & sisters. Moon.

Rosa-Mendoza, Gladys. *What time is it? / Qué hora es?* ill. by Susan Chapman Calitri. Me & Mi, 2001. ISBN 978-0-9679748-9-7 Subj: Foreign languages. Format, unusual – board books. Time.

Rosales, Melodye Benson. *Leola and the honeybears* ill. by author. An African-American retelling of Goldilocks and the Three Bears. Scholastic, 1999. ISBN 978-0-590-38358-5 Subj: Animals – bears. Ethnic groups in the U.S. – African Americans. Folk & fairy tales.

'Twas the night b'fore Christmas: an African-American version ill. by author. Based on the original poem, A visit from St. Nicholas, by Clement C. Moore. Scholastic, 1996. ISBN 978-0-590-73944-3 Subj: Ethnic groups in the U.S. – African Americans. Holidays – Christmas. Poetry. Santa Claus.

Rose, Deborah Lee. *All the seasons of the year* ill. by Kay Chorao. Abrams, 2010. ISBN 978-0-8109-8395-3 Subj: Animals – cats. Emotions – love. Family life – mothers. Rhyming text. Seasons.

Birthday zoo ill. by Lynn Munsinger. Whitman, 2002. ISBN 978-0-8075-0776-6 Subj: Animals. Birthdays. Parties. Rhyming text. Toys. Zoos.

Into the A, B, sea ill. by Steve Jenkins. Scholastic, 2000. ISBN 978-0-439-09696-6 Subj: ABC books. Animals. Sea & seashore.

Ocean babies ill. by Hiroe Nakata. National Geographic, 2005. ISBN 978-0-7922-8312-6 Subj: Animals – babies. Sea & seashore.

Someone's sleepy ill. by Dan Andreasen. Abrams, 2013. ISBN 978-1-4197-0539-7 Subj: Bedtime. Family life – mothers. Rhyming text.

The spelling bee before recess ill. by Carey Armstrong-Ellis. Abrams, 2013. ISBN 978-1-4197-0847-3 Subj: Contests. Rhyming text. School. Sportsmanship.

The twelve days of kindergarten ill. by Carey Armstrong-Ellis. Abrams, 2003. ISBN 978-0-8109-4512-8 Subj: Counting, numbers. Cumulative tales. Poetry. School.

The twelve days of springtime: a school counting book ill. by Carey Armstrong-Ellis. Abrams, 2008. ISBN 978-0-8109-8330-4 Subj: Counting, numbers. Cumulative tales. School. Seasons – spring.

The twelve days of winter: a school counting book ill. by Carey Armstrong-Ellis. Abrams, 2006. ISBN 978-0-8109-5472-4 Subj: Counting, numbers. Seasons – winter.

Rose, Marion. *The Christmas tree fairy* ill. by Jason Cockcroft. Bloomsbury, 2005. ISBN 978-1-58234-668-7 Subj: Behavior – wishing. Fairies. Holidays – Christmas.

Rose, Naomi C. *Tashi and the Tibetan flower cure* ill. by author. Lee & Low, 2011. ISBN 978-1-60060-425-6 Subj: Communities, neighborhoods. Ethnic groups in the U.S. – Tibetan Americans. Family life – grandfathers. Illness.

Rosen, Michael. *Bear flies high* ill. by Adrian Reynolds. Bloomsbury, 2009. ISBN 978-1-59990-386-6 Subj: Activities – flying. Animals – bears. Fairs, festivals.

Bear's day out ill. by Adrian Reynolds. Bloomsbury, 2007. ISBN 978-1-59990-007-0 Subj: Animals – bears. Friendship.

Crow and Hawk ill. by John Clementson. Harcourt, 1995. ISBN 978-0-15-200257-2 Subj: Behavior – running away. Birds – crows. Birds – hawks. Folk & fairy tales. Indians of North America – Pueblo.

How the animals got their colors ill. by John Clementson. Harcourt, 1992. ISBN 978-0-15-236783-1 Subj: Animals. Concepts – color. Folk & fairy tales – pourquoi tales. Poetry.

Howler ill. by Neal Layton. Bloomsbury, 2004. ISBN 978-1-58234-851-3 Subj: Animals – dogs. Babies. Emotions – envy, jealousy. Humorous stories.

Red Ted and the lost things ill. by Joel Stewart. Candlewick, 2009. ISBN 978-0-7636-4537-3 Subj: Behavior – lost & found possessions. Toys – bears.

A Thanksgiving wish ill. by John Thompson. Blue Sky, 1999. ISBN 978-0-590-25563-9 Subj: Communities, neighborhoods. Death. Family life – grandparents. Holidays – Thanksgiving.

This is our house ill. by Bob Graham. Candlewick, 1996. ISBN 978-1-56402-870-9 Subj: Behavior – sharing. Character traits – selfishness. Homes, houses. Prejudice.

Tiny little fly ill. by Kevin Waldron. Candlewick, 2010. ISBN 978-0-7636-4681-3 Subj: Animals. Insects – flies. Jungle.

Totally wonderful Miss Plumberry ill. by Chinlun Lee. Candlewick, 2006. ISBN 978-0-7636-2744-7 Subj: Behavior – bad day. Careers – teachers. School.

We're going on a bear hunt ill. by Helen Oxenbury. Aladdin, 1992. ISBN 978-0-689-71653-9 Subj: Animals – bears. Games. Participation. Sports – hunting.

Rosen, Michael J. *Avalanche* ill. by David Butler. Candlewick, 1998. ISBN 978-0-7636-0589-6 Subj: ABC books. Animals – dogs. Rhyming text. Weather – snow.

Chanukah lights ill. by Robert Sabuda. Candlewick, 2011. ISBN 978-0-7636-5533-4 Subj: Format, unusual – toy & movable books. Holidays – Hanukkah.

Chanukah lights everywhere ill. by Melissa Iwai. Harcourt, 2001. ISBN 978-0-15-202447-5 Subj: Counting, numbers. Holidays – Hanukkah. Jewish culture. Religion.

The dog who walked with God ill. by Stan Fellows. Candlewick, 1998. ISBN 978-0-7636-0470-7 Subj: Animals – dogs. Creation. Indians of North America – Kato. Weather – floods.

A drive in the country ill. by Marc Burckhardt. Candlewick, 2007. ISBN 978-0-7636-2140-7 Subj: Activities – traveling. Family life.

Elijah's angel ill. by Aminah Brenda Lynn Robinson. Harcourt, 1992. ISBN 978-0-15-225394-3 Subj: Careers – woodcarvers. Ethnic groups in the U.S. – African Americans. Friendship. Holidays – Christmas. Holidays – Hanukkah. Jewish culture.

Night of the pumpkinheads ill. by Hugh McMahon. Penguin, 2011. ISBN 978-0-8037-3452-4 Subj: Contests. Holidays – Halloween.

Our eight nights of Hanukkah ill. by DyAnne DiSalvo. Holiday, 2000. ISBN 978-0-8234-1476-5 Subj: Holidays – Hanukkah. Jewish culture.

With a dog like that, a kid like me . . . ill. by Ted Rand. Dial, 2000. ISBN 978-0-8037-2059-6 Subj: Animals. Animals – dogs. Imagination.

Rosenberg, Liz. *A big and little alphabet* ill. by Vera Rosenberry. Orchard, 1997. ISBN 978-0-531-33050-0 Subj: ABC books. Animals.

The carousel ill. by Jim LaMarche. Harcourt, 1995. ISBN 978-0-15-200853-6 Subj: Animals – horses, ponies. Death. Emotions – grief. Family life – mothers. Family life – sisters. Imagination. Merry-go-rounds.

Eli's night-light ill. by Joanna Yardley. Orchard, 2001. ISBN 978-0-531-33316-7 Subj: Bedtime. Light, lights. Night. Rhyming text.

Nobody ill. by Julie Downing. Roaring Brook, 2010. ISBN 978-1-59643-120-1 Subj: Family life – parents. Imagination – imaginary friends. Morning.

On Christmas eve ill. by John Clapp. Roaring Brook, 2002. ISBN 978-0-7613-2707-3 Subj: Family life. Holidays – Christmas. Santa Claus. Weather – snow. Weather – storms.

Tyrannosaurus dad ill. by Matthew Myers. Roaring Brook, 2011. ISBN 978-1-59643-531-5 Subj: Dinosaurs. Family life – fathers.

We wanted you ill. by Peter Catalanotto. Roaring Brook, 2002. ISBN 978-0-7613-2661-8 Subj: Adoption. Family life – parents.

Rosenberg, Madelyn. *Happy birthday, tree! a Tu B'Shevat story* ill. by Jana Christy. Whitman, 2012. ISBN 978-0-8075-3151-8 Subj: Ecology. Holidays – Tu B'Shevat. Jewish culture. Trees.

The Schmutzy Family ill. by Paul Meisel. Holiday House, 2012. ISBN 978-0-8234-2371-2 Subj: Days of the week, months of the year. Humorous stories. Jewish culture.

Rosenberg, Maxine B. *Mommy's in the hospital having a baby* photos by Robert Maass. Clarion, 1997. ISBN 978-0-395-71813-1 Subj: Babies. Birth. Family life – new sibling. Hospitals.

Rosenberry, Vera. *Run, jump, whiz, splash* ill. by author. Holiday, 1999. ISBN 978-0-8234-1378-2 Subj: Activities. Seasons.

Vera goes to the dentist ill. by author. Holt, 2002. ISBN 978-0-8050-6668-5 Subj: Careers – dentists. Health & fitness. Teeth.

Vera runs away ill. by author. Holt, 2000. ISBN 978-0-8050-6267-0 Subj: Behavior – running away. Family life.

Vera's baby sister ill. by author. Holt, 2005. ISBN 978-0-8050-7126-9 Subj: Family life – grandfathers. Family life – new sibling. Sibling rivalry.

Vera's first day of school ill. by author. Holt, 1999. ISBN 978-0-8050-5936-6 Subj: Character traits – shyness. Emotions – fear. School – first day.

Vera's Halloween ill. by author. Holt, 2008. ISBN 978-0-8050-8144-2 Subj: Behavior – lost. Holidays – Halloween.

When Vera was sick ill. by author. Holt, 1998. ISBN 978-0-8050-5405-7 Subj: Illness – chicken pox.

Who is in the garden? ill. by author. Holiday, 2001. ISBN 978-0-8234-1529-8 Subj: Animals. Gardens, gardening.

Rosenfeld, Dina Herman. *Five alive: my Yom Tov five senses* ill. by Tova Leff. Hachai, 2003. ISBN 978-1-929628-09-4 Subj: Holidays. Jewish culture. Senses.

Get well soon ill. by Rina Lyampe. Hachai, 2001. ISBN 978-1-929628-05-6 Subj: Illness. Jewish culture.

How in the world does bread come from the earth? ill. by Rina Lyampe. Hachai, 2002. ISBN 978-1-929628-06-3 Subj: Food. Religion. Rhyming text.

Rosenstock, Barb. *The camping trip that changed America: Theodore Roosevelt, John Muir, and our national parks* ill. by Mordicai Gerstein. Dial, 2012. ISBN 978-0-8037-3710-5 Subj: Camps, camping. Ecology. Parks. U.S. history.

Thomas Jefferson builds a library ill. by John O'Brien. Boyds Mills, 2013. ISBN 978-1-59078-932-2 Subj: Books, reading. Libraries. U.S. history.

Rosenthal, Amy Krouse. *Al Pha's bet* ill. by Delphine Durand. Penguin, 2011. ISBN 978-0-399-24601-2 Subj: ABC books. Language. Royalty – kings.

Bedtime for Mommy ill. by LeUyen Pham. Bloomsbury, 2010. ISBN 978-1-59990-341-5 Subj: Bedtime. Family life – mothers.

Chopsticks ill. by Scott Magoon. Hyperion, 2012. ISBN 978-1-4231-0796-5 Subj: Friendship. Humorous stories.

Christmas cookies: bite-size holiday lessons ill. by Jane Dyer. HarperCollins, 2008. ISBN 978-0-06-058024-7 Subj: Behavior. Character traits. Holidays – Christmas.

Cookies: bite-size life lessons ill. by Jane Dyer. HarperCollins, 2006. ISBN 978-0-06-058081-0 Subj: Activities – baking, cooking. Behavior. Character traits. Etiquette. Food.

Duck! Rabbit! ill. by Tom Lichtenheld. Chronicle, 2009. ISBN 978-0-8118-6865-5 Subj: Animals – rabbits. Birds – ducks. Optical illusions.

Exclamation mark ill. by Tom Lichtenheld. Scholastic, 2013. ISBN 978-0-545-43679-3 Subj: Character traits – being different. Character traits – individuality. Language. Self-concept.

I scream, ice cream! a book of wordles ill. by Serge Bloch. Chronicle, 2013. ISBN 978-1-4521-0004-3 Subj: Language.

It's not fair! ill. by Tom Lichtenheld. HarperCollins, 2008. ISBN 978-0-06-115257-3 Subj: Behavior – dissatisfaction. Character traits – questioning. Rhyming text.

Little Hoot ill. by Jen Corace. Chronicle, 2008. ISBN 978-0-8118-6023-9 Subj: Bedtime. Birds – owls.

Little Oink ill. by Jen Corace. Chronicle, 2009. ISBN 978-0-8118-6655-2 Subj: Animals – pigs. Character traits – cleanliness.

Little Pea ill. by Jen Corace. Chronicle, 2005. ISBN 978-0-8118-4658-5 Subj: Food.

The OK book ill. by Tom Lichtenheld. HarperCollins, 2007. ISBN 978-0-06-115255-9 Subj: Self-concept.

One of those days ill. by Rebecca Doughty. Penguin, 2006. ISBN 978-0-399-24365-3 Subj: Behavior – bad day.

One smart cookie: bite-size lessons for the school years and beyond ill. by Jane Dyer and Brooke Dyer. HarperCollins, 2010. ISBN 978-0-06-142970-5 Subj: Activities – baking, cooking. Behavior. Character traits. Food. Self-concept.

Plant a kiss ill. by Peter H. Reynolds. HarperCollins, 2011. ISBN 978-0-06-198675-8 Subj: Behavior – sharing. Emotions – love. Kissing.

Spoon ill. by Scott Magoon. Hyperion, 2009. ISBN 978-1-4231-0685-2 Subj: Character traits – individuality.

This plus that: life's little equations ill. by Jen Corace. HarperCollins, 2011. ISBN 978-0-06-172655-2 Subj: Behavior. Concepts. Counting, numbers.

Wumbers: it's a word cr8ed with a number! ill. by Tom Lichtenheld. Chronicle, 2012. ISBN 978-1-4521-1022-6 Subj: Counting, numbers. Language.

Yes Day! ill. by Tom Lichtenheld. HarperCollins, 2009. ISBN 978-0-06-115259-7 Subj: Behavior – resourcefulness. Behavior – wishing. Character traits – questioning. Holidays.

Rosenthal, Betsy R. *Which shoes would you choose?* ill. by Nancy Cote. Penguin, 2010. ISBN 978-0-399-25013-2 Subj: Clothing – shoes. Rhyming text.

Rosenthal, Eileen. *Bobo the sailor man!* ill. by Marc Rosenthal. Atheneum, 2013. ISBN 978-1-4424-4443-0 Subj: Animals – cats. Behavior – lost & found possessions. Sailors. Toys.

I must have Bobo! ill. by Marc Rosenthal. Simon & Schuster, 2011. ISBN 978-1-4424-0377-2 Subj: Animals – cats. Behavior – lost & found possessions. Toys.

I'll save you Bobo! ill. by Marc Rosenthal. Atheneum, 2012. ISBN 978-1-4424-0378-9 Subj: Activities – storytelling. Animals – cats. Toys.

Rosenthal, Marc. *Archie and the pirates* ill. by author. HarperCollins, 2009. ISBN 978-0-06-144164-6 Subj: Animals – monkeys. Friendship. Pirates.

Phooey! ill. by author. HarperCollins, 2007. ISBN 978-0-06-075248-4 Subj: Behavior – boredom. Cumulative tales. Humorous stories.

Roslonek, Steve. *The shape song swingalong* ill. by David Sim. Barefoot, 2011. ISBN 978-1-84686-671-5 Subj: Activities – drawing. Concepts – shape. Songs.

Rosoff, Meg. *Jumpy Jack and Googily* ill. by Sophie Blackall. Holt, 2008. ISBN 978-0-8050-8066-7 Subj: Animals – snails. Emotions – fear. Friendship. Humorous stories. Monsters.

Wild boars cook ill. by Sophie Blackall. Holt, 2008. ISBN 978-0-8050-7523-6 Subj: Activities – baking, cooking. Animals. Behavior – misbehavior. Food. Humorous stories.

Ross, Dave. *A book of hugs* ill. by Laura Rader. HarperCollins, 1999. ISBN 978-0-06-028147-2 Subj: Emotions.

A book of kisses ill. by Laura Rader. HarperCollins, 2000. ISBN 978-0-06-028453-4 Subj: Emotions.

Ross, Eileen. *The Halloween showdown* ill. by Lynn Rowe Reed. Holiday, 1999. ISBN 978-0-8234-1395-9 Subj: Animals. Animals – cats. Holidays – Halloween. Witches.

Ross, Fiona. *Chilly Milly Moo* ill. by author. Candlewick, 2011. ISBN 978-0-7636-5693-5 Subj: Animals – bulls, cows. Character traits – being different.

Ross, Gayle. *How Turtle's back was cracked* ill. by Murv Jacob. Dial, 1995. ISBN 978-0-8037-1729-9 Subj: Animals – wolves. Behavior – boasting. Folk & fairy tales. Indians of North America – Cherokee. Reptiles – turtles, tortoises.

The legend of the Windigo: a tale from native North America ill. by Murv Jacob. Dial, 1996. ISBN 978-0-8037-1898-2 Subj: Folk & fairy tales. Indians of North America – Algonquin. Indians of North America – Windigos. Insects – mosquitoes. Monsters.

Ross, Michael Elsohn. *Earth cycles* ill. by Gustav Moore. Millbrook, 2001. ISBN 978-0-7613-1815-6 Subj: Concepts. Day. Earth. Night. Seasons.

Mama's milk ill. by Ashley Wolff. Ten Speed, 2007. ISBN 978-1-58246-181-6 Subj: Animals. Babies. Family life – mothers. Rhyming text.

Mexican Christmas photos by Felix Rigau. Carolrhoda, 2002. ISBN 978-0-87614-601-9 Subj: Foreign lands – Mexico. Holidays – Christmas.

Play with me ill. by Julie Downing. Tricycle, 2009. ISBN 978-1-58246-255-4 Subj: Activities – playing. Animals. Family life – parents. Rhyming text.

Ross, Tom. *Eggbert, the slightly cracked egg* ill. by Rex Barron. Putnam, 1994. ISBN 978-0-399-22416-4 Subj: Careers – artists. Character traits – individuality. Eggs.

Ross, Tony. *The boy who cried wolf* ill. by author. Dial, 1991. ISBN 978-0-8037-0193-9 Subj: Animals – wolves. Behavior – lying. Behavior – trickery. Folk & fairy tales.

Centipede's 100 shoes ill. by author. Holt, 2003. ISBN 978-0-8050-7298-3 Subj: Clothing – shoes. Crustaceans – centipedes, millipedes.

I don't want to go to the hospital! ill. by author. Andersen, 2013. ISBN 978-1-46771-155-5 Subj: Hospitals. Royalty – princesses.

I want a party! ill. by author. Andersen, 2011. ISBN 978-0-7613-8089-4 Subj: Parties. Royalty – princesses.

I want my light on! a Little Princess story ill. by author. Andersen, 2010. ISBN 978-0-7613-6443-6 Subj: Bedtime. Emotions – fear. Ghosts. Royalty – princesses.

I want my tooth ill. by author. Kane/Miller, 2005. ISBN 978-1-929132-85-0 Subj: Royalty – princesses. Teeth.

I want to do it myself! a Little Princess story ill. by author. Andersen, 2011. ISBN 978-0-7613-7412-1 Subj: Camps, camping. Royalty – princesses.

I want to win! a Little Princess story ill. by author. Andersen, 2012. ISBN 978-0-7613-8993-4 Subj: Contests. Royalty – princesses.

I want two birthdays! ill. by author. Andersen, 2010. ISBN 978-0-7613-5495-6 Subj: Birthdays. Royalty – princesses.

Rossell, Judith. *Oliver* ill. by author. HarperCollins, 2012. ISBN 978-0-06-202210-3 Subj: Character traits – questioning. Imagination.

Ruby and Leonard and the great big surprise ill. by author. IPG/Little Hare, 2010. ISBN 978-1-921272-96-7 Subj: Activities – baking, cooking. Animals – mice. Birthdays. Family life – brothers & sisters.

Rossetti-Shustak, Bernadette. *I love you through and through* ill. by Caroline Jayne Church. Scholastic, 2005. ISBN 978-0-439-67363-1 Subj: Emotions – love. Format, unusual – board books. Rhyming text. Self-concept.

Rossiter, Nan Parson. *Sugar on snow* ill. by author. Dutton, 2002. ISBN 978-0-525-46910-0 Subj: Family life – brothers. Farms. Food.

Rostoker-Gruber, Karen. *Bandit* ill. by Vincent Nguyen. Marshall Cavendish, 2008. ISBN 978-0-7614-5382-6 Subj: Animals – cats. Behavior – running away. Moving.

Bandit's surprise ill. by Vincent Nguyen. Marshall Cavendish, 2010. ISBN 978-0-7614-5623-0 Subj: Animals – babies. Animals – cats. Behavior – sharing.

Ferret fun ill. by Paul Ratz de Tagyos. Marshall Cavendish, 2011. ISBN 978-0-7614-5817-3 Subj: Animals – cats. Animals – ferrets. Pets.

Roth, Carol. *All aboard to work — choo-choo!* ill. by Steve Lavis. Whitman, 2009. ISBN 978-0-8075-0271-6 Subj: Animals. Careers. Rhyming text. Trains.

Little Bunny's sleepless night ill. by Valeri Gorbachev. NorthSouth, 1999. ISBN 978-0-7358-1070-9 Subj: Animals – rabbits. Behavior – dissatisfaction. Friendship. Sleep.

The little school bus ill. by Pamela Paparone. NorthSouth, 2002. ISBN 978-0-7358-1647-3 Subj: Animals. Buses. Rhyming text. School.

Ten dirty pigs / Ten clean pigs ill. by Pamela Paparone. NorthSouth, 1999. ISBN 978-0-7358-1090-7 Subj: Animals – pigs. Bedtime. Counting, numbers. Format, unusual.

Where's my mommy? ill. by Sean Julian. NorthSouth, 2012. ISBN 978-0-7358-4032-4 Subj: Animals – cats. Family life – mothers. Farms.

Will you still love me? ill. by Daniel Howarth. Whitman, 2010. ISBN 978-0-8075-9114-7 Subj: Animals. Emotions – love. Family life – mothers. Family life – new sibling. Rhyming text.

Roth, Judith L. *Goodnight, dragons* ill. by Pascal Lemaître. Hyperion, 2012. ISBN 978-1-4231-4190-7 Subj: Dragons. Sleep.

Roth, Roger. *Fishing for Methuselah* ill. by author. HarperCollins, 1998. ISBN 978-0-06-027592-1 Subj: Friendship. Sports – fishing. Tall tales.

Roth, Ruby. *V is for vegan: the ABCs of being kind* ill. by author. North Atlantic Books, 2013. ISBN 978-1-58394-649-7 Subj: ABC books. Character traits – kindness to animals. Food. Health & fitness. Rhyming text.

Roth, Susan L. *Babies can't eat kimchee!* (Patz, Nancy)

The biggest frog in Australia ill. by author. Simon & Schuster, 1996. ISBN 978-0-689-80490-8 Subj: Foreign lands – Australia. Frogs & toads. Tall tales.

Cinnamon's day out: a gerbil adventure ill. by author. Dial, 1998. ISBN 978-0-8037-2323-8 Subj: Animals – gerbils. Behavior – running away.

Do re mi: if you can read music, thank Guido d'Arezzo ill. by author. Houghton, 2007. ISBN 978-0-618-46572-9 Subj: Music.

Great big guinea pigs ill. by author. Bloomsbury, 2006. ISBN 978-1-58234-724-0 Subj: Animals – guinea pigs. Prehistory.

Hands around the library: protecting Egypt's treasured books by Susan L. Roth and Karen Leggett

Abouraya ill. by Susan L. Roth. Dial, 2012. ISBN 978-0-8037-3747-1 Subj: Books, reading. Foreign lands – Egypt. Libraries. Violence, nonviolence.

Happy birthday Mr. Kang ill. by author. National Geographic, 2001. ISBN 978-0-7922-7723-1 Subj: Behavior – wishing. Birds. Character traits – freedom. Cities, towns. Ethnic groups in the U.S. – Chinese Americans. Family life – grandfathers.

Kanahena: a Cherokee story ill. by reteller. St. Martin's, 1988. ISBN 978-0-312-01722-4 Subj: Animals – wolves. Folk & fairy tales. Indians of North America – Cherokee.

Listen to the wind: the story of Dr. Greg and three cups of tea (Mortenson, Greg)

Night-time numbers: a scary counting book ill. by author. Barefoot, 1999. ISBN 978-1-84148-001-5 Subj: Bedtime. Counting, numbers. Night. Rhyming text.

Parrots over Puerto Rico by Susan L. Roth and Cindy Trumbore ill. by Susan L. Roth. Lee & Low, 2013. ISBN 978-1-62014-004-8 Subj: Birds – parakeets, parrots. Ecology. Foreign lands – Puerto Rico.

Rothenberg, Joan Keller. *Inside-out grandma* ill. by author. Hyperion, 1995. ISBN 978-0-7868-2092-4 Subj: Clothing. Family life – grandmothers. Folk & fairy tales. Holidays – Hanukkah. Jewish culture. Religion.

Matzah ball soup ill. by author. Hyperion, 1999. ISBN 978-0-7868-2170-9 Subj: Family life – sisters. Food. Holidays – Passover. Jewish culture.

Rothstein, Gloria. *Sheep asleep* ill. by Lizzy Rockwell. HarperCollins, 2003. ISBN 978-0-06-029106-8 Subj: Animals – sheep. Bedtime. Counting, numbers. Rhyming text.

Rotner, Shelley. *The A.D.D. book for kids* by Shelley Rotner and Sheila M. Kelly; photos by author. Millbrook, 2000. ISBN 978-0-7613-1722-7 Subj: Behavior. Disabilities – ADD.

Boats afloat photos by author. Orchard, 1998. ISBN 978-0-531-33112-5 Subj: Boats, ships. Transportation.

The body book by Shelley Rotner and Steve Calcagnino; photos by author. Orchard, 2000. ISBN 978-0-531-33256-6 Subj: Anatomy.

The buzz on bees: why are they disappearing? by Shelley Rotner and Anne Love Woodhull; photos by author. Holiday House, 2010. ISBN 978-0-8234-2247-0 Subj: Ecology. Insects – bees.

Citybook photos by Ken Kreisler. Orchard, 1994. ISBN 978-0-531-06837-3 Subj: Cities, towns. Rhyming text.

Every season by Shelley Rotner and Anne Love Woodhull; photos by author. Macmillan, 2007. ISBN 978-1-59643-136-2 Subj: Nature. Seasons.

Everybody works by Shelley Rotner and Ken Kreisler; photos by author. Millbrook, 2003. ISBN 978-0-7613-1751-7 Subj: Activities – working. Careers.

Faces photos by Ken Kreisler. Macmillan, 1994. ISBN 978-0-02-777887-8 Subj: Anatomy – faces. Character traits – individuality.

Feeling thankful by Shelley Rotner and Sheila M. Kelly; photos by author. Millbrook, 2000. ISBN 978-0-7613-1918-4 Subj: Emotions.

Hold the anchovies! by Shelley Rotner and Julia Pemberton Hellums; photos by author. Orchard, 1996. ISBN 978-0-531-08857-9 Subj: Activities – baking, cooking. Food.

Homer (deGroat, Diane)

I'm adopted! by Shelley Rotner and Sheila M. Kelly; photos by author. Holiday House, 2011. ISBN 978-0-8234-2294-4 Subj: Adoption.

Lots of grandparents by Shelley Rotner and Sheila M. Kelly; photos by author. Millbrook, 2001. ISBN 978-0-7613-2313-6 Subj: Emotions – love. Family life – grandparents.

Lots of moms by Shelley Rotner and Sheila M. Kelly; photos by author. Dial, 1996. ISBN 978-0-8037-1892-0 Subj: Ethnic groups in the U.S. Family life – mothers.

Parts photos by author. Walker, 2001. ISBN 978-0-8027-8754-5 Subj: Concepts. Picture puzzles. Rhyming text.

Pick a pet by Shelley Rotner and Cheo García; photos by author. Orchard, 1999. ISBN 978-0-531-33147-7 Subj: Animals. Pets.

Senses at the seashore photos by author. Lerner, 2006. ISBN 978-0-7613-2897-1 Subj: Sea & seashore – beaches. Senses.

Senses in the city photos by author. Lerner, 2008. ISBN 978-0-8225-7502-3 Subj: Cities, towns. Senses.

Shades of people by Shelley Rotner and Sheila M. Kelly; photos by author. Holiday, 2009. ISBN 978-0-8234-2191-6 Subj: Anatomy – skin. Concepts – color. Ethnic groups in the U.S.

What can you do? by Shelley Rotner and Sheila M. Kelly; photos by author. Millbrook, 2001. ISBN 978-0-7613-2119-4 Subj: Activities. Character traits – individuality. Self-concept.

What's love? by Shelley Rotner and Deborah Carlin; photos by author. Roaring Brook, 2009. ISBN 978-1-59643-362-5 Subj: Emotions – love.

Wheels around photos by author. Houghton, 1995. ISBN 978-0-395-71815-5 Subj: Wheels.

Where does food come from? by Shelley Rotner and Gary Goss; photos by author. Lerner, 2006. ISBN 978-0-7613-2935-0 Subj: Food.

Rotter, Charles. *Seals* ill. with photos. Child's World, 2001. ISBN 978-1-56766-891-9 Subj: Animals – seals. Science.

Walruses ill. with photos. Child's World, 2001. ISBN 978-1-56766-894-0 Subj: Animals – walruses. Science.

Rouillard, Wendy. *Barnaby's bunny* ill. by author. Scholastic, 2003. ISBN 978-0-439-33307-8 Subj: Animals. Animals – bears. Eggs. Pets. School.

Rounds, Glen. *Cowboys* ill. by author. Holiday, 1991. ISBN 978-0-8234-0867-2 Subj: Cowboys, cowgirls. U.S. history – frontier & pioneer life.

Once we had a horse ill. by author. Holiday, 1996. ISBN 978-0-8234-1241-9 Subj: Animals – horses, ponies.

Sod houses on the Great Plains ill. by author. Holiday, 1995. ISBN 978-0-8234-1162-7 Subj: Family life. Homes, houses. U.S. history – frontier & pioneer life.

Rouss, Sylvia A. *The littlest frog* ill. by Holly Hannon. Pitspopany, 2001. ISBN 978-1-930143-12-8 Subj: Foreign lands – Egypt. Frogs & toads. Jewish culture.

The littlest pair ill. by Holly Hannon. Pitspopany, 2001. ISBN 978-1-930143-17-3 Subj: Character traits – cooperation. Insects – termites. Religion – Noah.

Sammy Spider's first day of school ill. by Katherine Janus Kahn. Lerner, 2009. ISBN 978-0-8225-8583-1 Subj: Jewish culture. School – first day. Spiders.

Sammy Spider's first Passover ill. by Katherine Janus Kahn. Kar-Ben, 1995. ISBN 978-0-929371-81-8 Subj: Holidays – Passover. Jewish culture. Religion. Spiders.

Sammy Spider's first Shabbat ill. by Katherine Janus Kahn. Kar-Ben, 1997. ISBN 978-1-58013-007-3 Subj: Jewish culture. Religion. Spiders.

Sammy Spider's first Shavuot ill. by Katherine Janus Kahn. Lerner, 2008. ISBN 978-0-8225-7224-4 Subj: Holidays – Shavuot. Jewish culture. Religion.

Sammy Spider's first Tu B'Shevat ill. by Katherine Janus Kahn. Kar-Ben, 2000. ISBN 978-1-58013-065-3 Subj: Holidays – Tu B'Shevat. Jewish culture. Spiders. Trees.

Sammy Spider's first Yom Kippur ill. by Katherine Janus Kahn. Kar-Ben, 2013. ISBN 978-0-7613-9195-1 Subj: Holidays – Yom Kippur. Jewish culture. Religion. Spiders.

Rovetch, Lissa. *Ook the book* ill. by Shannon McNeill. Chronicle, 2001. ISBN 978-0-8118-2660-0 Subj: Humorous stories. Language. Poetry. Tongue twisters.

Rowe, Jeannette. *Whose ears?* ill. by author. Little, 1998. ISBN 978-0-316-75932-8 Subj: Anatomy – ears. Animals. Format, unusual – toy & movable books.

Whose feet? ill. by author. Little, 1998. ISBN 978-0-316-75934-2 Subj: Anatomy – feet. Animals. Format, unusual – toy & movable books.

Whose nose? ill. by author. Little, 1998. ISBN 978-0-316-75933-5 Subj: Anatomy – noses. Animals. Format, unusual – toy & movable books.

Rowe, John A. *I want a hug* ill. by author. Minedition, 2007. ISBN 978-0-698-40064-1 Subj: Animals – porcupines. Emotions – loneliness. Hugging. Reptiles – alligators, crocodiles.

Moondog ill. by author. Minedition, 2005. ISBN 978-0-698-40031-3 Subj: Animals – dogs. Ecology. Moon. Space & space ships.

Rox, John. *I want a hippopotamus for Christmas* ill. by Bruce Whatley. HarperCollins, 2005. ISBN 978-0-06-058549-5 Subj: Animals – hippopotamuses. Holidays – Christmas. Songs.

Rozen, Anna. *The merchant of noises* ill. by Francois Avril. Godine, 2006. ISBN 978-1-56792-321-6 Subj: Careers – salespeople. Character traits – cleverness. Noise, sounds.

Rubel, Nicole. *A cowboy named Ernestine* ill. by author. Dial, 2001. ISBN 978-0-8037-2152-4 Subj: Cowboys, cowgirls. Tall tales.

Ham and Pickles: first day of school ill. by author. Harcourt, 2006. ISBN 978-0-15-205039-9 Subj: Animals – hamsters. Family life – brothers & sisters. School – first day.

No more vegetables! ill. by author. Farrar, 2002. ISBN 978-0-374-36362-8 Subj: Family life – mothers. Food. Gardens, gardening. Plants.

Rubin, Adam. *Dragons love tacos* ill. by Daniel Salmieri. Dial, 2012. ISBN 978-0-8037-3680-1 Subj: Dragons. Food.

Secret pizza party ill. by Daniel Salmieri. Dial, 2013. ISBN 978-0-8037-3947-5 Subj: Animals – raccoons. Crime. Food. Parties.

Those darn squirrels! ill. by Daniel Salmieri. Clarion, 2008. ISBN 978-0-547-00703-8 Subj: Animals – squirrels. Birds. Old age.

Those darn squirrels and the cat next door ill. by Daniel Salmieri. Clarion, 2011. ISBN 978-0-547-42922-9 Subj: Animals – cats. Animals – squirrels. Birds. Old age.

Those darn squirrels fly south ill. by Daniel Salmieri. Clarion, 2012. ISBN 978-0-547-67823-8 Subj: Activities – traveling. Animals – squirrels. Birds. Old age.

Rubin, C. M. *Eleanor, Ellatony, Ellencake, and me* ill. by Christopher Fowler. Gingham Dog, 2003. ISBN 978-1-57768-412-1 Subj: Family life. Names. Rhyming text. Self-concept.

Rubin, Susan Goldman. *Jean Laffite: the pirate who saved America* ill. by Jeff Himmelman. Abrams, 2012. ISBN 978-0-8109-9733-2 Subj: Pirates. U.S. history.

Matisse dance for joy ill. by author. Chronicle, 2008. ISBN 978-0-8118-6288-2 Subj: Activities – dancing. Art. Format, unusual – board books.

The yellow house: Vincent van Gogh and Paul Gauguin side by side ill. by Joseph A. Smith. Abrams, 2001. ISBN 978-0-8109-4588-3 Subj: Art. Careers – artists. Foreign lands – France.

Rubinger, Ami. *Dog number 1 dog number 10* ill. by author. Abbeville, 2011. ISBN 978-0-7892-1066-1 Subj: Animals – dogs. Counting, numbers. Rhyming text.

I dream of an elephant ill. by author. Abbeville, 2010. ISBN 978-0-7892-1058-6 Subj: Animals – elephants. Concepts – color. Rhyming text.

Rubinstein, Gary. *The girl who never made mistakes* (Pett, Mark)

Ruddell, Deborah. *Today at the Bluebird Cafe: a branchful of birds* ill. by Joan Rankin. Simon & Schuster, 2007. ISBN 978-0-689-87153-5 Subj: Birds. Poetry.

A whiff of pine, a hint of skunk: a forest of poems ill. by Joan Rankin. Simon & Schuster, 2009. ISBN 978-1-4169-4211-5 Subj: Animals. Nature. Poetry.

Who said coo? ill. by Robin Luebs. Simon & Schuster, 2010. ISBN 978-1-4169-8510-5 Subj: Animals – pigs. Bedtime. Birds – owls. Birds – pigeons. Character traits – cooperation.

Rueda, Claudia. *Huff and puff: can you blow down the houses of the three little pigs?* ill. by author. Abrams, 2012. ISBN 978-1-4197-0170-2 Subj: Animals – pigs. Animals – wolves. Character traits – cleverness. Format, unusual – toy & movable books. Participation.

Is it big or is it little? ill. by author. Eerdmans, 2013. ISBN 978-0-8028-5423-0 Subj: Animals – cats. Animals – mice. Concepts – opposites. Concepts – size.

Let's play in the forest while the wolf is not around ill. by author. Scholastic, 2006. ISBN 978-0-439-82323-4 Subj: Animals. Animals – wolves. Games. Songs.

My little polar bear ill. by author. Scholastic, 2009. ISBN 978-0-545-14600-5 Subj: Animals – polar bears. Behavior – growing up. Emotions – love. Family life – mothers. Foreign lands – Arctic.

No ill. by author. Groundwood, 2010. ISBN 978-0-88899-991-7 Subj: Animals – bears. Bedtime. Hibernation.

Ruelle, Karen Gray. *Bark park* ill. by author. Peachtree, 2008. ISBN 978-1-56145-434-1 Subj: Animals – dogs. Parks.

Ruiz-Flores, Lupe. *Alicia's fruity drinks / Las aguas frescas de Alicia* ill. by Laura Lacámara. Arte Publico/Pinata, 2012. ISBN 978-1-55885-705-6 Subj: Ethnic groups in the U.S. – Mexican Americans. Family life – mothers. Foreign languages. Health & fitness. Illness – diabetes.

Rule, Rebecca. *The iciest, diciest, scariest sled ride ever!* ill. by Jennifer Thermes. Islandport, 2012. ISBN 978-1-934031-88-9 Subj: Seasons – winter. Sports – sledding.

Rumford, James. *Chee-lin: a giraffe's journey* ill. by author. Houghton, 2008. ISBN 978-0-618-71720-0 Subj: Activities – traveling. Animals – giraffes. Foreign lands – China.

Dog-of-the-Sea-Waves ill. by author. Houghton, 2004. ISBN 978-0-618-35611-9 Subj: Animals – seals. Character traits – kindness to animals. Family life – brothers. Foreign languages. Friendship. Hawaii.

Don't touch my hat! ill. by author. Random House, 2007. ISBN 978-0-375-93782-1 Subj: Careers – sheriffs. Clothing – hats. Superstition. U.S. history – frontier & pioneer life.

The Island-below-the-star ill. by author. Houghton, 1998. ISBN 978-0-395-85159-3 Subj: Activities – traveling. Boats, ships. Family life – brothers. Hawaii. Islands.

Max and the dumb flower picture (Alexander, Martha G.)

Nine animals and the well ill. by author. Houghton, 2003. ISBN 978-0-618-30915-3 Subj: Animals. Character traits – pride. Character traits – vanity. Counting, numbers. Folk & fairy tales. Foreign lands – India. Gifts. Parties.

Rain school ill. by author. Harcourt, 2010. ISBN 978-0-547-24307-8 Subj: Foreign lands – Chad. School. Weather – rain.

Sequoyah ill. by author. Houghton, 2004. ISBN 978-0-618-36947-8 Subj: ABC books. Foreign languages. Indians of North America – Cherokee.

Silent music: a story of Baghdad ill. by author. Roaring Brook, 2008. ISBN 978-1-59643-276-5 Subj: Activities – writing. Foreign lands – Iraq. War.

There's a monster in the alphabet ill. by author. Houghton, 2002. ISBN 978-0-618-22140-0 Subj: ABC books. Foreign lands – Greece. Foreign languages. Language.

Tiger and turtle ill. by author. Roaring Brook, 2010. ISBN 978-1-59643-416-5 Subj: Animals – tigers. Behavior – fighting, arguing. Friendship. Reptiles – turtles, tortoises.

Runton, Andy. *Owly and Wormy: bright lights and starry nights!* ill. by author. Simon & Schuster, 2012. ISBN 978-1-4169-5775-1 Subj: Animals – worms. Birds – owls. Emotions – fear. Friendship. Night. Wordless.

Owly and Wormy: friends all aflutter! ill. by author. Simon & Schuster, 2011. ISBN 978-1-4169-5774-4 Subj: Animals – worms. Birds. Friendship. Insects – butterflies, caterpillars. Metamorphosis. Wordless.

Rusackas, Francesca. *Daddy all day long* ill. by Priscilla Burris. HarperCollins, 2004. ISBN 978-0-06-050285-0 Subj: Animals – pigs. Bedtime. Counting, numbers. Emotions – love. Family life – fathers. Family life – sons.

I love you all day long ill. by Priscilla Burris. HarperCollins, 2003. ISBN 978-0-06-050277-5 Subj: Animals – pigs. Family life – mothers. School – first day.

Rusch, Elizabeth. *A day with no crayons* ill. by Chad Cameron. Rising Moon, 2007. ISBN 978-0-87358-910-9 Subj: Careers – artists. Concepts – color.

Russell, Joan Plummer. *Aero and Officer Mike* photos by Kris Turner Sinnenberg. Boyds Mills, 2001. ISBN 978-1-56397-931-6 Subj: Animals – dogs. Animals – service animals. Careers – police officers.

Russell, Natalie. *Brown Rabbit in the city* ill. by author. Penguin, 2010. ISBN 978-0-670-01234-3 Subj: Animals – rabbits. Cities, towns. Friendship.

Moon rabbit ill. by author. Viking, 2009. ISBN 978-0-670-01170-4 Subj: Animals – rabbits. Cities, towns. Friendship.

Russo, Marisabina. *The big brown box* ill. by author. Greenwillow, 2000. ISBN 978-0-688-17097-4 Subj: Activities – playing. Behavior – sharing. Family life – brothers. Games. Imagination. Sibling rivalry.

The bunnies are not in their beds ill. by author. Random House, 2007. ISBN 978-0-375-93961-7 Subj: Animals – rabbits. Bedtime. Behavior – misbehavior.

Come back, Hannah ill. by author. Greenwillow, 2001. ISBN 978-0-688-17384-5 Subj: Babies. Family life – mothers.

Grandpa Abe ill. by author. Greenwillow, 1996. ISBN 978-0-688-14098-4 Subj: Death. Emotions – grief. Family life – grandfathers.

Hannah's baby sister ill. by author. Greenwillow, 1998. ISBN 978-0-688-15832-3 Subj: Babies. Family life – brothers & sisters. Family life – new sibling.

I will come back for you: a family in hiding during World War II ill. by author. Random House, 2011. ISBN 978-0-375-86695-1 Subj: Family life – grandmothers. Foreign lands – Italy. Holocaust. Jewish culture. War.

Mama talks too much ill. by author. Greenwillow, 1999. ISBN 978-0-688-16412-6 Subj: Cities, towns. Communities, neighborhoods. Family life – mothers. Shopping.

Peter is just a baby ill. by author. Eerdmans, 2012. ISBN 978-0-8028-5384-4 Subj: Animals – bears. Babies. Family life – brothers & sisters. Foreign languages.

The trouble with baby ill. by author. Greenwillow, 2003. ISBN 978-0-06-008925-2 Subj: Emotions – envy, jealousy. Family life – brothers & sisters. Toys – dolls.

Under the table ill. by author. Greenwillow, 1997. ISBN 978-0-688-14603-0 Subj: Activities – drawing. Behavior – misbehavior. Family life.

A very big bunny ill. by author. Random House, 2010. ISBN 978-0-375-84463-8 Subj: Animals – rabbits. Character traits – being different. Concepts – size. Friendship. School. Self-concept.

When mama gets home ill. by author. Greenwillow, 1998. ISBN 978-0-688-14986-4 Subj: Family life. Family life – mothers.

Ruurs, Margriet. *In my backyard* ill. by Ron Broda. Tundra, 2007. ISBN 978-0-88776-775-3 Subj: Animals. Nature.

My librarian is a camel: how books are brought to children around the world ill. with photos. Boyds Mills, 2005. ISBN 978-1-59078-093-0 Subj: Careers – librarians. Libraries. World.

My school in the rain forest: how children attend school around the world ill. with photos. Boyds Mills, 2009. ISBN 978-1-59078-601-7 Subj: School. World.

Wake up, Henry Rooster! ill. by Sean Cassidy. Fitzhenry & Whiteside, 2006. ISBN 978-1-55041-952-8 Subj: Birds – chickens.

When we go camping ill. by Andrew Kiss. Tundra, 2001. ISBN 978-0-88776-476-9 Subj: Camps, camping. Family life. Nature.

Ruzzier, Sergio. *Amandina* ill. by author. Roaring Brook, 2008. ISBN 978-1-59643-236-9 Subj: Animals – dogs. Character traits – perseverance. Character traits – shyness. Theater.

Bear and Bee ill. by author. Disney/Hyperion, 2013. ISBN 978-1-4231-5957-5 Subj: Animals – bears. Behavior – sharing. Insects – bees. Prejudice.

Hey, Rabbit! ill. by author. Roaring Brook, 2010. ISBN 978-1-59643-502-5 Subj: Animals – rabbits. Friendship. Imagination.

The little giant ill. by author. Geringer, 2004. ISBN 978-0-06-052952-9 Subj: Concepts – size. Dwarfs, midgets. Friendship. Giants.

The room of wonders ill. by author. Farrar, 2006. ISBN 978-0-374-36343-7 Subj: Animals – pack rats. Behavior – collecting things. Museums.

Ryan, Candace. *Ribbit rabbit* ill. by Mike Lowery. Walker, 2011. ISBN 978-0-8027-2180-8 Subj: Animals – rabbits. Friendship. Frogs & toads.

Ryan, Cheli Durán. *Hildilid's night* ill. by Arnold Lobel. Macmillan, 1986, ©1971. ISBN 978-0-02-777260-9 Subj: Caldecott award honor books. Night.

Ryan, Cheryl. *Red are the apples* (Harshman, Marc)

Ryan, Pam Muñoz. *Amelia and Eleanor go for a ride* ill. by Brian Selznick. Scholastic, 1999. ISBN 978-0-590-96075-5 Subj: Activities – flying. Airplanes, airports. U.S. history.

Armadillos sleep in dugouts: and other places animals live ill. by Diane deGroat. Hyperion, 1997. ISBN 978-0-7868-2222-5 Subj: Animals. Homes, houses. Rhyming text.

The crayon counting book by Pam Muñoz Ryan and Jerry Pallotta ill. by Frank Mazzola. Charlesbridge, 1996. ISBN 978-0-88106-955-6 Subj: Concepts – color. Counting, numbers. Rhyming text.

The flag we love ill. by Ralph Masiello. Charlesbridge, 1996. ISBN 978-0-88106-846-7 Subj: Poetry. U.S. history.

Hello, Ocean! ill. by Mark Astrella. Charlesbridge, 2001. ISBN 978-0-88106-987-7 Subj: Rhyming text. Sea & seashore – beaches. Senses.

Hello ocean / Hola mar ill. by Mark Astrella. Charlesbridge, 2003. ISBN 978-1-57091-372-3 Subj: Foreign languages. Rhyming text. Sea & seashore – beaches. Senses.

How do you raise a raisin? ill. by Craig Brown. Charlesbridge, 2003. ISBN 978-0-613-82657-0 Subj: Food. Science.

Mice and beans ill. by Joe Cepeda. Scholastic, 2001. ISBN 978-0-439-18303-1 Subj: Animals – mice. Birthdays. Family life – grandmothers. Foreign lands – Mexico. Foreign languages.

Mud is cake ill. by David McPhail. Hyperion, 2002. ISBN 978-0-7868-0501-3 Subj: Activities – playing. Family life – brothers & sisters. Imagination. Rhyming text.

Nacho and Lolita ill. by Claudia Rueda. Scholastic, 2005. ISBN 978-0-439-26968-1 Subj: Birds – swallows. Folk & fairy tales. Missions.

There was no snow on Christmas Eve ill. by Dennis Nolan. Hyperion, 2005. ISBN 978-0-7868-5492-9 Subj: Holidays – Christmas. Religion – Nativity. Rhyming text. Weather.

Tony Baloney ill. by Edwin Fotheringham. Scholastic, 2011. ISBN 978-0-545-23135-0 Subj: Birds – penguins. Family life – brothers & sisters.

When Marian sang: the true recital of Marian Anderson, the voice of a century ill. by Brian Selznick. Scholastic, 2002. ISBN 978-0-439-26967-4 Subj: Careers – singers. Ethnic groups in the U.S. – African Americans. Prejudice. U.S. history.

Ryder, Joanne. *Bear of my heart* ill. by Margie Moore. Simon & Schuster, 2007. ISBN 978-0-689-85947-2 Subj: Animals – bears. Emotions – love. Family life – mothers. Rhyming text.

Big bear ball ill. by Steven Kellogg. HarperCollins, 2002. ISBN 978-0-06-027956-1 Subj: Activities – dancing. Animals. Animals – bears. Rhyming text.

Chipmunk song ill. by Lynne Cherry. Dutton, 1987. ISBN 978-0-525-67191-6 Subj: Animals – chipmunks. Nature. Rhyming text.

Dance by the light of the moon ill. by Guy Francis. Hyperion, 2007. ISBN 978-0-7868-1820-4 Subj: Activities – dancing. Animals. Farms. Rhyming text. Songs.

Each living thing ill. by Ashley Wolff. Harcourt, 2000. ISBN 978-0-15-201898-6 Subj: Animals. Character traits – kindness to animals. Rhyming text.

A fawn in the grass ill. by Keiko Narahashi. Holt, 2001. ISBN 978-0-8050-6236-6 Subj: Animals. Rhyming text.

Jaguar in the rain forest ill. by Michael Rothman. Morrow, 1996. ISBN 978-0-688-12991-0 Subj: Animals – jaguars. Foreign lands – French Guiana. Jungle.

Little panda ill. with photos. Aladdin, 2001. ISBN 978-0-689-84310-5 Subj: Animals – babies. Animals – pandas. Zoos.

Mouse tail moon ill. by Maggie Kneen. Holt, 2002. ISBN 978-0-8050-6404-9 Subj: Animals – mice. Poetry.

My father's hands ill. by Mark Graham. Morrow, 1994. ISBN 978-0-688-09190-3 Subj: Anatomy – hands. Family life – fathers. Gardens, gardening. Insects.

A pair of polar bears: twin cubs find a home at the San Diego Zoo ill. with photos. Simon & Schuster, 2006. ISBN 978-0-689-85871-0 Subj: Animals – polar bears. Multiple births – twins. Zoos.

Panda kindergarten ill. by Katherine Feng. HarperCollins, 2009. ISBN 978-0-06-057850-3 Subj: Animals – pandas. Foreign lands – China. School.

Rainbow wings ill. by Victor Lee. Morrow, 2000. ISBN 978-0-688-14129-5 Subj: Activities – flying. Science.

Step into the night ill. by Dennis Nolan. Four Winds, 1988. ISBN 978-0-02-777951-6 Subj: Nature. Night. Poetry.

Toad by the road: a year in the life of these amazing amphibians ill. by Maggie Kneen. Holt, 2007. ISBN 978-0-8050-7354-6 Subj: Frogs & toads. Poetry. Seasons.

Tyrannosaurus time ill. by Michael Rothman. Morrow, 1999. ISBN 978-0-688-13683-3 Subj: Dinosaurs. Imagination.

The waterfall's gift ill. by Richard Jesse Watson. Sierra Club, 2001. ISBN 978-0-87156-579-2 Subj: Ecology. Forest, woods. Nature. Water.

Where butterflies grow ill. by Lynne Cherry. Dutton, 1989. ISBN 978-0-525-67284-5 Subj: Insects – butterflies, caterpillars. Metamorphosis. Nature. Science.

White bear, ice bear ill. by Michael Rothman. Morrow, 1989. ISBN 978-0-688-07175-2 Subj: Animals – polar bears. Foreign lands – Arctic. Nature.

Wild birds ill. by Susan Estelle Kwas. HarperCollins, 2003. ISBN 978-0-06-027739-0 Subj: Birds.

Won't you be my hugaroo? ill. by Melissa Sweet. Harcourt, 2006. ISBN 978-0-15-205778-7 Subj: Hugging. Rhyming text.

Rylant, Cynthia. *All I see* ill. by Peter Catalanotto. Watts, 1988. ISBN 978-0-531-08377-2 Subj: Activities – painting. Art. Friendship.

All in a day ill. by Nikki McClure. Abrams, 2009. ISBN 978-0-8109-8321-2 Subj: Day. Rhyming text.

Alligator boy ill. by Diane Goode. Harcourt, 2007. ISBN 978-0-15-206092-3 Subj: Reptiles – alligators, crocodiles. Rhyming text.

Appalachia: the voices of sleeping birds ill. by Barry Moser. Harcourt, 1991. ISBN 978-0-15-201605-0 Subj: Country.

Baby face: a book of love for baby ill. by Diane Goode. Simon & Schuster, 2008. ISBN 978-1-4169-4909-1 Subj: Babies. Emotions – love. Poetry.

Bear day ill. by Jennifer Selby. Harcourt, 1998. ISBN 978-0-15-201090-4 Subj: Animals – bears. Rhyming text.

Best wishes photos by Carlo Ontal. R.C. Owen, 1992. ISBN 978-1-878450-20-3 Subj: Activities – writing. Careers – writers. Family life.

The bird house ill. by Barry Moser. Blue Sky, 1998. ISBN 978-0-590-47345-3 Subj: Birds. Homes, houses. Orphans.

Birthday presents ill. by Suçie Stevenson. Watts, 1987. ISBN 978-0-531-08305-5 Subj: Behavior – sharing. Birthdays. Family life. Gifts.

Bless us all: a child's yearbook of blessings ill. by author. Simon & Schuster, 1998. ISBN 978-0-689-82370-1 Subj: Days of the week, months of the year. Religion. Rhyming text.

The bookshop dog ill. by author. Blue Sky, 1996. ISBN 978-0-590-54331-6 Subj: Animals – dogs. Character traits – kindness to animals. Friendship. Weddings.

Brownie and Pearl get dolled up ill. by Brian Biggs. Simon & Schuster, 2010. ISBN 978-1-4169-8631-7 Subj: Activities – playing. Animals – cats. Character traits – appearance.

Brownie and Pearl go for a spin ill. by Brian Biggs. Simon & Schuster, 2012. ISBN 978-1-4169-8633-1 Subj: Animals – cats. Automobiles.

Brownie and Pearl grab a bite ill. by Brian Biggs. Simon & Schuster, 2011. ISBN 978-1-4169-8634-8 Subj: Animals – cats. Food.

Brownie and Pearl hit the hay ill. by Brian Biggs. Simon & Schuster, 2011. ISBN 978-1-4169-8635-5 Subj: Animals – cats. Bedtime.

Brownie and Pearl make good ill. by Brian Biggs. Simon & Schuster, 2012. ISBN 978-1-4169-8636-2 Subj: Animals – cats. Behavior – mistakes.

Brownie and Pearl see the sights ill. by Brian Biggs. Simon & Schuster, 2010. ISBN 978-1-4169-8637-9 Subj: Animals – cats. Seasons – winter. Shopping.

Brownie and Pearl take a dip ill. by Brian Biggs. Simon & Schuster, 2011. ISBN 978-1-4169-8638-6 Subj: Animals – cats. Sports – swimming.

Bunny bungalow ill. by author. Harcourt, 1999. ISBN 978-0-15-201092-8 Subj: Animals – rabbits. Family life. Homes, houses. Rhyming text.

Christmas in the country ill. by Diane Goode. Blue Sky, 2002. ISBN 978-0-439-07334-9 Subj: Country. Family life – grandparents. Holidays – Christmas.

The cookie-store cat ill. by author. Blue Sky, 1999. ISBN 978-0-590-54329-3 Subj: Activities – baking, cooking. Animals – cats. Careers – bakers.

Dog Heaven ill. by author. Blue Sky, 1995. ISBN 978-0-590-41701-3 Subj: Angels. Animals – dogs. Death.

Give me grace: a child's daybook of prayers ill. by author. Simon & Schuster, 1999. ISBN 978-0-689-82293-3 Subj: Days of the week, months of the year. Religion. Rhyming text.

The great Gracie chase ill. by Mark Teague. Blue Sky, 2001. ISBN 978-0-590-10041-0 Subj: Animals – dogs. Cumulative tales.

If you'll be my Valentine ill. by Fumi Kosaka. HarperCollins, 2005. ISBN 978-0-06-009270-2 Subj: Activities – making things. Character traits – kindness. Emotions – love. Holidays – Valentine's Day. Letters, cards. Rhyming text.

In November ill. by Jill Kastner. Harcourt, 2000. ISBN 978-0-15-201076-8 Subj: Activities. Seasons – fall.

Little Whistle ill. by Tim Bowers. Harcourt, 2001. ISBN 978-0-15-201087-4 Subj: Animals – guinea pigs. Stores. Toys.

Little Whistle's Christmas ill. by Tim Bowers. Harcourt, 2003. ISBN 978-0-15-204590-6 Subj: Animals – guinea pigs. Holidays – Christmas. Letters, cards. Santa Claus. Stores. Toys.

Little Whistle's dinner party ill. by Tim Bowers. Harcourt, 2001. ISBN 978-0-15-201079-9 Subj: Animals – guinea pigs. Parties. Stores. Toys.

Little Whistle's medicine ill. by Tim Bowers. Harcourt, 2002. ISBN 978-0-15-201086-7 Subj: Animals – guinea pigs. Illness. Stores. Toys. Toys – soldiers.

Miss Maggie ill. by Thomas di Grazia. Dutton, 1983. ISBN 978-0-525-44048-2 Subj: Character traits – curiosity. Friendship.

Moonlight, the Halloween cat ill. by Melissa Sweet. HarperCollins, 2003. ISBN 978-0-06-029712-1 Subj: Animals – cats. Holidays – Halloween.

Mr. Griggs' work ill. by Julie Downing. Watts, 1989. ISBN 978-0-531-08369-7 Subj: Activities – working. Careers – postal workers. Character traits – pride. Post office.

Night in the country ill. by Mary Szilagyi. Bradbury, 1986. ISBN 978-0-02-777210-4 Subj: Animals. Country. Night.

Puppies and piggies ill. by Ivan Bates. Harcourt, 2008. ISBN 978-0-15-202321-8 Subj: Animals. Bedtime. Emotions – love. Rhyming text.

The relatives came ill. by Stephen Gammell. Bradbury, 1985. ISBN 978-0-02-777220-3 Subj: Activities – traveling. Caldecott award honor books. Family life.

Scarecrow ill. by Lauren Stringer. Harcourt, 1998. ISBN 978-0-15-201084-3 Subj: Country. Farms. Scarecrows.

Silver packages: an Appalachian Christmas story ill. by Chris Soentpiet. Orchard, 1997. ISBN 978-0-531-33051-7 Subj: Accidents. Careers – doctors. Character traits – generosity. Holidays – Christmas. Illness. Trains. Transportation.

Snow ill. by Lauren Stringer. Harcourt, 2008. ISBN 978-0-15-205303-1 Subj: Nature. Weather – snow.

The stars will still shine ill. by Tiphanie Beeke. HarperCollins, 2005. ISBN 978-0-06-054640-3 Subj: Nature. Rhyming text. World.

This year's garden ill. by Mary Szilagyi. Bradbury, 1984. ISBN 978-0-02-777970-7 Subj: Gardens, gardening.

The ticky-tacky doll ill. by Harvey Stevenson. Harcourt, 2002. ISBN 978-0-15-201078-2 Subj: Family life – grandmothers. School.

Tulip sees America ill. by Lisa Desimini. Blue Sky, 1998. ISBN 978-0-590-84744-5 Subj: Activities – traveling. Animals – dogs. Automobiles.

The whales ill. by author. Blue Sky, 1996. ISBN 978-0-590-58285-8 Subj: Animals – whales. Sea & seashore.

When I was young in the mountains ill. by Diane Goode. Dutton, 1982. ISBN 978-0-525-42525-0 Subj: Caldecott award honor books. Family life.

The wonderful happens ill. by Coco Dowley. Simon & Schuster, 2000. ISBN 978-0-689-83177-5 Subj: Emotions – happiness.

Rymond, Lynda Gene. *Oscar and the mooncats* ill. by Nicoletta Ceccoli. Houghton, 2007. ISBN 978-0-618-56316-6 Subj: Animals – cats. Imagination. Moon.

Sabuda, Robert. *Beauty and the beast: a pop-up book of the classic fairy tale* ill. by author. Simon & Schuster, 2010. ISBN 978-1-4169-6079-9 Subj: Animals. Character traits – appearance. Character traits – loyalty. Emotions – love. Folk & fairy tales. Format, unusual – toy & movable books. Magic.

The Blizzard's robe ill. by author. Atheneum, 1999. ISBN 978-0-689-31988-4 Subj: Activities – sewing. Foreign lands – Arctic. Mythical creatures. Northern lights. Sky.

The Christmas alphabet ill. by author. Orchard, 1994. ISBN 978-0-531-06857-1 Subj: ABC books.

Format, unusual – toy & movable books. Holidays – Christmas.

Encyclopedia prehistorica: dinosaurs by Robert Sabuda and Matthew Reinhart ill. by authors. Candlewick, 2005. ISBN 978-0-7636-2228-2 Subj: Dinosaurs. Format, unusual – toy & movable books. Prehistory.

Encyclopedia prehistorica: mega-beasts by Robert Sabuda and Matthew Reinhart ill. by authors. Candlewick, 2007. ISBN 978-0-7636-2230-5 Subj: Format, unusual – toy & movable books. Fossils. Prehistory. Science.

Encyclopedia prehistorica: sharks and other seamonsters by Robert Sabuda and Matthew Reinhart ill. by authors. Candlewick, 2006. ISBN 978-0-7636-2229-9 Subj: Fish – sharks. Format, unusual – toy & movable books. Fossils. Prehistory. Science. Sea & seashore.

Fairies and magical creatures (Reinhart, Matthew)

Gods and heroes (Reinhart, Matthew)

The movable Mother Goose by Robert Sabuda and Mother Goose ill. by Robert Sabuda. Simon & Schuster, 1999. ISBN 978-0-689-81192-0 Subj: Animals. Format, unusual – toy & movable books. Insects. Nursery rhymes.

Peter Pan: a pop-up adaptation of J.M. Barrie's original tale ill. by author. Simon & Schuster, 2008. ISBN 978-0-689-85364-7 Subj: Fairies. Folk & fairy tales. Format, unusual – toy & movable books. Imagination.

St. Valentine ill. by author. Macmillan, 1993. ISBN 978-0-689-31762-0 Subj: Holidays – Valentine's Day. Religion.

Tutankhamen's gift ill. by author. Atheneum, 1994. ISBN 978-0-689-31818-4 Subj: Foreign lands – Egypt. Gifts. Royalty – pharaohs.

Winter in white: a mini pop-up treat ill. by author. Simon & Schuster, 2007. ISBN 978-0-689-85365-4 Subj: Format, unusual – toy & movable books. Rhyming text. Seasons – winter.

Winter's tale: an original pop-up journey ill. by author. Simon & Schuster, 2005. ISBN 978-0-689-85363-0 Subj: Format, unusual – toy & movable books. Seasons – winter. Weather – snow.

Sacre, Antonio. *La Noche Buena: a Christmas story* ill. by Angela Dominguez. Abrams, 2010. ISBN 978-0-8109-8967-2 Subj: Ethnic groups in the U.S. – Cuban Americans. Family life – grandmothers. Holidays – Christmas.

A mango in the hand: a story told through proverbs ill. by Sebastià Serra. Abrams, 2011. ISBN 978-0-8109-9734-9 Subj: Character traits – generosity. Family life. Foreign lands – Cuba. Foreign languages.

Sadler, Judy Ann. *Sandwiches for Duke* ill. by Lorna Bennett. Stoddart, 2001. ISBN 978-0-7737-3313-8 Subj: Animals – dogs. Clothing – hats. Farms. Pets. Weather – storms.

Sadler, Marilyn. *Alistair in outer space* ill. by Roger Bollen. Prentice-Hall, 1984. ISBN 978-0-13-022369-2 Subj: Libraries. Space & space ships.

Alistair's time machine ill. by Roger Bollen. Prentice-Hall, 1986. ISBN 978-0-317-39621-8 Subj: Machines. School. Science. Space & space ships. Time.

Sadu, Itah. *Christopher changes his name* ill. by Roy Candy. Firefly, 1998. ISBN 978-1-55209-216-3 Subj: Ethnic groups in the U.S. – African Americans. Names.

Sáenz, Benjamin Alire. *A gift from papá Diego / Un regalo de papá Diego* ill. by Geronimo Garcia. Cinco Puntos, 1998. ISBN 978-0-938317-33-3 Subj: Birthdays. Ethnic groups in the U.S. – Mexican Americans. Family life – grandfathers. Foreign languages.

Grandma Fina and her wonderful umbrellas / La abuelita Fina y sus sombrillas maravillosas ill. by Geronimo Garcia. Cinco Puntos, 1999. ISBN 978-0-938317-46-3 Subj: Birthdays. Ethnic groups in the U.S. – Mexican Americans. Family life – grandmothers. Foreign languages. Umbrellas.

Safran, Sheri. *All kinds of families: a lift-the-flap book* ill. by Rachel Fuller. IPG/Trafalgar Square, 2011. ISBN 978-1-85707-756-8 Subj: Family life. Format, unusual – toy & movable books.

Sage, Alison. *Teddy bears cure a cold* (Gretz, Susanna)

Sage, Angie. *Molly and the birthday party* ill. by author. Peachtree, 2001. ISBN 978-1-56145-248-4 Subj: Birthdays. Format, unusual – toy & movable books. Gifts. Parties.

Monkeys in the jungle ill. by author. Dutton, 1989. ISBN 978-0-525-44466-4 Subj: Animals. Jungle. Rhyming text.

Sage, James. *Farmer Smart's fat cat* ill. by Russell Ayto. Chronicle, 2002. ISBN 978-0-8118-3502-2 Subj: Animals – cats. Animals – mice. Contests. Farms. Plants.

Mr. Beast: a monster fright in the night! ill. by Russell Ayto. Holt, 2005. ISBN 978-0-8050-7730-8 Subj: Food. Monsters.

Sahagun, Bernardino de. *Spirit child: a story of the Nativity* ill. by Barbara Cooney. Morrow, 1984. ISBN 978-0-688-02610-3 Subj: Folk & fairy tales. Foreign lands – Mexico. Holidays – Christmas. Religion – Nativity.

St. George, Judith. *So you want to be an explorer?* ill. by David Small. Penguin, 2005. ISBN 978-0-399-23868-0 Subj: Careers – explorers.

So you want to be president? ill. by David Small. Philomel, 2000. ISBN 978-0-399-23407-1 Subj: Caldecott award books. U.S. history.

Zarafa: the giraffe who walked to the king ill. by Britt Spencer. Philomel, 2009. ISBN 978-0-399-25049-1 Subj: Animals – giraffes. Foreign lands – Egypt. Foreign lands – France. Royalty – kings.

Saint James, Synthia. *The gifts of Kwanzaa* ill. by author. Whitman, 1994. ISBN 978-0-8075-2907-2 Subj: Ethnic groups in the U.S. – African Americans. Gifts. Holidays – Kwanzaa.

St. Pierre, Stephanie. *Cheetahs* ill. with photos. Heinemann, 2001. ISBN 978-1-58810-106-8 Subj: Animals – cheetahs. Science.

Jaguars ill. with photos. Heinemann, 2001. ISBN 978-1-58810-108-2 Subj: Animals – jaguars. Science.

Leopards ill. with photos. Heinemann, 2001. ISBN 978-1-58810-105-1 Subj: Animals – leopards. Science.

Lynx ill. with photos. Heinemann, 2001. ISBN 978-1-58810-109-9 Subj: Animals – lynx. Science.

Siberian tigers ill. with photos. Heinemann, 2001. ISBN 978-1-58810-110-5 Subj: Animals – tigers. Science.

What the sea saw ill. by Beverly Doyle. Peachtree, 2006. ISBN 978-1-56145-359-7 Subj: Animals. Ecology. Sea & seashore.

Sakai, Komako. *Emily's balloon* ill. by author. Chronicle, 2006. ISBN 978-0-8118-5219-7 Subj: Activities – ballooning. Friendship.

Mad at Mommy ill. by author. Scholastic, 2010. ISBN 978-0-545-21209-0 Subj: Animals – rabbits. Emotions – anger. Family life – mothers.

The snow day ill. by author. Scholastic, 2009. ISBN 978-0-545-01321-5 Subj: Animals – rabbits. Family life – mothers. Seasons – winter. Weather – snow.

Salariya, David. *All about me! a baby's guide to babies* photos by author. Random House, 2008. ISBN 978-0-375-84529-1 Subj: Babies. Format, unusual – board books.

Salas, Laura Purdie. *A leaf can be . . .* ill. by Violeta Dabija. Millbrook, 2012. ISBN 978-0-7613-6203-6 Subj: Imagination. Rhyming text. Trees.

Salat, Cristina. *Peanut's emergency* ill. by Tammie Lyon. Whispering Coyote, 2002. ISBN 978-1-57091-440-9 Subj: Behavior – lost. Ethnic groups in the U.S. – African Americans. Problem solving. Safety.

Salley, Coleen. *Epossumondas* ill. by Janet Stevens. Harcourt, 2002. ISBN 978-0-15-216748-6 Subj: Animals. Animals – possums. Behavior – misunderstanding. Clowns, jesters. Family life. Folk & fairy tales. Humorous stories.

Epossumondas plays possum ill. by Janet Stevens. Harcourt, 2009. ISBN 978-0-15-206420-4 Subj: Animals – possums. Emotions – fear. Mythical creatures – werewolves. Swamps.

Epossumondas saves the day ill. by Janet Stevens. Harcourt, 2006. ISBN 978-0-15-205701-5 Subj: Animals. Animals – possums. Folk & fairy tales. Humorous stories.

Who's that tripping over my bridge? by Coleen Salley and P. C. Asbjørnsen ill. by Amy Jackson Dixon. Pelican, 2002. ISBN 978-1-56554-890-9 Subj: Animals – goats. Character traits – cleverness. Mythical creatures – trolls.

Saltz, Gail. *Amazing you: getting smart about your private parts* ill. by Lynne Cravath. Button, 2005. ISBN 978-0-525-47389-3 Subj: Anatomy. Birth. Sex instruction.

Saltzberg, Barney. *All around the seasons* ill. by author. Candlewick, 2010. ISBN 978-0-7636-3694-4 Subj: Rhyming text. Seasons.

Andrew drew and drew ill. by author. Abrams, 2012. ISBN 978-1-4197-0377-5 Subj: Activities – drawing. Format, unusual – toy & movable books. Imagination.

Baby animal kisses ill. by author. Harcourt, 2001. ISBN 978-0-15-202635-6 Subj: Animals – babies. Format, unusual – toy & movable books. Kissing.

Cornelius P. Mud, are you ready for baby? ill. by author. Candlewick, 2009. ISBN 978-0-7636-3596-1 Subj: Animals – pigs. Babies. Family life – brothers.

Cornelius P. Mud, are you ready for bed? ill. by author. Candlewick, 2005. ISBN 978-0-7636-2399-9 Subj: Animals – pigs. Bedtime. Hugging.

Cornelius P. Mud, are you ready for school? ill. by author. Candlewick, 2007. ISBN 978-0-7636-2913-7 Subj: Animals – pigs. Kissing. School.

Crazy hair day ill. by author. Candlewick, 2003. ISBN 978-0-7636-1954-1 Subj: Animals – hamsters. Behavior – mistakes. Hair. School.

Hi, Blueberry! ill. by author. Harcourt, 2007. ISBN 978-0-15-205984-2 Subj: Animals – rabbits. Birthdays. Format, unusual – toy & movable books.

Hip, hip, hooray day! ill. by author. Harcourt, 2002. ISBN 978-0-15-202495-6 Subj: Animals –

hippopotamuses. Animals – rabbits. Birthdays. Friendship. Sports – roller skating.

I love cats ill. by author. Candlewick, 2005. ISBN 978-0-7636-2588-7 Subj: Animals – cats. Rhyming text.

I love dogs ill. by author. Candlewick, 2005. ISBN 978-0-7636-2587-0 Subj: Animals – dogs. Format, unusual – board books. Rhyming text.

Kisses: a pull, touch, lift, squeak, and smooch book! ill. by author. Harcourt, 2010. ISBN 978-0-15-206534-8 Subj: Emotions – love. Format, unusual – toy & movable books. Kissing. Rhyming text.

The problem with pumpkins ill. by author. Harcourt, 2001. ISBN 978-0-15-202489-5 Subj: Animals – hippopotamuses. Animals – rabbits. Clothing – costumes. Friendship. Holidays – Halloween.

Soccer mom from outer space ill. by author. Crown, 2000. ISBN 978-0-517-80064-5 Subj: Clothing – costumes. Family life – mothers. Sports – soccer.

Star of the week ill. by author. Candlewick, 2006. ISBN 978-0-7636-2914-4 Subj: Character traits – being different. Character traits – individuality. School. Self-concept.

Salzano, Tammi. *One little blueberry* ill. by Kat Whelan. Tiger Tales, 2011. ISBN 978-1-58925-859-4 Subj: Counting, numbers. Food. Insects.

One rainy day ill. by Hannah Wood. ME Media/ Tiger Tales, 2011. ISBN 978-1-58925-860-0 Subj: Birds – ducks. Concepts – color. Format, unusual – board books. Weather – rain.

One windy day ill. by Hannah Wood. Tiger Tales, 2012. ISBN 978-1-58925-875-4 Subj: Animals – foxes. Careers – postal workers. Concepts – opposites. Weather – wind.

Sampson, Michael R. *Adam, Adam, what do you see?* (Martin, Bill, Jr.)

Caddie, the golf dog ill. by Floyd Cooper. Tommy Nelson, 1999. ISBN 978-0-8499-5823-6 Subj: Animals – dogs. Character traits – kindness to animals. Weather – storms.

I love our Earth (Martin, Bill, Jr.)

Kitty Cat, Kitty Cat, are you going to school? (Martin, Bill, Jr.)

Kitty Cat, Kitty Cat, are you going to sleep? (Martin, Bill, Jr.)

Kitty Cat, Kitty Cat, are you waking up? (Martin, Bill, Jr.)

Little granny quarterback (Martin, Bill, Jr.)

The little squeegy bug (Martin, Bill, Jr.)

Rock it, sock it, number line (Martin, Bill, Jr.)

Swish! (Martin, Bill, Jr.)

Trick or treat? (Martin, Bill, Jr.)

Samuels, Barbara. *Aloha, Dolores* ill. by author. DK, 2000. ISBN 978-0-7894-2508-9 Subj: Activities – vacationing. Animals – cats. Contests. Family life – sisters. Hawaii.

Dolores meets her match ill. by author. Farrar, 2007. ISBN 978-0-374-31758-4 Subj: Animals – cats. Family life – brothers & sisters. Humorous stories. Pets.

Duncan and Dolores ill. by author. Bradbury, 1986. ISBN 978-0-02-778210-3 Subj: Activities. Animals – cats. Family life – sisters. Humorous stories.

Faye and Dolores ill. by author. Bradbury, 1985. ISBN 978-0-02-778120-5 Subj: Emotions – love. Sibling rivalry.

Happy birthday, Dolores ill. by author. Watts, 1989. ISBN 978-0-531-08391-8 Subj: Birthdays. Parties.

Happy Valentine's Day, Dolores ill. by author. Farrar, 2006. ISBN 978-0-374-32844-3 Subj: Animals – cats. Family life – brothers & sisters. Holidays – Valentine's Day. Humorous stories.

The trucker ill. by author. Farrar, 2010. ISBN 978-0-374-37804-2 Subj: Animals – cats. Toys. Trucks.

What's so great about Cindy Snappleby? ill. by author. Watts, 1992. ISBN 978-0-531-08579-0 Subj: Family life – sisters. Frogs & toads. Sibling rivalry.

Samuels, Jenny. *A nose like a hose* ill. by author. Scholastic, 2003. ISBN 978-0-439-37303-6 Subj: Anatomy – noses. Animals – elephants.

SanAngelo, Ryan. *Eddie spaghetti* ill. by Jackie Urbanovic. Boyds Mills, 2002. ISBN 978-1-56397-974-3 Subj: Communities, neighborhoods. Crime. Food. Imagination. Problem solving.

Sánchez, Enrique O. *Saturday market* (Grossman, Patricia)

Sandburg, Carl. *From daybreak to good night* ill. by Lynn Smith-Ary. Annick, 2001. ISBN 978-1-55037-681-4 Subj: Farms. Poetry.

The Huckabuck family and how they raised popcorn in Nebraska and quit and came back ill. by David Small. The text was originally published in 1923 by Harcourt, Brace & Company in the book Rootabaga stories by Carl Sandburg. Farrar, 1999. ISBN 978-0-374-33511-3 Subj: Careers – farmers. Family life. Farms. Fire. Humorous stories.

Sanders, Eve. *What's your name?* (Sanders, Marilyn)

Sanders, Marilyn. *What's your name?* by Marilyn Sanders and Eve Sanders; photos by author. Holiday, 1995. ISBN 978-0-8234-1209-9 Subj: ABC books. Names.

Sanders, Nancy. *D is for drinking gourd: an African American alphabet* ill. by E. B. Lewis. Sleeping Bear, 2007. ISBN 978-1-58536-293-6 Subj: ABC books. Ethnic groups in the U.S. – African Americans. Slavery. U.S. history.

Sanders, Rob. *Cowboy Christmas* ill. by John Manders. Random House, 2012. ISBN 978-0-375-86985-3 Subj: Activities – baking, cooking. Cowboys, cowgirls. Holidays – Christmas. Santa Claus.

Sanders, Scott R. *Crawdad Creek* ill. by Robert Hynes. National Geographic, 1999. ISBN 978-0-7922-7097-3 Subj: Ecology. Family life – brothers & sisters. Rivers.

A place called Freedom ill. by Thomas B. Allen. Atheneum, 1997. ISBN 978-0-689-80470-0 Subj: Character traits – freedom. Ethnic groups in the U.S. – African Americans. Slavery. U.S. history – frontier & pioneer life.

Warm as wool ill. by Helen Cogancherry. Bradbury, 1992. ISBN 978-0-02-778139-7 Subj: Animals – sheep. Clothing. U.S. history – frontier & pioneer life.

Sanders-Wells, Linda. *Maggie's monkeys* ill. by Abby Carter. Candlewick, 2009. ISBN 978-0-7636-3326-4 Subj: Family life – brothers & sisters. Imagination.

Sanderson, Ruth, reteller. *Cinderella* ill. by reteller. Little, 2002. ISBN 978-0-316-77965-4 Subj: Family life – stepfamilies. Folk & fairy tales. Royalty – princes. Sibling rivalry.

The enchanted wood ill. by author. Little, 1991. ISBN 978-0-316-77018-7 Subj: Folk & fairy tales. Royalty – princes.

The golden mare, the firebird, and the magic ring ill. by reteller. Little, 2001. ISBN 978-0-316-76906-8 Subj: Animals – horses, ponies. Folk & fairy tales. Foreign lands – Russia. Magic. Royalty – tsars.

Goldilocks (The three bears)

Papa Gatto ill. by author. Little, 1995. ISBN 978-0-316-77073-6 Subj: Animals – cats. Behavior – greed. Folk & fairy tales. Foreign lands – Italy. Royalty – princes.

Sandman, Rochel. *Perfect porridge* ill. by Chana Zakashansky-Zverev. Hachai, 2000. ISBN 978-0-922613-92-2 Subj: Character traits – generosity. Food. Foreign lands – Uzbekistan. Immigrants. War.

Sandved, Kjell Bloch. *The butterfly alphabet* ill. by author. Scholastic, 1996. ISBN 978-0-590-48003-1 Subj: ABC books. Insects – butterflies, caterpillars. Insects – moths.

Sanfield, Steve. *Snow* ill. by Jeanette Winter. Philomel, 1995. ISBN 978-0-399-22751-6 Subj: Rhyming text. Weather – snow.

Sanger, Amy Wilson. *First book of sushi* ill. by author. Tricycle, 2001. ISBN 978-1-58246-050-5 Subj: Activities – baking, cooking. Ethnic groups in the U.S. – Japanese Americans. Food. Format, unusual – board books. Rhyming text.

Sanromán, Susana. *Señora Reganoña* ill. by author. Douglas & McIntyre, 1998. ISBN 978-0-88899-320-5 Subj: Bedtime. Emotions – fear. Foreign lands – Mexico. Friendship. Night.

Sansone, Adele. *The little green goose* ill. by Alan Marks. NorthSouth, 1999. ISBN 978-0-7358-1072-3 Subj: Birds – geese. Character traits – being different. Dinosaurs. Family life.

San Souci, Daniel. *The Mighty Pigeon Club* ill. by author. Ten Speed, 2007. ISBN 978-1-58246-213-4 Subj: Birds – pigeons. Clubs, gangs.

The rabbit and the dragon king ill. by Eujin Kim Neilan. Boyds Mills, 2002. ISBN 978-1-56397-880-7 Subj: Animals – rabbits. Dragons. Folk & fairy tales. Foreign lands – Korea. Reptiles – turtles, tortoises. Sea & seashore.

San Souci, Robert D. *The birds of Killingworth* ill. by Kimberly Bulcken Root. Based on a poem by Henry Wadsworth Longfellow. Dial, 2002. ISBN 978-0-8037-2111-1 Subj: Birds. Ecology. Nature.

The boy and the ghost ill. by Brian Pinkney. Simon & Schuster, 1989. ISBN 978-0-671-67176-1 Subj: Ethnic groups in the U.S. – African Americans. Ghosts. Homes, houses.

Brave Margaret: an Irish adventure ill. by Sally Wern Comport. Simon & Schuster, 1999. ISBN 978-0-689-81072-5 Subj: Boats, ships. Folk & fairy tales. Foreign lands – Ireland. Gender roles. Giants. Sea & seashore.

Callie Ann and Mistah Bear ill. by Don Daily. Dial, 1999. ISBN 978-0-8037-1768-8 Subj: Character traits – cleverness. Ethnic groups in the U.S. – African Americans. Folk & fairy tales.

Cendrillon: a Caribbean Cinderella ill. by Brian Pinkney. Simon & Schuster, 1998. ISBN 978-0-689-80668-1 Subj: Folk & fairy tales. Foreign lands – Caribbean Islands.

Cinderella Skeleton ill. by David Catrow. Harcourt, 2000. ISBN 978-0-15-202003-3 Subj: Anatomy – skeletons. Family life – stepfamilies. Folk & fairy tales. Holidays – Halloween. Rhyming text. Royalty – princes. Sibling rivalry.

The enchanted tapestry ill. by László Gál. Dial, 1987. ISBN 978-0-8037-0306-3 Subj: Activities – weaving. Behavior – greed. Character traits – bravery. Family life – brothers. Folk & fairy tales. Foreign lands – China.

The faithful friend ill. by Brian Pinkney. Simon & Schuster, 1995. ISBN 978-0-02-786131-0 Subj: Caldecott award honor books. Folk & fairy tales. Foreign lands – Caribbean Islands. Foreign lands – Martinique.

Feathertop: based on the tale by Nathaniel Hawthorne ill. by Daniel San Souci. Doubleday, 1992. ISBN 978-0-385-42045-7 Subj: Behavior – trickery. Magic. Scarecrows. Witches.

The hired hand: an African-American folktale ill. by Jerry Pinkney. Dial, 1997. ISBN 978-0-8037-1297-3 Subj: Activities – working. Character traits – laziness. Ethnic groups in the U.S. – African Americans. Folk & fairy tales. Magic.

The Hobyahs ill. by Alexi Natchev. Doubleday, 1994. ISBN 978-0-385-30934-9 Subj: Animals – dogs. Folk & fairy tales. Foreign lands – England. Monsters. Rhyming text.

The house in the sky ill. by Wil Clay. Dial, 1996. ISBN 978-0-8037-1285-0 Subj: Folk & fairy tales. Foreign lands – Caribbean Islands. Homes, houses.

The legend of Scarface ill. by Daniel San Souci. Doubleday, 1987. ISBN 978-0-385-15874-9 Subj: Folk & fairy tales. Indians of North America – Blackfoot. Indians of North America – Siksika.

Little gold star ill. by Sergio Martinez. Morrow, 2000. ISBN 978-0-688-14781-5 Subj: Ethnic groups in the U.S. – Hispanic Americans. Family life – stepfamilies. Folk & fairy tales. Foreign languages. Religion. Sibling rivalry.

Little Pierre ill. by David Catrow. Harcourt, 2003. ISBN 978-0-15-202482-6 Subj: Character traits – cleverness. Concepts – size. Family life – brothers. Folk & fairy tales. Little people. Mythical creatures – ogres. Swamps.

Nicholas Pipe ill. by David Shannon. Dial, 1997. ISBN 978-0-8037-1765-7 Subj: Careers – fishermen. Emotions – love. Folk & fairy tales. Mythical creatures – mermaids, mermen. Sea & seashore.

Pedro and the monkey ill. by Michael Hays. Morrow, 1996. ISBN 978-0-688-13743-4 Subj: Animals – monkeys. Folk & fairy tales. Foreign lands – Philippines. Monsters.

Peter and the blue witch baby ill. by Alexi Natchev. Doubleday, 2000. ISBN 978-0-385-32269-0 Subj: Emotions – envy, jealousy. Folk & fairy tales. Foreign lands – Russia. Giants. Royalty – tsars. Sun. Witches.

The red heels ill. by Gary Kelley. Dial, 1995. ISBN 978-0-8037-1134-1 Subj: Careers – shoemakers. Folk & fairy tales. Magic. Witches.

Robin Hood and the golden arrow ill. by E. B. Lewis. Scholastic, 2010. ISBN 978-0-439-62538-8 Subj: Folk & fairy tales. Foreign lands – England. Sports – archery.

The samurai's daughter ill. by Stephen T. Johnson. Dial, 1992. ISBN 978-0-8037-1136-5 Subj: Character traits – bravery. Family life – fathers. Folk & fairy tales. Foreign lands – Japan.

The secret of the stones ill. by James Ransome. Fogelman, 2000. ISBN 978-0-8037-1640-7 Subj: Ethnic groups in the U.S. – African Americans. Folk & fairy tales. Foreign lands – Africa. Magic. Orphans.

The silver charm ill. by Yoriko Ito. Doubleday, 2002. ISBN 978-0-385-32159-4 Subj: Animals – dogs. Animals – foxes. Animals – mice. Folk & fairy tales. Foreign lands – Japan. Magic. Mythical creatures – ogres. Pets.

Six foolish fishermen ill. by Doug Kennedy. Hyperion, 2000. ISBN 978-0-7868-2335-2 Subj: Character traits – foolishness. Sports – fishing.

The snow wife ill. by Stephen T. Johnson. Dial, 1993. ISBN 978-0-8037-1410-6 Subj: Behavior – secrets. Folk & fairy tales. Foreign lands – Japan.

Song of Sedna ill. by Daniel San Souci. Doubleday, 1981. ISBN 978-0-385-15866-4 Subj: Eskimos. Folk & fairy tales.

Sootface: an Ojibwa Cinderella story ill. by Daniel San Souci. Delacorte, 1994. ISBN 978-0-385-31202-8 Subj: Character traits – meanness. Family life – sisters. Folk & fairy tales. Indians of North America – Ojibwa.

Sukey and the mermaid ill. by Brian Pinkney. Four Winds, 1992. ISBN 978-0-02-778141-0 Subj: Ethnic groups in the U.S. – African Americans. Folk & fairy tales. Mythical creatures – mermaids, mermen.

The talking eggs ill. by Jerry Pinkney. Dial, 1989. ISBN 978-0-8037-0619-4 Subj: Caldecott award honor books. Character traits – kindness. Eggs. Folk & fairy tales. Magic.

Two bear cubs: a Miwok legend from California's Yosemite Valley ill. by Daniel San Souci. Yosemite Assoc., 1997. ISBN 978-0-939666-87-4 Subj: Animals. Animals – bears. Animals – worms. Folk & fairy tales. Indians of North America – Miwok.

A weave of words ill. by Raúl Colón. Orchard, 1997. ISBN 978-0-531-33053-1 Subj: Activities – weaving. Folk & fairy tales. Foreign lands – Armenia. Gender roles. Royalty – kings. Royalty – queens.

The white cat ill. by Gennady Spirin. Watts, 1990. ISBN 978-0-531-08409-0 Subj: Animals – cats. Folk & fairy tales. Magic. Royalty.

Santa Claus is coming to town ill. by Laura Blanken Merer. HarperCollins, 2001. ISBN 978-0-694-01559-7 Subj: Format, unusual – toy & movable books. Holidays – Christmas. Music. Santa Claus. Songs.

Santangelo, Colony Elliott. *Brother Wolf of Gubbio* ill. by author. Handprint, 2000. ISBN 978-1-929766-07-9 Subj: Animals – wolves. Cities, towns. Religion.

Santa's little library of Christmas stories ill. by Vincent Douglas. McGraw-Hill, 2002. ISBN 978-1-58845-235-1 Subj: Format, unusual – board books. Holidays – Christmas. Santa Claus.

Santella, Andrew. *George Washington* ill. with photos. Compass Point, 2000. ISBN 978-0-7565-0014-6 Subj: U.S. history. War.

Santiago, Esmeralda. *A doll for Navidades* ill. by Enrique O. Sánchez. Scholastic, 2005. ISBN 978-0-439-55398-8 Subj: Family life. Foreign lands – Puerto Rico. Gifts. Holidays – Christmas. Toys – dolls.

Santore, Charles. *A stowaway on Noah's Ark* ill. by author. Random House, 2000. ISBN 978-0-679-98820-5 Subj: Animals. Animals – mice. Behavior – hiding. Boats, ships. Religion – Noah.

Three hungry pigs and the wolf who came to dinner ill. by author. Random House, 2005. ISBN 978-0-375-92946-5 Subj: Animals – pigs. Animals – wolves. Food.

Santoro, Lucio. *Wild oceans: a pop-up book with revolutionary technology* by Lucio Santoro and Meera Santoro ill. by Lucio Santoro. Simon & Schuster, 2010. ISBN 978-1-4169-8467-2 Subj: Format, unusual – toy & movable books. Sea & seashore.

Santoro, Meera. *Wild oceans: a pop-up book with revolutionary technology* (Santoro, Lucio)

Santoro, Scott. *Farm-fresh cats* ill. by author. HarperCollins, 2006. ISBN 978-0-06-078179-8 Subj: Animals – cats. Farms.

Isaac the Ice Cream Truck ill. by author. Holt, 1999. ISBN 978-0-8050-5296-1 Subj: Careers – firefighters. Trucks.

Which way to witch school? ill. by author. HarperCollins, 2010. ISBN 978-0-06-078181-1 Subj: Rhyming text. School. Witches.

Santos, Rosa. *Play date* ill. by Gioia Fiammenghi. Kane, 2001. ISBN 978-1-57565-105-7 Subj: Days of the week, months of the year. Family life.

Santucci, Barbara. *Anna's corn* ill. by Lloyd Bloom. Eerdmans, 2002. ISBN 978-0-8028-5119-2 Subj: Death. Emotions – grief. Family life – grandfathers. Memories, memory. Plants. Seeds.

Loon summer ill. by Andrea Shine. Eerdmans, 2001. ISBN 978-0-8028-5182-6 Subj: Birds – loons. Divorce. Family life – daughters. Family life – fathers.

Sarcone-Roach, Julia. *The secret plan* ill. by author. Knopf, 2009. ISBN 978-0-375-85858-1 Subj: Activities – playing. Animals – cats. Animals – elephants. Bedtime.

Subway story ill. by author. Random House, 2011. ISBN 978-0-375-85859-8 Subj: Sea & seashore. Trains.

Sartell, Debra. *Time for bed, Baby Ted* ill. by Kay Chorao. Holiday House, 2010. ISBN 978-0-8234-1968-5 Subj: Babies. Bedtime. Rhyming text.

Sasso, Sandy Eisenberg. *Butterflies under our hats* ill. by Joan Keller Rothenberg. Paraclete, 2006. ISBN 978-1-55725-474-0 Subj: Character traits – luck. Foreign lands – Poland. Hope. Jewish culture.

Cain and Abel: finding the fruits of peace ill. by Joan Keller Rothberg. Jewish Lights, 2001. ISBN 978-1-58023-123-7 Subj: Emotions – anger. Family life – brothers. Religion.

For heaven's sake ill. by Kathryn Kunz Finney. Jewish Lights, 1999. ISBN 978-1-58023-054-4 Subj: Family life – grandmothers. Friendship. Religion.

God said amen ill. by Avi Katz. Jewish Lights, 2000. ISBN 978-1-58023-080-3 Subj: Behavior – sharing. Character traits – pride. Character traits – vanity.

God's paintbrush ill. by Annette C. Compton. Jewish Lights, 1992. ISBN 978-1-879045-22-4 Subj: Religion.

In God's name ill. by Phoebe Stone. Jewish Lights, 1994. ISBN 978-1-879045-26-2 Subj: Names. Religion.

Naamah, Noah's wife ill. by Bethanne Andersen. Skylight Paths, 2002. ISBN 978-1-893361-56-0 Subj: Family life. Format, unusual – board books. Plants. Religion – Noah. Seeds.

Satoshi, Kako. *Little Daruma and little Tengu* ill. by author. Tuttle, 2002. ISBN 978-0-8048-3347-9 Subj: Emotions – envy, jealousy. Foreign lands – Japan. Friendship.

Sattler, Jennifer. *Chick 'n' Pug* ill. by author. Bloomsbury, 2010. ISBN 978-1-59990-534-1 Subj: Animals – dogs. Birds – chickens.

Chick 'n' Pug meet the Dude ill. by author. Bloomsbury, 2013. ISBN 978-1-59990-600-3 Subj: Animals – dogs. Birds – chickens.

Pig kahuna ill. by author. Bloomsbury, 2011. ISBN 978-1-59990-635-5 Subj: Animals – pigs. Emotions – fear. Sports – surfing.

Sylvie ill. by author. Random House, 2009. ISBN 978-0-375-85708-9 Subj: Birds – flamingos. Food.

Uh-oh, Dodo! ill. by author. Boyds Mills, 2013. ISBN 978-1-59078-929-2 Subj: Activities – walking. Behavior – misbehavior. Birds – dodos. Family life – mothers.

Saudo, Coralie. *My dad is big and strong, but . . .: a bedtime story* ill. by Kris DiGiacomo. Enchanted Lion, 2012. ISBN 978-1-59270-122-3 Subj: Bedtime. Family life – fathers.

Sauer, Tammi. *Bawk and roll* ill. by Dan Santat. Sterling, 2012. ISBN 978-1-4027-7837-7 Subj: Activities – dancing. Birds – chickens. Music.

Chicken dance ill. by Dan Santat. Sterling, 2009. ISBN 978-1-4027-5366-4 Subj: Activities – dancing. Birds – chickens. Contests. Humorous stories.

Cowboy camp ill. by Mike Reed. Sterling, 2005. ISBN 978-1-4027-2224-0 Subj: Behavior – bullying, teasing. Camps, camping. Character traits – individuality. Cowboys, cowgirls.

Me want pet! ill. by Bob Shea. Simon & Schuster, 2012. ISBN 978-1-4424-0810-4 Subj: Animals. Cavemen. Pets.

Mostly monsterly ill. by Scott Magoon. Simon & Schuster, 2010. ISBN 978-1-4169-6110-9 Subj: Character traits – being different. Character traits – individuality. Monsters. School.

Mr. Duck means business ill. by Jeff Mack. Simon & Schuster, 2011. ISBN 978-1-4169-8522-8 Subj: Animals. Birds – ducks. Character traits – compromising.

Nugget and Fang: friends forever—or snack time? ill. by Michael Slack. Harcourt, 2013. ISBN 978-0-547-85285-0 Subj: Behavior – resourcefulness. Character traits – helpfulness. Fish. Fish – sharks. Prejudice.

Oh, nuts! ill. by Dan Krall. Bloomsbury, 2012. ISBN 978-1-59990-466-5 Subj: Animals – chipmunks. Character traits – conceit. Zoos.

Princess in training ill. by Joe Berger. Harcourt, 2012. ISBN 978-0-15-206599-7 Subj: Camps, camping. Character traits – individuality. Royalty – princesses.

Saul, Carol P. *Barn cat* ill. by Mary Azarian. Little, 1998. ISBN 978-0-316-76113-0 Subj: Animals – cats. Counting, numbers. Rhyming text.

Saunders, Dave. *So slow!* by Dave Saunders and Julie Saunders ill. by Dave Saunders. Marshall Cavendish, 2001. ISBN 978-0-7614-5080-1 Subj: Animals. Animals – snails. Character traits – perseverance. Concepts – speed.

Saunders, Julie. *So slow!* (Saunders, Dave)

Saunders, Karen. *Baby Badger's wonderful night* ill. by Dubravka Kolanovic. Egmont, 2011. ISBN 978-1-60684-172-3 Subj: Animals – badgers. Emotions – fear. Family life – fathers. Night.

Sava, Donna Lynn. *Teddy bear dreams* ill. by Scott Sava. Ipicturebooks, 2002. ISBN 978-1-59019-128-6 Subj: Careers. Dreams. Imagination. Rhyming text. Toys – bears.

Savadier, Elivia. *No haircut today!* ill. by author. Macmillan, 2005. ISBN 978-1-59643-046-4 Subj: Emotions – fear. Hair.

Time to get dressed! ill. by author. Macmillan, 2006. ISBN 978-1-59643-161-4 Subj: Babies. Character traits – individuality. Clothing. Family life – fathers.

Will Sheila share? ill. by author. Roaring Brook, 2008. ISBN 978-1-59643-289-5 Subj: Behavior – sharing. Family life – grandmothers.

Savage, Stephen. *Little Tug* ill. by author. Roaring Brook, 2012. ISBN 978-1-59643-648-0 Subj: Boats, ships. Character traits – helpfulness.

Ten orange pumpkins ill. by author. Dial, 2013. ISBN 978-0-8037-3938-3 Subj: Counting, numbers. Holidays – Halloween. Rhyming text.

Where's Walrus? ill. by author. Scholastic, 2011. ISBN 978-0-439-70049-8 Subj: Animals – walruses. Behavior – running away. Careers – zookeepers. Clothing – hats. Disguises. Wordless.

Savitz, Harriet May. *The story blanket* (Wolff, Ferida)

Sawyer, Ruth. *Journey cake, ho!* ill. by Robert McCloskey. Viking, 1953. ISBN 978-0-670-40943-3 Subj: Caldecott award honor books. Cumulative tales. Folk & fairy tales. Poverty.

The remarkable Christmas of the cobbler's sons ill. by Barbara Cooney. Viking, 1994. ISBN 978-0-670-84922-2 Subj: Behavior – sharing. Folk & fairy tales. Foreign lands – Tyrol. Holidays – Christmas. Royalty – kings.

Say, Allen. *Allison* ill. by author. Houghton, 1997. ISBN 978-0-395-85895-0 Subj: Adoption. Animals – cats. Behavior – misbehavior. Emotions. Family life.

The bicycle man ill. by author. Houghton, 1982. ISBN 978-0-395-32254-3 Subj: Foreign lands – Japan. Sports – bicycling.

The boy in the garden ill. by author. Harcourt, 2010. ISBN 978-0-547-21410-8 Subj: Birds – cranes. Character traits – kindness. Foreign lands – Japan. Gardens, gardening.

Emma's rug ill. by author. Houghton, 1996. ISBN 978-0-395-74294-5 Subj: Activities – drawing. Ethnic groups in the U.S. – Japanese Americans. Imagination.

Erika-San ill. by author. Houghton, 2009. ISBN 978-0-618-88933-4 Subj: Foreign lands – Japan.

The favorite daughter ill. by author. Scholastic, 2013. ISBN 978-0-545-17662-0 Subj: Character traits – being different. Ethnic groups in the U.S. – Japanese Americans. Family life – daughters. Prejudice. School.

Grandfather's journey ill. by author. Houghton, 1993. ISBN 978-0-395-57035-7 Subj: Activities – traveling. Caldecott award books. Ethnic groups in the U.S. – Japanese Americans. Family life. Family life – grandfathers. Foreign lands – Japan.

Kamishibai man ill. by author. Houghton, 2005. ISBN 978-0-618-47954-2 Subj: Activities – storytelling. Foreign lands – Japan. Theater.

Once under the cherry blossom tree: an old Japanese tale ill. by author. HarperCollins, 1974. ISBN 978-0-06-025217-5 Subj: Folk & fairy tales. Foreign lands – Japan.

A river dream ill. by author. Houghton, 1988. ISBN 978-0-395-48294-0 Subj: Dreams. Family life. Illness. Sports – fishing.

Tea with milk ill. by author. Houghton, 1999. ISBN 978-0-395-90495-4 Subj: Ethnic groups in the U.S. – Japanese Americans. Foreign lands – Japan.

Tree of cranes ill. by author. Houghton, 1991. ISBN 978-0-395-52024-6 Subj: Family life – mothers. Foreign lands – Japan. Holidays – Christmas.

Sayles, Elizabeth. *The goldfish yawned* ill. by author. Holt, 2005. ISBN 978-0-8050-7624-0 Subj: Bedtime. Dreams. Rhyming text.

Sayre, April Pulley. *Army ant parade* ill. by Rick Chrustowski. Holt, 2002. ISBN 978-0-8050-6353-0 Subj: Foreign lands – Panama. Forest, woods. Insects – ants. Science.

The bumblebee queen ill. by Patricia J. Wynne. Charlesbridge, 2005. ISBN 978-1-57091-362-4 Subj: Insects – bees.

Dig, wait, listen ill. by Barbara Bash. Greenwillow, 2001. ISBN 978-0-688-16615-1 Subj: Animals. Desert. Frogs & toads. Science.

Eat like a bear ill. by Steve Jenkins. Holt, 2013. ISBN 978-0-8050-9039-0 Subj: Animals – bears. Days of the week, months of the year. Hibernation. Nature. Seasons.

Go, go, grapes! a fruit chant ill. by author. Simon & Schuster, 2012. ISBN 978-1-4424-3390-8 Subj: Food. Rhyming text.

Here come the humpbacks! ill. by Jamie Hogan. Charlesbridge, 2013. ISBN 978-1-58089-405-0 Subj: Animals – whales. Family life – mothers. Migration.

Home at last: a song of migration ill. by Alix Berenzy. Holt, 1998. ISBN 978-0-8050-5154-4 Subj: Animals. Migration.

Honk, honk, goose! Canada geese start a family ill. by Huy Voun Lee. Holt, 2009. ISBN 978-0-8050-7103-0 Subj: Birds – geese. Nature.

The hungry hummingbird ill. by Gay W. Holland. Millbrook, 2001. ISBN 978-0-7613-1951-1 Subj: Birds – hummingbirds. Food. Science.

Hush, little puppy ill. by Susan Winter. Holt, 2007. ISBN 978-0-8050-7102-3 Subj: Animals – dogs. Bedtime. Rhyming text.

If you should hear a honey guide ill. by S. D. Schindler. Houghton, 1995. ISBN 978-0-395-71545-1 Subj: Animals. Birds. Foreign lands – Africa. Insects – bees.

If you're hoppy ill. by Jackie Urbanovic. HarperCollins, 2011. ISBN 978-0-06-156634-9 Subj: Animals. Rhyming text.

It's my city ill. by Denis Roche. Greenwillow, 2001. ISBN 978-0-688-16916-9 Subj: Birthdays. Cities, towns. Family life – brothers & sisters. Rhyming text.

Let's go nuts! seeds we eat ill. by author. Simon & Schuster, 2013. ISBN 978-1-4424-6728-6 Subj: Food. Rhyming text.

Meet the howlers! ill. by Woody Miller. Charlesbridge, 2010. ISBN 978-1-57091-733-2 Subj: Animals – monkeys.

Noodle Man ill. by Stephen Costanza. Orchard, 2002. ISBN 978-0-439-29307-5 Subj: Food. Humorous stories.

Rah, rah, radishes! a vegetable chant photos by author. Simon & Schuster, 2011. ISBN 978-1-4424-2141-7 Subj: Food. Rhyming text.

The shape of Betts Meadow ill. by Joanne Friar. Millbrook, 2002. ISBN 978-0-7613-2115-6 Subj: Ecology. Poetry.

Splish! splash! animal baths ill. by author. Millbrook, 2000. ISBN 978-0-7613-1821-7 Subj: Activities – bathing. Animals.

Stars beneath your bed: the surprising story of dust ill. by Ann Jonas. HarperCollins, 2005. ISBN 978-0-06-057189-4 Subj: Character traits – cleanliness.

Trout are made of trees ill. by Kate Endle. Charlesbridge, 2008. ISBN 978-1-58089-137-0 Subj: Ecology. Fish. Trees.

Trout, trout, trout ill. by Trip Park. NorthWord, 2004. ISBN 978-1-55971-889-9 Subj: Fish. Rhyming text.

Turtle, turtle, watch out! ill. by Lee Christiansen. Orchard, 2000. ISBN 978-0-531-33285-6 Subj: Character traits – kindness to animals. Migration. Reptiles – turtles, tortoises.

Turtle, turtle, watch out! ill. by Annie Patterson. Charlesbridge, 2010. ISBN 978-1-58089-148-6 Subj: Character traits – kindness to animals. Migration. Reptiles – turtles, tortoises.

Vulture view ill. by Steve Jenkins. Holt, 2007. ISBN 978-0-8050-7557-1 Subj: Birds – vultures. Rhyming text.

Sayres, Brianna Caplan. *Where do diggers sleep at night?* ill. by Christian Slade. Random House, 2012. ISBN 978-0-375-86848-1 Subj: Bedtime. Machines. Rhyming text. Trucks.

Sazaklis, John. *Fowl play* ill. by Steven E. Gordon. HarperFestival, 2013. ISBN 978-0-06-188536-5 Subj: Birds. Character traits – bravery. Crime. Ecology. Format, unusual – graphic novels.

Scanlon, Elizabeth Garton. *All the world* ill. by Marla Frazee. Simon & Schuster, 2009. ISBN 978-1-4169-8580-8 Subj: Activities. Caldecott award honor books. Family life. Seasons – summer. World.

Happy birthday, Bunny! ill. by Stephanie Graegin. Simon & Schuster, 2013. ISBN 978-1-4424-0287-4 Subj: Animals – rabbits. Birthdays. Parties. Rhyming text.

Noodle and Lou ill. by Arthur Howard. Simon & Schuster, 2011. ISBN 978-1-4424-0288-1 Subj: Animals – worms. Birds. Friendship. Self-concept.

A sock is a pocket for your toes ill. by Robin Preiss-Glasser. HarperCollins, 2004. ISBN 978-0-06-029527-1 Subj: Clothing – pockets. Poetry. Rhyming text.

Think big! ill. by Vanessa Brantley Newton. Bloomsbury, 2012. ISBN 978-1-59990-611-9 Subj: Art. Rhyming text. Theater.

Scarry, Huck. *Looking into the Middle Ages* ill. by author. HarperCollins, 1985. ISBN 978-0-06-025224-3 Subj: Format, unusual – toy & movable books. Knights. Middle Ages.

Scarry, Richard. *Richard Scarry's best Christmas book ever!* ill. by author. Random House, 1981. ISBN 978-0-394-94936-9 Subj: Holidays – Christmas.

Richard Scarry's best first book ever! ill. by author. Random House, 1979. ISBN 978-0-394-94250-6 Subj: Concepts. Days of the week, months of the year.

Richard Scarry's please and thank you book ill. by author. Random House, 1973. ISBN 978-0-394-92681-0 Subj: Etiquette.

Schaap, Martine. *Mop and the birthday picnic* by Martine Schaap and Alex de Wolf ill. by Alex de Wolf. McGraw-Hill, 2000. ISBN 978-1-57768-882-2 Subj: Activities – picnicking. Animals – dogs. Birthdays. Multiple births – twins.

Mop's backyard concert by Martine Schaap and Alex de Wolf ill. by Alex de Wolf. McGraw-Hill, 2001. ISBN 978-1-57768-892-1 Subj: Animals – dogs. Multiple births – twins. Musical instruments – bands.

Mop's mountain adventure by Martine Schaap and Alex de Wolf ill. by Alex de Wolf. McGraw-Hill, 2000. ISBN 978-1-57768-881-5 Subj: Activities – playing. Animals – dogs. Imagination. Multiple births – twins.

Mop's treasure hunt by Martine Schaap and Alex de Wolf ill. by Alex de Wolf. McGraw-Hill, 2001. ISBN 978-1-57768-891-4 Subj: Animals – dogs. Family life – grandfathers. Maps. Multiple births – twins.

Schachner, Judith Byron. *Bits and pieces* ill. by author. Dial, 2013. ISBN 978-0-8037-3788-4 Subj: Animals – cats. Behavior – lost & found possessions.

The Grannyman ill. by author. Dutton, 1999. ISBN 978-0-525-46122-7 Subj: Animals – cats. Character traits – responsibility. Old age.

Skippyjon Jones and the big bones ill. by author. Penguin, 2007. ISBN 978-0-525-47884-3 Subj: Animals – cats. Animals – dogs. Dinosaurs.

Skippyjon Jones Cirque de Olé ill. by author. Dial, 2012. ISBN 978-0-8037-3782-2 Subj: Animals – cats. Animals – dogs. Careers – acrobats. Circus.

Skippyjon Jones class action ill. by author. Penguin, 2011. ISBN 978-0-525-42228-0 Subj: Animals – cats. Animals – dogs. School.

Skippyjon Jones in mummy trouble ill. by author. Penguin, 2006. ISBN 978-0-525-47754-9 Subj: Animals – cats. Animals – dogs. Mummies.

Skippyjon Jones, lost in spice ill. by author. Dutton, 2009. ISBN 978-0-525-47965-9 Subj: Animals – cats. Animals – dogs. Space & space ships.

Yo, Vikings ill. by author. Dutton, 2002. ISBN 978-0-525-46889-9 Subj: Birthdays. Boats, ships. Careers – explorers. Character traits – persistence. Vikings.

Schaefer, A. R. *Alexander Calder* ill. with photos. Heinemann, 2003. ISBN 978-1-4034-0287-5 Subj: Art. Careers – artists. Careers – sculptors.

Diego Rivera ill. with photos. Heinemann, 2003. ISBN 978-1-4034-0288-2 Subj: Art. Careers – artists. Foreign lands – Mexico.

Grandma Moses ill. with photos. Heinemann, 2003. ISBN 978-1-4034-0289-9 Subj: Art. Careers – artists.

Schaefer, Carole Lexa. *ABCers* ill. by Pierr Morgan. Viking, 2012. ISBN 978-0-670-01231-2 Subj: ABC books. Activities – playing. Language. Parks.

Big Little Monkey ill. by Pierre Pratt. Candlewick, 2008. ISBN 978-0-7636-2006-6 Subj: Animals. Animals – monkeys. Jungle.

The Bora-Bora dress ill. by Catherine Stock. Candlewick, 2005. ISBN 978-0-7636-1234-4 Subj: Clothing – dresses. Parties.

Cool time song ill. by Pierr Morgan. Penguin, 2005. ISBN 978-0-670-05928-7 Subj: Animals. Foreign lands – Africa.

Down in the woods at sleepytime ill. by Vanessa Cabban. Candlewick, 2000. ISBN 978-0-7636-0843-9 Subj: Activities – storytelling. Animals. Bedtime. Dreams. Family life – mothers. Forest, woods.

Down in the woods at sleepytime [board book] ill. by Vanessa Cabban. Candlewick, 2004. ISBN 978-0-7636-2566-5 Subj: Activities – storytelling. Animals. Bedtime. Dreams. Family life – mothers. Forest, woods. Format, unusual – board books.

Dragon dancing ill. by Pierr Morgan. Penguin, 2007. ISBN 978-0-670-06084-9 Subj: Activities – dancing. Dragons. Imagination.

Kids like us ill. by Pierr Morgan. Viking, 2008. ISBN 978-0-670-06290-4 Subj: Activities – playing. Imagination. School.

The little French whistle ill. by Emilie Chollat. Knopf, 2002. ISBN 978-0-375-91569-7 Subj: Family life – cousins. Family life – grandfathers. Whistles.

Snow pumpkin ill. by Pierr Morgan. Crown, 2000. ISBN 978-0-517-80016-4 Subj: Activities – playing. Ethnic groups in the U.S. Snowmen. Weather – snow.

Someone says ill. by Pierr Morgan. Viking, 2003. ISBN 978-0-670-03664-6 Subj: Bedtime. Day. Imagination. School – nursery.

Two scarlet songbirds ill. by Elizabeth Rosen. Knopf, 2001. ISBN 978-0-375-91022-7 Subj: Birds. Careers – composers. Music.

Who's there? ill. by Pierr Morgan. Penguin, 2011. ISBN 978-0-670-01241-1 Subj: Bedtime. Emotions – fear.

Schaefer, Lola M. *Airport* ill. with photos. Heinemann, 2000. ISBN 978-1-57572-515-4 Subj: Airplanes, airports. Careers.

Apartment ill. with photos. Heinemann, 2002. ISBN 978-1-4034-0258-5 Subj: Homes, houses.

Chinese New Year ill. with photos. Pebble, 2001. ISBN 978-0-7368-0660-2 Subj: Ethnic groups in the U.S. – Chinese Americans. Foreign lands – China. Holidays – Chinese New Year.

Cinco de Mayo ill. with photos. Pebble, 2001. ISBN 978-0-7368-0661-9 Subj: Ethnic groups in the U.S. – Mexican Americans. Foreign lands – Mexico. Holidays – Cinco de Mayo.

Construction site ill. with photos. Heinemann, 2000. ISBN 978-1-57572-516-1 Subj: Careers – construction workers.

Dental office ill. with photos. Heinemann, 2000. ISBN 978-1-57572-517-8 Subj: Careers – dentists. Teeth.

Frankie Stein ill. by Kevan Atteberry. Marshall Cavendish, 2007. ISBN 978-0-7614-5358-1 Subj: Character traits – being different. Family life. Monsters.

Frankie Stein starts school ill. by Kevan Atteberry. Marshall Cavendish, 2010. ISBN 978-0-7614-5656-8 Subj: Behavior – bullying, teasing. Character traits – being different. Friendship. Monsters. School – first day.

Hanukkah ill. with photos. Pebble, 2001. ISBN 978-0-7368-0662-6 Subj: Holidays – Hanukkah. Jewish culture. Religion.

Homes ABC ill. with photos. Heinemann, 2003. ISBN 978-1-4034-0260-8 Subj: ABC books. Homes, houses.

Homes 123 ill. with photos. Heinemann, 2003. ISBN 978-1-4034-0259-2 Subj: Counting, numbers. Homes, houses.

Hospital ill. with photos. Heinemann, 2000. ISBN 978-1-57572-519-2 Subj: Careers – doctors. Careers – nurses. Hospitals.

House ill. with photos. Heinemann, 2003. ISBN 978-1-4034-0261-5 Subj: Homes, houses.

An island grows ill. by Cathie Felstead. HarperCollins, 2006. ISBN 978-0-06-623930-9 Subj: Islands. Rhyming text. Volcanoes.

Just one bite: 11 animals and their bites at life size! ill. by Geoff Waring. Chronicle, 2010. ISBN 978-0-8118-6473-2 Subj: Animals. Food.

Kwanzaa ill. with photos. Pebble, 2001. ISBN 978-0-7368-0663-3 Subj: Ethnic groups in the U.S. – African Americans. Holidays – Kwanzaa.

Lifetime: the amazing numbers in animal lives ill. by Christopher Silas Neal. Chronicle, 2013. ISBN 978-1-4521-0714-1 Subj: Animals. Counting, numbers. Science.

Loose tooth ill. by Sylvie Wickstrom. HarperCollins, 2004. ISBN 978-0-06-052777-8 Subj: Family life. Rhyming text. Teeth.

Mobile home ill. with photos. Heinemann, 2003. ISBN 978-1-4034-0263-9 Subj: Homes, houses.

One special day: a story for big brothers and sisters ill. by Jessica Meserve. Hyperion, 2012. ISBN 978-1-4231-3760-3 Subj: Babies. Family life – brothers. Family life – new sibling.

Police station ill. with photos. Heinemann, 2000. ISBN 978-1-57572-520-8 Subj: Careers – detectives. Careers – police officers.

Supermarket ill. with photos. Heinemann, 2000. ISBN 978-1-57572-518-5 Subj: Careers – storekeepers. Food. Stores.

This is the sunflower ill. by Donald Crews. Greenwillow, 2000. ISBN 978-0-688-16414-0 Subj: Cumulative tales. Flowers. Nature. Plants. Rhyming text. Seeds.

Toolbox twins ill. by Melissa Iwai. Holt, 2006. ISBN 978-0-8050-7733-9 Subj: Family life – fathers. Rhyming text. Tools.

Tugboats ill. with photos. Heinemann, 2003. ISBN 978-1-4034-0262-2 Subj: Boats, ships. Homes, houses.

The Wright brothers ill. with photos. Pebble, 2000. ISBN 978-0-7368-0549-0 Subj: Airplanes, airports. Careers – inventors. U.S. history.

Schafer, Kevin. *Penguins A B C* ill. with photos. NorthWord, 2002. ISBN 978-1-55971-831-8 Subj: ABC books. Birds – penguins.

Penguins 1 2 3 ill. with photos. NorthWord, 2002. ISBN 978-1-55971-830-1 Subj: Birds – penguins. Counting, numbers.

Schafer, Milton. *That crazy Barb'ra* ill. by G. Brian Karas. Dial, 2003. ISBN 978-0-8037-2584-3 Subj: Behavior – bullying, teasing. Rhyming text. School.

Schanzer, Rosalyn. *How Ben Franklin stole the lightning* ill. by author. HarperCollins, 2003. ISBN 978-0-688-16994-7 Subj: Careers – inventors. Careers – scientists. Science. Tall tales. U.S. history.

The Old Chisholm Trail ill. by author. National Geographic, 2001. ISBN 978-0-7922-7559-6 Subj: Cowboys, cowgirls. Music. Songs. U.S. history.

Scharschmidt, Sherry. *Tuck me in!* (Hacohen, Dean)

Scheer, Julian. *By the light of the captured moon* ill. by Ronald Himler. Holiday, 2001. ISBN 978-0-8234-1624-0 Subj: Friendship. Moon. Seasons – summer.

Rain makes applesauce by Julian Scheer and Marvin Bileck ill. by Marvin Bileck. Holiday, 1964. ISBN 978-0-8234-0091-1 Subj: Caldecott award honor books. Humorous stories. Weather – rain.

Scheffler, Axel. *The big balloon* ill. by author. Candlewick, 2013. ISBN 978-0-7636-6372-8 Subj: Animals – mice. Animals – rabbits. Toys – balloons.

The little puddle ill. by author. Candlewick, 2011. ISBN 978-0-7636-5878-6 Subj: Animals – mice. Animals – rabbits. Behavior – mistakes. Toilet training.

The scary monster ill. by author. Candlewick, 2012. ISBN 978-0-7636-5918-9 Subj: Animals – mice. Animals – rabbits. Clothing – costumes. Friendship. Monsters.

The snowy day ill. by author. Candlewick, 2013. ISBN 978-0-7636-6607-1 Subj: Animals – mice. Animals – rabbits. Character traits – cooperation. Friendship. Snowmen. Weather – snow.

The super scooter ill. by author. Candlewick, 2011. ISBN 978-0-7636-5877-9 Subj: Activities – playing. Animals – mice. Animals – rabbits. Friendship.

Scheffler, Ursel. *Taking care of Sister Bear* ill. by Ulises Wensell. Doubleday, 1999. ISBN 978-0-385-32660-5 Subj: Animals – bears. Babies. Behavior – lost. Family life – brothers & sisters.

Who has time for Little Bear? ill. by Ulises Wensell. Doubleday, 1998. ISBN 978-0-385-32536-3 Subj: Animals – bears. Family life. Friendship.

Schembri, Pamela. *The secret lunch special* (Catalanotto, Peter)

Schertle, Alice. *The adventures of old Bo Bear* ill. by David Parkins. Chronicle, 2006. ISBN 978-0-8118-3476-6 Subj: Activities – playing. Character traits – cleanliness. Toys – bears.

Advice for a frog and other poems ill. by Norman Green. Lothrop, 1995. ISBN 978-0-688-13487-7 Subj: Animals. Animals – endangered animals. Frogs & toads. Poetry.

Button up! ill. by Petra Mathers. Harcourt, 2009. ISBN 978-0-15-205050-4 Subj: Animals. Clothing. Poetry.

Down the road ill. by E. B. Lewis. Browndeer, 1995. ISBN 978-0-15-276622-1 Subj: Country. Eggs. Ethnic groups in the U.S. – African Americans. Family life.

Goodnight, Hattie, my dearie, my dove ill. by Ted Rand. HarperCollins, 2002. ISBN 978-0-688-16023-4 Subj: Bedtime. Counting, numbers. Toys.

How now, brown cow? ill. by Amanda Schaffer. Browndeer, 1994. ISBN 978-0-15-276648-1 Subj: Animals – bulls, cows. Poetry.

I am the cat ill. by Mark Buehner. Lothrop, 1999. ISBN 978-0-688-13154-8 Subj: Animals – cats. Poetry.

Jeremy Bean's St. Patrick's Day ill. by Linda Shute. Lothrop, 1987. ISBN 978-0-688-04814-3 Subj: Behavior – hiding. Character traits – being different. Holidays – St. Patrick's Day. Parties. School.

Little Blue Truck ill. by Jill McElmurry. Harcourt, 2008. ISBN 978-0-15-205661-2 Subj: Friendship. Rhyming text. Trucks.

Little Blue Truck leads the way ill. by Jill McElmurry. Harcourt, 2009. ISBN 978-0-15-206389-4 Subj: Cities, towns. Rhyming text. Traffic, traffic signs. Trucks.

Little Frog's song ill. by Leonard Everett Fisher. HarperCollins, 1992. ISBN 978-0-06-020060-2 Subj: Behavior – lost. Frogs & toads.

The skeleton in the closet ill. by Curtis Jobling. HarperCollins, 2003. ISBN 978-0-688-17739-3 Subj: Anatomy – skeletons. Clothing. Rhyming text.

Very hairy bear ill. by Matt Phelan. Harcourt, 2007. ISBN 978-0-15-216568-0 Subj: Animals – bears. Hibernation. Seasons.

We ill. by Kenneth Addison. Lee & Low, 2007. ISBN 978-1-58430-060-1 Subj: Poetry. World.

Witch Hazel ill. by Margot Tomes. HarperCollins, 1991. ISBN 978-0-06-025141-3 Subj: Family life – brothers. Moon. Plants. Scarecrows.

Schick, Eleanor. *Mama* ill. by author. Marshall Cavendish, 2000. ISBN 978-0-7614-5060-3 Subj: Death. Emotions – grief. Family life – mothers. Illness. Memories, memory.

My Navajo sister ill. by author. Simon & Schuster, 1996. ISBN 978-0-02-781155-1 Subj: Friendship. Indians of North America – Navajo.

Navajo ABC (Tapahonso, Luci)

Schindel, John. *Busy penguins* by John Schindel and Jonathan Chester ill. with photos. Tricycle, 2000. ISBN 978-1-58246-016-1 Subj: Activities. Birds – penguins. Format, unusual – board books. Rhyming text.

Frog face, my little sister and me photos by Janet Delaney. Holt, 1998. ISBN 978-0-8050-5546-7 Subj: Family life – new sibling. Family life – sisters.

What did they see? ill. by Doug Cushman. Holt, 2003. ISBN 978-0-8050-6167-3 Subj: Animals. Format, unusual – toy & movable books. Mirrors.

Schindler, S. D. *Spike and Ike take a hike* ill. by author. Penguin/Nancy Paulsen, 2013. ISBN 978-0-399-24495-7 Subj: Activities – walking. Animals. Animals – coatis. Animals – hedgehogs.

Schlessinger, Laura. *But I waaannt it!* ill. by Daniel McFeeley. HarperCollins, 2000. ISBN 978-0-06-028775-7 Subj: Behavior – greed.

Dr. Laura Schlessinger's Growing up is hard ill. by Daniel McFeeley. HarperCollins, 2001. ISBN 978-0-06-029201-0 Subj: Behavior – growing up. Family life – fathers. Family life – sons.

Dr. Laura Schlessinger's Where's God? ill. by Daniel McFeeley. HarperCollins, 2003. ISBN 978-0-06-051909-4 Subj: Family life – grandfathers. Religion.

Why do you love me? by Laura Schlessinger and Martha Lewis Lambert ill. by Daniel McFeeley. HarperCollins, 1999. ISBN 978-0-06-027866-3 Subj: Emotions – love. Family life – mothers. Family life – sons.

Schmid, Eleonore. *Hare's Christmas gift* ill. by author. NorthSouth, 2000. ISBN 978-0-7358-1377-9 Subj: Animals – rabbits. Character traits – bravery. Religion – Nativity.

Schmid, Paul. *Hugs from Pearl* ill. by author. HarperCollins, 2011. ISBN 978-0-06-180434-2 Subj: Animals – porcupines. Hugging. Problem solving. School.

Oliver and his alligator ill. by author. Disney/Hyperion, 2013. ISBN 978-1-4231-7437-0 Subj: Character traits – shyness. Emotions – fear. Reptiles – alligators, crocodiles. School – first day.

Peanut and Fifi have a ball ill. by Randall De Sève. Dial, 2013. ISBN 978-0-8037-3578-1 Subj: Behavior – fighting, arguing. Behavior – sharing. Family life – sisters. Toys – balls.

Perfectly Percy ill. by author. HarperCollins, 2013. ISBN 978-0-06-180436-6 Subj: Animals – porcupines. Problem solving. Toys – balloons.

A pet for Petunia ill. by author. HarperCollins, 2011. ISBN 978-0-06-196331-5 Subj: Animals – skunks. Pets. Toys.

Petunia goes wild ill. by author. HarperCollins, 2012. ISBN 978-0-06-196334-6 Subj: Behavior – misbehavior. Family life – parents. Imagination.

Schmidt, Gary D., reteller. *The Great Stone Face* a tale by Nathaniel Hawthorne; ill. by Bill Farnsworth. Eerdmans, 2002. ISBN 978-0-8028-5194-9 Subj: Folk & fairy tales.

Schmidt, Karen Lee. *Carl's nose* ill. by author. Harcourt, 2006. ISBN 978-0-15-205049-8 Subj: Animals – dogs. Careers – meteorologists. Mountains. Weather.

Schneider, Christine M. *Horace P. Tuttle, magician extraordinaire* ill. by author. Walker, 2001. ISBN 978-0-8027-8789-7 Subj: Behavior – needing someone. Careers – magicians. Humorous stories.

I'm bored! ill. by Herve Pinel. Houghton, 2006. ISBN 978-0-618-65760-5 Subj: Animals – dogs. Behavior – boredom. Toys – bears.

Picky Mrs. Pickle ill. by author. Walker, 1999. ISBN 978-0-8027-8703-3 Subj: Food. Rhyming text. Self-concept.

Saxophone Sam and his snazzy jazz band ill. by author. Walker, 2002. ISBN 978-0-8027-8809-2 Subj: Activities – dancing. Family life – brothers & sisters. Music. Radios. Rhyming text.

Schneider, Howie. *Chewy Louie* ill. by author. Rising Moon, 2000. ISBN 978-0-87358-765-5 Subj: Animals – babies. Animals – dogs. Pets.

Fast 'n Snappy ill. by Jane Manning. Carolrhoda, 2004. ISBN 978-1-57505-539-8 Subj: Careers – postal workers. Crime. Frogs & toads. Humorous stories. Post office. Reptiles – alligators, crocodiles. U.S. history.

Wilky the White House cockroach ill. by author. Penguin, 2006. ISBN 978-0-399-24388-2 Subj: Insects – cockroaches.

Schneider, Josh. *Bedtime monsters* ill. by author. Clarion, 2013. ISBN 978-0-544-00270-8 Subj: Bedtime. Emotions – fear. Monsters.

You'll be sorry ill. by author. Houghton, 2007. ISBN 978-0-618-81932-4 Subj: Behavior – misbehavior. Family life – brothers & sisters. Weather – floods.

Schnitzlein, Danny. *The monster who ate my peas* ill. by Matt Faulkner. Peachtree, 2001. ISBN 978-1-56145-216-3 Subj: Food. Monsters. Rhyming text.

Schnitzler, Pattie L. *Widdermaker* ill. by Rick Sealock. Carolrhoda, 2002. ISBN 978-0-87614-647-7 Subj: Animals – bulls, cows. Animals – horses, ponies. Cowboys, cowgirls. Humorous stories. Tall tales. U.S. history – frontier & pioneer life.

Schnur, Steven. *Autumn* ill. by Leslie Evans. Clarion, 1997. ISBN 978-0-395-77043-6 Subj: ABC books. Poetry. Seasons – fall.

Night lights ill. by Stacey Schuett. Farrar, 2000. ISBN 978-0-374-35522-7 Subj: Counting, numbers. Light, lights. Night. Rhyming text.

Spring ill. by Leslie Evans. Clarion, 1999. ISBN 978-0-395-82269-2 Subj: ABC books. Poetry. Seasons – spring.

Spring thaw ill. by Stacey Schuett. Viking, 2000. ISBN 978-0-670-87961-8 Subj: Farms. Nature. Seasons – spring.

Summer ill. by Leslie Evans. Clarion, 2001. ISBN 978-0-618-02372-1 Subj: ABC books. Poetry. Seasons – summer.

The tie man's miracle ill. by Stephen T. Johnson. Morrow, 1995. ISBN 978-0-688-13463-1 Subj: Character traits – kindness. Clothing. Holidays – Hanukkah. Holocaust. Jewish culture.

Winter ill. by Leslie Evans. Clarion, 2002. ISBN 978-0-618-02374-5 Subj: ABC books. Poetry. Seasons – winter.

Schnur, Susan. *Tashlich at Turtle Rock* by Susan Schnur and Anna Schnur Fishman ill. by Alex Steele-Morgan. Lerner/Kar-Ben, 2010. ISBN 978-0-7613-4509-1 Subj: Holidays – Rosh Hashanah. Jewish culture.

Schoebinger, Chris. *Snow angels* (Randall, Angel)

Schoenherr, Ian. *Cat and mouse* ill. by author. HarperCollins, 2008. ISBN 978-0-06-136313-9 Subj: Activities – playing. Animals – cats. Animals – mice. Nursery rhymes. Rhyming text.

Don't spill the beans! ill. by author. HarperCollins, 2010. ISBN 978-0-06-172457-2 Subj: Animals – bears. Behavior – secrets. Birthdays. Rhyming text.

Pip and Squeak ill. by author. HarperCollins, 2007. ISBN 978-0-06-087253-3 Subj: Animals – mice. Animals – rabbits. Birthdays. Weather – snow.

Read it, don't eat it! ill. by author. HarperCollins, 2009. ISBN 978-0-06-172455-8 Subj: Animals. Books, reading. Libraries. Rhyming text.

Schoenherr, John. *Bear* ill. by author. Putnam, 1991. ISBN 978-0-399-22177-4 Subj: Alaska. Animals – bears. Nature.

Rebel ill. by author. Putnam, 1995. ISBN 978-0-399-22727-1 Subj: Birds – geese. Character traits – curiosity. Family life. Lakes, ponds.

Schofield, Jennifer. *Animal babies in grasslands* ill. with photos. Kingfisher, 2004. ISBN 978-0-7534-5789-4 Subj: Animals. Animals – babies.

Animal babies in polar lands ill. with photos. Kingfisher, 2004. ISBN 978-0-7534-5755-9 Subj: Animals. Animals – babies. Foreign lands – Antarctic. Foreign lands – Arctic.

Animal babies in ponds and rivers ill. with photos. Kingfisher, 2004. ISBN 978-0-7534-5790-0 Subj: Animals. Animals – babies. Lakes, ponds. Rivers.

Animal babies in rain forests ill. with photos. Kingfisher, 2004. ISBN 978-0-7534-5788-7 Subj: Animals. Animals – babies. Forest, woods.

Schomp, Virginia. *If you were a . . . ballet dancer* ill. with photos. Benchmark, 1998. ISBN 978-0-7614-0616-7 Subj: Activities – dancing. Ballet. Careers – dancers.

If you were a . . . ballplayer ill. with photos. Benchmark, 1999. ISBN 978-0-7614-0917-3 Subj: Careers. Sports.

If you were a . . . construction worker ill. with photos. Benchmark, 1998. ISBN 978-0-7614-0617-4 Subj: Careers – construction workers.

If you were a . . . doctor ill. with photos. Benchmark, 2001. ISBN 978-0-7614-1000-3 Subj: Careers – doctors.

If you were a . . . farmer ill. with photos. Benchmark, 2001. ISBN 978-0-7614-1001-0 Subj: Careers – farmers. Farms.

If you were a . . . musician ill. with photos. Benchmark, 2001. ISBN 978-0-7614-1002-7 Subj: Careers – musicians. Music.

If you were a . . . pilot ill. with photos. Benchmark, 1999. ISBN 978-0-7614-0919-9 Subj: Activities – flying. Careers – airplane pilots. Transportation.

If you were a . . . police officer ill. with photos. Benchmark, 1997. ISBN 978-0-7614-0614-3 Subj: Careers – police officers.

If you were a . . . teacher ill. with photos. Benchmark, 1999. ISBN 978-0-7614-0916-8 Subj: Careers – teachers. School.

If you were a . . . truck driver ill. with photos. Benchmark, 2001. ISBN 978-0-7614-1003-4 Subj: Careers – truck drivers. Trucks.

If you were a . . . veterinarian ill. with photos. Benchmark, 1998. ISBN 978-0-7614-0613-6 Subj: Animals. Careers – veterinarians.

If you were a . . . zookeeper ill. with photos. Benchmark, 2000. ISBN 978-0-7614-0918-2 Subj: Animals. Careers – zookeepers.

If you were an . . . astronaut ill. with photos. Benchmark, 1998. ISBN 978-0-7614-0618-1 Subj: Careers – astronauts. Space & space ships.

Schoonmaker, Elizabeth. *Square cat* ill. by author. Simon & Schuster, 2011. ISBN 978-1-4424-0619-3 Subj: Animals – cats. Character traits – individuality. Concepts – shape. Self-concept.

Schories, Pat. *Jack and the night visitors* ill. by author. Boyds Mills, 2006. ISBN 978-1-932425-33-8 Subj: Aliens. Animals – dogs. Space & space ships. Wordless.

Jack wants a snack ill. by author. Front Street, 2008. ISBN 978-1-59078-546-1 Subj: Animals – dogs. Wordless.

When Jack goes out ill. by author. Boyds Mills, 2010. ISBN 978-1-59078-652-9 Subj: Aliens. Animals – dogs. Wordless.

Schotter, Roni. *All about grandmas* ill. by Janice Nadeau. Dial, 2012. ISBN 978-0-8037-3714-3 Subj: Character traits – individuality. Family life – grandmothers. Foreign languages. Rhyming text.

The boy who loved words ill. by Giselle Potter. Random House, 2006. ISBN 978-0-375-93601-2 Subj: Language. Self-concept.

Captain Bob sets sail ill. by Joe Cepeda. Atheneum, 2000. ISBN 978-0-689-82081-6 Subj: Activities – bathing. Imagination. Pirates.

Captain Bob takes flight ill. by Joe Cepeda. Atheneum, 2003. ISBN 978-0-689-83388-5 Subj: Activities – flying. Character traits – orderliness. Imagination.

Captain Snap and the children of Vinegar Lane ill. by Marcia Sewall. Watts, 1989. ISBN 978-0-531-08397-0 Subj: Character traits – being different. Character traits – generosity. Character traits – kindness.

Doo-Wop Pop ill. by Bryan Collier. HarperCollins, 2008. ISBN 978-0-06-057968-5 Subj: Activities – singing. Careers – custodians, janitors. Character traits – confidence. Rhyming text. Self-concept.

Hanukkah! ill. by Marylin Hafner. Little, 1990. ISBN 978-0-316-77466-6 Subj: Holidays – Hanukkah. Jewish culture. Religion.

In the piney woods ill. by Kimberly Bulcken Root. Farrar, 2003. ISBN 978-0-374-33623-3 Subj: Death. Family life – grandfathers. Forest, woods. Trees.

Mama, I'll give you the world ill. by S. Saelig Gallagher. Random House, 2006. ISBN 978-0-375-93612-8 Subj: Beauty shops. Birthdays. Family life – mothers. Family life – single-parent families. Parties.

Passover! ill. by Erin Eitter Kono. Little, Brown, 2006. ISBN 978-0-316-93991-1 Subj: Holidays – Passover. Jewish culture. Religion.

Passover magic ill. by Marylin Hafner. Little, 1995. ISBN 978-0-316-77468-0 Subj: Holidays – Passover. Jewish culture. Religion.

Purim play ill. by Marylin Hafner. Little, 1998. ISBN 978-0-316-77518-2 Subj: Holidays – Purim. Jewish culture. Religion. Theater.

Room for Rabbit ill. by Cyd Moore. Clarion, 2003. ISBN 978-0-618-18183-4 Subj: Divorce. Family life – fathers. Family life – stepfamilies. Toys.

When the Wizzy Foot goes walking ill. by Mike Wohnoutka. Penguin, 2007. ISBN 978-0-525-47791-4 Subj: Behavior – misbehavior. Concepts – size. Giants. Rhyming text.

Schreck, Karen Halvorsen. *Lucy's family tree* ill. by Stephen Gassler. Tilbury, 2001. ISBN 978-0-88448-225-3 Subj: Adoption. Ethnic groups in the U.S. – Mexican Americans. Family life. Genealogy. School. Self-concept.

Schreiber, Georges. *Bambino the clown* ill. by author. Viking, 1947. Subj: Animals – sea lions. Caldecott award honor books. Clowns, jesters.

Schrock, Jan West. *Give a goat* ill. by Aileen Darragh. Tilbury, 2008. ISBN 978-0-88448-301-4 Subj: Animals – goats. Behavior – seeking better things. Character traits – generosity. Foreign lands – Uganda. School.

Schroeder, Alan. *Baby Flo: Florence Mills lights up the stage* ill. by Cornelius Van Wright. Lee & Low, 2012. ISBN 978-1-60060-410-2 Subj: Careers – singers. Ethnic groups in the U.S. – African Americans. U.S. history.

Minty: a story of young Harriet Tubman ill. by Jerry Pinkney. Dial, 1996. ISBN 978-0-8037-1888-3 Subj: Ethnic groups in the U.S. – African Americans. Prejudice. Slavery. U.S. history.

Ragtime Tumpie ill. by Bernie Fuchs. Little, 1989. ISBN 978-0-316-77497-0 Subj: Activities – dancing. Ethnic groups in the U.S. – African Americans.

Smoky Mountain Rose: an Appalachian Cinderella ill. by Brad Sneed. Dial, 1997. ISBN 978-0-8037-1734-3 Subj: Animals – pigs. Family life – stepfamilies. Folk & fairy tales.

The stone lion ill. by Todd L. W. Doney. Scribners, 1994. ISBN 978-0-684-19578-0 Subj: Behavior – greed. Character traits – honesty. Character traits – kindness. Character traits – selfishness. Folk & fairy tales. Foreign lands – Tibet.

Schroeder, Lisa. *Baby can't sleep* ill. by Viviana Garofoli. Sterling, 2005. ISBN 978-1-4027-2171-7 Subj: Animals – sheep. Babies. Bedtime. Counting, numbers. Rhyming text.

Schubert, Dieter. *Bear's eggs* (Schubert, Ingrid)

There's a crocodile under my bed! (Schubert, Ingrid)

There's always room for one more (Schubert, Ingrid)

The umbrella (Schubert, Ingrid)

Schubert, Ingrid. *Bear's eggs* by Ingrid Schubert and Dieter Schubert ill. by authors. Front Street, 1999. ISBN 978-1-886910-46-1 Subj: Animals – bears. Animals – hedgehogs. Birds – geese. Eggs.

There's a crocodile under my bed! by Ingrid Schubert and Dieter Schubert ill. by authors. Boyds Mills, 2005. ISBN 978-1-932425-48-2 Subj: Bedtime. Reptiles – alligators, crocodiles.

There's always room for one more by Ingrid Schubert and Dieter Schubert ill. by authors. Front Street, 2002. ISBN 978-1-886910-77-5 Subj: Animals. Animals – beavers. Friendship. Insects – butterflies, caterpillars. Sports – sailing.

The umbrella by Ingrid Schubert and Dieter Schubert ill. by authors. Lemniscaat, 2011. ISBN 978-1-9359-5400-2 Subj: Animals – dogs. Umbrellas. Wordless. World.

Schubert, Leda. *Ballet of the elephants* ill. by Robert Andrew Parker. Macmillan, 2006. ISBN 978-1-59643-075-4 Subj: Animals – elephants. Ballet.

Feeding the sheep ill. by Andrea U'Ren. Farrar, 2010. ISBN 978-0-374-32296-0 Subj: Activities – weaving. Animals – sheep. Family life – mothers. Farms. Rhyming text.

Here comes Darrell ill. by Mary Azarian. Houghton, 2005. ISBN 978-0-618-41605-9 Subj: Barns. Character traits – helpfulness. Communities, neighborhoods. Machines. Seasons. Tractors. Trucks.

Monsieur Marceau ill. by Gerard DuBois. Roaring Brook, 2012. ISBN 978-1-59643-529-2 Subj: Clowns, jesters. Foreign lands – France.

The Princess of Borscht ill. by Bonnie Christensen. Roaring Brook, 2011. ISBN 978-1-59643-515-5 Subj: Activities – baking, cooking. Family life – grandmothers. Illness. Jewish culture.

Reading to Peanut ill. by Amanda Haley. Holiday House, 2011. ISBN 978-0-8234-2339-2 Subj: Activities – writing. Animals – dogs. Books, reading. Character traits – perseverance.

Winnie all day long ill. by William Benedict. Candlewick, 2000. ISBN 978-0-7636-1041-8 Subj: Animals – dogs. Sleep.

Winnie plays ball ill. by William Benedict. Candlewick, 2000. ISBN 978-0-7636-1040-1 Subj: Animals – dogs. Birthdays. Toys – balls.

Schuch, Steve. *A symphony of whales* ill. by Peter Sylvada. Harcourt, 1999. ISBN 978-0-15-201670-8 Subj: Animals – whales. Character traits – helpfulness. Dreams. Foreign lands – Russia. Music.

Schuett, Stacey. *Somewhere in the world right now* ill. by author. Knopf, 1995. ISBN 978-0-679-96537-4 Subj: Geography. Time. World.

Schuh, Mari C. *Chickens on the farm* ill. with photos. Pebble, 2002. ISBN 978-0-7368-0991-7 Subj: Birds – chickens. Farms.

Cows on the farm ill. with photos. Pebble, 2002. ISBN 978-0-7368-0992-4 Subj: Animals – bulls, cows. Farms.

Pigs on the farm ill. with photos. Pebble, 2002. ISBN 978-0-7368-0993-1 Subj: Animals – pigs. Farms.

Sheep on the farm ill. with photos. Pebble, 2002. ISBN 978-0-7368-0994-8 Subj: Animals – sheep. Farms.

Schulman, Janet. *A bunny for all seasons* ill. by Mei-lo So. Knopf, 2003. ISBN 978-0-375-92256-5 Subj: Animals – rabbits. Gardens, gardening. Seasons.

Countdown to spring ill. by Meilo So. Knopf, 2002. ISBN 978-0-375-81364-1 Subj: Animals. Counting, numbers. Seasons – spring.

Pale Male: citizen hawk of New York City ill. by Meilo So. Knopf, 2008. ISBN 978-0-375-84558-1 Subj: Birds – hawks. Cities, towns.

10 Easter egg hunters: a holiday counting book ill. by Linda Davick. Random House, 2011. ISBN 978-0-375-86787-3 Subj: Counting, numbers. Eggs. Holidays – Easter. Rhyming text.

10 trick-or-treaters: a Halloween counting book ill. by Linda Davick. Random House, 2005. ISBN 978-0-375-95225-8 Subj: Counting, numbers. Holidays – Halloween. Rhyming text.

10 Valentine friends: a holiday counting book ill. by Linda Davick. Random House, 2011. ISBN 978-0-375-86967-9 Subj: Counting, numbers. Holidays – Valentine's Day. Rhyming text.

Schultz, Sam. *Animal antics: the beast jokes ever* ill. by Brian Gable. Carolrhoda, 2004. ISBN 978-1-57505-640-1 Subj: Animals. Riddles & jokes.

Monster mayhem ill. by Brian Gable. Carolrhoda, 2004. ISBN 978-0-8225-1169-4 Subj: Monsters. Riddles & jokes.

Schumaker, Ward. *Dance!* ill. by author. Harcourt, 1996. ISBN 978-0-15-200046-2 Subj: Activities – dancing. Animals. Rhyming text.

In my garden ill. by author. Chronicle, 2000. ISBN 978-0-8118-2689-1 Subj: Counting, numbers. Gardens, gardening.

Schur, Maxine Rose. *Day of delight* ill. by Brian Pinkney. Dial, 1994. ISBN 978-0-8037-1414-4 Subj: Foreign lands – Ethiopia. Jewish culture. Religion.

Schuurmans, Hilde. *Sydney won't swim* ill. by author. Whispering Coyote, 2001. ISBN 978-1-57091-476-8 Subj: Animals – badgers. Emotions – fear. Sports – swimming.

Schwab, Eva. *Robert and the Robot* ill. by author. Front Street, 2001. ISBN 978-1-886910-59-1 Subj: Character traits – orderliness. Robots.

Schwartz, Amy. *Annabelle Swift, kindergartner* ill. by author. Orchard, 1988. ISBN 978-0-531-08337-6 Subj: Character traits – pride. School – first day. Sibling rivalry.

Bea and Mr. Jones ill. by author. Bradbury, 1982. ISBN 978-0-87888-202-1 Subj: Behavior – imitation. Family life – fathers.

A beautiful girl ill. by author. Macmillan, 2006. ISBN 978-1-59643-165-2 Subj: Anatomy. Animals. Animals – elephants. Birds – robins. Character traits – appearance. Fish. Insects – flies.

Begin at the beginning: a little artist learns about life ill. by author. HarperCollins, 2005. ISBN 978-0-06-000112-4 Subj: Behavior – growing up.

The boys teams ill. by author. Atheneum, 2001. ISBN 978-0-689-84138-5 Subj: Activities. School – nursery.

Dee Dee and me ill. by author. Holiday House, 2013. ISBN 978-0-8234-2524-2 Subj: Family life – sisters. Self-concept.

How to catch an elephant ill. by author. DK, 1999. ISBN 978-0-7894-2579-9 Subj: Animals – elephants.

Lucy can't sleep ill. by author. Roaring Brook, 2012. ISBN 978-1-59643-543-8 Subj: Bedtime. Rhyming text. Sleep.

Oma and Bobo ill. by author. Bradbury, 1987. ISBN 978-0-02-781500-9 Subj: Animals – dogs. Family life – grandmothers.

Oscar: the big adventures of a little sock monkey by Amy Schwartz and Leonard S. Marcus ill. by Amy Schwartz. HarperCollins, 2006. ISBN 978-0-06-072622-5 Subj: Animals – monkeys. Animals – rabbits. Pets. School. Toys.

Some babies ill. by author. Orchard, 2000. ISBN 978-0-531-33287-0 Subj: Activities – storytelling. Bedtime. Family life.

Starring Miss Darlene ill. by author. Macmillan, 2007. ISBN 978-1-59643-230-7 Subj: Animals. Animals – hippopotamuses. Behavior – mistakes. Careers – actors. Self-concept. Theater.

Things I learned in second grade ill. by author. Tegen, 2004. ISBN 978-0-06-050937-8 Subj: Behavior – growing up. School.

Tiny and Hercules ill. by author. Roaring Brook, 2009. ISBN 978-1-59643-253-6 Subj: Animals – elephants. Animals – mice. Friendship.

Willie and Uncle Bill ill. by author. Holiday House, 2012. ISBN 978-0-8234-2203-6 Subj: Activities – babysitting. Family life – aunts, uncles.

Schwartz, Corey Rosen. *Hop! Plop!* by Corey Rosen Schwartz and Tali Klein ill. by Olivier Dunrea. Walker, 2006. ISBN 978-0-8027-8056-0 Subj: Activities – playing. Animals – elephants. Animals – mice. Friendship. Noise, sounds.

The three ninja pigs ill. by Dan Santat. Putnam, 2012. ISBN 978-0-399-25514-4 Subj: Animals – pigs. Rhyming text. Sports – karate. Sports – martial arts.

Schwartz, David M. *How much is a million?* ill. by Steven Kellogg. Lothrop, 1985. ISBN 978-0-688-04050-5 Subj: Concepts – size. Counting, numbers.

If you hopped like a frog ill. by James Warhola. Scholastic, 1999. ISBN 978-0-590-09857-1 Subj:

Animals. Concepts. Counting, numbers. Picture puzzles. Science.

Ready! set! measure! ill. by Steven Kellogg. HarperCollins, 2002. ISBN 978-0-06-623784-8 Subj: Concepts – measurement. Concepts – weight. Counting, numbers.

Where else in the wild? more camouflaged creatures concealed — and revealed by David M. Schwartz and Yael Schy; photos by Dwight Kuhn. Tricycle, 2009. ISBN 978-1-58246-283-7 Subj: Animals. Disguises. Format, unusual – toy & movable books. Poetry.

Where in the wild: camouflaged animals concealed and revealed: ear-tickling poems by David M. Schwartz and Yael Schy; photos by Dwight Kuhn. Ten Speed, 2007. ISBN 978-1-58246-207-3 Subj: Animals. Disguises. Format, unusual – toy & movable books. Poetry.

Schwartz, Henry. *How I captured a dinosaur* ill. by Amy Schwartz. Watts, 1989. ISBN 978-0-531-08370-3 Subj: Camps, camping. Dinosaurs. Pets. Prehistory.

Schwartz, Howard. *Gathering sparks* ill. by Kristina Swarner. Roaring Brook, 2010. ISBN 978-1-59643-280-2 Subj: Character traits – kindness. Character traits – responsibility. Family life – grandfathers. Jewish culture. Religion.

Schwartz, Joanne. *Our corner grocery store* ill. by Laura Beingessner. Tundra, 2009. ISBN 978-0-88776-868-2 Subj: Family life – grandparents. Stores.

Schwartz, Roslyn. *The mole sisters and the cool breeze* ill. by author. Annick, 2002. ISBN 978-1-55037-771-2 Subj: Animals. Animals – moles. Concepts – cold & heat. Family life – sisters.

The mole sisters and the fairy ring ill. by author. Annick, 2003. ISBN 978-1-55037-819-1 Subj: Activities – playing. Animals – moles. Family life – sisters.

The mole sisters and the piece of moss ill. by author. Annick, 1999. ISBN 978-1-55037-583-1 Subj: Animals – moles. Character traits – helpfulness. Character traits – optimism. Family life – sisters.

The mole sisters and the question ill. by author. Annick, 2002. ISBN 978-1-55037-769-9 Subj: Animals. Animals – moles. Family life – sisters.

The mole sisters and the rainy day ill. by author. Annick, 1999. ISBN 978-1-55037-611-1 Subj: Animals – moles. Family life – sisters. Sports – swimming. Weather – rain.

Tales from Parc la Fontaine ill. by author. Firefly, 2006. ISBN 978-1-55451-044-3 Subj: Animals. Nature. Parks.

The Vole brothers ill. by author. OwlKids, 2011. ISBN 978-1-926818-83-2 Subj: Animals – voles. Family life – brothers. Food.

Schwarz, Viviane. *The adventures of a nose* ill. by Joel Stewart. Candlewick, 2002. ISBN 978-0-7636-1674-8 Subj: Anatomy – noses. Emotions – happiness. Self-concept.

Shark and Lobster's amazing undersea adventure ill. by author. Candlewick, 2006. ISBN 978-0-7636-2910-6 Subj: Crustaceans – lobsters. Emotions – fear. Fish – sharks. Sea & seashore.

There are cats in this book ill. by author. Candlewick, 2008. ISBN 978-0-7636-3923-5 Subj: Activities – playing. Animals – cats. Format, unusual – toy & movable books.

There are no cats in this book ill. by author. Candlewick, 2010. ISBN 978-0-7636-4954-8 Subj: Animals – cats. Format, unusual – toy & movable books.

Timothy and the strong pajamas: a superhero adventure ill. by author. Scholastic, 2008. ISBN 978-0-545-03329-9 Subj: Character traits – bravery. Character traits – smallness. Clothing – pajamas.

Schweninger, Ann. *Autumn days* ill. by author. Viking, 1991. ISBN 978-0-670-82758-9 Subj: Animals – dogs. Seasons – fall.

Halloween surprises ill. by author. Viking, 1984. ISBN 978-0-670-35935-6 Subj: Animals – rabbits. Holidays – Halloween.

Valentine friends ill. by author. Viking, 1988. ISBN 978-0-670-81448-0 Subj: Animals – rabbits. Family life. Holidays – Valentine's Day.

Schy, Yael. *Where else in the wild? more camouflaged creatures concealed — and revealed* (Schwartz, David M.)

Where in the wild: camouflaged animals concealed and revealed: ear-tickling poems (Schwartz, David M.)

Scieszka, Jon. *Baloney, Henry P.* ill. by Lane Smith. Viking, 2001. ISBN 978-0-670-89248-8 Subj: Aliens. School. Space & space ships.

Battle Bunny by Jon Scieszka and Mac Barnett ill. by Matthew Myers. Simon & Schuster, 2013. ISBN 978-1-4424-4673-1 Subj: Activities – writing. Animals. Animals – rabbits. Birthdays. Books, reading.

The book that Jack wrote ill. by Daniel Adel. Viking, 1994. ISBN 978-0-670-84330-5 Subj: Cumulative tales. Nursery rhymes.

Cowboy and Octopus ill. by Lane Smith. Penguin, 2007. ISBN 978-0-670-91058-8 Subj: Cowboys, cowgirls. Friendship. Octopuses.

The frog prince, continued ill. by Steve Johnson. Viking, 1991. ISBN 978-0-670-83421-1 Subj: Folk &

fairy tales. Frogs & toads. Royalty – princes. Royalty – princesses. Witches.

Melvin might? ill. by David Shannon and Loren Long, et al. Simon & Schuster, 2008. ISBN 978-1-4169-4134-7 Subj: Behavior – worrying. Character traits – bravery. Character traits – helpfulness. Trucks.

Robot Zot! ill. by David Shannon. Simon & Schuster, 2009. ISBN 978-1-4169-6394-3 Subj: Humorous stories. Robots. Space & space ships.

Smash! Crash! ill. by David Shannon and Loren Long, et al. Simon & Schuster, 2008. ISBN 978-1-4169-4133-0 Subj: Friendship. Trucks.

The Stinky Cheese Man and other fairly stupid tales by Jon Scieszka and Lane Smith ill. by Lane Smith. Viking, 1992. ISBN 978-0-670-84487-6 Subj: Caldecott award honor books. Folk & fairy tales.

Truckery rhymes ill. by David Shannon and Loren Long, et al. Simon & Schuster, 2009. ISBN 978-1-4169-4135-4 Subj: Nursery rhymes. Trucks.

The true story of the three little pigs by A. Wolf, as told to Jon Scieszka ill. by Lane Smith. Viking, 1989. ISBN 978-0-670-82759-6 Subj: Animals – pigs. Animals – wolves. Folk & fairy tales.

Walt Disney's Alice in Wonderland ill. by Mary Blair. Disney, 2008. ISBN 978-1-4231-0728-6 Subj: Behavior – running away. Imagination.

Scillian, Devin. *Brewster the rooster* ill. by Lee White. Little, Brown, 2007. ISBN 978-1-58536-311-7 Subj: Birds – chickens. Glasses. Rhyming text.

Memoirs of a hamster ill. by Tim Bowers. Sleeping Bear, 2013. ISBN 978-1-58536-831-0 Subj: Animals – cats. Animals – hamsters. Pets.

Sciurba, Katie. *Oye, Celia! a song for Celia Cruz* ill. by Edel Rodriguez. Holt, 2007. ISBN 978-0-8050-7468-0 Subj: Careers – singers. Foreign lands – Cuba. Music.

Scott, Ann Herbert. *Hi!* ill. by Glo Coalson. Philomel, 1994. ISBN 978-0-399-21964-1 Subj: Behavior – unnoticed, unseen. Post office.

On mother's lap ill. by Glo Coalson. Rev. ed. Houghton, 1992. ISBN 978-0-395-58920-5 Subj: Behavior – needing someone. Emotions – love. Eskimos. Family life. Family life – mothers. Sibling rivalry.

On mother's lap [board book] ill. by Glo Coalson. Clarion, 2000. ISBN 978-0-618-05159-5 Subj: Behavior – needing someone. Emotions – love. Eskimos. Family life. Family life – mothers. Format, unusual – board books. Sibling rivalry.

Scott, Elaine. *Friends!* photos by Margaret Miller. Atheneum, 2000. ISBN 978-0-689-82105-9 Subj: Friendship.

Scott, Janine. *Let's eat* ill. with photos. Compass Point, 2003. ISBN 978-0-7565-0365-9 Subj: Food.

Let's get dressed ill. with photos. Compass Point, 2003. ISBN 978-0-7565-0366-6 Subj: Clothing.

Time to tell ill. with photos. Compass Point, 2003. ISBN 978-0-7565-0455-7 Subj: Time.

Scott, Nathan Kumar. *Mangoes and bananas* ill. by T. Balaji. Tara, 2006. ISBN 978-81-86211-06-9 Subj: Animals – deer. Animals – monkeys. Behavior – greed. Behavior – trickery. Folk & fairy tales. Foreign lands – Indonesia.

The sacred banana leaf: an Indonesian trickster tale ill. by Radhashyam Raut. Tara, 2008. ISBN 978-81-86211-28-1 Subj: Animals – deer. Behavior – trickery. Folk & fairy tales. Foreign lands – Indonesia.

Scotton, Rob. *Love, Splat* ill. by author. HarperCollins, 2008. ISBN 978-0-06-083157-8 Subj: Animals – cats. Holidays – Valentine's Day. School.

Merry Christmas, Splat ill. by author. HarperCollins, 2009. ISBN 978-0-06-083160-8 Subj: Animals – cats. Behavior – misbehavior. Holidays – Christmas.

Russell and the lost treasure ill. by author. HarperCollins, 2006. ISBN 978-0-06-059851-8 Subj: Activities – photographing. Animals – sheep.

Russell the sheep ill. by author. HarperCollins, 2005. ISBN 978-0-06-059848-8 Subj: Animals – sheep. Bedtime. Counting, numbers. Sleep.

Russell's Christmas magic ill. by author. HarperCollins, 2007. ISBN 978-0-06-059854-9 Subj: Animals – sheep. Character traits – helpfulness. Holidays – Christmas. Santa Claus.

Secret Agent Splat! ill. by author. HarperCollins, 2012. ISBN 978-0-06-197871-5 Subj: Animals – cats. Behavior – lost & found possessions. Careers – detectives.

Splat and the cool school trip ill. by author. HarperCollins, 2013. ISBN 978-0-06-213386-1 Subj: Animals – cats. School – field trips. Zoos.

Splat says thank you! ill. by author. HarperCollins, 2012. ISBN 978-0-06-197874-6 Subj: Animals – cats. Animals – mice. Character traits – kindness. Friendship. Illness.

Splat the cat ill. by author. HarperCollins, 2008. ISBN 978-0-06-083154-7 Subj: Animals – cats. Animals – mice. Humorous stories. School – first day.

Splat the cat: on with the show by Rob Scotton and Annie Auerbach ill. by Rob Scotton. HarperCollins, 2013. ISBN 978-0-06-209010-2 Subj: Animals – cats. School. Theater.

Splish, splash, Splat! ill. by author. HarperCollins, 2011. ISBN 978-0-06-197868-5 Subj: Animals –

cats. Emotions – fear. Friendship. Sports – swimming.

Scrimger, Richard. *Eugene's story* ill. by Gillian Johnson. Tundra, 2003. ISBN 978-0-88776-544-5 Subj: Activities – storytelling. Family life – brothers & sisters. Sibling rivalry.

Princess Bun Bun ill. by Johnson, Gillian. Tundra, 2002. ISBN 978-0-88776-543-8 Subj: Family life – aunts, uncles. Family life – brothers & sisters. Monsters. Royalty – princesses.

The scrubbly-bubbly car wash ill. by Cynthia Jabar. HarperCollins, 2003. ISBN 978-0-06-029486-1 Subj: Automobiles. Family life – fathers. Rhyming text.

Scruggs, Afi. *Jump rope magic* ill. by David Diaz. Blue Sky, 2000. ISBN 978-0-590-69327-1 Subj: Activities – jumping. Ethnic groups in the U.S. – African Americans. Games. Noise, sounds. Rhyming text.

Seabrooke, Brenda. *'Twas the day before Christmas: the story of Clement Clarke Moore's beloved poem* ill. by Delana Bettoli. Dutton, 2008. ISBN 978-0-525-47816-4 Subj: Activities – writing. Holidays – Christmas. Poetry.

Sears, William, M.D. *Baby on the way* ill. by Renée Williams-Andriani. Little, 2001. ISBN 978-0-316-78767-3 Subj: Babies. Birth.

Sears, William, M.D., et al. *Eat healthy, feel great* ill. by Renée Williams-Andriani. Little, 2002. ISBN 978-0-316-78708-6 Subj: Food. Health & fitness.

What baby needs ill. by Renée Williams-Andriani. Little, 2001. ISBN 978-0-316-78828-1 Subj: Babies. Family life – new sibling.

You can go to the potty ill. by Renée Williams-Andriani. Little, 2002. ISBN 978-0-316-78888-5 Subj: Behavior – growing up. Toilet training.

Seattle, Chief. *Brother eagle, sister sky* ill. by Susan Jeffers. Puffin, 2002. ISBN 978-0-14-230132-6 Subj: Ecology. Indians of North America – Suquamish.

Sebe, Masayuki. *Let's count to 100!* ill. by author. Kids Can, 2011. ISBN 978-1-55453-661-0 Subj: Counting, numbers.

100 animals on parade! ill. by author. Kids Can, 2013. ISBN 978-1-55453-871-3 Subj: Animals. Counting, numbers. Parades.

Sedaka, Marc. *Dinosaur pet* ill. by Tim Bowers. Imagine, 2012. ISBN 978-1-936140-36-7 Subj: Dinosaurs. Music.

Sedaka, Neil. *Waking up is hard to do* by Neil Sedaka and Howard Greenfield ill. by Daniel Miyares. Imagine, 2010. ISBN 978-1-936140-13-8 Subj: Morning. Reptiles – alligators, crocodiles. Songs.

Seder, Rufus Butler. *Waddle!* ill. by author. Workman, 2009. ISBN 978-0-7611-5112-8 Subj: Animals. Concepts – motion. Format, unusual – toy & movable books.

The Wizard of Oz: a Scanimation book ill. by author. Workman, 2011. ISBN 978-0-7611-6373-2 Subj: Format, unusual – toy & movable books. Wizards.

Seeber, Dorothea P. *A pup just for me . . . A boy just for me* ill. by Ed Young. Philomel, 2000. ISBN 978-0-399-23403-3 Subj: Animals – dogs. Behavior – needing someone. Format, unusual – toy & movable books. Pets. Rhyming text.

Seeger, Laura Vaccaro. *Black? White! Day? Night!* ill. by author. Macmillan, 2006. ISBN 978-1-59643-185-0 Subj: Concepts – opposites. Format, unusual – toy & movable books.

Bully ill. by author. Roaring Brook, 2013. ISBN 978-1-59643-630-5 Subj: Animals. Animals – bulls, cows. Behavior – bullying, teasing. Emotions – anger.

Dog and Bear: three to get ready ill. by author. Roaring Brook, 2009. ISBN 978-1-59643-396-0 Subj: Animals – dogs. Friendship. Toys – bears.

Dog and Bear: two friends, three stories ill. by author. Macmillan, 2007. ISBN 978-1-59643-053-2 Subj: Animals – dogs. Friendship. Toys – bears.

Dog and Bear: two's company ill. by author. Roaring Brook, 2008. ISBN 978-1-59643-273-4 Subj: Animals – dogs. Friendship. Toys – bears.

First the egg ill. by author. Macmillan, 2007. ISBN 978-1-59643-272-7 Subj: Caldecott award honor books. Concepts – change. Format, unusual – toy & movable books.

Green ill. by author. Roaring Brook, 2012. ISBN 978-1-59643-397-7 Subj: Caldecott award honor books. Concepts – color. Nature.

The hidden alphabet ill. by author. Roaring Brook, 2003. ISBN 978-0-7613-1941-2 Subj: ABC books. Format, unusual – toy & movable books. Picture puzzles.

I had a rooster: a traditional folk song ill. by author. Viking, 2001. ISBN 978-0-670-03521-2 Subj: Animals. Noise, sounds. Songs.

Lemons are not red ill. by author. Macmillan, 2004. ISBN 978-1-59643-008-2 Subj: Concepts – color. Format, unusual – toy & movable books.

One boy ill. by author. Roaring Brook, 2008. ISBN 978-1-59643-274-1 Subj: Activities – painting. Counting, numbers. Format, unusual. Language.

Walter was worried ill. by author. Macmillan, 2005. ISBN 978-1-59643-068-6 Subj: ABC books. Emotions. Language. Weather – storms.

What if? ill. by author. Roaring Brook, 2010. ISBN 978-1-59643-398-4 Subj: Animals – seals. Behavior – sharing. Friendship. Toys – balls.

Seeger, Pete. *Abiyoyo* ill. by Michael Hays. Macmillan, 1986. ISBN 978-0-02-781490-3 Subj: Folk & fairy tales. Magic. Monsters.

Abiyoyo returns by Pete Seeger and Paul DuBois Jacobs ill. by Michael Hays. Simon & Schuster, 2001. ISBN 978-0-689-83271-0 Subj: Careers – magicians. Folk & fairy tales. Foreign lands – South Africa. Giants. Magic.

The deaf musicians by Pete Seeger and Paul DuBois Jacobs ill. by R. Gregory Christie. Penguin, 2006. ISBN 978-0-399-24316-5 Subj: Careers – musicians. Disabilities – deafness. Music.

Some friends to feed: the story of Stone Soup by Pete Seeger and Paul DuBois Jacobs ill. by Michael Hays. Penguin, 2005. ISBN 978-0-399-24017-1 Subj: Careers – military. Character traits – cleverness. Folk & fairy tales. Food. Foreign lands – Germany.

Segal, John. *Alistair and Kip's great adventure* ill. by author. Simon & Schuster, 2008. ISBN 978-1-4169-0280-5 Subj: Activities – traveling. Animals – cats. Animals – dogs. Boats, ships.

Carrot soup ill. by author. Simon & Schuster, 2006. ISBN 978-0-689-87702-5 Subj: Animals – rabbits. Food. Gardens, gardening.

Far far away! ill. by author. Philomel, 2009. ISBN 978-0-399-25007-1 Subj: Animals – pigs. Behavior – running away. Family life – mothers.

The lonely moose ill. by author. Hyperion, 2007. ISBN 978-1-4231-0173-4 Subj: Animals – moose. Birds. Emotions – loneliness. Friendship.

Pirates don't take baths ill. by author. Penguin, 2011. ISBN 978-0-399-25425-3 Subj: Activities – bathing. Animals – pigs. Imagination.

Segal, Lore Groszmann. *Morris the artist* ill. by Boris Kulikov. Farrar, 2003. ISBN 978-0-374-35063-5 Subj: Activities – painting. Birthdays. Careers – artists. Gifts.

Seibert, Patricia. *Mush! across Alaska in the world's longest sled-dog race* ill. by Jan Davey Ellis. Millbrook, 1992. ISBN 978-1-56294-705-7 Subj: Alaska. Animals – dogs. Sports – racing. Sports – sledding.

Seibold, J. Otto. *Lost sloth* ill. by author. McSweeney's McMullens, 2013. ISBN 978-1-938073-35-9 Subj: Animals – sloths. Character traits – luck. Shopping. Stores.

Penguin dreams by J. Otto Seibold and Vivian Walsh ill. by J. Otto Seibold. Chronicle, 1999. ISBN 978-0-8118-2558-0 Subj: Activities – flying. Birds – penguins. Dreams. Foreign lands – Antarctic. Rhyming text.

Vunce upon a time by J. Otto Seibold and Siobhan Vivian ill. by J. Otto Seibold. Chronicle, 2008. ISBN 978-0-8118-6271-4 Subj: Holidays – Halloween. Monsters.

Seim, Donna Marie. *Where is Simon, Sandy? the story of a little donkey that wouldn't quit* ill. by Susan Spellman. PublishingWorks, 2008. ISBN 978-1-933002-73-6 Subj: Animals – donkeys. Character traits – perseverance. Foreign lands. Water.

Seinfeld, Jerry. *Halloween* ill. by James Bennett. Little, 2002. ISBN 978-0-316-13454-5 Subj: Holidays – Halloween. Memories, memory.

Seki, Sunny. *The tale of the lucky cat* ill. by author. East West, 2007. ISBN 978-0-9669437-5-7 Subj: Animals – cats. Character traits – luck. Folk & fairy tales. Foreign lands – Japan.

Selick, Henry. *Moongirl* ill. by Peter Chan. Candlewick, 2006. ISBN 978-0-7636-3068-3 Subj: Merry-go-rounds. Monsters. Moon. Sports – fishing.

Selig, Josh. *Red & Yellow's noisy night* ill. by Little Airplane Productions. Sterling, 2012. ISBN 978-1-4027-9070-6 Subj: Bedtime. Behavior – fighting, arguing. Concepts – color. Lullabies. Noise, sounds.

Selkowe, Valrie M. *Happy birthday to me!* ill. by John Sandford. HarperCollins, 2001. ISBN 978-0-688-16680-9 Subj: Animals. Animals – rabbits. Birthdays. Gardens, gardening.

Selsam, Millicent E. *How to be a nature detective* ill. by Marlene Hill Donnelly. HarperCollins, 1995. ISBN 978-0-06-023448-5 Subj: Animals. Nature.

Keep looking! by Millicent E. Selsam and Joyce Hunt ill. by Normand Chartier. Macmillan, 1988. ISBN 978-0-02-781840-6 Subj: Animals. Farms. Seasons – winter.

Selznick, Brian. *The invention of Hugo Cabret: a novel in words and pictures* ill. by author. Scholastic, 2007. ISBN 978-0-439-81378-5 Subj: Caldecott award books. Foreign lands – France. Mystery stories. Orphans. Robots.

Sendak, Maurice. *Alligators all around: an alphabet* ill. by author. HarperCollins, 1962. ISBN 978-0-06-025530-5 Subj: ABC books. Reptiles – alligators, crocodiles.

Bumble-ardy ill. by author. HarperCollins, 2011. ISBN 978-0-06-205198-1 Subj: Animals – pigs. Birthdays. Parties. Rhyming text.

Chicken soup with rice ill. by author. HarperCollins, 1962. ISBN 978-0-06-025535-0 Subj: Days of the week, months of the year.

Hector Protector, and As I went over the water ill. by author. HarperCollins, 1993. ISBN 978-0-06-028643-9 Subj: Nursery rhymes.

In the night kitchen ill. by author. HarperCollins, 1970. ISBN 978-0-06-026669-1 Subj: Caldecott award honor books. Dreams. Imagination.

Mommy? ill. by author. Paper engineering by Matthew Reinhart. Scholastic, 2006. ISBN 978-0-439-88050-3 Subj: Format, unusual – toy & movable books. Monsters.

One was Johnny: a counting book ill. by author. HarperCollins, 1962. ISBN 978-0-06-025540-4 Subj: Counting, numbers.

Outside over there ill. by author. HarperCollins, 1981. ISBN 978-0-06-025524-4 Subj: Activities – babysitting. Babies. Caldecott award honor books. Mythical creatures – goblins.

Pierre: a cautionary tale in five chapters and a prologue ill. by author. HarperCollins, 1962. ISBN 978-0-06-118009-5 Subj: Behavior – indifference. Character traits – individuality. Humorous stories. Rhyming text.

Seven little monsters ill. by author. HarperCollins, 1977. ISBN 978-0-06-025478-0 Subj: Counting, numbers. Monsters. Rhyming text.

The sign on Rosie's door ill. by author. HarperCollins, 1960. ISBN 978-0-06-025506-0 Subj: Activities – playing. Imagination.

Very far away ill. by author. HarperCollins, 1957. ISBN 978-0-06-025515-2 Subj: Animals. Behavior – needing someone. Behavior – running away.

Where the wild things are ill. by author. HarperCollins, 1963. ISBN 978-0-06-025521-3 Subj: Behavior – misbehavior. Caldecott award books. Imagination. Monsters.

Sendelbach, Brian. *The underpants zoo* ill. by author. Scholastic, 2011. ISBN 978-0-545-24935-5 Subj: Clothing – underwear. Rhyming text. Zoos.

Senior, Olive. *Birthday suit* ill. by Eugenie Fernandes. Annick, 2012. ISBN 978-1-55451-369-7 Subj: Behavior – growing up. Clothing.

Senisi, Ellen B. *All kinds of friends, even green* photos by author. Woodbine, 2002. ISBN 978-1-890627-35-5 Subj: Disabilities – physical disabilities. Reptiles – iguanas. School.

For my family, love, Allie photos by author. Whitman, 1998. ISBN 978-0-8075-2539-5 Subj: Family life. Food. Marriage, interracial.

Hurray for pre-K! photos by author. HarperCollins, 2000. ISBN 978-0-06-028897-6 Subj: Activities. Emotions. School – nursery.

Just kids: visiting a class for children with special needs photos by author. Dutton, 1998. ISBN 978-0-525-45646-9 Subj: Disabilities. School.

Senning, Cindy Post. *Emily's everyday manners* (Post, Peggy)

Emily's out and about book by Cindy Post Senning and Peggy Post ill. by Leo Landry. Collins, 2009. ISBN 978-0-06-111700-8 Subj: Etiquette. Family life – mothers.

Sensel, Joni. *Bears barge in* ill. by Christopher L. Bivins. Dream Factory, 2000. ISBN 978-0-9701195-0-6 Subj: Animals. Ecology. Rhyming text.

Senshu, Noriko. *Sonny's dream* ill. by author. Roads, 2000. ISBN 978-1-57174-215-5 Subj: Alaska. Animals – bears. Behavior – growing up. Dreams. Emotions – fear. Hibernation.

Serafini, Frank. *Looking closely across the desert* photos by author. Kids Can, 2008. ISBN 978-1-55453-211-7 Subj: Desert.

Looking closely along the shore photos by author. Kids Can, 2008. ISBN 978-1-55453-141-7 Subj: Participation. Picture puzzles. Sea & seashore. Senses – sight.

Looking closely around the pond photos by author. Kids Can, 2009. ISBN 978-1-55337-395-7 Subj: Lakes, ponds.

Looking closely inside the garden photos by author. Kids Can, 2008. ISBN 978-1-55453-210-0 Subj: Gardens, gardening. Plants.

Looking closely through the forest photos by author. Kids Can, 2008. ISBN 978-1-55453-212-4 Subj: Forest, woods.

Serfozo, Mary. *Rain talk* ill. by Keiko Narahashi. Macmillan, 1990. ISBN 978-0-689-50496-9 Subj: Noise, sounds. Weather – rain.

There's a square ill. by David A. Carter. Scholastic, 1996. ISBN 978-0-590-54426-9 Subj: Concepts – shape. Rhyming text.

What's what? a guessing game ill. by Keiko Narahashi. McElderry, 1996. ISBN 978-0-689-80653-7 Subj: Animals – dogs. Concepts – opposites. Ethnic groups in the U.S. – African Americans. Language.

Who said red? ill. by Keiko Narahashi. Macmillan, 1988. ISBN 978-0-689-50455-6 Subj: Concepts – color.

Who wants one? ill. by Keiko Narahashi. Macmillan, 1989. ISBN 978-0-689-50474-7 Subj: Counting, numbers. Rhyming text.

Whooo's there? ill. by Jeffrey Scherer. Random House, 2007. ISBN 978-0-375-84050-0 Subj: Animals. Birds – owls. Forest, woods. Night. Rhyming text.

Seskin, Steve. *A chance to shine* by Steve Seskin and Allen Shamblin ill. by R. Gregory Christie. Ten Speed, 2006. ISBN 978-1-58246-167-0 Subj: Ethnic groups in the U.S. – African Americans. Homeless. Songs.

Don't laugh at me by Steve Seskin and Allen Shamblin ill. by Glin Dibley. Tricycle, 2002. ISBN 978-1-58246-058-1 Subj: Character traits – individuality. Music. Songs.

Seto, Loretta. *Mooncakes* ill. by Renné Benoit. Orca, 2013. ISBN 978-1-45980-107-3 Subj: Ethnic groups in the U.S. – Chinese Americans. Fairs, festivals. Family life. Folk & fairy tales.

Seuling, Barbara. *Drip! drop!* ill. by Nancy Tobin. Holiday, 2000. ISBN 978-0-8234-1459-8 Subj: Water.

Flick a switch ill. by Nancy Tobin. Holiday, 2003. ISBN 978-0-8234-1729-2 Subj: Science.

From head to toe ill. by Edward Miller. Holiday, 2002. ISBN 978-0-8234-1699-8 Subj: Anatomy. Science.

Spring song ill. by Greg Newbold. Harcourt, 2001. ISBN 978-0-15-202317-1 Subj: Animals. Rhyming text. Seasons – spring.

Winter lullaby ill. by Greg Newbold. Browndeer, 1997. ISBN 978-0-15-201403-2 Subj: Animals. Seasons – winter.

Seuss, Dr. *And to think that I saw it on Mulberry Street* ill. by author. Random House, 1989, ©1937. ISBN 978-0-394-94494-4 Subj: Humorous stories. Imagination. Rhyming text.

Bartholomew and the Oobleck ill. by author. Random House, 1949. ISBN 978-0-394-90075-9 Subj: Caldecott award honor books. Humorous stories. Royalty.

The butter battle book ill. by author. Random House, 1984. ISBN 978-0-394-96580-2 Subj: Rhyming text. War.

Did I ever tell you how lucky you are? ill. by Richard Erdoes. Random House, 1973. ISBN 978-0-394-92719-0 Subj: Character traits – luck. Humorous stories. Problem solving. Rhyming text.

Gerald McBoing Boing ed. by Kate Klimo; ill. by author. Random House, 2000. ISBN 978-0-679-99140-3 Subj: Communication. Concepts. Humorous stories. Noise, sounds. Rhyming text. Senses.

Gerald McBoing Boing sound book ill. by author. Random House, 2003. ISBN 978-0-375-82443-2 Subj: Communication. Concepts. Format, unusual. Humorous stories. Noise, sounds. Participation. Rhyming text.

Happy birthday to you! ill. by author. Random House, 1959. ISBN 978-0-394-90076-6 Subj: Birthdays. Humorous stories. Rhyming text.

Horton hatches the egg ill. by author. Random House, 1940. ISBN 978-0-394-90077-3 Subj: Animals – elephants. Birds. Character traits – helpfulness. Eggs. Humorous stories. Rhyming text.

Horton hears a Who! ill. by author. Random House, 1954. ISBN 978-0-394-90078-0 Subj: Animals – elephants. Character traits – kindness. Humorous stories. Rhyming text.

How the Grinch stole Christmas ill. by author. Random House, 1957. ISBN 978-0-394-90079-7 Subj: Character traits – meanness. Holidays – Christmas. Humorous stories. Rhyming text.

Hunches in bunches ill. by author. Random House, 1982. ISBN 978-0-394-95502-5 Subj: Problem solving. Rhyming text.

I can lick 30 tigers today and other stories ill. by author. Random House, 1969. ISBN 978-0-394-90094-0 Subj: Animals – tigers. Humorous stories. Rhyming text.

I had trouble getting to Solla Sollew ill. by author. Random House, 1965. Subj: Activities – traveling. Humorous stories. Rhyming text.

If I ran the circus ill. by author. Random House, 1956. ISBN 978-0-394-90080-3 Subj: Circus. Humorous stories. Rhyming text.

If I ran the zoo ill. by author. Random House, 1950. ISBN 978-0-394-90081-0 Subj: Caldecott award honor books. Humorous stories. Rhyming text. Zoos.

The king's stilts ill. by author. Random House, 1939. ISBN 978-0-394-90082-7 Subj: Humorous stories. Rhyming text. Royalty – kings. Toys.

The Lorax ill. by author. Random House, 1971. ISBN 978-0-394-92337-6 Subj: Ecology. Humorous stories.

McElligot's pool ill. by author. Random House, 1947. ISBN 978-0-394-90083-4 Subj: Caldecott award honor books. Fish. Humorous stories. Imagination. Rhyming text.

Oh, the places you'll go! ill. by author. Random House, 1990. ISBN 978-0-679-90527-1 Subj: Self-concept.

On beyond zebra ill. by author. Random House, 1955. ISBN 978-0-394-90084-1 Subj: Humorous stories. Letters, cards. Rhyming text.

Scrambled eggs super! ill. by author. Random House, 1953. ISBN 978-0-394-90085-8 Subj: Food. Humorous stories. Rhyming text.

The Sneetches, and other stories ill. by author. Random House, 1961. ISBN 978-0-394-90089-6 Subj: Emotions – fear. Humorous stories. Rhyming text.

Thidwick, the big-hearted moose ill. by author. Random House, 1948. ISBN 978-0-394-90086-5 Subj: Animals – moose. Birds. Humorous stories. Rhyming text.

Seven, John. *The ocean story* ill. by Jana Christy. Picture Window, 2011. ISBN 978-1-4048-6785-7 Subj: Ecology. Sea & seashore. Water.

A year with friends ill. by Jana Christy. Abrams, 2013. ISBN 978-1-4197-0443-7 Subj: Days of the week, months of the year. Friendship. Seasons.

Seven spunky monkeys ill. by Lynn Munsinger. Harcourt, 2005. ISBN 978-0-15-202519-9 Subj: Activities. Animals – monkeys. Counting, numbers. Day. Rhyming text.

Sexton, Colleen A. *Let's meet Martin Luther King, Jr* ill. with photos. Chelsea, 2004. ISBN 978-0-7910-7322-3 Subj: Careers – clergy. Ethnic groups in the U.S. – African Americans. U.S. history.

Seymour, Dorothy Z. *Ann likes red* ill. by Nancy Meyerhoff. Purple House, 2001. ISBN 978-1-930900-12-7 Subj: Clothing – dresses. Concepts – color.

Shafer, Dana. *Mud Pie Annie: God's recipe for doing your best* (Buchanan, Sue)

Shah, Idries. *The boy without a name* ill. by Mona Caron. Hoopoe, 2000. ISBN 978-1-883536-20-6 Subj: Dreams. Folk & fairy tales. Foreign lands – Middle East. Magic. Names.

The clever boy and the terrible, dangerous animal ill. by Rose Mary Santiago. Hoopoe, 2000. ISBN 978-1-883536-18-3 Subj: Character traits – helpfulness. Emotions – fear. Folk & fairy tales. Foreign lands – Middle East.

Fatima the spinner and the tent ill. by Natasha Delmar. Hoopoe, 2006. ISBN 978-1-883536-42-8 Subj: Activities – weaving. Folk & fairy tales. Foreign lands.

The silly chicken ill. by Jeff Jackson. Hoopoe, 2000. ISBN 978-1-883536-19-0 Subj: Birds – chickens. Folk & fairy tales. Foreign lands – Middle East.

Shahan, Sherry. *Cool cats counting* ill. by Paula Barragán. August House, 2005. ISBN 978-0-87483-757-5 Subj: Animals. Counting, numbers.

Fiesta! a celebration of Latino festivals ill. by Paula Barragán. August House, 2009. ISBN 978-0-87483-861-9 Subj: Days of the week, months of the year. Foreign lands – Latin America. Holidays.

The jazzy alphabet ill. by Mary Thelen. Philomel, 2002. ISBN 978-0-399-23453-8 Subj: ABC books. Musical instruments. Rhyming text.

That's not how you play soccer, Daddy ill. by Tatjana Mai-Wyss. Peachtree, 2007. ISBN 978-1-56145-416-7 Subj: Family life – fathers. Sports – soccer.

Shakespeare, William. *To sleep, perchance to dream* ill. by James Mayhew. Scholastic, 2001. ISBN 978-0-439-29655-7 Subj: Poetry.

Shamblin, Allen. *A chance to shine* (Seskin, Steve)

Don't laugh at me (Seskin, Steve)

Shange, Ntozake. *Coretta Scott* ill. by Kadir Nelson. Amistad, 2009. ISBN 978-0-06-125364-5 Subj: Ethnic groups in the U.S. – African Americans. Poetry. Prejudice. U.S. history.

Ellington was not a street ill. by Kadir Nelson. Simon & Schuster, 2004. ISBN 978-0-689-82884-3 Subj: Ethnic groups in the U.S. – African Americans. Poetry.

Freedom's a-callin me ill. by Rod Brown. Amistad, 2012. ISBN 978-0-06-133741-3 Subj: Character traits – freedom. Ethnic groups in the U.S. – African Americans. Poetry. Slavery. U.S. history.

Whitewash ill. by Michael Sporn. Walker, 1997. ISBN 978-0-8027-8491-9 Subj: Ethnic groups in the U.S. – African Americans. Prejudice.

Shannon, David. *The amazing Christmas extravaganza* ill. by author. Blue Sky, 1995. ISBN 978-0-590-48090-1 Subj: Emotions – anger. Holidays – Christmas.

A bad case of stripes ill. by author. Blue Sky, 1998. ISBN 978-0-590-92997-4 Subj: Behavior. Character traits – individuality.

Bugs in my hair! ill. by author. Scholastic, 2013. ISBN 978-0-545-14313-4 Subj: Hair. Insects – lice.

David gets in trouble ill. by author. Blue Sky, 2002. ISBN 978-0-439-05022-7 Subj: Bedtime. Behavior – misbehavior.

David goes to school ill. by author. Blue Sky, 1999. ISBN 978-0-590-48087-1 Subj: Behavior – misbehavior. School.

David smells: a diaper David book ill. by author. Scholastic, 2005. ISBN 978-0-439-69138-3 Subj: Babies. Format, unusual – board books. Senses.

Demasiados juguetes / too many toys ill. by author. Scholastic, 2008. ISBN 978-0-545-07918-1 Subj: Family life. Foreign languages. Toys.

Duck on a bike ill. by author. Blue Sky, 2002. ISBN 978-0-439-05023-4 Subj: Animals. Birds – ducks. Sports – bicycling.

Good boy, Fergus! ill. by author. Scholastic, 2006. ISBN 978-0-439-49027-6 Subj: Animals – dogs. Behavior – misbehavior.

Jangles: a big fish story ill. by author. Scholastic, 2012. ISBN 978-0-545-14312-7 Subj: Activities –

storytelling. Family life – fathers. Fish. Sports – fishing. Tall tales.

No, David! ill. by author. Blue Sky, 1998. ISBN 978-0-590-93002-4 Subj: Behavior – misbehavior. Caldecott award honor books.

Oh, David! a diaper David book ill. by author. Scholastic, 2005. ISBN 978-0-439-68881-9 Subj: Babies. Behavior – misbehavior. Format, unusual – board books.

Oops! a diaper David book ill. by author. Scholastic, 2005. ISBN 978-0-439-68882-6 Subj: Babies. Format, unusual – board books. Language.

The rain came down ill. by author. Blue Sky, 2000. ISBN 978-0-439-05021-0 Subj: Behavior. Behavior – misunderstanding. Weather – rain. Weather – rainbows.

Too many toys ill. by author. Scholastic, 2008. ISBN 978-0-439-49029-0 Subj: Family life. Toys.

Shannon, George. *April showers* ill. by José Aruego and Ariane Dewey. Greenwillow, 1995. ISBN 978-0-688-13122-7 Subj: Activities – dancing. Frogs & toads. Weather – rain.

Busy in the garden ill. by Sam Williams. HarperCollins, 2006. ISBN 978-0-06-000464-4 Subj: Gardens, gardening. Poetry.

Frog legs: a picture book of action verse ill. by Amit Trynan. Greenwillow, 2000. ISBN 978-0-688-17047-9 Subj: Frogs & toads. Poetry.

Heart to heart ill. by Steve Björkman. Houghton, 1995. ISBN 978-0-395-72773-7 Subj: Animals – moles. Animals – squirrels. Friendship. Holidays – Valentine's Day.

Lizard's home ill. by José Aruego and Ariane Dewey. Greenwillow, 1999. ISBN 978-0-688-16003-6 Subj: Character traits – cleverness. Homes, houses. Reptiles – lizards. Reptiles – snakes.

Lizard's song ill. by José Aruego and Ariane Dewey. Greenwillow, 1981. ISBN 978-0-688-84310-6 Subj: Animals – bears. Reptiles – lizards. Songs.

Rabbit's gift ill. by Laura Dronzek. Harcourt, 2007. ISBN 978-0-15-206073-2 Subj: Animals. Animals – rabbits. Behavior – sharing. Folk & fairy tales. Friendship.

The Secret Chicken Club ill. by Deborah Zemke. Handprint, 2005. ISBN 978-1-59354-118-7 Subj: Animals – bulls, cows. Birds – chickens. Clubs, gangs.

Spring: a haiku story ill. by Malcah Zeldis. Greenwillow, 1996. ISBN 978-0-688-13889-9 Subj: Foreign lands – Japan. Poetry. Seasons – spring.

The surprise ill. by José Aruego and Ariane Dewey. Greenwillow, 1983. ISBN 978-0-688-02314-0 Subj: Animals – squirrels. Birthdays.

Tippy-toe chick, go ill. by Laura Dronzek. Greenwillow, 2003. ISBN 978-0-06-029824-1 Subj: Animals – dogs. Birds – chickens. Character traits – bravery.

Tomorrow's alphabet ill. by Donald Crews. Greenwillow, 1995. ISBN 978-0-688-13505-8 Subj: ABC books. Concepts.

Turkey Tot ill. by Jennifer K Mann. Holiday House, 2013. ISBN 978-0-8234-2379-8 Subj: Animals. Birds – turkeys. Character traits – persistence. Farms. Problem solving.

A very witchy spelling bee ill. by Mark Fearing. Harcourt, 2013. ISBN 978-0-15-206696-3 Subj: Contests. Witches.

White is for blueberry ill. by Laura Dronzek. HarperCollins, 2005. ISBN 978-0-06-029275-1 Subj: Concepts – color. Nature. Senses – sight.

Who put the cookies in the cookie jar? ill. by Julie Paschkis. Holt, 2013. ISBN 978-0-8050-9197-7 Subj: Activities – baking, cooking. Food. Rhyming text.

Shannon, Margaret. *Gullible's troubles* ill. by author. Houghton, 1998. ISBN 978-0-395-83933-1 Subj: Animals – guinea pigs. Behavior – trickery. Family life. Monsters.

The red wolf ill. by author. Houghton, 2002. ISBN 978-0-618-05544-9 Subj: Activities – knitting. Folk & fairy tales. Royalty – princesses.

Shannon, Molly. *Tilly the trickster* ill. by Ard Hoyt. Abrams, 2011. ISBN 978-1-4197-0030-9 Subj: Behavior – misbehavior.

Shannon, Terry Miller. *Tub toys* by Terry Miller Shannon and Timothy Warner ill. by Lee Calderon. Tricycle, 2002. ISBN 978-1-58246-066-6 Subj: Activities – bathing. Rhyming text. Toys.

Shapiro, J. H. *Magic trash: a story of Tyree Guyton and his art* ill. by Vanessa Brantley Newton. Charlesbridge, 2011. ISBN 978-1-58089-385-5 Subj: Art. Careers – artists. Cities, towns. Ethnic groups in the U.S. – African Americans.

Shapiro, Jody Fickes. *Family lullaby* ill. by Cathie Felstead. HarperCollins, 2007. ISBN 978-0-06-051482-2 Subj: Babies. Emotions – love. Family life.

Up, up, up! It's apple-picking time ill. by Kitty Harvill. Holiday, 2003. ISBN 978-0-8234-1610-3 Subj: Family life – grandparents. Farms. Food. Seasons – fall.

Shapiro, Lawrence E. *It's time to give up your pacifier* ill. by Hideko Takahashi. New Harbinger, 2008. ISBN 978-1-57224-585-3 Subj: Babies. Behavior – growing up.

Shapiro, Zachary. *We're all in the same boat* ill. by Jack E. Davis. Putnam, 2009. ISBN 978-0-399-24393-6 Subj: ABC books. Animals. Boats, ships. Religion – Noah. Weather – floods. Weather – rain.

Sharkey, Niamh. *The gigantic turnip* (Tolstoy, Aleksey Nikolayevich)

Santasaurus ill. by author. Candlewick, 2005. ISBN 978-0-7636-2671-6 Subj: Dinosaurs. Holidays – Christmas. Santa Claus.

Sharmat, Marjorie Weinman. *The best Valentine in the world* ill. by Lilian Obligado. Holiday, 1982. ISBN 978-0-8234-0440-7 Subj: Animals – foxes. Holidays – Valentine's Day.

Gila monsters meet you at the airport ill. by Byron Barton. Macmillan, 1980. ISBN 978-0-02-782450-6 Subj: Behavior – misunderstanding. Moving.

Hooray for Father's Day! ill. by John Wallner. Holiday, 1987. ISBN 978-0-8234-0637-1 Subj: Animals – mules. Holidays – Father's Day.

Hooray for Mother's Day! ill. by John Wallner. Holiday, 1986. ISBN 978-0-8234-0588-6 Subj: Birds – chickens. Holidays – Mother's Day.

I'm terrific ill. by Kay Chorao. Holiday, 1977. ISBN 978-0-8234-0282-3 Subj: Animals – bears. Character traits – conceit. Character traits – pride. Self-concept.

I'm the best ill. by Will Hillenbrand. Holiday, 1991. ISBN 978-0-8234-0859-7 Subj: Animals – dogs. Pets.

The 329th friend ill. by Cyndy Szekeres. Four Winds, 1992. ISBN 978-0-02-782259-5 Subj: Animals. Animals – raccoons. Counting, numbers. Friendship. Self-concept.

Sharmat, Mitchell. *Gregory, the terrible eater* ill. by José Aruego and Ariane Dewey. Four Winds, 1980. ISBN 978-0-590-07586-2 Subj: Animals – goats. Food.

Sharratt, Nick. *The foggy, foggy forest* ill. by author. Candlewick, 2008. ISBN 978-0-7636-3921-1 Subj: Forest, woods. Format, unusual. Humorous stories. Rhyming text.

Pants (Andreae, Giles)

Shark in the park ill. by author. Candlewick, 2002. ISBN 978-0-385-75008-0 Subj: Animals. Birds. Fish – sharks. Format, unusual – toy & movable books. Parks. Rhyming text.

What's in the witch's kitchen? ill. by author. Candlewick, 2011. ISBN 978-0-7636-5224-1 Subj: Format, unusual – toy & movable books. Rhyming text. Witches.

Shaskan, Stephen. *A dog is a dog* ill. by author. Chronicle, 2011. ISBN 978-0-8118-7896-8 Subj: Animals. Animals – dogs. Circular tales. Disguises. Rhyming text.

Shaskan, Trisha Speed. *Seriously, Cinderella is so annoying! the story of Cinderella as told by the wicked stepmother* ill. by Gerald Guerlais. Picture Window, 2011. ISBN 978-1-4048-6674-4 Subj: Family life – stepfamilies. Folk & fairy tales. Humorous stories.

Shavick, Andrea. *You'll grow soon, Alex* ill. by Russell Ayto. Walker, 2000. ISBN 978-0-8027-8736-1 Subj: Behavior – growing up.

Shaw, Charles Green. *It looked like spilt milk* ill. by author. HarperCollins, 1947. ISBN 978-0-06-025565-7 Subj: Concepts – shape. Games. Imagination. Participation. Sky. Weather – clouds.

Shaw, Greg. *Wake up, sleepy bear!* (Morton-Shaw, Christine)

Shaw, Hannah. *School for bandits* ill. by author. Random House, 2011. ISBN 978-0-375-86768-2 Subj: Animals – raccoons. Behavior – misbehavior. Character traits – helpfulness. Etiquette. School.

Sneaky Weasel ill. by author. Knopf, 2009. ISBN 978-0-375-85625-9 Subj: Animals – weasels. Behavior – bullying, teasing. Friendship.

Shaw, Mary. *Brady Brady and the big mistake* ill. by Chuck Temple. Fitzhenry & Whiteside, 2002. ISBN 978-0-7737-6304-3 Subj: Behavior – lost & found possessions. Behavior – misbehavior. Sports – hockey.

Brady Brady and the great rink ill. by Chuck Temple. Stoddart, 2002. ISBN 978-0-7737-6224-4 Subj: Activities – making things. Activities – working. Sports – hockey.

Brady Brady and the runaway goalie ill. by Chuck Temple. Stoddart, 2001. ISBN 978-0-7737-6225-1 Subj: Sports – hockey.

Brady Brady and the Twirlin' Torpedo ill. by Chuck Temple. Stoddart, 2002. Subj: Friendship. Gender roles. Sports – hockey.

Shaw, Nancy. *Raccoon tune* ill. by Howard Fine. Holt, 2003. ISBN 978-0-8050-6544-2 Subj: Animals – raccoons. Noise, sounds. Rhyming text.

Sheep blast off! ill. by Margot Apple. Houghton, 2008. ISBN 978-0-618-13168-6 Subj: Animals – sheep. Rhyming text. Space & space ships.

Sheep in a jeep ill. by Margot Apple. Houghton, 1986. ISBN 978-0-395-41105-6 Subj: Animals – sheep. Rhyming text.

Sheep in a shop ill. by Margot Apple. Houghton, 1991. ISBN 978-0-395-53681-0 Subj: Animals – sheep. Rhyming text. Shopping.

Sheep on a ship ill. by Margot Apple. Houghton, 1989. ISBN 978-0-395-48160-8 Subj: Animals – sheep. Boats, ships. Rhyming text.

Sheep out to eat ill. by Margot Apple. Houghton, 1992. ISBN 978-0-395-61128-9 Subj: Animals – sheep. Food. Rhyming text.

Sheep take a hike ill. by Margot Apple. Houghton, 1994. ISBN 978-0-395-68394-1 Subj: Animals – sheep. Rhyming text. Sports – hiking.

Sheep trick or treat ill. by Margot Apple. Houghton, 1997. ISBN 978-0-395-84168-6 Subj: Animals – sheep. Holidays – Halloween. Rhyming text.

Shaw, Natalie, adapt. *Olivia plans a tea party* ill. by Patrick Spaziante. Simon & Schuster, 2011. ISBN 978-1-4423-3962-0 Subj: Animals – pigs. Parties.

Shea, Bob. *Big plans* ill. by Lane Smith. Hyperion, 2008. ISBN 978-1-4231-1100-9 Subj: Behavior – misbehavior. Humorous stories. Imagination. School.

Cheetah can't lose ill. by author. HarperCollins, 2013. ISBN 978-0-06-173083-2 Subj: Animals – cats. Animals – cheetahs. Behavior – boasting. Behavior – trickery. Character traits – cleverness. Contests.

Dinosaur vs. bedtime ill. by author. Hyperion, 2008. ISBN 978-1-4231-1335-5 Subj: Bedtime. Dinosaurs.

Dinosaur vs. Santa ill. by author. Disney/Hyperion, 2012. ISBN 978-1-4231-6806-5 Subj: Dinosaurs. Holidays – Christmas.

Dinosaur vs. the library ill. by author. Hyperion/Disney, 2011. ISBN 978-1-4231-3338-4 Subj: Dinosaurs. Libraries.

Dinosaur vs. the potty ill. by author. Hyperion/Disney, 2010. ISBN 978-1-4231-3339-1 Subj: Dinosaurs. Toilet training.

I'm a shark ill. by author. HarperCollins, 2011. ISBN 978-0-06-199846-1 Subj: Emotions – fear. Fish – sharks.

New socks ill. by author. Little, Brown, 2007. ISBN 978-0-316-01357-4 Subj: Behavior – growing up. Birds – chickens. Character traits – confidence. Clothing – socks. Self-concept.

Oh, Daddy! ill. by author. HarperCollins, 2010. ISBN 978-0-06-173080-1 Subj: Animals – hippopotamuses. Family life – fathers.

Race you to bed ill. by author. HarperCollins, 2010. ISBN 978-0-06-170417-8 Subj: Bedtime. Rhyming text.

Unicorn thinks he's pretty great ill. by author. Disney/Hyperion, 2013. ISBN 978-1-4231-5952-0 Subj: Animals – goats. Emotions – envy, jealousy. Friendship. Mythical creatures – unicorns. Self-concept.

Shea, Kitty. *Out and about at the newspaper* ill. by Zachary Trover. Picture Window, 2006. ISBN 978-1-4048-1149-2 Subj: Careers – journalists.

Out and about at the post office ill. by Becky Shipe. Picture Window, 2004. ISBN 978-1-4048-0294-0 Subj: Careers – postal workers. Post office. School – field trips.

Out and about at the public library ill. by Zachary Trover. Picture Window, 2005. ISBN 978-1-4048-1150-8 Subj: Careers – librarians. Libraries.

Out and about at the science center ill. by Becky Shipe. Picture Window, 2004. ISBN 978-1-4048-0297-1 Subj: Museums. School – field trips. Science.

Out and about at the supermarket ill. by Becky Shipe. Picture Window, 2004. ISBN 978-1-4048-0295-7 Subj: Careers – storekeepers. Food. School – field trips. Stores.

Out and about at the vet clinic ill. by Becky Shipe. Picture Window, 2004. ISBN 978-1-4048-0296-4 Subj: Animals. Careers – veterinarians. Pets. School – field trips.

Shea, Pegi Deitz. *The boy and the spell* ill. by Serena Riglietti. Pumpkin House, 2007. ISBN 978-0-9646010-4-8 Subj: Emotions – anger. Music.

I see me! ill. by Lucia Washburn. HarperCollins, 2000. ISBN 978-0-694-01278-7 Subj: Babies. Family life. Format, unusual – board books. Rhyming text.

New moon ill. by Cathryn Falwell. Boyds Mills, 1996. ISBN 978-1-56397-410-6 Subj: Ethnic groups in the U.S. – Hispanic Americans. Family life – brothers & sisters. Moon.

The whispering cloth ill. by Anita Riggio. Stitched by You Yang. Caroline House, 1995. ISBN 978-1-56397-134-1 Subj: Activities – sewing. Ethnic groups in the U.S. – Hmong Americans. Family life – grandmothers. Foreign lands – Thailand. War.

Shea, Susan A. *Do you know which one will grow?* ill. by Tom Slaughter. Blue Apple, 2011. ISBN 978-1-60905-062-7 Subj: Behavior – growing up. Concepts – change. Format, unusual – toy & movable books. Rhyming text.

Sheather, Allan. *Neptune's nursery* (Toft, Kim Michelle)

One less fish (Toft, Kim Michelle)

Sheehan, Monica. *Love is you and me* ill. by author. Simon & Schuster, 2013. ISBN 978-1-442436-07-7 Subj: Emotions – love. Rhyming text.

Shelby, Anne. *Homeplace* ill. by Wendy Anderson Halperin. Orchard, 1995. ISBN 978-0-531-08732-9 Subj: Family life. Family life – grandmothers.

The man who lived in a hollow tree ill. by Cor Hazelaar. Atheneum, 2009. ISBN 978-0-689-86169-7 Subj: Old age. Trees.

Potluck ill. by Irene Trivas. Watts, 1991. ISBN 978-0-531-08519-6 Subj: ABC books. Ethnic groups in the U.S. Food.

Sheldon, Annette. *Big sister now: a story about me and our new baby* ill. by Karen Maizel. Magination, 2006. ISBN 978-1-59147-243-8 Subj: Babies. Family life – brothers & sisters. Family life – new sibling.

Sheldon, Dyan. *Under the moon* ill. by Gary Blythe. Dial, 1994. ISBN 978-0-8037-1670-4 Subj: Dreams. Indians of North America – Sioux.

Unicorn dreams ill. by Neil Reed. Dial, 1997. ISBN 978-0-8037-2284-2 Subj: Imagination. Mythical creatures – unicorns. School.

Shelton, Paula Young. *Child of the civil rights movement* ill. by Raul Colón. Random House, 2009. ISBN 978-0-375-84314-3 Subj: Ethnic groups in the U.S. – African Americans. Prejudice. U.S. history.

Shepard, Aaron. *The baker's dozen* ill. by Wendy Edelson. Atheneum, 1995. ISBN 978-0-689-80298-0 Subj: Careers – bakers. Character traits – generosity. Folk & fairy tales.

The crystal heart: a Vietnamese legend ill. by Joseph Daniel Fiedler. Atheneum, 1998. ISBN 978-0-689-81551-5 Subj: Folk & fairy tales. Foreign lands – Vietnam.

Forty fortunes: a tale of Iran ill. by Alisher Dianov. Clarion, 1999. ISBN 978-0-395-81133-7 Subj: Careers – fortune tellers. Folk & fairy tales. Foreign lands – Iran.

The gifts of Wali Dad ill. by Daniel San Souci. Atheneum, 1995. ISBN 978-0-684-19445-5 Subj: Behavior – wishing. Folk & fairy tales. Foreign lands – India. Foreign lands – Pakistan. Gifts.

Master man ill. by David Wisniewski. Lothrop, 2000. ISBN 978-0-688-13784-7 Subj: Folk & fairy tales – pourquoi tales. Foreign lands – Nigeria. Tall tales. Weather – lightning, thunder.

One-eye! Two-eyes! Three-eyes! a very Grimm fairy tale ill. by Gary Clement. Simon & Schuster, 2006. ISBN 978-0-689-86740-8 Subj: Animals – goats. Folk & fairy tales. Magic. Royalty – princes.

The princess mouse ill. by Leonid Gore. Atheneum, 2003. ISBN 978-0-689-82912-3 Subj: Animals – mice. Folk & fairy tales. Foreign lands – Finland. Royalty – princesses. Songs.

The sea king's daughter ill. by Gennady Spirin. Atheneum, 1997. ISBN 978-0-689-80759-6 Subj: Careers – musicians. Folk & fairy tales. Foreign lands – Russia. Mythical creatures. Sea & seashore.

Sheridan, Sara. *I'm me!* ill. by Margaret Chamberlain. Scholastic, 2011. ISBN 978-0-545-28222-2 Subj: Activities – playing. Family life – aunts, uncles. Imagination.

Sherman, Joanne. *Because it's my body* ill. by John Steven Gurney. S.A.F.E. for Children, 2002. ISBN 978-0-9711735-0-7 Subj: Child abuse. Communication. Senses – touch.

Sherman, Pat. *The sun's daughter* ill. by R. Gregory Christie. Clarion, 2005. ISBN 978-0-618-32430-9 Subj: Folk & fairy tales – pourquoi tales. Indians of North America – Iroquois. Sun.

Sherry, Kevin. *Acorns everywhere!* ill. by author. Dial, 2009. ISBN 978-0-8037-3256-8 Subj: Animals – bears. Animals – squirrels. Behavior – forgetfulness.

I'm the best artist in the ocean ill. by author. Dial, 2008. ISBN 978-0-8037-3255-1 Subj: Art. Careers – artists. Sea & seashore. Squid.

I'm the biggest thing in the ocean ill. by author. Penguin, 2007. ISBN 978-0-8037-3192-9 Subj: Concepts – size. Sea & seashore. Squid.

Sheth, Kashmira. *Monsoon afternoon* ill. by Yoshiko Jaeggi. Peachtree, 2008. ISBN 978-1-56145-455-6 Subj: Family life – grandfathers. Foreign lands – India. Weather – rain.

My Dadima wears a sari ill. by Yoshiko Jaeggi. Peachtree, 2007. ISBN 978-1-56145-392-4 Subj: Clothing. Ethnic groups in the U.S. – East Indian Americans. Family life – grandmothers.

Tiger in my soup ill. by Jeffrey Ebbeler. Peachtree, 2013. ISBN 978-1-56145-696-3 Subj: Animals – tigers. Books, reading. Family life – brothers & sisters. Imagination.

Shewchuk, Pat. *In Lucia's neighborhood* ill. by Marek Colek. Kids Can, 2013. ISBN 978-1-55453-420-3 Subj: Cities, towns. Communities, neighborhoods.

Shields, Carol Diggory. *The bugliest bug* ill. by Scott Nash. Candlewick, 2002. ISBN 978-0-7636-0784-5 Subj: Contests. Insects. Poetry. Spiders.

Day by day a week goes round ill. by True Kelley. Dutton, 1998. ISBN 978-0-525-45457-1 Subj: Activities. Days of the week, months of the year. Rhyming text.

I am really a princess ill. by Paul Meisel. Dutton, 1993. ISBN 978-0-525-45138-9 Subj: Behavior – imitation. Character traits – vanity. Family life. Imagination. Royalty – princesses. Self-concept.

I wish my brother was a dog ill. by Paul Meisel. Dutton, 1997. ISBN 978-0-525-45464-9 Subj: Animals

– dogs. Babies. Behavior – wishing. Emotions – anger. Family life – brothers. Family life – new sibling. Sibling rivalry.

Lucky pennies and hot chocolate ill. by Hiroe Nakata. Dutton, 2000. ISBN 978-0-525-46450-1 Subj: Family life – grandfathers.

Lunch money and other poems about school ill. by Paul Meisel. Dutton, 1995. ISBN 978-0-525-45345-1 Subj: Poetry. School.

Martian rock ill. by Scott Nash. Candlewick, 2000. ISBN 978-0-7636-0598-8 Subj: Aliens. Birds – penguins. Plants. Rhyming text. Space & space ships.

Month by month a year goes round ill. by True Kelley. Dutton, 1998. ISBN 978-0-525-45458-8 Subj: Days of the week, months of the year. Rhyming text. Seasons.

Saturday night at the dinosaur stomp ill. by Scott Nash. Candlewick, 1997. ISBN 978-1-56402-693-4 Subj: Activities – dancing. Dinosaurs. Prehistory. Rhyming text.

Wombat walkabout ill. by Sophie Blackall. Dutton, 2009. ISBN 978-0-525-47865-2 Subj: Animals – wombats. Counting, numbers. Foreign lands – Australia. Rhyming text.

Shields, Gillian. *Dogfish* ill. by Dan Taylor. Atheneum, 2008. ISBN 978-1-4169-7127-6 Subj: Fish. Pets.

Elephantantrum! ill. by Cally Johnson-Isaacs. Tiger Tales, 2013. ISBN 978-1-58925-126-7 Subj: Animals – elephants. Behavior – misbehavior. Emotions – anger.

Library Lily ill. by Francesca Chessa. Eerdmans, 2011. ISBN 978-0-8028-5401-8 Subj: Activities – playing. Books, reading. Friendship. Libraries.

When the world was waiting for you ill. by Anna Currey. Bloomsbury, 2011. ISBN 978-1-59990-531-0 Subj: Animals – rabbits. Family life – new sibling. Rhyming text.

Shindler, Ramon. *Found alphabet* by Ramon Shindler and Wojciech Graniczewski ill. by Anita Andrzejewska and Andrzej Pilichowski-Ragno. Houghton, 2005. ISBN 978-0-618-44232-4 Subj: ABC books. Rhyming text.

Shipton, Jonathan. *Baby baby blah blah blah!* ill. by Francesca Chessa. Holiday, 2009. ISBN 978-0-8234-2213-5 Subj: Activities – writing. Babies. Family life – new sibling.

How to be a happy hippo ill. by Sally Percy. Little Tiger, 1999. ISBN 978-1-888444-61-2 Subj: Animals – hippopotamuses. Family life – fathers.

No biting, horrible crocodile! ill. by Claudio Muñoz. Western, 1995. ISBN 978-0-307-17521-2 Subj: Behavior – bullying, teasing. Reptiles – alligators, crocodiles. School.

What if? ill. by Barbara Nascimbeni. Dial, 1999. ISBN 978-0-8037-2390-0 Subj: Imagination. Self-concept.

Shireen, Nadia. *Good little wolf* ill. by author. Random House, 2011. ISBN 978-0-375-86904-4 Subj: Animals – wolves. Character traits – individuality. Self-concept.

Hey, Presto! ill. by author. Knopf, 2012. ISBN 978-0-375-86905-1 Subj: Animals – cats. Animals – dogs. Fairs, festivals. Friendship. Magic.

Shirotani, Hideo. *Let's eat / Vamos a comer* ill. by author. Simon & Schuster, 1992. ISBN 978-0-671-76927-7 Subj: Food. Foreign languages. Format, unusual – board books.

Let's play ill. by author. Little & Woods, 1991. ISBN 978-1-56180-044-5 Subj: Activities – playing. Format, unusual – board books.

Let's take a walk / Vamos a caminar ill. by author. Simon & Schuster, 1992. ISBN 978-0-671-76929-1 Subj: Activities – walking. Foreign languages. Format, unusual – board books.

What color? / Qué color? ill. by author. Simon & Schuster, 1992. ISBN 978-0-671-76930-7 Subj: Concepts – color. Foreign languages. Format, unusual – board books.

Shoemaker, Marla K. *Art museum opposites* (Friedland, Katy)

Shollar, Leah. *A thread of kindness* ill. by Shoshana Mekibel. Hachai, 2000. ISBN 978-1-929628-01-8 Subj: Character traits – generosity. Jewish culture. Religion.

Shore, Diane Z. *Look both ways: a cautionary tale* by Diane Z. Shore and Jessica Alexander ill. by Teri Weidner. Bloomsbury, 2005. ISBN 978-1-58234-968-8 Subj: Animals – squirrels. Rhyming text. Safety.

This is the dream by Diane Z. Shore and Jessica Alexander ill. by James Ransome. HarperCollins, 2006. ISBN 978-0-06-055520-7 Subj: Ethnic groups in the U.S. – African Americans. Prejudice. Rhyming text. U.S. history.

This is the feast ill. by Megan Lloyd. HarperCollins, 2008. ISBN 978-0-06-623794-7 Subj: Holidays – Thanksgiving. Indians of North America – Wampanoag. Poetry.

Shoulders, Debbie. *D is for drum: a Native American alphabet* (Shoulders, Michael)

Shoulders, Michael. *The ABC book of American homes* ill. by Sarah S. Brannen. Charlesbridge, 2008. ISBN 978-1-57091-565-9 Subj: ABC books. Homes, houses.

D is for drum: a Native American alphabet by Michael Shoulders and Debbie Shoulders ill. by Irving Toddy. Sleeping Bear, 2006. ISBN 978-1-58536-274-5 Subj: ABC books. Indians of North America.

Goodnight Baby Bear ill. by Teri Weidner. Sleeping Bear, 2010. ISBN 978-1-58536-471-8 Subj: Animals – bears. Bedtime. Books, reading. Family life.

Say Daddy! ill. by Teri Weidner. Sleeping Bear, 2008. ISBN 978-1-58536-354-4 Subj: Animals – babies. Animals – bears. Books, reading.

Showers, Paul. *A drop of blood* ill. by Don Madden. Rev. ed. HarperCollins, 1989. ISBN 978-0-690-04717-2 Subj: Anatomy. Science.

Ears are for hearing ill. by Holly Keller. HarperCollins, 1990. ISBN 978-0-690-04720-2 Subj: Anatomy – ears. Science. Senses – hearing.

Hear your heart ill. by Holly Keller. HarperCollins, 2001. ISBN 978-0-06-025411-7 Subj: Anatomy. Noise, sounds. Science.

How you talk ill. by Megan Lloyd. Rev. ed. HarperCollins, 1992. ISBN 978-0-06-022768-5 Subj: Anatomy. Communication. Language.

The listening walk ill. by Aliki. Rev. ed. HarperCollins, 1991. ISBN 978-0-06-021638-2 Subj: Activities – walking. Noise, sounds. Senses – hearing.

Look at your eyes ill. by True Kelley. Rev. ed. HarperCollins, 1992. ISBN 978-0-06-020188-3 Subj: Anatomy – eyes. Ethnic groups in the U.S. – African Americans. Science. Senses – sight.

Sleep is for everyone ill. by Wendy Watson. HarperCollins, 1997. ISBN 978-0-06-025393-6 Subj: Animals. Bedtime. Dreams. Health & fitness. Science. Sleep.

Where does the garbage go? ill. by Randy Chewning. Rev. ed. HarperCollins, 1994. ISBN 978-0-06-021057-1 Subj: Careers – sanitation workers. Ecology. Science.

Your skin and mine ill. by Kathleen Kuchera. Rev. ed. HarperCollins, 1991. ISBN 978-0-06-022523-0 Subj: Anatomy – skin. Ethnic groups in the U.S. – African Americans.

Shreeve, Elizabeth. *Oliver at the window* ill. by Candice Hartsough McDonald. Front Street, 2009. ISBN 978-1-59078-548-5 Subj: Divorce. Moving. School.

Shriver, Maria. *What's wrong with Timmy?* ill. by Sandra Speidel. Little, 2001. ISBN 978-0-316-23337-8 Subj: Disabilities – mental disabilities. Friendship.

Shulevitz, Uri. *Dawn* ill. by author. Farrar, 1974. ISBN 978-0-374-31707-2 Subj: Camps, camping. Family life – grandfathers. Morning. Sun.

Dusk ill. by author. Farrar, 2013. ISBN 978-0-374-31903-8 Subj: Cities, towns. Family life – grandfathers. Light, lights. Night. Twilight.

How I learned geography ill. by author. Farrar, 2008. ISBN 978-0-374-33499-4 Subj: Behavior – seeking better things. Caldecott award honor books. Geography. Imagination. Maps. Poverty.

The magician by Uri Shulevitz and Isaac Loeb Peretz ill. by adapter. Adapted from the Yiddish of Isaac Loeb Peretz. Macmillan, 1985, ©1973. ISBN 978-0-02-782770-5 Subj: Holidays – Passover. Jewish culture. Magic. Religion.

One Monday morning ill. by author. Aladdin, 1986, ©1967. ISBN 978-0-684-13195-5 Subj: Cities, towns. Days of the week, months of the year. Imagination. Royalty.

Rain rain rivers ill. by author. Farrar, 1969. ISBN 978-0-374-36171-6 Subj: Rhyming text. Weather – rain.

Snow ill. by author. Farrar, 1998. ISBN 978-0-374-37092-3 Subj: Caldecott award honor books. Cities, towns. Nature. Weather – snow.

So sleepy story ill. by author. Farrar, 2006. ISBN 978-0-374-37031-2 Subj: Imagination. Music. Night. Sleep.

The treasure ill. by author. Farrar, 1978. ISBN 978-0-374-37740-3 Subj: Caldecott award honor books. Dreams. Folk & fairy tales.

What is a wise bird like you doing in a silly tale like this? ill. by author. Farrar, 2000. ISBN 978-0-374-38300-8 Subj: Birds. Character traits – freedom. Royalty – emperors. Tall tales.

When I wore my sailor suit ill. by author. Farrar, 2009. ISBN 978-0-374-34749-9 Subj: Imagination. Sailors.

Shulimson, Sarene. *Lights out Shabbat* ill. by Jeffrey Ebbeler. Lerner/Kar-Ben, 2012. ISBN 978-0-7613-7565-4 Subj: Family life – grandparents. Holidays. Jewish culture. Religion.

Shulman, Goldie. *Way too much challah dough* ill. by Vitaliy Romanenko. Hachai, 2006. ISBN 978-1-929628-23-0 Subj: Behavior – running away. Food. Jewish culture.

Shulman, Lisa. *The moon might be milk* ill. by Will Hillenbrand. Penguin, 2007. ISBN 978-0-525-47647-4 Subj: Activities – baking, cooking. Animals. Family life – grandmothers. Food. Moon.

Over in the meadow at the big ballet ill. by Sarah Massini. Penguin, 2007. ISBN 978-0-399-24289-2 Subj: Ballet. Birds – swans. Rhyming text.

Shulman, Mark. *A is for zebra* ill. by Tamara Petrosino. Sterling, 2006. ISBN 978-1-4027-3494-6 Subj: ABC books.

Aa is for Aardvark ill. by author. Sterling, 2005. ISBN 978-1-4027-2871-6 Subj: ABC books.

Gorilla Garage ill. by Vincent Nguyen. Marshall Cavendish, 2009. ISBN 978-0-7614-5461-8 Subj: Animals – gorillas. Automobiles. Careers – mechanics. Rhyming text.

Shute, Linda. *Clever Tom and the leprechaun* ill. by author. Lothrop, 1988. ISBN 978-0-688-07489-0 Subj: Folk & fairy tales. Mythical creatures – leprechauns.

Halloween party ill. by author. Lothrop, 1994. ISBN 978-0-688-11715-3 Subj: Holidays – Halloween. Parties. Rhyming text. Witches.

Shuter, Jane. *Henry Ford* ill. with photos. Heinemann, 2001. ISBN 978-1-57572-229-0 Subj: Automobiles. Careers – engineers.

Siberell, Anne. *Whale in the sky* ill. by author. Dutton, 1982. ISBN 978-0-525-44021-5 Subj: Animals – whales. Folk & fairy tales. Indians of North America.

Siddals, Mary McKenna. *Compost stew: an A to Z recipe for the earth* ill. by Ashley Wolff. Tricycle, 2010. ISBN 978-1-58246-316-2 Subj: ABC books. Ecology. Rhyming text.

I'll play with you ill. by David Wisniewski. Clarion, 2000. ISBN 978-0-395-90373-5 Subj: Activities – playing. Nature.

Millions of snowflakes ill. by Elizabeth Sayles. Clarion, 1998. ISBN 978-0-395-71531-4 Subj: Rhyming text. Weather – snow.

Morning song ill. by Elizabeth Sayles. Holt, 2001. ISBN 978-0-8050-6369-1 Subj: Morning.

Tell me a season ill. by Petra Mathers. Clarion, 1997. ISBN 978-0-395-71021-0 Subj: Concepts – color. Rhyming text. Seasons.

Sidjanski, Brigitte. *Little Chicken and Little Duck* ill. by author. Minedition, 2007. ISBN 978-0-698-40055-9 Subj: Birds – chickens. Birds – ducks. Friendship. Prejudice.

Sidman, Joyce. *Butterfly eyes and other secrets of the meadow* ill. by Beth Krommes. Houghton, 2006. ISBN 978-0-618-56313-5 Subj: Nature. Poetry. Riddles & jokes.

Just us two ill. by Susan Swan. Millbrook, 2000. ISBN 978-0-7613-1563-6 Subj: Animals. Animals – babies. Family life – fathers.

Meow ruff: a story in concrete poetry ill. by Michelle Berg. Houghton, 2006. ISBN 978-0-618-44894-4 Subj: Animals – cats. Animals – dogs. Poetry. Weather – storms.

Red sings from treetops: a year in colors ill. by Pamela Zagarenski. Houghton, 2009. ISBN 978-0-547-01494-4 Subj: Caldecott award honor books. Concepts – color. Poetry. Seasons.

Song of the water boatman: and other pond poems ill. by Beckie Prange. Houghton, 2005. ISBN 978-0-618-13547-9 Subj: Caldecott award honor books. Lakes, ponds. Nature. Poetry.

Swirl by swirl: spirals in nature ill. by Beth Krommes. Harcourt, 2011. ISBN 978-0-547-31583-6 Subj: Concepts – shape.

Ubiquitous: celebrating nature's survivors ill. by Beckie Prange. Houghton Mifflin, 2010. ISBN 978-0-618-71719-4 Subj: Nature. Poetry.

Siebert, Diane. *Cave* ill. by Wayne McLoughlin. HarperCollins, 2000. ISBN 978-0-688-16448-5 Subj: Caves. Rhyming text.

Heartland ill. by Wendell Minor. HarperCollins, 1989. ISBN 978-0-690-04732-5 Subj: Poetry. U.S. history.

Mojave ill. by Wendell Minor. HarperCollins, 1988. ISBN 978-0-690-04569-7 Subj: Desert. Poetry.

Plane song ill. by Vincent Nasta. HarperCollins, 1993. ISBN 978-0-06-021467-8 Subj: Airplanes, airports. Rhyming text.

Sierra ill. by Wendell Minor. HarperCollins, 1991. ISBN 978-0-06-021640-5 Subj: Nature. Poetry.

Train song ill. by Mike Wimmer. HarperCollins, 1990. ISBN 978-0-690-04728-8 Subj: Rhyming text. Trains.

Truck song ill. by Byron Barton. Crowell, 1984. ISBN 978-0-690-04411-9 Subj: Rhyming text. Trucks.

Siegel, Mark. *Moving house* ill. by author. Roaring Brook, 2011. ISBN 978-1-59643-635-0 Subj: Homes, houses. Moving.

Siegel, Randy. *Grandma's smile* ill. by DyAnne DiSalvo. Roaring Brook, 2010. ISBN 978-1-59643-438-7 Subj: Activities – traveling. Anatomy – faces. Behavior – lost & found possessions. Family life – grandmothers.

My snake Blake ill. by Serge Bloch. Roaring Brook, 2012. ISBN 978-1-59643-584-1 Subj: Pets. Reptiles – snakes.

Siegelson, Kim L. *In the time of the drums* ill. by Brian Pinkney. Hyperion, 1999. ISBN 978-0-7868-2386-4 Subj: Character traits – freedom. Ethnic groups in the U.S. – African Americans. Slavery.

Sierra, Judy. *Ballyhoo Bay* ill. by Derek Anderson. Simon & Schuster, 2009. ISBN 978-1-4169-5888-8 Subj: Art. Careers – artists. Ecology. Rhyming text. Sea & seashore – beaches.

The beautiful butterfly ill. by Victoria Chess. Clarion, 2000. ISBN 978-0-395-90015-4 Subj: Animals – mice. Folk & fairy tales. Foreign lands – Spain. Insects – butterflies, caterpillars. Royalty – kings. Weddings.

Born to read ill. by Marc Brown. Knopf, 2008. ISBN 978-0-375-84687-8 Subj: Books, reading. Rhyming text.

Counting crocodiles ill. by Will Hillenbrand. Harcourt, 1997. ISBN 978-0-15-200192-6 Subj: Animals – monkeys. Counting, numbers. Foreign lands – Asia. Reptiles – alligators, crocodiles.

The gift of the crocodile: a Cinderella story ill. by Reynold Ruffins. Simon & Schuster, 2000. ISBN 978-0-689-82188-2 Subj: Fairies. Family life – stepfamilies. Folk & fairy tales. Foreign lands – Indonesia. Reptiles – alligators, crocodiles.

The house that Drac built ill. by Will Hillenbrand. Harcourt, 1995. ISBN 978-0-15-200015-8 Subj: Cumulative tales. Holidays – Halloween. Homes, houses. Monsters. Rhyming text.

Mind your manners, B. B. Wolf ill. by J. Otto Seibold. Random House, 2007. ISBN 978-0-375-83532-2 Subj: Animals – wolves. Etiquette. Folk & fairy tales. Humorous stories. Libraries.

Monster Goose ill. by Jack E. Davis. Harcourt, 2001. ISBN 978-0-15-202034-7 Subj: Monsters. Nursery rhymes.

Preschool to the rescue ill. by Will Hillenbrand. Harcourt, 2001. ISBN 978-0-15-202035-4 Subj: Animals. Character traits – helpfulness. School – nursery.

The secret science project that almost ate school ill. by Stephen Gammell. Simon & Schuster, 2006. ISBN 978-1-4169-1175-3 Subj: Rhyming text. School. Science.

Sleepy little alphabet: a bedtime story from Alphabet Town ill. by Melissa Sweet. Knopf, 2009. ISBN 978-0-375-84002-9 Subj: ABC books. Bedtime. Rhyming text.

Suppose you meet a dinosaur: a first book of manners ill. by Tim Bowers. Knopf, 2012. ISBN 978-0-375-86720-0 Subj: Dinosaurs. Etiquette. Rhyming text. Shopping. Stores.

Tasty baby belly buttons ill. by Meilo So. Knopf, 1998. ISBN 978-0-679-99369-8 Subj: Folk & fairy tales. Foreign lands – Japan. Gender roles. Mythical creatures – ogres.

Tell the truth, B. B. Wolf ill. by J. Otto Seibold. Random House, 2010. ISBN 978-0-375-85620-4 Subj: Activities – storytelling. Animals – wolves. Character traits – honesty. Folk & fairy tales. Humorous stories.

Thelonius Monster's sky-high fly pie: a revolting rhyme ill. by Edward Koren. Random House, 2006. ISBN 978-0-375-93218-2 Subj: Food. Insects – flies. Monsters. Rhyming text.

There's a zoo in room 22 ill. by Barney Saltzberg. Harcourt, 2000. ISBN 978-0-15-202033-0 Subj: ABC books. Animals. Pets. Rhyming text. School.

'Twas the fright before Christmas ill. by Will Hillenbrand. Harcourt, 2002. ISBN 978-0-15-201805-4 Subj: Animals – mice. Cumulative tales. Dragons. Holidays – Christmas. Homes, houses. Monsters. Mythical creatures. Rhyming text.

We love our school! a read-together rebus story. Random House, 2011. ISBN 978-0-375-86728-6 Subj: Animals. Rebuses. Rhyming text. School – first day.

Wild about books ill. by Marc Brown. Knopf, 2004. ISBN 978-0-375-92538-2 Subj: Animals. Books, reading. Careers – librarians. Libraries. Rhyming text. Zoos.

Wild about you! ill. by Marc Brown. Knopf., 2012. ISBN 978-0-307-93178-8 Subj: Animals – babies. Rhyming text. Zoos.

Wiley and the Hairy Man ill. by Brian Pinkney. Lodestar, 1996. ISBN 978-0-525-67477-1 Subj: Character traits – cleverness. Ethnic groups in the U.S. – African Americans. Folk & fairy tales. Monsters.

Zoozical ill. by Marc Brown. Random House, 2011. ISBN 978-0-375-86847-4 Subj: Animals. Rhyming text. Theater. Zoos.

Sif, Birgitta. *Oliver* ill. by author. Candlewick, 2012. ISBN 978-0-7636-6247-9 Subj: Behavior – solitude. Character traits – being different. Friendship. Imagination. Toys.

Silbaugh, Elizabeth. *Raggedy Ann's birthday party book* ill. by Laura Francesca Filippucci. Simon & Schuster, 2001. ISBN 978-0-689-82850-8 Subj: Activities. Birthdays. Parties. Toys – dolls.

Sill, Cathryn. *About amphibians* ill. by John Sill. Peachtree, 2000. ISBN 978-1-56145-234-7 Subj: Frogs & toads. Reptiles.

About fish ill. by John Sill. Peachtree, 2002. ISBN 978-1-56145-256-9 Subj: Fish.

About hummingbirds: a guide for children ill. by John Sill. Peachtree, 2011. ISBN 978-1-56145-588-1 Subj: Birds – hummingbirds.

About insects ill. by John Sill. Peachtree, 2000. ISBN 978-1-56145-207-1 Subj: Insects.

About mammals ill. by John Sill. Peachtree, 1997. ISBN 978-1-56145-141-8 Subj: Animals.

About marsupials: a guide for children ill. by John Sill. Peachtree, 2006. ISBN 978-1-56145-358-0 Subj: Animals – marsupials.

About penguins ill. by John Sill. Peachtree, 2009. ISBN 978-1-56145-488-4 Subj: Birds – penguins.

Wetlands ill. by John Sill. Peachtree, 2008. ISBN 978-1-56145-432-7 Subj: Nature. Science.

Sillifant, Alec. *Farmer Ham* ill. by Mike Spoor. NorthSouth, 2007. ISBN 978-0-7358-2134-7 Subj: Animals – pigs. Birds – crows. Careers – farmers. Farms.

Silvano, Wendi. *Counting coconuts / Contando cocos* ill. by Marty Granius. Raven Tree, 2004. ISBN 978-0-9720192-6-2 Subj: Animals – monkeys. Counting, numbers. Foreign languages.

Just one more ill. by Ricardo Gamboa. All About Kids, 2002. ISBN 978-0-9700863-7-2 Subj: Activities – traveling. Buses. Foreign lands – South America. Mountains.

Turkey Claus ill. by Lee Harper. Amazon, 2012. ISBN 978-0-7614-6239-2 Subj: Birds – turkeys. Clothing – costumes. Holidays – Christmas. Santa Claus.

Turkey trouble ill. by Lee Harper. Marshall Cavendish, 2009. ISBN 978-0-7614-5529-5 Subj: Birds – turkeys. Clothing – costumes. Farms. Holidays – Thanksgiving.

What does the wind say? ill. by Joan M. Delehanty. NorthWord, 2006. ISBN 978-1-55971-954-4 Subj: Poetry. Rhyming text.

Silverhardt, Lauryn. *Happy Chinese New Year, Kai-lan!* ill. by Jason Fruchter and Aka Chikasawa. Simon & Schuster, 2009. ISBN 978-1-4169-8505-1 Subj: Ethnic groups in the U.S. – Chinese Americans. Friendship. Holidays – Chinese New Year.

Silverman, Erica. *Follow the leader* ill. by G. Brian Karas. Farrar, 2000. ISBN 978-0-374-32423-0 Subj: Activities – playing. Bedtime. Family life – brothers. Rhyming text.

Gittel's hands ill. by Deborah Nourse Lattimore. BridgeWater, 1996. ISBN 978-0-8167-3798-7 Subj: Character traits – kindness. Character traits – meanness. Holidays – Passover. Jewish culture. Religion.

The Halloween house ill. by Jon Agee. Farrar, 1997. ISBN 978-0-374-16768-4 Subj: Counting, numbers. Ghosts. Holidays – Halloween. Monsters. Rhyming text. Witches.

The Hanukkah hop! ill. by Steven D'Amico. Simon & Schuster, 2011. ISBN 978-1-4424-0604-9 Subj: Activities – dancing. Holidays – Hanukkah. Jewish culture. Rhyming text.

There was a wee woman . . . ill. by Rosanne Litzinger. Farrar, 2008. ISBN 978-0-374-38253-7 Subj: Character traits – smallness. Clothing – shoes. Homes, houses. Rhyming text.

Silverstein, Shel. *A giraffe and a half* ill. by author. HarperCollins, 1964. ISBN 978-0-06-025656-2 Subj: Cumulative tales. Humorous stories. Rhyming text.

The giving tree ill. by author. HarperCollins, 2003. ISBN 978-0-06-025666-1 Subj: Character traits – generosity. Rhyming text. Trees.

The missing piece ill. by author. HarperCollins, 1976. ISBN 978-0-06-025672-2 Subj: Character traits – individuality. Concepts – shape.

Simard, Rémy. *Hocus Pocus* (Desrosiers, Sylvie)

Simeon, Jean-Pierre. *This is a poem that heals fish* ill. by Olivier Tallec. Enchanted Lion, 2007. ISBN 978-1-59270-067-7 Subj: Fish. Pets. Poetry.

Simhaee, Rebeka. *Sara finds a mitzva* ill. by Michael Weber. Hachai, 2010. ISBN 978-1-929628-46-9 Subj: Behavior – lost & found possessions. Family life – grandmothers. Jewish culture.

Siminovich, Lorena. *Alex and Lulu: two of a kind* ill. by author. Candlewick, 2009. ISBN 978-0-7636-4423-9 Subj: Animals – cats. Animals – dogs. Character traits – being different. Friendship.

I like bugs ill. by author. Candlewick, 2010. ISBN 978-0-7636-4802-2 Subj: Counting, numbers. Format, unusual – board books. Insects.

I like vegetables ill. by author. Candlewick, 2011. ISBN 978-0-7636-5283-8 Subj: Concepts – opposites. Food. Format, unusual. Gardens, gardening.

Monkey see, look at me! ill. by author. Dial, 2012. ISBN 978-0-8037-3737-2 Subj: Animals. Animals – monkeys. Behavior – imitation.

Simmonds, Posy. *Baker cat* ill. by author. Red Fox, 2006. ISBN 978-0-09-945596-7 Subj: Activities – baking, cooking. Animals – cats. Animals – mice. Careers – bakers.

Simmons, Jane. *Bouncy bouncy Daisy* ill. by author. Little, 2003. ISBN 978-0-316-79570-8 Subj: Birds – ducks. Format, unusual – toy & movable books.

Come along, Daisy! ill. by author. Little, 1998. ISBN 978-0-316-79790-0 Subj: Behavior – lost. Birds – ducks. Family life. Nature.

Daisy and the Beastie ill. by author. Little, 2000. ISBN 978-0-316-79785-6 Subj: Animals. Birds – ducks. Family life – brothers & sisters. Farms.

Daisy and the egg ill. by author. Little, 1998. ISBN 978-0-316-79747-4 Subj: Birds – ducks. Eggs. Family life – brothers & sisters. Family life – new sibling.

Daisy says coo! ill. by author. Little, 2000. ISBN 978-0-316-79764-1 Subj: Animals. Birds – ducks. Format, unusual – board books. Noise, sounds.

Daisy says, "Here we go round the mulberry bush" ill. by author. Little, 2002. ISBN 978-0-316-79811-2 Subj: Activities. Birds – ducks. Format, unusual – board books. Participation. Songs.

Daisy says, "If you're happy and you know it" ill. by author. Little, 2002. ISBN 978-0-316-79940-9 Subj: Birds – ducks. Format, unusual – board books. Noise, sounds. Participation. Songs.

Daisy, the little duck with big feet ill. by author. Little, 2001. ISBN 978-0-316-79454-1 Subj: Birds – ducks. Format, unusual. Noise, sounds.

Daisy's day out ill. by author. Little, 2000. ISBN 978-0-316-79763-4 Subj: Birds – ducks. Format, unusual – board books. Noise, sounds.

Daisy's favorite things ill. by author. Little, 1999. ISBN 978-0-316-79762-7 Subj: Animals. Birds – ducks. Format, unusual – board books. Night. Rhyming text.

Daisy's hide-and-seek ill. by author. Little, 2001. ISBN 978-0-316-79616-3 Subj: Animals. Birds – ducks. Format, unusual – toy & movable books. Games. Noise, sounds.

The dreamtime fairies ill. by author. Little, 2002. ISBN 978-0-316-79523-4 Subj: Bedtime. Fairies. Sleep. Toys.

Ebb and Flo and the greedy gulls ill. by author. McElderry, 2000. ISBN 978-0-689-82484-5 Subj: Animals – dogs. Behavior – misunderstanding. Birds – seagulls. Sea & seashore.

Ebb and Flo and the new friend ill. by author. Little, 1999. ISBN 978-0-689-82483-8 Subj: Animals – dogs. Behavior – sharing. Birds – geese.

Go to sleep, Daisy ill. by author. Little, 1999. ISBN 978-0-316-79761-0 Subj: Bedtime. Birds – ducks. Dreams. Noise, sounds. Sleep.

Little Fern's first winter ill. by author. Little, 2001. ISBN 978-0-316-79667-5 Subj: Activities – playing. Animals. Animals – rabbits. Family life – brothers & sisters. Games. Weather – snow.

Quack, Daisy, quack! ill. by author. Little, 2002. ISBN 978-0-316-79587-6 Subj: Behavior – lost. Birds – ducks. Noise, sounds.

Splish splash Daisy ill. by author. Little, 2003. ISBN 978-0-316-79560-9 Subj: Birds – ducks. Format, unusual – board books. Puzzles.

Together ill. by author. Random House, 2007. ISBN 978-0-375-84339-6 Subj: Animals – dogs. Friendship.

Simmons, Steven J. *Alice and Greta: a tale of two witches* ill. by Cyd Moore. Charlesbridge, 1997. ISBN 978-0-88106-974-7 Subj: Character traits – kindness. Character traits – meanness. Magic. Witches.

Alice and Greta's color magic ill. by Cyd Moore. Knopf, 2001. ISBN 978-0-375-81245-3 Subj: Behavior – misbehavior. Concepts – color. Magic. Witches.

Greta's revenge ill. by Cyd Moore. Crown, 1999. ISBN 978-0-517-80051-5 Subj: Behavior – misbehavior. Magic. Witches.

Simms, Laura. *Rotten teeth* ill. by David Catrow. Houghton, 1998. ISBN 978-0-395-82850-2 Subj: Activities – storytelling. School. Teeth.

Simon, Annette. *Robot zombie Frankenstein!* ill. by author. Candlewick, 2012. ISBN 978-0-7636-5124-4 Subj: Concepts – shape. Monsters. Robots.

Simon, Charnan. *Big bad Buzz* ill. by Len Epstein. Child's World, 2006. ISBN 978-1-59296-617-2 Subj: Animals – dogs. Behavior – animals, dislike of. Character traits – bravery. Emotions – fear.

A greedy little pig ill. by Marcy Ramsey. Child's World, 2006. ISBN 978-1-59296-622-6 Subj: Animals – pigs. Behavior – greed.

Jeremy Jones, clumsy guy ill. by Cari Pillo. Child's World, 2006. ISBN 978-1-59296-619-6 Subj: Character traits – clumsiness.

Messy Molly ill. by Mernie Gallagher-Cole. Child's World, 2006. ISBN 978-1-59296-625-7 Subj: Behavior – lost & found possessions. Behavior – messy. Character traits – orderliness. Toys – bears.

Simon, Francesca. *Calling all toddlers* ill. by Susan Winter. Orchard, 1999. ISBN 978-0-531-30120-3 Subj: Activities – playing. Rhyming text.

Toddler time ill. by Susan Winter. Orchard, 2000. ISBN 978-0-531-30251-4 Subj: Activities. Poetry.

Simon, Norma. *All families are special* ill. by Teresa Flavin. Whitman, 2003. ISBN 978-0-8075-2175-5 Subj: Family life. School.

All kinds of children ill. by Diane Paterson. Whitman, 1999. ISBN 978-0-8075-0281-5 Subj: Character traits – individuality. Self-concept.

All kinds of families ill. by Joe Lasker. Whitman, 1976. ISBN 978-0-8075-0282-2 Subj: Family life.

How do I feel? ill. by Joe Lasker. Whitman, 1970. ISBN 978-0-8075-3414-4 Subj: Emotions. Family life. Multiple births – twins.

The saddest time ill. by Jacqueline Rogers. Whitman, 1986. ISBN 978-0-8075-7203-0 Subj: Death. Emotions – grief.

The story of Hanukkah ill. by Leonid Gore. HarperCollins, 1997. ISBN 978-0-06-027420-7 Subj: Holidays – Hanukkah. Jewish culture. Religion.

The story of Passover ill. by Erika Weihs. HarperCollins, 1997. ISBN 978-0-06-027063-6 Subj: Holidays – Passover. Jewish culture. Religion.

Why am I different? ill. by Dora Leder. Whitman, 1976. ISBN 978-0-8075-9075-1 Subj: Character traits – being different. Character traits – individuality. Self-concept.

Simont, Marc. *The goose that almost got cooked* ill. by author. Scholastic, 1997. ISBN 978-0-590-69075-1 Subj: Activities – flying. Birds – geese. Character traits – individuality. Farms.

The stray dog ill. by author. HarperCollins, 2001. ISBN 978-0-06-028934-8 Subj: Animals – dogs. Caldecott award honor books. Character traits – kindness to animals.

Simple gifts: a Shaker hymn ill. by Chris Raschka. Holt, 1998. ISBN 978-0-8050-5143-8 Subj: Animals. Birds. Forest, woods. Music. Songs.

Simple Simon. *The adventures of Simple Simon* ill. by Chris Conover. Farrar, 1987. ISBN 978-0-374-36921-7 Subj: Nursery rhymes.

Simpson, Lesley. *The Purim surprise* ill. by Peter Church. Kar-Ben, 2003. ISBN 978-1-58013-090-5 Subj: Birthdays. Family life – daughters. Family life – mothers. Holidays – Purim. Jewish culture. Moving.

Simpson-Enock, Sarah. *Mommy, Mommy, what's in your tummy? a lift-the-flap book* ill. by Linzi West. Frances Lincoln, 2009. ISBN 978-1-84507-931-4 Subj: Birth. Character traits – questioning. Family life. Format, unusual – toy & movable books.

Singer, Isaac Bashevis. *Why Noah chose the dove* ill. by Eric Carle. Farrar, 1974. ISBN 978-0-374-38420-3 Subj: Animals. Birds – doves. Boats, ships. Religion – Noah. Weather – floods. Weather – rain. Weather – rainbows.

Singer, Marilyn. *Boo hoo boo-boo* ill. by Elivia Savadier. HarperCollins, 2002. ISBN 978-0-694-01566-5 Subj: Accidents. Illness. Rhyming text.

The boy who cried alien ill. by Brian Biggs. Hyperion, 2012. ISBN 978-0-7868-3825-7 Subj: Aliens. Behavior – lying. Character traits – honesty. Rhyming text.

Caterpillars. Illus. EarlyLight, 2011. ISBN 978-0-9797455-7-7 Subj: Insects – butterflies, caterpillars.

City lullaby ill. by Carll Cneut. Houghton, 2007. ISBN 978-0-618-60703-7 Subj: Babies. Cities, towns. Counting, numbers. Noise, sounds. Rhyming text.

The company of crows ill. by Linda Saport. Clarion, 2002. ISBN 978-0-618-08340-4 Subj: Birds – crows. Poetry.

Creature carnival ill. by Gris Grimly. Hyperion, 2004. ISBN 978-0-7868-1877-8 Subj: Animals. Humorous stories. Mythical creatures. Poetry.

Didi and Daddy on the Promenade ill. by Marie-Louise Gay. Clarion, 2001. ISBN 978-0-618-04640-9 Subj: Activities – walking. Family life – daughters. Family life – fathers. Parks.

Eggs ill. by Emma Stevenson. Holiday House, 2008. ISBN 978-0-8234-1727-8 Subj: Eggs.

Every day's a dog's day: a year in poems ill. by Miki Sakamoto. Dial, 2012. ISBN 978-0-8037-3715-0 Subj: Animals – dogs. Holidays. Poetry.

First food fight this fall and other school poems ill. by Sachiko Yoshikawa. Sterling, 2008. ISBN 978-1-4027-4145-6 Subj: Poetry. School.

Fred's bed ill. by JoAnn Adinolfi. HarperCollins, 2001. ISBN 978-0-694-01451-4 Subj: Animals. Furniture – beds. Rhyming text.

I'm getting a checkup ill. by David Milgrim. Clarion, 2009. ISBN 978-0-618-99000-9 Subj: Careers – doctors. Health & fitness.

I'm your bus ill. by Evan Polenghi. Scholastic, 2009. ISBN 978-0-545-08918-0 Subj: Buses. Rhyming text. School.

Let's build a clubhouse ill. by Timothy Bush. Houghton, 2006. ISBN 978-0-618-30670-1 Subj: Character traits – cooperation. Clubs, gangs. Rhyming text. Tools.

Nine o'clock lullaby ill. by Frané Lessac. HarperCollins, 1991. ISBN 978-0-06-025648-7 Subj: Foreign lands. Time.

On the same day in March ill. by Frané Lessac. HarperCollins, 2000. ISBN 978-0-06-443528-4 Subj: Maps. Weather. World.

The one and only me ill. by Nicole Rubel. HarperCollins, 2000. ISBN 978-0-694-01279-4 Subj: Anatomy. Character traits – individuality. Family life.

Quiet night ill. by John Manders. Clarion, 2002. ISBN 978-0-618-12044-4 Subj: Animals. Camps, camping. Counting, numbers. Night. Noise, sounds.

Shoe bop! ill. by Hiroe Nakata. Dutton, 2008. ISBN 978-0-525-47939-0 Subj: Clothing – shoes. Rhyming text. Shopping.

Solomon sneezes ill. by Brian Floca. HarperCollins, 1999. ISBN 978-0-694-01748-5 Subj: Humorous stories. Rhyming text.

A stick is an excellent thing: poems celebrating outdoor play ill. by LeUyen Pham. Clarion, 2012. ISBN 978-0-547-12493-3 Subj: Activities – playing. Poetry.

Tallulah's Nutcracker ill. by Alexandra Boiger. Clarion, 2013. ISBN 978-0-547-84557-9 Subj: Ballet. Behavior – mistakes. Emotions – embarrassment. Holidays – Christmas.

Tallulah's solo ill. by Alexandra Boiger. Clarion, 2012. ISBN 978-0-547-33004-4 Subj: Ballet. Family life – brothers & sisters.

Tallulah's toe shoes ill. by Alexandra Boiger. Clarion, 2013. ISBN 978-0-547-48223-1 Subj: Activities – dancing. Ballet. Character traits – perseverance. Clothing – shoes.

Tallulah's tutu ill. by Alexandra Boiger. Clarion, 2011. ISBN 978-0-547-17353-5 Subj: Ballet. Character traits – perseverance.

Turtle in July ill. by Jerry Pinkney. Macmillan, 1989. ISBN 978-0-02-782881-8 Subj: Animals. Days of the week, months of the year. Nature. Poetry.

What is your dog doing? ill. by Kathleen Habbley. Simon & Schuster, 2011. ISBN 978-1-4169-7931-9 Subj: Animals – dogs. Rhyming text.

Singleton, Debbie. *The king who wouldn't sleep* ill. by Holly Swain. Andersen, 2012. ISBN 978-0-7613-8997-2 Subj: Behavior – trickery. Character traits – cleverness. Counting, numbers. Royalty – kings.

Sinykin, Sheri. *Zayde comes to live* ill. by Kristina Swarner. Peachtree, 2012. ISBN 978-1-56145-631-4 Subj: Death. Family life – grandfathers. Jewish culture. Religion.

Siomades, Lorianne. *Cuckoo can't find you* ill. by author. Boyds Mills, 2002. ISBN 978-1-56397-778-7 Subj: Animals. Behavior – lost & found possessions. Rhyming text.

The itsy bitsy spider ill. by author. Boyds Mills, 1999. ISBN 978-1-56397-727-5 Subj: Character traits – persistence. Nursery rhymes. Spiders.

Kangaroo and cricket ill. by author. Boyds Mills, 1999. ISBN 978-1-56397-780-0 Subj: Activities. Animals. Rhyming text.

Katy did it! ill. by author. Boyds Mills, 2009. ISBN 978-1-59078-602-4 Subj: Insects.

My box of color ill. by author. Boyds Mills, 1998. ISBN 978-1-56397-711-4 Subj: Animals. Concepts – color.

A place to bloom ill. by author. Boyds Mills, 1997. ISBN 978-1-56397-656-8 Subj: Behavior – sharing. Earth. Ecology. Rhyming text.

Three little kittens by Lorianne Siomades and Mother Goose ill. by reteller. Boyds Mills, 2000. ISBN 978-1-56397-845-6 Subj: Animals – cats. Animals – mice. Behavior – lost & found possessions. Clothing – gloves, mittens. Nursery rhymes.

Sirett, Dawn. *Love your world: how to take care of the plants, the animals, and the planet* ill. by Rachael Parfitt; photos by Howard Shooter, et al. DK, 2009. ISBN 978-0-7566-4590-8 Subj: Ecology. World.

Sís, Peter. *Ballerina* ill. by author. Greenwillow, 2001. ISBN 978-0-688-17944-1 Subj: Activities – dancing. Ballet. Careers – dancers. Imagination.

Beach ball ill. by author. Greenwillow, 1990. ISBN 978-0-688-09182-8 Subj: Concepts. Sea & seashore – beaches.

Dinosaur! ill. by author. Greenwillow, 2000. ISBN 978-0-688-17049-3 Subj: Dinosaurs. Imagination. Prehistory. Wordless.

Fire truck ill. by author. Greenwillow, 1998. ISBN 978-0-688-15878-1 Subj: Careers – firefighters. Counting, numbers. Format, unusual – toy & movable books. Trucks.

Follow the dream ill. by author. Knopf, 1991. ISBN 978-0-679-90628-5 Subj: Careers – explorers.

Madlenka ill. by author. Farrar, 2000. ISBN 978-0-374-39969-6 Subj: Behavior – growing up. Foreign lands. Imagination. Teeth.

Madlenka, soccer star ill. by author. Farrar, 2010. ISBN 978-0-374-34702-4 Subj: Communities, neighborhoods. Imagination. Sports – soccer.

An ocean world ill. by author. Greenwillow, 1992. ISBN 978-0-688-09068-5 Subj: Animals – whales. Sea & seashore. Wordless.

Play, Mozart, play ill. by author. HarperCollins, 2006. ISBN 978-0-06-112182-1 Subj: Careers – musicians. Music.

Ship ahoy! ill. by author. Greenwillow, 1999. ISBN 978-0-688-16644-1 Subj: Boats, ships. Imagination. Monsters. Sea & seashore. Wordless.

A small tall tale from the far Far North ill. by author. Farrar, 2001. ISBN 978-0-374-37075-6 Subj: Eskimos. Foreign lands – Arctic. Indians of North America – Inuit. Tall tales.

Starry messenger ill. by author. Farrar, 1996. ISBN 978-0-374-37191-3 Subj: Astronomy. Caldecott award honor books. Careers – astronomers. Space & space ships. Stars.

Tibet through the red box ill. by author. Farrar, 1998. ISBN 978-0-374-37552-2 Subj: Activities – traveling. Caldecott award honor books. Foreign lands – Tibet.

Train of states ill. by author. Greenwillow, 2004. ISBN 978-0-06-057838-1 Subj: Trains. U.S. history.

Trucks, trucks, trucks ill. by author. Greenwillow, 1999. ISBN 978-0-688-16276-4 Subj: Format, unusual – toy & movable books. Trucks.

The wall: growing up behind the Iron Curtain ill. by author. Farrar, 2007. ISBN 978-0-374-34701-7 Subj: Caldecott award honor books. Careers – artists. Foreign lands – Czechoslovakia.

Waving ill. by author. Greenwillow, 1988. ISBN 978-0-688-07160-8 Subj: Counting, numbers.

Sitomer, Alan Lawrence. *Daddies do it different* ill. by Abby Carter. Hyperion, 2012. ISBN 978-1-4231-3315-5 Subj: Family life – fathers.

Siy, Alexandra. *One tractor: a counting book* ill. by Jacqueline Rogers. Holiday, 2008. ISBN 978-0-8234-1923-4 Subj: Counting, numbers. Pirates. Rhyming text. Tractors.

Skalak, Barbara Anne. *Waddle, waddle, quack, quack, quack* ill. by Sylvia Long. Chronicle, 2005. ISBN 978-0-8118-4342-3 Subj: Behavior – lost. Birds – ducks. Rhyming text.

Skead, Robert. *Something to prove: the great Satchel Paige vs. rookie Joe DiMaggio* ill. by Floyd Cooper. Carolrhoda, 2013. ISBN 978-0-7613-6619-5 Subj: Ethnic groups in the U.S. – African Americans. Prejudice. Sports – baseball. U.S. history.

Skeers, Linda. *Tutus aren't my style* ill. by Anne Wilsdorf. Penguin, 2010. ISBN 978-0-8037-3212-4 Subj: Ballet. Character traits – appearance. Character traits – individuality.

Skinner, Daphne. *Albert keeps score* ill. by Deborah Melmon. Kane, 2012. ISBN 978-1-57565-449-2 Subj: Animals – mice. Counting, numbers.

All aboard! ill. by Jerry Smath. Kane, 2007. ISBN 978-1-57565-239-9 Subj: Activities – traveling. Time. Trains.

Henry keeps score ill. by Page Eastburn O'Rourke. Kane, 2001. ISBN 978-1-57565-102-6 Subj: Counting, numbers. Family life – brothers & sisters. Sibling rivalry.

The right place for Albert ill. by Deborah Melmon. Kane, 2012. ISBN 978-1-57565-446-1 Subj: Animals – cats. Animals – mice. Counting, numbers.

Tightwad Tod ill. by John Nez. Kane, 2001. ISBN 978-1-57565-109-5 Subj: Counting, numbers. Money.

Sklansky, Amy E. *The duck who played the kazoo* ill. by Tiphanie Beeke. Clarion, 2008. ISBN 978-0-618-42854-0 Subj: Birds – ducks. Friendship. Musical instruments.

Out of this world: poems and facts about space ill. by Stacey Schuett. Knopf, 2012. ISBN 978-0-375-86459-9 Subj: Poetry. Space & space ships.

Where do chicks come from? ill. by Pamela Paparone. HarperCollins, 2005. ISBN 978-0-06-028893-8 Subj: Birds – chickens. Eggs. Science.

Skolsky, Mindy Warshaw. *Hannah and the whistling tea kettle* ill. by Diane Palmisciano. DK, 2000. ISBN 978-0-7894-2602-4 Subj: Crime. Family life – grandparents. Gifts. Noise, sounds. Stores.

Skrypuch, Marsha Forchuk. *Enough* ill. by Michael Martchenko. Fitzhenry & Whiteside, 2000. ISBN 978-1-55041-509-4 Subj: Careers – farmers. Folk & fairy tales. Foreign lands – Ukraine.

Skultety, Nancy. *From here to there* ill. by Tammie Lyon. Boyds Mills, 2005. ISBN 978-1-59078-092-3 Subj: Careers – construction workers. Roads. Trucks.

Slack, Michael. *Elecopter* ill. by author. Holt, 2013. ISBN 978-0-8050-9304-9 Subj: Animals – elephants. Helicopters. Rhyming text.

Monkey truck ill. by author. Holt, 2011. ISBN 978-0-8050-8878-6 Subj: Animals. Animals – monkeys. Character traits – helpfulness. Jungle. Rhyming text.

Slade, Suzanne. *Climbing Lincoln's steps: the African American journey* ill. by Colin Bootman. Whitman, 2010. ISBN 978-0-8075-1204-3 Subj: Ethnic groups in the U.S. – African Americans. Prejudice. U.S. history.

The house that George built ill. by Rebecca Bond. Charlesbridge, 2012. ISBN 978-1-58089-262-9 Subj: Buildings. Homes, houses. U.S. history.

What's new at the zoo? an animal adding adventure ill. by Joan Waites. Sylvan Dell, 2009. ISBN 978-1-934359-93-8 Subj: Counting, numbers. Zoos.

What's the difference? an endangered animal subtraction story ill. by Joan Waites. Sylvan Dell, 2010. ISBN 978-1-60718-070-8 Subj: Animals – endangered animals. Counting, numbers.

Slangerup, Erik Jon. *Dirt Boy* ill. by John Manders. Whitman, 2000. ISBN 978-0-8075-4424-2 Subj: Activities – bathing. Behavior – running away. Family life – mothers. Health & fitness.

Slate, Jenny. *Marcel the shell with shoes on: things about me* by Jenny Slate and Dean Fleischer-Camp ill. by Amy Lind. Penguin, 2011. ISBN 978-1-59514-455-3 Subj: Imagination. Sea & seashore.

Slate, Joseph. *The great big wagon that rang* ill. by Craig Spearing. Marshall Cavendish, 2002. ISBN 978-0-7614-5108-2 Subj: Careers – farmers. Rhyming text. U.S. history.

I want to be free ill. by E. B. Lewis. Putnam, 2009. ISBN 978-0-399-24342-4 Subj: Ethnic groups in the U.S. – African Americans. Rhyming text. Slavery.

Little Porcupine's Christmas ill. by Felicia Bond. Geringer, 2001. ISBN 978-0-06-029533-2 Subj:

Animals. Animals – porcupines. Holidays – Christmas.

Miss Bindergarten celebrates the last day of kindergarten ill. by Ashley Wolff. Penguin, 2006. ISBN 978-0-525-47744-0 Subj: ABC books. Animals. Careers – teachers. Rhyming text. School.

Miss Bindergarten celebrates the 100th day of kindergarten ill. by Ashley Wolff. Dutton, 1998. ISBN 978-0-525-46000-8 Subj: Animals. Careers – teachers. Counting, numbers. Rhyming text. School.

Miss Bindergarten gets ready for kindergarten ill. by Ashley Wolff. Dutton, 1996. ISBN 978-0-525-45446-5 Subj: ABC books. Animals. Careers – teachers. School – first day.

Miss Bindergarten has a wild day in kindergarten ill. by Ashley Wolff. Penguin, 2005. ISBN 978-0-525-47084-7 Subj: ABC books. Animals. Behavior – bad day. Careers – teachers. Rhyming text. School.

Miss Bindergarten stays home from kindergarten ill. by Ashley Wolff. Dutton, 2000. ISBN 978-0-525-46396-2 Subj: ABC books. Animals. Careers – teachers. Illness – cold (disease). Rhyming text. School.

Miss Bindergarten takes a field trip with kindergarten ill. by Ashley Wolff. Dutton, 2001. ISBN 978-0-525-46710-6 Subj: ABC books. Animals. Careers – teachers. Rhyming text. School. School – field trips.

Story time for Little Porcupine ill. by Jacqueline Rogers. Marshall Cavendish, 2001. ISBN 978-0-7614-5073-3 Subj: Activities – storytelling. Animals – porcupines. Creation. Family life – fathers. Folk & fairy tales. Sun.

What star is this? ill. by Alison Jay. Penguin, 2005. ISBN 978-0-399-24014-0 Subj: Religion – Nativity. Rhyming text.

Who is coming to our house? ill. by Ashley Wolff. Putnam, 1988. ISBN 978-0-399-21537-7 Subj: Animals. Animals – mice. Religion. Rhyming text.

Slater, Dashka. *Baby shoes* ill. by Hiroe Nakata. Bloomsbury, 2006. ISBN 978-1-58234-684-7 Subj: Babies. Clothing – shoes. Concepts – color. Rhyming text.

Firefighters in the dark ill. by Nicoletta Ceccoli. Houghton, 2006. ISBN 978-0-618-55459-1 Subj: Bedtime. Careers – firefighters. Dreams.

The sea serpent and me ill. by Catia Chien. Houghton, 2008. ISBN 978-0-618-72394-2 Subj: Behavior – growing up. Mythical creatures.

Slater, Teddy. *Smooch your pooch* ill. by Arthur Howard. Scholastic, 2010. ISBN 978-0-545-16736-9 Subj: Animals – dogs. Rhyming text.

Slawson, Michele Benoit. *Signs for sale* ill. by Bagram Ibatoulline. Viking, 2002. ISBN 978-0-670-03568-7 Subj: Family life – daughters. Family life – fathers. Signs & signboards.

Sleator, William. *The angry moon* ill. by Blair Lent. Little, 1970. ISBN 978-0-316-78737-6 Subj: Caldecott award honor books. Folk & fairy tales. Indians of North America – Tlingit. Moon.

Slegers, Liesbet. *The child in the manger* ill. by author. Clavis, 2010. ISBN 978-1-60537-084-2 Subj: Holidays – Christmas. Religion.

Fall leaves ill. by author. Clavis, 2012. ISBN 978-1-60537-122-1 Subj: Format, unusual – board books. Seasons – fall.

Funny ears ill. by author. Clavis, 2011. ISBN 978-1-60537-088-0 Subj: Anatomy – ears. Animals. Format, unusual – board books.

Funny feet ill. by author. Clavis, 2011. ISBN 978-1-60537-089-7 Subj: Anatomy – feet. Animals. Format, unusual – board books.

Funny tails ill. by author. Clavis, 2011. ISBN 978-1-60537-090-3 Subj: Anatomy – tails. Animals. Format, unusual – board books.

Happy Easter! ill. by author. Clavis, 2012. ISBN 978-1-60537-114-6 Subj: Animals – rabbits. Eggs. Holidays – Easter.

Katie goes to the doctor ill. by author. Clavis, 2011. ISBN 978-1-60537-076-7 Subj: Careers – doctors.

Kevin goes to the library ill. by author. Clavis, 2011. ISBN 978-1-60537-075-0 Subj: Libraries.

Playing ill. by author. Clavis, 2011. ISBN 978-1-60537-091-0 Subj: Activities – playing. Format, unusual – board books.

Winter snow ill. by author. Clavis, 2012. ISBN 978-1-60537-123-8 Subj: Format, unusual – board books. Seasons – winter.

Sleigh bells and snowflakes comp. by Linda Bronson; ill. by Linda Bronson. Holt, 2002. ISBN 978-0-8050-6755-2 Subj: Holidays – Christmas. Poetry.

Slingsby, Janet. *Hetty's 100 hats* ill. by Emma Dodd. Good Books, 2005. ISBN 978-1-56148-456-0 Subj: Behavior – collecting things. Birthdays. Clothing – hats. Counting, numbers.

Hush-a-bye babies ill. by Andy Beckett. Barron's, 2001. ISBN 978-0-7641-5410-2 Subj: Animals. Bedtime. Noise, sounds. Sleep.

Sloat, Robert. *Rib-ticklers* (Sloat, Teri)

Sloat, Teri. *Farmer Brown goes round and round* ill. by Nadine Bernard Westcott. DK, 1999. ISBN 978-0-7894-2512-6 Subj: Animals. Farms. Noise, sounds. Rhyming text. Weather – tornadoes.

Farmer Brown shears his sheep: a yarn about wool ill. by Nadine Bernard Westcott. DK, 2000. ISBN 978-0-7894-2637-6 Subj: Animals – sheep. Farms. Rhyming text.

Hark! The aardvark angels sing ill. by author. Putnam, 2001. ISBN 978-0-399-23371-5 Subj: Angels. Animals – aardvarks. Holidays – Christmas. Music. Songs.

I'm a duck! ill. by author. Penguin, 2006. ISBN 978-0-399-24274-8 Subj: Behavior – growing up. Birds – ducks.

Patty's pumpkin patch ill. by author. Putnam, 1999. ISBN 978-0-399-23010-3 Subj: ABC books. Rhyming text.

Pieces of Christmas ill. by author. Holt, 2002. ISBN 978-0-8050-6355-4 Subj: Animals. Holidays – Christmas. Letters, cards. Rhyming text. Santa Claus.

Rib-ticklers by Teri Sloat and Robert Sloat ill. by authors. Lothrop, 1995. ISBN 978-0-688-12520-2 Subj: Animals. Riddles & jokes.

There was an old lady who swallowed a trout ill. by Reynold Ruffins. Holt, 1998. ISBN 978-0-8050-4294-8 Subj: Animals. Cumulative tales. Fish. Folk & fairy tales. Humorous stories. Rhyming text.

The thing that bothered Farmer Brown ill. by Nadine Bernard Westcott. Orchard, 1995. ISBN 978-0-531-08733-6 Subj: Animals. Careers – farmers. Insects – mosquitoes. Night. Noise, sounds. Rhyming text. Sleep.

This is the house that was tidy and neat ill. by R. W. Alley. Holt, 2005. ISBN 978-0-8050-6921-1 Subj: Character traits – cleanliness. Rhyming text.

Slobodkina, Esphyr. *Caps for sale* ill. by author. Addison-Wesley, 1940. ISBN 978-0-06-025778-1 Subj: Animals – monkeys. Careers – peddlers. Clothing – hats. Humorous stories. Participation.

Circus caps for sale ill. by author. HarperCollins, 2002. ISBN 978-0-06-029656-8 Subj: Animals – elephants. Careers – peddlers. Circus. Clothing – hats. Crime. Humorous stories. Participation.

Slonim, David. *He came with the couch* ill. by author. Chronicle, 2005. ISBN 978-0-8118-4430-7 Subj: Friendship. Furniture.

I loathe you ill. by author. Simon & Schuster, 2012. ISBN 978-1-4424-2244-5 Subj: Emotions – love. Family life – mothers. Monsters. Rhyming text.

Oh, Ducky ill. by author. Chronicle, 2003. ISBN 978-0-8118-3562-6 Subj: Behavior – lost & found possessions. Food. Toys.

Patch ill. by author. Roaring Brook, 2013. ISBN 978-1-59643-643-5 Subj: Animals – dogs. Pets.

Slovenz-Low, Madeline. *Lion dancer: Ernie Wan's Chinese New Year* (Waters, Kate)

Small, David. *George Washington's cows* ill. by author. Farrar, 1994. ISBN 978-0-374-32535-0 Subj: Animals. Rhyming text. U.S. history.

Imogene's antlers ill. by author. Crown, 1985. ISBN 978-0-517-55564-4 Subj: Animals. Character traits – appearance.

Smallcomb, Pam. *Earth to Clunk* ill. by Joe Berger. Penguin, 2011. ISBN 978-0-8037-3439-5 Subj: Aliens. Family life – brothers & sisters. Pen pals. School. Space & space ships.

I'm not ill. by Robert Weinstock. Random House, 2011. ISBN 978-0-375-86115-4 Subj: Character traits – individuality. Friendship. Self-concept.

Smalley, Elisa. *Zoe Sophia in New York: the mystery of the Pink Phoenix papers* (Mauner, Claudia)

Zoe Sophia's scrapbook (Mauner, Claudia)

Smallman, Steve. *Dragon stew* ill. by Lee Wildish. Good Books, 2010. ISBN 978-1-56148-695-3 Subj: Dragons. Rhyming text. Vikings.

The lamb who came for dinner ill. by Joelle Dreidemy. Tiger Tales, 2007. ISBN 978-1-58925-067-3 Subj: Animals – sheep. Animals – wolves. Friendship.

My dad! ill. by Sean Julian. Good Books, 2012. ISBN 978-1-56148-744-8 Subj: Animals – bears. Family life – fathers. Rhyming text.

The very greedy bee ill. by Jack Tickle. Tiger Tales, 2007. ISBN 978-1-58925-065-9 Subj: Behavior – greed. Behavior – sharing. Insects – bees.

Smalls, Irene. *Don't say ain't* ill. by Colin Bootman. Charlesbridge, 2003. ISBN 978-1-57091-381-5 Subj: Books, reading. Ethnic groups in the U.S. – African Americans. Family life. Prejudice. School.

My Nana and me ill. by Cathy Ann Johnson. Little, Brown, 2005. ISBN 978-0-316-16821-2 Subj: Activities – playing. Ethnic groups in the U.S. – African Americans. Family life – grandmothers.

My Pop Pop and me ill. by Cathy Ann Johnson. Little, Brown, 2006. ISBN 978-0-316-73422-6 Subj: Activities – baking, cooking. Ethnic groups in the U.S. – African Americans. Family life – grandfathers. Rhyming text.

Smalls-Hector, Irene. *Because you're lucky* ill. by Michael Hays. Little, 1997. ISBN 978-0-316-79867-9 Subj: Behavior – sharing. Emotions – envy, jealousy. Ethnic groups in the U.S. – African Americans. Family life – cousins. Friendship.

Beginning school ill. by Toni Goffe. Silver Pr., 1996. ISBN 978-0-382-39328-0 Subj: Ethnic groups in the U.S. – African Americans. School – first day.

Jenny Reen and the Jack Muh Lantern ill. by Keinyo White. Atheneum, 1996. ISBN 978-0-689-31875-7 Subj: Ethnic groups in the U.S. – African Americans. Holidays – Halloween. Slavery. U.S. history.

Jonathan and his mommy ill. by Michael Hays. Little, 1992. ISBN 978-0-316-79870-9 Subj: Activities – walking. Cities, towns. Communities, neighborhoods. Ethnic groups in the U.S. – African Americans. Family life – mothers.

Kevin and his dad ill. by Michael Hays. Little, 1999. ISBN 978-0-316-79899-0 Subj: Ethnic groups in the U.S. – African Americans. Family life – fathers. Rhyming text.

Smath, Jerry. *The animals' Christmas carol* by Jerry Smath and Charles Dickens ill. by Jerry Smath. An adaption of Charles Dickens' A Christmas Carol. BridgeWater, 2000. ISBN 978-0-8167-6940-7 Subj: Animals. Behavior – greed. Holidays – Christmas.

Sammy Salami ill. by author. Abrams, 2007. ISBN 978-0-8109-9350-1 Subj: Activities – traveling. Activities – vacationing. Animals – cats. Behavior – lost. Pets.

Smee, Nicola. *Clip-clop* ill. by author. Boxer, 2006. ISBN 978-1-905417-09-4 Subj: Animals. Concepts – speed.

Jingle-jingle ill. by author. Boxer, 2008. ISBN 978-1-906250-08-9 Subj: Animals. Seasons – winter. Sports – sledding.

No bed without Ted ill. by author. Bloomsbury, 2005. ISBN 978-1-58234-963-3 Subj: Bedtime. Behavior – lost & found possessions. Format, unusual – toy & movable books. Toys – bears.

What's the matter, Bunny Blue? ill. by author. Boxer, 2010. ISBN 978-1-906250-91-1 Subj: Animals – rabbits. Behavior – lost. Family life – grandmothers. Rhyming text.

Smet, Marian De. *I have two homes* ill. by Nynke Mare Talsma. Clavis, 2012. ISBN 978-1-60537-102-3 Subj: Divorce. Family life.

Smiley, Norene. *That stripy cat* ill. by Tara Anderson. Fitzhenry & Whiteside, 2007. ISBN 978-1-55005-164-3 Subj: Animals – cats.

Smith, Alex T. *Foxy and Egg* ill. by author. Holiday House, 2011. ISBN 978-0-8234-2330-9 Subj: Animals – foxes. Behavior – trickery. Eggs. Humorous stories.

Smith, Charles R. *Brick by brick* ill. by Floyd Cooper. Amistad, 2013. ISBN 978-0-06-192082-0 Subj: Buildings. Ethnic groups in the U.S. – African Americans. Slavery. U.S. history.

Dance with me ill. by Noah Jones. Candlewick, 2008. ISBN 978-0-7636-2246-6 Subj: Activities – dancing. Rhyming text.

I am the world ill. by Charles R. Smith. Simon & Schuster, 2013. ISBN 978-1-4424-2302-2 Subj: Ethnic groups in the U.S. Rhyming text. World.

I'll be there photos by author. Composed by Hal Davis, Berry Gordy, Jr., Bob West, & Willie Hutchinson;. Hyperion, 2001. ISBN 978-0-7868-0785-7 Subj: Babies. Format, unusual – board books. Music. Songs.

Loki and Alex photos by author. Dutton, 2001. ISBN 978-0-525-46700-7 Subj: Animals – dogs. Ethnic groups in the U.S. – African Americans.

My gal photos by author. Hyperion, 2001. ISBN 978-0-7868-0782-6 Subj: Babies. Format, unusual – board books. Music. Songs.

Smith, Cynthia Leitich. *Holler Loudly* ill. by Barry Gott. Penguin, 2010. ISBN 978-0-525-42256-3 Subj: Character traits – being different. Tall tales.

Jingle dancer ill. by Cornelius Van Wright and Ying-Hwa Hu. Morrow, 2000. ISBN 978-0-688-16242-9 Subj: Activities – dancing. Family life. Indians of North America.

Santa knows by Cynthia Leitich Smith and Greg Leitich Smith ill. by Steve Björkman. Penguin, 2006. ISBN 978-0-525-47757-0 Subj: Holidays – Christmas. Santa Claus.

Smith, Dana Kessimakis. *A brave spaceboy* ill. by Laura Freeman. Hyperion, 2005. ISBN 978-0-7868-0933-2 Subj: Imagination. Moving.

Smith, Danna. *Balloon trees* ill. by Laurie Allen Klein. Sylvan Dell, 2013. ISBN 978-1-60718-612-0 Subj: Activities – making things. Toys – balloons. Trees.

Pirate nap: a book of colors ill. by Valeria Petrone. Clarion, 2011. ISBN 978-0-574-57531-5 Subj: Concepts – color. Pirates. Rhyming text.

Smith, David J. *If America were a village: a book about the people of the United States* ill. by Shelagh Armstrong. Kids Can, 2009. ISBN 978-1-55453-344-2 Subj: Counting, numbers. U.S. history.

This child, every child: a book about the world's children ill. by Shelagh Armstrong. Kids Can, 2011. ISBN 978-1-55453-466-1 Subj: World.

Smith, Dian G. *Hanukkah lights* ill. by JoAnn E. Kitchel. Chronicle, 2001. ISBN 978-0-8118-3257-1 Subj: Holidays – Hanukkah. Jewish culture.

Smith, Greg Leitich. *Santa knows* (Smith, Cynthia Leitich)

Smith, Jada Pinkett. *Girls hold up this world* ill. by Donyell Kennedy-McCullough. Scholastic, 2005. ISBN 978-0-439-08793-3 Subj: Gender roles. Rhyming text. Self-concept.

Smith, Janice Lee. *Jess and the stinky cowboys* ill. by Lisa Thiesing. Dial, 2004. ISBN 978-0-8037-2641-3 Subj: Activities – bathing. Animals – dogs. Careers – police officers. Character traits – cleanliness. Cowboys, cowgirls. Tall tales. U.S. history – frontier & pioneer life.

Smith, Joseph A. *Circus train* ill. by author. Abrams, 2001. ISBN 978-0-8109-4148-9 Subj: Circus. Moving. Trains.

Smith, Kathryn. *Little Donkey's Christmas story* ill. by Amanda Wood. Candle Books, 2002. ISBN 978-1-85985-441-9 Subj: Animals – donkeys. Format, unusual – toy & movable books. Holidays – Christmas. Participation. Religion – Nativity.

Little Lamb's Christmas story ill. by Amanda Wood. Candle Books, 2002. ISBN 978-1-85985-442-6 Subj: Animals – sheep. Format, unusual – toy & movable books. Holidays – Christmas. Participation. Religion – Nativity.

Smith, Lane. *Abe Lincoln's dream* ill. by author. Roaring Brook, 2012. ISBN 978-1-59643-608-4 Subj: Ghosts. U.S. history.

Glasses . . . who needs 'em? ill. by author. Viking, 1991. ISBN 978-0-670-84160-8 Subj: Glasses. Senses – sight.

Grandpa Green ill. by author. Roaring Brook, 2011. ISBN 978-1-59643-607-7 Subj: Caldecott award honor books. Family life – great-grandparents. Gardens, gardening. Memories, memory. Old age.

It's a book ill. by author. Roaring Brook, 2010. ISBN 978-1-59643-606-0 Subj: Animals. Books, reading. Humorous stories.

John, Paul, George and Ben ill. by author. Hyperion, 2006. ISBN 978-0-7868-4893-5 Subj: Humorous stories. U.S. history.

Madam President ill. by author. Hyperion, 2008. ISBN 978-1-4231-0846-7 Subj: Behavior – seeking better things. Character traits – ambition. Gender roles. Humorous stories.

Pinocchio, the boy ill. by author. Viking, 2002. ISBN 978-0-670-03585-4 Subj: Fairies. Folk & fairy tales. Humorous stories. Puppets. Self-concept.

The Stinky Cheese Man and other fairly stupid tales (Scieszka, Jon)

Smith, Linda. *The inside tree* ill. by David Parkins. HarperCollins, 2010. ISBN 978-0-06-028241-7 Subj: Animals – dogs. Homes, houses. Humorous stories. Trees.

Mrs. Biddlebox ill. by Marla Frazee. HarperCollins, 2002. ISBN 978-0-06-028690-3 Subj: Activities – baking, cooking. Emotions. Food. Rhyming text.

Sir Cassie to the rescue ill. by Karen Patkau. Orca, 2003. ISBN 978-1-55143-243-4 Subj: Family life – brothers & sisters. Imagination. Knights.

When Moon fell down ill. by Kathryn Brown. HarperCollins, 2001. ISBN 978-0-06-029497-7 Subj: Animals – bulls, cows. Moon. Rhyming text.

Smith, Lois T. *Carrie and Carl play* ill. by author. Candlewick, 2007. ISBN 978-0-7636-1690-8 Subj: Activities – playing. Format, unusual – toy & movable books.

Smith, Maggie. *Counting our way to Maine* ill. by author. Orchard, 1995. ISBN 978-0-531-08734-3 Subj: Activities – traveling. Counting, numbers.

Dear Daisy, get well soon ill. by author. Crown, 2000. ISBN 978-0-517-80073-7 Subj: Counting, numbers. Days of the week, months of the year. Family life – mothers. Friendship. Illness – chicken pox. Toys.

Desser, the best ever cat ill. by author. Knopf, 2001. ISBN 978-0-375-91056-2 Subj: Animals – cats. Death. Emotions. Pets.

One naked baby: counting to ten and back again ill. by author. Random House, 2007. ISBN 978-0-375-83329-8 Subj: Babies. Counting, numbers. Rhyming text.

Paisley ill. by author. Knopf, 2004. ISBN 978-0-375-92164-3 Subj: Animals – elephants. Behavior – needing someone. Toys.

Pigs in pajamas ill. by author. Knopf, 2012. ISBN 978-0-375-84817-9 Subj: Animals – pigs. Rhyming text. Sleepovers.

This is your garden ill. by author. Crown, 1998. ISBN 978-0-517-70993-1 Subj: Gardens, gardening.

Smith, Marie. *N is for our nation's capital: a Washington, DC alphabet* by Marie Smith and Roland Smith ill. by Barbara L. Gibson. Sleeping Bear, 2005. ISBN 978-1-58556-148-3 Subj: ABC books. Cities, towns. U.S. history.

S is for Smithsonian: America's museum alphabet by Marie Smith and Roland Smith ill. by Gijsbert van Frankenhuyzen. Sleeping Bear, 2010. ISBN 978-1-58536-314-8 Subj: ABC books. Museums. U.S. history.

Z is for zookeeper: a zoo alphabet by Marie Smith and Roland Smith ill. by Henry Cole. Sleeping Bear, 2005. ISBN 978-1-58536-158-8 Subj: ABC books. Zoos.

Smith, Mavis. *'Twas the day after Thanksgiving* ill. by author. Simon & Schuster, 2002. ISBN 978-0-

689-85234-3 Subj: Animals – mice. Format, unusual – toy & movable books. Holidays – Thanksgiving. Rhyming text.

Smith, Roland. *N is for our nation's capital: a Washington, DC alphabet* (Smith, Marie)

S is for Smithsonian: America's museum alphabet (Smith, Marie)

Z is for zookeeper: a zoo alphabet (Smith, Marie)

Smith, Rosie. *Captain Pajamas* (Whatley, Bruce)

Smith, Stu. *The bubble gum kid* ill. by Julia Woolf. Running Press, 2006. ISBN 978-0-7624-2046-9 Subj: Behavior – bullying, teasing. Rhyming text.

Smith, Will. *Just the two of us* ill. by Kadir Nelson. Scholastic, 2001. ISBN 978-0-439-08792-6 Subj: Family life – fathers. Family life – sons. Music. Songs.

Smith, William Jay. *Around my room* ill. by Erik Blegvad. Farrar, 2000. ISBN 978-0-374-30406-5 Subj: Poetry.

Smothers, Ethel Footman. *Auntee Edna* ill. by Wil Clay. Eerdmans, 2001. ISBN 978-0-8028-5154-3 Subj: Activities – baking, cooking. Ethnic groups in the U.S. – African Americans. Food.

Smucker, Anna Egan. *Golden delicious: a Cinderella apple story* ill. by Kathleen Kemly. Whitman, 2008. ISBN 978-0-8075-2987-4 Subj: Food. U.S. history.

Smythe, Theresa. *Chester's colorful Easter eggs* ill. by author. Holt, 2013. ISBN 978-0-8050-9326-1 Subj: Animals – rabbits. Concepts – color. Eggs. Holidays – Easter.

Sneed, Brad. *Deputy Harvey and the ant cow caper* ill. by author. Penguin, 2005. ISBN 978-0-8037-3023-6 Subj: Careers – sheriffs. Crime. Insects – ants. Mystery stories. U.S. history – frontier & pioneer life.

Picture a letter ill. by author. Fogelman, 2002. ISBN 978-0-8037-2613-0 Subj: ABC books. Wordless.

Sneed, Dani. *My even day* (Fisher, Doris)

One odd day (Fisher, Doris)

Snell, Gordon. *'Twas the day after Christmas* ill. by Sean DeLonas. HarperCollins, 2003. ISBN 978-0-06-028952-2 Subj: Animals – mice. Holidays – Christmas. Humorous stories. Rhyming text.

Twelve days, a Christmas countdown ill. by Kevin O'Malley. HarperCollins, 2002. ISBN 978-0-06-028955-3 Subj: Cumulative tales. Holidays – Christmas. Music. Songs.

Snicket, Lemony. *The composer is dead* ill. by Carson Ellis. HarperCollins, 2009. ISBN 978-0-06-123627-3 Subj: Musical instruments – orchestras. Mystery stories.

The dark ill. by Jon Klassen. Little, Brown, 2013. ISBN 978-0-316-18748-0 Subj: Emotions – fear. Light, lights. Night.

13 words ill. by Maira Kalman. HarperCollins, 2010. ISBN 978-0-06-166465-6 Subj: Animals – dogs. Birds. Language.

Snyder, Betsy E. *I haiku you* ill. by author. Random House, 2012. ISBN 978-0-375-86750-7 Subj: Emotions – love. Poetry.

Sweet dreams lullaby ill. by author. Random House, 2010. ISBN 978-0-375-85852-9 Subj: Bedtime. Lullabies. Nature. Rhyming text.

Snyder, Carol. *We're painting* ill. by Lisa Jahn-Clough. HarperCollins, 2002. ISBN 978-0-694-01445-3 Subj: Activities – painting. Concepts – color. Concepts – shape.

Snyder, Dianne. *The boy of the three-year nap* ill. by Allen Say. Houghton, 1988. ISBN 978-0-395-44090-2 Subj: Behavior – trickery. Caldecott award honor books. Character traits – laziness. Folk & fairy tales.

Snyder, Laurel. *Baxter, the pig who wanted to be kosher* ill. by David Goldin. Tricycle, 2010. ISBN 978-1-58246-315-5 Subj: Animals – pigs. Jewish culture.

Good night, laila tov ill. by Jui Ishida. Random House, 2012. ISBN 978-0-375-96868-9 Subj: Camps, camping. Family life. Jewish culture. Rhyming text.

So, Meilo. *Gobble, gobble, slip, slop* ill. by author. Knopf, 2004. ISBN 978-0-375-92504-7 Subj: Animals – cats. Behavior – greed. Folk & fairy tales. Foreign lands – India.

So, Sungwan. *Shanyi goes to China* ill. with photos. Frances Lincoln, 2006. ISBN 978-1-84507-470-8 Subj: Foreign lands – China.

Sobat, Vera. *Little Bear and the big fight* (Langreuter, Jutta)

Little Bear brushes his teeth (Langreuter, Jutta)

Little Bear goes to kindergarten (Langreuter, Jutta)

Sobel, June. *The goodnight train* ill. by Laura Huliska-Beith. Harcourt, 2006. ISBN 978-0-15-205436-6 Subj: Bedtime. Rhyming text. Trains.

Shiver me letters: a pirate ABC ill. by Henry Cole. Harcourt, 2006. ISBN 978-0-15-216732-5 Subj: ABC books. Pirates. Rhyming text.

Sobol, Richard. *Adelina's whales* photos by author. Dutton, 2003. ISBN 978-0-525-47110-3 Subj: Animals – whales. Family life. Foreign lands – Mexico.

Sockabasin, Allen. *Thanks to the animals* ill. by Rebekah Raye. Tilbury, 2005. ISBN 978-0-88448-270-3 Subj: Animals. Babies. Behavior – lost. Family life – fathers. Indians of North America – Passamaquoddy.

Sokol, Edward. *Meet Stinky Magee* ill. by author. HarperCollins, 2000. ISBN 978-0-688-17416-3 Subj: Food. Magic. Toys – rocking horses.

Solheim, James. *Born yesterday: the diary of a young journalist* ill. by Simon James. Penguin, 2010. ISBN 978-0-399-25155-9 Subj: Activities – writing. Babies. Humorous stories.

Santa's secrets revealed ill. by Barry Gott. Carolrhoda, 2004. ISBN 978-1-57505-600-5 Subj: Holidays – Christmas. Santa Claus.

Soltis, Sue. *Nothing like a puffin* ill. by Bob Kolar. Candlewick, 2011. ISBN 978-0-7636-3617-3 Subj: Birds – puffins.

Soman, David. *The amazing adventures of Bumblebee Boy* by David Soman and Jacky Davis ill. by David Soman. Penguin, 2011. ISBN 978-0-8037-3418-0 Subj: Activities – playing. Family life – brothers. Imagination.

Ladybug Girl by David Soman and Jacky Davis ill. by David Soman. Dial, 2008. ISBN 978-0-8037-3195-0 Subj: Activities – playing. Imagination.

Ladybug Girl and Bingo by David Soman and Jacky Davis ill. by David Soman. Dial, 2012. ISBN 978-0-8037-3582-8 Subj: Animals – dogs. Behavior – lost & found possessions. Camps, camping. Imagination.

Ladybug Girl and Bumblebee Boy by David Soman and Jacky Davis ill. by David Soman. Dial, 2009. ISBN 978-0-8037-3339-8 Subj: Activities – playing. Friendship. Imagination.

Ladybug Girl and the big snow by David Soman and Jacky Davis ill. by David Soman. Dial, 2013. ISBN 978-0-8037-3583-5 Subj: Activities – playing. Imagination. Weather – snow.

Ladybug Girl and the Bug Squad by David Soman and Jacky Davis ill. by David Soman. Penguin, 2011. ISBN 978-0-8037-3419-7 Subj: Activities – playing. Character traits – cooperation. Friendship. Imagination.

Ladybug Girl at the beach by David Soman and Jacky Davis ill. by David Soman. Penguin, 2010. ISBN 978-0-8037-3416-6 Subj: Emotions – fear. Sea & seashore – beaches.

Somary, Wolfgang. *Night and the candlemaker* ill. by Simon Bartram. Barefoot, 2000. ISBN 978-1-84148-137-1 Subj: Night. Sleep.

Somers, Kevin. *Meaner than meanest* ill. by Diana Cain Bluthenthal. Hyperion, 2001. ISBN 978-0-7868-2498-4 Subj: Character traits – meanness. Magic. Witches.

Sones, Sonya. *Violet and Winston* by Sonya Sones and Bennett Tramer ill. by Chris Raschka. Dial, 2009. ISBN 978-0-8037-3234-6 Subj: Birds – ducks. Birds – swans. Friendship.

Sorel, Edward. *The Saturday kid* in collab. with Cheryl Carlesimo; ill. by author. McElderry, 1999. ISBN 978-0-689-82399-2 Subj: Behavior – bullying, teasing. Music. Musical instruments – violins.

Sorensen, Henri. *New Hope* ill. by author. Lothrop, 1995. ISBN 978-0-688-13926-1 Subj: Activities – traveling. Family life. U.S. history – frontier & pioneer life.

Soros, Barbara. *Tenzin's deer* ill. by Danuta Maya. Barefoot, 2003. ISBN 978-1-84148-811-0 Subj: Animals – deer. Character traits – kindness to animals. Foreign lands – Tibet. Illness.

Soto, Gary. *Chato and the party animals* ill. by Susan Guevara. Putnam, 2000. ISBN 978-0-399-23159-9 Subj: Animals – cats. Birthdays. Parties.

Chato goes cruisin' ill. by Susan Guevara. Penguin, 2005. ISBN 978-0-399-23974-8 Subj: Animals – cats. Animals – dogs. Boats, ships. Ethnic groups in the U.S. – Mexican Americans. Foreign languages. Illness.

Chato's kitchen ill. by Susan Guevara. Putnam, 1995. ISBN 978-0-399-22658-8 Subj: Animals – cats. Animals – dogs. Animals – mice. Cities, towns. Food. Foreign languages.

Lucky Luis ill. by Rhode Montijo. Putnam, 2012. ISBN 978-0-399-24504-6 Subj: Animals – rabbits. Character traits – luck. Ethnic groups in the U.S. – Mexican Americans. Sports – baseball. Superstition.

My little car / Mi carrito ill. by Pamela Paparone. Penguin, 2006. ISBN 978-0-399-23220-6 Subj: Automobiles. Ethnic groups in the U.S. – Mexican Americans. Family life – grandfathers. Foreign languages. Toys.

The old man and his door ill. by Joe Cepeda. Putnam, 1996. ISBN 978-0-399-22700-4 Subj: Character traits – helpfulness. Ethnic groups in the U.S. – Mexican Americans. Food. Foreign lands. Parties. Senses – hearing.

Snapshots from the wedding ill. by Stephanie Garcia. Putnam, 1997. ISBN 978-0-399-22808-7 Subj:

Ethnic groups in the U.S. – Mexican Americans. Family life. Weddings.

Too many tamales ill. by Ed Martinez. Putnam, 1993. ISBN 978-0-399-22146-0 Subj: Ethnic groups in the U.S. – Mexican Americans. Food. Foreign languages. Holidays – Christmas.

Souders, Taryn. *Whole-y cow! fractions are fun* ill. by Tatjana Mai-Wyss. Sleeping Bear, 2010. ISBN 978-1-58536-460-2 Subj: Animals – bulls, cows. Counting, numbers. Rhyming text.

Souhami, Jessica. *Foxy!* ill. by author. Frances Lincoln, 2013. ISBN 978-1-84780-218-7 Subj: Animals. Animals – foxes. Behavior – trickery. Folk & fairy tales.

The leopard's drum: an Asante tale from West Africa ill. by author. Little, 1995. ISBN 978-0-316-80466-0 Subj: Animals – leopards. Folk & fairy tales. Foreign lands – Africa.

The little, little house ill. by author. Frances Lincoln, 2006. ISBN 978-1-84507-108-0 Subj: Folk & fairy tales. Humorous stories. Problem solving.

Mrs. McCool and the giant Cuhullin ill. by author. Holt, 2002. ISBN 978-0-8050-6852-8 Subj: Behavior – fighting, arguing. Character traits – cleverness. Folk & fairy tales. Foreign lands – Ireland. Giants.

No dinner! the story of the old woman and the pumpkin ill. by author. Marshall Cavendish, 2000. ISBN 978-0-7614-5059-7 Subj: Animals. Animals – wolves. Behavior – trickery. Folk & fairy tales. Foreign lands – India.

Rama and the demon king ill. by reteller. DK, 1997. ISBN 978-0-7894-2450-1 Subj: Animals – monkeys. Folk & fairy tales. Foreign lands – India. Royalty – kings. Royalty – princes.

Sausages ill. by author. Frances Lincoln, 2006. ISBN 978-1-84507-397-8 Subj: Behavior – wishing. Character traits – foolishness. Folk & fairy tales. Food.

Soule, Jean Conder. *Never tease a weasel* ill. by George Booth. Random House, 2007. ISBN 978-0-375-83420-2 Subj: Animals. Behavior – bullying, teasing. Character traits – kindness to animals. Humorous stories. Rhyming text.

Southwell, Jandelyn. *The little country town* ill. by Kay Chorao. Holt, 2000. ISBN 978-0-8050-5711-9 Subj: Country. Night. Noise, sounds. Rhyming text. Senses – smell.

Spafford, Suzy. *Witzy's colors* ill. by author. Lyrick, 2001. ISBN 978-1-58668-055-8 Subj: Animals. Concepts – color. Format, unusual – toy & movable books.

Spalding, Andrea. *It's raining, it's pouring* ill. by Leslie Elizabeth Watts. Orca, 2001. ISBN 978-1-55143-186-4 Subj: Giants. Illness. Imagination. Weather – rain.

Solomon's tree ill. by Janet Wilson. Mask & Tsimshian designs by Victor Reece. Orca, 2002. ISBN 978-1-55143-217-5 Subj: Activities – storytelling. Indians of North America – Tsimshian. Masks. Trees.

Spang, Günter. *The ox and the Donkey* ill. by Loek Koopmans. NorthSouth, 2001. ISBN 978-0-7358-1516-2 Subj: Animals – donkeys. Animals – oxen. Holidays – Christmas. Religion – Nativity.

Spanyol, Jessica. *Carlo likes counting* ill. by author. Candlewick, 2002. ISBN 978-0-7636-1774-5 Subj: Animals – giraffes. Counting, numbers.

Speed, Toby. *Brave potatoes* ill. by Barry Root. Putnam, 2000. ISBN 978-0-399-23158-2 Subj: Activities – baking, cooking. Fairs, festivals. Plants.

Two cool cows ill. by Barry Root. Putnam, 1995. ISBN 978-0-399-22647-2 Subj: Animals – bulls, cows. Moon. Rhyming text.

Speirs, John. *The little boy's Christmas gift* ill. by author. Abrams, 2001. ISBN 978-0-8109-4399-5 Subj: Gifts. Holidays – Christmas. Religion – Nativity. Trees.

Spelman, Cornelia Maude. *Mama and Daddy Bear's divorce* ill. by Kathy Parkinson. Whitman, 1998. ISBN 978-0-8075-5221-6 Subj: Animals – bears. Divorce. Emotions. Emotions – love.

When I care about others ill. by Kathy Parkinson. Whitman, 2002. ISBN 978-0-8075-8889-5 Subj: Animals – bears. Behavior – sharing. Character traits – kindness. Emotions.

When I feel angry ill. by Nancy Cote. Whitman, 2000. ISBN 978-0-8075-8888-8 Subj: Animals – rabbits. Behavior. Emotions – anger.

When I feel sad ill. by Kathy Parkinson. Whitman, 2002. ISBN 978-0-8075-8891-8 Subj: Animals – guinea pigs. Emotions – sadness.

When I feel scared ill. by Kathy Parkinson. Whitman, 2002. ISBN 978-0-8075-8890-1 Subj: Animals – bears. Emotions – fear.

When I feel worried ill. by Kathy Parkinson. Whitman, 2013. ISBN 978-0-8075-8893-2 Subj: Animals – guinea pigs. Behavior – worrying.

When I miss you ill. by Kathy Parkinson. Whitman, 2004. ISBN 978-0-8075-8910-6 Subj: Animals – guinea pigs. Emotions – loneliness. Family life – parents.

Your body belongs to you ill. by Teri Weidner. Whitman, 1997. ISBN 978-0-8075-9474-2 Subj: Child abuse. Health & fitness. Safety.

Spence, Robert, III. *Clickety clack* ill. by Margaret Spengler. Viking, 1999. ISBN 978-0-670-87946-5 Subj: Animals. Noise, sounds. Rhyming text. Trains.

Sper, Emily. *Hanukkah: a counting book in English, Hebrew, and Yiddish* ill. by author. Scholastic, 2001. ISBN 978-0-439-28291-8 Subj: Counting, numbers. Foreign languages. Holidays – Hanukkah. Jewish culture. Religion.

The Passover seder ill. by author. Scholastic, 2003. ISBN 978-0-439-44312-8 Subj: Format, unusual – toy & movable books. Holidays – Passover. Jewish culture. Language. Religion.

Sperring, Mark. *The fairytale cake* ill. by Jonathan Langley. Scholastic, 2005. ISBN 978-0-439-68329-6 Subj: Birthdays. Books, reading. Food. Rhyming text.

Mermaid dreams ill. by The Pope Twins. Scholastic, 2006. ISBN 978-0-439-79610-1 Subj: Bedtime. Mythical creatures – mermaids, mermen. Sea & seashore.

The shape of my heart ill. by Alys Paterson. Bloomsbury, 2013. ISBN 978-1-59990-962-2 Subj: Concepts – shape. Family life – mothers. Rhyming text.

The sunflower sword ill. by Miriam Latimer. Andersen, 2011. ISBN 978-0-7613-7486-2 Subj: Dragons. Friendship. Knights.

Spetter, Jung-Hee. *Lily and Trooper's fall* ill. by author. Front Street, 1998. ISBN 978-1-886910-38-6 Subj: Activities – playing. Animals – dogs. Seasons – fall.

Lily and Trooper's spring ill. by author. Front Street, 1998. ISBN 978-1-886910-36-2 Subj: Activities – picnicking. Activities – playing. Animals – dogs. Seasons – spring.

Lily and Trooper's summer ill. by author. Front Street, 1998. ISBN 978-1-886910-37-9 Subj: Activities – playing. Animals – dogs. Seasons – summer.

Lily and Trooper's winter ill. by author. Front Street, 1998. ISBN 978-1-886910-39-3 Subj: Activities. Animals – dogs. Seasons – winter. Weather – rain. Weather – snow.

Spier, Peter. *Bored — nothing to do!* ill. by author. Doubleday, 1978. ISBN 978-0-385-13178-0 Subj: Airplanes, airports. Behavior – boredom. Humorous stories.

Gobble, growl, grunt ill. by author. Doubleday, 1971. ISBN 978-0-385-24094-9 Subj: Animals. Noise, sounds. Participation.

Noah's ark ill. by author. Doubleday, 1977. ISBN 978-0-385-12730-1 Subj: Animals. Boats, ships. Caldecott award books. Religion – Noah. Rhyming text. Weather – floods. Weather – rain. Wordless.

Oh, were they ever happy! ill. by author. Doubleday, 1978. ISBN 978-0-385-13176-6 Subj: Activities – painting. Concepts – color. Humorous stories.

People ill. by author. Doubleday, 1980. ISBN 978-0-385-13182-7 Subj: World.

Peter Spier's Christmas! ill. by author. Doubleday, 1983. ISBN 978-0-385-13183-4 Subj: Holidays – Christmas.

Peter Spier's circus! ill. by author. Doubleday, 1992. ISBN 978-0-385-41970-3 Subj: Circus.

Peter Spier's rain ill. by author. Doubleday, 1982. ISBN 978-0-385-15485-7 Subj: Weather – rain. Wordless.

We the people: the Constitution of the United States of America ill. by author. Doubleday, 1987. ISBN 978-0-385-23789-5 Subj: U.S. history.

Spilsbury, Louise. *Carrots* ill. with photos. Heinemann, 2002. ISBN 978-1-58810-616-2 Subj: Activities – baking, cooking. Food. Plants.

Oranges ill. with photos. Heinemann, 2002. ISBN 978-1-58810-618-6 Subj: Activities – baking, cooking. Food. Trees.

Peas ill. with photos. Heinemann, 2002. ISBN 978-1-58810-620-9 Subj: Activities – baking, cooking. Food. Plants.

Spinelli, Eileen. *The best story* ill. by Anne Wilsdorf. Dial, 2008. ISBN 978-0-8037-3055-7 Subj: Activities – writing. Contests. Libraries.

A big boy now ill. by Megan Lloyd. HarperCollins, 2012. ISBN 978-0-06-008673-2 Subj: Animals – rabbits. Behavior – growing up. Family life – fathers. Sports – bicycling.

Buzz ill. by Vincent Nguyen. Simon & Schuster, 2010. ISBN 978-1-4169-4925-1 Subj: Activities – flying. Insects – bees.

Callie Cat, ice skater ill. by Anne Kennedy. Whitman, 2007. ISBN 978-0-8075-1042-1 Subj: Animals – cats. Contests. Sports – ice skating.

City angel ill. by Kyrsten Brooker. Penguin, 2005. ISBN 978-0-8037-2821-9 Subj: Angels. Cities, towns. Rhyming text.

Cold snap ill. by Marjorie Priceman. Knopf, 2012. ISBN 978-0-375-85700-3 Subj: Communities, neighborhoods. Seasons – winter. Weather – cold. Weather – snow.

Coming through the blizzard ill. by Jenny Tylden-Wright. Simon & Schuster, 1999. ISBN 978-0-689-81490-7 Subj: Holidays – Christmas. Weather – blizzards.

Do you have a cat? ill. by Geraldo Valério. Eerdmans, 2010. ISBN 978-0-8028-5351-6 Subj: Animals – cats. Rhyming text.

Do you have a dog? ill. by Geraldo Valério. Eerdmans, 2011. ISBN 978-0-8028-5387-5 Subj: Animals – dogs. Rhyming text.

Heat wave ill. by Betsy Lewin. Harcourt, 2007. ISBN 978-0-15-216779-0 Subj: Days of the week, months of the year. Weather.

Here comes the year ill. by Keiko Narahashi. Holt, 2002. ISBN 978-0-8050-6685-2 Subj: Days of the week, months of the year. Rhyming text.

Hero cat ill. by Jo Ellen McAllister Stammen. Marshall Cavendish, 2006. ISBN 978-0-7614-5223-2 Subj: Animals – cats. Character traits – bravery. Fire.

Hug a bug ill. by Dan Andreasen. HarperCollins, 2008. ISBN 978-0-06-051832-5 Subj: Hugging. Rhyming text.

I know it's autumn ill. by Nancy Hayashi. HarperCollins, 2004. ISBN 978-0-06-029423-6 Subj: Rhyming text. Seasons – fall.

In my new yellow shirt ill. by Hideko Takahashi. Holt, 2001. ISBN 978-0-8050-6242-7 Subj: Birthdays. Clothing – shirts. Concepts – color. Gifts. Imagination.

Jonah's whale ill. by Giuliano Ferri. Eerdmans, 2012. ISBN 978-0-8028-5382-0 Subj: Animals – whales. Religion – Jonah.

Miss Fox's class earns a field trip ill. by Anne Kennedy. Whitman, 2010. ISBN 978-0-8075-5169-1 Subj: Animals – foxes. Counting, numbers. School – field trips.

Miss Fox's class gets it wrong ill. by Anne Kennedy. Whitman, 2012. ISBN 978-0-8075-5165-3 Subj: Animals – foxes. Behavior – gossip. Careers – teachers. School.

Miss Fox's class goes green ill. by Anne Kennedy. Whitman, 2009. ISBN 978-0-8075-5166-0 Subj: Animals – foxes. Ecology. School.

Miss Fox's class shapes up ill. by Anne Kennedy. Whitman, 2011. ISBN 978-0-8075-5171-4 Subj: Animals – foxes. Careers – teachers. Health & fitness – exercise. School.

Night shift daddy ill. by Melissa Iwai. Hyperion, 2000. ISBN 978-0-7868-2424-3 Subj: Activities – working. Family life – fathers. Night.

Now it is summer ill. by Mary Newell DePalma. Eerdmans, 2011. ISBN 978-0-8028-5340-0 Subj: Animals – mice. Family life. Seasons – fall. Seasons – summer.

Peace Week in Miss Fox's class ill. by Anne Kennedy. Whitman, 2009. ISBN 978-0-8075-6379-3 Subj: Animals. Animals – foxes. Behavior – seeking better things. School.

The perfect Christmas ill. by JoAnn Adinolfi. Holt, 2011. ISBN 978-0-8050-9702-4 Subj: Family life. Holidays – Christmas. Rhyming text.

Polar bear, arctic hare: poems of the frozen North ill. by Eugenie Fernandes. Boyds Mills, 2007. ISBN 978-1-59078-344-3 Subj: Animals. Foreign lands – Arctic. Poetry.

Princess Pig ill. by Tim Bowers. Knopf, 2009. ISBN 978-0-375-84571-0 Subj: Animals – pigs. Farms. Royalty – princesses. Self-concept.

Rise the moon ill. by Raúl Colón. Dial, 2003. ISBN 978-0-8037-2601-7 Subj: Moon. Night. Rhyming text.

A safe place called home ill. by Christy Hale. Marshall Cavendish, 2001. ISBN 978-0-7614-5085-6 Subj: Emotions – fear. Homes, houses. Rhyming text. Safety.

Silly Tilly ill. by David Slonim. Marshall Cavendish, 2009. ISBN 978-0-7614-5525-7 Subj: Animals. Birds – geese. Character traits – foolishness. Farms. Rhyming text.

Six hogs on a scooter ill. by Scott Nash. Orchard, 2000. ISBN 978-0-531-33212-2 Subj: Animals – pigs. Family life. Humorous stories. Theater. Transportation.

Somebody loves you, Mr. Hatch ill. by Paul Yalowitz. Aladdin, 1994. ISBN 978-0-689-71872-4 Subj: Behavior – mistakes. Careers – postal workers. Communities, neighborhoods. Emotions – loneliness. Friendship. Holidays – Valentine's Day.

Someday ill. by Rosie Winstead. Penguin, 2007. ISBN 978-0-8037-2941-4 Subj: Imagination.

Sophie's masterpiece ill. by Jane Dyer. Simon & Schuster, 1998. ISBN 978-0-689-80112-9 Subj: Art. Character traits – perseverance. Homes, houses. Spiders.

Summerbath, winterbath ill. by Elsa Warnick. Eerdmans, 2001. ISBN 978-0-8028-5179-6 Subj: Activities – bathing. Family life. Poetry. Seasons.

Thanksgiving at the Tappletons' ill. by Maryann Cocca-Leffler. Addison-Wesley, 1982. ISBN 978-0-201-15892-2 Subj: Animals – wolves. Behavior – sharing. Family life. Holidays – Thanksgiving. Humorous stories.

Together at Christmas ill. by Bin Lee. Whitman, 2012. ISBN 978-0-8075-8010-3 Subj: Animals – mice. Counting, numbers. Holidays – Christmas. Rhyming text. Weather – cold.

Wanda's monster ill. by Nancy Hayashi. Whitman, 2002. ISBN 978-0-8075-8656-3 Subj: Emotions – fear. Family life – grandmothers. Monsters. Problem solving.

What do angels wear? ill. by Emily Arnold McCully. HarperCollins, 2003. ISBN 978-0-06-028887-7 Subj: Activities. Angels. Rhyming text.

When Mama comes home tonight ill. by Jane Dyer. Simon & Schuster, 1998. ISBN 978-0-689-81065-7 Subj: Bedtime. Family life – mothers. Rhyming text.

When no one is watching ill. by David Johnson. Eerdmans, 2013. ISBN 978-0-8028-5303-5 Subj: Character traits – shyness. Friendship. Rhyming text. Self-concept.

When Papa comes home tonight ill. by David McPhail. Simon & Schuster, 2009. ISBN 978-1-4169-1028-2 Subj: Bedtime. Family life – fathers. Rhyming text.

When you are happy ill. by Geraldo Valério. Simon & Schuster, 2006. ISBN 978-0-689-86251-9 Subj: Emotions. Family life.

Spinelli, Jerry. *I can be anything!* ill. by Jimmy Liao. Little, Brown, 2010. ISBN 978-0-316-16226-5 Subj: Careers. Rhyming text.

My daddy and me ill. by Seymour Chwast. Knopf, 2003. ISBN 978-0-375-90606-0 Subj: Activities. Family life – fathers. Family life – sons.

Spinner, Stephanie. *It's a miracle* ill. by Jill McElmurry. Atheneum, 2003. ISBN 978-0-689-84493-5 Subj: Family life – grandmothers. Holidays – Hanukkah. Jewish culture.

Spires, Ashley. *Larf* ill. by author. Kids Can, 2012. ISBN 978-1-55453-701-3 Subj: Character traits – being different. Friendship. Mythical creatures.

Small Saul ill. by author. Kids Can, 2011. ISBN 978-1-55453-503-3 Subj: Character traits – being different. Character traits – smallness. Pirates.

Spires, Elizabeth. *The big meow* ill. by Cynthia Jabar. Candlewick, 2002. ISBN 978-0-7636-0679-4 Subj: Animals – cats. Animals – dogs. Noise, sounds.

Spirin, Gennady. *A apple pie* ill. by author. Penguin, 2005. ISBN 978-0-399-23981-6 Subj: ABC books. Nursery rhymes.

Martha ill. by author. Penguin, 2005. ISBN 978-0-399-23980-9 Subj: Birds – crows. Foreign lands – Russia.

Philipok retold by Ann Keay Beneduce; ill. by author. Philomel, 2000. ISBN 978-0-399-23482-8 Subj: Character traits – ambition. Foreign lands – Russia. School.

The twelve days of Christmas (The twelve days of Christmas. English folk song)

We three kings ill. by author. Simon & Schuster, 2007. ISBN 978-0-689-82114-1 Subj: Holidays – Christmas. Religion – Nativity. Songs.

Spohn, Kate. *By word of mouse* ill. by author. Bloomsbury, 2004. ISBN 978-1-58234-867-4 Subj: Animals – mice. Careers – artists. Family life – sisters.

Snow play ill. by author. Scholastic, 2001. ISBN 978-0-439-26713-7 Subj: Animals – bears. Family life – grandmothers. Format, unusual – board books. Rhyming text. Weather – snow.

The wet dry book ill. by author. Random House, 2002. ISBN 978-0-375-82186-8 Subj: Concepts. Rhyming text.

Spradlin, Michael P. *Baseball from A to Z* ill. by Macky Pamintuan. HarperCollins, 2010. ISBN 978-0-06-124081-2 Subj: ABC books. Sports – baseball.

Off like the wind! the first ride of the Pony Express ill. by Layne Johnson. Walker, 2010. ISBN 978-0-8027-9652-3 Subj: Careers – postal workers. U.S. history – frontier & pioneer life.

Springett, Martin. *Kate and Pippin* ill. by Isobel Springett. Holt, 2012. ISBN 978-0-8050-9487-9 Subj: Animals – deer. Animals – dogs.

Springman, I. C. *More* ill. by Brian Lies. Houghton Mifflin, 2012. ISBN 978-0-547-61083-2 Subj: Animals – mice. Behavior – collecting things. Birds – magpies.

Springstubb, Tricia. *Phoebe and Digger* ill. by Jeff Newman. Candlewick, 2013. ISBN 978-0-7636-5281-4 Subj: Babies. Behavior – bullying, teasing. Behavior – lost & found possessions. Family life – new sibling. Parks. Toys.

Sproule, Gail. *Singing the dark* ill. by Sheena Lott. Fitzhenry & Whiteside, 2001. ISBN 978-1-55041-648-0 Subj: Activities – singing. Bedtime. Night.

Spurling, Margaret. *Bilby moon* ill. by Danny Snell. Kane/Miller, 2001. ISBN 978-1-929132-06-5 Subj: Animals. Animals – mice. Desert. Foreign lands – Australia. Moon.

Spurr, Elizabeth. *In the garden* ill. by Manelle Oliphant. Peachtree, 2012. ISBN 978-1-56145-581-2 Subj: Format, unusual – board books. Gardens, gardening. Rhyming text.

A pig named Perrier ill. by Martin Matje. Hyperion, 2002. ISBN 978-0-7868-0302-6 Subj: Animals – pigs. Pets.

Pumpkin hill ill. by Whitney Martin. Holiday House, 2006. ISBN 978-0-8234-1869-5 Subj: Holidays – Halloween.

Two bears beneath the stairs ill. by Nadine Bernard Westcott. Simon & Schuster, 2002. ISBN 978-0-689-84759-2 Subj: Animals. Counting, numbers. Format, unusual – toy & movable books. Rhyming text.

Srinivasan, Divya. *Little Owl's night* ill. by author. Penguin, 2011. ISBN 978-0-670-01295-4 Subj: Animals. Birds – owls. Night.

Octopus alone ill. by author. Viking, 2013. ISBN 978-0-670-78515-5 Subj: Character traits – shyness. Friendship. Octopuses.

Staake, Bob. *Bluebird* ill. by author. Random House, 2013. ISBN 978-0-375-87037-8 Subj: Behavior – bullying, teasing. Birds – bluebirds. Death. Emotions – loneliness. Friendship. Wordless.

The donut chef ill. by author. Random House, 2008. ISBN 978-0-375-84403-4 Subj: Activities – baking, cooking. Careers – chefs, cooks. Rhyming text.

The first pup: the real story of how Bo got to the White House ill. by author. Feiwel & Friends, 2010. ISBN 978-0-312-61346-4 Subj: Animals – dogs. Pets.

Look! A book! ill. by author. Little, Brown, 2011. ISBN 978-0-316-11862-0 Subj: Books, reading. Picture puzzles. Rhyming text.

Look! Another book! ill. by author. Little, Brown, 2012. ISBN 978-0-316-20459-0 Subj: Books, reading. Picture puzzles. Rhyming text.

My little ABC book ill. by author. Simon & Schuster, 1998. ISBN 978-0-689-81659-8 Subj: ABC books. Format, unusual – board books.

My little color book ill. by author. Simon & Schuster, 2001. ISBN 978-0-689-83486-8 Subj: Concepts – color. Format, unusual – board books.

My little 1 2 3 book ill. by author. Simon & Schuster, 1998. ISBN 978-0-689-81660-4 Subj: Counting, numbers. Format, unusual – board books.

My little opposites book ill. by author. Simon & Schuster, 2001. ISBN 978-0-689-83487-5 Subj: Animals. Concepts – opposites. Format, unusual – board books.

Stadler, Alexander. *Beverly Billingsly borrows a book* ill. by author. Harcourt, 2000. ISBN 978-0-15-202510-6 Subj: Behavior – worrying. Books, reading. Careers – librarians. Libraries. Nightmares.

Beverly Billingsly takes a bow ill. by author. Harcourt, 2003. ISBN 978-0-15-216816-2 Subj: Music. School. Theater.

Beverly Billingsly takes the cake ill. by author. Harcourt, 2005. ISBN 978-0-15-205357-4 Subj: Activities – baking, cooking. Food. Imagination. Parties.

Stadler, John. *Catilda* ill. by author. Atheneum, 2003. ISBN 978-0-689-84728-8 Subj: Animals – cats. Behavior – lost & found possessions. Toys – bears.

The cats of Mrs. Calamari ill. by author. Orchard, 1997. ISBN 978-0-531-33020-3 Subj: Animals – cats. Animals – dogs. Cities, towns. Glasses. Weddings.

Take me out to the ball game: a pop-up book ill. by author. Simon & Schuster, 2005. ISBN 978-0-689-85917-5 Subj: Format, unusual – toy & movable books. Songs. Sports – baseball.

What's so scary? ill. by author. Orchard, 2001. ISBN 978-0-531-33301-3 Subj: Animals. Books, reading. Careers – artists.

Wilson and Miss Lovely: a back-to-school mystery ill. by author. Random House, 2009. ISBN 978-0-375-84478-2 Subj: Animals – rabbits. Careers – teachers. Monsters. School.

Stafford, Liliana. *Just dragon* ill. by Margaret Power. Cygnet Books, 2000. ISBN 978-1-876268-02-2 Subj: Boats, ships. Death. Emotions – grief. Family life – grandfathers. Kites.

The snow bear ill. by Lambert Davis. Scholastic, 2000. ISBN 978-0-439-26977-3 Subj: Animals – polar bears. Friendship. Indians of North America – Inuit. Weather – snow.

Staines, Bill. *All God's critters* ill. by Kadir Nelson. Simon & Schuster, 2009. ISBN 978-0-689-86959-4 Subj: Animals. Farms. Music. Songs.

Stainton, Sue. *The chocolate cat* ill. by Anne Mortimer. HarperCollins, 2007. ISBN 978-0-06-057245-7 Subj: Animals – cats. Food. Magic.

I love cats ill. by Anne Mortimer. HarperCollins, 2007. ISBN 978-0-06-085154-5 Subj: Animals – cats.

The lighthouse cat ill. by Anne Mortimer. Tegen, 2004. ISBN 978-0-06-009605-2 Subj: Animals – cats. Lighthouses. Weather – storms.

Santa's snow cat ill. by Anne Mortimer. HarperCollins, 2001. ISBN 978-0-06-623828-9 Subj: Animals – cats. Behavior – lost & found possessions. Cities, towns. Holidays – Christmas. Santa Claus.

Stalder, Päivi. *Ernest's first Easter* ill. by Frauke Weldin. NorthSouth, 2010. ISBN 978-0-7358-2241-2 Subj: Animals – rabbits. Eggs. Holidays – Easter.

Stampler, Ann Redisch. *Go home, Mrs. Beekman!* ill. by Marsha Gray Carrington. Dutton, 2008. ISBN 978-0-525-46933-9 Subj: Family life – mothers. Humorous stories. School – first day.

The rooster prince of Breslov ill. by Eugene Yelchin. Clarion, 2010. ISBN 978-0-618-98974-4 Subj: Birds – chickens. Folk & fairy tales. Jewish culture. Royalty – princes.

Shlemazel and the remarkable spoon of Pohost ill. by Jacqueline M. Cohen. Houghton, 2006. ISBN 978-

0-618-36959-1 Subj: Character traits – laziness. Character traits – luck. Folk & fairy tales. Jewish culture.

The wooden sword: A Jewish Folktale from Afghanistan ill. by Carol Liddiment. Whitman, 2012. ISBN 978-0-8075-9201-4 Subj: Careers – shoemakers. Folk & fairy tales. Foreign lands – Afghanistan. Jewish culture.

Stanley, Diane. *The Giant and the beanstalk* ill. by author. HarperCollins, 2004. ISBN 978-0-06-000011-0 Subj: Folk & fairy tales. Giants. Humorous stories. Nursery rhymes.

Goldie and the three bears ill. by author. HarperCollins, 2003. ISBN 978-0-06-000009-7 Subj: Animals – bears. Friendship. Homes, houses. Humorous stories.

Joining the Boston Tea Party ill. by Holly Berry. HarperCollins, 2001. ISBN 978-0-06-027068-1 Subj: Activities – traveling. Time. U.S. history.

Raising Sweetness ill. by G. Brian Karas. Putnam, 1999. ISBN 978-0-399-23225-1 Subj: Books, reading. Letters, cards. Orphans.

Rumpelstiltskin's daughter ill. by author. Morrow, 1997. ISBN 978-0-688-14328-2 Subj: Behavior – greed. Folk & fairy tales. Humorous stories.

Thanksgiving on Plymouth Plantation ill. by Holly Berry. Cotler, 2004. ISBN 978-0-06-027076-6 Subj: Activities – traveling. Holidays – Thanksgiving. Multiple births – twins. U.S. history.

The trouble with wishes ill. by author. HarperCollins, 2007. ISBN 978-0-06-055451-4 Subj: Behavior – wishing. Careers – sculptors.

Stanley, Fay. *The last princess* ill. by Diane Stanley. HarperCollins, 2001. ISBN 978-0-06-029215-7 Subj: Hawaii. Royalty – princes. Royalty – princesses. U.S. history.

Stanley, Malaika Rose. *Baby Ruby bawled* ill. by Ken Wilson-Max. Tamarind, 2011. ISBN 978-1-84-853017-1 Subj: Babies. Bedtime. Emotions. Family life.

Stanley, Mandy. *At the pool* ill. by author. Kingfisher, 2004. ISBN 978-0-7534-5747-4 Subj: Format, unusual – board books. Language. Sports – swimming.

Bloomer, the dog you can play with ill. by author. Orchard, 2001. ISBN 978-0-531-30311-5 Subj: Activities. Animals – dogs. Format, unusual – toy & movable books.

First word book ill. by author. Kingfisher, 2000. ISBN 978-0-7534-5272-1 Subj: Dictionaries. Language.

In the park ill. by author. Kingfisher, 2004. ISBN 978-0-7534-5750-4 Subj: Format, unusual – board books. Language. Pets.

Lettice the dancing rabbit ill. by author. Simon & Schuster, 2002. ISBN 978-0-689-84797-4 Subj: Activities – dancing. Animals – rabbits. Ballet.

Lettice the flower girl ill. by author. Simon & Schuster, 2006. ISBN 978-1-4169-1157-9 Subj: Animals – rabbits. Weddings.

Lettice the flying rabbit ill. by author. Simon & Schuster, 2004. ISBN 978-0-689-86234-2 Subj: Activities – flying. Airplanes, airports. Animals – rabbits.

On the move ill. by author. Kingfisher, 2004. ISBN 978-0-7534-5749-8 Subj: Automobiles. Format, unusual – board books. Transportation.

Perfect pets ill. by author. Kingfisher, 2004. ISBN 978-0-7534-5748-1 Subj: Format, unusual – board books. Pets.

Stanton, Karen. *Papi's gift* ill. by René King Moreno. Boyds Mills, 2007. ISBN 978-1-59078-422-8 Subj: Birthdays. Careers – migrant workers. Family life – fathers. Foreign lands – Latin America. Gifts.

Stanton, Melissa. *My pen pal, Santa* ill. by Jennifer A. Bell. Random House, 2013. ISBN 978-0-375-86992-1 Subj: Activities – writing. Holidays – Christmas. Letters, cards. Santa Claus.

Starishevsky, Jill. *My body belongs to me* ill. by Sara Muller. Safety Star Media, 2009. ISBN 978-0-9821216-0-3 Subj: Child abuse.

Starr, Meg. *Alicia's happy day* ill. by Ying-Hwa Hu and Cornelius Van Wright. Star Bright, 2002. ISBN 978-1-887734-85-1 Subj: Birthdays. Emotions – happiness. Ethnic groups in the U.S. – Hispanic Americans. Parties.

Staub, Leslie. *Bless this house* ill. by author. Harcourt, 2000. ISBN 978-0-15-201984-6 Subj: Animals. Bedtime. Earth. Ecology. Lullabies.

Stauffacher, Sue. *Nothing but trouble: the story of Althea Gibson* ill. by Greg Couch. Knopf, 2007. ISBN 978-0-375-83408-0 Subj: Ethnic groups in the U.S. – African Americans. Sports. U.S. history.

Stead, Philip C. *Bear has a story to tell* ill. by Erin E. Stead. Roaring Brook, 2012. ISBN 978-1-59643-745-6 Subj: Activities – storytelling. Animals. Animals – bears. Character traits – helpfulness. Hibernation. Seasons.

Hello, my name is Ruby ill. by author. Roaring Brook, 2013. ISBN 978-1-59643-809-5 Subj: Birds. Character traits – smallness. Friendship.

A home for Bird ill. by author. Roaring Brook, 2012. ISBN 978-1-59643-711-1 Subj: Birds. Clocks, watches. Frogs & toads.

Jonathan and the big blue boat ill. by author. Roaring Brook, 2011. ISBN 978-1-59643-562-9 Subj:

Activities – traveling. Behavior – lost. Boats, ships. Toys – bears.

A sick day for Amos McGee ill. by Erin E. Stead. Roaring Brook, 2010. ISBN 978-1-59643-402-8 Subj: Animals. Caldecott award books. Illness. Old age. Zoos.

Steedman, Judith. *Windy* (Mitchell, Robin)

Steele, Philip. *A knight's city.* Simon & Schuster, 2008. ISBN 978-1-4169-6124-6 Subj: Format, unusual – toy & movable books. Knights.

Trains: the slide-out, see-through story of world-famous trains and railroads ill. by Sebastian Quigley and Nicholas Forder. Kingfisher, 2010. ISBN 978-0-7534-6465-6 Subj: Format, unusual – toy & movable books. Trains.

Steen, Sandra. *Car wash* by Sandra Steen and Susan Steen ill. by G. Brian Karas. Putnam, 2001. ISBN 978-0-399-23369-2 Subj: Automobiles. Family life – fathers.

Steen, Susan. *Car wash* (Steen, Sandra)

Steffensmeier, Alexander. *Millie and the big rescue* ill. by author. Walker, 2013. ISBN 978-0-8027-3402-0 Subj: Animals – bulls, cows. Behavior – hiding. Farms. Games.

Millie in the snow ill. by author. Walker, 2008. ISBN 978-0-8027-9800-8 Subj: Animals – bulls, cows. Character traits – helpfulness. Holidays – Christmas. Weather – snow.

Millie waits for the mail ill. by author. Walker, 2007. ISBN 978-0-8027-9662-2 Subj: Animals – bulls, cows. Careers – postal workers. Farms. Letters, cards.

Steggall, Susan. *Busy boats* ill. by author. Frances Lincoln, 2011. ISBN 978-1-84780-074-9 Subj: Boats, ships.

The diggers are coming! ill. by author. Frances Lincoln, 2013. ISBN 978-1-84780-288-0 Subj: Careers – construction workers. Machines. Rhyming text. Trucks.

The life of a car ill. by author. Holt, 2008. ISBN 978-0-8050-8747-5 Subj: Automobiles.

Rattle and rap ill. by author. Frances Lincoln, 2009. ISBN 978-1-84507-703-7 Subj: Activities – traveling. Ethnic groups in the U.S. – African Americans. Trains. Transportation.

Red car, red bus ill. by author. Frances Lincoln, 2012. ISBN 978-1-84780-184-5 Subj: Concepts – color. Transportation.

Steig, Jeanne. *Fleas!* ill. by Britt Spencer. Philomel, 2008. ISBN 978-0-399-24756-9 Subj: Activities – trading. Cumulative tales. Humorous stories. Insects – fleas.

Steig, William. *The amazing bone* ill. by author. Farrar, 1976. ISBN 978-0-374-30248-1 Subj: Animals – pigs. Caldecott award honor books. Magic.

Brave Irene ill. by author. Farrar, 1986. ISBN 978-0-374-30947-3 Subj: Character traits – bravery. Character traits – perseverance. Seasons – winter. Weather – snow. Weather – storms.

Caleb and Kate ill. by author. Farrar, 1977. ISBN 978-0-374-31016-5 Subj: Animals – dogs. Magic. Witches.

Doctor De Soto ill. by author. Farrar, 1982. ISBN 978-0-374-31803-1 Subj: Animals – foxes. Animals – mice. Character traits – cleverness.

Doctor De Soto goes to Africa ill. by author. HarperCollins, 1992. ISBN 978-0-06-205003-8 Subj: Animals – elephants. Animals – mice. Careers – dentists. Foreign lands – Africa.

Farmer Palmer's wagon ride ill. by author. Farrar, 1974. ISBN 978-0-374-32288-5 Subj: Animals – donkeys. Animals – pigs. Humorous stories.

Gorky rises ill. by author. Farrar, 1980. ISBN 978-0-374-31752-2 Subj: Frogs & toads. Magic.

Pete's a pizza ill. by author. HarperCollins, 1998. ISBN 978-0-06-205157-8 Subj: Activities – playing. Family life – fathers. Food. Games. Imagination.

Potch and Polly ill. by Jon Agee. Farrar, 2002. ISBN 978-0-374-36090-0 Subj: Emotions – love.

Roland, the minstrel pig ill. by author. Simon & Schuster, 1988, ©1968. ISBN 978-0-671-66841-9 Subj: Animals – foxes. Animals – pigs. Music. Musical instruments – lutes. Royalty.

Solomon the rusty nail ill. by author. Farrar, 1985. ISBN 978-0-374-37131-9 Subj: Animals – cats. Animals – rabbits. Behavior – trickery. Magic.

Spinky sulks ill. by author. Farrar, 1988. ISBN 978-0-374-38321-3 Subj: Character traits – stubbornness. Emotions – happiness. Family life.

Sylvester and the magic pebble ill. by author. Simon & Schuster, 1995, ©1969. ISBN 978-0-689-80417-5 Subj: Animals. Animals – donkeys. Caldecott award books. Family life. Magic.

Tiffky Doofky ill. by author. Farrar, 1987. ISBN 978-0-374-37542-3 Subj: Animals – dogs. Careers – sanitation workers. Emotions – love. Magic.

Toby, what are you? ill. by Teryl Euvremer. HarperCollins, 2001. ISBN 978-0-06-205170-7 Subj: Activities – playing. Animals. Behavior – imitation. Family life. Games.

Toby, where are you? ill. by Teryl Euvremer. HarperCollins, 1997. ISBN 978-0-06-205082-3 Subj: Activities – playing. Animals. Behavior – hiding. Family life.

Toby, who are you? ill. by Teryl Euvremer. Cotler, 2004. ISBN 978-0-06-000706-5 Subj: Activities – picnicking. Animals. Family life – parents. Imagination.

The toy brother ill. by author. HarperCollins, 1996. ISBN 978-0-06-205079-3 Subj: Family life – brothers. Middle Ages. Science. Sibling rivalry.

When everybody wore a hat ill. by author. Cotler, 2003. ISBN 978-0-06-009701-1 Subj: Careers – writers. Careers – illustrators. Clothing – hats. Immigrants. Memories, memory.

Which would you rather be? ill. by Harry Bliss. Colter, 2002. ISBN 978-0-06-029654-4 Subj: Animals – rabbits. Clothing – hats.

Wizzil ill. by author. Farrar, 2000. ISBN 978-0-374-38466-1 Subj: Birds – parakeets, parrots. Careers – farmers. Character traits – kindness. Witches.

Yellow and pink ill. by author. Farrar, 1984. ISBN 978-0-374-38670-2 Subj: Toys – dolls.

The Zabajaba Jungle ill. by author. Farrar, 1987. ISBN 978-0-374-38790-7 Subj: Dreams. Jungle.

Zeke Pippin ill. by author. HarperCollins, 1994. ISBN 978-0-06-205076-2 Subj: Animals – pigs. Behavior – running away. Magic. Music. Musical instruments – harmonicas.

Stein, David Ezra. *Because Amelia smiled* ill. by author. Candlewick, 2012. ISBN 978-0-7636-4169-6 Subj: Character traits – kindness. Emotions – happiness. Foreign lands.

Cowboy Ned and Andy ill. by author. Simon & Schuster, 2006. ISBN 978-1-4169-0041-2 Subj: Animals – horses, ponies. Cowboys, cowgirls. Friendship. U.S. history – frontier & pioneer life.

Dinosaur kisses ill. by author. Candlewick, 2013. ISBN 978-0-7636-6104-5 Subj: Dinosaurs. Kissing.

Interrupting chicken ill. by author. Candlewick, 2010. ISBN 978-0-7636-4168-9 Subj: Bedtime. Birds – chickens. Caldecott award honor books. Humorous stories.

Leaves ill. by author. Penguin, 2007. ISBN 978-0-399-24636-4 Subj: Animals – bears. Hibernation. Seasons. Trees.

Love, Mouserella ill. by author. Penguin, 2011. ISBN 978-0-399-25410-9 Subj: Activities – writing. Animals – mice. Family life – grandmothers. Letters, cards.

Monster hug! ill. by author. Penguin, 2007. ISBN 978-0-399-24637-1 Subj: Activities – playing. Hugging. Monsters.

Ned's new friend ill. by author. Simon & Schuster, 2007. ISBN 978-1-4169-2490-6 Subj: Animals – horses, ponies. Cowboys, cowgirls. Emotions – envy, jealousy. Friendship. U.S. history – frontier & pioneer life.

The nice book ill. by author. Putnam, 2008. ISBN 978-0-399-25050-7 Subj: Animals. Etiquette.

Ol' Mama Squirrel ill. by author. Penguin/Nancy Paulsen, 2013. ISBN 978-0-399-25672-1 Subj: Animals – bears. Animals – squirrels. Character traits – assertiveness.

Pouch! ill. by author. Putnam, 2009. ISBN 978-0-399-25051-4 Subj: Animals – kangaroos. Behavior – growing up. Self-concept.

Stein, Eric. *White water* (Bandy, Michael S.)

Stein, Janet. *This little bunny can bake* ill. by author. Random House, 2009. ISBN 978-0-375-84313-6 Subj: Animals – rabbits. Behavior – messy. Careers – chefs, cooks. School.

Stein, Mathilde. *Brave Ben* ill. by Mies van Hout. Boyds Mills, 2006. ISBN 978-1-932425-64-2 Subj: Character traits – bravery. Emotions – fear.

The child cruncher ill. by Mies van Hout. Boyds Mills, 2008. ISBN 978-1-59078-635-2 Subj: Family life. Imagination. Monsters.

Mine! ill. by Mies van Hout. Boyds Mills, 2007. ISBN 978-1-59078-506-5 Subj: Behavior – sharing. Character traits – selfishness. Ghosts.

Monstersong ill. by Gerdien van der Linden. Boyds Mills, 2007. ISBN 978-1-932425-90-1 Subj: Animals – pigs. Bedtime. Monsters. Rhyming text.

Stein, Peter. *Bugs galore* ill. by Bob Staake. Candlewick, 2012. ISBN 978-0-7636-4754-4 Subj: Insects. Rhyming text.

Cars galore ill. by Bob Staake. Candlewick, 2011. ISBN 978-0-7636-4743-8 Subj: Automobiles. Rhyming text.

Stem, J. David. *Kay Thompson's Eloise in Hollywood* by J. David Stem and David Weiss ill. by Hilary Knight. Simon & Schuster, 2005. ISBN 978-0-689-84289-4 Subj: Activities – traveling. Behavior. Hotels.

Stemple, Heidi E. Y. *Not all princesses dress in pink* (Yolen, Jane)

Sleep, black bear, sleep (Yolen, Jane)

Stephens, Helen. *Ahoyty-toyty* ill. by author. Fickling, 2004. ISBN 978-0-385-75040-0 Subj: Activities – vacationing. Boats, ships. Etiquette. Friendship.

The big adventure of the Smalls ill. by author. Aladdin, 2012. ISBN 978-1-4424-5058-5 Subj: Behavior – lost & found possessions. Toys – bears.

Fleabag ill. by author. Holt, 2010. ISBN 978-0-8050-7975-2 Subj: Animals – dogs. Moving.

How to hide a lion ill. by author. Holt, 2013. ISBN 978-0-8050-9834-1 Subj: Animals – lions. Behavior – hiding things. Clothing – hats. Crime. Friendship.

I'm too busy ill. by author. DK, 1999. ISBN 978-0-7894-2606-2 Subj: Animals – cats. Format, unusual – board books.

Poochie-poo ill. by author. Fickling, 2003. ISBN 978-0-385-75018-9 Subj: Animals – dogs. Behavior – misbehavior.

Ruby and the muddy dog ill. by author. Kingfisher, 2000. ISBN 978-0-7534-5225-7 Subj: Animals – dogs. Character traits – cleanliness. Character traits – honesty. Character traits – responsibility.

Ruby and the noisy hippo ill. by author. Kingfisher, 2000. ISBN 978-0-7534-5226-4 Subj: Animals – hippopotamuses. Monsters. Noise, sounds.

What about me? ill. by author. DK, 1999. ISBN 978-0-7894-4840-8 Subj: Animals – cats. Emotions – envy, jealousy. Ethnic groups in the U.S. – African Americans. Friendship.

Stephens, J. Moria. *Persephone, the ladybug* ill. by author. Little, 2001. ISBN 978-0-316-81544-4 Subj: Family life – daughters. Family life – mothers. Flowers. Insects – ladybugs.

Steptoe, Javaka. *The Jones family express* ill. by author. Lee & Low, 2003. ISBN 978-1-58430-047-2 Subj: Activities – traveling. Ethnic groups in the U.S. – African Americans. Family life – aunts, uncles. Gifts. Letters, cards. Parties.

Steptoe, John. *Baby says* ill. by author. Lothrop, 1988. ISBN 978-0-688-07424-1 Subj: Activities – playing. Babies. Sibling rivalry.

Creativity ill. by E. B. Lewis. Clarion, 1997. ISBN 978-0-395-68706-2 Subj: Ethnic groups in the U.S. – African Americans. Ethnic groups in the U.S. – Puerto Rican Americans. Friendship. School.

Mufaro's beautiful daughters: an African tale ill. by author. Lothrop, 1987. ISBN 978-0-688-04046-8 Subj: Caldecott award honor books. Character traits – kindness. Character traits – meanness. Folk & fairy tales. Foreign lands – Africa. Royalty – kings.

Stevie ill. by author. HarperCollins, 1969. ISBN 978-0-06-025764-4 Subj: Ethnic groups in the U.S. – African Americans. Friendship.

The story of jumping mouse: a Native American legend ill. by author. Lothrop, 1984. ISBN 978-0-688-01903-7 Subj: Animals – mice. Caldecott award honor books. Folk & fairy tales. Frogs & toads. Magic.

Stern, Ellen. *I saw a bullfrog* ill. by author. Random House, 2003. ISBN 978-0-375-92173-5 Subj: Animals. Character traits – appearance. Imagination. Rhyming text.

Steven, Kenneth. *The biggest thing in the world* ill. by Melanie Mitchell. IPG/Lion, 2010. ISBN 978-0-7459-6204-7 Subj: Animals – polar bears. Character traits – questioning. Emotions – love. Family life – mothers.

Stevens, April. *Edwin speaks up* ill. by Sophie Blackall. Random House, 2011. ISBN 978-0-375-85337-1 Subj: Babies. Birthdays. Shopping.

Waking up Wendell ill. by Tad Hills. Random House, 2007. ISBN 978-0-375-83621-3 Subj: Communities, neighborhoods. Counting, numbers. Morning. Noise, sounds.

Stevens, Jan Romero. *Carlos and the skunk / Carlos y el zorrillo* ill. by Jeanne Arnold. Rising Moon, 1997. ISBN 978-0-87358-591-0 Subj: Animals – skunks. Farms. Foreign languages.

Carlos digs to China / Carlos excava hasta la China ill. by Jeanne Arnold. Rising Moon, 2001. ISBN 978-0-87358-764-8 Subj: Activities – baking, cooking. Activities – digging. Foreign lands – China. Foreign languages. Hotels.

Twelve lizards leaping: a new Twelve days of Christmas ill. by Christine Mau. Rising Moon, 1999. ISBN 978-0-87358-744-0 Subj: Cumulative tales. Holidays – Christmas. Music. Religion. Songs.

Stevens, Janet. *And the dish ran away with the spoon* by Janet Stevens and Susan Stevens Crummel ill. by Janet Stevens. Harcourt, 2001. ISBN 978-0-15-202298-3 Subj: Animals. Behavior – running away. Humorous stories. Nursery rhymes.

Cook-a-doodle-doo! by Janet Stevens and Susan Stevens Crummel ill. by Janet Stevens. Harcourt, 1999. ISBN 978-0-15-201924-2 Subj: Activities – baking, cooking. Animals. Birds – chickens. Food.

Find a cow now! by Janet Stevens and Susan Stevens Crummel ill. by Janet Stevens. Holiday House, 2012. ISBN 978-0-8234-2218-0 Subj: Animals – bulls, cows. Animals – dogs. Birds. Farms.

The great fuzz frenzy by Janet Stevens and Susan Stevens Crummel ill. by Janet Stevens. Harcourt, 2005. ISBN 978-0-15-204626-2 Subj: Animals – prairie dogs. Behavior – greed. Toys – balls.

Help me, Mr. Mutt! expert answers for dogs with people problems by Janet Stevens and Susan Stevens Crummel ill. by Janet Stevens. Harcourt, 2008. ISBN 978-0-15-204628-6 Subj: Activities – writing. Animals – dogs. Humorous stories. Letters, cards.

The little red pen by Janet Stevens and Susan Stevens Crummel ill. by Janet Stevens. Harcourt,

2011. ISBN 978-0-15-206432-7 Subj: Character traits – cooperation. Humorous stories. School.

My big dog by Janet Stevens and Susan Stevens Crummel ill. by Janet Stevens. Golden, 1999. ISBN 978-0-307-10220-1 Subj: Animals – cats. Animals – dogs. Behavior – running away. Friendship.

Old bag of bones ill. by author. Holiday, 1996. ISBN 978-0-8234-1215-0 Subj: Animals. Animals – coyotes. Folk & fairy tales. Indians of North America – Shoshone. Old age.

Tops and bottoms ill. by author. Harcourt, 1995. ISBN 978-0-15-292851-3 Subj: Animals – bears. Animals – rabbits. Behavior – trickery. Caldecott award honor books. Character traits – cleverness. Folk & fairy tales. Gardens, gardening.

Stevenson, Emma. *Hide-and-seek science: animal camouflage* ill. by author. Holiday House, 2013. ISBN 978-0-8234-2293-7 Subj: Animals. Disguises. Picture puzzles.

Stevenson, Harvey. *Big scary wolf* ill. by author. Clarion, 1997. ISBN 978-0-395-74213-6 Subj: Animals – wolves. Bedtime. Emotions – fear. Noise, sounds.

Looking at liberty ill. by author. HarperCollins, 2003. ISBN 978-0-06-000101-8 Subj: Careers – sculptors. Foreign lands – France. Immigrants. U.S. history.

Stevenson, James. *All aboard!* ill. by author. Greenwillow, 1995. ISBN 978-0-688-12439-7 Subj: Activities – traveling. Animals – mice. Fairs, festivals. Trains.

Brr! ill. by author. Greenwillow, 1991. ISBN 978-0-688-09211-5 Subj: Family life – grandfathers. Seasons – winter.

The castaway ill. by author. Greenwillow, 2002. ISBN 978-0-688-16966-4 Subj: Activities – flying. Activities – vacationing. Animals – mice. Animals – porcupines. Islands.

Christmas at Mud Flat ill. by author. Greenwillow, 2000. ISBN 978-0-688-17301-2 Subj: Animals. Holidays – Christmas.

"Could be worse!" ill. by author. Greenwillow, 1977. ISBN 978-0-688-84075-4 Subj: Family life. Family life – grandfathers. Farms. Monsters.

Don't make me laugh ill. by author. Farrar, 1999. ISBN 978-0-374-31827-7 Subj: Animals. Behavior. Humorous stories.

Emma ill. by author. Greenwillow, 1985. ISBN 978-0-688-04021-5 Subj: Behavior – trickery. Witches.

Fried feathers for Thanksgiving ill. by author. Greenwillow, 1986. ISBN 978-0-688-06676-5 Subj: Behavior – trickery. Character traits – meanness. Witches.

Fun, no fun ill. by author. Greenwillow, 1994. ISBN 978-0-688-11674-3 Subj: Careers – artists. Careers – writers. Concepts – opposites. Emotions.

Grandpa's great city tour: an alphabet book ill. by author. Greenwillow, 1983. ISBN 978-0-688-02324-9 Subj: ABC books. Activities – flying. Cities, towns. Family life – grandfathers. Wordless.

Grandpa's too-good garden ill. by author. Greenwillow, 1989. ISBN 978-0-688-08486-8 Subj: Family life – grandfathers. Gardens, gardening.

The great big especially beautiful Easter egg ill. by author. Greenwillow, 1983. ISBN 978-0-688-01791-0 Subj: Eggs. Family life – grandfathers.

Happy Valentine's Day, Emma! ill. by author. Greenwillow, 1987. ISBN 978-0-688-07358-9 Subj: Animals. Character traits – meanness. Holidays – Valentine's Day. Humorous stories. Witches.

Heat wave at Mud Flat ill. by author. Greenwillow, 1997. ISBN 978-0-688-14206-3 Subj: Animals. Weather. Weather – rain.

Higher on the door ill. by author. Greenwillow, 1987. ISBN 978-0-688-06637-6 Subj: Behavior – growing up. Family life – grandparents.

Howard ill. by author. Greenwillow, 1980. ISBN 978-0-688-84255-0 Subj: Behavior – lost. Birds – ducks. Friendship.

I meant to tell you ill. by author. Greenwillow, 1996. ISBN 978-0-688-14178-3 Subj: Behavior – growing up. Careers – artists. Careers – writers. Family life – daughters. Family life – fathers.

July ill. by author. Greenwillow, 1990. ISBN 978-0-688-08823-1 Subj: Family life – grandparents. Sea & seashore. Seasons – summer.

Monty ill. by author. Greenwillow, 1992. ISBN 978-0-688-11241-7 Subj: Animals – rabbits. Birds – ducks. Frogs & toads. Reptiles – alligators, crocodiles.

The most amazing dinosaur ill. by author. Greenwillow, 2000. ISBN 978-0-688-16433-1 Subj: Anatomy – skeletons. Animals. Animals – rats. Dinosaurs. Museums. Prehistory.

Mr. Hacker ill. by author. Greenwillow, 1990. ISBN 978-0-688-09217-7 Subj: Animals. Emotions – loneliness. Pets.

National worm day ill. by author. Greenwillow, 1990. ISBN 978-0-688-08772-2 Subj: Animals. Friendship.

No friends ill. by author. Greenwillow, 1986. ISBN 978-0-688-06507-2 Subj: Family life – grandfathers. Friendship. Moving.

No need for Monty ill. by author. Greenwillow, 1987. ISBN 978-0-688-07084-7 Subj: Animals. Reptiles – alligators, crocodiles. Transportation.

Quick! Turn the page! ill. by author. Greenwillow, 1990. ISBN 978-0-688-09309-9 Subj: Problem solving.

Rolling Rose ill. by author. Greenwillow, 1992. ISBN 978-0-688-10675-1 Subj: Activities. Activities – walking. Babies.

Sam the Zamboni man ill. by Harvey Stevenson. Greenwillow, 1998. ISBN 978-0-688-14485-2 Subj: Careers. Family life – fathers. Machines. Sports – hockey. Sports – ice skating.

The Sea View Hotel ill. by author. Greenwillow, 1978. ISBN 978-0-688-84168-3 Subj: Activities – vacationing. Animals – mice. Hotels.

The stowaway ill. by author. Greenwillow, 1990. ISBN 978-0-688-08620-6 Subj: Animals – mice. Boats, ships. Friendship.

That dreadful day ill. by author. Greenwillow, 1985. ISBN 978-0-688-04036-9 Subj: Family life – grandfathers. School – first day.

That terrible Halloween night ill. by author. Greenwillow, 1980. ISBN 978-0-688-94281-6 Subj: Family life – grandfathers. Holidays – Halloween.

That's exactly the way it wasn't ill. by author. Greenwillow, 1991. ISBN 978-0-688-09869-8 Subj: Family life – brothers. Family life – grandfathers. Sibling rivalry.

There's nothing to do! ill. by author. Greenwillow, 1986. ISBN 978-0-688-04699-6 Subj: Behavior – boredom. Family life – grandfathers.

A village full of valentines ill. by author. Greenwillow, 1995. ISBN 978-0-688-13603-1 Subj: Animals. Holidays – Valentine's Day.

We can't sleep ill. by author. Greenwillow, 1982. ISBN 978-0-688-01214-4 Subj: Animals. Bedtime. Family life – grandfathers. Sleep.

What's under my bed? ill. by author. Greenwillow, 1983. ISBN 978-0-688-02327-0 Subj: Bedtime. Emotions – fear. Family life – grandfathers. Furniture – beds.

When I was nine ill. by author. Greenwillow, 1986. ISBN 978-0-688-05943-9 Subj: Family life.

Which one is Whitney? ill. by author. Greenwillow, 1990. ISBN 978-0-688-09062-3 Subj: Animals. Fish. Sea & seashore.

Wilfred the rat ill. by author. Greenwillow, 1977. ISBN 978-0-688-84103-4 Subj: Animals – chipmunks. Animals – rats. Animals – squirrels. Friendship.

Will you please feed our cat? ill. by author. Greenwillow, 1987. ISBN 978-0-688-06848-6 Subj: Character traits – helpfulness. Family life – grandfathers. Pets.

The wish card ran out! ill. by author. Greenwillow, 1981. ISBN 978-0-688-84305-2 Subj: Behavior – wishing.

Worse than the worst ill. by author. Greenwillow, 1994. ISBN 978-0-688-12250-8 Subj: Animals – dogs. Behavior – misbehavior. Family life – aunts, uncles.

Worse than Willy! ill. by author. Greenwillow, 1984. ISBN 978-0-688-02597-7 Subj: Babies. Family life – grandfathers. Family life – new sibling. Imagination. Sibling rivalry.

The worst person in the world ill. by author. Greenwillow, 1978. ISBN 978-0-688-84127-0 Subj: Friendship.

The worst person in the world at Crab Beach ill. by author. Greenwillow, 1988. ISBN 978-0-688-07299-5 Subj: Friendship. Humorous stories. Sea & seashore – beaches.

The worst person's Christmas ill. by author. Greenwillow, 1991. ISBN 978-0-688-10211-1 Subj: Character traits – meanness. Holidays – Christmas.

Yard sale ill. by author. Greenwillow, 1996. ISBN 978-0-688-14127-1 Subj: Animals. Garage sales, rummage sales.

Yuck! ill. by author. Greenwillow, 1984. ISBN 978-0-688-03830-4 Subj: Magic. Witches.

Stevenson, Robert Louis. *Block city* ill. by Daniel Kirk. Simon & Schuster, 2005. ISBN 978-0-689-86964-8 Subj: Imagination. Poetry. Sea & seashore. Toys.

Block city ill. by Ashley Wolff. Dutton, 1988. ISBN 978-0-525-44399-5 Subj: Imagination. Poetry. Sea & seashore. Toys.

A child's garden of verses sel. by Cooper Edens; ill. by Cooper Edens. DK, 1997. ISBN 978-0-7894-2068-8 Subj: Poetry.

A child's garden of verses ill. by Diane Goode. Morrow, 1998. ISBN 978-0-688-14584-2 Subj: Poetry.

A child's garden of verses ill. by Jessie Willcox Smith. Children's Classics, 1995. ISBN 978-0-517-12397-3 Subj: Poetry.

A child's garden of verses ill. by Tasha Tudor. Simon & Schuster, 1999. ISBN 978-0-689-81882-0 Subj: Poetry.

The little land ill. by Kim Fernandes. Kids Can, 2002. ISBN 978-1-55337-385-8 Subj: Imagination. Poetry.

The moon ill. by Tracey Campbell Pearson. Farrar, 2006. ISBN 978-0-374-35046-8 Subj: Moon. Poetry.

The moon ill. by Denise Saldutti. HarperCollins, 1984. ISBN 978-0-06-025789-7 Subj: Family life. Moon. Night. Poetry. Sports – fishing.

Where go the boats? ill. by Max Grover. Browndeer, 1998. ISBN 978-0-15-201711-8 Subj: Activities – playing. Poetry.

Stewart, Amber. *Bedtime for Button* ill. by Layn Marlow. Scholastic, 2009. ISBN 978-0-545-12991-6 Subj: Animals – bears. Bedtime. Dreams. Family life – fathers.

I'm big enough ill. by Layn Marlow. Scholastic, 2007. ISBN 978-0-439-90666-1 Subj: Animals – rabbits. Behavior – growing up.

Little by little ill. by Layn Marlow. Scholastic, 2008. ISBN 978-0-545-06163-6 Subj: Animals – otters. Character traits – perseverance. Family life – brothers & sisters. Self-concept. Sports – swimming.

No babysitters allowed ill. by Laura Rankin. Bloomsbury, 2008. ISBN 978-1-59990-154-1 Subj: Activities – babysitting. Animals – rabbits. Emotions – fear.

Puddle's new school ill. by Layn Marlow. Barron's, 2011. ISBN 978-0-7641-4683-1 Subj: Birds – ducks. School – first day.

Rabbit ears ill. by Laura Rankin. Bloomsbury, 2006. ISBN 978-1-58234-959-6 Subj: Animals – rabbits. Character traits – cleanliness.

Too small for my big bed ill. by Layn Marlow. Barron's, 2013. ISBN 978-0-7641-6587-0 Subj: Animals – tigers. Bedtime. Character traits – smallness.

Stewart, Joel. *Addis Berner Bear forgets* ill. by author. Farrar, 2008. ISBN 978-0-374-30036-4 Subj: Animals – bears. Cities, towns. Homeless. Memories, memory. Music. Musical instruments – trumpets.

Dexter Bexley and the big blue beastie ill. by author. Holiday House, 2007. ISBN 978-0-8234-2068-1 Subj: Character traits – cleverness. Friendship. Monsters.

Stewart, Melissa. *A place for birds* ill. by Higgins Bond. Peachtree, 2009. ISBN 978-1-56145-474-7 Subj: Birds. Ecology.

A place for frogs ill. by Higgins Bond. Peachtree, 2010. ISBN 978-1-56145-521-8 Subj: Ecology. Frogs & toads.

Under the snow ill. by Constance R. Bergum. Peachtree, 2009. ISBN 978-1-56145-493-8 Subj: Animals. Seasons – winter. Weather – snow.

When rain falls ill. by Constance R. Bergum. Peachtree, 2008. ISBN 978-1-56145-438-9 Subj: Animals. Weather – rain.

Stewart, Paul. *The birthday presents* ill. by Chris Riddell. HarperCollins, 2000. ISBN 978-0-06-028279-0 Subj: Animals – hedgehogs. Animals – rabbits. Behavior – sharing. Birthdays. Gifts.

A little bit of winter ill. by Chris Riddell. HarperCollins, 1999. ISBN 978-0-06-028278-3 Subj: Animals – hedgehogs. Animals – rabbits. Friendship. Hibernation. Seasons – winter.

Rabbit's wish ill. by Chris Riddell. HarperCollins, 2001. ISBN 978-0-06-029518-9 Subj: Animals – hedgehogs. Animals – rabbits. Friendship. Weather – floods.

Stewart, Sarah. *The gardener* ill. by David Small. Farrar, 1997. ISBN 978-0-374-32517-6 Subj: Caldecott award honor books. Careers – bakers. Family life – aunts, uncles. Gardens, gardening. Letters, cards. U.S. history.

The journey ill. by David Small. Farrar, 2001. ISBN 978-0-374-33905-0 Subj: Activities – writing. Birthdays. Cities, towns. Ethnic groups in the U.S. – Amish.

The library ill. by David Small. Farrar, 1995. ISBN 978-0-374-34388-0 Subj: Books, reading. Libraries. Rhyming text.

The money tree ill. by David Small. Farrar, 1991. ISBN 978-0-374-35014-7 Subj: Money. Seasons. Trees.

The quiet place ill. by David Small. Farrar, 2012. ISBN 978-0-374-32565-7 Subj: Ethnic groups in the U.S. – Mexican Americans. Family life – aunts, uncles. Immigrants. Letters, cards.

Stewart, Shannon. *Sea crow* ill. by Liz Milkau. Orca, 2004. ISBN 978-1-55143-288-5 Subj: Emotions – fear. Family life – brothers & sisters. Disabilities – physical disabilities. Moving.

Stewig, John Warren. *The animals watched: an alphabet book* ill. by Rosanne Litzinger. Holiday House, 2007. ISBN 978-0-8234-1906-7 Subj: ABC books. Animals. Boats, ships. Religion – Noah. Weather – floods. Weather – rain.

Clever Gretchen ill. by Patricia Wittmann. Marshall Cavendish, 2000. ISBN 978-0-7614-5066-5 Subj: Character traits – cleverness. Devil. Folk & fairy tales. Magic.

King Midas ill. by Omar Rayyan. Holiday, 1999. ISBN 978-0-8234-1423-9 Subj: Behavior – greed. Folk & fairy tales. Foreign lands – Greece. Royalty – kings.

Making plum jam ill. by Kevin O'Malley. Hyperion, 2002. ISBN 978-0-7868-2402-1 Subj: Activities – baking, cooking. Family life – aunts, uncles. Farms. Food.

Mother Holly: a retelling from the Brothers Grimm ill. by Johanna Westerman. NorthSouth, 2001. ISBN 978-1-55858-926-1 Subj: Family life – sisters.

Family life – stepfamilies. Folk & fairy tales. Foreign lands – Germany.

Stone soup ill. by Margot Tomes. Holiday, 1991. ISBN 978-0-8234-0863-4 Subj: Character traits – cleverness. Folk & fairy tales. Food.

Stickland, Henrietta. *Dinosaur roar!* (Stickland, Paul)

A number of dinosaurs: a pop-up counting book (Stickland, Paul)

Stickland, Paul. *Bears* ill. by author. Ragged Bears, 2001. ISBN 978-1-929927-34-0 Subj: Animals – bears. Animals – sheep. Bedtime. Parties. Rhyming text. Toys.

Dinosaur roar! by Paul Stickland and Henrietta Stickland ill. by Paul Stickland. Dutton, 1994. ISBN 978-0-525-45276-8 Subj: Concepts – opposites. Dinosaurs. Prehistory. Rhyming text.

Dinosaur stomp! ill. by author. Dutton, 1996. ISBN 978-0-525-45591-2 Subj: Activities – dancing. Dinosaurs. Format, unusual – toy & movable books. Prehistory. Rhyming text.

A number of dinosaurs: a pop-up counting book by Paul Stickland and Henrietta Stickland. Illus. Sterling, 2010. ISBN 978-1-4027-6479-0 Subj: Counting, numbers. Dinosaurs. Format, unusual – toy & movable books.

Ten terrible dinosaurs ill. by author. Dutton, 1997. ISBN 978-0-525-45905-7 Subj: Counting, numbers. Dinosaurs. Prehistory. Rhyming text.

Truck jam ill. by author. Ragged Bears, 2000. ISBN 978-1-929927-03-6 Subj: Format, unusual – toy & movable books. Transportation. Trucks.

Stiegemeyer, Julie. *Gobble gobble crash! a barnyard counting bash* ill. by Valeri Gorbachev. Dutton, 2008. ISBN 978-0-525-47959-8 Subj: Birds – turkeys. Counting, numbers. Farms. Rhyming text.

Seven little bunnies ill. by Laura J. Bryant. Marshall Cavendish, 2010. ISBN 978-0-7614-5600-1 Subj: Animals – rabbits. Bedtime. Counting, numbers. Rhyming text.

Under the baobab tree ill. by E. B. Lewis. Zonderkidz, 2012. ISBN 978-0-310-72561-9 Subj: Family life – brothers & sisters. Foreign lands – Africa. Religion. Trees.

Stier, Catherine. *Bugs in my hair?!* ill. by Tammie Lyon. Whitman, 2008. ISBN 978-0-8075-0908-1 Subj: Insects – lice. School.

Stihler, Chérie B. *The giant cabbage turnip* ill. by Jeremiah Trammell. Sasquatch, 2003. ISBN 978-1-57061-357-9 Subj: Alaska. Animals. Animals – moose. Character traits – cooperation. Cumulative tales. Fairs, festivals. Friendship. Plants.

Stileman, Kali. *Roly-poly egg* ill. by author. ME Media/Tiger Tales, 2011. ISBN 978-1-58925-852-5 Subj: Birds. Eggs. Format, unusual – toy & movable books.

Snack time for Confetti ill. by author. ME Media/Tiger Tales, 2013. ISBN 978-1-58925-127-4 Subj: Birds. Food.

Stiles, Martha Bennett. *Island magic* ill. by Daniel San Souci. Atheneum, 1999. ISBN 978-0-689-80588-2 Subj: Family life – grandfathers. Islands. Nature.

Stille, Darlene R. *Police cars* ill. with photos. Compass Point, 2003. ISBN 978-0-7565-0290-4 Subj: Automobiles. Careers – police officers. Transportation. Trucks.

Tractors ill. with photos. Compass Point, 2003. ISBN 978-0-7565-0287-4 Subj: Tractors. Transportation.

Stills, Caroline. *The house of 12 bunnies* by Caroline Stills and Sarcia Stills-Blott ill. by Judith Rossell. Holiday House, 2012. ISBN 978-0-8234-2422-1 Subj: Animals – rabbits. Bedtime. Counting, numbers.

Stills-Blott, Sarcia. *The house of 12 bunnies* (Stills, Caroline)

Stillwell, Fred. *The airplane alphabet book* (Pallotta, Jerry)

Stimpson, Colin. *Jack and the baked beanstalk* ill. by author. Candlewick, 2012. ISBN 978-0-7636-5563-1 Subj: Careers – chefs, cooks. Folk & fairy tales. Food. Giants. Magic. Plants.

Sting [Musician]. *Rock steady* ill. by Hugh Whyte. HarperCollins, 2001. ISBN 978-0-06-029231-7 Subj: Animals. Boats, ships. Religion – Noah. Rhyming text. Weather – floods. Weather – rain. Weather – rainbows.

Stinson, Kathy. *The man with the violin* ill. by Dusan Petricic. Annick, 2013. ISBN 978-1-55451-565-3 Subj: Careers – musicians. Family life – mothers. Music. Musical instruments – violins.

A pocket can have a treasure in it ill. by Deirdre Betteridge. Annick, 2008. ISBN 978-1-55451-126-6 Subj: Family life – new sibling. Farms.

Stock, Catherine. *Alexander's midnight snack: a little elephant's ABC* ill. by author. Clarion, 1988. ISBN 978-0-89919-512-4 Subj: ABC books. Animals – elephants. Bedtime. Food.

The birthday present ill. by author. Bradbury, 1991. ISBN 978-0-02-788401-2 Subj: Birthdays. Parties.

Christmas time ill. by author. Bradbury, 1990. ISBN 978-0-02-788403-6 Subj: Family life – fathers. Holidays – Christmas.

Easter surprise ill. by author. Bradbury, 1991. ISBN 978-0-02-788371-8 Subj: Family life – mothers. Holidays – Easter.

Gugu's house ill. by author. Clarion, 2001. ISBN 978-0-618-00389-1 Subj: Careers – artists. Family life – grandmothers. Foreign lands – Zimbabwe. Weather – rain.

Halloween monster ill. by author. Bradbury, 1990. ISBN 978-0-02-788404-3 Subj: Activities. Emotions – fear. Holidays – Halloween.

A porc in New York ill. by author. Holiday House, 2007. ISBN 978-0-8234-1994-4 Subj: Activities – vacationing. Animals. Careers – farmers.

Secret Valentine ill. by author. Bradbury, 1991. ISBN 978-0-02-788372-5 Subj: Character traits – kindness. Holidays – Valentine's Day.

Thanksgiving treat ill. by author. Bradbury, 1990. ISBN 978-0-02-788402-9 Subj: Family life – grandfathers. Holidays – Thanksgiving.

Stockdale, Susan. *Bring on the birds* ill. by author. Peachtree, 2011. ISBN 978-1-56145-560-7 Subj: Birds. Rhyming text.

Fabulous Fishes ill. by author. Peachtree, 2008. ISBN 978-1-56145-429-7 Subj: Fish. Rhyming text.

Stripes of all types ill. by author. Peachtree, 2013. ISBN 978-1-56145-695-6 Subj: Concepts – patterns.

Stockland, Patricia M. *In the horse stall* ill. by Todd Ouren. Abdo, 2008. ISBN 978-1-60270-024-6 Subj: Animals – horses, ponies. Farms.

In the pig pen ill. by Todd Ouren. Abdo, 2008. ISBN 978-1-60270-025-3 Subj: Animals – pigs. Farms.

In the sheep pasture ill. by Todd Ouren. Abdo, 2008. ISBN 978-1-60270-026-0 Subj: Animals – sheep. Farms.

Stoeke, Janet Morgan. *The bus stop* ill. by author. Penguin, 2007. ISBN 978-0-525-47805-8 Subj: Buses. Rhyming text. School.

A friend for Minerva Louise ill. by author. Dutton, 1997. ISBN 978-0-525-45869-2 Subj: Babies. Behavior – mistakes. Birds – chickens.

A hat for Minerva Louise ill. by author. Dutton, 1994. ISBN 978-0-525-45328-4 Subj: Behavior – misunderstanding. Birds – chickens. Clothing.

Hide and seek ill. by author. Dutton, 1999. ISBN 978-0-525-46189-0 Subj: Animals. Behavior – hiding. Birds – chickens. Farms. Format, unusual – board books. Games.

It's library day ill. by author. Dutton, 2008. ISBN 978-0-525-47944-4 Subj: Libraries. Rhyming text. School.

The Loopy Coop hens ill. by author. Penguin, 2011. ISBN 978-0-525-42190-0 Subj: Birds – chickens. Farms.

The Loopy Coop hens: letting go ill. by author. Dial, 2013. ISBN 978-0-8037-3768-6 Subj: Birds – chickens. Humorous stories. Trees.

Minerva Louise ill. by author. Dutton, 1988. ISBN 978-0-525-44374-2 Subj: Behavior – misunderstanding. Birds – chickens.

Minerva Louise and the colorful eggs ill. by author. Penguin, 2006. ISBN 978-0-525-47633-7 Subj: Birds – chickens. Eggs. Holidays – Easter.

Minerva Louise and the red truck ill. by author. Dutton, 2002. ISBN 978-0-525-46909-4 Subj: Birds – chickens. Careers – construction workers. Trucks.

Minerva Louise at school ill. by author. Dutton, 1996. ISBN 978-0-525-45494-6 Subj: Behavior – misunderstanding. Birds – chickens. School.

Minerva Louise at the fair ill. by author. Dutton, 2000. ISBN 978-0-525-46439-6 Subj: Behavior – mistakes. Birds – chickens. Fairs, festivals.

Minerva Louise on Christmas Eve ill. by author. Penguin, 2007. ISBN 978-0-525-47857-7 Subj: Birds – chickens. Holidays – Christmas. Santa Claus.

Minerva Louise on Halloween ill. by author. Dutton, 2009. ISBN 978-0-525-42149-8 Subj: Birds – chickens. Holidays – Halloween.

Pip's trip ill. by author. Dial, 2012. ISBN 978-0-8037-3708-2 Subj: Birds – chickens. Character traits – bravery. Farms.

Waiting for May ill. by author. Penguin, 2005. ISBN 978-0-525-47098-4 Subj: Adoption. Family life – brothers & sisters. Foreign lands – China.

Stohner, Anu. *Brave Charlotte* ill. by Henrike Wilson. Bloomsbury, 2005. ISBN 978-1-58234-690-8 Subj: Animals – dogs. Animals – sheep. Behavior – resourcefulness. Character traits – bravery.

Brave Charlotte and the wolves ill. by Henrike Wilson. Bloomsbury, 2009. ISBN 978-1-59990-424-5 Subj: Animals – sheep. Animals – wolves. Character traits – bravery. Clubs, gangs.

Stohs, Anita. *An Easter alleluia* ill. by Joel Snyder. Concordia, 2003. ISBN 978-0-7586-0116-2 Subj: Holidays – Easter. Music. Religion. Rhyming text. Songs.

Stojic, Manya. *Rain* ill. by author. Crown, 2000. ISBN 978-0-517-80086-7 Subj: Animals. Cumulative tales. Foreign lands – Africa. Weather – rain.

Snow ill. by author. Knopf, 2002. ISBN 978-0-375-92348-7 Subj: Animals. Forest, woods. Seasons – winter. Weather – snow.

Wet pebbles under our feet ill. by author. Knopf, 2002. ISBN 978-0-375-91519-2 Subj: Family life – grandparents. Islands. Sea & seashore – beaches.

Stolz, Mary. *Emmett's pig* ill. by Garth Williams and Rosemary Wells. HarperCollins, 2003. ISBN 978-0-06-028746-7 Subj: Animals – pigs. Birthdays. Cities, towns.

Storm in the night ill. by Pat Cummings. HarperCollins, 1988. ISBN 978-0-06-025912-9 Subj: Ethnic groups in the U.S. – African Americans. Family life – grandfathers. Night. Weather – storms.

Zekmet, the stone carver ill. by Deborah Nourse Lattimore. Harcourt, 1988. ISBN 978-0-15-299961-2 Subj: Activities – working. Foreign lands – Egypt.

Stone, Lynn M. *Chickens have chicks* ill. with photos. Compass Point, 2000. ISBN 978-0-7565-0000-9 Subj: Animals – babies. Birds – chickens.

Farm buildings ill. with photos. Rourke, 2002. ISBN 978-1-58952-091-2 Subj: Buildings. Farms.

Farms old and new ill. with photos. Rourke, 2002. ISBN 978-1-58952-094-3 Subj: Family life. Farms.

Getting around ill. with photos. Rourke, 2002. ISBN 978-1-58952-110-0 Subj: Animals. Sea & seashore.

Life of the kelp forest ill. with photos. Rourke, 2002. ISBN 978-1-58952-112-4 Subj: Ecology. Sea & seashore.

Partners ill. with photos. Rourke, 2002. ISBN 978-1-58952-114-8 Subj: Animals. Behavior – sharing. Ecology. Symbiosis.

Pigs and piglets ill. with photos. Compass Point, 2000. ISBN 978-0-7565-0003-0 Subj: Animals – babies. Animals – pigs.

Stone, Tanya Lee. *D is for dreidel* ill. by Dawn Apperley. Price Stern Sloan, 2002. ISBN 978-0-8431-4576-2 Subj: ABC books. Holidays – Hanukkah. Jewish culture. Rhyming text.

Elizabeth leads the way: Elizabeth Cady Stanton and the right to vote ill. by Rebecca Gibbon. Holt, 2008. ISBN 978-0-8050-7903-6 Subj: Behavior – seeking better things. Character traits – assertiveness. Character traits – bravery. Gender roles. U.S. history.

Sandy's circus: a story about Alexander Calder ill. by Boris Kulikov. Viking, 2008. ISBN 978-0-670-06268-3 Subj: Art. Careers – artists. Circus.

Who says women can't be doctors? the story of Elizabeth Blackwell ill. by Marjorie Priceman. Holt, 2013. ISBN 978-0-8050-9048-2 Subj: Careers – doctors. Character traits – assertiveness. Character traits – perseverance. Gender roles. Self-concept. U.S. history.

Stoop, Naoko. *Red Knit Cap Girl* ill. by author. Little, Brown, 2012. ISBN 978-0-316-12946-6 Subj: Animals. Clothing – hats. Forest, woods. Moon.

Red Knit Cap Girl to the rescue ill. by author. Little, Brown, 2013. ISBN 978-0-316-22885-5 Subj: Activities – traveling. Animals – polar bears. Behavior – lost. Character traits – helpfulness.

Stott, Ann. *Always* ill. by Matt Phelan. Candlewick, 2008. ISBN 978-0-7636-3232-8 Subj: Character traits – questioning. Emotions – love. Family life – mothers.

I'll be there ill. by Matt Phelan. Candlewick, 2010. ISBN 978-0-7636-4711-7 Subj: Behavior – growing up. Emotions – love. Family life – mothers.

Stowell, Penelope. *The greatest potatoes* ill. by Sharon Watts. Hyperion, 2005. ISBN 978-0-7868-5113-3 Subj: Activities – baking, cooking. Careers – chefs, cooks. Ethnic groups in the U.S. Food. Restaurants.

Stower, Adam. *Silly doggy* ill. by author. Scholastic, 2012. ISBN 978-0-545-37323-4 Subj: Animals – bears. Pets.

Two left feet ill. by author. Bloomsbury, 2004. ISBN 978-1-58234-884-1 Subj: Activities – dancing. Character traits – clumsiness. Contests. Monsters.

Straaten, Harmen van. *Duck's tale* ill. by author. NorthSouth, 2007. ISBN 978-0-7358-2133-0 Subj: Animals. Birds – ducks. Books, reading. Friendship. Frogs & toads.

For me? ill. by author. NorthSouth, 2004. ISBN 978-0-7358-2163-7 Subj: Animals. Birds – ducks. Friendship. Frogs & toads. Letters, cards.

Strand, Keith. *Grandfather's Christmas tree* ill. by Thomas Locker. Silver Whistle, 1999. ISBN 978-0-15-201821-4 Subj: Birds – geese. Character traits – kindness to animals. Holidays – Christmas. U.S. history – frontier & pioneer life.

Strauss, Anna. *Hush, Mama loves you* ill. by Alice Priestley. Walker, 2002. ISBN 978-0-8027-8806-1 Subj: Character traits – helpfulness. Emotions. Family life – mothers.

Strauss, Linda Leopold. *The Elijah door: a Passover tale* ill. by Alexi Natchev. Holiday House, 2012. ISBN 978-0-8234-1911-1 Subj: Behavior – fighting, arguing. Friendship. Holidays – Passover. Jewish culture. Religion.

The princess gown ill. by Malene Laugesen. Houghton, 2008. ISBN 978-0-618-86259-7 Subj: Activities – sewing. Clothing – dresses. Royalty – princesses.

Strauss, Rochelle. *One well: the story of water on Earth* ill. by Rosemary Woods. Kids Can, 2007. ISBN 978-1-55337-954-6 Subj: Water.

Strauss, Susan. *When woman became the sea: a Costa Rican creation myth* ill. by Cristina Acosta. Beyond Words, 1998. ISBN 978-1-885223-85-2 Subj: Creation. Folk & fairy tales. Foreign lands – Costa Rica. Sea & seashore.

Street, Pat. *There's a frog in my throat: 312 animal sayings from the horse's mouth* (Leedy, Loreen)

Strete, Craig Kee. *How the Indians bought the farm* by Craig Kee Strete and Michelle Netten Chacon ill. by Francisco X. Mora. Greenwillow, 1996. ISBN 978-0-688-14131-8 Subj: Animals. Behavior – trickery. Farms. Indians of North America.

They thought they saw him ill. by José Aruego and Ariane Dewey. Greenwillow, 1996. ISBN 978-0-688-14195-0 Subj: Concepts – color. Reptiles – lizards.

Stringer, Lauren. *Winter is the warmest season* ill. by author. Harcourt, 2006. ISBN 978-0-15-204967-6 Subj: Seasons – winter.

Stroud, Bettye. *Belle, the last mule at Gee's Bend: a civil rights story* (Ramsey, Calvin Alexander)

Dance y'all ill. by Cornelius Van Wright and Ying-Hwa Hu. Marshall Cavendish, 2001. ISBN 978-0-7614-5065-8 Subj: Activities – dancing. Emotions – fear. Ethnic groups in the U.S. – African Americans. Farms. Reptiles – snakes.

Down home at Miss Dessa's ill. by Felicia Marshall. Lee & Low, 1996. ISBN 978-1-880000-39-7 Subj: Character traits – kindness. Ethnic groups in the U.S. – African Americans. Family life – sisters. Illness. Old age. Seasons – summer.

The leaving ill. by Cedric Lucas. Marshall Cavendish, 2001. ISBN 978-0-7614-5067-2 Subj: Ethnic groups in the U.S. – African Americans. Slavery.

The patchwork path ill. by Erin Susanne Bennett. Candlewick, 2005. ISBN 978-0-7636-2423-1 Subj: Character traits – freedom. Ethnic groups in the U.S. – African Americans. Maps. Quilts. Slavery.

Stryer, Andrea Stenn. *Kami and the yaks* ill. by Bert Dodson. Bay Otter, 2007. ISBN 978-0-9778961-0-3 Subj: Animals – yaks. Character traits – bravery. Foreign lands – Nepal. Disabilities – deafness.

Stuchner, Joan Betty. *Can hens give milk?* ill. by Joe Weissmann. Orca, 2011. ISBN 978-1-55469-319-1 Subj: Birds – chickens. Farms. Humorous stories. Jewish culture.

The Kugel Valley Klezmer Band ill. by Richard Row. Crocodile, 2001. ISBN 978-1-56656-430-4 Subj: Foreign lands – Canada. Jewish culture. Musical instruments – bands.

Sturges, Philemon. *How do you make a baby smile?* ill. by Bridget Strevens-Marzo. HarperCollins, 2007. ISBN 978-0-06-076072-4 Subj: Animals – babies. Rhyming text.

I love bugs ill. by Shari Halpern. HarperCollins, 2005. ISBN 978-0-06-056169-7 Subj: Insects. Rhyming text.

I love planes ill. by Shari Halpern. HarperCollins, 2003. ISBN 978-0-06-028899-0 Subj: Airplanes, airports.

I love school ill. by Shari Halpern. HarperCollins, 2004. ISBN 978-0-06-009285-6 Subj: Family life – brothers & sisters. Rhyming text. School – nursery.

I love tools! ill. by Shari Halpern. HarperCollins, 2006. ISBN 978-0-06-009288-7 Subj: Activities – making things. Homes, houses. Rhyming text. Tools.

I love trains ill. by Shari Halpern. HarperCollins, 2001. ISBN 978-0-06-028901-0 Subj: Rhyming text. Trains.

I love trucks! ill. by Shari Halpern. HarperCollins, 1999. ISBN 978-0-06-027819-9 Subj: Careers – truck drivers. Rhyming text. Trucks.

Ten flashing fireflies ill. by Anna Vojtech. North-South, 1995. ISBN 978-1-55858-421-1 Subj: Counting, numbers. Insects – fireflies. Night. Rhyming text.

This little pirate ill. by Amy Walrod. Penguin, 2005. ISBN 978-0-525-46440-2 Subj: Animals – pigs. Parties. Pirates. Rhyming text.

Waggers ill. by Jim Ishikawa. Penguin, 2005. ISBN 978-0-525-47116-5 Subj: Animals – cats. Animals – dogs. Rhyming text.

What's that sound, Woolly Bear? ill. by Joan Paley. Little, 1996. ISBN 978-0-316-82021-9 Subj: Insects. Insects – butterflies, caterpillars. Insects – moths. Metamorphosis. Noise, sounds.

Who took the cookies from the cookie jar? (Lass, Bonnie)

Sturgis, Brenda Reeves. *10 turkeys in the road* ill. by David Slonim. Marshall Cavendish, 2011. ISBN 978-0-7614-5847-0 Subj: Birds – turkeys. Careers – farmers. Circus. Counting, numbers. Rhyming text.

Stutson, Caroline. *By the light of the Halloween moon* ill. by Kevin Hawkes. Lothrop, 1993. ISBN 978-0-688-12046-7 Subj: Cumulative tales. Holidays – Halloween. Rhyming text.

Cats' night out ill. by Jon Klassen. Simon & Schuster, 2010. ISBN 978-1-4169-4005-0 Subj: Activities

– dancing. Animals – cats. Cities, towns. Night. Rhyming text.

Cowpokes ill. by Daniel San Souci. Lee & Shepard, 1999. ISBN 978-0-688-13974-2 Subj: Cowboys, cowgirls. Rhyming text.

Night train ill. by Katherine Tillotson. Roaring Brook, 2002. ISBN 978-0-7613-1598-8 Subj: Rhyming text. Trains.

Prairie primer A to Z ill. by Susan Condie Lamb. Dutton, 1996. ISBN 978-0-525-45163-1 Subj: ABC books. Family life. Farms. Rhyming text. U.S. history – frontier & pioneer life.

Stuve-Bodeen, Stephanie. *Elizabeti's doll* ill. by Christy Hale. Lee & Low, 1998. ISBN 978-1-880000-70-0 Subj: Emotions – love. Foreign lands – Tanzania. Imagination. Rocks. Toys – dolls.

Elizabeti's school ill. by Christy Hale. Lee & Low, 2002. ISBN 978-1-58430-043-4 Subj: Family life. Foreign lands – Tanzania. School – first day.

Mama Elizabeti ill. by Christy Hale. Lee & Low, 2000. ISBN 978-1-58430-002-1 Subj: Babies. Family life – brothers. Family life – new sibling. Foreign lands – Tanzania.

A small brown dog with a wet pink nose ill. by Linzie Hunter. Little, Brown, 2010. ISBN 978-0-316-05830-8 Subj: Animals – dogs. Behavior – resourcefulness. Pets.

We'll paint the octopus red ill. by Pam DeVito. Woodbine, 1998. ISBN 978-1-890627-06-5 Subj: Family life – brothers & sisters. Disabilities – Down syndrome.

Suen, Anastasia. *Air show* ill. by Cecco Mariniello. Holt, 2001. ISBN 978-0-8050-4952-7 Subj: Airplanes, airports.

Baby born ill. by Chih-wei Chang. Lee & Low, 1998. ISBN 978-1-880000-68-7 Subj: Babies. Behavior – growing up. Rhyming text.

Baby born [board book] ill. by Chih-wei Chang. Lee & Low, 1999. ISBN 978-1-880000-95-3 Subj: Babies. Behavior – growing up. Format, unusual – board books. Rhyming text.

Delivery ill. by Wade Zahares. Viking, 1999. ISBN 978-0-670-88455-1 Subj: Rhyming text. Transportation.

Man on the moon ill. by Benrei Huang. Viking, 1997. ISBN 978-0-670-87393-7 Subj: Moon. Space & space ships. U.S. history.

Raise the roof ill. by Elwood H. Smith. Viking, 2003. ISBN 978-0-670-89282-2 Subj: Buildings. Careers – construction workers. Family life. Homes, houses. Rhyming text.

Red light, green light ill. by Ken Wilson-Max. Harcourt, 2005. ISBN 978-0-15-202582-3 Subj: Automobiles. Rhyming text. Traffic, traffic signs. Transportation. Trucks.

Road work ahead ill. by Jannie Ho. Penguin, 2011. ISBN 978-0-670-01288-6 Subj: Activities – traveling. Rhyming text. Roads.

Subway ill. by Karen Katz. Viking, 2004. ISBN 978-0-670-03622-6 Subj: Rhyming text. Trains. Transportation.

Window music ill. by Wade Zahares. Viking, 1998. ISBN 978-0-670-87287-9 Subj: Activities – trading. Family life – mothers. Rhyming text. Trains.

Sugarman, Brynn Olenberg. *Rebecca's journey home* ill. by Michelle Shapiro. Lerner, 2006. ISBN 978-1-58013-157-5 Subj: Adoption. Family life. Foreign lands – Vietnam. Jewish culture.

Sullivan, Mary. *Ball* ill. by author. Houghton Mifflin, 2013. ISBN 978-0-547-75936-4 Subj: Activities – playing. Animals – dogs. Toys – balls.

Sullivan, Paula. *Todd's box* ill. by Nadine Bernard Westcott. Harcourt, 2004. ISBN 978-0-15-205093-1 Subj: Activities – walking. Behavior – collecting things. Family life – mothers. Family life – sons.

Sullivan, Sarah. *Dear Baby: letters from your big brother* ill. by Paul Meisel. Candlewick, 2005. ISBN 978-0-7636-2126-1 Subj: Babies. Family life – brothers & sisters. Letters, cards.

Once upon a baby brother ill. by Tricia Tusa. Farrar, 2010. ISBN 978-0-374-34635-5 Subj: Activities – storytelling. Activities – writing. Family life – new sibling. Sibling rivalry.

Summers, Kate. *Milly and Tilly: the story of a town mouse and a country mouse* (Aesop)

Milly's wedding ill. by Maggie Kneen. Dutton, 1999. ISBN 978-0-525-46046-6 Subj: Animals – mice. Emotions – love. Weddings.

Summers, Susan. *The fourth wise man* ill. by Jackie Morris. Based on the story by Henry Van Dyke. Dial, 1998. ISBN 978-0-8037-2312-2 Subj: Religion – Nativity.

The sun, the moon, and the stars ill. by Nancy Elizabeth Wallace. Houghton, 2003. ISBN 978-0-618-26353-0 Subj: Moon. Poetry. Stars. Sun.

Sunami, Kitoba. *How the fisherman tricked the genie* ill. by Amiko Hirao. Atheneum, 2002. ISBN 978-0-689-83399-1 Subj: Behavior – trickery. Careers – fishermen. Emotions – anger. Folk & fairy tales. Mythical creatures – genies.

Sundgaard, Arnold. *The lamb and the butterfly* ill. by Eric Carle. Watts, 1988. ISBN 978-0-531-08379-6 Subj: Animals – sheep. Character traits – freedom. Insects – butterflies, caterpillars.

Supree, Burton. *"Mother, mother I feel sick"* (Charlip, Remy)

Surat, Michele Maria. *Angel child, dragon child* ill. by Vo-Dinh Mai. Raintree, 1983. ISBN 978-0-940742-12-3 Subj: Ethnic groups in the U.S. – Vietnamese Americans. School.

Surovec, Yasmine. *I see Kitty* ill. by author. Roaring Brook, 2013. ISBN 978-1-59643-862-0 Subj: Animals – cats. Imagination.

Surplice, Holly. *Guinea pig party* ill. by author. Candlewick, 2012. ISBN 978-0-7636-6269-1 Subj: Animals – guinea pigs. Counting, numbers. Parties. Rhyming text.

Sussman, Joni Kibort. *My first Yiddish word book* ill. by Pépi Marzel. Lerner, 2009. ISBN 978-0-8225-8755-2 Subj: Jewish culture. Language.

Sutherland, Marc. *MacMurtrey's wall* ill. by author. Abrams, 2001. ISBN 978-0-8109-4494-7 Subj: Communities, neighborhoods. Sea & seashore. Weather – storms.

Sutton, Benn. *Hedgehug: a sharp lesson in love.* HarperCollins, 2011. ISBN 978-0-06-196101-4 Subj: Animals – hedgehogs. Holidays – Valentine's Day. Hugging.

Sutton, Jane. *Don't call me Sidney* ill. by Renata Gallio. Penguin, 2010. ISBN 978-0-8037-2753-3 Subj: Activities – writing. Animals. Animals – pigs. Names.

The trouble with cauliflower ill. by Jim Harris. Penguin, 2006. ISBN 978-0-8037-2707-6 Subj: Animals – koalas. Character traits – luck. Food. Friendship. Superstition.

Sutton, Sally. *Demolition* ill. by Brian Lovelock. Candlewick, 2012. ISBN 978-0-7636-5830-4 Subj: Careers – construction workers. Machines. Trucks.

Roadwork ill. by Brian Lovelock. Candlewick, 2008. ISBN 978-0-7636-3912-9 Subj: Careers – construction workers. Roads. Trucks.

Suzuki, David. *Salmon forest* by David Suzuki and Sarah Ellis ill. by Sheena Lott. Greystone, 2003. ISBN 978-1-55054-937-9 Subj: Ecology. Fish. Nature.

Swaim, Jessica. *The hound from the pound* ill. by Jill McElmurry. Candlewick, 2007. ISBN 978-0-7636-2330-2 Subj: Animals – dogs. Emotions – loneliness. Pets. Rhyming text.

Swain, Gwenyth. *I wonder as I wander* ill. by Ronald Himler. Eerdmans, 2003. ISBN 978-0-8028-5214-4 Subj: Careers – clergy. Careers – composers. Religion. Songs. U.S. history.

Johnny Appleseed ill. by Janice Lee Porter. Carolrhoda, 2001. ISBN 978-1-57505-519-0 Subj: Activities – traveling. Gardens, gardening. Tall tales. Trees. U.S. history – frontier & pioneer life.

Riding to Washington ill. by David Geister. Sleeping Bear, 2008. ISBN 978-1-58536-324-7 Subj: Ethnic groups in the U.S. – African Americans. U.S. history.

Swain, Ruth Freeman. *How sweet it is (and was)* ill. by John O'Brien. Holiday, 2003. ISBN 978-0-8234-1712-4 Subj: Food.

Underwear: what we wear under there ill. by John O'Brien. Holiday, 2008. ISBN 978-0-8234-1920-3 Subj: Clothing – underwear.

Swallow, Pamela Curtis. *Groundhog gets a say* ill. by Denise Brunkus. Penguin, 2005. ISBN 978-0-399-23876-5 Subj: Animals – groundhogs. Holidays – Groundhog Day.

Swamp, Jake. *Giving thanks* ill. by Erwin Printup, Jr. Lee & Low, 1995. ISBN 978-1-880000-15-1 Subj: Ecology. Indians of North America – Mohawk. Nature. Religion.

Swann, Brian. *The house with no door: African riddle-poems* ill. by Ashley Bryan. Harcourt, 1998. ISBN 978-0-15-200805-5 Subj: Folk & fairy tales. Foreign lands – Africa. Poetry. Riddles & jokes.

Swann, Rick. *Our school garden!* ill. by Christy Hale. Readers to Eaters, 2012. ISBN 978-0-9836615-0-4 Subj: Character traits – cooperation. Emotions – loneliness. Gardens, gardening. School.

Swanson, Diane. *The dentist and you* ill. with photos. Firefly, 2002. ISBN 978-1-55037-729-3 Subj: Careers – dentists. Health & fitness. Teeth.

The doctor and you ill. with photos. Firefly, 2001. ISBN 978-1-55037-673-9 Subj: Careers – doctors. Health & fitness.

Headgear that hides and plays ill. by Rose Cowles. Greystone, 2001. ISBN 978-1-55054-819-8 Subj: Anatomy – heads. Animals.

Noses that plow and poke ill. with photos. Greystone, 1999. ISBN 978-1-55054-715-3 Subj: Anatomy – noses. Animals.

Skin that slimes and scares ill. with photos. Greystone, 2001. ISBN 978-1-55054-817-4 Subj: Anatomy – skin. Animals.

Swanson, Susan Marie. *The first thing my mama told me* ill. by Christine Davenier. Harcourt, 2002. ISBN 978-0-15-201075-1 Subj: Birthdays. Family life – mothers. Names. Self-concept.

The house in the night ill. by Beth Krommes. Houghton, 2008. ISBN 978-0-618-86244-3 Subj: Caldecott award books. Homes, houses. Light, lights. Night.

To be like the sun ill. by Margaret Chodos-Irvine. Harcourt, 2008. ISBN 978-0-15-205796-1 Subj: Flowers. Nature. Seeds.

Sweeney, Jacqueline. *What about Bettie?* ill. by Blind Mice Studio; photos by G. K. Hart, et al. Benchmark, 2001. ISBN 978-0-7614-1118-5 Subj: Animals. Birds – ducks. Character traits – being different. Family life – brothers & sisters.

Sweeney, Joan. *Me and my family tree* ill. by Annette Cable. Crown, 1999. ISBN 978-0-517-70966-5 Subj: Family life. Genealogy.

Me and my senses ill. by Annette Cable. Crown, 2003. ISBN 978-0-375-91102-6 Subj: Senses.

Me and the measure of things ill. by Annette Cable. Crown, 2001. ISBN 978-0-375-91101-9 Subj: Concepts – measurement. Concepts – weight.

Me counting time ill. by Annette Cable. Crown, 2000. ISBN 978-0-517-80056-0 Subj: Concepts – measurement. Time.

Suzette and the puppy ill. by Jennifer Heyd Wharton. Barron's, 2000. ISBN 978-0-7641-5294-8 Subj: Animals – dogs. Careers – artists. Foreign lands – France. Parks.

Sweet, Melissa. *Balloons over Broadway: the true story of the puppeteer of Macy's Parade* ill. by author. Harcourt, 2011. ISBN 978-0-547-19945-0 Subj: Parades. Puppets. Toys – balloons.

Carmine: a little more red ill. by author. Houghton, 2005. ISBN 978-0-618-38794-6 Subj: ABC books. Activities – painting. Animals – dogs. Animals – wolves. Concepts – color. Family life – grandmothers. Folk & fairy tales.

Fiddle-i-fee ill. by adapter. Little, 1992. ISBN 978-0-316-82516-0 Subj: Animals. Cumulative tales. Farms. Music. Songs.

Tupelo rides the rails ill. by author. Houghton, 2008. ISBN 978-0-618-71714-9 Subj: Animals – dogs. Character traits – bravery. Homeless.

Sweetland, Nancy Rose. *If I could / Si yo pudiera* ill. by Robert Sweetland. Raven Tree, 2002. ISBN 978-0-9701107-7-0 Subj: Foreign languages. Imagination.

Yelly Kelly ill. by Robert Sweetland. Raven Tree, 2003. ISBN 978-0-9720192-0-0 Subj: Behavior. Etiquette.

Swender, Jennifer. *Fire drill* (Jacobs, Paul DuBois)

Swenson, Jamie A. *Boom! Boom! Boom!* ill. by David Walker. Farrar, 2013. ISBN 978-0-374-30868-1 Subj: Animals. Bedtime. Rhyming text. Weather – lightning, thunder. Weather – storms.

Swift, Hildegarde Hoyt. *The little red lighthouse and the great gray bridge* by Hildegarde Hoyt Swift and Lynd Ward ill. by Lynd Ward. Harcourt, 1942. Subj: Boats, ships. Bridges. Lighthouses.

Swinburne, Stephen R. *Armadillo trail* ill. by Bruce Hiscock. Boyds Mills, 2009. ISBN 978-1-59078-463-1 Subj: Animals – armadillos.

Guess whose shadow? ill. by author. Boyds Mills, 1999. ISBN 978-1-56397-724-4 Subj: Activities – photographing. Light, lights. Shadows.

Lots and lots of zebra stripes photos by author. Boyds Mills, 1998. ISBN 978-1-56397-707-7 Subj: Animals. Concepts – color. Concepts – patterns. Disguises. Nature.

Safe, warm, and snug ill. by José Aruego and Ariane Dewey. Harcourt, 1999. ISBN 978-0-15-201734-7 Subj: Animals. Animals – babies. Family life – parents.

Swallows in the birdhouse ill. by Robin Brickman. Millbrook, 1996. ISBN 978-1-56294-182-6 Subj: Activities – making things. Birds – swallows. Homes, houses.

Turtle tide: the ways of sea turtles ill. by Bruce Hiscock. Boyds Mills, 2005. ISBN 978-1-59078-081-7 Subj: Reptiles – turtles, tortoises.

Water for one, water for everyone ill. by Melinda Levine. Millbrook, 1998. ISBN 978-0-7613-0269-8 Subj: Animals. Counting, numbers. Foreign lands – Africa.

What color is nature? photos by author. Boyds Mills, 2002. ISBN 978-1-56397-967-5 Subj: Concepts – color. Nature.

What's a pair? What's a dozen? ill. by author. Boyds Mills, 2000. ISBN 978-1-56397-827-2 Subj: Concepts. Counting, numbers.

What's opposite? ill. by author. Boyds Mills, 2000. ISBN 978-1-56397-881-4 Subj: Concepts – opposites.

Whose shoes? a shoe for every job ill. by author. Boyds Mills, 2010. ISBN 978-1-59078-569-0 Subj: Careers. Clothing – shoes.

Swope, Sam. *Gotta go! Gotta go!* ill. by Sue Riddle. Farrar, 2000. ISBN 978-0-374-32757-6 Subj: Foreign lands – Mexico. Insects – butterflies, caterpillars. Migration.

Sykes, Julie. *Careful, Santa* ill. by Tim Warnes. Tiger Tales, 2002. ISBN 978-1-58925-023-9 Subj: Accidents. Animals. Holidays – Christmas. Santa Claus.

Dora's chicks ill. by Jane Chapman. Tiger Tales, 2002. ISBN 978-1-58925-015-4 Subj: Animals. Behavior – lost. Birds – chickens. Counting, numbers.

Dora's eggs ill. by Jane Chapman. Little Tiger, 1997. ISBN 978-1-888444-09-4 Subj: Animals. Birds – chickens. Birth. Eggs. Farms.

Hurry, Santa! ill. by Tim Warnes. Little Tiger, 1998. ISBN 978-1-888444-37-7 Subj: Behavior – promptness, tardiness. Holidays – Christmas. Santa Claus.

I don't want to take a bath! ill. by Tim Warnes. Little Tiger, 1997. ISBN 978-1-888444-20-9 Subj: Activities – bathing. Animals. Animals – tigers. Behavior – running away. Family life – mothers.

Little Rocket's special star ill. by Jack Tickle. Dutton, 2000. ISBN 978-0-525-46494-5 Subj: Astronomy. Birthdays. Science. Stars.

Little Tiger's big surprise ill. by Tim Warnes. Little Tiger, 1999. ISBN 978-1-888444-52-0 Subj: Animals – tigers. Emotions – anger. Emotions – envy, jealousy. Family life – new sibling.

Smudge ill. by Jane Chapman. Little Tiger, 1998. ISBN 978-1-888444-44-5 Subj: Animals. Animals – dogs. Weather – rain.

This and that ill. by Tanya Linch. Farrar, 1996. ISBN 978-0-374-37492-1 Subj: Animals – cats. Birth. Farms.

Wait for me, Little Tiger ill. by Tim Warnes. Tiger Tales, 2001. ISBN 978-1-58925-009-3 Subj: Activities – playing. Animals – tigers. Family life – brothers & sisters. Jungle.

Sylver, Adrienne. *Hot diggity dog: the history of the hot dog* ill. by Elwood H. Smith. Penguin, 2010. ISBN 978-0-525-47897-3 Subj: Activities – baking, cooking. Food.

Sylvester, Kevin. *Splinters* ill. by author. Tundra, 2010. ISBN 978-0-88776-944-3 Subj: Folk & fairy tales. Sports – hockey.

Symes, Ruth. *Harriet dancing* ill. by Caroline Jayne Church. Scholastic, 2008. ISBN 978-0-545-03204-9 Subj: Activities – dancing. Animals – hedgehogs. Insects – butterflies, caterpillars.

Little Rex, big brother ill. by Sean Julian. Whitman, 2010. ISBN 978-0-8075-4636-9 Subj: Character traits – smallness. Dinosaurs. Family life – brothers.

Symes, Sally. *Yawn* ill. by Nick Sharratt. Candlewick, 2011. ISBN 978-0-7636-5725-3 Subj: Animals. Bedtime.

Szekeres, Cyndy. *Cyndy Szekeres' learn to count, funny bunnies* ill. by author. Scholastic, 2000. ISBN 978-0-439-14994-5 Subj: Animals – rabbits. Counting, numbers. Format, unusual – board books. Rhyming text.

I can count 100 bunnies, and so can you! ill. by author. Scholastic, 1998. ISBN 978-0-590-38361-5 Subj: Animals – rabbits. Counting, numbers.

The mouse that Jack built ill. by author. Scholastic, 1997. ISBN 978-0-590-69197-0 Subj: Animals – mice. Clothing. Cumulative tales. Seasons – winter.

Toby! ill. by author. Simon & Schuster, 2000. ISBN 978-0-689-82645-0 Subj: Animals – mice. Behavior – boredom.

Toby's please and thank you ill. by author. Simon & Schuster, 2001. ISBN 978-0-689-84275-7 Subj: Animals – mice. Etiquette. Format, unusual – board books. Rhyming text.

Taback, Simms. *I miss you every day* ill. by author. Penguin, 2007. ISBN 978-0-670-06192-1 Subj: Emotions – loneliness. Emotions – love. Letters, cards. Rhyming text.

Joseph had a little overcoat ill. by author. Viking, 1999. ISBN 978-0-670-87855-0 Subj: Caldecott award books. Clothing – coats.

Kibitzers and fools: tales my zayda told me ill. by author. Penguin, 2005. ISBN 978-0-670-05955-3 Subj: Activities – storytelling. Folk & fairy tales. Jewish culture.

Postcards from camp ill. by author. Penguin, 2011. ISBN 978-0-399-23973-3 Subj: Activities – writing. Camps, camping. Format, unusual. Letters, cards.

Simms Taback's city animals ill. by author. Blue Apple, 2009. ISBN 978-1-934706-52-7 Subj: Animals. Cities, towns. Format, unusual – toy & movable books.

Simms Taback's farm animals ill. by author. Blue Apple, 2011. ISBN 978-1-60905-078-8 Subj: Animals. Farms. Format, unusual – toy & movable books.

Simms Taback's safari animals ill. by author. Blue Apple, 2008. ISBN 978-1-934706-19-0 Subj: Animals. Format, unusual – toy & movable books.

Tabby, Abigail. *Baby face* ill. by Dan Yaccarino. HarperCollins, 2001. ISBN 978-0-694-01530-6 Subj: Babies. Emotions. Format, unusual – toy & movable books.

Taber, Norman. *Rufus at work* (Taber, Tory)

Taber, Tory. *Rufus at work* by Tory Taber and Norman Taber ill. by authors. Walker, 2005. ISBN 978-0-8027-8984-6 Subj: Activities – working. Animals – cats.

Tada, Joni Eareckson. *Forever friends* by Joni Eareckson Tada and Melody Carlson ill. by Melody Carlson. Crossway, 2000. ISBN 978-1-58134-216-1 Subj: Friendship. Toys. Toys – dolls.

The incredible discovery of Lindsey Renee ill. by Irena Roman. Crossway, 2001. ISBN 978-1-58134-195-9 Subj: Character traits – generosity. Money. Religion.

Tada, Satoshi. *Mr. Beetle* ill. by author. Carolrhoda, 2001. ISBN 978-1-57505-561-9 Subj: Character traits – kindness to animals. Friendship. Insects – beetles.

Tafolla, Carmen. *Baby Coyote and the old woman / El coyotito y la viejita* ill. by Matt Novak. New ed. designed & ed. by Bryce Milligan. Wings, 2000. ISBN 978-0-930324-48-3 Subj: Animals – babies. Animals – coyotes. Ecology. Foreign languages. Format, unusual – board books. Old age.

Fiesta babies ill. by Amy Córdova. Tricycle, 2010. ISBN 978-1-58246-319-3 Subj: Babies. Ethnic groups in the U.S. – Mexican Americans. Fairs, festivals. Rhyming text.

What can you do with a paleta? ill. by Magaly Morales. Tricycle, 2009. ISBN 978-1-58246-221-9 Subj: Cities, towns. Ethnic groups in the U.S. – Mexican Americans. Food.

What can you do with a rebozo? ill. by Amy Córdova. Ten Speed, 2007. ISBN 978-1-58246-220-2 Subj: Clothing. Ethnic groups in the U.S. – Mexican Americans. Foreign lands – Mexico.

Tafuri, Nancy. *All kinds of kisses* ill. by author. Little, Brown, 2012. ISBN 978-0-316-12235-1 Subj: Animals. Family life – mothers. Kissing.

The ball bounced ill. by author. Greenwillow, 1989. ISBN 978-0-688-07871-3 Subj: Babies. Toys – balls.

The barn party ill. by author. Greenwillow, 1995. ISBN 978-0-688-04617-0 Subj: Animals. Barns. Birthdays. Parties.

The big storm: a very soggy counting book ill. by author. Simon & Schuster, 2009. ISBN 978-1-4169-6795-8 Subj: Animals. Counting, numbers. Weather – storms.

Blue goose ill. by author. Simon & Schuster, 2008. ISBN 978-1-4169-2834-8 Subj: Activities – painting. Concepts – color. Farms.

The brass ring ill. by author. Greenwillow, 1996. ISBN 978-0-688-14169-1 Subj: Activities – vacationing. Concepts – shape. Concepts – size.

The busy little squirrel ill. by author. Simon & Schuster, 2007. ISBN 978-0-689-87341-6 Subj: Animals – squirrels. Seasons – fall.

Counting to Christmas ill. by author. Scholastic, 1998. ISBN 978-0-590-27143-1 Subj: Activities – making things. Animals. Counting, numbers. Holidays – Christmas.

Do not disturb ill. by author. Greenwillow, 1987. ISBN 978-0-688-06542-3 Subj: Activities. Animals. Camps, camping. Family life. Night. Noise, sounds. Wordless.

The donkey's Christmas song ill. by author. Scholastic, 2002. ISBN 978-0-439-27313-8 Subj: Animals. Animals – donkeys. Holidays – Christmas. Noise, sounds. Religion – Nativity.

Early morning in the barn ill. by author. Greenwillow, 1983. ISBN 978-0-688-02329-4 Subj: Farms. Morning. Wordless.

Five little chicks ill. by author. Simon & Schuster, 2006. ISBN 978-0-689-87342-3 Subj: Animals – babies. Birds – chickens.

Follow me! ill. by author. Greenwillow, 1990. ISBN 978-0-688-08774-6 Subj: Animals – sea lions. Crustaceans – crabs.

Goodnight, my duckling ill. by author. Scholastic, 2005. ISBN 978-0-439-39881-7 Subj: Bedtime. Behavior – lost. Birds – ducks.

Have you seen my duckling? ill. by author. Greenwillow, 1984. ISBN 978-0-688-02798-8 Subj: Birds – ducks. Caldecott award honor books. Character traits – individuality.

I love you, little one ill. by author. Scholastic, 1997. ISBN 978-0-590-92159-6 Subj: Animals. Animals – babies. Emotions – love. Family life – mothers.

Junglewalk ill. by author. Greenwillow, 1988. ISBN 978-0-688-07183-7 Subj: Animals. Dreams. Imagination. Jungle. Wordless.

Mama's little bears ill. by author. Scholastic, 2002. ISBN 978-0-439-27311-4 Subj: Animals – bears. Family life – mothers.

Rabbit's morning ill. by author. Greenwillow, 1985. ISBN 978-0-688-04064-2 Subj: Animals. Animals – rabbits. Wordless.

Silly little goose! ill. by author. Scholastic, 2001. ISBN 978-0-439-06304-3 Subj: Animals. Birds – geese. Clothing – hats. Homes, houses.

Snowy flowy blowy ill. by author. Scholastic, 1999. ISBN 978-0-590-18973-6 Subj: Days of the week, months of the year. Rhyming text. Seasons.

This is the farmer ill. by author. Greenwillow, 1994. ISBN 978-0-688-09469-0 Subj: Animals. Careers – farmers. Cumulative tales. Farms.

What the sun sees / What the moon sees ill. by author. Greenwillow, 1997. ISBN 978-0-688-14493-7 Subj: Bedtime. Dreams. Format, unusual. Moon. Nature. Night. Sun.

Where did Bunny go? ill. by author. Scholastic, 2001. ISBN 978-0-439-16959-2 Subj: Animals –

rabbits. Behavior – hiding. Birds. Friendship. Games.

Where we sleep ill. by author. Greenwillow, 1987. ISBN 978-0-688-07189-9 Subj: Animals. Format, unusual – board books. Sleep.

Who's counting? ill. by author. Greenwillow, 1986. ISBN 978-0-688-06131-9 Subj: Animals. Animals – dogs. Counting, numbers. Farms.

Whose chick are you? ill. by author. HarperCollins, 2007. ISBN 978-0-06-082515-7 Subj: Birds. Birds – swans. Eggs. Family life – mothers.

Will you be my friend? ill. by author. Scholastic, 2000. ISBN 978-0-590-63782-4 Subj: Animals – rabbits. Birds. Friendship. Weather – storms.

Tagholm, Sally. *The frog* ill. by Bert Kitchen. Kingfisher, 2000. ISBN 978-0-7534-5215-8 Subj: Frogs & toads. Science.

Taibah, Nadia Jameel. *How many donkeys? an Arabic counting tale* (MacDonald, Margaret Read)

Takabayashi, Mari. *I live in Brooklyn* ill. by author. Houghton, 2004. ISBN 978-0-618-30899-6 Subj: Cities, towns. Family life. Seasons.

I live in Tokyo ill. by author. Houghton, 2001. ISBN 978-0-618-07702-1 Subj: Cities, towns. Family life. Foreign lands – Japan.

Talbott, Hudson. *It's all about me-ow: a young cat's guide to the good life* ill. by author. Penguin, 2012. ISBN 978-0-399-25403-1 Subj: Animals – babies. Animals – cats. Pets.

Tamar, Erika. *The garden of happiness* ill. by Barbara Lambase. Harcourt, 1996. ISBN 978-0-15-230582-6 Subj: Activities – painting. Cities, towns. Communities, neighborhoods. Flowers. Gardens, gardening.

Tan, Amy. *The Chinese Siamese cat* ill. by Gretchen Schields. Macmillan, 1994. ISBN 978-0-02-788835-5 Subj: Animals – cats. Foreign lands – China.

The moon lady ill. by Gretchen Schields. Macmillan, 1992. ISBN 978-0-02-788830-0 Subj: Behavior – wishing. Family life – grandmothers. Folk & fairy tales. Foreign lands – China. Moon.

Tanaka, Shinsuke. *Wings* ill. by author. Purple Bear, 2006. ISBN 978-1-933327-19-8 Subj: Anatomy – wings. Animals – dogs. Imagination. Wordless.

Tang, Greg. *Math appeal* ill. by Harry Briggs. Scholastic, 2003. ISBN 978-0-439-21046-1 Subj: Counting, numbers. Rhyming text.

Math fables: lessons that count ill. by Heather Cahoon. Scholastic, 2004. ISBN 978-0-439-45399-8 Subj: Counting, numbers. Rhyming text.

Math fables too: making science count ill. by Taia Morley. Scholastic, 2007. ISBN 978-0-439-78351-4 Subj: Animals. Counting, numbers. Rhyming text. Science.

Tankard, Jeremy. *Boo hoo Bird* ill. by author. Scholastic, 2009. ISBN 978-0-545-06570-2 Subj: Animals. Birds. Illness.

Grumpy Bird ill. by author. Scholastic, 2007. ISBN 978-0-439-85147-3 Subj: Animals. Behavior – bad day. Birds. Emotions.

Me hungry! ill. by author. Candlewick, 2008. ISBN 978-0-7636-3360-8 Subj: Animals. Food. Humorous stories. Prehistory. Sports – hunting.

Tanner, Suzy-Jane. *Tinyflock Nursery School* ill. by author. HarperCollins, 2004. ISBN 978-0-06-055723-2 Subj: Animals – babies. Animals – sheep. School – first day. School – nursery.

Tapahonso, Luci. *Navajo ABC* by Luci Tapahonso and Eleanor Schick ill. by Eleanor Schick. Macmillan, 1995. ISBN 978-0-689-80316-1 Subj: ABC books. Indians of North America – Navajo. Language.

Tarbescu, Edith. *Annushka's voyage* ill. by Lydia Dabcovich. Clarion, 1998. ISBN 978-0-395-64366-2 Subj: Ethnic groups in the U.S. – Russian Americans. Family life – fathers. Family life – sisters. Immigrants. Jewish culture. Religion.

The boy who stuck out his tongue: a Yiddish folk tale ill. by Judith Christine Mills. Barefoot, 2000. ISBN 978-1-84148-067-1 Subj: Character traits – stubbornness. Folk & fairy tales. Jewish culture.

Tarlow, Ellen. *Pinwheel days* ill. by Gretel Parker. Star Bright, 2007. ISBN 978-1-59572-059-7 Subj: Animals. Animals – donkeys. Friendship.

Tarpley, Natasha Anastasia. *Bippity Bop barbershop* ill. by E. B. Lewis. Little, 2002. ISBN 978-0-316-52284-7 Subj: Careers – barbers. Ethnic groups in the U.S. – African Americans. Family life – fathers. Family life – sons. Hair.

I love my hair! ill. by E. B. Lewis. Little, 1997. ISBN 978-0-316-52275-5 Subj: Ethnic groups in the U.S. – African Americans. Family life – mothers. Hair.

Joe-Joe's first flight ill. by E. B. Lewis. Knopf, 2003. ISBN 978-0-375-91053-1 Subj: Activities – flying. Careers – airplane pilots. Ethnic groups in the U.S. – African Americans. Imagination. Moon. Prejudice.

Tarpley, Todd. *How about a kiss for me?* ill. by Liza Woodruff. Penguin, 2010. ISBN 978-0-525-42235-8 Subj: Kissing. Rhyming text.

Ten tiny toes ill. by Marc Brown. Little, Brown, 2012. ISBN 978-0-316-12921-3 Subj: Anatomy –

toes. Babies. Behavior – growing up. Rhyming text.

Tarsky, Sue. *The busy building book* ill. by Alex Ayliffe. Putnam, 1998. ISBN 978-0-399-23137-7 Subj: Buildings.

Tashiro, Chisato. *Five nice mice* adapt. by Kate Westerlund; ill. by author. Minedition, 2007. ISBN 978-0-698-40058-0 Subj: Animals – mice. Frogs & toads. Music.

Tatcheva, Eva. *Witch Zelda's birthday cake* ill. by author. Abrams, 2001. ISBN 978-0-8109-4567-8 Subj: Birthdays. Food. Format, unusual – toy & movable books. Holidays – Halloween. Witches.

Tate, Don. *It jes' happened: when Bill Traylor started to draw* ill. by R. Gregory Christie. Lee & Low, 2012. ISBN 978-1-60060-260-3 Subj: Activities – drawing. Art. Ethnic groups in the U.S. – African Americans. Slavery. U.S. history.

Tatham, Betty. *Baby Sea Otter* ill. by Joan Paley. Holt, 2005. ISBN 978-0-8050-7504-5 Subj: Animals – babies. Animals – otters.

Penguin chick ill. by Helen Davie. HarperCollins, 2002. ISBN 978-0-06-028595-1 Subj: Animals – babies. Birds – penguins.

Taulbert, Clifton L. *Little Cliff and the cold place* ill. by E. B. Lewis. Dial, 2002. ISBN 978-0-8037-2558-4 Subj: Concepts – cold & heat. Foreign lands – Arctic.

Little Cliff and the porch people ill. by E. B. Lewis. Dial, 1999. ISBN 978-0-8037-2175-3 Subj: Communities, neighborhoods. Ethnic groups in the U.S. – African Americans. Family life. Food. Friendship. Magic.

Little Cliff's first day of school ill. by E. B. Lewis. Dial, 2001. ISBN 978-0-8037-2557-7 Subj: Emotions – fear. Ethnic groups in the U.S. – African Americans. Family life – great-grandparents. School – first day.

Tauss, Marc. *Superhero* ill. by author. Scholastic, 2005. ISBN 978-0-439-62734-4 Subj: Cities, towns. Ethnic groups in the U.S. – African Americans. Problem solving. Robots.

Tavares, Matt. *Becoming Babe Ruth* ill. by author. Candlewick, 2013. ISBN 978-0-7636-5646-1 Subj: Behavior – growing up. School. Sports – baseball.

Henry Aaron's dream ill. by author. Candlewick, 2010. ISBN 978-0-7636-3224-3 Subj: Ethnic groups in the U.S. – African Americans. Prejudice. Sports – baseball. U.S. history.

Mudball ill. by author. Candlewick, 2005. ISBN 978-0-7636-2387-6 Subj: Sports – baseball.

Oliver's game ill. by author. Candlewick, 2004. ISBN 978-0-7636-1852-0 Subj: Family life – grandfathers. Sports – baseball.

There goes Ted Williams: the greatest hitter who ever lived ill. by author. Candlewick, 2012. ISBN 978-0-7636-2789-8 Subj: Sports – baseball. U.S. history.

Zachary's ball ill. by author. Candlewick, 2000. ISBN 978-0-7636-0730-2 Subj: Sports – baseball.

Taxali, Gary. *This is silly!* ill. by author. Scholastic, 2010. ISBN 978-0-439-71836-3 Subj: Humorous stories. Rhyming text.

Taylor, Alastair. *Swollobog* ill. by author. Houghton, 2001. ISBN 978-0-618-04348-4 Subj: Animals – dogs. Humorous stories. Toys – balloons.

Taylor, Alice. *A child's treasury of Irish rhymes* ill. by Nicola Emoe. Barefoot, 1999. ISBN 978-1-902283-18-0 Subj: Foreign lands – Ireland. Nursery rhymes.

Taylor, Ann. *Baby dance* ill. by Marjorie van Heerden. HarperCollins, 1999. ISBN 978-0-694-01206-0 Subj: Activities – dancing. Activities – singing. Babies. Ethnic groups in the U.S. – African Americans. Family life – fathers. Format, unusual – board books.

Taylor, Barbara. *I wonder why zippers have teeth and other questions about inventions.* Kingfisher, 1995. ISBN 978-1-85697-670-1 Subj: Careers – inventors. Character traits – questioning. Inventions.

Taylor, Eleanor. *Beep, beep, let's go!* ill. by author. Bloomsbury, 2005. ISBN 978-1-58234-973-2 Subj: Animals. Animals – dogs. Sea & seashore.

Taylor, Harriet Peck. *Coyote and the laughing butterflies* ill. by author. Macmillan, 1995. ISBN 978-0-02-788846-1 Subj: Animals – coyotes. Indians of North America. Insects – butterflies, caterpillars. Lakes, ponds.

Secrets of the stone ill. by author. Farrar, 2000. ISBN 978-0-374-36648-3 Subj: Animals. Art. Caves. Indians of North America – Southwest. Petroglyphs.

Ulaq and the northern lights ill. by author. Farrar, 1998. ISBN 978-0-374-38063-2 Subj: Animals. Animals – foxes. Foreign lands – Arctic. Northern lights. Sky.

Taylor, Jane. *Twinkle, twinkle little star* ill. by Heather Collins. Kids Can, 2000. ISBN 978-1-55074-566-5 Subj: Fairies. Format, unusual – board books. Nursery rhymes. Sky. Songs. Stars.

Twinkle, twinkle, little star ill. by Michael Hague. Morrow, 1992. ISBN 978-0-688-11169-4 Subj: Fairies. Nursery rhymes. Sky. Songs. Stars.

Twinkle, twinkle little star ill. by Julia Noonan. Scholastic, 1992. ISBN 978-0-590-45566-4 Subj: Holidays – Christmas. Nursery rhymes. Santa Claus. Sky. Songs. Stars.

Twinkle, twinkle, little star ill. by Jerry Pinkney. Little, Brown, 2011. ISBN 978-0-316-05696-0 Subj: Animals – chipmunks. Nursery rhymes. Sky. Songs. Stars.

Taylor, Joanne. *Full moon rising* ill. by Susan Tooke. Tundra, 2002. ISBN 978-0-88776-548-3 Subj: Careers – farmers. Days of the week, months of the year. Moon.

Taylor, Sean. *Boing!* ill. by Bruce Ingman. Candlewick, 2004. ISBN 978-0-7636-2475-0 Subj: Health & fitness. Sports – gymnastics.

Crocodiles are the best animals of all ill. by Hannah Shaw. Frances Lincoln, 2009. ISBN 978-1-84507-904-8 Subj: Animals – donkeys. Behavior – boasting. Reptiles – alligators, crocodiles. Rhyming text.

The grizzly bear with the frizzly hair ill. by Hannah Shaw. Frances Lincoln, 2011. ISBN 978-1-84780-085-5 Subj: Animals – bears. Animals – rabbits. Behavior – trickery. Character traits – cleverness.

Huck runs amuck! ill. by Peter H. Reynolds. Penguin, 2011. ISBN 978-0-8037-3261-2 Subj: Animals – goats. Flowers.

The ring went zing! a story that ends with a kiss ill. by Jill Barton. Penguin, 2010. ISBN 978-0-8037-3311-4 Subj: Cumulative tales. Humorous stories.

Robomop ill. by Edel Rodriguez. Dial, 2013. ISBN 978-0-8037-3411-1 Subj: Character traits – cleanliness. Humorous stories. Robots.

When a monster is born ill. by Nick Sharratt. Macmillan, 2007. ISBN 978-1-59643-254-3 Subj: Babies. Behavior – growing up. Monsters.

The world champion of staying awake ill. by Jimmy Liao. Candlewick, 2011. ISBN 978-0-7636-4957-9 Subj: Bedtime. Toys.

Taylor, Shirley. *The cross in the egg* ill. by Wendell E. Hall. August House, 1999. ISBN 978-0-87483-549-6 Subj: Animals – rabbits. Eggs. Holidays – Easter. Religion.

Taylor, Theodore. *Hello, Arctic!* ill. by Margaret Chodos-Irvine. Harcourt, 2002. ISBN 978-0-15-201577-0 Subj: Animals. Foreign lands – Arctic. Seasons.

Taylor, Thomas. *Little Mouse and the big cupcake* ill. by Jill Barton. Boxer, 2010. ISBN 978-1-907152-47-4 Subj: Animals – mice. Behavior – sharing. Food.

Taylor-Butler, Christine. *Lamb's Easter surprise* ill. by Cathy Ann Johnson. Sterling, 2012. ISBN 978-1-4027-8622-8 Subj: Animals – sheep. Holidays – Easter. Rhyming text.

Tazewell, Charles. *The littlest angel* ill. by Deborah Lanino. Children's Press, 1998. ISBN 978-0-516-20433-8 Subj: Angels. Gifts. Holidays – Christmas. Religion – Nativity. Stars.

The littlest angel ill. by Paul Micich. Ideals, 1991. ISBN 978-0-8249-8516-5 Subj: Angels. Gifts. Holidays – Christmas. Religion – Nativity. Stars.

The littlest angel ill. by Rebecca Thornburgh. CandyCane, 2002. ISBN 978-0-8249-4224-3 Subj: Angels. Gifts. Holidays – Christmas. Religion – Nativity. Stars.

Tchana, Katrin. *Sense Pass King* ill. by Trina Schart Hyman. Holiday, 2002. ISBN 978-0-8234-1577-9 Subj: Character traits – cleverness. Folk & fairy tales. Foreign lands – Cameroon. Royalty – kings.

Teague, David. *Franklin's big dreams* ill. by Boris Kulikov. Hyperion/Disney, 2010. ISBN 978-1-4231-1919-7 Subj: Bedtime. Dreams. Night.

Teague, Mark. *Baby tamer* ill. by author. Scholastic, 1997. ISBN 978-0-590-67712-7 Subj: Activities – babysitting. Behavior. Circus. Ethnic groups in the U.S. – African Americans.

Dear Mrs. LaRue ill. by author. Scholastic, 2002. ISBN 978-0-439-20663-1 Subj: Activities – writing. Animals – dogs. Humorous stories. Letters, cards. Pets.

Detective LaRue ill. by author. Scholastic, 2004. ISBN 978-0-439-45868-9 Subj: Activities – writing. Animals – cats. Animals – dogs. Careers – detectives. Letters, cards.

Firehouse! ill. by author. Scholastic, 2010. ISBN 978-0-439-91500-7 Subj: Animals – dogs. Careers – firefighters.

Funny farm ill. by author. Orchard, 2009. ISBN 978-0-439-91499-4 Subj: Animals – dogs. Farms. Humorous stories.

LaRue across America: postcards from the vacation ill. by author. Scholastic, 2011. ISBN 978-0-439-91502-1 Subj: Activities – vacationing. Activities – writing. Animals – cats. Animals – dogs. Letters, cards.

LaRue for mayor: letters from the campaign trail ill. by author. Blue Sky, 2008. ISBN 978-0-439-78315-6 Subj: Animals – dogs. Character traits – ambition. Letters, cards. Pets.

The lost and found ill. by author. Scholastic, 1998. ISBN 978-0-590-84619-6 Subj: Behavior – lost & found possessions. Imagination. School.

One Halloween night ill. by author. Scholastic, 1999. ISBN 978-0-590-63803-6 Subj: Holidays – Halloween. Magic.

Pigsty ill. by author. Scholastic, 1994. ISBN 978-0-590-45915-0 Subj: Animals – pigs. Character traits – cleanliness. Character traits – orderliness.

The secret shortcut ill. by author. Scholastic, 1996. ISBN 978-0-590-67714-1 Subj: Behavior – promptness, tardiness. School.

The three little pigs and the somewhat bad wolf ill. by author. Scholastic, 2013. ISBN 978-0-439-91501-4 Subj: Animals – pigs. Animals – wolves. Folk & fairy tales. Friendship.

Tebbs, Victoria. *Noah's Ark story* ill. by Melanie Mitchell. Lion, 2010. ISBN 978-0-7459-4901-7 Subj: Animals. Boats, ships. Religion – Noah. Weather – floods. Weather – rain.

Teckentrup, Britta. *Big smelly bear* ill. by author. Boxer, 2007. ISBN 978-1-905417-37-7 Subj: Activities – bathing. Animals – bears. Character traits – cleanliness.

Grumpy cat ill. by author. Boxer, 2008. ISBN 978-1-905417-69-8 Subj: Animals – cats. Emotions – loneliness.

Little Wolf's song ill. by author. Boxer, 2010. ISBN 978-1-907152-33-7 Subj: Animals – wolves. Behavior – growing up. Behavior – bullying, teasing. Noise, sounds.

Teevin, Toni. *What to do? What to do?* ill. by Janet Pedersen. Houghton, 2006. ISBN 978-0-618-44632-2 Subj: Activities – baking, cooking. Birds. Emotions – loneliness.

Tegen, Katherine Brown. *Dracula and Frankenstein are friends* ill. by Doug Cushman. HarperCollins, 2003. ISBN 978-0-06-000116-2 Subj: Friendship. Holidays – Halloween. Monsters. Parties.

Snowman magic ill. by Brandon Dorman. HarperCollins, 2012. ISBN 978-0-06-201445-0 Subj: Magic. Seasons – winter. Snowmen. Weather – snow.

The story of the Easter Bunny ill. by Sally Anne Lambert. HarperCollins, 2005. ISBN 978-0-06-050712-1 Subj: Animals – rabbits. Holidays – Easter.

The story of the leprechaun ill. by Sally Anne Lambert. HarperCollins, 2011. ISBN 978-0-06-143086-2 Subj: Careers – shoemakers. Mythical creatures – leprechauns.

Tellis, Annabel. *If my dad were a dog* ill. by author; photos by Tracy Morgan. Scholastic, 2007. ISBN 978-0-439-91387-4 Subj: Animals – dogs. Family life – fathers. Humorous stories. Rhyming text.

Temple, Charles A. *Train* ill. by Larry Johnson. Houghton, 1996. ISBN 978-0-395-69826-6 Subj: Ethnic groups in the U.S. – African Americans. Rhyming text. Trains. Transportation.

Temple, Frances. *Tiger soup* ill. by author. Orchard, 1994. ISBN 978-0-531-08709-1 Subj: Animals – monkeys. Animals – tigers. Behavior – trickery. Folk & fairy tales. Foreign lands – Jamaica. Spiders.

ten Cate, Marijke. *The very best door of all* (Linders, Clara)

Tender moments in the wild ill. with photos. Moonstone, 2001. ISBN 978-0-9707768-0-8 Subj: Animals – babies. Family life – parents.

Terasaki, Stanley Todd. *Ghosts for breakfast* ill. by Shelly Shinjo. Lee & Low, 2002. ISBN 978-1-58430-046-5 Subj: Ethnic groups in the U.S. – Japanese Americans. Farms. Ghosts. Humorous stories.

Terry, Michael. *Rhino's horns* ill. by author. Bloomsbury, 2001. ISBN 978-0-7475-5051-8 Subj: Animals. Animals – rhinoceros. Self-concept.

Tessler, Manya. *Yuki's ride home* ill. by author. Bloomsbury, 2008. ISBN 978-1-59990-023-0 Subj: Character traits – bravery. Emotions – fear. Family life – grandmothers. Sports – bicycling.

Teyssèdre, Fabienne. *Joseph wants to read* ill. by author. Dutton, 2001. ISBN 978-0-525-46692-5 Subj: ABC books. Animals. Animals – monkeys. Careers – teachers. Jungle. School.

Thach, James Otis. *A child's guide to common household monsters* ill. by David Udovic. Boyds Mills, 2007. ISBN 978-1-932425-58-1 Subj: Emotions – fear. Monsters. Rhyming text.

Thaler, Mike. *Pig Little* ill. by Paige Miglio. Holt, 2006. ISBN 978-0-8050-6977-8 Subj: Animals – pigs. Sea & seashore – beaches.

Thayer, Ernest Lawrence. *Casey at the bat* ill. by Gerald Fitzgerald. Atheneum, 1995. ISBN 978-0-689-31945-7 Subj: Poetry. Sports – baseball.

Casey at the bat: a ballad of the Republic, sung in the year 1888 ill. by Christopher Bing. Handprint, 2000. ISBN 978-1-929766-00-0 Subj: Caldecott award honor books. Poetry. Sports – baseball.

Casey at the bat: a ballad of the Republic, sung in the year 1888 ill. by Patricia Polacco. Putnam, 1988. ISBN 978-0-399-21585-8 Subj: Poetry. Sports – baseball.

Thayer, Jane. *Part-time dog* ill. by Lisa McCue. HarperCollins, 2004. ISBN 978-0-06-029692-6 Subj: Animals – dogs. Behavior – sharing. Character traits – kindness to animals. Communities, neighborhoods.

The popcorn dragon ill. by Lisa McCue. Morrow, 1989. ISBN 978-0-688-08876-7 Subj: Dragons. Food. Friendship.

The puppy who wanted a boy ill. by Lisa McCue. Morrow, 1986. ISBN 978-0-688-05945-3 Subj: Animals – dogs. Holidays – Christmas.

Thayer, Tanya. *Counting money* ill. by author. Lerner, 2002. ISBN 978-0-8225-1258-5 Subj: Counting, numbers. Money.

Earning money ill. by author. Lerner, 2002. ISBN 978-0-8225-1259-2 Subj: Activities – working. Money.

Fall ill. by author. Lerner, 2002. ISBN 978-0-8225-1987-4 Subj: Seasons – fall.

Saving money ill. by author. Lerner, 2002. ISBN 978-0-8225-1260-8 Subj: Behavior – saving things. Money.

Spending money ill. by author. Lerner, 2002. ISBN 978-0-8225-1261-5 Subj: Money. Shopping.

Spring ill. by author. Lerner, 2002. ISBN 978-0-8225-1986-7 Subj: Seasons – spring.

Summer ill. by author. Lerner, 2002. ISBN 978-0-8225-1984-3 Subj: Seasons – summer.

Winter ill. by author. Lerner, 2002. ISBN 978-0-8225-1985-0 Subj: Seasons – winter.

Theodorou, Rod. *Across the solar system* ill. with photos. Heinemann, 2000. ISBN 978-1-57572-486-7 Subj: Planets. Space & space ships. Sun.

Bengal tiger ill. with photos. Heinemann, 2001. ISBN 978-1-57572-267-2 Subj: Animals – endangered animals. Animals – tigers.

Black rhino ill. with photos. Heinemann, 2001. ISBN 978-1-57572-262-7 Subj: Animals – endangered animals. Animals – rhinoceros.

Blue whale ill. with photos. Heinemann, 2001. ISBN 978-1-57572-263-4 Subj: Animals – endangered animals. Animals – whales.

Florida manatee ill. with photos. Heinemann, 2001. ISBN 978-1-57572-265-8 Subj: Animals – endangered animals. Animals – manatees.

Giant panda ill. with photos. Heinemann, 2001. ISBN 978-1-57572-264-1 Subj: Animals – endangered animals. Animals – pandas.

Mountain gorilla ill. with photos. Heinemann, 2001. ISBN 978-1-57572-266-5 Subj: Animals – endangered animals. Animals – gorillas.

Thermes, Jennifer. *Sam Bennett's new shoes* ill. by author. Carolrhoda, 2006. ISBN 978-1-57505-822-1 Subj: Behavior – growing up. Clothing – shoes. Family life. Farms. U.S. history.

When I was built ill. by author. Holt, 2001. ISBN 978-0-8050-6532-9 Subj: Family life. Homes, houses.

They followed a bright star ill. by Ulises Wensell. Based on a poem by Joan Alavedra. Putnam, 1994. ISBN 978-0-399-22706-6 Subj: Religion – Nativity. Stars.

Thiele, Bob. *What a wonderful world* (Weiss, George)

Thien, Madeleine. *The Chinese violin* ill. by Joe Chang. Whitecap, 2001. ISBN 978-1-55285-205-7 Subj: Foreign lands – Canada. Music. Musical instruments – violins.

Thiesing, Lisa. *Me and you: a mother-daughter album* ill. by author. Hyperion, 1998. ISBN 978-0-7868-2338-3 Subj: Family life – daughters. Family life – mothers.

Thimmesh, Catherine. *Friends: true stories of extraordinary animal friendships.* Harcourt, 2011. ISBN 978-0-547-39010-9 Subj: Animals. Friendship.

This little light of mine ill. by E. B. Lewis. Simon & Schuster, 2005. ISBN 978-0-689-83179-9 Subj: Ethnic groups in the U.S. – African Americans. Songs.

This place I know poems sel. by Georgia Heard ill. by eighteen renowned picture book artists. Candlewick, 2002. ISBN 978-0-7636-1924-4 Subj: Emotions – fear. Emotions – grief. Poetry. U.S. history.

Thisdale, François. *Nini* ill. by author. Tundra, 2011. ISBN 978-1-77049-270-7 Subj: Adoption. Foreign lands – China.

Thomas, Eliza. *The red blanket* ill. by Joe Cepeda. Scholastic, 2004. ISBN 978-0-439-32253-9 Subj: Adoption. Emotions – love. Ethnic groups in the U.S. – Chinese Americans. Family life – single-parent families.

Thomas, Frances. *One day, Daddy* ill. by Ross Collins. Hyperion, 2001. ISBN 978-0-7868-0732-1 Subj: Careers – explorers. Family life – parents. Monsters. Space & space ships.

Thomas, Jan. *A birthday for Cow!* ill. by author. Harcourt, 2008. ISBN 978-0-15-206072-5 Subj: Animals. Animals – bulls, cows. Birthdays. Food. Friendship.

Can you make a scary face? ill. by author. Simon & Schuster, 2009. ISBN 978-1-4169-8581-5 Subj: Frogs & toads. Imagination. Insects – ladybugs.

The doghouse ill. by author. Harcourt, 2008. ISBN 978-0-15-206533-1 Subj: Animals. Animals – dogs. Emotions – fear.

The Easter Bunny's assistant ill. by author. HarperCollins, 2012. ISBN 978-0-06-169286-4 Subj: Animals – rabbits. Eggs. Holidays – Easter.

Here comes the big, mean dust bunny! ill. by author. Simon & Schuster, 2009. ISBN 978-1-4169-9150-2 Subj: Activities – playing. Animals – cats. Humorous stories. Rhyming text.

Is everyone ready for fun? ill. by author. Simon & Schuster, 2011. ISBN 978-1-4424-2364-1 Subj: Animals – bulls, cows. Birds – chickens. Humorous stories.

Let's sing a lullaby with the Brave Cowboy ill. by author. Simon & Schuster, 2012. ISBN 978-1-4424-4276-4 Subj: Bedtime. Cowboys, cowgirls. Emotions – fear. Lullabies.

Pumpkin trouble ill. by author. HarperCollins, 2011. ISBN 978-0-06-169284-0 Subj: Animals – mice. Animals – pigs. Birds – ducks. Holidays – Halloween.

Rhyming dust bunnies ill. by author. Atheneum, 2009. ISBN 978-1-4169-7976-0 Subj: Humorous stories. Rhyming text.

Thomas, Jane Resh. *Celebration!* ill. by Raúl Colón. Hyperion, 1997. ISBN 978-0-7868-2160-0 Subj: Activities – picnicking. Ethnic groups in the U.S. – African Americans. Family life. Holidays – Fourth of July.

Lights on the river ill. by Michael Dooling. Hyperion, 1994. ISBN 978-0-7868-2003-0 Subj: Careers – migrant workers. Emotions. Ethnic groups in the U.S. – Mexican Americans. Family life. Farms. Poverty.

Saying good-bye to grandma ill. by Marcia Sewall. Clarion, 1988. ISBN 978-0-89919-645-9 Subj: Death. Emotions – grief. Family life – grandmothers.

Scaredy dog ill. by Marilyn Mets. Hyperion, 1996. ISBN 978-0-7868-0278-4 Subj: Animals – dogs. Character traits – kindness to animals. Character traits – perseverance. Family life – mothers. Pets.

Thomas, Joan G. *If Jesus came to my house* ill. by Lori McElrath-Eslick. HarperCollins, 2008. ISBN 978-0-06-083942-0 Subj: Behavior. Character traits. Religion.

Thomas, Joyce Carol. *The blacker the berry: poems* ill. by Floyd Cooper. HarperCollins, 2008. ISBN 978-0-06-025375-2 Subj: Ethnic groups in the U.S. – African Americans. Poetry.

Brown honey in broomwheat tea ill. by Floyd Cooper. HarperCollins, 1993. ISBN 978-0-06-021088-5 Subj: Ethnic groups in the U.S. – African Americans. Poetry.

Cherish me ill. by Nneka Bennett. HarperCollins, 1998. ISBN 978-0-694-01097-4 Subj: Character traits – individuality. Ethnic groups in the U.S. – African Americans. Poetry.

Crowning glory ill. by Brenda Joysmith. Cotler, 2002. ISBN 978-0-06-023474-4 Subj: Ethnic groups in the U.S. – African Americans. Family life. Hair. Poetry.

Gingerbread days ill. by Floyd Cooper. HarperCollins, 1995. ISBN 978-0-06-023472-0 Subj: Days of the week, months of the year. Ethnic groups in the U.S. – African Americans. Folk & fairy tales. Poetry.

The gospel Cinderella ill. by David Diaz. Amistad, 2004. ISBN 978-0-06-025388-2 Subj: Ethnic groups in the U.S. – African Americans. Family life – stepfamilies. Folk & fairy tales. Music. Swamps.

In the land of milk and honey ill. by Floyd Cooper. Amistad, 2012. ISBN 978-0-06-025383-7 Subj: Activities – traveling. Ethnic groups in the U.S. – African Americans. Trains. U.S. history.

Joy ill. by Pamela Johnson. Hyperion, 2001. ISBN 978-0-7868-0750-5 Subj: Emotions – happiness. Ethnic groups in the U.S. – African Americans. Family life – mothers. Family life – sons. Format, unusual – board books.

Shouting ill. by Annie Lee. Hyperion, 2007. ISBN 978-0-7868-0664-5 Subj: Activities – dancing. Religion.

You are my perfect baby ill. by Nneka Bennett. HarperCollins, 1999. ISBN 978-0-694-01096-7 Subj: Babies. Ethnic groups in the U.S. – African Americans. Family life – new sibling.

Thomas, Mark. *Clothes in Colonial America* ill. with photos. Children's Press, 2002. ISBN 978-0-516-23932-3 Subj: Clothing. U.S. history.

Fun and games in Colonial America ill. with photos. Children's Press, 2002. ISBN 978-0-516-23935-4 Subj: Games. U.S. history.

Work in Colonial America ill. with photos. Children's Press, 2002. ISBN 978-0-516-23934-7 Subj: Activities – working. U.S. history.

Thomas, Naturi. *Uh-oh! It's Mama's birthday!* ill. by Keinyo White. Whitman, 1997. ISBN 978-0-8075-8268-8 Subj: Birthdays. Ethnic groups in the U.S. – African Americans. Family life – mothers. Gifts.

Thomas, Pat. *My family's changing* ill. by Lesley Harker. Barron's, 1999. ISBN 978-0-7641-0995-9 Subj: Divorce. Family life.

Why is it so hard to breathe? a first look at asthma ill. by Lesley Harker. Barron's, 2008. ISBN 978-0-7641-3898-0 Subj: Illness – asthma.

Thomas, Patricia. *Firefly mountain* ill. by Peter Sylvada. Peachtree, 2007. ISBN 978-1-56145-360-3 Subj: Insects – fireflies. Night. Seasons – summer.

Red sled ill. by Chris L. Demarest. Boyds Mills, 2008. ISBN 978-1-59078-559-1 Subj: Night. Rhyming text. Seasons – winter. Sports – sledding.

Thomas, Peggy. *Snow dance* ill. by Paul Facklam. Pelican, 2008. ISBN 978-1-58980-478-4 Subj: Activities – dancing. Seasons – winter. Weather – snow.

Thomas, Shelley Moore. *A baby's coming to your house* photos by Eric Futran. Whitman, 2001. ISBN 978-0-8075-0502-1 Subj: Babies. Family life – new sibling.

A cold winter's Good Knight ill. by Jennifer Plecas. Dutton, 2008. ISBN 978-0-525-47964-2 Subj: Dragons. Etiquette. Knights. Seasons – winter.

A Good Knight's rest ill. by Jennifer Plecas. Penguin, 2011. ISBN 978-0-525-42195-5 Subj: Activities – vacationing. Dragons. Friendship. Knights.

Good night, Good Knight ill. by Jennifer Plecas. Dutton, 2000. ISBN 978-0-525-46326-9 Subj: Bedtime. Dragons. Knights. Magic. Royalty.

Putting the world to sleep ill. by Bonnie Christensen. Houghton, 1995. ISBN 978-0-395-71283-2 Subj: Bedtime. Cumulative tales. Night. Rhyming text.

Somewhere today: a book of peace photos by Eric Futran. Whitman, 1998. ISBN 978-0-8075-7546-8 Subj: Character traits – helpfulness.

Take care, Good Knight ill. by Paul Meisel. Penguin, 2006. ISBN 978-0-525-47695-5 Subj: Animals – cats. Books, reading. Character traits – helpfulness. Dragons. Knights.

Thomas, Valerie. *Winnie the witch* ill. by Korky Paul. HarperCollins, 2007. ISBN 978-0-06-117312-7 Subj: Animals – cats. Concepts – color. Witches.

Winnie's midnight dragon ill. by Korky Paul. HarperCollins, 2008. ISBN 978-0-06-117314-1 Subj: Animals – cats. Dragons. Magic. Witches.

Thomassie, Tynia. *Cajun through and through* ill. by Andrew Glass. Little, 2000. ISBN 978-0-316-84189-4 Subj: Family life – cousins.

Thompson, Colin. *Falling angels* ill. by author. Hutchinson, 2001. ISBN 978-0-09-176817-1 Subj: Activities – flying. Family life. Family life – grandmothers. Imagination.

Unknown ill. by Anna Pignataro. Walker, 2000. ISBN 978-0-8027-8731-6 Subj: Animals – dogs. Behavior – needing someone. Fire.

Thompson, Emma. *The further tale of Peter Rabbit* ill. by Eleanor Taylor. Warne, 2012. ISBN 978-0-7232-6910-6 Subj: Activities – traveling. Animals – rabbits. Foreign lands – Scotland.

Thompson, Kay. *Here comes Eloise!* (Cheshire, Marc)

Kay Thompson's Eloise ill. by Hilary Knight. 50th anniversary ed. Simon & Schuster, 2005. ISBN 978-0-689-82795-2 Subj: Behavior. Hotels.

Kay Thompson's Eloise at Christmastime ill. by Hilary Knight. Simon & Schuster, 1999. ISBN 978-0-689-83039-6 Subj: Holidays – Christmas. Hotels.

Kay Thompson's Eloise in Moscow ill. by Hilary Knight. 40th anniversary ed. Simon & Schuster, 2000. ISBN 978-0-689-83211-6 Subj: Activities – traveling. Foreign lands – Russia. Hotels.

Kay Thompson's Eloise takes a bawth (sic) ill. by Hilary Knight and Mart Crowley. Simon & Schuster, 2002. ISBN 978-0-689-84288-7 Subj: Activities – bathing. Hotels. Parties.

Kay Thompson's Eloise's what I absolutely love love love ill. by Hilary Knight. Simon & Schuster, 2005. ISBN 978-0-689-84965-7 Subj: Emotions – love. Hotels. Self-concept.

Thompson, Lauren. *The apple pie that Papa baked* ill. by Jonathan Bean. Simon & Schuster, 2007. ISBN 978-1-4169-1240-8 Subj: Cumulative tales. Food. Trees.

Ballerina dreams: a true story photos by James Estrin. Feiwel & Friends, 2007. ISBN 978-0-312-37029-9 Subj: Activities – dancing. Ballet. Disabilities – cerebral palsy.

Chew, chew, gulp! ill. by Jarrett J. Krosoczka. Simon & Schuster, 2011. ISBN 978-1-4169-9744-3 Subj: Food. Rhyming text.

The Christmas magic ill. by Jon J Muth. Scholastic, 2009. ISBN 978-0-439-77497-0 Subj: Holidays – Christmas. Magic. Santa Claus.

The forgiveness garden ill. by Christy Hale. Feiwel & Friends, 2012. ISBN 978-0-312-62599-3 Subj: Behavior – forgiving. Emotions – hate. Gardens, gardening. Violence, nonviolence.

Hop, hop, jump! ill. by Jarrett J. Krosoczka. Simon & Schuster, 2012. ISBN 978-1-4169-9745-0 Subj: Health & fitness – exercise. Rhyming text.

How many cats? ill. by Robin Eley. Hyperion, 2009. ISBN 978-1-4231-0801-6 Subj: Animals – cats. Counting, numbers. Rhyming text.

Leap back home to me ill. by Matthew Cordell. Simon & Schuster, 2011. ISBN 978-1-4169-0664-3

Subj: Family life – mothers. Frogs & toads. Rhyming text.

Little Quack ill. by Derek Anderson. Simon & Schuster, 2003. ISBN 978-0-689-84723-3 Subj: Animals – babies. Birds – ducks. Character traits – bravery. Counting, numbers.

Little Quack [board book] ill. by Derek Anderson. Simon & Schuster, 2005. ISBN 978-0-689-87645-5 Subj: Animals – babies. Birds – ducks. Character traits – bravery. Counting, numbers. Format, unusual – board books.

Little Quack: dial-a-duck ill. by Derek Anderson. Simon & Schuster, 2006. ISBN 978-1-4169-0932-3 Subj: Birds – ducks. Counting, numbers. Format, unusual – board books. Format, unusual – toy & movable books.

Little Quack's bedtime ill. by Derek Anderson. Simon & Schuster, 2005. ISBN 978-0-689-86894-8 Subj: Bedtime. Birds – ducks. Family life – mothers. Night.

Little Quack's hide and seek ill. by Derek Anderson. Simon & Schuster, 2004. ISBN 978-0-689-85722-5 Subj: Birds – ducks. Counting, numbers. Family life – mothers. Games.

Little Quack's hide and seek [board book] ill. by Derek Anderson. Simon & Schuster, 2007. ISBN 978-1-4169-0325-3 Subj: Birds – ducks. Counting, numbers. Family life – mothers. Format, unusual – board books. Games.

Little Quack's new friend ill. by Derek Anderson. Simon & Schuster, 2006. ISBN 978-0-689-86893-1 Subj: Activities – playing. Birds – ducks. Friendship. Frogs & toads. Lakes, ponds.

Love one another ill. by Elizabeth Uyehara. Scholastic, 2000. ISBN 978-0-590-31830-3 Subj: Holidays – Easter. Religion.

Mouse's first Christmas ill. by Buket Erdogan. Simon & Schuster, 1999. ISBN 978-0-689-82325-1 Subj: Animals – mice. Holidays – Christmas. Santa Claus.

Mouse's first Christmas [board book] ill. by Buket Erdogan. Simon & Schuster, 2002. ISBN 978-0-689-85141-4 Subj: Animals – mice. Format, unusual – board books. Holidays – Christmas. Santa Claus.

Mouse's first fall ill. by Buket Erdogan. Simon & Schuster, 2006. ISBN 978-0-689-85837-6 Subj: Animals – mice. Seasons – fall.

Mouse's first Halloween ill. by author. Simon & Schuster, 2000. ISBN 978-0-689-83176-8 Subj: Animals – mice. Holidays – Halloween.

Mouse's first snow ill. by Buket Erdogan. Simon & Schuster, 2005. ISBN 978-0-689-85836-9 Subj: Animals – mice. Family life – fathers. Seasons – winter. Weather – snow.

Mouse's first spring ill. by Buket Erdogan. Simon & Schuster, 2005. ISBN 978-0-689-85838-3 Subj: Animals – mice. Family life – mothers. Seasons – spring. Weather – wind.

One riddle, one answer ill. by Linda S. Wingerter. Scholastic, 2001. ISBN 978-0-590-31335-3 Subj: Counting, numbers. Riddles & jokes. Royalty – princesses.

One starry night ill. by Jonathan Bean. Simon & Schuster, 2011. ISBN 978-0-689-82851-5 Subj: Animals. Holidays – Christmas. Religion – Nativity.

Polar bear morning ill. by Stephen Savage. Scholastic, 2013. ISBN 978-0-439-69885-6 Subj: Animals – polar bears. Foreign lands – Arctic. Friendship.

Wee little bunny ill. by John Butler. Simon & Schuster, 2010. ISBN 978-1-4169-7937-1 Subj: Animals – babies. Animals – rabbits.

Wee little chick ill. by John Butler. Simon & Schuster, 2008. ISBN 978-1-4169-3468-4 Subj: Birds – chickens. Character traits – confidence. Character traits – smallness. Farms. Self-concept.

Wee little lamb ill. by John Butler. Simon & Schuster, 2009. ISBN 978-1-4169-3469-1 Subj: Animals. Animals – mice. Animals – sheep. Character traits – shyness.

Thompson, Richard. *The follower* ill. by Martin Springett. Fitzhenry & Whiteside, 2000. ISBN 978-1-55041-532-2 Subj: Cumulative tales. Days of the week, months of the year. Mystery stories. Rhyming text. Witches.

The night walker ill. by Martin Springett. Fitzhenry & Whiteside, 2003. ISBN 978-1-55041-672-5 Subj: Behavior – collecting things. Emotions – fear. Imagination. Night. Noise, sounds.

Thoms, Susan Collins. *Cesar takes a break* ill. by Rogé. Sterling, 2008. ISBN 978-1-4027-3653-7 Subj: Pets. Reptiles – iguanas. School.

Thomson, Bill. *Chalk* ill. by author. Marshall Cavendish, 2010. ISBN 978-0-7614-5526-4 Subj: Activities – drawing. Magic. Wordless.

Fossil ill. by author. Amazon/Two Lions, 2013. ISBN 978-1-4778-4700-8 Subj: Animals – dogs. Fossils. Wordless.

Thomson, Pat. *The squeaky, creaky bed* ill. by Niki Daly. Random House, 2003. ISBN 978-0-385-90856-6 Subj: Animals. Cumulative tales. Family life – grandparents. Furniture – beds. Noise, sounds.

Thomson, Sarah L. *Amazing whales* ill. with photos. HarperCollins, 2005. ISBN 978-0-06-054466-9 Subj: Animals – whales.

Around the neighborhood: a counting lullaby ill. by Jana Christy. Amazon Children's, 2012. ISBN

978-0-7614-6164-7 Subj: Animals. Communities, neighborhoods. Counting, numbers. Lullabies. Nursery rhymes.

Cub's big world ill. by Joe Cepeda. Harcourt, 2013. ISBN 978-0-544-05739-5 Subj: Animals – polar bears. Family life – mothers.

Pirates, ho! ill. by Stephen Gilpin. Marshall Cavendish, 2008. ISBN 978-0-7614-5435-9 Subj: Pirates. Rhyming text.

Stars and stripes ill. by Bob Dacey and Debra Bandelin. HarperCollins, 2003. ISBN 978-0-06-050417-5 Subj: U.S. history.

Tigers ill. with photos. HarperCollins, 2004. ISBN 978-0-06-054451-5 Subj: Animals – endangered animals. Animals – tigers.

What Lincoln said ill. by James Ransome. Collins, 2009. ISBN 978-0-06-084820-0 Subj: U.S. history.

Where do polar bears live? ill. by Jason Chin. HarperCollins, 2010. ISBN 978-0-06-157518-1 Subj: Animals – polar bears. Foreign lands – Arctic.

Thong, Roseanne. *Fly free!* ill. by Eujin Kim Neilan. Boyds Mills, 2010. ISBN 978-1-59078-550-8 Subj: Birds. Character traits – kindness. Foreign lands – Vietnam. Religion.

Gai see: what you can see in Chinatown ill. by Yangsook Choi. Abrams, 2007. ISBN 978-0-8109-9337-2 Subj: Ethnic groups in the U.S. – Chinese Americans. Rhyming text. Seasons. Stores.

Round is a mooncake ill. by Grace Lin. Chronicle, 2000. ISBN 978-0-8118-2676-1 Subj: Concepts – shape. Ethnic groups in the U.S. – Chinese Americans.

Round is a tortilla ill. by John Parra. Chronicle, 2013. ISBN 978-1-4521-0616-8 Subj: Concepts – shape. Ethnic groups in the U.S. – Hispanic Americans. Rhyming text.

Tummy girl ill. by Sam Williams. Holt, 2007. ISBN 978-0-8050-7609-7 Subj: Babies. Behavior – growing up. Rhyming text.

Wish: wishing traditions around the world ill. by Elisa Kleven. Chronicle, 2008. ISBN 978-0-8118-5716-1 Subj: Behavior – wishing.

Thornhill, Jan. *Is this Panama? a migration story* ill. by Soyeon Kim. OwlKids, 2013. ISBN 978-1-926973-88-3 Subj: Birds. Migration. Nature.

The rumor ill. by reteller. Maple Tree, 2002. ISBN 978-1-894379-39-7 Subj: Animals. Animals – rabbits. Behavior – misunderstanding. Cumulative tales. Emotions – fear. Folk & fairy tales. Foreign lands – India.

Wild in the city ill. by author. Sierra Club, 1996. ISBN 978-0-87156-910-3 Subj: Animals. Animals – cats. Birds. Cities, towns. Ecology. Night.

Thorpe, Kiki. *A comfy, cozy Thanksgiving* ill. by Tom Brannon. Based on the TV series Bear in the Big Blue House. Simon & Schuster, 2002. ISBN 978-0-689-85012-7 Subj: Animals. Animals – bears. Character traits – helpfulness. Holidays – Thanksgiving.

Lots of bots ill. by Ben Butcher. Disney, 2008. ISBN 978-1-4231-1052-1 Subj: Rhyming text. Robots.

Time to cha-cha-cha! ill. by Barry Goldberg. Simon & Schuster, 2000. ISBN 978-0-689-83431-8 Subj: Activities – dancing. Animals. Animals – bears. Musical instruments.

The three bears. *Goldilocks* by Ruth Sanderson; ill. by author. Little, Brown, 2009. ISBN 978-0-316-77885-5 Subj: Animals – bears. Folk & fairy tales.

Goldilocks and the three bears retold by Jan Brett; ill. by reteller. Dodd, 1987. ISBN 978-0-396-08925-4 Subj: Animals – bears. Folk & fairy tales.

Goldilocks and the three bears retold by Caralyn Buehner; ill. by Mark Buehner. Penguin, 2007. ISBN 978-0-8037-2939-1 Subj: Animals – bears. Folk & fairy tales.

Goldilocks and the three bears adapt. by Lorinda Bryan Cauley; ill. by adapter. Putnam, 1981. ISBN 978-0-399-20794-5 Subj: Animals – bears. Folk & fairy tales.

Goldilocks and the three bears by Emma Chichester Clark; ill. by author. Candlewick, 2010. ISBN 978-0-7636-4680-6 Subj: Animals – bears. Folk & fairy tales.

Goldilocks and the three bears retold by Valeri Gorbachev; ill. by reteller. NorthSouth, 2001. ISBN 978-0-7358-1438-7 Subj: Animals – bears. Folk & fairy tales.

Goldilocks and the three bears retold by Steven Guarnaccia; ill. by reteller. Abrams, 2000. ISBN 978-0-8109-4139-7 Subj: Animals – bears. Folk & fairy tales.

Goldilocks and the three bears retold by David McPhail; ill. by reteller. Scholastic, 1995. ISBN 978-0-590-48117-5 Subj: Animals – bears. Folk & fairy tales.

Goldilocks and the three bears adapt. by James Marshall; ill. by adapter. Dial, 1988. ISBN 978-0-8037-0543-2 Subj: Animals – bears. Caldecott award honor books. Folk & fairy tales.

Goldilocks and the three bears retold by Gerda Muller; ill. by reteller. Floris, 2011. ISBN 978-0-86315-795-0 Subj: Animals – bears. Folk & fairy tales.

Goldilocks and the three bears retold by Gennady Spirin; ill. by reteller. Marshall Cavendish, 2009. ISBN 978-0-7614-5596-7 Subj: Animals – bears. Folk & fairy tales.

Goldilocks and the three bears retold by Janet Stevens; ill. by reteller. Holiday, 1985. ISBN 978-0-8234-0608-1 Subj: Animals – bears. Folk & fairy tales.

The three bears adapt. by Byron Barton; ill. by adapter. HarperCollins, 1991. ISBN 978-0-06-020424-2 Subj: Animals – bears. Folk & fairy tales.

The three bears ill. by Paul Galdone. Seabury Pr., 1972. Subj: Animals – bears. Folk & fairy tales.

The three bears [board book] ill. by Thea Kliros. HarperCollins, 2003. ISBN 978-0-06-008238-3 Subj: Animals – bears. Folk & fairy tales. Format, unusual – board books.

The 3 bears and Goldilocks by Margaret Willey; ill. by Heather Solomon. Atheneum, 2008. ISBN 978-1-4169-2494-4 Subj: Animals – bears. Behavior – misbehavior. Folk & fairy tales.

The three little pigs. *The three little pigs* retold by Gavin Bishop; ill. by reteller. Scholastic, 1990. ISBN 978-0-590-43358-7 Subj: Animals – pigs. Animals – wolves. Character traits – cleverness. Folk & fairy tales.

The three little pigs ill. by Paul Galdone. Seabury Pr., 1970. Subj: Animals – pigs. Animals – wolves. Character traits – cleverness. Folk & fairy tales.

The three little pigs by Maggie Moore; ill. by Rob Hefferan. Picture Window, 2003. ISBN 978-1-4048-0071-7 Subj: Animals – pigs. Animals – wolves. Character traits – cleverness. Folk & fairy tales.

The three little pigs retold by Steven Kellogg; ill. by reteller. Morrow, 1997. ISBN 978-0-688-08732-6 Subj: Animals – pigs. Animals – wolves. Character traits – cleverness. Family life – mothers. Folk & fairy tales.

The three little pigs retold by David McPhail; ill. by reteller. Scholastic, 1995. ISBN 978-0-590-48118-2 Subj: Animals – pigs. Animals – wolves. Character traits – cleverness. Folk & fairy tales.

The three little pigs retold by James Marshall; ill. by reteller. Dial, 1989. ISBN 978-0-8037-0594-4 Subj: Animals – pigs. Animals – wolves. Character traits – cleverness. Folk & fairy tales.

The three little pigs ill. by Bernadette Watts. North-South, 2012. ISBN 978-0-7358-4058-4 Subj: Animals – pigs. Animals – wolves. Character traits – cleverness. Folk & fairy tales.

The three little pigs ill. by Margot Zemach. Farrar, 1988. ISBN 978-0-374-37527-0 Subj: Animals – pigs. Animals – wolves. Character traits – cleverness. Folk & fairy tales.

The three little pigs [board book] ill. by Thea Kliros. HarperCollins, 2003. ISBN 978-0-06-008236-9 Subj: Animals – pigs. Animals – wolves. Character traits – cleverness. Folk & fairy tales. Format, unusual – board books.

The three little pigs / Los tres cerditos adapt. by Merce Escardo i. Bas; ill. by Pere Joan. Chronicle, 2006. ISBN 978-0-8118-5063-6 Subj: Animals – pigs. Animals – wolves. Character traits – cleverness. Folk & fairy tales. Foreign languages.

The three little pigs and the big bad wolf retold by Glen Rounds; ill. by reteller. Holiday, 1992. ISBN 978-0-8234-0923-5 Subj: Animals – pigs. Animals – wolves. Character traits – cleverness. Folk & fairy tales. Rhyming text.

The three little pigs and the fox adapt. by William H. Hooks; ill. by S. D. Schindler. Macmillan, 1989. ISBN 978-0-02-744431-5 Subj: Animals – foxes. Animals – pigs. Birds – chickens. Character traits – cleverness. Folk & fairy tales.

Thurber, James. *The great Quillow* ill. by Steven Kellogg. Harcourt, 1994. ISBN 978-0-15-232544-2 Subj: Careers – toy makers. Character traits – being different. Character traits – cleverness. Giants. Toys.

Many moons ill. by Marc Simont. Harcourt, 1990. ISBN 978-0-15-251872-1 Subj: Clowns, jesters. Illness. Moon. Royalty – princesses.

Many moons ill. by Louis Slobodkin. Harcourt, 1943. ISBN 978-0-15-251873-8 Subj: Caldecott award books. Clowns, jesters. Illness. Moon. Royalty – princesses.

Thurlby, Paul. *Paul Thurlby's alphabet* ill. by author. Candlewick, 2011. ISBN 978-0-7636-5565-5 Subj: ABC books.

Paul Thurlby's wildlife ill. by author. Candlewick, 2013. ISBN 978-0-7636-6563-0 Subj: Animals.

Thurman, Kathryn K. *A garden for Pig* ill. by Lindsay Ward. Kane/Miller, 2010. ISBN 978-1-935279-24-2 Subj: Animals – pigs. Food. Gardens, gardening.

Thury, Frederick. *The last straw* ill. by Vlasta Van Kampen. Charlesbridge, 1999. ISBN 978-0-88106-152-9 Subj: Animals – camels. Gifts. Holidays – Christmas. Religion – Nativity.

Tibo, Gilles. *The cowboy kid* ill. by Tom Kapas. Tundra, 2000. ISBN 978-0-88776-473-8 Subj: Activities – flying. Animals – horses, ponies. Cowboys, cowgirls. Homeless. Imagination. Magic.

The grand journey of Mr. Man ill. by Luc Melanson. Dominique & Friends, 2001. ISBN 978-1-894363-78-5 Subj: Activities – traveling. Behavior – needing someone. Death. Emotions – grief. Toys – bears. War.

Tierney, Fiona. *Lion's lunch?* ill. by Margaret Chamberlain. Scholastic, 2010. ISBN 978-0-545-

17691-0 Subj: Activities – drawing. Animals – lions. Behavior – bullying, teasing. Jungle.

Tildes, Phyllis Limbacher. *Animals in camouflage* ill. by author. Charlesbridge, 2000. ISBN 978-0-88106-120-8 Subj: Animals. Disguises. Picture puzzles.

Billy's big-boy bed ill. by author. Whispering Coyote, 2002. ISBN 978-1-57091-475-1 Subj: Behavior – growing up. Toys – bears.

Eye guess: a fold-out guessing game ill. by author. Charlesbridge, 2005. ISBN 978-1-57091-650-2 Subj: Animals. Format, unusual – toy & movable books.

Tillman, Nancy. *The crown on your head* ill. by author. Feiwel & Friends, 2011. ISBN 978-0-312-64521-2 Subj: Animals. Character traits – individuality. Rhyming text. Self-concept.

On the night you were born ill. by author. Feiwel & Friends, 2006. ISBN 978-0-312-34606-5 Subj: Birth. Night.

The spirit of Christmas ill. by author. Feiwel & Friends, 2009. ISBN 978-0-312-54965-7 Subj: Holidays – Christmas. Rhyming text.

Tumford the terrible ill. by author. Feiwel & Friends, 2011. ISBN 978-0-312-36840-1 Subj: Animals – cats. Behavior – misbehavior. Rhyming text.

Tumford's rude noises ill. by author. Feiwel & Friends, 2012. ISBN 978-0-312-36841-8 Subj: Animals – cats. Behavior – misbehavior. Etiquette. Noise, sounds. Rhyming text.

Wherever you are: my love will find you ill. by author. Feiwel & Friends, 2010. ISBN 978-0-312-54966-4 Subj: Emotions – love. Rhyming text.

Timmers, Leo. *Bang* ill. by author. Gecko, 2013. ISBN 978-1-877579-18-9 Subj: Accidents. Animals. Transportation.

Crow ill. by author. Clavis, 2010. ISBN 978-1-60537-071-2 Subj: Birds. Birds – crows. Character traits – being different. Self-concept.

Who is driving? ill. by author. Bloomsbury, 2007. ISBN 978-1-59990-021-6 Subj: Activities – driving. Animals. Automobiles. Trucks.

Tingle, Tim. *When Turtle grew feathers: a folktale from the Choctaw nation* ill. by Stacey Schuett. August House, 2007. ISBN 978-0-87483-777-3 Subj: Animals – rabbits. Behavior – trickery. Folk & fairy tales. Indians of North America – Choctaw. Reptiles – turtles, tortoises. Sports – racing.

Tinkham, Kelly A. *Hair for Mama* ill. by Amy Bates. Penguin, 2007. ISBN 978-0-8037-2955-1 Subj: Emotions – love. Ethnic groups in the U.S. – African Americans. Hair. Illness – cancer.

Tirabosco, Tom. *At the same time* ill. by author. Kane/Miller, 2001. ISBN 978-1-929132-17-1 Subj: Activities. Books, reading.

Titcomb, Gordon. *The last train* ill. by Wendell Minor. Roaring Brook, 2010. ISBN 978-1-59643-164-5 Subj: Music. Songs. Trains.

Titherington, Jeanne. *Baby's boat* ill. by author. Greenwillow, 1992. ISBN 978-0-688-08556-8 Subj: Babies. Bedtime. Boats, ships. Lullabies. Sea & seashore.

A place for Ben ill. by author. Greenwillow, 1987. ISBN 978-0-688-06494-5 Subj: Babies. Emotions – loneliness. Family life – brothers. Family life – new sibling.

Pumpkin pumpkin ill. by author. Greenwillow, 1985. ISBN 978-0-688-50696-4 Subj: Gardens, gardening. Holidays – Halloween.

Where are you going, Emma? ill. by author. Greenwillow, 1988. ISBN 978-0-688-07082-3 Subj: Behavior – lost. Family life – grandfathers.

Titus, Eve. *Anatole* ill. by Paul Galdone. McGraw-Hill, 1957. Subj: Animals – mice. Caldecott award honor books. Foreign lands – France.

Anatole and the cat ill. by Paul Galdone. McGraw-Hill, 1957. Subj: Animals – cats. Animals – mice. Caldecott award honor books. Character traits – bravery. Foreign lands – France. Problem solving.

Tobias, Tobi. *Wishes for you* ill. by Henri Sorensen. HarperCollins, 2003. ISBN 978-0-688-10839-7 Subj: Behavior – wishing. Family life – parents.

Tobin, Jim. *Sue MacDonald had a book* ill. by Dave Coverly. Holt, 2009. ISBN 978-0-8050-8766-6 Subj: Books, reading. Language. Rhyming text. Songs.

The very inappropriate word ill. by Dave Coverly. Holt, 2013. ISBN 978-0-8050-9474-9 Subj: Behavior – misbehavior. Language. School.

Tobola, Deborah. *The big buck adventure* (Gill, Shelley)

Todd, Barbara. *The rainmaker* ill. by Rogé. Annick, 2003. ISBN 978-1-55037-775-0 Subj: Mythical creatures. Umbrellas. Weather – rain.

Todd, Mark. *Monster trucks* ill. by author. Houghton, 2003. ISBN 978-0-618-18208-4 Subj: Rhyming text. Trucks.

Start your engines ill. by author. Callaway, 2000. ISBN 978-0-935112-48-1 Subj: Animals. Automobiles. Counting, numbers. Sports – racing.

What will you be for Halloween? ill. by author. Houghton, 2001. ISBN 978-0-618-08803-4 Subj: Clothing – costumes. Holidays – Halloween. Monsters. Rhyming text.

Todd, Traci. *T is for tugboat: navigating the seas from A to Z* ill. by Sara Gillingham. Chronicle, 2008. ISBN 978-0-8118-6094-9 Subj: ABC books. Boats, ships.

Toft, Kim Michelle. *Neptune's nursery* by Kim Michelle Toft and Allan Sheather ill. by Kim Michelle Toft. Charlesbridge, 2000. ISBN 978-1-57091-391-4 Subj: Animals. Picture puzzles. Rhyming text. Science. Sea & seashore.

One less fish by Kim Michelle Toft and Allan Sheather ill. by Kim Michelle Toft. Charlesbridge, 1998. ISBN 978-0-88106-322-6 Subj: Counting, numbers. Fish. Picture puzzles. Rhyming text.

The world that we want ill. by author. Charlesbridge, 2005. ISBN 978-1-58089-114-1 Subj: Animals. Ecology. Format, unusual.

Tokuda, Wendy. *Humphrey the lost whale* by Wendy Tokuda and Richard Hall ill. by Hanako Wakiyama. Heian Intl, 1986. ISBN 978-0-89346-270-3 Subj: Animals – whales. Behavior – lost. Behavior – needing someone. Sea & seashore.

Tokuda, Yukihisa. *I'm a pill bug* ill. by Kiyoshi Takahashi. Kane/Miller, 2006. ISBN 978-1-929132-95-9 Subj: Crustaceans.

Tokunbo, Dimitrea. *The sound of Kwanzaa* ill. by Lisa Cohen. Scholastic, 2009. ISBN 978-0-545-01865-4 Subj: Ethnic groups in the U.S. – African Americans. Holidays – Kwanzaa.

Tolan, Stephanie S. *Bartholomew's blessing* ill. by Margie Moore. HarperCollins, 2004. ISBN 978-0-06-001198-7 Subj: Angels. Animals – foxes. Animals – mice. Holidays – Christmas. Religion – Nativity.

Tolhurst, Marilyn. *Somebody and the three Blairs* ill. by Simone Abel. Watts, 1991. ISBN 978-0-531-08478-6 Subj: Animals – bears. Folk & fairy tales.

Tolman, Marije. *The tree house* by Marije Tolman and Ronald Tolman ill. by authors. Boyds Mills, 2010. ISBN 978-1-59078-806-6 Subj: Animals. Homes, houses. Trees. Wordless.

Tolman, Ronald. *The tree house* (Tolman, Marije)

Tolstoy, Aleksey Nikolayevich. *The enormous turnip* ill. by Scott Goto. Harcourt, 2002. ISBN 978-0-15-204585-2 Subj: Animals. Character traits – cooperation. Cumulative tales. Farms. Folk & fairy tales. Foreign lands – Russia. Plants. Problem solving.

The gigantic turnip by Aleksey Nikolayevich Tolstoy and Niamh Sharkey ill. by Niamh Sharkey. Barefoot, 1999. ISBN 978-1-902283-12-8 Subj: Character traits – cooperation. Cumulative tales. Farms. Folk & fairy tales. Foreign lands – Russia. Plants. Problem solving.

Tom Thumb. *The adventures of Tom Thumb* adapt. by Marianna Mayer; ill. by Kinuko Y. Craft. SeaStar, 2001. ISBN 978-1-58717-065-2 Subj: Folk & fairy tales. Giants. Little people. Royalty – kings. Wizards.

Tom Thumb: a tale adapt. by Lidia Postma; ill. by adapter. Based on a tale by Charles Perrault. Schocken, 1983. ISBN 978-0-8052-3855-6 Subj: Folk & fairy tales. Little people.

Tom Tit Tot. *Tom Tit Tot: an English folk tale* ill. by Evaline Ness. Scribners, 1965. Subj: Caldecott award honor books. Folk & fairy tales. Magic. Names.

Tomecek, Steve. *Dirt* ill. by Nancy Woodman. National Geographic, 2002. ISBN 978-0-7922-8204-4 Subj: Nature. Science.

Stars ill. by Sachiko Yoshikawa. National Geographic, 2003. ISBN 978-0-7922-6955-7 Subj: Astronomy. Stars.

Tomlinson, Jill. *The owl who was afraid of the dark* ill. by Paul Howard. Candlewick, 2000. ISBN 978-0-7636-1562-8 Subj: Animals. Birds – owls. Emotions – fear. Night.

Tomp, Sarah Wones. *Red, white, and blue goodbye* ill. by Ann Barrow. Walker, 2005. ISBN 978-0-8027-8962-4 Subj: Careers – military. Family life – fathers.

Tompert, Ann. *A carol for Christmas* ill. by Laura Kelly. Macmillan, 1994. ISBN 978-0-02-789402-8 Subj: Animals – mice. Foreign lands – Austria. Holidays – Christmas. Songs.

Grandfather Tang's story ill. by Robert Andrew Parker. Crown, 1990. ISBN 978-0-517-57272-6 Subj: Animals – foxes. Family life – grandfathers. Foreign lands – China.

Just a little bit ill. by Lynn Munsinger. Houghton, 1993. ISBN 978-0-395-51527-3 Subj: Activities – playing. Animals – elephants. Animals – mice. Concepts. Cumulative tales.

Little Fox goes to the end of the world ill. by Laura J. Bryant. Marshall Cavendish, 2010. ISBN 978-0-7614-5703-9 Subj: Animals – foxes. Family life – mothers. Imagination.

Nothing sticks like a shadow ill. by Lynn Munsinger. Houghton, 1984. ISBN 978-0-395-35391-2 Subj: Animals – groundhogs. Animals – rabbits. Holidays – Groundhog Day. Shadows.

The pied piper of Peru ill. by Kestutis Kasparavicius. Boyds Mills, 2002. ISBN 978-1-56397-949-1 Subj: Animals – mice. Character traits – kindness to animals. Foreign lands – Peru. Religion.

Saint Nicholas ill. by Michael Garland. Boyds Mills, 2000. ISBN 978-1-56397-844-9 Subj: Folk & fairy tales. Religion. Santa Claus.

Saint Patrick ill. by Michael Garland. Boyds Mills, 1998. ISBN 978-1-56397-659-9 Subj: Foreign lands – Ireland. Religion.

Tonatiuh, Duncan. *Dear Primo: a letter to my cousin* ill. by author. Abrams, 2010. ISBN 978-0-8109-3872-4 Subj: Activities – writing. Ethnic groups in the U.S. – Mexican Americans. Family life – cousins. Foreign lands – Mexico. Letters, cards.

Diego Rivera: his world and ours ill. by author. Abrams, 2011. ISBN 978-0-8109-9731-8 Subj: Art. Careers – artists. Foreign lands – Mexico.

Pancho Rabbit and the coyote: a migrant's tale ill. by author. Abrams, 2013. ISBN 978-1-4197-0583-0 Subj: Activities – traveling. Animals – coyotes. Animals – rabbits. Careers – migrant workers. Family life – fathers.

Tone, Satoe. *The very big carrot* ill. by author. Eerdmans, 2013. ISBN 978-0-8028-5426-1 Subj: Animals – rabbits. Food. Imagination.

Topek, Susan Remick. *Ten good rules* photos by Tod Cohen. Lerner, 2007. ISBN 978-1-58013-209-1 Subj: Religion – Moses.

Torres, Leyla. *Liliana's grandmothers* ill. by author. Farrar, 1998. ISBN 978-0-374-35105-2 Subj: Family life – grandmothers. Foreign lands – Latin America. Quilts.

Saturday sancocho ill. by author. Farrar, 1995. ISBN 978-0-374-36418-2 Subj: Activities – baking, cooking. Activities – trading. Family life – grandmothers. Food. Foreign lands – Colombia.

Torres, Melissa A. *The great Christmas tree celebration* ill. by Barbara Lanza. Scholastic, 2001. ISBN 978-0-439-28200-0 Subj: Format, unusual – toy & movable books. Holidays – Christmas. Trees.

Torrey, Richard. *Almost* ill. by author. HarperCollins, 2009. ISBN 978-0-06-156166-5 Subj: Behavior – growing up.

Because ill. by author. HarperCollins, 2011. ISBN 978-0-06-156173-3 Subj: Behavior.

Why? ill. by author. HarperCollins, 2010. ISBN 978-0-06-156170-2 Subj: Character traits – curiosity. Character traits – questioning.

Tortillas and lullabies / Tortillas y cancioncitas ill. by Corazones Valientes. Greenwillow, 1998. ISBN 978-0-688-14629-0 Subj: Family life. Foreign lands – Central America. Foreign languages.

Toscano, Charles. *Papa's pastries* ill. by Sonja Lamut. Zonderkidz, 2010. ISBN 978-0-310-71602-0 Subj: Behavior – sharing. Character traits – generosity. Character traits – kindness. Food. Poverty.

Toten, Teresa. *Bright red kisses* ill. by Deirdre Betteridge. Annick, 2005. ISBN 978-1-55037-909-9 Subj: Character traits – helpfulness. Family life – mothers.

Tougas, Chris. *Art's supplies* ill. by author. Orca, 2008. ISBN 978-1-55143-920-4 Subj: Art. Humorous stories. Imagination.

Tourville, Amanda Doering. *A crocodile grows up* ill. by Michael Denman and William J. Huiett. Picture Window, 2006. ISBN 978-1-4048-3157-5 Subj: Reptiles – alligators, crocodiles.

A giraffe grows up ill. by Michael Denman and William J. Huiett. Picture Window, 2006. ISBN 978-1-4048-3158-2 Subj: Animals – giraffes.

A jaguar grows up ill. by Michael Denman and William J. Huiett. Picture Window, 2006. ISBN 978-1-4048-6159-9 Subj: Animals – giraffes.

Townsend, Emily Rose. *Arctic foxes* ill. with photos. Capstone, 2004. ISBN 978-0-7368-2356-2 Subj: Animals – foxes. Foreign lands – Arctic.

Deer ill. with photos. Capstone, 2004. ISBN 978-0-7368-2067-7 Subj: Animals – deer.

Owls ill. with photos. Capstone, 2004. ISBN 978-0-7368-2068-4 Subj: Birds – owls.

Penguins ill. with photos. Capstone, 2004. ISBN 978-0-7368-2357-9 Subj: Birds – penguins. Foreign lands – Antarctic.

Polar bears ill. with photos. Capstone, 2004. ISBN 978-0-7368-2358-6 Subj: Animals – polar bears. Foreign lands – Arctic.

Seals ill. with photos. Capstone, 2004. ISBN 978-0-7368-2359-3 Subj: Animals – seals. Sea & seashore.

Squirrels ill. with photos. Capstone, 2004. ISBN 978-0-7368-2069-1 Subj: Animals – squirrels.

Woodpeckers ill. with photos. Capstone, 2004. ISBN 978-0-7368-2070-7 Subj: Birds – woodpeckers.

Townsend, Michael. *Cute and cuter* ill. by author. Knopf, 2013. ISBN 978-0-375-85718-8 Subj: Animals – cats. Animals – dogs. Emotions – envy, jealousy. Pets.

Train, Mary. *Time for the fair* ill. by Karel Hayes. Down East, 2005. ISBN 978-0-89272-694-3 Subj: Character traits – patience. Fairs, festivals. Seasons.

Tramer, Bennett. *Violet and Winston* (Sones, Sonya)

Trapani, Iza. *Baa baa black sheep* by Iza Trapani and Mother Goose ill. by Iza Trapani. Whispering

Coyote, 2001. ISBN 978-1-58089-070-0 Subj: Animals. Animals – sheep. Friendship. Humorous stories. Nursery rhymes.

Baa baa black sheep [board book] by Iza Trapani and Mother Goose ill. by Iza Trapani. Whispering Coyote, 2002. ISBN 978-1-58089-089-2 Subj: Animals. Animals – sheep. Format, unusual – board books. Friendship. Humorous stories. Nursery rhymes.

The bear went over the mountain ill. by author. Sky Pony, 2012. ISBN 978-1-61608-510-0 Subj: Animals – bears. Seasons. Senses. Songs.

Haunted party ill. by author. Charlesbridge, 2009. ISBN 978-1-58089-246-9 Subj: Counting, numbers. Ghosts. Holidays – Halloween. Parties.

Here we go 'round the mulberry bush ill. by author. Charlesbridge, 2006. ISBN 978-1-57091-663-2 Subj: Gardens, gardening. Songs.

How much is that doggie in the window? words & music by Bob Merrill; ill. by author. G. Stevens, 1999. ISBN 978-0-8368-2486-5 Subj: Animals – dogs. Family life. Format, unusual – board books. Pets. Songs.

I'm a little teapot ill. by author. Whispering Coyote, 1996. ISBN 978-1-879085-99-2 Subj: Foreign lands. Imagination. Music. Participation. Songs.

The itsy bitsy spider ill. by author. G. Stevens, 1996. ISBN 978-0-8368-1550-4 Subj: Character traits – persistence. Music. Nursery rhymes. Songs. Spiders.

Jingle bells ill. by author. Charlesbridge, 2005. ISBN 978-1-58089-095-3 Subj: Holidays – Christmas. Music. Songs.

Row, row, row your boat ill. by author. Whispering Coyote, 1999. ISBN 978-1-58089-022-9 Subj: Animals. Animals – bears. Boats, ships. Family life. Pets. Rhyming text. Weather – storms.

Rufus and friends: school days ill. by author. Charlesbridge, 2010. ISBN 978-1-58089-248-3 Subj: Nursery rhymes. Picture puzzles.

Shoo fly! ill. by author. Whispering Coyote, 2000. ISBN 978-1-58089-052-6 Subj: Animals – mice. Family life. Insects – flies. Music. Songs.

What am I? ill. by author. Whispering Coyote, 1992. ISBN 978-1-879085-76-3 Subj: Animals. Games. Rhyming text.

Trenc, Milan. *Another night at the museum* ill. by author. Holt, 2013. ISBN 978-0-8050-8948-6 Subj: Animals. Humorous stories. Museums. Water.

Trent, Shanda. *Farmers' market day* ill. by Jane Dippold. ME Media/Tiger Tales, 2013. ISBN 978-1-58925-115-1 Subj: Careers – farmers. Rhyming text. Shopping. Stores.

Tresselt, Alvin R. *Autumn harvest* ill. by Roger Antoine Duvoisin. Lothrop, 1951. ISBN 978-0-688-51155-5 Subj: Holidays – Thanksgiving. Seasons – fall.

The gift of the tree ill. by Henri Sorensen. Original title: The dead tree. Lothrop, 1992. ISBN 978-0-688-10685-0 Subj: Ecology. Forest, woods. Trees.

Hide and seek fog ill. by Roger Antoine Duvoisin. Lothrop, 1965. ISBN 978-0-688-51169-2 Subj: Caldecott award honor books. Sea & seashore. Weather – fog.

The mitten: an old Ukrainian folktale ill. by Yaroslava. Adapt. from the version by E. Rachev. Lothrop, 1989, ©1964. ISBN 978-0-606-04277-2 Subj: Animals. Folk & fairy tales. Foreign lands – Ukraine.

Rain drop splash ill. by Leonard Weisgard. Lothrop, 1946. ISBN 978-0-688-51165-4 Subj: Caldecott award honor books. Cumulative tales. Science. Weather – rain.

Sun up ill. by Henri Sorensen. Lothrop, 1991. ISBN 978-0-688-08657-2 Subj: Farms. Sun. Weather.

Wake up, farm! ill. by Carolyn Ewing. Lothrop, 1991. ISBN 978-0-688-08655-8 Subj: Animals. Farms. Morning. Noise, sounds.

White snow, bright snow ill. by Roger Antoine Duvoisin. Lothrop, 1988, ©1947. ISBN 978-0-688-51161-6 Subj: Caldecott award books. Weather – snow.

Trewin, Trudie. *I lost my kisses* ill. by Nick Bland. Scholastic, 2008. ISBN 978-0-545-05557-4 Subj: Behavior – lost & found possessions. Family life. Kissing.

Tricarico, Christine. *Cock-a-doodle dance!* ill. by Rich Deas. Feiwel & Friends, 2012. ISBN 978-0-312-38251-3 Subj: Activities – dancing. Animals. Farms.

Trice, Linda. *Kenya's word* ill. by Pamela Johnson. Charlesbridge, 2006. ISBN 978-1-57091-887-2 Subj: Ethnic groups in the U.S. – African Americans. Language.

Trimble, Marcia. *Flower Green* ill. by Jill Dubin. Images Pr., 2002. ISBN 978-1-891577-67-3 Subj: Concepts – color. Flowers. Seasons.

Hello sun ill. by Susan Arciero. Images Pr., 2000. ISBN 978-1-891577-50-5 Subj: Activities – photographing. Activities – traveling. Animals – lions. Foreign lands – Africa.

Moonbeams for Santa ill. by Sid Bingham. Images Pr., 2001. ISBN 978-1-891577-89-5 Subj: Holidays – Christmas. Moon. Rhyming text. Santa Claus.

Peppy's shadow ill. by Will Pellegrini. Images Pr., 2003. ISBN 978-1-891577-70-3 Subj: Animals – dogs. Puppets. Theater.

Tripp, Paul. *Tubby the tuba* ill. by Henry Cole. Penguin, 2006. ISBN 978-0-525-47717-4 Subj: Frogs & toads. Musical instruments – orchestras. Musical instruments – tubas.

Trist, Glenda. *A child's book of prayers* ill. with photos. DK, 1999. ISBN 978-0-7894-3976-5 Subj: Religion.

Trivizas, Eugenios. *The three little wolves and the big bad pig* ill. by Helen Oxenbury. McElderry, 1993. ISBN 978-0-689-50569-0 Subj: Animals – pigs. Animals – wolves. Behavior – misbehavior. Folk & fairy tales. Homes, houses.

Troll, Ray. *Sharkabet* ill. by author. WestWinds, 2002. ISBN 978-1-55868-518-5 Subj: ABC books. Fish – sharks.

Trollinger, Patsi B. *Perfect timing: how Isaac Murphy became one of the world's greatest jockeys* ill. by Jerome Lagarrigue. Penguin, 2006. ISBN 978-0-670-06083-2 Subj: Animals – horses, ponies. Careers – jockeys. Ethnic groups in the U.S. – African Americans. Sports – racing.

Trotter, Deborah W. *How do you know?* ill. by Julie Downing. Houghton, 2006. ISBN 978-0-618-46343-5 Subj: Emotions – love. Family life – mothers. Weather – fog.

Trottier, Maxine. *A safe place* ill. by Judith Friedman. Whitman, 1997. ISBN 978-0-8075-7212-2 Subj: Child abuse. Family life – fathers. Family life – mothers. Safety.

Troupe, Quincy. *Little Stevie Wonder* ill. by Lisa Cohen. Houghton, 2005. ISBN 978-0-618-34060-6 Subj: Careers – musicians. Ethnic groups in the U.S. – African Americans. Disabilities – blindness. Poetry.

Trumbauer, Lisa. *The great reindeer rebellion* ill. by Jannie Ho. Sterling, 2009. ISBN 978-1-4027-4462-4 Subj: Animals. Animals – reindeer. Holidays – Christmas. Rhyming text. Santa Claus.

Trumbore, Cindy. *Parrots over Puerto Rico* (Roth, Susan L.)

Truss, Lynne. *Eats, shoots and leaves: why, commas really do make a diffeerence!* ill. by Bonnie Timmons. Penguin, 2006. ISBN 978-0-399-24491-9 Subj: Language.

Tryon, Leslie. *Albert's alphabet* ill. by author. Atheneum, 1991. ISBN 978-0-689-31642-5 Subj: ABC books. Activities – making things. Birds – ducks. School.

Albert's birthday ill. by author. Atheneum, 1999. ISBN 978-0-689-82296-4 Subj: Animals. Birds – ducks. Birthdays. Parties.

Albert's Christmas ill. by author. Atheneum, 1997. ISBN 978-0-689-81034-3 Subj: Animals. Birds – ducks. Holidays – Christmas. Rhyming text. Santa Claus.

Albert's Halloween: the case of the stolen pumpkins ill. by author. Atheneum, 1998. ISBN 978-0-689-81136-4 Subj: Animals. Birds – ducks. Careers – detectives. Holidays – Halloween. Mystery stories.

Albert's play ill. by author. Atheneum, 1992. ISBN 978-0-689-31525-1 Subj: Animals. Rhyming text. Theater.

Patsy says ill. by author. Atheneum, 2001. ISBN 978-0-689-82297-1 Subj: Animals. Animals – pigs. Etiquette. School.

Tschiegg, Anne-Sophie. *Mommy time* (Brami, Elisbeth)

Tseng, Grace. *White tiger, blue serpent* ill. by Jean Tseng and Mou-Sien Tseng. Lothrop, 1999. ISBN 978-0-688-12516-5 Subj: Activities – weaving. Animals – tigers. Folk & fairy tales. Foreign lands – China. Magic. Reptiles – snakes.

Tsubakiyama, Margaret. *Mei-Mei loves the morning* ill. by Cornelius Van Wright and Ying-Hwa Hu. Whitman, 1999. ISBN 978-0-8075-5039-7 Subj: Family life – grandparents. Foreign lands – China. Health & fitness – exercise.

Tuck, Justin. *Home-field advantage* ill. by Leonardo Rodriguez. Simon & Schuster, 2011. ISBN 978-1-4424-0369-7 Subj: Family life – sisters. Hair. Multiple births – twins.

Tucker, Kathy. *Do cowboys ride bikes?* ill. by Nadine Bernard Westcott. Whitman, 1997. ISBN 978-0-8075-1693-5 Subj: Character traits – questioning. Country. Cowboys, cowgirls. Rhyming text.

Do knights take naps? ill. by Nick Sharratt. Whitman, 2000. ISBN 978-0-8075-1695-9 Subj: Knights. Middle Ages. Rhyming text. Sleep.

Do pirates take baths? ill. by Nadine Bernard Westcott. Whitman, 1994. ISBN 978-0-8075-1696-6 Subj: Pirates. Rhyming text. Sea & seashore.

The leprechaun in the basement ill. by John Sandford. Whitman, 1999. ISBN 978-0-8075-4450-1 Subj: Clothing – shoes. Holidays – St. Patrick's Day. Mythical creatures – leprechauns.

The seven Chinese sisters ill. by Grace Lin. Whitman, 2003. ISBN 978-0-8075-7309-9 Subj: Dragons. Family life – sisters. Foreign lands – China.

Tucker, Lindy. *Porkelia: a pig's tale* ill. by author. Charlesbridge, 2011. ISBN 978-1-934133-28-6

Subj: Activities – dancing. Animals – pigs. Character traits – ambition. Rhyming text.

Tudor, Tasha. *The doll's Christmas* ill. by author. Simon & Schuster, 1999. ISBN 978-0-689-82809-6 Subj: Holidays – Christmas. Parties. Toys – dolls.

1 is one ill. by author. Walck, 1956. ISBN 978-0-02-688535-5 Subj: Caldecott award honor books. Counting, numbers.

Pumpkin moonshine ill. by author. Simon & Schuster, 2000. ISBN 978-0-689-82846-1 Subj: Farms. Food. Holidays – Halloween.

A tale for Easter ill. by author. Simon & Schuster, 2001, ©1941. ISBN 978-0-689-82844-7 Subj: Animals. Dreams. Eggs. Holidays – Easter.

Tullet, Hervé. *The book with a hole.* Abrams, 2011. ISBN 978-1-85437-946-7 Subj: Format, unusual. Imagination. Participation.

Press here ill. by author. Chronicle, 2011. ISBN 978-0-8118-7954-5 Subj: Format, unusual. Imagination. Participation.

Tulloch, Shirley. *Who made me?* ill. by Cathie Felstead. Augsburg Fortress, 2000. ISBN 978-0-8066-4045-7 Subj: Animals. Foreign lands – Africa. Religion.

Tunnell, Michael O. *Halloween pie* ill. by Kevin O'Malley. Lothrop, 1999. ISBN 978-0-688-16805-6 Subj: Food. Holidays. Magic. Monsters. Witches.

The joke's on George ill. by Kathy Osborn. Boyds Mills, 2001. ISBN 978-1-56397-970-5 Subj: Careers – artists. Friendship. Museums.

Mailing May ill. by Ted Rand. Greenwillow, 1997. ISBN 978-0-688-12879-1 Subj: Careers – postal workers. Family life – grandparents. Trains. Transportation. U.S. history.

Turhan, Sedat. *Monkey business: fun with idioms* (Hambleton, Laura)

Turkle, Brinton. *Deep in the forest* ill. by author. Dutton, 1976. ISBN 978-0-525-28617-2 Subj: Animals – bears. Folk & fairy tales. Wordless.

Do not open ill. by author. Dutton, 1981. ISBN 978-0-525-28785-8 Subj: Animals – cats. Behavior – trickery. Behavior – wishing. Monsters. Sea & seashore.

Thy friend, Obadiah ill. by author. Viking, 1969. ISBN 978-0-670-71229-8 Subj: Birds – seagulls. Caldecott award honor books. Character traits – kindness to animals. Ethnic groups in the U.S. – Amish. Seasons – winter. U.S. history.

Turner, Ann Warren. *Abe Lincoln remembers* ill. by Wendell Minor. HarperCollins, 2001. ISBN 978-0-06-027578-5 Subj: Memories, memory. U.S. history.

Angel hide and seek ill. by Lois Ehlert. HarperCollins, 1998. ISBN 978-0-06-027086-5 Subj: Angels. Picture puzzles. Religion. Rhyming text.

The Christmas house ill. by Nancy Edwards Calder. HarperCollins, 1994. ISBN 978-0-06-023429-4 Subj: Family life. Holidays – Christmas. Homes, houses. Poetry.

Dakota dugout ill. by Ronald Himler. Macmillan, 1985. ISBN 978-0-02-789700-5 Subj: Farms. U.S. history – frontier & pioneer life.

In the heart ill. by Salley Mavor. HarperCollins, 2001. ISBN 978-0-06-023731-8 Subj: Day. Poetry.

Nettie's trip south ill. by Ronald Himler. Macmillan, 1987. ISBN 978-0-02-789240-6 Subj: Activities – traveling. Behavior – disbelief. Ethnic groups in the U.S. – African Americans. Family life.

Pumpkin cat ill. by Amy Bates. Hyperion, 2004. ISBN 978-0-7868-0494-8 Subj: Animals – cats. Holidays – Halloween. Libraries.

Secrets from the dollhouse ill. by Raúl Colón. HarperCollins, 2000. ISBN 978-0-06-024567-2 Subj: Poetry. Toys – dolls.

Shaker hearts ill. by Wendell Minor. HarperCollins, 1997. ISBN 978-0-06-025370-7 Subj: Religion. Rhyming text. U.S. history.

Through moon and stars and night skies ill. by James Graham Hale. HarperCollins, 1990. ISBN 978-0-06-026190-0 Subj: Adoption.

When Mr. Jefferson came to Philadelphia ill. by Mark Hess. HarperCollins, 2003. ISBN 978-0-06-027580-8 Subj: U.S. history. War.

Turner, Barbara J. *Out and about at the orchestra* ill. by Anne McMullen. Picture Window, 2003. ISBN 978-1-4048-0040-3 Subj: Careers – musicians. Music. Musical instruments – orchestras.

Turner, Glennette Tilley. *An apple for Harriet Tubman* ill. by Susan Keeter. Whitman, 2006. ISBN 978-0-8075-0395-9 Subj: Ethnic groups in the U.S. – African Americans. Slavery. U.S. history.

Turner, Pamela S. *Hachiko* ill. by Yan Nascimbene. Houghton, 2004. ISBN 978-0-618-14094-7 Subj: Animals – dogs. Death. Foreign lands – Japan. Pets.

Turner, Sandy. *Grow up* ill. by author. Cotler, 2003. ISBN 978-0-06-000954-0 Subj: Behavior – growing up. Careers. Imagination.

Otto's trunk ill. by author. Cotler, 2003. ISBN 978-0-06-000957-1 Subj: Animals – elephants. Concepts – size. Self-concept.

Silent night ill. by author. Atheneum, 2001. ISBN 978-0-689-84156-9 Subj: Animals – dogs. Holidays – Christmas. Noise, sounds. Santa Claus.

Turner-Denstaedt, Melanie. *The hat that wore Clara B.* ill. by Frank Morrison. Farrar, 2009. ISBN 978-0-374-32794-1 Subj: Clothing – hats. Ethnic groups in the U.S. – African Americans. Family life – grandmothers.

Tusa, Tricia. *Bunnies in my head* ill. by author and young patients at the M.D. Anderson Cancer Center in Houston, Texas. Anderson Cancer Center, 1998. ISBN 978-0-9664551-8-2 Subj: Art. Children as illustrators. Illness – cancer. Imagination.

Follow me ill. by author. Harcourt, 2011. ISBN 978-0-547-27201-6 Subj: Activities – swinging. Concepts – color. Imagination.

Stay away from the junkyard! ill. by author. Macmillan, 1988. ISBN 978-0-02-789541-4 Subj: Art. Behavior – collecting things.

Tutu, Archbishop Desmond. *Desmond and the very mean word: a story of forgiveness* by Archbishop Desmond Tutu and Douglas Carlton Abrams ill. by A. G. Ford. Candlewick, 2013. ISBN 978-0-7636-5229-6 Subj: Behavior – forgiving. Emotions – anger. Foreign lands – South Africa. Prejudice. Sports – bicycling.

God's dream by Archbishop Desmond Tutu and Douglas Carlton Abrams ill. by LeUyen Pham. Candlewick, 2008. ISBN 978-0-7636-3388-2 Subj: Character traits – generosity. Character traits – helpfulness. Religion.

The twelve days of Christmas. English folk song. *The twelve days of Christmas* ill. by Jan Brett. Dodd, 1986. ISBN 978-0-396-08821-9 Subj: Cumulative tales. Holidays – Christmas. Music. Songs.

The 12 days of Christmas adapt. by Jane Cabrera; ill. by adapter. Holiday House, 2013. ISBN 978-0-8234-2870-0 Subj: Cumulative tales. Holidays – Christmas. Music. Songs.

The twelve days of Christmas ill. by Rachel Griffin. Barefoot, 2002. ISBN 978-1-84148-940-7 Subj: Cumulative tales. Holidays – Christmas. Music. Songs.

Twelve days of Christmas by Rachel Isadora; ill. by author. Penguin, 2010. ISBN 978-0-399-25073-6 Subj: Cumulative tales. Holidays – Christmas. Music. Songs.

The twelve days of Christmas ill. by Laurel Long. Penguin, 2011. ISBN 978-0-8037-3357-2 Subj: Cumulative tales. Holidays – Christmas. Music. Songs.

The twelve days of Christmas ill. by Ilse Plume. HarperCollins, 1990. ISBN 978-0-06-024738-6 Subj: Cumulative tales. Holidays – Christmas. Music. Songs.

The twelve days of Christmas ill. by Jane Ray. Candlewick, 2011. ISBN 978-0-7636-5735-2 Subj: Cumulative tales. Holidays – Christmas. Music. Songs.

The twelve days of Christmas by Gennady Spirin; ill. by author. Marshall Cavendish, 2009. ISBN 978-0-7614-5551-6 Subj: Cumulative tales. Holidays – Christmas. Music. Songs.

The twelve days of Christmas ill. by Vladimir Vagin. HarperCollins, 1998. ISBN 978-0-06-028399-5 Subj: Cumulative tales. Holidays – Christmas. Music. Songs.

The twelve days of Christmas [board book] ill. by Jan Brett. Putnam, 2004. ISBN 978-0-339-24329-3 Subj: Cumulative tales. Format, unusual – board books. Holidays – Christmas. Music. Songs.

Two little eyes and other action rhymes sel. by Grace Cook; ill. by Carol Thompson. Candlewick, 2000. ISBN 978-0-7636-0952-8 Subj: Counting, numbers. Participation. Rhyming text.

Twohy, Mike. *Outfoxed* ill. by author. Simon & Schuster, 2013. ISBN 978-1-4424-7392-8 Subj: Animals – foxes. Behavior – trickery. Birds – ducks. Character traits – cleverness.

Poindexter makes a friend ill. by author. Simon & Schuster, 2011. ISBN 978-1-4424-0965-1 Subj: Animals – pigs. Books, reading. Character traits – shyness. Friendship. Libraries.

Tyger, Rory. *Newton* ill. by author. Barron's, 2001. ISBN 978-0-7641-5390-7 Subj: Emotions – fear. Noise, sounds. Toys – bears.

Tyler, Anne. *Timothy Tugbottom says no!* ill. by Mitra Modarressi. Penguin, 2005. ISBN 978-0-399-24255-7 Subj: Character traits – stubbornness. Sleepovers.

Tyler, Jenny. *Big Pig on a dig* ill. by author. Usborne, 1999. ISBN 978-1-58086-182-3 Subj: Activities – digging. Animals – pigs. Maps.

Tyler, Michael. *The skin you live in* ill. by David Lee Csicsko. Chicago Children's Museum, 2005. ISBN 978-0-9759580-0-1 Subj: Anatomy – skin. Rhyming text. Self-concept.

Uchida, Yoshiko. *The bracelet* ill. by Joanna Yardley. Philomel, 1993. ISBN 978-0-399-22503-1 Subj: Ethnic groups in the U.S. – Japanese Americans. Friendship. Slavery. U.S. history.

The magic purse ill. by Keiko Narahashi. McElderry, 1993. ISBN 978-0-689-50559-1 Subj: Character traits – bravery. Clothing – handbags, purses. Folk & fairy tales. Foreign lands – Japan.

The two foolish cats ill. by Margot Zemach. Macmillan, 1987. ISBN 978-0-689-50397-9 Subj: Animals – cats. Folk & fairy tales. Food.

The wise old woman ill. by Martin Springett. McElderry, 1994. ISBN 978-0-689-50582-9 Subj: Character traits – wisdom. Folk & fairy tales. Foreign lands – Japan. Old age.

Udry, Janice May. *Let's be enemies* ill. by Maurice Sendak. HarperCollins, 1961. ISBN 978-0-06-026131-3 Subj: Behavior – fighting, arguing. Emotions – hate. Friendship.

The moon jumpers ill. by Maurice Sendak. HarperCollins, 1959. ISBN 978-0-06-026145-0 Subj: Caldecott award honor books. Moon. Twilight.

A tree is nice ill. by Marc Simont. HarperCollins, 1956. ISBN 978-0-06-026156-6 Subj: Caldecott award books. Poetry. Seasons. Trees.

What Mary Jo shared ill. by Eleanor Mill. Whitman, 1966. ISBN 978-0-8075-8842-0 Subj: Character traits – shyness. Ethnic groups in the U.S. Ethnic groups in the U.S. – African Americans. Family life – fathers. School.

Uegaki, Chieri. *Suki's kimono* ill. by Stéphane Jorisch. Kids Can, 2003. ISBN 978-1-55337-084-0 Subj: Character traits – being different. Clothing – kimonos. Ethnic groups in the U.S. – Japanese Americans. Family life – grandmothers. School – first day.

Uff, Caroline. *Happy birthday, Lulu* ill. by author. Walker, 2000. ISBN 978-0-8027-8751-4 Subj: Birthdays. Gifts. Parties.

Hello, Lulu ill. by author. Walker, 1999. ISBN 978-0-8027-8712-5 Subj: Clothing – shoes. Family life. Friendship. Pets.

Lulu's busy day ill. by author. Walker, 2000. ISBN 978-0-8027-8716-3 Subj: Activities. Family life.

Uhlberg, Myron. *Dad, Jackie, and me* ill. by Colin Bootman. Peachtree, 2005. ISBN 978-1-56145-329-0 Subj: Ethnic groups in the U.S. – African Americans. Family life – fathers. Disabilities – deafness. Sports – baseball.

Lemuel, the fool ill. by Sonja Lamut. Peachtree, 2001. ISBN 978-1-56145-220-0 Subj: Activities – traveling. Character traits – foolishness. Cities, towns. Sports – sailing.

Mad Dog McGraw ill. by Lydia Monks. Putnam, 2000. ISBN 978-0-399-23308-1 Subj: Animals – dogs. Problem solving.

The printer ill. by Henri Sorensen. Peachtree, 2003. ISBN 978-1-56145-483-9 Subj: Family life – fathers. Fire. Disabilities – deafness. Sign language.

A storm called Katrina ill. by Colin Bootman. Peachtree, 2011. ISBN 978-1-56145-591-1 Subj: Behavior – lost. Ethnic groups in the U.S. – African Americans. Musical instruments. Weather – floods. Weather – hurricanes.

Ulmer, Wendy. *A isn't for fox: an isn't alphabet* ill. by Laura Knorr. Sleeping Bear, 2008. ISBN 978-1-58536-319-3 Subj: ABC books. Rhyming text.

Umansky, Kaye. *I don't like Gloria!* ill. by Margaret Chamberlain. Candlewick, 2007. ISBN 978-0-7636-3202-1 Subj: Animals – cats. Animals – dogs. Emotions – envy, jealousy. Pets.

Underwood, Deborah. *A balloon for Isabel* ill. by Laura Rankin. HarperCollins, 2010. ISBN 978-0-06-177987-9 Subj: Animals – porcupines. Character traits – being different. School.

The Christmas quiet book ill. by Renata Liwska. Houghton Mifflin, 2012. ISBN 978-0-547-55863-9 Subj: Holidays – Christmas. Noise, sounds.

The loud book! ill. by Renata Liwska. Houghton Mifflin, 2011. ISBN 978-0-547-39008-6 Subj: Day. Noise, sounds.

Part-time princess ill. by Cambria Evans. Disney/Hyperion, 2013. ISBN 978-1-4231-2485-6 Subj: Bedtime. Family life. Imagination. Royalty – princesses.

The quiet book ill. by Renata Liwska. Houghton Mifflin, 2010. ISBN 978-0-547-21567-9 Subj: Animals. Behavior – solitude. Noise, sounds.

Ungar, Richard. *Rachel captures the moon* ill. by author. Adapt. from a story by Samuel Tenenbaum. Tundra, 2001. ISBN 978-0-88776-505-6 Subj: Folk & fairy tales. Jewish culture. Moon.

Rachel's gift ill. by author. Tundra, 2003. ISBN 978-0-88776-616-9 Subj: Activities – baking, cooking. Character traits – kindness. Holidays – Passover. Jewish culture. Religion.

Rachel's library ill. by author. Tundra, 2004. ISBN 978-0-88776-678-7 Subj: Cities, towns. Foreign lands – Poland. Jewish culture. Libraries.

Ungerer, Tomi. *Crictor* ill. by author. HarperCollins, 1958. ISBN 978-0-06-026181-8 Subj: Humorous stories. Reptiles – snakes.

Flix ill. by author. Roberts Rinehart, 1998. ISBN 978-1-57098-161-6 Subj: Animals – cats. Animals – dogs. Prejudice.

Moon man ill. by author. Phaidon Press, 2009. ISBN 978-0-7148-5598-1 Subj: Moon. Space & space ships.

Otto: the autobiography of a teddy bear ill. by author. Phaidon, 2010. ISBN 978-0-7148-5766-4 Subj: Foreign lands – Germany. Holocaust. Jewish culture. Toys – bears. War.

The three robbers ill. by author. Phaidon Press, 2008. ISBN 978-0-7148-4877-8 Subj: Crime. Orphans.

Unobagha, Uzoamaka Chinyelu. *Off to the sweet shores of Africa and other talking drum rhymes* ill. by Julia Cairns. Chronicle, 2000. ISBN 978-0-8118-2378-4 Subj: Foreign lands – Africa. Poetry.

Up the hill and down comp. by William Jay Smith; ill. by Allan Eitzen. Boyds Mills, 2003. ISBN 978-1-56397-028-3 Subj: Poetry.

Urban, Linda. *Mouse was mad* ill. by Henry Cole. Harcourt, 2009. ISBN 978-0-15-205337-6 Subj: Animals. Animals – mice. Emotions – anger.

Urbanovic, Jackie. *Duck and cover* ill. by author. HarperCollins, 2009. ISBN 978-0-06-121444-8 Subj: Behavior – running away. Birds – ducks. Pets. Reptiles – alligators, crocodiles.

Duck at the door ill. by author. HarperCollins, 2007. ISBN 978-0-06-121438-7 Subj: Birds – ducks. Character traits – individuality. Pets.

Duck soup ill. by author. HarperCollins, 2008. ISBN 978-0-06-121441-7 Subj: Activities – baking, cooking. Animals. Birds – ducks. Friendship. Humorous stories.

Sitting duck ill. by author. HarperCollins, 2010. ISBN 978-0-06-176583-4 Subj: Activities – babysitting. Animals – dogs. Birds – ducks.

Urbigkit, Cat. *A young shepherd* photos by author. Boyds Mills, 2006. ISBN 978-1-59078-364-1 Subj: Animals – sheep. Careers – ranchers. Careers – shepherds.

Urdahl, Catherine. *Emma's question* ill. by Janine Dawson. Charlesbridge, 2009. ISBN 978-1-58089-145-5 Subj: Behavior – worrying. Family life – grandmothers. Hospitals. Illness. Old age.

Polka-dot fixes kindergarten ill. by Mai S. Kemble. Charlesbridge, 2011. ISBN 978-1-57091-737-0 Subj: Behavior – misbehavior. Character traits – assertiveness. Friendship. School. Self-concept.

U'Ren, Andrea. *Pugdog* ill. by author. Farrar, 2001. ISBN 978-0-374-36149-5 Subj: Animals – dogs. Gender roles.

Uribe, Verónica. *Buzz buzz buzz* ill. by Gloria Calderón. Douglas & McIntyre, 2001. ISBN 978-0-88899-430-1 Subj: Animals. Insects – mosquitoes. Sleep.

Ursone, Adele. *The Christmas tugboat: how the Rockefeller Center Christmas tree came to New York City* (Matteson, George)

Uslander, Arlene. *That's what grandparents are for* ill. by Freddie Levin. Peel Productions, 2002. ISBN 978-0-939217-60-1 Subj: Family life – grandparents. Poetry.

Vaës, Alain. *The princess and the pea* (Andersen, Hans Christian)

Vagin, Vladimir, reteller. *The enormous carrot* ill. by reteller. Scholastic, 1998. ISBN 978-0-590-45491-9 Subj: Animals. Cumulative tales. Farms. Folk & fairy tales. Foreign lands – Russia. Plants. Problem solving.

Here comes the cat by Vladimir Vagin and Frank Asch ill. by authors. Scholastic, 1989. ISBN 978-0-590-41859-1 Subj: Animals – cats. Animals – mice. Foreign languages.

Vail, Rachel. *Flabbersmashed about you* ill. by Yumi Heo. Feiwel & Friends, 2012. ISBN 978-0-312-61345-7 Subj: Emotions – anger. Emotions – loneliness. Friendship. School.

Jibberwillies at night ill. by Yumi Heo. Scholastic, 2008. ISBN 978-0-439-42070-9 Subj: Bedtime. Emotions – fear.

Over the moon ill. by Scott Nash. Orchard, 1998. ISBN 978-0-531-33068-5 Subj: Animals. Moon. Nursery rhymes. Theater.

Piggy Bunny ill. by Jeremy Tankard. Feiwel & Friends, 2012. ISBN 978-0-312-64988-3 Subj: Animals – pigs. Character traits – individuality. Holidays – Easter. Self-concept.

Righty and Lefty: a tale of two feet ill. by Matthew Cordell. Scholastic, 2007. ISBN 978-0-439-63629-2 Subj: Anatomy – feet. Character traits – cooperation.

Sometimes I'm Bombaloo ill. by Yumi Heo. Scholastic, 2002. ISBN 978-0-439-08755-1 Subj: Emotions – anger. Family life – brothers & sisters.

Vainio, Pirkko. *The best of friends* ill. by author. NorthSouth, 2000. ISBN 978-0-7358-1151-5 Subj: Animals – bears. Animals – rabbits. Friendship.

The Christmas angel ill. by author. NorthSouth, 1995. ISBN 978-1-55858-500-3 Subj: Angels. Holidays – Christmas. Homeless. Music. Poverty.

Who hid the Easter eggs? ill. by author. NorthSouth, 2011. ISBN 978-0-7358-2304-4 Subj: Animals – squirrels. Behavior – hiding things. Eggs. Holidays – Easter.

Valckx, Catharina. *Lizette's green sock* ill. by author. Houghton, 2005. ISBN 978-0-618-45298-9 Subj: Birds. Clothing – socks.

Valdivia, Paloma. *Up above and down below* ill. by author. OwlKids, 2012. ISBN 978-1-926973-39-5 Subj: Character traits – being different. Character traits – individuality. World.

Valentina, Marina. *Lost in the roses* ill. by author. Red Cygnet, 2007. ISBN 978-1-60108-014-1 Subj: Birds – chickens. Flowers – roses.

Vallverdu, Josep. *Aladdin and the magic lamp / Aldino y la lampara maravillosa* ill. by Pep Montserrat. Chronicle, 2006. ISBN 978-0-8118-5061-2 Subj: Folk & fairy tales. Foreign lands – Arabia. Foreign languages. Magic.

Vamos, Samantha R. *Alphabet trucks* ill. by Ryan O'Rourke. Charlesbridge, 2013. ISBN 978-1-58089-428-9 Subj: ABC books. Rhyming text. Trucks.

Before you were here, mi amor ill. by Santiago Cohen. Viking, 2009. ISBN 978-0-670-06301-7 Subj: Babies. Family life. Foreign languages.

The cazuela that the farm maiden stirred ill. by Rafael López. Charlesbridge, 2011. ISBN 978-1-58089-242-1 Subj: Activities – baking, cooking. Animals. Cumulative tales. Farms. Food. Foreign languages.

Van Allsburg, Chris. *Bad day at Riverbend* ill. by author. Houghton, 1995. ISBN 978-0-395-67347-8 Subj: Activities – drawing. Imagination.

The garden of Abdul Gasazi ill. by author. Houghton, 1979. ISBN 978-0-395-27804-8 Subj: Animals – dogs. Behavior – misbehavior. Caldecott award honor books. Imagination. Magic.

Jumanji ill. by author. Houghton, 1981. ISBN 978-0-395-30448-8 Subj: Caldecott award books. Games. Imagination. Jungle.

The mysteries of Harris Burdick ill. by author. Houghton, 1984. ISBN 978-0-395-35393-6 Subj: Imagination.

The polar express ill. by author. Houghton, 1985. ISBN 978-0-395-38949-2 Subj: Caldecott award books. Holidays – Christmas. Imagination. Night. Santa Claus. Trains.

Probuditi! ill. by author. Houghton, 2006. ISBN 978-0-618-75502-8 Subj: Imagination. Magic.

Queen of the falls ill. by author. Harcourt, 2011. ISBN 978-0-547-31581-2 Subj: Character traits – bravery. Character traits – persistence. U.S. history.

The stranger ill. by author. Houghton, 1986. ISBN 978-0-395-42331-8 Subj: Behavior – forgetfulness. Country. Seasons – fall.

Two bad ants ill. by author. Houghton, 1988. ISBN 978-0-395-48668-9 Subj: Homes, houses. Insects – ants.

The widow's broom ill. by author. Houghton, 1992. ISBN 978-0-395-64051-7 Subj: Magic. Prejudice. Witches.

The wreck of the Zephyr ill. by author. Houghton, 1983. ISBN 978-0-395-33075-3 Subj: Boats, ships. Sailors. Weather – storms.

The Z was zapped ill. by author. Houghton, 1987. ISBN 978-0-395-44612-6 Subj: ABC books.

Zathura ill. by author. Houghton, 2002. ISBN 978-0-618-25396-8 Subj: Activities – playing. Family life – brothers. Games. Space & space ships.

Van Buren, David. *I love you as big as the world* ill. by Tim Warnes. Good Books, 2008. ISBN 978-1-56148-618-2 Subj: Animals – bears. Emotions – love. Family life. Rhyming text.

Van Camp, Katie. *CookieBot! a Harry and Horsie adventure* ill. by Lincoln Agnew. HarperCollins, 2011. ISBN 978-0-06-197445-8 Subj: Food. Imagination. Robots. Toys.

Harry and Horsie ill. by Lincoln Agnew. HarperCollins, 2009. ISBN 978-0-06-175598-9 Subj: Bubbles. Imagination. Space & space ships. Toys.

Vande Griek, Susan. *The art room* ill. by Pascal Milelli. Douglas & McIntyre, 2002. ISBN 978-0-88899-449-3 Subj: Art. Careers – artists.

Loon ill. by Karen Reczuch. Groundwood, 2011. ISBN 978-1-55498-077-2 Subj: Behavior – growing up. Birds – loons.

Van der Meer, Mara. *Can we play?* ill. by author. Abrams, 2002. ISBN 978-0-8109-0379-1 Subj: Activities – playing. Days of the week, months of the year. Family life. Format, unusual – toy & movable books.

Vander Zee, Ruth. *Always with you* ill. by Ronald Himler. Eerdmans, 2008. ISBN 978-0-8028-5295-3 Subj: Foreign lands – Vietnam. Orphans. War.

Van Dusen, Chris. *The circus ship* ill. by Chris Van Dusen. Candlewick, 2009. ISBN 978-0-7636-3090-4 Subj: Boats, ships. Circus. Rhyming text.

Down to the sea with Mr. Magee ill. by author. Chronicle, 2000. ISBN 978-0-8118-2499-6 Subj: Animals – dogs. Animals – whales. Boats, ships. Rhyming text. Sea & seashore. Sports – sailing.

King Hugo's huge ego ill. by author. Candlewick, 2011. ISBN 978-0-7636-5004-9 Subj: Behavior – boasting. Magic. Rhyming text. Royalty – kings. Self-concept.

Learning to ski with Mr. Magee ill. by author. Chronicle, 2010. ISBN 978-0-8118-7495-3 Subj: Animals – dogs. Rhyming text. Sports – skiing.

Randy Riley's really big hit ill. by author. Candlewick, 2012. ISBN 978-0-7636-4946-3 Subj: Behavior – resourcefulness. Character traits – cleverness. Rhyming text. Robots. Sports – baseball.

Van Eerbeek. *The world of baby animals* ill. with photos. Sterling, 2000. ISBN 978-0-8069-8058-4 Subj: Animals – babies.

The world of farm animals ill. with photos. Sterling, 2001. ISBN 978-0-8069-8461-2 Subj: Animals. Farms.

The world of wild animals ill. with photos. Sterling, 2001. ISBN 978-0-8069-8452-0 Subj: Animals.

Van Fleet, Matthew. *Fuzzy yellow ducklings* ill. by author. Dial, 1995. ISBN 978-0-8037-1759-6 Subj: Animals. Birds. Concepts – color. Concepts – shape. Format, unusual – toy & movable books.

Heads ill. by author. Simon & Schuster, 2010. ISBN 978-1-4424-0379-6 Subj: Animals. Format, unusual – toy & movable books.

Moo photos by Brian Stanton. Simon & Schuster, 2011. ISBN 978-1-4424-3503-2 Subj: Animals. Farms. Format, unusual – toy & movable books.

One yellow lion ill. by author. Dial, 1992. ISBN 978-0-8037-1099-3 Subj: Animals. Concepts – color. Counting, numbers. Format, unusual – toy & movable books.

Spotted yellow frogs ill. by author. Dial, 1998. ISBN 978-0-8037-2350-4 Subj: Animals. Concepts – color. Concepts – shape. Format, unusual – toy & movable books.

VanHecke, Susan. *An apple pie for dinner* ill. by Carol Baicker-McKee. Marshall Cavendish, 2009. ISBN 978-0-7614-5452-6 Subj: Activities – baking, cooking. Activities – trading. Family life – grandmothers. Food.

Van Kampen, Vlasta. *Bear tales* ill. by author. Annick, 2000. ISBN 978-1-55037-619-7 Subj: Animals – bears. Creation. Folk & fairy tales. Foreign lands – Czechoslovakia. Foreign lands – Russia.

It couldn't be worse ill. by author. Annick, 2003. ISBN 978-1-55037-783-5 Subj: Animals. Behavior – fighting, arguing. Family life. Folk & fairy tales. Humorous stories. Problem solving.

Van Laan, Nancy. *La boda: a Mexican wedding celebration* ill. by Andrea Arroyo. Little, 1996. ISBN 978-0-316-89626-9 Subj: Foreign lands – Mexico. Foreign languages. Indians of North America – Zapotec. Weddings.

Little baby Bobby ill. by Laura Cornell. Knopf, 1997. ISBN 978-0-679-94922-0 Subj: Behavior – running away. Humorous stories. Rhyming text. Toys – bears.

Little Fish lost ill. by Jane Conteh-Morgan. Atheneum, 1998. ISBN 978-0-689-81331-3 Subj: Animals. Family life – mothers. Fish. Foreign lands – Africa. Rhyming text.

The magic bean tree ill. by Beatriz A. Vidal. Houghton, 1998. ISBN 978-0-395-82746-8 Subj: Folk & fairy tales. Foreign lands – Argentina. Indians of South America – Quechua.

Mama rocks, Papa sings ill. by Roberta Smith. Knopf, 1995. ISBN 978-0-679-94016-6 Subj: Activities – babysitting. Babies. Counting, numbers. Cumulative tales. Foreign lands – Haiti. Rhyming text.

Moose tales ill. by Amy Rusch. Houghton, 1999. ISBN 978-0-395-90863-1 Subj: Animals. Animals – beavers. Animals – moose. Friendship. Weather – snow.

Nit-pickin' ill. by George Booth. Atheneum, 2008. ISBN 978-0-689-83898-9 Subj: Insects – lice. Rhyming text.

Possum come a-knocking ill. by George Booth. Knopf, 1990. ISBN 978-0-394-92206-5 Subj: Animals – possums. Cumulative tales. Family life. Rhyming text.

Rainbow crow ill. by Beatriz A. Vidal. Knopf, 1989. ISBN 978-0-394-99577-9 Subj: Birds – crows. Concepts – color. Creation. Fire. Folk & fairy tales. Indians of North America – Lenape.

Shingebiss: an Ojibwe legend ill. by Betsy Bowen. Houghton, 1997. ISBN 978-0-316-89627-6 Subj: Birds – ducks. Folk & fairy tales. Indians of North America – Ojibwa. Seasons – winter.

Sleep, sleep, sleep ill. by Holly Meade. Little, 1995. ISBN 978-0-316-89732-7 Subj: Animals. Foreign lands. Foreign languages. Lullabies. Sleep.

So say the little monkeys ill. by Yumi Heo. Atheneum, 1998. ISBN 978-0-689-81038-1 Subj: Animals – monkeys. Folk & fairy tales. Foreign lands – Brazil. Rhyming text.

This is the hat ill. by Holly Meade. Hyperion, 1995. ISBN 978-0-7868-1030-7 Subj: Animals. Circular tales. Clothing – hats. Rhyming text.

Tickle tum ill. by Bernadette Pons. Atheneum, 2001. ISBN 978-0-689-83143-0 Subj: Family life – mothers. Food. Games.

A tree for me ill. by Sheila White Samton. Knopf, 2000. ISBN 978-0-679-99384-1 Subj: Animals. Counting, numbers. Rhyming text. Trees.

When winter comes: a lullaby ill. by Susan Gaber. Atheneum, 2000. ISBN 978-0-689-81778-6 Subj: Animals. Lullabies. Seasons – winter.

Van Leeuwen, Jean. *Across the wide dark sea: the Mayflower journey* ill. by Thomas B. Allen. Dial, 1995. ISBN 978-0-8037-1167-9 Subj: Activities – traveling. Boats, ships. Pilgrims. Religion. U.S. history.

Benny and beautiful baby Delilah ill. by LeUyen Pham. Penguin, 2006. ISBN 978-0-8037-2891-2 Subj: Babies. Family life – new sibling.

Chicken soup ill. by David Gavril. Abrams, 2009. ISBN 978-0-8109-8326-7 Subj: Behavior – hiding. Birds – chickens. Farms. Food. Illness – cold (disease).

Five funny bunnies: three bouncing tales ill. by Anne Wilsdorf. Marshall Cavendish, 2012. ISBN 978-0-7614-6114-2 Subj: Animals – rabbits. Family life – brothers & sisters.

Going west ill. by Thomas B. Allen. Dial, 1992. ISBN 978-0-8037-1028-3 Subj: Family life. Moving. U.S. history – frontier & pioneer life.

Nothing here but trees ill. by Phil Boatwright. Dial, 1998. ISBN 978-0-8037-2180-7 Subj: Careers – farmers. Trees. U.S. history – frontier & pioneer life.

Papa and the pioneer quilt ill. by Rebecca Bond. Penguin, 2007. ISBN 978-0-8037-3028-1 Subj: Family life. Quilts. U.S. history – frontier & pioneer life.

Sorry ill. by Brad Sneed. Fogelman, 2001. ISBN 978-0-8037-2261-3 Subj: Behavior – fighting, arguing. Careers – farmers. Character traits – persistence. Family life – brothers.

The strange adventures of Blue Dog ill. by Marco Ventura. Dial, 1999. ISBN 978-0-8037-1878-4 Subj: Animals – dogs. Farms. Toys.

The tickle stories ill. by Mary Whyte. Dial, 1998. ISBN 978-0-8037-2049-7 Subj: Activities – storytelling. Bedtime. Family life. Family life – grandfathers.

Touch the sky summer ill. by Dan Andreasen. Dial, 1997. ISBN 978-0-8037-1820-3 Subj: Activities – vacationing. Family life. Family life – grandparents. Lakes, ponds. Seasons – summer.

"Wait for me!" said Maggie McGee ill. by Jacqueline Rogers. Fogelman, 2001. ISBN 978-0-8037-2357-3 Subj: Behavior – growing up. Concepts – size. Family life – brothers & sisters.

van Lieshout, Elle. *The wish* by Elle van Lieshout and Erik van Os ill. by Paula Gerritsen. Boyds Mills, 2007. ISBN 978-1-932425-91-8 Subj: Behavior – solitude. Behavior – wishing. Emotions – love. Tractors.

van Lieshout, Maria. *Backseat A-B-see* ill. by author. Chronicle, 2012. ISBN 978-1-4521-0664-9 Subj: ABC books. Activities – traveling. Automobiles. Signs.

Flight 1-2-3 ill. by author. Chronicle, 2013. ISBN 978-1-4521-1662-4 Subj: Airplanes, airports. Counting, numbers.

Hopper and Wilson ill. by author. Penguin, 2011. ISBN 978-0-399-25184-9 Subj: Animals – elephants. Animals – mice. Friendship. Sports – sailing.

Peep! a little book about taking a leap ill. by author. Feiwel & Friends, 2009. ISBN 978-0-312-36915-6 Subj: Birds – chickens. Emotions – fear. Self-concept.

Splash: a little book about bouncing back ill. by author. Feiwel & Friends, 2008. ISBN 978-0-312-36914-9 Subj: Animals – seals. Behavior – bad day.

Tumble! a little book about having it all ill. by author. Feiwel & Friends, 2010. ISBN 978-0-312-54859-9 Subj: Animals – bears. Behavior – sharing.

Van Nutt, Julia. *The monster in the shadows* ill. by Robert Van Nutt. Doubleday, 2000. ISBN 978-0-385-32565-3 Subj: Crime. Monsters. Shadows.

The mystery of Mineral Gorge ill. by Robert Van Nutt. Doubleday, 1998. ISBN 978-0-385-32562-2 Subj: Animals – pigs. Mystery stories.

Pignapped! ill. by Robert Van Nutt. Doubleday, 2000. ISBN 978-0-385-32559-2 Subj: Animals – pigs. Character traits – foolishness. Museums.

Pumpkins from the sky? ill. by Robert Van Nutt. Doubleday, 1999. ISBN 978-0-385-32568-4 Subj: Animals – pigs. Fairs, festivals. Weather – storms.

Skyrockets and snickerdoodles ill. by Robert Van Nutt. Doubleday, 2001. ISBN 978-0-385-32553-0 Subj: Activities – writing. Cities, towns. Holidays – Fourth of July. Sports – baseball.

van Os, Erik. *The wish* (van Lieshout, Elle)

Van Rynbach, Iris. *Five little pumpkins* ill. by author. Boyds Mills, 1995. ISBN 978-1-56397-452-6 Subj: Holidays – Halloween. Plants. Rhyming text.

Van Steenwyk, Elizabeth. *First dog Fala* ill. by Michael G. Montgomery. Peachtree, 2008. ISBN 978-1-56145-411-2 Subj: Animals – dogs. U.S. history.

Prairie Christmas ill. by Ronald Himler. Eerdmans, 2006. ISBN 978-0-8028-5280-9 Subj: Birth. Family life. Holidays – Christmas. U.S. history – frontier & pioneer life.

Van Woerkom, Dorothy. *Abu Ali counts his donkeys* ill. by Harry Horse. Candlewick, 2000. ISBN 978-0-7636-0956-6 Subj: Animals – donkeys. Counting, numbers.

Becky and the bear ill. by Margot Tomes. Putnam, 1975. ISBN 978-0-399-60924-4 Subj: Animals – bears. Character traits – bravery. U.S. history – frontier & pioneer life.

Donkey Ysabel ill. by Normand Chartier. Macmillan, 1978. ISBN 978-0-02-791280-7 Subj: Animals – donkeys. Humorous stories.

Harry and Shelburt ill. by Erick Ingraham. Macmillan, 1977. ISBN 978-0-02-791290-6 Subj: Animals – rabbits. Friendship. Reptiles – turtles, tortoises. Sports – racing.

Hidden messages ill. by Lynne Cherry. Crown, 1980. ISBN 978-0-517-53520-2 Subj: Communication. Insects. Science.

The rat, the ox and the zodiac: a Chinese legend ill. by Errol Le Cain. Crown, 1976. ISBN 978-0-517-51849-6 Subj: Animals. Animals – rats. Character traits – cleverness. Folk & fairy tales. Foreign lands – China. Zodiac.

Varela, Barry. *Gizmo* ill. by Ed Briant. Macmillan, 2007. ISBN 978-1-59643-115-7 Subj: Inventions. Machines. Rhyming text.

Varley, Susan. *Badger's parting gifts* ill. by author. Lothrop, 1984. ISBN 978-0-688-02703-2 Subj: Animals – badgers. Death. Friendship. Gifts.

Varon, Sara. *Chicken and Cat* ill. by author. Scholastic, 2006. ISBN 978-0-439-63406-9 Subj: Animals – cats. Birds – chickens. Friendship. Wordless.

Chicken and Cat clean up ill. by author. Scholastic, 2009. ISBN 978-0-439-63408-3 Subj: Animals – cats. Birds – chickens. Character traits – cleanliness. Wordless.

Vasilovich, Guy. *The 13 nights of Halloween* ill. by author. HarperCollins, 2011. ISBN 978-0-06-180445-8 Subj: Cumulative tales. Holidays – Halloween. Rhyming text. Songs.

Vaughan, Marcia Kapok. *Snap!* ill. by Sascha Hutchinson. Scholastic, 1996. ISBN 978-0-590-60377-5 Subj: Animals. Animals – kangaroos. Reptiles – alligators, crocodiles.

We're going on a ghost hunt ill. by Ann Schweninger. Harcourt, 2001. ISBN 978-0-15-202353-9 Subj: Ghosts. Holidays – Halloween. Imagination. Rhyming text.

Whistling Dixie ill. by Barry Moser. HarperCollins, 1995. ISBN 978-0-06-021029-8 Subj: Animals. Pets. Swamps.

Vaughan, Richard Lee. *Eagle boy* ill. by Lee Christiansen. Sasquatch, 2000. ISBN 978-1-57061-171-1 Subj: Birds – eagles. Folk & fairy tales. Indians of North America.

Vega, Denise. *Build a burrito: a counting book in English and Spanish* ill. by David Diaz. Scholastic, 2008. ISBN 978-0-439-44155-1 Subj: Counting, numbers. Food. Foreign languages.

Grandmother, have the angels come? ill. by Erin Eitter Kono. Little, Brown, 2009. ISBN 978-0-316-10663-4 Subj: Character traits – questioning. Family life – grandmothers. Foreign languages. Old age.

Veit, Barbara. *Who stole my house?* ill. by AnnaLaura Cantone. NorthSouth, 2007. ISBN 978-0-7358-2122-4 Subj: Animals – snails. Homes, houses.

Velasquez, Eric. *Grandma's gift* ill. by author. Walker, 2010. ISBN 978-0-8027-2082-5 Subj: Art. Ethnic groups in the U.S. – Puerto Rican Americans. Family life – grandmothers. Foreign languages. Gifts. Holidays – Christmas.

Grandma's records ill. by author. Walker, 2001. ISBN 978-0-8027-8760-6 Subj: Activities – storytelling. Ethnic groups in the U.S. – Puerto Rican Americans. Family life – grandmothers. Music.

Veldkamp, Tjibbe. *The school trip* ill. by Philip Hopman. Front Street, 2001. ISBN 978-1-886910-70-6 Subj: School – first day.

Venter, Liezl. *Understanding Sam and Asperger syndrome* (Niekerk, Clarabelle van)

Verboven, Agnes. *Ducks like to swim* ill. by Anne Westerduin. Orchard, 1997. ISBN 978-0-531-30054-1 Subj: Animals. Birds – ducks. Farms. Noise, sounds. Water. Weather – rain.

Verburg, Bonnie. *The kiss box* ill. by Henry Cole. Orchard, 2011. ISBN 978-0-545-11284-0 Subj: Activities – traveling. Animals – bears. Emotions – love. Family life – mothers. Kissing.

Verde, Susan. *The museum* ill. by Peter H. Reynolds. Abrams, 2013. ISBN 978-1-4197-0594-6 Subj: Art. Museums. Rhyming text.

Verdet, Andre. *All about time* ill. by Celine Bour-Chollet et al. Scholastic, 1995. ISBN 978-0-590-42795-1 Subj: Clocks, watches. Days of the week, months of the year. Format, unusual – toy & movable books. Seasons. Time.

Verdick, Elizabeth. *On-the-go time* ill. by Marieka Heinlen. Free Spirit, 2011. ISBN 978-1-57542-379-1 Subj: Character traits – helpfulness. Format, unusual – board books. Shopping.

Peep leap ill. by John Bendall-Brunello. Amazon/Two Lions, 2013. ISBN 978-1-4778-1640-0 Subj: Birds – ducks. Counting, numbers. Rhyming text.

Tails are not for pulling ill. by Marieka Heinlen. Free Spirit, 2005. ISBN 978-1-57542-180-3 Subj: Format, unusual – board books. Pets.

Vere, Ed. *Banana!* ill. by author. Holt, 2010. ISBN 978-0-8050-9214-1 Subj: Animals – monkeys. Behavior – sharing.

Bedtime for monsters ill. by author. Holt, 2012. ISBN 978-0-8050-9509-8 Subj: Bedtime. Monsters.

Chick ill. by author. Holt, 2010. ISBN 978-0-8050-9168-7 Subj: Birds – chickens.

Everyone's little ill. by author. Orchard, 2001. ISBN 978-0-531-30336-8 Subj: Animals – elephants. Concepts – size. Format, unusual – toy & movable books.

The getaway ill. by author. Simon & Schuster, 2007. ISBN 978-1-4169-4789-9 Subj: Animals – elephants. Animals – mice. Behavior – stealing.

Verma, Jatinder Nath. *The story of Divaali* ill. by Nilesh Mistry. Barefoot, 2002. ISBN 978-1-84148-936-0 Subj: Folk & fairy tales. Foreign lands – India. Holidays – Divali. Religion – Hinduism. Royalty – princes.

Vern, Alex. *Where do frogs come from?* ill. with photos. Harcourt, 2001. ISBN 978-0-15-216304-4 Subj: Frogs & toads. Science.

Vernick, Audrey. *Brothers at bat: the true story of an amazing all-brother baseball team* ill. by Steven Salerno. Clarion, 2012. ISBN 978-0-547-38557-0 Subj: Family life – brothers. Sports – baseball. U.S. history.

Is your buffalo ready for kindergarten? ill. by Daniel Jennewein. HarperCollins, 2010. ISBN 978-0-06-176275-8 Subj: Animals – buffaloes. School – first day.

She loved baseball: the Effa Manley story ill. by Don Tate. HarperCollins, 2010. ISBN 978-0-06-134920-1 Subj: Ethnic groups in the U.S. – African Americans. Gender roles. Prejudice. Sports – baseball. U.S. history.

Teach your buffalo to play drums ill. by Daniel Jennewein. HarperCollins, 2011. ISBN 978-0-06-176253-6 Subj: Animals – buffaloes. Musical instruments – drums. Noise, sounds.

Verstraete, Larry. *S is for scientists: a discovery alphabet* ill. by David Geister. Sleeping Bear, 2010. ISBN 978-1-58536-470-1 Subj: ABC books. Careers – scientists. Science.

Vestergaard, Hope. *Digger, dozer, dumper* ill. by David Slonim. Candlewick, 2013. ISBN 978-0-7636-5078-0 Subj: Machines. Poetry. Trucks.

Hillside lullaby ill. by Margie Moore. Penguin, 2006. ISBN 978-0-525-47215-5 Subj: Animals. Bedtime. Rhyming text.

Potty animals: what to know when you've gotta go! ill. by Valeria Petrone. Sterling, 2010. ISBN 978-1-4027-5996-3 Subj: Animals. Etiquette. Hygiene. Rhyming text. Toilet training.

What do you do when a monster says boo? ill. by Maggie Smith. Penguin, 2006. ISBN 978-0-525-47737-2 Subj: Monsters. Rhyming text.

Vetter, Jennifer Riggs. *Down by the station* ill. by Frank Remkiewicz. Ten Speed, 2009. ISBN 978-1-58246-243-1 Subj: Songs. Transportation.

Viau, Nancy. *Storm song* ill. by Gynux. Amazon, 2013. ISBN 978-1-4778-1646-2 Subj: Family life. Rhyming text. Weather – storms.

Vidal, Beatriz A. *Federico and the Magi's gift* ill. by author. Knopf, 2004. ISBN 978-0-375-92518-4 Subj: Behavior – misbehavior. Foreign lands – Latin America. Foreign languages. Holidays – Christmas.

Vidrine, Beverly Barras. *Easter Day alphabet* ill. by Alison Davis Lyne. Pelican, 2003. ISBN 978-1-58980-076-2 Subj: ABC books. Holidays – Easter. Religion.

Vigil-Piñón, Evangelina. *Marina's muumuu / El muumuu de Marina* ill. by Pablo Torrecilla. Piñata, 2001. ISBN 978-1-55885-350-8 Subj: Clothing. Ethnic groups in the U.S. Family life – grandmothers. Foreign languages. Hawaii.

Vigna, Judith. *Boot weather* ed. by Ann Fay; ill. by author. Whitman, 1988. ISBN 978-0-8075-0837-4 Subj: Activities – playing. Clothing – shoes. Imagination. Seasons – winter. Weather.

I wish my daddy didn't drink so much ed. by Ann Fay; ill. by author. Whitman, 1988. ISBN 978-0-8075-3523-3 Subj: Behavior – wishing. Family life – fathers. Illness.

My two uncles ill. by author. Whitman, 1995. ISBN 978-0-8075-5507-1 Subj: Birthdays. Family life – aunts, uncles. Family life – grandfathers. Homosexuality.

Saying goodbye to daddy ill. by author. Whitman, 1990. ISBN 978-0-8075-7253-5 Subj: Death. Emotions. Emotions – grief. Family life – fathers.

Vila, Laura. *Building Manhattan* ill. by author. Viking, 2008. ISBN 978-0-670-06284-3 Subj: Buildings. Cities, towns. U.S. history.

Villa, Alvaro F. *Flood* ill. by author. Capstone, 2013. ISBN 978-1-62370-001-0 Subj: Family life. Weather – floods. Wordless.

Villeneuve, Anne. *Loula is leaving for Africa* ill. by author. Kids Can, 2013. ISBN 978-1-55453-941-3 Subj: Behavior – running away. Careers – chauffeurs. Imagination.

The red scarf ill. by author. Tundra, 2010. ISBN 978-0-88776-989-4 Subj: Animals – moles. Behavior – lost & found possessions. Careers – magicians. Circus. Clothing – scarves.

Villnave, Erica Pelton. *Sophie's lovely locks* ill. by author. Marshall Cavendish, 2011. ISBN 978-0-7614-5820-3 Subj: Character traits – generosity. Hair.

Vincent, Gabrielle. *Ernest and Celestine at the circus* ill. by author. Greenwillow, 1989. ISBN 978-0-688-08685-5 Subj: Animals – bears. Animals – mice. Circus.

Ernest and Celestine's picnic ill. by author. Morrow, 1988, 1982. ISBN 978-0-688-07809-6 Subj: Activities – picnicking. Animals – bears. Animals – mice. Weather – rain.

Merry Christmas, Ernest and Celestine ill. by author. Greenwillow, 1984. ISBN 978-0-688-02606-6 Subj: Animals – bears. Animals – mice. Friendship. Holidays – Christmas. Parties.

Viorst, Judith. *Alexander and the terrible, horrible, no good, very bad day* ill. by Ray Cruz. Aladdin, 1987, ©1972. ISBN 978-0-689-71173-2 Subj: Behavior – bad day. Family life.

Alexander, who used to be rich last Sunday ill. by Ray Cruz. Atheneum, 1978. ISBN 978-0-689-30602-0 Subj: Money.

Alexander, who's not (do you hear me? I mean it!) going to move ill. by Robin Preiss-Glasser. Atheneum, 1995. ISBN 978-0-689-31958-7 Subj: Character traits – stubbornness. Family life. Moving.

The alphabet from Z to A: (with much confusion on the way) ill. by Richard Hull. Atheneum, 1994. ISBN 978-0-689-31768-2 Subj: ABC books. Games. Language. Poetry.

The good-bye book ill. by Kay Chorao. Atheneum, 1988. ISBN 978-0-689-31308-0 Subj: Activities – babysitting. Books, reading. Imagination.

I'll fix Anthony ill. by Arnold Lobel. HarperCollins, 1988, ©1969. ISBN 978-0-689-71202-9 Subj: Family life. Sibling rivalry.

Just in case ill. by Diana Cain Bluthenthal. Simon & Schuster, 2006. ISBN 978-0-689-87164-1 Subj: Behavior – worrying.

My mama says there aren't any zombies, ghosts, vampires, creatures, demons, monsters, fiends, goblins, or things ill. by Kay Chorao. Atheneum, 1973. ISBN 978-0-689-30102-5 Subj: Bedtime. Emotions – fear. Family life – mothers. Imagination. Monsters.

Nobody here but me ill. by Christine Davenier. Farrar, 2008. ISBN 978-0-374-35540-1 Subj: Behavior – misbehavior. Behavior – needing someone. Emotions – loneliness. Family life.

Rosie and Michael ill. by Lorna Tomei. Atheneum, 1974. ISBN 978-0-689-30418-7 Subj: Friendship.

Super-completely and totally the messiest ill. by Robin Preiss-Glasser. Atheneum, 2001. ISBN 978-0-689-82941-3 Subj: Character traits – cleanliness. Character traits – orderliness. Family life – sisters.

The tenth good thing about Barney ill. by Erik Blegvad. Atheneum, 1987, ©1971. ISBN 978-0-689-71203-6 Subj: Animals – cats. Careers – doctors. Death. Emotions – grief. Pets.

Vischer, Frans. *Fuddles* ill. by author. Simon & Schuster, 2011. ISBN 978-1-4169-9155-7 Subj: Animals – cats. Behavior – lost.

A very Fuddles Christmas ill. by author. Aladdin, 2013. ISBN 978-1-4169-9156-4 Subj: Animals – cats. Holidays – Christmas.

Vischer, Phil. *Sidney and Norman: a tale of two pigs* ill. by Justin Gerard. Thomas Nelson, 2006. ISBN 978-1-4003-0834-7 Subj: Animals – pigs. Emotions – love. Religion.

Viva, Frank. *Along a long road* ill. by author. Little, Brown, 2011. ISBN 978-0-316-12925-1 Subj: Sports – bicycling.

A long way away ill. by author. Little, Brown, 2013. ISBN 978-0-316-22196-2 Subj: Aliens. Format, unusual. Sea & seashore. Space & space ships. Squid.

A trip to the bottom of the world with Mouse ill. by author. TOON, 2012. ISBN 978-1-93517-919-1 Subj: Animals – mice. Foreign lands – Antarctic. Format, unusual – graphic novels.

Vivian, Siobhan. *Vunce upon a time* (Seibold, J. Otto)

Voake, Charlotte. *Ginger* ill. by author. Candlewick, 1997. ISBN 978-0-7636-0108-9 Subj: Animals – cats. Behavior – running away. Emotions – envy, jealousy.

Ginger and the mystery visitor ill. by author. Candlewick, 2010. ISBN 978-0-7636-4865-7 Subj: Animals – cats.

Hello twins ill. by author. Candlewick, 2006. ISBN 978-0-7636-3003-4 Subj: Family life – brothers & sisters. Multiple births – twins.

Here comes the train ill. by author. Candlewick, 1998. ISBN 978-0-7636-0438-7 Subj: Family life. Trains.

Pizza kittens ill. by author. Candlewick, 2002. ISBN 978-0-7636-1622-9 Subj: Animals – cats. Family life. Food.

Tweedle - dee - dee ill. by author. Candlewick, 2008. ISBN 978-0-7636-3797-2 Subj: Music. Seasons – spring. Songs.

Voake, Steve. *Insect detective* ill. by Charlotte Voake. Candlewick, 2010. ISBN 978-0-7636-4447-5 Subj: Gardens, gardening. Insects. Science.

Voce, Louise. *Over in the meadow* ill. by author. Candlewick, 1994. ISBN 978-1-56402-428-2 Subj: Animals. Counting, numbers. Nursery rhymes.

Volkmann, Roy. *Curious kittens* ill. by author. Random House, 2001. ISBN 978-0-385-32778-7 Subj: Animals – babies. Animals – cats. Sports – swimming.

Volkmer, Jane Anne, adapt. *Song of Chirimia / La Musica de la Chirimia* ill. by adapter. Carolrhoda, 1990. ISBN 978-0-87614-423-7 Subj: Folk & fairy tales. Foreign lands – Mexico. Foreign languages. Indians of Central America – Maya. Religion.

von Olfers, Sibylle. *Mother Earth and her children: a quilted fairy tale* ill. by Sieglinde Schoen Smith. Breckling, 2007. ISBN 978-1-933308-18-0 Subj: Nature. Quilts. Rhyming text. Seasons – spring.

von Roehl, Angela. *Snail started it!* (Reider, Katja)

Vorst, Rochel Groner. *The sukkah that I built* ill. by Elizabeth Victor-Elsby. Hachai, 2002. ISBN 978-1-929628-07-0 Subj: Holidays – Sukkot. Jewish culture. Religion.

Votaw, Carol. *Good morning, little polar bear* ill. by Susan Banta. NorthWord, 2005. ISBN 978-1-55971-932-2 Subj: Animals. Foreign lands – Arctic. Morning.

Waking up down under ill. by Susan Banta. NorthWord, 2007. ISBN 978-1-55971-976-6 Subj: Animals. Foreign lands – Australia. Rhyming text.

Votry, Kim. *Baby's first signs* (Waller, Curt)

More baby's first signs (Waller, Curt)

Vozar, David. *Yo, hungry wolf! a nursery rap* ill. by Betsy Lewin. Doubleday, 1993. ISBN 978-0-385-30452-8 Subj: Animals – wolves. Folk & fairy tales. Rhyming text.

Vrombaut, An. *Clarabella's teeth* ill. by author. Clarion, 2003. ISBN 978-0-618-33379-0 Subj: Animals. Friendship. Reptiles – alligators, crocodiles. Teeth.

Vulliamy, Clara. *Ellen and Penguin and the new baby* ill. by author. Candlewick, 1996. ISBN 978-1-56402-697-2 Subj: Babies. Family life – brothers. Family life – mothers. Family life – new sibling. Toys.

Small ill. by author. Clarion, 2001. ISBN 978-0-618-19459-9 Subj: Animals – mice. Family life – grandmothers. Sleepovers. Toys.

Vyner, Tim. *World team* ill. by author. Roaring Brook, 2002. ISBN 978-0-7613-2409-6 Subj: Geography. Sports – soccer. Time.

Waber, Bernard. *An anteater named Arthur* ill. by author. Houghton, 1967. ISBN 978-0-395-20336-1 Subj: ABC books. Animals – anteaters.

Bearsie Bear and the surprise sleepover party ill. by author. Houghton, 1997. ISBN 978-0-395-86450-0 Subj: Animals. Bedtime. Seasons – winter. Sleepovers.

Courage ill. by author. Houghton, 2002. ISBN 978-0-618-23855-2 Subj: Character traits – bravery.

Do you see a mouse? ill. by author. Houghton, 1995. ISBN 978-0-395-72292-3 Subj: Animals – mice. Behavior – disbelief. Hotels. Puzzles.

Evie and Margie ill. by author. Houghton, 2003. ISBN 978-0-618-34124-5 Subj: Animals – hippopotamuses. Careers – actors. Emotions – envy, jealousy. Friendship. School. Theater.

Fast food! gulp! gulp! ill. by author. Houghton, 2001. ISBN 978-0-618-14189-0 Subj: Animals. Food. Restaurants. Rhyming text.

Funny, funny Lyle ill. by author. Houghton, 1987. ISBN 978-0-395-43619-6 Subj: Behavior – misunderstanding. Family life. Reptiles – alligators, crocodiles.

Gina ill. by author. Houghton, 1995. ISBN 978-0-395-74279-2 Subj: Emotions – loneliness. Friendship. Moving. Rhyming text. Sports – baseball.

Ira says goodbye ill. by author. Houghton, 1988. ISBN 978-0-395-48315-2 Subj: Emotions. Friendship. Moving.

Ira sleeps over ill. by author. Houghton, 1972. ISBN 978-0-395-13893-9 Subj: Activities – playing. Bedtime. Friendship. Sleep. Toys – bears.

A lion named Shirley Williamson ill. by author. Houghton, 1996. ISBN 978-0-395-80979-2 Subj: Animals – lions. Behavior – running away. Flowers. Names. Zoos.

Lorenzo ill. by author. Houghton, 1961. Subj: Character traits – curiosity. Fish.

Lovable Lyle ill. by author. Houghton, 1969. ISBN 978-0-395-25378-6 Subj: Friendship. Reptiles – alligators, crocodiles.

Lyle and the birthday party ill. by author. Houghton, 1966. ISBN 978-0-395-15080-1 Subj: Birthdays. Emotions – envy, jealousy. Reptiles – alligators, crocodiles.

Lyle at Christmas ill. by author. Houghton, 1998. ISBN 978-0-395-91304-8 Subj: Animals – cats. Holidays – Christmas. Reptiles – alligators, crocodiles.

Lyle at the office ill. by author. Houghton, 1994. ISBN 978-0-395-70563-6 Subj: Activities – working. Reptiles – alligators, crocodiles.

Lyle finds his mother ill. by author. Houghton, 1974. ISBN 978-0-395-19489-8 Subj: Family life – mothers. Reptiles – alligators, crocodiles.

Lyle, Lyle Crocodile ill. by author. Houghton, 1965. ISBN 978-0-395-13720-8 Subj: Character traits – helpfulness. Reptiles – alligators, crocodiles.

Lyle walks the dogs: a counting book ill. by Paulis Waber. Harcourt, 2010. ISBN 978-0-547-22323-0 Subj: Activities – walking. Animals – dogs. Counting, numbers. Reptiles – alligators, crocodiles.

The mouse that snored ill. by author. Houghton, 2000. ISBN 978-0-395-97518-3 Subj: Animals – mice. Noise, sounds. Rhyming text. Sleep – snoring.

Waboose, Jan Bourdeau. *Firedancers* ill. by C. J. Taylor. Stoddart, 2000. ISBN 978-0-7737-3138-7 Subj: Activities – dancing. Family life – grandmothers. Indians of North America – Ojibwa. Night.

Morning on the lake ill. by Karen Reczuch. Kids Can, 1998. ISBN 978-1-55074-373-9 Subj: Family life – fathers. Indians of North America – Ojibwa. Nature.

SkySisters ill. by Brian Deines. Kids Can, 2000. ISBN 978-1-55074-697-6 Subj: Family life – sisters. Indians of North America – Ojibwa. Night. Northern lights. Sky.

Waddell, Martin. *Bee frog* ill. by Barbara Firth. Candlewick, 2007. ISBN 978-0-7636-3310-3 Subj: Behavior – running away. Frogs & toads. Imagination. Self-concept.

The big big sea ill. by Jennifer Eachus. Candlewick, 1994. ISBN 978-1-56402-066-6 Subj: Family life – mothers. Night. Sea & seashore.

Can't you sleep, Little Bear? ill. by Barbara Firth. Candlewick, 1992. ISBN 978-1-56402-007-9 Subj: Animals – bears. Bedtime. Emotions – fear. Family life – fathers. Night. Sleep.

Captain Small Pig ill. by Susan Varley. Peachtree, 2010. ISBN 978-1-56145-519-5 Subj: Animals – goats. Animals – pigs. Birds – turkeys. Boats, ships.

Farmer Duck ill. by Helen Oxenbury. Candlewick, 1992. ISBN 978-1-56402-009-3 Subj: Animals. Birds – ducks. Careers – farmers. Character traits – helpfulness. Farms.

Good job, Little Bear! ill. by Barbara Firth. Candlewick, 1999. ISBN 978-0-7636-0736-4 Subj: Animals – bears. Character traits – confidence. Character traits – helpfulness.

It's quacking time ill. by Jill Barton. Candlewick, 2005. ISBN 978-0-7636-2738-6 Subj: Animals – babies. Birds – ducks. Eggs.

A kitten called Moonlight ill. by Christian Birmingham. Candlewick, 2001. ISBN 978-0-7636-1176-7 Subj: Animals – cats. Behavior – lost. Family life – mothers.

Let's go home, Little Bear ill. by Barbara Firth. Candlewick, 1993. ISBN 978-1-56402-131-1 Subj: Animals – bears. Emotions – fear. Family life – fathers. Forest, woods. Noise, sounds.

Mimi's Christmas ill. by Leo Hartas. Candlewick, 1997. ISBN 978-0-7636-0413-4 Subj: Animals – mice. Behavior – worrying. Family life. Holidays – Christmas.

Night night Cuddly Bear ill. by Penny Dale. Candlewick, 2000. ISBN 978-0-7636-1195-8 Subj: Animals – bears. Bedtime. Family life. Toys – bears.

Owl babies ill. by Patrick Benson. Candlewick, 1992. ISBN 978-1-56402-101-4 Subj: Birds – owls. Emotions – fear. Family life – mothers. Night.

Owl babies [board book] ill. by Patrick Benson. Candlewick, 1996. ISBN 978-1-56402-965-2 Subj: Emotions – fear. Family life – mothers. Format, unusual – board books. Night.

The pig in the pond ill. by Jill Barton. Candlewick, 1992. ISBN 978-1-56402-050-5 Subj: Animals. Animals – pigs. Careers – farmers. Cumulative tales. Lakes, ponds. Sports – swimming.

Rosie's babies ill. by Penny Dale. Candlewick, 1999. ISBN 978-0-7636-0718-0 Subj: Family life – mothers. Family life – new sibling. Toys.

Sailor Bear ill. by Virginia Austin. Candlewick, 1992. ISBN 978-1-56402-040-6 Subj: Behavior – lost. Boats, ships. Sailors. Sea & seashore. Toys – bears.

Sam Vole and his brothers ill. by Barbara Firth. Candlewick, 1992. ISBN 978-1-56402-082-6 Subj: Animals – mice. Emotions – loneliness. Family life – brothers. Sibling rivalry.

Sleep tight, Little Bear ill. by Barbara Firth. Candlewick, 2005. ISBN 978-0-7636-2439-2 Subj: Animals – bears. Bedtime. Emotions – loneliness. Night. Sleep.

Small Bear lost ill. by Virginia Austin. Candlewick, 1996. ISBN 978-1-56402-871-6 Subj: Activities – traveling. Behavior – lost. Toys – bears.

Snow bears ill. by Sarah Fox-Davies. Candlewick, 2002. ISBN 978-0-7636-1906-0 Subj: Activities – playing. Animals – bears. Family life – mothers. Weather – snow.

Squeak-a-lot ill. by Virginia Miller. Greenwillow, 1991. ISBN 978-0-688-10245-6 Subj: Activities – playing. Animals – mice. Noise, sounds.

The Super Hungry Dinosaur ill. by Leonie Lord. Dial, 2009. ISBN 978-0-8037-3446-3 Subj: Animals – dogs. Dinosaurs. Emotions – anger.

Tom Rabbit ill. by Barbara Firth. Candlewick, 2001. ISBN 978-0-7636-1089-0 Subj: Activities – playing. Animals – rabbits. Bedtime. Emotions – fear. Farms. Toys.

We love them ill. by Barbara Firth. Lothrop, 1990. ISBN 978-0-688-09332-7 Subj: Animals – dogs. Animals – rabbits. Friendship.

Webster J. Duck ill. by David Parkins. Candlewick, 2001. ISBN 978-0-7636-1506-2 Subj: Animals. Behavior – lost. Birds – ducks. Family life – mothers.

When the teddy bears came ill. by Penny Dale. Candlewick, 1995. ISBN 978-1-56402-529-6 Subj: Babies. Family life – brothers & sisters. Family life – new sibling. Toys – bears.

Who do you love? ill. by Camilla Ashforth. Candlewick, 1999. ISBN 978-0-7636-0586-5 Subj: Animals – cats. Bedtime. Emotions – love.

Yum, yum, yummy ill. by John Bendall-Brunello. Candlewick, 1998. ISBN 978-0-7636-0477-6 Subj: Animals – bears. Behavior – bullying, teasing. Behavior – greed. Family life – mothers. Food.

Wade, Mary Dodson. *Cinco de Mayo* ill. with photos. Children's Press, 2003. ISBN 978-0-516-22664-4 Subj: Foreign lands – Mexico. Holidays – Cinco de Mayo. War.

No year of the cat ill. by Nicole Wong. Sleeping Bear, 2012. ISBN 978-1-58536-785-6 Subj: Animals – cats. Animals – rats. Folk & fairy tales. Foreign lands – China. Royalty – emperors. Zodiac.

Wadham, Tim. *The queen of France* ill. by Kady MacDonald Denton. Candlewick, 2011. ISBN 978-0-7636-4102-3 Subj: Family life – parents. Imagination. Royalty – queens.

Wadsworth, Ginger. *One tiger growls: a counting book of animal sounds* ill. by James M. Needham. Charlesbridge, 1999. ISBN 978-0-88106-273-1 Subj: Animals. Counting, numbers. Noise, sounds.

Waechter, Phillip. *Rosie and the nightmares* ill. by author. Handprint, 2005. ISBN 978-1-59354-130-9 Subj: Animals – rabbits. Emotions – fear. Monsters. Nightmares.

Wagner, Anke. *Tim's big move!* ill. by Eva Eriksson. NorthSouth, 2012. ISBN 978-0-7358-4090-4 Subj: Behavior – worrying. Concepts – change. Friendship. Moving. School. Toys.

Wagner, Karen. *Bravo, Mildred and Ed!* ill. by Janet Pedersen. Walker, 2000. ISBN 978-0-8027-8735-4 Subj: Animals – mice. Character traits – confidence. Friendship.

A friend like Ed ill. by Janet Pedersen. Walker, 1998. ISBN 978-0-8027-8663-0 Subj: Animals – mice. Concepts – opposites. Friendship.

Wagner, Rachel. *A friend for Einstein: the smallest stallion* (Cantrell, Charlie)

Wahl, Jan. *The art collector* ill. by Rosalinde Bonnet. Charlesbridge, 2011. ISBN 978-1-58089-270-4 Subj: Art. Behavior – collecting things.

Elf night ill. by Peter Weevers. Carolrhoda, 2002. ISBN 978-1-57505-512-1 Subj: Bedtime. Dreams. Mythical creatures – elves. Rhyming text.

The field mouse and the dinosaur named Sue ill. by Bob Doucet. Scholastic, 2000. ISBN 978-0-439-09984-4 Subj: Animals – mice. Dinosaurs. Museums. Prehistory.

I met a dinosaur ill. by Chris Sheban. Harcourt, 1997. ISBN 978-0-15-201644-9 Subj: Dinosaurs. Imagination. Museums. Prehistory. Rhyming text.

Little Johnny Buttermilk ill. by Jennifer Mazzucco. August House, 1999. ISBN 978-0-87483-559-5 Subj: Behavior. Character traits – cleverness. Folk & fairy tales. Foreign lands – England. Witches.

Mabel ran away with the toys ill. by Liza Woodruff. Whispering Coyote, 2000. ISBN 978-1-58089-059-5 Subj: Babies. Behavior – running away. Emotions – envy, jealousy. Family life – new sibling. Sibling rivalry.

Wahman, Joe. *Snowboy 1, 2, 3* ill. by Wendy Wahman. Holt, 2012. ISBN 978-0-8050-8732-1 Subj: Counting, numbers. Rhyming text. Seasons – winter. Snowmen. Weather – snow.

Wahman, Wendy. *A cat like that* ill. by author. Holt, 2011. ISBN 978-0-8050-8942-4 Subj: Animals – cats.

Don't lick the dog: making friends with dogs ill. by author. Holt, 2009. ISBN 978-0-8050-8733-8 Subj: Animals – dogs. Pets.

Waite, Judy. *Mouse, look out!* ill. by Norma Burgin. Dutton, 1998. ISBN 978-0-525-42031-6 Subj: Animals – cats. Animals – dogs. Animals – mice. Homes, houses. Rhyming text.

The stray kitten ill. by Gavin Rowe. Crocodile, 2000. ISBN 978-1-56656-356-7 Subj: Animals – cats. Behavior – growing up. Behavior – lost.

Waite, Michael P. *Jojofu* ill. by Yoriko Ito. Lothrop, 1996. ISBN 978-0-688-13661-1 Subj: Animals – dogs. Character traits – loyalty. Folk & fairy tales. Foreign lands – Japan.

Waiting for baby ill. by Rachel Fuller. Child's Play, 2010. ISBN 978-1-84643-275-0 Subj: Babies. Birth. Format, unusual – board books.

Wakeman, Daniel. *Ben's bunny trouble* ill. by Dirk van Stralen. Orca, 2007. ISBN 978-1-55143-611-1 Subj: Animals – rabbits. Space & space ships. Wordless.

Walburg, Lori. *The legend of the candy cane* ill. by James Bernardin. Zondervan, 2002. ISBN 978-0-310-70447-8 Subj: Folk & fairy tales. Food. Holidays – Christmas. Religion – Nativity.

Waldherr, Kris. *Harvest* ill. by author. Walker, 2001. ISBN 978-0-8027-8792-7 Subj: Gardens, gardening.

Waldman, Debby. *Room enough for Daisy* by Debby Waldman and Rita Feutl ill. by Cindy Revell. Orca, 2011. ISBN 978-1-55469-255-2 Subj: Behavior – messy. Behavior – sharing. Jewish culture.

A sack full of feathers ill. by Cindy Revell. Orca, 2006. ISBN 978-1-55143-332-5 Subj: Behavior – gossip. Folk & fairy tales. Jewish culture.

Waldman, Neil. *The starry night* ill. by author. Boyds Mills, 1999. ISBN 978-1-56397-736-7 Subj: Art. Careers – artists. Imagination.

They came from the Bronx ill. by author. Boyds Mills, 2001. ISBN 978-1-56397-891-3 Subj: Animals – buffaloes. Ecology. Family life – grandmothers. Indians of North America – Comanche. U.S. history. Zoos.

Waldron, Jan L. *Angel Pig and the hidden Christmas* ill. by David McPhail. Dutton, 2000. ISBN 978-0-525-45744-2 Subj: Animals – pigs. Holidays – Christmas. Rhyming text.

John Pig's Halloween ill. by David McPhail. Dutton, 1998. ISBN 978-0-525-45941-5 Subj: Animals – pigs. Emotions – fear. Holidays – Halloween. Monsters. Parties. Rhyming text.

Waldron, Kevin. *Mr. Peek and the misunderstanding at the zoo* ill. by author. Candlewick, 2010. ISBN 978-0-7636-4549-6 Subj: Animals. Behavior – misunderstanding. Behavior – worrying. Self-concept. Zoos.

Walker, Alice. *Finding the green stone* ill. by Catherine Deeter. Harcourt, 1991. ISBN 978-0-15-227538-9 Subj: Behavior. Character traits. Ethnic groups in the U.S. – African Americans. Rocks.

To hell with dying ill. by Catherine Deeter. Harcourt, 1987. ISBN 978-0-15-289075-9 Subj: Death. Ethnic groups in the U.S. – African Americans. Friendship.

Walker, Anna. *I love birthdays* ill. by author. Simon & Schuster, 2010. ISBN 978-1-4169-8320-0 Subj: Animals – zebras. Birthdays. Parties. Rhyming text.

I love my dad ill. by author. Simon & Schuster, 2010. ISBN 978-1-4169-8319-4 Subj: Animals – zebras. Family life – fathers. Rhyming text.

I love my mom ill. by author. Simon & Schuster, 2010. ISBN 978-1-4169-8318-7 Subj: Animals – zebras. Family life – mothers. Rhyming text.

Walker, Rob D. *Mama says: a book of love for mothers and sons* ill. by Leo Dillon and Diane Dillon. Scholastic, 2009. ISBN 978-0-439-93208-0 Subj: Family life. Foreign languages. Poetry. Religion. World.

Walker, Sally M. *Druscilla's Halloween* ill. by Lee White. Carolrhoda, 2009. ISBN 978-0-8225-8941-9 Subj: Holidays – Halloween. Old age. Transportation. Witches.

Freedom song: the story of Henry "Box" Brown ill. by Sean Qualls. HarperCollins, 2012. ISBN 978-0-06-058310-1 Subj: Character traits – freedom. Ethnic groups in the U.S. – African Americans. Slavery. U.S. history.

The Vowel family: a tale of lost letters ill. by Kevin Luthardt. Carolrhoda, 2008. ISBN 978-0-8225-7982-3 Subj: Humorous stories. Language.

Walker, Sarah. *Birds* (Gray, Samantha)

Wallace, Ian. *Chin Chiang and the dragon's dance* ill. by author. Atheneum, 1984. ISBN 978-0-689-50299-6 Subj: Emotions – fear. Ethnic groups in the U.S. – Chinese Americans. Family life – grandfathers. Holidays – Chinese New Year.

Wallace, Ivy. *Pookie* ill. by author. Collins, 2000. ISBN 978-0-00-198377-9 Subj: Activities – traveling. Animals. Animals – rabbits. Character traits – being different. Fairies.

Pookie believes in Santa Claus ill. by author. Collins, 2000. ISBN 978-0-00-198380-9 Subj: Animals. Animals – rabbits. Holidays – Christmas. Santa Claus.

Pookie puts the world right ill. by author. Collins, 2001. ISBN 978-0-00-664735-5 Subj: Animals. Animals – rabbits. Behavior – wishing. Seasons – winter.

Wallace, John. *Anything for you* ill. by Harry Horse. HarperCollins, 2004. ISBN 978-0-06-058129-9 Subj: Animals – bears. Bedtime. Family life – mothers.

Tiny Rabbit goes to a birthday party ill. by author. Holiday, 2000. ISBN 978-0-8234-1489-5 Subj: Animals – rabbits. Birthdays. Gifts. Parties.

Wallace, Joseph E. *Big and noisy Simon* ill. by Kevin O'Malley. Hyperion, 2001. ISBN 978-0-7868-2450-2 Subj: Animals – elephants. Behavior. Foreign lands – Africa. Noise, sounds.

Wallace, Karen. *I am an ankylosaurus* ill. by Mike Bostock. Simon & Schuster, 2005. ISBN 978-0-689-87318-8 Subj: Dinosaurs.

Scarlette Beane ill. by Jon Berkeley. Dial, 2000. ISBN 978-0-8037-2475-4 Subj: Food. Gardens, gardening. Magic. Nature. Plants.

Wallace, Mary. *I is for Inuksuk: an Arctic celebration* ill. by author. Maple Tree, 2009. ISBN 978-1-897349-57-1 Subj: Foreign lands – Arctic. Foreign languages.

Wallace, Nancy Elizabeth. *Alphabet house* ill. by author. Marshall Cavendish, 2005. ISBN 978-0-7614-5192-1 Subj: ABC books. Animals – rabbits.

Apples, apples, apples ill. by author. Winslow, 2000. ISBN 978-1-890817-19-0 Subj: Activities – baking, cooking. Animals – rabbits. Family life. Farms. Music. Songs.

Count down to clean up ill. by author. Houghton, 2001. ISBN 978-0-618-10130-6 Subj: Animals – rabbits. Character traits – cleanliness. Counting, numbers.

Fly, monarch! Fly! ill. by author. Marshall Cavendish, 2008. ISBN 978-0-7614-5425-0 Subj: Animals – rabbits. Insects – butterflies, caterpillars.

The kindness quilt ill. by author. Marshall Cavendish, 2006. ISBN 978-0-7614-5313-0 Subj: Character traits – kindness. Quilts.

Look! Look! Look! by Nancy Elizabeth Wallace and Linda K. Friedlaender ill. by Nancy Elizabeth Wallace. Marshall Cavendish, 2006. ISBN 978-0-7614-5282-9 Subj: Animals – mice. Art. Letters, cards.

Look! Look! Look! at sculpture ill. by author. Marshall Cavendish, 2012. ISBN 978-0-7614-6132-6 Subj: Animals – mice. Art. Letters, cards.

Paperwhite ill. by author. Houghton, 2000. ISBN 978-0-618-04283-8 Subj: Animals – rabbits. Flowers. Friendship. Gardens, gardening. Plants. Seasons – spring.

Planting seeds ill. by author. Marshall Cavendish, 2010. ISBN 978-0-7614-5643-8 Subj: Animals – rabbits. Counting, numbers. Gardens, gardening. Seeds.

Pond walk ill. by author. Marshall Cavendish, 2011. ISBN 978-0-7614-5816-6 Subj: Animals – bears. Lakes, ponds. Science.

Pumpkin day ill. by author. Marshall Cavendish, 2002. ISBN 978-0-7614-5128-0 Subj: Animals – rabbits. Farms. Food. Plants.

Rabbit's bedtime ill. by author. Houghton, 1999. ISBN 978-0-395-98266-2 Subj: Animals – rabbits. Bedtime. Rhyming text.

Ready, set, 100th day! ill. by author. Marshall Cavendish, 2011. ISBN 978-0-7614-5956-9 Subj: Animals – rabbits. Character traits – cooperation. Counting, numbers. Family life. School.

Recycle every day! ill. by author. Marshall Cavendish, 2003. ISBN 978-0-7614-5149-5 Subj: Animals – rabbits. Contests. Ecology. School.

Rocks! rocks! rocks! ill. by author. Marshall Cavendish, 2009. ISBN 978-0-7614-5528-8 Subj: Animals – bears. Rocks. Science.

Seeds! Seeds! Seeds! ill. by author. Marshall Cavendish, 2004. ISBN 978-0-7614-5159-4 Subj: Animals – bears. Family life – grandfathers. Seeds.

Shells! Shells! Shells! ill. by author. Marshall Cavendish, 2007. ISBN 978-0-7614-5332-1 Subj: Animals – bears. Sea & seashore – beaches.

Snow ill. by author. Western, 1995. ISBN 978-0-307-17562-5 Subj: Animals – rabbits. Family life – grandfathers. Weather – snow.

Snow [board book] ill. by author. Marshall Cavendish, 2007. ISBN 978-0-7614-5362-8 Subj: Animals – rabbits. Format, unusual – board books. Seasons – winter. Weather – snow.

Stars! Stars! Stars! ill. by author. Marshall Cavendish, 2009. ISBN 978-0-7614-5612-4 Subj: Animals – rabbits. Space & space ships. Stars.

Tell-a-bunny ill. by author. Winslow, 2000. ISBN 978-1-890817-29-9 Subj: Animals – rabbits. Birthdays. Parties.

The Valentine Express ill. by author. Marshall Cavendish, 2004. ISBN 978-0-7614-5183-9 Subj: Animals – rabbits. Holidays – Valentine's Day. School.

Wallen, Ila. *The moon in my room* ill. by Robert Sauber. Bent Willow, 2002. ISBN 978-0-9710627-0-2 Subj: Activities – storytelling. Animals. Animals – bears. Bedtime. Emotions – fear. Forest, woods. Problem solving. Rhyming text.

Waller, Curt. *Baby's first signs* by Curt Waller and Kim Votry ill. by Kim Votry. Gallaudet Univ. Pr., 2001. ISBN 978-1-56368-114-1 Subj: Books, reading. Format, unusual – board books. Disabilities – deafness. Sign language.

More baby's first signs by Curt Waller and Kim Votry ill. by Kim Votry. Gallaudet Univ. Pr., 2001. ISBN 978-1-56368-115-8 Subj: Books, reading. Format, unusual – board books. Disabilities – deafness. Sign language.

Wallner, Alexandra. *Beatrix Potter* ill. by author. Holiday, 1995. ISBN 978-0-8234-1181-8 Subj: Activities – drawing. Animals. Art. Careers – writers. Emotions – loneliness. Imagination.

Betsy Ross ill. by author. Holiday, 1994. ISBN 978-0-8234-1071-2 Subj: Activities – sewing. U.S. history.

Lucy Maud Montgomery: the author of Anne of Green Gables ill. by author. Holiday House, 2006. ISBN 978-0-8234-1549-6 Subj: Activities – writing. Books, reading.

Susan B. Anthony ill. by author. Holiday House, 2012. ISBN 978-0-8234-1953-1 Subj: Gender roles. U.S. history.

Walsh, Ellen Stoll. *Balancing act* ill. by author. Simon & Schuster, 2010. ISBN 978-1-4424-0757-2 Subj: Animals – mice. Concepts.

Dot and Jabber and the great acorn mystery ill. by author. Harcourt, 2001. ISBN 978-0-15-202602-8 Subj: Animals – mice. Animals – squirrels. Seeds. Trees.

Dot and Jabber and the mystery of the missing stream ill. by author. Harcourt, 2002. ISBN 978-0-15-216512-3 Subj: Animals – mice. Rivers.

For Pete's sake ill. by author. Harcourt, 1998. ISBN 978-0-15-200324-1 Subj: Birds – flamingos. Character traits – being different. Character traits – individuality. Reptiles – alligators, crocodiles.

Hamsters to the rescue ill. by author. Harcourt, 2005. ISBN 978-0-15-205202-7 Subj: Animals – hamsters. Behavior – lost & found possessions. Birds – seagulls. Crustaceans – crabs. Friendship. Sea & seashore – beaches.

Mouse count ill. by author. Harcourt, 1991. ISBN 978-0-15-256023-2 Subj: Animals – mice. Counting, numbers. Reptiles – snakes.

Mouse magic ill. by author. Harcourt, 2000. ISBN 978-0-15-200326-5 Subj: Animals – mice. Concepts – color. Magic. Wizards.

Mouse paint ill. by author. Harcourt, 1989. ISBN 978-0-15-256025-6 Subj: Activities – painting. Animals – mice. Behavior – hiding. Concepts – color.

Mouse shapes ill. by author. Harcourt, 2007. ISBN 978-0-15-206091-6 Subj: Animals – mice. Concepts – shape.

Pip's magic ill. by author. Harcourt, 1994. ISBN 978-0-15-292850-6 Subj: Animals. Emotions – fear. Magic. Night. Reptiles – salamanders.

You silly goose ill. by author. Harcourt, 1992. ISBN 978-0-15-299865-3 Subj: Animals – foxes. Animals – mice. Birds – geese.

Walsh, Joanna. *The biggest kiss* ill. by Judi Abbot. Simon & Schuster, 2011. ISBN 978-1-4424-2769-3 Subj: Kissing. Rhyming text.

The perfect hug ill. by Judi Abbot. Simon & Schuster, 2012. ISBN 978-1-4424-6606-7 Subj: Animals. Hugging. Rhyming text.

Walsh, Melanie. *Do donkeys dance?* ill. by author. Houghton, 2000. ISBN 978-0-618-00330-3 Subj: Activities. Animals. Nature.

Do lions live on lily pads? ill. by author. Houghton, 2006. ISBN 978-0-618-47300-7 Subj: Animals. Character traits – questioning. Homes, houses. Nature.

Do monkeys tweet? ill. by author. Houghton, 1997. ISBN 978-0-395-85081-7 Subj: Animals. Noise, sounds.

Hide and sleep ill. by author. DK, 1999. ISBN 978-0-7894-4820-0 Subj: Bedtime. Behavior – hiding. Games.

Living with Mom and living with Dad ill. by author. Candlewick, 2012. ISBN 978-0-7636-5869-4 Subj: Divorce. Family life – parents. Format, unusual – toy & movable books.

Monster, monster ill. by author. Candlewick, 2002. ISBN 978-0-7636-1669-4 Subj: Format, unusual – toy & movable books. Monsters.

Ned's rainbow ill. by author. DK, 2000. ISBN 978-0-7894-5623-6 Subj: Activities – painting. Weather – rainbows.

10 things I can do to help my world: fun and easy eco-tips ill. by author. Candlewick, 2008. ISBN 978-0-7636-4144-3 Subj: Ecology.

Walsh, Vivian. *Penguin dreams* (Seibold, J. Otto)

Walter, Mildred Pitts. *Brother to the wind* ill. by Leo Dillon and Diane Dillon. Lothrop, 1985. ISBN 978-0-688-03811-3 Subj: Activities – flying. Foreign lands – Africa.

Darkness ill. by Marcia Jameson. Simon & Schuster, 1995. ISBN 978-0-689-80305-5 Subj: Night. Shadows.

My mama needs me ill. by Pat Cummings. Lothrop, 1983. ISBN 978-0-688-01671-5 Subj: Emotions – loneliness. Ethnic groups in the U.S. – African Americans. Family life.

Two too much ill. by Pat Cummings. Bradbury, 1990. ISBN 978-0-02-792290-5 Subj: Emotions. Ethnic groups in the U.S. – African Americans. Family life – brothers & sisters.

Ty's one-man band ill. by Margot Tomes. Four Winds, 1980. ISBN 978-0-02-792300-1 Subj: Folk & fairy tales. Music. Musical instruments – bands.

Walter, Virginia. *"Hi, pizza man!"* ill. by Ponder Goembel. Orchard, 1995. ISBN 978-0-531-08735-0 Subj: Animals. Noise, sounds.

Walters, Catherine. *Are you there, Baby Bear?* ill. by author. Dutton, 1999. ISBN 978-0-525-46161-6 Subj: Animals – babies. Animals – bears. Family life – new sibling. Multiple births – twins.

The magical snowman ill. by Alison Edgson. Good Books, 2009. ISBN 978-1-56148-671-7 Subj: Animals – rabbits. Magic. Seasons – winter. Snowmen.

Play gently, Alfie Bear ill. by author. Dutton, 2002. ISBN 978-0-525-46885-1 Subj: Animals – bears. Family life – brothers & sisters. Family life – mothers.

When will it be spring? ill. by author. Dutton, 1998. ISBN 978-0-525-45881-4 Subj: Animals – bears. Character traits – patience. Family life – mothers. Hibernation. Nature. Seasons – spring. Seasons – winter.

Walters, Eric. *The matatu* ill. by Eva Campbell. Orca, 2012. ISBN 978-1-55469-301-6 Subj: Animals. Buses. Family life – grandfathers. Folk & fairy tales. Foreign lands – Kenya.

Walters, Virginia. *Are we there yet, Daddy?* ill. by S. D. Schindler. Viking, 1999. ISBN 978-0-670-87402-6 Subj: Activities – traveling. Automobiles. Family life – fathers. Maps. Rhyming text.

Walton, Rick. *Baby's first year!* ill. by Caroline Jayne Church. Penguin, 2011. ISBN 978-0-399-25025-5 Subj: Babies. Rhyming text.

The bear came over to my house ill. by James Warhola. Putnam, 2001. ISBN 978-0-399-23415-6 Subj: Animals – bears. Rhyming text.

Bertie was a watchdog ill. by Arthur Robins. Candlewick, 2002. ISBN 978-0-7636-1385-3 Subj: Animals – dogs. Concepts – size. Crime.

Bunny school: a learning fun-for-all ill. by Paige Miglio. HarperCollins, 2005. ISBN 978-0-06-057509-0 Subj: Animals – rabbits. Rhyming text. School.

Frankenstein: a monstrous parody ill. by Nathan Hale. Feiwel & Friends, 2012. ISBN 978-0-312-55366-1 Subj: Monsters. Rhyming text.

How can you dance? ill. by Ana López-Escrivá. Putnam, 2001. ISBN 978-0-399-23229-9 Subj: Activities – dancing. Rhyming text.

I need my own country! ill. by Wes Hargis. Bloomsbury, 2012. ISBN 978-1-59990-559-4 Subj: Behavior – misbehavior. Imagination.

Just me and 6,000 rats: a tale of conjunctions ill. by Mike Gordon and Carl Gordon. Gibbs Smith, 2007. ISBN 978-1-4236-0219-4 Subj: Animals – rats. Humorous stories. Language.

Little dogs say "Rough!" ill. by Henry Cole. Putnam, 2000. ISBN 978-0-399-23228-2 Subj: Animals. Noise, sounds. Rhyming text.

My two hands, my two feet ill. by Julia Gorton. Putnam, 2000. ISBN 978-0-399-23338-8 Subj: Anatomy – feet. Anatomy – hands. Communication.

Noah's square dance ill. by Thor Wickstrom. Lothrop, 1995. ISBN 978-0-688-11187-8 Subj: Activities – dancing. Animals. Boats, ships. Religion – Noah. Rhyming text. Weather – floods. Weather – rain.

One more bunny ill. by Paige Miglio. Lothrop, 2000. ISBN 978-0-688-16848-3 Subj: Animals – rabbits. Counting, numbers.

Pig, pigger, piggest ill. by Jimmy Holder. Gibbs Smith, 1997. ISBN 978-0-87905-806-7 Subj: Animals – pigs. Castles. Witches.

The remarkable friendship of Mr. Cat and Mr. Rat ill. by Lisa McCue. Penguin, 2006. ISBN 978-0-399-23899-4 Subj: Animals – cats. Animals – rats. Friendship. Gifts.

So many bunnies ill. by Paige Miglio. Lothrop, 1998. ISBN 978-0-688-13657-4 Subj: ABC books. Counting, numbers. Rhyming text. Sleep.

What do we do with the baby? ill. by Paige Miglio. HarperCollins, 2008. ISBN 978-0-06-008419-6 Subj: Animals – rabbits. Babies. Emotions – love.

Walty, Margaret. *Rock-a-bye baby: lullabies for bedtime* ill. by author. Barefoot, 1998. ISBN 978-1-902283-03-6 Subj: Bedtime. Lullabies. Music.

Wan, Joyce. *Hug you, kiss you, love you* ill. by author. Scholastic, 2013. ISBN 978-0-545-54045-2 Subj: Animals. Emotions – love. Family life. Format, unusual – board books.

Wang, Gabrielle. *The race for the Chinese zodiac* ill. by Sally Rippin. Candlewick, 2013. ISBN 978-0-7636-6778-8 Subj: Animals. Folk & fairy tales. Foreign lands – China. Royalty – emperors. Zodiac.

Wang, Xiaohong. *One year in Beijing* ill. by Grace Lin. China Sprout, 2006. ISBN 978-0-9747302-5-7 Subj: Days of the week, months of the year. Foreign lands – China.

Wangerin, Walter. *Angels and all children* ill. by Tim Ladwig. Augsburg Fortress, 2002. ISBN 978-0-8066-3712-9 Subj: Holidays – Christmas. Music. Religion.

Probity Jones and the Fear Not Angel ill. by Tim Ladwig. Paraclete, 2005. ISBN 978-1-55725-457-3 Subj: Angels. Ethnic groups in the U.S. – African Americans. Holidays – Christmas. Religion – Nativity.

Water come down ill. by Gerardo Suzán. Augsburg Fortress, 1999. ISBN 978-0-8066-3711-2 Subj: Babies. Family life. Religion.

Warburton, Tom. *1000 times no* ill. by author. HarperCollins, 2009. ISBN 978-0-06-154263-3 Subj: Behavior – misbehavior. Foreign languages.

Ward, B. J. *Farty Marty* ill. by Steven Kellogg. Simon & Schuster, 2013. ISBN 978-1-4424-3901-6 Subj: Animals – cats. Music. Rhyming text. Senses – smell.

Ward, Cindy. *Cookie's week* ill. by Tomie dePaola. Putnam, 1988. ISBN 978-0-399-21498-1 Subj: Animals – cats. Behavior – misbehavior. Days of the week, months of the year.

Ward, D. J. *What happens to our trash?* ill. by Paul Meisel. Collins, 2012. ISBN 978-0-06-168756-3 Subj: Careers – sanitation workers. Ecology.

Ward, Helen. *The dragon machine* ill. by Wayne Anderson. Dutton, 2003. ISBN 978-0-525-47114-1 Subj: Activities – flying. Dragons. Emotions – loneliness. Imagination.

The king of the birds ill. by author. Millbrook, 1997. ISBN 978-0-7613-0288-9 Subj: Activities – flying. Birds. Character traits – cleverness. Royalty – kings.

Little Moon Dog ill. by Wayne Anderson. Penguin, 2007. ISBN 978-0-525-47727-3 Subj: Animals – dogs. Fairies. Friendship. Moon.

Old shell, new shell ill. by author. Millbrook, 2002. ISBN 978-0-7613-2708-0 Subj: Animals. Crustaceans – crabs. Foreign lands – Australia. Sea & seashore.

The rooster and the fox ill. by author. Millbrook, 2003. ISBN 978-0-7613-2920-6 Subj: Animals – foxes. Birds – chickens. Character traits – cleverness. Character traits – pride. Character traits – vanity. Farms.

The tin forest ill. by Wayne Anderson. Dutton, 2001. ISBN 978-0-525-46787-8 Subj: Animals. Dreams. Ecology. Forest, woods. Jungle. Trees.

Ward, Jennifer. *Forest bright, forest night* ill. by Jamichael Henterly. Dawn, 2005. ISBN 978-1-58469-066-5 Subj: Animals. Forest, woods.

Over in the garden ill. by Kenneth J. Spengler. Rising Moon, 2002. ISBN 978-0-87358-793-8 Subj: Counting, numbers. Gardens, gardening. Insects. Music. Rhyming text. Songs.

Somewhere in the ocean by Jennifer Ward and T. J. Marsh ill. by Kenneth J. Spengler. Rising Moon, 2000. ISBN 978-0-87358-748-8 Subj: Animals – babies. Counting, numbers. Rhyming text. Sea & seashore.

There was an old monkey who swallowed a frog (Little old lady who swallowed a fly)

There was an old pirate who swallowed a fish (Little old lady who swallowed a fly)

Way up in the Arctic ill. by Kenneth J. Spengler. Rising Moon, 2007. ISBN 978-0-87358-928-4 Subj: Animals. Counting, numbers. Foreign lands – Arctic. Rhyming text.

Ward, Lindsay. *Please bring balloons* ill. by author. Dial, 2013. ISBN 978-0-8037-3878-2 Subj: Animals – polar bears. Foreign lands – arctic. Merry-go-rounds. Toys – balloons.

When Blue met Egg ill. by author. Dial, 2012. ISBN 978-0-8037-3718-1 Subj: Birds. Eggs. Seasons – winter. Weather – snow.

Ward, Lynd. *The biggest bear* ill. by author. Houghton, 1952. Subj: Animals – bears. Caldecott award books. Character traits – kindness to animals. Foreign lands – Canada. Pets.

The little red lighthouse and the great gray bridge (Swift, Hildegarde Hoyt)

Ward, Nick. *Come on Baby Duck* ill. by author. Good Books, 2004. ISBN 978-1-56148-447-8 Subj: Birds – ducks. Emotions – fear. Sports – swimming.

Don't eat the babysitter! ill. by author. Random House, 2006. ISBN 978-0-385-75062-2 Subj: Activities – babysitting. Family life – brothers & sisters. Fish – sharks.

Wardlaw, Lee. *The chair where bear sits* ill. by Russell Benfanti. Winslow, 2001. ISBN 978-1-890817-85-5 Subj: Accidents. Animals. Animals – bears. Babies. Character traits – clumsiness. Cumulative tales. Food. Rhyming text.

Red, white, and boom! ill. by Huy Voun Lee. Holt, 2012. ISBN 978-0-8050-9065-9 Subj: Activities – picnicking. Holidays – Fourth of July. Parades. Rhyming text.

Saturday night jamboree ill. by Barry Root. Dial, 2000. ISBN 978-0-8037-2189-0 Subj: Activities – babysitting. Activities – dancing. Family life.

Won Ton: a cat tale told in haiku ill. by Eugene Yelchin. Holt, 2011. ISBN 978-0-8050-8995-0 Subj: Animals – cats. Character traits – kindness to animals. Poetry.

Wargin, Kathy-jo. *Scare a bear* ill. by John Bendall-Brunello. Sleeping Bear, 2010. ISBN 978-1-58536-430-5 Subj: Animals – bears. Rhyming text.

Warhola, James. *If you're happy and you know it: jungle edition* ill. by author. Scholastic, 2007. ISBN 978-0-439-72766-2 Subj: Animals. Emotions – happiness. Jungle. Songs.

Uncle Andy's ill. by author. Putnam, 2003. ISBN 978-0-399-23869-7 Subj: Careers – artists. Family life. Family life – aunts, uncles.

Uncle Andy's cats ill. by author. Putnam, 2009. ISBN 978-0-399-25180-1 Subj: Animals – cats. Careers – artists.

Waring, Geoff. *Oscar and the bat: a book about sound* ill. by author. Candlewick, 2008. ISBN 978-0-7636-4025-5 Subj: Animals – bats. Animals – cats. Noise, sounds.

Oscar and the cricket: a book about moving and rolling ill. by author. Candlewick, 2008. ISBN 978-0-7636-4029-3 Subj: Animals – cats. Concepts – motion. Insects – crickets.

Oscar and the moth: a book about light and dark ill. by author. Candlewick, 2007. ISBN 978-0-7636-3559-6 Subj: Animals – cats. Day. Light, lights. Night. Shadows.

Waring, Richard. *Alberto the dancing alligator* ill. by Holly Swain. Candlewick, 2002. ISBN 978-0-7636-1953-4 Subj: Behavior – lost. Pets. Reptiles – alligators, crocodiles.

Hungry hen ill. by Caroline Jayne Church. HarperCollins, 2001. ISBN 978-0-06-623880-7 Subj: Animals – foxes. Birds – chickens.

Warner, Sunny. *The moon quilt* ill. by author. Houghton, 2001. ISBN 978-0-618-05583-8 Subj: Animals – cats. Death. Family life. Memories, memory. Quilts.

Warner, Timothy. *Tub toys* (Shannon, Terry Miller)

Warnes, Tim. *Daddy hug* ill. by Jane Chapman. HarperCollins, 2008. ISBN 978-0-06-058950-9 Subj: Animals. Family life – fathers. Hugging. Rhyming text.

Who's that? (Gamble, Isobel)

Warnick, Elsa. *Bedtime* ill. by author. Browndeer, 1998. ISBN 978-0-15-201471-1 Subj: Activities. Bedtime.

Warren, Rick, commentary. *The Lord's prayer* ill. by Richard Jesse Watson. Zonderkidz, 2011. ISBN 978-0-310-71086-8 Subj: Religion.

Warren, Sarah. *Dolores Huerta: a hero to migrant workers* ill. by Robert Casilla. Marshall Cavendish, 2012. ISBN 978-0-7614-6107-4 Subj: Behavior – seeking better things. Careers – migrant workers. Ethnic groups in the U.S. – Mexican Americans. U.S. history.

Warrick, Karen Clemens. *If I had a tail* ill. by Sherry Neidigh. Rising Moon, 2001. ISBN 978-0-87358-781-5 Subj: Anatomy – tails. Animals. Riddles & jokes.

Who needs that nose? ill. by Sherry Neidigh. NorthWord, 2004. ISBN 978-1-55971-887-5 Subj: Anatomy – noses. Animals. Riddles & jokes.

Warwick, Dionne. *Little Man* by Dionne Warwick and David Freeman Wooley ill. by Fred Willingham. Charlesbridge, 2011. ISBN 978-1-57091-731-8 Subj: Activities – working. Character traits – perseverance. Ethnic groups in the U.S. – African Americans. Money. Musical instruments – drums.

Washington, Donna L. *A big, spooky house* ill. by Jacqueline Rogers. Hyperion, 2000. ISBN 978-0-7868-0349-1 Subj: Animals – cats. Mythical creatures.

Li'l Rabbit's Kwanzaa ill. by Shane W. Evans. HarperCollins, 2010. ISBN 978-0-06-072816-8 Subj: Animals – rabbits. Holidays – Kwanzaa.

The story of Kwanzaa ill. by Stephen Taylor. HarperCollins, 1996. ISBN 978-0-06-024819-2 Subj: Ethnic groups in the U.S. – African Americans. Holidays – Kwanzaa. U.S. history.

Washington, Kathy Gates. *Three colors of Katie* ill. by Kathy Farina. College of Dupage, 2010. ISBN 978-1-932514-18-6 Subj: Ethnic groups in the U.S. Family life.

Washington, Ned. *When you wish upon a star* by Ned Washington and Leigh Harline ill. by Eric Puybaret. Imagine, 2011. ISBN 978-1-936140-35-0 Subj: Behavior – wishing. Dreams. Songs. Stars.

Watanabe, Shigeo. *Ice cream is falling!* ill. by Yasuo Ohtomo. Putnam, 1989. ISBN 978-0-399-21550-6 Subj: Animals – bears. Seasons – winter. Weather – snow.

Let's go swimming ill. by Yasuo Ohtomo. Putnam, 1990. ISBN 978-0-399-21896-5 Subj: Animals – bears. Family life – fathers. Sports – swimming.

Where's my daddy? ill. by Yasuo Ohtomo. Philomel, 1982. ISBN 978-0-399-20899-7 Subj: Animals – bears. Behavior – lost. Character traits – perseverance. Family life – fathers.

Waterhouse, Stephen. *Engines, engines* (Bruce, Lisa)

Waters, Kate. *Lion dancer: Ernie Wan's Chinese New Year* by Kate Waters and Madeline Slovenz-Low; photos by Martha Cooper. Scholastic, 1990. ISBN 978-0-590-43046-3 Subj: Activities – dancing. Ethnic groups in the U.S. – Chinese Americans. Holidays – Chinese New Year.

Waterton, Betty. *A bumblebee sweater* ill. by Kim LaFave. Fitzhenry & Whiteside, 2007. ISBN 978-1-55455-028-9 Subj: Activities – knitting. Clothing – sweaters. Theater.

Watkins, Angela Farris. *My Uncle Martin's big heart* ill. by Eric Velasquez. Abrams, 2010. ISBN 978-0-8109-8975-7 Subj: Ethnic groups in the U.S. – African Americans. Family life – aunts, uncles. U.S. history. Violence, nonviolence.

My Uncle Martin's words for America: Martin Luther King Jr.'s niece tells how he made a difference ill. by Eric Velasquez. Abrams, 2011. ISBN 978-1-4197-0022-4 Subj: Ethnic groups in the U.S. – African Americans. Prejudice. U.S. history. Violence, nonviolence.

Watson, Clyde. *Applebet: an ABC* ill. by Wendy Watson. Farrar, 1982. ISBN 978-0-374-30384-6 Subj: ABC books. Fairs, festivals. Rhyming text.

Valentine foxes ill. by Wendy Watson. Watts, 1988. ISBN 978-0-531-08400-7 Subj: Animals – foxes. Family life. Food. Holidays – Valentine's Day.

Watson, Jesse Joshua. *Hope for Haiti* ill. by author. Penguin, 2010. ISBN 978-0-399-25547-2 Subj: Earthquakes. Foreign lands – Haiti. Hope. Sports – soccer.

Watson, Renée. *Harlem's little blackbird: the story of Florence Mills* ill. by Christian Robinson. Random House, 2012. ISBN 978-0-375-86973-0 Subj: Careers – singers. Ethnic groups in the U.S. – African Americans. U.S. history.

A place where hurricanes happen ill. by Shadra Strickland. Random House, 2010. ISBN 978-0-375-85609-9 Subj: Cities, towns. Communities, neighborhoods. Weather – hurricanes.

Watson, Richard Jesse. *The boy who went ape* ill. by Benjamin James Watson. Scholastic, 2008. ISBN 978-0-590-47966-0 Subj: Animals – chimpanzees. Behavior – misbehavior. School – field trips.

Watson, Wendy. *Bedtime bunnies* ill. by author. Clarion, 2010. ISBN 978-0-547-22312-4 Subj: Animals – rabbits. Bedtime. Seasons – fall.

Boo! It's Halloween ill. by author. Clarion, 1992. ISBN 978-0-395-53628-5 Subj: Family life. Holidays – Halloween.

Happy Easter day! ill. by author. Clarion, 1993. ISBN 978-0-395-53629-2 Subj: Animals – cats. Family life. Holidays – Easter.

Holly's Christmas eve ill. by author. HarperCollins, 2002. ISBN 978-0-688-17653-2 Subj: Character traits – helpfulness. Friendship. Holidays – Christmas. Machines. Santa Claus.

Hurray for the Fourth of July ill. by author. Houghton, 1992. ISBN 978-0-395-53627-8 Subj: Family life. Holidays – Fourth of July. Poetry.

Thanksgiving at our house ill. by author. Houghton, 1991. ISBN 978-0-395-53626-1 Subj: Family life. Holidays – Thanksgiving. Nursery rhymes.

A Valentine for you ill. by author. Houghton, 1991. ISBN 978-0-395-53625-4 Subj: Emotions – love. Holidays – Valentine's Day. Poetry.

Watt, Mélanie. *Chester* ill. by author. Kids Can, 2007. ISBN 978-1-55453-140-0 Subj: Activities – drawing. Activities – writing. Animals – cats.

Chester's back! ill. by author. Kids Can, 2008. ISBN 978-1-55453-287-2 Subj: Activities – drawing. Activities – writing. Animals – cats.

Chester's masterpiece ill. by author. Kids Can, 2010. ISBN 978-1-55453-566-8 Subj: Activities – drawing. Activities – writing. Animals – cats.

Have I got a book for you! ill. by author. Kids Can, 2009. ISBN 978-1-55453-289-6 Subj: Animals – foxes. Books, reading. Careers – salespeople.

Leon the chameleon ill. by author. Kids Can, 2001. ISBN 978-1-55074-867-3 Subj: Character traits – being different. Concepts – color. Reptiles – chameleons.

Scaredy Squirrel ill. by author. Kids Can, 2006. ISBN 978-1-55337-959-1 Subj: Animals – squirrels. Character traits – bravery. Emotions – fear.

Scaredy Squirrel at night ill. by author. Kids Can, 2009. ISBN 978-1-55453-288-9 Subj: Animals – squirrels. Dreams. Emotions – fear. Night. Sleep.

Scaredy Squirrel at the beach ill. by author. Kids Can, 2008. ISBN 978-1-55453-225-4 Subj: Animals – squirrels. Emotions – fear. Sea & seashore – beaches.

Scaredy Squirrel goes camping ill. by author. Kids Can, 2013. ISBN 978-1-89478-686-7 Subj: Animals – squirrels. Camps, camping. Emotions – fear.

Scaredy Squirrel has a birthday party ill. by author. Kids Can, 2011. ISBN 978-1-55453-468-5 Subj: Animals – squirrels. Birthdays. Emotions – fear. Parties.

Scaredy Squirrel makes a friend ill. by author. Kids Can, 2007. ISBN 978-1-55453-181-3 Subj: Animals – dogs. Animals – squirrels. Emotions – fear. Emotions – loneliness. Friendship.

Scaredy Squirrel prepares for Christmas: a safety guide for scaredies ill. by author. Kids Can, 2012. ISBN 978-1-55453-469-2 Subj: Animals – squirrels. Emotions – fear. Holidays – Christmas.

Scaredy Squirrel prepares for Halloween: a safety guide for scaredies ill. by author. Kids Can, 2013. ISBN 978-1-89478-687-4 Subj: Animals – squirrels. Emotions – fear. Holidays – Halloween.

You're finally here! ill. by author. Hyperion/Disney, 2011. ISBN 978-1-4231-3486-2 Subj: Animals – rabbits. Behavior – misbehavior. Books, reading. Etiquette.

Watters, Debbie. *Where's Mom's hair? a family journey through cancer* by Debbie, Haydn, & Emmett Waters; photos by Sophie Hogan. Second Story, 2005. ISBN 978-1-896764-94-8 Subj: Family life – mothers. Hair. Illness – cancer.

Watterson, Carol. *An edible alphabet: 26 reasons to love the farm* ill. by Michela Sorrentino. Tricycle, 2011. ISBN 978-1-58246-421-3 Subj: ABC books. Farms.

Watts, Bernadette. *The smallest snowflake* ill. by author. NorthSouth, 2009. ISBN 978-0-7358-2258-0 Subj: Character traits – smallness. Seasons – winter. Weather – snow.

Watts, Frances. *Kisses for Daddy* ill. by David Legge. Trafalgar, 2008. ISBN 978-1-921272-43-1 Subj: Animals – bears. Bedtime. Family life – fathers. Kissing.

Watts, Leslie Elizabeth. *The Baabaasheep Quartet* ill. by author. Fitzhenry & Whiteside, 2005. ISBN 978-1-55041-890-3 Subj: Activities – singing. Animals – sheep. Cities, towns. Music.

You can't rush a cat (Bradford, Karleen)

Waugh, Peter. *The great cannon beach mouse caper* ill. by Don Sunderland. Educare, 2002. ISBN 978-0-944638-38-5 Subj: Activities – traveling. Animals – mice. Birds – seagulls. Family life. Sea & seashore – beaches.

Wax, Naomi. *Even firefighters go to the potty: a potty training lift-the-flap story* (Wax, Wendy)

Wax, Wendy. *Even firefighters go to the potty: a potty training lift-the-flap story* by Wendy Wax and Naomi Wax ill. by Stephen Gilpin. Simon & Schuster, 2008. ISBN 978-1-4169-2720-4 Subj: Careers. Format, unusual – toy & movable books. Toilet training.

A very mice Christmas photos by Jon Holderer. HarperCollins, 2003. ISBN 978-0-06-052321-3 Subj: Animals – mice. Format, unusual – board books. Holidays – Christmas. Rhyming text.

Wayland, April Halprin. *New Year at the pier: a Rosh Hashanah story* ill. by Stéphane Jorisch. Dial, 2009. ISBN 978-0-8037-3279-7 Subj: Holidays – Rosh Hashanah.

Wayne-von Königslöw, Andrea. *How do you read to a rabbit?* ill. by author. Annick, 2010. ISBN 978-1-55451-232-4 Subj: Animals. Books, reading.

We wish you a merry Christmas: a traditional Christmas carol ill. by Tracey Campbell Pearson. Dial, 1983. ISBN 978-0-8037-9400-9 Subj: Behavior – misbehavior. Holidays – Christmas. Songs.

Weatherford, Carole Boston. *The Beatitudes: from slavery to civil rights* ill. by Tim Ladwig. Eerdmans, 2010. ISBN 978-0-8028-5352-3 Subj: Ethnic groups in the U.S. – African Americans. Prejudice. Religion. Slavery. U.S. history.

Before John was a jazz giant: a song of John Coltrane ill. by Sean Qualls. Holt, 2008. ISBN 978-0-8050-7994-4 Subj: Careers – musicians. Ethnic groups in the U.S. – African Americans. Music. U.S. history.

Champions on the bench: the Cannon Street YMCA All Stars ill. by Leonard Jenkins. Penguin, 2007. ISBN 978-0-8037-2987-2 Subj: Ethnic groups in the U.S. – African Americans. Prejudice. Sports – baseball. U.S. history.

Freedom on the menu: the Greensboro sit-ins ill. by Jerome Lagarrigue. Penguin, 2005. ISBN 978-0-8037-2860-8 Subj: Ethnic groups in the U.S. – African Americans. Prejudice. Restaurants. U.S. history.

I, Matthew Henson: polar explorer ill. by Eric Velasquez. Walker, 2008. ISBN 978-0-8027-9688-2 Subj: Careers – explorers. Ethnic groups in the U.S. – African Americans. Foreign lands – Arctic. U.S. history.

Jazz baby ill. by Laura Freeman. Lee & Low, 2002. ISBN 978-1-58430-039-7 Subj: Activities – playing. Music. Rhyming text.

Juneteenth jamboree ill. by Yvonne Buchanan. Lee & Low, 1995. ISBN 978-1-880000-18-2 Subj: Ethnic groups in the U.S. – African Americans. Holidays – Juneteenth. Slavery. U.S. history.

Moses: when Harriet Tubman led her people to freedom ill. by Kadir Nelson. Hyperion, 2006. ISBN 978-0-7868-5175-1 Subj: Caldecott award honor books. Ethnic groups in the U.S. – African Americans. Slavery. U.S. history.

Weaver, Tess. *Cat jumped in!* ill. by Emily Arnold McCully. Houghton, 2007. ISBN 978-0-618-61488-2 Subj: Animals – cats. Behavior – misbehavior.

Frederick Finch, loudmouth ill. by Debbie Tilley. Clarion, 2008. ISBN 978-0-618-45239-2 Subj: Character traits – individuality. Contests. Fairs, festivals. Humorous stories. Noise, sounds.

Opera cat ill. by Andréa Wesson. Clarion, 2002. ISBN 978-0-618-09635-0 Subj: Activities – singing. Animals – cats. Careers – singers. Foreign lands – Italy.

Weber, Elka. *The Yankee at the seder* ill. by Adam Gustavson. Tricycle, 2009. ISBN 978-1-58246-256-1 Subj: Holidays – Passover. Holidays – Seder. U.S. history. War.

Weber, Linda Kay. *Louie Larkey and the bad dream patrol* ill. by Nora Hilb. Moon Mt, 2001. ISBN 978-0-9677929-3-4 Subj: Dreams. Toys. Toys – bears.

Webster, Christine. *Otter everywhere* ill. by Tim Nihoff. Candlewick, 2007. ISBN 978-0-7636-2921-2 Subj: Activities – picnicking. Animals – otters. Sports – swimming.

Webster, Sheryl. *Noodle's knitting* ill. by Caroline Pedler. Good Books, 2010. ISBN 978-1-56148-694-6 Subj: Activities – knitting. Animals – mice.

Wedeven, Carol. *The Easter cave* ill. by Len Ebert. Concordia, 2001. ISBN 978-0-570-07135-8 Subj: Holidays – Easter. Religion.

Weeks, Sarah. *Be mine, be mine, sweet valentine* ill. by Fumi Kosaka. HarperCollins, 2005. ISBN 978-0-694-01514-6 Subj: Format, unusual – toy & movable books. Gifts. Holidays – Valentine's Day. Rhyming text.

Bite me, I'm a book ill. by Jef Kaminsky. Random House, 2002. ISBN 978-0-375-81261-3 Subj: Babies. Books, reading. Format, unusual – board books. Humorous stories. Rhyming text.

Bite me, I'm a shape ill. by Jef Kaminsky. Random House, 2002. ISBN 978-0-375-81262-0 Subj: Babies. Concepts – shape. Format, unusual – board books. Rhyming text.

Bunny fun ill. by Sam Williams. Harcourt, 2008. ISBN 978-0-15-205838-8 Subj: Activities – playing. Animals – rabbits. Rhyming text.

Catfish Kate and the sweet swamp band ill. by Elwood H. Smith. Atheneum, 2009. ISBN 978-1-4169-4026-5 Subj: Animals. Books, reading. Character traits – compromising. Fish. Music. Musical instruments – bands. Swamps.

Counting Ovejas ill. by David Diaz. Simon & Schuster, 2006. ISBN 978-0-689-86750-7 Subj: Animals – sheep. Bedtime. Concepts – color. Counting, numbers. Foreign languages.

Crocodile smile ill. by Lois Ehlert. HarperCollins, 1994. ISBN 978-0-06-022867-5 Subj: Animals. Animals – endangered animals. Music. Songs.

Ella, of course! ill. by Doug Cushman. Harcourt, 2007. ISBN 978-0-15-204943-0 Subj: Animals – pigs. Ballet. Problem solving. Umbrellas.

I'm a pig ill. by Holly Berry. HarperCollins, 2005. ISBN 978-0-06-074344-4 Subj: Animals – pigs. Rhyming text. Self-concept.

Mrs. McNosh and the great big squash ill. by Nadine Bernard Westcott. Geringer, 2000. ISBN 978-0-694-01202-2 Subj: Gardens, gardening. Homes, houses. Plants. Rhyming text.

Mrs. McNosh hangs up her wash ill. by Nadine Bernard Westcott. Geringer, 1998. ISBN 978-0-694-01076-9 Subj: Humorous stories. Laundry.

My somebody special ill. by Ashley Wolff. Harcourt, 2002. ISBN 978-0-15-202561-8 Subj: Animals. Character traits – questioning. Emotions. Family life – parents. Rhyming text. School – nursery.

Oh my gosh, Mrs. McNosh! ill. by Nadine Bernard Westcott. Geringer, 2002. ISBN 978-0-06-008858-3 Subj: Animals – dogs. Behavior – running away. Humorous stories. Parks. Rhyming text.

Overboard! ill. by Sam Williams. Harcourt, 2006. ISBN 978-0-15-205046-7 Subj: Activities – playing. Animals – rabbits. Babies. Rhyming text.

Sophie Peterman tells the truth! ill. by Robert Neubecker. Simon & Schuster, 2009. ISBN 978-1-4169-8686-7 Subj: Babies. Family life – new sibling. Sibling rivalry.

Without you ill. by Suzanne Duranceau. Geringer, 2003. ISBN 978-0-06-027816-8 Subj: Birds – penguins. Family life – parents.

Woof: a love story ill. by Holly Berry. HarperCollins, 2009. ISBN 978-0-06-025007-2 Subj: Animals – cats. Animals – dogs. Emotions – love. Music. Musical instruments – trombones. Rhyming text.

Wegerif, Gay. *Up close* ill. by author. Abrams, 2013. ISBN 978-1-4197-0391-1 Subj: Animals. Format, unusual – board books. Picture puzzles.

Weigel, Jeff. *Atomic Ace (he's just my dad)* ill. by author. Whitman, 2004. ISBN 978-0-8075-3216-4 Subj: Family life – fathers. Rhyming text.

Weigelt, Udo. *Bear's last journey* ill. by Sibylle Kazeroid. NorthSouth, 2003. ISBN 978-0-7358-1800-2 Subj: Animals. Animals – bears. Death. Emotions – grief.

The Easter Bunny's baby ill. by Rolf Siegenthaler. NorthSouth, 2001. ISBN 978-0-7358-1442-4 Subj: Animals – rabbits. Behavior – mistakes. Birds – ostriches. Eggs. Family life – parents. Holidays – Easter.

It wasn't me ill. by Julia Gukova. NorthSouth, 2001. ISBN 978-0-7358-1524-7 Subj: Animals – ferrets. Animals – mice. Behavior – stealing. Birds – ravens. Crime.

Old Beaver ill. by Bernadette Watts. NorthSouth, 2002. ISBN 978-0-7358-1565-0 Subj: Animals. Animals – beavers. Old age. Self-concept.

Super Guinea Pig to the rescue ill. by Nina Spranger. Walker, 2007. ISBN 978-0-8027-9705-6 Subj: Animals – guinea pigs. Disguises. Pets. Television.

Who stole the gold? ill. by Julia Gukova. NorthSouth, 2000. ISBN 978-0-7358-1373-1 Subj: Animals. Animals – hamsters. Behavior – stealing. Friendship.

Weil, Lisl. *The candy egg bunny* ill. by author. Holiday, 1975. ISBN 978-0-8234-0250-2 Subj: Animals – rabbits. Holidays – Easter. Witches.

Weinberg, Larry. *The Forgetful Bears help Santa* ill. by Jason Wolff. Random House, 2002. ISBN 978-0-375-92291-6 Subj: Animals – bears. Behavior – forgetfulness. Holidays – Christmas. Humorous stories. Santa Claus.

Weinert, Matthias. *No bath, no cake! Polly's pirate party* ill. by author. NorthSouth, 2013. ISBN 978-0-7358-4112-3 Subj: Activities – bathing. Character traits – cleanliness. Hygiene. Parties. Pirates.

Weinstein, Ellen Slusky. *Everywhere the cow says "Moo!"* ill. by Kenneth Andersson. Boyds Mills, 2008. ISBN 978-1-59078-458-7 Subj: Animals. Foreign languages. Noise, sounds.

Weinstock, Robert. *Food hates you, too, and other poems* ill. by author. Hyperion, 2009. ISBN 978-1-4231-1391-1 Subj: Food. Poetry.

Weis, Carol. *When the cows got loose* ill. by Ard Hoyt. Simon & Schuster, 2006. ISBN 978-0-689-85166-7 Subj: Animals – bulls, cows. Behavior – misbehavior. Circus.

Weisburd, Stefi. *Barefoot: poems for naked feet* ill. by Lori McElrath-Eslick. Boyds Mills, 2008. ISBN 978-1-59078-306-1 Subj: Poetry. Seasons – summer.

Weiss, David. *Kay Thompson's Eloise in Hollywood* (Stem, J. David)

Weiss, Ellen. *I love you, Little Monster* ill. by Alli Arnold. Simon & Schuster, 2012. ISBN 978-1-4424-2850-8 Subj: Emotions – love. Family life – mothers.

Kitten castle (Friedman, Mel)

Playtime for twins ill. by Sam Williams. Simon & Schuster, 2012. ISBN 978-1-4424-3027-3 Subj: Activities – playing. Format, unusual – board books. Multiple births – twins.

The taming of Lola: a shrew story ill. by Jerry Smath. Abrams, 2010. ISBN 978-0-8109-4066-6 Subj: Animals – shrews. Behavior – misbehavior. Emotions – anger. Family life – cousins. Family life – grandmothers.

Weiss, George. *What a wonderful world* by George Weiss and Bob Thiele ill. by Ashley Bryan. Atheneum, 1995. ISBN 978-0-689-80087-0 Subj: Nature. Poetry. Puppets. Songs.

Weiss, Mitch. *The ghost catcher: a Bengali folktale* (Hamilton, Martha)

The hidden feast: a folktale from the American South (Hamilton, Martha)

Priceless gifts: a folktale from Italy (Hamilton, Martha)

Weiss, Nicki. *Where does the brown bear go?* ill. by author. Greenwillow, 1989. ISBN 978-0-688-07863-8 Subj: Animals. Bedtime. Night. Sleep. Toys.

Where does the brown bear go? [board book] ill. by author. Tupelo, 1998. ISBN 978-0-688-16388-4 Subj: Animals. Bedtime. Format, unusual – board books. Night. Sleep. Toys.

The world turns round and round ill. by author. Greenwillow, 2000. ISBN 978-0-688-17214-5 Subj: Clothing. Ethnic groups in the U.S. Rhyming text. World.

Weitekamp, Margaret A. *Pluto's secret: an icy world's tale of discovery* by Margaret A. Weitekamp and David DeVorkin ill. by Diane Kidd. Abrams, 2013. ISBN 978-1-4197-0423-9 Subj: Planets. Space & space ships.

Weitzman, Elizabeth. *Let's talk about when a parent dies* ill. by author. Rosen, 1996. ISBN 978-0-8239-2309-0 Subj: Death. Emotions – grief. Family life.

Weitzman, Jacqueline Preiss. *Superhero Joe* ill. by Ron Barrett. Simon & Schuster, 2011. ISBN 978-1-4169-9157-1 Subj: Character traits – bravery. Emotions – fear. Imagination.

Superhero Joe and the creature next door ill. by Ron Barrett. Simon & Schuster, 2013. ISBN 978-1-4424-1268-2 Subj: Emotions – fear. Friendship. Imagination.

You can't take a balloon into the Metropolitan Museum ill. by Robin Preiss-Glasser. Dial, 1998. ISBN 978-0-8037-2302-3 Subj: Art. Cities, towns. Family life – grandmothers. Museums. Toys – balloons. Wordless.

You can't take a balloon into the National Gallery ill. by Robin Preiss-Glasser. Dial, 2000. ISBN 978-0-8037-2303-0 Subj: Art. Cities, towns. Family life – grandmothers. Museums. Picture puzzles. Toys – balloons. Wordless.

Welch, Willy. *Dancing with Daddy* ill. by Liza Woodruff. Whispering Coyote, 1999. ISBN 978-1-

58089-020-5 Subj: Activities – dancing. Animals. Family life – fathers. Rhyming text. Trees.

Grumpy Bunnies ill. by Tammie Lyon. Charlesbridge, 2000. ISBN 978-1-58089-053-3 Subj: Animals – rabbits. Rhyming text. School.

Playing right field ill. by Marc Simont. Scholastic, 1995. ISBN 978-0-590-48298-1 Subj: Songs. Sports – baseball.

Weller, Frances Ward. *The angel of Mill Street* ill. by Robert J. Blake. Philomel, 1998. ISBN 978-0-399-23133-9 Subj: Accidents. Angels. Animals – dogs. Careers – musicians. Ethnic groups in the U.S. – Irish Americans. Holidays – Christmas. Weather – snow.

Welling, Peter J. *Andrew McGroundhog and his shady shadow* ill. by author. Pelican, 2001. ISBN 978-1-56554-711-7 Subj: Animals – groundhogs. Hibernation. Holidays – Groundhog Day. Shadows.

Shawn O'Hisser, the last snake in Ireland ill. by author. Pelican, 2002. ISBN 978-1-58980-014-4 Subj: Animals. Foreign lands – Ireland. Humorous stories. Mythical creatures – leprechauns. Reptiles – snakes.

Wellington, Monica. *Apple farmer Annie* ill. by author. Dutton, 2001. ISBN 978-0-525-46727-4 Subj: Careers – farmers. Farms. Food. Stores.

Bunny's first snowflake ill. by author. Dutton, 2000. ISBN 978-0-525-46464-8 Subj: Animals. Animals – rabbits. Format, unusual – board books. Seasons – winter. Weather – snow.

Colors for Zena ill. by author. Dial, 2013. ISBN 978-0-8037-3743-3 Subj: Concepts – color.

Mr. Cookie Baker ill. by author. Penguin, 2006. ISBN 978-0-525-47763-1 Subj: Activities – baking, cooking. Careers – bakers. Food.

Night rabbits ill. by author. Dutton, 1995. ISBN 978-0-525-45335-2 Subj: Animals – rabbits. Night. Weather – storms.

Pizza at Sally's ill. by author. Penguin, 2006. ISBN 978-0-525-47715-0 Subj: Activities – baking, cooking. Careers – chefs, cooks. Food. Restaurants.

Riki's birdhouse ill. by author. Dutton, 2009. ISBN 978-0-525-42079-8 Subj: Activities – making things. Birds. Homes, houses.

Squeaking of art, the mice go to the museum ill. by author. Dutton, 2000. ISBN 978-0-525-46165-4 Subj: Animals – cats. Animals – mice. Art. Museums.

Truck driver Tom ill. by author. Penguin, 2007. ISBN 978-0-525-47831-7 Subj: Careers – truck drivers. Transportation. Trucks.

Zinnia's flower garden ill. by author. Penguin, 2005. ISBN 978-0-525-47368-8 Subj: Flowers. Gardens, gardening.

Wells, Robert E. *Did a dinosaur drink this water?* ill. by author. Whitman, 2006. ISBN 978-0-8075-8839-0 Subj: Science. Water.

What's so special about planet Earth? ill. by author. Whitman, 2009. ISBN 978-0-8075-8815-4 Subj: Earth. Space & space ships.

Why do elephants need the sun? ill. by author. Whitman, 2010. ISBN 978-0-8075-9081-2 Subj: Animals – elephants. Science. Sun.

Wells, Rosemary. *The bear went over the mountain* ill. by author. Scholastic, 1998. ISBN 978-0-590-02910-0 Subj: Animals – bears. Mountains. Songs.

Bingo ill. by author. Scholastic, 1999. ISBN 978-0-590-02913-1 Subj: Animals – dogs. Format, unusual – board books. Music. Songs.

Bunny cakes ill. by author. Dial, 1997. ISBN 978-0-8037-2144-9 Subj: Activities – baking, cooking. Animals – rabbits. Family life – brothers & sisters. Family life – grandmothers.

Bunny mail ill. by author. Viking, 2004. ISBN 978-0-670-03630-1 Subj: Activities – picnicking. Animals – rabbits. Family life – brothers & sisters. Family life – grandmothers. Letters, cards.

Bunny money ill. by author. HarperCollins, 1997. ISBN 978-0-06-027258-6 Subj: Animals – rabbits. Family life – brothers & sisters. Family life – grandmothers. Money.

Bunny party ill. by author. Viking, 2001. ISBN 978-0-670-03501-4 Subj: Animals – rabbits. Birthdays. Family life – brothers & sisters. Family life – grandmothers. Parties. Toys.

Carry me! ill. by author. Hyperion, 2006. ISBN 978-0-7868-0396-5 Subj: Animals – rabbits. Emotions – love. Family life. Poetry.

Clean-up time ill. by author. Viking, 2009. ISBN 978-0-670-01171-1 Subj: Animals – rabbits. Bedtime. Character traits – cleanliness. Family life – brothers & sisters. Format, unusual – board books. Rhyming text.

Emily's first 100 days of school ill. by author. Hyperion, 2000. ISBN 978-0-7868-2443-4 Subj: Animals – rabbits. Counting, numbers. School – first day.

First tomato ill. by author. Dial, 1992. ISBN 978-0-8037-1175-4 Subj: Animals – rabbits. Gardens, gardening. Rhyming text. School.

Forest of dreams by Rosemary Wells and Susan Jeffers ill. by Susan Jeffers. Dial, 1988. ISBN 978-0-8037-0570-8 Subj: Nature. Seasons – spring. Seasons – winter.

Fritz and the mess fairy ill. by author. Dial, 1991. ISBN 978-0-8037-0983-6 Subj: Animals – skunks. Behavior – misbehavior. Character traits – cleanliness. Fairies.

Goodnight Max ill. by author. Viking, 2000. ISBN 978-0-670-88707-1 Subj: Animals – rabbits. Bedtime. Family life – brothers & sisters. Format, unusual – toy & movable books.

The gulps ill. by Marc Brown. Little, Brown, 2007. ISBN 978-0-316-01460-1 Subj: Health & fitness. Health & fitness – exercise. Self-concept.

Hands off, Harry! ill. by author. HarperCollins, 2011. ISBN 978-0-06-192112-4 Subj: Behavior – misbehavior. Problem solving. Reptiles – alligators, crocodiles. School.

Hazel's amazing mother ill. by author. Dial, 1985. ISBN 978-0-8037-0210-3 Subj: Animals. Animals – badgers. Behavior – misbehavior. Family life – mothers.

The house in the mail ill. by Dan Andreasen. Viking, 2002. ISBN 978-0-7894-2603-1 Subj: Family life. Homes, houses. U.S. history.

How many? How much? ill. by Michael Koelsch. Viking, 2001. ISBN 978-0-670-89652-3 Subj: Concepts. Counting, numbers. School – first day.

The island light ill. by author. Dial, 1992. ISBN 978-0-8037-1178-5 Subj: Animals – rabbits. Family life – fathers. Illness. Lighthouses.

The itsy-bitsy spider ill. by author. Scholastic, 1998. ISBN 978-0-590-02911-7 Subj: Birds – ducks. Format, unusual – board books. Songs. Spiders.

The language of doves ill. by Greg Shed. Dial, 1996. ISBN 978-0-8037-1471-7 Subj: Birds – doves. Birds – pigeons. Death. Family life – grandfathers. War.

Letters and sounds ill. by Michael Koelsch. Viking, 2001. ISBN 978-0-670-89651-6 Subj: ABC books. Communication. Language. School.

A lion for Lewis ill. by author. Dial, 1982. ISBN 978-0-8037-4686-2 Subj: Activities – playing. Imagination.

The little lame prince ill. by author. Dial, 1990. ISBN 978-0-8037-0789-4 Subj: Animals – pigs. Behavior – greed. Folk & fairy tales. Disabilities – physical disabilities. Royalty – princes.

Love waves ill. by author. Candlewick, 2011. ISBN 978-0-7636-4989-0 Subj: Activities – working. Animals – rabbits. Emotions – love. Family life – parents. Rhyming text.

Lucy comes to stay ill. by Mark Graham. Dial, 1994. ISBN 978-0-8037-1214-0 Subj: Animals – dogs. Pets.

McDuff and the baby ill. by Susan Jeffers. Hyperion, 1997. ISBN 978-0-7868-2258-4 Subj: Animals – dogs. Babies. Family life.

McDuff comes home ill. by Susan Jeffers. Hyperion, 1997. ISBN 978-0-7868-2259-1 Subj: Animals – dogs. Behavior – lost.

McDuff goes to school ill. by Susan Jeffers. Hyperion, 2001. ISBN 978-0-7868-2432-8 Subj: Animals – dogs. Communities, neighborhoods. Foreign languages. School.

McDuff moves in ill. by Susan Jeffers. Hyperion, 1997. ISBN 978-0-7868-2257-7 Subj: Animals – dogs. Behavior – needing someone.

McDuff saves the day ill. by Susan Jeffers. Hyperion, 2002. ISBN 978-0-7868-2311-6 Subj: Activities – picnicking. Animals – dogs. Family life. Food. Holidays – Fourth of July. Insects – ants.

McDuffs hide-and-seek ill. by Susan Jeffers. Hyperion, 2004. ISBN 978-0-7868-1935-5 Subj: Animals – dogs. Animals – rabbits. Format, unusual – toy & movable books. Games.

McDuff's new friend ill. by Susan Jeffers. Hyperion, 1998. ISBN 978-0-7868-2337-6 Subj: Animals – dogs. Holidays – Christmas. Santa Claus.

McDuff's wild romp ill. by Susan Jeffers. Hyperion, 2005. ISBN 978-0-7868-1930-0 Subj: Animals – cats. Animals – dogs.

Max and Ruby's bedtime book ill. by author. Penguin, 2010. ISBN 978-0-670-01141-4 Subj: Animals – rabbits. Family life – brothers & sisters. Family life – grandmothers.

Max and Ruby's Midas ill. by author. Dial, 1995. ISBN 978-0-8037-1783-1 Subj: Animals – rabbits. Behavior – greed. Family life – brothers & sisters. Food.

Max and Ruby's treasure hunt ill. by author. Viking, 2012. ISBN 978-0-670-06317-8 Subj: Animals – rabbits. Family life – brothers & sisters. Family life – grandmothers. Format, unusual – toy & movable books. Nursery rhymes. Participation.

Max cleans up ill. by author. Viking, 2000. ISBN 978-0-670-89218-1 Subj: Animals – rabbits. Babies. Character traits – cleanliness. Family life – brothers & sisters.

Max counts his chickens ill. by author. Penguin, 2007. ISBN 978-0-670-06222-5 Subj: Animals – rabbits. Counting, numbers. Holidays – Easter. Sibling rivalry.

Max's ABC ill. by author. Penguin, 2006. ISBN 978-0-670-06074-0 Subj: ABC books. Animals – rabbits.

Max's apples ill. by author. Grosset, 2009. ISBN 978-0-448-45262-3 Subj: Activities – baking, cooking. Animals – rabbits. Family life – brothers & sisters. Food.

Max's bath ill. by author. Dial, 1985. ISBN 978-0-8037-0162-5 Subj: Activities – bathing. Animals – rabbits. Format, unusual – board books.

Max's bedtime ill. by author. Dial, 1985. ISBN 978-0-8037-0160-1 Subj: Animals – rabbits. Bedtime. Format, unusual – board books. Sibling rivalry. Toys.

Max's birthday ill. by author. Dial, 1985. ISBN 978-0-8037-0163-2 Subj: Animals – rabbits. Birthdays. Format, unusual – board books. Toys.

Max's breakfast ill. by author. Dial, 1998. ISBN 978-0-8037-2273-6 Subj: Animals – rabbits. Character traits – patience. Format, unusual – board books. Sibling rivalry.

Max's bunny business ill. by author. Viking, 2008. ISBN 978-0-670-01105-6 Subj: Animals – rabbits. Family life – brothers & sisters. Money. Shopping.

Max's chocolate chicken ill. by author. Dial, 1999. ISBN 978-0-8037-2351-1 Subj: Animals – rabbits. Holidays – Easter. Seasons – spring. Sibling rivalry.

Max's Christmas ill. by author. Dial, 1986. ISBN 978-0-8037-0290-5 Subj: Animals – rabbits. Holidays – Christmas. Santa Claus.

Max's dragon shirt ill. by author. Dial, 1991. ISBN 978-0-8037-0945-4 Subj: Activities – babysitting. Animals – rabbits. Behavior – lost. Clothing. Family life – brothers & sisters. Stores.

Max's Easter surprise ill. by author. Grosset, 2008. ISBN 978-0-448-44783-4 Subj: Animals – rabbits. Family life – brothers & sisters. Holidays – Easter.

Max's first word ill. by author. Dial, 1979. ISBN 978-0-8037-6066-0 Subj: Animals – rabbits. Format, unusual – board books. Language.

Max's new suit ill. by author. Dial, 1979. ISBN 978-0-8037-6065-3 Subj: Animals – rabbits. Clothing. Format, unusual – board books.

Max's ride ill. by author. Dial, 1979. ISBN 978-0-8037-6069-1 Subj: Animals – rabbits. Format, unusual – board books. Language.

Max's toys: a counting book ill. by author. Dial, 1979. ISBN 978-0-8037-6068-4 Subj: Animals – rabbits. Counting, numbers. Format, unusual – board books. Toys.

Max's worm cake ill. by author. Grosset, 2009. ISBN 978-0-448-45086-5 Subj: Animals – rabbits. Animals – worms. Family life – brothers & sisters. Gardens, gardening.

Miracle melts down ill. by author. HarperCollins, 2012. ISBN 978-0-06-192115-5 Subj: Animals. Emotions – anger. School.

The miraculous tale of the two Maries ill. by Petra Mathers. Penguin, 2006. ISBN 978-0-670-05960-7 Subj: Foreign lands – France. Religion.

Morris's disappearing bag ill. by author. Viking, 1999. ISBN 978-0-670-88721-7 Subj: Animals – rabbits. Gifts. Holidays – Christmas.

Moss pillows ill. by author. Dial, 1992. ISBN 978-0-8037-1177-8 Subj: Animals – rabbits. Family life. Forest, woods. Rhyming text.

My kindergarten ill. by author. Hyperion, 2004. ISBN 978-0-7868-0833-5 Subj: Animals. Animals – rabbits. Days of the week, months of the year. Rhyming text. School.

Night sounds, morning colors ill. by David McPhail. Dial, 1994. ISBN 978-0-8037-1302-4 Subj: Activities. Family life. Seasons. Senses.

Noisy Nora ill. by author. Dial, 1997. ISBN 978-0-8037-1835-7 Subj: Animals – mice. Behavior – needing someone. Rhyming text.

Otto runs for President ill. by author. Scholastic, 2008. ISBN 978-0-545-03722-8 Subj: Animals – dogs. Behavior – seeking better things. Character traits – ambition. Character traits – practicality. School.

Otto se presenta para presidente / Otto runs for President ill. by author. Scholastic, 2008. ISBN 978-0-545-04182-9 Subj: Animals – dogs. Behavior – seeking better things. Character traits – ambition. Character traits – practicality. Foreign languages. School.

Peabody ill. by author. Dial, 1983. ISBN 978-0-8037-0005-5 Subj: Sibling rivalry. Toys – dolls.

Peek-a-boo ill. by author. Viking, 2009. ISBN 978-0-670-01167-4 Subj: Animals – rabbits. Family life – brothers & sisters. Format, unusual – board books. Games.

Read to your bunny ill. by author. Scholastic, 1998. ISBN 978-0-590-30284-5 Subj: Animals – rabbits. Books, reading. Rhyming text.

Red boots ill. by author. Viking, 2009. ISBN 978-0-670-01169-8 Subj: Animals – rabbits. Clothing – boots. Family life – brothers & sisters. Format, unusual – board books. Rhyming text. Weather – snow.

Ruby's beauty shop ill. by author. Viking, 2002. ISBN 978-0-670-03553-3 Subj: Animals – rabbits. Beauty shops. Family life – brothers & sisters. Family life – grandmothers.

Shopping ill. by author. Viking, 2009. ISBN 978-0-670-01168-1 Subj: Animals – rabbits. Family life – brothers & sisters. Format, unusual – board books. Shopping.

Shy Charles ill. by author. Dial, 1988. ISBN 978-0-8037-0564-7 Subj: Activities – babysitting. Animals – mice. Character traits – individuality. Family life. Rhyming text.

Small world of Binky Braverman ill. by Richard Egielski. Viking, 2003. ISBN 978-0-670-03636-3 Subj: Emotions – loneliness. Family life – aunts, uncles. Imagination.

Stanley and Rhoda ill. by author. Dial, 1978. ISBN 978-0-8037-8249-5 Subj: Activities – babysitting. Animals – mice. Sibling rivalry.

Time-out for Sophie ill. by author. Viking, 2013. ISBN 978-0-670-78511-7 Subj: Animals – mice. Behavior – misbehavior. Family life.

Timothy goes to school ill. by author. Viking, 2000. ISBN 978-0-670-89182-5 Subj: Animals – raccoons. Behavior – growing up. School – first day.

Yoko ill. by author. Hyperion, 1998. ISBN 978-0-7868-2345-1 Subj: Animals – cats. Animals – raccoons. Food. Prejudice. School.

Yoko finds her way ill. by author. Disney/Hyperion, 2013. ISBN 978-1-4231-6512-5 Subj: Airplanes, airports. Animals – cats. Foreign lands – Japan. Signs & signboards.

Yoko learns to read ill. by author. Hyperion/Disney, 2012. ISBN 978-1-4231-3823-5 Subj: Animals – cats. Books, reading. Ethnic groups in the U.S. – Japanese Americans. Family life – mothers.

Yoko writes her name ill. by author. Hyperion, 2008. ISBN 978-0-7868-0371-2 Subj: Activities – writing. Behavior – bullying, teasing. Ethnic groups in the U.S. – Japanese Americans. School.

Yoko's paper cranes ill. by author. Hyperion, 2001. ISBN 978-0-7868-2602-5 Subj: Animals – cats. Birds – cranes. Birthdays. Ethnic groups in the U.S. – Japanese Americans. Family life – grandmothers. Foreign lands – Japan.

Yoko's show-and-tell ill. by author. Hyperion/Disney, 2010. ISBN 978-1-4231-1955-5 Subj: Behavior – misbehavior. Ethnic groups in the U.S. – Japanese Americans. Gifts. School. Toys – dolls.

Weninger, Brigitte. *Bye-bye, Binky* ill. by Yusuke Yonezu. Minedition, 2007. ISBN 978-0-698-40048-1 Subj: Animals. Behavior – growing up.

Davy in the middle ill. by Eve Tharlet. NorthSouth, 2004. ISBN 978-0-7358-1934-4 Subj: Activities – babysitting. Animals – rabbits. Behavior – growing up. Character traits – helpfulness. Family life. Family life – brothers & sisters.

Davy, soccer star! ill. by Eve Tharlet. NorthSouth, 2008. ISBN 978-0-7358-2196-5 Subj: Animals – badgers. Animals – rabbits. Behavior – bullying, teasing. Contests. Sports – soccer.

Double birthday ill. by Stephanie Roehe. Minedition, 2005. ISBN 978-0-698-40015-3 Subj: Animals – mice. Birthdays. Gifts. Toys.

The elf's hat ill. by John A. Rowe. NorthSouth, 2000. ISBN 978-0-7358-1255-0 Subj: Animals. Clothing – hats. Cumulative tales. Fairies. Insects – fleas. Rhyming text.

Good-bye, Daddy! ill. by Alan Marks. NorthSouth, 1995. ISBN 978-1-55858-383-2 Subj: Divorce. Emotions. Family life – fathers. Toys – bears.

Good night, Nori ill. by Yusuke Yonezu. Minedition, 2007. ISBN 978-0-698-40065-8 Subj: Animals – cats. Bedtime.

Happy birthday, Davy ill. by Eve Tharlet. NorthSouth, 2000. ISBN 978-0-7358-1346-5 Subj: Animals – rabbits. Birthdays. Parties.

Happy Easter, Davy ill. by Eve Tharlet. NorthSouth, 2001. ISBN 978-0-7358-1436-3 Subj: Animals – rabbits. Gifts. Holidays – Easter.

A letter to Santa Claus ill. by Anne Möller. NorthSouth, 2000. ISBN 978-0-7358-1360-1 Subj: Holidays – Christmas. Letters, cards. Santa Claus.

Little apple ill. by Anne Möller. NorthSouth, 2001. ISBN 978-0-7358-1426-4 Subj: Food. Trees.

Merry Christmas, Davy! ill. by Eve Tharlet. NorthSouth, 1998. ISBN 978-1-55858-981-0 Subj: Animals. Animals – rabbits. Behavior – sharing. Holidays – Christmas.

Miko goes on vacation ill. by Stephanie Roehe. Penguin, 2006. ISBN 978-0-698-40017-7 Subj: Animals – mice. Friendship. Sea & seashore – beaches. Sports – swimming. Toys.

Miko wants a dog ill. by Stephanie Roehe. Minedition, 2006. ISBN 978-0-698-40016-0 Subj: Animals – mice. Pets.

"Mom, wake up and play!" ill. by Stephanie Roehe. Minedition, 2005. ISBN 978-0-689-40012-4 Subj: Animals – mice. Family life – mothers. Morning.

"No bath! No way!" ill. by Stephanie Roehe. Minedition, 2005. ISBN 978-0-689-40013-1 Subj: Activities – bathing. Animals – mice. Bedtime. Family life – mothers.

Precious water ill. by Anne Möller. NorthSouth, 2002. ISBN 978-0-7358-1514-8 Subj: Ecology. Nature. Water.

Special delivery ill. by Alexander Reichstein. NorthSouth, 2000. ISBN 978-0-7358-1318-2 Subj: Family life – mothers. Format, unusual – toy & movable books. Games.

What's the matter, Davy? ill. by Eve Tharlet. NorthSouth, 1998. ISBN 978-1-55858-900-1 Subj: Animals – rabbits. Behavior – lost & found possessions. Toys.

Why are you fighting, Davy? ill. by Eve Tharlet. NorthSouth, 1999. ISBN 978-0-7358-1074-7 Subj: Animals – rabbits. Behavior – fighting, arguing. Character traits – individuality. Friendship.

Will you mind the baby, Davy? ill. by Eve Tharlet. NorthSouth, 1997. ISBN 978-1-55858-732-8 Subj: Activities – babysitting. Animals – rabbits. Babies. Family life – new sibling.

Werner, Sharon. *Alphasaurs and other prehistoric types* by Sharon Werner and Sarah Forss ill. by

Sharon Werner. Blue Apple, 2012. ISBN 978-1-60905-193-8 Subj: ABC books. Dinosaurs.

West, Colin. *One day in the jungle* ill. by author. Candlewick, 1995. ISBN 978-1-56402-646-0 Subj: Animals. Cumulative tales. Jungle. Noise, sounds.

West, Judy. *Have you got my purr?* ill. by Tim Warnes. Dutton, 2000. ISBN 978-0-525-46390-0 Subj: Animals. Animals – cats. Behavior – lost & found possessions. Noise, sounds.

Westcott, Nadine Bernard. *The lady with the alligator purse* ill. by author. Little, 1988. ISBN 978-0-316-93135-9 Subj: Clothing – handbags, purses. Games. Humorous stories. Poetry.

Peanut butter and jelly: a play rhyme ill. by author. Dutton, 1987. ISBN 978-0-525-44317-9 Subj: Animals – elephants. Careers – bakers. Family life. Food. Rhyming text.

Skip to my Lou ill. by adapter. Little, 1989. ISBN 978-0-316-93137-3 Subj: Farms. Folk & fairy tales. Music. Songs.

There's a hole in the bucket ill. by adapter. HarperCollins, 1990. ISBN 978-0-06-026423-9 Subj: Animals. Farms. Music. Songs.

Weston, Carrie. *If a chicken stayed for supper* ill. by Sophie Fatus. Holiday House, 2007. ISBN 978-0-8234-2067-4 Subj: Animals – foxes. Behavior – misbehavior. Birds – chickens. Counting, numbers. Night.

The new bear at school ill. by Tim Warnes. Scholastic, 2008. ISBN 978-0-545-05783-7 Subj: Animals – bears. School.

Weston, Mark. *Honda: the boy who dreamed of cars* ill. by Katie Yamasaki. Lee & Low, 2008. ISBN 978-1-60060-246-7 Subj: Automobiles. Careers – inventors. Foreign lands – Japan.

Weston, Martha. *Tuck in the pool* ill. by author. Clarion, 1995. ISBN 978-0-395-65479-8 Subj: Animals – pigs. Emotions – fear. Sports – swimming.

Tuck's haunted house ill. by author. Clarion, 2002. ISBN 978-0-618-15966-6 Subj: Animals – pigs. Family life – brothers & sisters. Holidays – Halloween. Homes, houses. Monsters.

Wethered, Peggy. *Touchdown Mars! an ABC adventure* by Peggy Wethered and Ken Edgett ill. by Michael Chesworth. Putnam, 2000. ISBN 978-0-399-23214-5 Subj: ABC books. Animals – cats. Planets. Space & space ships.

Weulersse, Odile. *Nasreddine* ill. by Rebecca Dautremer. Eerdmans, 2013. ISBN 978-0-8028-5416-2 Subj: Behavior – bullying, teasing. Family life – fathers. Folk & fairy tales. Foreign lands – Middle East.

Wewer, Iris. *My wild sister and me* ill. by author. NorthSouth, 2011. ISBN 978-0-7358-4003-4 Subj: Activities – playing. Emotions – envy, jealousy. Family life – brothers & sisters.

Wharnsby-Ali, Dawud. *A picnic of poems in Allah's green garden* ill. by Shireen Adams. Islamic Foundation, 2011. ISBN 978-0-8603-7444-2 Subj: Poetry. Religion – Islam.

What a morning! the Christmas story in Black spirituals sel. and ed. by John M. Langstaff; ill. by Ashley Bryan. Musical arrangements by John Andrew Ross. McElderry, 1987. ISBN 978-0-689-50422-8 Subj: Holidays – Christmas. Music. Religion. Songs.

What will we do with the baby-o? rhymes & songs sel. by Theo Heras; ill. by Jennifer Herbert. Tundra, 2004. ISBN 978-0-88776-689-3 Subj: Rhyming text. Songs.

Whatley, Bruce. *Captain Pajamas* by Bruce Whatley and Rosie Smith ill. by Bruce Whatley. HarperCollins, 1999. ISBN 978-0-06-026614-1 Subj: Aliens. Animals – dogs. Imagination. Night. Sleep.

Clinton Gregory's secret ill. by author. Abrams, 2008. ISBN 978-0-8109-9364-8 Subj: Bedtime. Imagination.

Wait! No paint! ill. by author. HarperCollins, 2001. ISBN 978-0-06-028271-4 Subj: Animals – pigs. Animals – wolves. Behavior – carelessness. Careers – illustrators.

Wheatley, Nadia. *Luke's way of looking* ill. by Matt Ottley. Kane/Miller, 2001. ISBN 978-1-929132-18-8 Subj: Art. Careers – artists. Careers – teachers. Character traits – individuality. Imagination. Museums.

Wheeler, Eliza. *Miss Maple's seeds* ill. by author. Penguin/Nancy Paulsen, 2013. ISBN 978-0-399-25792-6 Subj: Character traits – kindness. Seeds.

Wheeler, Lisa. *Boogie knights* ill. by Mark Siegel. Atheneum, 2008. ISBN 978-0-689-87639-4 Subj: Knights. Monsters. Parties. Rhyming text.

Castaway cats ill. by Ponder Goembel. Simon & Schuster, 2006. ISBN 978-0-689-86232-8 Subj: Animals – cats. Behavior – lost. Rhyming text.

Dino-baseball ill. by Barry Gott. Carolrhoda, 2010. ISBN 978-0-7613-4429-2 Subj: Dinosaurs. Sports – baseball.

Dino-basketball ill. by Barry Gott. Carolrhoda, 2011. ISBN 978-0-7613-6393-4 Subj: Dinosaurs. Rhyming text. Sports – basketball.

Dino-football ill. by Barry Gott. Carolrhoda, 2012. ISBN 978-0-7613-6394-1 Subj: Dinosaurs. Rhyming text. Sports – football.

Dino-hockey ill. by Barry Gott. Carolrhoda, 2007. ISBN 978-0-8225-6191-0 Subj: Dinosaurs. Rhyming text. Sports – hockey.

Dino-soccer ill. by Barry Gott. Carolrhoda, 2009. ISBN 978-0-8225-9028-6 Subj: Dinosaurs. Rhyming text. Sports – soccer.

Dino-wrestling ill. by Barry Gott. Carolrhoda, 2013. ISBN 978-1-46770-212-6 Subj: Dinosaurs. Rhyming text. Sports – wrestling.

Hokey pokey: another prickly love story ill. by Janie Bynum. Little, Brown, 2006. ISBN 978-0-316-00090-1 Subj: Activities – dancing. Animals – hedgehogs. Animals – porcupines. Friendship.

Jam and jelly by Holly and Nellie ill. by Gijsbert van Frankenhuyzen. Sleeping Bear, 2002. ISBN 978-1-58536-109-0 Subj: Activities – working. Clothing – coats. Family life – mothers. Food. Plants.

Jazz baby ill. by R. Gregory Christie. Harcourt, 2004. ISBN 978-0-15-202522-9 Subj: Babies. Music. Rhyming text.

Mammoths on the move ill. by Kurt Cyrus. Harcourt, 2006. ISBN 978-0-15-204700-9 Subj: Animals – woolly mammoths. Rhyming text.

Old Cricket ill. by Ponder Goembel. Atheneum, 2003. ISBN 978-0-689-84510-9 Subj: Behavior. Birds – crows. Character traits – helpfulness. Insects – crickets.

The pet project: cute and cuddly vicious verses ill. by Zachariah OHora. Atheneum, 2013. ISBN 978-1-4169-7595-3 Subj: Animals. Pets. Rhyming text.

Porcupining ill. by Janie Bynum. Little, 2002. ISBN 978-0-316-98912-1 Subj: Animals – hedgehogs. Animals – porcupines. Behavior – needing someone. Emotions – loneliness.

Sixteen cows ill. by Kurt Cyrus. Harcourt, 2002. ISBN 978-0-15-202676-9 Subj: Animals – bulls, cows. Cowboys, cowgirls. Rhyming text.

Turk and Runt ill. by Frank Ansley. Atheneum, 2002. ISBN 978-0-689-84761-5 Subj: Birds – turkeys. Character traits – cleverness. Concepts – size. Family life – brothers. Food. Holidays – Thanksgiving.

Ugly pie ill. by Heather Solomon. Harcourt, 2010. ISBN 978-0-15-216754-7 Subj: Activities – baking, cooking. Animals – bears. Food.

Wool gathering ill. by Frank Ansley. Atheneum, 2001. ISBN 978-0-689-84369-3 Subj: Animals – sheep. Family life. Poetry.

Wheeler, Opal. *Sing in praise: a collection of the best loved hymns* ill. by Marjorie Torrey. Dutton, 1946. Subj: Caldecott award honor books. Music. Religion. Songs.

Sing Mother Goose ill. by Marjorie Torrey. Music by Opal Wheeler. Dutton, 1945. Subj: Caldecott award honor books. Music. Nursery rhymes. Songs.

Wheeler, Valerie. *Yes, please! No, thank you!* ill. by Glin Dibley. Sterling, 2006. ISBN 978-1-4027-3929-3 Subj: Character traits – questioning. Etiquette. Format, unusual – board books.

Whelan, Gloria. *The boy who wanted to cook* ill. by Steve Adams. Sleeping Bear, 2011. ISBN 978-1-58536-534-0 Subj: Activities – baking, cooking. Careers – chefs, cooks. Family life. Foreign lands – France. Restaurants.

Whippo, Walt. *Little white duck* ill. by Joan Paley. Lyrics by Walt Whippo; music by Bernard Zaritzky. Little, 2000. ISBN 978-0-316-03227-8 Subj: Animals. Birds – ducks. Music. Songs. Theater.

Whitaker, Suzanne George. *The daring Miss Quimby* ill. by Catherine Stock. Holiday, 2009. ISBN 978-0-8234-1996-8 Subj: Activities – flying. Careers – airplane pilots. Gender roles. U.S. history.

White, Alexina B. *Frisky brisky hippity hop* adapt. by Susan Lurie; photos by Murray Head. Holiday House, 2012. ISBN 978-0-8234-2410-8 Subj: Animals – squirrels. Rhyming text.

White, Becky. *Betsy Ross* ill. by Megan Lloyd. Holiday House, 2011. ISBN 978-0-8234-1908-1 Subj: Activities – sewing. Flags. Rhyming text. U.S. history.

White, Ellen Emerson. *Santa paws* ill. by Robert J. Blake. Scholastic, 2003. ISBN 978-0-439-32438-0 Subj: Animals – dogs. Character traits – helpfulness. Holidays – Christmas.

White, Kathryn. *Ruby's school walk* ill. by Miriam Latimer. Barefoot, 2010. ISBN 978-1-84686-275-5 Subj: Activities – walking. Family life – mothers. Imagination. Rhyming text. School.

When they fight ill. by Cliff Wright. Winslow, 2000. ISBN 978-1-890817-46-6 Subj: Behavior – fighting, arguing. Family life.

White, Linda. *Too many pumpkins* ill. by Megan Lloyd. Holiday, 1996. ISBN 978-0-8234-1245-7 Subj: Behavior – dissatisfaction. Food. Friendship.

Too many turkeys ill. by Megan Lloyd. Holiday House, 2010. ISBN 978-0-8234-2084-1 Subj: Birds – turkeys. Farms. Gardens, gardening.

White, Linda Arms. *Comes a wind* ill. by Tom Curry. DK, 2000. ISBN 978-0-7894-2601-7 Subj: Birthdays. Contests. Family life – brothers. Family life – mothers. Tall tales. Weather – wind.

White, Marsha. *Hooper has lost his owner* ill. by author. Little, 2002. ISBN 978-0-316-06561-0 Subj:

Animals – dogs. Behavior – lost & found possessions. Format, unusual – toy & movable books.

Whitehead, Jenny. *Lunch box mail and other poems* ill. by author. Holt, 2001. ISBN 978-0-8050-6259-5 Subj: Poetry. School.

Whitehead, Kathy. *Looking for Uncle Louie on the Fourth of July* ill. by Pablo Torrecilla. Boyds Mills, 2005. ISBN 978-1-59078-061-9 Subj: Careers – police officers. Family life – aunts, uncles. Holidays – Fourth of July. Motorcycles. Parades.

Whitehouse, Patricia. *Alligator* ill. with photos. Heinemann, 2003. ISBN 978-1-58810-903-3 Subj: Reptiles – alligators, crocodiles. Zoos.

Barn owls ill. with photos. Heinemann, 2003. ISBN 978-1-58810-877-7 Subj: Birds – owls.

Bats ill. with photos. Heinemann, 2003. ISBN 978-1-58810-878-4 Subj: Animals – bats.

Coyotes ill. with photos. Heinemann, 2003. ISBN 978-1-58810-879-1 Subj: Animals – coyotes.

Elephants ill. with photos. Heinemann, 2003. ISBN 978-1-58810-897-5 Subj: Animals – elephants. Zoos.

Fall ill. with photos. Heinemann, 2003. ISBN 978-1-58810-892-0 Subj: Seasons – fall.

Flamingo ill. with photos. Heinemann, 2003. ISBN 978-1-58810-901-9 Subj: Birds – flamingos. Zoos.

Hippopotamus ill. with photos. Heinemann, 2003. ISBN 978-1-58810-899-9 Subj: Animals – hippopotamuses. Zoos.

Opossums ill. with photos. Heinemann, 2003. ISBN 978-1-58810-880-7 Subj: Animals – possums.

Ostrich ill. with photos. Heinemann, 2003. ISBN 978-1-58810-887-6 Subj: Birds – ostriches. Zoos.

Raccoons ill. with photos. Heinemann, 2003. ISBN 978-1-58810-882-1 Subj: Animals – raccoons.

Rats ill. with photos. Heinemann, 2003. ISBN 978-1-58810-881-4 Subj: Animals – rats.

Sea lion ill. with photos. Heinemann, 2003. ISBN 978-1-58810-902-6 Subj: Animals – sea lions. Zoos.

Seasons ABC ill. with photos. Heinemann, 2003. ISBN 978-1-58810-895-1 Subj: ABC books. Seasons.

Seasons 1 2 3 ill. with photos. Heinemann, 2003. ISBN 978-1-58810-896-8 Subj: Counting, numbers. Seasons.

Spring ill. with photos. Heinemann, 2003. ISBN 978-1-58810-894-4 Subj: Seasons – spring.

Summer ill. with photos. Heinemann, 2003. ISBN 978-1-58810-891-3 Subj: Seasons – summer.

Tiger ill. with photos. Heinemann, 2003. ISBN 978-1-58810-904-0 Subj: Animals – tigers. Zoos.

What's awake? A B C ill. with photos. Heinemann, 2003. ISBN 978-1-58810-884-5 Subj: ABC books. Animals. Night.

What's awake? 1 2 3 ill. with photos. Heinemann, 2003. ISBN 978-1-58810-885-2 Subj: Animals. Counting, numbers. Night.

Winter ill. with photos. Heinemann, 2003. ISBN 978-1-58810-893-7 Subj: Seasons – winter.

Whiteley, Opal Stanley. *Only Opal: the diary of a young girl* sel. & adapt. by Jane Boulton; ill. by Barbara Cooney. An adapt. of The story of Opal. Philomel, 1994. ISBN 978-0-399-21990-0 Subj: Family life. Poetry. U.S. history – frontier & pioneer life.

Whitfield, Susan. *The animals of the Chinese zodiac* ill. by Philippa-Alys Browne. Crocodile, 1998. ISBN 978-1-56656-236-2 Subj: Animals. Foreign lands – China.

Whitford, Rebecca. *Little yoga: a toddler's first book of yoga* ill. by Martina Selway. Holt, 2005. ISBN 978-0-8050-7879-4 Subj: Health & fitness.

Sleepy little yoga: a toddler's sleepy book of yoga ill. by Martina Selway. Holt, 2007. ISBN 978-0-8050-8193-0 Subj: Health & fitness.

Whiting, Sue. *The firefighters* ill. by Donna Rawlins. Candlewick, 2008. ISBN 978-0-7636-4019-4 Subj: Careers – firefighters. Imagination. School.

Whitman, Candace. *Lines that wiggle* ill. by Steve Wilson. Blue Apple, 2009. ISBN 978-1-934706-54-1 Subj: Art. Monsters. Rhyming text.

Whitman, Sylvia. *Under the Ramadan moon* ill. by Sue Williams. Whitman, 2008. ISBN 978-0-8075-8304-3 Subj: Holidays – Ramadan. Religion – Islam.

Whittaker, Nicola. *Feet* ill. with photos. G. Stevens, 2002. ISBN 978-0-8368-3163-4 Subj: Anatomy – feet. Animals. Rhyming text.

Hair ill. with photos. G. Stevens, 2002. ISBN 978-0-8368-3164-1 Subj: Animals. Hair. Rhyming text.

Noses ill. with photos. G. Stevens, 2002. ISBN 978-0-8368-3165-8 Subj: Anatomy – noses. Animals.

Tails ill. with photos. G. Stevens, 2002. ISBN 978-0-8368-3166-5 Subj: Anatomy – tails. Animals.

Who took the cookie? ill. by Tom Brannon. Random House, 2002. ISBN 978-0-375-81606-2 Subj: Food. Format, unusual – board books. Puppets.

Why did the chicken cross the road? ill. by Jon Agee. Penguin, 2006. ISBN 978-0-8037-3094-6 Subj: Birds – chickens. Humorous stories.

Whybrow, Ian. *A baby for Grace* ill. by Christian Birmingham. Kingfisher, 1998. ISBN 978-0-7534-5142-7 Subj: Babies. Family life – new sibling. Family life – sisters.

Badness for beginners: a Little Wolf and Smellybreff adventure ill. by Tony Ross. Carolrhoda, 2005. ISBN 978-1-57505-861-0 Subj: Animals – wolves. Behavior – misbehavior. Family life – brothers & sisters.

Bella gets her skates on ill. by Rosie Reeve. Abrams, 2007. ISBN 978-0-8109-9416-4 Subj: Animals – rabbits. Behavior – worrying. Seasons – winter. Sports – ice skating.

Faraway farm ill. by Alex Ayliffe. Carolrhoda, 2006. ISBN 978-1-57505-938-9 Subj: Farms. Picture puzzles. Rhyming text.

Good night, monster ill. by Ken Wilson-Max. Knopf, 2001. ISBN 978-0-375-81579-9 Subj: Animals. Format, unusual – toy & movable books. Monsters.

Harry and the bucketful of dinosaurs ill. by Adrian Reynolds. First pub. in the U.S. by Orchard Books under the title Sammy and the dinosaurs in 1999. Random House, 2003. ISBN 978-0-375-82541-5 Subj: Activities – playing. Dinosaurs. Imagination. Names. Toys.

Harry and the dinosaurs at the museum ill. by Adrian Reynolds. Penguin, 2005. ISBN 978-0-375-83338-0 Subj: Behavior – lost. Dinosaurs. Museums. Toys.

Harry and the dinosaurs go to school ill. by Adrian Reynolds. Random House, 2007. ISBN 978-0-375-84180-4 Subj: Dinosaurs. School – first day. Toys.

Harry and the dinosaurs say "Raahh" ill. by Adrian Reynolds. Random House, 2004. ISBN 978-0-375-82542-2 Subj: Careers – dentists. Dinosaurs. Emotions – fear. Toys.

Harry and the snow king ill. by Adrian Reynolds. Levinson Books, 1997. ISBN 978-1-899607-85-3 Subj: Family life. Seasons – winter. Snowmen. Weather – snow.

Hello! Is this grandma? ill. by Deborah Allwright. Tiger Tales, 2008. ISBN 978-1-58925-072-7 Subj: Animals. Format, unusual – toy & movable books. Reptiles – alligators, crocodiles. Telephone.

Sammy and the robots ill. by Adrian Reynolds. Orchard, 2001. ISBN 978-0-531-30327-6 Subj: Family life – grandmothers. Format, unusual – toy & movable books. Hospitals. Illness. Robots. Toys.

Wish, change, friend ill. by Tiphanie Beeke. McElderry, 2002. ISBN 978-0-689-84930-5 Subj: Animals – pigs. Behavior – wishing. Birds – penguins. Books, reading. Snowmen.

Wick, Walter. *Can you see what I see? cool collections* photos by author. Scholastic, 2004. ISBN 978-0-439-61772-7 Subj: Animals. Dinosaurs. Games. Picture puzzles. Rhyming text. Seasons.

Can you see what I see? dream machine photos by author. Scholastic, 2003. ISBN 978-0-439-39950-0 Subj: Bedtime. Dreams. Morning. Picture puzzles. Rhyming text.

Can you see what I see? once upon a time photos by author. Scholastic, 2006. ISBN 978-0-439-61777-2 Subj: Folk & fairy tales. Picture puzzles. Rhyming text.

Can you see what I see? out of this world photos by author. Scholastic, 2013. ISBN 978-0-545-24468-8 Subj: Picture puzzles. Rhyming text. Space & space ships.

Can you see what I see? picture puzzles to search and solve photos by author. Scholastic, 2002. ISBN 978-0-439-16391-0 Subj: Picture puzzles. Rhyming text.

Can you see what I see? Seymour and the juice box boat photos by author. Scholastic, 2004. ISBN 978-0-439-61778-9 Subj: Animals. Boats, ships. Picture puzzles. Rhyming text.

Can you see what I see? Seymour makes new friends photos by author. Scholastic, 2006. ISBN 978-0-439-61780-2 Subj: Friendship. Picture puzzles. Rhyming text.

Can you see what I see? the night before Christmas photos by author. Scholastic, 2005. ISBN 978-0-439-76927-3 Subj: Holidays – Christmas. Picture puzzles. Poetry. Santa Claus.

Can you see what I see? toyland express photos by author. Scholastic, 2011. ISBN 978-0-545-24483-1 Subj: Picture puzzles. Toys.

Can you see what I see? treasure ship photos by author. Scholastic, 2010. ISBN 978-0-439-02643-7 Subj: Boats, ships. Picture puzzles. Rhyming text. Riddles & jokes.

Wickberg, Susan. *Hey Mr. Choo-Choo, where are you going?* ill. by Yumi Heo. Putnam, 2008. ISBN 978-0-399-23993-9 Subj: Rhyming text. Trains.

Wickstrom, Sylvie. *I love you, Mister Bear* ill. by author. HarperCollins, 2003. ISBN 978-0-06-029332-1 Subj: Family life. Toys – bears.

Wiebe, Rudy. *Hidden buffalo* ill. by Michael Lonechild. Red Deer, 2003. ISBN 978-0-88995-285-0 Subj: Animals – buffaloes. Dreams. Foreign lands – Canada. Indians of North America – Cree.

Wiener, Lori S., et al, compiler. *Be a friend: children who live with HIV speak* ill. by Lori S. Wiener.

Whitman, 1994. ISBN 978-0-8075-0590-8 Subj: Children as authors. Children as illustrators. Illness – AIDS.

Wiese, Kurt. *Fish in the air* ill. by author. Viking, 1948. Subj: Caldecott award honor books. Foreign lands – China. Humorous stories. Kites.

The five Chinese brothers (Bishop, Claire Huchet)

The story about Ping (Flack, Marjorie)

You can write Chinese ill. by author. Viking, 1945. Subj: Caldecott award honor books. Foreign languages.

Wiesmüller, Dieter. *The adventures of Marco and Polo* ill. by author. Walker, 2000. ISBN 978-0-8027-8729-3 Subj: Activities – traveling. Animals – monkeys. Birds – penguins.

In the blink of an eye ill. by author. Walker, 2002. ISBN 978-0-8027-8855-9 Subj: Anatomy – eyes. Animals. Picture puzzles.

Wiesner, David. *Art and Max* ill. by author. Clarion, 2010. ISBN 978-0-618-75663-6 Subj: Activities – painting. Art. Careers – artists. Reptiles – lizards. Self-concept.

Flotsam ill. by author. Houghton, 2006. ISBN 978-0-618-19457-5 Subj: Caldecott award books. Imagination. Sea & seashore – beaches.

Free fall ill. by author. Lothrop, 1988. ISBN 978-0-688-05584-4 Subj: Bedtime. Books, reading. Caldecott award honor books. Dragons. Dreams. Wordless.

Hurricane ill. by author. Houghton, 1990. ISBN 978-0-395-54382-5 Subj: Family life – brothers & sisters. Imagination. Weather – storms.

The loathsome dragon by David Wiesner and Kim Kahng ill. by David Wiesner. Clarion, 2005. ISBN 978-0-618-54359-5 Subj: Dragons. Folk & fairy tales. Magic. Royalty.

Mr. Wuffles! ill. by author. Clarion, 2013. ISBN 978-0-618-75661-2 Subj: Aliens. Animals – cats. Caldecott award honor books. Petroglyphs. Space & space ships. Wordless.

Sector 7 ill. by author. Clarion, 1999. ISBN 978-0-395-74656-1 Subj: Caldecott award honor books. School. Weather – clouds. Wordless.

The three pigs ill. by author. Clarion, 2001. ISBN 978-0-618-00701-1 Subj: Animals – pigs. Animals – wolves. Books, reading. Caldecott award books. Character traits – cleverness. Folk & fairy tales.

Tuesday ill. by author. Houghton, 1991. ISBN 978-0-395-55113-4 Subj: Activities – flying. Caldecott award books. Frogs & toads. Magic. Night.

Wigersma, Tanneke. *Baby brother* ill. by Nynke Mare Talsma. Boyds Mills, 2005. ISBN 978-1-932425-55-0 Subj: Babies. Family life – grandmothers. Family life – new sibling. Letters, cards.

Wight, Tamra. *The three grumpies* ill. by Ross Collins. Bloomsbury, 2003. ISBN 978-1-58234-840-7 Subj: Behavior – bad day. Emotions.

Wilbur, Helen L. *Z is for Zeus: a Greek mythology alphabet* ill. by Victor Juhasz. Sleeping Bear, 2008. ISBN 978-1-58536-341-4 Subj: ABC books. Mythical creatures.

Wilbur, Richard. *The disappearing alphabet* ill. by David Diaz. Harcourt, 1998. ISBN 978-0-15-201470-4 Subj: ABC books. Poetry.

Wilcox, Brad. *Hip, hip, hooray for Annie McRae!* ill. by Julie Olson. Gibbs Smith, 2001. ISBN 978-1-58685-058-6 Subj: Emotions – happiness.

Wilcox, Brian. *Full moon* by Brian Wilcox and Lawrence David ill. by Brian Wilcox. Random House, 2001. ISBN 978-0-385-32792-3 Subj: Birthdays. Cities, towns. Family life – grandmothers. Moon.

Wilcox, Leah. *Waking Beauty* ill. by Lydia Monks. Putnam, 2008. ISBN 978-0-399-24615-9 Subj: Folk & fairy tales. Humorous stories. Rhyming text.

Wild, Margaret. *Bobbie Dazzler* ill. by Janine Dawson. Kane/Miller, 2007. ISBN 978-1-933605-46-3 Subj: Animals – wallabies. Character traits – perseverance. Foreign lands – Australia.

Fox by Margaret Wild and Ron Brooks ill. by Ron Brooks. Kane/Miller, 2001. ISBN 978-1-929132-16-4 Subj: Animals – dogs. Animals – foxes. Birds – magpies. Emotions – envy, jealousy. Emotions – loneliness. Friendship.

Going home ill. by Wayne Harris. Scholastic, 1994. ISBN 978-0-590-47958-5 Subj: Activities – traveling. Dreams. Hospitals.

Harry and Hopper ill. by Freya Blackwood. Feiwel & Friends, 2011. ISBN 978-0-312-64261-7 Subj: Animals – dogs. Death. Emotions – grief.

Hush, hush! ill. by Bridget Strevens-Marzo. Little Hare, 2010. ISBN 978-1-921272-86-8 Subj: Animals – hippopotamuses. Bedtime.

Itsy-bitsy babies ill. by Jan Ormerod. Little Hare, 2010. ISBN 978-1-921541-36-0 Subj: Babies. Rhyming text.

Lucy Goosey ill. by Ann James. Little Hare, 2009. ISBN 978-1-921049-87-3 Subj: Birds – geese. Family life – mothers. Migration.

Midnight babies ill. by Ann James. Clarion, 1999. ISBN 978-0-618-10412-3 Subj: Activities – dancing. Babies. Night.

Mr. Nick's knitting ill. by Dee Huxley. Harcourt, 1989. ISBN 978-0-15-200518-4 Subj: Activities – knitting. Friendship. Hospitals. Illness.

Nighty night ill. by Kerry Argent. Peachtree, 2001. ISBN 978-1-56145-246-0 Subj: Animals. Bedtime.

Old Pig ill. by Ron Brooks. Dial, 1996. ISBN 978-0-8037-1917-0 Subj: Animals – pigs. Death. Family life – grandmothers. Old age.

Our granny ill. by Julie Vivas. Ticknor & Fields, 1994. ISBN 978-0-395-67023-1 Subj: Family life – grandmothers.

Piglet and Granny ill. by Stephen Michael King. Abrams, 2009. ISBN 978-0-8109-4063-5 Subj: Animals – pigs. Family life – grandmothers. Farms.

Piglet and Mama ill. by Stephen Michael King. Abrams, 2005. ISBN 978-0-8109-5869-2 Subj: Animals – pigs. Emotions – love. Family life – mothers. Farms.

Piglet and Papa ill. by Stephen Michael King. Abrams, 2007. ISBN 978-0-8109-1476-6 Subj: Animals – pigs. Emotions – love. Family life – fathers. Farms.

The pocket dogs ill. by Stephen Michael King. Scholastic, 2001. ISBN 978-0-439-23973-8 Subj: Accidents. Animals – dogs. Behavior – lost. Clothing.

Puffling ill. by Julie Vivas. Feiwel & Friends, 2009. ISBN 978-0-312-56570-1 Subj: Behavior – growing up. Birds – puffins. Family life – parents.

Rosie and Tortoise ill. by Ron Brooks. DK, 1999. ISBN 978-0-7894-2630-7 Subj: Animals – rabbits. Family life – new sibling.

Thank you, Santa ill. by Kerry Argent. Scholastic, 1992. ISBN 978-0-590-45805-4 Subj: Animals – polar bears. Foreign lands – Arctic. Foreign lands – Australia. Holidays – Christmas. Letters, cards.

Tom goes to kindergarten ill. by David Legge. Whitman, 2000. ISBN 978-0-8075-8012-7 Subj: Animals – pandas. Family life. School – first day.

Wilde, Oscar. *The happy prince* ill. by Jane Ray. Dutton, 1995. ISBN 978-0-525-45367-3 Subj: Cities, towns. Folk & fairy tales. Poverty. Royalty – kings.

The selfish giant ill. by S. Saelig Gallagher. Putnam, 1995. ISBN 978-0-399-22448-5 Subj: Character traits – kindness. Character traits – selfishness. Folk & fairy tales. Gardens, gardening. Giants. Seasons – spring.

The selfish giant retold by Fiona Waters; ill. by Fabian Negrin. Knopf, 2000. ISBN 978-0-375-90319-9 Subj: Character traits – kindness. Character traits – selfishness. Folk & fairy tales. Gardens, gardening. Giants. Seasons – spring.

The selfish giant ill. by Lisbeth Zwerger. Alphabet Pr., 1984. ISBN 978-0-907234-30-2 Subj: Character traits – kindness. Character traits – selfishness. Folk & fairy tales. Gardens, gardening. Giants. Seasons – spring.

Wilder, Laura Ingalls. *Going to town* ill. by Renée Graef. HarperCollins, 1994. ISBN 978-0-06-023013-5 Subj: Cities, towns. Family life – sisters. U.S. history – frontier & pioneer life.

My little house songbook ill. by Holly Jones. HarperCollins, 1995. ISBN 978-0-06-024295-4 Subj: Music. Songs. U.S. history – frontier & pioneer life.

Santa comes to little house ill. by Renée Graef. HarperCollins, 2001. ISBN 978-0-06-025939-6 Subj: Family life. Holidays – Christmas. Santa Claus. U.S. history – frontier & pioneer life.

Wildsmith, Brian. *Brian Wildsmith 1 2 3* ill. by author. Millbrook, 1995. ISBN 978-1-56294-905-1 Subj: Concepts – shape. Counting, numbers.

Brian Wildsmith's puzzles ill. by author. Millbrook, 1996. ISBN 978-0-7613-0052-6 Subj: Games.

A Christmas story ill. by author. Eerdmans, 1998. ISBN 978-0-8028-5173-4 Subj: Animals – donkeys. Holidays – Christmas. Religion – Nativity.

The Easter story ill. by author. Eerdmans, 2000, ©1993. ISBN 978-0-8028-5189-5 Subj: Animals – donkeys. Holidays – Easter. Religion.

Give a dog a bone ill. by author. Pantheon, 1985. ISBN 978-0-394-97709-6 Subj: Animals – dogs. Format, unusual.

Goat's trail ill. by author. Knopf, 1986. ISBN 978-0-394-98276-2 Subj: Animals. Animals – goats. Cumulative tales. Format, unusual. Noise, sounds.

Joseph ill. by author. Eerdmans, 1997. ISBN 978-0-8028-5161-1 Subj: Religion.

Jungle party ill. by author. Star Bright, 2006. ISBN 978-1-59572-052-8 Subj: Animals. Jungle. Reptiles – snakes.

The little wood duck ill. by author. Star Bright, 2006. ISBN 978-1-59572-042-9 Subj: Birds – ducks.

Mary ill. by author. Eerdmans, 2002. ISBN 978-0-8028-5231-1 Subj: Religion.

Wiles, Debbie. *Freedom summer* ill. by Jerome Lagarrigue. Atheneum, 2001. ISBN 978-0-689-82380-0 Subj: Ethnic groups in the U.S. – African Americans. Friendship. Prejudice.

Wiley, Thom. *One sheep, blue sheep* ill. by Ben Mantle. Scholastic, 2012. ISBN 978-0-545-40284-2 Subj: Animals – sheep. Concepts – color. Counting, numbers. Farms. Format, unusual – board books.

Wilhelm, Hans. *Bunny trouble* ill. by author. Scholastic, 1991. ISBN 978-0-590-63153-2 Subj: Animals – rabbits.

I'll always love you ill. by author. Crown, 1985. ISBN 978-0-517-55648-1 Subj: Animals – dogs. Death. Emotions – grief. Pets.

More bunny trouble ill. by author. Scholastic, 1989. ISBN 978-0-590-41589-7 Subj: Animals – foxes. Animals – rabbits. Eggs. Family life – brothers. Family life – sisters. Holidays – Easter.

Quacky Ducky's Easter egg ill. by author. HarperCollins, 2004. ISBN 978-0-06-053430-1 Subj: Birds – ducks. Eggs. Format, unusual – board books. Friendship. Holidays – Easter.

Quacky Ducky's Easter fun ill. by author. HarperCollins, 2004. ISBN 978-0-06-053431-8 Subj: Activities – painting. Birds – ducks. Format, unusual – board books. Holidays – Easter.

Schnitzel's first Christmas ill. by author. Simon & Schuster, 1991. ISBN 978-0-671-74494-6 Subj: Animals – dogs. Behavior – needing someone. Holidays – Christmas. Santa Claus.

Willard, Nancy. *The flying bed* ill. by John Thompson. Scholastic, 2007. ISBN 978-0-590-25610-0 Subj: Activities – flying. Behavior – greed. Careers – bakers. Foreign lands – Italy. Furniture – beds. Magic.

The Moon and Riddles Diner and the Sunnyside Café ill. by Chris Butler. Harcourt, 2001. ISBN 978-0-15-201941-9 Subj: Food. Poetry. Restaurants.

The mouse, the cat and Grandmother's hat ill. by Jenny Mattheson. Little, 2003. ISBN 978-0-316-94006-1 Subj: Animals – cats. Animals – mice. Birthdays. Family life – grandmothers. Parties. Rhyming text.

Pish posh, said Hieronymous Bosch ill. by Leo Dillon and Diane Dillon. Harcourt, 1991. ISBN 978-0-15-262210-7 Subj: Careers – artists. Poetry.

Shadow story ill. by David Diaz. Harcourt, 1999. ISBN 978-0-15-201638-8 Subj: Folk & fairy tales. Mythical creatures – ogres. Orphans. Shadows.

A visit to William Blake's inn: poems for innocent and experienced travelers ill. by Alice Provensen and Martin Provensen. Harcourt, 1981. ISBN 978-0-15-293822-2 Subj: Caldecott award honor books. Imagination. Poetry.

Willems, Mo. *Big Frog can't fit in: a pop out book* ill. by author. Hyperion, 2009. ISBN 978-1-4231-1436-9 Subj: Concepts – size. Format, unusual – toy & movable books. Frogs & toads.

City dog, country frog ill. by Jon J Muth. Hyperion, 2010. ISBN 978-1-4231-0300-4 Subj: Animals – dogs. Friendship. Frogs & toads. Seasons.

Don't let the pigeon drive the bus ill. by author. Hyperion, 2003. ISBN 978-0-7868-1988-1 Subj: Birds – pigeons. Caldecott award honor books. Careers – bus drivers. Humorous stories.

Don't let the pigeon stay up late! ill. by author. Hyperion, 2006. ISBN 978-0-7868-3746-5 Subj: Bedtime. Birds – pigeons. Humorous stories.

The duckling gets a cookie!? ill. by author. Hyperion, 2012. ISBN 978-1-4231-5128-9 Subj: Behavior – sharing. Birds – ducks. Birds – pigeons. Etiquette. Food. Humorous stories.

Edwina, the dinosaur who didn't know she was extinct ill. by author. Hyperion, 2006. ISBN 978-0-7868-3748-9 Subj: Dinosaurs. Self-concept.

Goldilocks and the three dinosaurs ill. by author. HarperCollins, 2012. ISBN 978-0-06-210418-2 Subj: Behavior – misbehavior. Dinosaurs. Folk & fairy tales. Humorous stories.

Knuffle Bunny: a cautionary tale ill. by author. Hyperion, 2004. ISBN 978-0-7868-1870-9 Subj: Animals – rabbits. Behavior – lost & found possessions. Caldecott award honor books. Laundry. Toys.

Knuffle Bunny free: an unexpected diversion ill. by author. HarperCollins, 2010. ISBN 978-0-0619-2957-1 Subj: Activities – traveling. Animals – rabbits. Behavior – lost & found possessions. Character traits – bravery. Toys.

Knuffle Bunny too: a case of mistaken identity ill. by author. Hyperion, 2007. ISBN 978-1-4231-0299-1 Subj: Animals – rabbits. Caldecott award honor books. School – nursery. Toys.

Leonardo the terrible monster ill. by author. Hyperion, 2005. ISBN 978-0-7868-5294-9 Subj: Friendship. Imagination. Monsters.

Naked mole rat gets dressed ill. by author. Disney, 2009. ISBN 978-1-4231-1437-6 Subj: Animals. Character traits – individuality. Clothing.

The pigeon finds a hot dog! ill. by author. Hyperion, 2005. ISBN 978-0-7868-5248-2 Subj: Birds – ducks. Birds – pigeons. Food. Humorous stories.

The pigeon has feelings, too! a smidgeon of pigeon ill. by author. Hyperion, 2005. ISBN 978-0-7868-3650-5 Subj: Birds – pigeons. Emotions. Format, unusual – board books. Humorous stories.

The pigeon loves things that go! a smidgeon of pigeon ill. by author. Hyperion, 2005. ISBN 978-0-7868-3651-2 Subj: Birds – pigeons. Format, unusual – board books. Transportation.

The pigeon wants a puppy! ill. by author. Hyperion, 2008. ISBN 978-1-4231-0960-0 Subj: Animals – dogs. Birds – pigeons. Pets.

That is not a good idea! ill. by author. HarperCollins, 2013. ISBN 978-0-06-220309-0 Subj: Animals – foxes. Behavior – trickery. Birds – geese.

Time to pee ill. by author. Hyperion, 2003. ISBN 978-0-7868-1868-6 Subj: Animals – mice. Toilet training.

Time to say "please"! ill. by author. Hyperion, 2005. ISBN 978-0-7868-5293-2 Subj: Animals – mice. Etiquette. Format, unusual – toy & movable books.

Willey, Margaret. *Clever Beatrice, an Upper Peninsula conte* ill. by Heather Solomon. Atheneum, 2001. ISBN 978-0-689-83254-3 Subj: Character traits – cleverness. Folk & fairy tales. Giants. Tall tales.

Clever Beatrice and the best little pony ill. by Heather Solomon. Atheneum, 2004. ISBN 978-0-689-85339-5 Subj: Animals. Animals – horses, ponies. Careers – bakers. Character traits – cleverness. Folk & fairy tales. Mythical creatures – lutins.

Clever Beatrice Christmas ill. by Heather Solomon. Atheneum, 2006. ISBN 978-0-689-87017-0 Subj: Character traits – cleverness. Holidays – Christmas. Santa Claus.

Thanksgiving with me ill. by Lloyd Bloom. Geringer, 1998. ISBN 978-0-06-027114-5 Subj: Family life – aunts, uncles. Holidays – Thanksgiving. Rhyming text.

The 3 bears and Goldilocks (The three bears)

Willhoite, Michael. *Daddy's roommate* ill. by author. Wonderland, 1990. ISBN 978-1-55583-178-3 Subj: Divorce. Family life – fathers. Family life – same-sex parents. Homosexuality.

Williams, Barbara. *Albert's gift for grandmother* ill. by Doug Cushman. Candlewick, 2006. ISBN 978-0-7636-2097-4 Subj: Birthdays. Family life – grandmothers. Gifts. Reptiles – turtles, tortoises.

Chester Chipmunk's Thanksgiving ill. by Kay Chorao. Dutton, 1974. ISBN 978-0-525-27655-5 Subj: Animals – chipmunks. Holidays – Thanksgiving.

Williams, Brenda. *Home for a tiger, home for a bear* ill. by Rosamund Fowler. Barefoot, 2007. ISBN 978-1-905236-81-7 Subj: Animals. Homes, houses. Rhyming text. Spiders.

The real princess: a mathemagical tale ill. by Sophie Fatus. Barefoot, 2008. ISBN 978-1-905236-88-6 Subj: Counting, numbers. Folk & fairy tales. Royalty. Royalty – princesses.

Williams, Carol Ann. *Booming Bella* ill. by Tatjana Mai-Wyss. Putnam, 2008. ISBN 978-0-399-24277-9 Subj: Noise, sounds. School – field trips. Self-concept.

Williams, Garth. *Benjamin's treasure* ill. by author and Rosemary Wells. HarperCollins, 2001. ISBN 978-0-06-028741-2 Subj: Animals – rabbits. Islands. Sea & seashore. Sports – fishing. Weather – storms.

Williams, Karen Lynn. *A beach tail* ill. by Floyd Cooper. Boyds Mills, 2010. ISBN 978-1-59078-712-0 Subj: Activities – drawing. Ethnic groups in the U.S. – African Americans. Sea & seashore – beaches.

Beatrice's dream: a story of Kibera slum. Frances Lincoln, 2011. ISBN 978-1-84780-019-0 Subj: Cities, towns. Foreign lands – Kenya. Poverty. School.

Galimoto ill. by Catherine Stock. Lothrop, 1990. ISBN 978-0-688-08790-6 Subj: Foreign lands – Africa. Toys.

My name is Sangoel by Karen Lynn Williams and Khadra Mohammed ill. by Catherine Stock. Eerdmans, 2009. ISBN 978-0-8028-5307-3 Subj: Communication. Ethnic groups in the U.S. – Sudanese Americans. Immigrants. Names.

Painted dreams ill. by Catherine Stock. Lothrop, 1998. ISBN 978-0-688-13902-5 Subj: Activities – painting. Foreign lands – Haiti. Problem solving.

Tap-tap ill. by Catherine Stock. Clarion, 1994. ISBN 978-0-395-65617-4 Subj: Clothing – hats. Family life – mothers. Foreign lands – Haiti. Stores. Trucks.

When Africa was home ill. by Floyd Cooper. Watts, 1991. ISBN 978-0-531-08525-7 Subj: Family life. Foreign lands – Africa. Friendship.

Williams, Laura E. *ABC kids* ill. by author. Philomel, 2000. ISBN 978-0-399-23370-8 Subj: ABC books.

The best winds ill. by Eujin Kim Neilan. Boyds Mills, 2006. ISBN 978-1-59078-274-3 Subj: Ethnic groups in the U.S. – Korean Americans. Family life – grandfathers. Kites.

The can man ill. by Craig Orback. Lee & Low, 2010. ISBN 978-1-60060-266-5 Subj: Character traits – generosity. Homeless.

Williams, Linda. *Horse in the pigpen* ill. by Megan Lloyd. HarperCollins, 2002. ISBN 978-0-06-028548-7 Subj: Animals. Family life – mothers. Farms. Rhyming text.

The little old lady who was not afraid of anything ill. by Megan Lloyd. Crowell, 1986. ISBN 978-0-690-04586-4 Subj: Cumulative tales. Emotions – fear. Scarecrows.

Williams, Rozanne Lanczak. *The coin counting book* ill. by author. Charlesbridge, 2001. ISBN 978-0-88106-325-7 Subj: Counting, numbers. Money. Rhyming text.

Williams, Sam. *Angel's Christmas cookies* ill. by author. HarperCollins, 2002. ISBN 978-0-06-029651-3 Subj: Angels. Animals – bears. Food. Holidays – Christmas. Mythical creatures – elves. Trees.

Snowy magic ill. by author. HarperCollins, 2002. ISBN 978-0-06-029652-0 Subj: Angels. Holidays – Christmas. Magic. Mythical creatures – elves. Weather – snow.

That's love ill. by Mique Moriuchi. Holiday House, 2007. ISBN 978-0-8234-2028-5 Subj: Emotions – love. Rhyming text.

Williams, Sherley Anne. *Girls together* ill. by Synthia Saint James. Harcourt, 1999. ISBN 978-0-15-230982-4 Subj: Activities – playing. Cities, towns. Ethnic groups in the U.S. – African Americans. Friendship.

Working cotton ill. by Carole M. Byard. Harcourt, 1992. ISBN 978-0-15-299624-6 Subj: Activities – working. Caldecott award honor books. Careers – migrant workers. Ethnic groups in the U.S. – African Americans. Family life.

Williams, Sue. *Dinnertime* ill. by Kerry Argent. Harcourt, 2001. ISBN 978-0-15-216471-3 Subj: Animals – foxes. Animals – rabbits. Counting, numbers. Rhyming text.

I went walking ill. by Julie Vivas. Harcourt, 1990. ISBN 978-0-15-200471-2 Subj: Activities – walking. Animals. Concepts – color. Rhyming text.

I went walking [board book] ill. by Julie Vivas. Harcourt, 1990. ISBN 978-0-15-205626-1 Subj: Activities – walking. Animals. Concepts – color. Format, unusual – board books. Rhyming text.

Let's go visiting ill. by Julie Vivas. Harcourt, 1998. ISBN 978-0-15-201823-8 Subj: Animals. Counting, numbers. Pets. Rhyming text.

Williams, Suzanne. *Library Lil* ill. by Steven Kellogg. Dial, 1997. ISBN 978-0-8037-1698-8 Subj: Books, reading. Careers – librarians. Tall tales.

My dog never says please ill. by Tedd Arnold. Dial, 1997. ISBN 978-0-8037-1681-0 Subj: Animals – dogs. Behavior – wishing. Family life.

Old MacDonald in the city ill. by Thor Wickstrom. Golden, 2002. ISBN 978-0-307-10685-8 Subj: Animals. Cities, towns. Counting, numbers. Insects. Rhyming text.

Ten naughty little monkeys ill. by Suzanne Watts. HarperCollins, 2007. ISBN 978-0-06-059904-1 Subj: Animals – monkeys. Counting, numbers. Rhyming text.

The witch casts a spell ill. by Barbara Olsen. Dial, 2002. ISBN 978-0-8037-2646-8 Subj: Holidays – Halloween. Music. Mythical creatures. Songs. Witches.

Williams, Treat. *Air show!* ill. by Robert Neubecker. Hyperion/Disney, 2010. ISBN 978-1-4231-1185-6 Subj: Airplanes, airports.

Williams, Vera B. *A chair for always* ill. by author. HarperCollins, 2009. ISBN 978-0-06-172279-0 Subj: Babies. Family life. Furniture – chairs.

A chair for my mother ill. by author. Greenwillow, 1982. ISBN 978-0-688-00915-1 Subj: Behavior – seeking better things. Caldecott award honor books. Family life. Furniture – chairs.

Cherries and cherry pits ill. by author. Greenwillow, 1986. ISBN 978-0-688-05146-4 Subj: Art. Ethnic groups in the U.S. – African Americans. Imagination.

"More more more," said the baby ill. by author. Greenwillow, 1991. ISBN 978-0-688-09174-3 Subj: Babies. Caldecott award honor books. Ethnic groups in the U.S. Family life.

Music, music for everyone ill. by author. Greenwillow, 1984. ISBN 978-0-688-20604-8 Subj: Family life. Family life – grandmothers. Illness. Music. Musical instruments – accordions.

Something special for me ill. by author. Greenwillow, 1983. ISBN 978-0-688-01807-8 Subj: Birthdays. Family life. Gifts.

Three days on a river in a red canoe ill. by author. Greenwillow, 1981. ISBN 978-0-688-84307-6 Subj: Boats, ships. Camps, camping.

Williams-Garcia, Rita. *Catching the wild waiyuuzee* ill. by Mike Reed. Simon & Schuster, 2000. ISBN 978-0-689-82601-6 Subj: Ethnic groups in the U.S. – African Americans. Hair. Imagination.

Willis, Jeanne. *The boy who lost his bellybutton* ill. by Tony Ross. DK, 2000. ISBN 978-0-7894-6164-3 Subj: Anatomy – navels. Animals. Animals – dogs. Jungle. Reptiles – alligators, crocodiles.

Cottonball Colin ill. by Tony Ross. Eerdmans, 2008. ISBN 978-0-8028-5331-8 Subj: Animals – mice. Behavior – growing up. Family life – mothers.

Delilah D. at the library ill. by Rosie Reeve. Houghton, 2007. ISBN 978-0-618-78195-9 Subj: Imagination. Libraries.

Do little mermaids wet their beds ill. by Penelope Jossen. Whitman, 2001. ISBN 978-0-8075-1668-3 Subj: Behavior. Behavior – bedwetting. Mythical creatures – mermaids, mermen. Rhyming text.

Fly, chick, fly! ill. by Tony Ross. Andersen, 2012. ISBN 978-1-46770314-7 Subj: Activities – flying. Behavior – growing up. Birds – owls. Emotions – fear.

Gorilla! Gorilla! ill. by Tony Ross. Simon & Schuster, 2006. ISBN 978-1-4169-1490-7 Subj: Animals

– gorillas. Animals – mice. Behavior – misunderstanding. World.

Hippospotamus ill. by Tony Ross. Andersen, 2012. ISBN 978-1-4677-0316-1 Subj: Animals. Animals – hippopotamuses. Humorous stories. Rhyming text.

I'm sure I saw a dinosaur ill. by Adrian Reynolds. Andersen, 2011. ISBN 978-0-7613-8093-1 Subj: Dinosaurs. Rhyming text. Sea & seashore – beaches.

Misery Moo ill. by Tony Ross. Holt, 2005. ISBN 978-0-8050-7672-1 Subj: Animals – bulls, cows. Animals – sheep. Emotions – happiness. Emotions – sadness. Friendship.

Mommy do you love me? ill. by Jan Fearnley. Candlewick, 2008. ISBN 978-0-7636-3470-4 Subj: Birds – chickens. Emotions – love.

Susan laughs ill. by Tony Ross. Holt, 2000. ISBN 978-0-8050-6501-5 Subj: Activities. Emotions. Disabilities – physical disabilities. Rhyming text.

Tadpole's promise ill. by Tony Ross. Simon & Schuster, 2005. ISBN 978-0-689-86524-4 Subj: Frogs & toads. Insects – butterflies, caterpillars. Metamorphosis.

That's not funny! ill. by Adrian Reynolds. Andersen, 2010. ISBN 978-0-7613-6445-0 Subj: Animals. Animals – hyenas. Humorous stories.

What did I look like when I was a baby? ill. by Tony Ross. Putnam, 2000. ISBN 978-0-399-23595-5 Subj: Babies. Behavior – growing up. Character traits – appearance.

The wheels on the bus: a read-along sing-along trip to the zoo ill. by Adam Stower. Barrons, 2012. ISBN 978-0-7641-6491-0 Subj: Animals. Buses. Music. Songs. Zoos.

Willis, Nancy Carol. *Red knot: a shorebird's incredible journey* ill. by author. Birdsong, 2006. ISBN 978-0-9662761-5-2 Subj: Birds – sandpipers. Migration.

Wilner, Isabel. *The baby's game book* ill. by Sam Williams. Greenwillow, 2000. ISBN 978-0-688-15916-0 Subj: Babies. Family life. Games.

A garden alphabet ill. by Ashley Wolff. Dutton, 1991. ISBN 978-0-525-44731-3 Subj: ABC books. Animals. Gardens, gardening. Rhyming text.

Wilson, Anna. *Over in the grasslands* ill. by Alison Bartlett. Little, 2000. ISBN 978-0-316-93910-2 Subj: Animals. Counting, numbers. Foreign lands – Africa. Poetry.

Wilson, Anne. *Masha and the firebird* (Bateson-Hill, Margaret)

Noah's ark ill. by author. Chronicle, 2002. ISBN 978-0-8118-3563-3 Subj: Animals. Boats, ships. Caldecott award honor books. Religion – Noah. Weather – floods. Weather – rain. Weather – rainbows.

Wilson, April. *April Wilson's magpie magic* ill. by author. Dial, 1999. ISBN 978-0-8037-2354-2 Subj: Activities – drawing. Birds – magpies. Concepts – color. Concepts – shape. Concepts – size. Wordless.

Wilson, Dorminster. *Mother scorpion country* (Rohmer, Harriet)

Wilson, Gina. *Ignis* ill. by P. J. Lynch. Candlewick, 2001. ISBN 978-0-7636-1623-6 Subj: Behavior – growing up. Dragons. Fire. Self-concept.

Wilson, Karma. *Animal strike at the zoo, it's true!* ill. by Margaret Spengler. HarperCollins, 2006. ISBN 978-0-06-057503-8 Subj: Animals. Rhyming text. Zoos.

Bear feels scared ill. by Jane Chapman. Simon & Schuster, 2008. ISBN 978-0-689-85986-1 Subj: Animals. Animals – bears. Behavior – lost. Emotions – fear. Friendship.

Bear feels sick ill. by Jane Chapman. Simon & Schuster, 2007. ISBN 978-0-689-85985-4 Subj: Animals. Animals – bears. Friendship. Illness.

Bear says thanks ill. by Jane Chapman. Simon & Schuster, 2012. ISBN 978-1-4169-5856-7 Subj: Animals. Animals – bears. Behavior – sharing. Etiquette. Rhyming text.

Bear stays up for Christmas ill. by Jane Chapman. McElderry, 2004. ISBN 978-0-689-85278-7 Subj: Animals. Animals – bears. Forest, woods. Hibernation. Holidays – Christmas. Rhyming text.

Bear's loose tooth ill. by Jane Chapman. Simon & Schuster, 2011. ISBN 978-1-4169-5855-0 Subj: Animals – bears. Rhyming text. Teeth.

The cow loves cookies ill. by Marcellus Hall. Simon & Schuster, 2010. ISBN 978-1-4169-4206-1 Subj: Animals – bulls, cows. Farms. Food. Rhyming text.

Dinos in the snow! ill. by Laura Rader. Little, Brown, 2005. ISBN 978-0-316-00948-5 Subj: Dinosaurs. Rhyming text. Seasons – winter. Weather – snow.

Don't be afraid, Little Pip ill. by Jane Chapman. Simon & Schuster, 2009. ISBN 978-0-689-85987-8 Subj: Birds – penguins. Emotions – fear. Sports – swimming.

Hello, Calico! ill. by Buket Erdogan. Simon & Schuster, 2007. ISBN 978-1-4169-1356-6 Subj: Animals – cats. Format, unusual – board books.

Hogwash! ill. by Jim McMullan. Little, Brown, 2011. ISBN 978-0-316-98840-7 Subj: Activities – bathing. Animals – pigs. Character traits – cleanliness. Farms. Rhyming text.

Horseplay ill. by Jim McMullan. Little, Brown, 2012. ISBN 978-0-316-93842-6 Subj: Activities – playing. Animals – horses, ponies. Careers – farmers. Farms. Rhyming text.

How to bake an American pie ill. by Raúl Colón. Simon & Schuster, 2007. ISBN 978-0-689-86506-0 Subj: Rhyming text. U.S. history.

Mama always comes home ill. by Brooke Dyer. HarperCollins, 2005. ISBN 978-0-06-057506-9 Subj: Animals. Family life – mothers. Rhyming text.

Mama, why? ill. by Simon Mendez. Simon & Schuster, 2011. ISBN 978-1-4169-4205-4 Subj: Animals – polar bears. Bedtime. Character traits – questioning. Rhyming text. Sky.

Moose tracks! ill. by Jack E. Davis. Simon & Schuster, 2006. ISBN 978-0-689-83437-0 Subj: Animals. Animals – moose. Rhyming text.

Mortimer's Christmas manger ill. by Jane Chapman. Simon & Schuster, 2005. ISBN 978-0-689-85511-5 Subj: Animals – mice. Holidays – Christmas. Religion – Nativity.

Mortimer's first garden ill. by Dan Andreasen. Simon & Schuster, 2009. ISBN 978-1-4169-4203-0 Subj: Animals – mice. Gardens, gardening. Religion.

Princess me ill. by Christa Unzner. Simon & Schuster, 2007. ISBN 978-1-4169-4098-2 Subj: Imagination. Rhyming text. Royalty – princesses. Toys.

Sakes alive! a cattle drive ill. by Karla Firehammer. Little, Brown, 2005. ISBN 978-0-316-98841-4 Subj: Activities – driving. Animals – bulls, cows. Rhyming text.

Sleepyhead ill. by John Segal. Simon & Schuster, 2006. ISBN 978-1-4169-1241-5 Subj: Animals – cats. Bedtime. Rhyming text. Toys – bears.

Sweet Briar goes to camp ill. by LeUyen Pham. Penguin, 2005. ISBN 978-0-8037-2971-1 Subj: Animals – porcupines. Animals – skunks. Camps, camping. Emotions – loneliness.

What's in the egg, Little Pip? ill. by Jane Chapman. Simon & Schuster, 2010. ISBN 978-1-4169-4204-7 Subj: Animals – babies. Birds – penguins. Eggs. Family life – new sibling.

Where is home, Little Pip? ill. by Jane Chapman. Simon & Schuster, 2008. ISBN 978-0-689-85983-0 Subj: Animals – babies. Behavior – lost. Birds – penguins. Foreign lands – Antarctic.

Who goes there? ill. by Anna Currey. Simon & Schuster, 2013. ISBN 978-1-4169-8002-5 Subj: Animals – mice. Emotions – fear. Noise, sounds.

Whopper cake ill. by Will Hillenbrand. Simon & Schuster, 2007. ISBN 978-0-689-83844-6 Subj: Activities – baking, cooking. Birthdays. Food. Rhyming text. Tall tales.

Wilson, Sarah. *Friends and pals and brothers, too* ill. by Leo Landry. Holt, 2008. ISBN 978-0-8050-7643-1 Subj: Family life – brothers. Friendship. Rhyming text. Seasons.

Love and kisses ill. by Melissa Sweet. Candlewick, 1999. ISBN 978-1-56402-792-4 Subj: Animals. Emotions – love. Rhyming text.

Wilson, Tony. *The princess and the packet of frozen peas* ill. by Sue deGennaro. Peachtree, 2012. ISBN 978-1-56145-635-2 Subj: Folk & fairy tales. Royalty – princes. Royalty – princesses.

Wilson-Max, Ken. *Fuhara means happy: a book of Swahili words* ill. by author. Hyperion, 2000. ISBN 978-0-7868-2480-9 Subj: Foreign lands – Kenya. Foreign languages.

Halala means welcome: a book of Zulu words ill. by author. Hyperion, 1998. ISBN 978-0-7868-0414-6 Subj: Foreign lands – South Africa. Foreign languages.

Max's starry night ill. by author. Hyperion, 2001. ISBN 978-0-7868-0553-2 Subj: Animals – elephants. Emotions – fear. Ethnic groups in the U.S. – African Americans. Stars.

Wimmer, Sonja. *The word collector* ill. by author. IPG/Cuento de Luz, 2012. ISBN 978-8-41524-134-8 Subj: Behavior – collecting things. Language.

Winans, CeCe, et al. *Colorful world* ill. by Melodee Strong. Maren Green, 2008. ISBN 978-1-934277-13-3 Subj: Character traits – individuality. Songs.

Winch, John. *Keeping up with Grandma* ill. by author. Holiday, 2000. ISBN 978-0-8234-1563-2 Subj: Activities. Family life – grandfathers. Family life – grandmothers.

Winer, Yvonne. *Birds build nests* ill. by Tony Oliver. Charlesbridge, 2002. ISBN 978-1-57091-500-0 Subj: Birds. Homes, houses.

Butterflies fly ill. by Karen Lloyd-Jones. Charlesbridge, 2001. ISBN 978-1-57091-446-1 Subj: Activities – flying. Insects – butterflies, caterpillars.

Frogs sing songs ill. by Tony Oliver. Charlesbridge, 2003. ISBN 978-1-57091-548-2 Subj: Behavior. Ecology. Frogs & toads. Noise, sounds.

Wing, Natasha. *Go to bed, monster!* ill. by Sylvie Kantorovitz. Harcourt, 2007. ISBN 978-0-15-205775-6 Subj: Activities – drawing. Bedtime. Imagination. Monsters.

How to raise a dinosaur ill. by Pablo Bernasconi. Running Press, 2010. ISBN 978-0-7624-3342-1 Subj: Dinosaurs. Format, unusual – toy & movable books. Pets.

Jalapeño bagels ill. by Robert Casilla. Atheneum, 1996. ISBN 978-0-02-793077-1 Subj: Ethnic groups in the U.S. Family life. Food. School.

The night before the night before Christmas ill. by Mike Lester. Grosset, 2002. ISBN 978-0-448-42872-7 Subj: Holidays – Christmas. Rhyming text.

Winget, Susan. *Sam the Snowman* ill. by author. HarperCollins, 2008. ISBN 978-0-06-114475-2 Subj: Character traits – generosity. Seasons – winter. Snowmen. Weather – snow.

Tucker's four-carrot school day ill. by author. HarperCollins, 2005. ISBN 978-0-06-054643-4 Subj: Animals – rabbits. Friendship. School – first day.

Winkelman, Barbara Gaines. *Puffer's surprise* ill. by Steven James Petruccio. Soundprints, 2003. ISBN 978-1-59249-032-5 Subj: Fish. Foreign lands – Galapagos Islands. Sea & seashore.

Sockeye's journey home ill. by Joanie Popeo. Soundprints, 2000. ISBN 978-1-56899-829-9 Subj: Ecology. Fish. Migration.

Winne, Joanne. *Blue in my world* ill. with photos. Children's Press, 2000. ISBN 978-0-516-23123-5 Subj: Concepts – color.

Green in my world ill. with photos. Children's Press, 2000. ISBN 978-0-516-23124-2 Subj: Concepts – color.

Let's get ready for Kwanzaa ill. with photos. Children's Press, 2001. ISBN 978-0-516-23175-4 Subj: Ethnic groups in the U.S. – African Americans. Holidays – Kwanzaa.

Red in my world Ill. with photos. Children's Press, 2001. ISBN 978-0-516-23126-6 Subj: Concepts – color.

Winnick, Karen B. *Barn sneeze* ill. by author. Children's Press, 2000. ISBN 978-1-56397-948-4 Subj: Animals. Noise, sounds.

Sybil's night ride ill. by author. Boyds Mills, 2000. ISBN 978-1-56397-697-1 Subj: Animals – horses, ponies. Night. U.S. history. War.

A year goes round ill. by author. Boyds Mills, 2001. ISBN 978-1-56397-898-2 Subj: Days of the week, months of the year. Poetry.

Winnie-the-Pooh's A B C ill. by Ernest H. Shepard. Inspired by A. A. Milne; created with Gallaudet University Pr.; sign language ill. by Lois A. Lehman; sign language consultant Lvey Pittle Wallace. Dutton, 2001. ISBN 978-0-525-46714-4 Subj: ABC books. Disabilities – deafness. Language. Senses – hearing. Sign language.

Winstead, Rosie. *Ruby and Bubbles* ill. by author. Penguin, 2006. ISBN 978-0-8037-3024-3 Subj: Behavior – bullying, teasing. Birds. Friendship. Pets.

Winter, Jeanette. *Angelina's island* ill. by author. Farrar, 2007. ISBN 978-0-374-30349-5 Subj: Emotions – loneliness. Ethnic groups in the U.S. – Jamaican Americans. Immigrants.

Biblioburro: a true story from Colombia ill. by author. Simon & Schuster, 2010. ISBN 978-1-4169-9778-8 Subj: Animals – donkeys. Books, reading. Foreign lands – Colombia. Libraries.

The Christmas tree ship ill. by author. Philomel, 1994. ISBN 978-0-399-22693-9 Subj: Boats, ships. Holidays – Christmas. Trees. U.S. history.

Cowboy Charlie ill. by author. Harcourt, 1995. ISBN 978-0-15-200857-4 Subj: Activities – playing. Art. Careers – artists. Cowboys, cowgirls. U.S. history – frontier & pioneer life.

Follow the drinking gourd ill. by author. Dragonfly Books, 1992. ISBN 978-0-679-81997-4 Subj: Ethnic groups in the U.S. – African Americans. Sailors. Slavery. Stars. U.S. history.

Henri's scissors ill. by author. Simon & Schuster, 2013. ISBN 978-1-4424-6484-1 Subj: Art. Careers – artists. Foreign lands – France. Illness. Old age.

Kali's song ill. by author. Random House, 2012. ISBN 978-0-375-87022-4 Subj: Cave dwellers. Character traits – individuality. Music. Sports – hunting.

The librarian of Basra: a true story from Iraq ill. by author. Harcourt, 2005. ISBN 978-0-15-205445-8 Subj: Careers – librarians. Foreign lands – Iraq. Libraries. War.

Mama: a true story, in which a baby hippo loses his mama during a tsunami, but finds a new home ill. by author. Harcourt, 2006. ISBN 978-0-15-205495-3 Subj: Animals – hippopotamuses. Family life – mothers. Reptiles – turtles, tortoises. Tsunamis.

My baby ill. by author. Farrar, 2001. ISBN 978-0-374-35103-8 Subj: Art. Babies. Behavior – growing up. Clothing. Foreign lands – Africa.

Nasreen's secret school: a true story from Afghanistan ill. by author. Beach Lane Books, 2009. ISBN 978-1-4169-9437-4 Subj: Behavior – secrets. Foreign lands – Afghanistan. Gender roles. School.

Niño's mask ill. by author. Dial, 2003. ISBN 978-0-8037-2807-3 Subj: Clothing – costumes. Fairs, festivals. Foreign lands – Mexico.

Once upon a time in Chicago ill. by author. Hyperion, 2000. ISBN 978-0-7868-2404-5 Subj: Careers – musicians. Music. Musical instruments – bands.

The tale of Pale Male: a true story ill. by author. Harcourt, 2007. ISBN 978-0-15-205972-9 Subj: Birds – hawks.

Wangari's trees of peace: a true story from Africa ill. by author. Harcourt, 2008. ISBN 978-0-15-206545-4 Subj: Character traits – responsibility. Ecology. Foreign lands – Kenya. Trees.

The watcher: Jane Goodall's life with the chimps ill. by author. Random House, 2011. ISBN 978-0-375-86774-3 Subj: Animals – chimpanzees. Careers – scientists. Foreign lands – Tanzania. Nature.

Winter, Jonah. *Barack* ill. by A. G. Ford. HarperCollins, 2008. ISBN 978-0-06-170392-8 Subj: Ethnic groups in the U.S. – African Americans. U.S. history.

Diego ill. by Jeanette Winter. Knopf, 1991. ISBN 978-0-679-91987-2 Subj: Art. Careers – artists. Foreign languages.

Dizzy ill. by Sean Qualls. Scholastic, 2006. ISBN 978-0-439-50737-0 Subj: Careers – musicians. Ethnic groups in the U.S. – African Americans. Music.

Here comes the garbage barge! ill. by Red Nose Studio. Random House, 2010. ISBN 978-0-375-95218-0 Subj: Boats, ships. Careers – sanitation workers.

Just behave, Pablo Picasso! ill. by Kevin Hawkes. Scholastic, 2012. ISBN 978-0-545-13291-6 Subj: Activities – painting. Art. Careers – artists.

Muhammad Ali: champion of the world ill. by François Roca. Random House, 2008. ISBN 978-0-375-83622-0 Subj: Ethnic groups in the U.S. – African Americans. Sports – boxing. U.S. history.

Sonia Sotomayor: a judge grows in the Bronx / la juez que creció en el Bronx ill. by Edel Rodriguez. Atheneum, 2009. ISBN 978-1-4424-0303-1 Subj: Careers – judges. Ethnic groups in the U.S. – Hispanic Americans. Foreign languages.

Winters, Kari-Lynn. *Gift days* ill. by Stephen Taylor. Fitzhenry & Whiteside, 2012. ISBN 978-1-55455-192-7 Subj: Character traits – perseverance. Family life – brothers & sisters. Foreign lands – Uganda. School.

Winters, Kay. *Abe Lincoln, the boy who loved books* ill. by Nancy Carpenter. Simon & Schuster, 2003. ISBN 978-0-689-82554-5 Subj: Books, reading. U.S. history.

The bears go to school ill. by Katherine Kirkland. Whitman, 2013. ISBN 978-0-8075-0592-2 Subj: Animals – bears. School.

The teeny tiny ghost ill. by Lynn Munsinger. HarperCollins, 1997. ISBN 978-0-06-025684-5 Subj: Emotions – fear. Ghosts. Holidays – Halloween.

The teeny tiny ghost and the monster ill. by Lynn Munsinger. HarperCollins, 2004. ISBN 978-0-06-028885-3 Subj: Contests. Ghosts. Monsters. School.

This school year will be the best! ill. by Renée Williams-Andriani. Penguin, 2010. ISBN 978-0-525-42775-4 Subj: School – first day.

Tiger trail ill. by Laura Regan. Simon & Schuster, 2000. ISBN 978-0-689-82323-7 Subj: Animals – tigers. Behavior – growing up. Nature.

Whooo's haunting the teeny tiny ghost? ill. by Lynn Munsinger. HarperCollins, 1999. ISBN 978-0-06-027359-0 Subj: Emotions – fear. Ghosts. Holidays – Halloween.

Wolf watch ill. by Laura Regan. Simon & Schuster, 1997. ISBN 978-0-689-80218-8 Subj: Animals. Animals – wolves. Behavior – growing up. Nature. Rhyming text.

Winthrop, Elizabeth. *As the crow flies* ill. by Joan Sandin. Clarion, 1998. ISBN 978-0-395-77612-4 Subj: Divorce. Family life – fathers.

Bear and Mrs. Duck ill. by Patience Brewster. Holiday, 1988. ISBN 978-0-8234-0687-6 Subj: Activities – babysitting. Animals – bears. Birds – ducks.

Bear's Christmas surprise ill. by Patience Brewster. Holiday, 1991. ISBN 978-0-8234-0888-7 Subj: Activities – babysitting. Animals – bears. Birds – ducks. Holidays – Christmas.

A child is born: the Christmas story ill. by Charles Mikolaycak. Holiday, 1983. ISBN 978-0-8234-0472-8 Subj: Holidays – Christmas. Religion – Nativity.

Halloween hats ill. by Sue Truesdell. Holt, 2002. ISBN 978-0-8050-6386-8 Subj: Clothing – hats. Holidays – Halloween. Parades. Rhyming text.

He is risen: the Easter story ill. by Charles Mikolaycak. Holiday, 1985. ISBN 978-0-8234-0547-3 Subj: Holidays – Easter. Religion.

I'm the Boss! ill. by Mary Morgan. Holiday, 1994. ISBN 978-0-8234-1113-9 Subj: Animals – dogs. Character traits – assertiveness. Family life.

Promises ill. by Betsy Lewin. Clarion, 2000. ISBN 978-0-395-82272-2 Subj: Emotions. Family life – daughters. Family life – mothers. Illness – cancer.

Shoes ill. by William Joyce. HarperCollins, 1986. ISBN 978-0-06-026592-2 Subj: Clothing – shoes. Rhyming text.

Sledding ill. by Sarah Wilson. HarperCollins, 1989. ISBN 978-0-06-026566-3 Subj: Rhyming text. Sports – sledding.

Squashed in the middle ill. by Pat Cummings. Holt, 2005. ISBN 978-0-8050-6497-1 Subj: Ethnic groups in the U.S. – African Americans. Family life. Self-concept. Sleepovers.

Vasilissa the beautiful ill. by Alexander Koshkin. HarperCollins, 1991. ISBN 978-0-06-021663-4 Subj: Folk & fairy tales. Foreign lands – Russia. Royalty. Toys – dolls. Witches.

Winton, Tim. *The deep* ill. by Karen Louise. Tricycle, 2000. ISBN 978-1-58246-024-6 Subj: Animals – dolphins. Emotions – fear. Nature. Sea & seashore. Sports – swimming.

Wisdom, Jude. *Whatever Wanda wanted* ill. by author. Fogelman, 2002. ISBN 978-0-8037-2693-2 Subj: Behavior. Character traits – selfishness. Islands. Kites.

Wise, Bill. *Silent star: the story of deaf major leaguer William Hoy* ill. by Adam Gustavson. Lee & Low, 2012. ISBN 978-1-60060-411-9 Subj: Disabilities – deafness. Sports – baseball. U.S. history.

Wise, William. *Dinosaurs forever* ill. by Lynn Munsinger. Dial, 2000. ISBN 978-0-8037-2114-2 Subj: Dinosaurs. Humorous stories. Poetry.

Zany zoo ill. by Lynn Munsinger. Houghton, 2006. ISBN 978-0-618-18891-8 Subj: Animals. Language. Zoos.

Wishinsky, Frieda. *Please, Louise!* ill. by Marie-Louise Gay. Groundwood, 2007. ISBN 978-0-88899-796-8 Subj: Animals – dogs. Behavior – wishing. Family life – brothers & sisters.

What's up, bear? a book about opposites ill. by Sean L. Moore. OwlKids, 2012. ISBN 978-1-926973-41-8 Subj: Activities – traveling. Concepts – opposites. Language. Toys – bears.

Where are you, Bear? a Canadian alphabet adventure ill. by Sean L. Moore. Owl Kids, 2010. ISBN 978-1-897349-91-5 Subj: ABC books. Foreign lands – Canada.

You're mean, Lily Jean! ill. by Kady MacDonald Denton. Whitman, 2011. ISBN 978-0-8075-9476-6 Subj: Activities – playing. Family life – sisters. Friendship.

Wisniewski, David. *Elfwyn's saga* ill. by author. Lothrop, 1990. ISBN 978-0-688-09590-1 Subj: Folk & fairy tales. Foreign lands – Iceland. Disabilities – blindness. Magic.

Golem ill. by author. Clarion, 1996. ISBN 978-0-395-72618-1 Subj: Caldecott award books. Folk & fairy tales. Foreign lands – Czechoslovakia. Jewish culture. Mythical creatures.

Rain player ill. by author. Houghton, 1991. ISBN 978-0-395-55112-7 Subj: Foreign lands – Central America. Foreign lands – Mexico. Games. Indians of Central America – Maya.

Sumo Mouse ill. by author. Chronicle, 2002. ISBN 978-0-8118-3492-6 Subj: Animals – mice. Careers – storekeepers. Crime. Foreign lands – Japan. Toys.

Sundiata: lion king of Mali ill. by author. Clarion, 1992. ISBN 978-0-395-61302-3 Subj: Disabilities. Folk & fairy tales. Foreign lands – Mali. Royalty – kings.

Tough cookie ill. by author. Lothrop, 1999. ISBN 978-0-688-15338-0 Subj: Food. Humorous stories.

The warrior and the wise man ill. by author. Lothrop, 1989. ISBN 978-0-688-07890-4 Subj: Character traits – wisdom. Folk & fairy tales. Foreign lands – Japan. Multiple births – twins. Royalty.

Withrow, Sarah. *Be a baby* ill. by Manuel Monroy. Groundwood, 2007. ISBN 978-0-88899-776-0 Subj: Babies. Bedtime. Lullabies.

Witte, Anna. *Lola's fandango* ill. by Micha Archer. Barefoot, 2011. ISBN 978-1-84686-174-1 Subj: Activities – dancing. Birthdays. Ethnic groups in the U.S. – Hispanic Americans. Family life – mothers.

The parrot Tico Tango ill. by author. Barefoot, 2004. ISBN 978-1-84148-243-9 Subj: Animals. Behavior – greed. Birds – parakeets, parrots. Cumulative tales. Jungle. Rhyming text.

Witter, Bret. *Dewey: there's a cat in the library!* (Myron, Vicki)

Wiviott, Meg. *Benno and the night of broken glass* ill. by Josée Bisaillon. Lerner/Kar-Ben, 2010. ISBN 978-0-8225-9929-6 Subj: Animals – cats. Foreign lands – Germany. Holocaust. Jewish culture.

Woelfle, Gretchen. *Katje the windmill cat* ill. by Nicola Bayley. Candlewick, 2001. ISBN 978-0-7636-1347-1 Subj: Animals – cats. Foreign lands – Holland. Weather – floods.

Wohl, Lauren L. *Matzoh mouse* ill. by Pamela Keavney. HarperCollins, 1991. ISBN 978-0-06-026581-6 Subj: Family life. Holidays – Passover. Jewish culture. Religion.

Wohlrabe, Sarah C. *Helping you heal, a book about nurses* ill. by Eric Thomas. Picture Window, 2004. ISBN 978-1-4048-0086-1 Subj: Careers – nurses.

Helping you learn, a book about teachers ill. by Eric Thomas. Picture Window, 2004. ISBN 978-1-4048-0084-7 Subj: Careers – teachers.

Wojciechowski, Susan. *The best Halloween of all* ill. by Susan Meddaugh. 2nd ed. Candlewick, 1998. ISBN 978-0-7636-0458-5 Subj: Clothing – costumes. Holidays – Halloween.

The Christmas miracle of Jonathan Toomey ill. by P. J. Lynch. Candlewick, 1995. ISBN 978-1-56402-320-9 Subj: Careers – woodcarvers. Friendship. Holidays – Christmas. Religion.

A fine St. Patrick's Day ill. by Tom Curry. Random House, 2004. ISBN 978-0-375-92386-9 Subj: Character traits – kindness. Contests. Holidays – St. Patrick's Day.

Wojtowycz, David. *Animal antics from 1 to 10* ill. by author. Holiday, 2000. ISBN 978-0-8234-1552-6 Subj: Animals. Counting, numbers. Hotels.

A cuddle for Claude ill. by author. Dutton, 2001. ISBN 978-0-525-46691-8 Subj: Animals – polar bears. Behavior – running away. Family life – grandmothers.

Elephant Joe, Brave Knight! a tale of knightly chivalrousness ill. by author. Random House, 2012. ISBN 978-0-307-93087-3 Subj: Animals – elephants. Dragons. Knights.

Wojtusik, Elizabeth. *Kitty up!* ill. by Sachiko Yoshikawa. Dial, 2008. ISBN 978-0-8037-3278-0 Subj: Animals – cats. Animals – dogs. Rhyming text.

Wolf, Alex de. *Mop and the birthday picnic* (Schaap, Martine)

Mop's backyard concert (Schaap, Martine)

Mop's mountain adventure (Schaap, Martine)

Mop's treasure hunt (Schaap, Martine)

Wolf, Jake. *Daddy, could I have an elephant?* ill. by Marylin Hafner. Greenwillow, 1996. ISBN 978-0-688-13295-8 Subj: Animals. Family life – fathers. Pets.

Wolf, Karina. *The Insomniacs* ill. by Sean Hilts and Ben Hilts. Putnam, 2012. ISBN 978-0-399-25665-3 Subj: Night. Sleep.

Wolf, Sallie. *Truck stuck* ill. by Andy Robert Davies. Charlesbridge, 2008. ISBN 978-1-58089-119-6 Subj: Rhyming text. Trucks.

Wolf, Winfried. *The Easter bunny* ill. by Agnès Mathieu. Dial, 1986. ISBN 978-0-8037-0239-4 Subj: Animals – rabbits. Holidays – Easter.

Wolfe, Myra. *Charlotte Jane battles bedtime* ill. by Maria Monescillo. Houghton, 2011. ISBN 978-0-15-206150-0 Subj: Bedtime. Pirates.

Wolff, Ashley. *Baby Bear counts one* ill. by author. Simon & Schuster, 2013. ISBN 978-1-4424-4158-3 Subj: Animals – bears. Counting, numbers. Hibernation. Seasons – winter.

Baby Bear sees blue ill. by author. Simon & Schuster, 2012. ISBN 978-1-4424-1306-1 Subj: Animals – bears. Concepts – color. Nature.

I call my grandma Nana ill. by author. Tricycle, 2009. ISBN 978-1-58246-251-6 Subj: Family life – grandmothers. Foreign languages. Names. Rhyming text.

I call my grandpa Papa ill. by author. Tricycle, 2009. ISBN 978-1-58246-252-3 Subj: Family life – grandfathers. Foreign languages. Names. Rhyming text.

Stella and Roy go camping ill. by author. Dutton, 1999. ISBN 978-0-525-45864-7 Subj: Camps, camping. Family life. Sibling rivalry.

When Lucy goes out walking: a puppy's first year ill. by author. Holt, 2009. ISBN 978-0-8050-8168-8 Subj: Animals – dogs. Days of the week, months of the year. Rhyming text.

Wolff, Ferida. *It is the wind* ill. by James Ransome. HarperCollins, 2005. ISBN 978-0-06-028192-2 Subj: Animals. Bedtime. Noise, sounds. Sleep.

On Halloween night by Ferida Wolff and Dolores Kozielski ill. by Dolores Avendaño. Tambourine, 1994. ISBN 978-0-688-12973-6 Subj: Clothing – costumes. Counting, numbers. Cumulative tales. Holidays – Halloween. Rhyming text. Witches.

The story blanket by Ferida Wolff and Harriet May Savitz ill. by Elena Odriozola. Peachtree, 2008. ISBN 978-1-56145-466-2 Subj: Behavior – sharing. Friendship.

Wolff, Nancy. *It's time for school with Tallulah* ill. by author. Holt, 2007. ISBN 978-0-8050-7962-3 Subj: Activities – playing. Animals – cats. School.

Tallulah in the kitchen ill. by author. Holt, 2005. ISBN 978-0-8050-7463-5 Subj: Activities – baking, cooking. Animals – cats. Food.

Wolff, Patricia Rae. *A new, improved Santa* ill. by Lynne Cravath. Orchard, 2002. ISBN 978-0-439-35249-9 Subj: Holidays – Christmas. Santa Claus. Self-concept.

The toll-bridge troll ill. by Kimberly Bulcken Root. Browndeer, 1998. ISBN 978-0-15-277665-7 Subj: Mythical creatures – trolls. Riddles & jokes. School.

Wolkstein, Diane. *The banza: a Haitian story* ill. by Marc Brown. Dial, 1981. ISBN 978-0-8037-0429-9 Subj: Animals – goats. Animals – tigers. Character traits – bravery. Folk & fairy tales. Music. Musical instruments – banjos.

The day Ocean came to visit ill. by Steve Johnson and Lou Fancher. Harcourt, 2001. ISBN 978-0-15-201774-3 Subj: Folk & fairy tales – pourquoi tales. Foreign lands – Africa. Moon. Sea & seashore. Sun.

Little Mouse's painting ill. by Mary Jane Begin. Morrow, 1992. ISBN 978-0-688-07610-8 Subj: Animals. Animals – mice. Careers – artists. Friendship.

Step by step ill. by Joseph A. Smith. Morrow, 1994. ISBN 978-0-688-10316-3 Subj: Friendship. Insects – ants. Insects – grasshoppers.

Sun Mother wakes the world ill. by Bronwyn Bancroft. HarperCollins, 2004. ISBN 978-0-688-13916-2 Subj: Australian aborigines. Creation. Folk & fairy tales. Foreign lands – Australia.

Wong, Benedict Norbert. *Lo and behold* ill. by author. Taiji, 2003. ISBN 978-0-9728192-0-6 Subj: Dragons. Ethnic groups in the U.S. – Chinese Americans. Family life. Food. Self-concept.

Lo and behold, good enough to eat ill. by author. Taiji, 2003. ISBN 978-0-9728192-1-3 Subj: Dragons. Ethnic groups in the U.S. – Chinese Americans. Family life. Food. Self-concept.

Wong, Janet S. *Buzz* ill. by Margaret Chodos-Irvine. Harcourt, 2000. ISBN 978-0-15-201923-5 Subj: Family life. Insects – bees. Noise, sounds.

The dumpster diver ill. by David Roberts. Candlewick, 2007. ISBN 978-0-7636-2380-7 Subj: Communities, neighborhoods. Ecology.

Grump ill. by John Wallace. McElderry, 2001. ISBN 978-0-689-83485-1 Subj: Babies. Family life – mothers. Rhyming text. Sleep.

Hide and seek ill. by Margaret Chodos-Irvine. Harcourt, 2005. ISBN 978-0-15-204934-8 Subj: Behavior – hiding. Counting, numbers. Rhyming text.

Homegrown house ill. by E. B. Lewis. Simon & Schuster, 2009. ISBN 978-0-689-84718-9 Subj: Homes, houses. Moving. Poetry.

This next New Year ill. by Yangsook Choi. Farrar, 2000. ISBN 978-0-374-35503-6 Subj: Ethnic groups in the U.S. Family life. Holidays – Chinese New Year.

The trip back home ill. by Bo Jia. Harcourt, 2000. ISBN 978-0-15-200784-3 Subj: Activities – traveling. Ethnic groups in the U.S. – Korean Americans. Family life. Foreign lands – Korea.

Woo, Alan. *Maggie's chopsticks* ill. by Isabelle Malenfant. Kids Can, 2012. ISBN 978-1-55453-619-1 Subj: Character traits – individuality. Character traits – persistence. Ethnic groups in the U.S. – Chinese Americans. Family life. Food.

Wood, Audrey. *Alphabet adventure* ill. by Bruce Wood. Blue Sky, 2001. ISBN 978-0-439-08069-9 Subj: ABC books. Behavior – lost & found possessions.

Alphabet rescue ill. by Bruce Wood. Scholastic, 2006. ISBN 978-0-439-85316-3 Subj: ABC books. Careers – firefighters. Trucks.

Birdsong ill. by Robert Florczak. Harcourt, 1997. ISBN 978-0-15-200014-1 Subj: Birds. Flowers. Songs.

The Birthday Queen ill. by Don Wood. Scholastic, 2013. ISBN 978-0-545-41474-6 Subj: Birthdays. Family life – mothers. Parties.

Blue sky ill. by author. Scholastic, 2012. ISBN 978-0-545-31610-1 Subj: Nature. Sky.

The Bunyans ill. by David Shannon. Blue Sky, 1996. ISBN 978-0-590-48089-5 Subj: Mythical creatures. Nature. Tall tales. U.S. history – frontier & pioneer life.

The Christmas adventure of Space Elf Sam ill. by Bruce Wood. Blue Sky, 1998. ISBN 978-0-590-03143-1 Subj: Aliens. Holidays – Christmas. Santa Claus. Space & space ships.

A cowboy Christmas ill. by Robert Florczak. Simon & Schuster, 2000. ISBN 978-0-689-82190-5 Subj: Accidents. Cowboys, cowgirls. Family life. Holidays – Christmas.

The deep blue sea: a book of colors ill. by Bruce Wood. Scholastic, 2005. ISBN 978-0-439-75382-1 Subj: Concepts – color. Sea & seashore.

A dog needs a bone ill. by author. Scholastic, 2007. ISBN 978-0-545-00005-5 Subj: Animals – dogs. Rhyming text.

Elbert's bad word ill. by author. Harcourt, 1988. ISBN 978-0-15-225320-2 Subj: Behavior – misbehavior. Family life. Language.

The flying dragon room ill. by Mark Teague. Blue Sky, 1996. ISBN 978-0-590-48193-9 Subj: Activities – making things. Imagination. Magic.

Heckedy Peg ill. by Don Wood. Harcourt, 1987. ISBN 978-0-15-233678-3 Subj: Behavior – talking to strangers. Character traits – cleverness. Days of the week, months of the year. Folk & fairy tales. Food. Witches.

It's Duffy time! ill. by Don Wood. Scholastic, 2012. ISBN 978-0-545-22089-7 Subj: Animals – dogs. Clocks, watches. Sleep. Time.

Jubal's wish ill. by Don Wood. Blue Sky, 2000. ISBN 978-0-439-16964-6 Subj: Behavior – wishing. Friendship. Frogs & toads. Reptiles – lizards.

King Bidgood's in the bathtub ill. by Don Wood. Harcourt, 1985. ISBN 978-0-15-242730-6 Subj: Activities. Activities – bathing. Caldecott award honor books. Humorous stories. Royalty – kings.

Little Penguin's tale ill. by author. Harcourt, 1989. ISBN 978-0-15-246475-2 Subj: Activities – dancing. Animals. Animals – whales. Birds. Birds – penguins. Foreign lands – Antarctic.

Merry Christmas, big hungry bear (Wood, Don)

Moonflute ill. by Don Wood. Harcourt, 1986. ISBN 978-0-15-255337-1 Subj: Bedtime. Moon. Night. Sleep.

The napping house ill. by Don Wood. Harcourt, 1984. ISBN 978-0-15-256708-8 Subj: Animals. Cumulative tales. Family life – grandmothers. Rhyming text. Sleep.

The napping house wakes up ill. by Don Wood. Harcourt, 1994. ISBN 978-0-15-200890-1 Subj: Animals. Family life – grandmothers. Format, unusual – toy & movable books. Insects – fleas. Rhyming text. Sleep.

Oh my baby bear! ill. by author. Harcourt, 1990. ISBN 978-0-15-257698-1 Subj: Animals – bears. Bedtime. Behavior – growing up.

Piggies (Wood, Don)

Piggies [board book] (Wood, Don)

Piggy Pie Po ill. by Don Wood. Harcourt, 2010. ISBN 978-0-15-202494-9 Subj: Animals – pigs. Rhyming text.

The rainbow bridge ill. by Robert Florczak. Harcourt, 1995. ISBN 978-0-15-265475-7 Subj: Animals – dolphins. Creation. Folk & fairy tales. Indians of North America – Chumash.

Silly Sally ill. by author. Harcourt, 1992. ISBN 978-0-15-274428-1 Subj: Activities – traveling. Animals. Cumulative tales. Rhyming text.

Silly Sally [board book] ill. by author. Harcourt, 2007. ISBN 978-0-15-205902-6 Subj: Activities – traveling. Animals. Cumulative tales. Format, unusual – board books. Poetry.

Sweet dream pie ill. by Mark Teague. Blue Sky, 1998. ISBN 978-0-590-96204-9 Subj: Bedtime. Dreams.

Ten little fish ill. by Bruce Wood. Blue Sky, 2004. ISBN 978-0-439-63569-1 Subj: Counting, numbers. Fish. Foreign lands – South Sea Islands. Rhyming text.

The Tickleoctopus ill. by Don Wood. Harcourt, 1994. ISBN 978-0-15-287000-3 Subj: Activities – playing. Cave dwellers. Family life. Mythical creatures.

Weird parents ill. by author. Dial, 1990. ISBN 978-0-8037-0649-1 Subj: Character traits – being different. Emotions – embarrassment. Family life.

When the root children wake up by Audrey Wood and Sibylle Von Olfers ill. by Ned Bittinger. Scholastic, 2002. ISBN 978-0-590-42517-9 Subj: Flowers. Insects. Nature. Seasons – spring. Songs.

Wood, Don. *Merry Christmas, big hungry bear* by Don Wood and Audrey Wood ill. by Don Wood. Blue Sky, 2002. ISBN 978-0-439-32092-4 Subj: Animals – mice. Behavior – sharing. Gifts. Holidays – Christmas. Shopping.

Piggies by Don Wood and Audrey Wood ill. by Don Wood. Harcourt, 1991. ISBN 978-0-15-256341-7 Subj: Animals – pigs. Games.

Piggies [board book] by Don Wood and Audrey Wood ill. by Don Wood. Harcourt, 1991. ISBN 978-0-15-205632-2 Subj: Animals – pigs. Format, unusual – board books. Games.

Wood, Douglas. *Aunt Mary's rose* ill. by LeUyen Pham. Candlewick, 2010. ISBN 978-0-7636-1090-6 Subj: Death. Family life – aunts, uncles. Flowers – roses. Gardens, gardening.

Grandad's prayers of the earth ill. by P. J Lynch. Candlewick, 1999. ISBN 978-0-7636-0660-2 Subj: Death. Emotions – grief. Family life – grandfathers. Nature.

No one but you ill. by P. J. Lynch. Candlewick, 2011. ISBN 978-0-7636-3848-1 Subj: Nature. Senses.

Nothing to do ill. by Wendy Anderson Halperin. Penguin, 2006. ISBN 978-0-525-47656-6 Subj: Activities – playing.

Old Turtle ill. by Cheng-Khee Chee. Pfeifer-Hamilton, 1991. ISBN 978-0-938586-48-7 Subj: Animals. Ecology. Religion.

The secret of saying thanks ill. by Greg Shed. Simon & Schuster, 2005. ISBN 978-0-689-85410-1 Subj: Emotions – happiness. Nature.

What dads can't do ill. by Doug Cushman. Simon & Schuster, 2000. ISBN 978-0-689-82620-7 Subj: Family life – fathers.

What grandmas can't do ill. by Doug Cushman. Simon & Schuster, 2005. ISBN 978-0-689-84647-2 Subj: Family life – grandmothers.

What moms can't do ill. by Doug Cushman. Simon & Schuster, 2000. ISBN 978-0-689-83358-8 Subj: Family life – mothers.

What teachers can't do ill. by Doug Cushman. Simon & Schuster, 2002. ISBN 978-0-689-84644-1 Subj: Careers – teachers. Dinosaurs. School.

When a dad says "I love you" ill. by Jennifer A. Bell. Simon & Schuster, 2013. ISBN 978-0-689-87532-8 Subj: Animals. Emotions – love. Family life – fathers.

Where the sunrise begins ill. by Wendy Popp. Simon & Schuster, 2010. ISBN 978-0-689-86172-7 Subj: Nature. Sun.

Wood, Jakki. *A hole in the road* ill. by author. Frances Lincoln, 2008. ISBN 978-1-84507-286-5 Subj: Careers – construction workers. Machines.

Moo moo, brown cow ill. by Rog Bonner. Harcourt, 1992. ISBN 978-0-15-200533-7 Subj: Animals. Animals – cats. Concepts – color. Counting, numbers. Farms.

Never say boo to a goose! ill. by Clare Beaton. Barefoot, 2002. ISBN 978-1-84148-255-2 Subj: Animals. Animals – cats. Birds – geese. Farms.

Wood, Michele. *Going back home* ill. by author. Children's Book Press, 1996. ISBN 978-0-89239-137-0 Subj: Art. Careers – artists. Ethnic groups in the U.S. – African Americans.

Wood, Muriel. *Old bird* (Morck, Irene)

Wood, Nancy C. *Mr. and Mrs. God in the creation kitchen* ill. by Timothy Basil Ering. Candlewick,

2006. ISBN 978-0-7636-1258-0 Subj: Creation. Religion.

Woodhull, Anne Love. *The buzz on bees: why are they disappearing?* (Rotner, Shelley)

Every season (Rotner, Shelley)

Woodruff, Elvira. *Can you guess where we're going?* ill. by Cynthia Fisher. Holiday, 1998. ISBN 978-0-8234-1387-4 Subj: Family life – grandfathers. Libraries.

The memory coat ill. by Michael Dooling. Scholastic, 1999. ISBN 978-0-590-67717-2 Subj: Clothing – coats. Ethnic groups in the U.S. – Russian Americans. Immigrants. Jewish culture. Memories, memory.

Small beauties: the journey of Darcy Heart O'Hara ill. by Adam Rex. Random House, 2006. ISBN 978-0-375-92686-0 Subj: Family life. Foreign lands – Ireland. Immigrants. U.S. history.

Woodson, Jacqueline. *Coming on home soon* ill. by E. B. Lewis. Putnam, 2004. ISBN 978-0-399-23748-5 Subj: Caldecott award honor books. Ethnic groups in the U.S. – African Americans. Family life – grandmothers. Family life – mothers. U.S. history. War.

Each kindness ill. by E. B. Lewis. Penguin, 2012. ISBN 978-0-399-24652-4 Subj: Behavior – bullying, teasing. Careers – teachers. Character traits – being different. Ethnic groups in the U.S. – African Americans. Poverty. School.

The other side ill. by E. B. Lewis. Putnam, 2001. ISBN 978-0-399-23116-2 Subj: Cities, towns. Prejudice. Seasons – summer.

Pecan pie baby ill. by Sophie Blackall. Penguin, 2010. ISBN 978-0-399-23987-8 Subj: Babies. Ethnic groups in the U.S. – African Americans. Family life – new sibling. Family life – single-parent families.

Show way ill. by Hudson Talbott. Penguin, 2005. ISBN 978-0-399-23749-2 Subj: Ethnic groups in the U.S. – African Americans. Family life – mothers. Quilts. Slavery. U.S. history.

Sweet, sweet memory ill. by E. B. Lewis. Hyperion, 2000. ISBN 978-0-7868-2191-4 Subj: Death. Emotions – grief. Ethnic groups in the U.S. – African Americans. Family life – grandparents. Memories, memory.

This is the rope: a story from the Great Migration ill. by James Ransome. Penguin/Nancy Paulsen, 2013. ISBN 978-0-399-23986-1 Subj: Ethnic groups in the U.S. – African Americans. Family life. Migration. U.S. history.

We had a picnic this Sunday past ill. by Diane Greenseid. Hyperion, 1997. ISBN 978-0-7868-2192-1 Subj: Activities – picnicking. Ethnic groups in the U.S. – African Americans. Family life.

Wooldridge, Connie Nordhielm. *The legend of Strap Buckner* ill. by Andrew Glass. Holiday, 2001. ISBN 978-0-8234-1536-6 Subj: Devil. Folk & fairy tales. Tall tales.

When Esther Morris headed west ill. by Jacqueline Rogers. Holiday, 2001. ISBN 978-0-8234-1597-7 Subj: Gender roles. U.S. history.

Wicked Jack ill. by Will Hillenbrand. Holiday, 1995. ISBN 978-0-8234-1101-6 Subj: Behavior – wishing. Character traits – meanness. Devil. Folk & fairy tales.

Wooley, David Freeman. *Little Man* (Warwick, Dionne)

Woolley, Catherine *see* Thayer, Jane

Wormell, Christopher. *Blue Rabbit and friends* ill. by author. Fogelman, 2000. ISBN 978-0-8037-2499-0 Subj: Animals. Animals – rabbits. Friendship. Homes, houses.

Blue Rabbit and the runaway wheel ill. by author. Fogelman, 2001. ISBN 978-0-8037-2508-9 Subj: Animals. Animals – rabbits. Sports – bicycling.

Henry and the fox ill. by author. Trafalgar, 2008. ISBN 978-0-224-07044-7 Subj: Birds – chickens. Character traits – confidence. Emotions – fear. Self-concept.

The new alphabet of animals ill. by author. Running Press, 2002. ISBN 978-0-7624-1347-8 Subj: ABC books. Animals.

Puff, puff, chugga-chugga ill. by author. McElderry, 2001. ISBN 978-0-689-83986-3 Subj: Animals. Trains.

Wormell, Mary. *Bernard the angry rooster* ill. by author. Farrar, 2001. ISBN 978-0-374-30670-0 Subj: Animals. Behavior – bad day. Birds – chickens. Emotions – anger.

Hilda Hen's happy birthday ill. by author. Harcourt, 1995. ISBN 978-0-15-200299-2 Subj: Animals. Birds – chickens. Birthdays. Farms.

Hilda Hen's search ill. by author. Harcourt, 1994. ISBN 978-0-15-200069-1 Subj: Birds – chickens. Eggs. Farms.

Why not? ill. by author. Farrar, 2000. ISBN 978-0-374-38422-7 Subj: Animals. Animals – babies. Animals – cats. Character traits – questioning. Farms.

Wortche, Allison. *Rosie Sprout's time to shine* ill. by Patrice Barton. Random House, 2011. ISBN 978-0-375-86721-7 Subj: Behavior – boasting. Emotions – envy, jealousy. Gardens, gardening. Plants. School.

Worth, Valerie. *Pug and other animal poems* ill. by Steve Jenkins. Farrar, 2013. ISBN 978-0-374-35024-6 Subj: Animals. Poetry.

Wright, Betty Ren. *The blizzard* ill. by Ronald Himler. Holiday, 2003. ISBN 978-0-8234-1656-1 Subj: Birthdays. School. Weather – blizzards.

Wright, Catherine. *Steamboat Annie and the thousand-pound catfish* ill. by Howard Fine. Philomel, 2001. ISBN 978-0-399-23331-9 Subj: Activities – singing. Fish. Tall tales.

Wright, Cliff. *Bear and ball* ill. by author. Chronicle, 2005. ISBN 978-0-8118-4819-0 Subj: Animals – bears. Format, unusual – board books. Rhyming text. Toys – balls.

Bear and kite ill. by author. Chronicle, 2005. ISBN 978-0-8118-4820-6 Subj: Animals – bears. Format, unusual – board books. Kites. Rhyming text.

Wright, Courtni Crump. *Journey to freedom* ill. by Gershom Griffith. Holiday, 1994. ISBN 978-0-8234-1096-5 Subj: Character traits – freedom. Ethnic groups in the U.S. – African Americans. Slavery. U.S. history.

Jumping the broom ill. by Gershom Griffith. Holiday, 1994. ISBN 978-0-8234-1042-2 Subj: Ethnic groups in the U.S. – African Americans. Slavery. U.S. history. Weddings.

Wagon train: a family goes west in 1865 ill. by Gershom Griffith. Holiday, 1995. ISBN 978-0-8234-1152-8 Subj: Activities – traveling. Ethnic groups in the U.S. – African Americans. U.S. history – frontier & pioneer life.

Wright, Danielle. *Japanese nursery rhymes: Carp streamers, Falling rain, and other traditional favorites* ill. by Helen Acraman. Tuttle, 2012. ISBN 978-4-80531-188-2 Subj: Foreign lands – Japan. Nursery rhymes.

Wright, Dare. *A gift from the lonely doll* ill. by author. Houghton, 2001. ISBN 978-0-618-07181-4 Subj: Clothing – scarves. Emotions – loneliness. Gifts. Holidays – Christmas. Toys – bears. Toys – dolls.

The lonely doll photos by author. Houghton, 1998. ISBN 978-0-395-90112-0 Subj: Emotions – loneliness. Toys – bears. Toys – dolls.

Wright, Joan Richards. *Bugs* (Parker, Nancy Winslow)

Wright, Joanna. *Bunnies on ice* ill. by Johanna Wright. Roaring Brook, 2013. ISBN 978-1-59643-404-2 Subj: Animals – rabbits. Character traits – confidence. Seasons. Self-concept. Sports – ice skating.

Wright, Maureen. *Barnyard fun* ill. by Paul Ratz de Tagyos. Amazon/Two Lions, 2013. ISBN 978-1-4778-1643-1 Subj: Animals. Animals – sheep. Farms. Holidays – April Fools' Day. Riddles & jokes.

Earth Day, birthday! ill. by Violet Kim. Marshall Cavendish, 2012. ISBN 978-0-7614-6109-8 Subj: Animals. Animals – monkeys. Birthdays. Ecology. Holidays – Earth Day. Rhyming text.

Sleep, Big Bear, sleep! ill. by Will Hillenbrand. Marshall Cavendish, 2009. ISBN 978-0-7614-5560-8 Subj: Animals – bears. Hibernation. Rhyming text. Seasons – winter.

Sneeze, Big Bear, sneeze ill. by Will Hillenbrand. Marshall Cavendish, 2011. ISBN 978-0-7614-5959-0 Subj: Animals – bears. Rhyming text. Seasons – fall. Weather – wind.

Sneezy the snowman ill. by Stephen Gilpin. Marshall Cavendish, 2010. ISBN 978-0-7614-5711-4 Subj: Clothing. Snowmen.

Wright, Michael. *Jake goes peanuts* ill. by author. Feiwel & Friends, 2010. ISBN 978-0-312-54967-1 Subj: Food. Rhyming text.

Jake starts school ill. by author. Feiwel & Friends, 2008. ISBN 978-0-312-36798-5 Subj: Emotions – fear. Rhyming text. School – first day.

Jake stays awake ill. by author. Feiwel & Friends, 2007. ISBN 978-0-312-36797-8 Subj: Bedtime. Rhyming text. Sleep.

Wu, Faye-Lynn. *Chinese and English nursery rhymes: share and sing in two languages* ill. by Kieren Dutcher. Tuttle, 2010. ISBN 978-0-8048-4094-1 Subj: Foreign languages. Nursery rhymes.

Wyart, Peter. *The shepherds' tale* (Dowley, Tim)

The wise men's tale (Dowley, Tim)

Wyeth, Sharon Dennis. *Always my dad* ill. by Raúl Colón. Knopf, 1995. ISBN 978-0-679-93447-9 Subj: Behavior – needing someone. Country. Ethnic groups in the U.S. – African Americans. Family life – fathers. Family life – grandparents.

The granddaughter necklace ill. by Bagram Ibatoulline. Scholastic, 2013. ISBN 978-0-545-08125-2 Subj: Activities – storytelling. Ethnic groups in the U.S. – African Americans. Family life – mothers. Genealogy. Jewelry. Memories, memory.

Something beautiful ill. by Chris Soentpiet. Doubleday, 1998. ISBN 978-0-385-32239-3 Subj: Cities, towns. Communities, neighborhoods. Ethnic groups in the U.S. – African Americans.

Wyndham, Robert. *The Chinese Mother Goose rhymes* (Mother Goose)

Wynne-Jones, Tim. *The boat in the tree* ill. by John Shelley. Boyds Mills, 2007. ISBN 978-1-932425-49-9 Subj: Adoption. Boats, ships. Family life – brothers & sisters. Sibling rivalry.

Xinran, Xue. *Motherbridge of love* ill. by Josée Masse. Barefoot, 2007. ISBN 978-1-84686-047-8 Subj: Adoption. Emotions – love. Family life – mothers. Poetry.

Xiong, Blia. *Nine-in-one Grr! Grr!* adapt. by Cathy Spagnoli; ill. by Nancy Hom. Children's Press, 1989. ISBN 978-0-89239-048-9 Subj: Animals – tigers. Folk & fairy tales. Foreign lands – Laos.

Yaccarino, Dan. *All the way to America: the story of a big Italian family and a little shovel* ill. by author. Random House, 2011. ISBN 978-0-375-86642-5 Subj: Careers – writers. Ethnic groups in the U.S. – Italian Americans. Immigrants. U.S. history.

The birthday fish ill. by author. Holt, 2005. ISBN 978-0-8050-7493-2 Subj: Birthdays. Fish. Pets.

Deep in the jungle ill. by author. Atheneum, 2000. ISBN 978-0-689-82235-3 Subj: Animals. Animals – lions. Behavior – dissatisfaction. Circus.

Doug unplugged ill. by author. Knopf, 2013. ISBN 978-0-375-86643-2 Subj: Cities, towns. Robots.

Every Friday ill. by author. Holt, 2007. ISBN 978-0-8050-7724-7 Subj: Family life – fathers.

The fantastic undersea life of Jacques Cousteau ill. by author. Knopf, 2009. ISBN 978-0-375-85573-3 Subj: Careers – oceanographers. Sea & seashore.

First day on a strange new planet ill. by author. Hyperion, 2000. ISBN 978-0-7868-2499-1 Subj: Aliens. Planets. School. Space & space ships.

Five little ducks ill. by author. HarperCollins, 2005. ISBN 978-0-06-073465-7 Subj: Animals. Birds – ducks. Format, unusual – board books. Rhyming text. Songs.

Good night, Mr. Night ill. by author. Harcourt, 1997. ISBN 978-0-15-201319-6 Subj: Bedtime. Dreams. Night.

If I had a robot ill. by author. Viking, 1996. ISBN 978-0-670-86936-7 Subj: Behavior. Family life. Robots.

Lawn to lawn ill. by author. Random House, 2010. ISBN 978-0-375-85574-0 Subj: Animals. Moving.

The lima bean monster ill. by Adam McCauley. Walker, 2001. ISBN 978-0-8027-8777-4 Subj: Food. Monsters.

New pet ill. by author. Hyperion, 2001. ISBN 978-0-7868-2500-4 Subj: Aliens. Pets. Planets. Space & space ships.

An octopus followed me home ill. by author. Viking, 1997. ISBN 978-0-670-87401-9 Subj: Animals. Octopuses. Pets.

Oswald ill. by author. Atheneum, 2001. ISBN 978-0-689-84252-8 Subj: Animals – dogs. Moving. Octopuses. Pets.

So big ill. by author. HarperCollins, 2001. ISBN 978-0-694-01509-2 Subj: Animals. Concepts – size. Format, unusual – toy & movable books. Games.

Unlovable ill. by author. Holt, 2001. ISBN 978-0-8050-6321-9 Subj: Animals – dogs. Friendship. Self-concept.

Zoom! Zoom! Zoom! I'm off to the moon! ill. by author. Scholastic, 1997. ISBN 978-0-590-95610-9 Subj: Moon. Rhyming text. Space & space ships.

Yacowitz, Caryn. *Pumpkin fiesta* ill. by Joe Cepeda. HarperCollins, 1998. ISBN 978-0-06-027659-1 Subj: Fairs, festivals. Foreign lands – Mexico. Gardens, gardening. Plants.

Yagawa, Sumiko. *The crane wife* ill. by Suekichi Akaba. Morrow, 1982. ISBN 978-0-688-00496-5 Subj: Activities – weaving. Birds – cranes. Character traits – kindness to animals. Folk & fairy tales. Foreign lands – Japan.

Yahgulanaas, Michael Nicoll. *The little hummingbird* ill. by author. Greystone, 2010. ISBN 978-1-55365-533-6 Subj: Birds – hummingbirds. Character traits. Ecology. Folk & fairy tales. Foreign lands – South America.

Yamada, Utako. *The story of Cherry the pig* ill. by author. Kane/Miller, 2007. ISBN 978-1-933605-25-8 Subj: Activities – baking, cooking. Animals – pigs. Contests. Foreign lands – Japan.

Yamaguchi, Kristi. *Dream big, little pig!* ill. by Tim Bowers. Sourcebooks, 2011. ISBN 978-1-4022-5275-4 Subj: Animals – pigs. Character traits – ambition. Character traits – persistence. Sports – ice skating.

It's a big world, little pig! ill. by Tim Bowers. Sourcebooks, 2012. ISBN 978-1-4022-6644-7 Subj: Animals. Animals – pigs. Contests. Sports – ice skating.

Yamasaki, Katie. *Fish for Jimmy: inspired by one family's experience in a Japanese American internment camp* ill. by author. Holiday House, 2013. ISBN 978-0-8234-2375-0 Subj: Ethnic groups in the U.S. – Japanese Americans. U.S. history. War.

Yamashita, Haruo. *Seven little mice go to school* ill. by Kazuo Iwamura. NorthSouth, 2011. ISBN 978-0-7358-4012-6 Subj: Animals – mice. Character traits – cleverness. Family life – mothers. School – first day.

Seven little mice have fun on the ice ill. by Kazuo Iwamura. NorthSouth, 2011. ISBN 978-0-7358-4048-5 Subj: Animals – mice. Family life – mothers. Seasons – winter. Sports – fishing.

Yamawaki, Yuriko. *Guri and Gura* (Nakagawa, Rieko)

Guri and Gura's special gift (Nakagawa, Rieko)

Yang, Belle. *Always come home to me* ill. by author. Candlewick, 2007. ISBN 978-0-7636-2899-4 Subj: Birds – doves. Family life – mothers. Foreign lands – China. Multiple births – twins.

Yankovic, Al. *My new teacher and me!* ill. by Wes Hargis. HarperCollins, 2013. ISBN 978-0-06-219203-5 Subj: Careers – teachers. Humorous stories. Rhyming text. School – first day.

When I grow up ill. by Wes Hargis. HarperCollins, 2011. ISBN 978-0-06-192691-4 Subj: Careers. Rhyming text. School.

Yarrow, Peter. *Day is done* ill. by Melissa Sweet. Sterling, 2009. ISBN 978-1-4027-4806-6 Subj: Animals. Bedtime. Songs.

Let's sing together! ill. by Terry Widener. Sterling, 2009. ISBN 978-1-4027-5963-5 Subj: Songs.

Puff, the magic dragon by Peter Yarrow and Leonard Lipton ill. by Eric Puybaret. Sterling, 2007. ISBN 978-1-4027-4782-3 Subj: Dragons. Music. Songs.

Yashima, Taro. *Crow boy* ill. by author. Viking, 1955. ISBN 978-0-670-24931-2 Subj: Caldecott award honor books. Character traits – shyness. Emotions – loneliness. Foreign lands – Japan. School.

Umbrella ill. by author. Viking, 1958. ISBN 978-0-670-73858-8 Subj: Birthdays. Caldecott award honor books. Cities, towns. Ethnic groups in the U.S. – Japanese Americans. Umbrellas. Weather – rain.

Yates, Louise. *Dog loves books* ill. by author. Random House, 2010. ISBN 978-0-375-86449-0 Subj: Animals – dogs. Books, reading.

Dog loves counting ill. by author. Knopf, 2013. ISBN 978-0-449-81342-3 Subj: Animals – dogs. Bedtime. Books, reading. Counting, numbers.

Dog loves drawing ill. by author. Knopf, 2012. ISBN 978-0-375-87067-5 Subj: Activities – drawing. Animals – dogs.

Yates, Philip. *Ten little mummies* ill. by G. Brian Karas. Viking, 2003. ISBN 978-0-670-03641-7 Subj: Counting, numbers. Foreign lands – Egypt. Mummies. Rhyming text.

Yee, Brenda Shannon. *Sand castle* ill. by Thea Kliros. Greenwillow, 1999. ISBN 978-0-688-16194-1 Subj: Castles. Cumulative tales. Sand. Sea & seashore.

Yee, Paul. *Bamboo* ill. by Shaoli Wang. Simply Read, 2006. ISBN 978-1-894965-53-8 Subj: Folk & fairy tales. Foreign lands – China.

Yee, Wong Herbert. *Big black bear* ill. by author. Houghton, 1993. ISBN 978-0-395-66359-2 Subj: Animals – bears. Behavior – misbehavior. Etiquette. Rhyming text.

Detective Small in the amazing banana caper ill. by author. Houghton, 2007. ISBN 978-0-618-47285-7 Subj: Animals. Careers – detectives. Crime. Rhyming text.

Eek! There's a mouse in the house ill. by author. Houghton, 1992. ISBN 978-0-395-62303-9 Subj: Animals. Cumulative tales. Homes, houses. Rhyming text.

Fireman Small ill. by author. Houghton, 1994. ISBN 978-0-395-68987-5 Subj: Animals. Animals – pigs. Careers – firefighters. Fire. Rhyming text.

Fireman Small, fire down below ill. by author. Houghton, 2001. ISBN 978-0-618-00707-3 Subj: Animals. Animals – pigs. Careers – firefighters. Fire. Hotels. Rhyming text.

Fireman Small to the rescue ill. by author. Houghton, 1998. ISBN 978-0-395-88122-4 Subj: Animals. Animals – pigs. Careers – farmers. Careers – firefighters. Fire. Rhyming text.

Hamburger Heaven ill. by author. Houghton, 1999. ISBN 978-0-395-87548-3 Subj: Activities – working. Animals. Animals – pigs. Food. Restaurants.

Mrs. Brown went to town ill. by author. Houghton, 1996. ISBN 978-0-395-75282-1 Subj: Animals. Homes, houses. Rhyming text.

The Officers' Ball ill. by author. Houghton, 1997. ISBN 978-0-395-81182-5 Subj: Activities – dancing. Animals. Animals – hippopotamuses. Careers – police officers. Crime. Rhyming text.

A small Christmas ill. by author. Houghton, 2004. ISBN 978-0-618-32612-9 Subj: Animals. Careers – firefighters. Holidays – Christmas. Rhyming text. Santa Claus.

Summer days and nights ill. by author. Holt, 2012. ISBN 978-0-8050-9078-9 Subj: Day. Ethnic groups in the U.S. – Asian Americans. Night. Rhyming text. Seasons – summer.

Tracks in the snow ill. by Herbert Yee Wong. Holt, 2003. ISBN 978-0-8050-6771-2 Subj: Animals. Nature. Rhyming text. Seasons – winter.

Who likes rain? ill. by Herbert Yee Wong. Holt, 2007. ISBN 978-0-8050-7734-6 Subj: Ethnic groups in the U.S. – Asian Americans. Games. Rhyming text. Seasons – spring. Weather – rain.

Yeh, Kat. *The magic brush: a story of love, family, and Chinese characters* ill. by Huy Voun Lee. Walker, 2011. ISBN 978-0-8027-2178-5 Subj: Activities – storytelling. Activities – writing. Death. Ethnic groups in the U.S. – Chinese Americans. Family life – grandfathers. Foreign languages.

Yektai, Niki. *Bears at the beach* ill. by author. Millbrook, 1996. ISBN 978-0-7613-0022-9 Subj: Animals – bears. Counting, numbers. Sea & seashore – beaches.

Bears in pairs ill. by Diane deGroat. Bradbury, 1987. ISBN 978-0-02-793691-9 Subj: Animals – bears. Concepts. Rhyming text.

Hi bears, bye bears ill. by Diane deGroat. Watts, 1990. ISBN 978-0-531-08458-8 Subj: Rhyming text. Toys – bears.

Yep, Laurence. *Auntie Tiger* ill. by Insu Lee. HarperCollins, 2009. ISBN 978-0-06-029551-6 Subj: Animals – tigers. Disguises. Family life – sisters. Folk & fairy tales. Foreign lands – China.

Dragon prince ill. by Kam Mak. HarperCollins, 1997. ISBN 978-0-06-024393-7 Subj: Dragons. Emotions – envy, jealousy. Family life – sisters. Folk & fairy tales. Foreign lands – China. Sibling rivalry.

The Khan's daughter ill. by Jean Tseng and Mou-Sien Tseng. Scholastic, 1997. ISBN 978-0-590-48389-6 Subj: Folk & fairy tales. Foreign lands – Mongolia. Monsters. Royalty – khans. Weddings.

The man who tricked a ghost ill. by Isadore Seltzer. BridgeWater, 1993. ISBN 978-0-8167-3030-8 Subj: Behavior – trickery. Foreign lands – China. Ghosts. Middle Ages.

The shell woman and the king ill. by Ming-Yi Yang. Dial, 1993. ISBN 978-0-8037-1394-9 Subj: Folk & fairy tales. Foreign lands – China. Magic. Royalty – kings.

Yerkes, Jennifer. *A funny little bird* ill. by author. Sourcebooks/Jabberwocky, 2013. ISBN 978-1-4022-8013-9 Subj: Animals – foxes. Birds. Character traits – appearance. Emotions – loneliness. Self-concept.

Yezerski, Thomas. *Meadowlands: a wetlands survival story* ill. by author. Farrar, 2011. ISBN 978-0-374-34913-4 Subj: Ecology. Nature.

Queen of the world ill. by author. Farrar, 2000. ISBN 978-0-374-36165-5 Subj: Birthdays. Family life – mothers. Family life – sisters. Sibling rivalry.

Yi, Hu Yong. *Good morning China* ill. by author. Macmillan, 2007. ISBN 978-1-59643-240-6 Subj: Foreign lands – China. Morning.

Yin. *Brothers* ill. by Chris Soentpiet. Penguin, 2006. ISBN 978-0-399-23406-4 Subj: Ethnic groups in the U.S. – Chinese Americans. Family life – brothers & sisters. Friendship. Immigrants. Stores. U.S. history.

Coolies ill. by Chris Soentpiet. Philomel, 2001. ISBN 978-0-399-23227-5 Subj: Ethnic groups in the U.S. – Chinese Americans. Family life – brothers. Immigrants. Prejudice. Trains. U.S. history.

Dear Santa, please come to the 19th floor ill. by Chris Soentpiet. Philomel, 2002. ISBN 978-0-399-23636-5 Subj: Behavior – worrying. Ethnic groups in the U.S. – Hispanic Americans. Disabilities – physical disabilities. Holidays – Christmas. Homes, houses. Santa Claus.

Yokococo. *Matilda and Hans* ill. by author. Candlewick, 2013. ISBN 978-0-7636-6434-3 Subj: Animals – cats. Behavior – misbehavior.

Yolen, Jane. *All in the woodland early: an ABC book* ill. by Jane Breskin Zalben. Music & lyrics by author. Collins-World, 1980. ISBN 978-0-529-05509-5 Subj: ABC books. Forest, woods.

All star! Honus Wagner and the most famous baseball card ever ill. by Jim Burke. Penguin, 2010. ISBN 978-0-399-24661-6 Subj: Sports – baseball.

All those secrets of the world ill. by Leslie A. Baker. Little, 1991. ISBN 978-0-316-96891-1 Subj: Concepts – perspective. Family life – fathers. War.

Baby Bear's big dreams ill. by Melissa Sweet. Harcourt, 2007. ISBN 978-0-15-205291-1 Subj: Animals – bears. Behavior – growing up. Rhyming text.

Baby Bear's books ill. by Melissa Sweet. Harcourt, 2006. ISBN 978-0-15-205290-4 Subj: Animals – bears. Books, reading. Rhyming text.

Baby Bear's chairs ill. by Melissa Sweet. Harcourt, 2005. ISBN 978-0-15-205114-3 Subj: Animals – bears. Bedtime. Family life – fathers. Rhyming text.

Before the storm ill. by Georgia Pugh. Boyds Mills, 1995. ISBN 978-1-56397-240-9 Subj: Activities – playing. Seasons – summer. Weather – storms.

Beneath the ghost moon ill. by Laurel Molk. Little, 1994. ISBN 978-0-316-96892-8 Subj: Animals – mice. Character traits – bravery. Holidays – Halloween. Rhyming text.

Come to the fairies' ball ill. by Gary A. Lippincott. Boyds Mills, 2009. ISBN 978-1-59078-464-8 Subj: Clothing – dresses. Fairies. Parties. Rhyming text.

Creepy monsters, sleepy monsters: a lullaby ill. by Kelly Murphy. Candlewick, 2011. ISBN 978-0-7636-4201-3 Subj: Bedtime. Monsters. Rhyming text.

The day Tiger Rose said goodbye ill. by Jim LaMarche. Random House, 2011. ISBN 978-0-375-86663-0 Subj: Animals – cats. Death.

Dimity Duck ill. by Sebastien Braun. Penguin, 2006. ISBN 978-0-399-24632-6 Subj: Activities – playing. Birds – ducks. Friendship. Frogs & toads. Rhyming text.

An egret's day: poems photos by Jason Stemple. Boyds Mills, 2010. ISBN 978-1-59078-650-5 Subj: Birds – herons. Poetry.

Elsie's bird ill. by David Small. Penguin, 2010. ISBN 978-0-399-25292-1 Subj: Birds – canaries. Emotions – loneliness. Moving. U.S. history – frontier & pioneer life.

The emperor and the kite ill. by Ed Young. Philomel, 1988, ©1967. ISBN 978-0-399-21499-8 Subj: Caldecott award honor books. Character traits – smallness. Family life – fathers. Foreign lands – China. Kites. Royalty – emperors.

The firebird ill. by Vladimir Vagin. HarperCollins, 2002. ISBN 978-0-06-028539-5 Subj: Ballet. Folk & fairy tales. Foreign lands – Russia. Magic. Mythical creatures. Royalty – princes. Wizards.

The flying witch ill. by Vladimir Vagin. HarperCollins, 2003. ISBN 978-0-06-028537-1 Subj: Careers – farmers. Character traits – cleverness. Folk & fairy tales. Foreign lands – Russia. Witches.

The girl in the golden bower ill. by Jane Dyer. Little, 1994. ISBN 978-0-316-96894-2 Subj: Folk & fairy tales. Orphans. Witches.

Grandma's hurrying child ill. by Kay Chorao. Harcourt, 2005. ISBN 978-0-15-201813-9 Subj: Babies. Birth. Family life – grandmothers.

Harvest home ill. by Greg Shed. Harcourt, 2000. ISBN 978-0-15-201819-1 Subj: Careers – farmers. Farms. Rhyming text.

How do dinosaurs clean their rooms? ill. by Mark Teague. Blue Sky, 2004. ISBN 978-0-439-64950-6 Subj: Character traits – orderliness. Dinosaurs. Format, unusual – board books. Rhyming text.

How do dinosaurs count to ten? ill. by Mark Teague. Blue Sky, 2004. ISBN 978-0-439-64949-0 Subj: Counting, numbers. Dinosaurs. Format, unusual – board books. Rhyming text.

How do dinosaurs eat their food? ill. by Mark Teague. Scholastic, 2005. ISBN 978-0-439-24102-1 Subj: Dinosaurs. Etiquette. Food. Rhyming text.

How do dinosaurs get well soon? ill. by Mark Teague. Blue Sky, 2003. ISBN 978-0-439-24100-7 Subj: Dinosaurs. Illness. Rhyming text.

How do dinosaurs go to school? ill. by Mark Teague. Scholastic, 2007. ISBN 978-0-439-02081-7 Subj: Dinosaurs. Rhyming text. School.

How do dinosaurs learn their colors? ill. by Mark Teague. Scholastic, 2006. ISBN 978-0-439-85653-9 Subj: Concepts – color. Dinosaurs. Rhyming text.

How do dinosaurs play with their friends? ill. by Mark Teague. Scholastic, 2006. ISBN 978-0-439-85654-6 Subj: Behavior. Dinosaurs. Friendship. Rhyming text.

How do dinosaurs say good night? ill. by Mark Teague. Blue Sky, 2000. ISBN 978-0-590-31681-1 Subj: Bedtime. Behavior. Dinosaurs. Rhyming text.

How do dinosaurs say Happy Chanukah? ill. by Mark Teague. Scholastic, 2012. ISBN 978-0-545-41677-1 Subj: Dinosaurs. Holidays – Hanukkah. Rhyming text.

How do dinosaurs say I love you? ill. by Mark Teague. Scholastic, 2009. ISBN 978-0-545-14314-1 Subj: Dinosaurs. Emotions – love. Rhyming text.

How do dinosaurs say I'm mad? ill. by Mark Teague. Scholastic, 2013. ISBN 978-0-545-14315-8 Subj: Dinosaurs. Emotions – anger. Rhyming text.

How do dinosaurs say Merry Christmas? ill. by Mark Teague. Scholastic, 2012. ISBN 978-0-545-41678-8 Subj: Dinosaurs. Holidays – Christmas. Rhyming text.

Hush, little horsie ill. by Ruth Sanderson. Random House, 2010. ISBN 978-0-375-85853-6 Subj: Animals – horses, ponies. Bedtime. Rhyming text.

Jane Yolen's Old MacDonald songbook musical arrangements by Adam Stemple; ill. by Rosekrans Hoffman. Boyds Mills, 1994. ISBN 978-1-56397-281-2 Subj: Animals. Cumulative tales. Farms. Music. Songs.

Johnny Appleseed: the legend and the truth ill. by Jim Burke. HarperCollins, 2008. ISBN 978-0-06-059135-9 Subj: Activities – traveling. Gardens, gardening. Tall tales. Trees. U.S. history – frontier & pioneer life.

King Long Shanks ill. by Victoria Chess. Harcourt, 1998. ISBN 978-0-15-200013-4 Subj: Character traits – pride. Character traits – vanity. Clothing.

Folk & fairy tales. Frogs & toads. Imagination. Royalty – kings.

Letting Swift River go ill. by Barbara Cooney. Little, 1992. ISBN 978-0-316-96899-7 Subj: Country. U.S. history. Water.

Mama's kiss ill. by Daniel Baxter. Chronicle, 2008. ISBN 978-0-8118-6683-5 Subj: Family life – mothers. Kissing. Rhyming text.

A mirror to nature: poems about reflection ill. by Jason Stemple. Boyds Mills, 2009. ISBN 978-1-59078-624-6 Subj: Nature. Poetry. Water.

Miz Berlin walks ill. by Floyd Cooper. Philomel, 1997. ISBN 978-0-399-22938-1 Subj: Activities – storytelling. Activities – walking. Ethnic groups in the U.S. – African Americans. Old age.

Moon ball ill. by Greg Couch. Simon & Schuster, 1999. ISBN 978-0-689-81095-4 Subj: Bedtime. Dreams. Space & space ships. Sports – baseball.

My brothers' flying machine ill. by Jim Burke. Little, 2003. ISBN 978-0-316-97159-1 Subj: Airplanes, airports. Careers – airplane pilots. Careers – inventors. Family life – brothers. U.S. history.

My father knows the names of things ill. by Stéphane Jorisch. Simon & Schuster, 2010. ISBN 978-1-4169-4895-7 Subj: Family life – fathers. Rhyming text.

My Uncle Emily ill. by Nancy Carpenter. Philomel, 2009. ISBN 978-0-399-24005-8 Subj: Careers – poets. Family life – aunts, uncles. U.S. history.

Naming Liberty ill. by Jim Burke. Philomel, 2008. ISBN 978-0-399-24250-2 Subj: Behavior – seeking better things. Ethnic groups in the U.S. – Russian Americans. Immigrants. Jewish culture. U.S. history.

Not all princesses dress in pink by Jane Yolen and Heidi E. Y. Stemple ill. by Anne-Sophie Lanquetin. Simon & Schuster, 2010. ISBN 978-1-4169-8018-6 Subj: Character traits – individuality. Gender roles. Rhyming text. Royalty – princesses.

Off we go! ill. by Laurel Molk. Little, 2000. ISBN 978-0-316-90228-1 Subj: Animals – babies. Family life – grandparents. Rhyming text.

Owl moon ill. by John Schoenherr. Philomel, 1987. ISBN 978-0-399-21457-8 Subj: Birds – owls. Caldecott award books. Family life – fathers. Forest, woods. Night.

Pegasus, the flying horse ill. by Ming Li. Dutton, 1998. ISBN 978-0-525-65244-1 Subj: Character traits – vanity. Folk & fairy tales. Mythical creatures. Mythical creatures – Pegasus.

Picnic with Piggins ill. by Jane Dyer. Harcourt, 1988. ISBN 978-0-15-261534-5 Subj: Activities – picnicking. Animals. Animals – pigs. Birthdays.

Piggins ill. by Jane Dyer. Harcourt, 1987. ISBN 978-0-15-261685-4 Subj: Animals. Animals – pigs. Behavior – stealing. Parties. Problem solving.

Raising Yoder's barn ill. by Bernie Fuchs. Little, 1998. ISBN 978-0-316-96887-4 Subj: Barns. Communities, neighborhoods. Ethnic groups in the U.S. – Amish. Farms.

Romping monsters, stomping monsters ill. by Kelly Murphy. Candlewick, 2013. ISBN 978-0-7636-5727-7 Subj: Activities – playing. Monsters. Rhyming text.

Sister Bear: a Norse tale ill. by Linda Graves. Marshall Cavendish, 2011. ISBN 978-0-7614-5958-3 Subj: Animals – bears. Folk & fairy tales. Holidays – Christmas. Mythical creatures – trolls.

Sky dogs ill. by Barry Moser. Harcourt, 1990. ISBN 978-0-15-275480-8 Subj: Animals – horses, ponies. Folk & fairy tales. Indians of North America – Blackfoot. Indians of North America – Siksika.

Sleep, black bear, sleep by Jane Yolen and Heidi E. Y. Stemple ill. by Brooke Dyer. HarperCollins, 2007. ISBN 978-0-06-081560-8 Subj: Animals. Bedtime. Hibernation. Lullabies. Seasons – winter.

Soft house ill. by Wendy Anderson Halperin. Candlewick, 2005. ISBN 978-0-7636-1697-7 Subj: Activities – playing. Animals – cats. Behavior – boredom. Family life – brothers & sisters.

The three bears holiday rhyme book ill. by Jane Dyer. Harcourt, 1995. ISBN 978-0-15-200932-8 Subj: Animals – bears. Holidays. Poetry.

Waking dragons ill. by Derek Anderson. Simon & Schuster, 2012. ISBN 978-1-4169-9032-1 Subj: Dragons. Rhyming text.

Welcome to the icehouse ill. by Laura Regan. Putnam, 1998. ISBN 978-0-399-23011-0 Subj: Animals. Foreign lands – Arctic. Nature. Science. Seasons.

Welcome to the river of grass ill. by Laura Regan. Putnam, 2001. ISBN 978-0-399-23221-3 Subj: Animals. Birds. Ecology. Swamps.

Welcome to the sea of sand ill. by Laura Regan. Putnam, 1996. ISBN 978-0-399-22765-3 Subj: Animals. Desert. Ecology. Plants. Poetry.

Where have the unicorns gone? ill. by Ruth Sanderson. Simon & Schuster, 2000. ISBN 978-0-689-82465-4 Subj: Ecology. Mythical creatures – unicorns. Rhyming text.

Wings ill. by Dennis Nolan. Harcourt, 1992. ISBN 978-0-15-297850-1 Subj: Activities – flying. Mythical creatures. Royalty – princes.

Yolleck, Joan. *Paris in the spring with Picasso* ill. by Marjorie Priceman. Random House, 2010. ISBN

978-0-375-83756-2 Subj: Art. Foreign lands – France. Parties.

Yoo, Paula. *Sixteen years in sixteen seconds: the Sammy Lee story* ill. by Dom Lee. Lee & Low, 2005. ISBN 978-1-58430-247-6 Subj: Ethnic groups in the U.S. – Asian Americans. Sports – Olympics.

Yoo, Taeeun. *The little red fish* ill. by author. Penguin, 2007. ISBN 978-0-8037-3145-5 Subj: Fish. Libraries. Magic.

You are a lion! and other fun yoga poses ill. by author. Penguin, 2012. ISBN 978-0-399-25602-8 Subj: Health & fitness. Imagination.

Yoon, Salina. *At the beach* ill. by author. Feiwel & Friends, 2011. ISBN 978-0-312-66303-2 Subj: Format, unusual – board books. Sea & seashore – beaches.

Do cows meow? ill. by author. Sterling, 2012. ISBN 978-1-4027-8956-4 Subj: Animals. Farms. Format, unusual – toy & movable books. Noise, sounds.

Do crocs kiss? ill. by author. Sterling, 2012. ISBN 978-1-4027-8955-7 Subj: Animals. Format, unusual – toy & movable books. Noise, sounds.

Opposnakes: a lift-the-flap book about opposites ill. by author. Simon & Schuster, 2009. ISBN 978-1-4169-7875-6 Subj: Concepts – opposites. Format, unusual – toy & movable books. Reptiles – snakes.

Penguin and Pinecone: a friendship story ill. by author. Walker, 2012. ISBN 978-0-8027-2843-2 Subj: Birds – penguins. Friendship.

Penguin in love ill. by author. Walker, 2013. ISBN 978-0-8027-3600-0 Subj: Activities – knitting. Behavior – lost & found possessions. Birds – penguins. Clothing – gloves, mittens. Emotions – love.

Penguin on vacation ill. by author. Walker, 2013. ISBN 978-0-8027-3397-9 Subj: Activities – vacationing. Birds – penguins. Friendship. Sea & seashore.

Yorinks, Arthur. *Christmas in July* ill. by Richard Egielski. HarperCollins, 1991. ISBN 978-0-06-020257-6 Subj: Behavior – lost & found possessions. Clothing. Holidays – Christmas. Santa Claus.

Company's coming ill. by David Small. Crown, 1988. ISBN 978-0-517-56751-7 Subj: Behavior – misunderstanding. Humorous stories. Space & space ships.

Company's going ill. by David Small. Hyperion, 2001. ISBN 978-0-7868-0415-3 Subj: Activities – baking, cooking. Aliens. Humorous stories. Planets. Space & space ships. Weddings.

Harry and Lulu ill. by Martin Matje. Hyperion, 1999. ISBN 978-0-7868-2276-8 Subj: Animals – dogs. Emotions – anger. Emotions – love. Foreign lands – France. Imagination. Toys.

Hey, Al ill. by Richard Egielski. Farrar, 1986. ISBN 978-0-374-33060-6 Subj: Animals – dogs. Behavior – running away. Caldecott award books. Dreams. Imagination.

Homework ill. by Richard Egielski. Walker, 2009. ISBN 978-0-8027-9585-4 Subj: Activities – writing. Homework.

The invisible man ill. by Doug Cushman. HarperCollins, 2011. ISBN 978-0-06-156148-1 Subj: Careers – storekeepers. Character traits – being different.

Louis the fish ill. by Richard Egielski. Farrar, 1980. ISBN 978-0-374-34658-4 Subj: Careers – butchers. Fish. Imagination.

The Miami giant ill. by Maurice Sendak. HarperCollins, 1995. ISBN 978-0-06-205069-4 Subj: Careers – explorers. Foreign lands – Italy. Giants. Jewish culture.

Quack! ill. by Adrienne Yorinks. Abrams, 2003. ISBN 978-0-8109-3548-8 Subj: Animals. Birds – ducks. Quilts. Space & space ships.

What a trip! ill. by Richard Egielski. Scholastic, 2008. ISBN 978-0-545-03611-5 Subj: Humorous stories. Imagination.

Whitefish Will rides again ill. by Mort Drucker. HarperCollins, 1994. ISBN 978-0-06-205037-3 Subj: Careers – sheriffs. U.S. history – frontier & pioneer life.

You and me ill. by Rachel Fuller. Child's Play, 2010. ISBN 978-1-84643-277-4 Subj: Family life – new sibling. Format, unusual – board books.

Youme. *Mali under the night sky: a Lao story of home* ill. by author. Cinco Puntos, 2010. ISBN 978-1-933693-68-2 Subj: Foreign lands – Laos. War.

Young, Amy. *Belinda and the glass slipper* ill. by author. Penguin, 2006. ISBN 978-0-670-06082-5 Subj: Activities – dancing. Anatomy – feet. Ballet.

Belinda begins ballet ill. by author. Penguin, 2007. ISBN 978-0-670-06244-7 Subj: Activities – dancing. Anatomy – feet. Ballet.

Belinda in Paris ill. by author. Penguin, 2005. ISBN 978-0-670-03693-6 Subj: Activities – dancing. Anatomy – feet. Ballet. Clothing – shoes. Foreign lands – France.

Belinda, the ballerina ill. by author. Viking, 2002. ISBN 978-0-670-03549-6 Subj: Activities – dancing. Anatomy – feet. Ballet.

Don't eat the baby! ill. by author. Viking, 2013. ISBN 978-0-670-78513-1 Subj: Babies. Family life – new sibling.

The mud fairy ill. by author. Bloomsbury, 2010. ISBN 978-1-59990-104-6 Subj: Character traits – being different. Fairies. Frogs & toads.

Young, Cybèle. *A few bites* ill. by author. Groundwood, 2012. ISBN 978-1-55498-295-0 Subj: Family life – brothers & sisters. Food.

A few blocks ill. by author. Groundwood, 2011. ISBN 978-0-88899-995-5 Subj: Behavior – resourcefulness. Family life – brothers & sisters. Imagination.

Ten birds ill. by author. Kids Can, 2011. ISBN 978-1-55453-568-2 Subj: Birds. Counting, numbers. Problem solving.

Ten birds meet a monster ill. by author. Kids Can, 2013. ISBN 978-1-55453-955-0 Subj: Birds. Counting, numbers.

Young, Ed. *Cat and Rat* ill. by author. Holt, 1995. ISBN 978-0-8050-2977-2 Subj: Animals – cats. Animals – rats. Folk & fairy tales. Foreign lands – China. Royalty – emperors. Zodiac.

Donkey trouble ill. by author. Atheneum, 1995. ISBN 978-0-689-31854-2 Subj: Animals – donkeys. Behavior – misunderstanding. Desert. Folk & fairy tales. Stores.

Hook ill. by author. Roaring Brook, 2009. ISBN 978-1-59643-363-2 Subj: Activities – flying. Birds – chickens. Birds – eagles. Character traits – being different. Character traits – persistence.

Little Plum ill. by author. Philomel, 1994. ISBN 978-0-399-22683-0 Subj: Character traits – cleverness. Character traits – smallness. Folk & fairy tales. Foreign lands – China.

Lon Po Po: a Red Riding Hood story from China ill. by author. Putnam, 1989. ISBN 978-0-399-21619-0 Subj: Animals – wolves. Caldecott award books. Folk & fairy tales. Foreign lands – China.

The lost horse ill. by author. Silver Whistle, 1998. ISBN 978-0-15-201016-4 Subj: Animals – horses, ponies. Folk & fairy tales. Foreign lands – China. Weather – storms.

Monkey King ill. by author. HarperCollins, 2001. ISBN 978-0-06-027950-9 Subj: Animals – monkeys. Behavior – trickery. Foreign lands – China.

Mouse match ill. by author. Silver Whistle, 1997. ISBN 978-0-15-201453-7 Subj: Animals – mice. Family life – fathers. Foreign lands – China. Format, unusual. Weddings.

My Mei Mei ill. by author. Penguin, 2006. ISBN 978-0-399-24339-4 Subj: Adoption. Emotions – love. Ethnic groups in the U.S. – Chinese Americans. Family life – brothers & sisters. Sibling rivalry.

Night visitors ill. by author. Philomel, 1995. ISBN 978-0-399-22731-8 Subj: Dreams. Folk & fairy tales. Foreign lands – China. Insects – ants.

Seven blind mice ill. by author. Putnam, 1992. ISBN 978-0-399-22261-0 Subj: Animals – elephants. Animals – mice. Caldecott award honor books. Days of the week, months of the year. Disabilities – blindness. Foreign lands – India. Senses – sight.

What about me? ill. by author. Philomel, 2002. ISBN 978-0-399-23624-2 Subj: Cumulative tales. Folk & fairy tales. Foreign lands – Middle East. Religion.

Young, Jessica. *My blue is happy* ill. by Catia Chien. Candlewick, 2013. ISBN 978-0-7636-5125-1 Subj: Concepts – color. Emotions.

Young, Judy. *H is for hook: a fishing alphabet* ill. by Gary Palmer. Sleeping Bear, 2008. ISBN 978-1-58536-347-6 Subj: ABC books. Sports – fishing.

Young, Ned. *Zoomer* ill. by author. HarperCollins, 2010. ISBN 978-0-06-170088-0 Subj: Activities – playing. Animals – dogs. Imagination.

Zoomer's out-of-this-world Christmas ill. by author. HarperCollins, 2013. ISBN 978-0-06-199959-8 Subj: Aliens. Animals – dogs. Character traits – generosity. Holidays – Christmas. Space & space ships.

Zoomer's summer snowstorm ill. by author. HarperCollins, 2011. ISBN 978-0-06-170092-7 Subj: Animals – dogs. Imagination. Weather – snow.

Young, Ruth. *Golden Bear* ill. by Rachel Isadora. Viking, 1992. ISBN 978-0-670-82577-6 Subj: Ethnic groups in the U.S. – African Americans. Friendship. Imagination. Rhyming text. Toys – bears.

Who says moo? ill. by Lisa Campbell Ernst. Viking, 1994. ISBN 978-0-670-85162-1 Subj: Animals. Character traits – questioning. Noise, sounds. Riddles & jokes.

Youngquist, Cathrene Valente. *The three Billygoats Gruff and Mean Calypso Joe* by Cathrene Valente Youngquist and P. C. Asbjørnsen ill. by Kristin Sorra. Atheneum, 2002. ISBN 978-0-689-82824-9 Subj: Animals – goats. Character traits – cleverness. Folk & fairy tales. Foreign lands – Caribbean Islands. Mythical creatures – trolls.

Yu, Li-Qiong. *A New Year's reunion* ill. by Cheng-Liang Zhu. Candlewick, 2011. ISBN 978-0-7636-5881-6 Subj: Activities – working. Family life – fathers. Foreign lands – China. Holidays – Chinese New Year.

Yum, Hyewon. *Last night* ill. by author. Farrar, 2008. ISBN 978-0-374-34358-3 Subj: Dreams. Emotions. Toys – bears. Wordless.

Mom, it's my first day of kindergarten! ill. by author. Farrar, 2012. ISBN 978-0-374-35004-8 Subj: Behavior – worrying. Family life – mothers. School – first day.

There are no scary wolves ill. by author. Farrar, 2010. ISBN 978-0-374-38060-1 Subj: Animals – wolves. Emotions – fear. Imagination.

This is our house ill. by author. Farrar, 2013. ISBN 978-0-374-37487-7 Subj: Family life. Homes, houses.

The twins' blanket ill. by author. Farrar, 2011. ISBN 978-0-374-37972-8 Subj: Behavior – sharing. Character traits – individuality. Family life – sisters. Multiple births – twins.

Zacharias, Ravi. *The merchant and the thief: a folktale from India* ill. by Laure Fournier. Zonderkidz, 2012. ISBN 978-0-310-71636-5 Subj: Folk & fairy tales. Foreign lands – India. Religion.

Zagwÿn, Deborah Turney. *Apple batter* ill. by author. Tricycle, 1999. ISBN 978-1-883672-92-8 Subj: Character traits – persistence. Family life. Food. Gardens, gardening. Sports – baseball. Trees.

The pumpkin blanket ill. by author. Celestial Arts, 1990. ISBN 978-0-89087-637-4 Subj: Behavior – growing up. Foreign lands – Canada. Gardens, gardening. Quilts.

The sea house ill. by author. Tricycle, 2002. ISBN 978-1-58246-030-7 Subj: Boats, ships. Family life – aunts, uncles. Seasons – summer.

Turtle spring ill. by author. Tricycle, 1998. ISBN 978-1-883672-53-9 Subj: Family life – new sibling. Hibernation. Reptiles – turtles, tortoises. Seasons.

The winter gift ill. by author. Tricycle, 2000. ISBN 978-1-883672-93-5 Subj: Family life – grandmothers. Holidays – Christmas. Memories, memory. Moving.

Zalben, Jane Breskin. *Baby Babka* ill. by Victoria Chess. Clarion, 2004. ISBN 978-0-618-23489-9 Subj: Babies. Family life. Family life – aunts, uncles. Family life – brothers & sisters.

Baby shower ill. by author. Roaring Brook, 2010. ISBN 978-1-59643-465-3 Subj: Dreams. Parties. Pets.

Beni's first Chanukah ill. by author. Holt, 1988. ISBN 978-0-8050-0479-3 Subj: Animals – bears. Family life. Friendship. Holidays – Hanukkah. Jewish culture.

Beni's first wedding ill. by author. Holt, 1998. ISBN 978-0-8050-4846-9 Subj: Animals – bears. Family life. Jewish culture. Weddings.

Hey, Mama Goose ill. by Emilie Chollat. Penguin, 2005. ISBN 978-0-525-47097-7 Subj: Homes, houses. Nursery rhymes. Rhyming text.

Mousterpiece ill. by author. Roaring Brook, 2012. ISBN 978-1-59643-549-0 Subj: Animals – mice. Art. Careers – artists. Imagination. Museums.

Pearl's eight days of Chanukah ill. by author. Simon & Schuster, 1998. ISBN 978-0-689-81488-4 Subj: Animals – sheep. Holidays – Hanukkah. Jewish culture. Religion.

Pearl's marigolds for grandpa ill. by author. Simon & Schuster, 1997. ISBN 978-0-689-80448-9 Subj: Animals – sheep. Death. Emotions – grief. Family life – grandfathers. Memories, memory.

Pearl's Passover ill. by author. Simon & Schuster, 2002. ISBN 978-0-689-81487-7 Subj: Family life. Holidays – Passover. Jewish culture.

Saturday night at the Beastro by Jane Breskin Zalben and Steven Zalben ill. by authors. HarperCollins, 2004. ISBN 978-0-06-029228-7 Subj: Food. Monsters. Parties. Rhyming text.

Zalben, Steven. *Saturday night at the Beastro* (Zalben, Jane Breskin)

Zamorano, Ana. *Let's eat!* ill. by Julie Vivas. Scholastic, 1997. ISBN 978-0-590-13444-6 Subj: Family life. Food. Foreign lands – Spain. Health & fitness.

Zane, Alexander. *The wheels on the race car* ill. by James Warhola. Scholastic, 2005. ISBN 978-0-439-59080-8 Subj: Animals. Automobiles. Songs. Sports – racing.

Zappa, Ahmet. *Because I'm your dad* ill. by Dan Santat. Hyperion/Disney, 2013. ISBN 978-1-4231-4774-9 Subj: Family life – fathers.

Zarins, Kim. *The helpful puppy* ill. by Emily Arnold McCully. Holiday House, 2012. ISBN 978-0-8234-2318-7 Subj: Animals – dogs. Farms.

Zecca, Katherine. *A puffin's year* ill. by author. Down East, 2007. ISBN 978-0-89272-742-1 Subj: Birds – puffins.

Zehler, Antonia. *Two fine ladies: tea for three* ill. by author. Random House, 2002. ISBN 978-0-613-84579-3 Subj: Activities – playing. Animals – bears. Family life – sisters. Friendship. Multiple births – twins.

Two fine ladies have a tiff ill. by author. Random House, 2001. ISBN 978-0-375-91104-0 Subj: Activities – playing. Behavior – fighting, arguing. Family life – sisters. Friendship. Multiple births – twins.

Zekauskas, Felicia. *Belly button boy* (Maloney, Peter)

His mother's nose (Maloney, Peter)

One foot two feet: an exceptional counting book (Maloney, Peter)

Zelch, Patti R. *Ready, set . . . wait! what animals do before a hurricane* ill. by Connie McLennan. Sylvan Dell, 2010. ISBN 978-1-60718-072-2 Subj: Animals. Weather – hurricanes.

Zelinsky, Paul O. *The maid and the mouse and the odd-shaped house* ill. by author. Dodd, 1981. ISBN 978-0-396-07938-5 Subj: Animals – mice. Folk & fairy tales. Homes, houses.

The wheels on the bus ill. by adapter. Paper engineering by Roger Smith. Dutton, 1990. ISBN 978-0-525-46506-5 Subj: Buses. Family life – grandmothers. Format, unusual – toy & movable books. Music. Songs.

Zemach, Harve. *Duffy and the devil: a Cornish tale* ill. by Margot Zemach. Farrar, 1973. ISBN 978-0-374-31887-1 Subj: Caldecott award books. Devil. Folk & fairy tales. Foreign lands – England.

The judge: an untrue tale ill. by Margot Zemach. Farrar, 1969. ISBN 978-0-374-33960-9 Subj: Caldecott award honor books. Careers – judges. Monsters. Rhyming text.

Zemach, Kaethe. *Ms. McCaw learns to draw* ill. by author. Scholastic, 2008. ISBN 978-0-439-82914-4 Subj: Activities – drawing. Careers – teachers. Disabilities. School.

Zemach, Margot. *Eating up Gladys* ill. by Kaethe Zemach. Scholastic, 2005. ISBN 978-0-439-66490-5 Subj: Behavior – bossy. Family life – brothers & sisters.

It could always be worse: a Yiddish folk tale ill. by author. Farrar, 1976. ISBN 978-0-374-33650-9 Subj: Caldecott award honor books. Folk & fairy tales. Humorous stories. Jewish culture. Problem solving.

Some from the moon, some from the sun ill. by author. Farrar, 2001. ISBN 978-0-374-39960-3 Subj: Nursery rhymes. Songs.

The three wishes: an old story ill. by adapter. Farrar, 1986. ISBN 978-0-374-37529-4 Subj: Behavior – wishing. Character traits – foolishness. Folk & fairy tales.

Zeman, Ludmila. *Sindbad: from the tales of the Thousand and one nights* ill. by author. Tundra, 1999. ISBN 978-0-88776-460-8 Subj: Folk & fairy tales. Foreign lands – Arabia. Sailors. Sea & seashore.

Zenz, Aaron. *Chuckling ducklings and baby animal friends* ill. by author. Walker, 2011. ISBN 978-0-8027-2191-4 Subj: Animals – babies.

Zepeda, Gwendolyn. *Growing up with tamales / Los tamales de Ana* ill. by April Ward. Piñata, 2008. ISBN 978-1-55885-493-2 Subj: Activities – baking, cooking. Ethnic groups in the U.S. – Hispanic Americans. Food. Foreign languages. Holidays – Christmas.

Zhang, Song Nan. *The ballad of Mulan* ill. by author. Pan Asian Publications, 1998. ISBN 978-1-57227-056-5 Subj: Foreign lands – China. Gender roles. War.

Zia, F. *Hot, hot roti for Dada-ji* ill. by Ken Min. Lee & Low, 2011. ISBN 978-1-60060-443-0 Subj: Activities – baking, cooking. Ethnic groups in the U.S. – East Indian Americans. Family life – grandfathers. Food.

Ziarnik, Natalie. *Madeleine's light: a story of Camille Claudel* ill. by Robert Dunn. Boyds Mills, 2012. ISBN 978-1-59078-855-4 Subj: Art. Careers – sculptors. Foreign lands – France. Gender roles.

Ziefert, Harriet. *ABC dentist* ill. by Liz Murphy. Blue Apple, 2008. ISBN 978-1-934706-31-2 Subj: ABC books. Careers – dentists.

Animal music ill. by Donald Saaf. Houghton, 1999. ISBN 978-0-395-95294-8 Subj: Animals. Music. Musical instruments – bands. Rhyming text.

Be fair, share! ill. by Pete Whitehead. Sterling, 2007. ISBN 978-1-4027-3422-9 Subj: Animals. Behavior – sharing.

Beach party! ill. by Simms Taback. Blue Apple, 2005. ISBN 978-1-59354-067-8 Subj: Animals. Concepts – motion. Format, unusual – board books. Rhyming text. Sea & seashore.

Bigger than Daddy ill. by Elliot Kreloff. Blue Apple, 2006. ISBN 978-1-59354-147-7 Subj: Concepts – size. Ethnic groups in the U.S. – African Americans. Family life – fathers.

The biggest job of all ill. by Lauren Browne. Blue Apple, 2005. ISBN 978-1-59354-100-2 Subj: Careers. Family life – mothers.

Birdhouse for rent ill. by Donald Dreifuss. Houghton, 2001. ISBN 978-0-618-04881-6 Subj: Birds – chickadees. Family life. Homes, houses.

A bunny is funny by Harriet Ziefert and Fred Ehrlich ill. by Todd McKie. Blue Apple, 2008. ISBN 978-1-934706-03-9 Subj: Animals. Poetry.

Bunny's lessons ill. by Barroux. Blue Apple, 2011. ISBN 978-1-60905-028-3 Subj: Animals – rabbits. Behavior. Emotions. Friendship. Toys.

Buzzy had a little lamb ill. by Emily Bolam. Blue Apple, 2005. ISBN 978-1-59354-068-5 Subj: Animals – donkeys. School. Toys.

By the light of the harvest moon ill. by Mark Jones. Blue Apple, 2009. ISBN 978-1-934706-69-5 Subj: Seasons – fall.

Circus parade ill. by Tanya Roitman. Blue Apple, 2005. ISBN 978-1-59354-088-3 Subj: Circus. Parades.

Clara Ann Cookie ill. by Emily Bolam. Houghton, 1999. ISBN 978-0-395-92324-5 Subj: Clothing. Family life – mothers. Rhyming text.

Clara Ann Cookie go to bed! ill. by Emily Bolam. Houghton, 2000. ISBN 978-0-395-97381-3 Subj: Bedtime. Rhyming text. Toys – bears.

Counting chickens ill. by Flensted. Blue Apple, 2010. ISBN 978-1-60905-033-7 Subj: Counting, numbers. Format, unusual.

A dozen ducklings lost and found ill. by Donald Dreifuss. Houghton, 2003. ISBN 978-0-618-14175-3 Subj: Animals – babies. Birds – ducks. Counting, numbers.

Families have together ill. by Deborah Zemke. Blue Apple, 2005. ISBN 978-1-59354-071-5 Subj: Family life. Rhyming text.

First He made the sun ill. by Todd McKie. Putnam, 2000. ISBN 978-0-399-23199-5 Subj: Creation. Religion. Rhyming text.

First Night ill. by S. D. Schindler. Putnam, 1999. ISBN 978-0-399-23120-9 Subj: Holidays – New Year's. Parades. Rhyming text.

From Kalamazoo to Timbuktu! ill. by Tanya Roitman. Blue Apple, 2005. ISBN 978-1-59354-091-3 Subj: Activities – traveling. Rhyming text. Transportation.

Fun Land fun! ill. by Yukiko Kido. Sterling, 2007. ISBN 978-1-4027-3416-8 Subj: Friendship. Parks – amusement.

Grandma, it's for you! ill. by Lauren Browne. Blue Apple, 2006. ISBN 978-1-59354-109-5 Subj: Activities – making things. Clothing – hats. Family life – grandmothers. Gifts.

Grandma's wedding album ill. by Karla Gudeon. Blue Apple, 2011. ISBN 978-1-60905-058-0 Subj: Family life – grandparents. Weddings.

Hanukkah haiku ill. by Karla Gudeon. Blue Apple, 2008. ISBN 978-1-934706-33-6 Subj: Format, unusual. Holidays – Hanukkah. Poetry.

Hats off for the Fourth of July! ill. by Gustaf Miller. Viking, 2000. ISBN 978-0-670-89118-4 Subj: Clothing – hats. Holidays – Fourth of July. Rhyming text.

Home for Navidad ill. by Santiago Cohen. Houghton, 2003. ISBN 978-0-618-34976-0 Subj: Family life – mothers. Foreign lands – Mexico. Foreign languages. Holidays – Christmas.

I swapped my dog ill. by Emily Bolam. Houghton, 1998. ISBN 978-0-395-89159-9 Subj: Animals. Animals – dogs. Cumulative tales. Farms. Rhyming text.

Knick-knack paddywhack ill. by Emily Bolam. Sterling, 2005. ISBN 978-1-4027-2292-9 Subj: Activities – making things. Animals – dogs. Counting, numbers. Cumulative tales. Format, unusual – board books. Songs.

Lights on Broadway: a theatrical tour from A to Z by Harriet Ziefert and Brian Stokes Mitchell ill. by Elliot Kreloff. Blue Apple, 2009. ISBN 978-1-934706-68-8 Subj: ABC books. Theater.

Lucy rescued ill. by Barroux. Blue Apple, 2012. ISBN 978-1-60905-187-7 Subj: Animals – dogs. Toys.

Lunchtime for a purple snake ill. by Todd McKie. Houghton, 2003. ISBN 978-0-618-31133-0 Subj: Activities – painting. Careers – artists. Concepts – color. Family life – grandfathers.

Messy Bessie: where's my homework ill. by Roger De Muth. Blue Apple, 2007. ISBN 978-1-59354-181-1 Subj: Animals – mice. Behavior – messy. Format, unusual. Picture puzzles. Rhyming text. School.

Mighty Max ill. by Elliot Kreloff. Blue Apple, 2008. ISBN 978-1-934706-36-7 Subj: Activities – playing. Imagination. Sea & seashore – beaches.

Mommies are for counting stars ill. by Cynthia Jabar. Putnam, 1999. ISBN 978-0-14-056552-2 Subj: Family life – mothers. Format, unusual – toy & movable books.

Mommy, I want to sleep in your bed! ill. by Elliot Kreloff. Blue Apple, 2005. ISBN 978-1-59354-103-3 Subj: Animals – dogs. Bedtime. Family life – mothers. Sleep.

Mother Goose manners ill. by Pascale Constantin. Blue Apple, 2008. ISBN 978-1-934706-02-2 Subj: Etiquette. Nursery rhymes.

Murphy jumps a hurdle ill. by Emily Bolam. Blue Apple, 2006. ISBN 978-1-59354-174-3 Subj: Animals – dogs. Character traits – perseverance. Sports.

Murphy meets the treadmill ill. by Emily Bolam. Houghton, 2001. ISBN 978-0-618-11357-6 Subj: Health & fitness – exercise. Pets.

My dog thinks I'm a genius ill. by Barroux. Blue Apple, 2011. ISBN 978-1-60905-059-7 Subj: Activities – painting. Animals – dogs.

My forever dress ill. by Liz Murphy. Blue Apple, 2009. ISBN 978-1-934706-45-9 Subj: Activities – sewing. Clothing – dresses. Ecology. Family life – grandmothers.

A new coat for Anna ill. by Anita Lobel. Knopf, 1988. ISBN 978-0-394-97426-2 Subj: Clothing – coats. Family life. War.

No kiss for Grandpa! ill. by Emilie Boon. Orchard, 2001. ISBN 978-0-531-30328-3 Subj: Animals – cats. Family life – grandfathers.

Ode to Humpty Dumpty ill. by Seymour Chwast. Houghton, 2001. ISBN 978-0-618-05047-5 Subj: Character traits – helpfulness. Emotions – grief. Nursery rhymes.

One red apple ill. by Karla Gudeon. Blue Apple, 2009. ISBN 978-1-934706-67-1 Subj: Nature. Trees.

A polar bear can swim: what animals can and cannot do ill. by Emily Bolam. Viking, 1998. ISBN 978-0-670-88056-0 Subj: Activities. Animals. Circular tales.

The princess and the peas and carrots ill. by Travis Foster. Blue Apple, 2012. ISBN 978-1-60905-250-8 Subj: Behavior – misbehavior. Character traits – perfectionism. Family life.

Pumpkin Pie ill. by Donald Dreifuss. Houghton, 2000. ISBN 978-0-618-04883-0 Subj: Animals – goats. Fairs, festivals. Farms.

Pushkin meets the bundle ill. by Donald Saaf. Atheneum, 1998. ISBN 978-0-689-81413-6 Subj: Animals – dogs. Babies. Family life.

Pushkin minds the bundle ill. by Donald Saaf. Atheneum, 2000. ISBN 978-0-689-83216-1 Subj: Activities – vacationing. Animals – dogs. Babies. Family life.

Robin, where are you? ill. by Noah Woods. Blue Apple, 2012. ISBN 978-1-60905-192-1 Subj: Activities. Birds. Character traits – patience. Family life – grandfathers. Format, unusual – toy & movable books.

Rockheads ill. by Todd McKie. Houghton, 2004. ISBN 978-0-618-34574-8 Subj: Activities. Counting, numbers. Rhyming text.

Someday we'll have very good manners ill. by Chris L. Demarest. Putnam, 2001. ISBN 978-0-399-23558-0 Subj: Etiquette.

Squarehead ill. by Todd McKie. Houghton, 2001. ISBN 978-0-618-08378-7 Subj: Concepts – shape. Dreams. Self-concept.

Surprise! ill. by Richard Brown. Sterling, 2007. ISBN 978-1-4027-3410-6 Subj: Character traits – generosity. Family life – mothers.

Talk, baby! ill. by Emily Bolam. Holt, 1999. ISBN 978-0-8050-6144-4 Subj: Activities – talking. Babies. Family life – new sibling. Format, unusual – toy & movable books.

That's what grandmas are for ill. by Amanda Haley. Blue Apple, 2006. ISBN 978-1-59354-098-2 Subj: Family life – grandmothers.

That's what grandpas are for ill. by Deborah Zemke. Blue Apple, 2006. ISBN 978-1-59354-097-5 Subj: Family life – grandfathers.

There was a little girl who had a little curl ill. by Elliot Kreloff. Blue Apple, 2006. ISBN 978-1-59354-161-3 Subj: Behavior – misbehavior. Character traits – appearance. Hair.

39 uses for a friend ill. by Rebecca Doughty. Putnam, 2001. ISBN 978-0-399-23616-7 Subj: Friendship.

Toes have wiggles, kids have giggles ill. by Rebecca Doughty. Putnam, 2002. ISBN 978-0-399-23617-4 Subj: Activities. Rhyming text.

Train song ill. by Donald Saaf. Orchard, 2000. ISBN 978-0-531-30204-0 Subj: Rhyming text. Trains.

Two little witches ill. by Simms Taback. Candlewick, 1996. ISBN 978-1-56402-621-7 Subj: Counting, numbers. Holidays – Halloween. Witches.

Waiting for baby ill. by Emily Bolam. Holt, 1998. ISBN 978-0-8050-5929-8 Subj: Babies. Family life – new sibling.

What do ducks dream? ill. by Donald Saaf. Putnam, 2001. ISBN 978-0-399-23358-6 Subj: Animals. Bedtime. Dreams. Farms. Rhyming text. Sleep.

What is part this, part that? ill. by Tom Slaughter. Blue Apple, 2013. ISBN 978-1-60905-309-3 Subj: Rhyming text. Riddles & jokes.

When I first came to this land ill. by Simms Taback. Putnam, 1998. ISBN 978-0-399-23044-8 Subj: Cumulative tales. Folk & fairy tales. Immigrants. Poverty. Songs.

Wiggle like an octopus ill. by Simms Taback. Blue Apple, 2011. ISBN 978-1-60905-072-6 Subj: Animals. Format, unusual – board books. Participation. Rhyming text. Sea & seashore.

William and the dragon ill. by Richard Brown. Blue Apple, 2005. ISBN 978-1-59354-089-0 Subj: Dragons. Rhyming text.

You and me: we're opposites ill. by Ethan Long. Blue Apple, 2009. ISBN 978-1-934706-48-0 Subj: Animals. Concepts – opposites. Zoos.

You can't buy a dinosaur with a dime ill. by Amanda Haley. Blue Apple, 2003. ISBN 978-1-929766-81-9 Subj: Counting, numbers. Money. Problem solving.

You can't taste a pickle with your ear ill. by Amanda Haley. Blue Apple, 2002. ISBN 978-1-929766-68-0 Subj: Senses.

Zimmerman, Andrea Griffing. *Fire engine man* ill. by David Clemesha. Holt, 2007. ISBN 978-0-8050-7905-0 Subj: Careers – firefighters. Family life – brothers & sisters.

My dog Toby by Andrea Griffing Zimmerman and David Clemesha ill. by True Kelley. Harcourt, 2000. ISBN 978-0-15-202014-9 Subj: Animals – dogs. Pets.

Train man ill. by David Clemesha. Holt, 2012. ISBN 978-0-8050-7991-3 Subj: Family life – brothers. Imagination. Trains.

Trashy town by Andrea Griffing Zimmerman and David Clemesha ill. by Dan Yaccarino. HarperCollins, 1999. ISBN 978-0-06-027140-4 Subj: Careers – sanitation workers. Cities, towns.

Zimmett, Debbie. *Eddie enough* ill. by Charlotte Murray Fremaux. Woodbine, 2001. ISBN 978-1-890627-25-6 Subj: Behavior. Disabilities – ADD. School.

Zion, Gene. *Harry, the dirty dog* ill. by Margaret Bloy Graham. HarperCollins, 1956. Subj: Activities – bathing. Animals – dogs. Behavior – running away.

No roses for Harry ill. by Margaret Bloy Graham. HarperCollins, 1958. ISBN 978-0-06-026891-6 Subj: Animals – dogs. Clothing.

Zoboli, Giovanna. *I wish I had . . .* ill. by Simona Mulazzani. Eerdmans, 2013. ISBN 978-0-8028-5415-5 Subj: Anatomy. Animals. Behavior – wishing. Imagination.

Zoehfeld, Kathleen Weidner. *Apples, apples* ill. by Christopher Santoro. HarperCollins, 2004. ISBN 978-0-06-053787-6 Subj: Animals – bears. Food. Format, unusual – board books. Seasons – fall. Trees.

Did dinosaurs have feathers? ill. by Lucia Washburn. HarperCollins, 2004. ISBN 978-0-06-029027-6 Subj: Birds. Dinosaurs.

Dinosaur tracks ill. by Lucia Washburn. HarperCollins, 2007. ISBN 978-0-06-029024-5 Subj: Dinosaurs. Fossils.

Dinosaurs big and small ill. by Lucia Washburn. HarperCollins, 2002. ISBN 978-0-06-027936-3 Subj: Concepts – size. Dinosaurs.

How mountains are made ill. by James Graham Hale. HarperCollins, 1995. ISBN 978-0-06-024510-8 Subj: Earth. Mountains. Science.

Secrets of the garden: food chains and the food web in our backyard ill. by Priscilla Lamont. Random House, 2012. ISBN 978-0-517-70990-0 Subj: Ecology. Food. Gardens, gardening. Science.

What lives in a shell? ill. by Helen Davie. HarperCollins, 1994. ISBN 978-0-06-022999-3 Subj: Animals. Science. Sea & seashore.

What's alive? ill. by Nadine Bernard Westcott. HarperCollins, 1995. ISBN 978-0-06-023444-7 Subj: Animals. Plants. Science.

Where did dinosaurs come from? ill. by Lucia Washburn. HarperCollins, 2011. ISBN 978-0-06-029022-1 Subj: Dinosaurs.

Zolkower, Edie Stoltz. *Too many cooks* ill. by Shauna Mooney Kawasaki. Kar-Ben, 2000. ISBN 978-1-58013-063-9 Subj: Activities – baking, cooking. Holidays – Passover. Jewish culture.

Zolotow, Charlotte. *The beautiful Christmas tree* ill. by Yan Nacimbene. Houghton, 1999. ISBN 978-0-395-91365-9 Subj: Holidays – Christmas. Trees.

The bunny who found Easter ill. by Helen Craig. Houghton, 1998. ISBN 978-0-395-86265-0 Subj: Animals – rabbits. Emotions – loneliness. Holidays – Easter.

Do you know what I'll do? ill. by Javaka Steptoe. HarperCollins, 2000. ISBN 978-0-06-027880-9 Subj: Babies. Behavior – growing up. Emotions – love. Ethnic groups in the U.S. – African Americans. Family life.

A father like that ill. by LeUyen Pham. HarperCollins, 2007. ISBN 978-0-06-027864-9 Subj: Ethnic groups in the U.S. – African Americans. Family life – fathers. Family life – single-parent families.

The hating book ill. by Ben Shecter. HarperCollins, 1969. ISBN 978-0-06-443197-2 Subj: Behavior – gossip. Emotions – hate. Friendship.

I know a lady ill. by James Stevenson. Greenwillow, 1984. ISBN 978-0-688-03837-3 Subj: Character traits – kindness. Old age.

I like to be little ill. by Erik Blegvad. HarperCollins, 1987. ISBN 978-0-690-04674-8 Subj: Behavior – growing up. Family life – mothers.

If it weren't for you ill. by G. Brian Karas. HarperCollins, 2006. ISBN 978-0-06-027875-5 Subj: Family life. Sibling rivalry.

The moon was the best ill. by Tana Hoban. Greenwillow, 1993. ISBN 978-0-688-09941-1 Subj: Moon.

Mr. Rabbit and the lovely present ill. by Maurice Sendak. HarperCollins, 1962. ISBN 978-0-06-026946-3 Subj: Animals – rabbits. Birthdays. Caldecott award honor books. Concepts – color. Family life – mothers. Holidays – Easter.

My friend John ill. by Amanda Harvey. Doubleday, 2000. ISBN 978-0-385-32651-3 Subj: Friendship.

My grandson Lew ill. by William Pène Du Bois. HarperCollins, 1974. ISBN 978-0-06-026961-6 Subj: Death. Emotions – grief. Family life. Family life – grandfathers.

The old dog ill. by James Ransome. HarperCollins, 1995. ISBN 978-0-06-024412-5 Subj: Animals – dogs. Death. Emotions – grief. Ethnic groups in the U.S. – African Americans. Pets.

The poodle who barked at the wind ill. by Valerie Coursen. Holt, 2002. ISBN 978-0-8050-6306-6 Subj: Animals – dogs. Noise, sounds. Pets.

The quarreling book ill. by Arnold Lobel. HarperCollins, 1963. ISBN 978-0-06-026976-0 Subj: Behavior – fighting, arguing. Cumulative tales. Emotions – anger. Weather – rain.

Say it! ill. by James Stevenson. Greenwillow, 1980. Subj: Activities – walking. Emotions – love. Family life – mothers. Nature. Seasons – fall.

The sleepy book ill. by Ilse Plume. Rev. ed. HarperCollins, 1988. ISBN 978-0-06-026968-5 Subj: Animals. Bedtime. Sleep.

Sleepy book ill. by Stefano Vitale. HarperCollins, 2001. ISBN 978-0-06-027873-1 Subj: Animals. Bedtime. Sleep.

Some things go together ill. by Ashley Wolff. Newly illustrated ed. HarperCollins, 1999. ISBN 978-0-694-01197-1 Subj: Emotions – love. Family life. Poetry.

Something is going to happen ill. by Catherine Stock. HarperCollins, 1988. ISBN 978-0-06-027029-2 Subj: Morning. Weather – snow.

The storm book ill. by Margaret Bloy Graham. HarperCollins, 1952. ISBN 978-0-06-027026-1 Subj: Caldecott award honor books. Emotions – fear. Weather. Weather – rain. Weather – rainbows.

Summer is . . . ill. by Ruth Lercher Bornstein. Crowell, 1983. ISBN 978-0-690-04304-4 Subj: Rhyming text. Seasons – summer.

This quiet lady ill. by Anita Lobel. Greenwillow, 1992. ISBN 978-0-688-09306-8 Subj: Family life – mothers.

A tiger called Thomas ill. by Diana Cain Bluthenthal. Hyperion, 2003. ISBN 978-0-7868-0517-4 Subj: Character traits – shyness. Emotions – loneliness. Holidays – Halloween.

A tiger called Thomas ill. by Catherine Stock. Lothrop, 1988. ISBN 978-0-688-06697-0 Subj: Character traits – shyness. Emotions – loneliness. Holidays – Halloween.

When the wind stops ill. by Stefano Vitale. HarperCollins, 1995. ISBN 978-0-06-026972-2 Subj: Bedtime. Nature. Night. Weather – wind.

William's doll ill. by William Pène Du Bois. HarperCollins, 1972. ISBN 978-0-06-027048-3 Subj: Family life. Family life – grandmothers. Toys – dolls.

Zonta, Pat. *Jessica's x-ray* ill. by Clive Dobson. Firefly, 2002. ISBN 978-1-55297-578-7 Subj: Hospitals. Illness.

Zucker, Jonny. *Apples and honey* ill. by Jan Barger Cohen. Barron's, 2002. ISBN 978-0-7641-2265-1 Subj: Holidays – Rosh Hashanah. Jewish culture.

Four special questions ill. by Jan Barger Cohen. Barron's, 2003. ISBN 978-0-7641-2267-5 Subj: Holidays – Passover. Jewish culture.

It's party time ill. by Jan Barger Cohen. Barron's, 2003. ISBN 978-0-7641-2268-2 Subj: Holidays – Purim. Jewish culture.

Zuckerberg, Randi. *Dot* ill. by Joe Berger. HarperCollins, 2013. ISBN 978-0-06-228751-9 Subj: Activities. Computers.

Zuckerman, Andrew. *Creature abc* photos by author. Chronicle, 2009. ISBN 978-0-8118-6978-2 Subj: ABC books. Animals.

Zuckerman, Linda. *I will hold you 'til you sleep* ill. by Jon J Muth. Scholastic, 2006. ISBN 978-0-439-43420-1 Subj: Emotions – love. Family life.

Zuffi, Stefano. *Art 123: count from 1 to 12 with great works of art.* Abrams, 2011. ISBN 978-1-4197-0100-9 Subj: Art. Counting, numbers. Rhyming text.

Zullo, Germano. *Line 135* ill. by Albertine. Chronicle, 2013. ISBN 978-1-4521-1934-2 Subj: Activities – traveling. Cities, towns. Country. Trains.

Little bird ill. by Albertine. Enchanted Lion, 2012. ISBN 978-1-59270-118-6 Subj: Activities – flying. Birds.

Zweibel, Alan. *Our tree named Steve* ill. by David Catrow. Penguin, 2005. ISBN 978-0-399-23722-5 Subj: Family life. Letters, cards. Trees.

Title Index

Titles appear in alphabetical sequence with the author's name in parentheses, followed by the page number of the full listing in the Bibliographic Guide. For identical title listings, the illustrator's name is given to further identify the version. In the case of variant titles, both the original and differing titles are listed.

A

B

C

D

E

F

G

H

I

J

K

L

M

N

O

P

Q

R

S

T

U

V

W

X

Y

Z

Illustrator Index

Illustrators appear alphabetically in boldface followed by their titles. Names in parentheses are authors of the titles when different from the illustrator. Page numbers refer to the full listing in the Bibliographic Guide.

A

B

C

D

E

F

G

H

I

J

K

L

M

N

O

P

Q

R

S

T

U

V

W

X

Y

Z

About the Authors

REBECCA L. THOMAS recently retired as an elementary school librarian, Shaker Heights City Schools, Ohio. She is the author of numerous reference books, including the *Popular Series Fiction* set for Libraries Unlimited (2009) and *Across Cultures* (Libraries Unlimited, 2007).

The late **CAROLYN W. LIMA** served as children's librarian at the San Diego Public Library, Branch Libraries Division, San Diego, California. She created previous editions of this best-selling subject guide to picture books.